The New Testament

from
26 Translations

General Editor

Curtis Vaughan, Th. D.

ZONDERVAN PUBLISHING HOUSE
Grand Rapids, Michigan

INTRODUCTION

In the prologue of the Paris edition of the 1538 Coverdale diglot (in Latin and English), Miles Coverdale wrote of the value of differing translations of the Scriptures:

> Now for thy part, most gentle reader, take in good worth that I here offer thee with a good will, and let this present translation be no prejudice to the other that out of the Greek have been translated afore, or shall be hereafter. For if thou open thine eyes and consider well the gift of the Holy Ghost therein, thou shalt see that *one translation declareth, openeth and illustrateth another, and that in many cases one is a plain commentary unto another.*

The New Testament From 26 Translations is sent forth in the firm belief that this is true.

The Bible which has enjoyed the most widespread and lasting acceptance in the English speaking world is the King James Version. It is marked by simplicity, dignity, and power of statement, and has for centuries been greatly used of God to nurture the faith of His people. But for all the merits of the King James Version, the modern Bible reader finds it increasingly difficult to understand its archaic style and diction.

The aim of the present volume is to clarify the meaning of the King James Version by the use of more recent translations of the biblical text. These serve somewhat as a commentary on the text of the older translation.

The King James Version is the base for this work, and it is the only translation which is quoted in its entirety. Other translations are included only when they differ significantly from the King James. Sometimes only a few words of a given translation of a single passage require quotation. In such instances, omitted material is indicated by ellipses marks (...). The text of the King James Version is set in bold face type, while other translations quoted appear under the King James in roman type.

All marks of punctuation in the King James Version are retained, but in other translations the punctuation marks at the end of the quoted phrase or clause are, as a rule, omitted. An exception to this is made whenever the punctuation mark seems to be required for complete understanding of the quotation.

Special styles of print (such as italics and bold face type) used in some of the versions are not reproduced. Because the use of such devices varies so widely, it is felt these might be a hindrance rather than a help in using this New Testament. For example, some translations use italics for words which have no equivalent in the Greek; others use italics for quotations from the Old Testament; still others use italics to bring out emphasis. In reading a complete copy of any given version, these are readily understood and are generally quite helpful, but they would not be intelligible in this work. Had they been reproduced here, a special note explaining their significance would be required for each separate entry.

Quotation marks are retained only when the translator employed them to call special attention to a word or phrase.

The reader will observe that the translators at times differ sharply in their renderings of the same passage. Often this simply indicates a difference of opinion in their understanding of the meaning of the original text. In other cases, however, the difference may be accounted for by the fact that the translators were not rendering the same text. Monsignor Ronald Knox's version, for example, is based on the Latin Vulgate, and George N. Lamsa has translated the Aramaic text. All other versions are based on the Greek text, but, at times, the Greek manuscripts themselves show significant variations. Where this is so, each translator must decide for himself which reading is nearest the original. "A translator of Holy Scripture," wrote Henry Alford, "must be absolutely colorless; ready to sacrifice the choicest text, and the plainest proof of doctrine, if the words are not those of what he is constrained in his conscience to receive as God's testimony."

The General Editor is pleased to acknowledge his indebtedness to Mr. Jack Hamm of Dallas, Texas, and to Dr. William H. Rossell, formerly Professor of Old Testament at Southwestern Baptist Theological Seminary, Fort Worth, Texas. It was Mr. Hamm who conceived the idea of a multi-version New Testament, and who in many other ways worked untiringly to make it a reality. Dr. Rossell laid the groundwork for this volume, and until his untimely death in July, 1964 was the General Editor. It is a source of deep regret that so soon after its initiation the work was deprived of his scholarly insight and linguistic proficiency.

A special debt of gratitude is owed also to Mr. Clare Zachry, Dr. Milford O. Rouse, Mr. J. C. Cantrell, Mr. Orville Rogers, Mr. James Erwin, Mr. Ben Land, Mr. David Wicker II and Mr.

W. Dewey Presley. Without the encouragement and generous financial support of these men, all devout Christians and leaders in the business community of Dallas, this project could not have been completed.

The prayer of all who have shared in the labor of producing *The New Testament From 26 Translations* is that God may seal it with His approval and be pleased to use it for the honor and glory of His name.

CURTIS VAUGHAN, TH.D.
General Editor

EDITORS

ACKNOWLEDGMENTS

Appreciation is expressed to the publishers for permission to reprint selections from the following translations of the New Testament:

BAKER BOOK HOUSE. *The Epistles of Paul* by W. J. Conybeare.

CAMBRIDGE UNIVERSITY PRESS in association with Evans Bros., Ltd. *The New Testament in Basic English.*

CONCORDIA PUBLISHING HOUSE. *The New Testament in the Language of Today* by William F. Beck. Copyright © 1963 by Concordia Publishing House.

DIVISION OF CHRISTIAN EDUCATION, NATIONAL COUNCIL OF THE CHURCHES OF CHRIST IN THE UNITED STATES OF AMERICA. *The Revised Standard Version of the Bible*, New Testament section. Copyright © 1952 by The Division of Christian Education, National Council of the Churches of Christ in the United States of America.

HARPER AND ROW PUBLISHERS, INC. and HODDER AND STOUGHTON, LTD. *The New Testament, A New Translation* by James Moffatt. Copyright © 1964 by James Moffatt. Used by permission of Harper and Row, Inc. and Hodder and Stoughton, Ltd.

HARPER AND ROW PUBLISHERS, INC. and JAMES CLARKE AND COMPANY LTD. *Weymouth's New Testament in Modern Speech* by Richard Francis Weymouth, as revised by J. A. Robertson. Published by special arrangement with James Clarke and Company Ltd., London. Reprinted by permission of Harper and Row Publishers, Inc. and James Clarke and Company Ltd.

A. J. HOLMAN COMPANY, A subsidiary of J. B. Lippincott Company. *The Holy Bible From Ancient Eastern Manuscripts* by George M. Lamsa. Copyright © 1940, 1957, 1961 by A. J. Holman Company.

THE JUDSON PRESS. *The New Testament in Modern English* translated by Helen Barrett Montgomery. Copyright © 1924, 1952 by the American Baptist Board of Education and Publication.

KREGEL PUBLICATIONS. *The Emphasized New Testament* by Joseph Bryant Rotherham.

THE LOCKMAN FOUNDATION. *The New American Standard Bible, New Testament.* Copyright © 1960, 1962, 1963 by The Lockman Foundation.

THE MACMILLAN COMPANY. *The New Testament in Modern English.* Copyright © 1958, 1959, 1960 by J. B. Phillips. *The Gospels* © 1952, 1957 by The Macmillan Company; *The Young Church in Action* © 1955 by The Macmillan Company; *Letters to Young Churches* © 1947, 1957 by The Macmillan Company; *The Book of Revelation* © 1957 by The Macmillan Company.

GEOFFREY BLES, LTD. *The New Testament in Modern English.* Copyright © 1960 by J. B. Phillips; *The Gospel in Modern English.* Copyright © 1952; *The Young Church in Action.* Copyright © 1955; *Letters to Young Churches.* Copyright © 1947; *The Book of Revelation.* Copyright © 1957.

MOODY BIBLE INSTITUTE. *The New Testament: A Translation in the Language of the People* by Charles B. Williams. Copyright © 1937 by Bruce Humphries, Inc. Copyright © renewed 1965 by Edith S. Williams.

MOODY BIBLE INSTITUTE. *The Twentieth Century New Testament.*

OXFORD UNIVERSITY PRESS and CAMBRIDGE UNIVERSITY PRESS. *The New English Bible: New Testament.* Copyright © 1961 by The Delegates of the Oxford University Press and The Syndics of the Cambridge University Press. Reprinted by permission.

PENGUIN BOOKS, LTD. *The Four Gospels* translated by E. V. Rieu. Copyright © 1953 by Penguin Press, Ltd.

CONTENTS

AN EXPLANATION OF ABBREVIATIONS

The complete text of the King James Version appears in bold face type. The translations used here may be identified by the following code:

ASV	—	The American Standard Version
RSV	—	The Revised Standard Version
NASB	—	The New American Standard Bible: New Testament
NEB	—	The New English Bible: New Testament
ABUV	—	The New Testament of Our Lord and Savior Jesus Christ, American Bible Union Version (John A. Broadus et al)
Alf	—	The New Testament (Henry Alford)
Bas	—	The New Testament in Basic English
Beck	—	The New Testament in the Language of Today (William F. Beck)
Ber	—	The Berkeley Version of the New Testament (Gerrit Verkuyl)
Con	—	The Epistles of Paul (W. J. Conybeare)
Gspd	—	The New Testament: An American Translation (Edgar J. Goodspeed)
Knox	—	The New Testament in the Translation of Monsignor Ronald Knox
Lam	—	The New Testament According to the Eastern Texts (George M. Lamsa)
Mof	—	The New Testament: A New Translation (James Moffatt)
Mon	—	The Centenary Translation: The New Testament in Modern English (Helen Barrett Montgomery)
Nor	—	The New Testament: A New Translation (Olaf M. Norlie)
Phi	—	The New Testament in Modern English (J. B. Phillips)
Rieu	—	The Book of the Acts (C. H. Rieu)
Rieu	—	The Four Gospels (E. V. Rieu)
Rhm	—	The Emphasized New Testament: A New Translation (J. B. Rotherham)
Tay	—	Living Letters: The Paraphrased Epistles; Living Gospels: The Paraphrased Gospels; Living Prophecies: The Minor Prophets Paraphrased and Daniel and the Revelation (Kenneth N. Taylor)
TCNT	—	The Twentieth Century New Testament
Wey	—	The New Testament in Modern Speech (Richard Francis Weymouth)
Wms	—	The New Testament: A Translation in the Language of the People (Charles B. Williams)
Amp	—	The Amplified New Testament

THE
GOSPEL ACCORDING TO MATTHEW

CHAPTER 1

1. The book of the generation of Jesus Christ,
A Genealogy of Jesus Christ — TCNT
The family tree of Jesus Christ — Wms
A record of the ancestry of Jesus Christ — Knox
the son of David, the son of Abraham.
who was the descendant of both David and Abraham — Phi

2. Abraham begat Isaac;
Abraham was the father of Isaac — TCNT
To Abraham was born Isaac — NASB
and Isaac begat Jacob; and Jacob begat Judas and his brethren;
... Judah ... — ASV

3. And Judas begat Phares and Zara of Thamar;
... Judah ... Perez ... Zerah ... Tamar — ASV
and Phares begat Esrom; and Esrom begat Aram;
... Perez ... Hezron ... Ram — ASV

4. And Aram begat Aminadab; and Aminadab begat Naasson;
... Ram ... Amminadab ... Nahshon — ASV
and Naasson begat Salmon;
... Nahshon ... — ASV

5. And Salmon begat Booz of Rachab;
... Boaz ... Rahab — ASV
and Booz begat Obed of Ruth; and Obed begat Jesse;
... Boaz ... — ASV

6. And Jesse begat David the king; and David the king begat Solomon of her that had been the wife of Urias;
... Solomon, whose mother was Uriah's widow — TCNT

7. And Solomon begat Roboam; and Roboam begat Abia; and Abia begat Asa;
... Rehoboam ... Abijah ... — ASV

8. And Asa begat Josaphat; and Josaphat begat Joram; and Joram begat Ozias;
... Jehoshaphat ... Uzziah — ASV

9. And Ozias begat Joatham; and Joatham begat Achaz; and Achaz begat Ezekias;
... Uzziah ... Jotham ... Ahaz ... Hezekiah — ASV

10. And Ezekias begat Manasses; and Manasses begat Amon; and Amon begat Josias;
... Hezekiah ... Manasseh ... Josiah — ASV

11. And Josias begat Jechonias and his brethren, about the time they were carried away to Babylon;
... at the period of the removal to Babylon — Wey

12. And after they were brought to Babylon, Jechonias begat Salathiel;
... Jechoniah ... Shealtiel — ASV
and Salathiel begat Zorobabel;
... Shealtiel ... Zerubbabel — ASV

13. And Zorobabel begat Abiud; and Abiud begat Eliakim; and Eliakim begat Azor;
... Zerubbabel ... — ASV

14. And Azor begat Sadoc; and Sadoc begat Achim; and Achim begat Eliud;

15. And Eliud begat Eleazar; and Eleazar begat Matthan; and Matthan begat Jacob;

16. And Jacob begat Joseph the husband of Mary, of whom was born Jesus, who is called Christ.
... Mary, who gave birth to Jesus called Messiah — NEB

17. So all the generations from Abraham to David are fourteen generations;
The genealogy of Jesus Christ may thus be traced for fourteen generations from Abraham to David — Phi
and from David until the carrying away into Babylon are fourteen generations; and from the carrying away into Babylon unto Christ are fourteen generations.

18. Now the birth of Jesus Christ was on this wise: When as his mother Mary was espoused to Joseph,
The birth of Jesus Christ took place as follows: — His mother Mary was engaged to Joseph — TCNT
before they came together,
but, while she was still a virgin—TCNT
before they were united in marriage — Wey

1

she was found with child of the Holy Ghost.

it was found that she was about to become a mother through the influence of the holy Spirit — Gspd

. . . by the power of the Holy Spirit — TCNT

19. Then Joseph her husband,

Joseph, her husband-to-be — Nor

being a just man,

being a man of principle — Rieu

. . . a religious man — TCNT

and not willing to make her a publick example,

yet not willing to expose her to shame — ABUV

was minded to put her away privily.

he decided to break off the engagement privately — Gspd

he decided to divorce her secretly — Beck

20. But while he thought on these things,

But while he was contemplating this step — Wey

But just as this thought occurred to him — Wms

But when he had considered this — NASB

behold, the angel of the Lord appeared unto him in a dream, saying,

lo! a messenger of the Lord . . . — Rhm

Joseph, thou son of David,

Joseph, descendant of David — Amp

fear not to take unto thee Mary thy wife:

do not be afraid to take Mary home with you as your wife — NEB

. . . for your wife — TCNT

for that which is conceived in her is of the Holy Ghost.

for the expected Child within her is by the Holy Spirit — Nor

her Child is from the Holy Spirit — Beck

21. And she shall bring forth a son, and thou shalt call his name JESUS:

. . . and you must name Him Jesus — Wms

. . . Jesus ('the Savior') — Phi

for he shall save his people from their sins.

for it is he who shall save his people from their sins — TCNT

22. Now all this was done, that it might be fulfilled which was spoken of the Lord by the prophet, saying,

Now all this had happened in fulfillment of what the Lord had spoken by the prophet . . . — Nor

23. Behold, a virgin shall be with child, and shall bring forth a son,

The maiden will be pregnant and will have a son — Gspd

Behold, a virgin will conceive and give birth to a son — Lam

Behold, the virgin . . . — ASV

and they shall call his name Emmanuel, which being interpreted is, God with us.

. . . — a word which means 'God is with us' — TCNT

24. Then Joseph being raised from sleep did as the angel of the Lord had bidden him,

And Joseph awaking from his sleep, did as the messenger of the Lord directed him — Rhm

and took unto him his wife:

and brought home his wife — Wey

25. And knew her not

but did not live with her as her husband — TCNT

but had no intercourse with her — Phi

till she had brought forth her firstborn son:

. . . brought forth a son — ASV

and he called his name JESUS.

and he named the child Jesus — Gspd

CHAPTER 2

1. Now when Jesus was born in Bethlehem of Judaea

After the birth of Jesus at Bethlehem in Judaea — TCNT

in the days of Herod the king,

in the reign of King Herod — TCNT

behold, there came wise men from the east to Jerusalem,

lo! wise men from eastern parts came

into Jerusalem — Rhm

some Astrologers from the East arrived in Jerusalem — TCNT

there arrived from the east a party of astrologers making for Jerusalem — Phi

2. Saying, Where is he that is born King of the Jews?

who began to ask . . . — Nor

. . . Where is he that hath been born king of the Jews — Rhm
. . . Where is the new-born King of the Jews — TCNT
and enquiring as they went: Where is the child born to be king of the Jews — Phi
for we have seen his star in the east,
For we saw his star when it rose—Wey
We have seen his star out in the east — Knox
We observed the rising of his star — NEB
and are come to worship him.
and have come to bow down to him — Rhm
and have come to do homage to him — TCNT

3. When Herod the king had heard these things,
And when Herod the king heard it — ASV
Reports of this soon reached the king — Wey
he was troubled, and all Jerusalem with him.
and greatly agitated not only him, but all the people of Jerusalem — Wey
he was deeply perturbed . . . — Phi
he became alarmed . . . — Beck

4. And when he had gathered all the chief priests and scribes of the people together,
. . . all the chief priests and rabbis of the people — Mon
. . . all the chief priests and learned men among the people — Knox
. . . all of the people's ruling priests and men trained in the Bible — Beck
he demanded of them
he inquired of them — ASV
he was enquiring of them — Rhm
he began to inquire of them — Mon
he kept asking them — Lam
where Christ should be born.
Where is the Christ to be born — Rhm

5. And they said unto him, In Bethlehem of Judaea:
. . . In Bethlehem belonging to Judaea — Mof
for thus it is written by the prophet,
for so it stands written in the words of the prophet — Wey
and they referred him to the prophecy which reads — NEB

6. And thou Bethlehem, in the land of Juda,
And thou Bethlehem, land of Judah — ASV
art not the least among the princes of Juda:
By no means the least honourable art thou among princely places in Judah — Wey
you are not insignificant in the eyes of the kings of Judah — Lam
You are not at all the least among the leading places of Judah — Wms
art by no means the least among the foremost in Juda — Rieu
for out of thee shall come a Governor,
since from you will come a leader — Beck
. . . Prince — Wey
. . . Ruler — Mon
that shall rule my people Israel.
Who shall be shepherd of my people Israel — ASV

7. Then Herod, when he had privily called the wise men,[1]
Herod next called the astrologers to meet him in private — NEB
enquired of them diligently
learned of them exactly — ASV
what time the star appeared.
the date of the appearance of the star — TCNT
the exact time of the star's appearing — Wey

8. And he sent them to Bethlehem, and said, Go and search diligently for the young child;
. . . Go! Find out all you can about the Child — Nor
. . . Go and search out exactly concerning the young child — ASV
he sent them to Bethlehem with orders to discover the truth in this matter of the child — Rieu
and when ye have found him,
and as soon as ye find it — Rhm
bring me word again,
report to me — Mof
that I may come and worship him also.
that I also may come and worship him — ASV

9. When they had heard the king, they departed;

---

[1]For "wise men" see Matt. 2:1.

They set out at the king's bidding —
NEB

The Astrologers heard what the King had to say, and then continued their journey — TCNT

and, lo, the star, which they saw in the east,

and behold, the same star . . . — Lam

and all at once the star which they had seen in the east — Knox

And there was the star they had seen when it rose! — Beck

went before them,

was going before them — Rhm

led them on — TCNT

went in front of them as they traveled — Phi

till it came and stood over where the young child was.

till it came to rest over the place where the child was — RSV

until at last it shone immediately above the place where the little child lay — Phi

10. **When they saw the star,**

When they caught sight of the star — Mof

they rejoiced with exceeding great joy.

the sight filled them with intense joy — Wey

they were thrilled with ecstatic joy — Wms

They were overwhelmed with joy — Rieu

Their joy knew no bounds! — TAY

11. **And when they were come into the house, they saw the young child with Mary his mother,**

on reaching the house . . . — Mof

and fell down, and worshipped him:

and fell at his feet and did homage to him — TCNT

And they fell on their knees and worshiped him — Phi

. . . prostrated themselves — Rhm

and when they opened their treasures,

Then they unpacked their treasures — TCNT

. . . treasure-chests — Wey

. . . caskets — Mof

they presented unto him gifts; gold, and frankincense, and myrrh.

and laid before him gifts of gold and frankincense and myrrh — Rieu

. . . offerings of gold, perfume, and spices — Bas

12. **And being warned of God in a dream**

and being instructed by dream — Rhm

And it was made clear to them by God in a dream — Bas

that they should not return to Herod,

forbidding them to go back to Herod — Knox

they departed into their own country another way.

they returned to their own country by another road — TCNT

they set out to their own country by another route — Wms

13. **And when they were departed,**

As soon as they had gone — Knox

behold, the angel of the Lord

. . . an angel of the Lord — ASV

. . . a messenger of the Lord — Rhm

appeareth to Joseph

appeared to Joseph — TCNT

in a dream, saying,

by dream . . . — Rhm

Arise, and take the young child and his mother,

Arise take unto thee the child and its mother — Rhm

Awake . . . — TCNT

and flee into Egypt,

and seek refuge in Egypt — TCNT

and escape to Egypt — Wey

and be thou there until I bring thee word:

and stay there until I bid you return — TCNT

for Herod will seek the young child to destroy him.

for Herod is about to seek the child to destroy it — Rhm

for Herod intends to make a search for the child, in order to put him to death — Mon

14. **When he arose, he took the young child and his mother by night,**

He rose up therefore, while it was still night . . . — Knox

and departed into Egypt:

and withdrew into Egypt — ABUV

and took refuge in Egypt — Gspd

and made their escape to Egypt — Wms

and departed for Egypt — NASB

15. **And was there until the death of Herod: that it might be fulfilled which was spoken of the Lord by the prophet,**

. . . in fulfillment of these words of the Lord in the Prophet — TCNT

. . . so as to fulfill what the Lord had said by the prophet — Wms

saying,

where he says — TCNT

Out of Egypt have I called my son.

. . . did I call my son — ASV

16. **Then Herod, when he saw that he was mocked of the wise men,**

. . . trifled with by the Astrologers — TCNT

. . . tricked by the astrologers — Gspd

. . . insulted by the Magi — Lam

. . . outwitted by the wise men — Ber

was exceeding wroth,

he was furiously angry — Mof

he fell into a passion — NEB

and sent forth, and slew all the children that were in Bethlehem,

. . . slew all the male children . . . — ASV

. . . massacred all the boys . . . — Wey

and sent a detachment to murder all the boy babies . . . — Ber

and in all the coasts thereof,

and in all the parts round about it — Bas

and in all that region — RSV

and the surrounding district — Phi

from two years old and under, according to the time which he had diligently enquired of the wise men.

. . . which he had exactly learned . . . — ASV

. . . guided by the date which he had ascertained from the Astrologers — TCNT

. . . calculating by the time he had ascertained from the magicians — Mof

. . . for that was the time he had learned from the astrologers by his inquiries — Gspd

17. **Then was fulfilled that which was spoken by Jeremy the prophet, saying,**

. . . through Jeremiah the prophet . . . — ASV

Then the saying was fulfilled which had been uttered by the prophet Jeremiah — Mof

Then the word of Jeremiah the prophet came true — Bas

18. **In Rama was there a voice heard, lamentation, and weeping, and great mourning,**

A cry was heard in Ramah, Wailing and bitter lamentation — Wey

In Ramah there was a sound of weeping and great sorrow — Bas

. . . Wailing and loud laments — Rieu

Rachel weeping for her children,

It was Rachel bewailing her children — Wey

and would not be comforted, because they are not.

And she refused to be comforted, because they were no more — Wey

and inconsolable . . . — Mof

. . . because they could not be brought back — Lam

. . . because they were dead — Nor

19. **But when Herod was dead,**

But as soon as Herod was dead — Knox

behold, an angel of the Lord appeareth in a dream to Joseph in Egypt,

lo! a messenger of the Lord appeareth by dream . . . — Rhm

20. **Saying, Arise,**

and said, Wake up — Gspd

and take the young child and his mother,

and take unto thee the child and its mother — Rhm

take the boy and his mother — Lam

and go into the land of Israel:

and be journeying into the land of Israel — Rhm

and make the trip to the land of Israel — Wms

and return to the land of Israel — Knox

for they are dead which sought the young child's life.

for those who were seeking the child's life are dead — Wey

because they who were attempting to take the young child's life are dead — Bas

for the men who threatened the child's life are dead — NEB

21. **And he arose,**

Then he awoke — Gspd

and took the young child and his mother,

took unto him the child and its mother — Rhm

took the boy and his mother — Lam

and came into the land of Israel.

and journeyed towards the land of Israel — Phi

22. **But when he heard**

But because he heard — Amp

that Archelaus did reign in Judaea in the room of his father Herod,

that Archelaus was reigning over Judaea . . . — ASV

. . . instead of his father Herod — Rhm

that Archelaus had succeeded his father Herod as King of Judaea — TCNT

he was afraid to go thither:

he was afraid to return there — Knox

notwithstanding,

and— ASV

being warned of God in a dream,

being warned of God in a dream—ASV

being instructed by dream — Rhm

being divinely instructed in a dream — ABUV

because he was divinely warned in a dream — Wms

God having given him news of the danger in a dream — Bas

he turned aside into the parts of Galilee:

he withdrew . . . — ASV

he took refuge . . . — Gspd

he went into the part of the country called Galilee . . . — TCNT

he withdrew into the region of Galilee — ABUV

23. And he came and dwelt in a city called Nazareth:

and came and fixed his dwelling . . . — Rhm

And there he settled in the town of Nazareth — TCNT

where he came to live in a town called Nazareth — Knox

that it might be fulfilled which was spoken by the prophets,

. . . through the prophets — ASV

in fulfillment of these words in the Prophets — TCNT

so that the word of the prophets might come true — Bas

thus fulfilling the old prophecy — Phi

He shall be called a Nazarene.

Jesus was to be called a man from Nazareth — Beck

CHAPTER 3

1. In those days

About that time — TCNT

came John the Baptist,

cometh John the Baptist — ASV

came John the Immerser — Rhm

John the Baptist began his mission — Rieu

John the Baptizer appeared — Beck

preaching

proclaiming — Rhm

and kept preaching — Wms

in the wilderness of Judaea,

in the wasteland of Judaea — Bas

in the Judean desert — Ber

2. And saying, Repent ye:

his theme was . . . — NEB

. . . Let your hearts be turned from sin — Bas

. . . You must change your hearts—PHI

and called on people for a change of heart — Rieu

for the kingdom of heaven is at hand.

for the kingdom of the heavens hath drawn near — Rhm

for the Kingdom of heaven is now close at hand — Wey

the Reign of heaven is near — Mof

for the kingdom of Heaven is upon you! — NEB

3. For this is he that was spoken of

For this is the one referred to — NASB

by the prophet Esaias, saying,

through Isaiah the prophet . . . — ASV

in the Prophet Isaiah, where he says — TCNT

The voice of one crying in the wilderness, Prepare ye the way of the Lord,

A voice of one crying aloud! In the wilderness prepare ye the way of the Lord — Rhm

. . . In the desert prepare a road for the Lord — Wey

Hark! Someone is shouting in the desert . . . — Gspd

. . . Get the road ready for the Lord — Wms

. . . in the wasteland . . . — Bas

make his paths straight.

level the paths for him — Mof

clear a straight path for him — NEB

4. And the same John had his raiment of camel's hair,

Now John himself . . . — ASV

This man John . . . — Wey

John wore clothing made of hair cloth — Gspd

John's clothing was a rough coat of camel's hair — NEB

and a leathern girdle about his loins;

with a belt of leather round his waist
— TCNT
**and his meat was locusts and wild
honey.**
and his food . . . — ASV
and he lived on dried locusts and wild
honey — Gspd
. . . grasshoppers and wild honey —
Beck
5. **Then**
At that time — TCNT
went out to him
were going forth unto him — Rhm
began to go out to him — Mon
continued to go out to him — Wms
flocked to him — Phi
Jerusalem, and all Judaea,
. . . people from Jerusalem and from
all Judaea — Wey
and all the region round about Jordan,
as well as the whole district of the Jordan — TCNT
and from the whole of the Jordan valley — Wey
even the whole Jordan district — Wms
6. **And were baptized of him in Jordan,**
and were being immersed in the Jordan
river by him — Rhm
and got baptized by him in the Jordan
— Mof
And they were given baptism by him
. . . — Bas
confessing their sins.
openly confessing their sins — Rhm
in acknowledgment of their sins—Gspd
as one by one they continued to confess
their sins — Wms
saying openly that they had done
wrong — Bas
7. **But when he saw many of the Pharisees and Sadducees**
When, however, John saw . . . — TCNT
come to his baptism,
coming unto his immersion — Rhm
coming to receive his baptism — TCNT
coming to attend his baptism — Rieu
he said unto them,
O generation of vipers,
Ye offspring of vipers — ASV
Broods of vipers! — Rhm
You brood of snakes! — Gspd
you serpent's brood — Phi
**who hath warned you to flee from the
wrath to come?**
Who hath prompted you to seek refuge
from the coming judgment — TCNT

Who was it that taught you . . . to flee
from the vengeance that draws near
— Knox
. . . from the wrath that is on its way
— Rieu
. . . from the wrath which is at hand —
Alf
. . . from the coming retribution—NEB
who warned you to run away from the
punishment waiting for you — Beck
8. **Bring forth therefore fruits meet for
repentance:**
Let your life, then, prove your repentance — TCNT
Then produce fruit that will be consistent with your professed repentance
— Gspd
Go and do something to show that your
hearts are really changed — Phi
Bring forth fruit proving you are penitent! — Nor
9. **And think not to say within yourselves,**
. . . to be saying within yourselves —
Rhm
instead of presuming to say to yourselves — Mof
and do not fancy that you can say to
yourselves — Ber
And do not cherish the thought — Rieu
And don't think that you can get by
with saying — Nor
We have Abraham to our father:
As our father we have Abraham —
Rhm
Abraham is our ancestor — TCNT
**for I say unto you, that God is able of
these stones to raise up children unto
Abraham.**
. . . that out of these very stones God is
able to raise descendants for Abra-
ham! — TCNT
. . . God can produce descendants for
Abraham right out of these stones —
Gspd
10. **And now also the ax is laid unto the
root of the trees:**
And even now the axe lieth at the root
of the trees — ASV
Behold, the axe is already placed . . .
— Lam
Yes, even now the axe is being applied
. . . — Nor
The axe is now ready to strike . . . —
Beck
therefore
so that — Wey

every tree which bringeth not forth good fruit
... fails to bear ... — TCNT
is hewn down, and cast into the fire.
is to be hewn down and into fire to be cast — Rhm
will be cut down and thrown into the fire — TCNT

11. **I indeed baptize you with water**
I indeed am immersing you in water — Rhm
As for me, I am baptizing you with water — Knox
unto repentance:
to teach repentance — TCNT
for repentance — Wey
in token of your repentance — Gspd
to picture your repentance — Wms
into repentance — Rieu
for a change of heart — Beck
because of repentance — Amp
as a sign of your repentance — Phi
but he that cometh after me
but He who is Coming after me—TCNT
is mightier than I,
is more powerful than I — TCNT
is greater than I — Rieu
whose shoes I am not worthy to bear:
and I am not fit even to remove his sandals — Mof
and I am not fit to carry his shoes — Gspd
he shall baptize you with the Holy Ghost, and with fire:
... in the Holy Spirit and in fire — ASV
he will immerse you in Holy Spirit and fire — Rhm
He will baptize you with the fire of the Holy Spirit — Phi

12. **Whose fan is in his hand,**
His winnowing-fan is in his hand — TCNT
His winnowing fork is in his hand — Gspd
He holds his winnowing-fan ready — Knox
He comes all ready to separate the wheat from the chaff — Phi
and he will throughly purge his floor,
and he will thoroughly cleanse his threshing-floor — ASV
he will make clean his grain — Bas
to sweep his threshing-floor clean — Knox
and gather his wheat into the garner;

and will gather his wheat into the granary — Rhm
and store his grain in the barn — TCNT
but he will burn up the chaff
but the straw he will burn — Mof
with unquenchable fire.
with inextinguishable fire — TCNT
with fire that never can be put out — Wms

13. **Then cometh Jesus from Galilee**
Just at that time ... — Wey
Then Jesus came on the scene from Galilee — Mof
to Jordan unto John, to be baptized of him.
... to be immersed by him — Rhm
to be baptized by John at the Jordan — Mof

14. **But John forbad him,**
But John tried to prevent him — TCNT
John protested — Wey
But John would have kept him back — Bas
But John sought to dissuade him — Rieu
But John protested strenuously ... — Amp
saying,
by saying — Wms
I have need to be baptized of thee,
I have need by thee to be immersed — Rhm
It is I, he said, that ought to be baptized by thee — Knox
I need you to baptize me — Phi
and comest thou to me?
why then do you come to me — TCNT
and dost thou come to me instead — Knox

15. **And Jesus answering said unto him, Suffer it to be so now:**
Let it be so for the present — TCNT
Let it be so on this occasion — Wey
Let Me have My way now — Beck
for thus it becometh us to fulfil all righteousness.
since it is fitting for us thus to satisfy every claim of religion — TCNT
for so we ought to fulfil every religious duty — Wey
this is how we should fulfil all our duty to God — Mof
for it is right for us to do everything that God requires — Gspd
for this is the fitting way for both of us to do our full duty to God — Wms

8

it is well that we should thus fulfil all due observance — Knox

for so it behooves us to fulfil all divine requirements — Ber

It is right for us to meet all the Law's demands — Phi

we do well to conform in this way with all that God requires — NEB

Then he suffered him.

Upon this, John consented — TCNT

Then John gave in to him — Mof

Then John agreed to his baptism — Phi

16. **And Jesus, when he was baptized,**

. . . having been immersed — Rhm

went up straightway out of the water:

he went right up out of the water — Gspd

and just as he came up from the water — TCNT

and, lo,

At that moment — Wey

and look! — Wms

the heavens were opened unto him,

the heavens opened — Wms

the heavens were laid open — Rieu

and he saw the Spirit of God descending like a dove,

. . . as a dove — ASV

and lighting upon him:

and coming upon him — Alf

and resting upon him — Knox

17. **And lo**

And with that — Knox

a voice from heaven, saying,

. . . out of the heavens, saying — ASV

This is my beloved Son, in whom I am well pleased.

This is my dearly-loved Son . . . — Bas

This is My Son, the Beloved in whom I delight — Ber

. . . in whom I rejoice — Rieu

. . . on whom my favour rests — NEB

. . . with whom I am pleased — Lam

This is My Son, whom I love and delight in — Beck

CHAPTER 4

1. **Then was Jesus led up of the spirit**

Jesus was guided by the Spirit — Gspd

into the wilderness

into the desert — Wey

into the waste land — Bas

to be tempted of the devil.

. . . by the adversary — Rhm

to be tested by the Evil One — Bas

2. **And when he had fasted forty days and forty nights,**

He didn't eat anything for forty days — Beck

he was afterward an hungred.

and afterwards he was famished — Gspd

He finally grew hungry — Ber

and so was starving — Rieu

3. **And when the tempter came to him, he said,**

And coming near, the tempter said to him — Rhm

If thou be the Son of God,

If you are God's Son — TCNT

If you really are the Son of God — Phi

command that these stones be made bread.

speak! that these stones may become loaves — Rhm

tell these stones to become loaves of bread — TCNT

4. **But he answered and said, It is written,**

Jesus replied by citing the Scripture — Rieu

Man shall not live by bread alone,

It is not on bread alone that man is to live — TCNT

Not on bread alone can man live — Wms

Bread is not man's only need — Bas

but by every word that proceedeth out of the mouth of God.

But on every declaration coming forth through the mouth of God — Rhm

there is life for him in all the words which proceed from the mouth of God — Knox

he lives on every word that God utters — NEB

5. **Then the devil taketh him up into the holy city,**

Then the adversary taketh him with him unto the holy city — Rhm

and setteth him on a pinnacle of the temple,

and, placing him on the parapet of the temple — TCNT

and made him stand on the summit of the Temple — Gspd

and had Him stand on the tip-top turret of the temple — Wms

... the highest point ... — Bas
... the cornice ... — Rieu
... the edge ... — Beck

6. And saith unto him,
suggesting to Him — Ber
If thou be the Son of God,
If thou art God's Son — Rhm
cast thyself down:
throw yourself down — Wey
jump down — Nor
for it is written,
for Scripture says — TCNT
He shall give his angels charge concerning thee:
To his messengers will he give charge
  ... — Rhm
He will give his angels commands about
  thee — TCNT
He has commanded His angels to look
  after You — Nor
**and in their hands they shall bear thee
  up,**
And they will lift you up with their
  hands — Gspd
In their hands they will keep you up —
  Bas
and they will support you in their arms
  — NEB
**lest at any time thou dash thy foot
  against a stone.**
So that you may never strike your foot
  against a stone! — Gspd
so that even your foot may not strike
  a stone — Lam
lest thou shouldst chance to trip on a
  stone — Knox
for fear you should strike your foot
  against a stone — NEB

7. Jesus said unto him, It is written again,
  ... But it is further written — Knox
Yes, retorted Jesus, and the scripture
  also says — Phi
**Thou shalt not tempt the Lord thy
  God.**
Thou shalt not put to the test ... —
  Rhm

8. Again,
The third time — TCNT
Once more — Mof
the devil taketh him
the adversary taketh him with him —
  Rhm
the devil conveyed him — Mof
up into an exceeding high mountain,
to the top of ... — Knox

and sheweth him
and pointed out to him — Rhm
**all the kingdoms of the world, and the
  glory of them;**
all the realms of the world and their
  grandeur — Mof
  ... and their splendour — TCNT
  ... and their magnificence — Phi

9. And saith unto him,
and he said unto him — ASV
suggesting to Him — Ber
All these things will I give thee,
Every bit of this I will give to you —
  Wms
if thou wilt fall down and worship me.
if you will kneel down and do me
  homage — Wey
if you will go down on your face and
  give me worship — Bas
if you will only fall down and do me
  homage — NEB

**10. Then saith Jesus unto him, Get thee
  hence, Satan:**
  ... Begone, Satan! — TCNT
  ... Go! Away with you, Satan! — Nor
  ... Go away, devil! — Beck
for it is written,
**Thou shalt worship the Lord thy
  God,**
Thou shalt do homage to the Lord thy
  God — TCNT
You must worship the Lord your God
  — Mof
and him only shalt thou serve.
And to him only render divine service
  — Rhm

11. Then the devil leaveth him,
  ... the adversary ... — Rhm
Then the Devil left him alone — TCNT
At this the devil left him — Mof
and, behold, angels came
and lo! messengers came near — Rhm
and ministered unto him.
and began ministering unto him—Rhm
and waited on him — Gspd
and continued to wait upon him —
  Wms

12. Now when Jesus had heard
Now when he heard — ASV
that John was cast into prison,
  ... was delivered up — ASV
  ... had been taken into custody—NASB
he departed into Galilee;
he withdrew into Galilee — ASV
He set out for Galilee — Wms
he went back to Galilee — Phi

13. **And leaving Nazareth,**
But He left Nazareth — Wms
he came and dwelt
and made His home — Wms
in Capernaum, which is upon the sea coast,
. . . by the sea — ASV
in Capernaum-by-the-Lake — Mon
. . . on the Sea of Galilee — NEB
in the borders of Zabulon and Nephthalim:
on the frontiers of . . . — Wey
within the borders of Zebulun and Naphtali — TCNT
in the Zebulun-Naphtali territory—Phi

14. **That it might be fulfilled which was spoken by Esaias the prophet,**
. . . through Isaiah the prophet — ASV
So that the word of the prophet Isaiah might come true — Bas
In this way Isaiah's prophecy came true — Phi
And so what the prophet Isaiah said was to come true — Beck
saying,

15. **The land of Zabulon, and the land of Nephthalim,**
Land of Zebulon and land of Naphtali — Rhm
by the way of the sea, beyond Jordan,
Toward the sea, beyond the Jordan — — ASV
lying to the sea, across the Jordan — Mof
Along the road to the sea . . . — Gspd
over by the sea . . . — Rieu
. . . this side of the Jordan — Nor
Galilee of the Gentiles;
Galilee of the nations — Rhm
Galilee of the heathen! — Gspd

16. **The people which sat in darkness**
. . . that were living in darkness — Gspd
saw great light;
have seen a brilliant light — Wey
will see a great light — Beck
and to them which sat in the region and shadow of death
And, for those who were dwelling in the shadow-land of Death — TCNT
for men abiding in a land where death overshadowed them — Knox
. . . in the shadowy region of death — Rieu
. . . in the land and in the shadow of death — Nor

light is sprung up.
To them did light spring up — ASV
Light rose on them — Rhm
a light will rise — Beck

17. **From that time**
From that time onwards — Knox
Jesus began to preach,
. . . began to proclaim — TCNT
. . . continued to preach — Wms
and to say, Repent:
. . . Let your hearts be turned from sin — Bas
. . . You must change your hearts — Phi
for the kingdom of heaven is at hand.
for the kingdom of the heavens hath drawn near — Rhm
. . . is close at hand — Wey
. . . has arrived — Phi
. . . is upon you — NEB
the Reign of heaven is near — Mof

18. **And Jesus, walking by the sea of Galilee,**
. . . walking round beside the sea of Galilee — Rhm
saw two brethren, Simon called Peter,
. . . Simon, also known as Peter — TCNT
. . . Simon, who was afterward called Peter — Gspd
. . . Simon who was surnamed Peter — Wms
and Andrew his brother,
casting a net into the sea:
casting a large fishing-net into the sea — Rhm
throwing a drag-net into the lake — Wey
about to cast a net into the sea — Nor
for they were fishers.

19. **And he saith unto them,**
so he said to them — Mof
Follow me,
Come and follow me — TCNT
Come ye after me — Alf
and I will make you fishers of men.
. . . set you to fish for men — TCNT
. . . make you into fishers of men — Knox
. . . teach you to catch men — Phi

20. **And they straightway left their nets,**
And they dropped their nets at once — Mof
And at once they abandoned their nets — Ber
and followed him.

11

21. And going on from thence,
Going further on — TCNT
he saw other two brethren,
. . . two other men who were also
brothers — TCNT
. . . two other brothers — RSV
**James the son of Zebedee, and John
his brother, in a ship with Zebedee
their father,**
. . . in the boat beside their father Zebe-
daeus — Mof
mending their nets;
putting in order their nets — Rhm
repairing their nets — Lam
and he called them.

22. And they immediately left the ship
And they, too, at once left their boat —
Nor
and their father, and followed him.

23. And Jesus went about all Galilee,
Then he made a tour through the whole
of Galilee — Mof
Jesus now moved about through the
whole of Galilee — Phi
teaching in their synagogues,
as He continued teaching in their synagogues — Wms
**and preaching the gospel of the king-
dom,**
and proclaiming the glad-message of
the kingdom — Rhm
proclaiming the Good News of the
Kingdom — TCNT
preaching the gospel of the Reign —
Mof
announcing the good news of the kingdom — Ber
. . . about the kingdom — Phi
**and healing all manner of sickness and
all manner of disease among the
people.**
and curing every kind of disease and
every kind of sickness . . . — TCNT
and curing any disease or sickness . . .
— Gspd

**24. And his fame went throughout all
Syria:**

And the report of him went forth into
all Syria — ASV
Word went all through Syria about him
— Gspd
so that his fame spread . . . — Knox
. . . all through the surrounding country — Mof
**and they brought unto him all sick peo-
ple that were taken with divers diseases and torments,**
. . . all who were sick with various diseases, especially those who were suffering with torturing diseases — Wms
. . . seized with many kinds of diseases
and torments — ABUV
. . . sufferers from every kind of illness,
racked with pain — NEB
**and those which were possessed with
devils,**
possessed with demons — ASV
those having evil spirits — Bas
including the devil-possessed — Phi
those under the power of demons —
Amp
and those which were lunatick,
and epileptic — ASV
and those who were out of their minds
— Bas
the insane — Phi
and those that had the palsy:
and paralyzed — Rhm
and those who had no power of moving
— Bas
and he healed them.
he healed them all — Mof

**25. And there followed him great multi-
tudes of people from Galilee,**
Great crowds followed him from Galilee — Mon
and from Decapolis,
from the Ten Towns — Mon
the district of the Ten Towns — TCNT
**and from Jerusalem, and from Judaea,
and from beyond Jordan.**
. . . and from beyond the river Jordan
— Phi
. . . and from Transjordan — NEB
. . . and the other side of the Jordan —
Beck

CHAPTER 5

1. And seeing the multitudes,
On seeing the crowds of people—TCNT
When he saw the crowds — Mon
he went up into a mountain:

Jesus went up the hill — TCNT
and when he was set,
and when he had sat down — ASV
his disciples came unto him:

2. And he opened his mouth, and taught them, saying,
... he began teaching them ... — Rhm
He proceeded to teach them, and said — Wey
he opened his lips to teach them ... — Gspd
Then he began his teaching by saying to them — Phi

3. Blessed are the poor in spirit:
Happy the destitute in spirit — Rhm
Blessed — happy, to be envied, and spiritually prosperous [that is, with life-joy and satisfaction in God's favor and salvation, regardless of their outward conditions] — are the poor in spirit (the humble; rating themselves insignificant) — Amp
... those who feel their spiritual need — Gspd
... they who sense spiritual poverty — Ber
How happy are the humble-minded — Phi
How blest are those who know that they are poor — NEB
for theirs is the kingdom of heaven.
... the kingdom of the heavens—Rhm
the Realm of heaven is theirs — Mof

4. Blessed are they that mourn:
Happy are those who are sad — Bas
How happy are those who know what sorrow means — Phi
How blest are the sorrowful — NEB
Blessed and enviably happy, [with a happiness produced by experience of God's favor and especially conditioned by the revelation of His matchless grace] are those who mourn — Amp
for they shall be comforted.
they will be consoled — Mof
for they will be given courage and comfort — Phi

5. Blessed are the meek: for they shall inherit the earth.
... the gentle ... — TCNT
... the patient ... — Knox
... the humble-minded, for they will possess the land! — Gspd
How blest are those of a gentle spirit ... — NEB
Blessed — happy, blithesome, joyous, spiritually prosperous [that is, with life-joy and satisfaction in God's favor and salvation, regardless of their outward conditions] — are the meek (the mild, patient, long-suffering), for they shall inherit the earth — Amp
... for the earth will be their heritage — Bas
Happy are those who claim nothing, for the whole earth will belong to them — Phi

6. Blessed are they which do hunger and thirst after righteousness:
... for goodness — Mof
... for uprightness — Gspd
... for being and doing right — Wms
... for justice — Lam
... for holiness — Knox
... to see right prevail — NEB
Happy are those whose heart's desire is for righteousness — Bas
Blessed and fortunate and happy and spiritually prosperous [that is, in that state in which the born-again child of God enjoys His favor and salvation] are those who hunger and thirst for righteousness (uprightness and right standing with God) — Amp
for they shall be filled.
... completely satisfied — Wey
for they shall be completely satisfied — Amp

7. Blessed are the merciful:
... the compassionate — Wey
... those who show mercy — Wms
Blessed — happy, to be envied, and spiritually prosperous [that is, with life-joy and satisfaction in God's favor and salvation, regardless of their outward conditions] — are the merciful — Amp
for they shall obtain mercy.
... receive compassion — Wey
... be shown mercy! — Gspd

8. Blessed are the pure in heart: for they shall see God.
... the clean in heart ... — Bas
Happy are the utterly sincere ... — Phi
Blessed — happy, enviably fortunate, and spiritually prosperous [that is, possessing the happiness produced by experience of God's favor and especially conditioned by the revelation of His grace, regardless of their outward conditions] are the pure in heart, for they shall see God — Amp

9. Blessed are the peacemakers:
... those who make peace — Phi
Blessed—enjoying enviable happiness, spiritually prosperous [that is, with life-joy and satisfaction in God's favor and salvation, regardless of their outward conditions] — are the makers and maintainers of peace — Amp

for they shall be called the children of God.
... acknowledged as sons of God — Wey
for they shall be called the sons of God — Amp
they will be ranked sons of God—Mof
God shall call them his sons — NEB

10. Blessed are they which are persecuted
Blessed and happy and enviably fortunate and spiritually prosperous [that is, in the state in which one enjoys and finds satisfaction in God's favor and salvation, regardless of his outward conditions], are those who are persecuted — Amp
... those who have endured persecution — Gspd

for righteousness' sake:
in the cause of righteousness — TCNT
for the sake of goodness — Mof
for their uprightness — Gspd
for being and doing right — Wms
for the sake of justice — Lam
for righteousness' sake (for being and doing right) — Amp

for theirs is the kingdom of heaven.
... the kingdom of the heavens — Rhm
for to them belongs the Kingdom of heaven — Wey
the Realm of heaven is theirs — Mof

11. Blessed are ye, when men shall revile you,
Blessed — happy, to be envied, and spiritually prosperous [that is, with life-joy and satisfaction in God's favor and salvation, regardless of your outward conditions] — are you when people revile you — Amp
... whensoever they may reproach you — Rhm
... taunt you — TCNT
... denounce you — Mof
... abuse you — Gspd
... give you a bad name — Bas

... when the time comes for people to revile you — Rieu
and persecute you,
and are cruel to you — Bas
and shall say all manner of evil against you falsely,
and say all kinds of evil things against you falsely — Amp
and have said every cruel thing about you falsely — Wey
and say all kinds of slanderous things against you — Phi
and keep on telling lies about you — Nor
for my sake.
on My account — Amp

12. Rejoice, and be exceeding glad:
Rejoice and exult — Rhm
Be joyful and triumphant — Wey
Keep on rejoicing and leaping for ecstacy — Wms
Be glad and light-hearted — Knox
Be glad then, yes, be tremendously glad — Phi
Accept it with gladness and exultation — NEB
for great is your reward in heaven:
... in the heavens — Rhm
for you will be richly rewarded in heaven — Gspd
since your reward is great in heaven — Rieu
for so persecuted they the prophets which were before you.
They persecuted the prophets before your time in exactly the same way — Phi

13. Ye are the salt of the earth:
It is you who are the Salt of the earth — TCNT
but if the salt have lost his savour,
... become tasteless — Rhm
... should lose its strength — TCNT
... become insipid — Mof
wherewith shall it be salted?
what will you use to restore its saltness — TCNT
what can make it salt again — Mof
what is there left to give taste to it — Knox
it is thenceforth good for nothing,
it is good for nothing any more—Rhm
but to be cast out,
save being cast out — Rhm
but is thrown away — TCNT

14

and to be trodden under foot of men.
to be trampled on by men — Rhm
and trodden on by the passers by—Wey
and stamped under foot — Phi
14. **Ye are the light of the world.**
It is you who are the Light of the world
  — TCNT
A city that is set on an hill cannot be hid.
A town that stands on a hill cannot be hidden — TCNT
a town cannot be hid if built on a hilltop — Wey
15. **Neither do men light a candle,**
... lamp ... — NEB
and put it under a bushel,
... under the corn-measure — TCNT
... under a bowl — Mof
... under a peck-measure — Gspd
... under the meal-tub — NEB
but on a candlestick;
but upon the lampstand — Rhm
... on its stand — Gspd
and it giveth light unto all that are in the house.
and it shineth ... — ASV
16. **Let your light so shine before men,**
In like manner ... — Rhm
Even so let your light shine ... — ASV
... before the eyes of your fellow-men — TCNT
Let your light shine like that in the sight of men — Phi
And you, like the lamp, must shed light among your fellows — NEB
that they may see your good works,
... the good you do — Mof
... the beauty of your life — Rieu
and glorify your Father which is in heaven.
... praise your Father who is in heaven — TCNT
... who is in the heavens — Rhm
17. **Think not**
Do not for a moment suppose — Wey
Never imagine — Mof
that I am come to destroy the law,
that I came to pull down the law — Rhm
... do away with the Law — TCNT
... annul the Law — Wey
or the prophets:
I am not come to destroy,
... to pull down — Rhm
... to do away with them — TCNT
I have not come to annul them — Wey

but to fulfil.
but to give them their completion — Wey
but to enforce them — Gspd
but to bring them to perfection—Knox
18. **For verily I say unto you,**
In solemn truth ... — Mon
Believe me — Knox
Indeed, I assure you — Phi
And I tell you for a fact — Nor
With all the earnestness I have I say — Tay
Till heaven and earth pass,
... pass away — ASV
... disappear — TCNT
as long as heaven and earth endure — Gspd
one jot or one tittle
not even the smallest letter, nor one stroke of a letter — TCNT
not one dotting of an *i* or crossing of a *t* — Gspd
not an iota, not a dot — RSV
not an *i* or the dot of an *i* — Beck
shall in no wise pass from the law,
... pass away from the law — Rhm
will be dropped from the Law — Gspd
till all be fulfilled.
until all has taken place — Wey
until it is all in force — Mof
... accomplished — Knox
until its purpose is complete — Phi
until all that must happen has happened — NEB
19. **Whosoever therefore shall break one of these least commandments,**
... relax ... — Rhm
Whoever therefore tries to weaken even one of these smallest commandments — Lam
Whoever, then, sets aside ... — Knox
... disregards the least significant of these commands — Ber
... breaks one of these commandments, even the least of them—TCNT
... a single one of these commands, were it even one of the least — Mof
Therefore the man who abolishes one of these little rules — Rieu
and shall teach men so,
he shall be called the least
will be the least-esteemed — TCNT
he shall be regarded as small — Lam
shall count for little — Rieu
he will have the lowest place — NEB

in the kingdom of heaven:
. . . of the heavens — Rhm
in the Realm of heaven — Mof
but whosoever shall do and teach them,
but whoever keeps them, and teaches
others to do so — TCNT
but whoever practices them . . . — Wey
the same shall be called great
will be esteemed great — TCNT
will be acknowledged as great — Wey
. . . ranked great — Mof
shall count for much — Rieu
in the kingdom of heaven.
. . . of the heavens — Rhm
in the Realm of heaven — Mof

20. **For I say unto you, That except your
righteousness shall exceed the righteousness of the scribes and Pharisees,**
For I assure you that unless your righteousness greatly surpasses . . . —
Wey
. . . unless your goodness . . . — Mof
. . . your justice . . . — Knox
. . . unless your uprightness is far superior to that of the scribes and
Pharisees — Gspd
. . . unless your religion is above that
of the Teachers of the Law, and
Pharisees — TCNT
. . . unless you show yourselves far better men than the Pharisees and the
doctors of the law — NEB
ye shall in no case enter into
you will certainly not find entrance —
Wey
you will never even enter — Gspd
the kingdom of heaven.
. . . of the heavens — Rhm
the Realm of heaven — Mof

21. **Ye have heard that it was said by them
of old time,**
. . . to our ancestors — TCNT
. . . to the ancients — Wey
Thou shalt not kill;
. . . commit murder — Rhm
and whosoever shall kill
. . . commit murder — Rhm
shall be in danger of the judgment:
shall be liable to answer for it to the
Court — TCNT
shall be answerable to the magistrate —
Wey
shall come up for sentence — Mof
he must answer for it before the court
of justice — Knox
shall be liable so that he cannot escape

the punishment imposed by the court
— Amp

22. **But I say unto you,**
I go further and I say to you — Rieu
**That whosoever is angry with his
brother without a cause**
that everyone who is angry with his
brother — ASV
Everyone who harbors malice . . . —
Wms
. . . continues to be angry . . . — Amp
Anyone who nurses anger against his
brother — NEB
shall be in danger of the judgment:
. . . answerable to the magistrate —
Wey
liable to condemnation by the court —
Mon
must stand trial — Phi
**and whosoever shall say to his brother,
Raca,**
. . . worthless one! — Rhm
. . . Raca (which means, I spit on you)
— Lam
. . . simpleton — Ber
. . . empty-head — Beck
and whoever pours contempt upon his
brother — TCNT
whoever maligns his brother — Mof
shall be in danger of the council:
. . . liable to the high council — Rhm
. . . answerable to the Sanhedrin—Wey
but whosoever shall say, Thou fool,
. . . Rebel! — Rhm
. . . You cursed fool! — Gspd
and anyone who looks down on his
brother as a lost soul — Phi
while whoever calls down curses upon
him — TCNT
shall be in danger of hell fire.
. . . liable unto the fiery gehenna —
Rhm
shall go to the fire of Gehenna — Mof
will have to answer for it in the fiery
pit! — Gspd
is himself heading straight for the fire
of destruction — Phi
is liable to find himself condemned to
hell — Rieu
shall be guilty enough to go into the
hell of fire — NASB

23. **Therefore if thou bring thy gift to the
altar,**
If, when you are about to offer your
gift at the altar — Nor

. . . art offering thy gift at the altar —
ASV
. . . in the very act of presenting your
gift at the altar — Wms
and there rememberest
if even there you remember — TCNT
you suddenly remember — NEB
**that thy brother hath ought against
thee;**
. . . has some grievance against you —
TCNT
. . . some ground of complaint against
thee — Knox
24. **Leave there thy gift before the altar,**
stop! Leave your gift right there before
the altar — Nor
and go thy way;
first be reconciled to thy brother,
first make peace with your brother —
Nor
make friends with your brother first —
Wey
first come to an understanding with
your brother — Ber
and then come and offer thy gift.
. . . be offering thy gift — Rhm
after which you may come back and
present your gift — Nor
25. **Agree with thine adversary quickly,**
Be ready to make friends with your
opponent — TCNT
Come to terms without delay . . . —
Wey
Try to get reconciled with your accuser
promptly — Lam
If any man has a claim against thee,
come to terms there and then —
Knox
If someone sues you, come to terms
with him promptly — NEB
whiles thou art in the way with him;
even when you meet him on your way
to court — TCNT
while you have the chance — Phi
**lest at any time the adversary deliver
thee to the judge,**
for fear that he should hand you over
. . . — TCNT
or he may hand you over . . . — Gspd
to prevent your opponent from handing you over to the judge — Mon
and the judge deliver thee to the officer,
. . . to the jailer — Mof
and thou be cast into prison.
26. **Verily I say unto thee,**
I tell you truly — Mon

Believe me — Knox
**Thou shalt by no means come out
thence,**
In nowise mayest thou come out from
thence — Rhm
You would certainly not get out from
there — Mon
thou shalt not be set at liberty — Knox
you will never get out — RSV
**till thou hast paid the uttermost farth-
ing.**
. . . very last farthing — Wey
. . . last half penny of your debt — Mof
. . . the last cent — Mon
. . . last fraction of a penny — Amp
27. **Ye have heard that it was said by them
of old time,**
. . . how it used to be said — Mof
You have heard the commandment —
Rieu
Thou shalt not commit adultery:
You may not have connection with another man's wife — Bas
Do not break the marriage vow! — Ber
28. **But I say unto you,**
I, however, say to you — TCNT
That whosoever looketh on a woman
that he who casts his eyes on a woman
— Knox
to lust after her
with an impure intention — TCNT
and cherishes lustful thoughts — Wey
so as to have an evil desire for her —
Wms
lustfully — Phi
**hath committed adultery with her al-
ready in his heart.**
has in his heart already broken the
marriage vow — Ber
29. **And if thy right eye offend thee,**
. . . is causing thee to stumble — Rhm
. . . is a snare to you — TCNT
. . . is to cause your fall — Wey
. . . is a hindrance to you — Mof
. . . entices you to sin — Mon
. . . is the occasion of thy falling into
sin — Knox
. . . leads you astray — Phi
pluck it out, and cast it from thee:
tear it out and away with it — Wey
**for it is profitable for thee that one of
thy members should perish,**
it is better for you that one member
should be destroyed — Wey
for it is better to have one part of your
body suffer loss — Wms

and not that thy whole body should be cast into hell.
and not to have the whole of it thrown into Hell — TCNT
... into gehenna ... — Rhm
... onto the rubbish heap — Phi

30. **And if thy right hand offend thee,**
... is causing thee to stumble — Rhm
... is a snare to you — TCNT
... is to cause your fall — Wey
... is a hindrance to you — Mof
... entices you to sin — Mon
if your right hand is your undoing — NEB
cut it off, and cast it from thee;
cut it off and away with it — Wey
cut it off and fling it away — NEB
for it is profitable for thee that one of thy members should perish,
it is better for you that one member should be destroyed — Wey
better to lose one of thy limbs — Knox
and not that thy whole body should be cast into hell.
and not to have the whole of it go down to Hell — TCNT
rather than that your whole body should go into Gehenna — Wey
than have it all go down to the pit! — Gspd
... to the rubbish heap — Phi

31. **It hath been said,**
It was also said — ASV
It used to be said — Mof
They were told — NEB
Whosoever shall put away his wife,
If any man puts away his wife — Wey
let him give her a writing of divorcement:
... a notice of separation — TCNT
... a written notice of divorce — Wey
... a note of dismissal — NEB

32. **But I say unto you,**
I, however, say to you — TCNT
But what I tell you is this — NEB
That whosoever shall put away his wife,
that Everyone who divorceth his wife — Rhm
saving for the cause of fornication,
... unfaithfulness — Rhm
for any reason except unchastity—Mof
for any other cause but the loss of her virtue — Bas
for any reason other than adultery — Nor

except for being sexually unfaithful — Beck
causeth her to commit adultery:
maketh her an adulteress — ASV
leads to her committing adultery — TCNT
makes her a partner in adultery — Beck
and whosoever shall marry her that is divorced
... a divorced woman — Rhm
... a wife who is thus divorced — Wms
committeth adultery.
also commits adultery — Phi
is living in adultery — Beck

33. **Again, ye have heard that it hath been said**
Once again ... — Mof
by them of old time,
to our ancestors — TCNT
to the ancients — Wey
Thou shalt not forswear thyself,
... break an oath — TCNT
you shall not lie in your oaths — Lam
Thou shalt not perjure thyself — Knox
but shalt perform unto the Lord thine oaths:
but thou shalt keep thine oaths as a debt due to the Lord — TCNT
but you must fulfil your oaths to the Lord — Gspd
thou shalt perform what thou hast sworn in the sight of the Lord — Knox

34. **But I say unto you,**
I, however, say to you — TCNT
Swear not at all;
you should not bind yourselves by any oath at all — Knox
neither by heaven;
neither by the heaven — ASV
for it is God's throne:

35. **Nor by the earth; for it is his footstool:**
... the footstool under His feet — Wey
neither by Jerusalem; for it is the city of the great King.

36. **Neither shalt thou swear by thy head,**
You may not take an oath ... — Bas
... by thine own head — Rhm
because thou canst not make one hair white or black.
for you cannot make a single hair — white or black — Phi

37. **But let your communication be, Yea, yea; Nay, nay:**

Let your words be simply Yes or No —
TCNT
Let your word be Yes for Yes, and No
for No — Knox
for whatsoever is more than these
And what goeth beyond these — Rhm
cometh of evil.
is of the evil one — ASV
springs from evil — Mof
has a taint of evil — Phi

38. Ye have heard that it hath been said,
You have heard the saying — Mof
You have heard of the principle —
Rieu
**An eye for an eye, and a tooth for a
tooth:**

39. But I say unto you,
I, however, say to you — TCNT
That ye resist not evil:
Resist not him that is evil — ASV
you are not to resist an injury — Mof
don't resist the man who wants to harm
you — Phi
**but whosoever shall smite thee on thy
right cheek,**
slaps you on one cheek — Wms
turn to him the other also.

40. And if any man will sue thee at the law,
and, when anyone wants to go to law
with you — TCNT
and take away thy coat,
. . . your under-garment — Wey
. . . your shirt — Mof
. . . tunic — Rhm
let him have thy cloke also.
let him take your outer one also —
Wey
. . . overcoat — Phi

**41. And whosoever shall compel thee to
go a mile,**
. . . impress thee to go one mile —
ABUV
And if anyone compels you to convey
a burden one mile — Wey
whoever forces you to go one mile —
Mof
If a man in authority makes you go one
mile — NEB
go with him twain.
go two miles with him of thy own accord — Knox

42. Give to him that asketh thee,
give to the man who begs from you —
Mof
. . . keeps on begging you — Wms

**and from him that would borrow of
thee**
And him who is desiring from thee to
borrow — Rhm
turn not thou away.
do not refuse — RSV
do not turn your back — NEB

43. Ye have heard that it hath been said,
You have heard the saying — Mof
You have heard that it used to be said
— Phi
Thou shalt love thy neighbour,
Be kind to your friend — Lam
and hate thine enemy.
. . . him who is against you — Bas

44. But I say unto you,
I, however, say to you — TCNT
But what I tell you is this — NEB
**Love your enemies, bless them that
curse you, do good to them that hate
you, and pray for them which despitefully use you, and persecute
you;**
Love your enemies, and pray for them
that persecute you — ASV
. . . and pray for your persecutors —
Wey
. . . and make prayer for those who are
cruel to you — Bas

**45. That ye may be the children of your
Father which is in heaven:**
that ye may be sons of your Father
who is in heaven — ASV
. . . who is in the heavens — Rhm
so that you may show yourselves true
sons of your Father in heaven —
Gspd
only so can you be . . . — NEB
for he maketh his sun to rise
who causeth his sun to shine — Lam
for his sun gives light — Bas
on the evil and on the good,
on evil and good — Rhm
upon sinners as well as saints — Mon
on people whether they are bad or
good — Beck
**and sendeth rain on the just and on the
unjust.**
. . . on just and unjust — Rhm
. . . upon honest and dishonest men
alike! — Phi
. . . whether they do right or wrong
— Beck

46. For if ye love them which love you,
. . . only those who love you — TCNT
what reward have ye?

what reward will you have — TCNT
what reward have you earned — Wey
what reward can you expect — Gspd
do not even the publicans the same?
Even the tax-gatherers do that, do they
not — Mon

47. **And if ye salute your brethren only,**
 . . . show courtesy to . . . — TCNT
And if you are polite to your brothers
and no one else — Gspd
And if you exchange greetings only
with your own circle — Phi
what do ye more than others?
what more than common are ye doing
— Rhm
are you doing anything remarkable —
Wey
does that give you any special distinction — Nor
do not even the publicans so?
 . . . the nations . . . — Rhm

do not the very pagans do as much —
Mof
Even the Gentiles do that, do they not
— Mon
 . . . the people of the world . . . —
Beck

48. **Be ye therefore perfect,**
Ye therefore shall be perfect — ASV
Ye therefore shall become perfect —
Rhm
You, however, are to be perfect —
Wey
Be then complete in righteousness —
Bas
You must therefore be all goodness —
NEB
You must become spiritually mature —
Nor
**even as your Father which is in heaven
is perfect.**
as your heavenly Father is perfect —
ASV

CHAPTER 6

1. **Take heed that ye do not your alms
before men,**
 . . . exercise your virtues in public —
Rieu
 . . . make a show of your religion before men — NEB
Be careful not to do your good deeds
in the sight of men — Mon
to be seen of them:
to be gazed at by them — Rhm
in order to be noticed — Mof
to attract the attention of people —
Wms
**otherwise ye have no reward of your
Father which is in heaven.**
 . . . the heavens — Rhm
if you do, your Father who is in
Heaven has no reward for you —
TCNT
else you forfeit your reward . . . — Ber

2. **Therefore when thou doest thine alms,**
 . . . acts of charity — TCNT
When then you give money to the poor
— Bas
do not sound a trumpet before thee,
do not have a trumpet blown in front
of you — TCNT
never blow your own horn in public —
Wms
do not make a noise about it — Bas

as the hypocrites do in the synagogues
and in the streets,
as the hypocrites are in the habit of doing . . . on the street corners — Wms
like those play-actors in the synagogues . . . — Phi
that they may have glory of men.
that they may be praised by others —
TCNT
so as to win applause from men — Mof
who make sure that men admire them
— Phi
Verily I say unto you,
I solemnly tell you — Wey
Believe me — Knox
They have their reward.
they are getting back their reward —
Rhm
they have received in full their reward
— Wey
that is all the reward they will get —
Gspd

3. **But when thou doest alms,**
But whenever you, a follower of mine,
do a deed of charity — Wms
**let not thy left hand know what thy
right hand doeth:**
your own left hand must not know
what your right hand is doing —
Gspd

thou shalt not so much as let thy left hand know what thy right hand is doing — Knox

4. That thine alms may be in secret:
... your charity ... — TCNT
... your giving ... — Bas
so secret is thy almsgiving to be — Knox
and thy father which seeth in secret
and your Father, who sees what is in secret — TCNT
and your Father — He who sees in secret — Wey
... who knows all secrets — Phi
himself shall reward thee openly.
... shall recompense thee — ASV
... will give it back to thee — Rhm
... will render you your due — Rieu

5. And when thou prayest,
... ye pray — ASV
thou shalt not be as the hypocrites are:
ye shall not be ... — ASV
you are not to behave as hypocrites do — TCNT
... like the false-hearted men — Bas
... like the play-actors — Phi
for they love to pray standing in the synagogues
for they love to stand and pray in the synagogues — ASV
who take pleasure in getting up and saying their prayers in the Synagogues — Bas
and in the corners of the streets,
or at the corners of the wider streets — Wey
and in the corners of the squares — Gspd
and on the important street corners — Ber
that they may be seen of men.
... shine before men — Rhm
to attract the attention of people — Wms
Verily I say unto you,
I solemnly tell you — Wey
believe me — Knox
They have their reward.
they are getting back their reward — Rhm
they have received in full their reward — Wey
that is all the reward they will get! — Gspd

6. But thou, when thou prayest,
But, when one of you prays — TCNT

But whenever you, follower of mine, pray — Wms
enter into thy closet,
... thine inner chamber — ASV
... thy secret chamber — Alf
go into your own room — Wey
go into a room by yourself — NEB
and when thou hast shut thy door,
and fastening thy door — Rhm
pray to thy Father which is in secret;
... who dwells in secret — TCNT
... who is there in the secret place — NEB
... who is with you when you're alone — Beck
pray to your Father, the Invisible — Ber
pray to your Father privately — Phi
and thy Father which seeth in secret
and your Father — He who sees in secret — Wey
... who sees what is secret — TCNT
... who sees what is done in secret — Knox
... who sees all private things — Phi
shall reward thee openly.
shall recompense thee — ASV
will render you your due — Rieu
will repay you — NASB

7. But when ye pray,
And in praying — ASV
use not vain repetitions,
do not repeat the same words over and over again — TCNT
do not repeat empty phrases — Gspd
you must not keep on repeating set phrases — Wms
don't rattle off long prayers — Phi
do not go babbling on — NEB
as the heathen do:
as is done by the Gentiles — TCNT
for they think that they shall be heard for their much speaking.
who think that by using many words they will obtain a hearing — TCNT
for they suppose that they will be heard in accordance with the length of their prayers — Wms
... by their eloquence — Knox

8. Be not ye therefore like unto them:
Do not copy them — Rieu
for your Father knoweth what things ye have need of,
After all, God, who is your Father, knows your needs — Phi
before ye ask him.

before ever you ask Him — Wey

9. After this manner therefore pray ye:
Let this be how you pray — Mof
This then is how you should pray — Rieu
Our Father which art in heaven,
... the heavens — Rhm
Our Heavenly Father — Phi
Hallowed be thy name.
May thy name be held holy — TCNT
thy name be revered — Mof
may your name be honoured — Phi

10. Thy kingdom come.
thy Reign begin — Mof
Thy will be done
Accomplished be thy will — Rhm
in earth, as it is in heaven.
as in heaven, so on earth — ASV
on earth as well as in heaven! — Gspd

11. Give us this day our daily bread.
... the bread that we shall need—TCNT
... our needful bread — Alf
... our bread for the day — Wey
... our bread for the morrow — Mof
Give us bread for our needs from day to day — Lam
Give us the bread of life today — Rieu

12. And forgive us our debts, as we forgive our debtors.
... shortcomings . . . those who have failed in their duty towards us — Wey
... offenses . . . offenders . . . — Lam
... trespasses . . . them that trespass against us — Knox
Forgive us what we owe to you, as we have also forgiven those who owe anything to us — Phi
Forgive us the wrong we have done, As we have forgiven those who have wronged us — NEB

13. And lead us not into temptation,
And do not subject us to temptation — Gspd
And let us not be put to the test — Bas
but deliver us from evil:[2] **For thine is the kingdom, and the power, and the glory, for ever. Amen.**
but rescue us from the Evil one — Wey
... from error — Lam

14. For if ye forgive men their trespasses,
... your fellow men . . . — Knox
... the wrongs they have done — NEB
. . . others when they offend you — Gspd

your heavenly Father will also forgive you:
Your Father who is in the heavens will forgive even you — Rhm

15. But if ye forgive not men their trespasses,
. . . others when they offend you—Gspd
neither will your Father forgive your trespasses.
not even your Father will forgive your offences — TCNT
. . . the wrongs you have done — NEB

16. Moreover when ye fast, be not, as the hypocrites, of a sad countenance:
. . . of sullen countenance — Rhm
. . . do not put on gloomy looks . . . — TCNT·
. . . do not look dismal . . . — RSV
. . . don't look like those miserable play-actors — Phi
for they disfigure their faces,
for they darken their looks — Rhm
for they look woebegone — Mof
for they neglect their personal appearance — Gspd
For they deliberately disfigure their faces — Phi
that they may appear unto men to fast.
to let men see that they are fasting — Mof
trying to make it show that they are fasting — Nor
Verily I say unto you,
I solemnly say to you — Wms
believe me — Knox
They have their reward.
they are getting back their reward — Rhm
they have received in full their reward — Wey
that is all the reward they will.get — Gspd

17. But thou, when thou fastest,
But, when one of you fasts — TCNT
But whenever you, follower of mine, fast — Wms
But do thou, at thy times of fasting — Knox
anoint thine head, and wash thy face;
pour perfume on your hair . . . — Wey
brush your hair . . . — Phi

---

[2]Manuscript evidence for the doxology following the word "evil" is now recognized as not adequately supported by original manuscripts.

18. That thou appear not unto men to fast,
that it may not be apparent to men that you are fasting — Wey
so that your fast may be seen not of men — Mof
but unto thy Father which is in secret:
. . . who dwells in secret — TCNT
. . . who is in the secret place — NEB
. . . who is with you when you're alone — Beck
. . . your heavenly Father, the Invisible — Ber
let it be a secret between you and your Father — Phi
and thy Father, which seeth in secret,
. . . who sees what is secret — TCNT
. . . who sees what is done in secret — Knox
. . . who knows all secrets — Phi
shall reward thee openly.
shall recompense thee — ASV
will render you your due — Rieu
will repay you — NASB

19. Lay not up for yourselves treasures upon earth,
Store up no treasures for yourselves on earth — Mof
Stop storing up your riches on earth — Wms
Don't pile up treasures on earth — Phi
where moth and rust doth corrupt,
. . . corrode — Mof
where the moth and wear-and-tear destroy — Wey
where there is moth and rust to consume it — Knox
where it grows rusty and moth-eaten — NEB
where it may be turned to dust by worms and weather — Bas
and where thieves break through and steal:
. . . dig through . . . — Rhm
. . . come in by force . . . — Bas
. . . and steal them — Gspd

20. But lay up for yourselves treasures in heaven,
But keep on storing up your riches in heaven — Wms
But keep your treasure in Heaven — Phi
where neither moth nor rust doth corrupt,
. . . corrode — Mof
where neither the moth nor wear-and-tear destroys — Wey

where moths and rust cannot destroy them — Gspd
where it will not be turned to dust — Bas
where there is no moth or rust to consume it — Knox
and where thieves do not break through nor steal:
. . . dig not through . . . — Rhm
. . . cannot break in and steal them — Gspd

21. For where your treasure is, there will your heart be also.
. . . your wealth . . . — Wey
For where your treasure lies, your heart will lie there too — Mof
Where your treasure-house is, there your heart is too — Knox
For wherever your treasure is, you may be certain that your heart will be there too! — Phi

22. The light of the body is the eye:
The lamp of the body . . . — ASV
if therefore thine eye be single,
so, if your Eye is generous — Mof
. . . is unclouded — TCNT
thy whole body shall be full of light.
the whole of your body will be illumined — Mof
. . . lighted up — Wey

23. But if thine eye be evil,
. . . is diseased — TCNT
but if your Eye is selfish — Mof
But if you have poor eyesight — Nor
thy whole body shall be full of darkness.
. . . in the dark — Rhm
the whole of your body will be darkened — Mof
If therefore the light that is in thee be darkness,
And, if the inner light is darkness — TCNT
If then the very source of light in you is darkness — Wms
If all the light you have is darkness — Phi
If then the very light in you [your conscience] is darkened — Amp
how great is that darkness!
how intense must that darkness be — TCNT
how dark is the darkness — Alf
then — what darkness it is! — Mof
the darkness is doubly dark — NEB

24. No man can serve two masters:
No slave can belong to two masters —
Gspd
**for either he will hate the one, and
love the other; or else he will hold
to the one,**
. . . attach himself to one — TCNT
. . . stand by the one — Mof
. . . be loyal to the one — Beck
and despise the other.
and make light of the other — Gspd
Ye cannot serve God and mammon.
You cannot serve both God and Money
— TCNT
You must serve God or money; you
cannot serve both — Knox

25. Therefore I say unto you,
That is why I say to you — TCNT
**Take no thought for your life, what ye
shall eat, or what ye shall drink;**
Do not be anxious about your life here
— what you can get to eat or drink
— TCNT
Stop worrying about your life, as to
what you will have to eat or drink —
Wms
put away anxious thoughts about food
and drink to keep you alive — NEB
**nor yet for your body, what ye shall
put on.**
. . . wondering what you will have to
wear — Gspd
Is not the life more than meat,
surely life means more than food —
Mof
Is not life itself a greater gift than food
— Knox
Is not the life more important than its
nourishment — Ber
and the body than raiment?
surely the body means more than
clothes! — Mof

26. Behold the fowls of the air:
Observe intently . . . — Rhm
. . . the birds which fly in the air — Wey
Look at the wild birds — Wms
**for they sow not, neither do they reap,
nor gather into barns;**
that they sow not . . . — ASV
yet your heavenly Father feedeth them.
. . . keeps on feeding them — Wms
Are ye not much better than they?
Aren't you much more valuable to him
than they are — Phi
Are you not of greater consequence
than they — Rieu

**27. Which of you by taking thought can
add one cubit unto his stature?**
But which of you with all his worry can
add a single hour to his life — Gspd
. . . add one cubit to his span of life —
RSV
. . . prolong his life a single moment —
TCNT
. . . add a single foot to his height —
Wey
Can any of you, however much he worries, make himself an inch taller —
Phi
Can any of you by worrying add anything to your life — Beck

28. And why take ye thought for raiment?
And why are ye anxious concerning
raiment — ASV
And why should you trouble over
clothing — Mof
**Consider the lilies of the field, how
they grow;**
See how the wild flowers grow — Gspd
Look at the wild lilies and learn how
they grow — Wms
they toil not, neither do they spin:
They neither work nor weave — Phi

**29. And yet I say unto you, That even
Solomon in all his glory was not arrayed like one of these.**
. . . in all his splendour . . . — TCNT
. . . didn't dress like one of these —
Beck

**30. Wherefore, if God so clothe the grass
of the field,**
But if God so beautifully dresses the
wild grass — Gspd
**which to day is, and to morrow is cast
into the oven,**
which is green today but tomorrow is
dry and thrown into the fire — Nor
shall he not much more clothe you,
is he not much more likely to clothe
you — Phi
O ye of little faith?
O men of little faith — TCNT
faint believers — Ber
you 'little-faiths' — Phi
slow though you are to trust him —
Rieu
O men, how little you trust him! —
Mof

31. Therefore take no thought, saying,
Do not then ask anxiously — TCNT
So don't worry and don't keep saying
— Phi

What shall we eat? or, What shall we
drink? or, Wherewithal shall we be
clothed?
... how are we to be clothed — Mof
... What shall we wear — Mon

32. (For after all these things do the Gentiles seek:)
All these are the things for which the
nations are seeking — TCNT
... are eagerly seeking — Mon
(pagans make all that their aim in life)
— Mof
It is for the heathen to busy themselves
over such things — Knox
The people of the world run after all
these things — Beck
for your heavenly Father knoweth that
ye have need of all these things.
and surely your heavenly Father well
knows ... — Wms

33. But seek ye first the kingdom of God,
and his righteousness;
But seek ye first his kingdom, and his
righteousness — ASV
But continue to seek first ... — Mon
Set your heart on his kingdom ... —
Phi
... and the righteousness that he requires — TCNT
... and his approval — Knox
pursue the Kingdom and God's goodness first — Rieu
First be eager to have God as your
King ... — Beck
But you must make his kingdom and

uprightness before him, your greatest care — Gspd
and all these things shall be added unto
you.
and these things shall all be given you
in addition — Wey
and all that will be yours over and
above — Mof
and all these things will come to you as
a matter of course — Phi

34. Take therefore no thought for the morrow:
Be not therefore anxious for the morrow — ASV
So never be troubled about to-morrow
— Mof
Do not fret, then, over tomorrow —
Knox
for the morrow shall take thought for
the things of itself.
for the morrow will be anxious for itself — ASV
for to-morrow will bring its own anxieties — TCNT
to-morrow will take care of itself —
Mof
... can take care of itself — Phi
Sufficient unto the day is the evil thereof.
Every day has trouble enough of its
own — TCNT
Take the trouble of the day as it comes
— Bas
for to-day, to-day's troubles are enough
— Knox
One day's trouble is enough for one
day — Phi

CHAPTER 7

1. Judge not,
Pass no more judgments upon other
people — Gspd
Stop criticizing others — Wms
that ye be not judged.
so that you may not be criticized yourselves — Wms
or you yourselves will be judged —
Knox

2. For with what judgment ye judge, ye
shall be judged:
For you will be judged by the standard
you judge by — Gspd
For exactly as you criticize others, you
will be criticized — Wms

and with what measure ye mete, it
shall be measured to you again.
and with what yardstick you measure
you will be measured — Ber
and the measure you give will be the
measure you get — RSV

3. And why beholdest thou the mote that
is in thy brother's eye,
Why do you keep watching the tiny
speck in your brother's eye — Wms
And why do you look at the straw ...
— TCNT
... splinter ... — Wey
How is it that thou canst see the speck
of dust ... — Knox

25

**but considerest not the beam that is in
thine own eye?**
while you pay no attention at all to
the beam in yours — TCNT
and are not aware of the beam . . . —
Knox
but are not concerned about the stick
. . . — Nor
and fail to see the plank . . . — Mof
. . . timber . . . — Wey
4. **Or how wilt thou say to thy brother,**
How can you say . . . — Mof
By what right wilt thou say . . . —
Knox
**Let me pull out the mote out of thine
eye;**
Allow me to take the splinter out of
your eye — Wey
Just let me get that speck out of your
eye — Gspd
**and, behold, a beam is in thine own
eye?**
when all the time there is a beam in
your own — TCNT
. . . the beam . . . — ASV
. . . the plank . . . — Mof
5. **Thou hypocrite,**
You fraud! — Phi
**first cast out the beam out of thine own
eye;**
begin by removing the beam from your
own eye — Rieu
. . . plank . . . — Mof
. . . log . . . — RSV
and then shalt thou see clearly
and then you can see well enough —
Wms
**to cast out the mote out of thy brother's
eye.**
how to take out the straw . . . — TCNT
. . . splinter . . . — Wey
. . . speck . . . — Gspd
. . . grain of dust . . . — Bas
6. **Give not that which is holy unto the
dogs,**
You must never give the things that are
sacred to dogs — Wms
**neither cast ye your pearls before
swine,**
and you must never throw your pearls
before hogs — Wms
or put your jewels before pigs — Bas
do not feed your pearls to pigs — NEB
**lest they trample them under their feet,
and turn again and rend you.**
lest they should trample them under

their feet, and then turn and attack
you — TCNT
otherwise they will trample them under
their feet and then turn and mangle
you — Wey
. . . and tear you in pieces — Gspd
7. **Ask, and it shall be given you;**
Ask and the gift will be yours — Mof
Keep on asking . . . — Wms
. . . your prayer shall be granted —
TCNT
seek, and ye shall find;
keep on seeking . . . — Wms
**knock, and it shall be opened unto
you:**
keep on knocking . . . — Wms
. . . and the door shall be opened to
you — TCNT
8. **For every one that asketh receiveth;**
. . . who keeps on asking . . . — Wms
For it is always the one who asks who
receives — Gspd
The one who asks will always receive
— Phi
and he that seeketh findeth;
and the one who searches . . . — Gspd
. . . who keeps on seeking . . . — Wms
. . . will always find — Phi
**and to him that knocketh it shall be
opened.**
. . . keeps on knocking — Wms
9. **Or what man is there of you,**
What human father among you—Wms
whom if his son ask bread,
who, if his son shall ask him for a loaf
— ASV
when his son asks him for a loaf—TCNT
will he give him a stone?
will offer him a stone — Wey
10. **Or if he ask a fish,**
or if he shall ask for a fish — ASV
or when he asks for a fish — TCNT
will he give him a serpent?
will offer him a snake — Wey
11. **If ye then, being evil,**
. . . wicked though you are — TCNT
. . . imperfect as you are — Wey
. . . in spite of your being bad — Wms
. . . who are evil — RSV
**know how to give good gifts unto your
children,**
know enough to give your children
what is good — Gspd
are able to give good things . . . — Bas
. . . what is good for them — Knox

how much more shall your Father
which is in heaven give good things
... who is in the heavens ... — Rhm
... give what is good — TCNT
... wholesome gifts — Knox
to them that ask him?
... who keep on asking Him — Wms

12. Therefore all things whatsoever ye
would that men should do to you, do
ye even so to them:
Whatever, therefore, you would have
men do to you, do you also to them
— Wey
Therefore, you must always treat other
people as you would like to have
them treat you — Gspd
Do for others everything you want
them to do for you — Beck
for this is the law and the prophets.
for that is the teaching of both the
Law and the Prophets — TCNT
for in this the Law and the Prophets
are summed up — Wey
that is the meaning of the Law and the
prophets — Mof
this is the essence of all true religion
— Phi

13. Enter ye in at the strait gate:
... through the narrow gate — Nor
for wide is the gate, and broad is the
way, that leadeth to destruction,
For the wide gate has a broad road
which leads to disaster — Phi
Broad and spacious is the road ... —
TCNT
... there is plenty of room on the
road ... — NEB
... which leads to ruin — Wey
... perdition — Knox
and many there be which go in thereat:
and many are they that enter in thereby — ASV
and many are those entering through it
— Ber
and there are many people going that
way — Phi

14. Because strait is the gate, and narrow
is the way, which leadeth unto life,
but how small is the gate, how narrow
the road that leads on to life—Knox
... and straitened the way ... — ASV
... and the road is hard ... — Gspd
The narrow gate and the hard road
lead out into life — Phi
and few there be that find it.

and how few there are that find it! —
Knox
and only a few are finding it — Phi

15. Beware of false prophets,
Be on the watch ... — Bas
... false religious teachers — Phi
which come to you in sheep's clothing,
men who come to you ... — Knox
... disguised as sheep — Gspd
but inwardly they are ravening wolves.
but beneath that disguise ... — Wey
but are really greedy wolves — Phi
... ravenous wolves — TCNT

16. Ye shall know them by their fruits.
By their fruits shall ye find them out
— Rhm
By the fruit of their lives ... — TCNT
You must recognize them ... — Wms
... by what they do — Beck
Do men gather grapes of thorns,
Can grapes be picked from briars —
NEB
... thornbushes — TCNT
or figs of thistles?
... a clump of thistles — Phi

17. Even so every good tree bringeth forth
good fruit;
In the same way, a good tree always
yields good fruit — NEB
... sound tree ... — TCNT
but a corrupt tree bringeth forth evil
fruit.
Whereas the worthless tree ... — Rhm
while any tree that is withered ... —
Knox
... sickly tree ... poor fruit — Wms

18. A good tree cannot bring forth evil
fruit,
A good tree is incapable of producing
bad fruit — Phi
A sound tree ... — TCNT
... poor fruit — Wms
neither can a corrupt tree bring forth
good fruit.
and a rotten tree cannot bear sound
fruit — Mof
... worthless tree ... — Rhm
... withered tree ... — Knox

19. Every tree that bringeth not forth good
fruit is hewn down, and cast into the
fire.

20. Wherefore by their fruits ye shall
know them.
Hence it is by the fruit of their lives
that you will know such men—TCNT
So you must recognize them ... .—Wms

27

. . . you will fully know them . . . —
Amp
. . . by what they do — Beck

21. Not every one that saith unto me,
It is not every one who keeps saying
to me — Phi
Lord, Lord,
Master! Master! — TCNT
shall enter into the kingdom of heaven;
. . . kingdom of the heavens — Rhm
. . . Realm of heaven — Mof
**but he that doeth the will of my Father
which is in heaven.**
but only he who does the will of my
Father . . . — TCNT
but only those who are obedient to my
Father who is in heaven — Wey
. . . who is in the heavens — Rhm
but the man who actually does my
Heavenly Father's will — Phi

22. Many will say to me in that day,
On 'That Day' . . . — TCNT
. . . when the Day comes — Rieu
Lord, Lord,
Master, Master — TCNT
have we not prophesied in thy name?
did we not prophesy by thy name —
ASV
was not it in your name that we taught
— TCNT
didn't we preach in your name — Phi
and in thy name have cast out devils?
and by thy name cast out demons —
ASV
**and in thy name done many wonderful
works?**
and by thy name . . . — ASV
. . . we did many miracles — TCNT
. . . works of power . . . — Rhm
. . . many wonder-works — Wms

23. And then will I profess unto them,
Then I will tell them to their face—NEB
. . . say . . . plainly — TCNT
. . . say . . . openly — Wms
Then I shall let them hear the truth —
Rieu
I never knew you:
Never have I acknowledged you —
Rhm
You were never friends of mine —
Knox
At no time did I recognize you — Rieu
depart from me,
Go from my presence — TCNT
out of my sight — NEB
ye that work iniquity.

you that traffic in wrong-doing — Knox
you have worked on the side of evil! —
Phi
you and your wicked ways — NEB
you who practice lawlessness — NASB
you who are so busy doing wrong —
Beck

**24. Therefore whosoever heareth these
sayings of mine,**
. . . listens to this teaching of mine —
TCNT
. . . words of mine — ASV
. . . commandments of mine — Knox
and doeth them,
and puts them into practice — Phi
and acts accordingly — Rieu
**I will liken him unto a wise man, which
built his house upon a rock:**
. . . a prudent man . . . — TCNT
. . . thoughtful man . . . — Ber
He is like a man who had the sense to
build his house on rock — NEB
. . . on a rocky foundation — Wms

25. And the rain descended,
The rain poured down — TCNT
and the floods came,
and the rivers over-flowed — Lam
the swollen torrents came — Wey
and the winds blew,
. . . howled — Nor
and beat upon that house;
and it fell not:
yet it did not fall — Wey
but it never collapsed — Ber
for it was founded upon a rock.
For it had been founded upon the rock
— Rhm
for its foundations were upon the rock
— TCNT
. . . on a rocky foundation — Wms

**26. And every one that heareth these say-
ings of mine,**
. . . listens to this teaching of mine —
TCNT
. . . words of mine — ASV
. . . commandments of mine — Knox
and doeth them not,
and does not follow them — Phi
and does not act accordingly — Rieu
**shall be likened unto a foolish man,
which built his house upon the sand:**
. . . imprudent man . . . — Wms
He is like a man who was foolish
enough to build his house on sand
— NEB

27. And the rain descended,
The rain poured down — TCNT
and the floods came,
and the rivers overflowed — Lam
the swollen torrents came — Wey
and the winds blew,
. . . howled — Nor
and beat upon that house;
and struck against that house — TCNT
and battered that house — Phi
and it fell:
till down it fell — Mof
and it collapsed — Ber
and great was the fall of it.
and disastrous was the fall — Wey
and mighty was the crash! — Mof
and its downfall was complete — Gspd
and what a fall it had! — Rieu
28. And it came to pass, when Jesus had ended these sayings,
By the time that Jesus had finished speaking — TCNT
When Jesus closed this address, the result was — Wms

the people were astonished at his doctrine:
the crowd was filled with amazement at his teaching — TCNT
the multitudes . . . — ASV
. . . were stunned . . . — Lam
. . . were astonished at the power behind his teaching — Phi
29. For he taught them as one having authority,
for He had been teaching them as one who had authority — Wey
for he was teaching them . . . — Rhm
. . . like an authority — Mof
. . . as one who had authority to teach — Wms
For his words had the ring of authority — Phi
and not as the scribes.
and not like their Teachers of the Law — TCNT
quite unlike those of their scribes — Phi
and not like their Bible scholars — Beck

CHAPTER 8

1. When he was come down from the mountain,
Upon descending from the hill country — Wey
great multitudes followed him.

2. And, behold, there came a leper and worshipped him,
And lo! a leper coming near began to bow down to him — Rhm
. . . fell on his knees before him — Gspd
And he saw a leper who came up, and bowed to the ground before him — TCNT
And there suddenly appeared a leper, who approached him and did obeisance — Rieu
saying,
Lord, if thou wilt, thou canst make me clean.
Master, if only you are willing . . . — TCNT
If you only choose, sir, you can cleanse me — Mof

3. And Jesus put forth his hand, and touched him,
And he stretched forth his hand . . . — ASV

Jesus stretched out his hand and placed it on the leper — Phi
saying,
saying as he did so — TCNT
I will;
I am willing — Rhm
Of course I want to — Phi
I will it — Rieu
be thou clean.
be clean again — NEB
And immediately his leprosy was cleansed.
Instantly . . . — TCNT
4. And Jesus saith unto him,
See thou tell no man;
Be careful not to say a word to anyone — TCNT
but go thy way,
shew thyself to the priest,
let the priest examine you — Beck
and offer the gift that Moses commanded,
and make the offering for your recovery that Moses prescribed — Phi
. . . which Moses directed — Rhm
for a testimony unto them.
as evidence of your cure — TCNT
to make the truth known to them — Knox

to show them you're well — Beck

5. And when Jesus was entered into Capernaum,
there came unto him a centurion,
... a Captain in the Roman army — TCNT
beseeching him,
and appealed to him — Mof
asking for his aid — Knox

6. And saying, Lord,
my servant lieth at home sick of the palsy,
my servant-boy is at home bed-ridden with paralysis — Wms
my slave at home is lying ill with paralysis — Mon
my boy is lying in the house, paralyzed — Lam
grievously tormented.
and is suffering terribly — TCNT
and racked with pain — NEB

7. And Jesus saith unto him,
I will come and heal him.
Am I to come and heal him? — Rieu

8. The centurion answered and said,
the Captain went on — TCNT
Lord,
Sir — TCNT
I am not worthy that thou shouldest come under my roof:
I am unworthy to receive you under my roof — TCNT
I'm not important enough for you to come under my roof — Phi
I am not qualified for You to come under my roof — NASB
but speak the word only,
but only say with a word — Rhm
if thou wilt only speak a word of command — Knox
Just give the order, please — Phi
and my servant shall be healed.
... manservant ... — TCNT
... servant-boy ... — Wms

9. For I am a man under authority,
For I also am a man ... — ASV
For I myself am a man under the order of others — TCNT
For I too man a man who derives his powers from above — Rieu
having soldiers under me:
and I say to this man,
... to this one — ASV
Go, and he goeth;
... and I know he'll go — Phi

and to another, Come, and he cometh;
... and I know he'll come — Phi
and to my servant,
... slave-boy — Wms
Do this, and he doeth it.
... and he'll always do it — Phi

10. When Jesus heard it, he marvelled,
... he was amazed — Lam
Jesus heard him with astonishment — NEB
and said to them that followed,
... those who accompanied him—Lam
Verily I say unto you,
I solemnly tell you — Wey
I have not found so great faith, no, not in Israel.
in no Israelite have I found faith as great as this — Wey
I have never met faith like this anywhere in Israel — Mof

11. And I say unto you, That many shall come from the east and west,
... from the rising and the setting sun —Rieu
and shall sit down with Abraham, and Isaac, and Jacob,
and take their places at the feast with Abraham ... — Gspd
and sit at my table with Abraham ... — Phi
And shall recline ... — Rhm
in the kingdom of heaven.
... Realm of heaven — Mof
... kingdom of the heavens — Rhm

12. But the children of the kingdom shall be cast out into outer darkness:
while the heirs to the Kingdom will be banished into the darkness outside — TCNT
... sons of the kingdom ... — ASV
while the sons of the Realm will pass outside, into the darkness — Mof
... will be put out into the dark — Bas
But those who should have belonged to the kingdom ... — Phi
there shall be weeping and gnashing of teeth.
there, there shall be weeping and grinding of teeth — TCNT
where there will be tears and bitter regret — Phi

13. And Jesus said unto the centurion,
... the Captain — TCNT
Go thy way;
Go home! — Ber

and as thou hast believed, so be it done
unto thee.
You shall find it just as you believe! —
Gspd
it must be done for you as you have
believed — Wms
and your reward shall be equal to your
faith — Rieu
And his servant was healed in the selfsame hour.
And the servant was healed in that
hour — ASV
... servant-boy ... — Wms
... recovered precisely at that time —
Wey
14. And when Jesus was come into Peter's
house, he saw his wife's mother laid,
and sick of a fever.
he saw Peter's mother-in-law ... —
TCNT
Jesus noticed that ... was down with
fever — Mof
... had been put to bed with a high
fever — Phi
15. And he touched her hand, and the
fever left her: and she arose, and ministered unto them.
... and began ministering unto him
— Rhm
... and began to see to their needs —
Phi
16. When the even was come,
In the evening — TCNT
they brought unto him
many that were possessed with devils:
many demoniacs — Wey
many who were under the power of
demons — Wms
a number of people who had evil spirits — Bas
and he cast out the spirits with his
word,
and with a word He drove out the evil
spirits — Nor
... the demons ... — Mon
and healed all that were sick:
Indeed, he healed all who were ill —
Phi
17. That it might be fulfilled which was
spoken by Esaias the prophet,
... through Isaiah ... — ASV
in fulfillment of these words in the
Prophet Isaiah — TCNT
In this way what the prophet Isaiah said
was to come true — Beck
saying,

Himself took our infirmities, and bare
our sicknesses.
He took our infirmities on himself, and
bore the burden of our diseases —
TCNT
... weaknesses ... diseases — Rhm
18. Now when Jesus saw great multitudes
about him,
Now Jesus, because he saw a crowd
about Him — Wms
he gave commandment to depart
gave orders to depart — Rhm
unto the other side.
to the other side of the lake — Phi
19. And a certain scribe came, and said
unto him,
And a Teacher of the Law came up to
him, and said — TCNT
A man trained in the Bible ... — Beck
Master,
Teacher — ASV
I will follow thee whithersoever thou
goest.
I will follow you anywhere — Mof
... wherever you are going! — Gspd
20. And Jesus saith unto him,
The foxes have holes,
... dens — Rhm
and the birds of the air have nests;
even the wild birds have roosts — Wms
... a resting-place — Bas
... lodging places — Amp
but the Son of man hath not where to
lay his head.
... owns no place to lay His head —
Ber
... has nowhere that he can call his
own — Phi
21. And another of his disciples said unto
him, Lord,
Master, said another, who was a disciple — TCNT
Another of his pupils said to him ...
— Rieu
... sir — Gspd
suffer me first to go and bury my
father.
allow me ... — Wey
give me leave to go home and bury my
father before I come — Knox
... give the last honours to my father
— Bas
... bury [care for till death] my father
— Amp
22. But Jesus said unto him,
... saith ... — ASV

31

Follow me;
Be following me — Rhm
and let the dead bury their dead.
and leave the dead to bury their own
    dead — ASV
23. **And when he was entered into a ship,**
    Then He went on board a boat — Wey
    his disciples followed him.
    his disciples accompanying him — Mon
24. **And, behold, there arose a great tempest in the sea,**
    Suddenly so great a storm came on
        upon the Sea — TCNT
    . . . a sudden storm . . . — Mon
    . . . on the lake — Wey
    insomuch that the ship was covered with the waves:
    that the waves broke right over the
        boat — TCNT
    so that the waves threatened to engulf
        the boat — Wey
    so that the boat was being swamped by
        the waves — RSV
    but he was asleep.
    but he remained asleep — Gspd
    but He Himself was asleep — NASB
25. **And his disciples came to him,**
    And they came to him — ASV
    and woke him, saying,
    Lord, save us:
    Save us, sir! — Gspd
    Save us, Lord — NASB
    we perish.
    we are lost! — TCNT
    we are drowning! — Wey
    we are going down! — Wms
26. **And he saith unto them,**
    Why are ye fearful,
    Why are you so easily frightened —
        Wey
    Why are you such cowards — Rieu
    O ye of little faith?
    How little you trust God! — Mof
    you little-faiths — Phi
    You trust Me so little! — Beck
    Then he arose,
    and rebuked the winds and the sea;
    and ordered the winds and the lake to
        be quiet — Beck
    and there was a great calm.
    . . . dead calm — NEB
27. **But the men marvelled, saying,**
    The men were amazed, and exclaimed
        — TCNT
    And the men were dumfounded . . .
        — Wms

. . . and kept saying — Phi
So that all asked in amazement—Knox
What manner of man is this,
Whence is this one — Rhm
What kind of a man is this — TCNT
that even the winds and the sea obey him!
that both the winds and the sea unto
    him give ear — Rhm
Why, the very winds and waves obey
    Him! — Wey
28. **And when he was come to the other side into the country of the Gergesenes,**
    . . . Gerasenes — Knox
    . . . Gadarenes — ASV
    in the region of Gadara — Gspd
    there met him two possessed with devils,
    Jesus met two men who were possessed
        by demons — TCNT
    . . . who had evil spirits — Bas
    . . . two lunatics — Lam
    . . . two possessed creatures — Knox
    two men possessed by demons . . .
        confronted him — Gspd
    coming out of the tombs,
    coming from among the tombs — Wey
    who were just coming out from the
        tombs — Wms
    . . . out of the burial places — Beck
    exceeding fierce, so that no man might pass by that way.
    They were so violent that no one was
        able to pass that way — TCNT
    so savage . . . — Rieu
    . . . that nobody dared to use that road
        — Phi
29. **And, behold, they cried out, saying,**
    Suddenly they shrieked out — TCNT
    What have we do to with thee,
    What have we in common with thee —
        Rhm
    What do you want with us — TCNT
    What business have we together—Lam
    Why dost thou meddle with us — Knox
    Jesus, thou Son of God?
    O Son of God — RSV
    art thou come hither to torment us before the time?
    . . . before the proper time — Phi
    . . . before the appointed time to torture
        us — Gspd
30. **And there was a good way off from them**

Now at some distance from them —
Wey
an herd of many swine feeding.
31. **So the devils besought him, saying,**
. . . demons . . . — ASV
and the foul spirits began begging Jesus
— TCNT
And the lunatics kept asking him . . .
— Lam
and the devils asked a favour of him —
Knox
**If thou cast us out, suffer us to go
away into the herd of swine.**
If you are going to heal us, permit us
to attack the herd of swine — Lam
. . . send us into that herd of swine —
Mon
32. **And he said unto them,
Go.**
Begone! — Mof
Then go! — Phi
**And when they were come out,
they went into the herd of swine:**
and went into the swine — ASV
and attacked the swine — Lam
**and, behold, the whole herd of swine
ran violently down a steep place into
the sea,**
whereupon the entire herd instantly
rushed down the steep into the lake
— Wey
and perished in the waters.
and were drowned — Phi
33. **And they that kept them fled,**
And they who were feeding them fled
— Rhm

At this the men who tended them ran
away — TCNT
The swineherds took to their heels —
Phi
and went their ways into the city,
and went away . . . — ASV
and told every thing,
carrying the news of all that had occurred — TCNT
There they poured out the whole story
— Phi
**and what was befallen to the possessed
of the devils.**
including what had happened to the
demoniacs — Wey
especially about the men plagued by
devils — Beck
. . . who were under the power of demons — Wms
. . . who had the evil spirits — BAS
. . . the madmen — NEB
34. **And, behold, the whole city came out
to meet Jesus:**
At the news the whole town went out
. . . — TCNT
At once all the citizens came out . . .
— Mon
. . . all the townspeople . . . — Knox
**and when they saw him, they besought
him that he would depart out of
their coasts.**
. . . to go away from their neighbourhood — TCNT
. . . to move out of their district — Mof
. . . to move away from their country
— Mon

CHAPTER 9

1. **And he entered into a ship,**
Accordingly He went on board — Wey
So Jesus re-embarked on the boat —
Phi
**and passed over, and came into his
own city.**
. . . home town — Wms
2. **And, behold,**
Immediately — Phi
**they brought to him a man sick of the
palsy,**
They were bringing . . . — Rhm
. . . a paralytic — Mof
some people brought to him a paralyzed man — TCNT
lying on a bed:
lying on a sleeping pad — Amp

and Jesus seeing their faith
And because He saw their faith — Wms
. . . the faith of the bearers — Mof
said unto the sick of the palsy;
. . . paralytic — Mof
Son, be of good cheer;
Courage, Child! — TCNT
Son, take heart — Bas
thy sins be forgiven thee.
thy sins are forgiven — ASV
. . . pardoned — Wey
3. **And, behold, certain of the scribes said
within themselves,**
. . . Teachers of the Law said to themselves — TCNT
. . . Bible scholars . . . — Beck
This man blasphemeth.

This man speaketh profanely! — Rhm
Such language is impious — Wey
This man has no respect for God — Bas

4. **And Jesus knowing their thoughts said,**
   Jesus read their minds, and said — Knox
   ... inward thoughts ... — Rhm
   Wherefore think ye evil in your hearts?
   Why do you cherish such wicked thoughts — TCNT
   Why must you have such evil thoughts in your minds — Phi

5. **For whether is easier,**
   For which is easier — ASV
   which command is more lightly given — Knox
   to say,
   Thy sins be forgiven thee;
   Thy sins are forgiven — ASV
   Yours sins are pardoned — Wey
   or to say,
   Arise and walk?
   Get up, and walk about — TCNT

6. **But that ye may know**
   But I would have you know — Gspd
   But to make it quite plain — Phi
   However, to teach you — Rieu
   But to convince you — NEB
   that the Son of man hath power on earth
   ... authority ... — ASV
   to forgive sins,
   to pardon sins — Wey
   (then saith he to the sick of the palsy,)
   ... paralyzed man — TCNT
   ... paralytic — Mof
   Arise, take up thy bed, and go unto thine house.
   Get up, take up your bed, and return to your home — TCNT
   ... thy couch ... — Rhm
   ... sleeping pad ... — Amp

7. **And he arose,**
   And the man sprang to his feet — Phi
   and departed to his house.
   and went to his home — TCNT

8. **But when the multitudes saw it,**
   When the crowd saw this — TCNT
   they marvelled,
   they were afraid — ASV
   they were awe-struck — TCNT
   and glorified God,
   and praised God — TCNT
   and ascribed the glory to God — Wey
   which had given such power unto men.

for giving such power to men — TCNT
... authority ... — ASV

9. **And as Jesus passed forth from thence,**
   As Jesus went along — TCNT
   he saw a man, named Matthew,
   ... called Matthew — TCNT
   ... Matthew by name — Nor
   sitting at the receipt of custom:
   presiding over the tax office — Rhm
   sitting at work in the customs-house — Knox
   sitting at a tax collection booth — Tay
   and he saith unto him, Follow me. And he arose, and followed him.

10. **And it came to pass,**
    And later on — TCNT
    as Jesus sat at meat in the house,
    as he sat ... — ASV
    ... was reclining ... — Rhm
    as Jesus was in the house sitting at the dinner table — Phi
    that Jesus sat down to a meal in this man's house — Rieu
    behold, many publicans and sinners
    many bad characters — tax-gatherers and others — NEB
    ... tax-gatherers and outcasts — TCNT
    ... tax-collectors and other disreputable people — Phi
    came and sat down with him and his disciples.
    had come to be guests with him ... — Mof
    ... were reclining together with Jesus ... — Rhm

11. **And when the Pharisees saw it,**
    The Pharisees noticed this — Wey
    they said unto his disciples,
    began to say ... — Rhm
    they kept saying ... — Mon
    Why eateth your Master with publicans and sinners?
    Why does your Teacher eat in the company of tax-gatherers and outcasts — TCNT
    ... tax-collectors and irreligious people — Gspd
    ... and men of bad repute — Nor

12. **But when Jesus heard that, he said unto them,**
    Jesus overheard it, and replied — Nor
    But when he heard it ... — ASV
    They that be whole need not a physician,
    It is not men in good health who require a doctor — Wey

but they that are sick.

13. **But go ye and learn what that meaneth,**
   . . . what that text means — NEB
   Suppose you go away and learn what
   this means — Phi
   I will have mercy, and not sacrifice:
   It is mercy that wins favour with me,
   not sacrifice — Knox
   . . . not offerings — Bas
   I like mercy and not mere sacrifice —
   Beck
   for I am not come to call the righteous,
   I did not come to invite the pious —
   Gspd
   . . . virtuous people — NEB
   but sinners to repentance.
   but sinners — ASV
   but the outcasts — TCNT
   but the irreligious — Gspd

14. **Then came to him the disciples of
   John, saying,**
   Then John's disciples approached him
   with the question — Phi
   Why do we and the Pharisees fast oft,
   . . . observe the fasts — Phi
   . . . fast a great deal — Mof
   but thy disciples fast not?
   but your disciples don't fast at all —
   Nor

15. **And Jesus said unto them,**
   **Can the children of the bridechamber
   mourn,**
   . . . sons of the bride-chamber . . . —
   ASV
   Can the bridegroom's friends mourn —
   TCNT
   Can wedding guests mourn — Gspd
   Will the friends of the newly-married
   man be sad — Bas
   The attendants of the bride-groom cannot mourn . . . can they — NASB
   **as long as the bridegroom is with
   them? but the days will come, when
   the bridegroom shall be taken from
   them,**
   . . . will be parted from them — TCNT
   and then shall they fast.
   they will certainly fast then — Phi
   that will be the time for them to fast —
   NEB

16. **No man putteth a piece of new cloth
   unto an old garment,**
   . . . a patch of unshrunk cloth . . . —
   Rhm
   . . . a patch of brand-new goods . . .
   — Wms

for that which is put in to fill it up
   taketh from the garment,
   for the shrinking of it teareth away
   from the garment — Rhm
   Otherwise, the added patch tears away
   some of the garment — Wey
   and the rent is made worse.
   and make the hole worse than ever —
   Gspd

17. **Neither do men put new wine into old
   bottles:**
   . . . wine-skins — ASV
   **else the bottles break, and the wine
   runneth out,**
   . . . skins burst . . . wine is spilled —
   ASV
   and the bottles perish:
   . . . skins . . . — ASV
   . . . are spoiled — Rhm
   but they put new wine into new bottles,
   . . . fresh wine-skins — ASV
   . . . unused skins — Rhm
   and both are preserved.
   . . . saved — Wey

18. **While he spake these things unto them,
   behold,**
   Just as he said this to them — Gspd
   there came a certain ruler,
   . . . a synagogue official — NASB
   a President of a Synagogue . . . — TCNT
   one of the Elders . . . — Rieu
   and worshipped him,
   and knelt before him — Mof
   saying, My daughter is even now dead:
   . . . just now died — Alf
   but come and lay thy hand upon her,
   Please come . . . — Phi
   and she shall live.
   . . . will be restored to life — TCNT

19. **And Jesus arose,**
   At this, Jesus got to his feet — Phi
   and followed him,
   was following him — Rhm
   and began to follow him — NASB
   and so did his disciples.

20. **And, behold, a woman, which was diseased with an issue of blood twelve
   years,**
   But meanwhile a woman, who had
   been suffering from haemorrhage —
   TCNT
   **came behind him, and touched the hem
   of his garment:**
   . . . border of his garment — ASV
   . . . tassel on His coat — Wms

... edge of his robe — Bas

21. For she said within herself,
... kept saying ... — Rhm
... to herself — Wey
If I may but touch his garment,
If only I touch his mantle — Rhm
... robe — Mof
I shall be whole.
I shall be made well — Rhm
I shall be all right — Phi

22. But when Jesus turned him about, and when he saw her, he said,
But Jesus turning and seeing her said — ASV
But Jesus turned right around and saw her — Phi
Daughter, be of good comfort;
Cheer up, my daughter — Phi
... Take courage! — Rhm
thy faith hath made thee whole.
thy faith hath brought thee healing — Knox
... made thee well — Rhm
And the woman was made whole from that hour.
And instantly ... — Mof
... completely cured from that moment — Phi

23. And when Jesus came into the ruler's house,
When Jesus reached the President's house — TCNT
... official's house — Mof
... Elder's house — Rieu
and saw the minstrels and the people making a noise,
... flute-players ... — ASV
... the players with their instruments ... — Bas
... mourners playing the flute ... — Knox
... and the disturbance the crowd was making — Gspd

24. He said unto them, Give place:
... Go away — TCNT
... That is enough — Lam
... Make room — Bas
for the maid is not dead, but sleepeth.
the little girl is not dead; she is asleep — TCNT
And they laughed him to scorn.
They began to laugh at him — TCNT
They laughed derisively at Him — Ber
And they were laughing at Him—NASB
But they all scoffed and sneered at Him — Tay

25. But when the people were put forth,
But when Jesus had forced the crowd to leave — Phi
he went in, and took her by the hand,
... and grasped her hand — Rhm
and the maid arose.
... maiden ... — Rhm

26. And the fame hereof went abroad into all that land.
The report of this spread through all that part of the country — TCNT
And this became the talk of the whole district — Phi

27. And when Jesus departed thence,
And as Jesus passed by ... — ASV
two blind men followed him,
he was delayed by two blind men — Lam
crying, and saying,
crying out ... — ASV
who kept calling out — TCNT
who shrieked — Mof
Thou son of David, have mercy on us.
Have mercy on us, thou Son of David — Rhm
Take pity on us ... — TCNT

28. And when he was come into the house,
When he had gone indoors — TCNT
... into his lodging — Knox
the blind men came to him:
the same blind men ... — Lam
and Jesus saith unto them,
... asked them — TCNT
Believe ye that I am able to do this?
Have you faith in my power to cure you — Rieu
Do you really believe ... — Wms
They said unto him, Yea, Lord.
They say ... — ASV
... Yes, sir — Mof
Yes, Master! they answered — TCNT

29. Then touched he their eyes, saying,
Upon that ... — TCNT
According to your faith be it unto you.
... be it done unto you — ASV
... it must be done for you — Wms
As you believe, so your prayer is granted — Mof
Have what your faith expects! — Gspd
Your faith shall not be disappointed — Knox
Your reward shall be equal to your faith — Rieu

30. And their eyes were opened;
And their sight was restored — Gspd

and Jesus straitly charged them, saying,
And Jesus strictly charged them ... —
ASV
Jesus sternly cautioned them — TCNT
And assuming a stern tone Jesus said
to them — Wey
See that no man know it.
Be careful to let no one know — Wey
See that no one learns of this — Ber
31. **But they, when they were departed,**
But they had no sooner gone out —
Knox
**spread abroad his fame in all that
country.**
made him known throughout the whole
of that land — Rhm
spread the story throughout the whole
district — Phi
sang his praises to everybody in the
countryside — Rieu
32. **As they went out, behold,**
Just as they were going out — TCNT
Hardly had they left Him when — Nor
they brought to him a dumb man possessed with a devil.
... a man without the power of talking
... — Bas
a dumb demoniac ... — Wey
... who was demented — Lam
33. **And when the devil was cast out,**
... demon ... — ASV
the dumb spake:
the dumb man could speak — Wey
the patient recovered his speech — NEB
and the multitudes marvelled, saying,
The people were astonished at this ...
— TCNT
... were dumfounded ... — Wms
And the crowds exclaimed in astonishment — Wey
It was never so seen in Israel.
Nothing like this has ever been seen
in Israel! — TCNT
34. **But the Pharisees said,**
... began to say — Rhm
... maintained — Wey
... kept saying — Mon
**He casteth out devils through the
prince of the devils.**
... by the help of the chief of the
demons — TCNT
... because he is in league with the
devil himself — Phi
It is by the power of the Prince of the
demons ... — Wey

35. **And Jesus went about all the cities and
villages,**
Then Jesus made a tour ... — Mof
... was going round ... — Rhm
... continued to go throughout ... —
Mon
**teaching in their synagogues, and
preaching the gospel of the kingdom,**
... and proclaiming the glad-message
of the kingdom — Rhm
... gospel of the Reign — Mof
**and healing every sickness and every
disease among the people.**
and healing all manner of disease and
all manner of sickness — ASV
36. **But when he saw the multitudes,**
As he saw the crowds — Mof
But the sight of the crowds of people
— Gspd
**he was moved with compassion on
them,**
his heart was moved with compassion
for them — TCNT
He was touched with pity ... — Wey
he was deeply moved ... — Phi
filled him with pity for them — Gspd
because they fainted, and were scattered abroad,
... distressed and scattered — ASV
... torn and thrown down — Rhm
... mangled and thrown to the ground
— Ber
... distracted and dejected — Wey
as sheep having no shepherd.
37. **Then saith he unto his disciples,
The harvest truly is plenteous,**
... abundant — TCNT
There is much grain — Bas
but the labourers are few;
... reapers ... — Wey
... are scarce — Wms
but not enough men to get it in — Bas
38. **Pray ye therefore the Lord of the
harvest,**
Therefore urge the owner of the harvest
— Lam
... the Lord to whom the harvest belongs — Knox
**that he will send forth labourers into
his harvest.**
... thrust forth ... — Rhm
to bring more laborers to his harvest —
Lam
... for the harvesting — Knox

CHAPTER 10

1. **And when he had called unto him his twelve disciples,**
And calling near . . . — Rhm
he gave them power against unclean spirits, to cast them out,
. . . impure spirits . . . — Rhm
. . . authority to expel evil spirits — Phi
and to heal all manner of sickness and all manner of disease.
and also to heal . . . — Mof
. . . every disease and every infirmity — Rhm
. . . disease . . . sickness — ASV

2. **Now the names of the twelve apostles are these; The first, Simon, who is called Peter,**
. . . also known as Peter — TCNT
and Andrew his brother; James the son of Zebedee,
. . . Zebediah — TCNT
and John his brother;

3. **Philip, and Bartholomew; Thomas, and Matthew the publican;**
. . . tax-collector — Rhm
. . . customs-officer — Rieu
James the son of Alphaeus, and Lebbaeus, whose surname was Thaddaeus;
and Thaddaeus — ASV
and Lebbaeus — Alf

4. **Simon the Canaanite,**
Simon, a member of the Zealot party — NEB
. . . the Cananaean — ASV
. . . the Patriot — Phi
and Judas Iscariot, who also betrayed him.
and Judas of Kerioth . . . — Rieu
. . . who also delivered him up — Rhm
. . . the Apostle who betrayed him — TCNT
. . . who afterward betrayed him — Gspd
. . . who later turned traitor — Phi

5. **These twelve Jesus sent forth, and commanded them, saying,**
These twelve Jesus sent on a mission . . . — Wey
. . . sent out as his Messengers . . . — TCNT
These twelve men Jesus despatched with the following instructions — Mof

Go not into the way of the Gentiles,
Do not go among the Gentiles — Mof
Don't turn off into any of the heathen roads — Phi
Do not stray into the pagan lands — Rieu
and into any city of the Samaritans enter ye not:

6. **But go rather to the lost sheep of the house of Israel.**
but, instead of that, go to the lost sheep of Israel's race — Wey
But above all, go to the sheep which are lost from the house of Israel — Lam
Concentrate on the lost sheep . . . — Phi
. . . the wandering sheep . . . — Bas

7. **And as ye go, preach, saying,**
Go and preach! . . . — Nor
. . . continue to preach — Wms
And wherever you go, let it be known that — Rieu
The kingdom of heaven is at hand.
The Reign of heaven is near — Mof
. . . has arrived — Phi

8. **Heal the sick,**
Keep on curing the sick — Wms
cleanse the lepers, raise the dead,
raise the dead, cleanse the lepers—ASV
bring back the dead to life . . . — Rieu
cast out devils:
. . . demons — ASV
freely ye have received, freely give.
You have received free of cost, give free of cost — TCNT

9. **Provide neither gold, nor silver,**
Do not accumulate . . . — Lam
Do not acquire . . . — NASB
nor brass in your purses,
nor copper for your belts — Rhm
nor copper to carry in your girdles — Wey
or even copper money for your purse — Wms

10. **Nor scrip for your journey,**
neither satchel . . . — Rhm
or a wallet for a collection-bag . . . — Amp
not even with a bag for the journey — TCNT
no pack for the road — NEB
neither two coats,
or a change of clothes — TCNT

nor extra inner garment — Wey
no second coat — NEB
neither shoes,
nor sandals — Rhm
no spare shoes — Knox
nor yet staves:
or even a staff — TCNT
for the workman is worthy of his meat.
for the worker is worth his food—TCNT
... deserves his rations — Mof
... maintenance — Rhm
the workman is worth his keep — Phi

11. **And into whatsoever city or town ye shall enter,**
enquire who in it is worthy;
inquire who is a deserving man — Wey
... worthy to be your host — Knox
ask who is trustworthy in it — Lam
and there abide till ye go thence.
and make his house your home till you leave the place — Wey

12. **And when ye come into an house, salute it.**
... wish it well — Gspd
... salute the family — Lam
... say, May peace be on this house — Bas

13. **And if the house be worthy,**
if the household is deserving — Mof
And if the family is trustworthy—Lam
... should prove deserving — Wms
let your peace come upon it:
let your blessing rest upon it — TCNT
the peace you wish it will come over it — Gspd
may your good wish for peace upon it come true — Wms
but if it be not worthy,
but if the household is undeserving — Mof
... not trustworthy — Lam
let your peace return to you.
let your blessing return upon yourselves — TCNT
may your good wish bring peace to yourselves — Wms

14. **And whosoever shall not receive you,**
And where no one will welcome you — Gspd
And whoever refuses to receive you — Wey
... take you in — Bas
nor hear your words,
or even to listen to your message — Wey
nor heed your words — NASB

when ye depart out of that house or city, shake off the dust of your feet.
... the very dust that is on your feet — Wey
... the dust of that place from your feet — Phi

15. **Verily I say unto you,**
I solemnly tell you — Wey
I promise you — Knox
It shall be more tolerable for the land of Sodom and Gomorrha
the doom of the land of Sodom and Gomorrha will be more bearable — TCNT
... more endurable ... — Wey
in the day of judgment, than for that city.
... than the doom of that town—TCNT

16. **Behold, I send you forth**
Remember it is I who am sending you out — Wey
... I am sending you out as my Messengers — TCNT
as sheep in the midst of wolves:
as sheep into the midst of wolves — Wey
be ye therefore wise as serpents,
prove yourselves therefore ... — Wey
Become ... — Rhm
... shrewd as serpents — NASB
and harmless as doves.
and yet innocent as doves — Knox
... blameless ... — TCNT
... guileless ... — Mof

17. **But beware of men:**
Be on your guard against your fellow men — TCNT
Do not put your trust in men — Knox
... mankind — Rieu
for they will deliver you up to the councils,
for they will betray you to courts of law — TCNT
they will hand you over to sanhedrins — Mof
and they will scourge you in their synagogues;
and whip you in their places of worship — Beck
and will flog you ... — Wey

18. **And ye shall be brought before governors and kings for my sake,**
and you will be dragged before governors ... — RSV
and you will even be put on trial ... — Wey

. . . before both governors and kings
. . . — Rhm
for a testimony against them and the Gentiles.
that you may witness for me before them and the nations — TCNT
. . . to them and to the Gentiles — ASV

19. **But when they deliver you up,**
Now, when they bring you up for trial — Mof
. . . betray you — TCNT
take no thought how or what ye shall speak:
never trouble yourselves about how to speak or what to say — Mof
do not give anxious thought to the manner and wording of your defense — Rieu
for it shall be given you in that same hour what ye shall speak.
for you will be told at the very moment what you ought to say — Gspd
words will be given you when the time comes — Knox

20. **For it is not ye that speak,**
For it will not be really you who are speaking — Phi
but the Spirit of your Father which speaketh in you.
. . . that is speaking through you — Mof

21. **And the brother shall deliver up the brother to death,**
Brother will betray brother to death — TCNT
and the father the child:
. . . his child — ASV
and the children shall rise up against their parents,
and children . . . against parents — ASV
. . . take a stand against their parents — Wms
and cause them to be put to death.
and will put them to death — Wey

22. **And ye shall be hated of all men**
And you will be objects of universal hatred — Wey
for my name's sake:
because you bear my name — Wms
for your allegiance to me — NEB
but he that endureth to the end
but he . . . who holds out to the very end — Mof
But he who perseveres to the end—Ber
shall be saved.
this one shall be saved — ABUV
will be safe and sound — Phi

23. **But when they persecute you in this city,**
Only, if they persecute you in one city — Knox
When they hunt you in one town — Beck
flee ye into another:
escape to the next — TCNT
flee to a different one — Wms
take refuge in another — Knox
for verily I say unto you,
In solemn truth I tell you — Mon
Ye shall not have gone over the cities of Israel,
You will not have come to the end of the towns of Israel — TCNT
you shall not finish converting all the cities of the house of Israel — Lam
till the Son of man be come.
before the Son of man comes — TCNT

24. **The disciple is not above his master,**
The learner is not superior to his teacher — Wey
nor the servant above his lord.
nor a servant . . . — ASV
any more than the servant . . . — Phi

25. **It is enough for the disciple that he be as his master,**
Enough for the learner to be on a level with his teacher — Wey
The pupil should be satisfied to become like his teacher — Wms
for what is good enough for the teacher is good enough for the disciple as well — Phi
and the servant as his lord.
. . . to be on a level with his master — Wey
If they have called the master of the house Beelzebub,
. . . head of the house . . . Baal-zebub — TCNT
. . . Beelzebul — Wey
. . . the 'Prince of Evil' — Phi
how much more shall they call them of his household?
how much worse names . . . — Gspd
how much more will they malign those of his household — RSV

26. **Fear them not therefore:**
. . . however — Wey
for there is nothing covered,
For nothing hath been covered — Rhm
There is nothing concealed — TCNT
that shall not be revealed;
. . . uncovered — Rhm

and hid, that shall not be known.
And hidden which shall not be made known — Rhm
nor any thing private which will not be made public — Phi

27. **What I tell you in darkness, that speak ye in light:**
. . . speak in day light — Wey
. . . you must utter in the open — Mof
. . . you must repeat in broad daylight — NEB
and what ye hear in the ear,
and what is whispered in your ear — TCNT
what you hear in a whisper — Mof
and what comes to your ear secretly — Bas
that preach ye upon the house tops
you must shout from the house-tops — NEB

28. **And fear not them which kill the body, but are not able to kill the soul:**
. . . powerless to kill . . . — Phi
but rather fear him which is able to destroy both soul and body
But rather you must keep on fearing Him . . . — Wms
in hell.
in gehenna — Rhm
in the pit — Gspd
in the fires of destruction — Phi

29. **Are not two sparrows sold for a farthing?**
. . . for a penny — ASV
and one of them shall not fall on the ground
Yet not one of them will fall to the ground — TCNT
. . . can fall to the ground — Gspd
without your Father.
without your Father's knowledge — TCNT
without your Father's permission — Beck

30. **But the very hairs of your head are all numbered.**
And as for you, he takes every hair of your head into his reckoning—Knox
. . . even the hairs . . . have all been numbered — Rhm
. . . are all counted — Gspd

31. **Fear ye not therefore,**
Away then with fear — Wey
Cease to be afraid! — Mon

ye are of more value than many sparrows.
. . . more consequence . . . — Ber

32. **Whosoever therefore shall confess me before men,**
. . . acknowledge me before his fellow men — TCNT
. . . publicly acknowledges me — Phi
him will I confess also before my Father which is in heaven.
I, too, will acknowledge . . . — TCNT
. . . before my Father who is in the heavens — Rhm

33. **But whosoever shall deny me before men,**
but, if any one disowns me before his fellow men — TCNT
him will I also deny
I, too, will disown him — TCNT
before my Father which is in heaven.
before My heavenly Father — Ber
. . . Father who is in the heavens — Rhm

34. **Think not that I am come to send peace on earth:**
Do not imagine . . . — TCNT
. . . that I came . . . — ASV
. . . to bring peace to the earth — Gspd
I came not to send peace, but a sword.
. . . thrust peace . . . — Rhm
. . . bring peace . . . — Gspd

35. **For I am come to set a man at variance against his father,**
For I came . . . — ASV
For I have come to bring division, a man against his father — Ber
Indeed I have come to sow discord between a man and his father — Rieu
. . . to turn a man against his father — Gspd
and the daughter against her mother,
. . . a daughter . . . — Rhm
and the daughter in law against her mother in law.
a young wife . . . — NEB

36. **And a man's foes shall be they of his own household.**
A man's enemies will be the members of his own household — TCNT
. . . those who live in his own house — Phi

37. **He that loveth father or mother more than me**
. . . cares more for . . . — NEB
. . . more than he loves me — Gspd

is not worthy of me:
is not good enough for me — Bas
does not deserve to be mine — Phi
**and he that loveth son or daughter
more than me**
. . . cares more for . . . — NEB
. . . more than he loves me — Gspd
is not worthy of me.
is not good enough for me — Bas
38. **And he that taketh not his cross, and
followeth after me,**
. . . and follow in my steps — TCNT
. . . and follow where I lead — Wey
is not worthy of me.
is not good enough for me — Bas
39. **He that findeth his life shall lose it:**
He that hath found his life . . . — Rhm
He who is concerned about his life . . .
— Lam
He who secures his own life . . . —
Knox
Anybody who gains his lower life will
lose the higher life — Wms
By gaining his life a man will lose it
— NEB
If you cling to your life you will lose
it — Tay
**and he that loseth his life for my sake
shall find it.**
and any body who loses his lower life
for my sake will gain the higher
life — Wms
it is the man who loses his life for my
sake that will secure it — Knox
by losing his life for my sake, he will
gain it — NEB
but if you give it up for Me, you will
save it! — Tay
40. **He that receiveth you receiveth me,**
. . . is receiving me — Mon
He that giveth welcome unto you Unto
me giveth welcome — Rhm
**and he that receiveth me receiveth him
that sent me.**

. . . is receiving Him who sent me —
Mon
. . . him who sent me as his Messenger
— TCNT
And he that unto me giveth welcome
Giveth welcome unto him that sent
me forth — Rhm
41. **He that receiveth a prophet in the
name of a prophet**
. . . giveth welcome unto . . . — Rhm
. . . the welcome due to a prophet —
Knox
. . . because he is a Prophet — TCNT
shall receive a prophet's reward;
will have the same reward as a prophet
— Gspd
**and he that receiveth a righteous man
in the name of a righteous man**
. . . giveth welcome . . . — Rhm
. . . good man, because he is a good
man — TCNT
he who gives a just man the welcome
due to a just man — Knox
. . . because he is upright — Gspd
shall receive a righteous man's reward.
will have the same reward as an upright man — Gspd
. . . a good man's reward — TCNT
42. **And whosoever shall give to drink
unto one of these little ones**
. . . lowly ones — TCNT
. . . the humblest of my disciples —
Gspd
**a cup of cold water only in the name
of a disciple,**
but a cup of cold water . . . because he
is a disciple — TCNT
verily I say unto you,
I tell you in solemn truth — Mon
he shall in no wise lose his reward.
he shall assuredly not lose his reward
—TCNT
. . . not go unrewarded — NEB

CHAPTER 11

1. **And it came to pass, when Jesus had
made an end of commanding his
twelve disciples,**
. . . had finished giving instructions to
. . . — Rhm
**he departed thence to teach and to
preach in their cities.**
he left that place in order to teach and
preach . . . — TCNT

. . . to proclaim His message in the
neighbouring towns — Wey
. . . in the towns in which they lived —
Phi

2. **Now when John had heard in the
prison the works of Christ,**
Now when John heard . . . — Gspd
. . . what the Christ was doing — TCNT

he sent two of his disciples,
he sent word by his disciples — RSV

3. **And said unto him, Art thou he that should come,**
   ... he that cometh — ASV
   ... the coming one — Rhm
   or do we look for another?
   Or a different one are we to expect — Rhm

4. **Jesus answered and said unto them, Go and shew John again those things which ye do hear and see:**
   Go and tell John the things ... — ASV

5. **The blind receive their sight,**
   ... are regaining their sight — Gspd
   and the lame walk,
   and cripples walk — Wey
   and the lame can walk — Gspd
   the lepers are cleansed,
   ... are being cured — Gspd
   and the deaf hear,
   and the deaf can hear — Gspd
   the dead are raised up,
   the dead are being raised — Gspd
   and the poor have the gospel preached to them.
   And the destitute are told the joyful tidings — Rhm
   and the good news is being given to those in need — Phi
   and beggars are proclaiming the Good News — Rieu

6. **And blessed is he,**
   ... happy is he — Rhm
   whosoever shall not be offended in me.
   whosoever shall find no occasion of stumbling in me — ASV
   who does not take offense at my claims — Wey
   who does not stumble on account of me — Lam
   who does not find me a stumbling-block — NEB

7. **And as they departed,**
   But as these were going their way — Rhm
   As they were about to leave — Nor
   Jesus began to say unto the multitudes concerning John,
   Jesus proceeded to say ... — Wey
   ... with reference to John — TCNT
   What went ye out into the wilderness to see?
   ... to gaze at — Rhm

What was it, he asked, that you expected to see when you went out into the wilderness — Knox
What was the spectacle that drew you to the wilderness — NEB
A reed shaken with the wind?
A reed swaying in the wind? No — Rieu
A reed-bed swept by the wind — NEB

8. **But what went ye out for to see? A man clothed in soft raiment?**
   Why then did you go out? To see a man clothed in soft raiment? — RSV
   ... dressed in silks and satins? — Wms
   behold, they that wear soft clothing are in kings' houses.
   Why, those who wear rich things are to be found in the courts of kings! — TCNT
   ... are in royal palaces — Mof

9. **But what went ye out for to see? A prophet?**
   But wherefore went ye out? to see a prophet? — ASV
   Then why did you go out? ... — Rieu
   yea, I say unto you, and more than a prophet.
   Let Me assure you, he's even more than a prophet — Beck
   ... someone even greater than a prophet — Rieu

10. **For this is he, of whom it is written,**
    This is the man of whom Scripture says — TCNT
    Behold,
    Attention! — Wms
    I send my messenger before thy face,
    I am myself sending my Messenger ... — TCNT
    ... on before you — Gspd
    which shall prepare thy way before thee.
    He will prepare the road ahead of you — Gspd
    who is to prepare thy way for thy coming — Knox

11. **Verily I say unto you,**
    Believe me — Knox
    Among them that are born of women
    among such as are born of women — Rhm
    there hath not risen a greater than John the Baptist:
    ... John the Immerser — Rhm
    ... John the Baptizer — Beck

no one greater than John the Baptist has ever appeared — Gspd
notwithstanding
and yet — Mof
he that is least in the kingdom of heaven is greater than he.
he that is but little . . . — ASV
the least in the Realm of heaven . . . — Mof
a humble member of the kingdom of Heaven . . . — Phi

12. **And from the days of John the Baptist until now**
. . . to this very hour — TCNT
Ever since the coming of John the Baptist — NEB
. . . John the Immerser . . . — Rhm
. . . John the Baptizer . . . — Beck
the kingdom of heaven suffereth violence,
. . . has been taken by force — TCNT
. . . has been enduring violent assault— Wey
men have been taking the Kingdom of Heaven by storm — Gspd
and the violent take it by force.
. . . men using force have been seizing it — TCNT
. . . are seizing it as a precious prize — Wms
these eager souls are storming it! — Mof
. . . violent men are trying to take it by force — Beck

13. **For all the prophets and the law prophesied until John.**
. . . pointed to John — Rieu
For the teaching of all the Prophets and of the Law continued till the time of John — TCNT
Till John, it was but prophesied, by all the prophets and the law — Mof
whereas all the prophets and the law, before John's time, could only speak of things that were to come — Knox

14. **And if ye will receive it,**
. . . are willing to receive it — ASV
. . . are ready to accept the idea—Gspd
this is Elias, which was for to come.
John is himself the Elijah who was destined to come — TCNT
. . . that was about to come — ABUV
John himself is the 'Elijah' who must come before the kingdom — Phi

15. **He that hath ears to hear, let him hear.**

He that hath ears let him hear — Rhm
The man who has ears to hear must use them! — Phi
If you have ears that can hear, then hear — NEB

16. **But whereunto shall I liken this generation?**
. . . compare the present generation — TCNT
But how can I show what the people of this generation are like — Phi
It is like unto children sitting in the markets,
. . . little children . . . — TCNT
. . . market places — ASV
and calling unto their fellows,
and calling out to their playmates — TCNT

17. **And saying, We have piped unto you, and ye have not danced;**
. . . We have played the flute to you . . . — Rhm
We played at weddings for you but you wouldn't dance — Phi
we have mourned unto you, and ye have not lamented.
we wailed, and ye did not mourn — ASV
We sang a lament . . . — Rhm
we played at funerals and you wouldn't cry! — Phi
. . . and you would not beat your breasts — Mof

18. **For John came neither eating nor drinking,**
For John came in the strictest austerity — Phi
and they say, He hath a devil.
. . . a demon — ASV
. . . he is crazy — Lam

19. **The Son of man came eating and drinking,**
. . . enjoying life — Phi
and they say, Behold a man gluttonous, and a winebibber,
. . . See this man! — given to gluttony and tippling — Wey
. . . Just look at Him! A glutton and a wine-drinker — Wms
a friend of publicans and sinners.
the companion of tax-collectors and irreligious people — Gspd
. . . tax-gatherers and outcasts! — TCNT
But wisdom is justified of her children.
And yet wisdom hath been justified of her works — Rhm

Ah well, wisdom stands or falls by her
own actions — Phi
And yet God's ways were proved to
have been wise by their results —
Rieu
And yet what a wise person does proves
he's right — Beck

20. Then began he to upbraid the cities
. . . reproach the towns — TCNT
**wherein most of his mighty works were
done,**
in which he had done his noblest
mighty works — Rhm
in which most of his miracles . . . —
TCNT
. . . his numerous wonders . . . — Gspd
because they repented not:
because they had not repented — TCNT

21. Woe unto thee, Chorazin!
A curse on you, Chorazin! — Wms
woe unto thee, Bethsaida!
A curse on you, Bethsaida! — Wms
**for if the mighty works, which were
done in you, had been done in Tyre
and Sidon,**
. . . miracles . . . — TCNT
. . . wonders . . . — Gspd
For if Tyre and Sidon had seen the
demonstrations of God's power
which you have seen — Phi
**they would have repented long ago in
sackcloth and ashes.**

22. But I say unto you,
Moreover . . . — Rhm
But mark my words — Rieu
**It shall be more tolerable for Tyre and
Sidon at the day of judgment, than
for you.**
the doom of Tyre and Sidon will be
more bearable than yours . . . —
TCNT
Tyre and Sidon will fare better than
you will . . . — Gspd

**23. And thou, Capernaum, which art ex-
alted unto heaven,**
. . . Will you exalt yourself to Heaven?
— TCNT
. . . even to heaven — Wey
. . . Are you to be exalted to the skies?
— Gspd
shalt be brought down to hell:
thou shalt go down unto Hades — ASV
You will go down among the dead! —
Gspd

**for if the mighty works, which have
been done in thee, had been done in
Sodom,**
. . . wonders . . . — Gspd
If Sodom had seen the miracles that
you have seen — Phi
it would have remained until this day.
that city would have survived unto now
— Wey

24. But I say unto you,
Moreover . . . — Rhm
But mark my words — Rieu
**That it shall be more tolerable for the
land of Sodom in the day of judgment, than for thee.**
that the land of Sodom will fare better
. . . — Gspd
the doom of Sodom will be more bearable . . . — TCNT

25. At that time Jesus answered and said,
At that season . . . — ASV
About that time . . . — Wey
I thank thee, O Father,
I openly give praise unto thee Father—
Rhm
Lord of heaven and earth,
**because thou hast hid these things
from the wise and prudent,**
that, though thou hast hidden these
things from the wise and learned —
TCNT
. . . from sages and men of discernment
— Wey
and hast revealed them unto babes.
and hast unveiled them . . . — Wey
. . . to the child-like! — TCNT

26. Even so, Father:
Be it so, Father — Knox
Yes, Father — Beck
for so it seemed good in thy sight.
for so it was well-pleasing in thy sight
— ASV
for such has been Thy gracious will —
Wey
I praise you for wanting it to be that
way — Beck

**27. All things are delivered unto me of my
Father:**
. . . have been delivered . . . — ASV
. . . handed over . . . — Wey
**and no man knoweth the Son, but the
Father;**
. . . fully knoweth . . . — Rhm
. . . perfectly knows . . . — Wms

neither knoweth any man the Father, save the Son,
. . . perfectly knows . . . — Wms
Neither doth any one fully know . . . — Rhm
and he to whomsoever the Son will reveal him.
and those to whom the Son may choose to reveal him — NEB
. . . deliberately wills to make Him known — Amp

28. **Come unto me, all ye that labour and are heavy laden,**
. . . all you toiling and burdened ones — Wey
. . . all of you who are weary and over-burdened — Phi
. . . all whose work is hard, whose load is heavy — NEB
and I will give you rest.

and I will refresh you — Mof
and I, yes, I, will lead you into rest — Wms

29. **Take my yoke upon you,**
Bend your necks to my yoke — NEB
and learn of me;
. . . from me — TCNT
and let me be your teacher — Bas
for I am meek and lowly in heart:
. . . gentle and lowly-minded — TCNT
and ye shall find rest unto your souls.
and you will find your souls refreshed — Mof

30. **For my yoke is easy, and my burden is light.**
for the yoke I offer you is a kindly one, and the load I ask you to bear is light — Gspd
For My yoke fits so easily that My burden is light — Nor

CHAPTER 12

1. **At that time**
At that season — ASV
About the same time — TCNT
Jesus went on the sabbath day through the corn;
. . . the grainfields — ASV
and his disciples were an hungred,
. . . became hungry — Wey
and began to pluck the ears of corn,
. . . to pull the heads of wheat — Wms
. . . to pluck the heads of grain — Nor
and to eat.

2. **But when the Pharisees saw it, they said unto him,**
Behold,
. . . Look! — TCNT
thy disciples do that which is not lawful to do upon the sabbath day.
. . . what the Law forbids them to do . . . — Wey
. . . on a Sabbath! — TCNT
. . . on a day of rest — Beck

3. **But he said unto them, Have ye not read what David did, when he was an hungred,**
. . . hungry — ASV
and they that were with him;
and his men — Wey

4. **How he entered into the house of God,**
. . . the tabernacle — Knox
and did eat the shewbread,
. . . the consecrated bread — TCNT

. . . the loaves set out there before God — Knox
which was not lawful for him to eat,
though it was not allowable . . .—TCNT
neither for them which were with him,
or his men — Wey
but only for the priests?
since only priests can do so — Phi

5. **Or have ye not read in the law,**
. . . the book of law — Lam
how that on the sabbath days the priests in the temple profane the sabbath and are blameless?
. . . violate the sabbath rest in the temple . . . — Knox
. . . are not guilty when they desecrate the sabbath — Mof
. . . can break the Sabbath and yet remain blameless — Phi

6. **But I say unto you,**
That in this place is one greater than the temple.
that one greater than the temple is here — ASV
Something greater than the temple is here — Rhm

7. **But if ye had known what this meaneth,**
. . . what the text means — NEB
And had you learnt the meaning of the words — TCNT
I will have mercy, and not sacrifice,

I have set my heart on mercy not on
sacrifice — Rieu
I require mercy, not sacrifice — NEB
I desire compassion, and not a sacrifice
— NASB
**ye would not have condemned the
guiltless.**
you would not have been so quick to
condemn the innocent — Phi
8. **For the Son of man is Lord even of the
sabbath day.**
. . . master of the Sabbath — Gspd
. . . sovereign over the Sabbath — NEB
The Son of Man has even the sabbath
at his disposal — Knox
9. **And when he was departed thence,**
Passing on — TCNT
he went into their synagogue:
10. **And, behold, there was a man which
had his hand withered.**
and there he saw a man with a withered hand — TCNT
. . . a shrivelled hand — Wey
. . . a deformed hand — Tay
**And they asked him, saying,
Is it lawful to heal on the sabbath
days?**
. . . to work a cure . . . — TCNT
that they might accuse him.
so that they might have a charge to
bring against him — TCNT
11. **And he said unto them,
What man shall there be among you,**
Which of you is there — Wey
that shall have one sheep,
if he had only one sheep — TCNT
**and if it fall into a pit on the sabbath
day,**
. . . into a hole . . . — Wey
will he not lay hold on it,
. . . catch hold of it — Mof
will not put out a helping hand — Bas
and lift it out?
12. **How much then is a man better than
a sheep?**
Is not a man, however, worth far more
than a sheep — Wey
And how much more a man is worth
than a sheep! — Gspd
**Wherefore it is lawful to do well on
the sabbath days.**
Therefore it is allowable to do good
. . . — TCNT
Thus it is right to do a kindness . . .
— Mof
. . . a work of mercy . . . — Knox

13. **Then saith he to the man,
Stretch forth thine hand.**
Hold out your hand! — Gspd
And he stretched it forth;
. . . held it out — Gspd
**and it was restored whole, like as the
other.**
and it had become as sound as the other
— TCNT
14. **Then the Pharisees went out,**
But . . . — Alf
and held a council against him,
and held a consultation . . . — ABUV
plotted against Jesus — TCNT
how they might destroy him.
with a view to put him to death — Gspd
how they could get rid of him altogether — Phi
15. **But when Jesus knew it, he withdrew
himself from thence:**
And Jesus perceiving it . . . — ASV
Aware of this, Jesus departed elsewhere
— Wey
. . . went away from that place — TCNT
and great multitudes followed him,
and many followed him — ASV
and he healed them all;
16. **And charged them**
but he warned them — TCNT
sternly forbidding them — Rieu
that they should not make him known:
not to blaze abroad His doings — Wey
that they should not make him conspicuous by their talk — Phi
lest they should make him manifest —
Rhm
17. **That it might be fulfilled which was
spoken by Esaias the prophet,**
. . . through Isaiah . . . — ASV
. . . in the Prophet Isaiah — TCNT
saying,
18. **Behold my servant, whom I have
chosen;**
Behold! the Servant of my Choice —
— TCNT
**my beloved, in whom my soul is well
pleased:**
. . . in whom my heart delights! — TCNT
I will put my spirit upon him,
I will breathe my spirit upon him —
TCNT
**and he shall shew judgment to the
Gentiles.**
And he shall announce a time of judgment . . . — TCNT

... proclaim religion to the Gentiles —
Mof

and he will preach justice to the peoples — Lam

19. He shall not strive, nor cry;

He shall not wrangle or shout — Mof

... nor cry aloud — ASV

**neither shall any man hear his voice
in the streets.**

... in the broadways — Wey

20. A bruised reed shall he not break,

A crushed reed ... — Wey

He will not break off a bent reed —
Gspd

and smoking flax shall he not quench,

Nor snuff out the smouldering wick —
NEB

The dimly burning wick ... — Mon

**till he send forth judgment unto vic-
tory.**

Until he urge on Justice to victory —
Rhm

Till he has brought the judgment to a
victorious issue — TCNT

until He has led on justice to victory
— Wey

till he carries religion to victory — Mof

till he has made righteousness overcome all — Bas

until the time when he crowns his judgment with victory — Knox

**21. And in his name shall the Gentiles
trust.**

And on his name shall the Gentiles rest
their hopes — TCNT

... find hope — Lam

And his name will bring hope to the
pagans — Rieu

**22. Then was brought unto him one pos-
sessed with a devil, blind, and dumb:**

... a demoniac ... — Wey

... a man whom a demon had made
blind and dumb — Rieu

... who was also dumb and blind —
Lam

and he healed him,

**insomuch that the blind and dumb
both spake and saw.**

so that ... — TCNT

**23. And all the people were amazed, and
said,**

And all the multitudes were beside
themselves and were saying — Rhm

... were dumfounded, and began to
say — Wms

At this time the whole crowd went
wild with excitement, and people
kept saying — Phi

Is not this the son of David?

Is it possible that this is the son of
David — TCNT

This man cannot be the Son of David,
can he — NASB

**24. But when the Pharisees heard it, they
said,**

... on hearing this remark said to each
other — Phi

This fellow doth not cast out devils,

... demons — ASV

**but by Beelzebub the prince of the
devils.**

by the power of Beelzebul ... — Wey

... who rules over the devils — Beck

only by the help of Baal-zebub the
chief of the demons — TCNT

25. And Jesus knew their thoughts,

And knowing their thoughts — ASV

Reading their thoughts — Ber

and said unto them,

**Every kingdom divided against itself
is brought to desolation;**

Every kingdom in which civil war rages
suffers desolation — Wey

... is on the way to destruction—Gspd

... is bound to collapse — Phi

**and every city or house divided against
itself shall not stand:**

and every city or house in which there
is internal strife will be brought low
— Wey

**26. And if Satan cast out Satan, he is di-
vided against himself;**

So, if Satan drives Satan out, he must
be divided against himself — TCNT

... he has begun to make war on himself — Wey

how shall then his kingdom stand?

how then can his realm stand — Mof

27. And if I by Beelzebub cast out devils,

Besides ... — Mof

... by Beelzebul's power ... — Wey

... am casting out the demons — Rhm

**by whom do your children cast them
out?**

by whose help is it that your own sons
drive them out — TCNT

... your disciples ... — Wey

what alliance do your sons make when
they do the same thing — Phi

therefore they shall be your judges.

You stand condemned by them — Rieu

If this is your argument, they themselves will refute you — NEB
28. **But if I cast out devils by the Spirit of
God,**
On the other hand . . . — Rieu
**then the kingdom of God is come unto
you.**
it is evident that . . . — Wey
Then doubtless has come upon you unawares the kingdom of God! — Rhm
then the Reign of God has reached you
already — Mof
. . . has overtaken you — Gspd
. . . has swept over you unawares!—Phi
29. **Or else how can one enter into a strong
man's house, and spoil his goods,**
. . . seize his goods — Rhm
. . . carry off his goods — TCNT
except he first bind the strong man?
without first securing him — TCNT
and then he will spoil his house.
Then he can rob his house — Mon
After that he can make a clean sweep
of his house — Wms
. . . will he ransack his house — Wey
30. **He that is not with me is against me;
and he that gathereth not with me
scattereth abroad.**
and anyone who does not join me in
gathering, scatters — Gspd
and he who does not take part with me
in getting people together, is driving
them away — Bas
31. **Wherefore I say unto you,**
Which leads me to say this — Rieu
For that reason I warn you — Nor
**All manner of sin and blasphemy shall
be forgiven unto men:**
. . . profane speaking . . . — Rhm
. . . slander . . . — TCNT
. . . abusive speech — Gspd
men will be forgiven for any sin or impious word — Wey
**but the blasphemy against the Holy
Ghost shall not be forgiven unto
men.**
. . . speaking profanely of the Spirit . . .
— Rhm
. . . abusive speech about the Spirit cannot be forgiven — Gspd
32. **And whosoever speaketh a word
against the Son of man, it shall be forgiven him: but whosoever speaketh
against the Holy Ghost, it shall not be
forgiven him,**
cannot be forgiven for it — Gspd

neither in this world, neither in the
world to come.
either in the present age, or in the age
to come — TCNT
33. **Either make the tree good, and his fruit
good; or else make the tree corrupt,
and his fruit corrupt:**
Either produce like a good tree with
good fruits; or produce like a bad
tree with bad fruits — Lam
You must choose between having a
good tree with good fruit and a rotten tree with rotten fruit — Phi
Either pronounce the tree a good one
and its fruit good or pronounce it
rotten and its fruit rotten — Rieu
for the tree is known by his fruit.
For you can tell a tree at once by its
fruit — Phi
34. **O generation of vipers,**
Ye offspring of vipers — ASV
O brood of vipers — Wey
**how can ye, being evil, speak good
things?**
how can you, evil as you are, say anything good — TCNT
how can you say anything good out of
your evil hearts — Phi
**for out of the abundance of the heart
the mouth speaketh.**
For what fills the heart will rise to the
lips — TCNT
It is from the heart's overflow . . . —
Knox
35. **A good man out of the good treasure
of the heart bringeth forth good things:**
The good man out of his good treasure
bringeth forth good things — ASV
. . . the good he has accumulated . . .
— Gspd
. . . the goodness stored in his heart —
Phi
**and an evil man out of the evil treas-
ure bringeth forth evil things.**
and the evil man out of his evil treasure . . . — ASV
. . . can utter nothing but what is evil
— Knox
. . . out of what he has accumulated
that is bad, brings out things that are
bad — Gspd
36. **But I say unto you, That every idle
word that men shall speak,**
. . . for every careless thing . . . — TCNT
. . . every useless expression . . .—Rhm
. . . thoughtless word . . . — NEB

49

they shall give account thereof in the day of judgment.

37. **For by thy words thou shalt be justified,**
    For each of you by his words . . . — Wey
    Out of your own mouth you shall be acquitted — Rieu
    and by thy words thou shalt be condemned.
    and out of your own mouth condemned — Rieu

38. **Then certain of the scribes and of the Pharisees answered, saying,**
    At this point, some Teachers of the Law and Pharisees interposed — TCNT
    .. some Bible scholars and Pharisees . . . — Beck
    Master, we would see a sign from thee.
    Teacher! We desire of thee a sign to behold — Rhm
    . . . a spectacular sign given by you — Wms
    . . . your token of proof! — Ber

39. **But he answered and said unto them, An evil and adulterous generation seeketh after a sign;**
    Only a wicked and faithless age insists upon a sign — Gspd
    . . . craves evidence — Ber
    and there shall no sign be given to it, but the sign of the prophet Jonas:
    . . . Jonah the prophet — ASV

40. **For as Jonas was three days and three nights in the whale's belly;**
    For, just as Jonah was inside the sea-monster . . . — TCNT
    . . . the stomach of the great fish — Bas
    so shall the Son of man be three days and three nights
    and in the same way the Son of Man . . . — NEB
    in the heart of the earth.

41. **The men of Nineveh shall rise in judgment with this generation,**
    Even the men of Nineveh . . . — Lam
    . . . when this generation is on trial . . . — NEB
    and shall condemn it:
    and find it guilty — Lam
    and will leave it without excuse — Knox
    because they repented at the preaching of Jonas;
    because they repented under the preaching of Jonah — Mon

for they turned to the message preached by Jonah — Wms
for they turned from their sins . . . — Nor
. . . at Jonah's proclamation — TCNT
and, behold, a greater than Jonas is here.
. . . something greater than Jonah here — Rhm
and here is more than a Jonah! — TCNT
and mark! there is One greater than Jonah here — Wey

42. **The queen of the south shall rise up in the judgment with this generation,**
    . . . will awake at the judgment . . . — Wey
    . . . when this generation is on trial — NEB
    and shall condemn it:
    and find it guilty — Lam
    and will leave it without excuse — Knox
    for she came from the uttermost parts of the earth
    . . . the ends of the earth — ASV
    to hear the wisdom of Solomon;
    and, behold, a greater than Solomon is here.
    . . . something greater than Solomon here — Rhm
    and here is more than a Solomon! — TCNT
    and mark! there is One greater than Solomon here — Wey

43. **When the unclean spirit is gone out of a man,**
    No sooner does a foul spirit leave a man — TCNT
    . . . impure spirit . . . — Rhm
    he walketh through dry places,
    than it passes through places where there is no water — TCNT
    passeth through waterless places — ASV
    it roams about in the desert — Wey
    seeking rest, and findeth none.
    in search of ease . . . — Mof

44. **Then he saith, I will return into my house from whence I came out; and when he is come,**
    he findeth it empty, swept, and garnished.
    it finds it unoccupied . . . and put in order — TCNT
    . . . and ready for use — Wms

45. **Then goeth he, and taketh with himself seven other spirits more wicked than himself,**

Then off it goes to fetch seven other spirits . . . — Mof
and they enter in and dwell there: and the last state of that man is worse than the first.
. . . proves to be worse than the first — TCNT
and in the end the man is worse off than he was before — Gspd
Even so shall it be also unto this wicked generation.
This is how it will be . . . — Mof
and that is just what will happen to this evil generation — Phi
. . . this present wicked age — Gspd

46. While he yet talked to the people,
While he was still speaking — Gspd
. . . to the multitudes — ASV
behold, his mother and his brethren stood without,
. . . were standing on the edge of the crowd — Wey
desiring to speak with him.
asking to speak to him — TCNT
trying hard to get to speak to Him —
Wms

47. Then one said unto him,[3]
Some one told him this — TCNT
Behold, thy mother and thy brethren stand without, desiring to speak with thee.
. . . seeking to speak to thee — ASV

48. But he answered and said unto him that told him, Who is my mother? and who are my brethren?
Who is a mother, who are brethren, to me — Knox

49. And he stretched forth his hand toward his disciples,
and pointing to his disciples — NEB
and said, Behold my mother and my brethren!
He added, See here are my mother and my brothers — Wey

50. For whosoever shall do the will of my Father which is in heaven, the same is my brother, and sister, and mother.
To obey my Father who is in heaven — that is to be my brother and my sister and my mother — Wey

CHAPTER 13

1. The same day went Jesus out of the house,
On that day . . . — ASV
Jesus went out of doors that day — Rieu
and sat by the sea side.
and was sitting . . . — Rhm
and seated himself . . . — Mof

2. And great multitudes were gathered together unto him,
And such great crowds gathered about him — Gspd
. . . crowded round Him — Wey
so that he went into a ship,
. . . he went aboard a small boat — Phi
and sat;
and was sitting — Rhm
and the whole multitude stood on the shore.

3. And he spake many things unto them in parables,
Then he told them many truths in parables — TCNT
. . . in figures — Gspd
. . . in the form of a story — Bas
. . . in parables — that is, stories by way of illustration — Amp

saying,
for example — Nor
Behold, a sower went forth to sow;
Picture the sower going out to sow — Rieu

4. And when he sowed,
and as he sowed — ASV
some seeds fell by the way side,
. . . along the path — TCNT
and the fowls came and devoured them up:
and the birds swooped down and gobbled them up — Phi

5. Some fell upon stony places,
. . . rocky places — TCNT
where they had not much earth:
where it had but scanty soil — Wey
and forthwith they sprung up, because they had no deepness of earth:
They sprang up quickly in the shallow soil — Phi
it sprouted quickly . . . — NEB
. . . having no depth of soil — TCNT
. . . because they had not sunk deep in the ground — Knox

---

[3]Now recognized as not adequately supported by original manuscripts.

6. **And when the sun was up, they were scorched;**
   . . . the young corn was scorched—NEB
   and because they had no root, they withered away.

7. **And some fell among thorns;**
   . . . into the brambles — TCNT
   and the thorns sprung up,
   and the thistles shot up — NEB
   and choked them:
   and smothered them — Knox
   and choked the life out of them — Phi

8. **But other fell into good ground,**
   . . . in rich soil — Wms
   and brought forth fruit,
   and bore a crop — Mof
   some an hundredfold, some sixtyfold, some thirtyfold.
   some a hundred times what had been sown . . . — Phi

9. **Who hath ears to hear, let him hear.**
   . . . let him listen to this — Mof
   The man who has ears to hear should use them! — Phi

10. **And the disciples came, and said unto him,**
    At this point the disciples came forward . . . — Rieu
    Why speakest thou unto them in parables?
    . . . in figures — Gspd
    . . . in stories — Wms

11. **He answered and said unto them,**
    Because it is given unto you to know the mysteries of the kingdom of heaven, but to them it is not given.
    To you . . . the knowledge of the hidden truths of the Kingdom of Heaven has been imparted . . . — TCNT
    . . . the open secrets of the Realm of heaven . . . — Mof
    Because you have been given the chance to understand the secrets of the kingdom of Heaven . . . but they have not — Phi

12. **For whosoever hath, to him shall be given, and he shall have more abundance:**
    For whoever holds, to him shall more be given . . . — Mon
    . . . and his supply will overflow—Wms
    For if a man has possessions, he will get more until he has more than enough — Nor

but whosoever hath not, from him shall be taken away even that he hath.
But if you don't have what you should have, even what you have will be taken away from you — Beck

13. **Therefore speak I to them in parables:**
    For this reason I put things into the form of stories — Bas
    because they seeing see not;
    because, though they have eyes, they do not see — TCNT
    because for all their seeing they do not see — Mof
    because they go through life with their eyes open, but see nothing — Phi
    and hearing they hear not, neither do they understand.
    and though they have ears, they do not hear or understand — TCNT
    and for all their hearing they neither hear nor understand — Mof
    . . . but understand nothing of what they hear — Phi
    . . . and the sense is not clear to them — Bas

14. **And in them is fulfilled the prophecy of Esaias,**
    In their case the prophecy of Isaiah is being fulfilled — Mof
    They are a fulfilment of Isaiah's prophecy — Gspd
    In them more and more Isaiah's prophecy is coming true — Beck
    which saith, By hearing ye shall hear, and shall not understand;
    . . . They shall surely hear and yet will not understand — Rhm
    . . . You will listen and listen, and never understand — Gspd
    . . . You will keep on hearing, but will not understand — NASB
    and seeing ye shall see, and shall not perceive:
    and surely see and yet not perceive — Rhm
    And, though you have eyes, you will see without ever perceiving — TCNT
    And you will look and look, and never see! — Gspd
    And you will keep on seeing, but will not perceive — NASB

15. **For this people's heart is waxed gross,**
    For this people's mind is stupefied — Wey

For this nation's mind has grown dull
— Gspd
... hath become dense — Rhm
... is made fat — Mon
and their ears are dull of hearing,
their ears are heavy of hearing — Mof
And they hear faintly with their ears —
Gspd
and their eyes they have closed;
Their eyes also have they closed —
TCNT
And they have shut tight their eyes —
Wms
**lest at any time they should see with
their eyes,**
Lest some day ... — TCNT
and hear with their ears,
and should understand with their heart,
And with their hearts should understand — Rhm
... in their mind ... — TCNT
and should be converted,
and turn again — Mof
and I should heal them.
So that I might heal them — Wey
for me to cure them — Mof

16. **But blessed are your eyes, for they see:**
But as for you ... — Wey
But how fortunate you are to have eyes
that see — Phi
... your eyes are privileged because
they see — Rieu
... for they are beginning to see —
Wms
and your ears, for they hear.
... for they are beginning to hear —
Wms

17. **For verily I say unto you,**
For I tell you in truth — Wey
Believe me — Phi
**That many prophets and righteous
men have desired to see those things
which ye see,**
... upright men ... — Gspd
... longed to see what you see — RSV
and have not seen them;
and could not see it — Gspd
**and to hear those things which ye hear,
and have not heard them.**
and could not hear it — Gspd

18. **Hear ye therefore the parable of the
sower.**
To you, then, I will explain the parable
of the sower — Wey
Listen to what the parable of the sower
means — Beck

19. **When any one heareth the word of the
kingdom,**
... the Message of the Kingdom —
TCNT
... the word by which the kingdom is
preached — Knox
and understandeth it not,
then cometh the wicked one,
... the Evil One — Wey
**and catcheth away that which was
sown in his heart.**
and snatcheth away ... — ASV
and robs him of the seed that has been
sown in his mind — Gspd
**This is he which received seed by the
way side.**
This is the man meant by the seed
which was sown along the path —
TCNT

20. **But he that received the seed into
stony places,**
And he that was sown upon the rocky
places — ASV
... the thin rocky soil — Wms
**the same is he that heareth the word,
and anon with joy receiveth it;**
and at once accepts it joyfully — TCNT
and accepts it at once with enthusiasm
— Mof

21. **Yet hath he not root in himself,**
but it takes no real root in him — Gspd
but as it strikes no root in him — NEB
but dureth for a while:
he stands for only a short time — TCNT
he cannot hold out long — Rieu
**for when tribulation or persecution
ariseth**
but when suffering comes or persecution ... — Wey
because of the word,
... the Message — TCNT
by and by he is offended.
he at once turns against it — Wey
he is at once repelled — Mof
he promptly recants — Rieu
he at once gives it up — Nor

22. **He also that received seed among
the thorns**
And he that was sown among the
thorns — ASV
is he that heareth the word;
this is he that heareth the word — ASV
and the care of this world,
and the anxiety of the age — Rhm
but the cares of life — TCNT

and then the worries of the time —
Gspd
and the deceitfulness of riches,
and the glamour of wealth — TCNT
and the delight of being rich — Mof
and the deception caused by riches —
Lam
and the lure of riches — Rieu
**choke the word, and he becometh un-
fruitful.**
completely choke the Message, so that
it gives no return — TCNT
put a stop to the growth of the word
... — Bas
23. **But he that received seed into the good
ground**
And he that was sown upon the good
ground — ASV
**is he that heareth the word, and under-
standeth it;**
He's one who continues to hear and
understand the Word — Beck
which also beareth fruit,
and really yields a return — TCNT
so goes on producing good things —
Beck
**and bringeth forth, some an hundred-
fold, some sixty, some thirty.**
producing in some cases a hundredfold,
in others sixty, in others thirty —
Rieu
... one a hundred, another sixty, and
another thirty times as much as was
sown — Beck
24. **Another parable put he forth unto
them, saying,
The kingdom of heaven**
... of the heavens — Rhm
The Realm of heaven — Mof
**is likened unto a man which sowed
good seed in his field:**
may be compared ... — Wey
... clean seed — Knox
25. **But while men slept,**
But while his men were asleep — Phi
**his enemy came and sowed tares
among the wheat,**
... and resowed weeds among the
wheat — Mof
and went his way.
and escaped — Rieu
26. **But when the blade was sprung up,**
So, when the blades of corn shot up —
TCNT
and brought forth fruit,
and formed the kernel — Mof

and yielded their ripened grain — Wms
then appeared the tares also.
... the weeds appeared as well — Mof
the darnel could be seen among it —
NEB
27. **So the servants of the householder
came and said unto him,**
... the owner's servants ... — TCNT
... the farmer's men ... — Wey
**Sir, didst not thou sow good seed in
thy field?**
... clean seed ... — Knox
from whence then hath it tares?
Where, then, do the tares in it come
from — TCNT
How then does it contain weeds — Mof
28. **He said unto them,
An enemy hath done this.**
Some blackguard has done this to spite
me — Phi
The servants said unto him,
... say ... — ASV
**Wilt thou then that we go and gather
them up?**
29. **But he said, Nay;**
But he saith ... — ASV
lest while ye gather up the tares,
... darnel — Rhm
ye root up also the wheat with them.
30. **Let both grow together until the harvest: and in the time of harvest I will
say to the reapers,
Gather ye together first the tares,**
... darnel — Wey
**and bind them in bundles to burn
them:**
... bundles ready to burn — Phi
but gather the wheat into my barn.
... in my granary — Mof
31. **Another parable put he forth unto
them, saying,
The kingdom of heaven**
The Realm of heaven — Mof
**is like to a grain of mustard seed,
which a man took, and sowed in his
field:**
32. **Which indeed is the least of all seeds:**
As a seed it is the smallest of them all
— Phi
... less than all seeds — ASV
**but when it is grown,
it is the greatest among herbs,**
it is greater than the herbs — ASV
... garden-plants — Rhm
it is larger than the herbs — TCNT

and becometh a tree,
yea, it grows into a tree — Wms
so that the birds of the air come and lodge in the branches thereof.
so large that wild birds come . . . — Mof
. . . the wild birds come and roost in its branches — TCNT

33. **Another parable spake he unto them; The kingdom of heaven**
. . . of the heavens — Rhm
The Realm of heaven — Mof
is like unto leaven,
is like some yeast — TCNT
is like dough — Mof
which a woman took, and hid in three measures of meal,
and worked into a bushel of flour — Wms
till the whole was leavened.
for it to work there till the whole is leavened — Wey
until the whole had risen — TCNT
enough to leaven the whole batch — Knox

34. **All these things spake Jesus unto the multitude in parables;**
. . . to the crowds . . . — Mof
. . . in the form of stories — Bas
and without a parable spake he not unto them:
indeed to them he used never to speak at all except in parables — TCNT
and told them nothing except in figures — Gspd

35. **That it might be fulfilled which was spoken by the prophet, saying,**
. . . through the prophet . . . — Rhm
in fulfilment of these words in the Prophet — TCNT
I will open my mouth in parables;
. . . in figures — Gspd
. . . in stories — Wms
I will utter things which have been kept secret from the foundation of the world.
I will bring up things hidden from the foundation! — Rhm
. . . from before all time — Bas
. . . from the beginning of the world — Knox
I will utter truths concealed since creation — Wms

36. **Then Jesus sent the multitude away,**
Then he left the multitudes — ASV

and went into the house:
. . . indoors — Mof
and his disciples came unto him, saying,
. . . with the request — Wey
Declare unto us the parable of the tares of the field.
Explain . . . — ASV
. . . the parable of the darnel . . . — Rhm
. . . the figure of the weeds in the field — Gspd

37. **He answered and said unto them, He that soweth the good seed is the Son of man;**

38. **The field is the world;**
. . . the whole world — Phi
the good seed are the children of the kingdom;
and the good seed, these are the sons of the kingdom — ASV
By the good seed is meant the People of the Kingdom — TCNT
but the tares are the children of the wicked one;
and the darnel seeds are the sons of the evil one — Rhm
The weeds are . . . — Gspd
. . . followers of the wicked one—Wms
The tares are the wicked — TCNT

39. **The enemy that sowed them is the devil;**
The blackguard who sowed them . . . — Phi
. . . the adversary — Rhm
the harvest is the end of the world;
The harvest-time is the close of the age — TCNT
and the reapers are the angels.

40. **As therefore the tares are gathered**
As then the darnel is collected together — Wey
. . . the weeds are gathered — Mof
Therefore, just as the tares are picked out — Lam
and burned in the fire;
. . . with fire — ASV
so shall it be in the end of this world.
This is what will happen at the close of the age — Gspd

41. **The Son of man shall send forth his angels,**
. . . will despatch his angels — Mof
and they shall gather out of his kingdom
and they will pick out . . . — Lam

and they will uproot from the kingdom
— Phi
all things that offend,
... that cause stumbling — ASV
all that hinders — TCNT
all causes of sin — Wey
all who are hindrances — Mof
everything that is spoiling it — Phi
all who lead others to do wrong — Beck
and them which do iniquity;
and those who live in sin — TCNT
and all who violate His laws — Wey

42. **And shall cast them into a furnace of
fire:**
... the fiery furnace — TCNT
**there shall be wailing and gnashing of
teeth.**
where they will be weeping and grinding of teeth — TCNT
where there will be tears and bitter regret — Phi

43. **Then shall the righteous shine forth as
the sun**
Then, at last, the just will shine out,
clear as the sun — Knox
... radiate like the sun — Ber
in the kingdom of their Father.
in the Realm of their Father — Mof
Who hath ears to hear, let him hear.
He that hath ears, let him hear — ASV
The man who has ears should use
them! — Phi
Let him who has ears be listening —
Amp

44. **Again, the kingdom of heaven**
The Realm of heaven — Mof
... of the heavens — Rhm
is like unto treasure hid in a field;
is like a hoard of money, buried in a
field — Gspd
**the which when a man hath found, he
hideth,**
which a man found and hid again —
TCNT
... and covered up — RSV
and for joy thereof
and by reason of his joy — Rhm
and then, in his delight ... — TCNT
goeth and selleth all that he hath,
... went ... sold ... — TCNT
... whatsoever he hath — Rhm
and buyeth that field.
... bought ... — TCNT

45. **Again, the kingdom of heaven**
... the Realm of heaven — Mof
... of the heavens — Rhm

is like unto a merchant man, seeking
goodly pearls:
... a merchant seeking beautiful pearls
— Rhm
... a merchant in search of choice
pearls — TCNT
... rare pearls — Knox

46. **Who, when he had found one pearl of
great price,**
... a single pearl of high price — Mof
... of exceptional value — Ber
**went and sold all that he had, and
bought it.**
went and gave all that he had in exchange for it — Bas

47. **Again, the kingdom of heaven**
... Realm of heaven — Mof
... of the heavens — Rhm
is like unto a net,
... a large drag-net — Rhm
that was cast into the sea,
let down into the sea — Wey
and gathered of every kind:
and caught fish of all kinds — TCNT

48. **Which, when it was full,**
they drew to shore,
they drew up on the beach — ASV
and sat down,
and gathered the good into vessels,
and sorted the good fish into baskets
— TCNT
but cast the bad away.
... the worthless ... — Rhm

49. **So shall it be at the end of the world:**
... close of the age — TCNT
... when the world is brought to an
end — Knox
the angels shall come forth,
The messengers will come forth—Rhm
**and sever the wicked from among the
just.**
and separate the wicked from among
the righteous — Rhm
... from the midst of the righteous —
ABUV
... from among the upright — Gspd

50. **And shall cast them into the furnace of
fire: there shall be wailing and gnashing of teeth.**[4]

51. **Jesus said unto them, Have ye understood all these things?**
Have you grasped all this — Knox
... all these stories — Wms

---

[4]Compare verse 42.

They say unto him, Yea, Lord.
. . . Yea — ASV

52. **Then said he unto them, Therefore every scribe which is instructed unto the kingdom of heaven**
. . . So every Teacher of the Law, who has received instruction about the Kingdom of Heaven — TCNT
. . . You can see, then . . . how every one who knows the Law and becomes a disciple of the kingdom of Heaven — Phi
. . . a learner in the kingdom of Heaven — NEB
. . . Realm of heaven — Mof
. . . of the heavens — Rhm
is like unto a man that is an householder,
must be like a rich man — Knox
should be like the master of a house — Nor
which bringeth forth out of his treasure things new and old.
who knows how to bring both new and old things out of his treasure-house — Knox
. . . from his stores . . . — TCNT

53. **And it came to pass, that when Jesus had finished these parables,**
Jesus concluded this series of parables — Wey
. . . figures — Gspd
. . . stories — Wms
he departed thence.
and then departed — Wey
he withdrew from that place — TCNT

54. **And when he was come into his own country,**
. . . to His own home town — Wms
and coming into his own city — Rhm
he taught them in their synagogue,
began teaching . . . — Rhm
where he continued teaching the people in their synagogues — Mon
insomuch that they were astonished, and said,

in such a manner that they were deeply impressed . . . — TCNT
so that with astonishment were they being struck and were saying — Rhm
till in their amazement they said — Phi
Whence hath this man this wisdom,
Where did he get this wisdom — TCNT
and these mighty works?
and the power to do these wonders — Gspd

55. **Is not this the carpenter's son?**
. . . the wood-worker's son — Bas
He's only the carpenter's son — Phi
is not his mother called Mary?
Isn't Mary his mother — Phi
and his brethren, James, and Joses, and Simon, and Judas?
. . . Joseph . . . — ASV

56. **And his sisters, are they not all with us?**
And his sisters, too — are not they all living among us — TCNT
Whence then hath this man all these things?

57. **And they were offended in him.**
And they began to find cause of stumbling in him — Rhm
These things proved a hindrance to their believing in him — TCNT
So they were repelled by him — Mof
But Jesus said unto them,
and this led him to say — NEB
A prophet is not without honour,
A prophet is not refused honor any where — Gspd
No prophet is insulted — Lam
save in his own country,
. . . home town — NASB
and in his own house.
and among his own family — Wey

58. **And he did not many mighty works there because of their unbelief.**
And he did not work many miracles there, because of their want of faith — TCNT
And He performed but few mighty deeds there . . . — Wey

CHAPTER 14

1. **At that time**
About that time — Wey
Just then — Mon
Herod the tetrarch
Prince Herod — TCNT
Herod the governor — Gspd

Herod, who ruled in that quarter — Knox
heard of the fame of Jesus,
heard the report concerning Jesus — ASV
heard what was told of Jesus — Knox

2. **And said unto his servants,**
 . . . attendants — TCNT
 This is John the Baptist;
 This must be John the Baptist — TCNT
 This is no other than John the Baptist
 — Knox
 . . . John the Baptizer! — Beck
 . . . John the Immerser — Rhm
 he is risen from the dead;
 he must be risen from the dead—TCNT
 **and therefore mighty works do shew
 forth themselves in him.**
 and that is why these miraculous powers are active in him — TCNT
 . . . the powers of performing miracles . . . — Amp
 . . . are working through him — Mof
 . . . within him — Rhm

3. **For Herod had laid hold on John,**
 It must be explained that Herod had
 arrested John — Rieu
 and bound him,
 put him in chains — TCNT
 **and put him in prison for Herodias'
 sake, his brother Philip's wife.**
 and put him out of the way by putting
 him in prison . . . — Wms
 . . . to please Herodias . . . — TCNT

4. **For John said unto him, It is not lawful for thee to have her.**
 whom John had been telling him he
 could not marry — Rieu
 because John kept telling him . . . —
 Mon
 . . . You have no right to be living with
 her — TCNT
 . . . to have her as your wife — Lam

5. **And when he would have put him to
 death,**
 And he would have liked to put him
 to death — Wey
 He was anxious to kill him — Mof
 he feared the multitude,
 but was afraid of popular feeling —
 Rieu
 because they counted him as a prophet.
 . . . looked on John as a Prophet —
 TCNT
 . . . accepted him as a prophet — Lam
 in whose eyes John was a prophet —
 NEB

6. **But when Herod's birthday was kept,**
 Then, at the celebration of Herod's
 birthday — Knox

the daughter of Herodias danced before them,
 . . . before his guests — TCNT
 . . . in public — Mof
 and pleased Herod.
 to the delight of Herod — Mof

7. **Whereupon he promised with an oath
 to give her whatsoever she would ask.**
 and so passionately promised to give
 her . . . — WMS
 . . . whatsoever she should ask for herself — Rhm

8. **And she, being before instructed of her
 mother, said,**
 . . . being put forward by her mother,
 saith — ASV
 . . . at the instigation of her mother . . .
 — Mof
 She had been prompted beforehand by
 her mother — Knox
 **Give me here John Baptist's head in a
 charger.**
 Give me . . . this moment . . . — Mof
 . . . here and now . . . — Phi
 Give me right here on a tray . . . —
 Lam
 . . . on a platter . . . —ASV
 . . . the head of John the Baptist —
 Beck
 . . . John the Immerser — Rhm

9. **And the king was sorry:**
 The king was distressed at this—TCNT
 . . . was shocked — Nor
 . . . grieved — Alf
 nevertheless for the oath's sake,
 yet because of his repeated oath—Wey
 and them which sat with him at meat,
 and of the guests at his table — TCNT
 . . . who reclined at table with him —
 ABUV
 he commanded it to be given her.
 he gave orders that she should have it
 — Rieu

10. **And he sent,**
 and beheaded John in the prison.
 and so had John beheaded . . .—Knox

11. **And his head was brought in a charger,**
 . . . on a platter — ASV
 and given to the damsel:
 . . . young girl — Mon
 and she brought it to her mother.
 and she carried it off to her mother —
 Knox

12. **And his disciples came, and took up
 the body,**
 . . . corpse — ASV

and buried it, and went and told Jesus.

. . . told the news to Jesus — Phi

13. **When Jesus heard of it,**
he departed thence by ship into a desert
place apart:
he withdrew from thence in a boat, to
a desert place apart — ASV
he retired privately in a boat to a lonely
spot — TCNT
. . . to an uninhabited and secluded
district — Wey
. . . to a deserted place where he could
be alone — Rieu
and when the people had heard there-
of,
. . . the multitudes . . . — ASV
. . . heard of his departure — Phi
they followed him on foot out of the
cities.
came out of their towns and went after
him on foot — Rieu
and came after him by land from the
towns — NEB

14. **And Jesus went forth, and saw a great**
multitude,
On getting out of the boat . . . — TCNT
As he went ashore . . . — RSV
So Jesus disembarking was faced by a
large crowd — Rieu
. . . throng — RSV
and was moved with compassion
toward them,
and he had compassion on them—ASV
and was very deeply moved — Phi
and he healed their sick.

15. **And when it was evening, his disciples**
came to him, saying,
As twilight fell . . . — Mon
This is a desert place,
. . . lonely spot — TCNT
. . . uninhabited place — Wey
and the time is now past;
and the best of the day is now gone
— Wey
and supper-time has passed already —
Rieu
send the multitude away,
send therefore . . . — Alf
dismiss the multitudes — ABUV
that they may go into the villages, and
buy themselves victuals.
. . . food — ASV

16. **But Jesus said unto them, They need**
not depart;
give ye them to eat.

it is for you to give them something
to eat — TCNT

17. **And they say unto him,**
We have here but five loaves, and two
fishes.
We have nothing here but . . . — Alf
. . . five loaves of bread and two fish
— Lam

18. **He said, Bring them hither to me.**

19. **And he commanded the multitude to**
sit down on the grass,
and He told all the people to sit down
. . . — Wey
. . . recline upon the grass — Rhm
and took the five loaves,
. . . loaves of bread — Lam
and the two fishes,
. . . two fish — Wey
and looking up to heaven,
he blessed,
and said the blessing — TCNT
he thanked God — Phi
and brake,
He broke up the loaves — Wey
and gave the loaves to his disciples,
. . . the disciples — ASV
and the disciples to the multitude.
and the disciples gave them to the multitudes — Alf
. . . distributed them . . . — Wey

20. **And they did all eat, and were filled:**
. . . and were fully satisfied — Wey
Every one had sufficient to eat — TCNT
They all ate to their hearts' content —
NEB
and they took up of the fragments that
remained twelve baskets full.
and they picked up enough of the broken pieces that were left to fill twelve
baskets — TCNT
and the scraps left over, which they
picked up, were enough to fill twelve
great baskets — NEB

21. **And they that had eaten were about**
five thousand men, beside women and
children.
. . . without counting women and children — TCNT

22. **And straightway Jesus constrained his**
disciples to get into a ship,
Immediately afterwards . . . — TCNT
As soon as this was done, he prevailed
upon his disciples . . . — Knox

and to go before him unto the other side,
and cross over in advance of him — TCNT
... to the opposite shore — Wey
while he sent the multitudes away.
till he should send ... — ASV
... home — Knox

23. **And when he had sent the multitudes away,**
When he had seen the people off — Rieu
he went up into a mountain apart to pray:
He climbed the hill to pray in solitude — Wey
... to be alone and pray — Beck
and when the evening was come, he was there alone.
... he was still there alone — Lam

24. **But the ship was now in the midst of the sea,**
The boat was by this time some miles from shore — TCNT
tossed with waves: for the wind was contrary.
distressed by the waves ... — ASV
at the mercy of the waves ... — Phi
battling with a head-wind and a rough sea — NEB

25. **And in the fourth watch of the night**
But towards daybreak — Wey
... when the night had reached its fourth quarter — Knox
Between three and six in the morning — NEB
Jesus went unto them,
he came unto them — ASV
... towards the disciples — TCNT
walking on the sea.

26. **And when the disciples saw him walking on the sea, they were troubled,**
... terrified — TCNT
... greatly alarmed — Wey
saying, It is a spirit;
... ghost — ASV
... phantom — Mon
and they cried out for fear.
and by reason of their fear they cried out — Rhm
and shrieked for fear — Mof
... with terror — Wey

27. **But straightway Jesus spake unto them,**
But Jesus at once spoke to them—TCNT
saying, Be of good cheer;
... Courage! — TCNT

... It's all right! — Phi
... All is well! — Rieu
it is I;
I AM — Amp
be not afraid.
stop being afraid — Wms

28. **And Peter answered him and said, Lord,**
... Master — TCNT
if it be thou, bid me come unto thee on the water.
... upon the waters — ASV
... across the water — Rieu

29. **And he said, Come.**
Come on, then, replied Jesus — Phi
And when Peter was come down out of the ship,
So Peter got down from the boat — TCNT
he walked on the water,
... over the water — Alf
... waters — ASV
to go to Jesus.
and went towards Jesus — TCNT

30. **But when he saw the wind boisterous,**
but, when he felt the wind — TCNT
Then, seeing how strong the wind was — Knox
he was afraid;
he lost courage — Knox
he panicked — Phi
and beginning to sink, he cried,
... he cried out — ASV
saying, Lord, save me.
Master! Save me! — TCNT

31. **And immediately Jesus stretched forth his hand,**
Instantly Jesus stretched out his hand — TCNT
and caught him,
and took hold of him — ASV
and said unto him,
and saith unto him — ASV
O thou of little faith,
How little you trust me! — Mof
You little-faith! — Phi
wherefore didst thou doubt?
Why did you falter — TCNT
What made you lose your nerve like that — Phi

32. **And when they were come into the ship, the wind ceased.**
... lulled — Wey

33. **Then they that were in the ship came and worshipped him,**

And they that were in the boat worshipped him — ASV
... threw themselves on their faces before him — TCNT
saying, Of a truth thou art the Son of God.
... You are indeed God's Son—TCNT
... a son of God — Rieu
34. And when they were gone over, they came into the land of Gennesaret.
they came to the land, unto Gennesaret — ASV
they came up the land into Gennesaret — Rhm
... the country of Genesar — Knox
35. And when the men of that place had knowledge of him,
... recognized him — Alf

they sent out into all that country round about, and brought unto him all that were diseased;
36. And besought him
and kept begging him — Mon
And they began to entreat Him — NASB
that they might only touch the hem of his garment:
merely to let them touch the tassel of his cloak — TCNT
... the fringe of his garment — ABUV
... the mere tassel of his robe — Mof
and as many as touched were made perfectly whole.
... were made whole — ASV
... were restored to perfect health — Wey

CHAPTER 15

1. Then came to Jesus scribes and Pharisees,
Then come ... — Alf
... Pharisees and Bible scholars ... — Beck
which were of Jerusalem,
... from Jerusalem — Alf
saying,
who inquired — Wey

2. Why do thy disciples transgress the tradition of the elders?
... keep transgressing ... — Mon
... break the rules handed down by our ancestors — Gspd
for they wash not their hands when they eat bread.
For they eat their bread without first washing their hands — Gspd
For they do not practice [ceremonially] washing ... — Amp

3. But he answered and said unto them,
... He retorted — Wey
Why do ye also transgress the commandment of God by your tradition?
And why do you yourselves transgress ... — NASB
... keep transgressing ... — Mon
... in the interest of your tradition — NEB
Why do you too break God's command for the sake of what has been handed down to you — Gspd

4. For God commanded, saying,
For God said — ASV
Honour thy father and mother:
and, He that curseth father or mother,
... speaketh evil of ... — ASV
let him die the death.
let him surely die! — Rhm
must certainly be put to death — Wms
dies without hope of reprieve — Knox
5. But ye say,
Whosoever shall say to his father or his mother,
It is a gift, by whatsoever thou mightest be profited by me;
That wherewith thou mightest have been profited by me is given to God — ASV
I am making a temple-offering of all the support you might have got from me — Rieu
What you would have gained from me is given to God — RSV
Anything of mine that might have been of use to you is given to God—Gspd
... is dedicated to God — Mof
6. And honour not his father or his mother, he shall be free.
does not have to provide for his father — Gspd
is in no way bound to honor his father — Mon
then father or mother can get no service from him — Knox
shall no longer be bound by filial duty — Rieu

Thus have ye made the commandment of God of none effect by your tradition.

So you have repealed the law of God to suit your own tradition — Mof

So you have nullified what God has said, for the sake of what has been handed down to you — Gspd

And so your tradition empties the commandment of God of all its meaning — Phi

7. Ye hypocrites,

You false ones — Bas

What hypocrisy! — NEB

well did Esaias prophesy of you, saying,

it was indeed of you that Isaiah prophesied when he said — Mof

Isaiah described you beautifully when he said — Phi

How right Isaiah was when he prophesied about you — Rieu

8. This people draweth nigh unto me with their mouth, and honoureth me with their lips;

This people honoreth me with their lips — ASV

... pays me lip-service — NEB

but their heart is far from me.

while their heart far off holdeth from me — Rhm

9. But in vain they do worship me,

Their worship of me is an empty show — Wms

teaching for doctrines the commandments of men.

Teaching as their doctrines the precepts of men — ASV

For the lessons they teach are but human precepts — Gspd

they make doctrines of the precepts of men — Rieu

10. And he called the multitude,

... called to him ... — ASV

and said unto them,

Hear, and understand:

Listen to this, and grasp what it means — Knox

... understand this thoroughly — Phi

11. Not that which goeth into the mouth defileth a man;

it is not what goeth into a man's mouth that makes him common or unclean — Phi

but that which cometh out of the mouth,

It is what comes out of a man's mouth — Phi

this defileth a man.

that does defile him! — TCNT

that makes him unclean — Wey

12. Then came his disciples, and said unto him,

Later ... — Phi

Then coming near his disciples say unto him — Rhm

Knowest thou that the Pharisees were offended, after they heard this saying?

Are you aware ... — Ber

Do you know that the Pharisees are deeply offended by what you said — Phi

... what You just said — Nor

... were shocked to hear you say that — Gspd

13. But he answered and said, Every plant, which my heavenly Father hath not planted, shall be rooted up.

... will be pulled up by the roots — Phi

14. Let them alone:

Let them say what they will — Knox

they be blind leaders of the blind.

they are blind guides — ASV

And if the blind lead the blind,

and if one blind man leads another — Mof

both shall fall into the ditch.

... a pit — ASV

15. Then answered Peter and said unto him, Declare unto us this parable.

... Explain the maxim for us — Wms

... Make the story clear to us — Bas

16. And Jesus said,

And he said — ASV

Are ye also yet without understanding?

Are ye also even yet without understanding — ABUV

... without discernment — Rhm

Have even you no understanding yet — Gspd

Are you, like them, still without wisdom — Bas

You too? Still so dull? — Rieu

17. Do not ye yet understand,

Perceive ye not — ASV

that whatsoever entereth in at the mouth

that any uncleanness which finds its way into a man's mouth — Knox goeth into the belly,

passes into the stomach — Wey

travels down into his belly — Knox

and is cast out into the draught?

and is afterwards ejected from the body
— Wey

**18. But those things which proceed out of
the mouth**

whereas all that comes out of his
mouth — Knox

come forth from the heart;

has its origins in the heart — NEB

come from his heart and mind — Phi

and they defile the man.

and it is these that defile the man —
Wey

and it is they that really make a man
unclean — Phi

**19. For out of the heart proceed evil
thoughts, murders,**

It is from the heart that his wicked
designs come, his sins of murder —
Knox

For it is from a man's mind that evil
thoughts arise — murder — Phi

. . . evil thoughts, such as . . . murder
— Lam

adulteries,

adultery — Wms

broken faith between the married —
Bas

fornications,

sexual vice — Mof

immorality — Gspd

unclean desires of the flesh — Bas

thefts,

stealing — Mof

false witness,

perjury — TCNT

blasphemies:

railings — ASV

profane speakings — Rhm

slander — Wey

**20. These are the things which defile a
man:**

. . . make a man unclean — Wey

. . . pollute a man — Gspd

**but to eat with unwashen hands de-
fileth not a man.**

but not eating with unwashed hands!
— Gspd

. . . without washing his hands properly! — Phi

As for eating with unwashed hands,
that defiles no one — Rieu

21. Then Jesus went thence,

Jesus then left that place — Mon

**and departed into the coasts of Tyre
and Sidon.**

and withdrew into . . . — ASV

. . . the country around Tyre and Sidon
— TCNT

22. And, behold, a woman of Canaan

. . . a Canaanitish woman — ASV

came out of the same coasts,

of that district . . . — TCNT

who came from the borderlands —
Rieu

and cried unto him,

began crying out — Rhm

and kept crying — Wey

wailing — Mof

crying at the top of her voice — Phi

**saying, Have mercy on me, O Lord,
thou son of David;**

Master, Son of David, pity me — Wey

**my daughter is grievously vexed with
a devil.**

. . . cruelly harassed by a demon —
Wey

. . . evil spirit — Mon

. . . seriously afflicted with insanity —
Lam

. . . in a terrible state — a devil has got
into her! — Phi

23. But he answered her not a word.

But he would not answer her a word
— Gspd

He gave her no word in answer —
Knox

**And his disciples came and besought
him,**

. . . urged him — Gspd

. . . began requesting him — Rhm

. . . kept beseeching him — Mon

saying, Send her away;

Rid us of her, they said — Knox

for she crieth after us.

She keeps calling out after us — TCNT

she is wailing behind us — Mof

she's still following us and calling out
— Phi

**24. But he answered and said, I am not
sent**

I was only sent, replied Jesus — Phi

**but unto the lost sheep of the house of
Israel.**

. . . the sheep which went astray from

. . . the wandering sheep . . . — Bas

. . . the house of Israel — Lam

25. Then came she and worshipped him,
Nevertheless . . . — Alf
. . . began bowing down to him — Rhm
. . . and threw herself at His feet — Wey
. . . knelt before him — Mof
. . . kept praying — Wms
saying, Lord, help me.
. . . Master, help me! — TCNT

26. But he answered and said,
It is not meet
It is not fair — TCNT
It is not right, you know — Phi
to take the children's bread,
. . . children's food — TCNT
and to cast it to dogs.
. . . little dogs — Rhm
. . . puppies — Beck

27. And she said, Truth, Lord:
No, sir, she said — Mof
yet the dogs eat of the crumbs which
fall from their masters' table.
for the dogs also eat . . . — Alf
and yet the house dogs usually eat . . .
— Wms
for even the pups eat . . . — Ber
but even the dogs live on the scraps
that fall from their master's table!
— Phi

28. Then Jesus answered and said unto her,
O woman, great is thy faith:
Hearing this Jesus replied, Woman,
what faith you have! — NEB
be it unto thee even as thou wilt.
it shall be as you wish — Phi
your prayer is granted as you wish —
Mof
And her daughter was made whole
from that very hour.
. . . was healed from that hour — ASV
. . . at once — NASB

29. And Jesus departed from thence,
and came nigh unto the sea of Galilee;
skirted the Sea of Galilee — Rieu
went along the shore . . . — Mon
and went up into a mountain,
. . . up the hillside — Mof
and after climbing a hill — Mon
and sat down there.
was sitting there — Rhm

30. And great multitudes came unto him,
having with them
bringing with them — Wey
those that were lame, blind, dumb,
maimed,
. . . lame, crippled, blind, or dumb —
TCNT

and many others,
and many other sufferers — NEB
and cast them down at Jesus' feet; and
he healed them:
They put them down . . . — TCNT

31. Insomuch that the multitude wondered,
and the crowd was astonished — TCNT
Great was the amazement of the people — NEB
when they saw the dumb to speak,
. . . the dumb speaking — ASV
the maimed to be whole,
the maimed with their hands perfect —
Wey
the lame to walk,
and the lame walking — ASV
the lame walking about — TCNT
and the blind to see:
and the blind seeing — ASV
and the blind with their sight restored
— TCNT
and they glorified the God of Israel.
. . . praised . . . — TCNT

32. Then Jesus called his disciples unto
him, and said, I have compassion on
the multitude,
But Jesus quietly called his disciples to
him. My heart goes out to this crowd,
he said — Phi
because they continue with me now
three days,
for they have already been with . . . —
TCNT
and have nothing to eat:
. . . nothing left to eat — Gspd
and I will not send them away fasting,
and I am unwilling to send them away
hungry — TCNT
lest they faint in the way.
lest by any means they faint . . . — Rhm
for they may give out on the way —
Gspd
. . . collapse on the way — Phi
or they will have no strength for the
journey — Bas

33. And his disciples say unto him,
Whence should we have so much bread
in the wilderness,
. . . loaves in such numbers — Rhm
. . . in this remote place — Wey
as to fill so great a multitude?
to satisfy so vast a multitude — Wey
to feed such a crowd — Gspd

34. And Jesus saith unto them, How many
loaves have ye?

And they said, Seven, and a few little fishes.

. . . and there are a few small fishes — NEB

35. And he commanded the multitude to sit down on the ground.

Then he told the people to settle down on the ground — Rieu

36. And he took the seven loaves and the fishes,
and gave thanks,

and, after saying the thanksgiving — TCNT

said a blessing — Rieu

and brake them,
and gave to his disciples, and the disciples to the multitude.

and then distributed them to the disciples, and they to the people — Wey

and began giving . . . — Rhm

37. And they did all eat, and were filled:

Every one had sufficient to eat — TCNT

They all ate to their hearts' content — NEB

and they took up of the broken meat that was left seven baskets full.

and the leftovers filled seven hampers — Ber

and the scraps left over, which they picked up, were enough to fill seven baskets — NEB

. . . seven large baskets — Mof

38. And they that did eat were four thousand men,
beside women and children.

without counting women and children — TCNT

39. And he sent away the multitude,

He then dismissed the people — Wey

and took ship,

and embarked in the ship — Alf

and came into the coasts of Magdala.

and went to the neighbourhood of Magadan — TCNT

and crossed to the region of Magedan — Knox

CHAPTER 16

1. The Pharisees also with the Sadducees came,

And the Pharisees and Sadducees . . . — ASV

and tempting desired him that he would shew them a sign from heaven.

and trying him asked . . . — ASV

and, to test Him, asked Him to show them some wonderful proof from heaven — Beck

. . . a spectacular sign from heaven — Wms

2. He answered and said unto them,[5]
When it is evening, ye say,
It will be fair weather: for the sky is red.

It will be fine weather, for the sky is as red as fire — TCNT

3. And in the morning, It will be foul weather to day: for the sky is red and lowring.

. . . It will be stormy today, for the sky is red and threatening — RSV

. . . The sky is red and angry — Rieu

O ye hypocrites, ye can discern the face of the sky;

You know how to interpret the appearance of the sky — RSV

The face of the heaven indeed ye learn to distinguish — Rhm

You hypocrites, who can tell the weather by looking at the sky — Rieu

but can ye not discern the signs of the times?

but you have no idea how to interpret the signs of the times! — Phi

yet you are unable to read the signs of the times! — TCNT

4. A wicked and adulterous generation

An evil and . . . — ASV

. . . faithless age — Gspd

. . . apostate generation — Wey

. . . immoral generation — Nor

seeketh after a sign;

asks for a sign — Knox

is hankering for a spectacular sign — Wms

demands a sign — Nor

and there shall no sign be given unto it, but the sign of the prophet Jonas.

. . . the sign of Jonah — ASV

---

[5]Verse 2b and verse 3 are now recognized as not adequately supported by original manuscripts.

And he left them, and departed.
And leaving them behind . . . — Rhm
So he went off and left them — NEB

5. **And when his disciples were come to the other side,**
Now the disciples had crossed to the opposite shore — TCNT
they had forgotten to take bread.
and had forgotten to take any bread — TCNT
. . . to bring along food — Ber

6. **Then Jesus said unto them, Take heed and beware of the leaven of the Pharisees and of the Sadducees.**
Presently Jesus said . . . — TCNT
. . . See that you have nothing to do with the leaven of the Pharisees and Sadducees — Knox
. . . Keep your eyes open, . . . and be on your guard against . . . — Phi

7. **And they reasoned among themselves, saying,**
And they began to deliberate . . . — Rhm
Discussing this with one another they decided — Rieu
But they were debating with one another, and saying — Gspd
It is because we have taken no bread.
We took no bread — ASV
that he must have been referring to their lack of bread — Rieu

8. **Which when Jesus perceived, he said unto them,**
But Jesus, aware of this, said — RSV
Knowing what was in their minds, Jesus said to them — NEB
Jesus noticed it and said — Gspd
But Jesus knew what they were thinking and rebuked them — Rieu
O ye of little faith, why reason ye among yourselves, because we have brought no bread?
Men of little faith, what is this anxiety in your minds, that you have brought no bread with you — Knox
for their want of faith. Why are you arguing about your lack of bread? he asked — Rieu
Why do you talk about bringing no bread? Where is your faith — NEB
. . . Have you so little faith — Wms
. . . How little trust you have in me! — Mof

9. **Do ye not yet understand, neither remember the five loaves of the five thousand,**
Do ye not yet perceive, . . . — ASV
Do you not yet see, nor remember . . . — TCNT
and how many baskets ye took up?
and the number of baskets you filled — Knox
. . . you carried away — Wey
and how many [small hand] baskets you gathered — Amp

10. **Neither the seven loaves of the four thousand, and how many baskets ye took up?**
. . . and the number of hampers you filled then — Knox
. . . and how many large basketfuls you took up — Mon
. . . and how many [large] provision baskets . . . — Amp

11. **How is it that ye do not understand that I spake it not to you concerning bread,**
How could you suppose that I was thinking of bread, when I said — Knox
How is it that you failed to perceive that I did not speak about bread? — RSV
How can you fail to see that I was not speaking about bread? — NEB
that ye should beware of the leaven of the Pharisees and of the Sadducees.
Have nothing to do with the leaven of the Pharisees and Sadducees? — Knox
Be on your guard, I said, against the leaven of the Pharisees and Sadducees — NEB

12. **Then understood they how that he bade them not beware of the leaven of bread,**
Then they realized that he had not told them to beware . . . — Mon
Then they grasped the fact . . . — Phi
Then it dawned on them . . . — Nor
but of the doctrine of the Pharisees and of the Sadducees.
but of the teaching . . . — ASV

13. **When Jesus came into the coasts of Caesarea Philippi,**
. . . the parts of Caesarea . . . — ASV
. . . the district of Caesarea . . . — RSV
. . . the neighbourhood of Caesarea . . . — TCNT

... the region of Caesarea ... — Ber
... the parts of Caesarea of Philip — Rhm
... the neighborhood of Philip's Caesarea — Beck

he asked his disciples, saying, Whom do men say that I the Son of man am?
Who do men say that the Son of man is — ASV
What do men say of the Son of Man?
Who do they think he is — Knox
Who do people say that the Son of Man is — TCNT

14. **And they said, Some say that thou art John the Baptist:**
... John the Immerser — Rhm
some, Elias; and others, Jeremias, or one of the prophets.
some, Elijah; and others, Jeremiah, or one of the prophets — ASV

15. **He saith unto them, But whom say ye that I am?**
But you, he said, who do you say that I am — TCNT

16. **And Simon Peter answered and said,**
Simon Peter replied — RSV
It was Simon Peter who answered — Rieu
Thou art the Christ, the Son of the living God.
You are the Messiah, . . . — NEB
You are the promised Savior . . . — Beck

17. **And Jesus answered and said unto him, Blessed art thou, Simon Bar-jona:**
Happy art thou, Simon Bar-yona — Rhm
You are privileged, Simon son of Jonah — Rieu
Simon son of Jonah, you are favoured indeed! — NEB
Simon . . . you are a fortunate man indeed! — Phi
for flesh and blood hath not revealed it unto thee, but my Father which is in heaven.
for human nature has not disclosed this to you . . . — Gspd
for mere human nature has not revealed this to you . . . — Wey
For no human being has revealed this to you, but my Father who is in heaven — TCNT

You did not learn that from mortal man; it was revealed to you by my heavenly Father — NEB

18. **And I say also unto thee,**
And I tell you — RSV
And I tell thee this is my turn — Knox
And I, yes I, tell you — Wms
That thou art Peter, and upon this rock I will build my church;
you are Peter, the Rock; and on this rock I will build my church — NEB
Your name is Peter, a rock, and upon this Rock I will build my Church — TCNT
your name from now on is to be Peter, Rock, and on a massive rock like this I will build my church — Wms
that you are Petros (a rock), and on this petra (rock) I will build my church — Mon
... my assembly — Rhm
and the gates of hell shall not prevail against it.
and the gates of Hades . . . — ASV
and the powers of death shall not subdue it — Gspd
and the forces of death shall never overpower it — NEB
and the doors of Sheol shall not shut in on it — Lam
and the powers of the underworld shall never overthrow it — Wms
—the Gates of Hell will not be stronger — Rieu
and the gates of hell shall not hold out against her — Ber
and the might of Hades shall not triumph over it — Wey

19. **And I will give unto thee the keys of the kingdom of heaven:**
... the kingdom of the heavens — Rhm
... the Realm of heaven — Mof
... the keys to the kingdom of heaven — Nor
and whatsoever thou shalt bind on earth shall be bound in heaven:
Whatever you forbid on earth, Heaven shall forbid — Rieu
Whatever you prohibit on earth will be prohibited in heaven — Mof
Whatever you forbid on earth will be held in Heaven to be forbidden — TCNT
and whatever you forbid on earth must be what is already forbidden in heaven — Wms

and whatever you shall bind on earth shall have been bound in heaven — NASB

and whatever you bind on earth shall remain bound in heaven — Wey

and whatsoever thou shalt loose on earth shall be loosed in heaven.

and whatever you allow on earth, Heaven shall allow — Rieu

and whatever you permit on earth will be permitted in heaven — Mof

and whatever you allow on earth will be held in Heaven to be allowed — TCNT

and whatever you permit on earth must be what is already permitted in heaven — Wms

and whatever you shall loose on earth shall have been loosed in heaven — NASB

and whatever you loose on earth shall remain loosed in heaven — Wey

20. Then charged he his disciples that they should tell no man that he was Jesus the Christ.

Then he strictly charged the disciples to tell no one that he was the Christ — RSV

Then he strictly forbade them to tell any man that he, Jesus, was the Christ — Knox

Then he warned the disciples not to tell anyone that He was the promised Savior — Beck

He then gave his disciples strict orders not to tell anyone that he was the Messiah — NEB

21. From that time forth began Jesus to shew unto his disciples,

It was then that Jesus Christ began to make it clear to his disciples — Rieu

It was just after that that Jesus Christ for the first time clearly taught His disciples — Wms

At that time Jesus Christ began to explain to his disciples — TCNT

After this, Jesus Christ kept pointing out to His disciples — Beck

how that he must go unto Jerusalem,

that he must of necessity go to Jerusalem — Rieu

that he had to go to Jerusalem — Wms

and suffer many things of the elders and chief priests and scribes,

and submit to many forms of suffering

at the hands of the elders, high priests, and scribes — Wms

. . . the Councillors, and Chief Priests, and Teachers of the Law — TCNT

. . . Bible scholars — Beck

and be killed, and be raised again the third day.

and be slain, — and on the third day arise — Rhm

and finally be killed; and be raised to life . . . — Phi

be put to death, and on the third day restored to life — Rieu

22. Then Peter took him, and began to rebuke him, saying,

And taking him aside Peter began to rebuke him, saying — Rhm

At this Peter took him by the arm and began to rebuke him: — NEB

Whereupon Peter, drawing him to his side, began remonstrating with him — Knox

And Peter took Him aside and began to chide Him, as he said — Wms

Peter, however, took Him aside and protestingly said to him — Nor

But Peter took Him aside and started to correct Him — Beck

Peter took him and began to reprove him for it — Mof

Then Peter took him aside and began to reprove him, saying — Mon

Be it far from thee, Lord: this shall not be unto thee.

Mercy on thee Lord! In no wise shall this befall thee — Rhm

God forbid, Lord! This shall never happen to you — RSV

Heaven save you, Lord! This shall not be your fate — Rieu

God forbid, Master! That shall never befall you — Mon

Heaven shield you, My Lord! This must never be your lot! — Wms

God bless you, Master! that can never happen to you! — Gspd

God be merciful to You, Lord! This must never happen to You! — Beck

Master, he said, please God that shall never be your fate! — TCNT

23. But he turned, and said unto Peter,

But Jesus turned his back on him and said — Rieu

Then Jesus turned around and said to Peter — Phi

Get thee behind me, Satan:
Out of my way, Satan! — Phi
Away with you, Satan! — NEB
Get out of my sight, you Satan! — Gspd
Get out of my way, you Satan! — TCNT
Get behind me, Satan — Rieu
thou art an offence unto me:
. . . a stumbling-block . . . — ASV
. . . a stone in my path — Knox
. . . a snare in my path — Rieu
. . . a hindrance to me — TCNT
You're tempting Me to sin — Beck
for thou savourest not the things that be of God, but those that be of men.
Because thou art not regarding the things of God but the things of men — Rhm
for you are not on the side of God, but of men — RSV
for these thoughts of thine are man's, not God's — Knox
because your thoughts are not God's thoughts, but men's — Wey
Your outlook is not God's, but man's — Mof
for you do not side with God, but with men — Gspd
because you are not intent on what pleases God, but what pleases men — Mon
for you look at things, not as God does, but as man does — TCNT

24. Then Jesus said unto his disciples, If any man will come after me,
. . . would come after me — ASV
. . . wishes to come after me — Mon
. . . has a mind to come my way—Knox
. . . wishes to walk in my steps — TCNT
. . . wishes to walk in my footsteps — Rieu
. . . wishes to be a follower of mine — NEB
. . . to walk behind me — Ber
let him deny himself,
. . . renounce self — TCNT
he must leave self behind — NEB
he must disregard himself — Gspd
he must say 'No' to self — Wms
and take up his cross, and follow me.
put his cross on his shoulders, and keep on following me — Wms

25. For whosoever will save his life shall lose it:
. . . would save his life . . . — ASV
The man who tries to save his life shall lose it — Knox

For the man who chooses to save his life will lose it — Rieu
Whoever cares for his own safety is lost — NEB
For he who wants to save his life will lose it — Mon
For whoever wants to save his higher life will have to give up his lower life — Wms
and whosoever will lose his life for my sake shall find it.
but if a man will let himself be lost for my sake, he will find his true self — NEB
and whoever gives up his lower life for my sake will find the higher life — Wms
it is the man who loses his life for my sake that will secure it — Knox

26. For what is a man profited,
How is a man the better for it — Knox
What will a man gain — NEB
For what advantage will a man have — Ber
What good will it do a man — TCNT
if he shall gain the whole world, and lose his own soul?
. . . and forfeit his life — ASV
. . . and lose his higher life — Wms
if he gains the whole world at the cost of his life — Gspd
. . . at the cost of losing his own soul — Knox
. . . at the cost of his true self — NEB
or what shall a man give in exchange for his soul?
. . . for his life — ASV
For a man's soul, what price can be high enough — Knox
Or what can a man give that is as precious as his life — Rieu
Or what can he give that will buy that self back — NEB
What will a man offer as an equivalent for his soul — Mof
What price would a man pay as ransom for his soul — Nor
What could a man offer to buy back his soul once he had lost it — Phi

27. For the Son of man shall come in the glory of his Father with his angels;
For it is ordained that the Son of Man shall come in his Father's glory with his Angels — Rieu
. . . is about to come in the glory of the Father . . . — Ber

. . . is going to come in His Father's splendor . . . — Wms

. . . and in the company of his angels — Phi

and then he shall reward every man according to his works.

. . . render to every . . . according to his deeds — ASV

. . . he will give back to . . . according to his practice — Rhm

and then he will repay every man for what he has done — RSV

and then he will give to every man what his actions deserve — TCNT

28. **Verily I say unto you, There be some standing here,**

Believe me, there are those standing here — Knox

In all truth I tell you, some of these standing here — Rieu

Solemnly I tell you, some of those who are standing here — Mon

which shall not taste of death, till they see the Son of man coming in his kingdom.

who shall in no wise taste of death . . . — ASV

will certainly live to see the Son of Man coming in His kingdom — Wms

will not know death till they have seen the Son of Man coming into his Kingdom — TCNT

will not taste death until they see the Son of Man come to reign! — Gspd

. . . coming to rule as King — Beck

CHAPTER 17

1. **And after six days Jesus taketh Peter, James, and John his brother, and bringeth them up into an high mountain apart,**

. . . and led them up a high mountain apart — RSV

. . . a high mountain where they were alone — Knox

. . . to the top of a high and lonely hill — Tay

2. **And was transfigured before them:**

And was transformed before them — Rhm

And in their presence His appearance was changed — Wms

There his whole appearance changed before their eyes — Phi

and his face did shine as the sun, and his raiment was white as the light.

. . . his garments became white as the light — ASV

. . . his clothes were white as light itself — Rieu

3. **And, behold, there appeared unto them Moses and Elias talking with him.**

. . . Moses and Elijah . . . — ASV

4. **Then answered Peter, and said unto Jesus,**

Peter blurted out — Tay

Lord, it is good for us to be here:

Lord! it is delightful for us to be here — Rhm

Master, it is good that we are here — Mon

Sir, it's wonderful that we can be here — Tay

if thou wilt, let us make here three tabernacles; one for thee, and one for Moses, and one for Elias.

if you wish, I will make three booths here, one for you and one for Moses and one for Elijah — RSV

. . . three arbours . . . — Knox

. . . three shelters . . . — Rieu

. . . three shrines . . . — Nor

. . . three tents . . . — TCNT

5. **While he yet spake, behold, a bright cloud overshadowed them:**

. . . lo! a brightly shining cloud overshadowed them — Rhm

. . . a luminous cloud . . . — Mon

. . . a bright cloud enveloped them — Rieu

and behold a voice out of the cloud, which said,

and a voice was heard from within the cloud, which said — Wey

This is my beloved Son, in whom I am well pleased; hear ye him.

. . . my Son the Beloved, in whom I delight,—Be hearkening to him—Rhm

. . . my Son, my Beloved. He is my Chosen. Listen to him! — Gspd

. . . my Beloved, on whom my favour rests; listen to him — NEB

6. **And when the disciples heard it, they fell on their face, and were sore afraid.**

. . . they prostrated themselves and were overcome with awe — Rieu

. . . they were dreadfully frightened and fell upon their faces — Gspd

At the sound of the voice the disciples fell on their faces in terror — NEB

7. And Jesus came and touched them, and said, Arise, and be not afraid.

. . . came near and roused them with his touch; Arise, he said, do not be afraid — Knox

8. And when they had lifted up their eyes, they saw no man, save Jesus only.

Then they looked up and saw no one there but Jesus himself — Rieu

And on raising their eyes they saw no one except Jesus all alone — Mof

9. And as they came down from the mountain, Jesus charged them, saying,

And as they were coming down from the mountain, Jesus commanded them, saying — ASV

. . . warned them . . . — Knox

. . . ordered them . . . — Mof

Tell the vision to no man, until the Son of man be risen again from the dead.

Do not tell anybody what you have seen . . . — Knox

. . . until after the Son of man has been raised from the dead — Mon

10. And his disciples asked him, saying, Why then say the scribes[6] that Elias must first come?

The disciples put a question to him: Why then do our teachers say that Elijah . . . — NEB

. . . must come before Christ — Knox

11. And Jesus answered and said unto them, Elias truly shall first come, and restore all things.

. . . Elijah indeed cometh, and shall restore all things — ASV

. . . and set everything right — NEB

. . . and set everything in order — Tay

. . . to reform everything — Gspd

. . . So Elijah is coming and will re-establish everything?— Rieu

12. But I say unto you, That Elias is come already,

. . . that Elijah just now came — Rhm

No, I say unto you that Elijah has come already — Rieu

and they knew him not, but have done unto him whatsoever they listed.

And they recognized him not, But did with him whatsoever they pleased — Rhm

. . . misused him at their pleasure — Knox

. . . they have worked their will on him — Mof

Likewise shall also the Son of man suffer of them.

In the same way, too, the Son of man is destined to undergo suffering at men's hands — TCNT

13. Then the disciples understood that he spake unto them of John the Baptist.

Then perceived the disciples that concerning John the Immerser he spake to them — Rhm

14. And when they were come to the multitude, there came to him a certain man, kneeling down to him, and saying,

When they rejoined the people . . . — Rieu

. . . a man ran up to Him and fell on his knees before Him. He said—Nor

15. Lord, have mercy on my son: for he is lunatick, and sore vexed:

Master, have pity . . . — Wey

. . . for he is epileptic, and suffereth grievously — ASV

. . . and suffers terribly — TCNT

. . . and has bad fits — NEB

. . . suffers excruciating pain — Wms

. . . has become worse — Lam

. . . for he is mentally deranged, and in great trouble — Tay

for ofttimes he falleth into the fire, and oft into the water.

he will often throw himself into the fire, and often into water — Knox

16. And I brought him to thy disciples, and they could not cure him.

17. Then Jesus answered and said, O faithless and perverse generation,

. . . O faithless and perverted generation! — Rhm

. . . O unbelieving and rebellious generation — Ber

. . . misguided generation — Knox

. . . O you unbelieving, obstinate people! — Gspd

how long shall I be with you? how long shall I suffer you? bring him hither to me.

how long shall I be with you? how

---

[6]For variant translations of "scribes" see Matt. 16:21.

long shall I bear with you? . . . —
ASV
How long can I put up with you?
Bring him here to me! — Wms

18. **And Jesus rebuked the devil; and he
departed out of him:**
And Jesus reproved the demon and it
came out of him — Gspd
And Jesus rebuked him; and the demon
went out of him — ASV
. . . rebuked the lad; the demon came
out of him — Rieu
**and the child was cured from that very
hour.**
. . . was cured instantly — RSV

19. **Then came the disciples to Jesus apart,
and said,**
But the disciples approached Jesus
privately and asked — Rieu
Afterwards, when they were alone, the
disciples came to Jesus and asked —
Knox
Why could not we cast him out?

20. **And Jesus said unto them, Because of
your unbelief:**
. . . Because of your little faith — ASV
He answered, Your faith is too weak
— NEB
Because of your lack of faith, said
Jesus — Rieu
**for verily I say unto you, If ye have
faith as a grain of mustard seed,**
In solemn truth I tell you . . . — Mon
I declare to you in truth . . . — Wey
I tell you this: if you have faith no bigger even than a mustard-seed — NEB
**ye shall say unto this mountain, Re-
move hence to yonder place;**
you have only to say to this mountain,
Remove from this place to that —
Knox
you can say to this mountain, Move
from this place to that! — Mon
and it shall remove;
and it will move — Mon
and it shall be removed — Rhm
**and nothing shall be impossible unto
you.**
and you will find nothing impossible —
Rieu
Then you can do anything — Beck

21. **Howbeit this kind goeth not out but
by prayer and fasting.[7]**
But there is no way of casting out such
spirits as this except by prayer and
fasting — Knox

But this kind is driven out by prayer
alone — Mon

22. **And while they abode in Galilee, Jesus
said unto them,**
As they were gathering[8] in Galilee,
Jesus said to them — RSV
While they were still together in Gali-
lee, Jesus told them — Knox
As they continued going from place to
place in Galilee, Jesus said to them
— Mon
**The Son of man shall be betrayed into
the hands of men:**
The Son of man shall be delivered up
into . . . — ASV
The Son of man is about to be betrayed
into . . . — Mon
The Son of man is to be given up into
the power of men. . . — NEB
The Son of man is destined to be be-
trayed into the hands of his fellow-
men — TCNT

23. **And they shall kill him, and the third
day he shall be raised again.**
. . . and on the third day will he arise
— Rhm
. . . he will come back to life — Rieu
And they were exceeding sorry.
And they were greatly distressed—RSV
And they were crushed with grief —
Wms
And they felt deeply distressed — Ber
And they were overcome with sorrow
— Knox
And they were grieved exceedingly —
Rhm

24. **And when they were come to Capernaum,**
On their arrival at Capernaum — NEB
When they reached Capharnahum —
Mof
**they that received tribute money came
to Peter,**
they that received the half-shekel came
to Peter — ASV
the collectors of the temple-tax came
up to Peter — TCNT
**and said, Doth not your master pay
tribute?**
. . . Doth not your teacher pay the half-
shekel — ASV

---

[7]Verse 21 is now recognized as not adequately
supported by original manuscripts.
[8]This represents a variant reading.

... Does not your Master pay the temple-tax — TCNT

25. He saith, Yes.

Yes, answered Peter — TCNT

And when he was come into the house, Jesus prevented him, saying,

And coming into the house Jesus anticipated him, saying — Rhm

Then he joined the rest indoors and was about to say something when Jesus spoke — Rieu

When Jesus reached home — he got there ahead of Simon — He asked him — Wms

And when he came home, Jesus spoke to him first, saying — RSV

But on Peter's entering the house, Jesus forestalled him, saying — Mon

What thinkest thou, Simon?

What is your idea, Simon — Ber

How does it seem to you, Simon—Mon

of whom do the kings of the earth take custom or tribute?

... dues or tax — Rhm

... customs or taxes — Knox

... tax or toll — NEB

... import or capitation taxes — Rieu

... duties or taxes — Wms

... taxes or tribute — TCNT

of their own children, or of strangers?

from their sons, or from strangers — ASV

On their citizens, or on foreigners — Rieu

from their own people, or from aliens — Mon

from their own children, or from others — Wey

against their own people, or against conquered foreigners — Tay

26. Peter saith unto him, Of strangers.[9] Jesus saith unto him, Then are the children free.

... Therefore, the sons are free. — ASV

... Well then, continued Jesus, their sons go free — TCNT

... So citizens are exempt — Rieu

... Then the family is exempt — Phi

27. Notwithstanding, lest we should offend them, go thou to the sea,

But, lest we cause them to stumble, ... — ASV

But as we do not want to cause difficulty for these people, ... — NEB

but still, that we may not influence them to do anything wrong, go down to the sea — Wms

Still, that we may not shock them, ... — TCNT

and cast an hook, and take up the fish that first cometh up;

... take the first fish that arises—TCNT

and when thou hast opened his mouth, thou shalt find a piece of money:

... thou shalt find a shekel — ASV

... you will find a silver coin — Rieu

... a piece of four drachmas — Mof

... a stater[10] — NASB

open its mouth, and you will find a piece of money — TCNT

that take, and give unto them for me and thee.

... on my account and yours — Rieu

take that and pay it in; it will meet the tax for us both — NEB

Take that, and give it to the collectors for both of us — TCNT

CHAPTER 18

1. At the same time came the disciples unto Jesus, saying,

In that hour came the disciples ... — ASV

At that time ... — RSV

Just then ... — Wey

On the same occasion ... — TCNT

Who is the greatest in the kingdom of heaven?

Who then is the greatest in the kingdom of the heavens — Rhm

Who really excels ... — Ber

Who is really greatest ... — Gspd

Who ranks higher than others ... — Wey

... in the Realm of heaven — Mof

2. And Jesus called a little child unto him, and set him in the midst of them,

And he called to him a little child, and ... — ASV

... had him stand among them — Gspd

---

[9]For variants see previous verse.
[10]This is the actual Greek word.

3. And said, Verily[11] I say unto you,

. . . In solemn truth I tell you — Mon

Except ye be converted, and become as little children,

Except ye turn, and . . . — ASV

Unless your hearts are changed and . . . — Rieu

ye shall not enter into the kingdom of heaven.

ye shall in no wise enter . . . — ASV

you will never enter . . . — RSV

you will never get into the Kingdom of Heaven at all — Gspd

4. Whosoever therefore shall humble himself as this little child, the same is greatest in the kingdom of heaven.

So then, whoever becomes as lowly as this little child is the greatest in . . . — Wms

Anyone, therefore, who is as unassuming as this child is the greatest in . . . — Gspd

5. And whoso shall receive one such little child in my name receiveth me.

And whosoever shall give welcome unto one such child as this . . . — Rhm

. . . for my sake . . . — Mon

. . . on my account . . . — Gspd

. . . for the sake of my Name . . . — TCNT

6. But whoso shall offend one of these little ones which believe in me,

but whoso shall cause one of these little ones that believe on me to stumble — ASV

but whoever causes one of these little ones . . . to sin — RSV

But as for the man who corrupts one of these little ones . . . — Rieu

But whoever leads one of these little ones . . . to do wrong — Wms

But whoever is a hindrance to one of these little ones . . . — Mof

But whoever leads astray one of these little ones . . . — Nor

it were better for him that a millstone were hanged about his neck,

it is profitable for him that a great millstone . . . — ASV

his best course would be to have a large millstone tied around his neck—Rieu

and that he were drowned in the depth of the sea.

and that he should be sunk in the depth . . . — ASV

7. Woe unto the world because of offences!

Woe unto the world because of occasions of stumbling — ASV

Alas for the world! by reason of the causes of stumbling — Rhm

Woe to the world for temptations to sin! — RSV

. . . for the hurt done to consciences! — Knox

Alas for the world and its corruption! — Rieu

A curse on the world for such influences to do wrong! — Wms

Alas for the world with its pitfalls! — Phi

for it must needs be that offences come; but woe to that man by whom the offence cometh!

. . . on whose account the tripping up occurs — Ber

In the nature of things there must be pitfalls, yet alas for the man who is responsible for them! — Phi

Temptation to do wrong is inevitable, but woe to the man who does the tempting — Tay

8. Wherefore if thy hand or thy foot offend thee, cut them off, and cast them from thee:

If thy hand or thy foot is an occasion of falling to thee . . . — Knox

If your hand or your foot is your undoing, cut it off and fling it away — NEB

But if thy hand or thy foot is causing thee to sin, cut it off, and cast it from thee — ABUV

If your hand or your foot is a hindrance to your faith; cut it off and throw it away — Phi

it is better for thee to enter into life halt or maimed,

it is seemly for thee to enter into life maimed or lame — Rhm

. . . crippled or maimed — Rieu

Better to enter heaven crippled — Tay

rather than having two hands or two feet to be cast into everlasting fire.

. . . into the eternal fire — ASV

. . . the age-abiding fire — Rhm

than to be in hell with both hands and feet — Tay

---

[11]For variant translations of "Verily" see Matt. 17:20.

9. **And if thine eye offend[12] thee, pluck it out, and cast it from thee:**

. . . gouge it out and throw it away — Tay

it is better for thee to enter into life with one eye, rather than having two eyes to be cast into hell fire.

. . . the hell of fire — ASV

. . . the fiery gehenna — Rhm

. . . the fire of Gehenna — Mof

. . . the pit of torture — Wms

. . . the fire of the rubbish heap — Phi

Better to enter heaven with one eye than to be in hell with two — Tay

10. **Take heed that ye despise not one of these little ones;**

See to it that you do not treat one of these little ones with contempt — Knox

Be careful not to look with scorn on a single one of these little children — Wms

for I say unto you, That in heaven their angels do always behold the face of my Father which is in heaven.

. . . That their messengers in the heavens do continually behold the face of my Father in the heavens — Rhm

. . . That in heaven their angels have uninterrupted access to my Father in heaven — Wms

11. **For the Son of man is come to save that which was lost.[13]**

12. **How think ye?**

What think you — TCNT

Tell me this — Knox

if a man have an hundred sheep, and one of them be gone astray,

. . . and one of them gets lost — Wms

doth he not leave the ninety and nine, and goeth into the mountains, and seeketh that which is gone astray?

Will he not leave the ninety-nine upon the mountains . . . — Rhm

. . . and go in search of the one that strayed — NEB

13. **And if so be that he find it, verily[14] I say unto you, he rejoiceth more of that sheep, than of the ninety and nine which went not astray.**

And if he succeeds in finding it, I tell you solemnly that he rejoices over it

more than over the ninety and nine that never strayed away — Mon

14. **Even so it is not the will of your Father which is in heaven,**

Thus there is no desire in the presence of my Father who is in the heavens — Rhm

You can understand then that it is never the will of your Father in Heaven — Phi

that one of these little ones should perish.

. . . should be lost — Rhm

15. **Moreover if thy brother shall trespass against thee,[15]**

And if thy brother sin against thee — ASV

Again, if your brother wrongs you — Wms

go and tell him his fault between thee and him alone:

go, show him his fault . . . — ASV

go and have it out with him in private — Rieu

Withdraw, convince him betwixt thee and him alone — Rhm

go, make clear to him his error between you and him in private — Bas

if he shall hear thee, thou hast gained thy brother.

If he listens to you, you have gained your brother — RSV

. . . you have won back your brother — Wms

. . . you will be the richer by a brother — Rieu

16. **But if he will not hear thee, then take with thee one or two more,**

But if he does not listen, take one or two others along with you — RSV

But if he refuses to listen, call in one or two other people — Rieu

that in the mouth of two or three witnesses every word may be established.

that every word may be confirmed by

---

[12]For variants of "offend" see verse 7.

[13]Now recognized as not adequately supported by original manuscripts.

[14]For variations of "verily" see Matt. 16:28.

[15]The words "against thee" are now recognized as not adequately supported by original manuscripts.

the evidence of two or three witnesses — RSV

17. And if he shall neglect to hear them, tell it unto the church:

And if he refuse to hear them . . . — ASV

But if he hear them amiss, Tell it to the assembly — Rhm

If he pays no attention to these, report the matter to the church — Rieu

. . . the congregation — Gspd

but if he neglect to hear the church,

And if even the assembly he hear amiss — Rhm

And if he pays no attention even to the church — Rieu

and if he will not listen even to the congregation — NEB

let him be unto thee as an heathen man and a publican.

. . . as the Gentile and the publican — ASV

. . . as a Gentile and a tax-collector — RSV

you must then treat him as you would a pagan or a tax-gatherer — NEB

18. Verily I say unto you, Whatsoever ye shall bind on earth shall be bound in heaven: and whatsoever ye shall loose on earth shall be loosed in heaven.[16]

19. Again I say unto you, That if two of you shall agree on earth as touching any thing that they shall ask,

Another truth. If any two of you on earth agree in making any prayer — Rieu

And again I tell you that if two of you on earth symphonize your praying concerning anything for which you have asked — Mon

it shall be done for them of my Father which is in heaven.

It shall be brought to pass for them from my Father who is in the heavens — Rhm

it will be granted them by my Father who is in heaven — Knox

it will be done for you by My heavenly Father — Ber

My heavenly Father will answer your prayer — Nor

20. For where two or three are gathered together in my name, there am I in the midst of them.

For wherever two or three are gathered

as my followers, I am there among them — Gspd

For wherever two or three have met as my disciples, I am right there with them — Wms

21. Then came Peter to him, and said, Lord, how oft shall my brother sin against me, and I forgive him? till seven times?

. . . Lord, how often am I to forgive my brother if he goes on wronging me? As many as seven times? — NEB

. . . Lord, how often do I have to forgive . . . — Beck

. . . Would seven times be enough? — Phi

22. Jesus saith unto him, I say not unto thee, Until seven times: but, Until seventy times seven.

No, replied Jesus, not seven times, but seventy times seven! — Phi

23. Therefore is the kingdom of heaven likened unto a certain king,

For this cause hath the kingdom of the heavens become like unto a man, a king — Rhm

as you may learn from this parable of the Kingdom of Heaven — Rieu

That is why the Realm of heaven may be compared to a king — Mof

Thus the kingdom of heaven may be compared to a king — Mon

which would take account of his servants.

who would make a reckoning with his servants — ASV

who wished to settle an account with his servants — Rhm

who planned to settle accounts with his agents — Ber

who wished to settle accounts with his slaves — Mon

24. And when he had begun to reckon,

And when he began to settle — Rhm

When he had started calling in his accounts — Phi

one was brought unto him, which owed him ten thousand talents.[17]

there was brought unto him a certain debtor of a thousand talents — Rhm

---

[16]See the various translations of Matt. 16:19b.

[17]There are wide variations in the estimated value of the talent, which was originally a *weight* and might be either silver or gold.

there appeared before him a man whose debt ran into millions — NEB

... three million pounds — Mof

... ten million dollars — Gspd

... fifteen million dollars — Mon

... millions of dollars — Phi

25. But forasmuch as he had not to pay,

and, as he could not pay — TCNT

But since he did not have the means to repay — NASB

his lord commanded him to be sold, and his wife, and children, and all that he had, and payment to be made.

his master ordered him to be sold toward the payment of his debt—RSV

26. The servant therefore fell down, and worshipped him, saying,

The servant therefore falling down began to do homage unto him, saying — Rhm

So the servant fell on his knees, imploring him — RSV

Lord, have patience with me, and I will pay thee all.

Give me time, and I will pay you every cent of it — Wms

27. Then the lord of that servant was moved with compassion,

The man's master was sorry for him — Rieu

And his master's heart was touched — Gspd

The king took pity on his subject—Nor

and loosed him, and forgave him the debt.

released him, and forgave him the debt — ASV

He let him go free, and cancelled the loan — Rieu

28. But the same servant went out, and found one of his fellowservants,

But as the man went off he met one of his fellow-servants — Rieu

But on his way out, that slave met a fellow slave — Mon

which owed him an hundred pence:

who owed him a hundred denarii — RSV

... ten pounds — TCNT

... a few pounds — NEB

who owed him fifty dollars — Mon

... a hundred dollars — Gspd

... a few dollars — Phi

and he laid hands on him, and took him by the throat, saying, Pay me that thou owest.

and he seized him and began to choke him, saying ... — NASB

Grabbing him by the throat, he said ... — Ber

29. And his fellowservant fell down at his feet, and besought him, saying, Have patience with me, and I will pay thee all.[18]

Then his fellow slave fell at his feet, ... — Mon

... and begged him ... — Gspd

30. And he would not: but went and cast him into prison, till he should pay the debt.

but he refused, and had him jailed ... — NEB

31. So when his fellowservants saw what was done, they were very sorry,

The rest of the servants were full of indignation when they saw this done — Knox

When his fellow servants saw what had taken place, they were greatly distressed — TCNT

... exceedingly angry — Wey

... horrified — Phi

and came and told unto their lord all that was done.

and went and made quite plain to their master all the things which had been done — Rhm

and they went and reported to their lord all that had taken place — RSV

and went to their master and laid the whole matter before him — TCNT

... told him the whole story — NEB

32. Then his lord, after that he had called him, said unto him,

And so he was summoned by his master, who said — Knox

At once his master called him and said — Wey

O thou wicked servant,

You scoundrel! — NEB

You contemptible slave! — Ber

You evil-hearted wretch! — Tay

I forgave thee all that debt, because thou desiredst me:

... because thou besoughtest me — ASV

I canceled all that debt for you, because you begged me — Ber

---

[18]Compare verse 26.

33. Shouldest not thou also have had compassion on thy fellowservant, even as I had pity on thee?

was it not thy duty to have mercy . . . as I had mercy on thee — Knox

Was it not proper that you, too, should have taken pity . . . as I took pity on you — Nor

34. And his lord was wroth, and delivered him to the tormenters, till he should pay all that was due unto him.

And his master, in anger, gave him over to be tortured until the debt was paid — Knox

And angrily his master handed him over to the scourgers until he should pay everything he owed him — Ber

. . . the jailers . . . — Gspd

. . . the torturers . . . — TCNT

And so angry was the master that he condemned the man to torture until he should pay the debt in full — NEB

35. So likewise shall my heavenly Father do also unto you,

And that is how my heavenly Father will deal with you — NEB

if ye from your hearts forgive not every one his brother their trespasses.

if brother does not forgive brother with all his heart — Knox

unless you each forgive your brother from your hearts — NEB

if each of you does not heartily forgive his brother — Ber

CHAPTER 19

1. And it came to pass, that when Jesus had finished these sayings,

. . . these words — ASV

. . . this discourse — Gspd

he departed from Galilee, and came into the coasts of Judaea beyond Jordan;

. . . the borders of Judaea beyond the Jordan — ASV

. . . the region of Judea beyond the Jordan — RSV

. . . that district of Judaea which is on the far side of the Jordan — Rieu

2. And great multitudes followed him; and he healed them there.

And great crowds thronged after Him, and He cured them there — Wms

3. The Pharisees also came unto him, tempting[19] him, and saying unto him, Is it lawful for a man to put away his wife for every cause?

There came unto him Pharisees, trying him, and saying, Is it lawful . . . — ASV

And Pharisees came up to him and tested him by asking, Is it lawful to divorce one's wife for any cause — RSV

. . . on any grounds one may allege — Rieu

4. And he answered and said unto them, Have ye not read, that he which made them at the beginning made them male and female,

. . . that the Creator made human be-

ings male and female in the beginning — Rieu

5. And said, For this cause shall a man leave father and mother, and shall cleave to his wife: and they twain shall be one flesh.

. . . and be joined to his wife, and the two shall become one — RSV

6. Wherefore they are no more twain, but one flesh.

So that they are no more two, but one flesh — ASV

It follows that they are no longer two individuals: they are one flesh—NEB

. . . no longer two separate people, but one — Phi

. . . not two, but one body — Lam

What therefore God hath joined together, let not man put asunder.

What God himself, then, has yoked together man must not separate—TCNT

Therefore, what God has joined together, man must not try to separate — Gspd

. . . must stop separating — Wms

It follows that man must not part what God has united — Rieu

7. They say unto him, Why did Moses then command to give a writing of divorcement, and to put her away?

. . . to give a writing of repudiation and to divorce — Rhm

Why then, they said, did Moses enjoin

---

[19]For variants of "tempting," see Matt. 16:1.

that a man give his wife a writ of separation, and then he might put her away — Knox

Why, then, they said, did Moses direct that a man should serve his wife with a notice of separation and divorce her — TCNT

. . . divorce his wife by note of dismissal — NEB

8. He saith unto them, Moses because of the hardness of your hearts suffered you to put away your wives:

. . . It was because you were so unteachable that Moses gave you permission to divorce your wives—NEB

. . . It was because of your moral perversity that Moses allowed you to divorce . . . — Wms

. . . because you knew so little of the meaning of love that Moses . . . — Phi

but from the beginning it was not so.

but it was not like that when all began — NEB

But it was not intended that way at the beginning — Nor

but originally there was no such thing — Beck

9. And I say unto you, Whosoever shall put away his wife,

But I tell you that anyone who divorces his wife — TCNT

except it be for fornication, and shall marry another, committeth adultery:

saving for unfaithfulness . . . — Rhm

except for unchastity . . . — RSV

on any ground but her unfaithfulness . . . — Gspd

for any reason except adultery . . . — Nor

and whoso marrieth her which is put away doth commit adultery.[20]

and he that marrieth her when she is put away . . . — ASV

10. His disciples say unto him, If the case of the man be so with his wife, it is not good to marry.

. . . If that is the position with husband and wife, it is better to refrain from marriage — NEB

. . . not expedient to marry — ASV

. . . better not to marry at all — Knox

. . . there is no advantage in getting married — Wms

. . . it is not worth getting married! — Phi

11. But he said unto them, All men cannot receive this saying, save they to whom it is given.

. . . Not all find room for the word, save they to whom it hath been given — Rhm

That conclusion, he said, cannot be taken in by everybody, but only by those who have the gift — Knox

. . . It is not everyone that can accept the ruling, but only those that hear the call — Rieu

. . . Not all people understand this saying; only those to whom it is given — Ber

. . . It is not every man who has the capacity to carry out this saying, but it is for those to whom the capacity has been given — Wms

. . . but only those on whom the grace has been bestowed — Wey

. . . True, but this truth is not practicable for everyone, it is only for those who have the gift — Mof

12. For there are some eunuchs, which were so born from their mother's womb:

Some men have always been unsuited for marriage, having been born that way — Nor

. . . incapable of marriage . . . — NEB

Some men, it is true, have from birth been disabled for marriage — TCNT

and there are some eunuchs, which were made eunuchs of men:

while others were made so by men — Rieu

. . . others have been disabled by their fellowmen — TCNT

Others, because they have been mutilated by men — Beck

and there be eunuchs, which have made themselves eunuchs for the kingdom of heaven's sake.

. . . for love of the kingdom of heaven — Knox

and there are people who have chosen that condition for the sake of . . . — Rieu

. . . have themselves renounced marriage for the sake of . . . — NEB

He that is able to receive it, let him receive it.

---

[20]This clause is now recognized as not adequately supported by original manuscripts.

take this in, you whose hearts are large enough for it — Knox

He that is able to find room, let him find room — Rhm

Let him that can, obey the call — Rieu

Whoever is able to get practical hold of it, let him get hold — Ber

Let him accept it who can — Gspd

Let anyone practise it for whom it is practicable — Mof

13. **Then were there brought unto him little children, that he should put his hands on them, and pray:**

They brought children for him to lay his hands on them with prayer—NEB

. . . put his hands on them in blessing — BAS

and the disciples rebuked them.

The disciples scolded them for it—NEB

and the disciples held them back — Ber

His disciples interfered — Mon

. . . found fault with those who had brought them — TCNT

. . . spoke sharply to them — Nor

. . . frowned on the parents' action — Phi

14. **But Jesus said, Suffer little children, and forbid them not, to come unto me:**

. . . Let the children come to me, and do not hinder them — RSV

for of such is the kingdom of heaven.

for to such belongeth the kingdom . . . — ASV

for of this kind the kingdom . . . is composed — Ber

for it is to the childlike that the kingdom of heaven belongs — Mon

15. **And he laid his hands on them, and departed thence.**

. . . and went on his way — Knox

16. **And, behold, one came and said unto him, Good Master, what good thing shall I do,**

Up came a man and said, . . . — Mof

And behold, one came to him and said, Teacher, what good . . . — ASV

that I may have eternal life?

. . . have life age-abiding — Rhm

. . . win eternal life — Knox

. . . secure eternal life — Ber

. . . inherit eternal life — Mon

. . . obtain Immortal Life — TCNT

. . . get everlasting life — Beck

17. **And he said unto him, Why callest thou me good?**

. . . Why askest thou me concerning that which is good — ASV

there is none good but one, that is, God:

One there is who is good — ASV

God is good, and he only — Knox

There is only one who is perfectly good — Wms

One is the Good — ABUV

but if thou wilt enter into life, keep the commandments.

But if thou desirest into life to enter, Be keeping the commandments — Rhm

18. **He saith unto him, Which?**

He asked Him, What sort of commandments — Wms

Jesus said, Thou shalt do no murder,

. . . Thou shalt not kill — ASV

Thou shalt not commit adultery, Thou shalt not steal,

Do not be untrue in married life, Do not take what is not yours — BAS

Thou shalt not bear false witness,

Thou shalt not perjure thyself — Rieu

You must not lie — Wms

Thou shalt not lie in giving evidence — Wey

19. **Honour thy father and thy mother: and, Thou shalt love thy neighbour as thyself.**

. . . as much as thyself — Wey

20. **The young man saith unto him, All these things have I kept from my youth up:**

. . . All these things have I observed — ASV

All of these, said the young man, I have carefully obeyed — Wey

what lack I yet?

Where do I still fall short — NEB

How do I still fall behind — Ber

What more is required — Mof

21. **Jesus said unto him, If thou wilt be perfect,**

. . . If thou hast a mind to be perfect — Knox

. . . If you wish to go the whole way — NEB

. . . to be complete — NASB

go and sell that thou hast, and give to the poor,

Withdraw! sell thy substance and give to the destitute — Rhm

go and sell your possessions and give
to the poor — Rieu

... the needy — Ber

and thou shalt have treasure in heaven:

... riches in heaven — NEB

and come and follow me.

... then come back and follow me —
Knox

... then come back here and follow
me — Wms

And come! be following me — Rhm

22. **But when the young man heard that
saying, he went away sorrowful:**

And the young man hearing this word
went away sorrowing — Rhm

But when the young man heard this
statement, he went away grieved —
NASB

... sad at heart — Knox

... in gloom — Rieu

... in deep distress — Wms

... he turned away crestfallen — Phi

for he had great possessions.

for he was one who owned much property — NASB

for he was a man of great wealth —
NEB

because he was very rich — Beck

23. **Then said Jesus unto his disciples,
Verily[21] I say unto you, That a rich
man shall hardly enter into the kingdom of heaven.**

... It is hard for a rich man to enter
into the kingdom of heaven — ASV

... In solemn truth I tell you that a
rich man will find it difficult to enter
the kingdom of heaven — Mon

24. **And again I say unto you, It is easier
for a camel to go through the eye of a
needle,**

I repeat, It is easier ... — NEB

**than for a rich man to enter into the
kingdom of God.[22]**

25. **When his disciples heard it, they were
exceedingly amazed,**

And hearing it the disciples were being
struck with the greatest astonishment
— Rhm

... were thrown into great bewilder-
ment — Knox

... were utterly dumbfounded — Ber

... completely astounded — Gspd

saying, Who then can be saved?

... can possibly be saved — Mof

26. **But Jesus beheld them, and said unto
them,**

And Jesus looking upon them said to
them — ASV

Jesus fastened his eyes on them, and
said to them — Knox

Jesus looked them in the face, and said
— NEB

and looking intently Jesus said unto
them — Rhm

**With men this is impossible; but with
God all things are possible.**

Such a thing is impossible to man's
powers, but to God all things are
possible — Knox

Humanly speaking it is impossible; but
with God anything is possible — Phi

27. **Then answered Peter and said unto
him, Behold, we have forsaken all, and
followed thee;**

Hereupon Peter took occasion to say,
And what of us who have forsaken
all, ... — Knox

... But we — we left everything, and
followed you — TCNT

... Look! we gave up everything ...
— Beck

what shall we have therefore?

what is left for us — Knox

What shall we get by that — Rieu

What then shall be our reward — Wey

What is that going to be worth to us —
Phi

28. **And Jesus said unto them, Verily I
say unto you, That ye which have followed me, in the regeneration when
the Son of man shall sit in the throne
of his glory,**

... in the new world, when the Son of
man shall sit on his glorious throne
— RSV

... in the new birth, when the Son of
man sits on the throne of his glory
— Knox

... When the world is born anew and
the Son of Man takes the throne of
his glory — Rieu

... in the world that is to be, when the
Son of Man is seated on his throne
in heavenly splendour — NEB

... in the New Creation ... — Mon

... in the new order of life ... — Wms

... in the new age ... — Ber

---

[21]See Matt. 17:20.

[22]Several versions have "heaven" instead of
"God."

... in the new age — the Messianic rebirth of the world — . . . — Amp

ye also shall sit upon twelve thrones, judging the twelve tribes of Israel.

you my followers will have thrones of your own, where you will sit as judges of the . . . — NEB

you that have followed me will also be seated, on twelve thrones, governing the twelve tribes . . . — Rieu

29. And every one that hath forsaken houses, or brethren, or sisters, or father, or mother, or wife,[23] or children, or lands,

And every one that hath left . . . — ASV

. . . or children or farms — NASB

for my name's sake, shall receive an hundredfold, and shall inherit ever-

lasting life.

. . . shall be many times repaid and come into eternal life — Rieu

. . . shall be refunded a hundred times and shall inherit eternal life — Ber

. . . will be rewarded a hundred times and will obtain everlasting life—Nor

. . . will receive many times as much, and will gain Immortal Life — TCNT

30. But many that are first shall be last; and the last shall be first.

But many will be first that were last, and last that were first — Knox

But many now first shall be last and many last shall be first — Ber

But many who are first now will be last then, and many who are now last will be first — Gspd

CHAPTER 20

1. For the kingdom of heaven is like unto a man that is an householder,

For the Kingdom of Heaven is like a landowner — Rieu

. . . like an employer — Gspd

. . . like a farmer — Phi

. . . like the master of a house — BAS

. . . resembles an estate manager — Ber

which went out early in the morning to hire labourers into his vineyard.

. . . at daybreak to hire laborers for work in his vineyard — Knox

2. And when he had agreed with the labourers for a penny a day, he sent them into his vineyard.

He agreed with the labourers to pay them a denarius a day, and sent them out into . . . — TCNT

He agreed with the laborers to pay them a dollar a day, and sent them to . . . — Gspd

and after agreeing to pay them the usual day's wage he sent them off to work — NEB

He agreed with them on the wage of a silver coin a day and sent them to work — Phi

When he had contracted with the laborers at twenty cents a day, he sent them off to his vineyard — Wms

3. And he went out about the third hour, and saw others standing idle in the marketplace,

Going out three hours later he saw some more men . . . — NEB

About nine o'clock he went out and saw other workmen in the bazaar without employment — Ber

. . . and saw some men in the town square, loafing, with nothing to do — Nor

4. And said unto them; Go ye also into the vineyard, and whatsoever is right I will give you.

. . . and I will pay you a fair wage — NEB

And they went their way.

so off they went — NEB

And they went — Wms

5. Again he went out about the sixth and ninth hour, and did likewise.

Again he went out about twelve o'clock and three o'clock, and did as before — Wms

At noon he went out again, and at three in the afternoon, and made the same arrangement as before — NEB

6. And about the eleventh hour he went out, and found others standing idle,

An hour before sunset he went out and found another group standing there — NEB

About five he went out again and found still others standing around — Wms

and saith unto them, Why stand ye here all the day idle?

---

[23]The words "or wife" are now recognized as not adequately supported by original manuscripts.

... all the day unemployed — Rhm
... and have done nothing all the day
— Knox

7. **They say unto him, Because no man hath hired us. He saith unto them, Go ye also into the vineyard;[24] and whatsoever is right, that shall ye receive.**

8. **So when even was come, the lord of the vineyard saith unto his steward,**
As evening fell . . . — Ber
When evening came, the master of the vineyard said to his bailiff — Mof
... owner ... manager — Wms
... owner ... foreman — Gspd
... owner ... overseer — Nor
Call the labourers, and give them their hire,
Send for the workmen and pay them their wages — Knox
beginning from the last unto the first.
beginning with the last, and ending with the first — TCNT

9. **And when they came that were hired about the eleventh hour,[25] they received every man a penny.[26]**

10. **But when the first came, they supposed that they should have received more; and they likewise received every man a penny.**
Now when the first came, they thought they would receive more; but each of them also received a denarius — RSV

11. **And when they had received it,**
As they took it — NEB
And on getting it — Mof
they murmured against the goodman of the house,
... against the householder — ASV
they began to grumble at their employer — TCNT
... were indignant with the rich man — Knox

12. **Saying, These last have wrought but one hour,**
... have spent but one hour — ASV
... worked only one hour — RSV
... These late-comers have done only one hour's work — NEB
and thou hast made them equal unto us,
... made no difference between them and us — Knox
yet you have put them on a level with us — NEB

and yet you have put them on the same footing with us — TCNT
and you've treated them exactly the same as us — Phi
which have borne the burden and heat of the day.
who have borne the burden of the day and the scorching heat — ASV
who have sweated the whole day long in the blazing sun! — NEB
who have borne the brunt of the day's work, and the heat — TCNT
who have done the heavy work of the day and have stood the midday heat — Gspd

13. **But he answered one of them, and said,**
He dealt with this by saying to one of them — Rieu
But he replied to one . . . — RSV
Friend, I do thee no wrong: didst not thou agree with me for a penny?[27]
... I am not treating you unfairly. Did not you agree with me for a denarius — TCNT

14. **Take that thine is, and go thy way:**
Take up that which is thine, and go thy way — ASV
Take what belongs to you, and go — TCNT
Take your due and go — Rieu
Take your pay and go home — NEB
Take your wage and begone! — Mon
I will give unto this last, even as unto thee.
it is my will to give . . .— ASV
it is my pleasure to . . . — Knox
I choose to give to this last man the same as to you — RSV

15. **Is it not lawful for me to do what I will with mine own?**
Am I not allowed to do what I choose with what belongs to me — RSV
May I not do what I like with my own people — Rieu
Have I not the right to do what I choose with my own property—Mon

---

[24]The words "and whatsoever is right, that shall ye receive" are now recognized as not adequately supported by original manuscripts.
[25]See verse 6.
[26]See verse 2.
[27]Compare verse 2.

Is thine eye evil, because I am good?

Or do you begrudge my generosity — RSV

Are you envious because I am liberal — TCNT

Must thou give me sour looks, because I am generous — Knox

Or is your eye envious because I am generous — NASB

Why be jealous because I am kind — NEB

16. **So the last shall be first, and the first last:[28] for many be called, but few chosen.[29]**

17. **And Jesus going up to Jerusalem took the twelve disciples apart in the way, and said unto them,**

And as Jesus was going up to Jerusalem, he took the twelve disciples aside, and on the way he said to them — RSV

When Jesus was about to go up to Jerusalem, he took the Twelve aside by themselves, and as they went he said to them — Mon

When Jesus was on the point of going up to Jerusalem, he gathered the twelve disciples round him by themselves, and said to them as they were on their way — TCNT

18. **Behold, we go up to Jerusalem;**

Listen! we are going up to Jerusalem — TCNT

Take notice! . . . — Ber

and the Son of man shall be betrayed unto the chief priests and unto the scribes,[30]

. . . shall be delivered unto . . . — ASV

. . . will be given up to . . . — NEB

. . . handed over to . . . — Gspd

and they shall condemn him to death,

. . . will sentence him . . . — Mof

19. **And shall deliver him to the Gentiles**

. . . hand him over to the foreign power — NEB

. . . unto the nations — Rhm

. . . to the pagans — Rieu

. . . to the heathen — Gspd

to mock, and to scourge, and to crucify him:

to mock and flog and crucify — Wms

to be made sport of, and to be whipped, and to be put to death on the cross — Bas

and the third day he shall rise again.

. . . he will come back to life — Rieu

20. **Then came to him the mother of Zebedee's children with her sons,**

. . . the mother of the sons of Zebedee with her sons — ASV

worshipping him, and desiring a certain thing of him.

bowing down, and asking something from him — Rhm

falling on her knees to make a request of him — Knox

kneeling and requesting something of Him — Ber

bowing to the ground, and begging a favour — TCNT

21. **And he said unto her, What wilt thou?**

. . . What do you want — RSV

. . . What is it you wish — NEB

She saith unto him, Grant that these my two sons may sit,

. . . Command that these . . . — ASV

. . . Promise me this . . . — Nor

. . . Please say that . . . — Phi

the one on thy right hand, and the other on the left, in thy kingdom.

one at . . . and the other at . . . — NEB

22. **But Jesus answered and said, Ye know not what ye ask.**

Jesus turned to the brothers and said, You do not understand . . . — NEB

None of you know what you are asking, said Jesus — Mon

. . . You do not know what you are asking for yourselves — Rieu

Are ye able to drink of the cup that I shall drink of,

. . . that I am about to drink — ASV

Can you drink what I am going to drink — Gspd

and to be baptized with the baptism that I am baptized with?[31] They say unto him, We are able.

We can, they replied — NEB

Yes, they exclaimed, we can — TCNT

23. **And he saith unto them, Ye shall drink indeed of my cup,**

---

[28]Compare Matt. 19:30.

[29]The clause "for many be called, but few chosen" is now recognized as not adequately supported by original manuscripts.

[30]See Matt. 16:21 for variants of the word "scribe."

[31]This question is now recognized as not adequately supported by original manuscripts.

... You shall certainly drink ... — Rieu

and be baptized with the baptism that I am baptized with:[32] **but to sit on my right hand, and on my left, is not mine to give,**

but a place on my right hand or my left ... — Knox

but as for the seats on my right hand and my left ... — Rieu

but it shall be given to them for whom it is prepared of my Father.

except unto those for whom it hath been prepared by my Father — Rhm

but belongs to those for whom it has been prepared by ... — Mon

it is for those for whom my Father has destined it — Knox

it is for those to whom it has already been assigned by my Father — NEB

they will be given to those for whom they have been prepared ... — Wms

24. And when the ten heard it, they were moved with indignation against the two brethren.

... were sorely displeased concerning the two brethren — Rhm

... grumbled about the two brothers — Rieu

... were highly indignant ... — Phi

25. But when Jesus called them unto him, and said, Ye know that the princes of the Gentiles exercise dominion over them,

... the rulers of the Gentiles lord it over them — ASV

... the rulers of the nations lord it over them — Rhm

... the rulers of the pagans exercise despotic powers — Rieu

... the heathen rulers are high-handed with their people — Nor

... in the world, rulers lord it over their subjects — NEB

and they that are great exercise authority upon them.

And the great ones wield authority over them — Rhm

and great men vaunt their power over them — Knox

and their superiors oppress them — Ber

And their great men tyrannize over them — Gspd

... their chiefs likewise rule as dictators — Nor

26. But it shall not be so among you:

with you it must be otherwise — Knox

but among you it's different — Ber

but whosoever will be great among you, let him be your minister;

but whosoever would become great among you shall be your minister — ASV

Among you, whoever wants to be great must be your servant — NEB

27. And whosoever will be chief among you, let him be your servant:

and whoever wants to take the first place among you, must be your slave — TCNT

... must be the willing slave of all — NEB

28. Even as the Son of man came not to be ministered unto, but to minister,

... not to be served, but to serve — TCNT

... not to be waited on, but to wait on other people — Gspd

and to give his life a ransom for many.

... and to surrender his life as a ransom ... — NEB

... a ransom price to set many free — Wms

... the redemption price for many — Wey

... instead of many — Rhm

29. And as they departed from Jericho, a great multitude followed him.

... an immense crowd ... — Wey

30. And, behold, two blind men sitting by the way side, when they heard that Jesus passed by,

... that Jesus was passing by — ASV

and two blind men, sitting by the side of the road, heard that it was Jesus who was passing by — Mon

cried out, saying, Have mercy on us, O Lord, thou son of David.

... Have mercy on us, Son of David — RSV

... Have pity on us, Master, son of David! — Mon

... You Son of David! Take pity on us, sir! — Gspd

31. And the multitude rebuked them, because they should hold their peace:

... that they should hold their peace — ASV

[32]These words are now recognized as not adequately supported by original manuscripts.

The crowd rebuked them, telling them to be silent — RSV

People told them to hold their tongues — Rieu

... sternly told them to be quiet—NASB

... berated them, demanding silence — Ber

... angrily tried to silence them — Wey

but they cried the more, saying,

but this only made them cry out all the louder — Rieu

Have mercy on us, O Lord, thou Son of David.

32. And Jesus stood still, and called them, and said,

And Jesus stopped and called them, saying — RSV

What will ye that I shall do unto you?

What do you want me to do for you — RSV

33. They say unto him, Lord, that our eyes may be opened.

... Sir, we want our sight — NEB

... Lord, let us see again — Phi

... Master, let our eyes be opened — Wey

34. So Jesus had compassion on them, and touched their eyes:

And Jesus in pity touched their eyes — RSV

... Jesus was deeply moved, and touched their eyes — NEB

and immediately their eyes received sight, and they followed him.

Their sight came back at once and they followed him — Rieu

and immediately they recovered their sight ... — TCNT

CHAPTER 21

1. And when they drew nigh unto Jerusalem, and were come to Bethphage, unto the mount of Olives, then sent Jesus two disciples,

... Jesus sent two disciples on ahead — Gspd

2. Saying unto them, Go into the village over against you,

... the village facing you — TCNT

... the village opposite— NEB

... the village that is ahead of you — Wms

and straightway ye shall find an ass tied, and a colt with her:

... you will at once find a donkey tethered ... — NEB

... a she-ass tethered, and a foal at her side — Knox

... an ass with a cord round her neck, and a young one with her — Bas

loose them, and bring them unto me.

untie them ... — RSV

untie her and lead her here for me — TCNT

3. And if any man say ought unto you,

If anyone says anything to you — RSV

ye shall say, The Lord hath need of them; and straightway he will send them.

you are to say this—The Master wants them; ... — TCNT

... and he will let you have them without more ado — Knox

... the Lord needs them but will send them back at once — Rieu

4. All this was done, that it might be fulfilled which was spoken by the prophet, saying,

Now this is to come to pass that it might be fulfilled which was spoken through the prophet, saying — ASV

This happened in fulfilment of the word spoken through the prophet: — Mon

5. Tell ye the daughter of Sion, Behold, thy King cometh unto thee,

Tell Zion's daughter, See, your king is coming to you — Ber

meek, and sitting upon an ass, and a colt the foal of an ass.

humble, and mounted on an ass, and on a colt, the foal of an ass — RSV

in gentleness, riding on an ass, riding on the foal of a beast of burden — NEB

6. And the disciples went, and did as Jesus commanded them,

... and did even as Jesus appointed them — ASV

... just as Jesus had directed them — NASB

7. And brought the ass, and the colt, and put on them their clothes,

... and saddled them with their garments — Knox

... laid their cloaks on them — NEB

... threw their outer garments on them — Wey

and they set him thereon.
and he sat thereon — ASV
and bade Jesus mount — Knox
and Jesus seated himself upon them — Gspd

8. **And a very great multitude spread their garments in the way;**
And the most part of the multitude ... — ASV
Most of the crowd spread their garments on the road — RSV
Crowds of people carpeted the road with their cloaks — NEB
others cut down branches from the trees, and strawed them in the way.
and some cut branches from the trees to spread in his path — NEB

9. **And the multitudes that went before, and that followed, cried, saying,**
And both those that went in front of him and those that came behind cried: — Rieu
... sang aloud — Wey
The crowds that led the way, as well as those that followed behind, kept shouting: — TCNT
Hosanna to the son of David: Blessed is he that cometh in the name of the Lord;
Welcome the Son of David! ... — Wms
God bless the Son of David! ... — Gspd
God save the Son of David! ... — TCNT
Hosanna in the highest.
Hosanna in the heaven above — Knox
God bless him from on high! — Gspd
Welcome Him from on high! — Wms

10. **And when he was come into Jerusalem, all the city was moved,**
... the city was stirred — ASV
... was startled — Rhm
... went wild with excitement — NEB
... was thrown into commotion—Wey
And as he entered Jerusalem a shock ran through the whole city — Phi
saying, Who is this?

11. **And the multitude said, This is Jesus the prophet of Nazareth of Galilee.**

12. **And Jesus went into the temple of God, and cast out all them that sold and bought in the temple, and over-** threw the tables of the money-chang-ers, and the seats of them that sold doves,
... tipped over the tables of the cash-iers ... — Nor
... the tables of the bankers, and the chairs of the pigeon-sellers — Knox

13. **And said unto them, It is written, My house shall be called the house of prayer;**
Scripture says — My house ...—TCNT
... shall be known for a house of prayer — Knox
but ye have made it a den of thieves.
But you turn it into a robbers' den — Rieu
... a bandits' cave — Lam

14. **And the blind and the lame came to him in the temple; and he healed them.**

15. **And when the chief priests and scribes[33] saw the wonderful things that he did,**
... the marvels that he wrought—Rhm
... the miracles he did — Nor
... works of power which he did — Bas
and the children crying in the temple, and saying, Hosanna to the son of David;[34] they were sore displeased,
... moved with indignation — ASV
... greatly angered at it — Knox
... chagrined — Ber
... became furious — Nor
... they didn't like it at all — Beck

16. **And said unto him, Hearest thou what these say? And Jesus saith unto them, Yea; have ye never read, Out of the mouth of babes and sucklings thou hast perfected praise?**
... Thou hast made the lips of chil-dren, of infants at the breast, vocal with praise — Knox
... Thou hast ordained thy praises to be sung by little children and babes at the breast — Rieu
... Out of the mouth of infants and nursing babes Thou hast prepared praise for Thyself — NASB

17. **And he left them, and went out of the city into Bethany; and he lodged there.**
Then he left them and went out of the city to Bethany, where he spent the night — Rieu

---

[33]For variants of "scribes" see Matt. 16:21.
[34]See verse 9.

18. Now in the morning as he returned into the city, he hungered.
. . . he felt hungry — NEB
. . . he became hungry — TCNT

19. And when he saw a fig tree in the way, he came to it, and found nothing thereon, but leaves only,
and seeing one fig-tree . . . — Rhm
. . . a lone fig-tree by the road . . . — NASB
. . . a solitary fig-tree by the road-side . . . — TCNT
and said unto it, Let no fruit grow on thee henceforward for ever.
. . . May you be barren forever — Rieu
. . . You shall never bear fruit any more — NEB
And presently the fig tree withered away.
And immediately . . . — ASV
And instantly . . . — Ber

20. And when the disciples saw it, they marvelled, saying,
The disciples were amazed at the sight . . . — NEB
. . . were dumfounded . . . — Wms
. . . exclaimed in astonishment — Wey
How soon is the fig tree withered away!
How did the fig tree immediately wither away? — ASV
How in a moment . . . has withered away! — Wey
How is it . . . that the tree has withered so suddenly? — NEB
How on earth did that fig tree wither away quite suddenly like that? — Phi

21. Jesus answered and said unto them, Verily[35] I say unto you, If ye have faith, and doubt not,
. . . have faith and do not hesitate — Knox
. . . have faith and do not waver — Rieu
. . . have faith without ever a doubt — TCNT
. . . believe and don't doubt — Beck
ye shall not only do this which is done to the fig tree,
you will be able to do more than I have done over the fig tree — Knox
. . . perform such a miracle as this . . . — Wey
but also if ye shall say unto this mountain, Be thou removed, and be thou cast into the sea; it shall be done.
. . . Be then taken up and cast into the sea . . . — ASV
. . . Be lifted from your place and be hurled . . . — NEB
. . . Up, cast yourself into the sea! . . . — Mon

22. And all things, whatsoever ye shall ask in prayer, believing, ye shall receive.
And whatever you ask in prayer, you will receive, if you have faith — RSV
Anything you ask for in prayer, believe, and you will get it — Beck

23. And when he was come into the temple, the chief priests and the elders of the people came unto him as he was teaching, and said,
Afterwards he came into the temple . . . — Knox
. . . and the chief priests and elders of the nation came to him with the question: — NEB
Upon his entering the Temple, the chief priests . . . stepped up to him . . . — Ber
By what authority doest thou these things? and who gave thee this authority?
By what authority are you acting like this? . . . — NEB
What authority have you for doing as you do? . . . — Gspd
. . . And who gave You the right to do them — Beck

24. And Jesus answered and said unto them, I also will ask you one thing, which if ye tell me, I in like wise will tell you by what authority I do these things.
. . . I too have a question to ask; if you can tell me the answer, I will tell you in return . . . — Knox

25. The baptism of John, whence was it? from heaven, or of men?
The immersion of John . . . — Rhm
. . . was it sanctioned by Heaven or by man — Rieu
Where did John's baptism come from? . . . — Gspd
. . . What was its origin? divine or human — TCNT
And they reasoned with themselves, saying,

---

[35]Compare Matt. 16:28.

But they began to deliberate . . . — Rhm

And they argued with one another — RSV

Whereupon they cast about in their minds — Knox

So they began debating . . . — Mon

If we shall say, From heaven; he will say unto us, Why did ye not then believe him?

26. **But if we shall say, Of men; we fear the people;**

If on the other hand we should say, It was purely human — well, frankly, we are afraid of . . . — Phi

. . . we fear the multitude — ASV

. . . we have reason to fear the people — Rieu

for all hold John as a prophet.

. . . regard John . . . — Mon

. . . consider John . . . — Gspd

. . . believe that John was a prophet — Nor

27. **And they answered Jesus, and said, We cannot tell.**

. . . We know not — ASV

. . . We have no idea — Bas

And he said unto them, Neither tell I you by what authority I do these things.

He, in his turn, said, And you will not learn from me what is the authority by which I do these things — Knox

Then I, he said, refuse to tell you what authority I have to do these things — TCNT

28. **But what think ye? A certain man had two sons;**

But give me your judgment . . . — Mon

. . . A man had two children — ABUV

And he came to the first, and said, Son, go work to day in my vineyard.

One day he went to the first-born and said to him, My boy, will you go and work . . . ? — Nor

29. **He answered and said, I will not: but afterward he repented, and went.**

He answering said, I will not; afterwards, smitten with regret, he went — Rhm

. . . but afterwards he changed his mind and went — NEB

30. **And he came to the second, and said likewise.**

In the meantime, the man had gone to his second son and put the same question to him — Nor

And he answered and said, I go, sir: and went not.

31. **Whether of them twain did the will of his father?**

Which of the two . . . — ASV

. . . did his father's pleasure — Bas

They say unto him, The first. Jesus saith unto them, Verily I say unto you, That the publicans and the harlots go into the kingdom of God before you.

. . . the tax-collectors and prostitutes are going into the Kingdom of God ahead of you — Gspd

32. **For John came unto you in the way of righteousness,**

. . . came to you walking in the way of uprightness — Wms

. . . came among you following all due observance — Knox

. . . came to show you the right way to live — NEB

. . . came to you on a mission of righteousness — Ber

. . . showed you God's way to be good — Mof

and ye believed him not; but the publicans and the harlots believed him: and ye, when ye had seen it, repented not afterward, that ye might believe him.

. . . even when you saw that, you would not relent, and believe him — Knox

. . . you did not change your minds and believe him — NEB

. . . And ye seeing it were not even smitten with regret afterwards so as to believe him — Rhm

33. **Hear another parable:**

Now listen to another story — Phi

There was a certain householder, which planted a vineyard, and hedged it round about,

. . . and built a fence around it — Wms

and digged a winepress in it, and built a tower,

and hewed out a wine-vat in it . . . — Wms

. . . and built a watchtower — Mof

and let it out to husbandmen, and went into a far country:

. . . to tenants . . . into another country — RSV

... to some vine-dressers, while he went on his travels — Knox

then leased it to some farmers and went abroad — Rieu

rented it out to workers and left home — Beck

34. And when the time of the fruit drew near,

And when the season of the fruits drew near — ASV

when vintage time approached — Ber

when the grapes were getting ripe — Beck

he sent his servants to the husbandmen, that they might receive the fruits of it.

... to receive his fruits — ASV

... to claim its revenues — Knox

... for his share of the produce—Rieu

35. And the husbandmen[36] took his servants, and beat one, and killed another, and stoned another.

... took his agents ... — Ber

... one they cruelly beat, one they killed, one they pelted with stones — Wey

36. Again, he sent other servants more than the first: and they did unto them likewise.

A second time the owner sent some servants ... — TCNT

... but they fared no better — Knox

37. But last of all he sent unto them his son, saying, They will reverence my son.

... They will surely respect my son — Wms

... They might feel ashamed before my son — Lam

38. But when the husbandmen saw the son, they said among themselves, This is the heir; come, let us kill him, and let us seize on his inheritance.

... and have his inheritance — RSV

... get all that is coming to him — Wms

... get possession of his estate — Nor

39. And they caught him, and cast him out of the vineyard, and slew him.

So they laid hands on him ... — Rieu

... flung him out ... and murdered him — NEB

40. When the lord therefore of the vineyard cometh, what will he do unto those husbandmen?[37]

When therefore the owner of the vineyard comes ... — RSV

... how do you think he will deal with those tenants — NEB

41. They say unto him, He will miserably destroy those wicked men,

... those miserable men — ASV

He will put those wretches to a miserable death — RSV

He will bring those bad men to a bad end — NEB

In vengeance he will put the scoundrels to death — Wms

He will kill ... without mercy — Phi

and will let out his vineyard unto other husbandmen, which shall render him the fruits in their seasons.

... who will pay him his due when the season comes — Knox

... let him have his share of the crop when the season comes — NEB

... who will promptly pay him the rent — Wms

... render the produce at the vintage season — Wey

42. Jesus saith unto them, Did ye never read in the scriptures, The stone which the builders rejected, the same is become the head of the corner: this is the Lord's doing, and it is marvellous in our eyes?

... the same was made the head of the corner ... — ASV

... the chief corner-stone ... — NASB

... and it is wonderful in our eyes — NEB

43. Therefore say I unto you, The kingdom of God shall be taken from you,

On that authority I tell you ... — Rieu

That, I tell you, is why ... — Gspd

and given to a nation bringing forth the fruits thereof.

... to a people who produce the kingdom's fruits — Rieu

... to a people who will pay a fair rent for it — Wms

... who will do its work — Beck

44. And whosoever shall fall on this stone shall be broken: but on whomsoever it shall fall, it will grind him to powder.[38]

---

[36]See verse 33.

[37]Compare verse 33.

[38]This verse is now recognized as not adequately supported by original manuscripts.

... it will scatter him as dust — ASV

... scatter him like chaff — Knox

whoever falls on that stone will be smashed, and on whom it falls, he shall be pulverized — Ber

45. And when the chief priests and Pharisees had heard his parables, they perceived that he spake of them.

... they realized that he was speaking of them — Rieu

... they saw that he was referring to them — NEB

46. But when they sought to lay hands on him,

But when they tried to arrest him — RSV

Yet, although eager to arrest him — TCNT

They wanted to grab him — Beck

they feared the multitude, because they took him for a prophet.

... the crowds, since they considered him a prophet — Ber

... the people, because they looked on him as a prophet — Rieu

CHAPTER 22

1. And Jesus answered and spake unto them again by parables, and said,

Addressing them later Jesus spoke once more in allegory — Rieu

... in figures — Gspd

2. The kingdom of heaven is like unto a certain king,

... may be compared to ... — RSV

which made a marriage for his son,

... a marriage feast ... — ASV

... gave a wedding reception ... — Wms

... prepared a feast for his son's wedding — NEB

3. And sent forth his servants to call them that were bidden

... his slaves ... — Beck

... with a summons to all those whom he had invited — Knox

to the wedding:

to the marriage feast — RSV

to the banquet — TCNT

and they would not come.

but they did not want to come — Mon

but they refused to come — Rieu

4. Again, he sent forth other servants, saying, Tell them which are bidden, Behold, I have prepared my dinner:

... See now! I have prepared this feast for you — NEB

... Tell the invited guests that I have my reception all ready — Wms

... I have prepared my breakfast — ABUV

my oxen and my fatlings are killed, and all things are ready:

... my fattened livestock are all butchered ... — NASB

... my cattle and fat beasts ... — TCNT

come unto the marriage.

Come along to the festivities — Phi

Come to the banquet — TCNT

Come to the marriage feast — RSV

5. But they made light of it, and went their ways,

But they still paid no heed, and went off on other errands — Knox

... sneered at it ... — Lam

one to his farm, another to his merchandise:

one to his estate, another to his business — Mof

one to his home in the country, another to his business — Wey

6. And the remnant took his servants, and entreated them spitefully, and slew them.

and the rest laid hold on his servants and treated them shamefully, and killed them — ASV

... attacked them brutally and killed them — NEB

... maltreated and murdered them — Mon

7. But when the king heard thereof, he was wroth:

The king fell into a rage when he heard of it — Knox

The king was furious — NEB

... was provoked to anger — Rhm

and sent forth his armies, and destroyed those murderers, and burned up their city.

he sent troops to kill those murderers and set their town on fire — NEB

8. Then saith he to his servants, The wedding is ready, but they which were bidden were not worthy.

. . . the guests I invited did not deserve the honour — NEB

. . . were not good enough for it — Phi

9. Go ye therefore into the highways,

. . . into the crossways of the roads — Rhm

. . . the country crossroads — Wms

. . . the thoroughfares — RSV

. . . the street corners — Knox

. . . where the roads leave the city — Gspd

. . . the meetings of the ways — Alf

and as many as ye shall find, bid to the marriage.

and invite everyone you find to the banquet — TCNT

. . . the marriage-feast — Rhm

. . . wedding reception — Wms

10. So those servants went out into the highways,

. . . into the streets — RSV

. . . the roads — Mof

and gathered together all as many as they found, both bad and good:

and collected all the people whom they found, whether bad or good — TCNT

. . . rogues and honest men — Knox

and the wedding was furnished with guests.

So the hall was packed with guests — NEB

The bridal-hall was filled . . . — TCNT

11. And when the king came in to see the guests,

. . . to view the guests — Rhm

. . . to see the company at table — NEB

. . . to inspect his guests — Mon

he saw there a man which had not on a wedding garment:

. . . who was not dressed for a wedding — Rieu

12. And he saith unto him, Friend, how camest thou in hither not having a wedding garment?

. . . how did you get in here without wedding clothes — Rieu

. . . without being properly dressed for the wedding — Phi

And he was speechless.

And he was put to silence — Rhm

And he made no reply — Knox

The man had nothing to say for himself — Rieu

But his lips were sealed — Mon

13. Then said the king to the servants,

. . . to the attendants — RSV

. . . the ministers — Rhm

Bind him hand and foot, and take him away,[39] and cast him into outer darkness;

. . . turn him out into the dark — NEB

. . . the darkness outside — Rhm

there shall be weeping and gnashing of teeth.

the place of wailing and grinding of teeth — NEB

where there will be weeping and grinding of teeth — TCNT

there he can weep and regret his folly — Phi

14. For many are called, but few are chosen.

Thus you see that many are called . . . — Rieu

For though many are invited . . . — NEB

15. Then went the Pharisees, and took counsel how they might entangle him in his talk.

Then the Pharisees went and made a plot to trap Him in argument—Wms

. . . conferred together as to how they might lay a snare for Jesus in the course of conversation — TCNT

. . . agreed on a plan to trap him in his own words — NEB

16. And they sent out unto him their disciples with the Herodians, saying,

. . . with men of Herod's party. They said — NEB

Master, we know that thou art true,

Teacher we know . . . — ASV

. . . that you are honest — Mon

. . . that you are in the habit of telling the truth — Wms

. . . that you are sincere — Nor

and teachest the way of God in truth,

. . . in all sincerity the way of God — Knox

. . . in all honesty the way of life that God requires — NEB

neither carest thou for any man:

. . . holdest no one in awe — Knox

and are not afraid of anyone — Mon

regardless of the consequences — Gspd

for thou regardest not the person of men.

---

[39]The words "take him away" are now recognized as not adequately supported by original manuscripts.

For thou lookest not unto the face of
men — Rhm

and you court no one's favor — Ber

for you are impartial — Gspd

17. Tell us therefore, What thinkest thou?

Give us your ruling on this — NEB

So give us your opinion — Gspd

**Is it lawful to give tribute unto Caesar,
or not?**

Are we justified or not, in paying the
capitation-tax — Rieu

are we or are we not permitted to pay
taxes to the Roman Emperor — NEB

Are we right in paying taxes to the Emperor, or not — TCNT

**18. But Jesus perceived their wickedness,
and said,**

But Jesus, aware of their malice, said
— RSV

Jesus, who knew their evil ways, replied — Rieu

Why tempt ye me, ye hypocrites?

Why make ye trial of me . . . — ASV

Why put me to the test . . . — RSV

Oh false ones, why are you attempting
to put me in the wrong — Bas

19. Shew me the tribute money.

. . . the coinage in which the tribute
is paid — Knox

. . . the legal coin — Ber

And they brought unto him a penny.[40]

**20. And he saith unto them, Whose is this
image and superscription?**

. . . Whose likeness and inscription is
this — RSV

. . . Whose head and title are these —
TCNT

**21. They say unto him, Caesar's. Then
saith he unto them, Render therefore
unto Caesar the things which are Caesar's; and unto God the things that are
God's.**

. . . Why then, give back to Caesar
what is Caesar's, and to God what is
God's — Knox

. . . Pay Caesar what is due to Caesar,
and God what is due to God — Rieu

. . . Then pay to the Emperor what belongs to the Emperor, and to God
what belongs to God — TCNT

**22. When they had heard these words, they
marvelled, and left him, and went
their way.**

This answer took them by surprise,
and they went away and left him
alone — NEB

His reply surprised and baffled them
and they went away — Tay

**23. The same day came to him the Sad-
ducees,**

On that day, too, he was approached
with a question by the Sadducees —
Knox

which say that there is no resurrection,

who say the dead don't rise — Beck

and asked him,

and set him a problem — Rieu

**24. Saying, Master, Moses said, If a man
die, having no children,**

saying, Teacher . . . — ASV

. . . If someone dies childless — Ber

**his brother shall marry his wife, and
raise up seed unto his brother.**

. . . must marry the widow, and raise
up children for his brother — RSV

**25. Now there were with us seven breth-
ren:**

Now we know of a case where there
were . . . — Rieu

**and the first, when he had married a
wife, deceased,**

the first married, and died — RSV

**and, having no issue, left his wife unto
his brother:**

and having no children left his wife
to his brother — RSV

**26. Likewise the second also, and the third,
unto the seventh.**

The same thing happened with the second, and the third, and so on with
all seven — NEB

27. And last of all the woman died also.

**28. Therefore in the resurrection whose
wife shall she be of the seven? for
they all had her.**

**29. Jesus answered and said unto them, Ye
do err, not knowing the scriptures, nor
the power of God.**

. . . Ye are deceiving yourselves . . . —
Rhm

. . . You are wrong because you know
neither the scripture nor the power
of God — RSV

**30. For in the resurrection they neither
marry, nor are given in marriage, but
are as the angels of God in heaven.**

. . . men do not marry, nor are women
given in marriage, but they are like
the angels in heaven — Mon

---

[40]See Matt. 20:2.

31. But as touching the resurrection of the dead,

But in this matter of the resurrection of the dead — Rieu

have ye not read that which was spoken unto you by God, saying,

did you never read what God himself said: — Knox

32. I am the God of Abraham, and the God of Isaac, and the God of Jacob? God is not the God of the dead, but of the living.

. . . He is not the God of dead men, but of living — TCNT

33. And when the multitude heard this, they were astonished at his doctrine.

. . . amazed by his teaching — Knox

. . . filled with admiration for his teaching — Rieu

. . . dumfounded at His teaching—Wms

. . .profoundly impressed by His answers — Tay

34. But when the Pharisees had heard that he had put the Sadducees to silence, they were gathered together.

. . . they put their heads together — Rieu

. . . they had a meeting — Wms

. . . they came up to him in a body — Phi

35. Then one of them, which was a lawyer,

. . . a student of the Law — TCNT

. . . an expert in the Law — Gspd

asked him a question, tempting him, and saying,

. . . trying him: — ASV

36. Master, which is the great commandment in the law?

Teacher . . . — ASV

. . . the most important commandment . . . — Rieu

37. Jesus said unto him, Thou shalt love the Lord thy God with all thy heart, and with all thy soul, and with all thy mind.

38. This is the first and great commandment.

. . . the great and first commandment — ASV

That is the greatest commandment. It comes first — NEB

. . . the greatest and foremost commandment — Wey

39. And the second is like unto it,

There is a second like it — Mof

. . . is like it in importance — Nor

Thou shalt love thy neighbour as thyself.

40. On these two commandments hang all the law and the prophets.

In these two commandments all the law is contained and the prophets—Rhm

On these . . . depend . . . — RSV

The whole of the Law and the Prophets is summed up in these two Commandments — Wey

41. While the Pharisees were gathered together, Jesus asked them,

The Pharisees by now had gathered round; and Jesus questioned them — Rieu

Turning to the assembled Pharisees Jesus asked them — NEB

42. Saying, What think ye of Christ? Whose son is he?

What is your opinion . . . — Knox

What about the Messiah? . . . — Tay

They say unto him, The son of David.

43. He saith unto them, How then doth David in spirit call him Lord, saying,

. . . in the Spirit . . . — ASV

. . . inspired by the Spirit . . . — RSV

. . . under the Spirit's influence . . . — Gspd

44. The LORD said unto my Lord,

. . . said to my Master — Knox

Sit thou on my right hand, till I make thine enemies thy footstool?

. . . Till I put thine enemies underneath thy feet — ASV

45. If David then call him Lord, how is he his son?

David calls Christ his Master; how can he be also his son? — Knox

46. And no man was able to answer him a word, neither durst any man from that day forth ask him any more questions.

no one could say a word in answer; nor did any one after that day venture to question him further — TCNT

CHAPTER 23

1. Then spake Jesus to the multitude, and to his disciples,

2. Saying, The scribes[41] and the Pharisees sit in Moses' seat:

. . . the place from which Moses used to teach — Knox

. . . now occupy the chair of Moses — TCNT

. . . speak with the authority of Moses — Phi

3. All therefore whatsoever they bid you observe, that observe and do;

so practice and observe whatever they tell you — RSV

but do not ye after their works:

but do not imitate their actions — Knox

but do not behave as they do — Ber

but do not follow their example—TCNT

for they say, and do not.

for they preach, but do not practice — RSV

for they tell you one thing and do another — Knox

4. For they bind heavy burdens and grievous to be borne, and lay them on men's shoulders;

They fasten up packs too heavy to be borne, . . . — Knox

They pile up back-breaking burdens . . . — Phi

but they themselves will not move them with one of their fingers.

they decline, themselves, to lift a finger to move them — TCNT

5. But all their works they do for to be seen of men:

. . . to be gazed at by men — Rhm

Whatever they do is done for show — NEB

they make broad their phylacteries, and enlarge the borders of their garments,

Boldly written are the texts they carry, and deep is the hem of their garments — Knox

They wear wide Scripture texts as charms, and they wear large tassels — Gspd

They widen their phylacteries, and lengthen the tassels — Mon

They act holy by wearing on their arms large prayer boxes with Scripture verses inside, and by lengthening the memorial fringes of their robes! — Tay

6. And love the uppermost rooms at feasts,

. . . the first couch in the chief meals — Rhm

. . . the place of honor at feasts — RSV

. . . the best places at banquets — Rieu

. . . seats of honor at dinner parties — Phi

and the chief seats in the synagogues,

and the front seats . . . — Mof

7. And greetings in the markets,

and respectful greetings . . . — NASB

to be greeted with honor in public places — Wms

and to be called of men, Rabbi, Rabbi.[42]

and to be addressed as "rabbi" — NEB

and to have men call them "Teacher" — Wms

8. But be not ye called Rabbi:

You are not to claim the title of Rabbi — Knox

Do not let people call you Rabbi — Rieu

You must not seek to be called by titles, such as Teacher — Nor

for one is your Master, even Christ, and all ye are brethren.

for one is your teacher . . . — ASV

9. And call no man your father upon the earth:

Do not call any man on earth "father" — NEB

Nor are you to call any man on earth your father — Knox

for one is your Father, which is in heaven.

for the Heavenly One is your Father — Wms

for you have one Father and he is in Heaven — Phi

10. Neither be ye called masters: for one is your Master, even Christ.

Neither be called leaders, for your leader is one the Christ — Rhm

Nor must you be called "teacher"; you have one Teacher, the Messiah — NEB

---

[41]For variants of "scribes" see Matt. 16:21.

[42]The Greek uses "Rabbi" only once.

. . . for Christ is your one Instructor — Ber

11. But he that is greatest among you shall be your servant.

. . . shall be to you a minister — Rhm
the only 'superior' among you is the one who serves the others — Phi

12. And whosoever shall exalt himself shall be abased;

. . . shall be humbled — ASV

and he that shall humble himself shall be exalted.

13. But woe unto you, scribes[43] and Pharisees, hypocrites!

A curse on you . . . — Wms
. . . scribes and Pharisees, false ones — Bas

for ye shut up the kingdom of heaven against men:

for you lock the doors of the Kingdom of Heaven in men's faces — Gspd

for ye neither go in yourselves, neither suffer ye them that are entering to go in.

You won't come into it yourselves, and when others try to come in, you won't let them — Beck

14. Woe unto you, scribes and Pharisees, hypocrites! for ye devour widows' houses, and for a pretence make long prayer: therefore ye shall receive the greater damnation.[44]

15. Woe unto you, scribes and Pharisees, hypocrites! for ye compass sea and land to make one proselyte,

. . . For you scour sea and land . . . — Mon
. . . because you travel about on sea and land . . . — NASB
. . . to make one convert — Rhm

and when he is made, ye make him twofold more the child of hell than yourselves.

And when it is done ye make him a son of gehenna twofold more than ye — Rhm
. . . twice as worthy of damnation as yourselves — Knox
. . . twice as fit for hell as you are yourselves — NEB
. . . twice as ripe for destruction . . . — Phi

16. Woe unto you, ye blind guides, which say,

Alas for you, blind leaders, who say — Rieu

Whosoever shall swear by the temple, it is nothing;

when a man swears by the Temple he is not committed — Rieu
. . . is not duty-bound — Wms
. . . his oath counts for nothing — TCNT

but whosoever shall swear by the gold of the temple, he is a debtor!

. . . he is bound by his oath — RSV
. . . he is obligated — Ber

17. Ye fools and blind:

You blind fools! — RSV

for whether is greater, the gold, or the temple that sanctifieth the gold?

For which is greater, the gold or the temple that has made the gold sacred — RSV
. . . more important . . . — NEB

18. And, Whosoever shall swear by the altar, it is nothing;[45] but whosoever sweareth by the gift that is upon it, he is guilty.

. . . he is bound by his oath — RSV
. . . he is obligated — Ber

19. Ye fools[46] and blind: for whether is greater, the gift, or the altar that sanctifieth[47] the gift?

You blind men! . . . — RSV

20. Whoso therefore shall swear by the altar, sweareth by it, and by all things thereon.

21. And whoso shall swear by the temple, sweareth by it, and by him that dwelleth therein.

. . . him who has made it his dwelling-place — Knox
. . . by the sanctuary and by him who dwells there — NEB

22. And he that shall swear by heaven, sweareth by the throne of God, and by him that sitteth thereon.

---

[43]See Matt. 16:21 for variants of "scribes."
[44]Verse 14 is now recognized as not adequately supported by original manuscripts.
[45]See verse 16.
[46]The words "Ye fools" are now recognized as not adequately supported by original manuscripts.
[47]See verse 17.

23. Woe unto you, scribes[48] and Pharisees, hypocrites!

Alas for you, scribes and Pharisees, you utter frauds! — Phi

for ye pay tithe of mint and anise and cummin,

for you tithe mint and dill and cummin — RSV

You pay tithes on mint, fennel and carraway seed — TCNT

for you make men give a tenth of all sorts of sweet-smelling plants — BAS

For you tithe down to the last mint leaf in your garden — Tay

and have omitted the weightier matters of the law,

and have left undone . . . — ASV

and have dismissed . . . — Rhm

. . . neglected . . . — RSV

. . . forgotten . . . — Knox

. . . overlooked the weightier demands . . . — NEB

but ignore the important things — Tay

judgment, mercy and faith:

justice, and mercy and faith — ASV

. . . mercy and honour — Knox

. . . and faithfulness — NASB

. . . and integrity — Gspd

. . . and fidelity — Ber

these ought ye to have done, and not to leave the other undone.

these it was binding to do, and those not to dismiss — Rhm

It is these ye should have practised, without neglecting the others — NEB

These last you ought to have put in practice, without neglecting the first — TCNT

24. Ye blind guides, which strain at a gnat, and swallow a camel.

. . . strain out the gnat . . . — ASV

Blind leaders! You filter your wine to get rid of a gnat, and you swallow a camel — Rieu

. . . strain off a midge, yet gulp down a camel — NEB

you call yourselves leaders, and yet you can't see an inch before your noses, for you filter out the mosquito and swallow the camel — Phi

25. Woe unto you, scribes and Pharisees, hypocrites! for ye make clean the outside of the cup and of the platter,

. . . scour the outward part . . . — Knox

. . . of the cup and bowl — Rieu

but within they are full of extortion and excess.

. . . plunder and intemperance — Rhm

. . . avarice and incontinence — Knox

. . . rapine and unbridled greed — Rieu

. . . robbery and self-indulgence — NEB

. . . rapacity and self-indulgence — Mof

. . . violent behavior and uncontrolled desire — BAS

26. Thou blind Pharisee, cleanse first that which is within the cup and platter, that the outside of them may be clean also.

27. Woe unto you, scribes[49] and Pharisees, hypocrites! for ye are like unto whited sepulchres,

. . . like white-washed tombs — RSV

. . . white-washed graves — Beck

which indeed appear beautiful outward,

they look well from outside — NEB

but are within full of dead men's bones, and of all uncleanness.

. . . all manner of corruption — Knox

. . . all kinds of filth — NEB

. . . all rottenness — Mon

. . . every kind of decay — Beck

28. Even so ye also outwardly appear righteous unto men,

Thus, you are law-abiding men to outside view — Rieu

outside you look like honest men — NEB

So to men you seem just — Mof

Outwardly, and to others, you have the look of religious men — TCNT

but within ye are full of hypocrisy and iniquity.

yet there is nothing but hypocrisy and wickedness within you — Rieu

but inside you are brim-full of hypocrisy and crime — NEB

. . . hypocrisy and lawlessness — Rhm

29. Woe unto you scribes and Pharisees, hypocrites! because ye build the tombs of the prophets, and garnish the sepulchres of the righteous,

. . . adorn the monuments of the righteous — RSV

. . . embellish the monuments of the saints — NEB

---

[48]See Matt. 16:21.

[49]See Matt. 16:21 for variants of "scribes."

. . . decorate monuments for the upright — Wms

. . . for the good men of the past — Phi

**30. And say, If we had been in the days
of our fathers,**

and as you do this say, Had we lived
in our fathers time — Rieu

and your boast is, If we had lived in
the time of our forefathers — Wey

. . . the days of our ancestors — TCNT

**we would not have been partakers with
them in the blood of the prophets.**

. . . taken part with them in shedding
the blood of the prophets — RSV

. . . taken part in murdering the prophets — Knox

**31. Wherefore ye be witnesses unto your-
selves,**

Thus you witness against yourselves —
RSV

By doing this you are furnishing evidence against yourselves — TCNT

**that ye are the children of them which
killed the prophets.**

. . . sons of those who murdered . . . —
RSV

. . . descendants of those . . . — Wey

**32. Fill ye up then the measure of your
fathers.**

. . . the measure of the guilt of your
fathers — NASB

Go on then, finish off what your fathers
began — NEB

Then fill up to the brim the cup of your
forefathers' guilt! — Wms

33. Ye serpents, ye generation of vipers,

. . . offspring of vipers — ASV

. . . brood of vipers — RSV

. . . seed of scorpions — Lam

**how can ye escape the damnation of
hell?**

. . . flee from the judgment of Gehenna
— Rhm

. . . escape being sentenced to hell —
RSV

How can you escape being sentenced to
the pit — Gspd

. . . the rubbish heap — Phi

**34. Wherefore, behold, I send unto you
prophets, and wise men, and scribes:**

Know now why I am sending you
prophets and wise and learned men
— Rieu

For this reason, I am going to keep on

sending you prophets and wise men
and scholars — Nor

. . . prophets, sages, and teachers—NEB

. . . men to speak God's Word, men
who are wise and know the Bible —
Beck

**and some of them ye shall kill and
crucify; and some of them shall ye
scourge in your synagogues,**

. . . flog in your synagogues — NEB

and persecute them from city to city,

. . . chase from town to town — Wey

. . . hound from city to city — NEB

**35. That upon you may come all the right-
eous blood shed upon the earth,**

so that you will make yourselves answerable for all . . . — Knox

and so, on you will fall the guilt of all
the innocent blood spilt on the
ground — NEB

that upon your heads may come every
drop of innocent blood spilt upon
the earth — Mon

**from the blood of righteous Abel unto
the blood of Zacharias son of Bara-
chias,**

. . . innocent Abel . . . — RSV

. . . Abel, the just . . . — Mon

**whom ye slew between the temple and
the altar.**

. . . murdered between the sanctuary
and the altar — RSV

. . . between the holy place and the
altar — Beck

**36. Verily I say unto you, All these things
shall come upon this generation.**

. . . come home to the present generation — TCNT

. . . will be laid at the doors of this
generation — Phi

. . . this age — Gspd

Believe me, this generation will bear
the guilt . . . — NEB

. . . this generation shall be held answerable for all of it — Knox

**37. O Jerusalem, Jerusalem, thou that kill-
est the prophets, and stonest them
which are sent unto thee,**

. . . the messengers that are sent to you
— Phi

**how often would I have gathered thy
children together,**

. . . have I longed to gather your children to me — Rieu

even as a hen gathereth her chickens under her wings, and ye would not!

... thou didst refuse it — Knox

... you would not let me — NEB

38. Behold, your house is left unto you desolate.

Lo! your house is left to you — Rhm

... forsaken and desolate — RSV

Look, look! there is your temple, forsaken by God — NEB

Now your house is abandoned by me! — Wms

Now I leave you to yourselves — Gspd

39. For I say unto you, Ye shall not see me henceforth, till ye shall say, Blessed is he that cometh in the name of the Lord.

... you will not see me again ... — RSV

... you shall never see me until ... — NEB

CHAPTER 24

1. And Jesus went out, and departed from the temple:

And Jesus went out from the temple, and was going on his way — ASV

... and was walking away — Phi

and his disciples came to him for to shew him the buildings of the temple.

... to point out to him the buildings of the temple — RSV

... called his attention to the Temple buildings — Wey

2. And Jesus said unto them, See ye not all these things?

... You see all this, do you not — RSV

verily I say unto you, There shall not be left here one stone upon another, that shall not be thrown down.

... I prophesy to you that not a block of stone here will be left standing on one another — Rieu

3. And as he sat upon the mount of Olives, the disciples came unto him privately, saying,

Afterwards, while he was sitting ... — Knox

Tell us, when shall these things be?

... when will this happen — NEB

and what shall be the sign of thy coming, and of the end of the world?

... sign of thy presence and the conclusion of the age — Rhm

how can we tell when You're coming back and the world will come to an end — Beck

4. And Jesus answered and said unto them, Take heed that no man deceive you.

... lead you astray — ASV

... See to it that no one misleads you — NASB

5. For many shall come in my name, saying, I am Christ; and shall deceive many.

... making use of my name ... — Knox

... claiming my name and saying, I am the Messiah ... — NEB

6. And ye shall hear of wars and rumours of wars:

... of revolutions and rumors of wars — Lam

And the time is coming when you will hear the noise of battles near at hand and the news of battles far away — NEB

see that ye be not troubled:

... not disturbed in mind — Knox

Beware of panic — Rieu

take care not to be scared out of your wits — Wms

see and do not be alarmed — Mof

for all these things must come to pass, but the end is not yet.

such things must happen ... — Knox

... but the end is still to come — NEB

7. For nation shall rise against nation, and kingdom against kingdom:

... will go to war with nation ... — Wms

and there shall be famines, and pestilences,[50] and earthquakes, in divers places.

... in this region or that — Knox

... here and there — Gspd

... in different parts of the world—Phi

8. All these are the beginning of sorrows.

---

[50]The words "and pestilences" are now recognized as not adequately supported by original manuscripts.

But all these things are the beginning of
travail — ASV

all this is but the beginning of the sufferings — RSV

With all these things the birth-pangs of
the new age begin — NEB

9. **Then shall they deliver you up to be
afflicted, and shall kill you:**

. . . deliver you up unto tribulation . . .
— ASV

. . . give you up to persecution . . . —
Knox

Those are the days when they will have
you put to torture and to death —
Rieu

**and ye shall be hated of all nations for
my name's sake.**

. . . hated by the pagan world because
you use my name — Rieu

. . . hated by all the Gentiles . . .—Mof

. . . because of your allegiance to me —
— NEB

all the world will be hating you because
you bear my name — Knox

10. **And then shall many be offended,**

. . . shall many stumble — ASV

. . . fall away — RSV

. . . lose heart — Knox

. . . recant — Rieu

. . . lose their faith — NEB

. . . turn against me — Wey

**and shall betray one another, and shall
hate one another.**

and deliver up one another, . . . — ASV

11. **And many false prophets shall rise,
and shall deceive[51] many.**

. . . false prophets will appear . . . —
Gspd

12. **And because iniquity shall abound,**

And because iniquity shall be multiplied — ASV

And because of lawlessness being
brought to the full — Rhm

and as lawlessness spreads — NEB

and because of the increasing crime-
wave — Wms

And because there will be more and
more wickedness — Beck

the love of many shall wax cold.

most men's love . . . — RSV

the charity of most men . . . — Knox

men's love for one another . . . — NEB

in most of you love will grow cold —
Mof

13. **But he that shall endure unto the end,
the same shall be saved.**

But he that hath endured throughout
. . . — Rhm

. . . holds out to the end . . . — NEB

. . . perseveres . . . — Ber

. . . stands firm . . . — Wey

14. **And this gospel of the kingdom shall
be preached in all the world**

And this glad message . . . will be proclaimed in all the inhabited earth —
Rhm

Moreover these good tidings . . . must
be proclaimed . . . — Rieu

and this good news . . . — Gspd

**for a witness unto all nations; and then
shall the end come.**

for a testimony . . . — ASV

to testify to all the heathen . . . — Gspd

to let the pagan nations know . . . —
Rieu

so that all nations may hear the truth;
only after that . . . — Knox

15. **When ye therefore shall see the abomination of desolation,**

. . . the desolating sacrilege — RSV

. . . the Foul Desecration — TCNT

. . . destructive desecration — Wms

. . . the appalling Horror — Mof

. . . the horrible thing — Tay

. . . the refuse of desolation — Lam

. . . the abomination laying waste the
land — Beck

**spoken of by Daniel the prophet, stand
in the holy place,**

. . . set up in the holy place — Knox

(whoso readeth, let him understand:)

. . . let him think — Rhm

(let him who reads this, recognize what
it means) — Knox

Reader, note this well — Rieu

— let the reader observe those words
— Wey

(anyone who reads this should understand it) — Beck

16. **Then let them which be in Judaea flee
unto the mountains.**

then those of you who are in Judaea
must take refuge in the mountains —
TCNT

. . . must take to the hills — NEB

. . . escape to the hills — Phi

17. **Let him that is on the house top not
come down to take any thing out of his
house:**

. . . to save his household goods—Rieu

---

[51]See verse 4.

If a man is on the roof, he must not
come down to fetch his goods — NEB
... must not waste time going into his
house to collect anything — Phi

18. **Neither let him which is in the field
return back to take his clothes.**
... pick up his cloak — Rieu
... turn back to get his coat — Mof

19. **And woe unto them that are with child,
and to them that give suck in those
days!**
It will go hard with women who are
with child, or have children at the
breast, in those days — Knox
Alas, in those days, for the woman with
a child in her womb or at her breast!
— Rieu

20. **But pray ye that your flight be not in
the winter, neither on the sabbath day:**

21. **For then shall be great tribulation,**
for that will be a time of great distress
— TCNT
**such as was not since the beginning of
the world to this time, no, nor ever
shall be.**
the like of which has not occurred from
the beginning of the world down to
the present time — no, nor ever will
again — TCNT
... and can never be again — Knox

22. **And except those days should be shortened,**
And if those days had not been shortened — RSV
If that time of troubles were not cut
short — NEB
there should no flesh be saved:
no human being would be saved — RSV
no living thing would have escaped —
Rieu
not a mortal could survive — Ber
not a soul would be saved alive — Mof
**but for the elect's sake those days shall
be shortened.**
but for the sake of God's chosen people ... — Wms
but for the sake of God's People a limit
will be put to them — TCNT

23. **Then if any man shall say unto you,
Lo, here is Christ, or there; believe it
not.**
If anyone at that time says ... — Wms
... Look, here is the Messiah ... —
NEB

24. **For there shall arise false Christs, and
false prophets,**

Impostors will come claiming to be
messiahs or prophets — NEB
**and shall shew great signs and won-
ders;**
... miracles and portents — Rieu
displaying wonderful signs and prodigies — Wey
**insomuch that, if it were possible, they
shall deceive the very elect.**
to mislead even God's chosen, if such
a thing were possible — NEB

25. **Behold, I have told you before.**
Mark well, I have given you warning
of it — Knox
You see, I've told you this before it
happens — Beck

26. **Wherefore if they shall say unto you,**
If anyone says to you then — Rieu
If they tell you — NEB
**Behold, he is in the desert; go not
forth:**
He is there in the wilderness, ... —
NEB
... do not stir abroad — Knox
**behold, he is in the secret chambers;
believe it not.**
Lo, he is in the inner rooms ... — RSV
... He is hiding in our midst ... —
Rieu

27. **For as the lightning cometh out of the
east, and shineth even unto the west;**
... and is seen even unto the west —
ASV
... leaps across the sky from east to
west — Rieu
**so shall also the coming of the Son of
man be.**
So shall be the presence of the Son of
Man — Rhm

28. **For wheresoever the carcase is, there
will the eagles be gathered together.**
Wherever the corpse is, there the vultures will gather — NEB
wherever there is a dead body, the vultures will flock — Gspd

29. **Immediately after the tribulation of
those days shall the sun be darkened,**
... the misery of those days ... — Mof
... the distress ... — TCNT
and the moon shall not give her light,
... will not shed her light — Mon
... will stop shining — Beck
**and the stars shall fall from heaven,
and the powers of the heavens shall
be shaken:**

... the mighty ones of heaven will be shaken — Rieu

... the celestial powers ... — NEB

... the forces of the sky ... — Gspd

... the orbs of the heavens ... — Mof

... the forces of the heavens will be convulsed — TCNT

30. And then shall appear the sign of the Son of man in heaven:

Then will appear in the heaven the sign that heralds the Son of Man — NEB

and then shall all the tribes of the earth mourn,

... all the peoples of the earth will beat their breasts — Rieu

... will make lamentation — NEB

... will wring their hands — Phi

and they shall see the Son of man coming in the clouds of heaven with power and great glory.

... great power and glory — Rhm

... in overwhelming power and splendor — Wms

... with an army and great glory—Lam

31. And he shall send his angels with a great sound of a trumpet,

... his messengers with a great trumpet — Rhm

and they shall gather together his elect from the four winds, from one end of heaven to the other.

... from north, south, east and west — from one extremity of the earth to the other — Wey

... from the four points of the compass, from one end of the sky to the other — Wms

... from one horizon to the other — Rieu

... from the verge of heaven to the verge of earth — Mof

32. Now learn a parable of the fig tree;

From the fig tree learn its lesson — RSV

Let the fig tree teach you a parable — Mof

When his branch is yet tender, and putteth forth leaves,

as soon as its branch becomes tender ... — RSV

when its tender shoots appear and are breaking into leaf — NEB

ye know that summer is nigh:

33. So likewise ye, when ye shall see all these things,

... all these signs — Wey

know that it is near, even at the doors.

... that the end is near ... — NEB

... at the very gates — RSV

... right at your door — Wms

34. Verily I say unto you, This generation shall not pass, till all these things be fulfilled.

... pass away till ... be accomplished — ASV

... the present generation will live to see it all — NEB

... this age shall not come to an end before ... — Nor

35. Heaven and earth shall pass away, but my words shall not pass away.

Though heaven and earth should pass away, my words will stand — Knox

Earth and sky will pass away ... — Gspd

36. But of that day and hour knoweth no man, no, not the angels of heaven, but my Father only.

about that actual day and time ... — Phi

... not even the angels of heaven, neither the Son[52] but the Father only — ASV

37. But as the days of Noe were, so shall also the coming of the Son of man be.

As things were in Noah's days, so will they be ... — NEB

38. For as in the days that were before the flood they were eating and drinking, marrying and giving in marriage,

... they ate and drank and married — NEB

until the day that Noe entered into the ark,

up to the very day when Noah entered the ark — Rieu

39. And knew not until the flood came, and took them all away;

and they were taken unawares, when the flood came and drowned them all — Knox

... and swept them all away — RSV

so shall also the coming of the Son of man be.

That is how it will be when the Son of Man comes — NEB

40. Then shall two be in the field; the one shall be taken, and the other left.

At that time, of two men on a farm, one will be taken ... — TCNT

---

[52]Some manuscripts and versions include the phrase "nor the Son."

41. Two women shall be grinding at the mill; the one shall be taken, and the other left.

... grinding with the handmill ... — Wms

... at the millstone ... — Mof

... at the grist-mill ... — Nor

42. Watch therefore: for ye know not what hour your Lord doth come.

Keep awake, then; for you do not know ... — NEB

... on what day your Lord cometh — ASV

43. But know this, that if the goodman of the house had known

... master of the house ... — ASV

... householder ... — RSV

... head of the house ... — NASB

in what watch the thief would come,

in what part of the night ... — RSV

what time of night the burglar was coming — NEB

he would have watched,

he would have stayed awake — Rieu

... been on the alert — NASB

and would not have suffered his house to be broken up.

... to be dug through — Rhm

... to be broken into — RSV

... and would not let his home be plundered — Lam

44. Therefore be ye also ready:

Wherefore ye also be getting ready — Rhm

... be vigilant yourselves — Rieu

... continue to be ready — Wms

for in such an hour as ye think not the Son of man cometh.

the Son of Man will come at an hour when you are not expecting him — Knox

it is just when you are least expecting him that the Son of Man will come — TCNT

45. Who then is a faithful and wise servant,

Which of you, then, is a faithful ... — Knox

... faithful and sensible slave — NASB

... the trusty servant, the sensible man — NEB

... the faithful, thoughtful slave — Gspd

... trustworthy, careful servant — TCNT

whom his lord hath made ruler over his household,

Whom the master hath appointed over ... — Rhm

... to direct his household — Rieu

... to manage his household staff — NEB

to give them meat in due season?

... their food at the proper time — RSV

... their daily food — Rieu

to issue their rations at the proper time — NEB

to provide their sustenance on time — Ber

46. Blessed is that servant, whom his lord when he cometh shall find so doing.

... who is found at his task when his master comes — NEB

... who is doing his work when his master drops in on him — Nor

47. Verily I say unto you, That he shall make him ruler over all his goods.

... set him over all that he hath — ASV

... make director of his whole estate — Rieu

... put him in charge of all his property — Ber

48. But and if that evil servant shall say in his heart,

But if that wicked servant says to himself — RSV

But if he is a bad servant and says ... — NEB

My lord delayeth his coming;

My lord tarrieth — ASV

My master is long in coming — Rieu

... is going to stay a long time — Gspd

49. And shall begin to smite his fellow-servants,

... to strike his fellow-workers — Ber

... to beat his fellow-slaves — Wms

and takes to bullying his fellow-servants — Rieu

and to eat and drink with the drunken;

to gluttony and drinking with the tipplers — Rieu

50. The lord of that servant shall come in a day when he looketh not for him,

The master will come back some day when ... — Gspd

and in an hour that he is not aware of,

... an hour when he knoweth not — ASV

... suddenly and unexpectedly — Phi

51. And shall cut him asunder,

... punish him — RSV

... cut him off — Knox

... cut him in pieces — NEB

... scourge him till his flesh is cut — Ber

and appoint him his portion with the hypocrites:
and consign him to the hypocrites' lot — Rieu

and assign him the fate of the impious — Mof
there shall be weeping and gnashing of teeth.[53]

CHAPTER 25

1. **Then shall the kingdom of heaven be likened unto ten virgins,**
. . . be compared to ten maidens — RSV
. . . be like ten bridesmaids — Gspd
which took their lamps,
. . . their torches — Rhm
and went forth to meet the bridegroom.

2. **And five of them were wise, and five were foolish.**
. . . foolish . . . prudent — NASB
. . . stupid . . . sensible — Mof
. . . thoughtless . . . thoughtful — Wms

3. **They that were foolish took their lamps, and took no oil with them:**
. . . but they took no extra oil — Beck

4. **But the wise took oil in their vessels with their lamps.**
. . . took some oil in flasks as well as in their lanterns — Rieu

5. **While the bridegroom tarried, they all slumbered and slept.**
As the bridegroom was late in coming they all dozed off to sleep — NEB
. . . grew drowsy and fell asleep—Gspd

6. **And at midnight there was a cry made,**
. . . there came a shout — Ber
Behold, the bridegroom cometh; go ye out to meet him.
Here is the bridegroom! . . . — NEB
. . . come ye forth to meet him — ASV

7. **Then all those virgins arose, and trimmed their lamps.**
with that all the girls got up . . . — NEB

8. **And the foolish said unto the wise, Give us of your oil; for our lamps are gone out.**
. . . are going out — ASV
. . . Share your oil with us, our lamps are burning low — Knox

9. **But the wise**[54] **answered, saying, Not so; lest there be not enough for us and you:**

. . . Peradventure there will not be enough . . . — ASV
. . . No, there will never be enough for us both — NEB
but go ye rather to them that sell, and buy for yourselves.
Go to the store and buy your own oil — Wms

10. **And while they went to buy, the bridegroom came; and they that were ready went in with him to the marriage:**
. . . the marriage-feast — ASV
. . . escorted him to the wedding—Knox
. . . entered the banquet-hall — Ber
and the door was shut.

11. **Afterward came also the other virgins,**[55] **saying,**
But presently the other girls returned . . . — Rieu
And then the other five came back . . . — NEB
Lord, Lord, open to us.
Sir, Sir, open . . . — NEB
Master, Master, open up . . . — Ber
Sir, please open! Let us in! — Nor

12. **But he answered and said, Verily I say unto you, I know you not.**
But he replied, Truly . . . I do not know you — RSV
. . . Believe me, I do not recognize you — Knox

13. **Watch**[56] **therefore, for ye know neither the day nor the hour wherein the Son of man cometh.**[57]

14. **For the kingdom of heaven is as a man travelling into a far country,**
. . . going into another country — ASV
The situation is like that of a man going abroad — Ber

---

[53]See Matt. 22:13.
[54]See verse 2.
[55]See verse 1.
[56]See Matt. 24:42.
[57]The words "wherein the Son of man cometh" are now recognized as not adequately supported by original manuscripts.

It's like a man going on a trip — Beck
who called his own servants,
. . . his trusted servants — Knox
. . . his domestic servants — Ber
. . . his slaves — Mon
and delivered unto them his goods.
. . . entrusted to them his property —
RSV
. . . committed his money to their
charge — Knox
. . . put his capital in their hands —
NEB

**15. And unto one he gave five talents, to
another two, and to another one;**
. . . five bags of gold . . . — NEB
. . . five thousand dollars . . . — Wms
. . . three thousand pounds . . . twelve
hundred . . . six hundred — Nor
. . . $10,000 . . .$4,000 . . . $2,000 —
Beck
**to every man according to his several
ability;**
to each according to his particular ability — Rhm
each according to his capacity — NEB
to everyone as he was able — BAS
and straightway took his journey.
then he went away — RSV
. . . left the country — NEB
. . . started on his long journey — Wms
. . . and went abroad — ABUV

**16. Then he that had received the five tal-
ents went and traded with the same,**
. . . employed them in business — NEB
. . . went out and invested it — Wms
and made them other five talents.
. . . a profit of five talents more — Knox
. . . and gained another five — Ber

**17. And likewise he that had received two,
he also gained another two.**
So did the man with two; he made another two — Rieu

**18. But he that had received one went and
digged in the earth, and hid his lord's
money.**
. . . and buried his master's money —
Wey

**19. After a long time the lord of those
servants cometh, and reckoneth with
them.**
. . . and settled accounts with them —
RSV

**20. And so he that had received five tal-
ents came and brought other five talents, saying,**
. . . came forward, bringing five talents

more . . . — RSV
. . . and produced the five they had
made . . . — NEB
**Lord, thou deliveredst unto me five tal-
ents: behold, I have gained beside
them five talents more.**
Sir, you let me have five talents . . . —
Rieu
Master, you entrusted . . . to me . . . —
NASB

**21. His lord said unto him, Well done,
thou good and faithful servant:**
. . . my excellent, faithful slave — Gspd
. . . you're a sound, reliable servant —
Phi
**thou hast been faithful over a few
things,**
. . . trustworthy in a small way — NEB
. . . faithful in the use of a small amount
— Wms
. . . you have proved you could be
trusted with a little — Beck
**I will make thee ruler over many
things:**
I will set you over much — RSV
. . . put you in charge of something big
— NEB
. . . entrust many things to your care —
Nor
enter thou into the joy of thy lord.
come and share your master's joy —
TCNT
. . . your master's delight — NEB
. . . your master's feast — Mof
Come and be happy with your master
— Beck

**22. He also that had received two talents
came and said, Lord, thou deliveredst
unto me two talents: behold, I have
gained two other talents beside them.**

**23. His lord said unto him, Well done,
good and faithful servant; thou hast
been faithful over a few things, I will
make thee ruler over many things: enter thou into the joy of thy lord.**

**24. Then he which had received the one
talent came and said,**
. . . came to him and gave an accounting — Nor
**Lord, I knew thee that thou art an hard
man,**
. . . a severe man — Wey
. . . a tight-fisted man — Nor
**reaping where thou hast not sown,
and gathering where thou hast not
strawed:**

. . . gathering where you did not win-
now — RSV

. . . had not threshed — Gspd

25. And I was afraid, and went and hid thy talent in the earth:

and overcome with fear I went away and hid thy talent in the ground — Rhm

. . . buried your talent in the ground — Wey

lo, there thou hast that is thine.

lo, thou hast thine own — ASV

here it is — you have what belongs to you — NEB

here is your money — Gspd

26. His lord answered and said unto him, Thou wicked and slothful servant,

. . . wicked servant and cowardly — Rhm

. . . You lazy rascal! — NEB

. . . You lazy, worthless servant! — TCNT

. . . Despicable and lazy slave! — Ber

thou knewest that I reap where I sowed not, and gather where I have not strawed:[58]

27. Thou oughtest therefore to have put my money to the exchangers,

. . . put my money to the bankers — ASV

. . . invested my money with the bankers — RSV

. . . put my money on deposit — NEB

and then at my coming I should have received mine own with usury.

. . . received back mine own with interest — ASV

. . . collected my principal with interest — Wms

. . . gotten my capital with interest — Mof

28. Take therefore the talent from him, and give it unto him which hath ten talents.

29. For unto every one that hath shall be given,

For, to him who has, more will be given — TCNT

For in every case more shall be given to the man who has — Rieu

and he shall have abundance:

and he shall be made to abound—Rhm

till he has enough and to spare — NEB

even till it overflows — Wms

but from him that hath not

but from him who is wanting — Ber

. . . who has virtually nothing — Nor

. . . who doesn't have what he should have — Beck

shall be taken away even that which he hath.

even his 'nothing' will be taken away — Phi

30. And cast ye the unprofitable servant into outer darkness:

Fling the useless servant out into the dark — NEB

. . . the worthless servant . . . — RSV

. . . the good-for-nothing slave . . . — Gspd

there shall be weeping and gnashing of teeth.[59]

where he can weep and wail over his stupidity — Phi

31. When the Son of man shall come in his glory,

. . . shall have come . . . — Alf

. . . in his splendor — Gpsd

and all the holy[60] **angels with him, then shall he sit upon the throne of his glory:**

. . . on his glorious throne — RSV

. . . on his splendid throne — Wms

32. And before him shall be gathered all nations;

. . . gathered into his presence — Wey

and he shall separate them one from another,

. . . he will divide men . . . — Knox

. . . will sort out the people . . . — Rieu

as a shepherd divideth his sheep from the goats:

33. And he shall set the sheep on his right hand, but the goats on the left.

34. Then shall the King say unto them on his right hand, Come, ye blessed of my Father,

. . . my Father's blessed ones — Wey

. . . You have my Father's blessing: come — NEB

inherit the kingdom prepared for you from the foundation of the world:

take possession of the kingdom . . . — Knox

. . . that has been ready for you since the world was made — NEB

---

[58]See verse 24.

[59]See Matt. 22:13.

[60]The word "holy" is now recognized as not adequately supported by original manuscripts.

... has been destined for you from the creation of the world — Gspd
... reserved for you ... — Phi

35. **For I was an hungred, and ye gave me meat:**
    ... hungry and ye gave me to eat —ASV
    ... you gave me food — RSV
    I was thirsty, and ye gave me drink: I was a stranger, and ye took me in:
    ... ye took me home — Rhm
    ... you welcomed me — RSV
    ... homeless and you brought me in — Rieu

36. **Naked, and ye clothed me:**
    When I had no clothes, you gave me clothes — Gspd
    I was sick, and ye visited me:
    ... and you cared for me — Knox
    ... came to my help — NEB
    I was in prison, and ye came unto me.
    ... you visited me — Ber

37. **Then shall the righteous answer him, saying,**
    Whereupon the just will answer — Knox
    Lord, when saw we thee an hungred, and fed thee? or thirsty, and gave thee drink?

38. **When saw we thee a stranger, and took thee in? or naked, and clothed thee?**

39. **Or when saw we thee sick, or in prison, and came unto thee?**

40. **And the King shall answer and say unto them,**
    And the King will reply — TCNT
    Verily I say unto you,[61] Inasmuch as ye have done it unto one of the least of these my brethren,
    ... you rendered such services to one of the humblest ... — Wey
    ... whatever you did for the humblest ... — Phi
    ... one of these my brethren, even the least — ASV
    ... my brothers, these little ones — Rieu

... my brothers here, however humble — NEB
ye have done it unto me.

41. **Then shall he say also unto them on the left hand, Depart from me, ye cursed,**
    ... The curse is upon you; go from my sight — NEB
    ... Begone from me, accursed ones — Ber
    into everlasting fire, prepared for the devil and his angels:
    into the eternal fire which is prepared ... — ASV
    ... destined for the devil ... — Gspd
    ... prepared for the adversary and his messengers — Rhm

42. **For I was an hungred, and ye gave me no meat: I was thirsty, and ye gave me no drink:**

43. **I was a stranger, and ye took me not in: naked and ye clothed me not: sick, and in prison, and ye visited me not.[62]**

44. **Then shall they also answer him, saying,**
    Whereupon they, in their turn, will answer — Knox
    Lord, when saw we thee an hungred, or athirst, or a stranger, or naked, or sick, or in prison, and did not minister unto thee?
    ... and fail to look after you — Rieu
    ... and did nothing for you — NEB
    ... and did not wait on you — Wms
    ... and didn't help you — Beck

45. **Then shall he answer them, saying, Verily I say unto you, inasmuch as ye did it not to one of the least of these, ye did it not to me.**
    ... when you refused it to one of the least of my brethren here ...—Knox

46. **And these shall go away into everlasting punishment: but the righteous into life eternal.**
    ... and the upright to everlasting life — Gspd

CHAPTER 26

1. **And it came to pass, when Jesus had finished all these sayings,**
    ... all these words — ASV
    ... this discourse — Gspd
    he said unto his disciples,

2. **Ye know that after two days is the**

feast of the passover,
    ... after two days the passover cometh — ASV

---

[61]See Matt. 16:28.
[62]See verses 35 and 36.

... the Passover is celebrated — Ber
and the Son of man is betrayed to be crucified.
... is delivered up ... — ASV

3. **Then assembled together the chief priests, and the scribes,[63] and the elders of the people, unto the palace of the high priest, who was called Caiaphas,**
Then the Chief Priests and the Councillors of the Nation met in the house of the High Priest ... — TCNT
... court of the high priest ... — ASV

4. **And consulted that they might take Jesus by subtilty, and kill him.**
... in order to arrest Jesus by stealth ... — RSV
... to get Jesus into their power by a strategem ... — Rieu
... to get hold of Jesus by some trick ... — Phi

5. **But they said, Not on the feast day, lest there be an uproar among the people.**
... Not during the feast, lest a tumult arise ... — ASV
... or there may be rioting ... — NEB

6. **Now when Jesus was in Bethany, in the house of Simon the leper,**
While Jesus was staying in Bethany ... — Mon
When Jesus came back to Bethany ... — Wms

7. **There came unto him a woman having an alabaster box of very precious ointment,**
... cruse of exceeding precious ointment — ASV
... jar of very expensive ointment — RSV
... small bottle of fragrant oil, very costly — NEB
... vial of very costly perfume — NASB
and poured it on his head, as he sat at meat.
... as he sat at table — RSV
... as he reclined at table — Mon
... while he was reclining — Lam

8. **But when his disciples saw it, they had indignation, saying,**
And the disciples seeing it were greatly displeased ... — Rhm
Observing it, the disciples said indignantly — Ber
To what purpose is this waste?
Why this waste — RSV

9. **For this ointment might have been sold for much, and given to the poor.**
... for a good sum, and the money given to the poor — NEB

10. **When Jesus understood it, he said unto them,**
But Jesus, aware of this, said ... — RSV
Jesus overheard and said ... — Rieu
Why trouble ye the woman?
Why vex ye the woman — Rhm
Why do you embarrass the woman — Ber
Why are you annoying the woman — Mon
Don't find fault with the woman — Nor
Why ... make this woman feel uncomfortable — Phi
for she hath wrought a good work upon me.
... a seemly work for me — Rhm
... done a beautiful thing to me — RSV
... a gracious thing ... — Wey
she did well to treat me so — Knox
she has done a kind act ... — Bas

11. **For ye have the poor always with you;**
... the poor among you always — NEB
but me ye have not always.
but you will not always have me—RSV

12. **For in that she hath poured this ointment on my body,**
In pouring this ointment ... — TCNT
she did it for my burial.
... to prepare me for burial — ASV
it was her way of preparing me for burial — NEB
she has acted in view of my burial — Mof

13. **Verily I say unto you, Wheresoever this gospel shall be preached in the whole world,**
In solemn truth I tell you ... — Mon
... wheresoever this glad-message shall be proclaimed ... — Rhm
... this Good News ... — TCNT
there shall also this, that this woman hath done, be told for a memorial of her.
that also which this woman hath done ... — ASV
... shall be told in its place, to preserve her memory — Knox

---

[63]The words "and the scribes" are now recognized as not adequately supported by original manuscripts.

... recounted, as her memorial to me
— Phi

what she has done will be told in memory of her — RSV

14. Then one of the twelve, called Judas Iscariot, went unto the chief priests,
... the man called Judas of Kerioth
... — Rieu

15. And said unto them, What will ye give me, and I will deliver him unto you?
... What are ye willing to give me, and I ... — ASV
... What will you pay me for handing him over ... — Knox
... What are you ready to give me for betraying him to you — Mon
And they covenanted with him for thirty pieces of silver.
And they weighed unto him thirty pieces ... — ASV
... paid him thirty pieces ... — RSV
... counted him out thirty pieces ... — Gspd
... agreed on ... and paid ... — Nor
... thirty shekels — Wey

16. And from that time he sought opportunity to betray him.
... watched for a chance to betray him — Ber

17. Now the first day of the feast of unleavened bread the disciples came to Jesus, saying unto him,
on the first of the days of unleavened bread ... — Rhm
on the first day of the Passover Feast ... — Wms
Where wilt thou that we prepare for thee to eat the passover?
... to eat the paschal meal — Knox
... for your Passover supper — NEB

18. And he said, Go into the city to such a man, and say unto him,
... Go to so-and-so in the town ... — Rieu
... Go to a certain man in the city ... — NEB
The Master saith, My time is at hand;
The Teacher saith ... — ASV
... my appointed time is near — NEB
I will keep the passover at thy house with my disciples.
With thee will I keep the passover ... — Rhm

19. And the disciples did as Jesus had appointed them;

... as Jesus had directed them — RSV
and they made ready the passover.

20. Now when the even was come, he sat down with the twelve.
Then late in the evening he took his place at the table ... — Phi
As twilight was falling, he reclined with ... — Ber
... was sitting at meat with the twelve disciples — ASV

21. And as they did eat, he said, Verily[64] I say unto you, that one of you shall betray me.
... will deliver me up — Rhm

22. And they were exceeding sorrowful,
They were full of sorrow — Knox
... deeply grieved — NASB
In great distress — NEB
Sick at heart — Rieu
and began every one of them to say unto him,
and began to say to him one after another — RSV
they exclaimed one after the other — NEB
Lord, is it I?
Can you mean me, Lord — NEB
It is not I, is it, Master — Mon

23. And he answered and said, He that dippeth his hand with me in the dish, the same shall betray me.
... He that dipped his hand ... — ASV
... One who has dipped ... into this bowl ... — NEB
... The man who just dipped ... — Gspd

24. The Son of man goeth as it is written of him:
... as the scripture foretells of him — Knox
but woe unto that man by whom the Son of man is betrayed!
but a curse will be upon that man ... — Wms
but alas for that man ... — NEB
it had been good for that man if he had not been born.
It would have been better for that man ... — RSV

25. Then Judas, which betrayed him, answered and said,
Then Judas spoke, the one who was to betray him — NEB

---

[64]For variants of "Verily" see Matt. 16:28.

Master, is it I?
Can it be I, Rabbi — Rhm
Surely it is not I, Rabbi — Mon
Master, perhaps it is I — Lam
He said unto him, Thou hast said.
He said to him, Is it not? — Mon
. . . It is you that have said it — Rieu
. . . The words are yours — NEB
. . . You are right — Gspd

26. **And as they were eating, Jesus took bread,**
And while they were still at table . . . — Knox
. . . took a loaf — Mon
. . . took a Passover loaf — Gspd
and blessed it, and brake it, and gave it to the disciples,
blessed God, broke it . . . — Rieu
and having said the blessing he broke it . . . — NEB
. . . broke it in pieces . . . — Gspd
and said, Take, eat; this is my body.
. . . eat this, it means my body — Mof

27. **And he took the cup,**
. . . a cup — ASV
. . . the wine-cup — Gspd
and gave thanks, and gave it to them, saying,
gave thanks to God, and handed it to them . . . — Rieu
Drink ye all of it;
Drink of it, all of you — RSV
You must all drink from it — Gspd

28. **For this is my blood of the new testament,**
. . . blood of the covenant — ASV
. . . my blood, the blood of the covenant — NEB
. . . my covenanted blood — Ber
. . . blood which ratifies the agreement — Gspd
which is shed for many for the remission of sins.
. . . poured out . . . for the forgiveness of sins — RSV
. . . to set many free from their sins — Phi

29. **But I say unto you, I will not drink henceforth of this fruit of the vine,**
I tell you I shall not drink again of this fruit . . . — RSV
. . . this produce of the vine — Mof
. . . this juice of the grape — TCNT
until that day when I drink it new with you in my Father's kingdom.
. . . a new kind of wine with you in the

Kingdom of my Father — Rieu
. . . drink it with you in a new way . . . — Beck
. . . drink it anew with you . . . — Lam

30. **And when they had sung an hymn,**
After singing the Passover Hymn—NEB
they went out into the mount of Olives.
. . . out of the city and up the Mount of Olives — Gspd

31. **Then saith Jesus unto them, All ye shall be offended because of me this night:**
. . . find cause of stumbling in me during this night — Rhm
. . . fall away because of me . . . — RSV
. . . lose courage over me . . . — Knox
. . . This very night you will all renounce your faith in me — Rieu
. . . turn against me — Wey
. . . You will all desert me to-night — Gspd
for it is written, I will smite the shepherd,
Do not the Scriptures say . . . — Rieu
. . . I will strike down the shepherd — NASB
and the sheep of the flock shall be scattered abroad.
. . . flock will be scattered in all directions — Wey

32. **But after I am risen again, I will go before you into Galilee.**
But after I am raised up . . . — ASV
. . . go back to Galilee to meet you — Wms

33. **Peter answered and said unto him, Though all men shall be offended**[65] **because of thee,**
Peter declared to him . . . — RSV
. . . Though all the rest feel scandalized . . . — Ber
. . . Even if all the others . . . — Nor
yet will I never be offended.
I shall never do so — Rieu
I will never deny you — Lam

34. **Jesus said unto him, Verily I say unto thee, That this night, before the cock crow,**
. . . tonight, before the rooster crows — Beck
thou shalt deny me thrice.
you will disown me three times—TCNT

---

[65]For variants of "offended" see verse 31.

35. Peter said unto him, Though I should die with thee,

Even though it be needful for me with thee to die — Rhm

Even if I have to die with you — Gspd

yet will I not deny thee.

I will never, never disown you — Nor

Likewise also said all the disciples.

All the disciples said the same thing too — NASB

And all . . . spoke the same way — Ber

In like manner protested all the disciples — Wey

36. Then cometh Jesus with them unto a place called Gethsemane, and saith unto his disciples,

. . . to a plot of land called Gethsemane . . . — Knox

. . . to a garden called Gethsemane . . . — TCNT

Sit ye here, while I go and pray yonder.

. . . while I go yonder and pray — ASV

. . . while I go over there to pray—NEB

37. And he took with him Peter and the two sons of Zebedee, and began to be sorrowful and very heavy.

. . . grieved and in great distress — RSV

. . . anguish and dismay came over him — NEB

. . . began to give way to his grief and distress of heart — Wms

. . . became sad and deeply depressed — Nor

. . . to be in terrible distress and misery — Phi

38. Then he saith unto them, My soul is exceeding sorrowful, even unto death:

. . . my soul is ready to die with sorrow — Knox

. . . My heart is ready to break with grief — NEB

. . . is crushed with anguish, even to the point of death — Wey

tarry ye here, and watch with me.

abide ye here . . . — ASV

wait here and stay awake with me — Rieu

you must stay here and keep watch with me — Gspd

39. And he went a little farther, and fell on his face, and prayed, saying,

And he went forward a little . . . — ASV

. . . went a little beyond them . . . — NASB

. . . walked on a few steps and threw himself upon his face, and in this attitude continued to pray — Wms

. . . prostrated himself in prayer — Rieu

O my Father, if it be possible, let this cup pass from me:

My Father . . . let this cup pass away from me — ASV

. . . let me be spared this cup — TCNT

nevertheless not as I will, but as thou wilt.

Yet, I pray, not what I want but what you want — Wms

. . . not my will but yours be done — Nor

40. And he cometh unto the disciples, and findeth them asleep, and saith unto Peter, What, could ye not watch with me one hour?

. . . So you had not the strength to stay awake with me for a single hour — Rieu

41. Watch and pray, that ye enter not into temptation:

Be watching and praying . . . — Rhm

. . . pray that you may be spared the test — NEB

. . . pray that you may not be exposed to trial — Gspd

the spirit indeed is willing, but the flesh is weak.

the spirit indeed is eager . . . — Rhm

man's spirit is willing but human nature is weak — Wms

. . . but the body is frail — Wey

42. He went away again the second time, and prayed, saying,

. . . went back again and prayed the second time — Knox

O my Father, if this cup may not pass away[66] from me, except I drink it, thy will be done.

43. And he came and found them asleep again: for their eyes were heavy.

. . . for they could hardly keep their eyes open — Gspd

. . . for they were very weary — Wey

44. And he left them, and went away again, and prayed the third time, saying the same words.

this time he went away without disturbing them . . . — Knox

. . . praying in the same words as before — Mof

---

[66]See verse 39.

. . . asking the same thing — Nor

45. Then cometh he to his disciples, and saith unto them, Sleep on now, and take your rest:

. . . Are you still sleeping and taking your rest? — RSV

. . . Still sleeping? Still taking your ease? — NEB

. . . Sleep and take your rest hereafter — Knox

behold, the hour is at hand,

as I speak the time draws near — Knox
See! The time has come — Wms
Hark! my time is close at hand — Wey

and the Son of man is betrayed into the hands of sinners.

46. Rise, let us be going:

Up now and let us go — Rieu
Rouse yourselves! Let us go — Mon

behold, he is at hand that doth betray me.

the traitor is upon us — NEB
here comes my betrayer — Wms

47. And while he yet spake, lo, Judas, one of the twelve, came,

Before he had finished speaking, Judas . . . appeared — Rieu

Just as he was speaking, Judas . . . came up — Gspd

Suddenly . . . there came Judas . . . — Nor

and with him a great multitude with swords and staves, from the chief priests and elders of the people.

. . . a large mob . . . — Mof
. . . a great rabble . . . — Nor
. . . a great crowd with swords and clubs . . . — RSV
. . . a great crowd armed with swords and cudgels . . . — NEB

48. Now he that betrayed him gave them a sign, saying,

The traitor had appointed them a signal — Knox

Whomsoever I shall kiss, that same is he: hold him fast.

The one I shall kiss is the man: seize him — RSV

49. And forthwith he came to Jesus, and said,

And he came up to Jesus at once . . . — RSV

So he went straight up to Jesus . . . — Rieu

Hail, Master; and kissed him.

Hail, Rabbi . . . — ASV

Greetings, Rabbi . . . — Ber
Peace to you, Rabbi . . . — Wey
Good evening, Rabbi, and affectionately kissed him — Wms

50. And Jesus said unto him, Friend, wherefore art thou come?

. . . Friend, do that for which thou art come — ASV

. . . Friend, why are you here? — RSV

. . . My man, do your errand — Mof

. . . Is it for this that you have come, my friend? — Lam

Then came they, and laid hands on Jesus, and took him.

And they came forward, laid hands on Jesus and arrested him — Rieu

. . . seized Jesus, and held him fast — NEB

51. And, behold, one of them which were with Jesus stretched out his hand, and drew his sword,

One of his companions . . . — Mof

. . . lifted a hand to draw his sword — Knox

. . . reached for his sword and drew it — NEB

and struck a servant of the high priest's, and smote off his ear.

and struck the slave of the chief priest, and cut off his ear — RSV

slashed at . . . — Phi

52. Then said Jesus unto him, Put up again thy sword into his place:

. . . Put your sword back into its place — RSV

for all they that take the sword shall perish with the sword.

for all who draw the sword shall die by the sword — Ber

53. Thinkest thou that I cannot now pray to my Father,

. . . that I cannot appeal to my Father — RSV

. . . that I cannot ask my Father for help — TCNT

and he shall presently give me

and he shall even now send me — ASV
. . . at once send to my aid — NEB
and have him furnish me on the spot — Wms

more than twelve legions of angels?

a greater force than fifty thousand angels — Rieu
one hundred thousand angels — Wms
thousands of angels — Tay

54. But how then shall the scriptures be

fulfilled, that thus it must be?

How, then, could the Bible be true when it says this must happen—Beck

But in that case how would the Scriptures be fulfilled, which say that this must be — TCNT

... that it must happen this way — Ber

55. In that same hour said Jesus to the multitudes,

At the same time Jesus spoke to the crowd — NEB

... spoke to the rabble — Nor

Are ye come out as against a thief with swords and staves for to take me?

You have come out to my arrest with swords and clubs, as if I were a robber — Knox

I sat daily with you teaching in the temple,

Day after day I sat ... — RSV

and ye laid no hold on me.

... you did not arrest me — Rieu

... you never laid a finger on me—Phi

56. But all this was done, that the scriptures of the prophets might be fulfilled.

All this was so ordained, to fulfil what was written by the prophets — Knox

The whole of this occurred in fulfilment of the Prophetic Scriptures — TCNT

But all this is happening as the prophets said it would — Phi

Then all the disciples forsook him, and fled.

Then the disciples all deserted him and ran away — NEB

57. And they that had laid hold on Jesus led him away to Caiaphas the high priest,

Jesus was led off under arrest ... — NEB

... to the house of Caiaphas the high priest — ASV

... into the presence of the high priest, Caiaphas — Knox

where the scribes and the elders were assembled.

... lawyers and elders ... — NEB

... teachers of the Law and Councillors ... — TCNT

... Bible scholars and the elders ... — Beck

58. But Peter followed him afar off unto the high priest's palace,

... unto the court of the high priest — ASV

... at a distance, as far as the courtyard ... — RSV

... right up to the high priest's courtroom — Nor

and went in, and sat with the servants,

and entered in, and sat with the officers — ASV

and going inside he sat with the guards — RSV

to see the end.

meaning to see the end of it all — NEB

to see the outcome — NASB

to see the issue — Wey

59. Now the chief priests, and elders,[67] and all the council,

... and the entire Sanhedrin — Ber

... the whole Jewish court — Beck

sought false witness against Jesus, to put him to death;

were casting about for evidence against Jesus, on which, though false, they could condemn him to death — Rieu

... some allegation against Jesus on which a death-sentence could be based — NEB

60. But found none: yea, though many false witnesses came, yet found they none.

and they found it not, though many false witnesses came — ASV

At the last came two false witnesses,

But afterward came two ... — ASV

until at last two false accusers came forward — Knox

61. And said, This fellow said, I am able to destroy the temple of God, and to build it in three days.

... This man claimed that he could pull down the Temple of God and in three days build it up again — Rieu

... pull down the shrine of God ... — Rhm

... tear down the sanctuary of God ... — Gspd

62. And the high priest arose, and said unto him, Answerest thou nothing? what is it which these witness against thee?

... Have you no answer to make? ... — RSV

... no answer to the accusations ... — Knox

---

[67]The words "and elders" are now recognized as not adequately supported by original manuscripts.

... Answerest thou not what it is which these witness against thee — Alf

63. But Jesus held his peace.

But Jesus was silent — Rhm
But Jesus kept silence — Rieu

And the high priest answered and said unto him,

And now the High Priest said — Rieu
... said to him openly — Knox
Again the high priest addressed him — Mon

I adjure thee by the living God,

I put thee on oath by the living God — Rhm
By the living God I charge you to tell us: — NEB

that thou tell us whether thou be the Christ, the Son of God.

Are you the Messiah, the Son of God? — NEB

64. Jesus saith unto him, Thou hast said:

... You have said so — RSV
... Thy own lips have said it — Knox
... The words are yours — Rieu
... I am He — Mon
... It is true — Gspd

nevertheless I say unto you, Hereafter ye shall see the Son of man

... The time has come when you will see ... — Rieu
... from now on, you will see ... — NEB
... shortly you shall see ... — Ber
... in future you will all see ... — Mof

sitting on the right hand of power, and coming in the clouds of heaven.

... at the right hand of Power ... — ASV
... the Power ... — Rieu
... the Almighty ... — Gspd

65. Then the high priest rent his clothes, saying,

... tore his robes ... — RSV
... rent asunder his garments ... — Rhm
... tore at his own clothing, shouting — Tay

He hath spoken blasphemy; what further need have we of witnesses?

He hath spoken profanely! ... — Rhm
He has blasphemed! ... — NASB
Impious words! ... — Wey
... What more evidence do we want? — Mof

behold, now ye have heard his blasphemy.

You have all heard Him say it! — Tay

66. What think ye?

What is your judgment — RSV
What is your opinion — NEB
What is your verdict — Mon
What is your decision — TCNT

They answered and said, He is guilty of death.

... He is worthy of death — ASV
... The penalty is death — Knox
... He deserves death — Ber
... He is doomed to death — Mof

67. Then did they spit in his face, and buffeted him;

... spat in his face and struck him with their fists — Rieu
... and struck him on his head — Lam

and others smote him with the palms of their hands,

and others struck him smartly — Rhm
and some slapped him — RSV
and others boxed his ears — Wms
... slapped him on the cheek with their open hands — Nor

68. Saying, Prophesy unto us, thou Christ, Who is he that smote thee?

... Shew thyself a prophet, Christ ... — Knox
... Now play the Prophet for us, you Christ! ... — TCNT
... Now, Messiah, if you are a prophet, tell us who hit you — NEB

69. Now Peter sat without in the palace:[68] and a damsel came unto him, saying,

... a female servant ... — Rhm
... a maid came up to him ... — RSV
... a serving-maid accosted him and said — NEB

Thou also wast with Jesus of Galilee.

... Jesus the Galilaean — ASV

70. But he denied before them all, saying,

Peter denied it in front of everyone — Rieu

I know not what thou sayest.

I do not know what you mean — RSV
I don't know what you are talking about — Nor

71. And when he was gone out into the porch, another maid saw him,

He went out to the gatehouse, where another maid saw him — Rieu
... out to the gateway ... — NEB

---

[68]See verse 58.

As he was going out into the vestibule, another girl noticed him — Ber
and said unto them that were there,
. . . said to the bystanders — RSV
This fellow was also with Jesus of Nazareth.
This fellow certainly was with Jesus the Nazarene! — Mon
72. **And again he denied with an oath, I do not know the man.**
. . . denied it, and even swore, . . . — Wms
73. **And after a while came unto him they that stood by, and said to Peter,**
. . . the bystanders came up and said to Peter — RSV
Surely thou also art one of them; for thy speech bewrayeth thee.
Of a truth thou also art one of them,

for thy speech maketh thee known — ASV
Certainly you are . . . for your accent betrays you — RSV
. . . your accent gives you away — NEB
. . . anyone can tell by the way you talk — Beck
74. **Then began he to curse and to swear, saying, I know not the man.**
. . . to invoke a curse on himself and to swear . . . — RSV
. . . to swear with the strongest oaths . . . — Gspd
And immediately the cock crew.
That moment a rooster crowed — Ber
75. **And Peter remembered the word of Jesus, which said unto him, Before the cock crow, thou shalt deny[69] me thrice. And he went out, and wept bitterly.**

CHAPTER 27

1. **When the morning was come,**
At daybreak — Knox
At dawn — Ber
all the chief priests and elders of the people took counsel against Jesus to put him to death:
. . . met in full council to decide on measures against Jesus that would secure his execution — Rieu
. . . met in conference to plan the death of Jesus — NEB

2. **And when they had bound him, they led him away, and delivered him to Pontius[70] Pilate the governor.**
. . . put him in chains, and led him off . . . — NEB
. . . marched him off with his hands tied . . . — Phi
. . . Pilate, the Procurator — Rieu
. . . Pilate, the Roman Governor — NEB

3. **Then Judas, which had betrayed him, when he saw that he was condemned,**
When Judas the traitor saw that Jesus had been condemned — NEB
Then Judas, who had betrayed Him, as he felt condemned — Wms
Then Judas, who betrayed him, seeing that Jesus was condemned — TCNT
repented himself,
being smitten with remorse — Rhm
felt sorry — Beck
deeply regretted what he had done — Tay

and brought again the thirty pieces of silver to the chief priests and elders,
. . . returned the thirty pieces . . . — NASB
. . . brought back the thirty shekels . . . — Wey

4. **Saying, I have sinned in that I have betrayed the innocent blood.**
. . . I have done wrong. I have brought an innocent man to his death — Rieu
And they said, What is that to us? see thou to that.
. . . That is your business, they said. Why should we care? — Rieu
. . . What does that matter to us? It is your affair, not ours — Mof

5. **And he cast down the pieces of silver in the temple, and departed,**
Whereupon Judas left the money as an offering in the temple and withdrew — Rieu
And he threw the pieces of silver into the sanctuary and departed — NASB
and went and hanged himself.

6. **And the chief priests took the silver pieces, and said, It is not lawful for to put them into the treasury,**
Taking up the money, the chief priests

---

[69]See verse 34.
[70]The word "Pontius" is now recognized as not adequately supported by original manuscripts.

argued: This cannot be put into the temple fund — NEB

because it is the price of blood.

. . . it is blood-money — NEB

7. **And they took counsel, and bought with them the potter's field, to bury strangers in.**

After discussing the matter they spent it on the purchase of the Potter's Field where foreigners could be buried — Rieu

. . . a burial place for people not belonging to the city — Wey

8. **Wherefore that field was called, The field of blood, unto this day.**

This explains the name 'Blood Acre' by which that field has been known ever since — NEB

9. **Then was fulfilled that which was spoken by Jeremy the prophet, saying,**

. . . through Jeremiah the prophet . . . — ASV

In this way fulfilment was given to the prophetic utterance of Jeremiah: — NEB

And they took the thirty pieces of silver, the price of him that was valued,

. . . the price of him on whom a price had been set — RSV

. . . the price of the Precious One — Rieu

. . . the price set on a man's head — NEB

whom they of the children of Israel did value;

whom certain of the children of Israel did price — ASV

whose price had been set by the children of Israel — NASB

whom they had priced and expelled from the sons of Israel — Mof

on whom some Israelites had set a price — Rieu

10. **And gave them for the potter's field, as the Lord appointed me.**

. . . as the Lord directed me — NEB

. . . as the Lord commanded me—TCNT

11. **And Jesus stood before the governor: and the governor asked him, saying,**

. . . the Procurator, who interrogated him — Rieu

Art thou the King of the Jews? And Jesus said unto him, Thou sayest.[71]

12. **And when he was accused of the chief priests and elders, he answered nothing.**

And to all the charges of the Chief Priests and Elders he made no reply — Rieu

13. **Then said Pilate unto him, Hearest thou not how many things they witness against thee?**

. . . Do you not hear what a case they are building up against you — Rieu

. . . what a mass of evidence . . . — Wey

14. **And he answered him to never a word;**

. . . gave him no answer, not even to one word — ASV

. . . made . . . no reply on any point whatever — Rieu

. . . did not answer a single one of their accusations . . . — Phi

insomuch that the governor marvelled greatly.

leaving him completely at a loss—Rieu

to the Governor's great astonishment — NEB

15. **Now at that feast the governor was wont to release unto the people a prisoner, whom they would.**

at every feast . . . — Alf

. . . was accustomed to release for the crowd any one prisoner whom they wanted — RSV

16. **And they had then a notable prisoner, called Barabbas.**

. . . a distinguished prisoner . . .—Rhm

. . . a notorious prisoner . . .— TCNT

. . . a man of some notoriety called Jesus[72] Bar-Abbas — NEB

. . . Barabbas, who was a popular hero — Rieu

17. **Therefore when they were gathered together, Pilate said unto them,**

So Pilate, when he was faced by the crowd, said — Rieu

Whom will ye that I release unto you?

Whom shall I release — Knox

which one do you want me to set free — Wms

Barabbas, or Jesus which is called Christ?

Jesus Bar-Abbas or Jesus called Messiah — NEB

. . . or Jesus, the so-called Christ — Gspd

---

[71]See the same expression in Matt. 26:64.

[72]The manuscript support for this is weak but several versions accept it.

18. For he knew that for envy they had delivered him.

. . . was well aware that they had brought him up for judgment because they were jealous — Rieu

. . . out of spite . . . — NEB

. . . through sheer malice — Phi

19. When he was set down on the judgment seat,

While he was still on the Bench—TCNT

. . . sitting in court — NEB

his wife sent unto him, saying,

his wife sent word to him — RSV

Have thou nothing to do with that just man:

Do not meddle with this innocent man — Knox

Let that righteous man alone — Beck

for I have suffered many things this day in a dream because of him.

I dreamed today that I suffered much on his account — Knox

I was much troubled on his account in my dreams last night — NEB

for I have just had a painful experience in a dream about him — Gspd

I went through agonies dreaming about him last night — Phi

20. But the chief priests and the elders persuaded the multitude that they should ask Barabbas, and destroy Jesus.

. . . prevailed on the crowd . . . — Gspd

. . . persuaded the mob to ask for Barabbas and demand Jesus' execution — Phi

21. The governor answered and said unto them,

. . . the governor openly asked them — Knox

The Governor, however, said to them: — TCNT

Whether of the twain will ye that I release unto you?

Which of the two will ye . . . — ASV

They said, Barabbas.

22. Pilate saith unto them, What shall I do then with Jesus which is called Christ?

. . . Jesus, the so-called Christ — Gspd

They all say unto him, Let him be crucified.

With one voice they answered, Crucify him! — NEB

They all shouted back . . . — Nor

23. And the governor said, Why, what evil hath he done?

And he said . . . — ASV

. . . But what crime has he committed — Rieu

. . . What harm has he done — NEB

But they cried out the more, saying, Let him be crucified.

. . . cried louder than ever . . . — Knox

. . . kept shouting the more fiercely . . . — Mon

But their voices rose to a roar . . . — Phi

24. When Pilate saw that he could prevail nothing,

. . . saw that he was getting nowhere — Ber

. . . saw that his efforts were unavailing — TCNT

but that rather a tumult was made,

but rather that a riot was beginning — RSV

and the uproar only became worse — Knox

but that instead confusion was increasing — Lam

he took water, and washed his hands before the multitude, saying,

. . . washed . . . in full view of the people, saying — NEB

I am innocent of the blood of this just person: see ye to it.

I am innocent of this man's blood: see to it yourselves — RSV

I have no part in the death of this innocent man; it concerns you only — Knox

I am not responsible for this bloodshed: you must answer for it — Wey

. . . do as you please — Lam

25. Then answered all the people, and said, His blood be on us, and on our children.

. . . on our heads and the heads of our children — Rieu

26. Then released he Barabbas unto them: and when he had scourged Jesus, he delivered him to be crucified.

. . . but he had Jesus flogged, and handed him over to be crucified — NEB

27. Then the soldiers of the governor took Jesus into the common hall,

. . . into the Praetorium — ASV

. . . into the judgment-hall — Rhm

. . . to the Residence — Rieu

. . . into the Governor's headquarters — NEB

... into the barracks — Wms

and gathered unto him the whole band of soldiers.

and gathered the whole battalion before him — RSV

... the whole detachment ... — Rieu

... the whole garrison ... — TCNT

28. **And they stripped him, and put on him a scarlet robe.**

... a scarlet scarf they put about him — Rhm

... put a purple cloak on him — Wms

... a red military cloak — TCNT

29. **And when they had platted a crown of thorns, they put it upon his head,**

And they twisted a thorny crown ... — Mon

... made a wreath of thorns ... — Gspd

and a reed in his right hand:

and a rod ... — Knox

... a cane ... — Rieu

... a stick ... — Gspd

and they bowed the knee before him, and mocked him, saying,

and they kneeled down ... — ASV

falling on their knees ... they jeered at him: — NEB

Hail, King of the Jews!

Joy to thee, King of the Jews! — Rhm

Long live the king of the Jews! — Gspd

30. **And they spit upon him, and took the reed, and smote him on the head.**

... took the rod from him and beat him over the head with it — Knox

... struck him on the head, again and again — Mon

31. **And after that they had mocked him, they took the robe off from him, and put his own raiment on him, and led him away to crucify him.**

And when they had finished making sport of him ... — Gspd

32. **And as they came out, they found a man of Cyrene, Simon by name: him they compelled to bear his cross.**

... compelled to go with them, that he might bear his cross — ASV

33. **And when they were come unto a place called Golgotha, that is to say, a place of a skull,**

... the place named after a skull — Knox

... (a place named from its likeness to a skull) — TCNT

... (which means Skull Hill) — Phi

34. **They gave him vinegar to drink mingled with gall:**

... wine to drink ... — ASV

... a drink of wine mixed with bitters — Mof

... mixed with some bitter drug — Phi

and when he had tasted thereof, he would not drink.

But after tasting it, he refused to drink it — Mon

after tasting it, he took no more — BAS

35. **And they crucified him, and parted his garments, casting lots:**

After fastening him to the cross they divided ... — NEB

that it might be fulfilled which was spoken by the prophet, They parted my garments among them, and upon my vesture did they cast lots.[73]

36. **And sitting down they watched him there;**

... and kept watch over him there — RSV

... and sat down there on guard — Wey

37. **And set up over his head his accusation written,**

... a written proclamation of his offence — Knox

... his charge in writing — Mof

... a notice stating why he was being punished — Beck

THIS IS JESUS THE KING OF THE JEWS.

38. **Then there were two thieves crucified with him, one on the right hand, and another on the left.**

At that time two robbers ... — Mon

... two bandits, one on either side of him — Phi

39. **And they that passed by reviled him, wagging their heads,**

The passers-by hurled abuse at him ... — NEB

... blasphemed against him, tossing their heads — Knox

... nodding their heads in derision — Mof

40. **And saying, Thou that destroyest the temple, and buildest it in three days, save thyself.**

---

[73]The latter part of verse 35 is not adequately supported by original manuscripts.

. . . You destroyer and reconstructor of the temple . . . — Ber

If thou be the Son of God, come down from the cross.

If you are really the Son of God . . . — Wms

41. Likewise also the chief priests mocking him, with the scribes[74] and elders, said,

. . . kept taunting him . . . — Mon

. . . made fun of him . . . — Mof

42. He saved others; himself he cannot save. If he be the King of Israel, let him now come down from the cross, and we will believe him.

43. He trusted in God; let him deliver him now, if he will have him:

. . . let God rescue him, if he wants him — NEB

. . . let Him take him off now, if he loves him . . . — Ber

. . . if he delights in him — ABUV

for he said, I am the Son of God.

44. The thieves also, which were crucified with him, cast the same in his teeth.

. . . cast upon him the same reproach— ASV

. . . flung the same taunts at Jesus — Rieu

Insults of the same kind were heaped on Him even by the robbers who were crucified with Him — Wey

45. Now from the sixth hour there was darkness over all the land unto the ninth hour.

. . . darkness spread over the whole countryside . . . — Phi

. . . over all the earth . . . — Knox

. . . from midday until three in the afternoon — NEB

. . . from twelve o'clock to three . . . — Mof

46. And about the ninth hour Jesus cried with a loud voice, saying, Eli, Eli, lama sabachthani? That is to say, My God, my God, why hast thou forsaken me?

And about three o'clock . . . — Ber

47. Some of them that stood there, when they heard that, said, This man calleth for Elias.

And some of the bystanders . . . said . . . This man is calling Elijah — RSV

48. And straightway one of them ran, and took a spunge, and filled it with vinegar,

. . . ran at once and fetched a sponge, which he soaked in sour wine — NEB

and put it on a reed, and gave him to drink.

. . . upon a rod, and offered to let him drink — Knox

. . . held it to his lips on the end of a cane — NEB

49. The rest said, Let be, let us see whether Elias will come to save him.

. . . Wait, let us see whether Elijah . . . — RSV

. . . Leave him alone and let us see if Elijah comes to the rescue — Rieu

50. Jesus, when he had cried again with a loud voice, yielded up the ghost.

. . . gave one more great cry, and died — Phi

. . . uttered a loud scream, and gave up his spirit — Mof

. . . yielded up his life — Rieu

. . . breathed his last — NEB

. . . dismissed his spirit — Ber

51. And, behold, the veil of the temple was rent in twain from the top to the bottom;

Immediately the curtain of the Sanctuary was torn in two . . . — Wey

Suddenly the Temple curtain was torn in two . . . — TCNT

and the earth did quake, and the rocks rent;

and the earth shook, and the rocks were split — RSV

52. And the graves were opened; and many of the bodies of the saints which slept arose,

and the tombs were opened . . . — ASV

. . . and many bodies arose out of them, bodies of holy men gone to their rest — Knox

. . . and the bodies of many of God's People who had fallen asleep rose — TCNT

. . . bodies of the buried saints arose — Ber

53. And came out of the graves after his resurrection,

and coming forth out of the tombs . . . — ASV

and went into the holy city, and appeared unto many.

. . . plainly appeared . . . — Rhm

---

[74]For variants of "scribes" see Matt. 16:21.

... where many saw them — NEB
... showed themselves ... — Gspd

54. Now when the centurion, and they that were with him, watching Jesus,
When the Roman captain and the soldiers who were with him ... — Mon
... and the men who were guarding Jesus — Rieu
saw the earthquake, and those things that were done,
... and what took place — RSV
... and the prodigies — Rieu
... and all that was happening — NEB
they feared greatly, saying, Truly this was the Son of God.
they were filled with awe, and said, Truly this was the Son of God—RSV
they became very frightened and said, Truly this was a son of God! — NASB

55. And many women were there beholding afar off,
... looking on from afar — RSV
... watching from a distance — NEB
which followed Jesus from Galilee, ministering unto him:
who had followed ... — ASV
... rendering Him service — Ber
... waiting on his needs — Bas

56. Among which was Mary Magdalene, and Mary the mother of James and Joses, and the mother of Zebedee's children.
... Mary of Magdala ... — Wms
... and Mary the mother of James and Joseph, and the mother of the sons of Zebedee — RSV

57. When the even was come,
Although it was now evening — Wms
Towards sunset — Wey
there came a rich man of Arimathaea, named Joseph,
... a rich man belonging to Ramah ... — TCNT
who also himself was Jesus' disciple:
who followed Jesus as a disciple like the rest — Knox
... had himself been a pupil of Jesus — Rieu

58. He went to Pilate, and begged the body of Jesus.
he personally went ... and requested the body of Jesus — Ber
... claimed the body ... — Rhm
Then Pilate commanded the body to be delivered.

... ordered it to be given to him — RSV

59. And when Joseph had taken the body, he wrapped it in a clean linen cloth,
... a clean linen shroud — RSV

60. And laid it in his own new tomb, which he had hewn out in the rock:
then he buried it in a new grave, which he had fashioned for himself out of the rock — Knox
... unused tomb ... — NEB
and he rolled a great stone to the door of the sepulchre, and departed.
... against the entrance, and went away — NEB
... a big boulder over the doorway ... — Wms

61. And there was Mary Magdalene,
... Mary of Magdala — Wms
and the other Mary, sitting over against the sepulchre.
... opposite the grave — NASB
... in front of the grave — TCNT

62. Now the next day, that followed the day of the preparation,
Now on the morrow, which is the day after the Preparation — ASV
Next day, the morning after that Friday — NEB
The next day — the Saturday after the day of Preparation — Beck
the chief priests and Pharisees came together unto Pilate,
... approached Pilate in a body—Rieu

63. Saying, Sir, we remember that that deceiver said, while he was yet alive,
Your Excellency, we recall how that impostor said ... — NEB
... we have in mind how that false man said ... — Bas
After three days I will rise again.
... I come back to life — Rieu
On the third day I will rise — Beck

64. Command therefore that the sepulchre be made secure unto the third day,
... that his tomb shall be securely guarded ... — Knox
... that precautions be taken at the tomb ... — Lam
lest his disciples come by night,[75] and steal him away,

---

[75]The words "by night" are now recognized as not adequately supported by original manuscripts.

so that his disciples cannot come . . .
— Gspd

**and say unto the people, He is risen
from the dead: so the last error shall
be worse than the first.**
. . . the last deception . . . — Rhm
. . . the last fraud . . . — RSV
. . . that delusion be worse than the
other was — Gspd
. . . be more dangerous than the old —
Knox

55. Pilate said unto them, Ye have a watch:
. . . you can have a guard — Rieu
. . . the guard is yours — Ber

. . . Take a guard of soldiers — Mof
go your way, make it as sure as ye can.
. . . secure it for yourselves, as ye know
how — Rhm
. . . as safe as you think necessary —
Phi

**66. So they went, and made the sepulchre
sure, sealing the stone, and setting a
watch.**
. . . by sealing the stone and setting a
guard — RSV
. . . by sealing the stone in the presence
of the guard — Mon

CHAPTER 28

**1. In the end of the sabbath, as it began
to dawn toward the first day of the
week,**
Now late on the sabbath day . . . — ASV
And late in the week when it was on
the point of dawning into the first
of the week — Rhm
After the Sabbath, as the first day of
the week began to dawn — TCNT
On the night after the sabbath, at the
hour when dawn broke on the first
day of the week — Knox
After the Sabbath, towards dawn on
the first day of the week — Rieu
. . . about daybreak on Sunday — NEB
**came Mary Magdalene and the other
Mary to see the sepulchre.**
. . . to contemplate the tomb — Knox
. . . to look at the grave — Rieu
. . . to look after the tomb — Nor

**2. And, behold, there was a great earth-
quake:**
Suddenly there was a violent earthquake — NEB
But to their surprise there had been a
great earthquake — Wey
And lo! a great commotion occurred
— Rhm
. . . a great trembling of the earth —
Knox
**for the angel of the Lord descended
from heaven, and came and rolled
back the stone from the door,[76] and
sat upon it.**
. . . and was sitting upon it — Rhm

**3. His countenance was like lightning,
and his raiment white as snow:**
His appearance was like lightning . . .
— ASV

His face shone like lightning . . . —
NEB
His appearance was as dazzling as light-
ning . . . — TCNT

**4. And for fear of him the keepers did
shake, and became as dead men.**
. . . the guards trembled . . . — RSV
The sentries shook . . . became like
corpses — Ber
. . . collapsed like dead men — Phi

**5. And the angel answered and said unto
the women, Fear not ye: for I know
that ye seek Jesus, which was crucified.**
. . . You need not be afraid; I know
well . . . — Knox

**6. He is not here: for he is risen, as he
said.**
. . . has come back to life, as He foretold — Wey
**Come, see the place where the Lord
lay.**
. . . where he lay — RSV
. . . where the Lord was buried—Knox

**7. And go quickly, and tell his disciples
that he is risen from the dead;**
And go, hasten to tell his disciples . . .
— Ber
Then run and tell his disciples . . . —
Wms
**and, behold, he goeth before you into
Galilee; there shall ye see him: lo,
I have told you.**
. . . that is my message for you — Knox
. . . that is what I had to tell you — NEB
. . . Remember, I have told you — Mon

---

[76]The words "from the door" are now recognized as not adequately supported by original
manuscripts.

8. And they departed quickly from the sepulchre with fear and great joy;

Leaving the tomb at once, in awe and great joy — Rieu

So off they hurried . . . frightened and yet in ecstacy — Wms

and did run to bring his disciples word.

. . . to report it to his disciples — NASB

. . . to break the news to His disciples — Wms

9. And as they went to tell his disciples,[77] behold, Jesus met them, saying, All hail.

Suddenly Jesus was there in their path. He gave them his greeting — NEB

. . . and said, Good morning! — Wms

. . . saying, Joy to you! — Rhm

. . . Peace be to you — Wey

And they came and held him by the feet, and worshipped him.

With that they came near to him, and clung to his feet, and worshipped him — Knox

and they came up and clasped his feet, falling prostrate before him — NEB

. . . and knelt before him — Ber

10. Then said Jesus unto them, Be not afraid: go tell my brethren that they go into Galilee,

. . . Dismiss all fear! Go and take word to my brethren . . . — Wey

. . . to go back to Galilee — Wms

. . . to set out for Galilee — TCNT

and there shall they see me.

11. Now when they were going, behold, some of the watch came into the city,

They had not finished their journey, when some of the guards reached the city — Knox

and shewed unto the chief priests all the things that were done.

and reported . . . all that had happened — Rieu

12. And when they were assembled with the elders, and had taken counsel,

After meeting with the elders and conferring together — NEB

These met with the elders and agreed on a plan — Beck

they gave large money unto the soldiers,

. . . a sum of money — RSV

. . . offered a rich bribe . . . — Knox

13. Saying, Say ye, His disciples came by night,

. . . Tell people, His disciples came . . . — RSV

. . . Let this, they said, be your tale . . . — Knox

. . . Your story must be . . . — Rieu

and stole him away while we slept.

14. And if this come to the governor's ears,

. . . be reported unto the governor — Rhm

if news of it reaches the governor — Gspd

. . . comes to a hearing before the governor — ABUV

we will persuade him, and secure you.

we will satisfy him and keep you out of trouble — RSV

. . . bear you harmless — Alf

. . . save you from anxiety — ABUV

. . . and declare that you are blameless — Lam

15. So they took the money, and did as they were taught:

. . . as they were instructed — Rhm

. . . as they were told — Mon

and this saying is commonly reported among the Jews until this day.

was spread abroad . . . and continueth until this day — ASV

and this story has been current in Jewish circles ever since — Rieu

. . . among the Jews from that day to this — TCNT

16. Then the eleven disciples went away into Galilee, into a mountain where Jesus had appointed them.

. . . the mountain to which Jesus had directed them — RSV

. . . where Jesus had arranged to meet them — Rieu

17. And when they saw him, they worshipped him:[78] but some doubted.

. . . some were unconvinced — Rieu

. . . though some were in doubt about it — Gspd

. . . were somewhat skeptical — Nor

18. And Jesus came and spake unto them, saying,

As Jesus approached them, He said, — Ber

. . . came forward to them . . . — Mof

---

[77]This clause is now recognized as not adequately supported by original manuscripts.
[78]See Matt. 28:9.

All power is given unto me in heaven and in earth.

All authority hath been given . . . — ASV

Full authority . . . has been committed to me . . . — NEB

19. Go ye therefore, and teach all nations,

Set forth and make all peoples your disciples — Rieu

. . . make disciples of all the nations — ASV

baptizing them in the name of the Father, and of the Son, and of the Holy Ghost:

immersing them into the name . . . — Rhm

20. Teaching them to observe all things whatsoever I have commanded you:

. . . to keep all the commandments I gave you — Rieu

. . . to keep every rule that I have given you — Nor

and, lo, I am with you alway, even unto the end of the world. Amen.

And, mind you, I am alongside you . . . — Ber

. . . all the days until the conclusion of the age — Rhm

. . . every day to the end of time — Rieu

. . . day by day, until the close of the Age — Wey

THE
GOSPEL ACCORDING TO MARK

CHAPTER 1

1. **The beginning of the gospel of Jesus Christ,**
   Beginning the Good News about Jesus Christ — Beck
   The First Word of the Good Tidings of . . . — Rieu
   the Son of God;[1]

2. **As it is written**
   Even as it is written — ASV
   it stands written — NEB
   In accordance with the Scripture — Rieu
   in the prophets,
   in Isaiah the prophet[2] — ASV
   Behold, I send my messenger
   Here is my herald whom I send — NEB
   See, I am sending My messenger — Wey
   Attention! I will send My messenger — Nor
   before thy face,
   before thee — Knox
   ahead of you — Ber
   which shall prepare thy way before thee.
   who shall prepare thy way — ASV
   to prepare the way for you — Mof

3. **The voice of one crying in the wilderness,**
   Hark! Someone is shouting in the desert — Gspd
   The voice of one crying aloud: in the desert — Wey
   Prepare ye the way of the Lord,
   Make the way ready for the Lord — Nor
   Get the Lord's way ready — Gspd
   Make ready a road for the Lord—Mon
   make his paths straight.
   clear a straight path for him — NEB
   level the paths for him — Mof
   make His beaten-tracks straight (level and passable) — Amp

4. **John did baptize in the wilderness,**
   John came, who baptized in the wilderness — ASV
   John the baptizer appeared in the wilderness — RSV
   John came, he who immersed in the wilderness — ABUV
   and preach the baptism of repentance
   proclaiming a baptism in token of repentance — NEB
   and preached repentance and baptism — Gspd
   proclaiming a baptism of the penitent — Wey
   and preached the immersion of repentance — ABUV
   and was preaching a baptism conditioned on repentance — Wms
   proclaiming baptism as the mark of a complete change of heart — Phi
   for the remission of sins.
   for the forgiveness of sins — NASB
   to have their sins forgiven — Beck
   to obtain the forgiveness of sins—Wms

5. **And there went out unto him all the land of Judaea,**
   And there kept going out to him (continuously) all the country of Judea — Amp
   and they flocked to him from the whole Judaean country-side — NEB
   and they of Jerusalem,
   and all they of Jerusalem — ASV
   and all the people of Jerusalem — RSV
   and were all baptized of him
   and they were baptized by him — RSV
   . . . immersed . . . — ABUV
   . . . being baptized . . . — NASB
   in the river of Jordan,
   in the river Jordan — ASV
   confessing their sins.
   acknowledging . . . — Gspd
   making open confession of . . . — Wey
   when they confessed . . . — Nor
   saying that they were sinners — Bas

6. **And John was clothed with camel's hair,**
   John wore clothing made of camel-hair — Rieu
   John was dressed in a rough coat of camel's hair — NEB
   and with a girdle of a skin about his loins;
   and with a leathern girdle . . . — Alf

---

[1]Now recognized as not adequately supported by original manuscripts.

[2]This reading is supported by some manuscripts.

with a leather belt about his waist —
Ber
and he did eat locusts and wild honey;
and he fed on locusts and wild honey
— NEB
and his food was . . . — Wey
and he lived on grasshoppers . . . —
Beck
and he ate locusts, and "honey of the
wood" — Mon

7. And preached, saying,
And he was preaching, and saying —
NASB
His proclamation was — NEB
The burden of his preaching was — Phi
He kept preaching the following mes-
sage — Wms
Here is a sample of his preaching: —
Tay
**There cometh one mightier than I after
me,**
There is coming after me one more
powerful than I — TCNT
There is one coming after me who is
greater than I — Bas
the latchet of whose shoes
the strap of Whose sandals — Amp
**I am not worthy to stoop down and
unloose.**
I am not even fit to stoop down and
untie — NASB

8. I indeed have baptized you with water:
I immersed you in water — ABUV
**but he shall baptize you with the Holy
Ghost.**
but he will immerse you in the Holy
Spirit — ABUV
but he will baptize you with the Holy
Spirit — RSV

9. And it came to pass in those days,
It was in those days — Gspd
It happened at that time — NEB
**that Jesus came from Nazareth of
Galilee,**
. . . in Galilee — NEB
that Jesus arrived from the Galilean
village of Nazareth — Phi
and was baptized of John in Jordan.
. . . by John in the Jordan — RSV
and was immersed . . . — ABUV

**10. And straightway coming up out of the
water,**
And just as he was coming up . . . —
Gspd
At the moment when he came up . . .
— NEB

All at once, as he came up . . . — Phi
he saw the heavens opened,
he saw the heavens rent asunder — ASV
he saw . . . opening — NASB
he saw the sky parting asunder — Wey
and the Spirit like a dove
and the Spirit, dovelike — Ber
descending upon him:
. . . towards him — Rieu
coming down to enter into him—Gspd

**11. And there came a voice from heaven,
saying,**
and a voice came out of the heavens —
ASV
And a voice spoke from heaven — NEB
and a voice came from the sky, saying
— Wey
Thou art my beloved Son,
Thou art my Son, my Beloved — NEB
You are My Son, whom I love — Beck
You are my dearly-loved Son — Bas
in whom I am well pleased.
in thee I am . . . — ASV
on thee my favour rests — NEB
You are my Chosen! — Gspd
in Thee I am delighted — Ber

12. And immediately
And straightway — ASV
Immediately after this — Nor
the spirit driveth him
the Spirit driveth him forth — ASV
. . . took Him out — Nor
. . . sent him out — Knox
. . . impelled Him to go out — Wey
. . . urged him forth — Rhm
into the wilderness.
into the desert — Mof
into the waste land — Bas

**13. And he was there in the wilderness
forty days,**
and there he remained for forty days
— NEB
And He stayed in the desert forty days
— Wms
tempted of Satan;
. . . by Satan — ABUV
while Satan tempted him — Phi
and was with the wild beasts;
He was among . . . — NEB
There He was surrounded by wild
beasts — Nor
there he lodged with the beasts—Knox
and the angels ministered unto him.
but the angels waited upon him — Wey
. . . continued to wait upon him—Wms

125

only the angels were there to care for him — Phi

and the Angels ministered to his wants — Rieu

14. Now after that John was put in prison,

Now after John was delivered up — ASV

And after John had been taken into custody — NASB

After John had been arrested — NEB

Jesus came into Galilee,

Jesus went to Galilee — Mof

preaching the gospel of the kingdom of God,

... the gospel of God — ASV

proclaiming ... — NEB

... the good news ... — Wms

... from God — Rieu

15. And saying, The time is fulfilled,

... The season ... — Rhm

saying, the time has come at last — Phi

The time is ripe — Wms

and the kingdom of God is at hand:

and the reign of God is near — Gspd

and God's kingdom is here — Beck

— the kingdom of God has arrived — Phi

repent ye,

You must change your hearts and minds — Phi

let your hearts be turned from sin — Bas

Turn from your sins — Tay

and believe the gospel.

... in the gospel — ASV

... this Good News — Wey

and put your trust in the Good News — Rieu

16. Now as he walked by the sea of Galilee,

And passing along by ... — ASV

As he was passing along the shore of the Sea of Galilee — Gspd

he saw Simon and Andrew his brother

... and Andrew the brother of Simon — ASV

casting a net into the sea:

at work with a casting-net — NEB

about to drop a large net into the water — Nor

casting a net (to and fro) in the sea — Amp

for they were fishers.

for they were fishermen — RSV

17. And Jesus said unto them,

Jesus said to them — NEB

Come ye after me,

Follow me — RSV

Come with me — NEB

Come, follow me — Gspd

and I will make you to become fishers of men.

... make you fishers of men — NEB

... make you fish for men — Mof

and I will teach you to catch men — Phi

18. And straightway they forsook their nets,

... they left the nets — ASV

At once they dropped their nets — Mof

and followed him.

and went after him — Mof

19. And when he was gone a little farther thence,

Going on a little — Ber

Walking a little farther — Rieu

he saw James the son of Zebedee, and John his brother,

who also were in the ship mending their nets.

they too were in their boat, mending their nets — Mof

who were in the boat overhauling their nets — NEB

these too were in their boat, repairing their nets — Knox

20. And straightway he called them:

And immediately ... — RSV

Them, too, He gave an immediate call — Ber

and they left their father Zebedee in the ship

... in the boat — RSV

with the hired servants,

with the hired hands — Ber

with the crew — Mof

and went after him.

and left to follow him — NASB

21. And they went into Capernaum;

So they came to Capernaum — Mon

They arrived at ... — Phi

They entered ... — Ber

and straightway on the sabbath day

and immediately on the Sabbath — NASB

and on the very first ... — Gspd

As soon as the sabbath came — Mof

he entered into the synagogue, and taught.

he went to the synagogue and began to teach — Wey

He would go into the synagogue and teach — Nor

22. And they were astonished at his doctrine:

. . . at his teaching — ASV

And they were dumbfounded at His teaching — Wms

They were amazed at his way of teaching — Phi

for he taught them as one that had authority,

he taught them with a note of authority — NEB

for he taught them like an authority — Mof

for He was teaching them like one who had authority to teach — Wms

and not as the scribes.

and not like the Bible scholars — Beck

. . . the Doctors of the Law — Rieu

23. And there was in their synagogue

Now there was in their Synagogue at the time — TCNT

And straightway there was in their synagogue — ASV

And at that very moment, there in their synagogue — Mon

a man with an unclean spirit;

a man under the control of a foul spirit — Gspd

a man in the grip of an evil spirit — Phi

and he cried out,

He shrieked — NEB

And he screamed — Beck

24. Saying, Let us alone;³

what have we to do with thee, thou Jesus of Nazareth?

What . . ., Jesus thou Nazarene — ASV

What have we in common with thee, Jesus of Nazareth — Rhm

What do you want of us, Jesus, you Nazarene — Gspd

art thou come to destroy us?

Have you come . . . — RSV

You've come to destroy us! — Beck

I know thee who thou art, the Holy One of God.

I know who you are — the Holy One of God — NEB

25. And Jesus rebuked him, saying,

Jesus reproved him, and said — Gspd

But Jesus cut him short and spoke sharply — Phi

Jesus spoke to him threateningly — Knox

Hold thy peace,

Be silent — RSV

Silence! — Gspd

Hold your tongue — Phi

and come out of him.

Get out of him — Gspd

26. And when the unclean spirit had torn him,

And the unclean spirit, convulsing him — ABUV

And the unclean spirit threw the man into convulsions — NEB

The foul spirit threw the man into a fit — TCNT

and cried with a loud voice,

and gave a loud cry — Gspd

and with a deafening shriek — Wms

he came out of him.

and left him — Phi

27. And they were all amazed,

They were all dumbfounded — NEB

And all were awe-struck — Wey

All were full of astonishment — Knox

insomuch that they questioned among themselves, saying,

and began to ask one another — NEB

they inquired among themselves — Ber

they kept discussing it . . . — Wms

What thing is this?

What is this — ASV

Whatever is this — Mof

What does this mean — Gspd

What on earth has happened — Phi

what new doctrine is this?

What new teaching is this — Nor

a new teaching! — ASV

Here is a new sort of teaching — Wey

for with authority commandeth he even the unclean spirits,

He gives orders with authority even to the foul spirits — Gspd

Why, he gives orders to evil spirits — Phi

He even tells unclean spirit what to do — Rieu

and they do obey him.

and they obey him — ASV

and they do what he says — Bas

28. And immediately his fame spread abroad

And the report of him went out straightway everywhere — ASV

³Now recognized as not adequately supported by original manuscripts.

And at once his fame spread everywhere — RSV

And his reputation spread like wild-
fire — Phi

**throughout all the region round about
Galilee.**

in all the region of Galilee round about
— ASV

throughout all the surrounding region
of Galilee — RSV

all over that part of Galilee — Wms

29. **And forthwith, when they were come
out of the synagogue,**

As soon as they left . . . — Wms

Direct from the synagogue — Ber

**they entered into the house of Simon
and Andrew,**

they went into the home of . . . — Beck

they went home with . . . — Wms

with James and John.

and James and John went with them —
NEB

accompanied by James and John — Phi

30. **But Simon's wife's mother lay sick of
a fever,**

And the mother-in-law of Simon was
lying sick with fever — ABUV

And Simon's mother-in-law was confined to her bed with a fever — Wms

and anon they tell him of her.

and straightway . . . — ASV

and immediately they told him of her
— RSV

They told him about her at once — NEB

31. **And he came and took her by the
hand,**

He came forward, took her . . . — NEB

So He went to her, and taking her hand
— Wey

whereupon he went close and took her
by the hand — Knox

and lifted her up;

and raised her up — ASV

and helped her to her feet — NEB

and immediately the fever left her,

and the fever left her — ASV

and she ministered unto them.

and she began to wait on them — Rieu

. . . to see to their needs — Phi

32. **And at even, when the sun did set,**

That evening, at sundown — RSV

. . . after sunset . . . — NEB

When the evening came, as the sun was
setting[4] — Phi

**they brought unto him all that were
diseased,**

. . . sick — ASV

people came and brought to him all the
sick — Mon

they kept bringing to him all who were
sick — Phi

**and them that were possessed with
devils.**

and those who were demon-possessed
— NASB

and those under the power of demons
— Amp

and the demoniacs — ABUV

33. **And all the city was gathered together
at the door.**

And the whole city . . . about the door
— RSV

and the whole town was there, gathered at . . . — NEB

so that the whole city stood crowding
there at . . . — Knox

34. **And he healed many that were sick of
divers diseases,**

. . . who were sick with various diseases
— RSV

. . . that were afflicted with diseases of
every sort — Knox

and cast out many devils;

. . . demons — ASV

In many cases he expelled evil spirits
— Phi

and suffered not the devils to speak,

and he would not permit the demons
. . . — RSV

but he would not allow them to say a
word — Phi

because they knew him.

because they knew who He was—NASB

because they recognized him — Knox

because they knew that he was Christ
— Gspd

35. **And in the morning,**

And in the early morning — NASB

Early in the morning — Wms

rising up a great while before day,

And rising very early, by night — ABUV

while it was still dark, He arose —
NASB

long before daylight, he got up—Gspd

**he went out, and departed into a soli-
tary place,**

and left the house, and went off to a
lonely spot — Gspd

---

[4]Based on a variant reading.

left the house and went off to a deserted place — Phi

and leaving the house, made his way into the open country — Rieu

and there prayed.

and remained there in prayer — NEB

there began to pray — TCNT

and there he gave himself up to prayer — Bas

36. And Simon and they that were with him

And Simon and his companions—Gspd

followed after him.

hunted for Him — NASB

searched him out — NEB

searched everywhere for Him — Wey

37. And when they had found him, they said unto him, All men seek for thee.

they say to him, All are seeking thee — ABUV

they told him, Everybody is looking for you — Mof

38. And he said unto them, Let us go into the next towns,

And he says to them, Let us go elsewhere, into the neighboring towns — ABUV

And he said to them, Let us go on to the next towns — RSV

He answered, Let us move on to the country towns in the neighbourhood — NEB

that I may preach there also:

so that I may tell my message there too — Phi

I have to proclaim my message there also — NEB

for therefore came I forth.

for to this end . . . — ASV

for that is why I came out — RSV

39. And he preached in their synagogues throughout all Galilee,

And he remained[5] preaching . . . — Alf

and he went throughout all Galilee, preaching in their synagogues — RSV

So He went all over Galilee . . . —Wms

and cast out devils.

and was casting the demons out—Rhm

40. And there came a leper to him,

Once he was approached by a leper — NEB

beseeching him, and kneeling down to him,

who knelt before him, begging his help — NEB

appealing to him on his knees — Gspd

beseeching him on bended knee — Mof

and saying unto him, If thou wilt, thou canst make me clean.

If you are willing, he said, you are able to cleanse me — Wey

saying to Him, If you want to, you can cure me — Wms

Oh, if only You will, You can make me clean — Nor

41. And Jesus, moved with compassion,

Jesus was filled with pity for him — Phi

put forth his hand, and touched him,

he stretched out his hand, and touched him — RSV

and stretched out his hand and placed it on the leper — Phi

and saith unto him, I will; be thou clean.

. . . be thou made clean — ASV

and says to him, I will; be cleansed — ABUV

saying, Of course I want to — you are clean — Phi

42. And as soon as he had spoken,[6] immediately the leprosy departed from him,

And immediately the leprosy left him — RSV

and he was cleansed.

and he was cured — Gspd

the man was healed — Nor

43. And he straitly charged him,

. . . strictly . . . — ASV

. . . sternly . . . — RSV

and then Jesus, after sternly warning him — TCNT

and forthwith sent him away;

immediately . . . — TCNT

and sent him away at once — RSV

Then he dismissed him — NEB

44. And saith unto him, See thou say nothing to any man:

Be sure you say nothing to anybody — NEB

and said to him: Be careful not to say anything to any one — TCNT

but go thy way, shew thyself to the priest,

but go show thyself to the priest — ASV

---

[5]Based on a variant reading.

[6]Now recognized as not adequately supported by original manuscripts.

but begone! show yourself ... — Gspd

but go, let the priest examine you — Beck

and offer for thy cleansing those things which Moses commanded,

and make the offering laid down by Moses for your cleansing — NEB

and make the offerings for your recovery which Moses prescribed — Phi

for a testimony unto them.

for a proof to the people — RSV

that will certify the cure — NEB

as evidence to the authorities — Phi

so that the people might be notified — Rieu

45. But he went out, and began to publish it much,

But he went out and began to talk freely about it — RSV

But the man went out and made the whole story public — NEB

and to blaze abroad the matter,

and to spread abroad ... — ASV

and to spread the news — RSV

he spread it far and wide — NEB

insomuch that Jesus could no more openly enter into the city,

so that Jesus could no longer openly enter into a city — ABUV

until Jesus could no longer show himself in any town — NEB

but was without in desert places:

but was out in the country — RSV

and had to stay outside in unfrequented places — Phi

but had to stay out in the barren wastelands — Tay

and they came to him from every quarter.

Even so, people kept coming to him from all quarters — NEB

and still the people kept coming to him from everywhere — Beck

CHAPTER 2

1. And again he entered into Capernaum

And when he entered again into Capernaum — ASV

When he re-entered Capernaum — Phi

after some days;

Some days later — Ber

several days afterward — NASB

and it was noised that he was in the house.

it was heard that he was at home — ABUV

the news went round ... — NEB

a rumour spread that he was in somebody's house — Phi

2. And straightway many were gathered together,

and such a crowd gathered — Gspd

and they flocked to him in such numbers — Rieu

insomuch that there was no room to receive them,

so that there was no longer room for them — ASV

so that it was impossible to hold them — Lam

no, not so much as about the door:

no, not even about the door — ASV

not even in front of the entrance — Lam

and he preached the word unto them.

and he was preaching the word to them — RSV

3. And they come unto him,

And they come — ASV

And they came — RSV

bringing one sick of the palsy,

bringing to him a paralytic — RSV

... a man who was paralyzed — Gspd

which was borne of four.

borne by four — ABUV

borne by four men — Alf

carried ... — Ber

4. And when they could not come nigh unto him for the press,

... for the crowd — ASV

And when they could not get near him because of the crowd — RSV

they uncovered the roof where he was:

they removed the roof above Him — NASB

... the tiles from the roof over Jesus' head — Phi

they dug through the clay roof over His head — Tay

and when they had broken it up,

and when they had broken through — NEB

and when they had made an opening — RSV

they let down the bed

they lowered the mat — Wey

... the stretcher — NEB
they let down the pallet — RSV
wherein the sick of the palsy lay.
on which the paralytic was lying — Ber

5. **When Jesus saw their faith,**
   ... noted ... — Nor
   Then Jesus, when he perceived their
   faith — Mon
   he said unto the sick of the palsy,
   he said to the paralytic — RSV
   Son, thy sins be forgiven thee.
   ... are forgiven — ASV
   My son, your sins ... — RSV
   My lad, your sins are forgiven! — Nor

6. **But there were certain of the scribes
   sitting there,**
   Now there were some lawyers ... —
   NEB
   There were some Bible scholars ... —
   Beck
   and reasoning in their hearts,
   questioning in their hearts — RSV
   and they thought to themselves — NEB

7. **Why doth this man thus speak blas-
   phemies?**
   Why doth this man thus speak? he
   blasphemeth — ASV
   Why does the fellow talk like that?
   This is blasphemy! — NEB
   What does the man mean by talking
   like this? It is blasphemy! — Mof
   who can forgive sins but God only?
   Who can forgive sins but God alone —
   RSV
   Who can possibly forgive sins but God
   — Phi

8. **And immediately when Jesus perceived
   in his spirit**
   Now Jesus at once felt in His spirit —
   Wms
   Jesus, at once aware, through his spiritual insight — Rieu
   **that they so reasoned within them-
   selves,**
   that they thus questioned ... — RSV
   that this was what they were thinking
   — NEB
   that they were pondering thus within
   themselves — Nor
   **he said unto them, Why reason ye
   these things in your hearts?**
   said to them, Why do you question
   thus ... — RSV
   said to them: Why do you harbour
   thoughts like these — NEB

said to them, Why must you argue like
this in your minds — Phi

9. **Whether is it easier to say to the sick
   of the palsy,**
   Which is easier ... — ASV
   Is it easier to say to this paralyzed man
   — NEB
   Which is the easier thing, to say to the
   paralytic — Rieu
   Thy sins be forgiven thee;
   Thy sins are forgiven — ASV
   You have forgiveness for your sins —
   Bas
   **or to say, Arise, and take up thy bed,
   and walk?**
   ... Get up, take your stretcher and
   walk — Rieu
   ... Stand up, take your bed and walk
   — NEB

10. **But that ye may know**
    But to let you know — Gspd
    But to convince you — NEB
    But to prove to you — Phi
    **that the Son of man hath power on
    earth to forgive sins,**
    ... hath authority ... — ASV
    ... has the right ... — NEB
    ... has authority to forgive sins while
    he is on earth — Knox
    (he saith to the sick of the palsy,)
    — he said to the paralytic — RSV
    — he turned to the paralyzed man —
    NEB

11. **I say unto thee, Arise,**
    I bid you rise — Mon
    I tell you, get up — Gspd
    I say to you, stand up — NEB
    and take up thy bed,
    take up your pallet — RSV
    take up your mat — Wey
    and go thy way into thine house.
    and go unto thy house — ASV
    and go home — RSV

12. **And immediately he arose, took up the
    bed,**
    And he arose, and straightway took up
    the bed — ASV
    And he got up, took his stretcher at
    once — NEB
    At once the man sprang to his feet,
    picked up his bed — Phi
    and went forth before them all;
    and went out ... — RSV
    and walked off in full view of them all
    — Phi

insomuch that they were all amazed,
so that all were amazed — ABUV
so that they were astounded — NEB
The result was that they were all dumfounded — Wms
They were all filled with awe — Rieu
and glorified God, saying,
gave the glory to God, and said — Wey
and acknowledged the power of God, saying — Gspd
and began to praise God and say — Wms
We never saw it on this fashion.
We never saw it thus — ABUV
We never saw the like — Knox
. . . anything like this — RSV

13. **And he went forth again by the sea side;**
Again Jesus went out along the lake — Beck
He left the town and walked once more beside the sea — Rieu
and all the multitude resorted unto him,
All the crowd came to him — NEB
and all the multitude were coming to Him — NASB
and the whole multitude kept coming to Him — Wey
and he taught them.
and he began teaching them — Rhm
and He was teaching them — NASB
and he continued to teach them — Phi

14. **And as he passed by,**
And as he was passing along — Gspd
Then, as He walked on farther — Nor
he saw Levi the son of Alphaeus sitting at the receipt of custom,
sitting at the place of toll — ASV
at his seat in the custom-house — NEB
sitting at the tax-office — ABUV
at work in . . . — Nor
and said unto him, Follow me.
and he said to him, Come with me — Bas
And he arose and followed him.
And he got up . . . — Gspd
. . . and went with him — Bas
And Levi jumped to his feet and went along! — Tay

15. **And it came to pass, that, as Jesus sat at meat in his house,**
And as he sat at table. . . — RSV
Now Levi was at table in his own house — Mof

Later, when Jesus was sitting at dinner in Levi's house — Phi
So it came about that Jesus sat down to a meal in this man's house — Rieu
many publicans and sinners
many tax-collectors and irreligious people — Gspd
a large number of tax-collectors and disreputable folk — Phi
many bad characters — tax-gatherers and others — NEB
sat also together with Jesus and his disciples:
sat down with Jesus . . . — ASV
were dining with Jesus . . . — NASB
for there were many, and they followed him.
. . . and they followed him about — Alf
for there were many of them who used to follow him — Mon
. . . of these and they had begun to follow him — Rieu
. . . of them among his followers — Gspd

16. **And when the scribes and Pharisees**
Some doctors of the law who were Pharisees — NEB
And when the scribes who belonged to the Pharisees' party — Wms
saw him eat with publicans and sinners,
when they saw that he was eating with the sinners and publicans — ASV
saw that he was eating with the sinners and tax-gatherers — NASB
noticed him eating in this bad company — NEB
they said unto his disciples,
began saying unto his disciples — Rhm
How is it that he eateth and drinketh with publicans and sinners?
Why does he eat with the . . . — ABUV
Why does he eat with tax-collectors . . . — RSV
He is eating and drinking with tax-gatherers and sinners! — Wey

17. **When Jesus heard it, he saith unto them,**
On hearing this, Jesus said to them — Mof
Jesus overheard and . . . — NEB
They that are whole have no need of the physician,
They who are well need not a physician — ABUV

Those who are strong have no need of a doctor — Mof
but they that are sick:
but those who are ill — Mof
I came not to call the righteous, but sinners to repentance.
. . . but sinners — RSV
I did not come to invite virtuous people . . . — NEB
. . . invite the pious but the irreligious — Gspd

18. **And the disciples of John and of the Pharisees used to fast:**
And John's disciples and the Pharisees were fasting — ASV
Now John's disciples and those of the Pharisees were keeping a fast — Wey
and they come and say unto him,
and the people came and said to him — RSV
. . . and asked him — Gspd
they approached him with another question — Rieu
Why do the disciples of John and of the Pharisees fast,
Why do John's disciples and the disciples of the Pharisees fast — ASV
Why is it that John's disciples . . . are fasting — NEB
Why is it that when John's disciples . . . are keeping the fast — Gspd
but thy disciples fast not?
but your disciples do not fast — RSV
yours are not keeping it — Gspd

19. **And Jesus said unto them,**
Jesus replied to them — Ber
Jesus asked them — Beck
Can the children of the bridechamber fast,
Can the sons of . . . — ASV
Can the wedding guests fast — RSV
Can the bridegroom's friends fast — Beck
while the bridegroom is with them?
. . . is beside them — Mof
. . . is in their company — Ber
as long as they have the bridegroom with them,
. . . beside them — Mof
they cannot fast.
there can be no fasting — NEB
fasting is impossible — Wey
Fasting is out of the question — Phi

20. **But the days will come,**
But there will come days — ABUV
But the time will come — NEB

when the bridegroom shall be taken away from them,
. . . is taken away . . . — RSV
and then shall they fast in those days.
. . . will they fast in that day — ASV
and on that day they will fast — NEB
and when that day comes . . . — Gspd
that will be the time for them to fast — Phi

21. **No man also seweth a piece of new cloth**
No man seweth a piece of undressed cloth — ASV
No one sews a piece of unfulled cloth — ABUV
No one sews a patch of unshrunk cloth — NEB
. . . of brand-new goods — Wms
on an old garment:
on an old coat — Gspd
on a worn out garment — Lam
else the new piece that filleth it up taketh away from the old,
else that which should fill it up taketh from it, the new from the old — ASV
if he does, the patch tears away from it, the new from the old — RSV
and the rent is made worse.
and a worse rent is made — ASV
and a worse tear . . . — RSV
and leaves a bigger hole — NEB

22. **And no man putteth new wine into old bottles:**
. . . wine-skins — ASV
And no one pours new wine into old skins — Rieu
else the new wine doth burst the bottles,
else the wine will burst the skins — ASV
if he does, the wine will burst the skins — RSV
and the wine is spilled, and the bottles will be marred:
and the wine perisheth, and the skins — ASV
and the wine is lost, and so are the skins — RSV
and both the wine and skins are lost — Wey
the wine is spilt and the skins are ruined — Phi
but new wine must be put into new bottles.
but they put new wine into fresh wine-skins — ASV

New wine has to be put into fresh skins
— Gspd

23. **And it came to pass, that he went through the corn fields on the sabbath day;**
. . . that he was going on the sabbath day through the grainfields — ASV
One sabbath he was going through the grainfields — RSV
One Sabbath He was walking through the wheatfields — Wey
and his disciples began, as they went, to pluck the ears of corn.
. . . began to make a way, plucking the ears of grain — ABUV
. . . began to pick the heads of wheat as they made their way through — Gspd

24. **And the Pharisees said unto him, Behold, why do they on the sabbath day that which is not lawful?**
Look at what they are doing on the sabbath! That is not allowed — Mof
Look at that! Why should they do what is forbidden on the Sabbath day — Phi

25. **And he said unto them, Have ye never read what David did,**
Did ye never read . . . — ASV
when he had need, and was an hungred,
. . . and was hungry — ASV
when he was in need and became hungry — NASB
he, and they that were with him?
he and his men — NEB
he and his companions — NASB

26. **How he went into the house of God in the days of Abiathar the high priest,**
when Abiathar was high priest — ASV

in the time of Abiathar the High Priest
— NEB
and did eat the shewbread,
and ate the showbread — ASV
and ate the bread of the Presence — RSV
and ate the consecrated loaves — NEB
. . . the Presentation Loaves — Gspd
which is not lawful to eat but for the priests,
which it is not lawful to eat except . . .
— ABUV
which is not lawful for any but the priests to eat — RSV
which no one except the priests is allowed to eat — Mon
and gave also to them which were with him?
and also shared them with his followers — Mof
and even gave them to his men — NEB

27. **And he said unto them, The sabbath was made for man, and not man for the sabbath:**
The Sabbath was made for the sake of man and not man for the Sabbath
— NEB
The sabbath was made to serve man and not man to keep the sabbath — Wms
The Sabbath came into being for mankind, not mankind for the Sabbath
— Rieu

28. **Therefore the Son of man is Lord also of the sabbath.**
so that . . . is lord even of the sabbath — ASV
That is why the Son of Man is master even of the Sabbath — Phi
therefore the Son of Man is sovereign even over the Sabbath — NEB

CHAPTER 3

1. **And he entered again into the synagogue;**
And He entered again into a synagogue
— NASB
and there was a man there which had a withered hand.
. . . who had his hand withered — ASV
there was a man there with one hand shrivelled up — Wey

2. **And they watched him,**
And they were watching him — ABUV
. . . closely — Gspd

whether he would heal him on the sabbath day;
to see . . . on the sabbath — RSV
that they might accuse him.
so that they could bring a charge against him — NEB
so as to have a complaint to bring against Him — Nor

3. **And he saith unto the man which had the withered hand,**
He told the man with the shrunken hand — Ber

Stand forth.
Arise, and come into the midst—ABUV
Come here — RSV
Rise and come forward — Mof
Get up in the crowd — Wms

4. And he saith unto them,
then he asked them — Mof
Is it lawful to do good on the sabbath days, or to do evil?
. . . on the sabbath day to do good, or to do harm — ASV
Is it right to help or to hurt on the sabbath — Mof
Which is right, to do good on the sabbath day, or to do harm — Knox
to save life, or to kill?
. . . or to take it — Wms
to save a life, or to kill — ASV
. . . or to destroy one — Wey
But they held their peace.
But they were silent — ABUV
There was a dead silence — Phi
They had nothing to say — NEB
But they made no answer — Gspd

5. And when he had looked round about on them with anger,
And after looking around at them . . . — NASB
And he, after an angry glance round the circle — Rieu
being grieved for the hardness of their hearts,
. . . at the hardening of their heart — ASV
hurt by their obstinacy — Gspd
sorry because their minds were closed — Beck
deeply distressed by their callousness — Phi
deeply disturbed by their indifference to human need — Tay
he saith unto the man,
He said to the man — NASB
Stretch forth thine hand.
Stretch out your hand — RSV
. . . arm — NEB
Hold out your hand! — Gspd
And he stretched it out:
And he stretched it forth — ASV
And he held it out — Gspd
and his hand was restored whole as the other.
and his hand was restored — ASV
and the hand was completely restored — Wey
. . . was at once . . . — Mon

and his arm was restored — NEB
6. And the Pharisees went forth,
. . . went out — ASV
The Pharisees walked straight out — Phi
Then the Pharisees left the synagogue — Gspd
and straightway took counsel with the Herodians against him,
and held a consultation . . . against Him — Wms
began plotting against him with the partisans of Herod — NEB
how they might destroy him.
how to destroy him — RSV
to devise some means of destroying Him — Wey
to see how they could make away with him — NEB

7. But Jesus withdrew himself with his disciples to the sea:
And Jesus with his disciples withdrew to the sea — ASV
Jesus went away to the lake-side with his disciples — NEB
And Jesus, accompanied by his disciples, withdrew towards the sea — Rieu
and a great multitude from Galilee followed him, and from Judaea,
and a vast throng of people followed him from Galilee, and from Judea — Wms

8. And from Jerusalem, and from Idumaea, and from beyond Jordan;
and Jerusalem, Idumaea and Transjordan — NEB
and they about Tyre and Sidon,
and from about Tyre and Sidon — RSV
and the neighbourhood of . . . — Mof
a great multitude,
a vast crowd — Wey
when they had heard what great things he did,
as they heard . . . he was doing—ABUV
hearing all that he did — RSV
as they kept hearing of the great things that He was doing — Wms
came unto him.
came to see him — NEB
came to join him — Rieu

9. And he spake to his disciples, that a small ship should wait on him
And he told his disciples to have a boat ready for him — RSV
Therefore He gave directions to His

disciples to keep a small boat always ready — Wey

because of the multitude, lest they should throng him.

because of the crowd, . . . crush him — RSV

to prevent his being crushed by the crowd — Gspd

10. For he had healed many;

For he cured so many people — Gspd

insomuch that they pressed upon him for to touch him, as many as had plagues.

that all who had any ailments pressed up to him to touch him — Gspd

that sick people of all kinds came crowding in upon him to touch him — NEB

11. And unclean spirits, when they saw him,

And the unclean spirits, whensoever they beheld him — ASV

And the foul spirits, whenever they saw Him — Wey

Evil spirits, as soon as they saw him — Phi

fell down before him, and cried, saying,

would fall at his feet and cry aloud — NEB

threw themselves down at His feet, screaming out — Wey

acknowledged his authority and screamed — Phi

Thou art the Son of God.

You are the Son of God! — NASB

12. And he straitly charged them

And he charged them much — ASV

And he strictly ordered them — RSV

But he warned them repeatedly — Phi

that they should not make him known.

not to tell who he was — Gspd

not to reveal His identity — NASB

13. And he goeth up into a mountain,

He then went up into the hill-country — NEB

And Jesus made his way up the hill — TCNT

and calleth unto him whom he would:

and calleth unto him whom he himself would — ASV

and called to him those whom he desired — RSV

and summoned those whom he wanted — Gspd

and they came unto him.

and they went unto him — ASV

and they went and joined him — NEB

These left their homes . . . — Rieu

14. And he ordained twelve,

And he appointed twelve — ASV

that they should be with him,

to be . . . — RSV

as his companions — NEB

to associate with him — Rieu

and that he might send them forth to preach,

whom he could send out . . . — Phi

whom he would send out to proclaim the Gospel — NEB

15. And to have power to heal sicknesses,[7] and to cast out devils:

and to have authority to cast out demons — ASV

with authority to expel the demons — Wey

16. And Simon he surnamed Peter;

So he appointed the Twelve:[8] to Simon he gave the name Peter — NEB

These were the Twelve he appointed: Peter (which was the new name he gave Simon) — Phi

17. And James the son of Zebedee, and John the brother of James;

then came the sons of Zebedee, James and his brother John — NEB

and he surnamed them Boanerges, which is, The sons of thunder:

to whom he gave the name Boanerges, Sons of Thunder — NEB

18. And Andrew, and Philip, and Bartholomew, and Matthew, and Thomas, and James the son of Alphaeus,

and Thaddaeus, and Simon the Canaanite,

and Thaddaeus and Simon the Cananaean — ASV

and Thaddaeus and Simon, a member of the Zealot party — NEB

Thaddaeus, Simon the Patriot — Phi

19. And Judas Iscariot, which also betrayed him:

And Judas, the man from Kerioth, who betrayed Him — Beck

And Judas of Kerioth, the man through

---

[7]The words "to heal sicknesses" are now recognized as not adequately supported by original manuscripts.

[8]"And he appointed the twelve" is based on a variant reading.

whose treachery he was arrested —
Rieu
and they went into an house.
And he cometh into a house — ASV
Then he went home — RSV
Then they went indoors — Mof

20. **And the multitude cometh together again,**
And again the crowd gathered — Gspd
so that they could not so much as eat bread.
so that they could not even eat — RSV
so that there was no opportunity for them even to snatch a meal — Wey

21. **And when his friends heard of it,**
When his family heard of this — NEB
When his relatives learned of it — Ber
they went out to lay hold on him:
. . . to restrain him — Knox
set out to seize Him by force — Wey
they set out to take charge of him — NEB
set out from home to take him into custody — Rieu
for they said, He is beside himself.
for they were saying, He has lost His senses — NASB
for they said, He must be mad! — Phi
. . . He is deranged! — Ber
for people were saying that he was out of his mind — NEB

22. **And the scribes which came down from Jerusalem said,**
The Scribes who had come down from Jerusalem were saying — Phi
The doctors of the law, too, . . ., said NEB
He hath Beelzebub,
He is possessed by Beelzebul — RSV
He has Beelzebul in him — Wey
and by the prince of the devils casteth he out devils.
and through the prince of the demons he casts out the demons — ABUV
and by the help of . . . He drives out the demons — Wms
and it is by the power of the Prince of the demons that he expels the demons — Wey

23. **And he called them unto him,**
And He called them to Himself — NASB
So he called them to come forward — NEB
and said unto them in parables,

and began speaking to them in parables — NASB
and addressed them allegorically — Rieu
How can Satan cast out Satan?
How is it possible for Satan to expel Satan — Wey

24. **And if a kingdom be divided against itself,**
If a kingdom is disunited — Gspd
If one part of a kingdom fights another — Beck
If a kingdom is divided by internal strife — Rieu
For if civil war breaks out in a kingdom — Wey
that kingdom cannot stand.
that kingdom cannot last — Gspd
that kingdom will come to destruction — Bas

25. **And if a house be divided against itself,**
if a household is divided . . . — NEB
and if a family splits into parties—Wey
that house cannot stand.
that house will not be able to stand — ASV
. . . will never stand — NEB
that family cannot continue — Wey

26. **And if Satan rise up against himself, and be divided,**
. . . has risen up against himself, and is divided — RSV
. . . is in rebellion against himself, he is divided — NEB
he cannot stand, but hath an end.
. . . but is coming to an end — RSV
and cannot stand; and that is the end of him — NEB
he cannot stand — his end has come — Rieu
. . . — his days are certainly numbered — Phi

27. **No man can enter into a strong man's house,**
On the other hand, no one can break . . . — NEB
Indeed, no one can go . . . — Wey
But one cannot break into the Strong One's house — Rieu
and spoil his goods,
and plunder . . . — ABUV
and make off with . . . — NEB
and carry off his property — Wey
and rob him — Nor

137

except he will first bind the strong man;

unless he first binds . . . — RSV

unless he has first tied . . . — NEB

and then he will spoil his house.

then indeed he may plunder his house — RSV

then he can ransack the house — NEB

after that he can make a clean sweep of his house — Wms

28. Verily I say unto you,

Truly . . . — RSV

I tell you this — NEB

I tell you the truth — Beck

In solemn truth I tell you — Mon

I assure you — Ber

All sins shall be forgiven unto the sons of men,

All their sins shall be forgiven . . . — ASV

all men's sins can be forgiven — Phi

and blasphemies wherewith soever they shall blaspheme:

and whatever blasphemies they utter — RSV

and all the abusive things they say — Gspd

and all the slanders that they utter — TCNT

29. But he that shall blaspheme against the Holy Ghost

but whosoever shall blaspheme against the Holy Spirit — ASV

but whoever slanders the Holy Spirit — NEB

But whoever reviles the holy Spirit — Gspd

hath never forgiveness,

has no forgiveness forever — ABUV

can never be forgiven — NEB

remains unforgiven to the end — TCNT

but is in danger of eternal damnation:

but is guilty of an eternal sin — ASV

. . . of a sin that has no end — Wms

he has to answer for an enduring sin — TCNT

30. Because they said, He hath an unclean spirit.

— for they had said, He has an unclean spirit — RSV

This was because they were saying, . . . — Knox

31. There came then his brethren and his mother,

Then his mother and his brothers arrived — Phi

and, standing without, sent unto him, calling him.

They stood outside the house and sent a message asking him to come out to them — Phi

32. And the multitude sat about him,

And a multitude was sitting about him — ASV

There was a crowd sitting around him — Gspd

and they said unto him,

and he was told — Mof

when they told Him — Wms

Behold, thy mother and thy brethren without seek for thee.

Your mother and your brothers are outside, asking for you — RSV

. . . looking for you — Phi

33. And he answered them, saying,

and he replied — RSV

Who is my mother, or my brethren?

Who are my mother and my brothers — Gspd

34. And he looked round about on them which sat about him,

And looking around on those who sat about him — RSV

And, fixing His eyes on the people who were sitting round Him in a circle — Wey

and said, Behold my mother and my brethren!

he said, Here are my mother and my brothers — NEB

35. For whosoever shall do the will of God,

Whoever does the will of God — RSV

For whoever does the things God wills — Amp

the same is my brother, and my sister, and mother.

is my brother, and sister, and mother — RSV

is brother and sister and mother to me — Phi

CHAPTER 4

1. And he began again to teach by the sea side:
On another occasion he began . . . by the lake-side — NEB
and there was gathered unto him a great multitude,
And a very large crowd gathered about him — RSV
A bigger crowd than ever collected around him — Phi
so that he entered into a ship,
so that he got into a boat — RSV
and sat in the sea;
and sat in it on the sea — RSV
and sat there, a little way from the shore — Gspd
and the whole multitude was by the sea on the land.
and all the people were on the shore close to the water — Wey
The people all stood on the shore, facing the sea — Rieu
with the whole crowd on the beach right down to the water's edge — NEB

2. And he taught them many things by parables,
Then he began teaching them in parables many things — Mon
He continued teaching them by many stories — Wms
and said unto them in his doctrine,
and said to them in his teaching — ABUV
. . . in the course of his teaching — Gspd
As he taught he said — NEB

3. Hearken; Behold, there went out a sower to sow:
Hearken: Behold, the sower went forth . . . — ASV
Listen! A sower went out . . . — RSV

4. And it came to pass, as he sowed,
And as he sowed — RSV
And it happened that . . . — NEB
some fell by the way side,
some seed fell beside the road — NASB
some seed fell along the path — RSV
and the fowls of the air came and devoured it up.
and the birds came and devoured it — ASV
and the birds came and gobbled it up — Phi

5. And some fell on stony ground,
Another part fell on the rocky ground — ABUV
Some of the seed fell among the rocks — Phi
where it had not much earth;
where it had little soil — NEB
where the soil was shallow — Knox
and immediately it sprang up,
and it shot up at once — Mof
and it sprouted quickly — NEB
because it had no depth of earth:
because the soil was not deep — Gspd

6. But when the sun was up,
and when the sun was risen — ASV
but when the sun rose — NEB
And after the sun had risen — NASB
it was scorched;
the young corn . . . — NEB
it got scorched — Mof
it was burned — Bas
and because it had no root,
and as it had no proper root — NEB
it withered away.
it became dry and dead — Bas
it dried up — Lam

7. And some fell among thorns,
Another part fell among the thorns — ABUV
Other seed fell among thorns — RSV
Some seed fell among thistles — NEB
Some of the seed fell among brambles — TCNT
Some fell among briers — Knox
and the thorns grew up, and choked it,
. . . grew and choked the life out of it — Phi
but the brambles shot up and completely choked it — TCNT
and it yielded no fruit.
. . . no grain — RSV
. . . no crop — NEB

8. And other fell on good ground,
And others fell into the good ground — ASV
And other seeds fell into good soil — RSV
Some fell in rich soil — Wms
and did yield fruit that sprang up and increased;
and yielded fruit, growing up and increasing — ASV
and yielded a crop, for it sprang up and grew — Ber

and brought forth, some thirty, and some sixty, and some an hundred.
. . . thirtyfold, and sixtyfold, and a hundredfold — ASV
which yielded thirty or sixty or even a hundred times as much as the seed — Phi

9. **And he said unto them,**
And he said — ASV
He added — Mof
He concluded by saying — Rieu

He that hath ears to hear, let him hear.
He who has . . . — RSV
If you have ears to hear, then hear — NEB
Let him who has ears listen! — Wms

10. **And when he was alone,**
And as soon as He was alone — NASB
Then when they were by themselves — Phi
when they had him to themselves — Rieu

they that were about him with the twelve
the Twelve and others who were round him — NEB
His followers, along with the Twelve — NASB
his close followers and the Twelve — Phi

asked of him the parable.
asked him concerning the parables — RSV
began asking about the parables—Mon

11. **And he said unto them,**
And he was saying to them — NASB
He went on to say to them — Mon
He replied — NEB

Unto you it is given
To you is given — ABUV
To you has been given — RSV
To you has been intrusted — Gspd

to know
the mystery of the kingdom of God:
the mystery . . . — ASV
the secret . . . — RSV
the open secret of the Realm of God — Mof
the secret of the reign of God — Gspd

but unto them that are without,
but for those outside — RSV
But to those who do not know the secret — Phi

all these things are done in parables:
all things . . . — ASV

everything is in parables — RSV
everything comes by way of parables — NEB
everything is presented in stories — Wms

12. **That seeing they may see, and not perceive;**
so that they may indeed see but not perceive — RSV
so that (as Scripture says) they may look and look, but see nothing — NEB

and hearing they may hear, and not understand;
and may indeed hear but not understand — RSV
they may hear and hear, but understand nothing — NEB

lest at any time they should be converted,
lest haply they should turn again — ASV
if perhaps they may turn — ABUV
lest they should turn again — RSV
otherwise they might turn to God — NEB

and their sins should be forgiven them.
and it should be forgiven them — ASV
and be forgiven — ABUV

13. **And he said unto them,**
So he said — NEB
Then he continued — Phi
He resumed — Rieu

Know ye not this parable?
Do you not understand this parable — RSV
If you do not understand this parable — Ber

and how then will ye know all parables?
How then will you understand all the parables — RSV
how will you grasp . . . — Ber
How then are you to understand any parable — NEB

14. **The sower soweth the word.**
What the sower sows is the word — Wey
What the sower sows is the message — Gspd

15. **And these are they by the way side,**
And these are the ones along the path — RSV

where the word is sown;
in whom . . . — Wey

in whose hearts the message falls —
Gspd

but when they have heard,
when they hear — RSV
as soon as they hear it — Phi
but no sooner have they heard it—NEB
Satan cometh immediately,
straightway cometh Satan — ASV
Satan comes at once — Wey
and taketh away the word
and snatches away the message — Ber
and carries off the Word — Rieu
that was sown in their hearts.
that has been sown in them — ABUV
. . . in their minds — Phi

16. And these are they likewise
And these in like manner are they —
ASV
It is the same with those — NEB
which are sown on stony ground;
that are sown on the rocky places —
ABUV
who receive the seed on rocky ground
— NEB
who, when they have heard the word,
who, when they hear the word — RSV
As soon as they hear the Word — Beck
Whenever they hear the Word — Mon
immediately receive it with gladness;
straightway receive it with joy — ASV
at once accept it joyfully — Wey

17. And have no root in themselves,
But they have no real roots — Phi
but it takes no real root in them—Gspd
but it strikes no root in them — NEB
and so endure but for a time:
but endure for a while — ASV
they have no staying-power — NEB
and they last only a little while — Gspd
they cannot hold out long — Rieu
**afterward, when affliction or persecu-
tion ariseth**
then, when tribulation or . . . — ASV
when there is trouble or persecution —
NEB
then, when suffering or persecution
comes — Wey
for the word's sake,
because of the word — ASV
on account of the Word — Rieu
immediately they are offended.
straightway they stumble — ASV
immediately they fall away — RSV
they stumble and fall — Wey
they give it up at once — Gspd

**18. And these are they which are sown
among thorns;**
And others are they that are sown
among the thorns — ASV
Others again receive the seed among
thistles — NEB
It is different with those sown among
the thorns — Gspd
such as hear the word,
these are they that have heard the word
— ASV
These are people who have listened to
the Word — Rieu
They are people who listen to the message — Gspd

19. And the cares of this world,
and the anxieties of the age — ABUV
but worldly cares — NEB
but the worries of the time — Gspd
the anxieties of life — Mon
and the deceitfulness of riches,
the lure of riches — Rieu
and the false glamour of wealth — NEB
the deceiving pleasures of being rich —
Wms
**and the lusts of other things entering
in,**
and the desires about other things, entering in — ABUV
and the desires for other things enter in
— NASB
and cravings for many other things
come in — TCNT
choke the word,
and choke the word — NASB
and completely choke the Message —
TCNT
to smother the word — Knox
and it becometh unfruitful.
and it proves . . . — RSV
. . . barren — NEB
and it yields nothing — Gspd
and it produces no crop in their lives —
Phi

**20. And these are they which are sown on
good ground;**
And there are those who receive the
word in good soil — NEB
The last are those that received the seed
on rich soil — Rieu
such as hear the word, and receive it,
. . . and accept it — ASV
who listen to the word and take it in —
Mof
they hear the word and welcome it —
NEB

141

the people who hear the Word and embrace it — Rieu

and bring forth fruit,

and bear fruit — ASV

and yield a return — Gspd

some thirtyfold, some sixty, and some an hundred.

thirtyfold, and sixtyfold, and a hundredfold — ASV

thirty, sixty, and a hundred times as much as was sown — Beck

21. **And he said unto them,**

And He was saying to them — NASB

He went on to say — Wey

Is a candle brought to be put under a bushel,

Is the lamp brought to be put under the bushel — ASV

Do you bring in the lamp to put it under the meal-tub — NEB

... under the peck-measure — Gspd

... under a bucket — Phi

... under the measuring-bowl — Rieu

or under a bed?

or under the bed — NEB

or under the couch — Rhm

and not to be set on a candlestick?

and not to be put on the stand — ASV

Is it not, that it may be put on the lamp-stand — ABUV

Surely it is brought to be set ... — NEB

Shouldn't it be put on a lampstand — Beck

22. **For there is nothing hid,**

For nothing is hidden — ABUV

For no one hides anything — Gspd

which shall not be manifested;

except that it should be manifested — ABUV

except for the purpose of sometime bringing it to light again — Gspd

neither was any thing kept secret,

nothing concealed — Mof

and people do not keep secrets — Wms

but that it should come abroad.

but that it should come to light — ASV

except to be revealed — Mof

except to tell them — Wms

23. **If any man have ears to hear,**

If any one has ears to hear — ABUV

If you have ears to hear — NEB

If a man has ears — Phi

let him hear.

let him listen! — Wms

then hear — NEB

he should use them — Phi

24. **And he said unto them,**

He also said — NEB

Then He added — Nor

Take heed what ye hear:

Take care what you listen to — NASB

Take note of what you hear — NEB

Be careful how you listen — Phi

Give your minds to what you hear — Rieu

with what measure ye mete,

the measure you give — RSV

the measure you deal out to others — Mof

it shall be measured to you:

will be the measure you get — RSV

will be dealt out to yourselves — Mof

and unto you that hear shall more be given.

and more shall be given unto you — ASV

and more will be added to you — ABUV

and still more will be given you — RSV

and you will receive extra — Mof

25. **For he that hath,**

For the man who has — NEB

For he who holds — Mon

to him shall be given:

will be given more — NEB

and he that hath not,

and the man who has not — NEB

but to him who does not have much — Nor

and he who holds not — Mon

from him shall be taken even that which he hath.

shall be deprived of what he has — Ber

will forfeit even what he has — NEB

even the little he has will be taken from him — Nor

from him will be taken even what he holds — Mon

26. **And he said,**

And He was saying — NASB

Then he said — Phi

Another saying of His was this — Wey

So is the kingdom of God,

The kingdom of God is — RSV

as if a man should cast seed into the ground;

... should scatter seed upon the ground — RSV

like a man scattering seed on the ground — Gspd

27. **And should sleep,**

he goes to bed at night — NEB

and then sleeps by night — TCNT

and rise night and day,
and gets up in the morning — NEB
and rises by day — TCNT
and the seed should spring and grow up,
... should spring up and grow — ASV
... should sprout and grow — RSV
while the seed sprouts and grows tall — Wey
he knoweth not how.
he knows not how — ABUV
without his knowing it — Gspd
though he has no idea how it happens — Phi

28. **For the earth bringeth forth fruit of herself;**
The earth bears fruit of itself — ABUV
The ground produces a crop by itself— NEB
The earth . . . without any help from anyone — Phi
first the blade, then the ear,
first a blade, then the ear of corn — Phi
first the blade, then the head — NASB
first the stalk . . . — Wms
after that the full corn in the ear.
after that the corn is full . . . — Alf
then the full grain . . . — ASV
then full-grown corn . . . — NEB
then fully developed wheat in the head — Gspd

29. **But when the fruit is brought forth,**
. . . is ripe — ASV
. . . offereth itself — Alf
But when the grain is ripe — RSV
But when the crop permits — NASB
immediately he putteth in the sickle,
at once he puts in . . . — RSV
he sends for the reapers without delay — Phi
because the harvest is come.
because the harvest-time has come — NEB
for the reaping time . . . — Wms
because the harvest stands ready — Amp

30. **And he said,**
He said also — Mof
Another saying of His was this — Wey
Then he continued — Phi
Whereunto shall we liken the kingdom of God?
To what can we liken . . . — TCNT
With what can we compare . . . — RSV
How shall we picture . . . — NEB

or with what comparison shall we compare it?
or in what parable shall we set it forth — ASV
or what parable shall we use for it — RSV
or by what parable shall we present it — NASB

31. **It is like a grain of mustard seed,**
It is like the mustard-seed — NEB
which, when it is sown in the earth,
which, when sown upon the ground — RSV
is less than all the seeds that be in the earth:
is the smallest of all the seeds on earth — RSV
. . . in the world — Wey

32. **But when it is sown,**
yet . . . — ASV
But once sown — NEB
it groweth up,
it comes up — Wms
it springs up — NEB
it shoots up — Knox
and becometh greater than all herbs,
and becomes the greatest of all shrubs — RSV
and grows taller than any other plant — NEB
and becomes larger than all the garden plants — NASB
and shooteth out great branches;
and puts forth large branches — RSV
and produces branches so large — Gspd
so that the fowls of the air may lodge under the shadow of it.
so that the birds of the air can make their nests in its shade — RSV
that the wild birds can roost under the shelter of it — Gspd

33. **And with many other parables spake he the word unto them,**
. . . he spoke the word to them — ABUV
. . . he would give them his message — NEB
as they were able to hear it.
so far as they were able to receive it — NEB
according to their capacity for receiving it — Wey
such as their minds could take in—Phi
such as they could listen to easily — Knox

34. **But without a parable spake he not unto them:**

He never spoke to them except in parables — NEB

He said nothing to them except in figures — Gspd

and to them it was his practise never to speak except in parables — Mon

and when they were alone,

but privately — ASV

and in private — ABUV

he expounded all things to his disciples.

to his own disciples he explained all things — ABUV

... he expounded all things — ASV

35. And the same day,

And on that day — ASV

when the even was come,

when evening came — ABUV

in the evening — NEB

he saith unto them,

he said to them — RSV

Let us pass over unto the other side.

... the opposite shore — Alf

Let us go across to the other side — ABUV

Let us cross over to the other side of the lake — NEB

36. And when they had sent away the multitude,

And leaving the crowd — RSV

and dismissing the multitude — Rhm

So, having got rid of the crowd — Rieu

they took him even as he was in the ship.

they took him with them, just as he was, in the boat — RSV

and took him away in the boat in which he was sitting — Gspd

And there were also with him other little ships.

And other boats were with him — ASV

and there were other boats accompanying him — NEB

accompanied by other small craft—Phi

37. And there arose a great storm of wind,

And a great storm of wind arose — RSV

A heavy squall came on — NEB

Then a violent storm came up — Beck

and the waves beat into the ship,

... were beating into the boat — ABUV

... broke over the boat — NEB

... splashed into the boat — Mof

... kept dashing into the boat — TCNT

so that it was now full.

so that the boat was now filling — ABUV

... was already filling — RSV

until it was all but swamped — NEB

38. And he was in the hinder part of the ship,

And he himself was in the stern — ASV

asleep on a pillow:

... on the cushion — ASV

with his head on the headrest, fast asleep — Rieu

and they awake him, and say unto him,

and they woke him and said to him — RSV

they roused him and said — NEB

They awoke him with the words — Phi

Master, carest thou not that we perish?

Teacher ... — ASV

Master, we are sinking! Do you not care — NEB

Master, don't you care that we're drowning — Phi

39. And he arose, and rebuked the wind,

And he awoke ... — ASV

So He roused Himself ... — Wey

And being aroused, He rebuked the wind — NASB

and said unto the sea, Peace, be still.

and said to the sea, Peace! Be still! — RSV

... Hush! Silence! — Gspd

And the wind ceased, and there was a great calm.

The wind dropped, and there was a dead calm — NEB

The wind sank, and there was a perfect calm — Wey

40. And he said unto them,

Then He asked them — Wms

Why are ye so fearful?

Why are you afraid — RSV

Why are you so timid — Wey

Why are you such cowards — NEB

how is it that ye have no faith?

have ye not yet[9] faith — ASV

have you still no faith — Wey

What happened to your faith — Phi

41. And they feared exceedingly,

They were very much frightened — Wms

And they were filled with awe — RSV

Then they were awestruck — Mon

---

[9]Based on a slightly different reading.

144

and said one to another,
and said to one another — RSV
and they kept saying to each other —
Phi
What manner of man is this,
Who then is this — ASV

Who can this be — NEB
Who is this anyway — Ber
that even the wind and the sea obey him?
even the wind and the waves do what he tells them! — Phi

CHAPTER 5

1. **And they came over unto the other side of the sea,**
So they came to the other side of the lake — NEB
So they arrived at the opposite shore . . . — Wey
into the country of the Gadarenes.
. . . of the Gergesenes[10] — Alf
. . . of the Gerasenes[11] — ASV
and landed in the region of Gerasa — Gspd

2. **And when he was come out of the ship,**
And when he had come out of the boat — ABUV
And as soon as he had disembarked — Knox
As he stepped ashore — NEB
immediately there met him out of the tombs
He was met by a man from the tombs — Nor
a man with an unclean spirit,
. . . possessed by . . . — NEB
. . . under the power of a foul spirit — Wms
. . . in the grip of an evil spirit — Phi
a man possessed by a demon — Tay

3. **Who had his dwelling among the tombs;**
. . . in the tombs — Alf
who lived among the tombs — RSV
He was living in the place of the dead — Bas
and no man could bind him,
and no one could any longer . . . — ABUV
He could no longer be controlled — NEB
It was no longer possible to restrain him — Phi
no, not with chains:
no, not with a chain — ASV
not even . . . — ABUV
even chains were useless — NEB

4. **Because that he had been often bound with fetters and chains,**

he had often been fettered and chained up — NEB
for many a time he had been left securely bound in fetters and chains — Wey
He had often been found with chains on hands and feet — Beck
and the chains had been plucked asunder by him,
. . . rent asunder . . . — ASV
but the chains he wrenched apart — RSV
but he had snapped his chains — NEB
but afterwards the chains lay torn link from link — Wey
and the fetters broken in pieces:
. . . he broke . . . — RSV
and broken the fetters — NEB
and the fetters in fragments — Wey
neither could any man tame him.
and no man had strength to tame him — ASV
No one was strong enough to master him — NEB
and no one could do anything with him — Phi

5. **And always, night and day,**
And so, unceasingly, night and day — NEB
All night and day — Mof
All through the night as well as in the day-time — Phi
he was in the mountains, and in the tombs,
in the tombs and in the mountains — ASV
among the tombs and on . . . — RSV
. . . and on the hill-sides — NEB
crying, and cutting himself with stones.
he was crying out, and . . . — ASV
shrieking, and mangling himself with sharp stones — Wey

---

[10]A few manuscripts have this reading.
[11]The word "Gerasenes" is used in some manuscripts.

screaming and cutting himself with sharp pieces of stone — Tay

6. But when he saw Jesus afar off,
And when he saw Jesus from afar — ASV
When he saw Jesus in the distance — NEB
And catching sight of Jesus . . . — Gspd
he ran and worshipped him,
. . . and bowed down to him — ABUV
. . . and flung himself down before him — NEB
. . . and threw himself at His feet — Wey

7. And cried with a loud voice, and said,
and crying out . . ., he said — RSV
shouting loudly — NEB
yelling at the top of his voice — Phi
What have I to do with thee,
What have you to do with me — RSV
What do you want with me — NEB
Why dost thou meddle with me—Knox
Jesus, thou Son of the most high God?
Jesus, Son of the Most High God—RSV
Jesus, Son of God Most High — Wey
I adjure thee by God,
In God's name — NEB
For God's sake — Phi
In God's name, I implore you — Gspd
that thou torment me not.
do not torment me — RSV
. . . torture . . . — Mof

8. For he said unto him,
For he had said to him — RSV
For He had been saying to him — NASB
For Jesus was saying — Mon
Come out of the man, thou unclean spirit.
. . . you unclean spirit! — NASB
Foul spirit, come out of the man — Wey

9. And he asked him, What is thy name?
And Jesus asked him, What is your name — RSV
And he answered, saying,
He replied — RSV
My name is Legion: for we are many.
. . . for there are many of us — Rieu
. . . there are so many of us — NEB

10. And he besought him much
And he begged him eagerly — RSV
and he begged Jesus again and again — TCNT
And they begged him earnestly — Gspd

that he would not send them away out of the country.
not to send them out . . . — RSV
. . . that country — Wms
not to expel them from the neighbourhood — Rieu

11. Now there was there nigh unto the mountains
. . . on the mountain side — ASV
There, at the foot of the mountain, was — Knox
Now there was on the hillside — Mon
a great herd of swine feeding.
a large herd of pigs feeding — NEB

12. And all the devils besought him, saying,
And they besought him, saying — ASV
and they begged him — RSV
And they entreated Him, saying—NASB
Send us into the swine,
. . . to the swine — RSV
. . . among the pigs — NEB
that we may enter into them.
so that we may enter them — NASB
let us enter them — RSV
and let us go into them — NEB
and we'll get into them — Phi

13. And forthwith Jesus gave them leave.
And He gave them permission — NASB
And the unclean spirits went out,
. . . came out — ASV
Then out came the unclean spirits — Mof
and entered into the swine:
and went into the pigs — NEB
and the herd ran violently down a steep place into the sea,
. . . rushed down the steep . . . — ASV
. . . the steep bank . . . — NASB
. . . stampeded down the cliff into the lake — Phi
(they were about two thousand;)
about two thousand of them — NASB
— about 2000 in number — Wey
and were choked in the sea.
and they were drowned . . . — ASV

14. And they that fed the swine fled,
The herdsmen fled — RSV
The swineherds fled — Wey
The men in charge of them took to their heels — NEB
and told it in the city, and in the country.
and reported it . . . — ABUV
and carried the news to the town and country-side — NEB

and spread the news in town and country — Wey

And they went out to see what it was that was done.
And people came to see . . . that had happened — RSV
So the people went out to see what . . . — Wey

15. And they come to Jesus,
. . . came . . . — RSV
They approached Jesus — Rieu
and see him that was possessed with the devil, and had the legion, sitting,
and saw the demoniac sitting there — RSV
and observed the man who had been demon-possessed sitting down—NASB
and clothed, and in his right mind:
clothed and of sane mind — Wey
properly clothed and perfectly sane — Phi
and they were afraid,
and they became frightened — NASB
and they were awe-struck — Wey

16. And they that saw it
And those who had seen it — RSV
And those who had been eye-witnesses — Mon
The spectators — NEB
told them how it befell to him that was possessed with the devil,
recounted to them how it befell the demoniac — ABUV
told what had happened to . . . — RSV
told them how the madman had been cured — NEB
and also concerning the swine.
and to the swine — RSV
and what happened to the pigs — NEB
and all about the pigs — Gspd

17. And they began to pray him
. . . beseech him — ASV
. . . beg Jesus — RSV
Then they began to implore Jesus — Phi
to depart out of their coasts.
. . . from their borders — ASV
. . . from their neighborhood — RSV
to leave the district — NEB

18. And when he was come into the ship,
And as he was entering into the boat — ASV
As he was stepping . . . — NEB
As He was embarking — Wey
he that had been possessed with the devil

the man who had been possessed with demons — RSV
prayed him that he might be with him.
besought . . . — ASV
begged . . . — RSV
kept begging to go with him — Mon

19. Howbeit Jesus suffered him not,
But he refused — RSV
But He would not allow it — Wey
but saith unto him, Go home to thy friends,
and said to him, Go home to your friends — RSV
. . . Go home to your own people — Gspd
and tell them how great things the Lord hath done for thee,
. . . how much the Lord has done for you — RSV
and report to them all that the Lord . . . — Gpsd
and hath had compassion on thee.
and how he had pity on thee — ABUV
and how he has had mercy on you — RSV
and how merciful He has been to you — Beck

20. And he departed,
And he went his way — ASV
So the man went off — Phi
and began to publish in Decapolis
and began to proclaim in the Decapolis — RSV
and spread the news in the Ten Towns — NEB
how great things Jesus had done for him:
how much Jesus had done for him — RSV
all that . . . — Mof
and all men did marvel.
and they were all amazed — NEB
and all were marvelling — Rhm
And they were all simply amazed—Phi

21. And when Jesus was passed over again by ship unto the other side,
. . . the opposite shore — Alf
. . . had crossed again in the boat to the other side — RSV
As soon as Jesus had returned by boat to the other shore — NEB
much people gathered unto him:
a great multitude was gathered unto him — ASV
a great crowd gathered about him — RSV

147

a great number of people had gathered to meet him — TCNT
and he was nigh unto the sea.
and he was beside the sea — RSV
so he remained . . . — Mof

22. And, behold, there cometh one of the rulers of the synagogue,
Then came . . . — RSV
the president of one of the synagogues came up — NEB
Jairus by name;
named Jairus — Ber
and when he saw him, he fell at his feet,
and on catching sight of him fell . . . — Mof
And when he saw Jesus, he knelt before him — Phi

23. And besought him greatly, saying,
and entreated him earnestly, saying — NASB
and appealed to him, saying — Gspd
and began earnestly to beseech him — Rieu
My little daughter lieth at the point of death:
. . . is at death's door — NEB
My little girl is dying — Phi
I pray thee, come and lay thy hands on her,
Come and lay your hands on her — RSV
I beg you to come . . . — NEB
that she may be healed; and she shall live.
that she may be made whole, and live — ASV
so that she may be made well, and live — RSV
to cure her and save her life — NEB
that she may recover and live — Mon

24. And Jesus went with him;
So Jesus . . . — NEB
and much people followed him, and thronged him.
and a great multitude . . ., and they thronged him — ASV
and a great crowd . . . and thronged about him — RSV
. . . kept following Him, and jostling Him — Wms

25. And a certain woman,
And there was a woman — RSV
which had an issue of blood twelve years,

who had had a flow of blood for twelve years — RSV
who had suffered many haemorrhages . . . — NEB

26. And had suffered many things of many physicians,
and had endured much at the hands . . . — NASB
and in spite of long treatment by doctors — NEB
and had spent all that she had,
. . . all her resources — Rieu
and was nothing bettered, but rather grew worse,
and was no better . . . — RSV
and was not at all benefited . . . — ABUV

27. When she had heard of Jesus,
when she heard about Jesus — Ber
She had heard the reports . . . — RSV
When she had news of the things which Jesus did — Bas
came in the press behind,
and came up behind him in the crowd — RSV
and came up behind him under cover of the crowd — Phi
she came up from behind through the crowd — Rieu
and touched his garment.
. . . his cloak — NEB
. . . his robe — Mof

28. For she said, If I may touch but his clothes,
. . . If I touch even his garments — ABUV
for she kept saying, If I can only touch His clothes — Wms
For she thought, If I just touch His garments — NASB
I shall be whole.
I shall be made whole — ASV
. . . made well — RSV
. . . healed — Ber

29. And straightway the fountain of her blood was dried up;
And immediately the hemorrhage ceased — RSV
. . . the flow of her blood was dried up — NASB
and she felt in her body that she was healed of that plague.
. . . of her disease — RSV
and she knew in herself that she was cured of her trouble — Phi

30. And Jesus, immediately knowing in himself

And straightway, Jesus, perceiving . . .
— ASV

At the same time Jesus, aware — NEB

Jesus, conscious at once — Rieu

that virtue had gone out of him,

that the power proceeding from him
had gone forth — ASV

that power had gone out of him — NEB

that healing power had passed from
him — Gspd

turned him about in the press,

turned about in the crowd — ABUV

swung around in the throng — Rieu

and said, Who touched my clothes?

. . . my garments — ASV

31. And his disciples said unto him,

His disciples replied — Phi

But the disciples kept saying to Him —
Wms

**Thou seest the multitude thronging
thee,**

You see the crowd pressing around you
— RSV

. . . pressing you on all sides — Ber

You can see this crowd jostling you —
Phi

and sayest thou, Who touched me?

and yet you ask . . . — NEB

32. And he looked round about

. . . around — ABUV

Meanwhile he was looking round —
NEB

But He continued looking about —
Wey

to see her that had done this thing.

to see who had done it — RSV

to catch sight of the woman who had
done this — Knox

33. But the woman fearing and trembling,

And the woman, trembling with fear —
NEB

until the woman, frightened and trembling — Wey

Then the woman, scared and shaking
all over — Phi

knowing what was done in her,

knowing what had been done to her —
ASV

when she grasped what had happened
to her — NEB

came and fell down before him,

. . . threw herself at His feet — Wey

and told him all the truth.

. . . the whole truth — RSV

. . . the whole story — Phi

34. And he said unto her,

Whereupon he said — Rieu

**Daughter, thy faith hath made thee
whole;**

. . . hath saved thee — Alf

Daughter, your faith has made you
well — RSV

. . . it is your faith that has healed you
— Phi

**go in peace, and be whole of thy
plague.**

go in peace, and be healed of your disease — RSV

Go in peace, free for ever from this
trouble — NEB

35. While he yet spake,

While he was yet speaking — ABUV

Before he had finished speaking — Rieu

Even as he spoke — Gspd

**there came from the ruler of the syna-
gogue's house certain which said,**

. . . from the ruler's house some who
said — RSV

men came from the house of the warden of the synagogue to tell him —
Mon

Thy daughter is dead:

Your daughter has died — NASB

**why troublest thou the Master any
further?**

why trouble the Teacher . . . — ABUV

why trouble the Rabbi further — NEB

**36. As soon as Jesus heard the word that
was spoken,**

And Jesus, overhearing the word
spoken — ABUV

But Jesus, not heeding the word spoken
— ASV

But Jesus paid no attention to what
was said — Wms

Jesus heard them say this but took no
notice — Rieu

**he saith unto the ruler of the syna-
gogue,**

said to the synagogue official — NASB

Be not afraid, only believe.

Fear not . . . — ASV

Have no fear; only believe! — Ber

Now don't be afraid, just go on believing! — Phi

37. And he suffered no man to follow him,

And he allowed no one . . . — RSV

He let no one go with him — Gspd

**save Peter, and James, and John the
brother of James.**

except Peter and the brothers James and John — Wey

38. And he cometh to the house of the ruler of the synagogue,
And they come . . . — ASV
They came to the house of the leader . . . — Gspd
and seeth the tumult,
and there He saw confusion — Wms
and Jesus noticed the hubbub — Phi
he was faced by a disorderly scene — Rieu
and them that wept and wailed greatly.
and many weeping and wailing greatly — ASV
and people . . . loudly — RSV
— people . . . incessantly — TCNT

39. And when he was come in, he saith unto them,
And entering in, He said to them — NASB
And He went into the house and said to them — Wms
Why make ye this ado, and weep?
Why do you make a tumult and weep — RSV
Why this crying and commotion — NEB
What is the meaning of all this confusion and crying — Gspd
the damsel is not dead, but sleepeth.
the child . . ., but is sleeping — ABUV

40. And they laughed him to scorn.
And they laughed at him — ABUV
And they jeered at Him — Wey
Then they began to laugh in His face — Wms
But when he had put them all out,
But he put them all outside — RSV
But he drove them all out — Gspd
he taketh the father and the mother of the damsel,
and took the child's father and mother — RSV
taking with him the child's . . . — Rieu
and them that were with him,
and his own companions — NEB
and entereth in where the damsel was lying.

and went in where the child was — RSV
and went into the room where . . . lying — Gspd

41. And he took the damsel by the hand, and said unto her,
Taking her by the hand he said to her — RSV
Then, taking hold of her hand . . . — NEB
Talitha cumi; which is, being interpreted,
Talitha cumi; which means — RSV
Talitha koum — which may be translated — Mof
Damsel, I say unto thee, arise.
Little girl, I say to you, arise — RSV
Get up, my child — NEB
Wake up, little girl — Phi

42. And straightway the damsel arose, and walked;
And immediately the girl got up and walked — RSV
. . . and began to walk — NASB
. . . and started walking around — Wms
for she was of the age of twelve years.
for she was twelve years old — ASV
And they were astonished with a great astonishment.
And immediately they were overcome with amazement — RSV
At that they were beside themselves . . . — NEB
The moment they saw it they were utterly amazed — Gspd

43. And he charged them straitly that no man should know it;
And he strictly charged them that no one should know this — RSV
He gave them strict orders to let no one hear about it — NEB
but Jesus repeatedly cautioned them not to let any one know of it — TCNT
and commanded that something should be given her to eat.
and told them to give her something to eat — Gspd

CHAPTER 6

1. And he went out from thence,
And He went out from there — NASB
He left that place — NEB
Then he left that district — Phi
and came into his own country;

and went to his home town — NEB
and went to his own part of the country — Rieu
and his disciples follow him.
. . . followed him — RSV

... went with him — Bas
accompanied by His disciples — Wey

2. And when the sabbath day was come,
When the Sabbath came round — Rieu
And on the sabbath — RSV
he began to teach in the synagogue:
**and many hearing him were aston-
ished, saying,**
And the many as they heard were astonished, saying — ABUV
and the large audience was astounded
— Mof
many, as they listened, were deeply
impressed — Mon
**From whence hath this man these
things?**
Whence hath this man these things —
ASV
Where did he get all this — Gspd
How did he come by all this — Knox
**and what wisdom is this which is given
unto him,**
How does he come to have such wisdom — Gspd
**that even such mighty works are
wrought by his hands?**
and what mean such mighty works
wrought . . . — ASV
And, such miracles are wrought
through his hands! — ABUV
and, How does he work such miracles
— NEB
— and what about these marvelous
things that he can do — Phi

3. Is not this the carpenter,
Is not this the wood-worker — Bas
He's only the carpenter — Phi
**the son of Mary, the brother of James,
and Joses, and of Juda, and Simon?**
the son of Mary, and brother of James,
and Joses, and Judas, and Simon —
ASV
and are not his sisters here with us?
And do not His sisters live here among
us — Wey
And they were offended at him.
And they took offense at him — RSV
And they were deeply offended with
him — Phi
And so they found a cause for stumbling over him — Wms
This proved a hindrance to their believing in him — TCNT

4. But Jesus said unto them,
Then Jesus said to them — Mof
A prophet is not without honour,

A prophet will always be held in honour — NEB
A prophet is treated with honor everywhere — Gspd
**but in his own country, and among his
own kin, and in his own house.**
except in his home town, and among
his kinsmen and family — NEB
except in his own country, and among
his own relatives, and in his own
home — Gspd

5. And he could there do no mighty work,
And he was not able to do any miracle
there — ABUV
**save that he laid his hands upon a few
sick folk, and healed them.**
except . . . on a few sick people, and
healed them — ABUV

**6. And he marvelled because of their un-
belief.**
And he wondered at their lack of faith
— Mon
He was astonished . . . — Mof
and he was taken aback by their want
of faith — NEB
**And he went round about the villages,
teaching.**
And he went in a circuit about . . . —
ABUV
So He went round the adjacent villages,
teaching — Wey
Then He made a circle of the villages
and continued teaching — Wms

7. And he called unto him the twelve,
he summoned the Twelve — NEB
**and began to send them forth by two
and two;**
. . . out two by two — RSV
and sent them out in pairs on a mission — NEB
**and gave them power over unclean
spirits;**
and he gave them authority over the
. . . — ASV

8. And commanded them
and he charged them — ASV
and instructed them — NEB
**that they should take nothing for their
journey,**
to take nothing for the journey — Wey
. . . for the road — Phi
save a staff only;
except a staff — RSV
except a stick — Wey
**no scrip, no bread, no money in their
purse:**

no bread, no bag, no money in their girdle — ABUV
no bread, no pack . . . — NEB

9. But be shod with sandals;
but to go shod with sandals — ASV
but to wear sandals — RSV
and not put on two coats.
but not a second coat — NEB
and not put on two tunics — RSV
and not to wear two shirts — Gspd

10. And he said unto them,
Also, he told them — Mof
In what place soever ye enter into an house,
Wheresoever ye enter into a house — ASV
Wherever you are, when you go into a house — Phi
When you enter a house anywhere — Rieu
there abide till ye depart from that place.
stay there until you leave . . . — Phi
. . . town — NASB

11. And whosoever shall not receive you, nor hear you,
And whatever community will neither receive you nor listen to you — Ber
And wherever they give you no welcome and no hearing — Knox
when ye depart thence,
when you leave it — Nor
as you leave — NEB
shake off the dust under your feet
. . . that is on your feet — RSV
shake the dust off your feet — NEB
for a testimony against them.
. . . to them — ABUV
in witness against them — Knox
as a protest against them! — Phi
as a warning to them — Gspd
Verily I say unto you, It shall be more tolerable for Sodom and Gomorrha in the day of judgment, than for that city.

12. And they went out,
So they set out — Wey
and preached that men should repent.
and called publicly for repentance — NEB
and preached that men should change their whole outlook — Phi

13. And they cast out many devils,
And they were casting out many demons — NASB

and from time to time cast many demons out — Rieu
and anointed with oil many that were sick,
. . . many sick people — ABUV
and healed them.
and cured them — Gspd

14. And king Herod heard of him;
King Herod heard of it — RSV
. . . of all this — Wey
(for his name was spread abroad:)
for his name had become known — ASV
for the fame of Jesus had spread—NEB
for Jesus' name was on everybody's lips — Rieu
and he said, That John the Baptist was risen from the dead,
. . . John the Baptizer is risen . . . — ASV
Some[12] said, John the baptizer has been raised . . . — RSV
And people were saying, John the Baptist has been raised to life — NEB
and therefore mighty works do shew forth themselves in him.
that is why these powers are at work in him — RSV
. . . are active in him — Knox

15. Others said, That it is Elias.
But others said, It is Elijah — ASV
Others asserted that he was Elijah — Phi
And others said, That it is a prophet,
. . . It is a prophet — ASV
Others again, He is a prophet — NEB
or as one of the prophets.
like one of the prophets of old — RSV

16. But when Herod heard thereof, he said,
. . . of it, he said — RSV
. . . of him he said — Gspd
It is John, whom I beheaded: he is risen from the dead.
John, whom I beheaded, has been raised — RSV
John has risen, the John I beheaded — Mof
It must be John, whom I beheaded, risen from the dead! — Phi

17. For Herod himself had sent forth and laid hold upon John,
For Herod had sent and seized John — RSV

---

[12]Following a slightly different reading.

For this same Herod had sent and arrested John — NEB

It must be explained that Herod himself . . . — Rieu

and bound him in prison for Herodias' sake,

. . . on account of his marriage to Herodias — Mof

and put him in prison, in chains, to please . . . — TCNT

his brother Philip's wife:

for he had married her.

whom he had married — Rieu

18. For John had said unto Herod,

For John had been saying to Herod — NASB

It is not lawful for thee to have thy brother's wife.

you have no right to your brother's wife — Mof

It is not right for you to be living with . . . — Gspd

19. Therefore Herodias had a quarrel against him,

And Herodias set herself against him — ASV

Therefore Herodias bore a grudge . . . — Wey

So Herodias had it in for him — Wms

and would have killed him;

and desired to kill him — ASV

and wanted . . . — RSV

. . . to have him executed — Phi

but she could not:

but she could not manage it — Mof

but she lacked the power — Rieu

20. For Herod feared John,

for Herod stood in awe of John — Mof

. . . had a deep respect for . . . — Phi

knowing that he was a just man and an holy,

. . . a righteous and holy man — ASV

. . . an upright and holy man — Gspd

and observed him;

and kept him safe — ASV

and preserved him — ABUV

so he protected John — Mof

so he kept him in custody — NEB

and when he heard him, he did many things,

And . . ., he was much perplexed — ASV

. . . talk, he was very much disturbed — Gspd

and heard him gladly.

and yet he . . . — RSV

. . . enjoyed hearing him — Phi

21. And when a convenient day was come,

But an opportunity came — RSV

An opportune time came — Ber

Herodias found her opportunity — NEB

that Herod on his birthday made a supper

when . . . gave a banquet — RSV

. . . held a feast on his birthday — Mof

to his lords, high captains, and chief estates of Galilee;

to his chief officials and commanders and the leading men of Galilee — NEB

22. And when the daughter of the said Herodias came in, and danced,

The daughter of Herodias herself came in . . . — Rieu

Herodias' own daughter . . . for them — Gspd

Her daughter came in and danced — NEB

and pleased Herod and them that sat with him,

it . . . and those reclining at table with him — ABUV

she pleased Herod and his guests — RSV

to the great delight of . . . — Phi

the king said unto the damsel,

and the king said to the girl — RSV

Ask of me whatsoever thou wilt,

Ask me for anything you please — Wey

. . . you want — Nor

. . . whatever you wish — RSV

and I will give it thee.

and I will give it to you — Wey

23. And he sware unto her,

And he swore to her — ABUV

. . . an oath to her — NEB

And he vowed to her — RSV

He even swore to her — Rieu

Whatsoever thou shalt ask of me,

Whatever you ask me — RSV

I will give it thee,

I will give you — RSV

unto the half of my kingdom.

even . . . — RSV

were it the half of my realm — Mof

up to half of my kingdom! — Phi

24. And she went forth,

She at once went out — Wey

She left the room — Wms

and said unto her mother,

and asked her mother — Wms

What shall I ask?

And she said, The head of John the Baptist.
... John the Baptizer — ASV

25. **And she came in straightway with haste unto the king,**
... immediately with haste to the king — RSV
And she hurried back at once ... — Gspd
and asked, saying,
with her request — NEB
and made her request — Wey
I will that thou give me by and by
I will that you forthwith give me — ASV
I want you to give me at once — RSV
... this minute — Phi
in a charger
on a platter — ASV
on a dish — ABUV
the head of John the Baptist.

26. **And the king was exceedingly sorry:**
... became exceedingly sorrowful — ABUV
The king was greatly distressed — NEB
... very vexed — Mof
And the king was full of remorse — Knox
yet for his oath's sake,
but for the sake of his oaths — ASV
but because of ... — RSV
but in view of his oath — Rieu
and for their sakes which sat with him,
and his guests — Gspd
and the presence of his guests — Phi
he would not reject her.
... refuse her — ABUV
he did not want to break his word to her — RSV
he was not prepared to break faith with her — Rieu

27. **And immediately the king sent an executioner,**
So he sent at once a soldier of the guard — Mon
and commanded his head to be brought:
with orders to bring John's head — NEB
and he went and beheaded him in the prison,
So he went ... — Wey

28. **And brought his head in a charger,**
... on a platter — ASV
... on a dish — ABUV
and gave it to the damsel:
... the girl — Gspd

and the damsel gave it to her mother.
and the girl ... — Gspd

29. **And when his disciples heard of it,**
When John's disciples heard the news — NEB
When his disciples heard what had happened — Phi
they came and took up his corpse,
... took his body — RSV
... removed the body — Nor
and laid it in a tomb.
... a grave — Beck
and put it in a tomb — Gspd

30. **And the apostles gathered themselves together unto Jesus,**
Now the apostles gathered to meet Jesus — Mof
The apostles returned to Jesus — RSV
... now rejoined Jesus — NEB
and told him
and they reported to him — ABUV
all things, both what they had done, and what they had taught.
... whatever they did, and whatever they taught — ABUV
all that they had done and taught — RSV
every detail of what ... — Phi
a full report of their doings and their teaching — Rieu

31. **And he said unto them,**
Then He said to them — Wey
Come ye yourselves apart into a desert place,
Come away by yourselves to a lonely place — RSV
... to some quiet place — Gspd
... to the solitude of the open country — Rieu
and rest a while:
and get a little rest — Mof
where you can rest quietly — NEB
for there were many coming and going,
For people were coming and going in large numbers — Gspd
for there were people coming and going incessantly — Phi
and they had no leisure so much as to eat.
and they had no opportunity even to eat — ABUV
and they had no time even for meals — Gspd

32. **And they departed into a desert place by ship privately.**

So they went away privately in the boat
to a lonely spot — Mof
So they set off by themselves in their
boat for a secluded place — Gspd
So they went off in their boat to a deserted spot where they could be alone
— Rieu

33. **And the people saw them departing,**
But many saw them leave — NEB
and many knew him,
and many knew them — ASV
and knew of it — Gspd
and recognized them — NEB
recognized Him — Nor
and ran afoot thither out of all cities,
and they ran together there on foot
from all the cities — ASV
and they ran there on foot . . . towns —
RSV
and hurried around by land from all
the neighboring towns — Gspd
and ran around the lake from all the
towns — Wms
**and outwent them, and came together
unto him.**[13]
and got there ahead of them — RSV
and arrived first — NEB

34. **And Jesus, when he came out,**
As he landed — RSV
When he came ashore — NEB
So when Jesus disembarked — Mof
saw much people,
he saw a great multitude — ABUV
. . . a great throng — RSV
. . . a large crowd — Phi
**and was moved with compassion
toward them,**
and he had compassion on them — ASV
and his heart went out to them — NEB
. . . was touched at the sight of them —
Gspd
. . . with pity for them — Phi
**because they were as sheep not having
a shepherd:**
. . . like sheep without a shepherd —
Wey
**and he began to teach them many
things.**
he proceeded to teach them at length
— Mof
and he had much to teach them — NEB

35. **And when the day was now far spent,**
As the day wore on — Phi
As the hour grew late — Ber
his disciples came unto him, and said,
. . . approached him and said — NEB

This is a desert place,
This is a lonely place — RSV
We are in a desolate spot — Rieu
We are right in the wilds here — Phi
and now the time is far passed:
and the day is now far spent — ASV
and it is getting late — Gspd

36. **Send them away,**
Dismiss them — ABUV
Let them go now — Phi
**that they may go into the country
round about, and into the villages,**
, to the farms and villages around —
Gspd
and buy themselves bread:
. . . something to eat — ABUV
and get some food for themselves —
Bas
for they have nothing to eat.[14]

37. **He answered and said unto them,**
But he answered them — RSV
He replied — Mof
Give ye them to eat.
You give them something to eat — RSV
It is for you to give them something
to eat — TCNT
You feed them! — Tay
And they say unto him,
They replied — NEB
**Shall we go and buy two hundred pen-
nyworth of bread,**
. . . two hundred shillings' worth of
bread — ASV
. . . two hundred denarii worth of bread
— RSV
Are we to go and buy fifty dollars'
worth of bread — Mon
and give them to eat?
and give it to them to eat — RSV
to give them a meal — NEB
and feed them — Ber

38. **He saith unto them,**
He asked them — Ber
How many loaves have ye?
How many loaves do you have on hand
— Nor
go and see.
Go and have a look — Phi
And when they knew, they say,

---

[13]The words "and came together unto him"
are now recognized as not adequately supported by original manuscripts.

[14]Now recognized as not adequately supported
by original manuscripts.

When they had found out, they said —
Mon

Five, and two fishes.
Five, and two fish — Gspd

39. **And he commanded them to make all
sit down**
And he made them all be seated —
Bas
Then he commanded them all to sit
down — RSV
And he commanded them all to recline
— NASB

by companies upon the green grass.
in groups on the green grass — NEB
in companies . . . — Wey
in rows . . . — Wms
in parties on the fresh grass — Gspd

40. **And they sat down in ranks,**
So they sat down in groups — RSV
And they threw themselves down . . .
— Gspd
and they settled down in squares —
Rieu

by hundreds, and by fifties.
a hundred or fifty to each — Rieu
a hundred rows of fifty each — NEB

41. **And when he had taken the five loaves
and the two fishes,**
Then he took the five loaves and the
two fish — Gspd

he looked up to heaven,
and looking up toward heaven — NASB

and blessed, and brake the loaves,
and blessed and broke . . . — ABUV
said the blessing, broke the loaves —
NEB
and blessed the loaves and broke them
in pieces — Wms

**and gave them to his disciples to set
before them:**
and kept giving to the disciples . . . —
ABUV
and gave them to the disciples to distribute — NEB

**and the two fishes divided he among
them all.**
and he divided the two fish . . . — RSV

42. **And they did all eat, and were filled.**
And they all ate, and were filled — ASV
. . . and were satisfied — ABUV
They all ate to their hearts' content —
NEB

43. **And they took up twelve baskets full
of the fragments,**
And they took up fragments enough to
fill twelve baskets — Alf

and twelve great basketfuls of scraps
were picked up — NEB

and of the fishes.
and of the fish — RSV
with what was left of the fish — NEB

44. **And they that did eat of the loaves**
And they who ate the loaves — ABUV

were about five thousand men.
were five . . . — ASV
numbered . . . — NEB

45. **And straightway he constrained his disciples to get into the ship,**
. . . to enter into the boat — ASV
As soon as it was over he made his disciples embark — NEB

**and to go to the other side before unto
Bethsaida,**
and go before him to the other side, to
Bethsaida — RSV
and cross to Bethsaida ahead of him —
NEB
and cross ahead of Him toward Bethsaida — Wms

while he sent away the people.
while he himself was dismissing the
multitude — ABUV
while he dismissed the crowd — RSV
leaving Him behind to dismiss . . . —
Wey

46. **And when he had sent them away,**
And after he had taken leave of them
— ASV
And after bidding them farewell —
NASB

he departed into a mountain to pray.
he went up on the mountain to pray —
Gspd
he went into the hills to pray — RSV

47. **And when even was come,**
And when evening came — ABUV
When it grew late — Phi
Twilight had already come — Knox

the ship was in the midst of the sea,
the boat was out on the sea — RSV
and the boat was already well out on
the water — NEB
the boat was half way across the Lake
— Wey

and he alone on the land.
and he was alone . . . — ABUV
. . . on shore — Gspd

48. **And he saw them toiling in rowing;**
And he saw that they were distressed
. . . — RSV
. . . that they were straining at the oars
— Gspd

for the wind was contrary unto them;
... was against them — RSV
Due to a contrary wind — Nor

and about the fourth watch of the night
Somewhere between three and six in the morning — NEB
and toward morning — Gspd
And in the small hours — Phi

he cometh unto them,
he came to them — Knox
He came towards them — Wey
he went out to them — Gspd
He started toward them — Wms

walking upon the sea,
walking on the sea — ASV
walking on the waters of the lake — Phi

and would have passed by them.
and he was purposing to pass by them — Alf
and made as if to pass them by — Knox

49. **But when they saw him walking upon the sea,**
... on the water — Phi

they supposed it had been a spirit,
... an apparition — Alf
they thought it was a ghost — RSV

and cried out:
and cried aloud — Rieu
and cried out with fear — Nor

50. **For they all saw him, and were troubled.**
... and were terrified — Gspd
for all had seen him, and were full of dismay — Knox

And immediately he talked with them,
But straightway ... — ABUV
But immediately he spoke to them — RSV

and saith unto them, Be of good cheer:
and said to them, Take courage — NASB
and said, All is well! — Rieu
he said to them, Take heart — Bas

it is I; be not afraid.
it is I, have no fear — Mof
it is I; do not be alarmed — Wey

51. **And he went up unto them into the ship;**
And he got into the boat with them — RSV
And he climbed aboard the boat with them — Phi

and the wind ceased:
and the wind dropped — NEB
... stopped — NASB
And the wind fell — Gspd

and they were sore amazed in themselves beyond measure,
And they were greatly amazed in themselves — ABUV
And they were utterly astounded — RSV
But they were scared out of their wits — Phi

and wondered.[15]

52. **For they considered not the miracle of the loaves:**
for they understood not concerning the loaves — ASV
for they had not understood the incident of the loaves — NEB
for they had not gained any insight from the incident of the loaves — NASB

for their heart was hardened.
but their hearts were hardened — RSV
their minds were closed — NEB
but their minds were blinded — Gspd
Even that miracle had not opened their eyes to see who he was — Phi

53. **And when they had passed over,**
... crossed over — ASV
So they finished the crossing — NEB
When they had crossed the lake — Nor

they came into the land of Gennesaret,
they came to land at Gennesaret — Mof

and drew to the shore.
and moored to the shore — ASV
and anchored there — ABUV
and tied up there — Phi

54. **And when they were come out of the ship,**
And when they got out of the boat — RSV
When they came ashore — NEB
And when they had disembarked — Mof

straightway they knew him,
immediately the people recognized him — RSV

55. **And ran through that whole region round about,**
and ran about the whole neighborhood — RSV
and they hurried all over the countryside — Gspd
And they scoured the whole district — Wey

---

[15]Now recognized as not adequately supported by original manuscripts.

and began to carry about in beds those
    that were sick,
... on beds those who were sick —
    ABUV
... to bring sick people on their pal-
    lets — RSV
and brought the sick on stretchers —
    NEB
where they heard he was.
where he was reported to be — NEB

56. And whithersoever he entered,
And wherever ... — ABUV
Wherever he went — NEB
into villages, or cities, or country,
to farmsteads, villages, or towns—NEB
they laid the sick in the streets,

... in the market-places — ASV
they would lay their invalids in the
    marketplace — Mof
they laid down their sick right in the
    roadway — Phi
**and besought him that they might
    touch if it were but the border of his
    garment:**
... that they might touch even the
    fringe ... — RSV
begging him to let them touch even the
    tassel of his robe — Mof
**and as many as touched him were
    made whole.**
... it were made well — RSV
and all who touched it were cured —
    Gspd

CHAPTER 7

**1. Then came together unto him the
    Pharisees,**
And now Jesus was approached by the
    Pharisees — Phi
One day the Pharisees came to him in
    a body — Mon
**and certain of the scribes, which came
    from Jerusalem.**
with some doctors of the law who had
    come ... — NEB
**2. And when they saw some of his dis-
    ciples eat bread**
and had seen that some of his disciples
    ate their bread — ASV
and noticed that ... were eating their
    food — NEB
**with defiled, that is to say, with un-
    washen, hands,**
with hands defiled, that is, unwashed —
    RSV
with "common" hands — meaning that
    they had not gone through a cere-
    monial washing — Phi
they found fault.[16]

3. For the Pharisees, and all the Jews,
For the Pharisees and the Jews in gen-
    eral — NEB
The Pharisees, and indeed all the Jews
    — Phi
except they wash their hands oft,
... diligently — ASV
except they carefully wash their hands
    — Alf
till they wash their hands up to the
    wrist — Mof
eat not,

never eat — NEB
decline to eat — Mof
holding the tradition of the elders.
observing ... — RSV
observe the rules handed down from
    their ancestors — Gspd
in obedience to an old-established tra-
    dition — NEB

4. And when they come from the market,
When they brought something from
    the market — Nor
except they wash, they eat not.
they would not eat it without first hav-
    ing purified it by sprinkling — Nor
And many other things there be,
And there are many other things —
    ABUV
and they have a good many other cus-
    toms — Wey
which they have received to hold,
which they have inherited and hold to
    — TCNT
which they hold to by tradition—Knox
**as the washing of cups, and pots,
    brasen vessels, and of tables.**
the washing of cups and pots and ves-
    sels of bronze — RSV
washing of cups and jugs and copper
    bowls — NEB

**5. Then the Pharisees and scribes asked
    him,**
... put this question to him — Mof
Why walk not thy disciples

---

[16]Now recognized as not adequately supported
by original manuscripts.

Why do not thy disciples walk — ABUV
Why do your disciples not live — RSV
according to the tradition of the elders,
. . . handed down by the forefathers to
be observed — Amp
but eat bread with unwashen hands?
but eat bread with defiled hands — ASV
but eat their food without purifying
their hands — Gspd

6. **He answered and said unto them,**
Well hath Esaias prophesied of you
hypocrites,
Rightly did Isaiah prophesy . . . — Wey
You hypocrites, Isaiah described you
beautifully — Phi
as it is written,
when he wrote — Phi
as it stands written — Amp
This people honoureth me with their
lips,
This people pays me lip-service — NEB
but their heart is far from me.
but their hearts are estranged from Me
— Ber

7. **Howbeit in vain do they worship me,**
their worship of me is in vain — NEB
. . . is but an empty show — Wms
teaching for doctrines the command-
ments of men.
Teaching as their doctrines the precepts
of men — ASV
they make doctrines of the precepts of
men — Rieu

8. **For laying aside the commandment of**
God,
Neglecting . . . — NASB
You give up what God has commanded
— Wms
ye hold the tradition of men,
you cling to what men hand down —
— Wms
as the washing of pots and cups: and
many other such like things ye do.[17]

9. **And he said unto them,**
He also said to them — NEB
Full well ye reject the commandment
of God,
You have a fine way of rejecting . . .
— RSV
How well you set aside . . . — NEB
that ye may keep your own tradition.
in order to maintain your tradition! —
NEB
. . . preserve your own tradition! —
Rieu

10. **For Moses said, Honour thy father**
and thy mother;
and, Whoso curseth father or mother,
and, He that speaketh evil of . . . — ASV
and again, He who reviles . . . — Wey
let him die the death:
let him surely die — ABUV
let him be executed — Ber

11. **But ye say,**
But you hold that — NEB
But you have a different ruling — Rieu
If a man shall say to his father or
mother,
If a man tell his father or his mother
— RSV
It is Corban, that is to say, a gift,
It is Corban, that is, a gift of God —
ABUV
I am making Korban (that is a temple-
offering)— Rieu
by whatsoever thou mightest be profit-
ed by me;
What you would have gained from me
— RSV
of all the support you might have got
from me — Rieu
he shall be free.
he is exempt — Ber

12. **And ye suffer him no more to do ought**
then you no longer permit him to do
anything — RSV
you forbid him to do anything more
— Rieu
for his father or his mother;

13. **Making the word of God of none ef-**
fect
making void the word of God — ASV
thus nullifying God's precept — Wey
so making the Word of God invalid
— Phi
and so you break the law of God —
Tay
through your tradition, which ye have
delivered:
by your tradition, which ye handed
down — ABUV
by your own tradition, handed down
among you — NEB
in order to protect your man-made
tradition — Tay
and many such like things do ye.
And many such things ye do — ABUV

---

[17]The latter half of this verse is now recognized as not adequately supported by original
manuscripts.

You have many such practices — Gspd
And many other things that you do are just like that — NEB

14. And when he had called all the people unto him,
And summoning the multitude again — NASB
Then he called the crowd close to him again — Phi
he said unto them,
and addressed them — Nor
Hearken unto me every one of you, and understand:
Hear me, all of you . . . — RSV
Listen to me now, . . ., and understand this — Phi

15. There is nothing from without a man,
There is nothing outside a man — RSV
. . . external to a man — Rieu
that entering into him can defile him:
which by going into him . . . — RSV
which can enter into him and make him 'common' — Phi
but the things which come out of him,
It is what comes out of a man — Gspd
those are they that defile the man.
that pollutes him — Gspd

16. If any man have ears to hear, let him hear.[18]

17. And when he was entered into the house from the people,
Now when he went indoors away from the crowd — Mof
When he had left the people and gone indoors — NEB
his disciples asked him concerning the parable.
. . . questioned him about the parable — NEB
. . . asked him what he meant by his figure — Gspd

18. And he saith unto them,
And He answered them — Wms
Are ye so without understanding also?
Are ye too so without understanding — ABUV
Are you as dull as the rest — NEB
Do ye not perceive,
do you not see — Wey
that whatsoever thing from without entereth into the man,
that nothing that goes into a man from the outside — Gspd
it cannot defile him;
cannot make him unclean — Wey
cannot pollute him — Gspd

19. Because it entereth not into his heart,
because it does not reach . . . — Wms
but into the belly,
. . . his stomach — Wey
and goeth out into the draught,
and goes out into the drain — ABUV
and passes out of the body altogether — Phi
purging all meats?
so that all food is clean enough — Phi
This he said, making all meats clean — ASV
(thus he declared all foods clean) — RSV
Thus He was making and declaring all foods (ceremonially) clean — Amp

20. And he said,
He went on to say — Gspd
That which cometh out of the man,
It is what comes out of a man — Wey
that defileth the man.
that makes him unclean — Wey
that pollutes him — Gspd

21. For from within, out of the heart of men,
For from inside, out of a man's heart — NEB
proceed evil thoughts, adulteries, fornications, murders,
come . . ., fornication, theft, murder[19] — RSV
the designs of evil come: sexual vice, stealing . . . — Mof

22. Thefts, covetousness, wickedness, deceit, lasciviousness,
adultery, coveting, . . ., licentiousness — RSV
. . . lust, malice, deceit, sensuality — Mof
. . . self-seeking, malice, double-dealing, licentiousness — Rieu
an evil eye, blasphemy, pride, foolishness:
jealousy, slander, arrogance, and folly — Rieu
envying, . . ., recklessness — Mof

23. All these evil things come from within,
. . . proceed from within — ASV
all these evils issue . . . — Mof

---

[18]Now recognized as not adequately supported by original manuscripts.
[19]Manuscripts vary somewhat in word order here.

All these wicked things come from the
inside — Ber
and defile the man.
and make a man unclean — Wey
and defile the person — Ber

24. **And from thence he arose,**
Then he left that place — NEB
**and went into the borders of Tyre and
Sidon,**
and departed . . . of Tyre[20] — Alf
and entered into an house,
And he went into a certain house —
Gspd
and would have no man know it:
and wanted no one to know where he
was — Phi
and he would have liked to remain unrecognized — NEB
but he could not be hid.
but He could not escape observation —
Wey
But it proved impossible to remain hidden — Phi

25. **For a certain woman,**
But straightway a woman — ASV
Almost at once a woman — NEB
**whose young daughter had an unclean
spirit,**
whose little daughter was possessed by
a foul spirit — Gspd
heard of him,
heard about him — Gspd
and came and fell at his feet:
. . . and cast herself . . . — Rieu
arrived and prostrated herself before
him — Phi

26. **The woman was a Greek,**
Now the woman was a Gentile — NASB
She was a heathen who spoke Greek —
Wms
a Syrophenician by nation;
. . . by race — ASV
and had been born in Syro-Phenicia —
Wms
and she besought him
And she begged him — RSV
She asked him repeatedly — Rieu
**that he would cast forth the devil out
of her daughter.**
to cast the demon . . . — Rieu

27. **But Jesus said unto her,**
And he said to her — ABUV
And He was saying to her — NASB
Let the children first be filled:
. . . be satisfied — ABUV

You must let the children have all they
want first — Phi
**for it is not meet to take the children's
bread,**
for it is not right . . . — Gspd
it is not fair . . . — NEB
and to cast it unto the dogs.
and to throw it to the little dogs — Ber
and throw it to the house-dogs — Rieu

28. **And she answered and said unto him,**
But . . . to him — ASV
She took this up and said — Rieu
Yes, Lord:
True, Sir — Wey
yet the dogs under the table
but even . . . — Wey
yet the house-dogs . . . — Rieu
eat of the children's crumbs.
do pick up . . . — Mof
eat what the children leave — Gspd

29. **And he said unto her,**
He replied — Wey
For this saying go thy way;
Thanks to that saying you may go in
peace — Rieu
the devil is gone out of thy daughter.
the demon has . . . — ABUV
The evil spirit has left your daughter —
Phi

30. **And when she was come to her house,**
So she went home — Mof
And when she returned home — NEB
she found the devil gone out,
she found it was so; the demon had
gone — Nor
and her daughter laid upon the bed.
and the daughter was resting on her
bed — Nor

31. **And again, departing from the coasts
of Tyre and Sidon,**
And again he set out from the borders
of Tyre, and came through Sidon —
ASV
On his return journey from Tyrian territory he went by way of Sidon —
NEB
he came unto the sea of Galilee,
**through the midst of the coasts of
Decapolis.**
through the region of the . . . — RSV
crossing the district of the Ten Towns
— Gspd

---

[20]Some manuscripts lack the reference to
Sidon.

32. And they bring unto him one that was deaf,

And they brought to him a man who . . . — Gspd

and had an impediment in his speech;

and hardly able to speak — Gspd

and unable to speak intelligibly — Phi

who stammered — Mof

and they beseech him to put his hand upon him.

and they implored him to put his hand upon him — Phi

33. And he took him aside from the multitude,

and he took him aside privately — ASV

He took the man away from the crowd by himself — Rieu

and put his fingers into his ears,

. . . in the man's ears — Gspd

and he spit, and touched his tongue;

and touched his tongue with saliva — Ber

34. And looking up to heaven, he sighed,

Then, looking up toward heaven, He sighed — Ber

Then, looking up to Heaven, he gave a deep sigh — Phi

and saith unto him,

and said to him — RSV

Ephphatha, that is, Be opened.

Ephphatha! which means Be opened — TCNT

35. And straightway[21] his ears were opened,

and the string of his tongue was loosed,

and the bond . . . — ASV

and his tongue was released — Gspd

. . . was untied — Wms

the impediment to his speech was removed — Rieu

and he spake plain.

and he began to talk plainly — TCNT

36. And he charged them that they should tell no man:

Jesus forbade them to tell anyone — NEB

but the more he charged them,

. . . forbade them — Mof

. . . insisted — TCNT

so much the more a great deal they published it;

the more abundantly they published it — ABUV

. . . they spread the news far and wide — Gspd

37. And were beyond measure astonished, saying,

People were absolutely amazed, and kept saying — Phi

He hath done all things well:

How perfectly he has done everything! — Rieu

How wonderfully . . .! — Phi

Everything He does is wonderful—Tay

he maketh both the deaf to hear, and the dumb to speak.

he maketh even . . . — ASV

He actually makes the deaf hear and the dumb speak — Mof

He even corrects deafness and stammering! — Tay

CHAPTER 8

1. In those days the multitude being very great,

. . . when there was again a great multitude — ASV

. . . when again a great crowd had gathered — RSV

During these days there was once more a great concourse of people — Rieu

and having nothing to eat,

and they had . . . — ASV

Jesus called his disciples unto him,

he called unto him his disciples — ASV

and saith unto them,

and said to them — Gspd

2. I have compassion on the multitude,

I feel sorry for all these people — NEB

I am deeply moved concerning the people — Ber

My heart goes out to this crowd — Phi

because they have now been with me three days,

because they continue with me now . . . — ASV

and have nothing to eat:

and they have no food left — Phi

3. And if I send them away fasting to their own houses,

. . . to their home — ASV

And if I send them home hungry — Gspd

---

[21]Now recognized as not adequately supported by original manuscripts.

they will faint by the way:
. . . in the way — ABUV
they will collapse on the way — Phi
for divers of them came from far.
and some of them have come a long
distance — TCNT
for . . . are a long way from home —
Wms

4. And his disciples answered him,
His disciples replied — Mof
**From whence can a man satisfy these
men with bread**
Whence shall one be able to fill these
men . . . — ASV
How can one feed these men . . . —
RSV
Where could anyone find the food to
feed them — Phi
here in the wilderness?
in this remote place — Wey
in this lonely place — NEB

**5. And he asked them,
How many loaves have ye?**
How many loaves have you — Gspd
And they said, Seven.
and they answered, Seven — NEB

**6. And he commanded the people to sit
down on the ground:**
So he ordered the crowd to recline . . .
— Mof
**and he took the seven loaves,
and gave thanks, and brake,**
said a blessing, and broke them into
pieces — Rieu
**and gave to his disciples
to set before them;**
to distribute among the crowd — Nor
**and they did set them before the peo-
ple.**
and they passed them to the people —
Gspd
and they served it out . . . — NEB

7. And they had a few small fishes:
They had also a few small fish — Wey
**and he blessed,
and commanded to set them also before them.**
and told the disciples to pass them also
to the people — Gspd

8. So they did eat, and were filled:
And they ate, and were satisfied—ABUV
They all ate to their hearts' content —
NEB
**and they took up of the broken meat
that was left seven baskets.**

. . . of the broken pieces left over
seven baskets full — RSV
and they picked up the leftovers, seven
goodsized baskets full — Ber

**9. And they that had eaten were about
four thousand:**
The people numbered about . . . — NEB
and he sent them away.
And he dismissed them — ABUV
Jesus sent them home — Phi

**10. And straightway he entered into a
ship**
and immediately he got into . . . — RSV
**with his disciples,
and came into the parts of Dalmanu-
tha.**
. . . the district . . . — Mon

11. And the Pharisees came forth,
Then the Pharisees came out — NEB
The Pharisees now sallied out — Rieu
and began to question with him,
and engaged him in discussion — NEB
and began to dispute with him — Rieu
seeking of him a sign from heaven,
asking Him for . . . — Wey
tempting him.
trying him — ASV
by way of testing him — Mon
Just to put Him to a test — Nor

**12. And he sighed deeply in his spirit, and
saith,**
Deeply sighing in His very soul, He
said — Ber
He sighed deeply to himself and said
— NEB
**Why doth this generation seek after a
sign?**
What makes this generation want a sign
— Phi
Why do the men of to-day ask for a
sign — Wey
verily I say unto you,
I tell you truly — Mof
I assure you that — Nor
**There shall be no sign be given unto
this generation.**
no sign shall be given to . . . — RSV

13. And he left them,
Then he left them — Mon
With that . . . — Rieu
and entering into the ship again
he embarked again — ABUV
went on board again — Wey
departed to the other side.
. . . the opposite shore — Alf
and crossed to the other side — Gspd

14. **Now the disciples had forgotten to take bread,**
    Now they had forgotten to bring bread — RSV
    neither had they in the ship with them more than one loaf.
    and had only one loaf with them in the boat — Mof

15. **And he charged them, saying,**
    Jesus spoke seriously to them — Phi
    He began to warn them — NEB
    Take heed, beware of the leaven of the Pharisees,
    Look out! Avoid . . . — Nor
    Keep your eyes open! Be on your guard against the 'yeast' of the Pharisees — Phi
    and of the leaven of Herod.
    and the 'yeast' of Herod! — Phi

16. **And they reasoned among themselves, saying,**
    . . . one with another, saying — ASV
    And they discussed it with one another, saying — RSV
    And this sent them into earnest consultation among themselves — Phi
    It is because we have no bread.
    because they had brought no bread — Phi

17. **And when Jesus knew it,**
    And Jesus perceiving it — ASV
    And he noticed it — Gspd
    Knowing what was in their minds — NEB
    he saith unto them,
    he asked them — NEB
    Why reason ye, because ye have no bread?
    What makes you discuss the fact that you did not take bread along — Nor
    Why all this discussion about bringing no bread — Phi
    perceive ye not yet, neither understand?
    Do you not yet see nor understand — Gspd
    Have you no inkling yet? Do you still not understand — NEB
    Don't you understand or grasp what I say even yet — Phi
    have ye your heart yet hardened?
    Are your faculties benumbed — Rieu
    Are you so dull of mind — Wey
    Are your minds closed — NEB

18. **Having eyes, see ye not?**
    You have eyes; can't you see — Nor
    and having ears, hear ye not?
    You have ears; can't you hear — Nor
    and do ye not remember?
    And have you no memory — Nor

19. **When I brake the five loaves among five thousand,**
    When I broke . . . the five thousand — ABUV
    When I broke up . . . for the 5000 men — Wey
    how many baskets full of fragments took ye up?
    how many basketfuls of scraps did you pick up — NEB
    They say unto him, Twelve.
    They said to him, Twelve — Gspd

20. **And when the seven among four thousand,**
    And when the seven for the 4000 — Wey
    how many baskets full of fragments took ye up?
    how many basketfuls of broken pieces . . . — ASV
    And they said, Seven.

21. **And he said unto them,**
    Then He asked — Nor
    How is it that ye do not understand?
    Do ye not yet understand — ASV
    And does that still mean nothing to you — Phi

22. **And he cometh to Bethsaida;**
    And they came to . . . — Gspd
    and they bring a blind man unto him,
    and the people brought him a blind man — Rieu
    and besought him to touch him.
    and they entreated Him to touch him — Wey

23. **And he took the blind man by the hand,**
    And he took hold of . . . — ASV
    So He took the blind man . . . — Nor
    and led him out of the town;
    and brought him out of the village — ASV
    and led him outside the village — Phi
    and when he had spit on his eyes,
    then, after spitting . . . — Mof
    Then he moistened his eyes with saliva — Phi
    and put his hands upon him,
    he laid his hands on him — Mof
    he asked him if he saw ought.

and asked whether he could see anything — NEB

and asked him, Do you see anything
— Gspd

he asked: Can you distinguish anything — Rieu

24. And he looked up, and said,

The man's sight began to come back,
and he said — NEB

I see men as trees, walking.

I see men; for I behold them as trees,
walking — ASV

I see the people, for they look to me
like trees, only they are moving
about — Gspd

I can see people. They look like trees
— only they are walking about —
Phi

**25. After that he put his hands again upon
his eyes,**

Then Jesus put his hands on his eyes
once more — Phi

and made him look up:

and he looked intently — RSV

and the man stared in front of him —
Mof

and his sight came into focus — Phi

and the man saw clearly — Rieu

and he was restored,

and now he was cured — NEB

This time his sight was restored — Nor

and saw every man clearly.

and saw all things . . . — ASV

and saw everything sharp and clear —
Phi

and he could now distinguish even distant objects well — Rieu

**26. And he sent him away to his house,
saying,**

So He sent him home, and added —
Wey

**Neither go into the town, nor tell it
to any in the town.**[22]

Do not even enter into the village —
ASV

27. And Jesus went out, and his disciples,

Then Jesus and his disciples went away
— Gspd

And Jesus went on with his disciples —
RSV

into the towns of Caesarea Philippi;

into the villages . . . — ASV

and by the way he asked his disciples,

and on the way . . . — ASV

On the way there He was asking His
disciples — Wms

saying unto them, Whom do men say
that I am?

Who do people say . . . — Wey

Who are men saying . . . — Phi

**28. And they answered, John the Baptist:
but some say, Elias;**

and others, Elijah — ASV

and others, One of the prophets.

29. And he saith unto them,

And he asked them — Gspd

But whom say ye that I am?

But who say . . . — ASV

But you, who do you say . . . — Nor

But what about you — who do you say
that I am — Phi

**And Peter answereth and saith unto
him,**

Peter replied — NEB

It was Peter who answered him — Rieu

Thou art the Christ.

You are the Messiah — NEB

30. And he charged them

And Jesus admonished them — Rieu

And he warned them — Gspd

Then he gave them strict orders — NEB

that they should tell no man of him.

. . . no one concerning him — ABUV

that they must not tell this about Him
to anyone — Nor

31. And he began to teach them,

And now for the first time He told
them — Wey

**that the Son of man must suffer many
things,**

. . . must go through much suffering —
Gspd

. . . must of necessity suffer many things
— Amp

and be rejected of the elders,

be repudiated by the Elders — Rieu

and be disowned by the elders — Wms

and of the chief priests, and scribes,

and the chief priests, and the scribes —
ASV

**and be killed, and after three days rise
again.**

and be put to death, and on the third
day rise to life — Wey

32. And he spake that saying openly.

And he spoke the . . . — ABUV

he spoke of this quite freely — Mof

He dwelt on this pronouncement in the
plainest terms — Rieu

---

[22]The last clause is now recognized as not
adequately supported by original manuscripts.

And without any reserve He was telling
them this fact — Wms
And Peter took him,
whereupon . . . aside — Wey
At this . . . by the arm — NEB
and began to rebuke him.
. . . to remonstrate with him — Rieu
. . . to reprove him for it — Gspd

33. **But when he had turned about and
looked on his disciples,**
but he turned on him and noticing his
disciples — Mof
But Jesus swung round, and facing his
disciples — Rieu
he rebuked Peter, saying,
Get thee behind me, Satan:
Get behind me, Satan! — Rieu
Out of my way, Satan! — Phi
Away with you, Satan — NEB
Get out of my sight, you Satan! —
Gspd
**for thou savourest not the things that
be of God,**
for thou mindest not the things of God
— ASV
for thou thinkest not . . . — ABUV
for your thoughts are not God's
thoughts — Wey
Your outlook is not God's — Mof
you are not looking at things from
God's point of view — Phi
but the things that be of men.
but the things of men — ASV
but men's — Wey
but man's — Mof
but from man's — Phi

34. **And when he had called the people
unto him**
Then, summoning the crowd — Ber
with his disciples also,
with his disciples — ASV
as well as his disciples — NEB
he said unto them,
Whosoever will come after me,
If any man would come after me —
ASV
If any one wishes to . . . — ABUV
If anyone wants to be my disciple —
Wms
. . . to follow in my footsteps — Phi
let him deny himself,
let him renounce self — Wey
he must say 'No' to self — Wms
he must give up all right to himself —
Phi
and take up his cross,

put the cross on his shoulders — Wms
and follow me.
and come with me — NEB
and so be my follower — Wey
and keep on following me — Wms

35. **For whosoever will save his life shall
lose it;**
For whoever wants to preserve his own
life will lose it — Gspd
Whoever cares for his own safety is
lost — NEB
but whosoever shall lose his life
and whoever loses his life — Gspd
for my sake and the gospel's,
for me and for the good news — Gspd
the same shall save it.
will save it — RSV
will preserve it — Gspd

36. **For what shall it profit a man,**
For what does it . . . — ABUV
For what good does it do a man —
Gspd
How is a man the better for it — Knox
if he shall gain the whole world,
and lose his own soul?
and forfeit his life — ASV
and yet part with . . . — Gspd

37. **Or what shall a man give in exchange
for his soul?**
For what can a man give in return for
his life — RSV
What could a man offer as an equivalent for his soul — Mof
For what could a man give to buy back
his life — Wey
or what can a man give that is as
precious as . . . Rieu

38. **Whosoever therefore shall be ashamed
of me**
For whoever is . . . — ABUV
If anyone is ashamed of acknowledging me — Knox
and of my words
and of my teachings — Wey
**in this adulterous and sinful genera-
tion;**
in this wicked and godless age — NEB
in this apostate and sinful age — Wey
**of him also shall the Son of man be
ashamed,**
the Son of man also shall be ashamed
of him — ASV
**when he cometh in the glory of his
Father**
when he comes back in his Father's
glory — Gspd

... splendor — Wms
with the holy angels.
and of the holy angels — NEB

with the holy angels around him — Phi

CHAPTER 9

1. And he said unto them,
He went on to say — Wey
Verily I say unto you,
Truly, I say to you — RSV
I solemnly say to you — Wms
In all truth I tell you — Rieu
That there be some of them that stand here,
There are some of those standing here — ABUV
some of you who stand here — Gspd
which shall not taste of death,
who shall in no wise ... — ASV
will certainly live — Gspd
till they have seen the kingdom of God
until they see ... — ABUV
to see the reign of God — Gspd
come with power.
after it has come ... — NASB
present in all its power — Knox

2. And after six days
Six days later — NEB
Jesus taketh with him Peter, and James, and John,
Jesus took with him Peter and James and John — RSV
Jesus selected Peter, James and John — Rieu
and leadeth them up into an high mountain
and led them up a ... — RSV
apart by themselves:
where they were alone — NEB
and he was transfigured before them.
and in their presence he was transfigured — NEB
... His appearance underwent a change — Wey
His whole appearance changed before their eyes — Phi

3. And his raiment became shining,
and his garments became glistering — ASV
... glistening — RSV
his clothes became dazzling white — NEB
exceeding white as snow;
exceeding white — ASV
intensely white — RSV
as white as white could be — Wms

so as no fuller on earth can white them.
whiter than any earthly bleaching could make them — Phi

4. And there appeared unto them Elias with Moses:
And Elijah appeared to them, accompanied by Moses — Gspd
They saw Elijah appear, and Moses with him — NEB
and they were talking with Jesus.
... to Jesus — RSV
and stood there in conversation with Jesus — Phi

5. And Peter answered and said to Jesus,
Whereupon Peter said to Jesus — Rieu
Peter burst out to Jesus — Phi
Master, it is good for us to be here:
Rabbi ... — ASV
Master, it is well that we are here — RSV
Master, how good it is that we are here! — Gspd
Master, it is wonderful for us to be here! — Phi
Teacher, this is wonderful! — Tay
and let us make three tabernacles;
... booths — ABUV
let us put up three tents — Mof
Shall we make three shelters — NEB
one for thee, and one for Moses, and one for Elias.
one for you and one for Moses and one for Elijah — Gspd

6. For he wist not what to say;
For he knew not what to answer — ASV
He really did not know what to say — Phi
for they were sore afraid.
for they became ... — ASV
they were so frightened — Gspd
for they were overcome with awe — Rieu
they were all scared stiff — Tay

7. And there was a cloud that overshadowed them:
And there came a cloud overshadowing them — ASV

And a cloud came and overshadowed them — Gspd

And a cloud formed, over-shadowing them — Knox

Then a cloud appeared, casting its shadow over them — NEB

and a voice came out of the cloud, saying,

This is my beloved Son:

This is my Son, the Beloved — Wey

... my Beloved — Gspd

This is My dearly-loved Son — Phi

hear him.

hear ye him — ASV

listen to him — RSV

8. And suddenly, when they had looked round about,

And suddenly looking around — RSV

And now suddenly, when they looked around — NEB

they saw no man any more,

they saw no one there — Mof

they saw that there was now no one with them — Gspd

save Jesus only with themselves.

but Jesus alone ... — NEB

but Jesus alone — Gspd

9. And as they came down from the mountain,

And as they were coming down ... — ASV

On their way down the mountain — NEB

he charged them that they should tell no man

he forbade them to tell anyone — Mof

he cautioned them to let no one know — Gspd

he warned them not to tell anybody — Phi

what things they had seen,

what they had seen — RSV

till the Son of man were risen from the dead.

until the Son of Man should rise ... — Gspd

... had risen ... — NEB

10. And they kept that saying with themselves,

This order they obeyed — Mof

They seized upon those words — NEB

And they held that caution fast in their minds — Wms

So they kept the matter to themselves — RSV

questioning one with another

questioning — RSV

discussing with one another — NASB

debating with themselves — Mof

what the rising from the dead should mean.

what is the rising from the dead — ABUV

what the rising from the dead meant — RSV

what the "rising from the dead" could mean — Phi

11. And they asked him, saying,

And they put a question to him — NEB

Why say the scribes that Elias must first come?

Why do the scribes say that first Elijah must come — RSV

... that Elijah has to come first—Gspd

... that Elijah must come before Christ — Phi

12. And he answered and told them,

And he said to them — ABUV

He replied — NEB

Elias verily cometh first, and restoreth all things;

Elijah indeed comes first, and restores ... — ABUV

Yes, Elijah does come first to set everything right — NEB

Elijah does come first, and reforms everything — Gspd

and how it is written of the Son of man,

and how it is written of the Son of man — ASV

Yet how is it that the scriptures say of ... — NEB

But what does the Scripture say about the Son of Man — Phi

that he must suffer many things,

that he should suffer ... — ASV

that he is to endure great sufferings — NEB

This: that he must go through much suffering — Phi

and be set at nought.

and be rejected — Mof

and be treated with contempt — RSV

and have his claims rejected! — Phi

13. But I say unto you,

But I tell you — RSV

That Elias is indeed come,

Elijah has already come — Wms

and they have done unto him whatsoever they listed,

and they did to him whatever they
wished — ABUV
and they did to him whatever they
pleased — RSV
and they have worked their will upon
him — NEB
as it is written of him.
as was foretold about him in the Scriptures — Rieu

14. And when he came to his disciples,
And when they came to the disciples —
ASV
When they came back . . . — NEB
When they reached . . . — Mof
Then as they rejoined the other disciples — Phi
he saw a great multitude about them,
they saw a large crowd surrounding
them — NEB
they found them in the center of a large
crowd — Rieu
and the scribes questioning with them.
and scribes arguing with them — RSV
and a party of Scribes disputing with
them — Wey

15. And straightway all the people,
. . . all the multitude — ASV
And immediately all the crowd — RSV
when they beheld him,
when they saw him — ASV
at the sight of Jesus — Rieu
were greatly amazed,
were overcome with awe — Knox
and running to him saluted him.
and ran up to him and greeted him —
RSV
and they ran forward to welcome him
— NEB

16. And he asked the scribes,
And he asked them — ASV
What question ye with them?
What are you discussing with them —
RSV
What is this argument about — NEB
What are you arguing about with my
disciples — Rieu

**17. And one of the multitude answered
and said,**
. . . answered him — ASV
A man from the crowd . . . — Mof
A man in the crowd spoke up — NEB
**Master, I have brought unto thee my
son,**
Teacher, I brought unto thee my son
— ASV
Master, I brought my son to you — Phi

which hath a dumb spirit;
with an evil spirit that makes him dumb
— Rieu
He is possessed by a spirit which makes
him speechless — NEB

**18. And wheresoever he taketh him, he
teareth him:**
And wherever it lays hold of him, it
tears him — ABUV
Wherever it seizes him, it convulses
him — Wms
Whenever it attacks him, it dashes him
to the ground — NEB
**and he foameth, and gnasheth with his
teeth, and pineth away:**
and he foams at the mouth, grinds his
teeth, and goes rigid — NEB
**and I spake to thy disciples that they
should cast him out;**
I asked your disciples to cast it out —
Rieu
I begged your disciples to expel it —
Wey
and they could not.
and they were not able — ASV
but they were powerless — Knox
but they failed — NEB

19. He answereth him, and saith,
He answered him and said — Gspd
O faithless generation,
O unbelieving . . .! — Ber
O you unbelieving people — Gspd
What an unbelieving and perverse gen-
eration! — NEB
how long shall I be with you?
how long must I . . . — Wey
How long . . . before you will believe
— Phi
How much longer must I be with you
— Rieu
how long shall I suffer you?
how long shall I bear with you — ASV
How long must I endure you — NEB
. . . put up with you — Gspd
. . . bear your lack of faith — Phi
bring him unto me.
Bring him to me — ABUV

20. And they brought him unto him:
So they brought the boy to him — Mon
and when he saw him,
And the spirit, when he saw Jesus —
Wey
and as soon as the spirit . . . — Phi
straightway the spirit tare him;
. . . convulsed him — ABUV

immediately it convulsed the boy —
RSV

instantly threw the boy into convulsions — Ber

and he fell on the ground,

... to the ground — Mon

so that he fell on ... — Ber

and wallowed foaming.

and rolled about, foaming at the mouth — Wey

and kept rolling over and ... — Wms

and there he writhed, ... — Phi

21. And he asked his father,

Jesus asked the boy's father — Gspd

How long is it ago since this came unto him?

... has this been happening to him — Knox

... has he had this — RSV

... has he been like this — Gspd

And he said, Of a child.

... From a child — ASV

... From his childhood — Gspd

It began when he was a child, said the father — Rieu

22. And ofttimes it hath cast him into the fire,

and often it has thrown ... — Wey

and into the waters,

or into water — NEB

or into pools of water — Wey

to destroy him:

to make an end of him — NEB

to finish him off — Phi

but if thou canst do any thing;

but if you can do anything — RSV

But if there is anything you can do — Gspd

have compassion on us, and help us.

have pity on us and help us — RSV

23. Jesus said unto him,

If thou canst believe,[23]

If there is anything I can do! — Gspd

all things are possible to him that believeth.

... who believes — RSV

Anything can be done for one ... — Mof

Everything is possible for one who has faith — Gspd

24. And straightway the father of the child cried out,

At once the father of the boy ... — Mof

Whereupon ... cried aloud — Knox

and said with tears,[24]

Lord,[25] **I believe;**

I have faith — NEB

I do believe — Wey

help thou mine unbelief.

help me where faith falls short — NEB

Help me to believe more! — Phi

25. When Jesus saw that the people came running together,

Then Jesus, seeing that a crowd was rapidly gathering — Wey

Jesus saw then that the crowd was closing in upon them — NEB

he rebuked the foul spirit,

so he rebuked the unclean spirit — NEB

he spoke sharply to the evil spirit — Phi

saying unto him, Thou dumb and deaf spirit,

saying to it ... — RSV

... You deaf and dumb spirit — NASB

I charge thee, come out of him,

I command you ... — Wey

and enter no more into him.

and never enter him again — Rieu

26. And the spirit cried,

And it gave a cry — Gspd

Then it gave a shriek — Wms

The spirit gave a loud scream — Phi

and rent him sore,

it threw the boy into fit after fit — Wey

and convulsed him terribly — Gspd

and came out of him:

and left him — Nor

and he was as one dead;

And he became as one dead — ABUV

and the boy was like a corpse — RSV

and he lay there ... — Knox

insomuch that many said, He is dead.

in fact, many said ... — NEB

so that most of the bystanders said ... — Phi

27. But Jesus took him by the hand, and lifted him up;

But Jesus grasped his hand and made him rise — Gspd

... took his hand and raised him to his feet — NEB

and he arose.

and he stood up — Gspd

---

[23]Some manuscripts omit "believe."

[24]The last two words are now recognized as not adequately supported by original manuscripts.

[25]"Lord" is now recognized as not adequately supported by original manuscripts.

and then he stood on his own feet —
Phi

28. And when he was come into the house,
And when he had entered . . . — RSV
When he had gone indoors — Rieu
When he had gone home — Gspd
his disciples asked him privately,
and his disciples had him to themselves,
they asked him — Rieu
Why could not we cast him out?
Why were we unable to drive it out —
Phi
Why couldn't we drive out the spirit —
Beck

29. And he said unto them,
He answered them — Wms
**This kind can come forth by nothing,
but by prayer and fasting.**[26]
This kind cannot be expelled, except
through prayer — Ber
. . . be driven out by anything but
prayer — RSV

**30. And they departed thence, and passed
through Galilee;**
And they went forth from thence, . . .
— ASV
And going forth . . ., they were passing
along through Galilee — ABUV
They now left that district and made
a journey through Galilee — NEB
**and he would not that any man should
know it.**
Jesus wished it to be kept secret — NEB
He did not want anyone to know of
their journey — Mof
and he sought to remain unrecognized
— Rieu

**31. For he taught his disciples, and said
unto them,**
For he was teaching . . ., and saying
unto them — Alf
for he was explaining to his disciples
that — Mon
**The Son of man is delivered into the
hands of men,**
. . . will be delivered . . . — RSV
. . . is now to be given up into the power
of men — NEB
and they shall kill him;
and they will execute him — Ber
and after that he is killed,
and when He has been killed — NASB
he shall rise the third day.
after three days he shall rise again —
ASV
. . . he will come back to life — Rieu

32. But they understood not that saying,
But they did not understand what he
meant — Gspd
But they were completely mystified by
this saying — Phi
and were afraid to ask him.
and were afraid to question Him —
Wey

33. And he came to Capernaum:
And they . . . — ASV
and being in the house he asked them,
and when he was . . . — ASV
and when he was indoors . . . — NEB
**What was it that ye disputed among
yourselves by the way?**
. . . you were discussing on the way —
Gspd
What were you arguing about on the
road — Mof

34. But they held their peace:
But they were silent — ABUV
But they had nothing to say — Wms
They held their tongues — Rieu
**for by the way they had disputed
among themselves,**
for on the road they had been disputing
— Mof
for on the way they had been discussing
with one another — Gspd
who should be the greatest.
who was . . . — ASV

35. And he sat down, and called the twelve,
Seating Himself, He summoned the
twelve — Ber
and saith unto them,
and said to them — Phi
If any man desire to be first,
If any one wishes . . . — ABUV
**the same shall be last of all, and serv-
ant of all.**
he must be . . . — RSV
he must make himself . . . — NEB

36. And he took a child,
And he took a little child — ASV
and set him in the midst of them:
and put him . . . — RSV
and made him stand among them —
Gspd
and stood him in front of them all —
Phi
**and when he had taken him in his
arms,**

---

[26]The words "and fasting" are now recognized
as not adequately supported by original manuscripts.

and folding it in his arms — ABUV
and putting his arms round him — Phi
he said unto them,

37. Whosoever shall receive one of such children in my name,
Whoever receives one such child . . . — RSV
Whoever for my sake receives one such young child — Wey
Whoever welcomes one child like this on my account — Gspd
receiveth me:
receives me — ABUV
welcomes me — Rieu
and whosoever shall receive me,
and whoever receives me — ABUV
and whoever welcomes me — Rieu
receiveth not me, but him that sent me.
receives . . ., but him who . . . — ABUV
welcomes not me but him who has . . . — Gspd
is welcoming not only me but the One Who sent me! — Phi

38. And John answered him, saying,
John said to him — Gspd
Then . . . — Phi
Master, we saw one casting out devils in thy name,
Teacher, we saw a man using your name to drive out demons — Wms
and he followeth not us:[27]
and we forbad him, because he followeth not us.
and we forbad him, because he was not following us — RSV
but he does not follow us, and so we stopped him — Mof
and tried to stop him since he was not one of us — Rieu

39. But Jesus said, Forbid him not:
Jesus said, Do not stop him — NEB
But Jesus said, Do not hinder him — NASB
Jesus said, Do not try to stop him — Wms
for there is no man which shall do a miracle in my name,
. . . mighty work . . . — ASV
for there is no one who will use my name to do a mighty act — Gspd
that can lightly speak evil of me.
and be able quickly to . . . — ASV
and be able the next minute . . . — Wey

40. For he that is not against us
For whoever . . . — Wms

is on our part.
is for us — ASV
is on our side — Phi

41. For whosoever shall give you a cup of water to drink in my name, because ye belong to Christ,
because ye are Christ's — ASV
because you bear the name of Christ — RSV
because you are followers of the Messiah — NEB
verily I say unto you,
I tell you truly — Mof
I assure you — Phi
he shall not lose his reward.
he shall in no wise . . . — ASV
he will certainly not . . . — Wey
he will not fail to get . . . — Wms

42. And whosoever shall offend one of these little ones that believe in me,
And whosoever shall cause . . . on me to stumble — ASV
Whoever causes . . . who believe in me to sin — RSV
And whoever causes one of these humble believers to fall — Gspd
it is better for him that a millstone were hanged about his neck,
it were . . . if a great millstone . . . — ASV
it would be better for him . . . were hung round his neck — RSV
and he were cast into the sea.
. . . thrown . . . — RSV

43. And if thy hand offend thee,
And if thy hand cause thee to stumble — ASV
And if your hand causes you to sin — RSV
If your hand proves a snare to you — TCNT
. . . is your undoing — NEB
cut it off:
it is better for thee to enter into life maimed,
. . . for you to enter into life crippled — NASB
than having two hands to go into hell,
than with two hands to go to hell — RSV
than keep your two hands and go to Gehenna — Mof

---

[27]Now recognized as not adequately supported by original manuscripts.

than go with both your hands to the pit — Gspd

into the fire that never shall be quenched:

into the unquenchable fire — ASV

into the fire that cannot be put out — Gspd

44. Where their worm dieth not, and the fire is not quenched.[28]

45. And if thy foot offend thee,

. . . cause thee to stumble — ASV

And if your foot causes you to sin — RSV

And if it is your foot that leads you astray — NEB

cut it off:

it is better for thee to enter halt into life,

. . . for you to enter life lame — RSV

. . . crippled — Ber

. . . on one foot — Phi

than having two feet to be cast into hell,

than with two feet to be thrown . . . — RSV

than possessing both your feet to be thrown into Gehenna — Wey

than to keep both your feet and be thrown into the pit — Wms

into the fire that never shall be quenched:[29]

46. Where their worm dieth not, and the fire is not quenched.[30]

47. And if thine eye offend thee,

. . . cause thee to stumble — ASV

And if your eye causes you to sin — RSV

Or if your eye should cause you to fall — Wey

And if your eye leads you astray — Phi

pluck it out:

cast it out — ASV

tear it out — NEB

gouge it out! — Tay

it is better for thee to enter into the kingdom of God with one eye,

. . . for you to enter the kingdom of God one-eyed — Ber

than having two eyes to be cast into hell fire:

than with two eyes to be thrown into hell — RSV

than to keep both eyes and be . . . — NEB

than keep your two eyes and be thrown into Gehenna — Mof

48. Where their worm dieth not,

where the devouring worm never dies — NEB

where the worm that feeds upon them . . . — Gspd

where decay never stops — Phi

and the fire is not quenched.

. . . never put out — Mof

. . . never goes out — Phi

49. For every one shall be salted with fire,

Everyone has to be consecrated by the fire of the discipline — Mof

Everyone must be seasoned with fire — Gspd

and every sacrifice shall be salted with salt.[31]

50. Salt is good:

Salt is a good thing — NEB

Salt is excellent — Mof

but if the salt have lost his saltness,

. . . loses its saltness — NEB

. . . should become tasteless — Wey

. . . loses its flavor — Nor

wherewith will ye season it?

how will you . . . — RSV

what will you use to . . . — Gspd

what can you do to restore its flavor — Phi

Have salt in yourselves,

You must . . . — Phi

So don't lose your flavor! — Tay

and have peace one with another.

and be at peace . . . — ASV

and live at peace with one another — Wey

---

[28]This verse is now recognized as not adequately supported by original manuscripts.

[29]Now recognized as not adequately supported by original manuscripts.

[30]See note on verse 44.

[31]Now recognized as not adequately supported by original manuscripts.

CHAPTER 10

1. And he arose from thence,
Then he left — Mof
Then he got up and left Galilee — Phi
and cometh into the coasts of Judaea
and went to the territory . . . — Mof
He came into the outskirts of Judea —
Nor
by the farther side of Jordan:
and beyond the Jordan — ASV
and Transjordan — NEB
and the people resort unto him again;
and multitudes come together . . . —
ASV
and crowds gathered to him again —
RSV
Again crowds flocked to Him — Ber
and, as he was wont,
and again, as his custom was — RSV
he taught them again.
he taught them — RSV
He began to teach them — Wms

**2. And the Pharisees came to him, and
asked him,**
And there came Pharisees questioning
Him — Ber
**Is it lawful for a man to put away his
wife?**
. . . to divorce his wife — RSV
Is it right for a man . . . — Phi
tempting him.
This was to tempt him — Mof
— seeking to entrap Him — Wey

3. And he answered and said unto them,
So he replied — Mof
He asked in return — NEB
What did Moses command you?
What ruling did Moses give you — Ber

4. And they said,
They answered — NEB
**Moses suffered to write a bill of di-
vorcement,**
Moses allowed a man to write a certificate of divorce — RSV
Moses allowed men to write a divorce-
notice — Phi
and to put her away.
and to send his wife away — Wey
and to let her go — Ber
and then to dismiss her — Phi

**5. And Jesus answered and said unto
them,**
But Jesus said to them — Gspd
**For the hardness of your heart he
wrote you this precept.**

It was to suit your hard hearts that
Moses wrote such a command as
that — Knox
It was on account of your perversity
that he laid down that law for you
— Gspd

6. But from the beginning of the creation
but in the beginning, at the creation —
NEB
God made them male and female.

**7. For this cause shall a man leave his
father and mother,**
for this reason a man shall leave . . .
— RSV
and cleave to his wife;
and be joined to his wife — RSV
and be made one with his wife — NEB
and be wedded to his wife — Nor

8. And they twain shall be one flesh:
and the two shall become . . . — ASV
**so then they are no more twain, but
one flesh.**
It follows that they are no longer two
individuals: they are one flesh—NEB
So that in body they are no longer two
people but one — Phi

**9. What therefore God hath joined to-
gether, let not man put asunder.**
What God has . . ., man must not sep-
arate — NEB
It follows that man must not part what
God has united — Rieu
Therefore, what God has joined to-
gether man must stop separating —
Wms

10. And in the house
When they were indoors again — NEB
When they reached the house — Gspd
Back in their lodgings — Rieu
**his disciples asked him again of the
same matter.**
the disciples began questioning Jesus
again on the same subject — Wey

11. And he saith unto them,
And he said to them — Gspd
**Whosoever shall put away his wife,
and marry another,**
Whoever puts away . . ., and marries
another — ABUV
Whoever divorces . . . — RSV
committeth adultery against her.

12. And if a woman[32] shall put away her husband, and be married to another,
so too, if she divorces her husband and marries another — NEB
she committeth adultery.
she is an adulteress — Gspd

13. And they brought young children to him,
And they were bringing unto him little children — ASV
Then some people came to him bringing . . . — Phi
that he should touch them:
to have him . . . — Gspd
that He might lay His hands on them — Nor
and his disciples rebuked those that brought them.
and the disciples rebuked them — ASV
. . . scolded them for it — NEB
but the disciples interfered — Wey

14. But when Jesus saw it,
When Jesus noticed that — Ber
he was much displeased,
he was moved with indignation — ASV
he was indignant — RSV
he was angry — Bas
and said unto them,
and told them — Ber
Suffer the little children to come unto me,
Let . . . come to me — Wey
and forbid them not:
. . . hinder . . . — Alf
do not try to stop them — NEB
— never stop them! — Phi
for of such is the kingdom of God.
for to such belongeth . . . — ASV
for to those who are childlike the Kingdom of God belongs — Wey

15. Verily I say unto you,
I tell you truly — Mof
Believe me — Rieu
Whosoever shall not receive the kingdom of God as a little child,
Whoever does not receive . . . like a child — RSV
whoever will not submit to the Realm of God . . . — Mof
he shall not enter therein.
he shall in no wise . . . — ASV
shall not enter it — RSV
will never get into it at all — Mof

16. And he took them up in his arms,
And he folded them in his arms — ABUV

And he put his arms around them — NEB
And so he embraced them — Knox
put his hands upon them,
laid his . . . — NEB
. . . one by one — Wms
and blessed them.
. . . lovingly — Wey
and gave them a blessing — Nor
and called down blessings upon them — Rieu

17. And when he was gone forth into the way,
And as he was going forth . . . — ASV
. . . setting out on his journey — RSV
As he began to take the road again — Phi
there came one running,
a man ran up — RSV
a stranger . . . — NEB
a man came running up to him — Gspd
and kneeled to him,
and knelt before him — RSV
and knelt at his feet — Gspd
and asked him,
Good Master, what shall I do that I may inherit eternal life?
Good Teacher, what must I do to . . . — RSV
Good Master, . . . to make sure of . . . — Gspd

18. And Jesus said unto him,
And Jesus answered him — Wms
Why callest thou me good?
Why do you call me good — Gspd
there is none good but one, that is, God.
none is good save one, even God — ASV
No one is good but God alone — RSV

19. Thou knowest the commandments,
Do not commit adultery,[33]
Do not kill,
Do not murder — Gspd
Do not steal,
Do not bear false witness,
do not give false evidence — NEB
Defraud not,
Do not cheat — Phi
Honour thy father and mother.
Give honour to your father and mother — Bas

[32]Some manuscripts have "she."
[33]This command and the next are reversed in some manuscripts.

175

20. And he answered and said unto him,
He replied — Ber
Master, all these have I observed from my youth.
Teacher, all these things . . . — ASV
Master, I have obeyed all these commandments ever since I was a child — Gspd

21. Then Jesus beholding him loved him,
And Jesus looking upon him loved him — ASV
Jesus, looking at him, prized him dearly — Ber
Jesus looked steadily at him, and his heart warmed towards him — Phi
and said unto him,
and told him — Ber
One thing thou lackest:
You lack one thing — RSV
One thing remains for you to do — Rieu
go thy way, sell whatsoever thou hast,
go, sell what you have — RSV
go and sell all you possess — NEB
and give to the poor,
give the money to the poor — Mof
and give the proceeds to the poor — Wey
and thou shalt have treasure in heaven:
and you will have . . . — Mof
and then you will have riches . . . — Gspd
and come, take up the cross, and follow me.
and come, follow me — ASV
and come back and be a follower of mine — Gspd

22. And he was sad at that saying,
But his countenance fell at the saying — ASV
At these words his brow darkened — Wey
But the man's face clouded at these words — TCNT
He received these words with a sombre look — Rieu
and went away grieved:
and he went away sorrowful — RSV
. . . much cast down — Gspd
and went away in gloom — Rieu
for he had great possessions.
for he had a great deal of property — Gspd
for he was a man of great wealth — NEB

23. And Jesus looked round about,

. . . looked around — RSV
Then Jesus looked round at them all — Phi
and saith unto his disciples,
and said to . . . — Mof
How hardly shall they that have riches
How difficult it is for those who have money — Mof
How hard it will be for the wealthy — NEB
enter into the kingdom of God!
to enter the . . .! — NEB
to get into the . . .! — Wms

24. And the disciples were astonished at his words.
. . . were amazed . . . — ASV
The disciples were staggered by these words — Phi
His disciples were startled at this statement — Wms
But Jesus answereth again,
but Jesus insisted — NEB
so he repeated — Mof
but Jesus spoke to them once more — Ber
and saith unto them,
Children, how hard is it for them that trust in riches[34]
My sons, how difficult it is — Mof
Children, you don't know how hard it can be — Phi
to enter into the kingdom of God!
to get into . . . — Gspd

25. It is easier for a camel
. . . for a rope[35] — Lam
to go through the eye of a needle,
to pass through . . . — NEB
to get through a needle's eye — Mof
than for a rich man to enter into the kingdom of God.
. . . to get into . . . — Gspd

26. And they were astonished out of measure,
. . . exceedingly — ASV
They were more astonished than ever — NEB
At this statement their astonishment knew no bounds — Phi
saying among themselves,
and said to him — RSV
and said to one another — NEB
Who then can be saved?

---

[34]The last six words are now recognized as not adequately supported by original manuscripts.
[35]A few manuscripts have "cable," which resembles the Greek word for camel.

Then who ever can . . . — Mof
Then who can possibly be saved — Phi

27. And Jesus looking upon them saith,
Jesus looked at them and said — Gspd
Jesus looked them · in the face . . . — NEB
Jesus looked straight at them . . . — Phi
With men it is impossible,
For men it is . . . — Mof
Humanly speaking . . . — Phi
but not with God:
but not for God — NEB
for with God all things are possible.
to God everything is . . . — NEB
anything is possible for God — Mof

28. Then Peter began to say unto him,
At this Peter spoke — NEB
Peter started to say to him — Gspd
Then Peter burst out — Phi
Lo, we have left all, and have followed thee.
Well, we have left our all and followed you — Mof
Look, we have given up everything and have followed You — Ber
What of us, who have forsaken all, and followed thee? — Knox

29. And Jesus answered and said,
Verily I say unto you,
I tell you solemnly — Mon
I assure you — Ber
There is no man that hath left house,
there is no one who has given up home — NEB
or brethren, or sisters, or father, or mother,
or brothers . . . — Gspd
or wife,[36] or children, or lands,
and children and farms — Wms
or children or property — Phi
for my sake, and the gospel's,
. . . and for the gospel — RSV
for me and for the good news — Gspd

30. But he shall receive an hundredfold now in this time,
but will receive a hundred times as much now in this present life — Wey
who will not receive a hundred fold now in this time — RSV
houses, and brethren, and sisters, and mothers, and children, and lands, with persecutions;
. . . — and persecutions besides — NEB
. . . — though not without persecution — Phi

and in the world to come eternal life.
and in the age to come . . . — ABUV
and in the next world . . . — Phi

31. But many that are first shall be last;
But many who are first will . . . — NEB
But many who are now first . . . — Wey
and the last first.
and many who are last will be first — Mof
and the last now will then be the first — Phi

32. And they were in the way going up to Jerusalem;
And they were on the road, . . . — RSV
They were now on their way . . . — Phi
and Jesus went before them:
and Jesus was walking ahead of them — RSV
Jesus leading the way — NEB
and they were amazed;
and the disciples were filled with awe — NEB
They were puzzled and bewildered at this — Phi
They went in consternation — Rieu
and as they followed, they were afraid.
and they that followed . . . — ASV
while those who followed behind . . . — NEB
and their followers too had their fears — Rieu
and the company who followed were afraid — Mof
And he took again the twelve,
So once again he took the twelve aside — Mof
He let the Twelve come up with him once more — Rieu
and began to tell them what things should happen unto him,
he . . . what was to happen to him — RSV
and began to tell them what was going to befall Him — Wms

33. Saying, Behold, we go up to Jerusalem;
You see, he said; we are going up . . . — Rieu
and the Son of man shall be delivered
and the Son of Man will be given up — NEB
. . . will be handed over — Gspd
. . . will be betrayed — Mof

---

[36]The words "or wife" are now recognized as not adequately supported by original manuscripts.

177

unto the chief priests, and unto the scribes;

to . . . and the doctors of the law — NEB

to the ruling priests and the Bible scholars — Beck

and they shall condemn him to death,

They are going to . . . — Phi

they will sentence him to death — Mof

and shall deliver him to the Gentiles:

and will hand Him over . . . — Wey

and hand him over to the foreign power — NEB

. . . to pagans — Phi

34. And they shall mock him,

and they will ridicule him — Gspd

who will jeer at him — Phi

and they will make sport of Him — Wms

and shall scourge him,

and flog him — Gspd

and shall spit upon him,

and spit at him — Phi

and shall kill him:

and put Him to death — Wey

and the third day he shall rise again.

and after three days . . . — ASV

But . . . he will rise again — Phi

35. And James and John, the sons of Zebedee,

Thereupon . . . — Knox

come unto him, saying,

approached him and said — NEB

came to Him with a request — Nor

Master, we would that thou shouldest do for us whatsoever we shall desire.

Teacher, we want you to do for us whatever we ask of you — RSV

Master, we should like you to do us a favour — NEB

. . . we want you to grant us a special request — Phi

. . . we beg you to grant us a wish, whatever it may be — Rieu

36. And he said unto them,

He asked then — Wms

What would ye that I should do for you?

What do you want me to . . . — Gspd

37. They said unto him,

They said to him — Mof

Grant unto us that we may sit,

Give us permission to sit — Phi

one on thy right hand, and the other on thy left hand,

one at your right hand and one at your left — Gspd

in thy glory.

in your triumph — Gspd

in your splendor — Wms

when thou art glorified — Knox

38. But Jesus said unto them,

But Jesus told them — Ber

Ye know not what ye ask:

You do not know what you are asking — Mof

You do not realize what you are asking for — Wms

can ye drink of the cup that I drink of?

Can you drink the cup I have to drink — Mof

and be baptized with the baptism that I am baptized with?

or undergo the baptism I have to undergo — Mof

or endure the baptism of agony that I am to endure — Wms

39. And they said unto him, We can.

. . . We are able — ASV

Yes, we can, they replied — Phi

And Jesus said unto them,

Then Jesus told them — Phi

Ye shall indeed drink of the cup that I drink of;

Then you shall drink the cup that I am drinking — Gspd

and with the baptism that I am baptized withal shall ye be baptized:

and suffer the baptism I suffer — Rieu

and you will undergo the baptism by which I am being baptized! — Phi

40. But to sit on my right hand and on my left hand

but to sit at my right hand or at my left — RSV

is not mine to give;

is not for me to grant — NEB

but it shall be given to them for whom it is prepared.

it will be for those for whom it has been reserved — Wey

it is for those to whom it has already been assigned — NEB

— these belong to the men for whom they have been destined — Mof

41. And when the ten heard it,

When the other ten heard of this — Gspd

they began to be much displeased with James and John.

. . . indignant at . . . — RSV

they were at first very indignant at . . .
— Gspd

42. **But Jesus called them to him, and saith unto them,**
so Jesus called them and said — Mof
. . . all to him, and said — Phi
Ye know that they which are accounted to rule over the Gentiles
You know that those who are supposed to . . . — RSV
You know the so-called rulers of the Gentiles — Mof
You know that the acknowledged rulers of the pagans — Rieu
You know that in the world the recognized rulers — NEB
exercise lordship over them;
lord it over them — ASV
exercise despotic powers — Rieu
and their great ones exercise authority upon them.
. . . men make them feel their authority — Wey
. . . men tyrannize over them — Gspd

43. **But so shall it not be among you:**
It is not so with you — Rieu
That is not the way with you — NEB
But it shall not be so among you — RSV
But it must not be so . . . — Phi
but whosoever will be great among you,
but whoever would be . . . — RSV
among you, whoever wants to be great — NEB
shall be your minister:
must be your servant — Gspd
must become the servant of you all — Phi
. . . the willing slave of all — NEB

44. **And whosoever of you will be the chiefest, shall be servant of all.**
and whoever wants to take the first place among you must be the servant of all — TCNT
and whoever wishes to be the first of you must be the slave of all — Rieu
and whoever wants to hold the first position among you must be everybody's slave — Wms

45. **For even the Son of man came not to be ministered unto,**
For the Son of man also . . . to — ABUV
for the Son of man himself has not come to be served — Mof
. . . to be waited on — Gspd

For even I, the Man from Heaven, am not here to be served — Tay
but to minister,
but to serve — RSV
but to wait on other people — Gspd
but to help others — Tay
and to give his life a ransom for many.
and to give His life as the redemption-price . . . — Wey
. . . as a ransom for (instead of) many — Amp
. . . to free many others — Gspd

46. **And they came to Jericho:**
Then they reached Jericho — Mof
and as he went out of Jericho
and as he was leaving Jericho — RSV
with his disciples and a great number of people,
. . . and a great multitude — ASV
. . . and a large crowd — NEB
blind Bartimaeus, the son of Timaeus, sat by the highway side begging.
the son of Timaeus, Bartimaeus, a blind beggar, was sitting by the way side — ASV
Bartimaeus, (that is, the son of Timaeus) a blind beggar, was sitting in his usual place by the side of the road — Phi

47. **And when he heard that it was Jesus of Nazareth,**
. . . Jesus the Nazarene — ASV
he began to cry out, and say,
he began to shout — NEB
Jesus, thou son of David,
Son of David! Jesus! — Mof
have mercy on me.
have pity on me — Wey
take pity on me! — Gspd

48. **And many charged him**
And many rebuked him — ASV
And many were sternly telling him — NASB
that he should hold his peace:
to be quiet — NASB
to hold his tongue — Rieu
but he cried the more a great deal,
but he shouted all the more — NEB
but he only cried out all the louder — Wey
Thou son of David, have mercy on me.
Son of David, have pity on me — NEB
. . . take pity on me! — Ber

49. **And Jesus stood still,**
And Jesus stopped — RSV
So Jesus stopped — Nor

and commanded him to be called.
and said, Call him — ABUV
. . . Call him here — Gspd
And they call the blind man, saying unto him,
Then they called . . . and told him — Mof
They summoned . . ., saying to him — Nor
Be of good comfort,
Be of good cheer — ABUV
Take heart — RSV
Courage! — Mof
It's all right now — Phi
rise; he calleth thee.
rise, he is calling you — RSV
stand up; . . . — NEB
Get up, He is calling for you — Wms

50. **And he, casting away his garment,**
And throwing off his mantle — RSV
At this he threw off his coat — Phi
rose, and came to Jesus.
he sprang up and came to Jesus — RSV
jumped to his feet and . . . — Phi

51. **And Jesus answered and said unto him,**
Jesus spoke to him and said — Mof

What wilt thou that I should do unto thee?
What do you want me to do for you — Mof
The blind man said unto him,
. . . replied — Ber
Lord, that I might receive my sight.
Master, let me receive . . . — RSV
. . . regain . . . — Gspd
Rabboni, I want to regain . . . — Mof
Oh, Master, let me see again — Phi
O Teacher, . . ., I want to see! — Tay

52. **And Jesus said unto him,**
Then Jesus said — Mof
Go thy way; thy faith hath made thee whole.
Go your way; your faith has made you well — RSV
Go; your faith has cured you — NEB
Go! your faith has restored you — Ber
And immediately he received his sight,
Instantly he regained his sight — Wey
And all at once he could see again — Wms
and followed Jesus in the way.
. . . him on the road — NEB
and began to follow Jesus along the road — Wms

CHAPTER 11

1. **And when they came nigh to Jerusalem,**
. . . drew near . . . — RSV
When they were approaching . . . — Knox
unto Bethphage and Bethany,
and had arrived at Bethphage and Bethany — Wey
at the mount of Olives,
near . . . — Gspd
on the slopes of . . . — Phi
he sendeth forth two of his disciples,
he sent . . . — RSV
he dispatched . . . — Mof
he sent . . . ahead — Rieu

2. **And saith unto them,**
and said to them — RSV
with these instructions — Phi
Go your way into the village over against you:
Go into the village opposite you — RSV
Go to the village that lies in front of you — Gspd
Go into the village just ahead of you — Phi

and as soon as ye be entered into it,
and immediately on entering it — Wey
and, just as you enter — NEB
ye shall find a colt tied,
you will find a colt tethered — Mof
you'll find a young donkey tied up — Beck
whereon never man sat;
on which no one has ever sat — RSV
that has never been ridden — Gspd
loose him, and bring him.
untie it and bring it — RSV
. . . here — Wey

3. **And if any man say unto you,**
And if any one says to you — ABUV
If anyone asks — NEB
Why do ye this?
Why are you doing this — RSV
What are you doing there — Ber
say ye that the Lord hath need of him;
say, The Lord has need of it — RSV
say, Our Master needs it — NEB
and straightway he will send him hither.
. . . back hither — ASV

and will send it back here without delay — Wey

and will promptly return it here again — Nor

and he will let you have it without more ado — Knox

4. And they went their way,

And they departed — Rhm

So they went off — NEB

and found the colt

and found a colt — ABUV

and found a young ass — Wey

tied by the door without in a place where two ways met;

tethered outside a door in the street — Mof

tied ... at a street corner — Wms

tied by an outside door at a street crossing — Nor

and they loose him.

and they untied it — RSV

and they started to untie it — Beck

5. And certain of them that stood there said unto them,

but some of the bystanders said to them — Mof

What do ye, loosing the colt?

What are you doing, untying ... — Gspd

What do you mean by untethering that colt — Mof

What are you trying to do, untying ... — Mon

6. And they said unto them even as Jesus had commanded:

They answered as Jesus had told them — NEB

And they answered them as Jesus had bidden — Knox

And they told them what Jesus had said — RSV

and they let them go.

and the men allowed them to go—Mof

... let them take it — Gspd

7. And they brought the colt to Jesus,

So ... — Wey

Then ... — Ber

and cast their garments on him;

and threw ... over it — Wey

and saddled it with their garments — Knox

and he sat upon him.

— and he took his seat upon him — Rhm

and He mounted — Wey

and Jesus sat upon it — Ber

8. And many spread their garments in the way:

... upon the way — ASV

Many of the people spread out their coats in his path — Phi

Then many spread their garments to carpet the road — Wey

and others cut down branches off the trees,

while others cut branches from the fields — Nor

and others cut straw ... — Gspd

and strawed them in the way.

and spread them ... — Nor

and scattered it in his path — Gspd

9. And they that went before,

while those who led the way — Wey

Then those in front — Wms

and they that followed,

and those who ... — Wey

and those behind Him — Wms

cried, saying,

were crying aloud — Rhm

kept shouting — Wey

Hosanna;

Hosanna! — Mof

God bless him! — Gspd

Welcome Him! — Wms

God save Him! — Phi

Glory — Bas

Our Saviour — Beck

Blessed is he that cometh in the name of the Lord:

... who comes ...! — RSV

Blessings on him ...! — NEB

Blessed is He who is coming in the Lord's name! — Beck

10. Blessed be the kingdom of our father David,

... reign ... — Gspd

that cometh in the name of the Lord:

which is coming! — Gspd

Hosanna in the highest.

... in the heavens! — NEB

... in high heaven! — Mof

God save him from on high! — TCNT

11. And Jesus entered into Jerusalem, and into the temple:

So He came ... and entered the Temple — Wey

And he entered Jerusalem, and went into ... — RSV

So . . . and the temple-enclosure — Rieu

and when he had looked round about upon all things,

MARK 11

... round at everything — RSV
and looked it all over — Gspd
where he looked at the whole scene —
NEB
and now the eventide was come,
the hour being now late — ABUV
but, as it was . . . — NEB
and, as night was approaching — Ber
**he went out unto Bethany with the
twelve.**
he went away with the twelve to Bethany — Mof

12. **And on the morrow,**
Next day — Mof
On the following day — RSV
when they were come from Bethany,
when they had come out . . . — ABUV
after they had left Bethany — NEB
he was hungry:
he hungered — ASV
he felt hungry — Mof
Jesus became hungry — TCNT

13. **And seeing a fig tree afar off having
leaves,**
And seeing in the distance a fig tree in
leaf — RSV
**he came, if haply he might find any
thing thereon:**
he went to see if he could find anything
on it — RSV
he walked up to it . . . any fruit on it —
Phi
**and when he came to it, he found noth-
ing but leaves;**
But when he reached it . . . — Rieu
for the time of figs was not yet.
for it was not the season of figs — ASV
. . . for figs — RSV

14. **And Jesus answered and said unto it,**
And he spoke to the tree and said to it
— Gspd
and he dealt with the tree by saying to
it — Rieu
**No man eat fruit of thee hereafter for
ever.**
May no one eat fruit from thee any
more forever — ABUV
. . . ever eat fruit from you again—RSV
Nobody shall ever eat fruit from you!
— Phi
And his disciples heard it.
And the disciples heard him say it —
Phi
And his disciples were listening — NEB

15. **And they come to Jerusalem:**
Then they came . . . — Mof

and Jesus went into the temple,
and he entered into . . . — ASV
**and began to cast out them that sold
and bought in the temple,**
and began driving out those who
bought and sold . . . — NEB
**and overthrew the tables of the money-
changers,**
Then He upset the money-changers'
tables — Wms
and the seats of them that sold doves;
and the stalls of those who . . . — Mof
and the seats of those who sold pigeons
— RSV

16. **And would not suffer that any man**
and he would not allow anyone—Gspd
**should carry any vessel through the
temple.**
to carry anything . . . — Gspd
to carry his wares . . . — Knox
to use the temple court as a thorough-
fare for carrying goods — NEB

17. **And he taught, saying unto them,**
Then he began to teach them, and said
— NEB
Is it not written,
Does not the Scripture say — Gspd
**My house shall be called of all nations
the house of prayer?**
. . . a house of prayer for all the na-
tions — ASV
but ye have made it a den of thieves.
. . . a den of robbers — ASV
But you have turned it into a thieves'
kitchen! — Phi
But you have made it a robbers' cave
— NEB

18. **And the scribes and chief priests heard
it,**
The chief priests and doctors of the
law heard of this — NEB
This came to the ears of the scribes and
high priests — Mof
**and sought how they might destroy
him:**
and sought some means of making
away with him — NEB
and they cast about for a way of destroying him — Gspd
and they began to seek means . . . —
Mon
and they kept looking for some way to
destroy Him — Wms
for they feared him,
for they were afraid of him — Mof
They were really afraid of him — Nor

because all the people was astonished at his doctrine.

for all the multitude was astonished at his teaching — ASV

because the whole crowd was spell-bound by . . . — NEB

for all the people were amazed at what he taught — Gspd

for his teaching had captured the imagination of the people — Phi

19. And when even was come,

And every evening — ASV

And whenever it became late — ABUV

And whenever evening came — NASB

he went out of the city.

they went forth out . . . — ABUV

they would go out . . . — NASB

he and his disciples used to go out . . . — Gspd

20. And in the morning, as they passed by,

And as they passed by in the morning — ASV

Early next morning, as they passed by — NEB

One morning as they were walking along — Phi

they saw the fig tree dried up from the roots.

. . . withered away from the roots — ASV

. . . withered away to its roots — RSV

. . . withered root and branch — Rieu

21. And Peter calling to remembrance saith unto him,

And Peter remembered and said to him — RSV

Then Peter remembered, and exclaimed — Mon

Master, behold, the fig tree which thou cursedst is withered away.

Rabbi, look, the fig-tree which you cursed has withered — NEB

Master, look, the fig-tree that you cursed is all shrivelled up! — Phi

Master, look! The fig tree which You doomed has withered away! — Amp

22. And Jesus answering saith unto them,

Jesus answered them — Mof

Have faith in God.

Take hold on God's faithfulness — Mon

23. For verily I say unto you,

For I assure you — Ber

I solemnly say to you — Wms

That whosoever shall say unto this mountain,

whoever says to this mountain — RSV

Be thou removed,

Be thou taken up — ASV

Be lifted from your place — NEB

Move! — Nor

and be thou cast into the sea;

and throw yourself . . . — Wms

and hurl yourself . . . — Mon

and shall not doubt in his heart,

and does not . . . — RSV

and does not waver . . . — Rieu

and has not a doubt in his mind — Mof

and has no inward doubts — NEB

but shall believe that those things which he saith shall come to pass;

but believes that what he says will . . . — RSV

but stedfastly believes . . . will happen — Wey

but believes . . . is happening — NEB

. . . is done — Rieu

he shall have whatsoever he saith.

he shall have it — ASV

it shall be granted him — Wey

it will be done for him — RSV

24. Therefore I say unto you,

That is why I tell you — Wey

What things soever ye desire, when ye pray,

whatever you pray about and ask for — Phi

whatever you ask in prayer — RSV

believe that ye receive them,

. . . you will[37] receive it — Nor

. . . ye have received — Alf

and ye shall have them.

and you will — RSV

and it will be yours — NEB

25. And when ye stand praying,

And whenever you . . . — RSV

Also, whenever you stand up to pray — Mof

forgive, if ye have ought against any:

forgive whatever wrong any man has done you — Knox

you must forgive anything that you are holding against anyone else — Phi

that your Father also which is in heaven may forgive you your trespasses.

so that your Father in heaven may forgive you the wrongs you have done — NEB

---

[37]Based on a slightly different reading.

and your Heavenly Father will forgive you your sins — Phi

26. But if ye do not forgive, neither will your Father which is in heaven forgive your trespasses.[38]

27. And they come again to Jerusalem:

Once more they entered Jerusalem — Ber

and as he was walking in the temple,

... in the temple court — NEB

there come to him the chief priests, and the scribes, and the elders,

the chief priests and scribes and elders came to him — Knox

the Chief Priests, elders and Scribes approached him — Phi

28. And say unto him,

And began saying to Him — NASB

By what authority doest thou these things?

... are you doing these things — RSV

What authority have you for doing as you do — Gspd

By what authority are you acting — Rieu

and who gave thee this authority to do these things?

or who gave you this authority to do them — RSV

And who gave you a right to do as you are doing — Gspd

And who gave you permission to do these things — Phi

29. And Jesus answered and said unto them,

Jesus replied — Rieu

I will also ask of you one question,

Let me ask you ... — Gspd

I will ask you for a statement — Rieu

and answer me,

and I will tell you by what authority I do these things.

... I am acting — Rieu

30. The baptism of John, was it from heaven, or of men?

Was John's baptism from heaven or from men — Gspd

John's baptism — was it sanctioned by Heaven or by man — Rieu

The baptism of John: was it from God or from men — NEB

answer me.

Tell me that. — Phi

31. And they reasoned with themselves, saying,

This set them arguing among themselves — NEB

So they debated the matter with one another — Wey

They turned this over in their minds, saying to themselves — Rieu

If we shall say, From heaven;

If we say, from God — NEB

he will say, Why then did ye not believe him?

he will ask us, ... have faith in him — Rieu

32. But if we shall say, Of men;

But shall we say, From men? — RSV

But how can we say, From men? — Nor

they feared the people:

— they were afraid of the people — RSV

For ... — Nor

for all men counted John, that he was a prophet indeed.

for all men verily held John to be a prophet — ASV

for all held that John was a real prophet — RSV

for everyone was convinced that John was a prophet — Rieu

33. And they answered and said unto Jesus,

So they replied to Jesus — Mof

We cannot tell.

We know not — ASV

We do not know — Gspd

And Jesus answering saith unto them,

Jesus replied to them — Ber

Neither do I tell you by what authority I do these things.

Then neither will I tell you ... I act — NEB

CHAPTER 12

1. And he began to speak unto them by parables.

Then He began to speak to them in parables — Wey

A certain man planted a vineyard,

A man once ... — Gspd

There was a man who ... — Knox

and set an hedge about it,

---

[38]Now recognized as not adequately supported by original manuscripts.

and set a hedge around it — RSV
and put a wall round it — NEB
and fenced it in — Gspd
and digged a place for the winefat,
and dug a wine-vat — ABUV
dug a pit for the wine-press — Mon
and built a tower,
and built a watch-tower — Wey
and let it out to husbandmen,
then rented it out to some tenants — Nor
then he leased it to vinedressers — Mof
and went into a far country.
and left the neighborhood — Gspd
and went into another country — ASV
and went abroad — NEB

2. **And at the season**
   At the proper time — TCNT
   At vintage-time — Wey
   At the end of the season — Phi
   he sent to the husbandmen a servant,
   he sent a slave to the tenants — Gspd
   he sent an agent to the workers — Ber
   that he might receive from the husbandmen
   to get from them — RSV
   to collect . . . — NEB
   of the fruit of the vineyard.
   some of the proceeds . . . — Mon
   a share of the vintage — Wey
   his share of the produce — NEB

3. **And they caught him, and beat him,**
   And they took him . . . — ASV
   But they seized and thrashed him — Rieu
   and sent him away empty.
   and sent him back empty-handed — Gspd

4. **And again he sent unto them another servant;**
   A second time the owner sent a servant to them — TCNT
   He then sent another on the same errand — Nor
   and at him they cast stones, and wounded him in the head
   and him they wounded in the head — ASV
   And they beat him over the head — Gspd
   whom they beat about . . . — NEB
   and sent him away shamefully handled.
   and treated him shamefully — RSV
   and treated outrageously — NEB
   and insulted — Mof

5. **And again he sent another;**
   So he . . . — NEB
   and him they killed,
   but him they murdered — Phi
   and many others; beating some, and killing some.
   and so with many others, some they beat and some they killed — RSV
   And so they treated many others; some they flogged and some . . . — Mof

6. **Having yet therefore one son, his well-beloved,**
   He had yet one, a beloved son — ASV
   . . . one beloved son — Alf
   He had now only one left to send, his own dear son — NEB
   he sent him also last unto them, saying,
   finally he sent him to them, saying — RSV
   he sent him to them last of all, thinking — Gspd
   They will reverence my son.
   . . . respect . . . — Rieu
   . . . surely respect my own son — Phi

7. **But those husbandmen said among themselves,**
   But those vinedressers said to themselves — Mof
   But those tenants said to one another — RSV
   But those tenant-farmers . . . — Nor
   This is the heir;
   This is his heir — Gspd
   This fellow is the future owner — Phi
   come, let us kill him,
   come on . . . — Mof
   and the inheritance shall be ours.
   and the property will be ours — NEB
   and then we'll get the inheritance — Beck
   and everything that he would get will come to us! — Phi

8. **And they took him, and killed him,**
   So they seized him . . . — Wey
   Accordingly, they pounced on him and murdered him — Nor
   So they got hold of him . . . — Phi
   and cast him out of the vineyard.
   and flung his body outside . . . — Wey
   and dumped . . . — Nor

9. **What shall therefore³⁹ the lord of the vineyard do?**
   What will the owner . . . — Rieu

---

³⁹Some manuscripts do not have this word.

he will come and destroy the husband-men,

. . . and put the tenants to death — NEB

. . . and destroy the men who were working his vineyard — Phi

and will give the vineyard unto others.

and will hand it over to others — Phi

and lease the vineyard . . . — Ber

10. **And have ye not read this scripture;**

Have ye not read even . . . — ASV

Can it be that you have never read this text — NEB

The stone which the builders rejected

The very stone . . . — Mon

That stone which the builders threw away — Wms

is become the head of the corner:

The same was made . . . — ASV

has become . . . — RSV

. . . the main corner-stone — NEB

11. **This was the Lord's doing,**

This was from the Lord — ASV

This came . . . — Gspd

This is the work of the Lord — Wms

This corner-stone has come from the Lord — TCNT

and it is marvellous in our eyes?

And is wonderful . . . — ABUV

and a wonder to our eyes — Mof

And seems marvelous to us — Gspd

and admirable in our eyes — Rieu

12. **And they sought to lay hold on him,**

And they made attempts to take him — Bas

And they tried to arrest him — RSV

Then they began to look for a way to . . . — NEB

but feared the people:

but they were afraid of . . . — Gspd

. . . popular feeling — NEB

for they knew that he had spoken the parable against them:

for they perceived that he spake . . . — ASV

They knew he had meant the parable for them — Mof

for they knew perfectly well that he had aimed this parable at them—Phi

and they left him, and went their way.

and they left him, and went away — ASV

so they left him alone . . . — NEB

so they let him be and withdrew—Rieu

13. **And they send unto him certain of the**

Pharisees and of the Herodians,

But they sent some of the Pharisees and Herodians — Mof

A number of Pharisees and men of Herod's party were sent — NEB

Their next step was to send to Him some of the Pharisees and of Herod's partisans — Wey

to catch him in his words.

that they might catch him in talk — ASV

to set a trap for him in the course of conversation — TCNT

to trap him with a question — NEB

. . . in an argument — Phi

14. **And when they were come, they say unto him,**

And they came and said to him — RSV

They came up . . . — Mof

Master, we know that thou art true,

Teacher, . . . you are true — RSV

Master, . . . you tell the truth — Gspd

Teacher, we know you are sincere — Mof

Master, you are an honest man, we know — NEB

and carest for no man:

and fearless — Mof

regardless of the consequences — Gspd

and not partial to anyone — Ber

You are not prejudiced for or against a man — Nor

and that you are not swayed by men's opinions of you — Phi

for thou regardest not the person of men,

for you pay no regard to a man's position — TCNT

you do not court human favour — Mof

Obviously you don't care for human approval — Phi

but teachest the way of God in truth:

but of a truth teachest the way of God — ASV

but truly teach . . . — RSV

you teach in all honesty the way of life that God requires — NEB

Is it lawful to give tribute to Caesar, or not?

. . . to pay taxes . . . — RSV

Is it right . . . — Mof

Is it lawful to pay a poll-tax . . . — NASB

Are we or are we not permitted to pay taxes to the Roman Emperor — NEB

15. **Shall we give, or shall we not give?**

Must we give, or must we not give —
Alf
Should we pay them, or should we not
— RSV
Shall we pay, or shall we refuse to
pay — Wey
**But he, knowing their hypocrisy, said
unto them,**
But he, detecting . . ., replied — Rieu
But he saw their trick and said to them
— Mof
But he saw through their pretense, and
. . . — Gspd
He saw how crafty their question was,
and said — NEB
Why tempt ye me?
Why make ye trial of me — ASV
Why put me to the test — RSV
Why try to ensnare me — Wey
Why try this trick on me — Phi
bring me a penny, that I may see it.
. . . a denarius, . . . — RSV
. . . a coin, and let me look at it — RSV
Fetch me a silver piece . . . — NEB

16. And they brought it.
So they brought one — Mof
And he saith unto them,
Then He asked them — Wms
**Whose is this image and superscrip-
tion?**
Whose likeness and inscription is this
— RSV
Whose head is this, and whose inscrip-
tion — NEB
Whose head and title is this — Gspd
And they said unto him, Caesar's.
Caesar's, they replied — Wey
And they told him, The emperor's —
Gspd

17. And Jesus answering said unto them,
And Jesus said to them — ABUV
**Render to Caesar the things that are
Caesar's,**
Then give to Caesar what belongs to
Caesar — Phi
Pay Caesar what is due to Caesar —
NEB
Give back to Caesar what is Caesar's
— Knox
and to God the things that are God's.
. . . what is due to God — Rieu
And they marvelled at him.
And they marvelled greatly . . . — ASV
And they heard him with astonish-
ment — NEB
— a reply which staggered them — Phi

18. Then come unto him the Sadducees,
Then came up some Sadducees — Mon
The next to come to him were some of
the . . . — Rieu
which say there is no resurrection;
who maintain . . . — Ber
a sect which denies that there is any
. . . — Wey
and they asked him, saying,
and put a question to him — Mof
Their question was this: — NEB
19. Master, Moses wrote unto us,
. . . Moses prescribed for us — Knox
Teacher, Moses gave us a law — Wms
Master, Moses laid it down for us —
NEB
If a man's brother die,
that if . . . died — Gspd
that if a man with a brother dies—Rieu
**and leave his wife behind him, and
leave no children,**
and leaves a wife, but leaves no child
— RSV
that his brother should take his wife,
his brother should marry his widow —
Rieu
the man must take the wife — RSV
and raise up seed unto his brother.
. . . children for his brother — RSV
. . . a family . . . — Wey
and beget children in the dead brother's
name — Knox
and so provide him with descendants
— Rieu
20. Now there were seven brethren:
There were seven brothers — ABUV
and the first took a wife,
The eldest married a wife — Wms
and dying left no seed.
and died leaving no offspring — Mof
. . . without issue — Mon
. . . childless — Knox
21. And the second took her,
Then . . . married her — Ber
and died, neither left he any seed:
and died without leaving any child —
Gspd
and he too died without issue — NEB
and the third likewise.
and the third did the same — Wey
The same thing happened with the
third — Phi
**22. And the seven had her,[40] and left no
seed:**

---

[40]Now recognized as not adequately supported
by original manuscripts.

and the seven left no seed — ASV

And not one of the seven left a child — Wms

In fact all seven died without issue — Rieu

last of all the woman died also.

Finally the woman herself died — Phi

23. **In the resurrection therefore, when they shall rise,**[41]

In the resurrection — ASV

At . . . — TCNT

whose wife shall she be of them?

. . . will she be — Wey

for the seven had her to wife.

. . . for a wife — ABUV

. . . as wife — RSV

since all seven had married her — NEB

24. **And Jesus answering said unto them,**

Jesus said to them — Mof

Jesus replied — Phi

Do ye not therefore err,

Is it not for this cause that ye err — ASV

. . . on this account . . . — ABUV

Is not this why you are wrong — RSV

because ye know not the scriptures, neither the power of God?

that . . . , nor . . . — ASV

that you know neither the scriptures . . . — RSV

25. **For when they shall rise from the dead,**

For when people rise . . . — Gspd

For when they have risen . . . — Wey

they neither marry, nor are given in marriage;

men do not marry and women are not . . . — Wey

men and women do not marry — NEB

but are as the angels which are in heaven.

but are as angels in heaven — ASV

but they live as angels do . . . — Gspd

26. **And as touching the dead, that they rise:**

But . . . , that they are raised — ASV

As for the dead being raised — Mof

have ye not read in the book of Moses,

have you never read . . . — Wey

how in the bush God spake unto him, saying,

in the place concerning the Bush, how God spake unto him, saying — ASV

in the passage about the bush, how God said to him — Gspd

I am the God of Abraham, and the God of Isaac, and the God of Jacob?

I, the God of Abraham . . . — Rieu

27. **He is not the God of the dead, but the God of the living:**

. . . but of the living — ASV

God is not God of the dead . . . — NEB

ye therefore do greatly err.

ye do greatly err — ASV

You are greatly mistaken — NEB

you are quite wrong — RSV

You are entirely wrong — Gspd

That is where you made your great mistake! — Phi

28. **And one of the scribes came,**

. . . came up — RSV

Then . . . approached him — Phi

and having heard them reasoning together,

and heard them arguing — Gspd

He had been listening to the discussion — Phi

and perceiving that he had answered them well, asked him,

and seeing that he answered . . . — RSV

and noticing how well Jesus had answered them, he put this question to him — Phi

Which is the first commandment of all?

What commandment is the first of all — ASV

What is the chief of all the commands — Mof

Which commandment is most important to all — Nor

29. **And Jesus answered him,**

Jesus replied — Mon

The first of all the commandments is,

The first is — ASV

The chief one is: — Mof

Hear, O Israel; The Lord our God is one Lord:

. . . The Lord our God, the Lord is one — ASV

. . . The Lord your God is the only Lord — NEB

30. **And thou shalt love the Lord thy God**

love the Lord your God — NEB

and you must . . . — Mof

with all thy heart, and with all thy soul,

with all your heart, and with all your soul — RSV

---

[41]This clause is now recognized as not adequately supported by original manuscripts.

with your whole heart, your whole soul
— Gspd

**and with all thy mind, and with all thy
strength:**

and with all your mind, . . . your
strength — RSV

your whole mind, and your whole
strength — Gspd

this is the first commandment.[42]

31. And the second is like,[43] namely this,

The second is this — ASV

A second . . . — ABUV

**Thou shalt love thy neighbour as thy-
self.**

Love your neighbour as yourself — NEB

You must love . . . — Mof

. . . as you do yourself — Gspd

**There is none other commandment
greater than these.**

There is no . . . — ABUV

No other commandment is greater than
these — Phi

32. And the scribe said unto him,

The scribe then remarked — Nor

Well, Master, thou hast said the truth:

Of a truth, Teacher, thou hast well said
— ASV

You are right, Teacher; you have truly
said — RSV

Really, Master, you have finely said —
Gspd

**for there is one God; and there is none
other but he:**

that he is one . . . — ASV

that God is one and beside him there
is no other — NEB

that he stands alone, and there is none
but he — Gspd

**33. And to love him with all the heart, and
with all the understanding,**

Also, . . . with the whole heart, with
the whole understanding — Mof

and to love Him with the whole of our
hearts, the whole of our intelligence
— Phi

**and with all the soul, and with all the
strength,**

and with all the strength — ASV

and with all one's power — Rieu

and the whole of our energy — Phi

and to love his neighbour as himself,

and to love one's neighbour as oneself
— Mof

. . . no less than oneself — Wey

**is more than all whole burnt offerings
and sacrifices.**

is much more . . . — ASV

is infinitely more important than all
these burnt-offerings and sacrifices —
Phi

**34. And when Jesus saw that he answered
discreetly, he said unto him,**

wisely . . . — RSV

When Jesus saw how sensibly he answered . . . — NEB

Then Jesus, observing his intelligent response, said to him — Ber

**Thou art not far from the kingdom of
God.**

You are not far from the kingdom of
God! — Phi

**And no man after that durst ask him
any question.**

After that no one ventured to put any
more questions to him — Mof

After this, no one dared to pester Him
with catch-questions — Nor

**35. And Jesus answered and said, while he
taught in the temple,**

and Jesus went on to say, as . . . — NEB

As Jesus was teaching in the Temple,
he answered them and said — Gspd

While he was teaching in the Temple
courts, Jesus in his turn asked—Mon

As Jesus was teaching in the temple,
He came back at them with the question — Ber

**How say the scribes that Christ is the
son of David?**

. . . the Christ . . . — ASV

How can the scribes say that the Christ
is David's son — Mof

How can the Doctors of the Law maintain that the Messiah is a son of
David — Rieu

**36. For David himself said by the Holy
Ghost,**

David himself said in the Holy Spirit
— ASV

. . . inspired by the Holy Spirit, declared — RSV

. . . under the guidance of . . ., said —
Wms

David himself was moved by the Holy
Spirit to say — Knox

The Lord said to my Lord,

Sit thou on my right hand,

---

[42]Now recognized as not adequately supported
by original manuscripts.

[43]The word "like" is now recognized as not
adequately supported by original manuscripts.

Sit at . . . — RSV

till I make thine enemies thy footstool.

. . . the footstool of thy feet — ASV

till I put thy enemies under thy feet —
RSV

**37. David therefore himself calleth him
Lord;**

David himself calls him "Lord"—Wey

and whence is he then his son?

so how is he his son — RSV

how can he also be David's son — NEB

— where do they get the idea that he
is his son — Phi

**And the common people heard him
gladly.**

And the great multitude . . . — Alf

And the great throng listened to Him
with delight — Ber

The vast crowd heard this with great
delight — Phi

38. And he said unto them in his doctrine,

And in his teaching he said — ASV

And in the course of his teaching . . .
— Mof

He said as he taught them — NEB

Beware of the scribes,

Be on your guard against the Scribes —
Wey

. . . the Doctors of the Law — Rieu

which love to go in long clothing,

who desire to walk in long robes — ASV

who love to walk up and down . . . —
NEB

They like to parade about . . . — Nor

**and love salutations in the market-
places,**

and to be saluted with respect in public
places — Gspd

and having their hands kissed in the
market-place — Knox

39. And the chief seats in the synagogues,

and the best seats . . . — RSV

and to have the front seats . . . — Gspd

and the uppermost rooms at feasts:

and the places of honor . . . — RSV

and the choice places at the banquets
— Ber

and the best places at dinner-parties! —
Phi

40. Which devour widows' houses,

they prey upon the property of widows
— Mof

These are the men who eat up . . . —
NEB

. . . who live on widows' property—Phi

They are the men that rob widows of
their homes — TCNT

and for a pretence make long prayers:

and then mask their wickedness by
making long prayers — Wey

and to cover it up make long prayers!
— Gspd

and seek to justify themselves by making lengthy prayers — Rieu

these shall receive greater damnation.

. . . condemnation — ASV

All the heavier will their sentence be!
— Mof

They are only adding to their own punishment! — Phi

**41. And Jesus sat over against the treas-
ury,**

And he sat down opposite . . . — RSV

Then he sat down in front of the col-
lection-box — Wms

**and beheld how the people cast money
into the treasury:**

and watched the multitude putting
money . . . — RSV

watching as people dropped their
money into the chest — NEB

and many that were rich cast in much.

and many rich people were putting in
large sums — Gspd

42. And there came a certain poor widow,

but one poor widow came — TCNT

Then a poor widow came up — Phi

**and she threw in two mites, which
make a farthing.**

who dropped in two tiny coins, together
worth a farthing — NEB

and put in two copper coins, which
make a penny — RSV

**43. And he called unto him his disciples,
and saith unto them,**

Summoning His disciples, He told them
— Ber

So He called His disciples to Him and
said — Wey

Verily I say unto you,

I assure you — Ber

**That this poor widow hath cast more
in, than all they which have cast into
the treasury:**

this poor widow has put in more than
all those who are contributing to the
treasury — RSV

. . . than all the others — Phi

**44. For all they did cast in of their abun-
dance;**

for they all did cast in of their superfluity — ASV

for they have all put in a contribution
out of their surplus — Mof

For they all gave of what they had to
spare — Gspd

**but she of her want did cast in all that
she had, even all her living.**

but she out of her poverty has put in

everything she had, her whole living
— RSV

but she out of her need has thrown in
all she possessed — all she had to
live on — Wey

she, with so little to give, put in all that
she had, her whole livelihood —
Knox

CHAPTER 13

1. And as he went out of the temple,
As he was leaving . . . — NEB

one of his disciples saith unto him,
. . . exclaimed — Wey

**Master, see what manner of stones and
what buildings are here!**
Look, Teacher, what wonderful stones
and what wonderful buildings!—RSV
Look, Master. What mighty blocks of
stone! What marvelous buildings!
— Rieu

2. And Jesus answering said unto him,
Jesus replied to him — Ber

Seest thou these great buildings?
Do you see . . . — Gspd
Are you looking in wonder at . . . —
Wms

**there shall not be left one stone upon
another,**
there shall not be left here . . . — ASV
not one stone will be left here resting
upon another — Wey
Not a single stone will be left standing
on another — Phi

that shall not be thrown down.
. . . torn down — Gspd

**3. And as he sat upon the mount of
Olives over against the temple,**
As he was sitting on the Mount of
Olives opposite . . . — Gspd
Then while he was sitting on the slope
of the Mount of Olives facing . . . —
Phi
Later, as he sat in view of the Temple,
on the Mount of Olives — Rieu

**Peter and James and John and Andrew
asked him privately,**
Peter, James, John, and Andrew asked
him, apart from the others — Gspd

4. Tell us, when shall these things be?
Tell us, when will this be — RSV
. . . when is this to happen — Mof

**and what shall be the sign when all
these things shall be fulfilled?**

. . . when these things are all about to
be accomplished — ASV
What will be the sign when the fulfilment of all this is at hand — NEB

**5. And Jesus answering them began to
say,**
And Jesus began to say unto them —
ASV
So Jesus began to tell them — Phi
So Jesus began: — Mof

Take heed lest any man deceive you:
. . . that no man lead you astray — ASV
Take care that no one misleads you —
Wey

6. For many shall come in my name,
Many will come claiming my name —
NEB
. . . under my name — Gspd
. . . making use of my name — Knox
. . . bearing the name Messiah — Wms

saying, I am Christ;
saying, I am he — Alf
and say, Here I am — Phi

and shall deceive many.
and shall lead many astray — ASV
and will mislead many — Mon

**7. And when ye shall hear of wars and
rumours of wars,**
When you hear the noise of battle near
at hand and the news of battles far
away — NEB

be ye not troubled:
do not be alarmed — RSV
. . . frightened — NASB
. . . dismayed — Mon

for such things must needs be;
these things must needs come to pass
— ASV
they must . . . — ABUV
They have to come — Gspd
Such things are bound to happen—Phi

but the end shall not be yet.
but the end is not yet — ASV
. . . in sight — Nor

but the end is still to come — NEB

8. For nation shall rise against nation,

For nation will make war upon nation — NEB

Nation will take up arms against nation — Phi

and kingdom against kingdom:

kingdom upon kingdom — NEB

and kingdom against kingdom — Phi

and there shall be earthquakes in divers places,

there will be earthquakes in various places — ABUV

. . . here and there — Mof

. . . in many places — NEB

and there shall be famines and troubles:

there shall be famines — ASV

and famines, too — Mof

these are the beginnings of sorrows.

these things are the beginning of travail — ASV

. . . birth-pangs — ABUV

this is but the beginning of the sufferings — RSV

With these things the birth-pangs of the new age begin — NEB

9. But take heed to yourselves:

As for you, be on your guard — NEB

Look out for yourselves — Ber

You yourselves must keep your wits about you — Phi

for they shall deliver you up to councils;

Men will hand you over to Sanhedrins — Mof

They will drag you into court — Rieu

and in the synagogues ye shall be beaten:

and you will be flogged in synagogues — Ber

and ye shall be brought before rulers and kings for my sake,

and you shall stand before governors and kings . . . — RSV

. . . on my account — Rieu

for a testimony against them.

. . . unto them — ASV

to bear your witness to them — Phi

to witness to them for me — Mon

10. And the gospel must first be published among all nations.

. . . be preached unto all the nations — ASV

— for before the end comes the Gospel

must be proclaimed to all the nations — Phi

11. But when they shall lead you, and deliver you up,

And when they shall lead you to judgment . . . — ASV

When they are taking you off to trial — Gspd

So when you are arrested and taken away — NEB

take no thought beforehand what ye shall speak,

do not be anxious beforehand . . . — ASV

do not worry what you are going to say — Phi

neither do ye premeditate:[44]

but whatsoever shall be given you in that hour, that speak ye:

but say whatever is given you in that hour — RSV

— simply say the words you are given when the time comes — Phi

for it is not ye that speak, but the Holy Ghost.

for it will not be you who speak, but the Holy Spirit — Wey

12. Now the brother shall betray the brother to death,

And brother shall deliver up brother . . . — ASV

Brother will betray brother . . . — NEB

Men will hand over their brothers for execution — Rieu

and the father the son;

. . . his child — ASV

and a father his own child — Phi

and children shall rise up against their parents,

. . . will turn against their . . . — Gspd

and shall cause them to be put to death.

and kill them — Ber

and condemn them to death — Phi

and send them to their death — Rieu

13. And ye shall be hated of all men for my name's sake:

You will be hated by everyone, because you bear my name — Gspd

There will come a time when the whole world will hate you because you are known as my followers — Phi

---

[44]Now recognized as not adequately supported by original manuscripts.

All will hate you for your allegiance to me — NEB

but he that shall endure unto the end,
but he that hath endured . . . — Alf
but he who endures to . . . — RSV
but whoever perseveres to the finish — Ber
but he that endures to the uttermost — Rieu
the same shall be saved.
will be saved — RSV

14. **But when ye shall see the abomination of desolation,**
But when you see "the abomination of desolation" — NEB
. . . the desolating sacrilege — RSV
spoken of by Daniel the prophet,[45]
standing where it ought not,
. . . he . . . — ASV
standing where he has no right to stand — Gspd
set up where it ought not to be — RSV
usurping a place which is not his — NEB
(let him that readeth understand,)
(let the reader note this) — Mof
then let them that be in Judaea flee to the mountains:
let those in Judaea take refuge in the hills — Rieu
then those who are in Judaea must take to . . . — NEB

15. **And let him that is on the house top not go down into the house,**[46]
a man on the housetop must not go down — Gspd
neither enter therein, to take any thing out of his house:
nor enter in . . . — ASV
nor enter his house, to take anything away — RSV
and go indoors to save any of his household goods — Rieu

16. **And let him that is in the field not turn back again**
and . . . not turn back — RSV
for to take up his garment.
to pick up his coat — Ber

17. **But woe to them that are with child,**
And alas for the pregnant women — Mon
and to them that give suck in those days!
and for those that are nursing their infants in those days! — Mon

18. **And pray ye that your flight be not in the winter.**

And pray ye that it be not in the winter — ASV
Pray that it may not happen in winter — RSV

19. **For in those days shall be affliction,**
For those days shall be tribulation — ASV
. . . will be a time of distress — ABUV
. . . will bring distress — NEB
such as was not from the beginning of the creation which God created
such as there hath not been the like . . . — ASV
such as never was since the beginning of God's creation — Ber
unto this time, neither shall be.
until now; neither shall be — Ber
. . . and never will be again — Gspd

20. **And except that the Lord had shortened those days,**
And if the Lord had not shortened the days — Alf
And, had not the Lord put a limit to those days — TCNT
no flesh should be saved:
no human being would be saved — RSV
not a single soul would escape — TCNT
no living thing could survive — NEB
but for the elect's sake, whom he hath chosen,
However, for the sake of his own, whom he has . . . — NEB
but for the sake of His elect . . . for Himself — Wey
he hath shortened the days.
he has cut short the time — NEB
he did limit them — TCNT

21. **And then if any man shall say to you,**
And then if any one says . . . — RSV
Lo, here is Christ;
. . . the Christ — ASV
Look, here is the Messiah — NEB
or, lo, he is there;
or, Lo, there — ASV
or, Look, there he is! — RSV
believe him not:
do not believe it — Mof

22. **For false Christs and false prophets shall rise,**
. . . will appear — Gspd

---

[45]Now recognized as not adequately supported by original manuscripts.
[46]The words "into the house" are now recognized as not adequately supported by original manuscripts.

Impostors will come claiming to be messiahs or prophets — NEB

and shall shew signs and wonders,

and perform . . . — Mof

and they shall produce . . . — NEB

and display signs and marvels — TCNT

to seduce, if it were possible, even the elect.

that they might lead astray, if possible, the elect — ASV

to mislead the elect if they can — Mof

. . . God's chosen, if such a thing were possible — NEB

23. **But take ye heed:**

Be on your guard! — Ber

You must keep your eyes open! — Phi

behold, I have foretold you all things.

behold, I have told you all things beforehand — ASV

I have forewarned you of everything — Rieu

I am giving you this warning before it happens — Phi

24. **But in those days, after that tribulation,**

. . . when that misery is over — Gspd

. . . after that time of trouble — Bas

the sun shall be darkened,

. . . will turn dark — Wms

and the moon shall not give her light,

. . . will not shed its light — Gspd

. . . will cease to shine — Nor

25. **And the stars of heaven shall fall,**

. . . shall be falling from heaven — ASV

the stars will come falling from the sky — Rieu

. . . shall be fading from heaven — Ber

and the powers that are in heaven shall be shaken.

the celestial powers will . . . — NEB

and the powers of heaven will rock on their foundations — Phi

26. **And then shall they see the Son of man**

Then men shall behold the Son of Man — Nor

coming in the clouds with great power and glory.

. . . on the clouds in overwhelming power and splendor — Wms

27. **And then shall he send his angels,**

. . . forth the angels — ASV

and shall gather together his elect from the four winds,

and gather his chosen . . . — NEB

. . . together His elect from north, south, east, and west — Wey

to summon His chosen together from every quarter — Phi

from the uttermost part of the earth to the uttermost part of heaven.

— from the furthest bounds of earth and heaven — Wey

from one end of the world to the other — Gspd

from furthest earth to highest heaven — Phi

28. **Now learn a parable of the fig tree;**

Now from the fig tree learn her parable — ASV

From the fig tree learn its lesson — RSV

Learn a lesson from the fig-tree — NEB

When her branch is yet tender, and putteth forth leaves,

. . . is now become tender, and putteth forth its leaves — ASV

When its tender shoots appear and are breaking into leaf — NEB

as soon as ever her branches are full of sap and bursting into leaf — Mon

ye know that summer is near:

you know summer is at hand — Mof

29. **So ye in like manner, when ye shall see these things come to pass,**

even so ye also, when ye see these things coming to pass — ASV

So when you see these things happening — Gspd

know that it is nigh, even at the doors.

know ye that he is nigh . . . — ASV

you know that he is near, at the very gates — RSV

you may know that the end is near, at the very door — NEB

30. **Verily I say unto you,**

I tell you truly — Mof

I solemnly say to you — Wms

that this generation shall not pass,

This generation shall not pass away — ASV

the present generation will not . . . — Mof

this present age will not have passed — Phi

till all these things be done.

until all these things be accomplished — ASV

before all these things take place — RSV

until all these things begin to happen — Mon

31. **Heaven and earth shall pass away:**

Sky and earth will pass away — Wey

but my words shall not pass away.

my words will never . . . — NEB

but what I have told you will stand — Phi

32. But of that day and that hour knoweth no man,

No one knows anything about that day or hour — Mof

no, not the angels which are in heaven,

not even the angels in heaven — ASV

neither the Son, but the Father.

nor the Son, but only the Father — RSV

not even the Son . . . — Mof

33. Take ye heed, watch and pray:

Take heed, watch — RSV

Be alert, be wakeful — NEB

Take care, be on the alert, and pray — Wey

Keep looking, keep alert — Wms

for ye know not when the time is.

You do not know when the moment comes — NEB

for you do not know when it will happen — Wey

since you do not know the appointed time — Rieu

34. For the Son of man is as a man taking a far journey,

[It is] as a man taking a journey — Alf

It is like a man going on . . . — RSV

who left his house, and gave authority to his servants,

when he leaves home and puts his servants in charge — RSV

and to every man his work,

each with his own work to do — NEB

to each his particular task — Wms

and commanded the porter to watch.

and commands the doorkeeper to be on the watch — RSV

and has ordered . . . on the look-out for his return — Phi

35. Watch ye therefore:

Watch therefore — ASV

Keep awake, then — NEB

Just so must you keep a look-out — Phi

Keep a sharp lookout! — Tay

for ye know not when the master of the house cometh,

for you know not . . . is coming — Wey

at even, or at midnight, or at the cock-crowing, or in the morning:

at evening . . . — ABUV

in the evening . . ., or toward daybreak or early in the morning — Gspd

36. Lest coming suddenly he find you sleeping.

Beware lest He should arrive unexpectedly and find you asleep — Wey

— otherwise He might come unexpectedly and find you sound asleep — Phi

37. And what I say unto you I say unto all, Watch.

. . . I say to everyone: Keep awake — NEB

CHAPTER 14

1. After two days was the feast of the passover,

Now two days later was the feast of the Passover — Mon

It was now two days before the Passover — RSV

and of unleavened bread:

and the feast of Unleavened Bread — RSV

and the chief priests and the scribes sought how they might take him by craft,

. . . with subtlety — ASV

were seeking how to seize Him by stealth — NASB

were trying to think of some trick by which they could get Jesus into their power — Phi

and put him to death.

and kill him — ASV

and have him put to death — Mof

2. But they said, Not on the feast day,

for they said, Not during the feast — ASV

lest there be an uproar of the people.

. . . a tumult . . . — RSV

or the people will riot — Rieu

3. And being in Bethany in the house of Simon the leper,

And while he was . . . — ASV

Now when He was at Bethany . . . — Wey

as he sat at meat,

as he was reclining at table — ABUV

there came a woman having an alabaster box of ointment of spikenard very precious;

. . . having an alabaster cruse of ointment of pure nard very costly — ASV

a woman came in carrying a small bottle of very costly perfume, oil of pure nard — NEB

and she brake the box, and poured it on his head.

and she crushed the flask, and poured it over . . . — ABUV

4. **And there were some that had indignation within themselves, and said,**

. . . among themselves, saying — ASV

Some of those present were highly indignant and muttered — Phi

Whereupon some of them exchanged indignant comments — Rieu

Why was this waste of the ointment made?

To what purpose hath this waste . . . been made — ASV

Why was the ointment thus wasted — — RSV

Why this waste — NEB

What was the use of wasting the perfume like that — Gspd

5. **For it might have been sold for more than three hundred pence,**

For this ointment . . . denarii — RSV

This ointment . . . for three hundred pieces of silver — Knox

and have been given to the poor.

and the money given . . . — NEB

And they murmured against her.

And they angrily rebuked her — ABUV

And they reproached her — RSV

So they upbraided her — Mof

And they chided her — Ber

So they kept on grumbling at her — Wms

6. **And Jesus said, Let her alone;**

But . . . — ASV

why trouble ye her?

Why must you make trouble for her — NEB

Why are you annoying her — Mof

Why do you embarrass her — Ber

she hath wrought a good work on me.

She has done a good deed to me—Wms

It is a fine thing she has done for me — NEB

She has done a beautiful thing to me — Mof

7. **For ye have the poor with you always,**

You have the poor among you always — Rieu

and whenever ye will ye may do them good:

and you can help them whenever you like — NEB

but me ye have not always.

but you will not always have me — Mof

8. **She hath done what she could:**

She did . . . — Alf

She has done all she could — Gspd

she is come aforehand to anoint my body to the burying.

she hath anointed my body beforehand for the burying — ASV

she anointed . . . for my burial — Alf

— she has anticipated the perfuming of my body for burial — Mof

9. **Verily I say unto you,**

And I tell you in all truth — Rieu

Wheresoever this gospel shall be preached throughout the whole world,

wherever the gospel is preached in . . . — RSV

wherever, in the whole world, the Good News is proclaimed — TCNT

this also that she hath done shall be spoken of for a memorial of her.

what she has done will also be told, in memory of her — Gspd

the thing this woman did will also be spoken of, so that she shall not be forgotten — Rieu

10. **And Judas Iscariot, one of the twelve,**

Judas of Kerioth, one of the Twelve — Rieu

Then Judas Iscariot, who was one of the twelve — RSV

went unto the chief priests,

went away . . . — ASV

went off to . . . — Ber

to betray him unto them.

that he might deliver him unto them — ASV

11. **And when they heard it, they were glad,**

When they heard what he had to say they were delighted — Rieu

They gladly listened to his proposal — Wey

They were delighted to hear it — Mof

and promised to give him money.

. . . to pay him for it — Mof

And he sought how he might conveniently betray him.

. . . deliver him up — Alf

And he sought an opportunity to betray him — RSV

So he was watching for an opportunity to betray him to them — Gspd

12. And the first day of unleavened bread,
On the first day of the festival of Unleavened Bread — Gspd
when they killed the passover,
... sacrificed ... — ASV
— the day for killing the Passover lamb — Wey
his disciples said unto him,
His disciples asked Him — Wey
Where wilt thou that we go and prepare that thou mayest eat the passover?
Where do you want us to go and make the preparations for you to eat the Passover — Phi
Where do you wish us to go and arrange for you to eat the Passover — Rieu

13. And he sendeth forth two of his disciples,
And he sendeth two ... — ASV
So he sent out two of his disciples — NEB
and saith unto them,
with these instructions — Phi
Go ye into the city,
Go into ... — ASV
and there shall meet you a man bearing a pitcher of water:
and a man carrying a jar of water will meet you — RSV
and you will be met by a man carrying a jug of water — Rieu
follow him.

14. And wheresoever he shall go in,
And wherever he goes in — ABUV
and whatever house he goes into — Mof
say ye to the goodman of the house,
say to the master ... — ASV
say ye to the owner ... — Alf
say to the man ... — Gspd
The Master saith, Where is the guestchamber,
The Teacher saith, Where is my guestchamber — ASV
The Teacher says, ... my guest room — RSV
where I shall eat the passover with my disciples?
where I am to eat ... — RSV
where I can eat the Passover supper ... — Gspd

15. And he will shew you a large upper room furnished and prepared:

And he will himself ... and ready — ASV
And he will show you a large upstairs room all ready with the furnishings that we need — Phi
there make ready for us.
prepare the passover for us there — Mof

16. And his disciples went forth, and came into the city,
And the disciples set out and went to the city — RSV
and found as he had said unto them:
and found everything just as He had told them — Wey
and they made ready the passover.
... prepared ... — RSV
and they got the Passover supper ready — Wms

17. And in the evening he cometh with the twelve.
When it was evening he came with the Twelve — Gspd

18. And as they sat and did eat, Jesus said,
... and were eating ... — ASV
As they were at table eating ... — Mof
And while they were sitting there, right in the middle of the meal, Jesus remarked — Phi
Verily I say unto you, One of you which eateth with me shall betray me.
... One of you shall betray me, even he that eateth with me — ASV
I tell you in truth that one of you will betray me — one who is eating with me — Wey

19. And they began to be sorrowful,
And they were hurt — Gspd
At this they were dismayed — NEB
Their hearts sank — Rieu
and to say unto him one by one, Is it I?
... one after another, Is it I? — RSV
... Surely, not I? — Mon
and another said, Is it I?[47]

20. And he answered and said unto them,
He said to them — RSV
It is one of the twelve,
that dippeth with me in the dish.
he that ... — ASV
the man who dips his food with me in the bowl — Rieu

---

[47]Now recognized as not adequately supported by original manuscripts.

one who is dipping bread in the same dish with me — RSV

21. The Son of man indeed goeth, as it is written of him:

The Son of Man is going the way appointed for him in the scriptures — NEB

but woe to that man by whom the Son of man is betrayed!

but alas for the man . . . — Gspd

but a curse will be on that man by whom He is betrayed — Wms

good were it for that man if he had never been born.

. . . not been born — ASV

It would have been better for that man if he had never been born — Gspd

22. And as they did eat,

And as they were eating — ASV

During supper — NEB

Jesus took bread, and blessed, and brake it,

he took bread, and when he had blessed, he brake it — RSV

. . . and having said the blessing, he broke it — NEB

He took a loaf, blessed it, and broke it — Wey

. . . and blessed it, and broke it in pieces — Wms

and gave to them, and said,

and gave it to them, with the words — Phi

Take, eat: this is my body.

Take ye: this is my body — ASV

Take this. It is my body — Gspd

Take this, it means my body — Mof

23. And he took the cup,

Then He took a cup — Wey

and when he had given thanks, he gave it to them:

and after thanking God he gave it to them — Mof

and they all drank of it.

. . . from it — Gspd

24. And he said unto them,

He told them — Beck

This is my blood of the new testament,

. . . of the covenant — ASV

This means my covenant-blood — Mof

This represents my blood which ratifies the covenant — Wms

which is shed for many.

which is to be poured out on behalf of many — Wey

25. Verily I say unto you,

I tell you truly — Phi

I tell you in solemn truth — Mon

I will drink no more of the fruit of the vine,

I shall not drink again . . . — RSV

I will never drink the produce of the vine again — Mof

until that day that I drink it new in the kingdom of God.

till I drink the new wine . . . — Wey

till the day when I drink a new kind of wine . . . — Rieu

26. And when they had sung an hymn,

After singing the hymn — Gspd

After singing the Passover Hymn — NEB

Then they sang a psalm — Rieu

they went out into the mount of Olives.

. . . of the city and up the Mount of Olives — Gspd

27. And Jesus saith unto them,

Then Jesus told them — Beck

All ye shall be offended because of me this night:

All ye shall be offended — ASV

You will all be disconcerted — Mof

. . . turn against me — Beck

. . . desert me — Gspd

. . . fall away — RSV

. . . fall from your faith — NEB

for it is written, I will smite the shepherd,

for it stands written, I will strike the shepherd down — NEB

and the sheep shall be scattered.

and the sheep shall be scattered abroad — Phi

28. But after that I am risen,

Howbeit, after I am raised up — ASV

But after I am raised to life again — Gspd

I will go before you into Galilee.

I will precede you . . . — Rieu

29. But Peter said unto him,

Peter answered — NEB

Although all shall be offended, yet will not I.

Even though they all fall away,[48] I will not — RSV

30. And Jesus saith unto him,

Jesus told him — Ber

Verily I say unto thee,

I tell you in truth — Wey

---

[48]See verse 27 for varied renderings of this expression.

I solemnly say to you — Wms
That this day, even in this night,
today, this very night — NEB
before the cock crows twice,
thou shalt deny me thrice.
you will deny me three times — RSV
you yourself will disown me . . .! —
Gspd

31. But he spake the more vehemently,
But he kept saying most vehemently —
ABUV
But he insisted and repeated — NEB
But Peter kept on emphatically saying
— Wms
But Peter kept protesting passionately
— Mon
. . . protesting, with increasing vehem-
ence — Rieu
If I should die with thee,
Even if I must die with you — NEB
I will not deny thee in any wise.
I will by no means deny thee — ABUV
I will never disown you — NEB
Likewise also said they all.
And they all said the same — Mof
. . . kept saying the same thing — Wms

**32. And they came to a place which was
named Gethsemane:**
Then they came to a place called Gethsemane — Mof
and he saith to his disciples,
and he told . . . — Mof
Sit ye here, while I shall pray.
. . . while I pray — ASV
Sit down here till I have prayed — Wey

**33. And he taketh with him Peter and
James and John,**
And he took with him . . . — RSV
**and began to be sore amazed, and to
be very heavy;**
. . . greatly amazed, and sore troubled
— ASV
. . . greatly distressed and troubled —
RSV
and he began to feel distress and dread
— Gspd
and He began to be deeply distressed
and depressed — Nor
Horror and dismay came over him —
NEB

34. And saith unto them,
**My soul is exceeding sorrowful unto
death:**
My heart is heavy to the point of
death — Rieu
. . . is crushed with anguish . . . — Wey

. . . is ready to break with grief — NEB
tarry ye here, and watch.
abide . . . — ASV
stay here and watch — Mof
wait here and keep awake — Wey

35. And he went forward a little,
Then he walked forward a little way
— Phi
and fell on the ground,
and fell to the earth — Mof
and threw himself on the ground —
Gspd
and prayed that, if it were possible,
and began to pray that . . . — TCNT
and prayed that if possible — Ber
and prayed repeatedly that, if it were
possible — Mon
the hour might pass from him.
this hour might pass him by — NEB
he might be spared the hour of trial —
Gspd
He might be spared that time of agony
— Wey
he might not have to face the ordeal —
Phi

36. And he said, Abba, Father,
and he said, Abba! Father! — Wey
. . . Abba! that is, Father — Gspd
Dear Father, he said — Phi
all things are possible unto thee;
You can do anything — Nor
take away this cup from me:
remove . . . — ASV
please — let me not have to drink this
cup — Phi
**nevertheless not what I will, but what
thou wilt.**
Yet, I pray, not what I want but what
you want! — Wms
but even so let not my pleasure, but
yours be done — Bas

**37. And he cometh, and findeth them
sleeping,**
He came back and found them asleep
— NEB
Then he came and found them fast
asleep — Phi
and said unto Peter,
so he said to Peter — Mof
Simon, sleepest thou?
Simon, are you asleep — RSV
couldest not thou watch one hour?
Were you not able to keep awake a
single hour — Wey
Could you not keep watch one hour —
Mon

38. Watch ye and pray, lest ye enter into temptation.

Watch and pray, that ye enter not . . . — ASV

Keep watch, all of you, and pray that you may not come . . . — Mon

Watch and pray, all of you, that you may not have to face temptation — Phi

The spirit truly is ready, but the flesh is weak.

the spirit indeed is willing . . . — ASV

The spirit is eager . . . — Rieu

Your spirit is willing, but human nature is weak — Phi

39. And again he went away, and prayed,

Once more he went away and prayed — NEB

and spake the same words.

using the very same words — Wey

40. And when he returned, he found them asleep again,
(for their eyes were heavy,)

for they could hardly keep their eyes open — Gspd

for they were very weary — Wey

neither wist they what to answer him.

and they knew not what . . . — ASV

and they did not know how . . . — NEB

. . . what to say for themselves — Phi

41. And he cometh the third time, and saith unto them,

Then he came for the third time and said to them — Mof

When he came back . . ., he said to them — Gspd

Sleep on now, and take your rest:

Sleep on the remaining time, and take your rest — ABUV

Sleep and take your rest hereafter — Knox

Are you still sleeping and taking your rest? — Gspd

it is enough, the hour is come;

Enough! The hour has come — NEB

No more of that! The hour . . . — Mof

It is over. My hour is come — Mon

behold, the Son of man is betrayed into the hands of sinners.

See! the Son of Man . . . of wicked men — Gspd

now you are going to see the Son of Man betrayed into the hands of evil men! — Phi

See, the Son of Man is about to be betrayed into the hands of sinners! — Nor

42. Rise up, let us go;

Arise, let us be going — ASV

Up! let us go forward! — NEB

lo, he that betrayeth me is at hand.

see, my betrayer . . . — RSV

here is my betrayer close . . . — Mof

Look! Here comes my betrayer! — Gspd

43. And immediately, while he yet spake,

And straightway, while he was yet speaking — ABUV

Suddenly, while he was still speaking — NEB

Just at that moment . . . — Gspd

And indeed, while the words were still on his lips — Phi

cometh Judas, one of the twelve,

Judas came . . . — RSV

Judas, one of the Twelve, appeared — NEB

and with him a great multitude with swords and staves,

. . . a crowd with swords and clubs — RSV

. . . was a great mob armed with . . . — Nor

from the chief priests and the scribes and the elders.

44. And he that betrayed him had given them a token, saying,

Now the betrayer . . . a sign, saying — RSV

Now the traitor had agree with them upon a signal — NEB

Whomsoever I shall kiss, that same is he;

The one I shall kiss is the man — RSV

The one I kiss is your man — NEB

take him, and lead him away safely.

. . . and lead him away securely—ABUV

Seize him and get him safely away — Mof

hold him fast, and take him away under guard — Knox

45. And as soon as he was come, he goeth straightway to him, and saith,

So when he arrived he at once went up to him and said — Mof

So when he came he went straight up to Jesus and said — Gspd

Master, master; and kissed him.

Rabbi! and kissed Him affectionately — Wey

Master! and he kissed Him ardently —
Nor

Rabbi! and openly kissed him — Rhm

46. And they laid their hands on him, and took him.

Then they seized him and held him fast — NEB

and they laid hands on him and arrested him — Rieu

47. And one of them that stood by drew a sword,

But one of the bystanders drew his sword — Gspd

and smote a servant of the high priest,

. . . the servant . . . — ASV

and struck the slave . . . — RSV

and cut off his ear.

slashing off . . . — Phi

shearing off . . . — Rieu

48. And Jesus answered and said unto them,

Then Jesus spoke to them — Phi

Are ye come out, as against a thief,

Have you come out, as if after a robber — TCNT

with swords and with staves to take me?

with swords and clubs to arrest me — Wms

49. I was daily with you in the temple teaching,

I have been among you day after day in the Temple teaching — Gspd

Day after day I was with you as I taught in the temple — Beck

and ye took me not:

and you never seized me — Gspd

and you did not lay hands on me—NEB

and you never laid a finger on me — Phi

and you did not arrest me — Rieu

but the scriptures must be fulfilled.

but this is done that the scriptures might be fulfilled — ASV

But let the Scriptures be fulfilled! — Gspd

50. And they all forsook him, and fled.

Then the disciples all deserted him and ran away — NEB

51. And there followed him a certain young man,

And a young man followed him — RSV

One young man, however, began following him — Mon

having a linen cloth cast about his naked body;

with only a linen sheet thrown round his body — Mof

who wore nothing but a linen shirt — Phi

and the young men laid hold on him:

and they seized him — Gspd

They tried to arrest him — TCNT

52. And he left the linen cloth,

but he slipped out of . . . — NEB

but he left the shirt in their hands — Phi

and fled from them naked.

and ran away naked — RSV

and took to his heels stark naked — Phi

53. And they led Jesus away to the high priest:

Then . . . to the High Priest's house — NEB

and with him were assembled all the chief priests and the elders and the scribes.

where the chief priests, elders, and doctors of the law were all assembling — NEB

54. And Peter followed him afar off,

Peter followed him at a distance — Mof

And Peter followed, too, at a long distance — Nor

And Peter had followed him at a distance — RSV

even into the palace of the high priest:

right into the courtyard . . . — Gspd

until he was inside the high priest's courtyard — Ber

and he sat with the servants,

and he was sitting with the officers — ASV

. . . with the guards — RSV

and there he remained, sitting among the attendants — NEB

There he sat down with the temple-police — Rieu

and warmed himself at the fire.

warming himself . . . — NEB

. . . in the light of the fire — Mon

55. And the chief priests and all the council sought for witness against Jesus

. . . and all the Sanhedrin were seeking for testimony against Jesus — ABUV

Meanwhile the Chief Priests and the whole Council were casting about for evidence against Jesus — Rieu

to put him to death;

to warrant a death-sentence — NEB

and found none.
but failed to find any — NEB
But they failed completely — Phi

56. **For many bare false witness against him,**
. . . testified falsely against him—ABUV
Many gave false evidence . . . — NEB
There were plenty of people ready to give false testimony against him — Phi
but their witness agreed not together.
but their evidence was contradictory — Phi
but their statements did not tally — NEB

57. **And there arose certain,**
And certain ones rose up — ABUV
Then some came forward as witnesses — Wey
Some took the witness stand — Wms
and bare false witness against him, saying,
and testified falsely . . . — ABUV
and gave false testimony against him to this effect — Gspd

58. **We heard him say,**
We ourselves have heard him say — Gspd
I will destroy this temple that is made with hands,
I will pull down this Sanctuary built by human hands — Wey
and within three days I will build another made without hands.
. . . not made with hands — RSV
. . . with no hand of man to help me — Knox

59. **But neither so did their witness agree together.**
And not even so . . . — ASV
But even so their statements did not tally — Rieu
But even in this matter their testimony did not agree — Wms

60. **And the high priests stood up in the midst,**
Then the High Priest stood up in his place — NEB
Then the high priest got up and came forward into the center — Gspd
and asked Jesus, saying,
and questioned Jesus — TCNT
Answerest thou nothing?
what is it which these witness against thee?

What about this evidence against you — Mof

61. **But he held his peace, and answered nothing.**
But he was silent . . . — ABUV
But He remained silent, and gave no reply — Wey
Again the high priest asked him, and said unto him,
Once more the High Priest put a question to him — Rieu
Art thou the Christ, the Son of the Blessed?
. . . the Son of the blessed God — Knox
Are you the Messiah, the Son of the Blessed One — NEB

62. **And Jesus said, I am:**
and ye shall see the Son of man sitting on the right hand of power,
. . . sitting at the right hand of Power — ASV
and you will all see the Son of Man seated at the right hand of the Almighty — Gspd
and coming in the clouds of heaven.
. . . with the clouds of heaven — ASV
. . . amid . . . — Wey
. . . on the clouds of the sky — Nor

63. **Then the high priest rent his clothes, and saith,**
Then the High Priest tore his robes and cried — Phi
What need we any further witnesses?
What further need have we of witnesses — ASV
Need we call further witnesses — NEB
What more evidence do we want — Mof

64. **Ye have heard the blasphemy:**
Ye heard his blasphemy — Alf
You have heard his blasphemy for yourselves — Knox
Did you hear his blasphemy? — Gspd
what think ye?
What is your opinion — Rieu
. . . verdict — Mon
. . . decision — RSV
What do you think now — Wms
And they all condemned him to be guilty of death.
. . . worthy of death — ASV
And their verdict was that he deserved to die — Phi
Their judgment was unanimous: that he was guilty and should be put to death — NEB

65. And some began to spit on him,
... started to spit at him — Gspd
and to cover his face,
and to blindfold him — Mof
and to buffet him,
and to hit Him with their fists — Wms
and to smite him ... — Alf
and to say unto him, Prophesy:
and crying, Prove that you are a
prophet — Wey
saying, Now prophesy who hit you! —
Phi
and said to him, Now say what is to
come — Bas
**and the servants did strike him with
the palms of their hands.**
The attendants treated him to cuffs and
slaps — Mof
The officers too struck Him with open
hands — Wey
Even the servants who took him away
slapped his face — Phi

**66. And as Peter was beneath in the
palace,**
... in the court — ASV
... below in the courtyard — RSV
**there cometh one of the maids of the
high priest:**
a maidservant of the high priest came
along — Mof

**67. And when she saw Peter warming
himself,**
And when she noticed ... — Mof
she looked upon him, and said,
She looked closely at him, and said —
Phi
she took a good look at him, and said
— Nor
**And thou also wast with Jesus of Naz-
areth.**
Thou also wast with the Nazarene, even
Jesus — ASV
You were with this Jesus of Nazareth
too! — Gspd
You were there too, with this man from
Nazareth, this Jesus — NEB

68. But he denied, saying,
But he denied it, saying — Gspd
**I know not, neither understand I what
thou sayest.**
I neither know nor understand what
you mean — RSV
I don't know him and I don't know
what you're talking about — Phi
**And he went out into the porch; and
the cock crew.**

Then he went outside into the porch
— NEB
... into the passage — Mof
And then he went out into the fore-
court — Wey
And he walked out into the gateway —
Phi

69. And a maid saw him again,
And the maid saw him — ASV
and began to say to them that stood by,
and began again ... — ASV
... to say to the bystanders — RSV
This is one of them.
This man is one of them — RSV
This fellow ... — Gspd

70. And he denied it again.
A second time he repeatedly denied it
— Wey
**And a little after, they that stood by
said again to Peter,**
After a little the by-standers began to
say to Peter again — Mon
Surely thou art one of them:
To be sure, you are one of them —
Mof
**for thou art a Galilaean, and thy
speech agreeth thereto.**
Why, you are a Galilean! — Mof
You must be; you are a Galilean —
NEB

**71. But he began to curse and to swear,
saying,**
... to swear with the strongest oaths —
Gspd
And he fell to calling down curses on
himself and swearing — Knox
But he began to invoke a curse on himself and to swear — RSV
I know not this man of whom ye speak.
I do not know this man of whom you
speak — RSV
I tell you I don't know the man you're
talking about — Phi

72. And the second time the cock crew.
And straightway the second time ... —
ASV
And immediately the cock crowed a
second time — RSV
At that moment the cock crowed for
the second time — Mof
**And Peter called to mind the word that
Jesus said unto him,**
And Peter remembered how Jesus had
said to him — Gspd
and Peter remembered Jesus telling
him — Beck

Before the cock crow twice, thou shalt deny me thrice.

. . . crows twice, you will deny me three times — RSV

. . . you will disown me three times! — Gspd

And when he thought thereon, he wept.

As he considered that, he wept audibly — Ber

And he broke down and wept — RSV

and he burst into tears — Mof

And he started to cry — Beck

CHAPTER 15

1. And straightway in the morning

The first thing in the morning — Rieu

And as soon as it was morning — RSV

At earliest dawn — Wey

the chief priests held a consultation with the elders and scribes and the whole council,

. . . with the elders and scribes, and the whole council, held a consultation — ASV

the Chief Priests called together a committee of elders, Scribes, and members of the whole Council — Phi

and bound Jesus,

put Jesus in chains — TCNT

and carried him away,

and led him away — RSV

and took him away — Gspd

and delivered him to Pilate.

and delivered him up . . . — ASV

and handed him over . . . — NEB

2. And Pilate asked him,

So Pilate questioned him — Wey

Art thou the King of the Jews?

Are you the king of the Jews — Mof

And he answering said unto him, Thou sayest it.

He answered, Yes — Gspd

He replied, Certainly — Mof

And he answered him, You have said so — RSV

To which he replied, The words are yours — Rieu

In reply Jesus said, It is as you say — Mon

3. And the chief priests accused him of many things:

. . . brought many charges against him — NEB

And the high priests kept heaping accusations upon him — Gspd

And the chief priests began to accuse Him harshly — NASB

but he answered nothing.[49]

4. And Pilate asked him again, saying,

Pilate questioned him again — NEB

So . . . — Phi

Answerest thou nothing?

Have you no answer to make — Gspd

Have you no reply whatsoever . . . — Rieu

Have you nothing to say in your defence — NEB

behold how many things they witness against thee.

. . . they accuse thee of — ASV

See how many charges they bring against you — RSV

Listen to all their accusations — Phi

5. But Jesus yet answered nothing;

But Jesus no more answered anything — ASV

But Jesus made no further answer — RSV

so that Pilate marvelled.

. . . wondered — ABUV

. . . was astonished — Wms

6. Now at that feast he released unto them one prisoner,

Now at the feast he used to release . . . — ASV

Now it was Pilate's custom at festival-time to release a prisoner — Phi

whomsoever they desired.

whom they asked of him — ASV

whom they petitioned for — Gspd

at the people's request — NEB

7. And there was one named Barabbas,

And at this time a man named Barabbas — Wey

Now there was a man called Barabbas — Rieu

which lay bound with them that had made insurrection with him,

was in prison among the insurgents — Wey

among some revolutionaries — Gspd

confined with the insurrectionists — Ber

---

[49]Now regarded as not adequately supported by original manuscripts.

who had committed murder in the insurrection.
... in the uprising — Ber
... in a recent outbreak — Phi

8. And the multitude crying aloud[50] began to desire him
... went up and began to ask him — ASV
And the crowd came up and began to ask Pilate — RSV
So the people came crowding up, asking Pilate — Wey

to do as he had ever done unto them.
to do as he always did ... — Alf
for the usual favor — Gspd

9. But Pilate answered them, saying,
so Pilate replied to them — Ber
Pilate asked them — Gspd

Will ye that I release unto you the King of the Jews?
Do you want me to release for you ... — RSV
... to set free the king of the Jews — Phi

10. For he knew that the chief priests had delivered him for envy.
For he perceived that for envy the chief priests had delivered him up — ASV
For he could see that it was out of sheer spite that the High Priests had handed Him over — Wey
for he had begun to realize that the hierarchy had brought him up for judgment because they were jealous — Rieu

11. But the chief priests moved the people,
... stirred up the multitude — ASV
... incited the crowd — NEB
that he should rather release Barabbas unto them.
to ask him to release Barabbas rather than Jesus — NEB
to get them to demand Barabbas' release instead — Phi

12. And Pilate answered and said again unto them,
Pilate asked them again — Mof
Then Pilate came back at them again — Ber
What will ye then that I shall do unto him
What then shall I do unto him — ASV
Then what shall I do with the man — RSV
whom ye call the King of the Jews?

13. And they cried out again, Crucify him.
Whereupon they shouted again, Crucify him — Mof
They shouted back, Crucify him! — Gspd

14. Then Pilate said unto them,
But Pilate replied — Phi
Why, what evil hath he done?
Why, what harm has he done — NEB
Why, what wrong ... — Mon
But, what crime has he committed — Wey
And they cried out the more exceedingly, Crucify him.
But they cried out the more, Crucify him — Alf
But they shouted all the more, Crucify him — RSV
They shouted all the louder, Crucify him! — NEB
But their voices rose to a roar, Crucify him! — Phi

15. And so Pilate, willing to content the people,
So Pilate, wishing to satisfy the crowd — RSV
So Pilate, in his desire to satisfy the mob — NEB
And so Pilate, determined to humour the multitude — Knox
released Barabbas unto them,
released for them Barabbas — RSV
set Barabbas free for them — Rieu
and delivered Jesus, when he had scourged him, to be crucified.
and having scourged Jesus, he delivered him ... — RSV
and after having Jesus flogged, he handed him over for crucifixion — Rieu

16. And the soldiers led him away into the hall, called Praetorium;
... within the court, which is the Praetorium — ASV
... inside the palace (that is, the praetorium) — RSV
Then the soldiers took him inside the courtyard (the Governor's headquarters) — NEB
The soldiers then took Jesus away into the court-yard — that is the Government House — TCNT

---

[50]Some translations lack "crying aloud," which in the Greek closely resembles "came up" in its form.

and they called together the whole band.
and called together the whole company — NEB
and they called together the whole battalion — RSV
where they mustered the entire detachment — Ber
where they had called together their whole military unit — Nor

17. **And they clothed him with purple,**
. . . in a purple cloak — RSV
And they dressed him up . . . — Gspd
and platted a crown of thorns, and put it about his head,
and plaited . . ., and placed it on his head — Mon
and after weaving a crown of thorns, they put it on Him — NASB
and made a wreath of thorns and crowned him with it — Gspd
and twisting some thorn-twigs into a crown, they put it on his head — Phi

18. **And began to salute him,**
and they began to acclaim him — Gspd
. . . to shout at Him — Wms
Then they began to greet him — Phi
Hail, King of the Jews!
Long live the king of the Jews!—Gspd
Hail, Your Majesty — King of the Jews! — Phi

19. **And they smote him on the head with a reed,**
. . . his head with a reed — ASV
And they struck . . . — RSV
They beat him about the head with a cane — NEB
And they kept hitting Him on the head with a stick — Wms
and did spit upon him,
and spat . . . — ASV
. . . at him — Gspd
and kept spitting on Him— Wms
and bowing their knees worshipped him.
and then knelt and paid mock homage to him — NEB
and on bending knees they kept doing Him homage — Wms

20. **And when they had mocked him,**
When they had finished their mockery — NEB
Then, after making fun of him — Mof
When they had finished making sport of him — Gspd

they took off the purple from him,
they stripped him of the purple cloak — RSV
and put his own clothes on him,
and dressed him again in his own clothes — Phi
and led him out to crucify him.
Then they took him out of the city . . . — Gspd

21. **And they compel one Simon a Cyrenian,**
They forced Simon a Cyrenian — Mof
They compelled Simon, a native of Cyrene in Africa — Phi
who passed by, coming out of the country,
who was passing by on his way in from the country — Rieu
who was on his way from the fields at the time — Phi
the father of Alexander and Rufus, to bear his cross.
to carry . . . — Mof

22. **And they bring him unto the place Golgotha,**
Thus they brought him to the place called Golgotha — Rieu
which is, being interpreted, The place of a skull.
which, being translated, means 'Skull-ground' — Wey
(which means the place of a skull) — RSV
(which means Skull Hill) — Phi

23. **And they gave him to drink wine mingled with myrrh:**
And they offered him wine . . . — ASV
And they tried to give him wine mixed . . . — NASB
They offered him drugged wine—Gpsd
but he received it not.
but he did not take it — RSV
but he would not take it — Mof
but He refused it — Nor

24. **And when they had crucified him,**
Then they crucified him — Mof
Then they fastened him to the cross — NEB
Then they nailed Him . . . — Nor
they parted his garments,
and divided his garments among them — RSV
and distributed his clothes among themselves — Mof
and parcelled out his clothes — Rieu

casting lots upon them, what every man should take.

casting lots for them, to decide what each should take — RSV

drawing lots for them to decide each man's share — Mof

25. And it was the third hour, and they crucified him.

It was nine o'clock in the morning when they . . . — Wey

The hour of the crucifixion was nine in the morning — NEB

26. And the superscription of his accusation was written over,

and the inscription giving the charge against him read — NEB

The words of the charge against him, written over his head, ran thus — TCNT

THE KING OF THE JEWS.

27. And with him they crucify two thieves;

. . . two robbers — ASV

They also crucified two bandits at the same time — Phi

the one on his right hand, and the other on his left.

one on each side of him — Phi

28. And the scripture was fulfilled, which saith, And he was numbered with the transgressors.[51]

29. And they that passed by railed on him,

The passers-by hurled abuse at him: — NEB

People who passed by kept insulting Him — Nor

And the passers-by kept jeering at him — Mon

. . . kept hissing at Him— Wms

wagging their heads, and saying,

shaking their heads and saying — Gspd

nodding at him in derision and calling — Mof

Ah, thou that destroyest the temple,

Ha! . . . — ASV

Aha! You who would destroy the temple — RSV

and buildest it in three days,

and build it . . . — RSV

and rebuild it . . . — Mon

30. Save thyself, and come down from the cross.

Come down from the cross and save yourself! — NEB

Now save yourself by coming down from the cross — Wms

why not come down from the cross and save yourself? — Phi

31. Likewise also the chief priests mocking said among themselves with the scribes,

In like manner also the chief priests mocking him among themselves with the scribes said — ASV

So too the chief priests and doctors of the law jested with one another: — NEB

. . . with the Doctors of the Law, exchanged derisive comments — Rieu

The chief priests and religious leaders were also standing around joking about Jesus — Tay

He saved others; himself he cannot save.

He saved others, but he cannot save himself! — Gspd

32. Let Christ the King of Israel descend now from the cross,

Let the Christ, . . ., now come down . . . — ASV

Let this Christ, the king of Israel, come down from the cross now — Gspd

The Christ? The King of Israel? The idea! If so, let him come down from the cross — Nor

that we may see and believe.

Let us see that and we will believe! — — Mof

And they that were crucified with him reviled him.

. . . reproached him — ASV

They also who had been crucified with Jesus kept reviling him — Mon

Even those who were crucified with him taunted him — NEB

33. And when the sixth hour was come,

. . . had come — RSV

When twelve o'clock came — Mof

At midday — NEB

there was darkness over the whole land until the ninth hour.

darkness covered . . . till three o'clock — Mof

darkness spread over the whole earth, lasting till three o'clock — Nor

34. And at the ninth hour Jesus cried with a loud voice, saying,

and at three o'clock Jesus gave a loud cry — Mof

and at three Jesus cried aloud — NEB

[51]Now regarded as not adequately supported by original manuscripts.

207

Eloi, Eloi, lama sabachthani?

Eli, Eli, lema sabachthani — NEB

which is, being interpreted,

In translation this means — Nor

which means — Gspd

My God, my God, why hast thou for-saken me?

. . . why did You forsake me — Phi

35. And some of them that stood by, when they heard it, said,

On hearing this some of the bystanders said — Mof

Behold, he calleth Elias.

. . . Elijah — ASV

36. And one ran and filled a spunge full of vinegar,

A man came running with a sponge, soaked in sour wine — NEB

and put it on a reed,

and put it on the end of a stick — Gspd

and gave him to drink, saying,

and gave it to him . . . — RSV

and held it to his lips — NEB

Let alone; let us see whether Elias will come to take him down.

Let him alone! Let's see if Elijah will come and take him down! — Phi

37. And Jesus cried with a loud voice, and gave up the ghost.

And Jesus, uttering a loud cry, ex-pired — ABUV

But Jesus let out a great cry, and died — Phi

And Jesus uttered a loud cry, and breathed his last — RSV

38. And the veil of the temple was rent in twain

And the curtain of the temple was torn in two — Mof

from the top to the bottom.

from top to bottom — Wey

39. And when the centurion, which stood over against him,

. . . who stood by over against him — ASV

Now when the army-captain who stood facing him — Mof

saw that he so cried out, and gave up the ghost, he said,

seeing that he so expired, said — ABUV

saw how he died, he said — Phi

seeing his death and the manner of it, said — Rieu

Truly this man was the Son of God.

This man surely must have been a son of God! — Gspd

40. There were also women looking on afar off:

There were some women also watching from a distance — Gspd

among whom was Mary Magdalene, and Mary the mother of James the less and of Joses, and Salome;

among them Mary of Magdala, Mary the mother of the younger James and of Joseph, and Salome — Gspd

. . . Mary the mother of the younger James, Mary the mother of Joses, and Salome — Phi

41. (Who also, when he was in Galilee, followed him, and ministered unto him;)

who had followed him when he was in Galilee and ministered to his wants — Rieu

and many other women which came up with him unto Jerusalem.

besides several other women who had come up to Jerusalem with Him — Wms

42. And now when the even was come,

And when evening had come — RSV

because it was the preparation,

. . . the Preparation — ASV

since it was the day of Preparation — RSV

that is, the day before the sabbath,

(that is, the day before the Sabbath) — NEB

43. Joseph of Arimathaea, an honourable counsellor,

Joseph of Arimathea, a respected mem-ber of the council — RSV

. . . an honorable member of the San-hedrin — Ber

Joseph from Arimathea, an important member of the Jewish court — Beck

which also waited for the kingdom of God,

who also himself was looking for the . . . — ASV

who was himself living in expectation of the reign of God — Gspd

came, and went in boldly unto Pilate, and craved the body of Jesus.

bravely went in to Pilate and asked for . . . — NEB

took courage and went to Pilate and asked for . . . — RSV

dared to go to Pilate and ask for Jesus' body — Beck

44. And Pilate marvelled if he were already dead:

And Pilate wondered . . . — RSV

Pilate wondered whether he could have died so soon — Rieu

. . . was surprised to hear that he was already dead — NEB

and calling unto him the centurion,

and summoning . . . — RSV

he asked him whether he had been any while dead.

. . . he was already dead — RSV

45. And when he knew it of the centurion,

. . . he learned it . . . — ASV

And when he heard the centurion's report — NEB

having ascertained the fact from the centurion — Wey

he gave the body to Joseph.

he granted the corpse to Joseph — ASV

he gave Joseph permission to take the body — Gspd

46. And he bought fine linen,

And he bought a linen cloth — ASV

. . . linen shroud — RSV

. . . linen sheet — Gspd

. . . linen winding-sheet — Phi

and took him down, and wrapped him in the linen,

. . . from the cross and wrapped him in the sheet — Gspd

and laid him in a sepulchre which was hewn out of a rock,

Then he laid him in a tomb cut out of the rock — NEB

and rolled a stone unto the door of the sepulchre.

and he rolled a stone against the door of the tomb — ASV

and rolled a stone against the entrance — NEB

47. And Mary Magdalene and Mary the mother of Joses beheld where he was laid.

And Mary of Magdala and Mary the mother of Joseph were watching and saw where he was laid — NEB

CHAPTER 16

1. And when the sabbath was past,

When the Sabbath was over — Wey

Mary Magdalene, and Mary the mother of James, and Salome, had bought sweet spices,

. . . bought spices — ASV

. . . bought aromatic oils — NEB

that they might come and anoint him.

so that they might go and anoint him — RSV

intending to go . . . — NEB

2. And very early in the morning the first day of the week,

And very early on the first day . . . — ASV

they came unto the sepulchre at the rising of the sun.

just after[52] sunrise, they came to the tomb — NEB

3. And they said among themselves,

and they kept saying to one another — Mon

Who shall roll us away the stone from the door of the sepulchre?

Who will roll away the stone for us from the door of the tomb — RSV

. . . from the entrance to the tomb — Wey

4. And when they looked, they saw that the stone was rolled away:

But then, looking up, they saw that the stone was already rolled back — Wey

for it was very great.

. . . very large — RSV

it was of immense size — Wey

(for it was a very large boulder) — Mof

5. And entering into the sepulchre,

And entering the tomb — RSV

And when they went into the tomb — Gspd

they saw a young man sitting on the right side,

they saw a youth sitting on the right — Mof

clothed in a long white garment;

clothed in a white robe — ABUV

wearing a . . . — Knox

and they were affrighted.

and they were amazed — ASV

. . . dumbfounded — NEB

They were bewildered — Mof

They were terrified — Wey

6. And he saith unto them, Be not affrighted:

---

[52]Some manuscripts use the word "after" rather than "at" sunrise.

And he said to them, Do not be amazed
— RSV

But he said to them, There is no need
to be startled — Phi

. . . Be not terrified! — Ber

**Ye seek Jesus of Nazareth, which was
crucified:**

ye seek Jesus, the Nazarene, who hath
been crucified — ASV

Are you looking for Jesus the Nazarene, who was crucified? — Rieu

he is risen; he is not here:

He has risen . . . — Mof

behold the place where they laid him.

see . . . — RSV

See! the place where they laid him! —
Rhm

See! here is the spot where they laid
Him — Wms

7. **But go your way, tell his disciples and
Peter**

But go, tell . . . — ASV

But go and give this message to his
disciples and Peter: — NEB

that he goeth before you into Galilee:

that he is going before you to Galilee
— RSV

He will go on before you into Galilee
— NEB

that he will be in Galilee before you
— Phi

**there shall ye see him, as he said unto
you.**

you shall see him there, as he told you
— Mof

you will . . ., just as he told you —
Gspd

8. **And they went out quickly, and fled
from the sepulchre;**

And they went out, and fled from the
tomb — ASV

The women came out . . . — Rieu

for they trembled and were amazed:

for trembling and astonishment had
come upon them — ASV

for they were all trembling and bewildered — Gspd

They were trembling with excitement
— Phi

neither said they any thing to any man;

and they said nothing to any one —
ASV

for they were afraid.

for they were afraid to do so — Gspd

for they were afraid of . . .[53] — Mof

9. **Now when Jesus was risen early the
first day of the week,**

Now after his resurrection, early on
the first day of the week — Mon

When he had risen from the dead early
on Sunday morning — NEB

**he appeared first to Mary Magdalene,
out of whom he had cast seven devils.**

from whom he had cast out seven
demons — ASV

from whom He had driven out seven
evil spirits — Nor

10. **And she went and told them that had
been with him,**

She went and reported it to those who
. . . — ABUV

as they mourned and wept.

while they were mourning and weeping — Gspd

as they sat in grief and tears — Nor

11. **And they, when they had heard that
he was alive,**

But when they heard . . . — RSV

But they, when they were told that he
lived — Rieu

and had been seen of her, believed not.

and had been seen by her, did not believe it — Mon

12. **And after that he appeared in another
form unto two of them,**

Later he appeared in a different guise
. . . — NEB

After that, he appeared in the form of
a stranger . . . — Knox

**as they walked, and went into the
country.**

. . . on their way into the country —
ASV

as they were walking along, going into
the country — Nor

13. **And they went and told it unto the
residue:**

They went back and told the rest —
Gspd

neither believed they them.

but they would not believe them —
Gspd

but again no one believed them — NEB

14. **Afterward he appeared unto the eleven
as they sat at meat,**

Still later He appeared to the Eleven

---

[53]The text of Mark was apparently broken
off here. While many manuscripts have the
remaining verses, these witnesses are not of
superior quality.

themselves as they were sitting at table — Phi
Afterward he appeared . . ., as they were eating — Mon
and upbraided them with their unbelief and hardness of heart,
. . . for their unbelief . . . — RSV
and reproached them for their incredulity and dullness — NEB
and reproved them for their lack of faith and their stubbornness — Wms
because they believed not them which had seen him after he was risen.
because they had not believed those who saw him after he had risen — RSV
for they would not believe those who had seen Him after He had risen — Nor

15. And he said unto them,
Then he said to them — Phi
Go ye into all the world,
Go forth to every part of the world — NEB
Go the whole world over — Wey
and preach the gospel to every creature.
. . . to the whole creation — ASV
and proclaim the gospel to all mankind — Wey

16. He that believeth and is baptized shall be saved;
He who believes it and is baptized will be saved — Gspd
but he that believeth not shall be damned.
but he that disbelieveth shall be condemned — ASV
but he who will not believe . . . — Mof

17. And these signs shall follow them that believe;
. . . shall accompany . . . — ASV
And signs like these will attend those who believe — Gspd
Faith will bring with it these miracles: — NEB
In my name shall they cast out devils;
. . . demons — ASV
by my name they shall expel demons — Wey

they shall speak with new tongues;
they will speak in foreign tongues — Gspd
they will speak in tongues that are strange to them — Knox

18. They shall take up serpents;
. . . pick up . . . — RSV
they shall take up venomous snakes — Wey
and if they drink any deadly thing, it shall not hurt them;
and even if they drink any deadly poison, it shall do them no harm whatever — Wey
they shall lay hands on the sick, and they shall recover.
they will . . . and make them well — Mof

19. So then after the Lord had spoken unto them,
So after talking with them — NEB
he was received up into heaven,
the Lord Jesus was taken up . . . — NEB
was caught up . . . — Gspd
and sat on the right hand of God.
and sat down at . . . — ASV

20. And they went forth, and preached every where,
But they went out . . . — Ber
Then . . . — Wms
After this . . . — Nor
the Lord working with them,
while the Lord worked with them — Gspd
and confirming the word with signs following.
. . . by the signs that followed — ASV
. . . their message by the signs that attended it — Gspd
. . . the Word by the miracles that attested their work — Rieu
Amen.[54]

[54]Some ancient witnesses have, after verse 8, the following: But they reported briefly to Peter and his companions all they had been told. And afterward Jesus himself sent out by them from the east to the west the sacred and incorruptible message of eternal salvation — Gspd

THE
GOSPEL ACCORDING TO LUKE

CHAPTER 1

1. Forasmuch as many have taken in hand

Inasmuch as many have undertaken — RSV

Many writers have undertaken — NEB

As a number of attempts have been made — Bas

to set forth in order a declaration of those things

to draw up a narrative concerning those matters — ASV

to compile a narrative of the things — RSV

to draw up an account of the events — NEB

which are most surely believed among us,

which have been fulfilled among us — ASV

that have happened among us — NEB

that have certainly taken place among us — Ber

that are received with full assurance among us — Wey

2. Even as they delivered them unto us,

following the traditions handed down to us — NEB

exactly as these have been handed down to us . . . — Mof

on the authority of those — Wey

which from the beginning were eyewitnesses,

by the original eyewitnesses — NEB

who were from the beginning eyewitnesses — Wey

and ministers of the word;

and servants of the Gospel — NEB

and became devoted to the service of the word — Wey

3. It seemed good to me also,

. . . fitting . . . — NASB

And so I in my turn — NEB

having had perfect understanding of all things from the very first,

having traced the course of all things accurately from the first — ASV

having followed all things closely for some time past — RSV

having investigated everything carefully from the beginning — NASB

as one who has gone over the whole course of these events in detail — NEB

since I was accurately acquainted with everything from its inception — Ber

having kept in close touch with the whole course of these events — Rieu

to write unto thee in order,

to write an orderly account for you — RSV

to write it out for you in consecutive order — NASB

to write a connected narrative for you — NEB

. . . a factual account in a connected way — Nor

most excellent Theophilus,

4. That thou mightest know the certainty of those things,

. . . the truth concerning the things — RSV

. . . the exact truth about the things — NASB

so as to give you authentic knowledge about the matters — NEB

so that you may be reliably informed about the things — Gspd

to let you know the solid truth . . . — — Mof

in order that you may be able to satisfy yourself of the accuracy of the story — TCNT

wherein thou hast been instructed.

of which you have been informed — RSV

by which you were made a convert — Lam

which you have been taught by word of mouth — Mon

which you have heard from the lips of others — TCNT

5. There was in the days of Herod, the King of Judaea,

when Herod was King in the country of the Jews — Beck

a certain priest named Zacharias, of the course of Abia:

. . . of the division of the priesthood named after Abijah — NEB

. . . of the Abia week in the series — Ber

and his wife was of the daughters of Aaron, and her name was Elisabeth.

His wife was also of priestly descent
. . . — NEB

6. And they were both righteous before God,

Both of them were upright and devout
— NEB

. . . well approved in God's sight —
Knox

In God's eyes they were righteous —
Nor

walking in all the commandments and ordinances of the Lord blameless.

walking blamelessly in all the commandments and requirements of the Lord — NASB

blamelessly observing all . . . — NEB

as they lived blamelessly according to all the rules and regulations of the Lord — Beck

for they kept all His commandments and rules; they were blameless — Nor

7. And they had no child, because that Elisabeth was barren, and they both were now well stricken in years.

. . . advanced in years — RSV

. . . well on in years . . . — NEB

8. And it came to pass, that while he executed the priest's office before God

now while he was serving as priest before God — RSV

once, when . . . he was there to take part in divine service — NEB

in the order of his course,

when his division was on duty — RSV

when it was the turn of his division — NEB

in the sequence of his series — Ber

in his Order's week of Temple service — Rieu

9. According to the custom of the priest's office,

. . . priesthood — RSV

according to the priests' practice — Gspd

his lot was to burn incense when he went into the temple of the Lord.

his lot was to enter . . . and burn incense — ASV

it fell to him by lot to enter the temple of the Lord and burn incense — RSV

10. And the whole multitude of the people was praying without

all the throng of the people were outside praying — Gspd

at the time of incense.

It was the hour of incense offering — NEB

11. And there appeared unto him an angel of the Lord, standing on the right side of the altar of incense.

Then he saw the Lord's angel standing . . . — Beck

. . . a messenger of the Lord . . . — Rhm

12. And when Zacharias saw him, he was troubled, and fear fell upon him.

At this sight Zechariah was startled . . . — NEB

When Zacharias saw him, he was terribly agitated and a sense of awe swept over him — Phi

13. But the angel said unto him, Fear not, Zacharias: for thy prayer is heard;

. . . your prayer has been heard — NEB

and thy wife Elisabeth shall bear thee a son, and thou shalt call his name John.

. . . John [meaning God is favourable] — Amp

14. And thou shalt have joy and gladness; and many shall rejoice at his birth.

Your heart will thrill with joy and many will be glad that he was born — NEB

He will be your joy and delight . . . — Beck

15. For he shall be great in the sight of the Lord,

for he is to be high in the Lord's favour — Knox

He will be one of God's great men — Phi

and shall drink neither wine nor strong drink;

. . . no wine or fermented drink — Wey

and he shall be filled with the Holy Ghost, even from his mother's womb.

From his very birth he will be filled with the Holy Spirit — NEB

. . . from the hour of his birth — Mon

16. And many of the children of Israel shall he turn to the Lord their God.

and he will bring many Israelites to the Lord their God — NEB

17. And he shall go before him in the spirit and power of Elias

He will go before him as forerunner, possessed by the spirit . . . — NEB

And it is he who will go as a forerunner before Him . . . — NASB

ushering in his advent in the spirit and power of an Elias — Knox

to turn the hearts of the fathers to the children,

to reconcile father and child — NEB

to move fathers to love their children — Beck

and the disobedient to the wisdom of the just;

to convert the rebellious to the ways of the righteous — NEB

and the disobedient to think as righteous men — Beck

and the unyielding into the prudence of the righteous — Rhm

to make ready a people prepared for the Lord.

. . . for the Lord a people prepared for him — ASV

to prepare a people that shall be fit for the Lord — NEB

. . . perfectly ready for the Lord — Gspd

18. And Zacharias said unto the angel, Whereby shall I know this?

. . . How can I be sure of this — NEB

. . . How shall I know this for certain — NASB

. . . By what shall I know this — ABUV

. . . In what way can I be assured of this — Ber

for I am an old man, and my wife well stricken in years.

19. And the angel answering said unto him, I am Gabriel, that stand in the presence of God;

. . . in attendance upon God — NEB

and am sent to speak unto thee, and to shew thee these glad tidings.

. . . to bring thee these good tidings — ASV

. . . to bring you this good news — TCNT

20. And, behold, thou shalt be dumb, and not able to speak, until the day that these things shall be performed,

But now listen! you will lose your powers of speech and remain silent until . . . — NEB

because thou believest not my words, which shall be fulfilled in their season.

. . . though at their proper time my words will be proved true — NEB

21. And the people waited for Zacharias, and marvelled that he tarried so long in the temple.

. . . were waiting . . . and they marvelled while he tarried in the temple — ASV

. . . and they wondered at his delay in the temple — RSV

. . . were surprised he was staying so long in the holy place — Beck

22. And when he came out, he could not speak unto them: and they perceived that he had seen a vision in the temple:

. . . they realized that he had seen a vision . . . — NASB

for he beckoned unto them, and remained speechless.

and he continued making signs unto them, and remained dumb — ASV

He could but stand there making signs to them . . . — Knox

He tried to speak to them by signs — Nor

He could only nod to them . . . — Rieu

23. And it came to pass, that, as soon as the days of his ministration were accomplished, he departed to his own house.

And when his time of service was ended, he went to his home — RSV

. . . he left for home — Ber

24. And after those days his wife Elisabeth conceived, and hid herself five months, saying,

she kept herself in seclusion . . . — NASB

25. Thus hath the Lord dealt with me in the days wherein he looked on me, to take away my reproach among men.

. . . my disgrace . . . — NASB

. . . the disgrace I have endured . . . — Gspd

. . . my shame . . . — Bas

. . . my humiliation . . . — Ber

The Lord did this for me, she said. I was feeling ashamed among people, but He was kind and helped me, and I don't have to feel ashamed any more — Beck

26. And in the sixth month the angel Gabriel was sent from God unto a city of Galilee, named Nazareth,

Five months later . . . — Beck

27. **To a virgin espoused to a man whose name was Joseph, of the house of David;**
    ... betrothed ... — ASV
    ... engaged ... — NASB
    ... who was to be married ... — Bas
    and the virgin's name was Mary.
28. **And the angel came in unto her, and said, Hail, thou that art highly favoured, the Lord is with thee: blessed art thou among women.**
    ... Hail, O favored one ... — RSV
29. **And when she saw him, she was troubled at his saying, and cast in her mind what manner of salutation this should be.**
    ... and considered in her mind what sort of a greeting this might be — RSV
    ... and wondered what his greeting meant — Gspd
30. **And the angel said unto her, Fear not, Mary: for thou hast found favour with God.**
    ... Have no fear, Mary, for you have God's approval — Bas
    ... for God has been gracious to you — NEB
    ... God loves you dearly — Phi
31. **And, behold, thou shalt conceive in thy womb, and bring forth a son, and shalt call his name JESUS.**
    ... and you must call his name ... — Mof
32. **He shall be great, and shall be called the Son of the Highest:**
    ... Son of the Most High — RSV
    and the Lord God shall give unto him the throne of his father David:
    ... the throne of His forefather David — Wms
    ... the throne of His ancestor David — Beck
33. **And he shall reign over the house of Jacob for ever; and of his kingdom there shall be no end.**
    ... his reign will have no end — Gspd
34. **Then said Mary unto the angel, How shall this be, seeing I know not a man?**
    ... I have no husband — RSV
    ... since I am a virgin — NASB
    ... for I am not married — Nor
35. **And the angel answered and said unto her, The Holy Ghost shall come upon thee, and the power of the Highest shall overshadow thee:**

... The Holy Spirit shall come upon thee ... — ASV
... The Holy Spirit will come over you ... — Gspd
therefore also that holy thing which shall be born of thee shall be called the Son of God.
wherefore also that which is to be born shall be called holy, the Son of God — ASV
therefore the child to be born will be called holy, The Son of God — RSV
36. **And, behold, thy cousin Elisabeth, she hath also conceived a son in her old age:**
    Look, there is your kinswoman Elisabeth! ... — Mof
    Your relative Elisabeth, old as she is, is going to have a child — Nor
    and this is the sixth month with her, who was called barren.
    ... who was said to be barren — Gspd
37. **For with God nothing shall be impossible.**
    For no word of God shall be void of power — ASV
    for God's promises can never fail—NEB
    Because no word of God shall be without power — ABUV
    For there is nothing which God is not able to do — Bas
    to prove that nothing can be impossible with God — Knox
38. **And Mary said, Behold the handmaid of the Lord; be it unto me according to thy word.**
    ... I am the Lord's slave. Let it be as you say — Gspd
    And the angel departed from her.
39. **And Mary arose in those days, and went into the hill country with haste, into a city of Juda;**
    ... the mountain district ... — ABUV
    ... the uplands ... — NEB
    ... the highlands ... — Nor
40. **And entered into the house of Zacharias, and saluted Elisabeth.**
    ... greeted ... — Ber
41. **And it came to pass, that, when Elisabeth heard the salutation of Mary, the babe leaped in her womb; and Elisabeth was filled with the Holy Ghost:**
    And as Elisabeth listened to Mary's greeting ... — Ber
42. **And she spake out with a loud voice, and said,**

and she exclaimed with a loud cry —
RSV

Then she said, with great feeling—Nor

**Blessed art thou among women, and
blessed is the fruit of thy womb.**

blessed is your unborn child! — Mon

43. And whence is this to me,

And why is this granted me — RSV

Who am I — Gspd

How have I deserved to be thus visited
— Knox

Why am I so honored — Nor

**that the mother of my Lord should
come to me?**

To have the mother of my Lord come
to me — Gspd

**44. For, lo, as soon as the voice of thy
salutation sounded in mine ears,**

Just think, when the voice of your
greeting reached my ears — Ber

Why, as soon as ever the voice of thy
greeting sounded in my ears — Knox

the babe leaped in my womb for joy.

45. And blessed is she that believed:

Happy will she be who had faith — Bas

Blessed art thou for thy believing —
Knox

Oh, how happy is the woman who believes in God — Phi

I too was happy in the trust I felt —
Rieu

**for there shall be a performance of
those things which were told her
from the Lord.**

. . . a fulfilment of the things . . . — ASV

that the things which the Lord has said
to her will be done — Bas

for he does make his promise to her
come true — Phi

**46. And Mary said, My soul doth magnify
the Lord,**

. . . My soul exalts the Lord — NASB

. . . Tell out my soul the greatness of
the Lord — NEB

. . . My heart extols the Lord — Gspd

. . . My heart is overflowing with praise
of my Lord — Phi

**47. And my spirit hath rejoiced in God
my Saviour.**

. . . rejoices in . . . — RSV

. . . is glad in . . . — Bas

. . . delights in . . . — Beck

. . . exults in . . . — Gspd

. . . has found joy in . . . — Knox

. . . has joy in . . . — Mof

. . . triumphs in . . . — Wey

**48. For he hath regarded the low estate of
his handmaiden:**

So tenderly has he looked upon his
servant, humble as she is — NEB

. . . has had pity on . . . — Bas

. . . has had regard for the humble state
of His bondslave — NASB

**for, behold, from henceforth all gen-
erations shall call me blessed.**

And from this hour all ages will count
me blessed — Mon

After this all the people who ever shall
be . . . — Phi

**49. For he that is mighty hath done to me
great things; and holy is his name.**

For the Almighty has done wonders
for me . . . — Gspd

**50. And his mercy is on them that fear
him from generation to generation.**

And his mercy is unto generations and
generations On them that fear him
— ASV

From age to age his mercy rests on
those who reverence him — TCNT

51. He hath shewed strength with his arm;

He has done mighty deeds with His
arm — NASB

**he hath scattered the proud in the
imagination of their hearts.**

. . . put to flight those who have pride
in their hearts — Bas

. . . swept away the high and mighty —
Phi

. . . routed the proud-minded — Gspd

. . . driven the proud astray in the conceit of their hearts — Knox

the arrogant of heart and mind he has
put to rout — NEB

He scatters the proud with their own
devices — TCNT

**52. He hath put down the mighty from
their seats,**

. . . torn imperial powers from their
thrones — NEB

. . . put down princes from their thrones
— ASV

. . . pushed strong rulers from their
thrones — Beck

. . . dragged dynasts from their thrones
— Rieu

and exalted them of low degree.

. . . those who were humble — NASB

and lifted up lowly people — Beck

**53. He hath filled the hungry with good
things;**

Hungry men he filled with good—ABUV

and the rich he hath sent away empty.
... with nothing in their hands — Bas

54. He hath holpen his servant Israel, in remembrance of his mercy;
... that he might remember mercy — ASV
... because He wants to remember His mercy — Beck

55. As he spake to our fathers, to Abraham, and to his seed for ever.
... his posterity for ever — RSV
... his offspring for ever — Mon

56. And Mary abode with her about three months, and returned to her own house.

57. Now Elisabeth's full time came that she should be delivered; and she brought forth a son.
Now the time had come for Elisabeth to give birth ... — NASB

58. And her neighbours and her cousins heard how the Lord had shewed great mercy upon her;
... her relatives ... — NASB
... her kindred heard that the Lord had dealt in great mercy with her — ABUV
and they rejoiced with her.
they were as delighted as she was — NEB
they shared her happiness — Ber

59. And it came to pass, that on the eighth day they came to circumcise the child;
A week later they went to circumcise the child — TCNT
and they called him Zacharias, after the name of his father.
and they were going to call him Zacharias, after his father — NASB

60. And his mother answered and said,
but his mother spoke up ... — NEB
but his mother demurred ... — Ber
... his mother intervened ... — Rieu
Not so; but he shall be called John.

61. And they said unto her,
They argued with her — Ber
There is none of thy kindred that is called by this name.
There is no one among your relatives ... — NASB

62. And they made signs to his father,
Then they motioned to his father — Ber
how he would have him called.
as to what he wanted him called — NASB

63. And he asked for a writing table,
... a writing tablet — ASV
and wrote, saying, His name is John. And they marvelled all.
They were all astonished — Nor
which greatly surprised everybody — Phi

64. And his mouth was opened immediately, and his tongue loosed, and he spake, and praised God.
... and he began to speak in praise of God — NASB
... and he spoke out blessing God — Mof

65. And fear came on all that dwelt round about:
All who lived round them were overawed — Beck
and all these sayings were noised abroad throughout all the hill country of Judaea.
... these happenings became matters of conversation ... — Ber
... were talked about through all the hill country of Judea — RSV

66. And all they that heard them laid them up in their hearts, saying, What manner of child shall this be!
What then shall this child be? — ASV
What then will this child turn out to be? — NASB
Just what is this boy going to become? — Nor
And the hand of the Lord was with him.

67. And his father Zacharias was filled with the Holy Ghost, and prophesied, saying,
... uttered a divine message, saying — Gspd
... uttered this prophecy: — NEB

68. Blessed be the Lord God of Israel; for he hath visited and redeemed his people,
... has come to his people and made them free — Bas
... has cared for his people, and wrought their redemption — Mof

69. And hath raised up an horn of salvation for us in the house of his servant David;
and has raised up a deliverer of victorious power from the house of his servant David — NEB
He has given a descendant of His serv-

ant David To be our victorious Savior — Beck

And he has produced a mighty Savior for us . . . — Gspd

he has raised up a strong saviour for us . . . — Mof

He has raised up a sceptre of salvation for us . . . — Knox

. . . a standard of salvation . . . — Phi

Forging a weapon of salvation . . . — Rieu

70. **As he spake by the mouth of his holy prophets, which have been since the world began:**

. . . from of old — RSV

according to the promise which he made by the lips of holy men who have been his prophets . . . — Knox

71. **That we should be saved from our enemies, and from the hand of all that hate us;**

Salvation from our enemies, . . . — ASV

Salvation, yes, from our foes, from all who hate us — Nor

72. **To perform the mercy promised to our fathers,**

To show mercy towards our fathers — ASV

To make true the mercy which was promised to our ancestors — Ber

to deal mercifully with our fathers — Mof

Dealing pitifully with our forefathers — Wey

and to remember his holy covenant;

and keeping his sacred agreement — Gspd

by remembering . . . — Knox

. . . his holy agreement — Phi

73. **The oath which he sware to our father Abraham,**

Such was the oath he swore . . . — NEB

He had sworn an oath . . . — Knox

74. **That he would grant unto us, that we being delivered out of the hand of our enemies might serve him without fear,**

To rescue us from our enemies And let us serve Him without fear — Beck

that he would enable us to live without fear in his service, delivered from the hand of our enemies . . . — Knox

75. **In holiness and righteousness before him, all the days of our life.**

in holiness and uprightness, unafraid, in his own presence all our lives — Gspd

passing all our days in holiness, and approved in his sight — Knox

76. **And thou, child, shalt be called the prophet of the Highest:**

. . . a prophet . . . — Ber

for thou shalt go before the face of the Lord to prepare his ways;

for you will be the Lord's forerunner . . . — NEB

for you will go in advance of the Lord . . . — Ber

. . . to make his way ready — Gspd

going before the Lord to clear his way for him — Knox

77. **To give knowledge of salvation unto his people**

To tell His people they can be saved — Beck

thou wilt make known to his people the salvation — Knox

by the remission of their sins,

in the forgiveness of their sins — RSV

that is to release them from their sins — Knox

78. **Through the tender mercy of our God;**

Because of the heart of mercy of our God — ABUV

for in the tender compassion of our God — NEB

Because our God is merciful — Beck

Because the heart of our God is merciful — Gspd

Such is the merciful kindness of our God — Knox

Because of the yearning compassion of the mercy . . . — Rhm

whereby the dayspring from on high hath visited us,

when the day shall dawn upon us from on high — RSV

with which the Sunrise from on high shall visit us — NASB

by which the light of dawn beams on us from on high — Ber

which has bidden him to come to us, like a dawning from on high — Knox

whereby a new day . . . will break on us — Wey

the morning sun from heaven will rise upon us — NEB

79. **To give light to them that sit in darkness**

to shine on those who live in darkness — NEB

to shine on those sitting in darkness — Ber

and in the shadow of death,
... under the cloud of death — NEB
... the shadows of death — Lam
... under the shadow of death — Phi
to guide our feet into the way of peace.
to direct our feet into the path of peace — Wey
80. And the child grew, and waxed strong in spirit,
... continued to grow, and to become strong ... — NASB

and was in the deserts
and he lived out in the wilds — NEB
and he lived in lonely places — Phi
And he lived in the waste lands — Rieu
till the day of his shewing unto Israel.
... the day of his public appearance ... — NASB
... the day when he proclaimed himself ... — Gspd
till the day when he publicly announced himself to Israel — Rieu

CHAPTER 2

1. And it came to pass in those days,
About that time — TCNT
that there went out a decree from Caesar Augustus,
an edict was issued by the Emperor Augustus — TCNT
that all the world should be taxed.
... enrolled — ASV
that a census should be taken of all the inhabited earth — NASB
that a census should be taken of the whole Empire — TCNT
for a general registration throughout the Roman world — NEB
2. (And this taxing was first made when Cyrenius was governor of Syria.)
This was the first enrolment made when Quirinius was governor of Syria — ASV
(This was the first census taken while Quirinius was Governor of Syria) — TCNT
This was the first registration of its kind; it took place when Quirinius was governor of Syria — NEB
This was the first census, and it was taken while ... — Beck
3. And all went to be taxed, every one into his own city.
And all went to enrol themselves, every one to his own city — ASV
... to be enrolled ... — RSV
And every one went to his own town to be registered — TCNT
Everybody went to register, each to his own town — Beck
All must go and give in their names, each in his own city — Knox
4. And Joseph also went up from Galilee, out of the city of Nazareth, into Judaea, unto the city of David, which is called Bethlehem;

Among others Joseph went up from the town of Nazareth in Galilee to Bethlehem, the town of David, in Judaea — TCNT
(because he was of the house and lineage of David:)
because he belonged to the family and house of David — TCNT
5. To be taxed with Mary his espoused wife,
to enrol himself with Mary, who was betrothed to him — ASV
to be registered with Mary, who was engaged to become his wife — TCNT
in order to register, along with Mary ... — NASB
being great with child.
who was about to become a mother — TCNT
She was pregnant — NEB
6. And so it was, that, while they were there, the days were accomplished that she should be delivered.
And it came to pass ... the days were fulfilled ... — ASV
... the days were completed for her to give birth — NASB
While they were there her time came — TCNT
And while they were there the time came for her baby to be born — Tay
7. And she brought forth her firstborn son,
and she gave birth to her first child, a son — TCNT
and wrapped him in swaddling clothes,
She wrapped Him in a blanket — Tay
and folding him in linen — Bas
she swathed him round — TCNT
and laid him in a manger,
she put him to rest in the place where the cattle had their food — Bas

. . . in a stall for cattle — Mof

because there was no room for them in the inn.

because there was no room for them to lodge in the house — NEB

8. And there were in the same country shepherds abiding in the field,

There were shepherds not far away . . . — Beck

In that same country-side were shepherds out in the open fields — TCNT

keeping watch over their flock by night.

guarding their flocks of sheep — Tay

9. And, lo, the angel of the Lord came upon them,

And an angel of the Lord stood by them — ASV

. . . flashed upon them — Mof

. . . suddenly stood by them — TCNT

and the glory of the Lord shone round about them:

the splendor of the Lord blazed round them — Phi

and they were sore afraid.

and they were terribly frightened — NASB

and they were terror-stricken — Phi

and they were seized with fear — TCNT

10. And the angel said unto them,

But the angel reassured them . . . — Tay

Fear not: for, behold, I bring you good tidings of great joy, which shall be to all people.

Do not be afraid; I have good news for you: there is great joy coming to the whole people — NEB

Stop being afraid . . . — Wms

Don't be afraid! . . . I bring you the most joyful news ever announced, and it is for everyone! — Tay

11. For unto you is born this day in the city of David a Saviour, which is Christ the Lord.

Today in the city of David a deliverer has been born to you — the Messiah, the Lord — NEB

. . . the Lord Christ himself — Knox

. . . who is the Anointed Lord — Mon

. . . who is to be your Messiah and Lord — Wms

12. And this shall be a sign unto you;

This is the sign by which you are to know him — Knox

And this is the sign unto you — ASV

Ye shall find the babe wrapped in swaddling clothes, lying in a manger.

you will find a babe . . . — RSV

You will find the infant swathed, and lying in a manager — TCNT

you will find a baby all wrapped up . . . — NEB

13. And suddenly there was with the angel a multitude of the heavenly host praising God, and saying,

. . . a throng of the heavenly army . . . — Gspd

. . . an army of the troops of heaven . . . — Amp

Suddenly the angel was joined by a vast host of others—the armies of heaven — praising God: — Tay

14. Glory to God in the highest,

. . . in the highest [heavens] — Amp

Glory to God on high — TCNT

and on earth peace, good will toward men.

. . . among men with whom he is pleased — RSV

And on earth his peace for men on whom his favour rests — NEB

. . . peace toward men of his good pleasure — ABUV

and peace on earth to men that are God's friends — Knox

. . . among men who please him — Mon

and on earth peace among men in whom he finds pleasure — TCNT

15. And it came to pass, as the angels were gone away from them into heaven,

Now, when the angels had left them and gone back to Heaven — TCNT

the shepherds said one to another, Let us now go even unto Bethlehem,

. . . Let us go at once to Bethlehem — TCNT

. . . let us go straight to Bethlehem — NASB

and see this thing which is come to pass, which the Lord hath made known unto us.

and see this thing that has happened, of which the Lord has told us — TCNT

Let's see this wonderful thing that has happened . . . — Tay

The Lord has told us what has happened. Let's go to Bethlehem and see it — Beck

16. **And they came with haste, and found Mary, and Joseph, and the babe lying in a manger.**

So they went quickly ... — TCNT

... with all speed ... — NEB

They hurried over there and searched until they found . . . — Beck

17. **And when they had seen it, they made known abroad the saying which was told them concerning this child.**

The shepherds told everyone what had happened and what the angel had said to them about this child — Tay

18. **And all they that heard it wondered at those things which were told them by the shepherds.**

And all those to whose ears it came were full of wonder at the things said by the keepers of the sheep — Bas

Those who heard what the shepherds had to say were amazed — Nor

All who heard the shepherds were astonished at their story — TCNT

19. **But Mary kept all these things,**

... sayings — ASV

while Mary treasured up all that they said — TCNT

But Mary quietly treasured all these things in her heart — Tay

and pondered them in her heart.

pondering them . . . — ASV

and gave much thought to them — Bas

and mused upon it — Mof

and turned them over in her mind—Phi

and often thought about them — Tay

often dwelling on it in her mind — Wey

often pondering on them in her heart — Mon

20. **And the shepherds returned, glorifying and praising God**

And the shepherds went back, giving glory and praise to God — TCNT

Meanwhile the shepherds went back to their flock, . . . — Rieu

for all the things that they had heard and seen, as it was told unto them.

for what they had heard and seen; it had all happened as they had been told — NEB

... it was just as they had been told — Beck

for the news they had heard and the sight which confirmed it — Rieu

21. **And when eight days were accomplished for the circumcising of the child,**

Eight days after the birth of the child, when it was time to circumcise him — TCNT

When eight days had passed, and the time had come to circumcise him — Mon

his name was called JESUS, which was so named of the angel before he was conceived in the womb.

he received the name Jesus — the name given him by the angel before his conception — TCNT

... before his birth — Bas

... before his birth was first expected — Gspd

22. **And when the days of her purification according to the law of Moses were accomplished,**

... their purification . . . — ASV

When the time came for Mary's purification offering at the Temple . . . — Tay

Then after their purification had been completed in accordance with the Law of Moses — NEB

they brought him to Jerusalem, to present him to the Lord;

his parents took the child up to Jerusalem . . . — TCNT

23. **(As it is written in the law of the Lord, Every male that openeth the womb shall be called holy to the Lord;)**

. . . Every first-born male shall be deemed to belong to the Lord — NEB

... shall be considered consecrated to the Lord — Gspd

... shall be dedicated to the Lord — TCNT

24. **And to offer a sacrifice according to that which is said in the law of the Lord, A pair of turtledoves, or two young pigeons.**

and also to make an offering as stated in the law of the Lord: . . . — NEB

25. **And, behold, there was a man in Jerusalem, whose name was Simeon; and the same man was just and devout,**

... righteous and devout — ASV

... upright and devout — NEB

waiting for the consolation of Israel:

looking for . . . — ASV

who lived in constant expectation of the Consolation of Israel — TCNT

constantly expecting the Messiah to come — Tay

one who watched and waited for the restoration of Israel — NEB

waiting for the one who would comfort Israel — Beck

expecting Israel's Consoler — Ber

lived in the belief that Israel would one day be comforted — Rieu

and the Holy Ghost was upon him.

and he was under the guidance of the Holy Spirit — Wms

26. And it was revealed unto him by the Holy Ghost, that he should not see death,

It had been revealed to him by the Holy Spirit . . . — TCNT

. . . disclosed to him by the Holy Spirit . . . — NEB

before he had seen the Lord's Christ.

until he had seen the Lord's Christ — TCNT

. . . the Lord's Messiah — NEB

until he had seen Him — God's anointed King — Tay

27. And he came by the Spirit into the temple:

. . . in the Spirit . . . — ASV

. . . inspired by the Spirit . . . — RSV

. . . led by the Spirit . . . — Mon

Moved by the Spirit, Simeon came into the Temple Courts — TCNT

The Holy Spirit had impelled him to go to the Temple that day — Tay

and when the parents brought in the child Jesus, to do for him after the custom of the law,

. . . what was customary under the law — TCNT

. . . to perform the legal ritual for Him — Ber

and so, when Mary and Joseph arrived to present the baby Jesus to the Lord in obedience to the law — Tay

28. Then took he him up in his arms, and blessed God, and said,

. . . praised God, and said — NEB

29. Lord, now lettest thou thy servant depart in peace, according to thy word:

This day, Master, thou givest thy servant his discharge in peace; now thy promise is fulfilled — NEB

Lord, . . . now I can die content! For I have seen Him as You promised me I would! — Tay

30. For mine eyes have seen thy salvation,

For I have seen with my own eyes the deliverance — NEB

for mine eyes have seen thy saving power — Mof

31. Which thou hast prepared before the face of all people;

which thou hast made ready in full view of all the nations — NEB

which thou hast prepared in the sight of all nations — TCNT

32. A light to lighten the Gentiles, and the glory of thy people Israel.

A light to bring light to the Gentiles . . . — TCNT

A light for revelation to the Gentiles . . . — ASV

A light that will be a revelation to the heathen . . . — NEB

A light of revelation for the heathen, and a glory to your people Israel! — Gspd

33. And Joseph and his mother marvelled at those things which were spoken of him.

. . . were lost in wonder at all that was said about him — Rieu

. . . were full of wonder at what was being said . . . — NEB

Joseph and Mary just stood there, marveling at what was being said about Jesus — Tay

34. And Simeon blessed them,

Simeon gave them his blessing — TCNT

and said unto Mary his mother, Behold, this child is set for the fall and rising again of many in Israel;

. . . many in Israel will stand or fall because of him — NEB

. . . This child is destined to cause the fall and rise of many in Israel — Gspd

. . . to set many in Israel on the downward or the upward path — Rieu

and for a sign which shall be spoken against;

and for a sign to be opposed — NASB

. . . a sign which men reject — NEB

. . . a sign against which hard words will be said — Bas

. . . a portent that will be much debated — Gspd

. . . a sign which men will refuse to acknowledge — Knox

. . . a sign for man's attack — Mof

and to be a controversial figure — Nor

and to set up a standard which many will attack — Phi

and to serve as a revelation which will be disputed — Rieu

35. (Yea, a sword shall pierce through thy own soul also,)

and you too shall be pierced to the heart — NEB

and pain, like a sword, will go through your own soul too — Beck

that the thoughts of many hearts may be revealed.

and thus the secret thoughts of many will be laid bare — NEB

to show what they're thinking in their hearts — Beck

to bring out the secret aims of many a heart — Mof

and the inmost thoughts of many shall be brought into the light of day — Rieu

36. And there was one Anna, a prophetess, the daughter of Phanuel, of the tribe of Aser:

There was also a Prophetess named Hannah, . . . — TCNT

she was of a great age, and had lived with an husband seven years from her virginity;

She was a very old woman, who had lived seven years with her husband after she was first married — NEB

She was advanced in age, having lived with her husband seven years, after her girlhood — Mon

37. And she was a widow of about four-score and four years, which departed not from the temple,

and she had been a widow even unto fourscore and four years . . . — ASV

and then as a widow to the age of eighty-four . . . — NASB

and then being a widow even for four-score and four years. She departed not from the temple — Mon

but served God with fastings and prayers night and day.

but worshipped day and night in fastings and intercessions — Ber

38. And she coming in that instant gave thanks likewise unto the Lord,

At that moment she came up, and began publicly to thank God — TCNT

She, too, came forward just then . . . — Beck

and spake of him to all them that looked for redemption in Jerusalem.

and talked about the child to all who were looking for the liberation of Jerusalem — NEB

and spoke of the child to all that patiently waited for the deliverance of Israel — Knox

. . . to all in Jerusalem who were longing for salvation — Nor

and publicly proclaiming the Messiah's arrival to everyone in Jerusalem who had been awaiting the coming of the Savior — Tay

39. And when they had performed all things according to the law of the Lord,

When the child's parents had done everything enjoined by the Law of the Lord — TCNT

. . . everything prescribed in the law . . . — NEB

they returned into Galilee, to their own city Nazareth.

they returned to Galilee to their own town of Nazareth — TCNT

40. And the child grew, and waxed strong in spirit, filled with wisdom:

The child grew big and strong and full of wisdom — NEB

and the grace of God was upon him.

and the favor of God . . . — RSV

and God's love was with Him — Beck

with God's blessing resting on him — Gspd

and God poured out His blessings on Him — Tay

41. Now his parents went to Jerusalem every year at the feast of the passover.

Now it was the practice of his parents to go . . . — NEB

42. And when he was twelve years old, they went up to Jerusalem after the custom of the feast.

and when he was twelve, they made the pilgrimage as usual — NEB

43. And when they had fulfilled the days, as they returned, the child Jesus tarried behind in Jerusalem; and Joseph and his mother knew not of it.

and as they were returning after spending the full number of days . . . — NASB

when the festive season was over and they started for home . . . — NEB

44. But they, supposing him to have been in the company, went a day's journey; and they sought him among their kinfolk and acquaintance.

... in the caravan ... — NASB
They thought He was with the others who were travelling with them ... — Beck

45. And when they found him not, they turned back again to Jerusalem, seeking him.

46. And it came to pass, that after three days they found him in the temple,
It was not till the third day that they found him in the Temple Courts — TCNT
... two days later ... — Beck
sitting in the midst of the doctors, both hearing them, and asking them questions.
... sitting among the Teachers, now listening to them, now asking them questions — TCNT
... the scholars ... — Mof
... the Rabbis ... — Mon

47. And all that heard him were astonished at his understanding and answers.
... at his intelligence and his answers — TCNT
... at his powers of comprehension and at the answers that he gave — NEB

48. And when they saw him, they were amazed:
His parents were amazed to see Him there — Beck
and his mother said unto him, Son, why hast thou thus dealt with us?
... My child, why have you treated us like this — TCNT
behold, thy father and I have sought thee sorrowing.
... have been looking for you anxiously — RSV
... have been searching for you in great distress — TCNT
... in great anxiety — NEB
Think what anguish of mind thy father and I have endured searching for thee — Knox

Your father and I have been frantic, searching for You everywhere — Tay

49. And he said unto them, How is it that ye sought me?
What made you search for me? he answered — TCNT
wist ye not that I must be about my Father's business?
knew ye not that I must be in my Father's house — ASV

50. And they understood not the saying which he spake unto them.
And his words seemed strange to them — Bas

51. And he went down with them, and came to Nazareth, and was subject unto them:
... and continued to be under their authority — NEB
... and submitted himself to their control — TCNT
... and he was always obedient to them — Mon
but his mother kept all these sayings in her heart.
and his mother treasured all that was said in her heart — TCNT
but his mother kept treasuring up all these incidents in her heart — Mon
... kept in her heart the memory of all this — Knox
... stored up in her memory all that had occurred — Rieu

52. And Jesus increased in wisdom and stature,
And Jesus was ever advancing in wisdom and in stature — Mon
And Jesus grew in wisdom as he grew in years — TCNT
and in favour with God and man.
he grew also in the love of God and of those who knew him — Phi
and won the approval of God and all people — Beck
and gained the blessing of God and men — TCNT
and was loved by God and man — Tay

CHAPTER 3

1. Now in the fifteenth year of the reign of Tiberius Caesar, Pontius Pilate being governor of Judaea, and Herod being tetrarch of Galilee, and his brother Philip tetrarch of Ituraea and of the
region of Trachonitis, and Lysanias the tetrarch of Abilene,
... the reign of the Emperor Tiberius, when Pontius Pilate was Governor of Judaea, Herod Ruler of Galilee,

his brother Philip Ruler of the territory comprising Ituraea and Trachonitis, and Lysanius Ruler of Abilene — TCNT

2. Annas and Caiaphas being the high priests,

and when Annas and Caiaphas were High Priests — TCNT

the word of God came unto John the son of Zacharias

the message of God came to John . . . — Wms

a command from God came to John . . . — TCNT

in the wilderness.

in the waste land — Bas

3. And he came into all the country about Jordan,

. . . the region . . . — ASV

. . . the whole district of the Jordan — TCNT

. . . all over the Jordan valley . . . — NEB

preaching the baptism of repentance

and preached: Repent and be baptised — Beck

proclaiming a baptism upon repentance — TCNT

proclaiming an immersion of repentance — Rhm

preaching the immersion of repentance — ABUV

preaching a baptism conditioned on repentance — Wms

preaching that people should be baptized to show that they had turned to God and away from their sins — Tay

for the remission of sins;

for the forgiveness of sins — TCNT

to have your sins forgiven — Beck

to obtain the forgiveness of sins — Wms

unto remission of sins — ABUV

4. As it is written in the book of the words of Esaias the prophet,

As it is written in the book of the discourses of Isaiah the prophet: — Rhm

As it is written in the book of the prophet Isaiah — Mon

This was in fulfilment of what is said in the writings of the Prophet Isaiah — TCNT

saying, The voice of one crying in the wilderness,

A voice of one crying aloud! In the desert — Rhm

Someone will be calling in the wilderness: — Beck

A voice of one shouting in the desert: — Ber

Hark! Someone is shouting in the desert — Gspd

Prepare ye the way of the Lord, make his paths straight.

Make ye ready . . . — ASV

Get the road ready for the Lord, Make the paths straight for Him — Wms

Prepare the way for God, make straight paths for him — Mon

5. Every valley shall be filled,

Every ravine shall be filled up — Mon

Every chasm shall be filled up — Rhm

Fill up the valleys! — Tay

and every mountain and hill shall be brought low;

Every hill and mountain shall be laid low — Mon

. . . shall be levelled — TCNT

Level the mountains! — Tay

and the crooked shall be made straight,

The winding ways shall be straightened — TCNT

The corners shall be straightened — NEB

And the crooked places shall become straight — Rhm

Straighten the curves! — Tay

and the rough ways shall be made smooth;

and the rugged places smooth ways — Rhm

and the rough roads made smooth — TCNT

and the rough places made into smooth roads — Knox

Smooth out the ruts! — Tay

6. And all flesh shall see the salvation of God.

And all mankind shall see the salvation of God — TCNT

All people must see how God saves them — Beck

And all mankind is to see how God can save — Gspd

And every living thing shall see The saving hand of God — Rieu

7. Then said he to the multitude that came forth to be baptized of him,

And John said to the crowds that went to be baptized by him: — TCNT

So John used to say to the crowd of those who were going out to be baptized by him: — Mon

He said therefore to the multitudes that went out to be immersed by him — ABUV

O generation of vipers,

Ye offspring of vipers — ASV

Brood of vipers — ABUV

You brood of snakes! — Gspd

who hath warned you to flee from the wrath to come?

. . . the coming retribution — NEB

. . . the wrath that is on its way — Rieu

. . . the punishment waiting for you — Beck

who has prompted you to seek refuge from the coming judgement — TCNT

8. **Bring forth therefore fruits worthy of repentance,**

. . . that befit repentance — RSV

. . . in keeping with your repentance — NASB

Then prove your repentance by the fruit it bears — NEB

Then produce fruits in harmony with your repentance — Ber

. . . fruits consistent with your professed repentance — Gspd

Then bring forth fruit befitting your penitence — Mon

You say that you are sorry? Produce the fruits of repentance — Nor

Let your lives, then, prove your repentance — TCNT

and begin not to say within yourselves,

and do not begin to say among yourselves — TCNT

And don't start telling yourselves — Beck

And do not think of saying to yourselves — Rieu

instead of beginning to say to yourselves — Mof

We have Abraham to our father:

We have Abraham as our father—Mon

Abraham is our ancestor — TCNT

for I say unto you, That God is able of these stones to raise up children unto Abraham.

. . . God can produce descendants for Abraham right out of these stones! — Gspd

. . . out of these very stones God is able to raise descendants for Abraham! — TCNT

9. **And now also the ax is laid unto the root of the trees:**

And even now . . . — ASV

. . . is lying all ready at the root of the trees — Mof

But time is short, the axe lies ready at the root of the trees — Rieu

every tree therefore which bringeth not forth good fruit is hewn down, and cast into the fire.

. . . felled and thrown into the fire — — Ber

10. **And the people asked him, saying, What shall we do then?**

. . . What then must we do — ASV

11. **He answereth and saith unto them, He that hath two coats, let him impart to him that hath none;**

. . . share with him who has none — TCNT

and he that hath meat, let him do likewise.

if you have extra food, give it away to those who are hungry — Tay

12. **Then came also publicans to be baptized,**

Even tax-gatherers came to be baptized — TCNT

And there came even tax-collectors to be immersed — Rhm

. . . tax-farmers . . . — Bas

and said unto him, Master, what shall we do?

. . . How shall we prove to you that we have abandoned our sins — Tay

13. **And he said unto them, Exact no more than that which is appointed you.**

. . . Stop collecting any more than is prescribed for you — Wms

. . . collect no more than you have been ordered to — NASB

. . . Do not make an attempt to get more money than the right amount — Bas

14. **And the soldiers likewise demanded of him, saying, And what shall we do?**

The soldiers also repeatedly questioned him, saying . . . — Mon

. . . And we — what are we to do — TCNT

And he said unto them, Do violence to no man, neither accuse any falsely; and be content with your wages.

. . . Molest ye no one, neither accuse falsely; and be content with your supplies — Rhm

. . . Rob no one by violence or by false accusation, . . . — RSV

. . . No bullying; no blackmail; make do with your pay — NEB

. . . Don't use threats or blackmail to get money from anyone, . . . — Beck

. . . Do not extort money by intimidating or informing, . . . — Ber

15. And as the people were in expectation,

Then, while the people were in suspense — TCNT

. . . on the tiptoe of expectation — NEB

and all men mused in their hearts of John, whether he were the Christ, or not;

and all men reasoned in their hearts concerning John, whether perhaps he were the Christ — ASV

and were all debating with themselves whether John could be the Christ — TCNT

all wondering about John whether perhaps he was the Messiah — NEB

16. John answered, saying unto them all,

John gave them their answer by saying publicly — Knox

I indeed baptize you with water;

I indeed immerse you with water — ABUV

As for me, I baptize . . . — NASB

I indeed in water am immersing you — Rhm

but one mightier than I cometh, the latchet of whose shoes I am not worthy to unloose:

but there is coming one more powerful than I, and I am not fit even to unfasten his sandals — TCNT

. . . I'm not good enough to untie His shoe straps — Beck

he shall baptize you with the Holy Ghost and with fire:

he will immerse you in the Holy Spirit and fire — ABUV

He will baptize you with fire — with the Holy Spirit — Tay

17. Whose fan is in his hand,

His winnowing-fork is in his hand — Wms

His shovel is ready in hand — NEB

and he will throughly purge his floor,

and He will clean out His threshing-floor — Wms

and will gather the wheat into his garner;

. . . into his granary — Rhm

and store the grain in his barn — TCNT

but the chaff he will burn with fire unquenchable.

. . . with inextinguishable fire — TCNT

18. And many other things in his exhortation preached he unto the people.

With many other exhortations therefore preached he good tidings . . . — ASV

In this and in many other ways he made his appeal to the people and announced the good news — NEB

. . . he exhorted and continued telling his glad-message unto the people — Rhm

And so with many other challenging words he was telling the people the good news — Beck

. . . he declared the gospel to the people — Wey

19. But Herod the tetrarch, being reproved by him for Herodias his brother Philip's wife, and for all the evils which Herod had done,

but Herod the governor . . . — Gspd

. . . rebuked by him over the affair of his brother's wife . . . — NEB

When John was showing Herod . . . how wrong he was with regard to his brother's wife . . . — Beck

20. Added yet this above all, that he shut up John in prison.

he, on top of everything, locked John up in prison — Beck

he crowned them all by confining John to prison — Ber

21. Now when all the people were baptized, it came to pass,

Now it came to pass when all the people had been immersed — ABUV

During a general baptism of the people — NEB

that Jesus also being baptized, and praying, the heaven was opened,

that as Jesus also had been immersed and was praying, the heaven was opened — ABUV

when Jesus too had been baptized and was praying — NEB

22. And the Holy Ghost descended in a bodily shape like a dove upon him,

and the Holy Spirit descended, in a visible form, like a dove, upon him TCNT

227

and a voice came from heaven, which said, Thou art my beloved Son; in thee I am well pleased.

. . . Thou art my Son the Beloved, in thee I delight — Rhm

. . . on thee my favour rests — NEB

. . . You are my Son, my Beloved! You are my chosen! — Gspd

. . . You are My much loved Son, yes, My delight — Tay

23. **And Jesus himself began to be about thirty years of age, being (as was supposed) the son of Joseph,**

When Jesus began his work he was about . . . — NEB

Jesus was about 30 years old when He began His public ministry. He was known as the son of Joseph — Tay

. . . He was regarded as the son of Joseph — TCNT

which was the son of Heli,

Joseph's father was Heli — Tay

24. **Which was the son of Matthat, which was the son of Levi, which was the son of Melchi, which was the son of Janna, which was the son of Joseph,**

Which was the son of Matthat, which was the son of Levi, which was the son of Melchi, which was the son of Jannai, which was the son of Joseph — Alf

25. **Which was the son of Mattathias, which was the son of Amos, which was the son of Naum, which was the son of Esli, which was the son of Nagge,**

which was the son of Mattathias, which was the son of Amos, which was the son of Nahum, which was the son of Esli, which was the son of Naggae — Alf

26. **Which was the son of Maath, which was the son of Mattathias, which was the son of Semei, which was the son of Joseph, which was the son of Juda,**

Which was the son of Maath, which was the son of Mattathias, which was the son of Semein, which was the son of Josech, which was the son of Joda — Alf

27. **Which was the son of Joanna, which was the son of Rhesa, which was the son of Zorobabel, which was the son of Salathiel, which was the son of Neri,**

Which was the son of Joanan, which was the son of Rhesa, which was the son of Zorobabel, which was the son

of Salathiel, which was the son of Neri — Alf

. . . Johanan . . . Rhesa . . . Zerubbabel . . . Shealtiel . . . Neri — NEB

28. **Which was the son of Melchi, which was the son of Addi, which was the son of Cosam, which was the son of Elmodam, which was the son of Er,**

Which was the son of Melchi, which was the son of Addi, which was the son of Cosam, which was the son of Elmodam, which was the son of Er — Alf

29. **Which was the son of Jose, which was the son of Eliezer, which was the son of Jorim, which was the son of Matthat, which was the son of Levi,**

Which was the son of Jesus, which was the son of Eliezer, which was the son of Jorim, which was the son of Maththat, which was the son of Levi — Alf

. . . Joshua . . . Eliezer . . . Jorim . . . Matthat . . . Levi — NEB

30. **Which was the son of Simeon, which was the son of Juda, which was the son of Joseph, which was the son of Jonan, which was the son of Eliakim,**

Which was the son of Simeon, which was the son of Juda, which was the son of Joseph, which was the son of Jonam, which was the son of Eliakim — Alf

31. **Which was the son of Melea, which was the son of Menan, which was the son of Mattatha, which was the son of Nathan, which was the son of David,**

Which was the son of Melea, which was the son of Mennas, which was the son of Mattatha, which was the son of Nathan, which was the son of David — Alf

32. **Which was the son of Jesse, which was the son of Obed, which was the son of Booz, which was the son of Salmon, which was the son of Naasson,**

Which was the son of Jesse, which was the son of Obed, which was the son of Boaz, which was the son of Salmon, which was the son of Naasson — Alf

33. **Which was the son of Aminadab, which was the son of Aram, which was the son of Esrom, which was the son of Phares, which was the son of Juda,**

Which was the son of Aminadab, which

was the son of Admin, which was the son of Arni, which was the son of Esrom, which was the son of Phares, which was the son of Judah — Alf

34. Which was the son of Jacob, which was the son of Isaac, which was the son of Abraham, which was the son of Thara, which was the son of Nachor,

Which was the son of Jacob, which was the son of Isaac, which was the son of Abraham, which was the son of Thara, which was the son of Nachor — Alf

35. Which was the son of Saruch, which was the son of Ragau, which was the son of Phalec, which was the son of Heber, which was the son of Sala,

Which was the son of Saruch, which was the son of Ragau, which was the son of Phalec, which was the son of Heber, which was the son of Sala — Alf

. . . Serug . . . Reu . . . Peleg . . . Eber . . . Shelah — NEB

36. Which was the son of Cainan, which was the son of Arphaxad, which was

the son of Sem, which was the son of Noe, which was the son of Lamech,

Which was the son of Cainam, which was the son of Arphaxad, which was the son of Sem, which was the son of Noe, which was the son of Lamech — Alf

Cainan . . . Arpachshad . . . Shem . . . Noah . . . Lamech — ASV

37. Which was the son of Mathusala, which was the son of Enoch, which was the son of Jared, which was the son of Maleleel, which was the son of Cainan,

Which was the son of Mathusala, which was the son of Enoch, which was the son of Jared, which was the son of Maleleel, which was the son of Cainan — Alf

. . . Methuselah . . . Enoch . . . Jared . . . Mahalaleel . . . Cainan — ASV

38. Which was the son of Enos, which was the son of Seth, which was the son of Adam, which was the son of God.

Which was the son of Enos, which was the son of Seth, which was the son of Adam, which was the Son of God — Alf

CHAPTER 4

1. And Jesus being full of the Holy Ghost returned from Jordan,

And Jesus, full of the Holy Spirit, returned from the Jordan — ASV

and was led by the Spirit into the wilderness,

and was led about by the Spirit . . . — NASB

. . . up and down the wilderness — NEB

and was led in the Spirit in the desert — Rhm

2. Being forty days tempted of the devil.

during forty days being tempted of the devil — ASV

For forty days, being tested by the Evil One — Bas

. . . being tempted by the adversary — Rhm

And in those days he did eat nothing: and when they were ended, he afterward hungered.

All that time he had nothing to eat, and at the end of it he was famished — NEB

. . . and, when it was over, he became hungry — TCNT

3. And the devil said unto him, If thou be the Son of God, command this stone that it be made bread.

. . . tell this stone to become bread — Mon

4. And Jesus answered him, saying, It is written,

And Jesus answered him: Scripture says — TCNT

That man shall not live by bread alone, but by every word of God.

Man cannot live on bread alone — NEB

Bread is not man's only need — Bas

It is not on bread alone that man is to live — TCNT

5. And the devil, taking him up into an high mountain, shewed unto him all the kingdoms of the world in a moment of time.

And he led him up, and showed him . . . — ASV

Next the devil led him up and showed

229

him in a flash all the kingdoms of the world — NEB

Then he lifted Jesus up and showed him all the realms of the universe in a single instant — Mof

6. And the devil said unto him, All this power will I give thee, and the glory of them:

. . . To thee will I give all this authority and the glory of them — ASV

. . . I will give you all this power and all their splendor — Wms

. . . I will give You all this domain and its glory — NASB

. . . and the glory that goes with it — NEB

. . . all this power and magnificence — Phi

for that is delivered unto me;

for it has been handed over to me — NASB

for it has been put in my hands — NEB

. . . turned over to me — Gspd

and to whomsoever I will I give it.

and I give it to whom I will — RSV

. . . to anyone I please — Gspd

7. If thou therefore wilt worship me, all shall be thine.

You have only to do homage to me and it shall all be yours — NEB

8. And Jesus answered and said unto him, Get thee behind me, Satan:[1] for it is written,

And Jesus answered and said unto him, It is written — ASV

Jesus answered him by citing the Scripture — Rieu

Thou shalt worship the Lord thy God, and him only shalt thou serve.

You shall do homage to the Lord your God and worship him alone — NEB

The Lord thy God shalt thou worship, And unto him alone render divine service — Rhm

9. And he brought him to Jerusalem, and set him on a pinnacle of the temple, and said unto him,

The Devil next led him into Jerusalem, and, placing him on the parapet of the Temple, said: — TCNT

. . . and set him upon the pinnacle of the temple, — and said — Rhm

. . . the highest point . . . — Bas

. . . ledge . . . — Phi

. . . cornice . . . — Rieu

. . . a gable . . . — Amp

If thou be the Son of God, cast thyself down from hence;

. . . throw yourself down from here — TCNT

10. For it is written, He shall give his angels charge over thee, to keep thee:

for Scripture says, He will give his angels orders to take care of you — NEB

Unto his messengers will he give command concerning thee, To keep vigilant watch over thee — Rhm

11. And in their hands they shall bear thee up,

They will support you in their arms — Lam

lest at any time thou dash thy foot against a stone.

lest thou shouldst chance to trip on a stone — Knox

12. And Jesus answering said unto him, It is said, Thou shalt not tempt the Lord thy God.

Yes, said Jesus, but Scripture says also this . . . — Nor

. . . You may not put the Lord your God to the test — Bas

13. And when the devil had ended all the temptation,

. . . completed every temptation — ASV

. . . finished tempting him in every way — Knox

So, after exhausting on him every kind of temptation — Mon

he departed from him for a season.

. . . until an opportune time — RSV

. . . until a fitting season — Rhm

. . . biding his time — NEB

. . . till another time — Gspd

. . . till a fresh occasion should present itself — Rieu

14. And Jesus returned in the power of the Spirit into Galilee:

Then Jesus, armed with the power of the Spirit, returned to Galilee—NEB

and there went out a fame of him through all the region round about.

and a report concerning him went out . . . — RSV

and reports about him spread through the whole countryside — NEB

---

[1]The words "Get thee behind me, Satan" are now recognized as not adequately supported by original manuscripts.

15. And he taught in their synagogues, being glorified of all.

and he began to teach in their synagogues, and was glorified by all — Mon

. . . and was praised by all — NASB

. . . and all men sang his praises — NEB

16. And he came to Nazareth, where he had been brought up:

. . . where he had been as a child — Bas

and, as his custom was, he went into the synagogue on the sabbath day, and stood up for to read.

. . . and stood up to read the Scriptures — TCNT

. . . got up to give a reading — Bas

17. And there was delivered unto him the book of the prophet Esaias.

and was handed the scroll of the prophet Isaiah — NEB

And when he had opened the book, he found the place where it was written,

And unrolling the book . . . — ABUV

18. The Spirit of the Lord is upon me, because he hath anointed me to preach the gospel to the poor;

. . . For he has consecrated me to preach the good news to the poor — Gspd

. . . To tell glad tidings unto the destitute — Rhm

he hath sent me to heal the brokenhearted,[2] to preach deliverance to the captives,

He hath sent me forth — To proclaim to captives a release — Rhm

. . . To announce to prisoners, You are free — Beck

. . . to tell captives they can be free — Nor

and recovering of sight to the blind,

to the blind, You will see again — Beck

And new eyes for the blind — Rieu

to set at liberty them that are bruised,

. . . those who are oppressed — RSV

. . . downtrodden — NASB

. . . to let the broken victims go free — NEB

To free those whom tyranny has crushed — Wey

Setting the shattered free — Rieu

19. To preach the acceptable year of the Lord.

To proclaim the welcome year of the Lord — Rhm

. . . the favorable year . . . — NASB

. . . the year of the Lord's favour — NEB

. . . that the year of the Lord's good pleasure is come — Bas

to proclaim a year when men may find acceptance with the Lord — Knox

20. And he closed the book, and he gave it again to the minister, and sat down.

And rolling up the book . . . — ABUV

And folding up the scroll . . . — Rhm

. . . gave it back to the attendant . . . — ASV

And the eyes of all them that were in the synagogue were fastened on him.

The eyes of the whole congregation were riveted upon him — Rieu

21. And he began to say unto them, This day is this scripture fulfilled in your ears.

. . . in your hearing — RSV

. . . in your very hearing this text has come true — NEB

. . . Today, while you're listening, what is written here has come true — Beck

22. And all bare him witness, and wondered at the gracious words which proceeded out of his mouth.

There was a general stir of admiration; they were surprised that words of such grace should fall from his lips — NEB

All who were present spoke well of him and were astonished at the beautiful words that fell from his lips — TCNT

And they said, Is not this Joseph's son?

23. And he said unto them, Ye will surely say unto me this proverb, Physician, heal thyself:

. . . No doubt you will quote the proverb to me . . . — NEB

. . . you will remind me of the saying . . . — TCNT

whatsoever we have heard done in Capernaum, do also here in thy county.

. . . do here in your home town as well — NASB

24. And he said, Verily I say unto you, No prophet is accepted in his own country.

---

[2]The words "to heal the brokenhearted" are now recognized as not adequately supported by original manuscripts.

I tell you in solemn truth, he added
. . . — Mon

. . . No prophet is welcome in his home
town — NASB

. . . is recognized . . . — NEB

**25. But I tell you of a truth, many widows
were in Israel in the days of Elias,**

In very truth I tell you . . . in the days
of Elijah — Mon

**when the heaven was shut up three
years and six months,**

**when great famine was throughout all
the land;**

and a severe famine prevailed throughout the country — TCNT

and famine lay hard over the whole
country — NEB

**26. But unto none of them was Elias sent,
save unto Sarepta, a city of Sidon,
unto a woman that was a widow.**

. . . Elijah . . . Zarephath . . . — ASV

**27. And many lepers were in Israel in the
time of Eliseus the prophet; and none
of them was cleansed, saving Naaman
the Syrian.**

. . . Elisha . . . — ASV

**28. And all they in the synagogue, when
they heard these things, were filled with
wrath,**

At these words the whole congregation
were infuriated — NEB

. . . became enraged — TCNT

**29. And rose up, and thrust him out of
the city,**

They broke up the gathering, . . . —
Rieu

And rising up, . . . — Rhm

. . . they drove Jesus out of the town
— TCNT

**and led him unto the brow of the hill
whereon their city was built, that
they might cast him down headlong.**

. . . in order to throw him down the
cliff — NASB

. . . meaning to hurl him over the edge
— NEB

**30. But he passing through the midst of
them went his way,**

But he walked straight through them
all, and went away — NEB

**31. And came down to Capernaum, a city
of Galilee, and taught them on the
sabbath days.**

. . . and continued to teach the people
. . . — Mon

**32. And they were astonished at his doc-
trine:**

And they were being struck with astonishment at his teaching — Rhm

They were deeply impressed by his
teaching — Mon

for his word was with power.

for his word was with authority — ASV

for what he said had the note of authority — NEB

for his words had the ring of authority
— Rieu

**33. And in the synagogue there was a man,
which had a spirit of an unclean devil,**

. . . that had a spirit of an unclean
demon — ASV

. . . possessed by a devil, an unclean
spirit — NEB

and cried out with a loud voice,

He shrieked at the top of his voice —
NEB

**34. Saying, Let us alone; what have we
to do with thee, thou Jesus of Nazareth?**

saying, Ha! Jesus of Nazareth, what
business have you with us — Mon

Let be! What have we in common with
thee, O Jesus Nazarene! — Rhm

Stop! What do you want with us, Jesus
of Nazareth — TCNT

**art thou come to destroy us? I know
thee who thou art; the Holy One of
God.**

**35. And Jesus rebuked him, saying, Hold
thy peace, and come out of him.**

. . . Be silent! . . . — TCNT

. . . Hold your tongue . . . — Rieu

**And when the devil had thrown him in
the midst,**

And when the demon had thrown the
man down before them — Mon

. . . hurled him into the crowd — Beck

. . . threw him into a convulsion before them all — Knox

he came out of him, and hurt him not.

**36. And they were all amazed, and spake
among themselves, saying, What a
word is this!**

And they were all lost in amazement
and kept saying to one another:
What words are these? — TCNT

. . . they began discussing with one another and saying, What is this message? — NASB

. . . What is there in this man's words?
— NEB

for with authority and power he commandeth the unclean spirits, and
they come out.

He gives orders with authority and
power . . . — NEB

. . . gives orders authoritatively and
effectually . . . — Gspd

37. And the fame of him went out into
every place of the country round
about.

So the news spread, and he was the talk
of the whole district — NEB

38. And he arose out of the synagogue,
and entered into Simon's house. And
Simon's wife's mother was taken with
a great fever;

. . . a high fever — RSV

and they besought him for her.

. . . they asked him to help her — NEB

39. And he stood over her, and rebuked
the fever; and it left her:

He went to her, and, bending over her,
ordered the fever to leave . . . —
Beck

and immediately she arose and ministered unto them.

. . . and began to wait on them — NASB

40. Now when the sun was setting, all they
that had any sick with divers diseases
brought them unto him;

At sunset all who had friends suffering
from one disease or another . . . —
NEB

and he laid his hands on every one of
them, and healed them.

41. And devils also came out of many,

And demons . . . — ASV

crying out, and saying, Thou art Christ
the Son of God.

crying aloud . . . — Rhm

shouting . . . — NEB

And he rebuking them suffered them
not to speak:

These he sternly forbade to speak —
Rieu

for they knew that he was Christ.

because they knew He was the promised Savior — Beck

42. And when it was day, he departed and
went into a desert place:

. . . a lonely place — RSV

and the people sought him, and came
unto him, and stayed him, that he
should not depart from them.

But the people went in search of him,
and when they came where he was
they pressed him not to leave them
— NEB

but the people flocked out to find Him
. . . — Wey

and the crowds continued to look for
Him; they overtook Him, and tried
to keep Him from leaving them —
Wms

43. And he said unto them, I must preach
the kingdom of God to other cities
also:

. . . I must preach good tidings of the
Kingdom of God . . . — ASV

for therefore am I sent.

for I was sent for this purpose — NASB

44. And he preached in the synagogues of
Galilee.

So for some time He preached in the
synagogues of Judaea — Wey

CHAPTER 5

1. And it came to pass, that, as the people pressed upon him to hear the word
of God, he stood by the Lake of Gennesaret,

Now it came to pass, while the multitude pressed upon him and heard the
word of God, that he was standing
by the lake of Gennesaret — ASV

One day as he stood by the Lake of
Gennesaret, and the people crowded
upon him to listen to the word of
God — NEB

2. And saw two ships standing by the
lake:

he noticed two boats lying at the water's
edge — NEB

. . . close to the shore — TCNT

. . . drawn up on the beach — Phi

but the fishermen were gone out of
them, and were washing their nets.

the fishermen had disembarked . . . —
Mon

3. And he entered into one of the ships,
which was Simon's, and prayed him
that he would thrust out a little from
the land.

. . . and asked him to put out a little
from the land — ASV

And he sat down, and taught the people out of the ship.

. . . and began teaching the multitudes . . . — NASB

. . . then he went on teaching the crowds . . . — NEB

4. **Now when he had left speaking, he said unto Simon,**

When he was through speaking . . . — Lam

Launch out into the deep, and let down your nets for a draught.

Push off into deep water, and all throw out your nets for a haul — TCNT

. . . for a catch — RSV

5. **And Simon answering said unto him, Master, we have toiled all the night, and have taken nothing:**

. . . we worked hard all night and caught nothing — NASB

. . . we were hard at work all night and caught nothing at all — NEB

nevertheless at thy word I will let down the net.

but, at your bidding, I will throw out the nets — TCNT

but if you say so, . . . — NEB

but just because of your word . . . — Lam

However, I will take your word for it and lower the nets — Rieu

6. **And when they had this done, they inclosed a great multitude of fishes:**

They did so, and netted an enormous catch of fish — Rieu

. . . and made a big haul of fish — NEB

. . . and enclosed such a great shoal of fish — TCNT

and their net brake.

and their nets began to split — NEB

that their nets began to break — TCNT

that their nets started tearing — Ber

7. **And they beckoned unto their partners, which were in the other ship,**

So they signalled to their partners in the other boat — TCNT

And they made signs to their partners in the other boat — Rhm

that they should come and help them. And they came, and filled both the ships, so that they began to sink.

. . . and loaded both boats to the point of sinking — NEB

. . . filled both the boats to sinking point — Phi

8. **When Simon Peter saw it, he fell down at Jesus' knees, saying,**

At seeing this, Simon Peter fell down and caught Jesus by the knees — Knox

. . . fell on his knees before Jesus and said — Phi

Depart from me; for I am a sinful man, O Lord.

Go, Lord, leave me, sinner that I am! — NEB

Leave me to myself, Lord, I am a sinner — Knox

I beg you . . . leave me alone . . . — Lam

Keep away from me Lord, for I'm only a sinful man — Phi

9. **For he was astonished, and all that were with him, at the draught of the fishes which they had taken:**

For amazement overcame him . . . — Rhm

. . . at the catch of fish which they had taken — RSV

For he and all who were with him were lost in amazement at the haul of fish which they had made — TCNT

10. **And so was also James, and John, the sons of Zebedee, which were partners with Simon. And Jesus said unto Simon, Fear not;**

from henceforth thou shalt catch men.

henceforth you will be catching men — RSV

From now on, you're going to catch men — Beck

from now your catch will be men — Mof

henceforth shalt thou be taking men that they may live — Rhm

From now on you'll be fishing for the souls of men! — Tay

11. **And when they had brought their ships to land, they forsook all, and followed him.**

Then running their boats to shore . . . Ber

. . . they left all . . . — ASV

12. **And it came to pass, when he was in a certain city, behold a man full of leprosy:**

. . . while he was in one of the cities . . . — ASV

. . . he came upon a man who was far gone in leprosy — Knox

He was once in a certain town, where there happened to be a man covered with leprosy — NEB

who seeing Jesus fell on his face, and besought him, saying,

When the leper saw Jesus, he threw himself on his face and implored his help: — TCNT

Lord, if thou wilt, thou canst make me clean.

... if you are willing ... — NASB

... if only you will ... — NEB

... if You want to ... — Beck

If only you choose, sir, you can cure me! — Gspd

13. And he put forth his hand, and touched him, saying, I will: be thou clean.

... be thou made clean — ASV

... I am willing: Be cleansed! — Rhm

... Indeed I will; be clean again — NEB

... I want to, He said, Be clean!—Beck

... I do choose! Be cured! — Gspd

And immediately the leprosy departed from him.

Instantly the leprosy left the man — TCNT

Whereupon all at once his leprosy passed from him — Knox

14. And he charged him to tell no man:

... warned him not to tell anyone of it — Knox

but go, and shew thyself to the priest, and offer for thy cleansing, according as Moses commanded,

... and make offerings for your purification as Moses prescribed — Ber

for a testimony unto them.

for a proof to the people — RSV

that will certify your cure — NEB

to show them that you're well — Beck

to give people notice — Ber

to make the truth known to them — Knox

as evidence of your cure — TCNT

15. But so much the more went there a fame abroad of him:

But the news of Him was spreading ever further — NASB

But all the more the report about him continued to spread — Mon

and great multitudes came together to hear, and to be healed by him of their infirmities.

... were gathering to hear ...— NASB

... gathered to hear him and be cured of their ailments — NEB

16. And he withdrew himself

But He Himself would often slip away — NASB

From time to time he would withdraw — NEB

Jesus, however, habitually withdrew — Ber

And he would steal away from them — Knox

into the wilderness, and prayed.

to lonely places for prayer — NEB

17. And it came to pass on a certain day, as he was teaching,

And it came to pass on one of those days, that he was teaching — ASV

that there were Pharisees and doctors of the law sitting by, which were come out of every town of Galilee, and Judaea, and Jerusalem:

the Pharisees and Bible teachers were sitting there. They had come from every village in Galilee and Judea and from Jerusalem — Beck

and the power of the Lord was present to heal them.

... was with him to heal the sick — NEB

... wrought in him to heal — Alf

18. And, behold, men brought in a bed a man which was taken with a palsy:

... some men were carrying on a bed a man who was paralysed — NASB

... a man who was ill without power of moving — Bas

... a paralytic on a quilt-bed ... — Lam

and they sought means to bring him in, and to lay him before him.

They tried to bring him in ... — NEB

they tried to carry him inside ... — Mof

19. And when they could not find by what way they might bring him in because of the multitude,

And not finding any way to bring him in because of the crowd — NASB

they went upon the house top, and let him down through the tiling with his couch into the midst before Jesus.

they went up on the roof and let him down through the tiles with his stretcher, right in the center, in front of Jesus — NASB

... bed and all, into the middle of the company ... — NEB

So they went up on the roof above him, took off some tiles and lowered the sick man down into the middle of the crowd, still on his sleeping mat, right in front of Jesus! — Tay

20. **And when he saw their faith, he said unto him, Man, thy sins are forgiven thee.**

. . . your sins have been forgiven you — Rieu

21. **And the scribes and the Pharisees began to reason, saying,**

Then the Bible scholars and the Pharisees began to argue, saying — Beck

. . . began to question . . . — RSV

. . . began saying to themselves — NEB

. . . began to turn this over in their minds — Rieu

Who is this which speaketh blasphemies? Who can forgive sins, but God alone?

Who is this fellow with his blasphemous talk . . . — NEB

. . . who has no respect for God . . . — Bas

22. **But when Jesus perceived their thoughts,**

. . . questionings — RSV

. . . fully knowing their reasonings — Alf

. . . cavilings — Mon

. . . understood what they were thinking about — Nor

. . . the way in which they were debating — TCNT

he answering said unto them, What reason ye in your hearts?

Why do you harbour thoughts like these — NEB

Why argue in your hearts — Mof

What is this cavil in your hearts — Mon

23. **Whether is easier, to say, Thy sins be forgiven thee; or to say, Rise up and walk?**

Which is easier to say, Your sins are forgiven, or to say, Rise and walk — Mon

24. **But that ye may know that the Son of man hath power upon earth to forgive sins,**

. . . authority on earth . . . — ASV

But to convince you that the Son of Man has the right on earth . . . — NEB

(he said unto the sick of the palsy,) I say unto thee, Arise, and take up thy couch, and go into thine house.

. . . and go home — RSV

. . . pick up your mat and walk home — Ber

25. **And immediately he rose up before them,**

At once he was up their presence — Ber

Instantly the man sprang to his feet — Phi

and took up that whereon he lay,

. . . picked up the couch he had been lying on — Rieu

and departed to his own house, glorifying God.

and went home praising God — Rieu

26. **And they were all amazed, and they glorified God,**

And astonishment seized one and all and they began glorifying God — Rhm

And amazement took hold on all . . . — ASV

Sheer amazement gripped every man . . . — Phi

They were all dumbfounded and praised God — Rieu

The people, one and all, were lost in amazement . . . — TCNT

and were filled with fear,

. . . with awe — RSV

saying, We have seen strange things to day.

. . . You would never believe the things we have seen to-day — NEB

. . . To-day we have seen wonders — Lam

. . . We have seen unaccountable things today — Rhm

. . . We have seen incredible things to-day — Mof

. . . We have seen marvelous things to-day! — TCNT

. . . We never thought . . . to see what we have seen to-day — Rieu

27. **And after these things he went forth,**

Going outdoors after this — Ber

and saw a publican, named Levi, sitting at the receipt of custom:

. . . a tax-collector . . . at the tax-office — RSV

. . . a tax-farmer . . . at the place where taxes were taken — Bas

. . . at the place of toll — ASV

he noticed Levi, a tax collector, sitting at the toll-house — Ber

and he said unto him, Follow me.

. . . come and be one of My disciples — Tay

28. And he left all, rose up, and followed him.

And abandoning everything . . . — Rieu

And giving up his business . . . — Bas

29. And Levi made him a great feast in his own house:

. . . gave a big reception for Him . . . — NASB

. . . put on a great reception . . . — Nor

. . . gave a great entertainment . . . — TCNT

and there was a great company of publicans and of others that sat down with them.

among the guests was a large party of tax-gatherers . . . — NEB

and there was a crowded company of publicans and others who were their fellow-guests — Knox

30. But their scribes and Pharisees murmured against his disciples,

. . . began grumbling at His disciples — NASB

. . . muttered indignantly about this to Jesus' disciples — Phi

. . . made this a bone of contention with his disciples — Rieu

saying, Why do ye eat and drink with publicans and sinners?

. . . with tax-collectors and irreligious people — Gspd

. . . with tax-gatherers and outcasts — TCNT

31. And Jesus answering said unto them, They that are whole need not a physician; but they that are sick.

. . . It is not the healthy that need a doctor, but the sick — NEB

32. I came not to call the righteous, but sinners to repentance.

I have not come to invite virtuous people, but to call sinners to repentance — NEB

I have not come to invite the pious . . . — Gspd

33. And they said unto him, Why do the disciples of John fast often, and make prayers, and likewise the disciples of the Pharisees;

. . . John's disciples are much given to

fasting and the practice of prayer . . . — NEB

but thine eat and drink?

but yours eat and drink right along — Ber

34. And he said unto them, Can ye make the children of the bridechamber fast, while the bridegroom is with them?

. . . Can you make wedding guests fast . . . — RSV

. . . You cannot make the attendants of the bridegroom fast . . . — NASB

. . . Can you persuade the men of the bridegroom's company to fast . . . — Knox

. . . Can you make the bridal party fast . . . — Mon

35. But the days will come,

But other days will come . . . — Gspd

No, the days will come . . . — Knox

when the bridegroom shall be taken away from them, and then shall they fast in those days.

36. And he spake also a parable unto them;

He pictured it to them this way — Beck

Then he gave them this illustration — Phi

Then He told them a short story — Wms

No man putteth a piece of a new garment upon an old;

No one tears a piece from a new garment and puts it on an old garment — RSV

No one tears a piece from a new cloak to patch an old one — NEB

if otherwise, then both the new maketh a rent,

else he will rend the new — ASV

if he does he will tear the new — RSV

and the piece that was taken out of the new agreeth not with the old.

and the piece from the new will not match the old — RSV

37. And no man putteth new wine into old bottles;

. . . wineskins — ASV

else the new wine will burst the bottles, and be spilled, and the bottles shall perish.

. . . and the skins will be destroyed — RSV

38. But new wine must be put into new bottles;

No, we must pour new wine into fresh
wineskins — Rieu

But new wine into unused wineskins
must be poured — Rhm

Fresh skins for new wine! — NEB

and both are preserved.

... both are kept safe — Knox

**39. No man also having drunk old wine
straightway desireth new: for he saith,**

No man after drinking old wine wishes
for new ... — TCNT

The old is better.

The old is good enough — NASB

The old is preferable — Ber

The old suits me — Rieu

CHAPTER 6

**1. And it came to pass on the second sab-
bath after the first,[3]**

... on a sabbath — ASV

... on a certain Sabbath — NASB

... on the next sabbath — Knox

that he went through the corn fields;

... through the wheat fields — Mon

... through grainfields — Beck

**and his disciples plucked the ears of
corn, and did eat, rubbing them in
their hands.**

and his disciples were plucking the ears
of corn, rubbing them in their hands,
and eating them — NEB

His disciples were picking the heads of
grain, rubbing them in their hands,
and eating them — Beck

**2. And certain of the Pharisees said unto
them,**

**Why do ye that which is not lawful to
do on the sabbath days?**

... what is forbidden on the Sabbath
— NEB

... something you shouldn't do on a
day of rest — Beck

... what is not allowed on the Sabbath
— Ber

**3. And Jesus answering them said, Have
ye not read so much as this, what
David did,**

... Have ye not read even this, what
David did — ASV

... Have you not even read ... — NASB

... So you have not read ... — NEB

**when he was an hungred, and
they which were with him;**

when he was hungry ... — ASV

when he and his men were hungry —
NEB

**4. How he went into the house of God,
and did take and eat the shewbread,**

... the bread of the Presence — RSV

... the consecrated bread — NASB

... the loaves laid before God — Beck

... the loaves of presentation — Ber

... the loaves set forth before God —
Knox

... the bread that was on the table of
the Lord — Lam

**and gave also to them that were with
him;**

and gave it to his companions — NASB

and gave his men some — Beck

and he shared with his companions —
Ber

**which it is not lawful to eat but for the
priests alone?**

... for any but the priests to eat —
RSV

though priests alone were allowed to
eat them, and no one else — NEB

**5. And he said unto them, That the Son
of man is Lord also of the sabbath.**

... is sovereign even over the Sabbath
— NEB

... is master of the Sabbath — Gspd

... has even the sabbath at his disposal
— Knox

**6. And it came to pass also on another
sabbath, that he entered into the
synagogue and taught:**

On another Sabbath he had gone to
synagogue and was teaching — NEB

**and there was a man whose right hand
was withered.**

There happened to be a man in the
congregation ... — NEB

... whose right hand was deformed —
Tay

**7. And the scribes and Pharisees watched
him, whether he would heal on the
sabbath day;**

The Teachers of the Law and the Pharisees watched Jesus closely, to see ...
— TCNT

... were watching Him closely, to see
... — NASB

---

[3]Some manuscripts do not contain the words
"the second after the first."

. . . were on the watch to see . . . — Wey

that they might find an accusation against him.

. . . find how to accuse him — ASV

hoping to have a charge to bring against him — Rieu

so they might trump up some charge against him — Ber

8. **But he knew their thoughts,**

But he knew what they were thinking — Beck

But he knew their reasonings — Rhm

He was all along aware of their thoughts — Mon

and said to the man which had the withered hand, Rise up, and stand forth in the midst.

. . . Stand up and come out into the middle — TCNT

. . . Come and stand here — RSV

. . . Arise and come forward! — NASB

. . . Stand up and take the center — Ber

. . . Get up and stand in front — Gspd

. . . Come and stand here where everyone can see — Tay

And he arose and stood forth.

So he got up and stood there — Wms

9. **Then said Jesus unto them, I will ask you one thing;**

. . . I put the question to you: — NEB

. . . I want to ask you — Ber

Is it lawful on the sabbath days to do good, or to do evil?

if it is allowed to do good or evil on the Sabbath — Ber

Are we permitted on the Sabbath to choose between doing good and doing evil — Rieu

to save life, or to destroy it?

to save a life . . . — Ber

to save a life or to let it perish — TCNT

10. **And looking round about upon them all, he said unto the man,**

And glancing round at them all in anger . . . — Mof

Then, after looking at each of them in turn . . . — Rieu

Stretch forth thy hand.

Stretch out your hand — TCNT

Hold out your hand — Ber

And he did so: and his hand was restored whole as the other.

. . . was made well — Bas

. . . was made healthy again — Beck

. . . was fully restored — Ber

11. **And they were filled with madness;**

. . . with rage — NASB

. . . beside themselves with anger — NEB

. . . perfectly furious — Gspd

. . . were wild with rage — Tay

and communed one with another what they might do to Jesus.

and discussed with one another . . . — RSV

and began to discuss among themselves . . . — NEB

and began to plot His murder — Tay

12. **And it came to pass in those days, that he went out into a mountain to pray, and continued all night in prayer to God.**

During this time he went out one day into the hills . . . — NEB

It was in those days that he went up on the mountain . . . — Gspd

13. **And when it was day, he called unto him his disciples:**

When day broke . . . — NEB

and of them he chose twelve, whom also he named apostles;

14. **Simon, (whom he also named Peter,) and Andrew his brother, James and John, Philip and Bartholomew,**

15. **Matthew and Thomas, James the son of Alphaeus, and Simon called Zelotes,**

. . . the Zealot — RSV

. . . known as the Zealot — TCNT

16. **And Judas the brother of James, and Judas Iscariot, which also was the traitor.**

. . . who became the traitor — ASV

. . . who became a traitor — NASB

. . . who turned traitor — NEB

17. **And he came down with them, and stood in the plain,**

. . . and stood on a level place — ASV

With them he came down the hill and stood on a level spot — Mof

. . . till he reached a level place — Mon

and the company of his disciples, and a great multitude of people out of all Judaea and Jerusalem, and from the sea coast of Tyre and Sidon, which came to hear him, and to be healed of their diseases;

18. **And they that were vexed with unclean spirits: and they were healed.**

Those who were tormented by unclean spirits were healed also — Mon

And those who were troubled with foul spirits were cured — Gspd

19. And the whole multitude sought to touch him:

and every one in the crowd was trying to touch him — TCNT

. . . struggled to touch him — Rieu

for there went virtue out of him, and healed them all.

for power came forth from him . . . — ASV

20. And he lifted up his eyes on his disciples, and said,

Then turning to his disciples . . . — NEB

Then Jesus looked steadily at his disciples . . . — Phi

Blessed be ye poor: for yours is the kingdom of God.

How blest are you who are poor . . . — NEB

Happy ye poor . . . — ABUV

Happy ye destitute . . . — Rhm

How happy are you who own nothing . . . — Phi

21. Blessed are ye that hunger now:

Happy . . . — Rhm

for ye shall be filled.

. . . satisfied — NASB

. . . completely satisfied — Wms

Blessed are ye that weep now: for ye shall laugh.

for you are going to laugh — Phi

22. Blessed are ye, when men shall hate you, and when they shall separate you from their company,

. . . exclude you — RSV

. . . ostracize you — NASB

. . . outlaw you — NEB

. . . put you away from among them — Bas

. . . discriminate against you — Lam

. . . excommunicate you — Mof

and shall reproach you, and cast out your name as evil, for the Son of man's sake.

and detest all you stand for because you are loyal to the Son of Man — Phi

23. Rejoice ye in that day, and leap for joy: for, behold, your reward is great in heaven:

On that day be glad and dance for joy . . . — NEB

Be glad when that happens, and leap for joy . . . — Gspd

for in the like manner did their fathers unto the prophets.

for in the same way their fathers used to treat the prophets — NASB

for just so their forefathers behaved to the prophets — Wey

24. But woe unto you that are rich!

But unhappy are you who have wealth . . . — Bas

Alas, however, for you who are wealthy — Ber

But a curse on you who are rich . . . — Wms

But, oh, the sorrows that await the rich! — Tay

for ye have received your consolation.

for you are receiving your comfort in full — NASB

you have had your time of happiness — NEB

you get all the comforts you will ever get — Mof

For they have had their happiness down here — Tay

25. Woe unto you that are full! for ye shall hunger.

Alas for you who are sated now . . . — TCNT

. . . who are well-fed now . . . — NASB

. . . who have plenty to eat . . . — Gspd

Woe unto you that laugh now! for ye shall mourn and weep.

. . . for you will know sorrow and tears — Phi

26. Woe unto you, when all men shall speak well of you!

. . . when all mankind applaud you — Rieu

. . . when all men give you their approval — Bas

. . . when everybody says nice things about you — Phi

for so did their fathers to the false prophets.

just so did their fathers treat the false prophets — NEB

27. But I say unto you which hear, Love your enemies, do good to them which hate you,

But to you who hear me I say . . . — NEB

28. Bless them that curse you,

and pray for them which despitefully use you.

. . . which abuse you — RSV

. . . who treat you spitefully — NEB

. . . who insult you — ABUV

. . . who treat you insultingly — Knox

. . . who compel you to carry burdens — Lam

29. And unto him that smiteth thee on the one cheek offer also the other;
To the man that strikes you on the cheek, turn the other also — Gspd
and him that taketh away thy cloke forbid not to take thy coat also.
. . . withhold not thy coat also — ASV
. . . do not withhold your shirt from him either — NASB
. . . keep not back your undergarment — Ber

30. Give to every man that asketh of thee; and of him that taketh away thy goods ask them not again.
. . . whoever takes away what is yours, do not demand it back — NASB
. . . demand no restitution — Rieu

31. And as ye would that men should do to you, do ye also to them likewise.
And just as you want men to treat you, treat them in the same way — NASB
Treat others as you would like them to treat you — NEB

32. For if ye love them which love you, what thank have ye?
. . . what credit is that to you — RSV
. . . what grace do you practice — Ber
. . . what merit is there in that — Gspd
for sinners also love those that love them.

33. And if ye do good to them which do good to you, what thank have ye? for sinners also do even the same.
If you help those who help you, how should anyone be specially pleased with you. Sinners do that too — Beck

34. And if ye lend to them of whom ye hope to receive,
If you lend anything to those from whom you expect to get something — Beck
what thank have ye?
what thanks will be due to you — TCNT
what merit is there in that — Gspd
for sinners also lend to sinners, to receive as much again.
. . . in order to receive back the same amount — NASB
Even sinners lend to each other if they are to be repaid in full — NEB

35. But love ye your enemies, and do good, and lend,
hoping for nothing again;
. . . without expecting any return — NEB
. . . never despairing — Gspd
and your reward shall be great, and ye shall be the children of the Highest:
and you will have a rich reward . . . — NEB
for he is kind unto the unthankful and to the evil.
since He is kind to people who don't thank Him . . . — Beck
. . . to the wicked and the cruel — Lam

36. Be ye therefore merciful, as your Father also is merciful.
Be compassionate . . . — Rieu
Be full of pity . . . — Bas
. . . sympathetic, tender, responsive . . . — Amp

37. Judge not, and ye shall not be judged:
And do not pass judgment . . . — NASB
Then stop criticizing others . . . — Wms
condemn not, and ye shall not be condemned:
and do not condemn . . . — NASB
stop condemning others . . . — Wms
forgive, and ye shall be forgiven:
pardon, and you will be pardoned — NASB
acquit, and you will be acquitted — NEB
Make allowances for others and people will make allowances for you — Phi

38. Give, and it shall be given unto you;
Give, and gifts will be yours — Knox
Give, and others will give to you — TCNT
good measure, pressed down, and shaken together, and running over, shall men give into your bosom.
A generous measure, pressed and shaken down, and running over, will they pour into your lap — TCNT
. . . into your robe — Lam
For with the same measure that ye mete withal it shall be measured to you again.
For the measure you give will be the measure you get back — RSV
For with the yardstick you use for measuring, you in turn shall be measured — Ber

39. And he spake a parable unto them,
And he gave them teaching in the form of a story — Bas
He pictured it to them in this way — Beck
And he used a figure, saying — Gspd

Then he gave them an illustration — Phi

Can the blind lead the blind? shall they not both fall into the ditch?

. . . a pit — ASV

. . . a hole — Gspd

40. The disciple is not above his master:

A pupil . . . — NASB

. . . his teacher — ASV

Pupils are no better than their teacher — Rieu

but every one that is perfect shall be as his master.

but every one when he is fully taught will be like his teacher — RSV

but everyone, when his training is complete, will reach his teacher's level — NEB

training only leaves them like him — Rieu

41. And why beholdest thou the mote that is in thy brother's eye,

. . . the tiny speck . . . — Wms

. . . the speck of sawdust . . . — NEB

. . . the splinter . . . — Mon

. . . the straw . . . — TCNT

but perceivest not the beam that is in thine own eye?

. . . the log — RSV

. . . the great plank . . . — NEB

. . . the heavy girder . . . — Wms

42. Either how canst thou say to thy brother,

Or how can you say to your brother — Mon

Brother, let me pull out the mote that is in thine eye,

Brother, just let me get that speck out of your eye — Gspd

when thou thyself beholdest not the beam that is in thine own eye?

when you cannot see the girder in your own eye — Wms

Thou hypocrite,

O false one — Bas

You hypocrite — Wms

You fraud — Phi

You actor — pretender — Amp

cast out first the beam out of thine own eye, and then shalt thou see clearly to pull out the mote that is in thy brother's eye.[4]

begin by removing the beam from your own eye . . . — Rieu

43. For a good tree bringeth not forth corrupt fruit; neither doth a corrupt tree bring forth good fruit.

There is no such thing as a good tree bearing worthless fruit . . . — TCNT

For no good tree gives bad fruit . . . — Bas

For sound trees do not bear bad fruit . . . — Gspd

44. For every tree is known by his own fruit.

. . . is judged by . . . — Bas

A tree is identified by the kind of fruit it produces — Tay

For of thorns men do not gather figs,

People do not gather figs off thorn bushes . . . — TCNT

nor of a bramble bush gather they grapes.

. . . or grapes from blackberry plants — Bas

. . . a bunch of grapes from a blackberry bush — Phi

45. A good man out of the good treasure of his heart bringeth forth that which is good;

A good man produces good from the store of good within himself — NEB

A good man does good because of the good things stored in his heart — Nor

and an evil man out of the evil treasure of his heart bringeth forth that which is evil:

. . . expresses evil out of his evil accumulations — Ber

. . . from his heart's store of wickedness — Knox

. . . from his own stores of evil — Phi

for of the abundance of the heart his mouth speaketh.

for the mouth speaks from that which fills his heart — NASB

for the words which the mouth utters come from the overflowing of the heart — NEB

For a man's words will always express what has been treasured in his heart — Phi

What fills a man's heart will rise to his lips — TCNT

46. And why call ye me, Lord, Lord, and do not the things which I say?

---

[4]See verse 41 for other translations of "mote" and "beam."

. . . keep calling me . . . and never do . . . — NEB

. . . and do not practice what I tell you — Wms

47. Whosoever cometh to me, and heareth my sayings, and doeth them,

. . . hears my words and acts upon them — NASB

Everyone who comes to me and continues to listen to my words and practices their teaching — Wms

I will shew you to whom he is like:

I will show you to whom he may be compared — TCNT

48. He is like a man which built an house, and digged deep, and laid the foundation on a rock:

he is like a man that would build a house, who dug, dug deep . . . — Knox

. . . who digged and deepened . . . — Rhm

and when the flood arose, the stream beat vehemently upon that house, and could not shake it: for it was founded upon a rock.

Then, when a flood came, the river swept down upon that house, but had

no power to shake it, because it had been built well — TCNT

. . . the stream brake against that house . . . — ASV

. . . the river burst against that house . . . — NASB

. . . the water came up and the river was driving against that house . . . — Bas

. . . the torrent dashed against that house . . . — Beck

49. But he that heareth, and doeth not, is like a man that without a foundation built an house upon the earth;

. . . who built a house on the ground without a foundation — RSV

. . . without a base for it — Bas

against which the stream did beat vehemently, and immediately it fell;

. . . straightway it fell in — ABUV

. . . collapsed at once — Gspd

The river swept down upon it, and the house immediately collapsed — TCNT

and the ruin of that house was great.

and fell with a great crash — NEB

and the wreck of that house was complete — Gspd

And what a fall it had! — Rieu

CHAPTER 7

1. Now when he had ended all his sayings in the audience of the people,

. . . completed all His discourse in the hearing of the people — NASB

. . . finished all He had to say to the people who heard Him — Beck

. . . imparted to the listening people all he wished to say — Rieu

he entered into Capernaum.

2. And a certain centurion's servant, who was dear unto him, was sick,

A Captain in the Roman army had a slave whom he valued, and who was seriously ill — TCNT

and ready to die.

and at the point of death — ASV

indeed he was at death's door — Rieu

3. And when he heard of Jesus, he sent unto him the elders of the Jews, beseeching him that he would come and heal his servant.

. . . and save his servant — ASV

. . . save the life of his slave — NASB

4. And when they came to Jesus, they besought him instantly, saying,

When they found Jesus, they earnestly implored him to do so — TCNT

. . . pressed their petition earnestly: — NEB

. . . made their request warmly . . . — Bas

. . . urged Him strongly with the plea — Ber

That he was worthy for whom he should do this:

He is worthy to have you do this for him — RSV

He deserves this favour from you — NEB

He deserves to have this done for him — Ber

The man is one who has deserved this kindness at your hands — Rieu

5. For he loveth our nation,

he is a good friend of our race — Knox

and he hath built us a synagogue.

and himself built us our synagogue — ASV

and at his own expense built . . . — Alf

6. Then Jesus went with them. And when he was now not far from the house, the centurion sent friends to him, saying unto him,

Jesus went with them and had nearly reached the house when the centurion sent him a message by some friends — Rieu

Lord, trouble not thyself:

Lord, don't bother — Beck

Lord, take no further trouble — Ber

Master, do not take any more trouble — Gspd

. . . do not put yourself out — Rieu

for I am not worthy that thou shouldest enter under my roof:

it is not for me to have you under my roof — NEB

for I am not a suitable person to have you under my roof — Gspd

I'm not important enough for you to come to my house — Phi

7. Wherefore neither thought I myself worthy to come unto thee:

therefore I did not presume to come to you — RSV

And I had the feeling that I was not even good enough to come to you — Bas

That is why I did not think I was fit to come to you — Gspd

I didn't think I was fit to come to you in person — Phi

but say in a word, and my servant shall be healed.

Simply say the word and have my boy cured — Ber

Just give the order, please . . . — Phi

8. For I also am a man set under authority, having under me soldiers,

I know, for in my position I am myself under orders, with soldiers under me — NEB

I'm only a man who has to obey orders, but I have soldiers under me — Beck

I too know what it is to obey authority . . . — Knox

For I am myself under the orders of others, and I have soldiers under me — Gspd

I am used to working under orders . . . — Phi

For I too am a man who derives his powers from above, with soldiers under me — Rieu

and I say unto one, Go, and he goeth; and to another, Come, and he cometh; and to my servant, Do this, and he doeth it.

and I tell one to go and he goes . . . and my slave to do something and he does it — Gspd

9. When Jesus heard these things, he marvelled at him,

. . . he admired the man — NEB

. . . He was astounded at him — Wms

These words amazed Jesus — Phi

and turned him about, and said unto the people that followed him,

and turned and said to the multitude . . . — ASV

I say unto you, I have not found so great faith, no, not in Israel.

I tell you nowhere, even in Israel, have I found faith like this — NEB

I have never found faith like this anywhere, even in Israel — Phi

I tell you, I have not found, in a single case among the Jews, so great faith as this — Wms

10. And they that were sent, returning to the house, found the servant whole that had been sick.

And when the messengers went back to the house they found the slave well — Gspd

. . . found the servant in perfect health — Wey

11. And it came to pass the day after, that he went into a city called Nain;

. . . he happened to go . . . — Gspd

and many of his disciples went with him, and much people.

attended by his disciples and a great multitude of people — Knox

12. Now when he came nigh to the gate of the city, behold, there was a dead man carried out,

Just as he approached the gate of the town . . . — TCNT

. . . he met a funeral — NEB

the only son of his mother, and she was a widow: and much people of the city was with her.

. . . a sizeable crowd from the city was with her — NASB

. . . many of the townspeople were there with her — NEB

. . . The usual crowd of fellow townsmen was with her — Phi

13. **And when the Lord saw her, he had compassion on her,**

 . . . he felt deep sympathy for her — Ber

 . . . his heart went out to her — NEB

 and said unto her, Weep not.

 . . . Weep no more — Rieu

14. **And he came and touched the bier: and they that bare him stood still.**

 . . . touched the coffin; and the bearers came to a halt — NASB

 He went up to the open coffin and touched it . . . — Beck

 . . . The pallbearers stopped — Ber

 And he said, Young man, I say unto thee, Arise.

 . . . Get up — Bas

15. **And he that was dead sat up, and began to speak.**

 Then the corpse sat up . . . — Mof

 And he delivered him to his mother.

 and He presented him . . . — Ber

16. **And there came a fear on all:**

 They were all overawed — Beck

 Everyone was awe-struck — TCNT

 Awe took hold of everyone — Ber

 Profound and reverent fear seized them all — Amp

 and they glorified God, saying,

 and began praising God — TCNT

 they gave God the glory . . . — Ber

 That a great prophet is risen up among us;

 A Prophet, a great Prophet, has risen . . . — Wey

 and, That God hath visited his people.

 And again, God has shown his care for his people — NEB

 and, God has come to help His people — Beck

 and God has not forgotten his people — Gspd

17. **And this rumour of him went forth throughout all Judaea, and throughout all the region round about.**

 The story of what he had done ran through all parts of Judaea . . . — NEB

 And before long, all over Judaea and in all the adjoining lands, they were speaking of Jesus — Rieu

18. **And the disciples of John shewed him of all these things.**

 John too was informed of all this by his disciples — NEB

19. **And John calling unto him two of his disciples sent them to Jesus, saying, Art thou he that should come? or look we for another?**

20. **When the men were come unto him, they said, John the Baptist hath sent us unto thee, saying,**

 Art thou he that should come? or look we for another?

 Are you he who is to come or shall we look for another — RSV

 Are you the one who is to come, or are we to expect some other — NEB

 Art thou the Coming One . . . — ABUV

 Is it thy coming that was foretold, or are we yet waiting for some other — Knox

 . . . or must we keep on looking for another — Nor

21. **And in that same hour he cured many of their infirmities and plagues, and of evil spirits; and unto many that were blind he gave sight.**

 There and then he cured many sufferers from disease . . . — NEB

 At the very time of their visit . . . — Knox

 Jesus at that moment was healing . . . — Mof

22. **Then Jesus answering said unto them, Go your way, and tell John what things ye have seen and heard;**

 Then he gave them his answer: . . . — NEB

 how that the blind see, the lame walk, the lepers are cleansed, the deaf hear, the dead are raised,

 to the poor the gospel is preached.

 the poor have good news preached to them — RSV

 poor men have good tidings preached to them — ABUV

 The destitute are told the glad message — Rhm

23. **And blessed is he, whosoever shall not be offended in me.**

 . . . shall find no occasion of stumbling in me — ASV

 . . . does not find me a stumbling-block — NEB

 . . . who has no doubts about me — Bas

 . . . who finds nothing that repels him in me — Gspd

 . . . who does not lose confidence in me — Knox

. . . who is repelled by nothing in me
— Mof
. . . who never loses faith in me — Phi
. . . who does not take offence at my
claims — Wey

24. **And when the messengers of John
were departed, he began to speak unto
the people concerning John.**
. . . He began to address the throngs
regarding John — Ber
. . . he took occasion to speak of John
— Knox
**What went ye out into the wilderness
for to see?**
What was the spectacle that drew you
to the wilderness — NEB
What do you go out into the waste land
to see — Bas
what did you go out to see in the desert
— Ber
A reed shaken with the wind?
A reed-bed swept by the wind — NEB
A patch of reeds swaying in the wind
— Nor
. . . waving in the breeze — Phi

25. **But what went ye out for to see? A man
clothed in soft raiment?**
. . . A man dressed in silks and satins
— Wms
. . . elegantly dressed — Ber
. . . arrayed in soft robes — Mof
**Behold, they which are gorgeously ap-
parelled,**
. . . splendidly clothed — NASB
. . . those stylishly dressed — Ber
. . . proudly dressed — Knox
. . . handsomely clothed — Nor
and live delicately, are in kings' courts.
and live in luxury . . . — NASB

26. **But what went ye out for to see? A
prophet?**
**Yea, I say unto you, and much more
than a prophet.**
Yes, indeed, and far more than a
prophet — NEB
Let me assure you, far more than a
prophet — Beck

27. **This is he, of whom it is written, Behold, I send my messenger before thy
face, which shall prepare thy way before thee.**
He is the man of whom Scripture says,
Here is my herald . . . — NEB
John is the man about whom it is written . . . — Wey

28. **For I say unto you, Among those that
are born of women there is not a
greater prophet than John the Baptist:**
I tell you there is not a mother's son
greater than John — NEB
**but he that is least in the kingdom of
God is greater than he.**
yet he that is but little . . . — ASV
. . . the least important . . . — Ber
. . . one who is of little importance . . .
— Gspd
. . . a humble member of the kingdom
. . . — Phi
. . . the lowliest . . . — TCNT

29. **And all the people that heard him, and
the publicans,**
**justified God, being baptized with the
baptism of John.**
acknowledged God's justice, having
been baptised . . . — NASB
praised God, for they had accepted
John's baptism — NEB
. . . having been immersed with John's
immersion — ABUV
admitted that God was right . . . —
Beck
acknowledged the justice of God's demands by accepting baptism from
John — Gspd
proved the wisdom of God's ways
when they accepted baptism by John
— Rieu

30. **But the Pharisees and lawyers rejected
the counsel of God against themselves,
being not baptized of him.**
. . . rejected God's purpose for themselves . . . — NASB
. . . rejected what God had planned for
them . . . — Beck
. . . thwarted God's purpose for them
by refusing baptism . . . — Ber
. . . frustrated God's plan for them . . .
— Knox
. . . suppressed the will of God in themselves . . . — Lam

31. **And the Lord said, Whereunto then
shall I liken the men of this generation? and to what are they like?**
. . . How can I describe the people of
this generation? . . . — NEB

32. **They are like unto children sitting in
the marketplace, and calling one to
another, and saying,**
. . . sitting in a bazaar . . . — Ber
. . . boys who sit in the street . . . —Lam
. . . in the public square . . . — Wey

We have piped unto you, and ye have
not danced; we have mourned to
you, and ye have not wept.
We piped unto you . . . we wailed . . .
— ASV
we played the flute . . . we sang a dirge
. . . — NASB
we played a tune on the flute . . . we
sang a funeral song . . . — Beck
we played at weddings . . . we played
at funerals . . . — Phi

33. For John the Baptist came neither eat-
ing bread nor drinking wine; and ye
say,
He hath a devil.
He has a demon — Mon
He is possessed — NEB
There's a devil in him — Beck
He is insane — Lam
he is crazy — Phi

34. The Son of man is come eating and
drinking; and ye say, Behold a gluttonous man,
. . . a glutton — RSV
. . . See this man! given to gluttony —
Wey
. . . Just look at Him! A glutton—Wms
and a winebibber,
and tippling — Wey
and a drunkard — RSV
and a wine-drinker — ABUV
a friend of publicans and sinners!
A friend of tax-collectors and sinners
— Rhm
the companion of tax-collectors and irreligious people — Gspd

35. But wisdom is justified of all her children.
Yet wisdom is vindicated by . . . —
NASB
And yet God's wisdom is proved right
by all who are her children — NEB
. . . vindicated by all who are really
wise — Gspd
. . . justified by all its works — Lam
Ah, well, wisdom's reputation is entirely in the hands of her children
— Phi
. . . vindicated by all who are truly wise
— Wms
. . . shown to be true . . . — Amp

36. And one of the Pharisees desired him
that he would eat with him.
. . . invited him to dinner — NEB
And he went into the Pharisee's house,
and sat down to meat.

. . . took his place at table — NEB
. . . lay down for the meal — Beck
and entering into the house of the
Pharisee he reclined — Rhm

37. And, behold, a woman in the city,
which was a sinner,
. . . a woman who was living an immoral life in the town — NEB
. . . a woman known in the town as a
bad woman — Phi
. . . a woman who was an outcast in the
town — TCNT
when she knew that Jesus sat at meat
in the Pharisee's house, brought an
alabaster box of ointment,
. . . an alabaster flask of ointment —
RSV
. . . brought oil of myrrh in a small
flask — NEB
. . . a pot of ointment — Knox
. . . an alabaster-jar of perfume—Rhm

38. And stood at his feet behind him weeping, and began to wash his feet with
tears, and did wipe them with the hairs
of her head, and kissed his feet, and
anointed them with the ointment.
She took her place behind him . . . —
NEB

39. Now when the Pharisee which had bidden him saw it, he spake within himself, saying,
When his host the Pharisee saw this
. . . — NEB
This man, if he were a prophet, would
have known who and what manner
of the woman this is that toucheth
him:
If this fellow were a real prophet he
would know . . . — NEB
Had this man been 'The Prophet' . . .
— TCNT
for she is a sinner.
. . . an immoral woman — Wey

40. And Jesus answering said unto him,
Simon, I have somewhat to say unto
thee.
Jesus took him up and said . . . — NEB
In answer to his thoughts Jesus said . . .
— Wey
And he saith, Master, say on.
Speak on, Master, said he — NEB
. . . Proceed, Master — Gspd

41. There was a certain creditor which had
two debtors:
Two men owed a money-lender some
money — Beck

the one owed five hundred pence, and
the other fifty.

... shillings ... — ASV

... denarii ... — RSV

... silver pieces ... — NEB

... denaries ... — ABUV

... dollars ... — Ber

... pounds ... — Mof

**42. And when they had nothing to pay, he
frankly forgave them both.**

... he let them both off — NEB

**Tell me therefore, which of them will
love him most?**

Now which of them will love him more
— Beck

... will be more attached to him —
Gspd

**43. Simon answered and said, I suppose
that he, to whom he forgave most.**

... I should think the one that was let
off most — NEB

... the one who had the bigger debt
cancelled — Beck

... the one who had the greater debt
discharged — Knox

... the one who has been more generously treated — Phi

**And he said unto him, Thou hast right-
ly judged.**

... You are right — NEB

... Exactly — Phi

**44. And he turned to the woman, and said
unto Simon, Seest thou this woman? I
entered into thine house, thou gavest
me no water for my feet: but she hath
washed my feet with tears, and wiped
them with the hairs of her head.**

... you did not give me even water
for my feet ... — Lam

... you provided no water to wash my
feet ... — Phi

45. Thou gavest me no kiss:

... no kiss of greeting — Knox

There was no warmth in your greeting
— Phi

but this woman since the time I came
in hath not ceased to kiss my feet.

But she from the moment I came in has
not left off tenderly kissing my feet
— Wey

**46. My head with oil thou didst not
anoint: but this woman hath anointed
my feet with ointment.**

You did not put any oil upon my head,
but she has put perfume on my feet
— Gspd

... cheap oil ... costly perfume ...
— Amp

**47. Wherefore I say unto thee, Her sins,
which are many, are forgiven; for she
loved much:**

... her great love proves that her many
sins have been forgiven — NEB

**but to whom little is forgiven, the same
loveth little.**

where little has been forgiven, little
love is shown — NEB

But the man with little to be forgiven
loves me but little — Gspd

... has little love — Mof

But the man who has little to be forgiven has only a little love to give —
Phi

**48. And he said unto her, Thy sins are for-
given.**

**49. And they that sat at meat with him
began to say within themselves,**

The other guests began to ask themselves ... — NEB

Who is this that forgiveth sins also?

Who does this man think he is, going
around forgiving sins — Tay

**50. And he said to the woman, Thy faith
hath saved thee; go in peace.**

By your faith you have salvation ...
— Bas

It is your faith which has saved you ...
— Gspd

CHAPTER 8

**1. And it came to pass afterward, that he
went throughout every city and village,**

And it came to pass soon afterwards
... — ASV

Soon afterward he went on through
cities and villages — RSV

After this he went journeying from

town to town and village to village
— NEB

... he went about by city and village
— ABUV

Subsequently he traveled from one
town ... to another ... — Ber

Not long after this incident ... — Phi

preaching and shewing the glad tidings of the kingdom of God: and the twelve were with him,

... the good tidings ... — ASV

... the good news ... — RSV

... the good news of the Reign of God ... — Mof

proclaiming and delivering the glad message of the kingdom of God ... — Rhm

2. **And certain women, which had been healed of evil spirits and infirmities,**

... set free from evil spirits and infirmities — NEB

Mary called Magdalene, out of whom went seven devils,

Mary, known as Mary of Magdala (from whom seven demons had been expelled) — TCNT

3. **And Joanna the wife of Chuza Herod's steward,**

... (Chuza was King Herod's business manager and was in charge of his palace and domestic affairs) — Tay

and Susanna, and many others, which ministered unto him of their substance.

who provided for them out of their means — RSV

who were contributing to their support out of their private means — NASB

who gave him of their wealth for his needs — Bas

They supported ... with their property — Beck

who used to look after his comfort from their own resources — Phi

4. **And when much people were gathered together, and were come to him out of every city,**

And when a great crowd came together and people from town after town came to him — RSV

People were now gathering in large numbers ... — NEB

he spake by a parable:

5. **A sower went out to sow his seed: and as he sowed, some fell by the way side;**

... beside the road — NASB

... along the footpath — NEB

and it was trodden down, and the fowls of the air devoured it.

... birds of the heaven ... — ASV

... was walked on, and the birds of the air ate it — Ber

... the wild birds ate it up — TCNT

6. **And some fell upon a rock;**

... on rocky soil — NASB

and as soon as it was sprung up, it withered away, because it lacked moisture.

and as it grew up it withered away ... — RSV

and when it came up it became dry and dead ... — Bas

and they sprang up fast but dried out ... — Nor

7. **And some fell among thorns;**

... in among thistles — NEB

... among briars — Phi

... in the middle of brambles — TCNT

and the thorns sprang up with it, and choked it.

... and it had no room for growth — Bas

8. **And other fell on good ground,**

... into good soil — NEB

... where the soil was good — Knox

and sprang up, and bare fruit an hundredfold.

... produced a crop a hundred times as great — NASB

... produced a hundred times as much as was sown — Beck

... a hundred times what had been sown — Phi

And when he had said these things, he cried, He that hath ears to hear, let him hear.

... You have ears to hear. Then listen! — Beck

... Let the man who has ears to hear use them — Phi

9. **And his disciples asked him, saying, What might this parable be?**

And his disciples put questions to him about the points of the story — Bas

10. **And he said, Unto you it is given to know the mysteries of the kingdom of God:**

... You have been given the chance to understand the secrets ... — Phi

... the hidden truths ... — TCNT

but to others in parables;

but to others they are given in stories — Bas

... in the form of figures — Gspd

that seeing they might not see, and hearing they might not understand.

in order that they may look but see nothing, hear but understand nothing — NEB

... the sense will not be clear to them
— Bas

so that they go through life with their
eyes open and see nothing ... — Phi

11. Now the parable is this:
This is what the parable means — NEB
Now this is the point of the story —
Bas
The seed is the word of God.

**12. Those by the way side are they that
hear;**
The ones along the path are those who
have heard — RSV
Those on the road are the people who
hear — Mof
**then cometh the devil, and taketh away
the word out of their hearts, lest
they should believe and be saved.**
but the devil comes along and takes its
message from their hearts ... — Nor

**13. They on the rock are they, which,
when they hear, receive the word with
joy:**
The stony ground represents those who
enjoy listening to sermons — Tay
Those 'on the rock' are people who on
hearing the word welcome it with
enthusiasm — Mof
... who accept the message with great
delight — Phi
... with joy welcome the word — Rhm
**and these have no root, which for a
while believe,**
... they are believers for a while —
NEB
... for a time indeed they believe —
Mon
but somehow the message never really
gets through to them and doesn't
take root and grow — Tay
and in time of temptation fall away.
but in time of testing they desert —
NEB
and in time of trial fall away ... —
ABUV
and when the test comes they give up
— Bas
... they lose faith — Phi
and when trials come, recant — Rieu

**14. And that which fell among thorns are
they, which, when they have heard, go
forth, and are choked with cares and
riches and pleasures of this life,**
... as they go on their way they are
choked with worries ... — NASB
... but their further growth is checked

by cares and wealth ... — NEB
... but as they go along, worries ...
choke them — Beck
... and then choke themselves with
worries and riches ... — Lam
... but as time goes on they are overcome by the passing cares of life ...
— Nor
and bring no fruit to perfection.
and their fruit does not mature — RSV
and they bring nothing to maturity —
NEB
and bring no fruit to perfection — ABUV
so that they never ripen — Mof

**15. But that on the good ground are they,
which in an honest and good heart,**
... with a good and true heart — Bas
... in a good and well-disposed heart
— Ber
... in the true goodness of their hearts
— Rieu
... with open minds and in a right spirit
— Wey
having heard the word, keep it,
hearing the word, hold it fast — RSV
and bring forth fruit with patience.
and go on faithfully producing good
things — Beck
and endure, and yield a harvest —
Knox
and so bear fruit steadfastly — Mof
and go on steadily producing a good
crop — Phi
and in their constancy bear fruit —
Rieu

**16. No man, when he hath lighted a can-
dle,**
... after lighting a lamp — RSV
**covereth it with a vessel, or putteth it
under a bed;**
covers it over with a container ... —
NASB
... with a dish ... — Gspd
... with a pot ... — Wms
puts a cover over it ... — Bas
hides it under a jar ... — Beck
**but setteth it on a candlestick, that
they which enter in may see the
light.**
... on a stand ... — ASV
No, you put it on a lampstand ... —
Beck

**17. For nothing is secret, that shall not be
made manifest;**
For nothing is hidden that shall not become evident — NASB

. . . become public — NEB

. . . become perfectly plain — Phi

neither any thing hid, that shall not be known and come abroad.

. . . and come to light — NASB

. . . and brought into the open — NEB

. . . which will not become as clear as daylight — Phi

18. **Take heed therefore how ye hear:**

So be careful in what frame of mind you listen — Rieu

for whosoever hath, to him shall be given;

and whosoever hath not, from him shall be taken

even that which he seemeth to have.

. . . even that which he thinketh he hath — ASV

19. **Then came to him his mother and his brethren, and could not come at him for the press.**

. . . for the crowd — ASV

. . . because of the great number of people — Bas

20. **And it was told him by certain which said, Thy mother and thy brethren stand without, desiring to see thee.**

. . . are standing outside . . . — NEB

. . . are standing at the edge of the crowd . . . — Ber

21. **And he answered and said unto them, My mother and my brethren are these which hear the word of God, and do it.**

. . . and act upon it — NEB

. . . those who hear and practice the word of God — Ber

. . . those who listen to God's teaching and do what it bids — TCNT

22. **Now it came to pass on a certain day, that he went into a ship with his disciples: and he said unto them, Let us go over unto the other side of the lake. And they launched forth.**

23. **And as they sailed he fell asleep:**

and there came down a storm of wind on the lake; and they were filled with water, and were in jeopardy.

And a storm of wind came down on the lake, and they were filling with water, and were in danger — RSV

. . . a fierce gale of wind descended . . . and they began to be swamped and to be in danger — NASB

. . . a heavy squall struck the lake; they began to ship water and were in grave danger — NEB

. . . a windstorm broke loose over the lake . . . — Nor

24. **And they came to him, and awoke him, saying, Master, master, we perish.**

They went to him and roused him . . . — NEB

Then he arose, and rebuked the wind and the raging of the water:

. . . and the surging waves — NASB

. . . and the turbulent waters — NEB

. . . disciplined the wind and the surging of the water — Ber

. . . reproved the wind and the rough water — Gspd

. . . rebuked the wind and the angry waves — Nor

and they ceased, and there was a calm.

and they quieted down . . . — Lam

and they died down and everything was still — Phi

25. **And he said unto them, Where is your faith? And they being afraid wondered, saying one to another,**

What manner of man is this! for he commandeth even the winds and water,

Who is He? He orders even the winds and the water — Beck

Who is He, anyway, to give orders . . . — Ber

Whatever can he be . . . — Mof

Just who is this . . . — Nor

Who can He be . . . — Wms

and they obey him.

and they do what he says — Bas

26. **And they arrived at the country of the Gadarenes, which is over against Galilee.**

. . . Gerasenes . . . — ASV

. . . Gergesenes, which is opposite Galilee — NEB

. . . in the neighbourhood of Gerasa, which is just across the lake from Galilee . . . — Gspd

27. **And when he went forth to land,**

And as he stepped out on land — RSV

there met him out of the city a certain man, which had devils long time,

. . . who had demons in him . . . — TCNT

and ware no clothes, neither abode in any house, but in the tombs.

. . . lived not in a house but among the tombs — RSV

. . . lived homeless among the tombs — Knox

251

28. **When he saw Jesus, he cried out, and fell down before him, and with a loud voice said, What have I to do with thee, Jesus, thou Son of God most high? I beseech thee, torment me not.**

   . . . What do you want with me . . . — NEB

   . . . Let me alone, Jesus . . . — Beck

   . . . What have we in common . . . — Lam

   . . . What business have you with me? . . . — Mof

   . . . What have I in common with thee . . . — Rhm

29. **(For he had commanded the unclean spirit to come out of the man. For oftentimes it had caught him: and he was kept bound with chains and in fetters; and he brake the bands,**

   and was driven of the devil into the wilderness.)

   and with the devil in charge made off to the solitary places — NEB

   and go off into the desert with the devil at his heels — Phi

   impelled by the demon, escape into the desert — Wey

30. **And Jesus asked him, saying, What is thy name? And he said, Legion: because many devils were entered into him.**

   . . . Six thousand, he answered . . . — Beck

31. **And they besought him that he would not command them to go out into the deep.**

   . . . into the abyss — ASV

   . . . into the bottomless pit — Beck

32. **And there was there an herd of many swine feeding on the mountain:**

   . . . on the hillside — RSV

   . . . a huge drove of swine grazing on the mountainside — Ber

   and they besought him that he would suffer them to enter into them.

   And he suffered them.

   And He gave them permission — NASB

33. **Then went the devils out of the man, and entered into the swine: and the herd ran violently down a steep place into the lake,**

   . . . rushed down the steep bank . . . — NASB

   . . . down a sharp slope . . . — Bas

   . . . stampeded down the cliff . . . — Beck

and were choked.

   . . . were drowned — ASV

34. **When they that fed them saw what was done, they fled, and went and told it in the city and in the country.**

   When the herdsmen saw what had happened . . . — RSV

35. **Then they went out to see what was done;**

   and the people came out to see for themselves — NEB

   and came to Jesus, and found the man, out of whom the devils were departed, sitting at the feet of Jesus, clothed, and in his right mind:

   . . . clothed and in the full use of his senses . . . — Bas

   . . . dressed and sane . . . — Ber

   . . . properly dressed and quite composed . . . — Phi

   and they were afraid.

   . . . and they were struck with fear — Rhm

36. **They also which saw it told them by what means he that was possessed of the devils was healed.**

   The spectators told them how the madman had been cured — NEB

   . . . how the lunatic was healed — Lam

37. **Then the whole multitude of the country of the Gadarenes round about besought him to depart from them; for they were taken with great fear:**

   . . . for they were gripped with great fear . . . — NASB

   . . . for they felt thoroughly frightened . . . — Ber

   . . . for they were terrified — TCNT

   and the whole population of the Gerasene district, seized by panic, asked him to go away — Rieu

   and he went up into the ship, and returned back again.

38. **Now the man out of whom the devils were departed he sought him that he might be with him: but Jesus sent him away, saying,**

   And the man from whom the demons had gone forth began to beg of him that . . . — Rhm

39. **Return to thine own house,**

   Go home — Beck

   Go back to your home — TCNT

   and shew how great things God hath done unto thee.

and declare how much God has done
for you — RSV

and broadcast all that God has done
for you — Ber

**And he went his way, and published
throughout the whole city how great
things Jesus had done unto him.**

The man went all over the town spreading the news . . . — NEB

**40. And it came to pass, that, when Jesus
was returned, the people gladly received him: for they were all waiting
for him.**

On his return, Jesus was welcomed by
the people . . . — TCNT

Now when Jesus returned the crowd
welcomed him . . . — RSV

. . . for they were all expecting him —
Rhm

**41. And, behold, there came a man named
Jairus, and he was a ruler of the synagogue:**

. . . an official of the synagogue — ASB

. . . president of the synagogue — NEB

. . . A synagog leader — Beck

. . . a director of the synagogue — Ber

**and he fell down at Jesus' feet, and besought him that he would come into
his house:**

and falling down near the feet of Jesus
he began beseeching him to enter
into his house — Rhm

**42. For he had one only daughter, about
twelve years of age and she lay a dying.**

. . . an only daughter . . . — RSV

because he had an only-begotten
daughter about twelve years old,
and she was dying — Rhm

**But as he went the people thronged
him.**

. . . he could hardly breathe for the
crowds — NEB

. . . the people were pushing to be near
him — Bas

**43. And a woman having an issue of blood
twelve years,**

. . . a flow of blood . . . — RSV

. . . a hemorrhage . . . — NASB

**which had spent all her living upon
physicians, neither could be healed
of any,**

. . . had spent on doctors all she had
. . . — Ber

**44. Came behind him, and touched the
border of his garment:**

. . . the fringe . . . — RSV

. . . the tassel . . . — TCNT

**and immediately her issue of blood
stanched.**

. . . the flowing of her blood was
stopped — Bas

**45. And Jesus said, Who touched me?
When all denied, Peter and they that
were with him said, Master, the multitude throng thee and press thee,**

. . . the multitudes press thee and crush
thee — ASV

. . . the crowds are hemming you in
and pressing upon you! — NEB

. . . you are surrounded by people jostling you — Rieu

and sayest thou, Who touched me?

**46. And Jesus said, Somebody hath touched
me: for I perceive that virtue is gone
out of me.**

. . . Someone did touch Me, for I was
aware that power had gone out of
Me — NASB

**47. And when the woman saw that she was
not hid,**

. . . that she had not escaped notice —
Rhm

. . . seeing that she was detected — NEB

**she came trembling, and falling down
before him, she declared unto him
before all the people for what cause
she had touched him, and how she
was healed immediately.**

she came shaking with fear . . . — Bas

**48. And he said unto her, Daughter, be of
good comfort: thy faith hath made thee
whole; go in peace.**

. . . Daughter, Cheer up! Your faith has
healed you . . . — Ber

. . . it is your faith which has healed
you . . . — Phi

**49. While he yet spake, there cometh one
from the ruler of the synagogue's
house, saying to him, Thy daughter is
dead; trouble not the Master.**

. . . the Teacher — ASV

. . . trouble the Rabbi no further — NEB

**50. But when Jesus heard it, he answered
him, saying, Fear not: believe only,
and she shall be made whole.**

But Jesus heard, and interposed . . . —
NEB

**51. And when he came into the house, he
suffered no man to go in, save Peter,
and James, and John, and the father
and the mother of the maiden.**

. . . he did not allow anyone to go in with him except . . . — TCNT

52. And all wept, and bewailed her:
And they were all weeping and beating themselves for her — Rhm
but he said, Weep not; she is not dead, but sleepeth.
. . . Stop weeping, for she has not died, but is asleep — NASB

53. And they laughed him to scorn, knowing that she was dead.
But they only laughed at him . . . — NEB
And they laughed aloud at him . . . — Knox
This drew a scornful laugh from them, for they had seen her die — Phi
Then they began to laugh in His face . . . — Wms

54. And he put them all out, and took her

by the hand, and called, saying, Maid, arise.
. . . Get up, my child — NEB
. . . Rise, little girl — Mof

55. And her spirit came again, and she arose straightway: and he commanded to give her meat.
. . . something to eat — NEB

56. And her parents were astonished: but he charged them that they should tell no man what was done.
and warned her parents, who were beside themselves with wonder, to let no one hear of what had befallen — Knox
Her parents were amazed, but Jesus impressed on them that they were not to tell any one what had happened — TCNT
And her parents were beside themselves . . . — Rhm

CHAPTER 9

1. Then he called his twelve disciples together, and gave them power and authority over all devils,
. . . and gave them power and authority to overcome all the devils — NEB
. . . to deal with every kind of demon — Rieu
and to cure diseases.

2. And he sent them to preach the kingdom of God,
. . . to proclaim the kingdom of God . . . — TCNT
. . . to preach the Reign of God . . . — Mof
and to heal the sick.

3. And he said unto them, Take nothing for your journey,
neither staves, nor scrip,
. . . no staff, nor bag . . . — RSV
. . . neither stick nor pack . . . — NEB
. . . neither a stick nor a purse . . . — Phi
. . . no staff, no knapsack . . . — Rieu
. . . neither staff nor satchel . . . — Rhm
neither bread, neither money; neither have two coats apiece.

4. And whatsoever house ye enter into, there abide, and thence depart.
. . . stay there and take your leave from there — NASB
. . . and go on from there — NEB
. . . let that house be your resting-place

till you go away — Bas
. . . stay there and leave it only when you leave the town — Rieu

5. And whosoever will not receive you, when ye go out of that city,
As for those who will not receive you, when you leave their town — NEB
And wherever they deny you a welcome, as you leave the city — Knox
shake off the very dust from your feet for a testimony against them.
. . . as a warning to them — Beck
. . . as a protest against them — TCNT
. . . in witness against them — Knox
. . . as a demonstration against them — Rieu

6. And they departed, and went through the towns, preaching the gospel, and healing every where.
. . . telling the good news everywhere and healing the sick — Beck
. . . proclaiming the Good Tidings . . . — Rieu
. . . delivering the glad message . . . — Rhm

7. Now Herod the tetrarch heard of all that was done by him: and he was perplexed,
Now Prince Herod heard . . . and did not know what to make of it — NEB
And Herod, who was prince in that quarter . . . — Knox

When Herod the tetrarch heard . . . he
was quite at a loss — Mof
All these things came to the ears of
Herod . . . and caused him acute
anxiety — Phi
**because that it was said of some, that
John was risen from the dead;**
because he was told by some . . . —
Ber

8. **And of some, that Elias had appeared;
and of others,**
by some that Elijah had appeared, and
by others — RSV
**that one of the old prophets was risen
again.**
that one of the ancient prophets had
arisen — Mof
that one of the old-time prophets had
come back — Phi
that some prophet of the ancients . . .
— Rhm

9. **And Herod said, John have I behead-
ed: but who is this, of whom I hear
such things?**
And he desired to see him.
And he kept trying to see Him — NASB
And he was eager to see him — Knox
And he tried to find away of seeing
Jesus — Phi

10. **And the apostles, when they were returned, told him all that they had done.**
And now the apostles came back and
told Jesus . . . — Knox
**And he took them, and went aside pri-
vately into a desert place belonging
to the city called Bethsaida.**
He took them away with Him . . . in
order to be alone — Beck
And he took them and quietly retired
to a town called Bethsaida — Gspd

11. **And the people, when they knew it,
followed him:**
But the people recognized him and followed him in the crowds — TCNT
**and he received them, and spake unto
them of the kingdom of God, and
healed them that had need of healing.**
and he welcomed them . . . — RSV
He received them kindly . . . — Mon

12. **And when the day began to wear away,
then came the twelve, and said unto
him,**
When evening was drawing on . . . —
NEB

Towards the end of the day . . . — Beck
**Send the multitude away, that they
may go into the towns and country
round about, and lodge,**
**and get victuals: for we are here in a
desert place.**
and get provisions; for we are here in
a lonely place — RSV
. . . for we are in the desert here — Nor
. . . for we're quite in the wilds here —
Phi

13. **But he said unto them, Give ye them
to eat.**
. . . It is for you to give them something to eat — TCNT
. . . You give them something to eat —
RSV
**And they said, We have no more but
five loaves and two fishes; except we
should go and buy meat for all this
people.**
. . . unless we are to go and buy food
for all these people — RSV
. . . you don't expect us to go and buy
food for all these people? — Ber

14. **For they were about five thousand
men. And he said to his disciples,
Make them sit down by fifties in a
company.**
. . . in companies of about fifty each —
ASV
. . . recline in companies of fifty—ABUV
. . . in rows of about fifty — Mof
. . . Have them seated in groups of fifty
each — Nor

15. **And they did so, and made them all sit
down.**
. . . and got them all seated — NEB

16. **Then he took the five loaves and the
two fishes, and looking up to heaven,
he blessed them, and brake, and gave
to the disciples to set before the multitude.**
. . . he blessed them, broke them in
pieces, and began giving to his disciples to apportion among the crowd
— Mon

17. **And they did eat, and were all filled:**
They all ate to their heart's content —
NEB
. . . and had enough — Gspd
**and there was taken up of fragments
that remained to them twelve baskets.**
And they took up what was left over,

LUKE 9

twelve baskets of broken pieces —
RSV
and when the scraps they left were
picked up, they filled twelve great
baskets — NEB
. . . [small hand] baskets — Amp
18. **And it came to pass, as he was alone
praying, his disciples were with him:
and he asked them, saying,**
. . . praying in solitude . . . — ABUV
When in his season of private prayer
the disciples joined Him, He asked
them — Ber
Whom say the people that I am?
Who do the multitudes say that I am
— Rhm
19. **They answering said, John the Baptist;
but some say, Elias; and others say,
that one of the old prophets is risen
again.**
. . . but others say Elijah . . . — RSV
20. **He said unto them, But whom say ye
that I am?**
But you, he went on, who do you say
that I am — TCNT
**Peter answering said, The Christ of
God.**
. . . God's Messiah — NEB
. . . The Savior whom God has sent —
Beck
. . . the Christ whom God has anointed
— Knox
. . . God's Anointed — Rieu
21. **And he straitly charged them, and
commanded them to tell no man that
thing;**
Then he gave them strict orders not to
tell this to anyone — NEB
And he laid a strict charge upon them
. . . — Knox
22. **Saying, The Son of man must suffer
many things,**
. . . has to undergo great sufferings —
NEB
. . . is to be much ill-used — Knox
**and be rejected of the elders and chief
priests and scribes,**
. . . the elders, ruling priests, and Bible
scholars — Beck
. . . The Councillors, and Chief Priests,
and Teachers of the Law — TCNT
**and be slain, and be raised the third
day.**
23. **And he said to them all, If any man
will come after me,**
. . . If you want to follow Me — Beck

. . . If any man has a mind to come my
way — Knox
. . . If any man wishes to walk in my
steps — TCNT
. . . If any man chooses to be my disciple — Wms
let him deny himself,
he must leave self behind — NEB
he must disregard himself — Gspd
let him renounce self — Knox
he must give up all right to himself —
Phi
he must say 'No' to self — Wms
**and take up his cross daily, and follow
me.**
day after day he must take up his cross
. . . — NEB
carry his cross every day and keep close
behind me — Phi
put the cross on his shoulders daily, and
continue to follow me — Wms

24. **For whosoever will save his life shall
lose it:**
Whoever cares for his own safety is lost
— NEB
For whoever chooses to save his lower
life will lose his higher life — Wms
**but whosoever will lose his life for my
sake, the same shall save it.**
but if a man will let himself be lost
for my sake, that man is safe — NEB
but whoever gives up his lower life for
my sake will save his higher life —
Wms
25. **For what is a man advantaged, if he
gain the whole world,**
What will a man gain by winning the
whole world — NEB
How is a man the better for gaining
the whole world — Knox
Why, what benefit is it to a man to
have gained . . . — Wey
and lose himself, or be cast away?
and loses or forfeits himself — RSV
at the cost of his true self — NEB
but is himself destroyed or lost — Nor
26. **For whosoever shall be ashamed of me
and of my words, of him shall the Son
of man be ashamed,**
If you're ashamed of Me and what I
say, then the Son of Man will be
ashamed of you — Beck
**when he shall come in his own glory,
and in his Father's, and of the holy
angels.**

when he comes with the glory of his father, accompanied by . . . — Lam

27. But I tell you of a truth, there be some standing here, which shall not taste of death, till they see the kingdom of God.
. . . shall in no wise taste of death . . . — ASV
. . . will not know death . . . — TCNT
. . . will certainly live to see the kingdom of God — Wms

28. And it came to pass about an eight days after these sayings, he took Peter and John and James, and went into a mountain to pray.
About eight days after this conversation . . . — NEB
It was about a week after all this was said . . . — Knox

29. And as he prayed, the fashion of his countenance was altered,
. . . the appearance of his face altered — Mof
. . . His face took on a great change — Nor

and his raiment was white and glistering.
. . . became dazzling white — RSV
. . . white and radiant — ABUV
and his clothing had the brilliance of a lightning flash — Rieu

30. And, behold, there talked with him two men, which were Moses and Elias:
Suddenly there were two men talking with him . . . — NEB
And all at once two men were talking with Jesus; they were Moses and Elijah — TCNT

31. Who appeared in glory,
seen now in glory — Knox
who appeared in a vision of glory — Mof
revealed in heavenly splendour — Phi
who appeared in splendor — Wms
. . . splendor and majesty and brightness — Amp

and spake of his decease which he should accomplish at Jerusalem.
. . . his departure, the destiny he was to fulfil . . . — NEB
. . . conversed with Him about His exodus . . . — Ber
. . . the death which he was to achieve . . . — Knox
. . . the way he must take and the end he must fulfil — Phi

32. But Peter and they that were with him were heavy with sleep:
. . . had been in a deep sleep — NEB

and when they were awake, they saw his glory,
but when they awoke . . . — NEB
but they kept awake and saw . . . — Alf
waking up, they saw . . . — Beck
but waking up they saw his glorious appearance — Gspd

and the two men that stood with him.

33. And it came to pass, as they departed from him,
And as these were moving away from Jesus — NEB
At the moment of their parting from Him — Ber
And just as these were parting from him — Knox

Peter said unto Jesus, Master, it is good for us to be here:
. . . how good it is that we are here — NEB
. . . it is wonderful for us to be here — Phi

and let us make three tabernacles;
. . . three booths . . . — ASV
. . . three shelters . . . — NEB
. . . three huts . . . — Gspd
. . . three arbours . . . — Knox
. . . three tents . . . — Mof
. . . three shrines . . . — Nor

one for thee, and one for Moses, and one for Elias:

not knowing what he said.
not realizing what he was saying — NASB
But he spoke at random — Knox

34. While he thus spake, there came a cloud, and overshadowed them:
. . . a cloud formed and began to overshadow them — NASB
. . . a cloud came down and enveloped them — TCNT
The words were still on his lips when there came a cloud which cast a shadow over them — NEB
But while he was thus speaking, there came a cloud which spread over them — Wey

and they feared as they entered into the cloud.
. . . when they saw Moses and Elijah enter into the cloud — Lam
. . . when the others disappeared in the cloud — Nor

they saw those others disappear into the cloud and were terrified — Knox

35. And there came a voice out of the cloud,

and from the cloud came a voice — TCNT

There came a voice from within the cloud — Wey

saying, This is my beloved Son: hear him.

. . . my Son, my Chosen; listen to him! — RSV

. . . This is my Son, whom I have chosen . . . — Alf

36. And when the voice was past, Jesus was found alone.

When the voice had spoken, Jesus was seen to be alone — NEB

And with the dying away of the voice . . . — Ber

And they kept it close, and told no man in those days any of those things which they had seen.

. . . kept silence and at that time told nobody . . . — NEB

. . . breathed never a word . . . — Phi

37. And it came to pass, that on the next day, when they were come down from the hill, much people met him.

. . . he was met by a large crowd — NEB

38. And, behold, a man of the company cried out, saying,

. . . a man from the multitude . . . — ASV

All at once there was a shout from a man in the crowd — NEB

And now we have a man from the crowd shouting out — Phi

and out of the gathering came a man's voice — Rieu

Master, I beseech thee, look upon my son: for he is mine only child.

. . . look at my son, I implore you . . . — NEB

I entreat thee . . . look with favour upon my son . . . — Knox

Master, please come and look at my son . . . — Phi

39. And, lo, a spirit taketh him, and he suddenly crieth out;

. . . he suddenly screams — NASB

. . . he gives a sudden cry — Rieu

and it teareth him that he foameth again,

it convulses him till he foams — RSV

and throws him into convulsions with foaming at the mouth — NEB

and bruising him hardly departeth from him.

and as it mauls him, it scarcely leaves him — NASB

and when it goes away from him at last, he is marked as from blows — Bas

then it goes away, but only with a pang which lacerates him — Knox

and as the convulsions slowly subside, it leaves him shattered — Rieu

and does not leave him till it has well nigh covered him with bruises — Wey

40. And I besought thy disciples to cast him out; and they could not.

And I begged your disciples to drive it out . . . — Gspd

. . . to get rid of it . . . — Phi

41. And Jesus answering said, O faithless and perverse generation,

. . . O unbelieving and perverted generation — NASB

. . . Ah, faithless and misguided generation — Knox

. . . You really are an unbelieving and difficult people — Phi

. . . O you unbelieving and stubborn people of the times — Wms

how long shall I be with you, and suffer you? Bring thy son hither.

. . . and endure you all . . . — NEB

. . . put up with you . . . — Phi

42. And as he was yet a coming, the devil threw him down, and tare him.

. . . the demon tare him and mangled him — Rhm

. . . dashed him to the ground, and threw him into a convulsion — NASB

. . . and cruelly convulsed him — Mon

And Jesus rebuked the unclean spirit,

. . . gave sharp orders to the unclean spirit — Bas

. . . checked . . . — Knox

. . . reprimanded . . . — Phi

. . . reproved . . . — Wms

and healed the child, and delivered him again to his father.

43. And they were all amazed at the mighty power of God.

And they were all being struck with astonishment at the majesty of God — Rhm

And how astonished they all were at

the evidence of God's great power
— Ber

All were astounded at this grand display of God — Mof

But while they wondered every one at all things which Jesus did, he said unto his disciples,

44. Let these sayings sink down into your ears:

What I now say is for you: ponder my words — NEB

Listen carefully to what I say — Beck

You must store up these teachings in your minds — Gspd

Mark these words and remember them — Nor

You . . . should have these words ringing in your ears — Rieu

for the Son of man shall be delivered into the hands of men.

. . . is going to be given up into the power of men — NEB

. . . is about to be delivered . . . — ABUV

. . . is soon to be betrayed . . . — Knox

45. But they understood not this saying, and it was hid from them, that they perceived it not:

. . . it had been hidden from them so that they should not perceive its drift — NEB

. . . indeed it was concealed from them, in order that they might not comprehend it — Gspd

. . . something made it impossible for them to understand it — Phi

and they feared to ask him of that saying.

46. Then there arose a reasoning among them, which of them should be greatest.

And an argument arose among them . . . — RSV

A dispute . . . — NEB

. . . a questioning . . . — Knox

47. And Jesus, perceiving the thought of their heart, took a child, and set him by him,

Jesus knew what was passing in their minds, so he took a child . . . — NEB

Jesus, who saw what was occupying their thoughts . . . — Knox

. . . the dispute that was in their hearts . . . — Mon

48. And said unto them, Whosoever shall receive this child in my name receiveth me:

. . . If you welcome this little child . . . you welcome Me — Beck

and whosoever shall receive me receiveth him that sent me:

for he that is least among you all, the same shall be great.

You see, if anyone is least of all of you, he is great — Beck

For the lowliest among you all, he is truly great — Ber

For it is the lowliest of you all who is great — Mof

49. And John answered and said, Master, we saw one casting out devils in thy name;

. . . using your name to cast out evil spirits — Rieu

and we forbad him, because he followeth not with us.

. . . we tried to hinder him . . . — NASB

. . . as he was not one of us we tried to stop him — NEB

50. And Jesus said unto him, Forbid him not: for he that is not against us is for us.

. . . Do not stop him . . . — NEB

. . . You must not stop him . . . — Phi

. . . Do nothing of the kind . . . — Rieu

51. And it came to pass, when the time was come that he should be received up,

As the time was drawing near for Him to be taken up to heaven — Beck

. . . the days before he should be taken back into Heaven were running out — Phi

he stedfastly set his face to go to Jerusalem,

Jesus set his face resolutely in the direction of Jerusalem — TCNT

He showed He was determined to go . . . — Beck

He made up His mind firmly to go . . . — Nor

52. And sent messengers before his face:

and he sent on messengers in advance — TCNT

and they went, and entered into a village of the Samaritans, to make ready for him.

. . . to make arrangements for him — NASB

53. And they did not receive him, because his face was as though he would go to Jerusalem.

259

... because he was making for Jerusalem — NEB

... because he was clearly going to Jerusalem — Bas

... because his journey was in the direction of ... — Knox

54. And when his disciples James and John saw this, they said,

Lord, wilt thou that we command fire to come down from heaven, and consume them, even as Elias did?

Our Lord, would you be willing that we command ... — Lam

55. But he turned, and rebuked them, and said,

... and sternly corrected them ... — Beck

... and spoke disapprovingly to them ... — Nor

Ye know not what manner of spirit ye are of.

You do not understand what spirit it is you share — Knox

56. For the Son of man is not come to destroy men's lives, but to save them. And they went to another village.

57. And it came to pass, that, as they went in the way, a certain man said unto him, Lord, I will follow thee whithersoever thou goest.

As they went on their journey, a man said ... — Knox

As the little company made its way along the road ... — Phi

58. And Jesus said unto him, Foxes have holes, and birds of the air have nests;

, ... and the fowl of the sky a shelter — Lam

... and the wild birds have their nests — Mon

but the Son of man hath not where to lay his head.

but the Son of Man has nowhere to lay his head — TCNT

59. And he said unto another, Follow me. But he said, Lord, suffer me first to go and bury my father.

... and give the last honours to my father — Bas

... and bury (await the death of) my father — Amp

60. Jesus said unto him, Let the dead bury their dead:

... Let those without eternal life concern themselves with things like that — Tay

but go thou and preach the kingdom of God.

... and give news of the kingdom of God — Bas

... go you and announce, far and wide, the kingdom of God — Mon

61. And another also said, Lord, I will follow thee; but let me first go bid them farewell, which are at home at my house.

... but first let me say good-bye to my family — TCNT

... permit me first to entrust my household to someone — Lam

62. And Jesus said unto him, No man, having put his hand to the plow, and looking back, is fit for the kingdom of God.

... and then keeps looking back ... — NEB

... and looks back (to the things behind) ... — Amp

CHAPTER 10

1. After these things the Lord appointed other seventy[5] also,

After this, the Lord appointed seventy-two other disciples — TCNT

... a further seventy-two — NEB

Later on the Lord commissioned seventy other disciples — Phi

and sent them two and two before his face into every city and place, whither he himself would come.

... was about to come — ASV

... ahead of Him ... where He himself was going to come — NASB

... in pairs to every town and place he was going to visit himself — NEB

... every town and community where He planned to visit — Ber

2. Therefore said he unto them, The harvest truly is great, but the labourers are few:

... is plentiful ... — RSV

... The crop is heavy ... — NEB

... is rich, indeed ... — Ber

---

[5]Some manuscripts read "seventy," others "seventy-two."

. . . is abundant enough . . . — Gspd

pray ye therefore the Lord of the harvest, that he would send forth labourers into his harvest.

You must beg the owner to send labourers to harvest his crop — NEB

Ask the Owner of the crop to send out workers to bring in his grain — Beck

You must ask the Lord to whom the harvest belongs . . . — Knox

3. Go your ways: behold, I send you forth as lambs among wolves.

Be on your way. And look, I am sending you like lambs among wolves — NEB

. . . Notice that I am sending you as lambs into the midst of wolves — Ber

Go then, and remember, I am sending you out to be like lambs . . . — Knox

4. Carry neither purse, nor scrip, nor shoes; and salute no man by the way.

. . . no purse, no bag, no sandals . . . — RSV

. . . no purse or pack, and travel barefoot. Exchange no greetings on the road — NEB

. . . no bag for money, or for food . . . — Bas

5. And into whatsoever house ye enter, first say, Peace be to this house.

. . . May there be peace in this house — Beck

. . . begin by praying for a blessing on it — TCNT

6. And if the son of peace be there, your peace shall rest upon it:

And if a man of peace is there . . . — NASB

If a peaceful person lives there . . . — Ber

If there is anyone there who loves peace . . . — Gspd

and if those who dwell there are men of good will . . . — Knox

Then, if anyone there is deserving of a blessing . . . — TCNT

if not, it shall turn to you again.

but if there is not, it will come back to you — Gspd

If not, it will come back and rest on you — Rieu

7. And in the same house remain, eating and drinking such things as they give:

And in that very house abide . . . — ABUV

Stay at the same house . . . — Gspd

for the labourer is worthy of his hire.

. . . deserves his wages — RSV

. . . has a right to his reward — Bas

. . . earns his pay — Beck

. . . has a right to his maintenance — Knox

Go not from house to house.

Do not keep moving from house to house — NASB

Do not change from home to home — Ber

8. And into whatsoever city ye enter, and they receive you, eat such things as are set before you:

When you go into any town and the people welcome you . . . — Beck

9. And heal the sick that are therein, and say unto them, The kingdom of God is come nigh unto you.

. . . has come close to you — NEB

. . . is close upon you — Gspd

. . . The Reign of God is nearly on you — Mof

. . . is at your door — Wey

10. But into whatsoever city ye enter, and they receive you not,

But if you go into a town where they will not have you — Bas

But when you find the people of a town unfriendly — Rieu

go your ways out into the streets of the same, and say,

go out into its streets and say — TCNT

11. Even the very dust of your city, which cleaveth on us, we do wipe off against you:

. . . which clings to our feet, we wipe off to your shame — NEB

. . . in protest against you — Beck

notwithstanding be ye sure of this, that the kingdom of God is come nigh unto you.

Only take note of this . . . — NEB

But understand this . . . — Gspd

But it is still true that the kingdom of God has arrived — Phi

12. But I say unto you, that it shall be more tolerable in that day for Sodom, than for that city.

. . . more bearable for Sodom on the great Day . . . — NEB

. . . on that Day Sodom will fare better than that town — Gspd

. . . on the day of reckoning it will go easier for Sodom . . . — Nor

... when the Day comes, Sodom will have less to suffer ... — Rieu

... on that day the punishment will be lighter for Sodom ... — Wms

13. **Woe unto thee, Chorazin! woe unto thee, Bethsaida! for if the mighty works had been done in Tyre and Sidon, which have been done in you, they had a great while ago repented, sitting in sackcloth and ashes.**

Alas for you, Chorazin! ... — TCNT

A curse is on you ... — Bas

14. **But it shall be more tolerable for Tyre and Sidon at the judgment, than for you.**

Yet the doom of Tyre and Sidon will be more bearable at the Judgement than yours — TCNT

15. **And thou, Capernaum, which art exalted to heaven, shalt be thrust down to hell.**

... Shalt thou be exalted to heaven? Thou shalt be brought down unto Hades — ASV

... exalted to the skies? No, brought down to the depths — NEB

... You will go down among the dead — Gspd

... are you on your way up to heaven? I tell you you will go crashing down to hell — Phi

16. **He that heareth you heareth me;**

Whoever listens to you listens to me — NEB

and he that despiseth you despiseth me; and he that despiseth me despiseth him that sent me.

and he who oppresses you ... — Lam

and the man who has no use for you has no use for me either ... — Phi

17. **And the seventy returned again with joy, saying,**

The seventy-two came back jubilant ... — NEB

... came back delighted ... — Gspd

When the seventy-two returned, they exclaimed joyfully — TCNT

Lord, even the devils are subject unto us through thy name.

... the use of your name brings the very demons under our control — Rieu

Master, even the demons submit to us when we use your name — TCNT

... when we utter your name — Wey

18. **And he said unto them, I beheld Satan as lightning fall from heaven.**

... I was watching Satan fall from heaven like lightning — NASB

... I watched how Satan fell, like lightning, out of the sky — NEB

I watched Satan fall from heaven like a lightning flash — Mon

Yes, returned Jesus, I was watching and saw Satan fall from heaven like a flash of lightning — Phi

I kept my eyes on Satan, he replied. He fell, like lightning from the sky — Rieu

... I have had visions of Satan, fallen, like lightning from the heavens — TCNT

19. **Behold, I give unto you power to tread on serpents and scorpions, and over all the power of the enemy: and nothing shall by any means hurt you.**

And now you see that I have given you power ... — NEB

Now listen! I have given you authority ... — Nor

It is true that I have given you power ... — Phi

20. **Notwithstanding in this rejoice not, that the spirits are subject unto you;**

Nevertheless, what you should rejoice over is not that the spirits are subject to you — NEB

However, do not cheer because the spirits submit to you — Ber

However, the important thing is not that demons obey you — Tay

Yet it is not your power over evil spirits which should give you joy — Phi

However, you must stop rejoicing over the fact that the spirits are submitting to you — Wms

but rather rejoice, because your names are written in heaven.

but that your names are registered as citizens of heaven — Tay

21. **In that hour Jesus rejoiced in spirit, and said,**

... rejoiced in the Holy Spirit ... — RSV

... exulted in the Holy Spirit ... — NEB

... he was inspired with joy ... — Gspd

At this time Jesus was filled with gladness by the Holy Spirit ... — Knox

... was filled by the Holy Spirit with rapturous joy — Wey

I thank thee, O Father, Lord of heaven and earth,

I openly give praise unto thee, Father! Lord of heaven and earth! — Rhm

that thou hast hid these things from the wise and prudent,

... from the learned and wise — NEB

... from wise and discerning men — ABUV

... from wise and intelligent people — Beck

... from sages and men of understanding — Wey

and hast revealed them unto babes:

... to simple folk — Rieu

... to little children — Wms

... to babes — the childish, unskilled and untaught — Amp

even so, Father; for so it seemed good in thy sight.

yea, Father, for such was thy gracious will — RSV

Yes, Father, such was your choice — NEB

Yes, Father, I praise you for wanting it to be that way — Beck

Yes, I thank you, Father, for choosing to have it so — Gspd

Yes, Father, this was all according to Your good pleasure — Nor

Indeed, I thank thee, Father, for having chosen this way — Rieu

22. **All things are delivered to me of my Father: and no man knoweth who the Son is, but the Father;**

Everything is entrusted to me by my Father ... — NEB

Everything has been put into my hands by my Father ... — Phi

and who the Father is, but the Son, and he to whom the Son will reveal him.

... to whom the Son may choose to reveal him — NEB

... to whom it is the Son's good pleasure to reveal him — Knox

23. **And he turned him unto his disciples, and said privately, Blessed are the eyes which see the things that ye see:**

Turning to his disciples in private he said, Happy the eyes that see what you are seeing! — NEB

Then he turned to his disciples and said to them quietly: How fortunate

you are to see what you are seeing! — Phi

24. **For I tell you, that many prophets and kings have desired to see those things which ye see, and have not seen them;**

... have wished to see what you see and could not see it — Gspd

and to hear those things which ye hear, and have not heard them.

25. **And, behold, a certain lawyer stood up, and tempted him, saying,**

... stood up to put him to the test ... — RSV

... came forward to put this test question ... — NEB

... and put a searching question to him ... — Rieu

Master, what shall I do to inherit eternal life?

... what must I do to make sure of eternal life — Gspd

26. **He said unto him, What is written in the law? how readest thou?**

Jesus said, What is written in the Law? What is your reading of it — NEB

... What does the law say, in your reading of it — Bas

... and what has your reading taught you — Phi

27. **And he answering said, Thou shalt love the Lord thy God with all thy heart, and with all thy soul, and with all thy strength, and with all thy mind;**

... with your whole heart, your whole soul, your whole strength, your whole mind ... — Gspd

and thy neighbour as thyself.

28. **And he said unto him, Thou hast answered right; this do, and thou shalt live.**

... That is the right answer ... — NEB

29. **But he, willing to justify himself,**

But he wanted to vindicate himself — NEB

But he, desiring to put himself in the right — Bas

But he, wishing to justify his question — Gspd

Anxious to make an excuse for himself, however — Mof

But he, trying to justify himself for asking — Nor

And he, determined to acquit himself of reproach — Amp

said unto Jesus, And who is my neighbour?

30. And Jesus answering said, A certain man went down from Jerusalem to Jericho,

. . . A man was on his way from Jerusalem down to Jericho — NEB

and fell among thieves,

and the bandits attacked him — Lam

fell into the hands of brigands — Rieu

which stripped him of his raiment, and wounded him,

. . . took his clothing and gave him cruel blows — Bas

and departed, leaving him half dead.

and left him with little life remaining in him, and they went away — Lam

31. And by chance there came down a certain priest that way:

Now by chance a priest was going down that road — RSV

Just at that time a priest happened to go along that road — Beck

and when he saw him, he passed by on the other side.

. . . on the other side of the road — Gspd

32. And likewise a Levite, when he was at the place, came and looked on him, and passed by on the other side.

So did also a Levite who came to the place . . . — Beck

A Levite also came on the scene . . . — Phi

33. But a certain Samaritan, as he journeyed, came where he was:

. . . who was on a journey came upon him — NASB

. . . who was travelling that way . . . — Gspd

and when he saw him, he had compassion on him,

. . . was moved to pity — NEB

. . . he pitied him — Gspd

and at the sight of him he was touched to pity — Phi

and was filled with compassion directly he saw him — Rieu

34. And went to him, and bound up his wounds, pouring in oil and wine, and set him on his own beast, and brought him to an inn, and took care of him.

He went up and bandaged his wounds . . . — NEB

He went to him and dressed his wounds . . . — Wey

35. And on the morrow when he departed, he took out two pence,

. . . two shillings — ASV

. . . two denarii — RSV

. . . two silver pieces — NEB

. . . two dollars — Ber

. . . some money — Nor

. . . ten shillings — Phi

. . . four shillings — TCNT

. . . a half-dollar — Wms

. . . [two days' wages] — Amp

and gave them to the host, and said unto him,

. . . to the innkeeper . . . — RSV

Take care of him; and whatsoever thou spendest more, when I come again, I will repay thee.

Look after him; and if you spend any more, I will repay you on my way back — NEB

. . . when I come again I will give you whatever more is needed — Bas

. . . I will refund when I come back — Ber

36. Which now of these three, thinkest thou, was neighbour unto him that fell among the thieves?

. . . proved neighbor to the man . . . — RSV

. . . proved to be a neighbor to the man who fell into the robbers' hands — NASB

. . . was really neighbor . . . — Ber

37. And he said, He that shewed mercy on him.

. . . The one who showed him kindness — NEB

. . . The one who was kind enough to help him — Beck

. . . The man who took pity on him — Gspd

. . . The man who gave him practical sympathy — Phi

Then said Jesus unto him, Go, and do thou likewise.

. . . Go and do the same — NASB

. . . Go and do as he did — NEB

. . . Then you go and give the same — Phi

. . . Go and practice it yourself — Wms

38. Now it came to pass, as they went, that he entered into a certain village:

While they were on their way Jesus came to a village — NEB

and a certain woman named Martha received him into her house.

where a woman named Martha made him welcome in her home — NEB

39. And she had a sister called Mary, which also sat at Jesus' feet, and heard his word.

. . . and listened to his teaching — TCNT

. . . and stayed there listening to his words — NEB

. . . who settled down at the Lord's feet and was listening to what he said — Phi

40. But Martha was cumbered about much serving,

. . . distracted with much serving — RSV

. . . distracted with all her preparations — NASB

. . . distracted by her many tasks — NEB

. . . had her hands full of the work of the house — Bas

. . . worried about all she had to do for them — Beck

. . . got worried about much housework — Ber

. . . was so busy attending to them that she grew worried — Mof

. . . concerned about all she had to do — Nor

. . . was very worried about her elaborate preparations — Phi

. . . was busy and distracted in attending to her guests — Wey

and came to him, and said, Lord, dost thou not care

and she burst in saying, Lord don't you mind — Phi

She stopped in front of him and said, Lord is it nothing to you — Rieu

So she went up to Jesus and said, Master do you approve — TCNT

so she came up suddenly and said, Lord, do you not care — Wms

that my sister hath left me to serve alone?

. . . has left me to get on with the work by myself — NEB

. . . has let me do all the work — Bas

bid her therefore that she help me.

Tell her then to help me — RSV

Tell her to come and lend a hand — NEB

Come, tell her to take hold of her end of the work along with me — Mon

Please tell her to come and help me — Nor

41. And Jesus answered and said unto her, Martha, Martha, thou art careful and troubled about many things:

. . . you are worried and bothered about so many things — NASB

. . . you are fretting and fussing about so many things — NEB

. . . thou art anxious and troublest thyself . . . — Alf

. . . you worry and fuss about a lot of things — Beck

. . . you are anxious and bustling about many matters — Ber

. . . how many cares and troubles thou hast — Knox

. . . you are worried and excited about many things — Lam

42. But one thing is needful:

but only a few things are necessary, really only one — NASB

but our wants are few, indeed there is only one thing that we need — Gspd

but one thing is more necessary — Lam

Only a few things are really needed, perhaps only one — Phi

but there is one thing which you lack — Rieu

and Mary hath chosen that good part,

. . . the good portion — Alf

. . . the best part of all — Knox

. . . the most important thing — Phi

The part that Mary has chosen is best — NEB

which shall not be taken away from her.

and she is not to be dragged away from it — Mof

and you must not tear her away from it — Phi

and she shall not be deprived of it — Wey

CHAPTER 11

1. And it came to pass, that, as he was praying in a certain place, when he ceased, one of his disciples said unto him, Lord, teach us to pray, as John also taught his disciples.

As he was praying in a certain place

and paused, one of His disciples said to Him . . . — Ber

. . . after his prayer was over . . . — Knox

2. And he said unto them, When ye pray, say,

He said: Let this be your prayer: —
Rieu

Our Father which art in heaven,

Father — ASV

Hallowed be thy name.

may your name be kept holy — Bas

May thy name be held holy — TCNT

your name be revered — Gspd

may Your name be honored — Phi

Thy kingdom come.

thy Reign begin — Mof

Thy will be done, as in heaven, so in earth.

Let thy will be done . . . — Lam

Your will be done — held holy and revered . . . — Amp

3. Give us day by day our daily bread.

. . . every day bread for our needs — Bas

Daily grant us our food for the coming day — Ber

. . . our bread for the morrow, day by day — Mof

. . . each day the bread that we shall need — TCNT

. . . day after day our bread for the day — Wey

Continue giving us day by day our daily bread — Wms

4. And forgive us our sins; for we also forgive every one that is indebted to us.

. . . For we too forgive all who have done us wrong — NEB

. . . for we ourselves forgive everyone who wrongs us — TCNT

And lead us not into temptation;

And bring us not . . . — ASV

And let us not be put to the test — Bas

and keep us clear of temptation — Phi

but deliver us from evil.

but rescue us from evil — Ber

. . . from error — Lam

5. And he said unto them, Which of you shall have a friend, and shall go unto him at midnight, and say unto him, Friend, lend me three loaves;

. . . Suppose one of you shall have a friend . . . — NASB

. . . Let us say that one of you has a friend . . . — Ber

6. For a friend of mine in his journey is come to me,

. . . has turned up at my house — NEB

. . . on a trip has dropped in on me — Beck

. . . has come to my house from a distance — Wey

and I have nothing to set before him?

. . . to offer him — NEB

. . . and I do not have a thing . . . — Nor

. . . no food to put in front of him — Phi

. . . for him to eat — Wey

7. And he from within shall answer and say, Trouble me not: the door is now shut, and my children are with me in bed; I cannot rise and give thee.

. . . Do not bother me . . . I cannot get up and give you anything — RSV

. . . my children with me are in bed; I can not rise . . . — ABUV

. . . Don't bother me with your troubles . . . — Phi

. . . Don't put me to the trouble. I locked up long ago . . . — Rieu

. . . Do not pester me. The door is now barred . . . — Wey

. . . Stop bothering me . . . — Wms

8. I say unto you, Though he will not rise and give him, because he is his friend, yet because of his importunity he will rise and give him as many as he needeth.

. . . because of his persistence . . . — NASB

. . . the very shamelessness of the request will make him get up . . . — NEB

. . . if he keeps on making his request . . . — Bas

. . . shameless asking will make him rise . . . — Knox

. . . if he persists, he will rouse himself . . . — Phi

9. And I say unto you, Ask, and it shall be given you; seek, and ye shall find; knock, and it shall be opened unto you.

. . . ask, and you will receive . . . — NEB

. . . ask, and what you ask will be given you . . . — Gspd

. . . keep on asking . . . keep on seeking . . . keep on knocking . . . — Wms

10. For every one that asketh receiveth; and he that seeketh findeth; and to him that knocketh it shall be opened.

for every asker . . . every seeker . . . — Ber

For it is always the one who asks who receives . . . — Gspd

For everyone who keeps on asking . . . keeps on seeking . . . keeps on knocking . . . — Wms

11. If a son shall ask bread of any of you that is a father, will he give him a stone?
And of which of you that is a father shall his son ask a loaf . . . — ASV
Which of you fathers . . . — Gspd
or if he ask a fish, will he for a fish give him a serpent?
. . . will instead hand him a snake — Ber

12. Or if he shall ask an egg, will he offer him a scorpion?
Or a scorpion if he asked for an egg — Nor
. . . make him a present of a scorpion — Phi

13. If ye then, being evil, know how to give good gifts unto your children:
If you, then, bad as you are . . . — NEB
. . . in spite of your being bad . . . — Wms
how much more shall your heavenly Father give the Holy Spirit to them that ask him?
is not your Father much more ready to give from heaven, his gracious Spirit . . . — Knox
. . . to those who continue to ask Him — Wms

14. And he was casting out a devil, and it was dumb.
On one occasion He was expelling a dumb demon — Wey
And it came to pass, when the devil was gone out, the dumb spake;
. . . the man had the power of talking — Bas
. . . found speech — Knox
. . . when the demon was expelled the man could speak — Nor
and the people wondered.
And the multitudes marvelled — Rhm

15. But some of them said, He casteth out devils through Beelzebub the chief of the devils.
. . . by Beelzebub, the prince of demons — RSV
. . . the ruler of evil spirits — Bas
. . . because he is in league with Beelzebub, the chief of the evil spirits — Phi

16. And others, tempting him, sought of him a sign from heaven.
. . . by way of a test, demanded . . . — NEB
. . . meaning to test Him . . . demanded . . . some wonderful proof . . . — Beck

17. But he, knowing their thoughts, said unto them, Every kingdom divided against itself is brought to desolation;
. . . is laid waste — RSV
. . . goes to ruin — NEB
. . . if one part of any kingdom fights against another part, it loses its people — Beck
. . . Any kingdom that is disunited is on the way to destruction — Gspd
. . . in which a civil war rages, goes to ruin — Wey
. . . is in the process of destruction — Wms
. . . is doomed — Phi
. . . kingdoms are brought to ruin by internal strife — Rieu
and a house divided against a house falleth.
and a divided household falls — NEB
and a house divided against a house falls — ABUV
and a house in which there is division comes to destruction — Bas
so does the quarreling home go down — Ber
house after house falls down — Mof
and a disunited household will collapse — Phi

18. If Satan also be divided against himself, how shall his kingdom stand?
If, then, Satan is at war with himself, how will he keep his kingdom? . . . — Bas
If the devil fights against himself . . . — Beck
And how do you suppose that Satan's kingdom can stand firm if he is at war with himself — Knox
And if Satan disagrees with Satan . . . — Phi
And if Satan is engaged in conflict with himself . . . — Wey
because ye say that I cast out devils through Beelzebub.

19. And if I by Beelzebub cast out devils, by whom do your sons cast them out?
. . . by whom do your own people drive them out — NEB
. . . who helps your sons drive them out — Beck

... who is your sons' ally when they do the same thing — Phi

therefore shall they be your judges.

so let them be your judges — Bas

They can settle that question for you — Phi

20. **But if I with the finger of God cast out devils,**

But, if it is by the hand of God that I drive out demons — TCNT

no doubt the kingdom of God is come upon you.

... has overtaken you — Bas

then it must be that the kingdom of God has suddenly appeared among you — Knox

then the Reign of God has reached you already — Mof

... has swept over you unawares — Phi

it would seem that the kingdom of God confronts you — Rieu

21. **When a strong man armed keepeth his palace,**

... fully armed guardeth his own court — ASV

... his own homestead — NASB

... is on guard over his castle — NEB

... his courtyard — Lam

... fully aroused keeps guard over his homestead — Mon

his goods are in peace:

his possessions are safe — NEB

22. **But when a stronger than he shall come upon him, and overcome him,**

but, when one still stronger has attacked and overpowered him—TCNT

he taketh from him all his armour wherein he trusted, and divideth his spoils.

he taketh from him his whole armor ... — ASV

... all his armor on which he relied, and distributes his plunder — NASB

... his instruments of war in which he has put his faith, and makes division of his goods — Bas

23. **He that is not with me is against me: and he that gathereth not with me scattereth.**

... and he who will not give me help in getting people together is driving them away — Bas

... and anyone who doesn't help me gather scatters — Beck

24. **When the unclean spirit is gone out of a man, he walketh through dry places,**

... passeth through waterless places — ASV

seeking rest;

in search of a place to stay — Nor

in search [of a place] of rest (release, refreshing, ease) — Amp

and finding none, he saith, I will return unto my house whence I came out.

... I will go back to the house I left — Mof

25. **And when he cometh, he findeth it swept and garnished.**

... and put in order — RSV

... swept clean and tidy — NEB

... and decorated — Beck

... and orderly — Ber

... unoccupied, cleaned, and all in order — Gspd

... swept out, and neatly set in order — Knox

... warm and well furnished — Lam

... and ready for use — Wms

26. **Then goeth he, and taketh to him seven other spirits more wicked than himself; and they enter in, and dwell there:**

... they all come in and settle down — NEB

... and they all go in and make themselves at home — Phi

and the last state of that man is worse than the first.

... becometh worse ... — ASV

27. **And it came to pass, as he spake these things, a certain woman of the company lifted up her voice, and said unto him, Blessed is the womb that bare thee, and the paps which thou hast sucked.**

... the breasts which thou didst suck — ASV

... Happy is the mother who bore you and nursed you — Beck

... what a blessing for a woman to have brought you into the world and nursed you — Phi

28. **But he said, Yea rather, blessed are they that hear the word of God, and keep it.**

... No, happy are those who hear ... — NEB

... Yes, but a far greater blessing to hear the word of God and obey it — Phi

29. **And when the people were gathered thick together, he began to say,**
    As the crowds increased, Jesus began to speak: — TCNT
    With the crowds swarming round him he went on to say — NEB
    This is an evil generation: they seek a sign; and there shall no sign be given it, but the sign of Jonas the prophet.

30. **For as Jonas was a sign unto the Ninevites, so shall also the Son of man be to this generation.**
    As Jonah became a proof to the people of Nineveh . . . — Beck

31. **The queen of the south shall rise up in the judgment with the men of this generation, and condemn them:**
    At the judgement, when the men of this generation are on trial. . . — NEB
    for she came from the utmost parts of the earth to hear the wisdom of Solomon; and, behold, a greater than Solomon is here.
    . . . from the ends of the earth . . . — Bas

32. **The men of Nineve shall rise up in the judgment with this generation, and shall condemn it:**
    and ensure their condemnation — NEB
    and will leave it without excuse — Knox
    for they repented at the preaching of Jonas; and, behold, a greater than Jonas is here.
    . . . and what is here is greater than Jonah — NEB

33. **No man, when he hath lighted a candle, putteth it in a secret place,**
    . . . a lamp . . . in a cellar — ASV
    . . . in a cupboard — Phi
    neither under a bushel, but on a candlestick, that they which come in may see the light.
    nor under a peck-measure, but on the lampstand . . . — NASB
    or under a grain-measure but on top of a stand . . . — Ber
    or under a bucket . . . — Phi

34. **The light of the body is the eye:**
    Thy body has the eye for its lamp — Knox
    therefore when thine eye is single, thy whole body also is full of light;
    . . . is clear . . . — NASB

. . . is true . . . — Bas
. . . is healthy . . . — Beck
When your eyes are sound . . . — NEB
. . . when your eye [your conscience] is sound and fulfilling its office . . . — Amp
but when thine eye is evil, thy body also is full of darkness.
. . . is bad . . . — NASB
. . . is defective . . . is darkened — Ber

35. **Take heed therefore that the light which is in thee be not darkness.**
    See to it then that the light you have is not darkness — NEB
    So take care! Your very light may be darkness! — Gspd
    Take good care then, that this principle of light which is in thee is light, not darkness — Knox
    Look! perhaps your very light is dark — Mof
    So be on guard that the very source of light in you is not darkness — Wms

36. **If thy whole body therefore be full of light, having no part dark,**
    If you have light for your whole body with no trace of darkness — NEB
    the whole shall be full of light, as when the bright shining of a candle doth give thee light.
    it shall be wholly illumined, as when the lamp illumines you with its rays — NASB
    it will all be as bright as when a lamp flashes its rays upon you — NEB
    it will all be as light as a lamp makes things for you by its light — Gspd

37. **And as he spake, a certain Pharisee besought him to dine with him:**
    When he had finished speaking, a Pharisee invited him to dinner — NEB
    and he went in, and sat down to meat.
    and Jesus went in and took his place at table — TCNT

38. **And when the Pharisee saw it, he marvelled that he had not first washed before dinner.**
    . . . bathed himself . . . — ASV
    The Pharisee noticed with surprise that he had not begun by washing before the meal — NEB
    The Pharisee noticed, to his astonishment, that Jesus omitted the ceremonial washing before breakfast — TCNT

39. And the Lord said unto him, Now do ye Pharisees make clean the outside of the cup and the platter;

. . . You Pharisees! You clean the outside . . . — NEB

. . . You Pharisees do, it is true, clean the outside of the cup and of the plate — TCNT

but your inward part is full of ravening and wickedness.

. . . full of extortion . . . — ASV

. . . full of rapacity . . . — ABUV

but inside you there is nothing but greed and wickedness — NEB

while all within is running with avarice and wickedness — Knox

but your inner life is filled with rapacity and malice — Mof

40. Ye fools, did not he that made that which is without make that which is within also?

. . . Did not he who made the outside make the inside also — ABUV

41. But rather give alms of such things as ye have; and, behold, all things are clean unto you.

But let what is in the cup be given in charity, and all is clean — NEB

Just give your heart in helping the poor, and you'll find everything clean — Beck

But give your inmost light as charity, and you will immediately find everything clean — Gspd

But dedicate once for all your inner self, and at once you will have everything clean — Wms

42. But woe unto you, Pharisees!

but a curse on you Pharisees — Wms

for ye tithe mint and rue and all manner of herbs,

you make men give a tenth of every sort of plant — Bas

that will award God his tithe, though it be of mint or rue or whatever herb you will — Knox

and pass over judgment and the love of God:

. . . justice . . . — ASV

and give no thought to right . . . — Bas

and fail to be just and love God—Beck

and leave on one side justice and the love of God — Knox

these ought ye to have done, and not to leave the other undone.

. . . without neglecting the others — RSV

. . . without omitting the former — Mof

. . . it need not mean leaving the lesser duties undone — Phi

43. Woe unto you, Pharisees! for ye love the uppermost seats in the synagogues, and greetings in the markets.

. . . and salutations in the market places — RSV

. . . and having men bow down to you in public — Phi

. . . and to be greeted in the markets with respect — TCNT

. . . and you like to be bowed to in places of public resort — Wey

44. Woe unto you, scribes and Pharisees, hypocrites! for ye are as graves which appear not,

. . . like concealed tombs — NASB

. . . like unmarked graves — NEB

. . . like unsuspected tombs — Mof

. . . like tombs which lie hidden — Wey

and the men that walk over them are not aware of them.

45. Then answered one of the lawyers, and said unto him, Master, thus saying thou reproachest us also.

. . . you are insulting us too — NEB

. . . you give a bad name to us as to them — Bas

. . . you affront us also — Gspd

. . . thou art bringing us too into contempt — Knox

46. And he said, Woe unto you also, ye lawyers! for ye lade men with burdens grievous to be borne,

. . . Yes, you lawyers, it is no better with you! For you load men with intolerable burdens — NEB

. . . Yes, and I do blame you experts in the Law! For you pile up backbreaking burdens for men to bear — Phi

and ye yourselves touch not the burdens with one of your fingers.

you yourselves do not put so much as one finger to them — Bas

and you do not personally [even gently] touch the burdens . . . — Amp

47. Woe unto you! for ye build the sepulchres of the prophets,

. . . for you make resting-places for the bodies of the prophets — Bas

. . . for you build memorial tombs . . . — Phi

and your fathers killed them.

48. Truly ye bear witness that ye allow the deeds of your fathers:

So ye are witnesses and consent unto the works . . . — ASV

and so testify that you approve of the deeds . . . — NEB

You thus attest and countenance your fathers' deeds — Rieu

for they indeed killed them, and ye build their sepulchres.

49. Therefore also said the wisdom of God, I will send them prophets and apostles, and some of them they shall slay and persecute:

The Wisdom of God therefore says . . . Ber

And that is why God in his Wisdom said . . . — Rieu

50. That the blood of all the prophets, which was shed from the foundation of the world, may be required of this generation;

so that the people of today may be punished for the blood of all the prophets poured out since the world was made — Beck

51. From the blood of Abel unto the blood of Zacharias,

from the blood of Abel down to the blood of Zechariah — TCNT

which perished between the altar and the temple:

. . . the altar and the sanctuary — ASV

. . . the altar and the House of God — Mof

verily I say unto you, It shall be required of this generation.

52. Woe unto you, lawyers! for ye have taken away the key of knowledge; ye entered not in yourselves, and them that were entering in ye hindered.

. . . and those who were on their way in, you stopped — NEB

. . . and you got in the way of those who were going in — Bas

53. And as he said these things unto them, the scribes and the Pharisees began to urge him vehemently,

. . . began to press him hard — RSV

. . . began to be very hostile — NASB

. . . came round him angrily — Bas

. . . undertook to heckle Him fiercely — Ber

. . . resolved to hunt him down mercilessly — Knox

. . . commenced to follow him closely — Mof

. . . determined to pursue Him relentlessly — Nor

. . . began to regard him with bitter animosity — Phi

. . . began to assail him fiercely — NEB

. . . gave vent to their animosity — Rieu

and to provoke him to speak of many things:

and to ply him with a host of questions — NEB

questioning him about more things — Bas

and cross-examined Him about many things — Beck

and to draw Him out by cross-questioning on many points — Ber

and to browbeat him with a multitude of questions — Knox

and began to catechise him about this and that — Rieu

and trying to make him speak off-hand concerning many things — Rhm

54. Laying wait for him,

laying snares — NEB

And watching him — Bas

And they plotted against him in many ways — Lam

plotting, as if in ambush — Wms

and seeking to catch something out of his mouth, that they might accuse him.

to catch at something he might say — RSV

to catch him with his own words — NEB

to trap Him in something He might say — Beck

to pounce on some incriminating remark — Phi

to catch him in some compromising statement — Rieu

to catch some unguarded expression from His lips — Wey

CHAPTER 12

1. In the mean time, when there were gathered together an innumerable multitude of people,

Meanwhile the people had come streaming towards Him by thousands — Wey

insomuch that they trode one upon another,

packed so close that they were treading on one another — NEB

so that they were trampling one another underfoot — Wey

he began to say unto his disciples first of all,

But He paid attention first of all to His disciples — Nor

Beware ye of the leaven of the Pharisees, which is hypocrisy.

Be on your guard against the leaven — that is, the hypocrisy — of the Pharisees — TCNT

2. **For there is nothing covered, that shall not be revealed;**

What is veiled will all be revealed — Knox

For there is nothing covered up which is not going to be exposed — Phi

neither hid, that shall not be known.

nor anything kept secret which will not become known — TCNT

3. **Therefore whatsoever ye have spoken in darkness shall be heard in the light;**

Hence all that you have said in the dark will be heard in the light—TCNT

... will be repeated in the light of day — Knox

and that which ye have spoken in the ear in closets

and what you have whispered within closed doors — Wey

... in private rooms — RSV

shall be proclaimed upon the house tops.

will be announced from the roofs — Beck

shall be published ... — Ber

will be shouted ... — Phi

4. **And I say unto you my friends,**

To you who are my friends I say — TCNT

I tell you, as friends of mine — Phi

Be not afraid of them that kill the body,

never be afraid of ... — Wms

and after that have no more that they can do.

and then can't do any more — Beck

5. **But I will forewarn you**

But I will suggest to you — Rhm

I will show you — TCNT

But I will make clear to you — Bas

whom ye shall fear:

whom ye should fear — Rhm

of whom you should be afraid — TCNT

the one you must fear — Beck

whom you ought to fear — Mon

the only one you need to fear — Phi

Fear him, which after he hath killed hath power to cast into hell;

... hath authority to cast into gehenna — Rhm

... to fling you into Hell — TCNT

... to hurl you into the pit — Gspd

... to throw you into destruction! — Phi

yea, I say unto you, Fear him.

Yes, fear Him, I say — Rieu

Believe me, he is the one to fear — NEB

Yes, I tell you, fear Him! — NASB

6. **Are not five sparrows sold for two farthings,**

Do not sparrows sell five for two cents — Gspd

... for a penny — TCNT

... for two nickels — Ber

The market price of five sparrows is two cents, isn't it? — Phi

and not one of them is forgotten before God?

... has escaped God's notice — TCNT

and God has every one of them in mind — Bas

7. **But even the very hairs of your head are all numbered.**

... are all counted — Wey

... have all been counted by God! — Wms

... he takes every hair ... into his reckoning — Knox

... every single hair ... is numbered — Rieu

Fear not therefore:

Away with fear — Wey

Stop being afraid — Wms

ye are of more value than many sparrows.

you are more precious than ... — Wey

you are worth far more than sparrows — Mof

8. **Also I say unto you,**

And this I want you to know — Nor

Whosoever shall confess me before men,

everyone who owns me before men — Wms

... who gives witness to me ... — Bas

... who publicly acknowledges me — Phi

him shall the Son of man also confess
... the Son of Man will own — Wms
I, the Son of Man, will acknowledge — Phi

before the angels of God:
before the messengers of God — Rhm

9. But he that denieth me before men
... who disowns me ... — TCNT
... says ... that he has no knowledge of me — Bas
... who publicly disowns me — Phi
But he that disowns me to the world — Rieu

shall be denied before the angels of God.
... will find himself disowned ... — Phi

10. And whosoever shall speak a word against the Son of man,
Whoever shall make a statement ... — Ber
Anyone who speaks against ... — Phi

it shall be forgiven him:
will be forgiven for it — Mof
for him there is forgiveness — Ber

but unto him that blasphemeth against the Holy Ghost
... who against the Holy Spirit speaketh profanely — Rhm
... who slanders the Holy Spirit—TCNT
... who reviles the holy Spirit — Gspd
... who speaks abusively about ... — Wms
... who says evil words against ... — Bas

it shall not be forgiven.
will never obtain forgiveness — Wey

11. And when they bring you
When they bring you to trial — Knox
When they hale you — Rieu

unto the synagogues, and unto magistrates, and powers,
before the synagogues, and the rulers and the authorities — ASV
before the Synagogue Courts ... — TCNT
before synagogues and state authorities — NEB

take ye no thought
be not anxious — ASV
you must have no anxiety — Gspd
do not anxiously ponder — Wey
do not trouble yourselves about — Mof
do not worry about — Mon

how or what thing ye shall answer,
the manner or matter of your defence — Wey
the wording and the lines of your defence — Rieu
how you will conduct your defence — NEB

or what ye shall say:
nor what you are to say — Wey

12. For the Holy Ghost shall teach you in the same hour
... will make clear to you ... — Bas
... will instruct you when the time comes — Knox
... at that very moment — Wey

what ye ought to say.
what words to use — Knox
what is the right thing for you to say — Phi

13. And one of the company said unto him,
a man in the crowd said to Jesus — TCNT

Master, speak to my brother,
Teacher, ... — TCNT

that he divide the inheritance with me.
... give me my share of our inheritance — Mof
... share his legacy with me — Phi
... share the estate with me — Rieu
... divide the family property with me — NEB

14. And he said unto him,
But He refused, saying — Nor

Man, who made me a judge or a divider over you?
He replied, My good man ... — NEB
... who appointed me a judge or a property divider ... — Lam
... or an arbiter between you — TCNT
... or umpire ... — Wms

15. And he said unto them, Take heed, and beware of covetousness:
... See and keep clear of covetousness in every shape and form — Mof
... be on your guard against all covetousness — Wey
... Take care! You must be on your guard against every form of greed — Gspd
... Beware! Don't always be wishing for what others have — Tay

for a man's life consisteth not in the abundance of the things which he possesseth.

for even in the height of his prosperity a man's true Life does not depend on what he has — TCNT

for even when a man has more than enough, his wealth does not give him life — NEB

for not even when one has an abundance does his life consist of his possessions — NASB

16. And he spake a parable unto them, saying,

Then He told them a story, as follows — Wms

The ground of a certain rich man brought forth plentifully:

. . . one year produced abundantly — Rieu

. . . yielded a heavy crop — Knox

17. And he thought within himself, saying,

and he reasoned . . . — ASV

And he began to deliberate within himself . . . — Rhm

and he debated . . . — Wey

So he began to argue with himself — Wms

What shall I do,

What am I to do? — Wey

because I have no room

I have not the space — NEB

for I have nowhere — TCNT

for I have no place — Wey

where to bestow my fruits?

to store my crops in — Knox

to store this harvest of mine — Phi

18. And he said, This will I do:

I know what I'll do — Phi

I will pull down my barns, and build greater;

I will tear down my barns and build larger ones — Gspd

. . . my granaries . . . — Mof

. . . my storehouses and build them bigger — NEB

and there will I bestow all my fruits and my goods.

large enough to store all my crops . . . — Nor

and garner all my grain . . . — Rieu

I will store up all my harvest . . . — Wey

Then I'll have room enough! — Tay

19. And I will say to my soul, Soul, thou hast much goods laid up for many years;

. . . you have ample possessions . . . — Wey

. . . you have great wealth stored up . . . — Gspd

. . . plenty of good things put by . . . — TCNT

. . . many goods laid up for many years — ABUV

. . . you have a great amount of goods in store . . . — Bas

. . . Come, soul, thou hast goods in plenty . . . — Knox

take thine ease, eat, drink, and be merry.

Take it easy . . . — Ber

Relax! Eat, drink and have a good time! — Phi

take life easy . . . — NEB

. . . enjoy yourself merrily — Amp

20. But God said unto him, Thou fool,

. . . O you shortsighted — Lam

. . . Simpleton — Ber

this night thy soul shall be required of thee:

this very night your life is being demanded — TCNT

. . . thou must render up thy soul — Knox

. . . they are coming to reclaim your soul — Rieu

tonight you die — Beck

then whose shall those things be, which thou hast provided?

who then will be the owner of . . . — Bas

who will be master now of . . . — Knox

you have made your money — who will get it now — NEB

21. So is he that layeth up treasure for himself,

So fares the man who . . . — Mof

So that is what comes to the man who . . . — Bas

. . . who amasses treasure for himself — Wey

. . . who continues to pile up possessions for himself — Wms

. . . who hoards things for himself — Phi

and is not rich toward God.

but has no riches in God — Wey

instead of gaining the riches of God — Mof

and has not wealth in the eyes of God — Bas

and remains a pauper in the sight of God — NEB

and are not rich to the glory of God —
TCNT

22. And he said unto his disciples,
Then turning to His disciples He said
— Wey

Therefore I say unto you,
For this cause I say unto you — Rhm
That is why I tell you — Phi

**Take no thought for your life, what
ye shall eat;**
Be not anxious . . . — ASV
Stop worrying . . . — Wms
. . . put away anxious thoughts . . . —
NEB
. . . about the life here . . . — TCNT
. . . do not worry about life, wondering
what . . . — Gspd
. . . what you are to eat — Wey
. . . do not fret over your life, how to
support it with food — Knox

**neither for the body, what ye shall put
on.**
and for your persons, what you are to
put on — Wey
or about your body, wondering what
. . . — Gspd
And stop bothering about what clothes
you will need — Phi

23. The life is more than meat,
life is something more than food —
Mof
Life is more important than food —
Gspd

and the body is more than raiment.
. . . is something more than clothes —
Mof
. . . more important than . . . — Phi

**24. Consider the ravens: for they neither
sow nor reap;**
Think of the crows! . . . — Gspd
Just look at the ravens . . . — Nor
see how the ravens never sow or reap
— Knox

**which neither have storehouse nor
barn; and God feedeth them:**
. . . God continues to feed them—Wms

**how much more are ye better than
the fowls?**
of how much more value are ye . . . —
ASV
how much more important . . . — Lam
and how much more precious are you
. . . — TCNT
By how much do ye excel the birds —
Rhm

have you not an excellence far beyond
theirs — Knox

25. And which of you with taking thought
. . . by being anxious — ASV
. . . by worrying — Wms
. . . for all his fretting — Knox

can add to his stature one cubit?
. . . a single hour to his life — Gspd
. . . a moment to his years — Rieu
can prolong his life a moment — TCNT

**26. If ye then be not able to do that thing
which is least,**
and if you cannot manage . . . — Mof
. . . even a very little thing — Wey
. . . alter the least little thing — Rieu
And if you are powerless to do so small
a thing — Knox

why take ye thought for the rest?
why are ye anxious . . . — ASV
why should you worry about the rest
— Gspd
why fret about the rest — Rieu

27. Consider the lilies how they grow:
Look at the lilies . . . — Wey
Look how the lilies . . . — Mof

they toil not, they spin not;
. . . neither work nor weave — Phi

**and yet I say unto you, that Solomon
in all his glory was not arrayed like
one of these.**
. . . even Solomon in all his splendour
was not robed . . . — TCNT
. . . in all his magnificence . . . — Wey
. . . in all his grandeur was never robed
. . . — Mof
. . . in all his splendor was never dressed
. . . — Gspd

28. If then God so clothe the grass,
But if God thus adorneth . . . — Rhm
. . . so gorgeously dresses . . . — Wms

**which is to day in the field, and to mor-
row is cast into the oven;**
that blooms to-day and to-morrow is
feeding the oven — Wey
which is alive in the field today . . . —
RSV
which flowers in the field today and is
burned in the stove tomorrow — Phi
that are here today and gone tomorrow
— Tay

how much more will he clothe you,
How much rather you — Rhm
will he not be much more ready to
clothe you — Knox

O ye of little faith?
faint-believers! — Ber

you little-faiths — Phi

slow though you are to trust him — Rieu

How little faith you have! — NEB

O men, how little you trust him!— Mof

29. **And seek not ye what ye shall eat, or what ye shall drink,**

So you must stop seeking . . . — Wms

You must not set your heart on . . . — Phi

. . . what you are to have to eat or drink — Gspd

neither be ye of doubtful mind.

And be not held in suspense — Rhm

and do not waver between hope and fear — Wey

and let not your mind be disturbed by these things — Lam

and be harassed no more — Rieu

and be not tossed about with cares — ABUV

30. **For all these things do the nations of the world seek after:**

pagans make food and drink their aim in life — Mof

For all these things are the very things the nations of the world are greedily trying to get — Wms

The whole heathen world is busy about getting food and drink — Phi

All mankind scratches for its daily bread — Tay

and your Father knoweth that ye have need of these things.

but you have a Father who knows that you need them — NEB

31. **But rather seek ye the kingdom of God;**

But you must strive to find his kingdom — Gspd

But let your chief care be for . . . — Bas

No, make it your first care to find . . . — Knox

No, set your heart on . . . — Phi

Only be eager to have Him as your King — Beck

and all these things shall be added unto you.

. . . shall be yours without the asking — Knox

. . . will be supplied you besides — Ber

your food and drink will come as a matter of course — Phi

32. **Fear not, little flock;**

Dismiss your fears . . . — Wey

for it is your Father's good pleasure to give you the kingdom.

for your Father delighteth to give you the kingdom — Rhm

. . . plans to give you . . . — Phi

. . . has decided to . . . — Beck

. . . has determined to give you his kingdom — Knox

33. **Sell that ye have, and give alms;**

Sell your possessions . . . — Rhm

. . . what belongs to you . . . — TCNT

. . . and give to the poor — Nor

Sell your property and give to charity — Wms

provide yourselves bags which wax not old,

make for yourselves purses . . . — ASV

. . . that never wear out — Mof

so providing yourselves with a purse that time cannot wear holes in — Knox

a treasure in the heavens that faileth not,

an inexhaustible treasure . . . — TCNT

. . . that does not run short — Lam

. . . which will be yours for ever — Bas

a treasure-house that does not fail . . . — Rieu

. . . that will never be used up . . . — Beck

where no thief approacheth, neither moth corrupteth.

that no thief can get at, no moth destroy — Mof

where thief doth not draw near and moth doth not spoil — Rhm

where no thief reaches or moth ruins — Ber

34. **For where your treasure is, there will your heart be also.**

And your heart will be where your treasure is — Nor

35. **Let your loins be girded about,**

Make yourselves ready — TCNT

You must keep your belts tight—Wms

Be ready, dressed as for a journey — Bas

Be ready for action, with belts fastened — NEB

and your lights burning;

and your lamps burning — ASV

36. **And ye yourselves like unto men that wait for their lord, when he will return from the wedding;**

and be ye yourselves like unto . . . — ASV

. . . men who wait to welcome . . . — Phi

. . . for their master to come home . . . — Gspd

that when he cometh and knocketh, they may open unto him immediately.

ready to let him in the moment he arrives and knocks — NEB

37. Blessed are those servants,

Happy are those slaves — Mon

whom the lord when he cometh shall find watching:

. . . will find on the watch for him — Wms

. . . finds on the alert . . . — Ber

verily I say unto you, that he shall gird himself,

I promise you . . . — Knox

I assure you . . . — Ber

I tell you, in solemn truth, that He will tie an apron round him — Wey

. . . he will tighten his belt — Wms

and make them to sit down to meat,

and bid them take their places at table — TCNT

and will come forth and serve them.

and come forward . . . — Mof

. . . and wait upon them — TCNT

38. And if he shall come in the second watch, or come in the third watch,

. . . before or after midnight — Wms

Whether it is late at night, or in the early morning that he comes — TCNT

and find them so,

if he finds all as it should be — TCNT

and finds them thus alert — Mof

and finds them on the watch — Gspd

blessed are those servants.

happy are those slaves — Mon

they are most fortunate — Ber

39. And this know,

But of this be taking note — Rhm

This you do know — TCNT

Of this be sure — Wey

But understand this — Ber

that if the goodman of the house had known

that if the master . . . — ASV

. . . the owner . . . — Rieu

what hour the thief would come,

just when the burglar was coming — Beck

he would have watched, and not have suffered his house to be broken through.

. . . and would not have let his house be broken into — TCNT

. . . his house to be digged through — Rhm

40. Be ye therefore ready also:

So be ready yourselves — Mof

Be vigilant yourselves — Rieu

Hold yourselves ready, then — NEB

You, too, get ready — Beck

for the Son of man cometh at an hour when ye think not.

for when you are least expecting him the Son of Man will come — TCNT

41. Then Peter said unto him,

Peter asked Him — Ber

Lord, speakest thou this parable unto us,

. . . are you addressing this parable to us — Wey

. . . do you intend this parable specially for us — NEB

. . . do you mean this figure for us — Gspd

. . . with reference to us — TCNT

. . . for our benefit — Nor

or even to all?

or to every one — TCNT

42. And the Lord said, Who then is that faithful and wise steward,

. . . Well, where is the trusty, thoughtful steward . . . — Mof

. . . the manager that can be trusted and has good sense — Beck

whom his lord shall make ruler over

whom his master will put in charge of — Wey

. . . will put in control of — Bas

. . . will entrust with the care of — Knox

his household,

his establishment — TCNT

his family — Bas

his servants — NEB

to give them their portion of meat

to give out supplies — Mof

to supply their food allowance — Ber

in due season?

at the proper times — Wey

at stated times — Nor

43. Blessed is that servant,

Happy will that servant be — TCNT

whom his lord when he cometh

. . . when he comes home — TCNT

when his master comes back — Nor

shall find so doing.

finds in the faithful discharge of these duties — Rieu

44. Of a truth I say unto you,
I promise you — Knox
that he will make him ruler over
... will put him in charge of — TCNT
He will put him in control of — Bas
he will promote him to look after —
Phi
... will make him director of — Rieu
... will make him manager of — Beck
all that he hath.
all his possessions — Rhm
the whole of his property — TCNT
his whole estate — Rieu

45. But and if that servant say in his heart,
But if that slave says to himself—Wms
... if that manager ... — Nor
My lord delayeth his coming;
My master is a long time coming —
TCNT
... is not coming back for a long time
— Gspd
... is putting off his arrival — Ber
... is delayed in coming — RSV
... takes his time about returning —
Phi
... is late in coming — Amp
**and shall begin to beat the menservants
and maidens,**
and falls to beating the men and the
maids — Knox
and takes to bullying the boys and
maids — Rieu
**and to eat and drink, and to be
drunken;**
feasting and taking overmuch wine —
Bas
eating and drinking himself drunk —
Knox
to gluttony and wine and getting drunk
— Rieu

46. The lord of that servant will come
that servant's master ... — TCNT
... will come back — Gspd
**in a day when he looketh not for him,
and at an hour when he is not
aware,**
on some day when he expects nothing
... — Knox
... at an hour of which he has no idea
— Ber
... at a moment unforeseen — Nor
... suddenly and unexpectedly ... —
Phi
and will cut him in sunder,
... cut him in two — Mof
... tear him to pieces — Rieu

... will flog him severely — TCNT
... will severely punish him — Lam
and will appoint him his portion with
assign him his place among — TCNT
make him share the lot of — Wey
assign him the fate of — Mof
give him his share with — Wms
consign him to — Rieu
the unbelievers.
the untrustworthy — TCNT
the traitors' lot — Rieu

**47. And that servant, which knew his
lord's will,**
... knows his master's wishes — TCNT
... knew his master's program — Ber
... his master's plan — Phi
**and prepared not himself, neither did
according to his will,**
but does not get ready or act upon them
— Gspd
neither got ready for the program nor
worked it out — Ber
yet made no attempt to carry them out
— NEB
shall be beaten with many stripes.
will have many strokes of the lash —
Knox
will be flogged with many blows of the
lash — Nor

48. But he that knew not,
while one who does not know his master's wishes — TCNT
he who had not been told — Wey
**and did commit things worthy of
stripes,**
and did what deserves a beating—Mof
committed punishable faults — Rieu
though he has done wrong — Phi
yet earned a beating — Knox
shall be beaten with few stripes.
will receive but few lashes — Wey
will be let off lightly — Phi
For unto whomsoever much is given,
Where a man has been given much —
NEB
From anyone who has been given
much — Gspd
of him shall be much required:
much will be expected — TCNT
Much will be demanded — Wms
**and to whom men have committed
much,**
and the more a man has had entrusted
to him — NEB
to whom people have intrusted much
— Gspd

And he to whom they committed much
— Rhm
of him they will ask the more.
the more will be demanded — TCNT
something extra shall be asked — Rieu
people will demand even more — Nor
49. I am come
I came — ASV
to send fire on the earth;
to build a fire upon . . . — Mon
to set the world on fire — Rieu
and what will I,
and what can I wish — Rhm
if it be already kindled?
if it were already started — Beck
50. But I have a baptism
But an immersion have I — Rhm
to be baptized with;
to be immersed with — Rhm
to undergo — Wey
and how am I straitened
how am I pent up — Wey
how I am pressed with anguish — Wms
how impatient am I — Knox
how strained I feel — Ber
how hampered I am — NEB
till it be accomplished!
till it is all over! — Mof
till that has been achieved! — Rieu
until the ordeal is over! — NEB
51. Suppose ye
Is it your opinion — Bas
that I am come
that I came here — Rieu
to give peace on earth?
to establish peace . . . — NEB
to grant peace . . . — NASB
I tell you, Nay;
Not peace, I tell you — Gspd
I tell you, not so at all — Wms
No, I tell you, no — Rieu
but rather division:
but rather discord — Wms
. . . dissension — Wey
52. For from henceforth
For from now on — Gspd
there shall be five in one house divided,
. . . five persons split into parties —
Wey
a family of five . . . will be on opposite sides — Bas
three against two, and two against three.
Three will form a party against two
. . . — Wey

three in favor of Me, and two against
Me — Tay
53. The father shall be divided against the son, and the son against the father;
A father will decide one way about Me,
his son, the other — Tay
the mother against the daughter, and the daughter against the mother;
. . . opposed to . . . — TCNT
. . . at variance with . . . — Knox
. . . will side against . . . — Rieu
. . . will be set against . . . — Nor
mother and daughter will disagree —
Tay
the mother in law against her daughter in law, and the daughter in law against her mother in law.
54. And he said also to the people,
And he said to the crowds — Gspd
When ye see a cloud rise out of the west,
. . . cloud banking up in the west —
NEB
straightway ye say,
at once you remark — Ber
There cometh a shower;
A thunderstorm is coming — Rhm
That means rain — Nor
and so it is.
and come it does — TCNT
55. And when ye see the south wind blow,
when you feel . . . — Mof
ye say, There will be heat; and it cometh to pass.
A scorching heat will there be . . . —
Rhm
. . . it will be very hot, and hot it is —
Rieu
There will be a heat-wave, and there is
— NEB
56. Ye hypocrites,
You frauds! — Phi
ye can discern
ye know how to interpret — ASV
You know how to read — Wey
. . . to decipher — Mof
. . . to analyze — NASB
the face of the sky and of the earth;
the aspect of . . . — Wey
the look of . . . — Mof
but how is it that ye do not discern
. . . interpret — ASV
. . . decipher — Mof
. . . estimate the meaning of — Ber
. . . analyze — NASB
this time?

the present crisis — Wms
the times you live in — Knox
this fateful hour — NEB

57. Yea, and why even of yourselves judge ye not
Does not your own experience teach you — Knox
Why can you not do better still and out of your own conscience judge — Rieu
what is right?
to make the right decision — Knox
aright — Rieu
what is the right course — NEB

58. When thou goest
When, for instance, you are going — TCNT
with thine adversary
with your opponent — TCNT
to the magistrate,
before a magistrate — TCNT
to court — Wms
as thou art in the way,
on the way there — Mof
before you get there — Rieu
while you have the chance — Phi
give diligence
take pains — Rhm
do your best — TCNT
do your utmost — Mof

make an effort — RSV
bestir yourself — Rieu
try hard — Nor
that thou mayest be delivered from him;
to get a release from him — Rhm
to be quit of his claim — Knox
to settle with him — RSV
lest he hale thee to the judge,
. . . drag thee along . . . — Rhm
. . . hurry you off to . . . — Gspd
. . . rush you . . . — Wms
. . . haul you up . . . — Rieu
and the judge deliver thee to the officer,
. . . turn you over to the sheriff — Wms
. . . to the constable — Gspd
. . . to the police officer — Phi
. . . to the bailiff of the court — TCNT
and the officer cast thee into prison.
. . . put you in jail — NEB

59. I tell thee, thou shalt not depart thence,
Be sure of this, thou wilt find no discharge from it — Knox
. . . you will never get out — Mof
And there, I am sure, you would have to stay — Nor
till thou hast paid the very last mite.
. . . the very last fraction of a cent — TCNT

CHAPTER 13

1. There were present at that season
Just at that time — TCNT
It was just at this moment that — Phi
About this time — Tay
some that told him of the Galilaeans,
some people had come to tell Jesus about the Galilaeans — TCNT
whose blood Pilate had mingled with their sacrifices.
. . . with that of the beasts they had sacrificed — Rieu

2. And Jesus answering said unto them,
He asked in reply — Wey
Suppose ye that these Galilaeans
Are you of the opinion that . . . — Bas
Do you imagine that . . . — NEB
were sinners above all the Galilaeans,
were worse sinners than any other Galilaeans — TCNT
. . . than the mass of the . . . — Wey
because they suffered such things?
because this happened to them — Wey

because these things were done to them — Bas
because this befell them — Knox
because they suffered this fate — Rieu

3. I tell you, Nay:
I assure you it was not so — Wey
No, not at all! And listen! — Nor
but, except ye repent,
if your hearts are not changed — Bas
ye shall all likewise perish.
you will all come to the same end — Bas
you will all perish in much the same way — Rieu
You will all die just as miserable a death — Phi

4. Or those eighteen, upon whom the tower in Siloam fell, and slew them,
Or those eighteen men at Siloam on whom the tower fell, killing them all — TCNT
. . . who were killed . . . when the tower collapsed upon them — Phi

think ye that they were sinners
Are you imagining . . . — Phi
. . . they were worse offenders — Mof
. . . there was a heavier account against them — Knox
. . . they are proved to have been greater transgressors — Rieu
. . . worse culprits — NASB
. . . more guilty — NEB
above all men that dwelt in Jerusalem?
than all the other people living in Jerusalem — NEB

5. I tell you, Nay:
No, they were not — Nor
but, except ye repent,
unless your whole outlook is changed! — Phi
ye shall all likewise perish.
. . . come to an end in the same way — Bas
. . . die as tragically — Phi

6. He spake also this parable;
He used this figure — Gspd
And he went on to speak . . . — Rhm
. . . this story: — Wms
A certain man had a fig tree planted in his vineyard;
. . . growing in his vineyard — TCNT
and he came and sought fruit thereon, and found none.
. . . in search of fruit on it . . . — Mof
. . . but didn't find any — Beck

7. Then said he unto the dresser of his vineyard,
. . . to his gardener — TCNT
. . . to the vineyard hand — Rieu
Behold, these three years I come
Here have I come for three years — Mof
Look here! for three years I have been coming — Wms
seeking fruit on this fig tree,
expecting fruit on . . . — Phi
in the hope of fruit — Rieu
and find none:
without finding any — TCNT
and never found any — Phi
cut it down; why cumbereth it the ground?
. . . Why doth it make even the ground useless — Rhm
. . . Why should it rob the soil — TCNT
. . . take up space — Mof
. . . waste the ground — Gspd
. . . Why should it be a useless charge upon the land — Knox

. . . exhaust the soil — Ber
. . . clutter up the ground for nothing — Rieu

8. And he answering said unto him, Lord, let it alone this year also,
. . . Master, don't touch it this year — Phi
. . . Leave it, sir, just one more year — Wms
till I shall dig about it,
and I will have the earth turned up round it — Bas
and dung it:
and throw in manure — Rhm
and fertilized it — Mon

9. And if it bear fruit, well:
Then, if it bears in future, well and good — TCNT
perhaps it will bear fruit — Knox
and if not, then after that thou shalt cut it down.
. . . then you shall cut it down — Wey
. . . it will be time to cut it down then — Knox

10. And he was teaching in one of the synagogues on the sabbath.
There was a sabbath day on which he was preaching . . . — Knox

11. And, behold, there was a woman
and he saw before him . . . — TCNT
which had a spirit of infirmity eighteen years,
. . . had had a sickness caused by a spirit — Gspd
. . . had suffered from a weakening spirit — Ber
. . . had suffered under some influence that disabled her — Knox
. . . had been ill from some psychological cause — Phi
possessed by a spirit that had crippled her . . . — NEB
. . . afflicted with rheumatism . . . — Lam
and was bowed together,
She was bent double — TCNT
and could in no wise lift up herself.
and wholly unable to raise herself — TCNT
and could not straighten herself up at all — Gspd
quite unable to stand up straight — NEB

12. And when Jesus saw her,
. . . noticed her — Mof
As soon as Jesus saw her — Wms

he called her to him,
He called her over — NASB
**and said unto her, Woman, thou art
loosed**
... you are released — TCNT
... thou art rid — Knox
... liberated — Ber
... set free — Phi
from thine infirmity.
from your weakness — TCNT
from your illness — Phi
... your trouble — NEB

13. **And he laid his hands on her: and immediately she was made straight,**
... stood upright — Wey
... became erect — Mof
... she straightened herself up — Wms
... was raised upright — Knox
and glorified God.
and began glorifying God — Rhm

14. **And the ruler of the synagogue**
But the President of the Synagogue —
TCNT
... synagogue director — Ber
... governor of the ... — Rieu
answered with indignation,
took the matter up. He was indignant — Rieu
in his vexation ... spoke out — Gspd
**because that Jesus had healed on the
sabbath day,**
... had worked the cure on the Sabbath — TCNT
and said unto the people,
retorted to the crowd — Ber
announced to the congregation — Phi
**There are six days in which men ought
to work:**
... six days on which work ought to be
done — TCNT
... six working-days — NEB
... six workdays to be observed —
Ber
... to do your work — Beck
in them therefore come and be healed,
... get yourselves cured — Wey
and not on the sabbath day.
... on the day of rest — Rhm

15. **The Lord then answered him, and said,
Thou hypocrite,**
... O you false men! — Bas
... What hypocrites you are! — NEB
... You play actors — Amp
**doth not each one of you on the sab-
bath loose his ox or his ass from the
stall,**

every single one of you unties his ox
or his ass from the stall on the Sabbath day — Phi
On the Sabbath, do you not one and
all loose your ox or donkey from
the manger — Rieu
... from the feeding trough — Ber
and lead him away to watering?
and take it out to drink — TCNT

16. **And ought not this woman,**
... was it not right for ... — Wms
... was it wrong ... — Knox
... was it not necessary for her — Lam
being a daughter of Abraham,
daughter of Abraham as she is — Wey
**whom Satan hath bound, lo, these
eighteen years,**
... held tied up, mind you, ... — Ber
whom you all know Satan has kept
bound ... — Phi
who has been in the bondage of Satan
— think of it! — for ... — Nor
**be loosed from this bond on the sab-
bath day?**
to have been released ... — TCNT
delivered ... from bonds like these —
Knox
... untied of her bond — Ber

17. **And when he had said these things,**
even while He was saying this — Wms
all his adversaries
His opponents — Wms
all his antagonists — Rieu
all those who had taken sides against
Him — Nor
were ashamed:
were being put to shame — Rhm
were blushing with shame — Wms
felt ashamed — Ber
were covered with confusion — NEB
and all the people rejoiced
the mass of the people were delighted
— NEB
... were rejoicing — Rhm
... felt glad — Ber
the crowd was thrilled — Phi
**for all the glorious things that were
done by him.**
to see all the wonderful things ... —
TCNT
... continually done by Him — Wey

18. **Then said he,**
He went on to say, therefore — Rhm
This led him to say — Mon
Unto what is the kingdom of God like?

What does the kingdom of God resemble — Ber

and whereunto shall I resemble it?

What illustration can I use to make it plain to you — Phi

19. It is like a grain of mustard seed,

. . . like a grain of mustard — ABUV

. . . like a mustard-seed — Wey

which a man took, and cast into his garden;

. . . has taken and planted in . . . — Knox

and it grew, and waxed a great tree;

The seed grew and became a tree — TCNT

soon it grows into a tall bush — Tay

and the fowls of the air lodged in the branches of it.

the wild birds roosted . . . — TCNT

. . . nested . . . — Mon

. . . made nests . . . — RSV

20. And again he said, Whereunto shall I liken the kingdom of God?

. . . What comparison shall I find for . . . — Knox

. . . With what should I compare . . . — Beck

the Reign of God — Mof

21. It is like leaven,

. . . like some yeast — TCNT

which a woman took and hid in three measures of meal,

. . . covered in three pecks of flour — — TCNT

. . . in a bushel of flour — Gspd

. . . put out of sight in three portions of flour — Ber

. . . conceals in three pounds of wheat-meal — Rieu

till the whole was leavened.

to work there till . . . — Wey

until the whole had risen — TCNT

. . . fermented — Beck

enough to leaven the whole batch — Knox

22. And he went through the cities and villages,

And he was journeying on city by city and village by village — Rhm

Jesus went through towns and villages — TCNT

teaching,

teaching as he went — TCNT

and journeying toward Jerusalem.

and making progress unto . . . — Rhm

steadily proceeding towards . . . — Wey

23. Then said one unto him,

. . . someone asked Him — Wey

Lord, are there few that be saved?

Is it only a few, sir, who are saved — Mof

Lord, are only a few people being saved — Rieu

. . . in the path of Salvation — TCNT

And he said unto them,

His answer was — NEB

24. Strive to enter in

You must strain every nerve . . . — Gspd

You must struggle on to get in — Wms

Fight your way in — Knox

You must do your utmost to get in — Phi

Vie with each other to come in — Rieu

at the strait gate:

through the narrow door — Alf

for many, I say unto you, will seek to enter in,

. . . will try to find a way in — Wey

and shall not be able.

and will not succeed — Gspd

And they will not have the power — Rieu

but will not be able to make it — Nor

25. When once the master of the house is risen up, and hath shut to the door,

but when the head of the house has locked the door — Tay

From the hour when . . . — Lam

. . . has got up and shut the door — TCNT

and ye begin to stand without, and to knock at the door,

Then if you stand outside knocking — Tay

and you, still outside, give blows on the door — Bas

. . . knock . . . again and again — Wms

saying, Lord, Lord, open unto us;

pleading, Lord, open the door for us — Tay

. . . let us in — Bas

and he shall answer and say unto you,

But this will be his answer — Knox

I know you not whence ye are:

I do not know you. Where do you come from? — Rieu

26. Then shall ye begin to say,

. . . you will plead — Wey

You will then proceed to say — Mof

Thereupon you will fall to protesting — Knox

We have eaten and drunk in thy presence,

We have been entertained with you — Gspd

We sat at table with you — NEB

we have had meals with you — Phi

and thou hast taught in our streets.

. . . in our broadways . . . — Rhm

27. But he shall say, I tell you,

and his reply will be — TCNT

I know you not whence ye are;

I know nothing of you, nor whence you come — Knox

depart from me,

Leave my presence — TCNT

Begone from me — Wey

Get away from me — Gspd

Be off, you scoundrels! — Phi

Out of my sight — NEB

all ye workers of iniquity.

you that traffic in . . . — Knox

all of you, you and your wicked ways! — NEB

28. There shall be weeping and gnashing of teeth,

There shall be the weeping and the gnashing of teeth — ASV

. . . weeping in that place, and gnashing of teeth — Rieu

At that time there will be tears and bitter regret — Phi

There you will weep and grind your teeth — Gspd

when ye shall see

as soon as ye see — Rhm

Abraham, and Isaac, and Jacob, and all the prophets, in the kingdom of God,

. . . inside the Kingdom . . . — Wey

and you yourselves thrust out.

while you yourselves are being driven outside — TCNT

and find yourselves thrown out — Rieu

. . . excluded, outside! — Phi

29. And they shall come from the east, and from the west, and from the north, and from the south,

Yes, and people will come . . . — Mof

and shall sit down in the kingdom of God.

and take their places at the banquet in the Kingdom of God — TCNT

to take their ease in . . . — Knox

30. And, behold, there are last which shall be first,

Take notice that . . . — Nor

And mark! some now last will be first — Wey

There are some at the back now who will be in front then — Phi

and there are first which shall be last.

and some now first will be last — Wey

31. The same day there came certain of the Pharisees,

In that very hour . . . — ASV

Just then some Pharisees came up to Jesus — TCNT

saying unto him,

who warned Him — Wey

Get thee out,

Get out from here — Mon

Leave this place — Wey

and depart hence:

and continue your journey — Wey

for Herod will kill thee.

Herod means to kill you — Wey

. . . has a mind to . . . — Knox

. . . is out to . . . — NEB

32. And he said unto them, Go ye, and tell that fox,

. . . take this message to that fox — Wey

Behold, I cast out devils, and I do cures to day and to morrow,

Listen: today and tomorrow I shall be casting out devils and working cures — NEB

Here I am, driving out demons and performing cures, today and tomorrow — Gspd

You may take it that to-day and to-morrow I cast out demons and bring my work of healing to an end — Rieu

and the third day I shall be perfected.

. . . I shall have done — TCNT

. . . I finish — Wey

. . . I complete my task — Mof

. . . I will be through — Gspd

. . . I finish my course — Mon

. . . I am to reach my consummation — Knox

. . . my own end is achieved — Rieu

. . . I reach my goal — NEB

33. Nevertheless I must walk to day, and to morrow, and the day following:

But I must journey on . . . — Mof

Yet to you I admit that I am bound to travel on . . . — Rieu

for it cannot be

it is not conceivable — Wey

it would never do — Mof

it is unthinkable — NEB

that a prophet perish out of Jerusalem.
for a prophet to meet his death, except
at Jerusalem — Knox

**34. O Jerusalem, Jerusalem, which killest
the prophets, and stonest them that are
sent unto thee;**
Jerusalem, Jerusalem, still murdering
the prophets, and stoning the messengers that are sent to thee — Knox
**how often would I have gathered thy
children together,**
. . . have I longed to gather your children around me . . . — Gspd
. . . have I desired . . . — Wey
. . . I have yearned . . . — Wms
**as a hen doth gather her brood under
her wings,**
like a bird gathering her brood together
. . . — Phi
and ye would not!
but you refused! — Gspd
but you would never have it — Phi
but you would not let me — NEB
but you say no! — Nor

**35. Behold, your house is left unto you
desolate:**
. . . your house is abandoned to you —
Wey
Now I leave you to yourselves — Gspd
Now your house is abandoned to its
fate! — Wms
. . . your house is forsaken — RSV
Now, all that is left is yourselves, and
your house — Phi
Look, look! there is your temple, forsaken by God — NEB
**and verily I say unto you, Ye shall not
see me,**
I tell you that you will never see me
again — Wey
. . . you shall see nothing of me —
Knox
until the time come when ye shall say,
till the day comes when . . . — Mof
until the time comes . . . — Knox
**Blessed is he that cometh in the name
of the Lord.**
Blessings on him who . . . — NEB

CHAPTER 14

**1. And it came to pass, as he went into
the house**
It happened . . . when he went into the
house — Mon
. . . when he had gone . . . — Alf
of one of the chief Pharisees
of one of the rulers of the Pharisees —
ASV
of one of the Rulers of the Pharisee
party — Wey
of a member of the council who was
a Pharisee — Gspd
to eat bread on the sabbath day,
to dine — TCNT
to take a meal — Wey
that they watched him.
. . . were narrowly watching him —
Rhm
. . . were watching him closely — TCNT
. . . were watching Him carefully —
Beck

**2. And, behold, there was a certain man
before him which had the dropsy.**
Here his eye was met by the sight of a
man who had the dropsy — Knox
Right in front of him was a man afflicted with . . . — Phi

**3. And Jesus answering spake unto the
lawyers and Pharisees, saying,**

This led Jesus to ask the experts in the
Law and the Pharisees — Beck
. . . addressing the Students of the Law
and the . . . — TCNT
Is it lawful
Is it allowable — TCNT
Well, is it right — Phi
Is it permitted — NEB
to heal on the sabbath day?
to work a cure . . . — TCNT
to cure people . . . — Wey
to make people well . . . — Bas
. . . on a day of rest or not — Beck

4. And they held their peace.
But there was no reply — Phi
And he took him,
. . . took hold of the man — TCNT
He then took the patient — Ber
and healed him,
cured him — Wey
made him well — Bas
and let him go;
and dismissed him — Rhm
and sent him away — TCNT

5. And answered them, saying,
And he turned on them, and said —
Knox
**Which of you shall have an ass or an
ox fallen**

Which of you, finding that his son[6] or his ox has fallen — TCNT

Among yourselves, whose son, or whose ox, shall fall — Alf

into a pit,

into a well — ASV

into a water-hole — Bas

and will not straightway pull him out on the sabbath day?

wouldn't you rescue him without the slightest hesitation . . . — Phi

will he hesitate to haul it up . . . — NEB

and will not straightway pull him up on the day of rest — Rhm

6. And they could not answer him again to these things.

And they had no answer to that question — Bas

And they could not contradict that — Ber

This they could not dispute — Mof

7. And he put forth a parable to those which were bidden,

. . . told a parable to the guests — Mof

. . . gave . . . this illustration: — Gspd

. . . told . . . the following story: — Wms

. . . he spoke this lesson: — Ber

Then he gave a little word of advice to the guests — Phi

when he marked

observing — Rhm

when he noticed — Wey

how they chose out

. . . were choosing . . . for themselves — TCNT

. . . picked out — Mof

. . . began choosing — Mon

. . . were trying to secure — NEB

the chief rooms; saying unto them,

the first couches . . . — Rhm

the places of honor . . . — RSV

8. When thou art bidden of any man to a wedding,

. . . invited to a wedding reception — Phi

. . . unto a marriage feast — Rhm

sit not down in the highest room;

do not recline on the first couch — Rhm

do not sit down in the best seat — Mon

. . . in the place of honor — Nor

lest a more honourable man than thou

for fear that someone of higher rank — TCNT

in case a more distinguished guest than yourself — Mof

. . . a more important man . . . — Bas

one more highly esteemed by your host . . . — Ber

. . . a more eminent man than you — RSV

be bidden of him;

has been invited — Mof

9. And he that bade thee and him come and say to thee,

and he who invited you both will come and say to you — TCNT

Give this man place;

Make room for this man — TCNT

Give your place to . . . — Bas

. . . you must give up your seat for . . . — Phi

and thou begin with shame

. . . in confusion — TCNT

. . . with mortification — Mon

. . . in embarrassment — Wms

. . . with a blush — Knox

Then you will look foolish as you begin — NEB

and then in disgrace you proceed — NASB

to take the lowest room.

the last place to occupy — Rhm

to take the lowliest place — Ber

to sit in the humblest place — Phi

10. But when thou art bidden,

But when you are invited anywhere — Gspd

when you receive an invitation — NEB

go and sit down in the lowest room;

pass on and fall back into the last place — Rhm

go straight to the lowest place and sit down there — Knox

go and take your seat in an inconspicuous place — Phi

that when he that bade thee cometh, he may say unto thee,

that when your host comes . . . — Wey

Friend, go up higher:

. . . come close up higher — Rhm

Move higher up, my friend — Mof

. . . come to a better place — Gspd

. . . go higher than this — Knox

Come on, my dear fellow, we have a much better seat than this for you — Phi

---

[6]Alternative reading.

then shalt thou have worship
Then shalt thou have honour — Rhm
So you will be shown consideration —
Gspd
That is the way to be important — Phi
. . . you will have distinction — Nor
**in the presence of them that sit at meat
with thee.**
in the eyes of all your fellow-guests —
TCNT
before all that sit down in thy company
— Knox
. . . all who sit at table with you —
RSV

11. For whosoever exalteth himself
. . . who gives himself a high place —
Bas
. . . makes himself prominent — Ber
If you honor yourself — Beck
shall be abased;
shall be humbled — ASV
you'll be humbled — Beck
and he that humbleth himself
and he that abaseth himself — Rhm
the man who makes himself insignificant — Phi
shall be exalted.
shall be set high — Ber
will find himself important — Phi

**12. Then said he also to him that bade
him,**
. . . he went on to say . . . — Rhm
. . . to his host — Mof
**When thou makest a dinner or a sup-
per,**
When you put on a dinner or supper —
Nor
. . . give a breakfast or a dinner—TCNT
. . . a dinner or a supper — Rhm
. . . a luncheon or a dinner party —
Phi
**call not thy friends, nor thy brethren,
neither thy kinsmen, nor thy rich
neighbours;**
stop the social custom of inviting your
friends or your brothers or your relatives or your rich neighbors — Wms
. . . or your well-to-do neighbors — Ber
lest they also bid thee again,
. . . invite you in return — TCNT
. . . ask you back again — NEB
and a recompence be made thee.
and so repay your hospitality — Wey
and you get repaid — Mof

13. But when thou makest a feast,
No, when you entertain — TCNT

. . . when you give a reception — Wms
. . . when you give a party — Phi
**call the poor, the maimed, the lame,
the blind:**
make it your habit to invite people that
are . . . — Wms
. . . the poor, crippled, . . . — Beck
. . . the poor, the disabled, . . . — Amp
invite the destitute, the tried, the lame,
the blind — Rhm

14. And thou shalt be blessed;
and then you will be happy indeed —
TCNT
. . . you will have a blessing — Bas
then blessing will be yours — Ber
That way lies real happiness for you
— Phi
for they cannot recompense thee:
because they have no means of repay-
ing you — Wey
for these cannot make thee any return
— Knox
for thou shalt be recompensed
but you will be repaid . . . — Wey
thy reward will come . . . — Knox
at the resurrection of the just.
in the resurrection of the righteous —
Rhm
. . . of the upright — Gspd

**15. And when one of them that sat at meat
with him heard these things, he said
unto him,**
On hearing this, one of His fellow
guests . . . — Wey
. . . one of those who were at table
with him . . . — Bas
Blessed is he that
Happy will he be who — TCNT
Happy is he who — Beck
What happiness for a man — Phi
Blessed is everyone who — NASB
What a privilege it would be — Tay
shall eat bread in the kingdom of God.
feasts in the Realm of God — Mof
shall be at the banquet in the Kingdom
of God — Gspd
dines in . . . — Rieu
to get into the Kingdom of God! —
Tay

16. Then said he unto him,
But He told him — Ber
A certain man made a great supper,
A man was once giving a great dinner
— TCNT
Once upon a time, a man planned a
big dinner party — Phi

and bade many:
. . . invited a large number of guests —
Wey
. . . sent out many invitations — Knox

17. And sent his servant at supper time
and he sent out his servant at the hour
of the supper — Rhm
and at the time for the banquet he sent
his servant — RSV
Toward supper time a servant was
sent — Nor
to say to them that were bidden,
to say unto the invited — Rhm
with a message for his guests — NEB
. . . to remind them — Nor
Come; for all things are now ready.
Come, it's ready now! — Beck

18. And they all with one consent
. . . with one mind — ABUV
. . . without exception — Wey
. . . all alike — Mof
. . . all in the same attitude — Wms
. . . unanimously — Ber
. . . as one man — Phi
But they all, everyone of them — Nor
began to make excuse.
proceeded to decline — Mof
gave reasons why they were not able
to come — Bas
**The first said unto him, I have bought
a piece of ground,**
. . . a field — TCNT
. . . a farm — Mof
. . . some land — Phi
and I must needs go and see it:
I am forced . . . — Lam
I simply must go . . . — Ber
I've got to go out . . . — Beck
and am obliged to go and look at it —
TCNT
I pray thee have me excused.
Please excuse me — Wms
. . . count me excused — Knox
Please let me be excused — Rieu
please accept my apologies — NEB

**19. And another said, I have bought five
yoke of oxen,**
. . . five pairs of bullocks — TCNT
. . . five teams of oxen — Beck
and I go to prove them:
and I am on my way to try them —
TCNT
. . . to examine them — Gspd
. . . to make a test of them — Bas
. . . to try them out — Phi

I pray thee have me excused.
Please convey my apologies — Phi

**20. And another said, I have married a
wife,**
. . . I am just married — TCNT
and therefore I cannot come.
and for that reason I am unable to
come — TCNT
It is impossible for me to . . . — Wey

**21. So that servant came, and shewed his
lord these things.**
So the slave went back, and reported
this to his master — Gspd
. . . reported these answers to his master — Wms
**Then the master of the house being
angry**
. . . provoked to anger — Rhm
whereupon the host fell into a rage
— Knox
. . . was extremely annoyed — Phi
. . . was enraged — Mof
and it stirred his anger — Wey
said to his servant,
**Go out quickly into the streets and
lanes of the city,**
Quick, go out to . . . — Mof
. . . into the broadways and . . . — Rhm
. . . and alleys of the town — TCNT
**and bring in hither the poor, and the
maimed, and the halt, and the blind.**
. . . the poor, and the crippled . . . —
TCNT
. . . the poor and the disabled . . . —
Amp
and get . . . the lame and blind to come
— Nor
and the destitute and tried, and blind
and lame bring thou in here — Rhm

**22. And the servant said, Lord, it is done
as thou hast commanded,**
. . . your order has been carried out —
TCNT
. . . I have done what you told me, sir
— Phi
. . . Master, it's done as you ordered —
Beck
and yet there is room.
but there is room left still — Knox
. . . there are still empty places — Phi
. . . still room for more — Rieu

**23. And the lord said unto the servant, Go
out into the highways and hedges,**
the master said . . . — Mof
. . . go out among the highways and
fences — Rhm

. . . to the high roads and hedge-rows
— Wey
. . . on the roads, and among the hedges
— Gspd
. . . upon the highways and byways —
Nor
. . . out into the country lanes and out
behind the hedges — Tay
and compel them to come in,
and press people to come in — Mof
and make people come in — TCNT
. . . urge them . . . — Lam
and give them no choice but to . . . —
Knox
and force them . . . — Ber
that my house may be filled.
to fill up my house — Mof
I want my house to be full — NEB

24. **For I say unto you,**
for I tell you all — TCNT
**That none of those men which were
bidden**
not one of those invited guests — Mon
. . . who were first invited — Knox
shall taste of my supper.
shall get a taste of . . . — Wms

25. **And there went great multitudes with
him:**
On His journey vast crowds attended
Him — Wey
. . . were . . . travelling with him —
Mof
. . . were going along with him — Mon
. . . followed Him — Nor
and he turned, and said unto them,
and all at once He turned and . . . —
Wms
He turned around and spoke to them
— Nor

26. **If any man come to me,**
Anyone that comes to me — Rieu
Anyone who wants to be My follower
— Tay
**and hate not his father, and mother,
and wife, and children, and brethren, and sisters,**
without hating his own . . . — Gspd
without prizing far less dearly . . . —
Ber
without 'hating' his father . . . — Phi
and does not, in comparison, hate . . .
— Nor
must love Me far more than he does
his own father . . . — Tay
yea, and his own life also,
and what is more, . . . — ABUV

yes, and even his own life — RSV
yes, more than his own life — Tay
he cannot be my disciple.
he can be no disciple of mine — TCNT
otherwise he cannot be My disciple —
Tay

27. **And whosoever doth not bear his cross,**
. . . take up his own cross — Gspd
. . . persevere in carrying . . . — Wms
. . . shoulder his cross — Rieu
and come after me,
and walk in my steps — TCNT
and thus follow after me — Wms
cannot be my disciple.
cannot be a disciple of mine — Mof

28. **For which of you, intending to build**
. . . has a mind to build . . . — Knox
a tower,
a farm-building — Amp
**sitteth not down first, and counteth the
cost,**
. . . calculate the expense — Mof
. . . estimate the cost — Gspd
. . . to figure out the expense — Ber
. . . work out the cost of it — Phi
whether he have sufficient to finish it?
to see if he has enough money to complete it — Mof
to see if he has the means to complete
it — Mon
to see if he can afford to finish it —
Phi

29. **Lest haply, after he hath laid the foundation,**
Lest, perchance, . . . — Wms
Otherwise, when he has laid a foundation — RSV
and is not able to finish it,
and is not able to go on with it to the
end — Bas
and his resources fail before the end —
Rieu
all that behold it
all the spectators — Mof
everyone watching — Rieu
all the onlookers — NEB
begin to mock him,
. . . to jeer at him — Wey
. . . make fun of . . . — Mof
. . . ridicule . . . — Gspd
. . . make sport of . . . — Wms

30. **Saying, This man began to build,**
. . . Here is a man . . . — TCNT
. . . started to erect a building — Gspd
. . . made a start at building — Bas
and was not able to finish.

but he couldn't finish the job! — Nor

31. Or what king, going to make war against another king,

... marching to encounter ... in war — Wey

... setting out to wage war on ... — Rieu

... going to engage in conflict with ... — Amp

sitteth not down first, and consulteth

will not sit down first and take counsel — ASV

whether he be able with ten thousand to meet him

whether ... he can meet the onset of one — Knox

whether with ten thousand men he can face the one — Rieu

that cometh against him with twenty thousand?

who is coming at him with twice that number — Rieu

32. Or else, while the other is yet a great way off,

and, if he cannot ... — TCNT

And if he decides he can't ... — Phi

... long before the enemy approaches — NEB

he sendeth an ambassage,

he sends representatives — Bas

he despatches envoys — Knox

... a delegation — Ber

and desireth conditions of peace.

and asks on what terms he will make peace — Gspd

and asks for terms — NEB

33. So likewise, whosoever he be of you

This applies to everyone of you: — Nor

And so with every one of you — TCNT

In just that way, no one of you — Gspd

that forsaketh not

biddeth not farewell — Alf

doth not bid adieu unto — Rhm

who does not say goodbye to — Gspd

is not ready to give up — Bas

all that he hath,

all his own possessions — Rhm

all that belongs to him — Wey

all his goods — Mof

he cannot be my disciple.

he cannot be a disciple of mine — TCNT

34. Salt is good:

Salt, as I have said ... — Rieu

Yes, salt is good — TCNT

... excellent indeed — Mof

but if the salt have lost his savour,

... salt itself should lose its strength — TCNT

... become tasteless — Rhm

... becomes insipid — Mof

... itself deteriorates — Rieu

wherewith shall it be seasoned?

how will you restore its flavour — Wey

how can that strength be restored — Wms

what is there left to give taste to it — Knox

how shall its saltness be restored — RSV

35. It is neither fit for the land, nor yet for the dunghill;

It is no use for either soil or dunghill — Mof

It is fit neither for the ground nor the manure heap — Gspd

It is fit for neither soil nor manure — Wms

... nor for fertilizing — Lam

but men cast it out.

it is flung out — Mof

People simply throw it away — Nor

it is thrown out — Lam

He that hath ears to hear, let him hear.

... let him listen to this — Mof

Let him who has ears to hear with give heed! — Wms

CHAPTER 15

1. Then drew near unto him all the publicans and sinners

Now all the publicans and sinners were drawing near ... — ASV

But all the tax-collectors and the sinners ... — Rhm

... were everywhere in the habit of coming close to Him — Wey

... and notorious sinners ... — Wms

... and irreligious people ... — Gspd

... and the outcasts were consorting with him — Rieu

for to hear him.

to hear what he had to say — Phi

to hear him speak — Rieu

2. And the Pharisees and scribes murmured,

... began to complain — Mon

... began grumbling among themselves — NEB

. . . kept muttering and indignantly complaining — Amp
. . . found fault — TCNT
. . . and the Doctors of the Law shook their heads at one another — Rieu
But the Pharisees and the Bible scholars grumbled — Beck

saying, This man receiveth sinners,
This fellow, they said, welcomes sinners — NEB
Here is a man . . . that entertains . . . — Knox
This man always welcomes outcasts . . . they complained — TCNT
. . . irreligious people — Gspd
. . . notorious sinners — Wms

and eateth with them.
and even eats his meals with them — Phi

3. And he spake this parable unto them, saying;
So in speaking to them he used this figure: — Gspd
. . . told them the following story: — Wms
He answered them with this parable: — NEB

4. What man of you, having an hundred sheep, if he lose one of them, doth not leave the ninety and nine in the wilderness,
. . . out in the open country — TCNT
. . . in their desert pasture — Wey
. . . in the open — Lam
. . . alone where they are — Ber

and go after that which is lost, until he find it?
and continue to look for the lost one until he finds it — Wms

5. And when he hath found it,
And when he does find it — Knox

he layeth it on his shoulders, rejoicing.
How delighted he is then! He lifts it on to his shoulders — NEB

6. And when he cometh home,
and so goes home — Knox
and, on reaching home — TCNT
and home he goes — NEB

he calleth together his friends and neighbours,
to call his friends and neighbours together — NEB

saying unto them, Rejoice with me;
Rejoice with me! he cries — NEB
. . . Congratulate me — Gspd
. . . Be glad with me — Bas

. . . Come and celebrate with me — Phi

for I have found my sheep which was lost.
I found . . . — Beck
. . . that sheep of mine . . . — Phi
. . . my sheep — the one I had lost — Wey

7. I say unto you, that likewise
I tell you that in the same way — Wey

joy shall be in heaven
there will be more rejoicing in Heaven — TCNT

over one sinner that repenteth,
over a single sinner . . . — Mof
when one sinner is turned away from his wrongdoing — Bas

more than over ninety and nine just persons,
. . . righteous . . . — ASV
. . . upright people — Gspd
. . . law-abiding people — Rieu

which need no repentance.
who stand in no need of . . . — Ber
. . . a change of heart — Bas

8. Either what woman having ten pieces of silver,
Or again, what woman who has ten silver coins — TCNT

if she lose one piece,
at losing one of them — Ber

doth not light a candle, and sweep the house,
does she not light the lamp, sweep out the house — NEB
does she not light a lamp and scour the house — Mof

and seek diligently till she find it?
and look in every corner till she has found it — NEB
and search carefully until she finds it — TCNT
. . . anxiously . . . — Mon
. . . relentlessly . . . — Rieu
. . . from top to bottom . . . — Phi

9. And when she hath found it,
And when she does find it — Knox

she calleth her friends and her neighbours together, saying,
gathers her women-friends and . . . — Mof

Rejoice with me;
Congratulate me — Wey
Be glad with me — Bas
Come and celebrate with me — Phi

for I have found the piece which I

had lost.

I found . . . — Beck

. . . that coin I lost — Phi

10. **Likewise, I say unto you, there is joy
in the presence of the angels of God**

In just that way, I tell you . . . — Gspd

I can tell you it is that way also among
. . . — Nor

. . . the messengers of God — Rhm

Such, I assure you, is the jubilation of
God's Angels — Rieu

over one sinner that repenteth.

over one outcast . . . — TCNT

over a single sinner . . . — Mof

. . . whose heart is changed — Phi

over one sinner repenting — Rhm

11. **And he said, A certain man had two
sons:**

He further said . . . — Ber

. . . There was a man who had two sons
— Wey

12. **And the younger of them said to his
father,**

**Father, give me the portion of goods
that falleth to me.**

. . . the share of the property . . . —
Wey

. . . of the estate . . . — Knox

. . . which is coming to me — Mon

And he divideth unto them his living.

So he divided his means among them
— Mof

. . . between the two of them — Phi

So he apportioned to them his means of
living — Ber

So the father divided the property between them — TCNT

13. **And not many days after the younger
son gathered all together,**

Not many days later, the younger son
sold off everything — Mof

A few days later the younger son got
together all that he had — TCNT

. . . turned the whole of his share into
cash — NEB

. . . cashed in all he had — Beck

**and took his journey into a far coun-
try,**

left home for a country far away—
Rhm

and went abroad to a distant land —
Mof

and there wasted his substance

and there he squandered his inheritance — TCNT

. . . scattered his wealth — Lam

. . . his fortune — Knox

with riotous living.

with reckless living — Alf

in living unsavingly — Mon

by living a dissolute life — TCNT

in the wildest extravagance — Phi

14. **And when he had spent all,**

And when he had run through all his
money — Phi

After he had spent all that he had —
TCNT

**there arose a mighty famine in that
land;**

a severe famine set in throughout that
land — Mof

a terrible famine visited . . . — Ber

. . . struck that country — Wms

and he began to be in want.

. . . to feel the pinch of want — Wey

. . . found himself in want — Knox

. . . faced starvation — Rieu

15. **And he went and joined himself to**

. . . and engaged himself to — TCNT

. . . attached himself to — Mof

So he hired himself to — Wey

. . . imposed himself upon — Ber

a citizen of that country;

one of the local landowners — NEB

and he sent him into his fields

who put him on his farm — Knox

to feed swine.

to give the pigs their food — Bas

to feed the pigs — Phi

to mind the pigs — NEB

16. **And he would fain have filled his belly**

And he was longing to be filled — Mon

And often he craved to fill himself —
Wms

He even longed to satisfy his hunger
— TCNT

He got to the point of longing to stuff
himself — Phi

with the husks that the swine did eat:

with the bean-pods on which the pigs
were feeding — TCNT

. . . were eating — Rhm

and no man gave unto him.

and not a soul gave him anything —
Phi

17. **And when he came to himself, he said,**

But when he came to his senses . . . —
Mof

This brought him to himself . . . —
Rieu

**How many hired servants of my
father's**

How many of my father's hired hands
— Ber
... paid servants — NEB
have bread enough and to spare,
have more than enough to eat — Mof
... an abundance of food — Nor
and I perish with hunger!
and here am I perishing ... — Mof
and here I am starving! — Ber

18. **I will arise and go to my father, and will say unto him,**
I will be up and off to my father ... — Mof
Father, I have sinned against heaven,
... I sinned ... — TCNT
and before thee.
and against you — TCNT
and in your eyes — Gspd

19. **And am no more worthy**
No longer am I worthy — Rhm
... fit — TCNT
I no longer deserve — Wey
to be called thy son:
to be called a son of thine — Rhm
make me as one of thy hired servants.
treat me as ... — Wey
take me on as one of your hired hands
— Ber
... paid servants — NEB

20. **And he arose, and came to his father.**
... and went on his way to his father
— Knox
So he set out for his father's house —
NEB
But when he was yet a great way off,
But, while he was still a long way off
— TCNT
... far away — Mof
... at a distance — Lam
his father saw him, and had compassion,
... and was deeply moved — TCNT
... and his heart was moved with pity
for him — Wms
... and took pity on him — Knox
... and his heart went out to him —
Phi
and ran,
He ran to meet him — NEB
and fell on his neck,
and threw his arms round his neck —
TCNT
flung his arms round him — NEB
and kissed him.
gave him a kiss — Bas

21. **And the son said unto him, Father, I**

have sinned against heaven, and in thy sight, and am no more worthy to be called thy son.
... to be recognized as a son of yours
— Amp
... I don't deserve to be called your
son any more ... — Phi[7]

22. **But the father said to his servants,**
... to his slaves — Gspd
But the father turned to his servants
and said — TCNT
Bring forth the best robe, and put it on him;
Quick! bring forth a robe — the best!
and put on him — Rhm
and put a ring on his hand, and shoes on his feet:
give him a ring for ... and sandals for
... — Mof

23. **And bring hither the fatted calf, and kill it;**
get the calf we are fattening ... —
Gspd
get that calf we've fattened ... — Phi
and let us eat, and be merry:
and we will have a feast and a celebration! — Phi
and let us have a feast to celebrate the
day — NEB

24. **For this my son was dead,**
for here is my son who was dead —
TCNT
for this is my son — I thought he was
dead — Phi
and is alive again;
and he's alive again — Phi
and has come to life again — Wey
he was lost, and is found.
I thought I had lost him, and he's
found! — Phi
And they began to be merry.
... to celebrate — Gspd
... to get the festivities going — Phi
and so they began their merry-making
— Knox

25. **Now his elder son was in the field:**
Meanwhile ... was out in the fields —
TCNT
... out on the farm — Wey
and as he came and drew nigh to the house,

---

[7]Compare verses 18,19 and note how Phillips shows that the "prepared speech" was interrupted.

as he approached the house on his way
back — Rieu

he heard musick and dancing.
. . . the sound of . . . — Nor

26. And he called one of the servants
So he called one of the servants . . .
across to him — Phi
. . . one of the lads — Wey
and asked
and began to inquire — Mon
what these things meant.
what it all meant — TCNT
what was going on — Nor

**27. And he said unto him, Thy brother is
come;**
. . . Thy brother has come back—Knox
. . . has arrived — Mof
**and thy father hath killed the fatted
calf,**
. . . the calf he has been fattening —
Gspd
. . . has had the fat calf killed — Wey
because he hath received him
glad to have him restored — Knox
because he has got him back — Mof
. . . has got him home again — Phi
safe and sound.
alive and well — Gspd

28. And he was angry,
This made him angry — TCNT
At this he fell into a rage — Knox
But he was furious — Phi
and would not go in:
and did not care to go in — Rieu
and would not go into the house —
Gspd
**therefore came his father out, and in-
treated him.**
. . . began to entreat him — Rhm
. . . attempted to plead with him—Mon
. . . tried to win him over — Knox

29. And he answering said to his father,
Then he burst out: — Phi
but he retorted — NEB
Lo, these many years do I serve thee,
look at all the years I have been serving
you — TCNT
. . . I have been slaving for you — Mon
**neither transgressed I at any time thy
commandment:**
I have never disobeyed a commandment of yours — Mon
and yet thou never gavest me a kid,
. . . as much as a young goat — Nor
**that I might make merry with my
friends:**

. . . entertain my friends — Gspd
. . . celebrate with my friends — Wms
for a feast with my friends — NEB

30. But as soon as this thy son was come,
But when this son of yours came —
Mon
. . . turns up — NEB
But here comes that son of yours —
Rieu
**which hath devoured thy living with
harlots,**
. . . has swallowed up his patrimony
. . . — Knox
after running through your money with
his women — NEB
. . . with women of the street — Gspd
when he and his harlots have got
through your estate — Rieu
thou hast killed for him the fatted calf.
then you go and kill the fattened calf
for him! — Nor
. . . in his honour — Knox
for him you kill the calf we've fattened! — Phi

31. And he said unto him, Son,
You, my dear son, . . . — Wey
My boy, . . . — Rieu
thou art ever with me,
you and I are always together — Mof
you have been with me all the time —
Gspd
and all that I have is thine.
And all that is mine is thine — Rhm
. . . is already thine — Knox
and everything I have is yours — Phi

**32. It was meet that we should make
merry, and be glad:**
We were bound to . . . — Wey
But we had to celebrate and show our
joy — Phi
but for this merry-making and rejoicing there was good reason — Knox
How could we help celebrating this
happy day? — NEB
for this thy brother was dead,
for here is your brother who was dead
— TCNT
for this brother of yours . . . — Wey
For this is your brother; I thought he
was dead — Phi
because your brother was dead—Gspd
and is alive again;
and has come to life — Gspd
and was lost, and is found.
I thought he was lost—and he is found!
— Phi

CHAPTER 16

1. And he said also unto his disciples,
And he went on to say . . . — Rhm
He further told . . . — Ber
There was a certain rich man, which had a steward;
. . . who employed a manager — Nor
. . . an accountant — Tay
and the same was accused unto him
whose agent was reported to him — Phi
and this steward was maliciously accused to him — TCNT
he received complaints that this man — NEB
. . . charges were brought to him — RSV
that he had wasted his goods.
. . . mismanaging his property — Phi
. . . squandering . . . — Gspd

2. And he called him, and said unto him,
So he called him in . . . — Gspd
he sent for him . . . — Knox
How is it that I hear this of thee?
What is this that I am hearing . . . — Wms
give an account of thy stewardship;
Give in your accounts — TCNT
Send in your agency accounts — Rieu
Hand in an account of your management — Ber
Produce your accounts — NEB
Turn in the account of your stewardship — RSV
Make an accounting for your conduct of my affairs — Gspd
for thou mayest be no longer steward.
for I cannot let you hold it any longer — Wey
for you cannot act as . . . — TCNT
. . . manager any longer — Gspd
You cannot be my agent any longer — Rieu

3. Then the steward said within himself,
And the manager of the estate said to himself — Amp
What shall I do?
What am I to do — TCNT
for my lord taketh away from me the stewardship:
now that my employer deprives me of my managership — Ber
now that my employer is taking . . . — Phi
. . . my position away from me — Gspd
. . . is depriving me of my employment — Rieu

I cannot dig;
Dig I cannot — Rhm
I have not strength to dig — TCNT
I am too weak . . . — Mof
. . . for field labour — Wey
. . . to dig ditches — Nor
to beg I am ashamed.
I can't sink to begging — Phi
and too proud to beg — NEB

4. I am resolved what to do,
Ah! I see what to do — Wey
Say! I know what . . . — Nor
that, when I am put out of the stewardship,
when I am deposed from . . . — Mof
. . . removed from my position — Gspd
when I have lost the agency — Rieu
. . . when I am discharged from my management — Ber
they may receive me into their houses.
people may give me a home in their houses — Wey
I know how to make them welcome me to their houses — Rieu

5. So he called every one of his lord's debtors unto him,
Then he called in . . . — Gspd
. . . every single one of his master's debtors — Mof
. . . every one of his employer's tenants — Rieu
. . . one by one — Wey
and said unto the first, How much owest thou unto my lord?
. . . are you in debt to . . . — Wey
. . . What rent do you have to pay my employer — Rieu

6. And he said, An hundred measures of oil.
A hundred barrels of . . . — Mof
Eight hundred gallons of . . . — Gspd
. . . olive oil — Tay
And he said unto him, Take thy bill,
Here is your agreement, he said—TCNT
Take your lease, he said — Rieu
and sit down quickly,
sit right down — Gspd
and write fifty.
alter it to . . . — Wey
. . . four hundred! — Gspd

7. Then said he to another, And how much owest thou?
. . . And you, what is your rent — Rieu

And he said, An hundred measures of wheat.

... A hundred sacks ... — Ber

One thousand bushels ... — TCNT

And he said unto him, Take thy bill,

Here is your agreement, he said—TCNT

Take your lease, ... — Rieu

and write fourscore.

change it to ... — Mon

make it eight hundred — TCNT

8. And the lord commended

His master complimented — TCNT

... applauded — NEB

the unjust steward,

this dishonest agent — Rieu

this knavish steward — Knox

because he had done wisely:

on the shrewdness of his action—TCNT

for acting so astutely — NEB

for looking ahead — Mof

because he had been so careful for his own future — Phi

because he acted with shrewd business sense — Wms

for the children of this world

... men of the world — TCNT

For the worldly — NEB

are in their generation

in dealing with their fellow-men — TCNT

in their relation to their own age — Gspd

in dealing with their contemporaries — Phi

in their dealings with their own kind — Rieu

in temporal matters — Nor

wiser than

act with more business sense — Wms

are more astute — NEB

the children of light.

those who have the Light — TCNT

the men who enjoy spiritual light — Wms

the other-worldly — NEB

9. And I say unto you,

And my counsel to you is — Knox

Make to yourselves friends

Win friends for yourselves — TCNT

of the mammon of unrighteousness;

by the right use of your money, which so easily tends to wrongdoing — Wms

with the money that's often used in wrong ways — Beck

your worldly wealth — NEB

from out of this dishonest world—Rieu

that, when ye fail,

so that, when it comes to an end[8] — TCNT

so that when money is a thing of the past — NEB

they may receive you

your friends may welcome you—Wms

into everlasting habitations.

to the tents that never perish — Wey

to the eternal abodes — Mof

to the tents of eternity — Rieu

into an eternal home — NEB

10. He that is faithful in that which is least

... trustworthy in the smallest matter — TCNT

... faithful with a trifle — Mof

... dependable ... — Wms

... over a little sum — Knox

... in the little things — Phi

is faithful also in much:

is dependable also in a large deal — Wms

... in the big things — Phi

... in the important — Ber

... with a large trust — Mof

and he that is unjust in the least

he who plays false over a little sum — Knox

... who cheats in the little things — Phi

... who is dishonest in small matters — Nor

is unjust also in much.

... dishonest with a large trust — Mof

... in a large deal — Wms

11. If therefore ye have not been faithful

So, if you have proved untrustworthy — TCNT

... could not be trusted — Knox

in the unrighteous mammon,

with the 'dishonest money,' — TCNT

in your use of ... — Bas

in matters of deceitful riches — Ber

to deal with the wicked wealth of this world — Phi

in your dealings with the dishonest world — Rieu

with the wealth of this world — NEB

in money matters — Nor

who will commit to your trust

... entrust to you — Wey

---

[8]An alternative reading.

how can you ever be trusted with —
Mof
the true riches?
the true good — Wey
that which is really good — Beck

12. **And if ye have not been faithful**
if you have proved untrustworthy —
TCNT
in that which is another man's,
with what belongs to another — Wey
with what was only lent to you —
Knox
in handling another's wealth — Rieu
**who shall give you that which is your
own?**
what is really our own — TCNT
. . . what belongs to you — Gspd
. . . anything for your personal possession — Ber
. . . property to have as your own —
Nor

13. **No servant can serve two masters:**
No house-servant can be a slave to . . .
— Wms
. . . can belong to . . . — Gspd
**for either he will hate the one, and
love the other;**
He is bound to hate one and love the
other — Phi
or else he will hold to the one,
. . . attach himself to one — TCNT
. . . cling to the one — Mon
. . . will be devoted to one — Wms
. . . will support the one — Ber
or give his loyalty to one — Phi
and despise the other.
think nothing of the second — NEB
Ye cannot serve God and mammon.
. . . be the slave both of God and of
gold — Mon
. . . God and the power of money at
the same time — Phi

14. **And the Pharisees also, who were
covetous,**
. . . lovers of money — Rhm
. . . who were fond of money — Mof
heard all these things:
were listening to . . . — NASB
All this was said within hearing of the
Pharisees — TCNT
and they derided him.
and were openly sneering at him —
Rhm
and they were scoffing at Him — NASB
bitterly jeering at Him — Wey
and they ridiculed him — Gspd

were making sport of him — Bas
and poured scorn on him — Knox
and turned up their noses at Him —
Beck

15. **And he said unto them, Ye are they
which justify yourselves before men;**
. . . You are always courting the approval of men — Knox
. . . You are the people who impress
your fellow men with your righteousness — NEB
but God knoweth your hearts:
. . . can read your hearts — TCNT
but God sees through you — NEB
**for that which is highly esteemed
among men**
What is lofty in the view of man —
Mof
what the world esteems — Rieu
what sets itself up to be admired by
men — NEB
is abomination in the sight of God.
loathsome . . . — Mof
detestable . . . — Wms
disgusting . . . — Lam

16. **The law and the prophets were until
John:**
. . . sufficed until the time of . . . —
TCNT
. . . continued until John came — Wey
. . . lasted till John — Mof
. . . were in force until John's day —
Phi
**since that time the kingdom of God is
preached,**
from that time the gospel of the kingdom of God is preached — ASV
. . . the gospel of . . . has been spreading
— Wey
and every man presseth into it.
and anyone presses in — Mof
and everyone has been crowding into it
— Gspd
and everyone is storming his way into
it — Rieu
and they come crowding in — Nor

17. **And it is easier for heaven and earth
to pass,**
. . . sky and earth . . . — Wey
. . . to disappear — TCNT
. . . come to an end — Bas
than one tittle of the law
. . . one stroke of a letter in the Law —
TCNT
. . . one dotting of an *i* in . . . — Gspd
. . . one dot or stroke . . . — NEB

... the smallest detail ... — Wey
to fail.
to lapse — Wey
to become void — RSV
to become a dead letter — Phi
to be deleted — Rieu
to lose its force — NEB

18. **Whosoever putteth away his wife,**
Everyone who divorces his wife—TCNT
Any man who divorces his wife — Wey
and marrieth another,
... marries another woman — TCNT
... marries someone else — Mon
committeth adultery:
is an adulterer — TCNT
is untrue in married life — Bas
is living in adultery — Beck
and whosoever marrieth her that is put away from her husband
... marries a divorced woman — TCNT
committeth adultery.
is an adulterer — TCNT
is untrue in married life — Bas
he too is an adulterer — Knox
is living in adultery — Beck

19. **There was a certain rich man, which was clothed in purple and fine linen,**
... who used to dress in ... — Wms
... and he habitually dressed in ... — NASB
and fared sumptuously every day:
making merry day by day brilliantly — Rhm[9]
feasted every day in great splendour — TCNT
... in dazzling luxury — Wms
... in great magnificence — NEB

20. **And there was a certain beggar named Lazarus,**
... utterly destitute man ... —Amp
which was laid at his gate,
who lay ... — Knox
at his outer door ... — Wey
full of sores,
he was a mass of ulcers — Mof

21. **And desiring to be fed with**
longing to make a meal off — Wey
eager to satisfy his hunger with—Gspd
always craving to get a square meal from — Wms
the crumbs which fell from the rich man's table:
the scraps falling on the floor ... — Wey
moreover the dogs came and licked his sores.

Nay, the dogs, too, used to come and ... — Wey
Even the dogs, as they came along, ... — Ber

22. **And it came to pass, that the beggar died,**
In course of time ... — Wey
and was carried by the angels
and was carried away ... — Gspd
... was borne away by ... — Rieu
into Abraham's bosom:
to be Abraham's bosom companion — — Wms
to Abraham's arms — Rieu
the rich man also died, and was buried;
The rich man died too, ... — Mof

23. **And in hell**
And in Hades — ASV
And from among the dead — Phi
he lift up his eyes, being in torments,
he looked up in his torment — TCNT
... in constant tortures as he was — Wms
and seeth Abraham afar off,
and saw Abraham at a distance—TCNT
and Lazarus in his bosom.
... resting in his arms — Wey
and Lazarus at his side — TCNT

24. **And he cried, and said, Father Abraham,**
And he called to him and said ... — Gspd
And he gave a cry and said ... — Bas
have mercy on me,
take pity on me — Wey
and send Lazarus, that he may dip the tip of his finger in water, and cool my tongue;
... to wet the tip of his finger ... — Rieu
for I am tormented in this flame.
for I am suffering agony ... — TCNT
for I am in anguish ... — ASV
... here in the flames! — Gspd

25. **But Abraham said, Son,**
... Child — TCNT
remember that thou in thy lifetime receivedst thy good things,
... received in full your blessings — Wms
... you got all the bliss when you were alive — Mof
and likewise Lazarus evil things:

---

[9]Compare Luke 15:23,32.

just as Lazarus got the ills of life —
  Mof
. . . had his misfortunes in his — Gspd
but now he is comforted,
but now he has his consolation here —
  TCNT
he is in comfort now — Mof
now he is being cheered here — Ber
and thou art tormented.
and you are in pain — Bas
. . . in anguish — ASV

26. And beside all this,
But that is not all . . . — NEB
**between us and you there is a great
  gulf fixed:**
. . . there lies a great chasm — TCNT
. . . a great gulf yawns . . . — Mof
. . . a great chasm has been fixed — RSV
**so that they which would pass from
  hence to you cannot;**
in order that those who wish . . . may
  not be able — NASB
**neither can they pass to us, that would
  come from thence.**
and that none may cross over from
  thence to us — ASV

**27. Then he said, I pray thee therefore,
father, that thou wouldest send him to
my father's house:**
For this reason, I beg you, father, to
  send him . . . — Wms

**28. For I have five brethren; that he may
testify unto them,**
. . . earnestly warn them — Wey
. . . strongly warn . . . — Ber
. . . to tell them the whole truth — Rieu
lest they also come
so that they may not also come — Rieu

into this place of torment.
into this place of suffering — Knox
. . . of pain — Bas
to this place of misery — Nor

**29. Abraham saith unto him, They have
Moses and the prophets:**
. . . the writings of . . . — TCNT
let them hear them.
. . . hearken unto them — Rhm
. . . listen to them — TCNT
. . . give ear to what they say — Bas

30. And he said, Nay, father Abraham:
They will not do that, father Abraham
  — Knox
**but if one went unto them from the
  dead,**
but if only a man from the dead go to
  them — Lam
but if a messenger comes to them . . .
  — Knox
. . . from the grave — Rieu
they will repent.
. . . change completely — Phi

**31. And he said unto him, If they hear
not Moses and the prophets,**
. . . If unto Moses and the Prophets
  they do not hearken — Rhm
. . . If they do not listen to . . . — TCNT
. . . give attention to . . . — Bas
If they are deaf to . . . — Wey
neither will they be persuaded,
. . . be moved — Bas
. . . be convinced — Mof
. . . be led to believe — Wey
. . . will pay no heed — NEB
though one rose from the dead.
even if someone rises . . . — Gspd

CHAPTER 17

**1. Then said he unto the disciples, It is
impossible but that offences will come:**
. . . It is inevitable that there should be
  snares — TCNT
. . . that causes of stumbling should
  occur — Wey
. . . Temptations of sin are sure to come
  — RSV
**but woe unto him, through whom they
come!**
but woe betide the man . . . — NEB
. . . who is responsible for them — Phi

2. It were better for him that
It profiteth him if — Rhm
Better for him if — Wey

**a millstone were hanged about his
neck, and he cast into the sea,**
with a millstone hanging round his
  neck he had been hurled into the sea
  — Wey
than that he should offend
. . . hurt the conscience of — Knox
. . . be an obstacle to — Ber
one of these little ones.
a single one of . . . — Rieu
. . . these humble people — Gspd

3. Take heed to yourselves:
Give attention to yourselves — Bas
Keep good watch over yourselves —
  Knox

If thy brother trespass against thee,
If your brother sins — Mof
rebuke him;
reprove him — TCNT
check him — Mof
remonstrate with him — Gspd
call him to task — Ber
solemnly tell him so — Amp
and if he repent, forgive him.
and if he is sorry . . . — Wey

4. **And if he trespass against thee seven times in a day,**
Even if seven times a day he sin against thee — Rhm
. . . he wrongs you . . . — TCNT
and seven times in a day turn again to thee,
and comes back to you seven times — Ber
and returns to you seven times — NASB
but turns to you every time — TCNT
saying, I repent; thou shalt forgive him.
with the words, "I am sorry!" . . . — Ber
. . . you must forgive him — TCNT

5. **And the apostles said unto the Lord, Increase our faith.**
. . . Give us more faith — Alf

6. **And the Lord said, If ye had faith as a grain of mustard seed,**
. . . If ye have faith . . . — Rhm
. . . faith the size of a grain of . . . — Mof
ye might say unto this sycamine tree,
. . . to this black-mulberry tree — Wey
Be thou plucked up by the root, and be thou planted in the sea;
Pull yourself up by the roots and plant yourself in the sea — Phi
and it should obey you.
and it would have obeyed you — ABUV
and instantly it would obey you — Wey

7. **But which of you, having a servant plowing or feeding cattle,**
. . . following the plough, or herding the sheep — Knox
will say unto him by and by, when he is come from the field,
. . . from the farm — Wey
Go and sit down to meat?
Come straight in and sit down to your meal — Phi
. . . and take your place at table — TCNT

8. **And will not rather say unto him,**
instead of telling him — Ber
Make ready wherewith I may sup,
Get something ready for my supper — Ber
and gird thyself, and serve me,
then tuck up your clothes and wait on me at table — Rieu
till I have eaten and drunken;
till I have finished my dinner — Wey
while I am eating and drinking — TCNT
and afterward thou shalt eat and drink?
then you shall have yours — Wey
After that you can have your own meal — Rieu

9. **Doth he thank that servant because he did things that were commanded him? I trow not.**
He does not thank the slave . . . does he? — NASB

10. **So likewise ye,**
Well, it is the same with you — Mof
And so with you . . . — TCNT
when ye shall have done all those things which are commanded you,
. . . all the orders given you — Wey
. . . all the work you were given — Rieu
say, We are unprofitable servants:
. . . We are worthless slaves — Wms
. . . We are good-for-nothing slaves — Gspd
. . . There is no merit in our service — Wey
we have done that which was our duty to do.
we have merely done our duty — Wey
. . . what we ought to have done — Wms

11. **And it came to pass, as he went to Jerusalem,**
Now it happened in the course of . . . — Mof
. . . the journey to Jerusalem — ABUV
that he passed through the midst of Samaria and Galilee.
. . . was passing along the borders of . . . — ASV
. . . crossed the boundary between . . . — Phi
. . . was travelling through the borderlands of . . . — NEB

12. **And as he entered into a certain village,**
And as he was entering into . . . — Rhm

there met him ten men that were lepers,

ten men that were lepers came towards him — Knox

which stood afar off:

who stood at a distance — Mof

they stopped at a distance — Beck

13. And they lifted up their voices, and said,

and called across to him — Rieu

Jesus, Master, have mercy on us.

Jesus, Rabbi, take pity on us — Wey

14. And when he saw them, he said unto them,

When Jesus saw them . . . — TCNT

So as soon as He saw them . . . — Wms

Go shew yourselves unto the priests.

Go and present yourselves to . . . — Nor

Go and let the priests examine you — Beck

And it came to pass, that, as they went,

And while on their way to do this — Wey

And while they were going — Wms

they were cleansed.

they were cured — Gspd

15. And one of them, when he saw that he was healed, turned back,

. . . when he saw that he had been healed, . . . — NASB

. . . returned — Rhm

and with a loud voice glorified God,

glorifying God . . . — Wey

. . . at the top of his voice — Phi

with a great cry of praise to God—Rieu

praising God aloud — NEB

16. And fell down on his face at his feet, giving him thanks: and he was a Samaritan.

and fell prostrate . . . — Rhm

and threw himself at Jesus' feet with his face to the ground . . . — Knox

17. And Jesus answering said, Were there not ten cleansed?

. . . Were not all the ten made clean — TCNT

but where are the nine?

But the nine — where are they — TCNT

18. There are not found that returned to give glory to God,

Were none found returning . . . — ABUV

Can it be true that none of them . . . — Rieu

save this stranger.

except this foreigner — TCNT

. . . this one of another race — Rhm

19. And he said unto him, Arise, go thy way:

. . . Get up and go on your way—Wms

thy faith hath made thee whole.

. . . has brought thee recovery — Knox

20. And when he was demanded of the Pharisees,

Now having been questioned by the Pharisees — NASB

when the kingdom of God should come,

as to when . . . was coming — NASB

he answered them and said, The kingdom of God cometh not with observation:

. . . in a way that admits of observation — TCNT

. . . The Kingdom of God isn't ushered in with visible signs! — Tay

. . . does not so come that you can watch closely for it — Wey

. . . with visible display — Wms

. . . with signs to be observed — RSV

21. Neither shall they say,

there will be no saying — Knox

and so people will not say — Wms

Lo here! or, lo there!

Look, here it is! or There it is!—TCNT

for, behold, the kingdom of God is within you.

and the reason why is this — the Kingdom of God is within you — Rieu

for the Reign of God is now in your midst — Mof

. . . is among you — Alf

22. And he said unto the disciples,

Then, turning to His disciples, He said — Wey

The days will come, when ye shall desire

The time will come when . . . — Wms

. . . you will long and long in vain — Mof

to see one of the days of the Son of man,

to enjoy, but for a day, the Son of Man's presence — Knox

to see again a single day of . . . — Phi

for one glimpse of the Son of Man — Rieu

and ye shall not see it.

and it will not be granted you — Knox

23. And they shall say to you, See here; or, see there:

People will say to you There he is! or Here he is! — TCNT

go not after them, nor follow them.

But make no move . . . — Nor

. . . or go off in pursuit — Rieu

Stay where you are and don't go off looking for him — Phi

24. **For as the lightning, that lighteneth**

For just as the lightning when it flashes — Wey

For like the lightning-flash — NEB

out of the one part under heaven, shineth unto the other part under heaven;

shines from one end of the sky to the other — Gspd

shoots across the sky — Wey

lights up the sky from one side to the other — RSV

lights the heavens from horizon to horizon — Rieu

lights up the earth from end to end — NEB

so shall also the Son of man be in his day.

. . . when He comes — Wms

so the Son of Man will come — Rieu

25. **But first must he suffer many things,**

But before that happens . . . — Phi

. . . He has to . . . — Wms

. . . it is his destiny to . . . — Rieu

. . . undergo much suffering — TCNT

and be rejected of this generation.

and he must be rejected by the present generation — TCNT

. . . be disowned by this age — Wms

. . . be repudiated by . . . — NEB

26. **And as it was in the days of Noe,**

Just as it happened . . . — Lam

. . . in Noah's time — Rieu

As things were in Noah's days — NEB

so shall it be also

life will be — Phi

all will be — Knox

things will happen — Rieu

in the days of the Son of man.

In the time of the coming of the Son of Man — Phi

27. **They did eat, they drank, they married wives, they were given in marriage,**

People went on eating, drinking . . . — Gspd

. . . taking wives and giving wives — Wey

until the day that Noe entered into the ark,

up to the very day on which . . . — TCNT

and the flood came, and destroyed them all.

. . . and made an end of them all — NEB

28. **Likewise also as it was in the days of Lot;**

It will be just the same as it was . . . — Phi

So too, what happened in the time of Lot will be repeated — Rieu

they did eat, they drank, they bought, they sold, they planted, they builded:

they went on eating, drinking . . . — Gspd

they were feasting and trading . . . — Bas

29. **But the same day that Lot went out of Sodom**

but, on the very day on which Lot came out of Sodom — TCNT

it rained fire and brimstone from heaven,

the Lord sent down a rain of . . . — Lam

. . . fire and sulphur from the skies — TCNT

fire and brimstone rained from heaven — RSV

and destroyed them all.

and made an end of them all — NEB

30. **Even thus shall it be**

Exactly so will it be — Wey

That is how it will be — Phi

in the day when the Son of man is revealed.

on the day on which . . . — TCNT

. . . the veil is lifted from the Son . . . — Wey

. . . the Son of Man appears — Gspd

. . . is brought into the light — Rieu

31. **In that day, he which shall be upon the house top, and his stuff in the house,**

On that day, if a man is on his housetop and his goods in the house — TCNT

. . . with his belongings inside . . . — Ber

let him not come down

he must not go down — Mof

to take it away:

to save them — Rieu

to carry them out — Wms

to pick them up — NEB

and he that is in the field,
and equally . . . — Ber
. . . on the farm — TCNT
And the man out in the fields — Phi
let him likewise not return back.
must beware of turning back — Knox
must not come back to the house —
Nor
32. **Remember Lot's wife.**
Bear in mind the wife of Lot! — Rhm
. . . what happened to Lot's wife —
Phi
33. **Whosoever shall seek**
Whoever tries — Mof
to save his life shall lose it;
to make his life his own . . . — Rhm
to conserve his life for himself . . . —
Ber
to gain his life . . . — RSV
and whosoever shall lose his life
the man who is prepared to lose his life
— Phi
shall preserve it.
shall revitalize it — Ber
shall give it a living birth — Rhm
34. **I tell you, in that night there shall be
two men in one bed;**
On that night, I tell you, there will be
two lying on one bed — Wey

**the one shall be taken, and the other
shall be left.**
one will be taken away . . . — Wey
35. **Two women shall be grinding together;**
. . . will be crushing grain . . . — Bas
. . . will be turning the grinding mill together — Phi
. . . at the same mill — Rieu
**the one shall be taken, and the other
left.**
one will be taken away . . . — Wey
36. **Two men shall be in the field; the one
shall be taken, and the other left.**[10]
37. **And they answered and said unto him,
Where, Lord?**
Where will it be, Master? interposed
the disciples — TCNT
**And he said unto them, Wheresoever
the body is,**
Where the dead body is, he replied —
Wey
. . . Wherever the corpse is — Lam
. . . Wherever there is carrion — Wms
**thither will the eagles be gathered to-
gether.**
there also will the vultures flock together — Wey
there the vultures will gather — Mof

CHAPTER 18

1. **And he spake a parable unto them to
this end,**
He gave them an illustration to show
— Gspd
. . . to make it clear — Rieu
that men ought always to pray,
how necessary it is for people always
to pray — Wms
and not to faint;
and not be faint-hearted — Rhm
and never despair — TCNT
and never to give up — Wms

2. **Saying, There was in a city a judge,**
Once upon a time . . . there was a magistrate in a town — Phi
**which feared not God, neither regard-
ed man:**
who had no fear of God and no respect
for man — Wey
who cared nothing for God or man
— NEB

3. **And there was a widow in that city;
and she came unto him,**

. . . and she came oft . . . — ASV
. . . kept coming . . . — ABUV
. . . went to him again and again —
TCNT
saying, Avenge me of mine adversary.
. . . Grant me justice against my opponent — TCNT
. . . Give me justice and protection from
. . . — Wms
. . . Please protect me from the man
who is trying to ruin me — Phi
and begged him to protect her from an
enemy of hers by giving judgement
against him — Rieu
4. **And he would not for a while:**
he was unwilling for a time — Rhm
. . . to do anything — Beck
. . . to help her — Nor
but afterward he said within himself,
but later on . . . — Ber

---

[10]Now recognized as not adequately supported
by original manuscripts. Compare Matt. 24:
40.

but in the end . . . — NEB

Though I fear not God, nor regard man;

Although neither God I reverence nor man I respect — Rhm

Although I am without fear of God or regard for man — TCNT

True, I care nothing for God or man — NEB

5. Yet because this widow troubleth me,

. . . annoyeth me — Rhm

. . . is bothering me — Mof

. . . is such a nuisance — Phi

I will avenge her,

I will vindicate her — Rhm

I will grant her justice — TCNT

I will see justice done to her — Mof

I will protect her — Gspd

I will give her redress — Knox

I shall give judgment in her favor — Phi

I will see her righted — NEB

lest by her continual coming she weary me.

to stop her from plaguing me with her endless visits — TCNT

6. And the Lord said,

Hear what the unjust judge saith.

Listen to what this iniquitous judge says! — TCNT

Did you note what this dishonest judge said to himself? — Nor

Notice how this dishonest magistrate behaved — Phi

Contrast the thoughts of this dishonest judge with those of God — Rieu

7. And shall not God avenge his own elect,

And God — will not he see that his own People . . . have justice done them — TCNT

which cry day and night unto him,

who continue to . . . — Wms

who appeal to him . . . — Phi

though he bear long with them?

though he holds his hand — TCNT

although He delays vengeance on their behalf — Wey

though he is long in doing it — Bas

patient as he is — Phi

8. I tell you that he will avenge them speedily.

He will . . . have justice done them . . . — TCNT

Yes, He will soon avenge their wrongs — Wey

. . . he will quickly see justice done to . . . — Mof

. . . he will make haste to provide it — Gspd

. . . he will give them redress with all speed — Knox

I assure you he will not delay in seeing justice done — Phi

. . . will indeed give judgement for them . . . — Rieu

Nevertheless when the Son of man cometh,

. . . when the Son of man does come — Mof

shall he find faith on the earth?

will he find faith left on . . . — Knox

. . . men on earth who believe in him — Phi

9. And he spake this parable

He addressed this parable — Wey

unto certain which trusted in themselves that they were righteous,

to some who relied on themselves . . . — Wey

. . . because they were righteous — Mon

to people who were satisfied that they were religious — TCNT

. . . that they themselves were upright — Wms

. . . were sure of their own goodness — Mof

. . . who felt secure in their own righteousness — Rieu

and despised others:

and thought nothing of others — Gspd

had . . . a very low regard for others — Nor

. . . the rest of the world — Knox

10. Two men went up into the temple to pray;

. . . for prayer — Bas

the one a Pharisee, and the other a publican.

. . . the other a tax-collector — Rhm

11. The Pharisee stood and prayed thus with himself,

The Pharisee, standing erect, prayed as follows by himself — Wey

The Pharisee stood forward and began praying to himself in this way — TCNT

. . . said this self-centered prayer — Wms

God, I thank thee, that I am not as other men are,

. . . the rest of mankind — Phi

extortioners, unjust, adulterers,
thieves, rogues, adulterers — TCNT
greedy, dishonest, or adulterous —
    Gspd
who steal and cheat and commit adult-
    ery — Knox
or even as this publican.
or, for that matter . . . — NEB
nor indeed like this tax-collector here
    — Rieu
12. **I fast twice in the week,**
. . . I go without food — Bas
. . . two days in the week — Gspd
I give tithes of all that I possess.
I give a tenth of everything I get to
    God — TCNT
I give away a tenth part of all my
    income — Phi
13. **And the publican, standing afar off,**
Meanwhile the tax-gatherer stood at a
    distance — TCNT
. . . standing far back — Wey
**would not lift up so much as his eyes
    unto heaven,**
was even unwilling to lift up his eyes to
    heaven — NASB
not venturing even to raise his eyes to
    . . . — TCNT
but smote upon his breast,
But kept smiting his own breast — Rhm
and with a gesture of despair — Phi
**saying, God be merciful to me a sin-
    ner.**
. . . O God, be propitiated unto me, the
    sinner! — Rhm
. . . O God, have mercy on me, sinner
    that I am — Wey
14. **I tell you, this man went down to his
    house**
. . . went home — TCNT
justified
accounted by God freed from guilt
    — Wey
accepted by God — Mof
with God's approval — Gspd
forgiven and accepted by God — Wms
acquitted of his sins — NEB
rather than the other:
and not the other — Wms
for every one that exalteth himself
. . . makes himself high — Bas
. . . honors himself — Beck
. . . who sets himself up as somebody
    — Phi
shall be abased;
will become a nobody — Phi

**and he that humbleth himself shall be
    exalted.**
. . . makes himself low . . . — Bas
. . . who makes himself nobody will
    become somebody — Phi
15. **And they brought unto him also in-
    fants,**
. . . were bringing . . . — ASV
. . . even their babies — TCNT
that he would touch them:
for him to touch them — TCNT
**but when his disciples saw it, they re-
    buked them.**
. . . they began to find fault with those
    who had brought them — TCNT
. . . reproved them for it — Gspd
. . . said sharp words to them — Bas
. . . sternly told them not to do it —
    Beck
16. **But Jesus called them unto him, and
    said,**
. . . called the little children to him
    — TCNT
Suffer little children to come unto me,
Permit the children . . . — Lam
Allow the little ones . . . — Ber
and forbid them not:
and stop preventing them from it —
    Wms
and stop hindering them — NASB
for of such is the kingdom of God.
for the kingdom of God belongs to
    their kind — Ber
17. **Verily I say unto you,**
I tell you in truth that — Wey
I tell you in solemn truth — Mon
Believe me — Knox
**Whosoever shall not receive the king-
    dom of God as a little child**
. . . shall not welcome . . . — Rhm
. . . as a little child does — Wms
shall in no wise enter therein.
will never get into it at all — Wms
18. **And a certain ruler asked him, saying,**
A member of the council . . . — Gspd
A man of the ruling class . . . — NEB
. . . asked Jesus this question — TCNT
Good Master,
Good Teacher — ASV
Good Rabbi — Wey
what shall I do to inherit eternal life?
by doing what shall I inherit life age-
    abiding — Rhm
what have I to do . . . — Bas
. . . to get possession of . . . — Wms
. . . to make sure of . . . — Gspd

19. **And Jesus said unto him, Why callest thou me good?**

Why are you calling me 'good'? said Jesus to him — Mon

I wonder why you call me good?.. — Phi

none is good, save one, that is, God.

No one is good, no one but God — Mof

20. **Thou knowest the commandments, Do not commit adultery,**

... Do not be untrue to your wife — Bas

Do not kill,

... put anyone to death — Bas

Do not steal,

... take what is not yours — Bas

Do not bear false witness,

... say what is false about others — TCNT

... lie in giving evidence — Wey

... perjure thyself — Rieu

Honour thy father and thy mother.

Practice honoring your father and ... — Wms

21. **And he said, All these have I kept**

I have observed all these ... — TCNT

All these, he replied, I have carefully obeyed — Wey

from my youth up.

from childhood — TCNT

ever since I was a child — Gspd

since I was quite young — Phi

22. **Now when Jesus heard these things,**

On receiving this answer — Wey

he said unto him, Yet lackest thou one thing:

... There is still one thing wanting in you — Wey

... left for you to do — Rieu

sell all that thou hast, and distribute unto the poor,

... distribute the money among the poor — Mof

and thou shalt have treasure in heaven:

so the treasure thou hast shall be in heaven — Knox

and come, follow me.

and come back and be a follower of mine — Gspd

23. **And when he heard this, he was very sorrowful:**

At these words his heart sank — NEB

The answer filled him with sadness — Knox

... he was much cast down — Gspd

... was filled with gloom — Rieu

... became encompassed with grief — Rhm

for he was very rich.

... extremely rich — TCNT

... surpassingly rich — Wms

24. **And when Jesus saw that he was very sorrowful, he said,**

Jesus looked at him, and said — Wey

How hardly shall they that have riches enter into the kingdom of God!

With what difficulty shall they who have money ... — Rhm

25. **For it is easier for a camel to go through a needle's eye,**

... squeeze through ... — Phi

than for a rich man to enter into the kingdom of God.

... to get into the Realm of God — Mof

26. **And they that heard it said,**

His listeners said — Ber

Who then can be saved?

Then who can possibly be saved — Phi

27. **And he said, The things which are impossible with men are possible with God.**

... What is impossible to man's power is possible to God — Knox

... What men can't do God can do — Beck

28. **Then Peter said, Lo, we have left all,**

... And what of us? we have forsaken all that was ours — Knox

But we, said Peter, we left what belonged to us — TCNT

... our very own, homes and all — Wms

and followed thee.

to become your followers — NEB

29. **And he said unto them, Verily I say unto you,**

I tell you in truth ... — Wey

... I solemnly say to you — Wms

... In solemn truth I tell you — Mon

There is no man that hath left house, or parents, or brethren, or wife, or children, for the kingdom of God's sake,

... who has given up home or wife or brothers or parents or children for the Kingdom of God — Gspd

... the Realm of God — Mof

30. **Who shall not receive manifold more**

... many times as much — TCNT

... ever so much more — Mof

... many times their worth — Knox

in this present time,
in this life — Wey

and in the world to come life ever-lasting.
and in the age that is coming life age-abiding — Rhm
and everlasting life in the hereafter — Nor

31. Then he took unto him the twelve, and said unto them,
And taking aside the twelve he said unto them — Rhm
Gathering the Twelve round him, Jesus said to them — TCNT
Then He drew the twelve to Him and said — Wey

Behold, we go up to Jerusalem,
Listen to me. We are now going up to . . . — Phi
See, we are on our way to . . . — Mon

and all things that are written by the prophets concerning the Son of man
and all the predictions of the prophets regarding the Son of man — Mof
and everything that was foretold for the Son of Man through the Prophets — Rieu

shall be accomplished.
will be fulfilled — Wey
will there be carried out — Nor

32. For he shall be delivered unto the Gentiles,
For he will be delivered up unto the nations — Rhm
. . . handed over to . . . — Wey
. . . turned over to the heathen — Wms
. . . to the pagans — Rieu
. . . to the foreign power — NEB

and shall be mocked,
and ridiculed — Gspd
and sport made of Him — Wms
he is going to be jeered at — Phi

and spitefully entreated, and spitted on:
and insulted and spit upon — Rhm
outraged, and spat upon — Wey
ill-treated . . . — Mof
maltreated . . . — NEB

33. And they shall scourge him,
they will flog him — Gspd

and put him to death:
and execute Him — Ber

and the third day he shall rise again.
. . . will rise to life again — Wey

34. And they understood none of these things:

They could make nothing of all this — Knox

and this saying was hid from them,
and this statement was an insoluble riddle to them — Wms
The words were a mystery to them — Wey
. . . were obscure to them — Gspd
its meaning was concealed from them — NEB

neither knew they the things which were spoken.
they did not even begin to grasp what He meant — Wms
they had no idea of what he meant — Phi
. . . what he was talking about — NEB

35. And it came to pass, that as he was come nigh unto Jericho,
. . . as he was drawing near . . . — Rhm

a certain blind man sat by the way side begging:
. . . was sitting beside the road . . . — Rhm

36. And hearing the multitude pass by,
. . . a multitude moving along — Rhm
. . . a crowd going by — TCNT
. . . a crowd of travellers on the road — Rieu

he asked what it meant.
he inquired what it was all about — Ber
. . . what was the matter — TCNT
. . . what was happening — Rieu

37. And they told him, that Jesus of Nazareth passeth by.
so they informed him . . . — Ber
And they told him — Jesus of Nazareth is passing by! — Rhm

38. And he cried, saying,
Then, at the top of his voice he cried out — Wey
he shouted out — TCNT

Jesus, thou son of David, have mercy on me.
. . . take pity on me! — TCNT

39. And they which went before rebuked him, that he should hold his peace:
Those who were in front kept telling him to be quiet — TCNT
And those who led the way were sternly telling him to be quiet — NASB
Those in front reproved him and tried to silence him — Wey
. . . tried to hush his cries — Phi
. . . told him sharply to hold his tongue — NEB

but he cried so much the more,

. . . continued to call out the louder
— TCNT

. . . shouted all the more — Mof

But that made him call out all the more
— Phi

Thou son of David, have mercy on me.

. . . take pity on me! — TCNT

40. And Jesus stood,

Then Jesus stopped — TCNT

. . . stood quite still — Phi

**and commanded him to be brought
unto him:**

and ordered that he be led to Him
— Amp

**and when he was come near, he asked
him,**

And, when he had come close up to
him, Jesus asked him — TCNT

**41. Saying, What wilt thou that I shall do
unto thee?**

What do you want me to do for you
— TCNT

**And he said, Lord, that I may receive
my sight.**

And he said — Lord! . . . that I may
recover sight! — Rhm

. . . that I might see again — Mon

Sir, I want my sight back, he answered
— NEB

**42. And Jesus said unto him, Receive thy
sight:**

. . . Recover your sight — TCNT

. . . See again! — Wms

. . . Have back your sight — NEB

thy faith hath saved thee.

your faith has delivered you — TCNT

. . . has cured you — Wey

. . . has brought thee recovery — Knox

43. And immediately he received his sight,

And instantly he recovered sight —
Rhm

. . . he saw again — Wms

No sooner were the words spoken than
the man regained his sight — Wey

His sight came back immediately —
Rieu

and followed him, glorifying God:

and began to follow him glorifying
God — Rhm

. . . giving thanks to God — Gspd

. . . giving God the glory — Nor

**and all the people, when they saw it,
gave praise unto God.**

. . . gave glory to God — TCNT

and all the people gave praise to God
for what they had seen — NEB

CHAPTER 19

**1. And Jesus entered and passed through
Jericho.**

And he entered and was passing
through . . . — ASV

**2. And, behold, there was a man named
Zacchaeus,**

There was a man there, called Zac-
cheus — Mon

. . . known by the name of . . . — TCNT

**which was the chief among the publi-
cans, and he was rich.**

the principal tax-collector, a rich man
— Gspd

. . . the head of the tax collectors . . .
— Nor

. . . superintendent of taxes . . — NEB

. . . a commissioner of taxes . . . — TCNT

**3. And he sought to see Jesus who he
was;**

And he kept trying to see what sort of
man Jesus was — Mon

. . . to see who Jesus was — Gspd

. . . to distinguish which was Jesus —
Knox

and could not for the press,

But he could not see Him because of
the crowd — Nor

because he was little of stature.

as he was so small in stature — Wms

4. And he ran before,

So he ran on ahead — TCNT

and climbed up into a sycomore tree

. . . mulberry tree — TCNT

to see him:

to get a sight of him — Mof

just to get a glimpse of Him — Wms

to catch sight of him — Knox

for he was to pass that way.

. . . was about to pass that way — Wey

. . . was going to take that way across
the town — Rieu

**5. And when Jesus came to the place, he
looked up, and saw him, and said unto
him,**

As soon as . . . — Wey

But when Jesus reached the spot . . .
— Mof

Zacchaeus, make haste, and come down;

... come down quickly — Wey

... come down at once — Mof

for to day I must abide at thy house.

for I am due to stay at your home today — Ber

I must be your guest today — Phi

You must be my host to-day — Rieu

6. And he made haste, and came down,

He hurried down — Ber

He climbed down as fast as he could — NEB

and received him joyfully.

and welcomed him gladly — Mof

and took him home with him rejoicing — Rieu

and was happy to welcome Him — Beck

7. And when they saw it, they all murmured, saying,

But the bystanders muttered their disapproval ... — Phi

... began muttering with indignation — Wey

... began to complain: — TCNT

... began to grumble ... — Wms

... shook their heads — Rieu

At this there was a general murmur of disapproval — NEB

That he was gone to be guest with a man that is a sinner.

He has gone to stay with an irreligious man! — Gspd

Now he has gone to stay with a real sinner — Phi

He has gone to be the guest of a notorious sinner — Tay

8. And Zacchaeus stood, and said unto the Lord;

So Zacchaeus stopped and said ... — Mof

But Zacchaeus took his stand ... — Rieu

... and addressing the Lord said — Wey

Behold, Lord,

Listen, Master! — TCNT

Here and now, Master — Wey

Here and now, sir — NEB

the half of my goods I give to the poor;

... unto the destitute I give — Rhm

I am giving half my fortune ... — Rieu

... the half of all I have ... — Mof

... to charity — NEB

and if I have taken any thing from any man by false accusation,

and if I have wrongfully exacted ... — ASV

if I have defrauded any one of anything — TCNT

... cheated ... — Mof

... swindled ... — Phi

I restore him fourfold.

I am restoring it ... — Mon

and making fourfold restitution ... — Rieu

I pledge myself to repay to him four times the amount — Wey

I am ready to repay ... — NEB

9. And Jesus said unto him,

... said of him — Mof

Jesus said, pointing to him, — Ber

Jesus turned to him and said — Knox

This day is salvation come to this house,

... to this household — Rieu

forsomuch as he also is a son of Abraham.

for he too is a real descendant of ... — Wms

10. For the Son of man is come

For the Son of man came — ASV

That is what the Son of Man has come for — Knox

What did the Son of Man come for but — Rieu

to seek and to save that which was lost.

to search for those who are lost and to save them — TCNT

to seek and to save the people that are lost — Wms

11. And as they heard these things,

Then as the crowd still listened attentively — Phi

While these words were ringing in their ears — Rieu

he added and spake a parable,

Jesus went on to tell them a parable — TCNT

... went on to give them an illustration — Gspd

he added this parable — Mon

because he was nigh to Jerusalem,

... because he had now nearly reached ... — Knox

and because they thought

... were of the opinion — Bas

... they imagined — Mof

that the kingdom of God should immediately appear.

God's Reign would instantly come into
view — Mof

... was on the point of appearing —
Phi

... was going to ... — Wey

... dawn at any moment — NEB

that instantly was the kingdom of God
to shine forth — Rhm

12. He said therefore,

**A certain nobleman went into a far
country**

A man of noble family travelled to a
distant country — Wey

... went on a long journey abroad
— NEB

**to receive for himself a kingdom, and
to return.**

to obtain the rank of king, ... — Wey

to obtain royal power for himself and
then return — Mof

to receive his appointment to a Kingdom ... — TCNT

to have himself made king ... — Rieu

13. And he called his ten servants,

And he summoned ten slaves of his
— Mon

and delivered them ten pounds,

and gave unto them ten minas — Rhm

and gave them each twenty dollars
— Gspd

and gave them each a pound — Rieu

and said unto them, Occupy

... Use this money to trade with — Phi

... Buy and sell with these — Amp

till I come.

while I am away — Knox

14. But his citizens hated him,

But his subjects ... — TCNT

Now his countrymen ... — Wey

Now the people of his country ... —
Rieu

... continued to hate him — Wms

and sent a message after him,

and sent envoys ... — TCNT

and sent a deputation ... — Wey

... a delegation ... — Gspd

**saying, We will not have this man to
reign over us.**

We do not want this man ... — Gspd

... to become king over us — Wms

We object to ... — Mof

... this man as our King — TCNT

**15. And it came to pass, that when he was
returned, having received the kingdom,**

However, back he came as king — NEB

... when he came back as king — Knox

On his return, after having been appointed king — TCNT

... after he had obtained the sovereignty — Wey

**then he commanded these servants to
be called unto him,**

he directed that the servants ... — TCNT

... be summoned before him — Wey

to whom he had given the money,

to whom he had entrusted ... — Knox

that he might know

that he might find out — Mof

**how much every man had gained by
trading.**

what business they had done — Mof

their success in trading — Wey

what profit each had made — NEB

16. Then came the first, saying,

Now the first one presented himself
and said — Ber

**Lord, thy pound hath gained ten
pounds.**

Lord! thy mina hath made ten minas
— Rhm

Your twenty dollars has made two
hundred, sir — Gspd

... your coin has increased ten-fold
— Nor

**17. And he said unto him, Well, thou good
servant:**

... Well done, ... — Phi

Splendid, my good fellow, ... — Phi

... Wonderful! ... — Nor

**because thou hast been faithful in a
very little,**

As you have proved trustworthy in a
very small matter — TCNT

You proved you could be trusted ...
— Beck

... about a very small amount — Gspd

... dependable in a very small business
— Wms

have thou authority over ten cities.

I appoint you governor over ... —
TCNT

I am going to put you in charge of ...
— Phi

**18. And the second came, saying, Lord,
thy pound hath gained five pounds.**

... Thy mina, lord, hath made five
minas — Rhm

... Your twenty dollars has made a
hundred, sir — Gspd

... Your coin has increased to five
— Nor

19. And he said likewise to him, Be thou also over five cities.

. . . You shall be over five cities — Mon

. . . Thou too shalt have authority, over five cities — Knox

20. And another came, saying,

Then the one who was different came and said — Beck

Lord, behold, here is thy pound,

. . . thy mina — Rhm

Here is your coin, Sir — Nor

which I have kept laid up in a napkin:

I have kept them put away in a handkerchief — TCNT

which I have kept wrapt up in a cloth — Wey

21. For I feared thee,

For I lived in constant dread of you — Wms

I have been scared — Phi

because thou art an austere man:

you are such a hard man — Mof

. . . a stern man — TCNT

. . . a severe man — Wey

. . . a harsh man . . . — Rhm

knowing how exacting a man thou art — Knox

. . . a tight-fisted man — Nor

thou takest up that thou layedst not down,

picking up what you never put down — Mof

thou dost claim what thou didst never venture — Knox

you draw out what you never put in — NEB

You take what you didn't deposit — Beck

getting something for nothing — Phi

and reapest that thou didst not sow.

and you get grain you didn't sow — Beck

22. And he saith unto him, Out of thine own mouth will I judge thee,

By your own words . . . I will judge you — Wey

. . . I will condemn you . . . — RSV

. . . I will sentence you — Wms

. . . I will convict you by what you have said yourself — Mof

. . . I take thy judgement from thy own lips — Knox

. . . your own words condemn you — Phi

thou wicked servant.

you worthless servant — TCNT

You rascal of a servant — Mof

You good-for-nothing servant — Ber

You scoundrel — Phi

Thou knewest that I was an austere man,

You knew perfectly well, did you, . . . — Phi

taking up that I laid not down, and reaping that I did not sow:[11]

23. Wherefore then gavest not thou my money into the bank,

Why then did you not put . . . — Wey

. . . on deposit — NEB

that at my coming

In that case, when I came back — Wms

and then when I returned — Phi

and at my coming — RSV

I might have required mine own with usury?

I should have collected it with interest — RSV

I should have withdrawn it with interest — Rieu

24. And he said unto them that stood by,

. . . to the bystanders — Mof

. . . the others who were near — Bas

And to his attendants . . . Rieu

Take from him the pound,

Take from him the mina — Rhm

Take the coin from him — Nor

Take the twenty dollars away from him — Gspd

and give it to him that hath ten pounds.

and give it to the fellow who has . . . — Phi

. . . the ten minas — Rhm

. . . the two hundred — Gspd

. . . the ten pounds — ASV

25. (And they said unto him, Lord, he hath ten pounds.)

Master, they said to him, he already has ten pounds — Mon

. . . ten minas — Rhm

. . . two hundred, sir! — Gspd

26. For I say unto you,

Nay, but I tell you — Knox

My answer to that is — Rieu

That unto every one which hath shall be given;

. . . more will be given — TCNT

and from him that hath not,

But as for the man who has nothing — Phi

---

[11]See verse 21.

311

even that he hath shall be taken away from him.
even his "nothing" will be taken away — Phi
even the little he has will be taken from him — Knox

27. **But those mine enemies,**
(The indignant king ended by saying,) but as for these enemies of mine — Amp
Then the angry king said, As to . . . — Nor
which would not that I should reign over them,
who refused . . . — Knox
. . . that I should become their king — Wey
who objected to me . . . — Mof
these men who would not have me as their King — TCNT
bring hither,
fetch them here — Ber
and slay them before me.
and slaughter them in my presence — Gspd
and slay them outright before me — Rhm
and execute them . . . — Ber
. . . before my eyes — Nor

28. **And when he had thus spoken,**
When he had finished this parable — — Rieu
he went before, ascending up to Jerusalem.
He continued on His way up to Jerusalem — Beck
he went on ahead of them . . . — Gspd
he went forward on his way up to . . . — Mof
he took the road and led the way up to Jerusalem — Rieu

29. **And it came to pass, when he was come nigh to Bethphage and Bethany,**
It was when Jesus had almost reached . . . — TCNT
at the mount called the mount of Olives,
close to the mountain which is called Olivet — Knox
he sent two of his disciples,
he sent two of his disciples on an errand — Knox

30. **Saying,**
. . . with these instructions — NEB
Go ye into the village over against you;

Go on to . . . — Wms
. . . the village facing us — TCNT
. . . the village just ahead of you — Phi
in the which at your entering
in which, just as you enter — Wms
ye shall find a colt tied,
. . . a foal tethered — TCNT
. . . hitched — Ber
whereon yet never man sat:
which no one has yet ridden — TCNT
loose him, and bring him hither.
untether it and bring it — Mof
untie it, and lead it here — TCNT

31. **And if any man ask you, Why do ye loose him?**
. . . Why are you untethering it — Mof
thus shall ye say unto him,
simply say — Wey
Because the Lord hath need of him.
Because the Lord needs it! — Ber

32. **And they that were sent went their way,**
So the two who were sent . . . — TCNT
. . . went off — Mof
. . . on their errand — NEB
and found even as he had said unto them.
and found things . . . — Wey
and found the colt standing there . . . — Knox
. . . exactly as he had told them — Mof

33. **And as they were loosing the colt,**
In fact, as . . . — Phi
While they were untying . . . — TCNT
. . . untethering it — Mof
the owners thereof said unto them,
its owners . . . — ABUV
. . . did say — Phi
Why loose ye the colt?
Why are you untethering . . . — Mof

34. **And they said,**
And the two disciples answered — TCNT
The Lord hath need of him.
Because the Lord needs it — Mof

35. **And they brought him to Jesus:**
Then they led it back to . . . — TCNT
and they cast their garments upon the colt,
threw their cloaks on . . . — TCNT
and they set Jesus thereon.
they mounted Jesus . . . — Mof
. . . on its back — Phi

36. **And as he went,**
As He was riding along — Beck
they spread their clothes in the way.

the people kept spreading their cloaks
. . . — TCNT
. . . under him on the road — Mof
they carpeted the road with their garments — Wey

37. And when he was come nigh,
When he had almost reached — TCNT
And as He was coming near — Beck
**even now at the descent of the mount
of Olives,**
where the Mount of Olives slopes
down — Nor
the whole multitude of the disciples
every one of the many disciples — TCNT
the whole throng of . . . — Gspd
**began to rejoice and praise God with
a loud voice**
began to praise God loudly and joyfully — Gspd
began in their joy to sing a loud song
of praise to God — Rieu
in their joy began to sing aloud the
praises of God — NEB
**for all the mighty works that they had
seen;**
for all the miracles . . . — TCNT
. . . that they had seen him do — Phi

**38. Saying, Blessed be the King that com-
eth in the name of the Lord:**
God bless the king who comes . . . —
Phi
Blessings on him who comes as king
. . . — NEB
**peace in heaven, and glory in the
highest.**
There is peace in heaven . . . — Phi
. . . glory in highest heaven! — NEB

**39. And some of the Pharisees from
among the multitude said unto him,**
. . . called to him from the crowd —
Rieu
Master, rebuke thy disciples.
Rabbi, . . . — Wey
. . . restrain . . . — Phi
. . . reprimand . . . — NEB
Teacher, tell your disciples to stop this
— Nor

**40. And he answered and said unto them,
I tell you that, if these should hold
their peace,**
. . . if these men are silent — TCNT
the stones would immediately cry out.
. . . will cry out instead — Knox
. . . will shout aloud — NEB
the very stones in the road would burst
out cheering! — Phi

**41. And when he was come near, he be-
held the city,**
. . . came still nearer to the city — Phi
And as he drew near, and caught sight
of . . . — Knox
When He came into full view of the
city — Wey
and wept over it,
he broke into loud weeping — Mon
. . . burst into tears . . . — Wms

**42. Saying, If thou hadst known, even
thou, at least in this thy day,**
. . . If only you had known, on this
great day — NEB
. . . Ah, if only you too to-day had
found — Rieu
. . . even at this eleventh hour . . . —
Phi
**the things which belong unto thy
peace!**
the road to peace — Rieu
what makes for peace! — Wey
on what your peace depends! — Mof
the ways that can bring thee peace! —
Knox
the conditions of peace — Rhm
but now they are hid from thine eyes.
But as it is . . . — Gspd
. . . it's hidden so that you can't see it
— Beck
But as things are, you were not allowed
to see it — Rieu

43. For the days shall come upon thee,
For a time is coming upon you — TCNT
**that thine enemies shall cast a trench
about thee,**
. . . will surround you with earthworks
— TCNT
. . . will throw up ramparts round you
— Mof
. . . will fix a palisade around you —
Rieu
. . . will set up siege-works against you
— NEB
. . . will build an embankment around
you — Nor
and compass thee round,
. . . encircle you — TCNT
and keep thee in on every side,
hem you in on all sides — TCNT
besiege you . . . — Mof
shut you in . . . — Gspd
press thee hard on every side — Knox
. . . at every point — NEB

**44. And shall lay thee even with the
ground,**

And will level thee with the ground —
Rhm
. . . raze you . . . to the ground — Mof
. . . will dash thee to the ground — Wey
. . . bring down in ruin . . . — Knox
and thy children within thee;
you and your children within your
walls — NEB
**and they shall not leave in thee one
stone upon another;**
yes, they will not leave you one stone
standing upon another — Phi
**because thou knewest not the time of
thy visitation.**
and all because thou didst not recognize the time of my visiting thee —
Knox
because you did not know when God
visited you! — Gspd
. . . when you were divinely visited —
Ber
. . . God's moment when it came —
NEB
45. And he went into the temple,
. . . into the Temple Courts — TCNT
**and began to cast out them that sold
therein, and them that bought;**
and proceeded to drive out the dealers
— Wey
. . . to throw out the traders there —
Phi
**46. Saying unto them, It is written, My
house is the house of prayer:**
saying as he did so: Scripture says —
. . . — TCNT
. . . And my house shall be a house of
prayer — ASV
but ye have made it a den of thieves.
but you have turned it into a thieves'
kitchen! — Phi
. . . a cave for robbers — Wms
. . . a cave of bandits — Lam

47. And he taught daily in the temple.
Jesus continued to teach each day in
the Temple Courts — TCNT
And he was teaching daily in the temple — ASV
. . . day by day . . . — Rhm
But the chief priests and the scribes
but the High-priests and the Scribes —
Rhm
Meanwhile the Chief Priests and the
Doctors of the Law — Rieu
the ruling priests, the Bible scholars —
Beck
and the chief of the people
and the leaders of the people — Beck
and the leading men among the people
— Knox
. . . the foremost men — ABUV
. . . the national leaders — Phi
. . . the business community — Tay
sought to destroy him,
were seeking to . . . — Rhm
were bent on destroying him — Rieu
were devising some means of destroying him — Wey
were all the time trying to get rid of
him — Phi
. . . to make away with him — Knox
**48. And could not find what they might
do:**
. . . any way of doing it — Wey
But they could not hit upon a way —
Rieu
. . . found they were helpless — NEB
**for all the people were very attentive
to hear him.**
for the people one and all were hanging upon him — Rhm
. . . listening to him — Mon
for the people, to a man, were hanging on his words — Rieu

CHAPTER 20

**1. And it came to pass, that on one of
those days, as he taught the people in
the temple, and preached the gospel,**
And it came to pass, on one of the
days, as he was teaching the people
. . ., and preaching the gospel — ASV
. . . in the Temple Courts . . . — TCNT
. . . and telling the good tidings — Rhm
the chief priests and the scribes
the High-priests . . . — Rhm

the ruling priests, Bible scholars —
Beck
. . . and Doctors of the Law — Rieu
came upon him
confronted him — TCNT
took a stand against Him — Wms
came up and interrupted him — Rieu
came upon him and accosted him — NEB
with the elders.
joined by the Councillors — TCNT

2. And spake unto him, saying,
and asked him this direct question —
Phi
**Tell us, by what authority doest thou
these things?**
Tell us what sort of authority you have
for doing as you do — Wms
Tell us, by what authority are you doing these things — Wey
**or who is he that gave thee this au-
thority?**
Or who gives You the right to do them
— Beck

3. And he answered and said unto them,
He replied to them — Ber
I will also ask you one thing;
. . . will put a question to you — Wey
I too have a question to ask — Knox
I will ask you for a statement — Rieu
and answer me:
Give me an answer to it — TCNT
and it is for you to answer it — Nor

4. The baptism of John,
The immersion of John — Rhm
It is about John's baptism — TCNT
Whence did John's baptism come —
Knox
John's baptism, now — tell me — Phi
was it from heaven, or of men?
was it of divine or of human origin —
TCNT
sanctioned by Heaven or by man —
Rieu
did it come from Heaven or was it
purely human — Phi

**5. And they reasoned with themselves,
saying,**
So they debated the matter with one
another — Wey
And they discussed it with one another
— RSV
This set them arguing among them-
selves — NEB
If we shall say, From heaven;
If we tell him it was from heaven —
Knox
**he will say, Why then believed ye him
not?**
. . . Why didn't you believe him —
Beck

6. But and if we say, Of men;
but if we say it was purely human —
Phi
all the people will stone us:
the people one and all . . . — Rhm
. . . will stone us to death — Gspd

**for they be persuaded that John was
a prophet.**
for they are convinced . . . — Wey
for they are certain . . . — Bas

**7. And they answered, that they could
not tell whence it was.**
. . . that they did not know its origin
— TCNT
. . . where it came from — Mof

**8. And Jesus said unto them, Neither tell
I you**
. . . And you will not learn from me —
Knox
. . . Nor am I going to tell you — Wms
by what authority I do these things.
what sort of authority I have for doing
as I do — Wms
by what authority these things I am
doing — Rhm

**9. Then began he to speak to the people
this parable;**
Then he turned to the people and told
them . . . — Phi
**A certain man planted a vineyard, and
let it forth**
. . . leased it — Mof
. . . rented it out — NASB
to husbandmen,
to tenant farmers — Wms
to some field workers — Bas
to vine-growers — NEB
**and went into a far country for a long
time.**
and went from home for a long time
— Rhm
and went abroad for a long while —
TCNT
while he went away to spend a long
time abroad — Knox

**10. And at the season he sent a servant to
the husbandmen,**
And in due season . . . — Rhm
At vintage-time . . . — Wey
At the proper time . . . — TCNT
**that they should give him of the fruit
of the vineyard:**
for them to give him a share of the
crop — Wey
that they should give him a share of
the produce of the vineyard — TCNT
. . . pay him his share of the vineyard's
revenues — Knox
**but the husbandmen beat him, and
sent him away empty.**
. . . beat him up . . . — Phi

315

. . . and sent him off with nothing —
Mof

. . . empty-handed — TCNT

11. And again he sent another servant:

He proceeded to send . . . — Mof

He tried again and sent . . . — NEB

**and they beat him also, and entreated
him shamefully,**

they beat him up as well, manhandling
him disgracefully — Phi

. . . handled him shamefully — ASV

. . . outrageously treated . . . — NEB

. . . and dishonouring him — Rhm

. . . showing their contempt by thrash-
ing him — Rieu

and they beat him and insulted him —
Wms

and sent him away empty.

and sent him back empty-handed —
Wms

12. And again he sent a third:

Still persisting, he sent them a third —
Rieu

He tried once more with a third — NEB

**and they wounded him also, and cast
him out.**

they drove him away wounded, like
the others — Knox

and threw him outside — TCNT

**13. Then said the lord of the vineyard,
What shall I do?**

Then the owner of the vineyard said,
What am I to do — Wey

**I will send my beloved son: it may be
they will reverence him when they
see him.**

. . . my own dear son . . . — NEB

. . . my cherished son . . . — Tay

. . . Maybe they will respect him—Rieu

14. But when the husbandmen saw him,

But, on seeing him, the tenants—TCNT

**they reasoned among themselves, say-
ing,**

began to deliberate one with another
. . . — Rhm

they talked the matter over with one
another — Phi

they put their heads together . . . —
Rieu

**This is the heir: come, let us kill him,
that the inheritance may be ours.**

. . . so that his inheritance may pass
into our hands — Knox

. . . so that the property may come to
us — NEB

. . . and make his inheritance ours —
Rieu

**15. So they cast him out of the vineyard,
and killed him.**

So they flung him out of . . . — Wey

**What therefore shall the lord of the
vineyard do unto them?**

. . . will the owner of . . . — Wey

**16. He shall come and destroy these hus-
bandmen, and shall give the vineyard
to others.**

He will come and destroy those vine-
dressers, and will give . . . — Mon

He will come and destroy the men
who were working his property, . . .
— Phi

. . . and let others have the vineyard
— Ber

**And when they heard it, they said,
God forbid.**

When they heard this, they said, May
it never be so! — Wms

. . . Heaven forbid! — TCNT

17. And he beheld them, and said,

But He glanced at them . . . — Wms

But he fastened his eyes on them . . .
— Knox

But he looked them straight in the eyes
. . . — Phi

But Jesus fixed his eyes on them . . . —
Rieu

What is this then that is written,

Why then, what is the meaning of those
words which have been written —
Knox

What does this mean in your Bible —
Beck

**The stone which the builders rejected,
the same is become the head of the
corner?**

. . . has become the main corner-stone
— NEB

**18. Whosoever shall fall upon that stone
shall be broken;**

Every one who falls on that stone will
be dashed to pieces — TCNT

. . . will be shattered — Mof

**but on whomsoever it shall fall, it will
grind him to powder.**

. . . it will scatter him as dust — ASV

. . . will be scattered like chaff — Gspd

. . . he shall be pulverized — Ber

**19. And the chief priests and the scribes
the same hour sought to lay hands on
him;**

The Bible scholars and . . . — Beck

... And the Scribes and the High-priests sought to thrust on him their hands in that very hour — Rhm
... tried to arrest Him ... — Wms
... made attempts to get their hands on him ... — Bas
... then and there — TCNT
... right then — Ber
and they feared the people:
but the crowd alarmed them — Rieu
for they perceived that he had spoken this parable against them.
For they realized ... — Ber
... that it was at them that he had aimed this parable — TCNT

20. And they watched him, and sent forth spies,
Having watched their opportunity, they afterwards sent some spies — TCNT
So they bode their time ... — Rieu
... and sent secret agents — NEB
which should feign themselves just men,
who pretended to be ... — TCNT
... men of honest purpose — Knox
suborned to pose as conscientious people — Rieu
that they might take hold of his words,
... catch Him in some statement — NASB
... fasten on some expression of His — Wey
... pounce on something he might say — Rieu
that so they might deliver him unto the power and authority of the governor.
and so enable them to give him up to the Governor's jurisdiction and authority — TCNT
which could be used to hand him over ... — Phi
as a pretext for handing him over ... — NEB
... to the jurisdiction and ... of the Procurator — Rieu

21. And they asked him, saying,
So they put a question to Him — Wey
Master, we know that thou sayest and teachest rightly,
Rabbi, ... — Wey
Teacher, we know that you are right in what you say and teach — TCNT
neither acceptest thou the person of any,

and that you do not take any account of a man's position — TCNT
and that you make no distinctions between one man and another — Wey
you never look to human favour—Mof
you are partial to no one — Ber
you pay deference to no one — NEB
You don't favor any special persons — Beck
but teachest the way of God truly:
but teach in all honesty the way of life that God requires — NEB
but teach the Way of God honestly — TCNT

22. Is it lawful for us to give tribute unto Caesar, or no?
Is it allowable ... — Rhm
Are we right in paying tribute to the Emperor or not — TCNT
Is it right ... — Mof
Are we or are we not permitted to pay taxes to the Roman Emperor — NEB

23. But he perceived their craftiness, and said unto them,
Seeing through their deceitfulness, Jesus said to them — TCNT
But he detected their trickery ... — Gspd
... the cunning of their scheme ... — Rieu
But observing their villainy, ... — Rhm
Why tempt ye me?

24. Shew me a penny.
... a denarius — ASV
... a silver piece — Knox
... a coin — Tay
Whose image and superscription hath it? They answered and said, Caesar's.
Whose head and title are on it? ... — TCNT
Whose likeness, whose name does it bear inscribed on it? ... — Knox
Whose face is this, and whose name is in the inscription? ... — Phi

25. And he said unto them, Render therefore unto Caesar the things which be Caesar's, and unto God the things which be God's.
... Well then! render the things of Caesar unto Caesar, And the things of God unto God — Rhm
... pay to the Emperor what belongs to the Emperor ... — TCNT
... what is due to ... — Rieu

26. And they could not take hold of his words before the people:

And they were unable to catch Him in a saying in the presence of the people — NASB

So his reply gave them no sort of handle that they could use against him publicly — Phi

Thus their attempt to catch him out in public failed — NEB

and they marvelled at his answer, and held their peace.

in their wonder at his reply, they held their tongues — TCNT

. . . so taken aback . . . — Phi

. . . they fell silent — NEB

27. Then came to him certain of the Sadducees,

Some of the Sadducees . . . came forward — Wey

Then he was approached . . . by some of the Sadducees — Knox

which deny that there is any resurrection:

who maintain that there is no resurrection — TCNT

and they asked him,

and put a question to him — Mof

They set him a problem — Rieu

28. Saying, Master, Moses wrote unto us,

. . . Teacher, Moses laid down for us in his writings — TCNT

. . . Rabbi, Moses made this a law for us — Wey

If any man's brother die, having a wife, and he die without children,

if a man's married brother dies . . . — Mof

. . . leaving a wife but no children, — Wey

. . . dies without issue — Knox

that his brother should take his wife,

the surviving brother must marry the widow — Knox

. . . should take the widow as his wife — TCNT

and raise up seed unto his brother.

and raise up a family for his brother — TCNT

. . . offspring . . . — Mof

. . . in the dead brother's name — Knox

and so provide his brother with descendants — Rieu

and carry on his brother's family—NEB

29. There were therefore seven brethren:

Well, there were once seven brothers — TCNT

and the first took a wife, and died without children.

of whom the eldest, after taking a wife, died childless — TCNT

. . . without issue — Knox

30. And the second took her to wife,

The second married his widow — Rieu

and he died childless.

31. And the third took her; and in like manner the seven also: and they left no children, and died.

and so did the third . . . — Rieu

. . . in fact, all the seven took her in turn . . . — Nor

. . . and so, too, did all seven — dying without children — TCNT

32. Last of all the woman died also.

Afterward the woman also died — ASV

The woman herself was the last to die — TCNT

33. Therefore in the resurrection whose wife of them is she?

. . . does the woman become — ABUV

Now, in this 'resurrection' whose wife is she of these seven men — Phi

. . . which of these will be her husband — Knox

for seven had her to wife.

for she belonged to all of them — Phi

34. And Jesus answering said unto them, The children of this world marry, and are given in marriage:

The men and women of this world, said Jesus, . . . — TCNT

. . . of this age . . . — Rhm

. . . marry women, and women are given to men in marriage — Lam

35. But they which shall be accounted worthy to obtain that world, and the resurrection from the dead,

but those who are counted worthy to reach that world and the resurrection from the dead — Mon

. . . that other world . . . — TCNT

. . . yonder world . . . — Mof

. . . to find a place in that other age and . . . — Wey

neither marry, nor are given in marriage:

take neither wife nor husband — Knox

there is no marrying, or being married — TCNT

36. Neither can they die any more:

For they cannot even die any more — Rhm

mortal no longer — Knox

they are not subject to death any longer — NEB

for they are equal unto the angels;

they will be as the angels in heaven are — Knox

in these respects they are like angels — Tay

and are the children of God, being the children of the resurrection.

and since they are reborn in the resurrection, are children of God — Wms

... now that the resurrection has given them birth — Knox

... for they have been raised up in new life from the dead — Tay

and, having shared in the resurrection, they are God's Sons — TCNT

37. Now that the dead are raised,

As to the fact that ... — TCNT

But that the dead do rise — Rhm

... that the dead are awakened — Rieu

even Moses shewed at the bush,

Even Moses disclosed at the bush — Rhm

Moses himself has told you of it in the passage about the burning bush — Knox

even Moses showed to be true in the story of the bush — Phi

even Moses shewed in the history of the bush — Alf

when he calleth the Lord the God of Abraham, and the God of Isaac, and the God of Jacob.

38. For he is not a God of the dead, but of the living:

... not the God of dead men ... — Gspd

It is of living men, not of dead men, that he is the God — Knox

for all live unto him.

for to him, all are alive — Mon

for him, all men are alive — Knox

and from His point of view all men are living — Tay

39. Then certain of the scribes answering, said,

... Doctors of the Law ... — Rieu

... Bible scholars ... — Beck

... Teachers of the Law ... — TCNT

Master, thou hast well said.

Well said, Teacher! — TCNT

Rabbi, you have spoken well — Wey

... that was a fine answer — Mof

40. And after that they durst not

For no longer were they daring — Rhm

for they did not venture — TCNT

And indeed nobody had the courage — Phi

ask him any question at all.

to put a single question to Him — Wey

to question him any further — TCNT

41. And he said unto them, How say they that Christ is David's son?

... How is it that people say that the Christ is to be David's son — TCNT

... What do they mean by saying ... — Knox

... How can people maintain that the Messiah is a son of David — Rieu

... a descendant of King David — Tay

42. And David himself saith in the book of Psalms,

For David himself saith ... — ASV

Why, David himself says ... — Wey

The Lord said unto my Lord,

... to my Master — Knox

God said to my Lord, the Messiah — Tay

Sit thou on my right hand,

Take your seat at ... — Bas

43. Till I make thine enemies thy footstool.

Until I put thy enemies as a stool for thy feet — TCNT

44. David therefore calleth him Lord, how is he then his son?

... calls Christ his Master ... — Knox

David is plainly calling him 'Lord' ... — Phi

... how can He be his son — Wey

How can the Messiah be both David's son and David's God at the same time — Tay

45. Then in the audience of all the people he said unto his disciples,

Then, while everybody was listening ... — Phi

And with all the people listening ... — Amp

46. Beware of the scribes,

Be on your guard against the Teachers of the Law — TCNT

... the Doctors of the Law — Rieu

... the Bible scholars — Beck

which desire to walk in long robes,

who enjoy walking round in ... — Phi

and love greetings in the markets,

and are fond of salutations in the markets — Rhm

and like to be greeted in the streets with respect — TCNT

love to be bowed to in places of public resort — Wey

. . . in places where people congregate — Amp

and the highest seats in the synagogues,

the best seats in the Synagogues — TCNT

the front seats in the . . . — Mof

and the chief rooms at feasts;

and places of honour at dinner — TCNT

. . . the best places at banquets — Mof

. . . at dinner-parties — Wey

47. Which devour widows' houses,

who swallow up the property of widows — Wey

they prey upon the property of widows — Mof

They rob poor widows of their homes — Nor

and for a shew make long prayers:

and by way of excuse make long prayers — Wey

and to cover it up . . . — Gspd

and make a pretence of saying long prayers — TCNT

while they say long prayers for appearance' sake — NEB

the same shall receive greater damnation.

. . . a heavier sentence — Rhm

CHAPTER 21

1. And he looked up, and saw the rich men casting their gifts into the treasury.

. . . into the treasury — Gspd

. . . into the offertory chests — Rieu

. . . in the chests of the temple treasury — NEB

2. And he saw also a certain poor widow

and noticed . . . — Mof

. . . a poverty-stricken . . . — Rieu

casting in thither two mites.

putting in two tiny coins — NEB

. . . two small coins, worth one cent — Nor

. . . two small copper coins — Tay

3. And he said, Of a truth I say unto you, that this poor widow hath cast in more than they all:

. . . Believe me . . . — Knox

. . . This destitute widow . . . — Rhm

. . . I tell you in all truth that this widow, poor as she is, has put in more than all the rest — Rieu

. . . more than all of them — RSV

4. For all these have of their abundance cast in unto the offerings of God:

For from what they could well spare they have all of them contributed to the offerings — Wey

for these people all contributed out of their surplus — Mof

But she of her penury

But she out of her deficiency — Rhm

. . . out of her neediness — Mof

she, with so little to give — Knox

whereas she, who has less than she needs — Rieu

hath cast in all the living that she had.

has thrown in all she had to live on — Wey

put in her whole livelihood — Knox

5. And as some spake of the temple, how it was adorned with goodly stones and gifts, he said,

When some of them spoke about the Temple being decorated with beautiful stones and offerings, Jesus said — TCNT

. . . embellished with beautiful stones and dedicated gifts . . . — Wey

6. As for these things which ye behold,

All this that you admire — Rieu

the days will come, in the which there shall not be left one stone upon another,

a time is coming when not a block of stone here will be left standing on another — Rieu

that shall not be thrown down.

without being torn down — Mof

7. And they asked him, saying, Master, but when shall these things be?

. . . But, Teacher, when will this be — TCNT

. . . Rabbi . . . — Wey

and what sign will there be

What sign will be given — Knox

when these things shall come to pass?

. . . are about to take place — Wey

. . . when this is near — TCNT

. . . for this to take place — Mof

... when it is due to happen — NEB

8. And he said, Take heed that ye be not deceived:
See to it ... that you are not misled — Wey
for many shall come in my name,
... making use of my name — Knox
saying, I am Christ;
professing, I am He — Wey
... Here I am — Knox
and the time draweth near:
or saying, The time is close at hand — Wey
... The Day is upon us — NEB
go ye not therefore after them.
Do not follow their lead — Rieu
Never follow men like that — Phi

9. But when ye shall hear of wars and commotions,
... and revolutions — Rhm
be not terrified:
do not fall into a panic — NEB
for these things must first come to pass;
These things are bound to happen first — NEB
but the end is not by and by.
... not immediately — ASV

10. Then said he unto them,
Then he continued: — Phi
Nation shall rise against nation, and kingdom against kingdom:
... will make war upon ... — NEB

11. And great earthquakes shall be in divers places, and famines, and pestilences;
there will be great earthquakes with famine and pestilence here and there — Mof
... plagues and famines in various places — TCNT
... in one land or another — Rieu
and fearful sights and great signs shall there be from heaven.
There shall be terrors and great portents from heaven — Mon
There will be horrors and great signs in the sky — Gspd

12. But before all these, they shall lay their hands on you, and persecute you,
But before all these things happen, ... — Mon
... men will arrest you ... — Gspd
delivering you up to the synagogues, and into prisons,
and hand you over to synagogues and prisons — Gspd
being brought before kings and rulers for my name's sake.
you will be dragged before ... — Mof
you will be haled before ... for your allegiance to me — NEB

13. And it shall turn to you for a testimony.
That will turn out an opportunity for you to bear witness — Mof
It will all lead to your testifying — Gspd
This will be your chance to witness for me — Phi

14. Settle it therefore in your hearts,
Make up your minds — TCNT
not to meditate before what ye shall answer:
that you will not rehearse your defence beforehand — Mof
Prepare no speeches in your own defence — Rieu

15. For I will give you a mouth and wisdom,
For I myself will give you power of utterance and a wisdom — NEB
for I will myself give you words and a wisdom — TCNT
... such eloquence and wisdom — Ber
... such wisdom of utterance — Gspd
which all your adversaries shall not be able to gainsay nor resist.
as all your opponents combined will not be able to resist and refute — Wms
... to withstand or reply to — Wey
... to meet or refute — Mof
... to withstand or contradict — RSV

16. And ye shall be betrayed both by parents, and brethren, and kinsfolks, and friends;
And ye will be delivered up even by parents ... — Rhm
... even by your parents and brothers and relations and friends — TCNT
and some of you shall they cause to be put to death.
... they will send to their death — Rieu

17. And ye shall be hated by all men
You are going to be ... — Rieu
... continuously hated ... — Wms
... by every one — TCNT
all the world will be hating you — Knox
for my name's sake.

because you bear my name — Gspd

because you use my name — Rieu

for confessing Me — Ber

for your allegiance to me — NEB

18. But there shall not an hair of your head perish.

And a hair of your head in nowise shall perish — Rhm

Yet not a single hair of your head shall be lost! — TCNT

19. In your patience possess ye your souls.

By your endurance shall ye gain your lives for a possession — Rhm

By standing firm you will win true life for yourselves — NEB

Hold out stedfast and you win your souls — Mof

It is by endurance that you will secure possession of your souls — Knox

By your endurance you will gain your lives — RSV

20. And when ye shall see Jerusalem compassed with armies,

. . . being surrounded . . . — Gspd

When you see armies closing round . . . — Rieu

then know that the desolation thereof is nigh.

then recognize that . . . — NASB

. . . her devastation . . . — Gspd

. . . is not far away — Mof

21. Then let them which are in Judaea flee to the mountains;

Then is the time for those who are in Judaea to fly to the hills — Phi

Then those of you who are in Judaea must take refuge in the mountains — TCNT

. . . must take to the hills — NEB

and let them which are in the midst of it depart out;

those who are in Jerusalem must leave at once — TCNT

. . . must get out of it — Gspd

those who live in town must evacuate the city — Nor

and let not them that are in the countries enter thereinto.

and those who are in the country places . . . — TCNT

. . . must not try to get into the city — Phi

22. For these be the days of vengeance,

because this is the time of retribution — NEB

For those will be days of God's judgment — Tay

that all things which are written may be fulfilled.

when all that stands written is to be fulfilled — NEB

in fulfilment of all that is written in scripture — Mof

and the words of the ancient Scriptures written by the prophets will be abundantly fulfilled — Tay

23. But woe unto them that are with child, and to them that give suck, in those days!

Alas for the women who are pregnant and those who have nursing babies in those days! — Wms

Alas, in those days, for a woman with a child in her womb or at her breast! — Rieu

for there shall be great distress in the land, and wrath upon this people.

for sore anguish will come upon the land and Wrath on this people — Mof

for terrible misery shall be on the land and anger shall visit this people — Ber

For great calamity . . . and wrath . . . — Rieu

. . . bitter distress . . . and retribution . . . — Knox

. . . great distress . . . and a terrible judgement . . . — NEB

For there will be great distress upon this nation and wrath upon this people — Tay

24. And they shall fall by the edge of the sword,

. . . at the sword's point — NEB

The sword will cut them down — Beck

and shall be led away captive into all nations:

. . . into captivity all over the world — Knox

. . . into every pagan land — Rieu

and Jerusalem shall be trodden down of the Gentiles,

and Jerusalem will be under the heel of . . . — TCNT

and Jerusalem will be trampled under foot by the heathen — Gspd

. . . by foreigners — NEB

And pagan feet will tread Jerusalem — — Rieu

**until the times of the Gentiles be ful-
filled.**
until their day is over — TCNT
till the period of the Gentiles expires
— Mof
until the time of the heathen comes —
Gspd
until the time granted to the Gentile nations has run out — Knox
until the heathen's day is over — Phi
till pagan days are done — Rieu
until the time of heathen dominion will
have come to an end — Nor

**25. And there shall be signs in the sun,
and in the moon, and in the stars;**
And there shall be signs in sun and
moon and stars — ASV

and upon the earth distress of nations,
. . . anguish among the nations — Wey
On earth nations will stand helpless —
NEB
and on earth dismay among the
heathen — Gspd
and on the earth despair among the
nations — TCNT

**with perplexity; the sea and the waves
roaring;**
in perplexity at the roar of the sea and
the billows — Mon
not knowing which way to turn from
the roar and surge of the sea — NEB
confounded by the surge and thunder
of the sea — Rieu
perplexed by the roaring seas and
strange tides — Tay

26. Men's hearts failing them for fear,
men swooning with panic — Mof
men lifeless through fear — Mon
Men's courage will fail completely —
Phi

**and for looking after those things
which are coming on the earth:**
and foreboding of what is to befall the
universe — Mof
. . . the habitable earth — Mon
as they await the troubles that are over-
taking the whole world — Knox

**for the powers of heaven shall be
shaken.**
for the forces in the sky will shake —
Gspd
for the forces of the heavens will be
convulsed — TCNT

**27. And then shall they see the Son of
man coming in a cloud with power
and great glory.**

. . . with his full power and majesty —
Knox

**28. And when these things begin to come
to pass,**
When these events . . . — Nor
. . . begin to occur — TCNT

then look up, and lift up your heads;
straighten up, and . . . — Ber
straighten your backs and . . . — Rieu
stand upright and . . . — NEB
. . . look forward cheerfully — Beck

for your redemption draweth nigh.
for your release is not far distant —
Mof
because your liberation is near — NEB
for you will soon be free — Phi

29. And he spake to them a parable;
Then He pictured it this way: — Beck

Behold the fig tree, and all the trees;
Notice the . . . — Nor

30. When they now shoot forth,
as soon as they come out in leaf — RSV

ye see and know of your own selves
ye know of your own selves — Alf
you know, as you look at them, without being told — TCNT
you can see for yourselves — Mof

that summer is now nigh at hand.
. . . is coming — Gspd
. . . is in the offing — Ber

**31. So likewise ye, when ye see these
things come to pass,**
Even so ye also . . . — ASV
In the same way , . . — Rieu
So, whenever you see all this happen
— Mof
. . . these events taking place — Nor

**know ye that the kingdom of God is
nigh at hand.**
. be sure the Reign of God is at hand —
Mof

32. Verily I say unto you,
In solemn truth I tell you — Mon

This generation shall not pass away,
In nowise shall this generation pass
away — Rhm
. . . disappear — Phi

till all be fulfilled.
until all this has taken place — Phi

33. Heaven and earth shall pass away:
Earth and sky . . . — Gspd
. . . will come to an end — Bas

but my words shall not pass away.
but what I say . . . — Beck

... will stand — Knox
but my words never! — Mof

34. And take heed to yourselves,
Be on your guard — TCNT
But give attention to yourselves — Bas
Keep a watch on yourselves — NEB
lest at any time your hearts be over-charged
... overpowered — Mof
... loaded down — Gspd
lest your minds should ever be dulled — TCNT
... your faculties be numbed — Rieu
see to it that your minds are never clouded — Phi
with surfeiting, and drunkenness, and cares of this life,
with dissipation ... — Ber
with self-indulgence ... — Gspd
with revelry ... — Knox
by debauches or drunkenness or the anxieties of life — TCNT
and so that day come upon you unawares.
... catch you like the springing of a trap — Phi
... closes upon you suddenly like a trap — NEB
... and take you as in a net — Bas
and the Day catch you unawares like a fowler's noose — Rieu

35. For as a snare shall it come on all them that dwell on the face of the whole earth.
For come it will upon all who are living ... — TCNT
... that Day will dawn on each and every man — Rieu
... on all who are living anywhere — Gspd
... the whole world over — NEB

36. Watch ye therefore, and pray always,
But be watching ... — Rhm
Beware of slumbering ... — Wey

From hour to hour keep awake ... — Mof
But you must be vigilant ... — Gspd
Be on the alert ... — NEB
that ye may be accounted worthy to escape
that you may succeed in escaping — Mof
for the power to survive — Rieu
all these things that shall come to pass,
all that is destined to happen — TCNT
all these coming evils — Wey
all those impending events — Ber
all that lies before you — Knox
all these disasters that are on their way — Rieu
all these imminent troubles — NEB
and to stand before the Son of man.
... take your stand in the presence ... — Wey
... stand erect to meet the presence of ... — Knox

37. And in the day time he was teaching in the temple;
During the days, Jesus continued to teach in the Temple Courts — TCNT
... he was habitually in the Temple teaching — Mon
and at night he went out,
... went outside the city — Mof
and abode in the mount that is called the mount of Olives.
and spent the nights on the hill called the Mount of Olives — TCNT
... on the hill called Olivet — NEB

38. And all the people came early in the morning to him
... used to get up early to go to Him — Beck
And in the early morning the people flocked ... — NEB
in the temple, for to hear him.
to listen to him in the Temple Courts — TCNT

CHAPTER 22

1. Now the feast of unleavened bread drew nigh,
The festival of bread without yeast ... — Beck
... was approaching — Wey
which is called the Passover.
the paschal feast, as it is called — Knox
known as the Passover — TCNT

2. And the chief priests and scribes sought

And the High-priests and the Scribes were seeking — Rhm
and the Chief Priests and Doctors of the Law ... — Rieu
... and the Bible scholars ... — Beck
... continually sought means — Mon
how they might kill him;
how they were to ... — ABUV
to put him to death — Mon

... get him put to death — Mof
for they feared the people.
3. Then entered Satan into Judas
But now Satan found his way into the
heart of Judas — Knox
... took possession of Judas — TCNT
a diabolical plan came into the mind of
... — Phi
surnamed Iscariot,
who was known as Iscariot — TCNT
called the man from Kerioth — Beck
being of the number of the twelve.
who belonged to the Twelve — TCNT
a member of the Twelve — Gspd
**4. And he went his way, and communed
with**
And he went off ... — Gspd
... and had a discussion with — Bas
... to discuss ways and means with —
NEB
... unfolded a scheme he had — Rieu
the chief priests and captains,
the high priests and captains of the
Temple — Gspd
... and Commanders of the Temple
force — Rieu
... and officers of the temple police —
NEB
how he might betray him unto them.
as to how he should deliver Him up to
them — Wey
a method of getting Jesus into their
hands — Phi
... of putting Jesus into their power —
NEB
5. And they were glad,
They were delighted — Mof
and covenanted to give him money.
and made a bargain to pay him for it
— Wms
... to pay him in cash — Nor
6. And he promised,
He accepted their offer — Wey
and sought opportunity
and began to seek a favorable opportunity — Wms
... watched for a moment — Rieu
to betray him unto them
to hand him over — Knox
when he could arrest him for them —
Rieu
in the absence of the multitude.
without a disturbance — Gspd
without any commotion — Knox
without the interference of a crowd —
Rieu

without collecting a crowd — NEB
when He was away from the crowd —
Beck
**7. Then came the day of unleavened
bread,**
... of the festival of bread without
yeast — Beck
when the passover must be killed.
on which the Passover lambs had to
be killed — TCNT
— the day for the Passover lamb to be
sacrificed — Wey
8. And he sent Peter and John, saying,
and Jesus sent Peter and John on an
errand ... — Knox
... with instructions ... — Wey
**Go and prepare us the passover, that
we may eat.**
... prepare the Passover for us, that
we may eat it — Wey
... make preparations for us to eat
the Passover meal — Wms
**9. And they said unto him, Where wilt
thou that we prepare?**
... Where are we to get it ready —
Bas
... Where will you have us prepare it
— RSV
**10. And he said unto them, Behold, when
ye are entered into the city,**
Listen, he answered, when you have
got into the city — TCNT
You will no sooner have entered the
city, ... — Wey
**there shall a man meet you, bearing a
pitcher of water;**
a man carrying a pitcher of water will
meet you — TCNT
than you will meet a man carrying a
pitcher of water — Wey
... carrying a water-jug — Mon
**follow him into the house where he
entereth in.**
... into which he is entering — Rhm
**11. And ye shall say unto the goodman
of the house,**
And ye shall say unto the master of
the house — ASV
and say to the man of the house—Gspd
give this message to the householder —
NEB
... to the head of the house — Nor
The Master saith unto thee,
The Teacher saith ... — ASV
The Rabbi asks you — Wey
Where is the guestchamber,

Where is the guest-room — Bas

where I shall eat the passover with my disciples?

where I am to eat . . . — TCNT

. . . the Passover supper . . . — Gspd

12. And he shall shew you a large upper room furnished:

. . . a large upstairs room . . . — TCNT

. . . with couches spread — Mof

. . . with the necessary furniture — Gspd

there make ready.

There make your preparations — Wey

it is there that you are to make ready — Knox

13. And they went, and found as he had said unto them:

They went off . . . — Mof

. . . and found everything just as Jesus had told them — TCNT

. . . exactly as he had told them it would be — Phi

and they made ready the passover.

and they prepared the Passover supper — Gspd

and they made the Passover preparations — Phi

14. And when the hour was come,

When the time came for the evening meal — Rieu

he sat down,

Jesus took his place at table — TCNT

and the twelve apostles with him.

and the apostles sat down with him — Rieu

15. And he said unto them, With desire I have desired

. . . Earnestly have I longed — ABUV

. . . I have longed eagerly — Mof

. . . I have greatly desired — Gspd

. . . I have longed and longed — Knox

. . . With all my heart I have longed — Phi

. . . I have earnestly and intensely desired — Amp

to eat this passover with you

to share this paschal meal with you — Knox

before I suffer:

before my passion — Knox

16. For I say unto you, I will not any more eat thereof,

Believe me . . . — Phi

for I tell you that I certainly shall not eat one again — Wey

I will never eat the passover again — Mof

until it be fulfilled in the kingdom of God.

until all that it means is fulfilled in the . . . — Phi

until it has had its fulfilment in the . . . — TCNT

till its full meaning is brought out in . . . — Wey

until it finds its full fruition in the . . . — Wms

till the day of the perfect Passover in the . . . — Rieu

till the fulfilment of it in the Reign of God — Mof

17. And he took the cup,

And he received a cup — ASV

. . . a cup of wine — Wms

. . . a cup which was handed to him — Mof

and gave thanks,

after saying the thanksgiving — TCNT

and said, Take this, and divide it among yourselves:

. . . and share it among you — TCNT

. . . and distribute it among yourselves — Mof

18. For I say unto you, I will not drink of the fruit of the vine,

for I tell you, I shall from now on never again drink the fruit of the vine — Ber

. . . I shall not, after to-day, drink of the juice of the grape — TCNT

. . . I shall drink no more wine — Phi

until the kingdom of God shall come.

till such time as God's Reign comes — Mof

19. And he took bread,

And taking a loaf — Rhm

and gave thanks,

he gave thanks — Rhm

and, after saying the thanksgiving — TCNT

and brake it, and gave unto them, saying,

broke it in pieces, and gave it to them, saying — Gspd

broke it apart . . . — Tay

. . . with the words: — TCNT

This is my body[12] which is given for you:

---

[12]Some manuscripts omit the remainder of verse 19 and all of verse 20.

This means my body given up for your sake — Mof

this do in remembrance of me.

... in My memory — Ber

... for a commemoration of me — Knox

Do this to remember Me — Beck

20. **Likewise also the cup after supper, saying,**

And in the same way with the cup ... — TCNT

He handed them the cup in like manner, when the meal was over — Wey

And after they had eaten their supper, he dealt in the same way with the cup by saying — Rieu

This cup is the new testament

This cup of wine is the new covenant — Wms

This cup means the new ... — Mof

in my blood, which is shed for you.

made by my blood which is being poured out on your behalf — TCNT

ratified by my blood which is to be poured out on your behalf — Wey

21. **But, behold, the hand of him that betrayeth me**

Yet look! The hand of the man who is betraying me — Gspd

Yet see! the hand of the man ... — TCNT

... who is now engaged in ... — Amp

... delivering me up — Rhm

is with me on the table.

is at the table with me — Wey

rests on this table, at my side — Knox

lies with mine at this moment on the table — Phi

22. **And truly the Son of man goeth,**

... is going his way — Gspd

... moves to his end — Mof

as it was determined:

according to what is marked out — Rhm

by the way ordained for him — TCNT

as it has been decreed — Mof

on His pre-destined way — Wey

but woe unto that man by whom he is betrayed!

alas! for that man through whom he is being delivered up — Rhm

23. **And they began to enquire among themselves,**

Then they began questioning one another — TCNT

... to discuss with one another — Wey

They fell to surmising among themselves — Knox

which of them it was that should do this thing.

... who was to do this thing — NEB

who was about to do this thing — Rieu

24. **And there was also a strife among them,**

Then a jealous dispute broke out — NEB

A quarrel also rose among them — Mof

They even fell to wrangling — Rieu

And there was rivalry between them over the question — Knox

which of them should be accounted

as to which of them seemed to be — Rhm

... was thought to be — ABUV

... was considered and reputed to be — Amp

the greatest.

most important — Ber

25. **And he said unto them, The kings of the Gentiles exercise lordship over them;**

... of the nations lord it over them — Rhm

... of the heathen ... — Gspd

... of the pagans ... — Rieu

... In the world, kings lord it over their subjects — NEB

and they that exercise authority upon them are called benefactors.

... who wield authority over them ... — Rhm

and their authorities are given the title of Benefactor — Gspd

26. **But ye shall not be so:**

But with you it must not be so — TCNT

But you are not that way — Ber

but he that is greatest among you, let him be as the younger;

Your greatest man must become like a junior — Phi

With you, the senior must take the junior role — Rieu

and he that is chief, as he that doth serve.

your leader act the servant's part — Rieu

27. **For whether is greater,**

For which is greater — Rhm

For who is more important — Ber

For who is senior — Rieu

he that sitteth at meat, or he that serveth?

the diner ... — Rieu

. . . or the waiter — Ber

is not he that sitteth at meat?

Surely the diner — Rieu

Obviously, the man who sits down to dinner — Phi

. . . the master at the table — TCNT

but I am among you as he that serveth.

but I am in the midst of you . . . — ASV

. . . as he who waits — Wey

Yet it is I who play the servant's part among you — Rieu

28. **Ye are they which have continued with me in my temptations.**

. . . who have remained throughout with me in . . . — Rhm

You are the men who have stood by me in my trials — TCNT

. . . in all that I have gone through — Phi

. . . in the troubles that have tested Me — Beck

29. **And I appoint unto you a kingdom, as my Father hath appointed unto me;**

and, just as my Father has assigned me a Kingdom, I assign you places — TCNT

so, as my Father has assigned me royal power, I assign you the right — Mof

So just as my Father has conferred a kingdom on me, I confer on you the right — Gspd

. . . I endow you with the royal right — Rieu

and now I vest in you the kingship which my Father vested in me — NEB

And I covenant unto you — As my Father hath covenanted unto me — a kingdom — Rhm

30. **That ye may eat and drink at my table in my kingdom,**

to eat and drink at . . . — Gspd

and sit on thrones judging the twelve tribes of Israel.

and to sit on thrones and judge . . . — Gspd

31. **And the Lord said, Simon, Simon, behold,**

. . . Simon! Simon! listen — TCNT

. . . I tell you — Wey

. . . take heed — NEB

Satan hath desired to have you, that he may sift you as wheat:

Satan demanded to have . . . — RSV

. . . has obtained permission to have all of you to sift as wheat is sifted — Wey

. . . has claimed the right to sift you all like wheat — Mof

. . . has asked to have you all to sift like wheat — Phi

32. **But I have prayed for thee, that thy faith fail not:**

But I have entreated for thee . . . — Rhm

. . . made supplication . . . — Mon

. . . especially for you . . . — Wms

. . . that you may not lose your faith — Phi

and when thou art converted,

when, after a while . . . — Knox

. . . you have returned to me — TCNT

And you — once you have retraced your steps — Rieu

strengthen thy brethren.

it is for thee to be the support of thy brethren — Knox

33. **And he said unto him, Lord, I am ready to go with thee, both into prison, and to death.**

. . . with you I am prepared . . . — Rieu

. . . I am ready to bear thee company . . . — Knox

34. **And he said, I tell thee, Peter, the cock shall not crow this day, before that thou shalt thrice deny that thou knowest me.**

. . . A cock will not crow . . . — Rhm

. . . to-day till you have disowned all knowledge of me three times — TCNT

35. **And he said unto them, When I sent you**

. . . sent you out as my Messengers — TCNT

without purse, and scrip, and shoes,

. . . purse or satchel or sandals — Rhm

without purse, knapsack or sandals — Rieu

. . . purse, provision bag or shoes — Nor

barefoot without purse or pack — NEB

lacked ye any thing? And they said, Nothing.

you did not need anything, did you? They answered, Nothing at all — Wms

Did you go in want of anything? . . . — Knox

. . . No, not a thing — Phi

36. **Then said he unto them, But now, he that hath a purse, let him take it, and likewise his scrip:**
It is different now, he said; whoever has a purse had better take it with him, and his pack too — NEB
. . . and also a provision bag — Nor
. . . and a knapsack too — Rieu
and he that hath no sword, let him sell his garment, and buy one.
and he that hath none, let him sell his cloak, and buy a sword — ASV
and if you have no purse, sell your cloak and buy a sword — Rieu

37. **For I say unto you,**
Believe me — Knox
that this that is written must yet be accomplished in me,
what has been written about me must be fulfilled — Wms
that this saying of Scripture must find its fulfilment in me — Gspd
And he was reckoned
He was counted — TCNT
he was classed — Mof
He was rated — Gspd
He will be condemned — Tay
among the transgressors:
among the godless — TCNT
with lawless ones — Rhm
among criminals — Mof
with the outlaws — Wms
as a lawbreaker — Nor
as a criminal! — Tay
for the things concerning me have an end.
indeed, all that refers to me is finding its fulfilment — TCNT
Indeed, for me the course is run — Rieu

38. **And they said, Lord, behold, here are two swords.**
Look, Lord, . . . we have two swords here — NEB
And he said unto them, It is enough.
. . . That is enough — Lam
. . . Enough of this! — Gspd
Enough, enough! he said — Rieu

39. **And he came out,**
Leaving the house — Rieu
And he went out of the city — Gspd
and went, as he was wont,
and went, as his custom was — ASV
made his way as usual — TCNT
he went according to his custom — Rhm

. . . as He was in the habit of doing — Wms
. . . as he had often done before — Phi
to the mount of Olives; and his disciples also followed him.
. . . with his disciples following him — Gspd
. . . accompanied by the disciples — NEB

40. **And when he was at the place,**
When He had reached . . . — Nor
. . . his usual place — Phi
he said unto them, Pray
. . . Continue to pray — Wms
that ye enter not into temptation.
that you may not slip into . . . — Mof
. . . may not be subjected to trial — Gspd
. . . may not have to face temptation — Phi
. . . may be spared the hour of testing — NEB

41. **And he was withdrawn from them about a stone's cast,**
And he was torn from them about a stone's throw — Rhm
He Himself withdrew from them . . . — Wey
Then he went off by himself . . . — Phi
. . . about as far as you'd throw a stone — Beck
and kneeled down, and prayed,
sank to his knees, and prayed — Rieu
and bending his knees, he began to pray — Rhm
. . . he prayed repeatedly — Mon
. . . continued to pray — Wms

42. **Saying, Father, if thou be willing,**
. . . if it please thee — Mof
. . . if You wish — Beck
remove this cup from me:
spare me this cup — TCNT
nevertheless not my will, but thine, be done.
but let it not be as I want it . . . — Beck
Yet, not my will but always yours be done! — Wms

43. **And there appeared an angel unto him from heaven, strengthening him.**
And he had sight of . . . — Knox
. . . a messenger . . . — Rhm
. . . who gave him strength — Rieu

44. **And being in an agony**
And as He began to struggle inwardly — Beck
he fell into an agony — Mof

— an agony of distress having come upon Him — Wey

as his anguish became intense — TCNT

in anguish of spirit — NEB

he prayed more earnestly:

He continued to pray . . . — Nor

. . . with even greater vehemence — Rieu

. . . the more urgently — NEB

more intensely was he praying — Rhm

the force of his prayer became stronger — Bas

and his sweat was as it were great drops of blood falling down to the ground.

his perspiration became as if great drops of blood . . . — Rhm

. . . like clots of blood . . . — Wey

. . . dripping to the ground — Nor

The sweat upon him was like drops of blood streaming to the ground — Rieu

45. **And when he rose up from prayer, and was come to his disciples,**

. . . he came unto his disciples — ASV

he found them sleeping for sorrow,

only to find them asleep from sheer sorrow — Mof

. . . overwrought with sorrow — Knox

. . . worn out by grief — NEB

46. **And said unto them, Why sleep ye?**

. . . Why are ye slumbering — Rhm

. . . How can you sleep — Knox

rise and pray,

Get up and . . . — Mof

. . . keep praying — Wms

. . . go on praying — Phi

lest ye enter into temptation.

that you may not slip into . . . — Mof

. . . may not be subjected to trial! — Gspd

. . . may not have to face temptation — Phi

. . . that you may be spared the test — NEB

so that you may not be put to the test — Bas

47. **And while he yet spake,**

While he was still speaking — TCNT

He was still speaking when — Rieu

behold a multitude,

a crowd appeared in sight — TCNT

there came a mob — Mof

and he that was called Judas, one of the twelve, went before them,

. . . was leading them on — Rhm

Judas . . . was their guide — Wms

and drew near unto Jesus to kiss him.

He stepped up close to . . . — Nor

. . . to give him a kiss — Bas

48. **But Jesus said unto him, Judas, betrayest thou the Son of man with a kiss?**

. . . is it by a kiss that you . . . — TCNT

49. **When they which were about him saw**

. . . the supporters of Jesus . . . — Mof

. . . his followers . . . — NEB

what would follow,

what was going to happen — TCNT

what was coming — Gspd

what was afoot — Rieu

they said unto him, Lord, shall we smite with the sword?

. . . shall we use our swords — TCNT

. . . shall we strike out with . . . — Knox

50. **And one of them smote the servant of the high priest,**

And a certain one of them . . . — ASV

. . . did strike . . . — Mof

. . . struck a blow at . . . — Wey

. . . did slash at . . . — Phi

and cut off his right ear.

and took off . . . — Rhm

shearing off . . . — Rieu

51. **And Jesus answered and said, Suffer ye thus far.**

. . . Permit me to go as far as this! — Wms

. . . Permit them to go so far (as to seize Me) — Amp

. . . Stop! no more of this — NASB

No more of this! said Jesus — Rieu

And he touched his ear, and healed him.

and cured him by touching his ear — Mof

52. **Then Jesus said unto the chief priests, and captains of the temple, and the elders, which were come to him,**

Then, turning to . . . — TCNT

. . . the High-priests and . . . — Rhm

. . . the officers of the temple police . . . — NEB

. . . and elders (of the Sanhedrin) . . . — Amp

Be ye come out, as against a thief,

. . . as if to fight with a robber — Wey

. . . as though I were a brigand — Rieu

with swords and staves?

. . . and clubs — Rhm

. . . and cudgels — Wey

53. When I was daily with you in the temple,
I was close to you . . . — Knox
. . . day after day in the Temple Courts
— TCNT
ye stretched forth no hands against me:
you never stretched a hand . . . — Mof
you never laid a finger on me — Phi
but this is your hour, and the power of darkness.
But your time has come now . . . — Knox
. . . and the dark Power has its way — Mof
But this is your hour. Night takes command — Rieu
But this is your moment — the hour when darkness reigns — NEB
But you choose this hour, and the cover of darkness! — Gspd

54. Then took they him, and led him,
. . . arrested Him and led Him away — Wey
. . . seized him and . . . — Mon
and brought him into the high priest's house.
and marched him off . . . — Phi
. . . to the High Priest's palace — Rieu
And Peter followed afar off.
. . . was following . . . — Rhm
. . . at a distance — TCNT
. . . a good way behind — Wey

55. And when they had kindled a fire in the midst of the hall,
. . . had lit a fire in the centre of the court-yard — TCNT
. . . in the middle of the open square — Bas
and were set down together,
and had all sat down there — TCNT
and had seated themselves in a group round it — Wey
Peter sat down among them.
. . . was taking his seat among them — Mon
. . . in their circle — Ber

56. But a certain maid beheld him
A servant-girl . . . — Wms
. . . noticed him — Mof
as he sat by the fire,
. . . towards the light — Rhm
. . . near the blaze of the fire — TCNT
. . . in the light of the fire — ASV
. . . in the firelight — Knox

and earnestly looked upon him, and said,
peered into his face . . . — Phi
looked closely at . . . — Knox
took a long look at him . . . — Mof
took a good look at him . . . — Ber
fixed her eyes on him . . . — Wms
looking straight at him . . . — Beck
stared at him . . . — Rieu
with a sharp glance at him, she said — Mon
This man was also with him.
This fellow was with him, too! — Mon

57. And he denied him, saying,
But Peter denied it . . . — TCNT
Woman, I know him not.
I don't know him, girl! — Phi
No, ma'am, I do not know Him! — Nor
. . . I don't even know the man! — Tay

58. And after a little while another saw him, and said,
. . . some one else — a man . . . — TCNT
. . . noticed him . . . — Mof
. . . caught sight of him . . . — Knox
Thou art also of them.
You are one of them too! — Gspd
And Peter said, Man, I am not.
No, sir, I am not! — Nor

59. And about the space of one hour after
After an interval of about an hour — Wey
another confidently affirmed, saying,
. . . began stoutly to insist . . . — Rhm
. . . kept insisting . . . — Mon
. . . declared positively — TCNT
. . . emphatically asserted — Wms
. . . spoke up with confidence — Rieu
. . . spoke more strongly still — NEB
Of a truth this fellow also was with him:
That fellow really was with him — Mof
Unquestionably this fellow was with him — Ber
I am convinced . . . — Phi
It is a fact . . . — Rieu
for he is a Galilean.
For quite apart from other things, he is . . . — Rieu

60. And Peter said, Man, I know not what thou sayest.
. . . Sir . . . — Rieu
. . . I don't know what you're talking about — Phi
And immediately, while he yet spake,
At that moment . . . — NEB

And immediately, while he was still speaking — Mon

. . . while the words were on his lips — Knox

And at once, before he had finished — Rieu

the cock crew.

a cock crew — Rhm

there came the cry of a cock — Bas

61. And the Lord turned, and looked upon Peter.

. . . turned his head and looked straight at . . . — Phi

. . . swung round and looked at Peter intently — Rieu

. . . gave Peter a look — Bas

And Peter remembered the word of the Lord, how he had said unto him,

. . . recalled . . . — Amp

. . . the Lord's warning . . . — Ber

. . . how He had said to him — Wey

Before the cock crow,

Before a cock has crowed to-day — TCNT

thou shalt deny me thrice.

. . . disown me . . . — TCNT

you will have denied Me three times — Nor

62. And Peter went out, and wept bitterly.

. . . he went outside . . . — TCNT

. . . burst into bitter tears — Wms

63. And the men that held Jesus

. . . held Jesus in custody — Wey

. . . held Jesus prisoner — Knox

mocked him, and smote him.

kept making sport of him . . . — TCNT

flogged him and made fun of him — Mof

kept mocking him with blows — Rhm

. . . as they struck Him — Beck

beat Him in cruel sport — Wey

made a great game of knocking him about — Phi

64. And when they had blindfolded him, they struck him on the face, and asked him,

They covered his face and . . . — Beck

. . . and they kept asking him — NEB

saying, Prophesy, who is it that smote thee?

. . . Now play the Prophet, . . . — TCNT

Prove to us, . . . that you are a prophet, by telling us . . . — Wey

. . . Now, prophet, guess who hit you that time! — Phi

65. And many other things blasphemously spake they against him.

And that was only the beginning of the way they . . . — Phi

. . . went on heaping insults . . . — NEB

. . . blasphemous words against him — Knox

66. And as soon as it was day,

When day broke — Mof

the elders of the people and the chief priests and the scribes came together,

. . . the Council of Elders of the people . . . — NASB

. . . which included both chief priests and scribes, met — Phi

. . . both High-Priests and Scribes . . . — Rhm

the elders of the people, ruling priests, and Bible scholars had a meeting — Beck

and led him into their council, saying,

and marched him off to their own council . . . — Phi

They brought Jesus before their court . . . — Beck

. . . to their council chamber . . . — NASB

67. Art thou the Christ? tell us.

If you really are Christ . . . — Phi

. . . tell us so — TCNT

And he said unto them, If I tell you, ye will not believe:

. . . you will never believe me — Knox

. . . you will certainly not believe me — Rieu

68. And if I also ask you,

. . . put a question to . . . — Mof

ye will not answer me, nor let me go.

you will certainly not . . . — Rieu

. . . give an answer — Bas

69. Hereafter shall the Son of man sit on the right hand of the power of God.

But from now on . . . — Ber

But from this time forward . . . — Wey

. . . will be sitting . . . — Beck

. . . will be seated on the right hand of God Almighty — TCNT

70. Then said they all,

. . . they cried out with one voice — Wey

Art thou then the Son of God?

You, then, are the Son of God? — Wey

And he said unto them,

Ye say that I am.

Your own lips have said that I am —
Knox
As you say: I am He — Beck
It is you that say I am — Rieu
Ye say it; because I am — ABUV

71. **And they said,**
What need we any further witness?
Why do we need to call any more wit-
nesses — Phi
Why do we want any more evidence —
TCNT
for we ourselves have heard of his own
mouth.
. . . have heard it from his own lips —
Wey

CHAPTER 23

1. **And the whole multitude of them arose,**
. . . they all rose in a body — TCNT
The Council rose and without dispersing — Rieu
and led him unto Pilate.
and brought him before Pilate — ASV
took him off to Pilate — Rieu

2. **And they began to accuse him, saying,**
Here they began to make the following
charges against Him: — Wms
They opened the case against him by
saying — NEB
We found this fellow perverting the
nation,
. . . misleading our people — TCNT
. . . teaching our people sedition —
Rieu
and forbidding to give tribute to Cae-
sar,
preventing them from paying taxes to
the Emperor — TCNT
telling them that it is wrong to . . . —
Phi
saying that he himself is Christ a King.
claiming to be . . . — NEB
. . . the Christ, that is, a King — Rieu
. . . an anointed king — Rhm

3. **And Pilate asked him, saying, Art thou**
the King of the Jews?
. . . interrogated him . . . — Rieu
And he answered him and said, Thou
sayest it.
. . . Thy own lips have said it — Knox
. . . The words are yours — Rieu

4. **Then said Pilate to the chief priests**
and to the people,
But Pilate, turning to . . . — TCNT
. . . the High-priests and . . . — Rhm
. . . and to the crowd — Wey
I find no fault in this man.
I do not see anything to find fault with
in this man — TCNT
I cannot find anything criminal about
him — Mof
. . . anything blameworthy . . . — Wms
I do not find this person guilty — Rieu

5. **And they were the more fierce, saying,**
But they continued emphatically insisting — Wms
. . . they pressed their charge . . . — Phi
He stirreth up the people, teaching
throughout all Jewry,
He is exciting the . . . — Wms
He's a troublemaker among . . . — Phi
He rouses sedition among the people;
he has gone round the whole of Judaea preaching — Knox
beginning from Galilee to this place.
all the way from . . . — Phi
. . . Galilee (where he first started) to
this city — Wey

6. **When Pilate heard of Galilee, he asked**
whether the man were a Galilaean.
. . . heard the word "Galilee" . . . —
Mon

7. **And as soon as he knew that he be-**
longed unto Herod's jurisdiction,
. . . learning that He belonged to . . .
— Wey
. . . came under . . . — TCNT
having ascertained that he came from
a country under Herod's jurisdiction
— Rieu
he sent him to Herod, who himself also
was at Jerusalem at that time.
. . . turned him over to . . . — Gspd
. . . passed him on to . . . — Phi

8. **And when Herod saw Jesus, he was**
exceeding glad:
Herod was greatly delighted to see
Jesus — Mof
. . . was overjoyed . . . — Knox
To Herod the sight of Jesus was a great
gratification — Wey
for he was desirous to see him of a
long season,
for he had been wanting to see him for
a long time — TCNT

because he had heard many things of him; and he hoped to have seen some miracle done by him.

. . . had been hoping . . . — NEB

. . . to see some miracle performed by . . . — Wey

. . . some spectacular performance done . . . — Wms

. . . to witness some miracle of his — Knox

. . . to see some marvel at his hands — Rieu

9. Then he questioned with him in many words;

. . . put a number of questions to Him — Wey

. . . questioned him at some length — TCNT

. . . very thoroughly — Phi

but he answered him nothing.

. . . made no reply — TCNT

. . . gave him absolutely no reply — Phi

10. And the chief priests and scribes stood

And the High-priests and . . . — Rhm

. . . the Bible scholars . . . — Beck

. . . were standing there — Wey

. . . were standing around — Mon

and vehemently accused him.

and continually making accusations against him — Mon

making the most violent accusations — Phi

relentlessly denouncing him — Rieu

and pressed the case against him vigorously — NEB

11. And Herod with his men of war set him at nought,

. . . with his troops . . . — Alf

. . . and his guards made light of him — Gspd

. . . dismissed him as of no account — Rieu

and mocked him,

made sport of Him — Wey

and made fun of . . . — Mof

and ridiculed him — Gspd

and arrayed him in a gorgeous robe, and sent him again to Pilate.

dressed him up in a gorgeous cloak . . . — Phi

. . . in festal attire . . . — Knox

12. And the same day Pilate and Herod were made friends together:

And before the day was over . . . — Rieu

for before they were at enmity between themselves.

for before that there had been ill-will between them — TCNT

. . . long-standing enmity between them — Lam

. . . a standing feud between them — NEB

. . . they had been at daggers drawn — Phi

13. And Pilate, when he had called together the chief priests and the rulers and the people,

. . . called a meeting of . . . — Wms

. . . the High-priests and . . . — Rhm

. . . and the leading men, and the people — TCNT

. . . and the leading members of the council . . . — Gspd

14. Said unto them, Ye have brought this man unto me, as one that perverteth the people:

You brought this man before me charged with misleading . . . — TCNT

. . . on a charge of corrupting the loyalty of . . . — Wey

. . . as being an inciter to rebellion among . . . — Mof

. . . as a mischief-maker among . . . — Phi

and, behold, I, having examined him before you, have found no fault in this man touching those things whereof ye accuse him:

. . . I did not find this man to blame . . . — TCNT

. . . discovered . . . no ground for the accusations — Wey

. . . found nothing criminal . . . — Mof

. . . no substance in any of the charges . . . — Knox

. . . nothing in him to support your charges — NEB

15. No, nor yet Herod: for I sent you to him;

Nor did Herod find anything . . . — Nor

. . . for he sent him back unto us[13] — ASV

and, lo, nothing worthy of death is done unto him.

Indeed, he has done nothing to deserve the death penalty — Wms

---

[13]Variant reading.

Behold, nothing deserving death has been done by him — RSV

16. I will therefore chastise him, and release him.
So I will teach him a lesson and let him go — Gspd
I therefore propose to let him off with a flogging — NEB

17. (For of necessity he must release one unto them at the feast.)
(For he had to release them one convict at the feast.) — Ber
At the festival, he was obliged to grant them the liberty of one prisoner — Knox

18. And they cried out all at once, saying,
... began to shout as one man — TCNT
But there was a general outcry — NEB
Away with this man, and release unto us Barabbas:
Away with this fellow ... — Wms
... We want Barabbas set free! — Phi

19. (Who for a certain sedition made in the city, and for murder, was cast into prison.)
... for a riot that had broken out ... — TCNT
... for an insurrection started in the city ... — RSV

20. Pilate therefore, willing to release Jesus,
... in his desire to release Jesus — NEB
spake again to them.
once more addressed them — Wey
called to them again — TCNT

21. But they cried, saying, Crucify him, crucify him.
... they kept shouting back ... — Rieu
but they roared, To the cross, to the cross with him! — Mof

22. And he said unto them the third time, Why, what evil hath he done? I have found no cause of death in him:
... I found him guilty of no capital offence — Rieu
... nothing that deserves death — Wey
... nothing ... deserving the death penalty — Wms
I will therefore chastise him, and let him go.
So I will teach him a lesson and let him go — Gspd
... after due correction, I propose to let him go — Rieu
... let him off with a flogging — NEB

23. And they were instant with loud voices, requiring that he might be crucified.
But they continued to press him ... — Wms
... with frantic outcries ... — Wey
... at the top of their voices ... — Rieu
But they shouted him down ... — Phi
And the voices of them and of the chief priests prevailed.
and their clamour gained the day — TCNT
and their voices began to prevail — Rhm
and their shouts were overpowering Pilate — Beck

24. And Pilate gave sentence
... gave his decision — Bas
... pronounced the official decision — Phi
that it should be as they required.
that their request should be granted — Rhm
that their demand was to be carried out — Mof

25. And he released unto them
he set free — Wey
him that for sedition and murder was cast into prison,
... for rioting and murder — Phi
whom they had desired;
the man they were asking for — NASB
but he delivered Jesus to their will.
... turned Jesus over ... — Wms
... to be dealt with as they pleased — TCNT

26. And as they led him away,
... led him away to execution — NEB
they laid hold upon one Simon, a Cyrenian,
... seized a man named Simon ... — Gspd
... a native of Cyrene in Africa — Phi
coming out of the country,
on his way in from the country — TCNT
on his way home from the fields — Phi
and on him they laid the cross,
and they loaded him with ... — Knox
that he might bear it after Jesus.
for him to carry it behind Jesus — TCNT

27. And there followed him a great company of people,
... there was following him a great throng of people — Rhm

and of women, which also bewailed
and lamented him.

many being women who were beating
their breasts and wailing for him —
TCNT

28. **But Jesus turning unto them said,**
 ... turned round to the women ... —
 Rieu

 **Daughters of Jerusalem, weep not for
 me, but weep for yourselves, and for
 your children.**
 ... stop weeping for me ... — Wms
 ... let not your weeping be for me ...
 — Bas
 ... It is not for me that you should
 weep ... — Knox
 ... do not shed your tears for me ...
 — Phi

29. **For, behold, the days are coming, in
 the which they shall say, Blessed are
 the barren,**
 ... Happy are the childless women —
 Gspd
 ... who couldn't have children — Beck
 **and the wombs that never bare, and
 the paps which never gave suck.**
 and those who have never borne children or nursed them — TCNT

30. **Then shall they begin to say to the
 mountains, Fall on us; and to the hills,
 Cover us.**
 ... Cover us up! — Gspd
 ... Hide us! — Ber

31. **For if they do these things in a green
 tree,**
 If it goes so hard ... — Knox
 ... in moist wood — Rhm
 ... with the green wood — Wey
 what shall be done in the dry?
 what is to take place ... — ABUV
 ... when it is seasoned — Phi

32. **And there were also two other, malefactors, led with him to be put to
 death.**
 There were two others with him, criminals who were being led away to
 execution — NEB
 And two others also, who were criminals, were being led away to be put
 to death with Him — NASB

33. **And when they were come to the place,
 which is called Calvary,**
 When they had reached the place called
 'The Skull' — TCNT
 **there they crucified him, and the male-
 factors,**

... nailed Him to the cross ... — Wey
... crucified him there along with the
criminals — Mof

**one on the right hand, and the other
on the left.**
one on either side of him — Phi

34. **Then said Jesus, Father, forgive them;**
 Jesus meanwhile was saying ... —
 Knox
 ... kept saying ... — Mon
 for they know not what they do.
 ... what they are doing — TCNT
 **And they parted his raiment, and cast
 lots.**
 And in dividing his garments among
 them, they cast lots — ABUV
 They parcelled out his clothing and
 cast lots for the shares — Rieu

35. **And the people stood beholding.**
 ... staring — Ber
 ... watching — RSV
 **And the rulers also with them derided
 him, saying,**
 even the rulers ... — Mof
 ... were sneering ... — Rhm
 ... repeatedly taunted him ... — Mon
 He saved others; let him save himself,
 He saved other people ... — Phi
 ... let Him now rescue Himself—Amp
 if he be Christ, the chosen of God.
 if this fellow ... — Mon
 ... really is the Christ of God, His
 Chosen One — Wms
 ... the man of God's selection — Bas

36. **And the soldiers also mocked him,**
 ... made a jest at his expense — Rieu
 ... made sport of him — Wey
 ... made fun of him — Mof
 **coming to him, and offering him vine-
 gar,**
 ... bringing him common wine — TCNT
 ... presenting sour wine to him — Phi

37. **And saying, If thou be the king of the
 Jews, save thyself.**

38. **And a superscription also was written
 over him in letters of Greek, and
 Latin, and Hebrew, THIS IS THE
 KING OF THE JEWS.**
 For there was a notice above his head,
 This is ... — Gspd
 ... a placard ... — Wms

39. **And one of the malefactors which
 were hanged**
 ... one of the criminals who had been
 hung there — Mon
 railed on him,

kept reviling him — Mon

fell to blaspheming against him—Knox

covered him with abuse — Phi

saying, If thou be Christ, save thyself and us.

... Save yourself and us as well — Mof

40. **But the other answering rebuked him, saying,**

... intervened — Rieu

... checked him — Mof

... answered sharply — NEB

Dost not thou fear God, seeing thou art in the same condemnation?

... are under the same sentence of condemnation — RSV

... are suffering the same penalty — Gspd

... condemned to die like him — Rieu

41. **And we indeed justly;**

And we indeed are suffering justly — Wey

And it's fair enough for us — Phi

For us it is plain justice — NEB

for we receive the due reward of our deeds:

for we are only reaping our deserts — TCNT

for we are receiving due retribution — Mon

for we've only got what we deserve — Phi

but this man hath done nothing amiss.

but this man never did anything wrong in his life — Phi

42. **And he said unto Jesus,**

... went on to say — Jesus! — Rhm

Lord, remember me when thou comest into thy kingdom.

do not forget me when you have come to your Kingdom — TCNT

... to your throne — NEB

... to reign — Mof

43. **And Jesus said unto him, Verily I say unto thee,**

... In solemn truth I tell you — Mon

To day shalt thou be with me in paradise.

this very day ... — TCNT

44. **And it was about the sixth hour,**

By this time it was about twelve o'clock — Mof

... nearly mid-day — TCNT

and there was a darkness over all the earth

a darkness came over the whole country — TCNT

... fell upon ... — Lam

... overspread the ... — Nor

until the ninth hour.

lasting till three in the afternoon — TCNT

45. **And the sun was darkened,**

the sun's light failing — ASV

the sun being eclipsed — TCNT

and the veil of the temple was rent in the midst.

the curtain of the Sanctuary ... — Wey

... was split in two — Phi

... was ripped through the middle — Nor

46. **And when Jesus had cried with a loud voice, he said,**

... with a loud cry ... — TCNT

Father, into thy hands I commend my spirit:

... I commit ... — TCNT

... entrust ... — Wey

and having said thus, he gave up the ghost.

After uttering these words ... — Wey

... he expired — Mof

And with these words, he died — Phi

47. **Now when the centurion saw what was done, he glorified God,**

The Roman captain on seeing what had happened ... — TCNT

... began to glorify God — Rhm

saying, Certainly this was a righteous man.

... Beyond all doubt ... — NEB

... Certainly this man was innocent — Alf

... That was indeed a good man! — Phi

48. **And all the people that came together**

And all the crowds ... — Wey

... who had flocked there — Rieu

... who had collected — TCNT

to that sight,

for this spectacle — Ber

to see the sight — TCNT

beholding the things which were done,

after seeing all that had occurred — Wey

smote their breasts, and returned.

went home beating their breasts—TCNT

returned to the city ... — Wey

were returning ... — Mon

... in deep distress — Phi

49. **And all his acquaintance, and the women that followed him from Galilee, stood afar off,**

But all His acquaintances, and the women who had been His followers after leaving Galilee, continued standing at a distance — Wey

beholding these things.
watching all this — TCNT

50. And, behold, there was a man named Joseph, a counsellor;
. . . a member of the Jewish council — Phi

and he was a good man, and a just:
who bore a good and upright character — TCNT

51. (The same had not consented to
. . . had not concurred in — Wey
. . . had not voted for — Mof
. . . not approved of — Rieu

the counsel and deed of them;)
the decision and action of the Council — TCNT
their plan of action — Mof
their policy and the action they had taken — NEB

he was of Arimathaea, a city of the Jews:
he belonged to . . . — Mof

who also himself waited for the kingdom of God.
. . . lived in expectation of . . . — TCNT
. . . who looked forward to . . . — NEB
. . . was on the lookout for the Reign of God — Mof
. . . was on the watch for the kingdom of God — Mon

52. This man went unto Pilate, and begged the body of Jesus.
. . . made a request for . . . — Bas

53. And he took it down, and wrapped it in linen,

. . . took it down from the cross . . . — Gspd
Then he took it down and wrapped it in a linen shroud — RSV

and laid it in a sepulchre that was hewn in stone,
and laid Him in a tomb cut into the rock — NASB

wherein never man before was laid.
where no one as yet was lying — Rhm

54. And that day was the preparation,
It was the day of the Preparation—Mof
It was Friday — NEB

and the sabbath
and the day of rest — Beck

drew on.
was just dawning — Mof
was about to begin — NEB

55. And the women also, which came with him from Galilee, followed after,
. . . who had come with Jesus . . . followed close behind — Wey

and beheld the sepulchre,
. . . observed the tomb — Rhm
. . . took note of the tomb — NEB

and how his body was laid.
. . . was placed — Wey
. . . and the position of the body—Mof

56. And they returned, and prepared spices and ointments;
. . . went home . . . — TCNT
. . . spices and perfumes — Rhm

and rested the sabbath day according to the commandment.
. . . on Saturday . . . — Beck
. . . took their rest . . . — Bas
. . . remained quiet . . . — Nor
. . . in obedience to . . . — Wey

CHAPTER 24

1. Now upon the first day of the week, very early in the morning,
but in the deep dawn of the first day . . . — Mon
. . . at the first signs of dawn . . . — Phi
. . . in the dim light of dawn . . . — Rieu

they came unto the sepulchre,
the women . . . — Nor
. . . resorted to the tomb — Ber

bringing the spices which they had prepared,
taking with them the aromatic spices — Phi

and certain others with them.

There were some others with them — Nor

2. And they found the stone rolled away from the sepulchre.
The boulder they found rolled away from the tomb — Mof
They discovered that the stone had been rolled away — Phi

3. And they entered in, and found not the body of the Lord Jesus.
. . . but they looked in vain for . . . — Rieu

4. And it came to pass, as they were much perplexed thereabout,

. . . were at a loss to account for this — TCNT

. . . were puzzling over this — Mof

. . . were in doubt about it — Bas

behold, two men stood by them in shining garments:

when suddenly there stood by them two men whose raiment flashed like lightning — Wey

two men in dazzling robes suddenly took their stand beside them — Wms

5. And as they were afraid, and bowed down their faces to the earth,

The women were overcome with fear and lowered their eyes — Rieu

. . . became afraid . . . — ABUV

. . . were terrified . . . — Wey

they said unto them, Why seek ye the living among the dead?

. . . Why search among the dead for one who lives — NEB

. . . Why seek ye the Living One with the dead — Rhm

6. He is not here, but is risen:

. . . has come back to life — Wey

remember how he spake unto you when he was yet in Galilee,

. . . while He was still in Galilee — Wey

. . . before he left Galilee — TCNT

7. Saying, The Son of man must be delivered

. . . It is necessary that the Son of Man be given over — Nor

into the hands of sinful men, and be crucified, and the third day rise again.

into the power of sinful men . . . — NEB

8. And they remembered his words,

. . . recollected . . . — Mon

. . . recalled . . . — Wms

. . . called to mind . . . — Rieu

9. And returned from the sepulchre,

and they went back from the tomb — Gspd

and told all these things unto the eleven, and to all the rest.

bringing news of all this . . . — Knox

10. It was Mary Magdalene, and Joanna, and Mary the mother of James, and other women that were with them, which told these things unto the apostles.

The women concerned were . . . — Rieu

11. And their words seemed to them as idle tales,

What they said seemed to the Apostles mere nonsense — TCNT

and they believed them not.

. . . continued to disbelieve the women — Wms

. . . were minded to disbelieve them — Rhm

12. Then arose Peter, and ran unto the sepulchre;

and stooping down, he beheld the linen clothes laid by themselves,

and peering in saw nothing but the linen wrappings — Rieu

. . . saw the graveclothes lying by themselves — Knox

and departed, wondering in himself at that which was come to pass.

so he went away home, wondering what had happened — Wey

And he came away amazed — Rieu

13. And, behold, two of them went that same day to a village called Emmaus, which was from Jerusalem about threescore furlongs.

. . . about seven miles from Jerusalem — TCNT

14. And they talked together

and they were conversing one with another — Rhm

of all these things which had happened.

about all these events — Wey

15. And it came to pass, that, while they communed together and reasoned,

They were still conversing and debating together, when — Knox

While they were absorbed in their serious talk and discussion — Phi

Jesus himself drew near, and went with them.

Jesus himself overtook them and walked beside them — Mof

. . . and began walking beside them — Mon

16. But their eyes were holden that they should not know him.

But their eyes continued to be held that they should not recognize him even for an instant — Mon

But a spell was on their eyes — they did not recognize him — Rieu

but something held their eyes from seeing who it was — NEB

17. And he said unto them, What manner of communications are these that ye have one to another,

. . . What talk is this you exchange between you — Knox

. . . What is all this discussion that you are having — Phi

as ye walk, and are sad?

as you are walking? And they stood still, looking sad — NASB

. . . They stopped, looking downcast — Mof

. . . They halted, their faces full of gloom — NEB

. . . They stopped, their faces drawn with misery — Phi

. . . Disconcerted, they came to a halt — Rieu

18. And the one of them, whose name was Cleopas, answering said unto him, Art thou only a stranger in Jerusalem,

. . . Are you a stranger lodging alone in Jerusalem — Wey

. . . Are you staying by yourself at Jerusalem — TCNT

. . . Are you the only visitor to Jerusalem — Gspd

. . . You must be the only person in all Jerusalem — Tay

and hast not known the things which are come to pass there in these days?

who has not heard of . . . — Wms

. . . what has lately happened in the city — Wey

. . . what has just happened there — Rieu

. . . the things that have happened there within the last few days — TCNT

19. And he said unto them, What things?

. . . What kind of things? — ABUV

And they said unto him, Concerning Jesus of Nazareth,

. . . Oh, all about Jesus, from Nazareth — Phi

which was a prophet mighty in deed and word before God and all the people:

who had proved himself a prophet . . . — Rieu

. . . powerful in work and word . . . — Wey

. . . strong in action and utterance . . . — Mof

. . . strong in what he did and what he said . . . — Phi

. . . in practice and in preaching . . . — Ber

who, in the eyes of God and all the people, was a Prophet, whose power

was felt in both his words and actions — TCNT

whose words and acts had power with God, and with all the people — Knox

20. And how the chief priests and our rulers

. . . High-priests . . . — Rhm

. . . and our leading men — TCNT

delivered him to be condemned to death,

turned him over . . . — Wms

. . . unto a sentence of death — Rhm

. . . for execution — Phi

and have crucified him.

and so crucified him — Knox

and had him crucified — Gspd

21. But we trusted that it had been he which should have redeemed Israel:

We however were hoping that he was the one destined to redeem Israel! — Rhm

. . . who was about to ransom Israel — Wey

. . . to liberate Israel — NEB

and beside all this, to day is the third day since these things were done.

but now, to crown it all . . . — Knox

. . . three days have already passed . . . — Ber

. . . since all this happened — Phi

but he is dead, and that is three days ago! — Mof

22. Yea, and certain women also of our company made us astonished,

And what is more . . . — TCNT

. . . some women of our number gave us a surprise — Mof

. . . disturbed us profoundly — Phi

which were early at the sepulchre;

They went to the tomb at daybreak — TCNT

. . . early this morning — Gspd

23. And when they found not his body,

not finding the body of Jesus there — TCNT

. . . failed to find his body — NEB

they came, saying, that they had also seen a vision of angels,

and returned with a story . . . — NEB

which said that he was alive.

. . . that he lives — Ber

24. And certain of them which were with us went to the sepulchre,

Some of our people went straight off to the tomb — Phi

and found it even so as the women had said:

and found everything just as the women had said — TCNT

. . . exactly as the women had said — Mof

but him they saw not.

but of him they saw nothing — Knox

25. **Then he said unto them, O fools, and slow of heart**

O dull-witted men, He replied, with minds so slow — Wey

. . . O men sluggish in mind and slow in heart to — Wms

. . . O simpletons, with hearts so slow — Ber

. . . Too slow of wit, too dull of heart — Knox

to believe all that the prophets have spoken:

to rest your faith upon . . . — Rhm

to put your trust in . . . — Rieu

26. **Ought not Christ to have suffered these things,**

Was not the Christ bound to undergo this suffering — TCNT

Was there not a necessity for the Christ thus to suffer — Wey

Was it not inevitable that . . . — Phi

and to enter into his glory?

and then enter . . . — Wey

27. **And beginning at Moses and all the prophets,**

Then, going back to Moses and the whole line of the prophets — Knox

. . . starting from Moses and through all the prophets — Ber

he expounded unto them in all the scriptures

. . . interpreted to them . . . — ASV

. . . explained to them . . . — TCNT

. . . in every part of the scriptures — NEB

the things concerning himself.

the passages that referred to himself — TCNT

28. **And they drew nigh unto the village, whither they went:**

. . . the village they were making for — Rieu

and he made as though he would have gone further.

He pretended to be going further on — Mof

he acted as though he were going on — Gspd

He gave the impression that he meant to go on farther — Phi

29. **But they constrained him, saying,**

. . . pressed him not to do so . . . — TCNT

. . . urged him not to, and said — Gspd

Abide with us:

Stay with us — TCNT

for it is toward evening, and the day is far spent.

It is nearly evening . . . — Phi

evening draws on . . . — NEB

. . . and the sun is already low — TCNT

. . . it is far on in the day — Knox

. . . the day is nearly over — Wey

And he went in to tarry with them.

So he went indoors to stay . . . — Phi

30. **And it came to pass, as he sat at meat with them,**

After he had taken his place at table with them — TCNT

he took bread, and blessed it,

. . . and said the blessing — TCNT

. . . gave thanks — Phi

and brake, and gave to them.

broke it and passed it to them — Phi

. . . and offered it to them — Knox

. . . was handing it to them — Wey

31. **And their eyes were opened,**

. . . were instantly opened — Wms

Their eyes opened wide — Phi

Now their eyes could see — Nor

and they knew him;

. . . recognized him — TCNT

and he vanished out of their sight.

. . . became invisible for them — Ber

. . . disappeared from their sight — TCNT

32. **And they said one to another,**

. . . said to each other — TCNT

Did not our heart burn within us,

Were not our hearts . . . burning within us — Wey

Did we not feel our hearts on fire — NEB

while he talked with us by the way,

while he was talking to us on the road — TCNT

and while he opened to us the scriptures?

opening up the scriptures for us — Mof

as He went on explaining . . . — Wms

. . . the Bible to us — Beck

33. **And they rose up the same hour, and returned to Jerusalem,**

So they rose and without an hour's delay returned to Jerusalem — Wey

And they got to their feet without delay . . . — Phi

and found the eleven gathered together, and them that were with them,

. . . the eleven and their friends all gathered — Mof

. . . and their companions all together — TCNT

34. Saying, The Lord is risen indeed,

. . . that the Lord had really risen — Mof

. . . It is true: the Lord has risen — NEB

and hath appeared to Simon.

and Simon saw Him — Beck

35. And they told what things were done in the way,

Then the two men . . . — Beck

. . . themselves began to tell . . . — Wms

. . . the story of their encounter in the road — Knox

. . . the story of their walk — Phi

And they began to relate their experiences on the road — NASB

. . . what had happened on the road — Gspd

Then they gave their account of the events of their journey — NEB

and how he was known of them in breaking of bread.

. . . had been recognized by them . . . — Wey

. . . when he broke the loaf — Mof

. . . while He was breaking the bread — Beck

36. And as they thus spake,

While they were still talking about these things — TCNT

Just as they were speaking — Mof

They were telling their story, when — Rieu

Jesus himself stood in the midst of them,[14] and saith unto them, Peace be unto you.

he himself stood among them — Gspd

there he was, standing among them — NEB

37. But they were terrified and affrighted,

They were scared and terrified — Mof

Startled, and in the utmost alarm — Wey

. . . and panic stricken — Gspd

But they shrank back in terror — Phi

and supposed that they had seen a spirit.

they began to imagine that upon a spirit they were looking — Rhm

they thought they were looking at a ghost — Wey

. . . an apparition — Knox

38. And he said unto them, Why are ye troubled?

. . . Why are you upset — Mof

. . . Why are you so disturbed — Gspd

. . . Why such alarm — Wey

and why do thoughts arise in your hearts?

and why are doubts arising . . . — Wms

And why are such questionings in your minds — Wey

39. Behold my hands and my feet, that it is I myself:

Look at . . . and you will know that it is I — TCNT

handle me, and see;

Feel me, and look at me — TCNT

for a spirit hath not flesh and bones, as ye see me have.

ghosts have no flesh or bones . . . — Phi

. . . as you see that I have — TCNT

. . . as ye behold me having — ABUV

40. And when he had thus spoken, he shewed them his hands and his feet.

41. And while they yet believed not for joy, and wondered,

. . . were still disbelieving for sheer joy and still wondering about it — Wms

Even yet they could not believe it, for sheer joy; they were lost in wonder — Mof

They were still unconvinced, still wondering, for it seemed too good to be true — NEB

Then, while they were still doubtful, and bewildered with joy — Knox

he said unto them, Have ye here any meat?

. . . anything to eat — ASV

42. And they gave him a piece of a broiled fish, and of an honeycomb.

43. And he took it, and did eat before them.

. . . in their presence — Wey

. . . while they watched Him — Beck

44. And he said unto them, These are the words which I spake unto you,

This is what I told you, he said — TCNT

---

[14]Some texts omit the words "and saith unto them, Peace be unto you."

Here and now are fulfilled the words that I told you — Phi

... This is what I meant by saying — NEB

while I was yet with you,

while I still walked in your company — Knox

that all things must be fulfilled, which were written in the law of Moses, and in the prophets, and in the psalms, concerning me.

... must come true ... — Gspd

... had to be fulfilled ... — Wms

45. Then opened he their understanding,

Then he enlightened their minds — Knox

that they might understand the scriptures,

so that they might continue to understand ... — Wms

... the meaning of ... — TCNT

46. And said unto them, Thus it is written, and thus it behoved Christ to suffer,

... Scripture says that the Christ should suffer — TCNT

and to rise from the dead the third day:

And arise from among the dead on the third day — Rhm

47. And that repentance and remission of sins

... repentance for forgiveness of sins — TCNT

... repentance leading to the forgiveness of ... — Gspd

And that teaching about a change of heart ... — Bas

should be preached in his name

should be proclaimed on his authority — TCNT

among all nations, beginning at Jerusalem.

to all the nations ... — TCNT

to all the heathen ... — Gspd

48. And ye are witnesses of these things.

You are eyewitnesses of ... — Phi

it is you who are the witnesses to all this — NEB

To this you must bear testimony — Mof

49. And, behold,

And mark this: — NEB

I send the promise of my Father upon you:

I am sending forth ... — Rhm

... that which my Father has promised — TCNT

... my Father's promised gift to rest upon you — Wey

... Him whom My Father promised — Beck

but tarry ye in the city of Jerusalem,

But you, on your part, must stay right here in the city — Wms

until ye be endued with power from on high.

until ye be clothed with power ... — ASV

until you have been invested with power from above — TCNT

until you are armed with the power from above — NEB

50. And he led them out as far as to Bethany,

He took them out with him as far as Bethany — Rieu

and he lifted up his hands, and blessed them.

where ... with uplifted hands ... — Phi

... gave them a blessing — Bas

51. And it came to pass, while he blessed them,

As he was in the act of blessing them — TCNT

he was parted from them,[15] and carried up into heaven.

he left them ... — TCNT

52. And they worshipped him,

So they bowed down to worship him — Knox

and returned to Jerusalem with great joy:

and greatly rejoicing went back to Jerusalem — Rieu

53. And were continually in the temple, praising and blessing God. Amen.

where they spent all their time within the temple, blessing God — Mof

---

[15]Some Greek manuscripts omit the words "and carried up into heaven."

THE
GOSPEL ACCORDING TO JOHN

CHAPTER 1

1. In the beginning was the Word,
Originally was the Word — Rhm
The Logos existed in the very beginning — Mof
From the first the Word was in being — Bas
At the beginning God expressed himself — Phi
When all things began, the Word already was — NEB
and the Word was with God, and the Word was God.
. . . the Logos was with God, the Logos was divine — Mof
. . . was face to face with God . . . — Mon
. . . God had the Word abiding with him . . . — Knox
. . . the Word was divine — Gspd
. . . was God Himself — Wms
. . . what God was, the Word was — NEB

2. The same was in the beginning with God.
. . . was originally with God — Rhm
He was with God from the first — Bas
He . . . was face to face with God in the beginning — Wms
and he existed with God from the beginning — Phi

3. All things were made by him;
Through him all things came into being — TCNT
everything came into existence through him — Gspd
All creation took place through him — Phi
Everything came to be by his hand — Lam
and without him was not any thing made that was made.
. . . came into existence not even one thing — Rhm
no existence came into being apart from him — Mof
no single thing was created without him — NEB

4. In him was life;
In him appeared life . . . — Phi
What came to be in him was Life . . . — Rieu

It was by Him that life began to exist — Wms
and the life was the light of men.
and that life was the light of mankind — Gspd
and this life was the Light for men — Mof
this Life was the Light of men — Nor

5. And the light shineth in darkness;
. . . goes on shining . . . — Bas
. . . continues to shine . . . — Wms
. . . still shines . . . — TCNT
. . . shines on . . . — Wey
His life is the light that shines through the darkness — Tay
and the darkness comprehended it not.
and the darkness apprehended it not — ASV
. . . has not overcome it — RSV
. . . has not put it out — Beck
. . . did not appropriate it — Ber
and the darkness can never extinguish it — Tay

6. There was a man sent from God,
There came a man, sent from God — ASV
. . . arose a man . . . — Rhm
. . . appeared a man . . . — NEB
. . . with a message from God — Gspd
. . . sent forth from God — Rieu
whose name was John.

7. The same came for a witness, to bear witness of the Light,
. . . for testimony, to bear witness to the light — RSV
. . . for the purpose of witnessing . . . — Mof
. . . to tell about the Light — Nor
He came to tell the truth about the Light — Beck
that all men through him might believe.
. . . through him all men might learn to believe — Knox
. . . everyone through him might come to believe — Wms
. . . all might become believers through him — NEB
so that all men might have faith through him — Bas

8. He was not that Light, but was sent to bear witness of that Light.

He was not himself the Light . . . —
Ber

This man was not the Light . . . — Rieu

. . . he was sent to give witness about
the light — Bas

. . . as a personal witness to that light
— Phi

. . . to testify of the light — ABUV

**9. That was the true Light, which light-
eth every man that cometh into the
world.[1]**

. . . which enlightens every man coming into the world — TCNT

. . . which shines upon every man as he
comes . . . — Phi

There was the true light, even the light
which lighteth every man, coming
. . . — ASV

. . . which, coming into the world, enlightens every man — NASB

The true light . . . was coming into the
world — ABUV

The Light . . . was on its way into the
world — Rieu

**10. He was in the world, and the world
was made by him,**

He came into the world . . . — Gspd

he entered the world . . . — Mof

. . . and the world was made through
him — ASV

. . . came into existence through him —
Wey

. . . owed its being to him — NEB

and the world knew him not.

. . . didn't know Him — Beck

. . . and did not recognize him — Mof

. . . treated him as a stranger — Knox

11. He came unto his own,

. . . unto his own possessions — Alf

. . . to his own creation — Mon

. . . to His own world — Nor

. . . to what was his own — Knox

. . . to the things which were his — Bas

and his own received him not.

. . . they that were his own received
him not — ASV

. . . his own people . . . — Rhm

. . . his own folk welcomed him not —
Mon

12. But as many as received him,

But to all who did receive him — Gspd

But to those who did accept Him — Ber

. . . who welcomed him — Beck

Yet . . . to as many as took him — Rieu

**to them gave he power to become the
sons of God,**

. . . the right to become children of God
— ASV

. . . authority . . . — Rhm

. . . the privilege of becoming . . . —
Wey

. . . he empowered to become the children of God — Knox

even to them that believe on his name:

. . . to those who trust in his name —
Mon

. . . to those who had faith in his name
— Bas

. . . to those who have yielded him
their allegiance — NEB

. . . to those who . . . rely on — His
name — Amp

**13. Which were born, not of blood, nor of
the will of the flesh,**

. . . not of the blood of parents or of
a sexual desire — Beck

. . . not from blood, or from an impulse
of the flesh — Bas

. . . not born of any human stock . . .
— NEB

. . . who owe their birth neither to human blood, nor to physical urge —
Ber

nor of the will of man, but of God.

. . . through the will of a human father
. . . — Wey

. . . from the impulse of . . . man's desire . . . — Bas

nor to human design, but to God —
Ber

14. And the Word was made flesh,

. . . became flesh — Rhm

. . . became a human being — Phi

and dwelt among us,

and tarried among us — Mof

And pitched his tent among us — Rhm

and came to dwell among us — Knox

and lived among us — Phi

**(and we beheld his glory, the glory as
of the only begotten of the Father,)**

. . . the glory of the Only Son sent from
the Father — TCNT

. . . glory as of the Only Begotten . . .
— NASB

. . . such glory as befits the Father's
only Son — NEB

. . . such honor as an only son receives
. . . — Gspd

---

[1]It is uncertain whether the phrase "that cometh into the world" modifies "Light" or
"man."

... the splendor as of a father's only son — Phi

full of grace and truth.
Full of favour and truth — Rhm
full of grace and reality — Mof
abounding in blessing and truth — Gspd

15. **John bare witness of him, and cried, saying,**
John beareth witness ... and crieth ... — Alf
... gave testimony ... cried aloud ... — Wey
This was he of whom I spake,
This is he of whom I spoke — Nor
This was the One of whom I said — Ber
He that cometh after me is preferred before me:
my successor has taken precedence of me — Mof
... has a higher rank than I — NASB
He who comes after me ranks before me — RSV
for he was before me.
because He existed before me — Wms
... he was ever First — TCNT
... he was when I was not — Knox
... he existed before I was born — Phi

16. **And of his fulness have all we received,**
from his abundance we have all had a share ... — Gspd
... his bounty ... received ... — Wms
from all that is in Him ... — Beck
and grace for grace.
one grace after another — Ber
favour against favour — Rhm
Gift after gift of love — TCNT
blessing after blessing — Gspd

17. **For the law was given by Moses, but grace and truth came by Jesus Christ.**
... grace and reality are ours through Jesus Christ — Mof
... were realized through Jesus Christ — NASB
but Jesus Christ brought love and truth — Beck

18. **No man hath seen God at any time; the only begotten Son, which is in the bosom of the Father,**
... God, only begotten, who is in the bosom of the Father[2] — Mon
... the divine One, the only Son ... — Mof

... who is God and close to the Father's heart — Beck
... in the intimate presence of the Father — Nor
... God's only Son ... nearest to the Father's heart — NEB
he hath declared him.
He hath interpreted him — Rhm
he has made him known — RSV
has himself become our interpreter — Knox

19. **And this is the record of John,**
And this is the witness of John — ASV
... the testimony ... — RSV
when the Jews sent priests and Levites from Jerusalem to ask him, Who art thou?
... to ask him who he was — Wey
... to ask — Who are you? — TCNT

20. **And he confessed, and denied not;**
He admitted without denial — Ber
He admitted with complete candor — Phi
but confessed, I am not the Christ.
he frankly admitted ... — Wms
... I am not the Messiah — NEB
... I'm not the promised Savior — Beck

21. **And they asked him, What then? Art thou Elias?**
... Are you Elijah — Gspd
And he saith, I am not.
Art thou that prophet?
... the Prophet — ABUV
Are you the prophet we await — NEB
And he answered, No.

22. **Then said they unto him, Who art thou?**
that we may give an answer to them that sent us.
Let us have an answer for those who sent us — RSV
We must give an answer to those who sent us — Nor
What sayest thou of thyself?
What do you say concerning yourself — Lam
What can you tell us of yourself — Rieu

23. **He said, I am the voice of one crying in the wilderness, Make straight the way of the Lord,**
... Straighten the Lord's way — Gspd

---

[2]Represents a variant reading.

. . . Make the road straight for the Lord
— Wms

. . . Get ready for the coming of the
Lord! — Tay

as said the prophet Esaias.

just as Isaiah the prophet said — Ber

24. **And they which were sent were of the
Pharisees.**

25. **And they asked him, and said unto
him, Why baptizest thou then,**

They questioned him again . . . — Nor

and their next question was . . . — TCNT

. . . Why then dost thou immerse —
Rhm

. . . Then why are you baptizing — RSV

**if thou be not that Christ, nor Elias,
neither that prophet?**

. . . the promised savior . . . — Beck

. . . nor the Prophet — NASB

. . . the Messiah, nor Elijah, nor the
prophet — NEB

26. **John answered them, saying, I baptize
with water:**

. . . I immerse in water — ABUV

. . . I am only baptizing in water —
Gspd

**but there standeth one among you,
whom ye know not;**

. . . with whom you are not acquainted
— Wms

. . . whom you do not recognize — Mon

27. **He it is, who coming after me is preferred before me,**

. . . taketh place before me — Alf

. . . takes rank before me — Knox

. . . is put before me — Nor

**whose shoe's latchet I am not worthy
to unloose.**

. . . to unfasten his sandal — TCNT

. . . to undo his shoes — Bas

I am not fit to untie the string of his
sandal — Mof

28. **These things were done in Bethabara[3]
beyond Jordan, where John was baptizing.**

29. **The next day John seeth Jesus coming
unto him, and saith, Behold the Lamb
of God,**

which taketh away the sin of the world.

who is to take away . . . — Wey

who is to remove . . . — Gspd

who takes and bears away the sin of the
world — Mon

30. **This is he of whom I said, After me
cometh a man which is preferred before me: for he was before me.[4]**

31. **And I knew him not: but that he
should be made manifest to Israel,**

. . . that he might be revealed . . . —
RSV

. . . that he might be openly shown . . .
— Mon

It is true I have not known him, yet it
was to make him known to the people of Israel — Phi

**therefore am I come baptizing with
water.[5]**

32. **And John bare record, saying,**

. . . testified further . . . — Ber

. . . gave further evidence . . . — Amp

**I saw the Spirit descending from
heaven like a dove, and it abode
upon him.**

. . . and it remained upon him — Alf

I have seen the Spirit come down like
a dove from Heaven and rest upon
him — Phi

33. **And I knew him not: but he that sent
me to baptize with water, the same
said unto me, Upon whom thou shalt
see the Spirit descending, and remaining on him, the same is he which baptizeth with the Holy Ghost.**

. . . immerseth in the Holy Spirit —
ABUV

34. **And I saw, and bare record that this
is the Son of God.**

. . . have testified . . . — ABUV

. . . have declared my belief . . . — TCNT

. . . Since when, I have been testifying
that this is the Elect of God — Rieu

. . . and I declare publicly before you
all that . . . — Phi

35. **Again the next day after John stood,
and two of his disciples;**

On the morrow John was standing . . .
. . . — ASV

. . . with two of his disciples — NEB

36. **And looking upon Jesus as he walked,**

After gazing intently on Jesus as he
walked about — Mon

. . . watching Jesus as he walked by —
Knox

he saith, Behold the Lamb of God!

Look at the Lamb of God! — Beck

There is the Lamb of God — NEB

Look, this is the Lamb of God — Knox

---

[3]Nearly all modern versions give "Bethany,"
not "Bethabara."

[4]Compare verses 15 and 27 for these phrases.

[5]Compare verses 25 and 26 on "baptize."

37. **And the two disciples heard him speak, and they followed Jesus.**

38. **Then Jesus turned, and saw them following, and saith unto them, What seek ye?**
    . . . What are you looking for — Ber
    . . . What do you want — Mof
    They said unto him, Rabbi, (which is to say, being interpreted, Master,) where dwellest thou?
    . . . Rabbi . . . Teacher . . . — ASV
    . . . where are you staying — RSV

39. **He saith unto them, Come and see. They came and saw where he dwelt, and abode with him that day: for it was about the tenth hour.**
    . . . remained with him . . . — Alf
    . . . about four in the afternoon — Wms

40. **One of the two which heard John speak, and followed him, was Andrew, Simon Peter's brother.**

41. **He first findeth his own brother Simon, and saith unto him, We have found the Messias, which is, being interpreted, the Christ.**
    . . . which means Christ, the Anointed One — Mon

42. **And he brought him to Jesus. And when Jesus beheld him, he said,**
    . . . Jesus gazed at him . . . — Mof
    . . . And Jesus, looking at him closely . . . — Rieu
    . . . Looking at him fixedly . . . — Knox
    Thou art Simon the son of Jona: thou shalt be called Cephas, which is by interpretation, A stone.
    You are Simon the son of John; you shall be called Cephas (which translated means Peter) — NASB
    From now on your name shall be Cephas (which means Peter, or Rock) — Wms

43. **The day following Jesus would go forth into Galilee, and findeth Philip, and saith unto him, Follow me.**
    . . . he wished to go forth . . . — ABUV
    . . . decided to go . . . — RSV

44. **Now Philip was of Bethsaida, the city of Andrew and Peter.**

45. **Philip findeth Nathanael, and saith unto him, We have found him, of whom Moses in the law, and the prophets, did write, Jesus of Nazareth, the son of Joseph.**
    . . . spoken of by Moses in the Law, and by the prophets — NEB

46. **And Nathanael said unto him, Can there any good thing come out of Nazareth? Philip saith unto him, Come and see.**

47. **Jesus saw Nathanael coming to him, and saith of him, Behold an Israelite indeed,**
    . . . one who belongs to the true Israel — Knox
    . . . a true son of Israel — Bas
    in whom is no guile!
    in whom there is not deceit — TCNT

48. **Nathanael saith unto him, Whence knowest thou me?**
    . . . Where did You get to know me — Beck
    . . . How do you know me — RSV
    Jesus answered and said unto him, Before that Philip called thee, when thou wast under the fig tree, I saw thee.
    . . . When you were under that fig tree . . . I saw you — Mof

49. **Nathanael answered and saith unto him, Rabbi, thou art the Son of God; thou art the King of Israel.**
    . . . Teacher . . . Son of God . . . King of Israel — Nor

50. **Jesus answered and said unto him, Because I said unto thee, I saw thee under the fig tree, believest thou?**
    . . . Is it because I told you . . . that you have faith? — Rieu
    You believe because I told you . . . — Beck
    . . . You have faith because I said to you . . .[6] — Bas
    thou shalt see greater things than these.

51. **And he saith unto him, Verily, verily, I say unto you, Hereafter ye shall see heaven open,**
    . . . you will see the heaven opened — NASB
    . . . opened wide — Wey
    and the angels of God ascending and descending upon the Son of man.
    . . . messengers of God . . . — Rhm
    . . . going up and coming down upon . . . — Wms

---

[6]Bas and Beck treat this as a statement. Modern editors of the Greek text mark it a question.

CHAPTER 2

1. **And the third day there was a marriage in Cana of Galilee;**
   Two days afterwards . . . — Knox
   . . . there was a wedding . . . — TCNT
   and the mother of Jesus was there:

2. **And both Jesus was called, and his disciples, to the marriage.**
   . . . Jesus was invited . . . — ABUV
   . . . with his disciples . . . — Bas

3. **And when they wanted wine, the mother of Jesus saith unto him, They have no wine.**
   And when the wine failed . . . — ASV
   . . . the supply of wine gave out . . . — Phi

4. **Jesus saith unto her,**
   Woman, what have I to do with thee?
   . . . What part can I take with thee, O woman — Rhm
   . . . why dost thou trouble me with that — Knox
   . . . What is it to me and to you . . . — Lam
   . . . Do not try to direct me — Gspd
   . . . Your concern, mother, is not mine — NEB
   mine hour is not yet come.
   My time is not here yet — Ber
   It isn't the right time yet — Beck
   It is not yet time for me to act — Gspd

5. **His mother saith unto the servants, Whatsoever he saith unto you, do it.**

6. **And there were set there six water pots of stone,**
   after the manner of the purifying of the Jews,
   . . . for the Jewish ceremonial cleansing — Phi
   . . . for the religious washings of the Jews — Beck
   containing two or three firkins apiece.
   each holding twenty or thirty gallons — RSV
   large enough to hold twenty gallons or more — Wey

7. **Jesus saith unto them, Fill the water-pots with water. And they filled them up to the brim.**

8. **And he saith to them, Draw out now, and bear unto the governor of the feast.**
   . . . Now take a dip and carry it to the table-manager! — Ber
   . . . dip out some and bring it to the head steward — Nor
   And they bare it.
   So they took him some — Wms

9. **When the ruler of the feast had tasted the water that was made wine,**
   . . . the water now become wine . . . — Alf
   and knew not whence it was:
   . . . not knowing its source — NEB
   (but the servants which drew the water knew;) the governor of the feast called the bridegroom,

10. **And saith unto him, Every man at the beginning doth set forth good wine; and when men have well drunk,**
    . . . when men have had plenty to drink — Phi
    then that which is worse:
    . . . the inferior — Rhm
    . . . the poorer kind — Rieu
    but thou hast kept the good wine until now.

11. **This beginning of miracles did Jesus in Cana of Galilee,**
    This beginning of his signs . . . — ASV
    this earliest of his signs. . . — Ber
    and manifested forth his glory;
    . . . revealed his glory — TCNT
    . . . demonstrated his power — Phi
    and his disciples believed on him.
    . . . his disciples put their faith in him — Bas
    . . . his disciples' faith in him was fixed — Rieu

12. **After this he went down to Capernaum, he, and his mother, and his brethren, and his disciples: and they continued there not many days.**
    . . . they did not stay there long — NEB
    . . . there they stayed for a few days — Knox

13. **And the Jews' passover was at hand, and Jesus went up to Jerusalem,**

14. **And found in the temple those that sold oxen and sheep and doves, and the changers of money sitting:**
    . . . seated inside the temple, dealers in cattle . . . — Mof.
    . . . the money-changers sitting at their tables — Gspd

15. **And when he had made a scourge of small cords,**
    So he plaited a scourge of rushes — Mon

... made a lash out of cords — Wms

he drove them all out of the temple, and the sheep, and the oxen;

... with the sheep and oxen — Bas

... men, sheep, oxen and all — Rieu

and poured out the changers' money, and overthrew the tables;

16. And said unto them that sold doves, Take these things hence;

... Take these things away — RSV

make not my Father's house a house of merchandise.

Make not my Father's house a house of trade — Mon

... a market-house — TCNT

17. And his disciples remembered that it was written, The zeal of thine house hath eaten me up.

... Zeal for thy house shall eat me up — ASV

... Concern for God's House will be My undoing! — Tay

... jealousy for the honor of thy house ... — Knox

... shall consume me — Ber

18. Then answered the Jews and said unto him, What sign shewest thou unto us, seeing that thou doest these things?

... What sign of authority do you show us ... — Nor

... What authority can you show us ... — Wey

... for acting in this way — Mof

19. Jesus answered and said unto them, Destroy this temple, and in three days I will raise it up.

... Demolish this Sanctuary ... — Wey

... in three days I will restore it — Nor

20. Then said the Jews, Forty and six years was this temple in building, and wilt thou rear it up in three days?

It has taken forty-six years to build this temple ... — NEB

... Could you in three days put it up again — Rieu

21. But he spake of the temple of his body.

But He meant the sanctuary of His body — Wms

But he was speaking of his body as the sanctuary — Gspd

22. When therefore he was risen from the dead,

... had been raised from among ... — Rhm

After his resurrection — NEB

his disciples remembered that he had said this unto them: and they believed the scripture, and the word which Jesus had said.

23. Now when he was in Jerusalem at the passover, in the feast day,

... at the Passover feast — RSV

many believed in his name,

many came to trust in him — TCNT

many became believers — Wey

when they saw the miracles which he did.

beholding his signs ... — ASV

... observed the signs which he wrought — Ber

24. But Jesus did not commit himself unto them,

... did not trust himself unto them — ASV

... would not give them his confidence — Knox

because he knew all men,

by reason of his understanding them all — Rhm

because he understood every man — Lam

25. And needed not that any should testify of man:

and had no need of anybody's evidence about men — Gspd

He didn't need to be told about anyone — Beck

for he knew what was in man.

he understood human nature — Phi

for He knew mankind to the core — Tay

CHAPTER 3

1. There was a man of the Pharisees, named Nicodemus, a ruler of the Jews:

... a leading man among the Jews — TCNT

... a member of the Jewish Council — Gspd

2. The same came to Jesus by night, and

said to him, Rabbi, we know that thou art a teacher come from God:

... thou hast come from God as a teacher — ABUV

... you have come from God to teach us — Mof

for no man can do these miracles that

thou doest, except God be with him.
no one can do these signs . . . — ASV
. . . if God is not with him — Rieu

3. **Jesus answered and said unto him, Verily, verily, I say unto thee,**
. . . In truth I tell you — TCNT
. . . I most solemnly say — Wms
. . . I tell you in all truth — Rieu
. . . With all the earnestness I possess I tell you this: — Tay
Except a man be born again,
unless one is born anew — RSV
. . . born from above — Rhm
without a new birth — Bas
he cannot see the kingdom of God.
no one can see God's Realm — Mof
he cannot see . . . (and experience) — the kingdom . . . — Amp

4. **Nicodemus saith unto him, How can a man be born when he is old? can he enter the second time into his mother's womb, and be born?**

5. **Jesus answered, Verily, verily, I say unto thee,**
I assure you — Phi
In truth I tell you — NEB
Except a man be born of water and of the Spirit,
if anyone isn't born of water and the Spirit — Beck
unless a man is born from water and from spirit — Phi
unless a man owes his birth to Water and Spirit — TCNT
he cannot enter into the kingdom of God.
he can't get into God's kingdom — Beck

6. **That which is born of the flesh is flesh; and that which is born of the Spirit is spirit.**
Flesh gives birth to flesh . . . — Phi
What is born by natural birth is a thing of nature . . . — Knox
. . . it is spirit that gives birth to spirit — NEB
. . . whatever is born of the Spirit is spiritual — Wms

7. **Marvel not that I said unto thee, Ye must be born again.[7]**
Do not be astonished . . . — Rieu

8. **The wind bloweth where it listeth,**
. . . where it will — Alf
. . . wherever it pleases — Beck
and thou hearest the sound thereof,

. . . the voice of it — ASV
and you hear its voice — Mon
but canst not tell whence it cometh, and whither it goeth:
but you do not know . . . — TCNT
. . . where it comes from and where it goes — Bas
so is every one that is born of the Spirit.
It is the same with everyone . . . — Ber
Nor can you tell how a man is born . . . by the Spirit — Phi

9. **Nicodemus answered and said unto him, How can these things be?**
Nicodemus said to him, How can this be — RSV
How is all this possible? asked Nicodemus — Wey

10. **Jesus answered and said unto him, Art thou a master of Israel, and knowest not these things?**
. . . the teacher . . . and understandest not . . . — ASV
. . . a teacher . . . do not know . . . — Nor

11. **Verily, verily, I say unto thee, We speak that we do know,**
What we know we speak — Rhm
We know what we are talking about — Gspd
and testify that we have seen;
and bear witness of that which we have seen — ASV
and ye receive not our witness.
yet you all reject our evidence — Wey
yet you refuse our testimony — Mof

12. **If I have told you earthly things,**
. . . things which happen on this earth . . . — Phi
and ye believe not,
. . . none of you believe me — Mon
how shall ye believe, if I tell you of heavenly things?

13. **And no man hath ascended up to heaven, but he that came down from heaven, even the Son of man which is in heaven.**
. . . the Son of Man whose home is in heaven — Ber
And yet the Son of man, descended from heaven, is the only one who has ever ascended into heaven — Mof

---

[7]Compare verse 3.

14. **And as Moses lifted up the serpent in the wilderness, even so must the Son of man be lifted up:**
    And just as Moses in the desert lifted the serpent on the pole, the Son of Man must be lifted up — Wms
15. **That whosoever believeth in him should not perish, but have eternal life.**
    . . . everyone who trusts in Him . . . — Wms
    . . . whoever has faith may have in him eternal life — Bas
16. **For God so loved the world,**
    . . . had such love for the world — Bas
    . . . loved the world so dearly — Mof
    that he gave his only begotten Son,
    . . . the Son, the Only Son — Rieu
    . . . His Only Son — Wms
    . . . His only-begotten (unique) Son — Amp
    that whosoever believeth in him should not perish,
    . . . whoever trusts in him . . . — Mon
    . . . may not be lost — TCNT
    . . . shall not die — Nor
    so that no one who believes in him should be lost — Gspd
    but have everlasting life.
17. **For God sent not his Son into the world to condemn the world;**
    . . . to judge the world — ASV
    . . . to pass sentence on it — Mof
    but that the world through him might be saved.
    . . . that the world might find salvation . . . — Knox
    but to save it — through him — Phi
18. **He that believeth on him is not condemned: but he that believeth not is condemned already,**
    . . . is not judged . . . hath been judged already — ASV
    . . . shall not be condemned . . . — TCNT
    . . . has already received his sentence — Wms
    because he hath not believed in the name of the only begotten Son of God.[8]
19. **And this is the condemnation,**
    And the basis of the judgment is this — Gspd
    The ground of his condemnation is this — TCNT
    that light is come into the world,
    that the light has come into the world — ASV

and men loved darkness rather than light,
    . . . men preferred the darkness to the Light — TCNT
    and people have loved the darkness more than the light — Ber
    because their deeds were evil.
    for their works were evil — ASV
    because their deeds have been wicked — Wey
20. **For every one that doeth evil hateth the light,**
    . . . every wrongdoer hates the light — Wey
    Bad men all hate the light — NEB
    For every one who practices evil, hates the light — Ber
    neither cometh to the light, lest his deeds should be reproved.
    and does not come to the light . . . — NASB
    . . . lest his actions be exposed — Mon
    and keeps away from the light . . . — Ber
    . . . for fear their practices should be shown up — NEB
21. **But he that doeth truth cometh to the light,**
    . . . he who acts up to the truth . . . — TCNT
    . . . the man who lives the truth . . . — Rieu
    But he who does what is true comes to the light — RSV
    that his deeds may be made manifest, that they are wrought in God.
    to make it plain that all he has done has been done through God — Phi
    so that his works may be seen . . . — Beck
    . . . that they are done through God — Lam
22. **After these things came Jesus and his disciples into the land of Judaea;**
    . . . the country parts of Judaea — TCNT
    . . . the Judean district — Ber
    and there he tarried with them, and baptized.
    and there he tarried with them, and immersed — ABUV
    he remained with them for some time and baptized — Rieu

---

[8]Compare John 1:14,18; 3:16.

He was spending time with them and baptizing — NASB

he stayed there with them and kept baptizing people — Wms

23. **And John also was baptizing in Aenon near to Salim, because there was much water there:**

. . . immersing in Aenon . . . many waters were there — ABUV

. . . many streams there — Mon

and they came, and were baptized.

and they were coming and being immersed — Rhm

and people were constantly coming for baptism — NEB

24. **For John was not yet cast into prison.**

For John had not yet been put in prison — RSV

This was before John's imprisonment — NEB

25. **Then there arose a question between some of John's disciples and the Jews**

. . . on the part of John's disciples with a Jew — Alf

about purifying.

about religious cleansing — Beck

about the ceremony of purifying—Lam

26. **And they came unto John, and said unto him, Rabbi, he that was with thee beyond Jordan, to whom thou bearest witness,**

. . . to whom thou has borne witness — ASV

. . . whom you vouched for — Rieu

behold, the same baptizeth, and all men come to him.

behold, he immerses, and all are coming to him — ABUV

notice, he baptizes, and they all flock to him — Ber

. . . is baptizing, and everybody is going to him — TCNT

27. **John answered and said, A man can receive nothing, except it be given him from heaven.**

. . . A man can claim nothing . . . — Nor

. . . A man can get only what Heaven has given him — Beck

. . . A man can have only what God gives him — NEB

28. **Ye yourselves bear me witness, that I said, I am not the Christ,**

You can bear me out, that I said . . . — Mof

. . . I am not the Messiah — NEB

but that I am sent before him.

I have been sent in advance of him — Gspd

but I have been sent as his forerunner — Phi

29. **He that hath the bride is the bridegroom: but the friend of the bridegroom, which standeth and heareth him, rejoiceth greatly because of the bridegroom's voice:**

. . . is overjoyed at hearing the bridegroom's voice — NEB

this my joy therefore is fulfilled.

such is my joy, and it is complete — Bas

this joy of mine has been made full — NASB

30. **He must increase, but I must decrease.**

He must grow greater, but I must grow less — Wey

31. **He that cometh from above is above all:**

He who comes from above is above all others — Gspd

. . . is greater than all others — Bas

he that is of the earth is earthly, and speaketh of the earth:

the man who belongs to earth talks the language of earth — Knox

. . . is earth-minded and speaks from an earthly standpoint — Ber

he that cometh from heaven is above all.

32. **And what he hath seen and heard, that he testifieth;**

He states what he has seen and what he heard — TCNT

He bears witness to what he has seen and heard — RSV

and no man receiveth his testimony.

yet no one accepts his testimony — Mof

yet no one believes His witness — Nor

33. **He that hath received his testimony hath set to his seal that God is true.**

. . . hath set his seal to this, that God is true — ASV

. . . has thereby acknowledged that God is true — Gspd

. . . has certified . . . that God is true — Wms

34. **For he whom God hath sent speaketh the words of God: for God giveth not the Spirit by measure unto him.**

. . . it is not by measure that he gives the Spirit — RSV

. . . for He gives the Spirit without measure — NASB

. . . God does not give the Spirit sparingly — Mon

35. **The Father loveth the Son, and hath given all things into his hand.**

. . . has given him control over everything — Mof

. . . has entrusted him with all authority — NEB

36. **He that believeth on the Son hath everlasting life:**

Whoever trusts . . . possesses eternal life — Wms

He who has faith in the Son has eternal life — Bas

and he that believeth not the Son shall not see life;

but he that disbelieves the Son . . . — ABUV

he who does not obey the Son . . . — RSV

but he who disobeys the Son shall not see life — Mon

but the wrath of God abideth on him.

he lives under the anger of God — Phi

God's displeasure hangs over him continually — Knox

CHAPTER 4

1. **When therefore the Lord knew how the Pharisees had heard that Jesus made and baptized more disciples than John,**

. . . was making and baptizing . . . — ASV

. . . was making more disciples and baptizing a greater number than John — Knox

2. **(Though Jesus himself baptized not,**

though Jesus Himself was not baptizing — Wms

but his disciples,)

but His disciples were — NASB

3. **He left Judaea, and departed again into Galilee.**

4. **And he must needs go through Samaria.**

He had to pass through Samaria — RSV

5. **Then cometh he to a city of Samaria, which is called Sychar, near to the parcel of ground that Jacob gave to his son Joseph.**

. . . piece of land . . . — ABUV

. . . plot of land . . . — TCNT

. . . near the field that Jacob gave to . . . Joseph — Gspd

6. **Now Jacob's well was there. Jesus therefore, being wearied with his journey,**

. . . so Jesus, tired out with His journey — Wey

sat thus on the well:

sat down beside it, just as he was — Phi

and it was about the sixth hour.

It was then about mid-day — TCNT

7. **There cometh a woman of Samaria to draw water:**

. . . a Samaritan woman came . . . — Rieu

Jesus saith unto her, Give me to drink.

. . . Let Me have a drink — Ber

8. **(For his disciples were gone away unto the city to buy meat.)**

. . . to buy food — ASV

. . . to buy provisions — Wey

9. **Then saith the woman of Samaria unto him, How is it that thou, being a Jew, askest drink of me, which am a woman of Samaria?**

. . . What? You are a Jew, and you ask me for a drink — me, a Samaritan! — Mof

for the Jews have no dealings with the Samaritans.

(For Jews do not associate with Samaritans) — TCNT

(Jews and Samaritans . . . do not use vessels in common) — NEB

10. **Jesus answered and said unto her, If thou knewest the gift of God,**

. . . what it is God gives — Knox

. . . the generosity of God — Rieu

. . . If you had known the free gift of God — Mon

and who it is that saith to thee, Give me to drink;

and who is asking you for a drink — Mof

thou wouldest have asked of him, and he would have given thee living water.

you would have been the one to ask Him . . . — Wms

11. **The woman saith unto him, Sir, thou hast nothing to draw with, and the well is deep:**

. . . you have nothing to draw water with . . . — Phi

. . . you have no bucket and this well is deep — NEB

from whence then hast thou that living water?

where will you obtain the living water — Nor

Where can you get your living water — Gspd

12. **Art thou greater than our father Jacob, which gave us the well,**

. . . our forefather Jacob . . . — Wey

. . . our ancestor Jacob who gave us the well — TCNT

and drank thereof himself, and his children, and his cattle?

13. **Jesus answered and said unto her, Whosoever drinketh of this water shall thirst again:**

. . . will get thirsty again — Beck

. . . Anyone who drinks this water will be thirsty again — Mof

14. **But whosoever drinketh of the water that I shall give him shall never thirst;**

. . . shall never thirst any more — Mon

. . . will never, no never, be thirsty again — Wms

but the water that I shall give him shall be in him a well of water springing up into everlasting life.

. . . a fountain of water . . . eternal life — Alf

. . . a spring of water welling up to eternal life — RSV

For my gift will become a spring in the man himself, welling up into eternal life — Phi

15. **The woman saith unto him, Sir, give me this water, that I thirst not,**

. . . so that I may never again be thirsty — Nor

neither come hither to draw.

nor have to come all the way for drawing water — Ber

16. **Jesus saith unto her, Go, call thy husband, and come hither.**

17. **The woman answered and said, I have no husband. Jesus said unto her, Thou hast well said, I have no husband:**

. . . All too true! Jesus said — Tay

18. **For thou hast had five husbands; and he whom thou now hast is not thy husband:**

. . . the man you are now living with . . . — Gspd

in that saidst thou truly.

You have spoken the truth in saying that — Wey

19. **The woman saith unto him, Sir, I perceive that thou art a prophet.**

20. **Our fathers[9] worshipped in this mountain;**

and ye say, that in Jerusalem is the place where men ought to worship.

and yet you Jews say . . . — TCNT

whereas you Jews declare the proper place for worship is at Jerusalem — Mof

21. **Jesus saith unto her, Woman, believe me, the hour cometh,**

. . . the time is coming — Phi

when ye shall neither in this mountain, nor yet at Jerusalem, worship the Father.

when you will worship the Father neither on this mountain nor in Jerusalem — Rieu

22. **Ye worship ye know not what:**

. . . that which ye know not — ASV

You worship something you know nothing about — Gspd

we know what we worship:

we are worshipping what we do know — Mof

we worship that which we know — ASV

for salvation is of the Jews.

for the salvation of mankind is to come from our race — Phi

It is from the Jews that salvation comes — NEB

23. **But the hour cometh, and now is, when the true worshippers shall worship the Father in spirit and in truth:**

. . . when genuine worshipers . . . — Ber

. . . will worship the Father in Spirit and in reality — Mof

. . . in the true way of the spirit — Bas

for the Father seeketh such to worship him.

the Father is looking for such people to worship Him — Beck

for it is such worshipers the Father wants — Nor

24. **God is a Spirit:**

God is Spirit — ABUV

and they that worship him must worship him in spirit and in truth.

---

[9]"Fathers" meaning "ancestors," compare verse 12.

... must worship him in Spirit and in reality — Mof

25. The woman saith unto him, I know that Messias cometh, which is called Christ:

... the Messiah, who is called the Christ ... — TCNT

... the Christ, the Anointed One ... — Amp

when he is come, he will tell us all things.

... He will make everything plain to us — Ber

... he will teach us everything — Lam

26. Jesus saith unto her, I that speak unto thee am he.

... I am He — I, who am talking to you! — Nor

27. And upon this came his disciples, and marvelled that he talked with the woman:

... that he was speaking with a woman — ASV

... were surprised to find Him talking with a woman — Wey

yet no man said, What seekest thou? or, Why talkest thou with her?

but no one asked her what she wanted, or asked Jesus why he was talking with her — Rieu

28. The woman then left her water pot, and went her way into the city, and saith to the men,

29. Come, see a man, which told me all things that ever I did: is not this the Christ?

... Could this be the Messiah — NEB

... He is not the Christ, is he — Wms

... Do you suppose he is the Christ — Gspd

30. Then they went out of the city, and came unto him.

... and were coming to him — ASV

... and started to come to Jesus — Phi

They left town and made their way to see Him — Wey

31. In the mean while his disciples prayed him, saying, Master, eat.

... the disciples kept urging him ... — Mon

... the disciples had been begging him to eat — Rieu

32. But he said unto them, I have meat to eat that ye know not of.

... I have food ... — Rhm

... I have nourishment ... — Ber

... of which you have no knowledge — Bas

33. Therefore said the disciples one to another, Hath any man brought him ought to eat?

... Has anyone brought him anything to eat — ABUV

... Can anyone have brought him anything to eat — TCNT

34. Jesus saith unto them, My meat is to do the will of him that sent me, and to finish his work.

... to complete his work — Rhm

... My food ... to accomplish His work — NASB

... My nourishment comes from doing the will of God who sent Me, and finishing His work — Tay

35. Say not ye, There are yet four months, and then cometh harvest?

You have a saying, have you not ... — Mof

... In four months more the harvest comes — Wms

behold, I say unto you, Lift up your eyes, and look on the fields; for they are white already to harvest.

... raise your eyes and observe the fields ... — Ber

... and see them already whitening for the harvest — Rieu

36. And he that reapeth receiveth wages,

The reaper is already getting his wages — Mof

The reaper is drawing his pay — NEB

and gathereth fruit unto life eternal:

and gathering the harvest for eternal life — Gspd

and gathering in sheaves for Immortal Life — TCNT

that both he that soweth and he that reapeth may rejoice together.

37. And herein is that saying true, One soweth, and another reapeth.

38. I sent you to reap that whereon ye bestowed no labour:

... where you had not worked before — Beck

I sent you to reap a crop on which you had not toiled — Mon

other men laboured, and ye are entered into their labours.

... it is their labours you have inherited — Knox

... you step in to benefit from their work — Ber

39. And many of the Samaritans of that city believed on him for the saying of the woman, which testified,
. . . because of the woman's testimony — RSV
He told me all that ever I did.
He told me all the story of my life — Rieu

40. So when the Samaritans were come unto him,
they besought him that he would tarry with them:
they went on to request him to abide with them — Rhm
they asked Him to stay with them — Beck
they began asking him to remain with them — Mon
and he abode there two days.
and he did stay there two days — Gspd

41. And many more believed because of his own word;

42. And said unto the woman,
Now we believe, not because of thy saying:
Now we have faith, but not because of your story — Bas
We no longer believe in Him simply because of your statement — Wey
for we have heard him ourselves,
and know that this is indeed the Christ,[10] the Saviour of the world.
. . . this is indeed the Saviour of the world — ASV
. . . this is in truth the Saviour of the world — ABUV
. . . he is really the Savior of the world — Gspd

43. Now after two days he departed thence, and went into Galilee.

44. For Jesus himself testified, that a prophet hath no honour in his own country.
. . . in his own country a prophet goes unhonoured — Knox
. . . a prophet has no honor in his own fatherland — Nor

45. Then when he was come into Galilee, the Galilaeans received him,
. . . the Galileans welcomed him—Rhm
having seen all the things that he did at Jerusalem at the feast:
They had seen all He did at the festival in Jerusalem — Beck
for they also went unto the feast.

46. So Jesus came again into Cana of Galilee, where he made the water wine.
And there was a certain nobleman, whose son was sick at Capernaum.
. . . a certain officer, whose son was sick in Capernaum — Nor
At Capernaum there was an official whose son was ill — RSV

47. When he heard that Jesus was come out of Judaea into Galilee, he went unto him, and besought him that he would come down, and heal his son: for he was at the point of death.

48. Then said Jesus unto him,
Except ye see signs and wonders, ye will not believe.
Will none of you ever believe without seeing signs and portents? — NEB

49. The nobleman saith unto him, Sir, come down ere my child die.
. . . Come down, sir, before my boy is dead — Mof
Lord, come down . . . before my little boy dies — Beck

50. Jesus saith unto him, Go thy way; thy son liveth.
. . . thy son is to live — Knox
. . . Your boy is going to live — Wms
. . . Go, your son is living — TCNT
And the man believed the word that Jesus had spoken unto him, and he went his way.

51. And as he was now going down, his servants met him, and told him, saying, Thy son liveth.
. . . saying, that his son lived — ASV
. . . and told him that his son was living — RSV

52. Then enquired he of them the hour when he began to amend.
. . . at what hour he had shown improvement — Wey
. . . the hour when he became better — Bas
And they said unto him, Yesterday at the seventh hour the fever left him.
. . . Yesterday at one o'clock the fever left him — Ber
. . . The fever left him yesterday at one o'clock in the afternoon — Phi

---

[10]The words "the Christ" are now recognized as not adequately supported by original manuscripts.

53. So the father knew that it was at the same hour, in the which Jesus said unto him, Thy son liveth:
and himself believed, and his whole house.
And he and his whole household believed in Jesus — Gspd
and he and his whole household became believers — Wey

54. This is again the second miracle that Jesus did, when he was come out of Judaea into Galilee.
. . . the second sign which Jesus performed . . . — NEB
. . . the second occasion on which Jesus gave a sign . . . — TCNT
Thus once again Jesus wrought a miracle after leaving Judaea for Galilee — Rieu

CHAPTER 5

1. After this there was a feast of the Jews;
Some time later came one of the Jewish feast days — Phi
. . . one of the Jewish religious holidays — Tay
and Jesus went up to Jerusalem.
and Jesus travelled up to Jerusalem — Rieu

2. Now there is at Jerusalem by the sheep market a pool, which is called in the Hebrew tongue Bethesda, having five porches.
. . . in Hebrew called Beth-zatha . . . — RSV
. . . near the Sheep-gate . . . five colonnades — Gspd

3. In these lay a great multitude of impotent folk, of blind, halt, withered, waiting for the moving of the water.
. . . a multitude of them that were sick . . . — ASV
. . . in which a crowd of invalids . . . lay . . . — Ber

4. For an angel went down at a certain season into the pool, and troubled the water: whosoever then first after the troubling of the water stepped in was made whole of whatsoever disease he had.[11]

5. And a certain man was there, which had an infirmity thirty and eight years.
Among them was a man who had been crippled for thirty-eight years — NEB
And there was one man there who had been an invalid for thirty-eight years — Wey

6. When Jesus saw him lie,
When Jesus saw him lying there — NASB
and knew that he had been now a long time in that case,
and knew that he had been there a long time — Mon

and knowing that he had been ill for a long time — Rieu
he saith unto him, Wilt thou be made whole?
. . . Do you wish to be cured — TCNT
. . . Do you want to become well — Ber

7. The impotent man answered him, Sir, I have no man, when the water is troubled, to put me into the pool:
. . . I have no one to put me into the pool when the water is disturbed — Wey
but while I am coming, another steppeth down before me.
And while I'm trying to get there, somebody else steps in ahead of me — Beck

8. Jesus saith unto him, Rise, take up thy bed, and walk.
. . . Get up, take your bed and go — Bas
. . . Rise, take up your pallet, and walk — RSV
. . . take up your bed and go walking away — Mon
. . . Stand up, roll up your sleeping mat and go on home! — Tay

9. And immediately the man was made whole,
And at once the man was healed — RSV
And immediately the man became well — NASB
and took up his bed,
and walked:
and began to walk — Rhm
and went to walking — Wms
and on the same day was the sabbath.
Now it was the sabbath on that day — ASV

---

[11]The last phrase of verse 3 ("waiting . . . water") and verse 4 are now recognized as not adequately supported by original manuscripts.

This happened on a Sabbath day — Phi

10. The Jews therefore said unto him that was cured, It is the sabbath day:

it is not lawful for thee to carry thy bed.

it is against the Law . . . — Gspd

. . . for you to carry your pallet — NASB

you have no right to carry the mat — Ber

11. He answered them, He that made me whole, the same said unto me, Take up thy bed, and walk.

. . . The man who healed me told me to take up my bed and walk — Mon

12. Then asked they him, What man is that which said unto thee, Take up thy bed, and walk?

. . . Who is the man that said . . . — ASV

. . . Who was it that told you; Lift it and walk — Mof

13. And he that was healed wist not who it was:

But he . . . knew not who it was — ASV

for Jesus had conveyed himself away,

for Jesus had withdrawn — RSV

a multitude being in that place.

since there was a crowd at the place — Wms

14. Afterward Jesus findeth him in the temple, and said unto him, Behold, thou art made whole:

. . . See now, you have been cured — Rieu

. . . Now that you have been made well — Nor

sin no more, lest a worse thing come unto thee.

Do not go on sinning, lest a worse thing befall you — Mon

leave your sinful ways . . . — NEB

. . . or something worse might happen to you — Phi

15. The man departed, and told the Jews that it was Jesus, which had made him whole.

16. And therefore did the Jews persecute Jesus,

This was why the Jews used to persecute Jesus — Gspd

And that was why the Jews began to persecute Jesus — TCNT

and sought to slay him,[12]

because he had done these things on the sabbath day.

because these things he had been doing on Sabbath — Rhm

because He persisted in doing such things on the sabbath — Wms

17. But Jesus answered them, My Father worketh hitherto,

. . . My Father worketh even until now — Alf

. . . has continued working until now — Mon

. . . My Father is working still — RSV

and I work.

and so I am working — Beck

18. Therefore the Jews sought the more to kill him,

And for this the Jews wanted the more to kill him — Lam

This made the Jews all the more eager to kill him — TCNT

because he not only had broken the sabbath,

because not only did he not keep the Sabbath — Bas

but said also that God was his Father,

but also kept saying that God was His Father — Wms

but was calling God his own Father — Rhm

making himself equal with God.

treating himself as equal to God — Knox

thus putting himself on an equality with God — Gspd

19. Then answered Jesus and said unto them, Verily, verily, I say unto you, The Son can do nothing of himself,

. . . the Son can do nothing by himself — NEB

. . . the Son can do nothing of his own accord — Mof

but what he seeth the Father do:

nothing but what he sees the Father doing — Mof

but only what he sees the Father doing — RSV

he does only what he sees the Father doing — TCNT

for what things soever he doeth, these also doeth the Son likewise.

what the Father does is what the Son does in his turn — Knox

whatever the Father does the Son does it in the same way — Bas

---

[12]This phrase is now recognized as not adequately supported by original manuscripts.

20. For the Father loveth the Son, and sheweth him all things that himself doeth:

... lets him see everything that he himself is doing — Gspd

... shows Him everything He is doing — Beck

and he will shew him greater works than these,

And He will show Him still greater works than these — Nor

that ye may marvel.

to fill you with wonder — Phi

21. For as the Father raiseth up the dead, and quickeneth them;

For as the Father raises the dead, and makes them alive — ABUV

... and gives them life — Rieu

... makes them live — Ber

even so the Son quickeneth whom he will.

even so the Son also giveth life to whom he will — ASV

so the Son makes anyone live whom he chooses — Mof

22. For the Father judgeth no man,

The Father himself does not judge any man — TCNT

The Father is no man's judge — Phi

The Father judges no one — RSV

but hath committed all judgment unto the Son:

but he has entrusted all judgement to the Son — Lam

but He has entrusted the passing of judgement wholly to the Son — Wey

but has left all judgement to the Son — Rieu

23. That all men should honour the Son, even as they honour the Father.

so that all may reverence the Son just as they reverence the Father — Knox

so that all men may honor the Son equally with the Father — Phi

He that honoureth not the Son honoureth not the Father which hath sent him.

Whoever refuses to honor the Son ... — Gspd

... does not honour the Father who sent him — Mof

to deny reverence to the Son is to deny reverence to the Father — Knox

24. Verily, verily, I say unto you, He that heareth my word, and believeth on him that sent me,

... has faith in him who sent me — Bas

... and puts his trust in him who sent me — NEB

hath everlasting life,

has eternal life — RSV

and shall not come into condemnation;

and does not come under judgement — Wey

he will incur no sentence of judgment — Mof

He does not have to face judgment — Phi

but is passed from death unto life.

but hath passed out of death into life — ASV

but has already passed out of Death into Life — TCNT

for he has already come out of death into life — Nor

25. Verily, verily, I say unto you, The hour is coming, and now is, when the dead shall hear the voice of the Son of God:

... the dead will hear a call from the Son of God — Rieu

... the dead shall hearken unto the voice of the Son of God — Rhm

... the dead will listen to the voice of the Son of God — Mof

and they that hear shall live.

and all who hear shall come to life — NEB

and when they have heard it they will live — Phi

26. For as the Father hath life in himself;

For the Father, being as He is the source of Life — Rieu

For just as the Father is self-existent — Gspd

so hath he given to the Son to have life in himself;

so also has he granted to the Son to have life in himself — Mon

he has given self-existence to the Son — Gspd

has made the Son the source of Life — Rieu

27. And hath given him authority to execute judgment also,

and has given Him authority to act as Judge — Ber

he has also been given the right to pass judgement — NEB

because he is the Son of man.

because he is a son of man — ASV

because he is Son of man — ABUV

28. Marvel not at this:

No, do not be surprised — Phi

This should not surprise you — Beck

for the hour is coming, in the which all that are in the graves shall hear his voice,

. . . all that are in the tombs shall hear his voice — ASV

. . . all who are in their graves will hear Him calling — Beck

29. And shall come forth;

they that have done good, unto the resurrection of life;

They who the good things have done . . . — Rhm

those whose actions have been good . . . — Knox

. . . to the resurrection that is Life — Rieu

Those who have done good will rise to live — Beck

and they that have done evil, unto the resurrection of damnation.

and they that practised evil . . . — ABUV

But they who the corrupt things have practised . . . — Rhm

. . . to the resurrection of judgment — ASV

. . . will rise again to be judged — Nor

but those who have done wrong will rise to face judgment — Phi

30. I can of mine own self do nothing:[13]

as I hear, I judge: and my judgment is just;

As I listen, I judge . . . — Mon

I judge as I am informed — Ber

and My judgment is fair — Ber

I judge as I am bidden, and my verdict is just — NEB

because I seek not mine own will, but the will of the Father which hath sent me.[14]

for I am not trying to do my own will . . . — Wms

because my aim is not to do my own will . . . — TCNT

. . . but the will of him that sent me — ASV

for I am not seeking to do what I please, but what pleases him who has sent me — Gspd

31. If I bear witness of myself,

If I testify in my own behalf — Knox

If I alone testify about Myself — Beck

my witness is not true.

My testimony is not valid — Nor

my evidence cannot be accepted—Wey

My testimony is not reliable — Ber

32. There is another that beareth witness of me;

It is someone else who testifies to me — Gspd

I have Another to bear testimony to me — Mof

and I know that the witness which he witnesseth of me is true.

. . . the testimony which he bears to me is trustworthy — TCNT

. . . the evidence he bears for me is valid — Mof

33. Ye sent unto John, and he bare witness unto the truth.

34. But I receive not testimony from man:

Not that I rely on human testimony — NEB

but these things I say, that ye might be saved.

I only say these things so that you may have salvation — Bas

I only mention this that you may be saved — Mon

35. He was a burning and a shining light:

He was the burning and shining lamp — Rhm

He was the Lamp that was burning and shining — TCNT

and ye were willing for a season to rejoice in his light.

and you chose to rejoice for a while in his light — Mof

and you were glad enough for a time to enjoy the light he gave — Rieu

and for a while you wanted to enjoy his light — Beck

36. But I have greater witness than that of John:

But I have a higher testimony than John's — Phi

for the works which the Father hath given me to finish,

for the work which the Father has given me to bring to completion — Mon

for the works which the Father has given Me to accomplish — NASB

---

[13]Compare verse 19.

[14]The words "the Father" are now recognized as not adequately supported by original manuscripts.

the same works that I do,

the works themselves which I am doing — Rhm

the activities in which I am engaged — Ber

bear witness of me, that the Father hath sent me.

37. And the Father himself, which hath sent me, hath borne witness of me.

And the Father who sent Me, He has borne witness of Me — NASB

The Father who sent Me — He testified about Me — Beck

Ye have neither heard his voice at any time, nor seen his shape.

. . . neither heard his voice . . . nor seen his form — ASV

But you have never heard his voice, nor seen his appearance — Lam

38. And ye have not his word abiding in you:

And you have not kept his word in your hearts — Bas

But his word has found no home in you — NEB

and you do not keep his message in your hearts — Gspd

for whom he hath sent, him ye believe not.

for you refuse to believe Him whom He has sent — Wey

39. Search the scriptures;

Ye search the scriptures — ASV

You pore over the scriptures — Knox

You keep on searching the Scriptures — Wms

for in them ye think ye have eternal life:

in the belief that through them you get eternal life — Bas

for you imagine that you will find eternal life in them — Phi

and they are they which testify of me.

and it is these that bear witness of Me — NASB

yet they testify about Me! — Beck

40. And ye will not come to me, that ye might have life.

And ye are not willing to come to me . . . — ABUV

and . . . you refuse to come to me to have Life — TCNT

yet you do not want to come to Me in order to have life — Ber

41. I receive not honour from men.

I accept no credit from men — Mof

I take no praise from men — Rieu

I do not look to men for honour — NEB

42. But I know you, that ye have not the love of God in you.

But I know that in your hearts you do not really love God — Wey

43. I am come in my Father's name,

I have come in my Father's name — ABUV

I came here in my Father's name — Rieu

and ye receive me not:

and you give me no welcome — Knox

and you will not accept me — Phi

and you reject me — Rieu

if another shall come in his own name,

if another comes self-accredited — NEB

. . . with no other authority but himself — Bas

him ye will receive.

you will accept him! — Mof

you will give him your approval — Bas

44. How can ye believe, which receive honour one of another,

. . . when you receive glory from one another — NASB

. . . you who are always accepting honor from one another — Wms

. . . while you are for ever looking for one another's approval — Phi

and seek not the honour that cometh from God only?

and the glory that cometh from the only God ye seek not — ASV

and do not desire the honour which comes from the only God — TCNT

45. Do not think that I will accuse you to the Father:

Do not imagine that I will accuse you before the Father — Ber

there is one that accuseth you, even Moses, in whom ye trust.

. . . the very Moses on whom you have set your hope — NEB

There is already one who accuses you — Moses, whom you trust — Beck

46. For had ye believed Moses, ye would have believed me: for he wrote of me.

47. But if ye believe not his writings, how shall ye believe my words?

CHAPTER 6

1. **After these things Jesus went over the sea of Galilee, which is the sea of Tiberias.**
   . . . otherwise called the Lake of Tiberias — TCNT

2. **And a great multitude followed him, because they saw his miracles which he did on them that were diseased.**
   . . . they beheld the signs which he did on them that were sick — ASV
   . . . the wonderful cures that He had worked upon the ailing — Nor

3. **And Jesus went up into a mountain, and there he sat with his disciples.**
   And so Jesus went up on the hill and was sitting there with His disciples — Wms

4. **And the passover, a feast of the Jews, was nigh.**
   Now the passover was near, the feast of the Jews — Rhm
   The Jewish festival of the Passover was near — Beck

5. **When Jesus then lifted up his eyes, and saw a great company come unto him,**
   On looking up and seeing a large crowd approach — Mof
   he saith unto Philip, Whence shall we buy bread, that these may eat?
   . . . Where are we to buy bread . . . — TCNT
   . . . for all these people — Bas
   . . . Where can we buy food for these people to eat — Gspd

6. **And this he said to prove him: for he himself knew what he would do.**
   He said this to test him, for he himself knew what he intended to do — Mon

7. **Philip answered him, Two hundred pennyworth of bread is not sufficient for them,**
   . . . Two hundred denaries worth . . . is not enough . . . — ABUV
   . . . Forty or fifty dollars' worth . . . will not be enough . . . — Nor
   that every one of them may take a little.
   for everybody to get even a morsel — Mof
   for each of them to get just a little — Beck

8. **One of his disciples, Andrew, Simon Peter's brother, saith unto him,**

9. **There is a lad here, which hath five barley loaves, and two small fishes:**
   There is a little lad who has . . . and a couple of fish — Mon
   There is a boy here . . . — Gspd
   . . . with five barley-cakes and two fishes — Ber
   but what are they among so many?

10. **And Jesus said, Make the men sit down.**
    . . . Make the people recline — Rhm
    . . . Get the people to lie down — Mof
    . . . Make the people settle down — Rieu
    Now there was much grass in the place. So the men sat down, in number about five thousand.
    . . . So the men reclined, to the number of about five thousand — Rhm

11. **And Jesus took the loaves; and when he had given thanks,**
    he distributed to the disciples, and the disciples[15] to them that were set down;
    he distributed to those who were reclining — ABUV
    and likewise of the fishes as much as they would.
    so also the fish, as much as they wanted — RSV

12. **When they were filled, he said unto his disciples,**
    And when they had had enough . . . — Bas
    When all were fully satisfied . . . — Wey
    Gather up the fragments that remain, that nothing be lost.
    Gather up the broken pieces that remain . . . — ASV
    Collect the pieces that are left over . . . — Phi
    . . . so that nothing will be wasted — Beck

13. **Therefore they gathered them together,**
    So they gathered them up — Rhm
    And they collected them — Rieu
    and filled twelve baskets with the fragments of the five barley loaves,

---

[15]The words "to the disciples, and the disciples" are now recognized as not adequately supported by original manuscripts.

and filled twelve baskets with the broken pieces . . . — Phi

and filled twelve hand-baskets . . . — Nor

. . . with pieces of the five barley-cakes — Ber

which remained over and above unto them that had eaten.

which were left over by them who had eaten — Rhm

which were more than the eaters wanted — Wms

14. Then those men, when they had seen the miracle that Jesus did, said,

When the men saw this sign of Jesus' power . . . — Phi

When the people saw what a miracle he had done they began to say — Rieu

This is of a truth that prophet that should come into the world.

. . . the prophet that is to come into the world — Alf

Beyond doubt, this is the prophet who is to come . . . — Knox

15. When Jesus therefore perceived that they would come and take him by force, to make him a king,

. . . that they were about to come and carry him off by force . . . — Wey

. . . seize him to proclaim him king — NEB

he departed again into a mountain himself alone.

. . . withdrew again into the mountain himself alone — ASV

Jesus withdrew again to the hills by himself — RSV

16. And when even was now come, his disciples went down unto the sea,

But when evening came . . . — Rhm

. . . his disciples went down to the Sea — TCNT

17. And entered into a ship, and went over the sea toward Capernaum.

and entering into a boat, were going over the sea . . . — ABUV

and embarking in a boat they started across the sea . . . — Mof

And it was now dark, and Jesus was not come to them.

By this time it had become dark . . . — Wey

. . . yet Jesus had not come back to them — Nor

18. And the sea arose by reason of a great wind that blew.

the Sea, too, was getting rough . . . — TCNT

. . . because a strong wind was blowing — Phi

and the sea was getting up under a strong wind — Mof

19. So when they had rowed about five and twenty or thirty furlongs,

After they had rowed three or four miles — Mon

they see Jesus walking on the sea, and drawing nigh unto the ship: and they were afraid.

they saw Jesus . . . and approaching the ship . . . — Rieu

they saw Jesus walking on the lake . . . and they were terrified — Beck

20. But he saith unto them, It is I; be not afraid.

But He told them, It is I; have no fear — Ber

21. Then they willingly received him into the ship:

And after this they were glad to take him into the boat — TCNT

and immediately the ship was at the land whither they went.

And in a moment the boat came to the shore . . . — Beck

and immediately the boat reached the shore they were making for — Mon

22. The day following, when the people which stood on the other side of the sea

On the morrow the multitude that stood on the other side of the sea — ASV

Next morning the crowd who were still standing about on the other side of the Lake — Wey

saw that there was none other boat there, save that one where into his disciples were entered,[16]

saw that there was no other boat there but one — ABUV

saw that there had been only one boat there — RSV

and that Jesus went not with his disciples into the boat,

and that Jesus had not gone aboard with his disciples — Mof

---

[16]The phrase "whereinto . . . entered" is now recognized as not adequately supported by original manuscripts.

but that his disciples were gone away alone;

but that they had gone away without Him — Beck

23. (Howbeit there came other boats from Tiberias nigh unto the place

But some boats from Tiberias landed near the place — Gspd

Some other small boats . . . landed quite near the place — Phi

where they did eat bread, after that the Lord had given thanks:)

. . . after the Lord's thanksgiving — Ber

. . . after the Lord had blessed it — Rieu

24. When the people therefore saw that Jesus was not there, neither his disciples, they also took shipping,

. . . the multitude . . . embarked on these boats — Knox

. . . they also got into boats — Nor

and came to Capernaum, seeking for Jesus.

25. And when they had found him on the other side of the sea, they said unto him, Rabbi, when camest thou hither?

. . . Teacher, when did you get here — Wms

26. Jesus answered them and said, Verily, verily, I say unto you, Ye seek me,

. . . you are looking for me — Mon

not because ye saw the miracles,

not because you saw signs — NASB

but because ye did eat of the loaves, and were filled.

but because you ate that bread . . . — Gspd

. . . and had plenty — Wms

. . . and had your fill — Mof

27. Labour not for the meat which perisheth,

Work not for the food that perishes — ABUV

Stop toiling for the food that perishes — Wms

but for that meat which endureth unto everlasting life,

but for the food which endures to eternal life — NASB

but rather for the food that lasts forever — Nor

which the Son of man shall give unto you:

for him hath God the Father sealed.

for he it is upon whom the Father has set the seal of his authority — NEB

For upon the same hath the Father . . . set his seal — Rhm

for God the Father has certified Him — Ber

28. Then said they unto him, What shall we do, that we might work the works of God?

. . . What must we do to perform the works that God demands — Wms

. . . What are the works God wants us to do — Beck

29. Jesus answered and said unto them, This is the work of God,

. . . The work that God would have you do — TCNT

. . . This is the service God asks of you — Knox

that ye believe on him whom he hath sent.

have faith in him whom God has sent — Bas

that you . . . rely on . . . His Messenger — Amp

is to believe in him whom God sent as his messenger — TCNT

30. They said therefore unto him, What sign shewest thou then,

. . . What sign then will you work — Ber

. . . What sign can you give us to see — NEB

that we may see, and believe thee?

which we may see, and so believe you — TCNT

for us to see and so come to believe you — Gspd

what dost thou work?

What works are you going to do — Wms

What is your wonder-work — Nor

31. Our fathers did eat manna in the desert; as it is written, He gave them bread from heaven to eat.

Our forefathers ate manna in the desert . . . — Phi

32. Then Jesus said unto them, Verily, verily, I say unto you, Moses gave you not that bread from heaven;

. . . It was not Moses that gave you the bread out of heaven — ASV

. . . the bread that comes from heaven is not what Moses gave you — Knox

but my Father giveth you the true bread from heaven.

but my Father is giving you the bread — the true bread . . . — Wey but My Father gives you the real heavenly food — Ber

33. For the bread of God is he which cometh down from heaven,

for the bread of God is what comes down from heaven — Mon

and giveth life unto the world.

34. Then said they unto him, Lord, evermore give us this bread.

Ah, Lord, they said, give us that bread for ever! — Bas

35. And Jesus said unto them, I am the bread of life: he that cometh to me shall never hunger;

. . . will never be hungry — Phi

and he that believeth on me shall never thirst.

. . . will never again be thirsty — Mof

. . . will never be in need of drink — Bas

36. But I said unto you, That ye also have seen me,[17] and believe not.

as I have said already, you have seen me . . . — TCNT

as I said, you have seen . . . — Rieu

. . . and still you have no faith — Bas

37. All that the Father giveth me shall come to me;

All that which the Father is giving me . . . — Rhm

Everything the Father gives Me will come to Me — Beck

and him that cometh to me I will in no wise cast out.

and the man who comes to me I will never turn away — NEB

. . . I will certainly not cast out — Ber

38. For I came down from heaven, not to do mine own will,

. . . not to carry out my own will — Mof

. . . not to do what I want — Phi

but the will of him that sent me.

39. And this is the Father's[18] will which hath sent me,

And this is the will of him that sent me — ASV

and his will is this — TCNT

that of all which he hath given me I shall lose nothing, but should raise it up again at the last day.

that I should lose none of all that He has given me, but should raise them to life on the last day — Wms

40. And this is the will of him that sent me, that every one which seeth the Son, and believeth on him,

For this is the will of my Father[19] . . . — ASV

. . . that everyone who sees the Son and has faith in him — Rieu

may have everlasting life: and I will raise him up at the last day.

41. The Jews then murmured at him,

. . . began to murmur concerning him — Rhm

. . . began to find fault — Mon

because he said, I am the bread which came down from heaven.

42. And they said, Is not this Jesus, the son of Joseph, whose father and mother we know? how is it then that he saith, I came down from heaven?

43. Jesus therefore answered and said unto them, Murmur not among yourselves.

. . . Cease to mutter to each other — Rieu

. . . Do not whisper thus to one another — Knox

. . . Stop grumbling to one another — Phi

44. No man can come to me, except the Father which hath sent me draw him:

. . . unless the Father who sent me draws him — RSV

. . . without being attracted to me by the Father — Knox

and I will raise him up at the last day.

45. It is written in the prophets, And they shall be all taught of God.

. . . And they will all have teaching from God — Bas

. . . They shall all be taught by God — Lam

Every man therefore that hath heard, and hath learned of the Father, cometh unto me.

Every one that hath heard from the Father, and hath learned, cometh unto me — ASV

Everyone that has heard the Father's words and learnt them comes to me — Rieu

46. Not that any man hath seen the Father, save he which is of God, he hath seen the Father.

---

[17]Some manuscripts and translations omit "me."

[18]Some manuscripts omit "Father" in verse 39, but include it in verse 40.

[19]See verse 39, footnote.

47. Verily, verily, I say unto you, He that believeth on me hath everlasting life.
I tell you the truth, if you believe, you have everlasting life — Beck

48. I am that bread of life.
I am the bread that gives life — Gspd
I am the Life-giving Bread — TCNT

49. Your fathers did eat manna in the wilderness, and are dead.
Your fathers ate the manna in the wilderness, and they died — ASV

50. This is the bread which cometh down from heaven,
The bread which comes down from heaven is such bread — Bas
the bread that comes down from heaven is such — Mof
that a man may eat thereof, and not die.
that one who eats it will never die — Gspd
that he who eats of it never dies — Knox

51. I am the living bread which came down from heaven: if any man eat of this bread, he shall live for ever:
and the bread that I will give is my flesh, which I will give for the life of the world.
moreover, the bread which I will give is my flesh, given for the life of the world — Mon
Moreover the bread which I will give for the life of the world is my flesh — Wey

52. The Jews therefore strove among themselves, saying,
The Jews therefore contended with one another, saying — ABUV
Then the Jews began to dispute among themselves, saying — Mon
This led to an angry debate among the Jews — Wey
Then the Jews wrangled with each other — Ber
How can this man give us his flesh to eat?

53. Then Jesus said unto them, Verily, verily, I say unto you,
. . . With all the earnestness I possess I tell you this: — Tay
Except ye eat the flesh of the Son of man, and drink his blood,
If you do not take the flesh of the Son of man for food, and if you do not take his blood for drink — Bas

Unless you do eat the body of the Son of Man and drink his blood — Phi
ye have no life in you.
you have no inner life — Ber
ye have no life in yourselves — ASV
you have no self-existent life — Gspd
you are not really living at all — Phi

54. Whoso eateth my flesh, and drinketh my blood,
whoever continues to eat my flesh and drink my blood — Wms
He who takes my flesh for his food, and drinks my blood — TCNT
He who feeds on my flesh and drinks my blood — Mof
hath eternal life; and I will raise him up at the last day.
Hath life age-abiding . . . — Rhm

55. For my flesh is meat indeed, and my blood is drink indeed.
For my flesh is true food, and my blood is true drink — Rhm
For my flesh is real food and my blood is real drink — Wms

56. He that eateth my flesh, and drinketh my blood, dwelleth in me, and I in him.
. . . abides in me, and I in him — ABUV
. . . dwells continually in me and I dwell in him — NEB
. . . remains united to me and I remain united to him — Gspd

57. As the living Father hath sent me, and I live by the Father:
. . . and I live by reason of the Father — Alf
. . . and I have life because of the Father — Bas
. . . and I live through Him — Rieu
so he that eateth me, even he shall live by me.
so he that eateth me, he also shall live because of me — ASV
so he who takes me for his food . . . — TCNT
. . . will have life because of me — Bas
so also shall the one who feeds on Me live through Me — Nor

58. This is that bread which came down from heaven:
Such is the bread which has come down from heaven — Knox
This is the Bread that came down from heaven — Beck

not as your fathers did eat manna, and are dead:[20]

not such as your ancestors ate, and yet died — TCNT

Your fathers ate a different kind, and died — Rieu

it is unlike that which your forefathers ate — for they ate and yet died — Wey

he that eateth of this bread

He that feedeth upon this bread — Rhm

Whoever continues to eat this bread — Wms

shall live for ever.

will have life for ever — Bas

will live eternally — Knox

59. These things said he in the synagogue, as he taught in Capernaum.

He spoke thus while teaching in a synagogue at Capernaum — TCNT

Jesus said all these things while teaching in the synagogue at Capernaum — Phi

60. Many therefore of his disciples, when they had heard this, said, This is an hard saying; who can hear it?

. . . This is hard to accept. Who can listen to such teaching — Wey

. . . This is a harsh teaching! Who can listen to it — Gspd

. . . This is hard to take in! Who can listen to talk like this — Mof

. . . This is more than we can stomach! Why listen to such words — NEB

61. When Jesus knew in himself that his disciples murmured at it,

But as Jesus naturally knew . . . — Wms

Then Jesus, knowing intuitively . . . — Phi

. . . that His disciples were complaining about this — Beck

. . . that His disciples grumbled at this — NASB

Jesus, conscious within himself that his disciples were finding fault with him about this teaching — Mon

he said unto them, Doth this offend you?

. . . Doth this cause you to stumble — ASV

. . . Is this a stumbling block to you — ABUV

. . . Does this shock you — NEB

62. What and if ye shall see the Son of man ascend up where he was before?

What then if ye should behold the Son of man ascending up where he was before — Alf

Then what would you say if you saw the Son of Man ascend to where he came from — Rieu

63. It is the Spirit that quickeneth; the flesh profiteth nothing:

It is the spirit that giveth life . . . — ASV

. . . The flesh confers no benefit whatever — Wey

The spirit is the life-giver; the flesh is of no value — Bas

It is the Spirit that gives Life; mere flesh is of no avail — TCNT

the words that I speak unto you, they are spirit, and they are life.

The words I have uttered to you are spirit and life — Mof

The messages I bring you are spirit and life — Ber

The things which I have told you are spiritual and are life — Phi

64. But there are some of you that believe not.

For Jesus knew from the beginning who they were that believed not, and who should betray him.

Jesus said this because he had known from early days which were the unbelievers and who it was that would betray him — Rieu

For Jesus knew from the start who were the unbelievers and who would be His betrayer — Ber

65. And he said, Therefore said I unto you, that no man can come unto me, except it were given unto him of my Father.

. . . no one is able to come to me unless he is allowed by the Father — Mof

. . . unless it is granted him by the Father — RSV

. . . This is why I told you that no one can come to me, unless enabled by the Father — TCNT

66. From that time many of his disciples went back,

As a result of this many of his disciples withdrew — NASB

As a result many of His disciples went back to their old life — Beck

and walked no more with him.

---

[20]The word "manna" is now recognized as not adequately supported by original manuscripts.

and walked no more in his company —
Knox

and stopped accompanying Him —
Wms

and no longer went about with him —
RSV

67. Then said Jesus unto the twelve, Will ye also go away?

. . . Do ye also wish to go away — Alf

. . . Do you also want to leave me —
NEB

68. Then Simon Peter answered him, Lord, to whom shall we go?
thou hast the words of eternal life.

The words you have are words of eternal life — Mof

Your teachings tell us of eternal Life
— Wey

Immortal Life is in your teaching —
TCNT

You alone have the words that give eternal life — Tay

69. And we believe and are sure that thou art that Christ, the Son of the living God.[21]

And we have believed and know that thou art the Holy One of God —
ASV

and we believe and are satisfied that

you are the Holy One of God —
Gspd

and we have believed, and have come to know, that you are the Holy One of God — RSV

70. Jesus answered them, Have not I chosen you twelve,

. . . Did I not choose you twelve — Alf

and one of you is a devil?

yet even of you one is an enemy —
Mon

yet from among you one is an adversary — Rhm

yet, even of you, one is playing the 'Devil's' part — TCNT

71. He spake of Judas Iscariot the son of Simon:

But he was speaking of Judas, son of Simon Iscariot — ABUV

He meant Judas son of Simon of Kerioth — Rieu

He meant Judas, the son of Simon, the man from Kerioth — Beck

for he it was that should betray him, being one of the twelve.

for the same was about to deliver him up . . . — Rhm

for he, one of the twelve, was to betray him — RSV

for he . . . was planning to betray Him — Nor

CHAPTER 7

1. After these things Jesus walked in Galilee:

After this, Jesus moved about in Galilee — Phi

After this Jesus went about in Galilee
— RSV

After this Jesus moved from place to place in Galilee — Wey

for he would not walk in Jewry,

for he was not willing to walk in Judaea — ABUV

He did not wish to stay in Judea — Nor

He didn't want to travel in Judea —
Beck

because the Jews sought to kill him.

because the Jews were eager to put him to death — TCNT

because the Jews were determined to kill him — Rieu

because the Jews were looking for a chance to kill him — NEB

2. Now the Jews' feast of tabernacles was at hand.

As the Jewish festival of booths was near — Mof

However, the Jewish Feast of Booths was near — Ber

3. His brethren therefore said unto him, Depart hence, and go into Judaea,

So his brothers said to him . . . — RSV

. . . You must leave here and go to Judea — Wms

that thy disciples also may see the works that thou doest.

so that thy disciples also may see thy doings — Knox

to let your disciples also see the things you are doing — Gspd

---

[21]Some manuscripts use the words "the Holy One of God" instead of "Christ, the Son of the living God."

let Your disciples see the deeds You do — Nor

4. For there is no man that doeth any thing in secret, and he himself seeketh to be known openly.

For no one does a thing privately . . . — TCNT

. . . when he is trying to be known to the public — Wms

For no man works in secret if he seeks to be known openly — RSV

If thou do these things, show thyself to the world.

Since you are doing these deeds . . . — Wey

. . . let yourself be seen by all men — Bas

Since you can do these deeds, display yourself to the world — Mof

5. For neither did his brethren believe in him.

For not even His brothers were believing in Him — NASB

6. Then Jesus said unto them, My time is not yet come:

. . . My time has not yet arrived — Ber

. . . It is not yet the right time for me — Phi

. . . It is not yet time for me to do so — Wms

but your time is alway ready.

Your opportunity is always ready to hand — Knox

whereas for you one day is as good as another — Rieu

but any time is suitable for you — Nor

7. The world cannot hate you; but me it hateth,

It is impossible for the world to hate you . . . — Gspd

the world cannot be expected to hate you . . . — Knox

. . . but me it does hate — Mon

The world has no excuse for hating you; but me it hates — Rieu

because I testify of it, that the works thereof are evil.

for I testify against it, that its works are wicked — Nor

because I show the world how evil its deeds really are — Phi

8. Go ye up unto this feast:

Go to the feast yourselves — RSV

I go not up yet unto this feast;[22]

I am not going to this Festival yet — TCNT

I am not going up to this festival — NEB

for my time is not yet full come.

because my time is not yet fulfilled — ASV

because my time has not fully come — Bas

for it is not quite time for me to go — Wms

9. When he had said these words unto them, he abode still in Galilee.

And having said these things to them, He stayed in Galilee — NASB

10. But when his brethren were gone up, then went he also up unto the feast,

But when his brothers had gone up to the feast, then he also went up — ABUV

not openly, but as it were in secret.

not publicly, but as it were in secret — ASV

. . . but as though he did not wish to be observed — Gspd

not publicly, but in private — RSV

11. Then the Jews sought him at the feast, and said, Where is he?

The Jews were looking for him at the feast, and asked, Where can he be — Knox

12. And there was much murmuring among the people concerning him:

and there were many whispers about him among the people — TCNT

and there was much disputing about him among the crowd — Mon

And there was an undercurrent of discussion about him among the crowds — Phi

for some said, He is a good man: others said, Nay; but he deceiveth the people.

. . . Others said, Not so: he is imposing on the people — Wey

. . . others that He was not, but was misleading the masses — Wms

13. Howbeit no man spake openly of him for fear of the Jews.

But no one spoke of him in public, for fear of the Jews — Gspd

14. Now about the midst of the feast Jesus went up into the temple, and taught.

However, half-way through the Festival . . . — Rieu

---

[22]The witness of the Greek manuscripts is divided: some read "not yet," while others equally good read simply "not."

When the festival was half over . . . —
Mof

. . . Jesus went up to the Temple and
began to teach — Mon

15. **And the Jews marvelled, saying,**

The Jews therefore wondered . . . —
ABUV

The Jews were amazed . . . — Phi

**How knoweth this man letters, having
never learned?**

How is it that this man knows his letters . . . — Gspd

How can this uneducated fellow manage to read — Wey

How is it . . . that this untrained man
has such learning — NEB

How can He know so much when He's
never been to our schools — Tay

16. **Jesus answered them, and said, My
doctrine is not mine, but his that sent
me.**

. . . My teaching is not my own; it is his
who sent me — TCNT

. . . The learning which I impart is not
my own, it comes from him who
sent me — Knox

17. **If any man will do his will, he shall
know of the doctrine,**

If any man be willing to do his will, he
shall know concerning the teaching
— Alf

If any one wills to do God's will he
shall know concerning my teaching
— Mon

**whether it be of God, or whether I
speak of myself.**

whether it is from God or originates
with me — Wey

whether my teaching is from God or
whether I merely speak on my own
authority — Phi

18. **He that speaketh of himself seeketh
his own glory:**

He who talks on his own authority
aims at his own credit — Mof

The man who teaches on his own authority is seeking glory for himself
— Rieu

**but he that seeketh his glory that sent
him, the same is true,**

but whoever seeks the honor of him
who sent him is sincere — Wms

But He who wants to glorify the One
who sent Him tells the truth — Beck

but he who seeks his sender's honor is
sincere — Ber

and no unrighteousness is in him.

and there is no deception in his heart
— Lam

there is no dishonesty in him — Knox

and in him there is no falsehood — RSV

19. **Did not Moses give you the law, and
yet none of you keepeth the law?**

Was not it Moses who gave the Law?
Yet not one of you obeys it! — TCNT

Did not Moses give you the Law? And
yet not a man of you obeys the Law
— Mof

Why go ye about to kill me?

Else, why do you want to kill me —
Mof

If so, why are you trying to kill me —
Wms

Why have you a desire to put me to
death — Bas

20. **The people answered and said, Thou
hast a devil: who goeth about to kill
thee?**

. . . You have a demon! . . . — Mon

. . . You are possessed! . . . — NEB

. . . You must be mad! Who is trying
to kill you — Phi

21. **Jesus answered and said unto them, I
have done one work, and ye all marvel.**

. . . There is one action of mine which
has astounded you all — Knox

. . . I did one deed which made you
wonder — Nor

. . . I have done just one deed, and you
are all astonished at it — Gspd

22. **Moses therefore gave unto you circumcision;**

Well then, Moses gave you the rite of
circumcision — Wey

**(not because it is of Moses, but of the
fathers;)**

(not that it came from Moses but from
our ancestors) — Beck

**and ye on the sabbath day circumcise
a man.**

and you will circumcise a man even on
the Sabbath — Phi

23. **If a man on the sabbath day receive
circumcision, that the law of Moses
should not be broken;**

When a man receives circumcision on
a Sabbath to prevent the Law of
Moses from being broken — TCNT

But if a man is circumcised on the
Sabbath so as to comply with Moses'
law — Rieu

are ye angry at me, because I have made a man every whit whole on the sabbath day?

do you feel bitter toward Me . . . — Beck

how can you be angry with me . . . — Mon

. . . because I made a man completely well on the Sabbath — Rieu

. . . because on the sabbath I made a man's whole body well — RSV

24. **Judge not according to the appearance, but judge righteous judgment.**

Don't judge according to appearances, but make honest judgments — Nor

Stop judging superficially; you must judge fairly — Wms

25. **Then said some of them of Jerusalem, Is not this he, whom they seek to kill?**

26. **But, lo, he speaketh boldly, and they say nothing unto him.**

But here he is, speaking out boldly . . . — Wey

. . . and they have not a word to say to him — NEB

Do the rulers know indeed that this is the very Christ?

Can it be that the rulers indeed know that this is the Christ — ASV

Perhaps our elders have found out . . . — Lam

Is it possible that our rulers really know him to be the Messiah — Rieu

27. **Howbeit we know this man whence he is:**

But then, we know this man's origins — Knox

But then, we know this man and where he comes from — Phi

but when Christ cometh, no man knoweth whence he is.

But the Messiah — if He ever comes — no one will know from where He comes — Nor

and when the Christ appears, no one will know where he comes from — RSV

28. **Then cried Jesus in the temple as he taught, saying,**

So Jesus called out as He taught in the temple — Ber

Ye both know me, and ye know whence I am:

Yes, you know me, and you know where I am from — Wey

and I am not come of myself,

But I have not come on my own initiative — Mof

and I have not come on my own accord — Gspd

but he that sent me is true, whom ye know not.

but the One who has sent me exists as the Real One . . . — Wms

I was sent to you by One who is true . . . — Nor

but He who sent me is trustworthy, and him you do not know — Mon

29. **But I know him; for I am from him, and he hath sent me.**

30. **Then they sought to take him:**

Then they had a desire to take him — Bas

And now they were ready to seize him — Knox

Then they were anxious to arrest Him — Ber

but no man laid hands on him, because his hour was not yet come.

but no one touched him . . . — TCNT

but nobody laid a hand on Him . . . — Beck

. . . because he was not yet ready — Gspd

. . . because his appointed hour had not yet come — NEB

31. **And many of the people believed on him, and said, When Christ cometh,**

. . . When the Messiah comes — NEB

. . . When the promised Savior comes — Beck

will he do more miracles than these which this man hath done?

will he do more signs than this man has done — RSV

32. **The Pharisees heard that the people murmured such things concerning him;**

. . . heard the crowd whispering these things . . . — Phi

This discussion of the people came to the ears of the Pharisees — Bas

and the Pharisees and the chief priests sent officers to take him.

the high priests and the Pharisees despatched attendants to arrest him — Mof

. . . to seize him — ABUV

33. **Then said Jesus unto them, Yet a little while am I with you,**

. . . I shall be with you but a little longer — TCNT

... For a little while longer I am with you — NASB

and then I go unto him that sent me.

and then I am going back to Him who has sent me — Wms

and then I go my way to Him who sent me — Wey

34. **Ye shall seek me, and shall not find me: and where I am, thither ye cannot come.**

You'll be looking for Me and won't find me . . . — Beck

. . . where I am you cannot come — RSV

35. **Then said the Jews among themselves, Whither will he go, that we shall not find him?**

Where does this fellow intend to go, so that we shall not find him — Mon

will he go unto the dispersed among the Gentiles, and teach the Gentiles?

Is he off to the Dispersion among the Greeks, to teach the Greeks — Mof

He is not going to our people scattered among the Greeks, . . . to teach the Greeks, is He — Wms

36. **What manner of saying is this that he said,**

What is this saying that he said — Alf

What can it mean, this saying of his — Knox

Ye shall seek me, and shall not find me: and where I am, thither ye cannot come?

37. **In the last day, that great day of the feast,**

On the last and greatest day of the festival — NEB

On the final and most important day of the Feast — Ber

Jesus stood and cried, saying,

Jesus stood up and called out — Nor

Jesus stood up and proclaimed — RSV

If any man thirst, let him come unto me, and drink.

38. **He that believeth on me, as the scripture hath said,**

out of his belly shall flow rivers of living water.

. . . from within him shall flow rivers of living water — ABUV

Out of the heart of the one who believes in Me there will flow . . . — Nor

Out from his innermost being springs and rivers of living water shall flow (continuously) — Amp

39. **(But this spake he of the Spirit, which they that believe on him should receive:**

And this he spoke concerning the Spirit . . . — ABUV

. . . which they that believe in him were about to receive — Alf

He referred to the Spirit which those who believed in Him were to receive — Wey

for the Holy Ghost was not yet given; because that Jesus was not yet glorified.)

for the Spirit had not yet come . . . — TCNT

. . . because Jesus had not yet been raised to glory — Knox

. . . because Jesus had not yet been exalted — TCNT

40. **Many of the people therefore, when they heard this saying, said, Of a truth this is the Prophet.**

. . . This really is the prophet — Ber

. . . Without doubt this man is the Prophet — Mon

41. **Others said, This is the Christ. But some said, Shall Christ come out of Galilee?**

. . . Can the Messiah come from Galilee — Rieu

. . . What! Is the Christ to come from Galilee — Gspd

42. **Hath not the scripture said, That Christ cometh of the seed of David,**

. . . that Christ will be descended from David — Phi

Do not the Writings say that the Christ comes from the seed of David — Bas

and out of the town of Bethlehem, where David was?

and from Bethlehem, the village where David was — ASV

. . . the village . . . where David lived — Wms

43. **So there was a division among the people because of him.**

So there was a dissension among the people on His account — Wey

Thus the people disagreed about him — Rieu

44. And some of them would have taken him; but no man laid hands on him.

45. Then came the officers to the chief priests and Pharisees; and they said unto them, Why have ye not brought him?

The attendants went back to the high priests and Pharisees . . . — Gspd

When the officers came back to the high priests and Pharisees, they were asked, Why didn't you bring him back with you — Nor

46. The officers answered, Never man spake like this man.

. . . No man ever spoke as this man speaks! — Ber

47. Then answered them the Pharisees, Are ye also deceived?

The Pharisees retorted, Are you misled as well — Mof

48. Have any of the rulers or of the Pharisees believed on him?

Did a single one of our leading men believe in him, or a single Pharisee — Rieu

Have any of the authorities or of the Pharisees believed in him — RSV

49. But this people who knoweth not the law are cursed.

As for this mob who do not understand the Law . . . — Mon

But this crowd . . . is damned anyway! — Phi

As for this rabble . . . they are accursed — Wey

50. Nicodemus saith unto them, (he that came to Jesus by night, being one of them,)

51. Doth our law judge any man, before it hear him, and know what he doeth?

. . . unless it first hear from him, and know what he does — ABUV

Does our Law pass judgement on a man without first giving him a hearing, and finding out what he has been doing — TCNT

52. They answered and said unto him, Art thou also of Galilee?

. . . You are not from Galilee, too, are you — Wms

Search, and look: for out of Galilee ariseth no prophet.

Study and you will find that no prophet is to appear from Galilee — Gspd

Search the record . . . — Wms

. . . out of Galilee a prophet is not to arise — Rhm

. . . the Prophet doesn't come from Galilee — Beck

53. And every man went unto his own house.

CHAPTER 8

1. Jesus went unto the mount of Olives.[23]

2. And early in the morning he came again into the temple, and all the people came unto him; and he sat down, and taught them.

. . . He seated Himself, and was teaching them — Wey

3. And the scribes and Pharisees brought unto him a woman taken in adultery;

. . . brought in a woman detected in adultery — NEB

. . . a woman who had been caught in adultery — TCNT

and when they had set her in the midst,

They made her stand in front — Phi

and, placing her in the center — Ber

4. They say unto him, Master, this woman was taken in adultery, in the very act.

. . . Teacher, this woman hath been caught in the very act of committing adultery — Rhm

5. Now Moses in the law commanded us, that such should be stoned:

Now Moses, in the law, commanded us to stone such women to death — TCNT

In the Law, Moses ordered us to stone such women — Beck

but what sayest thou?

what then do You say — NASB

But you, what do you say — Mon

6. This they said, tempting him, that they might have to accuse him.

They said this to test him . . . — Mof

. . . so they might trump up a charge against Him — Ber

They were trying to trap Him, so that they might find something against Him — Nor

---

[23] John 7:53—8:11 is now recognized as not adequately supported by original manuscripts.

But Jesus stooped down, and with his finger wrote on the ground, as though he heard them not.

... having stooped down, was writing ... — ABUV

But Jesus stooped down and began to write on the ground with His finger — Nor

7. So when they continued asking him, he lifted up himself, and said unto them,

But as they persisted in their questioning ... — Phi

... he raised himself and said to them — Mon

He that is without sin among you, let him first cast a stone at her.

Let the sinless man among you be the first to throw a stone at her — Wey

Whichever of you is free from sin ... — Knox

8. And again he stooped down, and wrote on the ground.

9. And they which heard it, being convicted by their own conscience,[24] went out one by one,

Convicted by their conscience as they heard Him, they went out one by one — Beck

But they ... went away conscience-stricken one after the other — Ber

beginning at the eldest, even unto the last:

beginning with the older men ... — Mof

and Jesus was left alone, and the woman standing in the midst.

and Jesus was left alone with the woman standing before him — RSV

10. When Jesus had lifted up himself, and saw none but the woman, he said unto her,

Then Jesus raised Himself up and, seeing no one there except the woman ... — Nor

Then, raising His head, Jesus said to her — Wey

Woman, where are those thine accusers?[25] hath no man condemned thee?

Woman, where are your accusers? ... — Ber

Woman, where are they? Did no one condemn you — NASB

11. She said, No man, Lord. And Jesus said unto her, Neither do I condemn thee: go, and sin no more.

... go thy way; from henceforth sin no more — ASV

... Go, and never sin again — Mon

12. Then spake Jesus again unto them, saying, I am the light of the world: he that followeth me shall not walk in darkness,

... No follower of mine shall wander in the dark — NEB

... Whoever continues to follow me need never walk in darkness — Wms

but shall have the light of life.

but will live his life in the light — Phi

he will possess the light which is life — Knox

for living light will flood your path — Tay

13. The Pharisees therefore said unto him, Thou bearest record of thyself; thy record is not true.

... the witness you give is about yourself: your witness is not true — Bas

... your testimony is not valid — Ber

14. Jesus answered and said unto them, Though I bear record of myself, yet my record is true: for I know whence I came, and whither I go;

... for I know where I came from, and where I am going — NASB

but ye cannot tell whence I come, and whither I go.

But as for you, you have no idea where I come from or where I am going — Phi

15. Ye judge after the flesh; I judge no man.

You judge by worldly standards ... — NEB

You judge in a human way, a way in which I don't judge anybody — Beck

16. And yet if I judge, my judgment is true:

... my judgment is trustworthy — Mon

... my decision is right — Bas

... you can depend on My judgment — Beck

for I am not alone, but I and the Father[26] that sent me.

---

[24]This phrase is omitted by some manuscripts and translations.

[25]The words "thine accusers" are now recognized as not adequately supported by original manuscripts.

[26]Some editions of the Greek text omit "Father."

because I am not alone, but the Father who sent me is with me — TCNT

. . . but I and He that sent me judge together — Rieu

because I am not by myself — there is myself and the Father who sent me — Mof

17. **It is also written in your law, that the testimony of two men is true.**

18. **I am one that bear witness of myself, and the Father that sent me beareth witness of me.**

I am a witness for Myself . . . — Ber

. . . and the Father who sent me testifies concerning me — ABUV

19. **Then said they unto him, Where is thy Father? Jesus answered, Ye neither know me, nor my Father:**

. . . You know my Father as little as you know me — Wey

if ye had known me, ye should have known my Father also.

If you knew Me, you would know My Father — Beck

20. **These words spake Jesus in the treasury, as he taught in the temple: and no man laid hands on him; for his hour was not yet come.**

21. **Then said Jesus again unto them, I go my way, and ye shall seek me, and shall die in your sins: whither I go, ye cannot come.**

22. **Then said the Jews, Will he kill himself? because he saith, Whither I go, ye cannot come.**

23. **And he said unto them, Ye are from beneath; I am from above: ye are of this world; I am not of this world.**

24. **I said therefore unto you, that ye shall die in your sins:**

for if ye believe not that I am he, ye shall die in your sins.

for unless you believe that I am the Christ — Wms

For unless you believe that I am who I am — Phi

. . . you will die under the curse of your sins — Wms

. . . you will die with your sins upon you — Knox

25. **Then said they unto him, Who art thou?**

You — who are you? they asked — Wey

And Jesus saith unto them, Even the same that I said unto you from the beginning.[27]

. . . Even what I have told you from the beginning — RSV

. . . Why ask exactly what I have been telling you? — TCNT

. . . Why should I talk to you at all? — Mof

. . . What should I tell you first? — Beck

26. **I have many things to say and to judge of you:**

I have still much that concerns you to speak of and to pass judgement on — TCNT

. . . many judgments I could pass on you — Knox

I have much to say and to judge about you — Ber

but he that sent me is true; and I speak to the world those things which I have heard of him.

But He who sent me is faithful . . . — Nor

yet he who sent me is truthful . . . — Gspd

but My Sender is reliable . . . — Ber

. . . and I declare to the world what I have heard from him — RSV

27. **They understood not that he spake to them of the Father.**

28. **Then said Jesus unto them, When ye have lifted up the Son of man, then shall ye know that I am he,**

. . . then you will know that I am He — Mon

. . . you will recognize that it is myself you look for — Knox

. . . you will know then who I am — Mof

and that I do nothing of myself; but as my Father hath taught me, I speak these things.

. . . but speak as the Father has instructed me — Gspd

I do nothing on my own authority, but in all that I say, I have been taught by my Father — NEB

. . . I say exactly what my Father has instructed me to say — Wms

29. **And he that sent me is with me: the Father hath not left me alone; for I**

---

[27]Variant reading.

do always those things that please him.
. . . because at all times I do the things which are pleasing to him — Bas
. . . for I am busy all the time in pleasing Him — Rieu
. . . for I always do what is acceptable to him — NEB

30. **As he spake these words, many believed on him.**

31. **Then said Jesus to those Jews which believed on him, If ye continue in my word,**
. . . If ye abide in my word — ASV
. . . If you live in My Word — Beck
. . . If you are faithful to what I have said — Phi
. . . As for you, if you hold fast to my teaching — Wey
. . . If you adhere to My teaching — Ber
. . . If you dwell within the revelation I have brought — NEB
then are ye my disciples indeed;
ye are truly my disciples — ABUV
you are really disciples of mine — Gspd

32. **And ye shall know the truth,**
and you shall find out the Truth—TCNT
And you will have knowledge of what is true — Bas
you will understand the truth — Mof
and the truth shall make you free.
and that very truth will make you free — Lam
and the truth will set you free — Wms

33. **They answered him, We be Abraham's seed, and were never in bondage to any man:**
. . . We are descendants of Abraham . . . — RSV
. . . and have never yet been in slavery to any one — TCNT
. . . have never been anybody's slaves — Beck
how sayest thou, Ye shall be made free?
why do you say, You will become free — Bas
What do you mean by saying that we shall be freed — Rieu

34. **Jesus answered them, Verily, verily, I say unto you, Whosoever committeth sin is the servant of sin.**
. . . everyone who acts sinfully is the slave of sin — Knox

. . . everyone who lives in sin is a slave to sin — Beck

35. **And the servant abideth not in the house for ever:**
And a slave does not remain in the home always — TCNT
Now a slave does not remain always in his master's house — Wey
. . . does not remain permanently in the household — Mon
but the Son abideth ever.
A son stays forever — Beck
the son of the house does — Mof
it is the son that stays for ever — Rieu

36. **If the Son therefore shall make you free, ye shall be free indeed.**
So if the Son makes you free . . . — RSV
. . . you will be truly free — Bas
So if the Son liberates you, then you are unquestionably free — Ber

37. **I know that ye are Abraham's seed; but ye seek to kill me, because my word hath no place in you.**
. . . because my word hath not free course in you — ASV
. . . gaineth no ground in you — Alf
. . . makes no headway among you! — Mof
. . . findeth no place in you — Rhm
. . . because my words find no room in your hearts — Rieu

38. **I speak that which I have seen with my Father: and ye do that which ye have seen with your father.**
. . . and you are practicing what you have learned from your father — Wms
. . . are acting as you have learned . . . — Mon
. . . you are revealing in action . . . — NEB
. . . what you have learnt from your father — TCNT

39. **They answered and said unto him, Abraham is our father. Jesus saith unto them, If ye were Abraham's children, ye would do the works of Abraham.**
. . . If you are children of Abraham, said Jesus, act as Abraham acted — Rieu
. . . If ye were children of Abraham . . . — ABUV
. . . it is Abraham's deeds that you would be doing — Wey

40. But now ye seek to kill me,

as it is, you are designing to kill me — Knox

but now you want to kill me — Mof

But instead you are trying to kill me — Gspd

a man that hath told you the truth, which I have heard of God:

a man who told you the truth, as I heard it from God — NEB

... which He learned from God — Ber

a man who has taught you the truth he had from God — Rieu

this did not Abraham.

this is not what Abraham did — RSV

Abraham would never have done that — Phi

41. Ye do the deeds of your father.

You are practicing what your real father does — Wms

You are doing what your own father does — TCNT

Then said they to him, We be not born of fornication;

... We are not illegitimate children — Gspd

... We were not born illegitimately — Nor

We weren't born outside of marriage ... — Beck

we have one Father, even God.

We have one Father, who is God — Rieu

... one Father — God himself — TCNT

God is our father, and God alone — NEB

42. Jesus said unto them, If God were your Father,

... If God had been your father — Rhm

... If God were really your Father — Phi

ye would love me:

you would have love for me — Bas

you would welcome me gladly — Knox

for I proceeded forth and came from God;

for I proceeded forth and am now come from God — Mon

for I proceeded and came forth from God — RSV

for I came out from God, and now am here — TCNT

neither came I of myself, but he sent me.

43. Why do ye not understand my speech?

Why is it that you do not understand what I say — Gspd

... that you misunderstand ... — Wms

Why do you not understand My language — Ber

Why are my words not clear to you — Bas

even because ye cannot hear my word.

It is because you cannot bear to listen to my Message — TCNT

Because you are unable to listen to what I am saying — Mof

Because you cannot comprehend my thought — Rieu

... my revelation is beyond your grasp — NEB

44. Ye are of your father the devil,

Ye are of your father — the adversary — Rhm

Your father is the devil — Beck

and the lusts of your father ye will do:

and you desire to do what gives him pleasure — Wey

and you are determined to do what your father loves to do — TCNT

and you want to do your father's lustful desires — Nor

He was a murderer from the beginning,

He always was a murderer — Phi

He was a murderer from the very start — Wms

... a manslayer from the very beginning — Mon

and abode not in the truth,

and standeth not in the truth — ASV

He did not stand by the truth — Nor

and is not rooted in the truth — NEB

and he did not go in the true way — Bas

because there is no truth in him.

because truth is not in him — Mon

the truth will have nothing to do with him — Phi

When he speaketh a lie, he speaketh of his own:

When he says what is false ... — Bas

... he does what is natural to him — TCNT

When he lies, he speaks according to his own nature — RSV

for he is a liar, and the father of it.

... and the father of lies — Mof

45. And because I tell you the truth, ye believe me not.

And it is because I speak the truth that you will not believe me — Phi

Now, because I tell the truth, you don't believe Me — Beck

46. Which of you convinceth me of sin?

Who of you can prove me guilty of sin — Wms

Can any of you convict me of sin — Knox

Which of you can prove me in the wrong — NEB

And if I say the truth, why do ye not believe me?

Why then, if I am speaking the truth, do you not believe me — Mon

If I say what is true, why have you no belief in me — Bas

47. He that is of God heareth God's words:

He who comes from God listens to God's teaching — TCNT

The man who belongs to God listens to God's words — Knox

Only he who is a child of God listens . . . — Wey

ye therefore hear them not, because ye are not of God.

you do not listen to them, because you do not belong to God — Mof

You don't give ear . . . because you are not His children — Nor

It is because you are not His children that you do not hear — Rieu

48. Then answered the Jews, and said unto him, Say we not well that thou art a Samaritan, and hast a devil?

. . . Do we not say rightly . . . — NASB

. . . that you are a Samaritan and have a demon — RSV

. . . and are possessed — Gspd

49. Jesus answered, I have not a devil;

. . . I am not possessed by a demon — Wey

. . . There's no devil in Me — Beck

. . . I have not an evil spirit — Bas

but I honour my Father, and ye do dishonour me.

I am honoring my Father, and you are trying to dishonor me — Phi

. . . and you insult me — Rieu

but I have respect for my Father, and you have no respect for me — Gspd

50. And I seek not mine own glory:

However, I am not seeking honor for myself — Wms

I . . . am not in search of glory for myself — Bas

I do not care about my own glory — NEB

there is one that seeketh and judgeth.

there is one who is seeking my honour . . . — TCNT

there is One who cares for my credit, and he is judge — Mof

There's One who wants Me to have it, and He's the Judge — Beck

51. Verily, verily, I say unto you, If a man keep my saying, he shall never see death.

. . . if any one keeps my word, he will never behold death — ABUV

. . . he that cherishes my word . . . — Rieu

. . . anyone who observes My teaching . . . — Ber

. . . he will never experience death — Gspd

52. Then said the Jews unto him, Now we know that thou hast a devil.

. . . Now we know that you're mad — Phi

. . . that you are under the power of a demon — Wms

Abraham is dead, and the prophets;

Abraham died, and the prophets — ASV

and thou sayest, If a man keep my saying, he shall never taste of death.

. . . If any one lays my Message to heart, he will never know death — TCNT

53. Art thou greater than our father Abraham, which is dead? and the prophets are dead?

. . . our father Abraham, who died? And the prophets died! — RSV

. . . our father Abraham? He died, and the prophets died — Nor

whom makest thou thyself?

Who are you making yourself out to be — Mon

What do you claim to be — NEB

54. Jesus answered, If I honoured myself, my honour is nothing:

. . . If I glorify myself, my glory is nothing — Alf

. . . such glory amounts to nothing — Wms

. . . would be worthless — Ber

it is my Father that honoureth me; of whom ye say, that he is your God:

it is my Father who gives me glory . . . — Bas

There is One who glorifies me — namely my Father . . . — Wey

... whom you claim as your God —
Knox
... the very one who you say is your
God — Phi

**55. Yet ye have not known him; but I
know him:**
And yet ye have not come to know
him.... — Rhm
You have never come to know Him
... — Nor
**and if I should say, I know him not,
I shall be a liar like unto you:**
Were I to say, I do not know him ...
— Mon
... I would be a liar like yourselves —
Mof
but I know him, and keep his saying.
but I do know him and I keep his word
— RSV
... cherish his word — Rieu
... I am true to his word — Knox

**56. Your father Abraham rejoiced to see
my day:**
... exulted that he should see ... —
Rhm
... rejoiced that he was to see my day
— RSV
... was extremely happy in the prospect of seeing ... — Ber
... rejoiced at the thought ... — Nor
... of seeing my coming — Gspd

... was delighted to know of My day
— Beck
and he saw it, and was glad.

**57. Then said the Jews unto him, Thou art
not yet fifty years old,**
The Jews protested ... — NEB
... you are not even fifty years old —
Nor
and hast thou seen Abraham?
How can you have seen Abraham —
NEB

**58. Jesus said unto them, Verily, verily, I
say unto you, Before Abraham was, I
am.**
... I most solemnly say to you ... —
Wms
... Before Abraham was born, I am
ASV
... I tell you that before Abraham was,
I AM! — Nor
... before there was an Abraham, I
AM! — Phi

**59. Then took they up stones to cast at
him: but Jesus hid himself, and went
out of the temple,**
... Jesus concealed himself ... — Mof
... made his way out of the Temple
unobserved — Rieu
**going through the midst of them, and
so passed by.**[28]

CHAPTER 9

**1. And as Jesus passed by, he saw a man
which was blind from his birth.**
And passing along ... — ABUV
And when he went on his way ... —
Bas
... he saw a man who had been blind
from birth — Rieu

**2. And his disciples asked him, saying,
Master, who did sin, this man, or his
parents, that he was born blind?**
... Rabbi, who sinned, this man, or
his parents ... — ASV
Master, whose sin caused this man's
blindness, ... his own or his parents
— Phi
... Teacher, for whose sin was this
man born blind, his own or that of
his parents — Wms

**3. Jesus answered, Neither hath this man
sinned, nor his parents:**

Neither he nor his parents were guilty
... — Knox
It is not that this man or his parents
sinned ... — NEB
... Neither he nor his parents had
sinned — Rieu
**but that the works of God should be
made manifest in him.**
but to show what God could do in his
case — Wms
It was to let God's work be shown
plainly in him — Nor
but to show the power of God at work
in him — Phi
**4. I must work the works of him that sent
me, while it is day:**
We must work ... day[29] — ASV

---
[28]These phrases are now recognized as not
adequately supported by original manuscripts.
[29]Variant reading.

While daylight lasts, we must be busy with the work of him who sent me — Mof

... we must practice the works of My Sender — Ber

the night cometh, when no man can work.

There cometh a night, when no one can work — Rhm

the night comes when no work may be done — Bas

5. **As long as I am in the world, I am the light of the world.**

When I am in the world ... — ASV

While I am in the world, I am the Light of the world — Ber

... I am a light for the world — Gspd

I am the world's light as long as I am in it — Phi

6. **When he had thus spoken, he spat on the ground, and made clay of the spittle,**

... Jesus spat on the ground, made clay with the saliva — TCNT

... made some mud with the saliva — Nor

... made a paste with the spittle — NEB

and he anointed the eyes of the blind man with the clay,

and smeared the clay on the man's eyes — Mon

and applied the clay to his eyes — NASB

then he spread the clay on the man's eyes — Knox

... daubed the mud on his eyes — Ber

7. **And said unto him, Go, wash in the pool of Siloam, (which is by interpretation, Sent.)**

He went his way therefore, and washed, and came seeing.

So he went and washed and returned enjoying sight — Ber

and when he came away he could see — Rieu

So he went ... and returned seeing — Wey

8. **The neighbours therefore, and they which before had seen him that he was blind,**

... that he was a beggar — ASV

... and those who previously saw him as a beggar — NASB

... to whom he had been a familiar sight as a beggar — Wey

... those who had known him by sight as a mendicant — Rieu

said, Is not this he that sat and begged?

... that sits and begs — ABUV

... the man who used to sit and beg — Gspd

9. **Some said, This is he:**

... Yes! It is he! — Gspd

... This is the man — Knox

others said, He is like him:

Others said no, though they saw a likeness — Rieu

... No, but he looks like him — Beck

... No, but it surely does look like him — Wms

but he said, I am he.

... I am the man — Mof

... Yes, I am the man — Knox

... I am the one — Ber

10. **Therefore said they unto him, How were thine eyes opened?**

... Then how does it happen that you can see — Gspd

Then how was your blindness cured? they asked — Phi

... How did you get your sight — Beck

11. **He answered and said, A man that is called Jesus made clay, and anointed mine eyes,**

He whose name is Jesus ... made clay and smeared my eyes with it — Wey

... The man called Jesus made a paste and smeared my eyes with it — NEB

and said unto me, Go to the pool of Siloam, and wash:

and told me to go to Siloam and wash — Rieu

... Go and make yourself clean in Siloam — Bas

... Go to Siloam and wash your eyes — TCNT

and I went and washed, and I received sight.

So I went and washed and obtained sight — Wey

... and that's how I got my sight! — Phi

... and when I had washed them I could see — Gspd

So I went there, and washed, and recovered my sight — Knox

12. **Then said they unto him, Where is he? He said, I know not.**

13. They brought to the Pharisees him that aforetime was blind.

. . . the man who had formerly been blind — RSV

. . . him who was formerly blind—NASB

. . . this man who had once been blind — Mof

14. And it was the sabbath day when Jesus made the clay, and opened his eyes.

. . . and made him able to see — Gspd

. . . and gave him his sight — Beck

(It should be noted that Jesus made the clay and restored his sight on a Sabbath day.) — Phi

15. Then again the Pharisees also asked him how he had received his sight. He said unto them, He put clay upon mine eyes, and I washed, and do see.

. . . He applied clay to my eyes . . . — NASB

. . . and I washed, and I see — ASV

. . . and I washed them, and now I can see — Mof

16. Therefore said some of the Pharisees, This man is not of God,

. . . This man is not from God — Alf

. . . This man cannot be from God — TCNT

. . . This is not a man of God — Ber

because he keepeth not the sabbath day.

because he keeps not the sabbath — ABUV

since he does not observe the Sabbath — Phi

Others said, How can a man that is a sinner do such miracles?

. . . How can a sinful man . . . — Rhm

. . . do such signs — ASV

. . . perform such wonderworks—Wms

And there was a division among them.

They were divided on this — Mof

So there was a disagreement among them — Ber

17. They say unto the blind man again, What sayest thou of him, that he hath opened thine eyes?

. . . seeing that he hath opened thine eyes — Alf

What have you to say about him for opening your eyes — Bas

He said, He is a prophet.

. . . I say he is a prophet — Mof

Why, he said, he must be a prophet — Knox

18. But the Jews did not believe concerning him, that he had been blind, and received his sight,

. . . did not believe about him that he was blind and had received his sight — Mon

. . . didn't believe the man had been blind and got his sight — Beck

. . . that the man had been blind and had gained his sight — NEB

until they called the parents of him that had received his sight.

till they had summoned and examined his parents — Rieu

until they had called his parents and questioned them — TCNT

till they called in the parents of the man whose eyes had been opened — Nor

19. And they asked them, saying, Is this your son, who ye say was born blind?

. . . whom you report as having been born blind — Ber

. . . Is this your son, and do you affirm that he was born blind — Wms

how then doth he now see?

How does it happen he can see now — Beck

If so, how is it then that he now can see — Wms

20. His parents answered them and said, We know that this is our son, and that he was born blind:

21. But by what means he now seeth, we know not; or who hath opened his eyes, we know not:

But we do not know how he now sees . . . — Nor

. . . or who gave him his sight — Beck

. . . or who has made him able to see — Gspd

he is of age; ask him: he shall speak for himself.

. . . He is a grown-up man; he can speak for himself — Phi

. . . he himself will give his own account of it — Wey

. . . He will tell his own story — Nor

Ask him — He is old enough — he will tell you . . . — TCNT

. . . he is old enough to give an answer for himself — Bas

22. These words spake his parents, because they feared the Jews:

They said this because of their fear of the Jews — Bas

His parents . . . because they were afraid of the Jews — Gspd

for the Jews had agreed already,

. . . had already settled among themselves — Wey

. . . had by now come to an agreement — Knox

for the Jewish authorities had already agreed — NEB

that if any man did confess that he was Christ,

that anyone who acknowledged Jesus as Messiah — NEB

that anyone who confessed him to be Christ — Mof

. . . who admitted that Christ had done this thing — Phi

he should be put out of the synagogue.

should be excommunicated — Mof

he should be excluded from the synagogues — Gspd

he should be expelled from the synagogue — Nor

23. **Therefore said his parents, He is of age; ask him.**

24. **Then again called they the man that was blind, and said unto him, Give God the praise:**

. . . Give glory unto God! — Rhm

. . . Speak the truth before God — NEB

we know that this man is a sinner.

this man, to our knowledge, is a sinner — Knox

this man, we know quite well, is only a sinner — Mof

This man we know is a sinful man — Gspd

25. **He answered and said, Whether he be a sinner or no, I know not:**

. . . I do not know about his being a sinful man — Gspd

. . . I don't know if He's a sinner — Beck

one thing I know, that, whereas I was blind, now I see.

But one thing I am certain about . . . — Bas

I do know one thing . . . — Wms

. . . that although I was blind, now I can see — TCNT

But I do know this—I was a blind man and I see — Rieu

26. **Then said they to him again, What did he to thee? how opened he thine eyes?**

. . . How did he give you your sight — TCNT

27. **He answered them, I have told you already, and ye did not hear:**

. . . and you would not listen — RSV

. . . Weren't you listening? — Phi

wherefore would ye hear it again? will ye also be his disciples?

why do ye wish to hear it again? . . . — ABUV

. . . Do you want to be disciples of his — Mof

. . . is it your desire to become his disciples — Bas

. . . You do not want to become His disciples too, do you — NASB

28. **Then they reviled him, and said, Thou art his disciple; but we are Moses' disciples.**

Then they stormed at him . . . — Mon

They became abusive . . . — Rieu

. . . You are that man's disciple, but we are disciples of Moses — Wey

29. **We know that God spake unto Moses: as for this fellow, we know not from whence he is.**

We do know that God spoke to Moses . . . — Wms

. . . But this fellow! We do not know where he comes from — Mon

. . . we don't even know where he came from — Phi

30. **The man answered and said unto them, Why herein is a marvellous thing, that ye know not from whence he is,**

. . . Well, there is something strange about this! . . . — Wms

. . . What a remarkable thing! . . . — Rieu

. . . here is a matter for astonishment . . . — Knox

. . . You have no knowledge where he comes from — Bas

. . . how strange that you do not know where He is from — Nor

and yet he hath opened mine eyes.

though he gave me the use of my eyes — Bas

and yet He gave me my sight — Beck

and yet he has made me able to see! — Gspd

31. **Now we know that God heareth not sinners:**

We know that God does not listen to sinful people — Gspd

. . . God does not answer the prayers of sinners — Knox

but if any man be a worshipper of God, and doeth his will, him he heareth.

he listens to anyone who is devout and obeys his will — NEB

but He does hear one who reverences Him and does His will — Ber

32. Since the world began was it not heard that any man opened the eyes of one that was born blind.

. . . it was never heard that any one opened the eyes of a man born blind — ASV

. . . Nobody has ever heard of anyone giving sight to a man born blind — Beck

33. If this man were not of God, he could do nothing.

34. They answered and said unto him, Thou wast altogether born in sins, and dost thou teach us?

. . . You were born in utter sin, and would you teach us — RSV

. . . You are altogether depraved . . . —Nor

. . . You were wholly begotten and born in sin . . . — Wey

. . . And so you would teach us — you, born in utter depravity! — Mof

And they cast him out.

And so they turned him out of the synagogue — Wms

So they excluded him from the synagogue — Gspd

Then they expelled him from the synagogue — NEB

35. Jesus heard that they had cast him out; and when he had found him, he said unto him, Dost thou believe on the Son of God?[30]

. . . Do you believe in the Son of man — RSV

36. He answered and said, Who is he, Lord, that I might believe on him?

. . . And who is he Sir, that I may believe . . . — Rhm

. . . Tell me who he is, sir, that I should put my faith in him — NEB

. . . so that I may have faith in him — Bas

37. And Jesus said unto him, Thou hast both seen him, and it is he that talketh with thee.

. . . You have seen him. He is talking to you — Rieu

. . . You have already seen him . . . — Mon

. . . in fact, He is talking with you now — Ber

38. And he said, Lord, I believe. And he worshipped him.

So he said, Lord, I believe! Then he worshiped Him — Wms

. . . then he kneeled before Him — Nor

39. And Jesus said, For judgment I am come into this world,

. . . I came into the world to bring judgment — Nor

. . . to put men to the test . . . — TCNT

. . . so that people might be set asunder — Rieu

. . . My coming into this world is itself a judgment — Phi

that they which see not might see; and that they which see might be made blind.

that those who are blind should see, and those who see should become blind — Knox

to make the sightless see, to make the seeing blind — Mof

those who cannot see have their eyes opened and those who think they can see become blind — Phi

40. And some of the Pharisees which were with him heard these words, and said unto him, Are we blind also?

41. Jesus said unto them, If ye were blind, ye should have no sin:

. . . you would be guilty of no sin — Gspd

. . . you would be blameless — Ber

. . . If you were blind, you would have no guilt — RSV

but now ye say, We see; therefore your sin remaineth.

but as a matter of fact you boast that you see . . . — Wey

But as it is, you say that you can see . . . — Rieu

. . . you cannot be rid of your guilt — Knox

but since you claim to have sight, your sin remains — Ber

But your guilt remains because you claim to know what you are doing — Tay

---

[30]Some translations read "Son of man."

CHAPTER 10

1. **Verily, verily, I say unto you, He that entereth not by the door into the sheepfold, but climbeth up some other way,**
   Truly, truly, I tell you, he who does not enter . . . by the gate . . . — Mof
   . . . into the place where the sheep are kept . . . — Bas
   Believe me when I tell you this; the man who climbs into the sheepfold by some other way . . . — Knox
   the same is a thief and a robber.
   . . . a thief and a brigand — Rieu
   . . . and an outlaw — Bas
   . . . and a rogue — Phi

2. **But he that entereth in by the door is the shepherd of the sheep.**
   The shepherd of the sheep enters by the door — Nor
   he who enters by the gate is the shepherd . . . — Mof
   It is the shepherd of the flock who goes in by the door — Phi

3. **To him the porter openeth;**
   The watchman opens the door to him — Gspd
   The doorkeeper opens the door to him — Wms
   and the sheep hear his voice:
   and the sheep listen to his voice — TCNT
   . . . are attentive to . . . — Knox
   And the sheep recognize his voice — Rieu
   and he calleth his own sheep by name, and leadeth them out.
   He calls his own sheep by their names and leads them out — Beck
   and he calls to his own sheep . . . — Gspd
   he says over the names of the sheep, and takes them out — Bas

4. **And when he putteth forth his own sheep, he goeth before them,**
   When he hath put forth all his own . . . — ASV
   When he has brought his own sheep all out, he walks at the head of them — Wey
   and the sheep follow him: for they know his voice.

5. **And a stranger will they not follow, but will flee from him:**
   But they will never come on behind a stranger . . . — Wms

. . . but will run away from him — TCNT
   If a stranger comes, they run away from him instead of following him — Knox
   for they know not the voice of strangers.
   because they do not recognize the call of strangers — Ber
   for they do not recognize strange voices — Phi

6. **This parable spake Jesus unto them:**
   This similitude spake Jesus unto them — Rhm
   This figure Jesus used with them — RSV
   Jesus spoke to them in this allegorical language — Wey
   Jesus gave them this illustration — Phi
   but they understood not what things they were which he spake unto them.
   but they did not understand what He meant by it — Wms
   but they did not catch the meaning of what He said to them — Ber

7. **Then said Jesus unto them again, Verily, verily, I say unto you, I am the door of the sheep.**
   . . . it is I who am the door of the sheepfold — Knox
   . . . I am the Sheep-gate — Rieu
   . . . I am the Door for the sheep — Beck

8. **All that ever came before me are thieves and robbers:**
   They were all thieves and robbers who came before Me — Nor
   Those others who have found their way in . . . — Knox
   . . . were thieves and outlaws — Bas
   but the sheep did not hear them.
   but the sheep did not listen to them — TCNT
   but the sheep would not obey them — Gspd

9. **I am the door:**
   by me if any man enter in, he shall be saved,
   if any one enter in through me . . . — ABUV
   if any man goes in through me he will have salvation — Bas
   If a man goes in through me, he will be safe and sound — Phi
   and shall go in and out, and find pasture.

he will come and go at will . . . — Knox
. . . and will get food — Bas

10. **The thief cometh not, but for to steal, and to kill, and to destroy:**
The thief never comes except to . . . — Mon
The thief comes only to take the sheep and to put them to death: he comes for their destruction — Bas
The thief's purpose is to steal, kill and destroy — Tay
I am come that they might have life, and that they might have it more abundantly.
I came that they may have life . . . — ASV
. . . and have it abundantly — RSV
. . . and have it overflowing in them — Beck
. . . and have it to the full — Mof
My purpose is to give eternal life — abundantly! — Tay

11. **I am the good shepherd: the good shepherd giveth his life for the sheep.**
. . . lays down his life for the sheep — ABUV
. . . will give his life for the sake of his sheep — Phi

12. **But he that is an hireling, and not the shepherd, whose own the sheep are not,**
The hired servant . . . — Mon
. . . who is no shepherd, and does not claim the sheep as his own — Knox
When a hired man, who . . . doesn't own the sheep — Beck
. . . not being a shepherd nor regarding the sheep as his own — Rieu
seeth the wolf coming, and leaveth the sheep, and fleeth;
leaves the sheep and flees when he sees the wolf coming — Nor
. . . leaves the sheep and runs away — Beck
deserts the sheep and runs when he sees . . . — Ber
and the wolf catcheth them, and scattereth the sheep.
and the wolf snatches them, and scattereth them — ASV
and the wolf teareth them . . . — Alf
. . . carries off some . . . and scatters the flock — Wms
. . . harries the sheep and scatters them — Knox

13. **The hireling fleeth, because he is an hireling, and careth not for the sheep.**
He flees because he is a hireling and cares nothing for the sheep — RSV
. . . just because he is a hired man, who has no interest in the sheep — Mof

14. **I am the good shepherd, and know my sheep, and am known of mine.**
. . . and I know my own, and my own know me — ABUV
. . . I know my own sheep and my sheep know me — NEB

15. **As the Father knoweth me, even so know I the Father: and I lay down my life for the sheep.**
. . . and I am giving my life for my sheep — Gspd
. . . and I lay down My life on behalf of the sheep — Ber

16. **And other sheep I have, which are not of this fold:**
I have other sheep too, that are not in this fold — Beck
. . . which do not belong to this fold — Mon
them also I must bring, and they shall hear my voice;
. . . and they will listen to my voice — Wey
. . . They will recognize my voice — Rieu
and there shall be one fold, and one shepherd.
and they shall become one flock, one shepherd — ASV
so there will be one flock and one Shepherd — Nor

17. **Therefore doth my Father love me, because I lay down my life, that I might take it again.**
This is why the Father loves me . . . — TCNT
. . . because I lay down my life, to receive it back again — NEB
. . . I am giving my life, but giving it to take it back again — Gspd

18. **No man taketh it from me, but I lay it down of myself.**
. . . but I lay it down of my own free will — Phi
. . . but I am giving it as a free gift — Wms
. . . I lay it down of my own accord — RSV

No one snatches it from Me; but I voluntarily lay it down — Ber

No one can kill me without My consent — I lay down My life voluntarily — Tay

I have power to lay it down, and I have power to take it again.

I have authority to lay it down . . . authority to take it again — ABUV

I am authorized to lay it down . . . — Wey

. . . and I have the right to take it back — Wms

This commandment have I received of my Father.

This authority I received from My Father — Nor

I received this injunction . . . — Ber

This is an order that I have received . . . — Phi

Such were my Father's orders — Rieu

19. **There was a division therefore again among the Jews for these sayings.**

20. **And many of them said, He hath a devil, and is mad; why hear ye him?**

. . . He has an evil spirit and is out of his mind . . . — Bas

. . . He has a demon, and is insane; why do you listen to Him — NASB

. . . He has a devil, and is crazy . . . — Nor

21. **Others said, These are not the words of him that hath a devil.**

. . . not the sayings of one possessed with a demon — ASV

. . . of a demoniac — ABUV

Can a devil open the eyes of the blind?

Can a devil give sight to the blind — Beck

Can a demoniac open the eyes of the blind — Mon

22. **And it was at Jerusalem the feast of the dedication, and it was winter.**[31]

The Feast of Reconsecration in Jerusalem came round . . . — Rieu

. . . the feast of the opening of the Temple. . . — Bas

. . . the time of the Rededication Festival . . . — Gspd

23. **And Jesus walked in the temple in Solomon's porch.**

. . . was walking . . . in the portico of Solomon — RSV

. . . in the Temple Courts, in the Colonnade of Solomon — TCNT

. . . in Solomon's Arcade — Rieu

. . . in Solomon's covered way — Bas

24. **Then came the Jews round about him, and said unto him,**

There the Jews surrounded Him . . . — Beck

So the Jews closed in on him . . . — Phi

So the Jews encircled Him and asked Him — Ber

How long dost thou make us to doubt?

How much longer . . . — Wms

. . . do you propose to keep us on tenterhooks — Rieu

How long dost thou hold us in suspense — ASV

If thou be the Christ, tell us plainly.

If you are the Messiah say so plainly — NEB

If you really are Christ, tell us so straight out! — Phi

If You're the promised Savior, tell us frankly — Beck

25. **Jesus answered them, I told you, and ye believed not:**

. . . I have told you, but you will not believe me — Knox

. . . I have said it and you have no belief — Bas

. . . I told you — and you have no faith — Rieu

the works that I do in my Father's name, they bear witness of me.

The works which I am doing on my Father's authority are my credentials — Wms

26. **But ye believe not, because ye are not of my sheep, as I said unto you.**

But you do not believe me, because you are not of my flock . . . — TCNT

. . . because you do not belong to my sheep . . . — Mof

27. **My sheep hear my voice,**

My sheep listen to My voice — Beck

My sheep recognize My voice — Tay

and I know them, and they follow me:

28. **And I give unto them eternal life; and they shall never perish,**[32]

neither shall any man pluck them out of my hand.

and no one shall snatch them out of my hand — ASV

---

[31]ASV, RSV, NASB and some others begin verse 23 with this clause.

[32]Compare John 3:15,16.

and none shall tear them out of my hand — Alf

nor shall any one wrest them from my hand — Wey

29. My Father, which gave them me, is greater than all;

My Father . . . is stronger than all — Mon

My Father . . . is all-powerful — Rieu

What my Father has given me is greater than all[33] — Wey

and no man is able to pluck them out of my Father's hand.

and no one can tear anything out of the Father's hands — Gspd

. . . can snatch them out of my Father's hand — Wms

so no one can kidnap them from Me — Tay

30. I and my Father are one.

31. Then the Jews took up stones again to stone him.

. . . once more took up stones to throw at Him — Nor

. . . again brought stones to throw at him — TCNT

32. Jesus answered them, Many good works have I shewed you from my Father;

. . . I have shown you many of My Father's benevolent doings — Ber

. . . many good deeds, done by my Father's power — NEB

for which of those works do ye stone me?

33. The Jews answered him, saying, For a good work we stone thee not; but for blasphemy;

. . . for no good work but for blasphemy — RSV

. . . not . . . for doing anything good, but for your impious talk — Gspd

. . . not for any good action . . . — TCNT

. . . but for evil words — Bas

and because that thou, being a man, makest thyself God.

and because you, who are only a man . . . — Wey

. . . are making yourself out to be God — Phi

because You, a man, claim to be God — Beck

34. Jesus answered them, Is it not written in your law, I said, Ye are gods?

. . . Is there not a saying in your law . . . — Bas

35. If he called them gods, unto whom the word of God came,

If those to whom God's word was addressed are called gods — Wey

and the scripture cannot be broken;

(and the Scripture cannot be annulled) — Mon

. . . cannot be set aside — Gspd

36. Say ye of him, whom the Father hath sanctified, and sent into the world,

Do you say of one whom the Father has consecrated . . . — TCNT

. . . to One whom the Father dedicated . . . — Ber

. . . to Me, whom the Father appointed for His holy purpose . . . — Beck

Thou blasphemest; because I said, I am the Son of God?

Thou speakest profanely . . . — Rhm

. . . because I said I am a son of God — Rieu

. . . because I said, I am God's Son — Mof

37. If I do not the works of my Father, believe me not.

If I am not acting as my Father would, do not believe me — NASB

. . . do not accomplish My Father's work . . . — Ber

If I'm not doing My Father's works, don't trust Me — Beck

38. But if I do, though ye believe me not, believe the works:

. . . then let my actions convince you where I cannot — Knox

. . . even if you don't trust Me, trust My works — Beck

. . . accept the evidence of my deeds — NEB

that ye may know, and believe,

so that you may see clearly and be certain — Bas

so that you may understand . . . more and more clearly — TCNT

that you may know and understand — ASV

that the Father is in me, and I in him.

that the Father is in union with me . . . — Wms

. . . and I am in union with the Father — Gspd

_____

[33]Represents a variant reading.

39. Therefore they sought again to take him; but he escaped out of their hand,
Again they tried to arrest Him, but He escaped from their hands — Beck

40. And went away again beyond Jordan into the place where John at first baptized: and there he abode.

41. And many resorted unto him,
And many came unto him — ASV
And people came to him in great numbers — Gspd
and said, John did no miracle: but all things that John spake of this man

were true.
. . . John indeed did no sign . . . — ASV
. . . While John performed no sign . . . — NASB
. . . all that he said about this man was true — Phi

42. And many believed on him there.
And many became believers in him in that place — Gspd
And many found faith in him there — Knox
And many came to the decision that He was the Messiah — Tay

CHAPTER 11

1. Now a certain man was sick, named Lazarus, of Bethany,
Now there was a man ill, Lazarus of Bethany — Mof
A certain man, Lazarus, lay ill at Bethany — Nor
the town of Mary and her sister Martha.
of the village of Mary and her sister Martha — ASV
the village where Mary and . . . Martha lived — Phi

2. (It was that Mary which anointed the Lord with ointment, and wiped his feet with her hair,
— it was that Mary who anointed the Lord with perfume . . . — Mon
It was the Mary who poured the perfume upon the Lord . . . — Wms
. . . and made his feet dry with her hair — Bas
. . . and dried his feet with her hair — Rieu
whose brother Lazarus was sick.)

3. Therefore his sisters sent unto him, saying, Lord, behold, he whom thou lovest is sick.
. . . he whom you hold dear is ill — Mon
. . . your dear friend is ill — Bas

4. When Jesus heard that, he said, This sickness is not unto death,
. . . This illness is not to end in death — Wey
. . . The end of this sickness is not death — Knox
but for the glory of God,
it is going to bring glory to God — Phi
but is to promote the glory of God — Wey

but is to honor God — Wms
the end of it is the glory of God — Mof
that the Son of God might be glorified thereby.
to bring glory to the Son of God — NEB
. . . the Son of God may be honoured through it — TCNT
it is to glorify God's Son — Beck

5. Now Jesus loved Martha, and her sister, and Lazarus.
. . . was a dear friend to . . . — Ber
. . . held in loving esteem . . . — Wms

6. When he had heard therefore that he was sick, he abode two days still in the same place where he was.
Yet, though He had heard that Lazarus was ill . . . — Nor
. . . He still remained two days in that same place . . . — Wey

7. Then after that saith he to his disciples, Let us go into Judaea again.

8. His disciples say unto him, Master, the Jews of late sought to stone thee;
. . . Rabbi, the Jews were but now seeking to stone thee — ASV
. . . threatening to stone thee — Knox
. . . as it is, the Jews want to stone you — Ber
and goest thou thither again?
and are you going there again — RSV

9. Jesus answered, Are there not twelve hours in the day?
. . . Is not the day twelve hours long — Gspd
. . . Does not the day have twelve hours — Wms
If any man walk in the day, he stumbleth not, because he seeth the light of this world.

Anyone can walk in day-time without
stumbling . . . — NEB

. . . for he has the daylight to see by —
Phi

. . . because he can see the light of the
sun — TCNT

10. **But if a man walk in the night, he
stumbleth, because there is no light in
him.**

. . . walks about in the night he will
stumble . . . — Nor

. . . for he lacks light — Mof

11. **These things said he: and after that he
saith unto them, Our friend Lazarus
sleepeth;**

. . . Our friend Lazarus has fallen
asleep — RSV

. . . is at rest now — Knox

**but I go, that I may awake him out of
sleep.**

but I'm going there to wake him up —
Beck

But I intend to go and wake him —
Rieu

12. **Then said his disciples, Lord, if he
sleep, he shall do well.**

. . . if he is fallen asleep, he will recover
— ASV

. . . he will get well — TCNT

13. **Howbeit Jesus spake of his death:**

Yet Jesus had spoken about his death
— ABUV

. . . had referred to his death — Gspd

. . . meant that he was dead — TCNT

**but they thought that he had spoken
of taking of rest in sleep.**

but they thought He meant he was only
sleeping — Beck

but they thought that He was speaking
of literal sleep — NASB

. . . they imagined he meant natural
sleep — Mof

14. **Then said Jesus unto them plainly,
Lazarus is dead.**

15. **And I am glad for your sakes that I
was not there, to the intent ye may
believe;**

And for your sakes and the sake of
your faith I am glad I was not there
— Rieu

. . . it will be for your good and for the
good of your faith — NEB

. . . it will help you to believe — Knox

nevertheless let us go unto him.

Come, let us go to him — Mon

And now, let us go to him — Phi

16. **Then said Thomas, which is called
Didymus, unto his fellow-disciples,**

. . . who was called 'The Twin' . . . —
TCNT

**Let us also go, that we may die with
him.**

17. **Then when Jesus came, he found that
he had lain in the grave four days already.**

. . . he found that he had been in the
tomb . . . — ASV

When Jesus arrived . . . he had already
been buried for four days — Ber

18. **Now Bethany was nigh unto Jerusalem, about fifteen furlongs off:**

. . . was near Jerusalem, about two
miles off — RSV

. . . was just under two miles from Jerusalem — NEB

19. **And many of the Jews came to Martha
and Mary, to comfort them concerning
their brother.**

and a good many . . . had come . . . to
offer them sympathy — Phi

. . . to console them . . . — ASV

. . . to express sympathy . . . — Wey

. . . to sympathize with them . . .—Wms

. . . to give them comfort about their
brother — Bas

20. **Then Martha, as soon as she heard
that Jesus was coming, went and met
him: but Mary sat still in the house.**

. . . but Mary remained sitting in the
house — Mon

. . . sat quietly at home — TCNT

21. **Then said Martha unto Jesus, Lord, if
thou hadst been here, my brother had
not died.**

. . . Lord, had you been here . . . —
Rieu

. . . my brother would not have died —
NASB

22. **But I know, that even now, whatsoever
thou wilt ask of God, God will give it
thee.**

. . . whatever you ask of God He will
grant you — Ber

. . . God will give you whatever you ask
from him — Phi

. . . God will give You anything You
ask Him — Beck

23. **Jesus saith unto her, Thy brother shall
rise again.**

. . . Your brother shall rise to life —
TCNT

. . . Your brother will come to life again — Bas

. . . Your brother will come back to life — Rieu

24. Martha saith unto him, I know that he shall rise again in the resurrection at the last day.

. . . at the resurrection. when the last day comes — Knox

. . . on the Last Day — Gspd

25. Jesus said unto her, I am the resurrection, and the life:

. . . I am myself resurrection and life — Mof

. . . the Resurrection and the Life — Nor

he that believeth in me, though he were dead, yet shall he live:

. . . though he die, yet shall he live — ASV

. . . Even though he die shall live again! — Rhm

. . . even if he has died, shall live — Wey

26. And whosoever liveth and believeth in me shall never die.

And all that live and have faith in me . . . — Rieu

and whoever has life, and has faith in me . . . — Knox

And no one who is living and has faith in me will ever see death — Bas

Believest thou this?

Do you believe this — RSV

Is this your faith — Bas

27. She saith unto him, Yea, Lord: I believe that thou art the Christ, the Son of God,

. . . the Messiah, the Son of God — NEB

. . . You are the promised Savior, God's Son — Beck

which should come into the world.

who was to come into the world — Wms

whom the world awaited — Rieu

28. And when she had so said, she went her way, and called Mary her sister secretly, saying, The master is come, and calleth for thee.

. . . The Teacher . . . — ASV

. . . is asking for you — Gspd

. . . The Master is here and has sent for you — Bas

29. As soon as she heard that, she arose quickly, and came unto him.

30. Now Jesus was not yet come into the town, but was in that place where Martha met him.

. . . had not yet come to the village . . . — RSV

. . . was still where Martha had met Him — Beck

31. The Jews then which were with her in the house, and comforted her,

. . . who were with her . . . and consoling her — Rhm

when they saw Mary, that she rose up hastily and went out, followed her,

when they saw her start up and leave the house . . . — NEB

. . . saw Mary rise quickly and go out . . . — RSV

saying, She goeth unto the grave to weep there.

supposing that she was going unto the tomb . . . — ASV

thinking she was going to the grave . . . — Beck

. . . going to the tomb to wail there — Wey

32. Then when Mary was come where Jesus was, and saw him, she fell down at his feet,

But Mary went to the place where Jesus was . . . — Nor

. . . she bowed down at His feet — Beck

. . . she dropped at his feet — Mof

. . . she threw herself at his feet — TCNT

saying unto him, Lord, if thou hadst been here, my brother had not died.[34]

33. When Jesus therefore saw her weeping, and the Jews also weeping which came with her,

When Jesus saw how she and the Jews . . . were wailing — Rieu

. . . sobbing, and the Jews likewise who accompanied her, sobbing — Mon

he groaned in the spirit, and was troubled.

was greatly moved in his spirit . . . — Alf

he groaned deeply, and was greatly distressed — TCNT

---

[34]Compare verse 21.

he was deeply moved and visibly distressed — Phi

he sighed heavily and was deeply moved — NEB

He was moved with indignation and deeply troubled — Tay

repressing a groan, and yet showing great agitation — Gspd

34. And said, Where have ye laid him? They say unto him, Lord, come and see.

35. Jesus wept.

Jesus burst into tears — Mof

Jesus shed tears — Gspd

And Jesus himself was weeping — Bas

Tears came to Jesus' eyes — Tay

36. Then said the Jews, Behold how he loved him!

. . . See! how tenderly he loved him! — Rhm

. . . How he must have loved him! — TCNT

. . . See how dear he was to him! — Bas

37. And some of them said, Could not this man, which opened the eyes of the blind, have caused that even this man should not have died?

. . . Was not he . . . also able to prevent this man from dying — Wey

. . . Could not he . . . have prevented his death — Ber

. . . have kept this man from dying — Nor

But some said, This fellow healed a blind man — why couldn't He keep Lazarus from dying — Tay

38. Jesus therefore again groaning in himself cometh to the grave.

. . . being deeply moved within, came to the tomb — NASB

. . . was once more shaken by emotion . . . — Rieu

It was a cave, and a stone lay upon it.

. . . and a stone lay against it — ASV

. . . a stone lay against the mouth of it — TCNT

. . . with a stone across the entrance — Rieu

39. Jesus said, Take ye away the stone.

. . . Move the stone away — Gspd

. . . Remove the stone — NASB

Martha, the sister of him that was dead, saith unto him, Lord, by this

time he stinketh:

. . . by this time the body decayeth — ASV

. . . by this time he is offensive — ABUV

. . . Lord, there is already an odor — Nor

. . . there must be a stench by now — Rieu

for he hath been dead four days.

for he has been four days in the tomb — Mon

. . . he has been there four days — NEB

40. Jesus saith unto her, Said I not unto thee, that, if thou wouldest believe,

. . . if you had faith — Bas

. . . if you will only believe — Mof

thou shouldest see the glory of God?[35]

thou wilt see God glorified — Knox

you would see the wonder of what God can do — Phi

41. Then they took away the stone from the place where the dead was laid.[36]

So they took away the stone — ABUV

And Jesus lifted up his eyes, and said,

. . . raised His eyes . . . — NASB

. . . looked upwards . . . — NEB

Father, I thank thee that thou hast heard me.

. . . I thank you for listening to me — Wms

. . . for having heard Me — Ber

42. And I knew that thou hearest me always:

though I knew that you always listen to me — Gspd

I know that you always hear me — Phi

I knew You always hear Me — Beck

but because of the people which stand by I said it,

but for the sake of the multitude which stand around . . . — Alf

. . . the crowd . . . standing about, I said it — Mon

but I said it because of these who are here — Bas

that they may believe that thou hast sent me.

that they may come to believe . . . — Wms

---

[35]Compare verse 4.

[36]The words "from the place where the dead was laid" are now recognized as not adequately supported by original manuscripts.

. . . that you have made me your messenger — Gspd

43. And when he thus had spoken, he cried with a loud voice, Lazarus, come forth.
. . . Jesus called in a loud voice . . . — TCNT
After He had said this, He called out loud . . . — Beck
. . . he raised his voice in a great cry . . . — NEB

44. And he that was dead came forth, bound hand and foot with grave-clothes:
The dead man came out, his hands and feet bound with bandages — RSV
Out came the one who had died . . . — Ber
. . . his hands and feet swathed in linen bands — NEB
and his face was bound about with a napkin.
and his face tied up with a towel — Mof
with a napkin over his face — Rieu
and a cloth about his face — Bas
and with his face muffled with a handkerchief — Gspd
Jesus saith unto them, Loose him, and let him go.
. . . Untie him, and let him go — Mon
. . . Undo him and let him go home — Rieu
. . . Unbind him, and let him go — RSV

45. Then many of the Jews which came to Mary, and had seen the things which Jesus did,
. . . who came to see Mary and who saw what Jesus had done — Wms
. . . who had come with Mary, and had seen what he did — Mon
believed on him.
became believers in Him — Wey

46. But some of them went their ways to the Pharisees, and told them what things Jesus had done.
. . . went away to the Pharisees . . . — ASV
. . . and reported to them all Jesus had done — Knox

47. Then gathered the chief priests and the Pharisees a council,
Then the ruling priests and the Pharisees called a meeting of the council — Beck
. . . a meeting of the Sanhedrin — Mof

Therefore, the Sanhedrin, or Great Council, was called together . . . — Nor
and said, What do we? for this man doeth many miracles.
. . . What are we to do . . . — Rhm
. . . What shall we do? For this fellow is doing many miracles — Nor
. . . is doing many signs — ABUV

48. If we let him thus alone, all men will believe on him:
If we let him go on this way . . . — Ber
If we leave him alone like this . . . — NEB
. . . we shall have everybody believing in him — Phi
. . . he will find credit everywhere — Knox
If we just let him be, the whole people will believe in him — Rieu
and the Romans shall come and take away both our place and nation.
. . . and blot out both our city and nation — Wms
. . . and take away from us both land and people — Nor
. . . and rob us of both our sacred place and of our people — Mon
. . . and destroy both our holy place and nation — RSV

49. And one of them, named Caiaphas, being the high priest that same year,
. . . who held the high priesthood in that year — Knox
But one of them, Caiaphas, that year's high priest — Ber
said unto them, Ye know nothing at all,
. . . You know nothing about it — Wey
. . . You have no perception at all — Knox
. . . You are utterly mistaken — TCNT
. . . You plainly don't understand what is involved here — Phi

50. Nor consider that it is expedient for us, that one man should die for the people,
nor do ye take account that it is expedient for you . . . — ASV
you do not understand that . . . — RSV
You do not realize that it is to your interest . . . — Gspd
and that the whole nation perish not.
instead of the whole nation being destroyed — Mof

rather than have the whole nation ruined — Ber

51. And this spake he not of himself:

Now he did not say this of his own accord — Mon

It was not of his own impulse that he thus spoke — Wey

Now he did not say this on his own authority — Wms

. . . on his own initiative — Phi

but being high priest that year, he prophesied that Jesus should die for that nation;

. . . he was inspired to say . . . — Gspd

. . . and his words were a prophecy . . . — Mof

. . . he uttered this prophecy from God . . . — Wms

. . . that Jesus should die for the nation — ASV

52. And not for that nation only, but that also he should gather together in one

. . . but for the gathering together in one body . . . — Nor

. . . but to gather in one fold — Rieu

. . . but in order to unite into one body . . . — Wey

the children of God that were scattered abroad.

. . . the widely scattered children of God — Mon

the scattered family of God — Rieu

It was a prediction that Jesus' death would not be for Israel only, but for all the children of God scattered around the world — Tay

53. Then from that day forth they took counsel together for to put him to death.

. . . they planned together to kill Him — NASB

. . . they schemed to put Jesus to death — Wey

So from that day on they plotted his death — NEB

54. Jesus therefore walked no more openly among the Jews;

. . . no longer appeared in public . . . — Mof

. . . no longer went about openly . . . — RSV

but went thence unto a country near to the wilderness,

but left that neighbourhood . . . — TCNT

but went away from there . . . — NASB

. . . and went to the district near the desert — Gspd

into a city called Ephraim, and there continued with his disciples.

to a town called Ephraim, and there remained . . . — Mon

. . . where he was for some time . . . — Bas

55. And the Jews' passover was nigh at hand: and many went out of the country up to Jerusalem before the passover,

The Jews' Passover was approaching . . . — Ber

. . . and many came from the country to Jerusalem . . . — Beck

to purify themselves.

to make themselves clean — Bas

to go through ceremonial cleansing — Phi

56. Then sought they for Jesus, and spake among themselves, as they stood in the temple,

These began to look for Jesus . . . — Rieu

So they kept looking for Jesus . . . — Wms

. . . and asking one another as they stood in the temple — Beck

. . . as they stood in the Temple Courts — TCNT

What think ye, that he will not come to the feast?

What is your opinion? Will he not come to the feast — Bas

. . . Perhaps he is not coming to the festival — NEB

What do you think? Will he come to the festival — Nor

57. Now both the chief priests and the Pharisees had given a commandment,

Now the High-priests and the Pharisees had given commands — Rhm

. . . had given orders — ABUV

that, if any man knew where he were, he should shew it,

that if anyone should learn where He was . . . — Wms

. . . he should inform them — Rieu

. . . should report it to them — Knox

. . . should let them know — RSV

that they might take him.

that they might seize him — ABUV

so that they might get hold of Him — Ber

so that they could arrest him — Phi

CHAPTER 12

1. Then Jesus six days before the pass-over came to Bethany,
Six days before the paschal feast, Jesus went . . . — Knox
Six days before the Passover festival, Jesus came . . . — NEB
where Lazarus was which had been dead,[37] whom he raised from the dead.
where Lazarus was whom Jesus raised from the dead — ASV
where Lazarus . . . was living — TCNT

2. There they made him a supper;
So they gave a dinner for him there — Mon
. . . a dinner in his honour — Rieu
and Martha served: but Lazarus was one of them that sat at the table with him.
and Martha waited tables . . . — Ber
. . . and Lazarus . . . reclined at table beside him — Mof

3. Then took Mary a pound of ointment of spikenard, very costly,
. . . pure nard, very precious — ASV
. . . choice spikenard perfume of great value — TCNT
. . . very costly, genuine spikenard-oint-ment — NASB
and anointed the feet of Jesus, and wiped his feet with her hair: and the house was filled with the odour of the ointment.
. . . the fragrance of the perfume — Mon
. . . the scent of the ointment — Rieu

4. Then saith one of his disciples, Judas Iscariot, Simon's son,
which should betray him,
the one who would betray Him — Tay

5. Why was not this ointment sold for three hundred pence, and given to the poor?
Why wasn't this perfume sold . . . — Beck
. . . for three hundred denarii . . . — RSV
That perfume was worth a fortune! It should have been sold and the money given to the poor! — Tay

6. This he said, not that he cared for the poor;
. . . not that for the destitute he cared — Rhm

. . . not from any concern for the poor — Knox
but because he was a thief, and had the bag,
. . . he had charge of the money-bag — Ber
. . . having charge of the money-box — Nor
. . . being in charge of the purse — TCNT
and bare what was put therein.
he used to pilfer what was put into it — NASB
he used to take . . . — Gspd
he . . . used to help himself from the contents — Phi

7. Then said Jesus, Let her alone: against the day of my burying hath she kept this.
. . . that she may keep it against the day . . . — Alf
. . . Suffer her to keep it against the day . . . — ASV
. . . let her keep what she has for the day . . . — Mof
. . . Let her do it for the day of My burial — Beck
. . . she has kept it for the day of My burial — Nor
. . . Let her alone. She did it in prep-aration for My burial — Tay

8. For the poor always ye have with you; but me ye have not always.

9. Much people of the Jews therefore knew that he was there:
The common people . . . learned . . . — ASV
A great number of the Jews heard that he was there — NEB
and they came not for Jesus' sake only, but that they might see Lazarus also, whom he had raised from the dead.
and came not only to see Jesus but also Lazarus . . . — NEB
. . . not merely to see Jesus but also to see Lazarus . . . — Nor

10. But the chief priests consulted that they might put Lazarus also to death;
. . . made plans to kill Lazarus, too — Ber
. . . plotted to kill Lazarus too — Mon

[37]The words "which had been dead" are now recognized as not adequately supported by original manuscripts.

. . . resolved to do away with Lazarus as well — NEB

11. Because that by reason of him many of the Jews went away, and believed on Jesus.

. . . he was the reason many Jews were going over to Jesus . . . — Beck

. . . were beginning to go off and find faith in Jesus — Knox

. . . many . . . were falling away and believing in Jesus — Rieu

12. On the next day much people that were come to the feast,

. . . a great multitude that had come . . . — ABUV

. . . a great crowd of those who were there for the festival — Nor

. . . the big crowd who had come up for the Passover — Mon

when they heard that Jesus was coming to Jerusalem,

. . . that Jesus was on the way . . . — — NEB

. . . that Jesus was coming into Jerusalem — Phi

13. Took branches of palm trees, and went forth to meet him,

got palm branches and went out to meet him — Gspd

plucked branches off the palms and went out . . . — Rieu

and cried, Hosanna: Blessed is the King of Israel that cometh in the name of the Lord.[38]

shouting, God save him! . . . — Phi

and kept on shouting: Blessings on Him! . . . — Wms

crying, Hosanna! Blessed be he who comes in the name of the Lord . . . — RSV

. . . Even the King of Israel! — Rhm

shouting, The Savior! God bless the King of Israel! Hail to God's Ambassador — Tay

14. And Jesus, when he had found a young ass, sat thereon; as it is written,

. . . finding a young donkey, sat on it . . . — NASB

. . . found a young donkey and mounted it . . . — Wms

15. Fear not, daughter of Sion: behold, thy King cometh, sitting on an ass's colt.

Have no fear, daughter of Zion! . . . — Ber

. . . See, your King comes . . . — Nor

. . . sitting on a donkey's colt! — Amp

16. These things understood not his disciples at the first:

. . . his disciples noticed not at the first — Rhm

At the time, his disciples did not understand — Rieu

but when Jesus was glorified, then remembered they that these things were written of him,

but, when Jesus had been exalted . . . — TCNT

only after Jesus had attained his glory . . . — Knox

. . . they remembered how this had been written of him — Ber

. . . they remembered that this was said of him in Scripture — Gspd

and that they had done these things unto him.

and what they had done to him — Mon

and that they had fulfilled it in His case — Wms

17. The people therefore that was with him when he called Lazarus out of his grave, and raised him from the dead, bare record.

The crowd that had been with him when he called Lazarus out of the tomb . . . — RSV

. . . related what they had witnessed — Wey

. . . were continually talking about him — Phi

18. For this cause the people also met him,

For this cause also the multitude went and met him — ASV

This, indeed, was why the crowd met him — TCNT

for that they heard that he had done this miracle.

because they had heard about this sign . . . — Mon

. . . that He had performed this wonder-work — Wms

19. The Pharisees therefore said among themselves, Perceive ye how ye prevail nothing?

. . . Ye observe that ye are profiting nothing — Rhm

. . . ye are effecting nothing — ABUV

---

[38]These clauses are transposed in some manuscripts.

. . . You see, you're not getting anywhere — Beck

. . . You see? There's nothing one can do! — Phi

behold, the world is gone after him.

The whole world has run after him! — Gspd

. . . has turned aside to follow him — Knox

20. **And there were certain Greeks among them that came up to worship at the feast:**

21. **The same came therefore to Philip, which was of Bethsaida of Galilee, and desired him, saying,**

So these came to Philip, who was from Bethsaida . . . — RSV

They approached Philip . . . with the request — Phi

. . . and appealed to him, saying — Mof

. . . and asked him — Ber

Sir, we would see Jesus.

Sir, we wish to see Jesus — ABUV

Sir, we should like to meet Jesus — Rieu

22. **Philip cometh and telleth Andrew: and again Andrew and Philip tell Jesus.**

Philip went and told Andrew . . . — Nor

. . . then together they went and told Jesus — TCNT

. . . then Andrew and Philip went to let Jesus know — Ber

23. **And Jesus answered them, saying, The hour is come,**

. . . The time is at hand — Nor

. . . has come — Wms

that the Son of man should be glorified.

for the Son of Man to achieve his glory — Knox

for the Son of man to be . . . exalted — Amp

24. **Verily, verily, I say unto you, Except a corn of wheat fall into the ground and die, it abideth alone:**

. . . a grain of wheat . . . — ASV

. . . if a kernel of wheat doesn't fall . . . — Beck

. . . it remains a single grain — Wms

. . . it remains a single kernel — Mon

. . . it remains solitary — TCNT

. . . it remains what it was — a single grain — Wey

but if it die, it bringeth forth much fruit.

but, if it dies, it becomes fruitful — TCNT

. . . it makes a rich yield — Wey

. . . it brings a good harvest — Phi

. . . it produces much grain — Beck

25. **He that loveth his life shall lose it; and he that hateth his life in this world**

The man who loves himself is lost . . . — NEB

. . . and he who has no care for his life in this world — Bas

. . . he who is an enemy to his own life . . . — Knox

shall keep it unto life eternal.

will keep it, so as to live eternally — Knox

shall keep it in eternity — Rieu

shall keep it forever and ever — Nor

will preserve it for eternal life — Mof

26. **If any man serve me, let him follow me;**

Let one who serves Me follow Me — Ber

If any one is ready to serve me, let him follow me — Mon

and where I am, there shall also my servant be:

because wherever I am My servant must be — Nor

and my servant also must go wherever I go — Wms

if any man serve me, him will my Father honour.

If a man is ready to serve me, my Father will honour him — TCNT

. . . becomes My servant, My Father will give him honor — Nor

27. **Now is my soul troubled; and what shall I say?**

Now my heart is troubled; what can I say — Gspd

And now my soul is distressed. What am I to say — Knox

Now my soul is in turmoil, and what am I to say — NEB

Father, save me from this hour:

Father, save me from this hour? — RSV

Father, bring me safe through this hour — TCNT

Father, save Me from what is going to happen? — Beck

but for this cause came I unto this hour.

No! It was for this purpose that I came . . . — Nor

No! I came to suffer this now — Beck

28. Father, glorify thy name.

Father, honor your own name! — Phi

Father, show the glory of thy Power — Rieu

Father, make thy name known — Knox

Then came there a voice from heaven, saying, I have both glorified it, and will glorify it again.

. . . I have given it glory, and I will give it glory again — Bas

. . . I have made it known, and will yet make it known — Knox

. . . I have honored it, and I will honor it again! — Gspd

29. The people therefore, that stood by, and heard it, said that it thundered:

The people that stood and listened said, It thundered! — Ber

The crowd of bystanders on hearing it said . . . — Wms

The crowd standing . . . said that it had thundered — RSV

others said, An angel spake to him.

30. Jesus answered and said, This voice came not because of me, but for your sakes.

. . . for my sake, but for your sakes — ASV

. . . This voice spoke for your sake, not mine — NEB

31. Now is the judgment of this world:

Now judgment is passed on this world — Nor

Now this world is on its trial — TCNT

The day of judgement for the world is here — Rieu

Sentence is now being passed on this world — Knox

Now is this world to be judged — Mof

now shall the prince of this world be cast out.

now will the Prince of this world be driven out — Wey

now shall the ruler of this world be expelled — Ber

. . . will be thrown out — Beck

Its evil genius is now to be expelled — Gspd

32. And I, if I be lifted up from the earth,

. . . when I am lifted up . . . — Mof

And once I have been lifted up . . . — Beck

Yes, if only I am lifted up . . . — Knox

will draw all men unto me.

will draw the whole creation to myself — Rieu

shall draw everyone to Myself — Ber

I will attract all men to myself — Knox

33. This he said, signifying what death he should die.

. . . pointing to the sort of death he would have — Bas

He indicated . . . the manner of his coming death — Rieu

34. The people answered him, We have heard out of the law that Christ abideth for ever:

. . . We have learned from the law . . . — Wms

. . . that the Christ is to remain here forever — Gspd

. . . Our Law teaches us that the Messiah continues for ever — NEB

and how sayest thou, The Son of man must be lifted up?

what do you mean by saying . . . — Mof

. . . the Son of Man is destined to be "lifted up" — Rieu

How can you say that the Son of man must be lifted up — RSV

who is this Son of man?

Who is that Son of Man — Wey

What Son of Man is this — Knox

What Messiah are You talking about — Tay

35. Then Jesus said unto them, Yet a little while is the light with you.

. . . The Light will be with you a little while longer — Nor

. . . For a little while the Light shines among you — Ber

. . . The Light will shine . . . for a little longer yet — Mof

. . . You will have the Light only a little while longer — Amp

Walk while ye have the light, lest darkness come upon you:

Travel on . . . — TCNT

Finish your journey while you still have the light . . . — Knox

Keep on living by it while you have the light . . . — Wms

. . . or darkness will overtake you — Beck

for he that walketh in darkness knoweth not whither he goeth.

he who journeys in darkness cannot tell which way he is going — Knox

. . . has no idea where he is going — Phi

36. **While ye have light, believe in the light,**
... trust to the light — NEB
... put faith in the Light — Ber
You must believe in the light while you have the light — Phi
Make use of the Light while there is still time — Tay
that ye may be the children of light.
so that you may become sons of Light — Nor
... men of light — NEB
... to become enlightened people — Beck
These things spake Jesus, and departed, and did hide himself from them.
After saying this, Jesus ... hid from them — Ber
With these words Jesus went away and hid from them — Mof

37. **But though he had done so many miracles before them, yet they believed not on him:**
Though he had done so many signs ... — RSV
In spite of the many signs which Jesus had performed in their presence ... — NEB
... they still had no belief in him — Bas
... they put no faith in Him — Ber

38. **That the saying of Esaias the prophet might be fulfilled, which he spake,**
so that the prophecy of Isaiah was fulfilled, when he said — Phi
in fulfilment of the words of ... Isaiah, where he says — TCNT
Lord, who hath believed our report?
... what they heard from us — Wms
... our account — Gspd
Lord, is there anyone who has believed our message — Knox
and to whom hath the arm of the Lord been revealed?
... the might of the Lord ... — TCNT
... the Lord's power ... — NEB

39. **Therefore they could not believe, because that Esaias said again,**
The reason why they could not believe is stated again by Isaiah — Nor
And the reason for their unbelief lay in another saying of Isaiah's — Rieu

40. **He hath blinded their eyes, and hardened their heart;**
... has calloused their hearts — Ber

... and made their hearts insensible — Mof
He has made ... their minds dull — Gspd
that they should not see with their eyes, nor understand with their heart,
so they may neither see ... nor understand ... — Ber
lest they should see ... and perceive ... minds — NEB
and be converted, and I should heal them.
and lest they should repent ... — Nor
... turn back to me ... — Knox
And turn to me to cure them — Wms
and turn for me to heal them — RSV

41. **These things said Esaias, when he saw his glory, and spake of him.**
... Isaiah, because he saw his glory ... — ASV
Isaiah said this because ... it was of him that he spoke — Gspd
Isaiah was referring to Jesus when he made this prediction, for he had seen a vision of the Messiah's glory — Tay

42. **Nevertheless among the chief rulers also many believed on him;**
... a number even of the authorities ... — Mof
Yet many even of their leading men believed in him — Rieu
but because of the Pharisees they did not confess him,
but would not acknowledge him on account of the Pharisees — NEB
but wouldn't say so publicly ... —Beck
lest they should be put out of the synagogue:

43. **For they loved the praise of men more than the praise of God.**
... valued honour from men more than honour from God — TCNT
... their reputation among men ... the approval of God — Nor
they preferred the approval of men to the approval of God — Mof

44. **Jesus cried and said, He that believeth on me, believeth not on me, but on him that sent me.**
... He who has faith in me, has faith not in me ... — Bas
... Whoever believes on Me, believes not only on Me ... — Nor
... The believer in Me does not believe in Me but in My Sender — Ber

... When a man believes in me, he believes in him who sent me rather than in me — NEB

45. And he that seeth me seeth him that sent me.

to see me is to see him who sent me — Knox

and he that has his eyes on me . . . — Rieu

. . . is seeing the one who sent me — Phi

46. I am come a light into the world, that whosoever believeth on me should not abide in darkness.

I have come as light into the world, so that no one who continues to believe in me can remain in darkness — Wms

47. And if any man hear my words, and believe not,

. . . and keep them not — ASV

. . . listens to my words and does not abide by them — Rieu

I judge him not:

it is not I who judge him — Mon

I don't condemn him — Beck

for I came not to judge the world, but to save the world.

for I have not come to judge but to save the world — Wms

because I didn't come to condemn . . . but to save . . . — Beck

48. He that rejecteth me, and receiveth not my words,

Whoever rejects me and refuses to accept my teachings — Gspd

The man who spurns me and rejects my words — Rieu

Whoever persistently rejects me and refuses to accept . . . — Wms

hath one that judgeth him:

has a judge already — TCNT

has a judge appointed to try him — Knox

Hath that which is to judge him — Rhm

the word that I have spoken, the same shall judge him in the last day.

The word that I spoke, that will judge him . . . — ABUV

the words I have spoken . . . — Wey

My spoken word, it shall sentence him . . . — Ber

the word I spoke is what will judge him at the last day — NASB

49. For I have not spoken of myself;

. . . of my own accord — Ber

. . . on My own initiative — NASB

For I have not spoken on my own authority — RSV

but the Father which sent me, he gave me a commandment, what I should say, and what I should speak.

. . . His own instruction as to what to say and how to speak — Rieu

. . . gave me orders what to say and how to say it — Bas

. . . told Me what to say and what to preach — Nor

50. And I know that his commandment is life everlasting:

. . . what he commands means eternal life — Phi

And I know that His instruction means eternal life — Rieu

whatsoever I speak therefore, even as the Father said unto me, so I speak.

therefore the things I speak, I speak just as the Father has told Me — NASB

. . . when I speak, I speak as the Father has told me — Mof

Therefore, whatever I say, I say only what the Father has taught me — TCNT

CHAPTER 13

1. Now before the feast of the passover, when Jesus knew that his hour was come

. . . Jesus already knew . . . — Knox

Before the festival of the Passover began, Jesus realized that the time had come — Phi

that he should depart out of this world unto the Father,

that he should remove out of this world . . . — Rhm

for Him to leave this world . . . — Wey

for him to pass from this world to the Father — Wms

having loved his own which were in the world,

and as He had loved His own in the world — Wms

He had always loved his own . . . —
NEB
. . . those who were his own . . . —TCNT
He had loved those friends of his who
were in the world — Rieu
he loved them unto the end.
and he loved them to the last — Gspd
showed forth his love to the end—Mon
. . . to the highest degree — Amp
and now he showed how utterly he
loved them — Rieu

2. And supper being ended,
And during supper — ASV
And supper being in progress — Rhm
so at supper — Mof
**the devil having now put into the heart
of Judas Iscariot, Simon's son, to
betray him;**
the Devil having already put . . . —
ABUV
the devil had suggested to Judas . . . —
Wms
. . . the idea of betraying Jesus . . . —
Beck
. . . that he should deliver him up —
Rhm

**3. Jesus knowing that the Father had
given all things into his hands,**
. . . had left everything in his hands —
Knox
. . . had entrusted everything to him —
NEB
**and that he was come from God, and
went to God;**
. . . had come from God and was going
back to God — Beck
. . . and was to return to God — TCNT
and that he had come from and was
going to God — Rieu

**4. He riseth from supper, and laid aside
his garments;**
. . . took off His outer clothes — Wms
. . . threw off His upper garments —
Wey
rose from the table, put away His robe
— Ber
and took a towel, and girded himself.
and tied a towel around him — Mof
and wrapped a towel round his waist —
Rieu
took a cloth . . . — Nor
. . . and fastened it round his waist —
Phi

**5. After that he poureth water into a
bason, and began to wash the disciples'
feet, and to wipe them**
He that is bathed . . . — ASV

. . . into a washbasin . . . — Nor
**with the towel wherewith he was
girded.**
with the towel that was about his waist
— Gspd

6. Then cometh he to Simon Peter:
So He approached Simon Peter — Ber
**and Peter saith unto him, Lord, dost
thou wash my feet?**
. . . Lord, do you wash my feet — RSV
. . . You, Master! Are you going to
wash my feet — TCNT
. . . Lord, is it for thee to wash my feet
— Knox
. . . Master, You shouldn't be washing
our feet like this! — Tay

**7. Jesus answered and said unto him,
What I do thou knowest not now; but
thou shalt know hereafter.**
. . . What I do is not clear to you now
. . . — Bas
. . . You do not realize now what I am
doing . . . — Phi
. . . but thou shalt understand after-
wards — Alf
. . . but by-and-by you will learn—Wms
. . . But later you will understand —
Beck

**8. Peter saith unto him, Thou shalt never
wash my feet.**
. . . I will never let you wash my feet
— NEB
No! . . . You'll never wash my feet —
Beck
. . . You shall never, never wash my
feet! — Ber
**Jesus answered him, If I wash thee not,
thou hast no part with me.**
Unless you let me wash you, Peter . . .
— Phi
. . . you have no share with me — Wey
. . . you will not share my lot — Mof
. . . you will have no fellowship with
Me — Nor

**9. Simon Peter saith unto him, Lord, not
my feet only, but also my hands and
my head.**
. . . Lord, do not stop with my feet . . .
— Wms
. . . but my hands and my face too! —
Gspd

**10. Jesus saith to him, He that is washed
needeth not save to wash his feet,**
He that is bathed . . . — ASV
. . . does not need to wash, except for
his feet — RSV

. . . only needs to have his feet washed — Mof

but is clean every whit: and ye are clean, but not all.

but is clean all over . . . — RSV

but is completely clean . . . — NASB

. . . And you are clean — though not all of you — Phi

. . . but not every one of you — Nor

11. **For he knew who should betray him;**

. . . who was going to betray him — Gspd

. . . who was false to him — Bas (he knew the traitor) — Mof

For he knew his betrayer — ABUV

therefore said he, Ye are not all clean.

that is why he said, You are not all clean — Knox

12. **So after he had washed their feet, and had taken his garments,**

Then, after washing their feet and putting on his robe again — Bas

. . . and redressing . . . — Ber

. . . and put on his clothes — Gspd

and was set down again,

and reclined again at table — ABUV

and resumed his place — RSV

he said unto them, Know ye what I have done to you?

. . . Do you understand . . . — Wey

. . . what I have been doing to you — Mon

. . . Do you realize what I have just done to you — Phi

13. **Ye call me Master and Lord:**

. . . Teacher and Lord — ASV

. . . "The Rabbi" and "The Master" — Wey

You call me Teacher and Master — Gspd

and ye say well; for so I am.

and rightly so, because I am — Ber

You are right, for I am all of that — Nor

and you are right: that is what I am — Mof

14. **If I then, your Lord and Master, have washed your feet;**

. . . the Lord and the Teacher . . . — ASV

. . . your Master and Rabbi . . . — Wey

ye also ought to wash one another's feet.

you surely ought to wash . . . — Ber

it is your duty to . . . — Rieu

you must be ready to wash one another's feet — Phi

15. **For I have given you an example,**

I have been setting you an example — Knox

that ye should do as I have done to you.

and you should do as I do to you—Nor

you are to do as I have done for you — NEB

16. **Verily, verily, I say unto you, The servant is not greater than his lord;**

. . . a slave is not greater than his master — Mon

. . . A servant is not superior to his master — Ber

neither he that is sent greater than he that sent him.

nor is a messenger greater than He who sent him — Nor

and no messenger is greater than the man who sends him — Gspd

17. **If ye know these things, happy are ye if ye do them.**

. . . blessed are you if you do them — RSV

If you know this, happy are you if you act upon it — NEB

. . . you will be blessed, if you do it — Nor

18. **I speak not of you all: I know whom I have chosen.**

. . . not concerning you all; I know whom I chose — ABUV

I do not mean all of you . . . — Wms

. . . I know the men of my choice — Mof

. . . the kind of men whom I picked out — Rieu

but that the scripture may be fulfilled,

but let the Scripture be fulfilled—Gspd

but I know that the Scriptures must be fulfilled — Wms

it is that the scripture may be fulfilled — RSV

He that eateth bread with me hath lifted up his heel against me.

He who is eating my bread . . .—Gspd

. . . has turned against me — NEB

He who eats my bread kicks me—Beck

19. **Now I tell you before it come,**

From this time I tell you, before it comes to pass — ABUV

From now on I'm telling you these things before they happen — Beck

that, when it is come to pass,
so that when it does occur — Ber
in order that when they do happen —
Wey

ye may believe that I am he.
you may believe that I am what I say
— Gspd
you may believe who I am — Mof
you may believe that I am He — Wey
. . . that I am the one I claim to be —
Phi

20. **Verily, verily, I say unto you, He that
receiveth whomsoever I send receiveth
me;**
. . . if you receive anyone I send, you
receive Me — Beck
. . . the man who welcomes one whom
I send, welcomes me — Knox
. . . whoever welcomes any messenger
of mine . . . — Gspd
**and he that receiveth me receiveth him
that sent me.**
and anyone who accepts me will be accepting . . . — Phi
and he who welcomes Me, welcomes
My Sender — Ber

21. **When Jesus had thus said, he was
troubled in spirit,**
On saying this, Jesus was disquieted in
spirit — Mof
. . . was greatly moved — Gspd
. . . was disturbed in spirit — Nor
. . . was inwardly disturbed — Ber
. . . was profoundly moved — Rieu
. . . he was clearly in anguish of soul —
Phi
and testified, and said,
and said solemnly . . . — Gspd
and made a declaration . . . — Rieu
and said with deep earnestness . . . —
Wey
**Verily, verily, I say unto you, that one
of you shall betray me.**
. . . One from among you will deliver
me up — Rhm
. . . it is one of you that will betray me!
— Gspd

22. **Then the disciples looked one on another, doubting of whom he spake.**
The disciples kept looking at one another . . . — Wms
. . . at a loss to know which of them
he meant — Knox
. . . wondering whom he meant—TCNT
. . . undecided to whom He referred —
Ber

23. **Now there was leaning on Jesus'
bosom one of his disciples,**
There was at the table reclining in
Jesus' bosom . . . — ASV
One of his disciples . . . was lying close
to the breast of Jesus — RSV
. . . was reclining close beside Jesus —
NEB
whom Jesus loved.
whom Jesus specially loved — Wms
he was the favourite of Jesus — Mof

24. **Simon Peter therefore beckoned to
him,**
. . . maketh a sign to him — Alf
. . . gestured to him — NASB
. . . motioned to him — Beck
**that he should ask who it should be of
whom he spake.**
to ask whom He meant — Beck
and asked him, Who is it he means —
Knox
to ask Him to tell of whom it was He
had spoken — Nor

25. **He then lying on Jesus' breast**
He leaning back, as he was, on Jesus'
breast — ASV
So lying thus, close to the breast of
Jesus — RSV
So that disciple just leaned back against
Jesus' breast — Mon
saith unto him, Lord, who is it?
and said to him, Lord, who is it — Mon

26. **Jesus answered, He it is, to whom I
shall give a sop, when I have dipped it.**
. . . He it is, for whom I shall dip the
morsel, and give it to him — ABUV
It is the one to whom I give this piece
of bread . . . — Nor
. . . after I have put it in the vessel —
Bas
. . . when I dip it in the dish — Mof
**And when he had dipped the sop, he
gave it to Judas Iscariot, the son of
Simon.**
So he dipped the piece of bread and
. . . gave it to Judas . . . — Gspd

27. **And after the sop Satan entered into
him.**
And after the mouthful, Satan entered
into him — Ber
After he had taken the piece of bread,
Satan entered his heart — Phi
**Then said Jesus unto him, That thou
doest, do quickly.**
. . . Do at once what you are going to
do — TCNT

. . . Do quickly what you are about to do — Nor

. . . The quicker you act the better — Rieu

28. Now no man at the table knew for what intent he spake this unto him.

None of those at table understood why . . . — Mof

Now it was not clear to anyone . . . why he said this to him — Bas

29. For some of them thought, because Judas had the bag,

because Judas had the money-bag — ABUV

. . . had charge of the money-box — Nor

since Judas kept the common purse — Knox

that Jesus had said unto him, Buy those things that we have need of against the feast;

. . . Buy what things we have need of for the feast — ASV

. . . Buy what we require for the Festival — Wey

that . . . Jesus meant that he was to buy some things needed for the Festival — TCNT

or, that he should give something to the poor.

or to give something to the poor — TCNT

or bidding him give some alms to the poor — Knox

30. He then, having received the sop, went immediately out: and it was night.

Then at once, after taking the bite of bread, he went out . . . — Ber

As soon as Judas had received the piece of bread, he went out into the night. — Nor

31. Therefore, when he was gone out, Jesus said, Now is the Son of man glorified,

. . . Now at last the Son of man is glorified — Mof

. . . Now is glory given to the Son of man — Bas

. . . Now the Son of Man has been exalted — TCNT

. . . Now comes the glory of the Son of Man — Phi

My time has come; the glory of God will soon surround Me — Tay

and God is glorified in him.

and God has been honored through him — Gspd

. . . has been exalted . . . — TCNT

and in his glory God is exalted — Knox

— and God shall receive great praise because of all that happens to Me — Tay

32. If God be glorified in him, God shall also glorify him in himself, and shall straightway glorify him.

Since, in his glory, God is exalted, it is for God to exalt him in his own glory — Knox

And God shall give Me His own glory — Tay

and will glorify Him without delay — Wey

yes, He will glorify Him now — Beck

33. Little children, yet a little while I am with you.

. . . I shall be with you only a little while — Nor

. . . I am with you but a little longer — Ber

Ye shall seek me:

Then you will be looking for me — Bas

and as I said unto the Jews, Whither I go, ye cannot come; so now say I to you.

and, as I told the Jews I tell you now . . . — Mof

. . . Where I am going you cannot follow — Gspd

34. A new commandment I give unto you, That ye love one another;

I give you a new commandment — Love one another — TCNT

Now I am giving you a new command — Love one another — Phi

as I have loved you, that ye also love one another.

. . . so you are to love one another — NEB

. . . you must love one another — Phi

35. By this shall all men know that ye are my disciples,

by this everyone will recognize that . . . — Mof

By this it will be clear to all men . . . — Bas

The mark by which all men will know you for my disciples — Knox

if ye have love one to another.

by your love for one another — Gspd

if you keep showing love for one another — Wms

because you have such love for one another — Phi

will be the love you bear one another — Knox

36. Simon Peter said unto him, Lord, whither goest thou?

... Lord, where are you going — RSV

Jesus answered him, Whither I go, thou canst not follow me now;

... I am going where you cannot follow me at present — Mof

... Where I am going you may not come with me now — Bas

but thou shalt follow me afterwards.

but later you will follow Me — Nor

but one day you will — NEB

though you will follow me later — Phi

37. Peter said unto him, Lord, why cannot I follow thee now?

I will lay down my life for thy sake.

I am ready to lay down my life ... — Knox

I'll give my life for you — Beck

I would lay down my life for you! — Phi

38. Jesus answered him, Wilt thou lay down thy life for my sake?

... Will you lay down your life for me — TCNT

... Will you indeed lay down your life for me — NEB

Verily, verily, I say unto thee, The cock shall not crow, till thou hast denied me thrice.

Believe me, by cock-crow thou wilt thrice disown me — Knox

... before the cock crows, you will three times disown me! — Wms

... The rooster shall not crow until you have thrice disclaimed Me — Ber

... till you have denied me three times — RSV

CHAPTER 14

1. Let not your heart be troubled:

... disquieted — Mof

... distressed — Knox

Your mind must not be troubled — Gspd

You must not let yourselves be distressed — Phi

Set your troubled hearts at rest — NEB

Don't be upset — Tay

ye believe in God, believe also in me.

believe in God, believe also in me — ASV

You trust in God, trust also in me — Mon

as you have faith in God, have faith in me — Knox

have faith in God and have faith in me — Bas

Trust God — and trust Me — Tay

2. In my Father's house are many mansions:

... abiding places — ABUV

... dwellings — TCNT

... resting-places — Rieu

There are many rooms in my Father's house — Gspd

if it were not so, I would have told you. I go to prepare a place for you.

Otherwise I would have told you. I am going to make ready a place for you — Nor

if it were not so, would I have told you that I go to prepare a place for you? — RSV

3. And if I go and prepare a place for you,

for I am going away to make ready a place for you — Wms

And though I do go away, to prepare you a home — Knox

I will come again, and receive you unto myself;

I am coming again, and will take you to myself — ABUV

I shall return and take you to be with me — TCNT

I'll come again and take you home with Me — Beck

I am coming back; and then I will take you to myself — Knox

that where I am, there ye may be also.

so that you may be where I am — Nor

4. And whither I go ye know, and the way ye know.

And where I am going, you all know the way — Wey

And you know the way to the place where I am going — Wms

As for my destination, you know the way — Rieu

And you know the way where I am going — RSV

5. Thomas saith unto him, Lord, we know not whither thou goest;

. . . we don't know where You are going — Nor

. . . we have no knowledge of . . . — Bas

. . . we do not know your destination — Rieu

and how can we know the way?

and how can we know what road you're going to take — Phi

how are we to know the way there — Knox

6. Jesus saith unto him, I am the way, the truth, and the life:

. . . I myself am the road . . . — Phi

. . . I am the way; I am truth and life — Knox

. . . I am the real and living way—Mof

. . . I am the way; I am the truth and I am life — NEB

no man cometh unto the Father, but by me.

. . . but through me — Alf

. . . except by means of me — Mof

No one can come to the Father except through me — Wms

7. If ye had known me, ye should have known my Father also:

If you had recognized me, you would have known my Father also — TCNT

If you had known who I am . . . — Phi

If you have learned to know Me, you'll know My Father too — Beck

and from henceforth ye know him, and have seen him.

from now on you know Him . . . — NASB

. . . you do know him and you have seen him — Gspd

8. Philip saith unto him, Lord, shew us the Father, and it sufficeth us.

. . . and it is enough for us — Ber

. . . and it will satisfy us — Gspd

. . . show us the Father; that's enough for us — Beck

. . . let us see the Father; that is all we ask — Knox

9. Jesus saith unto him, Have I been so long time with you,

. . . have I been with you all this time — Bas

. . . Have I been all this time among you — TCNT

and yet hast thou not known me, Philip?

without your recognizing Me, Philip! — Ber

and yet you do not understand me — Mof

without your really knowing me, Philip — Phi

he that hath seen me hath seen the Father;

Anyone who has seen me has seen the Father — NEB

He who has looked on Me, has looked on the Father — Ber

and how sayest thou then, Shew us the Father?

Why do you say, Let us see the Father — Bas

how can you say, Show us the Father — RSV

10. Believest thou not that I am in the Father,

Don't you believe . . . — Beck

. . . that I am in union with the Father — Gspd

and the Father in me?

and that the Father is in union with me — Wms

the words that I speak unto you I speak not of myself:

The things that I tell you all . . . — Wey

. . . I do not speak on my own authority — RSV

. . . I do not speak of my own accord — Mof

. . . on My own initiative — NASB

The words I speak to you are not my own words — Knox

I am not the source of the words that I say to you — Gspd

but the Father that dwelleth in me, he doeth the works.

but the Father abiding in me doeth his works — ASV

but the Father, who ever dwells in me . . . — Mon

. . . (is) doing his own work — NEB

the Father, who dwells in Me, carries on His activities — Ber

11. Believe me that I am in the Father, and the Father in me:

You must believe me . . . — Wms

. . . that I am in union with the Father . . . — TCNT

. . . and that the Father is in union with me — Gspd

Have faith that I am in the Father and that the Father is in me — Bas

or else believe me for the very works' sake.

. . . on account of the works themselves — ABUV

Or else believe Me on account of My works — Beck

Or else believe it because of the mighty miracles you have seen Me do — Tay

12. **Verily, verily, I say unto you, He that believeth on me,**

. . . He who puts his faith in me — Bas

. . . whoever perseveres in believing in me — Wms

. . . he who trusts in me — Mon

the works that I do shall he do also;

will do the very deeds I do — Mof

will do the very things I am doing — Nor

will be able to do what I do — Knox

can himself do the things that I am doing — Wms

and greater works than these shall he do;

and he shall do greater deeds than these — Wey

and he will do even greater things than these — Phi

because I go unto my Father.

since I am journeying to the Father — Rieu

for I am going away to the Father — Phi

13. **And whatsoever ye shall ask in my name, that will I do,**

And whatever request you make in my name . . . — Bas

Anything you ask for as followers of mine . . . — Gspd

and I will do whatever you ask in my name — Mof

and I will do anything you ask in My name — Beck

that the Father may be glorified in the Son.

. . . may be honoured . . . — TCNT

. . . may have glory . . . — Nor

that the Son may bring glory to the Father — Phi

for this will bring praise to the Father because of what I, the Son, will do for you — Tay

14. **If ye shall ask any thing in my name, I will do it.**

If you make any request of me . . . — Wey

Yes, I repeat it, anything you ask for as bearers of my name . . . — Wms

If you ask Me anything in My name, I will do it — NASB

Ask for anything in my name and I will do it — Rieu

15. **If ye love me, keep my commandments.**

. . . ye will keep my commandments — ASV

. . . you will obey my commands — NEB

. . . you will do what I order — Beck

If you love me, you will lay my commands to heart — TCNT

16. **And I will pray the Father, and he shall give you another Comforter,**

And I will ask the Father . . . — NASB

And I will request the Father . . . — Rhm

. . . to give you another Helper — Mof

. . . another Advocate — ABUV

. . . Counselor — RSV

. . . another to befriend you — Knox

. . . some one else to stand by you — Phi

that he may abide with you for ever;

to be with you always — Gspd

to stay with you forever — Ber

. . . to the end of time — Rieu

to remain with you to the end of the age — Wms

17. **Even the Spirit of truth;**

Even the Spirit of true knowledge — Bas

It is the truth-giving Spirit . . . — Knox

whom the world cannot receive,

whom the world cannot accept — Phi

for whom the world can find no room — Knox

That Spirit the world cannot receive — Wey

the world cannot receive him — Mof

because it seeth him not, neither knoweth him:

. . . does not see it or recognize it — Gspd

. . . neither observes nor understands Him — Ber

. . . neither sees him nor knows him — RSV

but ye know him; for he dwelleth with you, and shall be in you.

... because he abides with you ... — ABUV

... He remains by your side ... — Wey

... He lives with you ... — Beck

... for he is ever with you and within you — Mon

... he is with you now and will be in your hearts — Phi

18. I will not leave you comfortless:

I will not leave you desolate — ASV

... bereft — Rhm

... orphans — Alf

... fatherless — Nor

I will come to you.

I am coming back to you — Gspd

19. Yet a little while, and the world seeth me no more;

After a little while ... — NASB

... the world shall see me no more — Mon

but ye see me:

but you can see me — Knox

but you will still see me — TCNT

because I live, ye shall live also.

for I will live again — and you will too — Tay

20. At that day ye shall know that I am in my Father, and ye in me, and I in you.

At that time it will be clear to you ... — Bas

... that I am in union with my Father ... — Gspd

... that you are in me, and I am in you — Phi

21. He that hath my commandments, and keepeth them,

The man who has received my commands and obeys them — NEB

He that takes hold of my commandments and keeps them — Rieu

He who has My orders and observes them — Ber

he it is that loveth me: and he that loveth me shall be loved of my Father, and I will love him, and will manifest myself to him.

... and disclose myself to him — NEB

... and make myself real to him — Wms

... show Myself to him — Nor

... reveal myself to him — Wey

22. Judas saith unto him, not Iscariot,

Judas (not Iscariot) said to him — RSV

... (not the man from Kerioth) asked Him — Beck

... the other Judas, not Iscariot ... — NEB

Lord, how is it

Lord, what is come to pass — ASV

... what then has happened — NASB

Why is it, Lord — Wms

Lord, ..., what is behind your words — Rieu

that thou wilt manifest thyself unto us, and not unto the world?

that you are going to reveal yourself to us ... — TCNT

that you mean to disclose yourself to us alone ... — NEB

... are going to make yourself known to us ... — Phi

when you speak of showing yourself to us and not to the world — Rieu

23. Jesus answered and said unto him, If a man love me, he will keep my words:

... If any one loves me, he will keep my word — ABUV

... he will obey my word — Mof

... will observe my teaching — Gspd

... will cherish my word — Rieu

... Anyone who loves me will heed what I say — NEB

and my Father will love him, and we will come unto him, and make our abode with him.

... and make our home with him — Mon

... we will come to him and live with him — Gspd

... and make our dwelling with him — NEB

24. He that loveth me not keepeth not my sayings:

If one does not love, he does not keep My Word — Nor

No one who does not love me will observe my teaching — Gspd

Anyone who doesn't love Me doesn't do what I say — Beck

He who does not love me neglects my words — Rieu

and the word which ye hear is not mine, but the Father's which sent me.

25. These things have I spoken unto you, being yet present with you.

... while yet abiding with you — Alf

All this I have told you while I am still with you — Nor

26. But the Comforter, which is the Holy Ghost, whom the Father will send in my name,

But the Advocate, the Holy Spirit . . . — Rieu

he shall teach you all things, and bring all things to your remembrance, whatsoever I have said unto you.

. . . bring to your remembrance all that I said . . . — ASV

. . . will put you in mind of all things . . . — Rhm

. . . will remind you of all that I have told you — Ber

he will teach you all things, and will recall to your minds all that I have said to you — TCNT

27. Peace I leave with you, my peace I give unto you:

Peace is my bequest to you . . . — Knox

Peace is my parting gift to you, my own peace — NEB

I leave you peace; I give you my own peace — Gspd

Peace I bequeath to you . . . — Ber

not as the world giveth, give I unto you.

It is not the world's 'Peace' I give you — Mon

my gift is nothing like the peace of this world — Phi

such as the world cannot give — NEB

And the peace I give isn't fragile like the peace the world gives! — Tay

Let not your heart be troubled, neither let it be afraid.

Let not your hearts be disquieted . . . — Mof

. . . neither let it be fearful — ASV

Do not allow your hearts to be unsettled or intimidated — Ber

Do not let your heart be distressed, or play the coward — Knox

. . . be troubled, or dismayed — TCNT

Don't feel troubled or afraid — Beck

28. Ye have heard how I said unto you, I go away, and come again unto you.

You heard me say that I was going away and would return to you — TCNT

If ye loved me, ye would rejoice,

If you loved me, you would have rejoiced — RSV

. . . you should be glad — Nor

because I said, I go unto the Father: for my Father is greater than I.

. . . my Father has greater power than I — Knox

29. And now I have told you before it come to pass,

. . . before it takes place — RSV

that, when it is come to pass, ye might believe.

in order that when it happens . . . — Gspd

. . . you may have faith — Ber

30. Hereafter I will not talk much with you:

I will no longer talk much with you — ABUV

After this, I shall not say much to you — Nor

for the prince of this world cometh,

for the Prince of this world is on his way — Rieu

. . . the evil genius of the world . . . — Gspd

for the world's ruler comes — Ber

for the Prince of this world approaches — NEB

and hath nothing in me.

He has no hold on me — Mof

. . . nothing in common with me — TCNT

. . . no rights over me — NEB

. . . no power over me — RSV

He has no claim on Me — Beck

31. But that the world may know that I love the Father;

No, but the world must be convinced . . . — Knox

. . . must be taught . . . — Rieu

. . . must be shown . . . — NEB

but he is coming that the world may know . . . — Gspd

But I want the world to know that I love the Father — Beck

and as the Father gave me commandment, even so I do.

and am doing what the Father has ordered me to do — Wms

and that I do as He has commanded Me — Nor

. . . just as the Father commanded — Mon

Arise, let us go hence.

Come, let us go away — Gspd

Rise! Let us go away from here! — Ber

Get up now! Let us leave this place — Phi

CHAPTER 15

1. I am the true vine, and my Father is the husbandman.

... the real Vine ... — Mof

... and my Father is the vinedresser — RSV

... the gardener — NEB

... the cultivator — Wms

2. Every branch in me that beareth not fruit he taketh away:

Any unfruitful branch in me he takes away — TCNT

Any branch of mine that does not bear fruit ... — Gspd

... He prunes away — Ber

Every barren branch of mine he cuts away — NEB

and every branch that beareth fruit, he purgeth it,

... he cleanseth — Alf

... he prunes — RSV

the branch that does yield fruit, he trims clean — Knox

that it may bring forth more fruit.

to increase its yield — Phi

to make it bear more fruit — Beck

3. Now are ye clean through the word which I have spoken unto you.

Already ye are clean because of the word ... — ASV

You are already cleansed by means of the Word ... — Nor

You are pruned already because of the teaching ... — Gspd

4. Abide[39] in me, and I in you.

Remain in me, as I remain in you — Mof

Dwell in me, as I in you — NEB

Remain united to me, and I will remain united to you — TCNT

As the branch cannot bear fruit of itself, except it abide in the vine;

... without staying on the vine — Ber

... unless it shares the life of the vine — Phi

... if it does not continue in the vine — Wey

... if it is not still on the vine — Bas

no more can ye, except ye abide in me.

so neither can ye ... — ABUV

... if you do not live on in me — Knox

5. I am the vine, ye are the branches:

He that abideth in me, and I in him, the same bringeth forth much fruit:

Whoever remains in union with me and I in union with him will bear abundant fruit — Wms

... will be very fruitful — Gspd

for without me ye can do nothing.

for apart from me ... — ASV

separated from me ... — Knox

... you can do nothing at all — Rieu

6. If any man abide not in me,

The man who does not share my life — Phi

he is cast forth as a branch, and is withered;

he's thrown away like a branch and dries up — Beck

he is trimmed off like a dry branch ... — Nor

he is thrown aside like a branch ... — Mof

he will be cast outside, like a branch which is withered — Lam

and men gather them, and cast them into the fire, and they are burned.

Such branches they gather up ... — Wey

... and throw them into the fire and burn them — Gspd

7. If ye abide in me, and my words abide in you, ye shall ask what ye will, and it shall be done unto you.

If you remain in union with me and my words remain in you, you may ask whatever you please and you shall have it — Wms

8. Herein is my Father glorified, that ye bear much fruit;

This is how my Father will be glorified ... — Phi

My Father is honored in this ... — Ber

... by your bearing abundant fruit — Wey

so shall ye be my disciples.

and so prove to be my disciples — RSV

and show yourselves to be disciples of mine — Gspd

9. As the Father hath loved me, so have I loved you: continue ye in my love.

I have loved you just as the Father has

---

[39]The words rendered "abide" in verses 4-7, 10; "continue" in verse 9; and "remain" in verses 11 and 16 are from the same Greek word.

loved me. You must remain in my love — Wms

10. If ye keep my commandments, ye shall abide in my love; even as I have kept my Father's commandments, and abide in his love.

If you continue to keep my commands, you will remain in my love, just as I have kept my Father's commands and remain in His love — Wms

11. These things have I spoken unto you, that my joy might remain in you,

All this have I told you . . . — Knox

. . . so that my own joy may be yours — TCNT

. . . that the joy which I have had . . . — Wms

. . . so that you can share my joy — Phi

and that your joy might be full.

. . . may be made full — ASV

. . . may be complete — Rieu

and that your joy may become perfect — Wey

12. This is my commandment, That ye love one another, as I have loved you.

This is My instruction . . . — Ber

. . . Love one another as I have loved you — Beck

This is the law I give you . . . — Bas

. . . you are to love one another as I have loved you — Mof

13. Greater love hath no man than this,

No one can show greater love — Gspd

. . . can give greater proof of love — TCNT

There is no greater love than this — Lam

that a man lay down his life for his friends.

than by laying down his life for his friends — TCNT

than he who gives his life . . . — Beck

the giving of his life for his friends — Wms

14. Ye are my friends, if ye do whatsoever I command you.

. . . if you keep on doing what I command you to do — Wms

. . . if you do all I command you — Knox

15. Henceforth I call you not servants;

No longer do I call you servants — ASV

I no longer call you slaves — Mon

for the servant knoweth not what his lord doeth:

. . . does not know what his master is working out — Ber

. . . does not share his master's confidence — Phi

but I have called you friends;

for all things that I have heard of my Father I have made known unto you.

because I have passed on to you everything . . . — Rieu

. . . that I have learned from my Father — Mon

. . . I've told you everything I heard from My Father — Beck

16. Ye have not chosen me, but I have chosen you, and ordained you,

Ye did not choose me . . . — ASV

It was not you that picked me out, but I picked out you . . . — Rieu

. . . but I chose you and appointed you — Mon

that ye should go and bring forth fruit, and that your fruit should remain: that whatsoever ye shall ask of the Father in my name, he may give it you.

17. These things I command you, that ye love one another.

I am giving you these commands that you may love one another — TCNT

18. If the world hate you, ye know that it hated me before it hated you.

. . . you know that it has first hated me — Wey

If the world hates you, be sure that it hated me before it learned to hate you — Knox

19. If ye were of the world, the world would love his own:

If you belonged to the world . . . — Ber

. . . the world would love what it owned — Mof

. . . would love you as its own — Nor

but because ye are not of the world,

Because you do not belong to the world . . . — TCNT

but I have chosen you out of the world,

I picked you out of it — Rieu

because I have singled you out from the midst of the world — Knox

and I have selected you from the world — Ber

therefore the world hateth you.

— that is why the world hates you — TCNT

20. **Remember the word that I said unto you, The servant is not greater than his lord. If they have persecuted me, they will also persecute you; if they have kept my saying, they will keep yours also.**

Do you remember what I told you? A slave isn't greater than his master! Since they persecuted Me, naturally they will persecute you. And if they listened to Me, they will listen to you! — Tay

21. **But all these things will they do unto you for my name's sake,**

. . . on account of my name — Mof

. . . on my account — RSV

because they know not him that sent me.

. . . do not understand who has sent me — Gspd

. . . for they do not know My Sender — Ber

22. **If I had not come and spoken unto them, they had not had sin:**

. . . they would not have been guilty — Nor

. . . they would have had no sin to answer for — TCNT

. . . they would be innocent — Rieu

but now they have no cloke for their sin.

but now they have no excuse for their sin — ASV

23. **He that hateth me hateth my Father also.**

Whoever hates Me also hates My Father — Nor

To hate me is to hate my Father too — Knox

24. **If I had not done among them the works which none other man did,**

If I had not worked among them and accomplished . . . — NEB

. . . such work as no one else ever did — TCNT

. . . the works which no one else did — RSV

. . . things that no other man has ever done — Phi

they had not had sin:

they would be blameless — Ber

but now have they both seen and hated both me and my Father.

. . . have seen and also hated . . . — Wey

. . . and hated Me and My Father as well — NASB

. . . seen both me and my Father, and hated both of us — Rieu

25. **But this cometh to pass, that the word might be fulfilled that is written in their law,**

But the saying written in Law . . . must be fulfilled — Gspd

However, this text in their Law had to come true — NEB

It is to fulfill the word that is written in their law — RSV

They hated me without a cause.

26. **But when the Comforter is come, whom I will send unto you from the Father, even the Spirit of truth, which proceedeth from the Father,**

who issues from the Father — Mof

which goes out from the Father — Ber

who goes forth from the Father — Nor

he shall testify of me:

He will testify regarding Me — Ber

. . . bear witness concerning Me — Nor

he will speak plainly about me — Phi

27. **And ye also shall bear witness,**

and you too are witnesses — Mof

. . . are to be my witnesses — Knox

and you must bear testimony — Gspd

because ye have been with me from the beginning.

. . . from the start — Wms

because you have been with me from the first — Mon

CHAPTER 16

1. **These things have I spoken unto you, that ye should not be offended.**

. . . be caused to stumble — ASV

I have said all this to keep you from falling away — RSV

I told you this so that nothing will upset your faith — Beck

2. **They shall put you out of the synagogues:**

They will expel you from their Synagogues — TCNT

. . . excommunicate you . . . — Mon

. . . shut you out from . . . — Ber

yea, the time cometh, that whosoever

killeth you will think that he doeth
God service.

indeed, the hour is coming when whoever kills you . . . — RSV

. . . will think he is offering sacrifice to
God — ABUV

. . . that he is doing God's pleasure —
Bas

. . . will claim that he is performing an
act of worship to God — Knox

3. **And these things will they do unto you,
because they have not known the
Father, nor me.**

because they have never had any true
knowledge of the Father or of me —
Phi

because they have never come to know
God nor me — Wms

4. **But these things have I told you, that
when the time shall come,**

. . . that, when the time for them comes
— TCNT

. . . when the time for it arrives — Mof

**ye may remember that I told you of
them.**

you may recollect that I told you —
Wey

you may remember that I forewarned
you — Nor

**And these things I said not unto you
at the beginning,**

I have not spoken like this to you before — Phi

I did not tell you these things at the
start — Wms

I didn't tell you this at first — Beck

because I was with you.

5. **But now I go my way to him that sent
me;**

**and none of you asketh me, Whither
goest thou?**

and yet not one of you asks me —
Where are you going — TCNT

and none of you is interested in the
purpose of My going and none of
you seems to wonder why — Tay

6. **But because I have said these things
unto you, sorrow hath filled your
heart.**

. . . your hearts are filled with sorrow
— Ber

. . . you are so distressed — Phi

. . . grief has filled your hearts — Wey

7. **Nevertheless I tell you the truth;**

And yet I can say truly — Knox

Yet it is only the truth when I tell you
— Gspd

Yet I am only telling you the truth —
TCNT

It is expedient for you that I go away:

It is profitable for you that I depart —
Rhm

But it is good for you that I should go
away — Rieu

it is to your advantage . . . — Wey

**for if I go not away, the Comforter
will not come unto you;**

he who is to befriend you will not come
to you unless I do go — Knox

. . . your Advocate . . . — NEB

. . . the Helper . . . — NASB

. . . the Counselor will not come to you
— RSV

**but if I depart, I will send him unto
you.**

but if I go . . . — ASV

but, if I leave you . . . — TCNT

whereas, if I go, I will send him to you
— Mof

8. **And when he is come, he will reprove
the world**

. . . he will bring conviction to the
world — Gspd

. . . will make the world conscious —
Bas

. . . he will convince the world — RSV

. . . it will be for him to prove the world
wrong — Knox

**of sin, and of righteousness, and of
judgment:**

9. **Of sin, because they believe not on me;**

. . . because they have not faith in me
— Bas

. . . by their refusal to believe in me —
NEB

10. **Of righteousness, because I go to my
Father, and ye see me no more;**

about uprightness, as shown by my going away to the Father, where you
can no longer see me — Gspd

11. **Of judgment, because the prince of this
world is judged.**

. . . because the prince of this world
has been convicted — Nor

. . . as shown by the condemnation of
the evil genius of this world — Gspd

. . . for the Spirit that is ruling this
world has been condemned — TCNT

. . . because the ruler of this world is
judged — RSV

12. I have yet many things to say unto you, but ye cannot bear them now.

I have much more to tell you . . . — Rieu

. . . but you are not strong enough for it now — Bas

. . . but it would be too much for you now — Beck

13. Howbeit when he, the Spirit of truth, is come,

However, when the Spirit of truth comes — Mof

he will guide you into all truth:

he will guide you into all the truth — ABUV

. . . into everything that is true — Phi

. . . into every truth — Ber

he will guide you into the whole truth — Mon

for he shall not speak of himself;

. . . of his own accord — Mof

. . . on His own initiative — NASB

for he will not speak on his own authority — RSV

but whatsoever he shall hear, that shall he speak:

but will tell what he hears — Gspd

he will say whatever he is told — Mof

and he will shew you things to come.

and he will declare to you . . . — ABUV

. . . will disclose to you . . . — NASB

and will make known to you that which is to come — Mon

14. He shall glorify me:

And he will bring honour to me — Knox

He will enhance my glory — Rieu

He will bring glory to me — Phi

for he shall receive of mine,

for he will draw upon what is mine — Mof

. . . draw on my truth — Phi

. . . will be enriched from what is mine — Rieu

for he will take what is mine — RSV

and shall shew it unto you.

. . . declare . . . — ASV

. . . announce . . . — Rhm

and communicate it to you — Gspd

and disclose it to you — Mof

and reveal it to you — Nor

15. All things that the Father hath are mine:

All that the Father has belongs to me — Gspd

Whatever the Father has is Mine — Nor

therefore said I, that he shall take of mine, and shall shew it unto you.

and shall disclose it to you — NASB

and tell them to you — Wms

16. A little while, and ye shall not see me: and again, a little while, and ye shall see me, because I go to the Father.

17. Then said some of his disciples among themselves, What is this that he saith unto us,

. . . What does He mean by telling us — Wms

. . . What does this mean, that he is saying to us — Knox

Some of his disciples asked each other what he meant by saying — Rieu

A little while, and ye shall not see me: and again, a little while, and ye shall see me: and, Because I go to the Father?

18. They said therefore, What is this that he saith, A little while?

. . . What is the meaning of 'In a little' — Mof

. . . What does he mean by a little while — Ber

we cannot tell what he saith.

We do not know what he means — RSV

. . . what he is talking about — NASB

19. Now Jesus knew that they were desirous to ask him,

Jesus perceived that . . . — ASV

Jesus took note that . . . — Rhm

. . . they wanted to ask him — RSV

and said unto them, Do ye enquire among yourselves of that I said,

. . . Are you discussing among yourselves why I said — Nor

. . . Are you discussing what I said — NEB

A little while, and ye shall not see me: and again, a little while, and ye shall see me?

20. Verily, verily, I say unto you, That ye shall weep and lament,

. . . you will be weeping and wailing — Mon

. . . you will cry and mourn — Beck

but the world shall rejoice;

but the world will be glad — Wey

while the world feels glad — Ber

and ye shall be sorrowful, but your sorrow shall be turned into joy.

But though you will be plunged in grief
. . . — NEB

. . . your grief will be turned into gladness — Wms

21. **A woman when she is in travail hath sorrow, because her hour is come:**
The mother in childbirth has anguish
. . . — Ber
A woman in labour is in pain because her time has come — TCNT

but as soon as she is delivered of the child, she remembereth no more the anguish,
but when the baby is born, she forgets her pain — Wms
. . . she forgets her suffering — Rieu

for joy that a man is born into the world.
so glad is she that . . . — Knox
she's so happy a child was brought into the world — Beck

22. **And ye now therefore have sorrow:**
. . . have grief — Rhm
So you have sorrow now — RSV
So you, too, are sorrowful — Gspd

but I will see you again, and your heart shall rejoice,
. . . and then you will be joyful — NEB
. . . and then your hearts will be glad — Nor

and your joy no man taketh from you.
and no one shall be able to deprive you of that joy — Ber
and your joy shall no man snatch away from you — Mon
and no one will rob you of your joy — TCNT

23. **And in that day ye shall ask me nothing.**
. . . shall ask me no question — ASV
. . . you will not need to ask anything of me — Knox
. . . you will ask nothing of me — Rieu
At that time you won't need to ask Me for anything — Tay

Verily, verily, I say unto you, Whatsoever ye shall ask the Father in my name, he will give it you.
. . . If ye shall ask anything of the Father . . . — ASV
. . . he will give it you in my name — ABUV
. . . he will grant it to you in my Name — TCNT
. . . he will give you as my followers — Gspd

for you can go directly to the Father and ask Him, and He will give you what you ask because you use My name — Tay

24. **Hitherto have ye asked nothing in my name:**
As yet you have not asked for anything
. . . — Wey
So far you haven't asked for anything in My name — Beck
. . . as my followers — Gspd

ask, and ye shall receive,
ask now . . . — Phi
. . . and you shall receive . . . — Mon

that your joy may be full.
so that your joy may be complete — Nor
to bring you gladness in full measure — Knox
that your joy may be overflowing — Phi

25. **These things have I spoken unto you in proverbs:**
. . . in dark sayings — ASV
. . . in similitudes — ABUV
. . . veiled speech — Beck
. . . in figurative language — NASB

but the time cometh, when I shall no more speak unto you in proverbs,
. . . in parables — Knox
. . . when I shall speak to you in metaphor no longer — Rieu

but I shall shew you plainly of the Father.
. . . tell you openly . . . — Knox
. . . shall talk about My Father in plain words — Nor

26. **At that day ye shall ask in my name:**
. . . you shall pray in my name — Mon
. . . you will make your request in my name — NEB

and I say not unto you, that I will pray the Father for you:
and I do not say that I will intercede with the Father for you — TCNT
and I shall not have to ask the Father in your behalf — Nor

27. **For the Father himself loveth you,**
. . . dearly loveth you — Rhm
. . . tenderly loves you — Wms
. . . holds you dear — Wey
because ye have loved me,
Because ye have dearly loved me — Rhm
because you now tenderly love me — Wms

since you have become my friends —
Knox

**and have believed that I came out from
God.**

and have believed that I came forth
from the Father — ASV

**28. I came forth from the Father, and am
come into the world:**

From the Father I came and I entered
the world — Mof

I did come from the Father and have
entered the world — Ber

I left the Father and came into the
world — Beck

**again, I leave the world, and go to the
Father.**

Now I am leaving the world and going
back to the Father — Wms

I am leaving the world again . . . —
NASB

. . . and return to the Father — Phi

**29. His disciples said unto him, Lo, now
speakest thou plainly, and speakest no
proverb.**[40]

. . . Ah, now you are speaking plainly
. . . — RSV

. . . and are not using a figure of speech
— NASB

**30. Now are we sure that thou knowest all
things,**

Now know we . . . — ASV

. . . that You have the knowledge of
everything — Nor

**and needest not that any man should
ask thee:**

and need not wait for any one to question you — TCNT

and need no one to put questions to
you — Mof

and don't need anyone to tell You anything — Tay

**by this we believe that thou camest
forth from God.**

**31. Jesus answered them, Do ye now be-
lieve?**

. . . Do you believe that already—TCNT

**32. Behold, the hour cometh, yea, is now
come, that ye shall be scattered, every
man to his own, and shall leave me
alone:**

. . . you will all be scattered to your
homes . . . — Gspd

. . . each to his place . . . — Ber

The hour is coming — in fact, it is already here — when you will be scattered to the winds, every man for
himself, and I shall be left alone —
Nor

. . . and you'll leave Me alone — Beck

**and yet I am not alone, because the
Father is with me.**

. . . I am never alone . . . — Lam

Yet I am not really alone, for the
Father is with me — Phi

**33. These things I have spoken unto you,
that in me ye might have peace.**

. . . so that through me you may find
peace — Mon

. . . that you through union with me
may have peace — Wms

I have told you this so that you may
have peace in Me — Nor

In the world ye shall have tribulation:

. . . you are under pressure — Ber

. . . you have affliction — Wey

. . . you will find suffering — Rieu

. . . you will find trouble — TCNT

but be of good cheer;

but take courage! — Gspd

but be courageous — Mon

But keep up your courage — Wey

but be confident! — Ber

but, never lose heart — Phi

but cheer up! — Tay

I have overcome the world.

I have conquered the world — Wms

I have won the victory over the world
— Wey

CHAPTER 17

**1. These words spake Jesus, and lifted up
his eyes to heaven,**

Jesus said this, then raised His eyes
toward heaven — Ber

When Jesus had thus spoken, He lifted
His face toward heaven . . . — Nor

. . . Jesus looked up to heaven — Beck

and said, Father, the hour is come;

**glorify thy Son, that thy Son also
may glorify thee:**

. . . honour thy Son, that thy Son may
honour thee — TCNT

. . . give glory to your Son . . . may give
glory to you — Bas

---

[40]Compare verse 25.

... exalt ... and magnify Your Son ...
— Amp

2. As thou hast given him power over all flesh,

.. authority over all mankind — NASB

For thou hast made him sovereign over all mankind — NEB

that he should give eternal life to as many as thou hast given him.

3. And this is life eternal, that they might know thee the only true God,

... that they get to know thee, the only real God — Rhm

... to know thee who alone art truly God — NEB

And eternal life means knowing you as the only true God — Gspd

and Jesus Christ, whom thou hast sent.

and your Apostle Jesus Christ — Rieu

and Jesus the Christ whom You have sent — Nor

and knowing Jesus your messenger as Christ — Wms

4. I have glorified thee on the earth:

I have exalted thy glory on earth — Knox

I have given you glory ... — Bas

I have brought you honor upon the earth — Phi

I have finished the work which thou gavest me to do.

having accomplished the work ... — RSV

having done perfectly the work ... — Wey

by completing the work which thou hast given me to do — TCNT

I have completed the task Thou gavest Me to do — Ber

5. And now, O Father, glorify thou me with thine own self

... let me have glory with you — Bas

... honor me in your own presence — Phi

... glorify Me at Your side — Beck

... invest me at your side — Rieu

with the glory which I had with thee before the world was.

... which I enjoyed in thy presence before the world began — Mof

... before the world existed — Gspd

... when the world had not yet come to be — Rieu

... which I had with thee before the world was made — RSV

6. I have manifested thy name unto the men which thou gavest me out of the world:

I have revealed Thy name ... — Wey

... made known ... — Mon

... made your very self known ... — Wms

I have shown your self to the men whom you gave me ... — Phi

thine they were, and thou gavest them me;

they were thy own ... — TCNT

They belonged to thee, and have become mine ... — Knox

They were your men ... — Phi

At first they were yours, but now you have given them to me — Wms

and they have kept thy word.

and they have obeyed your message — Gspd

... have held to thy word — Mof

and they have obeyed Thy teaching — Wey

7. Now they have known that all things whatsoever thou hast given me are of thee.

They recognize now ... — TCNT

Now they have realized ... — Ber

... that whatever thou hast given me was from thee — Mon

... that you are indeed the source of all I have from you — Rieu

... that all thy gifts have come to me from thee — NEB

... everything You gave Me comes from You — Beck

8. For I have given unto them the words which thou gavest me;

... the declarations which thou gavest me — Rhm

... truths which Thou didst teach me — Wey

for I have given them the knowledge you bestowed on me — Rieu

and they have received them, and have known surely that I came out from thee,

and they have accepted them and have really understood ... — Ber

... and been convinced that I came from you — Gspd

... and they have come to know in reality ... — Wms

... have certain knowledge that I came from you — Bas

JOHN 17

and they have believed that thou didst send me.
and they have faith . . . — Bas
. . . are convinced that you did send me — Wms

9. **I pray for them: I pray not for the world,**
I have a request to make for them . . . — Gspd
I intercede for them; I am not interceding . . . — TCNT
. . . I am not praying for the world now — Wms
but for them which thou hast given me; for they are thine.

10. **And all mine are thine, and thine are mine;**
and all things that are mine are thine . . . — ASV
And all my possessions are thine . . . — Rhm
Yes, all who are Mine, are Thine . . . — Ber
and I am glorified in them.
and in them my glory is achieved — Knox
and through them has my glory shone — NEB
and I am glorified by them — Lam

11. **And now I am no more in the world,**
I am to be in the world no longer — Mof
. . . to stay . . . — NEB
I am remaining . . . — Knox
My presence in the world is over — Ber
but these are in the world, and I come to thee.
Holy Father, keep through thine own name those whom thou hast given me,
. . . preserve in Thy name those whom . . . — Ber
. . . protect by the power of thy name those whom . . . — NEB
. . . keep them true to Thy name, which . . . — Wey
. . . keep them by the power of thy Name which . . . — Mof
. . . protect them in your name, which you have given me — Lam
that they may be one, as we are.

12. **While I was with them in the world,[41] I kept them in thy name:**
. . . I kept them safe . . . — Nor

. . . I was keeping them in Thy name — NASB
. . . I kept them by the power that you gave me — Phi
those that thou gavest me I have kept,
and I protected them — Gspd
I have guarded them — RSV
and kept them safe — NEB
and none of them is lost,
and not one of them has come to destruction — Bas
but the son of perdition;
only the son of perdition — Mof
. . . the son of destruction — Rhm
except the one who was destined to be lost — Gspd
that the scripture might be fulfilled.

13. **And now come I to thee; and these things I speak in the world, that they might have my joy fulfilled in themselves.**
But now I am come to thee; and I am speaking thus, while still in the world, that they may have my own joy, in all its fulness in their hearts — TCNT

14. **I have given them thy word; and the world hath hated them, because they are not of the world, even as I am not of the world.**
I have given them Your commands. And the world hates them because they don't fit in with it, just as I don't — Tay

15. **I pray not that thou shouldest take them out of the world,**
I'm not asking You to take them out of the world — Beck
. . . remove them out of the world — Wey
but that thou shouldest keep them from the evil.
but . . . keep them from the evil one — ASV
. . . protect them from the Evil One — Rieu

16. **They are not of the world, even as I am not of the world.**
They are no more sons of the world than I am — Phi
They do not belong to the world, as I, too, do not . . . — Knox

---

[41]The words "in the world" are now recognized as not adequately supported by original manuscripts.

418

17. Sanctify them through thy truth:
Consecrate them in the truth — Rieu
make them holy by the truth — Phi
thy word is truth.
thy Message is Truth — TCNT

18. As thou hast sent me into the world, even so have I also sent them into the world.

19. And for their sakes I sanctify myself,
And on their behalf I hallow myself — Rhm
. . . I dedicate myself — Mon
And for them I make myself holy — Bas
that they also might be sanctified through the truth.
. . . that they too may be consecrated in the truth — Rieu
that they may be made holy by the truth — Phi
. . . may be thoroughly dedicated in the truth — Mon

20. Neither pray I for these alone,
But I am not thinking of them only — Rieu
But it is not only for them that I am interceding — TCNT
. . . do I make request — Rhm
I do not ask in behalf of these alone — NASB
but for them also which shall believe on me through their word;
but for all who will have faith in me . . . — Bas
. . . through their message — Wms
. . . those that are brought by their teaching to have faith in me — Rieu

21. That they all may be one; as thou, Father, art in me, and I in thee, that they also may be one in us:
May they all be one . . . — Nor
. . . Just as you, Father, live in me and I live in you . . . — Phi
Let them all be one. Just as you, Father, are in union with me and I am with you, let them be in union with us — Gspd
that the world may believe that thou hast sent me.
so that the world may be convinced . . . — Wms
so that all men may come to have faith that . . . — Bas

22. And the glory which thou gavest me I have given them; that they may be one, even as we are one:

23. I in them, and thou in me, that they may be made perfect in one;
I in union with them and thou with me . . . — TCNT
. . . so that they may be perfectly united — Wms
. . . may be made completely one — Nor
. . . perfectly unified — Gspd
. . . that they may be brought to perfect unity — Rieu
and that the world may know that thou hast sent me, and hast loved them, as thou hast loved me.
Then the world will learn . . . — NEB
that the world may recognize . . . — Ber
and the world may be sure that you sent me . . . — Wms
. . . may know You sent Me and loved them as You loved Me — Beck

24. Father, I will that they also, whom thou hast given me, be with me where I am;
Father, I desire that . . . — ASV
. . . that these, thy gift to me, may be beside me . . . — Mof
Father, I want those . . . to be with me where I am — Phi
that they may behold my glory, which thou hast given me: for thou lovedst me before the foundation of the world.
. . . for you loved me before the creation of the world — Gspd
. . . the beginning of the world — TCNT
. . . before the world was made — Beck

25. O righteous Father, the world hath not known thee: but I have known thee, and these have known that thou hast sent me.

26. And I have declared unto them thy name, and will declare it:
and I made known unto them thy name . . . — ASV
and I revealed to them and will reveal your Being — Rieu
I have made your self known to them and I will continue to do so — Phi
that the love wherewith thou hast loved me may be in them, and I in them.
so that the love . . . may be felt in them . . . — Wms
. . . may dwell in them . . . — Knox
. . . may be in their hearts . . . — Phi

CHAPTER 18

1. When Jesus had spoken these words,
When he had finished his prayer —
Rieu
After offering this prayer — Wey
**he went forth with his disciples over
the brook Cedron,**
he went forth . . . over the brook Kidron — ASV
. . . across the Kidron valley — RSV
. . . to a place across the Ravine of Cedars — Mon
**where was a garden, into the which he
entered, and his disciples.**
to an orchard . . . — Mof
There was a garden there . . . — Nor
. . . and he went into it with his disciples — Gspd

**2. And Judas also, which betrayed him,
knew the place:**
Judas, his betrayer, knew the place
well — Knox
Judas the Traitor also knew this place
— Mon
**for Jesus ofttimes resorted thither with
his disciples.**
for Jesus often met there with his disciples — RSV

**3. Judas then, having received a band of
men and officers from the chief priests
and Pharisees,**
So taking a party of soldiers as well as
some police . . . — Rieu
So after procuring troops and some attendants . . . — Mof
. . . and some Temple police . . . —
Mon
**cometh thither with lanterns and
torches and weapons.**
Judas came there with . . . — Mon

**4. Jesus therefore, knowing all things that
should come upon him,**
Jesus, fully realizing all that was going
to happen to him — Phi
. . . who knew all that was impending
for him — Rieu
. . . knowing exactly what was going to
happen to Him — Beck
**went forth, and said unto them, Whom
seek ye?**
. . . Who is it, he asked, you are looking
for — Knox

**5. They answered him, Jesus of Nazareth.
Jesus saith unto them, I am he. And**

**Judas also, which betrayed him, stood
with them.**
. . . Now Judas also . . . was standing
with them — Rhm
. . . Judas . . . was himself standing
there — Rieu
. . . And there stood Judas the traitor
with them — NEB
**6. As soon then as he had said unto them,
I am he, they went backward, and fell
to the ground.**
. . . they all shrank back . . . — Knox
. . . they stepped back . . . — Nor
When Jesus said I am he, they drew
back and fell to the ground — TCNT
**7. Then asked he them again, Whom seek
ye? And they said, Jesus of Nazareth.**
**8. Jesus answered, I have told you that I
am he:**
. . . I told you that I am he — ABUV
**if therefore ye seek me, let these go
their way:**
If, then, you are looking for me . . . —
Mon
. . . let these men go — Gspd
. . . let these escape — Ber
**9. That the saying might be fulfilled,
which he spake, Of them which thou
gavest me have I lost none.**
He did this to carry out the prophecy
He had just made . . . — Tay
**10. Then Simon Peter having a sword
drew it, and smote the high priest's
servant,**
. . . and struck the high priest's servant
— ASV
. . . the high priest's slave — RSV
and cut off his right ear.
shearing off his right ear — Rieu
The servant's name was Malchus.
**11. Then said Jesus unto Peter, Put up thy
sword into the sheath:**
. . . Sheathe your sword — Mof
. . . Put your sword into its scabbard —
Beck
**the cup which my Father hath given
me, shall I not drink it?**
Must I not drink the cup which the
Father has handed me — Wms
Shall I refuse to drink the cup . . . —
Wey
. . . which my Father himself has appointed for me — Knox
12. Then the band and the captain and the

officers of the Jews took Jesus, and bound him,

... seized Jesus and bound him — ASV
... arrested Jesus and put handcuffs on him — Wms

13. **And led him away to Annas first; for he was father in law to Caiaphas, which was the high priest that same year.**

14. **Now Caiaphas was he, which gave counsel to the Jews,**

that it was expedient that one man should die for the people.

that it would be to their interest if one man died for the whole people — NEB

that it was for their welfare that one should die for the people — Wms

15. **And Simon Peter followed Jesus, and so did another disciple:**

And Simon Peter and another disciple followed Jesus — ABUV

that disciple was known unto the high priest,

... being well-known to the High Priest — TCNT

This other disciple was an acquaintance of ... — Gspd

... was known personally to the High Priest — Phi

and went in with Jesus into the palace of the high priest.

... into the court ... — ASV
... the court of the high priest's palace — Mon
... into the high priest's courtyard — Beck

16. **But Peter stood at the door without.**

whereas Peter remained standing at the door outside — Rhm

Then went out that other disciple, which was known unto the high priest, and spake unto her that kept the door, and brought in Peter.

... and talked to the girl watching the door ... — Beck
... the doormaid ... — Nor
... spoke to the doorkeeper and brought Peter in — Mon

17. **Then saith the damsel that kept the door unto Peter, Art not thou also one of this man's disciples?**

The girl in charge of the door then said to Peter ... — Ber
... Aren't you one of this man's disciples — Nor

He saith, I am not.

18. **And the servants and officers stood there, who had made a fire of coals; for it was cold: and they warmed themselves:**

As it was cold the slaves and attendants had made a charcoal fire ... — Gspd
... and they were standing and warming themselves — RSV

and Peter stood with them, and warmed himself.

19. **The high priest then asked Jesus of his disciples, and of his doctrine.**

... and of his teaching — ASV
The High Priest questioned Jesus about his disciples and about what he taught — NEB

20. **Jesus answered him,**
I spake openly to the world;

I have spoken publicly to the world — Beck
I have spoken to all the world openly — Mon

I ever taught in the synagogue, and in the temple, whither the Jews always resort;

I have continually taught in some synagogue or in the Temple ... — Wey
... where all Jews meet together — Phi

and in secret have I said nothing.

21. **Why askest thou me?**

Why are you questioning me — Bas

ask them which heard me, what I have said to them:

question them who have heard what I spake ... — Rhm
Ask my hearers what I have said to them — Mof

behold, they know what I said.

These people here ... — Rieu
these witnesses here know what I said — Mon

22. **And when he had thus spoken, one of the officers which stood by struck Jesus with the palm of his hand,**

... one of the police struck him on the face — NEB
... gave Him a slap ... — Nor
... gave him a blow with his hand — TCNT

saying, Answerest thou the high priest so?

... Is that how you answer the high priest — RSV

421

. . . Is this the way to answer the high priest — Ber

23. Jesus answered him, If I have spoken evil, bear witness of the evil:

. . . If I have said anything wrong . . . — Mon

. . . give evidence of the wrong — Ber

. . . bring a charge against me — Rieu

. . . If I have said anything wrong, testify to it — Gspd

but if well, why smitest thou me?

but if what I have said is true . . . — Wms

. . . then why do you strike Me — Nor

24. Now Annas had sent him bound unto Caiaphas the high priest.

. . . sent Him, still bound, to Caiaphas . . . — Beck

. . . with his hands still tied . . . — Phi

And Annas sent Jesus, bound as he was, to Caiaphas . . . — Rieu

25. And Simon Peter stood and warmed himself. They said therefore unto him, Art thou also one of his disciples? He denied it, and said, I am not.

26. One of the servants of the high priest, being his kinsman whose ear Peter cut off,

. . . being a kinsman of him whose ear Peter cut off — ASV

saith, Did not I see thee in the garden with him?

. . . Didn't I see you in the garden with him — Nor

27. Peter then denied again; and immediately the cock crew.

. . . and at once the cock crowed — RSV

. . . and at that very moment . . .—Mon

. . . the rooster crowed — Ber

28. Then led they Jesus from Caiaphas unto the hall of judgment:

. . . to the Praetorium — Wey

. . . to the Government House — TCNT

. . . into the Governor's headquarters — NEB

and it was early;

It was now early morning — Phi

and they themselves went not into the judgment hall,

and the Jews refrained from entering . . . — Rieu

. . . the Government House themselves — TCNT

lest they should be defiled;

for fear that they would be contaminated — Phi

that they might not be ceremonially defiled — Mon

but that they might eat the passover.

and to be able to eat the Passover supper — Gspd

so they could eat the Passover meal — NEB

29. Pilate then went out unto them, and said, What accusation bring ye against this man?

. . . What have you to say against this man — Nor

. . . What is the charge you bring against this man — Wms

30. They answered and said unto him, If he were not a malefactor,

. . . If he had not been a criminal — Mof

. . . an evil-doer — NASB

we would not have delivered him up unto thee.

we would not have turned him over to you — Gspd

we should not have handed him over to you — Rieu

we would not have committed him to you — Ber

31. Then said Pilate unto them, Take ye him, and judge him according to your law.

. . . Take him yourselves . . . — Knox

. . . and try him by your own Law — TCNT

Pilate said, Take him away and try him by your own law — NEB

The Jews therefore said unto him, It is not lawful for us to put any man to death:

. . . We are not allowed . . . — Mon

. . . We are not permitted . . . — NASB

. . . We are not allowed to execute anyone — Rieu

But we want Him crucified, they said, and your approval is required—Tay

32. That the saying of Jesus might be fulfilled,

thus fulfilling Jesus' prophecy — Phi

in fulfilment of what Jesus had said — TCNT

This made it possible for the word of Jesus to be fulfilled — Wms

which he spake, signifying what death he should die.

. . . when he declared how he was to die — Gspd

. . . indicating the nature of His impending death — Ber

. . . the manner of his death — NEB

33. **Then Pilate entered into the judgment hall again, and called Jesus, and said unto him, Art thou the King of the Jews?**

34. **Jesus answered him, Sayest thou this thing of thyself, or did others tell it thee of me?**

. . . Do you ask me this on your own initiative . . . — Wms

. . . or did others say it about me — Bas

. . . Is that your own idea, or have others suggested it to you — NEB

35. **Pilate answered, Am I a Jew?**

. . . I am not a Jew, am I — NASB

. . . Do you take me for a Jew — Gspd

Thine own nation and the chief priests have delivered thee unto me:

No, your own people . . . have given you into my hands — Nor

It's your people and your chief priests who handed you over to me — Phi

what hast thou done?

36. **Jesus answered, My kingdom is not of this world:**

. . . My realm does not belong to this world — Mof

. . . My kingdom is not founded in this world — Phi

if my kingdom were of this world, then would my servants fight, that I should not be delivered to the Jews:

. . . my subjects would have fought . . . — Wey

. . . to prevent my being given up to the Jews — TCNT

but now is my kingdom not from hence.

But really the source of My kingdom is not here — Ber

. . . My kingdom is not of this realm — NASB

But in fact my kingdom is not founded on all this! — Phi

37. **Pilate therefore said unto him, Art thou a king then?**

You are a king, then? You! said Pilate — Mon

. . . So you are a king? — RSV

Jesus answered, Thou sayest that I am a king.

. . . It is you that say I am a king — Rieu

. . . "King" is your word — NEB

. . . I am, as you say, a King — Nor

To this end was I born, and for this cause came I into the world, that I should bear witness unto the truth.

I was born and came into the world to testify to the truth — Beck

What I was born for, what I came into the world for, is to bear witness of the truth — Knox

Every one that is of the truth heareth my voice.

Every one who is on the side of truth listens to my voice — TCNT

. . . who is a friend of the truth . . . — Wey

. . . who loves truth recognizes my voice — Phi

Every one who lives on truth listens to My voice — Ber

38. **Pilate saith unto him, What is truth? And when he had said this, he went out again unto the Jews, and saith unto them, I find in him no fault at all.**

. . . I find no crime in this man — Mon

. . . I don't find this Man guilty of anything — Beck

. . . I can find no ground for a charge against Him — Wms

39. **But ye have a custom, that I should release unto you one at the passover:**

But I have an arrangement with you . . . — Phi

. . . that I set someone free for you at the Passover — Beck

You have a custom of demanding . . . — Knox

. . . that I should release one prisoner to you . . . — Wey

will ye therefore that I release unto you the King of the Jews?

so, do you want me to liberate for you . . . — Ber

Do you wish me to release to you the King of the Jews — Mon

40. **Then cried they all again, saying,**

Then they shouted back — Gspd

Again the clamour rose — NEB

Then they yelled — Beck

Not this man, but Barabbas.

Not this fellow, but Barabbas — Ber

No, not him! Bar-Abbas! — Mof

Now Barabbas was a robber.

. . . a brigand — Rieu

. . . a bandit — Phi

Now Barabbas was an outlaw — Bas

CHAPTER 19

1. Then Pilate therefore took Jesus, and scourged him.

... had him flogged — Phi

... and let Him be lashed — Ber

... and had him whipped with cords — Bas

Then Pilate laid open Jesus' back with a leaded whip — Tay

2. And the soldiers platted a crown of thorns,

... a garland of thorns — Rieu

... wove a crown of thorns — Lam

... twisted thorn twigs into a crown — Phi

The soldiers twisted some thorns into a crown — Beck

and put it on his head, and they put on him a purple robe,

... clothed him in a purple robe — Rieu

... robed him in a purple cloak — NEB

... threw a purple cloak about him — Mon

... robed Him in royal purple — Tay

3. And said, Hail, King of the Jews!

and they came unto him, and said ... — ASV

They kept coming up to him and saying ... — TCNT

... Long life to the King of the Jews! — Bas

and kept marching up to Him and saying ... — Wms

... Joy to thee! O King of the Jews! — Rhm

and they smote him with their hands.

each one giving him a blow — Gspd

... struck Him blows with their hands — Nor

... gave him blow after blow ... — TCNT

... gave Him blows in the face — NASB

4. Pilate therefore went forth again, and saith unto them, Behold, I bring him forth to you, that ye may know

... Behold, I bring him out to you ... — ASV

... to let you know — Beck

... I am going to bring Him out to you ... — Wms

... to let you clearly understand — Wey

that I find no fault in him.

that I find not even one cause against him — Lam

... nothing with which he can be charged — TCNT

... no crime in him — RSV

I find him not guilty — Ber

5. Then came Jesus forth, wearing the crown of thorns, and the purple robe. And Pilate saith unto them, Behold the man!

... Lo! the Man! — Rhm

... See, there is the man — Wey

... Here is the man! — RSV

6. When the chief priests therefore and officers saw him, they cried out, saying,

The chief priests and their henchmen saw him and shouted — NEB

... they gave a loud cry — Bas

... raised the cry — Nor

the high priests and their attendants ... yelled ... — Mof

Crucify him, crucify him.

To the cross! to the cross! — Bas

Pilate saith unto them, Take ye him, and crucify him:

... Take him yourselves and put him on the cross — Bas

for I find no fault in him.

I do not find him guilty — Rieu

for I find no crime in him — ABUV

For my part, I find nothing with which he can be charged — TCNT

7. The Jews answered him, We have a law, and by our law he ought to die,

... We have a law of our own ... — Rieu

... and by our law he deserves death — Gspd

... he should be put to death — Nor

because he made himself the Son of God.

because he made himself out to be God's Son — Mon

... claimed to be the Son of God — Wey

8. When Pilate therefore heard that saying, he was the more afraid;

... he was more afraid than ever — Phi

... he became still more alarmed — TCNT

... he was more frightened than before — Gspd

Their use of this expression added to Pilate's fears — Rieu

9. **And went again into the judgment hall, and saith unto Jesus, Whence art thou?**
... Where are you from — RSV
... Where do you come from — Mof
... What is your origin — Wey
But Jesus gave him no answer.

10. **Then saith Pilate unto him, Speakest thou not unto me?**
... You do not speak to me? — NASB
... Do you refuse to speak to me — Wms
knowest thou not that I have power to crucify thee, and I have power to release thee?
Surely you know that I have authority to release you ... — NEB
... that I have it in my power either to release you or to crucify you — Wey

11. **Jesus answered, Thou couldest have no power at all against me,**
... no authority whatever over me — Lam
... You have no power whatever of your own — Ber
except it were given thee from above:
had it not been granted you from above — Wey
if Heaven had not empowered you — Rieu
if it was not given to you by God — Bas
therefore he that delivered me unto thee hath the greater sin.
That is why the man who handed Me over to you is guilty of a greater sin — Beck
... is more guilty than you are — Wey
and therefore the deeper guilt lies with the man who handed me over to you. — NEB

12. **And from thenceforth Pilate sought to release him:**
Upon this Pilate sought to release him — ASV
This made Pilate anxious to release him — TCNT
From that moment Pilate tried to release him — NEB
Because of this Pilate kept on trying to set Him free — Wms
but the Jews cried out, saying, If thou let this man go, thou art not Caesar's friend:

But the Jews kept up a steady roar ... — Rieu
... If you liberate him, you are no friend of Caesar's — Ber
... you are no friend of the emperor's! — Gspd
whosoever maketh himself a king speaketh against Caesar.
... sets himself against Caesar — RSV
... is a rebel against the Emperor — Mon
Any would-be king is disloyal to Caesar — Rieu
any man who claims to be a king is defying Caesar — NEB

13. **When Pilate therefore heard that saying, he brought Jesus forth, and sat down in the judgment seat**
On hearing what they said, Pilate brought Jesus out, and took his seat upon the Bench — TCNT
... and seated himself on the judgment seat — Nor
... had him sit in the judge's seat — Gspd
in a place that is called the Pavement, but in the Hebrew, Gabbatha.
... in a place which is called Lithostrotos ... — Knox
... the Stone Pavement ... — Lam
... The Pavement ('Gabbatha' in the language of the Jews) — NEB

14. **And it was the preparation of the passover,**
Now it was the day of Preparation of the Passover — RSV
and about the sixth hour:
and about the noon hour — Nor
about twelve o'clock — Ber
and he saith unto the Jews, Behold your King!

15. **But they cried out, Away with him, away with him, crucify him.**
At that the people shouted ... — TCNT
... Off with him! Off with him! Crucify him! — Mof
Pilate saith unto them, Shall I crucify your King?
... Must I crucify your king — Wms
... Am I to crucify your king — Gspd
The chief priests answered, We have no king but Caesar.
... We have no king but the emperor! — Wms

16. **Then delivered he him therefore unto them to be crucified.**

Thereupon he gave Jesus up into their hands . . . — Knox

Then at last, to satisfy them, he handed Jesus over to be crucified — NEB

And they took Jesus, and led him away.

17. **And he bearing his cross went forth into a place called the place of a skull,**

Carrying His cross, He came to a spot named the Place of the Skull . . . — Nor

. . . called Skull Place — Beck

which is called in the Hebrew Golgotha:

. . . in the Jews' language . . . — NEB

which the Jews called Golgotha — Beck

18. **Where they crucified him, and two other with him,**

There they crucified him, and two others — Phi

on either side one, and Jesus in the midst.

one on either side, and Jesus between — Lam

one on each side and Jesus in the middle — Gspd

19. **And Pilate wrote a title, and put it on the cross.**

. . . an inscription to be put on the cross — Mof

Pilate prepared a notice of the charge . . . — Rieu

. . . and had it fastened to the top of the cross — Wey

And the writing was, JESUS OF NAZARETH THE KING OF THE JEWS.

20. **This title then read many of the Jews: for the place where Jesus was crucified was nigh to the city:**

. . . the place . . . was near the city — RSV

and it was written in Hebrew, and Greek, and Latin.

21. **Then said the chief priests of the Jews to Pilate, Write not, The King of the Jews; but that he said, I am King of the Jews.**

. . . Do not put, The King of the Jews . . . — Bas

. . . write, This man said, I am the king of the Jews — Knox

22. **Pilate answered, What I have written I have written.**

. . . What I have written stands — Rieu

23. **Then the soldiers, when they had cru-**

cified Jesus, took his garments, and made four parts, to every soldier a part;

The soldiers . . . took His outer garments and made four parts . . . — NASB

. . . took his clothes and divided them into four shares — a share for each soldier — TCNT

. . . divided them into four parts, one for each soldier — Mof

and also his coat: now the coat was without seam, woven from the top throughout.

They also took his coat; but this was seamless . . . — Rieu

. . . The tunic was without seam, woven in one piece from top to bottom — Beck

24. **They said therefore among themselves, Let us not rend it, but cast lots for it, whose it shall be:**

. . . Let us not tear it, but cast lots for it . . . — RSV

. . . Let's draw lots. . . — Phi

. . . let us toss for it . . . — NEB

. . . let us draw for it to see who gets it — Wms

that the scripture might be fulfilled, which saith,

So that the Scripture was fulfilled . . . — Ber

They parted my raiment among them, and for my vesture they did cast lots.

They shared my garments among them, and cast lots for my clothing — NEB

These things therefore the soldiers did.

That was what the soldiers did — TCNT

25. **Now there stood by the cross of Jesus his mother, and his mother's sister, Mary the wife of Cleophas, and Mary Magdalene.**

Meanwhile near the cross of Jesus were standing his mother and his mother's sister, as well as Mary the wife of Clopas and Mary of Magdala — TCNT

26. **When Jesus therefore saw his mother, and the disciple standing by, whom he loved,**

So when Jesus saw . . . his favourite disciple standing near — Mof

he saith unto his mother, Woman, behold thy son!

. . . Mother, there is your son! — Bas

. . . (Dear) lady . . . — Amp

. . . Look, your son! — Wey

27. Then saith he to the disciple, Behold thy mother!

. . . There is your mother! — Beck

And from that hour that disciple took her unto his own home.

And from that moment . . . — Ber

. . . the disciple took her into his own keeping — Knox

. . . to his house — Bas

28. After this, Jesus knowing that all things were now accomplished, that the scripture might be fulfilled,

. . . knowing that all things are now finished . . . — ASV

. . . that everything had been done to fulfill the Scriptures — Nor

. . . so that the Writings might come true — Bas

saith, I thirst.

29. Now there was set a vessel full of vinegar:

. . . a bowl standing there full of common wine — TCNT

. . . a bowl of sour wine — Gspd

and they filled a spunge with vinegar,

So they soaked a sponge in the wine — Phi

and put it upon hyssop, and put it to his mouth.

and put it upon a stalk of hyssop . . . — Mon

. . . and brought it up to His mouth — NASB

so they . . . fixed it on a javelin[42] . . . — NEB

30. When Jesus therefore had received the vinegar, he said, It is finished:

As soon as Jesus had taken the wine, He said . . . — Wey

. . . All is finished! — TCNT

Jesus . . . said, The task is done — Rieu

and he bowed his head, and gave up the ghost.

. . . and yielded up his spirit — Knox

. . . and gave up his life — Rieu

31. The Jews therefore, because it was the preparation,[43] that the bodies should not remain upon the cross on the sabbath day,

. . . to prevent the bodies' hanging on the cross during the Sabbath — Mon

(for that sabbath day was an high day,)

because that sabbath day was a solemn one — Knox

. . . a particularly important Sabbath — Phi

besought Pilate that their legs might be broken, and that they might be taken away.

they asked Pilate to have the legs of the men broken and the bodies taken away — Beck

32. Then came the soldiers, and brake the legs of the first, and of the other which was crucified with him.

So the soldiers came and broke the legs . . . — RSV

. . . first of the one and then of the other . . . — Nor

33. But when they came to Jesus, and saw that he was dead already, they brake not his legs:

34. But one of the soldiers with a spear pierced his side, and forthwith came there out blood and water.

. . . and instantly blood and water came out — Ber

35. And he that saw it bare record, and his record is true;

and he knoweth that he saith true, that ye might believe.

and he knows that he is telling the truth . . . — Mon

36. For these things were done, that the scripture should be fulfilled, A bone of him shall not be broken.

37. And again another scripture saith, They shall look on him whom they pierced.

38. And after this Joseph of Arimathea, being a disciple of Jesus, but secretly for fear of the Jews,

besought Pilate that he might take away the body of Jesus:

requested Pilate . . . — Rhm

. . . for permission to take the body of Jesus — Mon

. . . to remove the body of Jesus — Wms

and Pilate gave him leave. He came therefore, and took the body of Jesus.

Pilate granted permission . . . — NASB

---

[42] The Greek words for "hyssop" and "javelin" are similar.

[43] Compare verse 14.

... So he went and removed the body — Mof

39. And there came also Nicodemus, which at the first came to Jesus by night, and brought a mixture of myrrh and aloes, about an hundred pound weight.

... bringing with him about seventy-five pounds of spices, myrrh and aloes mixed — Nor

... taking a roll of myrrh and aloes weighing about a hundred pounds — Gspd

40. Then took they the body of Jesus, and wound it in linen clothes with the spices,

... and wrapped it in bandages with the spices — Wms

... wrapped it with the spices in strips of linen — Rieu

as the manner of the Jews is to bury.

as the custom of the Jews is ... — ASV

... in preparing for burial — Nor

41. Now in the place where he was crucified there was a garden;

There was a garden near the place ... — Mon

... at the place ... — Wey

and in the garden a new sepulchre, wherein was never man yet laid.

... a new tomb ... — ASV

... in which no one had yet been laid — NASB

42. There laid they Jesus therefore because of the Jews' preparation day; for the sepulchre was nigh at hand.

so they put Jesus there, it being the Jewish day of Preparation ... — Mof

... and because the tomb was near — Lam

CHAPTER 20

1. The first day of the week cometh Mary Magdalene early, when it was yet dark, unto the sepulchre,

... unto the tomb — ASV

... Mary of Magdala went early to the tomb ... — Mof

and seeth the stone taken away from the sepulchre.

and sees the stone taken away out of the tomb — ABUV

... saw that the stone had been removed ... — TCNT

2. Then she runneth, and cometh to Simon Peter, and to the other disciple, whom Jesus loved,

So she came running ... — Mon

So she ran and went ... — RSV

and saith unto them, They have taken away the Lord out of the sepulchre, and we know not where they have laid him.

3. Peter therefore went forth, and that other disciple, and came to the sepulchre.

Then Peter and the other disciple set out on their way to the tomb — Nor

... left the city and started for the tomb — Wms

4. So they ran both together: and the other disciple did outrun Peter, and came first to the sepulchre.

... the other disciple ran faster than Peter ... — Gspd

... and was first to arrive at the tomb — Phi

5. And he stooping down, and looking in, saw the linen clothes lying;

As he stooped ... — Ber

... he saw the linen wrappings lying there ... — Nor

yet went he not in.

but did not enter — NEB

6. Then cometh Simon Peter following him, and went into the sepulchre, and seeth the linen clothes lie,

... and entered into the tomb ... — ASV

... and he gazed at the linen wrappings as they lay — Mon

7. And the napkin, that was about his head, not lying with the linen clothes, but wrapped together in a place by itself.

... but rolled up in a place by itself — Bas

... but apart, folded up into one place — Rhm

8. Then went in also that other disciple, which came first to the sepulchre,

... who had reached the tomb first ... — Wms

and he saw, and believed.

saw what had happened and believed — Phi

and saw and was convinced — Wey

9. For as yet they knew not the scripture,

For they did not yet understand from the scripture — Lam

. . . had not previously understood . . . — Wms

that he must rise again from the dead.

which showed that he must rise from the dead — NEB

10. Then the disciples went away again unto their own home.

11. But Mary stood without at the sepulchre weeping:

. . . stood weeping outside the tomb — RSV

and as she wept, she stooped down, and looked into the sepulchre.

. . . she stooped to look into the tomb — ABUV

12. And seeth two angels in white sitting,

. . . two angels in white raiment . . . — Wey

. . . clothed in white . . . — TCNT

the one at the head, and the other at the feet, where the body of Jesus had lain.

13. And they say unto her, Woman, why weepest thou?

. . . Lady, why do you weep — Rieu

She saith unto them, Because they have taken away my Lord, and I know not where they have laid him.

14. And when she had thus said, she turned herself back, and saw Jesus standing, and knew not that it was Jesus.

. . . she turned around . . . — NASB

. . . and saw Jesus standing there . . . — Mon

. . . but had no idea that it was Jesus — Bas

. . . but did not recognize Him — Wey

15. Jesus saith unto her, Woman, why weepest thou? whom seekest thou?

. . . Lady, why do you weep? Whom are you looking for — Rieu

She, supposing him to be the gardener, saith unto him, Sir, if thou have borne him hence,

. . . Sir, if you have carried him off — Ber

. . . taken Him away from here — Nor

tell me where thou hast laid him, and I will take him away.

16. Jesus saith unto her, Mary. She turned herself, and saith unto him, Rabboni;

Jesus says to her, Mary! . . . — ABUV

. . . She turned round, and exclaimed in Hebrew . . . — TCNT

. . . Rabbouni! — Rieu

which is to say, Master.

which is Hebrew for 'My Master' — NEB

which means, My Teacher! — Lam

17. Jesus saith unto her, Touch me not;

. . . Be not detaining me — Rhm

. . . Do not hold me — TCNT

. . . You must not cling to me — Gspd

for I am not yet ascended to my Father: but go to my brethren, and say unto them, I ascend unto my Father, and your Father; and to my God, and your God.

18. Mary Magdalene came and told the disciples that she had seen the Lord, and that he had spoken these things unto her.

19. Then the same day at evening, being the first day of the week, when the doors were shut where the disciples were assembled for fear of the Jews, came Jesus and stood in the midst,

. . . Jesus came among them — Bas

. . . Jesus came and stood among them — RSV

and saith unto them, Peace be unto you.

20. And when he had so said, he shewed unto them his hands and his side. Then were the disciples glad, when they saw the Lord.

. . . Then the disciples rejoiced . . . — ABUV

. . . were filled with joy at seeing the Lord — Wey

. . . were thrilled with joy over seeing their Lord — Wms

21. Then said Jesus to them again, Peace be unto you: as my Father hath sent me, even so send I you.

. . . As the Father has sent me as his Messenger . . . — TCNT

. . . I am sending you out in my turn — Knox

. . . so I am now sending you — Wms

22. And when he had said this, he breathed on them, and saith unto them, Receive ye the Holy Ghost:

. . . he breathed strongly . . . — Rhm

. . . Receive ye the Holy Spirit — ASV

23. Whose soever sins ye remit, they are remitted unto them;

If you forgive any men's sins, they are forgiven — Phi

If you get forgiveness for people's sins . . . — Wms

and whose soever sins ye retain, they are retained.

if you pronounce them unforgiven, unforgiven they remain — NEB

If you bind fast the sins for any, they remain bound — Wey

if you let people's sins fasten upon them, they will remain fastened upon them — Wms

24. But Thomas, one of the twelve, called Didymus,[44] was not with them when Jesus came.

25. The other disciples therefore said unto him, We have seen the Lord. But he said unto them, Except I shall see in his hands the prints of the nails, and put my finger into the print of the nails, and thrust my hand into his side,

. . . Unless I see his hands with the mark of the nails . . . — Mof

. . . and put my finger into the wound . . . — Wey

. . . and press my hand into his side — Rhm

I will not believe.

you will never make me believe — Knox

I refuse to believe it — Mof

26. And after eight days again his disciples were within, and Thomas with them: then came Jesus, the doors being shut, and stood in the midst, and said, Peace be unto you.

27. Then saith he to Thomas, Reach hither thy finger, and behold my hands;

. . . Come here and feel my hands with your finger — Rieu

. . . Look at my hands, put your finger here — Mof

and reach hither thy hand, and thrust it into my side:

and put out your hand, and place it in my side — RSV

and take your hand and put it in My side — Beck

and be not faithless, but believing.

Do not be an unbeliever, but believe — Rieu

You must not doubt, but believe — Phi

28. And Thomas answered and said unto him, My Lord and my God.

29. Jesus saith unto him, Thomas, because thou hast seen me, thou hast believed: blessed are they that have not seen, and yet have believed.

. . . Have you believed because you have seen me? . . . — RSV

. . . You believe because you have seen Me . . — Nor

. . . Blessed are those who believe without seeing — Ber

. . . Happy are those who have never seen me and yet have believed! — Phi

30. And many other signs truly did Jesus in the presence of his disciples, which are not written in this book:

His disciples saw Jesus do many other miracles that are not written in this book — Beck

31. But these are written, that ye might believe that Jesus is the Christ, the Son of God;

. . . so that you believe Jesus is the promised Savior . . . — Beck

. . . that Jesus is the . . . Anointed One . . . — Amp

and that believing ye might have life through his name.

and so that, having this faith you may have life . . . — Bas

and that through believing you may have life, as bearers of His name — Wms

. . . you may have life eternal in his Being — Rieu

. . . you may have life as his followers — Gspd

CHAPTER 21

1. After these things Jesus shewed himself again to the disciples at the sea of Tiberias;[45] and on this wise shewed he himself.

. . . and this is how he appeared to them — Knox

2. There were together Simon Peter, and Thomas called Didymus,[46] and Na-

[44]Compare John 11:16.
[45]Compare John 6:1.
[46]Compare John 11:16.

thanael of Cana in Galilee, and the sons of Zebedee, and two other of his disciples.

3. **Simon Peter saith unto them, I go a fishing.**
Simon Peter told them, I go off fishing! — Ber
They say unto him, We also go with thee.
. . . We will go with you — Nor
They went forth, and entered into a ship immediately; and that night they caught nothing.
Off they went and embarked in the boat . . . — Mof
They went out and got into the boat . . . — RSV

4. **But when the morning was now come, Jesus stood on the shore:**
Now just as day was breaking . . . — Wms
. . . Jesus stood on the beach — ASV
but the disciples knew not that it was Jesus.
. . . had no idea that . . . — Phi
. . . did not recognize that it was Jesus — Mon

5. **Then Jesus saith unto them, Children, have ye any meat?**
. . . Lads, you have no fish, have you — Wms
. . . have you got anything — Mof
They answered him, No.

6. **And he said unto them, Cast the net on the right side of the ship, and ye shall find. They cast therefore, and now they were not able to draw it for the multitude of fishes.**

7. **Therefore that disciple whom Jesus loved saith unto Peter, It is the Lord. Now when Simon Peter heard that it was the Lord, he girt his fisher's coat unto him, (for he was naked,)**
. . . girded on his outer garment . . . — ABUV
. . . he belted on his fisherman's coat, for he had taken it off — Wms
and did cast himself into the sea.
and plunged into the sea — Nor

8. **And the other disciples came in a little ship; (for they were not far from land, but as it were two hundred cubits,)**
The rest of the disciples came in the boat . . . — Mon
. . . for they were only about a hundred yards from shore — TCNT

dragging the net with fishes.
hauling in the net of fish — Ber

9. **As soon then as they were come to land, they saw a fire of coals there, and fish laid thereon, and bread.**
. . . they saw burning coals there . . . — Beck
. . . with fish cooking on it, and some bread — Mof

10. **Jesus saith unto them, Bring of the fish which ye have now caught.**
. . . Bring some of the fish you have just caught — Gspd

11. **Simon Peter went up, and drew the net to land full of great fishes, an hundred and fifty and three:**
and for all there were so many, yet was not the net broken.
and yet, although there were so many, the net had not been torn — TCNT

12. **Jesus saith unto them, Come and dine.**
. . . Come and break your fast — ASV
. . . Come and have your breakfast — Phi
And none of the disciples durst ask him, Who art thou?
Now none of the disciples dared ask him, Who are you — RSV
Not one of the disciples ventured to ask him who he was — TCNT
knowing that it was the Lord.

13. **Jesus then cometh, and taketh bread, and giveth them, and fish likewise.**

14. **This is now the third time that Jesus shewed himself to his disciples, after that he was risen from the dead.**
This makes the third time that Jesus appeared . . . — NEB
Thus Jesus appeared to his disciples a third time . . . — Knox

15. **So when they had dined,**
So when they had breakfasted — ABUV
When they had finished breakfast — RSV
Jesus saith to Simon Peter, Simon, son of Jonas, lovest thou me more than these?
. . . do you love me more than these others do — Mon
. . . are you more devoted to me than these others — Gspd
. . . do you love me more than these things — Lam
. . . more than all else — NEB

He saith unto him, Yea, Lord; thou knowest that I love thee.[47]

. . . you know that I am your friend — TCNT

. . . that you are dear to me — Mon

. . . that I love You dearly — Nor

He saith unto him, Feed my lambs.

. . . Tend My lambs — NASB

. . . Feed My lambs . . . — Beck

16. **He saith to him again the second time, Simon, son of Jonas, lovest thou me?**

. . . are you devoted to me — Gspd

He saith unto him, Yea, Lord; thou knowest that I love thee.

. . . you know that you are dear to me — Wey

. . . you know that I am your friend — Phi

He saith unto him, Feed my sheep.

. . . Shepherd my sheep — ABUV

. . . Keep my sheep — Alf

. . . Tend my sheep — RSV

17. **He saith unto him the third time, Simon, son of Jonas, lovest thou me?**[48] **Peter was grieved because he said unto him the third time, Lovest thou me?**

. . . Peter was hurt that he asked him a third time . . . — NEB

. . . Simon, son of John, are you my friend — TCNT

. . . Am I dear to you — Wey

And he said unto him, Lord, thou knowest all things; thou knowest that I love thee.

. . . Lord, you know everything . . . — Wms

. . . You must know that I love You dearly — Nor

. . . you know that you are dear to me — Mon

Jesus saith unto him, Feed my sheep.

18. **Verily, verily, I say unto thee, When thou wast young, thou girdedst thyself, and walkedst whither thou wouldest:**

. . . when you were younger, you used to dress yourself . . . — Phi

. . . and walk wherever you chose — Wey

but when thou shalt be old, thou shalt stretch forth thy hands, and another shall gird thee,

. . . you will stretch out your hands for some one to gird you — Mon

. . . and someone else will dress you — Phi

and carry thee whither thou wouldest not.

and bring you where you do not wish to go — NASB

and you will be taken where you have no wish to go — Mof

19. **This spake he, signifying by what death he should glorify God.**

Now this he spoke, signifying by what manner of death . . . — ABUV

He said this to show by what kind of death . . . — Beck

. . . by which he would give God glory — Bas

by which Peter was to honor God — Gspd

And, when he had spoken this, he saith unto him, Follow me.

. . . Keep on following me! — Wms

20. **Then Peter, turning about, seeth the disciple whom Jesus loved following;**

Peter turned and saw the disciple whom Jesus loved following them — Beck

which also leaned on his breast at supper, and said, Lord, which is he that betrayeth thee?

21. **Peter seeing him saith to Jesus, Lord, and what shall this man do?**

. . . Lord, what about this man — RSV

. . . And what about him, Lord — Mof

22. **Jesus saith unto him, If I will that he tarry till I come,**

. . . If I choose . . . — Mon

. . . that he remain until I come — Rhm

. . . that he should wait till I come — — TCNT

what is that to thee?

what concern is that of yours — Wey

is that your business — Phi

follow thou me.

You follow Me! — Ber

Your business is to follow Me — Nor

23. **Then went this saying abroad among the brethren, that that disciple should not die:**

As a result, word went round among the brethren . . . — Rieu

So the report got out . . . — Wms

. . . that this disciple was not to die — Knox

---

[47]Peter uses a word implying fond personal affection; Jesus' word implies commitment and devotion.

[48]Jesus here adopts Peter's word.

yet Jesus said not unto him, He shall not die; but, If I will that he tarry till I come, what is that to thee?

24. **This is the disciple which testifieth of these things,**

It is this disciple who bears testimony to these facts — Mon

This same disciple is our authority for these events — Rieu

It is this same disciple who attests what has here been written — NEB

and wrote these things: and we know that his testimony is true.

It is in fact he who wrote it . . . — NEB

. . . and we know well that his witness is truthful — Knox

. . . We know that his witness is reliable — Phi

25. **And there are also many other things which Jesus did, the which, if they should be written every one,**

. . . so many, indeed, that if every one were recorded — Nor

. . . If it were all to be recorded in detail — NEB

I suppose that even the world itself could not contain the books that should be written.

. . . the world would not have room for . . . — Beck

. . . the books which would have to be written — Knox

I do not think the world itself could hold the volumes they would fill — Rieu

Amen.

THE
ACTS OF THE APOSTLES

CHAPTER 1

1. The former treatise have I made, O Theophilus,
My dear Theophilus, In my first book I gave you some account — Phi
of all that Jesus began both to do and teach,
. . . did and taught as a beginning — Wey
. . . did and taught from the beginning — Gspd
. . . set out to do and teach — Knox

2. Until the day in which he was taken up,
. . . was received up — ASV
until the day of His ascension — Ber
. . . he was taken up to heaven — NEB
after that he through the Holy Ghost had given commandments
after that he had given commandment through the Holy Spirit — ASV
after giving instructions through the Holy Spirit — NEB
after He had by the Holy Spirit given orders — NASB
unto the apostles whom he had chosen:
to the special messengers of his choice — Phi

3. To whom also he showed himself alive
To them he presented himself alive — RSV
after his passion
after his death — Bas
After He had suffered death — Nor
after his suffering — NASB
by many infallible proofs,
in many convincing manifestations — Mon
. . . sure tokens — Rhm
. . . sure proofs — Wey
. . . convincing proofs — NASB
. . . convincing demonstrations — Amp
being seen of them forty days,
appearing unto them by the space of forty days — ASV
He appeared to them from time to time during forty days — TCNT
appearing to them over a period of forty days — NASB
and speaking of the things pertaining to the kingdom of God:
. . . discussing the affairs of God's realm — Mof

. . . discussing the interests of the kingdom of God — Ber
and speaking of the concerns of the kingdom of God — NASB

4. And, being assembled together with them,
And as he ate bread with them — Lam
as he sat at table with them — Knox
and while staying with them — RSV
while he was eating a meal with them — Phi
While he was in their company — NEB
commanded them that they should not depart from Jerusalem,
charged them . . . — ASV
instructed . . . — Gspd
gave them orders . . . — Bas
but wait for the promise of the Father,
but — To abide around the promise of the Father — Rhm
but to wait for the Father's promised gift — Wey
but to wait there for the fulfilment of the Father's promise — Knox
which, saith he, ye have heard of me.
the one of whom you have heard from me — Lam

5. For John truly baptized with water;
For John indeed immersed with water — Rhm
For John baptized people in water — Gspd
but ye shall be baptized with the Holy Ghost not many days hence.
But ye in the Holy Spirit shall be immersed — Rhm
but there is a baptism with the Holy Spirit which you are to receive . . . — Knox

6. When they therefore were come together,
On one occasion, when the Apostles had met together — TCNT
they asked of him, saying,
They . . . began to question him, saying — Rhm
they asked Jesus this question — TCNT
they began to ask him — Mon
they were asking him, saying — NASB
Lord, wilt thou at this time restore again the kingdom to Israel?

... is this the time when you are to establish once again the sovereignty of Israel — NEB

... are you now going to make Israel an independent kingdom again — Beck

7. And he said unto them,
He answered — NEB

It is not for you to know the times or the seasons,
It is not your business to learn times and dates — Wms

It is not your affair to know times or seasons — Ber

... the course and periods of time — Mof

... times and occasions — Mon

... times or epochs — NASB

... the things and events of time and their definite periods — Amp

which the Father hath put in his own power.
... hath set within his own authority — ASV

... has fixed by his own authority — RSV

8. But ye shall receive power, after that the Holy Ghost is come upon you:
But you shall receive power when the Holy Spirit has come upon you — NASB

and ye shall be witnesses unto me both in Jerusalem, and in all Judaea, and in Samaria, and unto the uttermost part of the earth.
and you shall be My witnesses both in Jerusalem, and in all Judea and Samaria, and even to the remotest part of the earth — NASB

... to the very ends of the earth — Gspd

9. And when he had spoken these things, while they beheld, he was taken up;
Jesus had no sooner said this than he was caught up before their very eyes — TCNT

... as they were looking on, he was lifted up — RSV

and a cloud received him out of their sight.
and a cloud caught him away from their eyes — Rhm

and a cloud closing beneath Him hid Him from their sight — Wey

and a cloud swept under Him and carried Him out of their sight — Wms

10. And while they looked stedfastly toward heaven as he went up,
And as they strained their eyes towards heaven, to watch his journey — Knox

They were still looking intently up to heaven, watching His departure — Nor

And as they were gazing intently into the sky while He was departing — NASB

behold, two men stood by them in white apparel;
suddenly there were two men in white garments standing by them — Wey

two men dressed in white suddenly stood beside them — Gspd

two men in white clothes were standing right beside them — Beck

11. Which also said,
who also said — ASV

Ye men of Galilee, why stand ye gazing up into heaven?
... why do you stand looking into the sky — NASB

this same Jesus, which is taken up from you into heaven,
This Jesus, who has been taken up from you into heaven — NASB

shall so come in like manner as ye have seen him go into heaven.
will come back in the same fashion, just as you have watched him going into heaven — Knox

will come in just the same way as you have watched Him go into heaven — NASB

12. Then returned they unto Jerusalem from the mount called Olivet,
Then they went back to Jerusalem from the hill called the Olive orchard — Gspd

which is from Jerusalem a sabbath day's journey.
which is near Jerusalem, a sabbath day's journey away — RSV

This was near Jerusalem, a little over a half mile away — Nor

13. And when they were come in,
When they got there — TCNT
When they reached the city — Wms
and when they had entered — RSV

they went into an upper room,
they went up to the upper room — RSV

435

they went to the room upstairs — NEB
they went to the second-floor room —
Beck
where abode
which was now their fixed place for
meeting — Wey
where they were staying — Gspd
**both Peter, and James, and John, and
Andrew,**
both Peter and John and James and
Andrew — ASV
**Philip, and Thomas, Bartholomew,
and Matthew, James the son of Alphaeus, and Simon Zelotes,**
. . . Simon the Zealot — ASV
. . . Simon who had been a Zealot —
Mof
and Judas the brother of James.
. . . Judas the son of James — ASV

14. **These all continued with one accord
in prayer and supplication,**
These all with one accord continued
stedfastly in prayer — ASV
All of these with one mind continued
earnest in prayer — Wey
They were all devoting themselves with
one mind to prayer — Gspd
All these engaged constantly and with
one mind in prayer — Ber
with the women,
together with some women — Wey
and Mary the mother of Jesus,
including Mary the mother of Jesus —
NEB
and with his brethren.

15. **And in those days Peter stood up in
the midst of the disciples, and said,**
. . . in the midst of the brethren . . . —
ASV
About this time, at a gathering of the
Brethren, Peter rose to speak —
TCNT
**(the number of names together were
about an hundred and twenty,)**
the company of persons was in all . . .
— RSV
and there was a multitude of persons
gathered together, about a hundred
and twenty — ASV
there was a crowd of about a hundred
and twenty persons all together —
Mof

16. **Men and brethren,**
Brethren — ASV
Brothers — TCNT

**this scripture must needs have been
fulfilled,**
it was necessary that the Scripture
should be fulfilled — Wey
**which the Holy Ghost by the mouth
of David spake before concerning
Judas,**
which the Holy Spirit foretold through
the lips of David . . . — Ber
**which was guide to them that took
Jesus.**
who acted as guide to those who arrested Jesus — Wey

17. **For he was numbered with us,**
for he was one of our number — Wms
Judas was one of us twelve — Beck
and had obtained part of this ministry.
and received his portion in this ministry — ASV
and having had his part allotted him
in this work of ours — TCNT
and a share in this ministry of ours fell
to his lot — Gspd

18. **Now this man purchased a field with
the reward of iniquity;**
. . . had bought a piece of land with
the payment for his treachery —
TCNT
. . . the wages of crime — Ber
. . . the proceeds of his infamy — Phi
. . . the price of his villainy — NEB
and falling headlong,
and falling from a height — TCNT
but swelling up — Mof
having fallen down head first — Nor
he burst asunder in the midst,
his body burst open — TCNT
he was ruptured in the middle — Nor
and all his bowels gushed out.
and all his vitals poured out — Gspd
and all his intestines poured out —
Wms

19. **And it was known unto all the dwellers at Jerusalem;**
And it became known . . . — ASV
Everybody living in Jerusalem heard
about it — Beck
**insomuch as that field is called in their
proper tongue,**
and so the field got its name, in their
language — TCNT
**Aceldama, that is to say, The field of
blood.**

20. **For it is written in the book of Psalms,
Let his habitation be desolate,**

Let their camping-place be deserted —
Knox
... dwelling ... — TCNT
... residence ... — Mof
... estate ... — Gspd
... homestead ... — Nor
and let no man dwell therein:
And let no one live in it — TCNT
and his bishoprick let another take.
and His office ... — RSV
... His work ... — Wey
... his charge — Mof
... his position — Gspd

21. **Wherefore of these men which have companied with us**
It is necessary, therefore, that of the men who have been with us — Wey
So one of the men who has been associated with us — Gspd
It would be wise to choose one of the men who has been with us — Nor
all the time that the Lord Jesus went in and out among us,
... moved about among us — TCNT

22. **Beginning from the baptism of John,**
from his baptism by John — TCNT
from John's ministry of baptism — NEB
unto that same day that he was taken up from us,
down to the day on which he was taken up away from us — TCNT
must one be ordained to be a witness with us of his resurrection.
must one become a witness ... — ASV
some one must be found to join us as a witness ... — TCNT
one of these men must join with us and become a witness to testify to His resurrection — Amp

23. **And they appointed two,**
And they put forward two — RSV
So they brought forward two men — Mof
Then they proposed two men — Gspd
Then they nominated two men — Wms
Joseph called Barsabas,
... who was known as Barsabbas — NEB

who was surnamed Justus,
and bore the added name of Justus — NEB
and Matthias.

24. **And they prayed, and said,**
and they offered this prayer — TCNT
Thou, Lord, which knowest the hearts of all men,
... knower of all hearts — Ber
shew whether of these two thou hast chosen,
show of these two the one whom thou hast chosen — ASV
show clearly which of these two ... — Wey
make clear which one of these two ... — Ber

25. **That he may take part of this ministry and apostleship,**
to take the place in this ministry ... — RSV
to fill the place in this apostolic ministry — Mof
to take this place of service as an apostle — Gspd
to take a share in this service as an apostle — Wms
to serve in this office of apostle — Beck
from which Judas by transgression fell,
from which Judas fell away — ASY
from which Judas turned aside — NASB
that he might go to his own place.
to go where he belonged — Gspd

26. **And they gave forth their lots;**
Then they drew lots between them — TCNT
Then they cast lots for them — Mof
and the lot fell upon Matthias;
and the decision was given for Matthias — Bas
and so Matthias was chosen — Beck
and he was numbered with the eleven apostles.
and ... he was added to the number of the eleven Apostles — TCNT
and a place with the eleven Apostles was voted to him — Wey
and he was enrolled with ... — RSV

CHAPTER 2

1. **And when the day of Pentecost was fully come,**
In the course of the Harvest Thanksgiving-day — TCNT

On the day of the Harvest Festival — Gspd
While the Day of Pentecost was running its course — NEB

they were all with one accord in one place.

they were all together in one place — RSV

the disciples had all met together — TCNT

2. And suddenly there came a sound from heaven

suddenly there came from the heavens a noise — TCNT

as of a rushing mighty wind,

as of the rushing of a mighty wind — — ASV

like that of a strong wind coming nearer and nearer — TCNT

like a violent blast of wind — Mof

like the rushing of a violent tempest blast — Amp

and it filled all the house where they were sitting.

3. And there appeared unto them cloven tongues like as of fire,

And there appeared unto them tongues parting asunder . . . — ASV

. . . tongues of what appeared to be flame, separating — TCNT

. . . tongues of what looked like fire, distributing themselves over the assembly — Wey

and it sat upon each of them.

so that one settled on each of them — TCNT

and on the head of each person a tongue alighted — Wey

one resting on the head of each — Mof

4. And they were all filled with the Holy Ghost,

. . . Holy Spirit — ASV

and began to speak with other tongues,

. . . in foreign tongues — Mof

. . . in foreign languages — Gspd

. . . in different tongues — Bas

. . . in different languages — Phi

as the Spirit gave them utterance.

as the Spirit prompted their utterances — TCNT

according as the Spirit gave them words to utter — Wey

as the Spirit enabled them to express themselves — Mof

as the Spirit granted them to utter divine things — Wms

. . . was giving unto them to be sounding forth — Rhm

. . . gave them power to proclaim His Message — Phi

5. And there were dwelling at Jerusalem Jews, devout men,

Now there were in Jerusalem sojourning Jews, reverent men — Rhm

There were then staying in Jerusalem religious Jews — TCNT

. . . devout Jews — Mof

. . . Jews, God-fearing men — Bas

. . . Jews of deep faith — Phi

. . . pious Jews — Nor

out of every nation under heaven.

from every part of the world — Wey

from many and distant lands — Mon

6. Now when this was noised abroad,

And when this sound was heard — ASV

So when this noise was heard — Wey

And when this speaking was heard — Nor

And when this sound occurred — NASB

the multitude came together, and were confounded,

the throng came together and were thrown into confusion — Rhm

they came crowding together and were amazed — Wey

the crowd rushed together in great excitement — Wms

. . . and they were bewildered — RSV

because that every man heard them speak in his own language.

because each of them heard the disciples speaking . . . — TCNT

7. And they were all amazed and marvelled,

They were beside themselves with wonder — Wey

All were amazed and astonished — Mof

saying one to another,

saying — ASV

Behold, are not all these which speak Galileans?

8. And how hear we every man in our own tongue, wherein we were born?

. . . our own language . . . — ASV

. . . in our own native language—TCNT

. . . in the language which was ours from our birth — Bas

9. Parthians, and Medes, and Elamites,

Some of us are Parthians, some Medes, some Elamites — TCNT

and the dwellers in Mesopotamia, and in Judaea, and Cappadocia, in Pontus, and Asia,

and some of us live in Mesopotamia . . . — TCNT

inhabitants of Mesopotamia . . .—Wey
residents in Mesopotamia . . . — Mof

**10. Phrygia, and Pamphylia, in Egypt, and
in parts of Libya about Cyrene,**

of Phrygia and Pamphylia, of Egypt
and of parts of Africa towards Cyrene — Wey

. . . Egypt and the parts of Libya belonging to Cyrene — RSV

and strangers of Rome,

some of us are visitors from Rome —
TCNT

transient dwellers from Rome — Wms

Jews and proselytes,

either Jews by birth or converts—TCNT

Jews and those who have accepted the
Jewish religion — Beck

11. Cretes and Arabians,

Cretans and Arabians — ASV

**we do hear them speak in our tongues
the wonderful works of God.**

We hear them speaking . . . — ASV

. . . about the majesty of God — Wey

. . . talking of the triumphs of God —
Mof

. . . the excellencies of God — Ber

. . . speaking of the magnificence of
God — Phi

**12. And they were all amazed, and were
in doubt,**

But they were all beside themselves,
and were utterly at a loss — Rhm

. . . utterly amazed and bewildered —
TCNT

. . . astounded and bewildered — Wey

. . . amazed and perplexed — RSV

. . . amazed and puzzled — Beck

**saying one to another, What meaneth
this?**

. . . What can this mean — Wey

. . . How will this turn out — Ber

. . . What can it all possibly mean —
Nor

13. Others mocking said,

But others said with a sneer — TCNT

But others, scornfully jeering, said —
Wey

But others in derision were saying —
Wms

But others, making sport of them, said
— Bas

Others said contemptuously — NEB

These men are full of new wine.

They are brimfull of sweet wine—Wey

They are running over with new wine
— Wms

They have been drinking — NEB

They are simply drunk with new wine
— Nor

14. But Peter, standing up with the eleven,

Then arose Peter, representing the
eleven — Ber

Then Peter, with the Eleven standing
by him — Phi

lifted up his voice, and said unto them,

. . . spoke forth unto them — ASV

addressed them in a loud voice — Wey

raised his voice and declared to them
— NASB

**Ye men of Judaea, and all ye that
dwell at Jerusalem,**

Men of Judaea, and all you inhabitants
of Jerusalem — Wey

Men of Judaea and residents in Jerusalem — Mof

Jewish men and Jerusalem residents —
Ber

Fellow Jews, and all you who live in
Jerusalem — NEB

be this known to you,

let me tell you what this means—TCNT

and hearken to my words:

and give ear unto my words — RSV

and mark my words — TCNT

and attend to what I say — Wey

and give close attention to my words —
Wms

**15. For these are not drunken, as ye
suppose,**

You are wrong in thinking that these
men are drunk — TCNT

**seeing it is but the third hour of the
day.**

indeed it is only nine in the morning!
— TCNT

**16. But this is that which was spoken by
the prophet Joel;**

But this is what was predicted by the
prophet Joel — Gspd

**17. And it shall come to pass in the last
days, saith God,**

And it shall be in the last days . . . —
ASV

This will happen in the last days . . . —
NEB

**I will pour out of my Spirit upon all
flesh:**

. . . on all mankind — TCNT

I will pour out upon everyone a portion of my spirit — NEB

**and your sons and your daughters shall
prophesy,**

... shall become Prophets — TCNT

... will speak God's Word — Beck

... prophesy — telling forth the divine counsels — Amp

and your young men shall see visions,

... visions (that is, divinely granted appearances) — Amp

and your old men shall dream dreams:

... dream [divinely suggested] dreams — Amp

18. **And on my servants and on my hand-maidens**

And even upon my men-servants and upon my maid-servants — Rhm

Even on the servants — for they are mine — both men and women — TCNT

on my very slaves and slave-girls — Mof

Even on your servants, men and women alike — Nor

I will pour out in those days of my Spirit;

At that time I will pour out My Spirit — Wey

and they shall prophesy:

... prophesy — telling forth the divine counsels and predicting future events pertaining especially to God's kingdom — Amp

19. **And I will shew wonders in heaven above,**

I will display marvels in the sky above — Wey

I will grant wonders in the sky above — NASB

I will give you startling wonders in the sky above — Beck

and signs in the earth beneath;

... on the earth below — TCNT

blood, and fire, and vapour of smoke:

... mist of smoke — TCNT

... cloud of smoke — Wey

... thick smoke — Gspd

... whirling smoke — Knox

... drifting smoke — NEB

... smoking vapor — Amp

20. **The sun shall be turned into darkness,**

The sun will become darkness — TCNT

... shall be changed into darkness — Mof

The sun will become dark — Bas

and the moon into blood,

And the moon blood-red — TCNT

before that great and notable day of the Lord come:

Before the day of the Lord come, That great and notable day — ASV

... the great and manifest day — Rhm

To usher in the day of the Lord—That great and illustrious day — Wey

ere the great, open Day of the Lord arrives — Mof

Before the coming of the great and glorious day of the Lord — Wms

before that great and conspicuous Day of the Lord arrives — Ber

before that great, resplendent day, the day of the Lord, shall come — NEB

21. **And it shall come to pass,**

And it shall be — RSV

And then — NEB

that whosoever shall call on the name of the Lord

... every one who invokes ... — TCNT

And whoever makes his prayer to the Lord — Bas

... Lord — that is, invoking, adoring and worshipping the Lord (Christ) — Amp

shall be saved.

22. **Ye men of Israel, hear these words;**

Men of Israel, listen to this — TCNT

Fellow Israelites, listen to what I say — Wms

Oh men of Israel, listen! — Tay

Jesus of Nazareth, a man approved of God among you

Jesus the Nazarene, a Man pointed out of God unto you — Rhm

... a man whose mission from God was proved — TCNT

... a man accredited to you from God ... — Wey

... a man whom God commended to you — Gspd

... a man attested to you by God — RSV

... a man singled out by God and made known to you — NEB

by miracles and wonders and signs, which God did by him in the midst of you,

... through him ... — Rhm

as ye yourselves also know:

as you personally know — Ber

23. **Him, being delivered by the determinate counsel and foreknowledge of God,**

him, being delivered up ... — ASV

... in accordance with God's definite

plan and with his previous knowledge — TCNT

. . . through God's settled purpose . . . — Wey

. . . in the predestined course of God's deliberate purpose — Mof

. . . by the fixed purpose and intention of God — Gspd

. . . by the deliberate will and plan of God — NEB

ye have taken, and by wicked hands
Ye by the hand of lawless men — ASV

. . . with the help of heathen men — TCNT

. . . by the hand of godless men — NASB

have crucified and slain:
did crucify and slay — ASV

nailed him to a cross and put him to death — TCNT

24. **Whom God hath raised up,**
But God has raised Him to life — Wey

having loosed the pains of death:
. . . the pangs of death — RSV

released him from the pangs of death — TCNT

by unfastening the cords of death — Ber

releasing him from the agony of death — Rieu

putting an end to the agony of death — NASB

because it was not possible that he should be holden of it.
it being impossible for death to retain its hold upon him — TCNT

It was not possible for him to be held fast by death — Wey

for death could not control him — Gspd

since it was impossible for him to be held by the power of death — Wms

there was nothing by which death could hold such a Man — Phi

it was not possible for death to master him — Rieu

because it could not be that death should keep him in its grip — NEB

25. **For David speaketh concerning him,**
I foresaw the Lord always before my face,
I beheld . . . — ASV

I saw the Lord always before me — RSV

I have had the Lord ever before my eyes — TCNT

I have ever fixed my eyes upon the Lord — Wey

I constantly regarded the Lord before me — Gspd

I always kept my eyes upon the Lord — Wms

I foresaw that the presence of the Lord would be with me always — NEB

I was always beholding the Lord in my presence — NASB

for he is on my right hand,
. . . at my right hand — RSV

that I should not be moved:
that I may not be shaken — Rhm

that I should not be disquieted — TCNT

so that I need not be disturbed — Nor

lest I be overthrown — Rieu

26. **Therefore did my heart rejoice,**
therefore my heart was glad — RSV

Therefore my heart was cheered — TCNT

For this my heart is gladdened — Ber

and my tongue was glad;
and my tongue rejoiced — ASV

and my tongue exulted — Rhm

. . . told its delight — TCNT

. . . rejoices — Gspd

. . . greatly rejoiced — ABUV

. . . is jubilant — Ber

. . . exulted exceedingly — Amp

moreover also my flesh shall rest in hope:
. . . shall dwell . . . — ASV

Yea further even my flesh shall encamp on hope — Rhm

Yes, even my body, too, will rest in hope — TCNT

My very body also shall pitch its tent in hope — Mon

And my body still lives in hope — Wms

my body, too, shall rest in confidence — Knox

27. **Because thou wilt not leave my soul in hell,**
Because thou wilt not leave my soul unto hades — ASV

For thou wilt not abandon my soul to the Place of Death — TCNT

Because thou wilt not forsake my soul in the grave — Mof

For you will not desert my soul in death — Gspd

neither wilt thou suffer thine Holy One to see corruption.

Nor give up Thy Holy One to undergo
decay — Wey

nor let thy holy one suffer decay —
Mof

You will not let your Holy One be destroyed — Gspd

Nor let thy loyal servant suffer corruption — NEB

28. **Thou hast made known to me the
ways of life;**

Thou hast shown me the path of life
— TCNT

**thou shalt make me full of joy with
thy countenance.**

. . . full of gladness . . . — RSV

Thou wilt fill me with happiness in
thy presence — TCNT

Thou wilt fill me with gladness in Thy
presence — Wey

thou wilt fill me with delight in thy
presence — Mof

I will be full of joy when I see your
face — Bas

Thou wilt fill me with good cheer in
Thy presence — Ber

You will fill Me with joy by being with
Me — Beck

And you will delight Me with the sight
of Your face — Nor

You will enrapture Me — diffusing My
soul with joy — with and in Your
presence — Amp

29. **Men and brethren,**

Brethren — ASV

Brother-men — Ber

Men and brother Jews — Phi

**let me freely speak unto you of the
patriarch David,**

I may say unto you freely . . . — ASV

it is allowable to say with freedom of
speech unto you concerning the patriarch David — Rhm

I can speak to you confidently about
. . . — TCNT

As to the patriarch David, I need hardly remind you — Wey

I can speak quite plainly to you . . . —
Mof

I can say this . . . without fear of contradiction — Knox

that he is both dead and buried,

That he both died and was buried —
ASV

**and his sepulchre is with us unto this
day.**

and his tomb is with us unto this day
— ASV

. . . we still have his tomb among us —
Wey

and his grave is here among us to this
very day — Gspd

30. **Therefore being a prophet,**

Speaking, then, as a Prophet — TCNT

It is clear therefore that he spoke as
a prophet — NEB

And so, because he was a prophet —
NASB

**and knowing that God had sworn with
an oath to him,**

. . . had solemnly sworn to him — TCNT

. . . had promised him with an oath —
Gspd

. . . had made a solemn vow — Rieu

**that of the fruit of his loins, accord-
ing to the flesh, he would raise up
Christ[1] to sit on his throne;**

that of the fruit of his loins he would
set one upon his throne — ASV

to set one of his descendants upon . . .
— TCNT

31. **He seeing this before spake of the resurrection of Christ,**

he foreseeing this . . . — ASV

David looked into the future and was
referring to . . . — TCNT

with prophetic foresight he spoke of
. . . — Wey

David saw what was ahead and said the
promised Savior would rise again —
Beck

that his soul[2] was not left in hell,

That neither was he left unto hades —
ASV

that he had not been abandoned to the
Place of Death — TCNT

to the effect that He was not left forsaken in the grave — Wey

for he was not deserted in death —
Gspd

. . . in the realm of the dead — Nor

He was not deserted when He was
dead — Beck

neither his flesh did see corruption.

nor did his flesh see corruption — ASV

---

[1]The words "according to the flesh, he would
raise up Christ" are now recognized as not
adequately supported by original manuscripts.
[2]The words "his soul" are now recognized as
not adequately supported by original manuscripts.

nor did His body undergo decay—Wey

and his body was not destroyed—Gspd

and His body did not experience decay — Beck

32. This Jesus hath God raised up,

It was this Jesus, whom God raised to life — TCNT

Jesus is this One, and God has now raised Him up — Nor

whereof we all are witnesses.

and of that fact we are ourselves all witnesses — TCNT

a fact to which all of us testify — Wey

as we all can bear witness — Mof

and to whose resurrection we are all witnesses — Gspd

a fact of which all of us are eyewitnesses! — Phi

33. Therefore being by the right hand of God exalted,

So then, now that he has been exalted to the right hand of God — TCNT

Being therefore lifted high by the right hand of God — Wey

Since he is by the mighty hand of God exalted — Mon

And now He sits on the throne of highest honor in heaven, next to God — Tay

and having received of the Father the promise of the Holy Ghost,

He has received from the Father the promised Holy Spirit — Wey

. . . the long-promised holy Spirit — Mof

. . . the promised gift of the Holy Spirit — TCNT

he hath shed forth this,

He hath poured forth this — ASV

and has poured forth that Spirit—Rieu

which ye now see and hear.

as you now see and hear for yourselves — TCNT

in your sight and hearing — Rieu

34. For David is not ascended into the heavens:

For it was not David who went up into Heaven — TCNT

For David did not go up to heaven — Gspd

David never ascended to Heaven—Phi

No, it was not David who ascended to heaven — Nor

but he saith himself,

Indeed he says himself — TCNT

The LORD said unto my Lord,

The Lord said to my master — TCNT

The Lord God said unto MY LORD — Rieu

Sit thou on my right hand,

Sit at my right hand — Wey

35. Until I make thy foes thy footstool.

Till I make thine enemies the footstool of thy feet — ASV

Till I put thy enemies as a footstool under thy feet — TCNT

36. Therefore let all the house of Israel know assuredly,

So let all Israel know beyond all doubt — TCNT

Therefore the whole nation of Israel must understand — Gspd

Without a shadow of doubt, then, let the whole house of Israel acknowledge — Ber

Let all Israel then accept as certain — NEB

that God hath made that same Jesus, whom ye have crucified, both Lord and Christ.

that God hath made him both Lord and Christ, this Jesus whom ye crucified — ASV

that God has made him both Master and Christ — this very Jesus whom you crucified — TCNT

37. Now when they heard this, they were pricked in their heart,

When the people heard this, they were conscience-smitten — TCNT

. . . it went straight to their hearts — Mof

. . . they were stung to the heart — Gspd

. . . they were stabbed to the heart — Wms

. . . they were moved to the depths of their hearts — Ber

. . . their consciences were stung — Knox

. . . they were cut to the heart — RSV

. . . they were pierced to the heart — NASB

. . . they felt crushed — Beck

and said unto Peter and to the rest of the apostles,

and said to Peter and the rest of the Apostles — TCNT

They asked Peter and the other apostles — Beck

Men and brethren, what shall we do?

What are we to do, Brothers — TCNT

Men and fellow Jews, what shall we do now — Phi

Friends, what are we to do — NEB

Fellow Jews, what should we do — Beck

38. Then Peter said unto them, Repent,

You must repent, Peter answered — TCNT

. . . Each one of you must turn from sin, return to God — Tay

. . . Repent — change your views, and purpose to accept the will of God in your inner selves instead of rejecting it — Amp

and be baptized every one of you in the name of Jesus Christ for the remission of sins,

— and, as an expression of it, let every one of you be baptized in the name of Jesus Christ — that you may have your sins forgiven — Wms

And let each one of you be immersed . . . into the remission of your sins — Rhm

and be immersed every one of you, in the name of Jesus Christ, unto remission of your sins — ABUV

. . . for the forgiveness of your sins — TCNT

. . . in order to have your sins forgiven — Gspd

. . . so that you may have your sins forgiven — Phi

. . . in the name of Jesus the Messiah . . . — NEB

and ye shall receive the gift of the Holy Ghost.

. . . the Holy Spirit — RSV

. . . the free-gift of the Holy Spirit — Rhm

and you will have the Holy Spirit given to you — Bas

then you also shall receive this gift, the Holy Spirit — Tay

39. For the promise is unto you, and to your children,

For the promise is for you . . . — TCNT

For to you belongs the promise . . . — Wey

For the promise is meant for you . . . — Mof

For it is to you and your children that this great Message comes — Phi

and to all that are afar off,

as well as to all those far away — Gspd

and to all those in distant times and places — Rieu

even as many as the Lord our God shall call.

. . . shall call unto him — ASV

every one whom the Lord our God calls to him — RSV

for anyone whom the Lord our God may call to himself — Mof

[even] to as many as the Lord our God invites and bids come to Himself — Amp

40. And with many other words did he testify and exhort, saying,

And with many different words bare he full witness, and went on exhorting them saying — Rhm

In many other ways Peter bore his testimony, and urged the people — TCNT

And with many more appeals he solemnly warned and entreated them, saying — Wey

With many more words he continued to testify and to plead with them — Wms

Peter continued his speech for a long time, and appealed to them repeatedly — Rieu

In these and many other words he pressed his case and pleaded with them — NEB

Save yourselves from this untoward generation.

. . . this crooked generation — ASV

Be saved from this perverse generation — Rhm

to find safety from that perverse age — TCNT

Escape from this perverse generation — Wey

. . . this false-minded generation — Knox

. . . this perverted generation — Phi

. . . this wicked generation — Nor

41. Then they that gladly received his word were baptized:

Those therefore, who joyfully welcomed his word . . . — Wey

So those who accepted what he said . . . — Mof

So all those who had taken his words to heart . . . — Knox

Then those, who welcomed his message, were baptized — Ber

and the same day there were added unto them about three thousand souls.

and about three thousand joined the disciples on that day alone — TCNT

and there were added that day about three thousand souls — RSV

and on that day alone . . . were added to the number of disciples — Phi

Thus . . . were added to the believers that day — Nor

42. And they continued stedfastly

And they went on to give constant attention — Rhm

They were regularly present — TCNT

and they were constant in attendance — Wey

They devoted themselves — Mof

These occupied themselves continually — Knox

They met constantly — NEB

And they were continually devoting themselves — NASB

They were loyal — Beck

And they steadfastly persevered, devoting themselves constantly — Amp

in the apostles' doctrine and fellowship,

in the apostles' teaching . . . — ASV

at the teaching of the Apostles and at the sharing of the offerings — TCNT

to the instruction given by the apostles and to fellowship — Mof

to the teaching and the society of the apostles — Gspd

to the teaching of the apostles and to fellowship with one another — Wms

learning the teaching of the Apostles, and joined in their fellowship — Phi

to hear the apostles teach, and to share the common life — NEB

and in breaking of bread, and in prayers.

in the breaking of bread and the prayers — ASV

as well as at the Breaking of the Bread and at the Prayers — TCNT

breaking bread and praying together — Mof

43. And fear came upon every soul:

A deep impression was made upon every one — TCNT

Awe came upon every one — Wey

Everyone felt a sense of awe — Gspd

A sense of reverence seized everyone — Wms

and every soul was struck with awe — Knox

A sense of awe was everywhere — NEB

And a sense of awe (reverential fear) . . . — Amp

and many wonders and signs were done by the apostles.

and many wonders and signs through means of the apostles were coming to pass — Rhm

and many marvels . . . were wrought by the Apostles — Wey

44. And all that believed were together, and had all things common;

All who had become believers in Christ agreed in having everything in common — TCNT

And all the believers kept together, and had everything in common — Wey

The believers all shared everything they had with one another — Gspd

. . . and held all they had as common goods to be shared by one another — Wms

All the faithful held together, and shared all they had — Knox

The believers all met together and had everything jointly — Ber

They lived as a community and shared everything — Rieu

45. And sold their possessions and goods, and parted them to all men, as every man had need.

And their possessions and goods were they selling, and distributing them unto all in so far as anyone had need — Rhm

And so they continued to sell their property and goods and to distribute the money to all, as anyone had special need — Wms

They would sell their lands and other property, and distribute the proceeds among all, just as any one from time to time had need — Mon

46. And they, continuing daily with one accord in the temple,

And daily giving attendance with one intent . . . — Rhm

Every day, too, they met regularly in the Temple Courts — TCNT

445

Daily they regularly frequented the temple with a united purpose — Ber

Day after day they met by common consent . . . — Phi

Every day they met in the Temple in unity of spirit — Rieu

All were one at heart as they went to the temple regularly every day — Beck

and breaking bread from house to house,

and breaking bread at home — ASV

and broke bread together in their own homes — Mof

they practiced breaking their bread together in their homes — Wms

Likewise they observed the breaking of bread in their homes — Nor

breaking bread in private houses — NEB

They had their meals in their homes — Beck

did eat their meat with gladness and singleness of heart,

they took their food . . . — ASV

they were partaking of food with exultation . . . — Rhm

partaking of their food in simple-hearted gladness — TCNT

they took their meals with great happiness and single-heartedness — Wey

they ate with a glad and simple heart — Mof

they partook of food with glad and generous hearts — RSV

sharing meals with simple joy — Phi

shared their meals with unaffected joy — NEB

they continued to eat their food with gladness and an undivided heart — Mon

47. Praising God, and having favour with all the people.

continually praising God, and winning respect from all the people — TCNT

. . . and enjoying the good will of all the people — Ber

And the Lord added to the church daily such as should be saved.

And the Lord added to them day by day those that were saved — ASV

Also day by day the Lord added to their number those whom He was saving — Wey

And every day the Lord continued to add to them the people who were being saved — Wms

while daily the Lord added to the group those who were being saved — Ber

and the Lord increased their community daily by new converts — Rieu

CHAPTER 3

1. Now Peter and John went up together into the temple

Now Peter and John were going up into . . . — ASV

at the hour of prayer, being the ninth hour.

for the hour of prayer — the ninth — Rhm

during the time of the three o'clock Prayers — TCNT

2. And a certain man lame from his mother's womb was carried,

. . . was being carried — Rhm

and, just then, some men were carrying there one who had been lame from his birth — Wey

Now a man who had been a cripple from birth used to be carried there — NEB

whom they laid daily at the gate of the temple which is called Beautiful,

. . . at the door . . . — ASV

The man used to be set down every day at the gate of the Temple called the Beautiful Gate — TCNT

to ask alms of them that entered into the temple;

to beg from the people as they went in — Wey

so he could beg the people for gifts as they went . . . — Beck

3. Who seeing Peter and John about to go into the temple asked an alms.

. . . asked to receive an alms — ASV

. . . was requesting to receive an alms — Rhm

. . . he kept asking them for alms — Mon

. . . he began asking to receive alms — NASB

4. And Peter, fastening his eyes upon him with John,

But Peter directed his gaze at him — RSV

But Peter looking steadfastly at him
 . . . — Rhm

Peter fixing his eyes on him, as did
 John also — Wey

Peter looked him straight in the eye,
 and so did John . . . — Wms

And Peter, along with John, fixed his
 gaze upon him . . . — NASB

said, Look on us.

 . . . Look straight at us! — Phi

5. And he gave heed unto them,

 The man gave them his attention —
 TCNT

 So he looked and waited — Wey

 So he watched them closely — Ber

 the man was all attention — NEB

 He turned in their direction — Rieu

**expecting to receive something of
 them.**

 . . . from them — RSV

 supposing they were going to give him
 something — Gspd

 Expecting a gift from them — NEB

**6. Then Peter said, Silver and gold have
 I none;**

 . . . I do not possess silver and gold —
 NASB

but such as I have give I thee:

 but I will give you what I do have —
 Mof

**In the name of Jesus Christ of Naz-
 areth rise up[3] and walk.**

 In the name of Jesus Christ of Nazareth, walk — ASV

 In the name of Jesus Christ of Nazareth, get up and walk! — Nor

**7. And he took him by the right hand,
 and lifted him up:**

 . . . raised him up — RSV

 And laying hold of him by the right
 hand he raised him up — Rhm

 Grasping the lame man . . . Peter lifted
 him up — TCNT

 Then he took him . . . and helped him
 up — Phi

 And grasping him . . . he pulled him to
 his feet — Rieu

**and immediately his feet and ancle
 bones received strength.**

 and instantly were his feet and ankles
 strengthened — Rhm

 Instantly his feet and ankles grew firm
 — Ber

8. And he leaping up stood, and walked,

 and leaping forward he stood, and
 walked — Rhm

and jumping up, he began to walk
 about — TCNT

he sprang up, stood on his feet, and
 started to walk — NEB

And with a leap, he stood upright and
 began to walk — NASB

and entered with them into the temple,

 and then went with them into the Temple Courts — TCNT

**walking, and leaping, and praising
 God.**

 walking, jumping, and praising God —
 TCNT

 where he walked about, leaping and
 praising God — Phi

**9. And all the people saw him walking
 and praising God:**

 All the people saw him walking about
 . . . — TCNT

**10. And they knew that it was he which
 sat for alms at the Beautiful gate of
 the temple:**

 And they began to recognize him, that
 the same was he who for the alms
 used to sit at the Beautiful Gate of
 the temple — Rhm

 and recognized him as the beggar who
 used to sit at the Beautiful Gate of
 the Temple — Rieu

**and they were filled with wonder and
 amazement at that which had happened unto him.**

 they were utterly astonished and
 amazed at what had happened to
 him — TCNT

 they were filled with awe and amazement . . . — Wey

 they were completely astounded and
 bewildered . . . — Wms

**11. And as the lame man which was
 healed[4] held Peter and John,**

 And he held fast Peter and John — ASV

 While he was still clinging to . . . —
 Wms

 And he would not let go of Peter and
 John — Knox

all the people ran together unto them

 all the people quickly gathered round
 them — TCNT

---

[3]The words "rise up" are now recognized as
not adequately supported by original manuscripts.

[4]The words "the lame man which was healed"
are now recognized as not adequately supported by original manuscripts.

in the porch that is called Solomon's,
in the portico called Solomon's — RSV
in the Colonnade called after Solomon — TCNT
in what was known as Solomon's Portico — Wey
in what was known as Solomon's Colonnade — Gspd
greatly wondering.
greatly amazed — Rhm
in the greatest astonishment — TCNT
awe-struck — Wey
in the utmost astonishment — Gspd
in utter amazement — Wms
beside themselves with wonder — Knox

12. **And when Peter saw it, he answered unto the people,**
On seeing this, Peter spoke to the people — TCNT
where Peter, seeing his opportunity, addressed them — Rieu
Ye men of Israel, why marvel ye at this?
Men of Israel, why do you wonder at this — RSV
Men of Israel, why are you surprised at this — Mof
... why does this astonish you — Knox
... what is there in this that so astonishes you — Rieu
or why look ye so earnestly on us,
or why fasten ye your eyes on us — ASV
Or upon us why are ye intently looking — Rhm
and why do you stare so at us — TCNT
Or why gaze at us — Wey
as though by our own power or holiness we had made this man to walk?
... power or godliness ... — Rhm
as though we, by any power or piety of our own, had enabled this man to walk — TCNT

13. **The God of Abraham, and of Isaac, and of Jacob,**
The God of Abraham and Isaac and Jacob — Rhm
the God of our fathers,
The God of our ancestors — TCNT
the God of our forefathers — Wey
hath glorified his Son Jesus;
glorified his servant Jesus — RSV
hath glorified his Servant Jesus — ASV
has done honour to his Servant Jesus — TCNT

Who has done this thing to honor His Servant Jesus — Phi
has given the highest honour to his servant Jesus — NEB
whom ye delivered up,
though you indeed surrendered him — TCNT
whom you yourselves betrayed — Wms
whom you committed for trial — NEB
and denied him in the presence of Pilate,
and denied before the face of Pilate — ASV
and disowned him even before Pilate — TCNT
and repudiated in Pilate's court — NEB
when he was determined to let him go.
when he had decided to release him — RSV
when Pilate's voice was for setting him free — Knox
after Pilate had decided to acquit him — Rieu
after he had made up his mind to set Him free — Nor

14. **But ye denied the Holy One and the Just,**
But ye denied the Holy and Righteous One — ASV
Yes, you disowned the holy and righteous One — Wey
but you repudiated the Holy and Just One — Mof
and desired a murderer to be granted unto you;
and asked for yourselves the release of a murderer! — TCNT
and asked as a favour the release of a murderer — Wey
You demanded the release of a murderer — Rieu

15. **And killed the Prince of life,**
But the Princely Leader of Life ye slew — Rhm
The very Guide to Life you put to death — TCNT
and you killed the pioneer of Life — Mof
and killed the very source of life — Gspd
while you killed the author of life — Knox
and murdered the Author of Life — Rieu

and killed him who has led the way to life — NEB

You killed the Lord and Giver of life — Beck

whom God hath raised from the dead;

Whom God raised from among the dead — Rhm

but God has raised Him from the dead — Wey

whereof we are witnesses.

To this we are witnesses — RSV

and of that fact we are ourselves witnesses — TCNT

as we can testify — Gspd

and we are here to bear witness of it — Knox

16. And his name through faith in his name hath made this man strong, whom ye see and know:

And by faith in his name hath his name . . . — ASV

And it is by faith in the name of Jesus, that this man, whom you all see and know, has — by his name — been made strong — TCNT

In virtue of faith in His name, His name has strengthened this man whom you behold and know — Wey

It is His name, that is, on condition of faith in His name — that has made strong again this man whom you see and recognize — Wms

Here is a man you all know by sight, who has put his faith in that name, and that name has brought him strength — Knox

And the name of Jesus, by awakening faith, has strengthened this man, whom you see and know — NEB

yea, the faith which is by him hath given him this perfect soundness in the presence of you all.

Yes, it is the faith inspired by Jesus that has made this complete cure of the man, before the eyes of you all — TCNT

and the faith which He has bestowed has entirely restored this man, as you can all see — Wey

it is the faith He inspires which has made the man thus hale and whole before you all — Mof

Yes, faith inspired by Him has given this man the perfect health you all see — Wms

And this faith has made him completely well, as you can all see for yourselves — NEB

17. And now, brethren, I wot that through ignorance ye did it, as did also your rulers.

And now, fellow Jews . . . — Beck

And now, brethren, I know that it was in ignorance . . . — Wey

Yet I know, brothers, that you did not know what you were doing, any more than your leaders did — Gspd

. . . you did not realize what you were doing . . . — Wms

. . . you had no idea what you were doing . . . — Phi

18. But those things, which God before had shewed by the mouth of all his prophets, that Christ should suffer, he hath so fulfilled.

But the things which God foreshowed by the mouth of all the prophets, that his Christ should suffer, he thus fulfilled — ASV

But it was in this way that God fulfilled all that he had long ago foretold, as to the sufferings of his Christ, by the lips of all the Prophets — TCNT

But in this way God has fulfilled the declarations He made through all the Prophets, that His Christ would suffer — Wey

19. Repent ye therefore, and be converted,

. . . and turn again — RSV

You must, therefore, repent and turn — Wey

So repent and turn to God — Gspd

Repent, then, and turn back to him — Knox

that your sins may be blotted out,

for your sins to be wiped away — TCNT

so that the record of your sins may be cancelled — Wey

to have your sins wiped out — Gspd

so that your sins may be completely taken away — Bas

when the times of refreshing shall come from the presence of the Lord;

so there may come seasons of refreshing . . . — ASV

to the end that in that case there may come seasons of refreshing from the face of the Lord — Rhm

and then better and brighter days will come direct from the Lord himself — TCNT

so that a breathing-space may be vouchsafed you — Mof
that times of revival may come . . . —
Wms
Then the Lord may grant you a time
of recovery — NEB

**20. And he shall send Jesus Christ, which
before was preached unto you:**
and that he may send the Christ who
hath been appointed for you, even
Jesus — ASV
And he may send forth him who had
been fore-appointed for you—Christ
Jesus — Rhm
and he will send you, in Jesus, your
long-appointed Christ — TCNT
and he will send Jesus, your destined
Christ — Gspd
and that he may send the Christ appointed for you, Jesus — RSV
. . . your destined Messiah, Jesus —
Rieu

21. Whom the heaven must receive
But Heaven must be his home — TCNT
Yet he must remain in heaven — Gspd
Yet heaven must retain him — Wms
**until the times of restitution of all
things,**
. . . of restoration of all things — ASV
. . . of the due establishment of all
things — Rhm
. . . of universal restoration — TCNT
. . . of the reconstitution of all things
— Wey
. . . of the great Restoration — Mof
. . . for the universal reformation —
Gspd
. . . when all things are put right —
Bas
. . . when all is restored anew — Knox
until the time for establishing all —
RSV
until the whole world is re-created —
Rieu
until the final recovery of all things
from sin — Tay
**which God hath spoken by the mouth
of all his holy prophets since the
world began.**
whereof God spake by the mouth of his
holy prophets that have been from
of old — ASV
of which God has spoken from the
earliest ages through the lips of His
holy Prophets — Wey

that God spake by the mouth of his
holy prophets from of old — RSV
Ages ago God spoke of this by the lips
of . . . — Mof
— from the most ancient time in the
memory of man — Amp
22. For Moses truly said unto the fathers,[5]
Moses indeed said — ASV
Moses, for instance, said long ago —
Tay
**A prophet shall the Lord your God
raise up unto you of your brethren,
like unto me;**
. . . from among your brethren, like
unto me — ASV
The Lord your God will raise up from
among your brothers a Prophet, as
he did me — TCNT
. . . as he raised me — Wey
. . . just as He appointed me — Nor
**him shall ye hear in all things whatso-
ever he shall say unto you.**
you must listen to whatever he may tell
you — Mof
You must attentively listen to everything that he tells you — Wms
Listen to everything he tells you —
Beck
**23. And it shall come to pass, that every
soul, which will not hear that prophet,**
And every one who refuses to listen to
the Prophet — Wey
And it shall be that every soul that
does not heed . . . — NASB
**shall be destroyed from among the
people.**
shall be utterly destroyed . . . — ASV
shall be exterminated from the People
— Mof
will be annihilated . . . — Gspd
**24. Yea, and all the prophets from Sam-
uel and those that follow after, as
many as have spoken,**
Yes, and all the Prophets from Samuel
onwards, and all of their successors
who taught the people — TCNT
All the prophets who have spoken
since Samuel — Nor
And likewise, all the prophets who
have spoken, from Samuel and his
successors onward — NASB
have likewise foretold of these days.

[5]The words "unto the fathers" are now recognized as not adequately supported by original
manuscripts.

they also told of these days — ASV
have also predicted these days — Wey

25. Ye are the children of the prophets,
Ye are the sons of the prophets — ASV
You are yourselves the heirs of the Prophets — TCNT
You are the descendants of the prophets — Gspd

and of the covenant which God made with our fathers,
. . . with your fathers — ASV
. . . with your ancestors — TCNT
and of the covenant which God covenanted . . . — Rhm
and the heirs of the agreement that God made with your forefathers — Gspd
and the heirs of the sacred compact . . . — Wms

saying unto Abraham,
when he said to Abraham — TCNT

And in thy seed shall all the kindreds of the earth be blessed.
In your descendants will all the nations . . . — TCNT
all families on earth shall be blessed in your offspring — Mof
Through a descendant of thine . . . — Rieu
And in your Descendant all the people . . . — Beck

26. Unto you first God,
It was for you first that God — TCNT
It is to you first that God — Wey
It is for you above all others that God — Rieu

having raised up his Son Jesus,[6]
having raised up his Servant — ASV
after raising His Servant from the grave — Wey

sent him to bless you,
sent him to you first, to bless you — RSV
Hath sent him forth, ready to bless you — Rhm
and sent him with blessings for you — TCNT

in turning away every one of you from his iniquities.
When you are turning away, each one, from your wickedness — Rhm
by turning each of you from his wicked ways — TCNT
by causing every one of you to turn from his wickedness — Wey
as each of you turns from his evil ways — Ber
by turning each of you from his sinful way of life — Rieu
each one of you who will turn away from your wicked ways — Nor

CHAPTER 4

1. And as they spake unto the people,
But as they were speaking . . . — Rhm
While Peter and John were still speaking to the people — TCNT
Before they had finished speaking to the crowd — Knox
While they were talking to the people — Beck

the priests,
the Chief Priests — TCNT

and the captain of the temple, and the Sadducees,
with the Officer in charge at the Temple . . . — TCNT
the Commander of the Temple Guard . . . — Wey
the military commander of the temple . . . — Wms
together with the Controller of the Temple . . . — NEB

came upon them,
came up to them — TCNT

came down upon them — Wms
surprised them — Ber
moved toward them — Phi
stepped up to them — Beck

2. Being grieved that they taught the people,
being sore troubled because they taught . . . — ASV
annoyed because they were teaching the people — RSV
being tired out because . . . — Rhm
They were much annoyed because they were teaching . . . — TCNT
highly incensed at their teaching . . . — Wey
greatly disturbed because they were teaching . . . — Gspd
indignant at their teaching the multitude — Knox

---

[6]The word "Jesus" is now recognized as not adequately supported by original manuscripts.

furious with them for teaching . . . — Rieu

exasperated at their teaching . . . — NEB

and preached through Jesus the resurrection from the dead.

and proclaimed in Jesus . . . — ASV

and announcing in Jesus the resurrection from among the dead — Rhm

and proclaiming Jesus as an instance of . . . — Mof

and declaring that in the case of Jesus there had been a . . . — Gspd

and for trying to prove the doctrine of the resurrection from the dead by quoting the case of Jesus — Rieu

and preaching that in Jesus the dead rise — Beck

3. And they laid hands on them,

They arrested the Apostles — TCNT

and put them in hold unto the next day:

and put them in ward unto the morrow — ASV

and put them in custody for the morrow — Rhm

and put them in prison till the next day — TCNT

and . . . jailed them overnight — Tay

for it was now eventide.

for it was already evening — RSV

as it was already evening — TCNT

4. Howbeit many of them which heard the word believed;

Many, however, of those who had heard their Message believed it — TCNT

But many of those who had heard the message became believers — NEB

and the number of the men was about five thousand.

. . . came to be about five thousand — ASV

and the number of the men alone mounted up to some five thousand — TCNT

5. And it came to pass on the morrow,

The next day — TCNT

Next morning — Mof

that their rulers, and elders, and scribes,

the leading men, Councillors, and Rabbis — TCNT

the leading members of the council . . . — Gspd

their magistrates . . . — Amp

their rulers, elders, and Bible scholars — Beck

6. And Annas the high priest, and Caiaphas, and John, and Alexander,

. . . Jonathan, Alexander — Rieu

and as many as were of the kindred of the high priest,

. . . of high-priestly descent — Rhm

and all the High Priest's relations — TCNT

and the other members of the High Priest's family — Wey

and whoever belonged to the high priest's clan — Ber

and all the Chief Priests — Rieu

were gathered together at Jerusalem.[7]

7. And when they had set them in the midst,

They had Peter and John brought before them — TCNT

So they made the Apostles stand forward — Wey

Then they made the men stand before them — Mon

and placing them in the center — Ber

They summoned the prisoners into their presence — Rieu

They brought the apostles before the court — NEB

they asked,

and began the examination — NEB

they enquired — RSV

and demanded of them — Wey

and repeatedly inquired of them — Wms

they asked them formally — Phi

By what power, or by what name, have ye done this?

By what power, or in what name . . . — ASV

In what power, or in what name, did ye do this — ABUV

By what authority, in whose name, . . . Mof

By what sort of power and authority . . . — Wms

By what power and on whose authority . . . — Rieu

By what power or authority have men like you done this — Gspd

8. Then Peter, filled with the Holy Ghost,

. . . the Holy Spirit — ASV

---

[7]In some manuscripts this clause appears in verse 5, and it is placed there in most modern translations.

. . . because he was filled . . . — Wms

. . . Guided by the Holy Spirit, Peter — Rieu

said unto them,

spoke as follows — TCNT

Ye rulers of the people, and elders of Israel,[8]

Ye rulers of the people, and elders — ASV

Leaders of the people and Councillors — TCNT

Rulers and elders of the people — Wey

Leaders of the people and members of the council — Gspd

O you rulers of the people, and men of authority — Bas

Honorable leaders and elders of our nation — Tay

9. If we this day be examined of the good deed done to the impotent man,

. . . are examined concerning a good deed done to an impotent man — ASV

. . . are to be examined for doing good to a sick man — Rhm

since we are on trial to-day for a kind act done to a helpless man — TCNT

if we are being cross-examined to-day upon a benefit rendered to a cripple — Mof

if we are on trial today for a benefit done to a sick man — NASB

by what means he is made whole;

In whom this man hath been made well — Rhm

as to how this man has been cured — Wey

by what means this man has been healed — RSV

10. Be it known unto you all, and to all the people of Israel,

So let me tell you all . . . — TCNT

you and the people of Israel must all understand — Mof

then you and all . . . should know — Ber

that by the name of Jesus Christ of Nazareth,

that it is by the authority of . . . — TCNT

that through the name of . . . — Wey

that it is through the power of . . . — Gspd

. . . in the name of Jesus Christ the Nazarene — Rhm

whom ye crucified, whom God raised from the dead,

. . . whom God raised from among the dead — Rhm

even by him doth this man stand here before you whole.

even in him . . . — ASV

it is, I say, by his authority that this man stands here before you cured — TCNT

through that name this man stands here before you in perfect health — Wey

. . . strong and well — Mof

. . . in prime condition — Ber

11. This is the stone which was set at nought of you builders,

He is the stone . . . — ASV

. . . scorned by you, the builders—TCNT

. . . treated with contempt . . . — Wey

. . . despised . . . — Mof

. . . rejected . . . — Gspd

. . . cast aside . . . — Mon

. . . thrown away . . . — Wms

which is become the head of the corner.

which was made . . . — ASV

but it has been made the Cornerstone — Wey

. . . the chief stone of the building — Bas

. . . the chief stone at the corner — Knox

. . . the keystone — NEB

12. Neither is there salvation in any other:

And in none other is there salvation — ASV

And Salvation comes through no one else — TCNT

There is no salvation by anyone else — Mof

In no one else can salvation be found — Phi

Salvation is through him alone — Rieu

No one else can save us — Beck

for there is none other name under heaven given among men, whereby we must be saved.

. . . wherein we must be saved — ASV

for there is no other Name in the whole world, given to men, to which we must look for our Salvation — TCNT

---

[8]The words "of Israel" are now recognized as not adequately supported by original manuscripts.

for no one else in all the wide world has been appointed among men as our only medium by which to be saved — Wms

In all the world he is the only means men have been given of finding the salvation we look for — Rieu

13. Now when they saw the boldness of Peter and John,

Now when they beheld . . . — ASV

And looking at Peter's boldness of speech and John's — Rhm

Seeing how boldly Peter and John spoke — TCNT

As they looked on . . . so fearlessly outspoken — Wey

. . . the glad fearlessness of Peter and John — Mon

. . . the courage . . . — Wms

. . . the freedom of speech . . . — Ber

. . . the complete assurance . . . — Phi

. . . the bold assurance . . . — Rieu

. . . the confidence . . . — NASB

and perceived that they were unlearned and ignorant men,

and having discovered that they were unlettered and obscure men — Rhm

. . . uneducated and obscure persons — TCNT

. . . illiterate persons, untrained in the schools — Wey

. . . uncultured persons and mere outsiders — Mof

. . . uneducated persons with no advantages — Gspd

. . . simple men, without learning — Knox

. . . men without schooling or skill — Ber

. . . uneducated, common men — RSV

. . . untrained laymen — NEB

they marvelled;

they began to marvel — Rhm

the Council was surprised — TCNT

They were astonished — Mof

They were amazed — Gspd

they wondered — RSV

they were staggered — Phi

The Council were dumfounded — Rieu

they began to wonder — NEB

and they took knowledge of them, that they had been with Jesus.

recognizing them also that they . . . — Rhm

and realized that they had been companions of Jesus — TCNT

and realized what being with Jesus had done for them! — Tay

and now they recognized them as having been . . . — Wey

then recognized them as former companions . . . — NEB

Then they realized these men had been with Jesus — Beck

14. And beholding the man which was healed standing with them,

seeing the man also standing with them, even the [man] who had been cured — Rhm

But since they saw . . . — Mon

However, confronted by the sight of the cured man standing at their side — Rieu

they could say nothing against it.

they had nothing wherewith to contradict — Rhm

they could find no effective reply — Phi

they could not contradict the fact or say anything in opposition — Amp

15. But when they had commanded them to go aside out of the council,

So they ordered them out of court — TCNT

But having commanded them to go aside out of the Sanhedrin — ABUV

So they ordered them to withdraw from the Sanhedrin — Wey

so they ordered them out of the council-chamber — Knox

they conferred among themselves,

and then began consulting together — TCNT

they proceeded to hold a consultation — Mof

they had a discussion among themselves — Bas

. . . discussed the matter among themselves — NEB

16. Saying, What shall we do to these men?

What are we going to do with these men — Phi

for that indeed a notable miracle hath been done by them is manifest to all them that dwell in Jerusalem;

. . . a notable sign . . . — Rhm

. . . a remarkable sign . . . — TCNT

. . . . an extraordinary wonder . . . — Gspd

. . . an unmistakable wonder-work . . . — Wms

. . . a noteworthy miracle . . . — NASB
and we cannot deny it.
and it is not possible to say that it is
not so — Bas
and we are powerless to deny it —
Knox

**17. But that it spread no further among
the people,**
Nevertheless lest it further spread
abroad . . . — Rhm
But to keep it from spreading farther
. . . — Gspd
But the news must not spread any
further — Knox
let us straitly[9] threaten them,
let us threaten them — ASV
let us warn them — TCNT
let us stop them by threats — Wey
let us severely threaten them — Wms
we must deter them by threats — Knox
we had better caution them — NEB
**that they speak henceforth to no man
in this name.**
that they are not to tell anyone in the
future about this Name — Mof
to say nothing to anyone else at all
about this person — Gspd
never again to speak to anyone in this
name — NEB

18. And they called them,
So they recalled the Apostles — Wey
So they called them back — Rieu
**and commanded them not to speak at
all nor teach in the name of Jesus.**
and charged them . . . — ASV
and ordered them altogether to give
up speaking or teaching . . . — Wey
. . . not to speak or teach a single sentence . . . — Mof
. . . to refrain from all public speaking
and teaching . . . — NEB

**19. But Peter and John answered and said
unto them,**
But Peter and John said in reply —
Mon
**Whether it be right in the sight of God
to hearken unto you more than unto
God, judge ye.**
Whether it is right, in God's eyes, to
listen to you rather than to him —
you must decide — TCNT
Decide for yourselves whether it is
right before God to obey you rather
than God — Mof
20. For we cannot but speak

as for us, we cannot help speaking of
— TCNT
Certainly we cannot give up speaking
— Mof
for we cannot keep from telling —Wms
It is impossible for us to refrain from
speaking — Knox
We cannot possibly give up speaking
— NEB
for we cannot stop speaking — NASB
**the things which we have seen and
heard.**

**21. So when they had further threatened
them,**
And when they had said more sharp
words to them — Bas
The court repeated the caution — NEB
they let them go,
the Council set them at liberty — TCNT
they turned them loose — Wms
and then freed them — Ber
**finding nothing how they might pun-
ish them,**
not seeing any safe way of punishing
them — TCNT
being quite unable to find any way of
punishing them — Mon
for they could find no pretext for punishing them — Rieu
finding no basis on which they might
punish them — NASB
because of the people:
on account of the people — Rhm
because of the attitude of the people —
Phi
**for all men glorified God for that
which was done.**
who were all giving honor to God for
what had happened — Gspd
Everybody was thanking God for what
had happened — Phi

**22. For the man was above forty years old,
on whom this miracle of healing was
shewed.**
the more so as the man who was the
subject of this miraculous cure was
more than forty years old — TCNT
for the man on whom this wonder of
healing had been done was more
than forty years old — Gspd

23. And being let go,
And when they had been let go — Rhm

---

[9]The word "straitly" is now recognized as not
adequately supported by original manuscripts.

455

After they had been set at liberty —
TCNT

After their release — Wey

As soon as the apostles were released
— Mon

they went to their own company,

they came unto their own friends —
Rhm

the apostles went to their companions
— Wms

they went back to their own group —
Nor

**and reported all that the chief priests
and elders had said unto them.**

and related what the high priests and
elders had said — Mof

. . . the high priests and members of
the council . . . — Gspd

24. **And when they heard that,**

When they had heard their story —
TCNT

**they lifted up their voice to God with
one accord,**

moved by a common impulse, they
raised their voice to God in prayer
— TCNT

one and all lifted up their voices to
God — Wey

the entire company raised their cry to
God — Mof

with one united prayer to God — Wms

they all, with one mind, made prayer
to God — Bas

they lifted their voices together to God
— RSV

they raised their voices to God in unity
of spirit — Rieu

they raised their voices as one man and
called upon God — NEB

and said, Lord, thou art God,[10]

and said, O Lord — ASV

. . . O Sovereign! — Rhm

O Sovereign Lord — TCNT

. . . Master — Gspd

Ruler of all — Knox

. . . Almighty God — Nor

**which hast made heaven, and earth,
and the sea, and all that in them is:**

thou that didst make . . . — ASV

it is thou who hast made sky . . . and
everything that is in them — TCNT

you are the Maker of . . . — Wms

25. **Who by the mouth of thy servant
David hast said,**

who by the Holy Spirit by the mouth
of our father David thy servant,
didst say[11] — ASV

and who by the lips of our ancestor,
thy servant David, speaking under
the influence of the holy Spirit, hast
said — TCNT

and didst say through the Holy Spirit
by the lips of our forefather David,
Thy servant — Wey

who said to our fathers by the holy
Spirit through the lips of thy servant
David — Mof

Why did the heathen rage,

Why did the Gentiles rage — ASV

Unto what end did nations rage—Rhm

Why are the nations so violently moved
— Bas

What means this turmoil among the
nations — Knox

and the people imagine vain things?

And the peoples . . . — ASV

And peoples busy themselves with
empty things — Rhm

And the nations form vain designs —
TCNT

and the peoples vainly conspire — Mof

and the peoples form futile plans —
Mon

And why are the thoughts of the people so foolish — Bas

why do the peoples cherish vain dreams
— Knox

And the People of Israel make vain
schemes — Rieu

and the peoples lay their plans in vain
— NEB

and the foolish nations plan their little
plots against Almighty God — Tay

26. **The kings of the earth stood up,**

. . . set themselves in array — ASV

. . . took their stand — Wms

. . . got ready — Ber

**and the rulers were gathered together
against the Lord,**

. . . assembled together . . . — ABUV

. . . mustered together . . . — Mof

. . . make common cause . . . — Knox

and against his Christ.

. . . his Anointed — ASV

. . . his Messiah — NEB

---

[10]The word "God" is now recognized as not
adequately supported by original manuscripts.
[11]Variant reading.

27. For of a truth against thy holy child Jesus,
for of a truth in this city[12] against thy holy Servant Jesus — ASV
whom thou hast anointed,
whom thou hast consecrated the Christ — TCNT
who was marked out by you as Christ — Bas
whom thou didst anoint as Messiah — NEB
Whom You consecrated by anointing — Amp
both Herod, and Pontius Pilate, with the Gentiles, and the people of Israel,
not Herod and Pontius Pilate only, but the nations and the people of Israel besides — TCNT
were gathered together,
They did . . . assemble — Wey
have gathered together — Rieu
made common cause — NEB
met and plotted together — Amp

28. For to do whatsoever thy hand and thy counsel determined before to be done.
. . . marked out beforehand . . . — Rhm
but only to do all that thy providence and thy will had already determined should be done — TCNT
to carry out what thy hand had traced, thy purpose had decreed — Mof
to carry out what your hand and will had destined should happen — Gspd
to do that which had been fixed before by your hand and your purpose — Bas
so accomplishing all that thy power and wisdom had decreed — Knox

29. And now, Lord, behold their threatenings;
. . . look upon their threats — RSV
. . . give heed to their threats — TCNT
. . . give attention to their threats — Wms
and grant unto thy servants,
and enable thy servants — TCNT
and give your slaves — Gspd
that with all boldness they may speak thy word,
to speak thy word with all boldness — RSV
with all freedom of utterance to be speaking . . . — Rhm

with all fearlessness, to tell thy Message — TCNT
to proclaim Thy word with fearless courage — Wey
with perfect courage to continue to speak your message — Wms
power to be preachers of your word without fear — Bas
to preach thy word confidently — Knox

30. By stretching forth thine hand to heal:
while thou stretchest forth thy hand to heal — ASV
and that signs and wonders may be done
and to give signs and marvels — Wey
and to perform miracles and wonders — Mof
and signs and wonders take place — NASB
by the name of thy holy child Jesus.
through the name of thy holy servant Jesus — RSV
through the power of thy holy Servant Jesus — TCNT
by the authority of your holy Servant Jesus — Wms

31. And when they had prayed,
And when they had made supplication — Rhm
And when their prayer was ended — Bas
When they had finished praying—Knox
the place was shaken where they were assembled together;
the place in which they were assembled was shaken — TCNT
the place where they were was violently moved — Bas
the place in which they had gathered rocked to and fro — Knox
their meeting-place shook — Ber
and they were all filled with the Holy Ghost,
. . . the Holy Spirit — RSV
and they were filled, one and all . . . — Rhm
and they spake the word of God with boldness.
and began speaking . . . with freedom of utterance — Rhm
and continued to tell God's Message fearlessly — TCNT

---

[12]"In this city" represents a variant reading.

and continued courageously to speak God's Message — Wms

preaching the word of God without fear — Bas

32. And the multitude of them that believed were of one heart and of one soul:

And the throng of them that believed had one heart and soul — Rhm

The whole body of those who had become believers in Christ were animated by one spirit — TCNT

Now the multitude of the believers . . . — Mon

Now there was but one heart and soul among the multitude of the believers — Mof

. . . in the vast number of those who had become believers — Wms

The host of believers were one in heart and soul — Ber

The community of the faithful were one, heart and soul — Rieu

neither said any of them that ought of the things which he possessed was his own;

Not one of them claimed any of his goods as his own — TCNT

not one of them considered anything his personal property — Mof

and not one of them said that any of the things which he had was his property only — Bas

no one claimed his belongings just for himself — Ber

And nobody called anything he had his own — Beck

but they had all things common.

but everything was held for the common use — TCNT

but everything they had was common property — Wey

they shared all they had with one another — Mof

but they shared everything that they had as common property — Wms

but everything was common property to all — Phi

33. And with great power gave the apostles witness of the resurrection of the Lord Jesus:

The Apostles continued with great power to bear their testimony to the resurrection of Jesus, their Master — TCNT

. . . with great effect . . . — Wey

. . . with great force — Phi

and great grace was upon them all.

great favour also was upon them all — Rhm

and divine help was given to them all abundantly — TCNT

and God's favor rested richly upon them — Gspd

and a wonderful spirit of generosity pervaded the whole fellowship — Phi

They were all held in high esteem — NEB

and abundant grace . . . — NASB

and much good will rested on all of them — Beck

34. Neither was there any among them that lacked:

There was not a needy person among them — RSV

Indeed, there was no poverty among them — TCNT

And, in fact, there was not a needy man among them — Wey

Nor was there any one of them in want — Mon

None of them was destitute — Knox

Not one among them suffered need — Ber

for as many as were possessors of lands or houses sold them,

for all who were owners of . . . — TCNT

. . . proceeded to sell them, one by one — Wms

and brought the prices of the things that were sold,

were bringing the prices of the things that were being sold — Rhm

and continued to bring the money received for the things sold — Wms

35. And laid them down at the apostles' feet:

and [were] laying them at the feet of the Apostles — Rhm

and gave it to the Apostles — Wey

and put them at the disposal of the apostles — Gspd

and distribution was made unto every man according as he had need.

and distribution was made unto each, according as any one had need — ASV

and then every one received a share in proportion to his needs — TCNT

it was then distributed according to each individual's need — Mof then distribution was continuously made to everyone in proportion to his need — Wms

so that each could have what share of it he needed — Knox

and they would be distributed to each, as anyone had need — NASB

36. And Joses, who by the apostles was surnamed Barnabas,

And Joseph . . . — ASV

. . . who had received from the Apostles the additional name of Barnabas — TCNT

(which is, being interpreted, The son of consolation,)

which is to be translated . . . — Rhm

. . . Son of exhortation — ASV

(which means, Son of encouragement) — RSV

which means The Preacher — TCNT

signifying Son of Encouragement — Wey

the sense of which is, Son of comfort — Bas

which means, the man of encouragement — Knox

a Levite, and of the country of Cyprus,

. . . a man of Cyprus by race — ASV

A Levite of Cyprian birth — TCNT

. . . a native of Cyprus — Wey

a Cyprian Levite — Ber

37. Having land, sold it,

having a field . . . — ASV

sold a farm that belonged to him — TCNT

he had an estate, which he sold—Knox

He sold a plot of land he owned — Rieu

and brought the money, and laid it at the apostles' feet.

and brought the proceeds and put them at the disposal of the apostles — Gspd

and brought the purchase-money to lay it . . . — Knox

and brought the proceeds which he deposited . . . — Ber

and handed the money to the Apostles — Rieu

CHAPTER 5

1. But a certain man named Ananias,

There was, however, a man named Ananias — TCNT

with Sapphira his wife,

in partnership with his wife Sapphira — Wms

sold a possession,

sold some property — TCNT

. . . a farm of his — Mon

. . . a piece of property — Wms

. . . an estate — Knox

2. And kept back part of the price,

and . . . kept back some of the proceeds — TCNT

but . . . dishonestly kept back part of the price received for it — Wey

appropriated some of the purchase-money — Mof

reserved part of the price for himself — Phi

he kept back a part of the selling price — Nor

his wife also being privy to it,

with her connivance — TCNT

his wife also being aware of it — ABUV

with her full knowledge and consent — Wey

and brought a certain part,

though he brought the rest — Wey

and brought only part of it — Gspd

and laid it at the apostles' feet.

and gave it to the Apostles — Wey

to put at the disposal of the apostles — Gspd

3. But Peter said, Ananias, why hath Satan filled thine heart to lie to the Holy Ghost,

. . . how is it that Satan has so taken possession of your heart, that you have defrauded the holy Spirit — TCNT

. . . that you should try to deceive the Holy Spirit — Wey

and to keep back part of the price of the land?

and dishonestly keep back part of the price paid you for this land — Wey

and covertly withdraw some of the field's price — Ber

4. Whiles it remained, was it not thine own?

While it remained, did it not remain thine own — ASV

While it was unsold, was it not your own — TCNT

When you had the land, was it not yours to keep — Rieu

and after it was sold, was it not in thine own power?

and when sold was it not in thine own authority — Rhm

. . . was not the money at your own disposal — TCNT

. . . was the money not yours to do as you pleased about it — Mof

. . . was not the money under your control — Gspd

why hast thou conceived this thing in thine heart?

How is it that you have cherished this design in your heart — Wey

How could you think of doing such a thing — Gspd

How could you have the heart to do such a thing — Wms

How is it that you have contrived this deed in your heart — RSV

What possessed you to do this — Rieu

thou hast not lied unto men, but unto God.

You have not defrauded men, but God — TCNT

You did not cheat men but God — Ber

5. **And Ananias hearing these words fell down, and gave up the ghost:**

And as Ananias heard these words he fell and expired — Rhm

. . . fell down dead — Wey

. . . fell down and died — Knox

. . . collapsed and died — Phi

. . . dropped dead — NEB

. . . fell down and breathed his last — NASB

and great fear came on all them that heard these things.

and every one who heard of it was appalled — TCNT

and all who heard the words were awestruck — Wey

and a strange awe seized everybody who heard it — Wms

And all who heard of it were terrified — Beck

6. **And the young men arose,**

But the younger men got up — TCNT

The younger men, however, rose — Wey

wound him up,

and wrapped him round — ASV

and after winding the body in a sheet — TCNT

and wrapped him in a shroud — Rieu

and covered his body — NEB

and carried him out, and buried him.

carried it out and buried it — TCNT

then carried him out of the city . . . — Rieu

and after carrying him out, they buried him — NASB

7. **And it was about the space of three hours after,**

And it came to pass, after about three hours interval — Rhm

After an interval of about three hours — RSV

About three hours later — Gspd

Now there elapsed an interval of about three hours — NASB

when his wife, not knowing what was done, came in.

. . . not knowing what had happened . . . — RSV

. . . quite unconscious of what had occurred . . . — Mof

. . . ignorant of what had occurred . . . — Ber

8. **And Peter answered unto her,**

Peter at once questioned her — Wey

Peter spoke directly to her — Phi

Peter turned to her and said — NEB

Tell me whether ye sold the land for so much?

Tell me! was it for so much ye gave up the field — Rhm

Is it true . . . that you sold the land for such and such a sum — TCNT

. . . was it for so much that you sold the estate — Knox

. . . were you paid such and such a price for the land — NEB

And she said, Yea, for so much.

Yes, she said, that was all we sold it for — Mof

And she said, Yes, that was the price — NASB

9. **Then Peter said unto her,**

Peter then came back at her — Ber

How is it that ye have agreed together

What is this conspiracy between you — Knox

Why did you both conspire — NEB

to tempt the Spirit of the Lord?

to try . . . — ASV

to put to the proof . . . — Rhm

to provoke . . . — TCNT

to put the Spirit of the Lord to the test — Wey

behold, the feet of them which have buried thy husband are at the door, and shall carry thee out.

Listen! The foot-steps of those who . . . — TCNT

There at the door are the footsteps of the men who . . . — Gspd

10. **Then fell she down straightway at his feet, and yielded up the ghost:**

And she fell down immediately at his feet . . . — ASV

And she fell instantly at his feet, and expired — Rhm

Instantly she fell down dead at his feet — Wey

Immediately she collapsed at Peter's feet and died — Phi

And suddenly she dropped dead at his feet — NEB

. . . and breathed her last — NASB

and the young men came in, and found her dead,

and when the young men came in, they . . . — Mon

and, carrying her forth, buried her by her husband.

. . . by her husband's side — TCNT

11. **And great fear came upon all the church, and upon as many as heard these things.**

And there came great fear upon the whole assembly . . . — Rhm

The whole Church and all who heard of these events were appalled — TCNT

The whole Church was awe-struck, and so were all who heard of this incident — Wey

So a strange awe seized the whole church . . . — Wms

Terror struck all the church and all who heard about it — Rieu

12. **And by the hands of the apostles were many signs and wonders wrought among the people;**

And through . . . were coming to pass . . . — Rhm

Many signs and wonders continued to occur among the people, through the instrumentality of the Apostles — TCNT

(and they were all with one accord in Solomon's porch.

whose custom it was to meet all together in the Colonnade of Solomon — TCNT

and by common consent they all met in Solomon's Portico — Wey

The community's meeting-place was now Solomon's Colonnade — Rieu

. . . in the porch or covered walk called Solomon's — Amp

13. **And of the rest durst no man join himself to them:**

but none of the rest ventured to stand by them — TCNT

But none of the others dared to attach themselves . . . — Wey

not a soul from the outside dared to join them — Mof

None of the others dared to associate with them — Gspd

None of the others dared to come too near them — Beck

but the people magnified them.

nevertheless the people continued to magnify them — Rhm

On the other hand, the people were full of their praise — TCNT

Yet the people held them in high honour — Wey

Though the people extolled them — Mof

. . . continued to hold them in high regard — Wms

the people held them in high esteem — Rieu

14. **And believers were the more added to the Lord, multitudes both of men and women.)**

and the more were being added when they believed in the Lord, throngs . . . — Rhm

while large numbers, both men and women, kept joining them more readily than ever as they became believers in the Master — TCNT

and still more were believers in the Lord added . . . — ABUV

and more and more believers in the Lord were joining them . . . — Mon

However, throngs of men and women who believed in the Lord were increasingly added — Ber

15. **Insomuch that they brought forth the sick into the streets,**

so that even into the broad-ways were they bringing . . . — Rhm

They went so far as to bring out their sick . . . — Ber

As a result of the miracles people even carried . . . — Rieu

to such an extent that they even carried . . . — NASB

and laid them on beds and couches,

. . . small couches and beds — Rhm

. . . mattresses and mats — TCNT

. . . beds and pallets — ABUV

. . . light couches or mats — Wey

. . . beds and mattresses — Mof

. . . beds and mats — Gspd

. . . little couches or pallets — Wms

. . . beds and stretchers — Rieu

. . . cots and mats — Nor

. . . cots and pallets — NASB

that at least the shadow of Peter passing by might overshadow some of them.

that, as Peter came by, at the least his shadow . . . — ASV

in the hope that, as Peter came, at least his shadow . . . — TCNT

16. **There came also a multitude out of the cities round about unto Jerusalem,**

And there also came together the multitude from the cities round about Jerusalem — ASV

Moreover even the throng of the cities all round Jerusalem was coming together — Rhm

The inhabitants, too, of the towns in the neighborhood of Jerusalem came in crowds — Wey

Crowds gathered even from the towns round Jerusalem — Mof

Even from towns outside Jerusalem the crowd came streaming in — Ber

bringing sick folks,

bringing sick people — TCNT

and them which were vexed with unclean spirits:

and such as were harassed by impure spirits — Rhm

and people troubled with unclean spirits — Mof

and those afflicted . . . — RSV

and all those who were suffering from evil spirits — Phi

and some who were troubled with foul demons — Nor

and they were healed every one.

who indeed were being cured one and all — Rhm

and they were all alike cured — TCNT

all of whom were healed — Mof

17. **Then the high priest rose up, and all they that were with him,**

On this the High Priest and all his supporters . . . were aroused — TCNT

This roused the High Priest. He and all his party — Wey

Now the high priest took a stand, and all his friends — Wms

This roused the high priest and those who thought with him — Knox

All this roused the High Priest and his allies — Phi

The High Priest and his circle . . . — Rieu

Then the High Priest and his colleagues . . . — NEB

(which is the sect of the Sadducees,)

who formed the party of the Sadducees — TCNT

and were filled with indignation,

and they were filled with jealousy — ASV

were filled with angry jealousy — Wey

. . . with bitter jealousy — Mof

they were insufferably jealous — Ber

were goaded into action by jealousy — NEB

18. **And laid their hands on the apostles,**

arrested the Apostles — TCNT

So they seized the apostles — Ber

and put them in the common prison.

and put them in public ward — ASV

and had them placed in custody — TCNT

. . . the public prison — ABUV

. . . the common jail — Gspd

. . . official custody — NEB

19. **But the angel of the Lord by night**

But an angel of the Lord . . . — ASV

. . . at night — RSV

. . . during the night — Wey

. . . in the night — Gspd

opened the prison doors,

and brought them forth, and said,

and leading them out said — Rhm

and let them out . . . — Mon

conducted them out . . . — Ber

20. **Go, stand and speak in the temple to the people all the words of this life.**

Be going your way, and taking your stand be speaking . . . all the declarations of this Life — Rhm

Go . . . and take your stand in the Temple Courts, and tell the people all you have to say about the new Life — TCNT

. . . and continue proclaiming . . . all this Message of Life — Wey

. . . and tell the people all about this new life — Gspd

. . . and tell the people everything about this Way of Life — Rieu

. . . and tell them about this new life and all it means — NEB

. . . the whole message of this Life — NASB

21. **And when they heard that, they entered into the temple early in the morning, and taught.**

about daybreak . . . — ASV

just before daybreak, and began to teach — Wey

at early dawn . . . — ABUV

about dawn . . . — Mof

But the high priest came, and they that were with him,[13]

and called the council together,

and had called together the Sanhedrin — Wey

they summoned the Sanhedrin — Mon

and convened the council — Nor

and all the senate of the children of Israel,

and the council of seniors belonging to the sons of Israel — Mof

and indeed the whole senate of the Israelites — Gspd

even the whole Senate of the sons of Israel — Ber

that is, the full senate of the Israelite nation — NEB

and sent to the prison to have them brought.

. . . the prison-house . . . — ASV

. . . the jail . . . — Phi

22. **But when the officers came, and found them not in the prison,**

But the officers that came . . . — ASV

But the officers who went did not find them . . . — TCNT

. . . the attendants . . . — Mof

. . . the police . . . — NEB

they returned, and told,

and they returned and reported — RSV

23. **Saying, The prison truly found we shut with all safety,**

We found the prison safely locked up — Mof

We found the prison securely locked up — Gspd

We found the prison-house locked quite securely — NASB

and the keepers standing without before the doors:

and the keepers standing at the doors — ASV

with the sentries posted at the doors — Mof

with the guards stationed at the doors — Mon

but when we had opened, we found no man within.

but on opening the doors we found no one inside — Mof

24. **Now when the high priest**[14] **and the captain of the temple and the chief priests heard these things,**

Now when the captain of the temple and the chief priests heard these words — RSV

they doubted of them whereunto this would grow.

they were much perplexed concerning them . . . — ASV

they were utterly at a loss concerning them — what perhaps this might come to — Rhm

were quite at a loss to know what to make of it — Mof

were at a loss to know what had become of them — Knox

they were utterly at a loss to know how this might turn out — Wms

they were completely mystified at the Apostles' disappearance and wondered what further developments there would be — Phi

. . . wondering what would happen next — Wey

25. **Then came one and told them, saying,**

And there came one and told them — ASV

However, someone came and reported to them — Mof

until an eye-witness told them — Knox

Behold, the men whom ye put in prison are standing in the temple, and teaching the people.

---

[13]See verse 17.

[14]The words "the high priest" are now recognized as not adequately supported by original manuscripts.

. . . are standing in the temple and teaching . . . — RSV

Look! the men you put in prison are there in the temple teaching the people — NEB

26. Then went the captain[15] with the officers,

and brought them without violence:

brought them not with violence—Rhm

. . . but without using violence — Wey

. . . not, however, by force — Mon

. . . but without using force — NEB

for they feared the people, lest they should have been stoned.

for they were afraid of being stoned by the people — RSV

27. And when they had brought them, they set them before the council:

and then brought them up before the Council — TCNT

So they brought them and set them before the Sanhedrin — Wey

They conducted them before the Sanhedrin — Mof

and the high priest asked them,

And the High-priest questioned them — Rhm

The High Priest demanded an explanation from them — TCNT

and the high priest examined them — Ber

and the High Priest began his examination — NEB

28. Saying, Did not we straitly command you that ye should not teach in this name?[16]

Did we not give you strict orders . . . not teach in this name — Nor

. . . We strictly charged you not to teach in this name — ASV

and, behold, ye have filled Jerusalem with your doctrine,

. . . with your teaching — RSV

And look what has happened — you have filled . . . — Phi

But, see! You have filled . . . — Nor

and intend to bring this man's blood upon us.

and are wishing to make us responsible for the death of this man — TCNT

and now want to bring on us the people's vengeance for this man's death — Wms

You are determined to lay this man's death at our door — Knox

and what is more you are determined to fasten the guilt of that Man's death upon us — Phi

And you want to get us punished for killing this Man — Beck

29. Then Peter and the other apostles answered and said,

But Peter and the apostles answered and said — ASV

Peter replied for himself and the apostles — NEB

We ought to obey God rather than men.

We must obey . . . — RSV

30. The God of our fathers raised up Jesus,

The God of our ancestors has raised Jesus from the grave — TCNT

The God of our forefathers has raised Jesus to life — Wey

whom ye slew and hanged on a tree.

whom ye slew, hanging him on a tree — ASV

whom you yourselves put to death, by hanging him on a cross — TCNT

whom you crucified and put to death — Wey

whom you slew by hanging him on a tree — Mon

whom you murdered by hanging Him on a cross of wood — Phi

31. Him hath God exalted with his right hand to be a Prince and a Saviour,

Him as a Princely-leader and Saviour hath God exalted unto his right hand — Rhm

It is this Jesus, whom God has exalted to his right hand, to be a Guide and a Saviour — TCNT

. . . as our pioneer and saviour — Mof

. . . as our leader and savior — Gspd

. . . as a ruler and a saviour — Bas

for to give repentance to Israel, and forgiveness of sins.

to give repentance to Israel, and remission of sins — ASV

to give Israel repentance and forgiveness of sins — TCNT

to give to Israel a change of heart and . . . — Bas

---

[15]For variants of "captain" and "officers" see verses 22,24.

[16]Some manuscripts have this as a statement, not a question, though many manuscripts show it as the latter.

to give Israel the chance to repent and find . . . — Rieu

32. And we are his[17] witnesses of these things;

And we are witnesses to the truth of this — TCNT

And we are witnesses of these things — ASV

We are witnesses of these events — Rieu

and so is also the Holy Ghost,

. . . the Holy Spirit — RSV

whom God hath given to them that obey him.

. . . unto them who are yielding obedience unto him — Rhm

. . . to those who are obedient to him — NEB

33. When they heard that, they were cut to the heart,

The members of the Council grew furious on hearing this — TCNT

And hearing it, they were convulsed with rage — ABUV

Infuriated at getting this answer — Wey

. . . they were furious — Gspd

. . . they were cut to the quick — Knox

. . . they were enraged — RSV

The words went through their hearts like a sword — Rieu

This touched them on the raw — NEB

and took counsel to slay them.

and were minded to slay them — ASV

they were disposed to kill the Apostles — Wey

and determined to destroy them — Ber

and planned to kill them — Nor

and were intending to slay them — NASB

34. Then stood there up one in the council,

But there stood up one in the council — ASV

But there stood up one in the Sanhedrin — ABUV

But one man stood up in the Assembly — Phi

But a member of the Council rose to his feet — NEB

a Pharisee, named Gamaliel, a doctor of the law,

. . . a law-teacher — Rhm

. . . a Teacher of the Law — TCNT

. . . a professor of law — Ber

had in reputation among all the people,

had in honor of all the people — ASV

honoured by all the people — Rhm

held in universal respect — TCNT

who was highly respected by all the people — Mof

highly regarded by all the people — Gspd

who was held in esteem by all the people — Knox

and commanded to put the apostles forth a little space;

and commanded to put the men[18] forth a little while — ASV

gave orders to put the men outside for a little — Rhm

and directed that the men should be taken out of court for a little while — TCNT

and ordered the men to be removed for a while — Gspd

35. And said unto them, Ye men of Israel,

Then he addressed the Assembly: Men of Israel — Phi

He then spoke to the Council, saying . . . — Nor

take heed to yourselves what ye intend to do as touching these men.

take heed to yourselves as touching these men, what ye are about to do — ASV

take care what you do with these men — RSV

be careful what you are about to do in dealing with these men — Wey

take care what you propose to do with these men — Gspd

think well what you mean to do with these men — Knox

be careful how you intend to treat these men — Ber

be cautious in deciding what to do with these men — NEB

36. For before these days rose up Theudas,

For it is not long ago that Theudas appeared — TCNT

For some time ago Theudas appeared — Gspd

---

[17]The word "his" is now recognized as not adequately supported by original manuscripts.
[18]Some manuscripts use the word "men" instead of "apostles."

ACTS 5

Remember that some time ago a man
called Theudas made himself conspicuous — Phi

boasting himself to be somebody;
giving himself out to be . . . — ASV
affirming himself to be . . . — Rhm
claiming to be . . . — TCNT
saying that he himself was . . . — ABUV
professing to be a person of importance
— Wey

**to whom a number of men, about four
hundred, joined themselves:**
unto whom was inclined a number of
men . . . — Rhm
and was joined by a body of some four
hundred men — TCNT
a number of men, about four hundred
of them, rallied to him — Mof
. . . espoused his cause — Wms
. . . gave their support — Bas
. . . adhered to him — Ber
and he had a following of four hundred
men — Phi
and attracted about four hundred followers — Rieu

who was slain;
He himself was killed — TCNT
. . . he was put to death — Nor

**and all, as many as obeyed him, were
scattered,**
. . . were dispersed — ASV
. . . as had been trusting in him were
disbanded — Rhm
and all his following scattered — TCNT
and all his followers were dispersed —
Wey
and his band was broken up — Bas
and all his supporters were dispersed —
Ber

and brought to nought.
and came to nought — ASV
and came to nothing — RSV
and wiped out — Mof
and disappeared — Gspd
and they vanished — Ber
and the movement came to nothing —
Phi

37. **After this man rose up Judas of
Galilee**
. . . Judas the Galilean — TCNT
in the days of the taxing,
in the days of the enrolment — ASV
at the time of the census — TCNT
at the time of the enrollment for the
Roman tax — Wms
in the days of the registration — Knox

and drew away much people after him:
and drew a people into revolt after him
— Rhm
and got people to follow him — TCNT
and was the leader in a revolt — Wey
and got people to desert to him — Mof
and raised a great following — Gspd
he persuaded the people to rebel under
his leadership — Knox
and raised a popular following — Ber
he also perished;
But he too was crushed — Rieu
and all, even as many as obeyed him,[19]
were dispersed;
. . . were scattered abroad — ASV

38. **And now I say unto you,**
And in this present case, my advice
to you is — TCNT
So I advise you to-day — Mof
So in the present case, I tell you—Gspd
**Refrain from these men, and let them
alone:**
not to interfere with these men, but to
let them alone — TCNT
Stand aloof from these men . . .—Rhm
keep away from these men . . . — Gspd
have nothing to do with these men . . .
— Knox
**for if this counsel or this work be of
men,**
for if these designs and these proceedings are only of human origin—TCNT
for if this scheme or work be of human
origin — Wey
for if this idea or movement is of
human origin — Gspd
For, if this program or movement has
its origin in man — Wms
If this is man's design or man's undertaking — Knox
it will come to nought:
it will be overthrown — ASV
it will come to nothing — Wey
it will collapse — Mof
it will go to pieces — Wms
it will fail — RSV
it will break down — Beck

39. **But if it be of God, ye cannot overthrow it;**
but if it is of God, ye will not be able
to overthrow them — ASV
. . . you will be powerless to put them
down — Wey

_____
[19]For this clause see verse 36.

466

. . . you will not be able to stop it —
Gspd

. . . you can never stop it — Wms

. . . you cannot defeat them — Phi

lest haply ye be found even to fight against God.

lest perhaps you find yourselves to be actually fighting against God — Wey

You may even find yourselves fighting God! — Mof

and you are in danger of fighting against God — Bas

and you risk finding yourselves at war with God — NEB

40. And to him they agreed:

And they were persuaded by him — Rhm

The Council followed his advice — TCNT

And to him they assented — ABUV

His advice carried conviction — Wey

They gave in to him — Mof

They were convinced by him — Gspd

So they took his advice — RSV

and when they had called the apostles, and beaten them,

and when they had called the apostles unto them . . . — ASV

and calling the Apostles in, had them flogged — TCNT

and after summoning the apostles and flogging them — Mof

they commanded that they should not speak in the name of Jesus, and let them go.

charged them not to speak . . . — ASV

warned them not to speak about the name . . . — Gspd

they charged them to stop speaking on the authority of Jesus, and then turned them loose — Wms

gave them strict injunctions not to speak of Jesus, and then set them free — Rieu

then they ordered them to give up speaking in the name of Jesus, and discharged them — NEB

. . . released them — Nor

41. And they departed from the presence of the council,

But the Apostles left the Council — TCNT

They, therefore, left the Sanhedrin — Wey

So they went out from before the council — Gspd

So they went on their way from . . . — NASB

The apostles left the court — Beck

rejoicing that they were counted worthy to suffer shame for his name.

. . . to suffer dishonor for the Name — ASV

. . . to suffer disgrace on behalf of the Name — Wey

. . . to bear humiliation for the sake of the Name — Phi

. . . to suffer indignity . . . — NEB

overjoyed at the honour of suffering dishonour for the Name — Rieu

42. And daily in the temple, and in every house,

And every day, in the temple and at home — ASV

. . . either in the Temple or in private houses — TCNT

. . . both in the temple and from house to house — Knox

they ceased not to teach and preach Jesus Christ.

. . . Jesus as the Christ — ASV

they ceased not to be teaching and telling the good news as to the Anointed Jesus — Rhm

. . . the Gospel of Jesus, the Messiah — Mon

their teaching and their preaching was continually of Jesus Christ — Knox

CHAPTER 6

1. And in those days,

About this time — TCNT

During this period — NEB

when the number of the disciples was multiplied,

. . . was multiplying — ASV

. . . was constantly increasing — TCNT

. . . kept growing — Ber

there arose a murmuring of the Grecians against the Hebrews,

. . . of the Grecian Jews . . . — ASV

complaints were made by the Greek-speaking Jews against the native Jews — TCNT a complaint was brought against those who spoke Aramaic by those who spoke Greek — Beck

because their widows were neglected in the daily ministration.

. . . were being overlooked in the daily distribution — TCNT

. . . distribution of food — Mof

. . . distribution of alms — Mon

. . . administration of relief — Knox

2. **Then the twelve called the multitude of the disciples unto them, and said,**

The Twelve, therefore, summoned the general body of the disciples and said to them — TCNT

The Twelve called a meeting of the community of disciples and addressed them — Rieu

It is not reason that we should leave the word of God,

It is not fit that we should forsake . . . — ASV

It will not do for us to neglect God's message — TCNT

It is not desirable that we should drop preaching the word of God — Mof

. . . neglect the teaching of God's word — Ber

It would be a grave mistake for us to neglect the word of God — NEB

and serve tables.

to attend to tables — TCNT

and attend to meals — Mof

to keep accounts — Gspd

to wait on tables — Wms

in order to make distribution of food — Bas

3. **Wherefore, brethren, look ye out among you**

. . . pick out from among yourselves — Wey

seven men of honest report,

. . . of good report — ASV

. . . who can be well-attested — Rhm

. . . of good reputation — Mof

. . . of good standing — Gspd

full of the Holy Ghost and wisdom,

full of the Spirit and of wisdom —-ASV

full of the Spirit, and of good practical sense — Wms

whom we may appoint over this business.

whom we will appoint over this need — Rhm

and we will appoint them to undertake this duty — Wey

and we will put them in charge of this matter — Gspd

and we will assign them to this business — Wms

and we will hand over the task to them — Rieu

4. **But we will give ourselves continually to prayer,**

But we will continue stedfastly in prayer — ASV

But, as for us, we will devote ourselves to prayer — Wey

Then we will give all our time . . . — Bas

Then we shall devote ourselves wholeheartedly . . . — Phi

. . . to conducting prayer — Rieu

and to the ministry of the word.

and in the ministry of the word — ASV

and to the delivery of the Message — TCNT

and the teaching of the word — Bas

and to the ministry of preaching — Knox

and preaching the gospel — Rieu

5. **And the saying pleased the whole multitude:**

And the saying was pleasing in the sight of all the throng — Rhm

This proposal was unanimously agreed to — TCNT

The suggestion met with general approval — Wey

This plan commended itself to the whole body — Mof

The whole group liked the idea — Beck

and they chose Stephen,

and they selected Stephen — Rhm

a man full of faith and of the Holy Ghost,

a man of firm faith and graced by the Holy Spirit — Rieu

and Philip, and Prochorus, and Nicanor, and Timon, and Parmenas, and Nicolas a proselyte of Antioch:

. . . Nicolaus . . . — ASV

and Nicholas of Antioch, a former convert to Judaism — TCNT

6. **Whom they set before the apostles:**

these men they presented to the apostles — Mof

These they set before the apostles — RSV

and when they had prayed, they laid their hands on them.

who then prayed and placed their hands on them — TCNT

and having prayed, they . . . — ABUV

and, after prayer, they . . . — Wey

7. And the word of God increased;

So God's Message spread — TCNT

Meanwhile God's word continued to spread — Wey

By now the word of God was gaining influence — Knox

and the number of the disciples multiplied in Jerusalem greatly;

. . . exceedingly — ASV

. . . rapidly — TCNT

and a great company of the priests were obedient to the faith.

and a large body of the priests accepted the Faith — TCNT

and a great multitude . . . were obeying the faith — ABUV

and a host of priests . . . — Mof

many of . . . had given their allegiance to . . . — Knox

and very many of . . . adhered to the Faith — NEB

8. And Stephen, full of faith and power,

. . . full of grace[20] and power — ASV

did great wonders and miracles among the people.

wrought great wonders and signs . . . — ASV

was doing . . . — ABUV

9. Then there arose certain of the synagogue, which is called the synagogue of the Libertines, and Cyrenians, and Alexandrians, and of them of Cilicia and of Asia,

But some members from the Synagogue known as that of the Freed Slaves and . . . as well as visitors from Cilicia and Roman Asia—TCNT

But some members of the synagogue called the Synagogue of Freedmen, comprising Cyrenians and Alexandrians and people from Cilicia and Asia — NEB

disputing with Stephen.

undertook to debate with Stephen — Gspd

tried debating with Stephen — Phi

10. And they were not able to resist the wisdom and the spirit by which he spake.

. . . to withstand the wisdom and the Spirit . . . — ASV

. . . to withstand his wisdom and inspiration — TCNT

but they could not cope with his good practical sense and the spiritual power . . . — Wms

but they were no match for Stephen's wisdom, and for the Spirit which then gave utterance — Knox

but found themselves quite unable to stand up against either his practical wisdom or the spiritual force with which he spoke — Phi

but could not hold their own against the inspired wisdom with which he spoke — NEB

11. Then they suborned men, which said,

Then they secretly instigated men, who said — RSV

Then they induced some men to say — TCNT

Then they privately put forward men who declared — Wey

They then instigated people to say — Mof

Thereupon they employed agents to say — Knox

In desperation they bribed men to allege — Phi

We have heard him speak blasphemous words against Moses, and against God.

. . . use abusive language about . . . — Gspd

We heard him slander Moses and God — Beck

12. And they stirred up the people,

In this way they excited the people — Wey

They aroused the people — Gspd

Having thus roused the feelings of the people — Knox

Thus they got the people wrought up — Ber

and the elders, and the scribes,

as well as the Councillors and Rabbis — TCNT

the elders, and the men of the Law — Beck

and came upon him, and caught him,

. . . and seized him — RSV

. . . and arrested him — TCNT

. . . seized him with violence — Wey

who rushed on him, dragged him away — Mof

---

[20]Variant reading.

they attacked and grabbed him — Ber

and brought him to the council,

and brought him to the Sanhedrin — ABUV

and marched him off before the Sanhedrin — Phi

and brought him before the court — Beck

13. **And set up false witnesses, which said,**

Here they brought forward false witnesses who declared — Wey

There they had witnesses stand up and lie — Beck

This man ceaseth not to speak blasphemous words against this holy place, and the law:

. . . to speak words against . . . — ASV

. . . is never done talking against . . . — Mof

. . . is never tired of uttering insults against . . . — Knox

. . . is always attacking the Temple and the Law — Rieu

14. **For we have heard him say,**

indeed, we have heard him declare — TCNT

Why, we have heard him say — Mof

that this Jesus of Nazareth shall destroy this place,

that Jesus, the Nazarene . . . — Wey

. . . will tear this place down — Gspd

. . . will demolish this place — Ber

and shall change the customs which Moses delivered us.

. . . handed down to us — TCNT

15. **And all that sat in the council, looking stedfastly on him,**

At once the eyes of all who were sitting in the Sanhedrin were fastened on him — Wey

As all those seated in the Sanhedrin gazed at him — Ber

Everyone in the Council-chamber gazed at Stephen — Rieu

The men seated in the council were all staring at Stephen — Nor

The eyes of all the members of the council were riveted upon Stephen — TCNT

And fixing their gaze on him, all who were sitting in the Council — NASB

saw his face as it had been the face of an angel.

and they saw his face looking like the face of an angel — TCNT

saw that his face shone like the face . . . — Mof

and his face appeared to them like the face . . . — NEB

CHAPTER 7

1. **Then said the high priest, Are these things so?**

Then the High Priest asked him, Are these statements true — Wey

. . . Are these charges true — Knox

. . . Is this so — RSV

2. **And he said, Men, brethren, and fathers, hearken;**

And he said, Brethren and fathers, hearken — ASV

. . . Brothers and Fathers, listen — TCNT

. . . Fellow Jews and fathers, listen — Beck

. . . fathers of this nation, listen to me — NEB

The God of glory appeared unto our father Abraham,

The Glorious God appeared to our ancestor . . . — TCNT

. . . our forefather . . . — Wey

when he was in Mesopotamia,

while . . . — Rhm

when he was living in . . . — Wey

when he was still in . . . — Mof

before he dwelt in Charran,

before he settled in Haran — TCNT

before he ever made his home in Haran — Wms

3. **And said unto him,**

and told him — Ber

Get thee out of thy country, and from thy kindred,

Leave your country and your kindred — TCNT

Leave your land and your countrymen — Mof

Leave your country and your relatives — Gspd

Go out of your land, and away from your family — Bas

and come into the land which I shall shew thee.

and go into whatever land I point out to you — Wey

. . . to which I direct thee — Knox

4. Then came he out of the land of the Chaldaeans,

Thereupon he left Chaldaea — Wey

So he left Chaldea — Mon

and dwelt in Charran:

. . . Haran — ASV

and from thence, when his father was dead,

and from there, after his father's death — TCNT

he removed him into this land, wherein ye now dwell.

God removed him into this land . . . — ASV

God shifted him . . . — Mof

God caused him to move into this country . . . — Gspd

God transferred him to this land . . . — Phi

God led him to migrate to this land . . . — NEB

he was led to this land . . . — Nor

5. And he gave him none inheritance in it,

God did not give him any property in it — TCNT

. . . no possession in it — Wey

He gave him no heritable property in it — Ber

Yet God gave him no part of it as an inheritance — Phi

He gave him nothing in it to call his own — NEB

Yet God did not give him any ownership in the land — Nor

no, not so much as to set his foot on:

not even a foot of ground — TCNT

not even a foot of the land — Mof

not a single foot — Gspd

not so much as a foot's space — Knox

not even a foot's length — RSV

yet he promised that he would give it to him for a possession,

And yet He promised to bestow the land as a permanent possession on him — Wey

. . . promised that it should eventually belong to him — Phi

and to his seed after him,

and for his descendants after him — TCNT

and his posterity . . . — Wey

and to his offspring . . . — Mof

when as yet he had no child.

though up to that time he had no children — TCNT

and promised this at a time when Abraham was childless — Wey

though at that time he had no descendant at all — Phi

6. And God spake on this wise,

What God said was this — TCNT

And this is what God told him — Knox

And God spoke to this effect — RSV

That his seed should sojourn in a strange land;

Abraham's descendants will live in a foreign country — TCNT

His descendants will be strangers, living in a foreign land — Gspd

. . . would live as strangers . . . — Knox

that his posterity would be aliens in a land belonging to others — RSV

and that they should bring them into bondage, and entreat them evil four hundred years.

. . . and treat them ill, four hundred years — ASV

where they will be enslaved and ill-treated for . . . — TCNT

. . . enslaved and oppressed . . . — Mof

. . . enslaved and misused . . . — Gspd

. . . enslaved and mistreated for . . . — NASB

7. And the nation to whom they shall be in bondage will I judge, said God:

But I will myself judge the nation, to which they shall be enslaved . . . — TCNT

And I will sentence the nation that has enslaved them . . . — Gspd

And whatever nation to which they shall be in bondage I myself will judge . . . — NASB

and after that shall they come forth,

and after that they will leave the country — TCNT

and at last they will escape — Knox

after that they shall come out free — Phi

and serve me in this place.

and render divine service unto me . . . — Rhm

and worship me in this very place — TCNT

and worship me on this spot — Gspd

8. And he gave him the covenant of circumcision:

. . . a covenant . . . — ABUV

And with Abraham He made the sacred compact of . . . — Wms

Then he made a covenant with Abraham, the covenant that ordained circumcision — Knox

and so Abraham begat Isaac, and circumcised him the eighth day;

and it was under these circumstances that Abraham became the father of Isaac . . . — TCNT

and under this Covenant he became the father of . . . — Wey

and Isaac begat Jacob; and Jacob begat the twelve patriarchs.

and Isaac became the father of Jacob; and Jacob of . . . — TCNT

Isaac had a son Jacob, and Jacob's sons were the founders of the Twelve Tribes — Rieu

9. And the patriarchs, moved with envy,

. . . moved with jealousy — ASV

The Patriarchs, out of jealousy—TCNT

sold Joseph into Egypt:

sold Joseph into slavery in Egypt — TCNT

and sold him as a slave into Egypt — Wms

sold Joseph as a slave, to be taken to Egypt — Knox

but God was with him,

10. And delivered him out of all his afflictions,

and rescued him out of all his tribulations — Rhm

and rescued him out of all his troubles — TCNT

and rescued him from his distress — Rieu

and gave him favour and wisdom in the sight of Pharaoh, king of Egypt;

and enabled him to win favour and a reputation for wisdom with Pharaoh . . . — TCNT

and allowing him to find favour for his wisdom with Pharaoh . . . — Mof

and enabled him to win favor and to show wisdom when he stood before Pharaoh . . . — Gspd

and won him favour and a name for wisdom with . . . — Knox

and he made him governor over Egypt and all his house.

who appointed him Governor of Egypt and of his whole household — TCNT

made him Governor of Egypt and put him in charge of his own entire household — Phi

. . . and all the royal household — Wey

Pharaoh made him governor of Egypt and controller of his household — Rieu

. . . appointed him chief administrator . . . — NEB

11. Now there came a dearth over all the land of Egypt and Chanaan,

Now there came a famine over all Egypt and Canaan — ASV

Then a famine spread over the whole of Egypt and Canaan — TCNT

and great affliction:

causing great distress — TCNT

attended with great misery — Mof

and there was great suffering — Gspd

which caused great suffering — Phi

and caused great hardship — NEB

and our fathers found no sustenance.

and our ancestors could find no food — TCNT

so that our ancestors could not find provender — Mof

and our forefathers could not find the simplest food — Wms

so that our fathers failed to find nourishment — Ber

12. But when Jacob heard that there was corn in Egypt,

. . . grain . . . — ASV

. . . food . . . — Mof

. . . wheat . . . — Ber

he sent out our fathers first.

he sent forth our fathers the first time — ASV

Jacob sent our ancestors there. This was their first visit — TCNT

Jacob sent our ancestors on their first visit to that country — Mof

13. And at the second time Joseph was made known to his brethren;

In the course of their second visit, Joseph made himself known to his brothers — TCNT

It was on their second visit that Joseph was recognized by his brothers — Phi

. . . Joseph told his brothers who he was — Beck

and Joseph's kindred was made known unto Pharaoh.

and Joseph's family became known to Pharaoh — RSV

and Joseph's race became manifest . . . — ASV

and Pharaoh learnt the parentage of Joseph — TCNT

and Pharaoh was informed of Joseph's lineage — Mof

and his ancestry became plain to Pharaoh — Phi

14. Then sent Joseph, and called his father Jacob to him,

Then Joseph sent an invitation to his father . . . — TCNT

and all his kindred, threescore and fifteen souls.

. . . all his relations, seventy-five persons in all — TCNT

and all his family, numbering seventy-five persons — Wey

15. So Jacob went down into Egypt,

and Jacob went south to Egypt — Mof

And Jacob moved down to Egypt — Nor

and died, he, and our fathers,

There he died and our ancestors too — TCNT

There he died, and so did our forefathers — Wey

where he and our fathers finished their course — Ber

16. And were carried over into Sychem,

. . . unto Shechem — ASV

and their bodies were removed to Shechem — TCNT

and they were carried back to Shechem — Gspd

and laid in the sepulchre that Abraham bought for a sum of money of the sons of Emmor the father of Sychem.

and laid in the tomb . . . for a price of silver of the sons of Hamor in Shechem — ASV

17. But when the time of the promise drew nigh,

Now just as the time of the promise was drawing near — TCNT

But as the time drew near for the fulfilment . . . — Wey

But as the promised time approached — Ber

which God had sworn to Abraham,

which God vouchsafed . . . — ASV

. . . had made . . . — TCNT

. . . promised . . . — ABUV

. . . had announced . . . — Ber

. . . had granted . . . — RSV

. . . had assured . . . — NASB

the people grew and multiplied in Egypt,

the people increased largely in numbers in Egypt — TCNT

the people became many times more numerous . . . — Wey

our nation in Egypt grew and increased in numbers — NEB

18. Till another king arose, which knew not Joseph.

till there arose another king over Egypt,[21] who . . . — ASV

till a new king, who knew nothing of Joseph, came to the throne — TCNT

. . . a different king . . . — Beck

. . . came to power . . . — Bas

19. The same dealt subtilly with our kindred,

. . . dealt craftily with our race — RSV

This king acted deceitfully towards our race — TCNT

He took a cunning method with our race — Mof

He took advantage of our people — Gspd

By taking a cunning advantage of our race — Wms

this king dealt treacherously with our race — Knox

He defrauded our race — Ber

This man cleverly victimized our race — Phi

He exploited our race — Nor

It was he who took shrewd advantage of our race — NASB

and evil entreated our fathers,

and ill-treated our fathers — ASV

and oppressed our forefathers — Wey

he oppressed our ancestors — Mof

was cruel to our fathers — Bas

and abused our fathers — Ber

and persecuted our forefathers — Rieu

and mistreated our fathers — NASB

so that they cast out their young children,

so as to cause their babies to be exposed — Rhm

making them abandon their own infants — TCNT

by forcing them to expose their infants — Mof

by forcing them to leave their babies out in the open — Rieu

to the end they might not live.

---

[21]"Over Egypt" represents a variant reading.

ACTS 7

that they might not be kept alive — RSV

so that they should not survive — TCNT

so that the race should die out — Phi

to die of exposure — Rieu

20. In which time Moses was born,
At this time Moses was born — RSV
At which season . . . — ASV
It was just at this time that . . . — TCNT
and was exceeding fair,
He was a wonderfully beautiful child — TCNT
and was beautiful before God[22]—ABUV
a divinely beautiful child — Mof
beautiful in God's sight — Ber
a child of remarkable beauty — Phi
He was a fine child, and pleasing to God — NEB
and nourished up in his father's house three months:
. . . reared . . . — TCNT
. . . cared for . . . — Wey
. . . brought up . . . — Mof
. . . nurtured in his parental home . . . — Ber
. . . nursed . . . — NEB

21. And when he was cast out,
but when he was exposed — Rhm
and, when he was abandoned — TCNT
At length he was cast out — Wey
then exposed to die — Rieu
Pharaoh's daughter took him up,
. . . rescued him — Rhm
. . . adopted him — Wey
. . . took him away — NASB
and nourished him for her own son.
and nourished him for herself as a son — Rhm
and reared him as her own son — TCNT
and brought him up as her own son — Wey
and brought him up to be her own son — Ber
. . . nurtured . . . — NASB
. . . raised him . . . — Beck

22. And Moses was learned in all the wisdom of the Egyptians,
. . . instructed . . . — ASV
. . . trained . . . — Rhm
. . . educated in all the learning . . . — TCNT
. . . educated in all the culture . . . — Mof
So Moses was educated in all the science and learning of the Egyptians — Ber

and was mighty in words and in deeds.
and he was mighty in his words and works — ASV
and showed ability in both speech and action — TCNT
and possessed great influence through his eloquence and his achievements — Wey
he was a strong man in speech and action — Mof
he was vigorous, too, in speech and in act — Knox
and became not only an excellent speaker but a man of action as well — Phi
and was a vigorous man, and forceful in his speech — Rieu
a powerful speaker and a man of action — NEB

23. And when he was full forty years old,
And when there was being fulfilled unto him a period of forty years — Rhm
When he was in his fortieth year — TCNT
And when he was nearly forty years old — ABUV
As he was rounding out his fortieth year — Wms
He was approaching the age of forty — NEB
it came into his heart to visit his brethren the children of Israel.
the thought came into his mind that he would visit his brother Israelites — TCNT
it occurred to him to visit his brethren the descendants of Israel — Wey
it entered his mind . . . — NASB

24. And seeing one of them suffer wrong,
and seeing one being wronged — Rhm
and seeing an Israelite ill-treated — TCNT
He saw one of them being badly treated — Mof
. . . being imposed upon — Wey
. . . being mistreated — Wms
. . . being attacked — Bas
. . . treated unfairly — Ber
he defended him,
he went to his help — TCNT
he took his part — Wey
he came to the rescue — Knox

[22]Variant reading.

474

and avenged him that was oppressed,

and avenged him that was getting worn out — Rhm

and secured justice for the ill-treated man — Wey

and paid rough justice . . . — Phi

and avenged the victim — NEB

and smote the Egyptian:

smiting . . . — ASV

by striking down . . . — TCNT

and gave the Egyptian a death-blow — Bas

by killing the Egyptian — Knox

by slaying . . . — Ber

25. **For he supposed his brethren would have understood**

He supposed that his brothers would understand — TCNT

He supposed his brethren to be aware — Wey

He thought . . . — Mof

how that God by his hand would deliver them:

that God through his hand would give them deliverance — Rhm

. . . was giving them deliverance — ASV

that God through his instrumentality . . . — Wms

that God was using him to rescue them — Phi

but they understood not.

but they failed to understand — Ber

but they did not understand — RSV

26. **And the next day he shewed himself unto them as they strove,**

And the day following he appeared unto them . . . — ASV

The next day he appeared on the scene again, as some of them were fighting — TCNT

. . . he came and found two of them fighting — Wey

. . . he came across two of them fighting — Gspd

. . . he came in sight when two of them were quarrelling — Knox

and would have set them at one again,

and would have reconciled them in peace — Rhm

and tried to make peace between them — TCNT

and tried to pacify them — Mof

and tried to bring them to make up their quarrel — NEB

saying, Sirs, ye are brethren;

. . . Men! ye are brothers! — Rhm

why do ye wrong one to another?

how is it that you are ill-treating one another — TCNT

why do you injure one another — Mof

why should you harm each other — Wms

why abuse each other — Ber

27. **But he that did his neighbour wrong thrust him away, saying,**

But he that was wronging his neighbour . . . — Rhm

The man who was ill-treating his fellow-workman pushed Moses aside with the words — TCNT

But the man who was doing the wrong resented his interference, and asked — Wey

But the aggressor thrust him off . . . — Gspd

Who made thee a ruler and a judge over us?

Who hath appointed thee to be . . . — Rhm

. . . ruler and umpire — Mof

Who made you our ruler and referee— Wms

28. **Wilt thou kill me, as thou didst the Egyptian yesterday?**

Do you mean to kill me as you killed . . . — Wey

Do you want to kill me as you killed . . . — RSV

29. **Then fled Moses at this saying,**

Alarmed at this question, Moses fled from the country — Wey

At this retort Moses fled — RSV

At that Moses fled — Mof

At this remark Moses fled — Ber

and was a stranger in the land of Madian,

and became a sojourner in the land of Midian — ASV

and became an exile in Midian—TCNT

and went and lived for a time in Midian — Gspd

and became an alien in the land of Midian — NASB

where he begat two sons.

in which country he had two sons born to him — TCNT

There he became the father of two sons — Wey

30. **And when forty years were expired,**

. . . were fulfilled — ASV

. . . had passed — RSV

At the end of forty years — TCNT
Forty years later — Knox
When forty years had passed — Wms
there appeared to him in the wilderness of mount Sina an angel of the Lord[23]
an angel appeared to him in the wilderness of Mount Sinai . . . — ASV
. . . in the Desert of Mount Sinai . . . — TCNT
. . . in the desert near Mount Sinai . . . — NEB
in a flame of fire in a bush.
in the flame of a burning thorn-bush — Mof

31. **When Moses saw it, he wondered at the sight:**
. . . marvelled . . . — Rhm
. . . was astonished . . . — TCNT
. . . was amazed . . . — Rieu
and as he drew near to behold it,
and as he was going near to observe — Rhm
but, on his going nearer to look at it more closely — TCNT
and as he drew near to consider it — ABUV
and as he approached to investigate — Ber
the voice of the Lord came unto him,
there came a voice of the Lord — ASV
the voice of the Lord said — Mof

32. **Saying, I am the God of thy fathers,**
I am the God of your ancestors — TCNT
I am the God of your forefathers — Wey
the God of Abraham, and the God[24] **of Isaac, and the God of Jacob.**
the God of Abraham, and of Isaac, and of Jacob — ASV
the God of Abraham, Isaac, and Jacob — TCNT
Then Moses trembled, and durst not behold.
Moses trembled all over, and did not dare to look — TCNT
Quaking with fear Moses did not dare to gaze — Wey
Moses was so terrified that he did not dare to look at the bush — Mof
Moses felt so shaken, he did not dare to investigate — Ber

33. **Then said the Lord to him,**
But the Lord said to him — Mof
Put off thy shoes from thy feet:

Loose the shoes from thy feet — ASV
Loose the sandals of thy feet — Rhm
Untie the sandals from your feet — Ber
Take off your shoes — Gspd
for the place where thou standest is holy ground.
for the spot on which you are standing . . . — Wey
. . . is sacred ground — Mof

34. **I have seen, I have seen the affliction of my people which is in Egypt,**
I have surely seen the affliction . . . — ASV
I have indeed seen the ill-treatment . . . — Rhm
I have indeed seen the oppression of my people, who are in Egypt — TCNT
Truly, I have seen the sorrows of my people in Egypt — Bas
The affliction of my people in Egypt is before my eyes continually — Knox
and I have heard their groaning,
. . . their groans — TCNT
. . . their lamenting — Knox
. . . their sighs — Rieu
and am come down to deliver them.
and have come down to rescue them — Rhm
and I have come down to deliver them — RSV
. . . to save them — Gspd
. . . to take them out — Nor
And now come, I will send thee into Egypt.
Come now, I will send you back to Egypt — Mof
. . . I will send you back to Egypt as my messenger — Wms

35. **This Moses whom they refused, saying,**
This same Moses, whom they had disowned with the words — TCNT
. . . whom they denied . . . — ABUV
. . . whom they rejected, asking him — Wey
. . . whom they pushed aside with the words — Rieu
. . . when they said — Mon
Who made thee a ruler and a judge?[25]

---

[23]The words "of the Lord" are now recognized as not adequately supported by original manuscripts.
[24]Some manuscripts do not repeat "the God."
[25]See verse 27.

the same did God send to be a ruler
and a deliverer
... a ruler and a saviour — Bas
this very man was commissioned as
ruler and liberator by God himself
— NEB
**by the hand of the angel which ap-
peared to him in the bush.**
with the hand ... — ASV
with the help of the angel ... — TCNT
by aid of the angel ... — Mof
by the agency of the angel ... — Rieu
speaking through the angel ... — NEB

36. **He brought them out,**
This man led them forth — ASV
He it was who led them out — TCNT
It was he who brought them out of
Egypt — Gspd
**after that he had shewed wonders and
signs in the land of Egypt,**
having wrought wonders and signs in
Egypt — ASV
after performing marvels and signs in
Egypt — Wey
by performing wonders and signs there
— Wms
working miracles and signs in Egypt —
NEB
**and in the Red sea, and in the wilder-
ness forty years.**
and at the Red Sea ... — Wey
... in the desert ... — Rhm

37. **This is that Moses, which said unto
the children of Israel,**
... who said ... — ASV
... unto the sons of Israel ... — Rhm
... to the people of Israel — TCNT
... to the descendants of Israel — Wey
... to the Israelites — RSV
**A prophet shall the Lord your[26] God
raise up unto you of your brethren,
like unto me; him shall ye hear.**
A prophet shall God raise up unto you
from among your brethren, like unto
me — ASV
God will raise up for you, from among
your brothers, a Prophet, as he
raised me up — TCNT
... just as He raised me up — Wey
... just as he appointed me — Nor

38. **This is he, that was in the church in
the wilderness with the angel that
spake to him in the mount Sina, and
with our fathers:**
... who appeared at the assembly in
the Desert ... — TCNT

This was the man who at the assembly
in the desert intervened between the
angel who spoke to him on mount
Sinai and our fathers — Mof
It was he who with the congregation in
the desert went between the angel
who spoke to him on Mount Sinai
and our forefathers — Gspd
**who received the lively oracles to give
unto us:**
... living oracles ... — ASV
... ever-living utterances to hand on to
us — Wey
... living Words ... — Mof
who ... received and communicated to
you utterances that still live — Gspd
... words of life ... — Knox

39. **To whom our fathers would not obey,**
to whom our fathers would not be
obedient — ASV
to whom our fathers were not willing
to become obedient — ABUV
Our forefathers, however, would not
submit to him — Wey
... would not listen to him — Gspd
by whom our fathers would not be controlled — Bas
To him our fathers did not want to
submit — Ber
Our fathers refused to obey him — RSV
But our forefathers would not accept
his leadership — NEB
but thrust him from them,
more than that, they rejected him —
TCNT
but spurned his authority — Wey
they pushed him aside — Mof
**and in their hearts turned back again
into Egypt,**
and hankered secretly after Egypt —
Mof
they turned their thoughts towards
Egypt — Knox

40. **Saying unto Aaron, Make us gods to
go before us:**
... that shall go before us — ASV
... Make gods for us, to march in
front of us — Wey
... Make gods for us, who will lead us
— Beck
**for as for this Moses, which brought
us out of the land of Egypt,**

[26]"The Lord your" and "him shall ye hear"
are now recognized as not adequately supported by original manuscripts.

477

... who led us forth ... — ASV

we wot not what is become of him.

we do not know what has become of him — TCNT

we don't know what has happened to him — Mof

41. And they made a calf in those days,

Moreover they made a calf at that time — Wey

They even made a calf ... — Gspd

So they fashioned a calf at this time — Knox

That was when they made the bull-calf — NEB

and offered sacrifice unto the idol,

and brought a sacrifice ... — ASV

... to this idol — Mof

and brought sacrifice to the image — Ber

and rejoiced in the works of their own hands.

and held festivities in honour of their own handiwork — TCNT

and kept rejoicing in the gods which their own hands had made — Wey

and held a celebration over what their own hands had made ... — Gspd

and got into a happy mood over their handiworks — Ber

and held a feast in honour of the thing their hands had made — NEB

42. Then God turned,

But God turned — ASV

So God turned away — TCNT

So God turned from them — Wey

and gave them up to worship the host of heaven;

and left them ... — Gspd

and abandoned them ... — Ber

... to serve ... — ASV

... the Starry Host — TCNT

as it is written in the book of the prophets,

as it stands written ... — NEB

O ye house of Israel, have ye offered to me slain beasts and sacrifices by the space of forty years in the wilderness?

Victims and sacrifices did ye offer unto me, forty years in the desert, O house of Israel — Rhm

... all those forty years in the Desert — TCNT

It was not to Me that you offered ... was it, O house of Israel — NASB

43. Yea, ye took up the tabernacle of Moloch,

Nay, you lifted up Moloch's tent — Wey

No, you offered me the tent of Moloch — Wms

No, you set up the tabernacle to Moloch — Nor

You took with you the tabernacle of Moloch — TCNT

and the star of your god Remphan,

And the star of the god Rephan—TCNT

and the star-symbol of Rephan your god — Mof

... Rompha — Gspd

figures which ye made to worship them:

The forms which ye made to bow down unto them — Rhm

The images which you had made to worship — TCNT

and I will carry you away beyond Babylon.

So I will exile you ... — TCNT

and I will remove you ... — RSV

So I will deport you ... — Gspd

I will banish you ... — NEB

44. Our fathers had the tabernacle of witness in the wilderness,

The tent of witness was with our fathers in the desert — Rhm

... the tabernacle of the testimony ... — ASV

... the tabernacle of Revelation ... — TCNT

In the desert our forefathers had the Tent of the Testimony — Gspd

... the tent in which God spake to His people — Beck

as he had appointed, speaking unto Moses,

even as he appointed who spake ... — ASV

according as he who was speaking ... gave instructions — Rhm

even as he directed ... — ABUV

as God gave orders to Moses — Bas

as God commanded when he told Moses — NEB

that he should make it according to the fashion that he had seen.

... according to the figure ... — ASV

... according to the model ... — Rhm

... in imitation of the model ... —Wey

... after the pattern ... — Mof

... after the design ... — Bas

45. Which also our fathers that came after

This Tabernacle, which was handed on to them — TCNT

which also our fathers in turn received — ABUV

That Tent was bequeathed to the next generation of our forefathers — Wey

Our fathers of the next generation — NEB

Our fathers who in turn inherited it — Nor

brought in with Jesus

. . . with Joshua — RSV

into the possession of the Gentiles,

when they entered on the possession of the nations — ASV

at the conquest of the nations — TCNT

when they were taking possession of the land of the Gentile nations — Wey

they dispossessed the nations — Gspd

whom God drave out before the face of our fathers,

that God thrust out . . . — ASV

which God thrust out before our fathers — RSV

for God drove them out as our ancestors advanced — Phi

unto the days of David;

and remained here down to the time of David — TCNT

So it continued till David's time — Wey

They used it till the time of David — Nor

46. Who found favour before God,

Who found favor in the sight of God — RSV

David won favour with God — TCNT

He won the approval of God — Gspd

who found grace before God — Ber

and desired to find a tabernacle for the God of Jacob.

and asked to find a habitation . . . — ASV

and asked permission to find a dwelling . . . — TCNT

and begged to be allowed to provide a dwelling . . . — Gspd

and longed to devise a resting-place for the God of Israel — Knox

47. But Solomon built him an house.

But it was Solomon who built a House for God — TCNT

but it was Solomon who came to build a house for Him — Wms

yet it was Solomon who built him a temple — Nor

48. Howbeit the most High dwelleth not in temples made with hands;

. . . does not dwell in anything hand-made — Ber

Yet it is not in buildings made by hands that the Most High dwells — TCNT

Yet of course the Most High does not live in man-made houses — Phi

as saith the prophet,

49. Heaven is my throne,

The heaven is my throne — ASV

The sky is a throne for me — TCNT

Heaven is the seat of my power — Bas

and earth is my footstool:

And the earth the footstool of my feet — ASV

And earth is a resting-place for my feet — Bas

what house will ye build me? saith the Lord:

What manner of house . . . — ASV

What kind of a house . . . — ABUV

or what is the place of my rest?

Or what place is there where I may rest — TCNT

Or what resting-place shall I have — Wey

On what spot could I settle — Mof

Or what place is there for My repose — NASB

50. Hath not my hand made all these things?

Did not my hand make . . . — RSV

Was it not my hand that made . . . — TCNT

Did not my hand make this universe — Mon

Are not all these things of my own making — NEB

51. Ye stiffnecked and uncircumcised in heart and ears,

You obstinate race, heathen in heart and ears — TCNT

You stubborn people, heathen in heart and ears — Gspd

O you stubborn people, hard of heart and hard of hearing — Rieu

How stubborn you are, heathen still at heart and deaf to the truth! — NEB

ye do always resist the Holy Ghost:

you are continually at strife with the Holy Spirit — Wey

you are forever resisting the Holy Spirit — TCNT

as your fathers did, so do ye.
your ancestors did it, and you are doing it still — TCNT
As with your fathers, so with you! — Mof
Just as your fathers did, so are you doing now — Phi
Like fathers, like sons — NEB

52. **Which of the prophets have not your fathers persecuted?**
Can you name a single prophet whom your fathers did not persecute — Phi
and they have slain them which shewed before of the coming of the Just One;
and they killed them that showed before of the coming of the Righteous One — ASV
They killed those who announced beforehand the coming . . . — Mof
They killed the men who foretold . . . — Wey
of whom ye have been now the betrayers and murderers:
whose betrayers and murderers you have now become — Wey
And here you have betrayed him, murdered him! — Mof

53. **Who have received the law by the disposition of angels,**
ye who received . . . as it was ordained by angels — ASV
. . . the Law as transmitted by angels — TCNT
. . . given through angels — Wey
. . . through mediation of angels — Ber
. . . as delivered by angels — RSV
. . . received the Law of God miraculously, by the hand of angels — Phi
and have not kept it.
and yet have not obeyed it — Wey

54. **When they heard these things,**
As they listened to this — TCNT
As they continued to listen to this address — Wms
While they were listening — Beck
they were cut to the heart,[27]
and they gnashed on him with their teeth.
and gnashed their teeth at Stephen — TCNT
and they ground their teeth at him in rage — Phi

55. **But he, being full of the Holy Ghost,**
. . . Holy Spirit — ASV

looked up stedfastly into heaven, and saw the glory of God,
fixed his eyes intently on the sky . . . — TCNT
gazed up at heaven . . . — Mof
he looked right into heaven . . . — Wms
and gazing intently up to heaven . . . — NEB
and Jesus standing on the right hand of God,
. . . at God's right hand — TCNT

56. **And said, Behold, I see the heavens opened,**
I can see heaven wide open, he said — Wey
Look, he said, I see heaven open — Mof
and the Son of man standing on the right hand of God.
and the Son of Man . . . at God's right hand — TCNT

57. **Then they cried out with a loud voice,**
But they . . . — ASV
At this, with a loud shout — TCNT
Upon this, with a loud outcry — Wey
But they uttered a great shout — Gspd
But they yelled at the top of their voices — Beck
and stopped their ears,
they stopped their ears — TCNT
they shut their ears — Mof
and held their ears — Wms
and put their fingers into their ears — Knox
and holding their hands to their ears — Ber
and covered their ears — NASB
and ran upon him with one accord,
and rushed upon him . . . — ASV
and rushed at him like one man — Mof
. . . in a body — Mon
Then they made one rush at him — NEB

58. **And cast him out of the city, and stoned him:**
forced him outside the city, and began to stone him — TCNT
and having cast him out of the city, they . . . — ABUV
dragged him out of the city . . . — Wey
and hustled him . . . — Phi
and, flinging him out of the city . . . — NEB

---

[27]See Acts 5:33.

and the witnesses laid down their
clothes at a young man's feet, whose
name was Saul.
... their garments ... — ASV
the witnesses throwing off their outer
garments and giving them into the
care of a young man called Saul —
Wey

**59. And they stoned Stephen, calling upon
God, and saying,**
And they continued stoning Stephen,
while he appealed to the Master —
TCNT
So they stoned Stephen, while he
prayed — Wey
As they stoned Stephen, he prayed —
Gspd
Lord Jesus, receive my spirit.
Jesus, Master ... — TCNT

**60. And he kneeled down, and cried with
a loud voice,**
Falling on his knees, he cried out loudly — TCNT

Then, rising on his knees, he cried
aloud — Wey
Then, on his knees, he cried in ringing
tones — Phi
Lord, lay not this sin to their charge.
Lord, do not reckon this sin against
them — Wey
... let not this sin stand against them
— Mof
... do not lay this sin up against them
— Gspd
... do not charge this sin on the book
against them — Wms
... do not hold this sin against them
— RSV
**And when he had said this, he fell
asleep.**
and with these words he fell asleep —
TCNT
With these words he slept the sleep of
death — Mof
... he went to his rest — Bas
... he fell asleep in the Lord — Knox

CHAPTER 8

**1. And Saul was consenting unto his
death.**
... was taking pleasure with them in
his death — Rhm
... fully approved of his murder —
Wey
... was altogether agreed to his murder
— Ber
... was in hearty agreement with putting him to death — NASB
**And at that time there was a great per-
secution against the church which
was at Jerusalem;**
And there arose on that day a great
persecution ... — ASV
On that very day a great storm of persecution burst upon the Church in
Jerusalem — Phi
**and they were all scattered abroad
throughout the regions of Judaea
and Samaria, except the apostles.**
and its members were all scattered ...
— TCNT
and all except the apostles were scattered ... — Wey
and all except the apostles were scattered about over the countryside of
Judaea and Samaria — Knox

**2. And devout men carried Stephen to his
burial,**

And devout men buried Stephen — ASV
Some religious men ... — TCNT
Some pious men ... — Gspd
And God-fearing men ... — Bas
While reverent men ... — Phi
and made great lamentation over him.
with loud lamentations for him —
TCNT
making a great weeping over him —
Bas

**3. As for Saul, he made havock of the
church,**
But Saul laid waste the church — ASV
But Saul began ravaging the church —
NASB
But Saul began to devastate the Church
— TCNT
entering into every house,
entering house after house — TCNT
by entering one house after another —
Mof
forcing himself into homes — Ber
**and haling men and women committed
them to prison.**
and dragging ... — ASV
and dragging off ... — Wey
and dragging people off, even women
... — Rieu

**4. Therefore they that were scattered
abroad**

481

Now those who were scattered in different directions — TCNT

They therefore that were dispersed — ABUV

But those who had taken flight — Bas

Those who had been driven away — Knox

went every where preaching the word.

went from place to place, with the Good News of the Message — TCNT

went through the land preaching the gospel — Mof

. . . spreading the gospel of God's Word — Wey

. . . with the happy tidings of the Word — Ber

5. **Then Philip went down to the city of Samaria,**

. . . to one of the cities of Samaria — Knox

. . . to a city of Samaria — RSV

and preached Christ unto them.

and proclaimed unto them the Christ — ASV

and there began proclaiming the Messiah — Rieu

6. **And the people with one accord gave heed unto those things which Philip spake,**

And the multitudes gave heed with one accord unto the things that were spoken by Philip — ASV

Crowds of people with one accord gave attention . . . — Wey

And the crowds attended like one man to what was said by Philip — Mof

The crowds unanimously attended to the teachings of Philip — Ber

hearing and seeing the miracles which he did.

when they heard, and saw the signs . . . — ASV

when they heard of, and saw the signs . . . — TCNT

listening to him and watching the miracles . . . — Mof

when they heard him and saw the signs . . . — RSV

7. **For unclean spirits, crying with loud voice, came out of many that were possessed with them:**

For from many of those that had unclean spirits, they came out, crying with a loud voice — ASV

For there were many cases of people with wicked spirits, where the spirits, with loud screams, came out of them — TCNT

For many of those under the power of foul spirits cried out and the spirits came out of them — Wms

and many taken with palsies, and that were lame, were healed.

and many who were paralyzed and lame were cured — TCNT

and many paralytics and lame persons were restored to health — Wey

8. **And there was great joy in that city.**

. . . much joy . . . — ASV

so that there was great rejoicing throughout that city — TCNT

9. **But there was a certain man, called Simon,**

. . . Simon by name — ASV

which beforetime in the same city used sorcery,

. . . magical arts — Rhm

who had been practising magic there — TCNT

. . . practicing witchcraft — Beck

and bewitched the people of Samaria,

and amazed . . . — ASV

and amazing the nation of Samaria — ABUV

and astonishing the Samaritans — Wey

to the utter astonishment of the Samaritan nation — Mof

who had kept the Samaritan people thrilled — Wms

and had swept the Samaritans off their feet — NEB

giving out that himself was some great one:

saying that himself was someone great — Rhm

pretending that he was more than human — Wey

and who made great pretensions — Gspd

and pretending to have great powers — Knox

10. **To whom they all gave heed, from the least to the greatest, saying,**

Every one, high and low, listened attentively to him — TCNT

To him people of all classes paid attention . . . — Wey

Everybody, high and low, kept running after him . . . — Wms

so that high and low hung upon his words — Knox

All classes flocked to him — Rieu

This man is the great power of God.

This man is the power of God which is called Great — ASV

This man, they used to say, must be that Power of God which men call The Great Power — TCNT

. . . the Power of God, known as the Great Power — Wey

He must be what is known as the Great Power of God! — Gspd

. . . The Mighty One of God — Rieu

11. And to him they had regard, because that of long time he had bewitched them with sorceries.

And they gave heed to him . . . — ASV

They attached themselves to him because he had dazzled them with his skill in magic for a considerable time — Mof

. . . amazed them with his magic — RSV

. . . thrilled them with his magical performances — Wms

. . . kept them excited with magic arts — Ber

They had been under the spell of his magic for so long that they were confirmed followers of his — Rieu

12. But when they believed Philip preaching the things concerning the kingdom of God, and the name of Jesus Christ,

. . . Philip's message of the good news of the Kingdom . . . — Wey

But when they believed Philip, who was preaching the glad tidings . . . — Mon

until Philip came and preached to them about God's kingdom. Then they found faith — Knox

they were baptized, both men and women.

men and women alike accepted baptism — Gspd

and were baptized, men and women alike — Knox

13. Then Simon himself believed also:

Indeed Simon himself believed — TCNT

Even Simon himself believed — RSV

and when he was baptized, he continued with Philip,

and after his baptism attached himself to Philip — TCNT

and after being baptized remained in close attendance on Philip — Wey

. . . devoted himself to Philip — Gspd

and was baptized, and thereupon was constantly in Philip's company — NEB

. . . after which he stayed by Philip faithfully — Nor

and wondered, beholding the miracles and signs which were done.

and beholding signs and great miracles wrought, he was amazed — ASV

and was full of amazement at seeing such signs and such great miracles performed — Wey

utterly astonished . . . — Mof

he was always thrilled . . . — Wms

He was carried away when he saw . . . — NEB

As he saw the signs and remarkable demonstrations of power which took place, he lived in a state of constant wonder — Phi

14. Now when the apostles which were at Jerusalem

. . . apostles at Jerusalem — RSV

heard that Samaria had received the word of God,

heard that the Samaritans had welcomed God's Message — TCNT

they sent unto them Peter and John:

they despatched Peter and John — Mof

15. Who, when they were come down, prayed for them, that they might receive the Holy Ghost:

On their arrival, they prayed that the Samaritans might receive the Holy Spirit — TCNT

. . . prayed for the believers to receive the Holy Spirit — Ber

16. (For as yet he was fallen upon none of them:

For He had not as yet fallen upon any of them — Wey

For until then the Spirit had not come upon any of them — NEB

only they were baptized in the name of the Lord Jesus.)

only they had been baptized into the name . . . — ASV

they had simply been baptized . . . — Mon

17. Then laid they their hands on them,

Then the Apostles laid their hands upon them — Wey

Then they put their hands on them — Bas

... placed their hands on them — Ber
and they received the Holy Ghost.

18. **And when Simon saw that through laying on of the apostles' hands the Holy[28] Ghost was given,**

    ... the Spirit was being given — Rhm

    When Simon saw that the Spirit was bestowed ... — NEB

    he offered them money,

    he brought them a sum of money — TCNT

19. **Saying, Give me also this power,**

    ... this authority — Rhm

    that on whomsoever I lay hands, he may receive the Holy Ghost.

    so that, if I place my hands upon any one, he may receive the Holy Spirit — TCNT

    to communicate the holy Spirit to anyone I lay my hands upon — Gspd

    so that if I were to put my hands on anyone he could receive ... — Phi

20. **But Peter said unto him, Thy money perish with thee,**

    ... Thy silver perish with thee — ASV

    ... Thy silver with thee go to destruction! — Rhm

    Take your money to perdition with you! ... — TCNT

    Perish your money and yourself ... — Wey

    ... Death to you and your money — Mof

    ... Go to destruction with your money — Gspd

    because thou hast thought that the gift of God may be purchased with money.

    because you have imagined that you can obtain God's free gift with money — Wey

    because you have supposed ... — Mon

    How dare you think you could buy the gift of God? — Phi

21. **Thou hast neither part nor lot**

    You have no share or part ... — TCNT

    in this matter:

    in our Message — TCNT

    in this religion — Mof

    in this movement — Gspd

    in these doings — Knox

    in this ministry — Phi

    for thy heart is not right in the sight of God.

    for your heart is not right with God — TCNT

... not sincere ... — Wms

... not true ... — Knox

... not straight ... — Ber

... not honest ... — Phi

for you are dishonest with God — NEB

22. **Repent therefore of this thy wickedness,**

    Let your heart be changed — Bas

    So, repent of this crookedness of yours — Ber

    Repent of your sin — Rieu

    and pray God,[29]

    ... pray the Lord — ASV

    ... beseech the Lord — Mon

    ... plead with the Lord — Ber

    if perhaps the thought of thine heart may be forgiven thee.

    that, if possible, you may be forgiven for such a thought — TCNT

    in the hope that the purpose which is in your heart may perhaps be forgiven you — Wey

    to forgive you for what you had in mind — Ber

23. **For I perceive that thou art in the gall of bitterness, and in the bond of iniquity.**

    for I see that you have fallen into the bitterness of envy and the fetters of sin — TCNT

    For I see you are a bitter poison and a pack of evil — Mof

    ... you are a bitter weed and a bundle of crookedness — Wms

    For I can see inside you, and I see a man bitter with jealousy and bound with his own sin — Phi

    I can see that you are doomed to taste the bitter fruit and wear the fetters of sin — NEB

    For I see that you are poisoned with envy and are a slave of wrong-doing — Nor

    I see you're turning to bitter poison and being chained by wickedness — Beck

24. **Then answered Simon, and said,**

    Simon replied — Mof

    Pray ye to the Lord for me,

    Entreat ye in my behalf unto the Lord — Rhm

    Beseech the Lord for me! — Mof

---

[28]The word "Holy" is now recognized as not adequately supported by original manuscripts.
[29]The word "God" is now recognized as not adequately supported by original manuscripts.

You plead with the Lord for me — Ber
Pray to the Lord for me yourselves — NASB

that none of these things which ye have spoken come upon me.

that nothing you have said may befall me — Mof

... may happen to me — Mon

25. And they, when they had testified and preached the word of the Lord,

... having fully borne witness and spoken ... — Rhm

So the Apostles, after giving a solemn charge and delivering the Lord's Word — Wey

After bearing their testimony to the word of the Lord and preaching it — Mof

So the apostles, after bearing solemn witness, and declaring the message of the Lord — Mon

Then after they had thoroughly testified and talked over the Lord's teachings — Ber

after having given earnest personal testimony ... — Nor

returned to Jerusalem,

began their return ... — Rhm

made their way back to Jerusalem — TCNT

they began their journey back — Knox

they took the road back ... — NEB

and preached the gospel in many villages of the Samaritans.

telling the Good News, as they went, in many Samaritan villages — TCNT

preaching the gospel to many villages of the Samaritans — RSV

evangelizing many Samaritan villages as they went — Mon

26. And the angel of the Lord spake unto Philip, saying,

Meanwhile an angel of the Lord had said to Philip — TCNT

Arise, and go toward the south unto the way that goeth down from Jerusalem unto Gaza,

Rise and proceed south to the road that runs down from Jerusalem to Gaza — Wey

Get up and go south, along the road from ... — Mof

... along the road that runs down from Jerusalem to Gaza — TCNT

... by the road that runs from ... — Gspd

... down the road which runs from ... — Phi

Rise up and go south. Take the road ... — Nor

which is desert.

the same is desert — ASV

(It is now deserted.) — TCNT

crossing the desert — Wey

(the desert-route) — Mof

(The town is now deserted.) — Gspd

this is the desert road — Wms

a lonely road — Ber

out in the desert — Phi

It is a deserted road — Beck

27. And he arose and went:

So he set out on his journey — TCNT

So he got up and went on his way — Mof

and, behold, a man of Ethiopia, an eunuch of great authority under Candace queen of the Ethiopians,

and on his way he came upon an official of high rank, in the service of Candance, Queen of the Abyssinians — TCNT

... a eunuch, a state-officer ... — ABUV

... an Ethiopian eunuch, a member of the court of ... — Gspd

... a high official of the Kandake, or Queen, of Ethiopia — NEB

who had the charge of all her treasure,

who was over all her treasure — ASV

He was her Treasurer — TCNT

as her treasurer — Wey

(he was her chief treasurer) — Mof

and had come to Jerusalem for to worship,

who had come to Jerusalem to worship — ASV

He had been to Jerusalem on a pilgrimage — NEB

28. Was returning, and sitting in his chariot read Esaias the prophet.

and he was returning and sitting in his chariot, and was reading the prophet Isaiah — ASV

was now on his way home, sitting in his carriage and reading ... — TCNT

... sitting in his carriage and reading aloud ... — NEB

29. Then the Spirit said unto Philip, Go near, and join thyself to this chariot.

Go up and join this chariot — RSV

... Go up and keep close to the carriage — TCNT

. . . Go up and contact that chariot — Ber

. . . Approach this carriage, and keep close to it — NEB

30. And Philip ran thither to him,

So Philip ran up — TCNT

and as Philip ran up — Ber

And when Philip had run up — NASB

and heard him read the prophet Esaias, and said,

and heard him reading Isaiah the prophet . . . — RSV

Understandest thou what thou readest?

Do you really understand what you are reading — TCNT

Is the sense of what you are reading clear to you — Bas

31. And he said, How can I, except some man should guide me?

. . . unless someone will explain it to me — TCNT

. . . puts me on the right track — Mof

. . . shall show me the way — Mon

. . . teaches me — Wms

. . . will give me the clue — NEB

And he desired Philip that he would come up and sit with him.

And he earnestly invited Philip to come up . . . — Wey

And he begged Philip to get up and sit beside him — Mof

. . . to climb in and to be seated with him — Ber

32. The place of the scripture which he read was this,

Now the passage of the scripture which he was reading was this — RSV

. . . the portion of Scripture . . . — Mon

He was led as a sheep to the slaughter;

As a sheep unto slaughter was he led — Rhm

Like a sheep he was led away to be slaughtered — Gspd

and like a lamb dumb before his shearer,

And as a lamb is mute in the hands of its shearer — TCNT

or a lamb before its shearer is dumb — RSV

And as a lamb is quiet when its wool is being cut — Bas

And as a lamb before its shearer is silent — NASB

so opened he not his mouth:

So he openeth not . . . — ASV

So he refrains from opening his lips — TCNT

So he made no sound — Bas

33. In his humiliation his judgment was taken away:

In his humiliation justice was denied him — RSV

In his lowly condition justice was denied him — TCNT

By humbling himself he had his doom removed — Mof

His sentence ended in his humiliation — Gspd

He was brought low, and all his rights taken away — Knox

In his humiliation he was deprived of his trial — Ber

Here he was humbled, but the judgment on him was reversed — Rieu

He has been humiliated and has no redress — NEB

When He humbles Himself, His condemnation will be taken away — Beck

and who shall declare his generation?

His generation who shall describe — Rhm

Who will tell the story of his age — TCNT

Who will make known His posterity — Wey

Who can tell his family — Mof

Who can tell of his times — Wms

Who will tell the story to His generation — Nor

And who will be able to calculate the number of his followers — Rieu

And who can express the wickedness of the people of His generation — Tay

for his life is taken from the earth.

For He is destroyed from among men — Wey

For His life is removed from the earth — Wms

For he is raised up to a life above the land of the living — Rieu

34. And the eunuch answered Philip, and said,

So the eunuch said to Philip — Mof

And the eunuch turned to Philip, and said — Knox

I pray thee, of whom speaketh the prophet this?

Will you tell me whom the Prophet is speaking about — TCNT

Tell me, about whom does the prophet say this — Knox

of himself, or of some other man?
himself, or someone else — TCNT

35. Then Philip opened his mouth, and began at the same scripture, and preached unto him Jesus.
And Philip opened his mouth, and beginning from this scripture . . . — ASV
Then Philip began, and taking this passage as his text, told him the Good News about Jesus — TCNT
. . . preached the gospel of Jesus to him — Mof

36. And as they went on their way,
Presently, as they were going along the road — TCNT
As they travelled on — Mof
As they continued down the road — Wms

they came unto a certain water:
they came to some water — TCNT

and the eunuch said, See, here is water; what doth hinder me to be baptized?
. . . what is to prevent my being baptized — TCNT
. . . What is there to keep me from being baptized — Wms
. . . what forbids my being immersed — ABUV

37. And Philip said, If thou believest with all thine heart, thou mayest. And he answered and said, I believe that Jesus Christ is the Son of God.[30]

38. And he commanded the chariot to stand still:
So he ordered the carriage to stop — TCNT
And he gave orders for the carriage to stop — Phi

and they went down both into the water, both Philip and the eunuch; and he baptized him.
. . . and he immersed him — ABUV
and they both went down into the water . . . — RSV
and Philip and the eunuch went down into the water, and Philip baptized him — Gspd

and both of them, Philip and the eunuch, went down into the water, and Philip baptized him — Mon

39. And when they were come up out of the water,
And when they came up . . . — RSV
But no sooner had they come up . . . — Wey

the Spirit of the Lord caught away Philip,
. . . snatched Philip away — Mon
. . . suddenly took Philip away — Wms
. . . hurriedly transported Philip — Ber
. . . caught up Philip — RSV

that the eunuch saw him no more:
and the eunuch . . . — ASV
That was the last the eunuch saw of him — Rieu

and he went on his way rejoicing.
With a glad heart he resumed his journey — Wey
so he went joyfully on his way — Ber

40. But Philip was found at Azotus:
Philip was found at Ashdod — TCNT
but Philip found himself at Azotus — Wey
As for Philip, he was next heard of at Azotus — Knox
Philip appeared at Azotus — NEB

and passing through he preached in all the cities, till he came to Caesarea.
and passing on . . . — RSV
. . . he preached the gospel to all the cities . . . — ASV
and as he went along, he told the Good News . . . — TCNT
and went on telling the good news in all the towns all the way to Caesarea — Gspd
and from thence he set out on a missionary journey through all the cities, ending up in Caesarea — Rieu
and toured the country, preaching in all the towns till he reached Caesarea — NEB

---

[30]Verse 37 is now recognized as not adequately supported by original manuscripts.

CHAPTER 9

1. **And Saul, yet breathing out threatenings and slaughter against the disciples of the Lord,**

   But Saul, yet breathing threatening . . . — ASV

   . . . still uttering murderous threats against . . . — TCNT

   Now Saul, whose every breath was a threat of destruction . . . — Wey

   went unto the high priest,

   called on the high priest — Ber

2. **And desired of him letters to Damascus to the synagogues,**

   and asked him for letters addressed to the Jewish congregations at Damascus — TCNT

   and begged from him letters addressed to the synagogues in Damascus — Wey

   that if he found any of this way, whether they were men or women,

   that if he found any that were of the Way . . . — ASV

   so that if he found any men or women there who belonged to the Way — Gspd

   authorizing him to arrest . . . — NEB

   he might bring them bound unto Jerusalem.

   . . . bring them in chains . . . — Wey

   he might have them put in chains and taken to . . . — TCNT

   he might take them as prisoners, to Jerusalem — Bas

3. **And as he journeyed, he came near Damascus:**

   And as he journeyed it came to pass that he drew nigh unto . . . — ASV

   While on his journey, as he was getting near . . . — TCNT

   As he traveled on he finally approached . . . — Wms

   and suddenly there shined round about him a light from heaven:

   suddenly a light from the sky flashed all round him — TCNT

4. **And he fell to the earth,**

   . . . upon the earth — ASV

   He fell to the ground — TCNT

   and heard a voice saying unto him, Saul, Saul, why persecutest thou me?

   . . . why are you persecuting me — TCNT

5. **And he said, Who art thou, Lord?**

   . . . Who are you, sir — Gspd

   And the Lord said, I am Jesus whom thou persecutest:

   . . . I am Jesus, whom you are persecuting — RSV

   it is hard for thee to kick against the pricks.[31]

6. **And he trembling and astonished said, Lord, what wilt thou have me to do? And the Lord said unto him,**

   Arise, and go into the city, and it shall be told thee what thou must do.

   . . . what you ought to do — Gspd

   . . . what thy work is — Knox

7. **And the men which journeyed with him stood speechless,**

   Meanwhile the men who travelled with Saul were standing dumb with amazement — Wey

   His fellow-travellers stood speechless — Mof

   Saul's travelling companions . . . —Rieu

   hearing a voice, but seeing no man.

   hearing the sound of the voice . . . — TCNT

8. **And Saul arose from the earth;**

   Saul got up from the ground — Mof

   and when his eyes were opened, he saw no man:

   . . . he saw nothing — ASV

   though his eyes were open, he could see nothing — TCNT

   but they led him by the hand, and brought him into Damascus.

   So his men led him by the hand till they got him into Damascus — TCNT

   They had to take him by the hand and lead him . . . — Gspd

9. **And he was three days without sight,**

   and for three days he was unable to see — TCNT

   and for three days he remained blind — Ber

   and neither did eat nor drink.

   and neither ate nor drank — RSV

10. **And there was a certain disciple at Damascus, named Ananias;**

    and to him said the Lord in a vision, Ananias.

---

[31]The last clause of verse 5 and the first half of verse 6 are not in the original manuscripts at this place. (Cf. Acts 22:10; 26:14.)

The Lord spake to this man in a dream
. . . — Phi

And he said, Behold, I am here, Lord.
. . . Yes, Master — TCNT
. . . Yes, Lord — Gspd
I am here, Lord . . . — Phi

11. **And the Lord said unto him, Arise, and go into the street which is called Straight,**
. . . and go to Straight Street — Wey
and enquire in the house of Judas for one called Saul, of Tarsus:
for, behold, he prayeth,
for he is even now praying — Wey
for he is there praying — Gspd
You will find him at prayer — NEB

12. **And hath seen in a vision[32] a man named Ananias coming in,**
And he hath seen a man named Ananias . . . — ASV
he has had a vision of a man named Ananias . . . — NEB
He has had a vision and seen a man named Ananias . . . — Gspd
and putting his hand on him, that he might receive his sight.
. . . to bring back his sight — Mof
. . . to restore his sight — Gspd

13. **Then Ananias answered, Lord, I have heard by many of this man,**
. . . I have heard from many people about this man — TCNT
how much evil he hath done to thy saints at Jerusalem:
and about the great mischief he has done . . . — Wey
especially the great suffering he has brought on your people in . . . — Wms
. . . your holy people in Jerusalem — Phi

14. **And here he hath authority from the chief priests to bind all that call on thy name.**
. . . to put in chains all those who invoke your name — TCNT
and here he is authorized by the High Priests to arrest . . . — Wey

15. **But the Lord said unto him, Go thy way:**
. . . Go — Wey
. . . Go on thy errand — Knox
for he is a chosen vessel unto me,
. . . my chosen instrument — TCNT
. . . the means I have chosen — Gspd

to bear my name before the Gentiles, and kings, and the children of Israel:
. . . before the heathen and their kings, and the people of Israel — TCNT
. . . before the Gentiles and their kings as well as before the sons of Israel — Mof
. . . the descendants of Israel — Gspd

16. **For I will shew him how great things he must suffer for my name's sake.**
For I am going to show him what he will have to endure for my sake — Gspd
Indeed, I myself will show him . . . — Phi

17. **And Ananias went his way, and entered into the house;**
And Ananias departed . . . — ASV
So Ananias went off and entered the house — Mof
and putting his hands on him said,
and laying . . . — ASV
Brother Saul, the Lord, even Jesus, that appeared unto thee in the way as thou camest, hath sent me,
Saul, my Brother, I have been sent by The Lord — by Jesus, who appeared to you on your way here — TCNT
. . . I have been sent by the Lord Jesus — Gspd
that thou mightest receive thy sight,
— so that you may recover your sight — TCNT
. . . regain your sight — Mof
and be filled with the Holy Ghost.
. . . the Holy Spirit — ASV

18. **And immediately there fell from his eyes as it had been scales:**
Instantly something like scales fell from Saul's eyes — TCNT
. . . what seemed to be scales — Wey
and he received sight forthwith,
and his sight was restored — TCNT
and he could see once more — Wey
he regained his sight — Mof
and arose, and was baptized.
Then he got up . . . — TCNT
and arose, and was immersed — ABUV
Upon this he rose and received baptism — Wey

19. **And when he had received meat, he was strengthened.**
and he took food and was strengthened — ASV

---

[32]Some manuscripts omit "in a vision."

and after he had taken food, felt his strength return — TCNT

. . . and regained his strength — Wey

Then was Saul certain days with the disciples which were at Damascus.

Then he remained some little time . . . — Wey

For several days . . . — Mof

20. **And straightway he preached Christ in the synagogues,**

. . . he proclaimed Jesus . . . — ASV

Soon he was proclaiming Jesus publicly in . . . — NEB

that he is the Son of God.

saying, He is the Son of God — RSV

21. **But all that heard him were amazed, and said;**

Everyone was astonished, and said — Gspd

All his hearers were staggered and kept saying — Phi

And all those hearing him continued to be amazed, and were saying — NASB

Is not this he that destroyed them which called on this name in Jerusalem,

Is not this he that in Jerusalem made havoc of them that called on this name — ASV

. . . harassed . . . — Wms

. . . brought ruin on . . . — Knox

. . . who went ravaging . . . — Ber

and came hither for that intent, that he might bring them bound unto the chief priests?

And who had also come here for the express purpose of having such persons put in chains and taking them before . . . — TCNT

and came down here with the sole object of taking back all such people as prisoners before the Chief Priests — Phi

22. **But Saul increased the more in strength,**

Saul's power, however, kept steadily increasing — TCNT

Saul, however, gained power more and more — Wey

Saul became more and more vigorous — Mof

But Saul grew more and more powerful — Gspd

But Saul was inspired with ever greater strength — Knox

But Saul went on from strength to strength — Phi

But Saul grew more and more forceful — NEB

and confounded the Jews which dwelt at Damascus,

and was confounding . . . — Rhm

and bewildered . . . — Gspd

and continued to put to utter confusion . . . — Wms

and silenced . . . — Knox

He put the Jewish residents in Damascus to confusion — Mof

proving that this is very Christ.

proving that Jesus was the Christ — RSV

by the proofs he gave that Jesus was the Christ — TCNT

with his proofs that Jesus is the Christ — Wey

by proving from the Scriptures that Jesus was the Messiah — Rieu

23. **And after that many days were fulfilled,**

Now when a considerable number of days were being fulfilled — Rhm

After some time had gone by — TCNT

after a number of days had elapsed — Mof

After several days had gone by — Wms

As the days mounted up — NEB

the Jews took counsel to kill him:

the Jews took counsel together . . . — ASV

the Jews laid a plot to kill Saul — TCNT

the Jews consulted together . . .—ABUV

. . . conspired to make away with him — Mof

. . . hatched a plot against his life — NEB

24. **But their laying await was known of Saul.**

but their plot became known to Saul — RSV

but information of their intention was given to him — Wey

but Saul found out about the plot — Gspd

but Saul got wind of their plot — Ber

And they watched the gates day and night to kill him.

and they were even narrowly watching the gates, both day and night, that they might kill him — Rhm and, although they kept watch on the gates . . . — Mof

They watched the city gates . . . — Gspd

Day and night they kept guarding the city gates, to murder him — Wms

25. Then the disciples took him by night, and let him down by the wall in a basket.

but the disciples taking him by night through the wall let him down, lowering him in a basket — Rhm

but his disciples let him down by night through an opening in the wall, lowering him in a basket — TCNT

. . . let him down over the wall — RSV

. . . by lowering him in a hamper-basket — Wms

. . . lowering him to the ground in a hamper — Knox

his disciples managed one night to let him down over the wall by lowering him in a basket — Mof

26. And when Saul[33] was come to Jerusalem,

And when he was come to Jerusalem — ASV

On his arrival at Jerusalem — TCNT

When he reached Jerusalem — Gspd

he assayed to join himself to the disciples:

and made several attempts to associate with the disciples — Wey

and tried to join the disciples — Mof

where he tried to attach himself to . . . — Knox

but they were all afraid of him, and believed not that he was a disciple.

. . . not believing that he was . . . — ASV

. . . unable to believe that he was really . . . — Mof

. . . they could not believe he was a true . . . — Knox

. . . not believing that his conversion was genuine — Rieu

27. But Barnabas took him, and brought him to the apostles,

Barnabas, however, introduced him to the apostles — TCNT

Barnabas, however, got hold of him and brought . . . — Mof

. . . took him up and presented him . . . — Wms

. . . took him by the hand and brought . . . — Knox

and declared unto them how he had seen the Lord in the way, and that he had spoken to him,

and told them the story of how Saul on his journey . . . — TCNT

. . . and heard his voice — NEB

and how he had preached boldly at Damascus in the name of Jesus.

and how in Damascus he had spoken out fearlessly . . . — TCNT

. . . he had fearlessly taught . . . — Wey

and how courageously he had spoken . . . — Wms

28. And he was with them coming in and going out at Jerusalem.

After that, Saul remained at Jerusalem, on familiar terms with the Apostles — TCNT

Henceforth Saul was one of them, going in and out of the city — Wey

After that, he associated with them freely in Jerusalem — Gspd

Saul now stayed with them, moving about freely in . . . — NEB

29. And he spake boldly in the name of the Lord Jesus,[34]

preaching boldly[35] in the name of the Lord — ASV

and disputed against the Grecians:

and he spoke and disputed against the Grecian Jews — ASV

talking and arguing with the Greek-speaking Jews — TCNT

and was speaking and disputing against the Grecian Jews — ABUV

And he often talked with the Hellenists and had discussions with them — Wey

he also held conversations and debates with the Hellenists — Mof

but they went about to slay him.

but they were seeking to kill him — ASV

But they kept trying to murder him — Wms

But they planned to murder him — NEB

[33]The word "Saul" is now recognized as not adequately supported by original manuscripts.
[34]The word "Jesus" is now recognized as not adequately supported by original manuscripts.
[35]See verse 27.

30. Which when the brethren knew,
And when the brethren knew it — ASV
But when the Brethren found this out — TCNT
they brought him down to Caesarea, and sent him forth to Tarsus.
and then sent him by sea to Tarsus — Wey

31. Then had the churches rest throughout all Judaea and Galilee and Samaria, and were edified;
So the church throughout all Judaea and Galilee and Samaria had peace, being . . . — ASV
. . . being built up — ABUV
. . . and became well-established — TCNT
. . . was consolidated — Mof
. . . continued to be built up spiritually — Wms
and walking in the fear of the Lord, and in the comfort of the Holy Ghost,
and, ordering its life by reverence for the Lord and help of the holy Spirit — TCNT
. . . the encouragement of the Holy Spirit — Wey
. . . stimulated by the holy Spirit — Gspd
. . . in the strengthening presence of the Holy Spirit — Phi
were multiplied.
They increased in membership — Nor

32. And it came to pass, as Peter passed throughout all quarters,
While travelling about in all directions, Peter — TCNT
Now Peter, as he went to town after town — Wey
As Peter was traveling about among them all — Gspd
In the course of a missionary journey through the whole region Peter — Rieu
he came down also to the saints which dwelt at Lydda.
went down to visit the People of Christ living at . . . — TCNT
. . . God's people at Lydda — Gspd
. . . the Brotherhood at Lydda — Rieu
. . . the holy people living in Lydda — Beck

33. And there he found a certain man named Aeneas,
And he found there a certain man, by name Aeneas — Rhm
which had kept his bed for eight years, and was sick of the palsy.
who had been bed-ridden for eight years with paralysis — TCNT
bedridden for eight years, a paralytic — Mon

34. And Peter said unto him, Aeneas, Jesus Christ maketh thee whole:
. . . Jesus Christ healeth thee — ASV
. . . cures you — TCNT
arise, and make thy bed.
Get up, and make your bed — TCNT
And he arose immediately.
Aeneas got up instantly — TCNT
He at once rose to his feet — Wey

35. And all that dwelt at Lydda and Saron saw him, and turned to the Lord.
and all the inhabitants of Lydda and the Plain of Sharon saw him, and came over to the Lord's side — TCNT
and all the inhabitants of Lydda and Sharon, those who turned to the Lord, saw him — Ber
. . . and so they turned to the Lord — Wms
. . . and were converted to the Lord — Rieu

36. Now there was at Joppa a certain disciple named Tabitha,
. . . a certain female disciple, by name Tabitha — Rhm
Among the disciples at Joppa was a woman called Tabitha — Wey
which by interpretation is called Dorcas:
or, as the name may be translated, Dorcas — Wey
which is in Greek Dorcas, that is gazelle — Gspd
this woman was full of good works and almsdeeds which she did.
Her life was full of the good and charitable actions which she was constantly doing — Wey
She had devoted herself to doing good and to acts of charity — Gspd
a woman bubbling over with helpful activities and practice of charities — Ber
She was always busy doing good and helping the poor — Nor

37. And it came to pass in those days, that she was sick, and died:

... that she fell sick ... — ASV

She happened to take ill and die at this time — Mof

whom when they had washed, they laid her in an upper chamber.

and when they had washed her, they ... — ASV

After washing her body they laid it out in a room upstairs — Wey

38. And forasmuch as Lydda was nigh to Joppa,

Lydda, however, being near Jaffa — Wey

As Joppa was near Lydda — Gspd

and the disciples had heard that Peter was there,

the disciples, hearing that Peter was there — ASV

the disciples, learning that ... — Ber

they sent unto him two men, desiring him that he would not delay to come to them.

sent two men unto him entreating him, Delay not to come on unto us — ASV

... Please come to us without delay — RSV

39. Then Peter arose and went with them.

And Peter, arising, went with them — Rhm

Peter started with them at once — TCNT

So Peter at once got up and ... — Wms

When he was come, they brought him into the upper chamber:

On his arrival they took him upstairs — Wey

On arrival they conducted him to the upper room — Ber

and all the widows stood by him weeping,

... came round him in tears — TCNT

and shewing the coats and garments which Dorcas made, while she was with them.

and showing him all the clothing and cloaks that Dorcas used to make ... — Wey

... the shirts and coats ... — Gspd

... the undergarments and coats ... — Ber

... the dresses and cloaks ... — Phi

... the inner and outer garments ... — Beck

40. But Peter put them all forth,

But Peter sent everybody out of the room — TCNT

Peter made them all leave the room — Nor

and kneeled, and prayed;

then he knelt down and prayed — Mof

and turning him to the body said, Tabitha, arise.

and turning to the body ... — ASV

And she opened her eyes: and when she saw Peter, she sat up.

She opened her eyes, and, seeing Peter, sat up — TCNT

Then she opened her eyes, and when she saw Peter ... — Wms

41. And he gave her his hand, and lifted her up,

Giving her his hand, Peter raised her up — TCNT

... he raised her to her feet — Wey

... helped her to her feet — Phi

and when he had called the saints and widows,

and calling in the believers and the widows — Gspd

... the members of the congregation and the widows — NEB

presented her alive.

he gave her back to them alive — Wey

he shewed her to them alive — Knox

42. And it was known throughout all Joppa;

And it became known ... — ASV

... all over Joppa — Mof

The news spread all over Joppa — NEB

and many believed in the Lord.

... on the Lord — ASV

and many came to believe in the Lord — Gspd

and many people were converted to the Lord — Rieu

43. And it came to pass, that he tarried many days in Joppa with one Simon a tanner.

Meanwhile Peter stayed some days in Jaffa with a tanner called Simon — TCNT

and Peter remained for a considerable time at Joppa, staying at the house of a man called Simon, a tanner — Wey

CHAPTER 10

1. There was a certain man in Caesarea called Cornelius,

There was then in Caesarea a man named Cornelius — TCNT

a centurion of the band called the Italian band,

a Captain in the regiment known as the Italian Regiment — TCNT

a centurion of a cohort . . . Italian cohort — ABUV

a captain in an Italian company of the Roman army — Nor

a captain in the troop called Italian — Beck

2. A devout man, and one that feared God with all his house,

a religious man and one who reverenced God, as also did all his household — TCNT

devout, and fearing God with all his house — ABUV

He was religious and God-fearing — and so was every member of his household — Wey

a pious man who worshipped the true God . . . — Knox

who like all his household was a pious observer of Jewish religious customs — Rieu

which gave much alms to the people,

He was liberal in his charities to the people — TCNT

He practiced liberal benevolences among . . . — Ber

He was generous in giving alms to the people of Israel — Rieu

He gave generously to help the Jewish people — NEB

and prayed to God alway.

. . . always — ASV

. . . constantly — TCNT

and was a real man of prayer — Phi

and regular in his prayers — Rieu

3. He saw in a vision evidently about the ninth hour of the day

He saw in a vision openly . . . — ASV

One afternoon, about three o'clock, he distinctly saw in a vision — TCNT

an angel of God coming in to him, and saying unto him, Cornelius.

an angel from God coming into his room, and calling him by name — TCNT

4. And when he looked on him, he was afraid, and said, What is it, Lord?

and he, fastening his eyes upon him, and being affrighted . . . — ASV

Looking steadily at him, and being much alarmed . . . — Wey

He stared at the angel in terror, saying . . . — Mof

. . . gazing at him in terror — Knox

What is it, Lord? he asked, gazing at him in terror — Knox

And he said unto him, Thy prayers and thine alms are come up for a memorial before God.

. . . Your prayers and your alms have risen before God as a sacrifice to be remembered — Mof

. . . Thy prayers and almsdeeds are recorded on high in God's sight — Knox

. . . have ascended as worthy to be remembered . . . — Ber

. . . have been observed and remembered by God — Rieu

5. And now send men to Joppa, and call for one Simon, whose surname is Peter:

Now send men to Joppa, for a man named Simon, who is also called Peter — Gspd

. . . invite over a man named Simon . . . — Wms

6. He lodgeth with one Simon a tanner,

the same is a guest . . . — Rhm

He is being entertained at the house of a tanner named Simon — Gspd

he is lodging with another Simon, a tanner — NEB

whose house is by the sea side:

who has a house close to the sea—Wey

whose house stands by the sea — Mof

he shall tell thee what thou oughtest to do.[36]

7. And when the angel which spake unto Cornelius was departed,

. . . who had been speaking with him had departed — Rhm

When the angel who spoke to him had left — Mof

he called two of his household servants,

---

[36]Now recognized as not adequately supported by original manuscripts.

calling two of the domestics — Rhm

he summoned . . . — Knox

and a devout soldier of them that waited on him continually;

and a religious soldier who was one of his constant attendants — TCNT

and a God-fearing soldier . . . — Wey

. . . who belonged to his personal retinue — Mof

and a military orderly who was a religious man — NEB

8. And when he had declared all these things unto them,

and having rehearsed . . . — ASV

. . . after telling them the whole story — TCNT

. . . having related everything to them — RSV

he sent them to Joppa.

. . . he sent them off . . . — Rhm

9. On the morrow, as they went on their journey,

. . . as those men were journeying — Rhm

The next day, while they were still on their journey — Wey

and drew nigh unto the city,

and just as they were getting near the town — TCNT

. . . not far from the town — Wms

. . . approaching the town — Ber

Peter went up upon the house top to pray about the sixth hour:

. . . about mid-day — TCNT

. . . about noon — Wey

10. And he became very hungry, and would have eaten:

. . . and desired to eat — ASV

. . . and wished to eat — Rhm

. . . and wanted something to eat — TCNT

. . . and wished for some food — Wey

but while they made ready,

and while they were making ready — Rhm

but, while they were preparing it — Wey

But as they were getting the meal ready — Mof

he fell into a trance,

there came upon him a trance — Rhm

a trance came over him — Mof

11. And saw heaven opened,

and he beholdeth the heaven opened — ASV

and saw that the sky was open — TCNT

He saw a rift in the sky — NEB

and he beheld the sky opened up — NASB

and a certain vessel descending unto him, as it had been a great sheet knit at the four corners, and let down to the earth:

and a certain vessel descending, as it were a great sheet, let down by four corners upon the earth — ASV

something like a great sail was descending, let down by its four corners towards the earth — TCNT

and what seemed to be an enormous sheet was descending, being let down to earth by ropes at the four corners — Wey

and a container coming down like a wide sheet let down to earth by the four corners — Ber

and a thing coming down that looked like a great sheet of sail-cloth. It was slung by the four corners, and was being lowered to the ground — NEB

12. Wherein were all manner of fourfooted beasts of the earth, and wild beasts,[37] and creeping things, and fowls of the air.

wherein were all manner of fourfooted beasts and creeping things of the earth and birds of the heaven — ASV

In it were all kinds of quadrupeds, reptiles, and birds — TCNT

. . . wild birds — Mof

In it he saw creatures of every kind, whatever walks or crawls or flies — NEB

13. And there came a voice to him, Rise, Peter; kill, and eat.

. . . Get up, Peter! Kill something and eat it! — Gspd

14. But Peter said, Not so, Lord;

. . . No, Sir, I cannot — TCNT

. . . On no account, Lord, he replied — Wey

. . . Never, Sir! — Gspd

. . . By no means, Lord — Ber

for I have never eaten any thing that is common or unclean.

---

[37]The words "and wild beasts" are now recognized as not adequately supported by original manuscripts.

for I have never eaten anything defiled and impure — TCNT

... unhallowed and unclean — Wey

... anything that was not ceremonially cleansed — Gspd

... undedicated and unclean — Ber

... impure or untouchable — Rieu

... profane or unclean — NEB

... unholy and unclean — NASB

... prohibited or unclean — Nor

15. And the voice spake unto him again the second time,

And a voice came ... — ASV

Once more the voice came to him — Ber

What God hath cleansed, that call not thou common.

... make not thou common — ASV

What God has pronounced pure ... you must not call defiled — TCNT

... you must not regard as unhallowed — Wey

16. This was done thrice:

This happened, in all, three times — TCNT

This took place three times — Wey

and the vessel was received up again into heaven.

and straightway the vessel was received up into heaven — ASV

and then suddenly it was all taken up into the sky — TCNT

and immediately the sheet was drawn up out of sight — Wey

17. Now while Peter doubted in himself what this vision which he had seen should mean,

... was much perplexed in himself ... — ASV

While Peter was still puzzling over the meaning of the vision he had seen — TCNT

... wondering as to the meaning ... — Wey

Peter was quite at a loss to know the meaning ... — Mof

While Peter was mulling over in his mind ... — Ber

... inwardly perplexed ... — RSV

... greatly perplexed in mind as to what the vision which he had seen might mean — NASB

behold, the men which were sent from Cornelius had made enquiry for Simon's house,

... having just asked the way to Simon's house — TCNT

and stood before the gate.

came to the door — Wey

They were in fact standing at the very doorway — Phi

appeared at the gate — NASB

18. And called, and asked whether Simon, which was surnamed Peter, were lodged there.

and called out to enquire if Simon, whose other name was Peter, was staying there — TCNT

calling out to ascertain whether Simon ... was a guest there — Ber

19. While Peter thought on the vision,

And as Peter was pondering over the vision — Rhm

... was earnestly considering the vision — ABUV

... was meditating on the vision — Wms

... was turning over the vision in his mind — Bas

... thinking deeply about the vision — Phi

... reflecting on the vision — NASB

the Spirit said unto him, Behold, three men seek thee.

... Behold, three men are looking for you — RSV

... Lo! two[38] men, seeking thee—Rhm

... There are two men looking for you at this moment — TCNT

... Some men are here looking for you — NEB

20. Arise therefore, and get thee down,

So get up and go down — TCNT

Get up and go downstairs — Phi

and go with them, doubting nothing:

and do not hesitate to go with them — TCNT

and go with them without any misgivings — Wey

and have no hesitation about accompanying them — Mof

for I have sent them.

for I have sent them myself — TCNT

for it was I who have sent them — Mof

---

[38]Variant reading.

21. **Then Peter went down to the men which were sent unto him from Cornelius;**[39] **and said,**

And Peter went down to the men, and said — ASV

So Peter went down and said to the men — Wey

Behold, I am he whom you seek:

I am the man you are looking for — TCNT

what is the cause wherefore ye are come?

What is your object in coming — TCNT

What is the reason for your coming — Gspd

What is the purpose of your coming — Wms

what is your errand — Knox

What brings you here — NEB

22. **And they said, Cornelius the centurion,**

. . . Cornelius, a colonel in the army — Wms

a just man, and one that feareth God,

a pious officer who reverences God — TCNT

an upright and God-fearing man — Wey

a man who worships the true God and keeps his law — Knox

a good-living and God-fearing man — Phi

and of good report among all the nation of the Jews,

and is well spoken of by the whole Jewish nation — TCNT

and a man of high reputation with all the Jewish nation — Wms

as all the Jewish people will testify — Knox

whose character can be vouched for by . . . — Phi

was warned from God by an holy angel to send for thee into his house,

. . . has been instructed by a holy angel to send . . . — TCNT

. . . has been divinely instructed . . . — Wey

. . . was directed . . . — Gspd

. . . was divinely directed . . . — NASB

and to hear words of thee.

and listen to what you have to say — — TCNT

and to listen to your message — Mon

and to listen to a message you would bring — Wms

23. **Then called he them in, and lodged them.**

Upon this Peter invited them in and entertained them — TCNT

So he took them in for the night — Bas

So he called them in to be his guests RSV

And on the morrow Peter went away with them,

. . . he arose[40] and went forth with them — ASV

The next day he set out with them — Wey

Next day he was up and off with them — Mof

But next day he got up and traveled with them — Ber

and certain brethren from Joppa accompanied him.

and some of the brothers in Joppa went along with him — Wms

accompanied by some members of the congregation at Joppa — NEB

and some fellow disciples from Joppa went along — Beck

24. **And the morrow after they**[41] **entered into Caesarea.**

and the following day he entered Caesarea — TCNT

and the day after that they reached Caesarea — Wey

and on the next day he reached Caesarea — Mof

And Cornelius waited for them,

. . . was waiting . . . — ASV

. . . was expecting them — Rhm

. . . was awaiting their arrival — Wey

and had called together his kinsmen and near friends.

having called together his kinsfolk and intimate friends — Rhm

. . . his kinsmen and close friends — RSV

25. **And as Peter was coming in, Cornelius met him,**

And when it came to pass that Peter entered . . . — ASV

So when Peter entered the city . . . — TCNT

---

[39]"Which were sent unto him from Cornelius" is now recognized as not adequately supported by original manuscripts.

[40]Variant reading.

[41]Some manuscripts have "they," others "he."

When Peter entered the house . . . — Wey

Peter was just going into the house when . . . — Mof

and fell down at his feet, and worshipped him.

and throwing himself at Peter's feet, bowed to the ground — TCNT

. . . did homage — Rhm

. . . and made obeisance to him — Gspd

. . . and did reverence to him — Ber

. . . and bowed to the ground in deep reverence — NEB

26. But Peter took him up, saying,

. . . raised him up . . . — ASV

. . . lifted him to his feet . . . — Gspd

. . . made him stand up — Beck

. . . roused him with the words — Phi

Stand up; I myself also am a man.

. . . I am only a man like you — TCNT

. . . I am only a man myself — Mof

Rise, I am a human being, too — Ber

. . . I am a man like anyone else — NEB

Stand up! I'm not a god! — Tay

27. And as he talked with him, he went in,

And conversing with him . . . — Rhm

Talking with him as he went, Peter entered the house — TCNT

As he continued to talk with him he went into the house — Wms

and found many that were come together.

where he found a large gathering of people — TCNT

and found a large company assembled — Wey

and found a great crowd had gathered — Wms

28. And he said unto them, Ye know how that it is an unlawful thing for a man that is a Jew to keep company, or come unto one of another nation;

You are aware . . . that it is forbidden for a Jew to be on intimate, or even visiting, terms with a foreigner — TCNT

. . . a Jew is strictly forbidden to associate with a Gentile or visit him — Wey

. . . a Jew is forbidden to associate with Gentiles or go into their houses — Rieu

but God hath shewed me that I should

not call any man common or unclean.[42]

and yet unto me hath God showed . . . — ASV

29. Therefore came I unto you without gainsaying,

. . . without raising any objection — TCNT

. . . without any demur — Mof

. . . without any hesitation — Gspd

. . . without question — Bas

as soon as I was sent for:

when I was sent for — ASV

I ask therefore for what intent ye have sent for me?

I therefore ask why you sent for me — Wey

Now I want to know what made you send for me — Phi

Will you tell me, please, why you have sent for me — Rieu

30. And Cornelius said,

Cornelius answered — Gspd

Four days ago I was fasting[43] until this hour;

Four days ago, until this hour — ASV

Just three days ago this very hour — TCNT

and at the ninth hour I prayed in my house,

I was keeping the ninth hour of prayer . . . — ASV

. . . observing the time of the three o'clock prayer — TCNT

I was praying in my house at three o'clock in the afternoon — Mof

I was home for my three o'clock worship — Ber

and, behold, a man stood before me in bright clothing,

. . . in bright apparel — ASV

. . . in dazzling clothing — TCNT

. . . in shining raiment — Wey

. . . in dazzling attire — Ber

31. And said, Cornelius, thy prayer is heard, and thine alms are had in remembrance in the sight of God.

. . . and your acts of charity have been remembered by God — Wey

. . . your charitable gifts . . . — Phi

. . . God has heard your prayer and re-

---

[42]For the meanings of "common" and "unclean" see verse 14.

[43]The word "fasting" is now recognized as not adequately supported by original manuscripts.

members your gifts to the poor —
Beck

32. Send therefore to Joppa, and call hither Simon, whose surname is Peter;
... and invite Simon ... — Wey
... and summon Simon ... — Mof

he is lodged in the house of one Simon a tanner by the sea side:[44]

who, when he cometh, shall speak unto thee.[45]

33. Immediately therefore I sent to thee;
So, I sent to you at once — RSV

and thou hast well done that thou art come.
and I thank you heartily for having come — Wey
and you have been kind enough to come — Mof
and you acted nobly to have come along — Ber
and you have been most kind in coming — Phi

Now therefore are we all here present before God,
That is why all of us are now assembled here in God's presence — Wey
So now we are all here in God's presence — Wms

to hear all things that are commanded thee of God.
to listen to what the Lord has commanded you to say — Wey
ready to listen to whatever charge the Lord has given thee — Knox
to hear all that the Lord has ordered you to say — NEB

34. Then Peter opened his mouth, and said,
Then Peter began to speak ... — Wey
Then Peter began and said — Mof
And opening his mouth, Peter said — NASB

Of a truth I perceive that God is no respecter of persons:

35. But in every nation he that feareth him, and worketh righteousness,
but that in every nation he who reverences him and does what is right — TCNT
but in every nation the man who reveres God and practices doing right — Wms

is accepted with him.
is acceptable to him — TCNT
... God is not one to show partiality — TCNT

... God makes no distinction between one man and another — Wey
... God has no favourites — Mof
Now I really understand that God shows no partiality — Gspd
I now thoroughly grasp the truth that God is not partial — Ber

36. The word which God sent unto the children of Israel,
God has sent his Message to the Israelite people — TCNT
... to the sons of Israel — ABUV
... to Israel's descendants — Gspd
... to the Israelites — NEB

preaching peace by Jesus Christ: (he is Lord of all:)
announcing the glad tidings of peace through ... — Rhm
by telling them the good news of peace through Jesus Christ — Wms

37. That word, I say, ye know, which was published throughout all Judaea,
ye yourselves know what hath come to pass throughout the whole of Judaea — Rhm
You know, yourselves, the story which spread through all Judaea — TCNT
you know how the message spread ... — Mon
You know the things that occurred up and down Judea — Ber
I need not tell you what happened lately all over the land of the Jews — NEB

and began from Galilee, after the baptism which John preached;
beginning in Galilee after the baptism which John proclaimed — Wey
though it began in Galilee ... — Knox

38. How God anointed Jesus of Nazareth with the Holy Ghost and with power:
even Jesus of Nazareth, how God anointed him with the Holy Spirit and with power — ASV
— the story, I mean, of Jesus of Nazareth, and how God consecrated him his Christ by enduing him with the Holy Spirit and with power — TCNT
You must have heard how God anointed Him with the power of the Holy Spirit — Phi

---

[44]See verse 6 for variations.
[45]Now recognized as not adequately supported by original manuscripts.

who went about doing good,

so that He went about doing good — Wey

who traversed the land doing good — Ber

and healing all that were oppressed of the devil;

and curing all who were under the power of . . . — TCNT

and curing all who were harassed by . . . — Mof

and curing all who were overpowered by . . . — Wms

and curing all those who were under the devil's tyranny — Knox

for God was with him.

because God was with him — Rhm

with God at his side — Knox

39. And we are witnesses of all things which he did both in the land of the Jews, and in Jerusalem;

. . . both in the Judaean country and in Jerusalem itself — Phi

whom they slew and hanged on a tree:[46]

40. Him God raised up the third day,

This Jesus God raised from the grave on the . . . — TCNT

But God raised Him to life on the third day — Amp

and shewed him openly;

and gave him to be made manifest — ASV

and enabled him to show himself openly — TCNT

and permitted him to appear — Wey

and allowed him to be seen — Mof

and caused him to be plainly seen — Gspd

and granted that he should become visible — NASB

41. Not to all the people,

not to the general public — Tay

not by all the Jews — Rieu

but unto witnesses chosen before of God, even to us,

. . . but to witnesses — men previously chosen by God — namely, to us — Wey

but by witnesses whom God had previously selected . . . — Mof

but by witnesses whom God had designated beforehand . . . — Gspd

but to us, the witnesses whom God had appointed beforehand — Knox

but to us witnesses previously selected of God — Ber

but to us who were chosen by God as witnesses — RSV

but just by us—God's specially chosen eye-witnesses — Rieu

who did eat and drink with him

but to us who ate and drank with Him — Tay

and we ate and drank with Him—Nor

after he rose from the dead.

after his resurrection from the dead — TCNT

after he had risen from the dead — Gspd

42. And he commanded us to preach unto the people,

And he charged us . . . — ASV

And he gave us a commission to preach . . . — Knox

. . . to proclaim . . . — Rhm

. . . to announce . . . — Gspd

. . . to herald . . . — Ber

and to testify

and solemnly declare — Wey

and bear solemn testimony — Gspd

that it is he which was ordained of God to be the Judge of quick and dead.

. . . appointed by God . . . — TCNT

. . . the Judge of the living and the dead — ASV

43. To him give all the prophets witness,

To Him all the prophets bear witness — Wey

It is to him that all the prophets testify — NEB

that through his name whosoever believeth in him shall receive remission of sins.

. . . forgiveness of sins — TCNT

that remission of sins is to be received through his name by every one that believeth on him — Rhm

44. While Peter yet spake these words,

While Peter was yet speaking these words — Rhm

Before Peter had finished saying these words — TCNT

Even while Peter was preaching this sermon — Nor

the Holy Ghost fell on all them which heard the word.

---

[46]See Acts 5:30.

the Holy Spirit fell upon all who were
hearing . . . — Rhm

the Holy Spirit came down on all who
heard the Word — Beck

the Holy Spirit came upon all who were
listening to his message — Nor

. . . as they heard the Word behind his
words — Rieu

**45. And they of the circumcision which
believed were astonished, as many as
came with Peter,**

And the faithful of the circumcision
who had come with Peter were
amazed — Rhm

And all the Jewish believers who had
come with Peter were astonished —
Wey

And the circumcised believers . . . —
Ber

And the believers from among the
circumcised . . . — RSV

**because that on the Gentiles also was
poured out the gift of the Holy
Ghost.**

that the gift of the holy Spirit had
actually been poured out on the
Gentiles — Mof

because the gift of the holy Spirit had
been showered upon the heathen too
— Gspd

**46. For they heard them speak with
tongues, and magnify God.**

for they could hear them speaking with
tongues and extolling God — TCNT

. . . speaking in tongues and extolling
the majesty of God — Wey

. . . speaking in foreign languages and
declaring the greatness of God —
Gspd

. . . speaking in tongues of ecstasy and
acclaiming the greatness of God —
NEB

. . . speaking in other languages and
praising God — Beck

Then answered Peter,

At this Peter asked — TCNT

Then Peter said openly — Knox

**47. Can any man forbid water, that these
should not be baptized,**

Can any one refuse the water for the
baptism of these people — TCNT

Who will grudge us the water for baptizing these men — Knox

Surely no one can refuse the water for
these to be baptized — NASB

**which have received the Holy Ghost
as well as we?**

now that they have received the holy
Spirit just as we did ourselves —
TCNT

since they have received the Holy Spirit
. . . — Wms

**48. And he commanded them to be bap-
tized in the name of the Lord.**

And he ordered . . . — Mof

So he directed that they should be baptized in the name of Jesus Christ —
TCNT

**Then prayed they him to tarry certain
days.**

after which they asked him to stay
there a few days longer — TCNT

Then they asked him to remain some
days — ABUV

Then they begged him to remain with
them for a time — Wey

CHAPTER 11

**1. And the apostles and brethren that
were in Judaea heard that the Gentiles
had also received the word of God.**

Now the Apostles and the brethren
who were throughout Judaea heard
that the nations also had welcomed
the word of God — Rhm

. . . that even the heathen had welcomed God's Message — TCNT

The apostles and other disciples in all
Judea heard: The non-Jewish peo-
ple, too, have accepted God's Word
— Beck

**2. And when Peter was come up to Jeru-
salem,**

. . . came up . . . — Rhm

. . . went up . . . — TCNT

. . . returned to . . . — Wey

they that were of the circumcision

those converts who held to circumcision — TCNT

the party of circumcision — Wey

the circumcision party — Mof

the advocates of circumcision — Gspd

the champions of circumcision — Wms

those insisting on circumcision — Ber

the stricter Jews — Rieu

those who were of Jewish birth — NEB
those who still held to the need of
  circumcision — Nor
contended with him,
began to find fault with him — Rhm
began attacking him — TCNT
took him to task — Gspd
disputed with him — Mon
began to bring charges against him
  — Wms
criticized him — RSV
took issue with him — NASB

3. **Saying, Thou wentest in to men uncircumcised, and didst eat with them.**
You went into the houses of men uncircumcised . . . and you ate with
  them — Wey
charging him with having visited and
  eaten with men who were not Jews
  — Gspd
. . . Why did you go to uncircumcised
  men and eat with them? — RSV

4. **But Peter rehearsed the matter from
the beginning, and expounded it by
order unto them, saying,**
But Peter began and expounded the
  matter unto them in order, saying
  — ASV
But Peter expounded the matter by
  order unto them from the beginning,
  saying — Alf
So Peter began, and explained the facts
  to them as they had occurred —
  TCNT
But Peter began and gave them an
  orderly account . . . — ABUV
Peter, however, explained the whole
  matter to them from the beginning
  — Wey
Then Peter proceeded to put the facts
  before them — Mof
Then Peter explained the matter to
  them from beginning to end — Gspd
Whereupon Peter told them the story
  point by point from the beginning
  — Knox
Peter then began to relate what had
  happened, in consecutive order —
  Nor

5. **I was in the city of Joppa praying:**
I was praying in the town of Joppa
  — Gspd
and in a trance I saw a vision,
and while in a trance . . . — TCNT
when I fell into a trance . . . — Knox

and while completely unconscious of
  my surroundings . . . — Phi
**A certain vessel descend, as it had been
a great sheet, let down from heaven
by four corners;[47]**
and it came even to me:
and it came right down to me — TCNT
and it came close to me — Wey

6. **Upon the which when I had fastened
mine eyes,**
into which steadfastly looking — Rhm
Looking closely at it — TCNT
On which looking intently — ABUV
and while I gazed at it — Mon
I considered, and saw
I began to observe, and saw — Rhm
I began to distinguish — TCNT
I examined it closely, and saw — Wey
and when I looked at it closely I saw
  — Phi
**fourfooted beasts of the earth, and
wild beasts, and creeping things, and
fowls of the air.**
quadrupeds, wild beasts, reptiles, and
  birds — TCNT
animals and beasts of prey . . . — RSV
. . . and the wild birds — Mof

7. **And I heard a voice saying unto me,**
And I heard also a voice . . . — ASV
Arise, Peter; slay and eat.
Rise, Peter; kill and eat — ASV
Get up, Peter! Kill something and eat
  it! — Gspd

8. **But I said, Not so, Lord:**
No, Sir, I cannot, I answered — TCNT
On no account, Lord, I replied — Wey
. . . Never, sir! — Gspd
. . . Never by any means, sir — Wms
**for nothing common or unclean hath
at any time entered into my mouth.[48]**

9. **But the voice answered me again from
heaven, What God hath cleansed, that
call not thou common.[49]**

10. **And this was done three times:**
This happened, in all, three times —
  TCNT
**and all were drawn up again into
heaven.**
when everything was drawn up again
  into the sky — TCNT

---

[47]See Acts 10:11.
[48]Compare Acts 10:14.
[49]Compare Acts 10:15.

Then all of it was pulled up to the
sky again — Beck

**11. And, behold, immediately there were
three men already come unto the
house where I was, sent from Caesarea
unto me.**

And, behold, forthwith three men
stood before the house in which we
were, having been sent . . . — ASV

Just at that moment three men, who
had been sent from Caesarea to find
me, reached the house where we
were staying — Gspd

12. And the spirit bade me go with them,
The Spirit told me to go with them —
TCNT

nothing doubting.
making no distinction — RSV
without hesitation — TCNT
without any misgivings — Wey
regardless of their nationality — Rieu

**Moreover these six brethren accom-
panied me,**
And there went with me these six
brethren also — Rhm
. . . these six brethren who are now
present — Wey

and we entered into the man's house:
and we entered the Centurion's house
— Wey
and we came into the man's home —
Beck

**13. And he shewed us how he had seen an
angel in his house, which stood and
said unto him,**
And he told us how he had seen the
angel standing in his house and saying — RSV
and he related to us . . . — Rhm
Then he described to us . . . — Wey
Then he announced to us . . . — Ber
And he reported to us . . . — NASB

**Send men to Joppa, and call for Simon,
whose surname is Peter;**[50]

**14. Who shall tell thee words, whereby
thou and all thy house shall be saved.**
. . . thou shalt be saved, thou and all
thy house — ASV
He will teach you truths by which
you and all your household will be
saved — Wey
he will declare to you a message by
which you will be saved . . . — RSV
he will give you the message through
which . . . — Ber

He will tell you how you can be saved;
yes, you and your whole household
— Nor

15. And as I began to speak,
I had just begun to speak, Peter con-
tinued — TCNT
And, said Peter, No sooner had I begun
to speak than — Wey
But in the beginning of my speech —
Ber
While I was beginning to tell them
this Message — Phi
Hardly had I begun speaking, when —
NEB

**the Holy Ghost fell on them, as on us
at the beginning.**
the Holy Spirit fell upon them, just as
He fell upon us at the first — Wey
. . . descended on them as he did originally on us — Rieu

**16. Then remembered I the word of the
Lord, how that he said,**
Then I remembered the Lord's words,
how he said — Wey
. . . the saying of the Lord — Mof
Then I was reminded of what the Lord
said to us — Knox

**John indeed baptized with water; but
ye shall be baptized with the Holy
Ghost.**
. . . with water . . . in the Holy Spirit
— ASV
. . . in water . . . in the Holy Spirit —
Gspd

**17. Forasmuch then as God gave them the
like gift as he did unto us,**
If then . . . — RSV
As, then, God had given them the
very same gift . . . — TCNT
. . . exactly the same gift . . . — Mof
. . . no less a gift . . . — NEB
. . . made them the same free gift . . .
— Knox
Now since God granted to them a gift
equal to ours — Ber

who believed on the Lord Jesus Christ;
when we believed . . . — ASV
after believing . . . — NASB

**what was I, that I could withstand
God?**
who was I that I should be able to
thwart God — TCNT

---

[50]Compare Acts 10:5.

who was I — how could I try — to
thwart God — Mof

who was I, what power had I, to stay
God's hand — Knox

who was I to try to stand in God's
way — Rieu

. . . to interfere with God — Gspd

18. When they heard these things,

On hearing this statement — TCNT

On hearing this — Wey

they held their peace,

they ceased to object — TCNT

they were silenced — RSV

they desisted — Mof

they made no further objection—Gspd

they quieted down — Ber

their doubts were silenced — NEB

they were satisfied — Nor

they were content — Knox

and glorified God, saying,

and broke out into praise of God —
TCNT

and they extolled the goodness of God
. . . — Wey

but they gave honor to God . . .—Gspd

but gave God the glory . . . — Wms

**Then hath God also to the Gentiles
granted repentance unto life.**

So even to the heathen . . . the repentance which leads to Life! — TCNT

So God has actually allowed the Gentiles to repent and live! — Mof

Then God has given even the heathen
repentance and the hope of life!
— Gspd

Then to the Gentiles as to us God has
given a change of heart, so that they
may have life — Bas

. . . life-giving repentance of heart . . .
— Knox

**19. Now they which were scattered abroad
upon the persecution that arose about
Stephen**

They therefore who had been scattered
abroad by reason of the tribulation
that took place on account of
Stephen — Rhm

The fugitives from the persecution that
had broken out over Stephen—Gspd

**travelled as far as Phenice, and Cy-
prus, and Antioch,**

made their way to Phoenicia . . . —
Wey

**preaching the word to none but unto
the Jews only.**

speaking the word to none save only
to Jews — ASV

telling the Message — but only to Jews
— TCNT

**20. And some of them were men of Cyprus
and Cyrene,**

And there were some from among
them, Cyprians and Cyrenians —
Rhm

But some of them were Cyprians and
Cyreneans — Wey

. . . natives of Cyprus and Cyrene —
Phi

**which, when they were come to An-
tioch,**

who, on coming to Antioch — Wey

who on reaching Antioch — Mof

and these, when they arrived at Antioch
— NEB

spake unto the Grecians,

spake unto the Greeks also — ASV

began to speak to the Greeks too —
Wms

began to speak to pagans as well—NEB

preaching the Lord Jesus.

announcing the glad-tidings as to the
Lord Jesus — Rhm

publishing the good news of the Lord
Jesus — ABUV

**21. And the hand of the Lord was with
them:**

The Lord's power was with them —
TCNT

The Lord's blessing was on them —
Rieu

**and a great number believed, and
turned unto the Lord.**

. . . that believed turned . . . — ASV

and there were a vast number who
believed and turned to the Lord —
Wey

**22. Then tidings of these things came unto
the ears of the church which was in
Jerusalem:**

And the report concerning them . . .
— ASV

And the matter was reported in the
hearing of the assembly . . . — Rhm

The news about them reached . . . —
TCNT

The story of this . . . — Knox

When word of it came to the attention
of . . . — Ber

**and they sent forth Barnabas, that he
should go as far as Antioch.**

and they sent forth Barnabas as far as

Antioch — ASV

and they despatched Barnabas to Antioch — Mof

. . . all the way to Antioch — Gspd

and they sent Barnabas on a mission to Antioch — Knox

23. Who, when he came, and had seen the grace of God, was glad,

On arriving he was delighted to see the grace of God — Wey

When he reached there and saw the favor God had shown them, he was delighted — Gspd

When he came there and saw how gracious God had been to them, he rejoiced — Nor

and exhorted them all, that with purpose of heart they would cleave unto the Lord.

and encouraged them all to make up their minds to be faithful to the Master — TCNT

and he encouraged them all to remain, with fixed resolve, faithful to the Lord — Wey

and he encouraged them all to be resolute and steadfast in their devotion to the Lord — Gspd

and continuously encouraged them all with hearty purpose to continue to be devoted to the Lord — Wms

and he made clear to them the need of keeping near the Lord with all the strength of their hearts — Bas

and . . . encouraged them all to remain loyal to the Lord with steady hearts — Ber

24. For he was a good man, and full of the Holy Ghost and of faith:

. . . an excellent man . . . — Gspd

. . . a splendid man . . . — Ber

and much people was added unto the Lord.

and the number of believers in the Lord greatly increased — Wey

Considerable numbers of people were brought in for the Lord — Mof

So a large number of people were united to the Lord — Wms

25. Then departed Barnabas to Tarsus, for to seek Saul:

And he went forth to Tarsus to seek for Saul — ASV

Afterwards Barnabas left for Tarsus to look for Saul — TCNT

Then Barnabas went over to Tarsus to seek out Saul — Gspd

26. And when he had found him, he brought him unto Antioch.

and when he had come across him . . . — Bas

And it came to pass, that a whole year they assembled themselves with the church,

. . . that even for a whole year they were gathered together with the church — ASV

. . . they were the guests of the Church — Wey

. . . they met with the church — Gspd

where for an entire year they conducted church meetings — Ber

. . . joining in the worship of the Church — Rieu

For a whole year the two of them lived in fellowship with the congregation there — NEB

and taught much people.

and taught a large number of people — TCNT

teaching a great multitude — Knox

. . . a large company of people — RSV

and gave instruction to large numbers — NEB

And the disciples were called Christians first in Antioch.

and it was in Antioch that the disciples first got the name of 'Christians' — TCNT

27. And in those days came prophets from Jerusalem unto Antioch.

About this time, some Prophets came to Antioch from Jerusalem — TCNT

At that time certain Prophets came down from Jerusalem to Antioch — Wey

28. And there stood up one of them named Agabus,

One of them, named Agabus, came forward — TCNT

and signified by the Spirit that there should be great dearth throughout all the world:

and, under the influence of the Spirit foretold . . . — TCNT

publicly predicted by the Spirit the speedy coming of a great famine throughout the world — Wey

showed by the Spirit that a severe famine was about to visit the whole world — Mof

ACTS 12

... prophesied through the Spirit ...
— Knox

which came to pass in the days of Claudius Caesar.

a famine which actually occurred in the reign of Claudius — TCNT

and this took place in the days of Claudius — RSV

29. **Then the disciples, every man according to his ability, determined to send relief unto the brethren which dwelt in Judaea:**

So the disciples, without exception, determined, in proportion to their means, to send something to help the Brethren living in Judaea — TCNT

So the disciples put aside money, every one in proportion to his means, for the relief of the brethren living in Judaea — Wey

Thereupon it was decided that each of

the disciples should contribute according to his means ... — Knox

... agreed to make a contribution ... — NEB

30. **Which also they did, and sent it to the elders by the hands of Barnabas and Saul.**

... sent it to the Officers of the Church ... — TCNT

... forwarding their contribution ... by Barnabas ... — Wey

... sending their contributions to the presbyters ... — Mof

... sending it to the rulers of the church — Bas

... they entrusted it to the hands of ... — Knox

... sending their contribution to the elders there personally through Barnabas ... — Phi

... sending it in charge of ... — NASB

CHAPTER 12

1. **Now about that time Herod the king**

It was at that time that King Herod — TCNT

stretched forth his hands to vex certain of the church.

put forth his hands to afflict ... — ASV

laid his hands upon certain ... to vex them — Alf

... to do them violence — Wey

... to harm ... — ABUV

laid violent hands upon some who belonged to the church — Gspd

arrested some ... — Wms

made cruel attacks on the Christians — Bas

exerted his authority to persecute some of those who belonged to the church — Knox

2. **And he killed James the brother of John with the sword.**

and James, John's brother, he beheaded — Wey

3. **And because he saw it pleased the Jews,**

And when he saw ... — ASV

Finding that this gratified the Jews — Wey

... was agreeable to the Jews — Wms

... was acceptable to the Jews — Knox

When he saw how the Jews liked that — Beck

he proceeded further to take Peter also.

he proceeded to seize Peter also — ASV

he went further and arrested Peter as well — TCNT

he took a next step ... — Nor

(Then were the days of unleavened bread.)

And those were the days of ... — ASV

(This was during the Festival of Unleavened Bread.) — TCNT

That was during the Passover days — Ber

4. **And when he had apprehended him,**

And when he had taken him — ASV

After seizing Peter — TCNT

He had him arrested — Wey

Having secured him — NEB

he put him in prison,

and put in jail — Gspd

and delivered him to four quaternions of soldiers to keep him;

and entrusted him to the keeping of four Guards of four soldiers each — TCNT

handing him over to the care of sixteen soldiers — Wey

with four squads of soldiers to guard him — Gspd

with a guard of four soldiers, relieved four times a day — Knox

506

under the charge of a guard of four sections, each consisting of four soldiers — Rieu

under a military guard, four squads of four men each — NEB

. . . four detachments, with four in each detachment . . . — Nor

intending after Easter to bring him forth to the people.

meaning to bring him up . . . — TCNT

meaning to produce him in public after the Passover — NEB

5. Peter therefore was kept in prison:

So Peter was closely guarded in prison — Mof

So Peter was kept in the jail — Gspd

but prayer was made without ceasing of the church unto God for him.

but meanwhile the prayers of the Church were being earnestly offered to God on his behalf — TCNT

but long and fervent prayer was offered . . . — Wey

but earnest prayer to God for him was persistently made by the church — Wms

but there was a continual stream of prayer going up to God from the church on his behalf — Knox

6. And when Herod would have brought him forth, the same night Peter was sleeping between two soldiers,

On the very night before the day on which Herod meant to bring him up for trial Peter was asleep . . . — TCNT

On the night before his trial . . . — Rieu

On the very night before Herod had planned to bring him forward . . . — NEB

bound with two chains:

handcuffed by two chains — Rieu

chained with double chains — Phi

and the keepers before the door kept the prison.

and sentries . . . — RSV

while there were sentries in front of the door, guarding the prison — TCNT

and guards were on duty outside the door — Wey

and watchmen were at the door, guarding the jail — Gspd

while guards maintained a strict watch on the doorway of the prison — Phi

7. And, behold, the angel of the Lord came upon him,

And, behold an angel of the Lord stood by him — ASV

All at once an angel . . . stood by him — TCNT

Suddenly an angel . . . stood by him — Wey

. . . flashed on him — Mof

and a light shined in the prison:

. . . shined in the cell — ASV

. . . shone in the room — Gspd

and the cell was ablaze with light — — NEB

and a light illuminated the building — Nor

and he smote Peter on the side, and raised him up,

and smiting the side of Peter he roused him up — Rhm

and, striking Peter on the side, he woke him — Wey

and by striking Peter on the side the angel woke him — Wms

then touching Peter in the side, he roused him — Ber

He tapped Peter on the side and woke him up — Phi

The angel woke Peter with a touch on the side — Rieu

He tapped Peter on the shoulder and woke him — NEB

saying, Arise up quickly.

saying as he did so: Get up quickly — TCNT

. . . Rise up speedily — ABUV

. . . Quick, get up! — Mof

. . . Get up! Quick! — Beck

And his chains fell off from his hands.

The chains dropped from his wrists — TCNT

. . . fell away from his wrists — NEB

8. And the angel said unto him,

Then the angel said — Bas

Gird thyself, and bind on thy sandals.

Put on your belt and your sandals — TCNT

Fasten your girdle . . . and tie on your sandals — Wey

Tighten your belt and put on your shoes — Wms

Dress yourself and put on your sandals — RSV

Do up your belt and put your shoes on — NEB

And so he did. And he saith unto him,

And he did so . . . — RSV

When Peter had done so, the angel added — TCNT

Cast thy garment about thee, and follow me.

Throw your cloak round you . . . — TCNT

Wrap your mantle around you and follow me — RSV

Put on your coat . . . — Mof

Put your coat round you and come with me — Bas

9. And he went out, and followed him;

Peter went out and followed the angel — TCNT

And he followed him out — Mof

So he kept following him out — Wms

And he went out and continued to follow — NASB

and wist not that it was true which was done by the angel;

and he knew not . . . — ASV

without knowing that what was happening under the angel's guidance was real — TCNT

yet could not believe that what the angel was doing was real — Wey

not realizing that what the angel did was real — Mof

having no idea that the angel's activity was real — Ber

not realizing the angel was actually doing this — Beck

but thought he saw a vision.

but supposed that he saw a vision — Wey

but imagining that he saw a vision — Mof

for he thought he was having a vision — Gspd

he thought he was dreaming it — Wms

he thought it was just a vision — NEB

10. When they were past the first and the second ward,

After passing the first Guard, and then a second — TCNT

And when they had gone past the first and second watchmen — Bas

But they passed the first guard-post, then the second — NEB

they came unto the iron gate that leadeth unto the city;

and at last came to the iron gate which led into the city — Wms

which opened to them of his own accord:

. . . of its own accord — RSV

. . . of itself — TCNT

and it automatically opened for them — Ber

and they went out, and passed on through one street;

When they had gone out, and had walked along one street — TCNT

and they passed out and proceeded one block — Wms

Walking out, they went along one block — Ber

. . . and walked the length of one street — NEB

and they went outside and up the street — Beck

and forthwith the angel departed from him.

and immediately . . . — RSV

and straightway . . . — ASV

all at once the angel left him — TCNT

and then suddenly the angel left him — Wey

the angel immediately left him — Mof

when suddenly the angel was absent from him — Ber

when the angel suddenly vanished from Peter's sight — Phi

11. And when Peter was come to himself, he said,

Peter coming to himself said — Wey

Then Peter came to his senses and said — Mof

As Peter recovered full consciousness . . . — Ber

Now I know of a surety,

Now I know of a truth — ASV

Now I know for certain — TCNT

Now I really know — Wms

Now I am sure — RSV

Now I know for sure — NASB

that the Lord hath sent his angel,

. . . hath sent forth his angel — ASV

and hath delivered me out of the hand of Herod,

and has rescued me from Herod's hands — TCNT

and rescued me from the power of Herod — Gspd

to rescue me from Herod's clutches — Rieu

and from all the expectation of the people of the Jews.

and from all that the Jewish people expected — TCNT

and from all that the Jewish people were expecting — RSV

... that the Jewish people were anticipating — Wey
... that the Jewish people were expecting to do to me — Wms
... that the people of the Jews hoped to see — Knox

12. And when he had considered the thing,
And when he was aware of it — Alf
As soon as he understood what had happened — TCNT
When he realized this — RSV
So, on reflection — Wey
When he grasped the situation — Mof
When he realized his situation — Gspd
After some thought — Knox
Having orientated himself — Ber
As the truth broke upon him — Phi
When he realized how things stood — NEB
Then, after thinking it over — Nor
he came to the house of Mary the mother of John,
he went ... — TCNT
he made for the house ... — NEB
whose surname was Mark:
whose other name was Mark — RSV
who was also called Mark — Gspd
the one called Mark — Beck
where many were gathered together praying.
where many were gathered together and were praying — RSV
where a considerable number were gathered together and praying — Rhm
... a large number ... — Wey
where a number had met for prayer — Mof
where a large company was at prayer — NEB

13. And as Peter knocked at the door of the gate,
And when he had knocked at the door of the porch — Rhm
On his knocking at the door in the gate — TCNT
When he knocked at the outer door — Gspd
... the door of the gateway — RSV
He gave a knock on the courtyard gate — Rieu
... the entrance gate — Beck
a damsel came to hearken, named Rhoda.

a maid came to answer ... — ASV
a maidservant ... — TCNT
a servant-girl ... — Wms
a girl named Rhoda came to the front to listen — Ber
a maid called Rose came to answer it — Rieu

14. And when she knew Peter's voice,
and recognizing the voice of Peter — Rhm
Recognizing Peter's voice — RSV
but as soon as she recognized Peter's voice — Mof
she opened not the gate for gladness, but ran in,
but in her joy, left the gate unopened, and ran in — TCNT
for very joy she did not open the door, but ran in — Wey
instead of opening the door she ran inside from sheer joy — Mof
in her joy she did not stop to open the door ... — Gspd
she ... was too overjoyed to open the gate for him ... — Knox
and told how Peter stood before the gate.
and told them that Peter was standing there — Wey
and reported that Peter was standing on the doorstep — Phi
and announced, Peter is standing at the gate — Beck

15. And they said unto her, Thou art mad.
... Thou art raving — Rhm
... You are crazy! — Gspd
... You are out of your mind! — NASB
But she constantly affirmed that it was even so.
She, however, kept on strongly declaring ... — Rhm
But she stoutly maintained that it was true — Wey
But she persistently insisted that it was so — Wms
But she insisted up and down that it was so — Ber
... kept insisting ... — NASB
Then said they, It is his angel.
It is his guardian angel, they said — Wey
... It must be his guardian angel — Knox

16. But Peter continued knocking:
Meanwhile Peter went on knocking — TCNT

But Peter kept on knocking — Mof

and when they had opened the door, and saw him, they were astonished.

and when they opened, they saw him and were amazed — RSV

until at last they opened the door and saw that it was really he, and were filled with amazement — Wey

so when they opened, they saw to their astonishment that it was he — Ber

and when they opened it and recognized him they were simply amazed — Phi

17. But he, beckoning unto them with the hand to hold their peace,

Peter made signs to them to be quiet — TCNT

But he motioned with his hand for silence — Wey

Calling for silence by a gesture of his hand — Knox

He waved his hand to quiet them down — Beck

declared unto them how the Lord had brought him out of the prison.

and then described to them . . . — Wey

and explained how the Lord had conducted him out of the prison — Ber

And he said, Go shew these things unto James, and to the brethren.

. . . Tell these things . . . — ASV

. . . Go report these things . . . — Alf

. . . Give the news . . . — Bas

Tell this to James and to the brethren — RSV

Report this to James and the members of the church — NEB

Tell James and the other Christians about this — Beck

And he departed, and went into another place.

And going out he went his way unto some other place — Rhm

Then he left the house, and went away . . . — TCNT

And off he went to another place — Mof

18. Now as soon as it was day,

And when it became day — Rhm

In the morning — TCNT

Now when day broke — Mof

At daybreak — Nor

there was no small stir among the soldiers,

. . . no small commotion . . . — Rhm

. . . no little consternation . . . — Ber

. . . great alarm . . . — Rieu

. . . great consternation . . . — NEB

. . . no small disturbance . . . — NASB

what was become of Peter.

over what had become of Peter — RSV

as to what could possible have become of Peter — TCNT

as to what could have happened to Peter — Phi

19. And when Herod had sought for him,

. . . had had search made for Peter — TCNT

Herod made inquiries for him — Mof

Herod made close search — NEB

and found him not,

and had failed to find him — TCNT

and could not find him — Wey

he examined the keepers,

he cross-questioned the Guard — TCNT

after cross-examining the guards — Mof

he examined the sentries — RSV

he had the guards tried — Rieu

so he interrogated the guards — NEB

and commanded that they should be put to death.

ordered them to be led away to death — Rhm

and ordered them away to execution — TCNT

And he went down from Judaea to Caesarea, and there abode.

and going down . . . stayed there — Rhm

Then he went down from Judea to Caesarea, and remained there — RSV

. . . and remained there — Wey

. . . where he spent some time — Mof

. . . and was spending time there — NASB

20. And Herod was highly displeased with them of Tyre and Sidon:

Now he was bitterly hostile to . . . — Rhm

Now the people of Tyre and Sidon had incurred Herod's violent displeasure — Wey

Now Herod was angry with the people of Tyre and Sidon — RSV

As there was a bitter feud between him and the inhabitants of Tyre and Sidon — Mof

Herod was very angry with . . . — Gspd

Now Herod cherished a bitter grudge against . . . — Wms

But he felt ugly toward . . . — Ber

He had for some time been furiously angry with . . . — NEB

He had a violent quarrel with . . . — Beck

but they came with one accord to him,

but they went together to him — TCNT

So they sent a large deputation to wait on him — Wey

they waited on him unanimously — Mof

So they came before him in a body — Gspd

They sent a joint embassy to him — Rieu

who now by common agreement presented themselves at his court — NEB

and, having made Blastus the king's chamberlain their friend,

and persuading Blastus who was over the bed-chamber of the king — Rhm

and having won over Blastus . . . — TCNT

and having secured the good will of Blastus, his treasurer — Wey

and after conciliating the royal chamberlain . . . — Mof

. . . the controller of the king's house — Bas

. . . the king's household steward — Nor

desired peace;

they asked for peace — ASV

they were suing for peace — Rhm

they begged Herod for a peaceful arrangement — TCNT

they begged the king to be friendly with them again — Wey

they asked for a reconciliation — Gspd

they pleaded for peace — Ber

because their country was nourished by the king's country.

. . . was fed . . . — ASV

because their country was dependent on the King's for its food supply — TCNT

21. And upon a set day

And on an appointed day . . . — Rhm

So a day was fixed . . . — Gspd

Herod, arrayed in royal apparel,

. . . putting on royal apparel — Rhm

. . . put on his state-robes — TCNT

. . . having arrayed himself in royal robes — Wey

sat upon his throne,

and seating himself upon the tribunal — Rhm

took his seat on the tribunal — Wey

and seated on the rostrum — NEB

and made an oration unto them.

began to make them a speech — TCNT

and was haranguing them — Wey

and made them an address — Gspd

made a public statement to them — Bas

22. And the people gave a shout, saying,

And the people shouted . . . — RSV

The people kept shouting — TCNT

and the assembled people raised the shout — Wey

and the people shouted in applause — Gspd

The mob shouted — Ber

It is the voice of a god, and not of a man.

The voice of a God, and not of a man — ASV

It is a god's voice, not a man's! — Mof

There is a god speaking, not a mere man! — Phi

23. And immediately the angel of the Lord smote him,

Instantly an angel of the Lord struck him — Wey

But the angel of the Lord struck him down immediately — Gspd

. . . struck him down with a deadly disease — Nor

because he gave not God the glory:

because he had usurped the honour due to God — NEB

and he was eaten of worms,

and becoming worm-eaten — Rhm

and being eaten up by worms — Wey

and his flesh was wasted away by worms — Bas

He was attacked by a violent internal disease — Rieu

and gave up the ghost.

he expired — Rhm

and died — RSV

24. But the word of God grew and multiplied.

And the word of the Lord went on growing and multiplying — Rhm

Meanwhile the Lord's Message kept extending, and spreading far and wide — TCNT

But the Lord's message continued to grow and spread — Gspd

And still the word of God grew strong and spread wide — Knox

But the word of the Lord continued to gain ground and increase its influence — Phi

25. And Barnabas and Saul returned from Jerusalem, when they had fulfilled their ministry,

. . . returned unto[51] Jerusalem . . . — Rhm

Barnabas and Saul returned, after visiting Jerusalem in the discharge of their commission — TCNT

When Barnabas and Saul had performed their mission to Jerusalem, they went back — Gspd

When Barnabas and Saul had finished their helpful service . . . Wms

Barnabas and Saul returned from Jerusalem, their mission of relief fulfilled — Knox

and took with them John, whose surname was Mark.

and took along with them John who was called Mark — Wms

bringing with them John whose other name was Mark — RSV

taking John Mark with them — NEB

CHAPTER 13

1. Now there were in the church that was at Antioch

Now there were at Antioch, in the church that was there — ASV

There were at Antioch, among the members of the Church there — TCNT

There were at Antioch, in the congregation there — NEB

certain prophets and teachers;

prophets and teachers — ASV

some Prophets and Teachers — TCNT

a number of prophets and teachers — Gspd

as Barnabas, and Simeon that was called Niger,

. . . Simeon who went by the name of Black — TCNT

and Lucius of Cyrene,

and Manaen, which had been brought up with Herod the tetrarch, and Saul.

. . . the foster-brother of Herod the tetrarch . . . — ASV

. . . foster-brother of Prince Herod . . . — TCNT

. . . who was an intimate friend of the governor . . . — Wms

. . . a childhood companion of Herod . . . — Ber

. . . a member of the court of Herod the tetrarch — RSV

2. As they ministered to the Lord, and fasted,

And as they were publicly ministering unto the Lord and fasting — Rhm

While they were worshipping the Lord . . . — TCNT

While they were keeping a fast and offering worship . . . — NEB

While the Christians were worshipping . . . — Beck

the Holy Ghost said,

the Holy Spirit said — RSV

Separate me Barnabas and Saul for the work whereunto I have called them.

Set apart for me . . . — ABUV

Separate now for Me . . . — Amp

Dedicate Barnabas and Saul for a special job I have for them! — Tay

3. And when they had fasted and prayed,

Then, when they . . . — ASV

So after fasting and prayer — Gspd

At this, after further fasting and prayer — Phi

and laid their hands on them,

and the laying on of hands — Wey

they sent them away.

and sent them on their way — TCNT

they let them go — Wey

and set them free for this work — Phi

they bade them farewell — Rieu

4. So they, being sent forth by the Holy Ghost,

So Barnabas and Saul, sent on this mission . . . — TCNT

They therefore, being thus sent out by the Holy Spirit — Wey

So these two, sent at the Holy Spirit's command — Phi

The two men, missionaries of the Holy Spirit — Rieu

Indeed, it was really the Holy Spirit who had sent them out — Nor

---

[51]Variant reading.

departed unto Seleucia;
went down to Seleucia — ASV
and from thence they sailed to Cyprus.
. . . they sailed away . . . — Alf
and from there sailed to Cyprus—Wey

5. And when they were at Salamis,
And arriving at Salamis — ABUV
On reaching Salamis — TCNT
they preached the word of God in the synagogues of the Jews:
they proclaimed . . . — ASV
they declared . . . — Rhm
they began to tell God's message in the Jewish Synagogues — TCNT
they began to announce . . . — Wey
and they had also John to their minister.
. . . as their attendant — ASV
. . . as their assistant — Wey
. . . as their helper — Nor

6. And when they had gone through the isle unto Paphos,
. . . the whole island . . . — RSV
They covered the whole island as far as Paphos — Mof
Traversing the entire island . . . — Ber
they found a certain sorcerer, a false prophet, a Jew,
they there met with a Jewish magician and false prophet — Wey
they came upon a certain magician, a Jewish false prophet — RSV
. . . a Jew who posed as a prophet — NEB
whose surname was Bar-jesus:
whose name was Bar-Jesus — ASV
whose real name was Barjoshua — TCNT
Bar-Jesus by name — Wey
named Barjesus — Gspd

7. Which was with the deputy of the country,
who was with the proconsul — ASV
He was at the court of the Governor — TCNT
who was a friend of the Proconsul — Wey
he belonged to the suite of the proconsul — Mof
He was attached to the governor — Gspd
He was in the retinue of the Governor — NEB
Sergius Paulus, a prudent man;

. . . a man of understanding — ASV
. . . a man of intelligence — RSV
. . . an intelligent man — Rhm
. . . a man of considerable intelligence — TCNT
. . . a man of keen intelligence — Wey
. . . a man of good sense — Knox
who called for Barnabas and Saul,
The same called unto him . . . — ASV
who sent for . . . — TCNT
He summoned . . . — Mon
who urgently invited . . . — Ber
and desired to hear the word of God.
and sought to hear . . . — RSV
and asked to be told God's Message — TCNT
and demanded to hear . . . — Mof
and wanted to hear . . . — NEB

8. But Elymas the sorcerer
. . . the magician — Alf
(for so is his name by interpretation)
for so, when translated, is his name — Rhm
for that is the meaning of the name — TCNT
for that is the translation of his name — Mof
for that is the sense of his name — Bas
as he called himself — Nor
withstood them,
opposed them — TCNT
put himself against them — Bas
began to argue with them — Rieu
was opposing them — NASB
seeking to turn away the deputy from the faith.
seeking to turn away the proconsul from the faith — RSV
seeking to turn aside the procounsul . . . — ASV
eager to divert the Governor's attention . . . — TCNT
and tried to prevent the Proconsul from accepting the faith — Wey
with the purpose of turning the ruler . . . — Bas
as he was anxious to stop the procounsul from being converted — Rieu

9. Then Saul, (who also is called Paul,)
But Saul who is also Paul — Rhm
However, Saul (who is the same as Paul) — TCNT
But Saul, whose other name is Paul — Bas

So Saul — that is, Paul — Ber

Paul, hitherto known as Saul — Rieu

Saul — hereafter called Paul — Nor

filled with the Holy Ghost,

filled with the Holy Spirit — ASV

because he was full of the Holy Spirit
— Wms

prompted by the Holy Spirit — Rieu

set his eyes on him,

fastened his eyes on him — ASV

fixed his eyes on him — Alf

looked steadily at him — Mof

looked him straight in the eye — Wms

looking hard at him — Bas

looked intently at him — RSV

eyed him closely — Phi

looked him in the face — NEB

looked squarely at him — Nor

10. **And said,**

O full of all subtilty and all mischief,

O full of all guile and all villany —
ASV

You incarnation of deceit and fraud!
— TCNT

You who are full of every kind of
craftiness and unscrupulous cunning
— Wey

You monster of underhandedness and
cunning — Gspd

You expert in every form of deception
and sleight-of-hand — Wms

O you, who are full of false tricks and
evil ways — Bas

You crafty villain — Rieu

You utter impostor and charlatan —
NEB

You professional deceiver and mischief
maker — Nor

thou child of the devil,

thou son of the devil — ASV

thou enemy of all righteousness,

and foe to all that is right — Wey

you enemy of all good — Mof

hating all righteousness — Bas

enemy of all honest dealing — Knox

**wilt thou not cease to pervert the right
ways of the Lord?**

Will you never cease diverting the
straight paths of the Lord — TCNT

Will you never stop trying to make the
Lord's straight paths crooked —
Gspd

will you never stop plotting against the
saving purposes of God — Ber

11. **And now, behold, the hand of the Lord
is upon thee,**

Listen! The hand . . . is upon you even
now — TCNT

See here, the Lord's hand will fall on
you — Mof

The Lord's hand is right upon you —
Gspd

And now, behold, the hand of the Lord
is upon you — RSV

Right now the hand . . . is upon you —
Wms

Now listen, the Lord Himself will
touch you — Phi

Look now, the hand of the Lord strikes
— NEB

**and thou shalt be blind, not seeing the
sun for a season.**

and you shall be blind for a time and
unable to see the sun — TCNT

**And immediately there fell on him a
mist and a darkness;**

and instantly . . . — Rhm

Immediately mist and darkness fell
upon him — RSV

In a moment a dark mist fell upon him
— Mof

Immediately a mist and then an utter
blackness came over his eyes — Phi

**and he went about seeking some to
lead him by the hand.**

and he felt about . . . — Alf

and going about he was seeking . . . —
Rhm

and he went feeling about for someone
to guide him — TCNT

and, as he walked about, he begged
people . . . — Wey

and he groped about for someone to
take him . . . — Mof

12. **Then the deputy, when he saw what
was done, believed,**

Then the proconsul seeing what had
happened . . . — Rhm

When the Governor saw what had happened, he became a believer in
Christ — TCNT

Then the proconsul believed, when he
saw what had happened — Mof

The proconsul was convinced when he
witnessed this scene — Rieu

**being astonished at the doctrine of the
Lord.**

being amazed at the teaching of the
Lord — Rhm

being greatly struck with the teaching about the Master — TCNT

and was thunderstruck at the Lord's teaching — Gspd

and overcome with awe at the Lord's teaching — Knox

for he was shaken to the core at the Lord's teaching — Phi

deeply impressed by what he had learned about the Lord — NEB

13. Now when Paul and his company loosed from Paphos,

. . . set sail . . . — ASV

. . . put to sea . . . — Alf

. . . put out to sea — Wey

they came to Perga in Pamphylia:

and went to . . . — TCNT

and John departing from them returned to Jerusalem.

Here John quit them . . . — Wms

. . . withdrawing from them . . . — Rhm

. . . left them . . . — TCNT

. . . separated himself from them . . . — Ber

14. But when they departed from Perga,

But they, passing through from Perga — ASV

The rest went on . . . — TCNT

But they themselves, passing through . . . — Wey

From Perga they continued their journey — NEB

they came to Antioch in Pisidia,

. . . Antioch of Pisidia — ASV

arrived at Pisidian Antioch — Mof

reached Pisidian Antioch — Knox

came to Antioch near Pisidia — Beck

and went into the synagogue on the sabbath day,

On Saturday they went into the synagog — Beck

and sat down.

and took their seats — TCNT

15. And after the reading of the law and the prophets

When the reading from . . . was finished — Knox

After the readings from the Law and the Prophets — Rieu

the rulers of the synagogue sent unto them, saying,

the Wardens of the synagogue . . . — Wey

the synagogue authorities . . . — Gspd

the leaders of the synagogue worship . . . — Wms

the officials of the synagogue . . . — NEB

the Presidents of the Synagogue sent them this message — TCNT

Ye men and brethren,

Brethren — RSV

Fellow Jews — Beck

if ye have any word of exhortation for the people, say on.

if there is in you a word of exhortation unto . . . — Rhm

if you have any word of exhortation for the people, say it — RSV

if you have any helpful words to address to the people, now is your opportunity — TCNT

. . . anything encouraging to say to the people, speak — Wey

. . . any word of counsel for . . . say it — Mof

. . . any appeal to make to . . . proceed — Gspd

. . . any message of encouragement for . . . you may speak — Wms

. . . in your hearts any word of encouragement for . . . let us hear it — Knox

16. Then Paul stood up, and beckoning with his hand said,

And Paul standing up and making a sign . . . — Rhm

So Paul rose and, motioning with his hand, spoke as follows . . . — TCNT

So Paul rose, and motioning . . . for silence . . . — Wey

Paul came forward and motioned for silence — Rieu

. . . and made a gesture . . . to claim audience — Knox

. . . and suggesting silence by a wave of . . . — Ber

Men of Israel,

Israelites — Wey

and ye that fear God,

and such as revere God! — Rhm

and all here who reverence God — TCNT

and all you who worship the true God — Knox

and Gentiles of the synagogue — Rieu

and you God-fearing people — Nor

give audience.

hearken — ASV

listen to me — TCNT
pay attention to me — Wey

17. The God of this people of Israel
... of this people Israel ... — RSV
chose our fathers,
selected our fathers — Ber
chose our ancestors — TCNT
chose our forefathers — Wey
and exalted the people when they dwelt as strangers in the land of Egypt,
and raised the position of the people during their stay in Egypt — TCNT
and made the people great during their stay in Egypt — Wey
made them a great nation while they were in Egypt — Rieu
When they were still living as aliens in Egypt he made them into a nation — NEB
he multiplied . . . as they sojourned in . . . — Mof
... when they sojourned in ... — ASV
and with an high arm brought he them out of it.
and with uplifted arm brought them out from it — TCNT
until with wondrous power He brought ... — Wey
stretching out his arm to deliver them from it — Knox
and led them out of Egypt with his mighty hand — Rieu

18. And about the time of forty years
And for about the time ... — ASV
For about forty years — TCNT
suffered he their manners in the wilderness.
carried he them as a nurse ... — Alf
he bore with them in the wilderness — RSV
he bore with them in the Desert — TCNT
as a nursing-father bare he them[52] ... — ASV
He fed them like a nurse in the desert — Wey
Then after he had taken care of them ... — Gspd
he bore with their ways ... — ABUV
he put up with their ways ... — Bas
he patiently endured their ways ... — Rieu

19. And when he had destroyed seven nations in the land of Chanaan,

Then, after overthrowing . . . Canaan — Wey
he divided their land to them by lot.
he gave them their land for an inheritance — ASV
he allotted their land to the people — TCNT
He divided that country among them as their inheritance — Wey
and settled them upon their land — Gspd
whose lands he gave them for an inheritance — Knox
He distributed their land by lot — Ber
and gave their country to His people as an inheritance — Beck

20. And after that he gave unto them judges about the space of four hundred and fifty years,[53] until Samuel the prophet.
and after these things he gave them judges until Samuel the prophet — ASV
Later on he gave them Judges, of whom the Prophet Samuel was the last — TCNT
and afterwards appointed judges for them ... — NEB
Judges ruled for about 450 years, and were followed by Samuel the prophet — Tay
By now some four hundred and fifty years had passed; and after this he appointed judges over them, up to the time ... — Knox

21. And afterward they desired a king:
... they asked for a king — RSV
And when, after a while, they demanded a king — TCNT
Next they asked for a king — Wey
Then it was that they begged for a king — Mof
and God gave unto them Saul the son of Cis,
... the son of Kish — ASV
a man of the tribe of Benjamin,
a Benjamite — Wey
by the space of forty years.
for the space of forty years — ASV
who reigned for forty years — TCNT

---

[52]Variant reading.
[53]Some translations place the words "about the space of four hundred and fifty years" at the end of verse 19.

who was their king for forty years —
Bas

22. And when he had removed him,
and setting him aside — Rhm
After removing him — TCNT
After deposing him — Mof
But God took the throne away from
him again — Beck
**he raised up unto them David to be
their king;**
he raised David to the throne — TCNT
He raised up David for their king —
Ber
**to whom also he gave testimony, and
said,**
Of whom he also said, bearing witness
— Rhm
of whom he testified and said — RSV
and he bore also this testimony to him
— TCNT
a man of whom God Himself bore witness in the words — Phi
sponsoring him with these words —
Rieu
giving him approval in these words —
NEB
I have found David the son of Jesse,
I have found in David, Jesse's son —
TCNT
a man after mine own heart,
a man I love — Wey
a man after my heart — RSV
a man dear to my heart — Bas
a man agreeable to my mind — Ber
which shall fulfil all my will.
who shall do all my will — ASV
who will carry out all my purposes —
TCNT
who will obey all My commands —
Wey
who will do all that I desire — Gspd
who will do all that my will requires —
Wms
who will do all my pleasure — Bas
who will carry out My whole program
— Ber
who will do all that I want him to —
Nor

23. Of this man's seed hath God
It was from this man's descendants that
God — TCNT
Of this man's posterity . . . — RSV
according to his promise
in fulfilment of His promise — Wey
as he had promised — Mof

according to the promise made to him
— Knox
raised unto Israel a Saviour, Jesus:
brought[54] unto Israel . . . — ASV
brought Israel a Saviour — in Jesus —
TCNT
given Israel a Saviour, Jesus — Nor
. . . a Savior in the person of Jesus —
Wms

**24. When John had first preached before
his coming**
John beforehand proclaiming before
the face of his coming — Rhm
Before his coming John had preached
— RSV
John had proclaimed, before Jesus
came among them — TCNT
in preparation for whose coming John
had preached — Gspd
**the baptism of repentance to all the
people of Israel.**
a baptism upon repentance, for all . . .
— TCNT
baptism as an expression of repentance,
for . . . — Wms
. . . the baptism which goes with a
change of heart — Bas
a baptism in which all the people of
Israel was to repent — Knox

25. And as John fulfilled his course,
. . . was fulfilling . . . — ASV
As John was drawing towards the end
of his career — TCNT
And as John was finishing his course
— RSV
But John, when he was fulfilling his
career — Wey
And as John was closing his career —
Mof
Toward the end of his career — Gspd
And John, when he was finishing his
race — Mon
And when John was completing his
work — Bas
he said,
he was saying — Rhm
he used to say — TCNT
used to speak thus — Wey
repeatedly asked the people — Mon
Whom think ye that I am? I am not he.
What suppose ye that I am? . . . — ASV
What do you think I am? I am not the
Christ — TCNT

---

[54]Variant reading.

What do you suppose me to be? I am not the Christ — Wey

I am not what you suspect me to be — Knox

But, behold, there cometh one after me,

No, but after me one is coming — RSV

no, he is coming after me — Mof

look rather for one who comes after me — Knox

whose shoes of his feet I am not worthy to loose.

the shoes of whose feet . . . to unloose — ASV

One of whom I am not worthy the sandals of his feet to loosen — Rhm

whose shoe, even, I am not worthy to untie — TCNT

whose sandal I am not worthy to unfasten — Wey

the shoes on whose feet I am not fit to untie — Gspd

26. **Men and brethren, children of the stock of Abraham,**

Brethren, sons of the family of Abraham — RSV

Brethren, sons of the stock of Abraham — Alf

Brethren! sons of the race of Abraham — Rhm

Brethren, descendants of the family of Abraham — Wey

Brothers! Descendants of the house of Abraham — Gspd

and whosoever among you feareth God,[55]

to you is the word of this salvation sent.

to us is the word of this salvation sent forth — ASV

it was to us that the Message of this Salvation was sent — TCNT

to us has the word of this salvation been sent — Wey

27. **For they that dwell at Jerusalem, and their rulers,**

For the people at Jerusalem and their leading men — TCNT

For those who live in Jerusalem . . . — RSV

because they knew him not,

not recognizing him — Rhm

failing to recognize Jesus — TCNT

refused to recognize him — Gspd

because they were ignorant of Him — Wms

nor yet the voices of the prophets which are read every sabbath day,

and not understanding the utterances of . . . — TCNT

they have fulfilled them in condemning him.

fulfilled these by condemning him — RSV

even though in condemning Him they fulfill these very prophecies! — Phi

by condemning Jesus did what their prophets predicted . . . — Beck

28. **And though they found no cause of death in him,**

They found no ground at all for condemning him to death — TCNT

Without having found Him guilty of any capital offence — Wey

though they could find him guilty of no crime that deserved death — Mof

For though they found no cause for putting him to death — Phi

Though they failed to find grounds for the sentence of death — NEB

yet desired they Pilate that he should be slain.

yet they asked of Pilate . . . — ASV

and yet demanded his execution from Pilate — TCNT

they urged Pilate to have Him put to death — Wey

they begged Pilate to have him put to death — Mof

29. **And when they had fulfilled all that was written of him,**

After carrying out everything written about him — TCNT

and, after carrying out all that had been predicted of him in scripture — Mof

When they had carried out everything that had been said about him in the Scriptures — Gspd

And when they had completed . . . — Phi

they took him down from the tree,

taking him down from the tree — Rhm

they took Jesus down from the cross — TCNT

and laid him in a sepulchre.

and laid him in a tomb — RSV

30. **But God raised him from the dead:**

. . . from among the dead — Rhm

---

[55]Compare verse 16.

31. And he was seen many days of them which came up with him from Galilee to Jerusalem,

Who appeared during many days unto them who . . . — Rhm

For many days he was seen by those who . . . — Mof

who are his witnesses unto the people.

who are now his witnesses . . . — ASV

and are now witnesses concerning Him to the Jews — Wey

They are now his witnesses before our nation — NEB

They are now telling the people the truth about Him — Beck

32. And we declare unto you glad tidings,

And we bring you good tidings — ASV

We, too, have the Good News to tell you — TCNT

So we now preach to you the glad news — Mof

So we are bringing you the joyful tidings — Ber

how that the promise which was made unto the fathers,

of the promise made unto the fathers — ASV

about the promise made to our ancestors — TCNT

about the promise made to our forefathers — Wey

that what God promised to the fathers — RSV

33. God hath fulfilled the same unto us their children,

that God hath fulfilled the same unto our[56] children — ASV

that our children have had the promise fulfilled to them by God to the very letter — TCNT

that God has amply fulfilled it to our children — Wey

has been fulfilled by God for us their children — Mof

this he has fulfilled to us their children — RSV

has now been carried out for us and our children — Rieu

God . . . has fulfilled it for the children — NEB

in that he hath raised up Jesus again;

by raising up Jesus — Rhm

by his raising Jesus from the grave — — TCNT

in raising up Jesus — ABUV

by raising Jesus to life — Gspd

as it is also written in the second psalm,

This is just what is said in the second Paslm — TCNT

just as the Scripture says in the second psalm — Gspd

as the second psalm describes — Rieu

as indeed it stands written, in the second Psalm — NEB

This is so stated also in the second Psalm — Nor

Thou art my Son, this day have I begotten thee.

My son art thou: I this day have begotten thee — Rhm

. . . today I have begotten thee — RSV

. . . This day thou hast been born to me — TCNT

. . . To-day I have become Thy Father — Wey

. . . today I have generated Thee — Ber

. . . Today I am Your Father — Beck

34. And as concerning that he raised him up from the dead,

And in that he raised him from among the dead — Rhm

As to his raising Jesus from the dead — TCNT

And as to His having raised Him from among . . . — Wey

And as a proof that he has raised . . . — Mof

Now as evidence that he has raised . . . — Gspd

But that he raised Him . . . — Ber

now no more to return to corruption,

no longer in danger of returning . . . — TCNT

never again to be in the position of one soon to return to decay — Wey

never to return to decay — Mof

never to turn to dust — Ber

he said on this wise,

this is what he said — TCNT

He speaks thus — Wey

He expressed this way — Ber

I will give you the sure mercies of David.

I will give you the holy and sure blessings of . . . — RSV

I will give you the sacred promises made to . . . — TCNT

---

[56]Variant reading.

I will give you the holy, the sure promises of . . . — ABUV

I will give you the holy and trustworthy promises made to . . . — Wey

I will give you the holiness of David that fails not — Mof

I will fulfil to you my sacred promises to . . . — Gspd

I will give you the blessings promised to David, holy and sure — NEB

35. **Wherefore he saith also in another psalm,**

For the same reason, too, in another Psalm, it is said — TCNT

Thou shalt not suffer thine Holy One to see corruption.

Thou wilt not give thy Holy One to see . . . — ASV

Thou wilt not give up . . . to undergo corruption — TCNT

. . . to undergo decay — Wey

You will not let your . . . experience decay — Wms

Thou wilt not allow thy faithful servant . . . — Knox

You will not let your Loved One experience decay — Beck

36. **For David, after he had served his own generation by the will of God,**

. . . after he had in his own generation served the counsel of God — ASV

David, of course, after obediently doing God's will in his own time — TCNT

. . . after having been useful to his own generation in accordance with God's purpose — Wey

. . . after serving God's purpose in his own generation — Mof

fell on sleep,

fell asleep — RSV

died — Mof

he by God's will went to his rest — Beck

and was laid unto his fathers,

and was gathered . . . — Alf

and was laid by the side of his ancestors — TCNT

was gathered to his forefathers — Wey

and rested with his fathers — Knox

and was buried with his fathers — Ber

and saw corruption.

and did undergo corruption[57] — TCNT

37. **But he, whom God raised again, saw no corruption.[58]**

38. **Be it known unto you therefore,**

Let it be known to you therefore — RSV

I would, therefore, have you know — — TCNT

Understand therefore — Wey

So you must understand — Mof

And so, let it be clear to you — Bas

Here is news for you — Knox

It should be clear then to you — Ber

And so you should know — Beck

men and brethren,[59]

that through this man is preached unto you the forgiveness of sins:

. . . is proclaimed unto you remission of sins — ASV

that our announcement is, that there is forgiveness of sins for you through Jesus — TCNT

that through this man forgiveness of sins is offered to you — Bas

39. **And by him all that believe are justified from all things,**

And by him every one that believes is freed from everything — RSV

. . . every one that believeth is justified . . . — ASV

and that, in union with him, all who believe in him are cleared from every charge — TCNT

and in Him every believer is absolved from all offences — Wey

and that through union with Him everyone of you who believes is given right standing with God and freed from every charge — Wms

It is through him that everyone who has faith is acquitted of everything — NEB

from which ye could not be justified by the law of Moses.

from which you could not be cleared under the Law of Moses — TCNT

from which you could not be absolved under . . . — Wey

from which you could not be freed by . . . — Wms

for which there was no acquittal under . . . — NEB

40. **Beware therefore, lest that come upon you, which is spoken of in the prophets;**

---

[57]See verse 35.

[58]See verses 33 and 35.

[59]See verse 15.

Take care, therefore, that what is said in the Prophets does not come true of you — TCNT

So take care that what is said in the prophets does not come upon you — Wms

So take care that these words of the prophets do not come true for you — Bas

So be careful the prophetic utterance does not become your experience — Ber

Take care then that this saying of the prophets should never apply to you — Phi

Now be careful, or what the prophets said will happen to you — Beck

41. Behold, ye despisers, and wonder, and perish:

See, ye despisers, and marvel and disappear — Rhm

Look, you despisers, then wonder and hide your heads — TCNT

Look, you disdainful folk, wonder at this and perish — Mof

Look, you scoffers! Then wonder and begone! — Gspd

Look, you scoffers! Then wonder and vanish away — Wms

for I work a work in your days,

For I am about to do a great work myself . . . — TCNT

Because I am carrying on a work in your time — Wey

for in your days I do a deed — Mof

For I am doing something in your times — Gspd

a work which ye shall in no wise believe,

A work which you will never believe — TCNT

a work which you will utterly refuse to believe — Wey

such as you would never believe — — Ber

though a man declare it unto you.

Though one relate it in full unto you — Rhm

even if told you in full — TCNT

even if it is made clear to you — Bas

even if it were described in full — Rieu

42. And when the Jews were gone out of the synagogue,[60]

And as they went out — ASV

And as they were going out — Rhm

As Paul and Barnabas were going out — TCNT

the Gentiles[61] besought that these words might be preached to them the next sabbath.

they besought that . . . might be spoken . . . — ASV

they kept on beseeching . . . — Rhm

the people begged for a repetition of this teaching . . . — TCNT

the people earnestly begged to have all this repeated to them on the following Sabbath — Wey

they were implored to preach the same message there . . . — Knox

43. Now when the congregation was broken up,

Now when the synagogue broke up — ASV

After the congregation had broken up — TCNT

Now when the meeting was ended — Bas

and when the synagogue was dismissed — Ber

And when the meeting of the synagogue broke up — RSV

After the congregation had dispersed — NEB

many of the Jews and religious proselytes

. . . devout proselytes — ASV

. . . converts who joined in their worship — TCNT

. . . devout converts from heathenism — Wey

. . . devout converts to Judaism — Gspd

. . . God-fearing Gentiles who had become Jews — Bas

followed Paul and Barnabas:

continued with . . . — Wey

went away with . . . — Gspd

allied themselves with . . . — Wms

accompanied . . . — Rieu

who, speaking to them,

who, in conversation with them — TCNT

persuaded them to continue in the grace of God.

---

[60]"The Jews" and "the synagogue" are now recognized as not adequately supported by original manuscripts.

[61]"Gentiles" is now recognized as not adequately supported by original manuscripts.

and urged them to continue in the grace of God — RSV

urged them to continue to rely on the mercy of God — TCNT

urged them to hold fast to the grace of God — Wey

. . . to continue to rely on the unmerited favor . . . — Wms

44. And the next sabbath day came almost the whole city together to hear the word of God.

. . . almost the whole population of the city . . . — Wey

. . . gathered to hear God's message — TCNT

45. But when the Jews saw the multitudes,

. . . the crowds of people — TCNT

. . . the crowds — Wey

they were filled with envy,

were filled with jealousy — Rhm

they became exceedingly jealous — TCNT

filled with angry jealousy — Wey

they were completely overcome by their jealousy — Wms

they became terribly jealous — Ber

they were filled with jealous resentment — NEB

and spake against those things which were spoken by Paul,

and contradicted what was spoken by Paul — RSV

and contradicted the things . . . — ASV

and kept contradicting Paul's statements — TCNT

contradicting[62] and blaspheming.

and blasphemed — ASV

in abusive language — TCNT

and abused him — Wey

and talked abusively — Ber

and reviled him — RSV

covering him with abuse — Phi

with violent abuse — NEB

46. Then Paul and Barnabas waxed bold, and said,

And Paul and Barnabas spoke out boldly . . . — RSV

. . . speaking boldly said — Rhm

. . . spoke out fearlessly . . . — TCNT

. . . spoke out plainly . . . — Gspd

. . . courageously spoke out — Wms

. . . answered them fearlessly — Rieu

Then, throwing off all reserve, Paul . . . said — Wey

At this Paul . . . did not mince their words but said — Phi

It was necessary that the word of God should first have been spoken to you:

We were bound to proclaim . . . to you first — Wey

God's message had to be told to you first — Gspd

. . . to you Jews first — Wms

but seeing ye put it from you,

Seeing ye thrust it from you — ASV

but since you reject it — TCNT

But since you spurn it — Wey

but as you push it aside — Mof

but because you will have nothing to do with it — Bas

since you repudiate it — NASB

and judge yourselves unworthy of everlasting life,

and thus condemn yourselves as unworthy of eternal life — NEB

lo, we turn to the Gentiles.

why, we turn to the heathen! — TCNT

well, we turn to the Gentiles — Wey

now and here we turn to the heathen — Wms

observe: we are turning to the Gentiles — Ber

we are now turning to the non-Jews — Beck

47. For so hath the Lord commanded us, saying,

For this is the Lord's order to us — TCNT

For these are the orders the Lord has given us — Gspd

Indeed the Lord has commanded us to do so in the words — Phi

For these are our instructions from the Lord — NEB

The Lord gave us a commission. It is this — Nor

I have set thee to be a light of the Gentiles,

I have set thee for a light . . . — ASV

I have destined thee for a light to the heathen — TCNT

I have placed Thee as a light to the Gentiles — Wey

I have made you a light for the heathen — Gspd

---

[62]The word "contradicting" is now recognized as not adequately supported by original manuscripts.

I have appointed thee . . . — Knox

that thou shouldest be for salvation unto the ends of the earth.

. . . unto the uttermost parts of the earth — ASV

To be the means of salvation to . . . — TCNT

in order that Thou mayest be a Saviour . . . — Wey

that you may bring salvation to the uttermost parts of the earth — RSV

to bring salvation to . . . — Mof

and a means of salvation to earth's farthest bounds — NEB

to save people all over the earth — Beck

48. And when the Gentiles heard this, they were glad,

And they of the nations hearing this began to rejoice — Rhm

On hearing this, the heathen were delighted — TCNT

The Gentiles listened with delight — Wey

And when the Gentiles heard this, they were glad — RSV

The heathen kept on listening and rejoicing — Wms

The Gentiles were overjoyed when they heard this — Nor

and glorified the word of the Lord:

and extolled God's message — TCNT

and praised God's message — Gspd

and giving the glory to God's message — Wms

they eulogized the Lord's message — Ber

and thanked God for His Message — Phi

and thankfully acclaimed the word of the Lord — NEB

and as many as were ordained to eternal life believed.

. . . as many as had become disposed for . . . — Rhm

and all who were predestined to eternal Life . . . — Wey

and all who were destined . . . — Gspd

and those marked out by God for . . . — Bas

as many as were appointed for . . . — Ber

49. And the word of the Lord was published throughout all the region.

. . . spread thoughout all the region — RSV

. . . was spread abroad . . . — ASV

. . . was being spread . . . — NASB

and the Lord's Message was carried . . . that district — TCNT

. . . went far and wide over the whole country — Mof

50. But the Jews stirred up the devout and honourable women,

. . . urged on the devout women of honorable estate — ASV

. . . urged on the devout women of the higher class — Rhm

. . . the devout women of rank — Alf

. . . roused the ladies of position who worshipped with them — TCNT

. . . influenced the gentlewomen of rank who worshipped with them — Wey

. . . incited the devout women of high rank — Mof

. . . stirred up the well-to-do religious women — Gspd

. . . the devout women of wealth — Ber

. . . the devout women of high standing — RSV

. . . the influential women attached to the synagogue — Rieu

. . . the most religious and respected women — Nor

and the chief men of the city,

and the leading men of the town — TCNT

and the leading citizens — Mon

and the men of first rank in town — Wms

and the outstanding men of the city — Ber

the city authorities — Rieu

and raised persecution against Paul and Barnabas,

and stirred up a persecution . . . — ASV

and so started a persecution . . . — Wms

and instigated persecution . . . — Ber

and succeeded in starting a persecution . . . — Phi

and expelled them out of their coasts.

and cast them out of their borders — ASV

and drove them out of their neighbourhood — TCNT

and drove them out of the district — Wey

and drove them out of their territory — Mof

51. But they shook off the dust of their feet against them,

And they, having shaken off . . . — ABUV

They, however, shook the dust off their feet in protest — TCNT

. . . as a protest against them — Wms

and came unto Iconium.

and went to Iconium — RSV

52. And the disciples were filled with joy,

leaving the disciples full of joy — TCNT

and as for the disciples, they were more and more filled with joy — Wey

But the disciples continued to be full of joy — Gspd

Their converts, however, continued in joy — Rieu

And the converts were filled with joy — NEB

and with the Holy Ghost.

And with the Holy Spirit — ASV

CHAPTER 14

1. And it came to pass in Iconium,

The same thing occurred in Iconium — TCNT

Their Iconium experience was similar — Ber

Much the same thing happened at Iconium — Phi

that they went both together into the synagogue of the Jews,

that they entered together . . . — ASV

where Paul and Barnabas went into the Jewish Synagogue — TCNT

the Apostles went together to the Jewish synagogue — Wey

similarly they went into the Jewish synagogue — NEB

and so spake,

and spoke in such a way — TCNT

and preached — Wey

and spoke with such power — Gspd

and preached in such a way — Knox

and spoke so well — Ber

and spoke with such conviction — Phi

and spoke to such purpose — NEB

and spoke in such a manner — NASB

that a great multitude both of the Jews and also of the Greeks believed.

that a large number of both Jews . . . believed them — TCNT

with the result that a great number . . . — Wey

that a great body . . . — Mof

that a great company . . . — RSV

that a big crowd . . . — Beck

2. But the unbelieving Jews

But the Jews that were disobedient — ASV

But the unpersuaded Jews — Rhm

But the Jews who refused to believe — TCNT

But the refractory Jews — Mof

But the Jews who refused their message — Gspd

But those Jews who had not the faith — Bas

The unconvinced Jews, however — Rieu

But the unconverted Jews — NEB

stirred up the Gentiles, and made their minds evil affected against the brethren.

stirred up the Gentiles and poisoned their minds against the brethren — RSV

stirred up the souls of the Gentiles and made them . . . — ASV

stirred up and embittered the minds of the Gentiles against the brethren — Alf

stirred up the heathen, and poisoned their minds . . . — TCNT

. . . against the Christians — NEB

. . . against the disciples — Nor

3. Long time therefore abode they

. . . they tarried there — ASV

Therefore Paul and Barnabas spent a considerable time there — TCNT

For a considerable time, however, Paul and Barnabas remained there — Wey

So they remained for a long time — RSV

In spite of this, however, they stayed there . . . — Wms

speaking boldly in the Lord,

speaking out fearlessly in dependence on the Lord — TCNT

speaking fearlessly about the Lord —
Mof

and continued to speak with courage
from the Lord — Wms

and spoke boldly and openly in reliance on the Lord — NEB

**which gave testimony unto the word
of his grace,**

who bare witness . . . — ASV

who supported the Message of his
mercy — TCNT

who attested the word of his grace —
Mof

who bore witness to his gracious message — Gspd

and he confirmed the message of his
grace — NEB

He gave His approval to the preaching
of His grace — Nor

who gave His approval to the words of
His love — Beck

**and granted signs and wonders to be
done by their hands.**

granting . . . — RSV

by permitting . . . to take place at their
hands — TCNT

by permitting signs and marvels to be
done by them — Wey

by allowing . . . to be performed by
them — Mof

4. **But the multitude of the city was
divided:**

But the townspeople were divided —
TCNT

At length the people of the city split
into parties — Wey

But the mass of the city's people was
divided — Mon

the common folk . . . were divided in
opinion — Knox

**and part held with the Jews, and part
with the apostles.**

some siding with the Jews, some with
the Apostles — TCNT

some supporting the Jews and others
the apostles — Rieu

5. **And when there was an assault made**

When an attempt was made — RSV

And when there was made an onset —
ASV

and when a movement was made —
TCNT

And when a hostile movement was
made — Wey

And when a violent attempt was made
— Bas

**both of the Gentiles, and also of the
Jews**

on the part of both heathen and Jews
— TCNT

by both Gentiles and Jews — Wey

with their rulers,

with their leading men — TCNT

with the sanction of their magistrates
— Wey

with the authorities — Gspd

in collaboration with the authorities
— Phi

with the connivance of the city authorities — NEB

**to use them despitefully, and to stone
them,**

to treat them shamefully . . . — ASV

to illtreat and stone them — TCNT

to insult . . . — Mof

to assault . . . — Knox

to abuse and to stone them — Ber

to molest them and to stone them —
RSV

to mistreat and to stone them — NASB

6. **They were ware of it,**

they became aware of it — ASV

the Apostles heard of it — TCNT

having become aware of it — Wey

the apostles got wind of it — Mon

When they became aware of this danger — Nor

they found out about it — Beck

**and fled unto Lystra and Derbe, cities
of Lycaonia,**

and fled unto the cities of Lycaonia,
Lystra and Derbe — ASV

and took refuge at Lystra and Derbe,
towns in Lycaonia —TCNT

made their escape into the Lycaonian
towns of . . . — Wey

**and unto the region that lieth round
about:**

and the region round about — ASV

and the neighbouring country — Wey

and to the surrounding country — Mof

and their suburbs — Ber

and the surrounding countryside — Phi

7. **And there they preached the gospel.**

where they continued to tell the Good
News — TCNT

and there they went on preaching the
good news — Gspd

where they continued to spread the good news — NEB

8. And there sat a certain man at Lystra,
Now at Lystra there was a man sitting — RSV

There used to sit in the streets of Lystra a man — TCNT

At Lystra there was a man sitting — Mof

impotent in his feet,
who had no power in his feet — TCNT

who had not the use of his feet — Gspd

lame in his feet — Mon

who had no strength in his feet — Wms

who could not use his feet — RSV

a crippled man — NEB

being a cripple from his mother's womb,
he had been lame from his birth — TCNT

a cripple from birth — Mon

lame from birth — NEB

who never had walked:
and had never walked at all — TCNT

who had never walked in his life — NEB

9. The same heard Paul speak:
He listened to Paul speaking — RSV

This man was listening to Paul speaking — TCNT

He was listening to Paul as he talked — Gspd

who stedfastly beholding[63] him,
who, fastening his eyes upon him — ASV

and perceiving that he had faith to be healed,
and seeing that he had faith to be made whole — ASV

. . . to be cured — Wey

. . . to be made well — Bas

10. Said with a loud voice,
said loudly — TCNT

he shouted aloud to him — Wms

Stand upright on thy feet.
Stand up on your feet — TCNT

Stand erect on your feet — Mof

Get on your feet and stand erect! — Wms

Stand up straight on your feet — Ber

And he leaped and walked.
And he sprang up and began to walk about — Rhm

The man jumped up, and began walking about — TCNT

11. And when the people saw what Paul had done,
The crowds of people, seeing what . . . — TCNT

Then the crowds, seeing . . . — Wey

The multitudes, seeing . . . — Knox

they lifted up their voices, saying in the speech of Lycaonia,
called out in the Lycaonian language — TCNT

rent the air with their shouts in the Lycaonian language — Wey

they shouted in the Lycaonian language — Mof

cried out in the Lycaonian dialect — Knox

they shouted in Lycaonian — Ber

they shouted, in their native Lycaonian — NEB

The gods are come down to us in the likeness of men.
The gods, made like unto men, have come . . . — Rhm

The Gods have made themselves like men and come down to us — TCNT

. . . in the form of men — Wey

. . . in human form — Mof

It is the gods, who have . . . in human shape — Knox

These men are gods in human bodies! — Tay

12. And they called Barnabas, Jupiter;
Barnabas they called Zeus — RSV

They called Barnabas 'Zeus'[64] — Wey

And they began to call Barnabas "Zeus" — Mon

and Paul, Mercurius, because he was the chief speaker.
and Paul, Mercury — ASV

and Paul, as being the principal speaker, 'Hermes'[65] — Wey

and Paul Hermes, since he was the chief spokesman — Mof

and they called Paul, because he led in the discourse, Hermes [God of speech] — Amp

. . . seeing that he was the leader of discourse — Rhm

---

[63]See the same verb form in Acts 1:10; 3:4,12; 6:15; 7:55; 10:4; 11:6; 13:9.

[64]"Jupiter" is the Latin for "Zeus," the national Greek god.

[65]"Mercurius" (Mercury) is the Latin for the Greek "Hermes."

... because he led the conversation — Ber

... because he was the spokesman — Rieu

13. Then the priest of Jupiter, which was before their city,

And the priest of Zeus, whose temple was in front of the city — RSV

The priest of Jupiter-beyond-the-Walls — TCNT

And the priest of Zeus — the temple of Zeus being just outside the city — Wey

The priest of the temple of Zeus that stood at the entrance to the town — Gspd

And the priest of the image of Jupiter ... — Bas

and the priest of Jupiter, Defender of the City — Knox

In fact, the city-priest for Zeus — Ber

What is more, the High Priest of Jupiter whose temple was at the gateway of the city — Phi

The Priest of Zeus from the temple outside the city — Rieu

brought oxen and garlands unto the gates,

brought bullocks and garlands to the gates — TCNT

... unto the doors of the house — Alf

and would have done sacrifice with the people.

... with the multitudes — ASV

with the intention of offering sacrifices — TCNT

and in company with the crowd was intending to offer sacrifices to them — Wey

to join the people in offering sacrifice — Ber

and prepared to offer public sacrifice — Rieu

14. Which when the apostles, Barnabas and Paul, heard of,

But when the apostles Barnabas and Paul heard of it — RSV

they rent their clothes,

they rent their garments — ASV

they tore their clothes — TCNT

they tore their robes — NASB

and ran in among the people,

and rushed out among the multitude — RSV

and sprang forth among the multitude — ASV

and rushed out into the crowd — TCNT

and made a dash among the crowds — Ber

crying out,

exclaiming — Wey

shouting — Mof

crying aloud — Knox

crying at the top of their voices — Phi

15. And saying, Sirs, why do ye these things?

Men! why these things are you doing — Rhm

Friends, why are you doing this — TCNT

Men, what is this you are doing — Mof

We also are men of like passions with you,

We are only men like you — TCNT

We also are but human beings with natures like yours — Wey

We are men with the same feelings as you — Bas

We too are mortal men like yourselves — Knox

We also are men, of like nature with you — RSV

We are human, with emotions as yourselves — Ber

We are human beings like you — Rieu

We are only human beings, no less mortal than you — NEB

We are also men of the same nature as you — NASB

and preach unto you

and bring you good tidings — ASV

and bring you good news — RSV

and we have come with the Good News — TCNT

The gospel we are preaching to you is — Mof

that ye should turn from these vanities

that from these vain things ye should be turning — Rhm

... these follies — TCNT

... such futile ways — Mof

... these empty things — Mon

... these foolish things — Wms

... these meaningless things — Phi

... such superstitions — Nor

unto the living God,

which made heaven, and earth, and the sea,

who made the heaven and the earth and the sea — ASV

who made the sky, the earth, the sea — TCNT

the Creator of earth and sky and sea — Wey

and all things that are therein:

and everything that is in them — TCNT

and all that they contain — Gspd

16. Who in times past suffered all nations to walk in their own ways.

who in the generations gone by . . . — ASV

. . . he permitted all the heathen to go their . . . — TCNT

In past generations he allowed all the nations to walk . . . — RSV

In bygone ages he allowed all nations to go their . . . — Mof

17. Nevertheless he left not himself without witness, in that he did good,

Yet he has not omitted to give you, in his kindly acts, evidence about himself — TCNT

and yet by His beneficence He has not left His existence unattested — Wey

though as the bountiful Giver he did not leave himself without a witness — Mof

though he did not fail to give some evidence about himself, through his kindness to you — Gspd

though even then he showed that he existed by the good things he gave you — Rieu

and yet he has not left you without some clue to his nature, in the kindness he shows — NEB

and gave us rain from heaven, and fruitful seasons,

and gave you from heaven rains and fruitful seasons — RSV

sending you, as he does, rain from Heaven and harvest — TCNT

in that He sends you . . . — Wey

. . . and crops in their seasons — NEB

filling our hearts with food and gladness.

filling your hearts . . . — ASV

and satisfying your desires with food and good cheer — TCNT

giving you food and joy to your heart's content — Mof

food for your bodies, and happiness for your hearts — Rieu

and gives you food and good cheer in plenty — NEB

filling you with food, and making you happy — Beck

18. And with these sayings scarce restrained they the people, that they had not done sacrifice unto them.

. . . the multitudes from doing sacrifice . . . — ASV

Even with this appeal they could hardly prevent the people from offering . . . — TCNT

Even with words like these they had difficulty in preventing the thronging crowd from . . . — Wey

Even by saying this it was all they could do to keep the crowds from sacrificing to them — Mof

19. And there came thither certain Jews from Antioch and Iconium,

Presently, however, there came some Jews . . . — TCNT

But now a party of Jews came . . . — Wey

But some of the Jews from . . . had followed them — Knox

Then Jews from . . . came on the scene — NEB

who persuaded the people,

and having persuaded the multitudes — ASV

who, after they had won over the people — TCNT

and, having won over the crowd — Wey

these won over the multitude to their side — Knox

who influenced the populace — Ber

and after turning the minds of the people against Paul — Phi

and, having stoned Paul, drew him out of the city,

they stoned Paul, and dragged him . . . — ASV

supposing he had been dead.

supposing that he was dead — RSV

thinking him to be dead — TCNT

under impression he was dead — Ber

and left him for dead — Rieu

20. Howbeit, as the disciples stood round about him,

But when the disciples had gathered round him — TCNT

But the disciples formed a circle about him — Wms

The converts formed a ring round him
— NEB
But when the disciples came and stood
around him — Beck
he rose up, and came into the city:
he got up and went back into the town
— TCNT
and he got up and went back to town
— Wms
he got up and entered the city — Ber
**and the next day he departed with
Barnabas to Derbe.**
and on the morrow he went forth . . .
— ASV
Next day he went off . . . — Mof
. . . he went on . . . — Gspd

21. **And when they had preached the gospel to that city,**
After telling the Good News throughout that town — TCNT
After proclaiming the gospel to the
people there — Wey
and had taught many,
and had made many disciples — RSV
and making a number of converts —
TCNT
and gaining a large number of converts
— Wey
and winning many converts — Mon
**they returned again to Lystra, and to
Iconium, and Antioch,**
they returned to Lystra and to Iconium,
and to Antioch — RSV
they retraced their steps to Lystra,
Iconium, and . . . — Wey
they turned back to . . . — Mof
they went back to . . . — Mon

22. **Confirming the souls of the disciples,**
reassuring the minds . . . — TCNT
Everywhere they strengthened the disciples — Wey
strengthening the souls of the disciples
— RSV
strengthening the hearts of the disciples — Wms
where they fortified the spirits of . . .
— Knox
reassuring the disciples spiritually —
Ber
They put fresh heart into the disciples
there — Phi
heartening the converts — NEB
**and exhorting them to continue in the
faith,**

beseeching them to abide in the faith
— Rhm
urging them to remain true to the Faith
— TCNT
by encouraging them to hold fast to the
faith — Wey
urging them to stand firm in the Faith
— Phi
and encouraging them to be true to
their religion — NEB
**and that we must through much trib-
ulation enter into the kingdom of
God.**
and that through many tribulations we
must enter . . . — ASV
and showing that it is only through
many troubles that we can enter the
Kingdom of God — TCNT
and warned them saying, It is through
many afflictions that we must make
our way into the Kingdom of God
— Wey
and reminding them that we have to
undergo many hardships to get into
the Kingdom . . . — Gspd
and telling them that we cannot enter
the kingdom of heaven without
many trials — Knox

23. **And when they had ordained them
elders in every church,**
And when they had appointed elders
for them in every church — RSV
They also appointed Officers for them
in . . . — TCNT
. . . they selected Elders by show of
hands — Wey
They chose presbyters for them in . . .
— Mof
They helped them select elders in each
church — Wms
. . . in each congregation — NEB
and had prayed with fasting,
and, after prayer and fasting — TCNT
and with prayer and fasting — Gspd
they commended them to the Lord,
entrusted them to the Lord — Mof
they committed them to the Lord —
Gspd
these were dedicated to the Lord —
Nor
on whom they believed.
on whom their faith rested — Wey
in whom they had put their faith —
Rieu

24. And after they had passed throughout Pisidia, they came to Pamphylia.

Paul and Barnabas then went through Pisidia, and came into Pamphylia — TCNT

Then they came through Pisidia to Pamphylia — Mof

After traveling through Pisidia, they reached Pamphylia — Ber

25. And when they had preached the word in Perga, they went down into Attalia:

. . . spoken the word . . . — RSV

and after telling the word at Perga . . . they came down to Attaleia — Wey

26. And thence sailed to Antioch,

and from there they sailed back to Antioch — Gspd

and from there set sail for Antioch — NEB

from whence they had been recommended to the grace of God for the work which they fulfilled.

whence they had been committed . . . — ASV

from which they had been commended to the help of God . . . — TCNT

. . . for the task which they had now completed — Phi

27: And when they were come,

And when they had arrived — Rhm

Upon their arrival — Wey

On arriving there — Wms

and had gathered the church together,

they gathered the church together — RSV

they called the Church together — Wey

they called a church meeting — Ber

and had called the congregation together — NEB

they rehearsed all that God had done with them,

and declared all that God had done with them — RSV

and gave an account of . . . with and through them — TCNT

and proceeded to report in detail all that God, working with them, had done — Wey

and gave a full account . . . — Rieu

. . . all that God had helped them to do — NEB

and how he had opened the door of faith unto the Gentiles.

and that he had opened a door . . . — ASV

especially how he had opened to the heathen a door to the Faith — TCNT

and how he had thrown open the gates of faith to the Gentiles — NEB

and how He had opened the door for the people who were not Jews so that they, too, might believe — Beck

28. And there they abode long time with the disciples.

and at Antioch they stayed with the disciples for a long time — TCNT

They spent a considerable time . . . — Mof

So they spent a good, long time . . . — Ber

CHAPTER 15

1. And certain men which came down from Judaea

But some men came down from Judea — RSV

A party of Jews from Judaea now arrived in Antioch — Rieu

But now some visitors came down from Judaea — Knox

And certain persons coming down from Judaea — Rhm

taught

and were teaching — Alf

began to teach — Rhm

tried to convince — Wey

and attempted to teach — Mon

the brethren, and said,

the brotherhood — NEB

the Christians — Beck

Except ye be circumcised

Unless you are circumcised — RSV

that, unless they were circumcised — TCNT

that without circumcision — Bas

after the manner of Moses,

after the custom of Moses — ASV

as Moses prescribed — Gspd

in accordance with Mosaic practice — NEB

in accordance with the custom enjoined by Moses — TCNT

ye cannot be saved.

they could not be saved — TCNT

there is no salvation — Bas

2. When therefore Paul and Barnabas had no small dissension and disputation with them,

Between these new-comers and Paul and Barnabas there was no little disagreement and controversy — Wey

Since Paul and Barnabas had experienced no little discussion and debate with them — Ber

And when Paul and Barnabas had no small dissension and debate with them — RSV

Paul and Barnabas vigorously opposed them and contested their doctrine — Rieu

Naturally Paul and Barnabas took a leading part in the discussion and disagreement that arose — Nor

This gave rise to a serious dispute, and much discussion between Paul and Barnabas and these men — TCNT

That brought them into fierce discussion and controversy with Paul and Barnabas — NEB

they determined that Paul and Barnabas,

and it reached such a point that it was necessary for Paul and Barnabas — Lam

the brethren appointed that Paul and Barnabas — ASV

it was arranged that Paul and Barnabas — Rhm

it was therefore settled that Paul and Barnabas — TCNT

And so it was arranged that these two — NEB

and certain other of them,

and others of their number — TCNT

and some other brethren — Wey

and some others from Antioch — NEB

should go up to Jerusalem

unto the apostles and elders about this question.

to consult the Apostles and Officers of the Church about the matter under discussion — TCNT

to see the apostles and presbyters at Jerusalem . . . — Mof

. . . about this dispute — Ber

. . . about the whole question — Phi

. . . concerning this issue — NASB

to confer with the apostles and elders about this question — Gspd

to settle the question with the Apostles and Elders — Rieu

3. And being brought on their way by the church,

They therefore being set forward by the Assembly — Rhm

So they set out, being accompanied for a short distance by the Church — Wey

The church sped them on their journey — Mof

The church saw them off upon their journey — Gspd

So they were endorsed and sent on by the church — Wms

So then, fitted out for their trip by the church — Ber

So, being sent on their way . . . — RSV

It was, in fact, the congregation that was sending them — Nor

they passed through Phenice and Samaria,

and they travelled through all Phoenicia and the territory of the Samaritans — Lam

and they made their way through Phoenicia and Samaria — TCNT

declaring the conversion of the Gentiles:

informing the brothers . . . that the Gentiles were turning to God — Mof

they told of the conversion of the heathen — Gspd

relating how the Gentiles were turning to God — Knox

reporting the conversion of the Gentiles — RSV

fully relating the conversion of them of the nations — Rhm

telling the story of the conversion of the Gentiles — TCNT

where they narrated in detail the conversion of the Gentiles — Ber

they told the whole story how the non-Jews were turning to God — Beck

and they caused great joy unto all the brethren.

to the great joy of all the Brethren — TCNT

and brought great rejoicing to all the brothers — Wms

and thus made all the brothers very happy — Ber

And all the brothers were overjoyed to hear about it — Phi

4. And when they were come to Jerusalem,

On their arrival at Jerusalem — TCNT

When they reached Jerusalem — Gspd

they were received of the church,

they were welcomed by the Assembly — Rhm

they were cordially received by the Church — Wey

they had a meeting with . . . — Bas

they were given a welcome . . . — Nor

they were heartily welcomed . . . — Amp

they were received by the congregation of the church — Rieu

and of the apostles and elders,
and they declared

and they rehearsed — ASV

and gave a full report — Rieu

and they recounted — Rhm

all things that God had done with them.

all that God had helped them to do — TCNT

all that God, working with them, had done — Wey

how great things God had wrought with them — ABUV

how God had been with them and what he had done — Mof

all that God had accomplished through them — Amp

5. But there rose up certain of the sect of the Pharisees which believed, saying,

Some of the Pharisees' party, who had become believers in Christ, came forward — TCNT

But certain men who had belonged to the sect of the Pharisees but were now believers — Mon

But some believers who belonged to the party of the Pharisees came forward and declared — Knox

But some who believed [that is, who acknowledged Jesus as their Savior and devoted themselves to Him] belonged to the sect of the Pharisees, and they rose up and said — Amp

That it was needful to circumcise them,

It is necessary to circumcise them — RSV

that they were bound to circumcise converts — TCNT

Gentiles must be circumcised — Mof

You must circumcise them — Lam

and to command them to keep the law of Moses.

and to charge them to keep the law of Moses — RSV

and to direct them to observe the Law of Moses — TCNT

6. And the apostles and elders came together

. . . were gathered together — ASV

. . . held a meeting — TCNT

for to consider of this matter.

to investigate this question — Mof

to consider this question — TCNT

to decide about this matter — Knox

to look into and consider . . . — Amp

7. And when there had been much disputing,

. . . much debate — RSV

. . . much questioning — ASV

After much discussion — TCNT

and, after a lively debate — Ber

After an exhaustive inquiry — Phi

Peter rose up, and said unto them,

Peter stood up and addressed them in these words — Phi

Men and brethren,

Brethren — RSV

My friends — NEB

Fellow Christians — Beck

ye know how that a good while ago

You . . . know well that long ago — TCNT

You will keep in mind that a good while back — Ber

Ye yourselves well know that in days long past — Rhm

God made choice among us,

. . . among you — ASV

God singled me out — TCNT

it was God's pleasure — Bas

God made a selection among you — Amp

that the Gentiles by my mouth

that through my mouth the nations — Rhm

that through my lips the Gentiles — TCNT

should hear the word of the gospel,

should hear word of the glad tidings — Rhm

should hear the Message of the Good News — TCNT

should hear the gospel message — Ber

and believe.

and so learn to believe — Knox

and become believers in Christ — TCNT

and believe — that is credit and place their confidence in it — Amp

8. And God, which knoweth the hearts,
... who knows men's hearts — Gspd
... who knows men's inmost thoughts — Phi
... who reads all hearts — TCNT
... the searcher of hearts — Bas
... who is acquainted with and understands ... — Amp
and the heart-observing God — Rhm
bare them witness,
gave His testimony in their favor — Wey
attested this — Mof
testified for them — Gspd
bore witness to them — RSV
gave them evidence — Ber
declared his acceptance of the Gentiles — TCNT
has assured them of his favour — Knox
showed his approval of them — Rieu
giving them the Holy Ghost,
by giving ... — TCNT
by bestowing ... — Wey
... the Holy Spirit — ASV
even as he did unto us;
just as he gave it to us — Mof
exactly as he did to us — Phi

9. And put no difference between us and them,
and he made no distinction ... — RSV
he made not the slightest distinction ... — Mof
And he did not discriminate ... — Lam
Making no division ... — Bas
He would not make any difference ... — Knox
purifying their hearts by faith.
but cleansed their hearts by faith — RSV
when he purified their hearts by their faith — TCNT
in that he cleansed ... — Wey
because he cleansed ... — Wms
he had removed all the uncleanness from their hearts when he gave them faith — Knox

10. Now therefore why tempt ye God,
... why make ye trial of God — ASV
... why are you proving God — Rhm
Why, then, do you now provoke God — TCNT

Then why do you now try to test God — Gspd
How is it, then, that you would now call God in question — Knox
Now then, why be a trial to God — Ber
Why then must you now strain the patience of God — Phi
to put a yoke upon the neck of the disciples,
by putting a yoke upon the neck of the disciples — RSV
by laying on the neck of these disciples a yoke — Wey
by trying to put on the shoulders of these disciples a burden — Phi
which neither our fathers nor we were able to bear?
such as we and our fathers have been too weak to bear — Knox
which was too heavy even for us and our forefathers to bear — Rieu
... our ancestors ... — TCNT
such as neither our forefathers nor now we [ourselves] were able to endure — Amp

11. But we believe that through the grace of the Lord Jesus Christ
... through the favour ... — Rhm
... it is through the loving-kindness ... — TCNT
... by the mercy ... — Gspd
... through the grace [the undeserved favor and mercy] of the Lord Jesus — Amp
we shall be saved,
we are saved — Alf
that we have been saved — TCNT
even as they.
in like manner as they — ASV
just as they are — Wms

12. Then all the multitude kept silence,
Every voice in the assembly was hushed — TCNT
Then the whole assembly remained silent — Wey
So the whole meeting was quieted — Mof
and gave audience to Barnabas and Paul,
and began to hearken unto ... — Rhm
as they listened to ... — TCNT
declaring what miracles and wonders
rehearsing what signs and wonders — ASV

relating how many signs and wonders
— Rhm

**God had wrought among the Gentiles
by them.**
God had done through them among
the Gentiles — RSV
which God had performed . . . — Mof
God had worked . . . — NEB
God had shown . . . — TCNT

13. And after they had held their peace,
After they had finished speaking —
TCNT
And when they had come to an end —
Bas

James answered, saying,
James addressed the Council — TCNT
James made this response — Gspd
James replied — RSV
James summed up — NEB

Men and brethren,[66]
hearken unto me:
hear what I have to say — TCNT
listen to me — Bas

14. Simeon hath declared
. . . hath fully told — Rhm
. . . has related — RSV
Simon has described — TCNT
. . . has explained — Mof

**how God at the first did visit the Gen-
tiles, to take out of them a people
for his name.**
the manner in which God first visited
the Gentiles, in order to take from
among them a people to bear his
Name — TCNT
how it was God's original concern to
secure a People from among the
Gentiles . . . — Mof
how God was first pleased to take
from among the Gentiles a people
for himself — Bas
how for the first time God has looked
with favour on the Gentiles, and
chosen from among them a people
dedicated to his name — Knox
how early God had in mind to gain
out of the Gentiles a people for His
name — Ber
the first occasion on which God visited
the Gentiles and took from them a
new chosen people to bear his name
— Rieu
how it first happened that God took
notice of the Gentiles, to choose

from among them a people to bear
his name — NEB
how God first came to the non-Jews to
get a people for Himself — Beck

15. And to this agree
This agrees with — Mof
This is in full agreement with — Phi
the words of the prophets;
what the prophets wrote — Phi
the language of the Prophets — Wey
the predictions of the prophets — Gspd
as it is written,
as Scripture has it — NEB

16. After this I will return,
Afterward . . . — Gspd
There will come a time when I shall
return — Nor
**and will build again the tabernacle of
David,**
I will set up again . . . — Lam
. . . the dwelling of David — RSV
. . . the tent of David — Rhm
. . . the House of David — TCNT
which is fallen down;
that hath fallen — Rhm
and I will build again the ruins thereof,
Its very ruins I will rebuild — TCNT
Even from its ruins I will rebuild it —
NEB
and I will set it up:
and set it up once more — TCNT
and raise it afresh — Knox
and restore it — Ber

17. That the residue of men
that the rest of men — RSV
that so the rest of mankind — TCNT
So that the men who remain — Lam
might seek after the Lord,
may seek out . . . — Rhm
may earnestly seek . . . — TCNT
may find the Lord — Knox
and all the Gentiles,
Even all the nations — Wey
. . . the heathen — Gspd
upon whom my name is called,
which are called by My name — Wey
who are called by my name — RSV
among whom my name is named —
Knox
who belong to me — Rieu
upon whom my name has been bestowed — TCNT

---

[66]Compare verse 7.

whom I have claimed for my own —
NEB

over whom my name has been invoked
— Ber

saith the Lord,
So said the Lord — Lam
The Lord says this — Ber

who doeth all these things.
who is the doer of all this — Knox
whose work it is — NEB

18. **Known unto God are all his works
from the beginning of the world.**
God has known from all eternity what
he does today — Knox
From eternity all His doings are known
— Ber

19. **Wherefore my sentence is,**
. . . my judgment is — RSV
In my judgement, therefore — TCNT
Therefore it is my opinion — Amp
For this reason my decision is — Bas
So I propose — Rieu

that we trouble not
we should not add to the difficulties of
— TCNT
that we should impose no irksome re-
strictions on — NEB
that we should not put obstacles in the
way and annoy and disturb — Amp

**them, which from among the Gentiles
are turned to God:**
those Gentiles who are turning to God
— TCNT
. . . who turn to God — RSV
. . . who have found their way to God
— Knox
the Gentile converts — Rieu

20. **But that we write unto them,**
. . . command them — Alf
Yet, let us send them written instructions — Wey
but instead write and tell them — Rieu
but instruct them by letter — NEB

**that they abstain from pollutions of
idols,**
to abstain from food that has been
polluted by being sacrificed to idols
— TCNT
to abstain from things polluted by
connexion with idolatry — Wey

and from fornication,
from impurity — TCNT
from sexual vice — Mof
immorality — Gspd
and from unchastity — Ber

and from things strangled,
and from what is strangled — ASV
from eating the flesh of strangled animals — TCNT
and from the flesh of animals put to
death in ways against the law — Bas

and from blood.
and from tasting blood — Mof

21. **For Moses of old time hath in every
city them that preach him,**
For Moses out of ancient generations
hath in every city them that proclaim
him — Rhm
For in every town, for generations past,
there have been those who preach
Moses — TCNT
As for Moses, ever since the earliest
times he . . . has preachers . . . to
expound him — Knox
For Moses will continue . . . to have
people . . . to proclaim his Law, as
he has had for generations — Rieu
Moses, after all, has never lacked
spokesmen in every town for generations past — NEB

**being read in the synagogues every
sabbath day.**
for he is read every sabbath in the
synagogues — RSV
seeing that in the synagogues every sabbath he is read — Rhm
read as he is in the Synagogue every
Sabbath — TCNT
where he is read aloud in the synagogues every sabbath — Mof

22. **Then pleased it the apostles and elders,**
Then it seemed good to the apostles
and elders — ASV
It was then decided by the Apostles and
the Officers — TCNT

with the whole church,
with the assent of the whole Church —
TCNT
with the approval of . . . — Wey
With the concurrence of the whole
church — Rieu

**to send chosen men of their own com-
pany to Antioch with Paul and
Barnabas;**
to choose men out of their company
and send them to Antioch with Paul
and Barnabas — ASV
to select representatives and send them
with Paul and Barnabas to Antioch
— Gspd

namely, **Judas surnamed Barsabas, and Silas,**

Those chosen were Judas (called Barsabas) and Silas — TCNT

chief men among the brethren:

who were leading men among the Brethren — TCNT

prominent members of the brotherhood — Mof

leading men among the brethren — Wey

leaders among the Christians — Ber

23. And they wrote letters by them after this manner;

with the following letter: — RSV

and they wrote thus by them — ASV

They were bearers of the following letter — TCNT

The apostles and elders and brethren send greeting

The apostles and the elders, brethren, . . . greeting — ASV

The Apostles and the Elder Brethren . . . wish joy — Rhm

The Apostles, and the Brothers who are the Officers of the Church — TCNT

We, the apostles and elders, send greetings as brothers — NEB

unto the brethren which are of the Gentiles in Antioch and Syria and Cilicia:

to the brothers from among the heathen in Antioch, Syria, and Cilicia — Wms

to the Gentile members of the Brotherhood in Antioch, Syria, and Cilicia — Rieu

to their non-Jewish fellow Christians in Antioch, Syria, and Cilicia—Beck

24. Forasmuch as we have heard,

As we have been informed — Wey

Since we have heard — RSV

Because we have knowledge — Bas

Having learned — Mof

that certain which went out from us

that some of our number — TCNT

that some of our number who visited you — Knox

have troubled you with words,

had upset you by their orations—TCNT

have disturbed you by their teaching — Wey

have caused great distress of spirit among you by spreading misleading doctrines — Rieu

have caused you trouble by their claims — Nor

subverting your souls,

dismantling your souls — Rhm

and unsettled your minds — TCNT

by continuing to unsettle your minds — Wms

putting your souls in doubt — Bas

unsettling your consciences — Knox

and they continue to upset you — Beck

saying, Ye must be circumcised, and keep the law:[67]

to whom we gave no such commandment:

although we gave them no instructions — RSV

unto whom we had given no instructions — Rhm

without instructions from us — TCNT

quite unauthorized by us — Mof

although we had given them no such commission — Knox

although we gave them no express orders or instructions [on the points in question] — Amp

25. It seemed good unto us, being assembled with one accord,

It seemed good unto us, having come to one accord — ASV

we met and decided — TCNT

we have unanimously decided — Wey

we have passed a unanimous resolution — Wms

meeting together with common purpose of heart, we have resolved — Knox

to send chosen men unto you

to choose men and send them to you — RSV

to select representatives and send them — Gspd

to send you outstanding men —-Ber

to send delegates back to you — Rieu

with our beloved Barnabas and Paul,

with our dear brothers . . . — TCNT

in company with our beloved friends . . . — Wey

26. Men that have hazarded their lives

men who have given up their lives — Rhm

. . . endangered . . . — Wey

. . . risked . . . — Mof

. . . dedicated . . . — Lam

---

[67]Now recognized as not adequately supported by original manuscripts.

... devoted ... — Rieu
... staked ... — Knox
who personally have jeopardized their
lives — Ber
who have sacrificed themselves — TCNT
who are living only — Beck
for the name of our Lord Jesus Christ.
in behalf of the name of our Lord
Jesus Christ — Rhm
for the sake of our Lord Jesus Christ —
Wey
to the cause of our Lord Jesus Christ
— Rieu

27. **We have sent therefore Judas and
Silas,**
So we are dispatching ... — Ber
The delegates we have sent are ... —
Rieu
**who shall also tell you the same things
by mouth.**
who also themselves by word of mouth
can tell you the same things — Rhm
and they will tell you by word of mouth
what we are now writing — TCNT
who will confirm the message ... —
Knox
who will personally announce these
things — Ber

28. **For it seemed good to the Holy Ghost,
and to us,**
We have, therefore, decided, under the
guidance of the Holy Spirit — TCNT
The holy Spirit and we have decided
— Mof
For it is the will of the Holy Spirit and
of us — Lam
It is the Holy Spirit's pleasure and ours
— Knox
**to lay upon you no greater burden
than these necessary things;**
to lay no further burden upon you beyond these necessary conditions —
TCNT
to lay upon you no burden heavier than
these necessary requirements — Wey
not to impose any extra burden on you,
apart from these essential requirements — Mof
not to lay upon you any burden but
this indispensable one — Gspd
that no burden should be laid upon you
beyond these, which cannot be
avoided — Knox
not to burden you more than is necessary — Beck

29. **That ye abstain from meats offered to
idols,**[68]
You are to avoid ... — Nor
Keep away from ... — Beck
and from blood,[69]
from flesh which still has the blood in
it — Rieu
from blood-meat — Knox
the eating of blood — Nor
and from things strangled,[70]
from the meat of animals that have
been strangled — Wms
from the flesh of animals killed by
strangling — Rieu
and from fornication:[71]
... sex impurity — Nor
... sexual sin — Beck
from which if ye keep yourselves,
If you guard yourselves against such
things — TCNT
If you keep yourselves free from these
things — Wey
ye shall do well.
it shall be well with you — ASV
you shall prosper — Rhm
you will have done your part — Knox
you will get along splendidly — Ber
you will make good progress — Phi
you will do right — Rieu
you will be doing right — NEB
Fare ye well.
Goodbye — Mof
Remain steadfast in our Lord — Lam
May you be happy — Bas
Farewell — be strong! — Amp

30. **So when they were dismissed,**
So when they were sent off — RSV
So the bearers of this letter were sent
on their way — TCNT
When the messengers were dispatched
— Mof
The delegates left as instructed — Rieu
they came to Antioch:
they came down to Antioch — ASV
arrived in Antioch — Ber
and reached Antioch — Rieu
they set out for Antioch — Nor
**and when they had gathered the mul-
titude together,**

---

[68]See verse 20.
[69]See verse 20.
[70]See verse 20.
[71]See verse 20.

and having gathered the congregation together — RSV

There they called a meeting of all the Brethren — TCNT

where they called together the whole assembly — Wey

and after gathering the whole body — Mof

they delivered the epistle:

they handed them the letter — Mof

31. **Which when they had read, they rejoiced for the consolation.**

And when they had read it, they rejoiced for the consolation — ASV

The reading of which caused great rejoicing by its encouraging contents — TCNT

The people read it, and were delighted with the comfort it brought them — Wey

When it had been read aloud the congregation were both relieved and delighted — Rieu

When the letter was read it gave them both comfort and joy — Nor

32. **And Judas and Silas, being prophets also themselves,**

Judas and Silas were themselves prophets — Gspd

. . . were themselves both inspired preachers — Phi

. . . prophets (inspired interpreters of the will and purposes of God) — Amp

exhorted the brethren with many words, and confirmed them.

exhorted the brethren with many words and strengthened them — RSV

with much discourse consoled and confirmed the brethren — Rhm

further encouraged the Brethren by many an address, and strengthened their faith — TCNT

gave the brothers much encouragement and strength by their words — Gspd

urged and warned and consoled and encouraged the brethren with many words and strengthened them—Amp

33. **And after they had tarried there a space,**

After some stay — TCNT

And having remained a while — ABUV

And when they had been there for some time — Bas

they were let go in peace from the brethren unto the apostles.

they were dismissed in peace from the brethren unto those that had sent them forth — ASV

they were dismissed with kind farewells from the Brethren, and returned to those who had sent them — TCNT

and when they left the Brotherhood and returned to those who had sent them, peace had been restored — Rieu

they were sent back by the brethren with [the greeting] Peace, to those who had sent them — Amp

34. **Notwithstanding it pleased Silas to abide there still.**[72]

35. **Paul also and Barnabas continued in Antioch,**

. . . remained . . . — RSV

. . . stayed on . . . — Mof

teaching and preaching the word of the Lord,

teaching and telling the joyful tidings . . . of the word of the Lord — Rhm

where they taught and . . . told the Good News of the Lord's Message — TCNT

continued to teach the Lord's message and to tell the good news — Wms

with many others also.

with the help of many others — TCNT

with a band of fellow-workers — Rieu

36. **And some days after**

Some time after this — TCNT

After a while — Wey

Paul said unto Barnabas, Let us go again

. . . Let us return now — ASV

. . . Let us go back — TCNT

and visit our brethren

to visit the brothers — Mof

and revisit . . . — Gspd

and look in on the brothers — Ber

and again visit and help and minister to . . . — Amp

in every city where we have preached the word of the Lord,

. . . we proclaimed . . . — RSV

. . . have told the Lord's Message — TCNT

---

[72]Now recognized as not adequately supported by original manuscripts.

in the various towns in which we have made known the Lord's word — Wey

and see how they do.
and see how they are — RSV
and see how they are prospering — TCNT
to see how they are getting on — Gspd

37. And Barnabas determined to take with them John,
. . . was minded to take . . . — ASV
. . . was bent on taking . . . — Wey
But Barnabas persisted in wanting to take along John — Wms
whose surname was Mark.
who was called Mark — ASV
whose other name was Mark — TCNT

38. But Paul thought not good to take him with them,
. . . felt that they ought not . . . — TCNT
But Paul did not approve . . . — Gspd
Paul, however, thought it wrong . . . — Rieu
who departed from them from Pamphylia,
who withdrew . . . — ASV
who had deserted . . . — TCNT
because he had left them when they were in Pamphylia — Lam
the one who had quit them in Pamphylia — Ber
and went not with them to the work.
instead of accompanying them on active service — Mof
and did not go on with them to the work — Wms
and was not prepared to go on with them in their work — Phi
and had not continued with them in the work — Nor

39. And the contention was so sharp between them,
And there arose a sharp contention . . . — RSV
And there arose an angry feeling . . . — Rhm
So there arose a sharp altercation . . . — Wey

They differed so sharply about it — Gspd
There was a sharp clash of opinion, so much so — Phi
The disagreement was so sharp — Wms
that they departed asunder one from the other:
. . . separated from each other — RSV
which resulted in their parting from one another — Wey
they parted company — Mof
that they went their separate ways — Phi
and resulted in their separating — Rieu
and so Barnabas took Mark, and sailed unto Cyprus;
and Barnabas took Mark and sailed for Cyprus — Wms

40. And Paul chose Silas,
. . . chose Silas for his companion — TCNT
and departed,
. . . set out — Wey
He started on his journey — NEB
being recommended by the brethren unto the grace of God.
being commended by the brethren to the grace of the Lord — RSV
committed unto the favour of the Lord by the brethren — Rhm
after he had been committed by the Brethren to the gracious care of the Lord — TCNT
his fellow Christians entrusting him to the Lord's love — Beck

41. And he went through Syria and Cilicia,
He made his way . . . — Mof
. . . travelled . . . — Gspd
His trip took him . . . — Nor
confirming the churches.
strengthening the Churches in the Faith — TCNT
establishing churches — Lam
bringing new strength to the congregations — NEB
where he established congregations — Nor

CHAPTER 16

1. Then came he to Derbe and Lystra:
Paul eventually reached . . . — Rieu
and, behold, a certain disciple was there,
At the latter place they found a disciple — TCNT
named Timotheus,
named Timothy — Ber
the son of a certain woman, which was a Jewess, and believed;

the son of a Jewess that believed — ASV

whose mother was a Jewess who had become a believer in Christ — TCNT

but his father was a Greek:

and a Gentile father — Knox

2. **Which was well reported of by the brethren that were at Lystra and Iconium.**

who was well attested . . . — Rhm

he was well spoken of . . . — RSV

He had a good reputation . . . — Mof

and who was well recommended . . . — Ber

3. **Him would Paul have to go forth with him;**

Wishing to take this man with him on his journey — TCNT

and took and circumcised him because of the Jews which were in those quarters:

Paul caused him to be circumcised on account of the Jews in that neighbourhood — TCNT

. . . out of consideration for the Jews . . . — NEB

In deference to the Jews of the area, he circumcised Timothy before they left — Tay

for they knew all that his father was a Greek.

for they one and all knew . . . — Rhm

4. **And as they went through the cities,**

As they travelled from town to town — TCNT

they delivered them the decrees for to keep, that were ordained of the apostles and elders which were at Jerusalem.

they were delivering unto them for observance the decrees which had been decided upon by the Apostles and Elders who were in Jerusalem — Rhm

they gave the Brethren the decisions which had been reached by the Apostles and Officers of the Church at Jerusalem, for them to observe — TCNT

they informed the communities of the decisions . . . and told them to carry them out — Rieu

5. **And so were the churches established in the faith,**

So the churches were strengthened in the faith — RSV

The assemblies therefore were being confirmed . . . — Rhm

so the churches through faith continued to grow in strength — Wms

In this way the faith of the churches was strengthened — Rieu

and increased in number daily.

and grew in number from day to day — Wey

and daily increased in membership — Nor

6. **Now when they had gone throughout Phrygia and the region of Galatia,**

And they went through the region of Phyrgia and Galatia — RSV

And they passed through the Phrygian and Galatian country — Rhm

They next went through the Phrygian district of Galatia — TCNT

and were forbidden of the Holy Ghost to preach the word in Asia,

having been forbidden of the Holy Spirit to speak the word in Asia — ASV

but were restrained by the Holy Spirit from delivering the Message in Roman Asia — TCNT

but were told by the Holy Spirit not to preach in Asia — Rieu

7. **After they were come to Mysia,**

And when they were come over against Mysia — ASV

When they reached the borders of Mysia — TCNT

When they got as far as Mysia — Mof

And when they had come opposite Mysia — RSV

When they came to a point east of Mysia — Rieu

and when they approached the Mysian border — NEB

they assayed to go into Bithynia:

they were attempting to journey into Bithynia — Rhm

they were about to enter Bithynia — Wey

they planned to enter . . . — Knox

. . . into the province of Bithynia — Rieu

but the Spirit suffered them not.

and the Spirit of Jesus suffered them not — ASV

but the Spirit of Jesus did not permit them — TCNT

8. And they passing by Mysia came down to Troas.
Passing through Mysia, they went down to Troas — TCNT
So, passing along Mysia, they came to Troas — Wey
So they crossed Mysia and went down to the sea at Troas — Knox
so they skirted Mysia and reached the coast at Troas — NEB

9. And a vision appeared to Paul in the night;
and there one night Paul saw a vision — TCNT
There stood a man of Macedonia, and prayed him, saying,
a man of Macedonia was standing beseeching him and saying — RSV
A Macedonian was standing and appealing to him — TCNT
a man from Macedonia kept standing and pleading with him in these words — Wms
Come over into Macedonia, and help us.
... and bring us succour! — Rhm

10. And after he had seen the vision,
As soon as he saw the vision — Mof
immediately we endeavoured to go into Macedonia,
Straightway we sought to go forth into Macedonia — ASV
... we looked for an opportunity to cross over to Macedonia — TCNT
we at once set about getting a passage to Macedonia — NEB
assuredly gathering that the Lord had called us
concluding that God had called us — RSV
convinced that God had called us — Phi
concluding that God had summoned us — Rhm
for to preach the gospel unto them.
to evangelize there — Ber

11. Therefore loosing from Troas,
Setting sail therefore from Troas — ASV
we came with a straight course to Samothracia,
we made a straight course to Samothrace — ASV

and ran before the wind to Samothrace — TCNT
and struck a bee line for Samothrace — Wms
and the next day to Neapolis;
and the day following to Neapolis — ASV
and on the morrow unto New City — Rhm
The next day we arrived in Neapolis — Mon

12. And from thence to Philippi,
From there we made our way to Philippi — TCNT
which is the chief city of that part of Macedonia, and a colony:
which is a city of Macedonia, the first of the district, a Roman colony — ASV
which is the first Macedonian city of the district, and a colony — Alf
a Roman garrison town, and the principal place in that part of Macedonia — Gspd
a Roman colony, the leading town in that part of Macedonia — Wms
a city of the first rank in that district of Macedonia ... — NEB
and we were in that city abiding certain days.
In that city we spent several days — TCNT
There we stayed for some time — Mon

13. And on the sabbath we went out of the city by a river side,
And on the day of rest we went forth outside the gate beside a river — Rhm
On Saturday we went out of the gate and along the river —Beck
where prayer was wont to be made;
where we supposed there was a place of prayer — RSV
where we had reason to believe there was a place for prayer — Wey
where we had an idea that there would be a place of prayer — Bas
and we sat down, and spake unto the women which resorted thither.
and sitting down we went on to speak unto the women who had come together — Rhm
Some women had already come together and there we sat down and talked to them — Nor

14. And a certain woman named Lydia,

Among them was a woman, named Lydia — TCNT

One who heard us was a woman named Lydia — RSV

a seller of purple,

a dealer in purple cloth — TCNT

in the purple dye trade — Rieu

of the city of Thyatira,

who belonged to the town of Thyatira — Mof

which worshipped God,

devout towards God — Rhm

who was accustomed to join in the worship of God — TCNT

She was a believer in God — Gspd

heard us:

listened to us — Mon

and she stayed to listen to us — Wms

She listened attentively — Rieu

whose heart the Lord opened,

The Lord touched this woman's heart — TCNT

and the Lord so moved upon her heart — Wms

that she attended unto the things which were spoken of Paul.

to give heed to what was said by Paul — RSV

so that she gave attention to the Message delivered by Paul — TCNT

that she accepted the message spoken by Paul — Wms

15. And when she was baptized, and her household,

And when she was immersed and her house — Rhm

. . . along with her household — Mof

And when she and her family had had baptism — Bas

she besought us, saying,

she urged us to become her guests — TCNT

she appealed to us, and said — Gspd

she earnestly entreated us, saying — Amp

If ye have judged me to be faithful to the Lord,

If ye have judged me to be a believer in the Lord — Rhm

If you are convinced I am a believer . . . — Mof

If in your opinion I am one really convinced [that Jesus is the Messiah and author of salvation], and that I

will be faithful to the Lord — Amp

come into my house, and abide there.

come into my house and be my guests — Bas

And she constrained us.

And she insisted on our doing so — TCNT

And she continued to insist that we do so — Wms

16. And it came to pass, as we went to prayer,

One day, as we were on our way to the Place of Prayer — TCNT

But it happened, as we were going to the prayer service — Ber

a certain damsel possessed with a spirit of divination met us,

a certain damsel having a spirit of Python met us — Rhm

we were met by a girl possessed by a divining spirit — TCNT

a slave girl met us possessed by a spirit of ventriloquism — Mof

. . . by a fortune-telling demon — Nor

a slave girl who was possessed by a spirit of divination — claiming to foretell future events and to discover hidden knowledge — Amp

which brought her masters much gain

who made large profits for her masters — TCNT

by soothsaying:

by her power of fortune-telling — Mof

17. The same followed Paul and us,

She used to follow after Paul and us — Mon

and cried, saying,

crying out again and again — Mon

shrieking — Mof

These men are the servants

. . . are slaves — Gspd

. . . bondservants — NASB

of the most high God,

of the Supreme God — NEB

of the Highest God — Nor

which shew unto us

who proclaim unto you — ASV

who indeed are declaring unto you — Rhm

and they are bringing you news of — TCNT

the way of salvation.

a way of salvation — TCNT

how to be saved — Rieu

18. And this did she many days.

And this she did for many days —
RSV

And this she continued to do for many
days — Rhm

This she persisted in for a considerable
time — Wey

She went on doing this day after day
— Rieu

**But Paul, being grieved, turned and
said to the spirit,**

But Paul was annoyed, and turned and
said to the spirit — RSV

But Paul, worn out and turning unto
the spirit said — Rhm

and then Paul, in a burst of irritation,
turned round . . . — Phi

until Paul could bear it no longer.
Rounding on the spirit he said —
NEB

**I command thee in the name of Jesus
Christ to come out of her.**

In the name of Jesus Christ I order
you out of her! — Mof

And he came out the same hour.

And it came out that very hour — ASV

That very moment the spirit left her
— TCNT

and there and then it came out of her
— Knox

**19. And when her masters saw that the
hope of their gains were gone,**

. . . that there was no hope of further
profit from her — TCNT

. . . that their hope of gain had also departed — Wey

they caught Paul and Silas,

they seized . . . — TCNT

they grabbed . . . — Ber

**and drew them into the marketplace
unto the rulers,**

and dragged them . . . before the rulers
— ASV

dragged them into the public square to
the authorities — TCNT

20. And brought them

and took them — TCNT

to the magistrates, saying,

to the chiefs of the police court. They
said — Wms

before the highest Roman officials . . .
— Beck

**These men, being Jews, do exceedingly
trouble our city,**

These men, Jews by origin, are disturbing the peace of our city — Knox

. . . are throwing our city into confusion
— NASB

21. And teach customs,

and are declaring customs — Rhm

They are advocating practices — Gspd

they're teaching religious ways — Beck

**which are not lawful for us to receive,
neither to observe, being Romans.**

which it is not allowable for us either
to accept or observe being Romans
— Rhm

which it would be illegal for us Roman
citizens to accept and practice —
Rieu

**22. And the multitude rose up together
against them:**

On this the mob rose as one man against
them — TCNT

The crowd, too, joined in the outcry
against them — Wey

This speech roused the feelings of the
crowd against Paul and Silas — Rieu

**and the magistrates rent off their
clothes,**

. . . stripped them of their clothing —
TCNT

. . . ordered them stripped — Wey

. . . tore off their garments — ABUV

. . . tore off the prisoners' clothes —
NEB

and commanded to beat them.

and ordered them to be beaten with
rods — TCNT

**23. And when they had laid many stripes
upon them,**

After beating them severely — TCNT

and, after severely flogging them —
Wey

they cast them into prison,

the Magistrates put them in prison —
TCNT

. . . flung them into prison — NEB

**charging the jailor to keep them
safely:**

with orders to the jailor to keep them
in safe custody — TCNT

and gave the jailor strict orders to keep
close watch of them — Gspd

. . . to guard them securely — Ber

. . . to keep them under close guard —
NEB

24. Who, having received such a charge,

On receiving so strict an order, the
jailor — TCNT

thrust them into the inner prison,

he put them into the inner prison — RSV

... in the inner dungeon — Nor

and made their feet fast in the stocks.

and secured their feet in the stocks — TCNT

with chains on their feet — Bas

25. And at midnight Paul and Silas prayed,

But about midnight Paul and Silas were praying — RSV

... were worshipping — Ber

and sang praises unto God:

and singing hymns unto God — ASV

and the prisoners heard them.

... were listening to them — ASV

26. And suddenly there was a great earthquake, so that the foundations of the prison were shaken:

suddenly there was an earthquake of such violence that the jail was shaken to its foundations — TCNT

and immediately all the doors were opened,

all the doors flew open — TCNT

At one stroke all the doors sprang open — Ber

... flew open simultaneously — Rieu

and every one's bands were loosed.

and the bonds of all were unfastened — Rhm

and all the prisoners' chains were loosened — TCNT

and the chains fell off every prisoner — Wey

and all the prisoners found their fetters unfastened — NEB

27. And the keeper of the prison awaking out of his sleep,

... jailor, being roused out of sleep — ASV

... startled out of his sleep — Amp

It woke up the jailor — Gspd

and seeing the prison doors open,

... wide open — Wey

he drew out his sword, and would have killed himself,

... and was about to kill himself ... — RSV

... intending to kill himself — TCNT

... and was on the point of killing himself — Wey

supposing that the prisoners had been fled.

because he thought ... — Mon

in the belief that the prisoners had escaped — TCNT

for he imagined that all the prisoners ... — Phi

28. But Paul cried out with a loud voice, saying,

But Paul at once shouted out to him — Wms

... shouted loudly to him — Wey

... at the top of his voice — Phi

Do thyself no harm: for we are all here.

Don't hurt yourself — we are all here! — Phi

29. Then he called for a light, and sprang in,

Calling for a light, the jailor rushed in — TCNT

and came trembling, and fell down before Paul and Silas,

and trembling for fear ... — ASV

and fell terror-stricken before ... — Ber

and flung himself trembling at the feet of Paul and Silas — TCNT

30. And brought them out, and said,

and leading them forth outside said — Rhm

Sirs, what must I do to be saved?

Gentlemen, ... — Gspd

Men, what is it necessary for me to do that I may be saved — Amp

31. And they said, Believe on the Lord Jesus Christ,

... Have faith in the Lord Jesus — Ber

... Put your trust in ... — NEB

... Believe in and on the Lord Jesus Christ — that is, give yourself up to Him, take yourself out of your own keeping and entrust yourself into His keeping — Amp

and thou shalt be saved, and thy house.

and you shall be saved, you and your household too — TCNT

and you will be saved; [and this applies both to] you and your household as well — Amp

32. And they spake unto him the word of the Lord,

Then they spoke to him of God's Message — TCNT

Then they explained to him the gospel of the Lord — Rieu

and to all that were in his house.

as well as to all who were in his house
— Wey

in the presence of the rest of his household — Rieu

**33. And he took them the same hour of
the night,**

At that very hour of the night he took
them — TCNT

And he, there and then, at dead of
night took them away — Knox

and washed their stripes;

he bathed them from their stripes —
Rhm

and washed their wounds — TCNT

and bathed [them because of their
bloody] wounds — Amp

**and was baptized, he and all his,
straightway.**

and was immersed, he and his, one
and all, on the spot — Rhm

and he himself and every one belonging to him were baptized without
delay — TCNT

and he and all the members of his
household at once were baptized —
Wms

**34. And when he had brought them into
his house,**

And he brought them up into his house
— ASV

he set meat before them,

and set food before them — ASV

and offered them food — Phi

and gave them a meal — Rieu

**and rejoiced, believing in God with all
his house.**

and rejoiced greatly with all his house,
having believed in God — ASV

and exulted . . . — Rhm

rejoicing that he, with all his household, had come to believe in God —
TCNT

and was filled with gladness with his
whole household, his faith resting in
God — Wey

overjoyed like all his household at having believed in God — Mof

and the hearts of the whole household
overflowed with joy at having found
God — Rieu

and he leaped much for joy and exulted
. . . — Amp

35. And when it was day,

In the morning — TCNT

When day broke — Mof

When daylight came — NEB

**the magistrates sent the serjeants, say-
ing,**

the magistrates sent the police, saying
— RSV

the praetors sent their lictors with the
order — Wey

the chiefs of the police court sent
policemen with the message — Wms

the officials sent attendants and said —
Beck

Let those men go.

Release those men — Wey

**36. And the keeper of the prison told this
saying to Paul,**

And the jailor reported the words to
Paul, saying — RSV

**The magistrates[73] have sent to let you
go:**

The Magistrates have sent an order
for your discharge — TCNT

. . . orders for you to be released —
Wey

now therefore depart, and go in peace.

so you had better leave the place at
once and go quietly away — TCNT

So you can take your leave and go
unmolested — Gspd

37. But Paul said unto them,

But Paul's answer to them was — TCNT

**They have beaten us openly uncon-
demned,**

They have flogged us in public without
trial — TCNT

being Romans,

though we are Roman citizens — TCNT

and have cast us into prison;

and have thrown us into prison —
RSV

and now do they thrust us out privily?

and now they are for sending us out
secretly! — TCNT

and are they now going to send us
away privately — Wey

and now they are going to get rid of
us secretly! — Mof

And now do they want to get rid of us
in this underhand way — Phi

and are they now to smuggle us out
privately — NEB

**nay verily; but let them come them-
selves and fetch us out.**

---

[73]For translations of "magistrates" see verses
20 and 35.

No, indeed! Let them come and take us out themselves — TCNT

. . . come in person and fetch us out — Wey

No! They must come in person and conduct us out — Rieu

I should say not! These should come themselves and take us out — Beck

38. And the serjeants told these words unto the magistrates:

This answer the lictors took back to the praetors — Wey

The officers then went and reported this demand to the magistrates — Nor

and they feared, when they heard that they were Romans.

and they were struck with fear when . . . — Rhm

who, on hearing that Paul and Silas were Roman citizens, were alarmed — TCNT

they were alarmed by this talk of Roman citizenship — Knox

39. And they came and besought them,

and went to the prison, and did their best to conciliate them — TCNT

Accordingly they came and apologized to them — Wey

and came and plead with them — Wms

and brought them out, and desired them to depart out of the city.

Then they took them out and begged them to leave the city — TCNT

Then they escorted them out and requested them to go away from the city — NEB

. . . they kept begging them to leave the city — NASB

40. And they went out of the prison,

So they left the prison — Mof

and entered into the house of Lydia:

and visited Lydia — RSV

and when they had seen the brethren,

where they saw the brothers — Ber

where they met their fellow-Christians — NEB

they comforted them, and departed.

they exhorted them . . . — Alf

and encouraged them, they left the place — TCNT

and gave them encouragement; then they set out on their journey — Knox

CHAPTER 17

1. And when they had passed through Amphipolis and Apollonia,

And travelling through . . . — Rhm

After passing through . . . — TCNT

they came to Thessalonica, where was a synagogue of the Jews:

. . . Here the Jews had a Synagogue — TCNT

2. And Paul, as his manner was, went in unto them,

. . . as his custom was . . . — ASV

and, following his usual custom, Paul joined them — TCNT

Following his usual practice, Paul went to their meetings — NEB

and three sabbath days reasoned with them out of the scriptures,

and for three sabbath days . . . from the scriptures — ASV

. . . addressed them, drawing his arguments from the Scriptures — TCNT

and for three weeks . . . — RSV

and on three Saturdays had Bible discussions with them — Beck

3. Opening and alleging,

He laid before them and explained — TCNT

explaining and quoting passages to prove — Mof

that Christ must needs have suffered, and risen again from the dead;

that it behooved the Christ to suffer, and to rise again . . . — ASV

that it was necessary for the Christ . . . — RSV

that the Christ must undergo suffering . . . — TCNT

that the sufferings of Christ and his rising from the dead were foreordained — Knox

and that this Jesus, whom I preach unto you, is Christ.

and [saying] This is the Christ — Jesus whom I am declaring unto you — Rhm

and It is this man, he declared, who is the Christ — this Jesus about whom I am telling you — TCNT

4. And some of them believed,

. . . were persuaded — RSV

. . . became believers — Nor

He convinced some of them — Gspd

and consorted with Paul and Silas;

and cast in their lot with Paul and Silas — Rhm

and attached themselves to . . . — Wey

and joined themselves to . . . — ABUV

and of the devout Greeks a great multitude,

as did also a large body of Greeks who were accustomed to join in the Jewish services — TCNT

including a great number of God-fearing Greeks — Wey

. . . of the Greek adherents of the synagogue — Rieu

and of the chief women not a few.

and a great number of women belonging to the leading families — TCNT

and by a considerable number of influential women — Phi

and many of the wives of the leading men — Rieu

5. **But the Jews which believed not, moved with envy,**

. . . moved with jealousy — ASV

But the Jews, in a fury of jealousy — Phi

took unto them certain lewd fellows of the baser sort,

. . . certain vile fellows of the rabble — ASV

. . . wicked fellows of the rabble — RSV

engaged some worthless fellows from the streets — TCNT

and taking to them, of the idlers in the market-place, some vicious men — ABUV

recruited some low fellows from the dregs of the populace — NEB

got some wicked rowdies to join them — Nor

and gathered a company, and set all the city on an uproar,

and gathered a mob . . . — Alf

and, getting a mob together, kept the city . . . — TCNT

. . . and threw the city into disorder — Rieu

and assaulted the house of Jason,

and besieging the house of Jason — Rhm

They attacked Jason's house — TCNT

and sought to bring them out to the people.

with the intention of bringing Paul and Silas before the Popular Assembly — TCNT

and searched for Paul and Silas, to bring them out before the assembly of the people — Wey

6. **And when they found them not,**

and, not finding them there — TCNT

And when they were not able to get them — Bas

they drew Jason and certain brethren

they proceeded to drag Jason and some of the Brethren — TCNT

they dragged forth Jason and the brethren who were there — Lam

unto the rulers of the city,

before the rulers . . . — ASV

. . . the City Magistrates — TCNT

. . . the politarchs — Mof

. . . the city fathers — Ber

. . . the city council — Knox

crying,

loudly accusing them — Wey

These that have turned the world upside down

They who have thrown the inhabited world into confusion — Rhm

These upsetters of the whole world — Mof

These fellows, who have turned the world topsy-turvy — Wms

These world revolutionists — Ber

are come hither also;

have now come here — TCNT

are here now — Beck

7. **Whom Jason hath received:**

unto whom Jason has given welcome — Rhm

and have been harboured by Jason! — TCNT

and Jason has taken them in — Gspd

. . . has received them to his house and privately protected them! — Amp

and these all do contrary to the decrees of Caesar,

They are all defying the decrees of the Emperor — TCNT

. . . are acting against the orders of Caesar — Bas

All these folk defy the edicts of Caesar — Knox

. . . flout the Emperor's laws — NEB

saying that there is another king, one Jesus.

They say that some one else is king — a man called Jesus — TCNT

claiming that there is another king — Jesus — Ber

8. **And they troubled the people and the rulers[74] of the city, when they heard these things.**

On hearing this, the people . . . were much concerned — TCNT

Great was the excitement among the crowd . . ., when they heard these charges — Wey

These words caused a great commotion in the mob, which affected the magistrates also — NEB

9. **And when they had taken security of Jason, and of the other,**

and . . . they took bail from Jason and the others — TCNT

Jason and the rest had to undertake to stand security for Paul and Silas' good behaviour — Rieu

they let them go.

they released them — ABUV

and turned them loose — Wms

10. **And the brethren immediately sent away Paul and Silas by night unto Berea:**

That very night the Brethren sent . . . off to Beroea — TCNT

As soon as darkness fell the members of the congregation sent . . . — NEB

who coming thither went into the synagogue of the Jews.

who, as soon as they arrived, went . . . — Alf

When they got there . . . — Mon

. . . they made their way to the Jewish synagogue — Knox

11. **These were more noble than those in Thessalonica,**

These Jews of Beroea were better disposed than . . . — TCNT

. . . of a nobler disposition than . . . — Wey

. . . more high-minded than . . . — Gspd

. . . proved more generous-minded . . . — Phi

. . . were more liberal-minded . . . — NEB

. . . were finer spirits . . . — Rieu

. . . were of a better breed than . . . — Knox

in that they received the word with all readiness of mind,

for they welcomed the Message with great readiness — TCNT

. . . accepted the message most eagerly — Phi

. . . were eager to hear . . . — Nor

. . . very eager to get the Word — Beck

and searched the scriptures daily,

examining — RSV

and made a daily study of the scriptures — Mof

whether those things were so.

to see if what was said was true — TCNT

to see whether it was as Paul stated — — Wey

to verify this new interpretation — Rieu

12. **Therefore many of them believed;**

As a consequence many of them became believers in Christ — TCNT

also of honourable women which were Greeks, and of men, not a few.

together with a large number of prominent Greeks, both women and men — Mof

as certain Greek women of fashion did, and not a few of the men as well — Knox

including outstanding Greek women and a goodly number of men — Ber

including quite a number of the influential Greek men and Women — Rieu

also many noble Greeks, women as well as men — Beck

13. **But when the Jews of Thessalonica**

As soon, however, as the Jews . . . — Wey

had knowledge

came to know — Rhm

found out — TCNT

had news — Bas

became aware — Beck

that the word of God was preached of Paul at Berea,

. . . had been declared by Paul . . . — Rhm

. . . was proclaimed . . . — ASV

that God's Message had been delivered by Paul at Beroea — TCNT

---

[74]See verse 6.

that Paul was proclaiming the word of God at Beroea as well — Mof

they came thither also,

they followed him there — Rieu

they came there too — RSV

and stirred up the people.

stirring up and troubling the multitude — ASV

exciting and disturbing the minds of the people — TCNT

and ceased not to stir up and alarm the people — Lam

stirring up and inciting the crowds — RSV

to cause trouble and spread alarm among the people — Phi

and incited the mob to a riot — Wey

to stir up trouble and rouse the rabble — NEB

14. And then immediately the brethren sent away Paul to go as it were to the sea:

. . . sent forth Paul to go as far as to the sea — ASV

. . . sent Paul on his way to the sea — RSV

. . . promptly sent Paul down to the sea-coast — Wey

. . . sent Paul away, to continue his journey up to the coast — Knox

but Silas and Timotheus abode there still.

. . . stayed behind there — Rhm

. . . remained where they were — Mof

. . . remained in that city — Lam

15. And they that conducted Paul

The men who went with Paul — Gspd

The men who accompanied Paul — Phi

Those who were caring for Paul — Mon

The friends who escorted Paul — TCNT

The men who acted as Paul's body-guard — Wms

brought him unto Athens:

brought him as far as Athens — RSV

took him all the way to Athens—Gspd

and receiving a commandment unto Silas and Timotheus for to come to him with all speed, they departed.

and after receiving a message for Silas and Timothy to join him as quickly as possible, they started on their return — TCNT

16. Now while Paul waited for them at Athens,

But while in Athens Paul was expecting them — Rhm

his spirit was stirred in him,

. . . was provoked within him — RSV

his soul was irritated — Mof

he was exasperated — Gspd

his soul was deeply vexed — Ber

his indignation was aroused — Rieu

his spirit was stirred to its depths — Wms

his heart was moved within him — Knox

when he saw the city wholly given to idolatry.

as he beheld the city full of idols — ASV

at seeing the whole city full of idols — TCNT

at the sight of the idols that filled the city — Mof

for he saw all the town full of images of the gods — Bas

seeing how the city was given to idols — Rhm

to see the city completely steeped in idolatry — Wms

17. Therefore disputed he in the synagogue with the Jews,

So he reasoned . . . — ASV

. . . argued . . . — TCNT

. . . had discussions . . . — Wey

and with the devout persons,[75]

and God-fearing Gentiles — Bas

and with those who joined in their worship — TCNT

and the devout proselytes — Mof

and the devout adherents — Ber

and the observers of Jewish religious customs — Rieu

and in the market[76] daily

and in the market-place every day — RSV

and he even argued daily in the open market-place — Phi

with them that met with him.

with them who happened to be at hand — Rhm

with any whom he happened to find — Gspd

with the passers-by — Phi

18. Then certain philosophers of the Epicureans, and of the Stoicks,

---

[75]Compare verse 4.

[76]Compare Acts 16:19.

And certain also of the Epicurean and Stoic philosophers — ASV

Among others some Epicurean and Stoic philosophers — TCNT

And some of those who were supporters of the theories of the Epicureans and Stoics — Bas

encountered him.

also came across him — Mof

also encountered him again and again — Mon

joined issue with him — TCNT

were disputing with him — ABUV

began to debate with him — Wms

crossed swords with him — Rieu

And some said,

And some were saying — Rhm

Some would ask — TCNT

What will this babbler say?

What would this babbler say — RSV

What might this picker of scraps wish to be saying — Rhm

What has this beggarly babbler to say — Wey

Whatever does the fellow mean with his scraps of learning — Mof

What is this rag-picker trying to make out — Gspd

What is this scraps-of-truth-picker trying to say — Wms

What do you suppose this chatterbox has to say — Nor

. . . this amateur talker . . . — Ber

. . . this cock sparrow . . . — Phi

. . . this dilettante . . . — Rieu

. . . this charlatan . . . — NEB

other some,

and others — Alf

while others would say — TCNT

Others said — Amp

He seemeth to be a setter forth of strange gods:

. . . a Preacher of foreign Deities — TCNT

. . . a proclaimer of foreign gods — ABUV

Of foreign demons he seemeth to be a declarer — Rhm

His business . . . seems to be to cry up some foreign gods — Wey

He seems to be trying to proclaim some more gods to us, and outlandish ones at that — Phi

because he preached unto them Jesus, and the resurrection.

(This was because he was telling the Good News about Jesus and the Resurrection) — TCNT

19. And they took him,

So they laid hold of him — TCNT

So they arrested him — Lam

So they took him by the sleeve—Knox

and brought him unto Areopagus, saying,

. . . unto Mars' hill . . . — Alf

and took him to the city auditorium and said — Wms

and brought him to the court house which is called Areopagus, and said to him — Lam

and brought him to the council of the Areopagus and said — Gspd

. . . to the Court of Areopagus — TCNT

and brought him to the Areopagus [Mars Hill auditorium] saying — Amp

May we know what this new doctrine, whereof thou speakest, is?

May we know what this new teaching is, which you present — RSV

May we hear what new teaching this is which you are giving — TCNT

May we know what is this novel teaching of yours — Mof

Will you make clear to us what is this new teaching of yours — Bas

Is it possible for us to learn what this new teaching is, about which you are talking — Ber

May we know what this novel — unheard of and unprecedented—teaching is which you are openly declaring — Amp

20. For thou bringest certain strange things to our ears:

For you bring some strange things to our ears — RSV

For the things you are saying sound strange to us — Wey

For you proclaim strange words to our ears — Lam

Thou dost introduce terms which are strange to our ears — Knox

What you say is unfamiliar . . . — Rieu

You are introducing ideas that sound strange . . . — NEB

. . . sound startling . . . — Wms

we would know therefore what these things mean.

we should like to know what they mean
— TCNT

we have a desire to get the sense of
them — Bas

We are consequently interested to
know what it means — Rieu

**21. (For all the Athenians and strangers
which were there**

(All Athenians and the foreigners staying in the city — TCNT

(Now everybody in Athens . . . — Beck

. . . and even foreign visitors to Athens
— Phi

. . . sojourning foreigners — Rhm

. . . foreigners who lived there — RSV

. . . foreigners living in Athens — Rieu

spent their time in nothing else,

unto nothing else were devoting their
leisure — Rhm

found no time for anything else—TCNT

**but either to tell, or to hear some new
thing.)**

than to be telling or hearing something
newer — Rhm

than repeating or listening to the latest
novelty.) — Mof

but communicating or listening to new
ideas.) — Rieu

but telling, or listening to, the last new
thing.) — TCNT

. . . something newer than the last —
Amp

**22. Then Paul stood in the midst of Mars'
hill,[77] and said,**

. . . taking his stand . . . — Rhm

. . . stood up in full view of the Areopagus . . . — Knox

Ye men of Athens,

Men of Athens — TCNT

Gentlemen of Athens — Phi

**I perceive that in all things ye are too
superstitious.**

in all things I perceive that ye are very
religious — ASV

on every hand I see signs of your being very devout — TCNT

I observe at every turn that you are a
most religious people — Mof

from every point of view I see that you
are extremely religious — Gspd

wherever I look I find you scrupulously
religious — Knox

my own eyes tell me that you are in all
respects an extremely religious people — Phi

I notice that you are in many ways interested in religion — Rieu

I see that in everything that concerns
religion you are uncommonly scrupulous — NEB

. . . very much given to the worship of
divinities — ABUV

. . . that you are most religious (very
reverent to demons) — Amp

23. For as I passed by,

For as I was going about — TCNT

. . . going here and there — Wms

. . . made my way here — Phi

. . . walked about — Lam

and beheld your devotions,

I observed the objects of your worship
— RSV

looking at your sacred shrines — TCNT

and viewed the houses of your idols
— Lam

in examining your monuments—Knox

I found an altar

I came upon an altar — TCNT

I actually came upon . . . — Mof

I even found . . . — Gspd

I particularly noticed an altar — Phi

with this inscription,

on which were inscribed the words —
Phi

with this writing on it — Bas

TO THE UNKNOWN GOD.

TO AN UNKNOWN GOD — ASV

THIS IS THE ALTAR OF THE UN-
KNOWN GOD — Lam

TO THE GOD OF WHOM THERE
IS NO KNOWLEDGE — Bas

TO GOD THE UNKNOWN — Phi

**Whom therefore ye ignorantly wor-
ship,**

What therefore you worship as unknown — RSV

What therefore ye worship in ignorance
— ASV

What therefore you in your ignorance
revere — Rhm

The Deity you worship but do not
know — Rieu

what you don't know and yet worship
— Beck

him declare I unto you.

this I set forth unto you — ASV

that I am now proclaiming to you —
TCNT

---

[77]For translations of "Mars' hill" see verse 19.

... am revealing to you — Knox
... announce to you — Ber
... can make known to you — Rieu

24. God that made

The God ... — ASV
God who created — Gspd
the world and all things therein,
the world and all things that are in it
— TCNT
the universe and everything in it —
Wey
the world and all that it contains —
Wms
seeing that he is Lord of heaven and earth,
— he, Lord as he is of Heaven and
earth — TCNT
since he is Lord ... — Gspd
dwelleth not in temples made with hands;
not in hand-made shrines doth dwell
— Rhm
is not housed in buildings made with
hands — Bas
does not live in ... — Gspd
does not dwell in sanctuaries built by
man — Wey
... man-made temples — Rieu

25. Neither is worshipped with men's hands, as though he needed any thing,
neither is he served by men's hands, as
though he needed any thing — ASV
nor by human hands is waited upon as
though in want of anything — Rhm
nor yet do human hands minister to his
wants, as though he needed anything
— TCNT
And is not dependent on the work of
men's hands, as if he had need of
anything — Bas
Nor can he ... lack anything, or need
the service of human hands — Rieu
seeing he giveth
seeing he himself giveth — ASV
for it is he who giveth — Mof
to all life, and breath, and all things;
... and everything else — Wms
... and all we have — Knox
... and every good thing — Nor
who gave life and breath, indeed everything, to all creatures — Rieu

26. And hath made of one blood all nations of men
And he made from one every nation of
men — RSV

And made all nations of men, (created) of one blood — Alf
He made all races of men from one
stock — TCNT
He caused to spring from one forefather people of every race — Wey
He created the first man and from him
all the races of men — Rieu
for to dwell on all the face of the earth,
and caused them to settle on all parts
of the earth's surface — TCNT
for them to live on the whole surface
of the earth — Wey
to dwell all over the earth — Mof
that now cover the face of the earth —
Rieu
and hath determined the times before appointed,
having determined allotted periods —
RSV
having determined their appointed seasons — ASV
marking out fitting opportunities —
Rhm
definitely appointing the pre-estab-
lished periods — Ber
He fixed the epochs of their history —
NEB
fixing a time for their rise and fall —
TCNT
And he has given to each the cycles it
was to pass through — Knox
after first fixing the dates of the rise
and fall of nations — Rieu
and he has appointed seasons by his
command — Lam
and the bounds of their habitation;
... limits of their settlements — TCNT
... boundaries of their abodes — Mof
... their territorial boundaries — Rieu
... boundaries they live in — Beck

27. That they should seek the Lord,
... should seek God — ASV
... search for God — TCNT
His purpose was that they should seek
God — Rieu
if haply they might feel after him, and find him,
if by any means they might feel their
way to him ... — TCNT
if perhaps they could grope for Him
... — Wey
on the chance of finding him in their
groping for him — Mof

and, it might be, touch and find him — NEB

in the hope that they might feel after him and find him — RSV

though he be not far from every one of us:

... is not far from each one of us — RSV

although in truth he is already not far ... — Rhm

Though indeed he is close to each one of us — Mof

28. **For in him we live, and move, and have our being;**

For in him we have life and motion and existence — Bas

For it is through union with him that ... — Gspd

as certain also of your own poets have said,

To use the words of some of your own poets — TCNT

Some of your own poets have endorsed this in the words — Phi

To quote even some of your own poets — Rieu

For we also are his offspring.

We too belong to His race — Mof

For we are his kindred — Lam

For indeed we are his children — Knox

You see, we are His children — Beck

29. **Forasmuch then as we are the offspring of God,**

So if we are God's children — Gspd

Now then, since we have our being from God — Beck

we ought not to think

we ought not to be supposing — Rhm

we must not think — TCNT

we ought not to imagine — Wey

it is not right for us to have the idea — Bas

that the Godhead is like unto gold, or silver, or stone,

that the Deity has any resemblance to anything made of gold, or silver, or stone — TCNT

that His nature resembles gold or silver or stone — Wey

that the divine nature can be represented in gold, or silver, or stone — Knox

graven by art and man's device.

— a work of human art and imagination — TCNT

a representation by the art and imagination of man — RSV

sculptured by the art and inventive faculty of man — Wey

wrought by human art and thought — Gspd

or anything humanly manufactured or invented — Ber

shaped by mortal hand and brain — Rieu

30. **And the times of this ignorance God winked at;**

... God overlooked — ASV

True, God looked with indulgence on the days of man's ignorance — TCNT

Such ages of ignorance God overlooked — Mof

God has shut his eyes to these passing follies of ours — Knox

However, while God paid no attention to those seasons of ignorance — Ber

Now while it is true that God has overlooked the days of ignorance — Phi

Such former ages of ignorance God, it is true, ignored and allowed to pass unnoticed — Amp

but now commandeth all men every where to repent:

but now he is announcing to every one everywhere the need for repentance — TCNT

but now he gives orders to all men in every place to undergo a change of heart — Bas

but now He charges all people everywhere to repent — that is, to change their minds for the better and heartily to amend their ways, with abhorrence for their past sins — Amp

31. **Because he hath appointed a day,**

... fixed a day — RSV

... set a day — Wms

... set aside a day — Rieu

in the which he will judge the world in righteousness

in which he is about to be judging the habitable world ... — Rhm

on which he intends to judge the world with justice — TCNT

on which he will have the world judged, and justly judged — NEB

by that man whom he hath ordained;

by a man whom he hath pointed out — Rhm

in the person of a man whom he has destined for this work — Wey

through a Man destined for the task
— Ber

by the standard of a man whom he has
appointed — Phi

by a man of his choosing — NEB

by the man who has been marked out
by him for this work — Bas

**whereof he hath given assurance unto
all men**

and of this he has given assurance to
all men — RSV

. . . has given proof of this to all —
Mof

He has made this credible to all —
Wms

of which he has given a sign to all men
— Ber

He has given everyone a good reason
to believe — Beck

**in that he hath raised him from the
dead.**

by raising him from among the dead
— Rhm

by giving him back from the dead —
Bas

**32. And when they heard of the resurrec-
tion of the dead,**

On hearing of a resurrection of the
dead — TCNT

When they heard Paul speak of a resurrection of dead men — Wey

When resurrection from the dead was
mentioned — Knox

some mocked:

. . . began to mock — TCNT

. . . began jeering — Wey

. . . sneered — Mof

. . . laughed outright — Phi

. . . began to laugh ironically — Rieu

**and others said, We will hear thee
again of this matter.**

but others said that they would hear

what he had to say about that another time — TCNT

. . . Let us go more fully into this another time — Bas

33. So Paul departed from among them.

And so Paul left the Court — TCNT

. . . the auditorium — Wms

And with that, Paul went away from
the meeting — Nor

So ended Paul's hearing in the Council
— Rieu

So with this mixed reaction Paul retired from the assembly — Phi

34. Howbeit certain men clave unto him,

But certain persons joining themselves
unto him — Rhm

A few, however, attached themselves
to him — Wey

But a few men associated with him —
Ber

Some of them, however, followed him
— Lam

. . . gave him their support — Bas

But some men were on his side and
joined him — Amp

and believed:

and became believers in Christ — TCNT

and were converted — Lam

among the which was

among whom also was — ASV

including — Mof

Dionysius the Areopagite,

Dionysius, one of the judges of Areopagus — Lam

. . . the Mars-hill judge — Rhm

. . . a member of the Court of Areopagus — TCNT

. . . a member of the Council — Wey

**and a woman named Damaris, and
others with them.**

. . . and several others — TCNT

. . . and some others — Gspd

CHAPTER 18

**1. After these things Paul departed from
Athens, and came to Corinth;**

Before long Paul left Athens and went
on to Corinth — Phi

On leaving Athens, Paul next went to
Corinth — TCNT

**2. And found a certain Jew named
Aquila,**

There he met a Jew . . . — TCNT

. . . came across . . . — Mof

. . . fell in with . . . — NEB

born in Pontus,

a man of Pontus by race — ASV

a native of Pontus — RSV

from the region of Pontus — Lam

**lately come from Italy, with his wife
Priscilla;**

He and his wife Priscilla had recently
come from Italy — Wey

. . . had recently arrived from Italy —
Mof

554

. . . had but recently migrated from Italy — Ber

(because that Claudius had commanded

in consequence of the order which had been issued by the Emperor Claudius — TCNT

all Jews to depart from Rome:)

all the Jews to leave Rome — RSV

expelling all the Jews from Rome — Wey

banishing . . . — Rieu

and came unto them.

Paul paid them a visit — TCNT

. . . went to see them — Gspd

. . . called on them — Ber

. . . approached them — Rieu

. . . accosted them — Mof

3. And because he was of the same craft,

. . . of the same trade — RSV

. . . of the same occupation — Ber

then, since they were brothers of the same craft — Knox

and because they made tents for a living just as he did — Beck

he abode with them,

. . . lodged with them — Wey

. . . stayed with them — Mof

. . . made his home with them — NEB

and wrought:

and worked — Alf

and they all worked together — Mof

and they carried on business together — NEB

and worked at his trade — Nor

for by their occupation they were tentmakers.

— their trade was tent-making — TCNT

(They were workers in leather by trade.) — Mof

. . . saddle makers . . . — Lam

. . . leather-workers — Rieu

4. And he reasoned in the synagogue every sabbath,

. . . began reasoning . . . — Rhm

Sabbath after Sabbath, he preached . . . — Wey

. . . he used to preach . . . — Mon

. . . gave addresses . . . — TCNT

. . . had discussions . . . — Bas

. . . held a disputation . . . — Knox

. . . argued . . . — Mof

and persuaded

and was persuading — Rhm

and tried to persuade — Mon

trying to convince — TCNT

and tried to win over — Wey

and won over — Ber

the Jews and the Greeks.

both Jews and Greeks — Rhm

both Jews and pagans — NEB

5. And when Silas and Timotheus were come from Macedonia,

But when Silas and Timothy came down from Macedonia — ASV

Now at the time when Silas and Timothy arrived . . . — Wey

By the time Silas and Timothy came south . . . — Mof

Paul was pressed in the spirit,

. . . constrained by the word — ASV

. . . occupied with preaching — RSV

. . . engrossed with the word — ABUV

. . . completely given up to the word — Bas

. . . completely possessed by the message — Ber

. . . began to be urged on in the word — Rhm

. . . was earnestly occupied in discoursing — Alf

. . . was hard pressed with teaching the word — Nor

. . . was preaching fervently — Wey

. . . was absorbed in preaching the message — Gspd

. . . devoted himself entirely to delivering the Message — TCNT

and testified to the Jews

bearing full witness unto the Jews — Rhm

earnestly maintaining before the Jews — TCNT

solemnly affirming to . . . — Wey

emphatically assuring . . . — Gspd

strongly urging upon . . . — Ber

arguing to . . . — Mof

showing the Jews as clearly as he could — Phi

using his own experience as evidence to convince the Jews — Rieu

that Jesus was Christ.

that the Christ was Jesus — RSV

that the Messiah was Jesus — Rieu

Jesus is the promised Saviour — Beck

6. And when they opposed themselves,

But as they began opposing — Rhm

However, as they set themselves against him — TCNT

But they set their faces against it —
Knox

However, when they turned against
him — Phi

and blasphemed,

and defaming — Rhm

and talked blasphemy — Knox

and blasphemed Christ — Rieu

and became abusive — TCNT

and abused him — Mof

and said evil words — Bas

and reviled him — RSV

he shook his raiment,

Paul shook his clothes in protest —
TCNT

until he shook the dust out of his garments — Knox

whereupon he rejected them with a
symbolic shake of his robes — Rieu

he shook out the skirts of his cloak
— NEB

**and said unto them, Your blood be
upon your own heads;**

. . . The responsibility for your fate be
upon your own heads — Rieu

I am clean:

Pure am I — Rhm

My conscience is clear — TCNT

I am not responsible — Wey

I am not to blame for it! — Gspd

I am innocent — Ber

from henceforth I will go

After this I will go — Gspd

From this time forward . . . — TCNT

From now on . . . — Mon

unto the Gentiles.

to the heathen — Gspd

to the non-Jews — Beck

7. And he departed thence,

So he left — TCNT

**and entered into a certain man's house,
named Justus, one that worshipped
God,[78]**

. . . a devout proselyte called Titus Justus — Mof

**whose house joined hard to the syn-
agogue.**

. . . was next door to . . . — RSV

**8. And Crispus, the chief ruler of the
synagogue,**

. . . the President . . . — TCNT

. . . leader . . . — Gspd

. . . warden . . . — Mon

. . . a leading man in the synagogue
— Rieu

. . . who held office in the synagogue
— NEB

**believed[79] on the Lord with all his
house;**

came to believe in the Lord, and so
did all his household — TCNT

became a believer . . . and so did all
his family — Wms

and many of the Corinthians

and many of the people of Corinth
— Gspd

hearing believed, and were baptized.

as they listened to Paul, became believers in Christ . . . — TCNT

hearing the word, had faith and were
given baptism — Bas

as they heard Paul, were converted and
baptized — Rieu

9. Then spake the Lord to Paul

And the Lord said to Paul — RSV

in the night by a vision,

by night through means of a vision
— Rhm

in a vision by night — Wey

in a night vision — Ber

Be not afraid,

Have no fear — TCNT

Dismiss your fears — Wey

Stop being afraid — Wms

Put aside your fears — Rieu

but speak, and hold not thy peace:

but continue to speak, and refuse to
be silenced — TCNT

speak on and never stop — Mof

go on with your preaching . . . — NEB

. . . and do not give up — Gspd

**10. For I am with thee, and no man shall
set on thee to hurt thee:**

. . . and no one shall attack you to injure you — Wey

. . . and none shall come near to do
thee harm — Knox

. . . shall assault you to your hurt —
Beck

. . . shall lift a finger to harm you —
Phi

. . . shall assail thee . . . — ABUV

for I have much people in this city.

There are many in this city who belong
to me — Phi

for there are many of my People in
this city — Rieu

---

[78]For the translations of "one that worshipped
God" see Acts 17:4,17.

[79]Compare Acts 16:31,34.

11. And he continued there a year and six months,

So he settled there for a year and a half — TCNT

And he stayed a year and six months — RSV

So he lived there . . . — Mon

. . . for eighteen months — Phi

teaching the word of God[80] among them.

and taught God's Message among the people — TCNT

12. And when Gallio was the deputy of Achaia,

. . . was proconsul of Achaia — ASV

. . . governor of Greece — TCNT

. . . became proconsul . . . — Wey .

. . . ruler . . . — Bas

the Jews made insurrection with one accord against Paul,

the Jews with one accord rose up against Paul — ASV

the Jews made a combined attack on Paul — TCNT

. . . a united attack . . . — RSV

. . . made a concerted move to overthrow Paul — Rieu

. . . without exception . . . — Mof

. . . unanimously . . . — Wms

and brought him to the judgment seat,

and dragged him . . . — Knox

. . . before the court — Wey

. . . the tribunal — Mof

. . . the Governor's Bench — TCNT

13. Saying, This fellow persuadeth men

charging him with persuading people — TCNT

This man, they said, is inducing people — Wey

declaring, This fellow advises the people — Ber

. . . This man is perverting men's minds — Phi

to worship God contrary to the law.

. . . in a way forbidden by the Law — TCNT

. . . in an unlawful manner — Wey

. . . in ways that violate our laws — Wms

. . . illegally — Rieu

14. And when Paul was now about to open his mouth,

Just as Paul was on the point of speaking — TCNT

. . . was about to begin his defense — Wey

Paul was all ready to speak, but before he could utter a word — Phi

Before Paul could open his lips — Gspd

Gallio said unto the Jews,

If it were a matter of wrong or wicked lewdness, O ye Jews,

If indeed it were a matter of wrong or of wicked villany . . . — ASV

Jews, if this were a case of misdemeanor or some serious crime — TCNT

If it had been some wrongful act or piece of cunning knavery . . . — Wey

If some misdemeanor or rascality were involved, Jews — Gspd

. . . some injustice or villainy . . . — ABUV

. . . of wrongdoing or vicious crime — RSV

. . . of some actual offense or crime — Rieu

reason would that I should bear with you:

there would be some reason for my listening patiently to you — TCNT

I should have reason to bear with you — RSV

I might reasonably have listened to you — Wey

I would welcome you properly — Lam

I would naturally take it up — Rieu

It would be only fair that I listen to you — Beck

15. But if it be a question of

But if they are questions about — ASV

but, since it is a dispute about — TCNT

but if it is some bickering about — NEB

words and names,

words and persons — Mof

words and titles — Gspd

and of your law,

and your own law — RSV

and law, that which ye have — Rhm

and your kind of Law — ABUV

your Jewish Law — NEB

look ye to it;

you can attend to them for yourselves — Mof

you will have to see to it yourselves — Wms

---

[80]On "word of God" see Acts 15:35.

then it is your own concern — Ber
settle the matter yourselves — Rieu
for I will be no judge of such matters.
I am not minded to be a judge of these
matters — ASV
I refuse to be a judge . . . — Wey
I decline to adjudicate upon matters
like that — Mof
I am not willing . . . — Mon
I flatly refuse . . . — Phi

16. **And he drave them from the judgment
seat.**[81]
And he had them ejected from the
court — Phi
He had the Jews cleared . . . — Rieu
. . . from his platform — Beck

17. **Then all the Greeks took Sosthenes,**
. . . laying hold of . . . — Rhm
. . . set upon . . . — TCNT
Then they all seized Sosthenes — Gspd
Thereupon there was a general onslaught upon Sosthenes — Knox
the chief ruler[82] **of the synagogue,
and beat him**
began to strike him — Rhm
and kept beating him — Wms
and gave him a beating — Rieu
before the judgment seat.[83]
in front of the courthouse — Phi
in full view of the bench — NEB
right before the governor — Nor
**And Gallio cared for none of those
things.**
. . . did not trouble himself about any
of these things — TCNT
. . . did not concern himself in the least
about this — Wey
. . . took no notice — Mof
. . . paid no attention to it — Gspd
. . . disregarded these things — Lam
. . . was indifferent to the whole affair
— Rieu

18. **And Paul after this tarried there yet
a good while,**
Paul remained there some time after
this — TCNT
. . . many days longer — RSV
. . . quite a while longer — Nor
. . . a while longer — Rieu
and then took his leave of the brethren,
said goodbye to the brothers — Mof
and sailed thence into Syria,
set sail for Syria — Rhm
and went by ship to Syria — Bas
and with him Priscilla and Aquila;

accompanied by Priscilla and Aquilla
— Mof
having shorn his head in Cenchrea:
but not before his head had been
shaved at Cenchreae — TCNT
He had cut off his hair at Cenchreae
— Wey
for he had a vow.
because he was under a vow — TCNT
. . . bound by a vow — Wey
for he had taken an oath — Bas
as part of a vow — Rieu

19. **And he came to Ephesus,**
And they came to Ephesus — RSV
They put into Ephesus — TCNT
and left them there:
and there Paul left his companions
behind — Wey
where he was to leave them — Rieu
**but he himself entered into the syna-
gogue,**
while he went personally in the synagogue — Ber
and reasoned[84] **with the Jews.**
and reasoned . . . — RSV
and spoke to the Jews — Lam
and debated with the Jews — Phi

20. **When they desired him**
And when they asked him — ASV
. . . requested him — Rhm
. . . begged him — Mon
. . . wanted him — Nor
to tarry longer time with them,
to prolong his stay — TCNT
to remain a longer time with them —
ABUV
to stay for a while — Mof
he consented not;
he declined — RSV
he said, No — Bas
he refused — Phi

21. **But bade them farewell, saying,**
but taking his leave of them, and saying — ASV
but he said goodbye to them, telling
them — Mof
**I must by all means keep this feast
that cometh in Jerusalem:**[85]

---

[81]On "judgment seat" see verse 12.
[82]See verse 8.
[83]See verse 12.
[84]See verse 4.
[85]Now recognized as not adequately supported
by original manuscripts.

but I will return again unto you,
I will come back again to you — TCNT
if God will.
please God — TCNT
if it is the will of God — Mof
And he sailed from Ephesus.
. . . took ship from Ephesus — Bas
. . . set sail from Ephesus — RSV
. . . left Ephesus by ship — Rieu

22. **And when he had landed at Caesarea,**
On reaching Caesarea — TCNT
and went down to Caesarea. Here he disembarked — Phi
and gone up, and saluted the church,
he went up to Jerusalem and exchanged greetings with the Church — TCNT
he went up to the capital to salute the church — Mof
. . . and paid his respects to the church — Gspd
he went down to Antioch.
and then went on to Antioch — Gspd

23. **And after he had spent some time there, he departed,**
. . . Paul set out on a tour — Wey
. . . he started out again — Gspd
and went over all the country of Galatia and Phyrgia[86] in order,
and went through . . . — ASV
and made a journey . . . — NEB
and made his way successively through . . . — Ber
and went from place to place through . . . — RSV
and travelled systematically through . . . — Gspd
and by a definite schedule travelled all over . . . — Wms
he set out on a tour through . . . — TCNT
strengthening all the disciples.
establishing . . . — ASV
imparting new strength to . . . — Wms
in order to strengthen . . . — Nor
strengthening the faith of all the disciples as he went — TCNT
making the disciples strong in the faith — Bas
confirming . . . — Alf
reassuring . . . — Gspd
putting new heart into . . . — Phi
. . . all the converts — NEB

24. **And a certain Jew named Apollos, born at Alexandria,**
. . . a native of Alexandria — Wey

. . . an Alexandrian by race — ASV
an eloquent man,
a learned man — Rhm
a man of culture — Mof
a gifted speaker — Phi
and mighty in the scriptures,
well versed in the scriptures — RSV
. . . well grounded in the scriptures — Knox
strong in his knowledge of the scriptures — Mof
and mighty in the Bible — Beck
and a great authority on the scriptures — Rieu
skilful in the use of the Scriptures — Gspd
came to Ephesus.

25. **This man was instructed in**
. . . had been instructed in — RSV
. . . had been orally taught — Rhm
He had been converted to — Lam
. . . had been trained in — Bas
the way of the Lord;
the Cause of the Lord — TCNT
and being fervent in the spirit,
. . . in spirit — ASV
and with burning zeal — TCNT
and with spiritual fervor — Wms
and glowing with the Spirit — Gspd
and burning in spirit — Bas
with fiery enthusiasm — Rieu
and being an enthusiastic soul — Nor
he spake and taught
he used to speak and teach — Wey
he preached and taught — Mof
he talked and taught — Gspd
diligently
painstakingly — Gspd
accurately — RSV
carefully — TCNT
the things of the Lord,
the facts about Jesus —TCNT
about the life of Jesus — Knox
the story of Jesus — Rieu
knowing only the baptism of John.
though all the baptism he knew was that of John — Mof
though he knew of no baptism but John's — TCNT

26. **And he began to speak boldly in the synagogue:**
This man began to speak out fearlessly . . . — TCNT

---

[86]On "the country of Galatia and Phrygia" see Acts 16:6.

In the synagogue he was very out-spoken at first — Mof

He spoke very confidently in the synagogue at first — Gspd

He began to speak freely in the synagogue — Ber

whom when Aquila and Priscilla had heard,

whereupon Priscilla and Aquilla, who had been listening — Knox

they took him unto them,

... took him home — TCNT

... invited him to their home — Rieu

... took him aside — Phi

... took him in hand — NEB

... made friends with him — Knox

and expounded unto him the way of God more perfectly.

and explained the Cause of God to him more carefully still — TCNT

and explained more accurately to him what the Way of God really meant — Mof

and gave him fuller teaching about ... — Bas

and expounded the new way to him in greater detail — NEB

27. **And when he was disposed to pass into Achaia,**

When he wanted to cross to Greece — TCNT

Then, as he had made up his mind to ... — Wey

He was meaning to continue his journey into Achaia — Knox

He expressed a wish to cross to Achaia — Rieu

the brethren wrote, exhorting the disciples to receive him:

... urgently wrote unto the disciples to welcome him — Rhm

... to the disciples in Corinth, begging them to give him a kindly welcome — Wey

the brethren encouraged him, and wrote to the disciples to receive him — RSV

the Brethren furthered his plans, and wrote to the disciples there to welcome him — TCNT

who, when he was come, helped them much which had believed through grace:

who arriving was very useful unto them who had believed with his gift — Rhm

On his arrival he proved of great assistance to those who had, through the loving-kindness of God, become believers in Christ — TCNT

His visit was a welcome reinforcement to the believers — Knox

On his arrival he proved a source of great strength to those who had believed through grace — Phi

When he arrived he proved of great help to the faithful through the grace that had been given him — Rieu

On his arrival there he was of great service to those who through God's favor had become believers — Gspd

to those who through grace — God's unmerited favor and mercy — had believed (adhered to, trusted in and relied on [Christ as Lord and Savior]) — Amp

28. **For he mightily convinced the Jews, and that publickly,**

... powerfully confuted ... — RSV

... vigorously confuted ... — TCNT

... publicly refuted the Jews with might and main — Mof

... successfully refuted the Jews in public — Wms

... was indefatigable in confuting the Jews — NEB

... spared no pains to refute ... — Knox

... in open debate he resoundingly refuted ... — Rieu

He was a powerful debater and openly refuted ... — Nor

... powerfully and in public overcame the Jews in argument — Wey

for with great force he came out ahead in his public discussions with the Jews — Ber

Publicly and vigorously he proved the Jews were wrong — Beck

shewing by the scriptures

proving by ... — TCNT

making clear from the holy Writings — Bas

quoting from the scriptures to prove — Phi

as he showed from the Bible — Beck

that Jesus was Christ.

that Jesus was the Christ — ASV

... is the Christ — ABUV

that Jesus is the promised Saviour — Beck

CHAPTER 19

1. **And it came to pass, that, while Apollos was at Corinth,**
During the stay of Apollos in Corinth — Wey
It was when Apollos was in Corinth that — Mof
Paul having passed through the upper coasts came to Ephesus:
... the upper country ... — RSV
Paul passed through the inland districts of Roman Asia, and went to Ephesus — TCNT
... through the hinterland ... — Mon
Paul travelled through the northern countries ... — Lam
Paul finished his journeys through the inland country ... — Knox
Paul, travelling by the higher route ... — Rieu
Paul travelled over the hills to get to Ephesus — Beck
and finding certain disciples,
There he found some disciples — TCNT
where he found a few disciples — Wey
He met some disciples there — Knox

2. **He said unto them,**
He asked them — Wey
Have ye received the Holy Ghost
Did you get the Holy Spirit — Bas
Was the Holy Spirit given to you — Knox
Did you receive the Holy Spirit — RSV
since ye believed?
when you first believed — Wey
on your becoming believers — Ber
At your conversion — Rieu
And they said unto him, We have not so much as heard whether there be any Holy Ghost.
... Nay! not even whether there is Holy Spirit did we hear — Rhm
No, they said, we never even heard of its existence — Mof
Why, they said, nobody even mentioned to us the existence of a Holy Spirit — Knox

3. **And he said unto them, Unto what then were ye baptized?**
What then was your baptism? Paul asked — TCNT
How then were you baptized? ... — Gspd
What baptism, then, did you receive? ... — Knox

Then what baptism were you baptized with? ... — Rieu
And they said, Unto John's baptism.
With John's baptism, they answered — Gspd

4. **Then said Paul, John verily baptized with the baptism of repentance,**
... John ... administered a baptism of repentance — Wey
... John's baptism was a baptism upon repentance — TCNT
... a baptism in token of repentance — Gspd
... a baptism that was an expression of repentance — Wms
... a baptism to show a change of heart — Phi
... a baptism that goes with a change of heart — Bas
... John baptized those who were sorry for their sins — Beck
saying unto the people,
telling the people — Mof
bidding the people — Wey
but he always told the people — Phi
that they should believe
to believe — Mof
that they were to have faith — Bas
that they must believe — Phi
to put their trust — NEB
on him which should come after him, that is, on Christ Jesus.
on One who was to come after him; namely, on Jesus — Wey

5. **When they heard this,**
On hearing this — RSV
they were baptized
... immersed — Rhm
... had themselves baptized — Mof
in the name of the Lord Jesus.
into the name of the Lord Jesus — ASV
into the Faith of the Lord Jesus — TCNT

6. **And when Paul had laid his hands upon them,**
and, after Paul had placed his hands on them — TCNT
And as Paul laid ... — Ber
and with the laying on of Paul's hands — Rieu
the Holy Ghost came on them;
the Holy Spirit descended upon them — TCNT

and they spake with tongues, and prophesied.

. . . began speaking with tongues and prophesying — Rhm

. . . began to speak with tongues and to preach — TCNT

and they spoke in foreign tongues and with prophetic inspiration — Gspd

and they had the power of talking with tongues, and became prophets — Bas

and they cried out in ecstasy and uttered prophecies — Rieu

and they started to talk in other languages and to speak God's Word — Beck

7. And all the men were about twelve.

There were about twelve of them in all — RSV

8. And he went into the synagogue,

Paul went to the synagogue there — TCNT

Then Paul made his way into the synagogue — Phi

and spake boldly for the space of three months,

and for three months spoke out fearlessly — TCNT

. . . continued to preach fearlessly — Wey

. . . spoke confidently — Gspd

. . . courageously spoke — Wms

. . . spoke openly . . . — Lam

. . . spoke with utmost confidence — Phi

. . . spoke boldly and freely — NEB

disputing and persuading

reasoning and persuading as to — ASV

giving addresses and trying to convince his hearers about — TCNT

arguing and persuading people about — Mof

holding discussions and trying to persuade them about — Gspd

persuasively discussing — Ber

arguing and pleading about — RSV

using both argument and persuasion as he talked of — Phi

the things concerning the kingdom of God.

the things concerning the kingdom of God — ASV

the Reign of God — Mof

the interests of the kingdom of God — Ber

9. But when divers were hardened, and believed not,

But when some were hardened and disobedient — ASV

. . . were hardening themselves and refusing to be persuaded — Rhm

. . . hardened their hearts and refused to believe — TCNT

. . . grew obstinate in unbelief — Wey

. . . grew stubborn and disobedient — Mof

grew harder and harder and refused to believe — Wms

But because some of the people were hard-hearted and would not give hearing — Bas

but spake evil of that way before the multitude,

denouncing the Cause before the people — TCNT

speaking evil of the new way before the whole congregation — NEB

speaking evil of the Way before the congregation — RSV

and, what is more, spoke offensively about the way in public — Phi

discrediting the way of the Lord in the eyes of the multitude — Knox

finding fault with . . . — Gspd

actually criticizing . . . — Wms

and cursed the way of God in the presence of the assembly — Lam

and slandered the Christian religion before the crowd — Beck

he departed from them,

he turned from them — Ber

and separated the disciples,

and withdrew his disciples — TCNT

and, taking with him those who were disciples — Wey

withdrew his converts — NEB

disputing[87] daily in the school of one Tyrannus.

and gave daily addresses in the lecture-hall of Tyrannus — TCNT

and continued his argument every day from eleven to four in the lecture-room of Tyrannus — Mof

and went on holding daily discussions in the schoolroom of Tyrannus — Ber

10. And this continued by the space of two years;

---

[87]On "disputing" see Acts 18:4.

And this took place for two years —
Rhm

This went on . . . — TCNT

. . . kept up . . . — Ber

Two years passed in this way — Rieu

**so that all they which dwelt in Asia
heard the word of the Lord Jesus,
both Jews and Greeks.**

. . . all who lived in Roman Asia, Jews
and Greeks alike, heard the Lord's
Message — TCNT

. . . all the inhabitants of the province
of Asia, Jews as well as Greeks . . .
— Wey

11. And God wrought special miracles

God did such extraordinary wonders
— Gspd

God also continued to do such wonder-
works — Wms

God gave most unusual demonstrations
of power — Phi

. . . special works of power — Bas

. . . miracles of an unusual kind — NEB

by the hands of Paul:

through Paul — Wey

by means of Paul — Mof

**12. So that from his body were brought
unto the sick handkerchiefs or aprons,**

so that people would carry home to the
sick handkerchiefs or aprons that
had touched his body — TCNT

Kerchiefs or aprons, for instance,
which Paul had handled, would be
carried to the sick — Wey

People even carried away towels or
aprons he had used — Mof

so that bits of linen or clothing from
his body were taken to people who
were ill — Bas

and the diseases departed from them,

and they would recover from their ailments — Wey

and at their touch sick folk were freed
from their diseases — Mof

and they were cured of their diseases
— Gspd

and the evil spirits went out of them.

and the wicked spirits were going out
— Rhm

. . . were driven out — Knox

. . . were made to go — Ber

and even the insane were restored —
Lam

**13. Then certain of the vagabond Jews,
exorcists,**

. . . of the wandering Jews, exorcists —
Rhm

. . . some itinerant Jews, who were
exorcists — TCNT

Some Jews who went from place to
place casting out demons — Gspd

. . . some wandering Jews who claimed
to be driving out the evil spirits —
Wms

Some Jews who made it their business
to go around and drive out evil
spirits — Beck

**took upon them to call over them
which had evil spirits the name of
the Lord Jesus,**

undertook to pronounce the name of
the Lord Jesus over those who had
evil spirits — RSV

. . . to use the Name of the Lord Jesus
over those who had wicked spirits
in them — TCNT

who undertook to invoke the name of
Jesus over those who had the evil
spirits — Wey

invoked the name of the Lord Jesus
over those who were possessed —
Lam

who attempted to invoke the name of
the Lord Jesus when dealing with
those who had evil spirits — Phi

also attempted to name the name of the
Lord Jesus over madmen with the
formula — Rieu

**saying, We adjure you by Jesus whom
Paul preacheth.**

. . . I command you by that Jesus . . .
— Wey

. . . whom Paul proclaimeth! — Rhm

. . . I conjure you in the name of Jesus,
the name that is preached by Paul
— Knox

. . . I solemnly implore and charge you
by the Jesus Whom Paul preaches!
— Amp

**14. And there were seven sons of one
Sceva, a Jew, and chief of the priests,**

The seven sons of Sceva, a Jewish Chief
Priest — TCNT

A Jewish high priest name Sceva had
seven sons — Gspd

Seven brothers, sons of a chief priest
called Sceva — Phi

There were seven sons of one Sceva, a
Jew of high-priestly family — Wey

which did so.

who did this — ASV
who were doing this — Wey
who were using this method — NEB
who were trying to do this — Nor
used to do this — Mof
practiced this — Ber

15. And the evil spirit answered and said,
But the evil spirit retorted — Mof
The reply of one evil spirit to them, however, was — Rieu
But on one occasion the evil spirit answered — Wms
Jesus I know,
Jesus indeed I am getting to know — Rhm
Jesus I acknowledge — TCNT
Jesus I recognize — Lam
and Paul I know;
and Paul I well-know — Rhm
. . . I understand — ABUV
. . . I have heard of — Mon
and I am acquainted with Paul — Phi
but who are ye?
but who on earth are you — Phi

16. And the man in whom the evil spirit was
Then the insane man — Lam
And the madman — Rieu
leaped on them,
sprang on them — TCNT
ran at them — Knox
flew at them — NEB
and overcame them,
mastered all of them — RSV
and mastered both of them — ASV
overpowered them all — Mof
and was stronger than the two of them — Bas
and got the better of them — Knox
and prevailed against them,
and so completely overpowered them — TCNT
and treated them with such violence — Wey
so that they fled out of that house naked and wounded.
. . . stripped of their clothes, and wounded — TCNT
. . . tattered and bruised — Gspd
. . . wounded, with their clothes torn off their backs — Phi

17. And this was known to all the Jews and Greeks also dwelling at Ephesus;
And this became known to all, both

Jews and Greeks, that dwelt at Ephesus — ASV
This incident came to the knowledge of all the Jews and Greeks living at Ephesus — TCNT
All the people of Ephesus, Jews as well as Greeks, came to know of this — Wey
and fear fell on them all,
they were all awe-struck — TCNT
There was widespread awe — Wey
They were all frightened — Beck
and alarm and terror fell on them all — Amp
and the name of the Lord Jesus was magnified.
and the Name of the Lord Jesus was held in the highest honour — TCNT
and they began to hold the name of the Lord Jesus in high honor — Wey
while the name of the Lord Jesus became highly respected — Phi
. . . was highly praised — Ber
. . . was extolled — RSV
and made the name . . . a name to be venerated — Rieu
and started to think very highly of the name . . . — Beck

18. And many that believed came,
Many, too, of them who had become believers in Christ came — TCNT
Many of those who had professed their faith — Phi
and confessed, and shewed their deeds.
confessing and declaring their deeds — ASV
confessing and divulging their practices — RSV
made public statement of their sins and all their acts — Bas
began openly to admit their former practices — Phi
with a full confession of their practices — TCNT
and openly confessed that they had been using magical spells — NEB
19. Many of them also which used curious arts
. . . that practiced magical arts — ASV
while a number of people, who had practiced magic — TCNT

brought their books together,
collected their books — TCNT
brought out their books — Gspd
made their books into a heap — Knox

and burned them before all men:
and burnt them publicly — TCNT
and burned them up before the public
gaze — Wms

and they counted the price of them,
The total value was reckoned — Wey
They added up the cost of these books
— Beck

**and found it fifty thousand pieces of
silver.**
they found it amounted to five thousand pounds — TCNT
it was found that they were worth two
thousand pounds — Mof
and found to be ten thousand dollars
— Gspd
. . . came to about twenty-five thousand
dollars — Nor
. . . worth fifty thousand denarii —
Beck

**20. So mightily grew the word of God and
prevailed.**
So irresistibly did the Lord's message
spread and prevail — TCNT
Thus mightily did the Lord's word
spread and triumph — Wey
So the Lord's message went on growing wonderfully in influence and
power — Gspd
In a way of just such power as this the
Lord's message kept on spreading
and increasing — Wms
So the word of the Lord was increased
very greatly and was full of power —
Bas
By such great victories the Word of the
Lord continued to spread and demonstrate its power — Rieu
. . . showed its power, spreading more
and more widely and effectively —
NEB

21. After these things were ended,
Sometime after these events — TCNT
When matters had reached this point
— Wey
With these aims accomplished — Ber
Paul purposed in the spirit,
Paul resolved — RSV
. . . determined in his own mind—Wey
. . . made up his mind — Lam
. . . resolved in his spirit — Mon
. . . under the Spirit's guidance, resolved
— Gspd
the Spirit moved Paul to plan — Rieu

**when he had passed through Mace-
donia and Achaia,**
to go through Macedonia and Greece
— TCNT
to revisit Macedonia and Greece —
Gspd
to go to Jerusalem,
and then make his way to Jerusalem —
TCNT
on his way to Jerusalem — Mof
**saying, After I have been there, I must
also see Rome.**
After I get there, he said, I must also
visit Rome — Mof
. . . I have a desire to see Rome — Bas

22. So he sent into Macedonia
and he dispatched . . . — Mof
two of them that ministered unto him,
two of his helpers — RSV
two of his assistants — Wey
Timotheus and Erastus;
**but he himself stayed in Asia for a
season.**
. . . remained for a while in Roman
Asia — Wey
. . . went on living in Asia for a time
— Bas
. . . in the province of Asia — NEB

23. And the same time
And about that time — ASV
But in process of time — Ber
But as time went on — Amp
During that time — Beck
there arose no small stir
. . . no small disturbance — Rhm
. . . no small commotion — Wey
. . . no small tumult — ABUV
. . . a great outcry — Bas
. . . a great riot — Nor
a big blowup developed — Tay
there was a great uprising — Lam
about that way.[88]
concerning the Christians — Tay

**24. For a certain man named Demetrius,
a silversmith,**
A silversmith named Demetrius —
TCNT
which made silver shrines for Diana,
who made models of the shrine of Artemis — TCNT
. . . silver boxes for the images of
Diana — Bas

[88]On the word "way" see Acts 18:25 and
19:9.

... miniature statuettes of Artemis —
Rieu

by manufacturing silver shrines of
Artemis — Wms

**brought no small gain unto the crafts-
men;**

brought no little business to the craftsmen — RSV

and so gave a great deal of work to the
artisans — Rhm

a business which brought great profits
to the craftsmen in his employ —
Wey

and provided the artisans with no small
income — Ber

25. Whom he called together

And now he called a meeting of these
— Knox

with the workmen of like occupation,

as well as the workmen engaged in
similar occupations — TCNT

with the other workmen of the same
trade — Bas

and workmen in allied trades — NEB

and others who did similar work —
Beck

and said,

and addressed them in these words —
Rieu

Sirs,

Men — RSV

Friends — Knox

Comrades — Rieu

ye know

you ought to know — Lam

you understand — Ber

that by this craft we have our wealth.

that our prosperity depends upon this
work — TCNT

that by this business we make our
money — Mon

that this trade is the source of our
wealth — Mof

we're getting a fine income from this
business — Beck

that this craft is our livelihood — Rieu

that our high standard of living depends on this industry — NEB

26. Moreover ye see and hear,

And you can see and hear for yourselves — Bas

If you use your eyes and ears you also
know — Phi

As your eyes and ears tell you — Rieu

that not alone at Ephesus, but almost

throughout all Asia,

that not only at Ephesus, but in almost
the whole of Roman Asia — TCNT

... the whole province of Asia — Wey

... practically throughout Asia — Phi

**this Paul hath persuaded and turned
away much people,**

... has persuaded and turned away a
considerable company of people —
RSV

... has convinced and won over great
numbers of people — TCNT

this fellow Paul has led away a vast
number of people — Wey

... persuaded a whole multitude to
change their allegiance — Knox

... has succeeded in changing the
minds of a great number of people
— Phi

... has won over large numbers of people to his way of thinking — Rieu

how this fellow Paul has won and
taken away a large crowd — Beck

**saying that they be no gods, which
are made with hands:**

by his assertion that those Gods which
are made by hands are not Gods at
all — TCNT

He declares that hand-made gods are
not gods at all — Mof

by persuading them that manufactured
gods are not real gods — Ber

**27. So that not only this our craft is in
danger to be set at nought;**

And not only is there danger that this
our trade come into disrepute — ASV

Now the danger is not only that we
will have our trade discredited —
Mof

There is a danger people will not only
reject our line of business — Beck

So that not only is this business of ours
likely to fall into discredit — TCNT

... will lose its reputation — Wms

... may be damaged in the opinion of
Men — Bas

**but also that the temple of the great
goddess Diana should be despised,**

but there is further danger that the
Temple of the great goddess Artemis
will be thought nothing of — TCNT

... may count for nothing — RSV

... will be regarded as worthless —
NASB

... be made of no account — ASV

... will fall into utter disrepute — Wey
... will cease to command respect —
NEB
... will be neglected — Gspd
... might come to be lightly regarded
— Phi
and her magnificence should be destroyed,
and that she may even be deposed from
her magnificence — RSV
also that even on the point of being
pulled down may be Her Majesty —
Rhm
and she will be degraded from her majestic glory — Mof
and the magnificence of her . . . will
be a thing of the past! — Gspd
will soon be dethroned from her majestic glory! — Wms
and so she . . . will have all her
grandeur destroyed — Nor
and then it will not be long before she
. . . is brought down from her divine
pre-eminence — NEB
and then she . . . will be robbed of her
glory — Beck
whom all Asia and the world worshippeth.
she who is now worshipped by the
whole province of Asia; nay, by the
whole world — Wey

28. **And when they heard these sayings,**
After listening to this harangue — Wey
As they listened — Ber
they were full of wrath,
the men were greatly enraged — TCNT
they all became furiously angry — Wey
This speech roused them to fury —
Rieu
and cried out, saying,
and began shouting — TCNT
and raised the cry — Mof
and cried out again and again — Mon
Great is Diana of the Ephesians.
Great is Artemis of the Ephesians! —
RSV

29. **And the whole city was filled with confusion:**
The commotion spread through the
whole city — TCNT
The riot and uproar spread through
the whole city — Wey
Then the city was agitated from end to
end — Ber

Soon the whole city was in an uproar
— Phi
... was in tumult — Lam
... was thrown into chaos — Rieu
and having caught Gaius and Aristarchus,
and having seized . . . — ASV
carrying off with them . . . — Rhm
dragging with them . . . — TCNT
**men of Macedonia, Paul's companions
in travel,**
Macedonians, fellow-travellers of Paul
— Rhm
two Macedonians who were Paul's
travelling companions — TCNT
**they rushed with one accord into the
theatre.**
and the people rushed together into the
amphitheatre — TCNT
They rushed like one man into the
amphitheatre — Mof
they jointly stormed the theatre —
Ber

30. **And when Paul would have entered in
unto the people,**
Paul wished to go into the amphitheatre and face the people — TCNT
Paul wished to go in among the crowd
— RSV
(Paul wanted to enter the popular assembly — Mof
Then Paul would have liked to go in
and address the people — Wey
the disciples suffered him not.
but the disciples would not let him —
RSV
... stopped him — Lam
... tried to prevent it — Knox
... would not hear of it — Nor

31. **And certain of the chief of Asia,**
And certain also of the Asiarchs — ASV
A few of the public officials, too —
Wey
And some of the delegates of Asia —
Knox
Even some of the dignitaries of the
province — NEB
while some of the chief religious officials of the province — TCNT
which were his friends,
because they were his friends — Lam
**sent unto him, desiring him that he
would not adventure himself into
the theatre.**
also sent to beg him . . . — Mof

sent him warning . . . — Ber
went and urged him . . . — NEB
. . . begging him not to risk his life
by entering . . . — Lam
sent repeated entreaties to him not to
trust himself inside — TCNT

**32. Some therefore cried one thing, and
some another:**
Meanwhile some were shouting one
thing and some another — TCNT
There was a hubbub of conflicting cries
— Rieu
for the assembly was confused;
. . . was all uproar and confusion —
Wey
for there was no order in the meeting
— Bas
for the mass meeting was just a tumult
— Ber
**and the more part knew not where-
fore they were come together.**
most of those present not even knowing why they had met — TCNT
and the greater part had no idea why
they had come together — Wey
and most of them could not tell what
had brought them together — Knox

**33. And they drew Alexander out of the
multitude,**
And they brought Alexander out . . .
— ASV
A man called Alexander . . . was
pushed into the forefront of the
crowd — Phi
Then some of the people crowded
around Alexander — Wey
Some of the crowd prompted Alexander — RSV
. . . called upon Alexander — Gspd
But some of the crowd explained the
trouble to Alexander — NEB
the Jews putting him forward.
the Jews thrusting him forward—Rhm
whom the Jews pushed to the front —
TCNT
whom the Jews had put forward —
RSV
since the Jews had pushed and urged
him forward — Amp
**And Alexander beckoned with the
hand,**
. . . motioning with his hand to get
silence — Wey
and he made a gesture with his hand —
Gspd

**and would have made his defence unto
the people.**
wanted to defend himself before the
people — Mof
and tried to give an account of himself
before the people — Knox
to show that he wanted to speak in
their defence to the people — TCNT
and was going to speak to the people in
their defence — Gspd

**34. But when they knew that he was a
Jew,**
But when they perceived that he was a
Jew — ASV
But recognizing . . . — Rhm
No sooner, however, did they see that
he was a Jew — Wey
**all with one voice about the space of
two hours cried out,**
one cry broke from them all, and they
continued shouting for two hours —
TCNT
then there arose from them all one roar
of shouting, lasting about two hours
— Wey
a single cry came from every mouth,
and for some two hours they kept on
shouting — Knox
they shouted as one man for about two
hours — Phi
they roared out in unison . . . and went
on doing so for about two hours —
Rieu
Great is Diana of the Ephesians.
Great is Artemis of Ephesus! Great is
Artemis of Ephesus! — Mof
Great Artemis of Ephesus! — Wms

35. And when the townclerk
When the Recorder — TCNT
. . . secretary of state — Mof
. . . mayor of the city — Lam
had appeased the people, he said,
had quieted the multitude . . . — ASV
having calmed the multitude, saith —
Rhm
had succeeded in quieting the crowd,
he said — TCNT
brought some order in the crowd . . .
— Ber
Ye men of Ephesus,
Ephesians — Rhm
Gentlemen of Ephesus — Phi
what man is there that knoweth not
why who is there of mankind that doth
not acknowledge — Rhm

who is there, I ask you, who needs to
be told — TCNT

who on earth does not know — Mof

who in the world could be ignorant of
the fact — Phi

all the world knows — NEB

**how that the city of the Ephesians is
a worshipper of the great goddess
Diana,**

that this city of Ephesus is the Warden
of the temple of the great Artemis
— TCNT

. . . is temple-keeper . . . — RSV

. . . is guardian of the temple . . . —
Alf

**and of the image which fell down
from Jupiter?**

and of the sacred stone that fell from
the sky — RSV

. . . statue which fell down from Zeus
— TCNT

. . . the stone that fell down from the
sky — Gspd

. . . the image which is Jupiter's offspring — Knox

. . . that symbol of her which fell from
heaven — NEB

**36. Seeing then that these things cannot
be spoken against,**

. . . be contradicted — RSV

As these are undeniable facts — TCNT

All this is beyond question — Mof

No one can dispute this — Rieu

ye ought to be quiet,

you ought to keep calm — TCNT

it becomes you to maintain your self-
control — Wey

you should compose yourselves — Ber

so there is no need for this uproar —
Rieu

and do nothing rashly.

and not act recklessly — Wey

and do nothing unwise — Bas

and do nothing which you might afterwards regret — Phi

37. For ye have brought hither these men,

The men you have brought here—Rieu

. . . brought here as culprits — NEB

which are neither robbers of churches,

who are neither robbers of temples —
ASV

who are guilty neither of sacrilege —
Mof

who are neither sacrilegious — RSV

though they have not been guilty of
disloyalty — Gspd

who are neither temple destroyers —
Ber

nor yet blasphemers of your goddess.

nor as defaming our goddess — Rhm

or of abusive speech against our goddess — Wms

nor have they reviled . . . — Lam

nor insulters of . . . — Ber

**38. Wherefore if Demetrius, and the crafts-
men which are with him,**

If, however, Demetrius and the artisans
who are acting with him — TCNT

. . . and his fellow tradesmen — Mof

have a matter against any man,

have against anyone an accusation —
Rhm

have a charge to make against anyone
— TCNT

have a case . . . — Lam

have a complaint . . . — Ber

the law is open,

the courts are open — RSV

there are Court Days — TCNT

terms of court are conducted — Ber

there are assizes held — Alf

the courts are in session — NASB

and there are deputies:

and there are proconsuls — RSV

there is a proconsul in the city — Lam

and there are appointed judges — Alf

let them implead one another.

let them accuse one another — ASV

let them bring their charges — Wey

let them bring charges against one another — RSV

. . . their charges and countercharges
— NEB

let both parties take legal proceedings
— TCNT

let them go to law — Wms

**39. But if ye enquire any thing concern-
ing other matters,**

But if you desire anything further —
Wey

But if you require anything beyond
that — Gspd

But if there are other matters into
which you wish to hold an inquiry
— Rieu

But if you want some other matter
cleared up — Nor

If, on the other hand, you have any
further question to raise — Knox

it shall be determined in a lawful assembly.

it shall be settled in the regular assembly — ASV

it must be settled in the legal assembly of the citizens — Mof

let it be taken up in the regular meeting — Bas

it will have to be dealt with in the statutory assembly — NEB

40. For we are in danger to be called in question for this day's uproar,

For I tell you we are in danger of being proceeded against for to-day's riot — TCNT

For in connection with today's proceedings there is danger of our being charged with attempted insurrection — Wey

For, truly, we are in danger of being made responsible for this day's trouble — Bas

We may easily be called to account for today's proceedings — Knox

As it is, we are likely to be accused of causing a riot because of today's meeting — Rieu

there being no cause whereby we may give an account of this concourse.

there being no cause for it: and as touching it we shall not be able to give account of this concourse — ASV

there being nothing to account for it; and in that case we shall be at a loss to give any reason for this disorderly gathering — TCNT

there having been no real reason for this riot; nor shall we be able to justify the behaviour of this disorderly mob — Wey

there is not a single reason we can give for this disorderly gathering — Mof

particularly as we have no real excuse to offer for this commotion — Phi

There is no justification for it, and if the issue is raised we shall be unable to give any explanation of this uproar — NEB

41. And when he had thus spoken,

With these words — TCNT

After this speech — Rieu

he dismissed the assembly.

he broke up the meeting — Knox

CHAPTER 20

1. And after the uproar was ceased,

When the confusion was over — Gspd

When the tumult had been quieted down — Ber

After this disturbance died down — Phi

Paul called unto him the disciples,

Paul sent for the disciples — ASV

Paul invited the disciples to see him — Ber

and embraced them,

and, with encouraging words, bade them goodbye — TCNT

and having exhorted and embraced them — ABUV

and comforted them and kissed them — Lam

and departed for to go into Macedonia.

and started on his journey to Macedonia — TCNT

and left for Macedonia — Ber

2. And when he had gone over those parts,

Passing through those parts — Rhm

After going through those districts — TCNT

As he made his journey through those districts — Phi

... those parts of the country — NEB

and had given them much exhortation,

and exhorting them with much discourse — Rhm

and speaking many encouraging words to the disciples — TCNT

and encouraging the people at length — Mof

and encouraging the brethren with many suggestions — Ber

speaking frequently and raising the spirits of the congregations — Rieu

he came into Greece,

and then came into Greece — Wey

3. And there abode three months.

There he spent three months — RSV

And when he had spent three months there — ASV

where he stayed three months — TCNT

And when the Jews laid wait for him,

and a plot was laid against him by the Jews — ASV

when he learnt that a plot had been laid against him by the Jews — TCNT

The Jews having planned to waylay him — Wey

because the Jews had made a secret design against him — Bas

as he was about to sail into Syria,

Just as he was going to sail for Syria — Gspd

he purposed to return through Macedonia.

he determined . . . — RSV

so he decided to return by way of Macedonia — TCNT

he changed his mind and returned by way of Macedonia — Wms

4. And there accompanied him into Asia Sopater of Berea;

He was accompanied by . . . — TCNT

The following were his fellow travelers as far as the province of Asia . . . — Nor

. . . Sopater of Beroea, the son of Pyrrhus — ASV

and of the Thessalonians, Aristarchus and Secundus;

Aristarchus and Secundus from Thessalonica — TCNT

and Gaius of Derbe, and Timotheus;

. . . Timothy — Rhm

and of Asia, Tychicus and Trophimus.

and the Asians, Tychicus and Trophimus — RSV

as well as by Tychicus and Trophimus of Roman Asia — TCNT

In addition there were Tychicus and Trophimus of Asia — Rieu

but Tychicus and Trophimus were from the province of Asia — Beck

5. These going before tarried for us at Troas.

But these had gone before and were waiting for us at Troas — ASV

These men went to Troas and waited for us there — TCNT

who[89] had gone on . . . — Rieu

6. And we sailed from Philippi

while we ourselves set sail from Philippi — Mon

after the days of unleavened bread,

after the Passover — TCNT

. . . festival of Unleavened Bread — Gspd

and came unto them to Troas in five days;

and joined them five days later at Troas — TCNT

and arrived at Troas in five days — Lam

and came to them at Troas. It took us five days to get there — Nor

where we abode seven days.

where we stayed for a week — TCNT

7. And upon the first day of the week,

When the new week began — Knox

On the Saturday night — NEB

On Sunday — Beck

when the disciples came together to break bread,

when we were gathered together to break bread — RSV

when we had met for the Breaking of Bread — TCNT

when we had come together for the holy meal — Bas

in our assembly for the breaking of bread — NEB

when we met for a meal — Beck

Paul preached unto them,

Paul . . . began preaching to them — Mon

Paul discoursed with them — ASV

Paul talked with them — RSV

Paul was holding a discussion with them — Rieu

ready to depart on the morrow;

intending to depart on the morrow — ASV

on the eve of his departure — Rieu

since he expected to leave the next day — Nor

and continued his speech until midnight.

and prolonged his speech until midnight — ASV

and he went on talking till after the middle of the night — Bas

8. And there were many lights in the upper chamber,

Now there were a good many torches in the upper room — Rhm

. . . a good many lamps in the upstairs room — TCNT

Now there was a great glow of light from the torches in . . . — Lam

there were many lamps burning . . . — Knox

where they were gathered together.

where we all were — Wey

where we had met — TCNT

---

[89]Variant reading.

. . . were assembled — ABUV

. . . had gathered — Rieu

9. And there sat in a window a certain young man named Eutychus,

And a youth by the name Eutychus . . . — Wey

. . . who was sitting in the window — Alf

. . . on the window sill — Phi

. . . on the window ledge — NEB

being fallen into a deep sleep:

borne down with deep sleep — ASV

was gradually overcome with great drowsiness — TCNT

became very drowsy — Gspd

grew more and more sleepy — NEB

the heaviness of sleep proved too much for him — Ber

and as Paul was long preaching,

And as Paul discoursed yet longer — ASV

while Paul preached at unusual length — Wey

As Paul still went on speaking — Knox

and as Paul's address went on and on — Mof

as Paul talked still longer — RSV

he sunk down with sleep,

being borne down by his sleep — ASV

and being overcome by sleep — RSV

being overpowered by sleep — Rhm

At last, quite overpowered by his drowsiness — TCNT

so as he sagged down in his sleep — Ber

until the young man finally dropped off to sleep — Rieu

At last he was completely overcome by sleep — NEB

and fell down from the third loft,

. . . from the third story — ASV

and fell three storeys to the ground — Rieu

and was taken up dead.

and was picked up for dead — TCNT

. . . a corpse — Mof

. . . lifeless — Ber

When they picked him up, he was dead — Rieu

10. And Paul went down,

Paul hastened down — Nor

and fell on him,

. . . bent over him — Lam

. . . stooped over him — Ber

. . . threw himself upon him — TCNT

. . . lay on him — Beck

and embracing him said,

took him in his arms and said — Bas

and folding him in his arms said — Wey

and holding him gently in his arms, said — Phi

Trouble not yourselves;

Do not be alarmed — RSV

Stop being alarmed — Wms

Do not be troubled — Bas

Have no anxiety — Ber

Make ye no ado — ASV

Do not be excited — Lam

Cease your wailing — Wey

Do not lament — Mof

Do not make an uproar — ABUV

Stop making such a fuss — Rieu

Stop this commotion — NEB

for his life is in him.

his life is still in him — Wms

he is still alive — TCNT

There is life in him — Rieu

He's alive — Beck

11. When he therefore was come up again,

And when Paul had gone up — RSV

And going up — Rhm

Then he went upstairs — TCNT

And when he was gone up — ASV

. . . had gone back up — NASB

and had broken bread, and eaten,

. . . broken the bread . . . — ASV

and breaking the loaf, and tasting — Rhm

and, after breaking and partaking of the Bread — TCNT

broke the bread, and took some food — Wey

to celebrate the breaking of bread and have a meal — Rieu

and talked a long while, even till break of day,

he talked with them at great length till daybreak — TCNT

and after a long conversation which was continued till daybreak — Wey

and after much conversation that lasted till the sun rose — Beck

so he departed.

and then left — TCNT

at last he parted from them — Wey

and so finally departed — Phi

12. And they brought the young man alive,

Meanwhile they had taken the lad away alive — TCNT

. . . taken the lad home alive — Wey

And they took the boy in, living — Bas

. . . when the young man rejoined them safe and sound — Rieu

and were not a little comforted.

and were greatly comforted — TCNT

much to their relief — Mof

and rejoiced over him exceedingly — Lam

for which they felt supremely cheered — Ber

There was great rejoicing — Rieu

and were not a little comforted and cheered and refreshed and encouraged — Amp

13. And we went before to ship,

We started first, went on board ship — TCNT

But going ahead to the ship — RSV

But we, going before him by ship — Bas

Meanwhile we had gone aboard the ship — Phi

and sailed unto Assos,

and sailed for Assos — TCNT

and sailed on ahead for Assos — Phi

there intending to take in Paul:

intending to take Paul on board there — TCNT

where we were to take Paul on board — Wms

intending to pick up Paul there — Phi

for so had he appointed,

. . . arranged — Rhm

This was by his own arrangement — TCNT

as he had commanded us — Lam

These were his instructions — Rieu

He had planned it that way — Nor

minding himself to go afoot.

intending himself to go by land — ASV

for he intended to travel by land — Mof

since he himself had planned to go overland — Phi

. . . by road — NEB

. . . on foot — Rhm

14. And when he met with us at Assos,

When he met us on our arrival at Assos — Phi

we took him in,

we took him on board — Rhm

and came to Mitylene.

and went on to Mitylene — TCNT

and sailed on to Mitylene — Wms

15. And we sailed thence, and came the next day over against Chios;

The day after we had sailed from there, we arrived off Chios — TCNT

We sailed on from there and the following day put in at a point opposite Chios — Rieu

. . . and arrived off the coast of Chios the next day — Phi

and the next day we arrived at Samos,

. . . touched at Samos — RSV

. . . put in at Samos — Alf

. . . thrust aside into Samos — Rhm

. . . crossed over to Samos — Mof

. . . docked at Samos — Ber

and on the second day we made Samos — NEB

the following day we struck across to Samos — Amp

and tarried at Trogyllium;[90]

and the next day we came to Miletus.

and we went on next day to Miletus — Mof

we came on the third day to Miletus — Bas

16. For Paul had determined to sail by Ephesus,

. . . had decided to sail past Ephesus — RSV

Paul's plan was to sail past Ephesus — Wey

Paul had made up his mind to . . . — Knox

Paul had sailed past Ephesus intentionally — Rieu

because he would not spend the time in Asia:

that he might not have to spend time in Asia — ASV

so as to avoid spending much time in Roman Asia — TCNT

so that he might not be kept in Asia — Bas

fearing he might be delayed there — Lam

to avoid any loss of time in Asia — Mof

with the idea of spending as little time as possible in Asia — Phi

for fear of having to waste time in Asia — Knox

for he hasted,

---

[90]Now recognized as not adequately supported by original manuscripts.

for he was hurrying — Gspd
He wanted to hurry on — Nor
for he was hastening — RSV
since he was very desirous — Wey
he was eager — Wms
He hoped — Phi
if it were possible for him,
if possible — TCNT
to be at Jerusalem the day of Pentecost.
against the day of Pentecost to arrive in Jerusalem — Rhm
to reach Jerusalem . . . by the Festival at the close of the Harvest — TCNT
. . . by the day of the Harvest Festival — Gspd
to celebrate the day of Pentecost at Jerusalem — Lam
to keep the day of Pentecost at Jerusalem — Knox

17. And from Miletus he sent to Ephesus,
From Miletus he sent a message to Ephesus — Knox
He did, however, send from Miletus to Ephesus — NEB
and called the elders of the church.
and called to him . . . — RSV
and summoned . . . — Alf
and called for the elders of the assembly — Rhm
and invited the Officers of the church to meet him — TCNT
asking the elders of the church to come to him — Rieu
to get the pastors of the church — Beck
. . . the Presbyters of the church — Mof
. . . the elders of the congregation — NEB

18. And when they were come to him,
Upon their arrival — Mof
and when they joined him — NEB
and when they had come out to him and gathered round him — Knox
he said unto them,
he spoke to them as follows: — TCNT
he told them — Ber
he addressed them in these words — Phi
Ye know,
You know well — TCNT
You yourselves can testify — Knox
You are well acquainted — Ber
I am sure you know — Phi
from the first day that I came into Asia,

from the first day that I set foot in Asia — ASV
ever since I set foot in Asia — Mof
. . . the province of Asia — Wey
after what manner I have been with you at all seasons,
after what manner I was with you all the time — ASV
the life that I always led among you — TCNT
the kind of life I lived among you the whole time — Wey
what my whole life has been like — Bas
about my way of life all the time I was with you — Rieu

19. Serving the Lord
and how I continued to serve the Lord — Wms
Doing the Lord's work — Bas
with all humility of mind,
with all lowliness of mind — ASV
most humbly — Gspd
without pride — Bas
and with many tears, and temptations,
and with tears and with trials — RSV
and with many a tear and many a trial — Mof
through all the sorrow and troubles — Bas
which befell me
which I encountered — Mof
to which I was subjected — Rieu
by the lying in wait of the Jews:
by the plots of the Jews — ASV
through the machinations of the Jews — NEB
because of the evil designs of the Jews — Bas

20. And how I kept back nothing that was profitable unto you, but have shewed you,
how I shrank not from declaring unto you anything that was profitable — ASV
I never shrank from telling you anything that could be helpful to you — TCNT
And yet I did not neglect to preach to you about those things that were good for your soul — Lam
and how I never failed you, when there was any need of preaching to you — Knox

You know that I kept back nothing that
was for your good: I delivered the
message to you — NEB

**and have taught you publickly, and
from house to house.**

and teaching you publicly and in your
homes — Rhm

or from teaching you both in public
and in private — TCNT

. . . in the streets and from house to
house — Lam

. . . in meetings and in homes — Beck

**21. Testifying both to the Jews, and also
to the Greeks,**

bearing full witness both to Jews and
to Greeks — Rhm

but earnestly urged . . . — Gspd

stressing to Jews and Greeks alike —
Rieu

With Jews and pagans alike I insisted
on — NEB

and how I earnestly warned Jews and
non-Jews — Beck

repentance toward God,

as to the repentance due unto God —
Rhm

the repentance that leads to God —
TCNT

repentance before God — Mof

the necessity of repentance before God
— Rieu

to turn to God in repentance — Gspd

to turn from sin to God — Beck

**and faith toward our Lord Jesus
Christ.**

and as to belief on our Lord Jesus —
Rhm

and trust in our Lord Jesus — NEB

**22. And now, behold, I go bound in the
spirit unto Jerusalem,**

And now, under spiritual constraint, I
am here on my way to Jerusalem —
TCNT

And now, as you see, I am on my way
to Jerusalem, under the constraint of
the Spirit — NEB

. . . for the Spirit compels me to go
there — Gspd

. . . because I am impelled by the Spirit
to do so — Wms

And now, you notice, I am bound by
the Spirit to go . . . — Ber

And now, as you see, I am going to
Jerusalem, a prisoner in spirit — Bas

. . . bound by the (Holy) Spirit and
obligated and compelled by the [con-
victions of my own] spirit — Amp

**not knowing the things that shall befall
me there:**

not knowing what will happen to me
there — TCNT

What will befall me there, I do not
know — Mof

and I have no idea of . . . — Nor

**23. Save that the Holy Ghost witnesseth in
every city,**

except that the Holy Spirit testifies to
me in every city — RSV

save that the Holy Spirit testifieth unto
me in every city — ASV

. . . from city to city doth bear me full
witness — Rhm

. . . in town after town the Holy Spirit
plainly declares to me — TCNT

. . . in every town I visit, the holy Spirit
warns me — Gspd

. . . makes clear to me — Bas

. . . emphatically assures me — Wms

knowing only that in every city the
Holy Spirit prophesies — Rieu

**saying that bonds and afflictions abide
me.**

. . . bonds and tribulations await me —
Rhm

. . . imprisonment and suffering are
awaiting me — Wey

. . . prison and pain . . . — Bas

. . . imprisonment and persecution . . .
— Gspd

24. But none of these things move me,

I care nothing for all that — Knox

However, I am not concerned about
anything — Ber

**neither count I my life dear unto my-
self,**

But I count my life as of no value unto
myself — Alf

But even the sacrifice of my life I count
as nothing — Wey

But my life does not matter — Gspd

But to me my life is nothing; I am not
afraid — Lam

But my life is of no importance to me
— Rieu

But then, I set no value on my own life
— Mof

**so that I might finish my course with
joy,**

if only I may complete the course
marked out for me — TCNT
as compared with the joy of finishing
my course — Mof
if only I can finish my race — Gspd
and the ministry,
. . . task — TCNT
and be faithful to the duty — Wey
and fulfilling the commission — Mof
and do the service — Gspd
**which I have received of the Lord
Jesus,**
that was allotted to me by the Lord
Jesus — TCNT
which the Lord Jesus has entrusted to
me — Wey
which the Lord Jesus assigned to me —
NEB
**to testify the gospel of the grace of
God.**
to bear full witness as to the good news
of the favour of God — Rhm
which was to declare the Good News
of the Love of God — TCNT
to attest . . . — Mof
of declaring . . . — Gspd
of faithfully telling . . . — Wms

25. **And now, behold, I know that ye all,**
And now, I tell you, I know that none
of you — TCNT
I know today that not one of you —
Mof
One word more: . . . — NEB
**among whom I have gone preaching
the kingdom of God,**
among whom I went about . . . — ASV
. . . as herald of the Kingdom — Ber
shall see my face no more.
will ever see my face again — TCNT
will ever see me again — Rieu

26. **Wherefore I take you to record this
day,**
. . . I testify unto you this day — ASV
. . . I take you to witness this day — Alf
Therefore I declare to you this day —
TCNT
Therefore I solemnly affirm to you to-
day — Wey
Therefore do I protest before you to-
day — Mof
And I ask you to bear me witness today
— Knox
That being so, I here and now declare
— NEB
**that I am pure from the blood of all
men.**

that I am clear from . . . — Mon
that I am innocent of the blood of all
of you — RSV
that I am guiltless of the blood of all
— Ber
that my conscience is clear in regard to
the fate of any of you — TCNT
that, should any of you perish, the responsibility is not mine — Wey
that I am not to blame for any man's
damnation — Rieu
that no man's fate can be laid at my
door — NEB
that I have no man's blood on my
hands — Knox

27. **For I have not shunned to declare
unto you**
For I shrank not from declaring unto
you — ASV
For I have not fallen short at all of
preaching to you — Ber
. . . announcing . . . — **Rhm**
. . . telling you — Mon
. . . proclaiming — Rieu
all the counsel of God.
the whole counsel of God — RSV
the whole purpose of God concerning
you — TCNT
God's purpose without reserve — Gspd
all the will of God — Lam
the complete will of God — **Phi**
God's whole plan — Wey

28. **Take heed therefore unto yourselves,**
Be watchful over yourselves — TCNT
Take care of . . . — Gspd
Give attention to . . . — Bas
Be on guard for yourselves — Ber
Keep a watchful eye on yourselves —
Rieu
and to all the flock,
and over the whole flock — TCNT
and for every flock — Phi
**over the which the Holy Ghost hath
made you overseers,**
in which the Holy Spirit hath set you
as overseers — Rhm
. . . hath made you bishops — ASV
. . . shepherds — Nor
of which the Holy Spirit has placed you
in charge — TCNT
of which the holy Spirit has appointed
you guardians — Mof
which the Holy Spirit has given into
your care — Bas
to feed the church of God,

to be shepherding the assembly of God — Rhm

shepherd the church of the Lord[91] — Mof

to give food to the church of God — Bas

to shepherd the church (that is, tend and feed and guide the church) — Amp

which he hath purchased with his own blood.

which he has bought . . . — Wey

for which he gave his blood — Bas

which he obtained with his own blood — RSV

which he acquired through means of the blood of his own — Rhm

which he won for himself at the cost of his life — TCNT

. . . at the price of his own blood — Knox

29. **For I know this, that after my departing**

I know that after my departing — ASV

. . . when I am gone — Wey

shall grievous wolves enter in among you,

there will enter . . . grievous wolves into your midst — Rhm

merciless wolves will get in among you — TCNT

violent wolves will break in among you — Wms

fierce wolves will attack you — Lam

cruel . . . — Wey

savage . . . — Gspd

evil . . . — Knox

monstrous . . . — Nor

ferocious . . . — Amp

not sparing the flock.

who will not spare the flock — TCNT

doing damage to . . . — Bas

that have no mercy on . . . — Ber

30. **Also of your own selves shall men arise,**

and from among your own selves . . . — RSV

yes, and men of your own number will arise — Mof

. . . will appear — Gspd

yes, and from among yourselves will emerge men — Rieu

Even from your own body there will be men coming forward — NEB

And even some of you men will start to — Beck

speaking perverse things,

speaking distorted things — Rhm

who will distort the truth — Rieu

and will teach perversions of truth — TCNT

who will seek with their perverse talk — Wey

who will give wrong teaching — Bas

who will come forward with a false message — Knox

and teach false doctrines — Nor

to draw away disciples after them.

trying to draw away the disciples and make them followers of themselves — Phi

to induce the disciples to break away and follow them — NEB

to seduce the disciples — Rieu

and find disciples to follow them — Knox

31. **Therefore watch,**

Wherefore, be on the watch — Rhm

. . . be on your guard — TCNT

. . . be on the alert — Wey

Keep, therefore, on the lookout — Ber

That is why I tell you to keep on the alert — Phi

and remember,

remembering — ASV

that by the space of three years

for three years — Rhm

I ceased not to warn every one night and day with tears.

night and day I never ceased even with tears to warn each one of you — TCNT

I never quit night and day to give each of you warning with my tears — Ber

I never failed . . . to warn every one of you, even with tears in my eyes — Phi

instructing every one of you continually, and with tears — Knox

night and day, I never cease to counsel each of you, and how I wept over you — NEB

. . . to watch over each one of you with tears — Mof

32. **And now, brethren, I commend you to God,**

---

[91]Mof makes this a command.

... I entrust you to God — Mof

... I commit you to the Lord — Gspd

... I give you into the care of God — Bas

... commit you to God — that is, I deposit you in His charge, entrusting you to His protection and care — Amp

and to the word of his grace,

and unto his word of favour — Rhm

and to the Message of his love — TCNT

and to his gracious word — Knox

and to the revelation of his grace — Rieu

which is able to build you up,

a Message which has the power to build up your character — TCNT

which will build you up — Gspd

which has power to build you up — NEB

... to make you strong — Bas

and to give you an inheritance

... the inheritance — RSV

... your place — TCNT

... your proper possession — Wms

... your salvation — Beck

among all them which are sanctified.

among all those who are sanctified — RSV

among all the hallowed ones — Rhm

among the saints — Wey

among all those made holy — Ber

to be shared by all who are made holy — Beck

among all the consecrated — Mof

among those whom God has consecrated — Gspd

among all God's consecrated people — Wms

among all those who have become Christ's People — TCNT

with all who live dedicated lives — Rieu

among all who are dedicated to him — NEB

33. I have coveted no man's silver, or gold, or apparel.

I never coveted anyone's gold or silver or clothing — TCNT

I desired no one's ... — ABUV

I have never asked for silver or gold or clothing from any man — Knox

I have set my mind on no one's ... — Ber

I have not wanted anyone's money or clothes for myself — NEB

34. Yea, ye yourselves know,

yourselves acknowledge — Rhm

you yourselves have seen — Bas

you will bear me out — Knox

that these hands have ministered unto my necessities,

that these hands of mine provided not only for my own wants — TCNT

that these hands supplied my needs — Ber

these hands worked for what I needed — Beck

and to them that were with me.

but for my companions also — TCNT

and for the people with me — Wey

and the needs of my companions — Rieu

35. I have shewed you all things,

I left nothing undone to show you — TCNT

In every way I have shown you — Wey

I showed you how this was the way — Mof

Always I have tried to show you — Knox

I have in every way pointed out to you — Ber

In all things I gave you an example — ASV

how that so labouring

that by so toiling — RSV

that, labouring as I laboured — TCNT

how, by working as I do — Wey

to work hard — Mof

that it is our duty so to work — Knox

ye ought to support the weak,

one must help the weak — RSV

succor the needy — Mof

you are to give help to the feeble — Bas

that one must provide for the poor — Rieu

and be the support of the weak — Knox

and to remember the words of the Lord Jesus,

remembering what was spoken by the Lord Jesus himself — Knox

how he said,

when he said — Phi

that he himself said — ASV

It is more blessed to give than to receive.

There is a greater blessing in giving than in getting — Bas

Happy is it rather to give than to receive — Rhm

It makes one happier to give than to be given to — Gspd

Happiness lies more in giving than in receiving — NEB

It is more blessed — makes one happier and more to be envied — to give than to receive— Amp

36. And when he had thus spoken,

When Paul had finished speaking — TCNT

With these words — Mof

When he had finished his talk — Nor

he kneeled down, and prayed with them all.

kneeling down with them all he prayed — Rhm

he fell on his knees with them all and prayed — Wms

he went down on his knees in prayer with them all — Bas

he knelt and prayed with the whole group — Rieu

37. And they all wept sore,

. . . much — Rhm

. . . freely — Ber

. . . aloud — Gspd

. . . abundantly — Knox

All were in tears — TCNT

They all broke into loud lamentation — Mof

Then there were loud cries of sorrow from them all — NEB

They all burst into tears — Rieu

and fell on Paul's neck, and kissed him,

and throwing their arms round Paul's neck, they kissed him again and again — TCNT

as they folded Paul in their arms and kissed him — NEB

. . . and kissed him lovingly — Wey

. . . affectionately — Gspd

38. Sorrowing most of all for the words which he spake,

. . . which he had spoken — ASV

deeply distressed by his saying — Rieu

sorrowing chiefly because he told them — Mof

grieving most of all over what he had said — TCNT

grieving most over what he had said — Knox

because they were especially pained at his saying — Wms

What saddened them most of all was his saying — Phi

It hurt them most of all that he had said — Beck

that they should see his face no more.

that they would never see his face again — TCNT

about never seeing his face again — Knox

And they accompanied him unto the ship.

And they brought him on his way unto the ship — ASV

And they brought him to the ship — RSV

CHAPTER 21

1. And it came to pass, that after we were gotten from them,

. . . that we were parted from them — ASV

And when at last we had parted from them — Alf

. . . having torn ourselves from them — Rhm

When the parting was over — Gspd

When he had finally said farewell to them — Phi

and had launched,

and had set sail — ASV

we came with a straight course unto Coos,

we ran before the wind to Cos — TCNT

we made a straight run to Cos — Mof

we struck a bee-line for Cos — Wms

and the day following unto Rhodes,

and the next day . . . — RSV

. . . we came to Rhodes — TCNT

and from thence unto Patara:

and from there to Patara — TCNT

2. And finding a ship sailing over unto Phenicia,

And having found a ship crossing over unto Phoenicia — ASV

Finding a ship bound for Phoenicia — Wey

And as there was a ship going to Phoenicia — Bas

we went aboard, and set forth.

. . . and set sail — RSV

. . . and put to sea — Wey

we embarked and set sail — Ber

3. Now when we had discovered Cyprus,
. . . had come in sight of Cyprus —
ASV
And sighting Cyprus — Rhm
we left it on the left hand,
and leaving it behind to the left —
Rhm
and sailed into Syria,
we held on our voyage to Syria — Rhm
we sailed for Syria — Mon
we went on to Syria — Bas
and landed at Tyre:
and put into Tyre — TCNT
and docked at Tyre — Ber
**for there the ship was to unlade her
burden.**
. . . was to discharge her cargo — Rhm
. . . was to unload her cargo — ABUV

4. And finding disciples,
And having found the disciples — ASV
And having sought the disciples — Alf
Having searched for the disciples and
found them — Wey
So we looked up the disciples there —
Gspd
Here we enquired for the brethren —
Knox
We went and found the disciples —
NEB
we tarried there seven days:
and remained there seven days — Rhm
and stayed a week with them — TCNT
who said to Paul
and they unto Paul began to say —
Rhm
and every day they said to Paul—Lam
and these disciples kept telling Paul —
Mon
They advised Paul — Ber
they warned Paul — TCNT
through the Spirit,
Speaking under the influence of the
Spirit — TCNT
led by the Spirit — Phi
prompted by the Holy Spirit — Amp
because of impressions made by the
Spirit — Wms
taught by the Spirit — Wey
Instructed by the Spirit — Gspd
that he should not go up to Jerusalem.
not to go on to Jerusalem — RSV
that he should not set foot in Jerusalem — ASV
not to proceed to Jerusalem — Wey

to abandon his visit to Jerusalem —
NEB

**5. And when he had accomplished those
days,**
However, when we had come to the
end of our visit — TCNT
When, however, our time was up —
Wey
But when our time ashore was ended —
NEB
we departed and went our way;
we went forth and continued our journey — Rhm
we left there and went on — Gspd
we had to leave them and continue our
journey — Rieu
**and they all brought us on our way,
with wives and children,**
all of them accompanying us with
wives and children — Rhm
all the disciples with their wives and
children escorting us — TCNT
They all came out to see us off, bringing their wives and children, accompanying us — Phi
till we were out of the city:
as far as outside the city — Rhm
out of the city — TCNT
till we got outside the town — Mof
**and we kneeled down on the shore,
and prayed.**[92]

**6. And when we had taken our leave one
of another,**
and bade each other farewell — ASV
and then said good-bye to one another
— TCNT
we said our last words to one another
— Bas
then embraced one another — Ber
And when we had kissed one another
goodbye — Lam
we tore ourselves from each other —
Rhm
we took ship;
we went on board the ship — RSV
and embarked in the ship — Alf
and they returned home again.
while they returned home — Wey
and they went home — Gspd

**7. And when we had finished our course
from Tyre, we came to Ptolemais,**
By sailing from Tyre to Ptolemais we
completed our voyage — Mof

_____
[92]See Acts 20:36.

Continuing our voyage we left Tyre and reached Ptolemais — Rieu

We continued our sailing, going from Tyre to Ptolemais — Beck

and saluted the brethren,

and we greeted the brethren — RSV

and exchanged greetings with the Brethren there — TCNT

and after paying our respects to the brothers — Ber

There we greeted our fellow Christians — Beck

Here we inquired after the welfare of the brethren — Wey

and abode with them one day.

and spent a day with them — TCNT

and stayed with them one day — Mon

and stayed the night with them — Rieu

8. And the next day we that were of Paul's company departed,

And on the morrow we . . . departed — ASV

The next day we left — TCNT

and came unto Caesarea:

and reached Caesarea — TCNT

and went on to Caesarea — Gspd

and proceeded to Caesarea — Phi

and we entered into the house of Philip the evangelist,

where we went to the house of Philip, the Missionary — TCNT

. . . were guests in the house of Philip, the preacher — Bas

. . . called at the home of . . . — Ber

which was one of the seven;

who was one of 'the Seven' — TCNT

who had been one of the seven deacons — Nor

and abode with him.

and stayed with him — RSV

and lodged with him — Knox

9. And the same man had four daughters, virgins,

Now this man had four virgin daughters — ASV

. . . four unmarried daughters — RSV

which did prophesy.

who prophesied — ASV

who had the gift of prophecy — TCNT

who were prophetesses — Wey

all of whom spoke by the Spirit of God — Phi

who spoke God's Word — Beck

10. And as we tarried there many days,

During our visit, which lasted several days — TCNT

Now during our somewhat lengthy stay — Wey

When we had been there several days — Rieu

While we were staying there longer than we had expected — Beck

there came down from Judaea a certain prophet, named Agabus.

11. And when he was come unto us, he took Paul's girdle,

He came to see us, and, taking Paul's girdle — TCNT

. . . Paul's belt — Gspd

and bound his own hands and feet, and said,

and putting it round his feet and hands, said — Bas

and, tying his feet and hands, he said — Ber

Thus saith the Holy Ghost,

This is what the Holy Spirit says — TCNT

Here is the word of the Holy Spirit: — Mof

These are the words of the Holy Spirit — NEB

So shall the Jews at Jerusalem bind the man that owneth this girdle,

The man whose this girdle is shall the Jews thus bind in Jerusalem — Rhm

The Jews at Jerusalem will bind the man who owns this belt like this — Gspd

This is how the Jews in Jerusalem will tie the man this belt belongs to — Beck

and shall deliver him into the hands of the Gentiles.

and will hand him over to the Gentiles — Wey

. . . to the heathen! — Gspd

12. And when we heard these things,

As soon as we heard these words — Wey

On hearing this — Ber

both we, and they of that place,

. . . and the brethren at Caesarea — Wey

. . . and the local disciples — Mof

. . . and those who were standing near — Mon

. . . and all the people there — Wms

. . . and our hosts — Knox

we as well as the local residents — NASB

besought him not to go up to Jerusalem.

began beseeching him . . . — Rhm

began to entreat Paul . . . — TCNT

begged him . . . — Gspd

implored Paul . . . — Knox

. . . not to continue on to Jerusalem — Rieu

begged and implored Paul to abandon his visit to Jerusalem — NEB

13. Then Paul answered,

It was then that Paul made the reply: — TCNT

His reply was — Wey

To which he answered — Knox

What mean ye to weep and to break mine heart?

What can you mean by thus unmanning me with your weeping — Wey

What do you mean by weeping and disheartening me — Mof

What do you mean by thus breaking my heart with your grief — Mon

. . . by lamenting and crushing my spirits — Knox

What do you achieve by weeping and discouraging me — Ber

. . . unnerving me with all your tears — Phi

Why all these tears? Why are you trying to weaken my resolutions—NEB

for I am ready not to be bound only,

. . . not only to be imprisoned — RSV

. . . not only to be a prisoner — Bas

. . . not only to go to Jerusalem and be put in chains — Wey

I am prepared not merely to be bound — Ber

I am prepared to be more than imprisoned — Rieu

but also to die at Jerusalem

but even to suffer death at Jerusalem — TCNT

but even to die . . . — RSV

I am even prepared to die at . . . — Rieu

for the name of the Lord Jesus.

in behalf of the name of . . . — Rhm

for the sake of the Lord Jesus! — Wey

14. And when he would not be persuaded,

So when he was not to be dissuaded — Wey

So as he would not yield — Gspd

And when he would not listen to us — Lam

Finding that he would not take our advice — Knox

we ceased, saying,

we said no more to him, only adding — TCNT

we ceased remonstrating with him and said — Wey

we held our peace, saying — ABUV

we acquiesced . . . — Mof

we stopped begging him, and said — Wms

we composed ourselves and said — Knox

we gave up and said — NEB

we fell silent, remarking — NASB

we were silent, and could only say — Beck

The will of the Lord be done.

Let the purpose of God be done — Bas

15. And after those days

At the end of our visit — TCNT

A few days afterwards — Wey

When the time came to an end — Knox

we took up our carriages,

we took up our baggage — ASV

we made ready — RSV

making ready what we had — Rhm

we packed our baggage — Wey

we got ready — Wms

we hired horses — Rieu

and went up to Jerusalem.

and continued our journey to Jerusalem — Wey

and started for Jerusalem — Mof

and we set out for Jerusalem — Rieu

and took the road up to Jerusalem — NEB

16. There went with us also certain of the disciples of Caesarea,

Some of the disciples from Caesarea . . . — TCNT

. . . also joined our party — Wey

and brought with them one Mnason of Cyprus,

to introduce us to one Mnason of Cyprus — Alf

to take us to the house of a Cypriot named Mnason — Knox

and they brought us to the house of Mnason, a native of Cyprus — Phi

They escorted us as far as the house
of Mnason, a Cypriot — Rieu
an old disciple,
an early disciple — RSV
one of the first disciples — Knox
one of the original disciples — Rieu
a . . . disciple of long standing — TCNT
a brother who was among the first
converts — Lam
a Christian from the early days — NEB
with whom we should lodge.
with whom we were to stay — TCNT
with whom we were to break our journey — Rieu

17. And when we were come to Jerusalem,
On our arrival at Jerusalem — TCNT
At length we reached Jerusalem —
Mon
the brethren received us gladly.
. . . gladly welcomed us — Rhm
the brethren there gave us a hearty
welcome — TCNT
. . . gave us a very warm welcome —
Phi
. . . were pleased to see us — Bas
we were warmly welcomed by the
brotherhood — Rieu
our fellow Christians eagerly welcomed
us — Beck

18. And the day following
And on the next day — Rhm
Paul went in with us unto James;
Paul went with us to see James — TCNT
we went with Paul to call on James —
Wey
. . . to visit James — Phi
Paul and the rest of us were received
by James — Rieu
and all the elders were present.
and all the Officers of the Church were
present — TCNT
. . . presbyters . . . — Mof
. . . elders of the church . . . — Wms
. . . had gathered — Knox
. . . attended — NEB
. . . came there too — Beck

19. And when he had saluted them,
After greeting them — TCNT
After exchanging greetings — Wey
Paul greeted them warmly — Gspd
And when he had said how glad he was
to see them — Bas
he declared particularly
he rehearsed one by one — ASV

he went on to narrate one by one —
Rhm
Paul related in detail — TCNT
. . . described in detail — Mof
he recounted to them step by step —
Ber
**what things God had wrought among
the Gentiles by his ministry.**
each of the things . . . — Rhm
all that God had done among the Gentiles through his efforts — TCNT
. . . for the Gentiles through his work
— Nor
. . . through his ministry — RSV
. . . through his service — Wms
through his work among the non-Jews
— Beck

20. And when they heard it,
When they heard his statement — Wey
and they, on hearing this account —
Phi
they glorified the Lord,
began glorifying God — Rhm
they began praising God — TCNT
they . . . gave glory to God — Wey
they adored and exalted and praised
and thanked God — Amp
and said unto him,
Then they said to him — Phi
They told him — Beck
Thou seest, brother,
. . . observest . . . — Rhm
You see, Brother — RSV
Brother, thou canst see for thyself —
Knox
You know, brother — Phi
**how many thousands of Jews there are
which believe;**
how many myriads . . . — Rhm
that the Jews who have become believers in Christ may be numbered
by tens of thousands — TCNT
and they are all zealous of the law:
. . . naturally earnest in upholding the
Jewish Law — TCNT
. . . zealots for the law — ABUV
. . . zealous supporters . . . — Knox
. . . zealous champions . . . — Wms
. . . ardent upholders . . . — Mof
and they all have a great respect for
the law — Bas
and every one of them is a staunch up-
holder of the law — Phi

21. And they are informed of thee,

and they have been told about you — RSV

Now they have heard it rumoured concerning thee — Rhm

Now what they have been told about you is — Wey

Now what they have been told about you, again and again, is — Mon

Now they have been given certain information about you — NEB

that thou teachest all the Jews which are among the Gentiles to forsake Moses,

that an apostacy art thou teaching from Moses unto all the Jews who are among the nations — Rhm

that you teach all Jews in foreign countries to forsake Moses — TCNT

that you teach all Jews who live among Gentiles to break away from Moses — Mof

. . . among the heathen to turn away from Moses — Gspd

. . . to turn their backs on Moses — Wms

. . . to give up the law of Moses — Bas

. . . to disregard the Law of Moses — Phi

that everywhere in the Gentile world you teach Jews to renounce the Law of Moses — Rieu

saying that they ought not to circumcise their children,

telling them not to . . . — RSV

and that you continue to tell them to stop circumcising . . . — Wms

instructing them not to . . . — Rieu

neither to walk after the customs.

or observe the customs — RSV

or even to observe Jewish customs — TCNT

. . . old-established customs — Wey

nor to follow the old customs — Mof

neither to follow after the customs of the law — Lam

. . . the cherished customs — Wms

and not to keep the old rules — Bas

or follow the other traditional customs — Rieu

to give up . . . following our way of life — NEB

22. What is it therefore?

What is to be done — Mof

What shall we do about it — Beck

Now, how about it — Ber

What then ought you to do — Wey

What is your duty, then — Wms

What do you plan to say — Rieu

What will happen — Knox

the multitude must needs come together:

Why, a multitude of them will assuredly gather round thee — Knox

A crowd of them will surely gather about you — Nor

In any event the congregation will meet — Ber

for they will hear that thou art come.

as they are certain to hear of your arrival — TCNT

They will be sure to hear you have arrived — Mof

for they will learn that you have arrived — Ber

for they are simply bound to hear . . . — Phi

for they will undoubtedly hear . . . — Rieu

23. Do therefore this that we say to thee:

Do what we are going to suggest — TCNT

Now, why not follow this suggestion of ours — Phi

We suggest that you take this course — Rieu

We have four men which have a vow on them;

. . . who of their own accord put themselves under a vow — TCNT

. . . who have vowed to purify themselves — Lam

. . . who are under a vow — Gspd

24. Them take,

Join these men — TCNT

Suppose you join them — Phi

Associate with these men — Wey

Take them along with you — Wms

and purify thyself with them,

be purified with them — Rhm

share their purification — TCNT

undergo the rites of purification with them — Gspd

and make a similar vow yourself — Rieu

and make yourself clean with them — Bas

and be at charges with them,

and bear their charges — Alf

and bear their expenses — TCNT

and pay their expenses — Wey

and bear the costs for them — ABUV
and make the necessary payments for them — Bas

that they may shave their heads:
of having their heads shaved — Wms
for the shaving of their heads — Knox
so that they may have their hair cut short — Phi
after which they may shave their heads — NEB

and all may know
and all shall know — ASV
and then all will see — TCNT
and everybody will understand — Mof
Then everyone will realize — Ber
This will prove to everyone — Rieu

that those things, whereof they were informed concerning thee, are nothing;
that the things which they have heard rumoured concerning thee are nothing — Rhm
that there is no truth in the things they have been told about you — TCNT
that what has been said against you is false — Lam
that there is no basis for the reports about you — Ber

but that thou thyself also walkest orderly, and keepest the law.
On the contrary thou thyself dost keep the ranks guarding the law — Rhm
but that on the contrary, you yourself rule your life in obedience to the Jewish Law — TCNT
but that, on the contrary, you are guided by obedience to the law — Mof
but that you yourself observe the Law — Gspd
but that you yourself are living as a constant observer of the law — Wms
but that you personally order your life in observance of the Law — Ber
but that you are a practising Jew and keep the Law yourself — NEB
but you live strictly according to the Law — Beck

25. As touching the Gentiles which believe,
As to the Gentiles who have become believers in Christ — TCNT
But as for the Gentiles who have believed — RSV
As for Gentile believers — Mof

On the part of Gentile believers — Ber
As for the Gentile converts — Rieu
About the non-Jews who now believe — Beck

we have written and concluded
We have sent a letter with our judgment — RSV
we wrote, giving judgment — ASV
we have sent our decision — TCNT
we sent word, deciding — ABUV
we have sent them our resolution — Wms
our letter conveyed to them our decision — Rieu

that they observe no such thing, save only[93]

that they keep themselves from things offered to idols, and from blood, and from strangled, and from fornication.[94]

26. Then Paul took the men,
On this Paul joined the men — TCNT
So Paul associated with the men — Wey
Then Paul took the men along with him — Wms

and the next day purifying himself with them[95]
and the next day, after placing himself under a vow similar to theirs — Rieu

entered into the temple,
went into the temple — ASV

to signify the accomplishment of the days of purification,
declaring the fulfillment of . . . — ASV
to declare the filling up of the days of purification — Rhm
and gave notice of the expiration of the period of purification — TCNT
to give notice of the date when the period of purification would end — NEB
announcing the completion of the days of the purification — ABUV
and gave notice of the time when the vow was to end — Rieu

until that an offering should be offered for every one of them.
and there he remained until the sacrifice for each one of them was offered — Wey

---

[93]Now recognized as not adequately supported by original manuscripts.
[94]See Acts 15:20,29.
[95]See verse 24.

until the time came for each to have sacrifice made on his behalf — Knox

— the time, that is to say, when the sacrifice could be offered for each one of them — Mof

and when the sacrifice for each of them was to be made — Rieu

27. And when the seven days were almost ended,

But, just as the seven days were drawing to a close — TCNT

And when the seven days were all but at an end — Knox

But just before the period of seven days was up — NEB

the Jews which were of Asia,

the Jews from Asia — RSV

the Jews from the province of Asia — Wey

when they saw him in the temple,

caught a glimpse of him in the temple — Wms

stirred up all the people,

and began to stir up all the crowd — Mon

stirred the crowd to a frenzy — Rieu

They excited the whole crowd into an uproar — Nor

and laid hands on him,

by seizing Paul — TCNT

and seized him — Wms

and grabbed hold of him — Ber

28. Crying out,

and shouting — TCNT

as they kept shouting — Wms

yelling — Beck

Men of Israel, help:

To the rescue, men of Israel! — Mof

. . . help! help! — Wms

. . . come to our help — Bas

. . . to our aid! — Ber

. . . come and help! — Rieu

This is the man,

Here is the man — Mof

This is the fellow — NEB

that teacheth all men every where against the people,

who goes everywhere preaching to everybody against the Jewish people — Wey

who goes about teaching everybody to despise our people — Knox

who everywhere talks treason against Israel — Rieu

who spreads his doctrine all over the world, attacking our people — NEB

and the law, and this place:

the Law, and this Temple — Rieu

our law, and this sanctuary — NEB

and further brought Greeks also into the temple,

and, what is more, he has actually brought Greeks into the Temple — TCNT

On top of all this . . . — NEB

. . . Gentiles even into the temple — Mon

. . . non-Jews . . . — Beck

and hath polluted this holy place.

. . . defiled . . . — RSV

. . . profaned . . . — Rhm

. . . desecrated . . . — Wey

and made this holy place unclean — Bas

profaning these sacred precincts — Knox

29. (For they had seen before with him in the city Trophimus an Ephesian,

For they had previously seen Trophimus the Ephesian in Paul's company in the city — TCNT

whom they supposed that Paul had brought into the temple.)

and were under the belief that Paul had taken him into the Temple — TCNT

and they thought that he had entered the temple with Paul — Lam

and surmised that Paul had brought him into the temple — Ber

and they supposed that he had brought the man into the temple — [that is], into the inner court [forbidden to Gentiles] — Amp

30. And all the city was moved,

And the whole city was set in motion — Rhm

. . . was stirred — TCNT

. . . was thrown into turmoil — Mof

. . . was thrown into confusion — Gspd

. . . was thrown into uproar — Mon

. . . was aroused — RSV

The excitement spread through the whole city — Wey

and the people ran together:

. . . quickly collected — TCNT

. . . rushed together — Mof

The Jews ran to the spot — Rieu

and people came running from all directions — NEB

and a mob collected — Phi

The mob surged together — Mon

and the crowd surged back and forth — Nor

and they took Paul,

and they laid hold on Paul — ASV

seized Paul — TCNT

and drew him out of the temple:

and dragged him out of the temple — RSV

pulling him out of the temple — Bas

and forthwith the doors were shut.

when the doors were immediately shut — TCNT

and the Temple gates were immediately closed — Wey

and the doors were slammed behind him — Phi

Immediately the gates were shut behind them — Rieu

31. And as they went about to kill him,

And as they were seeking to kill him — ASV

They were bent on killing him — TCNT

But while they were trying to kill Paul — Wey

While they set about killing him — Rieu

While they were clamouring for his death — NEB

tidings came unto the chief captain of the band,

when it was reported to the officer commanding the garrison — TCNT

word was taken up to the Tribune in command of the battalion — Wey

a report was taken up to the military tribune in command of the cohort — Rieu

a report came up to the commander of the Roman Cohort — NASB

when it was reported to the tribune who was in charge of about six hundred soldiers — Beck

that all Jerusalem was in an uproar.

... was in confusion — ASV

... was in a ferment — Wey

... was in a tumult — Gspd

... was out of control — Bas

... was in riot — Rieu

that the people were rioting all over Jerusalem — Nor

32. Who immediately took soldiers and centurions,

He instantly got together some officers and men — TCNT

So he at once got together some soldiers and captains — Wms

He at once summoned his troops, with their officers — Knox

Without a moment's delay ... — Phi

He immediately took a force of soldiers with their centurions — NEB

and ran down unto them:

and charged down upon the crowd — TCNT

and swept down upon them — Knox

and came down on the rioters at the double — NEB

and when they saw the chief captain[96] and the soldiers,

At the sight of ... — Wey

But as soon as they saw ... — Wms

they left beating of Paul.

they stopped hitting Paul — Rieu

33. Then the chief captain came near,

... went up to Paul — TCNT

... making his way to him — Wey

... stepped forward — NEB

and took him,

arrested him — TCNT

and seized him — Mof

took charge of him — Ber

and commanded him to be bound with two chains;

and ordered him to be bound with two chains — RSV

... to be doubly chained — TCNT

... with a double chain — Knox

... to be handcuffed on both sides — Rieu

... to be shackled with two chains — NEB

and demanded who he was, and what he had done.

and inquired ... — ASV

and began to inquire who he might be and what he had done — Rhm

34. And some cried one thing, some another, among the multitude:

Some of the crowd shouted one accusation against Paul and some another — Wey

Some of the crowd roared one thing ... — Mof

---

[96]For the translation of "chief captain" see verse 31.

The crowd started shouting out, some one thing, some another — Rieu

and when he could not know the certainty for the tumult,

and, as he could get no definite reply on account of the uproar — TCNT

until, as the uproar made it impossible for the truth to be ascertained — Wey

so, unable to get at the facts . . . — Ber

. . . because of the shouting that was going on — Phi

. . . because of the hubbub — Rieu

he commanded him to be carried into the castle.

he ordered Paul to be taken into the barracks — TCNT

. . . to be taken to headquarters — Lam

. . . into the army building — Bas

. . . into the Fort — Rieu

35. And when he came upon the stairs,

When Paul reached the steps — TCNT

When Paul was going up the steps — Mon

so it was, that he was borne of the soldiers

he had to be carried by the soldiers — Wey

he was actually being carried by the soldiers — TCNT

for the violence of the people.

because of the violence . . . — Alf

36. For the multitude of the people followed after, crying,

for the people were following in a mass, shouting out : — TCNT

for a tremendous crowd of people kept following them and shouting—Wms

for the mob of the people followed, crying — RSV

for the Jews were following him in a crowd yelling out — Rieu

for the whole crowd were at their back yelling — NEB

The mob was right behind them, yelling — Beck

Away with him.

Kill him! — TCNT

Put him to death — Knox

37. And as Paul was to be led into the castle,[97]

. . . about to be brought into the castle — ASV

Just as they were going to take him . . . — Gspd

he said unto the chief captain,[98]

Paul asked the centurion — Knox

May I speak unto thee?

May I say something unto thee — ASV

May I have a word with thee — Knox

Who said, Canst thou speak Greek?

And he said, Dost thou know Greek — ASV

You know Greek! said the commander — Mof

So you can talk Greek? he exclaimed — Rieu

38. Art not thou that Egyptian,

Then you are not the Egyptian — Mof

Are you not then [as I supposed] the Egyptian — Amp

which before these days madest an uproar,

who some time ago raised an insurrection — TCNT

who some years ago excited the riot — Wey

who before this got the people worked up against the government — Bas

. . . recently stirred up the rebellion — Ber

. . . a revolt — RSV

and leddest out into the wilderness four thousand men that were murderers?

and led the four thousand Bandits out into the wilderness — TCNT

of the 4000 cut-throats and led them out into the Desert — Wey

and led out into the wilderness the four thousand men of the Assassins — ASV

and led a force of four thousand terrorists out into the wilds — NEB

. . . four thousand dagger-men . . . — Beck

39. But Paul said, I am a man which am a Jew of Tarsus, a city in Cilicia,

But Paul said, I am a Jew, of Tarsus in Cilicia — ASV

No, said Paul, I am . . . — TCNT

. . . a native of Tarsus . . . — Mon

a citizen of no mean city:

. . . no obscure city — Rhm

. . . no unimportant city — Wey

. . . no insignificant city — Gspd

. . . a city of some note — TCNT

---

[97]On "castle" see verse 34.

[98]On "chief captain" see verse 31.

... a famous town — Mof
... a well-known city — Lam
... an important city — Beck
... not a bad city at all — Nor
and, I beseech thee, suffer me to speak
and I beg you to give me permission
to speak — TCNT
Please let me speak — Wms
Will you please allow me to . . .—Rieu
I ask your permission to . . . — NEB
unto the people.

40. **And when he had given him licence,**
The Commanding Officer gave his per-
mission — TCNT
He granted the request — Wms
And when he let him do so — Bas
So with his permission — Wey
Paul's request was granted — Rieu
Paul stood on the stairs,
Paul, standing on the steps — TCNT
Paul, from the steps — Bas
Paul took his stand on the steps —
Beck

**and beckoned with the hand unto the
people.**
waved with his hand unto the people
— Rhm
made signs with his hand to the people
— TCNT
and motioned to the people to be quiet
— Wey
and with a gesture called for the attention of the people — NEB
**And when there was made a great
silence,**
and when they had become quiet —
Gspd
As soon as quiet was restored — NEB
A great hush came over them — Mof
There was a deep silence — Knox
he spake unto them
he addressed them — Rhm
in the Hebrew tongue, saying,
in the Hebrew language, saying — RSV
in Aramaic — Rieu
in the Jewish language — NEB
in the Hebrew dialect — NASB

CHAPTER 22

1. **Men, brethren, and fathers,**
Brothers and Fathers — TCNT
**hear ye my defence which I make now
unto you.**
listen to the defence which I am about
to make — TCNT
listen to what I have to say in my defense — Gspd
give ear to the story of my life which
I now put before you — Bas
2. **(And when they heard that he spake
in the Hebrew tongue to them,**
... in the Hebrew language ... — Rhm
And on hearing him address them in
Hebrew — Wey
... in Aramaic — Rieu
... in their own language — NEB
they kept the more silence:
they were the more quiet — ASV
the silence became intense — RSV
the silence deepened — Rieu
they quieted down still more — Beck
and he saith,)
and Paul went on — TCNT
and he continued — Wms
so he proceeded — Ber
3. **I am verily a man which am a Jew,**
I am a Jew — RSV
I am a Jew born and bred — Ber

I am a true-born Jew — NEB
I am, without question, a Jew — Nor
born in Tarsus, a city in Cilicia,
a native of Tarsus in Cilicia — TCNT
of Tarsus in Cilicia by birth — Bas
yet brought up in this city
but nurtured in this city — Rhm
but I had my education in this city —
Bas
but raised in this city — Beck
at the feet of Gamaliel,
under the teaching of Gamaliel — Wey
educated at the feet of Gamaliel — Mof
under the care and guidance of Gamaliel — Lam
I received my training at the feet of
Gamaliel — Phi
... at the Academy of Gamaliel —
Rieu
**and taught according to the perfect
manner of the law of the fathers,**
instructed according to the strict manner . . . — ASV
trained after the strictness of our ancestral law — Rhm
educated according to the strict system
of our ancestral Law — TCNT
I was thoroughly trained in every point
of our ancestral law — NEB

being trained in the keeping of every detail of the law of our fathers — Bas

and I was schooled in the strictest observance of our fathers' law — Phi

and was zealous toward God,

being zealous for God — ASV

being a zealot for God — ABUV

I was as zealous in God's service — TCNT

I have always been ardent in God's service — NEB

I was as much on fire with zeal for God — Phi

I was full of religious fervour — Rieu

as jealous for the honour of the law — Knox

as ye all are this day.

as any of you who are here today — TCNT

like all of you today — Wey

4. **And I persecuted this way unto the death,**

In my persecution of this Cause I did not stop even at the taking of life — TCNT

And I made attacks on this Way, even to death — Bas

I am also the man who persecuted this Way to the death — Phi

I hunted to their death men and women who believed as I do now — Beck

. . . those who followed the new Way — Nor

binding and delivering into prisons both men and women.

I put in chains, and imprisoned, men and women alike — TCNT

continually binding both men and women and throwing them into prison — Wey

and chained and imprisoned the men and women who belonged to it — Rieu

5. **As also the high priest doth bear me witness, and all the estate of the elders:**

. . . the council of the elders — Alf

. . . and all the Eldership — Rhm

and to that the High Priest himself and all the council can testify — TCNT

as the high priest and the whole council will bear me witness — Gspd

To this the high priest and all the council of elders are witnesses — Mon

from whom also I received letters unto the brethren,

For I had letters of introduction from them to our fellow Jews at Damascus — TCNT

It was from them that I got letters to the brotherhood at Damascus — Mof

In fact, they gave me letters . . . — Gspd

. . . to our Jewish brethren there — Rieu

and went to Damascus,

unto Damascus was I journeying — Rhm

and I journeyed to Damascus — RSV

and I was on my way to that place — TCNT

and I went there — Gspd

and I set out for Damascus — Nor

to bring them which were there bound unto Jerusalem, for to be punished.

to bind those who had gathered there and bring them back to Jerusalem for punishment — Mof

to make fresh prisoners there and bring them . . . — Knox

6. **And it came to pass, that, as I made my journey,**

While I was still on my way — TCNT

Now as I neared Damascus on my journey — Mof

But on my way — Gspd

and was come nigh unto Damascus

just as I was getting close to Damascus — TCNT

and drew near to Damascus — RSV

just before I reached Damascus — Wms

about noon,[99]

at mid-day — TCNT

suddenly there shone from heaven a great light round about me.

suddenly out of heaven there flashed a great light all around me — Rhm

a great light from heaven suddenly shone about me — RSV

a sudden blaze of light from heaven shone round me — Wey

---

[99]Some translations place this phrase with the following clause.

... a brilliant light from heaven flashed round me — Mof
... an intense light ... beamed ... — Ber

7. And I fell unto the ground,
I dropped to the earth — Mof
And as I fell to the ground — Ber
and heard a voice saying unto me,
Then I heard ... — NEB
... a voice asking me — Beck
Saul, Saul, why persecutest thou me?
Saul! Saul! Why me art thou persecuting — Rhm
... why do you persecute me — RSV

8. And I answered, Who art thou, Lord?
Who are you? I asked — Mof
I answered, Who are you, sir — Gspd
... Tell me, Lord, who you are — NEB
And he said unto me,
Then the voice said — TCNT
he answered me — Mon
So he told me — Ber
I am Jesus of Nazareth, whom thou persecutest.
... the Nazarene, whom thou art persecuting — Rhm

9. And they that were with me saw indeed the light,
The men with me saw the light — TCNT
(My companions ... — Mof
... certainly saw ... — Ber
... naturally saw ... — Phi
... beheld the light, to be sure — NASB
and were afraid;[100]
were alarmed — Nor
but they heard not the voice of him that spake to me.
but did not hear the speaker's voice — TCNT
but the voice of him who spoke to me they did not understand — ABUV

10. And I said,
Then I said — TCNT
And I asked — Wey
What shall I do, Lord?
What am I to do, Lord — TCNT
What must I do, Lord — Knox
... sir — Gspd
And the Lord said unto me,
... answered — Wms
Arise, and go into Damascus;
Get up and go into Damascus — TCNT
Get up and continue your journey to Damascus — NEB
and there it shall be told thee

and there you shall be told — TCNT
and it will be made clear to you — Bas
of all things which are appointed for thee to do.
all that you have been appointed to do — TCNT
about all you are destined to do — Mof
... that has been laid out for you to do — Ber
... that has been assigned to you — Rieu
everything you are ordered to do — Beck

11. And when I could not see for the glory of that light,
But as I could not see clearly owing to ... — Rhm
In consequence of that dazzling light I could not see — TCNT
The glory of that light had blinded me — Knox
Due to the brilliancy of that intense light I was blinded — Ber
That light was so bright I couldn't see anything — Beck
being led by the hand of them that were with me,
but my companions led me by the hand — TCNT
... had to lead me by the hand — Gspd
guided by the hands of my companions — Ber
I came into Damascus.
till I reached Damascus — TCNT
and in this way I reached Damascus — Wms

12. And one Ananias,
There a man named Ananias — TCNT
And a certain Ananias — Wey
There, there was a man called Ananias — Phi
a devout man according to the law,
a strict observer of our Law — TCNT
a man devout in strict observance of the law — Wms
a man who was devout by the standard of the Law — NASB
a pious man who obeyed the Law — Wey
a God-fearing man who kept the law — Bas

---

[100]Now recognized as not adequately supported by original manuscripts.

a man devoted to the Law — Ber
a strict and devout Jew — Rieu

**having a good report of all the Jews
which dwelt there,**

well spoken of by . . . — RSV
who had a good reputation among all
the Jewish inhabitants — Mof
highly respected by . . . — Gspd

13. **Came unto me,**
came to see me — Gspd
called on me — Ber
and stood, and said unto me,
and standing by me said unto me —
ASV
Brother Saul, receive thy sight.
Saul, my Brother, recover your sight
— TCNT
Saul brother! look up — Rhm
. . . look up and see — Knox
. . . you may see again! — Phi
. . . see again! — Beck
And the same hour
And then and there — TCNT
I looked up upon him.
I recovered my sight and looked up at
him — TCNT
I was able to see him — Bas
I received my sight and saw him — ASV
I looked up at him and could see —
Rieu

14. **And he said, The God of our fathers
hath chosen thee,**
. . . hath appointed thee — ASV
. . . You have been marked out by the
God of our fathers — Bas
. . . Our father God has prepared you
before hand — Ber
that thou shouldest know his will,
to know his will — ASV
to get to know his will — Rhm
to learn his will — Gspd
to recognize his will — Ber
to learn what he wants — Beck
to have knowledge of his purpose—Bas
and see that Just One,
and see the Righteous One — ASV
to see his Righteous One — Gspd
**and shouldest hear the voice of his
mouth.**
and to hear words from his lips—TCNT
and hear Him speak — Wey
and to hear his very voice — NEB

15. **For thou shalt be his witness unto all
men**

. . . a witness for him unto all men —
ASV
. . . to all the world — TCNT
of what thou hast seen and heard.
of what you have just seen . . . — TCNT
of all that . . . — Lam

16. **And now why tarriest thou?**
And now why delay — Wey
. . . why do you wait — Mof
. . . why wait any longer — TCNT
Come then, why art thou wasting time
— Knox
Now then, why hesitate — Ber
arise, and be baptized,
. . . get thyself immersed — Rhm
Be baptized at once — TCNT
Get up and be baptized — Mof
and wash away thy sins,
and have thy sins bathed away — Rhm
be cleansed of your sins — Ber
calling on the name of the Lord.
and invoke his name — TCNT
by calling on His name — Wms
giving worship to his name — Bas
as you call on his name — Phi

17. **And it came to pass, that,**
One day — Rieu
when I was come again to Jerusalem,
when I had returned . . . — ASV
even while I prayed in the temple,
and was praying in the temple — Alf
and was at prayer in the temple — Bas
I was in a trance;
I fell into a trance — RSV
I saw a vision — Lam
my senses became more than naturally
clear — Bas
this happened: I experienced an ecstasy
— Ber
unconscious of everything else — Phi

18. **And saw him saying unto me,**
I saw Him and He said to me — Wey
I saw the Lord there speaking to me
— Knox
Make haste,
Hurry — Ber
Quick — Rieu
and get thee quickly out of Jerusalem:
and leave Jerusalem at once — TCNT
. . . with all speed — Knox
Leave Jerusalem as soon as you can —
Rieu
. . . without delay — NEB
**for they will not receive thy testimony
concerning me.**

for they will not accept your evidence about me — Mof

... not accept thy witness ... — Rhm

... not accept evidence about me from you — Rieu

... not accept the truth you tell about me — Beck

19. And I said, Lord,

Lord, I answered — TCNT

... I replied — Wey

But, Lord, I said — Mof

they know

they themselves know — ASV

these people know — TCNT

they surely know — Mof

that is because they know — Rieu

that I imprisoned and beat in every synagogue them that believed on thee:

that I was wont to imprison and beat ... — Alf

that I used to imprison and scourge in Synagogue after Synagogue ... — TCNT

how active I was in imprisoning, and flogging . . . those who believe in thee — Wey

that it was I who imprisoned and flogged . . . throughout the Synagogues — Mof

that I used to go through one synagogue after another, and to imprison and flog those who believed in you — Gspd

that it was I who imprisoned and manhandled . . . — Ber

20. And when the blood of thy martyr Stephen was shed,

... of Stephen thy witness ... — RSV

that when Stephen your witness was put to death — Bas

and because while the blood was streaming from your witness Stephen — Rieu

I also was standing by, and consenting unto his death,

... and approving — RSV

... and well pleased — ABUV

... and was in accord with his slayers — Lam

I was there, giving approval — Bas

and kept the raiment of them that slew him.

and guarding the mantles of . . . — Rhm

and took charge of the clothes of those who were murdering him — TCNT

... of them who stoned him — Lam

— why, I was even holding in my arms the outer garments of those who killed him — Phi

21. And he said unto me,

Depart:

Go — TCNT

Leave — Ber

Go immediately — Rieu

for I will send thee far hence unto the Gentiles.

because I unto nations afar off will send thee — Rhm

because I am to send you out and far away among the heathen — Wms

I mean to send thee on a distant errand to the Gentiles — Knox

... to a people who are not Jews — Beck

22. And they gave him audience unto this word,

Up to this word they listened to him — RSV

Up to this point the people had been listening to Paul — TCNT

Until they heard this last statement the people listened to Paul — Wey

The crowd listened to Paul till he came to the word 'Gentiles' — Rieu

Up to this point they had given him a hearing — NEB

and then lifted up their voices, and said,

but at these words they called out — TCNT

but now with a roar of disapproval they cried out — Wey

But at that they shouted — Mof

... roared out — Mon

Away with such a fellow from the earth: for it is not fit that he should live.

Kill him! A fellow like this ought not to have been allowed to live — TCNT

Kill him and get him out of the world! A creature like that ought not to be allowed to live! — Gspd

... It is a disgrace that he should live — Knox

Wipe him off the face of the earth! Such a man isn't fit to live — Rieu

Down with him! A scoundrel like that is better dead! — NEB

... For he ought not to live — RSV

23. And as they cried out,
... were crying out — Alf
As they were shouting — TCNT
And when they continued their furious shouts — Wey
They kept on yelling — Nor
and cast off their clothes,
and threw off their garments — ASV
tearing off their clothes — TCNT
and tearing their mantles — Rhm
and ripping their clothes — Phi
and shaking their clothes — Alf
and waved their garments — RSV
throwing their clothes into the air — Wey
and throwing their clothes about — Gspd
and threw dust into the air,
and cast dust into the air — ASV
and flinging dust about — Wey
and hurling dust into the air — Phi

24. The chief captain[101] commanded him to be brought into the castle,[102]
... ordered Paul to be taken into the Fort — TCNT
... commanded him to be brought into the barracks — RSV
and bade that he should be examined by scourging;
and directed that he should be examined under the lash — TCNT
and be examined by flogging — Wey
and told them to examine him by flogging — Wms
and questioned under the lash — Rieu
and told his men to get information from Paul by whipping him — Beck
saying that with scourging he should be put to the test — Rhm
that he might know
that he might find out — Rhm
in order to ascertain — Wey
in order to fully know — ABUV
to learn — Mon
to make him tell — Rieu
wherefore they cried so against him.
for what cause they so shouted against him — ASV
the reason for their outcry against him — TCNT
why the people shouted at him in this way — Mof
why they hooted at him that way — Ber

the reason for such an uproar against him — Phi

25. And as they bound him with thongs,
And when they had tied him up with the thongs — ASV
And as they bound him down with the thongs — Alf
But when they had stretched him out with the straps — Rhm
But just as they had tied him up to be scourged — TCNT
Paul said unto the centurion[103] that stood by,
... standing near — TCNT
... who stood over him — Lam
... who was present — Bas
... who was in charge — Knox
Is it lawful for you to scourge a man that is a Roman,
Is it legal for you to scourge a Roman citizen — TCNT
Are you allowed to scourge a Roman citizen — Mof
Can you legally flog a man who is a Roman citizen — Rieu
and uncondemned?
one too who is uncondemned — Wey
and one who is uncondemned at that — Wms
unconvicted — TCNT
and untried at that — Phi
and moreover has not been found guilty — NEB
and has not been sentenced — Knox

26. When the centurion heard that,
On hearing this question — Wey
he went and told the chief captain,[104] saying,
Take heed what thou doest:
What art thou about to do? — ASV
What are you intending to do? — Wey
What do you propose to do? — Gspd
Do you know what you are doing? — TCNT
Do you realize what you were about to do? — Phi
Be careful what you do — Lam
for this man is a Roman.
This man is a Roman citizen — TCNT

---

[101]See Acts 21:31 for translations of "chief captain."
[102]See Acts 21:34 for translations of "castle."
[103]For translations of "centurion" see Acts 21:32.
[104]On "chief captain" see Acts 21:31.

27. Then the chief captain came, and said unto him,
... came to Paul and asked him — Wey
... himself came up to Paul and said — Phi
Tell me, art thou a Roman?
... are you a Roman citizen — RSV
What is this? Thou art a Roman citizen? — Knox
Tell me, are YOU a Roman citizen? — Rieu
He said, Yea.
Yes, replied Paul — TCNT

28. And the chief captain answered,
Whereupon the colonel replied — Phi
the commander muttered — Tay
With a great sum obtained I this freedom.
I bought this citizenship for a large sum — RSV
I had to pay a heavy price for my position as citizen — TCNT
I paid a large sum for this citizenship — Wey
I got Roman rights for myself at a great price — Bas
It cost me a heavy sum to win this privilege — Knox
I am too, ..., and it cost me plenty! — Tay
And Paul said, But I was free born.
I am one by birth, rejoined Paul — TCNT
... But I was born a citizen — ABUV
Yes, but I was born to it — Rieu

29. Then straightway they departed from him which should have examined him:
The men who were to have examined Paul immediately drew back — TCNT
So the men who had been on the point of judicially examining him immediately left him — Wey
Then those who were about to scourge him ... — Mon
... left him alone — Lam
... moved away from him — Wey
... kept their hands off — Ber
... immediately let go of him — NASB
and the chief captain also was afraid,

... was struck with fear — Rhm
... was alarmed — TCNT
... felt worried — Ber
after he knew that he was a Roman,
when he found out ... — Rhm
finding that Paul was a Roman citizen — TCNT
on discovering that ... — Ber
and because he had bound him.
and that he had put him in irons — NEB
especially since he had him bound — Nor

30. On the morrow,
On the next day — TCNT
because he would have known the certainty
desiring to know the certainty — ASV
desiring to know the real reason — RSV
wishing to find out the real reason — TCNT
wishing to know exactly — Wey
determined to discover the truth — Knox
wherefore he was accused of the Jews,
as to why he was being accused by the Jews — Rhm
why Paul was denounced by the Jews — TCNT
of the charge which the Jews had brought against him — Lam
he loosed him from his bands,
... released him — Rhm
... had his chains taken off — TCNT
... had him unchained — Rieu
and commanded the chief priests and all their council to appear,
... to come together — ASV
... to assemble — Alf
he directed the Chief Priests and the whole of the High Council to assemble — TCNT
and brought Paul down,
and took Paul down — TCNT
and he brought Paul down — RSV
and set him before them.
and brought him before them — TCNT
placing him in front of them — Mof
to confront them with him — Knox
to face them — Ber

CHAPTER 23

1. **And Paul, earnestly beholding the council, said,**
   . . . looking steadfastly on the council, said — ASV
   . . . fixing his eyes upon the council, said — Alf
   Then Paul, fixing a steady gaze on the Sanhedrin, said — Wey
   . . . looking intently . . . — ABUV
   Paul looked straight at the council members and said — Nor
   Men and brethren,
   My brothers — Bas
   Fellow Jews — Beck
   I have lived in all good conscience before God until this day.
   I in all good conscience have used my citizenship for God . . . — Rhm
   for my part, I have always ordered my life before God, with a clear conscience, up to this very day — TCNT
   I have lived with a perfectly good conscience before God down to the present day — Mof
   All my life I have behaved myself with full loyalty of conscience towards God — Knox
   I have lived all my life and still live today . . . — NEB
   . . . in the presence of God with an altogether clear conscience — Ber
2. **And the high priest Ananias commanded them that stood by him**
   At this . . . ordered the men standing near — TCNT
   On hearing this . . . ordered those who were standing near Paul — Wey
   . . . ordered the attendants — Ber
   to smite him on the mouth.
   to strike him . . . — RSV
   to give him a blow . . . — Bas
3. **Then said Paul unto him,**
   whereupon Paul turned to him and said — TCNT
   Paul retorted — NEB
   God shall smite thee,
   God is about to be smiting thee — Rhm
   God will strike you — TCNT
   God is going to strike you — NASB
   It's you that God will strike — Rieu
   thou whited wall:
   You whited sepulcher — Mon
   you white-washed wall! — TCNT

you painted pigpen — Tay
O you hypocrite — Lam
you specious fraud — Rieu
for sittest thou to judge me after the law,
. . . according to the law — ASV
Are you sitting there to try me in accordance with law — TCNT
Do you sit as a judge to try me in accordance with law — Wms
How dare you sit there judging me by the Law — Phi
Do you use the Law to sit in judgement on me — Rieu
and commandest me to be smitten contrary to the law?
. . . unlawfully — Rhm
and yet, in defiance of law, order me to be struck — TCNT
and yet contrary to the law you order me to be struck — RSV
and you yourself break the Law by ordering me to be struck! — Wey
and yet in violation of the law you order . . . — Wms
and give orders for me to be struck, which is clean contrary to the Law — Phi
yet abuse the Law by ordering me to be struck — Rieu
4. **And they that stood by said,**
   The people standing near said to Paul — TCNT
   The bystanders said — Mof
   The bystanders objected — Nor
   Here the attendants interposed — Rieu
   Revilest thou God's high priest?
   Do you know that you are insulting God's High Priest — TCNT
   Would you revile God's high priest — RSV
   Do you rail at . . . — Wey
   Do you mean to insult . . . — Gspd
   Do you dare to insult God's High Priest — Phi
   Is that the way to talk to God's High Priest — Tay
5. **Then said Paul,**
   And Paul said — ASV
   Paul answered — Wms
   I wist not, brethren, that he was the high priest:
   I did not know . . . — RSV
   I knew not . . . — ASV

I was not aware . . . — Rhm
I had no idea that . . . — Bas
I could not tell that . . . — Knox

for it is written,
for Scripture says — TCNT
As the Scriptures say — Rieu
Scripture, I know, says — NEB
The Bible does say — Beck

Thou shalt not speak evil of the ruler of thy people.
Of a ruler of thy people shalt thou not speak injuriously — Rhm
You must not speak evil of any ruler of your people.) — Mof
You must not defame a ruler of the people — Ber
You must not abuse . . . — NEB

6. But when Paul perceived
Because Paul knew — Gspd
But when Paul saw — Bas
When Paul realized — Rieu
Now Paul was well aware — NEB

that the one part was Sadducees, and the other Pharisees,
that some of those present were Sadducees and other Pharisees — TCNT
that the Sanhedrin consisted partly of Sadducees and partly of Pharisees — Wey
that there were two factions among them, one of the Sadducees and the other of the Pharisees — Knox

he cried out in the council,
Paul shouted to them — Mof
shouted, right in the Sanhedrin — Ber
raised his voice and said to them — Phi
he began to cry out in the council chamber — Wms

Men and brethren, I am a Pharisee, the son of a Pharisee:
. . . a son of Pharisees — ASV
. . . and the son of Pharisees! — Gspd
. . . and my fathers were Pharisees before me — Knox

of the hope and resurrection of the dead
touching the hope and . . . — ASV
concerning the hope and . . . — Alf
with respect to the hope and . . . — RSV
It is on the question of hope for the dead and of their resurrection — TCNT
It is because of my hope of a resurrection of the dead — Wey

I am called in question.
I am on trial — RSV
that I am on my trial — TCNT
I am here to be questioned — Bas
I am accused — Ber
that I am indicted and being judged — Amp

7. And when he had so said,
As soon as he said this — TCNT
When he said that — Gspd
At this — Ber
At these words — Phi

there arose a dissension
a dispute arose — TCNT
a quarrel broke out — Mof
there was an argument — Bas

between the Pharisees and the Sadducees:
and the multitude was divided.
. . . the meeting . . . — Mof
. . . the court . . . — Wms
. . . the people . . . — Lam
. . . the assembly — RSV
and there was a sharp division of opinion among those present — TCNT
and the assembly took different sides — Wey
. . . was divided into two factions — Amp

8. For the Sadducees say
. . . hold — Gspd
. . . claim — Phi
. . . deny — Rieu

that there is no resurrection,
. . . no rising again — Rhm
. . . no such thing as a resurrection — TCNT
. . . no coming back from the dead — Bas
the possibility of the resurrection — Rieu

neither angel, nor spirit:
nor messenger nor spirit — Rhm
and that there is neither angel, nor spirit — TCNT
and no such thing as an angel or spirit — Wms
and the existence of angels and spirits — Rieu

but the Pharisees confess both.
while the Pharisees believe in them — TCNT
. . . acknowledge them all — Wey
. . . affirm them all — Mof

... confess the one as well as the other — Ber

... declare openly and speak out freely, acknowledging [their faith in] them both — Amp

9. And there arose a great cry:

... a great clamor — ASV

So a great uproar ensued — TCNT

So there was a vociferous yelling — Wms

Loud and confused shouting broke out — Rieu

So a great uproar broke out — NEB

The meeting became very noisy — Nor

and the scribes that were of the Pharisees' part

and some of the scribes of the Pharisees' part — ASV

and some of the teachers of the Law belonging to the Pharisees' party — TCNT

and some of the scribes on the side of the Pharisees — Bas

Some of the Bible scholars ... — Beck

arose, and strove, saying,

stood up and strove, saying — ASV

stood up and hotly protested — TCNT

sprang to their feet and fiercely contended — Wey

got up and insisted — Gspd

rose up and argued, saying — Lam

got up and argued vehemently — Ber

stood up and began to argue heatedly, saying — NASB

came forward to protest — Knox

jumped to their feet and protested violently — Phi

rose to their feet and heatedly joined the fray — Rieu

openly took sides and declared — NEB

stood up and thoroughly fought the case, ... declaring — Amp

We find no evil in this man:

Nothing bad find we in this man — Rhm

We find nothing whatever wrong in this man — TCNT

We find this man not guilty of any crime — Rieu

but if a spirit or an angel hath spoken to him,

And what if a spirit hath spoken to him, or an angel? — ASV

Suppose a spirit did speak to him, or an angel — TCNT

... has really spoken to him! — Wms

let us not fight against God.[105]

10. And when there arose a great dissension,

But when the dissension became violent — Mon

The dissension rose high — Knox

... was mounting — NEB

The dispute was becoming so violent — TCNT

Since the dispute kept getting hotter and hotter — Wms

But the discord grew so bitter — Ber

As the tension mounted — Phi

As the debate became very heated — Nor

The words occasioned such an outcry — Rieu

the chief captain,[106] **fearing lest Paul should have been pulled in pieces of them,**

... should be torn in pieces by them — ASV

commanded the soldiers to go down,

ordered the troops to go down — Rhm

... the troops to march down — Mof

... a detachment to march down — Ber

and to take him by force from among them,

and rescue him from them — TCNT

and get him away from them — Gspd

and take him out of their hands — Wms

and snatch him from their midst — Ber

and to bring him into the castle.[107]

and take him into the Fort — TCNT

and to bring him into the barracks — RSV

and to bring him safe to the soldiers' quarters — Knox

11. And the night following the Lord stood by him, and said,

That night the Lord came and stood by Paul, and said — TCNT

But that same night ... — Wms

Be of good cheer, Paul:

Be of good courage! — Rhm

Take courage — RSV

Courage! — TCNT

Have courage — Rieu

---

[105]Now recognized as not adequately supported by original manuscripts.

[106]On "chief captain" see Acts 21:31.

[107]On "castle" see Acts 21:34.

Keep up your courage — NEB
Paul, be brave — Nor
Be strong — Lam
Be of good heart — Bas
Do not lose heart — Knox
Take heart! — Ber

for as thou hast testified of me in Jerusalem,
You have borne witness for me in Jerusalem — TCNT
For as you have witnessed to my Cause at Jerusalem — NASB
You have witnessed the truth about me in Jerusalem — NEB
For just as you have given a full account of me in Jerusalem — Nor

so must thou bear witness also at Rome.
. . . testify also at Rome — ABUV
and now thou must carry the same witness to Rome — Knox
just so it is necessary for you to testify at Rome — Ber
you must bear witness in the same way in Rome — Rieu

12. And when it was day,
In the morning — TCNT
When day broke — Mof
At daybreak — Ber

certain of the Jews banded together,
. . . combined together — TCNT
. . . came together — Bas
. . . held a conclave — Knox
there were Jews who formed a plot — Ber
the Jews made a plot — RSV

and bound themselves under a curse,
. . . by an oath — RSV
and took an oath — TCNT
and solemnly swore — Wey
taking a solemn oath — Mof
and pledged themselves under an oath — Ber

saying that they would neither eat nor drink till they had killed Paul.
that they would not take food or drink till they had put Paul to death—Bas

13. And they were more than forty which had made this conspiracy.
. . . who this sworn-confederacy had formed — Rhm
There were more than forty in the plot — TCNT
. . . involved in this plot — Gspd

. . . who swore to carry out this plot — Beck
. . . who had sworn this oath — Mon
And more than forty of them took this oath — Bas

14. And they came to the chief priests and elders, and said,
. . . went to the Chief Priests and the Councillors . . . — TCNT
. . . approached . . . — Phi

We have bound ourselves under a great curse,
. . . taken a solemn oath — TCNT
. . . sworn ourselves to liability of a curse — Ber
. . . strictly bound ourselves by an oath — RSV
. . . made a sacred vow — Rieu

that we will eat nothing until we have slain Paul.
to taste nothing until we have killed Paul — ASV
not to touch food . . . — Mof
to eat nothing until . . . — Mon
to let nothing pass our lips . . . — Phi
to take no food till we have put Paul to death — Bas

15. Now therefore ye with the council
Now therefore do ye with the High-council — Rhm
So we want you now, with the consent of the Council — TCNT
Now then, you, in cooperation with the Sanhedrin — Ber
You therefore, along with the council — RSV
We want you, with the Sanhedrin — Rieu
It is now for you, acting with the council — NEB
We therefore ask you, together with the council — Nor

signify to the chief captain[108]
ask . . . — Mon
make it appear unto the captain — Rhm
to suggest to the Commanding Officer — TCNT
must inform . . . — Mof
must now notify . . . — Wms
send word to . . . — Ber
must make it plain to . . . — Phi

[108]On "chief captain" see Acts 21:31.

that he bring him down unto you to morrow,

that he should bring Paul down before you — TCNT

that you want him to bring Paul down to you — Phi

as though ye would enquire something more perfectly concerning him:

as though ye would judge of his case more exactly — ASV

. . . determine his matter more regularly — Alf

as if you meant to get more exact information about him — Beck

as though you intended to go more fully into his case — TCNT

on the pretext of a more thorough examination of his case — Rieu

as if you intended to inquire more minutely about him — Wey

and we, or ever he come near,

. . . before he comes near — ASV

. . . before he comes here — TCNT

Then we, if he comes anywhere near — Ber

are ready to kill him.

will be ready to make away with him — TCNT

are prepared to assassinate him — Wey

will be waiting to put him to death — Bas

shall be standing by ready to kill him — Phi

16. And when Paul's sister's son

However, the son of Paul's sister — TCNT

But Paul's nephew — Wey

Paul's sister had a son who — Knox

heard of their lying in wait,

hearing of the plot — TCNT

heard of the intended attack upon him — Wey

heard about their treacherous ambush — Mof

got wind of the ambush — Ber

learned about this ambush — Nor

he went and entered into the castle, and told Paul.

went to the Fort, and on being admitted, told Paul about it — TCNT

so he came along and entered the barracks to inform Paul — Ber

17. Then Paul called one of the centurions[109] unto him, and said,

. . . one of the Captains of the garrison and asked him — TCNT

Bring this young man unto the chief captain:[110]

This young man lead thou away unto . . . — Rhm

to take the lad to . . . — TCNT

Take this young man to . . . — Wey

Conduct this young man to . . . — Ber

for he hath a certain thing to tell him.

. . . something to tell him — ASV

for he has information to give him — Wey

18. So he took him, and brought him to the chief captain, and said,

The Captain went with the lad to the Commanding Officer, and said — TCNT

So the officer took him to the commander, saying — Mof

So he bade him follow and took him to . . . — Knox

. . . and brought him into the colonel's presence — Phi

Paul the prisoner called me unto him,

The prisoner Paul has summoned me — Mof

. . . made a request to me — Bas

. . . sent for me — NEB

and prayed me to bring this young man unto thee,

and asked me . . . — ASV

and begged me to bring this youth to you — Wey

who hath something to say unto thee.

as having somewhat to tell thee — Rhm

as he has something to tell you — Mof

19. Then the chief captain took him by the hand,

. . . taking him by the arm — Wey

. . . took his hand — Phi

and went with him aside privately, and asked him,

and going aside asked him privately — ASV

. . . began privately to ask — Rhm

and stepping aside where they could be alone . . . — Gspd

stepped to one side with him privately and inquired — Ber

and drew him aside (where they could not be overheard) . . . — Phi

What is that thou hast to tell me?

what it was he had to tell him — TCNT

---

[109]On "centurions" see Acts 21:32.

[110]On "chief captain" see Acts 21:31.

What have you to tell me — Wey

What is it which thou hast to report unto me — Rhm

What is the news you have for me — Mof

20. And he said,

He answered — Wms

And he replied — Phi

The Jews have agreed to desire thee

... to ask thee — ASV

... to request thee — Rhm

... have decided to ask you — Lam

... have planned to ask you — Rieu

that thou wouldest bring down Paul to morrow into the council,

to bring down Paul tomorrow into the council — ASV

to take Paul down before the Sanhedrin tomorrow — Rieu

as though they would enquire somewhat of him more perfectly.

on the plea of your making further inquiry into his case — TCNT

on the plea that they propose to examine his case in detail — Mof

as though you were going to examine his case more carefully — Wms

as though they were desirous to learn something more from him — Lam

as if they meant to examine his cause more precisely — Knox

as though they were going to inquire somewhat more thoroughly about him — RSV

pretending they want a more thorough inquiry — Rieu

on the pretext of obtaining more precise information about him — NEB

21. But do not thou yield unto them:

But do not give way to them — Bas

but do not you give in to them — Ber

You must not listen to them — Lam

Thou therefore do not be persuaded by them — Rhm

But do not let them persuade you — TCNT

I beg you not to comply — Wey

for there lie in wait for him of them more than forty men,

More than forty of them are lying in ambush for him — Mof

some of them will be lying in ambush, more than forty in number — Knox

which have bound themselves with an

oath,[111] **that they will neither eat nor drink**[112]

till they have killed him:

... made away with him — TCNT

... assassinated him — Wey

... murdered him — Mof

... destroyed him — Ber

and now are they ready,

and they are at this very moment in readiness — TCNT

they are all ready at this moment — Mof

and they are all set — Nor

looking for a promise from thee.

awaiting the promise ... — Rhm

counting upon your promise — TCNT

awaiting your consent — Mof

and are only waiting to get your promise — Gspd

all they want now is for you to give the order — Phi

22. So the chief captain then let the young man depart,

The chief captain therefore dismissed the young man — Rhm

So the Tribune sent the youth home — Wey

... sent the youth away — Gspd

and charged him,

cautioning him — TCNT

warning him — Knox

directing him — Gspd

with strict directions — Wms

with the strict advice — Nor

instructing him — NASB

with the injunction — Mon

See thou tell no man

Tell nobody — Mof

Do not let anyone know — Wey

Don't let a soul know — Phi

not to mention to anyone — TCNT

that thou hast shewed these things to me.

that thou hast signified these things to me — ASV

that he had given him that information — TCNT

that you have informed me of this — Mof

that he had notified him of this plot — Wms

---

[111]See verse 14.

[112]See verse 14.

that he had disclosed this information — Rieu

23. And he called unto him two centurions, saying,

Then he called two Captains, and ordered them — TCNT

He summoned two of the officers and said — Mof

. . . and gave them these orders — Rieu

Make ready two hundred soldiers to go to Caesarea,

. . . as far as Caesarea — RSV

to have two hundred men ready to go to Caesarea — TCNT

Get ready two hundred men . . . to march to Caesarea — Wey

Make preparations for 200 heavy infantry . . . to go . . . — Rieu

. . . to proceed to . . . — Phi

and horsemen threescore and ten, and spearmen two hundred,

and seventy horsemen . . . — Rhm

as well as seventy troopers and two hundred lancers — TCNT

. . . cavalry . . . light infantry — Wey

. . . mounted men . . . spearmen — Gspd

. . . cavalrymen . . . light armed troops — NEB

at the third hour of the night;

by nine o'clock that night — TCNT

starting at . . . tonight! — Wey

and have them ready to start at . . . — Beck

They will set out at the third hour of the night — Knox

24. And provide them beasts, that they may set Paul on,

and to have horses ready for Paul to ride — TCNT

He further told them to provide horses to mount Paul on — Wey

and bring him safe unto Felix the governor.

so that they might take him safely to . . . — TCNT

and conduct him safely to governor Felix — Ber

that he may ride through under safe escort to Felix the Governor — NEB

25. And he wrote a letter after this manner:

To him he wrote a letter, somewhat as follows: — TCNT

He also wrote a letter of which these were the contents: — Wey

to whom he sent the following letter — Wms

26. Claudius Lysias unto the most excellent governor Felix sendeth greeting.

Claudius Lysias sends his compliments to his Excellency Felix the Governor — TCNT

Greetings to His Excellency the Governor Felix from Claudius Lysias — Rieu

27. This man was taken of the Jews,

. . . was seized by the Jews — RSV

The man whom I send with this had been seized by the Jews — TCNT

This man, having been apprehended by the Jews — Rhm

When this man was set upon by the Jews — Ber

This man was caught by the Jews — Rieu

and should have been killed of them:

and was about to be slain of them — ASV

and was on the point of being killed by them — TCNT

and was within an inch of being murdered by them — Ber

then came I with an army,

when I came upon them with the soldiers — ASV

. . . came upon them with the force under my command — TCNT

. . . with my troop — Alf

. . . with my regiment — Nor

. . . with my men — Gspd

when I arrived with my troops — Phi

and rescued him,

and took him out of danger — Ber

and removed him — NEB

having understood that he was a Roman.

having learned . . . — RSV

as I learnt that he was a Roman citizen — TCNT

for I had been informed that . . . — Wey

as I had ascertained that . . . — Mof

since I had discovered . . . — Phi

28. And when I would have known

And desiring to know — ASV

And wishing to know — ABUV

Wishing to ascertain exactly — TCNT

Wishing to know with certainty — Wey

Anxious to find out — Mof

And desiring to get at — Bas

602

In the hope of discovering — Ber

the cause wherefore they accused him,

the ground of the charges they made against him — TCNT

the offence of which they were accusing him — Wey

the charge on which they accused him — RSV

the crime for which they were accusing him — ABUV

what charge they made against him — Gspd

the reason for their attack — Bas

I brought him forth into their council:

. . . down into their council — ASV

I took him down into their High-council — Rhm

I brought him before their Council — TCNT

. . . Sanhedrin — Wey

29. **Whom I perceived to be accused of questions of their law,**

whom I found to be accused about questions . . . — ASV

when I found that their charges were connected with questions of their own Law — TCNT

and I discovered that the charges had to do with . . . — Wey

where I found he was accused of matters relating to . . . — Mof

but to have nothing laid to his charge worthy of death or of bonds.

and that there was nothing alleged involving either death or imprisonment — TCNT

and that nothing was said against him which might be a reason for prison or death — Bas

He was not accused of any crime punishable by death or imprisonment — Rieu

but there was none for which he deserved to die or be in chains — Beck

30. **And when it was told me**

And when it was shown to me — ASV

And when it was disclosed — RSV

But when I was informed — Rhm

I was subsequently informed — Rieu

how that the Jews laid wait for the man,

that there would be a plot against the man — ASV

of a plot against the man, which was

about to be put into execution — TCNT

that a plot was being concocted against this man — Ber

that a conspiracy was preparing against the man — Alf

I sent straightway to thee,

I sent him to thee forthwith — ASV

I am sending him to you at once — TCNT

. . . without delay — Phi

and gave commandment to his accusers also

charging his accusers also — ASV

and I have directed . . . — TCNT

giving orders to these who are against him — Bas

At the same time I have notified his accusers — Phi

to say before thee what they had against him.

to speak against him before thee — ASV

to prosecute him before you — TCNT

to state before you the case they have against him — Wey

to present their charges against him before you — Gspd

that they must plead their case before thee — Knox

to bring their case before you — Rieu

Farewell.

31. **Then the soldiers, as it was commanded them, took Paul,**

The soldiers, in accordance with their orders, took charge of Paul — TCNT

. . . according to their instructions . . . — RSV

. . . acting on their orders . . . — Phi

The soldiers took Paul, as instructed — Rieu

and brought him by night to Antipatris.

and escorted him as far as Antipatris that night — Gspd

and, riding through the night, brought him down to Antipatris — Phi

32. **On the morrow they left the horsemen to go with him, and returned to the castle:**

On the next day, leaving the troopers to go on with him, they returned to the Fort — TCNT

The next day the infantry returned to

the barracks, leaving the cavalry to proceed with him — Wey

... leaving the troopers to ride on with him — Mon

... leaving the cavalry to escort him the rest of the way — NEB

33. Who, when they came to Caesarea,

and the others, entering into Caesarea — Rhm

On arriving at Caesarea — TCNT

They went into Caesarea — Phi

and delivered the epistle to the governor,

and delivered the letter . . . — RSV

handed the letter to the Governor — Rieu

presented Paul also before him.

set Paul before him — Rhm

and brought Paul before him — TCNT

and also handed Paul over to him — Mof

and turned Paul over to him, too — Wms

and conducted Paul into his presence — Rieu

34. And when the governor had read the letter,

As soon as Felix had read the letter — TCNT

Felix, after reading the letter — Wey

he asked of what province he was.

he inquired to what province Paul belonged — TCNT

and said, What part of the country do

you come from? — Bas

And when he understood that he was of Cilicia;

When he learned . . . — RSV

... that he came from Cilicia — TCNT

and finding it was Cilicia — Mof

35. I will hear thee, said he,

I will hear thee fully, said he — ASV

I myself will hear thee in full . . . — Rhm

he said: I will hear all you have to say — TCNT

... hear your case — Mon

... will give you a full hearing — Nor

when thine accusers are also come.

as soon as your accusers have arrived — TCNT

when the prosecution arrives — Rieu

when thy accusers, too, are present — Knox

And he commanded him to be kept

and he ordered him to be kept in custody — Mon

And he commanded him to be guarded — RSV

and gave orders that . . . he should be kept under guard — Rhm

... that he should be kept safe — Knox

in Herod's judgment hall.

in Herod's Government House — TCNT

in the praetorium of Herod — ABUV

at his headquarters in Herod's palace — NEB

CHAPTER 24

1. And after five days

Five days afterwards — TCNT

Five days later — Mof

Ananias the high priest descended with the elders,

the high priest Ananias came down with certain elders — ASV

the High Priest Ananias came down with some of the Councillors — TCNT

. . . came down to Caesarea with a number of Elders — Wey

... with a group of Elders — Rieu

and with a certain orator named Tertullus,

... a barrister named Tertullus — TCNT

... a pleader called . . . — Wey

... an attorney named . . . — Gspd

... a prosecuting attorney . . . — Wms

... an advocate . . . — Knox

... a spokesman . . . — RSV

who informed the governor against Paul.

and they made a statement to Felix against Paul — Bas

who made a complaint against Paul before Felix — Nor

to present their evidence against Paul to the governor — Ber

They stated to the Governor the case against Paul — Wey

2. And when he was called forth,

So Paul was sent for — Wey

... was summoned — Mof

When Paul had been called — Wms

Tertullus began to accuse him, saying,

and then Tertullus proceeded to accuse him — Mof

... began to impeach him as follows: — Wey
... began his indictment thus — Knox
... began his charge by saying — Nor
... began his speech for the prosecution — TCNT

Seeing that by thee we enjoy great quietness,
... much peace — ASV
Seeing that great peace we are obtaining through thee — Rhm
since through your efforts we enjoy perfect peace — Gspd
Because by you we are living in peace — Bas
It is through you that we enjoy perfect tranquility — Lam

and that very worthy deeds are done unto this nation by thy providence,
and that by thy providence evils are corrected for this nation — ASV
and through your wisdom wrongs are put right for this nation — Bas
and that reforms are being brought about for this nation through thy forethought — Rhm
and we owe it to your foresight that this nation is constantly securing reforms — TCNT
and as it is owing to your wise care that the state of this nation has been improved — Mof
and that through your foresight wonderful improvements have been the nation's fortune — Ber
and we know that it is due to your foresight that the nation enjoys improved conditions of living — Phi

3. **We accept it always, and in all places, most noble Felix, with all thankfulness.**
And we all, everywhere, receive your favors, O most excellent Felix — Lam
In all things and in all places we are conscious of our great debt to you ... — Bas
Your Excellency Felix, we are humbly grateful, now and always — Rieu

4. **Notwithstanding, that I be not further tedious unto thee,**
But — not to be tedious — TCNT
But not to weary you too much — Mon

But while I desire not to weary you with lengthy discussions — Lam
But I must not weary thee with more of this — Knox
But, that I may not weary you any further — NASB
But lest I too long detain thee — Rhm
I will not detain you unnecessarily — Rieu
However, not to take more of your precious time — Ber
Not to keep you too long — Beck

I pray thee
I entreat thee — ASV
I beseech thee — Rhm
I beg you — TCNT
I make a request to you — Bas
I simply want to ask you — Nor

that thou wouldest hear us of thy clemency a few words.
to hear us concisely in thy considerateness — Rhm
with your accustomed fairness, to listen to a brief statement of our case — TCNT
to grant us in your courtesy a brief hearing — Mof
to be kind enough to give us a brief hearing — Gspd
to listen to a few words from us—Mon
to hear in brief our humble complaint — Lam
in your kindness to hear us briefly — RSV
to listen, with your usual courtesy, while we briefly set forth the facts — Rieu

5. **For we have found this man a pestilent fellow,**
... a pest — Rhm
... a public pest — TCNT
The fact is, we have found this man is a perfect pest — Mof
... a source of mischief — Wey
... to be a veritable plague — Ber

and a mover of sedition among all the Jews throughout the world,
and a mover of insurrection ... — ASV
he stirs up sedition among the Jews all over the world — Mof
an inciter of insurrection among all the Jews of the empire — Mon
an organizer of insurrection among all the Jews in the whole world — Nor
and a disturber of the peace among all

the Jews throughout the empire —
Wey

he is one who stirs up disputes among
the Jews all the world over — TCNT

a fomenter of discord among . . . —
NEB

. . . who are scattered throughout the
world — Alf

**and a ringleader of the sect of the
Nazarenes:**

and the chief mover in the society of
the Nazarenes — Bas

. . . the Nazarene heretics — TCNT

. . . heresy of the Nazarenes — Mon

**6. Who also hath gone about to profane
the temple:**

who moreover assayed to profane the
temple — ASV

who also attempted to desecrate even
the temple — Rhm

He actually tried to desecrate . . . —
Mof

who, in addition, was attempting to
make the Temple unclean — Bas

whom we took,

on whom we also laid hold — ASV

whom we also seized — Rhm

but we caught him — TCNT

We of course arrested him — Rieu

**and would have judged according to
our law.**

and intended to try him according to
our own law — Knox

and would have sentenced him by our
Law — Ber

We wanted to try him by our own Law
— Rieu

**7. But the chief captain Lysias came upon
us, and with great violence took him
away out of our hands,**

. . . and by force took him . . . — Lam

. . . came on the scene and, with considerable violence . . . — Rieu

**8. Commanding his accusers to come
unto thee:**

and insisted that his accusers must appear before thee — Knox

and told the prosecution to bring their
case to you — Rieu

by examining of whom thyself

by examining him thyself — ASV

. . . on all these points — TCNT

Examine him for yourself — Mof

Interrogate him thyself — Knox

If you will personally cross-question
him — Ber

You will be able to question him —
Rieu

**mayest take knowledge of all these
things, whereof we accuse him.**

thou wilt be able . . . — ASV

. . . to ascertain the things of which we
are accusing him — Rhm

. . . to satisfy yourself as to the charges
which we are bringing against him —
TCNT

. . . to find out about all these charges
of ours against him — Mof

. . . to learn the truth as to all this we
allege against him — Wey

and verify the truth of all our charges
— Rieu

9. And the Jews also assented,

. . . joined in the charge — ASV

. . . joined in the attack — Rhm

. . . agreed — ABUV

. . . witnessed against him — Lam

. . . supported these accusations—Rieu

While Tertullus was speaking the Jews
kept joining in — Phi

saying that these things were so.

maintaining that these were the facts —
Wey

affirming that all this was so — RSV

declaring that such were the facts of
the case — Mof

and declared that all he said was exactly so — Ber

and bore out his statements — TCNT

declaring that these accusations were
true — Nor

**10. Then Paul, after that the governor had
beckoned unto him to speak, answered,**

And Paul answered, when the governor
had motioned him to be speaking —
Rhm

On a sign from the Governor, Paul
made his reply — TCNT

**Forasmuch as I know that thou hast
been of many years a judge unto
this nation,**

Well knowing thee to have been for
many years judge unto this nation —
Rhm

Knowing, as I do, for how many years
you have acted as Judge to this nation — TCNT

. . . have administered justice to this
nation — Wey

... in this province — NEB

I do the more cheerfully answer for myself:

I cheerfully make my defence — RSV

it is with confidence that I undertake my own defence — TCNT

I feel encouraged to make my defence — Mof

I find it easier to defend myself on these charges — Ber

11. Because that thou mayest understand,

seeing that thou art able to ascertain — Rhm

For you can easily ascertain — TCNT

... find out — Nor

as you can easily satisfy yourself — Gspd

for you can verify the fact — Wms

that there are yet but twelve days

that it is not more than twelve days — ASV

since I went up to Jerusalem for to worship.

from the time I came to Jerusalem to worship — Bas

since I went on a pilgrimage to Jerusalem — Rieu

12. And they neither found me

And they have not seen me — Bas

I was never found — Phi

in the temple disputing with any man,

... disputing with any opponent — Wey

debating with anyone in the Temple — Gspd

... holding discussions with any one — TCNT

neither raising up the people,

or stirring up a crowd — RSV

neither raising up the multitude — Alf

or causing a crowd to collect — TCNT

or creating a disturbance among the people — Gspd

or causing a riot — Mof

neither in the synagogues, nor in the city:

either in the synagogues or throughout the city — Rhm

— either in the Temple, or in the Synagogues, or about the city — TCNT

either in the synagogues or in the open air — Phi

13. Neither can they prove the things whereof they now accuse me.

They cannot furnish you with any proof of their present charges against me — Mof

and they are not able to give facts in support of the things they say against me now — Bas

And they cannot sustain the charges which they just made ... — Gspd

And they cannot establish the charges which they are now making against me — TCNT

Neither can they produce any evidence to substantiate these present charges — Ber

14. But this I confess unto thee,

This, however, I do acknowledge to you — TCNT

I certainly admit to you — Mof

I will say openly to you — Bas

I will freely admit to you, however — Phi

However, I admit this much — Rieu

that after the way which they call heresy,

that after the Way which they call a sect — ASV

that ... I follow the way of life that they call a sect — Gspd

that ... I follow what we call the way, and they call a sect — Knox

that it is as a believer of the Cause which they call heretical — TCNT

that in the way which they style a heresy — Wey

that ... after that Way, which to them is not the true religion — Bas

so worship I the God of my fathers,

so serve I the God of our fathers — ASV

so am I rendering divine service unto my fathers' God — Rhm

that I worship the God of my ancestors — TCNT

I continue to worship the God of my forefathers — Wms

believing all things which are written in the law and in the prophets:

believing all things which are according to the law, and which are written in the prophets — ASV

At the same time, I believe everything that is in accordance with ... —TCNT

believing everything that is taught in the Law or written ... — Wey

although in fact I believe in the scriptural authority of both the Law and the Prophets — Phi

15. And have hope toward God, which they themselves also allow,

having hope toward God, which they themselves also look for — ASV

and I have a hope that rests in God — a hope which they also cherish — TCNT

and in reliance on God I hold the hope which my accusers too accept — NEB

and trust God for the same thing they're looking for — Beck

that there shall be a resurrection of the dead, both of the just and unjust.

that a resurrection there shall certainly be both of righteous and unrighteous — Rhm

that there will one day be a resurrection of good and bad alike — TCNT

the hope that God will grant a resurrection to the good and the wicked alike — Rieu

16. And herein do I exercise myself,

This being so, I strive at all times — TCNT

This, too, is my own earnest endeavour — Wey

So I always take pains — RSV

In this I myself also take pains — ABUV

Hence I too endeavour — Mof

For this reason I labor — Lam

And in this I do my best — Bas

I therefore exert myself — Ber

With this hope before me I do my utmost — Phi

Accordingly, I, no less than they, train myself — NEB

to have always a conscience void of offence toward God, and toward men.

to have an unoffending conscience towards God and men, continually — Rhm

to keep my conscience clear before both God and man — TCNT

at all times to have no reason for shame before God or man — Bas

to have in all respects a clear conscience in my relations with God and with men — Ber

to live my whole life with a clear conscience . . . — Phi

to maintain always a blameless conscience . . . — NASB

17. Now after many years

Now after some years — RSV

Now after several years' absence — Wey

I came to bring alms to my nation, and offerings.

intending to do alms unto my nation I arrived, — also [to present] offerings — Rhm

I had come to bring charitable gifts . . ., and to make offerings — TCNT

. . . to bring a sum of money to my countrymen, and offer sacrifices — Wey

I came up with alms and offerings for my nation — Mof

I came to give help and offerings to my nation — Bas

18. Whereupon

amidst which — ASV

and it was while engaged in this — TCNT

While I was busy about these — Wey

While I was performing these duties — Wms

It was when I had just made these offerings — Knox

certain Jews from Asia found me purified in the temple,

that they found me in the Temple, after completing a period of purification — TCNT

they found me just as I had completed my rites of purification in the temple — Wms

neither with multitude, nor with tumult.

with no crowd, nor yet with tumult — ASV

but not with any crowd or disorder — TCNT

with no crowd about me and no uproar — Wey

I was not mixed up in any mob or riot — Mof

however, there was no crowd with me and no disturbance at all — Wms

19. Who ought to have been here before thee,

who should in my opinion have come before you — Phi

There were, however, some Jews from Roman Asia who ought to have been here before you — TCNT it is they who ought to have been in court — NEB

But some Jews from Asia—they ought to be here before you — RSV

and object,

and to make accusation — ASV

and to accuse me — Alf

and to have made any charge — TCNT

and to have been my prosecutors — Wey

if they had ought against me.

that they may have against me — TCNT

if they had any quarrel with me — Knox

if they knew anything tangible against me — Ber

20. Or else let these same here say,

Or else let these men themselves say — RSV

— or else let my opponents here say — TCNT

As they are not here, let these who are say — Rieu

if they have found any evil doing in me,

what wrong-doing they found — ASV

what misdemeanor they found me guilty of — Wey

what crime . . . — ABUV

what fault . . . — Mof

what misdeed . . . — NASB

when I stood before the council,

when I was before the Council — TCNT

. . . the Sanhedrin — Wey

when I was brought before the Council — NEB

21. Except it be for this one voice, that I cried standing among them,

except as to the one sentence that I shouted out as I stood among them — TCNT

Unless it was that one expression of which I made use when I shouted out as I stood among them — Wey

. . . one remark . . . — Ber

Yes, there was one thing they resented, for I cried out — Nor

Touching the resurrection of the dead I am called in question by you this day.

Concerning the raising of the dead am I to be judged this day by you — Rhm

It is about the resurrection of the dead

that I am on my trial before you to-day — TCNT

I am this day being judged on the question of the coming back from the dead — Bas

I am on trial before you today because I believe in . . . — Rieu

The true issue in my trial before you today is . . . — NEB

In regard to the resurrection of the dead I am indicted and on trial before you this day! — Amp

22. And when Felix heard these things,[113]

At this point Felix — Wey

having more perfect knowledge of that way,

having more exact knowledge concerning the Way — ASV

— though he had a fairly accurate knowledge of all that concerned the Cause — TCNT

who was fairly well informed about the new faith — Wey

who had a fairly clear conception of the principles involved in the Way — Wms

who had full information about this way — Knox

who was better acquainted with the Way than most people — Phi

who knew the Christian religion rather well — Beck

he deferred them, and said,

adjourned the case . . . with the promise — TCNT

. . . adjourned the trial, saying to the Jews — Wey

. . . adjourned the hearing, saying — Rieu

put them off . . . saying to the Jews — ABUV

he remanded Paul, telling the Jews — Mof

postponed the case, saying — Nor

When Lysias the chief captain[114] shall come down,

As soon as . . . — Rhm

. . . arrives — Phi

I will know the uttermost of your matter.

I will decide your case — RSV

---

[113]The words "heard these things" are now recognized as not adequately supported by original manuscripts.

[114]On "chief captain" see Acts 21:31.

I will determine your matter — ASV

... adjudge your matter — Alf

... give my decision in your case — TCNT

... go carefully into the matter — Mon

... diagnose your case more thoroughly — Ber

... try your case — Rieu

... finish the examination of your case — Nor

23. And he commanded a centurion to keep Paul,

And he gave order to the centurion that he should be kept in charge — ASV

So he gave orders to the Captain in charge of Paul to keep him in custody — TCNT

... that Paul was to be kept safely — Knox

... to keep Paul under open arrest NEB

... to guard him — Beck

and to let him have liberty,

and have a measure of liberty — Rhm

but to relax the regulations — TCNT

but should have some liberty — RSV

but to allow him some freedom — Mof

but left at his ease — Knox

but with relaxed rigor — Ber

but to grant him reasonable liberty — Phi

and that he should forbid none of his acquaintance to minister or come to him.

and not to forbid any of his friends to minister unto him — ASV

and not to prevent any of his personal friends from attending to his wants — TCNT

... from showing him kindness — Wey

... from looking after him — Gspd

and not to keep his friends from coming to see him — Bas

and none of his loved ones should be discouraged from rendering aid — Ber

... from seeing and helping him — Nor

24. And after certain days,

Some days later — TCNT

Not long after this — Wey

when Felix came with his wife Drusilla, which was a Jewess,

Felix brought along his wife Drusilla, a Jewess — Ber

Felix came again. His wife Drusilla, who was a Jew, was with him — Beck

he sent for Paul, and heard him concerning the faith in Christ.

and sending for Paul, listened to what he had to say about faith in Christ Jesus — TCNT

summoned Paul and listened to his exposition of the Faith in Christ — Rieu

25. And as he reasoned of righteousness,

But while Paul was speaking at length about righteousness — TCNT

... about justice — Wey

And as he argued about justice — RSV

But when he argued about morality — Mof

But as he talked of uprightness — Gspd

But when he discussed purity of life — Ber

But while Paul was talking about goodness — Phi

... the good life — Rieu

But when the discourse turned to questions of morals — NEB

temperance,

self control — ASV

continence — Knox

the mastery of passions — Ber

self-mastery — Mof

and judgment to come,

and the judgment to come — ASV

and the coming judgment — TCNT

and the future judgment — Wey

Felix trembled, and answered,

Felix was terrified, and answered — ASV

... was afraid ... — Alf

... became terrified, and interrupted him — TCNT

... became alarmed and exclaimed — NEB

Go thy way for this time;

For the present be going thy way — Rhm

... leave me — Wey

You may go for the present — Mof

For the time being you can go — Rieu

That will do for the present — NEB

when I have a convenient season,

and when I find an opportunity — Rhm

when I can find a moment — Mof

when I can find leisure — Knox

When I can spare the time — Ber

and when the right time comes — Bas

when it will be convenient for me — Nor

When I get a chance — Beck

I will call for thee.

I will send for thee — Rhm

I will summon you — RSV

26. He hoped also that money should have been given him of Paul,

at the same time also hoping that money would be given him by Paul — Rhm

At the same time he nursed a secret hope that Paul would pay him money — Phi

He was hoping, too, for a bribe from Paul — TCNT

that he might loose him:[115]

wherefore he sent for him the oftener,

and so he used to send for him frequently — TCNT

and for that reason he used to send for him very often — Gspd

and so he kept sending for him — Wms

and communed with him.

he used to converse with him — Rhm

and talk with him — TCNT

and courted his company — Knox

and talked things over with him — Ber

and talk privately with him, quite often — Rieu

27. But after two years

But when two years had elapsed — Mof

But at the close of two years — Wms

Porcius Festus came into Felix' room:

Felix was succeeded by Porcius Festus — RSV

another governor succeeded him, whose name was . . . — Lam

Porcius Festus took the place of Felix — Bas

and Felix, willing to shew the Jews a pleasure,

and desiring to gain favor with the Jews, Felix — ASV

. . . to gain popularity . . . — TCNT

and being desirous of gratifying the Jews, Felix — Wey

and as Felix wanted to ingratiate himself with . . . — Mof

and because he wished to curry favor with . . . — Mon

And Felix, to do the Jews a favor — Lam

left Paul bound.

he left Paul a prisoner — TCNT

. . . in custody — Mof

kept Paul in chains — Bas

CHAPTER 25

1. Now when Festus was come into the province, after three days he ascended from Caesarea to Jerusalem.

Three days after Festus had entered upon his Province, he left Caesarea and went up to Jerusalem — TCNT

Festus, having entered on his duties as governor of the province, three days later went up from Caesarea to Jerusalem — Wey

Three days after entering upon his provincial office, Festus went up from Caesarea to Jerusalem — Ber

2. Then the high priest and the chief men of the Jews

. . . leading men among the Jews — TCNT

. . . Jewish leaders — Mof

. . . Jewish elders — Wms

. . . most prominent Jews — Ber

. . . principal men of the Jews — RSV

informed him against Paul,

laid information before him against Paul — Rhm

informed him of the case against Paul — Phi

presented their charges against Paul — Gspd

appeared before him against Paul — Ber

and besought him,

and began to beseech him — Rhm

3. And desired favour against him,

asking for themselves a favour against him — Rhm

and asked a favour of him, to Paul's injury — TCNT

asking it as a favour, to Paul's prejudice — Wey

requesting a concession against Paul — NASB

that he would send for him to Jerusalem,

— to have Paul brought to Jerusalem — TCNT

to order Paul to come to Jerusalem — Gspd

laying wait in the way to kill him.

---

[115]Now recognized as not adequately supported by original manuscripts.

laying a plot to kill him on the way — ASV

making an ambush to kill him on the way — Rhm

All the while they were plotting to make away with him on the road — TCNT

They meant to lay in wait for him and kill him on the way — Mon

4. But Festus answered,

To which Festus replied — Ber

that Paul should be kept at Caesarea,

that Paul was in prison in Caesarea — TCNT

... would be kept in Caesarea — Beck

... was in safe keeping at Caesarea — Knox

that Paul was under guard ... — Ber

and that he himself would depart shortly thither.

... was going there very soon — Wey

... planned to leave for there soon — Amp

... meant to leave for Caesarea before long — Mof

... intended to go there shortly — RSV

5. Let them therefore, said he, which among you are able,

Let them therefore, saith he, that are of power among you — ASV

They therefore among you (saith he) who are in power — Rhm

... the men of weight among you — Alf

So let the influential men among you, he said — TCNT

Let those then, he said, who are in authority among you — Mon

I suggest that your leaders — Rieu

go down with me,

go there with me — NASB

accompany me — Rieu

and accuse this man, if there be any wickedness in him.

and if there be anything amiss in the man, let them accuse him — ASV

... charge him formally with it — TCNT

and charge him with whatever crime he has committed — Mof

and if he has done anything wrong prosecute him there — Rieu

6. And when he had tarried among them more than ten days,

After spending among them not more than eight or ten days — Rhm

After staying only eight or ten days there — Gspd

he went down unto Caesarea;

and the next day

and on the morrow — ASV

On the day after his arrival — Phi

sitting on the judgment seat

taking his place on the judgment seat — Rhm

he took his seat on the bench — TCNT

after taking his seat on the judge's bench — Wms

commanded Paul to be brought.

ordered ... — RSV

... to be brought before him — TCNT

... brought in — Wey

... brought up — NEB

and sent for Paul — Bas

7. And when he was come,

On Paul's appearance — TCNT

When he was brought in — Rieu

As soon as he arrived — Phi

the Jews which came down from Jerusalem stood round about,

the Jews who had come ... surrounded him — TCNT

... came round him — Bas

... collected round him — Ber

... stood up on all sides of him — Phi

and laid many and grievous complaints against Paul,

bringing against him many and grievous charges — ASV

and made many serious charges — TCNT

and presented their charges — numerous and weighty — Ber

and made a variety of serious charges — Rieu

and made all sorts of serious statements against him — Bas

... many grave accusations — Knox

which they could not prove.

which they failed to establish — TCNT

... were unable to substantiate — Wey

which they were not able to prove — Rhm

which were not supported by the facts — Bas

8. While he answered for himself,

While Paul said in his defense — ASV

Paul, in his defense, maintained — Phi

Paul's answer to the charge was — TCNT

In reply, Paul said — Wey

Paul's plea was: — NEB

Neither against the law of the Jews, neither against the temple, nor yet against Caesar, have I offended any thing at all.

. . . have I sinned at all — ASV

I have not committed any offense against the Jewish Law, or the Temple, or the Emperor — TCNT

I have committed no crime against the Law of the Jews, against the Temple, or against Caesar — Mon

9. But Festus, willing to do the Jews a pleasure,[116]

But Festus, because he was willing to do the Jews a favor — Lam

Festus, as he wished to gain popularity with the Jews — TCNT

But Festus, wishing to gain the goodwill of the Jews — Phi

Then Festus, in hope of winning the favor of the Jews — Nor

answered Paul, and said,

interrupted Paul with the question — TCNT

turned to Paul and asked — Rieu

Wilt thou go up to Jerusalem,

Art thou willing . . . — Rhm

Art thou ready . . . — Knox

Do you wish to . . . — RSV

Are you prepared to . . . — Phi

Do you want to . . . — Beck

and there be judged of these things before me?

and there concerning these things be judged of me — Rhm

and be tried on these charges before me there — TCNT

and there be put on trial [before the Jewish Sanhedrin] in my presence concerning these charges — Amp

10. Then said Paul, I stand at Caesar's judgment seat,

But Paul said, I am standing before . . . — RSV

No, replied Paul, I am standing at the Emperor's Bar — TCNT

. . . before the emperor's court — Gspd

. . . before the seat of Caesar's authority — Bas

I take my stand at Caesar's tribunal — Ber

where I ought to be judged:

where alone I ought to be tried — Wey

where I have a right to be tried — Knox

where I must be tried — Ber

and that is where I should be judged — Phi

to the Jews have I done no wrong,

I have not wronged the Jews — TCNT

I have done the Jews no injury of any sort — Wey

For I have committed no offense against the Jews — Rieu

Against the Jews I have committed no crime — NEB

as thou very well knowest.

as you yourself are well aware — TCNT

as you indeed know well enough — Wey

— you know that perfectly well — Mof

as you can easily see — Gspd

as you know better [than your question implies] — Amp

11. For if I be an offender,

If then I am a wrong-doer — ASV

If, however, I am breaking the law — TCNT

It comes to this: if I were a criminal — Phi

or have committed any thing worthy of death,

and have committed any offense deserving death — TCNT

and have done anything that deserves death — Gspd

and have done anything for which I ought to die — Mon

and had committed some crime which deserves the death penalty — Phi

. . . deserves the death sentence — Rieu

I refuse not to die:

I should not refuse to die — Lam

I am ready for death — Bas

I do not ask to escape the penalty — TCNT

I do not ask for a reprieve — Knox

I do not seek to escape death — RSV

I do not ask to escape the death penalty — NEB

I excuse not myself from dying — Rhm

I do not object to die — Mof

I would not appeal against it — Rieu

I am not begging to keep from dying — Wms

but if there be none of these things

but if none of these things is true — ASV

---

[116]On "willing to do the Jews a pleasure" see Acts 24:27.

But if there is no truth — Wey

But as in fact there is no truth — Phi

whereof these accuse me,

in the accusations of these people — TCNT

in what these men allege against me — Wey

in any of their charges against me — Mof

no man may deliver me unto them.

no man can give me up unto them — ASV

no man hath power to give me unto them as a favour — Rhm

no one can give me up to them — RSV

no man may deliver me to them just to please them — Lam

no man has the right to make them a present of my life — Knox

No one shall sacrifice me to gain their favour — Rieu

it is not open to anyone to hand me over as a sop to them — NEB

I will let no man turn me over to them — Nor

I appeal unto Caesar.

I appeal to the Emperor — TCNT

Let my cause come before Caesar — Bas

I make my appeal to Caesar — Ber

12. Then Festus, when he had conferred with the council,

Upon that, Festus, after conferring with his Council — TCNT

. . . having consulted with his council — ABUV

. . . after a conference with his advisors — Phi

. . . having conversed with the council — Rhm

answered,

decreed — Lam

pronounced — Rieu

replied to Paul — Phi

Hast thou appealed unto Caesar? unto Caesar shalt thou go.

You have appealed to the Emperor; to the Emperor you shall go — TCNT

You have said, Let my case come before Caesar; to Caesar you will go — Bas

You have appealed to Caesar; to Caesar you shall go — RSV

13. And after certain days

Some days later — TCNT

A short time after this — Wey

Now when several days had elapsed — NASB

king Agrippa and Bernice came unto Caesarea

Agrippa the king and Bernice arrived at Caesarea — ASV

to salute Festus.

and paid a visit of congratulation to Festus — TCNT

to pay a complimentary visit to Festus — Wey

as a greeting to Festus — ABUV

to pay their respects to Festus — Mof

on a state visit to Festus — Gspd

to pay official respects to Festus — Wms

to greet Festus — Lam

to bid Festus welcome — Ber

14. And when they had been there many days,

And as they tarried there many days — ASV

And as they were spending more days there — Rhm

and, as they were staying there for several days — TCNT

and, during their rather lengthy stay — Wey

And when they had been with him several days — Lam

They prolonged their stay for some days — Phi

Festus declared Paul's cause unto the king,

Festus laid Paul's case before the king . . . — RSV

Festus acquainted the king with Paul's situation — Ber

and this gave Festus opportunity of laying Paul's case before the king — Phi

and Festus referred Paul's case to the king — Rieu

saying, There is a certain man

There is a man here, he said — Gspd

I have a man here, he said — Phi

left in bonds by Felix:

left a prisoner by Felix — ASV

who was left in prison by Felix — Mof

left in custody by Felix — NEB

15. About whom, when I was at Jerusalem, the chief priests and the elders of the Jews informed me,[117]

---

[117]On "informed me" see Acts 24:1 and 25:2.

and when I went to Jerusalem the chief priests and elders of the Jews denounced him to me — Knox

... made allegations against him—Phi

desiring to have judgment against him.

demanding judgement against him — TCNT

and continued to ask for a judgment against him — Wms

asking for sentence against him — ASV

begging that sentence might be pronounced against him — Wey

claiming against him condemnation — Rhm

and demanded his condemnation — Mof

and asked me to condemn him — Beck

and asked for his conviction — Gspd

and asked me to pronounce him guilty Rieu

16. To whom I answered,

My answer to them was — TCNT

It is not the manner of the Romans

that it is not the custom of the Romans — ASV

the practice of Romans — TCNT

that with Romans it is not customary — Ber

to deliver any man to die,

to give up any man — ASV

to grant as a favour any man — Rhm

to give up any man to the accusers — TCNT

... for punishment — Wey

... to be slain — Lam

to pronounce a condemnation — Knox

to hand a man over gratuitously — Ber

to hand over an accused man — Rieu

before that he which is accused have the accusers face to face,

till the accused had met them face to face — TCNT

until his accusers come and accuse him face to face — Lam

until he has been face to face with those who are attacking him — Bas

until the accused man has been confronted with his accusers — Knox

and have licence to answer for himself

and have had opportunity to make his defence — ASV

... an opportunity of answering — TCNT

and give him a chance to defend himself — Lam

concerning the crime laid against him.

concerning the charge — RSV

... the accusations — Gspd

17. Therefore, when they were come hither,

When therefore they were come together here — ASV

So they met here — TCNT

So they foregathered here — Rieu

And so after they had assembled here — NASB

When, therefore, a number of them came here — Wey

without any delay on the morrow I sat on the judgment seat,[118]

I made no delay ... — RSV

and without loss of time I took my seat on the Bench the very next day — TCNT

I lost no time to occupy the judgment seat — Ber

and without delay, in fact on the next day, I took my place on the bench — Rieu

and commanded the man to be brought forth.

and ordered the man to be brought before me — TCNT

18. Against whom when the accusers stood up,

But, when his accusers came forward — TCNT

and standing up around him — ABUV

But when the case for the prosecution was opened — Rieu

they brought none accusation of such things

they brought no charge of such evil things — ASV

they brought no charge of wrong-doing — TCNT

they did not charge him with misdemeanours — Wey

they said nothing about such crimes — Bas

as I supposed:

which I had been suspecting — Rhm

such as I had expected — TCNT

as I had in mind — Bas

as I had anticipated — Phi

19. But had certain questions against him of their own superstition,

... their own religion — ASV

---

[118]On "judgment seat" see verse 6.

I found that there were certain questions in dispute between them about their own religion — TCNT

But they quarrelled with him about certain matters connected with their own religion — Wey

They merely had a quarrel with him about . . . — Wms

their controversies with him were concerned with scruples of their own — Knox

Rather, their dispute with him was in regard to their system of religion — Nor

But they had certain grievances against him relative to their own worship — Lam

and of one Jesus, which was dead,

and concerning one Jesus, who had died — Rhm

and about some dead man called Jesus — TCNT

and about someone called Jesus, a dead man — NEB

whom Paul affirmed to be alive.

whom Paul declared to be alive—TCNT

but, so Paul maintained, is now alive — Wey

Paul said he was alive — Mof

but whom Paul affirmed over and over was alive — Mon

but whom Paul claimed to be still alive — Phi

whom Paul alleged to be alive — NEB

20. And because I doubted of such manner of questions,

And I, being perplexed how to investigate concerning these things — ASV

And I being at a loss as to the inquiry into these things — Rhm

I was at a loss how to investigate such questions — Wey

And because I was not well acquainted with their controversy — Lam

And as I had not enough knowledge for the discussion of these things — Bas

As I felt uncertain about the proper investigation of such issues — Ber

Finding myself out of my depth in such discussions — NEB

I asked him whether he would go to Jerusalem,

I asked Paul if he were willing to go up to Jerusalem — TCNT

. . . if he would like to . . . — Gspd

I made the suggestion to him to go . . . — Bas

and there be judged of these matters.

and there be put upon his trial — TCNT

and there stand his trial on these matters — Wey

and be tried there on these charges — Mof

. . . on these issues — NEB

. . . on these complaints — Ber

21. But when Paul had appealed

Paul, however, appealed — TCNT

But Paul entered an appeal — Mof

to be reserved unto the hearing of Augustus,

to have his case reserved for the consideration of his August Majesty — TCNT

that his case be retained for examination by Augustus — Ber

for his case to be reserved for the decision of the emperor — Mof

to have his case reviewed for the decision of the Emperor — Mon

to be remanded in custody for His Imperial Majesty's decision — NEB

I commanded him to be kept

I ordered him to be kept — Rhm

. . . to be detained in custody — TCNT

. . . to remain in custody — Rieu

. . . to be held — Ber

. . . that he should be kept safe—Knox

till I might send him to Caesar.

until I could send him up unto Caesar — Rhm

22. Then Agrippa said unto Festus,

Agrippa remarked to Festus — Ber

I would also hear the man myself.

I also could wish to hear the man myself — ASV

I should like to hear this man myself — TCNT

I have a desire to give the man a hearing myself — Bas

I have often wished, myself, to hear this man speak — Knox

I have been wanting to hear this man myself — Phi

To morrow, said he, thou shalt hear him.

To-morrow, replied Festus, you shall — Wey

Tomorrow, he said, you may give him a hearing — Bas

23. And on the morrow,

So the next day — TCNT

Accordingly, the following day — Ber

when Agrippa was come, and Bernice,

when Agrippa and Bernice had come — TCNT

with great pomp,

in full state — TCNT

with great pomp and ceremony — Phi

with great display — Rhm

and was entered into the place of hearing,

and they had entered the audience-chamber — Rhm

and took their seats in the Audience Hall — Wey

and went into the audience room — Gspd

and entered into the court house—Lam

and made their entry into the hall of judgment — Knox

. . . the auditorium — NASB

with the chief captains,[119] **and principal men of the city,**

with the captains of thousands and men of distinction of the city — Rhm

. . . superior officers and the principal people . . . — TCNT

accompanied by the military commanders and the prominent civilians of the town — Mof

. . . high-ranking officers and the prominent citizens . . . — NEB

. . . and dignitaries of the city — Rieu

at Festus' commandment Paul was brought forth.

at the command of Festus Paul was brought in — ASV

by the order of Festus Paul was brought before them — TCNT

Then Festus gave the order and Paul was brought in — Beck

24. And Festus said, King Agrippa, and all men which are here present with us,

. . . King Agrippa and all here present — Mof

. . . King Agrippa and all you gentlemen here present with us — NEB

ye see this man,

ye observe this person — Rhm

You see before you the man — TCNT

you are looking at the person — Ber

about whom all the multitude of the Jews have dealt with me,

. . . made suit to me — ASV

concerning whom one and all the throng of Jews have interceded with me — Rhm

about whom the whole Jewish people have applied to me — TCNT

. . . sent to me — Mon

on whose account the whole constituency of the Jews have made complaint to me — Ber

whose case the Jewish community brought before me — Rieu

both at Jerusalem, and also here,

first in Jerusalem and then here — Rieu

crying that he ought not to live any longer.

loudly asserting that he ought not to be allowed to live — TCNT

They loudly insist he ought not to live any longer — Mof

crying out that he must not be allowed to live a day longer — Knox

clamouring for his execution — Rieu

loudly insisting that he had no right to remain alive — NEB

25. But when I found

For myself, I was satisfied — Knox

But I for my part discovered — Phi

But it was clear to me — NEB

that he had committed nothing worthy of death,

that he had not done anything deserving death — TCNT

. . . for which he deserved to die — Wey

that he had committed no capital crime — NEB

and that he himself hath appealed to Augustus,[120]

and as he himself appealed to the emperor — ASV

and as he himself has made a request to be judged by Caesar — Bas

I have determined to send him.

I decided to send him — RSV

. . . to Rome — Wey

26. Of whom I have no certain thing to write unto my lord.

Concerning whom anything certain to write unto my Lord I have not — Rhm

But I have nothing definite to write about him to my Imperial Master — TCNT

---

[119]On "chief captains" see Acts 21:31.

[120]On "Augustus" see verses 11,12,21.

But I do not know what to write Caesar concerning him — Lam

I have nothing substantial to write His Majesty — Ber

Frankly, I have nothing specific to write to the emperor about him — Phi

I don't have anything reliable to write our lord about him — Beck

Wherefore I have brought him forth before you,
and for that reason I have brought him before you all — TCNT

and specially before thee, O king Agrippa,
and particularly before you . . . — Ber

that, after examination had,
that, after examining him — TCNT
that, when he has been examined — Wey
. . . as a result of your cross-examination — Mof
so that when he is questioned — Lam
so that as a result of this preliminary inquiry — NEB
so that after the investigation has taken place — NASB

I might have somewhat to write.
I may find something which I can put into writing — Wey
there may emerge some charge which I may put in writing — Phi

27. For it seemeth to me unreasonable
For it seems to me absurd — TCNT
. . . ridiculous — Phi
. . . odd — Ber
For it is not proper — Lam
It makes no sense to me — Beck

to send a prisoner,
to forward a prisoner — Mof
to send a prisoner up for trial — Nor

and not withal to signify the crimes laid against him.
without at the same time stating the charges made against him — TCNT
not to indicate the charges against him — RSV
without specifying . . . — Wms
without writing down . . . — Lam
without making clear what there is against him — Bas
without reporting what he's accused of — Beck

CHAPTER 26

1. Then Agrippa said unto Paul,
Turning to Paul, Agrippa said — TCNT
Thou art permitted to speak for thyself.
You are at liberty to speak for yourself — TCNT
You have permission . . . — Wey
. . . to speak in your own defense — Gspd
You may put your case before us — Bas
You have permission to state your case — Rieu
Then Paul stretched forth the hand,
So Paul, with outstretched arm — Wey
So Paul, with that characteristic gesture of the hand — Phi
So Paul, extending his hand — Nor
and answered for himself:
and made his defence — ASV
went on to make his defence — Rhm
and began his defence — TCNT
made his answer, saying: — Bas
2. I think myself happy, king Agrippa,
King Agrippa I have been counting myself happy — Rhm

I have been congratulating myself, King Agrippa — TCNT
I think myself fortunate . . . — Wey
because I shall answer for myself this day before thee
that I am to make my defence before thee this day — ASV
in being able to defend myself to-day before you — Mof
that it is before you that I am to defend myself today — Gspd
in making my defense before thee personally today — Phi
touching all the things whereof I am accused of the Jews:
with regard to the charges brought against me by the Jews — TCNT
As regards all the accusations brought against me . . . — Wey
against all the charges which the Jews have preferred against me — Wms
3. Especially because I know thee to be expert
because you are especially familiar — RSV

Especially as thou art well versed —
Rhm

for you are so thoroughly acquainted
— Ber

The more so because you are expert —
Bas

especially as you have expert knowledge — Rieu

No one is more familiar than thou —
Knox

**in all customs and questions which are
among the Jews:**

in all the Jewish customs and questions
— Rhm

. . . that prevail among the Jews —
Wey

in all questions that have to do with
the Jews and their ways — Bas

with the customs of the Jews, and their
controversies — Knox

. . . customs and problems — Ber

in all Jewish matters, both our customs
and our disputes — NEB

**wherefore I beseech thee to hear me
patiently.**

I beg you therefore to give me a patient
hearing — TCNT

Pray listen to me then with patience —
Mof

So I make my request to you to give
me a hearing to the end — Bas

4. My manner of life from my youth,

My life, then, from my youth upwards
— TCNT

The kind of life I have lived from . . .
— Wey

What my life was like when boyhood
was over — Knox

**which was at the first among mine own
nation at Jerusalem,**

which was from the beginning among
mine own nation and at Jerusalem
— ASV

was passed, from the very first, among
my own nation, and in Jerusalem —
TCNT

as exemplified in my early days among
. . . — Wey

which from its commencement was
formed among my nation, even in
Jerusalem — Rhm

spent from the first among my own
people and in Jerusalem — Knox

know all the Jews.

and is within the knowledge of all Jews
— TCNT

is known to all the Jews — Wey

is familiar to all Jews — NEB

5. Which knew me from the beginning,

having knowledge of me from the first
— ASV

and they have always known — TCNT

They are fully aware — Ber

They have known for a long time —
RSV

They have known all the time — Phi

if they would testify,

— if they please to bear witness —
Rhm

— if they choose to give evidence —
TCNT

— if they would but testify to the fact
— Wey

— as they could testify if they wanted
to — Rieu

if they chose to admit it — Mof

if they want to tell the truth — Beck

**that after the most straitest sect of our
religion**

that according to the strictest sect of
our own religion — Rhm

that in accordance with the very strictest form of our religion — TCNT

I lived a Pharisee.

I lived a true Pharisee — TCNT

I lived as a Pharisee — NEB

my life was that of a Pharisee — Wey

6. And now I stand and am judged

And now I stand here to be judged —
ASV

Even now . . . I stand here on my trial
— TCNT

**for the hope of the promise made of
God unto our fathers:**

for the hope of the promise unto our
fathers being brought to pass by God
— Rhm

because of my hope in the promise
given by God to our ancestors —
TCNT

because of a hope that I hold in a
promise that God made to our forefathers — Phi

**7. Unto which promise our twelve tribes,
instantly serving God day and night,
hope to come.**

unto which promise our twelve tribes,
earnestly serving God . . . hope to
attain — ASV

unto which hope our twelve-tribed nation with intensity night and day rendering divine service is hoping to attain — Rhm

— a promise which our Twelve Tribes, by earnest service night and day, hope to see fulfilled — TCNT

the promise which our twelve tribes, worshipping day and night, hope to have made good to them — Wey

And which our twelve tribes expect to realize with a devotion that continues night and day — Ber

the very promise which our twelve tribes, ardently worshipping God day and night, hope to see fulfilled! — Rieu

Our twelve tribes . . . expect to see this promise come true — Beck

For which hope's sake, king Agrippa, I am accused of the Jews.

It is for this hope, your Majesty, that I am accused — and by Jews themselves! — TCNT

And I am actually impeached by Jews for this hope, O king! — Mof

And this is the hope, my lord king, for which the Jews call me to account — Knox

8. Why should it be thought a thing incredible with you,

Why is it judged incredible with you — ASV

Why do you all hold it incredible — TCNT

Why is it deemed with all of you a thing past belief — Wey

Why do you Jews of all people find it impossible to believe — Rieu

that God should raise the dead?

if God doth raise the dead — ASV

that God can raise . . . — Lam

for God to make the dead come to life again — Bas

9. I verily thought with myself,

I myself, it is true, once thought it — TCNT

Fact is that I was possessed of the idea — Ber

I myself was convinced — RSV

Anyway, at the time I was convinced — Rieu

that I ought to do many things contrary to the name of Jesus of Nazareth.

that against the name of Jesus the Nazarene it was needful many hostile things to bring about — Rhm

my duty to oppose in every way the Name of . . . — TCNT

a duty to be active in hostility to the name of Jesus, the Nazarene — Wey

to take extreme measures in hostility to the name . . . — Wms

to defy, in many ways, the name of . . . — Knox

that it was my duty to combat the influence of . . . — Rieu

10. Which thing I also did in Jerusalem:

and I actually did so at Jerusalem — TCNT

and many of the saints did I shut up in prison,

I myself threw many of the People of Christ into prison — TCNT

and numbers of the saints I put in prison — Bas

and I had many of God's people imprisoned — Phi

I locked up many of the holy people in prison — Beck

having received authority from the chief priests;

having received the necessary authority . . . — Alf

by authority from the chief priests — RSV

Acting on the authority of the Chief Priests — TCNT

armed with authority received from . . . — Wey

under powers granted me by . . . — Knox

and when they were put to death,

. . . done to death — Knox

. . . executed — Ber

. . . condemned to death — Mon

. . . on trial for their lives — Phi

and when it was proposed to put them to death — TCNT

I gave my voice against them.

I voted against them — Mof

I cast my vote against them — RSV

I gave my decision against them — Bas

I voted for their execution — Rieu

11. And I punished them oft in every synagogue,

And punishing them oftentimes in all the synagogues — ASV

there was not a synagogue where I did not often punish them — Mof

and many a time in all the synagogues I had them punished — Gspd

and I tortured them in every synagogue — Lam

In every synagogue I often administered torture — Rieu

Time after time, in every synagogue, I tried by punishments — TCNT

and compelled them to blaspheme;

and forced them to blaspheme — Wey

thus compelling them to blaspheme the name of Jesus — Lam

forcing them to say things against God — Bas

I strove to make them blaspheme — ASV

and tried to force them to say impious things — Gspd

and tried to force them to use abusive language — Wms

to make them recant by blaspheming Christ — Rieu

to make them renounce their faith — NEB

and being exceedingly mad against them,

So frantic was I against them — TCNT

and in my wild fury — Wey

. . . frantic fury — Mof

. . . mad fury — Mon

In my mad rage against them — Gspd

. . . raging fury against them — RSV

In an excess of fanaticism — Rieu

Indeed, my fury rose to such a wild pitch — NEB

And in my burning zeal and furious rage against them — Nor

and being furiously enraged against them — NASB

I persecuted them even unto strange cities.

I also went to other cities to persecute them — Lam

I persecuted them as far as foreign cities — Ber

that I extended my persecution to foreign cities — NEB

I went on to pursue them as far as even the outlying cities — Rhm

that I pursued them even to towns beyond our borders — TCNT

I even pursued them to distant towns — Gspd

I chased them even to foreign towns — Wey

and I hounded them to distant cities — Phi

I hunted them down even to foreign cities — Beck

I harassed (troubled, molested, persecuted) them . . . — Amp

12. Whereupon as I went to Damascus

It was while I was travelling to Damascus on an errand of this kind — TCNT

While thus engaged, I was travelling one day to Damascus — Wey

I was on the way to Damascus for this purpose — Lam

On one such occasion I was travelling to Damascus — NEB

with authority and commission from the chief priests,

entrusted with full powers by the Chief Priests — TCNT

armed with authority and a commission from the High Priests — Wey

authorized and commissioned by . . . — Gspd

with authority based on a commission from . . . — Wms

with authority and approval of . . . — Ber

authorized and appointed by . . . — Beck

13. At midday, O king, I saw in the way

that at midday, your Majesty, I saw right in my path — TCNT

and on the journey, at noon, O King, I saw — Wey

a light from heaven, above the brightness of the sun,

from heaven, above the splendour of the sun . . . a light — Rhm

coming from the heavens, a light brighter than the glare of the sun — TCNT

. . . brighter than the brightness of the sun — Wey

a light from heaven more dazzling than the sun — Mof

. . . more brilliant than the sun — Ber

shining round about me and them which journeyed with me.

flash round me and my fellow-travellers — Mof

which shone about me and my companions — Knox

blazing about me and my fellow-travellers — Phi

14. **And when we were all fallen to the earth,**
We all fell to the ground — TCNT
I heard a voice speaking unto me,
and then I heard a voice — TCNT
a voice came to me — Bas
and saying in the Hebrew tongue,
saying unto me in the Hebrew language — ASV
and saying in the Hebrew tongue (Aramaic) — Lam
asking me in the Jewish language — Beck
Saul, Saul, why persecutest thou me?
. . . why are you persecuting me — TCNT
Saul! Saul! Why do you continue to persecute me — Wms
. . . why are you attacking me so cruelly — Bas
it is hard for thee to kick against the pricks.
You cannot kick against the goad! — Gspd
You hurt yourself by kicking at the goad — Mof
You only hurt yourself by kicking against the goad — Rieu
By kicking against the goads you are punishing yourself — TCNT
You are finding it painful to kick against the ox-goad — Wey
It is hard on you to kick against the goad — Ber
It is hurting you to keep on kicking . . . — Wms
It is not easy for you to kick against your own conscience — Phi
It will be hard for you to rebel and resist — Nor

15. **And I said, Who art thou, Lord?**[121]
And he said, I am Jesus whom thou persecutest.[122]

16. **But rise, and stand upon thy feet:**
but get up and stand upright — TCNT
for I have appeared unto thee for this purpose,
for to this end have I appeared unto thee — ASV
for I have come to you for this purpose — Bas
for I have shown myself to you for a reason — Phi

to make thee a minister and a witness
to appoint you to serve and bear witness — RSV
to appoint thee a minister and a witness — ASV
. . . an attendant and a witness — Rhm
. . . a servant and a witness — TCNT
. . . to my service as a witness — Mof
. . . to serve me and to testify — Gspd
both of these things which thou hast seen,
both of the things wherein thou hast seen me — ASV
to the things in which you have seen me — RSV
both as to the things you have already seen — Wey
of what you have seen of me today — Phi
of those revelations of me which you have already had — TCNT
of this vision of me — Rieu
and of those things in the which I will appear unto thee;
and to those in which I will appear to you — RSV
and of those in which I shall yet appear to you — TCNT
and those which I shall yet enable you to see — Wms
and the visions to come — Rieu
and also of what I will reveal to you — Nor
and what you will see whenever I appear to you — Beck

17. **Delivering thee from the people, and from the Gentiles,**
Rescuing thee from among the people, and from among the nations — Rhm
I will rescue you from the People and also from the Gentiles — Mof
I will rescue you from the Jews and from the Gentiles — Rieu
I will be thy Deliverer from the hands of thy people, and of the Gentiles — Knox
I will save you from your people and from the heathen — Gspd
I will keep you safe . . . — Bas
unto whom now I send thee,
Unto whom I am sending thee — Rhm
to whom I now send you — TCNT

---

[121]See Acts 22:8.
[122]See Acts 22:8.

For to the Gentiles I am sending you
— Rieu

to whom I am going to send you —
Wms

18. To open their eyes,

that their eyes may be opened — Mof

**and to turn them from darkness to
light,**

that they may turn . . . — ASV

and that they may turn from darkness
to light — Mof

turning them from the dark to light —
Bas

**and from the power of Satan unto
God,**

. . . authority of Satan . . . — Rhm

. . . dominion of Satan . . . — ABUV

. . . Satan's control . . . — Gspd

**that they may receive forgiveness of
sins,**

. . . remission of sins — ASV

. . . pardon for their sins — TCNT

so that they may have their sins forgiven — Gspd

**and inheritance among them which
are sanctified[123] by faith that is in
me.**

. . . by the faith respecting me — Rhm

. . . by faith in me — TCNT

and have a possession among . . . —
Wms

and take their place with those whose
lives have been made holy by their
faith in me — Rieu

and get a share of what the people
enjoy who are made holy by believing in Me — Beck

19. Whereupon, O king Agrippa,

After that, King Agrippa — TCNT

**I was not disobedient unto the heav-
enly vision:**

I did not fail to obey the heavenly
vision — TCNT

I could not disobey that heavenly
vision — Wms

I did not go against the vision from
heaven — Bas

**20. But shewed first unto them of Damas-
cus,**

but declared both to them of Damascus first — ASV

But . . . I carried tidings — Both to
them in Damascus first — Rhm

but I proceeded to preach first to the
people in Damascus — Wey

I turned first to the inhabitants of
Damascus — NEB

but first I told . . . — Beck

**and at Jerusalem, and throughout all
the coasts of Judaea,**

and Jerusalem, and then through the
whole of Judaea — TCNT

then to the people in Jerusalem and
all the rest of Judaea — Rieu

and Jerusalem, then the whole country
of the Jews — Beck

and then to the Gentiles,

and unto the nations — Rhm

and to the Gentiles as well — TCNT

and even to the heathen — Gspd

and finally to the Gentiles — Rieu

and I preached even to the Gentiles —
Nor

**that they should repent and turn to
God,**

repentance and conversion to God —
TCNT

the necessity of turning to God and repenting — Rieu

to turn from sin to God — Beck

and do works meet for repentance.

doing works worthy of repentance —
ASV

performing deeds appropriate to repentance — NASB

and so act as befits men who are penitent — Knox

might give, in their works, the fruits of
a changed heart — Bas

and a life befitting that repentance —
TCNT

and live lives consistent with such repentance — Wey

and live lives to prove their change of
heart — Phi

and demonstrating that repentance by
deeds — Rieu

**21. For these causes the Jews caught me
in the temple,**

For this cause the Jews seized me . . .
— RSV

That is why . . . — TCNT

It was on this account that . . . — Wey

For these very things the Jews arrested
me . . . — Wms

On account of these facts the Jews
grabbed me . . . — Ber

---

[123]On "inheritance" and "them which are
sanctified" see Acts 20:32.

and went about to kill me.

and assayed to kill me — ASV

and tried to kill me — Wey

and wanted to kill me — Lam

and kept on trying to kill me — Wms

and were attempting to slay me with their own hands — Rhm

and made attempts upon my life — TCNT

22. Having therefore obtained help of God, I continue unto this day, witnessing unto small and great,

However, I have received help from God to this very day and so stand here and bear my testimony to high and low alike — TCNT

But God has helped me to this very day, and behold I stand and testify to the humble and to the great — Lam

And so, by God's help, I am here today, witnessing to small and great — Bas

But thanks to God's help, I still stand here today, bearing my witness . . . — Knox

But by the grace of God I am still alive today to bear my witness to one and all — Rieu

I have stood firm until now, and have solemnly exhorted . . . — Wey

saying none other things than those which the prophets and Moses did say should come:

saying nothing but what . . . — RSV

claiming nothing else than . . . — Nor

— without adding a word to what the Prophets, as well as Moses, declared should happen — TCNT

adding nothing to what the prophets and Moses foretold should take place — Phi

Yet there is nothing in my message which goes beyond what the prophets spoke of . . . as things to come — Knox

saying nothing contrary to Moses and the Prophets, but the very things which they said were to take place — Lam

23. That Christ should suffer,

how that the Christ must suffer — ASV

how that the Christ was to be a suffering Christ — Wey

that the Messiah would have to die — Rieu

and that he should be the first that should rise from the dead, and should shew light unto the people, and to the Gentiles.

and how that he first by the resurrection of the dead should proclaim light both . . . — ASV

and that, by rising from the dead, he was destined to be the first to bring news of light, not only to our nation, but also to . . . — TCNT

and being the first to rise from the dead he was to proclaim a message of light both to the Jewish people and to the Gentiles — Wey

and by being the first . . . — Gspd

. . . would announce the dawn to Israel and to the Gentiles — NEB

24. And as he thus spake for himself,

. . . thus made his defence — RSV

Now as he was saying these things in his defence — Rhm

As he was defending himself in this way — Beck

When he brought this forward in his defence — Mof

And when he made his answer in these words — Bas

Festus said with a loud voice,

Festus called out loudly — TCNT

Festus exclaimed in a loud voice — Wey

Festus burst out — Phi

Festus shouted at the top of his voice — NEB

Paul, thou art beside thyself;

Paul, thou art mad — ASV

Paul, you are raving mad — Mon

You are raving, Paul! — Rhm

Paul, you are out of your mind — Bas

Paul, you are insane! — Nor

You're crazy, Paul! — Beck

You are going crazy, Paul! — Wms

much learning doth make thee mad.

thy much learning is turning thee mad — ASV

your great learning is driving you mad — TCNT

. . . is driving you mad — RSV

. . . is turning your brain — Wey

. . . is driving you insane — Mof

. . . is driving you crazy — Wms

. . . has made you unbalanced — Bas

Much study has made you mad — Lam

your excessive study has turned you to frenzy — Ber

too much study is driving you mad —
NEB

25. But he said, I am not mad, most noble[124] **Festus;**

I am not raving . . . — Rhm

Paul answered, I am not going crazy . . . — Wms

. . . I am not out of my mind — Ber

but speak forth the words of truth and soberness.

but the declaration of truth and soberness am I sounding forth — Rhm

on the contrary, the statements that I am making are true and sober — TCNT

I am speaking words of sober truth — Wey

. . . the straight truth — Wms

I speak nothing but the sober truth — Phi

26. For the king knoweth of these things,

Indeed, the King knows about these matters — TCNT

Why, the king is well aware of this! — Mof

And King Agrippa is also familiar with these things — Lam

. . . is well versed in these matters — NEB

before whom also I speak freely:

and I can speak to him with freedom — Gspd

therefore I dare speak to him more freely — Nor

. . . speak boldly — Alf

and to him I speak freely — RSV

so I speak before him without constraint — TCNT

so that I unreservedly address him — Ber

To the king I can speak without the slightest hesitation — Mof

and this is why I am speaking openly before him — Lam

that is why I speak with such confidence in his presence — Knox

for I am persuaded

I am sure — TCNT

I do not believe — Wey

I am convinced — Rieu

that none of these things are hidden from him;

that there is nothing whatever of what I have been telling him that has escaped his attention — TCNT

that any detail of them has escaped his notice — Wey

any of these things are unknown to him — Ber

that he can be unaware of any of these facts — NEB

all this is common knowledge to him — Bas

None of this . . . is news to him — Knox

for this thing was not done in a corner.

for it did not happen in a corner! — Gspd

for they were not done in secret — Lam

it was not in some secret corner that all this happened — Knox

27. King Agrippa, believest thou the prophets?

. . . do you believe the Prophets — Wey

. . . you believe the prophets, don't you — Nor

I know that thou believest.

I know you do — TCNT

28. Then Agrippa said unto Paul,

. . . answered — Wey

. . . remarked — Mof

But Agrippa turned to Paul — Ber

Agrippa countered Paul's question by saying — Rieu

Almost thou persuadest me to be a Christian.

With little effort you almost persuade me to become a Christian — Lam

A little more and you will be making me a Christian — Bas

You are with a little effort convincing enough to make me a Christian — Ber

Much more of this . . . and you will be making me a Christian — Phi

With but little persuasion thou wouldest fain make me a Christian — ASV

You are soon trying to make a Christian of me — TCNT

At this rate, . . . it won't be long before you believe you have made a Christian of me! — Mof

In a short time you think to make me a Christian! — RSV

You are in a hurry to persuade me and make a Christian of me! — Gspd

You think it will not take much to win

[124]On "most noble" see Acts 24:3.

me over and make a Christian of me — NEB

Lightly art thou persuading thyself that thou canst make me a Christian — Alf

In brief, you are confident that you can make me a Christian — Wey

In short, you are doing your best to persuade me to become a Christian — Mon

You think it a small task to make a Christian of me — just offhand to induce me with little ado and persuasion, at very short notice — Amp

29. And Paul said, I would to God, that not only thou, but also all that hear me this day, were both almost, and altogether

And Paul said, I would to God, that whether with little or with much, not only thou, but also all that hear me this day, might become — ASV

And Paul answered, — I could pray unto God that both almost and altogether, not only thou but all they who are hearing me this day might become — Rhm

Whether it is soon or late . . . — TCNT

And Paul said, I could pray God, that both in some degree and in a great degree, not only thou, but also all that hear me this day, may become — ABUV

Why, said Paul, it would be my prayer to God that, whether it were with much ado or little . . . — Knox

Ah, replied Paul, whether it means 'much more' or 'only a little,' I would to God . . . — Phi

. . . that I could persuade you, either in one word or many — Rieu

such as I am, except these bonds.

just what I am myself — except for these chains — TCNT

in my condition — not including these shackles — Ber

30. And when he had thus spoken,[125]
the king rose up, and the governor, and Bernice,

Then the king rose to his feet and so did . . . — Phi

With that the king rose, and with him the Governor . . . — NEB

and they that sat with them:

and those who had been sitting with them — TCNT

and the rest of the company — Rieu

31. And when they were gone aside,

and after leaving the room — Gspd

and stepping to one side — Ber

and, after retiring — TCNT

they talked between themselves, saying,

they spoke to one another, saying — ASV

. . . discussed the case among themselves — TCNT

they discussed the matter among themselves and agreed — Phi

This man doeth nothing worthy of death or of bonds.

There is nothing . . . deserving death or imprisonment in this man's conduct — TCNT

This man is guilty of no fault . . . — Knox

. . . punishable by death or even imprisonment — Nor

32. Then said Agrippa unto Festus,

Agrippa remarked to Festus — Phi

This man might have been set at liberty,

. . . released — Rhm

. . . set free — Mon

He might easily have been discharged — Phi

if he had not appealed unto Caesar.[126]

CHAPTER 27

1. And when it was determined that we should sail into Italy,

As it was decided that we were to sail to Italy — TCNT

And now word was given for the voyage to Italy — Knox

Once it had been decided that we were to be sent to Italy — Rieu

they delivered Paul and certain other prisoners unto one named Julius, a centurion of Augustus' band.

Paul and some other prisoners were put

---

[125]Now recognized as not adequately supported by original manuscripts.
[126]See Acts 25:11,12.

in charge of a Captain of the Augustan Guard, named Julius — TCNT

they handed over Paul and a few other prisoners into the custody of Julius, an officer of the Augustan battalion — Wey

. . . who belonged to the Augustan Cohort — Knox

Paul and some other prisoners were handed over to an officer of the Imperial regiment called Julius — Mof

. . . to a centurion named Julius, of the emperor's own regiment — Phi

2. And entering into a ship of Adramyttium,

And embarking in a ship of Adramyttium — RSV

And going on board . . . — Rhm

We embarked on a ship sailing from Adramyttium — Phi

we launched, meaning to sail by the coasts of Asia;

about to sail along the coasts of Asia, we put to sea — ABUV

which was about to sail unto the places on the coast of Asia, we put to sea ASV

which was on the point of sailing to the ports along the coast of Roman Asia, and put to sea — TCNT

which was bound for the Asiatic seaports, we set sail — Mof

that was going to sail to the ports on the coast of the province of Asia, and we started out — Beck

one Aristarchus, a Macedonian of Thessalonica, being with us.

Aristarchus, a Macedonian from Thessalonica, went with us — TCNT

3. And the next day we touched at Sidon.

And on the next day we put into Zidon — Rhm

. . . landed at Sidon — ABUV

And on the day after we came to Sidon — Bas

. . . docked at Sidon — Ber

. . . made a stop at Sidon — Nor

And Julius courteously entreated Paul,

and Julius treated Paul kindly — RSV

where Julius treated Paul in a friendly manner — TCNT

. . . with consideration — NASB

. . . with thoughtful kindness — Wey

. . . humanely — ABUV

and gave him liberty to go unto his friends

and allowed him to go to see his friends — TCNT

. . . to visit his friends — Wey

and permitted him to go to his friends — ABUV

to refresh himself.

and receive their hospitality — TCNT

and enjoy their care — Wey

to get any care he needed — Beck

and rest — Lam

4. And when we had launched from thence,

And putting to sea from thence — ASV

After setting sail from there — Wms

When we set sail again — Rieu

Leaving Sidon — NEB

we sailed under Cyprus, because the winds were contrary.

we sailed under the lee of Cyprus, because . . . — ASV

we had to sail under the lee of Cyprus, as the wind was against us — Mof

we sailed along the south coast of Cyprus, . . . — Ber

contrary winds forced us to keep to the sheltered side of Cyprus — Rieu

5. And when we had sailed over the sea of Cilicia and Pamphylia,

And when we had sailed across the sea which is off Cilicia and Pamphylia — ASV

and, after crossing the sea of . . . — TCNT

and, sailing the whole length of the sea that lies off . . . — Wey

Then, when we had crossed the gulf that lies off the coasts of . . . — Phi

we came to Myra, a city of Lycia.

we reached Myra in Lycia — TCNT

we landed at . . . — Ber

6. And there the centurion found a ship of Alexandria sailing into Italy;

. . . sailing for Italy — RSV

. . . on her way to Italy — TCNT

. . . bound for Italy — Wey

and he put us therein.

and put us on board of her — TCNT

. . . transferred us to that — Ber

7. And when we had sailed slowly many days,

For several days our progress was slow — TCNT

It took several days of slow and difficult sailing — Wey

We had a slow voyage for many days after this — Knox

For several days we beat slowly to windward — Phi

For a good many days we made little headway — NEB

and scarce were come over against Cnidus,

and were come with difficulty over against Cnidus — ASV

and it was only with difficulty that we arrived off Cnidus — TCNT

for us to come off Cnidus — Wey

we made Gnidus with difficulty — Knox

and only just succeeded in arriving off Cnidus — Phi

we managed to reach a point off Cnidus — Rieu

we were hard put to it to reach Cnidus — NEB

the wind not suffering us,

As the wind was still unfavorable — TCNT

for the wind was against us — Bas

with the wind beating us back — Knox

from which point, as the wind did not allow us to get on by the direct course — Wey

the wind was not suffering us to get on — Rhm

. . . not suffering us to put in — ABUV

then, as the wind checked our progress — Mof

Then as the wind kept us from going on — Gspd

then, checked by the wind — Ber

Then, since the wind was still blowing against us — Phi

we sailed under[127] Crete, over against Salmone;

we ran under the lee of Crete off Salmone — Wey

we had to sail around Crete toward the city of Salmone — Lam

we went under cover of Crete, in the direction of Salmone — Bas

we sailed south of Crete off Salmone — Ber

so we made for Salmone and the shelter of Crete — Rieu

and so, starting at Cape Salmone, we sailed on the sheltered side of Crete — Beck

8. And, hardly passing it,

And with difficulty coasting along it — ASV

And with difficulty, by keeping close in shore — TCNT

and, hugging the coast, struggled on — NEB

And sailing down the side of it — Bas

And though hardly making any headway — Nor

came unto a place which is called The fair havens;

we reached a place called Fair Havens — TCNT

and finally reached . . . — Wms

to a place called Fair Havens — NEB

nigh whereunto was the city of Lasea.

near the town of Lasea — Wey

not far from the town of Lasea — Mof

9. Now when much time was spent,

And when a considerable time had passed — Rhm

As a great deal of time had now passed — Gspd

Much time had now been wasted — Knox

As much time had been lost — RSV

Our voyage thus far had occupied a long time — Wey

By this time it was far on in the season — Mof

and when sailing was now dangerous,

and sailing was already dangerous — Rhm

and the navigation being now unsafe — Wey

and the journey was now full of danger — Bas

and it was risky to go on with the voyage — NEB

because the fast was now already past,

because the Fast was now already gone by — ASV

(for the autumn Fast was past) — Mof

because it was late in the year — Bas

as even the Fast of the Atonement was past — Rieu

the fall festival was already over—Nor

even the day of fasting had already gone by — Beck

Paul admonished them,

Paul began to advise — Rhm

and so Paul gave this warning: — TCNT

Paul warned them — Wey

---

[127]On "sailed under" see verse 4.

10. And said unto them,
  by saying — Wms
  Sirs, I perceive
  My friends, I see — TCNT
  Gentlemen . . . — Gspd
  that this voyage will be with hurt and much damage,
  that the voyage will be with injury and much loss — ASV
  . . . will be attended with danger and heavy loss — Wey
  . . . with hardship and serious loss — Mof
  that this voyage is likely to end in disaster and heavy loss — Gspd
  . . . will be beset with hardship and with great loss — Lam
  . . . will involve hardship and considerable damage — Ber
  that this voyage will be disastrous; it will mean grave loss — NEB
  not only of the lading and ship,
  not only of the cargo and of the ship — Rhm
  not only of our freight and of the vessel — Knox
  but also of our lives.
  but to our own lives also — TCNT
  and there will be loss of life as well — Rieu
  but also of life — NEB
  but even of our persons — Rhm
11. Nevertheless the centurion[128] believed
  . . . listened to — Lam
  . . . paid more attention to — RSV
  . . . gave more heed to — ASV
  . . . was more persuaded by — Rhm
  . . . let himself be persuaded by — Wey
  . . . was more influenced by — TCNT
  . . . put confidence in — Ber
  . . . put his faith in — Nor
  the master and the owner of the ship,
  the captain and the owner — TCNT
  by the pilot and by the owner — Wey
  by the pilot and the captain — Gspd
  the helmsman and the master — Knox
  more than those things which were spoken by Paul.
  than by what was said by Paul — TCNT
  rather than by anything Paul could say — Mof
  rather than by Paul's arguments — Wey
  rather than in Paul's suggestions — Ber
12. And because the haven was not commodious to winter in,
  and as the harbour was inconvenient

for wintering in — Wey
  . . . not a suitable one to winter in — TCNT
  Moreover, since the harbor is unsuitable for a ship to winter in — Phi
  . . . was not well situated for wintering in — ABUV
  . . . was badly placed for wintering in — Mof
  . . . was not fit to winter in — Gspd
  . . . was ill adapted for winter quarters — Mon
  the more part advised to depart thence also,
  the more part advised to put to sea from thence — ASV
  the majority were in favour of continuing the voyage — TCNT
  . . . favoured sailing on — Rieu
  the majority reached a decision to put out to sea from there — NASB
  if by any means they might attain to Phenice,
  if by any means they could reach Phoenix — ASV
  in the hope of being able to reach Phoenix — TCNT
  on the chance that somehow they could reach Phoenix — RSV
  and there to winter;
  to winter — Alf
  for the winter — Bas
  and spend the winter there — NASB
  which is an haven of Crete,
  Phoenix is a harbour of Crete — TCNT
  another harbour in Crete — Rieu
  and lieth toward the south west and north west.
  exposed south-west and north-west — NEB
  facing west-south-west and west-north-west — Gspd
  and looketh in the direction of the south-west and north-west winds — Alf
  looking north-east and south-east — ASV
  open to the north-east and south-east — TCNT
  facing north-east and south-east — Wey
13. And when the south wind blew softly,
  So when a light wind sprang up from the south — TCNT

---

[128]On "centurion" see Acts 21:32.

When a moderate southerly breeze sprang up — Mof

When a light breeze from the south began to blow — Wms

supposing that they had obtained their purpose,

so that they supposed they were now sure of their purpose — Wey

thinking their purpose was about to be realized — Wms

thinking that they had found their opportunity — TCNT

thinking their object was within reach — Gspd

they imagined that it answered their purpose — Rieu

they supposed that their plan was favorable — Nor

thinking they had obtained just what they wanted — Phi

they thought that their purpose was as good as achieved — NEB

they thought they could reach their destination as they had desired — Lam

they felt they could easily make it — Beck

loosing thence,

they weighed anchor — RSV

they let the ship go — Bas

and setting sail — Rieu

they sailed close by Crete.

and sailed along Crete, close in shore — ASV

and kept along the coast of Crete, close in shore — TCNT

and ran close along the coast of Crete — Gspd

and coasted along, hugging the shores of Crete — Phi

14. But not long after

But shortly afterwards — TCNT

But very soon — Gspd

But before long — Phi

there arose against it a tempestuous wind, called Euroclydon.

there beat down from it a tempestuous wind, which is called Euraquilo — ASV

there blew from the shore . . . — Alf

a hurricane came down on us off the land — a north-easter, as it is called — TCNT

a furious north-east wind, coming down from the mountains, burst upon us — Wey

. . . swept down from the land — RSV

down rushed a hurricane of a wind called Euroclydon — Mof

a violent wind, which they call Northeaster, rushed down from it — Gspd

a furious wind . . . rushed down from the island — Mon

a gale of a wind struck the ship, the wind called Euraquilo — Knox

a violent wind [of the character of a typhoon] . . . — Amp

. . . tore down from the land-ward side — NEB

a hurricane . . . dashed down from Crete — Beck

15. And when the ship was caught,

The ship was caught by it — TCNT

The ship was snatched along by it — Wms

And when the ship got into the grip of it — Bas

and could not bear up into the wind,

and could not face the wind — RSV

and since she could not be brought up into the wind — Phi

and we not being able to bring her head to the wind — Rhm

so, unable to head against the wind — Ber

we let her drive.

we gave way to it, and were driven — ASV

so we had to give way and let her drive before it — TCNT

so we gave way and let her run before it — Gspd

so we gave up and let her drift — Ber

we let her go and were borne along — Rhm

16. And running under a certain island which is called Clauda,

And running under the lee of a small island called Cauda — RSV

And sailing near the side of . . . — Bas

Running south of a small island . . . — Ber

As we passed under the shelter of . . . — Nor

we had much work to come by the boat:

we were able, with difficulty, to secure the boat — ASV

we were able, though it was hard work, to make the ship's boat safe — Bas

and with a struggle managed to get the ship's boat under control — NEB

and with a struggle managed to get
hold of the small boat — Beck

17. Which when they had taken up,
and when they had hoisted it up — ASV
and after hoisting it on board — TCNT
they used helps, undergirding the ship;
the men frapped the ship — TCNT
they used frapping-cables to undergird
the ship — Wey
they used ropes . . . — Mof
. . . to brace the ship — Gspd
they put cords under and round the
ship — Bas
and then passed cables round the ship
to reinforce it — Rieu

**and, fearing lest they should fall into
the quicksands,**
and, fearing lest they should be cast
upon the Syrtis — ASV
But, afraid of being driven on to the
Syrtis Sands — TCNT
and in fear of being stranded on the
Syrtis — Mof
Fearing they would run on the great
sandbank near Africa — Beck
But from fear that they would be
thrown upon the Syrtis quicksands
— Nor

strake sail,
. . . lowered the gear — RSV
. . . let down the sea anchor — NASB
. . . lowered the sail — Wms
. . . lowered our topgear — Alf
. . . lowered the yard — TCNT
. . . lowered the mainsail — NEB
. . . shortened sail — Phi

and so were driven.
and let her drive — NEB
and then drifted — TCNT
and let the ship drift — Gspd
and went running before the wind —
Bas
and were carried before the wind —
Rieu
and lay to, drifting — Phi

**18. And we being exceedingly tossed with
a tempest,**
So violently were we tossed by the
storm — TCNT
As we were being terribly battered by
the storm — Mof
because we were so violently beaten by
the storm — Wms
And as we labored exceedingly with the
storm — ASV

But, as the storm was still violent —
Wey
And still fighting the storm with all
our strength — Bas
The storm continued to lash us — Rieu
as we were making very heavy weather
— NEB

the next day they lightened the ship;
the next day they began to throw the
freight overboard — ASV
. . . began to throw the cargo overboard
— Rhm
and the next day they jettisoned some
of the cargo — Rieu
. . . we threw our belongings into the
sea — Lam

19. And the third day
and, on the following day — TCNT
while two days later — Mof

**we cast out with our own hands the
tackling of the ship.**
they cast out with their own hands . . .
— RSV
threw out the ship's tackle with their
own hands — TCNT
they let all the sailing apparatus go
over the side — Bas
they deliberately threw the spare tackle
overboard — Rieu

**20. And when neither sun nor stars in
many days appeared,**
As neither sun nor stars were visible
for several days — TCNT
And as we had not seen the sun or
stars for a long time — Bas
Then, when for many days there was
no glimpse of sun or stars — Phi
For days on end there was no sign of
either sun or stars — NEB

and no small tempest lay on us,
and, as the gale still continued severe
— TCNT
and the terrific gale still harassed us —
Wey
and the storm continued to rage —
Gspd
and a great tempest still beat upon us
— Mon
and we were still in the grip of the
gale — Phi
and the storm continued unabated —
Rieu

**all hope that we should be saved was
then taken away.**
. . . was now taken away — ASV

all hope of our being saved was at last abandoned — TCNT

... was gradually abandoned — NASB

and at last we had to give up all hope of being saved — Mof

the last ray of hope was now vanishing — Wey

and our last hopes of coming through alive began to fade — NEB

21. But after long abstinence

And when there had been long abstinence from food — Alf

And when they had been long without food — ASV

It was then, when they had gone a long time without food — TCNT

Since hardly anybody wanted to eat — Beck

Paul stood forth in the midst of them, and said,

that Paul came forward, and said — — TCNT

Paul got up among them, and said — Gspd

Sirs, ye should have hearkened unto me,

My friends, you should have listened to me — TCNT

Gentlemen, you ought to have listened to me — Gspd

and not have loosed from Crete,

and not have set sail from Crete — ASV

and to have gained this harm and loss.

and have gotten this injury and loss — ASV

and so incurred this injury and damage — TCNT

Then there would never have been this loss and damage — Rieu

You would then have escaped this suffering and loss — Wey

22. And now I exhort you to be of good cheer:

I now bid you cheer up — Mof

And even now I advise you to cheer up — Ber

Yet, even as things are, I urge you not to lose courage — TCNT

But now take courage — Wey

Even now, I beg you to keep up your courage — Gspd

I now bid you to take heart — RSV

But now I urge you not to lose heart — NEB

for there shall be no loss of any man's life among you,

for there will not be a single life lost among you — TCNT

but of the ship.

but only of the ship — ASV

— only the ship — TCNT

though we shall lose the ship — Phi

23. For there stood by me this night the angel of God, whose I am, and whom I serve,

... an angel of the God whose I am, whom also I serve — ASV

For last night an angel of the God to whom I belong, and whom I serve, stood by me — TCNT

For this very night there stood by me an angel of the God to whom I belong and whom I worship — RSV

24. Saying, Fear not, Paul;

saying — Be not afraid Paul! — Rhm

... Have no fear, Paul — TCNT

... Dismiss all fear, Paul — Wey

... Stop being afraid, Paul — Wms

thou must be brought before Caesar:

thou must stand before Caesar — ASV

you must appear before the Emperor — TCNT

it is ordained that you shall appear before the Emperor — NEB

it is necessary for you to stand before Caesar — Amp

and, lo,

and note this — Wey

and see! — Gspd

and listen! — Wms

Behold — Mon

and be assured — Ber

God hath given thee all them that sail with thee.

God has granted to thee as a favour all them who are sailing with thee — Rhm

God has granted thee the safety of all thy fellow-voyagers — Knox

And for your sake God will save the lives of all on board — Rieu

25. Wherefore, sirs, be of good cheer:

Cheer up, men! — Mof

Wherefore be of good courage, Sirs! — Rhm

Therefore, courage, my friends! — TCNT

So take heart, men — RSV

for I believe God,

I have faith in God — Rieu

for I have confidence in my God — Wms

I trust in God — Knox

that it shall be even as it was told me.
that everything will happen exactly as I have been told — TCNT
and believe that what I was told will come true — Rieu

26. Howbeit we must be cast upon a certain island.
though we have to be cast ashore on some island — NEB
But we still have to be wrecked on an island — Rieu
We shall, however, have to be driven on some island — TCNT
But we are to be stranded on a certain island — Wey
But we shall have to run on some island — RSV

27. But when the fourteenth night was come,
. . . had come — Rhm
. . . arrived — Mof
It was now the fourteenth night of the storm — TCNT
as we were driven up and down in Adria,
. . . driven to and fro in the sea of Adria — ASV
and we were drifting about in the Adriatic Sea — TCNT
while we were still drifting across the Mediterranean — Rieu
about midnight the shipmen deemed
. . . surmised — ASV
. . . the sailors suspected — Rhm
. . .began to suspect — TCNT
. . . sensed — Phi
. . . had the feeling — Rieu
that they drew near to some country;
that they were drawing near to some country — ASV
That they were drawing near land — TCNT
that we were nearing land — Phi
that there was land ahead — Gspd

28. And sounded,
On taking soundings — Mof
So they cast the sounding lead — Lam
So they hove the lead — Wey
. . . let down the lead — Bas
. . . dropped the lead — Beck
and found it twenty fathoms:
and found twenty fathoms — RSV
and found the water 120 feet deep — Beck

and when they had gone a little further,
and after a little space — ASV
and a little further on — Mof
after a short interval — NEB
they sounded again,
they took another sounding — NASB
and found it fifteen fathoms.
and it was ninety feet — Bas

29. Then fearing lest we should have fallen upon rocks,
. . . lest haply we should be cast ashore on rocky ground — ASV
. . . that we might be cast ashore on a rugged coast — NEB
. . . lest haply on rocky places we should be wrecked — Rhm
Then, as they were afraid of our being driven upon some rocky coast — TCNT
Then for fear of possibly running on rocks — Mof
So, for fear that we might be hurled on the rocks — Phi
. . . might fall off [our course] onto rocks — Amp
they cast four anchors out of the stern,
they let go four anchors from the stern — ASV
they dropped four anchors from the stern — Gspd
they threw out . . . —Mon
they let down four hooks from the back of the ship — Bas
and wished for the day.
and wished that day would come — ABUV
and kept wishing for daylight to come — Wms
and longed for daylight — TCNT
. . . for break of day — Ber
and waited anxiously for daylight — Gspd
and began praying that day might dawn — Rhm
. . . for morning to come — Beck

30. And as the shipmen were about to flee out of the ship,
And as the sailors were seeking to flee out of the ship — ASV
And when the sailors were trying to flee from the ship — Mon
when they had let down the boat into the sea,
and had lowered the boat . . . — RSV

. . . had already lowered the ship's boat . . . — NEB

They had even lowered . . . —Mof

and actually lowered . . . — Gspd

and they got as far as letting a boat down . . . — Phi

under colour as though they would have cast anchors out of the fore-ship,

by pretext as though out of the prow they had been about to reach anchors — Rhm

on pretence of running out anchors from the bows — TCNT

under pretext of going to cast anchor from the prow — Ber

pretending that they were going to take out anchors from the front of the ship and let them down — Beck

under pretense that they were going in it to make fast the ship to the land — Lam

31. Paul said to the centurion[129] and to the soldiers,

But Paul, addressing Julius and the soldiers, said — Wey

Except these abide in the ship,

Unless the sailors remain on board — TCNT

Unless these men remain on the ship — Mon

If you do not keep these men in the ship — Bas

ye cannot be saved.

you will not be safe — Bas

Your lives will be sacrificed — Wey

there is no hope of your being saved — Phi

you have no chance of being saved — Rieu

you can none of you come off safely — NEB

you can't be rescued — Beck

32. Then the soldiers cut off the ropes of the boat,

Upon that the soldiers cut the ropes which held the boat — TCNT

and let her fall off.

and let her fall away — Rieu

and let her drift away — TCNT

and let it drop — Knox

and let it go — RSV

33. And while the day was coming on,

And as day was dawning — Wey

As day began to break — Knox

Just before daybreak — Mof

And when dawn was near — Bas

Then while everyone waited for the day to break — Phi

Paul besought them all to take meat, saying,

. . . to take some food, saying — ASV

Paul kept urging them all to take something to eat — Gspd

Paul gave them all orders to take food, saying — Bas

This day is the fourteenth day that ye have tarried

. . . that ye wait — ASV

It is a fortnight today . . . that, owing to your anxiety — TCNT

This is the fourteenth day . . . that you have been on the strain — Wey

For fourteen days now you have been uninterruptedly on the alert — Ber

You have had fourteen days of suspense — Rieu

For the last fourteen days . . . you have lived in suspense — NEB

For fourteen days today you have been constantly waiting — Wms

and continued fasting, having taken nothing.

and have fasted, eating little or nothing — Wey

fasting, having eaten nothing — Mon

you have gone without food, taking nothing — TCNT

and going without food, not even taking a bit — Wms

without a proper meal — Mof

that you have not had time to eat — Nor

34. Wherefore I pray you to take some meat:

. . . I beseech you to take some food — ASV

So I urge you to take something to eat — TCNT

I therefore strongly advise you to take some food — Wey

So I implore you to eat something — Ber

for this is for your health:

. . . for your safety — ASV

your safety depends on it — TCNT

your lives depend on it — NEB

This is essential for your safety — Wey

---

[129]On "centurion" see Acts 21:32.

it will sustain your health — Ber

it will give you strength — RSV

for there shall not an hair fall from the head of any of you.

for there shall not a hair perish . . . — ASV

for not one of you will lose even a hair of his head — TCNT

For not a hair of your head will go to ruin — Ber

35. **And when he had thus spoken, he took bread,**

And when he had said this, and had taken bread — ASV

And having said these things and taken a loaf — Rhm

With these words he took some bread — TCNT

and gave thanks to God in presence of them all:

he gave thanks unto God before all — Rhm

and, after saying the thanksgiving to God before them all — TCNT

he gave praise to God before them all — Bas

and gave thanks to God in front of everyone — Rieu

and when he had broken it, he began to eat.

and he brake it, and began to eat — ASV

broke it in pieces, and began to eat — TCNT

36. **Then were they all of good cheer,**

The men all felt cheered — TCNT

Then they all cheered up — Mof

. . . took heart — Bas

. . . found courage — Knox

This raised the spirits of all — Wey

and they also took some meat.

and themselves also took food — ASV

and had something to eat themselves — TCNT

37. **And we were in all in the ship two hundred threescore and sixteen souls.**

. . . two hundred and seventy-six souls — Alf

There were two hundred and seventy-six of us, crew and passengers on board — Wey

— all told there were 276 of us on board — Ber

38. **And when they had eaten enough,**

After satisfying their hunger — TCNT

After eating a hearty meal — Wey

when they had eaten as much as they wanted — NEB

they lightened the ship,

they further lightened the ship — TCNT

they began to lighten the ship — Mon

and cast out the wheat into the sea.

throwing out . . . — ASV

by throwing the grain . . . — TCNT

by dumping the wheat into the sea — Ber

39. **And when it was day,**

And when day came — Rhm

In the morning — Beck

they knew not the land:

they could not recognize the land — Rhm

they could not recognize the coast — Wey

they tried in vain to recognize the land — Mon

no one recognized the land — Phi

they could not make out what land it was — TCNT

they found that the coast was strange to them — Knox

but they discovered

but they perceived — ASV

But they noticed — Wey

but gradually could see — Beck

a certain creek with a shore,

a certain bay with a beach — ASV

. . . with a sloping beach — Knox

. . . with a sandy shore — Phi

a certain creek in which there was a beach — TCNT

an inlet with a sandy beach — Wey

an inlet of the sea with a floor of sand — Bas

into the which they were minded,

and they took counsel — ASV

they consulted — TCNT

and they began conferring — Mon

on which they determined — ABUV

and made up their minds — Knox

on which they planned — RSV

if it were possible, to thrust in the ship.

whether they could drive the ship upon it — ASV

if it were possible, to run the ship aground — Alf

as to whether they could run this ship safely into it — TCNT

if possible, to bring the ship ashore — RSV

to beach the ship if they could — Phi

40. And when they had taken up the anchors,
And casting off the anchors — ASV
And when they had cut away the anchors — Alf
they committed themselves unto the sea,
they left them in the sea — ASV
and abandoned the anchors — TCNT
they let them go into the sea — Rhm
and threw them into the sea — Lam
and dropping them in the sea — Ber
and trusted themselves to the mercy of the sea — Knox
and loosed the rudder bands,
at the same time loosing the bands of the rudders — ASV
while the crew unlashed the ropes that tied the rudders — Mof
. . . loosening the lashings of the rudders — Rhm
. . . unlashed the gear of the steering oars — TCNT
. . . cut the ropes which held the steering oars — Phi
. . . untied the ropes that held up the steering oars — Beck
and hoised up the mainsail to the wind,
and hoisting up the foresail to the wind — ASV
then they hoisted the topsail . . . — Lam
spread out the foresail to catch the wind — Beck
and made toward shore.
they made for the beach — RSV
and headed toward shore — Mof
and let her drive to the beach — NEB
and steered the ship to the shore — Beck

41. And falling into a place where two seas met,
But lighting upon a place where two seas met — ASV
But striking a reef where two seas met — NASB
But the ship struck on a shoal between two deep places in the sea — Lam
They got, however, into a kind of channel — TCNT
But they struck a shoal — Gspd
They struck a bank in the water — Beck
But now, finding that they were running into a cross sea — Knox

But unluckily they encountered a spot where two currents met — Rieu
But they found themselves caught between cross-currents — NEB
they ran the ship aground;
they stranded the ship — Wey
they drove the ship aground — Mof
they grounded the ship where they were — Knox
and the forepart stuck fast,
and the foreship struck — ASV
and her prow sticking fast — ABUV
The prow jammed — Mof
and the foreward part rested upon the bottom — Lam
and the front part was fixed in the sand — Bas
So the prow settled — Ber
and remained unmoveable,
and could not be moved — TCNT
and remained fixed — Mon
but the hinder part was broken
but the stern began to break up — ASV
. . . began to go to pieces — Wey
. . . was going to pieces — ABUV
but the back part was broken — Bas
while the stern was being pounded to pieces — NEB
with the violence of the waves.
under the violent pounding of the waves — Nor
under the strain — TCNT
under the heavy hammering of the sea — Wey
under the beating of the waves — Mof
by the force of the waves — Bas
by the surf — RSV

42. And the soldiers' counsel was
The advice of the soldiers was — TCNT
And it was the plan of the soldiers — ABUV
It was then the soldiers' idea — Ber
Now the soldiers recommended — Wey
. . . proposed — Gspd
. . . were planning — Mon
. . . had in mind — Nor
to kill the prisoners,
that the prisoners should be killed — TCNT
that they should kill the prisoners — ABUV
lest any of them should swim out, and escape.
for fear that any of them should swim away and make their escape — TCNT

so that no one would get away by swimming — Bas

for fear that any of them should dive overboard and escape — Knox

43. But the centurion,[130] **willing to save Paul,**

... desiring to save Paul — ASV

... anxious to save Paul — TCNT

kept them from their purpose;

prevented their carrying out their intention — TCNT

and commanded that they which could swim

and ordered that those who could swim — TCNT

should cast themselves first into the sea,

... overboard — RSV

should be the first to jump into the sea — TCNT

to jump overboard first — Gspd

to leap off first — Ber

to throw themselves overboard first — RSV

and get to land:

and get first to the land — ASV

and make their way to land — Knox

and try to reach shore — TCNT

and make for shore — Ber

and strike out for the shore — Nor

44. And the rest,

and that the rest should follow — TCNT

Of the rest, some were ferried across — Knox

some on boards,

... on planks — ASV

and some on broken pieces of the ship.

and some on other things from the ship — ASV

or pieces of wreckage — Mof

and others should grab anything they could find on the ship — Nor

And so it came to pass,

In these various ways — TCNT

In this way it turned out — Mof

that they escaped all safe to land.

that all were brought safely through on to the land — Rhm

everyone managed to get safely ashore — TCNT

they all got safely to land — Wey

all reached land in safety — Knox

they all reached land and safety — Rieu

CHAPTER 28

1. And when they were escaped,

And when we were escaped — ASV

After our escape — Gspd

And when we were safely through — Rhm

When we were all safe — TCNT

Once we were safely ashore —Rieu

then they knew that the island was called Melita.

then we knew ... — ASV

we found that the island was called Malta — TCNT

... discovered ... — Wey

... ascertained ... — Mon

we recognized the island. It was Malta — Rieu

2. And the barbarous people shewed us

And the natives shewed us — Alf

The foreign-speaking people showed us — Mon

And the barbarians who inhabited it showed us — Lam

The rough islanders treated us with — NEB

no little kindness:

uncommon kindness — NEB

marked ... — TCNT

no common philanthropy — Rhm

remarkable friendliness — Ber

for they kindled a fire,

for they lit a fire — TCNT

building a bonfire on the beach — Tay

and received us every one,

and took us all under shelter — TCNT

and made us all welcome — Wey

and took us in — Bas

because of the present rain,

because of the rain that had set in — Rhm

because it was raining — Bas

because of the pelting rain— Wey

for the rain had set in — Rieu

... driving rain — Phi

... downpouring rain — Wms

and because of the cold.

and was cold — TCNT

and the cold — Wey

3. And when Paul had gathered a bundle of sticks,

---

[130]On "centurion" see Acts 21:32.

Paul had collected a bundle of faggots
— Knox

. . . a bundle of dry sticks — Rieu

Paul had got together an armful of
sticks — NEB

. . . an armful of dry branches — Beck

and laid them on the fire,

and had thrown them . . . — Wey

and was placing them . . . — Rieu

there came a viper out of the heat,

a viper came out by reason of the heat
— ASV

. . . crawled out of them because of the
heat — Gspd

a snake came out . . . — Bas

When a viper, roused by the warmth,
came out of them — Rieu

As he did so a viper crawled out of
the heat — Nor

and fastened on his hand.

and fastened itself . . . — Wey

and fastened its fangs on his hand —
Rieu

and wound itself around his hand —
Nor

4. **And when the barbarians[131] saw the
venomous beast hang on his hand,**

. . . the venomous creature hanging
from his hand — ASV

. . . the reptile hanging on his hand —
Mon

The islanders, seeing the snake hanging
on to his hand — NEB

they said among themselves,

. . . one to another — ASV

No doubt this man is a murderer,

Evidently this man is a murderer —
TCNT

Beyond doubt . . . — Wey

This man must be a murderer! — Mof

a murderer, no doubt! — Tay

whom, though he hath escaped the sea,

whom, though he hath escaped from
the sea — ASV

whom, though brought safely through
out of the sea — Rhm

for, though he has been saved from
the sea — TCNT

he has escaped death by drowning —
Rieu

yet vengeance suffereth not to live.

yet Justice hath not suffered to live —
ASV

Justice has not allowed him to live —
TCNT

but justice has caught up with him all
the same — Rieu

but divine vengeance would not let
him live — Knox

5. **And he shook off the beast into the
fire,**

But he only shook the creature off into
the fire — Gspd

But he simply shook the reptile . . . —
Wms

But Paul shook his hand and threw the
viper . . . — Lam

and felt no harm.

and suffered no harm — ABUV

and came to no harm — Rieu

and was not a whit the worse — Mof

without suffering any ill effect — Phi

6. **Howbeit they looked when he should
have swollen,**

But they expected that he would have
swollen — ASV

The natives were expecting inflamation
to set in — TCNT

They expected to see him swell up —
Gspd

They still expected that any moment
he would swell up — NEB

The natives kept on looking for him to
swell up — Wms

or fallen down dead suddenly:

or to fall down suddenly dead — Rhm

or suddenly drop dead — Wms

but after they had looked a great while,

but when they were long in expectation
— ASV

but after waiting for a long time —
TCNT

but when they had waited a long time
— RSV

and saw no harm come to him,

and beheld nothing amiss come to him
— ASV

and had observed nothing unusual happening to him — Rhm

and saw no misfortune come to him
— RSV

they changed their minds,

. . . their talk — Lam

. . . their opinion — Bas

and said that he was a god.

and began to say . . . — Rhm

and said over and over . . . — Mon

and declared that he must be a god —
Knox

---

[131]On "barbarians" see verse 2.

7. In the same quarters were possessions of the chief man of the island, whose name was Publius;

Now in the neighborhood of that place were lands belonging to the chief man of the island, named Publius — ASV

In that neighborhood there was an estate belonging to the Governor of the island, whose name was Publius — TCNT

In the same part of the island there were lands . . . Wey

Near this place there was an estate belonging to the chieftain of the island . . . — Rieu

. . . the leading citizen . . . — Knox

. . . the chief magistrate . . . — NEB

who received us,

and he gladly received us — Lam

who making us welcome — Rhm

who welcomed us to his house — Wey

and lodged us three days courteously.

and entertained us three days courteously — ASV

for three days hospitably entertained us — Rhm

and for three days generously made us his guests — Wey

8. And it came to pass,

And it so happened — Rhm

that the father of Publius lay sick

. . . was lying prostrate — Rhm

. . . was lying ill — Wey

of a fever and of a bloody flux:

of fever and dysentery — ASV

of dysentery and attacks of fever — Wey

suffering from recurrent bouts of fever and dysentery — NEB

with a disease of the stomach — Bas

to whom Paul entered in,

So Paul went to see him — TCNT

and prayed, and laid his hands on him, and healed him.

and, after praying, he placed his hands on him and cured him — TCNT

and put his hands on him with prayer, and made him well — Bas

and prayed, and healed him with the laying on of hands — Rieu

9. So when this was done,

And when this happened — Rhm

After this — TCNT

Because this cure was performed — Wms

others also, which had diseases in the island, came, and were healed:

all the people in the island who had any illness came to Paul and were cured — TCNT

the rest of the sick folk in the island also came and got cured — Mof

The rest of the sick people on the island kept coming to him and by degrees were cured—Wms

10. Who also honoured us with many honours;

They also loaded us with honours — Wey

There also showed us honor in many ways — Nor

They also showed us every kind of respect — Ber

They also presented us with many gifts — TCNT

They made us rich presents — Mof

As a result we were showered with gifts — Tay

and when we departed,

and when we were departing — Alf

and when we sailed — RSV

and when at last we sailed — Wey

and when the time came for us to sail — Phi

they laded us with such things as were necessary.

they put on board such things as we needed — ASV

they supplied all our needs — Ber

they put supplies on board for us — Wey

they ladened us with provisions — Lam

they provided us with everything that we needed — Gspd

11. And after three months

Three months later — Gspd

Three months passed before — Wey

we departed in a ship of Alexandria,

we set sail in a ship of Alexandria — ASV

we sailed on an Alexandrian ship — Gspd

we put to sea in . . . —Ber

which had wintered in the isle,

which had been at the island for the winter — Bas

whose sign was Castor and Pollux.

whose sign was The Twin Brothers — ASV

whose ensign was — The Twin Brothers — Rhm

Its name was "The Twin Brothers" — Mon

and had the Twin Sons of Zeus for her figure-head — TCNT

It ran in front a figure of the Twin Sons of Zeus — Beck

named from its figurehead the Heavenly Twins — Rieu

It was called the Dioscuri, after the twin brothers Castor and Pollux — Nor

12. And landing at Syracuse,

And touching at Syracuse — ASV

We docked at . . . — Ber

We put in at . . . —TCNT

On our way we put in at Syracuse — Nor

we tarried there three days.

and stayed there three days — TCNT

and spent three days there — Rieu

13. And from thence we fetched a compass,

then we weighed anchor — Gspd

After weighing anchor and leaving there — Wms

And from thence we fetched a circuit — ASV

and from there we made a circuit — following the coast — Amp

From there we worked round — Wey

From thence we circled round — Lam

and from there we worked to windward — TCNT

and came to Rhegium:

and arrived at Rhegium — RSV

we reached Rhegium — Rhm

and so got to Rhegium — TCNT

and after one day

A day later — TCNT

Next day — Mof

When we had spent a day there — Knox

the south wind blew,

. . . sprang up — ASV

. . . began to blow — Wms

. . . blew in our favor — Lam

and we came the next day to Puteoli:

and on the second day we came to Puteoli — RSV

and took us to Puteoli in two days— TCNT

and the following day we arrived at Puteoli — Gspd

and we made Puteoli on the second day out — Knox

14. Where we found brethren,

There we found some of the Brethren — TCNT

. . . fellow-Christians — NEB

and were desired to tarry with them seven days:

and were invited . . . — RSV

and were entreated . . . — ASV

and were urged to stay a week with them — TCNT

and they begged us . . . Wms

who prevailed on us to stay . . . — Knox

and so we went toward Rome.

and thus towards Rome we came — Rhm

Then on to Rome we went — Ber

And so we came to Rome — RSV

after which we went on to Rome — TCNT

And so we ended our journey at Rome — Knox

In this way we finally reached Rome Wms

15. And from thence, when the brethren heard of us,

. . . heard the tidings concerning us — Rhm

. . . heard of our arrival — Alf

The Brethren there had heard about us — TCNT

As the local brothers had heard about us — Mof

The Brotherhood there, hearing about us — Rieu

The brothers there had had news of our coming — Gspd

The Christians there . . . — NEB

they came to meet us as far as Appii forum, and The three taverns:

and came out as far as the Market of Appius and the Three Taverns to meet us — TCNT

. . . the Market of Appius and Three Inns . . . — NASB

and came as far as the Market Town of Appius and the Three Shops to meet us — Beck

. . . to welcome us — Rieu

whom when Paul saw,

And as soon as Paul caught sight of them — Wms

he thanked God, and took courage.

he gave thanks to God and took renewed courage — Nor

... and was greatly encouraged—Gspd
... and felt encouraged — Beck
... and was much cheered — TCNT
gave praise to God and took heart —
Bas

16. And when we came to Rome,
And when we entered into Rome — ASV
When we finally entered Rome — Mon
On our reaching Rome — TCNT
When at length we reached Rome —
Nor

**the centurion delivered the prisoners
to the captain of the guard:**[132]
**but Paul was suffered to dwell by him-
self with a soldier that kept him.**
Paul was allowed to live by himself except for the soldier who was in
charge of him — TCNT
Paul was allowed to have his own residence which he shared with ... —
Knox
Paul received permission to live by
himself, guarded by a soldier — Wey
and the centurion gave permission to
Paul to live where he pleased ... —
Lam
... to live alone with the soldier who
was guarding him — Phi

**17. And it came to pass, that after three
days**
Three days after our arrival — TCNT
Three days later — Mof
**Paul called the chief of the Jews to-
gether:**
Paul sent and called the Jewish leaders
— Lam
he called together the local leaders of
the Jews — RSV
Paul invited the leading Jews to meet
him — TCNT
... to come to see him — Gspd
and when they were come together,
... they came together — Rhm
... had assembled — Knox
... had gathered — RSV
he said unto them,
he spoke to them as follows: — TCNT
Men and brethren,
Brothers — TCNT
Brother men — Ber
Fellow Jews — Beck
**though I have committed nothing
against the people,**
though I had done nothing against the
people — ASV

although I had done nothing hostile to
the interests of our nation — TCNT
... nothing prejudicial to our people —
Wey
though I had not been disloyal to our
people — Rieu
or customs of our fathers,
or to our ancestral customs — TCNT
or contrary to the customs of our forefathers — Wey
or the ways of our fathers — Bas
or the traditions of our fathers — Rieu
**yet was I delivered prisoner from Jeru-
salem into the hands of the Romans.**
yet I was sent from Jerusalem as a
prisoner, and handed over to the
Romans — TCNT
yet I was turned over to the Romans
as a prisoner at Jerusalem — Gspd
I am here as a prisoner from Jerusalem.
I was handed over to the authority
of the Romans — Rieu
yet I was made a prisoner at Jerusalem
and delivered into the hands of the
Romans — Nor

18. Who, when they had examined me,
They examined me — Gspd
After examining me — Wms
who, after they had sharply questioned
me — Wey
And the Romans after investigating my
case — Rieu
would have let me go,
desired to set me at liberty — ASV
were minded to ... — Rhm
were ready to release me — TCNT
were willing to ... — Wey
were prepared to ... — Phi
intended to let me go free — Rieu
and would have liked to release me —
NEB
**because there was no cause of death
in me.**
... nothing worthy of death in me —
Rhm
... nothing in my conduct deserving
death — TCNT
as I had done nothing to deserve death
— Rieu
as I was innocent of any crime that
deserved death — Mof
because there was no reason for the
death penalty in my case — RSV

---

[132]Now recognized as not adequately supported by original manuscripts.

since no capital charge lay against me — Knox

19. But when the Jews spake against it,
... made protest against it — Bas
... cried out against it — Knox
... objected — RSV
But, as the Jews opposed my release — TCNT
But the Jews opposed this course — Rieu
But owing to the opposition of the Jews — Wey

I was constrained to appeal unto Caesar;
I was compelled ... — Alf
I had to put my cause into Caesar's hands — Bas
and I had no option but to appeal to the Emperor — NEB

not that I had ought to accuse my nation of.
— not as though against my own nation I had anything to bring by way of accusation — Rhm
— not that I'm accusing my people of anything — Beck
— not, indeed, that I had any charge to make against my own nation — TCNT

20. For this cause therefore
This, then, is my reason — TCNT
This is the reason why — Mon
But it is because of this accusation of the Jews — Phi

have I called for you, to see you, and to speak with you:
did I entreat you to see and to speak with me — ASV
for urging you to come to see me and talk with me — TCNT
I begged you all to see and speak with me — Mon
I have invited you here, that I might see you and speak to you — Wey

because that for the hope of Israel
for on behalf of ... — Alf
for on account of ... — Rhm
since it is because of the hope of Israel — RSV
In actual fact it is on account of ... — Phi
because I share Israel's hope — Mof
It is because I hope as Israel hopes — Knox

I am bound with this chain.
this chain have I about me — Rhm
that I wear this chain — Wey
that I have to wear this chain — Gspd

21. And they said unto him,
At this they said to him — Knox

We neither received letters out of Judaea concerning thee,
We ... have not had any letter about you from Judaea — TCNT

neither any of the brethren that came
nor did any of the brethren come hither — ASV
nor have any of our fellow Jews come — TCNT
and no brother has come here — Mof
and not one of our Jewish brothers has come — Wms
nor have any of the brethren who have come from Jerusalem — Lam
nor have any of the brothers arrived — Ber
and no Jew coming here — Beck

shewed or spake any harm of thee.
and report or speak any harm of thee — ASV
and reported or said anything bad about you — TCNT
... anything to your disadvantage — Wey
with any bad report or story about you — Mof
with a bad report or gossip about you — Ber
with any report or gossip to your discredit — NEB

22. But we desire to hear of thee what thou thinkest:
But we deem it well that from thee we should hear what are thine opinions — Rhm
We ask nothing better than to hear what thy opinions are — Knox
... what it is that you believe — Wey
But we shall be glad to hear from you what your views are — TCNT
But we want to hear you state your views — Gspd
But we think it fitting to let you tell us what your views are — Wms
We think it only right to let you tell your own story — Mof
But we are eager to hear from you what it is you believe — Mon

for as concerning this sect,
for with regard to this sect — TCNT

for as far as this sect is concerned — Gspd

for so far as this heresy is concerned — Ber

for as to this form of religion — Bas

we know

it is known to us — ASV

we are well aware — TCNT

all we know is — Wey

it is known by all of us — Wms

we understand — Gspd

that every where it is spoken against.

that it is spoken against on all sides — TCNT

that there are objections to it on all hands — Mof

that serious objections have been raised to it everywhere — Phi

that everywhere it is denounced — Gspd

that no one has a good word to say for it — NEB

23. And when they had appointed him a day,

And having arranged with him a day — Rhm

there came many to him into his lodging;

they came to him into his lodging in great number — ASV

came in large numbers to see him at the place where he was lodging — Wms

and a large group of them came to his lodgings — Rieu

to whom he expounded and testified the kingdom of God,

unto whom he proceeded to expound, bearing full witness as to the kingdom of God — Rhm

when Paul proceeded to lay the subject before them. He bore his testimony to the Kingdom of God — TCNT

And then he solemnly explained to them the Kingdom of God — Wey

he explained the Reign of God to them from personal testimony — Mof

he expounded his beliefs, speaking in witness of the Kingdom of God — Rieu

He dealt at length with the whole matter; he spoke urgently of the kingdom of God — NEB

persuading them concerning Jesus,

and tried to convince them about Jesus — TCNT

and having discourses with them about Jesus — Bas

attempting to persuade them about Jesus — Ber

both out of the law of Moses, and out of the prophets,

by arguments drawn from the Law of Moses and from the Prophets — TCNT

by appealing to . . . — NEB

from morning till evening.

from dawn till dusk — Knox

— speaking from morning till evening — TCNT

24. And some believed the things which were spoken,

Some began to believe what he said — Mon

and some hearkened to his words — Lam

. . . were in agreement with what he said — Bas

. . . were persuaded by the things that were spoken — Rhm

Some were inclined to accept what he said — TCNT

Some indeed were convinced by his reasonings — Ber

and some believed not.

and some disbelieved — ASV

others refused to believe — Wey

others, however, rejected it — TCNT

. . . remained sceptical — Rieu

. . . remained in doubt — Nor

25. And when they agreed not among themselves,

So as they disagreed among themselves — TCNT

Unable to agree among themselves — Wey

disagreeing among themselves — Lam

When they could not reach agreement among themselves — Phi

they departed,

. . . began to leave — Rhm

. . . began to disperse — TCNT

. . . began to go — Mon

. . . started to leave — Gspd

they at last left him — Wey

the meeting broke up — Rieu

after that Paul had spoken one word,

but not before Paul had spoken a parting word to them, saying — Wey

when Paul added this one word — Mof

after Paul had said this one thing — Bas

after Paul had made one statement —
RSV

after one last word from Paul — Rieu

Well spake the Holy Ghost

True, indeed, was the declaration made
by the Holy Spirit — TCNT

The Holy Spirit spoke the truth —
Beck

The Holy Ghost was right in saying —
RSV

It was an apt word that the holy Spirit
spoke — Mof

by Esaias the prophet unto our fathers,

through Isaiah the prophet unto your
fathers — ASV

. . . to your ancestors — TCNT

26. **Saying, Go unto this people, and say,**
— Go to this nation and say — TCNT

When he said, Go and tell this people
— Mof

Hearing ye shall hear,

By hearing ye shall hear — ASV

You shall surely hear — Rhm

You shall indeed hear — RSV

You will hear with your ears — TCNT

You will hear and hear — Wey

You will listen, and listen — Gspd

You will keep on hearing — NASB

and shall not understand;

and shall in no wise understand — ASV

and yet will in nowise understand —
Rhm

without ever understanding — TCNT

but never understand — Mof

but not catch the meaning — Ber

and seeing ye shall see,

And will look and look — Wey

You will see and see — Mof

you will watch and watch — Knox

You shall see with your eyes — Rieu

And, though you have eyes, you will
see — TCNT

And you will keep on seeing — NASB

and not perceive:

and shall in no wise perceive — ASV

without ever perceiving — TCNT

and yet will in nowise perceive — Rhm

but never perceive — Mof

and by no means see — Wey

and never see! — Gspd

but the sense will not be clear to you
— Bas

. . . not see — not perceive, have knowledge of or become acquainted with
what you look at, at all — Amp

27. **For the heart of this people is waxed
gross,**

. . . hath become dense — Rhm

. . . fat — Bas

For the mind of this nation has grown
dense — TCNT

. . . has grown callous — Wey

. . . is obtuse — Mof

For this people's soul has grown dull
— Wms

. . . is hardened — Lam

For the hearts of this people have lost
their feeling — Rieu

and their ears are dull of hearing,

Their hearing has become dull — Wey

And with their ears heavily have they
heard — Rhm

Their ears are heavy of hearing — Mof

. . . slow in hearing — Bas

. . . slow to listen — Knox

And they hear faintly with their ears —
Gspd

. . . scarcely hear . . . — Wms

. . . hardly hear . . . — Nor

They have ears that are hard of hearing
— Rieu

their ears are dull — NEB

and their eyes have they closed;

and they have shut their eyes — Gspd

and they keep their eyes shut — Knox

and their eyes are closed — NEB

lest they should see with their eyes,

lest haply they should perceive with
their eyes — ASV

lest someday . . . — TCNT

so as never to . . . — Gspd

for fear they might . . . — Nor

Otherwise, their eyes might see — NEB

so that their eyes don't see — Beck

and hear with their ears,

and give hearing with their ears — Bas

their ears hear — NEB

and understand with their heart,

and in their mind they should understand — TCNT

and become wise in their hearts — Bas

and their heart understand — NEB

and should be converted,

and should turn again — ASV

and turn to me — Wms

and return — Rhm

and turn about — Ber

and repent before me — Lam

and be turned again to me — Bas

and then they might turn again — NEB

and I should heal them.
for me to heal them — RSV
so as to let Me heal them — Nor
— When I would certainly heal them
— Rhm
so that I might make them well — Bas
And let me cure them! — Gspd
and I should forgive them — Lam

28. Be it known therefore unto you,
Understand, then — TCNT
Let it be known to you then — RSV
Let it be plainly understood then —
Phi
You should know — Beck
Therefore I want you to know — Nor
Be assured, therefore — Wey
Therefore take notice — NEB
**that the salvation of God is sent unto
the Gentiles,**
that this salvation . . . — Alf
that this message of God's salvation has
been sent to the heathen — Gspd
and that they will hear it.
and they will listen — TCNT
they, at any rate, will give heed — Wey
and they, at least, will listen to it —
Knox

**29. And when he had said these words,
the Jews departed, and had great reasoning among themselves.**[133]

**30. And Paul dwelt two whole years in his
own hired house,**
For two whole years Paul stayed in a
house which he rented for himself —
TCNT
After this Paul lived for fully two years
in private hired rooms — Wey
. . . in a lodging hired at his own expense — Knox
and received all that came in unto him,

and made welcome all who were coming in unto him — Rhm
welcoming all who came to see him —
TCNT
. . . to visit him — Mof
31. Preaching the kingdom of God,
proclaiming . . . — Rhm
he preached the Reign of God — Mof
He continued to preach the kingdom of
God — Mon
**and teaching those things which con-
cern the Lord Jesus Christ,**
and teaching about the Lord Jesus
Christ — TCNT
and to teach about the Lord Jesus
Christ — Mon
and teaching the facts about . . . — NEB
. . . the truths that concern our . . . —
Knox
and boldly taught the truth about . . .
— Beck
**with all confidence, no man forbid-
ding him.**
with all boldness, none forbidding him
— ASV
openly and unhindered — Gspd
with all freedom of speech, without
hindrance — Rhm
with perfect fearlessness, unmolested
— TCNT
with all boldness, quite unmolested —
Mof
without let or hindrance — Wey
and with that perfect, unfettered freedom of speech — Wms
without fear, and no orders were given
that he was not to do so — Bas
with utmost freedom and without hindrance from anyone — Phi

---

[133]Now recognized as not adequately supported by original manuscripts.

THE EPISTLE OF PAUL TO THE ROMANS

CHAPTER 1

1. Paul, a servant of Jesus Christ,
Paul, a bondsman of . . . — Con
Paul, a slave of . . . — Gspd
called to be an apostle,
an Apostle by the selection of God —
Bas
a called Apostle — Con
called as a messenger — Phi
separated unto the gospel of God,
set apart for the service of the Gospel
— NEB
set apart to publish the Glad-tidings of
God — Con
. . . to [preach] the Gospel (good news)
of and from God — Amp

2. (Which he had promised afore
which he promised beforehand — RSV
which he promised long ago — Gspd
by his prophets in the holy scriptures,)
through his prophets . . . — ASV

**3. Concerning his Son Jesus Christ our
Lord,**
It is about his Son: . . . it is about Jesus
Christ our Lord — NEB
The Gospel is centered in God's Son.
. . . . He is our Lord, Jesus Christ —
Phi
**which was made of the seed of David
according to the flesh;**
who was born of David's offspring by
natural descent — Mof
who was born of the seed of David according to the flesh — ASV
on the human level he was born of
David's stock — NEB
who, as to his human nature, was descended from David — TCNT
who as to the flesh (His human nature)
was descended from David — Amp

**4. And declared to be the Son of God
with power,**
and installed as Son of God with power
— Mof
and designated Son of God in power —
RSV
And decisively declared Son of God —
Gspd
who was declared with power to be the
Son of God — NASB
who was instated as the Son of God
with power — ABUV

Who was distinguished as the Son of
God — by power — Rhm
but . . . was declared Son of God by a
mighty act — NEB
but . . . was miraculously designated
Son of God — TCNT
but . . . was miraculously marked out
as . . . — Wey
and . . . was openly designated the Son
of God in power — in a striking,
triumphant and miraculous manner
— Amp
according to the spirit of holiness,
by the Spirit of Holiness — Mof
on the level of the Spirit — the Holy
Spirit — NEB
in his holiness of spirit — Gspd
in respect of the sanctified spirit that
was his — Knox
as to the spirit of holiness within him
— TCNT
on the holy spiritual side — Wms
by the resurrection from the dead:
in that he rose from . . . — NEB
by being raised from . . . — Gspd
because he arose from . . . — Lam

5. By whom we have received
through whom we received — ASV
grace and apostleship,
the undeserved gift of apostleship —
Ber
the grace of apostleship — Knox
favour and apostleship — Rhm
the favour of my commission — Mof
God's favor and a commission as an
apostle in His name — Wms
**for obedience to the faith among all na-
tions, for his name:**
unto obedience of faith among all the
nations for his name's sake — ASV
to bring about the obedience of faith
for the sake of his name among all
the nations — RSV
to urge obedience and faith among all
the heathen — Gspd
to win men to the obedience that
springs from faith among all the
Gentiles — Wey
to urge upon all the heathen obedience
inspired by faith — Wms
all over the world, men must be taught
to honour his name by paying him

the homage of their faith — Knox

6. Among whom are ye also the called of Jesus Christ:

including yourselves who are called to belong to Jesus Christ — RSV

Among whom ye also are numbered, being called by Jesus Christ — Con

among whom you too as called ones belong to Jesus Christ — Wms

7. To all that be in Rome, beloved of God, called to be saints:

To all God's beloved in Rome, who are called to be saints — RSV

to all who are beloved of God in Rome, called as saints — NASB

to all of you in Rome whom God loves and has called to be his dedicated people — NEB

Grace to you and peace from God our Father, and the Lord Jesus Christ.

Favour to you, and peace, . . . — Rhm

God our Father and the Lord Jesus Christ bless you and give you peace — Gspd

8. First, I thank my God

I must begin by telling you how I thank God — Phi

through Jesus Christ for you all, that your faith is spoken of throughout the whole world.

that your faith is proclaimed . . . — ASV

because your faith is being proclaimed . . . — NASB

because all over the world they are telling the story of your faith — NEB

because [the report of] your faith is made known to all the world and is commended everywhere — Amp

9. For God is my witness,

For God . . . bears me witness — Ber

As God is my witness — Gspd

Before God . . . I assure you — Phi

I call God to witness — Wey

whom I serve with my spirit

. . . in my spirit — ASV

. . . with my spiritual self — Ber

. . . with the worship of my spirit—Con

to whom I offer the humble service of my spirit — NEB

to whom I address the inner worship of my heart — Knox

to whom I render holy service in my spirit — Mon

whom I serve with all my heart — Phi

to whom I render priestly and spiritual service — Wey

in the gospel of his Son,

in proclaiming the Glad-tidings of His Son — Con

that without ceasing I make mention of you always in my prayers;

how unceasingly I make mention of you, always in my prayers — ASV

how continually I make mention of you in my prayers — NEB

I never fail to mention you when I pray — Gspd

10. Making request,

asking that — RSV

never failing to ask — Knox

always entreating — Mon

and one of the things I keep on praying for is — Tay

if by any means now at length I might have a prosperous journey by the will of God to come unto you.

if . . . I may be prospered by the will of God to come unto you — ASV

that somehow by God's will I may now at last succeed in coming to you — RSV

that if there be place for it in the will of God, I may some day be sped on my way to visit you — Ber

that, if it be possible, I might now at length have a way open to me . . . to come and visit you — Con

that now at length, if such be his will, the way may be made clear for me to come to you — Mon

11. For I long to see you,

For I am yearning to see you — Ber

that I may impart unto you some spiritual gift,

in order to impart to you some spiritual help — Wey

in the hope that I may have some spiritual gift to share with you — Knox

to the end ye may be established;

to strengthen you — RSV

to make you strong — NEB

for your confirmation — Ber

for the establishment of your steadfastness — Con

and so give you fresh strength — TCNT

12. That is, that I may be comforted together with you by the mutual faith both of you and me.

... comforted in you, each of us by the other's faith, both yours and mine — ASV

I mean that we may be mutually strengthened by your faith and mine — Ber

or rather that both you and I may find encouragement in each other's faith — TCNT

I mean when I'm with you I'll be encouraged by your faith and you by mine — Beck

13. Now I would not have you ignorant, brethren,

And I do not want you to be unaware, ... — NASB

I want you to know, Brothers — TCNT

that oftentimes I purposed to come unto you,

that I have often intended to come to you — RSV

that I have often planned to visit you — Nor

(but was let hitherto,)

(and was hindered hitherto) — ASV

(but thus far have been prevented) — RSV

(but something has always prevented me) — Phi

(but God did not let me) — Tay

that I might have some fruit among you also,

in order that I may reap some harvest among you — RSV

that I might find among you some fruit of my labours — TCNT

even as among other Gentiles.

even as in the rest of the Gentiles — ASV

as I do among the other non-Jewish people — Beck

as well as among the rest of the heathen — Gspd

as I have already among the other nations — TCNT

14. I am debtor

I have a duty — TCNT

I am under obligation — RSV

both to the Greeks, and to the barbarians;

both to Greeks and to barbarians — ASV

both to civilized peoples and heathen nations — Tay

to Greeks and non-Greeks — Nor

to the cultured and to the uncultured — Amp

both to the wise, and to the unwise.

both to the wise and to the foolish — ASV

learned and simple — Knox

to the cultured and to the uncultured — Mon

to the educated and uneducated alike — Tay

15. So, as much as in me is,

As far as I am able — Bas

As far as my ability will carry me — Phi

So, as far as I can — Wms

So, to the fullest extent of my ability — Tay

And so, for my part — TCNT

I am ready to preach the gospel

I am eager to bring the good news — Beck

I am ready to declare the Glad-tidings — Con

I am willing and eagerly ready to preach the Gospel — Amp

to you that are at Rome also.

to you in Rome as I have to others — Knox

16. For I am not ashamed of

For I am proud of — Mof

For [even in the chief city of the world] I am not ashamed of — Con

the gospel of Christ:[1]

the Glad-tidings of Christ — Con

the joyful message — Rhm

for it is the power of God unto salvation to every one that believeth;

It is the saving power of God for everyone who has faith — NEB

It is an instrument of God's power, that brings salvation to all who believe in it — Knox

to the Jew first, and also to the Greek.

17. For therein is the righteousness of God revealed

For in it there is a revelation of the Divine Righteousness — TCNT

For in the gospel a righteousness which comes from God is revealed — Wey

For in the good news God's way of man's right standing with Him is uncovered — Wms

---

[1]The words "of Christ" are now recognized as not adequately supported by original manuscripts.

In it God's way of uprightness is disclosed — Gspd

In it is shown God's plan to justify us — Nor

It reveals God's way of justifying us — Knox

I see in it God's plan for imparting righteousness to men — Phi

because here is revealed God's way of righting wrong — NEB

from faith to faith:

faith first and last — Knox

a way that starts from faith and ends in faith — NEB

which springs from Faith, and which Faith receives — Con

a process begun and continued by their faith — Phi

resulting from faith and leading on to faith — TCNT

the Way of faith that leads to greater faith — Wms

as it is written,

as Scripture says — TCNT

The just shall live by faith.

He who through faith is righteous shall live — RSV

he shall gain life who is justified through faith — NEB

The upright will have life because of his faith — Gspd

Through faith the righteous man shall find Life — TCNT

18. For the wrath of God is revealed from heaven

On the other hand, God's indignation . . . — Ber

So, too, there is a revelation from Heaven of the Divine Wrath — TCNT

For we see divine retribution revealed from heaven — NEB

For God's anger is breaking forth from heaven — Gspd

For God's wrath is ever being revealed from heaven — Mon

For God's anger from heaven is being uncovered — Wms

against all ungodliness and unrighteousness of men,

against every form of ungodliness and wickedness on the part of those men — TCNT

against the impiety and wrong-doing of the men — Knox

against all impiety and injustice of men — Nor

falling upon all the godless wickedness of men — NEB

who hold the truth in unrighteousness;

who hold back the truth in unrighteousness — ABUV

who keep down the truth [which they know] by the wickedness whereby they live — Con

who smother the truth by their unrighteousness — Mon

who, by their wicked lives, are stifling the truth — TCNT

who through their wickedness suppress the truth — Wey

who . . . repress and hinder the truth and make it inoperative — Amp

whose wrong-doing denies his truth its full scope — Knox

19. Because that which may be known of God

because that which is known of God — ASV

Because that which can be known of God — Con

is manifest in them;

lies plain before their eyes — NEB

is manifested in their hearts — Con

is clear to their minds — Knox

is manifest among them — Mon

is plain to them — TCNT

is clear to their inner moral sense — Wms

for God hath shewed it unto them.

for God manifested it unto them — ASV

God himself having shown it to them — Con

God himself has made it clear to them — Knox

20. For the invisible things of him

For . . . his invisible things — Alf

For . . . those things of God which the eye is unable to see — Bas

His invisible qualities — Ber

for . . . his invisible nature — Mof

God's invisible attributes — TCNT

His invisible perfections — Wey

For . . . His invisible characteristics — Wms

from the creation of the world

since the creation of the world — ABUV

ever since the world was made — Con

are clearly seen, being understood by the things that are made,

are clearly seen, being perceived through the things that are made — ASV have been visible . . . to the eye of reason, in the things he has made — NEB

are to be seen and studied in his works — TCNT

have been made intelligible and clearly visible by His works — Wms

have been clearly perceptible and understandable through the things He has made — Nor

even his eternal power and Godhead;

even his everlasting power and divinity — ASV

namely, his eternal power and deity — RSV

his eternal power and divine character — Gspd

his eternal power and his divineness — — Knox

his everlasting power and divine being — Mof

namely, His eternal power and divine nature — Wey

so that they are without excuse:

that they may be without excuse — ASV

so that men have no excuse — TCNT

There is therefore no possible defence for their conduct — NEB

thus leaving these men without a rag of excuse — Phi

21. Because that, when they knew God,

because although they knew God — Con

They knew all the time that there is a God — Phi

And although men knew that God exists — Nor

they glorified him not as God, neither were thankful;

they did not honor him as God or give thanks to him — RSV

they have refused to honour him as God, or to render him thanks — NEB

yet they did not offer him as God either praise or thanksgiving — TCNT

but became vain in their imaginations, and their foolish heart was darkened.

but became vain in their reasonings, and their stupid heart was darkened — ABUV

Hence all their thinking has ended in futility, and their misguided minds are plunged in darkness — NEB

their thoughts turned to worthless things, and their ignorant hearts were darkened — Beck

in their reasonings they went astray after vanity, and their senseless heart was darkened — Con

they became fantastic in their notions, and their senseless hearts grew benighted — Knox

Rather, they busied themselves with silly speculations about Him, and their stupid minds groped about in the dark — Nor

they have indulged in their futile speculations until their stupid minds have become dark — Gspd

22. Professing themselves to be wise, they became fools,

Affirming themselves to be wise . . . — ABUV

They boast of their wisdom, but they have made fools of themselves — NEB

Behind a façade of "wisdom" they became just fools — Phi

Though claiming to be wise, they made fools of themselves — Wms

23. And changed the glory of the uncorruptible God

and they have exchanged the glory of the immortal God — Wey

and forsook the glory of the imperishable God — Con

and exchanged the majesty of . . . — Mon

They even altered the glory of God immortal — Ber

exchanging the splendour of immortal God — NEB

into an image made like to corruptible man, and to birds, and fourfooted beasts, and creeping things.

for images resembling mortal man or birds or animals or reptiles — RSV

for an image shaped like mortal man, even for images like birds, beasts, and creeping things — NEB

for idols graven in the likeness of perishable men, or of birds and beasts, and creeping things — Con

24. Wherefore God also gave them up to uncleanness through the lusts of their own hearts,

Wherefore God delivered them up in the desires of their hearts to uncleanness — ABUV

Wherefore God gave them up in the covetings of their hearts unto impurity — Rhm

And so God, letting them follow the lusts of their hearts, gave them up to live immorally — Beck

Therefore God abandoned them to impurity, letting them follow the cravings of their hearts — TCNT

And so God let them go ahead into every sort of sex sin, and do whatever they wanted to — Tay

So God has given them up, in their hearts' lust, to sexual vice — Mof

For this reason God has given them up to the vileness of their own desires — NEB

and therefore God gave them up — to be the playthings of their own foul desires — Phi

That is why God abandoned their lustful hearts to filthy practices — Knox

to dishonour their own bodies between themselves:

that their bodies should be dishonored among themselves — ASV

so they degrade their own bodies with one another — Wms

25. **Who changed the truth of God into a lie,**

because they exchanged the truth about God for a lie — RSV

because they have bartered away the true God for a false one — NEB

These men deliberately forfeited the truth of God and accepted a lie — Phi

for they had substituted a lie for the truth about God — TCNT

and worshipped and served the creature more than the Creator,

. . . rather than the Creator — ASV

reverencing and worshipping the creature in preference to the Creator — Knox

and reverenced and worshipped the things made instead of the Maker — Con

who is blessed for ever. Amen.

who alone is worthy to be worshipped for ever and ever, amen — Phi

who is to be praised for ever. Amen — TCNT

26. **For this cause God gave them up unto vile affections:**

. . . unto vile passions — ASV

For this cause God delivered them up to shameful passions — ABUV

God therefore handed them over to disgraceful passions — Phi

and, in return, God abandoned them to passions which brought dishonour to themselves — Knox

That is why God has given them up to passions of dishonor — Mon

for even their women did change the natural use into that which is against nature:

For even their females exchanged away the natural use into that which is against nature — Rhm

Their women exchanged natural relations for unnatural — RSV

Their women exchanged natural for unnatural intercourse — Knox

Even the women among them perverted the natural use of their bodies to the unnatural — TCNT

their women have exchanged the natural function of sex for what is unnatural — Mof

even their women turned against God's natural plan for them and indulged in sex sin with each other — Tay

27. **And likewise also the men, leaving the natural use of the woman,**

and the men likewise gave up natural relations with women — RSV

In like manner also even the males, leaving the natural use of the female — Rhm

but the men also, in the same way, neglecting sexual intercourse with women — Wey

burned in their lust one toward another;

Flamed out in their eager desire for one another — Rhm

were consumed with passion for one another — TCNT

have burned fiercely in their lust for one another — Wey

were swept into lustful passions for one another — Phi

and were ablaze with passion for one another — Mon

were burnt up with desire for each other — Knox

and have run wild with lust toward one
another — Lam

**men with men working that which is
unseemly,**

men committing shameless acts with
men — RSV

males behave indecently with males —
NEB

men with men working abomination —
Con

men with men practising shameless acts
— Mon

and receiving in themselves that recompence of their error which was meet.

and receiving in themselves that recompense of their error which was due
— ASV

receiving in their own persons the due
penalty for their error — RSV

and are paid in their own persons the
fitting wage of such perversion —
NEB

and incurred in their own persons the
inevitable penalty of their own perverseness — TCNT

**28. And even as they did not like to retain
God in their knowledge,**

And even as they refused to have God
in their knowledge — ASV

. . . they did not choose to retain God
in their knowledge — ABUV

And since they did not see fit to acknowledge God — RSV

Moreover, since they considered themselves too high and mighty to acknowledge God — Phi

And just as they refused to recognize
God any longer — Gspd

**God gave them over to a reprobate
mind,**

. . . to an outcast mind — Con

God abandoned them to depraved
thoughts — TCNT

God delivered them up to a reprobate
mind — ABUV

God gave them up to a base mind —
RSV

. . . to minds that He did not approve
— Wms

. . . unto a disapproved mind — Rhm

God has abandoned them to unworthy
impulses — Gspd

he allowed them to become the slaves
of their degenerate minds — Phi

to do those things which are not convenient;

to do those things which are not fitting
— ASV

to improper conduct — RSV

to perform unmentionable deeds — Phi

to be doing the things that are not becoming — Rhm

to do those things which were indecent
— Mon

to practices that were improper—Wms

**29. Being filled with all unrighteousness,
fornication,[2] wickedness, covetousness,
maliciousness;**

They are filled with all unrighteousness, fornication, depravity, covetousness, maliciousness — Con

They revel in every kind of wrongdoing, wickedness, greed, and depravity — Gspd

**full of envy, murder, debate, deceit,
malignity; whisperers,**

They overflow with envy, murder,
strife. . . . They are whisperers —
Con

They are full of envy, murder, quarreling, deceit, and ill-nature. They are
gossips — Gspd

They are versed in every kind of injustice, knavery, impurity, avarice, and
ill-will . . . — Knox

30. Backbiters, haters of God,

backbiters, hateful to God — ASV

Slanderers, hated of God — Alf

defamers, loathed by God — Mof

slanderers, abhorrent to God — Gspd

stabbers-in-the-back, God-haters—Phi

scandal-mongers . . . — NEB

despiteful, proud, boasters,

insolent, haughty, boastful — ASV

They overflowed with insolent pride
and boastfulness — Phi

**inventors of evil things, disobedient to
parents,**

inventors of vices, unto parents unyielding — Rhm

ingenious in evil, undutiful — Gspd

inventors of wickedness; undutiful to
parents — Con

and their minds teemed with diabolical
invention. They scoffed at duty to
parents — Phi

they invent new kinds of mischief, they
show no loyalty to parents — NEB

---

[2]The word "fornication" is now recognized as
not adequately supported by original manuscripts.

31. Without understanding, covenant-breakers,

They were undiscerning, untrustworthy — TCNT

destitute of sense, faithless — Wey

devoid of conscience, false to their word — Mof

conscienceless, treacherous — Gspd

foolish, faithless — RSV

They were without sense, without faith — Mon

without natural affection, implacable, unmerciful:

without affection, and without pity — Wey

callous, merciless — Mof

unloving, and unpitying — Gspd

heartless, ruthless — RSV

32. Who knowing the judgment of God, that they which commit such things are worthy of death,

who, knowing the ordinance of God, that they that practise such things are worthy of death — ASV

Who, indeed, having acknowledged the righteous sentence of God . . . — Rhm

Who knowing the decree of God, whereby all that do such things are worthy of death — Con

In short, though knowing well the sentence which God pronounces against such deeds as deserving death — Wey

Yet, with the just decree of God before their minds, they never grasped the truth that those who so live are deserving of death — Knox

They were fully aware of God's penalty for these crimes — Tay

not only do the same, but have pleasure in them that do them.

not only commit the sins, but delight in their fellowship with sinners — Con

not only are they guilty of them themselves, but they even applaud those who do them — TCNT

yet they went right ahead and did them anyway, and encouraged others to do them, too — Tay

CHAPTER 2

1. Therefore thou art inexcusable, O man, whosoever thou art that judgest:

Wherefore thou art without excuse, . . . — ASV

Therefore you have nothing to say in your own defence, whoever you are who set yourself up as a judge — TCNT

for wherein thou judgest another, thou condemnest thyself;

for in judging thy neighbor thou condemnest thyself — Con

For at whatever point you condemn others you automatically condemn yourself — Phi

for thou that judgest doest the same things.

. . . dost practise the same things — ASV

You, the judge, are habitually practising the very same things — Mon

2. But we are sure that the judgment of God is according to truth against them which commit such things.

. . . against them that practise such things — ASV

And we know that God judges them who do such things, not by their words, but by their deeds — Con

"We know that God's judgment against those who practise such vices is in accord with the truth," you say? — Mon

And we know that God's judgment falls unerringly upon those who do them — TCNT

and we know that God's judgment falls rightly upon those who commit such sins — Wey

We know the doom of God falls justly upon those who practise such vices — Mof

God's judgment, we know, is utterly impartial in its action against such evildoers — Phi

3. And thinkest thou this, O man, that judgest them which do such things, and doest the same, that thou shalt escape the judgment of God?

You who judge those that do such things and yet are yourself guilty of them — do you suppose that you of all men will escape God's judgement — TCNT

What makes you think that you, who so readily judge the sins of others, can consider yourself beyond the judgment of God — Phi

4. Or despisest thou the riches of his goodness and forbearance and long-suffering;

Or the riches of his kindness and forbearance and long-suffering dost thou despise — Rhm

or does the rich abundance of His kindness . . . cause thee to despise Him — Con

Or do you think lightly of his abundant kindness, patience, and forbearance — TCNT

Or is it that thou art presuming on that abundant kindness of his, which bears with thee and waits for thee — Knox

Are you, perhaps, misinterpreting God's generosity and patient mercy toward you as weakness on his part — Phi

not knowing that the goodness of God leadeth thee to repentance?

and art thou ignorant that God, by His kindness [in withholding punishment], strives to lead thee to repentance — Con

not realizing that his kindness is meant to lead you to repentance — TCNT

and fail to see that God's kindness ought to induce you to repent — Gspd

without recognizing that God's kindness is meant to lead you to a change of heart — NEB

5. But after thy hardness and impenitent heart

Because of the hardness and impenitence of your heart — Lam

But in line with your obstinacy and impenitence of heart — Ber

But according to thy hardness and [thine] impenitent heart — Rhm

In the stubbornness of your impenitent heart — Wey

treasurest up unto thyself wrath

Art treasuring up for thyself anger — Rhm

art treasuring up against thyself a store of wrath — Con

you are laying up for yourself a treasure of wrath — Lam

against the day of wrath and revelation of the righteous judgment of God;

on the Day of Wrath, when the justice of God will burst forth — Gspd

which will be manifested in the day of wrath, even the day when God will reveal to the sight of men the righteousness of His judgment — Con

6. Who will render to every man according to his deeds:

For He will pay to all their due, according to their deeds — Con

for he will give to every man what his actions deserve — TCNT

7. To them who by patient continuance in well doing seek for glory and honour and immortality, eternal life:

to them that by patience in well-doing seek for glory and honor and incorruption, eternal life — ASV

To those who with insistent good behavior strive for excellence, genuine worth, and immortality, He awards eternal life — Ber

to those who with steadfast endurance in well-doing seek glory and honor incorruptible, He will give eternal life — Con

To those who, by perseverance in doing good, aim at glory, honour, and all that is imperishable, he will give immortal life — TCNT

8. But unto them that are contentious,

but unto them that are factious — ASV

But to them that seek their own — Alf

but for men of guile — Con

while on the self-willed — Wey

but self-seeking people — Gspd

for those who rebel against God's plan of life — Phi

but for those who are governed by selfish ambition — NEB

and do not obey the truth, but obey unrighteousness,

who are disloyal to the truth and responsive only to what is wrong — Gspd

who are always resisting the right and yielding to the wrong — Wms

indignation and wrath,

shall be wrath and indignation — ASV

there will fall wrath and anger — Wey

there will be wrath and fury — RSV

there will be the fury of retribution — NEB

9. Tribulation and anguish,

distress and despair — TCNT
crushing distress and anguish — Gspd
Suffering and affliction — Lam
Trouble and sorrow — Bas
There will be grinding misery — NEB
upon every soul of man that doeth evil,
upon every human being who persists
in wrong-doing — TCNT
for every human soul who works on the
side of evil — Phi
of the Jew first, and also of the Gentile;
of the Jew first, and also of the Greek
— ASV

10. **But glory, honour, and peace, to every man that worketh good,**
But glory and honor and peace shall
be given to every man who does the
work of good — Con
But distinction and honor and peace
to all who do what is good — Ber
But glory and honor and heart-peace
shall be awarded to every one who
(habitually) does good — Amp
to the Jew first, and also to the Gentile:
to the Jew first, and also to the Greek
— ASV

11. **For there is no respect of persons with God.**
since God shows no partiality — TCNT
For God pays no attention to this
world's distinctions — Wey
There are no human preferences with
God — Knox
For God has no favourites — NEB

12. **For as many as have sinned without law shall also perish without law:**
For they who have sinned without [the
knowledge of] the Law shall perish
without [the punishment of] the Law
— Con
All who sin without having the Law
will perish without regard to the Law
— Gspd
those who have sinned outside the pale
of the Law of Moses will perish outside its pale — NEB
and as many as have sinned in the law shall be judged by the law;
and as many as have sinned under the
law . . . — ASV
and all who sin while subject to Law
will be judged by the Law — Wey
those who have been sinners with the
law for their rule will be judged with
the law for their rule — Knox

13. **(For not the hearers of the law are just before God,**
For it is not those who hear the Law
read who are righteous in the sight
of God — Wey
For merely hearing the Law read does
not make a man upright in the sight
of God — Gspd
but the doers of the law shall be justi-fied.
But the doers of law shall be declared
righteous — Rhm
but the doers of the Law shall be
counted righteous — Con
but it is those who obey it that will be
pronounced righteous — TCNT
it is those who obey the Law who will
be acquitted — Mof
but men who practice the law will be
recognized as upright — Wms

14. **For when the Gentiles, which have not the law,**
(for when Gentiles that have not the
law — ASV
When Gentiles who have no law—Wey
When heathen who have no Law —
Gspd
When the gentiles, who have no knowledge of the Law — Phi
do by nature the things contained in the law,
do instinctively what the Law requires
— TCNT
obey by natural instinct the commands
of the Law — Mon
these, having not the law,
are a law unto themselves:
show that they have a law in themselves — Phi

15. **Which shew the work of the law writ-ten in their hearts,**
in that they show . . . — ASV
since they manifest . . . — Con
they exhibit the effect of the Law written on their hearts — Mof
for they show the demands of the Law
written upon their hearts — TCNT
They show that what the law requires
is written on their hearts — RSV
their conscience also bearing witness,
their consciences corroborating it —
TCNT
their sense of right and wrong giving
witness to it — Bas

Their own consciences endorse the existence of such a law — Phi

and their thoughts the mean while accusing or else excusing one another;)

and their inward thoughts, answering one to the other, accuse, or else defend them — Con

and their moral judgments alternately accuse or perhaps defend them — Wey

and when they dispute with one another they find themselves condemning this, approving that — Knox

16. In the day when God shall judge the secrets of men

on the day when God passes judgement on men's inmost lives — TCNT

on that Day when . . . God . . . judges what men have kept secret — Gspd

by Jesus Christ according to my gospel.

by Jesus Christ, according to the Gladtidings which I preach — Con

as the Good News that I tell declares that he will do through Christ Jesus — TCNT

through Christ Jesus in agreement with the Gospel I preach — Ber

which, according to the Gospel that I preach, will be through Jesus Christ — Nor

17. Behold, thou art called a Jew,

But if thou bearest the name of a Jew — ASV

Suppose you call yourself a Jew — Gspd

Now you, my reader, who bear the name of Jew — Phi

and restest in the law,

and resteth upon the law — ASV

and are relying upon Law — TCNT

trust on the law — Lam

take your stand upon the Law — Phi

and you feel secure in the law — Nor

rest comfortably in your Law — Beck

and makest thy boast of God,

and boastest of God's favor — Con

and boast of belonging to God — TCNT

pride yourself in God — Wey

and boast of your relation to God — RSV

you brag that you are His special friends — Tay

18. And knowest his will,

And have knowledge of his desires — Bas

know what he wants — Beck

and approvest the things that are more excellent,

And testing the things that differ—Rhm

and givest judgment upon good and evil — Con

have learnt to appreciate the finer moral distinctions — TCNT

and with a sense of what is vital in religion — Mof

can tell what is right — Gspd

discern what things are of moment — Knox

being instructed out of the law;

having been carefully instructed from the Law — TCNT

from hearing the Law read — Gspd

by being instructed in the law — Wms

because the law has taught thee—Knox

19. And art confident that thou thyself art a guide of the blind,

and believest thyself to be . . . — ABUV

and have persuaded yourself that you are a guide to the blind — Wey

a light of them which are in darkness,

a light to their darkness — Knox

20. An instructor of the foolish, a teacher of babes,

a corrector of the foolish, . . . — ASV

A trainer of the simple . . . — Rhm

an instructor of the unintelligent, and a teacher of the childish — TCNT

admonishing the fool, instructing the simple — Knox

which hast the form of knowledge and of the truth in the law.

having in the law the form of knowledge and of the truth — ASV

possessing in the Law the perfect pattern of knowledge and of truth — Con

for in the law you have the framework of knowledge and the essentials of truth — Nor

because in the Law you have the outline of all Knowledge and Truth — TCNT

. . . you have the embodiment of knowledge and truth — Mof

21. Thou therefore which teachest another, teachest thou not thyself?

Why, then, you teacher of others, do not you teach yourself — TCNT

you then who teach your fellow-man, do you refuse to teach yourself — Wey

thou that preachest a man should not steal, dost thou steal?

Do you preach against stealing, and yet steal — TCNT

You who cry out against stealing, do you steal — Wey

22. **Thou that sayest a man should not commit adultery, dost thou commit adultery?**

Do you forbid adultery, and yet commit adultery — TCNT

Will you warn men against adultery, and yet practice it yourself — Gspd

You who keep saying that a man should not commit adultery, do you commit adultery — Mon

You denounce the practice of adultery, but are you sure of your own purity — Phi

thou that abhorrest idols, dost thou commit sacrilege?

. . . dost thou rob temples — ASV

Do you loathe idols, and yet plunder temples — TCNT

23. **Thou that makest thy boast of the law,**

thou that gloriest in the law — ASV

You who pride yourself in the Law — Wey

through breaking the law dishonourest thou God?

through thy transgression of the law dishonorest thou God — ASV

do you habitually dishonor God through your transgressions of the Law — Mon

24. **For the name of God is blasphemed among the Gentiles through you,**

Why, it is owing to you that the name of God is maligned among the Gentiles — Mof

For the name of God is continually blasphemed among the Gentiles because of you — Mon

The name of God . . . has become a reproach among the Gentiles, because of you — Knox

No wonder . . . the world hates God because of you — Tay

as it is written.

even as it is written — ASV

as Scripture says — TCNT

as Holy Writ declares — Wey

There is, you know, a verse of scripture to that effect — Phi

25. **For circumcision verily profiteth, if thou keep the law:**

Circumcision has its value, if you are obeying the Law — TCNT

For Circumcision indeed profiteth, if thou be a doer of the law — ASV

Circumcision will help you only if you observe the Law — Gspd

That most intimate sign of belonging to God that we call circumcision does indeed mean something if you keep the law — Phi

Being a Jew is worth something if you obey God's laws — Tay

but if thou be a breaker of the law,

. . . a transgressor of the law — ASV

but if you habitually break the Law — Mon

But if you flout the Law — Phi

thy circumcision is made uncircumcision.

your circumcision is no better than uncircumcision — TCNT

your circumcision counts for nothing — Wey

you might as well be uncircumcised — Gspd

you are to all intents and purposes uncircumcising yourself — Phi

you are no better off than the heathen — Tay

26. **Therefore if the uncircumcision keep**

And if the heathen obey — Tay

the righteousness of the law,

the ordinances of the law — ASV

the righteous requirement of the law — Rhm

the decrees of the Law — Con

the just demands of the law — Wms

shall not his uncircumcision be counted for circumcision?

will not he, although not circumcised, be regarded by God as if he were — TCNT

will he not be counted as though he were a Jew — Wms

27. And shall not uncircumcision which is by nature, if it fulfil the law, judge thee,

Moreover, is it not plain to you that those who are physically uncircumcised, and yet keep the Law, are a continual judgment upon you — Phi

In fact, those heathen will be much better off than you Jews — Tay

who by the letter and circumcision dost transgress the law?

who with the letter and circumcision art a transgressor of the law — ASV

who with Scripture and circumcision dost break the Law — Con

who, for all your written Law and your circumcision, are yet a breaker of the Law — TCNT

who have kept the letter of the law by being circumcised but are otherwise lawbreakers — Nor

28. For he is not a Jew, which is one outwardly;

For not he who is one in appearance is a Jew — Rhm

For a man who is only a Jew outwardly is not a real Jew — TCNT

neither is that circumcision, which is outward in the flesh:

nor is outward bodily circumcision real circumcision — TCNT

and true circumcision is not that which is outward and bodily — Wey

and the real circumcision is not something physical and external — Gspd

29. But he is a Jew, which is one inwardly;

The real Jew is the man who is a Jew in soul — TCNT

The real Jew is the man who is a Jew on the inside — Wms

The true Jew is one who belongs to God in heart — Phi

A real Jew is anyone whose heart is right with God — Tay

and circumcision is that of the heart,

true circumcision is achieved in the heart — Knox

and true circumcision is heart-circumcision — Wey

in the spirit, and not in the letter;

a spiritual and not a literal thing — TCNT

according to the spirit, not the letter of the law — Knox

directed not by written precepts but by the Spirit — NEB

whose praise is not of men, but of God.

Such a man receives his praise not from men, but from God — Gspd

for God's, not for man's approval — Knox

CHAPTER 3

1. What advantage then hath the Jew?

But if this be so, what advantage has the Jew — Con

What is the advantage, then, of being a Jew — TCNT

or what profit is there of circumcision?

and what has been the profit of circumcision — Con

Or, what benefit does circumcision confer — Wms

What value was there in circumcision — Knox

2. Much every way:

Great in every way — TCNT

A great deal, from every point of view — Gspd

chiefly, because that unto them were committed

first of all, that they were intrusted with — ASV

the oracles of God.

God's utterances — TCNT

the scriptures of God — Mof

3. For what if some did not believe?

For what if some were without faith — ASV

Even supposing that some of them have proved untrustworthy — Mof

shall their unbelief make the faith of God without effect?

shall their want of faith make of none effect the faithfulness of God — ASV

will their want of faith make God break faith — TCNT

4. God forbid:

It is not to be thought of — Knox

Not at all — Wms

That be far from us — Con

Of course not! — Phi

May it never be! — NASB

Far be it! — Rhm
Never! — Mof
By no means! — Gspd
Certainly not! — NEB
Heaven forbid! — TCNT

yea, let God be true, but every man a liar;
God must prove true, though every man prove a liar — TCNT
Let us think of God as true, even if every living man be proved a liar — Phi

as it is written,
as the Scripture says — Gspd

That thou mightest be justified in thy sayings,
That thou mightest be declared righteous in thy words — Rhm
That thou mayest be vindicated in thy pleadings — Mof
That you may be shown to be right in what you say — Gspd
When thou speakest thou shalt be vindicated — NEB

and mightest overcome when thou art judged.
And win your case when you go into court — Gspd
and win the verdict when thou art on trial — NEB
and gain thy cause when men would judge thee — TCNT
and prevail when you are judged [by sinful men] — Amp

5. But if our unrighteousness commend the righteousness of God,
establisheth the righteousness of God — Alf
makes God's righteousness all the clearer — TCNT
sets God's righteousness in a clearer light — Wey
serves to magnify God's righteousness — Nor

what shall we say?
what are we to infer — Mof

Is God unrighteous who taketh vengeance?
Will God be wrong in inflicting punishment — TCNT
(Does that mean that God does wrong in punishing us for it — Knox
Is it fair, then, for Him to punish us when our sins are helping Him — Tay

(I speak as a man)
— I use a human analogy — Wey
(I am putting it in ordinary human terms) — Gspd

6. God forbid:[3]
Never! — Mof

for then how shall God judge the world?
for [if this punishment be unjust] how shall God judge the world — Con
that would mean that God has no right to judge the world — Knox

7. For if the truth of God hath more abounded through my lie unto his glory;
But if the truth of God through my lie abounded unto his glory — ASV
But, if my falsehood redounds to the glory of God, by making his truthfulness more apparent — TCNT
But, you say, if a falsehood of mine has brought great honor to God by bringing out his truthfulness — Gspd

why yet am I also judged as a sinner?
why am I still condemned as a sinner — Wms
I on my side do not deserve to be condemned as a sinner — Knox

8. And not rather, (as we be slanderously reported, and as some affirm that we say,) Let us do evil, that good may come?
Why should we not say — as some people slanderously assert that we do say — Let us do evil that good may come — TCNT
why should we not (as we are slanderously reported, and as some affirm that we say,) do evil, that good may come — ABUV
And why not do evil that good may come? — as some people slanderously charge us with saying — RSV

whose damnation is just.
The condemnation of such men is indeed just — TCNT
Such arguments are rightly condemned — Mon

9. What then? are we better than they?
What shall we say then [having gifts above the Gentiles]? have we the pre-eminence over them — Con

[3]See verse 4 for other translations of this phrase.

What follows, then? Are we Jews in any way superior to others — TCNT

What then? Are we Jews any better off — RSV

What then? Are we Jews at a disadvantage — Wey

What then? are we worse off than they — Bas

Well, then, has either side the advantage — Knox

No, in no wise:

Not at all! — Rhm

for we have before proved both Jews and Gentiles, that they are all under sin;

for we before brought the charge against both Jews and Gentiles, that . . . — Alf

for we have already charged all, both Jews and Gentiles, with the guilt of sin — Con

We have already charged Jews and Greeks all alike with being under the control of sin — Gspd

Our indictment against both Jews and Greeks was that all alike were in subjection to sin — TCNT

For I have shown above that all men from Jews to Greeks are under the condemnation of sin — Phi

for we have already shown that all men alike are sinners, whether Jews or Gentiles — Tay

10. As it is written,

As Scripture says — TCNT

The scriptures endorse this fact plainly enough — Phi

There is none righteous, no, not one:

There is not a single man who is upright — Gspd

There is not an innocent man among them, no, not one — Knox

11. There is none that understandeth,

There is none that discerneth — Rhm

there is none that seeketh after God.

not one who is searching for God! — TCNT

12. They are all gone out of the way,

They have all turned aside — ASV

All have swerved from the right path — Mon

all alike are on the wrong course — Knox

they are together become unprofitable;

one and all have gone wrong — Mof

they are one and all worthless — Gspd

Every one of them has become corrupt — Mon

all are wasted lives — Knox

they have become utterly useless — Ber

there is none that doeth good, no, not one.

. . . no, not so much as one — ASV

not one of them acts honourably, no, not one — Knox

There is no one to show kindness; no, not one — NEB

13. Their throat is an open sepulchre;

Their throats are like opened graves — TCNT

Their mouths are gaping tombs—Knox

Their talk is foul and filthy like the stench from an open grave — Tay

with their tongues they have used deceit;

they are treacherous with their tongues — Mof

They use their tongues to deceive — Gspd

Their tongues are loaded with lies — Tay

the poison of asps is under their lips:

the poison of snakes is under their lips — Bas

Everything they say has in it the sting and poison of deadly snakes — Tay

14. Whose mouth is full of cursing and bitterness:

And their mouths are full of bitter curses — TCNT

Their talk overflows with curses and calumny — Knox

15. Their feet are swift to shed blood:

They are quick to kill — Tay

They run hot-foot to shed blood — Knox

16. Destruction and misery are in their ways:

Distress and trouble dog their steps — TCNT

Ruin and wretchedness mark their paths — Gspd

Wherever they go they leave misery and trouble behind them — Tay

17. And the way of peace have they not known:

and of the path of peace they have no experience — Ber

And they have never known what it is to try to be kind and good — Tay

18. There is no fear of God before their eyes.

They do not keep the fear of God before their eyes — Knox

And reverence for God does not enter their thoughts — NEB

They care nothing about God nor what He thinks of them — Tay

19. Now we know that what things soever the law saith,

Now we know that whatever the law says — ABUV

it saith to them who are under the law:

is addressed to those who are under its authority — TCNT

that every mouth may be stopped,

that every mouth may be silenced — Wey

that every excuse may die on the lips of him who makes it — Phi

so that no one may have anything to say in self-defence — NEB

so that [the murmurs and excuses of] every mouth may be hushed — Amp

and all the world may become guilty before God.

. . . may be subject to condemnation before God — ABUV

and all the world may be brought under the judgment of God — ASV

and that the whole world may await sentence from God — Wey

and the whole world be made accountable to God — Gspd

and everyone in the world may realize his guilt before God — Nor

20. Therefore by the deeds of the law there shall no flesh be justified in his sight:

because by the works of the law . . . — ASV

No human creature can become acceptable in his sight by observing the law — Knox

Because no human creature can be brought into right standing with God by observing the Law — Wms

For no human being can be made upright in the sight of God by observing the Law — Gspd

for by the law is the knowledge of sin.

for through the law cometh the knowledge of sin — ASV

for it is Law that shows what sin is — TCNT

All that the Law can do is make men conscious of sin — Gspd

indeed it is the straightedge of the Law that shows us how crooked we are — Phi

for His laws make us see that we are sinners — Tay

21. But now the righteousness of God without the law is manifested,

But now apart from the law a righteousness of God hath been manifested — ASV

But now, not by the Law, but by another way, God's righteousness is brought to light — Con

But now, quite apart from any law, a righteousness coming from God has been fully brought to light — Mon

But now God's way of giving men right standing with Himself has come to light; a way without connection with the law — Wms

But, in these days, God's way of justification has at last been brought to light; one which . . . stands apart from the law — Knox

But now God has shown us a different way to heaven — not by being "good enough" and trying to keep his laws — Tay

being witnessed by the law and the prophets;

though the Law and the Prophets bear witness to it — Gspd

22. Even the righteousness of God

even a righteousness of God — ABUV

the Divine righteousness — TCNT

I mean a righteousness coming from God — Mon

It is God's way of uprightness — Gspd

God's way of justification — Knox

God's own way of giving men right standing with Himself — Wms

God's own way of making men righteous — Nor

which is by faith of Jesus Christ unto all and upon all them that believe:

through faith in Jesus Christ unto all them that believe — ASV

which is bestowed, through faith in Jesus Christ, upon all . . . who believe in him — TCNT

which comes by believing in Jesus Christ. And it is meant for all who have faith — Mof

for there is no difference:
for there is no difference [between Jew and Gentile] — Con
No distinction is made — Wey

23. For all have sinned,
All alike have sinned — Knox
and come short of the glory of God;
all alike are unworthy of God's praise — Knox
and none have attained the glorious likeness of God — Con
and all fall short of God's glorious ideal — TCNT
and lack the glory which comes from God — Mon
and fall short in being any glory to God — Ber
and are deprived of the divine splendour — NEB

24. Being justified freely by his grace
but they are justified for nothing by his grace — Mof
but they are now being justified by his free grace — Mon
And justification comes to us as a free gift of his grace — Knox
Being declared righteous freely by his favour — Rhm
but are acquitted freely by His grace — Wey
but by his mercy they are made upright for nothing — Gspd
And they may have righteousness put to their credit, freely, by his grace — Bas
but anybody may have right standing with God as a free gift of His undeserved favor — Wms
through the redemption that is in Christ Jesus:
through the ransom which is paid in Christ Jesus — Con
through the deliverance found in Christ Jesus — TCNT
through the salvation which is in Jesus Christ — Lam
through his act of liberation in the person of Christ Jesus — NEB

25. Whom God hath set forth to be a propitiation through faith in his blood,
Whom God set forth as a propitiatory covering . . . — Rhm
For him hath God set forth, in His blood to be a propitiatory sacrifice by means of Faith — Con

For God set him before the world, to be, by the shedding of his blood, a means of reconciliation through faith — TCNT
For God openly set him forth for himself as an offering of atonement through faith, by means of his blood — Mon
For God designed him to be the means of expiating sin by his sacrificial death, effective through faith — NEB
whom God put forward as an expiation by his blood, to be received by faith — RSV
God has appointed him as the means of propitiation, a propitiation accomplished by the shedding of his blood, to be received and made effective in ourselves by faith — Phi
to declare his righteousness for the remission of sins that are past, through the forbearance of God;
thereby to manifest the righteousness of God; because in His forbearance God had passed over the former sins of men in the times that are gone by — Con
to make clear his righteousness when, in his pity, God let the sins of earlier times go without punishment — Bas
Which was for vindication of His righteousness in forgiving the sins that previously were committed under God's forbearance — Ber
This was to show God's righteousness, because in his forbearance he had passed over former sins — RSV
This was to vindicate his own justice (for in his forbearance, God passed over men's former sins) — Gspd

26. To declare, I say, at this time his righteousness:
With a view to a showing forth of his righteousness in the present season — Rhm
to vindicate his justice at the present time — Gspd
that is, to demonstrate His justice at the present time — Wey
for the exhibition of his righteousness in this present time — ABUV
that he might be just, and the justifier of him which believeth in Jesus.
That he might be righteous even when declaring righteous him that hath faith in Jesus — Rhm

that he himself might be just, and yet the justifier of him who has faith in Jesus — Mon

27. Where is boasting then?

Where, then, is the boasting [of the Jew] — Con

Then what becomes of our boasting — Mof

Where then is there room for boasting — Wey

What reason, then, is there for pride — Bas

Then what can we boast about doing to earn our salvation — Tay

It is excluded.

It has been shut out — Con

It is ruled out absolutely — Mof

Nothing at all — Tay

By what law? of works? Nay; but by the law of faith.

By what manner of law? of works? Nay: but by a law of faith — ASV

By what sort of Law? A Law requiring obedience? No, a Law requiring faith — TCNT

On what principle? On the principle of doing deeds? No, on the principle of faith — Mof

28. Therefore we conclude that a man is justified by faith without the deeds of the law.

For we conclude that a man is pronounced righteous on the ground of faith, quite apart from the obedience to Law — TCNT

For we deem that a man is accounted righteous by faith, apart from fulfilment of the Law — Wey

For we hold that a man is brought into right standing with God by faith, that observance of the law has no connection with it — Wms

So it is that we are saved by faith in Christ and not by the good things we do — Tay

29. Is he the God of the Jews only? is he not also of the Gentiles?

Or is God the God of Jews only? is he not the God of Gentiles also — ASV

Does God belong to the Jews alone? Does he not belong to the heathen too — Gspd

Yes, of the Gentiles also:

Yea, He is the God of the Gentiles also — Con

30. Seeing it is one God, which shall justify the circumcision by faith, and uncircumcision through faith.

if so be that God is one, and he shall justify . . . — ASV

For God is one [for all men], and He will justify . . . — Con

God treats us all the same; all, whether Jews or Gentiles, are approved if they have faith — Tay

31. Do we then make void the law through faith?

Do we then make the law of none effect through faith — ASV

Is this using faith to overthrow law — Gspd

Why, then? Do we nullify the law through faith — Lam

Does that mean that we are using faith to rob the law of its force — Knox

God forbid:[4]

Heaven forbid! — TCNT

Not for one moment! — Mof

Far from it — Gspd

On the contrary — RSV

yea, we establish the law.

We uphold the Law — Mof

This confirms the Law — Gspd

we are setting the law on its right footing — Knox

We put the Law in its proper place — Phi

CHAPTER 4

1. What shall we say then that Abraham our father, as pertaining to the flesh, hath found?

. . . that Abraham, our forefather, hath found according to the flesh — ASV

What, then, can we say that our father

Abraham gained by the fleshly ordinance — Con

But if so, what can we say about Abra-

---

[4]See Rom. 3:4 for other translations of this phrase.

ham, our forefather by natural descent — Mof

Now how does all this affect the position of our ancestor Abraham — Phi

2. For if Abraham were justified by works,

If he was pronounced righteous as the result of obedience — TCNT

For if he was made upright by what he did — Gspd

he hath whereof to glory; but not before God.

he hath ground of boasting. But he hath none before God — Alf

he has a ground of boasting. But he has no ground of boasting with God — Con

then he would have something to boast about. But from God's point of view Abraham had no basis at all for pride — Tay

**3. For what saith the scripture?
Abraham believed God,**

Abraham put his faith in God — Knox

Abraham had faith in God — Gspd

and it was counted unto him for righteousness.

and it was set down to his account as righteousness — Mon

and his faith was regarded by God as righteousness — TCNT

and it was credited to him as uprightness — Gspd

. . . as right standing with God — Wms

and that is why God cancelled his sins and declared him just and righteous — Tay

4. Now to him that worketh is the reward not reckoned of grace, but of debt.

Now if a man earn his pay by his work, it is not counted to him as a favor, but it is paid him as a debt — Mon

Now to one who works, his wages are not reckoned as a gift but as his due — RSV

Now if a man does a piece of work, his wages are not 'counted' as a favour; they are paid as a debt — NEB

5. But to him that worketh not, but believeth on him that justifieth the ungodly,

but a man who has no work to offer, but has faith in him who can make the ungoldly upright — Gspd

Whereas unto him that worketh not but believeth on him that declareth righteous the ungodly — Rhm

But if without any work to his credit he simply puts his faith in him who acquits the guilty — NEB

his faith is counted for righteousness.

his faith is reckoned as righteousness — Rhm

his faith is regarded by God as righteousness — TCNT

his faith is credited to him as righteousness — Wey

6. Even as David also describeth the blessedness of the man,

Even as David also pronounceth blessing upon the man — ASV

In precisely the same way David speaks of the blessing pronounced . . . — TCNT

Just as David also affirmeth the happiness of the man — Rhm

unto whom God imputeth righteousness without works,

unto whom God reckoneth righteousness apart from works — Rhm

whom God credits with righteousness apart from his actions — Wey

7. Saying, Blessed are they whose iniquities are forgiven,

Happy they whose lawlessnesses have been forgiven — Rhm

Blessed are those whose wrong-doings have been forgiven — TCNT

Happy are they whose violations of the Law . . . — Gspd

and whose sins are covered.

and over whose sins a veil has been drawn! — TCNT

and whose sins are wiped away — Lam

all their transgressions buried away — Knox

and put out of sight — Tay

8. Blessed is the man to whom the Lord will not impute sin.

Blessed the man whom the Lord will never regard as sinful! — TCNT

Happy is the man whose sin the Lord will take no account of! — Gspd

Happy are they whose sin the Lord does not charge against him! — Wms

Yes, what joy there is for anyone whose sins are no longer counted against him — Tay

9. Cometh this blessedness then upon the circumcision only, or upon the uncircumcision also?

Is this blessing, then, for the circumcised alone? or does it not belong also to the uncircumcised — Con

Now does this happiness come to the Jews alone, or to the heathen peoples too — Wms

for we say that faith was reckoned to Abraham for righteousness.

for we say, his faith was reckoned to Abraham for righteousness — Con

We say that — Abraham's faith was regarded by God as righteousness — TCNT

What we say is, Abraham's faith was credited to him as uprightness — Gspd

For we say, Abraham's faith was credited to him as right standing — Wms

10. How was it then reckoned?

Under what circumstances, then, did this take place — TCNT

when he was in circumcision, or in uncircumcision?

Was it after he was circumcised, or before — Gspd

Not in circumcision, but in uncircumcision.

Not after he was circumcised, but before — Gspd

11. And he received the sign of circumcision,

And he received circumcision as an outward sign of inward things — Con

and he was afterward given the mark of circumcision — Gspd

Circumcision was only given to him as a token — Knox

The circumcision ceremony was a sign that Abraham already had faith and that God had already accepted him — Tay

a seal of the righteousness of the faith which he had yet being uncircumcised:

as a seal of that justification which came to him through his faith while he was still uncircumcised — Knox

a seal of the faith-righteousness which he had while he was in uncircumcision — Mon

as the stamp of God's acknowledgment of the uprightness based on faith that was his before he was circumcised — Gspd

as a witness of the faith which he had before he underwent circumcision — Bas

to confirm the righteousness he got by believing before he was circumcised — Beck

— to attest the righteousness due to the faith of an uncircumcised man — TCNT

that he might be the father of all them that believe, though they be not circumcised;

in order that he might be the father of all who have faith in God even when uncircumcised — TCNT

so that he might be the father of all uncircumcised believers — Ber

The purpose was to make him the father of all who believe without being circumcised — RSV

that righteousness might be imputed unto them also:

To the end [the same] righteousness might be reckoned unto them—Rhm

that they also may be regarded by God as righteous — TCNT

that they might have their faith credited to them as right standing with God — Wms

12. And the father of circumcision to them who are not of the circumcision only,

He is the father of circumcision to those who are not merely circumcised — Mon

and at the same time he is the father of such of the circumcised as do not rely upon their circumcision alone — NEB

As well as the father of the Jews who are not only circumcised — Beck

but who also walk in the steps of that faith of our father Abraham, which he had being yet uncircumcised.

but who also follow our father Abraham in that faith which he had while still uncircumcised — TCNT

but follow our forefather Abraham's example in the faith he had before he was circumcised — Gspd

13. For the promise, that he should be the heir of the world, was not to Abraham, or to his seed, through the law,

For the promise to Abraham and his seed that he should inherit the world came not by the Law — Con

The promise made to Abraham and his descendants — that they should possess the earth — was given, not because of their keeping the law — Nor

but through the righteousness of faith.

but through the uprightness that resulted from his faith — Gspd

but through the righteousness due to faith — TCNT

but through faith-righteousness — Mon

but because of the righteousness which had its roots in faith — Phi

but because of justification by faith — Nor

14. For if they which are of the law be heirs,

For if it is adherents of the Law who are heirs — Mof

For if it is those who rely on Law who are heirs — Wey

faith is made void, and the promise made of none effect:

Faith is made of no account, and the promise is brought to nought — Con

faith is nullified and the promise amounts to nothing! — Gspd

faith is empty and the promise becomes void — Mon

then faith is useless and the promise counts for nothing — Wey

then faith is futile and the promise is abrogated — Ber

then faith is robbed of its meaning and the promise comes to nothing! — TCNT

15. Because the law worketh wrath:

because the Law brings [not blessings but] punishment — Con

For we have already noted that the Law can produce no promise, only the threat of wrath to come — Phi

For where there is law there is wrath — Nor

for where no law is, there is no transgression.

but, where no Law exists, no breach of it is possible — TCNT

16. Therefore it is of faith, that it might be by grace;

That is why it depends on faith, in order that the promise may rest on grace — RSV

That is why all turns upon faith; it is to make the promise a matter of favour — Mof

The promise was made on the ground of faith, in order that it might be a matter of sheer grace — NEB

to the end the promise might be sure to all the seed;

that so the promise [not being capable of forfeiture] might stand firm to all the seed of Abraham — Con

thus the promise is made good to all Abraham's posterity — Knox

and be guaranteed to all his descendants — RSV

not to that only which is of the law, but to that also which is of the faith of Abraham;

not to his children of the Law alone, but to the children of his Faith — Con

not merely to those who rely on the Law, but also to those who rely on a faith like Abraham's — Wey

not only that posterity of his which keeps the law, but that which imitates his faith — Knox

who is the father of us all,

17. (As it is written, I have made thee a father of many nations,) before him whom he believed,

as the Scripture says, I have made you the father of many nations. The promise is guaranteed in the very sight of God in whom he had faith — Gspd

That is what the Scriptures mean when they say that God made Abraham the father of many nations. God will accept all people in every nation who trust God as Abraham did — Tay

even God,

who quickeneth the dead,

who gives life to the dead — TCNT

who can make the dead live — Phi

and calleth those things which be not as though they were.

and calls into existence the things that do not exist — RSV

and speaks of future events with as much certainty as though they were already past — Tay

and speak his word to those who are yet unborn — Phi

18. **Who against hope believed in hope,**

who past hope upon hope believed — Rhm

With no ground for hope, Abraham, sustained by hope, put faith in God — TCNT

Abraham, hoping against hope, had faith — Gspd

that he might become the father of many nations, according to that which was spoken, So shall thy seed be.

to the end that he might become a father of . . . — ASV

and so became the father of many nations, in fulfilment of the Scripture, So countless shall your descendants be — Gspd

19. **And being not weak in faith, he considered not his own body now dead, when he was about an hundred years old, neither yet the deadness of Sarah's womb:**

And without being weakened in faith he considered his own body now as good as dead (he being about a hundred years old), and the deadness of Sarah's womb — ASV

His faith never quailed, even when he noted the utter impotence of his own body (for he was about a hundred years old) or the impotence of Sarah's womb — Mof

Though he was nearly a hundred years old, yet his faith did not fail him, even when he thought of his own body, then utterly worn out, and remembered that Sarah was past bearing children — TCNT

20. **He staggered not at the promise of God through unbelief;**

yet, looking unto the promise of God, he wavered not through unbelief — ASV

and yet he never staggered in doubt at the promise of God — Wms

but was strong in faith,

but waxed strong through faith — ASV

On the contrary, his faith gave him strength — TCNT

giving glory to God;

and he praised God for this blessing before it ever happened — Tay

21. **And being fully persuaded that,**

and being absolutely certain that — Wey

fully convinced that — Knox

in the full assurance that — Gspd

in the firm conviction that — TCNT

what he had promised, he was able also to perform.

God was able to do what he had promised — Gspd

22. **And therefore it was imputed to him for righteousness.**

And therefore his faith was regarded as righteousness — TCNT

Hence his faith was counted to him as righteousness — Mof

For this reason also his faith was credited to him as righteousness — Wey

23. **Now it was not written for his sake alone, that it was imputed to him;**

It was not on his account alone that these words, "it was credited to him," were written — Gspd

24. **But for us also, to whom it shall be imputed,**

But for our sake also, unto whom it shall be reckoned — ASV

but also with reference to us. Our faith, too, will be regarded by God in the same light — TCNT

if we believe on him that raised up Jesus our Lord from the dead;

who believe on him that raised Jesus our Lord from the dead — ASV

if we have faith in him who . . .—TCNT

25. **Who was delivered for our offences, and was raised again for our justification.**

who was delivered up for our trespasses, and . . . — ASV

who was delivered up because of our offences, and was raised to life for our acquittal — Wey

Him who was delivered up because of our transgressions, and was raised because of our justification — NASB

CHAPTER 5

1. **Therefore being justified by faith,**

. . . having been justified . . . — NASB

. . . declared righteous . . . — Rhm

Since we stand justified as the result of faith — Mon

we have peace with God through our

Lord Jesus Christ:

let us have peace . . . — Alf

let us enjoy the peace we have . . . — Mof

let us continue to enjoy the peace we have . . . — Mon

let us grasp the fact that we have peace . . . — Phi

let us enjoy peace with God through Jesus Christ, our Lord — TCNT

2. **By whom also we have access by faith into this grace wherein we stand,**

through whom also we have had our access by faith . . . — ASV

Through whom also we have had our introduction by our faith into this favour wherein we stand — Rhm

and rejoice in hope of the glory of God.

and we exult in hope of the glory of God — Con

and triumph in the hope of God's glory — Mof

So let us exult in our hope of attaining God's glorious ideal — TCNT

And let us glory in our hope of sharing the glory of God — Gspd

And we rejoice in the hope of beholding the glory of God — Nor

Let us exult in the hope of the divine splendour that is to be ours — NEB

and we confidently and joyfully look forward to actually becoming all that God has had in mind for us to be — Tay

3. **And not only so, but we glory in tribulations also:**

And not only so, but we even glory in our tribulations — Alf

. . . but we also rejoice in our tribulations — ASV

. . . we exult also in our sufferings — Con

. . . let us exult in our afflictions also ABUV

Not only so, but we triumph even in our troubles — Mof

This doesn't mean, of course, that we have only a hope of future joys — we can be full of joy here and now even in our trials and troubles — Phi

knowing that tribulation worketh patience;

. . . perfects patience in us — Lam

. . . worketh steadfastness — ASV

. . . brings about perseverance — NASB

for we know that trouble works fortitude — Mon

. . . produces endurance — Gspd

4. **And patience, experience,**

and endurance, approval — Alf

and endurance strength of character— TCNT

endurance, ripeness of character—Wey

and endurance, tested character — Wms

and endurance brings proof that we have stood the test — NEB

and experience, hope:

and character produces hope — Mof

and this proof is the ground of hope — NEB

5. **And hope maketh not ashamed;**

and our hope cannot shame us in the day of trial — Con

and that hope never disappoints — TCNT

Nor does this hope delude us — Knox

because the love of God is shed abroad in our hearts by the Holy Ghost which is given unto us.

Because the love of God has been poured forth in our hearts . . . — ABUV

since God's love floods our hearts through the holy Spirit which has been given to us — Mof

6. **For when we were yet without strength,**

For while we were yet helpless [in our sins] — Con

while we were still powerless to help ourselves — Knox

When we were utterly helpless with no way of escape — Tay

in due time Christ died for the ungodly.

Christ at the appointed time died for sinners — Con

Christ, in God's good time, died on behalf of the godless — TCNT

at the decisive moment Christ died for us godless men — Gspd

7. **For scarcely for a righteous man will one die:**

Why, a man will hardly die for the just — Mof

Why, a man will hardly give his life for an upright person — Gspd

Now it is an extraordinary thing for one to give his life even for an upright man — Amp

yet peradventure for a good man some would even dare to die.

(although some, perchance, would even endure death for the good) — Con

though once in a while a man is brave enough to die for a generous friend — Wms

though perhaps for a noble and lovable and generous benefactor someone might even dare to die — Amp

8. **But God commendeth his love toward us, in that, while we were yet sinners, Christ died for us.**

But God commendeth his own love toward us . . . — ASV

But God demonstrates His own love . . . — NASB

But he giveth proof of his own love toward us . . . — Alf

But God proves his love for us by the fact that Christ died for us when we were still sinners — Gspd

Yet the proof of God's amazing love is this: that it was while we were sinners that Christ died for us—Phi

9. **Much more then, being now justified by his blood,**

Much more, then, now that we have been pronounced righteous by virtue of the shedding of his blood — TCNT

Much more, then, now that we have been acquitted by His blood — Wey

we shall be saved from wrath through him.

shall we be saved through him from the wrath [to come] — Alf

it is far more certain that through him we shall be saved from God's anger — Gspd

10. **For if, when we were enemies, we were reconciled to God by the death of his Son,**

For if while we were hostile we were reconciled to Him through . . . — Wey

If while were His enemies we were made God's friends by the death of His Son — Beck

much more, being reconciled, we shall be saved by his life.

it is far more certain that now that we are reconciled we shall be saved through sharing in his life — Gspd

surely now that we are reconciled we may be perfectly certain of our salvation through his living in us — Phi

it is much more certain that since we have been reconciled we shall finally be saved through His new life — Wms

it is much more [certain], now that we are reconciled, that we shall be saved [daily delivered from sin's dominion] through His [resurrection] life — Amp

11. **And not only so, but we also joy in God through our Lord Jesus Christ,**

Not only so, but we triumph in God . . . — Mof

Nor is this our hope only for the time to come; but also [in our present sufferings] we exult in God . . . — Con

And not only that, but this too: we shall continue exulting in God . . . — Wms

by whom we have now received the atonement.

by whom we have now received reconciliation with God — Con

through whom we have now obtained our reconciliation — Mon

12. **Wherefore, as by one man sin entered into the world, and death by sin;**

This, therefore, is like the case when, through one man [Adam], sin entered into the world, and by sin death — Con

So here is the comparison: As through one man sin came into the world, and death as the consequence of sin — Wms

and so death passed upon all men,

and so death spread to all mankind — Con

and thus death pervaded the whole human race — NEB

for that all have sinned:

because all men sinned — Gspd

because all had sinned — Mon

for no one was himself free from sin — Phi

13. **(For until the law sin was in the world:**

For before the Law was given [by

Moses], there was sin in the world
— Con

To be sure, sin was in the world earlier
than the Law — Ber

**but sin is not imputed when there is
no law.**

but sin is not reckoned against the sinner, when there is no law [forbid-
ding it] — Con

but sin cannot be charged against a
man where no Law exists — TCNT

though I suppose, technically speaking, it was not "sin" where there was
no law to define it — Phi

**14. Nevertheless death reigned from Adam
to Moses,**

Nevertheless death, the complement of
sin, held sway over mankind . . . —
Phi

and yet we see death reigning in the
world from Adam's time to the time
of Moses — Knox

**even over them that had not sinned
after the similitude of Adam's transgression,**

even over those whose sin was not a
breach of law, as Adam's was —
TCNT

even over those who had not sinned
as Adam had, in the face of an express command — Gspd

**who is the figure of him that was to
come.**

And Adam foreshadows that One to
come — TCNT

Now Adam is a type of Him who was
to come — Mon

Adam, the first man, corresponds in
some degree to the man who was
to come — Phi

**15. But not as the offence, so also is the
free gift.**

But far greater is the gift than was the
transgression — Con

but the gift is very different from the
trespass — Mof

But the free gift is not like the transgression — Mon

But God's act of grace is out of all
proportion to Adam's wrongdoing
— NEB

**For if through the offence of one many
be dead,**

For if by the trespass of the one the
many died — ASV

for if by the sin of the one man
[Adam] death came upon the many
— Con

For, if by reason of the offence of the
one man the whole race died —
TCNT

For if one man's offense made the
mass of mankind die — Gspd

**much more the grace of God, and the
gift by grace, which is by one man,
Jesus Christ, hath abounded unto
many.**

much more did the grace of God and
his free gift abound unto the many
by the grace of the one man Jesus
Christ — Alf

Much more the favour of God and the
free-gift in favour . . . unto the many
superabounded — Rhm

the grace of God and the free gift
which comes by the grace of the
one man Jesus Christ overflowed
far more richly upon the rest of men
— Mof

much more in the grace of the one
man Jesus Christ has the freeness
of God's bounty overflowed unto the
many — Con

far more were the loving-kindness of
God, and the gift given in the lov-
ing-kindness of the one man, Jesus
Christ, lavished upon the whole race
— TCNT

God's mercy and his gift given through
the favor of the one man Jesus
Christ have far more powerfully
affected mankind — Gspd

its effect is vastly exceeded by the grace
of God and the gift that came to so
many by the grace of the one man,
Jesus Christ — NEB

**16. And not as it was by one that sinned,
so is the gift:**

Moreover, the boon [of God] exceeds
the fruit of Adam's sin — Con

There is a contrast, too, between the
gift and the results of the one man's
sin — TCNT

Nor is there any comparison between
the gift and the effects of that one
man's sin — Gspd

And the effect of the gift of God was
greater than the effect of the offence
of Adam — Lam

for the judgment was by one to con-

demnation, but the free gift is of many offences unto justification.

for the judgment came of one unto condemnation, but the free gift came of many trespasses unto justification — ASV

for the doom came out of one offence, a sentence of condemnation; but the gift comes, out of many offences, a sentence of acquittal — Con

for while the sentence ensuing on a single sin resulted in doom, the free gift ensuing on many trespasses issues in acquittal — Mof

That sentence arose from the act of one man, and was for condemnation; but God's gift arose out of many offenses and results in acquittal — Gspd

17. For if by one man's offence death reigned by one;

For if the reign of death was established by the one man [Adam], through the sin of him alone — Con

For if through the transgression of the one, death reigned as king through the one — Mon

If one man by his sin made death a king — Beck

And if death began its reign through one man, owing to one man's fault — Knox

The sin of this one man, Adam, caused death to be king over all — Tay

much more they which receive abundance of grace and of the gift of righteousness shall reign in life by one, Jesus Christ.)

far more shall the reign of life be established in those who receive the overflowing fulness of the free gift of righteousness by the one man Jesus Christ — Con

all the more will those who receive God's overflowing mercy and gift of uprightness live and reign through the one individual Jesus Christ — Gspd

to a much greater degree will those who continue to receive the overflow of His unmerited favor and His gift of right standing with Himself, reign in real life through one, Jesus Christ — Wms

18. Therefore as by the offence of one judgment came upon all men to condemnation;

Therefore, as the fruit of one offence reached to all men, and brought upon them condemnation — Con

Well then, as one man's trespass issued in doom for all — Mof

To conclude then: As the one fall affected all men for their condemnation — Ber

even so by the righteousness of one the free gift came upon all men unto justification of life.

so, too, a single decree of righteousness resulted for all mankind in that declaration of righteousness which brings Life — TCNT

so also the result of a single deed of righteousness is a life-giving acquittal for all mankind — Wey

so through one righteous act there is for all men a justified life — Ber

so one man's act of righteousness leads to acquittal and life for all men — RSV

19. For as by one man's disobedience

For, as through the disobedience of the one man — TCNT

many were made sinners,

the many were constituted sinners — ABUV

the whole race was rendered sinful — TCNT

the many were placed in the position of sinners — Ber

all were made sinners — Beck

so by the obedience of one

so, too, through the obedience of the one — TCNT

shall many be made righteous.

will the many be constituted righteous — ABUV

the mass of mankind will be made righteous — Wey

the whole race will be rendered righteous — TCNT

20. Moreover the law entered, that the offence might abound.

And the Law was added, that sin might abound — Con

Law slipped in to aggravate the trespass — Mof

Then law slipped in, and multiplied the offense — Gspd

The introduction of the law caused sin to increase — Lam

But the Law came in, [only] to expand and increase the trespass [making it more apparent and exciting opposition] — Amp

But where sin abounded, grace did much more abound:

But where the sin abounded the favour greatly superabounded — Rhm

but where sin abounded, the gift of grace has overflowed beyond [the outbreak of sin] — Con

But, where sins were multiplied, the loving-kindness of God was lavished the more — TCNT

sin increased, but grace surpassed it by far — Mof

Yet, though sin is shown to be wide and deep, thank God his grace is wider and deeper still! — Phi

But where sin was thus multiplied, grace immeasurably exceeded it — NEB

21. That as sin hath reigned unto death,

in order that, just as Sin had reigned in the realm of Death — TCNT

so that just as sin had reigned through death — Gspd

in order that as sin has reigned and brought death — Wey

The whole outlook changes — sin used to be the master of men and in the end handed them over to death — Phi

even so might grace reign through righteousness unto eternal life by Jesus Christ our Lord.

so also grace might rule as king in righteousness which issues in eternal life — Mon

now grace is the ruling factor, with righteousness as its purpose and its end the bringing of men to the eternal Life of God through Jesus Christ our Lord — Phi

CHAPTER 6

1. What shall we say then?

Then what shall we conclude — Gspd

Shall we continue in sin, that grace may abound?

shall we persist in sin that the gift of grace may be more abundant—Con

Shall we sin to our heart's content and see how far we can exploit the grace of God — Phi

2. God forbid.[5]

How shall we, that are dead to sin, live any longer therein?

How shall we, who died to sin, live . . . — ABUV

We have died, once for all, to sin; can we breathe its air again — Knox

3. Know ye not, that so many of us as were baptized into Jesus Christ were baptized into his death?

Or, are ye ignorant, that all we who were immersed into Christ Jesus were immersed into his death — ABUV

or have you forgotten that all of us, when we were baptized into fellowship with Christ Jesus, were baptized into fellowship with His death —Con

Do you not know that all of us who have been baptized into union with Christ Jesus have been baptized into his death — Gspd

4. Therefore we are buried with him by baptism into death:

We were buried therefore with him through our baptism into his death — Alf

We were buried therefore with him through the immersion into his death — ABUV

Our baptism in his death made us share his burial — Mof

that like as Christ was raised up from the dead

that, just as Christ was raised from the dead — TCNT

by the glory of the father,

by a manifestation of the Father's power — TCNT

by the Father's glorious power—Wey

in the splendour of the Father — NEB

even so we also should walk in newness of life.

---

[5]See Rom. 3:4 for a variety of translations of this phrase.

we too might live and move in the new sphere of Life — Mof

we also should live an entirely new life — Wey

so we too might habitually live and behave in newness of life — Amp

5. For if we have been planted together in the likeness of his death,

For if we have been grafted into the likeness of His death — Con

For if we have become united with the likeness of his death — ABUV

For if we have grown into union with him by undergoing a death like his — Gspd

For if we have been united with him in a death like his — RSV

For if we have become one with Him by sharing in His death — Wey

we shall be also in the likeness of his resurrection:

so shall we also share His resurrection — Con

so we shall also be united with him in the likeness of his resurrection — Mon

we shall also be one with Him by sharing in His resurrection — Wey

surely we shall share a resurrection life like His — Wms

we shall certainly be united with him in a resurrection like his — RSV

6. Knowing this, that our old man is crucified with him,

For we know that our old man was crucified with Christ — Con

This we know — that our old self was nailed to the cross with Him—Wey

Let us never forget that our old selves died with him on the cross — Phi

We know that the man we once were has been crucified with Christ — NEB

that the body of sin might be destroyed,

In order that the sinful body might be made powerless— Rhm

in order that the body, the stronghold of Sin, might be rendered powerless — TCNT

in order that our sinful nature might be neutralized — Wey

in order that [our] body, [which is the instrument] of sin, might be made

ineffective and inactive for evil — Amp

that henceforth we should not serve sin.

that so we should no longer be in bondage to sin — ASV

that we might no longer be the slaves of sin — Con

7. For he that is dead is freed from sin.

for he that hath died is justified from sin — ASV

For the man who has so died has been pronounced righteous and released from Sin — TCNT

(for once dead, a man is absolved from the claims of sin) — Mof

for a dead man can safely be said to be immune to the power of sin—Phi

8. Now if we be dead with Christ,

But if we died with Christ — ASV

Now, if we have shared the death of Christ — Con

we believe that we shall also live with him.

we believe that we shall also share His life — Con

9. Knowing that Christ being raised from the dead dieth no more;

. . . Christ, once raised from the dead, will never die again — Gspd

death hath no more dominion over him.

Death over him no more hath lordship — Rhm

Death has power over him no longer — TCNT

death's power to touch him is finished — Phi

10. For in that he died, he died unto sin once:

For the death that he died, he died unto sin once — ASV

For the death that he died was a death to sin, once and for all — TCNT

For by the death He died He once for all ended His relation to sin — Wms

but in that he liveth, he liveth unto God.

but the life that he liveth, he liveth unto God — ASV

but He lives [forever] unto God—Con

the life he now lives is a life in relation to God — Gspd

but now He lives forever in unbroken fellowship with God — Tay

11. Likewise reckon ye also yourselves to be dead indeed unto sin, but alive unto God

So let it be with you — regard yourselves as dead to sin, but as living for God — TCNT

So you must think of yourselves as dead to sin but alive to God—Gspd

So you too must consider yourselves as having ended your relation to sin but living in unbroken relation to God — Wms

In the same way look upon yourselves as dead to the appeal and power of sin but alive and sensitive to the call of God — Phi

through Jesus Christ our Lord.

In Christ Jesus — ASV

through union with Christ Jesus — TCNT

because you are in Christ Jesus—Beck

12. Let not sin therefore reign

Accordingly sin must not continue to reign — Wms

Therefore let not sin rule as king — Mon

in your mortal body,

in your death-doomed body — Rhm

that ye should obey it in the lusts thereof.

causing you to obey its lusts — Con

and compel you to obey its cravings TCNT

that ye should obey its desires — ABUV

to make you subject to its appetites — Knox

13. Neither yield ye your members as instruments of unrighteousness unto sin:

nor present your members to sin as weapons of unrighteousness—ABUV

Do not continue to present any part of your body to sin to be used as a weapon of unrighteousness — Mon

and no longer offer your faculties as instruments of wickedness for sin to use — Wey

Do not offer any part of your bodies to Sin, in the cause of unrighteousness — TCNT

you must not let sin have your members for the service of vice — Mof

and you must not offer the parts of your bodies to sin as the instruments of wrong — Gspd

Don't let sin keep on using your organs as tools for doing wrong — Beck

but yield yourselves unto God, as those that are alive from the dead,

but once for all offer yourselves to God (as those who, though once dead, now have Life) — TCNT

But, like men rescued from certain death, put yourselves in God's hands — Phi

put yourselves at the disposal of God, as dead men raised to life — NEB

you must dedicate yourselves to God as men who have been brought from death to life — Mof

and your members as instruments of righteousness unto God.

and the various parts of your bodies to be used as weapons of righteousness — Mon

and devote every part of your bodies to the cause of righteousness—TCNT

and let God use your organs as tools for doing what is right — Beck

14. For sin shall not have dominion over you:

for sin shall not have the mastery over you — Con

. . . must no longer control you—Gspd

. . . shall not be lord over you — Wey

. . . is not meant to be your master — Phi

for ye are not under the law, but under grace.

for you are not under the rule of law, but under the rule of grace — Mon

for you are not governed by Law, but by grace — Ber

15. What then? shall we sin, because we are not under the law, but under grace?

What then? Shall we commit an act of sin because . . .—Mon

What follows, then? Are we to sin because we are living under the reign of Love and not of Law — TCNT

God forbid.[6]

16. Know ye not, that to whom ye yield yourselves servants to obey, his servants ye are to whom ye obey;

Know ye not that He to whose service you give yourselves is your real master — Con

---

[6]See Rom. 3:4 for other translations of this phrase.

Surely you know that, when you offer yourselves as servants, to obey any one, you are the servants of the person whom you obey — TCNT

Don't you know that when you submit to someone as master and obey him, you become his slave — Nor

whether of sin unto death, or of obedience unto righteousness?

whether sin, whose end is death, or obedience, whose end is righteousness — Con

and this is true whether you serve sin, with death as its result; or obedience, with righteousness as its results — NEB

17. But God be thanked, that ye were the servants of sin,

But thanks be to God, that, whereas ye were servants of sin — ASV

But, thank God! though you were once slaves of sin — Gspd

but ye have obeyed from the heart

you have now yielded a hearty obedience to — Wey

that form of doctrine which was delivered you.

the standard of teaching to which you were introduced — Ber

that form of teaching whereunto ye were delivered — ASV

the teaching whereby you were moulded anew — Con

that form of doctrine under which you were placed — TCNT

18. Being then made free from sin, ye became the servants of righteousness.

and when you were freed from the slavery of sin, you became the bondsmen of righteousness — Con

19. I speak after the manner of men because of the infirmity of your flesh:

(I use this human analogy to bring the truth home to your weak nature.) — Mof

(I use an everyday illustration because human nature grasps truth more readily that way.) — Phi

I speak this way, using the illustration about slaves, because it makes it easy to understand — Tay

for as ye have yielded your members servants to uncleanness and to iniquity unto iniquity;

Once you offered every part of your bodies to the service of impurity,

and of wickedness, which leads to further wickedness — TCNT

For just as you before gave up the parts of your bodies in slavery to vice and greater and greater license — Gspd

For just as you formerly offered the parts of your bodies in slavery to impurity and to ever increasing lawlessness — Wms

even so now yield your members servants to righteousness unto holiness.

even so now present your members as servants to righteousness unto sanctification — ASV

Now, in the same way, offer them to the service of Righteousness, which leads to holiness — TCNT

so now you must surrender your faculties into slavery to righteousness, unto deeds of holiness — Mon

so you must now put them at the service of righteousness, with holiness as your goal — Wey

20. For when ye were the servants of sin, ye were free from righteousness.

For when you were the slaves of sin, you were free from the service of righteousness — Con

. . . you were under no subjection to righteousness — Mon

When you were slaves of sin, you weren't free to serve righteousness as your master — Beck

21. What fruit had ye then in those things whereof ye are now ashamed?

Well, what did you gain then by it all? Nothing but what you are now ashamed of! — Mof

But what were the fruits that you reaped from those things of which you are now ashamed — Wms

And what harvest were you then reaping, from acts which now make you blush — Knox

for the end of those things is death.

Why, they result in death! — Gspd

None, for they end in death — Wms

In the long run those things mean one thing only — death — Phi

22. But now being made free from sin, and become servants to God,

But now, being freed from the bondage of sin, and enslaved to the service of God — Con

Now that you are free from the claims of sin, and have become God's slaves instead — Knox

But now, freed from the commands of sin and bound to the service of God — NEB

ye have your fruit unto holiness, and the end everlasting life.

. . . unto sanctification, and the end eternal life — ASV

your fruit is growth in holiness, and its end is life eternal — Con

the fruit that you reap is an ever-increasing holiness, and the end Immortal Life — TCNT

your gain is consecration, and the end

of that is life eternal — Mof

the immediate result is consecration, and the final destiny is eternal life — Wms

23. For the wages of sin is death;

Sin pays its servants: the wage is death — Phi

but the gift of God is eternal life through Jesus Christ our Lord.

but the free gift of God . . . — ASV

but the gift of God is Immortal Life, through union with Christ Jesus, our Lord — TCNT

but God gives to those who serve him: his free gift is eternal life through Christ Jesus our Lord — Phi

CHAPTER 7

1. Know ye not, brethren, (for I speak to them that know the law,)

[I say that you are not under the Law]; or are you ignorant, brethren (for I speak to those who know the Law) — Con

Do you not know, brothers — for I am speaking to men who know what law is — Gspd

You must surely be aware, brethren (for I am speaking to men who have some knowledge of law) — Knox

how that the law hath dominion over a man as long as he liveth?

that the dominion of the Law over men lasts only during their life — Con

That law governs a person only during his lifetime — Mon

that legal claims are only binding on a man so long as he is alive — Knox

2. For the woman which hath an husband

thus the married woman — Con

A wife, for instance — Wey

is bound by the law to her husband so long as he liveth;

is bound by the Law to her husband while he lives — Con

but if the husband be dead,

but if the husband die — ASV

she is loosed from the law of her husband.

the marriage law no longer applies to her — Gspd

the law which bound her to him has lost its hold upon her — Con

3. So then if, while her husband liveth, she be married to another man, she shall be called an adulteress:

she will be counted an adulteress—Con

she becomes an adulteress — Lam

she incurs the stigma of adultery — Phi

she will incur the charge of adultery — NEB

but if her husband be dead, she is free from that law;

but, if her husband dies, the law has no further hold on her — TCNT

so that she is no adulteress, though she be married to another man.

. . . even if she unites herself with another man — Mon

4. Wherefore, my brethren, ye also are become dead to the law by the body of Christ;

It is the same in your case, my brothers. The crucified body of Christ made you dead to the Law — Mof

Well, brethren, you too have undergone death, as far as the law is concerned, in the person of Christ crucified — Knox

So you, my friends, have died to the law by becoming identified with the body of Christ — NEB

So, my brothers, you too in the body of Christ have ended your relation to the law — Wms.

Wherefore you also, my brethren, were made dead to the Law by [union with] the body of Christ — Con

Your "husband," your master, used to be the Jewish law; but you "died," as it were, with Christ on the cross — Tay

that ye should be married to another, even to him who is raised from the dead,

so that you may belong to another husband, who was raised from the dead — Gspd

and you are free to give yourselves in marriage, so to speak, to another, the one who was raised from the dead — Phi

that we should bring forth fruit unto God.

in order that we might bear fruit for God — Gspd

that you may be productive for God — Phi

5. For when we were in the flesh,

For while we obeyed our lower natures — Wey

When we were living merely earthly lives — TCNT

For when we were unspiritual — Mof

the motions of sins,

the sinful passions — ASV

the sinful cravings — Mof

the stirrings of sins — Alf

which were by the law,

occasioned by the Law — Con

aroused by the Law — TCNT

excited by the Law — Mof

did work in our members to bring forth fruit unto death.

were active in our members so as to bring forth fruit unto death — Alf

were active in every part of our bodies, with the result that our bodies bore fruit for Death — TCNT

operated through the organs of our bodies . . . —Gspd

. . . leading us to bring forth fruit unto death — Con

were constantly operating in our natural powers — in our bodily organs, in the sensitive appetites and wills of the flesh — so that . . . — Amp

6. But now we are delivered from the law, that being dead wherein we were held;

But now we have been discharged from the law, having died to that wherein we were held — ASV

But now we have received full release from the law by dying [in that] wherein we used to be held fast — Rhm

But now that we have died [with Christ] the Law wherein we were formerly held fast has lost its hold upon us — Con

But now the Law no longer applies to us; we have died to what once controlled us — Gspd

But now we have been released from the Law, because we are dead to that in which we were held — Mon

But now we are discharged from the law, dead to that which held us captive — RSV

that we should serve in newness of spirit, and not in the oldness of the letter.

so that we serve in newness of the spirit, and not in oldness . . . — ASV

so that we serve in newness of the Spirit, and not . . . — ABUV

so that we render a service which is new and spiritual, not old and ceremonial — Wey

so that we are no longer in the old bondage of the letter, but in the new service of the spirit — Con

and so we serve under new, spiritual conditions, not under old, written regulations — TCNT

and now you can really serve God; not in the old way, mechanically obeying a set of rules, but in the new way, with all of your hearts and minds — Tay

so that we serve not under the old written code but in the new life of the Spirit — RSV

and we are free to serve God not in the old obedience to the letter of the Law, but in a new way, in the Spirit — Phi

7. What shall we say then?

Then what shall we conclude — Gspd

Is the law sin?

That Law and sin are the same thing — TCNT

Is the Law itself a sinful thing — Wey

God forbid.[7]

---

[7]See Rom. 3:4 for various translations of this phrase.

Nay, I had not known sin, but by the law:

Howbeit, I had not known sin, except through the law — ASV

On the contrary, I should not have learnt what sin is, had it not been for Law — TCNT

But it must in fairness be admitted that I should never have had sin brought home to me but for the Law — Phi

No, the law is not sinful but it was the law that showed me my sin — Tay

for I had not known lust, except the law had said, Thou shalt not covet.

for I had not known coveting, except . . . — ASV

For example, I should never have felt guilty of the sin of coveting if I had not heard the Law saying Thou shalt not covet — Phi

For example, only when the Law said, Don't lust, did I know how wrong it is to lust — Beck

8. **But sin, taking occasion by the commandment, wrought in me all manner of concupiscence.**

but sin, finding occasion, wrought in me through the commandment all manner of coveting — ASV

But sin took advantage of the Commandment to arouse in me every form of covetousness — TCNT

That command gave sin an opening, and it led me to all sorts of covetous ways — Gspd

But when sin had gained a vantage-ground, by means of the commandment, it stirred up within me all manner of lust — Mon

Sin found its rallying point in that command and stirred within me every sort of evil desire — Wms

But sin made that command a fulcrum that effected in me all sorts of covetousness — Ber

Through that commandment sin found its opportunity, and produced in me all kinds of wrong desires — NEB

For without the law sin was dead.

for apart from the law sin is dead — ASV

for where there is no consciousness of Law sin shows no sign of life — TCNT

For sin, in the absence of the Law, has no chance to function technically as "sin" — Phi

9. **For I was alive without the law once:**

And I was alive apart from law at one time — Rhm

And I felt that I was alive before, when I knew no law — Con

There was a time when I myself, unconscious of Law, was alive—TCNT

There was a time when I, too, did not have the law, and I was, so to speak, "alive" — Nor

but when the commandment came,

but when the Commandment was brought home to me — TCNT

sin revived, and I died.

sin awoke and then I died — Gspd

sin rose to life, and I died — Con

sin sprang into life, while I — died! — TCNT

the sense of sin found new life, and with that, I died — Knox

I realized that I had broken the law and was a sinner, doomed to die — Tay

10. **And the commandment, which was ordained to life,**

and the very commandment whose end is life — Con

The commandment designed to bring me life — Wey

I found to be unto death.

I found was a sentence to death — Phi

brought me death — Wey

11. **For sin, taking occasion by the commandment, deceived me, and by it slew me.**

For sin, finding occasion, through the commandment beguiled me, and through it slew me — ASV

For sin seized the advantage, and by means of the commandment beguiled me, and also put me to death — Wey

Sin fooled me by taking the good laws of God and using them to make me guilty of death — Tay

The command gave an impulse to sin, sin beguiled me and used the command to kill me — Mof

12. **Wherefore the law is holy, and the commandment holy,**

So the Law itself is holy, and each command is holy — Gspd

and just, and good.

and righteous and good — Mon

just, and for our good — Mof

13. Was then that which is good made death unto me?

Do I say, then, that Good became to me Death — Con

Did that which is good, then, bring death to me — RSV

But didn't the law cause my doom? How then can it be good — Tay

God forbid.[8]

But sin, that it might appear sin, working death in me by that which is good;

It was sin that did so, so that it might be recognized as sin, because even through something that was good it effected my death — Gspd

It was sin that killed me, and thereby sin exposed its true character: it used a good thing to bring about my death — NEB

that sin by the commandment might become exceeding sinful.

. . . might become sinful beyond measure — RSV

that the unutterable malignity of sin might become plain through the commandment — Mon

that by means of the commandment the unspeakable sinfulness of sin might be plainly shown — Wey

and so, through the commandment, sin became more sinful than ever — NEB

and in this way the Commandment showed how intensely sinful sin is — TCNT

14. For we know that the law is spiritual: but I am carnal, sold under sin.

I however am a creature of flesh, . . . — Rhm

but for me, I am carnal, a slave sold into the captivity of sin — Con

but I am unspiritual, sold to sin — Wey

15. For that which I do I allow not:

. . . I know not — ASV

For that which I am working out I do not approve — Rhm

I do not understand my own actions — TCNT

for what I would, that do I not; but what I hate, that do I.

for I do not what I would, but what I hate — Con

For I am so far from habitually doing what I want to do that I find myself doing the very thing that I hate — TCNT

I do not act as I desire to act; on the contrary, I do what I detest — Mof

I do not act as I would, but I do what I loathe — Wey

16. If then I do that which I would not,

But if I am always doing what I do not want to do — Wms

But if my will is against my deeds — Con

Now when I act against my wishes — Mof

I consent unto the law that it is good.

. . . right — Rhm

I thereby acknowledge the goodness of the Law — Con

This means I agree that the Law is right — Mof

17. Now then it is no more I that do it,

This being so, the action is no longer my own — TCNT

but sin that dwelleth in me.

but that of Sin which is within me — TCNT

it is sin, which has possession of me — Gspd

but it is sin which has its home in me — Mon

but sin which dominates me — Lam

18. For I know that in me (that is, in my flesh,) dwelleth no good thing:

I know that there is nothing good in me — I mean in my earthly nature — TCNT

For I know that in me, that is, in my lower self, nothing good has its home — Wey

Of this I am certain, that no principle of good dwells in me, that is, in my natural self — Knox

I know I am rotten through and through so far as my old sinful nature is concerned — Tay

for to will is present with me; but how to perform that which is good I find not.

---

[8]See Rom. 3:4 for other translations of this phrase.

I can will, but I cannot do, what is right — Gspd

for the wish to do right is there but not the power — Wey

No matter which way I turn I can't make myself do right. I want to but I can't — Tay

19. For the good that I would I do not:
For the good that I desire I do not — Alf

I do not do the good things that I want to do — Gspd

but the evil which I would not, that I do.

but the evil which I do not intend to do, that I am ever practising—Mon

I do the wrong things that I do not want to do — Gspd

20. Now if I do that I would not,
Now if my own will is against my deeds — Con

Well, if I act against my wishes—Mof

it is no more I that do it,

it is no more I myself who do them — Con

the action is no longer my own—TCNT

clearly it is no longer I who am the agent — NEB

it is not I that am acting — Gspd

but sin that dwelleth in me.

it is sin, which has possession of me — Gspd

but sin which has its home in me — Mon

it must be the sinful principle that dwells in me — Knox

21. I find then a law,
So I find it to be a law [of my being] — Amp

So this is my experience of the Law: — Mof

I discover this principle, then: — NEB

that, when I would do good, evil is present with me.

I desire to do what is right, but wrong is all that I can manage — Mof

that when I want to do right, only the wrong is within my reach — NEB

that I who want to do right am dogged by what is wrong — Gspd

When I want to do right, the wrong is always in my way — Wms

22. For I delight in the law of God after the inward man:

I have in fact a sympathetic pleasure in the law of God . . . — Rhm

for I consent gladly to the law of God in my inner man — Con

At heart I delight in the Law of God — TCNT

For in accordance with my better inner nature I approve God's law — Wms

For I joyfully concur with the law of God in the inner man — NASB

I love to do God's will so far as my new nature is concerned — Tay

My inner nature agrees with the divine law — Gspd

For in my inmost self all my sympathy is with the law of God — Wey

23. But I see another law in my members,
but I see a different law in my members — ASV

but all through my body I see another principle — Gspd

but I see another power operating in my lower nature — Wms

But there is something else deep within me, in my lower nature — Tay

warring against the law of my mind,

waging war with the law of my will — Mon

in conflict with the law of my reason — Gspd

which wages war against the disposition of my conscience — Knox

battling against the principles which my reason dictates — Ber

and bringing me into captivity

which makes me a prisoner — Gspd

and so I am handed over as a captive — Knox

to the law of sin which is in my members.

to that law of sin which is in my bodily faculties — Mon

to the power of sin which is operating in my lower nature — Wms

to that disposition towards sin which my lower self contains — Knox

24. O wretched man that I am!
Pitiable creature that I am — Knox

It is an agonizing situation — Phi

who shall deliver me from the body of this death?

Who shall rescue me out of this body doomed to death — Rhm

Who can save me from this doomed body — Gspd

Who can save me from this deadly lower nature — Wms

who is to set me free from a nature thus doomed to death — Knox

and who on earth can set me free from the clutches of my own sinful nature — Phi

25. I thank God through Jesus Christ our Lord.

I thank God [that He has now delivered me] through Jesus Christ our Lord — Con

Thank God, there is deliverance through Jesus Christ, our Lord! — TCNT

Thank God ! it is done through Jesus Christ our Lord! — Gspd

God! to whom be thanks through Jesus Christ our Lord! — Wey

Nothing else than the grace of God, through Jesus Christ our Lord — Knox

Thank God — He has done it through our Lord Jesus Christ! — Beck

O thank God! — He will! through Jesus Christ, the Anointed One, our Lord! — Amp

So then with the mind I myself serve the law of God; but with the flesh the law of sin.

So in my higher nature . . . in my lower nature . . . — Wms

So mentally I am a slave to God's law, but physically to the law of sin — Gspd

If I am left to myself, my conscience is at God's disposition, but my natural powers are at the disposition of sin — Knox

In a word then, I myself, subject to God's law as a rational being, am yet, in my unspiritual nature, a slave to the law of sin — NEB

So you see how it is: my new life tells me to do right, but the old nature that is still inside me loves to sin — Tay

CHAPTER 8

1. There is therefore now no condemnation to them which are in Christ Jesus,

Thus there is no doom now for those who are . . . — Mof

So there is no condemnation any more for those who are in union with . . . — Gspd

So then there is no condemnation at all . . . — Wms

The conclusion of the matter is this: there is no condemnation for those who are united with . . . — NEB

who walk not after the flesh, but after the Spirit.[9]

2. For the law of the Spirit of life in Christ Jesus

For the law of the spirit of life . . . — Rhm

For the new spiritual principle of life . . . — Phi

for through your union with Christ Jesus, the law of the life-giving Spirit — TCNT

for the Spirit's law — life in Christ Jesus — Wey

hath made me free

has set you free — TCNT

lifts me out — Phi

from the law of sin and death.

from the principle of sin and death — Knox

from the power of sin and death — Wms

from the rule of sin that kills — Beck

of the old vicious circle of sin and death — Phi

3. For what the law could not do, in that it was weak through the flesh, God sending his own Son in the likeness of sinful flesh, and for sin, condemned sin in the flesh:

For God has done what the Law could not do, weakened as it was by the flesh. By sending his own Son in the likeness of sinful flesh, and on account of sin, he condemned sin in the flesh — Mon

What Law could not do, in so far as our earthly nature weakened its action, God did, by sending his own Son, with a nature resembling our sinful nature, to atone for sin — TCNT

What the law could never do, because our lower nature robbed it of all po-

---

[9]Now recognized as not adequately supported by original manuscripts.

tency, God has done: by sending his own Son in a form like that of our sinful nature, and as a sacrifice for sin, he has passed judgment against sin within that very nature — NEB

For what was impossible to the Law — thwarted as it was by human frailty — God effected. Sending His own Son in the form of sinful humanity to deal with sin, God pronounced sentence upon sin in human nature — Wey

. . . He has signed the death-warrant of sin in our nature — Knox

4. That the righteousness of the law

that the ordinance of the law — ASV

In order that the righteous requirement of the law — Rhm

to the end that the decrees of the law — Con

might be fulfilled in us,

might be satisfied in us — TCNT

might be fully met in our case—Gspd

who walk not after the flesh, but after the Spirit.

who live now in obedience, not to our earthly nature, but to the Spirit — TCNT

since we live not on the physical but on the spiritual plane — Gspd

For our lives are ruled not by our lower, but by our spiritual natures — Wey

whose conduct, no longer under the control of our lower nature, is directed by the Spirit — NEB

5. For they that are after the flesh do mind the things of the flesh;

They who follow their earthly nature are earthly minded — TCNT

people who are controlled by the physical think of what is physical—Gspd

For they who live after the flesh, give their attention to the things of the flesh — Mon

If men comply with their lower nature, their thoughts are shaped by the lower nature — Wey

but they that are after the Spirit the things of the Spirit.

and people who are controlled by the spiritual think of what is spiritual — Gspd

but they who live after the Spirit mind spiritual things — Con

But they who live after the spirit, give their attention to spiritual things — Mon

and those who follow the Spirit have their interests in the Spirit — Mof

but those who follow after the Holy Spirit find themselves doing those things that please God — Tay

6. For to be carnally minded is death; but to be spiritually minded is life and peace.

The interests of the flesh mean death, the interests of the Spirit mean life and peace — Mof

For the mind of the flesh is death; but the mind of the Spirit is life and peace — ASV

But to set the mind on the flesh brings death, whereas to set the mind on the Spirit brings life and peace — Nor

7. Because the carnal mind is enmity against God:

because the mind of the flesh . . . — ASV

for the interests of the flesh are hostile to God — Mof

for the mind set on the flesh is hostile to God — RSV

For the outlook of the lower nature is enmity with God — NEB

The mind which is interested only in carnal things is enmity to God — Nor

This is so because the fleshly mind hates God — Beck

for it is not subject to the law of God,

for it doth not submit itself to the law of God — Alf

for it does not subject itself to the law of God — ABUV

for it refuses to obey God's law — Gspd

neither indeed can be.

indeed it cannot obey it — Gspd

8. So then they that are in the flesh

So, those controlled by the flesh—Ber

They moreover who in flesh have their being — Rhm

Those who obey the lower nature — Wey

And they who are earthly minded — Mon

cannot please God.

cannot satisfy God — Mof

cannot be acceptable to God — Knox

9. But ye are not in the flesh, but in the Spirit,

But ye have not your being in flesh but in spirit — Rhm

You, however, are not controlled by the flesh, but by the Spirit — Ber

if so be that the Spirit of God dwell in you.

since the Spirit of God lives within you — TCNT

if God's Spirit has really taken possession of you — Gspd

if the Spirit of God has His home within you — Wms

Now if any man have not the Spirit of Christ,

Unless a man has the Spirit of Christ — TCNT

he is none of his.

he does not belong to Christ — TCNT

he is not a Christian at all — Tay

10. And if Christ be in you,

But if Christ is in you — Mon

the body is dead because of sin;

although your bodies must die because of sin — Wms

though your bodily self is dead because of sin — Mon

though the body is a dead thing owing to Adam's sin — Mof

but the Spirit is life because of righteousness.

yet your spirit is life, because of righteousness [which dwells within it] — Con

your spirit is full of life because of righteousness — Mon

your spirits are now enjoying life because of right standing with God — Wms

yet the spirit is life itself because you have been justified — NEB

11. But if the Spirit of him that raised up Jesus from the dead dwell in you,

lives within you — TCNT

has taken possession of you — Gspd

he that raised up Christ from the dead shall also quicken your mortal bodies

shall make alive [even] your death-doomed bodies — Rhm

shall endow with life also your dying bodies — Con

will also make your dying bodily self live — Mon

by his Spirit that dwelleth in you.

because of his Spirit that dwells in you — ABUV

through his Spirit that has taken possession of you — Gspd

by his indwelling Spirit in your lives — Mon

12. Therefore, brethren, we are debtors, not to the flesh, to live after the flesh.

Therefore, brethren, we are bound not to the Flesh, that we should live after the Flesh [but to the Spirit] — Con

So then, Brothers, we owe nothing to our earthly nature, that we should live in obedience to it — TCNT

Well then, my brothers, we owe a duty — but it is not to the flesh! — Mof

It follows, my friends, that our lower nature has no claim upon us; we are not obliged to live on that level — NEB

13. For if ye live after the flesh,

If you live in obedience to your earthly nature — TCNT

for if you live under the control of the physical — Gspd

for if you go on living according to the flesh — Mon

ye shall die:

ye must die — ASV

ye are about to die — Rhm

you are doomed to die — Con

you are on the road to death — Mof

but if ye through the Spirit do mortify the deeds of the body,

but if by the Spirit ye put to death . . . — ASV

but if by the Spirit you keep putting to death . . . — Mon

But if by the Spirit you put to death all the base pursuits of the body — NEB

but if, by the power of the Spirit, you put an end to the evil habits of the body — TCNT

ye shall live.

14. For as many as are led by the Spirit of God, they are the sons of God.

For all who are led by God's Spirit, and they alone, are the sons of God — Con

For only those are sons of God who are led by God's Spirit — Mon

Those who follow the leading of God's Spirit are all God's sons — Knox

15. For ye have not received the spirit of bondage again to fear;

. . . a spirit of servitude leading back into fear — Rhm

It is not a consciousness of servitude that has been imparted to you, to fill you with fear again — Gspd

For you did not receive the spirit of a slave, to fill you once more with fear — TCNT

For you have not received a Spirit of bondage, that you should go back again to the state of slavish fear — Con

but ye have received the Spirit of adoption,

But ye have received a spirit of sonship — Rhm

but the consciousness of adopted sons — Wms

but a Spirit which makes us sons—NEB

whereby we cry, Abba, Father.

wherein we cry [unto God], saying, Father — Con

in which we cry out, My Father, my dear Father! — Mon

enabling us to cry Abba! Father!—NEB

16. The Spirit itself beareth witness with our spirit,

The Spirit himself thus assures our spirit — Knox

The Spirit himself endorses our inward conviction — Phi

In that cry the Spirit of God joins with our spirit in testifying — NEB

For His Holy Spirit speaks to us deep in our hearts, and tells us — Tay

that we are the children of God:

17. And if children, then heirs; heirs of God, and joint-heirs with Christ;

If we are his children we share his treasures, and all that Christ claims as his will belong to all of us as well! — Phi

if so be that we suffer with him, that we may be also glorified together.

presuming we suffer jointly, so that we may also enjoy glory jointly — Ber

since we share Christ's sufferings in order that we may also share his Glory — TCNT

but to share his glory, we must now be sharing his sufferings — Mon

if we share his sufferings now in order to share his splendour hereafter — — NEB

18. For I reckon that the sufferings of this present time

I consider . . . — RSV

For I reckon that the sufferings we now endure — NEB

are not worthy to be compared with the glory which shall be revealed in us.

are nothing worth, when set against the glory which shall soon be revealed unto us — Con

not to be compared with the glory that is to burst upon us — Gspd

bear no comparison with the splendour, as yet unrevealed, which is in store for us — NEB

19. For the earnest expectation of the creature waiteth for the manifestation of the sons of God.

For the eager outlook of creation ardently awaiteth the revealing of . . . — Rhm

For the longing of the creation looks eagerly for the time when [the glory of] the sons of God shall be revealed — Con

All creation is yearning, longing to see the manifestation of the sons of God — Wey

For the creation waits with eager longing for the revealing of . . . — RSV

For . . . creation . . . waits expectantly . . . for God's sons to be made known — waits for the revealing, the disclosing of their sonship — Amp

The whole creation is on tiptoe to see the wonderful sight of the sons of God coming into their own — Phi

20. For the creature was made subject to vanity,

. . . to decay — Con

. . . imperfection — TCNT

. . . futility — Wey

. . . the bondage of transitoriness—Ber

not willingly, but by reason of him who hath subjected the same in hope,

Not by choice . . . — Rhm

not for some deliberate fault of its own . . . — Knox

not by its own choice, but because of

him who made it so; yet always
there was hope — NEB

not of its own will, but by reason of
him who subjected it, in hope—ASV

not of its own will but by the will of
him who subjected it in hope; —
RSV

21. Because the creature itself also

because the universe itself — NEB

And the hope is that in the end the
whole of created life — Phi

shall be delivered from

will be rescued from — Phi

the bondage of corruption

its bondage to decay — Gspd

its slavery to death — Con

the shackles of mortality — NEB

the tyranny of change and decay—Phi

**into the glorious liberty of the children
of God.**

into the liberty of the glory of the
children of God — ASV

into the freedom which belongs to the
glory of the children of God—Mon

and shall gain the freedom of the sons
of God when they are glorified —
Con

and gain the glorious freedom of
God's children — Mof

and enter upon the liberty and splendour of . . . — NEB

**22. For we know that the whole creation
groaneth and travaileth in pain together until now.**

Up to the present, we know, the whole
created universe groans in all its
parts as if in the pangs of childbirth
— NEB

To this day, we know, the entire creation sighs and throbs with pain —
Mof

For we know that the whole of creation is moaning with the pangs of
childbirth until this hour — Wey

For we know that the whole creation
is groaning together, and suffering
the pangs of labor, which have not
yet brought forth the birth — Con

The whole of nature, as we know,
groans in a common travail all the
while — Knox

It is plain to anyone with eyes to see
that at the present time all created
life groans in a sort of universal
travail — Phi

23. And not only they, but ourselves also,

And even we Christians — Tay

which have the firstfruits of the Spirit,

who have received the Spirit for the
firstfruits [of our inheritance]—Con

who have the Spirit as a foretaste of
the future — Mof

to whom the Spirit is given as firstfruits of the harvest to come — NEB

though we have the first-fruits of the
Spirit — ABUV

**even we ourselves groan within our-
selves,**

even we ourselves are groaning inwardly — Con

**waiting for the adoption, to wit, the
redemption of our body.**

longing for the adoption that shall ransom our body from its bondage —
Con

while we eagerly await our full adoption as Sons — the redemption of
our bodies — TCNT

as we wait for full sonship in the redemption of our bodies — Wey

as we await that right of sonship that
involves our bodily redemption —
Ber

while we wait for that redemption of
our bodies which will mean that at
last we have realized our full sonship in him — Phi

24. For we are saved by hope:

For in hope were we saved — ASV

For our salvation lies in hope — Con

We were saved with this hope ahead
— Mof

For we have been saved, though only
in hope — NEB

When we were saved we had this hope
— Nor

but hope that is seen is not hope:

But hope beheld is not hope — Rhm

Now when an object of hope is seen,
there is no further need to hope —
Mof

Hope would not be hope at all if its
object were in view — Knox

hope always means waiting for something that we do not yet possess —
Phi

**for what a man seeth, why doth he
yet hope for?**

for who hopeth for that which he seeth
— ASV

for why should a man hope for what he already sees — Wey

for if we see it, why should we yet hope — Lam

(for a man who already has something doesn't need to hope and trust that he will get it.) — Tay

25. But if we hope for that we see not,

but if we hope for things not seen — Con

And if we are hoping for something still unseen — Knox

then do we with patience wait for it.

we steadfastly endure the present, and long earnestly for the future — Con

then we need endurance to wait for it — Knox

with perseverance we wait eagerly for it — NASB

we keep on patiently waiting for it — Wms

we wait for it with patience and composure — Amp

26. Likewise

And in like manner — ASV

In the selfsame way — Rhm

the Spirit also helpeth our infirmities:

the Spirit supports us in our weakness — TCNT

the Spirit also takes hold with us in our weakness — Mon

the Spirit comes to the aid of our weakness — Knox

The Spirit of God not only maintains this hope within us, but helps us in our present limitations — Phi

for we know not what we should pray for as we ought:

We do not even know how to pray as we should — TCNT

for we do not know what and how we ought to pray — Ber

. . . what is right and proper for us to pray for — Lam

. . . what prayer to offer nor how to offer it worthily as we ought — Amp

but the Spirit itself maketh intercession for us with groanings which cannot be uttered.

. . . maketh intercession with sighings unutterable — Rhm

. . . makes intercession for us with groans [for deliverance] which words cannot utter — Con

. . . pleads for us with inexpressible yearnings — Gspd

but the Spirit Himself intercedes on our behalf with sighs too deep for words — Ber

but through our inarticulate groans the Spirit himself is pleading for us — NEB

27. And he that searcheth the hearts

And God who searches our inmost being — NEB

knoweth what is the mind of the Spirit,

knows [though it be unspoken] what is the desire of the Spirit — Con

knoweth what is preferred by the Spirit — Rhm

knows what the Spirit's meaning is — TCNT

because he maketh intercession for the saints according to the will of God.

since the Spirit pleads before God for the saints — Mof

because he pleads for God's own people in God's own way — NEB

because His intercessions for the saints are in harmony with God's will — Wey

28. And we know that all things work together for good to them that love God,

Now we know that all things continually work together for good to those who love God — Mon

But we do know that God causes all things to work together for the good of those who love him — TCNT

We know that in everything God works with those who love him . . . to bring about what is good — Gspd

We know also that those who love God . . . have his aid and interest in everything — Mof

Moreover we know that to those who love God . . . everything that happens fits into a pattern for good — Phi

We know that in everything God works for good with those who love him — RSV

Yes, we know that all things go on working together for the good of those who keep on loving God — Wms

to them who are the called according to his purpose.

ROMANS 8

and are called according to His plan
— Beck
those who have been called in terms
of his purpose — Mof
who are called in accordance with
God's purpose — Wms

29. For whom he did foreknow,
For whom he fore-approved — Rhm
For those whom God chose from the
first — TCNT
For those whom he had marked out
from the first — Gspd
For those on whom He set His heart
beforehand — Wms
he also did predestinate
he also foreordained — ASV
He also fore-appointed — Rhm
He marked off as His own — Wms
**to be conformed to the image of his
Son,**
to be made like to the pattern of His
Son — Con
to be made like his Son — Gspd
to share the likeness of His Son—Wey
to be moulded into the image of his
Son — Knox
that he might be
so that his Son might be — TCNT
the firstborn among many brethren.
the eldest of a great brotherhood —
Mon
the Eldest in a vast family of brothers
— Wey
the eldest among many Brothers —
TCNT

30. Moreover whom he did predestinate,
and whom he foreordained — ASV
. . . fore-appointed — Rhm
and those whom He marked off as His
own — Wms
He chose them long ago — Phi
them he also called:
when the time came he called them —
Phi
**and whom he called,
them he also justified:**
the same he also declared righteous —
Rhm
He also made righteous — Ber
He has also acquitted — Wey
he makes upright — Gspd
He brings into right standing with
Himself — Wms
**and whom he justified,
them he also glorified.**

them he also made glorious — Rhm
he also brought to Glory — TCNT
he has also given his splendour — NEB

**31. What shall we then say to these
things?**
Then what shall we conclude from this
— Gspd
In face of all this, what is there left to
say — Phi
**If God be for us, who can be against
us?**
If God is on our side, who can there
be against us — TCNT
Just this — If God is for us, what does
it matter who may be against us —
Nor

**32. He that spared not his own Son, but
delivered him up for us all,**
but gave Him up for us all — Con
**how shall he not with him also freely
give us all things?**
will he not, then, with him, freely give
us all things — TCNT
surely He will give us everything besides! — Mof
and with this gift how can he fail to
lavish upon us all he has to give —
NEB

**33. Who shall lay any thing to the charge
of God's elect?**
Who shall bring an accusation against
the chosen ones of God — Rhm
What accuser can harm God's chosen
— Con
Who will bring a charge against any
of God's People — TCNT
Who would dare to accuse us, whom
God has chosen — Phi
It is God that justifieth.
He who pronounces them righteous is
God! — TCNT
Will God, who acquits them — Wey

34. Who is he that condemneth?
What judge can doom us — Con
Who then will condemn us — Tay
It is Christ that died,
It is Christ Jesus that died — ASV
Will Christ who died? — Mon
Will Christ? NO! For He is the One
Who died for us — Tay
yea rather, that is risen again,
yes, rather, that was raised from the
dead — ASV
what is more, who rose again — Ber
who is even at the right hand of God,

687

who is also at the right hand of God
— ABUV
. . . reigns in power for us — Phi
. . . is sitting at the place of highest
honor next to God — Tay
who also maketh intercession for us.
and is even pleading on our behalf —
TCNT
and indeed pleads our cause — NEB

35. **Who shall separate us from the love
of Christ?**
Who can separate us . . . — Con
What can ever part us . . . — Mof
shall tribulation, or distress,
Will trouble, or difficulty — TCNT
shall tribulation, or anguish — ASV
Can anguish or calamity — Mof
Can trouble or misfortune — Gspd
Can suffering, or straitness of distress
— Con
**or persecution, or famine, or naked-
ness, or peril, or sword?**
or persecution, or famine, or nakedness or the peril of our lives, or the
swords of our enemies — Con

36. **As it is written,**
Even as it is written — ASV
As the Scripture says — Gspd
**For thy sake we are killed all the day
long;**
we face death at every moment —
Knox
**we are accounted as sheep for the
slaughter.**
We were accounted . . . — ASV
reckoned no better than sheep marked
down for slaughter — Knox
we are regarded as sheep to be slaughtered — RSV

37. **Nay, in all these things we are more
than conquerors**
Yet amidst all these things we more
than conquer — TCNT
And yet in all these things we keep on
gloriously conquering — Wms

No, in all these things we win an overwhelming victory — Phi
through him that loved us.
through him who has proved his love
for us — Phi

38. **For I am persuaded,**
For I am certain — Mof
. . . convinced — Gspd
. . . fully persuaded — Mon
. . . have full assurance — Wms
I have become absolutely convinced
— Phi
**that neither death, nor life, nor angels,
nor principalities, nor powers, nor
things present, nor things to come,**
that there is nothing in death or life,
in the realm of spirits or superhuman
powers, in the world as it is or the
world as it shall be, in the forces
of the universe — NEB
that neither death nor life, neither
messenger of Heaven nor monarch
of earth, neither what happens today
nor what may happen tomorrow . . .
— Phi

39. **Nor height, nor depth, nor any other
creature,**
neither the height above us nor the
depth beneath us, nor any other created thing — Knox
nor things above, nor things below,
nor any power in the whole creation
— Con
neither a power from on high nor a
power from below, nor anything else
in God's whole world — Phi
**shall be able to separate us from the
love of God, which is in Christ Jesus
our Lord.**
will be able to separate us from the
love of God, which comes to us in
Christ Jesus our Lord — Knox
. . . the love of God revealed in Christ
Jesus, our Lord! — TCNT
. . . the love God has shown in Christ
Jesus our Lord! — Gspd

CHAPTER 9

1. **I say the truth in Christ, I lie not, my
conscience also bearing me witness in
the Holy Ghost.**
I am speaking the truth as one in union
with Christ; it is no lie; and my
conscience, enlightened by the Holy

Spirit, bears me out when I say —
TCNT
I am speaking the truth as a Christian,
and my own conscience, enlightened
by the Holy Spirit, assures me it is
no lie — NEB

2. That I have great heaviness and continual sorrow in my heart.

that I have great sorrow and unceasing pain . . . — ASV

That I have great grief and incessant travail . . . — Rhm

. . . and unceasing anguish in my heart — ABUV

when I say that I am greatly pained and my heart is constantly distressed — Gspd

that there is a great weight of sorrow upon me, and that my heart is never free from pain — TCNT

3. For I could wish that myself were accursed from Christ

For I could wish that I myself were anathema from Christ — ASV

yea, I could wish that I myself were cast out from Christ as an accursed thing — Con

I could have wished myself accursed and banished from Christ — Mof

For I was on the point of praying to be accursed from Christ — Mon

Indeed, I could even wish that I myself might be sentenced to separation from Christ — Nor

for my brethren, my kinsmen according to the flesh:

on behalf of my brethren . . . — Alf

for the sake of my brothers, my natural kinsmen — Mof

if that would benefit my brethren, my own kinsmen by race — Knox

4. Who are Israelites;

For they are Israelites — TCNT

to whom pertaineth the adoption, and the glory, and the covenants,

to whom belongeth . . . — Alf

. . . the adoption as sons, the visible Presence, the Covenants — TCNT

and to them belong the rights of sonship, God's glorious presence, the divine agreements — Gspd

whom God adopted for His children, whose were the glory of the Shechinah and the Covenants — Con

they were made God's sons; theirs is the splendour of the divine presence, theirs the covenants — NEB

and the giving of the law, and the service of God, and the promises;

the revealed Law, the Temple worship, and the promises — TCNT

5. Whose are the fathers,

the patriarchs are theirs — Mof

They are descended from the Patriarchs — TCNT

and of whom as concerning the flesh Christ came,

and from them physically Christ came — Gspd

and from them in respect of His human lineage came the Christ — Wey

and of their race, according to the flesh, is the Christ — RSV

who is over all, God blessed for ever. Amen.

(Blessed for evermore be the God who is over all! Amen.) — Mof

God who is over all be blessed for ever. Amen — RSV

May God, supreme above all, be blessed for ever! Amen — NEB

who is exalted above all, God blessed throughout the ages. Amen — Wey

who is God over all, blessed for ever. Amen — Alf

who rules as God over all things, blessed for ever, Amen — Knox

Who now rules over all things and is blessed of God forever — Tay

who is over all, God, blessed forever, Amen — Mon

6. Not as though the word of God hath taken none effect.

But it is not as though the word of God hath come to nought — ASV

It is not, however, as though the word of God had failed — Rhm

And yet it is not as if God's promise had failed of its effect — Knox

Now this does not mean that God's word to Israel has failed — Phi

It doesn't mean God failed to do what He said — Beck

For they are not all Israel, which are of Israel:

For not everybody that is descended from Israel really belongs to Israel — Wms

7. Neither, because they are the seed of Abraham, are they all children:

nor because all are the seed of Abraham, are they all the children of Abraham — Con

they are not all children of Abraham because they are Abraham's descendants — Mon

but, In Isaac shall thy seed be called.

but he was told, The line of Isaac will

be called your descendants — Gspd

The promise was, In Isaac shall thy posterity be called — Mon

8. That is, They which are the children of the flesh, these are not the children of God:

That is, it is not the children of the flesh that are the children of God — ASV

This means that it is not the children born in the course of nature who are God's Children — TCNT

That is to say, it is not his physical descendants who are the children of God — Gspd

This means that not all of Abraham's children are children of God — Tay

but the children of the promise are counted for the seed.

. . . are reckoned as a seed — Rhm

. . . are reckoned as his true offspring — Mof

. . . are counted his true descendants — Wms

but it is the children born in fulfilment of the Promise who are to be regarded as Abraham's descendants — TCNT

9. For this is the word of promise,

For this word was of promise — Alf

For these words are the words of a promise — TCNT

For this is what the promise said — Gspd

At this time will I come, and Sarah shall have a son.

When I come back at this time next year, Sarah will have a son — Gspd

At the time fixed I will come, and . . . — NEB

Next year I will give you and Sarah a son (Isaac) — Tay

10. And not only this; but when Rebecca also had conceived by one, even by our father Isaac;

Nor is that all. There is also the case of Rebecca, when she was about to bear children to our ancestor Isaac — TCNT

11. (For the children being not yet born, neither having done any good or evil,

For before the children were born or had done anything either good or bad — Gspd

and though the children were still unborn and had done nothing either good or bad — Mof

that the purpose of God according to election might stand, not of works, but of him that calleth;)

in order to carry out God's purpose of selection, which depends not on what men do but on his calling them — Gspd

in order that God's electing purpose might stand, based not on their actions but on His calling them — Wey

so that God's purpose might stand out clearly as his own choice, with no action of theirs to account for it, nothing but his will, from whom the call came — Knox

(to confirm the divine purpose in election, which depends on the call of God, not on anything man does) — Mof

12. It was said unto her,
The elder shall serve the younger.

that the elder [son] should serve the younger [son] — Amp

13. As it is written,

As the Scripture says — Gspd

and that accords with the text of Scripture — NEB

So it is that we read — Knox

Jacob have I loved, but Esau have I hated.

I have been a friend to Jacob, and an enemy to Esau — Knox

To Jacob I was drawn, but Esau I repudiated — Ber

14. What shall we say then? Is there unrighteousness with God?

Then are we to infer that there is injustice in God — Mof

What do we conclude? That God is guilty of injustice — Gspd

Does this mean God is unjust — Beck

God forbid.[10]

15. For he saith to Moses,
I will have mercy on whom I will have mercy,

I will have mercy on whom I choose to have mercy — Mof

and I will have compassion on whom I will have compassion.

---

[10]See Rom. 3:4 for other translations of this phrase.

I will have compassion on whom I choose to have compassion — Mof

and take pity on the man on whom I choose to take pity — Gspd

16. So then it is not of him that willeth, nor of him that runneth, but of God that sheweth mercy.

You see, it is not a question of human will or effort but of the divine mercy — Mof

So, then, all depends, not on human wishes or human efforts, but on God's mercy — TCNT

17. For the scripture saith unto Pharaoh, Even for this same purpose have I raised thee up, that I might shew my power in thee,

It was for this that I raised you up, to display my power in you — Mof

It was for this very purpose that I raised thee to the throne, to show my power by my dealings with thee — TCNT

For this very purpose I set you up high, to present in you the evidence of my power — Ber

I have raised you to your position for the very purpose of displaying my power in dealing with you — Gspd

and that my name might be declared throughout all the earth.

... might be published abroad in all the earth — ASV

so that my name may be proclaimed in all the earth — RSV

and to make my name known throughout the world — TCNT

and to spread news of my name over all the earth — Mof

and to spread my fame over all the the world — NEB

18. Therefore hath he mercy on whom he will have mercy, and whom he will he hardeneth.

So, then, where God wills, he takes pity, and where he wills, he hardens the heart — TCNT

Thus he not only shows mercy as he chooses, but also makes men stubborn as he chooses — NEB

19. Thou wilt say then unto me,

Perhaps you will say to me — TCNT

Why doth he yet find fault?

Why does God still blame us — Con

For who hath resisted his will?

for who can resist His will — Con

For his purpose who hath withstood — Rhm

since there is no resisting his will — Knox

Who can oppose his will — Mof

Who is able to go against his purpose — Bas

Who of us, by resisting, can change His purpose — Nor

20. Nay but, O man, who art thou that repliest against God?

Nay, but who art thou, friend, to bandy words with God — Knox

Nay, but who are you, a mere man, to cavil against God — Wey

However, O man, who are you to question God — Lam

On the contrary, who are you, my friend, to answer back to God — Gspd

But who are you, my man, to speak back to God — Mof

I might rather ask Who are you who are arguing with God — TCNT

Shall the thing formed say to him that formed it,

Can a thing that is molded say to its maker — Gspd

Is the pot to ask the potter — Knox

Will what is molded say to its molder — RSV

Why hast thou made me thus?

Why did you make me like this — TCNT

21. Hath not the potter power over the clay;

Has not the potter absolute power over his clay — TCNT

Has not the potter a right over the clay — ABUV

Is not the potter free to do what he will with the clay — Knox

of the same lump to make one vessel unto honour, and another unto dishonour?

so that out of the same lump he makes one thing for better, and another for common, use — TCNT

Has he no right to make out of the same lump one vessel for a noble purpose, another for a menial — Mof

the right to make from the same lump one thing for exalted uses and another for menial ones — Gspd

. . . one vessel for ornamental purposes, another for degrading service — Wms

22. What if God, willing to shew his wrath, and to make his power known,

But what if God (though willing to show forth His wrath, and to make known His power) — Con

What if God, though desirous to display his anger and show his might — Mof

And what if God, while having the will to make manifest His anger and to show His power — Wey

May it not be that God, though he must sooner or later expose his wrath against sin and show his controlling hand — Phi

endured with much longsuffering

bore most patiently with — TCNT

has tolerated most patiently — Mof

has shown great patience toward — Gspd

yet endured, with much long-suffering — Mon

the vessels of wrath fitted to destruction:

. . . fitted for perdition — ABUV

the objects of his displeasure, though they were fit only to be destroyed — TCNT

the objects of his anger, ripe and ready to be destroyed — Mof

the objects of his vengeance, fit only for destruction — Knox

the agents that deserve wrath and are maturing for destruction — Ber

23. And that he might make known the riches of his glory on the vessels of mercy,

And what if thus He purposed to make known . . . — Con

so as to make known his surpassing glory in dealing with the objects of his mercy — TCNT

and did so in order to make known the full wealth of his splendour upon vessels which were objects of mercy — NEB

which he had afore prepared unto glory,

whom he prepared beforehand for glory — TCNT

whom he has made ready beforehand to receive glory — Mof

whom he has prepared from the beginning to share his glory — Gspd

24. Even us, whom he hath called,

And such are we, whom He has called — Con

that is, for us whom he has called — Mof

not of the Jews only, but also of the Gentiles?

from among the Gentiles as well as the Jews — Mof

not only from among the Jews but from among the heathen — Gspd

25. As he saith also in Osee,

This, indeed, is what he says in the Book of Hosea — TCNT

I will call them my people, which were not my people;

Those who were not my people I will call my people — Mon

and her beloved, which was not beloved.

and her who was not beloved, I will call 'my beloved' — RSV

26. And it shall come to pass, that in the place where it was said unto them, Ye are not my people;

And in the very place where they were told, You are no people of mine — Gspd

there shall they be called the children of the living God.

There they shall be called Sons of the living God — Mon

27. Esaias also crieth concerning Israel,

Moreover . . . — Alf

And Isaiah cries aloud over Israel — TCNT

But Isaiah makes this proclamation about Israel: — NEB

Though the number of the children of Israel be as the sand of the sea,

Though the Israelites be countless as the sands of the sea — NEB

a remnant shall be saved:

it is the remnant that shall be saved — ASV

[only] the remnant shall be saved — Con

only a remnant of them shall escape — TCNT

only a small part will get salvation — Bas

28. For he will finish the work, and cut it short in righteousness: because a short work will the Lord make upon the earth.

For the Lord will do a work on the earth, Completing it and cutting it short — ABUV

for the Lord will execute his word upon the earth, finishing it and cutting it short — ASV

For the Lord will execute his sentence upon the world, fully and without delay — TCNT

for the Lord will carry out his sentence on earth with rigour and dispatch — Mof

for the Lord will hold a final and summary reckoning upon the earth — Wey

For the Lord will execute His sentence upon the earth, quickly ending His dealings, justly cutting them short — Tay

29. And as Esaias said before,

Even as Isaiah says in an earlier place — Wey

It is as Isaiah predicted — Amp

Except the Lord of Sabaoth had left us a seed,

If the Lord of hosts had not left us a seed — Rhm

Had not the Lord of Hosts spared some few of our race to us — TCNT

Had not the Lord of hosts left us with some descendants — Mof

Were it not that the Lord, the God of Hosts, had left us some survivors — Wey

If the Lord of Hosts had not left us a stock to breed from — Knox

we had been as Sodoma, and been made like unto Gomorrha.

we would have fared like Sodom, we would have been like Gomorrha — Mof

we would have been like Sodom and Gomorrha — Bas

30. What shall we say then?

Then what do we conclude — Gspd

To what conclusion does this bring us — Wey

That the Gentiles,

We say that the Gentiles — Con

That Gentiles — Mof

That heathen — Gspd

which followed not after righteousness,

who never had the Law's standard of righteousness to guide them — Phi

who never aimed at righteousness — Mof

have attained to righteousness,

Have laid hold of righteousness — Rhm

have grasped it — Wey

nevertheless achieved it — NEB

obtained righteousness — ABUV

even the righteousness which is of faith.

A righteousness, however, which is by faith — Rhm

a righteousness which was the result of faith — TCNT

...which was produced by faith — Gspd

...dependent on faith — Wey

...conditioned on faith — Wms

...that comes through faith — Ber

that is, they attained justification by faith — Nor

31. But Israel, which followed after the law of righteousness,

But Israel, on the other hand, though seeking justification by law — Nor

but that the house of Israel, though they sought a law of righteousness — Con

but that Israel who pursued the righteousness which is based on law — RSV

while Israel, straining after a law that should bring uprightness — Gspd

...who was in pursuit of a Law that could give righteousness — Wey

hath not attained to the law of righteousness.

failed to discover one — TCNT

did not arrive at [such] a law — ABUV

did not come up to it — Gspd

did not succeed in fulfilling that law — RSV

failed to reach the goal of righteousness — Phi

32. Wherefore?

And why — Con

Why was this — Knox

Because they sought it not by faith,

Because their principle was not faith — Ber

Because they did not pursue it through faith — RSV

Because their efforts were not based on faith — NEB

but as it were by the works of the law.

but on what they could do — Mof

but through doing certain things — Gspd

but thought to gain it by works — Mon

but as if it were based on works — RSV

but thought they could get it by works — Beck

For they stumbled at that stumblingstone;

They stumbled against the stone of stumbling — ABUV

... that stone that makes people stumble — Gspd

... the stone that occasions stumbling — Ber

33. As it is written,

As Scripture says — TCNT

Behold, I lay in Sion a stumblingstone and rock of offence:

See, I place a Stumbling-block in Zion — a Rock which shall prove a hindrance — TCNT

Here I lay a stone in Sion that will make men stumble, even a rock to trip them up — Mof

and whosoever believeth in him shall not be ashamed.

And he that believeth on him shall not be put to shame — ASV

And he who believes in him shall have no cause for shame — TCNT

and no man that hath faith in Him shall be confounded — Con

yet he whose faith rests upon it shall never be disappointed — Wey

CHAPTER 10

1. Brethren, my heart's desire and prayer to God for Israel is,

Brothers, the longing of my heart and my prayer to God is for my countrymen — Mon

Brothers, my heart's good will goes out for them, and my prayer to God is — Wms

that they might be saved.

2. For I bear them record that they have a zeal of God,

I can testify that they are zealous for the honour of God — TCNT

For I testify for them, that they have a zeal for God — ABUV

I can vouch for their zeal for God — Mof

I can testify to their sincere devotion to God — Gspd

I bear witness that they possess an enthusiasm for God — Wey

For I give witness of them that they have a strong desire for God — Bas

I know from experience what a passion for God they have — Phi

but not according to knowledge.

but not according to correct knowledge — Rhm

but they are not guided by true insight — TNCT

but it is not an intelligent devotion — Gspd

only it is a zeal without knowledge — Mon

3. For they being ignorant of God's righteousness,

For, being ignorant of the righteousness that comes from God — RSV

for because they knew not the righteousness of God — Con

Not knowing the righteousness God gives — Beck

They did not recognize God's way of justification — Knox

and going about to establish their own righteousness,

and seeking to establish . . . — ASV

and in their eagerness to set up a righteousness of their own — TCNT

have not submitted themselves unto

they refused to accept with submission — TCNT

They would not surrender to — Mof

they refused to conform to — Gspd

they have the wrong attitude to receive — Phi

the righteousness of God.[11]

4. For Christ is the end of the law for righteousness to every one that believeth.

For the end of the Law is Christ, that all may attain righteousness who have faith in Him — Con

For Christ marks the termination of law, so that now anyone who has

---

[11]See Rom. 1:17 for other translations of this phrase.

faith may attain uprightness — Gspd

For Christ has brought Law to an end, so that righteousness may be obtained by every one who believes in him — TCNT

Christ has superseded the law, bringing justification to anyone who will believe — Knox

For to every believer Christ is an end of law as a means of righteousness — Mon

For Christ has put an end to law as a way to right standing for everyone who puts his trust in Him — Wms

For Christ means the end of the struggle for righteousness-by-the-Law for everyone who believes in him — Phi

For Christ is to every believer the completion of the Law that brings righteousness — Ber

For the consummation of Law is Christ, to bring righteousness to every believer — Wey

5. For Moses describeth

For Moses writes concerning — Con

the righteousness which is of the law,

the righteousness which is based on the law — RSV

the righteousness required by the Law — Wey

law-righteousness — Mof

the law-way to right standing with God — Wms

That the man which doeth those things shall live by them.

those who practise it will find Life through it — TCNT

Anyone who can perform it, shall live by it — Mof

The man who does this shall gain life by it — NEB

that if a man does what the law commands, he will live — Nor

6. But the righteousness which is of faith

But the righteousness which results from faith — TCNT

. . . the uprightness that springs from faith — Gspd

. . . the righteousness based on faith — Wey

. . . the faith-way to right standing — Wms

. . . the justification which comes from faith — Knox

speaketh on this wise,

speaks in this way — Mon

says something like this: — Phi

Say not in thine heart, Who shall ascend into heaven?

Do not say, Who will scale heaven for us — Knox

(that is, to bring Christ down from above:)

that is, Who can bring down Christ from heaven — Con

(as if we had to bring Christ down to earth) — Knox

7. Or, Who shall descend into the deep?

nor say, Who shall descend into the abyss — Con

or, Who will go down into the depths below — TCNT

(that is, to bring up Christ again from the dead.)

that is, Who can raise up Christ from the dead? — Con

(as if we had to bring Christ back from the dead) — Knox

8. But what saith it?

But what does it say — Mon

No, what it does say is this: — Mof

The word is nigh thee, even in thy mouth, and in thy heart:

God's message is close to you, on your lips and in your mind — Gspd

The Word (God's message in Christ) is near you, on your lips and in your heart — Amp

. . . is already within easy reach of each of us; in fact, it is as near as our own hearts and mouths — Tay

that is, the word of faith, which we preach;

that is, the Word Faith which we proclaim, saying — Con

. . . the word which we are publishing about the faith — Wey

. . . the message about faith that we preach — Gspd

which means The Message of Faith which we proclaim — TCNT

That is the very word of faith which we preach: — Mon

9. That if thou shalt confess with thy mouth the Lord Jesus,

Confess with your mouth "Jesus is Lord" — Mon

because if thou shalt confess with thy mouth Jesus as Lord — ASV

For, if with your lips you acknowledge the truth of the Message that JESUS IS LORD — TCNT

and it says, in effect, If you openly admit by your own mouth that Jesus Christ is the Lord — Phi

and shalt believe in thine heart

and with your mind you believe — Gspd

and in your heart believe (adhere to, trust in and rely on the truth) — Amp

that God hath raised him from the dead, thou shalt be saved.

10. **For with the heart man believeth unto righteousness;**

For faith unto righteousness is in the heart — Con

for with his heart man believes and is justified — Mof

For with their minds men believe and are made upright — Gspd

For in their hearts people exercise the faith that leads to right standing — Wms

The heart has only to believe, if we are to be justified — Knox

For it is believing in the heart that makes a man righteous before God — Phi

and with the mouth confession is made unto salvation.

and confession unto salvation is from the mouth — Con

with his mouth he confesses and is saved — Mof

and with their lips they make the acknowledgment which means salvation — Wms

and it is stating his belief by his own mouth that confirms his salvation — Phi

11. **For the scripture saith,**
Whosoever believeth on him shall not be ashamed.

Whosoever believeth on him shall not be put to shame — ASV

No man that hath faith in Him shall be confounded — Con

No one who believes in him shall have cause for shame — TCNT

... will ever be disappointed — Mof

12. **For there is no difference between the Jew and the Greek:**

For no distinction is made between the Jew and the Greek — TCNT

for there is no distinction between Jew and Gentile — Con

Jew and Greek are on the same footing — Wey

And that "whosoever" means anyone, without distinction between Jew or Greek — Phi

for the same Lord over all is rich unto all that call upon him.

for the same Lord is Lord of all, and is rich unto all that call upon him — ASV

because the same [Jesus] is Lord over all, and He gives richly to all who call upon Him — Con

the same Lord is Lord over all, rich in blessing to all who call upon Him — Wey

for they all have the same Lord, and he is generous to all who call upon him — Gspd

for all have the same Lord, and he is bountiful to all who invoke him — TCNT

For all have the same Lord whose boundless resources are available to all who turn to him in faith — Phi

for the same Lord is over them all, because He is infinitely kind to all who call upon Him — Wms

the same Lord is Lord of all and bestows his riches upon all who call upon him — RSV

all alike have one Lord, and he has enough and to spare for all those who call upon him — Knox

13. **For whosoever shall call upon the name of the Lord shall be saved.**

For everyone who calls upon the name of the Lord will be saved — Wms

14. **How then shall they call on him**

But how are men to call upon him — RSV

in whom they have not believed?

in whom they have put no faith — Con

in whom they have not learnt to believe — TCNT

if they have not believed in him — Gspd

and how shall they believe in him

... put faith in Him — Con

and how are they to believe ... — ABUV

of whom they have not heard?

whom they never heard — Con

whose words they have not heard — TCNT

if they have never heard him — Gspd

and how shall they hear without a preacher?

And how are they to hear his words unless some one proclaims him — TCNT

And how are they ever to hear, without a preacher — Mof

. . . without someone to spread the news — NEB

. . . unless someone tells them — Tay

15. And how shall they preach, except they be sent?

And how shall they bear the tidings if no messengers be sent forth — Con

And how can men preach unless they are sent — Mof

And how could anyone spread the news without a commission to do so — NEB

And how can men [be expected to] preach unless they are sent — Amp

as it is written,

So we read in scripture — Knox

As Scripture says — TCNT

How beautiful are the feet of them that preach the gospel of peace,[12] and bring glad tidings of good things!

. . . that bear Glad-tidings of peace, that bear Glad-tidings of good things! — Con

How beautiful are the feet of them that bring glad tidings of good things! — ASV

How pleasant is the coming of men with glad, good news! — Mof

How welcome is the coming of those who bring good news! — Gspd

. . . of those who tell of peace, who tell of good news — Knox

16. But they have not all obeyed the gospel.

Yet some have not hearkened to the Glad-tidings — Con

It is true, they have not all accepted the good news — Gspd

But, some will say, they have not all hearkened to the gospel — Wey

For Esaias saith,

For Isaiah says — ABUV

No, for Isaiah asks — Wey

Lord, who hath believed our report?

. . . who has put faith in what we told — Wms

. . . who has believed our teaching — TCNT

. . . our message — Wey

. . . what we have told — Gspd

17. So then faith cometh by hearing,

So faith comes from hearing what is told — Gspd

. . . from a message heard — Mon

. . . from what is heard — RSV

We conclude that faith is awakened by the message — NEB

and hearing by the word of God.

and that hearing comes through the message about Christ — Gspd

and what is heard comes by the preaching of Christ — RSV

. . . by the preaching [of the message that came from the lips] of Christ — Amp

and the message is the word of Christ — Phi

18. But I say,

But I ask — TCNT

Have they not heard?

have they not heard [the voice of the teachers] — Con

had they no opportunity to hear — Gspd

did the news never come to them — Knox

Yes verily,

Indeed they have — RSV

their sound went into all the earth,

Their voices have gone all over the earth — Gspd

the utterance fills every land — Knox

[for the Scripture says,] Their voice [that of nature bearing God's message] has gone out to all the earth — Amp

and their words unto the ends of the world.

the message reaches the ends of the world — Knox

and their words to the bounds of the inhabited world — NEB

19. But I say,

But again I ask — TCNT

Did not Israel know?

did not Israel know [the purpose of God] — Con

---

[12] The words "that preach the gospel of peace" are now recognized as not adequately supported by original manuscripts.

Did Israel not understand — Mof

did Israel fail to understand — Gspd

can it be that Israel failed to recognize the message — NEB

First Moses saith,

And my answer must be that they did. For Moses says — Phi

yea, it is said first by Moses — Con

Listen to Moses first. He says — Wey

Why, there is a saying that goes back to Moses — Knox

In reply, I first cite Moses, who says — NEB

I will provoke you to jealousy by them that are no people,

I will make you jealous against them which are no people — Con

I will make you jealous of a nation that is no nation — Mof

I will use a nation that is no nation to stir your envy — NEB

and by a foolish nation I will anger you.

With a nation void of understanding will I anger you — ASV

Against an undiscerning nation I will arouse your anger — TCNT

20. **But Esaias is very bold, and saith,**

And Isaiah, more daring still, puts

these words into the mouth of God — Phi

And next, let Isaiah speak. He is very bold when he says — Nor

I was found of them that sought me not;

I was found by those who were not seeking me — TCNT

I was made manifest unto them that asked not after me.

I made myself known to those who were not inquiring of me — TCNT

I was clearly shown to those who never asked about me — NEB

21. **But to Israel he saith,**

But of Israel he says — RSV

All day long I have stretched forth my hands

unto a disobedient and gainsaying people.

unto a people unyielding and contradicting — Rhm

to a disobedient and obstinate people — Gspd

to a self-willed and fault-finding people — Wey

to a people that refuses obedience and cries out against me — Knox

to an unruly and recalcitrant people — NEB

CHAPTER 11

1. **I say then, Hath God cast away his people?**

. . . Did God cast off his people — ASV

. . . God has not disowned His people, has He — Wms

I ask then, has God repudiated his people — Gspd

I say, then, — must we think that God has cast off His people — Con

God forbid. [13]

By no means! — RSV

For I also am an Israelite,

For I myself am an Israelite — TCNT

Why, I am an Israelite myself — Mof

of the seed of Abraham, of the tribe of Benjamin.

a descendant of Abraham, . . . — TCNT

. . . a member of the tribe of Benjamin — Mof

2. **God hath not cast away his people**

God has not repudiated his people — Gspd

No, God has not disowned His people — Wms

which he foreknew.

whom he foreapproved — Rhm

whom he chose from the first — TCNT

which he had marked out from the first — Gspd

on whom He set His heart beforehand — Wms

the people whose destiny he himself appointed — Phi

which he acknowledged of old as his own — NEB

Wot ye not what the scripture saith of Elias?

Or know ye not . . . of Elijah — ASV

Do you not know what Scripture says in the case of Elijah — Wey

. . . in the Elijah incident — Ber

Have you forgotten the words of Scrip-

---

[13]See Rom. 3:4 for other translations of this phrase.

ture in the story of Elijah — TCNT

how he maketh intercession to God against Israel, saying,

how he pleadeth with God against Israel: — ASV

how he complains to God . . . — Ber

3. Lord, they have killed thy prophets, and digged down thine altars;

. . . they have demolished thine altars — Mof

and I am left alone,

and I only am left — Alf

I am the only one left — Gspd

and they seek my life.

And they are seeking my life! — Rhm

and they are trying to kill me — Wms

4. But what saith the answer of God unto him?

But what was the divine response — TCNT

But what does the oracle say to him — NEB

I have reserved to myself seven thousand men, who have not bowed the knee to the image of Baal.

I have left for myself seven thousand men, who have not bowed the knee to Baal — ASV

I have kept for myself . . . — RSV

I have left myself seven thousand men who have never knelt to Baal! — Gspd

. . . who have not done homage to Baal — NEB

There are seven thousand men I have kept true to myself, with knees that never bowed to Baal — Knox

5. Even so then at this present time also

So likewise at this present time — Con

And so in our own time, too — TCNT

there is a remnant according to the election of grace.

A remnant by way of an election of favour hath come into being — Rhm

there is a remnant [of the house of Israel] chosen by gift of grace — Con

there is to be found a remnant of our nation selected by God in love — TCNT

there has come to be a remnant — a selection by grace — Wey

there is a remnant (a small believing minority), selected (chosen) by grace — Amp

a remnant remains, in accordance with God's unmerited favor — Wms

6. And if by grace, then is it no more of works:

But if their choice be the gift of grace, it can no more be deemed the wage of works — Con

But if it is by grace, it is no longer on the basis of men's deeds — Wey

But if it is by His unmerited favor, it is not at all conditioned on what they have done — Wms

otherwise grace is no more grace.

else favour no longer proveth to be favour! — Rhm

for the gift that is earned is no gift — Con

otherwise grace would cease to be grace — Mof

But if it be of works, then it is no more grace: otherwise work is no more work.[14]

or if it be gained by works, it is no longer the gift of grace; for work claims wages, and not gifts — Con

7. What then?

What are we to infer from this — Mof

So this is the situation: — Tay

Israel hath not obtained that which he seeketh for;

Why, that Israel as a nation failed to secure what it was seeking — TCNT

Israel has failed to obtain what it is still in search for — Wms

most of the Jews have not found the favor of God they are looking for — Tay

but the election hath obtained it,

but the chosen have won it — Con

while those whom God selected did secure it — TCNT

only this chosen remnant has attained it — Knox

but the selected few have achieved it — NEB

and the rest were blinded

. . . were hardened — ASV

. . . have become callous — Wey

The rest were made blind to the truth — NEB

8. (According as it is written,

as Scripture says — TCNT

---

[14]These words are now recognized as not adequately supported by original manuscripts.

699

God hath given them the spirit of slumber,

God gave them a spirit of stupor — ASV

God has thrown them into a state of spiritual insensibility — Gspd

God has given them over to an attitude of insensibility — Wms

God brought upon them a numbness of spirit — NEB

God has numbed their senses — Knox

God has given them a deadness of mind — TCNT

eyes that they should not see, and ears that they should not hear;) unto this day.

. . . that they should not hear, unto this very day — ASV

eyes that are not to see and ears that are not to hear — and it is so to this very day — TCNT

with eyes that cannot see and ears that cannot hear, that has lasted down to this day — Gspd

he gave them blind eyes and deaf ears, and so it is still — NEB

9. And David saith,

Similarly David says — NEB

Let their table be made a snare, and a trap,

May their feasts prove a snare and a trap to them — TCNT

Let their good food and other blessings trap them into thinking all is well between themselves and God — Tay

and a stumblingblock, and a recompence unto them:

A hindrance and a retribution — TCNT

Their ruin and their retribution — Gspd

To make them fall and get what they deserve — Beck

a pitfall and a just retribution — rebounding as a boomerang upon them — Amp

10. Let their eyes be darkened, that they may not see,

let their eyes be dim, so that they cannot see — Knox

and bow down their back alway.

And do thou always make their backs to bend — TCNT

Make their backs bend forever under their burden! — Gspd

Make their backs stoop for ever — Wey

11. I say then,

I ask then — TCNT

Have they stumbled that they should fall?

Did they stumble in order that they might fall — Rhm

Did God make His Jewish people stumble like this for the purpose of bringing disaster to them — Tay

Was their stumbling to result in their fall — TCNT

has their stumbling led to their absolute ruin — Gspd

Have they stumbled so as to fall — Mon

Have they stumbled irretrievably — Wey

they did not stumble so as to fall in utter ruin, did they — Wms

Was this fall of theirs an utter disaster — Phi

God forbid:[15]

By no means! — RSV

but rather through their fall salvation is come unto the Gentiles,

But by their trespass. . . . — ABUV

On the contrary, through their falling away Salvation has reached the Gentiles — TCNT

Through their false step salvation has gone to the heathen — Gspd

the result of their false step has been to bring the Gentiles salvation — Knox

His purpose was to make His salvation available to the Gentiles — Tay

for to provoke them to jealousy.

to provoke them to rivalry — ABUV

so as to make the Israelites jealous — Gspd

so that they might be moved to envy — Bas

and the result of that must be to rouse the Jews to emulate them — Knox

and then the Jews would be jealous and begin to want God's salvation for themselves — Tay

12. Now if the fall of them be the riches of the world,

Now if their trespass is . . . — ABUV

Now if their stumbling enriches the world — Con

and if their lapse is the enrichment of the world — Wey

---

[15]See Rom. 3:4 for other translations of this phrase.

Now if the whole world became rich
as a result of God's offer of salvation, when the Jews stumbled over
it and turned it down — Tay

**and the diminishing of them the riches
of the Gentiles;**

and their diminution ... — ABUV

and their loss ... — ASV

and their overthrow becomes the enrichment of heathen peoples — Wms

and their defection proved such a benefit to the gentiles — Phi

and if the lessening of their gain gives
wealth to the Gentiles — Con

and their defeat has enriched the
heathen — Gspd

if the Gentiles have been enriched by
their default — Knox

how much more their fulness?

how much more must their fulness do!
— Con

how much more will result from their
full restoration! — TCNT

what an enrichment will follow their
reinstatement! — Wey

how much richer the result will be
when the full quota of Jews comes
in! — Wms

think what tremendous advantages their
fulfilling of God's plan could mean!
— Phi

think how much greater a blessing the
world will share in later on when the
Jews too come to Christ — Tay

13. For I speak to you Gentiles,

But I speak to you that are Gentiles. —
ASV

Now a word to you who are Gentiles.
— Phi

**inasmuch as I am the apostle of the
Gentiles, I magnify mine office:**

Inasmuch then as I am an apostle of
Gentiles, I glorify my ministry —
ASV

. . . to Gentiles, I take pride in my
ministry — Wey

Being myself an Apostle to the Gentiles, I exalt my office — TCNT

as an apostle to the Gentiles I lay great
stress on my office — Mof

**14. If by any means I may provoke to
emulation them which are my flesh,**

if by any means I may provoke to
jealousy ... — ASV

in the hope that I may stir my countrymen to rivalry — TCNT

and might save some of them.

and so save some of them — Wms

and in that way save some of them —
Tay

**15. For if the casting away of them be the
reconciling of the world,**

For, if their being cast aside has meant
the reconciliation of the world —
TCNT

For if their rejection and exclusion
from the benefits of salvation were
[overruled] for the reconciliation of
a world to God — Amp

**what shall the receiving of them be,
but life from the dead?**

what must the gathering of them in be
but ... — Con

what will their restoration be but life
out of death — Mon

what can it mean but that the dead will
live — Beck

what will their admission mean? Why,
it will be life from the dead! — Mof

what will their acceptance and admission mean? [It will be nothing short
of] life from the dead! — Amp

**16. For if the firstfruit be holy, the lump is
also holy:**

If the first handful of dough is holy,
so is the whole mass — TCNT

When the first loaf is consecrated, the
whole batch is consecrated with it —
Knox

Now if the first-fruits of the dough
[Abraham and the Patriarchs] are
holy, so also is the whole mass [their
descendants] — Mon

**and if the root be holy, so are the
branches.**

... hallowed ... — Con

... consecrated .. — Mof

And if the root of a tree [Abraham] is
holy, so also are the branches [his
descendants] — Mon

**17. And if some of the branches be broken
off,**

But if some of the branches were
broken off — ASV

**and thou, being a wild olive tree, wert
graffed in among them,**

and you who were only a wild olive
shoot have been grafted in — Gspd

and you, a wild olive shoot, were
grafted in their place — RSV

**and with them partakest of the root
and fatness of the olive tree;**

and didst become partaker with them of the root of the fatness of the olive tree — ASV

and came to share with them the root which is the source of the richness of the cultivated olive — TCNT

and made to share the root and richness of the olive — Con

... the rich growth of the olive stem — Mof

18. Boast not against the branches.

glory not over the branches — ASV

exult not over ... — ABUV

you must not look down upon ... — Gspd

do not be uplifted in pride over ... — Bas

do not be arrogant toward ... — NASB

don't let yourself feel superior to those former branches — Phi

That is no reason why thou shouldest boast thyself better than the branches — Knox

But if thou boast, thou bearest not the root, but the root thee.

but if thou gloriest, ... — ASV

but — if thou art boastful — thou bearest not the root, but the root thee — Con

But, if you do exult over them, remember that you do not support the root, but the root supports you — TCNT

remember, in thy mood of boastfulness, that thou owest life to the root, not the root to thee — Knox

19. Thou wilt say then,

You may make the natural retort — Phi

The branches were broken off, that I might be graffed in.

Branches were broken off, that I might be grafted in — ASV

20. Well; because of unbelief they were broken off,

Very well; but it was for lack of faith that they ... — Wms

True enough, but it was for want of faith that they were cut away—Knox

That is true; but it was for their want of faith that they were broken off — Gspd

and thou standest by faith.

and by thy faith thou standest in their place — Con

And you owe your position to your faith — Mof

and you only stand through your faith — Wey

Be not highminded, but fear:

You ought not to feel proud; you ought to be afraid — Gspd

Stop your haughty thinking; rather continue to be reverent — Wms

So do not become proud, but stand in awe — RSV

Put away your pride, and be on your guard — NEB

21. For if God spared not the natural branches, take heed lest he also spare not thee.

... neither will he spare thee — ASV

22. Behold therefore the goodness and severity of God:

Fix your gaze, therefore, on the goodness and the ... — Mon

Consider both the kindness and the ... — Mof

Behold then God's kindness and severity — ABUV

There is graciousness, then, in God, and there is severity — Knox

You must try to appreciate both the kindness and the strict justice of God — Phi

on them which fell, severity; but toward thee, goodness, if thou continue in his goodness:

if thou continue steadfast to His goodness — Con

if thou continue in his kindness—ABUV

provided you adhere to that kindness — Mof

provided that you continue responsive to that kindness — Wey

otherwise thou also shalt be cut off.

otherwise you in your turn will be pruned away — Gspd

23. And they also,
if they abide not still in unbelief,

if they continue not in their unbelief — ASV

if they persist not in their faithlessness — Con

if they do not cling to their unbelief — Gspd

shall be graffed in:
for God is able to graff them in again.

for God has the power to graft ... — Gspd

for God is able to graft them in where they were before — Con

24. For if thou wert cut out of the olive tree which is wild by nature,
For if thou wast cut out of that which is by nature a wild olive tree — ASV
and wert graffed contrary to nature into a good olive tree:
and wast grafted against nature into the fruitful olive — Con
and grafted, contrary to nature, into a cultivated olive tree — RSV
how much more
how much easier — Gspd
how much more readily — Wey
shall these, which be the natural branches,
be graffed into their own olive tree?
be grafted into the fruitful stock from whence they sprang! — Con
be grafted back into their parent tree — TCNT

25. For I would not, brethren, that ye should be ignorant of
For I would not, brethren, have you ignorant of — ASV
this mystery,
the truth, hitherto hidden — TCNT
this hidden truth — Mon
this secret — Mof
this sacred secret — Rhm
this uncovered secret — Wms
God's secret plan — Phi
lest ye should be wise in your own conceits;
Lest within yourselves ye be presumptuous — Rhm
to keep you from thinking too well of yourselves — Gspd
so that you will not feel proud and start bragging — Tay
that blindness in part is happened to Israel,
that a hardening in part hath befallen Israel — ASV
. . . a partial insensibility . . . — Mof
. . . partial blindness . . — Wey
. . . temporary insensibility . . . — Wms
that blindness has fallen upon a part of Israel — Con
that blindness of heart has to some degree befallen Israel — Lam
that the callousness which has come over Israel is only partial — TCNT
until the fulness of the Gentiles be come in.
Until the full measure of the nations shall come in — Rhm

until the full body of the Gentiles shall have come in — Con
until the great mass of the Gentiles has come in — Wey
until the full number of the Gentiles come in — RSV

26. And so all Israel shall be saved:
And then all Israel shall be saved — TCNT
and so in that way all Israel will be saved — Wms
Once this has happened, all Israel . . . — Phi
then the whole of Israel will find salvation — Knox
as it is written,
as Scripture says — TCNT
There shall come out of Sion the Deliverer,
The Deliverer will come from Zion — RSV
and shall turn away ungodliness from Jacob:
He will banish . . . — TCNT
He will remove all . . . — Wey

27. For this is my covenant unto them,
And they shall see the fulfilment of my Covenant — TCNT
And this will be my agreement with them — Gspd
And this is the Covenant I will grant them — Wey
when I shall take away their sins.
When I have taken away . . . — TCNT
when I take away . . . — RSV

28. As concerning the gospel,
As touching the joyful-message — Rhm
In the preaching of the gospel — Knox
From the stand-point of the Good News — TCNT
In respect of the Glad-tidings — Con
they are enemies for your sakes:
they are enemies of God — which is to your advantage — Mof
they are treated as enemies of God on your account — Gspd
God rejects them, to make room for you — Knox
but as touching the election, they are beloved for the fathers' sakes.
but in respect of God's choice, they are His beloved for their fathers' sake — Con
but from the stand-point of God's selection, they are dear to him on account of the Patriarchs — TCNT

but in his elective purpose he still welcomes them, for the sake of their fathers — Knox

29. For the gifts and calling of God are without repentance.

. . . are not repented of — ASV

. . . cannot be repented of — Alf

for no change of purpose can annul God's gifts and call — Con

For God never regrets his gifts or his Call — TCNT

for God does not change his mind about those to whom he gives his blessings or sends his call — Gspd

For God does not withdraw his gift and his call — Lam

for the gifts and the call of God are irrevocable — RSV

30. For as ye in times past have not believed God,

. . . were disobedient to God — ASV

For just as ye at one time had not yielded unto God — Rhm

You were once rebels — Knox

yet have now obtained mercy through their unbelief:

but now have obtained mercy by their disobedience — ASV

And yet now have received mercy by their refusal to yield — Rhm

but have now found mercy in the day of their disobedience — TCNT

31. Even so have these also now not believed,

. . . now been disobedient — ASV

So these also have now refused to yield — Rhm

they are rebels now — Knox

that through your mercy they also may obtain mercy.

that by the mercy shown to you they also may now obtain mercy — ASV

but some day they will share in God's mercy upon you — Tay

32. For God hath concluded them all in unbelief,

For God hath shut up all unto disobedience — ASV

For God had consigned all men to disobedience — Mof

For God has locked up all in the prison of disobedience — Mon

that he might have mercy upon all.

that to all alike he may show mercy — TCNT

33. O the depth of the riches both of the wisdom and knowledge of God!

Oh! the depth of the riches and wisdom and knowledge of God! — Rhm

What a fathomless depth lies in the wisdom and knowledge of God! — Mof

How inexhaustible God's resources, wisdom, and knowledge are! — Gspd

Frankly, I stand amazed at the unfathomable complexity of God's wisdom and God's knowledge — Phi

Oh what a wonderful God we have! How great are His wisdom and knowledge and riches — Tay

how unsearchable are his judgments, and his ways past finding out!

. . . and his ways past tracing out! — ASV

How inscrutable His judgments, how trackless His footsteps! — Wey

how inscrutable are his judgements, how undiscoverable his ways! — Knox

How inscrutable his judgments! How mysterious his methods! — Mof

How unfathomable his decisions are, and how untraceable his ways! — Gspd

How unfathomable are his judgments, and how unsearchable his paths! — Mon

How could man ever understand his reasons for action, or explain his methods of working? — Phi

34. For who hath known the mind of the Lord? or who hath been his counsellor?

Who has ever known the Lord's thoughts, or advised him — Gspd

35. Or who hath first given to him,

Or who has advanced anything to him — Gspd

and it shall be recompensed unto him again?

that he should deserve a recompense — Con

so that he may claim a recompense — TCNT

So as to receive payment in return — Mon

and so earned his favours — Knox

36. For of him, and through him, and to him, are all things:

For from him, and through him, and

for him, are all things — ABUV

For from him everything comes; through him everything exists; and in him everything ends! — Gspd

All things find in him their origin, their

impulse, the centre of their being — Knox

Source, Guide, and Goal of all that is — NEB

to whom be glory for ever. Amen.

CHAPTER 12

1. I beseech you therefore, brethren,

I exhort you . . . — Con

I entreat you . . . — TCNT

I appeal to you . . . — Gspd

I plead with you . . . — Wey

I beg you . . . — Wms

I appeal to you therefore, brethren, and beg of you — Amp

by the mercies of God,

in view of God's mercies — Ber

through the compassions of God — Rhm

because of God's compassion — Nor

in view of [all] the mercies of God — Amp

that ye present your bodies a living sacrifice,

to offer your very selves to him: a living sacrifice — Con

to make a decisive dedication of your bodies as a living sacrifice — Wms

to make a decisive dedication of your bodies — presenting all your members and faculties — as a living sacrifice — Amp

holy, acceptable unto God,

consecrated and acceptable to God — Mof

holy, well pleasing to God — ABUV

dedicated and fit for his acceptance — NEB

consecrated to God and worthy of his acceptance — Knox

holy (devoted, consecrated) and well pleasing to God — Amp

which is your reasonable service.

. . . spiritual service — ASV

. . . rational service — ABUV

. . . reasonable worship — Con

. . . spiritual worship — RSV

. . . spiritual service of worship — NASB

as an act of intelligent worship — Phi

This is your reasonable service of worship — Mon

which is the worship it is right for you to give him — Bas

this is the worship due from you as rational creatures — Knox

which is your reasonable (rational, intelligent) service and spiritual worship — Amp

2. And be not conformed to this world:

And be not fashioned according to this world — ASV

And be not configuring yourselves unto this age — Rhm

Do not live according to the fashions of the times — Nor

You must not adopt the customs of this world — Gspd

Do not imitate the way of this world — Lam

Stop living in accordance with the customs of this world — Wms

Don't let the world around you squeeze you into its own mold — Phi

Do not be conformed to this world — this age, fashioned after and adapted to its external, superficial customs — Amp

but be ye transformed by the renewing of your mind,

but be ye transfigured in the renewing of your mind — Alf

but by your new attitude of mind be transformed — Gspd

but by the new ideals that mold your minds continue to transform yourselves — Wms

but let God remold your minds from within — Phi

but let yourselves be transformed by a renewing of your minds — Beck

but be transformed by the complete change that has come over your minds — TCNT

But be ye transformed (changed) by the [entire] renewal of your mind — by its new ideals and its new attitude — Amp

that ye may prove what is that good, and acceptable, and perfect will of God.

that ye may discern what is the will of God, good and well pleasing, and perfect — Alf

so that you may discern what God's will is — all that is good, acceptable, and perfect — TCNT

so as to find and follow God's will; that is, what is good, well-pleasing to Him, and perfect — Wms

— so that you may prove [for yourselves] what is the good and acceptable and perfect will of God, even the thing which is good and acceptable and perfect [in His sight for you] — Amp

3. **For I say, through the grace given unto me, to every man that is among you,**

For through the grace bestowed upon me [as Christ's Apostle], I warn every man among you — Con

by the favor that God has shown me, I would tell every one of you — Gspd

In virtue of my office, I tell every one of your number — Mof

not to think of himself more highly than he ought to think;

not to think too highly of himself — Gspd

not to value himself unduly — Wey

not to estimate himself above his real value — Wms

but to think soberly,

but so to think as to think soberly — ASV

but to think reasonably — Gspd

he must take a sane view of himself — — Mof

but to make a sober estimate — Wey

but to think with sober judgment — RSV

but try to have a sane estimate of your capabilities — Phi

but think your way to a sober estimate — NEB

according as God hath dealt to every man the measure of faith.

according to the measure of faith which God has given him — Con

corresponding to the degree of faith which God has assigned to each — Mof

judging himself by the degree of faith God has allowed him — Gspd

measuring your value by how much faith God has given you — Tay

4. **For as we have many members in one body,**

For, just as in the human body there is a union of many parts — TCNT

and all members have not the same office:

and not all the members have the same function — Mon

and each part has its own function — TCNT

5. **So we, being many, are one body in Christ,**

so we, by our union in Christ, many though we are, form but one body — TCNT

and every one members one of another.

and fellow-members one of another — Con

and we are individually parts of one another — Gspd

and are dependent on one another — Bas

and each acts as the counterpart of another — Knox

each one of us being a part of the whole and mutually dependent on the other parts — Nor

6. **Having then gifts differing according to the grace that is given to us,**

We have gifts that differ with the favor that God has shown us — Gspd

Having gifts that differ according to the grace given to us, let us use them: — RSV

The gifts we possess differ as they are allotted to us by God's grace, and must be exercised accordingly: — NEB

whether prophecy, let us prophesy according to the proportion of faith;

He that has the gift of prophecy, let him exercise it according to the proportion of his faith — Con

if our gift is to preach, let our preaching correspond to our faith — TCNT

If a man is a prophet, let him prophesy as far as the measure of his faith will let him — Knox

the gift of inspired utterance, for example, in proportion to a man's faith — NEB

7. **Or ministry, let us wait on our ministering:**

He that has the gift of ministration, let him minister — Con

if it is practical service, let us mind our service — Mof

If your gift is that of serving others, serve them well — Tay

or he that teacheth, on teaching;

let the teacher labor in teaching — Con

the teacher must mind his teaching — Mof

Let the teacher give himself to his teaching — Mon

8. Or he that exhorteth, on exhortation:

and if our gift be the stimulating of the faith of others let us set ourselves to it — Phi

and one who has the gift of stirring speech should use it to stir his hearers — NEB

If you can encourage, encourage — Beck

The preacher should see to it that his sermons are strong and helpful — Tay

he that giveth, let him do it with simplicity;

. . . with liberality — ASV

Let the man who gives in charity do so with a generous heart — TCNT

He who gives, let him do it with singleness of mind — Mon

. . . with sincerity — Lam

If God has given you money, be generous in helping others with it — Tay

he that ruleth, with diligence;

He who rules, let him rule diligently — Con

let him who is in authority exercise due diligence — TCNT

one who presides should be zealous — Wey

if you are a leader, exert yourself to lead — NEB

he that sheweth mercy, with cheerfulness.

he who does acts of mercy . . . — RSV

and one who gives help should do it cheerfully — Wey

He who shows pity, let him show it gladly — Con

and he who shows mercy must be cheerful — Mon

And if yours is the gift of kindness to others, do it cheerfully — Tay

9. Let love be without dissimulation.

. . . without hypocrisy — ASV

. . . sincere — TCNT

. . . unfeigned — ABUV

Your love must be genuine — Gspd

Abhor that which is evil;

Regard evil with horror — Wey

Hate what is wrong — Gspd

cleave to that which is good.

cling to the right — TCNT

wed yourselves to what is good — Mon

keep on holding to what is right — Wms

10. Be kindly affectioned one to another with brotherly love;

In love of the brethren be tenderly affectioned one to another — ASV

Be affectionate in your love for the brotherhood — Gspd

Be affectionate towards each other, as the love of brothers demands — Knox

love one another with brotherly affection — RSV

Be devoted to one another in brotherly love — NASB

Love one another tenderly as fellow Christians — Beck

in honour preferring one another;

in honor let each set his neighbor above himself — Con

in showing respect, set an example of deference to one another — TCNT

eager to show one another honor — Gspd

outdo one another in showing honor — RSV

11. Not slothful in business;

Let your diligence be free from sloth — Con

never flagging in zeal — TCNT

never slack in earnestness — Wms

I would see you unwearied in activity — Knox

not lagging behind in diligence — NASB

Never be lazy in your work — Tay

fervent in spirit;

Be glowing in spirit — Mon

Have your spirits aglow — Wey

on fire with the Spirit — Gspd

be aglow with the Spirit — RSV

serving the Lord;

be true bondsmen of your Lord — Con

Slave for the Master — Mon

12. Rejoicing in hope;

In your hope be joyful — Con

let your hope be a joy to you — Mof

Let hope keep you joyful — NEB

patient in tribulation;

patient under affliction — Wey

in your sufferings be steadfast — Con

in affliction enduring — ABUV

steadfast in time of trouble — Gspd

continuing instant in prayer;

continuing steadfastly in prayer — ASV

in prayer perserving — Rhm

persistent in prayer — Gspd

steadfastly maintain the habit of prayer — Phi

in your prayers be unwearied — Con

13. **Distributing to the necessity of saints;**

relieving the wants of Christ's people — TCNT

providing generously for the needs of the saints — Knox

given to hospitality.

Make a practice of hospitality — Mof

And show hospitality to the stranger — Con

pursuing the practice of hospitality — Amp

14. **Bless them which persecute you: bless, and curse not.**

Bless those who make a practice of persecuting you; bless them instead of persecuting them — Mof

Call down blessings on your persecutors — blessings, not curses — NEB

If someone harms you, don't curse him; pray that God will bless him — Tay

15. **Rejoice with them that do rejoice, and weep with them that weep.**

With the joyful be joyful, and mourn with the mourners — NEB

Share the happiness of those who are happy, and the sorrow of those who are sad — Phi

When others are happy, be happy with them. If they are sad, share their sorrow — Tay

16. **Be of the same mind one toward another.**

Be of one mind amongst yourselves — Con

Live in harmony with one another — Gspd

Have full sympathy with one another — Mon

Have equal regard for one another — NEB

Mind not high things, but condescend to men of low estate.

do not be haughty, but associate with the lowly — RSV

Set not your mind on high things, but condescend to things that are lowly — ASV

Do not be too ambitious, but accept humble tasks — Gspd

Do not let your thoughts be highflown, but accommodate yourselves to humble ways — Wey

do not aspire to eminence, but willingly adjust yourselves to humble situations — Ber

Set not your mind on high things, but be carried away with the lowly — ABUV

instead of being ambitious, associate with humble folk — Mof

Don't become snobbish, but take a real interest in ordinary people — Phi

Avoid being haughty; mingle with the lowly — Nor

Be not wise in your own conceits.

Do not be wise in your own estimation — NASB

Do not think too highly of yourselves — TCNT

Do not be conceited — Gspd

And don't think you know it all! — Tay

17. **Recompense to no man evil for evil.**

Never return injury for injury — TCNT

Provide things honest in the sight of all men.

Take thought for things honorable in the sight of all men — ASV

but take thought for what is noble in the sight of all — RSV

Aim to do what is honorable in the eyes of all — Mon

determine on the noblest ways in dealing with all people — Ber

See that you are above reproach in the eyes of everyone — Gspd

18. **If it be possible, as much as lieth in you,**

If you can, so far as it depends on you — Wey

As far as your responsibility goes — Phi

live peaceably with all men.

be at peace with all men — ASV

19. **Dearly beloved, avenge not yourselves,**

Never take vengeance into your own hands, my dear friends — Phi

but rather give place unto wrath:

but let the wrath of God have its way — Mof

but leave room for God's anger — Gspd

but leave the field clear for God's wrath
— Mon

allow retribution to run its course —
Knox

for it is written,

for the Scripture says — Gspd

Vengeance is mine;

Vengeance belongeth unto me — ASV

Vengeance is for me — Knox

I will repay, saith the Lord.

20. **Therefore if thine enemy hunger, feed him;**

But there is another text: If your

enemy is hungry, feed him — NEB

if he thirst, give him drink:

for in so doing thou shalt heap coals of fire on his head.

for in this way you will make him feel a burning sense of shame — Mof

21. **Be not overcome of evil, but overcome evil with good.**

Never be conquered by evil, but conquer evil with good — TCNT

Never let evil get the better of you; get the better of evil by doing good — Mof

CHAPTER 13

1. **Let every soul be subject unto**

Let every man submit himself to — Con

Let every one obey — TCNT

the higher powers.

the authorities that are over him — ABUV

the authorities of government — Con

its lawful superiors — Knox

the governing authorities — RSV

the government that is over him—Beck

For there is no power but of God:

For there is no authority save by God — Rhm

for all authority comes from God — Con

For no Authority exists except by the will of God — TCNT

for no authority can exist without the permission of God — Gspd

the powers that be are ordained of God.

The authorities that now exist have been appointed by God — Mon

the existing authorities have been established by him — Gspd

2. **Whosoever therefore resisteth the power,**

So that he that sets himself against the authority — ABUV

Hence anyone who resists authority — Mof

resisteth the ordinance of God:

is opposing the divine order — Mof

sets himself in opposition to what God has ordained — Gspd

is a rebel against the ordinance of God — Knox

is resisting God's appointment — Wey

is resisting a divine institution — NEB

and they that resist

shall receive to themselves damnation.

will bring judgment upon themselves — Con

will incur sentence — Wey

will get the penalty due them — Wms

will get punishment for themselves — Bas

3. **For rulers are not a terror to good works, but to the evil.**

For civil authorities are not a terror to [people of] good conduct, but to [those of] bad behavior — Amp

The man who does right has nothing to fear from the magistrates, as the wrongdoer has — Gspd

For government, a terror to crime, has no terrors for good behaviour — NEB

Wilt thou then not be afraid of the power?

And wouldest thou have no fear of the power — ASV

Do you want to have no reason to fear the Authorities — TCNT

Do you want to have no dread of the civil authorities — Wms

do that which is good, and thou shalt have praise of the same:

Then do what is good, and you will win their praise — TCNT

Then practice doing right, and you will be commended for it — Wms

Then continue to do right and you will win their approval — NEB

4. **For he is the minister of God to thee for good.**

For the magistrate is God's minister to thee for good — Con

For they are God's servants appointed for your good — TCNT

for they are God's agents to do you good — Gspd

The officer is God's servant for your protection — Phi

But if thou do that which is evil,

But if you are a wrong-doer — Mon

be afraid;

you may well be afraid — TCNT

you have reason to be alarmed — Phi

for he beareth not the sword in vain:

for not by chance does he bear the sword [of justice] — Con

for the sword they carry is not without meaning — TCNT

for they do not carry swords for nothing — Gspd

for he is the minister of God, a revenger to execute wrath upon him that doeth evil.

for he is a minister of God, an avenger for wrath to him that doeth evil — ASV

They are God's servants to inflict his punishments on those who do wrong — TCNT

for they are God's agents of punishment, for retribution on the offender — NEB

5. Wherefore ye must needs be subject,

You are bound, therefore, to obey — TCNT

Wherefore it is necessary to submit yourselves — ABUV

not only for wrath, but also for conscience sake.

not only for fear of punishment . . . — Wey

not only through fear of God's punishments, but also as a matter of conscience — TCNT

not only to escape God's wrath, but as a matter of principle — Gspd

not simply because it is the safest, but because it is the right thing to do — Phi

6. For this cause pay ye tribute also:

This, too, is the reason why you pay taxes — Mon

It is right, too, for you to pay taxes — Phi

for they are God's ministers, attending continually upon this very thing.

tax-gatherers are ministers of God, de-

voting their energies to this very work — Wey

for the civil authorities are God's official servants faithfully devoting themselves to this very end — Wms

7. Render therefore to all their dues:

Pay them all what is due them — Gspd

Discharge your obligations to all men — NEB

tribute to whom tribute is due; custom to whom custom;

tribute to one, taxes to another — Mof

— tribute to the man entitled to receive it, taxes to the man entitled to receive them — Gspd

tax to whom tax is due, toll to whom toll — Wey

pay your taxes and import duties gladly — Tay

fear to whom fear; honour to whom honour.

respect where respect is due, and honour where honour is due — TCNT

8. Owe no man any thing, but to love one another:

Owe no debt to any man, save the debt of love alone — Con

Leave no debt unpaid except the standing debt of mutual love — Wey

for he that loveth another

for he that loveth his neighbor — ASV

hath fulfilled the law.

has fully satisfied the Law — Gspd

has done all that the law demands — Knox

has obeyed the whole Law in regard to his neighbor — Phi

9. For this,

For the Law which says — Mon

For the commandments — Gspd

Thou shalt not commit adultery, Thou shalt not kill,

You must not commit adultery, You must not murder — Gspd

Thou shalt not steal, Thou shalt not bear false witness,[16] Thou shalt not covet;

You must not steal, You must not covet — Gspd

and if there be any other commandment,

---

[16]The words "Thou shalt not bear false witness" are now recognized as not adequately supported by original manuscripts.

it is briefly comprehended in this saying, namely,

it is summed up in this word, namely — ASV

Thou shalt love thy neighbour as thyself.

10. Love worketh no ill to his neighbor:

Love never wrongs a neighbor — TCNT

therefore love is the fulfilling of the law.

love therefore is the fulfilment of the law — ASV

Therefore Love fully satisfies the Law — TCNT

10. Love worketh no ill to his neighbour:

This do, knowing the season wherein we stand — Con

Carry out these injunctions because you know the crisis that we are in — Mon

Live thus, realizing the situation — Wey

Meanwhile, make no mistake about the age we live in — Knox

Besides this you know what hour it is — RSV

This I say, because you know the crisis that we have reached — TCNT

that now it is high time to awake out of sleep:

that already it is time for you . . . — ASV

that it is already the hour for you to awaken from sleep — NASB

for the time has already come for you to rouse yourselves from sleep — TCNT

it is time to wake up to reality — Phi

for now is our salvation nearer than when we believed.

For salvation (final deliverance) is nearer to us now than when we first believed — Amp

12. The night is far spent,

The night is far advanced — ABUV

The night is nearly over — Phi

the day is at hand:

the day is almost here — Mof

day is about to dawn — Wey

let us therefore cast off the works of darkness,

Let us therefore put off . . . — ABUV

So let us lay aside the deeds of darkness — Wey

and let us put on the armour of light.

and let us put on the weapons of light — ABUV

let us arm ourselves for the fight of the day — Phi

13. Let us walk honestly,

Let us walk becomingly — ASV

let us live decorously — Mof

Let us live honorably — Gspd

Let us behave with decency — NEB

as in the day;

as befits the day — Ber

as in the open light of day — Mof

not in rioting and drunkenness,

not in revelling and . . . — ASV

. . . carousing and . . . — Gspd

Not in revellings and in drunken bouts — Rhm

not in chambering

not in lewdness — ABUV

not in prostitution — Ber

not in sexual promiscuity — NASB

and wantonness,

and wanton deeds — Rhm

and indecency — Gspd

and debauchery — Wey

and sensuality — NASB

not in strife and envying.

not in quarrelling and jealousy — TCNT

14. But put ye on the Lord Jesus Christ,

But clothe yourselves with . . . — Con

But put on as your armour . . . — Wey

and make not provision for the flesh, to fulfil the lusts thereof.

and spend no thought on your earthly nature, to satisfy its cravings — TCNT

and make no provision for the passions of your lower nature — Wey

and put a stop to gratifying the evil desires that lurk in your lower nature — Wms

CHAPTER 14

1. Him that is weak in the faith receive ye,

. . . in his faith receive into your fellowship — Con

Treat people who are overscrupulous in

their faith like brothers — Gspd

Welcome a man of weak faith — Mof

but not to doubtful disputations.

not for decisions of disputes — ABUV

but not for the purpose of deciding

doubtful points — Mon

but not for disputes over opinions — RSV

but not for the purpose of passing judgement on their scruples — TCNT

2. For one believeth that he may eat all things:

One man hath faith to eat all things — ASV

One man's faith allows him to eat anything — Wey

For instance, one man will have faith enough to eat all kinds of foods — NEB

another, who is weak, eateth herbs.

while a man of weaker faith eats only vegetables — Wey

while the overscrupulous man eats nothing but vegetables — Gspd

3. Let not him that eateth despise him that eateth not;

. . . set at nought him that eateth not — ASV

The eater should not feel contempt for the abstainer — Ber

The meat eater should not despise the vegetarian — Phi

The man who will eat anything must not look down on the man who abstains from some things — Gspd

and let not him which eateth not

nor let him who abstains — Con

judge him that eateth:

censure the eater — Wey

for God hath received him.

. . . has accepted him — Wey

. . . has welcomed him — Mof

God, after all, has found room for him — Knox

4. Who art thou that judgest another man's servant?

Who are you, that you should pass judgement on the servant of another — TCNT

Who are you to criticize the servant of Another — Mof

to his own master he standeth or falleth.

It is for his own master to say whether he succeeds or fails — Gspd

It is his own master's business whether he stands or falls — Wms

Yea, he shall be holden up:

Yea, he shall be made to stand — ASV

And stand he will — TCNT

and he will succeed — Gspd

for God is able to make him stand.

for the Lord hath power to make him stand — ASV

for his Master has . . . — Mon

God is well able to give him a sure footing — Knox

5. One man esteemeth one day above another:

Again, one man considers some days to be more sacred than others — TCNT

Then again, this man rates one day above another — Mof

One man makes a distinction between this day and that — Knox

another esteemeth every day alike.

while another considers all days to be alike — TCNT

while that man rates all days alike — Mof

Let every man be fully persuaded in his own mind.

Let each man be fully assured . . . — ASV

Every one ought to be fully convinced . . . — TCNT

On such a point everyone should have reached conviction in his own mind — NEB

On questions of this kind everyone must decide for himself — Tay

6. He that regardeth the day,

He who observes a day — TCNT

the man who values a particular day — Mof

regardeth it unto the Lord;

does it in the Lord's honor — Gspd

observes it for the Lord's sake — Wey

observes it to the Master's honour — TCNT

and he that regardeth not the day, to the Lord he doth not regard it.[17]

He that eateth, eateth to the Lord,

He, again, who eats meat eats it to the Master's honour — TCNT

and he who eats eats for the Lord's sake — Wey

for he giveth God thanks;

since he thanks God for his food — Mof

and he that eateth not, to the Lord he eateth not,

---

[17]This clause is now recognized as not adequately supported by original manuscripts.

and he who abstains, abstains unto the
Lord — Con

and the man who abstains does it in
the Lord's honor — Gspd

and the abstainer abstains for the
Lord's sake — Wey

and giveth God thanks.

and he too thanks God — Mof

7. For none of us liveth to himself,

There is not one of us whose life concerns himself alone — TCNT

None of us lives only to himself —
Gspd

. . . for himself alone — NEB

None of us lives as his own master —
Knox

and no man dieth to himself.

and not one of us whose death concerns
himself alone — TCNT

and none of us dies only to himself —
Gspd

and equally no one of us dies, for himself alone — NEB

and none of us dies as his own master
— Knox

8. For whether we live,

for, if we live — TCNT

While we live — Knox

we live unto the Lord;

we are responsible to the Lord — Gspd

we always live in relation to the Lord
— Wms

our life is for the Master — TCNT

we live as the Lord's servants — Knox

and whether we die,

and, if we die — TCNT

when we die — Knox

we die unto the Lord:

we are responsible to him — Gspd

our death is for the Master — TCNT

we always die in relation to the Lord —
Wms

we die as the Lord's servants — Knox

**whether we live therefore, or die, we
are the Lord's.**

So then, whether we live or die, we belong to our Lord — Mon

in life and in death, we belong to the
Lord — Knox

**9. For to this end Christ both died, and
rose, and revived,**

For to this end Christ died and lived
again — ASV

For this purpose Christ died and became alive again — Mon

For this was the purpose of Christ's
dying and coming to life — Wey

**that he might be Lord both of the dead
and living.**

that he might be Lord over both the
dead and the living — TCNT

10. But why dost thou judge thy brother?

And who art thou, to pass judgment
on . . . — Knox

But you, why do you find fault with
your brother — Wey

But you [the abstainer], why do you
pass judgment on your brother —
Mon

**or why dost thou set at nought thy
brother?**

And you, why do you look down upon
your brother — Mof

Or you again [the non-abstainer], why
do you despise yours — Mon

And you, sir, why do you hold your
brother in contempt — NEB

Who art thou, to mock at thy brother
— Knox

**for we shall all stand before the judg-
ment seat of Christ.**

. . . the Bar of God — TCNT

All of us will have to stand before the
tribunal of God — Mof

We shall all have to stand before God
for judgment — Gspd

11. For it is written,

For Scripture says — TCNT

**As I live, saith the Lord, every knee
shall bow to me,**

As surely as I live, says the Lord, every
knee will bend before me — Gspd

and every tongue shall confess to God.

and every tongue shall acknowledge
God — Con

. . . shall give praise to God — RSV

**12. So then every one of us shall give ac-
count of himself to God.**

Each of us then will have to answer for
himself to God — Mof

It is to God alone that we have to answer for our actions — Phi

**13. Let us not therefore judge one another
any more:**

So let us stop criticizing one another
— Mof

So let us no longer pass judgment on
. . . — Mon

but judge this rather,

but let this rather be your judgment —
Con

Rather let this be your resolve — TCNT

that no man put a stumblingblock or an occasion to fall in his brother's way.

never to put any hindrance or obstacle in your brother's way — Gspd

not to trip up or entangle a brother's conscience — Knox

do nothing to make a brother stumble or fall — Phi

14. I know, and am persuaded by the Lord Jesus,

. . . in the Lord Jesus — ASV

Through my union with the Lord Jesus, I know and am persuaded — TCNT

I know and as a follower of the Lord Jesus I am convinced — Gspd

I am absolutely convinced, as a Christian — NEB

that there is nothing unclean of itself:

That nothing is profane of itself — Rhm

. . . is defiled of itself — ABUV

that in itself nothing is 'impure' — Wey

that nothing is intrinsically unholy — Phi

but to him that esteemeth any thing to be unclean, to him it is unclean.

but whatever a man thinks unclean is unclean to him — Con

A thing is 'defiling' only to him who holds it to be so — TCNT

but any food is "unclean" for one who considers it "unclean" — Mon

15. But if thy brother be grieved with thy meat,

For if because of meat thy brother is grieved — ASV

. . . because of food . . . — ABUV

If your brother is being injured because you eat a certain food — Mof

If your habit of unrestricted diet seriously upsets your brother — Phi

now walkest thou not charitably.

thou walkest no longer in love — ASV

you are not living by the standard of love — Wms

No longer by the rule of love art thou walking — Rhm

your life is not governed by love — Gspd

you are no longer following the guidance of love — Wey

Destroy not him with thy meat, for whom Christ died.

Do not, by what you eat, ruin a man for whom Christ died — TCNT

. . . persist in destroying . . . — Mon

Do not by your eating bring disaster to . . . — NEB

16. Let not then your good be evil spoken of:

Therefore do not let what is a boon to you and others bring reproach — Wey

So do not let what is good to you be spoken of as evil — RSV

Do not let what is right for you become a matter of reproach — TCNT

What for you is a good thing must not become an occasion for slanderous talk — NEB

17. For the kingdom of God is not meat and drink;

. . . does not mean food and drink — RSV

The Reign of God is not a matter of eating and drinking — Mof

For the Kingdom of God does not consist in . . . — Wey

but righteousness, and peace, and joy in the Holy Ghost.

but of righteousness and peace and gladness through the presence of the Holy Spirit — TCNT

. . . peace, and happiness through the possession of the holy Spirit — Gspd

it means rightness of heart, finding our peace and our joy in the Holy Spirit — Knox

18. For he that in these things serveth Christ is acceptable to God, and approved of men.

For he that herein serveth Christ is well-pleasing to God, and approved of men — ASV

He who serves the Christ in this way pleases God, and wins the approval of his fellow men — TCNT

19. Let us therefore follow after the things which make for peace,

So then, let us pursue . . . — ABUV

So let us keep on pursuing the things that . . . — Wms

Let us, therefore, keep before us whatever will contribute to peace — Gspd

Let our aim, then, be peace — Knox

and things wherewith one may edify another.

And the things which belong to the up-building one of another — Rhm

and our mutual upbuilding — Wms

20. For meat destroy not the work of God.

Overthrow not for meat's sake the work of God — ASV

Do not for the sake of meat undo the work of God — Alf

Do not, for the sake of food, be tear-ing down God's work — Mon

Don't ruin God's work just for food — Beck

All things indeed are pure;

All things indeed [in themselves] are pure — Con

All food indeed is ceremonially clean — Mon

but it is evil for that man who eateth with offence.

but it can be harmful to the man who eats it with a guilty conscience — Phi

but it is evil for that man who by eat-ing makes another stumble — ABUV

yet, if a man eats so as to put a stum-bling-block in the way of others, he does wrong — TCNT

but it is wrong for any one to make others fall by what he eats — RSV

21. It is good neither to eat flesh, nor to drink wine, nor any thing

The right course is not to eat meat, nor to drink wine, nor to do anything — Mon

We should be willing to be both veg-etarians and teetotalers — Phi

whereby thy brother stumbleth,[18] or is offended, or is made weak.

whereby thy brother is caused to stum-ble — Rhm

22. Hast thou faith? have it to thyself be-fore God.

Hast thou faith [that nothing is un-clean]? keep it for thine own comfort before God — Con

Certainly keep your own conviction on the matter, as between yourself and God — Mof

The faith that you have, keep between

yourself and God — RSV

Your personal convictions [on such matters] exercise as in God's pres-ence, keeping them to yourself — Amp

Happy is he that condemneth not him-self in that thing which he alloweth.

. . . that judgeth not himself in that which he approveth — ASV

Happy the man who does not censure himself in the deeds he approves — Wey

Happy the person who has no qualms of conscience in what he allows him-self to do — Ber

he is a fortunate man who has no mis-givings about what he allows himself to eat — Mof

23. And he that doubteth is damned if he eat,

But he that doubteth is condemned if he eats — ASV

But one who has misgivings stands self-condemned if he eats — Wey

But if anyone has doubts about eating and then eats, that condemns him at once — Mof

But he who has misgivings, and yet eats meat, is condemned already — Mon

Yet if a man eats meat with an uneasy conscience about it, you may be sure he is wrong to do so — Phi

because he eateth not of faith: for whatsoever is not of faith is sin.

it was not faith that induced him to eat, and any action that is not based on faith is a sin — Mof

for he is not following his convictions, and anything that does not rest on conviction is wrong — Gspd

For his action does not spring from his faith, and when we act apart from our faith we sin — Phi

For whatever does not originate and proceed from faith is sin — that is, whatever is done without a convic-tion of its approval by God is sinful — Amp

---

[18]The words "or is offended, or is made weak" are now recognized as not adequately sup-ported by original manuscripts.

CHAPTER 15

1. We then that are strong ought to bear the infirmities of the weak,

It is the duty of us who are strong to put up with the weaknesses of those who are immature — Gspd

No, we who are bold in our confidence ought to bear with the scruples of those who are timorous — Knox

We who are strong ought to bear with the failings of the weak — RSV

We who are strong have to be a support to the feeble — Bas

and not to please ourselves.

not to insist on having our own way — Knox

2. Let every one of us please his neighbour for his good to edification.

Each of us ought to give way to his neighbour, where it serves a good purpose by building up his faith — Knox

Let each one of us please his neighbor for that which is good, unto edifying — ASV

. . . for his good, to upbuilding — ABUV

. . . with a view to edification — Alf

Let each of us please his neighbor for good ends, to build him up — Con

Every one of us should please his neighbor for his good, to help him grow — Beck

Everyone of us must try to please his neighbor, to do him good, and help in his development — Gspd

3. For even Christ pleased not himself;

For indeed Christ did not seek His own pleasure — Wey

but, as it is written,

On the contrary, as Scripture says of him — TCNT

The reproaches of them that reproached thee fell on me.

The abuses of those who abused you fell on me — Ber

4. For whatsoever things were written aforetime were written for our learning,

Whatever was written in the Scriptures in days gone by was written for our instruction — TCNT

that we through patience and comfort of the scriptures might have hope.

that through patience and through comfort of the scriptures we might have hope — ASV

so that, through patient endurance, and through the encouragement drawn from the Scriptures, we might hold fast to our hope — TCNT

that by steadfast endurance, and by the counsel of the Scriptures, we may hold fast our hope — Con

5. Now the God of patience and consolation

Now the God of patience and of comfort — ASV

And may God, the source of all fortitude and all encouragement — NEB

Now may the God who gives perseverance and encouragement — NASB

grant you to be likeminded one toward another according to Christ Jesus:

. . . to be of one mind together, according to the will of Christ — Con

. . . to be united in sympathy in Christ — TCNT

. . . to be in full sympathy with one another, in accordance with the example of Jesus Christ — Mon

6. That ye may with one mind and one mouth glorify God, even the Father of our Lord Jesus Christ.

that with one accord ye may with one mouth glorify the God and Father of our Lord Jesus Christ — ASV

that you may unite in a chorus of praise and glory to . . .! — Mof

that together you may with one voice glorify . . . — RSV

7. Wherefore receive ye one another,

Therefore welcome one another — Wey

as Christ also received us to the glory of God.

even as Christ also received you . . . — ASV

just as Christ has welcomed you, to promote the glory of God — Wey

8. Now I say that Jesus Christ was a minister to the circumcision

My meaning is that Christ has become a servant to the circumcised — Wey

For I say that Christ has been made a minister of the Circumcision [the People of Israel] — Mon

for the truth of God,

in order to prove God's honesty — Mof

in behalf of God's truth — ABUV
to show God's truthfulness — Gspd
in vindication of God's truth — Mon
to confirm the promises made unto the fathers:
in order to confirm the promises given to the patriarchs — RSV
to make valid His promises to our forefathers — Wms
in carrying out the promises made to our forefathers — Gspd

9. And that the Gentiles might glorify God for his mercy;
and so that the Gentiles also should praise God for his mercy — Mon
as it is written,
As Scripture says — TCNT
For this cause I will confess to thee among the Gentiles,
... I will acknowledge thee ... — Con
Therefore will I give praise unto thee ... — ASV
and sing unto thy name.
And sing in honour of thy Name — TCNT
and sing psalms to Thy name — Ber

10. And again he saith,
And again it says — TCNT
Rejoice, ye Gentiles, with his people.
Be glad, ye Gentiles, in company with his people — Wey

11. And again, Praise the Lord, all ye Gentiles; and laud him, all ye people.
And let all the peoples praise him — ASV
... extol him — ABUV
... repeat his praise — Rhm
And let all nations sing his praises — Gspd
and greatly sing His praises, all you peoples — Ber

12. And again, Esaias saith,
And again, Isaiah saith — ASV
There shall be a root of Jesse,
... a Scion of the house of Jesse — TCNT
The descendant of Jesse will come — Gspd
The root of Jesse shall come — RSV
and he that shall rise to reign over the Gentiles;
And he who rises up to rule over ... — ABUV
in him shall the Gentiles trust.
On him shall the Gentiles hope — ASV
... rest their hopes — TCNT

... build their hopes — Wey
The heathen will set their hopes on him — Gspd

13. Now the God of hope
May God, who inspires our hope — TCNT
... the source of hope — Gspd
... the giver of hope — Wey
... the fountain of hope — Ber
May the God of your hope — Amp
fill you with all joy and peace in believing,
fill you with perfect happiness and peace in your faith — Gspd
so fill you with perfect joy and peace through your continuing faith — Wms
that ye may abound in hope,
that you may be overflowing with hope — Mon
that ... your whole life and outlook may be radiant with hope — Phi
through the power of the Holy Ghost.
in the power of the Holy Spirit — ASV

14. And I myself also am persuaded of you, my brethren,
... am confident regarding you, my brothers — Mon
Personally I am satisfied about you, my brethren — Amp
that ye also are full of goodness,
that ye yourselves are full of goodness — ASV
filled with all knowledge,
furnished with all Christian learning — TCNT
amply furnished with knowledge — Ber
richly supplied with perfect knowledge — Wms
fully equipped with every kind of knowledge — Beck
able also to admonish one another.
and well able to give advice to one another — TCNT
and well qualified to instruct one another — Gspd
and competent to counsel one another — Wms

15. Nevertheless, brethren, I have written the more boldly unto you in some sort,
But I write the more boldly unto you in some measure — ASV
But I have written very boldly to you on some points — NASB

Yet I have written to you somewhat boldly in parts [of this letter] — Con

as putting you in mind,

by way of refreshing your memories — TCNT

by way of reminding you — Mon

to remind you [rather than to teach you] — Con

because of the grace that is given to me of God,

... that was given me from God—NASB

because of the charge with which God has entrusted me — TCNT

because of the favor God has shown me — Gspd

16. That I should be the minister of Jesus Christ to the Gentiles,

... a public minister of Christ Jesus unto the nations — Rhm

in making me a minister of Christ Jesus to the heathen peoples — Wms

... a priest of Christ Jesus unto the Gentiles — Mon

ministering the gospel of God,

Doing priestly service with the glad-message of God — Rhm

to act as a priest of God's good news — Gspd

with God's gospel for my priestly charge — Knox

in the priestly service of the gospel of God — RSV

my priestly service is the preaching of the gospel of God — NEB

that the offering up of the Gentiles might be acceptable,

In order that the offering up of the nations might prove to be acceptable — Rhm

so that the Gentiles, when offered before him, may be an acceptable sacrifice — Mon

being sanctified by the Holy Ghost.

hallowed by the working of the Holy Spirit — Con

made holy by the Holy Spirit — Ber

because consecrated by the Holy Spirit — Mon

17. I have therefore whereof I may glory through Jesus Christ in those things which pertain to God.

I have therefore my glorying in Christ Jesus in things pertaining to God — ASV

I have then my boast in Christ Jesus concerning the things of God—Mon

It is, then, through my union with Christ Jesus that I have a proud confidence in my work for God — TCNT

In Christ Jesus, then, I have reason to be proud of my work for God — RSV

18. For I will not dare to speak of any of those things which Christ hath not wrought by me,

For I will venture to speak only of those things which Christ wrought through me — ABUV

I will venture to speak of those things alone in which I have been Christ's instrument — NEB

to make the Gentiles obedient, by word and deed,

to bring the Gentiles into his allegiance, ... — NEB

to bring the Gentiles to obedience, by word and work — ABUV

19. Through mighty signs and wonders, by the power of the Spirit of God;

through the power displayed in signs and marvels, and through the power of the Holy Spirit — TCNT

in the power of signs and wonders, in the power of the Holy Spirit — ASV

so that from Jerusalem, and round about unto Illyricum,

So that starting from Jerusalem and as far round as Illyricum — Amp

I have fully preached the gospel of Christ.

I have proclaimed without reserve ... — Mon

I have fulfilled my task in bearing the Glad-tidings of Christ — Con

I have told in full the Good News of the Christ — TCNT

I have completed the preaching of the good news of Christ — Gspd

20. Yea, so have I strived to preach the gospel, not where Christ was named,

yea, making it my aim so to preach the gospel, not where Christ was already named — ASV

And thus I aspired to preach ... — NASB

In all this it has been my ambition to preach the good news only where Christ's name was unknown — Gspd

lest I should build upon another man's foundation:

so as not to build on foundations other men had laid — Gspd

21. But as it is written,
But as Scripture says — TCNT
To whom he was not spoken of, they shall see:
They to whom no tidings of him came shall see — Alf
They who have never been told of him will see — Gspd
and they that have not heard shall understand.
And they who have never heard will understand — Gspd

22. For which cause also I have been much hindered from coming to you.
Wherefore also I have been hindered these many times from coming unto you — Rhm
That is why I have so often been prevented from coming to you — TCNT
This [ambition] is the reason why I have so frequently been hindered from coming to visit you — Amp

23. But now having no more place in these parts,
But now having no longer a place in these regions — ABUV
But now that I have no longer room enough [for my labors] in these parts — Con
But now, since I no longer have any room for work in these regions — RSV
and having a great desire these many years to come unto you;
and having a longing . . . — ABUV
and since I have longed for many years to come to you — RSV

24. Whensoever I take my journey into Spain, I will come to you[19]:
Whenever I go to Spain; — ABUV
for I trust to see you in my journey,
— for I hope in passing through to see you — ABUV
and to be brought on my way thitherward by you,
and to be sped forward by you — Mof
and be helped forward by you — Wey
and to be sent there with your support — NEB
and to be aided on my journey there by you — Amp
if first I be somewhat filled with your company.
after I have enjoyed your company for a while — Mof

after I have enjoyed being with you for a while — Gspd
after I have had the satisfaction of seeing you all — Phi

25. But now I go unto Jerusalem to minister unto the saints.
Just now, however, I am on my way to Jerusalem, to take help to Christ's People there — TCNT

26. For it hath pleased them of Macedonia and Achaia
For the provinces of Macedonia and Achaia have willingly undertaken — Con
For Macedonia and Greece have determined — Gspd
. . . were delighted — Wms
to make a certain contribution
for the poor saints which are at Jerusalem.
for the poor among the saints that are at Jerusalem — ASV
for the destitute of the saints who are in Jerusalem — Rhm
for the poor among God's people in Jerusalem — Gspd

27. It hath pleased them verily; and their debtors they are.
Yea, it hath been their good pleasure; . . . — ASV
Yes, they were glad to do so; and indeed it is a duty which they owe to them — TCNT
Yes, it has been their good pleasure, and their debt, too — Mon
Yes, they have thought it good, and in fact it was a debt they owed them — Wey
For if the Gentiles have been made partakers of their spiritual things,
. . . spiritual riches — Mon
For if the Gentiles have shared in their spiritual things — ABUV
their duty is also to minister unto them in carnal things.
they owe it to them also to minister to them [the Jews] in worldly goods — Mon
they ought also to be of service to them in material blessings — RSV

28. When therefore I have performed this,
. . . finished this task — Con

---

[19]The words "I will come to you" are now recognized as not adequately supported by original manuscripts.

... completed this mission — Amp

... accomplished this — ASV

When I have settled this matter—TCNT

and have sealed to them this fruit,

and have secured to them [the poor at Jerusalem] the fruit of this collection — Mon

and seen this contribution safely into their possession — Gspd

and delivered the proceeds under my own seal — NEB

I will come by you into Spain.

I will start for Spain, and come to you on the way — Gspd

29. And I am sure that, when I come unto you,

And I know that, . . . — ASV

I shall come in the fulness of the blessing of the gospel of Christ.

... in the fulness of the blessing of Christ — ASV

I will come with Christ's fullest blessing — Gspd

it will be with a full measure of blessing from Christ — TCNT

... with rich blessing from Christ — Wey

30. Now I beseech you, brethren,

I beg you, brothers — Gspd

I appeal to you, brethren — RSV

for the Lord Jesus Christ's sake,

by our Lord Jesus Christ — ASV

and for the love of the Spirit,

and by the love of the Spirit — ASV

and by the love which the Spirit gives — Con

and by the love which His Spirit inspires — Wey

that ye strive together with me in your prayers to God for me;

that you agonize with me in your prayers to God on my behalf — Ber

to help me in my conflict with your prayers to God on my behalf — Con

to help me in my struggle by your prayers to God on my behalf—Mon

to unite with me in earnest wrestling in prayer to God in my behalf — Amp

to wrestle with me in prayers to God on my behalf — Wms

be my allies in the fight; pray to God for me — NEB

31. That I may be delivered from them that do not believe in Judaea;

... them that are disobedient in Judaea — ASV

... them who do not yield in Judaea — Rhm

... unbelievers in Judaea — Mof

That I may be rescued from those in Judaea who reject the Faith — TCNT

and that my service which I have for Jerusalem may be accepted of the saints;

and that the service which I have undertaken for Jerusalem may be favorably received by the Saints — Con

and that my ministry for Jerusalem may prove acceptable to the saints — ABUV

32. That I may come unto you with joy by the will of God,

... in joy through the will of God — ASV

so that, God willing, I may be able to come to you with a joyful heart — TCNT

and may with you be refreshed.

and together with you find rest — ASV

and may be refreshed in your companionship — Con

and enjoy some rest among you — TCNT

33. Now the God of peace be with you all. Amen.

May God, the giver of peace, . . . — TCNT

CHAPTER 16

1. I commend unto you Phebe our sister,

Let me introduce our sister Phoebe — Mof

which is a servant of the church which is at Cenchrea:

who is a ministering servant of . . . — Con

who is a deaconness in the church at Cenchrea — Wms

2. That ye receive her in the Lord, as becometh saints,

Welcome her in the Lord as holy people should — Beck

In order that ye may give her welcome in the Lord in a manner worthy of the saints — Rhm

720

and I ask that you give to her a Christian welcome — one worthy of Christ's People — TCNT

and that ye assist her in whatsoever business she hath need of you:

And stand by her in any matter wherein she may have need of you — Rhm

and give her any help she may require — Mof

for she hath been a succourer of many, and of myself also.

for she herself also hath been a helper of many, and of mine own self — ASV

For she also hath proved to be a defender of many, . . . — Rhm

For she has herself been a protector of many, including myself — Gspd

She has proved herself a staunch friend to me and to many others — TCNT

3. Greet Priscilla and Aquila

Salute Prisca and Aquila — ASV

Remember me to . . . — Gspd

Give my love to . . . — Bas

Shake hands for me with . . . — Phi

my helpers in Christ Jesus:

my fellow-workers in . . . — ASV

4. Who have for my life laid down their own necks:

who risked their own lives to save mine — TCNT

who once risked their very necks for my life — Wms

unto whom not only I give thanks, but also all the churches of the Gentiles.

but also all the assemblies of the nations — Rhm

5. Likewise greet the church that is in their house.

[Salute] also the assembly at their house — Rhm

My greetings, also, to the congregation which meets at their house — Knox

[Remember me] also to the church [that meets] in their house — Amp

Salute my well-beloved Epaenetus, who is the firstfruits of Achaia[20] unto Christ.

. . . the firstfruits of Asia unto Christ — ASV

the first in Asia to be reaped for Christ — Mof

the first man in Roman Asia to believe in Christ — Mon

who was the earliest convert to Christ in the province of Asia — Wey

6. Greet Mary, who bestowed much labour on us.

. . . on you — ASV

. . . who has laboured strenuously for you — Wey

. . . who has toiled so hard for you — Wms

7. Salute Adronicus and Junia,

. . . and Junias — ASV

my kinsmen, and my fellowprisoners,

. . . and my fellow-captives — Rhm

my countrymen and once my fellowprisoners — TCNT

who are of note among the apostles,

They are noted men among the missionaries — Gspd

they are outstanding men among the messengers — Phi

who also were in Christ before me.

and who became Christians before I did — TCNT

8. Greet Amplias my beloved in the Lord.

Remember me to Ampliatus, my dear Christian friend — Gspd

9. Salute Urbane, our helper in Christ, and Stachys my beloved.

. . . Urbanus our fellow-worker in Christ . . . — ASV

10. Salute Apelles approved in Christ.

. . . the approved in Christ — ASV

. . . tested and tried in Christ — Mon

. . . who has been tried and found trustworthy in Christ's work — Con

Salute that tried Christian, Apelles — Mof

Remember me to that veteran Christian, Apelles — Gspd

Salute them which are of Aristobulus' household.

. . . those who belong to the household of Aristobulus — Mof

11. Salute Herodian my kinsman.

. . . my countryman Herodian — TCNT

Greet them that be of the household of Narcissus, which are in the Lord.

. . . the Christians in the household of Narcissus — TCNT

12. Salute Tryphena and Tryphosa, who labour in the Lord.

---

[20]Some manuscripts read "Achaia"; others have "Asia."

. . . who work hard in the Lord —
Mof

. . . who are ever toiling in the Lord
— Mon

Salute the beloved Persis,

Salute Persis the beloved — ASV

which laboured much in the Lord.

who has toiled terribly in the Lord's
service — Mon

13. **Salute Rufus chosen in the Lord,**

. . . the chosen in the Lord — ASV

. . . the elect in the Lord — ABUV

. . . eminent in the Lord — RSV

. . . that eminent Christian, Rufus —
TCNT

. . . that choice Christian, Rufus — Mof

and his mother and mine.

and [her who is] his mother and mine
— Alf

. . . his mother, who has been a mother
to me also — TCNT

14. **Salute Asyncritus, Phlegon, Hermas,
Patrobas, Hermes,**

. . . Hermas . . . Hermas — ASV

and the brethren which are with them.

and the brothers who meet with them
Gspd

and the brothers who are associated
with them — Mon

15. **Salute Philologus, and Julia, Nereus,
and his sister, and Olympas,**

and all the saints which are with them.

and all the holy people who are with
them — Beck

and all God's people who meet with
them — Gspd

and all the saints associated with them
— Mon

16. **Salute one another with an holy kiss.**

Greet one another with a sacred kiss —
TCNT

. . . a consecrated kiss — Wms

The churches of Christ salute you.

All the churches of Christ . . . — ASV

All the assemblies of the Christ . . . —
Rhm

all Christ's congregations send you
their greetings — NEB

17. **Now I beseech you, brethren,**

. . . exhort . . . — ABUV

. . . urge . . . — TCNT

. . . beg . . . — Mof

. . . entreat . . . — Knox

. . . appeal . . . — RSV

. . . implore . . . — Phi

**mark them which cause divisions and
offences**

mark them that are causing the divisions and occasions of stumbling —
ASV

to keep your eye on those who stir up
dissensions and put hindrances in
your way — Mof

to take note of those who create dissensions and difficulties — RSV

**contrary to the doctrine which ye have
learned;**

in opposition to the instruction which
you were given — Gspd

and avoid them.

and turn away from them — ASV

dissociate yourselves from them — TCNT

18. **For they that are such serve not our
Lord Jesus Christ,**

. . . our Lord Christ — ASV

but their own belly;

but are slaves to their own appetites —
TCNT

they are slaves of their own base desires
— Mof

**and by good words and fair speeches
deceive the hearts of the simple.**

and by their smooth and fair speech
they beguile the hearts of the innocent — ASV

and through their kind and smooth
speech deceive the hearts of the
guileless — ABUV

with their plausible and pious talk they
beguile the hearts of unsuspecting
people — Mof

and they seduce the minds of innocent
people with smooth and specious
words — NEB

and by fair and flattering words they
deceive the hearts of the simple-
minded — RSV

19. **For your obedience is come abroad
unto all men.**

The fame of your obedience has spread
everywhere — NEB

I am glad therefore on your behalf:

I rejoice therefore over you — ASV

**but yet I would have you wise unto
that which is good,**

but I want you to be well versed in all
that is good — TCNT

yet I should wish you to be experts in
goodness — NEB

and simple concerning evil.

Yet pure as to what is evil — Rhm

and innocent in what is evil — Wey

and guileless as to what is evil — RSV

but simpletons in evil — NEB

20. And the God of peace shall bruise Satan under your feet shortly.

And God, the giver of peace, will before long crush Satan under your feet — TCNT

The grace of our Lord Jesus Christ be with you. Amen.

The grace of our Lord Jesus be with you! — NEB

21. Timotheus my workfellow, and Lucius, and Jason, and Sosipater, my kinsmen, salute you.

Timothy my fellow-worker saluteth you; and Lucius and Jason and Sosipater, my kinsmen — ASV

Timothy, my fellow-worker sends you his greetings, and Lucius, Jason, and Sosipater, my countrymen, send theirs — TCNT

22. I Tertius, who wrote this epistle, salute you in the Lord.

(I Tertius, who took this letter down, add my Christian greetings.) — NEB

23. Gaius mine host, and of the whole church, saluteth you,

Gaius, who is the host, not of me alone, but also of the whole Church, salutes you — Con

My host Gaius, who extends his hospitality to the whole church, sends you his greeting — TCNT

There are also greetings to you from Gaius, my host, with whom the congregation meets — Nor

Erastus the chamberlain of the city saluteth you,

Erastus the treasurer of the city . . . — ASV

and Quartus a brother.

and Quartus the brother — ASV

and our brother Quartus — Gspd

24. The grace of our Lord Jesus Christ be with you all. Amen.[21]

25. Now to him that is of power to stablish you

. . . who is able to strengthen you — TCNT

Now unto him who hath power to establish you — Rhm

according to my gospel,

as promised in the Good News — TCNT

according to my Glad-tidings — Con

and the preaching of Jesus Christ,

— Even the proclamation of Jesus Christ — Rhm

and the preaching about Jesus Christ — Gspd

and in accordance with the message preached about Jesus Christ — Wms

according to the revelation of the mystery,

According to the revelation of a sacred secret — Rhm

in accordance with the revelation of that hidden purpose — TCNT

which was kept secret since the world began,

which hath been kept in silence through times eternal — ASV

26. But now is made manifest,

but has now been brought to light — Con

and by the scriptures of the prophets, according to the commandment of the everlasting God, made known to all nations

and at the command of the eternal God made known through the writings of the prophets to all the heathen — Gspd

for the obedience of faith:

for obedience to the faith — ABUV

to secure submission to the Faith — TCNT

to lead them to obedience and faith — Gspd

to win them to obedience inspired by faith — Wms

27. To God only wise, be glory through Jesus Christ for ever. Amen.

— to the one wise God be glory forever through Jesus Christ. Amen — Gspd

— to God who alone is wise, through Jesus Christ, be glory for endless ages! Amen — NEB

to the only wise God, through Jesus Christ, to whom be the glory for ever. Amen — ASV

---

[21]Verse 24 is now recognized as not adequately supported by original manuscripts.

THE FIRST EPISTLE OF PAUL TO THE CORINTHIANS

CHAPTER 1

1. Paul, called to be an apostle of Jesus Christ through the will of God,

From Paul, apostle of Jesus Christ by God's call and by God's will — NEB

Paul commissioned by the will of God as a messenger of Christ Jesus — Phi

and Sosthenes our brother,

together with our colleague Sosthenes — NEB

and Sosthenes, a Christian brother — Phi

2. Unto the church of God which is at Corinth,

Unto the assembly of God which is in Corinth — Rhm

to the congregation of God's people at Corinth — NEB

to them that are sanctified in Christ Jesus,

even them that are sanctified in Christ Jesus — ASV

to those who are consecrated by union with Christ Jesus — Gspd

called to be saints,

and called as God's people — Gspd

and called to become His people — TCNT

claimed by him as his own — NEB

with all that in every place call upon the name of Jesus Christ our Lord,

like those anywhere who call . . . — Gspd

along with all men everywhere who invoke the name of . . . — NEB

both theirs and ours:

their Lord and ours — ASV

their Master and ours — TCNT

3. Grace be unto you, and peace,

spiritual blessing and peace to you — Wms

. . . His blessings, and great peace of heart and mind — Tay

from God our Father, and from the Lord Jesus Christ.

from God our Father and the Lord Jesus Christ — ASV

4. I thank my God always on your behalf,

I thank my God always concerning you — ASV

I give praise to my God for you at all times — Bas

for the grace of God which is given you by Jesus Christ;

by reason of . . . — Rhm

because of the grace of God which was given you in Christ Jesus — RSV

for what the gift of his grace in Christ Jesus has meant to you — Phi

for the spiritual blessing given you by God through union with Christ Jesus — Wms

5. That in every thing ye are enriched by him,

because you have in everything been richly blessed through union with Him — Wms

that in every way you were enriched in him — RSV

in him you have received a wealth of all blessing — Mof

in all utterance, and in all knowledge;

with full power of expression and with adequate knowledge — Ber

from the words on your lips to the understanding in your hearts — Phi

full power to speak of your faith, and full insight into its meaning — Mof

6. Even as the testimony of Christ was confirmed in you:

So your experience has confirmed the testimony that I bore to Christ — Gspd

all of which verifies the testimony we bore to Christ when we were with you — Mof

7. So that ye come behind in no gift;

so that you are not lacking in any spiritual gift — RSV

And thus there is no gift in which you are deficient — TCNT

waiting for the coming of our Lord Jesus Christ:

during this time of waiting for his final appearance — Phi

as you eagerly look for our Lord Jesus Christ to appear again — Beck

looking earnestly for the time when our Lord Jesus Christ shall be revealed to sight — Con

8. Who shall also confirm you unto the end,

He will see to it that you will be able to hold out to the end — Nor

He will keep you steadfast in the faith to the end — Phi

he will insure your complete vindication — Gspd

that ye may be blameless in the day of our Lord Jesus Christ.

so that nobody can accuse you of anything on the day . . . —Beck

that ye may be unreprovable in the day of our Lord Jesus Christ — ASV

so that when his day comes you need fear no condemnation — Phi

9. God is faithful,

God is utterly dependable — Phi

God is entirely trustworthy — Wms

by whom ye were called unto the fellowship of his Son Jesus Christ our Lord.

through whom you have been given a part with his son . . . —Bas

who called you to share in the life of his Son . . . —NEB

10. Now I beseech you, brethren,

Fellow Christians . . . I urge you — Beck

Only I entreat you, brethren — Knox

by the name of our Lord Jesus Christ,

through the name of our Lord Jesus Christ — ASV

by all that our Lord Jesus Christ means to you — Phi

that ye all speak the same thing,

to agree in what you profess — TCNT

to agree in what you say — Gspd

and that there be no divisions among you;

and not allow yourselves to be split up into parties — Phi

and that you do not split up in factions — Nor

but that ye be perfectly joined together

All together you should be achieving a unity — Phi

but to be knit together — Mon

in the same mind and in the same judgment.

in your understanding and judgment — Beck

— of one mind and of one opinion — TCNT

I plead with you to be of the same mind, all seeing things from the same point of view — Tay

11. For it hath been declared unto me of you, my brethren,

For it hath been signified unto me concerning you, . . . — ASV

For it has been made clear to me, my brethren — Amp

by them which are of the house of Chloe,

. . . the Chloe family — Ber

by Chloe's people — RSV

that there are contentions among you.

that party feeling exists among you — TCNT

that there are strifes among you—Rhm

12. Now this I say, that every one of you saith,

each of you, I mean, has a cry of his own — Knox

I mean that each of you has his party-cry — Mof

I am of Paul; and I of Apollos;

I belong to Paul, or I belong to Apollos, — RSV

I am a follower of Paul, another, And I, of Apollos — Gspd

I am for Paul, I am for Apollo—Knox

Paul certainly is my leader, or But Apollos is mine — Ber

I belong to Paul's party, another, And I belong to Apollos' party — Wms

and I of Cephas;

I belong to Peter — Beck

. . . for Peter — Tay

and I of Christ.

. . . I owe my faith to Christ alone — Phi

. . . and some that they alone are the true followers of Christ — Tay

13. Is Christ divided?

What are you saying? Is there more than one Christ — Phi

Is Christ, the Messiah, divided into parts — Amp

And so, in effect, you have broken Christ into many pieces — Tay

You have rent the Christ in pieces! — TCNT

was Paul crucified for you?

Paul was not crucified for you, was he — NASB

or were ye baptized in the name of Paul?

Or were you immersed into the name of Paul — ABUV

You were not baptized in the name of Paul, were you — Wms

14. I thank God that I baptized none of you, but Crispus and Gaius;

Thank God, I never baptized one of you . . . — NEB

I give thanks that I immersed no one of you . . . — ABUV

I give thanks that none of you did I immerse . . . — Rhm

15. Lest any should say that I had baptized in mine own name.

. . . ye were immersed . . . — ABUV

lest any man should say that ye were baptized into my name — ASV

so that none of you can claim baptism in my name — Ber

16. And I baptized also the household of Stephanas:

Yea! I immersed the house of Stephanas also — Rhm

besides, I know not whether I baptized any other.

. . . I immersed any other — ABUV

but I can't remember anyone else — Phi

17. For Christ sent me not to baptize, but to preach the gospel:

For Christ sent me not to be immersing, But to be telling the good news — Rhm

For Christ sent me forth as His Apostle, not to baptize, but to publish Glad-tidings — Con

For Christ did not send me to see how many I could baptize, but to proclaim the gospel — Phi

not with wisdom of words,

not with an orator's cleverness — Knox

and not with eloquent wisdom — RSV

lest the cross of Christ should be made of none effect.

lest the cross of Christ should be made void — ASV

or the Cross of Christ might seem an empty thing — Gspd

18. For the preaching of the cross is to them that perish foolishness;

For the word of the cross . . . — ASV

To those who count their own ruin, the message of the cross is but folly — Knox

For the discourse that concerneth the Cross . . . — Rhm

. . . to those who are in the process of being destroyed — Wms

The Message of the Cross is indeed mere folly to those who are in the path to Ruin — TCNT

Those who are doomed to perish find the story of the cross sheer folly — Mof

but unto us which are saved it is the power of God.

. . . to those whom He is saving . . . — Wey

. . . it means all the power of God — Gspd

but to us who are in the path of Salvation it is the very power of God — TCNT

but to us who are being saved from that death, it is nothing less than the power of God — Phi

19. For it is written, I will destroy the wisdom of the wise,

Scripture says . . . — NEB

As it says in the Holy Writings . . . — Bas

. . . I will render useless the wisdom of the learned — Ber

. . . I will bring the philosophy of the philosophers to naught — TCNT

. . . I will destroy all human plans of salvation no matter how wise they seem to be — Tay

and will bring to nothing the understanding of the prudent.

And the discernment of the discerning will I bring to nought — ASV

and set aside the keenness of the sagacious — Ber

and ignore the best ideas of men, even the most brilliant of them — Tay

20. Where is the wise? where is the scribe?

. . . philosopher . . . — Gspd

. . . sage . . . — Mof

. . . where the Teacher of the Law — TCNT

where is the disputer of this world?

. . . logician . . . — Wms

or your subtle debater — limited, all of them, to this passing age — NEB

hath not God made foolish the wisdom of this world?

Has not God made the wisdom of this world look foolish — Phi

Has not God shown that the wisdom of this world is utter folly — Nor

Has not God made foolish the philosophy of the world — Mon

21. For after that in the wisdom of God the world by wisdom knew not God,

For since in accordance with the wisdom of God the world had never in reality, by means of its wisdom, come to know God — Wms

For God in his wisdom saw to it that the world would never find God through human brilliance — Tay

As God in his wisdom ordained, the world failed to find him by its wisdom — NEB

it pleased God by the foolishness of preaching to save them that believe.

it was God's good pleasure . . . — ASV

. . . His message, which the world calls foolish and silly . . . — Tay

. . . to save people who put their faith in Him — Wms

. . . to save those who believe in Christ! — TCNT

it pleased God through the folly of what we preach to save those who believe — RSV

22. For the Jews require a sign,

seeing that the Jews ask for signs — ASV

Jews continue to ask for miracles — Mon

and the Greeks seek after wisdom:

and Greeks pursue . . . — Amp

. . . an intellectual panacea — Phi

Greeks are ever wanting philosophy — Mon

23. But we preach Christ crucified,

But we come preaching a crucified Messiah — Mon

we preach about Christ dying to save them — Tay

unto the Jews a stumblingblock,

Unto Jews indeed an occasion of stumbling — Rhm

a message that is a trap-stick to the Jews — Wms

and unto the Greeks foolishness;

and absurd to the heathen — Gspd

and sheer nonsense to the gentiles — — Phi

24. But unto them which are called, both Jews and Greeks,

But God has opened the eyes of those called to salvation . . . — Tay

Christ the power of God, and the wisdom of God.

. . . The Center of God's wise plan for their salvation — Tay

25. Because the foolishness of God is wiser than men;

what seems foolish in God is wiser than men — Bas

This so-called foolish plan of God is far wiser than the wisest plan of the wisest man — Tay

and the weakness of God is stronger than men.

the weakness that springs from God surpasses human strength — Ber

what seems feeble in God is stronger than men — Bas

26. For ye see your calling, brethren,

For consider, brothers, what happened when God called you — Gspd

My brothers, think what sort of people you are, whom God has called—NEB

how that not many wise men after the flesh,

There are not many among you who are wise, as men reckon wisdom — TCNT

not many of you were wise according to worldly standards — RSV

Few of you are men of wisdom, by any human standard — NEB

not many mighty, not many noble, are called:

nor many of the ruling class, nor many from the noblest families — Phi

not many in positions of power, not many born of noble parents — Beck

27. But God hath chosen the foolish things of the world to confound the wise;

But God has chosen what the world calls foolish to shame the wise — Phi

. . . the world's simpletons to shame the learned — Ber

. . . that he might put to shame them that are wise — ASV

and God hath chosen the weak things of the world to confound the things which are mighty;

. . . what the world calls weak to shame the strong — Phi

. . . the world's weaklings to shame the strong — Ber

. . . that he might put to shame the things which are strong — ABUV

28. And base things of the world, and things which are despised, hath God chosen,

God has chosen what the world holds base and contemptible — Knox

God also has chosen the world's lowborn and contemptibles — Ber

and God chose what the world counts poor and insignificant — TCNT

And God chose people of humble birth and despised of men — Nor

yea, and things which are not,

and what it thinks does not exist — Wms

— things that to it are unreal — TCNT

to bring to nought things that are:

to nullify its realities — Gspd

to overthrow the existing order — NEB

to put a stop to what it thinks exists — Wms

29. **That no flesh should glory in his presence.**

. . . before God — ASV

And so there is no place for human pride in the presence of God — NEB

so that in his presence no human being might have anything to boast of — Gspd

30. **But of him are ye in Christ Jesus,**

So you owe it all to him through union with Christ Jesus — Wms

He is the source of your life in Christ Jesus — RSV

But thanks to Him you are in Christ Jesus — Wey

who of God is made unto us wisdom,

who was made unto us wisdom from God — ASV

He has become our wisdom from God — Wey

and righteousness, and sanctification, and redemption:

. . . our means of right standing . . . — Wms

that is, our righteousness and consecration and redemption — Mof

31. **That, according as it is written,**

so that the scripture might be fulfilled — Knox

as it is said in the Holy Writings — Bas

He that glorieth, let him glory in the Lord.

If anyone is going to boast, let him only boast of what the Lord has done — Tay

If a man is proud, let him be proud of the Lord — NEB

CHAPTER 2

1. **And I, brethren, when I came to you,**

. . . fellow-Christians . . . — Beck

came not with excellency of speech or of wisdom,

without any high pretensions to eloquence, or to philosophy — Knox

I did not come with pretensions to eloquence or learning — Nor

declaring unto you the testimony of God.

proclaiming unto you the testimony of God — RSV

I declared the attested truth of God — NEB

Declaring unto you the mystery[1] of God — Rhm

. . . God's uncovered secret — Wms

2. **For I determined not to know any thing among you,**

You may as well know now that it was my secret determination to concentrate entirely — Phi

For I had decided that while I was with you I would speak of nothing — Nor

save Jesus Christ, and him crucified.

but the knowledge of Jesus Christ alone . . . — Con

. . . and him as one who had been crucified! — Rhm

on Jesus Christ himself and the fact of his death upon the cross — Phi

3. **And I was with you in weakness,**

And in my intercourse with you, I was filled with weakness — Con

It was with distrust of myself . . . — Knox

Indeed, when I came among you, I was weak — TCNT

and in fear, and in much trembling.

and full of fears, and in great anxiety — TCNT

full of anxious fear . . . — Knox

nervous and shaking with fear — NEB

4. **And my speech and my preaching**

My Message and my Proclamation — TCNT

The word I spoke, the gospel I proclaimed — NEB

was not with enticing words of man's wisdom,

did not sway you with subtle arguments — NEB

were not delivered in the persuasive language of philosophy — TCNT

I didn't use clever talk to persuade you — Beck

---

[1]Variant reading.

but in demonstration of the Spirit and of power:

they were attended with proof and power given by the Spirit — Wms

but with the convincing power of the Spirit — Wey

but God's power was in my words, proving to those who heard them that the message was from God — — Tay

5. That your faith should not stand in the wisdom of men,

that your faith might have its foundation not in the wisdom of men — Con

Plainly God's purpose was that your faith should not rest upon man's cleverness — Phi

so that your faith should be based, not on the philosophy of man — TCNT

but in the power of God.

but upon the power of God — Phi

6. Howbeit we speak wisdom among them that are perfect:

. . . among them that are fullgrown — ASV

We do, of course, speak wisdom among those who are spiritually mature — Phi

yet not the wisdom of this world, nor of the princes of this world,

although it is not a wisdom of this age or of the rulers of this age — RSV

but it is not the wisdom of these times nor of the leaders of this age — Nor

that come to nought:

who are doomed to pass away — RSV

which are declining to their end — NEB

7. But we speak the wisdom of God in a mystery, even the hidden wisdom,

. . . a wisdom that came from God, once a covered secret but now uncovered — Wms

but it is God's wisdom that I speak, whereof the secret is made known to His people — Con

which God ordained before the world unto our glory;

which God foreordained before the worlds unto our glory — ASV

which God marked off as His plan for bringing us to glory — Wms

But which God had intended for our glory before time began — Nor

8. Which none of the princes of this world knew:

. . . leaders of the present age has learnt — Wey

. . . had come to know — Rhm

None of the rulers of the present age understands it — Mon

for had they known it, they would not have crucified the Lord of glory.

9. But as it is written, Eye hath not seen,

. . . Things which eye saw not — ASV

But, in the words of Scripture, Things beyond our seeing — NEB

nor ear heard, neither have entered into the heart of man,

no ear has ever heard, and no human heart ever conceived — Nor

things beyond our hearing, things beyond our imagining — NEB

the things which God hath prepared for them that love him.

. . . that has God made ready . . . — Ber

10. But God hath revealed them unto us by his Spirit:

But God has given us the revelation of these things through his Spirit — Bas

Yet God has unveiled them to us by his Spirit — Mon

for the Spirit searcheth all things,

For the Spirit explores everything — NEB

for the Spirit fathoms all things — TCNT

yea, the deep things of God.

even the depths of God — RSV

even the inmost depths of God's being — TCNT

11. For what man knoweth the things of a man,

For who among men knoweth the things of a man — ASV

For what human being can understand a man's thoughts — Gspd

save the spirit of man which is in him?

except that person himself — Tay

except his own inner spirit — Beck

even so the things of God knoweth no man, but the Spirit of God.

Thus even the things of God hath no one come to know . . . — Rhm

So also no one comprehends the thoughts of God except the Spirit of God — RSV

Just so no one but the Spirit of God can understand the thoughts of God — Wms

12. Now we have received, not the spirit of the world,

We have not received the spirit that belongs to this world — Wms

but the Spirit which is of God;
. . . which comes forth from God — Mon

but the Spirit that comes from God — Wms

that we might know the things that are freely given to us of God.
that we might understand the gifts bestowed on us by God — RSV

that we might get insight into the blessings God has graciously given us — Wms

13. **Which things also we speak, not in words which man's wisdom teacheth,**
And we speak of these gifts, not in language taught by human philosophy — TCNT

And we tell and explain this mystery in words not taught by human learning — Nor

Of these high themes we speak in words not taught by human philosophy — Mon

but which the Holy Ghost teacheth;
but those which the Holy Spirit teaches us — Phi

in the very words given us by the Holy Spirit — Tay

comparing spiritual things with spiritual.
combining spiritual things with spiritual words — ASV

explaining spiritual things to spiritual men — Con

interpreting spiritual things to spiritual men — ABUV

matching what is spiritual with what is spiritual — Knox

14. **But the natural man receiveth not the things of the Spirit of God:**
the natural man rejects the teaching of God's Spirit — Con

An unspiritual man does not accept the things the Spirit of God teaches — Wms

for they are foolishness unto him: neither can he know them,

. . . he cannot get to know them—Rhm

for to him it is mere folly; he cannot grasp it — TCNT

for they are nonsense to him; and he cannot understand them — Wms

— they just don't make sense to him — Phi

because they are spiritually discerned.
because it is to be understood only by spiritual insight — TCNT

because they are appreciated by spiritual insight — Wms

because you must have the Spirit to see their real value — Beck

because it takes spiritual insight to see its true value — Gspd

15. **But he that is spiritual judgeth all things,**
A man gifted with the Spirit can judge the worth of everything — NEB

If you have the Spirit, you can find out the real value of everything — Beck

But he who is spiritual appraises all things — NASB

But the man with spiritual insight is able to understand everything — TCNT

yet he himself is judged of no man.
but his own true value no unspiritual man can see — Gspd

while he is properly valued by none — Ber

although he himself is understood by no one — TCNT

16. **For who hath known the mind of the Lord, that he may instruct him?**
For who has comprehended the mind of the Lord as to be able to instruct him — TCNT

For who has ever known the Lord's thoughts, so that he can instruct him — Gspd

But we have the mind of Christ.
. . . we who are spiritual have the very thoughts of Christ! — Phi

We, however, have the very mind of Christ — TCNT

Well, our thoughts are Christ's thoughts — Mof

CHAPTER 3

1. **And I, brethren, could not speak unto you as unto spiritual,**
. . . as I would to healthy Christians — Tay

Fellow Christians, I couldn't talk to you as spiritual people — Beck

. . . as men with spiritual insight — TCNT

but as unto carnal,
I had to treat you as creatures of flesh and blood — Gspd
I had to deal with you on the merely natural plane — NEB
even as unto babes in Christ.
as babies in Christian living — Gspd
You were little children in Christ's nursery — Knox
as merely baby Christians — Wms
— mere infants in the Faith of Christ — TCNT

2. I have fed you with milk, and not with meat:
I gave you milk to drink, not meat to eat — Nor
And my practice has been to feed you, as it were, with milk and not with meat — Phi
for hitherto ye were not able to bear it,
for you were not then able to take it — TCNT
for you could not take it — Nor
You were unable to digest meat in those days — Phi
neither yet now are ye able.
And even now you still have to be fed on milk — Tay
Why, you cannot take it even now — Wms

3. For ye are yet carnal:
you are still worldly — TCNT
you are still of a worldly attitude — Ber
For you are still . . . controlled by your own desires — Tay
for whereas there is among you envying, and strife, and divisions,
. . . there is among you jealousy and strife — ASV
. . . jealousy and party feeling — TCNT
are ye not carnal, and walk as men?
. . . and do ye not walk after the manner of men — ASV
you are living on the purely human level of your lower nature — NEB
are you not worldly-minded and do you not behave like the unconverted — Ber
is it not true that you are worldly, and are acting merely as other men do — TCNT

4. For while one saith,
I am of Paul; and another, I am of Apollos;[2]

quarreling about whether I am greater than Apollos and dividing the church — Tay
are ye not carnal?
are ye not men — ASV
you shew that nature is still alive, that you are guided by human standards — Knox
are you not unchanged men — Ber

5. Who then is Paul, and who is Apollos,
What then is Apollos? and what is Paul — ASV
but ministers by whom ye believed,
No more than servants through whom you came to believe — Phi
Just servants through whom you came to have faith — Gspd
Men by whose help you came to believe — Beck
Servants through whom you were led to accept the Faith — TCNT
even as the Lord gave to every man?
and each as the Lord gave to him — ASV
each doing the work that God allotted to him — Nor
and was it not the Lord who gave to each of them the measure of his success — Con
and that only as the Lord helped each of you — TCNT

6. I have planted, Apollos watered; but God gave the increase.
I did the planting, Apollos did the watering, but it was God who kept the plants growing — Wms
. . . but God was causing the growth — NASB

7. So then neither is he that planteth any thing,
. . . deserves credit — Ber
. . . deserves the credit — Lam
. . . counts for much — TCNT
neither he that watereth;
but God that giveth the increase.
but only God who gives the growth — RSV
but God the grower — Ber
but God is everything in keeping the plants growing — Wms

8. Now he that planteth and he that watereth are one:

---

[2]Compare I Cor. 1:12.

. . . are working as a team, with the same aim — Tay

. . . are working for the same end — Bas

The planter and the waterer are one in aim — Wms

and every man shall receive his own reward according to his own labour.

. . . shall receive his wages . . . — RSV

. . . will get his own pay in accordance with his own work — Wms

9. **For we are labourers together with God:**

For we are God's fellow-workers — ASV

for we are God's men, working together — Beck

for we belong to God as His fellow-workers — Wms

ye are God's husbandry, ye are God's building.

you belong to God as His field to be tilled, as His building to be built — Wms

you are a field of God's tilling, a structure of God's design — Knox

10. **According to the grace of God which is given unto me, as a wise master-builder,**

in accordance with God's unmerited favor given to me . . . — Wms

In His love God gave me a work to do, and so as an expert master builder — Beck

I have laid the foundation, and another buildeth thereon.

I laid a foundation, and another man is building upon it — RSV

I . . . laid the foundation, and someone else is putting up the building — NEB

But let every man take heed how he buildeth thereupon.

Whoever he is, let him be careful how he builds — Mof

I say only this, let the builder be careful how he builds! — Phi

11. **For other foundation can no man lay than that is laid,**

For there is no other base for the building but that which has been put down — Bas

The foundation is laid already, and no one can lay another — Phi

which is Jesus Christ.

for it is Jesus Christ himself — Phi

12. **Now if any man build upon this foundation**

Whatever is used by those who build upon this foundation — TCNT

gold, silver, precious stones, wood, hay, stubble;

. . . costly stones . . . — ASV

. . . stones of great price, wood, dry grass, cut stems — Bas

. . . grass and straw — Nor

13. **Every man's work shall be made manifest:**

the character of each one's work will come to light — Wms

the quality of each man's work will become known — TCNT

for the day shall declare it, because it shall be revealed by fire;

for the Day will disclose it . . . — RSV

for the Day will show it. For the Day will break in fire — Gspd

the day will show it plainly enough, for the day will arise in a blaze of fire — Phi

and the fire shall try every man's work of what sort it is.

and the fire will test the quality of everyone's work — Gspd

and the fire will test the worth of each man's work — NEB

Everyone's work will be put through the fire so that all can see whether or not it keeps its value — Tay

14. **If any man's work abide which he hath built thereupon,**

If the work which any man has built on the foundation survives — RSV

He whose building stands unharmed — Con

If any man's work — the building he has made — stands the test — Mon

he shall receive a reward.

he shall receive wages — Alf

he will have his pay — Gspd

shall receive payment for his labor — Con

15. **If any man's work shall be burned, he shall suffer loss:**

But if the house he has built burns up . . . — Tay

he whose work is burned down shall forfeit his reward — Con

But if a man's work be destroyed under the test, he loses it all — Phi

but he himself shall be saved;
yet so as by fire.
> but like a man escaping through a wall
> of flames — Tay
> he will be snatched from the very
> flames — Mof
> but only as though he were pulled out
> of the fire — Nor

16. Know ye not that ye are the temple of God,
> . . . God's temple — Con
> Do you not know that you are God's
> sanctuary — Mon

and that the Spirit of God dwelleth in you?
> and that God's Spirit has his home in
> you — TCNT
> . . . has His permanent home in you —
> Wms
> God's Spirit makes his home in you —
> Gspd
> and that you form a shrine wherein
> God's Spirit dwells — Con

17. If any man defile the temple of God, him shall God destroy:
> If anybody desecrates the temple of
> God, God will bring him to ruin —
> Knox
> If any man ruin the temple of God,
> God shall ruin him — Con

for the temple of God is holy, which temple ye are.
> For God's temple is sacred to Him . . .
> — Wms
> For the temple of God is sacred, and
> that is what you are — Gspd
> for the Temple of God is sacred, and
> so also are you — TCNT

18. Let no man deceive himself.
> Let no one be deceiving himself —
> Rhm
> Let no one be under any illusion over
> this — Phi

If any man among you seemeth to be wise in this world,
> If any one of you imagines that he is
> wiser than the rest of you, in what
> this world calls wisdom — Gspd
> If any one of you supposes that he is
> wise in the philosophy of the present
> age — Mon

let him become a fool, that he may be wise.
> be a fool rather than let it hold you
> back from the true wisdom from
> above — Tay
> let him become foolish that he may
> become wise — NASB

19. For the wisdom of this world is foolishness with God.
> for the wisdom of this world is folly
> in God's estimation — Ber
> For this world's cleverness is stupidity
> to God — Phi

For it is written, He taketh the wise in their own craftiness.
> Scripture says, He traps the wise in their
> own cunning — NEB
> . . . God uses man's own brilliance to
> trap him — Tay

20. And again, The Lord knoweth the thoughts of the wise, that they are vain.
> . . . the reasonings . . . — ASV
> . . . The Lord taketh note of the specu-
> lations of the wise . . . — Rhm
> . . . The Lord knows the deliberations
> of the learned, how futile they are
> — Ber
> . . . The Lord sees how fruitless are the
> deliberations of the wise — TCNT

21. Therefore let no man glory in men.
> . . . repose his confidence . . . — Knox
> So then let no one be boasting in men
> — Rhm
> Therefore let none of you make his
> boast in men — Con

For all things are yours;
> Everything belongs to you! — Phi

22. Whether Paul, or Apollos, or Cephas,
> He has given you Paul and Apollos
> and Peter as your helpers — Tay

or the world, or life, or death, or things present, or things to come;
> He has given you the whole world to
> use, and life and even death are your
> servants to bring you to Christ. He
> has given you all of the present and
> all of the future — Tay

all are yours;
> all of them belong to you — NEB

23. And ye are Christ's; and Christ is God's.
> But you belong to Christ, and Christ
> belongs to God — Gspd

CHAPTER 4

1. Let a man so account of us, as of the ministers of Christ,

... As officers of Christ — Rhm

Let a man regard us in this manner, as servants of Christ — NASB

We must be regarded as Christ's underlings — NEB

Let men look upon us as Christ's servants — TCNT

and stewards of the mysteries of God.

... the hidden truths of God — TCNT

... the sacred secrets of God — Rhm

and managers authorized to distribute the secret truths of God — Gspd

and trustees to handle God's uncovered truths — Wms

2. Moreover it is required in stewards, that a man be found faithful.

Here ... — ASV

Now in this matter of trustees, the first and final requirement is that they should prove trustworthy — Wms

And it is the prime requisite in a trustee that he should prove worthy of his trust — Phi

Now then, you demand of any manager that he can be trusted — Beck

Now what we look for in stewards is that they should be trustworthy — TCNT

3. But with me it is a very small thing that I should be judged of you, or of man's judgment:

For my part, if I am called to account by you or by any human court of judgement, it does not matter to me in the least — NEB

But it weighs very little with me that I am judged by you or by any human tribunal — TCNT

yea, I judge not mine own self.

I don't even trust my own judgment on this point — Tay

I do not even pass judgment on myself — Nor

4. For I know nothing by myself;

For I know nothing against myself — ASV

My conscience does not, in fact, reproach me — Knox

I know not that I am guilty of unfaithfulness — Con

yet am I not hereby justified:

Nevertheless not hereby am I declared righteous — Rhm

this does not prove that I am innocent — Gspd

but he that judgeth me is the Lord.

5. Therefore judge nothing before the time, until the Lord come,

The moral of this is that we should make no hasty or premature judgments ... — Phi

So do not criticize at all; the hour of reckoning has still to come ... — Mof

So, don't judge anything too early. Wait till the Lord comes — Beck

who both will bring to light the hidden things of darkness,

he will bring into the light of day all that at present is hidden in darkness — Phi

For he will light up the darkness that now hides things — Gspd

and will make manifest the counsels of the hearts:

and he will expose the secret motives of men's hearts — Phi

and to reveal life's inner aims and motives — Mof

and bring to the light the plans people have in their hearts — Beck

and then will every man have praise of God.

and then everyone will get from God the praise he deserves — Gspd

Every man will then receive from God Himself the praise that is his due — Nor

6. And these things, brethren, I have transferred to myself and to Apollos for your sakes;

... I have taken Apollos and myself as examples of these things — Bas

... that you may profit by it — Nor

I have used myself and Apollos above as an illustration ... — Phi

Fellow Christians, in a special way of speaking I have referred only to myself and Apollos — Beck

that ye might learn in us not to think of men above what is written,

so that you might learn from what I have said about us ... — Phi

... not to go beyond what the Scriptures permit — Nor

so that, from our example, you may learn to observe the precept — Keep to what is written, — TCNT

that no one of you be puffed up for one against another.

so that you may stop boasting in favor of . . . — Wms

so you may not be arrogant champions of one teacher against another — — Wey

that none of you may speak boastfully of one teacher to the disparagement of another — TCNT

7. For who maketh thee to differ from another?

After all, friend, who is it that gives thee this pre-eminence — Knox

For who makes any one of you superior to others — TCNT

and what hast thou that thou didst not receive?

What powers hast thou, that did not come to thee by gift — Knox

What do you possess that has not been given you — Mof

now if thou didst receive it,

If then you really received it all as a gift — NEB

why dost thou glory, as if thou hadst not received it?

why do you boast as if it had been gained, not given — Mof

why boast of it as if it were something you had achieved yourself — Phi

8. Now ye are full, now ye are rich,

Already are ye filled, already ye are become rich — ASV

You Corinthians have your heart's desire already, have you? You have heaven's rich bliss already! — Mof

Are you all so soon satisfied? Are you so soon rich? — TCNT

ye have reigned as kings without us:

ye have come to reign without us — ASV

Have you begun to reign without us? — TCNT

Have you ascended your thrones without us to join you? — Wms

Have you already taken possession of your kingdom without our help? — Nor

and I would to God ye did reign, that we also might reign with you.

How I wish you had the kingdom, so we might reign with you! — Ber

I wish you had entered it, so that we might share it with you! — Gspd

9. For I think that God hath set forth us the apostles last,

. . . God has exhibited us apostles at the very end of the procession — Gspd

as it were appointed to death:

like criminals condemned to die — Con

like the men condemned to die in the arena — Gspd

We are like men condemned to death in the arena — NEB

like doomed gladiators in the arena! — Mof

as men doomed to death — TCNT

for we are made a spectacle unto the world, and to angels, and to men.

put on display at the end of a victor's parade, to be stared at by men and angels alike — Tay

to be gazed at in a theatre by the whole world, both men and angels — Con

10. We are fools for Christ's sake, but ye are wise in Christ;

For Christ's sake we are held as fools, while you through union with Christ are men of wisdom — Wms

We, for Christ's sake, are 'fools,' but you, by your union with Christ, are men of discernment — TCNT

we are weak, but ye are strong;

ye are honourable, but we are despised.

ye have glory, but we have dishonor — ASV

You are honored, but we are despised — Beck

11. Even unto this present hour we both hunger, and thirst,

Up to the present moment, we have suffered hunger and thirst — Nor

and are naked, and are buffeted, and have no certain dwellingplace;

. . . we are ill-clad and knocked about, we are waifs — Mof

poorly dressed, beaten, homeless — Beck

12. And labour, working with our hands:

We toil to exhaustion with our own hands — Ber

We still have to work for our living by manual labor — Phi

being reviled, we bless;

we meet abuse with blessings — TCNT

Men curse us, but we return a blessing — Phi

curses we meet with blessings — Con
being persecuted, we suffer it:
we meet persecution with endurance — — TCNT
they make our lives miserable, but we take it patiently — Phi

13. **Being defamed, we entreat:**
when we are slandered by them we try to conciliate them — Wms
we are made as the filth of the world, and are the offscouring of all things unto this day.
We are considered as worthless filth . . . — Nor
To this moment we are considered the scum of the earth, the scrapings of everyone's feet — Ber

14. **I write not these things to shame you,**
It is with no wish to shame you that I am writing like this — TCNT
I do not write this to make you blush with shame — Wms
but as my beloved sons I warn you.
but to admonish you as my beloved children — ASV
but to give you counsel as my dear children — Wms

15. **For though ye have ten thousand instructors in Christ,**
. . . tutors . . . — ASV
. . . teachers in the Christian faith — Phi
yet have ye not many fathers:
but you have only one father — NEB
for in Christ Jesus I have begotten you through the gospel.
For it was I myself who became your father through your union with Christ Jesus, which resulted from my telling you the good news — Wms
for in this matter of union with Christ, I became your father, through preaching the good news to you — Gspd

16. **Wherefore I beseech you, be ye followers of me.**
. . . be ye imitators of me — ASV
that is why I implore you to follow the footsteps of me your father — Phi
I exhort you therefore, become imitators of me — ABUV

17. **For this cause have I sent unto you Timotheus,**
who is my beloved son, and faithful in the Lord,
For he is one of those I won to Christ,

a beloved and trustworthy child in the Lord — Tay
who is a dear son to me and a most trustworthy Christian — NEB
who shall bring you into remembrance of my ways which be in Christ,
who will remind you of my principles of behavior in Christ Jesus — Ber
he will remind you of my methods of teaching the Faith of Christ Jesus — TCNT
as I teach every where in every church.
. . . in all our congregations — NEB
. . . in every assembly — Rhm

18. **Now some are puffed up, as though I would not come to you.**
. . . have been filled with arrogance . . . — Con
. . . are filled with self-importance because they think I am not coming to Corinth — NEB
. . . thinking that I am afraid to come and deal with you — Tay

19. **But I will come to you shortly, if the Lord will,**
But I will come to you I will, and that soon, if it please the Lord — Mon
and will know, not the speech of them which are puffed up, but the power.
I'll find out whether these proud men are just big talkers or whether they really have God's power — Tay
and then I will test, not the fine words of those who hold me in contempt, but the powers they can shew — Knox

20. **For the kingdom of God is not in word, but in power.**
For mighty deeds, not empty words, are the tokens of God's kingdom — Con
For God's reign does not show itself in talk but in power — Mof
for the Kingdom of God does not consist in talking but doing — Wms

21. **What will ye? shall I come unto you with a rod,**
. . . a rod of discipline — Mof
Choose, then: am I to come to you with a rod in my hand — NEB
What is your desire? Must I come to you with the rod — Con
or in love, and in the spirit of meekness?
. . . a spirit of gentleness — ASV
or in a loving and gentle spirit — TCNT

CHAPTER 5

1. It is reported commonly that there is fornication among you,

It is actually reported . . . — ASV

. . . that there is sexual immorality among you — Phi

Everybody is talking about the terrible thing that has happened there among you — Tay

and such fornication as is not so much as named among the Gentiles,

something so wicked that even the heathen don't do it — Tay

immorality of a kind that even pagans condemn — Phi

that one should have his father's wife.

that a man co-habits with his father's wife — Wms

for a man is living with his father's wife — RSV

2. And ye are puffed up,

And you are arrogant! — RSV

And you can still be proud of yourselves! — NEB

and have not rather mourned, that he that hath done this deed might be taken away from you.

instead of being overwhelmed with grief at having to expel from your number the man who had done this — Gspd

instead of being sorry for it, and seeing to it that the man who has done this be removed from your membership — Wms

Shouldn't you be overwhelmed with sorrow and shame? The man who has done such a thing should certainly be expelled from your fellowship — Phi

3. For I verily, as absent in body, but present in spirit,

For my part, I am present with you in spirit even though I am absent from you in body — Nor

have judged already, as though I were present,

and my judgement . . .is already given, as if I were indeed present — NEB

and I assure you as solemnly as if I were actually present before your assembly that I have already pronounced judgment — Phi

concerning him that hath so done this deed,

on the one who thus behaved — Ber

4. In the name of our Lord Jesus Christ,

by the authority of our Lord Jesus — Wms

when ye are gathered together,

Call an assembly — Knox

When you are assembled — RSV

and my spirit, with the power of our Lord Jesus Christ,

at which I will be present in spirit . . . — Knox

My spirit and the power of our Lord Jesus will be with you — Beck

5. To deliver such an one unto Satan for the destruction of the flesh,

. . . for the destruction of his lower nature — Wms

. . . for the destruction of his fleshly lusts — Con

. . . that what is sensual in him may be destroyed — TCNT

that man should be left to the mercy of Satan so that while his body will experience the destructive powers of sin — Phi

that the spirit may be saved in the day of the Lord Jesus.

in the hope that this will wake him up and save his soul before it is too late — Tay

so that his spirit may have forgiveness in the day of the Lord Jesus — Bas

6. Your glorying is not good.

Your ground for boasting about such a case is not good — Wms

Your pride in your church is lamentably out of place — Phi

Your boasting is unseemly — TCNT

Know ye not that a little leaven leaveneth the whole lump?

Don't you know a little yeast makes the whole dough sour — Beck

7. Purge out therefore the old leaven,

Cleanse out the old leaven — ABUV

Clear out every bit of the old yeast — Phi

that ye may be a new lump, as ye are unleavened.

. . . for in fact you are free from that leaven — Wey

so that you may be as a lump of fresh dough, unleavened — Nor

and then you will be bread of a new

baking, as it were unleavened Passover bread — NEB

For even Christ our passover is sacrificed for us:

For indeed our Passover has begun; the sacrifice is offered — Christ himself — NEB

We Christians have had a Passover Lamb sacrificed for us — none other than Christ himself! — Phi

8. **Therefore let us keep the feast, not with old leaven,**

Let us, therefore, celebrate the festival . . . — RSV

. . . not with the leaven of former days — TCNT

neither with the leaven of malice and wickedness; but with the unleavened bread of sincerity and truth.

. . . purity and honesty of intent — Knox

. . . of unadulterated truth — Phi

9. **I wrote unto you in an epistle not to company with fornicators:**

. . . not to mix with those who live in sexual sin — Beck

I wrote you in my letter to stop associating with sexually immoral people — Wms

10. **Yet not altogether with the fornicators of this world,**

I didn't mean, of course, that you were to have no contact at all with the immoral of this world — Phi

But I had not in mind the sinners who are outside the church — Bas

I didn't mean you should altogether keep away from people who live in sexual sin in this world — Beck

or with covetous, or extortioners, or with idolaters;

any more than with its greedy graspers, or its idolaters — Wms

or who are covetous and grasping . . . — TCNT

the avaricious, the thievish . . . — Mon

for then must ye needs go out of the world.

for it is not possible to keep away from such people without going out of the world completely — Bas

since otherwise you would need to get

out of . . . human society altogether! — Amp

11. **But now I have written unto you not to keep company,**

. . . not to be mixing yourselves up — Rhm

Now what I really meant was for you to stop associating with — Wms

if any man that is called a brother be a fornicator,

if a pretended brother is lewd — Ber

. . . anyone who calls himself a Christian but lives in sexual sin — Beck

or covetous, or an idolater, or a railer, or a drunkard, or an extortioner;

or if he is a miser, an idolater, a slanderer, a drunkard, or a swindler — Nor

or avaricious or idolatrous or scurrilous or drunken or grasping — Wey

or a swindler, an idolater, a man with a foul tongue, a drunkard, or a thief — Phi

with such an one no not to eat.

with such a person you must even stop eating — Wms

— no, not even to sit at table with such people — TCNT

12. **For what have I to do to judge them also that are without?**

What business of mine is it to judge outsiders — Ber

Is it my business to judge those who are outside the church — Beck

do not ye judge them that are within?

But surely it is your business to judge those who are inside the church — Phi

You are judges within the fellowship — NEB

13. **But them that are without God judgeth.**

God alone can judge those who are outside — Phi

Therefore put away from among yourselves that wicked person.

You must expel that wicked person from your membership — Wms

It is your plain duty to expel from your church this wicked man! — Phi

Root out the evil-doer from your community — NEB

CHAPTER 6

1. Dare any of you, having a matter against another,

Would any of you, having a lawsuit against his brother — Lam

Can it be that, when one of you has a dispute with another, he dares — TCNT

go to law before the unjust,

to go to law in a sinful pagan court — Mof

to bring it before a court of unrighteous men — Beck

to have his case tried before the heathen — TCNT

and not before the saints?

instead of the community of God's people — NEB

instead of laying it before God's people — Gspd

2. Do you not know that the saints shall judge the world?

It is God's people who are to judge the world; surely you know that — NEB

Do you not know that the saints are to manage the world — Mof

and if the world shall be judged by you,

are ye unworthy to judge the smallest matters?

are you incompetent to adjudicate upon trifles — Mof

are you unfit to try the most trivial cases — TCNT

3. Know ye not that we shall judge angels?

Don't you realize that we Christians are going to judge and reward the angels — Tay

Do you not know that we are to manage angels — Mof

how much more things that pertain to this life?

How much more, mere matters of business! — NEB

How much more, then, of these matters of everyday life — Nor

4. If then ye have judgments of things pertaining to this life,

If therefore you have such business disputes — NEB

when you have these common quarrels to decide — Knox

set them to judge who are least esteemed in the church.

you would do better to appoint the most insignificant of your own number as judges — Knox

Give the arbitration of them to the very least esteemed in your church — Con

do you set them to judge who are of no account in the church? — ASV

how can you entrust jurisdiction to outsiders, men who count for nothing in our community? — NEB

Why then go to outside judges who are not even Christians? — Tay

5. I speak to your shame.

. . . to move you to shame — ASV

I say this deliberately to rouse your sense of shame — Phi

Is it so, that there is not a wise man among you?

Are you really unable to find among your number one man with enough sense — Phi

no, not one that shall be able to judge between his brethren?

capable of deciding between a man and his brother — Mon

who could decide a dispute between members of the brotherhood — Mof

6. But brother goeth to law with brother,

No, one Christian sues another — Beck

But brother with brother sueth for judgment — Rhm

and that before the unbelievers.

and that before unbelieving judges — Nor

7. Now therefore there is utterly a fault among you, because ye go to law one with another.

Nay, already it is altogether a defect in you, that you have lawsuits one with another — ASV

Without going any further, suing one another means you have utterly failed — Beck

Even to have law-suits with one another at all, is in itself, evidence of defeat — Mof

Why do ye not rather take wrong?

How is it that you do not prefer to put up with wrong — Knox

Why not just accept mistreatment and leave it at that — Tay

why do ye not rather suffer yourselves to be defrauded?

It would be far more honoring to the Lord to let yourself be cheated — Tay

Why don't you rather let yourselves be robbed — Beck

8. Nay, ye do wrong, and defraud, and that your brethren.

On the contrary, you yourselves inflict wrong and fraud . . . — Wey

You practice wrongdoing and robbing others, and that your brothers—Wms

Instead of this, you wrong and cheat others yourselves — yes, even your brothers — TCNT

9. Know ye not that the unrighteous shall not inherit the kingdom of God?

Surely you know that the unjust will never come into possession of . . . — NEB

Have you forgotten that the kingdom of God will never belong to the wicked — Phi

Do not you know that wrong-doers will have no share in God's Kingdom — TCNT

Be not deceived: neither fornicators, nor idolaters,

Stop being misled; people who are sexually immoral . . . — Wms

. . . Nobody who lives in sexual sin or worships idols — Beck

Make no mistake. Neither the licentious, nor idolaters — Wey

nor adulterers, nor effeminate, nor abusers of themselves with mankind,

none who are guilty either of adultery or of homosexual perversion — NEB

10. Nor thieves, nor covetous, nor drunkards, nor revilers,

who steal, are greedy, get drunk, slander — Beck

or thieves or greedy graspers . . . — Wms

. . . slanderers — Ber

nor extortioners, shall inherit the kingdom of God.

or the rapacious shall have any share in the kingdom of God — Phi

or swindlers, will possess the kingdom of God — NEB

11. And such were some of you:

And these are just the characters some of you used to be — Wms

Some of you once belonged to these classes — Nor

but ye are washed,

But you have cleansed yourselves from all that — Phi

but now your sins are washed away — Tay

but ye are sanctified,

you became Christ's people! — TCNT

you have been dedicated to God — NEB

you are set apart to God — Tay

but ye are justified in the name of the Lord Jesus, and by the Spirit of our God.

you are now in right standing with God . . . — Wms

and He has accepted you because of what the Lord Jesus and the Spirit of our God have done for you — Tay

12. All things are lawful unto me,

I am free to do anything, you say—NEB

Everything is allowable to me — Wey

Everything is permitted me — Ber

All things are lawful for me? — Mon

but all things are not expedient:

. . . profitable — Wey

Yes, but not all things are good for me — Mon

but that does not mean that everything is good for me to do — Phi

all things are lawful for me,

All things are lawful for me? — Mon

but I will not be brought under the power of any.

Yes, but I will not let myself be enslaved by the power of any — Mon

they shall not bring me under their power — Con

I will not be mastered by anything — Ber

but I must not abdicate my own liberty — Knox

but I will not be enslaved by anything — RSV

13. Meats for the belly, and the belly for meats:

Food is meant for our animal nature, and our animal nature claims its food; true enough — Knox

Food is meant for the stomach and the stomach craves food — Nor

but God shall destroy both it and them.

but God will eventually cause both of them to cease their work — Nor but God has no permanent purpose for either — Phi

Now the body is not for fornication,

The body is not intended for sexual immorality — Wms

The body is not made for sexual sin — Beck

but for the Lord; and the Lord for the body.

but for the service of the Lord, and the Lord is for the body to serve — Wms

it was made for God, and God is the answer to our deepest longings — Phi

14. **And God hath both raised up the Lord,**

And God who made the Lord Jesus come back from the dead — Bas

and, as God has raised the Lord—TCNT

and will also raise up us by his own power.

so he will raise up us also by the exercise of his power — TCNT

will also raise us mortal men by his power — Phi

15. **Know ye not that your bodies are members of Christ?**

. . . are members of the Body of Christ — Nor

Do you not know that your bodies are parts of Christ Himself — Wms

shall I then take the members of Christ,

and make them the members of an harlot?

to make them members of a prostitute — Ber

. . . of a loose woman — Bas

God forbid.

Heaven forbid! — TCNT

No, never! — Ber

Never! — RSV

16. **What? know ye not that he which is joined to an harlot is one body?**

And don't you know that if a man joins himself to a harlot that she becomes a part of him and he becomes a part of her — Tay

Do you not know that he who joins himself to a prostitute becomes one body with her — RSV

for two, saith he, shall be one flesh.

For, God says, . . . — Phi

The Bible says, The two will be one flesh — Beck

17. **But he that is joined unto the Lord is one spirit.**

But the man who is in union with the Lord is spiritually one with Him — Wms

While a man who is united with the Lord is one with him in spirit—Mon

18. **Flee fornication.**

Keep on running from sexual immorality! — Wms

Avoid sexual looseness like the plague! — Phi

Every sin that a man doeth is without the body;

Every other sin which a man commits is outside the body — RSV

Every other sinful thing a man does hurts someone else — Tay

The root of sin is not in the body (but in the soul) — Con

but he that committeth fornication sinneth against his own body.

but this is sinning against his own body — Tay

yet the fornicator sins against his own body — Con

19. **What? know ye not that your body is the temple of the Holy Ghost**

Have you forgotten . . . — Phi

. . . a shrine . . . — NEB

. . . a sanctuary . . . — Mon

. . . Holy Spirit — ASV

which is in you, which ye have from God,

who is in you, whom ye have from God — ABUV

He lives within you, a gift from God the Father — Nor

and ye are not your own?

so that you are no longer your own masters — Knox

you do not belong to yourselves — Ber

20. **For ye are bought with a price:**

you have been bought and paid for — Gspd

A great price was paid to ransom you — Knox

therefore glorify God in your body,

So use every part of your body to give glory back to God — Tay

Therefore, honour God in your bodies — TCNT

and in your spirit, which are God's.[3]

---

[3]Now recognized as not adequately supported by original manuscripts.

CHAPTER 7

1. Now concerning the things whereof ye wrote unto me:

To come to the subjects of your correspondence — Ber

Now for the questions in your letter — Mof

As for the questions you raised in your letter — Knox

It is good for a man not to touch a woman.

— it is good for a man not to have sex relations with a woman — Beck

It is indeed an excellent thing for a man to have no intercourse with a woman — Mof

It would be well for a man to remain single — TCNT

2. Nevertheless, to avoid fornication,

but because there is so much immorality — Mon

Nevertheless, because of the danger of immorality — Lam

But because of the temptation to impurity — Nor

let every man have his own wife, and let every woman have her own husband.

3. Let the husband render unto the wife due benevolence:

The husband should give to his wife her conjugal rights — RSV

let the husband live in the intercourse of affection with his wife — Con

and likewise also the wife unto the husband.

and the wife equally must give the husband his due — NEB

4. The wife hath not power of her own body, but the husband:

The wife does not have the right to do as she pleases with her own body; the husband has his right to it — Wms

The wife has not authority over her own body, but the husband — ABUV

The wife does not have sole authority over her own person, for she belongs to her husband — Nor

The wife cannot claim her body as her own; it is her husband's — NEB

and likewise also the husband hath not power of his own body, but the wife.

5. Defraud ye not one the other,

Do not withhold sexual intercourse from one another — Mof

You husbands and wives must stop refusing each other what is due—Wms

Stop depriving one another — NASB

except it be with consent for a time,

except when both of you consent to do so . . . — Lam

unless it is only temporary and by mutual consent — Mon

that ye may give yourselves to fasting[4] and prayer;

that you may give yourselves without disturbance to prayer — Con

That ye may have leisure for prayer — Rhm

so that your minds may be free for prayer — TCNT

that you may devote yourselves to prayer — NASB

and come together again,

But afterward you should resume relations as before — Phi

till you again live as man and wife — TCNT

that Satan tempt you not for your incontinency.

lest, through your fleshly passions, Satan should tempt you to sin — Con

lest through your lack of self-control Satan begin to tempt you to sin — Mon

6. But I speak this by permission, and not of commandment.

. . . concession . . . — ASV

I say this by way of concession; I am not imposing a rule upon you — Knox

But as I say this, I'm yielding to you, not ordering you — Beck

7. For I would that all men were even as myself.

I would that every one lived as I do — Mon

I should like to have everyone be just as I am myself — Gspd

But every man hath his proper gift of God,

but each one has only the gift God gave him — Beck

---

[4]"Fasting" is now recognized as not adequately supported by original manuscripts.

but I realize that everyone has his own particular gift from God — Phi

one after this manner, and another after that.

one of one kind and one of another — RSV

one this gift and another that — NEB

8. I say therefore to the unmarried and widows,

It is good for them if they abide even as I.

it is a good thing to remain unattached, as I am — Phi

9. But if they cannot contain, let them marry:

but if they cannot restrain their passions . . . — Ber

but if you can't control yourselves, get married — Beck

for it is better to marry than to burn.

For it is better to marry than to be aflame with passion — RSV

. . . than to be consumed with passion — TCNT

I think it is far better for them to be married than to be tortured by unsatisfied desire — Phi

for marriage is better than the fever of passion — Wey

for it is better to marry than to burn with passionate desire — Nor

10. And unto the married I command, yet not I, but the Lord,

To those already married my instructions are — and they are not mine, but the Lord's — Gspd

My command — or rather, the Lord's command — to the married is—Nor

To the married, not I, but the Lord gives commandment — Con

Let not the wife depart from her husband:

that the wife be not separated from her husband — Alf

that the wife should not leave her husband — NASB

11. But and if she depart, let her remain unmarried,

(but if she be already parted, let her remain single — Con

but if she be actually separated . . . — Alf

(if she has done so, let her remain as she is — TCNT

or be reconciled to her husband:

or else be reconciled with him;) — Con

or else be reconciled to her husband) — TCNT

and let not the husband put away his wife.

And a husband must not divorce his wife — Gspd

A husband is not, in similar circumstances, to divorce his wife — Phi

12. But to the rest speak I, not the Lord:

To the rest I say this, as my own word, not as the Lord's — NEB

To the rest of the people I myself would say — though the Lord Himself has said nothing about it—Wms

if any brother hath a wife that believeth not,

that if any brother has a wife who is an unbeliever — RSV

For a brother who has a non-Christian wife — Phi

and she be pleased to dwell with him, let him not put her away.

and she is willing to live with him . . . — Gspd

. . . agrees to live with him . . . — Beck

. . . he should not divorce her — RSV

and she is well pleased to dwell with him Let him not leave her — Rhm

13. And the woman which hath an husband that believeth not, and if he be pleased to dwell with her, let her not leave him.

14. For the unbelieving husband is sanctified by the wife,

An unbelieving man married to such a woman serves a holy purpose — Beck

For, through his wife, the husband who is an unbeliever has become associated with Christ's People — TCNT

For the husband who is not a believer is consecrated through union with his wife — Gspd

For the heathen husband now belongs to God through his Christian wife — NEB

For the unbelieving husband is, in a sense, consecrated by being joined to the person of his wife — Phi

For perhaps the husband who isn't a Christian may become a Christian with the help of his Christian wife — Tay

and the unbelieving wife is sanctified by the husband:

else were your children unclean; but now are they holy.

Were it otherwise, their offspring would be born under a stain . . . — Knox

Otherwise your children would not belong to God. Whereas in fact they do — NEB

Otherwise your children would be 'defiled' but, as it is, they belong to Christ's People — TCNT

Otherwise, if the family separates, the children might never come to know the Lord. But for a family to stay together may, in God's plan, result in the children's salvation — Tay

15. But if the unbelieving depart, let him depart.

If, however, the unbeliever is determined to separate, let him do so — Wey

If on the other hand the heathen partner wishes for a separation, let him have it — NEB

A brother or a sister is not under bondage in such cases:

in such a case the brother or sister is not bound — RSV

. . . is under no compulsion — NEB

in such cases the Christian brother or sister is not tied to marriage — Mof

but God hath called us to peace.

for God intended that we live together in peace — Nor

It is to a life of peace that God has called you — Mof

16. For what knowest thou, O wife, whether thou shalt save thy husband?

and after all how can you, who are a wife, know whether you will be able to save your husband or not — Phi

For after all, there is no assurance to you wives that your husbands will be saved if they stay — Tay

Think of it: as a wife you may be your husband's salvation — NEB

or how knowest thou, O man, whether thou shalt save thy wife?

17. But as God hath distributed to every man, as the Lord hath called every one, so let him walk.

Only, let every one lead the life which the Lord has assigned to him, and in which God has called him — RSV

Only, whatever the condition which the Lord has assigned to each indi-

vidual — and whatever his condition when God called him — in that let him continue — Wey

Only, everybody must continue to live in the station which the Lord assigned to him, in that in which God called him — Wms

I would add this — that each one should fill the place that God has assigned to him and to which the Lord has called him — Nor

And so ordain I in all churches.

And so in all the assemblies I ordain — Rhm

That is what I teach in all our congregations — NEB

This is the rule that I lay down in every Church — TCNT

18. Is any man called being circumcised?

Was any one at the time of his call already circumcised — RSV

Was a man called with the marks of circumcision on him — NEB

let him not become uncircumcised.

Let him not seek to remove the marks of circumcision — RSV

Let him not try to disguise it — Wey

Let him not efface it — Ber

Is any called in uncircumcision? let him not be circumcised.

Was any one at the time of his call uncircumcised? Let him not seek circumcision — RSV

19. Circumcision is nothing, and uncircumcision is nothing,

For neither circumcision counts for anything nor uncircumcision — RSV

. . . has no value . . . — Ber

but the keeping of the commandments of God.

obedience to God's commandments is everything — Wey

all that matters is keeping God's commands — Gspd

20. Let every man abide in the same calling wherein he was called.

Whatever be the condition of life in which he was called, in that let him continue — Mon

Every one must remain in the condition of life where he was called — Mof

21. Art thou called being a servant?

. . . a slave — Alf

. . . a bond-servant — ASV

Were you a slave when you heard the call — Phi

. . . when you became a Christian — Bas

care not for it:

Stop letting that annoy you — Wms

Never mind — RSV

Don't let that worry you — Phi

but if thou mayest be made free, use it rather.

nay, even if thou canst become free, use it rather — ASV

Even if you can gain your freedom, make the most of your present condition instead — Gspd

But if you can gain your freedom, avail yourself of the opportunity — RSV

though if you find the opportunity to become free you had better take it — Phi

22. **For he that is called in the Lord, being a servant, is the Lord's freeman:**

For the man who as a slave received the call to be a Christian . . . — NEB

When a slave is called . . . he becomes the Lord's freedman — Nor

For a slave who has been called to union with the Lord is a freedman of the Lord — Gspd

likewise also he that is called, being free, is Christ's servant.

When a free man is called he becomes the Lord's slave — Nor

In the same way, if you are free when you are called, you are Christ's slave — Beck

23. **Ye are bought with a price;**

You have been bought and paid for — Gspd

You have been redeemed, at tremendous cost — Phi

be not ye the servants of men.

stop becoming slaves to men — Wms

Do not let yourselves become slaves to men — TCNT

24. **Brethren, let every man, wherein he is called, therein abide with God.**

Brothers, let every one remain in the condition in which he was when he was called, in close communion with God — TCNT

My brothers, let every one of us continue to live his life with God in the state in which he was when he was called — Phi

25. **Now concerning virgins I have no commandment of the Lord:**

Concerning you virgin daughters . . . — Con

Now as far as young unmarried women are concerned, I must confess that I have no direct commands from the Lord — Phi

yet I give my judgment, as one that hath obtained mercy of the Lord to be faithful.

. . . as one who has been moved by the Lord's mercy to be faithful — Con

but I tell you my opinion, and it is that of a man whom the Master in his mercy has made worthy to be trusted — TCNT

. . . and it is that of a man who, through the Lord's mercy, is deserving of your confidence — Mon

Nevertheless I give you my considered opinion as one who is, I think, to be trusted after all his experience of God's mercy — Phi

26. **I suppose therefore that this is good for the present distress,**

I think, then, that, in view of the time of suffering that has now come upon us — TCNT

. . . by reason of the distress that is upon us — ASV

. . . in view of the time of suffering now imminent — Mon

. . . by reason of the present necessity — Alf

I say, that it is good for a man so to be.

it would be an excellent plan for you to remain as you are — Mof

what I have already said is best — that a man should remain as he is — TCNT

27. **Art thou bound unto a wife? seek not to be loosed.**

Are you married? Stop trying to get a divorce — Wms

Are you tied to a wife? Never try to untie the knot — Mof

Art thou loosed from a wife? seek not a wife.

Are you unmarried? Stop looking for a wife — Wms

But if you aren't married, don't rush into marriage at this time — Tay

28. **But and if thou marry, thou hast not sinned;**

But if you marry, you do not sin — RSV

and if a virgin marry, she hath not sinned.

and if a girl marries she does not sin — RSV

Nevertheless such shall have trouble in the flesh: but I spare you.

Such people, however, will have trouble in worldly affairs . . . — Mon

. . . and I would spare you — ASV

Yet those who marry will have worldly trouble, which I would like to spare you — Gspd

Yet I do believe that those who take this step are bound to find the married state an extra burden in these critical days, and I should like you to be as unencumbered as possible — Phi

29. But this I say, brethren, the time is short:

. . . the time is shortened — ASV

. . . The opportunity is contracted — Rhm

. . . The appointed time has grown very short — Gspd

. . . the time we live in will not last long — NEB

All our futures are so foreshortened, indeed — Phi

What I mean, Brothers, is this: — The time is short — TCNT

it remaineth, that both they that have wives be as though they had none;

so let those who have wives live as if they had none — Mof

From now on even those who have wives had better live as if they had none — Nor

For that reason those who have wives should stay as free as possible for the Lord — Tay

that those who have wives should live, so to speak, as though they had none! — Phi

30. And they that weep, as though they wept not;

sadness . . . should not keep anyone from doing God's work — Tay

those who weep must forget their tears — Knox

And for those who are in sorrow, to give no signs of it — Bas

There is no time to indulge in sorrow — Phi

and they that rejoice, as though they rejoiced not;

and for those who rejoice not to make it known — Nor

no time for enjoying our joys — Phi

and they that buy, as though they possessed not;

those who buy must renounce possession — Knox

those who buy have no time to enjoy their possessions — Phi

If you buy anything, act as if you didn't have it — Beck

31. And they that use this world, as not abusing it:

. . . as not using it to the full — ASV

and those who mix in the world, as though they were not absorbed in it — Gspd

While you use the world, don't try to get out of it all you can — Beck

And those who are busy with worldly affairs must not be overly absorbed in them — Nor

and indeed their every contact with the world must be as light as possible — Phi

for the fashion of this world passeth away.

for this world as we see it is passing away — TCNT

for the present scheme of things is rapidly passing away — Phi

32. But I would have you without carefulness.

. . . free from cares — ASV

. . . free from all anxieties — Mon

I don't want you to worry — Beck

He that is unmarried careth for the things that belong to the Lord,

. . . is anxious about the Master's Cause — TCNT

The unmarried man is free to concern himself with the Lord's affairs — Phi

The cares of the unmarried man are fixed upon the Lord — Con

how he may please the Lord:

his aim is to please the Lord — NEB

and he strives to please the Lord — Con

and about how to please the Lord — Nor

33. But he that is married careth for the things that are of the world,

But the married man is sure to be concerned also with matters of this world — Phi

But a married man can't do that so well; he has to think about his responsibilities down here on earth — Tay

But once he's married, he worries about earthly things — Beck

how he may please his wife.

his aim is to please his wife — NEB

and so his devotion is divided — Wms

— so he is torn in two directions . . . — Mof

34. There is a difference[5] also between a wife and a virgin.

You find the same difference in the case of the unmarried and the married woman — Phi

and is divided. So also the woman who is unmarried and the virgin — ASV

The unmarried woman careth for the things of the Lord,

So a woman who is free of wedlock, or a virgin, is concerned with the Lord's claim — Knox

Again, the woman who is a widow, or the maid, is anxious about the Lord's business — Mon

that she may be holy both in body and in spirit:

her aim is to be dedicated to him in body as in spirit — NEB

striving to be pure both in body and in spirit — TCNT

is anxious to please the Lord in all she is and does — Tay

but she that is married careth for the things of the world,

once married, she is anxious about worldly affairs — Mof

Whereas the married woman is concerned with the world's claim — Knox

But once she is married, she worries about earthly things — Beck

how she may please her husband.

her aim is to please her husband — NEB

how best to satisfy her husband — Mof

desiring to please her husband — TCNT

35. And this I speak for your own profit;

I say this for your own benefit — RSV

I am saying this to help you — Tay

not that I may cast a snare upon you,

I have no wish to keep you on a tight rein — NEB

not to try to keep you from marrying — Tay

not with any intention of putting a halter around your necks — TCNT

but for that which is comely,

I am thinking of what is suitable for you — Knox

but in order to secure for the Master seemly . . . devotion — TCNT

but to promote what is seemly — NASB

and that ye may attend upon the Lord without distraction.

so that your service to God may be as far as possible free from worldly distractions — Phi

and to secure your undivided devotion to the Lord — RSV

and so that you may be able to give all your attention to the things of the Lord — Bas

36. But if any man thinketh that he behaveth himself uncomely toward his virgin,

. . . his virgin daughter — ASV

If, however, a father thinks that he is not acting fairly by his unmarried daughter — TCNT

But if any man think that he is treating his virgin daughter in an unseemly manner — Con

If one thinks that he is not behaving properly toward his betrothed — RSV

But if a man thinks he is not acting properly toward the girl to whom he is engaged — Gspd

. . . to the maid who is his spiritual bride — Mof

But if a man has a partner in celibacy and feels that he is not behaving properly towards her — NEB

if she pass the flower of her age, and need so require,

and she is getting older and wants to marry — Tay

when she is past her youth, and if under these circumstances her marriage ought to take place — TCNT

in leaving her unmarried beyond the flower of her age, and so the matter is urgent — Mon

especially as she is beginning to lose her first youth and the emotional strain is considerable — Phi

if his passions are too strong . . . — Gspd

---

[5]Some versions place a period after the word "difference."

if his passions are strong, and it has to be — RSV

if, that is, his instincts are too strong for him, and something must be done — NEB

let him do what he will, he sinneth not: let them marry.

let him do what she desires . . . — Wms

let him do what his heart tells him to do — let them be married; there is no sin in that — Phi

let him do what she desires; he commits no sin; she and her suitor should be allowed to marry — Wey

let him do as he wishes, and marry her. There is no sin in that — Nor

37. Nevertheless he that standeth stedfast in his heart,

On the other hand, a father, who has definitely made up his mind — TCNT

Yet for the man of steadfast purpose — Phi

But the man who is strong in mind and purpose — Bas

having no necessity, but hath power over his own will,

who, instead of being forced against his will — Mof

and is under no compulsion, but is free to carry out his own wishes — Mon

who is able to bear the strain and has his own desires well under control — Phi

and has so decreed in his heart that he will keep his virgin, doeth well.

and who has determined to keep his daughter unmarried, does well — Mon

and who has come to the decision, in his own mind, to keep his unmarried daughter at home, will be doing right — TCNT

and then determines to keep his betrothed untouched — Nor

and has determined in his heart, to keep her as his betrothed he will do well — RSV

and if he has decided in his own mind to preserve his partner in her virginity, he will do well — NEB

has determined in himself to keep his maid a spiritual bride — that man will be doing the right thing — Mof

38. So then he that giveth her in marriage doeth well;

. . . giveth his own virgin daughter in marriage . . . — ASV

So he that gives his daughter in marriage is doing right — Mon

So that he who marries his betrothed does well — RSV

Thus, he who marries his partner does well — NEB

but he that giveth her not in marriage doeth better.

and he who does not give his virgin daughter in marriage does even better — Lam

and he who keeps her unmarried will be doing better — Mon

But if he doesn't marry her, he'll be doing better — Beck

and he who refrains from marriage will do better — RSV

39. The wife is bound by the law as long as her husband liveth;

. . . bound by the law of wedlock . . . — Con

The wife is a part of her husband as long as he lives — Tay

but if her husband be dead, she is at liberty to be married to whom she will;

but if her husband be fallen asleep, she is at liberty to be married to whom she wishes — ABUV

but if the husband should pass to his rest, the widow is free to marry any one she wishes — TCNT

only in the Lord.

so long as he is a Christian — Gspd

only in a Christian way — Ber

provided the marriage is within the Lord's fellowship — NEB

40. But she is happier if she so abide, after my judgment:

In my opinion she would be happier to remain as she is, unmarried — Phi

It is my judgment, however, that she will enjoy life better by remaining single — Ber

and I think also that I have the Spirit of God.

And I think I am here expressing not only my opinion, but the will of the Spirit as well — Phi

and I think I have God's spirit as well as other people — Gspd

I, too, lay claim to have the Spirit of God — Nor

CHAPTER 8

1. Now as touching things offered unto idols,

Now to deal with the matter of meat which has been sacrificed to idols — Phi

Now about food consecrated to heathen deities — NEB

we know that we all have knowledge.

Of course we all have knowledge, as you say — NEB

We know that every one of us has some knowledge of the matter — Wms

We presuppose that we all have knowledge — Ber

Knowledge puffeth up, but charity edifieth.

Knowledge makes arrogant . . . — NASB

Knowledge breeds conceit, while love builds up character — TCNT

but we should remember that while knowledge may make a man look big, it is only love that can make him grow to his full stature — Phi

2. And if any man think that he knoweth any thing,

If anyone thinks he knows all the answers — Tay

If anybody claims to have superior knowledge — Knox

If a man thinks that he already has knowledge — Mon

he knoweth nothing yet as he ought to know.

he still has a lot to learn — Phi

he does not yet truly know as he ought to know — Mon

he has not yet reached that knowledge which he ought to have reached — TCNT

3. But if any man love God, the same is known of him.

. . . God is known by him — Wms

but if he loves God, he is opening his whole life to the Spirit of God — Phi

But if he loves God, he will have knowledge of God — Nor

But if a man loves God, God knows him — Beck

4. As concerning therefore the eating of those things that are offered in sacrifice unto idols,

Well then, about eating this consecrated food — NEB

Relative, then, to the food that has been dedicated to idols — Ber

Concerning then the eating of idol-sacrifices — Rhm

we know that an idol is nothing in the world,

. . . an idol is not really a god — Tay

Of course, as you say, a false god has no existence in the real world — NEB

we know well that an idol has no real existence in the universe — Mon

we know that an idol-god has no real existence in the world — Nor

and that there is none other God but one.

and there is only one God — Beck

but there is no other God. God is One. — Nor

5. For though there be that are called gods,

So-called gods there may be — Mof

For even if there are so-called gods — NASB

It is true that men have supposed that there are so-called "gods" — Nor

whether in heaven or in earth,

both in heaven and in earth — Phi

both in the sky and down here on earth — Tay

(as there be gods many, and lords many,)

gods and lords galore in fact — Phi

indeed there are plenty of such gods and lords — Gspd

We hear of many such gods and many such lords — Nor

6. But to us there is but one God, the Father, of whom are all things, and we in him;

. . . from whom are all things and for whom we exist — RSV

. . . the source of all things and the goal of our living — Wms

. . . who is the origin of all things, and the end of our being — Knox

and one Lord Jesus Christ,

and there is only one Lord, Jesus Christ — Nor

by whom are all things, and we by him.

Who made everything and gives us life — Tay

749

through whom everything was made and through whom we live — Gspd

7. Howbeit there is not in every man that knowledge:

But this knowledge of ours is not shared by all men — Phi

But not everybody knows this — Beck

This knowledge of God is not shared by everyone — Nor

for some with conscience of the idol until this hour

on the contrary, there are some who still have a conscientious fear of the idol — Con

But some by their familiarity until even now with the idol — Rhm

But some, through being hitherto accustomed to idols — RSV

eat it as a thing offered unto an idol;

as an idol-sacrifice eat it — Rhm

and think the meat an idolatrous sacrifice — Con

still regard the meat as food sacrificed to a god — Nor

eat this food with a sense of its heathen consecration — NEB

and their conscience being weak is defiled.

and so their consciences, because they are overscrupulous, are contaminated — Wms

and their conscience, being weak, is polluted by the eating — NEB

their conscience is not easy, and so incurs guilt — Knox

8. But meat commendeth us not to God:

Now our acceptance by God is not a matter of meat — Phi

Now our food cannot change our place in God's sight — Con

God's approval of us is not based on the food we take — Bas

Just remember that God doesn't care whether we eat it or not — Tay

for neither, if we eat, are we the better; neither, if we eat not, are we the worse.

If we abstain we do not lose anything, and if we eat we do not gain anything — Mof

We lose nothing by not eating and gain nothing by eating — Beck

We have no advantage with Him by eating, and we do not fall short by abstaining — Nor

9. But take heed lest by any means this liberty of yours become a stumbling-block to them that are weak.

. . . become a stumbling block to overscrupulous people — Wms

But be careful, or weak Christians may fall into sin because you do as you please — Beck

You must be careful that your freedom to eat meat does not in any way hinder anyone whose faith is not as robust as yours — Phi

10. For if any man see thee which hast knowledge sit at meat in the idol's temple,

. . . reclining at table in an idol's temple — Mon

For if somebody sees you, who have an intelligent view of this matter, partaking of a meal in an idol's temple — Wms

If a weak character sees you sitting down to a meal in a heathen temple — you, who have knowledge — NEB

shall not the conscience of him which is weak be emboldened to eat those things which are offered to idols;

are you not encouraging the man with a delicate conscience to do the same — Phi

will that really fortify his weak conscience? Will it not embolden him to violate his scruples of conscience by eating food that has been offered to idols — Mof

will not his conscience, if he is a weak man, become so hardened that he, too, will eat food offered to idols — TCNT

11. And through thy knowledge shall the weak brother perish,

For this overscrupulous brother . . . is ruined by what you call your knowledge — Gspd

He is ruined, this weak man, ruined by your 'enlightened mind' — Mof

Surely you would not want your superior knowledge to bring spiritual disaster to a weaker brother — Phi

for whom Christ died?

for whose sake Christ died — ASV

12. But when ye sin so against the brethren,

By sinning in this way against the brotherhood — Mof

But when you sin against your fellow
Christians in this way — Beck
and wound their weak conscience,
and damage the weak consciences of
your brethren — Phi
by injuring their doubtful consciences
— Knox
and wounding their too scrupulous consciences — Gspd
and in ever and again wounding their
weak consciences — Mon
ye sin against Christ.
you really sin against Christ — Phi
you are sinning against Christ — Mon
then you sin against Christ himself —
Nor
13. Wherefore, if meat make my brother

to offend,
So if eating meat offered to idols is going to make my brother sin — Tay
So if food makes my fellow Christian
sin — Beck
**I will eat no flesh while the world
standeth,**
I will abstain from flesh meat perpetually — Knox
I will never eat meat again — NASB
In nowise will I eat flesh unto the age
that abideth — Rhm
lest I make my brother to offend.
rather than be the occasion of my
brother's sin — Knox
I don't want to give him a reason for
sinning — Beck

CHAPTER 9

1. Am I not an apostle?
Is there any doubt that I am a genuine
messenger — Phi
Is it denied that I am an Apostle —
Con
am I not free?
any doubt that I am a free man — Phi
Is it denied that I am free from man's
authority — Con
Am I not free — unrestrained and exempt from any obligation — Amp
have I not seen Jesus Christ our Lord?
Have I not seen Jesus our Lord with
my own eyes — Phi
Is it denied that I have seen the Lord
— Con
are not ye my work in the Lord?
Is it denied that you are the fruits of
my labor in the Lord — Con
Are you not the product of my work
in the Lord's service — Gspd
Are not you yourselves my work
achieved in union with the Lord —
TCNT
**2. If I be not an apostle unto others, yet
doubtless I am to you:**
Even if other people should refuse to
recognize my divine commission,
yet to you at any rate I shall always
be a true messenger — Phi
If others do not accept me as an apostle, you at least are bound to do so
— NEB
**for the seal of mine apostleship are ye
in the Lord.**
for you are yourselves the seal which

stamps the reality of my apostleship
... — Con
for you are living proof of God's call
to me — Phi
for you yourselves, by virtue of your
union with the Lord, are proof of
my apostleship — Wms
**3. Mine answer to them that do examine
me is this:**
This is my defense to those who would
examine me — RSV
this is my answer to those who question
my authority — Con
That is how I vindicate myself to my
critics — Wey
**4. Have we not power to eat and to
drink?**
Have we no right to eat and drink at
the expense of the churches — Mof
Have we not a right to be provided with
food and drink — Knox
Can't I claim the same privilege the
other apostles do of being a guest in
homes — Tay
**5. Have we not power to lead about a
sister, a wife,**
Have I no right to take a Christian wife
about with me — NEB
Do they deny my right to carry a believing wife with me on my journeys
— Con
May we not take along with us on our
journeys a Christian sister, or a wife
— Nor
as well as other apostles, and as the

brethren of the Lord, and Cephas?

like the other messengers, like other Christian brothers, and like Cephas — Phi

as the rest of the apostles and the Lord's brothers and Peter do — Mon

as the other Apostles and the Master's brothers and Kephas all do — TCNT

6. Or I only and Barnabas, have not we power to forbear working?

Or is it only Barnabas and I who have no right to refrain from working for a living — RSV

Are Barnabas and I the only ones not allowed to leave their ordinary work to give time to the ministry — Phi

Must Barnabas and I alone keep working for our living, while you supply these others — Tay

7. Who goeth a warfare any time at his own charges?

Did you ever hear of a man serving in the army at his own expense — NEB

Who ever goes to war without looking to someone to be responsible for his payment — Bas

Does a soldier ever pay his own expenses — Beck

Does any one ever serve as a soldier at his own expense — TCNT

who planteth a vineyard, and eateth not of the fruit thereof?

Who plants a vineyard without eating any of its fruits — RSV

What husbandman plants a vineyard without sharing in its fruit — Con

Does anyone plant a vineyard and not eat of its grapes — Beck

or who feedeth a flock, and eateth not of the milk of the flock?

What shepherd tends his flock and does not taste the milk — Mon

Who takes care of sheep without drinking of their milk — Nor

8. Say I these things as a man?

I am not speaking these things according to human judgment, am I—NASB

Do I speak these things after the manner of men — ASV

Human arguments, you say? — Mof

This is, I know, an argument from everyday life — Phi

or saith not the law the same also?

but it is a principle endorsed by the Law — Phi

Does not the Law endorse the same principle — Amp

9. For it is written in the law of Moses, Thou shalt not muzzle the mouth of the ox that treadeth out the corn.

. . . when it is treading out the grain — RSV

. . . A threshing ox shall not be muzzled — NEB

Doth God take care for oxen?

must we suppose that God is making provision for oxen — Knox

Do you think God was thinking only about oxen when He said this — Tay

10. Or saith he it altogether for our sakes?

Does he not speak entirely for our sake — RSV

or saith he it assuredly for our sake — ASV

Is he not clearly speaking in our interest — Gspd

For our sakes, no doubt, this is written:

Surely we are included! You might even say that the words were written for us — Phi

Of course this law was written in our interest — Gspd

that he that ploweth should plow in hope;

because the ploughman needs to plough in hope — Mof

and that he that thresheth in hope should be partaker of his hope.

and he that thresheth, to thresh in the hope of partaking — ASV

and the thresher as he threshes should have some hope of an ultimate share in the harvest — Phi

11. If we have sown unto you spiritual things,

If we unto you the things of the Spirit have sown — Rhm

If we have sown for you the seed of spiritual things — Phi

If I have sown for you the seeds of spiritual good — Mon

We have been busy planting spiritual seed in you — Nor

is it a great thing if we shall reap your carnal things?

is it too much if we reap your material benefits — RSV

is it too much to expect from you a material harvest — NEB

is it too great for us to reap a material support from you — Wms

Is it a hardship for you if we reap some of your material harvest — Nor

12. If others be partakers of this power over you, are not we rather?

If you allow others these rights, have not we a stronger claim — NEB

If other teachers possess that right over you, do not we possess it much more — Wey

Nevertheless we have not used this power; but suffer all things,

But I have availed myself of no such right. On the contrary, I put up with all that comes my way — NEB

Yet I have not used my right, but forego every claim — Con

lest we should hinder the gospel of Christ.

rather than put an obstacle in the way of the gospel of Christ — RSV

lest I should by any means hinder the course of Christ's Glad-tidings—Con

so that I may not in any way hinder the progress of Christ's gospel — Mon

13. Do ye not know that they which minister about holy things

You know (do you not?) that those who perform the temple service — NEB

Are you not aware that those who conduct the temple service — Ber

Are you ignorant of the fact that those who minister sacred things — Phi

live of the things of the temple?

get their living from the temple—Wms

get their daily bread from the temple — Nor

take part of the sacred food of the Temple for their own use — Phi

get their food from the temple — RSV

and they which wait at the altar are partakers with the altar?

and those who attend regularly to the altar . . . — NASB

and as attendants at the altar get their share of the sacrifices — Mof

and those who serve at the altar share in the sacrificial offerings — RSV

14. Even so hath the Lord ordained

On the same principle the Lord has ordered — Phi

So, too, the Master has appointed — Mon

In the same way, the Lord commanded — RSV

that they which preach the gospel should live of the gospel.

. . . the heralds of the gospel live by preaching the gospel — Knox

That they who the glad message tell Should of the glad-message live — Rhm

That those who proclaim the gospel should get their living by the gospel — RSV

15. But I have used none of these things:

But for my part, I have never availed myself of any of these rights — Mon

But I have made no use of any of these rights — RSV

But I have never taken advantage of any such right — NEB

neither have I written these things, that it should be so done unto me:

nor do I intend to claim it in this letter — NEB

nor am I writing this to secure any such provision — RSV

And I am not writing this now so that I may become an illustration of this — Gspd

for it were better for me to die,

I had rather die! — NEB

I would die sooner than — Mof

than that any man should make my glorying void.

than let anyone deprive me of this, my source of pride — Mof

No one shall make my boast an empty boast — NEB

16. For though I preach the gospel, I have nothing to glory of:

What I am proud of is not the mere preaching of the gospel — Mof

Proclaiming the gospel gives me no ground of boasting — Mon

for necessity is laid upon me:

Necessity compels me to do that — Nor

for I am compelled to do so by order of my Master — Con

yea, woe is unto me, if I preach not the gospel!

for a curse is on me if I do not — Bas

It would mean Woe is me! if I did not preach the Gospel — Nor

17. For if I do this thing willingly, I have a reward:

For were my service of my own free choice, I might claim wages to reward my labour — Con

If I do this work because I choose to do so then I am entitled to a reward — Phi

If I were volunteering my services of my own free will, then the Lord would give me a special reward — Tay

but if against my will,

but since I serve by compulsion — Con

but if I do it because I must — Gspd

a dispensation of the gospel is committed unto me.

it is no more than for a steward to discharge his trust — Mof

I am a slave intrusted with a stewardship — Con

I am entrusted with a commission — RSV

18. What is my reward then? Verily that, when I preach the gospel,

What can I expect in the way of reward? . . . — Phi

What then is my reward? Just this: When I tell the good news — Beck

In that case, what pay should I get? My pay is this, that in my preaching — Nor

I may make the gospel of Christ without charge,

to make the Glad-tidings free of cost — Con

I won't let it cost anybody anything — Beck

to present the Good News free of all cost — TCNT

that I abuse not my power in the gospel.

so as not to use to the full my right in the gospel — ASV

that I might forego my right as an Evangelist — Con

and so make but a sparing use of the rights which it gives me — TCNT

19. For though I be free from all men,

. . . from the authority of all men — Con

In this way no one has any claim on me — Nor

I am not bound to obey anyone just because he pays my salary — Tay

yet have I made myself servant unto all,

I brought myself under bondage to all — ASV

yet I have freely and happily become a servant of any and all — Tay

yet I have made myself everyone's slave — Phi

that I might gain the more.

that I might win more men to Christ — Phi

in the hope of winning as many converts as possible — Wey

20. And unto the Jews I became as a Jew,

To Jews I have become like a Jew — Mof

With the Jews I lived like a Jew — Knox

that I might gain the Jews;

that I might win Jews for Christ — Nor

to win over Jews — Mof

to them that are under the law, as under the law,

when I am with Gentiles who follow Jewish customs and ceremonies . . . — Tay

. . . I put myself in the position of being under the Law — Phi

to those who are subject to Law I became like a man subject to Law — though I was not myself subject to Law — TCNT

. . . not being myself under the law[6] — ASV

that I might gain them that are under the law;

21. To them that are without law, as without law,

to men who have no written law . . . — Wms

To those who have no Law I became like a man who has no Law — TCNT

When with the heathen I agree with them as much as I can — Tay

(being not without law to God, but under the law to Christ,)

except of course that I must always do what is right as a Christian — Tay

This did not mean that I did not recognize the law of God, but it meant that I was under the law of Christ — Nor

that I might gain them that are without law.

to win those who have no Law — TCNT

22. To the weak became I as weak,

To the overscrupulous I have become overscrupulous — Gspd

With the scrupulous, I behaved myself like one who is scrupulous — Knox

---

[6]Variant reading.

that I might gain the weak:

to win the scrupulous — Knox

I am made all things to all men,

I have, in short, been all things to all sorts of men — Phi

Indeed, I have become everything in turn to men of every sort — NEB

Yes, whatever a person is like, I try to find common ground with him — Tay

that I might by all means save some.

in the hope that by all possible means . . . — Wey

. . . by any and by all means . . . — Mon

so that in one way or another . . . — NEB

that by every possible means I might win some to God — Phi

23. And this I do for the gospel's sake,

But I do it all to advance the Gospel — Ber

I am still doing this for the sake of the Gospel — Nor

that I might be partaker thereof with you.

that I may become a fellow-partaker of it — NASB

That a joint-partaker thereof I may become — Rhm

for the blessing I myself receive when I see them come to Christ — Tay

24. Know ye not that they which run in a race run all,

. . . those racing in the stadium all run, to be sure — Ber

. . . in a race all the runners compete — RSV

You know (do you not?) that at the sports all the runners run the race — NEB

but one receiveth the prize?

but only one wins the prize — Phi

So run, that ye may obtain.

run, then, for victory — Knox

Well, you ought to run with your minds fixed on winning the prize! — Phi

You must run in such a way that you can get the prize — Wms

25. And every man that striveth for the mastery is temperate in all things.

. . . practices rigid self-control in training — Wms

— and every man who strives in the matches trains himself by all manner of self-restraint — Con

But every man in training is temperate in all things — Wey

Anyone who enters a contest goes into strict training — Beck

Now they do it to obtain a corruptible crown;

. . . a crown that fades — Knox

. . . to win a wreath that will soon wither — Gspd

In such a race the winner receives a perishable wreath — Nor

but we an incorruptible.

we, a wreath that never fades — NEB

— we, a crown that cannot fade — Con

but the one we compete for will never wither — Gspd

but in the Christian race the prize is an imperishable crown — Nor

26. I therefore so run, not as uncertainly;

I, therefore, run not like a racer uncertain of his goal — Con

So I run straight to the goal with purpose in every step — Tay

So I run with a clear goal ahead of me — Beck

So I keep on running, but not aimlessly — Nor

so fight I, not as one that beateth the air:

I fight to win. I'm not just shadow-boxing or playing around — Tay

that is the way I fight, not like one who punches the air — Wms

I am no shadowboxer; I really fight! — — Phi

27. But I keep under my body, and bring it into subjection:

But I keep on beating and bruising my body and making it my slave — Wms

I bruise my body and make it my slave — Wey

lest that by any means, when I have preached to others,

so that I, after I have summoned others to the race — Wms

lest I, who have called others to the contest — TCNT

I myself should be a castaway.

I myself should be disqualified — RSV

I should myself fail shamefully of the prize — Con

CHAPTER 10

1. Moreover, brethren, I would not that ye should be ignorant,

I want you to know, brethren — RSV

You should understand, my brothers — NEB

I want you to know, fellow Christians — Beck

how that all our fathers were under the cloud,

. . . protected by the cloud — Gspd

God made them safe and guided them by sending a cloud . . . ahead of them — Tay

that our fathers all marched out of Egypt under the pillar of cloud — Nor

and all passed through the sea;

. . . went securely . . . — Wms

. . . passed safely . . . — Gspd

and all passed through the Red Sea — Nor

2. And were all baptized unto Moses

. . . immersed . . . — ABUV

all, as it were, accepted baptism as followers of Moses — Gspd

they all underwent baptism as followers of Moses — TCNT

in the cloud and in the sea;

3. And did all eat of the same spiritual meat;

. . . the same supernatural food — TCNT

. . . food of the Spirit — Beck

4. And did all drink the same spiritual drink:

for they drank of that spiritual Rock that followed them;

they continued to drink . . . — Wms

they used to drink . . . — Gspd

. . . the supernautral Rock . . . — RSV

. . . the attending spiritual rock — Ber

and that Rock was Christ.

5. But with many of them God was not well pleased:

. . . the great majority of them . . . — Amp

. . . God was not at all satisfied — Wms

Yet most of them lost God's favor — Con

And yet, most of them were not accepted by God — NEB

for they were overthrown in the wilderness.

For they were strewed along in the desert — Rhm

and their dead bones lay strewn about in the wilderness — Nor

for the desert was strewn with their corpses — NEB

6. Now these things were our examples,

Now, these things were shadows of our own case — Con

Now in these events our ancestors stand as examples to us — Phi

These events are examples to us, warning us — Nor

to the intent we should not lust after evil things, as they also lusted.

to keep us from hankering after what is evil . . . — Wms

to teach us not to long for evil things as our forefathers longed — TCNT

that we should not crave evil things, as they also craved — NASB

We were not to set our hearts, as some of them set their hearts, on forbidden things — Knox

7. Neither be ye idolaters, as were some of them;

Now stop being idolaters, as some of them were — Wms

So do not worship false gods as some of them did — Nor

as it is written, The people sat down to eat and drink,

. . . After resting and feasting — Bas

and rose up to play.

the people got up to take their pleasure — Bas

then got up to dance in worship of the golden calf — Tay

And they rose up for idol dances — Mon

8. Neither let us commit fornication,

Let us stop practicing immorality — Wms

Let us not sin sexually — Beck

as some of them committed,

and fell in one day three and twenty thousand.

. . . fell dead . . . — Gspd

. . . were killed . . . — Knox

. . . came to their end . . . — Bas

9. Neither let us tempt Christ,

Let us stop trying the Lord's patience — Wms

Neither let us make trial of the Lord
— ASV

Nor must we presume on the Lord —
Mof

Let us not go too far in testing the
Lord's patience — Beck

as some of them also tempted,
and were destroyed of serpents.

with the result that they were, one after
another, destroyed by the snakes —
TCNT

they were killed for it by the snakes —
Gspd

10. Neither murmur ye,

and do not say evil things against the
Lord — Bas

You must stop grumbling — Wms

Don't complain — Beck

as some of them also murmured,
and were destroyed of the destroyer.

for that is why God sent his Angel to
destroy them — Tay

only to be destroyed by the Destroying
angel — Mof

the angel of death killed them — Beck

11. Now all these things happened unto
them for ensamples:

Now these things were happening to
them typically — Mon

But these things by way of type were
happening to them — Rhm

Now all these things befell them as
shadows of things to come — Con

Now these things which happened to
our ancestors are illustrations of the
way in which God works — Phi

and they are written for our admoni-
tion,

and were recorded for our benefit as a
warning — NEB

and were recorded to serve as a caution
to us — TCNT

upon whom the ends of the world are
come.

in whose lives the climax of the ages
has been reached — Wms

who are the heirs of the ages which
have gone before us — Phi

For upon us the fulfilment of the ages
has come — NEB

12. Wherefore let him that thinketh he
standeth

so then let him who imagines that he
is standing so securely — Mon

I mean this, that he who is sure he
stands safely — Nor

So let the man who feels sure of his
standing today — Phi

take heed lest he fall.

be careful that he does not fall tomorrow — Phi

beware! You may fall — NEB

13. There hath no temptation taken you

So far you have faced no trial — NEB

No temptation has come your way —
Phi

but such as is common to man:

that is not common to all mankind —
TCNT

beyond what man can bear — NEB

that is too hard for flesh and blood to
bear — Phi

but God is faithful,

God can be depended on — Gspd

God is faithful to His promises — Con

And you can trust God — Beck

God will not fail you — TCNT

who will not suffer you to be tempted
above that ye are able:

not to allow you to suffer any temptation beyond your powers of endurance — Phi

He will not let you be tested more than
you can stand — Beck

and he will not let you be tempted beyond your strength — RSV

but will with the temptation also make
a way to escape,

But when you are tested, He will also
make a way out — Beck

He will see to it that every temptation
has a way out — Phi

He will show you how to escape temptation's power — Tay

that ye may be able to bear it.

so that you can come through it victoriously — Nor

that ye may be able to hold out — Rhm

that ye may be able to endure it —
ASV

14. Wherefore, my dearly beloved, flee
from idolatry.

. . . keep on running from idolatry —
Wms

So then, my beloved, continually flee
from idolatry — Mon

And so, my dear friends, keep away
from the worship of idols — Beck

15. I speak as to wise men:

I speak to you as men of discernment
— TCNT

I appeal to your intelligence — Ber

I appeal to your good sense — Gspd

I speak as to sensible men — RSV

judge ye what I say.

Look now and see for yourselves whether what I am about to say is true — Tay

Make up your minds about what I say — Gspd

Form your own judgement on what I say — NEB

16. The cup of blessing which we bless,

When we ask the Lord's blessing upon our drinking from the cup of wine at the Lord's Table — Tay

Does not the consecrated cup which we bless — Gspd

is it not the communion of the blood of Christ?

. . . a sign of our sharing in the blood of Christ — Wms

mean that in drinking it we share in the blood of Christ — Gspd

this means, doesn't it, that all who drink it are sharing together the blessing of Christ's blood — Tay

is it not a common participation in the blood of Christ — Mon

is it not the blood of Christ that we share with Him — Nor

The bread which we break, is it not the communion of the body of Christ?

. . . is it not a common participation in the body of Christ — Mon

. . . is it not the body of Christ that we also share with Him — Nor

. . . shows that we are sharing together in the benefits of His body which was broken for us — Tay

Is not the loaf which we break a sign of our sharing in the body of Christ — Wms

17. For we being many are one bread, and one body:

Because there is one bread, we who are many are one body — RSV

Because there is one loaf, we, many as we are, are one body — Gspd

Though we are many, the one loaf makes us all one body — Nor

for we are all partakers of that one bread.

for it is one loaf of which we all partake — NEB

since we all participate in the One Bread — Ber

for we all do share in the one loaf — Mon

18. Behold Israel after the flesh:

Or look at Israel, God's people by nature — Knox

Look at the Israelites in their practices — Wms

Consider the practice of Israel — RSV

Behold Israel whose observance is after the flesh — Lam

are not they which eat of the sacrifices partakers of the altar?

do you not see that those who eat of the sacrifices are in partnership with the altar — Con

And the Jewish priests, when they ate of the animals brought to God as sacrifices, were showing that they were partners with God — Tay

19. What say I then?

Then what do I mean — Wms

What am I trying to say — Tay

that the idol is any thing,

Am I saying that the idols to whom the heathen bring sacrifices are really alive and are real gods — Tay

that an idol is anything but an idol — NEB

Am I saying that an idol-god really exists — Nor

or that which is offered in sacrifice to idols is any thing?

or that meat offered to an idol is really changed thereby — Con

or that food sacrified to idols has some value — Nor

20. But I say, that the things which the Gentiles sacrifice,

No, what I imply is that anything pagans offer in sacrifice — Mof

No, these sacrifices of the non-Jews — Beck

Not at all! I say emphatically that gentile sacrifices — Phi

they sacrifice to devils, and not to God:

they sacrifice to demons, and not to God — ASV

are really offering it to evil spirits and not to God at all — Knox

are offered to demons and to a Being who is no God — TCNT

and I would not that ye should have fellowship with devils.

and I would not that ye should have communion with demons — ASV

I do not want you to be partners with demons — RSV

21. Ye cannot drink the cup of the Lord, and the cup of devils:

... and the cup of demons — RSV

It is not possible for you, at the same time, to take the cup of the Lord and the cup of evil spirits — Bas

ye cannot be partakers of the Lord's table, and of the table of the devils.

You cannot partake of the table of the Lord and the table of demons — RSV

You cannot be a guest at both the Lord's Supper and at the table of devils — Nor

22. Do we provoke the Lord to jealousy?

What! do we intend to rouse the Lord's jealousy — Mof

Or are we trying to make the Lord jealous — Beck

Or are we trying to stir up God's anger — Nor

are we stronger than he?

Surely, we are not stronger than He, are we — Nor

We are not stronger than He, are we — NASB

23. All things are lawful for me,

Everything is permissible for people — Wms

We are free to do anything, you say — NEB

All things are lawful, you say? — Mon

but all things are not expedient:

but not all things are helpful — RSV

but not everything can be done without harm — Knox

but not everything is good for others — Beck

All things are lawful for me but all things edify not.

but not all things build up the church — Con

Yes, but everything does not build up character — TCNT

but everything is not constructive — Phi

but does everything help the building of the community? — NEB

24. Let no man seek his own,

Let no man, then, set his own advantage as his objective — Phi

No one should always be looking after his own welfare — Wms

Let not each one be always seeking his own ... good — Mon

but every man another's wealth.

but also that of his neighbor — Wms

but everybody for the good of the other person — Beck

but rather let each one seek the good of others — Nor

25. Whatsoever is sold in the shambles, that eat,

Eat anything for sale in the meat market — Gspd

You may eat anything sold in the meat-market — NEB

asking no question for conscience sake:

without making inquiries to satisfy your scruples — TCNT

and don't ask any questions or let your conscience trouble you — Beck

without question of right or wrong — Bas

without raising any question, as far as conscience is concerned — Gspd

26. For the earth is the Lord's, and the fulness thereof.

For the earth is the Lord's, and everything in it — RSV

The whole earth and all that is in it belongs to the Lord — Phi

27. If any of them that believe not bid you to a feast, and ye be disposed to go;

If a pagan asks you to dinner and you want to go — Phi

If an unbeliever invites you to his house and you consent to go — TCNT

whatsoever is set before you, eat,

feel free to eat whatever is set before you — Phi

eat whatever is put before you — NEB

asking no question for conscience sake.

without making inquiries to satisfy your scruples — TCNT

don't ask any questions or let your conscience trouble you — Beck

without raising any question, as far as conscience is concerned — Gspd

28. But if any man say unto you, This is offered in sacrifice unto idols,

... used in idolatrous worship — Knox

... This has been offered in sacrifice — ASV

But if your host should say straight out, This meat has been offered to an idol — Phi

eat not for his sake that shewed it, and for conscience sake:

make it your rule not to eat of it ... — Wms

... on account of the man who told you and his conscientious scruples — Gspd

then, for the sake of the speaker and his scruples, do not eat it — TCNT

for the earth is the Lord's, and the fulness thereof:[7]

29. Conscience, I say, not thine own, but of the other:

I do not say your scruples, but his — TCNT

thy neighbor's conscience, I say, not thine own — Con

I mean his conscience, not yours — RSV

for why is my liberty judged of another man's conscience?

What? you say, is my freedom to be called in question by another man's conscience — NEB

But, you may object, why should my freedom be decided upon another's scruples of conscience — Mon

What good is there in doing what I please if someone else's conscience condemns it — Beck

Why then should my personal freedom be limited by another's conscience — Wms

30. For if I by grace be a partaker,

If I partake with thankfulness — ASV

If I give thanks for what I eat — Beck

If I eat after giving thanks — Mon

why am I evil spoken of for that for which I give thanks?

why am I called a sinner for that which I eat with thanksgiving — Con

why am I blamed for eating food over

which I have said grace — NEB

why should I let myself be denounced for eating what I thank God for — Beck

31. Whether therefore ye eat, or drink, or whatsoever ye do, do all to the glory of God.

do everything to glorify God — Beck

You should always give God the glory — Nor

32. Give none offence, neither to the Jews,

Give no occasion of stumbling, either to Jews — ASV

Stop being stumbling blocks to Jews — Wms

Don't be the reason for others to sin, whether they are Jews — Beck

nor to the Gentiles, nor to the church of God.

... or to the assembly of God — Rhm

or Gentiles or Christians — Tay

33. Even as I please all men in all things,

just as I myself am in the habit of pleasing everybody in everything — Wms

for I, also, try to please everybody in everything — TCNT

just as I try to please all men in everything I do — RSV

not seeking mine own profit, but the profit of many,

I do not strive for personal profit, but seek the good of as many as possible — Nor

without considering my own advantage but their advantage — Phi

not doing ... what is best for me, but what is best for them — Tay

that they may be saved.

CHAPTER 11

1. Be ye followers of me, even as I also am of Christ.

Be ye imitators of me, even as I also am of Christ — ASV

Pattern after me as I pattern after Christ — Ber

2. Now I praise you, brethren, that ye remember me in all things,

I must give you credit for remembering what I taught you — Phi

I prize and praise you for always remembering me — Wms

I want to give you credit, brethren, for not forgetting me — Nor

and keep the ordinances, as I delivered them to you.

and held fast the traditions, even as I delivered them to you — ASV

and keep unchanged the rules which I delivered to you — Con

and for upholding the traditions that I passed on to you — Nor

3. But I would have you know, that the head of every man is Christ; and the head of the woman is the man; and

---

[7]Now recognized as not adequately supported by original manuscripts.

the head of Christ is God.

But there is one matter I want to remind you about: that a wife is responsible to her husband; her husband is responsible to Christ; and Christ is responsible to God — Tay

But I am anxious that you should understand that the Christ is the Head of every man . . . — TCNT

4. Every man praying or prophesying,

Any man who offers prayer or explains the will of God — Gspd

If a man prays or preaches — Phi

if a man should pray or prophesy in the congregation — Con

Any man . . . when praying or preaching in public — TCNT

having his head covered,

with a veil over his head — Con

dishonoureth his head.

disgraces . . . — Gspd

he would bring shame on his head — Con

dishonours him who is his Head — TCNT

**5. But every woman that prayeth or prophesieth[8]
with her head uncovered dishonoureth her head:**

with her head unveiled . . . — ASV

. . . disgraces her head — Gspd

. . . brings shame upon her head—Knox

. . . is just as much a disgrace — Phi

. . . dishonours her husband — Tay

for that is even all one as if she were shaven.

for it is one and the same thing as if she were shaven — ASV

she is no better than the woman who has her head shaved — Knox

for that is to make herself like one of the shameless women who shave their heads — TCNT

6. For if the woman be not covered, let her also be shorn:

For if a woman will not veil herself, then she should cut off her hair — RSV

if she cast off her veil, let her shave her head at once — Con

but if it be a shame for a woman to be shorn or shaven,

If she admits that a woman is disgraced when her hair is cut short or shaved — Knox

But, since to cut her hair short, or shave it off, marks her as one of the shameless women — TCNT

let her be covered.

let her be veiled — ASV

let her keep her veil on her head—Con

7. For a man indeed ought not to cover his head,

. . . not to have his head veiled — ASV

. . . has no need to veil his head—Knox

forasmuch as he is the image and glory of God:

for he represents the person and glory of God — Nor

he represents the likeness and supremacy of God — Mof

for he has been from the beginning the likeness of God and the reflection of his glory — TCNT

but the woman is the glory of the man.

but woman is the reflection of man's glory — TCNT

but a woman represents the glory of man — Nor

the woman represents the supremacy of man — Mof

8. For the man is not of the woman; but the woman of the man.

For man did not originally spring from woman, but woman was made out of man — NEB

Man does not originate from woman, but woman from man — Wey

The first man didn't come from woman, but the first woman came out of man — Tay

9. Neither was the man created for the woman;

. . . on account of the woman — ABUV

. . . for the woman's sake — Ber

Man was not created originally for the sake of woman — Phi

but the woman for the man.

but woman was created for the sake of man — Phi

10. For this cause ought the woman to have power on her head

. . . a sign that she is under man's authority — Tay

and therefore it is woman's duty to have a sign of authority on her head — NEB

---

[8]See verse 4 for variations of "prayeth or prophesieth."

For this reason a woman ought to bear on her head an outward sign of man's authority — Phi

because of the angels.

on account of the angels, if of nobody else — Gspd

especially out of respect for the angels — Wms

because of her (guardian) angels — Mon

because of the presence of the angels — TCNT

11. Nevertheless neither is the man without the woman,

Not that . . . man has any place apart from woman — Knox

man is not independent of woman — Nor

Woman is . . . essential to man — NEB

neither the woman without the man, in the Lord.

. . . in union with the Lord — Gspd

. . . in their fellowship with the Lord — Con

. . . from the Lord's point of view — Wms

in Christ's fellowship man is . . . essential to woman — NEB

in the Lord woman is not independent of man — RSV

12. For as the woman is of the man,

For just as the woman was created out of man — Nor

For as the woman originates from the man — NASB

even so is the man also by the woman;

so man is now born of woman — RSV

so also man has his birth through woman — Wey

but all things of God.

and all things originate from God — NASB

but everything comes ultimately from God — Wey

13. Judge in yourselves:

Judge for yourselves — RSV

Judge of this matter by your own feeling — Con

is it comely that a woman pray unto God uncovered?

is it becoming that a woman pray to God unveiled — ABUV

Is it fitting that a woman should pray to God in public with her head uncovered — TCNT

Do you think it right and proper for a woman to pray to God bareheaded — Phi

14. Doth not even nature itself teach you, that, if a man have long hair, it is a shame unto him?

. . . it is a dishonor to him — ASV

Isn't there a natural principle here, that makes us feel that long hair is disgraceful to a man — Phi

Does not nature itself teach you it is degrading for a man to wear long hair — Wms

15. But if a woman have long hair, it is a glory to her:

. . . it is an added grace to her — Knox

But for a woman to have long hair is different; that is her pride — Nor

for her hair is given her for a covering.

We feel this because the long hair is the cover provided by nature for the woman's head — Phi

because her hair has been given her instead of a veil — Mon

16. But if any man seem to be contentious,

. . . seems anxious to dispute the matter — Ber

. . . presumes to raise objections on this point — Mof

If, however, any one still thinks it right to contest the point — TCNT

we have no such custom,

well, I acknowledge no other mode of worship — Mof

I can say that we have no such custom (of women going bareheaded) — Nor

I for my part recognize no other practice in worship than this — Gspd

neither the churches of God.

or in any of the congregations of God's people — NEB

Nor yet the assemblies of God — Rhm

17. Now in this that I declare unto you I praise you not,

But in the following instructions I do not commend you — RSV

In giving you these injunctions I must mention a practice which I cannot commend — NEB

But in giving you the following injunction I cannot commend you — Mof

And, while instructing you, let me mention one thing about which I cannot give you praise — Nor

that ye come together not for the better, but for the worse.

for holding your assemblies in a way
that does harm, not good — Knox

your solemn assemblies are for evil
rather than for good — Con

**18. For first of all, when ye come together
in the church,**

. . . when you meet as a congregation
Gspd

. . . when your congregation assembles
— Con

To begin with . . . when you meet as a
church — TCNT

For, in the first place, when you assemble as a church — RSV

**I hear that there be divisions among
you;**

I hear that divisions exist among you
— ABUV

I am told that cliques prevail — Mof

Everyone keeps telling me about the
arguing that goes on in these meetings, and the divisions developing
among you — Tay

and I partly believe it.

and I think there must be truth in what
I hear — Phi

to some extent I believe it — Ber

and I can just about believe it — Tay

and I believe there is some truth in it —
Mon

**19. For there must be also heresies among
you,**

For there must be cliques among you
— Phi

for dissensions are necessary — NEB

For there must necessarily be differences of opinion among you — Wey

**that they which are approved may be
made manifest among you.**

in order that those who have God's approval may be clearly seen among
you — Bas

If genuine Christians are to be recognized — Mof

so that those who are true metal may
be distinguished from the rest —
Knox

that those who are genuine among you
may be recognized — RSV

**20. When ye come together therefore into
one place,**

When therefore ye assemble yourselves
together — ASV

So when you hold your meetings —
Wms

this is not to eat the Lord's supper.

it is impossible for you to eat the Lord's
Supper — NEB

it is not possible to eat the Lord's supper — ASV

**21. For in eating every one taketh before
other his own supper:**

for each begins to eat . . . his own supper, before any thing has been given
to others — Con

each comer hastens to eat the supper
he has brought for himself — Knox

each of you is in a rush to eat his own
supper — Wms

**and one is hungry, and another is
drunken.**

and one has not enough food, and another is the worse for drink — Bas

with the result that one has too little to
eat, and another has too much to
drink! — TCNT

**22. What? have ye not houses to eat and to
drink in?**

**or despise ye the church of God, and
shame them that have not?**

Or the assembly of God do ye despise
. . . — Rhm

Or do you mean to show your contempt for the church of God, and to
humiliate those who have nothing —
Gspd

Or, are you trying to show your contempt for the church of God and trying to humiliate those who have no
houses — Wms

**What shall I say to you? shall I praise
you in this? I praise you not.**

Am I to commend this sort of conduct?
Most certainly not! — Phi

What am I to say? Can I commend
you? On this point, certainly not! —
NEB

What ought I to say to you? Praise
you? No, I cannot approve — Nor

**23. For I have received of the Lord that
which also I delivered unto you,**

For the tradition which I handed on to
you came to me from the Lord himself — NEB

I passed on to you what I received of
the Lord himself — Mof

For I myself received from the Lord
the account which I have in turn
given to you — TCNT

That the Lord Jesus the same night in which he was betrayed took bread:

How that the Lord Jesus In the night when he was being delivered up took a loaf — Rhm

that the Lord Jesus, on the night of his arrest, took bread — NEB

24. And when he had given thanks, he brake it, and said,

He gave thanks, broke it, and said — Beck

And when He had given thanks, He broke it and gave it to His disciples, saying — Nor

Take, eat; this is my body, which is broken for you:

This means my body broken for you — Mof

This is my body which takes your place — Gspd

This is my own body given on your behalf — TCNT

this do in remembrance of me.

do this in memory of me — Mof

Do this to remember me — Beck

25. After the same manner also he took the cup, when he had supped, saying,

. . . cup of wine . . . — Tay

Similarly, when supper was ended, he took the cup saying — Phi

This cup is the new testament in my blood:

. . . the new agreement ratified by my blood — Gspd

. . . established and set in motion by my blood — Tay

This cup means the new covenant ratified by my blood — Mof

this do ye, as oft as ye drink it, in remembrance of me.

Whenever you drink it, do this as a memorial of me — NEB

26. For as often as ye eat this bread, and drink this cup,

ye do shew the Lord's death till he come.

you are heralding . . . — Knox

. . . re-telling the message . . . — Tay

you commemorate our LORD'S death until he come — Lam

you are telling how the Lord died, till He comes — Beck

you proclaim the Lord's death until he comes — RSV

27. Wherefore whosoever shall eat this bread,

and drink this cup of the Lord, unworthily,

. . . in the wrong spirit — Bas

. . . in an unworthy way — Wms

or drinks the cup of the Lord in an unworthy manner — RSV

shall be guilty of the body and blood of the Lord.

will be guilty of desecrating the body and blood of the Lord — NEB

will be guilty of profaning the body and blood of the Lord — Gspd

must answer for a sin against the body and blood of the Lord — Mon

28. But let a man examine himself,

. . . have a self-examination — Ber

. . . test himself — Mof

. . . be proving himself — Rhm

Let each man look into his own heart — TCNT

and so let him eat of that bread,

and only then should he eat the bread — Phi

and only in this way should he eat any of the bread — Wms

and only then eat of the bread — TCNT

and drink of that cup.

29. For he that eateth and drinketh unworthily,

eateth and drinketh damnation to himself,

is condemned for his eating and drinking — Beck

eats and drinks condemnation to himself — Mon

brings a judgement upon himself by his eating and drinking — TCNT

not discerning the Lord's[9] body.

if he does not discern the Body — NEB

if he does not judge the body rightly — NASB

without a proper sense of the Body — Mof

30. For this cause many are weak and sickly among you,

That is why many of you are weak and ill — RSV

It is this careless participation which is the reason for the many feeble and sickly Christians in your church — Phi

and many sleep.

---

[9]The word "Lord's" is now recognized as not adequately supported by original manuscripts.

and some have died — RSV

and the explanation of the fact that many of you are spiritually asleep — Phi

31. For if we would judge ourselves,

If we only judged our own lives truly — Mof

If you carefully examine yourselves before eating — Tay

If, however, we were judging ourselves aright — Mon

we should not be judged.

32. But when we are judged,

But if punishment does come — Bas

But if the Lord judges us — Beck

but through our condemnation by the Lord — Mon

we are chastened of the Lord,

he is disciplining us — NEB

we are being disciplined by the Lord — Wms

we are undergoing discipline — TCNT

we are trained — Mon

that we should not be condemned with the world.

that we may not incur, as the world incurs, damnation — Knox

to save us if possible from being condemned along with the wicked world — Nor

so that we may not be condemned along with the world — Mon

33. Wherefore, my brethren,

So then, my fellow Christians — Beck

when ye come together to eat,

whenever you come together for this meal — Mon

when you come to celebrate the Lord's Supper — Nor

tarry one for another.

wait for one another — TCNT

34. And if any man hunger, let him eat at home;

those who are hungry had best eat at home — Knox

Those of you who are hungry should first eat your meal at home — Nor

that ye come not together unto condemnation.

that your coming together be not unto judgment — ASV

you must not gather, only to incur condemnation — Mof

so that he won't bring punishment upon himself when you meet together — Tay

And the rest will I set in order when I come.

I will settle in detail the matters that remain, when I come — Wms

The other details I will settle when I come — TCNT

There are other questions which I shall try to settle in person when I come — Nor

CHAPTER 12

1. Now concerning spiritual gifts, brethren,

... special abilities ... — Tay

Concerning those who exercise Spiritual Gifts, brethren — Con

Fellow Christians, ... about the gifts of the Spirit — Beck

I would not have you ignorant.

I do not want you to be uninformed — RSV

I do not want to leave you in the dark — Ber

it is not right for you to be without teaching — Bas

I don't want any misunderstanding about them — Tay

2. Ye know that ye were Gentiles,

You know how, in the days when you were still pagan — NEB

You know that in the days of your

heathenism — Con

You know that there was a time when you were Gentiles — TCNT

carried away unto these dumb idols,

you were blindly led astray to worship dumb and senseless idols [by those who pretended to gifts from heaven] — Con

you were swept off to those dumb heathen gods — NEB

you were in the habit of going off ... after idols that could not speak — Wms

you went after images without voice or power — Bas

even as ye were led.

just the way you had been taught — Nor

just as you happened to be led — TCNT

wherever you might be led — Wms

3. Wherefore I give you to understand,
Wherefore I make known unto you —
ASV
For this reason I must impress upon
you — NEB
For that reason, I want you to know
this: — Nor
But now you are meeting people who
claim to speak messages from the
Spirit of God. How can you know
whether they are really inspired by
God or whether they are fakes? Here
is the test: — Tay
**that no man speaking by the Spirit of
God calleth Jesus accursed:**
that no one who says A curse on Jesus!
can be speaking under the influence
of the Spirit of God — NEB
if you are moved by God's Spirit, you
don't say, Jesus is cursed — Beck
**and that no man can say that Jesus
is the Lord, but by the Holy Ghost.**
. . . without being under the influence
of the Holy Spirit — Gspd
. . . unless he is inspired by the Holy
Spirit — Con
and only if you are moved by the Holy
Spirit can you say, Jesus is the Lord
— Beck

4. Now there are diversities of gifts,
. . . distinctive gifts of grace — Ber
Gifts differ — TCNT
Now gifts are given to different persons
— Beck
but the same Spirit.
but it is the same Spirit who gives them
— Phi
but the same Spirit gives them all —
Con

**5. And there are differences of adminis-
trations,**
and there are varieties of service —
RSV
There are different ways of serving God
— Phi
ways of serving differ — TCNT
and [they are given for] various minis-
trations — Con
but the same Lord.
but all to serve the same Lord — Con
but it is the same Lord who is served
— Gspd

6. And there are diversities of operations,
. . . varieties of things accomplished —
Ber

the working whereby they are wrought
is various — Con
there are varieties of activities — Wms
results differ — TCNT
And again, there are different ways of
doing things — Nor
And there are varieties of effects —
NASB
**but it is the same God which worketh
all in all.**
but it is the same God who achieves his
purposes through them all — Phi
but God who produces them all in us
all is the same — Gspd
but it is the same God who does all
things by putting energy in us all —
Wms
yet the God who brings about every result is in every case the same — TCNT

**7. But the manifestation of the Spirit is
given to every man to profit withal.**
Each man is given his gift by the Spirit
that he may use it for the common
good — Phi
But the gift whereby the Spirit becomes
manifest is given to each for profit
of all — Con
Now, the Spirit shows Himself to each
one to make him useful — Beck

**8. For to one is given by the Spirit the
word of wisdom;**
. . . message of wisdom — Ber
The Spirit gives one person the ability
to speak of wisdom — Beck
**to another the word of knowledge by
the same Spirit;**
another, by the same Spirit, receives
the power to express knowledge —
Gspd
. . . the ability to speak intelligently —
Beck
to another a word of insight by the
same Spirit — Mon

9. To another faith by the same Spirit;
another, from his union with the same
Spirit receives faith — Gspd
to one in the same Spirit, special faith
— Wey
**to another the gifts of healing by the
same Spirit;**
to another the ability to heal . . . — Phi
. . . the ability to cure the sick — Gspd
to another power to cure diseases by
the one Spirit — TCNT

10. To another the working of miracles;
. . . miraculous powers — Mof

... the powers which work Miracles —
Con

... supernatural powers — TCNT

to another prophecy;

... prophetic insight — Wms

... inspiration in preaching — Gspd

... the gift of preaching — TCNT

to another discerning of spirits;

... the power of discriminating between spirits — Wey

... the power to discriminate between the true Spirit and false spirits — Wms

... the gift of distinguishing between true and false inspiration — TCNT

to another divers kinds of tongues;

Another can talk strange languages — Beck

... various ecstatic utterances — Gspd

Still another person is able to speak in languages he never learned — Tay

to another the interpretation of tongues;

Another can tell the meaning of languages — Beck

others, who do not know the language either, are given power to understand what he is saying — Tay

11. But all these worketh that one and the selfsame Spirit,

all these abilities one and the same spirit energizes — Ber

But the one and same Spirit accomplishes all these achievements — Wms

dividing to every man severally as he will.

who apportions to each one individually as he wills — RSV

apportioned to each of us just as the Spirit chooses — Gspd

distributing to each individual exactly as He pleases — Ber

12. For as the body is one, and hath many members,

As the human body, which has many parts, is a unity — Phi

A man's body is all one, though it has a number of different organs—Knox

A man's body is a unity, though it has many members — Nor

and all the members of that one body, being many, are one body:

and those parts, despite their multiplicity, constitute one single body — Phi

so also is Christ.

So it is with the body of Christ — Tay

13. For by one Spirit are we all baptized into one body,

For indeed we were all brought into one body by baptism, in the one Spirit — NEB

For through the baptism of the one Spirit we were all formed into one body — Bas

For in one Spirit we were all immersed into one body — ABUV

For in the communion of one Spirit we all were baptized into one body — Con

whether we be Jews or Gentiles, whether we be bond or free;

whether we are Jews or Greeks, whether slaves or free men — NEB

and have been all made to drink into one Spirit.

and we have all had experience of the same Spirit — Phi

and we have all been imbued with one Spirit — Ber

and that one Spirit was poured out for all of us to drink — Beck

and all have been given to drink at one Source, and the one Spirit — Nor

14. For the body is not one member but many.

For the body does not consist of one member but of many — RSV

A body is not one single organ, but many — NEB

The human body, I repeat, consists not of one part, but of many — TCNT

15. If the foot shall say, Because I am not the hand, I am not of the body;

I do not belong to the body — RSV

therefore I belong not to the body — Con

is it therefore not of the body?

that would not make it any less a part of the body — RSV

does it belong to the body any the less for that — Knox

16. And if the ear shall say, Because I am not the eye, I am not of the body; is it therefore not of the body?[10]

17. If the whole body were an eye, where were the hearing?

---

[10]Compare verse 15.

... where would the hearing come in
— Ber

... how could we hear — Wms

If the whole were hearing,

If the whole body were an ear — RSV

If the body were all ear — NEB

where were the smelling?

how could we smell — Wms

where would the sense of smell be —
TCNT

18. **But now hath God set the members every one of them in the body,**

But as it is, God arranged the organs in the body, each of them — RSV

But God has arranged all the parts in the one body — Phi

as it hath pleased him.

as he chose — RSV

as he wished them to be — Gspd

each one of them according to His own plan — Nor

19. **And if there were all one member,**

If all were a single organ — RSV

where were the body?

how could there be a body at all — Phi

there would not be a body at all — NEB

20. **But now are they many members,**

in fact, however, there are many different organs — NEB

yet but one body.

21. **And the eye cannot say unto the hand, I have no need of thee: nor again the head to the feet, I have no need of you.**

22. **Nay, much more those members of the body,**

On the contrary, the parts of the body — RSV

Quite the contrary: those organs of the body — NEB

which seem to be more feeble, are necessary:

which seem to be weaker are indispensable — RSV

that are considered most delicate are indispensable — Gspd

23. **And those members of the body, which we think to be less honourable,**

... considered ignoble — Ber

... we think common — Gspd

And those organs of the body which we regard almost devoid of honor — Nor

upon these we bestow more abundant honor;

are the very parts we invest with special honour — Mof

we dress with special honor — Beck

we surround with special honour — TCNT

and our uncomely parts have more abundant comeliness.

Our poor-looking members, too, receive extra adornment — Ber

and the less beautiful parts are adorned with greater beauty — Con

The parts which do not look beautiful have a deeper beauty in the work they do — Phi

24. **For our comely parts have no need:**

such as our good-looking members do not require — Ber

whereas the beautiful need no adornment — Con

but God hath tempered the body together,

But God has combined the various parts of the body — NEB

God has established a harmony in the body — Knox

and so God has built up the body harmoniously — Nor

having given more abundant honour to that part which lacked:

giving great honor to its apparently inferior parts — Wms

giving special honor to that which needed it most — Knox

giving special honour to the humbler parts — NEB

by giving importance of function to the parts which lack apparent importance — Phi

25. **That there should be no schism in the body;**

... no clash ... — Gspd

that there might be no division in the body — ABUV

that there may be no discord in the body — RSV

that the body should work together as a whole — Phi

but that the members should have the same care one for another.

... have a common concern for one another — Mof

all the different parts were to make each other's welfare their common care — Knox

but that all the members might enter-

tain the same anxiety for one another — Wey

26. And whether one member suffer, all the members suffer with it;
If one member suffers, all suffer to-
gether — RSV
Then, if one of the parts suffers pain,
all the other parts feel that pain —
Nor

or one member be honoured, all the members rejoice with it.
all rejoice together — RSV
all the others are happy with it — Beck
all the other parts find some joy in it —
Nor

27. Now ye are the body of Christ,
Together you are the Body of Christ
— TCNT

and members in particular.
and individually members of it — RSV
and members with assigned parts — Ber
and each . . . is a separate and necessary part — Tay
and everyone has his place in it—Beck

28. And God hath set some in the church,
That is, God has set people within the
church — Mof
And God hath indeed set certain in the
assembly — Rhm
Within our community God has appointed — NEB
God has given us different positions in
the church — Knox

first apostles,
first some to be his messengers — Phi

secondarily prophets,
. . . some to be preachers of power —
Phi
. . . inspired preachers — Gspd

thirdly teachers,

after that miracles,
then miracle-workers — NEB
then he has given supernatural powers
— TCNT

then gifts of healings,
then healers — RSV
then those with ability to heal the sick
— Amp

helps,
helpers — RSV
assistants — Ber
those who help others — Tay

governments,
administrators — RSV
organizers — Phi
power to guide them — NEB

wise guides — Bas
Those who can get others to work together — Tay
managers — Beck

diversities of tongues.
the gift of ecstatic utterance of various
kinds — NEB
various languages — Ber
Those who speak in languages they
have never learned — Tay
ecstatic speakers — Wms
those who can talk strange languages
— Beck

29. Are all apostles?
All are not apostles, are they — NASB
Not all are apostles, are they — Wms

are all prophets?
. . . preachers — Phi
Not all are prophets, are they — Wms
All are not prophets, are they — NASB

are all teachers? are all workers of miracles?
. . . can every one have supernatural
powers — TCNT
. . . miracle workers — Ber
Not all are teachers, are they? Not all
are wonder-workers, are they —
Wms
All are not teachers, are they? All are
not workers of miracles, are they —
NASB

30. Have all the gifts of healing?
Not all are people with power to cure
the sick, are they — Wms
All do not have the gifts of healings,
do they — NASB

do all speak with tongues?
Not all are ecstatic speakers, are they
— Wms
All do not speak with tongues, do they
— NASB
Can all talk strange languages — Beck
or speak foreign languages — Nor

do all interpret?
Not all can explain ecstatic speaking,
can they — Wms
All do not interpret, do they — NASB
Do all translate — Rhm

31. But covet earnestly the best gifts:
. . . the greatest gifts — Alf
aim hard for the choicest graces —
Ber
You should set your hearts on the best
spiritual gifts — Phi

and yet shew I unto you a more ex-cellent way.

... something else that is better than any of them — Tay

Yet I can still show you a way beyond all comparison the best — TCNT

And yet I will go on to show you a still higher path — Mof

but I shall show you a way which surpasses them all — Phi

CHAPTER 13

1. Though I speak with the tongues of men and of angels,

Even though I speak in every human and angelic language — Ber

If I can speak the languages of men and even of angels — Gspd

and have not charity,

but have not love — RSV

and have not love in my heart — Lam

I am become as sounding brass, or a tinkling cymbal.

I am only a noisy gong or a clashing cymbal — Gspd

... or a clanging cymbal — Mof

I am no better than echoing bronze, or the clash of cymbals — Knox

2. And though I have the gift of prophecy,

Even if I speak God's Word — Beck

Even though I have the gift of preaching — TCNT

I may have the powers of prophecy — Knox

and understand all mysteries, and all knowledge;

and know all sacred secrets ... — Rhm

and know every kind of hidden truth and have every kind of knowledge — Beck

And know all secret truths, and knowledge in its every form — Wms

no secret hidden from me, no knowledge too deep for me — Knox

and though I have all faith, so that I could remove mountains,

I may have such absolute faith that I can move hills from their place — Mof

and if I had perfect faith so I could remove mountains — Nor

and have not charity,

... love — RSV

I am nothing.

I am useless — Ber

I would still be worth nothing — Tay Tay

3. And though I bestow all my goods to feed the poor,

I may distribute all I possess in charity — Mof

If I should dole out everything I have for charity — Wms

Even if I give away all that I have to feed the hungry — Beck

and though I give my body to be burned,

... to be burnt at the stake — Knox

if I were burned alive for preaching the Gospel — Tay

and have not charity,

but have not love — RSV

it profiteth me nothing.

It goes for nothing — Knox

It avails me nothing — Mon

I am not in the least benefited — Ber

4. Charity suffereth long, and is kind;

Love is very patient, very kind — Mof

... Is gracious — Rhm

This love of which I speak is slow to lose patience — it looks for a way of being constructive — Phi

charity envieth not; charity vaunteth not itself,

Love never boils with jealousy ... — Wms

... it is neither anxious to impress — Phi

Love knows no jealousy, love makes no parade — Mof

Love is never envious, never boastful — TCNT

is not puffed up,

it is not arrogant — RSV

nor conceited — NEB

It does not put on airs — Gspd

nor does it cherish inflated ideas of its own importance — Phi

5. Doth not behave itself unseemly,

is never rude — Mof

or unmannerly — Ber

It isn't indecent — Beck

seeketh not her own,

never selfish — Mof

Love does not insist on its own way — RSV

It does not insist on its rights — Gspd

Love is never self-seeking — TCNT

does not pursue selfish aims — Nor
is not easily provoked, thinketh no evil;
... Love bears no malice — Mon
never provoked, never reckons up her wrongs — TCNT
not quick to take offence. Love keeps no score of wrongs — NEB
it is not irritable or resentful — RSV
It is not touchy. It does not keep account of evil — Phi

6. Rejoiceth not in iniquity,
rejoiceth not in unrighteousness — ASV
takes no pleasure in wrongdoing — Bas
does not gloat over other men's sins — NEB
love is never glad when others go wrong — Mof
but rejoiceth in the truth;
but rejoices at the victory of truth — Knox
but joyfully sides with the truth — Wey
But always glad when truth prevails — Wms
but delights in the truth — NEB

7. Beareth all things, believeth all things,
She can overlook faults ... — Wey
... has unquenchable faith — Ber
always slow to expose, always eager to believe the best — Mof
It bears up under anything. It exercises faith in everything — Wms
There is nothing love cannot face; there is no limit to its faith — NEB
Love knows no limit to its endurance, no end to its trust — Phi
hopeth all things,
always hopeful — Mof
hopes under all circumstances — Ber
It keeps up hope in everything — Wms
endureth all things.
ever patient — TCNT
endures without limit — Ber
It gives us power to endure everything — Wms

8. Charity never faileth:
Love will never come to an end — NEB
Love never disappears — Mof
Love shall never pass away — Con
but whether there be prophecies, they shall fail;
... they shall be done away — ASV
... it will be superseded — Mof
The time will come when we outgrow prophecy — Knox

But, whether it be the gift of preaching, it will be done with — TCNT
whether there be tongues, they shall cease;
If now exist ecstatic speakings, they will cease — Wms
Or strange languages, they will stop — Beck
whether there be knowledge, it shall vanish away.
... it will soon be set aside — Wms
as for knowledge, it will be superseded — Mof
knowledge will be swept away — Knox
Whether gaining of knowledge It shall be done away — Rhm

9. For we know in part,
For our knowledge is fragmentary — Ber
Our knowledge, our prophecy, are only glimpses of the truth — Knox
we only know bit by bit — Mof
We learn only a part of anything — Beck
and we prophesy in part.
and the prophet's word gives only a part of what is true — Bas
and what we prophesy is incomplete — Wms
and our preaching is incomplete — TCNT

10. But when that which is perfect is come,
But as soon as that which is complete is come — Rhm
when the time of fulfillment comes — Knox
when wholeness comes — NEB
then that which is in part shall be done away.
then the fragmentary becomes antiquated — Ber
the imperfect will be superseded — Mof
that is the end of the incomplete — Phi
then the need for these inadequate special gifts will come to an end — Tay

11. When I was a child, I spake as a child,
... I used to speak as a child — Rhm
I understood as a child, I thought as a child:
to prefer as a child, To reason as a child — Rhm
I felt as a child ... — ASV
I entertained child interests — Ber
think like a child, plan like a child — Beck

but when I became a man, I put away childish things.

but on becoming a man I was through with childish ways — Ber

... I gave up childish ways — RSV

... I have outgrown childish ways — Knox

When I grew up, I had finished with childish things — NEB

12. **For now we see through a glass, darkly;**

For now we see in a mirror, and are baffled — Mon

At present we seem to see only blurred reflections in a mirror — Nor

As yet we see, in a mirror, dimly — TCNT

We can see and understand only a little about God now, as if we were peering at His reflection in a poor mirror — Tay

At present we only see the baffling reflections in a mirror — Mof

but then face to face:

but then — face to face! — TCNT

but someday we are going to see Him in His completeness, face to face — Tay

now I know in part; but then shall I know even as also I am known.

at present I am learning bit by bit ... — Mof

now I know in fragments ... — Mon

As yet my knowledge is incomplete, but then I shall know in full, as I have been fully known — TCNT

... but then shall I know fully even as also I was fully known — ASV

... I shall recognize God as he recognizes me — Knox

... just as clearly as God sees into my heart right now — Tay

... we shall understand as completely as we are understood — Ber

At present all I know is a little fraction of the truth, but the time will come when I shall know it as fully as God now knows me! — Phi

13. **And now abideth faith, hope, charity, these three;**

... these are the great three — Gspd

There are three things — faith, hope, love — that keep on forever — Tay

In a word, there are three things that last for ever: faith, hope, and love — NEB

but the greatest of these is charity.

but the most important of these is love — Beck

CHAPTER 14

1. **Follow after charity,**

Keep on pursuing love — Wms

Make love your aim — Mof

Hotly pursue this love — Mon

Make love your great quest — Ber

Seek this Love earnestly — TCNT

and desire spiritual gifts,

while you set your heart on the gifts of the Spirit — Phi

but still keep cultivating your spiritual gifts — Wms

Make ... spiritual gifts your aspiration — Knox

but rather that ye may prophesy.

The highest gift you can wish for is to be able to speak the messages of God — Phi

and above all prophecy — NEB

and especially inspired preaching — Gspd

and especially to speak God's Word — Beck

above all the gift of preaching — TCNT

2. **For he that speaketh in an unknown tongue speaketh not unto men,**

When a man is using the language of ecstacy he is talking ... not with men — NEB

When a man talks a strange language, he doesn't talk to people — Beck

but unto God: for no man understandeth him;

... no one catches the meaning — Ber

howbeit in the spirit he speaketh mysteries.

yet in spirit he is speaking of hidden truths — TCNT

Although in spirit he is speaking sacred secrets — Rhm

he is no doubt inspired, but he speaks mysteries — NEB

3. **But he that prophesieth**

On the other hand, when a man prophesies — NEB

But the inspired preacher — Gspd

But he who preaches — TCNT

speaketh unto men to edification,

is speaking to his fellow men words that will build up faith — TCNT

he is talking to men, and his words have power to build — NEB

does his fellow-men good — Gspd

gives people a constructive . . . message — Ber

is helping others grow in the Lord — Tay

and exhortation, and comfort.

and encouragement and consolation — RSV

they stimulate and they encourage — NEB

to encourage and comfort them—Beck

4. **He that speaketh in an unknown tongue edifieth himself;**

. . . may strengthen his own faith — Knox

When you talk a strange language, you encourage yourself — Beck

Anyone who speaks ecstatically does himself good — Gspd

but he that prophesieth edifieth the church.

. . . Buildeth up an assembly — Rhm

while he who preaches builds up the faith of the Church — TCNT

But when you speak God's Word, you help the church grow — Beck

but it is prophecy that builds up a Christian community — NEB

5. **I would that ye all spake with tongues, but rather that ye prophesied:**

. . . rather that you all preached the word of God — Phi

I want you all to talk strange languages, but I would rather have you speak God's Word — Beck

I would like for all of you to speak in ecstasy, but I would rather that you prophesy — Wms

for greater is he that prophesieth than he that speaketh with tongues,

The man who speaks with real prophetic insight renders greater service . . . — Wms

. . . is more useful . . . — Gspd

It is more important to speak God's Word than strange languages—Beck

A Preacher is of more account than he who speaks in tongues — TCNT

except he interpret, that the church may receive edifying.

Unless indeed he translate That the assembly may receive upbuilding — Rhm

unless he interprets what he says so that the faith of the congregation may be strengthened — Nor

unless indeed he can explain its meaning, and so help to build up the community — NEB

6. **Now, brethren, if I come unto you speaking with tongues,**

For suppose I came to you, my brothers, speaking with tongues — Phi

what shall I profit you, except I shall speak to you either by revelation,

how can I help you unless I tell you what God has told me — Beck

what good shall I do you, unless what I say contains something by way of revelation — NEB

. . . unless my words convey some revelation — TCNT

how shall I benefit you unless I bring you some revelation — RSV

or by knowledge, or by prophesying, or by doctrine?

or enlightenment, . . . or instruction — NEB

or knowledge, or take the form of preaching or teaching — TCNT

some knowledge in spiritual things, some message from God, or some teaching about the Christian life — Phi

7. **And even things without life giving sound, whether pipe or harp,**

Even musical instruments . . . are examples of the need to speak plain English rather than in unknown languages — Tay

Even in the case of inanimate objects which are capable of making sound, such as a flute or harp — Phi

except they give a distinction in the sounds,

unless each note is sounded clearly — Tay

unless the notes are quite distinct — TCNT

how shall it be known what is piped or harped?

no one will recognize the tune — Tay

how can we recognize what melody flute or harp is playing — Knox

how can we understand their music —
Con

8. For if the trumpet give an uncertain sound,

if the bugle does not sound a call distinct and clear — Wms

Unless the bugle note is clear — Phi

And if the bugle gives an indistinct sound — RSV

who shall prepare himself to the battle?

how shall the soldier prepare himself for battle — Con

who will be called to arms — Phi

9. So likewise ye, except ye utter by the tongue words easy to be understood,

. . . if you . . . say words that have no sense — Bas

In the same way, if you don't talk with a clear meaning — Beck

Therefore, in speaking, you too must use a language that men can understand — Nor

So with yourselves; if you in a tongue utter speech that is not intelligible — RSV

how shall it be known what is spoken? for ye shall speak into the air.

You will be talking to the winds—Wey

you will be pouring words into the empty air! — Mof

10. There are, it may be, so many kinds of voices in the world,

How many different kinds of sound there are, or may be, in the world! — NEB

and none of them is without signification.

Nothing is altogether soundless — NEB

and not one of them fails to convey meaning — TCNT

And not one unspoken — Rhm

11. Therefore if I know not the meaning of the voice,

Well then, if I do not know the meaning of the sound the speaker makes — NEB

but if I do not know the meaning of the language — RSV

If, then, I do not catch the significance of an expression — Ber

But if I do not understand the meaning of a language — Nor

I shall be unto him that speaketh a barbarian,

I shall appear to the speaker to be talking gibberish — Mof

I shall be a foreigner to those who speak it — TCNT

I shall be a foreigner to the speaker — RSV

and he that speaketh shall be a barbarian unto me.

his words will be gibberish to me — NEB

and to my mind he will be talking gibberish himself — Mof

and the speaker a foreigner to me — RSV

12. Even so ye, forasmuch as ye are zealous of spiritual gifts,

So with yourselves; since you are eager for manifestations of the Spirit — RSV

You are, I know, eager for gifts of the Spirit — NEB

Since you have set your hearts on spiritual gifts — Knox

So since you are ambitious for spiritual endowments — Gspd

seek that ye may excel to the edifying of the church.

be eager to excel in such as will build up the faith of the Church — TCNT

strive that your abundant possession of them may build up the church — Con

ask for them in abundant measure, but only so as to strengthen the faith of the church — Knox

13. Wherefore let him that speaketh in an unknown tongue pray that he may interpret.

Therefore, the man who speaks in ecstasy must pray . . . — Wms

. . . that he may be able to interpret what he utters — Con

. . . should pray for the power to interpret his message — Nor

If then you talk a strange language, pray to be able to explain it — Beck

14. For if I pray in an unknown tongue,

If I pray in a strange language — Beck

If, when praying, I use the gift of tongues — TCNT

my spirit prayeth,

my spirit indeed prays — TCNT

but my understanding is unfruitful.

but my mind is helping nobody—Gspd

but I don't know what I am saying — Tay

but my mind is a blank — TCNT

15. What is it then?
What then follows — Wey
What then is my conclusion — TCNT
I will pray with the spirit, and I will pray with the understanding also:
. . . I will pray with my mind in action too — Wms
. . . and also in ordinary language everybody understands — Tay
. . . but also pray so as to be understood — Beck
I will sing with the spirit, and I will sing with the understanding also.
. . . also in ordinary language, so I can understand the praise I am giving — Tay
. . . ecstatically . . . intelligently . . . — Gspd

16. Else when thou shalt bless with the spirit,
how shall he that occupieth the room of the unlearned say Amen at thy giving of thanks,
. . . an ordinary person who is there . . . — Beck
. . . the man in the congregation who is without your gift . . . — TCNT
He that filleth up the place of the ungifted person How shall he say the Amen . . . — Rhm
how can those who are ungifted say amen to your thanksgiving — Phi
seeing he understandeth not what thou sayest?
since they do not know what you are talking about — Phi
when he does not know what you mean — Wey

17. For thou verily givest thanks well,
To be sure, you are giving thanks well enough — Ber
You are, indeed, doing right to give thanks — Wms
It is well enough for you to give thanks that way — Nor
but the other is not edified.
the other's faith is not strengthened — Knox
but your neighbor is not built up — Wms
but your fellow man is not enlightened — Lam

18. I thank my God,
I speak with tongues more than ye all:
I talk in strange languages more than any of you — Beck
I offer thanksgiving to God in private, speaking in Tongues . . . more than any of you — Con
that I have a greater gift of tongues than any of you — Phi
I speak in ecstasy more than any of you — Gspd

19. Yet in the church I had rather speak five words with my understanding,
. . . in the assembly . . . — Alf
. . . I would rather say five words that can be understood — Beck
But in the public congregation I would rather speak five words with my mind in action — Wms
but in the congregation I would rather speak five intelligible words — NEB
that by my voice I might teach others also,
in order to instruct the people too — Wms
than ten thousand words in an unknown tongue.
than ten thousand words in a tongue which nobody understands — Phi
than ten thousand words in a language nobody understands — Beck
than ten thousand words in ecstasy — — Wms

20. Brethren, be not children in understanding:
. . . in mind — ASV
Brothers, stop being children in intelligence — Wms
Do not be content to think childish thoughts — Knox
howbeit in malice be ye children,
be babes in evil — RSV
but as to evil, keep on being babies — Wms
Keep the innocence of children — Knox
but in understanding be men.
but at least be grown-up in your thinking — NEB
but mentally be mature — Gspd
but in your understanding be full grown — ABUV
but in understanding show yourselves men — TCNT

21. In the law it is written,
With men of other tongues and other lips will I speak unto this people;
In strange languages and by the mouth of foreigners I will speak to these people — Beck

**and yet for all that will they not hear
me, saith the Lord.**

and even then they will not listen to
me, says the Lord — RSV

and even so they will not heed me, says
the Lord — NEB

**22. Wherefore tongues are for a sign, not
to them that believe,**

that means that tongues are a sign of
God's power . . . — Phi

. . . ecstatic speaking . . . — Gspd

. . . not to them who have faith — Bas

. . . not a help to God's children — Tay

Then strange languages are not meant
to warn believers — Beck

but to them that believe not:

but to the unbelieving — ASV

but to interest the unsaved — Tay

**but prophesying serveth not for them
that believe not,**

. . . inspired preaching . . . — Gspd

while God's Word isn't meant for unbelievers — Beck

while the gift of preaching is intended
as a sign, not for those who do not
believe in Christ — TCNT

but for them which believe.

**23. If therefore the whole church be come
together into one place,**

So if the whole congregation is assembled — NEB

suppose at a meeting of the whole
church — Ber

If then the whole assembly come together with one consent — Rhm

**and all speak with tongues, and there
come in those that are unlearned,
or unbelievers,**

and all are using the strange tongues of
ecstasy . . . — NEB

. . . and outsiders or unbelievers enter
— RSV

. . . and men come in who are both un-
instructed and without faith — Phi

. . . and some men who are without the
gift, or who are unbelievers, come in
— TCNT

. . . and ungifted men or unbelievers
enter — NASB

and all talk strange languages and then
some ordinary people or unbelievers
come in — Beck

will they not say that ye are mad?

. . . demented — Ber

. . . raving — Rhm

. . . fanatical — Lam

won't they say you're crazy — Beck

24. But if all prophesy,

if they are all inspired to preach —
Gspd

But suppose they all gave testimony —
Ber

But if all speak God's Word — Beck

**and there come in one that believeth
not, or one unlearned,[11]**

**he is convinced of all, he is judged of
all:**

all these sermons will convince him
of the fact that he is a sinner, and
his conscience will be pricked by
everything he hears — Tay

he is convicted in his conscience by
every speaker, he feels himself
judged by all — Con

he is convinced of his sin by them all,
he is called to account by them all
— Gspd

**25. And thus are the secrets of his heart
made manifest;**

the secrets of his heart are disclosed —
RSV

and the secrets of his heart are laid
bare — NEB

all that is kept hidden in his heart will
be revealed — Knox

the secret depths of his heart are laid
open — Con

**and so falling down on his face he will
worship God,**

**and report that God is in you of a
truth.**

declaring that God is among you indeed — ASV

publicly confessing that God is indeed
among you — Knox

26. How is it then, brethren?

Then what is our conclusion . . . —
Wms

Then what is the right course, brothers
— Gspd

To sum up, my friends — NEB

**when ye come together, every one of
you hath**

whenever you meet let everyone be
ready to contribute — Phi

Whenever you meet together, each con-
tributes something — Mon

Whenever you assemble, there is not
one of you who is not ready either
with — Wey

---

[11]Compare verse 23.

a psalm,

a hymn — RSV

with a song of praise — Wey

hath a doctrine,

. . . a lesson — RSV

. . . a piece of teaching — Phi

. . . a sermon — Wey

hath a tongue,

. . . a strange language — Beck

. . . an ecstatic utterance — NEB

hath a revelation,

. . . a spiritual truth — Phi

others will . . . tell some special information God has given him — Tay

hath an interpretation.

or an explanation — Beck

hath a translation — Rhm

Let all things be done unto edifying.

. . . for the common good — Bas

Let all things be done to upbuilding — ABUV

Everything should be done to make your church strong in the faith — Phi

everything . . . must be useful to all, and build them up in the Lord — Tay

everything shall be constructive — Ber

27. **If any man speak in an unknown tongue,**

If you talk a strange language — Beck

If anybody speaks in ecstasy — Wms

let it be by two, or at the most by three, and that by course;

let it be limited to two or three people at the most, and have one speak at a time — Gspd

there must be only two, or three at most, and let one speak at a time — Wms

and let one interpret.

and let the same interpreter explain the words of all — Con

and someone explain what he says — Gspd

and let someone give the sense — Bas

28. **But if there be no interpreter,**

But if no one is present who understands what they are saying — Tay

But if there be none to translate — Rhm

let him keep silence in the church;

they must not speak out loud — Tay

and let him speak to himself, and to God.

they may talk silently to themselves and to God — Tay

29. **Let the prophets speak two or three,**

Don't have more than two or three preachers either — Phi

Two or three should speak God's Word — Beck

The number of prophets to speak should be limited to two or three — Nor

and let the other judge.

while the others think over what has been said — Phi

while the rest weigh what is said — Gspd

let the others be judges of what they say — Bas

30. **If any thing be revealed to another that sitteth by,**

But should a message of truth come to one who is seated — Phi

But if a revelation be made to another sitting by — ASV

But if, while someone is prophesying, someone else receives a message or idea from the Lord he must not interrupt — Tay

let the first hold his peace.

then the original speaker should stop talking — Phi

for one person should stop before another begins to speak — Tay

31. **For ye may all prophesy one by one,**

For in this way you can all preach to one another, as you are inspired — Gspd

For it is possible for all to give testimony, each in his turn — Ber

You can all speak God's Word one after another — Beck

that all may learn,

so that the whole congregation may receive instruction — NEB

and all may be comforted.

and everyone will have his faith stimulated — Phi

and all may receive encouragement — Ber

and all may be stimulated — Nor

32. **And the spirits of the prophets are subject to the prophets.**

The spirit of a true preacher is under that preacher's control — Phi

Remember that a person who has a message from God has the power to stop himself and wait his turn — Tay

777

and the gift of prophecy does not take from the prophets the control of their own spirits — Con

33. For God is not the author of confusion, but of peace,

for the God who inspired them is not a God of disorder . . . — NEB

For God is a God not of disorder but of harmony — Mof

as in all churches of the saints.

such is the teaching I give in all the churches of the saints — Knox

This custom prevails in the Churches of Christ's People — TCNT

As in all congregations of God's people — NEB

As in all the assemblies of the saints — Rhm

As in all the churches of the holy people — Beck

34. Let your women keep silence in the churches:

women should not address the meeting — NEB

. . . during the church meeting — Tay

At the meetings of the Church married women should remain silent — TCNT

for it is not permitted unto them to speak;

but they are commanded to be under obedience, as also saith the law.

they must . . . take a secondary place . . . — Ber

but should keep their place as the law directs — NEB

but let them be in subjection, as also saith the law — ASV

35. If they will learn any thing,

If there is something they want to know — NEB

if they have a desire for knowledge about anything — Bas

let them ask their husbands at home: for it is a shame for women to speak in the church.

It is a shocking thing that a woman should address the congregation — NEB

for it is wrong for women to express their opinions in church meetings — Tay

for it is unbecoming for a married woman to speak at a meeting of the church — TCNT

For, it is considered a disgrace for women to speak in the church — Nor

36. What? came the word of God out from you?

What! did God's Message to the world originate with you — TCNT

You challenge this rule? Pray, did God's word start from you — Mof

Do I see you questioning my instructions? Are you beginning to imagine that the word of God originated in your church — Phi

or came it unto you only?

or that you have a monopoly of God's truth — Phi

Are you the only people it has reached — Mof

37. If any man think himself to be a prophet, or spiritual,

. . . claims to be inspired to preach, or have any other spiritual endowment — Gspd

. . . claims to have the prophetic spirit, or any other spiritual gift — Wms

If anyone thinks he speaks for God or has the Spirit — Beck

If anyone claims to be inspired or a prophet — NEB

let him acknowledge that the things that I write unto you

let him prove it by recognizing that this message of mine to you — Knox

are the commandments of the Lord.

has the Lord's authority — NEB

is the Lord's injunction — Ber

38. But if any man be ignorant,

If any one does not recognize this — RSV

But if any man refuse this acknowledgement — Con

If anyone pays no attention to it — Gspd

let him be ignorant.

he himself should not be recognized — NEB

let him refuse it at his peril — Con

pay no attention to him — Gspd

well, we will leave him in his ignorance — Tay

39. Wherefore, brethren, covet to prophesy,

. . . cultivate the gift of prophetic speaking — Wms

. . . set your hearts on being inspired to preach — Gspd

So, my fellow Christians, be eager to speak God's Word — Beck

In conclusion then, my brothers, set your heart on preaching the word of God — Phi

and forbid not to speak with tongues.

while not forbidding the use of tongues — Phi

and don't try to keep anyone from talking strange languages — Beck

but stop preventing others from speaking in ecstasy — Wms.

40. Let all things be done decently and in order.

. . . with propriety and in orderly fashion — Ber

. . . suitably and with right order — Knox

Everything must always be done in a proper and orderly way — Wms

CHAPTER 15

1. Moreover, brethren, I declare unto you the gospel which I preached unto you,

Now let me remind you, brothers, of the essence of the good news which I proclaimed to you — Wms

Now I want to remind you, brothers, of the form in which I presented to you the good news I brought — Gspd

Now I would remind you, brethren, in what terms I preached to you the gospel — RSV

which also ye have received, and wherein ye stand;

in which you are at present standing — Phi

on which your faith is based — Bas

your faith is squarely built upon this wonderful message — Tay

on which you have taken your stand — Mon

2. By which also ye are saved,

. . . are being saved — Alf

. . . your salvation is being worked out — Phi

and which is now bringing you salvation — NEB

and through which you are to be saved — Wms

if ye keep in memory what I preached unto you,

I would remind you of the very words that I used in telling it to you, since you are still holding fast to it — TCNT

if ye hold fast the word which I preached unto you — ASV

if you cling to the words I used in telling it to you — Beck

provided you adhere to my statement of it — Mof

unless ye have believed in vain.

unless, of course, your faith had no meaning behind it at all — Phi

unless of course you never really believed it in the first place — Tay

unless your faith at first was spurious — Wms

and since it was not in vain that you became believers in Christ — TCNT

3. For I delivered unto you first of all that which I also received,

. . . as of first importance . . . — RSV

First and foremost, I handed on to you the facts which had been imparted to me — NEB

For I passed on to you, among the primary principles of the good news, what I had received — Wms

I transmitted to you before all else what had also been transmitted to me — Wey

how that Christ died for our sins according to the scriptures;

. . . as the Scriptures foretold — Gspd

. . . as it says in the Writings — Bas

4. And that he was buried, and that he rose again the third day according to the scriptures:

. . . (as the Scriptures had foretold) — TCNT

. . . as the Bible said he would — Beck

he came back from the dead as it says in the Writings — Bas

5. And that he was seen of Cephas,

And that he appeared to Cephas — ASV

then of the twelve:

. . . by the eleven apostles — Knox

by the rest of The Twelve — Tay

6. After that, he was seen of above five hundred brethren at once;

. . . simultaneously — Ber

of whom the greater part remain unto this present,

the majority of whom survive to this day — Mof

of whom the greater part are living at this present time — Con

but some are fallen asleep.

though some have died — Mof

though some have gone to their rest — Knox

7. After that, he was seen of James;

Then he appeared to James — RSV

then of all the apostles.

8. And last of all he was seen of me also,

In the end he appeared even to me — NEB

as of one born out of due time.

by this so-called abortion of an apostle — Mof

as though I had been born almost too late for this — Tay

who am, as it were, the abortion — TCNT

9. For I am the least of the apostles,

. . . least important . . . — Gspd

. . . least worthy . . . — Tay

For I belong to the lowest rank of the apostles — Wms

For I am the meanest of the Apostles — TCNT

that am not meet to be called an apostle,

not deserving the name of apostle — Ber

and am not fit to bear the title apostle — Wms

I who am unworthy of the name of Apostle — TCNT

because I persecuted the church of God.

. . . I once persecuted . . . — Wms

Because I persecuted the assembly of God — Rhm

because of my cruel attacks on the church of God — Bas

10. But by the grace of God I am what I am:

But whatever I am now it is all because God poured out such kindness and grace upon me — Tay

But by God's unmerited favor I have become what I am — Wms

God's love made me what I am — Beck

and his grace which was bestowed upon me was not in vain;

. . . has not been without fruit — Knox

. . . was not ineffective — Ber

. . . not without results — Tay

and His unmerited favor shown to me

was not bestowed for nothing — Wms

but I laboured more abundantly than they all:

. . . toiled more extensively . . . — Wms

I have worked harder than any of them — Gspd

For I did more work than all of them — Bas

I have actually done more work than all of the others — Nor

on the contrary, in my labours I have outdone them all — NEB

yet not I, but the grace of God which was with me.

. . . but God's unmerited favor working with me — Wms

. . . that is joined with me — Ber

yet actually I wasn't doing it, but God worked through me, helping and blessing me — Tay

11. Therefore whether it were I or they,

So then, whether preached by me, or them — Con

It makes no difference who worked the hardest, I or they — Tay

At any rate, whether I or they have done most — Mof

so we preach, and so ye believed.

this has been the message and this has been the foundation of your faith — Phi

the important thing is that we preached the Gospel to you, and you believed it — Tay

this is the way we preach and the way that you came to believe — Wey

12. Now if Christ be preached that he rose from the dead,

If you believe what we preach, that Christ rose from the dead — Tay

how say some among you that there is no resurrection of the dead?

how can certain individuals among us . . . — Mof

. . . no resurrection of dead men — ABUV

. . . that there is no such thing as a resurrection of the dead — Gspd

how can some of you deny that there is any resurrection — Phi

13. But if there be no resurrection of the dead,

If there is no such thing as a resurrection of the dead — Wey

then is Christ not risen:

then Christ must still be dead — Tay

14. And if Christ be not risen,
And if He is still dead — Tay
then is our preaching vain,
. . . useless — Tay
. . . groundless — Knox
then our proclamation is without meaning — TCNT
there is nothing in our message — Gspd
and your faith is also vain.
. . . gone for nothing — Mof
. . . groundless — Knox
and our faith without meaning — TCNT
there is nothing in our faith either —
— Gspd

15. Yea, and we are found false witnesses of God;
More than that, we are detected in bearing false witness against God — Mon
Moreover, we are found guilty of false witness against God — Con
we are found guilty of misrepresenting God — Gspd
we apostles are all liars — Tay
because we have testified of God that he raised up Christ:
because we testified against God . . . — Beck
because we testified in respect to God . . . — ABUV
whom he raised not up, if so be that the dead rise not.
and that is utterly false if it should be true that the dead do not, in fact, rise again! — Phi

16. For if the dead rise not,
then is not Christ raised:
then Christ is still dead — Tay

17. And if Christ be not raised,
your faith is vain;
your faith is futile — RSV
your faith is a mere delusion — Wms
your faith is folly — TCNT
your faith is worthless — NASB
ye are yet in your sins.
and you are still in your old state of sin — NEB
you are still under the control of your sins — Gspd
you are back in your sins — Knox
and your sins have never been forgiven — Phi

18. Then they also which are fallen asleep in Christ are perished.

. . . who have fallen asleep in trust in Christ have perished — Gspd
Yes, even those who have fallen asleep, though in union with Christ, have perished — Wms
Moreover those who have died believing in Christ are utterly dead and gone — Phi
And those who died trusting in Christ to save them are lost forever — Nor

19. If in this life only we have hope in Christ,
Truly, if our hope in Christ were limited to this life only — Phi
If the hope we have learned to repose in Christ belongs to this world only — Knox
And if our hopes in Christ applied only to this life, and not beyond — Nor
we are of all men most miserable.
we are of all men most pitiable — ASV
then we are unhappy beyond all other men — Knox

20. But now is Christ risen from the dead,
But the glorious fact is that Christ did rise from the dead — Phi
But the truth is, Christ was raised to life — NEB
and become the firstfruits of them that slept.
he has become the very first to rise of all who sleep the sleep of death — Phi
and has become the first of millions now dead who will come back to life again some day — Tay
the first in the harvest of those who are sleeping in their graves — Beck

21. For since by man came death,
Death came . . . because of what one man (Adam) did — Tay
For since it was through a man that death resulted — Wms
Just as death came into the world through a man — Nor
by man came also the resurrection of the dead.
and it is because of what this other man (Christ) has done that now there is resurrection from the dead — Tay
it was also through a man that the resurrection of the dead resulted — Wms
a man also brought resurrection of the dead — NEB

22. For as in Adam all die,

> For just as because of their relation to Adam all men die — Gspd
>
> For just as all men die by virtue of their descent from Adam — Wms
>
> For, as through union with Adam all men die — TCNT
>
> As members of a sinful race all men die — Phi

even so in Christ shall all be made alive.

> so because of their relation to Christ they will be brought to life again — Gspd
>
> so all such as are in union with Christ will be made alive again — Wms
>
> so through union with the Christ will all be made to live — TCNT
>
> as members of the Christ of God all men shall be raised to life — Phi

23. But every man in his own order:

> ... in his own rank — Knox
>
> ... in his own division — Mof
>
> Each, to be sure, in his turn — Ber

Christ the firstfruits;

> with Christ the very first — Phi

afterward they that are Christ's at his coming.

> then when Christ comes back, all His people will become alive again — Tay
>
> then, when He comes, those who belong to Christ — Beck

24. Then cometh the end,

> Then, and not till then, comes the end — Phi
>
> Full completion comes after that — Knox

when he shall have delivered up the kingdom to God, even the Father;

> when he hands over his royal power to God the Father — Mof
>
> when He is to surrender the Kingship to God the Father — Wey
>
> when Christ ... hands over the kingdom to God the Father — Phi

when he shall have put down all rule and all authority and power.

> after destroying ... — RSV
>
> after abolishing every kind of domination ... — NEB
>
> when he has abolished all other government and all authority and power — Wey
>
> after annulling every ruler and all government and power — Ber

> after he has put an end to every other government, authority and power — Beck

25. For he must reign,

> Christ's reign will and must continue — Phi
>
> He must be king — Ber
>
> since He must rule as King — Beck

till he hath put all enemies under his feet.

> until every enemy has been conquered — Phi
>
> until He has destroyed all His enemies — Tay
>
> until God has put all his enemies under his feet — TCNT

26. The last enemy that shall be destroyed is death.

> and the last enemy to be abolished is death — NEB
>
> Death is the last enemy to be stopped — Wms
>
> As the last enemy, Death is done away with — ABUV

27. For he hath put all things under his feet.

> For God has put all things in subjection under his feet — RSV
>
> for everything is to be reduced to subjection and put under Christ's feet — Gspd
>
> For the rule and authority over all things has been given to Christ by His Father — Tay

But when he saith all things are put under him,

> but in that quotation, All things are put under him — Mon

it is manifest that he is excepted, which did put all things under him.

> it is quite obvious that God, who brings them all under subjection to Christ, is himself excepted — Phi
>
> except of course Christ does not rule over the Father Himself, Who gave Him this power — Tay
>
> it is self-evident that God who reduced everything to subjection, is not included — Nor

28. And when all things shall be subdued unto him,

> And when all things have been subjected unto him — ASV
>
> and when that subjection is complete — Knox

When Christ has finally won the battle
against all his enemies — Tay

then shall the Son also himself be subject unto him that put all things under him,

. . . He . . . will put Himself also under
His Father's orders — Tay

. . . shall subject Himself to the One
whom all obey — Ber

then shall the Son acknowledge himself
subject to God the Father, who gave
the Son power over all things — Phi

then the Son himself will also become
subject to God, who had given Him
power over everything — Nor

that God may be all in all.

. . . utterly supreme — Tay

. . . everything to everyone — Mof

so that God will remain all in all —
Nor

Thus, in the end, shall God be wholly
and absolutely God — Phi

29. Else what shall they do which are baptized for the dead,

Otherwise, what do people mean by
having themselves baptized on behalf
of the dead — Gspd

then what point is there in people baptizing themselves for those who are
gone — Tay

Else what will they do who are immersed for the dead — ABUV

Otherwise what will those do who are
baptized for the dead — Wey

if the dead rise not at all? why are they then baptized for the dead?

If the dead are not raised at all, why
are people baptized on their behalf
— RSV

30. And why stand we in jeopardy every hour?

And I too, why do I put my life to
hazard every hour — Con

Besides, why do we live dangerously
every moment — Ber

. . . face peril hour after hour — Knox

Why also do we apostles take such
risks every hour — Wey

31. I protest by your rejoicing which I have in Christ Jesus our Lord,

I swear it, Brothers, by the pride in you
that I feel through my union with
Christ Jesus, our Lord — TCNT

I affirm this, brethren, by my glorying
in you, as I justly do in Christ Jesus
our Lord — Wey

as surely as I ascribe my glorying in
you, brother, to Christ Jesus our
Lord — Ber

By the very pride I take in you,
brothers, through our union with
Christ Jesus — Gspd

I swear it by my pride in you, my
brothers — for in Christ Jesus our
Lord I am proud of you — NEB

I die daily.

I myself run the risk of dying every
single day — Wms

that death is daily at my side — Knox

Not a day but I am at death's door! —
Mof

that I face death every day of my life!
— Phi

32. If after the manner of men I have fought with beasts at Ephesus,

. . . wild beasts, those men of Ephesus
— Tay

If, as the saying is, I fought wild beasts
at Ephesus — NEB

And if, to use the popular expression,
I have fought with wild beasts here
in Ephesus — Phi

If like other men I have fought with
wild animals in Ephesus — Beck

If with only human hopes I had fought
in the arena at Ephesus — TCNT

what advantageth it me, if the dead rise not?

What do I gain . . .? If the dead are
not raised — RSV

what is the good of an ordeal like that
if there is no life after this one —
Phi

And what value is there . . . if it is only
for what I gain in this life down here
— Tay

let us eat and drink; for to morrow we die.

let us take our pleasure in feasting, for
tomorrow we come to an end — Bas

why not say, Let us eat and drink, for
tomorrow we die — Nor

33. Be not deceived:

Don't let yourselves be deceived —Phi

Don't be fooled by those who say such
things — Tay

Don't be misled by such reasonings —
Nor

Do not be tricked by false words —
Bas

evil communications corrupt good manners.

Bad company ruins good habits—Beck

Bad company ruins character — Gspd

Bad company ruins morals — RSV

Bad company is the ruin of a good character — NEB

34. Awake to righteousness, and sin not;

. . . and quit sinning — Ber

Awake to soberness righteously, and sin not — ASV

Sober up, as is right, and stop sinning — Wms

Come to your senses and stop sinning — Nor

for some have not the knowledge of God:

There are some who know nothing of God — NEB

for some of you are utterly ignorant about God — Gspd

for some of you . . . are without any true knowledge of God — Wms

For . . . some of you are not even Christians at all and have never really known God — Tay

I speak this to your shame.

You should be ashamed that I have to write like this at all! — Phi

I say it to shame you — ABUV

I say this to make you feel ashamed — Beck

35. But some man will say,

But perhaps someone will ask — Phi

How are the dead raised up?

How is the resurrection achieved—Phi

and with what body do they come?

and with what manner of body do they come — ASV

With what sort of body do the dead arrive — Phi

what kind of body will they be wearing when they appear — Knox

36. Thou fool, that which thou sowest is not quickened, except it die:

Simpleton! . . . — Ber

A senseless question! . . . — NEB

You foolish man! . . . — RSV

Now that is talking without using your minds! In your own experience you know that a seed does not germinate without itself dying — Phi

37. And that which thou sowest, thou sowest not that body that shall be,

. . . it has not the form it is going to have — Gspd

And when you sow the seed you are

not sowing the body that it will become — Mon

and when the green shoot comes up out of the seed, it is very different from the seed you first planted — Tay

but bare grain, it may chance of wheat, or some other grain:

but a bare kernel . . . — RSV

but is a naked grain, of wheat (it may be) or something else — Wms

38. But God giveth it a body as it hath pleased him,

and God clothes it with the body of his choice — NEB

But God gives it a body as he plans — Ber

it is for God to embody it according to his will — Knox

and to every seed his own body.

each kind of seed a body of its own — Mof

and to every seed the body of its own proper plant — Con

to each seed its special body — TCNT

39. All flesh is not the same flesh:

For not all flesh is alike — RSV

Then again, even in this world, all flesh is not identical — Phi

All forms of life are not the same — TCNT

but there is one kind of flesh of men, another flesh of beasts,

but there is one kind for men, another for animals — RSV

there is flesh of men, flesh of beasts — NEB

Human beings have one kind of flesh, animals have another — Beck

another of fishes, and another of birds.

40. There are also celestial bodies, and bodies terrestrial:

. . . heavenly bodies . . . earthly bodies — Gspd

bodies that belong to heaven and bodies that belong to earth — Knox

There are bodies which exist in this world, and bodies which exist in the heavens — Phi

but the glory of the celestial is one,

and the splendour of the heavenly bodies is one thing — NEB

but the beauty of heavenly bodies is of one kind — Gspd

and the glory of the terrestrial is another.

the splendour of the earthly, another — NEB

and the beauty of earthly bodies is of another kind — Gspd

41. There is one glory of the sun, and another glory of the moon,

The sun has a splendour of its own, the moon another splendour — NEB

The sun is glorious in one way and the moon in another way — Ber

and another glory of the stars:

for one star differeth from another star in glory.

. . . in brightness — NEB

. . . in beauty — Gspd

. . . in brilliancy — Ber

in fact, each star differs from every other star in its splendor — Nor

42. So also is the resurrection of the dead.

That is how it will be when the dead rise — Beck

It is sown in corruption;

. . . decomposition — Ber

. . . a perishable body — NASB

When the body is sown, it decays — Beck

it is raised in incorruption:

. . . an imperishable body — NASB

. . . free from decay — Gspd

when it rises, it can't decay — Beck

43. It is sown in dishonour; it is raised in glory:

. . . humiliation . . . splendor — Gspd

. . . shame . . . glory — Bas

The bodies we now have embarrass us for they become sick and die; but they will be full of glory when we come back to life again — Tay

sown disfigured, it rises beautiful — TCNT

it is sown in weakness; it is raised in power:

feeble when it is planted, it comes again in power — Bas

Yes, they are weak, dying bodies now, but when we live again they will be full of strength — Tay

44. It is sown a natural body;

. . . physical body — Gspd

The body sown is animal — Mon

. . . just human bodies — Tay

it is raised a spiritual body.

. . . superhuman — Tay

It is raised a body of the spirit — Rhm

There is a natural body, and there is a spiritual body.

As surely as there is a human body, there is also a spiritual body — TCNT

45. And so it is written, The first man Adam was made a living soul;

. . . became a human being — TCNT

. . . a living creature — Gspd

. . . Adam, the first man, was made a natural living being — Beck

the last Adam was made a quickening spirit.

The last Adam became a life-giving spirit — ASV

46. Howbeit that was not first which is spiritual,

Observe, the spiritual does not come first — NEB

It was not the principle of spiritual life that came first — Knox

but that which is natural;

but the physical — RSV

natural life came first — Knox

but the animal — Wey

and afterward that which is spiritual.

47. The first man is of the earth, earthy:

Man the first is from the earth, material — Mof

The first man was made of earthly clay — Con

The first man is made of the soil of the ground — Beck

the second man is the Lord[12] from heaven.

Man the second is from heaven — Mof

48. As is the earthy, such are they also that are earthy:

Those earth-minded are like the one from the earth — Ber

The nature of that earth-born man is shared by his earthly sons — Knox

The nature of the man made of dust is repeated in all men — all made of dust — Nor

and as is the heavenly, such are they also that are heavenly.

and the heavenly man is the pattern of all the heavenly — NEB

the nature of the heaven-born man, by his heavenly sons — Knox

and those heaven-minded are like the One from heaven — Ber

the nature of the Man from heaven is

---

[12]The words "the Lord" are now recognized as not adequately supported by original manuscripts.

repeated in those who are of heaven
— Nor

49. And as we have borne the image of the earthy,

and it remains for us, who once bore the stamp of earth — Knox

... the likeness of material man—Mof

... of the man of dust — RSV

So that just as we have been made like the material pattern — Phi

and as we have reflected the likeness of him who was made of dust — Wms

we shall also bear the image of the heavenly.

so shall we be made like the Heavenly pattern — Phi

so we shall wear the likeness of the heavenly man — NEB

to bear the stamp of heaven — Knox

so we shall some day have a body like Christ's — Tay

50. Now this I say, brethren,

I tell you this, brethren — RSV

What I mean, my brothers, is this — NEB

that flesh and blood cannot inherit the kingdom of God;

the Kingdom of God cannot be enjoyed by flesh and blood — Knox

it is utterly impossible for flesh and blood to possess the kingdom of God — Phi

an earthy body made of flesh and blood cannot get into God's kingdom — Tay

Our physical bodies cannot take part in the kingdom of God — Wms

neither doth corruption inherit incorruption.

nor does the perishable inherit the imperishable — RSV

and decay will not share in what is imperishable — Gspd

These perishable bodies of ours are not the right kind to live forever — Tay

what is decaying will never take part in what is immortal — Wms

51. Behold, I shew you a mystery;

Take notice: I am telling you a secret — Ber

Lo, I tell you a secret truth — Mon

Listen, I will tell you God's hidden purpose! — TCNT

Lo! a sacred secret unto you do I declare — Rhm

We shall not all sleep, but we shall all be changed.

not all of us are to die ... — Mof

... we shall all be given new bodies — Tay

... but we shall all be transformed — TCNT

52. In a moment, in the twinkling of an eye, at the last trump: for the trumpet shall sound,

and the dead shall be raised incorruptible,

... imperishable — RSV

... beyond the reach of corruption — Phi

... will rise immortal — NEB

... will suddenly become alive with new bodies that will never, never die — Tay

and we shall be changed.

and we who are still alive shall suddenly be utterly changed — Phi

we who are still alive shall suddenly have new bodies too — Tay

we, also, shall be transformed — TCNT

53. For this corruptible must put on incorruption,

This perishable being must be clothed with the imperishable — NEB

For this body which comes to destruction will be made free from the power of death — Bas

For this decaying part of us must put on the body that can never decay — Wms

For this perishable body of ours must put on an imperishable form—TCNT

and this mortal must put on immortality.

and this part capable of dying must put on the body that can never die — Wms

and this dying body a deathless form — TCNT

And this mortal clothe itself with immortality — Rhm

54. So when this corruptible shall have put on incorruption,[13] and this mortal shall have put on immortality,

then shall be brought to pass the saying that is written,

then will happen what is written — Beck

---

[13]Compare verse 53.

then will the words of Scripture come to pass — Mon

Death is swallowed up in victory.

Death has been triumphantly destroyed — Gspd

Death is overcome by life — Bas

55. O death, where is thy sting?

. . . Where is now your sting — Tay

For where now, O death, is your power to hurt us — Phi

O grave, where is thy victory?

O death . . . — ASV

. . . what then of your victory — Tay

Where now, O grave, is the victory you hoped to win — Phi

56. The sting of death is sin;

It is sin which gives death its sting — Phi

You can never hurt us again, for our sin, which gives you your power over us, will be gone — Tay

and the strength of sin is the law.

and it is the Law which gives sin its strength — Phi

the law, which reveals our sins, is no longer upon us — Tay

57. But thanks be to God,

But thank God! — Beck

But unto God be thanks — Rhm

which giveth us the victory through our Lord Jesus Christ.

The victory is ours . . . He makes it ours by our Lord Jesus Christ — Mof

58. Therefore, my beloved brethren, be ye stedfast, unmovable,

Since future victory is sure . . . — Tay

. . . continue to be firm, incapable of being moved — Wms

. . . be strong in purpose — Bas

. . . hold your ground . . . — Mof

Stand firm, then, my dear fellow Christians, and let nothing move you — Beck

always abounding in the work of the Lord,

as you busy yourselves . . . — Phi

always devote yourselves to . . . — Gspd

and work for the Lord always, work without limit — NEB

at all times aboundingly active in the Lord's service — Ber

forasmuch as ye know that your labour is not in vain in the Lord.

because you know that your labor in the service of the Lord is never thrown away — Wms

since you know that in the Lord your labour cannot be lost — NEB

for you know that, in union with him, your toil is not in vain — TCNT

aware that your labor in the Lord is not futile — Ber

you know that nothing you do for the Lord is ever wasted as it would be if there were no resurrection — Tay

CHAPTER 16

1. Now concerning the collection for the saints,

. . . in aid of God's people — NEB

Now as far as the fund for Christians in need is concerned — Phi

With reference to the collection for Christ's people — TCNT

Now about the contribution for God's people — Wms

Now . . . about the money you are collecting to send to the Christians in Jerusalem — Tay

as I have given order to the churches of Galatia, even so do ye.

you should follow my directions to our congregations in Galatia — NEB

you better do as I suggested to the churches of Galatia — Ber

follow the plan which I have prescribed for the Galatian churches — Knox

carry out the same arrangements as I made for the churches of Galatia — Mof

2. Upon the first day of the week

Every Sunday — NEB

On the first day of every week — Wms

let every one of you lay by him in store,

let each of you personally set aside — Ber

each of you must put aside and store up something — Wms

each of you should at home lay aside some money . . . and save it — Beck

as God hath prospered him,

in proportion to his gains — NEB

How much depends on how much the Lord has helped you earn — Tay

according to his financial ability — Nor

that there be no gatherings when I
come.

that no collections be made when I
come — ASV

so that there will be no need for collections when I come — Phi

3. **And when I come, whomsoever ye
shall approve by your letters,**

I will furnish credentials for those
whom you select — Mof

Then, on my arrival, I shall give letters of recommendation to the persons you have selected — Nor

**them will I send to bring your liberal-
ity unto Jerusalem.**

. . . your gift of charity . . . — Wms

. . . your benevolence — Con

I will send . . . to carry your gift to
Jerusalem — RSV

and send them on with your contribution to Jerusalem — Nor

4. **And if it be meet that I go also,**

If it seems advisable that I should go
also — RSV

If it seems right for me to go as well —
Phi

or if there seem sufficient reason for
me also to go thither — Con

they shall go with me.

5. **Now I will come unto you, when I
shall pass through Macedonia: for I do
pass through Macedonia.**

I will visit you after passing through
Macedonia, for I intend to pass
through Macedonia — RSV

6. **And it may be that I will abide,**

and perhaps I will stay with you — RSV

I am likely to stay a while — Ber

the chances are, I shall spend some
time with you — Mof

yea, and winter with you,

or even spend the winter — RSV

**that ye may bring me on my journey
whithersoever I go.**

it will be for you to put me on my way
to my next stage, whatever it be —
Knox

so that you may speed me forward on
any journey that lies before me —
Mof

so you may help me on to whatever
points I may visit — Wms

7. **For I will not see you now by the way;**

I don't wish to see you now, for it
would merely be in passing — Phi

I do not want this to be a flying visit
— NEB

This is no occasion for a mere passing
visit with you — Knox

but I trust to tarry a while with you,

I hope to spend some time with you —
RSV

if the Lord permit.

if it is the Lord's will — Phi

8. **But I will tarry at Ephesus until Pentecost.**

. . . until the Harvest Festival — Gspd

I intend, however, staying at Ephesus
till the Festival at the close of the
Harvest — TCNT

9. **For a great door and effectual is
opened unto me,**

for a door that offers wide and effective
service stands open before me—Wey

For I have an opportunity here that is
great and calls for work — Wms

a great opportunity lies open to me,
plain to view — Knox

for I have a great and promising opportunity here — Gspd

for I have wide opportunities here for
active service — Mof

for there is a great opportunity of doing useful work — Phi

and there are many adversaries.

and there is much opposition — NEB

and many opponents — Ber

and strong forces oppose me — Knox

and there are many to thwart me—Mof

10. **Now if Timotheus come, see that he
may be with you without fear:**

. . . make him feel quite at home with
you — Mof

. . . be careful to give him no cause of
fear in your intercourse with him —
Con

If Timothy comes, take care that he has
no cause for feeling anxious while
he is with you — TCNT

**for he worketh the work of the Lord,
as I also do.**

for he is devoted to the Lord's work,
just as I am — Gspd

He is doing the Master's work no less
than I am — TCNT

11. **Let no man therefore despise him:**

. . . slight him — Ber

He is not to be treated with disrespect
— Knox

and there is therefore no reason to look down on him — Phi

So let no one disparage him — Mof

but conduct him forth in peace, that he may come unto me:

But set him forward on his journey in peace . . . — ASV

Send him happily on his way to join me — NEB

for I look for him with the brethren.

since I am waiting for him with our friends — NEB

because I am expecting him with the other Christians — Beck

12. As touching our brother Apollos, I greatly desired him to come unto you with the brethren:

. . . I have earnestly urged him to go to see you — Wms

. . . I have repeatedly urged him to accompany the brethren who are coming to you — Wey

As for our brother Apollos, I strongly urged him to visit you with the other brethren — RSV

but his will was not at all to come at this time;

but he is quite resolved not to do so at present — Wey

and find him quite unready to go now — Ber

but it was definitely not God's will for him to do so then — Phi

He didn't think it was God's time — Tay

but he will come when he shall have convenient time.

He will come, however, when he has a good opportunity — Wey

13. Watch ye, stand fast in the faith,

Keep your eyes open for spiritual danger . . . — Tay

. . . stand firm in your faith — Gspd

Be on your guard, stand firm in the faith — Nor

quit you like men, be strong.

be courageous, be strong — RSV

be valiant . . . — Lam

keep on acting like men; continue to grow in strength — Wms

14. Let all your things be done with charity.

Let all your affairs be in an atmosphere of love — Ber

Let everything you do be done in a loving spirit — TCNT

Let all your acts be done in love — ABUV

Let all your affairs in love be carried on — Rhm

15. I beseech you, brethren, (ye know the house of Stephanas,

I ask this favor of you . . . — Mof

I have another request to make to you, Brothers. You remember Stephanas and his household — TCNT

that it is the firstfruits of Achaia,

. . . first to be converted in Greece — Gspd

. . . was the first to be reaped in Achaia — Mof

how they were the earliest Greek converts — Wey

and that they have addicted themselves to the ministry of the saints,)

Well, they have made up their minds to devote their lives to looking after Christian brothers — Phi

how they have devoted themselves to supplying the needs of the saints — Knox

and that they have devoted themselves to the service of God's people — Wms

16. That ye submit yourselves unto such,

You should yield obedience to their kind — Ber

I want you to enlist under such leaders — Gspd

I beg you to put yourselves under leaders like these — Wms

and to every one that helpeth with us, and laboureth.

and to extend your recognition to all their helpers and workers — Phi

and indeed to everyone who labours hard at our common task — NEB

as well as to every fellow-worker and earnest toiler — Ber

and to every one who shares their work and toils hard — Wey

and to every one that works with us, and labors — ABUV

and under anyone who cooperates with you and helps in the Lord's work — Nor

17. I am glad of the coming of Stephanas and Fortunatus and Achaiacus:

for that which was lacking on your part they have supplied.

because they have done what you had no chance to do — NEB

because they have supplied what you lacked — Wms

for they have made up for your absence — Ber

for they have done what was needed to make your work complete — Bas

18. For they have refreshed my spirit and yours:

They are a tonic to me and to you — Phi

They have cheered my heart, and yours too — Gspd

for they have lightened my spirit and yours — Con

therefore acknowledge ye them that are such.

for which cause give respect to such people — Bas

Such men deserve your recognition — Knox

You must deeply appreciate such men — Wms

Recognize the worth of such men as these — TCNT

19. The churches of Asia salute you.

The assemblies of Asia . . . — Rhm

. . . in the province of Asia . . . — Beck

. . . in Roman Asia . . . — TCNT

. . . wish to be remembered — Gspd

. . . send their love to you — Bas

Greetings from the congregations in Asia — NEB

Aquila and Priscilla salute you much in the Lord,

. . . send you their special Christian greetings — Gspd

. . . salute you most heartily . . . — Ber

. . . their loving salutation . . . — Con

with the church that is in their house.

. . . which assembles at their house — Con

with the congregation that meets in their house — Lam

with the assembly meeting in their house — Rhm

20. All the brethren greet you.

All the brethren salute you — ASV

All the Christians greet you — Beck

All the brethren wish to be remembered — Nor

Greet ye one another with an holy kiss.

. . . sacred kiss — Gspd

. . . the kiss of the saints — Knox

Salute one another with a holy kiss — ASV

And give each other a loving handshake when you meet — Tay

I should like you to shake hands all round as a sign of Christian love — Phi

21. The salutation of me Paul with mine own hand.

The final greeting is mine — Paul's — with my own hand — Wms

I, Paul, add this greeting in my own handwriting — TCNT

22. If any man love not the Lord Jesus Christ, let him be Anathema Maranatha.

If anyone doth not dearly love the Lord Let him be anathema [that is, accursed]; Maran atha [that is, The Lord cometh,] — Rhm

. . . God's curse be on him . . . — Mof

. . . be held accursed . . . — Knox

. . . let him be accursed. Our Lord, come! — RSV

23. The grace of our Lord Jesus Christ be with you.

May God's love and favor rest upon you — Tay

The spiritual blessing of the Lord Jesus Christ be with you — Wms

May the Lord Jesus love you! — Beck

24. My love be with you all in Christ Jesus. Amen.

My love to all of you who are in union with Christ Jesus — TCNT

My love be with you all in union with Christ Jesus — Wms

. . . So be it — Bas

THE SECOND EPISTLE OF PAUL TO THE CORINTHIANS

CHAPTER 1

1. Paul, an apostle of Jesus Christ by the will of God,

. . . God's messenger for Christ Jesus . . . — Phi

. . . appointed by God to be Jesus Christ's messenger — Tay

and Timothy our brother,

. . . Timothy the brother — Rhm

unto the church of God which is at Corinth,

to the congregation of God's people at Corinth — NEB

Unto the assembly of God which is in Corinth — Rhm

with all the saints which are in all Achaia:

. . . all Christians throughout Achaia — Phi

. . . all God's people all over Greece — Gspd

. . . all Christ's people throughout Greece — TCNT

. . . all who are dedicated to him . . . — NEB

. . . all the holy people everywhere in Greece — Beck

2. Grace be to you and peace from God our Father, and from the Lord Jesus Christ.

Favour unto you, and peace . . . — Rhm

spiritual blessing and peace . . . — Wms

3. Blessed be God, even the Father of our Lord Jesus Christ, the Father of mercies, and the God of all comfort;

Thanks be to God . . . — Con

Praise be to the God and Father of our Lord Jesus Christ, the all-merciful Father, the God whose consolation never fails us! — NEB

4. Who comforteth us in all our tribulation,

Who encourageth us . . . — Rhm

who consoles us in our every trouble — Ber

who comforts me in all my distress — Mof

. . . in every sorrow I have — Wms

. . . in all our affliction — ASV

that we may be able to comfort them which are in any trouble,

so that we in turn may be able to com-fort others in any trouble of theirs — NEB

so that I am able to comfort people who are in any distress — Mof

by the comfort wherewith we ourselves are comforted of God.

and to share with them the consolation we ourselves receive from God—NEB

5. For as the sufferings of Christ abound in us, so our consolation also aboundeth by Christ.

For as we share abundantly in Christ's sufferings, so through Christ we share in comfort too — RSV

The sufferings of Christ, it is true, over-flow into our lives; but there is over-flowing comfort, too, which Christ brings to us — Knox

As Christ's cup of suffering overflows, and we suffer with him, so also through Christ our consolation over-flows — NEB

For as we have more than our share of suffering for Christ, so also through Christ we have more than our share of comfort — Wey

For just as Christ's (own) sufferings fall to our lot [as they overflow upon His disciples, and we share and experience them] abundantly, so through Christ comfort and conso-lation and encouragement are also [shared and experienced] abundantly by us — Amp

6. And whether we be afflicted, it is for your consolation and salvation,

If distress be our lot, it is the price we pay for your consolation, for your salvation — NEB

If I am in trouble, it is to bring you comfort and salvation — Gspd

Have we trials to endure? It all makes for your encouragement, for your salvation — Knox

This means that if we experience trou-ble we can pass on to you comfort and spiritual help — Phi

which is effectual in the enduring of the same sufferings which we also suffer: or whether we be comforted, it is for your consolation and sal-vation.

or whether we are comforted, it is for your comfort which worketh in the patient enduring of the same sufferings which we also suffer — ASV

and if we are comforted, it is for your comfort, which you experience when you patiently endure the same sufferings that we suffer — RSV

if I am comforted, it is in the interests of your comfort, which is effective as it nerves you to endure the same sufferings as I suffer myself — Mof

if our lot be consolation, it is to help us to bring you comfort, and strength to face with fortitude the same sufferings we now endure — NEB

7. And our hope of you is stedfast,

Our hope for you is unshaken — RSV

And our hope for you is firmly grounded — NEB

My hope for you is well founded — Wms

Our hope for you . . . is ever unwavering — Amp

knowing, that as ye are partakers of the sufferings, so shall ye be also of the consolation.

for we know that as you share in our sufferings, you will also share in our comfort — RSV

partners of our sufferings, you will be partners of our encouragement too — Knox

for I know that as you are comrades in my sufferings, so also are you comrades in my comfort — Mon

for we know that if you have part in the suffering, you have part also in the divine consolation — NEB

8. For we would not, brethren, have you ignorant of our trouble which came to us in Asia,

About our affliction which came upon us in the province of Asia, we would have you know, brethren — Wey

Now I would like you to know about the distress which befell me in Asia . . . — Mof

For I do not want you, brothers, to misunderstand the distress that I experienced in Asia — Gspd

For I do not want you to be uninformed . . . — Wms

For we do not want you to be unaware . . . — NASB

Make no mistake, brethren, about the trial which has been befalling us in Asia — Knox

that we were pressed out of measure, above strength,

we were weighed down exceedingly, beyond our power — ASV

we were burdened altogether beyond our strength — TCNT

we were exceedingly depressed, quite beyond endurance — Wey

I was crushed, crushed far beyond what I could stand — Mof

I was so utterly and unendurably crushed — Gspd

it was something that overburdened us beyond our strength — Knox

At that time we were completely overwhelmed; the burden was more than we could bear — Phi

The burden of it was far too heavy for us to bear — NEB

insomuch that we despaired even of life:

so that we renounced all hope even of life — Wey

I feared I would never live through it — Tay

in fact we told ourselves that this was the end — Phi

9. But we had the sentence of death in ourselves,

It seemed to us as though we had been sentenced to death — Nor

Indeed, we personally passed the sentence of death on ourselves — Ber

Nay, by my own self I was already doomed to death — Con

Indeed, we had the presentiment that we must die — TCNT

Indeed, for ourselves we could find no outcome but death — Knox

Yes, we ourselves have had the answer of death in ourselves — Bas

that we should not trust in ourselves, but in God which raiseth the dead:

But this was to make me rely not on myself but on the God who raises the dead — Mof

the purpose of this was to make us lose confidence in ourselves and place it in God, who is able even to raise the dead — Nor

10. Who delivered us from so great a death, and doth deliver:

who delivered us out of so great a death, and will deliver — ASV

he rescued me from so terrible a death, he rescues still — Mof

It is he who has preserved us, and is preserving us, from such deadly peril — Knox

. . . from so imminent a death . . . — TCNT

. . . such mortal peril . . . — NEB

in whom we trust that he will yet deliver us;

on whom we have set our hope that he will also still deliver us — ASV

in whom I have hope that He will still deliver me for the time to come — Con

for in him we have placed our hopes of future deliverance — TCNT

and I rely upon him for the hope that he will continue to rescue me — Mof

yes, and I expect Him to do it again and again — Tay

11. Ye also helping together by prayer for us,

while you lend us your aid by entreaty for us — Wey

Let me have your co-operation in prayer — Mof

Only you, too, must help us with your prayers — Knox

You also can work together with us, and for us, by your prayers — Nor

and here you can join us and help by praying for us — Phi

that for the gift bestowed upon us by the means of many persons thanks may be given by many on our behalf.

that thanksgivings may from many tongues be offered up on my behalf, for the blessing gained to me by many prayers — Con

And then many lips will give thanks on our behalf for the blessing granted us in answer to many prayers — TCNT

so that thanksgivings may arise from many on our behalf for the boon granted to us at the intercession of many — Wey

so that many will give thanks on our behalf for the blessings granted us in answer to many prayers — RSV

so that the good that is done to us in answer to many prayers will mean

eventually that many will thank God for our preservation — Phi

Then, with so many people praying for our deliverance, there will be many to give thanks on our behalf for the gracious favour God has shown toward us — NEB

12. For our rejoicing is this, the testimony of our conscience,

. . . our glorying . . . — ASV

. . . our boasting . . . — Rhm

. . . our proud confidence . . . — NASB

For my boast is what my conscience tells me — Gspd

It is our boast, made in all good conscience — Knox

The reason for our exultation is the witness of our conscience — Ber

We boast of this, and our conscience backs us up — Nor

Now it is a matter of pride to us — endorsed by our conscience — Phi

that in simplicity and godly sincerity,

. . . in holiness and sincerity of God — ASV

. . . in godly honesty and singleness of mind — Con

. . . from pure motives and in sincerity before God — Wms

. . . in holiness and with pure motives before God — Wey

. . . with singleheartedness and sincerity in God's sight — Knox

not with fleshly wisdom, but by the grace of God,

not in the strength of carnal wisdom, but in the strength of God's grace — Con

. . . worldly policy . . . — TCNT

. . . worldly wisdom . . . — Wey

. . . worldly cunning . . . — Mof

. . . human cunning . . . — Nor

. . . worldly shrewdness . . . — Gspd

. . . human cleverness . . . — Beck

. . . earthly wisdom . . . — RSV

we have had our conversation in the world, and more abundantly to youward.

we behaved ourselves . . . — ASV

I have dealt with the world, and above all with you — Con

we have conducted ourselves in the world, and above all in our relations with you — Mon

we have behaved in the world generally, but specially toward you — Ber

13. **For we write none other things unto you, than what ye read or acknowledge;**

For I write nothing else to you but what you read openly, yea, and what you acknowledge inwardly — Con

We never write anything to you other than what you read in public and acknowledge — TCNT

We write to you nothing different from what you read, or indeed recognize as true — Wey

You don't have to read between the lines of my letters; you can understand them — Mof

For what I am writing to you is only what you can read and understand — Gspd

And we mean by our letters nothing else than what you read in them, and understand us to mean — Knox

Our letters to you have no double meaning — they mean just what you understand them to mean when you read them — Phi

and I trust ye shall acknowledge even to the end;

Yes, I trust you will understand the full meaning of my letters — Mof

and I hope you will understand it fully — Gspd

. . . perfectly — Wms

and I trust that you will admit this even to the end of this letter — Nor

I hope that you will come to understand us better — Knox

14. **As also ye have acknowledged us in part,**

just as you have partly understood us — Ber

as you have partly understood the meaning of my life — Mof

as you have to some extent understood us — Beck

as I believe some of you have understood me — Phi

that we are your rejoicing,

. . . your glorying . . . — ASV

. . . your theme of boasting . . . — Rhm

. . . your reason for boasting . . . — Wey

. . . your source of pride . . . — Mof

. . . your pride and joy . . . — Lam

. . . your chief pride . . . — Knox

even as ye also are ours in the day of the Lord Jesus.

15. **And in this confidence I was minded to come unto you before,**

With this conviction in my mind, I planned to come and see you first — TCNT

Relying on this I meant to visit you first — Mof

It was because I was sure of this that I wanted to come to see you before going anywhere else — Gspd

It was because I felt so confident about all this that I had intended to come first of all to you — NEB

. . . our original plan was to pay you a visit first — Phi

that ye might have a second benefit;

so that your pleasure might be doubled — TCNT

so that you might receive a twofold joy — Wey

to let you have a double delight — Mof

to give you a double pleasure — Gspd

that you might have a pleasure twice over — Mon

to give you a double opportunity of spiritual profit — Knox

so that you might enjoy a double blessing — Ber

. . . a second joy — Rhm

. . . the benefit of a double visit — NEB

so that you would enjoy two visits — Nor

16. **And to pass by you into Macedonia, and to come again out of Macedonia unto you,**

to visit you both on my way to Macedonia, and to come to you again on my return from Macedonia — TCNT

and of you to be brought on my way toward Judaea.

and of you to be set forward on my journey into Judaea — ASV

so as to be sped by you on my journey to Judaea — Mof

and you would see me off on my way to Judea — Nor

and to be escorted from you to Judea — Ber

17. **When I therefore was thus minded, did I use lightness?**

Am I accused, then, of forming this purpose in levity and caprice — Con

As this was my plan, where, pray, did I show any fickleness of purpose — TCNT

Was it vacillating of me to want to do that — Gspd

When I thus made up my mind, do you suppose I did it lightly — Knox

When I wanted to do this, was I trifling — Beck

Now because I changed my original plan was I being unstable and capricious — Amp

or the things that I purpose, do I purpose according to the flesh,

Or the plans which I form — do I form them on worldly principles — Wey

When I propose some plan, do I propose it in a worldly way — Mof

Do I make my plans like a worldly man — Gspd

Or, do I make my plans in accordance with worldly notions — Wms

Can it be said of me that the plans I form are formed by motives of human prudence — Knox

Or do you think that my plans are formed on mere impulse — TCNT

that with me there should be yea yea, and nay nay?

so that in the same breath I say Yes and No — TCNT

ready to mean no as well as yes — Mof

to have my Yes mean No, if I want it so — Wms

saying, Yes, today, and, No, tomorrow Bas

so that it is first Yes, I will, and then, No, I will not, with me — Knox

saying yes, yes, and changing to no, no, according to circumstance — Nor

saying yes and meaning no — Phi

18. **But as God is true, our word toward you was not yea and nay.**

As God is faithful, the message we delivered to you is not one which hesitates between Yes and No — Knox

As surely as God is faithful, our word to you was not of the yes-and-no variety — Nor

Yet as God is faithful, my words to you are no [deceitful] mixture of yea and nay — Con

As surely as God can be relied on, there has been no equivocation about our message to you — Gspd

. . . the language in which we address

you is not an ambiguous blend of Yes and No — NEB

19. **For the Son of God, Jesus Christ, who was preached among you by us, even by me and Silvanus and Timotheus, was not yea and nay,**

. . . was never a blend of Yes and No — NEB

. . . never wavered between Yes and No — TCNT

but in him was yea.

it is always Yes with Him — Wey

but in him is the everlasting Yes — Mon

he is the divine Yes — Phi

With him it was, and is, Yes — NEB

20. **For all the promises of God in him are yea,**

For all the promises of God have their Yes in Him — Wey

For, many as were the promises of God, in Christ is the Yes that fulfils them — TCNT

for in him is the yes that affirms all the promises of God — Mof

for to all the promises of God he supplies the Yes that confirms them — Gspd

Every promise of God finds its affirmative in Him — Phi

He is the Yes pronounced upon God's promises, every one of them — NEB

and in him Amen, unto the glory of God by us.

that is why, when we give glory to God, it is through him that we say our Amen — Knox

Therefore, through Christ again, let the Amen rise, through us, to the glory of God — TCNT

wherefore also through him is the Amen . . . — ASV

and therefore through Him we utter the Amen . . . — Wey

Hence it is through him that we affirm our amen in worship . . . — Mof

and through him can be said the final amen . . . — Phi

21. **Now he which stablisheth us with you in Christ, and hath anointed us, is God;**

And he who has established me with you in the Anointed One, and has anointed me, is God — Mon

And if you and we belong to Christ,

guaranteed as his and anointed, it is all God's doing — NEB

We owe our position in Christ to this God of positive promise: it is he who has consecrated us to this special work — Phi

But it is God who makes us as well as you secure through union with Christ . . . — Wms

It is God who gives both us and you our certainty in Christ . . . — Knox

For it is God who has confirmed our faith and your faith in Christ . . . — Nor

. . . and has commissioned us — RSV

22. Who hath also sealed us, and given the earnest of the Spirit in our hearts.

who stamped me with his seal and gave me the Spirit as a pledge in my heart — Mof

And He has set His seal upon us . . . — Con

. . . and gave us his Spirit in our hearts as a pledge of future blessings — TCNT

. . . as a guarantee — Wey

. . . as a first installment of future rewards — Wms

. . . as a pledge of what is to come — NEB

. . . and given us the foretaste of his Spirit in our hearts — Knox

. . . and gave us in our hearts the Spirit's security deposit — Ber

23. Moreover I call God for a record upon my soul,

But I call upon God as a witness against my own soul — Rhm

But I call God to witness against me — RSV

But for my own part, I call God to witness, as my soul shall answer for it — Con

But, as my life shall answer for it, I call God to witness — TCNT

But I call God as my soul's witness — Wey

With my soul as the forfeit I call this God to witness — Knox

I appeal to God to witness what I am going to say — NEB

that to spare you I came not as yet unto Corinth.

that it was to spare you that I deferred my visit to Corinth — TCNT

that to spare you I have delayed my coming to Corinth — Ber

24. Not for that we have dominion over your faith, but are helpers of your joy:

I do not mean that we are to dictate to you with regard to your faith; on the contrary, we work with you for your true happiness — TCNT

Not that we would domineer over your faith; rather, we would help you to achieve happiness — Knox

Not that we have lordship over your faith . . . — ASV

Not that we lord it over your faith . . . — Mof

Not that we are the masters of you and your faith . . . — Gspd

We are not trying to dominate you and your faith . . . — Phi

Do not think we are dictating the terms of your faith . . . — NEB

I speak not as though your faith was enslaved to my authority . . . — Con

for by faith ye stand.

for in faith ye stand fast — ASV

for your faith is steadfast — Con

for as to your faith you stand firm — Wey

you have a standing of your own in the faith — Mof

your hold on the faith is secure enough — NEB

You stand on your own feet in your faith — Beck

CHAPTER 2

1. But I determined this with myself,

But I have resolved — Wey

For I made up my mind — Gspd

For I have definitely decided — Wms

On this I was resolved in my own mind — Knox

that I would not come again to you in heaviness.

that I would not pay you another painful visit — Phi

not again to visit you in grief — Con

that I would not come again to you with sorrow — ASV

2. For if I make you sorry, who is he

then that maketh me glad, but the same which is made sorry by me?

for if I cause you grief, who is there to cause me joy, but those whom I have grieved — Con

For if I pain you, then who is to give me pleasure? None but the very people I am paining! — Mof

For what point is there in my depressing the very people who can give me such joy — Phi

3. And I wrote this same unto you,

So I wrote as I did — TCNT

And for this very reason I wrote to you — Con

This is what I said in my letter — Gspd

And those were the very terms in which I wrote to you — Knox

This is precisely the point I made in my letter — NEB

The real purpose of my previous letter was — Phi

lest, when I came, I should have sorrow from them of whom I ought to rejoice;

so that when I came I might not be pained by those who should have made me rejoice — RSV

that I might not receive grief from those who ought to give me joy — Con

that when I did come I might not be made sad by the very people who ought to make me glad — Wms

I didn't want to come and be made sad by those who should have made me happy — Beck

having confidence in you all, that my joy is the joy of you all.

for I felt sure that it was true of you all that my joy was in every case yours also — TCNT

I relied on you all, I felt sure that my joy would be a joy for everyone of you — Mof

I felt confidence in you all, I knew that what made me happy would make you happy too — Knox

and I had sufficient confidence in you all to know that for me to be happy is for all of you to be happy — NEB

I have such confidence in you that my joy depends on all of you — Phi

4. For out of much affliction and anguish of heart I wrote unto you with many tears;

. . . in deep affliction and anguish of spirit . . . — Wey

. . . in sore distress and misery of heart . . . — Mof

. . . in great trouble and distress of mind . . . — Gspd

. . . in deep distress and with a heart of anguish . . . — Ber

That letter I sent you came out of great distress and anxiety; how many tears I shed as I wrote it — NEB

not that ye should be grieved, but that ye might know the love which I have more abundantly unto you.

But I never meant to cause you pain; I wanted you rather to know the love, the more than ordinary love, that I have for you — NEB

not to give you pain, but to let you see how intense a love I have for you — TCNT

. . . but in the hope of showing you how brimful my heart is with love for you — Wey

. . . but to convince you of my love, my special love for you — Mof

5. But if any have caused grief, he hath not grieved me, but in part: that I may not overcharge you all.

If the behaviour of a certain person has caused distress, it does not mean so much that he has injured me, but that to some extent (I do not wish to exaggerate) he has injured all of you — Phi

If a certain individual has been causing pain, he has been causing pain not so much to me as to all of you — at any rate (for I am not going to overstate the case) to a section of you — Mof

. . . but in part (that I press not too heavily) to you all — ASV

. . . but some of you; [some, I say,] that I may not press too harshly upon all — Con

. . . he has, to some extent — not to be too severe — pained every one of you — TCNT

. . . but in some measure — not to put it too severely — to you all — RSV

. . . but, in some measure, all of you, so that I must not be too hard on him — Knox

. . . to some extent, not to labour the

point, it has been done to you all —
NEB

6. Sufficient to such a man is this punishment, which was inflicted of many.

This punishment inflicted on him by so many of you is punishment enough for the man I speak of — Knox

. . . inflicted on him by the sentence of the majority . . . — Con

The penalty on which the general meeting has agreed has met the offence well enough — NEB

7. So that contrariwise ye ought rather to forgive him, and comfort him,

so that now you must take the opposite course, and forgive and encourage him — TCNT

Something very different is called for now: you must forgive the offender and put heart into him — NEB

lest perhaps such a one should be swallowed up with overmuch sorrow.

lest he should be overwhelmed by the excess of his sorrow — Con

lest perhaps he be driven to despair by his excess of grief — Wey

else he may be overwhelmed by despair — Ber

8. Wherefore I beseech you that ye would confirm your love toward him.

So I entreat you to assure him of your love — TCNT

. . . to reaffirm your love for him — RSV

. . . to restore him to his place in your affections — Gspd

. . . fully to reinstate him in your love — Wey

9. For to this end also did I write, that I might know the proof of you, whether ye be obedient in all things.

For my aim in writing was simply to test you, to see if you were absolutely obedient — Mof

. . . to ascertain whether you might be relied upon to be obedient in everything — TCNT

. . . to test your loyalty . . . — Knox

My previous letter was something of a test — I wanted to make sure that you would follow my orders implicitly — Phi

I wrote, I may say, to see how you stood the test, whether you fully accepted my authority — NEB

10. To whom ye forgive any thing, I forgive also:

When you forgive a man anything, I forgive him, too — TCNT

But anyone who has your forgiveness has mine too — NEB

for if I forgave any thing, to whom I forgave it, for your sakes forgave I it in the person of Christ;

Indeed, for my part, whatever I have forgiven (if I have had to forgive anything) I have forgiven for your sakes, in the presence of Christ — TCNT

. . . in the sight of Christ — Con

. . . as before Christ — Phi

11. Lest Satan should get an advantage of us:

We don't want Satan to win any victory here — Phi

lest Satan should overreach us — Ber

to keep Satan from getting the better of us — Gspd

to keep us from being worsted by Satan — Wms

. . . we will not be outsmarted by Satan — Tay

for we are not ignorant of his devices.

for well I know his manoeuvres — Mof

. . . his designs — Bas

. . . his schemings — Ber

. . . his wiles — NEB

. . . how resourceful he is — Knox

12. Furthermore, when I came to Troas to preach Christ's gospel,

Now when I came to Troas for the gospel of Christ — ASV

. . . to preach the good news of the Christ there — Gspd

and a door was opened unto me of the Lord,

even though in the Lord's providence a door should open before me — Wey

even though there was an opening for serving the Master — TCNT

though I had a wide opportunity in the Lord — Mof

and found a great opportunity open to me in the Lord's service — Knox

although there was an obvious God-given opportunity — Phi

13. I had no rest in my spirit,

I had no relief for my spirit — ASV

I could get no peace of mind — TCNT

because I found not Titus my brother:

because there was no sign of brother
Titus — Phi

because I didn't find Titus, my fellow
worker — Beck

**but taking my leave of them, I went
from thence into Macedonia.**

So I said goodbye to them and went on
to Macedonia — Gspd

so I bade them farewell . . . — Wey

. . . and pressed on into Macedonia —
Knox

14. **Now thanks be unto God, which always causeth us to triumph in Christ,**

. . . who always leadeth us in triumph
in Christ — ASV

. . . who leads me on from place to
place in the train of his triumph —
Con

. . . who, through our union with Christ,
leads us in one continual triumph —
TCNT

. . . who in Christ ever leads us in His
triumphal procession — Wey

. . . Who in Christ always leads us in
triumph — as trophies of Christ's
victory — Amp

Wherever I go, thank God, he makes
my life a constant pageant of triumph in Christ — Mof

**and maketh manifest the savour of his
knowledge by us in every place.**

and uses us to spread the sweet odour
of the knowledge of him in every
place — TCNT

displaying everywhere through us the
sweetness of the knowledge of Him
— Wey

diffusing the perfume of his knowledge
everywhere by me — Mof

and who evidences through us in every
place the fragrance that results from
knowing Him — Ber

and everywhere uses us to reveal and
spread abroad the fragrance of the
knowledge of himself — NEB

and makes our knowledge of him
spread throughout the world like a
lovely perfume — Phi

15. **For we are unto God a sweet savour
of Christ, in them that are saved, and
in them that perish:**

For we are the fragrance of Christ
ascending to God . . . — TCNT

We are indeed the incense offered by
Christ to God, both for those who
are on the way to salvation, and for

those who are on the way to perdition — NEB

We are Christ's incense offered to God,
making manifest both those who are
achieving salvation and those who
are on the road to ruin — Knox

. . . among those who are being saved
and those who are perishing — RSV

Yes, I am the fragrance of Christ to
God, diffused among those who are
being saved and who are perishing
alike — Gspd

16. **To the one we are the savour of death
unto death; and to the other the savour
of life unto life.**

to the one an odour of death that leads
to death, and to others an odour of
life that leads to life — Wey

to the one a deadly fragrance that
makes for death, to the other a vital
fragrance that makes for life — Mof

to the latter it is a deadly fume that
kills, to the former a vital fragrance
that brings life — NEB

To the latter it seems like the deathly
smell of doom; to the former it has
the refreshing fragrance of life itself
— Phi

And who is sufficient for these things?

But who is equal to such a task — TCNT

And for such service as this who is
competent — Wey

And who is qualified for this career —
Mof

Who is qualified for this task — Gspd

Now, who is competent to preach that
way — Nor

Who could think himself adequate for
a responsibility like this — Phi

17. **For we are not as many, which corrupt
the word of God:**

For we are not, as the many, driving
a petty trade with the word of God
— Rhm

For I seek not profit (like most) by setting the word of God to sale — Con

Unlike many people, we are not in
the habit of making profit out of
God's Message — TCNT

Unlike most teachers, we do not adulterate God's word — Wey

For I am no peddler of God's message,
like most men — Gspd

for I am not like most, trafficking in the
word of God — Mon

For we are not like the great number

who make use of the word of God for profit — Bas

For we do not, like so many, peddle an adulterated message of God — Ber

At least we don't peddle an impure Word of God like many others — Beck

but as of sincerity, but as of God, in the sight of God speak we in Christ.

but as men of sincerity, as commissioned by God, in the sight of God we speak in Christ — RSV

when we declare the word we do it in sincerity, as from God and in God's sight, as members of Christ — NEB

but I speak from a single heart, from the command of God, as in God's presence, and in fellowship with Christ — Con

but like a man of sincerity, like a man that is sent from God and living in His presence, in union with Christ I speak His message — Wms

but in Christ we talk sincerely as men who come from God and stand before God — Beck

CHAPTER 3

1. Do we begin again to commend ourselves?

Do you say that we are beginning to commend ourselves once more — Wey

You will say, perhaps, that we are making a fresh attempt to recommend ourselves to your favour — Knox

Are we beginning all over again to produce our credentials — NEB

or need we, as some others, epistles of commendation to you, or letters of commendation from you?

Do I need, like some people, to be commended by written certificates either to you or from you — Mof

Do we need, as some apparently do, to exchange testimonials before we can be friends — Phi

. . . letters of introduction . . . — NEB

2. Ye are our epistle written in our hearts, known and read of all men:

Why, you yourselves are the letter we carry about with us, written in our hearts, for all to recognize and read — Knox

Why, you are my certificate yourselves . . . — Mof

You are my letter of recommendation . . . — Wms

You yourselves are our testimonial, written in our hearts and yet open for anyone to inspect and read — Phi

No, you are all the letter we need, a letter written on our heart; any man can see it for what it is and read it for himself — NEB

3. Forasmuch as ye are manifestly declared to be the epistle of Christ

a letter coming manifestly from Christ — Con

All can see that you are a letter from Christ — TCNT

You are an open letter from Christ — Knox

ministered by us,

penned by us — Wey

written by us — Phi

delivered by us — TCNT

transcribed by me — Mon

produced by my service — Wms

the fruit of our work — Bas

prepared by us — Beck

committed to my charge — Con

written not with ink, but with the Spirit of the living God; not in tables of stone, but in fleshy tables of the heart.

. . . in tables that are hearts of flesh — ASV

. . . not on tablets of stone but on tablets of human hearts — RSV

4. And such trust have we through Christ to God-ward:

Such is the confidence I have through Christ in the presence of God—Wms

It is in full reliance upon God, through Christ, that we make such claims — NEB

Such, through Christ, is the confidence in which we make our appeal to God — Knox

5. Not that we are sufficient of ourselves to think any thing as of ourselves;

not thinking myself sufficient to gain

wisdom by my own reasonings — Con

I do not mean that we are fit to form any judgement by ourselves, as if on our own authority — TCNT

not that of ourselves we are competent to decide anything of our own judgment — Wey

It is not that I am qualified to form any judgment by myself — Mof

Not that I am of myself qualified to claim anything as originating with me — Gspd

Not that I am sufficient in myself to reach any conclusion in my own wisdom — Mon

Not as if we were able by ourselves to do anything for which we might take the credit — Bas

not because we possess self-sufficiency to form personal judgments — Ber

Not that we are in any way confident of our own resources — Phi

There is no question of our being qualified in ourselves: we cannot claim anything as our own — NEB

but our sufficiency is of God;

but our competency comes from God — Wey

Such qualification as we have comes from God — NEB

all our ability comes from God—Knox

6. Who also hath made us able ministers of the new testament;

who also made us sufficient as ministers of a new covenant — ASV

He has also made us competent servants of a new covenant — Wey

. . . competent to serve as ministers of the New Covenant — Nor

and he has further qualified me . . . — Mof

. . . to dispense his new covenant — NEB

It is he who makes us competent administrators of the new agreement — Phi

not of the letter, but of the spirit:

of which the substance is not a written Law, but a Spirit — TCNT

which is not a written code but a Spirit — Wey

which is not a written but a spiritual covenant — Wms

It is a spiritual, not a written law — Knox

a covenant expressed not in a written document, but in a spiritual bond — NEB

for the letter killeth, but the spirit giveth life.

For the written Law means death, but the Spirit gives life — TCNT

for the letter of the law punishes with death . . . — Lam

for the written law condemns to death . . . — NEB

The letter of the law leads to the death of the soul; the Spirit of God alone can give life to the soul — Phi

7. But if the ministration of death, written and engraven in stones, was glorious,

But if the service that brings death — its code being engraved in writing upon stones — came with glory — Wey

. . . the dispensation of death . . . — RSV

. . . was brought into existence with glory — Rhm

. . . was ushered in with such splendor — Gspd

. . . was introduced with a splendor — Wms

. . . was inaugurated with divine splendour — NEB

. . . was invested with glory — Mof

. . . was promulgated to men in a dazzling cloud — Knox

so that the children of Israel could not stedfastly behold the face of Moses for the glory of his countenance; which glory was to be done away:

That splendour, though it was soon to fade, made the face of Moses so bright that the Israelites could not gaze steadily at him — NEB

so that the people of Israel could not look Moses in the face, for the brightness of it, although that brightness soon passed away — Knox

so magnificent that the Israelites were unable to look unflinchingly at Moses' face, for it was alight with heavenly splendor . . . — Phi

. . . a glory even then fading — Mon

. . . a glory which was only for a time — Bas

. . . — a transient lustre — Wey

8. How shall not the ministration of the spirit be rather glorious?

how far more glorious must the ministration of the spirit be — Con

will not the service of the Spirit be far more glorious — Wey

surely the administration of the Spirit must be invested with still greater glory — Mof

how much more shall the ministry of the Spirit abide in glory — Mon

How much more dazzling, then, must be the brightness in which the spiritual law is promulgated to them — Knox

will not the dispensation of the Spirit be attended with greater splendor — RSV

can we not see what a much more glorious thing is the new administration of the Spirit of Life — Phi

9. For if the ministration of condemnation be glory,

For if the service which pronounces doom had glory — Wey

If there was glory in the administration that condemned — Mof

For if there was splendor in the dispensation of condemnation — RSV

If splendour accompanied the dispensation under which we are condemned — NEB

much more doth the ministration of righteousness exceed in glory.

far more glorious still is the service which offers righteousness — Wey

then the administration that acquits abounds far more in glory — Mof

there must be more splendour yet in the proclamation of our acquittal — Knox

how much richer in splendour must that one be under which we are acquitted — NEB

how much greater and more glorious is the service of the Spirit, causing justification — Nor

how infinitely more splendid is it to administer a system which ends in making men good — Phi

10. For even that which was made glorious had no glory in this respect, by reason of the glory that excelleth.

Indeed, that which then had glory has lost its glory, because of the glory which surpasses it — TCNT

For, in fact, that which was so glorious has no glory at all in comparison with the surpassing glory — Wey

For an account of its surpassing splendor, what was once so splendid has now no splendor at all — Wms

indeed, what once seemed resplendent seems by comparison resplendent no longer, so much does the greater splendour outshine it — Knox

Indeed, the splendour that once was is now no splendour at all; it is outshone by a splendour greater still — NEB

Indeed, in view of this fact, what once had splendor [the glory of the Law in the face of Moses] has come to have no splendor at all, because of the overwhelming glory that exceeds and excels it [the glory of the Gospel in the face of Jesus Christ] — Amp

11. For if that which is done away was glorious, much more that which remaineth is glorious.

For if that which passeth away was with glory, much more that which remaineth is in glory — ASV

And, if that which was to pass away was attended with glory, far more will that which is to endure be surrounded with glory — TCNT

For if that which was to be abolished came with glory, much more is that which is permanent arrayed in glory — Wey

if what faded had its glory, then what lasts will be invested with far greater glory — Mof

For if what faded away came with splendor, how much more splendid what is permanent must be — Gspd

For if that which was soon to fade had its moment of splendour, how much greater is the splendour of that which endures — NEB

12. Seeing then that we have such hope,

Having therefore such a hope — ASV

Such is the ground of our confidence — Knox

we use great plainness of speech:

we use great boldness of speech — ASV

we speak with all plainness — TCNT

we speak without reserve — Wey

I use great freedom of speech — Mon

we keep nothing back — Bas

we are quite frank and open in our ministry — Phi

13. And not as Moses, which put a veil over his face,

unlike Moses, who used to throw a veil over his face — Wey

. . . who used to cover his face with a veil — Mon

It is not for us to use veiled language, as Moses veiled his face — Knox

that the children of Israel could not stedfastly look to the end of that which is abolished:

. . . on the end of that which was passing away — ABUV

that the sons of Israel might not see the end of that fading brightness — Con

to prevent the Israelites from gazing at the disappearance of what was passing away — TCNT

to hide from the gaze of the children of Israel the passing away of what was but transitory — Wey

. . . the last rays of a fading glory — Mof

. . . the passing of a fading glory — Mon

. . . the end of the fading splendor — RSV

He did it so that the people of Israel might not go on gazing at the features of the old order, which was passing away — Knox

14. But their minds were blinded:

. . . hardened — ASV

. . . dulled — Mof

. . . had been made insensitive — NEB

. . . have been closed — Beck

. . . dullness has crept over their senses — Knox

for until this day remaineth the same veil untaken away in the reading of the old testament;

so to this day, whenever the Old Covenant is being read, the same veil is still there, still unlifted — Nor

for even today when the old agreement is read to them there is still a veil over their minds — Phi

. . . when they read in their synagogues the ancient covenant . . . — Con

. . . at the public reading of the Old Covenant . . . — TCNT

which veil is done away in Christ.

only for those who are in union with

Christ does it pass away — TCNT

for only through union with Christ is it removed — Gspd

. . . it has been abrogated in Christ — Knox

because only through Christ is it taken away — RSV

though the veil has actually been lifted by Christ — Phi

because only in Christ is the old covenant abrogated — NEB

15. But even unto this day, when Moses is read, the veil is upon their heart.

Yes, alas, even to this day there is still a veil over their hearts when the writings of Moses are read — Phi

16. Nevertheless when it shall turn to the Lord, the veil shall be taken away.

But whenever they return to the Lord, the veil is withdrawn — Wey

However, as Scripture says of Moses, whenever he turns to the Lord the veil is removed — NEB

There must be a turning to the Lord first, and then the veil will be taken away — Knox

. . . when their heart turns to the Lord . . . — Con

. . . whenever a man turns to the Lord . . . — TCNT

whenever anybody turns to the Lord . . . . — Wms

17. Now the Lord is that Spirit; and where the Spirit of the Lord is, there is liberty.

Now the Lord means the Spirit, and where the Spirit of the Lord is, freedom is — Wey

The Spirit we have been speaking of is the Lord . . . — Knox

Now the Lord of whom this passage speaks is the Spirit . . . — NEB

18. But we all, with open face beholding as in a glass the glory of the Lord,

But all of us who are Christians have no veils on our faces, but reflect like mirrors the glory of the Lord — Phi

. . . with unveiled face beholding as in a mirror . . . — ASV

. . . seeing, as if reflected in a mirror . . . — TCNT

. . . we all mirror . . . — Mof

. . . reflecting like a mirror . . . — Mon

. . . we can be mirrors that brightly reflect the glory of the Lord — Tay

are changed into the same image from glory to glory, even as by the Spirit of the Lord.

We are transfigured in ever-increasing splendor into his own image, and the transformation comes from the Lord who is the Spirit — Phi

. . . from one degree of splendor to another . . . — Gspd

. . . even as from the Lord the Spirit — ASV

. . . Even as from a Spirit that is Lord — Rhm

CHAPTER 4

1. Therefore seeing we have this ministry, as we have received mercy, we faint not;

Being entrusted, then, by God's mercy with this ministry, we do not play the coward — Knox

Seeing then that we have been entrusted with this commission, which we owe entirely to God's mercy, we never lose heart — NEB

. . . I discharge it with no faint-hearted fears — Con

. . . I never give up — Wms

. . . we are not despondent — Ber

. . . nothing can daunt us — Phi

. . . we do not get discouraged — Amp

2. But have renounced the hidden things of dishonesty.

but we have renounced the hidden things of shame — ASV

. . . the secret dealings of shame — Con

. . . the secrecy prompted by shame — TCNT

. . . the secrecy which means shame — Wey

I disown those practices which very shame conceals from view — Mof

. . . disgraceful, underhanded ways — Gspd

. . . all underhanded, disgraceful methods — Wms

. . . all shameful concealment — Knox

. . . the deeds that men hide for very shame — NEB

. . . the secret ways that anybody should feel ashamed of — Beck

not walking in craftiness, nor handling the word of God deceitfully;

I walk not in the paths of cunning, I adulterate not the word of God — Con

refusing to adopt crafty ways, or to tamper with God's Message — TCNT

I do not go about it craftily; I do not falsify the word of God — Mof

We don't use trickery . . . — Beck

no clever tricks, no dishonest manipulation of the Word of God — Phi

we neither practise cunning nor distort the word of God — NEB

but my manifestation of the truth commending ourselves to every man's conscience in the sight of God.

but openly setting forth the truth, as in the sight of God, I commend myself to the conscience of all men — Con

but by clear statement of the truth we commend ourselves to every human conscience before God — Wey

I state the truth openly and so commend myself to every man's conscience before God — Mof

it is by making the truth publicly known that we recommend ourselves to the honest judgement of mankind, as in God's sight — Knox

only by declaring the truth openly do we recommend ourselves, and then it is to the common conscience of our fellow-men and in the sight of God — NEB

3. But if our gospel be hid, it is hid to them that are lost:

And even if our gospel is veiled, it is veiled in them that perish — ASV

If, indeed, our gospel is veiled, the veil is on the heart of those who are perishing — Wey

If the meaning of my preaching of the good news is veiled at all, it is so only in the case of those who are on the way to destruction — Gspd

4. In whom the god of this world hath blinded the minds of them which believe not,

whose unbelieving minds the God of this world has blinded — Con

men whose minds have been blinded by the God of this Age, unbelievers as they are — TCNT

In their case, the god of this world has blinded the minds of the unbelievers — Gspd

lest the light of the glorious gospel of Christ, who is the image of God, should shine unto them.

that the light of the gospel of the glory of Christ, who is the image of God, should not dawn upon them — ASV

so that the glorious gospel of Christ, God's image, cannot reach them with the rays of its illumination — Knox

... the light from the Good News of the glory of the Christ ... — TCNT

... the light of the good news of the glorious Christ ... — Gspd

... cannot dawn upon them and bring them light — NEB

5. For we preach not ourselves, but Christ Jesus the Lord; and ourselves your servants for Jesus' sake.

(It is Christ Jesus as Lord, not myself, that I proclaim; I am simply a servant of yours for Jesus' sake.) — Mof

For it is not myself but Christ Jesus that I am proclaiming as Lord; I am only a slave of yours for Jesus' sake — Gspd

... Christ Jesus as Lord, and ourselves as your servants ... — ASV

... and about ourselves we simply say that we are your servants for Jesus' sake — Nor

6. For God, who commanded the light to shine out of darkness, hath shined in our hearts,

Seeing it is God, that said, Light shall shine out of darkness, who shined in our hearts — ASV

For God who said, Light shall shine out of darkness, has shone within my heart — Mof

The same God who bade light shine out of darkness has kindled a light in our hearts — Knox

God, who first ordered light to shine in darkness, has flooded our hearts with his light — Phi

For the same God who said, Out of darkness let light shine, has caused his light to shine within us — NEB

to give the light of the knowledge of the glory of God in the face of Jesus Christ.

so that we should bring out into the light the knowledge of the glory of God, seen in the face of Christ — TCNT

to give me the light of the knowledge of God's glory, that is on the face of Christ — Gspd

whose shining is to make known his glory as he has revealed it in the features of Jesus Christ — Knox

to give the light of revelation — the revelation of the glory of God in the face of Jesus Christ — NEB

to bring you the light of knowing God's glory ... — Beck

... in the person of Christ — Lam

7. But we have this treasure in earthen vessels,

But this treasure is lodged in a body of fragile clay — Con

But I possess this treasure in a frail vessel of earth — Mof

This priceless treasure we hold, so to speak, in a common earthenware jar — Phi

We are no better than pots of earthenware to contain this treasure — NEB

... fragile earthen pots — Wey

... a mere earthen jar — Gspd

... perishable earthenware — Knox

... utensils of mere clay — Ber

... bodies of clay — Nor

that the excellency of the power may be of God, and not of us.

that the exceeding greatness of the power may be of God, and not from ourselves — ASV

that its all-prevailing power may be seen to come from God, and not to be our own — TCNT

it must be God, and not anything in ourselves, that gives it its sovereign power — Knox

— an evidence that the unparalleled power is of God, and not from us — Ber

and this proves that such transcendent power does not come from us, but is God's alone — NEB

8. We are troubled on every side, yet not distressed;

we are pressed on every side, yet not straitened — ASV

I am hard pressed, yet not crushed — Con

Though hard pressed on every side, we are never hemmed in — TCNT

Troubles are round us on every side, but we are not shut in — Bas

For ourselves, we are being hampered everywhere, yet still have room to breathe — Knox

We are hedged in from every side, but we live no cramped lives — Ber

we are perplexed, but not in despair;

bewildered, but never at our wits' end — NEB

are hard put to it, but never at a loss — Knox

9. Persecuted, but not forsaken;

Pursued, but not abandoned — Rhm

We are persecuted, but we never have to stand it alone — Phi

hunted, we are never abandoned to our fate — NEB

We are hunted down, but God never abandons us — Tay

cast down, but not destroyed;

though struck down, never killed — TCNT

struck down, we are not left to die — NEB

always getting a knockdown, but never a knockout — Wms

we are struck down to the ground, but never struck out and destroyed — Amp

10. Always bearing about in the body the dying of the Lord Jesus,

wherever I go, I am being killed in the body as Jesus was — Mof

always being exposed to death as Jesus was — Wms

we carry about continually in our bodies the dying state of Jesus — Knox

Every day we experience something of the death of Jesus — Phi

Wherever we go we carry death with us in our body, the death that Jesus dies — NEB

that the life also of Jesus might be made manifest in our body.

so that the life of Jesus may be visible in my mortal nature — Gspd

so that the living power of Jesus may be manifested in our bodies too — Knox

so that we may also know the power of the life of Jesus in these bodies of ours — Phi

that in this body also life may reveal itself, the life that Jesus lives — NEB

11. For we which live are alway delivered unto death for Jesus' sake,

For I, in the midst of life, am daily given over to death for the sake of Jesus — Con

For we, alive though we are, are continually surrendering ourselves to death for the sake of Jesus — Wey

For continually, while still alive, we are being surrendered into the hands of death, for Jesus' sake — NEB

that the life also of Jesus might be made manifest in our mortal flesh.

that in my dying flesh the life whereby Jesus conquered death might show forth its power — Con

so that the living power of Jesus may be manifested in this mortal nature of ours — Knox

12. So then death worketh in us, but life in you.

So, then, death working in me works life in you — Con

In me then death is active, in you life — Mof

We are always facing death, but this means that you know more and more of life — Phi

13. We having the same spirit of faith, according as it is written, I believed, and therefore have I spoken: we also believe, and therefore speak;

Yet having the same spirit of faith whereof it is written I believed, and therefore did I speak, I also believe, and therefore speak — TCNT

But since our spirit of faith is the same, therefore — as it is written, I believed and so I spoke — I too believe and so I speak — Mof

I spoke my mind, says the scripture, with full confidence, and we too speak our minds with full confidence — Knox

Our faith is like that mentioned in the scripture . . . — Phi

14. Knowing that he which raised up the Lord Jesus shall raise up us also by Jesus, and shall present us with you.

sure that He who raised the Lord Jesus will raise me too with Jesus and set me at your side in his presence — Mof and we know for certain that he who raised the Lord Jesus from death shall also raise us with Jesus. We shall all stand together before him — Phi

. . . and shall call me into His presence together with you — Con

. . . and will set us with you in His presence — Wey

. . . and summon us, like you, before him — Knox

. . . and will have us stand with you before Him — Ber

. . . and bring us to his presence, and you with us — NEB

15. For all things are for your sakes,

for all [my sufferings] are on your behalf — Con

It is all in your interests — Mof

For it is all for your benefit — Gspd

For we go through all things on account of you — Bas

All this is to help you — Beck

that the abundant grace might through the thanksgiving of many redound to the glory of God.

that the loving-kindness of God, spreading from heart to heart, may cause yet more hearts to overflow with thanksgiving, to his glory — TCNT

in order that grace may increase with the increased number who receive it, and cause abundant thanksgiving to the glory of God — Wey

so that the more grace abounds, the more thanksgiving may rise and redound to the glory of God — Mof

in order that as God's favor reaches greater and greater numbers, it may result in more and more thanksgiving in praise of God — Gspd

because the greater the number to whom the grace is given, the greater is the praise to the glory of God — Bas

so that grace made manifold in many lives may increase the sum of gratitude which is offered to God's glory — Knox

so that, as the abounding grace of God is shared by more and more, the greater may be the chorus of thanksgiving that ascends to the glory of God — NEB

so that God's love, as it spreads will move more and more people to overflow with thanks to God's glory — Beck

16. For which cause we faint not;

Therefore, as I said, we do not lose heart — TCNT

No wonder we do not lose heart! — NEB

So I never give up — Wms

No, we do not play the coward — Knox

That is why we are not discouraged — Beck

but though our outward man perish, yet the inward man is renewed day by day.

No, even though outwardly we are wasting away, yet inwardly we are being renewed day by day — TCNT

though the outward part of our nature is being worn down, our inner life is refreshed from day to day — Knox

The outward man does indeed suffer wear and tear, but every day the inward man receives fresh strength — Phi

17. For our light affliction, which is but for a moment,

For the momentary lightness of the tribulation — Rhm

The light burden of our momentary trouble — TCNT

For our light and transitory affliction — Wey

The slight trouble of the passing hour — Mof

For our present trouble, which is only for a short time — Bas

Our troubles are slight and short-lived — NEB

These troubles and sufferings of ours are, after all, quite small and won't last very long — Tay

worketh for us a far more exceeding and eternal weight of glory;

is preparing for us, in measure transcending thought, a weight of imperishable glory — TCNT

is achieving for us, beyond all proportions, an eternal weight of glory — Wey

results in a solid glory past all comparison — Mof

is piling up for me an eternal blessedness beyond all comparison — Gspd continues to accumulate for me a solid and eternal glory far beyond any comparison — Wms

brings with it a reward multiplied every way, loading us with everlasting glory — Knox

are winning for us a permanent, glorious and solid reward out of all proportion to our pain — Phi

and the outcome an eternal glory which outweighs them far — NEB

18. **While we look not at the things which are seen, but at the things which are not seen:**

Meanwhile I look not to things seen, but to things unseen — Con

if only we will fix our eyes on what is unseen, not on what we can see — Knox

for the things which are seen are temporal; but the things which are not seen are eternal.

for the things that are seen pass away, but the things that are unseen endure for ever — Con

for what is seen is transient, but what is unseen is imperishable — TCNT

The visible things are transitory: it is the invisible things that are really permanent — Phi

For the visible things are temporary . . . — Rhm

for the things which are seen are for a time . . . — Alf

for the things that are seen are for a season . . . — ABUV

What we can see, lasts but for a moment . . . — Knox

CHAPTER 5

1. **For we know that if our earthly house of this tabernacle were dissolved,**

. . . if our earthly tent-dwelling should be taken down — Rhm

. . . if the tent which is my earthly house be destroyed — Con

. . . if our tent — that earthly body which is now our home — is taken down — TCNT

. . . if our earthly tent dwelling should be dismantled — Ber

. . . if the earthly frame that houses us today should be demolished — NEB

we have a building of God, an house not made with hands, eternal in the heavens.

we have in heaven a building from God, a house not made by human hands, but eternal — Wey

God will provide me a building in heaven to live in, not built by human hands but eternal — Gspd

we have a permanent house in Heaven, made, not by man, but by God — Phi

we possess a building which God has provided — a house not made by human hands, eternal, and in heaven — NEB

2. **For in this we groan,**

In this one, indeed, we sigh — Wey

This makes me sigh with longing — Gspd

In this present frame we sigh with deep longing — Phi

earnestly desiring to be clothed upon with our house which is from heaven:

desiring to cover my earthly raiment with the robes of my heavenly mansion — Con

longing to put over it our heavenly dwelling — TCNT

yearning to be under cover of my heavenly habitation — Mof

we yearn to have our heavenly habitation put on over this one — NEB

3. **If so be that being clothed we shall not be found naked.**

sure that, when we have put it on, we shall never be found discarnate — TCNT

since I am sure that once so covered I shall not be 'naked' at the hour of death — Mof

for if I do, I shall never find myself disembodied — Gspd

4. **For we that are in this tabernacle do groan, being burdened:**

For we who are in this 'tent' sigh under our burden — TCNT

Yes, if we tent-dwellers here go sighing and heavy-hearted — Knox

As long as we are clothed in this temporary dwelling we have a painful longing — Phi

So while we are in this tent, we sigh, feeling oppressed — Beck

not for that we would be unclothed, but clothed upon,

not desiring to put off our [earthly] clothing, but to put over it [our heavenly] raiment — Con

unwilling to take it off, yet wishing to put our heavenly body over it — TCNT

not that I want to be stripped, no, but to be under cover of the other — Mof

because I do not want to be stripped of it, but to put on the other over it — Gspd

it is not because we would be stripped of something; rather we would clothe ourselves afresh — Knox

not that we would be unclothed, but that we would be further clothed — RSV

not because we want just to get rid of these "clothes," but because we want to know the full cover of the permanent house that will be ours — Phi

because we do not want to have the old body stripped off. Rather our desire is to have the new body put on over it — NEB

that mortality might be swallowed up of life.

that this our dying nature might be swallowed up by life — Con

so that all that is mortal may be absorbed in Life — TCNT

our mortal nature must be swallowed up in life — Knox

so that our mortal part may be absorbed into life immortal — NEB

and have life swallow up our death — Beck

5. Now he that hath wrought us for the selfsame thing is God,

For this, nothing else, God was preparing us — Knox

God himself has shaped us for this very end — NEB

And He who has prepared me for this very end is God — Con

And he who formed us for this very purpose is God — Wey

who also hath given unto us the earnest of the Spirit.

who has also given us his Spirit as a pledge — TCNT

who has given us His Spirit as guarantee — Wey

because He has given me the Spirit as the first installment of future bliss — Wms

when he gave us the foretaste of his Spirit — Knox

6. Therefore we are always confident,

Being therefore always of good courage — ASV

We have therefore an unfailing confidence — Wey

Come what may, then, I am confident — Mof

So I am always cheerful and confident — Wms

We take heart, then, continually — Knox

knowing that, whilst we are at home in the body, we are absent from the Lord:

knowing that, while our home is in the body, we are absent from our home with the Lord — TCNT

since we recognize that our spirits are exiled from the Lord's presence so long as they are at home in the body — Knox

We realize that being "at home" in the body means that to some extent we are "away" from the Lord — Phi

7. (For we walk by faith, not by sight:)

For we guide our lives by faith, and not by what we see — TCNT

for we guide ourselves by faith and not by external appearance — Wey

(for I have to lead my life in faith, without seeing him) — Mof

8. We are confident, I say, and willing rather to be absent from the body, and to be present with the Lord.

And in this confidence we would gladly leave our home in the body, and make our home with the Lord — TCNT

9. Wherefore we labour,

Wherefore also we make it our aim — ASV

Therefore I strive earnestly — Con

Therefore . . . our one ambition is — TCNT

Hence also I am eager — Mof

that, 'whether present or absent, we may be accepted of him.

whether at home or absent, to be well-pleasing unto him — ASV whether in banishment or at home . . . — Con

whether in our home or absent from our home . . . — TCNT

whether in the body or away from it . . . — Mof

whether at home or in exile . . . — Mon

10. For we must all appear before the judgment seat of Christ;

For we must all be made manifest . . . — ASV

For at the Bar of the Christ we must all appear in our true characters — TCNT

for we have all to appear without disguise before the tribunal of Christ — Mof

All of us have a scrutiny to undergo before Christ's judgement-seat — Knox

that every one may receive the things done in his body, according to that he hath done, whether it be good or bad.

that each may reap the results of the life which he has lived in the body, in accordance with his actions — whether good or worthless — TCNT

each to be requited for what he has done with his body, well or ill — Mof

each to be repaid with good or evil for the life he has lived in the body — Gspd

so that each one may receive good or evil, according to what he has done in the body — RSV

that each may get his pay for what he has done, whether it be good or bad — Wms

11. Knowing therefore the terror of the Lord, we persuade men;

Therefore, because we know the fear inspired by the Lord, it is true that we are trying to win men — TCNT

Knowing then what the fear of the Lord means, we endeavour to win men — Wey

If I 'appeal to the interests of men,' then, it is with the fear of the Lord before my mind — Mof

It is with this knowledge of what the fear of the Lord means that I appeal to men — Gspd

All our persuading of men, then, is with this solemn fear of God in our minds — Phi

but we are made manifest unto God; and I trust also are made manifest in your consciences.

yet my uprightness is manifest in the sight of God; and I hope also that it is manifested by the witness of your consciences — Con

but our motives are plain to God; and I hope that in your inmost hearts they are plain to you also — TCNT

What I am is plain to God without disguise, plain also, I trust, to your own conscience — Mof

God recognizes us for what we are, and so I hope, does your better judgement — Knox

God already knows what we really are, and I hope you, too, are clearly conscious of it — Beck

To God our lives lie open, as I hope they also lie open to you in your heart of hearts — NEB

12. For we commend not ourselves again unto you, but give you occasion to glory on our behalf,

We are not commending ourselves again to you, but are furnishing you with a ground of boasting on our behalf — Wey

We are not "commending ourselves" again to you, but rather are giving you cause for pride in us — TCNT

This is not 'recommending myself to you again'; it is giving you an incentive to be proud of me — Mof

We are not requesting your approval, but we are giving you the chance of taking pride in us — Bas

that ye may have somewhat to answer them which glory in appearance, and not in heart.

so that you may have an answer ready for those who pride themselves on appearances and not on character — TCNT

so that you may have a reply ready for those who boast openly but yet insincerely — Wey

which you can use against men who are proud of externals instead of the inward reality — Mof

to use in answering men who pride themselves on external advantages and not on sincerity of heart — Gspd

that you may have something to say to those who are constantly prating about external privileges and are not concerned about the state of the heart — Wms

so that you may be able to answer those who pride themselves on a man's position and not on his heart — RSV

then you will have something to say to those whose pride is all in outward show and not in inward worth — NEB

13. For whether we be beside ourselves, it is to God:

For if I be mad, it is for God's cause — Con

For if I was out of my senses, as they say, it was between God and me — Gspd

Are these wild words? Then take them as addressed to God — Knox

Are we insane to say such things about ourselves? If so, it is to bring glory to God — Tay

or whether we be sober, it is for your cause.

or if we are in our senses, it is for your good — Wey

Or sober sense? Then take them as addressed to yourselves — Knox

14. For the love of Christ constraineth us;

It is the love of Christ which compels us — TCNT

For the love of Christ overmasters us — Wey

It is Christ's love that controls me — Gspd

The very spring of our actions is the love of Christ — Phi

For the love of Christ leaves us no choice — NEB

because we thus judge, that if one died for all, then were all dead:

since we have thus concluded, that One died for all, and hence all died — Wey

convinced that as One has died for all, then all have died — Mof

because we are of the opinion that if one was put to death for all, then all have undergone death — Bas

and this is the conviction we have reached; if one man died on behalf of all, then all thereby became dead men — Knox

We look at it like this: if one died for all men then, in a sense, they all died — Phi

15. And that he died for all, that they which live should not henceforth live unto themselves, but unto him which died for them, and rose again.

His purpose in dying for all was that men, while still in life, should cease to live for themselves, and should live for him who for their sake died and was raised to life — NEB

Christ died for us all, so that being alive should no longer mean living with our own life, but with his life who died for us and has risen again — Knox

16. Wherefore henceforth know we no man after the flesh:

For ourselves, then, from this time forward, we refuse to regard anyone from the world's standpoint — TCNT

Therefore for the future we know no one simply as a man — Wey

Once convinced of this, then, I estimate no one by what is external — Mof

and therefore, henceforward, we do not think of anybody in a merely human fashion — Knox

From now on, therefore, we regard no one from a human point of view — RSV

This means that our knowledge of men can no longer be based on their outward lives — Phi

With us therefore worldly standards have ceased to count in our estimate of any man — NEB

yea, though we have known Christ after the flesh, yet now henceforth know we him no more.

yea, though once my view of Christ was carnal, yet now it is no longer carnal — Con

Even if we once thought of Christ from the standpoint of the world, yet now we do so no longer — TCNT

Even if we have known Christ simply as a man, yet now we do so no longer — Wey

even though I once estimated Christ by what is external, I no longer estimate him thus — Mof

811

even if we used to think of Christ in a human fashion, we do so no longer —Knox

even though we once regarded Christ from a human point of view, we regard him thus no longer — RSV

(indeed, even though we knew Christ as a man we do not know him like that any longer) — Phi

Once I mistakenly thought of Christ that way, merely as a human being like myself. How differently I feel now! — Tay

17. Therefore if any man be in Christ, he is a new creature:

Whosoever, then, is in Christ, is a new creation — Con

Therefore, if any one is in union with Christ, he is a new being — TCNT

There is a new creation whenever a man comes to be in Christ — Mof

For if a man is in Christ he becomes a new person altogether — Phi

So if any man is in Christ, he is in a new world — Bas

When anyone is united to Christ, there is a new world — NEB

old things are passed away; behold, all things are become new.

the old things are passed away; behold, they are become new — ASV

his old being has passed away, and behold, all has become new — Con

His old life has passed away; a new life has begun! — TCNT

the old state of things has passed away; a new has come — Wey

what is old has gone, the new has come — Mof

his old life has disappeared, everything has become new about him — Knox

the old has passed away, behold, the new has come — RSV

the past is finished and gone, everything has become fresh and new — Phi

the old order has gone, and a new order has already begun — NEB

18. And all things are of God, who hath reconciled us to himself by Jesus Christ, and hath given to us the ministry of reconciliation;

But all comes from God, for He it is who reconciled me to Himself by Jesus Christ, and charged me with the ministry of reconciliation—Con

It is all the doing of the God who has reconciled me to himself through Christ and has permitted me to be a minister of his reconciliation — Mof

But all things are of God, who has made us at peace with himself through Christ, and has given us the work of making peace — Bas

But God has done it all. When we were His enemies, through Christ He made us His friends and gave us the work of making friends of enemies — Beck

From first to last this has been the work of God. He has reconciled us men to himself through Christ, and he has enlisted us in this service of reconciliation — NEB

19. To wit, that God was in Christ, reconciling the world unto himself,

to proclaim that God, in Christ, was reconciling the world to himself — TCNT

to tell how in Christ God was reconciling the world to Himself — Wey

— how God through Christ reconciled the world to himself — Gspd

That is, that God was in Christ making peace between the world and himself — Bas

What I mean is, that God was in Christ reconciling the world to himself — NEB

not imputing their trespasses unto them;

instead of debiting men's offenses against them — Wms

not counting their sins against them — Phi

no longer holding men's misdeeds against them — NEB

reckoning their sins no more against them — Con

not charging men's transgressions to their account — Wey

not putting their sins to their account — Bas

and hath committed unto us the word of reconciliation.

and having ordained me to speak the word of reconciliation — Con

and having given to us the preaching of this news of peace — Bas

and entrusted to us the message of reconciliation — RSV

20. Now then we are ambassadors for Christ, as though God did beseech you by us:

Therefore I am an ambassador for Christ, as though God exhorted you by my voice — Con

It is, then, on Christ's behalf that we are acting as ambassadors, God, as it were, appealing to you through us — TCNT

So I am an envoy for Christ, God appealing by me, as it were — Mof

It is for Christ, therefore, that I am an envoy, seeing that God makes his appeal through me — Gspd

So we are the representatives of Christ, as if God was making a request to you through us — Bas

we pray you in Christ's stead, be ye reconciled to God.

We implore you on Christ's behalf — Be reconciled to God — TCNT

As one representing Christ I beg you, be reconciled to God — Wms

we entreat you in Christ's name, make your peace with God — Knox

As his personal representative we say, Make your peace with God — Phi

21. For he hath made him to be sin for us, who knew no sin;

Him who knew no sin he made to be sin on our behalf — ASV

For our sakes he made him to be sin who himself knew nothing of sin — Mof

For him who had no knowledge of sin God made to be sin for us — Bas

For God caused Christ, who had never sinned, to be sin for us — Nor

For God caused Christ, who himself knew nothing of sin, actually to be sin for our sakes — Phi

Christ was innocent of sin, and yet for our sake God made him one with the sinfulness of men — NEB

that we might be made the righteousness of God in him.

that we might be changed into the righteousness of God in Christ — Con

so that we, through union with him, might become the Righteousness of God — TCNT

so that through union with Him we might come into right standing with God — Wms

so that in him we might be turned into the holiness of God — Knox

so that in Him we might receive justification from God — Nor

so that in Christ we might be made good with the goodness of God — Phi

CHAPTER 6

1. We then, as workers together with him, beseech you also that ye receive not the grace of God in vain.

As God's fellow-worker, I appeal to you, too, not to accept the favor of God and then waste it — Gspd

And now, to further that work, we entreat you not to offer God's grace an ineffectual welcome — Knox

As cooperators with God himself we beg you, then, not to fail to use the grace of God — Phi

As men who are working with God we plead with you: Don't let God's love be wasted on you — Beck

Sharing in God's work, we urge this appeal upon you: you have received the grace of God; do not let it go for nothing — NEB

2. (For he saith, I have heard thee in a time accepted, and in the day of salva-

tion have I succoured thee:

. . . At the time for acceptance I listened to thee, And on the day of deliverance I helped thee — TCNT

. . . I have heard you in the time of favour, and helped you on the day of salvation — Mof

(I have answered thy prayer, he says, in a time of pardon, I have brought thee help in a day of salvation — Knox

God's own words are: In the hour of my favour I gave heed to you; On the day of deliverance I came to your aid — NEB

behold, now is the accepted time; behold, now is the day of salvation.)

Now is the time for acceptance! Now is the day of deliverance! — TCNT

Well, here is the time of favour, here is the day of salvation.) — Mof

And here is the time of pardon; the day of salvation has come already — Knox

The hour of favour has now come; now, I say, has the day of deliverance dawned — NEB

3. Giving no offence in any thing, that the ministry be not blamed:

Never do we put an obstacle in any one's way, that no fault may be found with our ministry — TCNT

We give no cause for stumbling of any sort, lest our ministry should incur discredit — Wey

4. But in all things approving ourselves as the ministers of God,

No, we are trying to commend ourselves under all circumstances, as God's ministers should — TCNT

On the contrary, we seek to commend ourselves as God's servants in every way — Wey

But in everything making it clear that we are the servants of God — Bas

Indeed we want to prove ourselves genuine ministers of God whatever we have to go through — Phi

In fact, in everything we do we try to show that we are true ministers of God — Tay

in much patience, in afflictions, in necessities, in distresses,

in many an hour of endurance, in troubles, in hardships, in difficulties — TCNT

by great endurance, by afflictions, distresses, anguish — Wey

by our steadfast endurance: in hardships and dire straits — NEB

5. In stripes, in imprisonments, in tumults,

in floggings, in imprisonments, in riots — TCNT

In scourgings, in bonds, . . . — Lam

under the lash, in prison, in the midst of tumult — Knox

flogged, imprisoned, mobbed — NEB

We have been beaten, put in jail, faced angry mobs — Tay

in labours, in watchings, in fastings;

in toils, in sleepless nights . . . — TCNT

toiling, sleepless, starving — Mof

in labors, in sleepless watching, in hunger and thirst — Mon

when we are tired out, sleepless, and fasting — Knox

worked to exhaustion, stayed awake through sleepless nights of watching, and gone without food — Tay

6. By pureness, by knowledge, by longsuffering,

with innocence, insight, patience—Mof

with purity, understanding, patience — Mon

We have to be pure-minded, enlightened, forgiving — Knox

through innocence, knowledge, and endurance of wrongs — Ber

We recommend ourselves by the innocence of our behaviour, our grasp of truth, our patience — NEB

. . . forbearance — RSV

by kindness, by the Holy Ghost, by love unfeigned,

. . . kindness, . . . holiness of spirit, . . . genuine love — Gspd

through kindness by the Holy Spirit in unpretended love — Ber

and kindliness; by gifts of the Holy Spirit, by sincere love — NEB

in graciousness . . . — Rhm

7. By the word of truth, by the power of God, by the armour of righteousness on the right hand and on the left,

speaking the word of truth, working with the power of God, fighting with the weapons of righteousness, both for attack and for defence — Con

speaking the plain truth, and living by the power of God. Our sole defense, our only weapon, is a life of integrity — Phi

by truthful speech . . . by the weapons of righteousness in right hand and left — Wey

We must rely on the truth of the Word . . . — Nor

8. By honour and dishonour, by evil report and good report: as deceivers, and yet true;

through good report and evil; through honor and through infamy; counted as a deceiver, yet being true — Con

amid honour and disrepute, amid slander and praise; regarded as deceivers, yet proved to be true — TCNT

through honour and ignominy, through calumny and praise; regarded as impostors, and yet true men — Wey

By glory and by shame, by an evil name and a good name; as untrue, and still true — Bas

now honoured, now slighted, now traduced, now flattered. They call us deceivers, and we tell the truth — Knox

9. As unknown, and yet well known;

as unknown [by men], yet acknowledged [by God] — Con

The world ignores us, but we are known to God — Tay

as dying, and, behold, we live;

as ever dying, yet behold I live; as chastened by suffering, yet not destroyed — Con

at the point of death, yet here I am alive, punished, but not dead yet — Gspd

10. As sorrowful, yet alway rejoicing; as poor, yet making many rich; as having nothing, and yet possessing all things.

grieved but always glad, a 'pauper' but the means of wealth to many, without a penny but possessed of everything — Mof

sad men, that rejoice continually; beggars, that bring riches to many; disinherited, and the world is ours — Knox

We know sorrow, yet our joy is inextinguishable. We have nothing to bless ourselves with, yet we bless many others with true riches. We are penniless, and yet in reality we have everything worth having — Phi

. . . penniless, we own the world — NEB

11. O ye Corinthians, our mouth is open unto you, our heart is enlarged.

We are speaking freely to you, Corinthians; we throw our hearts wide open to you — Knox

I have kept nothing back from you, men of Corinth; I have opened my heart to you — Gspd

Corinthians, we address you frankly with wide-open hearts — Ber

Oh, our dear friends in Corinth, we are hiding nothing from you and our hearts are absolutely open to you — Phi

Men of Corinth, we have spoken very frankly to you; we have opened our heart wide to you all — NEB

12. Ye are not straitened in us, but ye are straitened in your own bowels.

You find no narrowness in my love, but the narrowness is in your own — Con

there is room there for you, yet there is not room, in your love, for us — TCNT

There is no want of affection for you in us; the want is in your own affections — Wey

There is no narrowness in my love; but the narrowness is in your own — Mon

It is not our feelings to you which are narrow, but yours to us — Bas

It is not our fault, it is the fault of your own affections, that you feel constraint with us — Knox

Our affections toward you are not restricted, but rather, you are restricted in your affections — Nor

Any stiffness between us must be on your side, for we assure you there is none on ours — Phi

On our part there is no constraint; any constraint there may be is in yourselves — NEB

13. Now for a recompence in the same, (I speak as unto my children,) be ye also enlarged.

I pray you therefore in return for my affection (I speak as to my children), let your hearts be opened in like manner — Con

Can you not in return — I appeal to you as I should to children — open your hearts to us? — TCNT

Then as a fair return — I speak as to my children — let your hearts be opened also — Wey

A fair exchange now, as the children say! Open your hearts wide to me — Mof

Pay us back in the same coin (I am speaking to you as to my children); open your hearts wide too — Knox

Do reward me (I talk to you as though you were my own children) with the same complete candor! — Phi

In fair exchange then (may a father speak so to his children?) open wide your hearts to us — NEB

14. Be ye not unequally yoked together with unbelievers:

Do not enter into inconsistent relations with those who reject the Faith — TCNT

Avoid unsuitable connections with unbelievers — Wey

Keep out of all incongruous ties with unbelievers — Mof

Stop forming intimate and inconsistent relations with unbelievers — Wms

Do not be mismated with unbelievers — Nor

for what fellowship hath righteousness with unrighteousness? and what communion hath light with darkness?

For what is there in common between righteousness and lawlessness? Or what partnership has light with darkness — Wey

What common interest can there be between goodness and evil? How can light and darkness share life together — Phi

15. **And what concord hath Christ with Belial? or what part hath he that believeth with an infidel?**

And what agreement is there between Christ and the Evil One? or what part has one who has faith with one who has not — Bas

How can there be harmony between Christ and the devil? What can a believer have in common with an unbeliever — Phi

. . . or what can those who accept the Faith have in common with those who reject it — TCNT

16. **And what agreement hath the temple of God with idols? for ye are the temple of the living God;**

And what agreement hath a temple of God with idols? for we are a temple of the living God — ASV

What common ground can idols have with the temple of God? For we, remember, are ourselves living temples of the living God — Phi

as God hath said, I will dwell in them, and walk in them; and I will be their God, and they shall be my people.

17. **Wherefore come out from among them, and be ye separate, saith the Lord, and touch not the unclean thing; and I will receive you,**

Come out, then, from among them, the Lord says to us, separate yourselves from them, and do not even touch what is unclean . . . — Knox

18. **And will be a Father unto you, and ye shall be my sons and daughters, saith the Lord Almighty.**

CHAPTER 7

1. **Having therefore these promises, dearly beloved, let us cleanse ourselves from all filthiness of the flesh and spirit,**

With these promises, dear friends, let us purify ourselves from everything that pollutes either body or spirit — TCNT

As these great promises are ours, beloved, let us cleanse ourselves from everything that contaminates either flesh or spirit — Mof

Such are the promises, beloved, that await us. Why then, let us purge ourselves clean from every defilement of flesh and spirit — Knox

perfecting holiness in the fear of God.

and, in deepest reverence for God, aim at perfect holiness — TCNT

let us be fully consecrated by reverence for God — Mof

and by reverence for God make our

consecration complete — Gspd

Let us prove our reverence for God by consecrating ourselves to him completely — Phi

2. **Receive us;**

Make room for us in your hearts — TCNT

we have wronged no man, we have corrupted no man, we have defrauded no man.

In no instance have we ever wronged, or harmed, or taken advantage of, anyone — TCNT

Not one of you has ever been wronged or ruined or cheated by us — Phi

3. **I speak not this to condemn you: for I have said before, that ye are in our hearts to die and live with you.**

I am not saying this to blame you, for as I have already said, I hold you in my heart to live together and to die together — Mon

I am not finding fault with you when I say this; I have told you before now, we hold you so close in our hearts that nothing in life or in death can part us from you — Knox

I do not want to blame you. Why, as I have told you before, the place you have in our heart is such that, come death, come life, we meet it together — NEB

4. Great is my boldness of speech toward you, great is my glorying of you:

Great is my confidence toward you, great is my boasting on your behalf — Alf

I have the utmost confidence in you; I am always boasting about you — TCNT

I am perfectly frank with you. I have great pride in you — NEB

I am filled with comfort, I am exceeding joyful in all our tribulation.

I am full of encouragement and, in spite of all our troubles, my heart is overflowing with happiness—TCNT

I am full of encouragement, nay, I cannot contain myself for happiness, in the midst of all these trials of mine — Knox

In all our many troubles my cup is full of consolation, and overflows with joy — NEB

5. For, when we were come into Macedonia, our flesh had no rest,

For even after our arrival in Macedonia we could get no relief for body or mind — Wey

For I got no relief from the strain of things, even when I reached Macedonia — Mof

Even when we reached Macedonia there was still no relief for this poor body of ours — NEB

but we were troubled on every side; without were fightings, within were fears.

on every side there have been troubles — conflicts without, anxieties within — TCNT

it was trouble at every turn, wrangling all around me, fears in my own mind — Mof

there was trouble at every turn, quarrels all around us, forebodings in our heart — NEB

6. Nevertheless God, that comforteth those that are cast down, comforted us by the coming of Titus;

But God, who encourages the downcast, has encouraged us by the arrival of Titus — TCNT

Nevertheless he that comforteth the lowly . . . — ASV

But the God who comforts the dejected . . . — Mof

But the God who comforts the downhearted comforted me by the coming of Titus — Mon

But there is one who never fails to comfort those who are brought low; God gave us comfort, as soon as Titus came — Knox

7. And not by his coming only, but by the consolation wherewith he was comforted in you,

And it is not only by his arrival that we are encouraged, but also by the encouragement which he received from you — TCNT

Yes, and by more than his arrival, by the comfort which you had been to him — Mof

It was not only that he came; he inspired us with that courage he had derived from you — Knox

And it wasn't merely his coming that cheered us, but the comfort you had given him — Phi

when he told us your earnest desire, your mourning, your fervent mind toward me; so that I rejoiced the more.

and the tidings which he brought of your longing for my love, your mourning for my reproof, your zeal for my cause; so that my sorrow has been turned into joy — Con

for he tells us of your strong affection, your penitence, and your zeal on my behalf — so that I am happier still — TCNT

as he reported to us your eager affection, your grief, and your jealousy on my behalf, so that I rejoiced more than ever — Wey

for he gave me such a report of how you longed for me, how sorry you were, and how eagerly you took my part, that it added to my delight — Mof for he could tell us of your eagerness to help, your deep sympathy and keen interest on my behalf. All that made me doubly glad to see him — Phi

8. **For though I made you sorry with a letter, I do not repent, though I did repent: for I perceive that the same epistle hath made you sorry, though it were but for a season.**

For though I grieved you in my letter, I do not regret it; but though I did regret it (for I see that grief was caused you by that letter, though but for a season) — Con

In fact, if I did pain you by that letter, I do not regret it. I did regret it when I discovered that my letter had pained you even for the time being — Mof

Yes, even if I caused you pain by my letter, I am not sorry for it. Perhaps I was tempted to feel sorry, when I saw how my letter had caused you even momentary pain — Knox

For although my letter had hurt you I don't regret it now (as I did, I must confess, at one time). I can see that the letter did upset you, though only for a time — Phi

Even if I did wound you by the letter I sent, I do not now regret it. I may have been sorry for it when I saw that the letter had caused you pain, even if only for a time — NEB

9. **Now I rejoice, not that ye were made sorry, but that ye sorrowed to repentance:**

I now rejoice; not because you were grieved, but because your grief led you to repentance — Con

but I am glad now — not glad that you were pained but glad that your pain induced you to repent — Mof

but now I am glad; not glad of the pain, but glad of the repentance the pain brought with it — Knox

and now I am glad I sent it, not because I want to hurt you but because it made you grieve for things that were wrong — Phi

but now I am happy, not that your feelings were wounded but that the wound led to a change of heart — NEB

for ye were made sorry after a godly manner, that ye might receive damage by us in nothing.

For it was God's will that you should feel sorrow, in order that you should not suffer loss in any way at our hands — TCNT

for your pain was such as God accepts, so that you received no injury from us in any respect — Wey

for you took it as God meant you to do, so that you should not lose anything at all through me — Gspd

In other words, the result was to make you sorry as God would have had you sorry, and not merely to make you offended by what we said — Phi

for yours was a holy sorrow . . . — Bas

. . . so that you were not in any way the losers through what we had done — Knox

10. **For godly sorrow worketh repentance to salvation not to be repented of:**

For the work of godly sorrow is repentance not to be repented of, leading to salvation — Con

For the pain that God approves results in a repentance that leads to salvation and leaves no regrets — Gspd

For the sorrow that relates the sorrower to God works out a repentance that leads to salvation such as is never regretted — Ber

For godly grief produces a repentance that leads to salvation and brings no regret — RSV

For the wound which is borne in God's way brings a change of heart too salutary to regret — NEB

but the sorrow of the world worketh death.

but the work of worldly sorrow is death — Con

but the sorrow the world produces results in death — Wms

whereas the world's remorse leads to death — Knox

it is the world's sorrow that is such a deadly thing — Phi

but the hurt which is borne in the world's way brings death — NEB

11. **For behold this selfsame thing, that ye sorrowed after a godly sort, what carefulness it wrought in you,**

For see what results that other sorrow

— sorrow in accordance with God's will — has had in your case. What earnestness it produced! — TCNT

See how earnest this God-given pain has made you! — Gspd

For notice how serious this God-related grief has made you — Ber

You can look back now and see how the hand of God was in that sorrow. Look how seriously it made you think — Phi

yea, what clearing of yourselves, yea, what indignation, yea, what fear,

what eagerness to clear yourselves from blame . . . — Con

how eager it made you to prove your innocence . . . — Phi

what vindication of yourselves . . . — NASB

. . . what wrath against sin . . . — Bas

. . . how disgusted with wrong . . . — Beck

. . . how angered you were, how apprehensive! — NEB

what explanations! what strong feeling! what alarm! — TCNT

how you disowned the guilt; the indignation you felt, the fear that overcame you — Knox

yea, what vehement desire, yea, what zeal, yea, what revenge!

how eager to see me . . . — Gspd

. . . how loyal to me, how determined to punish the offender! — Wms

. . . yea, what exacting of punishment! — Alf

. . . what readiness to punish! — TCNT

. . . how ready to vindicate me — Ber

how you missed me, how you took my part, how you righted the wrong done — Knox

Look how it made you long for my presence, how it stirred up your keenness for the faith, how ready it made you to punish the offender! — Phi

How your longing for me awoke, yes, and your devotion and your eagerness to see justice done! — NEB

In all things ye have approved yourselves to be clear in this matter.

You have cleared yourselves altogether from every stain of guilt in this matter — Con

You have completely wiped away reproach from yourselves in the matter — Wey

At every point you have cleared yourselves in the matter — Wms

12. Wherefore, though I wrote unto you, I did it not for his cause that had done the wrong, nor for his cause that suffered wrong,

So my letter was written to you, not on account of the offender nor for the sake of the injured party — Mof

I wrote to you, but really not so much on account of the man who was doing wrong nor for the sake of the one who was suffering wrong — Nor

And so, although I did send you that letter, it was not the offender or his victim that most concerned me — NEB

but that our care for you in the sight of God might appear unto you.

but to make you conscious, in the sight of God, of your own earnest care for us — TCNT

but in order to let you realize before God how seriously you do care for me — Mof

but rather to let you see yourselves, as before God, how devoted to us you really are — Nor

but to let you see for yourselves, in the sight of God, how deeply you really do care for us — Phi

My aim in writing was to help to make plain to you, in the sight of God, how truly you are devoted to us — NEB

13. Therefore we were comforted in your comfort: yea, and exceedingly the more joyed we for the joy of Titus, because his spirit was refreshed by you all.

Therefore we have been comforted: and in our comfort we joyed the more exceedingly . . . — ASV

This, therefore, is the ground of my comfort; but besides my consolation on your account, I was beyond measure rejoiced by the joy of Titus . . . — Con

And it is this that has encouraged us. In addition to the encouragement that this gave us, we were made far happier still by the happiness of

Titus; for his heart has been cheered by you all — TCNT

. . . because his mind has been set at rest by you all — RSV

This is what encouraged us. While we were encouraged, we were much more delighted to see how happy Titus was because all of you had cheered him up — Beck

14. For if I have boasted any thing to him of you, I am not ashamed;

For if in anything I have gloried to him on your behalf, I was not put to shame — ASV

Although I have been boasting a little to him about you, you did not put me to shame — TCNT

I had told him of my pride in you, and I have not been disappointed — Mof

I had boasted to Titus of the confidence I felt in you, and you did not play me false — Knox

You see, I had told him of my pride in you, and you have not let me down — Phi

but as we spake all things to you in truth, even so our boasting, which I made before Titus, is found a truth.

but, just as everything we had said to you was true, so our boasting to Titus about you has also proved to be the truth — TCNT

No, just as all I have had to say to you has been true, so all I said about you to Titus, all my pride in you, has also proved true — Mof

but as we said nothing to you but what was true, so the good things which I said to Titus about you were seen by him to be true — Bas

no, the boast I had made to Titus proved true, as true as the message

which I had delivered to you — Knox

15. And his inward affection is more abundant toward you, whilst he remembereth the obedience of you all, how with fear and trembling ye received him.

And his heart is more than ever drawn towards you, while he calls to mind the obedience of you all, and the fear and trembling wherewith you received him — Con

And his affection for you is all the greater, as he remembers the deference that you all showed him, and recalls how you received him with anxious care — TCNT

And his love to you is the more increased by his memory of you all, how you gave way to his authority, and how you took him to your hearts with fear and honour — Bas

He bears a most affectionate memory of you, of the submissiveness you all shewed, of the anxious fear with which you received him — Knox

Titus himself has a much greater love for you, now that he has seen for himself the obedience you gave him, and the respect and reverence with which you treated him — Phi

16. I rejoice therefore that I have confidence in you in all things.

I rejoice that in all things you give me ground for courage — Con

I am glad that I can feel perfect confidence in you — TCNT

I rejoice that I have complete confidence in you — Wey

It gives me great joy to see you answering to my good opinion of you in every way — Bas

I am profoundly glad to have my confidence in you so fully proved — Phi

CHAPTER 8

1. Moreover, brethren, we do you to wit of the grace of God bestowed on the churches of Macedonia;

I desire, brethren, to make known to you the manifestation of God's grace, which has been given in the churches of Macedonia — Con

I must tell you, brothers, how the favor of God has been shown in the churches of Macedonia — Gspd

Fellow Christians, we want you to know what God's gift of love has done in the churches of Macedonia — Beck

2. How that in a great trial of affliction the abundance of their joy and their deep poverty abounded unto the riches of their liberality.

For in the heavy trial which has proved their steadfastness, the fulness of their joy has overflowed, out of the depth of their poverty, in the richness of their liberality — Con

how, tried though they were by many a trouble, their overflowing happiness, and even their deep poverty, resulted in a flood of generosity — TCNT

Amid a severe ordeal of trouble, their overflowing joy and their deep poverty together have poured out a flood of rich generosity — Mof

The troubles they have been through have tried them hard, yet in all this they have been so exuberantly happy that from the depths of their poverty they have shown themselves lavishly open-handed — NEB

3. For to their power, I bear record, yea, and beyond their power they were willing of themselves;

They have given (I bear them witness) not only according to their means, but beyond their means, and that of their own free will — Con

For I give them witness, that as they were able, and even more than they were able, they gave from the impulse of their hearts — Bas

I can testify that of their own accord they undertook to do all they could, and more than they could — Knox

I can guarantee that they were willing to give to the limit of their means, yes and beyond their means, without the slightest urging from me or anyone else — Phi

4. Praying us with much intreaty that we would receive the gift, and take upon us the fellowship of the ministering to the saints.

With earnest entreaty they begged from us the favour of sharing in this service to the saints — Wey

they begged us, most urgently, to allow them the privilege of helping to supply the needs of the saints — Knox

In fact they simply begged us to accept their gifts and so let them share the honor of supporting their brothers in Christ — Phi

5. And this they did, not as we hoped, but first gave their own selves to the Lord, and unto us by the will of God.

They indeed exceeded our expectations. First of all they gave themselves to the Lord, and to us as God willed — Wey

They have done more than I expected; they gave themselves to the Lord, to begin with, and then (for so God willed it) they put themselves at my disposal — Mof

Nor was their gift, as I must confess I had expected, a mere cash payment. Instead they made a complete dedication of themselves first to the Lord and then to us, as God's appointed ministers — Phi

6. Insomuch that we desired Titus, that as he had begun, so he would also finish in you the same grace also.

This led us to urge Titus that, as he had been the one who commenced the work, so he should complete among you this act of beneficence also — Wey

This has led me to ask Titus to complete the arrangements for the same gracious contribution among yourselves, as it was he who started it — Mof

7. Therefore, as ye abound in every thing, in faith, and utterance, and knowledge, and in all diligence, and in your love to us, see that ye abound in this grace also.

And, remembering how you excel in everything — in faith, in teaching, in knowledge, in unfailing earnestness, and in the affection that we have awakened in you — I ask you to excel also in this expression of your love — TCNT

You excel in so much already, in faith, in power of utterance, in knowledge of the truth, in devotion of every kind, in your loving treatment of us; may this gracious excellence be yours too — Knox

. . . surely you should show yourselves equally lavish in this general service! — NEB

8. I speak not by commandment, but by occasion of the forwardness of others, and to prove the sincerity of your love.

I am not laying a command upon you, but I am making use of the earnestness shown by others to test the genuineness of your affection—TCNT

I am not saying this in the spirit of a command, but I am simply trying to test the genuineness of your love by the enthusiasm of others — Wms

I say this not as a command, but to prove by the earnestness of others that your love also is genuine — RSV

This is not meant as an order; by telling you how keen others are I am putting your love to the test — NEB

9. For ye know the grace of our Lord Jesus Christ, that, though he was rich, yet for your sakes he became poor, that ye through his poverty might be rich.

(You know how gracious our Lord Jesus Christ was; rich though he was, he became poor for the sake of you, that by his poverty you might be rich.) — Mof

(You do not need to be reminded how gracious our Lord Jesus Christ was; how he impoverished himself for your sakes, when he was so rich, so that you might become rich through his poverty) — Knox

10. And herein I give my advice:

But in this matter I give my opinion — Wey

But I will tell you what I think about it — Mof

Here is my considered opinion on the matter — NEB

for this is expedient for you, who have begun before, not only to do, but also to be forward a year ago.

for it becomes you to do thus, inasmuch as you began not only the contribution, but the purpose of making it, before others, in the year which is passed — Con

it is to your interest to go on with this enterprise, for you started it last year, you were the first not merely to do anything but to want to do anything — Mof

you can claim that as your due, since it was you who led the way, not only in acting, but in proposing to act, as early as last year — Knox

it is best for you now to complete what a year ago you began not only to do but to desire — RSV

I think it would be a good thing for you, who were the first a year ago to think of helping, as well as the first to give, to carry through what you then intended to do — Phi

11. Now therefore perform the doing of it; that as there was a readiness to will, so there may be a performance also out of that which ye have.

Now, therefore, fulfil your purpose by your deeds, that as you then showed your readiness of will, so now you may finish the work, according to your means — Con

And now I want you to complete the work, so that its completion may correspond with your willing readiness — in proportion, of course, to your means — TCNT

Now finish doing it too, so that your readiness to finish it may be just like your readiness to start it, in accordance with what you have — Wms

It remains for you now to complete your action; readiness of the will must be completed by deeds, as far as your means allow — Knox

Finish it, then, as well as you can, and show that you can complete what you set out to do with as much efficiency as you showed readiness to begin — Phi

Now I want you to go on and finish it: be as eager to complete the scheme as you were to adopt it, and give according to your means — NEB

12. For if there be first a willing mind, it is accepted according to that a man hath, and not according to that he hath not.

For, where there is willingness, a man's gift is valued by its comparison with what he has, and not with what he has not — TCNT

If only one is ready to give according to his means, it is acceptable; he is not asked to give what he has not got — Mof

After all, the important thing is to be willing to give as much as we can — that is what God accepts, and no one is asked to give what he has not got — Phi

If you're eager to give, God accepts you according to what you have, not

according to what you don't have
— Beck

13. For I mean not that other men be eased, and ye burdened:

I do not mean to be easy upon others and hard upon you — Gspd

Of course, I don't mean that others should be relieved to an extent that leaves you in distress — Phi

There is no question of relieving others at the cost of hardship to yourselves — NEB

14. But by an equality, that now at this time your abundance may be a supply for their want, that their abundance also may be a supply for your want: that there may be equality:

but, by equalizing matters, to secure that, on the present occasion, what you can spare may supply their need, so that at another time what they can spare may supply your need, and thus matters may be equalized — TCNT

but that by way of reciprocity, your surplus should at the present juncture contribute to their deficiency, in order that their surplus may in turn contribute to your deficiency, so that there may be reciprocity — Wey

15. As it is written, He that had gathered much had nothing over; and he that had gathered little had no lack.

as Scripture has it, The man who got much had no more than enough, and the man who got little did not go short — NEB

16. But thanks be to God, which put the same earnest care into the heart of Titus for you.

I thank God for inspiring Titus with the same keen interest in your welfare that I have — TCNT

Thank God, he puts the same devotion to you that I feel into Titus' heart — Gspd

But thanks be to God, who kindles in the heart of Titus the same enthusiasm for you that I have — Wms

Thank God Titus feels the same deep concern for you as we do! — Phi

17. For indeed he accepted the exhortation; but being more forward, of his own accord he went unto you.

for he not only has consented to my desire, but is himself very zealous in the matter, and departs to you of his own accord — Con

for he has responded to my appeal, but he goes to you really of his own accord, he is so devoted to you — Gspd

For while he gladly gave ear to our request, he was interested enough to go to you from the impulse of his heart — Bas

He not only accepted our appeal, but was so enthusiastic about it that, of his own accord, he went to you — Nor

18. And we have sent with him the brother, whose praise is in the gospel throughout all the churches;

Along with him I am sending that brother whose services to the gospel are praised by all the churches — Mof

I am sending with him the well-known brother whose praise for spreading the good news is ringing through all the churches — Wms

And I have sent as his companion the brother who is with him . . . — Con

. . . who is highly praised as a gospel preacher in all the churches — Tay

19. And not that only, but who was also chosen of the churches to travel with us with this grace, which is administered by us

And more than that, he was chosen by the vote of the Churches to travel with us in our administration of this generous gift — Wey

What is more, he has been appointed by the churches to travel with me in the interests of this generous undertaking, which I am superintending — Gspd

he, too, is the man whom the churches have appointed to be our companion in this gracious ministry of ours — Knox

Moreover they have duly appointed him to travel with us and help in this beneficent work — NEB

to the glory of the same Lord, and declaration of your ready mind:

to honor the Lord and to show our readiness to help — Gspd

for the Lord's own glory and for ex-
pediting our work — Ber

for the glory of the Lord and to show
our good will — RSV

to the glory of the Lord himself — Mof

20. Avoiding this, that no man should blame us in this abundance which is administered by us:

For I guard myself against all suspicion which might be cast upon me
in my administration of this bounty
with which I am charged — Con

What we are specially guarding against
is that any fault should be found
with us in regard to our administration of this charitable fund — TCNT

They were anxious that no suspicion
should be aroused against us, with
these great sums to handle — Knox

We want to guard against any criticism
of our handling of this generous gift
— NEB

21. Providing for honest things, not only in the sight of the Lord, but also in the sight of men.

for we are trying to make arrangements
which shall be right, not only in the
eyes of the Lord, but also in the eyes
of men — TCNT

I aim at being above reproach not only
from God but also from men —
Mof

and [we want] to be absolutely above-
board not only in the sight of God
but in the eyes of men — Phi

for our aims are entirely honourable,
not only in the Lord's eyes, but also
in the eyes of men — NEB

22. And we have sent with them our brother, whom we have oftentimes proved diligent in many things,

The brother whom I have sent likewise
with them is one whom I have put to
the proof in many trials, and found
always zealous in the work — Con

Along with them I am also sending our
brother: I have had ample proof of
his keen interest on many occasions
— Mof

I send with them another brother of
ours whose devotion we have often
tested in many ways — Gspd

And, to accompany these, we are sending a brother of whose eagerness we

have had good proof, in many ways
and upon many occasions — Knox

With these men we are sending another
of our company whose enthusiasm
we have had many opportunities of
testing — NEB

but now much more diligent, upon the great confidence which I have in you.

but who is now yet more zealous from
the full trust which he has in you —
Con

now he is more eager than ever, such
is the confidence he feels in you —
Knox

23. Whether any do enquire of Titus, he is my partner and fellowhelper concerning you:

If I must say anything about Titus, he
is my intimate companion, and he
shares my work for you — TCNT

As for Titus, he is my partner and
comrade in my labours for you —
Wey

As for Titus, he is my associate and
your fellow worker — Ber

or our brethren be enquired of, they are the messengers of the churches, and the glory of Christ.

while these brothers of ours represent
the churches, and are a credit to
Christ — Gspd

or our brethren, — they are apostles of
the churches . . . — Alf

. . . ambassadors of the churches . . . —
Con

while these brothers of ours, the representatives of the churches . . . — Wms

as for these brethren of ours, they are
the envoys of the churches . . . —
Knox

as for our brethren, they are messengers of the churches . . . — ABUV

if it is our Brothers, they are delegates
of the Churches, an honour to Christ
— TCNT

24. Wherefore shew ye to them, and be-fore the churches, the proof of your love, and of our boasting on your be-half.

So let them have proof of how you can
love, and of my reasons for being
proud of you; it will be a proof read
by the churches — Mof

So you must give proof to them before all the churches of your love, and justify my pride in you — Gspd

So do let them, and all the churches,

see how genuine is your love, and justify all the nice things we have said about you! — Phi

CHAPTER 9

1. For as touching the ministering to the saints, it is superfluous for me to write to you:

For of your ministration to the saints [at Jerusalem] it is needless that I should write to you — Con

It is really unnecessary for me to write to you about this fund for your fellow-Christians — Gspd

And indeed, to write and tell you about the collection for the saints would be waste of time — Knox

I realize that I really don't even need to mention this to you, about helping God's people — Tay

2. For I know the forwardness of your mind,

For I know your readiness — ASV

I know, of course, your willingness to help — TCNT

I know well your eagerness — Knox

for which I boast of you to them of Macedonia, that Achaia was ready a year ago;

and boast of it to the Macedonians on your behalf, saying that Achaia has been ready ever since last year — Con

I am proud of it: Achaia, I tell them, was all ready last year — Mof

Indeed I have told the Macedonians with some pride that Achaia was ready to undertake this service twelve months ago — Phi

I speak of it with pride to the Macedonians: I tell them that Achaia had everything ready last year — NEB

and your zeal hath provoked very many.

and it was really your zeal that stimulated most of them — TCNT

and your ardour has stimulated the majority of them — Wey

and your enthusiasm has been a stimulus to most of them — Gspd

and most of them have been fired by your zeal — NEB

3. Yet have I sent the brethren, lest our boasting of you should be in vain in

this behalf; that, as I said, ye may be ready:

But I have sent the brethren, lest my report of you in this matter should be turned into an empty boast; that you may be truly ready, as I declared you to be — Con

Still, I send the brethren in order that in this matter our boast about you may not prove hollow; so that, as I told them, you may be ready—Wey

At the same time I am sending these brothers just in case my pride in you should prove an empty boast in this particular instance; I want you to be "all ready," as I have been telling them that you would be — Mof

4. Lest haply if they of Macedonia come with me, and find you unprepared, we (that we say not, ye) should be ashamed in this same confident boasting.

Otherwise, if any Macedonians were to come with me, and find you unprepared, we — to say nothing of you — should feel ashamed of our present confidence — TCNT

for if I bring with me men from Macedonia and they find you are not prepared, what a disgrace it will be to us, let alone you, after all the confidence we have shown! — NEB

5. Therefore I thought it necessary to exhort the brethren, that they would go before unto you, and make up beforehand your bounty, whereof ye had notice before, that the same might be ready, as a matter of bounty, and not as of covetousness.

Therefore I think it necessary to urge the Brothers to go to you in advance, and to complete the arrangements for the gift, which you have already promised, so that it may be ready, as a gift, before I come, and not look as if it were being given under pressure — TCNT

That is why I have thought it necessary to ask the brethren to visit you first, and see that the free offering you have already promised is prepared beforehand. Only it is to be a free offering, not a grudging tribute — Knox

This is my reason, then, for urging the brothers to visit you before I come myself, so that they can get your promised gift ready in good time. But, having let you into my confidence, I should like it to be a spontaneous gift, and not money squeezed out of you by what I have said — Phi

. . . that your promised gift may be ready as a real act of grace, and not as something extorted from you — Wey

. . . I want it to be forthcoming as a generous gift, not as money wrung out of you — Mof

. . . and thus it would be a willing gift and not a begrudged obligation — Nor

6. But this I say, He which soweth sparingly shall reap also sparingly; and he which soweth bountifully shall reap also bountifully.

[Remember] this: he who sows sparingly and grudgingly will also reap sparingly and grudgingly, and he who sows generously and that blessings may come to someone, will also reap generously and with blessings — Amp

Remember the saying — Scanty sowing, scanty harvest; plentiful sowing, plentiful harvest — TCNT

. . . and he which soweth with blessings shall reap also with blessings — Alf

. . . and he who sows generously will reap a generous harvest — Mof

7. Every man according as he purposeth in his heart, so let him give; not grudgingly or of necessity: for God loveth a cheerful giver.

Everyone must give what he has made up his mind to give, not reluctantly or under compulsion; God loves a man who is glad to give — Gspd

Let everyone give as his heart tells him . . . — Phi

. . . and not with pain or constraint . . . — Wey

. . . there should be no reluctance, no sense of compulsion . . . — NEB

8. And God is able to make all grace abound toward you; that ye, always having all sufficiency in all things, may abound to every good work:

And God is able to give you an overflowing measure of all good gifts, that all your wants of every kind may be supplied at all times, and you may give of your abundance to every good work — Con

God has power to shower all kinds of blessings upon you, so that, having, under all circumstances and on all occasions, all that you can need, you may be able to shower all kinds of benefits upon others — TCNT

God is able to bless you with ample means, so that you may always have quite enough for any emergency of your own and ample besides for any kind act to others — Mof

God has the power to supply you abundantly with every kind of blessing, so that, with all your needs well supplied at all times, you may have something to spare for every work of mercy — Knox

After all, God can give you everything that you need, so that you may always have sufficient both for yourselves and for giving away to other people — Phi

And it is in God's power to provide you richly with every good gift; thus you will have ample means in yourselves to meet each and every situation, with enough and to spare for every good cause — NEB

9. (As it is written, He hath dispersed abroad; he hath given to the poor: his righteousness remaineth for ever.

as it is written, He scatters his gifts to the poor broadcast, his charity lasts for ever — Mof

as the Scripture says, He scatters his gifts to the poor; his uprightness will never be forgotten — Gspd

as the Scripture says: He has generously given to the poor, his deeds of charity go on for ever — Wms

Scripture says of such a man: He has lavished his gifts on the needy, his benevolence stands fast for ever — NEB

II CORINTHIANS 9

10. **Now he that ministereth seed to the sower both minister bread for your food, and multiply your seed sown, and increase the fruits of your righteousness;)**

And God, who supplies seed for the sower and bread for eating, will supply you with seed and multiply it, and will increase the benefits wrought by your almsgiving — Wey

He who gives seed to the sower and turns that seed into bread to eat will give you the seed of generosity to sow and, for harvest, the satisfying bread of good deeds done — Phi

... he will increase the crop of your charities — Mof

... and increase the harvest springing up from your almsgiving — Mon

... and enlarge the harvest which your deeds of charity yield — Wms

11. **Being enriched in every thing to all bountifulness, which causeth through us thanksgiving to God.**

being enriched with all good things, that you may give ungrudgingly; causing thanksgiving to God from those to whom I bear your gifts — Con

The more you are enriched by God, the more scope will there be for generous giving, and your gifts, administered through us, will mean that many will thank God — Phi

12. **For the administration of this service not only supplieth the want of the saints, but is abundant also by many thanksgivings unto God;**

For the ministration of this service not only fills up the measure of the necessities of the saints, but also overflows beyond it, in many thanks to God — Con

For the rendering of a public service such as this, not only relieves the needs of your fellow-Christians, but also results in the offering to God of many a thanksgiving — TCNT

For the rendering of this service does more than supply the wants of God's people; it results in a wealth of thanksgiving to God — Gspd

... it yields, besides, a rich harvest of thanksgiving in the name of the Lord — Knox

... It also results in an overflowing tide of thanksgiving to God — Phi

13. **Whiles by the experiment of this ministration they glorify God for your professed subjection unto the gospel of Christ, and for your liberal distribution unto them, and unto all men;**

while by the experience of this ministration they glorify God for the subjection of your confession unto the gospel of Christ, and for the liberality of your contribution unto them, and unto all — Alf

while they praise God for the proof thus given of the obedience wherewith you have consented to the Glad-tidings of Christ, and for the single-mindedness of your liberality both to them, and to all — Con

Through the evidence afforded by the service thus rendered, you cause men to praise God for your fidelity to your profession of faith in the Good News of Christ, as well as for the liberality of your contributions for them and for all others — TCNT

By the evidence of this service you procure glory to God for your loyalty to your profession of the gospel of Christ, and for the liberality of your contributions for them and for all — Wey

Under the test of this service, you will glorify God by your obedience in acknowledging the gospel of Christ, and by the generosity of your contribution for them and for all others — RSV

For through the proof which this affords, many will give honour to God when they see how humbly you obey him and how faithfully you confess the gospel of Christ; and will thank him for your liberal contribution to their need and to the general good — NEB

14. **And by their prayer for you, which long after you for the exceeding grace of God in you.**

Moreover, in their prayers for you they express the earnest longings of their love towards you, caused by the surpassing grace of God manifest in you — Con

827

and they will intercede, too, on your behalf, as the abundant measure of grace which God bestows on you warms their hearts towards you — Knox

And as they join in prayer on your behalf, their hearts will go out to you because of the richness of the grace which God has imparted to you — NEB

15. Thanks be unto God for his unspeakable gift.

Thank God, then, for his indescribable generosity to you! — Phi

. . . for his inestimable gift! — TCNT

. . . for his indescribable gift! — Gspd

. . . for his incomparable gift — Lam

. . . for his inexpressible gift! — RSV

. . . for his gift beyond words! — NEB

CHAPTER 10

1. Now I Paul myself beseech you by the meekness and gentleness of Christ,

Now I am going to appeal to you personally, by the gentleness and sympathy of Christ himself — Phi

. . . on the basis of Christ's gentleness and considerateness — Ber

. . . by the gentleness and reasonableness of Christ — Wey

. . . by the gentleness and forbearance of Christ — Gspd

. . . by the humble-heartedness and selflessness of Christ — Mon

. . . by the gentleness and fairness of Christ — Wms

. . . by the gentleness and courtesy of Christ — Knox

. . . with the gentleness and kindness of Christ — Beck

. . . by the gentleness and magnanimity of Christ — NEB

who in presence am base among you, but being absent am bold toward you:

I who in your presence am lowly among you, but being absent am of good courage toward you — ASV

the Paul who is humble enough to your face when he is with you, but outspoken enough when he gets away from you — Mof

the Paul who is so humble when face to face with you, but so bold in dealing with you when he is far away! — Gspd

the man who is so different when he meets you face to face, and deals so boldly with you at a distance — Knox

I, so feeble (you say) when I am face to face with you, so brave when I am away — NEB

2. But I beseech you, that I may not be bold when I am present with that confidence, wherewith I think to be bold against some, which think of us as if we walked according to the flesh.

I implore you not to drive me to show my boldness when I do come, by the confident tone which I expect to have to adopt towards some of you, who are expecting to find us influenced in our conduct by earthly motives — TCNT

I beg you not to make me take as bold an attitude when I come, as I count on taking toward some people who suspect me of acting from worldly motives — Gspd

What I ask is, that you will not force me to deal boldly with you when we meet. I have my own grounds for confidence, and with these I may well be counted a match for those who think we rely on merely human powers — Knox

For I am afraid otherwise that I shall have to do some plain speaking to those of you who will persist in reckoning that our activities are on the purely human level — Phi

3. For though we walk in the flesh, we do not war after the flesh:

For although we live in the world, it is no worldly warfare that we are waging — Wey

Human indeed we are, but it is in no human strength that we fight our battles — Knox

Weak men we may be, but it is not as such that we fight our battles — NEB

4. (For the weapons of our warfare are not carnal, but mighty through God to the pulling down of strong holds;)

The weapons we wield are not merely human, but divinely potent to demolish strongholds — NEB

5. Casting down imaginations, and every high thing that exalteth itself against the knowledge of God,

We are engaged in confuting arguments and pulling down every barrier raised against the knowledge of God — TCNT

I demolish theories and any rampart thrown up to resist the knowledge of God — Mof

Yes, we can pull down the conceits of men, and every barrier of pride which sets itself up against the true knowledge of God — Knox

Our battle is to bring down every deceptive fantasy and every imposing defense that men erect against the true knowledge of God — Phi

we demolish sophistries⁴ and all that rears its proud head against the knowledge of God — NEB

We are destroying speculations ... — NASB

and bringing into captivity every thought to the obedience of Christ;

and causing every thought to come under the authority of Christ — Bas

we make every mind surrender to Christ's service — Knox

we compel every human thought to surrender in obedience to Christ — NEB

6. And having in a readiness to avenge all disobedience, when your obedience is fulfilled.

And when the obedience of your church shall be complete, I am ready to punish all who may be disobedient — Con

and are fully prepared to punish every act of rebellion, when once your submission is complete — TCNT

I am prepared to court-martial anyone who remains insubordinate, once your submission is complete — Mof

Once we are sure of your obedience, we shall not shrink from dealing with those who refuse to obey — Phi

and we are prepared to punish all rebellion when once you have put yourselves in our hands — NEB

... when once your submission has been put beyond question — Mon

7. Do ye look on things after the outward appearance?

Ye look at the things that are before your face — ASV

You look at the outward appearance of things — TCNT

Open your eyes to what is before your face — Wey

Look at this obvious fact — Mof

Look these facts in the face — Mon

Look at what is before your eyes — RSV

Do look at things which stare you in the face! — Phi

If any man trust to himself that he is Christ's, let him of himself think this again, that, as he is Christ's, even so are we Christ's.

Let any one, who is confident that he belongs to Christ, reflect, for himself, again upon the fact — that we belong to Christ no less than he does — TCNT

There may be someone who takes credit to himself for being the champion of Christ; if so, let him reflect further that we belong to Christ's cause no less than himself — Knox

So-and-So considers himself to belong to Christ. All right; but let him reflect that we belong to Christ every bit as much as he — Phi

8. For though I should boast somewhat more of our authority, which the Lord hath given us for edification, and not for your destruction, I should not be ashamed:

For though I should glory somewhat abundantly concerning our authority (which the Lord gave me for building you up, and not for casting you down), I shall not be put to shame — ASV

Even supposing I were to boast somewhat freely of my authority (and the Lord gave it to me for building you up, not for demolishing you), I would feel quite justified — Mof

You may think that I have boasted unduly of my authority (which the Lord gave me, remember, to build you up, not to break you down), but I don't think I have done anything to be ashamed of — Phi

9. That I may not seem as if I would terrify you by letters.

I say this, lest you should imagine that I am writing empty threats — Con

It must not be thought that I try to overawe you when I write — Knox

So you must not think of me as one who scares you by the letters he writes — NEB

10. For his letters, say they, are weighty and powerful;

For they say, His letters are impressive and forceful — Wms

Don't bother about his letters, some say. He sounds big, but it's all noise — Tay

but his bodily presence is weak, and his speech contemptible.

but his personality is weak and his delivery is beneath contempt — Mof

but his personal appearance is insignificant and as a speaker he amounts to nothing — Gspd

When he gets here you will see that there is nothing great about him, and you have never heard a worse preacher — Tay

11. Let such an one think this, that, such as we are in word by letters when we are absent, such will we be also in deed when we are present.

Let such a man assure himself that the words which I write while absent I will bear out by my deeds when present — Con

Such people had better understand that when I arrive and take action I will do just as I say I will in my letters when I am far away — Gspd

I warn those who speak thus that, when we visit you, our actions will not belie the impression which our letters make when we are at a distance — Knox

12. For we dare not make ourselves of the number, or compare ourselves with some that commend themselves:

For we have not the boldness to pair or compare ourselves with some of those who commend themselves — ABUV

I do not indeed venture to class or compare myself with certain individuals who approve of themselves —Gspd

Of course, we shouldn't dare include ourselves in the same class as those who write their own testimonials, or even to compare ourselves with them! — Phi

but they measuring themselves by themselves, and comparing themselves among themselves, are not wise.

All they are doing, of course, is to measure themselves by their own standards or by comparisons within their own circle, and that doesn't make for accurate estimation, you may be sure — Phi

Their trouble is that they are only comparing themselves with each other, and measuring themselves against their own little ideas — Tay

but when they measure themselves by their own yardstick and compare themselves with themselves, they don't show good sense — Beck

What fools they are to measure themselves by themselves, to find in themselves their own standard of comparison! — NEB

13. But we will not boast of things without our measure, but according to the measure of the rule which God hath distributed to us, a measure to reach even unto you.

We, however, will not boast beyond our due limits, but will keep within the limit of the field which God has assigned to us as a limit, which reaches even to you — Wey

and so my boasting never goes beyond the limit — it is determined by the limits of the sphere marked out for me by God. That sphere stretches to include yourselves — Mof

With us there will be no attempt to boast beyond our proper sphere; and our sphere is determined by the limit God laid down for us, which permitted us to come as far as Corinth — NEB

. . . Our goal is to measure up to God's plan for us, and this plan includes our working there with you — Tay

14. For we stretch not ourselves beyond our measure, as though we reached not unto you: for we are come as far as to you also in preaching the gospel of Christ:

There is no straining of authority on our part, as though it did not extend to you. For we were the first to come to you with the gospel of Christ — Wey

I am not overstepping the limit, as if you lay beyond my sphere; I was the very first to reach you with the gospel of Christ — Mof

Nobody can say that we are encroaching, that you lie beyond our orbit; our journeys in preaching Christ's gospel took us all the way to you — Knox

We are not going too far when we claim you as part of our work program, for we were the first to come to you with the Gospel of Christ — Tay

We are not overstretching our commission, as we should be if it did not extend to you, for we were the first to reach Corinth in preaching the gospel of Christ — NEB

15. Not boasting of things without our measure, that is, of other men's labours;

I do not boast beyond my limits in a sphere where other men have done the work — Mof

Not taking credit to ourselves for what is not our business, that is, for the work of others — Bas

Our pride is not in matters beyond our proper sphere nor in the labors of other men — Phi

We are not trying to claim credit for the work someone else has done among you — Tay

And we do not boast of work done where others have laboured, work beyond our proper sphere — NEB

but having hope, when your faith is increased, that we shall be enlarged by you according to our rule abundantly,

but we entertain the hope that, as your faith grows, our field of activity among you may be enlarged till it goes beyond you — Wey

my hope rather is that the growth of your faith will allow me to enlarge the range of my appointed sphere — Mof

we hope to attain still further vantage-points through you — Knox

but we entertain the hope that your growing faith shall enlarge our sphere of influence so greatly with your help — Ber

No, our hope is that your growing faith will mean the expansion of our sphere of action — Phi

16. To preach the gospel in the regions beyond you,

and we may preach the gospel in the districts beyond you — Wey

and to preach the gospel in lands that lie beyond you — Mof

without going beyond our province, and preach the gospel further afield — Knox

that we may evangelize those beyond you — Ber

so that before long we shall be preaching the gospel in districts beyond you — Phi

and not to boast in another man's line of things made ready to our hand.

without trespassing on the sphere assigned to others, or boasting of what has been already done — TCNT

not boasting in another man's field about work already done by him — Wey

without having to boast over work already done in another's field — Gspd

17. But he that glorieth, let him glory in the Lord.

Meantime, He that boasteth, let him boast in the Lord — Con

But let the man who boasts, boast about the Lord — Gspd

18. For not he that commendeth himself is approved, but whom the Lord commendeth.

For a man is proved worthy, not when he commends himself, but when he is commended by the Lord — Con

For it is not the man who approves himself who is really approved; it is the man of whom the Lord approves — Gspd

For the Lord's approval of a man is not dependent on his opinion of himself, but on the Lord's opinion of him — Bas

It is not self-commendation that matters; it is winning the approval of God — Phi

CHAPTER 11

1. Would to God ye could bear with me a little in my folly: and indeed bear with me.

Would that ye could bear with me in a little foolishness: but indeed ye do bear with me — ASV

I wish you could put up with a little of my foolishness — please try! — Phi

2. For I am jealous over you with godly jealousy:

for I feel a divine jealousy on your behalf — Mof

. . . with a jealousy of God — Con

. . . with God's own jealousy — Wey

for I have espoused you to one husband, that I may present you as a chaste virgin to Christ.

because I betrothed you to one only husband, even to Christ, that I might present you unto Him in virgin purity — Con

for in my eyes you are like a fresh, unspoiled girl whom I am presenting as fiancée to your true husband — Phi

3. But I fear, lest by any means, as the serpent beguiled Eve through his subtilty, so your minds should be corrupted from the simplicity that is in Christ.

but I fear lest, as Eve was beguiled by the craftiness of the serpent, so your imagination should be corrupted, and you should be seduced from your singleminded faithfulness to Christ — Con

But I am afraid that just as the serpent by his cunning deceived Eve, your thoughts will be led astray from their single-hearted fidelity to Christ — Gspd

But I am afraid that as the serpent deceived Eve by his cunning, your thoughts will be led astray from a sincere and pure devotion to Christ — RSV

4. For if he that cometh preacheth another Jesus, whom we have not preached, or if ye receive another spirit, which ye have not received, or another gospel, which ye have not accepted, ye might well bear with him.

For, if some new-comer is proclaiming a Jesus other than him whom we proclaimed, or if you are receiving a Spirit different from the Spirit which you received, or a Good News different from that which you welcomed, then you are marvellously tolerant! — TCNT

You put up with it all right, when some interloper preaches a second Jesus (not the Jesus I preached), or when you are treated to a Spirit different from the Spirit you once received, and to a different gospel from what I gave you! — Mof

Some new-comer preaches to you a different Christ, not the one we preached to you; he brings you a spirit other than the spirit you had from us, a gospel other than the gospel you received; you would do well, then, to be patient with me — Knox

5. For I suppose I was not a whit behind the very chiefest apostles.

for I reckon myself no whit behind your super-eminent Apostles — Con

I do not regard myself as in any way inferior to the most eminent Apostles! — TCNT

For I think that I am not in the least inferior to these superfine apostles of yours — Gspd

For I consider myself not a single bit inferior to those surpassingly superior apostles of yours! — Wms

I claim to have done no less than the very greatest of the apostles — Knox

Yet I cannot believe I am in the least inferior to these extra-special messengers of yours — Phi

6. But though I be rude in speech, yet not in knowledge;

Yea, though I be unskilled in the arts of speech, yet I am not wanting in the gift of knowledge — Con

Though I am no trained orator, yet I am not without knowledge — TCNT

I am no speaker, perhaps, but knowledge I do possess — Mof

Although I am untrained as an orator, yet I am not so in the field of knowledge — Wms

Even if I lack skill in rhetoric, I certainly do not lack in knowledge — Ber

Perhaps I am not a polished speaker, but I do know what I am talking about — Phi

but we have been throughly made manifest among you in all things.

nay, in every way we have made this manifest unto you in all things — ASV

indeed we made this perfectly clear to you in every way — TCNT

I never failed to make myself intelligible to you — Mof

at all times we have made known to you the full truth — NEB

7. Have I committed an offence in abasing myself that ye might be exalted, because I have preached to you the gospel of God freely?

Did I sin in abasing myself that you might be exalted, in that I proclaimed God's gospel to you without reward — Wey

But perhaps I did wrong in taking a humble place that you might have a high one — I mean in preaching the gospel of God to you for nothing! — Mof

Did I do wrong in taking a lowly place to let you have an exalted one, in that I preached the good news about God to you without accepting any pay — Wms

Unless perhaps you think I did wrong to honour you by abasing myself, since I preached God's gospel to you at no charge to yourselves — Knox

Or was this my offence, that I made no charge for preaching the gospel of God, lowering myself to help in raising you — NEB

8. I robbed other churches, taking wages of them, to do you service.

I robbed other churches, letting them pay me so that I could work for you! — Gspd

I took money from other churches as payment for my work, so that I might be your servant — Bas

As a matter of fact I was only able to do this by robbing other churches, for it was what they paid me that made it possible to minister to you free of charge — Phi

It is true that I took toll of other con-

gregations, accepting support from them to serve you — NEB

9. And when I was present with you, and wanted, I was chargeable to no man: for that which was lacking to me the brethren which came from Macedonia supplied:

and when I was present with you and was in want, I was not a burden on any man; for the brethren, when they came from Macedonia, supplied the measure of my want — ASV

And when I was with you and my resources failed, I was a dead-weight on no one; for the brethren, when they came from Macedonia, fully supplied my wants — Wey

Even when I lacked the actual necessities of life while I was with you, I was a burden to no one; for whatever I lacked, the brothers from Macedonia supplied, when they came — Mon

I was penniless when I visited you, but I would not cripple any of you with expenses; the brethren came from Macedonia to relieve my expenses — Knox

Then while I was with you, if I ran short I sponged on no one; anything I needed was fully met by our friends who came from Macedonia — NEB

and in all things I have kept myself from being burdensome unto you, and so will I keep myself.

Thus I kept myself, as I intend to keep myself, from being a burden to you in any way — Mof

10. As the truth of Christ is in me, no man shall stop me of this boasting in the regions of Achaia.

As the truth of Christ lives in me, no one in all the country of Achaia shall silence this boast of mine — Knox

By the truth of Christ within me, no one shall stop my being proud of this independence through all Achaia — Phi

11. Wherefore? because I love you not? God knoweth.

Why? Because I do not love you? God knows that I do! — TCNT

Why? Because I have no love for you?
let God be judge — Bas

Does this mean that I do not love you?
God knows it doesn't — Phi

12. **But what I do, that I will do, that I may cut off occasion from them which desire occasion; that wherein they glory, they may be found even as we.**

No, I intend to go on as I am doing, in order to checkmate those who would fain make out that in the apostolate of which they boast they work on the same terms as I do — Mof

And I shall keep on doing as I am, in order to cut the ground from under the feet of those who want an opportunity to show themselves on a level with me in the matters of which they boast — Wms

No, I shall continue to do as I have done, so as to cut away the ground from those who would gladly boast that they are no different from myself — Knox

And I shall go on doing as I am now, to cut the ground from under those who would seize any chance to put their vaunted apostleship on the same level as ours — NEB

13. **For such are false apostles, deceitful workers, transforming themselves into the apostles of Christ.**

Men of this stamp are sham apostles, dishonest workmen, assuming the garb of apostles of Christ — Wey

'Apostles'? They are spurious apostles, false workmen — they are masquerading as 'apostles of Christ' — Mof

God's messengers? They are counterfeits of the real thing, dishonest practitioners, "God's messengers" only by their own appointment — Phi

14. **And no marvel; for Satan himself is transformed into an angel of light.**

No wonder they do, for Satan himself masquerades as an angel of light — Mof

15. **Therefore it is no great thing if his ministers also be transformed as the ministers of righteousness; whose end shall be according to their works.**

So it is no surprise if his ministers also masquerade as ministers of right-

eousness. Their doom will answer to their deeds — Mof

It is only to be expected that his agents shall have the appearance of ministers of righteousness — but they will get their deserts one day — Phi

16. **I say again, Let no man think me a fool; if otherwise, yet as a fool receive me, that I may boast myself a little.**

I repeat, no one should think me a fool, but if you do, show me at least the patience you would show a fool, and let me have my little boast like the others — Gspd

Once more I appeal to you, let none of you think me vain; or, if it must be so, give me a hearing in spite of my vanity, and let me boast a little in my turn — Knox

Once more, let me advise you not to look upon me as a fool. Yet if you do, then listen to what this "fool" has to boast about — Phi

17. **That which I speak, I speak it not after the Lord, but as it were foolishly, in this confidence of boasting.**

But, in so doing, I speak not in the spirit of the Lord, but, as it were, in folly, while we stand upon this ground of boasting — Con

I am not speaking here as a Christian, but like a fool, if it comes to bragging — NEB

18. **Seeing that many glory after the flesh, I will glory also.**

for, since many are boasting in the spirit of the flesh, I will boast likewise — Con

So many people brag of their earthly distinctions that I shall do so too — NEB

19. **For ye suffer fools gladly, seeing ye yourselves are wise.**

Wise as you are, you find pleasure in tolerating fools — Wey

You put up with fools so readily, you who know so much! — Mof

From your heights of superior wisdom I am sure you can smile tolerantly on a fool — Phi

20. **For ye suffer, if a man bring you into bondage, if a man devour you, if a man take of you, if a man exalt himself, if a man smite you on the face.**

You tolerate a man even when he enslaves you, when he plunders you, when he gets you into his power, when he puts on airs of superiority, when he strikes you in the face! — TCNT

Why, you let other people tyrannize over you, prey upon you, take advantage of you, vaunt their power over you, browbeat you — Knox

Oh, you're tolerant, all right! You don't mind, do you, if a man takes away your liberty, spends your money, takes advantage of you, puts on airs or even smacks your face? — Phi

21. I speak as concerning reproach, as though we had been weak. Howbeit whereinsoever any is bold, (I speak foolishly,) I am bold also.

I admit, to my shame, that we have been weak. But whatever the subject on which others are not afraid to boast — though it is foolish to say so — I am not afraid either! — TCNT

I am quite ashamed to say that I was not equal to that sort of thing! Let them vaunt as they please, I am equal to them (mind, this is the rôle of a fool!) — Mof

I am almost ashamed to say that I never did brave strong things like that to you. Yet in whatever particular they enjoy such confidence I (speaking as a fool, remember) have just as much confidence — Phi

And we, you say, have been weak! I admit the reproach. But if there is to be bravado (and here I speak as a fool), I can indulge in it too — NEB

To my shame, I must say, we were too weak for that! . . . — RSV

22. Are they Hebrews? so am I. Are they Israelites? so am I. Are they the seed of Abraham? so am I.

23. Are they ministers of Christ? (I speak as a fool) I am more;

Are they ministers of Christ? (I speak as one beside himself) I more — ASV

Are they 'Servants of Christ'? Though it is madness to talk like this, I am more so than they — TCNT

Are they servants of Christ? (I speak as if I were out of my senses.) Much more I — Wey

They say they serve Christ? But I have served Him far more! (Have I gone mad to boast like this?) — Tay

in labours more abundant, in stripes above measure, in prisons more frequent, in deaths oft.

I have had more of toil, more of imprisonment! I have been flogged times without number. I have been often at death's door — TCNT

with measureless toils and imprisonments, with excessive floggings and facing death so frequently— Ber

24. Of the Jews five times received I forty stripes save one.

Five times at the hands of the Jews I have received one short of forty lashes — Mon

25. Thrice was I beaten with rods, once was I stoned, thrice I suffered shipwreck, a night and a day I have been in the deep;

Three times I have been scourged by the Romans; once I have been stoned; three times have I been shipwrecked; a night and a day have I been adrift in the open sea — Mon

26. In journeyings often, in perils of waters, in perils of robbers, in perils by mine own countrymen, in perils by the heathen, in perils in the city, in perils in the wilderness, in perils in the sea, in perils among false brethren;

In my travels I have been in constant danger from rivers and floods, from bandits, from my own countrymen, and from pagans. I have faced danger in city streets, danger in the desert, danger on the high seas, danger among false Christians — Phi

My journeys have been many. I have been through dangers from rivers, dangers from robbers, dangers from my own people . . . — TCNT

27. In weariness and painfulness, in watchings often, in hunger and thirst, in fastings often, in cold and nakedness.

I have been through toil and hardship. I have passed many a sleepless night; I have endured hunger and thirst; I have often been without food; I have known cold and nakedness — TCNT

I have known exhaustion, pain, long vigils, hunger and thirst, doing with-

out meals, cold and lack of clothing — Phi

. . . often I have shivered with cold,
without enough clothing to keep me
warm — Tay

**28. Beside those things that are without,
that which cometh upon me daily, the
care of all the churches.**

Omitting what is besides, my care day
by day, my anxiety for all the
churches — Alf

And, not to speak of other things, there
is my daily burden of anxiety about
all the Churches — TCNT

In addition to all the other things . . .
— Bas

Besides these experiences from the outside . . . — Ber

Apart from all external trials I have
the daily burden of responsibility for
all the churches — Phi

**29. Who is weak, and I am not weak? who
is offended, and I burn not?**

Who is weak, but I share his weakness?
Who is caused to fall, but I burn with
indignation — Con

Who is weak without my being weak?
Whose conscience is hurt without my
being fired with indignation — Gspd

**30. If I must needs glory, I will glory of
the things which concern mine infirmities.**

If boast I must, it shall be of things

which display my weakness — Wey

But if I must brag, I would rather brag
about the things that show how weak
I am — Tay

**31. The God and Father of our Lord Jesus
Christ, which is blessed for evermore,
knoweth that I lie not.**

The God and Father of the Lord Jesus
— he who is for ever blessed —
knows that I am speaking the truth
— TCNT

The God and Father of our Lord Jesus
Christ, to whom be praise for ever,
is witness that the things which I say
are true — Bas

the God who is Father of our Lord
Jesus Christ . . . — Knox

**32. In Damascus the governor under Are-
tas the king kept the city of the Damascenes with a garrison, desirous to
apprehend me:**

(At Damascus the ethnarch of king
Aretas had patrols out in the city of
the Damascenes to arrest me — Mof

When I was in Damascus, the Governor under King Aretas had the gates
of that city guarded, so as to arrest
me — TCNT

**33. And through a window in a basket was
I let down by the wall, and escaped his
hands.**

but I was lowered in a basket from a
loophole in the wall, and so managed to escape his clutches.) — Mof

CHAPTER 12

**1. It is not expedient for me doubtless to
glory. I will come to visions and revelations of the Lord.**

I must boast! It is unprofitable; but I
will pass to visions and revelations
given by the Lord — TCNT

If we are to boast (although boasting
is out of place), I will go on to the
visions and revelations the Lord has
granted me — Knox

**2. I knew a man in Christ above fourteen
years ago, (whether in the body, I cannot tell; or whether out of the body, I
cannot tell: God knoweth;) such an one
caught up to the third heaven.**

I know a man in Christ who fourteen
years ago was caught up to the third
heaven — whether in the body or

out of the body I do not know, God
knows — RSV

I know a man in Christ who, fourteen
years ago, had the experience of being caught up into the third Heaven.
I don't know whether it was an actual physical experience; only God
knows that — Phi

**3. And I knew such a man, (whether in
the body, or out of the body, I cannot
tell: God knoweth;)**

I simply know that in the body or out
of the body (God knows which)
— Mof

**4. How that he was caught up into para-
dise, and heard unspeakable words,
which it is not lawful for a man to
utter.**

this man was caught up to paradise and heard sacred secrets which no human lips can repeat — Mof

5. Of such an one will I glory: yet of myself I will not glory, but in mine infirmities.

Of an experience like that I am prepared to boast, but not of myself personally — not except as regards my weaknesses — Mof

I am honestly proud of an experience like that, but I have made up my mind not to boast of anything personal, except of what may be called my weaknesses — Phi

6. For though I would desire to glory, I shall not be a fool; for I will say the truth:

If I should choose to boast, I should not be guilty of empty vanity, for I should speak the truth — Con

It would not be vanity, if I had a mind to boast about such a man as that; I should only be telling the truth — Knox

but now I forbear, lest any man should think of me above that which he seeth me to be, or that he heareth of me.

but I forbear to speak, that I may not cause any man to think of me more highly than when he sees my deeds or hears my teaching — Con

But I will refrain from it, for I do not want anyone to be influenced by the wonderful character of these revelations to think more of me than is justified by my words or conduct — Gspd

But I refrain, because I should not like anyone to form an estimate of me which goes beyond the evidence of his own eyes and ears — NEB

7. And lest I should be exalted above measure through the abundance of the revelations, there was given to me a thorn in the flesh, the messenger of Satan to buffet me, lest I should be exalted above measure.

It was for this reason, and to prevent my thinking too highly of myself, that a thorn was sent to pierce my flesh — an instrument of Satan to discipline me — so that I should not think too highly of myself — TCNT

And so, to keep me from being unduly elated by the magnificence of such revelations, I was given a sharp pain in my body which came as Satan's messenger to bruise me; this was to save me from being unduly elated — NEB

8. For this thing I besought the Lord thrice, that it might depart from me.

three times over I prayed the Lord to relieve me of it — Mof

Three times I begged the Lord to have him leave me alone — Beck

9. And he said unto me, My grace is sufficient for thee: for my strength is made perfect in weakness.

but He has said to me, My grace suffices for you, for power is perfected in weakness — Wey

but he told me, My grace is enough for thee; my strength finds its full scope in thy weakness — Knox

but his answer was: My grace is all you need; power comes to its full strength in weakness — NEB

Most gladly therefore will I rather glory in my infirmities, that the power of Christ may rest upon me.

Most gladly therefore will I rather glory in my infirmities in order that the power of Christ may overshadow me — Wey

More than ever, then, I delight to boast of the weaknesses that humiliate me, so that the strength of Christ may enshrine itself in me — Knox

I shall therefore prefer to find my joy and pride in the very things that are my weakness; and then the power of Christ will come and rest upon me — NEB

10. Therefore I take pleasure in infirmities, in reproaches, in necessities, in persecutions, in distresses for Christ's sake: for when I am weak, then am I strong.

That is why I delight in weakness, ill-treatment, hardships, persecutions, and difficulties, when borne for Christ. For, when I am weak, then it is that I am strong! — TCNT

I am well content with these humiliations of mine, with the insults, the hardships, the persecutions, the times of difficulty I undergo for Christ;

when I am weakest, then I am strongest of all — Knox

I can even enjoy weaknesses, suffering, privations, persecutions and difficulties for Christ's sake. For my very weakness makes me strong in him — Phi

11. **I have become a fool in glorying; ye have compelled me: for I ought to have been commended of you:**

I have been making a fool of myself, but you forced me to do it, when you ought to have been expressing your approval of me — Gspd

I have been making a fool of myself boasting. But you forced me to do it, for any praise of me should have come from you — Nor

I am being very foolish, but it was you who drove me to it; my credentials should have come from you — NEB

for in nothing am I behind the very chiefest apostles, though I be nothing.

For I am not a bit inferior to your superfine apostles, even if I am nobody! — Gspd

No, I have done no less than the very greatest of the apostles, worthless as I am — Knox

For I am not really in the least inferior, nobody as I am, to these extraspecial messengers — Phi

Even if I'm nothing, I wasn't in any way inferior to your "super" apostles — Beck

12. **Truly the signs of an apostle were wrought among you in all patience, in signs, and wonders, and mighty deeds.**

The marks, at least, of an Apostle were seen in the deeds which I wrought among you, in signs, and wonders, and miracles, with steadfast endurance of persecution — Con

The signs that mark a true apostle were most patiently shown when I was among you, in signs, wonders, and marvels — Gspd

The marks of a true apostle were there, in the work that I did among you, which called for such constant fortitude, and was attended by signs, marvels, and miracles — NEB

13. **For what is it wherein ye were inferior**

to other churches, except it be that I myself was not burdensome to you? forgive me this wrong.

In what respect have you been worse used than other Churches, except that I myself was not a dead-weight upon you? Forgive this injustice! — Wey

What makes you feel so inferior to other churches? Is it because I have not allowed you to support me financially? My humblest apologies for this great wrong! — Phi

14. **Behold, the third time I am ready to come to you; and I will not be burdensome to you: for I seek not yours, but you:**

See, I am now for the third time prepared to visit you, and I will not be a dead-weight on you. I desire not your money, but yourselves — Wey

This is the third time I have made preparations for visiting you, and I do not intend to cripple you with expenses; what I claim is yourselves, not anything you can give — Knox

Now I am coming to you again, the third time; and it is still not going to cost you anything, for I don't want your money. I want you! — Tay

for the children ought not to lay up for the parents, but the parents for the children.

Children don't have to put by their savings for their parents; parents do that for their children — Phi

parents should make provision for their children, not children for their parents — NEB

15. **And I will very gladly spend and be spent for you;**

And I will most gladly spend and be utterly spent for the good of your souls — Wey

So in my own case, I will most happily spend my money and myself for your sakes — Wms

though the more abundantly I love you, the less I be loved.

. . . Do you love me less because I love you so much? — Beck

If I love you so intensely, am I the less to be loved? — Wey

16. **But be it so, I did not burden you:**

nevertheless, being crafty, I caught you with guile.

You will admit that I was not a burden to you, but you say that I was "crafty" and caught you "by a trick"! — TCNT

Ah, you say, that may be; I did not lay any charge on you myself, but I preyed upon you by roundabout means, like the knave I am — Knox

17. Did I make a gain of you by any of them whom I sent unto you?

Did I defraud you of your wealth by some of the messengers whom I sent to you — Con

I did not make any money out of you through anybody that I sent to you, did I — Wms

I have not exploited you through anyone I sent you, have I — Ber

Who, of the men I have sent you, was used by me to defraud you — NEB

18. I desired Titus, and with him I sent a brother.

I actually begged Titus to go, and sent the well-known brother with him — Wms

Did Titus make a gain of you? walked we not in the same spirit? walked we not in the same steps?

Titus did not make any money out of you, did he? Did not he and I act in the same spirit, and take the very same steps — Wms

You don't think Titus made anything out of you, do you? Yet didn't I act in the same spirit as he, and take the same line as he did — Phi

19. Again, think ye that we excuse ourselves unto you? we speak before God in Christ: but we do all things, dearly beloved, for your edifying.

You are thinking all this time that we are making our defence to you. Really it is before God in Christ that we speak. But, beloved, it is all with a view to your upbuilding — Wey

It may seem to you that all this time we have been attempting to put ourselves in the right; but we are saying these things before God in Christ. For all things, dear brothers, are for your profit — Bas

Are you thinking all this time that I am trying to justify myself in your eyes? Actually I am speaking in Christ before God himself, and my only reason for so doing is to help you in your spiritual life — Phi

20. For I fear, lest, when I come, I shall not find you such as I would, and that I shall be found unto you such as ye would not:

For I fear lest perchance when I come I should find you not such as I could wish, and that you also should find me other than you desire — Con

I'm afraid I may come and find you different from what I want you to be, and you may find me different from what you want me to be — Beck

lest there be debates, envyings, wraths, strifes, backbitings, whisperings, swellings, tumults:

I am afraid that I may find quarrelling, jealousy, ill-feeling, rivalry, slandering, back-biting, self-assertion, and disorder — TCNT

that there will be dissension, rivalry, ill humour, factiousness, backbiting, gossip, self-conceit, disharmony — Knox

21. And lest, when I come again, my God will humble me among you, and that I shall bewail many which have sinned already, and have not repented of the uncleanness and fornication and lasciviousness which they have committed.

I am afraid lest, on my next visit, my God may humble me in regard to you, and that I may have to mourn over many who have long been sinning, and have not repented of the impurity, immorality, and sensuality, in which you have indulged — TCNT

I have the fear that on this new visit God has humiliation in store for me when we meet; that I shall have tears to shed over many of you, sinners of old and still unrepentant, with a tale of impure, adulterous, and wanton living — Knox

CHAPTER 13

1. This is the third time I am coming to you. In the mouth of two or three witnesses shall every word be established.

This will be my third visit to you. Any charge must be sustained by the evidence of two or three witnesses — Gspd

2. I told you before, and foretell you, as if I were present, the second time; and being absent now I write to them which heretofore have sinned, and to all other, that, if I come again, I will not spare:

I warned you already, on my second visit, and I warn you now before I come, both you who sinned some time ago and the rest of you as well, that I will spare no one if I come back —-Mof

I give you now, still absent, the warning of my second visit; I have told you before, and tell you now, both those who have sinned already and all the rest of you, that I will show no leniency next time I come — Knox

3. Since ye seek a proof of Christ speaking in me, which to you-ward is not weak, but is mighty in you.

Thus you shall have the proof you seek of the power of Christ, who speaks in me; for He shows no weakness towards you, but works mightily among you — Con

That will prove to you that I am indeed a spokesman of Christ. It is no weak Christ you have to do with, but a Christ of power — Mof

4. For though he was crucified through weakness, yet he liveth by the power of God. For we also are weak in him, but we shall live with him by the power of God toward you.

Weakness brought him to the cross, but the power of God brought him life; and though it is in our weakness that we are united to him, you will find us too, as he is, alive with God's power — Knox

He was "weak" enough to be crucified, yes, but he lives now by the power of God. I am weak as he was weak, but I am strong enough to deal with

you for I share his life by the power of God — Phi

His weak, human body died on the cross, but now he lives by the mighty power of God; we, too, are weak in our bodies, as He was, but now we live and are strong, as He is, and have all of God's power to use — Tay

5. Examine yourselves, whether ye be in the faith; prove your own selves. Know ye not your own selves, how that Jesus Christ is in you, except ye be reprobates?

Put yourselves to the proof, to see whether you are holding the Faith. Test yourselves. Surely you recognize this fact about yourselves — that Jesus Christ is in you! Unless indeed you cannot stand the test! — TCNT

You should be looking at yourselves to make sure that you are really Christ's. It is yourselves that you should be testing, not me. You ought to know by this time that Christ is in you, unless you are not real Christians at all — Phi

6. But I trust that ye shall know that we are not reprobates.

But I hope that you will recognize that we can stand the test — TCNT

And when you have applied your test, I am confident that you will soon find that I myself am a genuine Christian — Phi

7. Now I pray to God that ye do no evil; not that we should appear approved, but that ye should do that which is honest, though we be as reprobates.

Yet I pray to God that you may do no evil; desiring not that my own power may be clearly proved, but that you may do right, although I should seem unable to abide the proof — Con

But we pray God that you may not do wrong — not that we may appear to have met the test, but that you may do what is right, though we may seem to have failed — RSV

Our prayer to God is that we may not have to hurt you; we are not concerned to be vindicated ourselves; we want you to do what is right, even if we should seem to be discredited — NEB

8. For we can do nothing against the truth, but for the truth.

We have no power at all against the Truth, but we have power in the service of the Truth — TCNT

The powers we have are used in support of the truth, not against it — Knox

For we have no power to act against the truth, but only for it — NEB

9. For we are glad, when we are weak, and ye are strong: and this also we wish, even your perfection.

I rejoice, I say, when I am powerless [against you], and you are strong; yea, the very end of my prayers is your perfect reformation — Con

I am glad to be weak if you are strong; mend your ways, that is all I beg of you — Mof

and we are best pleased when we have no power against you, and you are powerless yourselves. That is what we pray for, your perfection—Knox

We are glad to be weak if it means that you are strong. Our ambition for you is true Christian maturity — Phi

10. Therefore I write these things being absent, lest being present I should use sharpness, according to the power which the Lord hath given me to edification, and not to destruction.

For this reason I write thus while absent, that when present I may not have to act severely in the exercise of that authority which the Lord has given me for building up, and

not for pulling down — Wey

Hence the tone of this letter, so that when I do come I shall not be obliged to use that power of severity which God has given me — though even that is not meant to break you down but to build you up — Phi

11. Finally, brethren, farewell.

Finally, brethren, we wish you all joy — Knox

And now, Brothers, good-bye — TCNT

Be perfect, be of good comfort, be of one mind, live in peace; and the God of love and peace shall be with you.

Aim at perfection; take courage; agree together; live in peace. And then God, the source of all love and peace, will be with you — TCNT

Perfect your lives, listen to the appeal we make, think the same thoughts, keep peace among yourselves . . . — Knox

12. Greet one another with an holy kiss.

Greet one another with the kiss of saints — Knox

Greet one another with the kiss of peace — NEB

A handshake all round, please! — Phi

13. All the saints salute you.

All God's people send you greetings — NEB

All the Christians here send greeting — Phi

14. The grace of the Lord Jesus Christ, and the love of God, and the communion of the Holy Ghost, be with you all. Amen.

The grace of the Lord Jesus Christ, the love of God and the fellowship that is ours in the Holy Spirit be with you all — Phi

THE
EPISTLE OF PAUL TO THE GALATIANS

CHAPTER 1

1. Paul, an apostle, (not of men, neither by man, but by Jesus Christ, and God the Father, who raised him from the dead;)

From Paul, an Apostle whose commission is not from men and is given, not by man, but by Jesus Christ and God the Father who raised him from the dead — TCNT

From Paul, an apostle, not by human appointment or by human commission, but by commission from Jesus Christ and from God the Father who raised him from the dead — NEB

2. And all the brethren which are with me, unto the churches of Galatia:

I and the group of friends now with me send greetings to the Christian congregations of Galatia — NEB

... the assemblies of Galatia — Rhm

3. Grace be to you and peace from God the Father, and from our Lord Jesus Christ,

Favour unto you and peace ... — Rhm

May God, our Father, and the Lord Jesus Christ, bless you and give you peace — TCNT

4. Who gave himself for our sins, that he might deliver us from this present evil world, according to the will of God and our Father:

For Christ, to rescue us from this present wicked age, gave himself for our sins, in accordance with the will of our God and Father — TCNT

... to rescue us from the evil world that surrounds us ... — Knox

5. To whom be glory for ever and ever. Amen.

to whom be ascribed all glory for ever and ever. Amen — TCNT

6. I marvel that ye are so soon removed from him that called you into the grace of Christ unto another gospel:

I am amazed that you are so readily deserting for a different gospel Him who called you by the grace of Christ — Wey

I am amazed that you are so quickly turning away from him who called

you by the mercy of Christ, to some different good news — Gspd

I am dumbfounded that you have so quickly deserted Him who called you into the grace of Christ, and have gone over to a different "gospel" — Nor

I am amazed that you are so soon shifting your ground, and deserting him who called you ... — Mon

I am astonished ... — TCNT

I marvel that thus quickly ye are moving away from him that called you in the favour of Christ, Unto a different glad-message — Rhm

7. Which is not another;

For other gospel there is none — Wey

Not, of course, that it is or ever could be another gospel — Phi

which is really no Good News at all — TCNT

but there be some that trouble you, and would pervert the gospel of Christ.

It simply means that certain individuals are unsettling you; they want to distort the gospel of Christ — Mof

but there are obviously men who are upsetting your faith with a travesty of the gospel of Christ — Phi

But then, I know that there are people who are harassing you, and who want to pervert the Good News of Christ — TCNT

... to change the glad-message of Christ — Rhm

8. But though we, or an angel from heaven, preach any other gospel unto you than that which we have preached unto you, let him be accursed.

Now even though it were myself or some angel from heaven, whoever preaches a gospel that contradicts the gospel I preached to you, God's curse be on him! — Mof

... let him be anathema — ASV

... may he be damned! — Phi

9. As we said before, so say I now again, If any man preach any other gospel unto you than that ye have received, let him be accursed.

We have said it before, and I repeat it now — if anyone is preaching to you good news that contradicts the good news you have already received, a curse upon him! — Gspd

Let me repeat what I have just said: If anyone shall proclaim to you a gospel different from what you have received, let there be a curse on him! — Nor

10. For do I now persuade men, or God? or do I seek to please men? for if I yet pleased men, I should not be the servant of Christ.

Is it man's favour or God's that I try to gain? Or am I seeking to please men? If I were still a man-pleaser, I should not be Christ's servant — Wey

Do you think it is man's favour, or God's, that I am trying to win now? Shall I be told, now, that I am courting the good will of men? If, after all these years, I were still courting the favour of men, I should not be what I am, the slave of Christ — Knox

Does my language now sound as if I were canvassing for men's support? Whose support do I want but God's alone? Do you think I am currying favour with men? If I still sought men's favour, I should be no servant of Christ — NEB

11. But I certify you, brethren, that the gospel which was preached of me is not after man.

I would remind you, Brothers, that the Good News which I told is no mere human invention — TCNT

For I tell you plainly, brothers, that the good news that I preached is not a human affair — Gspd

12. For I neither received it of man, neither was I taught it, but by the revelation of Jesus Christ.

For indeed it was not from man that I received or learnt it, but by a revelation from Jesus Christ — Wey

No man gave it to me, no man taught it to me; it came to me as a direct revelation from Jesus Christ — Phi

13. For ye have heard of my conversation in time past in the Jews' religion,

For you have heard of my former behavior in the days of my Judaism — Con

You have heard of my early career in Judaism — Wey

You have heard what my manner of life was when I was still a practising Jew — NEB

how that beyond measure I persecuted the church of God, and wasted it:

how I persecuted the Church of God with fanatical zeal and, in fact, did my best to destroy it — Phi

— how furiously I persecuted the Church of God, and made havoc of it — Wey

How that exceedingly was I persecuting the assembly of God and laying it waste — Rhm

how I persecuted beyond measure the Church of God, and strove to root it out — Con

14. And profited in the Jews' religion above many my equals in mine own nation, being more exceedingly zealous of the traditions of my fathers.

And I made progress in the Jewish religion beyond many of mine own age among my countrymen . . . — Alf

and how, in my devotion to Judaism, I surpassed many of my contemporaries among my own people in my intense earnestness in upholding the traditions of my ancestors — TCNT

going further in my zeal as a Jew than many of my own age and race, so fierce a champion was I of the tradition handed down by my forefathers — Knox

I was one of the most religious Jews of my own age in the whole country, and tried as hard as I possibly could to follow all the old, traditional rules of my religion — Tay

15. But when it pleased God, who separated me from my mother's womb, and called me by his grace,

But when God, who had set me apart even before my birth, and who called me by his love — TCNT

But when the time came for God (who had chosen me from the moment of my birth, and then called me by his grace) — Phi

16. To reveal his Son in me, that I might preach him among the heathen; immediately I conferred not with flesh and blood:

saw fit to reveal his Son in me, so that I might tell the Good News of him among the Gentiles, then at once, instead of consulting any human being — TCNT

to reveal his Son within me so that I might proclaim him to the non-Jewish world, I did not, as might have been expected, talk over the matter with any human being — Phi

17. Neither went I up to Jerusalem to them which were apostles before me; but I went into Arabia, and returned again unto Damascus.

or even going up to Jerusalem to see those who were Apostles before me, I went into Arabia, and came back again to Damascus — TCNT

I did not even go to Jerusalem to meet those who were God's messengers before me — no, I went away to Arabia and later came back to Damascus — Phi

18. Then after three years I went up to Jerusalem to see Peter, and abode with him fifteen days.

. . . to become acquainted with Cephas . . . — ASV

Then, when three years had passed, I did go up to Jerusalem, to visit Peter, and I stayed a fortnight there in his company — Knox

19. But other of the apostles saw I none, save James the Lord's brother.

but I did not see any of the other apostles, except James, the Lord's brother — Knox

20. Now the things which I write unto you, behold, before God, I lie not.

Be sure that in writing this to you I am speaking the truth, as in the sight of God — Wey

(I am writing to you the sheer truth, I swear it before God!) — Mof

(And I declare before God I'm writing you no lie.) — Beck

21. Afterwards I came into the regions of Syria and Cilicia:

After that, I went to the districts of Syria and Cilicia — Gspd

22. And was unknown by face unto the churches of Judaea which were in Christ:

I was still personally unknown to the Christian churches of Judea — Gspd

But the Christians in Judea still didn't know what I looked like — Tay

23. But they had heard only, That he which persecuted us in times past now preacheth the faith which once he destroyed.

they only heard people say, The man who once persecuted us is now preaching the good news of the faith he tried to destroy — Gspd

24. And they glorified God in me.

and they praised God for me — Gspd

And they gave glory to God because of me — Tay

CHAPTER 2

1. Then fourteen years after I went up again to Jerusalem with Barnabas, and took Titus with me also.

Fourteen years later . . . — Beck

2. And I went up by revelation,

At that time I went up in obedience to a revelation — Con

(It was in consequence of a revelation that I went up at all) — Mof

I went up under the guidance of a divine revelation — Wms

and communicated unto them that gospel which I preach among the Gentiles, but privately to them which were of reputation, lest by any means I should run, or had run, in vain.

and I put before them the gospel which I proclaim among the Gentiles. I did this in private to the leaders of the Church, for fear that I was running or should have run in vain — Wey

I submitted the gospel I am in the habit of preaching to the Gentiles, submitting it privately to the authorities, to make sure that my course of action would be and had been sound — Mof

and I gave a full exposition of the gospel which I preach among the gentiles. I did this first in private conference with the church leaders, to make sure that what I had done was acceptable to them — Phi

. . . I talked privately to the leaders of the church so that they would all understand just what I had been teaching and, I hoped, agree that it was right — Tay

3. But neither Titus, who was with me, being a Greek, was compelled to be circumcised:

But although Titus, my companion, was a Greek, they did not compel even him to be circumcised — Mon

And they did agree; they did not even demand that Titus, my companion, should be circumcised, though he was a Gentile — Tay

4. And that because of false brethren unawares brought in, who came in privily to spy out our liberty which we have in Christ Jesus, that they might bring us into bondage:

This question came up because of some false brethren who had been smuggled into the meeting secretly, and who slipped in to spy on the freedom that we have in Christ Jesus, so as to bring us into bondage again — Nor

In fact, the suggestion would never have arisen but for the presence of some pseudo-Christians, who wormed their way into our meeting to spy on the liberty which we enjoy in Christ Jesus, and then attempted to tie us up with rules and regulations — Phi

5. To whom we gave place by subjection, no, not for an hour; that the truth of the gospel might continue with you.

— why, we did not for a moment yield submission to them, that the Truth of the Good News might be yours always! — TCNT

But we refused to yield for a single instant to their claims; we were determined that the truth of the gospel should hold good for you — Mof

We did not give those men an inch, for the truth of the gospel for you and all gentiles was at stake — Phi

but not for one moment did I yield to their dictation; I was determined that the full truth of the Gospel should be maintained for you — NEB

6. But of these who seemed to be somewhat, (whatsoever they were, it maketh no matter to me: God accepteth no man's person:) for they who seemed to be somewhat in conference added nothing to me:

But from those who were held in chief reputation — it matters not to me of what account they were — God is no respecter of persons — those (I say) who were the chief in reputation gave me no new instruction — Con

Further, from the reputed leaders (whether they were men of importance or not matters nothing to me; God recognizes no external distinction) — from these reputed leaders I received no new suggestions — Wey

And as far as the leaders of the conference were concerned (I neither know nor care what their exact position was: God is not impressed with a man's office), they had nothing to add to my gospel — Phi

But as for the men of high reputation (not that their importance matters to me: God does not recognize these personal distinctions) — these men of repute, I say, did not prolong the consultation — NEB

Then, with respect to those who were considered leaders at the Council . . . — Nor

7. But contrariwise, when they saw that the gospel of the uncircumcision was committed unto me, as the gospel of the circumcision was unto Peter;

On the contrary, they saw that I had been entrusted with the Good News for the Gentiles, just as Peter had been for the Jews — TCNT

In fact they recognized that the gospel for the uncircumcised was as much my commission as the gospel for the circumcised was Peter's — Phi

8. (For he that wrought effectually in Peter to the apostleship of the circumcision, the same was mighty in me toward the Gentiles:)

For he who gave Peter power for his mission to the Jews gave me, also, power to go to the Gentiles — TCNT

for He who had been at work in Peter

for an apostleship to the Jews had also been at work in me for the Gentiles — Wey

(for he who equipped Peter to be an apostle of the circumcised equipped me as well for the uncircumcised) — Mof

For the God who had done such great work in Peter's ministry for the Jews was plainly doing the same in my ministry for the gentiles — Phi

9. **And when James, Cephas, and John, who seemed to be pillars, perceived the grace that was given unto me, they gave to me and Barnabas the right hands of fellowship; that we should go unto the heathen, and they unto the circumcision.**

and when they recognized the favor God had shown me, James, Cephas, and John, who were regarded as pillars of the church, pledged Barnabas and me their co-operation, with the understanding that we should work among the heathen and they among the Jews — Gspd

And so, recognizing the grace God had given me, they joined their right hands in fellowship with Barnabas and myself; the Gentiles were to be our province, the circumcised theirs — Knox

Recognizing, then, the favour thus bestowed upon me, those reputed pillars of our society, James, Cephas, and John, accepted Barnabas and myself as partners, and shook hands upon it, agreeing that we should go to the Gentiles while they went to the Jews — NEB

10. **Only they would that we should remember the poor; the same which I also was forward to do.**

provided only, that we should remember the poor, which I have accordingly endeavored to do with diligence — Con

Only it was their desire that we should give thought to the poor; which very thing I had much in mind to do — Bas

The only suggestion they made was that we should not forget the poor — and with this I was, of course, only too ready to agree — Phi

11. **But when Peter was come to Antioch, I withstood him to the face, because he was to be blamed.**

But when Peter visited Antioch, I opposed him to his face, because his conduct condemned him — Wey

. . . for he stood self-condemned — TCNT

12. **For before that certain came from James, he did eat with the Gentiles:**

Before certain persons came from James, he had been in the habit of eating with the Gentile converts — TCNT

It happened like this. Until the arrival of some of James' companions, he, Peter, was in the habit of eating his meals with the gentiles — Phi

but when they were come, he withdrew and separated himself, fearing them which were of the circumcision.

but when they came, he began to withdraw and hold aloof, for fear of offending those who still held to circumcision — TCNT

After they came, however, he withdrew and ate separately from the gentiles — out of sheer fear of what the Jews might think — Phi

. . . for fear of the circumcision party — Wey

13. **And the other Jews dissembled likewise with him; insomuch that Barnabas also was carried away with their dissimulation.**

The rest of the Jews were no less false to their principles; Barnabas himself was carried away by their insincerity — Knox

So the rest of the Jews played the hypocrite along with him, with the result that even Barnabas was carried away by their hypocrisy — Ber

14. **But when I saw that they walked not uprightly according to the truth of the gospel, I said unto Peter before them all, If thou, being a Jew, livest after the manner of Gentiles, and not as do the Jews, why compellest thou the Gentiles to live as do the Jews?**

But, when I saw that they were not dealing straightforwardly with the Truth of the Good News, I said to Peter, before them all, If you, who were born a Jew, adopt Gentile customs, instead of Jewish, why are you trying to compel the Gentile converts to adopt Jewish customs — TCNT

So, when I found that they were not following the true path of the gospel, I said to Cephas in front of them all, Since thou, who art a born Jew, dost follow the Gentile, not the Jewish way of life, by what right dost thou bind the Gentiles to live like Jews — Knox

But when I saw that their conduct did not square with the truth of the Gospel . . . — NEB

15. We who are Jews by nature, and not sinners of the Gentiles,

We, though we are Jews by birth and not outcasts of Gentile origin—TCNT

We are Jews by birth, and not unhallowed Gentiles — Con

We ourselves are Jews by birth and not heathen sinners — Wms

16. Knowing that a man is not justified by the works of the law, but by the faith of Jesus Christ, even we have believed in Jesus Christ, that we might be justified by the faith of Christ, and not by the works of the law:

but since we know that a man is justified simply by faith in Jesus Christ and not by doing what the Law commands, we ourselves have believed in Christ Jesus so as to get justified by faith in Christ and not by doing what the Law commands — Mof

and yet, because we know that a man does not come into right standing with God by doing what the law commands, but by simple trust in Christ, we too have trusted in Christ Jesus, in order to come into right standing with God by simple trust in Christ and not by doing what the law commands — Wms

We, like anyone else, had to learn to believe in Jesus Christ, so that we might be justified by faith in Christ, not by observance of the law — Knox

for by the works of the law shall no flesh be justified.

— for by doing what the Law commands no person shall be justified — Mof

because by doing what the law commands no man can come into right standing with God — Wms

Observance of the law cannot win acceptance for a single human creature — Knox

17. But if, while we seek to be justified by Christ, we ourselves also are found sinners,

But what if, while seeking to be justified in Christ, we have indeed reduced ourselves to the sinful state of unhallowed Gentiles? — Con

If it is discovered that in our quest for justification in Christ we are 'sinners' as well as the Gentiles — Mof

By putting our hopes of justification in Christ, we took our rank as guilty creatures like the rest — Knox

Now if, as we seek the real truth about justification, we find we are as much sinners as the gentiles — Phi

is therefore Christ the minister of sin? God forbid.

does that make Christ an agent of sin? Never! — Mof

does that mean that Christ makes us sinners? Of course not! — Phi

18. For if I build again the things which I destroyed, I make myself a transgressor.

For, if I rebuild the very things that I pulled down, I prove myself to have done wrong — TCNT

But if I attempt to build again the whole structure of justification by the Law then I do, in earnest, make myself a sinner — Phi

19. For I through the law am dead to the law, that I might live unto God.

I, indeed, through Law became dead to Law, in order to live for God — TCNT

For under the Law I "died," and now I am dead to the Law's demands so that I may live for God — Phi

20. I am crucified with Christ: nevertheless I live; yet not I, but Christ liveth in me: and the life which I now live in the flesh I live by the faith of the Son of God, who loved me, and gave himself for me.

I have been put to death on the cross with Christ; still I am living; no longer I, but Christ is living in me;

and that life which I now am living in the flesh I am living by faith, the faith of the Son of God, who in love for me, gave himself up for me — Bas

with Christ I hang upon the cross, and yet I am alive; or rather, not I; it is Christ that lives in me. True, I am living, here and now, this mortal life; but my real life is the faith I have in the Son of God, who loved me, and gave himself for me — Knox

As far as the Law is concerned I may consider that I died on the cross with Christ . . . — Phi

21. I do not frustrate the grace of God: for if righteousness come by the law, then Christ is dead in vain.

I do not nullify the grace of God; for if acquittal from guilt comes through the Law, then Christ died in vain — Wey

I am not annulling God's grace; no, but if saving righteousness comes by way of the Law, then indeed Christ's death was useless — Mof

I do not spurn the grace of God. If we can be justified through the law, then Christ's death was needless — Knox

CHAPTER 3

1. O foolish Galatians, who hath bewitched you, that ye should not obey the truth,

Foolish Galatians! Who has been fascinating you — TCNT

O senseless Galatians, who has bewitched you — Mof

Senseless Galatians, who is it that has cast a spell on you, that you should refuse your loyalty to the truth — Knox

You stupid Galatians! You must have been bewitched — NEB

before whose eyes Jesus Christ hath been evidently set forth, crucified among you?

— you before whose very eyes Jesus Christ was depicted upon the cross — TCNT

you who had Jesus Christ the crucified placarded before your very eyes — Mof

you, before whom Jesus Christ has been exposed to view on his cross — Knox

— you before whose eyes Jesus Christ was openly displayed upon his cross! — NEB

before whose eyes Jesus Christ was so graphically presented as crucified — Ber

before whose eyes Jesus Christ was publicly portrayed as crucified — RSV

2. This only would I learn of you, Received ye the Spirit by the works of the law, or by the hearing of faith?

One question I would ask you. When

you received the Spirit, was it from the works of the Law, or the preaching of faith — Con

This one question I would ask you: Is it on the ground of obeying the Law that you received the Spirit, or is it because you heard and believed — Wey

I simply want to ask you one thing: did you receive the Spirit by doing what the Law commands or by believing the gospel message — Mof

Let me be content with asking you one question, Was it from observance of the law that the Spirit came to you, or from obeying the call of faith — Knox

3. Are ye so foolish? having begun in the Spirit, are ye now made perfect by the flesh?

Are you so senseless? Having begun in the Spirit, would you now end in the flesh — Con

Surely you can't be so idiotic as to think that a man begins his spiritual life in the Spirit and then completes it by reverting to outward observances — Phi

Can it be that you are so stupid? You started with the spiritual; do you now look to the material to make you perfect — NEB

4. Have ye suffered so many things in vain? if it be yet in vain.

Have you experienced so much to no purpose — if indeed it has been to no purpose — Wey

Have all your great experiences been
in vain — if vain indeed they should
be — NEB

**5. He therefore that ministereth to you
the Spirit, and worketh miracles among
you, doeth he it by the works of the
law, or by the hearing of faith?**

Whence, I say, are the gifts of Him
who furnishes you with the fulness
of the Spirit, and works in you the
power of miracles? From the deeds
of the Law, or from the preaching
of Faith — Con

He who supplies you abundantly with
his Spirit and endows you with such
powers — does he do this as the result of obedience to Law? or as the
result of your having listened with
faith — TCNT

When God lavishes his Spirit on you
and enables you to perform miracles,
what is the reason for it? Your observance of the law, or your obedience to the call of faith — Knox

**6. Even as Abraham believed God, and
it was accounted to him for righteousness.**

Even as Abraham had faith in God,
and it was put to his account as righteousness — Bas

Look at Abraham: he put his faith in
God, and that faith was counted to
him as righteousness — NEB

**7. Know ye therefore that they which are
of faith, the same are the children of
Abraham.**

Know, therefore, that they only are the
sons of Abraham who are children
of Faith — Con

So you see, the real descendants of
Abraham are the men of faith —
Gspd

Can you not see, then, that all those
who "believe God" are the real "sons
of Abraham"? — Phi

**8. And the scripture, foreseeing that God
would justify the heathen through
faith, preached before the gospel unto
Abraham, saying, In thee shall all nations be blessed.**

Besides, Scripture anticipated God's
justification of the Gentiles by faith,
when it announced the gospel beforehand to Abraham in these terms:
All nations shall be blessed in thee
— Mof

There is a passage in scripture which,
long beforehand, brings to Abraham
the good news. Through thee all the
nations shall be blessed; and that passage looks forward to God's justification of the Gentiles by faith —
Knox

**9. So then they which be of faith are
blessed with faithful Abraham.**

So we see that those who rest on faith
are blessed with believing Abraham
— Wey

So the men of faith share the blessing
of Abraham and his faith — Gspd

So then those who are of faith have a
part in the blessing of Abraham who
was full of faith — Bas

So those who believe are blessed with
Abraham, who believed — Beck

**10. For as many as are of the works of the
law are under the curse:**

Those who take their stand on observance of the law are all under a curse
— Knox

All who rely on obedience to Law are
under a curse — TCNT

**for it is written, Cursed is every one
that continueth not in all things
which are written in the book of the
law to do them.**

for the Scripture says, Cursed be anyone who does not stand by everything that is written in the Book of
the Law and obey it — Gspd

Cursed be everyone (we read) who
does not persist in carrying out all
that this book of the law prescribes
— Knox

**11. But that no man is justified by the
law in the sight of God, it is evident:**

And it is manifest that no man is
counted righteous in God's judgment
under the conditions of the Law —
Con

... declared righteous ... — Rhm

And indeed, that the law cannot make
a man acceptable to God is clear
enough — Knox

It is evident that no one is ever justified
before God in terms of law — NEB

for, The just shall live by faith.

for it is written, By faith shall the righteous live — Con

It is faith, we are told, that brings life
to the just man — Knox

because we read, he shall gain life who is justified through faith — NEB

12. And the law is not of faith: but, The man that doeth them shall live in them.

and the Law has nothing to do with faith. It teaches that he who does these things shall live by them — Wey

The Law, however, does not rest on faith, but on works — He who does them shall live by them — Nor

And the Law is not a matter of faith at all but of doing . . . — Phi

13. Christ hath redeemed us from the curse of the law, being made a curse for us: for it is written, Cursed is every one that hangeth on a tree:

Christ ransomed us from the curse pronounced in the Law, by taking the curse on himself for us, for Scripture says — Cursed is any one who is hanged on a tree — TCNT

From this curse invoked by the law Christ has ransomed us, by himself becoming, for our sakes, an accursed thing; we read that, There is a curse on the man who hangs on a gibbet — Knox

14. That the blessing of Abraham might come on the Gentiles through Jesus Christ; that we might receive the promise of the Spirit through faith.

Thus, in Christ Jesus, the blessing of Abraham was to be imparted to the Gentiles, so that we, through faith, might receive the promised gift of the Spirit — Knox

God's purpose is therefore plain: that the blessing promised to Abraham might reach the gentiles through Jesus Christ, and the promise of the Spirit might become ours by faith — Phi

15. Brethren, I speak after the manner of men;

Brethren, I will take an illustration from every-day life — Wey

Brothers, I am going to use a human illustration: — Wms

Brethren, let me take an argument from common life — Knox

Though it be but a man's covenant, yet if it be confirmed, no man disannulleth, or addeth thereto.

Even a human covenant when once ratified, no one can set aside or amplify — Wey

Even a human contract, once it has been ratified, no one can annul or change — Wms

A valid legal disposition made by an ordinary human being cannot afterwards be set aside; no one can make fresh provisions in it — Knox

Even in ordinary life, when a man's will and testament has been duly executed, no one else can set it aside or add a codicil — NEB

16. Now to Abraham and his seed were the promises made. He saith not, And to seeds, as of many; but as of one, And to thy seed, which is Christ.

Now it was to Abraham that the promises were made, 'and to his offspring.' It was not said 'to his offsprings,' as if many persons were meant, but the words were 'to thy offspring,' showing that one person was meant — and that was Christ — TCNT

Now the promises were pronounced to Abraham and to his 'issue'. It does not say 'issues' in the plural, but in the singular, 'and to your issue'; and the 'issue' intended is Christ — NEB

17. And this I say, that the covenant, that was confirmed before of God in Christ, the law, which was four hundred and thirty years after, cannot disannul, that it should make the promise of none effect.

My point is this: — An agreement already confirmed by God cannot be cancelled by the Law, which came four hundred and thirty years later, so as to cause the promise to be set aside — TCNT

And this is my contention; the law, coming into being four hundred and thirty years afterwards, cannot unmake the disposition which God made so long ago, and cancel the promise — Knox

What I am saying is this: a testament, or covenant, had already been validated by God; it cannot be invalidated, and its promises rendered ineffective, by a law made four hundred and thirty years later — NEB

18. For if the inheritance be of the law, it is no more of promise: but God gave it to Abraham by promise.

If our heritage is the result of Law, then it has ceased to be the result of a promise. Yet God conferred it on Abraham by a promise — TCNT

For if the receiving of the promised blessing were now made to depend on the Law, that would amount to a cancellation of the original "contract" which God made with Abraham as a promise — Phi

19. Wherefore then serveth the law?

What, then, you ask, was the use of the Law — TCNT

Where then lies the point of the Law — Phi

It was added because of transgressions, till the seed should come to whom the promise was made;

It was a later addition, to make men conscious of their wrong-doings and intended to last only till the coming of that 'offspring' to whom the promise had been made — TCNT

It was an addition made to underline the existence and extent of sin until the arrival of the "seed" to whom the promise referred — Phi

and it was ordained by angels in the hand of a mediator.

and it was enacted by the ministration of angels through the hands of [Moses, who was] a mediator [between God and the people] — Con

also, it was transmitted by means of angels through the agency of an intermediary — Mof

enacted through the agency of angels in the person of an intermediary — Wms

It was promulgated through angels, and there was an intermediary — NEB

20. Now a mediator is not a mediator of one, but God is one.

Now where a mediator is, there must be two parties. But God is one [and there is no second party to His promise] — Con

but an intermediary is not needed for one party acting alone, and God is one — NEB

But when God gave His promise to Abraham, He did it by Himself alone, without angels or Moses in between — Tay

21. Is the law then against the promises of God? God forbid:

Is the Law then opposed to the promises of God? God forbid! — Wey

Is the law an infringement, then, of God's promises? That is not to be thought of — Knox

Does the Law, then, frustrate the promise of God? No, certainly not — Nor

for if there had been a law given which could have given life, verily righteousness should have been by the law.

for if a law had been given which could have conferred life, righteousness would certainly have come by the Law — Wey

Doubtless, if a law had been given that was capable of imparting life to us, it would have been for the law to bring us justification — Knox

Surely, if a law had been given which could have given spiritual life, then justification would indeed have come by that law — Nor

22. But the scripture hath concluded all under sin, that the promise by faith of Jesus Christ might be given to them that believe.

But the words of Scripture represent the whole world as being in bondage to sin, so that the promised blessing, dependent, as it is, upon faith in Jesus Christ, may be given to those who have faith in him — TCNT

but Scripture has consigned all without exception to the custody of sin, in order that the promise due to faith in Jesus Christ might be given to those who have faith — Mof

But, in Scripture, the Law makes all men guilty of sin, so that what was promised, based on faith in Jesus Christ, might be given to those who believe in Him — Nor

But, as things are, the scripture has all men "imprisoned" for their sins, because they are found guilty by the Law, that to men in such condition the promise might come to release all who believe in Jesus Christ — Phi

23. But before faith came, we were kept under the law, shut up unto the faith which should afterwards be revealed.

But before Faith came we were shut up in prison, in ward under the Law, in preparation for the Faith which should afterwards be revealed—Con

Before the coming of faith we were all imprisoned under the power of the Law, with our only hope of deliverance the faith that was to be shown to us — Phi

24. Wherefore the law was our schoolmaster to bring us unto Christ, that we might be justified by faith.

Thus, even as the slave who leads a child to the house of the schoolmaster, so the Law has led us to [our teacher] Christ, that by Faith we might be justified — Con

So that the Law has proved a tutor to discipline us for Christ, that through faith we may be justified — Wey

Or, to change the metaphor, the Law was like a strict governess in charge of us until we went to the school of Christ and learned to be justified by faith in him — Phi

So that the law was our custodian until Christ came . . . — RSV

25. But after that faith is come, we are no longer under a schoolmaster.

But now that faith has come, we are no longer in the charge of the attendant — Gspd

Once we had that faith we were completely free from the governess's authority — Phi

26. For ye are all the children of God by faith in Christ Jesus.

For in Christ Jesus you are all sons of God through your faith — Gspd

For now that you have faith in Christ Jesus you are all sons of God — Phi

27. For as many of you as have been baptized into Christ have put on Christ.

For all of you who were baptized into union with Christ clothed yourselves with Christ — TCNT

(for all of you who had yourselves baptized into Christ have taken on the character of Christ) — Mof

. . . have put on the family likeness of Christ — Phi

28. There is neither Jew nor Greek, there is neither bond nor free, there is neither male nor female: for ye are all one in Christ Jesus.

All distinctions between Jew and Greek, slave and freeman, male and female, have vanished; for in union with Christ you are all one — TCNT

You are no longer Jews or Greeks or slaves or free men or even merely men or women, but you are all the same — you are Christians, you are one in Christ Jesus — Tay

29. And if ye be Christ's, then are ye Abraham's seed, and heirs according to the promise.

And since you belong to Christ, it follows that you are Abraham's offspring and, under the promise, sharers in the inheritance — TCNT

And if you belong to Christ, then you are indeed Abraham's children; the promised inheritance is yours — Knox

But if you thus belong to Christ, you are the 'issue' of Abraham, and so heirs by promise — NEB

CHAPTER 4

1. Now I say, That the heir, as long as he is a child, differeth nothing from a servant, though he be lord of all;

Now I say that so long as an heir is a child, he in no way differs from a slave, although he is the owner of everything — Wey

I mean this: As long as the heir is a minor, he is no better than a slave, although he is the owner of all the property — Gspd

Consider this: one who comes into his property while he is still a child has no more liberty than one of the servants, though all the estate is his — Knox

But remember this, that if a father dies and leaves great wealth for his little son, that child is not much better off than a slave until he grows up, even though he actually owns everything his father had — Tay

2. But is under tutors and governors until the time appointed of the father.

but he is under guardians and trustees until the time his father has appointed — Wey

he is under the control of guardians and trustees, until he reaches the age prescribed by his father — Knox

He has to do what his guardians and managers tell him to, until he reaches whatever age his father set — Tay

3. Even so we, when we were children, were in bondage under the elements of the world:

And so we also [who are Israelites] when we were children were in bondage, under our childhood's lessons of outward ordinances — Con

And so it is with us: when we were under age, as it were, we were slaves to the puerile teaching of this world — TCNT

So when we were spiritually under age, we were slaves to the world's crude notions — Wms

So it was with us; in those childish days of ours we toiled away at the schoolroom tasks which the world gave us, till the appointed time came — Knox

So it is with us. When we were children we were like slaves learning the elements of world knowledge — Nor

And so it was with us. During our minority we were slaves to the elemental spirits of the universe — NEB

4. But when the fulness of the time was come, God sent forth his Son, made of a woman, made under the law.

but when the full time came, God sent his Son — born a woman's child, born subject to Law — TCNT

Then God sent out his Son on a mission to us. He took birth from a woman, took birth as a subject to the law — Knox

5. To redeem them that were under the law, that we might receive the adoption of sons.

that He might redeem from their slavery the subjects of the Law, that we might be adopted as the sons of God — Con

that he might redeem those who were under the authority of the Law and lead us into becoming, by adoption, true sons of God — Phi

to purchase freedom for the subjects of the law, in order that we might attain the status of sons — NEB

6. And because ye are sons, God hath sent forth the Spirit of his Son into your hearts, crying, Abba, Father.

And because you are sons, God has sent into our hearts the spirit of his Son, with the cry, Abba! that is, Father — Gspd

It is because you really are his sons that God has sent the Spirit of his Son into our hearts to cry Father, dear Father — Phi

7. Wherefore thou art no more a servant, but a son; and if a son, then an heir of God through Christ.

So you are no longer a slave, but a son; and if a son, then an heir, made so by God — Gspd

8. Howbeit then, when ye knew not God, ye did service unto them which by nature are no gods.

But formerly, when you knew not God, you were in bondage to gods that have no real being — Con

In those days, when you were ignorant of God, you were in servitude to gods who are really no gods at all — Mof

Before you Gentiles knew God you were slaves to so-called gods that did not even exist — Tay

9. But now, after that ye have known God, or rather are known of God, how turn ye again to the weak and beggarly elements, whereunto ye desire again to be in bondage?

But now that you have found God — or, rather, have been found by him — how is it that you are turning back to that poor and feeble puerile teaching, to which yet once again you are wanting to become slaves — TCNT

Now you have recognized the true God, or rather, the true God has recognized you. How is it that you are going back to those old schoolroom tasks of yours, so abject, so ineffectual, eager to begin your drudgery all over again — Knox

But now, after you have learned to know God, or rather, after God came to know you as His own, how can you turn back to the weak and helpless elemental false gods, whose slaves you want to be once more — Nor

. . . how is it you are turning back again to the weak and worthless rudimentary notions to which you are once more willing to be enslaved — Wey

. . . to the weak and beggarly elemental spirits . . . — RSV

. . . how can you revert to dead and sterile principles and consent to be under their power all over again — Phi

10. Ye observe days, and months, and times, and years.

You are scrupulous in keeping Days and Months and Seasons and Years! — TCNT

11. I am afraid of you, lest I have bestowed upon you labour in vain.

You make me fear that the labour which I have spent on you may have been wasted — TCNT

12. Brethren, I beseech you, be as I am; for I am as ye are: ye have not injured me at all.

Take my position, I beg you, brothers, just as I once took yours! You took no advantage of me then — Gspd

Stand by me; I have taken my stand with you. I appeal to you, brethren. You have never treated me amiss — Knox

I do beg you to follow me here, my brothers. I am a man like yourselves, and I have nothing against you personally — Phi

13. Ye know how through infirmity of the flesh I preached the gospel unto you at the first.

though you know that it was because of an illness that I preached the good news to you that first time — Gspd

Why, when I preached the gospel to you in the first instance, it was, you remember, because of outward circumstances which were humiliating to me — Knox

You know how handicapped I was by illness when I first preached the gospel to you — Phi

14. And my temptation which was in my flesh ye despised not, nor rejected; but received me as an angel of God, even as Christ Jesus.

yet you neither scorned nor loathed the bodily infirmity which was my trial; but you welcomed me as an angel of God, yea, even as Christ Jesus — Con

And as for what must have tried you in my condition, it did not inspire you with scorn or disgust, but you welcomed me as if I had been an angel of God — or Christ Jesus himself! — TCNT

Those outward circumstances of mine were a test for you, which you did not meet with contempt or dislike . . . — Knox

You didn't shrink from me or let yourselves be revolted at the disease which was such a trial to you . . . — Phi

and you resisted any temptation to show scorn or disgust at the state of my poor body . . . — NEB

15. Where is then the blessedness ye spake of? for I bear you record, that, if it had been possible, ye would have plucked out your own eyes, and have given them to me.

Why, then, did you think yourselves so happy? (for I bear you witness that, if it had been possible, you would have torn out your own eyes and given them to me) — Con

You congratulated yourselves. Now, what has become of all that? . . . — Mof

What has become of your blessed good will? . . . — Nor

What has happened to that fine spirit of yours? . . . — Phi

Where is that happy spirit that we felt together then? . . . — Tay

Have you forgotten how happy you thought yourselves in having me with you? . . . — NEB

16. Am I therefore become your enemy, because I tell you the truth?

Am I your enemy to-day, because I have been honest with you — Mof

And have I now made myself your enemy by being honest with you — NEB

17. They zealously affect you, but not well;

yea, they would exclude you, that ye might affect them.

They [who call me so] show zeal for you with no good intent; they would shut you out from others, that your zeal may be for them alone — Con

Certain people are seeking your favour, but with no honourable object. No indeed, they want to isolate you, so that you will have to seek their favour — TCNT

These men make much of you — yes, but for dishonest ends; they want to debar you from us, so that you may make much of them — Mof

Oh, I know how keen these men are to win you over, but can't you see that it is for their own ends? They would like to see you and me separated altogether, and have your zeal all to themselves — Phi

18. But it is good to be zealously affected always in a good thing, and not only when I am present with you.

Now it is a fine thing to have special attention paid you, if it is done sincerely and unceasingly, and not only when I am with you — Wms

It is always a fine thing to have people interested in you, if it is for a right cause, and not only when I am going to be with you — Nor

For a good purpose it is always good to be made much of, and not only when I am present with you — RSV

Don't think I'm jealous — it is a grand thing that men should be keen to win you, whether I'm there or not, provided it is for the truth — Phi

It is a fine thing when people are nice to you with good motives and sincere hearts, especially if they aren't doing it just when I am with you! — Tay

19. My little children, of whom I travail in birth again until Christ be formed in you,

my dear children — you for whom I am again enduring a mother's pains, till a likeness of Christ shall have been formed in you — TCNT

For my children you are, and I am in travail with you over again until you take the shape of Christ — NEB

20. I desire to be present with you now,

and to change my voice; for I stand in doubt of you.

I would that I were present with you now, that I might change my tone; for you fill me with perplexity — Con

would that I could be with you at this moment, and alter my tone, for I am at my wits' end about you! — Mof

How I wish I could be there with you right now and not have to reason with you like this, for at this distance I frankly don't know what to do — Tay

21. Tell me, ye that desire to be under the law, do ye not hear the law?

Tell me, you who want to be still subject to Law — Why do you not listen to the Law — TCNT

22. For it is written, that Abraham had two sons, the one by a bondmaid, the other by a freewoman.

For the Scripture says that Abraham had two sons, one by the slave-girl, and one by the free woman — Gspd

23. But he who was of the bondwoman was born after the flesh; but he of the freewoman was by promise.

But the child of the slave-girl was born in the ordinary course of nature, while the child of the free woman was born in fulfillment of the promise — Gspd

24. Which things are an allegory: for these are the two covenants; the one from the mount Sinai, which gendereth to bondage, which is Agar.

Now, all this is allegorical; for these two women are the two covenants; the first given from Mount Sinai, whose children are born into bondage, which is Hagar — Con

All this is allegorical; for the women represent two Covenants. One originates on Mount Sinai, and bears children destined for slavery. This is Hagar — Wey

25. For this Agar is mount Sinai in Arabia, and answereth to Jerusalem which now is, and is in bondage with her children.

(for the word Hagar in Arabia signifies Mount Sinai); and she answers to the earthly Jerusalem, for she is in bondage with her children — Con

for the name Hagar stands for Mount Sinai in Arabia, and corresponds to the present Jerusalem, which is in bondage together with her children — Wey

26. But Jerusalem which is above is free, which is the mother of us all.

But the heavenly Jerusalem is the free woman; she is our mother — NEB

27. For it is written, Rejoice thou barren that bearest not; break forth and cry, thou that travailest not: for the desolate hath many more children than she which hath an husband.

For Scripture says, Rejoice, O barren woman who never bore child; break into a shout of joy, you who never knew a mother's pangs; for the deserted wife shall have more children than she who lives with the husband — NEB

28. Now we, brethren, as Isaac was, are the children of promise.

As for ourselves, Brothers, we, like Isaac, are children born in fulfilment of a promise — TCNT

29. But as then he that was born after the flesh persecuted him that was born after the Spirit, even so it is now.

Yet at that time the child born in the course of nature persecuted the child born by the power of the Spirit; and it is the same now — TCNT

30. Nevertheless what saith the scripture? Cast out the bondwoman and her son: for the son of the bondwoman shall not be heir with the son of the freewoman.

Yet what does the Scripture say? Drive the slave-girl and her son away, for the slave-girl's son shall not share the inheritance with the son of the free woman — Gspd

31. So then, brethren, we are not children of the bondwoman, but of the free.

So, brothers, we are children not of a slave but of one who is free — Gspd

You see, then, my brothers, we are no slave-woman's children; our mother is the free woman — NEB

CHAPTER 5

1. Stand fast therefore in the liberty wherewith Christ hath made us free, and be not entangled again with the yoke of bondage.

For freedom did Christ set us free: stand fast therefore, and be not entangled again in a yoke of bondage — ASV

With freedom did Christ make us free; stand fast therefore, and be not held again with a yoke of bondage — ABUV

Christ has made us completely free; stand fast then, and do not again be hampered with the yoke of slavery — Wey

With her freedom Christ hath made you free . . . — Rhm

This is the freedom with which Christ has freed us . . . — Gspd

2. Behold, I Paul say unto you, that if ye be circumcised, Christ shall profit you nothing.

The word of Paul is your warrant for this; if you are for being circumcised, Christ is of no value to you at all — Knox

Listen! I, Paul, say this to you as solemnly as I can: if you consent to be circumcised then Christ will be of no use to you at all . . . — Phi

3. For I testify again to every man that is circumcised, that he is a debtor to do the whole law.

Once again I would warn anyone who is accepting circumcision that he thereby engages himself to keep all the precepts of the law — Knox

. . . I testify again to every man who submits to circumcision, that he thereby lays himself under obligation to fulfil the whole Law — Con

4. Christ is become of no effect unto you, whosoever of you are justified by the law: ye are fallen from grace.

Ye are severed from Christ, ye who would be justified by the law . . . — ASV

If you rest your righteousness on the Law, you are cut off from Christ . . . — Con

You are for justification by the Law? Then you are done with Christ, you have deserted grace — Mof

You people who propose to be made upright by law have finished with Christ; you have lost your hold upon God's favor — Gspd

If you try to be justified by the Law you automatically cut yourself off from the power of Christ; you put yourself outside the range of his grace — Phi

When you seek to be justified by way of law, your relation with Christ is completely severed: you have fallen out of the domain of God's grace — NEB

Ye are separated from Christ, whoever of you are being justified by law; ye are fallen away from grace — ABUV

5. For we through the Spirit wait for the hope of righteousness by faith.

For we, by the help of the Spirit, are eagerly waiting for the fulfilment of our hope — that we may be pronounced righteous as the result of faith — TCNT

All our hope of justification lies in the spirit; it rests on our faith — Knox

For to us, our hope of attaining that righteousness which we eagerly await is the work of the Spirit through faith — NEB

6. For in Jesus Christ neither circumcision availeth any thing, nor uncircumcision; but faith which worketh by love.

in Christ Jesus circumcision is not valid, neither is uncircumcison, but only faith active in love — Mof

For in union with Christ Jesus, neither circumcision nor the want of it counts for anything, but only faith acting through love — Gspd

once we are in Christ, circumcision means nothing, and the want of it means nothing; the faith that finds its expression in love is all that matters — Knox

7. Ye did run well; who did hinder you that ye should not obey the truth?

You were running the race well: who has cast a stumbling-block in your way? who has turned you aside from your obedience to the truth — Con

You were doing splendidly . . . — Mof

You were making such progress! — Gspd

8. This persuasion cometh not of him that calleth you.

The counsel which you have obeyed came not from Him who called you — Con

The persuasion brought to bear on you does not come from him who calls you — TCNT

Not he who called you; this pressure comes from elsewhere — Knox

Whatever persuasion he used, it did not come from God who is calling you — NEB

9. A little leaven leaveneth the whole lump.

A little yeast will make all the dough rise — Gspd

A little yeast makes the whole dough sour — Beck

But it only takes one wrong person among you to infect all the others — Tay

10. I have confidence in you through the Lord, that ye will be none otherwise minded: but he that troubleth you shall bear his judgment, whosoever he be.

As for me, I rely upon you, in the Lord, that you will not be led astray; but he that is troubling you, whosoever he be, shall bear the blame — Con

I am confident in the Lord that you will not take a different view. The man who is unsettling you will have to pay the penalty for it, no matter who he is — Gspd

I am fully confident in the Lord that you will be of the same mind with me, leaving the disturbers of your peace, be they who they may, to answer for it — Knox

I feel confident in the Lord that you will not take any fatal step. But whoever it is who is worrying you will have a serious charge to answer one day — Phi

11. And I, brethren, if I yet preach circumcision, why do I yet suffer persecution? then is the offence of the cross ceased.

But if I myself [as they say] still preach circumcision, why am I still persecuted? for if I preach circumcision, then the cross, the stone at which they stumble, is done away — Con

As for myself, brethren, if it is true that I preach the need of circumcision, why am I persecuted? If I did, the preaching of the cross would no longer give offence — Knox

And as for me, my brothers, if I were still advocating circumcision (as some apparently allege!), why am I still suffering persecution? I suppose if I would only recommend this little rite all the hostility which the preaching of the cross provokes would disappear! — Phi

12. I would that they were even cut off which trouble you.

I could even wish that the people who are unsettling you would go further still and mutilate themselves—TCNT

I wish those who are so eager to cut your bodies would cut themselves off from you altogether — Phi

As for these agitators, they had better go the whole way and make eunuchs of themselves! — NEB

13. For, brethren, ye have been called unto liberty; only use not liberty for an occasion to the flesh, but by love serve one another.

For you, brethren, have been called to freedom; only make not your freedom a vantage-ground for the Flesh, but rather enslave yourselves one to another by the bondage of love — Con

. . . Only do not make your freedom an incentive to your lower nature . . . — Wey

. . . an excuse for the gratification of your lower nature . . . — Wms

. . . licence for your lower nature . . . — NEB

. . . an opportunity for self-indulgence . . . — TCNT

Yes, brethren, freedom claimed you when you were called. Only, do not let this freedom give a foothold to corrupt nature; you must be servants still, serving one another in a spirit of charity — Knox

14. For all the law is fulfilled in one word, even in this; Thou shalt love thy neighbour as thyself.

Indeed, the whole Law has been summed up in this one precept . . . — TCNT

For all the law is made complete in one word . . . — Bas

15. But if ye bite and devour one another, take heed that ye be not consumed one of another.

But, if you are continually wounding and preying upon one another, take care that you are not destroyed by one another — TCNT

But if freedom means merely that you are free to attack and tear one another to pieces, be careful that it doesn't mean that between you, you destroy your fellowship altogether— Phi

But if you go on fighting one another, tooth and nail, all you can expect is mutual destruction — NEB

16. This I say then, Walk in the Spirit, and ye shall not fulfil the lust of the flesh.

This is what I have to say: — Let your steps be guided by the Spirit, and then you will never gratify the cravings of your earthly nature — TCNT

I mean, lead the life of the Spirit; then you will never satisfy the passions of the flesh — Mof

Here is my advice. Live your whole life in the Spirit and you will not satisfy the desires of your lower nature — Phi

17. For the flesh lusteth against the Spirit, and the Spirit against the flesh: and these are contrary the one to the other: so that ye cannot do the things that ye would.

for the desire of the Flesh fights against the Spirit, and the desire of the Spirit fights against the Flesh; and this variance tends to hinder you from doing what you wish to do — Con

For these cravings of our earthly nature conflict with the Spirit, and the Spirit with our earthly nature—they are two contrary principles — so that you cannot do what you wish—TCNT

. . . and that is why you cannot do all that your will approves — Knox

. . . so that what you will to do you cannot do — NEB

18. But if ye be led of the Spirit, ye are not under the law.

But, if you follow the guidance of the Spirit, you are not subject to Law — TCNT

It is by letting the spirit lead you that you free yourselves from the yoke of the law — Knox

When you are guided by the Holy Spirit you need no longer force yourself to obey Jewish laws — Tay

19. Now the works of the flesh are manifest; which are these; Adultery, fornication, uncleanness, lasciviousness,

The sins of our earthly nature are unmistakeable. They are sins like these —unchastity, impurity, indecency— TCNT

Now the deeds of the flesh are quite obvious, such as sexual vice, impurity, sensuality — Mof

Anyone can see the kind of behaviour that belongs to the lower nature: fornication, impurity, and indecency — NEB

20. Idolatry, witchcraft, hatred, variance, emulations, wrath, strife, seditions, heresies,

idolatry, witchcraft; enmities, strife, jealousy, passionate anger; intrigues, divisions, sectarian parties — Con

idolatry and sorcery; quarrels, a contentious temper, envy, fits of rage, selfish ambitions, dissensions, party intrigues — NEB

21. Envyings, murders, drunkenness, revellings, and such like:

envy, drunkenness, carousing, and the like — Gspd

of the which I tell you before, as I have also told you in time past, that they which do such things shall not inherit the kingdom of God.

I warn you as I did before that people who do such things will have no share in the Kingdom of God — Gspd

22. But the fruit of the Spirit is love, joy, peace, longsuffering, gentleness, goodness, faith,

The Spirit, on the other hand, brings a harvest of love, joy, peace; forbearance, kindness, benevolence; good faith — Wey

The Spirit, however, produces in human life fruits such as these: love, joy, peace, patience, kindness, generosity, fidelity — Phi

23. Meekness, temperance: against such there is no law.

meekness, self-restraint. Against such things there is no law — Wey

tolerance and self-control — and no law exists against any of them — Phi

24. And they that are Christ's have crucified the flesh with the affections and lusts.

Now those who belong to Christ Jesus have crucified the lower nature with its passions and appetites — Wey

Those who belong to Christ Jesus have crucified their old nature with all that it loved and lusted for — Phi

Those who belong to Christ have nailed their natural evil desires to His cross and crucified them there — Tay

25. If we live in the Spirit, let us also walk in the Spirit.

If we live by the Spirit, let our steps be guided by the Spirit — Con

If we are living now by the Holy Spirit's power, let us follow the Holy Spirit's leading in every part of our lives — Tay

If the Spirit is the source of our life, let the Spirit also direct our course — NEB

26. Let us not be desirous of vain glory, provoking one another, envying one another.

Let us not become vainglorious, provoking one another to strife, regarding one another with envy — Con

Then we won't need to look for honors and popularity, which lead to jealousy and hard feelings — Tay

We must not be conceited, challenging one another to rivalry, jealous of one another — NEB

CHAPTER 6

1. Brethren, if a man be overtaken in a fault, ye which are spiritual, restore such an one in the spirit of meekness; considering thyself, lest thou also be tempted.

Brothers, if anybody is caught in the very act of doing wrong, you who are spiritual, in the spirit of gentleness, must set him right; each of you continuing to think of yourself, for you may be tempted too — Wms

Even if a man should be detected in some sin, my brothers, the spiritual ones among you should quietly set him back on the right path, not with any feeling of superiority but being yourselves on guard against temptation — Phi

If a man should do something wrong, my brothers, on a sudden impulse, you who are endowed with the Spirit must set him right again very gently. Look to yourself, each one of you: you may be tempted too — NEB

2. Bear ye one another's burdens, and so fulfil the law of Christ.

Practise bearing one another's burdens, and in this way carry out the law of Christ — Wms

Bear the burden of one another's failings . . . — Knox

Help one another to carry these heavy loads . . . — NEB

3. For if a man think himself to be something, when he is nothing, he deceiveth himself.

For if any one thinks himself to be somebody when he is nobody, he is deluding himself — Wey

When a man thinks he is something big, he is really nothing at all; he is fooling himself — Nor

If a man thinks he is "somebody," he is deceiving himself, for that very thought proves that he is nobody — Phi

If anyone thinks he is too great to stoop to this, he is fooling himself. He is really a nobody — Tay

4. But let every man prove his own work, and then shall he have rejoicing in himself alone, and not in another.

let everyone bring his own work to the test — then he will have something to boast about on his own account, and not in comparison with his fellows — Mof

Everyone should examine his own conduct; then he will be able to take the measure of his own worth; no need to compare himself with others — Knox

Let every man learn to assess properly the value of his own work and he can then be glad when he has done something worth doing without depending on the approval of others — Phi

Let everyone be sure that he is doing his very best, for then he will have the personal satisfaction of work well-done, and won't need to compare himself with someone else — Tay

5. For every man shall bear his own burden.

For everyone will have to bear his own load of responsibility — Mof

Each of us, then, will have his own load to carry — Knox

For every one must "shoulder his own pack" — Phi

Each of us must bear some faults and burdens of his own. For none of us is perfect! — Tay

6. Let him that is taught in the word communicate unto him that teacheth in all good things.

Moreover, let him who is receiving instruction in the Word give to his instructor a share in all the good things which he possesses — Con

Let those who receive instruction in the word share with their instructors all temporal blessings — Wey

The man under Christian instruction should be willing to contribute toward the livelihood of his teacher — Phi

7. Be not deceived; God is not mocked: for whatsoever a man soweth, that shall he also reap.

Make no mistake about it; you cannot cheat God. A man will reap what he sows — Knox

Don't be under any illusion: you cannot make a fool of God! A man's harvest in life will depend entirely on what he sows — Phi

8. For he that soweth to his flesh shall of the flesh reap corruption; but he that soweth to the Spirit shall of the Spirit reap life everlasting.

The man who now sows for his own Flesh shall reap therefrom a harvest doomed to perish; but he who sows for the Spirit shall from the Spirit reap the harvest of eternal life — Con

He who sows for his lower nature will from that nature reap destruction; but he who sows for the Spirit will from that Spirit reap Life eternal — Wey

If he sows seed in the field of his lower nature, he will reap from it a harvest of corruption, but if he sows in the field of the Spirit, the Spirit will bring him a harvest of eternal life — NEB

9. And let us not be weary in well doing: for in due season we shall reap, if we faint not.

Never let us grow tired of doing what is right, for if we do not faint we shall reap our harvest at the opportune season — Mof

Let us not grow tired of doing good, for, unless we throw in our hand, the ultimate harvest is assured — Phi

And let us not get tired of doing what is right, for after a while we will reap a harvest of blessing if we don't get discouraged and give up — Tay

10. As we have therefore opportunity, let us do good unto all men, especially unto them who are of the household of faith.

Let us practise generosity to all, while the opportunity is ours; and above all, to those who are of one family with us in the faith — Knox

That's why whenever we can we should always be kind to everyone, and especially to our Christian brothers — Tay

11. Ye see how large a letter I have written unto you with mine own hand.

See what large letters I make, when I write to you with my own hand! — Gspd

Here is some bold lettering for you, written in my own hand — Knox

You see these big letters? I am now writing to you in my own hand — NEB

12. As many as desire to make a fair shew in the flesh, they constrain you to be circumcised; only lest they should suffer persecution for the cross of Christ.

Those who wish to appear to advantage in regard to outward observances are the very people who are trying to compel you to be circumcised; and they do it only to avoid being persecuted for the cross of Jesus, the Christ — TCNT

Those who want to make a pleasing appearance in worldly fashion, are the very ones who would force circumcision on you, for the simple reason that so they may escape persecution on account of the cross of Christ — Ber

Those teachers of yours who are trying to force you to be circumcised are doing it for just one reason: so that they can be popular and avoid the persecution they would get if they admitted that the cross of Christ alone can save — Tay

13. For neither they themselves who are circumcised keep the law; but desire to have you circumcised, that they may glory in your flesh.

Why, even the circumcision party do not observe the Law themselves! They merely want you to get circumcised, so as to boast over your flesh! — Mof

Why, they do not even observe the law, although they adopt circumcision; they are for having you circumcised, so as to make a display of your outward conformity — Knox

. . . that your obedience to the fleshly ordinance may give them a ground of boasting — Con

. . . so that they can boast of you as members of their party — Wms

. . . in order that they can boast that you are their disciples — Tay

14. But God forbid that I should glory, save in the cross of our Lord Jesus Christ, by whom the world is crucified unto me, and I unto the world.

But I never want to boast of anything but the cross of our Lord Jesus Christ, on which the world has been crucified to me and I have been to the world — Gspd

Yet God forbid that I should boast about anything or anybody except the cross of our Lord Jesus Christ, which means that the world is a dead thing to me and I am a dead man to the world! — Phi

15. For in Christ Jesus neither circumcision availeth any thing, nor uncircumcision, but a new creature.

For neither is circumcision nor the omission of it anything; but a new nature is everything — TCNT

861

For neither circumcision nor the lack of it is important, but a new creation counts — Ber

For in Christ it is not circumcision nor uncircumcision that counts, but the power of a new birth — Phi

It doesn't make any difference now whether we have been circumcised or not; what counts is whether we really have been changed into new and different people — Tay

Circumcision is nothing; uncircumcision is nothing; the only thing that counts is new creation! — NEB

16. And as many as walk according to this rule, peace be on them, and mercy, and upon the Israel of God.

May all who rule their conduct by this principle find peace and mercy — they who are the Israel of God — TCNT

Now peace and mercy be on all who walk by this rule; that is, on the true Israel of God — Wms

To all who live by this principle, to the true Israel of God, may there be peace and mercy! — Phi

17. From henceforth let no man trouble me: for I bear in my body the marks of the Lord Jesus.

Let nobody interfere with me after this, for I bear on my body the scars that mark me as a slave of Jesus — Gspd

. . . for I bear the marks of Jesus branded on my body — TCNT

. . . for I bear branded on my body the owner's stamp of the Lord Jesus — Mof

. . . for I bear in my body the brand-marks of Jesus' ownership — Ber

. . . for I bear the marks of Jesus branded on my body — NEB

18. Brethren, the grace of our Lord Jesus Christ be with your spirit. Amen.

May the blessing of Jesus Christ, our Lord, rest on your souls, Brothers. Amen — TCNT

THE
EPISTLE OF PAUL TO THE EPHESIANS

CHAPTER 1

1. Paul, an apostle of Jesus Christ by the will of God,

Paul, an apostle of Christ Jesus through the will of God — ASV

Paul, messenger of Christ Jesus by God's will — Phi

From Paul, apostle of Christ Jesus, commissioned by the will of God — NEB

to the saints which are at Ephesus, and to the faithful in Christ Jesus:

to the saints [who are in Ephesus] faithful in Christ Jesus — Wey

To the saints who are also faithful in Christ Jesus — RSV

to all faithful Christians at Ephesus (and other places where this letter is read) — Phi

To Christ's People [at Ephesus] who are faithful to him — TCNT

to God's people at Ephesus, believers incorporate in Christ Jesus — NEB

2. Grace be to you, and peace,

may grace and peace be granted to you — Wey

grace and peace be yours — Knox

from God our Father, and from the Lord Jesus Christ.

3. Blessed be the God and Father of our Lord Jesus Christ,

Praise be to the God and Father of our Lord Jesus Christ — Phi

who hath blessed us with all spiritual blessings in heavenly places in Christ:

who has blessed us on high with every spiritual blessing, in Christ — TCNT

who has crowned us with every spiritual blessing in the heavenly realms in Christ — Wey

. . . with every spiritual blessing, higher than heaven itself — Knox

. . . that heaven itself enjoys — Nor

4. According as he hath chosen us in him before the foundation of the world,

even as . . . He chose us as His own in Christ before the creation of the world — Wey

For consider what he has done — before the foundation of the world he chose us . . . in Christ — Phi

For he chose us in our union with Christ before the creation of the universe — TCNT

that we should be holy and without blame before him in love:[1]

to be consecrated and above reproach in his sight in love — Gspd

to be saints, to be blameless in his sight, for love of him — Knox

to become . . . his holy and blameless children living within his constant care — Phi

to be dedicated, to be without blemish in his sight, to be full of love — NEB

that we might be holy and blameless in his sight, living in the spirit of love — TCNT

5. Having predestinated us unto the adoption of children by Jesus Christ to himself,

having foreordained us unto adoption as sons . . . — ASV

marking us out beforehand . . . — Knox

He destined us in love to be his sons through Jesus Christ — RSV

He planned . . . that we should be adopted as his own children through Jesus Christ — Phi

and he destined us . . . to be accepted as his sons — NEB

From the first he destined us . . . to be adopted as Sons through Jesus Christ — TCNT

according to the good pleasure of his will,

in his good-will towards us — TCNT

such being his gracious will and pleasure — Wey

according to the purpose of his will — RSV

He has done what in His kindness He planned to do — Beck

because it pleased Him and was His kind intent — Amp

6. To the praise of the glory of his grace,

to the praise of the splendour of His grace — Wey

---

[1]Some translations put "in love" with the thought of verse 5. Note the rendering of RSV.

Thus he would manifest the splendour of that grace — Knox

that we might learn to praise that glorious generosity of his — Phi

that the glory of his gracious gift . . . might redound to his praise — NEB

and so to enhance that glorious manifestation of his loving-kindness — TCNT

wherein he hath made us accepted in the beloved.

which he freely bestowed on us in the Beloved — ASV

. . . in the beloved One — Alf

with which He has enriched us in the beloved One — Wey

by which he has taken us into his favour in the person of his beloved Son — Knox

which has made us welcome in the everlasting love he bears toward the Beloved — Phi

which he gave us in The Beloved — TCNT

7. In whom we have redemption through his blood,

It is in Him, and through the shedding of His blood, that we have our deliverance — Wey

It is through him, at the cost of his own blood, that we are redeemed — Phi

For in Christ our release is secured . . . through the shedding of his blood — NEB

the forgiveness of sins, according to the riches of his grace;

the forgiveness of our trespasses . . . — ASV

the forgiveness of our transgressions . . . — Alf

the forgiveness of our offences — so abundant was God's grace — Wey

freely forgiven through that full and generous grace — Phi

and our sins are forgiven . . . Therein lies the richness of God's free grace — NEB

8. Wherein he hath abounded toward us

which he made to abound toward us — ASV

which He . . . lavished upon us — Wey

that has overflowed upon us — Knox

which has overflowed into our lives — Phi

in all wisdom and prudence;

in a full stream of wisdom and discernment — Knox

and opened our eyes to the truth — Phi

imparting full wisdom and insight — NEB

accompanied by countless gifts of wisdom and discernment — TCNT

9. Having made known unto us the mystery of his will,

when He made known to us the secret of His will — Wey

to make known to us the hidden purpose of his will — Knox

For God has allowed us to know the secret of his plan — Phi

when he made known to us his hidden purpose — TCNT

according to his good pleasure which he hath purposed in himself:

It was his loving design — Knox

and it is this: he purposes in his sovereign will — Phi

— such was his will and pleasure determined beforehand — NEB

according to His kind intention . . . — NASB

And this is in harmony with God's merciful purpose — Wey

10. That in the dispensation of the fulness of times he might gather together in one all things in Christ,

unto a dispensation of the fulness of the times, to sum up all things in Christ — ASV

unto the dispensation of the fulness of the times, to gather up together all things in Christ — Alf

for the government of the world when the times are ripe for it — the purpose which He has cherished in His own mind of restoring the whole creation to find its one Head in Christ — Wey

to give history its fulfilment by resuming everything in him — Knox

as a plan for the fulness of time, to unite all things in him — RSV

that all human history shall be consummated in Christ — Phi

in view of that Divine Order which was to mark the completion of the ages, when he should make everything . . . centre in him — TCNT

with a view to an administration suitable to the fulness of the times, that

EPHESIANS 1

is, the summing up of all things in Christ — NASB

both which are in heaven, and which are on earth;
everything that exists in Heaven or earth — Phi
all in heaven and on earth — NEB
even in him:
In him, I say — TCNT

11. **In whom also we have obtained an inheritance,**
in whom we were also made his inheritance — Alf
In Him too we have been made heirs — Wey
And here is the staggering thing — that in all which will one day belong to him we have been promised a share — Phi
for by our union with him we became God's Heritage — TCNT

being predestinated according to the purpose of him
having been foreordained . . . — ASV
having been chosen beforehand in accordance with the intention of Him — Wey
singled out beforehand to suit his purpose — Knox
(since we were long ago destined for this by the one — Phi
as was decreed in his design — NEB
having from the first been destined for this in the intention of him — TCNT

who worketh all things after the counsel of his own will:
whose might carries out in everything the design of His own will — Wey
for it is he who is at work everywhere, carrying out the designs of his will — Knox
who achieves his purposes by his sovereign will) — Phi
whose purpose is everywhere at work — NEB
who, in all that happens, is carrying out his own fixed purpose — TCNT

12. **That we should be to the praise of his glory,**
that we should be devoted to the extolling of His glorious attributes — Wey
we were to manifest his glory — Knox
that we . . . should cause his glory to be praised — NEB

that we should enhance his glory — TCNT

who first trusted in Christ.
who were the first to fix our hopes on Christ — Wey
— we who have been the first to rest our hopes on the Christ — TCNT

13. **In whom ye also trusted, after that ye heard the word of truth, the gospel of your salvation:**
in whom ye also, having heard the word of the truth, the gospel of your salvation — ASV
In whom are ye also, having heard the word of truth, the gospel of your salvation — Alf
in him you too were called, when you listened to the preaching of the truth, that gospel which is your salvation — Knox
And you, too, by your union with him, after you had heard the Message of the Truth, the Good News of your salvation — TCNT

in whom also after that ye believed, ye were sealed with that holy Spirit of promise,
— in whom, having also believed, ye were sealed with the Holy Spirit of promise — ASV
were . . . stamped with the promised Holy Spirit as a guarantee of purchase — Phi
— you believed in him and were sealed as his by receiving the holy Spirit, which he had promised — TCNT

14. **Which is the earnest of our inheritance**
who is an earnest of our inheritance — Con
And the Spirit is a pledge of our future heritage — TCNT
that Spirit being a pledge and foretaste of our inheritance — Wey
who is the first installment of our inheritance — Wms
who is given as a pledge of our inheritance — NASB

until the redemption of the purchased possession,
unto the redemption of God's own possession — ASV
given to redeem that which He hath purchased — Con

865

until the day when God completes the redemption of what he has paid for as his own — Phi

with a view to the redemption of God's own possession — NASB

fore-shadowing the full redemption of God's own People — TCNT

unto the praise of his glory.

Unto his glorious praise — Rhm

— to enhance his Glory — TCNT

and so manifest God's glory — Knox

to his praise and glory — NEB

15. Wherefore I also,

And therefore I — TCNT

For this cause I also — ASV

after I heard of your faith in the Lord Jesus,

because I have heard ... — RSV

ever since I heard of the faith in the Lord Jesus which prevails among you — TCNT

and love unto all the saints,

and the love which ye show toward all the saints — ASV

and the practical way in which you are expressing it[2] toward fellow Christians — Phi

and of your confidence in all Christ's People — TCNT

16. Cease not to give thanks for you,

offer never-ceasing thanks on your behalf — Wey

making mention of you in my prayers;

while I make mention of you in my prayers — Wey

remembering you in my prayers — RSV

and I never give up praying for you — Phi

17. That the God of our Lord Jesus Christ, the Father of glory,

... the Father most glorious — Mon

... the Father to whom glory belongs — Knox

My prayer is that the God of Jesus Christ our Lord, the all-glorious Father — TCNT

may give unto you the spirit of wisdom and revelation

... a spirit of wisdom and revelation — ASV

to give you a spirit of wisdom and of insight — Con

will give you spiritual wisdom and the insight — Phi

may inspire you with wisdom and true insight — TCNT

may grant you the Spirit to give wisdom and revelation — Wms

in the knowledge of him:

through an intimate knowledge of himself — Mon

through a growing knowledge of Him — Wms

through a fuller knowledge of himself — TCNT

to know more of him — Phi

by which there comes the knowledge of him — NEB

18. The eyes of your understanding being enlightened;

having the eyes of your heart enlightened — ASV

and that the eyes of your heart may be flooded with light — Mon

that you may receive that inner illumination of the spirit — Phi

that your minds may be so enlightened — TCNT

that ye may know what is the hope of his calling,

that you may realize the hope given by God's Call — TCNT

so that you may know what is the hope which His call to you inspires — Wey

and what the riches of the glory of his inheritance in the saints,

and how gloriously rich his inheritance is among God's people — Gspd

how gloriously rich God's portion in His people is — Wms

how rich in glory is that inheritance of his found among the saints — Knox

— the magnificence and splendor of the inheritance promised to Christians — Phi

what the wealth and glory of the share he offers you among his people in their heritage — NEB

the wealth of the glory of his heritage among Christ's People — TCNT

19. And what is the exceeding greatness of his power to us-ward who believe,

---

[2]Referring to "faith," Phi translates a Greek text which does not contain the word "love."

and the transcendent greatness of the power which he is able to exercise in dealing with us who believe in him — TCNT

and what the transcendent greatness of His power in us believers — Wey

and how surpassingly great his power is for us who believe — Gspd

and how tremendous is the power available to us who believe in God — Phi

and how vast the resources of his power open to us who believe — NEB

according to the working of his mighty power,

according to the working of the might of his strength — Alf

as seen in the working of His infinite might — Wey

like the mighty strength — Gspd

as seen in the energy of that resistless might — Mon

measured by His tremendously mighty power — Wms

The same mighty power — TCNT

20. Which he wrought in Christ, when he raised him from the dead,

which he exercised in raising Christ from the dead — Mon

which he accomplished in Christ . . . — RSV

which he exerted in Christ . . . — NEB

was exerted upon the Christ, when he raised the Christ from the dead — TCNT

and set him at his own right hand in the heavenly places,

and he made him sit . . . — Alf

and gave him the place of supreme honor in Heaven — Phi

when he enthroned him at his right hand in the heavenly realms — NEB

and caused him to sit at his right hand on high — TCNT

21. Far above all principality, and power, and might, and dominion,

above all rule, and authority, and power, and lordship — Alf

exalting him above all Angels and Archangels of every rank — TCNT

high above all other government and authority and power and dominion — Wey

infinitely superior to any conceivable command — Phi

and every name that is named,

and above every name that can be named — TCNT

and every title of sovereignty used — Wey

yea, far above every other title that can be conferred — Wms

and any title of sovereignty that can be named — NEB

not only in this world, but also in that which is to come:

whether in the present age, or in the age to come — TCNT

22. And hath put all things under his feet,

And He put all things under His feet — Con

He has put everything under his dominion — Knox

God has placed everything under the power of Christ — Phi

and gave him to be the head over all things to the church,

and gave Him to be sovereign head of the Church — Con

and has appointed Him universal and supreme Head of the Church—Wey

and made him the indisputable head of the church — Gspd

and made him the head to which the whole Church is joined — Knox

and has set him up as head of everything for the Church — Phi

and gave him to the Church as its supreme Head — TCNT

23. What is his body,

for the Church is Christ's Body — TCNT

the fulness of him that filleth all in all.

the Fulness of Him who fills all things everywhere with Himself — Con

and is filled by him who fills all things everywhere with his presence — TCNT

the completeness of Him who everywhere fills the universe with Himself — Wey

filled by him who fills everything everywhere — Gspd

the completion of him who everywhere and in all things is complete — Knox

and in that body lives fully the one who fills the whole universe — Phi

the fullness of him who himself receives the entire fullness of God — NEB

CHAPTER 2

1. And you hath he quickened,

And you, likewise, He raised from death to life — Con

And so God has given life to you (Gentiles) also — Mon

who were dead in trespasses and sins;

when ye were dead through your trespasses and sins — ASV

who were dead by reason of your trespasses and your sins — Alf

He found you dead men; such were your transgressions, such were the sinful ways you lived in — Knox

2. Wherein in time past ye walked according to the course of this world,

For at one time you lived in sin, following the ways of the world — TCNT

which were once habitual to you while you walked in the ways of this world — Wey

in the midst of which you once lived under the control of the present age of the world — Gspd

in which you passed your lives after the way of the world — Mon

in which you once lived in accordance with the spirit of this present world — Wms

That was when you followed the fashion of this world — Knox

according to the prince of the power of the air,

and obeyed the Ruler of the Powers of the Air — Con

and obeyed its unseen ruler — Phi

in subjection to the Ruler of the Powers of the air — TCNT

and the master-spirit of the air — Gspd

and the mighty prince of the air — Wms

when you owned a prince whose domain is in the lower air — Knox

when you obeyed the commander of the spiritual powers of the air — NEB

the spirit that now worketh in the children of disobedience:

. . . who is still at work among the disobedient — TCNT

(who is still operating in those who do not respond to the truth of God) — Phi

the spirit now at work among God's rebel subjects — NEB

of the spirit that is now working in the sons of disobedience — NASB

3. Among whom also we all had our conversation in times past in the lusts of our flesh,

And it was among them that we all once lived our lives, indulging the cravings of our earthly nature — TCNT

among whom we also all had our way of life in times past — Alf

Among them we too once all passed our lives — Wey

We all lived among them once, indulging our physical cravings — Gspd

among whom all of us, we Jews as well as you heathen, once lived while gratifying the cravings of our lower nature — Wms

We too, all of us, were once of their company; our life was bounded by natural appetites — Knox

Among these we all once lived in the passions of our flesh — RSV

fulfilling the desires of the flesh and of the mind;

. . . and of our imagination — Con

obeying the impulses of our lower nature and its thoughts — Gspd

carrying out the dictates of our senses and temperament — Mon

and carrying out the desires prompted by that earthly nature and by our own thoughts — TCNT

and we did what corrupt nature of our own calculation would have us to do — Knox

and followed the impulses and imaginations of our evil nature — Phi

and were by nature the children of wrath, even as others.

Our very nature exposed us to the Divine Wrath, like the rest of mankind — TCNT

and were in our original state deserving of anger like all others — Wey

and by nature we were doomed to God's wrath like other men — Gspd

with God's displeasure for our birthright, like other men — Knox

In our natural condition we, like the rest, lay under the dreadful judgement of God — NEB

4. But God, who is rich in mercy,
Yet God, in his abundant compassion — TCNT
How rich God is in mercy — Knox

for his great love wherewith he loved us,
because of his great love . . . — Alf
because of the intense love . . . — Wey
with what an excess of love he loved us! — Knox

5. Even when we were dead in sins,
. . . dead in our trespasses — Alf
even though we were dead because of our offences — TCNT
though dead because of our shortcomings — Wms
Our sins had made dead men of us — Knox

hath quickened us together with Christ,
called us to share the life of Christ — Con
gave Life to us in giving Life to the Christ — TCNT
made us . . . live again with the Christ — Gspd
and he, in giving life to Christ, gave life to us too — Knox

(by grace ye are saved;)
(by grace have ye been saved) — ASV
(By God's loving-kindness you have been saved) — TCNT
it is by His unmerited favor that you have been saved — Wms
— it is, remember, by grace and not by achievement that you are saved — Phi

6. And hath raised us up together, and made us sit together in heavenly places in Christ Jesus:
and in Christ Jesus He raised us up with Him from the dead, and seated us with Him in the heavens — Con
raised us with Him from the dead, and enthroned us with Him in the heavenly realms as being in Christ Jesus — Wey
— and has lifted us right out of the old life to take our place with him in Christ Jesus in the Heavens — Phi
And, through our union with Christ Jesus, God raised us up with him, and caused us to sit with him on high — TCNT
And he raised us with Christ, and through our union with Christ Jesus made us sit down with him in heaven — Gspd

7. That in the ages to come he might shew the exceeding riches of his grace
in order that, . . ., he might display in the ages to come the boundless wealth of his loving-kindness — TCNT
. . . the transcendent riches of His grace — Wey
to show the incomparable wealth of his mercy throughout the ages to come — Gspd
He would have all future ages see, . . ., the surpassing richness of his grace — Knox
Thus he shows for all time the tremendous generosity of the grace — Phi
so that he might display in the ages to come how immense are the resources of his grace — NEB

in his kindness toward us through Christ Jesus.
in kindness toward us in Christ Jesus — ASV
by his goodness to us in Christ Jesus — TCNT
in that clemency which he shewed us in Christ Jesus — Knox
and kindness he has expressed toward us in Christ Jesus — Phi

8. For by grace are ye saved through faith;
. . . have ye been saved through faith — ASV
Yes, it was grace that saved you, with faith for its instrument — Knox
It was nothing you could or did achieve — it was God's gift of grace which saved you — Phi
For it is by his grace you are saved, through trusting him — NEB
For it is by God's loving-kindness that you have been saved, through your faith — TCNT

and that not of yourselves:
It is not due to yourselves — TCNT
It is not by your own action — Gspd
it did not come from yourselves — Knox

it is not your own doing — NEB

it is the gift of God:

the gift is God's — TCNT

of God is the gift — Alf

9. Not of works,

not won by works — Con

It is not due to obedience to Law — TCNT

It has not been earned — Gspd

It is not the result of what anyone can do — Wms

not from any action of yours — Knox

not because of works — RSV

not as a result of works — NASB

lest any man should boast.

so that it may be impossible for any one to boast — Wey

so that no one can boast of it — Gspd

or there would be room for pride — Knox

10. For we are his workmanship,

For we are his handiwork — Alf

For we are God's own handiwork — Wey

For he has made us — Gspd

For He has made us what we are — Wms

No, we are his design — Knox

created in Christ Jesus unto good works,

. . . for good works — ASV

. . . to do good works — Con

creating us through our union with Christ Jesus for the life of goodness — Gspd

God has created us in Christ Jesus, pledged to such good actions — Knox

created, by our union with Christ Jesus, for the good actions — TCNT

because He has created us through our union with Christ Jesus for doing good deeds — Wms

which God hath before ordained that we should walk in them.

which God afore prepared . . . — ASV

in doing which God had pre-arranged that we should spend our lives — TCNT

which He has pre-destined us to practise — Wey

which God has predestined us to live — Gspd

which God predestined us to make our daily way of life — Mon

as he has prepared beforehand, to be the employment of our lives—Knox

11. Wherefore remember, that ye being in time past Gentiles in the flesh,

Wherefore remember that you, who once were reckoned among carnal Gentiles — Con

Remember, therefore, that you were once Gentiles yourselves, as your bodies showed — TCNT

. . . once physically heathen — Gspd

. . . once heathen in a physical sense — Wms

. . . Gentiles, according to all outward reckoning — Knox

Do not lose sight of the fact that you were born Gentiles — Phi

who are called Uncircumcision by that which is called the Circumcision in the flesh made by hands;

known by those whose bodies were circumcised as "the uncircumcised" — Phi

you, 'the uncircumcised' so called by those who are called 'the circumcised' (but only with reference to an outward rite)— NEB

you were called 'The Uncircumcised' by those who were called 'The Circumcised' — circumcised only by the hand of man! — TCNT

12. That at that time ye were without Christ,

. . . separate from Christ — ASV

. . . shut out from Christ — Con

. . . had no connection with Christ — Gspd

In those days there was no Christ for you — Knox

Remember that you were at that time far from Christ — TCNT

being aliens from the commonwealth of Israel,

you were shut out from the citizenship of Israel — TCNT

estranged from . . . — Wey

outlaws from . . . — Knox

utter strangers to God's chosen community, Israel — Phi

excluded from the commonwealth of Israel — NASB

and strangers from the covenants of promise,

you were strangers to the Covenants founded on God's Promise — TCNT

with no share by birth in the covenants which are based on the promises — Wey

strangers to the sacred compacts made
by God's promise — Wms

strangers to every covenant, with no
promise to hope for — Knox[3]

you had no knowledge of, or right to,
the promised agreements — Phi

outside of God's covenants and the
promise that goes with them — NEB

**having no hope, and without God in
the world:**

you were in the world without hope
and without God — TCNT

and you had no hope and no God, in
all the world — Wey

with the world about you, and no God
— Knox

You had nothing to look forward to
and no God to whom you could turn
— Phi

13. **But now in Christ Jesus ye who**

But now, through your union with
Christ Jesus, you who — TCNT

sometimes were far off

aforetime were far off — Alf

... so far away — Wey

were once outside the pale — Phi

are made nigh by the blood of Christ.

... in the blood of Christ — ASV

... through the blood of Christ — Con

have, by the shedding of the blood of
the Christ, been brought near—TCNT

through the blood of Christ ... are
with us inside the circle of God's
love in Christ Jesus — Phi

14. **For he is our peace,**

He is our bond of peace — Knox

He it is who is our Peace — TCNT

For Christ is our living peace — Phi

who hath made both one,

He made the two divisions of mankind
one — TCNT

He who has made Jew and Gentile one
— Wey

he has made the two nations one —
Knox

He has made a unity of the conflicting
elements of Jew and gentile — Phi

who made both groups into one —
NASB

**and hath broken down the middle wall
of partition between us;**

... the wall which parted us — Con

... the wall which kept us apart—Wms

... the hostile dividing wall — Wey

and broke down the barrier of the dividing wall — NASB

broke down the barrier that separated
them — TCNT

15. **Having abolished in his flesh the enmity, even the law of commandments
contained in ordinances;**

... the law of the commandments
(consisting) in ordinances — Alf

for, in His flesh, He destroyed the
ground of our enmity, the law of
enacted ordinances — Con

and in his human nature put an end to
the cause of enmity between them
— the Law with its injunctions and
ordinances — TCNT

through His human nature He has put
a stop to the hostility between us,
namely, the law with its commands
and decrees — Wms

... He has put an end to the law with
its decrees — Knox

... for he annulled the law with its
rules and regulations — NEB

By his sacrifice he removed the hostility of the Law, with all its commandments and rules — Phi

**for to make in himself of twain one
new man,**

that he might create in himself of the
two ... — ASV

in order to create, through union with
himself, from Jew and Gentile, one
New Man — TCNT

His design was to unite the two sections of humanity in Himself so as
to form one new man — Wey

that he might create in himself one new
man in place of the two — RSV

so making peace;

thus producing peace — Phi

and thus make peace — TCNT

16. **And that he might reconcile both unto
God in one body by the cross,**

both sides, united in a single body, he
would reconcile to God through his
cross — Knox

... by the sacrifice of one body on the
cross — Phi

---

[3]Compare Knox's rendering of the next
phrase.

This was his purpose, to reconcile the two in a single body to God through the cross — NEB

having slain the enmity thereby:

. . . their enmity thereby — Con

when . . . he had destroyed their mutual enmity — TCNT

and to kill the feud between them — Gspd

on which he slew our enmity — Mon

after He had killed the hostility through it — Wms

inflicting death, in his own person, upon the feud — Knox

thereby bringing the hostility to an end — RSV

and by this act made utterly irrelevant the antagonism between them — Phi

by it having put to death the enmity — NASB

17. And came and preached peace to you which were afar off, and to them that were nigh.

. . . glad tidings of peace . . . — Alf

He came with the Good News of peace . . . — TCNT

So He came and proclaimed the gospel of peace . . . — Wey

So he came preaching Peace to you (Gentiles) . . . and Peace to us (Jews) . . . — Mon

. . . his message was of peace . . . — Knox

Then he came and told both you who were far from God and us who were near that the war was over — Phi

18. For through him we both have access by one Spirit unto the Father.

. . . our access in one Spirit unto the Father — ASV

. . . power to approach the Father in the fellowship of one Spirit — Con

for it is by Him that both of us now have an introduction to the Father — Wms

for it is through him that we, the Jews and the Gentiles, united in the one Spirit, are now able to approach the Father — TCNT

19. Now therefore

So then — ASV

Take notice then — Mon

It follows, then — TCNT

ye are no more strangers and foreigners,

that you are no longer strangers and aliens — TCNT

. . . mere foreigners or persons excluded from civil rights — Wey

. . . no longer exiles, then, or aliens — Knox

. . . no longer outsiders or aliens — Phi

. . . no longer aliens in a foreign land — NEB

but fellow-citizens with the saints,

but are fellow-citizens with Christ's People — TCNT

On the contrary you share citizenship with the saints — Wey

the saints are your fellow-citizens — Knox

but fellow citizens with every other Christian — Phi

and of the household of God;

you belong to God's household — Knox

and members of God's household — Con

20. And are built upon the foundation of the apostles and prophets,

built up upon the foundation of the apostles and prophets — Alf

You have been built up upon the foundation laid by the Apostles and Prophets — TCNT

You are a building which has been reared on the foundation of the Apostles and Prophets — Wey

Firmly beneath you is the foundation, God's messengers and prophets — Phi

Jesus Christ himself being the chief corner stone:

the actual foundation-stone being Christ Jesus himself — Phi

Christ Jesus himself being the cornerstone — TCNT

21. In whom all the building fitly framed together

. . . each several building . . . — ASV

United in him, every part of the building, closely joined together — TCNT

in union with whom the whole fabric, truly bonded together — Wey

Through him every part of the building is closely united — Gspd

In union with Him the whole building is harmoniously fitted together — Wms

in whom the whole structure is joined together — RSV

In him each separate piece of building, properly fitting into its neighbor — Phi

In him the whole building is bonded together — NEB

groweth unto an holy temple in the Lord:

and grows into . . . — RSV

is growing unto . . . — Alf

grows into a temple hallowed by the indwelling of the Lord — Con

is rising so as to form a holy sanctuary in the Lord — Wey

and grows into a temple sacred through its relation to the Lord — Gspd

and continues to grow into a sacred temple through its union with the Lord — Wms

as it grows into a temple, dedicated to the Lord — Knox

will grow into a Temple, consecrated by its union with the Lord — TCNT

22. In whom ye also are builded together

in whom ye also being builded together — Alf

And in Him, not others only, but you also are built up together — Con

And, through union in him, you also are being built up together — TCNT

and in him you, too, are continuously built together — Mon

and you yourselves, in union with Him, in fellowship with one another, are being built up — Wms

in him you too are being built in with the rest — Knox

in whom you also are built into it — RSV

for an habitation of God through the Spirit.

. . . in the Spirit — ASV

to make a house wherein God may dwell by the presence of His Spirit — Con

to be a dwelling-place for God through the Spirit — TCNT

to become a fixed abode for God through the Spirit — Wey

so that God may find in you a dwelling-place for his Spirit — Knox

into a spiritual dwelling for God — NEB

CHAPTER 3

1. For this cause I Paul,

Wherefore I, Paul — Con

This is why I, Paul — Gspd

With this in mind, I fall on my knees; I, Paul — Knox

It is in this great cause that I, Paul — Phi

With this in mind I make my prayer, I, Paul — NEB

the prisoner of Jesus Christ for you Gentiles,

the prisoner of Christ Jesus . . . — ASV

who, for maintaining the cause of you Gentiles, am the prisoner of Jesus Christ — Con

the prisoner of Jesus, the Christ, for the sake of you Gentiles — TCNT

whom Jesus the Christ has made a prisoner for the sake of you heathen — Gspd

. . . for the sake of the heathen — Wms

. . . for the love of you Gentiles—Knox

2. If ye have heard of the dispensation of the grace of God which is given me to you-ward:

for I suppose that you have heard of the stewardship of God's grace, which was given me for you — Con

— for you have heard, I suppose, of the responsible charge with which God entrusted me for your benefit—TCNT

— if at least you have heard how I dealt with the mercy of God that was given me for you — Gspd

You will have been told how God planned to give me a special grace for preaching to you — Knox

— assuming that you have heard of the stewardship of God's grace that was given to me for you — RSV

For you must have heard how God gave me grace to become your minister — Phi

3. How that by revelation he made known unto me the mystery;

and also that it was by direct revelation that the hidden purpose of God was made known to me — TCNT

in that by a revelation the truth hitherto kept secret was made known to me — Wey

and how the secret was made known to me by revelation — Gspd

how a revelation taught me the secret
— Knox

and how he allowed me to understand
his secret by giving me a direct revelation — Phi

(as I wrote afore in few words,

(as I have already shortly written to
you — Con

as I have already briefly told you —
TCNT

I have been setting out briefly here —
Knox

I have already written a brief account
of this — NEB

4. Whereby, when ye read,

so that, when you read — Con

And, by reading what I have written
— TCNT

By means of that explanation, as you
read it — Wey

When you read this — RSV

And by referring to this — NASB

**ye may understand my knowledge in
the mystery of Christ)**

ye can perceive . . . — ASV

you will be able to judge how far I
understand this hidden purpose of
God in Christ — TCNT

you can judge of my insight into the
truth of Christ — Wey

you will be able to understand my insight into the secret about the Christ
— Wms

. . . how well I have mastered this
secret of Christ's — Knox

**5. Which in other ages was not made
known unto the sons of men,**

which in other generations . . . — ASV

which, in the generations of old . . . —
Con

In former generations it was not made
known to mankind — TCNT

which in earlier ages . . . to the human
race — Wey

which in past ages . . . to mankind —
Gspd

This secret was hidden to past generations of mankind — Phi

In former generations this was not
disclosed to the human race — NEB

**as it is now revealed unto his holy
apostles and prophets by the Spirit;**

. . . in the Spirit — ASV

as it has now been revealed by the in-

dwelling of the Spirit, to His holy
apostles and prophets — Con

as fully as it has now been revealed by
the Spirit to the Apostles and Prophets among Christ's People — TCNT

but it has now . . . been made plain to
God's consecrated messengers and
prophets — Phi

but now it has been revealed by inspiration to his dedicated apostles
and prophets — NEB

**6. That the Gentiles should be fellow-
heirs, and of the same body,**

to wit, that the Gentiles are fellow-
heirs, and fellow-members of the
body — ASV

. . . joined in the same body — Alf

to wit, that the Gentiles are heirs of the
same inheritance, and members of
the same body — Con

I mean the truth that the Gentiles are
joint heirs with us Jews, and that
they form one body with us — Wey

. . . the heathen are fellow-heirs with
the Jews . . . — Gspd

namely, that in Christ Jesus the Gentiles form one body with us [the
Jews], and are coheirs — Mon

and it is this: that . . . — Knox

that . . . the Gentiles are co-heirs with
us and members of one Body—TCNT

and partakers of his promise

and fellow-partakers of the promise —
ASV

and partakers of the same promise —
Con

and that they share with us in God's
Promise — TCNT

and have the same interest as we have
in the promise — Wey

and equal partners in God's promise
— Phi

in Christ by the gospel:

by union with Christ Jesus and through
the Good News — TCNT

7. Whereof I was made a minister,

. . . a ministering servant — Con

. . . a worker — Gspd

for which I was called to serve — Wms

Of this Good News I became a minister
— TCNT

**according to the gift of the grace of
God**

in virtue of the charge with which God
entrusted me — TCNT

by the grace he gave me — Phi

given unto me by the effectual working of his power.

. . . in the full measure of His mighty working — Con

bestowed on me by the energy of his power — Mon

. . . by the exercise of his power—Wms

(and he gives it in all the effectiveness of his power) — Knox

and by the power with which he equipped me — Phi

in the exercise of his power — TCNT

8. Unto me, who am less than the least of all saints,

To me, the very least of all his people — Gspd

Yes, to me, whom am less than the least of all Christ's People — TCNT

Yes, to me, less than the least of all Christians — Phi

is this grace given,

was this grace given — ASV

has this work been graciously entrusted — Wey

was this charge entrusted! — TCNT

yet I was the one chosen — Tay

that I should preach among the Gentiles

that I might preach as good news to the heathen — Wms

Unto the nations to announce the glad-message — Rhm

of making known to the Gentiles — Knox

to preach to the Gentiles — RSV

for this special joy of telling the Gentiles the Glad News of — Tay

to tell the Gentiles the Good News of — TCNT

the unsearchable riches of Christ;

the untraceable riches of the Christ — — Rhm

the boundless wealth to be found in the Christ — TCNT

the exhaustless wealth of Christ—Wey

the fathomless wealth of Christ — Mof

the incalculable riches of Christ — Phi

the endless treasures available to them in Christ — Tay

9. And to make all men see what is the fellowship of the mystery,

and to enlighten all men what is the dispensation of the mystery — Alf

And to bring to light — What is the administration of the sacred secret — Rhm

and to bring light to all, that they might behold what is the stewardship of the mystery — Con

and to make clear what is God's way of working out that hidden purpose — TCNT

and to show all men in a clear light what my stewardship is — Wey

and enlighten all men upon the new order of that divine secret — Mof

and should make all men see the new dispensation of that secret purpose — Mon

and to make clear how is to be carried out the trusteeship of this secret — Wms

and to make all men understand the meaning of this secret — Nor

and of bringing to light how this hidden purpose was to be put into effect — NEB

And to explain to everyone that God is the Saviour of the Gentiles too — Tay

which from the beginning of the world hath been hid in God, who created all things by Jesus Christ:

which for ages hath been hid in God who created all things — ASV

which had been hidden away from the ages in God who did all things create — Rhm

which from the first had been concealed in the mind of the Creator of all things — TCNT

which from all the ages lay concealed in the mind of God, the Creator of all things — Wey

which God the Creator of all concealed from eternity — Mof

just as He who made all things had secretly planned from the very beginning — Tay

which, from the ages of old, has been hid in God, the maker of all things — Con

10. To the intent that now unto the principalities and powers in heavenly places

And His reason? . . . — Tay

In order that now . . . — Rhm

875

so that now to the Archangels and to all the Powers on high — TCNT

in order that . . . to the powers and authorities in the heavenly realms — Wey

The purpose is that all the angelic powers — Phi

might be known by the church the manifold wisdom of God,

. . . through the church . . . — ASV

. . . through means of the assembly . . . — Rhm

should be made known the all-embracing wisdom of God — TCNT

— concealed in order that the Church might now be used to display . . . the innumerable aspects of God's wisdom — Wey

. . . the many-sided wisdom of God — Gspd

. . . the many phases of God's wisdom — Wms

. . . the subtlety of God's wisdom — Knox

should now see the complex wisdom of God's plan being worked out through the Church — Phi

. . . the supreme wisdom of God — Nor

11. According to the eternal purpose which he purposed in Christ Jesus our Lord:

. . . in the Christ, even Jesus our Lord — Alf

. . . the plan of the ages which he made in the anointed Jesus our Lord — Rhm

in accordance with that purpose which runs through all the ages and which he has now accomplished in Jesus, the Christ, our Master — TCNT

. . . which God executed in the gift of Christ Jesus our Lord — Wms

This was according to the eternal purpose which he has realized in Christ Jesus our Lord — RSV

in conformity to that timeless purpose which he centered in Christ Jesus, our Lord — Phi

Just as He had always planned to do through Jesus Christ our Lord — Tay

12. In whom we have boldness and access with confidence by the faith of him.

in whom we have boldness and access in confidence through our faith in him — ASV

In whom we have our freedom of speech and introduction with assurance through the faith of him — RSV

in whom we can approach without fear to God in trustful confidence, through faith in Him — Con

and in union with him, and through our trust in him, we find courage to approach God with confidence — TCNT

through whom, as we have faith in him, we enjoy our confidence of free access — Mof

Now we can come fearlessly right into God's presence, assured of His glad welcome when we come with Christ and trust in Him — Tay

who gives us all our confidence, bids us come forward, emboldened by our faith in him — Knox

In him we have access to God with freedom, in the confidence born of trust in him — NEB

13. Wherefore I desire that ye faint not at my tribulations for you,

Wherefore I ask . . . — ASV

Wherefore I pray that I may not faint under my sufferings for you — Con

Therefore I beg you not to be disheartened at the sufferings that I am undergoing for your sakes — TCNT

Do not, then, lose courage . . . — Nor

So please don't lose heart at what they are doing to me here — Tay

which is your glory.

which are your glory — ASV

for they redound to your honour — TCNT

for it does you honor — Gspd

Indeed, you should be honored — Phi

14. For this cause I bow my knees unto the Father of our Lord Jesus Christ,

. . . I bend my knees . . . — Con

. . . on bended knee I beseech . . . — Wey

For this reason, then, I kneel before the Father — TCNT

With this in mind, then, I fall on my knees . . . — Knox

When I think of the wisdom and scope of His plan I fall down on my knees and pray to the Father — Tay

15. Of whom the whole family in heaven and earth

from whom every family . . . — ASV

From whom every fatherhood . . . — Rhm

from whom all 'fatherhood' in Heaven and on earth — TCNT

is named,

takes its title — Knox

derives its name — TCNT

16. That he would grant you, according to the riches of his glory,

. . . in proportion to the wealth of his glory — TCNT

. . . in accordance with the wealth of His glorious perfections — Wey

. . . out of his wealth of glory — Gspd

. . . in accordance with the riches of His perfect character — Wms

. . . out of the glorious richness of his resources — Phi

to be strengthened with might by his Spirit in the inner man;

to be strengthened by His Spirit with power permeating your inmost being — Wey

a mighty increase of strength by his Spirit in the inner man — Mof

. . . in your inner nature — Gspd

to know the strength of the Spirit's inner reinforcement — Phi

the mighty inner strengthening of His Holy Spirit — Tay

17. That Christ may dwell in your hearts by faith;

so that the Christ, through your faith, may make his home within your hearts in love — TCNT

that Christ may actually live . . . — Phi

And I pray that Christ will be more at home in your hearts . . . — Tay

that ye, being rooted and grounded in love,

to the end that ye . . . — ASV

so that having your roots deep and your foundations strong in love — Wey

and I pray that you, now firmly rooted and established — TCNT[4]

And I pray that you, firmly fixed in love yourselves — Phi

May your roots go down deep into the soil of God's marvelous love — Tay

18. May be able to comprehend with all saints

may be strong to apprehend . . . — ASV

may be fully able . . . — Alf

may be mighty enough to grasp firmly . . . — Rhm

may receive power to grasp . . . — Nor

may, with all Christ's People, have the power to comprehend — TCNT

what is the breadth, and length, and depth, and height;

what is the breadth and length and height and depth — ASV

in all its width and length and height and depth — TCNT

the dimensions — Nor

19. And to know the love of Christ, which passeth knowledge,

and to understand — though it surpasses all understanding — the love of the Christ — TCNT

and may know the love of Christ which transcends all knowing — Mon

. . . which is really beyond human understanding — Nor

and to know for yourselves that love so far beyond our comprehension — Phi

and to experience this love for yourselves . . . — Tay

that ye might be filled with all the fulness of God.

. . . unto all the fulness of God — ASV

and so be filled to the full with God himself — TCNT

. . . with the entire fulness of God — Mof

. . . with all the completion God has to give — Knox

. . . through all your being with God himself — Phi

that you may be filled up to all the fulness of God — NASB

And so at last you will be filled up with God Himself — Tay

20. Now unto him that is able to do exceeding abundantly above

. . . able to do far more than — TCNT

. . . able to do infinitely beyond — Wey

. . . can do unutterably more than — Gspd

---

[4]TCNT construes "in love" with the preceding phrase.

... surpassingly more than — Wms

... immeasurably more than — NEB

all that we ask or think,

anything that we can ask or conceive
— TCNT

all our highest prayers or thoughts —
Wey

all our hopes and dreams — Knox

... we would ever dare to ask or even
dream of — Tay

**according to the power that worketh
in us,**

... the power which doth energise itself within us — Rhm

by the power at work within us —
RSV

through his power which is at work
within us — TCNT

21. **Unto him be glory in the church by
Christ Jesus**

... in the church and in Christ Jesus
— ASV

to him be all glory through the Church
and through Christ Jesus — TCNT

may he be glorified in the Church, and
in Christ Jesus — Knox

May He be given glory . . . because of
His master plan of salvation for the
church through Christ Jesus — Tay

**throughout all ages, world without
end.**

unto all generations for ever and ever
— ASV

even to all the generations of the age
of ages — Con

for all generations, age after age —
TCNT

to the last generation of eternity —
Knox

forever and ever through endless ages
— Tay

Amen.

CHAPTER 4

1. **I therefore, the prisoner of the Lord,
beseech you**

... the prisoner in the Lord . . . —
ASV

I urge you, then — I who am a prisoner
in the Master's cause — TCNT

... prisoner for the Lord's sake —
Wey

As God's prisoner, then, I beg you —
Phi

I beg you — I, a prisoner here in jail
for serving the Lord — Tay

**that ye walk worthy of the vocation
wherewith ye are called,**

... of the calling . . . — ASV

to live lives worthy of the Call that
you have received — TCNT

to live lives worthy of the summons
you have received — Gspd

to live and act in a way worthy of those
who have been chosen for such wonderful blessings as these — Tay

as God has called you, live up to your
calling — NEB

2. **With all lowliness**

with perfect modesty — Mof

with perfect humility — Gspd

and meekness,

and gentleness — Con

**with longsuffering, forbearing one an-
other in love;**

... Bearing one with another in love
— Rhm

patient, bearing lovingly with one another — TCNT

patient, too, in bearing with one another's faults, as charity bids —
Knox

making allowances for one another because you love one another — Phi

3. **Endeavouring to keep**

giving diligence to keep — ASV

earnestly striving to maintain — Alf

continuing with eager earnestness to
maintain — Wms

eager to maintain — RSV

**the unity of the Spirit in the bond of
peace.**

The oneness of the Spirit in the uniting-
bond of peace — Rhm

the unity of the Spirit, bound together
with the bond of peace — Con

in the bond of peace the unity given by
the Spirit — TCNT

... by binding peace upon yourselves
— Mof

... through the tie of peace — Gspd

4. **There is one body, and one Spirit,**

You are one body and one spirit —
Con

There is but one Body and one Spirit
— TCNT

You are one body, with a single Spirit — Knox

even as ye are called in one hope of your calling;

even as you were called to share one common hope — Con

just as there was but one hope set before you when you received your Call — TCNT

as also when you were called you had one and the same hope held out to you — Wey

. . . one hope that belongs to your call — Mof

just as there is but one hope resulting from the call you have received — Wms

5. One Lord, one faith, one baptism,

. . . one immersion — Rhm

There is but one Lord, one Faith, one baptism — TCNT

with the same Lord, the same faith, the same baptism — Knox

6. One God and Father of all,

There is but one God and Father of all — TCNT

with the same God, the same Father, all of us — Knox

you have one God and Father of all — Con

who is above all, and through all, and in you all.

who is over all, and works through all, and dwells in all — Con

— the God who is over all, pervades all, and is in all — TCNT

who rules over all, acts through all, and dwells in all — Wey

who is above all beings, pervades all things, and lives in all of us — Knox

who is the one over all, the one working through all and the one living in all — Phi

7. But unto every one of us is given grace

. . . his own special grace — Knox

. . . special abilities — Tay

But unto each one of us was the grace given — ASV

Every one of us, however, has been entrusted with some charge — TCNT

Yet to each of us individually His grace was given — Wey

His favor has been bestowed upon each one of us — Wms

But each one of us has been given his gift — NEB

according to the measure of the gift of Christ.

. . . the free-gift of the Christ — Rhm

measured out with the munificence of Christ — Wey

in Christ's generous measure — Gspd

out of the rich diversity of Christ's giving — Phi

his due portion of Christ's bounty — NEB

each in accordance with the extent of the gift of Christ — TCNT

8. Wherefore he saith,

Wherefore it is written: — Con

That is why it is said — TCNT

Concerning this the Scripture says — Wms

(That is why we are told — Knox

When he ascended up on high,

When He went up on high — Con

He has mounted up on high — Knox

He ascended into the heights — NEB

he led captivity captive,

he led captives captive — Alf

he led his captives into captivity — TCNT

he led a host of captives — Gspd

he has captured his spoil — Knox

With captives in his train — NEB

took prisoners — Beck

and gave gifts unto men.

he has brought gifts to men — Knox

and gave gifts to people — Beck

9. (Now that he ascended,

Now this, He ascended — ASV

Now this "he ascended" — Mon

Now that word "He went up," — Con

Now surely this 'going up' — TCNT

Now, the word 'ascended' — NEB

In saying, "He ascended," — RSV

(Note the implication here — to say that Christ "ascended" — Phi

Now this expression, "He ascended," — NASB

what is it but that he also descended first

what is it — save — That he also descended — Rhm

what saith it, but that He first came down — Con

must imply that he had already gone down — TCNT

what does it mean but that He had first descended — Wey

implies that he also descended — Mon

into the lower parts of the earth?

into the under parts of the earth — Rhm

to the earth below —Con

into the world beneath — TCNT

that is, from the height of Heaven to the depth of this world — Phi

to the lowest level, down to the very earth — NEB

to the under-regions of the earth — Nor

10. **He that descended is the same also that ascended up far above all heavens,**

Yea, He who came down is the same who is gone up, far above all the heavens — Con

It is he who went down who has also gone up above all the heavens — Gspd

The very One that went down has gone up, too, far above all the heavens — Wms

And he who so went down is no other than he who has gone up, high above all the heavens — Knox

The one that made this descent is identically the same person as he who has now ascended high above the very Heavens — Phi

He who went down is the same as he who went up — up beyond the highest Heaven — TCNT

that he might fill all things.)

that he might fill all things with his presence — TCNT

in order to fill the universe — Wey

to fill creation with his presence — Knox

that the whole universe from lowest to highest might know his presence — Phi

that He might be the ruler over all things everywhere — Tay

11. **And he gave some, apostles; and some, prophets;**

And he gave some to be apostles; and some, prophets — ASV

And he it is who gave to the Church Apostles, Prophets — TCNT

And He Himself appointed some to be apostles, some to be prophets—TCNT

It is he who made some men apostles, some prophets — Mon

And his gifts were that some should be apostles, some to be prophets—Wey

His "gifts unto men" were varied. Some he made his messengers, some prophets — Phi

and some, evangelists; and some, pastors and teachers;

some as missionaries . . . — Gspd

. . . And some, shepherds and teachers Rhm

Missionaries, Pastors, and Teachers — TCNT

others to be evangelists, or pastors, or teachers — Knox

some preachers of the gospel; to some he gave the power to guide and teach his people — Phi

12. **For the perfecting of the saints, for the work of the ministry,**

With a view to the fitting of the saints for the work of ministering — Rhm

for the perfecting of the saints, to labor in their appointed service — Con

to fit his People for the work of the ministry — TCNT

in order fully to equip His people for the work of serving — Wey

in order to equip the saints for the work of serving — Mon

for the immediate equipment of God's people for the work of service — Wms

to equip God's people for work in his service — NEB

in order to get His holy people ready to serve as workers — Beck

His gifts were made that Christians might be properly equipped for their service — Phi

for the edifying of the body of Christ:

unto the building up . . . — ASV

for the ultimate building up . . . — Wms

13. **Till we all come in the unity of the faith,**

till we all attain unto the unity of the faith — ASV

Until we all advance into . . . — Rhm

till we all attain the same faith — Con

till we all of us arrive at oneness in faith — Wey

Until finally we all believe alike about our salvation — Tay

And this shall continue, until we all attain to that unity which is given by faith — TCNT

and of the knowledge of the Son of God,

and of the perfect knowledge . . . — Alf

. . . the personal knowledge . . . — Rhm

and by a fuller knowledge of the Son of God — TCNT

and knowledge of the Son of God — Con

unto a perfect man, unto the measure of the stature of the fulness of Christ:

unto a fullgrown man . . . — ASV

and reach the stature of manhood, and be of ripe age to receive the fulness of Christ — Con

until we reach the ideal man — the full standard of the perfection of the Christ — TCNT

and at mature manhood and the stature of full-grown men in Christ — Wey

and reach mature manhood, and that full measure of development found in Christ — Gspd

to mature manhood, measured by nothing less than the full stature of Christ — NEB

14. That we henceforth be no more children,

. . . infants — Rhm

. . . babes — Wey

Then we shall no longer be like infants — TCNT

tossed to and fro, and carried about with every wind of doctrine,

tossed as waves . . . — Alf

Billow-tossed and shifted round . . . — Rhm

tossed to and fro, and blown round by every shifting current of teaching — Con

tossed backward and forward, blown about by every breath of human teaching — TCNT

nor shall we resemble mariners tossed on the waves and carried about with every changing wind of doctrine — Wey

. . . driven before the wind of each new doctrine — Knox

. . . whirled about by every fresh gust of teaching — NEB

. . . driven by every windy thing that is taught — Beck

by the sleight of men, and cunning craftiness, whereby they lie in wait to deceive;

by the sleight of men, in craftiness, after the wiles of error — ASV

in the sleight of men, in cunning craftiness according to the wily manner of error — ABUV

through the trickery and the craftiness of men, towards the snares of error — TCNT

tricked by the sleight of men, and led astray into the snares of the cunning — Con

that human subtlety, human skill in fabricating lies, propounds — Knox

dupes of crafty rogues and their deceitful schemes — NEB

according to men's cleverness and unscrupulous cunning, that makes use of every shifting device to mislead — Wey

through the trickery of men with their ingenuity in inventing error — Gspd

by the cunning of men, by their craftiness in deceitful wiles — RSV

and the jockeying of men who are expert in the crafty presentation of lies — Phi

. . . their crafty presentation of error as truth — Nor

by the trickery of men, by craftiness in deceitful scheming — NASB

15. But speaking the truth in love,

but being followers of truth in love — Alf

But pursuing truth May in love—Rhm[5]

But we shall lovingly hold to the truth — Wey

We are to follow the truth, in a spirit of charity — Knox

but that we should live in truth and love — Con

Rather, let our lives lovingly express truth in all things — speaking truly, dealing truly, living truly — Amp

may grow up into him in all things, which is the head, even Christ:

and should grow up in every part to the measure of His growth, who is our head, even Christ — Con

---

[5]Rhm connects "in love" with the phrase that follows.

16. From whom the whole body fitly joined together and compacted by that which every joint supplieth, according to the effectual working in the measure of every part, maketh increase of the body unto the edifying of itself in love.

Dependent on Him, the whole body — its various parts closely fitting and firmly adhering to one another — grows by the aid of every contributory ligament, with power proportioned to the need of each individual part, so as to build itself up in a spirit of love — Wey

For from him the whole Body, closely joined and knit together by the contact of every part with the source of its life, derives its power to grow, in proportion to the vigour of each individual part; and so is being built up in a spirit of love — TCNT

from whom the whole body, joined and knit together by every joint with which it is supplied, when each part is working properly, makes bodily growth and upbuilds itself in love — RSV

. . . as a harmonious structure knit together by the joints . . . — Phi

17. This I say therefore, and testify in the Lord,

. . . protesting in the Lord — Rhm

. . . and adjure you in the Lord — Con

. . . and affirm together with the Lord — NASB

This, then, as one in union with the Lord, I say to you and urge upon you: — TCNT

So what I mean and insist upon in the Lord's name is this — Gspd

Let me say this, then, speaking for the Lord — Tay

that ye henceforth walk not as other Gentiles walk, in the vanity of their mind,

. . . even as the nations walk . . . — Rhm

. . . with their frivolity of mind — Gspd

. . . who make vain fancies their rule of life — Knox

. . . with their good-for-nothing notions — NEB

to live no longer like other Gentiles, whose minds are filled with folly — Con

Do not continue to live such purposeless lives as the Gentiles live—TCNT

18. Having the understanding darkened,

with their powers of discernment darkened — TCNT

Their minds are clouded with darkness — Knox

. . . they live blindfold — Phi

Their wits are beclouded — NEB

Their understanding is darkness itself — Nor

being alienated from the life of God

estranged from the life of God — Con

cut off from . . . — TCNT

having no share in . . . — Wey

they are strangers to the life that is in God — NEB

excluded from the life of God — NASB

. . . the life God gives — Beck

through the ignorance that is in them,

because of the ignorance . . . — ASV

because ignorance prevails among them — NEB

because of the blindness of their heart:

. . . the hardening of their heart — ASV

. . . the insensibility of their normal nature — Wey

. . . their obstinacy of heart — Gspd

. . . their minds gave grown hard as stone — NEB

. . . their closed minds — Beck

By reason of their hearts being turned into stone — Rhm

19. Who being past feeling have given themselves over unto lasciviousness,

. . . unto wantonness — Alf

Lost to all sense of shame, they have abandoned themselves to licentiousness — TCNT

for they have become callous, and abandoned themselves to sensuality — Gspd

for in their recklessness they have abandoned themselves to sensuality — Wms

and so, in despair, they have given themselves to incontinence — Knox

They have stifled their consciences and then surrendered themselves to sensuality — Phi

Dead to all feeling, they have abandoned themselves to vice — NEB

to work all uncleanness with greediness.

unto making a trade of all impurity with greed — Rhm

in order to practise every kind of impurity without restraint — TCNT

greedily indulging in every kind of profligacy — Wey

which leads to excessive practices of all sorts of immorality — Wms

practicing any form of impurity which lust can suggest — Phi

20. But ye have not so learned Christ;

But far different is the lesson you learnt from the Christ — TCNT

That is not the way you have been taught what Christ means — Gspd

But that isn't the way Christ taught you! — Tay

21. If so be that ye have heard him, and have been taught by him,

if, that is, you really listened to him, and through union with him were taught — TCNT

at least if you have really become acquainted with him and been instructed in him — Gspd

as the truth is in Jesus:

and this is true Christian teaching — Wey

the truth as it is seen in Jesus — Wms

the Truth, as it is to be found in Jesus — TCNT

22. That ye put off concerning the former conversation the old man,

That ye were to strip off — as regardeth the former behaviour — the old man — Rhm

For you learnt with regard to your former way of living that you must cast off your old nature — TCNT

... your original evil nature — Wey

... your old self — Gspd

No, what you learned was to fling off the dirty clothes of the old way of living — Phi

which is corrupt according to the deceitful lusts;

that waxeth corrupt ... — ASV

who corrupteth himself ... — Rhm

whose way is destruction, following the desires which deceives — Con

which, yielding to deluded passions, grows corrupt — TCNT

which is going to ruin ... — Gspd

which is on the way to destruction ... — Wms

the self that wasted its aim on false dreams — Knox

which were rotted through and through with lust's illusions — Phi

which, deluded by its lusts, is sinking towards death — NEB

23. And be renewed in the spirit of your mind;

... by the Spirit ... — Alf

You must adopt a new attitude of mind — Gspd

and, with yourselves mentally and spiritually remade — Phi

that the very spirit of your minds must be constantly renewed — TCNT

24. And that ye put on the new man,

and that you must clothe yourselves in that new nature — TCNT

... that new and better self — Wey

to put on the clean fresh clothes of the new life — Phi

which after God is created in righteousness and true holiness.

which was created to resemble God, with the righteousness and holiness springing from the Truth — TCNT

which was made by God's design for righteousness and the holiness which is no illusion — Phi

which is created to be like God ... — Beck

25. Wherefore putting away lying,

... stripping off what is false — Rhm

Away with falsehood, then — Knox

Finish, then, with lying — Phi

speak every man truth with his neighbour:

... truth to his fellow man — Wey

for we are members one of another.

For we are united to one another like the parts of a body — TCNT

... intimately related to one another in Christ — Phi

membership of the body binds us to one another — Knox

26. Be ye angry, and sin not:

If angry, beware of sinning — Wey

If you do get angry, you must stop sinning in your anger — Wms

Do not let resentment lead you into sin — Knox

If you are angry, don't sin by nursing your grudge — Tay

let not the sun go down upon your wrath:

the sunset must not find you still angry — Knox

Never go to bed angry — Phi

do not let sunset find you still nursing it — NEB

27. Neither give place to the devil.

and give no opportunity to the Devil — TCNT

you must not give the devil a chance — Gspd

don't give the devil that sort of foothold — Phi

leave no loop-hole for the devil — NEB

28. Let him that stole steal no more:

Let him that stealeth . . . — Alf

Let the stealer . . . — Rhm

Let the robber rob no more — Con

He who has been a thief must steal no more — Wey

If you used to be a thief . . . — Phi

but rather let him labour, working with his hands the thing which is good,

but rather let him toil with his hands at honest work — TCNT

rather he must keep on working and toiling with his own hands at some honest vocation — Wms

you must learn to make an honest living — Phi

that he may have to give to him that needeth.

. . . impart to him that hath need — Alf

so that he may have something of which he can give the needy a share — Wey

so that he may have something to share with any one in want — TCNT

. . . something to contribute to the needy — Wms

29. Let no corrupt communication proceed out of your mouth,

. . . corrupt speech . . . — ASV

. . . putrid discourse . . . — Rhm

Let no unwholesome words ever pass your lips — Wey

Never let any foul word pass your lips — TCNT

but that which is good to the use of edifying,

but such as is good for edifying as the need may be — ASV

. . . good for the building up of the need — Alf

but only such as is good for edifying, as fits the occasion — RSV

but only such good words as the occasion demands — TCNT

but let all your words be good for benefiting others according to the need of the moment — Wey

that it may minister grace unto the hearers.

so that they may be a means of blessing to the hearers — Wey

which God can use to help other people — Phi

that they may be a help to those who hear them — TCNT

30. And grieve not the holy Spirit of God,

You must not offend God's holy Spirit — Gspd

do not distress God's holy Spirit — Knox

And never grieve . . . — Ber

Never hurt . . . — Phi

Don't cause the Holy Spirit sorrow — Tay

whereby ye are sealed unto the day of redemption.

in whom ye were sealed . . . — ASV

for it was through that Spirit that God sealed you as his, against the Day of Redemption — TCNT

. . . in preparation for the day of Redemption — Wey

with which you have been marked for the Day of Redemption — Gspd

He is, remember, the personal pledge of your eventual full redemption — Phi

for that Spirit is the seal with which you were marked for the day of our final liberation — NEB

31. Let all bitterness, and wrath, and anger, and clamour, and evil speaking,

. . . railing — ASV

. . . brawling, and abusive language — TCNT

. . . loud insulting language — Wey

. . . no more violent assertiveness, no more slander — Phi

be put away from you,

be banished from among you — TCNT

be unknown among you — Wey

with all malice:

as well as all malice — TCNT

32. And be ye kind one to another,
Be generous to one another — NEB
tenderhearted,
tenderly affectionate — Rhm
be understanding — Phi
forgiving one another, even as God for Christ's sake hath forgiven you.

ready to forgive one another, just as God, in Christ, forgave you — TCNT
Be as ready to forgive others as . . . — Phi
forgiving one another, just as God has forgiven you because you belong to Christ — Tay

CHAPTER 5

1. Be ye therefore followers of God, as dear children;
. . . imitators of God, as beloved children — ASV
Therefore imitate God, as his dear children — TCNT
Therefore be followers of God's example, as the children of His love — Con
As God's favoured children, you must be like him — Knox
As children copy their fathers you, as God's children, copy him — Phi
2. And walk in love, as Christ also hath loved us,
. . . loved you — ASV
and live a life of love, following the example of the Christ — TCNT
and practice living in love . . . — Wms
Let love guide your footsteps . . . — Nor
and hath given himself for us an offering and a sacrifice to God for a sweetsmelling savour.
who loved you and gave himself for you as an offering and a sacrifice to God, that should be fragrant and acceptable — TCNT
and gave Himself to God as a sacrifice to take away your sins. And God was pleased, for Christ's love for you was like a sweet perfume to Him — Tay
3. But fornication, and all uncleanness,
As for unchastity and every kind of impurity — TCNT
But sexual vice . . . — Wms
As for debauchery . . . — Knox
or covetousness,
and the itch to get your hands on what belongs to other people — Phi
or ruthless greed — NEB
let it not be once named among you,
. . . not even be named . . . — ASV
— don't even talk about such things — Phi

as becometh saints;
as befits Christ's People — TCNT
4. Neither filthiness, nor foolish talking, nor jesting,
And shamelessness . . . — Rhm
nor shameful conduct . . . — TCNT
nor filthiness, nor buffoonery, nor ribald jesting — Con
There must be no indecency or foolish or scurrilous talk — Gspd
. . . suggestive jesting — Wms
. . . smartness in talk — Knox
. . . nor levity — RSV
No coarse, stupid, or flippant talk — NEB
Dirty stories, foul talk and coarse jokes — Tay
which are not convenient:
. . . not befitting — ASV
— these are not for you — Tay
Which things are beneath you — Rhm
— all that is unbecoming — Gspd
they are wholly out of place among you — TCNT
— they are all alike discreditable — Wey
but rather giving of thanks.
but a sense of all that we owe to God — Phi
5. For this ye know, that no whoremonger, nor unclean person, nor covetous man, who is an idolater,
For this ye know of a surety . . . — ASV
For of this you may be sure — that no one who is unchaste or impure or greedy of gain (for to be greedy of gain is idolatry) — TCNT
For be well assured that no fornicator or immoral person and no profligate — or in other words idol-worshipper — Wey
hath any inheritance in the kingdom of Christ and of God.
. . . any place awaiting him . . . — TCNT
. . . any share awaiting him . . . — Wey

6. Let no man deceive you with vain words:

... mislead you ... — Con

... with empty words — ASV

... with specious arguments — TCNT

... shallow arguments — NEB

Stop letting anyone deceive you with groundless arguments — Wms

Do not allow anyone to cheat you with empty promises — Knox

Don't let anyone fool you on this point, however plausible his argument — Phi

for because of these things cometh the wrath of God upon the children of disobedience.

... the sons of disobedience — ASV

... the anger of God upon the sons of obstinacy — Rhm

7. Be not ye therefore partakers with them.

... co-partners with them — Rhm

you do ill to throw in your lot with them — Knox

Don't even associate with such people — Tay

8. For ye were sometimes darkness,

... once darkness — ASV

... sheer darkness — Gspd

... all darkness — Knox

For though once your heart was full of darkness — Tay

but now are ye light in the Lord:

now it is full of light from the Lord — Tay

now, in the Lord, you are all daylight — Knox

walk as children of light:

As children of light be walking — Rhm

Live and act as sons of Light — Wey

You must live as men native to the light — Knox

Live like men who are at home in daylight — NEB

9. (For the fruit of the Spirit is in all goodness and righteousness and truth;)

(for the fruit of the light ...) — ASV

for the outcome of life in the Light may be seen in every form of goodness, righteousness, and sincerity — TCNT

for the effect of the Light ... — Wey

for the product of the light ... — Wms

The light produces in men quite the opposite of sins like these — everything that is wholesome and good and true — Phi

for where light is, there all goodness springs up, all justice and truth — NEB

10. Proving what is acceptable unto the Lord.

... well-pleasing unto the Lord — ASV

and learn in your own experience what is fully pleasing to the Lord — Wey

Let your lives be living proofs of the things which please God — Phi

always trying to find out what is pleasing to the Lord — TCNT

11. And have no fellowship with the unfruitful works of darkness,

Take no part in deeds of Darkness, from which no good can come — TCNT

Steer clear of the activities of darkness — Phi

but rather reprove them.

but rather even reprove them — ASV

yea, rather expose their foulness — Con

... set your faces against them — Wey

but show them up for what they are — NEB

12. For it is a shame even to speak of those things which are done of them in secret.

It is degrading even to speak of the things continually done by them in secret — TCNT

for it is disgraceful ... — NASB

their secret actions are too shameful even to bear speaking of — Knox

13. But all things that are reproved are made manifest by the light:

But all things become visible when they are exposed by the light — NASB

But all things when they are reproved are made manifest by the light — ASV

All such actions, when exposed, have their true character made manifest by the Light — TCNT

But everything can be tested by the light and thus be shown in its true colours — Wey

yet when anything is exposed by the light, it is made visible — Gspd

For light is capable of showing up everything for what it really is — Phi

for whatsoever doth make manifest is light.

for everything that is made manifest is light — ASV

for whatsoever is made manifest becomes light — Con

for whatever shines of itself is light — Wey

and anything that is made visible is light — Gspd

It is even possible (after all, it happened with you!) for light to turn the thing it shines upon into light also — Phi

and everything thus illumined is all light — NEB

14. **Wherefore he saith,**
    . . . it saith — Rhm

    Thus God speaks through the scriptures — Phi

    And so the hymn says — NEB

    And that is why it is said — TCNT

    Awake thou that sleepest,

    Rise, sleeper — Wey

    — Sleeper, awake! — TCNT

    Wake up, sleeper! — Gspd

    and arise from the dead, and Christ shall give thee light.

    . . . Christ shall shine upon thee — ASV

    . . . the Christ shall give thee light! — TCNT

    . . . Christ will dawn upon you! — Gspd

    . . . Christ will make day dawn on you — Wms

15. **See then that ye walk circumspectly,**

    Look therefore carefully how ye walk — ASV

    Take heed then how ye walk strictly — Alf

    . . . exactly how ye are walking — Rhm

    See, then, that you walk without stumbling — Con

    Take great care, then, how you live — TCNT

    Live life, then, with a due sense of responsibility — Phi

    not as fools, but as wise,

    not unwisely, but wisely — TCNT

    Do not act thoughtlessly, but like sensible men — Gspd

not thoughtlessly but thoughtfully — Wms

like sensible men, not like simpletons — NEB

16. **Redeeming the time, because the days are evil.**

    buying up opportunities . . . — Alf

    making the most of every opportunity; for these are evil days — TCNT

    Make the best use of your time, despite all the difficulties of these days — Phi

17. **Wherefore be ye not unwise,**

    . . . foolish — ASV

    Therefore do not grow thoughtless — TCNT

    So stop becoming senseless — Wms

    No, you cannot afford to be reckless — Knox

    but understanding what the will of the Lord is.

    but have discernment . . . — Rhm

    but try to understand . . . — TCNT

    but learn to know . . . — Con

18. **And be not drunk with wine, wherein is excess;**

    . . . riot — ASV

    . . . debauchery — RSV

    . . . wild living — Beck

    And be not getting drunk with wine in which is dissoluteness — Rhm

    Do not drink wine to excess, for that leads to profligacy — TCNT

    Do not indulge in much wine — a thing in which excess is so easy — Wey

    Stop getting drunk on wine, for that means profligacy — Wms

    Do not besot yourselves with wine; that leads to ruin — Knox

    Don't get your stimulus from wine (for there is always the danger of excessive drinking) — Phi

    Do not give way to drunkenness and the dissipation that goes with it — NEB

    but be filled with the Spirit;

    But be getting filled in Spirit — Rhm

    but seek to be filled with the Spirit of God — TCNT

    . . . drink deeply of . . . — Wey

    . . . drink deep in the Spirit — Mon

    but ever be filled with the Spirit — Wms

    but let the Spirit stimulate your souls — Phi

19. Speaking to yourselves in psalms and hymns and spiritual songs,

and speak to one another in psalms and hymns and sacred songs — TCNT

your tongues unloosed in psalms and hymns and spiritual music — Knox

Express your joy in singing among yourselves . . . — Phi

singing and making melody in your heart to the Lord;

Singing and striking the strings with your heart unto the Lord — Rhm

and make melody with the music of your hearts, to the Lord — Con

Sing and make music in your hearts . . . — TCNT

and with your hearts sing and play music to the Lord — Beck

20. Giving thanks always for all things

Always give thanks for everything — TCNT

continue giving thanks for everything — Wms

give thanks every day for everything — NEB

unto God and the Father in the name of our Lord Jesus Christ;

. . . to God, even the Father . . . — ASV

Unto your God and Father . . . — Rhm

21. Submitting yourselves one to another in the fear of God.

subjecting yourselves . . . in the fear of Christ — ASV

. . . in reverence of Christ — Rhm

. . . out of reverence for Christ — Mon

and, as you stand in awe of Christ, submit to each other's rights—Knox

Honor Christ by submitting to each other — Tay

22. Wives, submit yourselves unto your own husbands, as unto the Lord.

. . . subordinate yourselves . . . — Gspd

Wives should submit to their husbands . . . — TCNT

You wives must learn to adapt yourselves to your husbands, as you submit yourselves to the Lord — Phi

23. For the husband is the head of the wife,

The man is the head to which the woman's body is united — Knox

For a man is the Head of his wife — TCNT

For a husband is in charge of his wife — Tay

even as Christ is the head of the church:

in the same way that . . . — Phi

in the same way Christ is in charge of His body the church — Tay

and he is the saviour of the body.

His body, which He saves — Con

he, the Saviour on whom the safety of his body depends — Knox

which is His body that He saves — Beck

24. Therefore as the church is subject unto Christ,

But as the Church submits to the Christ — TCNT

so let the wives be to their own husbands in every thing.

so also married women should be entirely submissive to their husbands — Wey

So you wives must willingly obey your husbands in everything — Tay

25. Husbands, love your wives, even as Christ also loved the church, and gave himself for it;

and gave himself up for it — ASV

. . . up to death for her — Wey

26. That he might sanctify and cleanse it

. . . sanctify it, having cleansed it — ASV

to make her holy, after purifying her — TCNT

to consecrate her, after cleansing her — Gspd

To make her holy and clean — Tay

with the washing of water by the word,

by the laver of the water in the word — Alf

with the bath of water in declaration — Rhm

by the indwelling of the word of God — Con

by the Washing with the Water, according to his promise — TCNT

with the baptismal water by the word — Wey

with the bath in water through her confession of him — Gspd

through His word, as pictured in the water bath — Wms

through the baptism of his Word — Phi

by water and word — NEB

washed by baptism and God's word —
Tay

**27. That he might present it to himself a
glorious church,**

. . . in stainless glory — Con

. . . in all her beauty — TCNT

. . . as a splendid bride — Wms

. . . all glorious — NEB

. . . as something wonderful — Beck

**not having spot, or wrinkle, or any
such thing;**

with no spot or wrinkle or blemish of
any kind — TCNT

without a blot or wrinkle or anything
like it — Wms

no stain, no wrinkle, no such disfigurement — Knox

**but that it should be holy and without
blemish.**

. . . and faultless — TCNT

. . . perfect — Phi

**28. So ought men to love their wives as
their own bodies.**

That is how husbands ought to love
their wives — as if they were their
own bodies — TCNT

He that loveth his wife loveth himself.

. . . is really loving himself — TCNT

. . . is but loving himself — Knox

The love a man gives his wife is the
extending of his love for himself to
enfold her — Phi

**29. For no man ever yet hated his own
flesh;**

. . . his own body — TCNT

. . . his own person — Gspd

. . . his own physical person — Wms

It is unheard of, that a man should
bear ill-will to his own flesh — Knox

but nourisheth and cherisheth it,

But every one feeds his body and cares
for it — TCNT

but he feeds and fosters it — Wms

no, he keeps it fed and warmed —
Knox

even as the Lord the church:

and that is what Christ does for his
body, the Church — Phi

and that is how Christ treats the church
— NEB

**30. For we are members of his body, of his
flesh, and of his bones.[6]**

because we are members of his body —
ASV

. . . parts of his body — Gspd

. . . limbs of his body — Knox

**31. For this cause shall a man leave his
father and mother,**

For this reason . . . — Wey

Therefore . . . — Gspd

Thus it is that (in the words of Scripture) . . . — NEB

and shall be joined unto his wife,

and shall cleave unto . . . — Con

and be united to . . . — TCNT

and cling to . . . — Wey

attach himself to . . . — Gspd

and they two shall be one flesh.

. . . a single body — NEB

32. This is a great mystery:

This mystery is great — ASV

This sacred secret is great — Rhm

In this there is a profound truth —
TCNT

This is a great truth hitherto kept
secret — Wey

The marriage relationship is doubtless
a great mystery — Phi

I know this is hard to understand —
Tay

There's a great truth hidden here —
Beck

**but I speak concerning Christ and the
church.**

I mean the truth concerning . . . — Wey

I understand it of Christ . . . — Gspd

and I take it to mean . . . — RSV

but I am speaking of something deeper
still — the marriage of Christ and
his Church — Phi

I give it as a picture of . . . — Nor

but it is an illustration of . . . — Tay

**33. Nevertheless let every one of you in
particular so love his wife even as
himself;**

Nevertheless do ye also severally love
each one his own wife . . . — ASV

But as for you individually, you must
each one of you love his own wife
exactly as if she were yourself —
Mon

In practice what I have said amounts
to this: let . . . — Phi

So again I say, a man must love his
wife as a part of himself — Tay

**and the wife see that she reverence her
husband.**

---

[6]The words "of his flesh, and of his bones" are
now recognized as not adequately supported
by original manuscripts.

and the wife be careful to respect . . .
— TCNT
and the wife must see to it that she

deeply respects her husband — obeying, praising and honoring him —
Tay

CHAPTER 6

1. **Children, obey your parents in the Lord:**
   Children, obey your parents, as children of the Lord — TCNT
   Children, as Christians, obey your parents — Gspd
   for this is right.
   . . . it is your duty — Knox
   . . . the right thing for you to do — Phi

2. **Honour thy father and mother;**
   You must honor . . . — Gspd
   which is the first commandment with promise;
   . . . accompanied with a promise — Gspd
   . . . with a promise to make it good — Wms
   . . . to contain a promise — Phi
   this is an important commandment with a promise — Beck

3. **That it may be well with thee,**
   so that thou mayest prosper — TCNT
   and thou mayest live long on the earth.
   And thou shalt be long-lived . . . — Rhm
   and thou shalt live long to enjoy the land — Knox

4. **And, ye fathers,**
   You parents, too — Wms
   provoke not your children to wrath:
   fret not your children to anger — Alf
   vex not your children — Con
   don't overcorrect . . . — Phi
   do not irritate your children — TCNT
   must stop exasperating your children — Wms
   do not rouse your children to resentment — Knox
   must not goad your children to resentment — NEB
   but bring them up in the nurture and admonition of the Lord.
   but nurture them in the chastening and admonition . . . — ASV
   but bring them up with Christian discipline and instruction — TCNT
   . . . in such training and correction as befits the servants of the Lord — Con

. . . with the sort of education and counsel the Lord approves — Wms
. . . which belong to a Christian upbringing — NEB
but raise them by letting the Lord train and correct them — Beck

5. **Servants, be obedient to them that are your masters according to the flesh,**
   Slaves . . . — Mon
   Bondsmen, obey your earthly masters — Con
   . . . your human masters — Phi
   with fear and trembling, in singleness of your heart, as unto Christ;
   . . . in simplicity of your heart, as unto Christ — Alf
   with anxiety and self-distrust, in singleness of heart . . . — Con
   with anxious care, giving them ungrudging service, as if obeying the Christ — TCNT
   with respect and eager anxiety to please and with simplicity of motive, as if you were obeying Christ — Wey
   in reverence and awe, with sincerity of heart . . . — Gspd
   . . . as service rendered to Christ himself — Phi

6. **Not with eyeservice, as menpleasers;**
   not only when their eyes are on you . . . — TCNT
   not with mere external service . . . — Gspd
   not serving them as though they were watching you — Wms
   not with that show of service which tries to win human favour — Knox
   not with the idea of currying favor with men — Phi
   but as the servants of Christ, doing the will of God from the heart;[7]
   but as slaves of Christ, who are trying to carry out the will of God — TCNT
   . . . conscientiously doing what you believe to be the will of God for you — Phi

---

[7]Some translations connect "from the heart" with the phrase that follows.

. . . do wholeheartedly the will of God — NEB

. . . with all your heart — Nor

7. With good will doing service,

from the heart with good will doing service — Alf

From the soul with good will rendering service — Rhm

With good will fulfilling your service — Con

Give your service heartily and cheerfully — TCNT

Do your duties heartily and willingly Gspd

slaving with good-will from your heart — Mon

Heartily and cheerfully keep on working as slaves — Wms

Yours must be a slavery of love — Knox

Do good work with good will — Nor

as to the Lord, and not to men:

as working for the Master and not for men — TCNT

. . . not just for men — Nor

8. Knowing that whatsoever good thing any man doeth, the same shall he receive of the Lord,

for you know that every one will be rewarded by the Master for any honest work that he has done — TCNT

. . . will be repaid by the Lord for every task well done — Knox

. . . for his good conduct — Gspd

whether he be bond or free.

whether he is a slave or a freeman — TCNT

9. And, ye masters, do the same things unto them, forbearing threatening:

And ye, masters, do in like manner by them, and abstain from threats — Con

. . . treat your slaves in the same spirit. Give up threatening them — TCNT

. . . act toward your slaves on the same principles, and refrain from threats — Wey

. . . cease to threaten them — Gspd

. . . deal with them accordingly; there is no need to threaten them — Knox

knowing that your Master also is in heaven;

knowing that he who is both their Master and yours is in heaven — ASV

for you know that their real Lord and yours . . . — Wms

neither is there respect of persons with him.

and that before him there is no distinction of rank — TCNT

. . . he will show no partiality — Gspd

who makes no distinction between master and man — Phi

and he has no favourites — NEB

and He doesn't prefer one to another — Beck

10. Finally, my brethren, be strong in the Lord,

Finally, be strong in the Lord — ASV

Just one thing more . . . — Nor

Henceforth, be ye strengthened . . . — Alf

. . . be empowering yourselves . . . — Rhm

. . . let your hearts be strengthened . . . — Con

For the future, find strength in your union with the Lord — TCNT

I have no more to say, brethren, except this; draw your strength from the Lord — Knox

and in the power of his might.

and in the strength . . . — ASV

and in the grasp . . . — Rhm

and in the conquering power . . . — Con

and in the power which His supreme might imparts — Wey

in the power of his boundless resource — Phi

and in the power which comes from his might — TCNT

from that mastery which his power supplies — Knox

11. Put on the whole armour of God,

. . . the complete armour of God — Rhm

. . . the full armour of God — TCNT

. . . all the armour which God provides — NEB

You must wear all the weapons in God's armoury — Knox

that ye may be able to stand against the wiles of the devil.

. . . against the strategies of the adversary — Rhm

. . . the cunning of the devil — Knox

. . . the devices of the devil — NEB

. . . the schemes of the devil — NASB

so that you can successfully resist all the devil's methods — Phi

so that you may be able to stand your ground against the stratagems of the Devil — TCNT

12. For we wrestle not against flesh and blood,

For our wrestling . . . — ASV

Because our struggle . . . — Rhm

For the adversaries with whom we wrestle . . . — Con

For ours is no struggle against enemies of flesh and blood — TCNT

For our contest is not with human foes alone — Wms

For our fight is not against any physical enemy — Phi

but against principalities, against powers, against the rulers of the darkness of this world,

. . . against the world-rulers of this darkness — ASV

. . . the Sovereigns of this present darkness — Con

. . . the master-spirits of this dark world — Gspd

. . . cosmic powers of this dark world — Wms

. . . those who have the mastery of the world in these dark days — Knox

. . . great evil princes of darkness who rule this world — Tay

but against all the various Powers of Evil that hold sway in the Darkness around us — TCNT

but with the despotisms, the empires, the forces that control and govern this dark world — Wey

against spiritual wickedness in high places.

. . . the spiritual hosts of wickedness in the heavenly places — ASV

the spirits of evil in the heavens — Con

against the Spirits of Wickedness on high — TCNT

— the spirited hosts of evil arrayed against us in the heavenly warfare — Wey

with malign influences in an order higher than ours — Knox

and spiritual agents from the very headquarters of evil — Phi

against huge numbers of wicked spirits in the spirit world — Tay

13. Wherefore take unto you the whole armour of God,[8]

For this cause take up . . . — Rhm

Wherefore, take up with you to the battle . . . — Con

Therefore put on . . . — Wey

Therefore you must wear . . . — Phi

that ye may be able to withstand in the evil day,

In order that ye may receive power to withstand . . . — Rhm

that you may be able to withstand them . . . — Con

. . . stand your ground . . . — Wey

. . . in the day when evil attacks you — Wms

that, when the evil day comes, you may be able to withstand the attack — TCNT

. . . resist evil in its day of power — Phi

and having done all, to stand.

and having overthrown them all, to stand unshaken — Con

and, having fought to the end, still stand your ground — TCNT

and, having fought to the end, to remain victors on the field — Wey

and when it is all over to hold your ground — Gspd

and, after having completely finished the contest, to hold your own — Wms

and be found still on your feet, when all the task is over — Knox

14. Stand therefore, having your loins girt about with truth,

Stand your ground, then, with truth for your belt — TCNT

. . . girt with the belt of truth — Con

. . . first fastening round you the girdle . . . — Wey

. . . with your waist encircled . . . — Wms

. . . with truth as your belt — Phi

. ·. Buckle on the belt of truth — NEB

and having on the breastplate of righteousness;

for coat of mail put on integrity — NEB

and put on uprightness as your coat of mail — Gspd

. . . the breastplate of uprightness — Wey

---

[8]Compare verse 11.

the breastplate of justice fitted on —
Knox

**15. And your feet shod with the prepara-
tion of the gospel of peace;**

. . . with the readiness of the gospel . . .
— Alf

. . . in readiness to publish the gospel
. . . — Knox

. . . the readiness of the glad-message of
peace — Rhm

and put on your feet the preparation
the good news of peace supplies —
Wms

and having shod your feet with the
equipment of the gospel . . . — RSV

and with the readiness to serve the
Good News of Peace as shoes for
your feet — TCNT

and shod as ready messengers of the
Glad tidings of peace — Con

16. Above all, taking the shield of faith,

Besides all these, take on the shield
which faith provides — Wms

At every onslaught take up faith for
your shield — TCNT

Above all be sure you take . . . — Phi

. . . the great shield of faith — Wey

**wherewith ye shall be able to quench
all the fiery darts of the wicked.**

. . . the evil one — ASV

. . . all the ignited darts of the wicked
one — Rhm

for with it you will be able to extinguish all the flaming darts of the Evil
One — TCNT

. . . all the flaming missiles . . . — Gspd

. . . to put out all the fire-tipped arrows
shot by . . . — Wms

. . . every burning missile the enemy
hurls at you — Phi

17. And take the helmet of salvation,

And receive . . . — Alf

and take salvation for your helmet —
Gspd

take the helmet salvation provides —
Wms

and the sword of the Spirit,

and take the sword the Spirit wields
— Wms

which is the word of God:

which is what God hath spoken —
Rhm

which is the Message of God —TCNT

which is the voice of God — Gspd

**18. Praying always with all prayer and
supplication in the Spirit,**

with all prayer and supplication praying at all seasons in the Spirit — ASV

Continue to pray at every season with
all earnestness of supplication in the
Spirit — Con

Pray with unceasing prayer and entreaty at all times in the Spirit —
Wey

Use every kind of prayer and entreaty,
and at every opportunity pray in the
Spirit — Gspd

Give yourselves wholly to prayer and
entreaty; pray on every occasion in
the power of the Spirit — NEB

Pray all the time. Ask God for anything in line with the Holy Spirit's
wishes — Tay

**and watching thereunto with all per-
severance and supplication for all
saints;**

Be intent upon this, with unwearying
perseverance and supplication for all
Christ's People — TCNT

and be always on the alert to seize
opportunities for doing so, with unwearied persistence and entreaty on
behalf of all the saints — Wey

be ever on the alert with perfect devotion and entreaty for all God's
people — Wms

keep awake to that end with all perseverance; offer your supplication
for all the saints — Knox

Plead with Him, reminding Him of
your needs, and keep praying earnestly for all Christians everywhere
— Tay

**19. And for me, that utterance may be
given unto me, that I may open my
mouth boldly,[9]**

and on my behalf, that utterance may
be given unto me in opening my
mouth — ASV

— and on my behalf also, that, when
I begin to speak, words may be
given me — TCNT

. . . that I may be granted the right
words when I open my mouth — NEB

. . . I'll be told what to say — Beck

---

[9]Some translations construe "boldly" with the
phrase that follows.

to make known the mystery of the gospel,
to make known with boldness the mystery of the gospel — ASV
With freedom of utterance to make known the sacred secret — Rhm
and may boldly and freely make known his hidden purpose — NEB
so that I may fearlessly make known the inmost truth of the Good News — TCNT
so that, outspoken and fearless, I may make known the truths (hitherto kept secret) of the gospel — Wey
. . . the open secret of the good news — Wms
. . . that His salvation is for the Gentiles too — Tay

20. For which I am an ambassador in bonds:
. . . in chains — ASV
. . . in fetters — Con
on behalf of which I am an Ambassador — in chains! — TCNT
. . . an envoy, and in prison — Gspd
that therein I may speak boldly, as I ought to speak.
That therein I may use freedom of utterance as it is needful for me to speak — Rhm
Pray that I may declare it boldly, as I ought to speak — Con
Pray that, in telling it, I may speak fearlessly as I ought — TCNT
. . . have the courage to speak . . . — Gspd
. . . as courageously as I ought — Wms
. . . as is my plain and obvious duty — Phi

21. But that ye also may know my affairs,
But that you, as well as others, may be informed of my concerns — Con
. . . what is happening to me — Beck
and how I do,
what I am accomplishing — Rhm
how I am — Wms
Tychicus, a beloved brother and faithful minister in the Lord,

. . . faithful servant . . . — Con
. . . our dear Brother and faithful helper in the Master's cause — TCNT
. . . and trustworthy helper in the Lord's work — NEB
shall make known to you all things:
will tell you everything — TCNT
will tell you all about it — Gspd
will give you all the information — Wms

22. Whom I have sent unto you for the same purpose,
. . . for this very purpose — ASV
I am sending him to you on purpose — TCNT
that is the reason why . . . — Knox
that ye might know our affairs,
. . . get to know . . . — Rhm
. . . may learn all about us — TCNT
. . . exactly how we are — Phi
to let you have news of me — Knox
and that he might comfort your hearts.
. . . may encourage your hearts — Rhm
. . . may cheer your hearts — TCNT
and to put fresh heart into you — NEB
and to bring courage to your hearts — Knox

23. Peace be to the brethren,
. . . to all Christian brothers — Phi
. . . to the brotherhood — NEB
and love with faith,
and love linked with faith — TCNT
and love combined with faith — Wey
from God the Father and the Lord Jesus Christ.
from God our Father . . . — Rhm

24. Grace be with all them that love our Lord Jesus Christ in sincerity. Amen.
. . . with a love incorruptible — ASV
. . . with incorruptness — Rhm
. . . with an undying love — TCNT
. . . with an immortal love — Knox
God's blessing be with all who have an unfailing love for . . . — Gspd
God's grace be with all who love our Lord Jesus Christ, grace and immortality — NEB

THE
EPISTLE OF PAUL TO THE PHILIPPIANS

CHAPTER 1

1. Paul and Timotheus,
... Timothy — ASV
the servants of Jesus Christ,
bondsmen of Jesus Christ — Con
bondservants of Christ Jesus — Wey
... slaves ... — Gspd
to all the saints in Christ Jesus which are at Philippi,
To all Christ's People at Philippi — TCNT
to all God's people in union with Christ Jesus who are at Philippi — Wms
to all those of God's people, incorporate in Christ Jesus, who live at Philippi — NEB
to all who are holy in Christ Jesus in Philippi — Beck
with the bishops and deacons:
with overseers and ministers — Rhm
with the Presidents and Assistant-Officers — TCNT
with the ministers of the Church and their assistants — Wey
with the superintendents and assistants — Gspd
to the elders and deacons — Mon

2. Grace be unto you, and peace, from God our Father, and from the Lord Jesus Christ.
Favour ... — Rhm
spiritual blessing ... — Wms

3. I thank my God upon every remembrance of you,
... upon all my remembrance of you — ASV
... on occasion of all my remembrance ... — Rhm
Every recollection that I have of you is a cause of thankfulness to God — TCNT

4. Always in every prayer of mine for you all
always in every supplication of mine on behalf ... — ASV
in every petition of mine in your behalf — Mon
making request with joy,
making my supplication ... — ASV
— and my prayers are full of joy — TCNT
finding a joy in offering it — Wey

I am offering my prayer with joy — Mon

5. For your fellowship in the gospel
... in furtherance of the gospel — ASV
on account of your contribution unto the glad-message — Rhm
over your cooperation in the good news — Gspd
thankful for your partnership in the gospel — RSV
from the first day until now;
... until the present — Rhm
... to this moment — Ber

6. Being confident of this very thing,
Being persuaded ... — Rhm
And I am confident accordingly — Con
For of this I am quite sure — TCNT
Of this I am fully persuaded — Mon
that he which hath begun a good work in you
that he by whom the good work was started in you — Bas
that he who has inspired this generosity in you — Knox
will perform it until the day of Jesus Christ:
will perfect it ... — ASV
... up to the day of ... — Alf
will complete it in readiness for ... — TCNT
will go on completing it until ... — Mon
will bring it to completion by the day ... — NEB
will keep right on helping you grow in His grace until His task within you is finally finished on that day when Jesus Christ returns — Tay
will continue until the day of Jesus Christ — right up to the time of His return—developing [that good work] and perfecting and bringing it to full completion in you — Amp

7. Even as it is meet for me to think this of you all,
even as it is right for me to be thus minded on behalf of you all — ASV
And I am justified in having this confidence about you all — Wey
And I have a right to think this way about you — Wms

It is quite appropriate for me to have you all in mind this way — Ber

because I have you in my heart;

because you have me in your heart — Alf

because you have a warm place in my heart — TCNT

you are close to my heart — Knox

because you hold me in such affection — NEB

inasmuch as both in my bonds,

. . . in my imprisonment — Con

whether shut up in prison — Wms

both when I have been in chains — Nor

and in the defence and confirmation of the gospel,

. . . the glad-message — Rhm

and in the work of defending and establishing the Good News — TCNT

or out defending and vindicating the good news — Wms

and also when I have been free to defend and vindicate the gospel — Nor

ye are all partakers of my grace.

ye all are partakers with me of grace — ASV

. . . joint partakers of my favour — Rhm

We have shared together the blessings of God — Tay

8. For God is my record,

. . . witness — ASV

how greatly I long after you all

that I yearn over you all — TCNT

how I never stop yearning for all of you — Wms

how my love goes out to you . . . — Bas

in the bowels of Jesus Christ.

in the tender mercies of Christ Jesus — ASV

in the tender heart . . . — Alf

in the tender affections . . . — Rhm

with the deep-felt affection . . . — Ber

with tender Christian affection — Wey

with the affection of Christ Jesus himself — Mof

9. And this I pray,

And it is my prayer — Mon

And what I pray for is this — TCNT

that your love may abound yet more and more

—that your love may grow yet stronger and stronger — TCNT

that you will overflow more and more with love for others — Tay

in knowledge and in all judgment;

. . . discernment — ASV

. . . understanding — Con

in personal knowledge and all perception — Rhm

10. That ye may approve things that are excellent;

that ye may discern . . . — Alf

. . . may be putting to test the things that differ — Rhm

. . . may distinguish the things that differ — ABUV

teaching you to distinguish good from evil — Con

enabling you to have a sense of what is vital — Mof

so that you may always approve the better things — Wms

that you may learn to prize what is of value — Knox

and may thus bring you the gift of true discrimination — NEB

until you are able to appreciate all moral distinctions — TCNT

that ye may be sincere and without offence

. . . incorrupt and may give no occasion of stumbling — Rhm

. . . unsullied and blameless — Ber

And I pray, too, that you may be kept pure and blameless — TCNT

so that you may be men of transparent character, and may be blameless — Wey

and to be inwardly clean, no one being able to criticize you — Tay

till the day of Christ;

in preparation for the day of Christ — Wey

as you face the day of Christ — Ber

from now until our Lord returns — Tay

11. Being filled with the fruits of righteousness, which are by Jesus Christ,

bearing a rich harvest of that righteousness which comes through Jesus Christ — TCNT

your life all covered with the harvest of righteousness which Jesus Christ produces — Mof

with your lives filled with the fruits which uprightness produces through Jesus Christ — Gspd

as Jesus Christ has filled your life with
  righteous works — Beck
unto the glory and praise of God.
by which you glorify and praise God
  — Beck

12. **But I would ye should understand,**

  Now I would have you know — ASV
  Now it is my purpose to make clear to
    you — Bas
  I hasten to assure you — Knox
  **brethren, that the things which hap-
    pened unto me**
  . . . that the things which relate unto
    myself — Rhm
  . . . that what I have gone through —
    Wey
  **have fallen out rather unto the further-
    ance of the gospel:**
  . . . the advancement of the glad-mes-
    sage — Rhm
  have tended rather to the furtherance
    than hindrance of the Glad-tidings
    — Con
  has turned out to the furtherance of the
    gospel rather than otherwise — Wey
  has been a great boost in getting out
    the Good News concerning Christ —
    Tay
  has actually only served to advance
    and give a renewed impetus to the
    [spreading of the] good news — of
    the Gospel — Amp

13. **So that my bonds in Christ are mani-
    fest in all the palace, and in all other
    places.**

  So that my chains have become well
    known in the name of Christ,
    throughout the whole Praetorium,
    and to all the rest — Con
  throughout the whole of the praetorian
    guard and everywhere else it is rec-
    ognized that I am imprisoned on
    account of my connexion with Christ
    — Mof
  so that throughout the imperial guard
    and everywhere else my shackles
    have become known in union with
    Christ — Ber
  so that my imprisonment in the cause
    of Christ . . . — NASB
  It has even become evident, not only to
    all the Imperial Guard, but to every
    one else, that it is for Christ's sake
    that I am in chains — TCNT

For everyone around here, including
  all the soldiers over at the barracks,
  know my chains are simply because
  I am a Christian — Tay

14. **And many of the brethren in the Lord,
    waxing confident by my bonds,**

  And besides this, most of our Brothers
    have gained confidence in the Lord
    through my chains — TCNT
  And so most of the brethren in the
    Lord assured by my bonds — Rhm
  and most of the brothers in the Lord,
    made confident in the Lord through
    my imprisonment — Mon
  **are much more bold to speak the word
    without fear.**
  are becoming more abundantly bold to
    be fearlessly speaking the word of
    God — Rhm
  and now venture with far greater free-
    dom to speak of God's Message
    fearlessly — TCNT

15. **Some indeed preach Christ even of
    envy and strife;**

  It is true that some do proclaim the
    Christ out of jealousy and opposi-
    tion — TCNT
  Some indeed actually preach Christ out
    of envy and contentiousness — Wey
  . . . jealousy and partisanship — Gspd
  Some, of course, are preaching the
    Good News because they are jealous
    of the way God has used me — Tay
  and some also of good will:
  but there are others who proclaim him
    from good-will — TCNT

16. **The one preach Christ of contention,**
  . . . from a spirit of intrigue — Con
  . . . from motives of rivalry — Wey
  . . . in a factious spirit — TCNT
  . . . for their own ends — Mof
  not sincerely,
  Not purely — Rhm
  not with pure intent — ABUV
  with mixed motives — Mof
  **supposing to add affliction to my
    bonds:**
  supposing to rouse up tribulation with
    my bonds — Rhm
  thinking to stir up persecution against
    me in my imprisonment — Con
  thinking to add to the pain of my
    chains — TCNT
  imagining that they are making my im-
    prisonment harder to bear — Gspd

just because they hope to make my
chains gall me worse — Knox

17. But the other of love,
   knowing that I am set for the defence
   of the gospel.
   ... am appointed to defend the Glad-
   tidings — Con
   knowing that I have been appointed
   to plead the cause of the Good News
   — TCNT
   for they know that God has put me
   where I am to defend our right to
   preach the good news — Gspd

18. What then?
   What does it matter, however — Wey
   notwithstanding, every way,
   Only that in some way or other —
   TCNT
   whether in pretence, or in truth,
   either with assumed or with real earnestness — TCNT
   either perversely or in honest truth —
   Wey
   from false motives or honest ones —
   Gspd
   for ulterior ends or honestly — Mof
   Christ is preached;
   ... proclaimed — ASV
   ... announced — Con
   and I therein do rejoice, yea, and will
   rejoice.

19. For I know that this shall turn to my
   salvation
   The outcome of all this, I know, will
   be my release — Mof
   for I know that . . . all this will turn
   out for my highest welfare — Gspd
   For I know that . . . all these things
   will ultimately turn out for . . . —
   Lam
   ... will turn out for my safety — Ber
   ... turn out victoriously for me—Beck
   through your prayer,
   ... supplication — ASV
   and the supply of the Spirit of Jesus
   Christ,
   and the giving of the stored wealth of
   the Spirit . . . — Bas
   and the help of the Spirit of Jesus
   Christ — Gspd

20. According to my earnest expectation
   and my hope,
   ... my eager outlook and hope —
   Rhm

And this will fulfil my earnest expectation and hope — TCNT
that in nothing I shall be ashamed,
... be put to shame — ASV
that I shall have no cause for shame —
TCNT
that I shall never disgrace myself —
Gspd
that I shall never be put to the blush
— Knox
but that with all boldness, as always,
... with all freedom of speech . . . —
Rhm
... with unfailing courage . . . — TCNT
... by my all-conquering courage . . .
— Wms
so now also Christ shall be magnified
in my body,
... Christ will be honored in my body
— RSV
whether it be by life, or by death.
whether by my life or by my death —
TCNT

21. For to me to live is Christ,
   For to me living means Christ — Wms
   For to me life is Christ — TCNT
   As life means Christ to me — Mof
   and to die is gain.
   so death means gain — Mof
   and dying brings gain — Wms
   and if I die I should merely gain more
   of him — Phi
   and dying — well, that's better yet! —
   Tay

22. But if I live in the flesh, this is the fruit
   of my labour:
   But if to live in the flesh, — if this
   shall bring fruit from my work —
   ASV
   But since to live means a longer stay
   on earth, that implies more labour
   for me — Wey
   But if living on here means having my
   labor bear fruit — Gspd
   If, however, my being alive physically
   means for me fruitful service — Ber
   but what if my living on in the body
   may serve some good purpose? —
   NEB
   But what if living on in this mortal
   body is the only way to harvest what
   I have sown? — Knox
   yet what I shall choose I wot not.
   ... I make not known — Rhm
   ... I cannot tell — Wey

Then which to choose I cannot tell! —
TCNT

Which then am I to choose? — NEB

so I can say nothing as to my personal
preference—I cannot choose—Amp

23. **For I am in a strait betwixt two,**
I am held in constraint . . . — Rhm

But between the two I am in perplexity
— Con

I am in a dilemma between the two —
Mof

I am in a hard position between two —
Bas

I feel the pressure from both sides —
Ber

I am perplexed either way! — TCNT

**having a desire to depart, and to be
with Christ;**

My strong desire is to depart and be
with Christ — Mof

I have a strong desire to break camp
and to be with Christ — Mon

which is far better:

24. **Nevertheless to abide in the flesh is
more needful for you.**
. . . in my flesh is more necessary . . .
— Alf

25. **And having this confidence,**
Yes, I am confident that this is so —
TCNT

Convinced of this — RSV

**I know that I shall abide and continue
with you all**

and I know that I shall remain, and
shall go on working side by side with
you all — Wey

for your furtherance and joy of faith;

to promote your progress and joy in
the Faith — TCNT

to help you to develop and to be glad
in your faith — Gspd

to the happy furtherance of your faith
— Knox

26. **That your rejoicing may be more abundant in Jesus Christ for me**

that your glorying may abound in
Christ Jesus in me — ASV

that in me your matter of boasting may
abound in Christ Jesus — Alf

so that . . . you, in your union with
Christ Jesus, may find in me fresh
cause for exultation — TCNT

so that in me you may have ample
cause to glory in Christ — RSV

So you can look forward to making
much of me as your minister in
Christ — Phi

by my coming to you again.

through my presence with you again —
ASV

27. **Only let your conversation be**
Only let your manner of life be —
ASV

Only conduct yourselves — Alf

Only . . . be using your citizenship —
Rhm

Only, do lead a life that is — Mof

Under all circumstances let your lives
be — TCNT

Be sure to conduct yourselves as citizens of Christ — Ber

Whatever happens, show yourselves
citizens — Gspd

as it becometh the gospel of Christ:

worthy of the gospel . . . — ASV

that are worthy of the gospel — Ber

**that whether I come and see you, or
else be absent, I may hear of your
affairs,**

so that whether I come and see you or
am absent, I may hear of you — RSV

that ye stand fast in one spirit,

that you are standing firm, animated by
one spirit — TCNT

**with one mind striving together for
the faith of the gospel:**

with one soul joining for the combat
along with the faith . . . — Rhm

and joining with one heart in a common struggle for the Faith taught by
the Good News — TCNT

and with one mind, fighting shoulder
to shoulder for the faith of the gospel
— Wey

and that with one purpose you are continuing to cooperate in the fight for
faith in the good news — Wms

28. **And in nothing terrified by your adversaries:**

. . . your opposers — Rhm

. . . its adversaries — Con

Never be scared for a second by your
opponents — Mof

Never in the slightest degree be frightened by . . . — Wms

not for a moment intimidated . . . —
Ber

Shew a bold front at all points to your
adversaries — Knox

and not caring two straws for your enemies — Phi

which is to them an evident token of perdition,

for their enmity is to them an evidence of perdition — Con

To them this will be a sign of their Destruction — TCNT

your fearlessness is a clear omen of ruin for them — Mof

Your fearlessness will be to them a sure token of impending destruction — Wey

but to you of salvation, and that of God.

but to you it will be a sure token of your salvation — a token coming from God — Wey

and of your own salvation — at the hands of God — Mof

29. For unto you it is given in the behalf of Christ,

Because to you it was granted . . . — ABUV

For you have had the privilege granted you on behalf of Christ — Wey

not only to believe on him,

. . . have faith in him — Bas

but also to suffer for his sake;

but to undergo pain . . . — Bas

30. Having the same conflict which ye saw in me,

. . . contest . . . — Rhm

. . . hard struggle . . . — TCNT

maintaining, as you do, the same kind of conflict that you once saw in me — Wey

Take your part in the same struggle that you have seen me engage in — Gspd

while you wage the same conflict which you once saw in me — Mon

Your battle is my own battle; you saw how I fought it once — Knox

We are in this fight together. You have seen me suffer for Him in the past — Tay

and now hear to be in me.

and which you hear that I am maintaining still — TCNT

and you have heard how I am fighting it now — Knox

CHAPTER 2

1. If there be therefore any consolation in Christ,

. . . exhortation . . . — ASV

If, then, you can be entreated in Christ — Con

So by all the stimulus of Christ — Mof

So by whatever appeal there is in our relation to Christ — Gspd

So, if there is any appeal in our union with Christ — Wms

If, then, any encouragement comes through union with Christ — TCNT

Is there any such thing as Christians cheering each other up? — Tay

if any comfort of love,

if any consolation . . . — ASV

if any encouragement from love — ABUV

if there is any persuasive power in love — TCNT

if you can be persuaded, by love — Con

by every incentive of love — Mof

Do you love me enough to want to help me? — Tay

if any fellowship of the Spirit,

if any communion . . . — Alf

. . . common sharing . . . — Wey

by all your participation in the Spirit — Mof

if we have any common share in the Spirit — Wms

if there is any communion with the Spirit — TCNT

Does it mean anything to you that we are brothers in the Lord, sharing the same Spirit? — Tay

if any bowels and mercies,

if any tender mercies and compassions — ASV

if any tenderness and compassions — Alf

if any affection and compassion — NASB

by all your affectionate tenderness — Mof

Are your hearts tender and sympathetic at all? — Tay

2. Fulfil ye my joy,

fill up my cup of joy — Wms

do make my best hopes for you come true — Phi

Then make me truly happy — Tay

that ye be likeminded,

That the same thing ye esteem — Rhm

by living in harmony — Mon

by your mutual identity of purpose — Ber

having the same love, being of one accord, of one mind.

having the same love, with united souls being of one mind — Alf

united in mutual love, with harmony of feeling giving your minds to one and the same object — Wey

by fostering the same disposition of love, your hearts beating in unison, your minds set on one purpose — Wms

live together in love, as though you had only one mind and one spirit between you — Phi

3. Let nothing be done through strife or vainglory;

. . . through faction or through vainglory — ASV

in nothing following self-seeking nor vainglory — Alf

Do nothing in a spirit of intrigue or vanity — Con

never acting for private ends or from vanity — Mof

Stop acting from motives of selfish strife or petty ambition — Wms

doing nothing through envy or through pride — Bas

Nothing should be done in a factious spirit or from vanity — TCNT

Do nothing from selfishness or empty conceit — NASB

but in lowliness of mind

but, with true humility — Wey

but modestly — Gspd

but with low thoughts of self — Bas

let each esteem other better than themselves.

practice treating one another as your superiors — Wms

each of you should . . . regard others as of more account than himself — TCNT

let each one of you regard one another as more important than himself — NASB

4. Look not every man on his own things,

Seek not your private ends alone — Con

Stop looking after your own interests only — Wms

but every man also on the things of others.

but let every man seek likewise his neighbor's good — Con

but practice looking out for the interests of others too — Wms

5. Let this mind be in you, which was also in Christ Jesus:

Have this mind . . . — ASV

Let the same disposition be in you . . . — Wey

Treat one another with the same spirit as you experience in Christ Jesus — Mof

Have the same attitude that Christ Jesus had — Gspd

Let Christ Jesus be your example as to what your attitude should be — Phi

Let this same attitude and purpose and [humble] mind be in you which was in Christ Jesus. — Let Him be your example in humility — Amp

Think just as Christ Jesus thought — Beck

6. Who, being in the form of God,

who, existing in the form of God — ASV

Who in form of God subsisting — Rhm

Though the divine nature was his from the beginning — TCNT

who, though from the beginning he had the nature of God — Mon

For he, who has always been God by nature — Phi

His nature is, from the first, divine — Knox

thought it not robbery to be equal with God:

counted not the being on an equality with God a thing to be grasped — ASV

did not reckon equality with God something to be forcibly retained — Mon

and yet he did not see, in the rank of Godhead, a prize to be coveted — Knox

did not cling to his prerogatives as God's equal — Phi

yet he did not look upon equality with God as above all things to be clung to — TCNT

7. But made himself of no reputation,

but emptied himself — ASV

but impoverished himself — TCNT

but laid it aside — Gspd

but stripped Himself [of His glory] —
Con

but stripped himself [of all privileges
and rightful dignity] — Amp

**and took upon him the form of a
servant,**

and took upon Him the form of a slave
— Con

. . . the nature of a bondservant —
Wey

and consented to take on the nature
of a slave — Nor

by taking the nature of a servant —
TCNT

and was made in the likeness of men:

being changed into the likeness of man
— Con

born in human guise — Mof

and became like human beings — Ber

and to be born like other men — Nor

8. **And being found in fashion as a man,**

And having appeared in the guise of
men — Con

Then he appeared among us as a man
— TCNT

And being recognized as truly human
— Wey

and appearing in human form — Mof

**he humbled himself, and became
obedient unto death,**

. . . even unto death — ASV

He abased Himself and showed obedience, even unto death — Con

He humbled Himself and even stooped
to die — Wey

He finally humiliated Himself in obedience so as to die — Wms

. . . and lived obediently to the extreme
of death — Ber

even the death of the cross.

yea death upon a cross — Rhm

going so far as to actually die a criminal's death on a cross — Tay

9. **Wherefore God also hath highly exalted him,**

Wherefore God also exalted him exceedingly — Alf

. . . uplifted him far on high — Rhm

And that is why God raised him to the
very highest place — TCNT

**and given him a name which is above
every name:**

and bestowed on him . . . — Alf

and gave him the Name which stands
above all other names — TCNT

and has conferred on Him the Name
which is supreme above every other
name — Wey

10. **That at the name of Jesus every knee
should bow,**

so that in adoration of the Name of
Jesus every knee should bend —
TCNT

. . . everyone should kneel — Gspd

of things in heaven, and things in earth,

Of beings . . . — Rhm

of all who dwell in heaven, in earth —
Con

in heaven and on earth — Gspd

and things under the earth;

. . . underground — Rhm

or under the earth — Con

and of those in the underworld — Wey

and in the underworld — Gspd

11. **And that every tongue should confess**

. . . might openly confess — Rhm

. . . may give witness — Bas

**that Jesus Christ is Lord, to the glory
of God the Father.**

12. **Wherefore, my beloved,**

Therefore, my dearly-loved friends —
Wey

as ye have always obeyed,

. . . were always obedient — Alf

. . . always followed up my suggestions
— Ber

. . . always so careful to follow my instructions — Tay

**not as in my presence only, but now
much more in my absence,**

not simply as though I were with you,
but all the more because I am away
— Gspd

**work out your own salvation with fear
and trembling.**

. . . reverence and trepidation — Ber

. . . reverence and self-distrust — Mon

. . . with anxious care — TCNT

carry out with fear and trembling your
own salvation — Alf

with reverence and awe make every effort to insure your salvation —
Gspd

so now with reverence and awe keep
on working clear down to the finishing point of your salvation — Wms

labour earnestly, I say, to make sure
of your own salvation — Wey

13. For it is God which worketh in you both to will and to do of his good pleasure.

For it is God who energiseth within you both the desiring and the energising — Rhm

For it is God Himself whose power creates within you both the desire and the power to execute His gracious will — Wey

who makes you willing and gives you the energy to do what He wants — Beck

for it is God who works in you both will and deed — Con

Remember it is God who, in his kindness, is at work within you, enabling you both to will and to work — TCNT

For it is God who in his good-will is at work in your hearts, inspiring your will and your action — Gspd

14. Do all things without murmurings and disputings:

. . . murmurings and questionings — ASV

. . . complaining or arguing — Beck

. . . grumbling and faultfinding — Amp

In all that you do, avoid discontent and dissension — TCNT

15. That ye may be blameless and harmless,

. . . faultless and inviolate — Rhm

. . . guileless — Con

. . . innocent — Beck

the sons of God, without rebuke,

children of God without blemish — ASV

children of God blameless — Rhm

— irreproachable children of God — Wey

— faultless children of God — TCNT

in the midst of a crooked and perverse nation,

in the midst of an evil-disposed and perverse generation — TCNT

in a twisted and foolish generation — Bas

living in a warped and diseased world — Phi

among whom ye shine as lights in the world;

. . . ye are seen as lights . . . — ASV

. . . ye appear as luminaries . . . — Rhm

. . . ye shine like stars . . . — Con

. . . you are seen as heavenly lights . . . — Wey

in which you are seen shining like stars in a dark world — TCNT

16. Holding forth the word of life;

offering to men the Message of Life — TCNT

holding out to them the word of Life — Wey

For you are to them the light of life — Lam

holding fast the word of life — RSV

as you cling to the Word of Life — Beck

that I may rejoice in the day of Christ,

that I may have whereof to glory . . . — ASV

that you may give me ground of boasting . . . — Con

It will then be my glory . . . — Wey

so that I can be proud of you . . . — Mof

Then I can boast on the day of Christ — Beck

that I have not run in vain, neither laboured in vain.

that I did not run my course for nothing, or toil for nothing — TCNT

because neither my career nor my labor has been a failure — Wms

17. Yea, and if I be offered upon the sacrifice and service of your faith,

Yea, if I am being poured out . . . — Alf

Nay! If I am even to be poured out as a drink-offering upon the sacrifice and public ministry of your faith — Rhm

But though my blood be poured forth upon the ministration of the sacrifice of your faith — Con

Nay, even if my life is being poured as a libation upon the sacrificial offering of your faith — Wey

Even if my life is to be poured out as a libation as you offer your faith in a service of sacrifice to God — Gspd

In fact, even if my lifeblood must be poured out for a sacrifice to nurture your faith — Ber

And yet, even if, when your faith is offered as a sacrifice to God, my lifeblood must be poured out in addition — TCNT

I joy, and rejoice with you all.

still I shall rejoice and share the joy of you all — TCNT

I joy, and congratulate you all — Alf

I rejoice for myself, and rejoice with you all — Con

18. For the same cause also do ye joy, and rejoice with me.

And in like manner do ye also joy, and congratulate me — Alf

and do you also rejoice and share my joy — TCNT

And I bid you also share my gladness, and congratulate me — Wey

Likewise you also should be glad and rejoice with me — RSV

. . . and congratulate me on [my share in] it — Amp

19. But I trust in the Lord Jesus

But I hope . . . — ASV

to send Timotheus shortly unto you,

. . . Timothy . . . — ASV

that I also may be of good comfort,

. . . good courage — Alf

. . . cheered — Wey

that I also may be at ease — Lam

when I know your state.

when I have ascertained the things that concern you — Rhm

by getting good news of you — Wey

20. For I have no man likeminded,

. . . of equal soul — Rhm

. . . as interested as I am — Lam

For I have no one else as near of my own attitude — Ber

For I have no one else of kindred spirit — NASB

who will naturally care for your state.

who will care truly . . . — ASV

who will naturally be careful about . . . — Alf

who would take a genuine interest in your welfare — TCNT

21. For all seek their own,

They are all pursuing their own aims — TCNT

Everybody is selfish — Mof

Everyone else seems to be worrying about his own plans — Tay

not the things which are Jesus Christ's.

. . . which are of Christ Jesus — Alf

22. But ye know the proof of him,

. . . the trials which have proved his worth — Con

. . . what Timothy has proved himself to be — TCNT

. . . Timothy's approved worth — Wey

. . . his proved character — ABUV

. . . his tested character — Wms

But his quality is clear to you — Bas

that, as a son with the father,

that, as a child serveth a father — ASV

how like a son in fellowship with his father — Wms

he hath served with me in the gospel.

. . . in the furtherance of the gospel — ASV

hath he done service for the glad message — Rhm

he hath shared my servitude, to proclaim the Glad-tidings — Con

he has toiled with me like a slave in preaching the good news — Wms

23. Him therefore I hope to send presently,

. . . without delay — Con

. . . immediately — ABUV

so soon as I shall see how it will go with me.

As soon as I can look off from the things that concern myself — Rhm

just as soon as I can see how my case is going to turn out — Gspd

when I have had time to see how I stand — Knox

Whenever I am through attending to these personal matters of mine — Ber

24. But I trust in the Lord

I am assured, however . . . — Rhm

Really, I am trusting that by the help of the Lord — Wms

that I also myself shall come shortly.

that I shall myself also come to you before long — Wey

I soon shall come myself — Wms

25. Yet I supposed it necessary to send to you Epaphroditus,

Yet I deem it important to send Epaphroditus to you now — Wey

my brother, and companion in labour, and fellowsoldier,

. . . and fellow-worker and fellow-soldier — ASV

he is my brother and comrade both in labour and in arms — Wey

but your messenger, and he that ministered to my wants.

but your apostle, and minister to my need — Alf

and he was also your messenger to help me in my need — TCNT

26. For he longed after you all, and was full of heaviness, because that ye had heard that he had been sick.

for he has been homesick for you all, and distressed at your having heard of his illness — Mon

. . . and was sore troubled — ASV

27. For indeed he was sick nigh unto death:

And, indeed, he had a sickness which brought him almost to death — Con

And I can assure you that his illness very nearly proved fatal — TCNT

but God had mercy on him;

but God had compassion on, him — Con

But God had pity on him — TCNT

and not on him only, but on me also, lest I should have sorrow upon sorrow.

that I might not have . . . — Alf

. . . the sorrow of losing him to add to my sufferings — Phi

28. I sent him therefore the more carefully,

. . . the more diligently — ASV

. . . the more anxiously — Alf

The more promptly therefore have I sent him — Rhm

I am therefore all the more eager to send him — Wey

that, when ye see him again, ye may rejoice,

that you may have the joy of seeing him again — Con

in the hope that when you see him

again you may be glad — Wey

and that I may be the less sorrowful.

and my own sorrow be lightened — TCNT

and I may feel more relieved — Gspd

. . . may be relieved from anxiety — Lam

29. Receive him therefore in the Lord with all gladness;

. . . with heartfelt Christian joy—Wey

So give him a hearty Christian welcome — Wms

and hold such in reputation:

and hold such men in honour — Alf

and hold in honor men like him—Wms

30. Because for the work of Christ he was nigh unto death,

For it was owing to his devotion to the Master's work that he was at the point of death — TCNT

not regarding his life,

hazarding his life — ASV

having risked his own life — TCNT

hazarding his very life — Mon

to supply your lack of service toward me.

that he might supply all which you could not do, in ministering to me — Con

in endeavoring to make good any deficiency that there might be in your service to me — Wey

to make up your lack of opportunity to minister to me — Wms

to do for me in person what distance prevented you all from doing — Phi

CHAPTER 3

1. Finally, my brethren,

For the rest, my brethren — Rhm

In conclusion, my Brothers — TCNT

One more thing . . . — Nor

rejoice in the Lord.

be joyful . . . — Wey

continue to be glad that you are in union with the Lord — Wms

delight yourselves in the Lord — Phi

All joy be yours in your union with the Lord — TCNT

To write the same things to you, to me indeed is not grievous,

. . . irksome — ASV

To repeat the same warnings is not wearisome to me — Con

It doesn't bore me to repeat a piece of

advice like this — Phi

I never get tired of telling you this — Tay

but for you it is safe.

and it is safe for you — Con

while so far as you are concerned it is a safe precaution — Wey

and for you it is reassuring — Ber

and it is good for you to hear it again and again — Tay

2. Beware of dogs,

Beware of backbiters — Lam

Look out for those dogs [the Judaizers] — Amp

beware of evil workers,

. . . mischievous workers — Rhm

. . . the Evil Workmen — Con

beware of the concision.

... mutilation — Rhm

... the men who mutilate themselves! — TCNT

... the incision-party! — Mof

... the false circumcision — NASB

... their disfigurement — Knox

Look out for these who demand circumcision — Nor

look out for men who circumcise only their bodies — Beck

3. For we are the circumcision,

For it is we who are the circumcised — TCNT

We are, remember, truly circumcised — Phi

which worship God in the spirit,

who worship by the Spirit of God — ASV

Who in the Spirit of God are doing divine service — Rhm

— we whose worship is prompted by the Spirit of God — TCNT

when we worship God by the Spirit — Phi

and rejoice in Christ Jesus,

who exult in Christ Jesus — TCNT

who take pride in Christ Jesus only — Wms

priding ourselves only on Christ Jesus — Gspd

and have no confidence in the flesh.

and trust not in the flesh — Alf

and why do not rely upon external privileges — TCNT

... in outward ceremonies — Wey

and not relying on physical advantages — Gspd

4. Though I might also have confidence in the flesh.

I have, however, some basis for confidence in the flesh — Ber

though I, if any man, have cause to rely even upon them — TCNT

If any other man thinketh that he hath whereof he might trust in the flesh, I more:

If any other man thinks that he has ground of confidence in the flesh, I have more — Con

If any one thinks he can rely upon external privileges, far more can I! — TCNT

However, if a man thinks his hope is on things of the flesh, I have more hope than he has — Lam

Yet if anyone ever had reason to hope that he could save himself, it would be I — Tay

5. Circumcised the eighth day,

I was circumcised when eight days old — TCNT

... on the eighth day after birth — Mof

of the stock of Israel,

I am an Israelite by race — TCNT

a member of the race of Israel — Wey

of the tribe of Benjamin,

an Hebrew of the Hebrews;

I am a Hebrew, and the child of Hebrews — TCNT

I was the Hebrew son of Hebrew parents — Mof

I was in fact a full-blooded Jew — Phi

as touching the law, a Pharisee;

Measured by the standard set by the law, I was a Pharisee — Wms

6. Concerning zeal, persecuting the church;

... the assembly — Rhm

in point of ardour a persecutor of the church — Mof

in bitter hate I was cruel to the church — Bas

touching the righteousness which is in the law, blameless.

as to righteousness of the Law, unblameable — Con

immaculate by the standard of legal righteousness — Mof

as to the righteousness which comes through Law, blameless — Wey

and by the Law's standard of uprightness, no fault could be found in me — Gspd

I kept all the righteousness of the law to the last detail — Bas

in legal rectitude, faultless — NEB

according to the law so righteous nobody could find any fault in me — Beck

7. But what things were gain to me,

But what was once gain to me — Con

But all the things which I once held to be gains — TCNT

But all such assets — NEB

those I counted loss for Christ.

those for Christ's sake have I counted loss — Alf

I have now, for Christ's sake, come to count as loss — TCNT

I have written off because of Christ — NEB

8. Yea doubtless, and I count all things but loss

... to be loss — ASV

Nay, I even reckon all things as pure loss — Wey

More than that, I count everything as loss — TCNT

for the excellency of the knowledge of Christ Jesus my Lord:

for the sake of the exceeding value of the knowledge of Christ Jesus my Lord — TCNT

because of the priceless privilege of knowing ... — Wey

because of the surpassing worth of knowing ... — RSV

in view of the surpassing value of knowing ... — NASB

for whom I have suffered the loss of all things,

I have put aside all else — Tay

And for his sake I have lost everything — TCNT

and do count them but dung,

and count it as refuse — TCNT

and think it rubbish — Gspd

counting it worth less than nothing — Tay

that I may win Christ.

if I may but gain Christ — TCNT

in order that I can have Christ — Tay

9. And be found in him,

and be found at death in him — Mof

and be known to be united with him — Gspd

and be actually in union with Him — Wms

For now my place is in him — Phi

not having mine own righteousness, which is of the law,

possessing no legal righteousness of my own — Mof

not having a supposed right standing which depends on my doing what the law commands — Wms

not having a righteousness of my own derived from the Law — NASB

no longer counting on being saved by being good enough or by obeying God's laws — Tay

but that which is through the faith of Christ,

but that which arises from faith in Christ — Wey

but the righteousness which comes through faith in Christ — TCNT

the righteousness which is of God by faith:

— the righteousness which is derived from God and is founded on faith — TCNT

... which comes from God, founded upon faith — Mon

the real right standing with God which originates from Him and rests on faith — Wms

10. That I may know him,

To get to know him — Rhm

[For my determined purpose is] that I may know Him — Amp

I long to know Christ — Wey

That I may have knowledge of him — Bas

and the power of his resurrection,

and of the power by which he came again from the dead — Bas

and the power which is in His resurrection — Wey

and experience the power of His resurrection — Nor

... the power outflowing from His resurrection — Amp

that is, the power of His resurrection — Wms

and the fellowship of his sufferings,

and all that it means to share his sufferings — TCNT

and to share in His sufferings — Wey

and so to share with Him in His sufferings — Wms

being made conformable unto his death;

becoming conformed unto his death — ASV

... to the likeness of his death — Alf

sharing the likeness of His death — Con

and die even as He died — Wey

with my nature transformed to die as he died — Mof

as to be continuously transformed by His death — Wms

11. If by any means I might attain

so that I may perhaps attain as he did — Phi

if somehow I will get to be one of those
— Beck

in the hope that I may attain — Wey

in the hope of attaining, in some measure — Wms

unto the resurrection of the dead.

to the earlier resurrection which is from among the dead — Rhm

the resurrection that lifts me out from among the dead — Wms

the reward of life from the dead — Bas

who will rise from the dead — Beck

to the [spiritual and moral] resurrection [that lifts me] out from among the dead [even while in the body]—Amp

12. Not as though I had already attained,

Not that I have already received — Rhm

Not that I have already won — Con

Not that I have already laid hold of it — TCNT

either were already perfect:

I have not yet reached perfection — NEB

or that I am already made perfect — TCNT

or am already at the goal — Beck

but I follow after, if that I may apprehend that for which also I am apprehended of Christ Jesus.

but I press on, if so be that I may lay hold on that for which also I was laid hold on by Christ Jesus — ASV

but I press forward to appropriate it, because I have been appropriated myself by Christ Jesus — Mof

but I am pressing on to see if I can capture it, because I have been captured by Jesus Christ — Gspd

I only press on, in hope of winning the mastery as Christ Jesus has won the mastery over me — Knox

but I press onward, if indeed I might lay hold on that for which Christ also laid hold on me — Con

13. Brethren, I count not myself to have apprehended:

Brothers, I do not consider that I have captured it yet — Gspd

. . . I am still not all I should be — Tay

. . . I don't think I have it in my hands — Beck

but this one thing I do,

but here is my one aspiration — Wms

But I do concentrate on this — Phi

forgetting those things which are behind,

— forgetting what lies behind — TCNT

and reaching forth unto those things which are before,

and stretching forward to the things which are before — ASV

and straining every nerve for that which lies in front — TCNT

14. I press toward the mark

. . . the goal — ASV

With the goal in view I press on — Rhm

I push on to secure — Wey

I strain to reach the end of the race — Tay

for the prize of the high calling of God in Christ Jesus.

. . . the upward calling . . . — Rhm

for the prize of God's heavenly calling in Christ Jesus — Con

the prize of God's heavenward call . . . — Wey

for the prize to which God through Christ Jesus calls us upward — Gspd

and receive the prize for which God is calling us up to heaven because of what Christ Jesus did for us — Tay

eager for the prize, God's heavenly summons in Christ Jesus — Knox

15. Let us therefore, as many as be perfect, be thus minded:

As many therefore as are full-grown Let this be our resolve — Rhm

Let us all, then, who are ripe in understanding, be thus minded — Con

Let all of us, then, whose faith is mature, think thus — TCNT

. . . who are mature believers cherish these thoughts — Wey

I hope all of you who are mature Christians will see eye-to-eye with me on these things — Tay

All of us who are spiritually adult should set ourselves this sort of ambition — Phi

Therefore let those of you who are perfect think these things over — Lam

and if in any thing ye be otherwise minded,

and if you disagree on some points — Tay

and if you reason in any other way — Lam

God shall reveal even this unto you.

God will make this clear to you — Gspd

you will find that this is the attitude which God is leading you to adopt — Phi

I believe that God will make it plain to you — Tay

16. Nevertheless, whereto we have already attained, let us walk by the same rule, let us mind the same thing.

Only, we must let our steps be guided by such truth as we have attained — Mof

However, we must continue to live up to that degree of success that we have already reached — Wms

But whatever be the point that we have already reached, let us persevere in the same course — Wey

Only let us hold true to what we have already attained and walk and order our lives by that — Amp

17. Brethren, be followers together of me,

Brethren, be ye imitators together of me — ASV

. . . unite in following my example — TCNT

Copy me, brothers, one and all of you — Mof

and mark them which walk so as ye have us for an ensample.

And keep an eye on them who thus are walking, — Even as ye have us for an ensample — Rhm

and mark those who walk according to my example — Con

and notice those who live by the example you get from me — Mof

and keep your eyes on those who practice living by the pattern we have set for you — Wms

. . . as you have it exemplified in us — Ber

18. (For many walk, of whom I have told you often, and now tell you even weeping, that they are the enemies of the cross of Christ:

For there are many — as I used often to tell you, and am now telling you even with tears — who live and walk as the enemies of the cross of Christ — Mon

. . . who are living in enmity to the cross of Christ — TCNT

. . . who practice living as the enemies of . . . — Wms

. . . who behave as though they hated the cross of Christ — Nor

19. Whose end is destruction, whose God is their belly,

whose end is perdition . . . — ASV

These men are heading for utter destruction . . . — Phi

The end of such men is Ruin; for their appetites are their God — TCNT

Their doom is destruction, their stomach is their god — Wms

Their future is eternal loss for their god is good food — Tay

and whose glory is in their shame,

They are proud of what they should be ashamed of — Tay

who mind earthly things.)

Who upon earthly things are resolved — Rhm

whose mind is set on earth things — Con

they are absorbed in earthly matters — Gspd

and their minds are feeding on earthly things — Wms

and this world is the limit of their horizon — Phi

20. For our conversation is in heaven;

For our citizenship . . . — ASV

For our country is in the heavens — Alf

For my life abides in heaven — Con

But the State of which we are citizens is in Heaven — TCNT

We, however, are free citizens of Heaven — Wey

But we are a colony of heaven — Mof

But the commonwealth to which we belong is in heaven — Gspd

But we are citizens of Heaven — Phi

from whence also we look for the Saviour, the Lord Jesus Christ:

whence also we wait for a Saviour . . . — ASV

from which also we expect the Lord Jesus Christ as Deliverer — Ber

our outlook goes beyond this world to the hopeful expectation of the savior who will come from Heaven, the Lord Jesus Christ — Phi

21. Who shall change our vile body,

who shall fashion anew the body of our humiliation — ASV

Who will transfigure our humbled body
— Rhm

He will make our poor bodies over —
Gspd

When He comes back He will take
these dying bodies of ours — Tay

**that it may be fashioned like unto his
glorious body,**

that it may be conformed to the body
of his glory — ASV

and give it a form like that of his own
resplendent body — NEB

and change them into glorious bodies
like His own — Tay

**according to the working whereby he
is able even to subdue all things unto
himself.**

according to the working of his power
. . . — Alf

in the exercise of the power which He
has even to subject all things to Himself — Wey

by the exertion of the power that He
has . . . — NASB

using the same mighty power that He
will use to conquer all else everywhere — Tay

CHAPTER 4

1. **Therefore, my brethren dearly beloved
and longed for,**

So then, my dear Brothers, whom I am
longing to see — TCNT

. . . for whom I cherish love and longing — Mof

my joy and crown,

my delight and prize — Knox

my delight and my crown (wreath of
victory) — Amp

**so stand fast in the Lord, my dearly
beloved.**

this is how you are to stand firm in the
Lord, O my beloved — Mof

by the help of the Lord keep on standing firm, dearly loved friends —
Wms

in this way stand firm in the Lord, dear
friends — Ber

My beloved friends, stay true to the
Lord — Tay

2. **I beseech Euodias, and beseech Syn-
tyche,**

I exhort Euodia, and I exhort Syn-
tyche — ASV

I appeal to . . . — Ber

**that they be of the same mind in the
Lord.**

On the same thing to be resolved in the
Lord — Rhm

to live in harmony as fellow-Christians
— TCNT

to be of one mind, as sisters in Christ
— Wey

to agree in the Lord — Mof

to make up your differences as Christians should — Phi

3. **And I intreat thee also, true yokefel-
low,**

And I solemnly beg you, my true comrade — Wms

And I make request to you, true helper
in my work — Bas

Yes, and I ask thee, who sharest the
yoke so loyally — Knox,

And I ask you, my true teammate —
Tay

**help those women which laboured with
me in the gospel,**

to help them [to be reconciled]; for
they strove earnestly in the work of
the Glad-tidings with me — Con

to help them, remembering that they
toiled by my side in spreading the
Good News — TCNT

to help these women, for they shared
my toil in connexion with the gospel
— Wey

keep on co-operating with those two
women, because they shared with me
the struggle in spreading the good
news — Wms

**with Clement also, and with other my
fellowlabourers, whose names are in
the book of life.**

and so, too, did Clement and my other
fellow-workers, whose names are in
the Book of Life — TCNT

4. **Rejoice in the Lord alway:**

. . . at all times — Con

Always be glad in the Lord — Wey

All joy be yours at all times in your
union with the Lord — TCNT

By the help of the Lord always keep up
the glad spirit — Wms

Delight yourselves in the Lord — Phi
Be happy in the Lord always — Beck
and again I say, Rejoice.
Again I say, goodbye — Gspd

5. Let your moderation be known unto all men.
Let your forbearance . . . — ASV
Let your considerateness . . . — Rhm
Let your humility . . . — Lam
Let your forbearing spirit be plain to every one — TCNT
Let your reasonableness be recognized by every one — Mon
Give proof to all of your courtesy — Knox
Have a reputation for gentleness — Phi
Let your magnanimity be manifest to all — NEB
The Lord is at hand.
. . . is near — Rhm
. . . is coming soon — Gspd
never forget the nearness of our Lord — Phi

6. Be careful for nothing;
In nothing be anxious — ASV
Let no care trouble you — Con
Do not worry about anything — Mon
Entertain no worry — Ber
but in every thing by prayer and supplication with thanksgiving let your requests be made known unto God.
but under all circumstances, by prayer and entreaty joined with thanksgiving, make your needs known to God — TCNT
but by prayer and earnest pleading together with thanksgiving let your requests be unreservedly made known before God — Wey
tell God every detail of your needs in earnest and thankful prayer — Phi

7. And the peace of God,
which passeth all understanding,
which transcends all our powers of thought — Wey
that surpasses all our dreams — Mof
which is deeper than all knowledge — Bas
which surpasses all comprehension — NASB
shall keep your hearts and minds through Christ Jesus.
shall guard your hearts and your thoughts in Christ Jesus — ASV

will . . . be a garrison to guard your hearts and minds in Christ Jesus — Wey
through your union with Christ Jesus . . . will guard your minds and thoughts — Gspd
shall garrison and mount guard over . . . — Amp

8. Finally, brethren,
In conclusion, Brothers — TCNT
Here is a last piece of advice — Phi
whatsoever things are true,
all that rings true — Knox
whatsoever things are honest,
. . . honorable — ASV
. . . dignified — Rhm
whatever is worthy of reverence—Mon
whatsoever things are just, whatsoever things are pure,
what is right, what is pure — Gspd
whatsoever things are lovely,
. . . endearing — Con
. . . amiable — Gspd
. . . lovable — TCNT
whatsoever things are of good report;
whatever is high-toned — Mof
whatever is kindly spoken — Ber
whatever is gracious — RSV
. . . kindly — Gspd
. . . the fine, good things in others — Tay
if there be any virtue, and if there be any praise,
— if there is any virtue or anything deemed worthy of praise — Wey
whatever is lofty and whatever is praiseworthy — Ber
if there is any excellence . . . — RSV
if virtue and honour have any meaning — TCNT
think on these things.
The same be taking into account — Rhm
— be such your treasures — Con
there let your thoughts dwell — TCNT
cherish the thought of these things — Wey
let this be the argument of your thoughts — Knox

9. Those things, which ye have both learned, and received, and heard, and seen in me, do:
Let all that you learnt and received and heard and saw in me fashion your conduct — Wey

That which you were taught and learned, and which you heard and saw in me, — be that your practice — Con

Model your conduct on what you have learned from me, on what I have told you and shown you — Phi

All that you learnt and received and heard and saw in me put into practice continually — TCNT

and the God of peace shall be with you.

and then God, the giver of peace, will be with you — TCNT

10. But I rejoiced in the Lord greatly,

I was very glad, as a Christian — Gspd

How grateful I am and how I praise the Lord — Tay

that now at the last your care of me hath flourished again;

that now at length ye have revived your thought for me — ASV

. . . ye have revived again in your care for me — Alf

when I found that now, after so long a time, your care for me has borne fruit again — Con

that now once more your care for me blossomed afresh — Mon

to have your interest in my welfare revived again after so long — Wms

because of late your thoughtfulness toward me came to life again — Ber

wherein ye were also careful, but ye lacked opportunity.

wherein ye did indeed take thought . . . — ASV

though your care indeed never failed . . . — Con

The interest indeed you had, but not the opportunity — TCNT

for what you lacked was never the care but the chance of showing it — Mof

for you have always been interested but you have had no opportunity to show it — Gspd

11. Not that I speak in respect of want:

I do not refer to this through fear of privation — Wey

Not that I have anything to complain of — Gspd

Do not think that I am saying this under pressure of want — TCNT

for I have learned, in whatsoever state I am, therewith to be content.

. . . in whatsoever circumstances I am to be independent — Rhm

for I indeed have learned, whatever be my outward experiences, to be content — Wey

for I have learned how to be contented with the condition I am in — Gspd

for I am able, wherever I am, to be dependent on myself — Bas

for I have learned to make ends meet in whatever situation I am — Ber

For I, however I am placed, have learnt to be independent of circumstances — TCNT

12. I know both how to be abased,

I know also how to be in low estate — Alf

I know how to face humble circumstances — TCNT

I know how to live when things are difficult — Phi

I know how to get along with humble means — NASB

I can bear either abasement — Con

and I know how to abound:

or abundance — Con

And I know what it is to have more than enough — Rhm

and I know how to face prosperity — TCNT

and how to live amid abundance — Wey

. . . how to enjoy plenty — Gspd

every where and in all things I am instructed both to be full and to be hungry,

in everything and in all things have I learned the secret both to be filled and to be hungry — ASV

. . . Both to be well fed, And to be hungering — Rhm

In all things, and amongst all men, I have been taught the secret, to be full or to be hungry — Con

I have learned the secret, in all circumstances, of either getting a full meal or of going hungry — Wms

Into all and every human experience I have been initiated — into plenty and hunger — TCNT

In general and in particular I have learned the secret of facing either plenty or poverty — Phi

I have been very thoroughly initiated into the human lot with all its ups and downs — NEB

both to abound and to suffer need.
into prosperity and want — TCNT

13. **I can do all things through Christ which strengtheneth me.**

I have strength for all things in him which giveth me power — Alf

Nothing is beyond my power in the strength of him who makes me strong! — TCNT

I am ready for anything through the strength of the one who lives within me — Phi

14. **Notwithstanding ye have well done,**

Yet I thank you — Wey

But it was very kind of you — Gspd

Still, I think that you did the right thing — Nor

Yet you acted nobly — TCNT

that ye did communicate with my affliction.

in contributing to the help of my affliction — Con

in sharing my troubles — TCNT

for taking your share in my troubles — Wey

15. **Now ye Philippians know also, that in the beginning of the gospel,**

... in the early days of the Good News — TCNT

... at the first preaching of the gospel — Wey

... in the early days of my mission — NEB

... in the beginning of my Gospel ministry — Nor

when I departed from Macedonia,

— at the time when I had just left Macedonia — TCNT

no church communicated with me as concerning giving and receiving, but ye only.

no church had fellowship with me in the matter of giving and receiving but ye only — ASV

no Church, with the one exception of yourselves, had anything to do with me as far as giving and receiving are concerned — TCNT

no church but yours went into partnership and opened an account with me — Gspd

no church but yours went into partnership with me to open an account of credit and debits — Wms

16. **For even in Thessalonica ye sent once and again unto my necessity.**

... you sent once and again to relieve my need — Con

... you sent more than once to relieve my wants — TCNT

17. **Not because I desire a gift:**

It is not money I am anxious for — Mof

but I desire fruit that may abound to your account.

but I seek the fruit which accrues therefrom to your account — Con

but I am anxious to see the abundant return that will be placed to your account — TCNT

what I am anxious for is the interest that accumulates in this way to your divine credit! — Mof

I set store by the rich increase that stands to your credit — Knox

but I seek for the profit which increases to your account — NASB

but I seek and am eager for the fruit which increases to your credit — the harvest of blessing that is accumulating to your account — Amp

18. **But I have all, and abound:**

... and more than enough — Alf

But I have all which I require, and more than I require — Con

I have enough of everything, and to spare — TCNT

You have paid me in full, and more too — Gspd

I am full,

My wants are fully satisfied — TCNT

I am fully supplied — Con

having received of Epaphroditus the things which were sent from you,

now that I have received from Epaphroditus the gifts which you sent me — TCNT

an odour of a sweet smell, a sacrifice acceptable, well pleasing to God.

they are like the sweet fragrance of a sacrifice which is acceptable and pleasing to God — TCNT

It is like fragrant incense, just such a sacrifice as God welcomes and approves — Gspd

your generosity is like a lovely fragrance, a sacrifice that pleases the very
heart of God — Phi

19. **But my God shall supply all your need**
   . . . every need of yours — ASV
   And it is He who will supply all your
   needs — Tay
   **according to his riches in glory by
   Christ Jesus.**
   out of the greatness of his wealth . . .
   — TCNT
   in the fulness of His glorious riches in
   Christ Jesus — Con
   from his glorious resources in Christ
   Jesus — Phi
   from His riches in glory, because of
   what Christ Jesus has done for you
   — Tay

20. **Now unto God and our Father be
   glory for ever and ever. Amen.**
   . . . unto the ages of ages. Amen — Con

21. **Salute every saint in Christ Jesus.**
   Give my greeting to every one of the
   People of Christ Jesus — TCNT

Remember me to all my fellow-Chris-
tians — Gspd
Greetings to every true Christian —
Phi
Say Hello for me to all the Christians
there — Tay
Greet everyone who is holy . . . —
Beck
**The brethren which are with me greet
you.**
The brethren (my associates) . . . —
Amp
. . . wish to be remembered to you —
Gspd

22. **All the saints salute you,**
   All Christ's people here . . . — TCNT
   **chiefly they that are of Caesar's house-
   hold.**
   especially the Imperial slaves — Mof
   especially those who belong to the
   emperor's household — Gspd

23. **The grace of our Lord Jesus Christ be
   with you all. Amen.**
   . . . your spirit — Alf
   . . . your spirits — Con

THE
EPISTLE OF PAUL TO THE COLOSSIANS

CHAPTER 1

1. Paul, an apostle of Jesus Christ by the will of God,

... an apostle of Christ Jesus through the will of God — ASV

... by God's purpose — Knox

... commissioned by the will of God — NEB

... chosen by God — Tay

and Timotheus our brother,

And Timothy my brother — Rhm

and our colleague Timothy — NEB

and our fellow worker Timothy—Beck

2. To the saints and faithful brethren in Christ which are at Colosse:

Unto the holy and faithful brethren in Christ ... — Rhm

... the devoted and steadfast Christian brothers ... — Gspd

to the consecrated and faithful brothers at Colossae who are in union with Christ — Wms

To Christ's People at Colossae — the Brothers who are faithful to him — TCNT

Grace be unto you, and peace, from God our Father and the Lord Jesus Christ.

... from God our Father — ASV

Favour unto you and peace from our God and Father — Rhm

spiritual blessing and peace to you ... — Wms

3. We give thanks to God and the Father of our Lord Jesus Christ,

I give continual thanks to God the Father of ... — Con

we never fail to thank God ... — TCNT

praying always for you,

Whenever we pray ... — TCNT

constantly praying ... — Wey

Every time we pray ... — Wms

4. Since we heard of your faith in Christ Jesus,

having heard ... — ASV

now that we have heard ... — TCNT

because we have heard ... — Wey

for what we have heard ... — Gspd

and of the love which ye have to all the saints,

... the love which you cherish ... — Wey

... for all his People — TCNT

5. For the hope which is laid up for you in heaven,

because of the hope ... — ASV

... treasured up ... — Wey

... which awaits its fulfilment in Heaven — TCNT

Both spring from the hope stored up for you in heaven — NEB

whereof ye heard before in the word of the truth of the gospel;

whereof you heard the promise in the truthful Word of the glad-tidings — Con

You heard of this hope originally in ... — Mof

6. Which is come unto you, as it is in all the world; and bringeth forth fruit, as it doth also in you,

which is come unto you; even as it is also in all the world bearing fruit and increasing, as it doth in you also — ASV

— bearing fruit and growing, as it does, through all the world, just as it did among you — TCNT

For it has reached you, and remains with you, just as it has also spread through the whole world yielding fruit there and increasing — Wey

which is come to you, as it is through all the world; and everywhere it bears fruit and grows, as it does also among you — Con

And just as it is spreading through the whole world, bearing fruit and increasing, so also is it among you — Mon

since the day ye heard of it, and knew the grace of God in truth:

From the day when ye heard and came personally to know the favour of God in truth — Rhm

from the very day that you heard of God's loving-kindness, and understood what that loving-kindness really is — TCNT

... and recognized it for what in truth it is — NEB

7. As ye also learned of Epaphras our dear fellowservant,

And thus you were taught by Epaphras my fellow-bondsman — Con

... my dear fellow-slave — Gspd

... who is in the same service as we are — Phi

... our beloved co-worker — Nor

who is for you a faithful minister of Christ;

who is a faithful minister of Christ on our behalf — ASV

who, as a minister of Christ, faithfully represents us — TCNT

a minister of Christ who is faithful to your interests — Mof

who is loyally serving Christ in our place — Beck

8. Who also declared unto us your love in the Spirit.

Who also hath made evident unto us your love in spirit — Rhm

And it is he who declared to me your love for me in the Spirit — Con

and who tells us of the love with which the Spirit has inspired you — TCNT

... has awakened in you — Gspd

9. For this cause we also, since the day we heard it, do not cease to pray for you,

That is why ... — Gspd

... from the day we heard of you ... — Rhm

and to desire that ye might be filled with the knowledge of his will

... the personal knowledge of his will — Rhm

... clear knowledge of what his will is — Gspd

and to ask of God that you may fully attain to the knowledge of His will — Con

... that you may possess that deeper knowledge ... — TCNT

in all wisdom and spiritual understanding;

In all spiritual wisdom and discernment — Rhm

which comes through all true spiritual wisdom and insight — TCNT

by being given spiritual insight and understanding — Phi

and to make you wise about spiritual things — Tay

10. That ye might walk worthy of the Lord unto all pleasing,

... to His full satisfaction — Wms

... waiting continually on his pleasure — Knox

so that you may lead a life that is worthy of the Lord and give him entire satisfaction — Mof

... bring joy to his heart — Phi

Then you will live lives worthy of the Master, and so please God in every way — TCNT

being fruitful in every good work,

bearing fruit ... — ASV

Your lives will be fruitful in every kind of good action — TCNT

... in active goodness of every kind — NEB

by perennially bearing fruit in every good enterprise — Wms

and increasing in the knowledge of God;

and grow continually in ... — Con

all the time learning to know God better and better — Tay

and your character will grow through a fuller knowledge of God — TCNT

11. Strengthened with all might, according to his glorious power,

strengthened with all power according to the might of his glory — ASV

With all power being empowered According to the grasp of his glory — Rhm

You will be made strong at all points with a strength worthy of the power manifested in his Glory — TCNT

Since his power is so glorious, may you be strengthened with strength of every kind — Wey

May his glorious might nerve you with full power — Mof

unto all patience and longsuffering with joyfulness;

unto all endurance and long-suffering with joy — Rhm

— strong to endure with patience, and even with gladness, whatever may befall you — TCNT

and be prepared for cheerfully enduring all things with patience and long-suffering — Wey

for the cheerful exercise of endurance and forbearance — Gspd

for the cheerful exercise of unlimited patience and perseverance — Ber so that you will find yourselves able to pass through an experience and endure it with joy — Phi

for the attaining of all steadfastness and patience, joyously[1] — NASB

12. Giving thanks unto the Father, which hath made us meet

. . . made you sufficient — Rhm

. . . fitted us — Con

. . . qualified us — Mof

. . . entitled you — Gspd

to be partakers of the inheritance of the saints in light:

for the portion of . . . — Alf

for your share in . . . — Rhm

. . . the lot which awaits Christ's People in the realms of Light — TCNT

to share the light which saints inherit — Knox

to share the lot of those who are living in the light — Phi

13. Who hath delivered us from the power of darkness,

Who hath rescued us out of the authority of the darkness — Rhm

. . . from the dominion of . . . — Con

. . . from the tyranny of . . . — TCNT

. . . the control of . . . — Ber

. . . the darkness and gloom of Satan's kingdom — Tay

and hath translated us into the kingdom of his dear Son:

and has removed us into . . . — TCNT

and reestablished us in . . . — Phi

. . . the kingdom of the Son of his love — ASV

and transplanted us into the kingdom of his beloved Son — Con

14. In whom we have redemption through his blood,

. . . our redemption — ASV

and through whom we have found deliverance — TCNT

by whom we have been ransomed from captivity — Gspd

Who bought our freedom — Tay

even the forgiveness of sins:

even the remission . . . — Alf

which means the forgiveness of our sins — Wms

through having our sins forgiven — Gspd

15. Who is the image of the invisible God,

. . . the visible expression of . . . — Phi

. . . the very incarnation of . . . — TCNT

. . . the exact likeness of . . . — Wms

. . . the unseen God — Rhm

. . . the true likeness of the God we cannot see — Knox

the firstborn of every creature:

First-born and Head of all creation — TCNT

His firstborn Son who existed before any created thing — Wms

his is the primacy over all created things — NEB

16. For by him were all things created,

For in Him was created the universe — Wey

that are in heaven, and that are in earth, visible and invisible,

whether spiritual or material, seen or unseen — Phi

of things in heaven and on earth, things seen and things unseen — Wey

whether they be thrones, or dominions, or principalities, or powers:

— Angels and Archangels and all the Powers of Heaven — TCNT

the spirit world with its kings and kingdoms, its rulers and authorities — Tay

all things were created by him, and for him:

. . . through him, and unto him — ASV

In fact, every single thing was created through, and for, him — Phi

the whole universe has been created through and for him — NEB

all were made by Christ for His own use and glory — Tay

17. And he is before all things,

he takes precedence of all — Knox

He was before all else began — Tay

So He existed before all things — Wms

and by him all things consist.

and they all in him hold together — Rhm

and in Him all things subsist — Con

and all things unite in him — TCNT

and in and through Him the universe is one harmonious whole — Wey

and all coheres in him — Mof

and he sustains and embraces them all — Gspd

---

[1]NASB construes "joyously" with the following phrase.

18. And he is the head of the body, the church:

... the assembly — Rhm

He too is that head whose body is the Church — Knox

who is the beginning, the firstborn from the dead;

The Firstborn from the dead, he is to the Church the Source of its life — TCNT

in virtue of his primacy as the first to be born from the dead — Mof

it begins with him, since his was the first birth out of death — Knox

Life from nothing began through him, and life from the dead began through him — Phi

He is its origin, the first to return from the dead — NEB

that in all things he might have the preeminence.

that he, in all things, may stand first — TCNT

... occupy the foremost place — Wey

... have first place — Ber

and he is, therefore, justly called the Lord of all — Phi

to be in all things alone supreme—NEB

so that He is first in everything — Tay

19. For it pleased the Father that in him should all fulness dwell;

For He willed that in Himself all the Fulness of the universe should dwell — Con

For it pleased the Father that in him the divine nature in all its fulness should dwell — TCNT

... the whole of the divine perfections ... — Wey

It was in him that the full nature of God chose to live — Phi

For in him the complete being of God, by God's own choice, came to dwell — NEB

For God wanted all of Himself to be in His Son — Tay

20. And, having made peace through the blood of his cross,

by him to reconcile all things unto himself;

through him ... — ASV

... fully to reconcile ... — Rhm

... to win back all things ... into union with himself — Knox

It was through His Son that God cleared a path for everything to come to him — Tay

by him, I say, whether they be things in earth, or things in heaven.

... all on earth and all in heaven alike — Mof

21. And you, that were sometime alienated and enemies in your mind by wicked works,

And you, being in time past alienated and enemies in your mind in your evil works — ASV

And you Who at one time were estranged and enemies in your mind in your wicked works — Rhm

And you, likewise, who once were estranged from Him, and with your mind at war with Him, when you lived in wickedness — Con

And it pleased God that you, once estranged from him and hostile towards him in your thoughts, intent only on wickedness — TCNT

You, too, were once estranged from him; your minds were alienated from him by a life of sin — Knox

... you were his enemies in heart and mind, and your deeds were evil — NEB

yet now hath he reconciled

— but now he has reconciled you — TCNT

yet now He has brought you back as His friends — Tay

22. In the body of his flesh through death,

in his body of flesh through means of his death — Rhm

by the sacrifice of Christ's earthly body in death — TCNT

through dying in his human body — Gspd

by Christ's death in his body of flesh and blood — NEB

to present you holy and unblameable and unreproveable in his sight:

to present you holy and blameless and unaccusable before him — Rhm

... consecrated, faultless, and blameless in His presence — Wms

so that he may present you before himself as dedicated men, without blemish and innocent in his sight — NEB

23. If ye continue in the faith grounded and settled,

provided that . . . — Alf

if, indeed, you be steadfast in your faith, with your foundation firmly grounded and immovably fixed — Con

if only you remain true to your Faith, firm and immovable — TCNT

This reconciliation assumes, of course, that you maintain a firm position in the faith — Phi

and be not moved away from the hope of the gospel, which ye have heard,

and not suffering yourselves to be shifted away from the hope of the Glad-tidings which you heard — Con

never abandoning the hope held out in the Good News to which you listened — TCNT

never to be dislodged from . . . — NEB

and which was preached to every creature which is under heaven;

. . . in all creation . . . — ASV

. . . all over the world — Wms

and which, indeed, the whole world is now having an opportunity of hearing — Phi

whereof I Paul am made a minister;

. . . a ministering servant — Con

. . . a worker — Gspd

And I, Paul, have the joy of telling it to others — Tay

24. Who now rejoice in my sufferings for you,

And even now I rejoice in the afflictions which I bear for your sake — Con

It is now my happiness to suffer for you — NEB

and fill up that which is behind of the afflictions of Christ in my flesh

and fill up on my part that which is lacking . . . — ASV

and am filling up the things that lack of the tribulations of the Christ in my flesh — Rhm

and in my own person I supplement the afflictions endured by the Christ — TCNT

I would make up the full sum of all that Christ has to suffer in my person — Mof

This is my way of helping to complete, in my poor human flesh, the full tale

of Christ's afflictions still to be endured — NEB

and in my body am enduring what still needs to be endured of Christ's sorrows — Beck

for his body's sake, which is the church:

In behalf of his body . . . — Rhm

25. Whereof I am made a minister,

Of which I have become minister — Rhm

whereof I was made a servant — Con

according to the dispensation of God which is given to me for you,

According to the administration of God . . . — Rhm

in virtue of the office with which God entrusted me — TCNT

to minister in the stewardship which God gave me for you [Gentiles] — Con

by the divine commission which has been granted me in your interests — Mof

in accordance with the trusteeship God entrusted to me for you — Wms

to fulfil the word of God;

to fill up the word of God — Rhm

to make a full presentation of God's message — Mof

that I might prove among you the universal message of God — Wms

to complete the preaching of his word among you — Knox

to tell His secret plan to you Gentiles — Tay

26. Even the mystery which hath been hid from ages and from generations,

. . . for ages and generations — ASV

The sacred secret . . . — Rhm

the open secret, covered up from the people of former ages and generations — Wms

For He has had a secret for centuries and generations past — Tay

but now is made manifest to his saints:

. . . shown openly . . . — Con

. . . disclosed . . . — Gspd

. . . uncovered . . . — Wms

but which is now as clear as daylight to those who love God — Phi

27. To whom God would make known

. . . was pleased to make known — ASV

. . . willed to manifest — Con

. . . has chosen to make known — Gspd

... wanted to tell — Beck

what is the riches of the glory of this mystery among the Gentiles;

what is the glorious wealth of this sacred secret among the nations — Rhm

the surpassing glory of that hidden Truth when proclaimed among the Gentiles — TCNT

... the full wonder and splendor of his secret plan ... — Phi

how rich among the non-Jews is the glory of this hidden truth: — Beck

which is Christ in you, the hope of glory:

— Christ among you! Your hope of glory! — TCNT

... the promise of glorification — Gspd

... the hope of all the glorious things to come — Phi

28. **Whom we preach,**

Him I am ever proclaiming — Mon

So, naturally, we proclaim Christ! — Phi

warning every man,

admonishing ... — ASV

and teaching every man in all wisdom;

... with all the wisdom that we possess — TCNT

... with ample wisdom — Wms

... in the whole range of wisdom — Ber

... all that we know about him — Phi

that we may present every man per-

fect in Christ Jesus:

... complete in Christ — Rhm

... full grown ... — Con

... perfected by union with ... — TCNT

... mature through union with ... — Wms

... perfect because of what Christ has done for each of them — Tay

29. **Whereunto I also labour,**

Unto which I am even toiling — Rhm

To this end ... I exert all my strength — Wey

That is what I am working for — Gspd

For this I labor [unto weariness] — Amp

striving according to his working, which worketh in me mightily.

earnestly contending ... — Alf

... in reliance upon the power of Him who is mightily at work within me — Wey

... by His active energy which is mightily working in me — Wms

Contending according to his energy which is energising itself in me with power — Rhm

with all the strength that God gives me — Phi

struggling like an athlete by His power that is working mightily in me — Beck

striving with all the superhuman energy which He so mightily enkindles and works within me — Amp

CHAPTER 2

1. **For I would that ye knew what great conflict I have for you,**

For I would have you know how greatly I strive for you — ASV

... what a fight I am putting up for you — Gspd

... what a battle I am fighting for you — Wms

... what anxiety I feel over you — Knox

... how strenuous are my exertions for you — NEB

and for them at Laodicea,

and for as many as have not seen my face in the flesh;

and for all who do not know me personally — Gspd

... have never met me — Phi

... have never set eyes on me — NEB

... haven't seen me face to face—Beck

2. **That their hearts might be comforted,**

... cheered — Wey

... braced — Amp

May their hearts be encouraged! — Mof

I want them to continue in good heart — NEB

being knit together in love,

being bound to one another by love — TCNT

... welded together in love — Wey

... well ordered in love — Knox

... united by love — Gspd

May they learn the meaning of love! — Mof

and in the unity of love — NEB

and unto all riches of the full assurance of understanding,

and keeping in view the full blessed-ness of a firm conviction — TCNT

How I long for you to grow more certain in your knowledge and more sure in your grasp — Phi

and to come to the full wealth of conviction which understanding brings — NEB

advancing towards an abounding wealth of understanding — Wey

May they have all the wealth of conviction that comes from insight! — Mof

to the acknowledgement of the mystery of God, and of the Father, and of Christ;

that they may know the mystery of God, even Christ — ASV

Unto a personal knowledge of the sacred secret of God, — Christ — Rhm

. . . a perfect knowledge of God's hidden Truth, even Christ himself — TCNT

so that they may finally reach the fullest knowledge of the open secret, Christ Himself — Wms

resulting in a true knowledge of God's mystery, that is, Christ Himself — NASB

For God's secret plan, now at last made known, is Christ Himself — Tay

May they learn to know that open secret of God, the Father of Christ — Mof

3. In whom are hid all the treasures of wisdom and knowledge.

In Him all the treasures of wisdom and knowledge are stored up, hidden from view — Wey

. . . all treasures of wisdom and knowledge are to be found — Gspd

In Him all the treasures of [divine] wisdom, [of comprehensive insight into the ways and purposes of God], and [all the riches of spiritual] knowledge and enlightenment are stored up and lie hidden — Amp

4. And this I say, lest any man should beguile you with enticing words.

. . . mislead you . . . — Con

. . . delude you with persuasiveness of speech — ASV

This I say in order that no one may be

reasoning you aside with plausible discourse — Rhm

I say this to prevent any one from deceiving you by plausible arguments — TCNT

. . . plausible sophistry — Wey

. . . specious arguments — Gspd

. . . lead you astray with high-flown talk — Knox

. . . fool you with smooth talk — Tay

5. For though I be absent in the flesh, yet am I with you in the spirit,

For though I am far away in person, still I am with you in spirit — Wms

. . . absent from you in body . . . — Wey

. . . physically absent . . . — Ber

joying and beholding your order,

and am delighted to witness your good discipline — Wey

. . . your steadiness — Mof

. . . your harmony — Gspd

. . . your fine order — Wms

and the stedfastness of your faith in Christ.

and the solid front presented by your faith in Christ — Wey

and the solid firmness of . . . — Rhm

and the solidity of . . . — Gspd

and the unbroken front resulting from your faith in Christ — TCNT

6. As ye have therefore received Christ Jesus the Lord, so walk ye in him:

So just as you once accepted the Christ, Jesus, as your Lord, you must live in vital union with him — Gspd

Go on, then, ordering your lives in Christ Jesus our Lord, according to the tradition you have received of him — Knox

And now just as you trusted Christ to save you, trust Him too for each day's problems; live in vital union with Him — Tay

7. Rooted and built up in him, and stablished in the faith,

. . . And making yourselves sure in your faith — Rhm

having the roots of your being firmly planted in Him, and continually building yourselves up in Him, and always being increasingly confirmed in the faith — Wey

Let your roots grow down into Him and draw up nourishment from Him.

See that you go on growing in the Lord, and become strong and vigorous in the truth — Tay

as ye have been taught,

abounding therein with thanksgiving.

overflowing with faith and thanksgiving — TCNT

overflowing with gratitude — Knox

8. Beware lest any man spoil you through philosophy and vain deceit,

Be taking heed lest there shall be anyone leading you off as a spoil . . . — Rhm

Take care there is not some one who will carry you away by his 'philosophy' — a hollow sham! — TCNT

Take care lest there be any one who leads you away as prisoners by means of his philosophy and idle fancies — Wey

Beware of anyone getting hold of you by means of a theosophy which is specious make-believe — Mof

Take care that nobody captures you by the idle fancies of his so-called philosophy — Wms

Take care not to let anyone cheat you with his philosophizings, with empty phantasies — Knox

Be careful that nobody spoils your faith through intellectualism or high-sounding nonsense — Phi

Be on your guard; do not let your minds be captured by hollow and delusive speculations — NEB

after the tradition of men, after the rudiments of the world, and not after Christ.

According to the instruction of men, According to the first principles of the world, — And not according to Christ — Rhm

following the tradition of men, the outward lessons of childhood, not the teaching of Christ — Con

following, as it does, mere human traditions, and dealing with puerile questions of this world, and not with Christ — TCNT

following human traditions and the world's crude notions instead of following Christ — Wey

on lines of human tradition, corresponding to the Elemental spirits of the world and not to Christ — Mof

guided by human tradition, following material ways of looking at things, instead of following Christ — Gspd

following human tradition and the world's crude notions instead of Christ — Wms

He may set forth some human tradition, or some theory about the nature of the universe, but not the teachings of Christ — Nor

built on men's thoughts and ideas, instead of on what Christ has said — Tay

9. For in him dwelleth all the fulness of the Godhead bodily.

. . . in bodily form — Con

For in Christ the Godhead in all its fulness dwells incarnate — TCNT

. . . all the fullness of Deity continues to live embodied — Wms

Yet it is in him that God gives a full and complete expression of himself (within the physical limits that he set himself in Christ) — Phi

For in Christ there is all of God in a human body — Tay

10. And ye are complete in him,

. . . filled full . . . — Alf

and in him ye are made full — ASV

and in Him you have your Fulness — Con

and, by your union with him, you also are filled with it — TCNT

So you have everything when you have Christ, and you are filled with God through your union with Christ — Tay

which is the head of all principality and power:

he is the fountain head from which all dominion and power proceed — Knox

who is the authority over all authorities, and the supreme power over all powers — Phi

He is the highest ruler over every other power — Tay

11. In whom also ye are circumcised with the circumcision made without hands,

. . . not done by hand — Rhm

. . . not man's handiwork — Knox

. . . not by any physical act — Phi

. . . not by a bodily operation — Tay

in putting off the body of the sins[2] of the flesh by the circumcision of Christ:

in the putting off of the body of the flesh — ASV

when you threw off the tyranny of the earthly body, and received the circumcision of Christ — TCNT

when you threw off your sinful nature in the circumcision of Christ — Wey

but by being set free from the sins of the flesh by virtue of Christ's circumcision — Phi

In the circumcision of Christ you were set free from your sinful nature — Nor

12. Buried with him in baptism,

. . . in your immersion — Rhm

you, by baptism, have been united with his burial — Knox

wherein also ye are risen with him through the faith of the operation of God,

wherein you were also raised with him through faith in the working of God — ASV

wherein also you were made partakers of His resurrection, through the faith wrought in you by God — Con

. . . and all this because you have faith in the tremendous power of God — Phi

. . . through your faith in the omnipotence of God — TCNT

who hath raised him from the dead.

. . . from among the dead — Rhm

13. And you, being dead in your sins and the uncircumcision of your flesh,

. . . through your trespasses . . . — ASV

. . . by your offences . . . — Rhm

. . . through your misdeeds . . . — Gspd

and you also, when you were dead in the transgressions and uncircumcision of your flesh — Con

And to you, who once were dead, by reason of your sins and your uncircumcised nature — TCNT

hath he quickened together with him, having forgiven you all trespasses;

God raised to share His life. For He forgave us all our transgressions — Con

— to you God gave Life in giving life to Christ! He pardoned all our sins! — TCNT

14. Blotting out the handwriting of ordinances that was against us, which was contrary to us,

having blotted out the bond written in ordinances . . . — ASV

He cancelled the bond which stood against us — the bond that consisted of ordinances — and which was directly hostile to us! — TCNT

canceled the note that stood against us, with its requirements — Wms

Christ has utterly wiped out the damning evidence of broken laws and commandments which always hung over our heads — Phi

and took it out of the way, nailing it to his cross;

— all these obligations he set aside when he nailed them to the cross — Mof

swept it out of the way, by nailing it to the cross — Knox

and has completely annulled it by nailing it over his own head on the cross — Phi

He took this list of sins and destroyed it by nailing it to Christ's cross — Tay

15. And having spoiled principalities and powers,

And He disarmed the Principalities and the Powers [which fought against Him] — Con

He rid himself of all the Powers of Evil — TCNT

And the hostile princes and rulers He stripped off from Himself — Wey

and the dominions and powers he robbed of their prey — Knox

and then, having drawn the sting of all the powers ranged against us — Phi

On that cross he discarded the cosmic powers and authorities — NEB

he made a shew of them openly, triumphing over them in it.

He made of them an open example, Celebrating a triumph over them thereby — Rhm

and put them to open shame, leading them captive in the triumph of Christ — Con

---

[2]The words "of the sins" are now recognized as not adequately supported by original manuscripts.

and held them up to open contempt, when he celebrated his triumph over them on the cross! — TCNT

made a public display of them, triumphing over them by the cross — Wms

he exposed them, shattered, empty and defeated, in his final glorious triumphant act! — Phi

16. Let no man therefore judge you in meat, or in drink,

Therefore, suffer not any man to condemn you for what you eat or drink — Con

Therefore suffer no one to sit in judgement on you as to eating or drinking — Wey

Do not, then, allow any one to take you to task on questions of eating or drinking — TCNT

or in respect of an holyday, or of the new moon, or of the sabbath days:

. . . a sabbath day — ASV

. . . sabbaths — Con

or in the matter of annual or monthly or weekly festivals — TCNT

17. Which are a shadow of things to come;

All that is the mere shadow of what is to be — Mof

all these were but shadows cast by future events — Knox

All these things have at most only a symbolical value — Phi

These things are only the shadow of what is to come — TCNT

That was only a shadow of something that was to follow — Gspd

but the body is of Christ.

the substance is in the Christ — TCNT

the reality is found in Christ — Gspd

the solid fact is Christ — Phi

The One foreshadowed is Christ — Nor

18. Let no man beguile you of your reward in a voluntary humility and worshipping of angels,

Let no man rob you of your prize by a voluntary humility and worshipping of the angels — ASV

. . . lay down rules for you as he pleases, with regard to fasting and any cult of angels — Mof

Stop letting anyone, in gratuitous humility and worship of angels, defraud you as an umpire — Wms

You must not allow anyone to cheat you by insisting on a false humility which addresses its worship to angels — Knox

You are not to be disqualified by the decision of people who go in for self-mortification and angel-worship — NEB

Let no one defraud you of salvation's victory prize . . . — Ber

Let no man succeed in his wish to defraud you of your prize, persuading you to self-humiliation, and worship of the angels — Con

Nor let any man cheat you of your joy in Christ by persuading you to make yourselves "humble" and fall down and worship angels — Phi

intruding into those things which he hath not seen, vainly puffed up by his fleshly mind,

dwelling in the things which he hath seen, vainly puffed up . . . — ASV

Such a man busies himself with his visions, and without reason is rendered conceited by his merely human intellect — TCNT

taking his stand on the visions he has seen, and idly puffed up with his unspiritual thoughts — Wey

Such a man takes his stand upon false visions; his is the ill-founded confidence that comes of human speculation — Knox

Such a man, inflated by an unspiritual imagination, is pushing his way into matters he knows nothing about — Phi

who brags of visions and, though empty, is inflated by his worldly mind — Ber

19. And not holding the Head,

and in his cleverness forgetting the head — Phi

He fails to maintain union with the Head — TCNT

He doesn't cling to the Head — Beck

Such a one does not keep his hold upon Christ, the Head — Wey

from which all the body by joints and bands having nourishment ministered, and knit together,

from whom the whole body, by the joints which bind it, draws full supplies for all its needs, and is knit together — Con

from whom the body, in all its parts nourished and strengthened by its points of contact and its connexions — Wey

from which the whole body, when supplied and united through its joints and sinews — Wms

on whom all the body depends, supplied and unified by joint and ligament — Knox

increaseth with the increase of God.

Groweth with the growth of God — Rhm

and increases in a godly growth — Con

grows with a growth that God produces — Wms

and grows according to God's laws of growth — Phi

grows according to God's design — NEB

20. **Wherefore if ye be dead with Christ from the rudiments of the world,**

If ye died . . . — ASV

If ye have died together with Christ from the first principles of the world — Rhm

If, then, when you died with Christ, you put away the childish lessons of outward things — Con

Since, with Christ, you became dead to the puerile teaching of this world — TCNT

If you have died with Christ and have escaped from the world's rudimentary notions — Wey

If you have died with Christ to material ways of looking at things — Gspd

If, by dying with Christ, you have parted company with worldly principles — Knox

why, as though living in the world, are ye subject to ordinances,

why, as though living in the world, do ye subject yourselves to ordinances — ASV

. . . submit yourselves to decrees — Con

. . . submit to rules and regulations — Mof

Then why behave as though you were still living the life of the world? Why let people dictate to you: — NEB

why do you submit, as though your life were still that of the world, to such ordinances as — TCNT

21. **(Touch not; taste not; handle not;**

Handle not, nor taste, nor touch — ASV

"hold not, taste not, touch not" — Con

'Do not handle this'; 'Do not taste that'; 'Do not touch that other thing' — Wey

22. **Which all are to perish with the using;)**

Which things are all for decay and in the using up — Rhm

— forbidding the use of things which are all made to be consumed in the using — Con

For all the things referred to in them cease to exist when used — TCNT

after the commandments and doctrines of men?

You are following mere human directions and instructions — TCNT

all based on the will and the word of men — Knox

23. **Which things have indeed a shew of wisdom in will worship,**

These rules indeed have an appearance of wisdom, where there is self-imposed worship — Wey

Such practices pass for wisdom, with their self-imposed devotions — Gspd

They will win you, no doubt, the name of philosophers, for being so full of scruple — Knox

I know that these regulations look wise with their self-inspired efforts at worship — Phi

Such prohibitions appear reasonable where there is a desire for self-imposed service — TCNT

and humility, and neglecting of the body;

. . . and severity to the body — ASV

. . . torturings of the body — Wms

and so-called 'humility,' and harsh treatment of the body — TCNT

their self-humiliation, and ascetic discipline — Gspd

their policy of self-humbling, and their studied neglect of the body — Phi

not in any honour to the satisfying of the flesh.

but are not of any value against the indulgence of the flesh — ASV

but . . . are of no value to check the indulgence of fleshly passions — Con but they are of no value, they simply pamper the flesh! — Mof

but they are all forgotten, when nature asks to be gratified — Knox

But in actual practice they do honor,

not to God, but to man's own pride — Phi

but are of no real value against the indulgence of our earthly nature — TCNT

CHAPTER 3

1. If ye then be risen with Christ,

If ye then were raised . . . — ASV

So if you have been raised to life in fellowship with Christ — Wms

Were you not raised to life with Christ? — NEB

If, then, you were partakers of Christ's resurrection — Con

seek those things which are above,

keep on seeking the things above — Wms

you must lift your thoughts above — Knox

reach out for the highest gifts of Heaven — Phi

Then aspire to the realm above — NEB

where Christ sitteth on the right hand of God.

where Christ is, enthroned at God's right hand — Wey

where Christ reigns in power — Phi

2. Set your affection on things above,

Give your minds to the things that are above — Wey

Practice occupying your minds with . . . — Wms

You must be heavenly-minded — Knox

Give your heart to the heavenly things — Phi

let your thoughts dwell on that higher realm — NEB

not on things on the earth.

not earthly-minded — Knox

not to the passing things of earth — Phi

don't spend your time worrying about things down here — Tay

3. For ye are dead,

For ye died — ASV

you have undergone death — Knox

For, as far as this world is concerned, you are already dead — Phi

I repeat, you died — NEB

and your life is hid with Christ in God.

and your life is now hidden in God through your fellowship with Christ — Wms

and your true life is a hidden one in God, through Christ — Phi

4. When Christ, who is our life, shall appear,

. . . shall be manifested — ASV

When Christ appears — He is our true Life — Wey

One day, Christ, the secret center of our lives, will show himself openly — Phi

then shall ye also appear with him in glory.

then shall ye also with him be manifested . . . — ASV

you too will appear to be glorified in fellowship with Him — Wms

and you will all share in that magnificent dénouement — Phi

5. Mortify therefore

Put to death therefore — ASV

So treat as dead — Gspd

So once for all put to death — Wms

Make dead therefore — Rhm

You must deaden, then — Knox

your members which are upon the earth;

your earthward inclinations — Wey

your lower, earthly nature — Wms

fornication, uncleanness, inordinate affection,

sexual immorality, impurity, passion — Wms

sexual immorality, dirty-mindedness, uncontrolled passion — Phi

fornication, indecency, lust — NEB

evil concupiscence, and covetousness,

unholy desire, and all greed — Wey

evil desire, and the lust for other people's goods — Phi

which is idolatry:

for that is a form of idolatry — Wey

6. For which things' sake the wrath of God cometh on the children of disobedience:

It is on account of these very sins that God's wrath is coming — Wey

. . . God's anger is coming — Gspd

... God's dreadful judgement is impending — NEB

These are what bring down God's vengeance on the unbelievers — Knox

7. In the which ye also walked some time,

wherein ye also once walked — ASV

and you also were once addicted to them — Wey

You too used to practice these sins — Wms

and such was your own behaviour — Knox

when ye lived in them.

while you were living under their power — Wey

when you used to live that sort of life — Wms

8: But now ye also put off all these;

but now do ye also put them all away — ASV

But now you must rid yourselves of every kind of sin — Wey

But now you too must once for all put them all aside — Wms

anger, wrath, malice, blasphemy, filthy communication out of your mouth.

— anger and passionate outbreaks, ill-will, evil-speaking, foul-mouthed abuse — so that these may never soil your lips — Wey

— anger, rage, malice, and abusive, filthy talk from your lips — Wms

resentment, anger, spite, insults, foul-mouthed utterance — Knox

— anger, rage, spite, rough, abusive talk — these must be banished from your lips — Gspd

9. Lie not one to another,

Stop lying ... — Wms

do not tell lies at one another's expense — Knox

seeing that ye have put off the old man with his deeds;

... with his doings — ASV

Having stript off the old man together with his practices — Rhm

Get rid of your old self and its habits — TCNT

you have stripped off the old nature with its practices — Mof

... the old self, and the habits that went with it — Knox

... the old man and all he did — Phi

10. And have put on the new man,

and clothe yourselves with that new self — TCNT

and put on the new nature — Mof

and have begun life as the new man — Phi

which is renewed in knowledge after the image of him that created him:

that is being renewed ... — ASV

Who is being moulded afresh unto personal knowledge ... — Rhm

which is being remoulded into full knowledge so as to become like Him who created it — Wey

which is in the process of being made new in the likeness of its Creator — Wms

that is being refitted all the time for closer knowledge, so that the image of the God who created it is its pattern — Knox

who is out to learn what he ought to be according to the plan of God — Phi

11. Where there is neither Greek nor Jew, circumcision nor uncircumcision, Barbarian, Scythian, bond nor free:

where there cannot be ... — ASV

In that new life there is no distinction between Greek and Jew, circumcised and uncircumcised, barbarian, Scythian, slave, freeman — TCNT

In that new creation there can be neither ... — Wey

In it there is no room for ... — Mof

In this new relation there is no Greek and Jew ... — Wms

In this new man of God's design there is no distinction between Greek and Hebrew, Jew or gentile, foreigner or savage, slave or free man — Phi

— a renewal in which there is no distinction between Greek and Jew ... — NASB

Here, what matters is not Greek and Jew, the circumcised and the uncircumcised ... — Gspd

In this new life one's nationality or race or education or social position is unimportant. Such things mean nothing — Tay

but Christ is all, and in all.

Christ is everything and everywhere — Mof

but Christ is everything and in us all — Gspd

there is nothing but Christ in any of us — Knox

Christ is all that matters, for Christ lives in them all — Phi

whether a person has Christ is what matters, and He is equally available to all — Tay

but Christ is all! — and in all! — TCNT

12. Put on therefore, as the elect of God, holy and beloved,

... as God's chosen people ... — Con

... God's picked representatives of the new humanity, purified and beloved of God himself — Phi

Therefore, as God's People, consecrated and dear to him, clothe yourselves with — TCNT

Then put on the garments that suit God's chosen people, his own, his beloved: — NEB

bowels of mercies, kindness, humbleness of mind,

tenderness of heart, kindness, self-humiliation — Con

an heart of pity ... — Alf

Tender affections of compassion, graciousness ... — Rhm

be merciful in action, kindly in heart, humble in mind — Phi

meekness, longsuffering;

gentleness, forbearance — TCNT

Accept life, and be most patient — Phi

13. Forbearing one another, and forgiving one another,

you must bear with one another's faults, be generous to each other — Knox

if any man have a quarrel against any:

... thinks himself aggrieved by his neighbor — Con

when there is any ground for complaint — TCNT

even as Christ forgave you, so also do ye.

... the Master ... — TCNT

just as the Lord has freely forgiven you, so must you also do — Wms

the Lord's generosity to you must be the model of yours — Knox

14. And above all these things put on charity,

And over all the rest put on the robe of love — Con

And above all you must be loving — Mof

And, to crown all this ... — Knox

which is the bond of perfectness.

which binds together and completes the whole — Con

for that is the girdle which makes all complete — TCNT

for love is the link of the perfect life — Mof

which binds everything together in perfect harmony — RSV

for love is the golden chain of all the virtues — Phi

15. And let the peace of God rule in your hearts,

And let the peace of Christ act as umpire ... — Rhm

Let the Peace that the Christ gives decide all doubts within your hearts — TCNT

... settle all questionings ... — Wey

Let the ruling principle in your hearts be Christ's peace — Gspd

to the which also ye are called in one body;

for you also were called to the enjoyment of peace as members of one Body — TCNT

that is why you have been called as members of the one Body — Mof

remembering that as members of the one body you were called to live in harmony — Phi

and be ye thankful.

And show yourselves thankful — TCNT

And practice being thankful — Wms

Learn, too, to be grateful — Knox

16. Let the word of Christ dwell in you richly in all wisdom;

... richly; in all wisdom — ASV

... remain as a rich treasure in your hearts. In all wisdom — Wey

Let Christ's teaching live in your hearts, making you rich in the true wisdom — Phi

Remember what Christ taught and let His words enrich your lives and make you wise — Tay

teaching and admonishing one another in psalms and hymns and spiritual songs,

teach and train one another with ... — Mof

Teach and help one another along the right road with ... — Phi teach them to each other and sing them out in . . . — Tay

singing with grace in your hearts to the Lord.

With gratitude raising song . . . — Rhm

praise God with thankful hearts — Mof

singing God's praises with joyful hearts — Phi

singing to the Lord with thankful hearts — Tay

17. **And whatsoever ye do in word or deed, do all in the name of the Lord Jesus,**

. . . in dependence on the Lord Jesus — Mof

. . . as followers of the Lord Jesus — Gspd

. . . with reference to the Lord Jesus — Wms

. . . as a representative of the Lord Jesus — Tay

giving thanks to God and the Father by him.

and through Him continue to give thanks to God the Father — Wms

18. **Wives, submit yourselves unto your own husbands,**

. . . be in subjection . . . — ASV

. . . adapt yourselves to . . . — Phi

as it is fit in the Lord.

for that is your duty as Christians — Gspd

as the service of the Lord demands — Knox

as befits those who belong to the Lord — TCNT

19. **Husbands, love your wives,**

Married men, be affectionate to . . . — Wey

and be not bitter against them.

don't let bitterness or resentment spoil your marriage — Phi

and never treat them harshly — TCNT

20. **Children, obey your parents in all things:**

Children, always obey your parents — TCNT

. . . at every point — Mof

for this is well pleasing unto the Lord.

for that is pleasant to see in those who belong to the Lord — TCNT

for this pleases the Lord right well — Mof

for that is commendable in Christians — Gspd

it is a gracious sign of serving the Lord — Knox

for at your age this is one of the best things you can do to show your love for the Lord — Phi

21. **Fathers, provoke not your children to anger,**

. . . vex not your children — Con

. . . do not fret and harass your children — Wey

. . . avoid irritating . . . — Mof

. . . don't overcorrect . . . —Phi

. . . stop exasperating . . . — Wms

and you, parents, must not rouse your children to resentment — Knox

lest they be discouraged.

. . . disheartened — Rhm

lest their spirit should be broken — Con

or you may make them sullen and morose — Wey

lest they become dispirited — Mof

. . . grow up feeling inferior and frustrated — Phi

. . . become discouraged and quit trying — Tay

22. **Servants, obey in all things your masters according to the flesh;**

. . . your masters here below at every point — Mof

. . . give your masters full obedience — Knox

Slaves, your job is to obey your masters — Phi

not with eyeservice, as menpleasers; but in singleness of heart, fearing God:

. . . fearing the Lord — ASV

not only when their eyes are upon you, as if you had but to please men, but giving them ungrudging service, in your reverence for the Master — TCNT

do not work simply when their eye is upon you, like those who court human favour, but serve them with a single heart, out of reverence for your Lord and Master — Mof

not with the idea of currying favor, but as a sincere expression of your devotion to the Lord — Phi

23. **And whatsoever ye do, do it heartily,**

. . . work heartily — ASV

Whatever you do, do it with all your heart — Wms

... with a will — Knox

... put your whole heart and soul into it — Phi

Whatever you are doing, let your hearts be in your work — Wey

as to the Lord, and not unto men;

as for the Lord ... — Con

as if working for the Master ... — TCNT

24. Knowing that of the Lord ye shall receive the reward of the inheritance:

... the recompense of ... — ASV

remember, you are to receive from the Lord the inheritance which is your due — Mof

for you know that it is from the Lord that you are going to get your pay in the form of an inheritance — Wms

... the portion he has allotted you in return — Knox

for ye serve the Lord Christ.

so keep on serving ... — Wms

... Christ, the Master — TCNT

Unto the Lord Christ are ye in service — Rhm

Think of Christ as the master you are working for — Gspd

since you are actually employed by the Lord Christ — Phi

25. But he that doeth wrong shall receive for the wrong which he hath done:

... acteth unrighteously ... — Rhm

... will reap the wrong ... — TCNT

... will be paid back ... — Mof

But the wicked man will be punished for his misdeeds — Phi

Dishonesty will be requited — NEB

and there is no respect of persons.

and there will be no partiality — TCNT

and he has no favourites — NEB

with God there are no merely earthly distinctions — Wey

there will be no favour shown — Mof

... no exceptions — Wms

... no human preferences — Knox

and naturally no distinction will be made between master and man — Phi

He has no special favorites who can get away with shirking — Tay

CHAPTER 4

1. Masters, give unto your servants that which is just and equal;

... just and equitable treatment — Knox

... deal rightly and justly with your bondsmen — Con

... do what is right and fair ... — TCNT

knowing that ye also have a Master in heaven.

... a Master of your own in heaven — Mof

... a heavenly employer — Phi

2. Continue in prayer,

Continue stedfastly in ... — ASV

Persevere in ... — Con

Devote yourselves to ... — TCNT

Be earnest and unwearied in ... — Wey

and watch in the same with thanksgiving;

maintain your zest for prayer by thanksgiving — Mof

and wide awake about it when you give thanks — Gspd

be both alert and thankful as you pray — Phi

with mind awake and thankful heart — NEB

Give your whole mind to it, and also offer thanksgiving — TCNT

3. Withal praying also for us,

Include us in your prayers, please — Phi

And by all means, pray also for us — Nor

and at the same time, pray for us — TCNT

that God would open unto us a door of utterance,

that God may open unto us a door for the word — ASV

that God may give us an opening for our Message — TCNT

... a door for preaching — Wey

to speak the mystery of Christ,

... the sacred secret ... — Rhm

... the open secret about Christ — Wms

... the truths hidden in the Christ — TCNT

for which I am also in bonds:

— the truths for which I am in chains! — TCNT

... in custody — Mof

... kept in prison — Gspd

4. That I may make it manifest, as I ought to speak.

... declare it openly ... — Con

... make the secret plain ... — NEB

... as it is my duty to do — Wey

... which I know is my duty — Phi

Pray that I may unfold it as I should — Mof

in order to make it evident why I have to tell it — Wms

5. Walk in wisdom toward them that are without,

Conduct yourselves with wisdom ... — Con

... toward non-Christians — Phi

Show tact in your behaviour to the outside world — TCNT

Behave wisely in relation to ... — Wey

Let Christian wisdom rule your behaviour to ... — Mof

Be wise in all your contacts with ... — Tay

Be prudent in your behaviour towards those not of your company — Knox

redeeming the time.

making the most of every opportunity — TCNT

seizing your opportunities — Wey

make the very most of your time — Mof

using your time to the best possible advantage — Ber

Make the most of your chances to tell others the Good News — Tay

6. Let your speech be alway with grace, seasoned with salt,

... always be kindly ... — TCNT

... seasoned with the salt of grace — Wey

... that is, with winsomeness — Wms

... with an edge of liveliness — Knox

Let your talk always have a saving salt of grace about it — Mof

Always put your message attractively, and yet pointedly — Gspd

Speak pleasantly to them, but never sentimentally — Phi

Let your conversation be always gracious, and never insipid — NEB

that ye may know how ye ought to answer every man.

understanding how to give to every man a fitting answer — Con

and learn how to answer any question put to you — Mof

and be prepared to give every inquirer a fitting answer — Gspd

study how best to talk with each person you meet — NEB

7. All my state shall Tychicus declare unto you,

All that concerns me will be made known to you by Tychicus — Con

You will hear how things go with me from Tychicus — Knox

... all about my present circumstances — Phi

who is a beloved brother, and a faithful minister and fellowservant in the Lord:

our much-loved brother, a trusty assistant and fellow-servant with us in the Lord's work — Wey

... fellow-bondslave in the Lord — NASB

... He is a hard worker and serves the Lord with me — Tay

8. Whom I have sent unto you for the same purpose,

... this very purpose — ASV

... for the express purpose — Gspd

This is partly why I am sending him to you — Phi

that he might know your estate, and comfort your hearts;

that ye may know our state, and that he may comfort your hearts — ASV

... learn our circumstances ... give you encouragement — TCNT

... how we are faring ... cheer your hearts — Wey

to give me news of you, and to bring courage to your hearts — Knox

... put fresh heart into you — NEB

9. With Onesimus, a faithful and beloved brother,

who is one of you.

your fellow-countryman — Con

who is one of your own number — Gspd

They shall make known unto you all things which are done here.

... all that is going on here — TCNT

... how things stand here — Knox

... all the news here — NEB

... everything that is happening here — Beck

Between them they will tell you of conditions and activities here — Phi

10. Aristarchus my fellowprisoner saluteth you,
> . . . sends you his greeting — TCNT
> . . . wishes to be remembered to you — Gspd
> . . . who is also in prison here, sends greetings — Phi

and Marcus, sister's son to Barnabas,
and Mark, the cousin of Barnabas — ASV
so does Mark . . . — NEB
. . . the kinsman of Barnabas — Knox

(touching whom ye received commandments:
. . . received instructions — TCNT
I believe I told you before about him — Phi

if he come unto you, receive him;)
. . . give him a welcome — Wey
. . . make him welcome — TCNT

11. And Jesus, which is called Justus,
Joshua, who is called Justus, also sends his greetings — TCNT

who are of the circumcision. These only are my fellowworkers unto the kingdom of God, which have been a comfort unto me.
These are the only converts from Judaism who have worked with me for the kingdom of God; I have found them a great comfort — TCNT
. . . but what a help they have been! — Phi

12. Epaphras, who is one of you,
> . . . your fellow-countryman — Con
> . . . one of your own number — Gspd
> . . . another member of your church — Phi

a servant of Christ, saluteth you,
a slave of Christ Jesus . . . — Gspd

always labouring fervently for you in prayers,
ever contending on your behalf in his prayers — Con
always most earnest in your behalf in his prayers — TCNT
always wrestling on your behalf . . . — Wey
He prays hard for you all the time — NEB

that ye may stand perfect and complete in all the will of God.
that in ripeness of understanding, and full assurance of belief, you may abide steadfast in all the will of God — Con
praying that you may stand firm, with a matured faith and with a sure conviction of all that is in accordance with God's will — TCNT
hoping that you will stand firm in the perfect achievement of all that is God's will for you — Knox

13. For I bear him record,
I can vouch for him — Knox
From my own observation I can tell you — Phi

that he hath a great zeal for you,
. . . much labor . . . — ASV
. . . deep interest . . . — TCNT
how great his toiling for you is — Wms
that he has a real passion for your welfare — Phi

and them that are in Laodicea, and them in Hierapolis.
and the brothers in Laodicea and Hierapolis — Gspd

14. Luke, the beloved physician, and Demas, greet you.
. . . our dear doctor . . . — TCNT
Luke, the doctor and dear friend . . . — Beck

15. Salute the brethren which are in Laodicea, and Nymphas, and the church which is in his house.[3]
. . . in their house — ASV
. . . the Church that meets at her house — TCNT
. . . the congregation who meet in her house — Phi

16. And when this epistle is read among you,
cause that it be read also in the church of the Laodiceans;
provide that it be read also . . . — Con
see that . . . — TCNT
have it read . . . — Gspd
see that it is read out . . . — Knox

and that ye likewise read the epistle from Laodicea.
and that you in return read the one . . . — NEB
. . . that is coming from there — Gspd
And read the letter I wrote to them — Tay

---

[3]Some manuscripts read "her house" and "their house."

17. And say to Archippus,

A brief message to Archippus: — Phi

Take heed to the ministry which thou hast received in the Lord, that thou fulfil it.

God ordained you to your work — see that you don't fail him! — Phi

Attend to the duty entrusted to you in the Lord's service, and discharge it to the full — NEB

God called you into His service — Oh, do not fail Him! — Nor

18. The salutation by the hand of me Paul.

The salutation of me Paul with mine own hand — ASV

I, Paul, add this greeting in my own handwriting — TCNT

The farewell is in my own hand, from Paul — Gspd

My personal greeting to you written by myself — Phi

Remember my bonds.

. . . my chains — Con

Remember I am in prison — Mof

Remember my fetters — RSV

Don't forget I'm in prison — Phi

Grace be with you. Amen.

THE FIRST
EPISTLE OF PAUL TO THE THESSALONIANS

CHAPTER 1

1. Paul, and Silvanus, and Timotheus,

... Timothy — RSV

unto the church of the Thessalonians

unto the assembly . . . — Rhm

to the church assembled at Thessalonica — Knox

which is in God the Father and in the Lord Jesus Christ:

in union with God the Father and the Lord Jesus Christ — TCNT

Grace be unto you, and peace, from God our Father, and the Lord Jesus Christ:

May God bless you and give you peace — TCNT

May blessing and peace of heart . . . — Tay

2. We give thanks to God always for you all,

I give continual thanks . . . — Con

making mention of you in our prayers;

continually mentioning [you when engaged] in our prayers — Amp

3. Remembering without ceasing your work of faith,

we never fail to recall the efforts that have resulted from your faith — TCNT

constantly bearing in mind . . . — NASB

. . . your energetic faith — Gspd

And without intermission recall your active faith — Ber

We cannot forget . . . how your work came from your faith — Nor

and labour of love, and patience of hope

your unwearied love . . . — Knox

. . . and endurance of hope — Rhm

. . . and the steadfastness of your hope — Con

the toil prompted by your love, and the patient endurance sustained by your hope — TCNT

your loving service, and your unwavering expectation — Gspd

in our Lord Jesus Christ,

in the sight of God and our Father;

before our God and Father — ASV

in the presence of . . . — Con

as we appear before God our Father — Nor

4. Knowing, brethren beloved, your election of God.

Brethren, beloved by God, I know how God has chosen you — Con

[O] brethren beloved by God, we recognize and know that He has selected (chosen) you — Amp

. . . that you have been marked out by God's purpose — Bas

Brothers, whom God loves, we know that he has chosen you — TCNT

5. For our gospel came not unto you in word only,

How that our glad-message . . . — Rhm

for my Glad-tidings . . . — Con

Our preaching to you did not depend upon mere argument — Knox

because the Good News that we brought came home to you, not merely as so many words — TCNT

When we brought you the Good News, it was not just meaningless chatter to you — Tay

but also in power, and in the Holy Ghost, and in much assurance;

but also in power; with the might of the Holy Spirit, and with the full assurance of belief — Con

but with a power and a fulness of conviction due to the Holy Spirit — TCNT

but in power also, and in the Holy Spirit, and with deep conviction — Mon

. . . with full conviction — RSV

but as a message with power behind it — the effectual power, in fact, of the Holy Spirit — Phi

What we told you produced a powerful effect upon you, for the Holy Spirit gave you great and full assurance that what we said was true — Tay

as ye know what manner of men we were among you for your sake.

even as ye know what manner of men we showed ourselves toward you . . . — ASV

. . . we proved among you for your sakes — Alf

As you, likewise, know the manner in

which I behaved myself among you, for your sakes — Con

You know indeed the sort of men we became among you . . . — Wey

For you know the life we lived among you for your good — TCNT

6. And ye became followers of us, and of the Lord,

And ye became imitators of us . . . — ASV

Moreover, you followed in my steps, and in the steps of the Lord — Con

having received the word in much affliction,

Giving welcome unto the word In much tribulation — Rhm

and, in spite of much suffering, you welcomed the Message — TCNT

after receiving the word amid severe affliction — Wey

because you welcomed our message . . . in spite of the painful persecutions it brought you — Wms

with joy of the Holy Ghost:

with joy which came from the Holy Spirit — Con

with joy inspired by the Holy Spirit — RSV

7. So that ye were ensamples to all that believe

so that ye became an example . . . — Alf

. . . unto all who were coming to the faith — Rhm

And thus you have become patterns to all the believers — Con

thus you have become a model for all believers — NEB

in Macedonia and Achaia.

throughout Macedonia and Greece — TCNT

8. For from you sounded out the word of the Lord

For it was from you that the Lord's Message resounded — TCNT

You have become a sort of sounding-board from which the word of the Lord has rung out — Phi

And now the Word of the Lord has spread out from you — Tay

From Thessalonica the word rang out — NEB

not only in Macedonia and Achaia, but also in every place your faith to God-ward is spread abroad;

. . . is gone forth — ASV

. . . but the fact of your faith has been broadcast everywhere — Ber

. . . but the story of your belief in God has gone everywhere — Gspd

throughout Macedonia and Greece; and, more than that, your faith in God has become known far and wide — TCNT

and not in Macedonia and Achaia alone, but everywhere your faith in God has reached men's ears — NEB

so that we need not to speak any thing.

We never need to speak about it — Mof

No words of ours are needed — NEB

So we [find that we] never need to tell people anything [further about it] — Amp

9. For they themselves shew of us what manner of entering in we had unto you,

For they themselves report concerning us . . . — RSV

For others are telling of their own accord, concerning me, what welcome you gave me — Con

For they themselves give the news of how we came among you — Bas

People tell us of their own accord about the visit we paid to you — Mof

and how ye turned to God from idols to serve the living and true God;

and how you turned from your idols to God, to be bondservants of the true and ever-living God — Wey

. . . to serve a living and a real God — Mof

. . . to be slaves of a true and living God — Mon

10. And to wait for his Son from heaven,

and to await the return from heaven of His Son — Wey

whom he raised from the dead,

even Jesus, which delivered us from the wrath to come.

even Jesus, who delivereth us . . . — ASV

— Jesus, our Deliverer from God's coming wrath — Wey

— Jesus: Who is to rescue us out of the anger that is coming — Rhm

even Jesus our deliverer from the coming wrath — Con

— Jesus, our deliverer from the punishment which is impending — TCNT

Jesus who delivers us from the wrath
to come — RSV

. . . who personally delivered us from
the judgment which hung over our
heads — Phi

CHAPTER 2

**1. For yourselves, brethren, know our
entrance in unto you, that it was not
in vain:**

For, you know yourselves, brethren,
that my coming amongst you was
not fruitless — Con

For you yourselves, brethren, know
that our visit to you did not fail of
its purpose — Wey

**2. But even after that we had suffered
before, and were shamefully entreated,
as ye know, at Philippi,**

But though we had previously suffered
and been insulted, even as ye know,
in Philippi — Rhm

but after I had borne suffering and outrage (as you know) at Philippi —
Con

Far from it; after all the injury and outrage which to your knowledge we
had suffered at Philippi — NEB

we were bold in our God

we had courage in our God — RSV

we had the courage, by the help of our
God — TCNT

**to speak unto you the gospel of God
with much contention.**

. . . conflict — ASV

to tell you God's Good News in spite
of great opposition — TCNT

**3. For our exhortation was not of deceit,
nor of uncleanness, nor in guile:**

For our exhortation is not in error . . .
— ASV

Our appeal to you was not based on a
delusion, nor was it made from unworthy motives, or with any intention of misleading you — TCNT

And as you will remember, we did not
make our appeal by advocating false
doctrines, nor did we have any impure motives or practice any sort of
deceit — Nor

4. But as we were allowed of God

But even as we have been approved
of God — ASV

But as God has proved my fitness —
Con

We have passed God's scrutiny—Knox

**to be put in trust with the gospel, even
so we speak;**

to be entrusted with the Good News,
therefore we tell it — TCNT

**not as pleasing men, but God, which
trieth our hearts.**

not seeking to please men, but God,
who proves our hearts — Con

not to satisfy men, but to satisfy the
God who tests our hearts — Mof

not to please men, but to please God,
who is testing my motives — Mon

not to please men, but to please God,
Who tests our hearts (expecting
them to be approved) — Amp

not to ingratiate ourselves with men,
but to please God . . . — Ber

**5. For neither at any time used we flat-
tering words, as ye know,**

Never at any time, as you know, did
we use the language of flattery —
TCNT

Never once did we try to win you with
flattery, as you very well know —
Tay

We never resorted to flattery (you
know that) — Mof

**nor a cloke of covetousness; God is
witness:**

Nor a pretext for greed — God is witness! — Rhm

nor hide covetousness under fair pretence, (God is witness) — Con

nor to any pretext for self-seeking
(God is witness to that) — Mof

or make false professions to hide selfish aims. God will bear witness to
that — TCNT

**6. Nor of men sought we glory, neither
of you, nor yet of others,**

we never sought honour from men,
from you or from anybody else —
Mof

neither did we seek plaudations from
men, either from you or from others
— Ber

**when we might have been burden-
some, as the apostles of Christ.**

... have claimed authority ... — ASV

Though we could have assumed dignity ... — Rhm

although, as Apostles of Christ, we might have burdened you with our support — TCNT

though we might have made demands as apostles of Christ — RSV

although as Christ's envoys we might have made our weight felt — NEB

7. But we were gentle among you,

But we behaved gently when we were among you — Amp

But we lived among you with a childlike simplicity — TCNT

Instead we were mild-mannered in your circle — Ber

On the contrary I showed myself among you as gentle as a mother — Mon

even as a nurse cherisheth her children:

like as when a nursing-mother cherisheth her own children — Alf

when she tenderly nurses her own children — Mon

8. So being affectionately desirous of you,

Thus yearning after you — Rhm

We loved you dearly — Tay

so in my fond affection — Con

we were willing to have imparted unto you, not the gospel of God only, but also our own souls, because ye were dear unto us.

it was my joy to give you not only the Glad-tidings of God, but my own life also, because you were dear to me — Con

we were willing, not only to share with you God's good news, but to lay down our very lives too for you, all because you were so dearly loved by us — Wms

9. For ye remember, brethren, our labour and travail:

... my toilsome labours — Con

for labouring night and day,

Night and day we used to work at our trades — TCNT

because we would not be chargeable unto any of you,

that we might not burden any of you — RSV

we preached unto you the gospel of God.

we heralded to you God's Gospel — Ber

while we proclaimed to you God's Good News — TCNT

10. Ye are witnesses, and God also, how holily and justly and unblameably we behaved ourselves among you that believe:

... how holy, and just, and unblameable were my dealings towards you that believe — Con

You will bear witness, and God also, that our relations with you who believed in Christ were pure, and upright, and beyond reproach — TCNT

... how devoutly and uprightly and blamelessly we behaved ourselves toward you believers — NASB

11. As ye know how we exhorted and comforted and charged every one of you, as a father doth his children,

as ye know how we dealt with ... — ASV

Indeed, you know that, like a father with his own children, we used to encourage and comfort every one of you, and solemnly plead with you — TCNT

Even as ye know how unto each one of you we were as a father unto his own children, consoling you and soothing and calling to witness — Rhm

As you well know, we dealt with you one by one, as a father deals with his children, appealing to you by encouragement, as well as by solemn injunctions — NEB

12. That ye would walk worthy of God,

That ye might walk worthily of God — Alf

to live lives worthy of the God — NEB

who hath called you unto his kingdom and glory.

who invites you to share His own Kingdom and glory — Wey

... and the glorious blessedness [into which true believers will enter after Christ's return] — Amp

13. For this cause also thank we God without ceasing,

Wherefore I also give continual thanks to God — Con

because, when ye received the word of God which ye heard of us,

That when ye received a spoken word from us — which was God's — Rhm

because, in receiving the teaching that you had from us — TCNT

ye received it not as the word of men,

you accepted it . . . — RSV

ye welcomed it — not as a human word — Rhm

but as it is in truth, the word of God,

but as the message of God, as it really is — Wms

but as what it really is — the teaching of God — TCNT

which effectually worketh also in you that believe.

Which is also inwardly working itself in you who believe — Rhm

which has living power in you who have faith — Bas

— exercising its [superhuman] power in those who adhere to and trust in and rely on it — Amp

which is even now doing its work within you who believe in Christ — TCNT

14. For ye, brethren, became followers of the churches of God which in Judaea are in Christ Jesus:

. . . became imitators of . . . — ASV

. . . began to follow the example of . . . — Mon

You took for your model, brethren, the churches of God which are assembled in Judaea in the name of Jesus Christ — Knox

You have fared like the congregations in Judaea, God's people in Christ Jesus — NEB

For you, brothers, followed the example of God's churches in Judea that are in union with Christ Jesus — Gspd

for ye also have suffered like things of your own countrymen,

inasmuch as you suffered the like persecution from your own countrymen — Con

seeing that you endured the same ill-treatment . . . — Wey

For when you suffered at the hands of your fellow countrymen you were sharing the experience of the Judaean Christian churches — Phi

even as they have of the Jews:

which they endured from the Jews — Con

15. Who both killed the Lord Jesus, and their own prophets,

. . . Jesus the Lord . . . — Alf

and have persecuted us;

and drove us out — RSV

and who have driven me forth [from city to city] — Con

who harassed ourselves — Mof

and they please not God,

a people displeasing to God — Con

and are contrary to all men:

and to show themselves foes of all men — Amp

and enemies to all mankind — Con

16. Forbidding us to speak to the Gentiles

Hindering us from speaking unto the nations — Rhm

And try to keep us from talking to the non-Jews — Beck

who would hinder me from speaking to the Gentiles — Con

that they might be saved,

with a view to their Salvation — TCNT

for fear some might be saved — Tay

to fill up their sins alway:

continuing always to fill up the measure of their sins — Con

and so are always increasing the measure of their iniquity — TCNT

They continue always to fill up the measure of their sins — Mon

Alas, they are always piling up their sins to the limit — Nor

for the wrath is come upon them to the uttermost.

But anger hath overtaken them at length — Rhm

but the wrath [of God] has overtaken them to destroy them — Con

But God's judgement has overtaken them at last! — TCNT

Now God is angry with them forever — Beck

17. But we, brethren, being taken from you for a short time

. . . being bereaved of you . . . — ASV

. . . although torn from you for a short season — Mon

in presence, not in heart,

— in person, not in spirit — Wey

endeavoured the more abundantly to see your face with great desire.

endeavoured all the more with intense
longing to see you face to face —
Wey

made eager efforts to behold you face
to face with strong longing — Mon

18. **Wherefore we would have come unto
you, even I Paul, once and again;**

Wherefore we desired to come unto
you . . . — Rhm

And so we wanted to come to you —
I Paul again and again — Wey

That is why we made up our minds to
go to see you — at least I, Paul, did,
more than once — TCNT

but Satan hindered us.

And Satan thwarted us — Rhm

but Satan put difficulties in our way
— TCNT

19. **For what is our hope, or joy, or crown
of rejoicing?**

. . . glorying — ASV

. . . boasting — RSV

For what is my hope, or joy? What is
the victor's wreath in which I exult
— Mon

**Are not even ye in the presence of our
Lord Jesus Christ at his coming?**

. . . at His appearing — Con

What but your own selves in the presence of our Lord Jesus, at his coming! — Mon

It is you! Yes, you will bring us much
joy as we stand together before our
Lord Jesus Christ when He comes
back again — Tay

20. **For ye are our glory and joy.**

For you are my pride and my delight
— Mon

You are our pride and our delight! —
TCNT

CHAPTER 3

1. **Wherefore when we could no longer
forbear,**

Wherefore no longer concealing our
anxiety — Rhm

So when we could endure it no longer
— Wey

**we thought it good to be left at Athens
alone;**

We were well-pleased to be left in
Athens alone — Rhm

I determined willingly . . . — Con

2. **And sent Timotheus, our brother, and
minister of God, and our fellowlabourer in the gospel of Christ,**

and sent Timothy, our brother and
God's minister in the gospel of
Christ — ASV

. . . God's minister in the service of
Christ's Good News — Wey

**to establish you, and to comfort you
concerning your faith:**

. . . and to exhort you on behalf of your
faith — Alf

to strengthen you, and to encourage
you in your faith — TCNT

to strengthen your faith and encourage
you — Tay

to strengthen and establish, exhort and
comfort and encourage you in your
faith — Amp

3. **That no man should be moved by
these afflictions:**

. . . might be disquieted in . . . — Alf

. . . might be shrinking back in these
tribulations — Rhm

that none of you should waver in these
afflictions — Con

that none of you might be unnerved by
your present trials — Wey

We did not want any of you to lose
heart at the troubles you were going
through — Phi

**for yourselves know that we are ap-
pointed thereunto.**

since you know yourselves that such is
our appointed lot — Con

Troubles are our lot, you know that
well — Mof

You know yourselves that this is what
we must expect — Gspd

because you see that these things are
part of God's purpose for us — Bas

for you yourselves know that we have
been destined for this — NASB

4. **For verily, when we were with you,
we told you before that we should
suffer tribulation;**

we told you beforehand — We are destined to suffer tribulation — Rhm

we warned you beforehand that we
were certain to encounter trouble —
TCNT

. . . that we were going to be pressed
with difficulties — Wms

even as it came to pass, and ye know.

as you know that it befell — Con

5. For this cause, when I could no longer forbear,

... no longer concealing my anxiety — Rhm

Therefore, since I could no longer endure the uncertainty — TCNT

On this account, when I could no longer bear the suspense — Nor

I sent to know your faith,

... to learn tidings of your faith — Con

... [how you were standing the strain, and endurance of] your faith—Amp

... to know the condition of your faith — Wey

lest by some means the tempter have tempted you,

Lest by any means he that tempteth should have tempted you — Rhm

it might be that the tempter of souls had been tempting you — Knox

and our labour be in vain.

and in vain should have been our toil — Rhm

and our labour had been thrown away — Mof

6. But now when Timotheus came from you unto us,

But when Timothy came even now unto us from you — ASV

But now that Timothy has come straight from you to us — Phi

and brought us good tidings of your faith and charity,

... love — ASV

with a glowing account of your faith and love — Phi

and that ye have good remembrance of us always,

and that you still keep an affectionate remembrance of me — Con

and that you are still holding me in affectionate remembrance — Mon

desiring greatly to see us, as we also to see you:

and want to see us just as much as we want to see you — Tay

7. Therefore, brethren, we were comforted over you

For this cause were we consoled, brethren, over you — Rhm

in all our affliction and distress by your faith:

in all our necessity and tribulation through your faith — Rhm

in all of our crushing troubles and suffering here — Tay

8. For now we live, if ye stand fast in the Lord.

For it is new life to us to know that you are holding fast to the Lord — TCNT

For now I am really living, if you are standing firm in the Lord — Mon

It brings to us renewed life ... — Nor

9. For what thanks can we render to God again for you,

How can we thank God enough — TCNT

For how great is the praise which we give to God for you — Bas

for all the joy wherewith we joy for your sakes before our God;

for all the happiness that you are giving us in the sight of our God — TCNT

for all the happiness you made me feel in the presence of God — Gspd

and how great the joy with which we are glad because of you before our God — Bas

10. Night and day praying exceedingly

praying earnestly night and day — RSV

Night and day making very abundant entreaties — Rhm

that we might see your face, and might perfect

... and might fill up — Alf

... and fit in the things — Rhm

... and might round out to completeness — Wms

to see you personally and to adjust — Ber

that which is lacking in your faith?

the defects of your faith — Alf

whatever may be imperfect and lacking in your faith — Amp

what is yet wanting in your faith — Con

what needs advancement in your faith — Ber

11. Now God himself and our Father,

Now may our God and Father himself — RSV

and our Lord Jesus Christ, direct our way unto you.

... make straight our way unto you — Rhm

... speed us on our journey to you — Knox

12. **And the Lord make you to increase and abound in love one toward another, and toward all men,**

And for you, may the Lord fill you to overflowing with love for one another and for every one — TCNT

The Lord make you grow in love and overflow with it for one another and for everybody — Beck

and as for you, may the Lord give you a rich and an even richer love for one another and for all men — Knox

even as we do toward you:

May the Lord make your love for one another and for all men wide and full like my love for you — Gspd

13. **To the end he may stablish your hearts unblameable in holiness**

... establish ... — ASV

... confirm your hearts faultless in holiness — Rhm

so that your hearts may be strong and faultlessly pure — Gspd

so that your hearts may be strong and free from all sin — Bas

and so may He give you inward strength to be holy and without a fault — Beck

before God, even our Father,

before our God and Father — ASV

at the coming of our Lord Jesus Christ with all his saints.

In the Presence ... — Rhm

at the appearing ... — Con

when our Lord Jesus Christ returns with all who belong to Him — Tay

CHAPTER 4

1. **Furthermore then we beseech you, brethren,**

Finally then, ... — ASV

For the rest, brethren, we request — Rhm

and exhort you by the Lord Jesus,

... in the name of the Lord Jesus — Con

and beg you, in the face of our union with the Lord Jesus — Wms

that as ye have received of us how ye ought to walk and to please God,

that, as I taught you how to walk that you might please God — Con

to follow our instructions about the way you are to live, so as to satisfy God — Mof

to continue advancing in the ideal you caught from us, how to behave in a way that pleases God — Ber

so ye would abound more and more.

but you are to excel in it still further — Mof

to continue to live this life better and better — Wms

that you live more and more closely to that ideal — Tay

2. **For ye know what commandments we gave you by the Lord Jesus.**

For you are aware of the instructions which we gave you ... — Wms

... by the authority of the Lord Jesus — Con

For you know what charges I laid upon you through the Lord Jesus — Mon

3. **For this is the will of God,**

For this is a thing willed of God — Rhm

For this is God's purpose — TCNT

even your sanctification,

that you should be holy — NEB

that you should be pure — TCNT

that you should be consecrated — Gspd

— separated and set apart for pure and holy living — Amp

that ye should abstain from fornication:

... unchastity — Rhm

that you should keep yourselves from fornication — Con

abstaining from all immorality — TCNT

that you abstain from sexual vice — Mof

4. **That every one of you should know how to possess his vessel**

... acquire ... — Alf

that each of you should learn to master his own body — Con

each of you recognizing the duty of taking one woman for his wife — TCNT

that each of you shall know how to procure himself a wife — Wey

in sanctification and honour;

in holiness and honor — RSV

purely and honourably — TCNT

in consecration and honor — Amp

5. **Not in the lust of concupiscence,**

not in the passion of lust — RSV

Not in the lust of carnal desire — Alf

Not with a passion of coveting — Rhm

and not for the mere gratification of his passions — TCNT

even as the Gentiles which know not God:

. . . the nations . . . — Rhm

. . . the heathen . . . — Con

6. That no man go beyond and defraud his brother in any matter:

That no man transgress, and wrong his brother in the matter — ASV

that you never cheat in this matter by taking another man's wife — Tay

No one is to wrong or defraud his brother in this matter — Gspd

and that no man may make attempts to get the better of his brother in business — Bas

You cannot break this rule without in some way cheating your fellow men — Phi

because that the Lord is the avenger of all such,

because the Lord is an avenger in all these things — RSV

All such the Lord will punish — Con

because the Lord will pay you back terribly for this — Tay

as we also have forewarned you and testified.

Even as we before told you and solemnly called you to witness — Rhm

as we told you before, in the most solemn terms — Gspd

7. For God hath not called us unto uncleanness, but unto holiness.

. . . not for uncleanness, but in sanctification — Alf

For God's Call to us does not permit of an impure life, but demands purity — TCNT

For God's purpose in His call to us is that our way of living should not be sinful, but sinless — Nor

For God has not called us for the purpose of impurity, but in sanctification — NASB

For God has not called us to impurity, but to consecration [to dedicate ourselves to the most thorough purity] — Amp

8. He therefore that despiseth, despiseth not man, but God,

. . . that rejecteth, rejecteth . . . — ASV

Therefore he who disregards this warn-

ing disregards, not man, but God — TCNT

who hath also given unto us his holy Spirit.

. . . his Spirit, which is holy — Alf

9. But as touching brotherly love ye need not that I write unto you:

But concerning love of the brethren . . . — ASV

for ye yourselves are taught of God to love one another.

. . . are God-taught . . . — Rhm

10. And indeed ye do it toward all the brethren which are in Macedonia:

As you show by deeds towards all the brethren . . . — Con

. . . in the whole of Macedonia — Rhm

but we beseech you, brethren, that ye increase more and more;

But I exhort you, brethren, to abound still more — Con

Yet, Brothers, we urge you to still further efforts — TCNT

We beg you, brothers, to continue to live better and better — Wms

11. And that ye study to be quiet,

And to be ambitious to be quiet — Rhm

Make it your ambition to live quietly — TCNT

also, endeavour to live quietly — Mof

Let it be a point of honour with you to keep calm — Knox

and to do your own business,

and to be attending to your own affairs — Rhm

and to work with your own hands, as we commanded you;

even as we charged you — ASV

12. That ye may walk honestly toward them that are without,

That ye should walk reputably . . . — Rhm

so that your conduct may win respect from those outside the Church — TCNT

so that you may live influentially with the outsiders — Wms

So that you may bear yourselves becomingly . . . — Amp

and that ye may have lack of nothing.

. . . need of nothing — ASV

and be dependent on nobody — RSV

and that you may need help from no man — Con

13. **But I would not have you to be ignorant, brethren,**

We would like you, brothers, to understand — Mof

We do not want you to be under any misapprehension, brothers — Gspd

But it is our desire, brothers, that you may be certain — Bas

But we do not want you to be uninformed, brethren — NASB

And now, dear brothers, I want you to know — Tay

concerning them which are asleep,

. . . that fall asleep — ASV

. . . which are sleeping — Alf

with regard to those who have passed to their rest — TCNT

about those who sleep in death — NEB

what happens to a Christian when he dies — Tay

that ye sorrow not, even as others which have no hope.

lest you should mourn, as do the rest who have no hope — Wey

that you may not grieve as others do who have no hope — RSV

14. **For if we believe that Jesus died and rose again, even so them also which sleep in Jesus will God bring with him.**

. . . which fell asleep through Jesus . . . — Alf

So also will God bring forth with him them who have fallen asleep through Jesus — Rhm

so also will God, through Jesus, bring back those who sleep, together with Him — Con

15. **For this we say unto you by the word of the Lord,**

This we tell you on the authority of the Lord — TCNT

For on the Lord's own authority we mean to say — Wms

that we which are alive and remain unto the coming of the Lord

. . . unto the Presence of the Lord — Rhm

that we who are alive, and are left until the coming of the Lord — RSV

that we who are living, who survive to the appearing of the Lord — Con

that those of us who are still living at the Coming of the Lord — TCNT

shall not prevent them which are asleep.

shall in no wise precede . . . — ASV

shall in no wise gain an advantage over them which fell asleep — Alf

shall in no way precede [into His presence] or have any advantage at all over those who have previously fallen asleep [in Him in death] — Amp

shall not come before those who sleep — Con

will not anticipate those who have passed to their rest — TCNT

16. **For the Lord himself shall descend from heaven with a shout, with the voice of the archangel, and with the trump of God:**

Because the Lord himself With a word of command With a chief-messenger's voice And with a trumpet of God Shall descend from heaven — Rhm

For, with a loud summons, with the shout of an archangel, and with the trumpet-call of God, the Lord himself will come down from heaven — TCNT

For the Lord himself shall descend from heaven with the shout of war, the Archangel's voice, and the trumpet of God — Con

One word of command, one shout from the archangel, one blast from the trumpet of God and the Lord himself will come down from heaven! — Phi

and the dead in Christ shall rise first:

Then those who died in union with Christ shall rise first — TCNT

17. **Then we which are alive and remain shall be caught up together with them in the clouds,**

first the Christian dead will rise, then we who are left alive shall join them, caught up in the clouds — NEB

. . . on clouds — Gspd

. . . among the clouds — Con

to meet the Lord in the air: and so shall we ever be with the Lord.

to meet the Lord in the air. Thus we shall always be with the Lord — NEB

18. **Wherefore comfort one another with these words.**

So then be consoling one another with these words — Rhm

. . . with what I have told you — TCNT

Tell one another this for your consolation — Knox

CHAPTER 5

1. But of the times and the seasons, brethren,

But concerning the times and the seasons, brethren — ASV

But as for times and dates — Wey

As regards the course and periods of time, brothers — Mof

Now as to the times and epochs, brethren — NASB

ye have no need that I write unto you.

. . . that anything be written to you — Mon

2. For yourselves know perfectly

For you are yourselves keenly aware — Ber

that the day of the Lord so cometh as a thief in the night.

. . . will come as a robber in the night — Con

. . . will come as unexpectedly as a burglary to a householder — Phi

3. For when they shall say, Peace and safety;

As soon as they begin to say . . . — Rhm

and while men say Peace and Safety — Con

When people say, such peace and security! — Wms

. . . Peace and tranquility — Lam

When people are saying All is quiet and safe — TCNT

then sudden destruction cometh upon them,

Then suddenly upon them cometh destruction — Rhm

catastrophe will sweep down upon them as suddenly and inescapably — Phi

destruction shall come upon them in a moment — Con

it is then that . . . Ruin comes suddenly upon them — TCNT

as travail upon a woman with child;

as the pangs of travail upon a woman with child — Con

as birth pangs to a pregnant woman — Phi

Just as the birth-throe unto her that is with child — Rhm

like pains on a woman who is going to have a baby — Beck

and they shall not escape.

and they shall find no escape — Con

4. But ye, brethren, are not in darkness, that that day should overtake you as a thief.

that The Day should come upon you as the robber on sleeping men — Con

that the day should surprise you like a thief — Wey

. . . should come upon you like a bandit — Mon

that the daylight should take you by surprise as if you were thieves — TCNT

5. Ye are all the children of light, and the children of the day:

. . . all sons of light, and sons of day — ASV

we are not of the night, nor of darkness.

We belong neither to night nor darkness — Wey

we do not belong to the night and its darkness — Knox

We have nothing to do with night, or darkness — TCNT

6. Therefore let us not sleep, as do others;

We must not sleep on, then, like the rest of the world — Knox

So then, let us not take our rest as others do — Bas

Let us then never fall into the sleep that stupefies the rest of the world — Phi

but let us watch and be sober.

but let us keep awake and be sober — RSV

but let us be self-controlled and awake — Bas

but let us be on our guard and composed — Ber

but let us be alert and sober — NASB

but let us keep awake (alert, watchful, cautious and on our guard) . . . — Amp

No, let us be watchful and self-controlled — TCNT

7. For they that sleep sleep in the night; and they that be drunken are drunken in the night.

for they who slumber, slumber in the night; and they who are drunken, are drunken in the night — Con

night is the sleeper's time for sleeping, the drunkard's time for drinking — Knox

for those who sleep, sleep at night, and those who get drunk, are drunk at night — Wey

8. But let us, who are of the day, be sober,

But let us, who belong to the Day, control ourselves — TCNT

but we, who belong to daylight, must keep sober — NEB

putting on the breastplate of faith and love;

clad in faith and love as our coat of mail — Mof

armed with faith and love for breastplate — NEB

and for an helmet, the hope of salvation.

and helmeted with the hope of salvation — Gspd

with the hope of salvation as our helmet — Mof

9. For God hath not appointed us to wrath,

For God has not destined us for wrath — RSV

God has not destined us to incur His anger — Wey

For God appointed us not to reap His wrath — Wms

For God has not destined us to the terrors of judgement — NEB

For God did not choose us to condemn us — Phi

but to obtain salvation by our Lord Jesus Christ,

But unto acquiring . . . — Rhm

but to the full attainment of salvation through . . . — NEB

but to save us for the sake of our Lord Jesus Christ — Nor

but that we might secure his salvation through Jesus Christ our Lord — Phi

10. Who died for us,

that, whether we wake or sleep,

in order that whether we be watching or sleeping — Rhm

in order that whether we are keeping vigil [in life] or sleeping [in death] — Mon

so that whether we are still alive or are dead [at Christ's appearing] — Amp

we should live together with him.

we share his life — Phi

we . . . might live in company with him — NEB

11. Wherefore comfort yourselves together,

. . . exhort one another — ASV

. . . be consoling one another — Rhm

Then encourage one another — Beck

and edify one another, even as also ye do.

and build each other up . . . — ASV

and try to build up one another's characters, as indeed you are doing — TCNT

12. And we beseech you, brethren,

Now we request you . . . — Rhm

to know them which labour among you,

to acknowledge those . . . — Con

. . . who are toiling among you — Rhm

to value those who toil among you — TCNT

to respect those who work with you — Gspd

to pay deference to those who work among you — Knox

to appreciate the men who are with you — Beck

and are over you in the Lord, and admonish you;

and preside over . . . — Alf

and are your leaders in the Lord's service, and give you counsel — TCNT

presiding over you in the Lord and maintaining discipline — Mof

who are over you in the Lord to keep order among you — Bas

13. And to esteem them very highly in love for their work's sake.

hold them in special esteem and affection, for the sake of their work — Mof

And be at peace among yourselves.

And maintain peace . . . — Con

Live in peace . . . — Mon

14. Now we exhort you, brethren,

We entreat you also, brothers — TCNT

warn them that are unruly,

admonish the disorderly — ASV

admonish the careless — NEB

admonish the idle — RSV

keep a check upon loafers — Mof

warn the vagabonds — Knox

admonish (warn and seriously advise) those who are out of line . . . — Amp

comfort the feebleminded,

encourage the fainthearted — ASV

Soothe them of little soul — Rhm

encourage the timid — Con

cheer up the despondent — Gspd

comfort those who are frightened — Tay

support the weak,

help the weak — RSV

support the waverers — Knox

give a helping hand to the weak — TCNT

be patient toward all men.

be longsuffering . . . — ASV

be patient with all — Con

lose patience with none — Mon

15. See that none render evil for evil unto any man;

Take care that none of you ever pays back wrong for wrong — TCNT

Be sure that no one repays a bad turn by a bad turn — Phi

but ever follow that which is good,

. . . be pursuing . . . — Rhm

but strive to do good always — Con

but always follow the kindest course — TCNT

you must aim always at what is best — Knox

both among yourselves, and to all men.

one toward another, and toward all — ASV

with one another, and with every one — TCNT

among yourselves and in the world at large — Phi

16. Rejoice evermore.

Rejoice always — RSV

Be happy in your faith at all times — Phi

Always be joyful — TCNT

17. Pray without ceasing.

Never give up praying — Gspd

Pray constantly — RSV

never cease to pray — TCNT

Be unceasing in prayer — praying perseveringly — Amp

18. In every thing give thanks:

continue to give thanks, whatever be your lot — Con

under all circumstances give thanks to God — TCNT

Thank God whatever happens — Gspd

Make it a habit to thank God for everything — Wms

for this is the will of God in Christ Jesus concerning you.

For this is a thing willed of God . . . — Rhm

this is what God expects of you all in Christ Jesus — Knox

If you follow this advice you will be working out the will of God expressed to you in Christ Jesus — Phi

19. Quench not the Spirit.

Quench not [the manifestation] of the Spirit — Con

Do not put out the light of the Spirit — TCNT

Do not extinguish the Spirit's fire — Ber

Do not stifle the voice of the Spirit — TCNT

Do not stifle the utterances of the Spirit — Knox

Do not stifle inspiration — NEB

20. Despise not prophesyings.

Think not meanly of prophesyings — — Con

do not make light of prophetic gifts — TCNT

do not despise prophetic utterance — Ber

do not hold prophecy in low esteem — Knox

Do not scoff at those who prophesy — Tay

21. Prove all things;

try all [which the prophets utter] — Con

but test everything — RSV

Bring everything to the test — TCNT

but continue to prove all things until you can approve them — Wms

and yet you must scrutinize it all carefully — Knox

hold fast that which is good.

cling to what is good — TCNT

What is comely hold ye fast — Rhm

retaining only what is good — Knox

22. Abstain from all appearance of evil.

. . . wickedness — Rhm

hold yourselves aloof from every form of evil — Con

shun every form of evil — TCNT

and rejecting all that has a look of evil about it — Knox

23. And the very God of peace sanctify you wholly;

and the God of peace himself . . . — ASV

. . . hallow you completely — Rhm

May the God of peace consecrate you through and through — Mof

and I pray God your whole spirit and soul and body be preserved blameless

... be kept sound and blameless — RSV

... be preserved entire, without blame — ASV

... be kept altogether faultless — Mon

unto the coming of our Lord Jesus Christ.

at the appearing of ... — Con

24. **Faithful is he that calleth you,**

He who calls you will not fail you — TCNT

who also will do it.

he will complete his work — TCNT

He will fulfil my prayer — Con

25. **Brethren, pray for us.**

26. **Greet all the brethren with an holy kiss.**

... with a sacred kiss — TCNT

Give a handshake all round — Phi

27. **I charge you by the Lord**

I adjure ... — ASV

I give orders in the name of the Lord — Bas

that this epistle be read unto all the holy brethren.

to have this letter read to all the Brethren — TCNT

28. **The grace of our Lord Jesus Christ be with you. Amen.**

947

THE SECOND
EPISTLE OF PAUL TO THE THESSALONIANS

CHAPTER 1

1. Paul, and Silvanus, and Timotheus,
Paul, Silas, and Timothy — TCNT

unto the church of the Thessalonians
to the church assembled at Thessalonica — Knox
Unto the assembly of Thessalonians — Rhm
to the congregation of Thessalonians — NEB

in God our Father and the Lord Jesus Christ:
in union with God our Father . . . — TCNT
founded on God our Father . . . — Phi
who belong to God our Father . . . — NEB
kept safe in God our Father — Tay

2. Grace unto you, and peace, from God our Father and the Lord Jesus Christ.
May God, the Father, and the Lord Jesus Christ bless you and give you peace — TCNT
Grace (unmerited favor) be to you and heart peace from . . . — Amp

3. We are bound to thank God always for you, brethren, as it is meet,
. . . as is fitting — Con
Brothers, it is our duty always to thank God about you, as is but right — TCNT
We owe a constant debt of thanksgiving to God, brethren, on your behalf; we have good reason for it — Knox

because that your faith groweth exceedingly,
because your faith is growing abundantly — RSV
considering the wonderful growth of your faith — TCNT
when your faith thrives so well — Knox
because your faith increases mightily — NEB
because your faith is greatly enlarged — NASB

and the charity of every one of you all toward each other aboundeth;
and because, without exception, your love for one another is continually increasing — TCNT
and your mutual love, one and all, is increasing — Mof

and your love for one another exceeds all measure — Knox
and the love you have, each for all and all for each, grows ever greater — NEB

4. So that we ourselves glory in you in the churches of God
So that we ourselves in you are boasting in the assemblies of God — Rhm
So much is this the case that we ourselves speak with pride, before the Churches of God — TCNT
so that we are always boasting of you among the churches of God — Wms
. . . among the congregations of God's people — NEB

for your patience and faith in all your persecutions and tribulations that ye endure:
for your steadfastness and faith in all your persecutions and in the afflictions which you are enduring — RSV
for your patient endurance and faith, in spite of your persecutions and crushing sorrows which you are enduring — Wms
because your faith remains so steadfast under all your persecutions, and all the troubles you endure — NEB
for your steadfastness — your unflinching endurance and patience — and your firm faith in the midst of all the persecutions and crushing distresses and afflictions under which you are holding up — Amp
. . . in spite of all the crushing troubles and hardships you are going through — Tay

5. Which is a manifest token of the righteous judgment of God,
A proof of the righteous judgment of God — Rhm
These persecutions will vindicate the justice of God's judgement — TCNT
For these are a plain token of God's righteous judgement — Wey
They are proof positive of God's equity — Mof
This is a proof of God's justice in judging — Gspd
This is evidence of the righteous judgment of God — RSV

948

These qualities show how justly the judgment of God works out in your case — Phi

See how this brings out the justice of God's judgement — NEB

This is a clear proof of God's justice in judging — Nor

that ye may be counted worthy of the kingdom of God, for which ye also suffer:

and will result in your being reckoned worthy of God's Kingdom, for the sake of which you are now afflicted — TCNT

His aim being to let you show yourselves worthy of His kingdom — Wms

Without doubt he intends to use your suffering to make you worthy . . . — Phi

for he is using your sufferings to make you ready for His kingdom — Tay

6. Seeing it is a righteous thing with God to recompense tribulation to them that trouble you;

since God deems it just to inflict suffering upon those who are now inflicting suffering upon you — TCNT

since God considers it but just to repay with trouble those who trouble you — Mof

. . . to repay with suffering those who are making you suffer — Gspd

. . . to repay with crushing sorrows those who cause you these crushing sorrows — Wms

It is surely just that God should balance the account by sending trouble to those who trouble you — NEB

For after all it is only just for God to repay with affliction those who afflict you — NASB

7. And to you who are troubled rest with us,

and to give relief to you who are suffering, as well as to us — TCNT

and to give rest to you who are being crushed with sorrows, along with us — Wms

when the Lord Jesus shall be revealed from heaven with his mighty angels,

By the revealing of the Lord Jesus from heaven With his messengers of power — Rhm

at the Appearing . . . — TCNT

at the unveiling . . . — Wms

8. In flaming fire taking vengeance on them that know not God,

in flaming fire. Then he will inflict punishment upon those who refuse to know God — TCNT

in a blaze of fire, and takes vengeance on the godless — Gspd

in flaming fire, inflicting vengeance upon those who do not know God — RSV

with fire flaming about him, as he pours out vengeance on those who do not acknowledge God — Knox

It will bring full justice in dazzling flame upon those who have refused to know God — Phi

dealing out retribution to those who do not know God — NASB

Bringing judgment on those who do not wish to know God — Tay

and that obey not the gospel of our Lord Jesus Christ:

And them who decline to hearken unto the glad-message of our Lord Jesus — Rhm

and [upon those] who ignore and refuse to obey the Gospel of our Lord Jesus Christ — Amp

and upon those who turn a deaf ear to the Good News of Jesus, our Lord — TCNT

that is, those who will not listen to . . . — Wms

and who refuse to submit to His plan to save them through our Lord Jesus Christ — Tay

9. Who shall be punished

Who indeed a penalty shall pay — Rhm

they shall receive their righteous doom — Con

These men will pay the penalty — TCNT

Their punishment will be — Phi

They will be punished — Tay

with everlasting destruction from the presence of the Lord,

of everlasting Ruin — banished from the presence of the Lord — TCNT

with eternal ruin and exclusion from . . . — Gspd

of eternal destruction as exiles from . . . — Wms

949

eternal exclusion from the radiance of the face of the Lord — Phi

in everlasting hell, forever shut away from the face of the Lord — Tay

by being taken away from the Lord — Beck

and from the glory of his power;

and from the glorious manifestation of his might — TCNT

and the majesty of his power — Knox

and the glorious majesty of his power — Phi

and the splendour of his might — NEB

never to see the glory of His power — Tay

10. When he shall come to be glorified in his saints,

Whensoever he shall come To be made all-glorious in his saints — Rhm

when he comes to be honoured in his People — TCNT

when . . . He comes to be glorified in His consecrated ones — Wms

when he comes to shew how glorious he is in his saints — Knox

But to those whom he has made holy his coming will mean splendor unimaginable — Phi

and to be admired in all them that believe

and to be marvelled at . . . — ASV

and [He will] be marveled at and admired [in His glory reflected] in all who have believed . . . — Amp

and to be revered in all who have learnt to believe — TCNT

how marvellously he has dealt with all the faithful — Knox

It will be a breath-taking wonder to all who believe — Phi

and adored among all believers — NEB

(because our testimony among you was believed) in that day.

. . . our witness . . . — Rhm

on that day (for our testimony has found confirmation in your lives) — Mof

on that day . . . — because our testimony has been confidently accepted among you — Wms

in that day . . .; [and you are of that number], for you believed my testimony — Con

11. Wherefore also we pray always for you,

To which end . . . — RSV

In view of this great prospect . . . — Phi

With this in view, our constant prayer for you is — TCNT

And so we keep on praying for you — Tay

that our God would count you worthy of this calling,

. . . your calling — ASV

. . . the Call that you have received — TCNT

. . . His call — Wey

and fulfil all the good pleasure of his goodness,

and may fulfil every good resolve — RSV

and fulfil every desire of goodness — ASV

and mightily perfect within you all the content of goodness — Con

and by his power make perfect your delight in all goodness — TCNT

and by his power to fulfil every good resolve — Mof

and mightily bring to fulfilment every good purpose — NEB

and the work of faith with power:

and every work of faith, with power — ASV

and the efforts that have resulted from your faith — TCNT

all the activity of your faith — Knox

and every act inspired by faith — NEB

12. That the name of our Lord Jesus Christ may be glorified in you,

. . . may be made all-glorious in you — Rhm

Then . . . will the name of Jesus, our Lord, be honoured in you — TCNT

We pray that the name of our Lord Jesus may become more glorious through you — Phi

and ye in him, according to the grace of our God and the Lord Jesus Christ.

and you through union with Him, in accordance with the favor of God and the Lord Jesus Christ — Wms

and that you may share something of his glory — all through the grace of our God and the Lord Jesus Christ — Phi

CHAPTER 2

1. Now we beseech you, brethren, by the coming of our Lord Jesus Christ,

Now we do implore you, by the very certainty of the coming of . . . — Phi

Now we beseech you, brethren, touching the coming of . . . — ASV

But concerning the appearing of our Lord Jesus Christ . . . I beseech you, brethren — Con

As to the Coming of our Lord Jesus Christ . . . we beg you, Brothers — TCNT

But there is one entreaty we would make of you, brethren, as you look forward to the time when our Lord Jesus Christ will come — Knox

and by our gathering together unto him,

and our gathering together to meet him — Con

and our muster before him — Mof

and our assembling to meet him — RSV

and our being gathered to meet him — TCNT

and gather us in to himself — Knox

2. That ye be not soon shaken in mind, or be troubled,

That ye be not quickly tossed from your mind nor be put in alarm — Rhm

not rashly to be shaken from your soberness of mind, nor to be agitated — Con

not lightly to let your minds become unsettled, nor yet to be disturbed — TCNT

Not to allow your minds to be quickly unsettled or disturbed or kept excited or alarmed — Amp

Do not be terrified out of your senses all at once, and thrown into confusion — Knox

to keep your heads and not be thrown off your balance — Phi

do not suddenly lose your heads or alarm yourselves — NEB

neither by spirit, nor by word, nor by letter as from us,

either by spirit, or by rumor, or by letter attributed to me — Con

by any revelation, or by any message, or by any letter, purporting to come from us — TCNT

whether by some message by the Spirit or by some saying or letter that is claimed as coming from me — Wms

by an alleged revelation of the Spirit, or by some remark or letter attributed to us — Nor

as that the day of Christ is at hand.

. . . the day of the Lord is just at hand — ASV

. . . the day of the Lord hath set in — Rhm

to the effect that the Day of the Lord is come — TCNT

alleging that the Day of the Lord is already here — NEB

3. Let no man deceive you by any means:

Let no man beguile you in any wise — ASV

Let nobody delude you into this belief, whatever he may say — Mof

for that day shall not come, except there come a falling away first,

for before that day, the falling away must first have come — Con

for it cannot come unless the apostasy comes first — Wey

for that cannot take place until the great revolt occurs — Wms

It will not come till the Rebellion takes place first of all — Mof

For it will not come until after the Great Apostasy — TCNT

That day will not come before there arises a definite rejection of God — Phi

That day cannot come before the final rebellion against God — NEB

For that day will not come until two things happen: first, there will be a time of great rebellion against God — Tay

and that man of sin be revealed, the son of perdition;

And there be revealed the man of lawlessness, The son of destruction — Rhm

and the appearing of that Incarnation of Wickedness, that Lost Soul — TCNT

and the representative of lawlessness is uncovered, the one who is doomed to destruction — Wms

951

the champion of wickedness must first appear, destined to inherit perdition — Knox

when wickedness will be revealed in human form, the man doomed to perdition — NEB

and then the man of rebellion will come — the son of hell — Tay

4. Who opposeth and exalteth himself above all that is called God, or that is worshipped;

Who opposes and exalts himself so proudly and insolently against and over all that is called God or that is worshiped — Amp

who opposes himself and exalts himself against all that is called God, and against all worship — Con

who sets himself against and exalts himself above every so-called god or object of worship — Wey

who vaunts himself above and against every so-called god or object of worship — Mof

This is the rebel who is to lift up his head above every divine name, above all that men hold in reverence — Knox

so proudly insolent toward everything called God or worshiped — Ber

He rises in his pride against every god, so called, every object of men's worship — NEB

He will defy every god there is, and tear down every other object of adoration and worship — Tay

so that he as God sitteth in the temple of God, shewing himself that he is God.

even to seat himself in the temple of God, and openly declare himself a God — Con

actually seating himself in the temple of God with the proclamation that he himself is God — Mof

till at last he enthrones himself in God's temple, and proclaims himself as God — Knox

He will go in and sit as God in the temple of God, claiming that he is God Himself — Tay

5. Remember ye not, that, when I was yet with you, I told you these things?

Do you not remember that when I was

still with you, I often told you this — Con

. . . I used to speak to you of all this — TCNT

. . . I mentioned this to you repeatedly — Nor

6. And now ye know what withholdeth that he might be revealed in his time.

And now ye know that which restraineth, to the end that he may be revealed in his own season — ASV

And now you know the hindrance why he is not yet revealed, in his own season — Con

And you know now what the restraining influence is which prevents his appearing before his appointed time — TCNT

So now you know the power that is holding him back, that he is to be unveiled at His own appointed time — Wms

At present there is a power (you know what I mean) which holds him in check, so he may not shew himself before the time appointed to him — Knox

You will probably also remember how I used to talk about a "restraining power" which would operate until the time should come for the emergence of this man — Phi

you must now be aware of the restraining hand which ensures that he shall be revealed only at the proper time — NEB

7. For the mystery of iniquity doth already work:

For the secret of lawlessness already is inwardly working itself — Rhm

For the mystery of lawlessness — that hidden principle of rebellion against constituted authority — is already at work in the world — Amp

Wickedness, indeed, is already at work in secret — TCNT

For the secret power of lawlessness is already at work — Wms

meanwhile, the conspiracy of revolt is already at work — Knox

For already the secret power of wickedness is at work — NEB

only he who now letteth will let, until he be taken out of the way.

only there is one that restraineth now, until he be taken out of the way — ASV

but only until he who at present restrains it is removed out of the way — TCNT

only, he who checks it now will be able to check it, until he is removed from the enemy's path — Knox

but its activities are restricted until what I have called the "restraining power" is removed — Phi

secret only for the present until the Restrainer disappears from the scene — NEB

but the evil work is held in check and will be held back until the time when He who now restrains will be set aside — Nor

8. And then shall that Wicked be revealed,

And then shall be revealed the lawless one — ASV

Then will 'Wickedness Incarnate' appear — TCNT

Then the embodiment of disobedience will make his appearance — Gspd

Then the representative of lawlessness will be uncovered — Wms

And then the lawless man will appear in person — Mof

whom the Lord shall consume with the spirit of his mouth,

whom the Lord Jesus shall slay with the breath of his mouth — ASV

But the Lord Jesus will blast him by the breath of his mouth — Nor

and shall destroy with the brightness of his coming:

and destroy him by his appearing and his coming — RSV

and bring to nought by the manifestation of his coming — ASV

And paralyse with the forthshining of his Presence — Rhm

and annihilate him by the splendour of his Coming — TCNT

and annihilate by the radiance of his coming — NEB

and put a stop to his operations by His appearance and coming — Wms

9. Even him, whose coming is after the working of Satan

that is, the representative of lawless-

ness, whose coming is in accordance with the working of Satan — Wms

But the appearance of that lawless one shall be in the strength of Satan's working — Con

For at the Coming of the Lord there will be great activity on the part of Satan — TCNT

He will come, when he comes, with all Satan's influence to aid him — Knox

The lawless man is produced by the spirit of evil — Phi

It is through the cunning of Satan that this man of sin will come — Nor

with all power and signs of lying wonders,

With all manner of mighty work and signs and wonders of falsehood — Rhm

in the form of all kinds of deceptive miracles, signs, and marvels — TCNT

with his plenitude of power and pretended signs and wonders — Wms

there will be no lack of power, of counterfeit signs and wonders — Knox

and aimed with all the force, wonders and signs that falsehood can devise — Phi

and Satan will furnish him with every sort of power and with pretended signs and miracles — Nor

10. And with all deceivableness of unrighteousness in them that perish;

and all the delusions of unrighteousness, for those who are in the way of perdition — Con

and with all wicked deception for those who are to perish — RSV

To those involved in this dying world he will come with evil's undiluted power to deceive — Phi

and all the deception that sinfulness can impose on those doomed to destruction — NEB

because they received not the love of the truth, that they might be saved.

since they refuse to love the Truth that would save them — Mof

because they did not open their minds to love the truth, so as to find salvation — NEB

11. And for this cause God shall send them strong delusion,

. . . a working of error — ASV

. . . a fatal delusion — Wey

... an active delusion — Mof
... a misleading influence — Gspd
... the full force of evil's delusion — Phi
... powerful heresies among them — Nor

that they should believe a lie:
... believe that lie — Wey
... put faith in falsehood — Mof
... put their faith in an utter fraud — Phi
... the lie — NEB
and let them believe lies — Nor

12. **That they all might be damned**
... judged — ASV
... condemned — Con
... doomed — Mof
who believed not the truth,
who refused credence to the truth — Knox
who refuses to believe the Truth — TCNT
but had pleasure in unrighteousness.
but delight in wickedness — TCNT
but have preferred disobedience—Gspd
and have made evil their playfellow — Phi

13. **But we are bound to give thanks alway to God for you,**
... it is our duty always to thank God ... — TCNT
brethren beloved of the Lord,
brethren whom the Lord has so favoured — Knox
brothers, loved by the Lord as you are — Ber
because God hath from the beginning[1] chosen you to salvation
because God has chosen you as the first to be reaped for salvation — Mof
God has picked you out as the first-fruits in the harvest of salvation — Knox
because God chose you from the beginning to be saved — RSV
for, from the first, God chose you for Salvation — TCNT
through sanctification of the Spirit and belief of the truth:
through the purifying influence of the Spirit, and your belief in the Truth — TCNT
by sanctifying your spirits and convincing you of his truth — Knox

14. **Whereunto he called you by our gospel,**
it was for this that he called you by our gospel — Mof
[It was] to this end that He called you through our Gospel — Amp
It was his call that you followed when we preached the gospel to you — Phi
For this purpose He called you by the good news we tell — Beck
to the obtaining of the glory of our Lord Jesus Christ.
to attain to the glory of our Lord Jesus Christ — TCNT
to gain the glory of ... — Mof
so that you may share in the glory of ... — Gspd
so that you may possess for your own the splendour of ... — NEB

15. **Therefore, brethren, stand fast,**
Stand firm then, Brothers — TCNT
and hold the traditions which ye have been taught,
... the instructions ... — Rhm
... the teaching which has been delivered to you — Con
and hold to the rules which you have learned from us — Mof
and keep a tight grip on the teachings you have received from us — Wms
and hold on! Be loyal to the teachings we passed on to you — Phi
whether by word, or our epistle.
whether by my words or by my letters — Con
either by word of mouth or by letter — RSV
orally or by letter — Mof

16. **Now our Lord Jesus Christ himself, and God, even our Father, which hath loved us,**
who has shewn such love to us—Knox
and hath given us everlasting consolation
and gave us eternal comfort — RSV
and, in his loving-kindness, gave us unfailing consolation — TCNT
and good hope through grace,
and a hope that cannot fail — Con
and good ground for hope — TCNT
and a well-founded hope — Gspd

17. **Comfort your hearts,**

---

[1]Some manuscripts read "first-fruits" instead of "from the beginning."

Console your hearts — Rhm
inspire you with courage — Phi
**and stablish you in every good word
and work.**
and strengthen you to do and say all

that is right — TCNT
and strengthen you in every good thing
you do or say — Wms
and fortify you in every good deed
and word! — NEB

CHAPTER 3

1. **Finally, brethren, pray for us, that the
word of the Lord may have free
course,**
... may run — ASV
... may hold its onward course — Con
... may spread rapidly — TCNT
... may speed on — Mof
... may continue to spread — Wms
... may go forward unhindered — Phi
and be glorified, even as it is with you:
and be received everywhere with honour, as it was among you — TCNT
and be extolled ... — Wey
and prove its glorious power ...—Wms
and bring him glory ... — Phi
and triumph wherever it goes, winning
converts everywhere as it did when
it came to you — Tay
and be glorified (extolled) and triumph, even as [it has done] with you
— Amp

2. **And that we may be delivered from
unreasonable and wicked men:**
and that we may be preserved from
wrong-headed and wicked men —
TCNT
... saved from unjust and wicked men
— Gspd
... unprincipled and wicked men —
Wms
... unbalanced and malicious people
— Ber
and that we may be preserved from
malicious interference — Knox
for all men have not faith.
... hold the faith — Rhm
the faith does not reach all hearts —
Knox

3. **But the Lord is faithful,**
But the Lord is to be relied on — Gspd
But the Lord keeps faith with us —
Knox
**who shall stablish you, and keep you
from evil.**
he will give you strength, and guard
you from Evil — TCNT
... give you strength and protect you
from the evil one — Gspd

... fortify you and guard you from the
evil one — NEB

4. **And we have confidence in the Lord
touching you,**
We have faith in you through the Lord
— Gspd
We are sure of you in the Lord —
Knox
We feel perfect confidence about you,
in the Lord — NEB
And I rely on you in the Lord — Con
**that ye both do and will do the things
which we command you.**
that you practice and will practice what
we suggested — Ber
that you are following and will follow
my precepts — Con

5. **And the Lord direct your hearts into
the love of God,**
But may the Lord guide your hearts
... — Rhm
... into ever deeper understanding of
his love — Phi
May the Lord guide you into a realization of God's love for you — Wms
and into the patient waiting for Christ.
... the patience of Christ — ASV
... the steadfastness of Christ — Con
and into the steadfastness and patience
of Christ in waiting for His return
— Amp

6. **Now we command you, brethren, in
the name of our Lord Jesus Christ,**
We urge you, Brothers ... — TCNT
Brothers, we charge you ... — Mof
**that ye withdraw yourselves from every
brother that walketh disorderly,**
that you keep away from any brother
who is living in idleness — RSV
to avoid any Brother who is living an
ill-ordered life — TCNT
to stand aloof from every brother
whose life is disorderly — Wey
to shun any brother who is loafing —
Mof
to hold yourselves aloof from any
brother who is living as a shirker —
Wms

to have nothing to do with any brother who lives a vagabond life — Knox

don't associate with the brother whose life is undisciplined — Phi

and not after the tradition which he received of us.

. . . they received . . . — ASV

which is not in agreement with the teaching that you received from us — TCNT

and who despises the teaching we gave you — Phi

7. For yourselves know how ye ought to follow us:

. . . how ye ought to imitate us — ASV

For you know yourselves the way to follow my example — Con

. . . how to copy us — Mof

for we behaved not ourselves disorderly among you;

When we were with you, our life was not ill-ordered — TCNT

we did not loaf in your midst — Mof

we were no vagabonds ourselves — Knox

our lives among you were never undisciplined — Phi

we were no idlers among you — NEB

you never saw us loafing — Tay

8. Neither did we eat any man's bread for nought;

nor did we eat any one's bread without paying for it — TCNT

we did not take free meals from anyone — Mof

we did not accept board and lodging from anyone without paying for it — NEB

but wrought with labour and travail night and day,

no, toiling hard at our trade, we worked night and day — Mof

instead, we did hard and heavy work night and day — Ber

we toiled and drudged, we worked for a living night and day — NEB

that we might not be chargeable to any of you:

so as not to be a burden upon any of you — TCNT

so as not to impose on any of you — Ber

to avoid the slightest expense to any of you — Phi

9. Not because we have not power,

This was not because we had not a right to receive support — TCNT

not that we are obliged to do so — Knox

but to make ourselves an ensample unto you to follow us.

. . . imitate us — ASV

but our object was to give you a pattern for you to copy — TCNT

. . . for you to imitate — Con

but as a model for your own behaviour — Knox

10. For even when we were with you, this we commanded you,

For when I was with you I often, gave you this rule: — Con

Indeed, when we were with you, what we urged upon you was — TCNT

The charge we gave you on our visit was — Knox

When we were actually with you we gave you this principle to work on: — Phi

. . . we laid down the rule: — NEB

that if any would not work, neither should he eat.

that the man who refuses to work must be left to starve — Knox

the man who will not work shall not eat — NEB

11. For we hear that there are some which walk among you disorderly,[2]

We hear that there are among you people who are living ill-ordered lives — TCNT

working not at all, but are busybodies.

At nothing working, yet too busily working! — Rhm

neglecting their own work, and meddling with that of others — Con

busybodies instead of busy — Mof

neglecting their own business to mind other people's — Knox

never doing a stroke of work, and busy only in other people's affairs — Phi

12. Now them that are such we command and exhort by our Lord Jesus Christ,

. . . we urge and entreat . . . — TCNT

Now with the authority of the Lord Jesus Christ we charge and exhort such people — Gspd

---

[2]See verse 6 for translation of "disorderly."

Our order to such men, indeed our appeal by the Lord Jesus Christ, is — Phi

that with quietness they work, and eat their own bread.

to attend quietly to their business, and earn their own living — TCNT

to settle down to work and eat the food they have earned themselves — Phi

to work quietly for their living — NEB

that they work in quietness and earn their own food and other necessities — Amp

13. But ye, brethren, be not weary in well doing.

But you, Brothers, must not grow weary of doing what is right — TCNT

. . . must not get tired of doing right — Gspd

And the rest of you — don't get tired of honest work! — Phi

14. And if any man obey not our word by this epistle,

If any man be disobedient to my written word — Con

If any one disregards what we have said in this letter — TCNT

If anybody refuses to listen to what we have said in our letter — Knox

. . . does not follow up our messages . . . — Ber

note that man,

take special note of that man — NASB

he is to be a marked man — Knox

and have no company with him,

and avoid his company — TCNT

do not associate with him — Mof

and stop having anything to do with him — Wms

that he may be ashamed.

till he is ashamed of himself — Knox

15. Yet count him not as an enemy,

Yet do not think of him as an enemy — TCNT

Do not look upon him as an enemy — — Gspd

You must not regard him as an enemy — Wms

but admonish him as a brother.

but caution him as you would a Brother — TCNT

but warn him as . . . — Gspd

correcting him like . . . — Knox

but reprimand him as . . . — Phi

but give him friendly advice, as one of the family — NEB

16. Now the Lord of peace himself give you peace

May the Lord, from whom all peace comes, himself give you his peace — TCNT

always by all means.

at all times in all ways — ASV

in all ways and at all seasons — Con

continually, whatever comes — Mof

in every circumstance — NASB

no matter what happens — Tay

The Lord be with you all.

May he be with you all — TCNT

17. The salutation of Paul with mine own hand, which is the token in every epistle:

I, Paul, add this greeting in my own handwriting. It is my signature to every letter — TCNT

. . . this authenticates all my letters — NEB

. . . for proof that it really is from me — Tay

so I write.

This is how I write — TCNT

This is my handwriting — Wms

18. The grace of our Lord Jesus Christ be with you all. Amen.

May the blessing of our Lord Jesus Christ be with you all — TCNT

The favour of our Lord Jesus Christ be with you all — Rhm

THE
FIRST EPISTLE OF PAUL TO TIMOTHY

CHAPTER 1

1. Paul, an apostle of Jesus Christ

Paul, an apostle (special messenger) of Christ Jesus — Amp

Paul, Jesus Christ's messenger — Phi

by the commandment of God our Saviour,

according to the commandment of God our Saviour — ASV

by order of God . . . — Gspd

By injunction of God . . . — Rhm

by appointment of God . . . — Wey

and Lord Jesus Christ, which is our hope;

and Christ Jesus, our Hope — TCNT

and of Christ Jesus, the Messiah, our Hope — Amp

and by Jesus Christ our Lord — our only hope — Tay

2. Unto Timothy, my own son in the faith:

to Timothy, my true child in the faith — NASB

to Timothy my genuine child in faith — Wms

. . . his true-born son . . . — NEB

. . . my real son by faith — Beck

Grace, mercy and peace,

Favour mercy peace — Rhm

spiritual blessing, mercy, and peace be with you — Wms

from God our Father and Jesus Christ our Lord.

From God the Father and Christ Jesus . . . — ASV

. . . God, the Father, and Christ Jesus, our Lord — TCNT

3. As I besought thee to abide still at Ephesus,

Even as I exhorted thee to remain in . . . — Rhm

As I besought thee to continue in . . . — ABUV

I begged you to remain on in . . . — Wey

As I urged you . . . — RSV

when I went into Macedonia,

when I was going into . . . — ASV

. . . was on my way to . . . — Alf

. . . was setting out for . . . — Con

just before I went to . . . — Phi

that thou mightest charge some

that thou mightest command certain persons — Con

that you may instruct certain people there — TCNT

that you might caution certain persons — Wey

to warn certain teachers — Wms

that they teach no other doctrine,

not to teach a different doctrine — ASV

not to teach strange views — Gspd

against teaching novelties — Mof

not to be teaching heterodoxy — Mon

to stop inventing new doctrines — Phi

4. Neither give heed to fables and endless genealogies,

nor to be paying attention to myths and interminable genealogies — Mon

to stop devoting themselves to myths and never-ending pedigrees — Wms

and not to busy themselves with stories and endless records of ancestors — Beck

against occupying their minds with legends and . . . — Knox

which minister questions,

which promote speculations — RSV

which further disputes — ABUV[1]

which bring arguings — Rhm

which furnish ground for disputation — Con

— wild ideas that stir up questions and arguments — Tay

rather than godly edifying which is in faith:

rather than God's stewardship, which is in faith — ABUV

rather than that stewardship of God which is with faith — Rhm

rather than acceptance by faith of God's administration — Ber

rather than a stewardship entrusted by God, a stewardship which is in faith — Mon

rather than to further that divine plan which is revealed in the Faith — TCNT

instead of helping people accept God's plan of faith — Tay

---

[1]Alternative reading.

. . . acceptance in faith of God's provision for salvation — Wey

so do.

[so I do now.] — ABUV

Do so still — Wey

5. Now the end of the commandment is charity

But the end of the charge is love — ASV

The end at which our warning aims is charity — Knox

But the goal of our instruction is love — NASB

The object to be secured by such caution is the love — Wey

Whereas the aim of the Christian discipline is the love — Mof

out of a pure heart, and of a good conscience, and of faith unfeigned:

from a pure heart and a good conscience and a faith without hypocrisy — NASB

that rises out of a pure heart, a clear conscience, and undisguised faith — Ber

that issues from a pure heart and a good conscience and sincere faith — RSV

6. From which some having swerved

from which some erring — ABUV

From these some have deviated—Wey

For some men, straying from these things — NASB

Certain persons by swerving from these — RSV

Some people have stepped aside from these things — Wms

But certain individuals have missed the mark on this very matter — Amp

But these teachers have missed this whole idea — Tay

have turned aside unto vain jangling;

have turned off into empty talk — Ber

and turned to fruitless talking — Wms

have gone astray into a wilderness of words — NEB

. . . unto vain babbling — Alf

. . . into vain arguments and discussions and purposeless talk — Amp

and have lost their way in empty reasoning — Wey

7. Desiring to be teachers of the law;

wishing to be teachers of the law — ABUV

They are ambitious to be teachers. . . — Wey

understanding neither what they say,

— Not understanding either what they say — Rhm

even though they do not understand either what they are saying — NASB

but they have no idea either of the meaning of the words they use — Mof

yet they fail to realize the meaning of their own words — Phi

nor whereof they affirm.

nor about what they positively affirm — ABUV

or the things about which they make such confident assertions — Wms

or the things they so confidently express — Beck

or of the themes on which they harp — Mof

8. But we know that the law is good,

Now we know that excellent is the law — Rhm

But we know that the Law is admirable — Ber

if a man use it lawfully;

if one put it to a lawful use — Rhm

when used legitimately — TCNT

if a man makes a right use of it — Bas

if it is used as it was meant to be used — Beck

9. Knowing this,

as knowing this — ASV

recognizing — NEB

keeping this in mind — Ber

and be aware of this — Alf

that the law is not made for a righteous man,

that a law is not enacted for a righteous man — Wey

that the law is not laid down for the just — RSV

That to a righteous man law doth not apply — Rhm

that law is not intended for upright men — Gspd

. . . the upright and just, who are in right standing with God — Amp

but for the lawless and disobedient,

but for the lawless and insubordinate — Alf

. . . the lawless and disorderly — TCNT

. . . lawless and unruly men — ABUV

... those who are lawless and rebellious — NASB

... the wicked and rebellious — Lam

... those who have no respect for law and order — Bas

for the ungodly and for sinners,

for the impious and sinful — Con

for the irreligious and sinful — Mon

for irreligious and wicked people — TCNT

for ungodly and sinful — ABUV

the godless and sinful — Wms

for unholy and profane,

for the irreverent and the profane — Mof

for the impious and profane — Ber

the irreligious and worldly — NEB

the godless and profane — Wey

for the unholy and those who have no religion — Bas

those who live unholy lives and insult holy things — Beck

for murderers of fathers and murderers of mothers, for manslayers,

for smiters of fathers and smiters of mothers, ... — Alf

for patricides and matricides; for homicides — Ber

for those who lay violent hands on father or mother, for murderers — Knox

Yes, the Law is directed against the sort of people who attack their own parents, who kill their fellows — Phi

for those who illtreat their fathers or mothers, for murderers — TCNT

10. For whoremongers, for them that defile themselves with mankind,

for fornicators, for abusers of themselves with men — ASV

for the immoral, for sexual perverts — Mon

for fornicators, sodomites — Con

and immoral men and homosexuals — NASB

men who sin sexually with women or with other men — Beck

for menstealers, for liars, for perjured persons,

slave-dealers, liars, perjurers — Con

kidnapers, falsifiers, perjurers — Ber

... those who lie or swear to lies — Beck

... liars, and false witnesses — Wey

and if there be any other thing that is contrary to sound doctrine;

and for whatever else is opposed to the wholesome teaching — Wey

And if anything else unto the healthful teaching is opposed — Rhm

and those who do any other things against the right teaching — Bas

— in fact all whose behaviour flouts the wholesome teaching — NEB

and for whatever else is opposed to sound Christian teaching — TCNT

... that opposes sound moral teaching Nor

11. According to the glorious gospel of the blessed God,

according to the gospel of the glory of the blissful God — ABUV

According to the glad-message of the glory of the happy God — Rhm

in accordance with the glorious gospel of the blessed God — RSV

which conforms with . . . the gospel which tells of the glory of God in his eternal felicity — NEB

— as is taught in the glorious Good News of the ever-blessed God — TCNT

as set forth in the glorious good news of . . . — Gspd

as measured by the glorious good news of . . . — Wms

which was committed to my trust.

with which I was entrusted — Alf

which was given into my care — Bas

12. And I thank Christ Jesus our Lord, who hath enabled me,

I thank him that enabled me, even Christ Jesus our Lord — ASV

I thank him who gave me power, Christ . . . — ABUV

Grateful am I unto him that empowered me . . . — Rhm

I give thanks to him that put strength in me, even Christ Jesus our Lord — Alf

who has made me equal to the task, . . . — NEB

I am thankful to Christ Jesus, our Lord, who has been my strength — TCNT

How I thank our Lord Jesus Christ, the source of all my strength — Knox

for that he counted me faithful,

In that faithful he accounted me —
Rhm

— because He has judged me faithful
— Wey

for thinking me trustworthy — Gspd

for shewing confidence in me — Knox

He thought I could be trusted — Beck

. . . considered me reliable — Nor

. . . deemed me worthy — Ber

for judging me worthy of this trust —
NEB

putting me into the ministry;

appointing me to his service — ASV

and appointed me to do His work —
Beck

appointing me to [this stewardship of]
the ministry — Amp

by appointing me to his ministry —
TCNT

**13. Who was before a blasphemer, and a
persecutor, and injurious:**

though I was before a blasphemer, and
a persecutor, and an insulter — Alf

Though formerly a defamer and persecutor and insulter — Rhm

me who was formerly a slanderer, a
persecutor, and an oppressor — Ber

. . . and a wanton aggressor — Mof

. . . and an insolent foe — Nor

. . . and a doer of outrage — Con

though I was previously guilty of blasphemy and persecution and wanton
outrage — Wey

— although in the past I had met him
with abuse and persecution and outrage — NEB

but I obtained mercy,

Nevertheless mercy was shown me —
Rhm

because I did it ignorantly in unbelief.

because I had acted ignorantly, in unbelief — Wey

because without knowledge I acted in
unbelief — Rhm

because in my unbelief I had acted out
of ignorance — Mof

because what I did was done in the
ignorance of a man without faith —
Phi

because I didn't know what I was doing, for I didn't know Christ at that
time — Tay

**14. And the grace of our Lord was ex-
ceeding abundant**

Yet exceeding abundant was the favour
of our Lord — Rhm

and the grace of our Lord was more
than abundant — Wey

and the loving-kindness of our Lord
was boundless — TCNT

. . . abounded beyond measure — Con

. . . overflowed for me — RSV

. . . flooded my life — Mof

. . . was lavished upon me — NEB

The grace of the Lord came upon me
in a full tide — Knox

**with faith and love which is in Christ
Jesus.**

. . . with the faith and love which are
found in Christ Jesus — NASB

with the faith and love which are ours
in . . . — NEB

with faith and love that rest in . . . —
Ber

along with the faith and love that
Christ Jesus inspires — Mof

together with faith and love that union
with Christ Jesus brings — Gspd

of faith and love, the love that is in
Christ Jesus — Knox

15. This is a faithful saying,

Faithful is the saying — ASV

Faithful the saying! — Rhm

It is a trustworthy statement — NASB

It is a saying to be trusted — Wms

It is a sure word — Mof

True is the saying — Wey

Reliable is the message — Ber

and worthy of all acceptation,

entitled to the fullest acceptance —
Gspd

and deserving of wholehearted acceptance — Ber

and what a welcome it deserves —
Knox

and deserving of universal acceptance
— Wey

**that Christ Jesus came into the world
to save sinners;**

That Christ Jesus came into the world
sinners to save — Rhm

— Christ Jesus entered the world to
rescue sinners — Phi

of whom I am chief.

Of whom the chief am I — Rhm

among whom I am foremost — Wey

and among them I stand first — NEB

I am the worst of them — Beck

961

And there is no greater sinner than I!
— TCNT

16. Howbeit for this cause I obtained mercy,

Nevertheless on this account was mercy shewn me — Rhm

Yet mercy was shown me for the express purpose — TCNT

that in me first

that in me as chief — ASV

in order that in me as the foremost — Wey

that . . . in my case, beyond all others — TCNT

so that in me first of all — Knox

Jesus Christ might shew forth all long-suffering,

. . . shew forth his entire longsuffering — Rhm

. . . shew forth the whole of his longsuffering — Alf

. . . display the fulness of His patience — Wey

. . . display His unlimited patience — Ber

. . . demonstrate how vast is His patience — Nor

. . . exhibit . . . his exhaustless patience — TCNT

. . . give the extreme example of his patience — Knox

. . . demonstrate His perfect patience — NASB

for a pattern to them

for an ensample of them — ASV

for an example to [encourage] those — Amp

as a striking example for those — Wey

as an illustration for those — Mon

a typical illustration of it for all — Mof

and that I might be typical of all — NEB

which should hereafter believe on him to life everlasting.

that should thereafter believe on him unto eternal life — ASV

who would afterwards rest their faith on Him with a view to . . . — Wey

about to believe on him unto life age-abiding — Rhm

who were afterwards to believe on him and attain Immortal Life — TCNT

17. Now unto the King eternal, immortal, invisible, the only wise God,

But unto the King of the ages, the immortal, the invisible, the only God — Alf

Now to the King eternal, ever-living, unseen, the only God — Bas

Now to the King of the ages, the incorruptible, invisible, only God — ABUV

Now to the king of all worlds, . . . — NEB

. . . who alone is God — Wey

be honour and glory for ever and ever. Amen.

Be honour and glory unto the ages of ages. Amen! — Rhm

— be honor and glory through the endless ages! Amen! — Nor

be ascribed honour and glory . . . — TCNT

. . . for ever and ever. So be it — Bas

18. This charge I commit unto thee, son Timothy,

This, then, is the charge that I lay upon you, Timothy, my Child — TCNT

This order I give to you, Timothy my son — Bas

This command I entrust to you, . . . — NASB

I transmit these injunctions to you, Timotheus my son — Mof

This is the instruction which I entrust to you, my son Timothy — Wms

according to the prophecies which went before on thee,

according to the prophecies which led the way to thee — ASV

in accordance with the prophecies previously made concerning thee — NASB

in accordance with the prophetic utterances which pointed to you — RSV

in agreement with the previous prophecies that bear on yourself — Ber

in accordance with what was predicted of you — TCNT

. . . what the prophets said who first directed me to you — Mof

. . . prophetic intimations which I formerly received concerning you — Amp

that thou by them mightest war a good warfare.

that thou mayest war in them the good warfare — Alf

that by them you may fight the good fight — NASB

so that you may with their aid put up a splendid fight — Ber

that you may, aided by them, continue to fight the good fight — Wms

that being equipped with them you may . . . — Wey

that in the strength thereof thou mayest . . . — Con

that inspired by them you may wage the good warfare — RSV

— Fight the good fight in the spirit of those predictions — TCNT

19. Holding faith, and a good conscience;

having faith, and a good conscience — ABUV

possessed of faith and a clear conscience — Ber

holding fast to . . . — Wey

by keeping your hold on . . . — Wms

armed with faith and . . . — NEB

Cling tightly to your faith in Christ and always keep your conscience clear — Tay

which some having put away

which some having thrust from them — ASV

which some have rejected — NASB

which certain individuals have cast aside — Mon

for some have thrust the latter aside — Wms

It was through spurning conscience that certain persons — NEB

Certain individuals have scouted the good conscience — Mof

Some, through refusing this duty — Knox

concerning faith have made shipwreck:

made shipwreck concerning the faith — ASV

and suffered shipwreck in regard to their faith — NASB

and, as far as their faith is concerned, have run their ships on the rocks — Phi

and have had their faith ruined—Gspd

and thus come to grief over their faith — Mof

as regards the Faith, some have wrecked their lives — TCNT

20. Of whom is Hymenaeus and Alexander;

Among whom are Hymenaeus and Alexander — Con

Hymenaeus and Alexander are two examples of this — Tay

whom I have delivered unto Satan,

whom I have given over to Satan — Mon

whom I turned over . . . — Gspd

that they may learn not to blaspheme.

that they might be taught not to blaspheme — ASV

so they may be disciplined not to speak profanely — Ber

to be so disciplined that they will stop their abusive speech — Wms

to be disciplined so that they may no longer blaspheme — Lam

that they may be taught by chastisement not to blaspheme — Alf

blaspheme — Alf

. . . taught by punishment not to blaspheme — Con

. . . not to slander holy things — Beck

That will teach them to stop their blasphemous ongoings! — Mof

CHAPTER 2

1. I exhort therefore, that, first of all,

I exhort therefore, first of all, that — ASV

First of all then, I am urging, that — Mon

I urge you, as most important of all — Beck

Well, my very first counsel is that — Mof

supplications, prayers, intercessions, and giving of thanks,

petitions, prayers, intercessions, and thanksgivings — TCNT

supplications, prayers, petitions, and thanksgivings — Wey

earnest requests, humble entreaties, intercessions and . . . — Nor

be made for all men;

be made on behalf of all men — NASB

be offered regularly for all men—Mon

should be offered for all mankind — Knox

2. For kings, and for all that are in authority;

In behalf of kings and all them who are in eminent station — Rhm for kings and all who hold high positions — Ber

for sovereigns and all in high office — NEB

for emperors, and all who are in authority — Gspd

for kings and rulers in positions of responsibility — Phi

that we may lead a quiet and peaceable life

that we may lead a tranquil and quiet life — ASV

In order that an undisturbed and quiet life we may lead — Rhm

that we may live peaceful and tranquil lives — Wey

so that we may have a calm and quiet life — Bas

that [outwardly] we may pass a quiet and undisturbed life [and inwardly] a peaceable one — Amp

in all godliness and honesty.

in all godliness and gravity — ASV

in all godliness and decorum — ABUV

with all reverence and dignity — Ber

in perfect piety and seriousness—Wms

godly and respectful in every way — RSV

in a deeply religious and reverent spirit — TCNT

in full observance of religion and high standards of morality — NEB

3. **For this is good and acceptable in the sight of God our Saviour;**

For this is good and pleasing in the eyes of our Saviour God — Mon

This is comely and acceptable before our Saviour God — Rhm

Such praying is wholesome and is welcome in the presence of God our Saviour — Ber

Such prayer is right, and approved by God . . . — NEB

It is good to do this, and it pleases God . . . — Gspd

4. **Who will have all men to be saved,**

who would have all men to be saved — ASV

who wishes all mankind to be saved — Wey

who desires all men . . . — Mof

who wants all persons . . . — Ber

For He longs for all . . . — Tay

who is ever willing for all mankind . . . — Wms

whose will it is that all men should find salvation — NEB

and to come unto the knowledge of the truth.

And unto a personal knowledge of truth to come — Rhm

and come into full knowledge of the truth — Mon

and attain to a full knowledge of the Truth — TCNT

and to come to an understanding of . . . — Ber

and to come to an increasing knowledge of . . . — Wms

and come to realize the truth — Phi

and be led to recognize the truth — Knox

and increasingly to perceive and recognize and discern and know precisely and correctly the [divine] Truth: — Amp

5. **For there is one God,**

There is but one God — TCNT

That there [is only] one God — Amp

For God is one — Mon

and one mediator between God and men, the man Christ Jesus;

one mediator also between God and men, himself man, Christ Jesus — ASV

and one intermediary between God and men — the man Christ Jesus—Gspd

and one go-between of God and of men, . . . — Ber

and one peacemaker between God and men, . . . — Bas

and one is mediator between God and man, . . . — Mon

and [only] one mediator between . . . — Amp

and One who brings God and men together, . . . — Beck

6. **Who gave himself a ransom for all,**

who gave Himself as a ransom for all — Wey

Who gave himself a ransom in behalf of all — Rhm

who sacrificed himself to win freedom for all mankind — NEB

Who gave himself as an offering for all — Bas

to be testified in due time.

The testimony in its own fit times — Rhm

the testimony borne at the proper time
— NASB

the testimony to be given in due season — ABUV

a testimony which came in due time — Lam

— a fact testified to at its own appointed time — Wey

and this was announced at the right times — Beck

— in due time this was attested — Mof

witness of which was to be given at the right time — Bas

This is the message which at the proper time God gave to the world — Tay

This must be our testimony, as opportunities present themselves — TCNT

7. Whereunto I am ordained a preacher, and an apostle,

For this I was appointed a herald and apostle — Ber

Unto which I have been appointed proclaimer and apostle — Rhm

and for which purpose I was appointed a preacher and . . . — Wms

And of this testimony I was appointed . . . — Con

Of this fact I have been made . . . — Wey

(I speak the truth in Christ, and lie not;)

(I speak the truth, I lie not) — ASV

— I am telling the truth; I do not falsify — Ber

— Truth I speak I utter no falsehood — Rhm

(what I say is true, not false) — Bas

(I make no false claims, I am only recalling the truth) — Knox

a teacher of the Gentiles in faith and verity.

A teacher of nations in faith and truth — Rhm

— a teacher of the heathen in the realm of faith and truth — Wms

— to teach the heathen faith and truth — Gspd

to instruct the nations in the true faith — NEB

to teach . . . the gentile world to believe and know the truth — Phi

and to show them God's plan of salvation through faith — Tay

8. I will therefore

I desire therefore — ASV

My wish, then, is — Mon

I am minded therefore — Rhm

that men pray every where,

that the men pray in every place — ASV

that in every place the men should offer up prayers — Con

that it should be the custom everywhere for the men to lead the prayers — TCNT

that everywhere prayers be said by the men of the congregation — NEB

. . . at any meeting of the church — Mof

lifting up holy hands, without wrath and doubting.

Uplifting hands of lovingkindness Apart from anger and disputings — Rhm

lifting to heaven holy hands which are kept unstained by anger and dissension — Wms

with hands reverently uplifted, avoiding heated controversy — TCNT

lifting up their hands in holiness, putting away anger and disputation — Con

as without anger and disputing they lift up dedicated hands — Ber

. . . not in a mood of anger or argument — Beck

9. In like manner also,

In the same way — Rhm

In similar spirit — Ber

I also desire — TCNT

in like manner also the women — Mon

So, too, with the women — Knox

that women adorn themselves in modest apparel,

that women adorn themselves, in becoming apparel — ABUV

that the women — In seemly attire . . . be adorning themselves — Rhm

the women shall dress themselves . . . in becoming attire — Ber

I desire women to clothe themselves in suitable apparel — Mon

that the women should come in seemly apparel — Con

. . . in orderly apparel — Alf

. . . in becoming manner — NEB

. . . with appropriate dress — TCNT

. . . in proper clothes — Gspd

with shamefacedness and sobriety;

with shamefastness and sobriety — ASV

with modesty and soberness — ABUV
with modesty and self-restraint — Con
modestly and discreetly — Nor
modestly and prudently — Ber
modest and refined — Lam
modestly and sensibly — Gspd
with a quiet and serious air — Bas
adorning themselves with reverence
and self-restraint — Mon
and their demeanor should be modest
and serious — Phi

not with broided hair, or gold,
not with braided hair, and gold — ASV
and not with wreaths or gold ornaments for the hair — TCNT
Not with plaitings and ornamentation
of gold — Rhm
not with [elaborate] hair arrangement
or gold — Amp
not with elaborate hair-styles, not
decked out with gold — NEB
The adornment of a Christian woman
is not a matter of an elaborate coif-
fure — Phi

or pearls, or costly array;
or pearls or costly raiment — ASV
or pearls or expensive dresses — Wms
or pearls, or rich clothes — Knox
or jewels or robes of great price — Bas
or pearls or expensive finery — Mof
expensive clothes or valuable jewelry
— Phi

10. **But (which becometh women professing godliness)**
but — as befits women making a claim
to godliness — Wey
but, as is appropriate for women who
profess to be religious — Gspd
but as (becomes women proclaiming
godliness) — Mon
as is right for women who are living in
the fear of God — Bas
. . . women who profess to be pious —
Wms
. . . women who lay claim to piety —
Knox
. . . women who profess reverential fear
for and devotion to God — Amp

with good works.
through good works — ASV
by means of good works — Alf
with good deeds — Mof
— with good actions — TCNT
with the ornament of good works —
Con

clothed with good works — Bas

11. **Let the woman learn in silence with
all subjection.**
Let a woman in quietness be learning
in all submission — Rhm
A woman shall quietly learn with complete submission — Ber
Let a woman quietly receive instruction
with entire submissiveness — NASB
Let a woman quietly take the place of
a learner and be under authority —
Bas
A married woman must learn in quiet
and in perfect submission — Wms
A woman must listen quietly in church
and be perfectly submissive — Mof
A woman should listen silently to her
teachers, and show them all deference — TCNT
A woman should learn quietly and
humbly — Phi

12. **But I suffer not a woman to teach, nor
to usurp authority over the man,**
But I do not allow a woman to teach
or exercise authority over a man —
NASB
But teaching — unto a woman I do not
permit, Nor yet to have authority
over a man — Rhm
But I suffer not the woman to teach,
nor yet to rule over the man — Alf
. . . to teach, nor to have dominion over
a man — ASV
. . . to teach, nor to claim authority,
over the man — Con
. . . to teach, neither to domineer over
a man — Ber
. . . to teach or dictate to men — Mof
. . . to teach, and issue commands to
her husband — Knox
I do not permit a married woman to
practice teaching or domineering
over a husband — Wms
I never let women teach men or lord
it over them — Tay

but to be in silence.
but to be in quietness — ASV
but to remain quiet — NASB
instead, she is to keep still — Ber
but she must remain silent — Wey
she is to remain in quietness and keep
silence [in religious assemblies] —
Amp

13. **For Adam was first formed, then Eve.**

For Adam was created first, and Eve afterwards — NEB

(My reasons are that man was created before woman — Phi

Why? Because God made Adam first, and afterwards He made Eve — Tay

14. And Adam was not deceived,

and Adam was not beguiled — ASV

nor is it Adam that went astray — Knox

And Adam was not taken by deceit — Bas

It was not Adam who was deceived by the serpent — Nor

And Adam was not fooled by Satan — Tay

but the woman being deceived was in the transgression.

but the woman being beguiled hath fallen into transgression — ASV

but the woman, deluded as she was, experienced the transgression — Ber

it was the woman who was deluded and fell into sin — Gspd

but his wife was thoroughly deceived, and became involved in transgression — Wey

. . . having been wholly deceived hath come to be in transgression — Rhm

. . . being taken by the deceit hath become a transgressor — Alf

. . . being tricked, became a wrong-doer — Bas

. . . yielding to deception, fell into sin — NEB

woman was led astray, and was involved in transgression — Knox

15. Notwithstanding she shall be saved in childbearing,

But she shall be saved through child-bearing — ABUV

but she shall be saved through her child-bearing — ASV

But women will find their salvation in motherhood — TCNT

Notwithstanding she will be saved by the Child-bearing — Mon

But she shall be preserved through the bearing of children — NASB

However, women will get safely through childbirth — Mof

But women will be saved by the bearing of children — Con

Yet woman will find her salvation in child-bearing — Knox

So God sent pain and sorrow to women when their children are born, but He will save their souls — Tay

if they continue in faith and charity and holiness

if they abide in faith, and love, and sanctification — ABUV

if they continue to live in faith, love, and purity — Wms

if they continue to be faithful and loving and holy — Mof

if they continue to have faith and to be loving and holy — Gspd

if they never abandon faith, love, or holiness — TCNT

if the women continue in faith and love and sanctity — NASB

with sobriety.

with soberness — ABUV

with sobermindedness — Alf

with modesty — RSV

with self-restraint — Con

blended with good sense — Wms

and use good judgment — Beck

CHAPTER 3

1. This is a true saying,[2]

There is a popular saying: — NEB

If a man desire the office of a bishop,

if any man aspires to the office of overseer — NASB

If any one longs for the office of bishop — ABUV

If anyone for oversight is eager — Rhm

If a man seeketh the office of a bishop — ASV

When a man aspires to be a Presiding-Officer in the Church — TCNT

. . . the office of superintendent — Gspd

. . . the office of a minister — Mon

. . . the office of pastor — Wms

Whoever aspires to the office of overseer — Ber

To aspire to leadership — NEB

he desireth a good work.

A noble work doth he covet — Rhm

he is aspiring to a noble task — Mon

it is a fine work he desires to do — NASB

---

[2]See I Tim. 1:15.

he is ambitious for a noble task — TCNT
desires an excellent work — Wms
sets his heart on a fine work — Gspd
is out for a splendid task — Ber
is an honourable ambition — NEB

2. A bishop then must be blameless,

The bishop therefore must be without reproach — ASV

It is needful then for the overseer to be irreproachable — Rhm

The Presiding-Officer should be a man of blameless character — TCNT

A superintendent must be a man above reproach — Gspd

. . . must be one with whom no fault can be found — Knox

. . . must give no grounds for accusation but must be above reproach — Amp

. . . must be of blameless reputation — Phi

. . . must be a good man whose life cannot be spoken against — Tay

the husband of one wife,

one wife's husband — Ber
must have only one wife — Wms
faithful to his one wife — NEB
he must be married only once — Mof

vigilant, sober, of good behaviour,

temperate, sober-minded, orderly—ASV
temperate, prudent, respectable — NASB
temperate, sensible, dignified — RSV
he must be temperate, master of himself, unruffled — Mof
living a temperate, discreet, and well-ordered life — TCNT
sober, self-restrained, orderly — Con
self-controlled, serious-minded, having respect for order — Bas
. . . and leading an orderly (disciplined) life — Amp

given to hospitality,

hospitable — Alf
opening his house freely to guests — Bas
[he must be] hospitable—showing love for and being a friend to the believers, especially strangers or foreigners — Amp

apt to teach;

skilled in teaching — Con
and with a gift for teaching — Wey
qualified to teach — Ber
and a good teacher — NEB
apt in teaching — Alf

a ready teacher — Bas

3. Not given to wine, no striker, not greedy of filthy lucre;

no brawler, no striker — ASV
not addicted to wine or pugnacious — NASB
not a hard drinker nor given to blows — Wey
Not given to wine, not combative — Amp
neither a drunkard nor a fist-fighter — Ber
He must be neither intemperate nor violent — Phi
. . . not ready to wound — Rhm
. . . He must not be quarrelsome—Nor

but patient, not a brawler, not covetous;

but gentle, not contentious, no lover of money — ASV
but forbearing, averse to strife, not a money-lover — ABUV
But considerate averse to contention not fond of money — Rhm
but gentle, not pugnacious, . . . — Wey
but of a forbearing disposition, avoiding quarrels, . . . — NEB
but genial, conciliatory, not after money — Ber
. . . peaceable, and liberal — Con
. . . neither quarrelsome nor grasping — Knox
. . . not be a controversialist nor must he be fond of money-grabbing — Phi

4. One that ruleth well his own house,

Over his own house presiding well — Rhm
presiding beautifully over his own house — Ber
ruling his own household well — Con
managing his own house well — Gspd
able to manage his own household properly — Mof
He should manage his own family well — Beck
He must be one who is a good head to his own family — Knox

having his children in subjection with all gravity;

Having children in submission with all dignity — Rhm
keeping his children under control with true dignity — Wey

having his children in subjection with all decorum — ABUV

with perfect seriousness keeping his children under control — Wms

keeping his children submissive and respectful in every way — RSV

and whose children are kept under control and well-behaved — TCNT

and keep his children ever under control and thoroughly well behaved — Mon

5. (For if a man know not how to rule his own house,

(but if one knows not how to preside over his own house — ABUV

If a man does not know how to manage his own household — Wey

if he can not superintend his own home affairs — Nor

— for if a man does not know how to conduct his own household — Gspd

. . . how to control his own family — NEB

. . . can't make his own little family behave — Tay

if a man has not learned how to manage his own household — Knox

how shall he take care of the church of God?)

how shall he take charge of a church of God — Mon

How of an assembly of God shall he take care — Rhm

how can he look after a congregation of God's people — NEB

will he know how to govern God's church — Knox

6. Not a novice,

Not a new convert — Rhm

He must not be a recent convert — Mon

He must not be a beginner in the faith — Phi

. . . not be a new Christian — Tay

lest being lifted up with pride

lest being puffed up — ASV

Lest being beclouded — Rhm

for fear he should be blinded with pride — Wey

lest being besotted with pride — Alf

or else becoming conceited — Wms

for fear that, through his high opinion of himself — Bas

or he may be carried away by vanity — Knox

because he might be proud of being chosen so soon — Tay

or he may [develop a beclouded and stupid state of mind] as the result of pride — Amp

he fall into the condemnation of the devil.

into the sentence of the adversary he fall — Rhm

he fall into the judgment of the devil — Alf

and fall into the condemnation incurred by the devil — NASB

and come under the same condemnation as the Devil — Wey

and fall under similar sentence as the devil — Ber

and incurs the doom passed on the devil — Mof

and incur criticism from slanderous people — Gspd

7. Moreover he must have a good report of them which are without;

It is needful moreover to have an honourable testimony also from them who are without — Rhm

But he must also have a good testimony from those outside — ABUV

He should also be well spoken of by outsiders — TCNT

And he is to have a good name among those outside the church — Bas

He must also enjoy a favorable reputation . . . — Ber

. . . have a good reputation with the non-Christian public — NEB

. . . be a man of good standing with outsiders — Gspd

. . . bear a good character, too, in the world's eyes — Knox

lest he fall into reproach and the snare of the devil.

that he fall not into reproach and a snare of the Devil — ABUV

Lest into reproach he fall and the snare of the adversary — Rhm

or else he may incur reproach and fall into the devil's trap — Wms

so he may not be involved in slander and get snared by . . . — Ber

so that he may not be exposed to scandal and get caught in the devil's snare — NEB

that he may not incur censure and so fall into . . . — TCNT

or he may fall into disgrace and ... — Beck

or he may get into disgrace and be entrapped by the slanderers — Gspd

8. Likewise must the deacons be grave,

In like manner the deacons [must be] worthy of respect — Amp

Ministers in the same way — Dignified — Rhm

So, too, Assistant-Officers should be serious — TCNT

In the same way the helpers in the church should be serious — Beck

Deacons, in the same way, must be men of serious demeanour — Wey

... men of serious outlook — Phi

... men of high principle — NEB

By the same token are deacons to be honorable — Ber

not doubletongued, not given to much wine,

not indulging in double talk, given neither to excessive drinking — NEB

not shifty and double talkers but sincere in what they say, ... — Amp

not false in word, not given to taking much wine — Bas

straightforward men, not addicted to wine — Gspd

sincere in their talk, not addicted to strong drink — Wms

... They too should be temperate — Phi

not greedy of filthy lucre;

or fond of sordid gain — NASB

not greedy of base gain — Rhm

not greedy for ill-gotten gains — Ber

or to questionable money-making — TCNT

nor to money-grubbing — NEB

nor greedy for base gain — craving wealth and resorting to ignoble and dishonest methods of getting it — Amp

9. Holding the mystery of the faith in a pure conscience.

Holding the sacred secret of the faith in. . . — Rhm

but they must continue to hold the open secret of faith with . . . — Wms

but holding the divine truth of the faith with . . . — Gspd

they must maintain the divine truth of the faith with . . . — Mof

but with a pure conscience keeping

hold on the hidden truth of the faith — Ber

. . . who hold the deep truths of the Faith and have a . . . — TCNT

These must be men who combine a clear conscience with a firm hold on the deep truths of our faith — NEB

10. And let these also first be proved;

And let them also be tested first — RSV

Let these first be examined — Lam

They too, should first be tested till approved — Wms

And these, too, must undergo probation — Wey

No less than bishops, they must first undergo a scrutiny — NEB

and let them also be tried and investigated and proved first — Amp

then let them use the office of a deacon, being found blameless.

Then let them be ministering being unaccusable — Rhm

then let them serve as deacons, being without reproach — ABUV

and only appointed to their Office if no objection is raised against them — TCNT

and after trial be made Deacons, if they are found irreproachable—Con

and afterwards, if there is no fault to be found with them, they can serve as assistants — Gspd

and then, if they are of unblemished character, let them serve as deacons — Wey

then if they prove themselves blameless let them serve as deacons — RSV

11. Even so must their wives be grave,

Women in like manner must be grave — ASV

Women must likewise be dignified — NASB

[The] women likewise must be worthy of respect and serious — Amp

Women, in the same way, must be serious-minded — Wey

Women are to be serious in behaviour — Bas

Deaconesses likewise must be grave — Mon

The deaconesses too must be serious — Wms

Their wives, likewise, must be women of gravity — Con

Similarly must the wives be honorable
— Ber

Their wives should share their serious
outlook — Phi

**not slanderers, sober, faithful in all
things.**

not given to slandering, but temperate
and altogether trustworthy — Ber

who will not talk scandal, sober and
trustworthy in every way — NEB

not gossips; they must be temperate,
and perfectly trustworthy — Gspd

not malicious gossips, but temperate,
faithful in all things — NASB

saying no evil of others, controlling
themselves, true in all things — Bas

and must be women of discretion and
self-control — women who can be
trusted — Phi

**12. Let the deacons be the husbands of
one wife,**

Let the deacons be appointed from
those who have not been polyga-
mous — Lam

A deacon must be faithful to his one
wife — NEB

Let ministers be . . . — Rhm

Assistant-Officers should be faithful
husbands — TCNT

The assistants must be only once married — Gspd

**ruling their children and their own
houses well.**

presiding well over their children and
their own houses — ABUV

fitly ruling their children and their own
households — Con

and they must manage their children
and their households properly—Mof

admirable managers of their children
and of their own homes — Ber

and they should have happy, obedient
families — Tay

**13. For they that have used the office of a
deacon well**

For they who have ministered well —
Rhm

For those who render good service —
Wms

Those who have filled that post with
honour — TCNT

For they that have served well as deacons — ASV

Because those who rendered helpful
service as deacons — Ber

For those who have well performed
the office of a Deacon — Con

For deacons with a good record of
service — NEB

purchase to themselves a good degree,

gain to themselves a good standing —
ASV

are gaining an honorable position for
themselves — Mon

obtain for themselves a good standing-
place — Alf

a good degree for themselves are acquiring — Rhm

do take a worthwhile step upward for
themselves — Ber

win a good position for themselves —
Mof

may claim a high standing — NEB

. . . a good reputation — Nor

. . . a sure footing — Knox

**and great boldness in the faith which
is in Christ Jesus.**

and great confidence in the faith that is
in Christ Jesus — NASB

as well as much fearless confidence in
the faith of Christ Jesus — Mon

and become free from fear in the faith
which is . . . — Bas

and great freedom of speech in the
faith that is . . . — Rhm

and acquire great boldness of speech
in their faith in . . . — Wey

and the right to speak openly on matters of the Christian faith — NEB

as well as great confidence through the
faith that they place in Christ Jesus
— TCNT

and great boldness in proclaiming that
faith, which is founded on Christ
Jesus — Knox

14. These things write I unto thee,

These things unto thee I am writing —
Rhm

but I am writing these instructions to
you — RSV

hoping to come unto thee shortly:

hoping to come to you before long —
NASB

in the hope of shortly coming to you —
Ber

though I am hoping before long to
come to see you — Wey

**15. But if I tarry long, that thou mayest
know**

but if I delay, that thou mayest know
— ABUV

but in case I am delayed, I write so
that you may know — NASB

in case I am detained, to let you see —
Mof

But if I am long in coming, this will
make clear to you — Bas

But, for fear I may be hindered, I now
write, so that . . . — Wey

So that if I don't come for awhile you
will know — Tay

**how thou oughtest to behave thyself
in the house of God,**

how one ought to conduct himself in
the household of God — NASB

How it behoveth in a house of God to
behave oneself — Rhm

how men ought to behave themselves
in . . . — ASV

how people ought to conduct themselves in . . . — Wms

how you ought to behave in the household of God — Mon

what your conduct ought to be in . . .
— TCNT

how people should behave in God's
family — Beck

which is the church of the living God,

The which is an assembly of a Living
God — Rhm

(for such is the Church of the living
God) — Con

— the Church of the ever-living God
— Mon

the pillar and ground of the truth.

the pillar and foundation of the truth
— Gspd

. . . and support of the truth — Ber

. . . and buttress of the truth — Wey

. . . and bulwark of the Truth — Mof

. . . and mainstay of the truth — Mon

. . . and stay — the prop and support —
of the Truth — Amp

. . . and base of what is true — Bas

. . . and foundation upon which the
truth rests — Knox

16. **And without controversy great is the
mystery of godliness:**

And confessedly great is the mystery of
godliness — Alf

And by common confession great is
. . . — NASB

And confessedly great is the sacred
secret of godliness — Rhm

And, confessedly, the hidden truth of
godliness is great — Ber

Undoubtedly the mystery of our religion is a great wonder — Wms

And great beyond all question is the
mystery of our religion — NEB

No one can deny the profundity of the
divine truth of our religion! — Gspd

And who does not admit how profound
is the divine truth of our religion? —
Mof

God was manifest in the flesh,

Who was made manifest in flesh —
Rhm

— He who appeared in the flesh —
Wey

He in flesh was manifested — Mon

He (God) was made visible in human
flesh — Amp

He who was seen in the flesh — Bas

He was revealed in our nature — TCNT

. . . made visible in human form —
Wms

. . . showed himself as a human being
— Phi

justified in the Spirit,

Was declared righteous in spirit—Rhm

Pronounced righteous in spirit — TCNT

Was vindicated in the Spirit — NASB

In the Spirit was attested — Mon

was proved righteous by the Spirit —
Wey

was given God's approval in the spirit
Bas

was proved spotless and pure in His
Spirit — Tay

seen of angels,

appeared to angels — ABUV

Was made visible unto messengers —
Rhm

beheld by angels — Con

preached unto the Gentiles,

Preached among the nations — ASV

Among the Gentiles heralded — Mon

He was proclaimed among the heathen
— Gspd

of whom the good news was given
among the nations — Bas

believed on in the world,

Was believed on in [the] world — Rhm

He was trusted in throughout the world
— Wms

believed in by the world — Ber

received up into glory.

Received up in glory — ASV

And in glory taken up — Mon
and received back into the glory of Heaven — Phi

and was received up again to His glory in heaven — Tay
glorified in high heaven — NEB

CHAPTER 4

1. Now the Spirit speaketh expressly,
Now the Spirit expressly declares — Wey
But the Spirit explicitly says — NASB
But the Spirit says distinctly — Ber
But the Spirit says clearly — Bas
God's Spirit specifically tells us — Phi
We are expressly told by inspiration — Knox

that in the latter times some shall depart from the faith,
that in later times some shall fall away from . . . — ASV
that in after times some will desert from . . . — NEB
that, in later days, there will be some who abandon . . . — Knox
That in later seasons some will revolt from . . . — Rhm
. . . certain people will rebel against the faith — Mof
. . . some in the church will turn away from Christ — Tay

giving heed to seducing spirits, and doctrines of devils;
paying attention to deceitful spirits and doctrines of demons — NASB
giving heed to deceiving spirits and the teachings of demons — Wey
because they continuously give their attention to deceiving spirits and the things that demons teach — Wms
and devote their attention to misleading spirits, and . . . — TCNT
and give their minds to subversive doctrines inspired by devils — NEB
they will yield to deluding spirits and demonic teachings — Ber

2. Speaking lies in hypocrisy;
in hypocrisy speaking falsehood—Rhm
in the hypocrisy of speakers of lies — Alf
by means of the hypocrisy of liars — NASB
through the pretensions of liars — Gspd
and this through the hypocrisy of men who teach falsely — Wey
who will make use of the hypocrisy of lying teachers — TCNT

Through the false ways of men whose words are untrue — Bas
They will be taught by men who are lying hypocrites — Nor
These teachers will tell lies with straight faces — Tay

having their conscience seared with a hot iron;
whose consciences are seared (cauterized) — Amp
of men having their own consciences seared with a brand — Alf
whose own consciences are seared as with a branding iron — Ber
whose conscience is hardened as if by a searing-iron — Knox
whose consciences are as dead as seared flesh — Phi
branded in their own conscience as with a hot iron — ASV
. . . branded with the devil's sign—NEB
. . . as the devil's slaves — Beck

3. Forbidding to marry, and commanding to abstain from meats,
hindering marriage, enjoining abstinence from meats — Con
forbidding people to marry, and insisting on abstinence from foods —Wey
Who prohibit marriage, and demand abstinence from foods — Lam
and they discourage marriage and enjoin abstinence from certain kinds of foods — TCNT
They will say it is wrong to be married and wrong to eat meat — Tay

which God hath created to be received with thanksgiving
which God created unto participation with thanksgiving — Alf
which God has created to be partaken of with thankfulness — Wey
. . . to be gratefully shared in — NASB
. . . to be enjoyed with thanksgiving — NEB
though God created these foods to be enjoyed thankfully — TCNT

of them which believe and know the truth.
for them that believe and have full knowledge of . . . — Alf

for those who believe and understand
. . . — Ber

by them who believe and personally
know . . . — Rhm

by those who hold the Faith and have
attained a full knowledge of the
Truth — TCNT

. . . and have a clear knowledge of
. . . — Mon

4. For every creature of God is good,

Because every creature of God . . . —
Alf

For everything that God has created
. . . — Wey

and nothing to be refused,

and nothing is to be rejected — ASV

And nothing to be cast away — Rhm

and there is nothing that need be rejected — TCNT

and nothing is to be tabooed — Mof

and nothing is evil — Bas

if it be received with thanksgiving;

If with thanksgiving it be received —
Rhm

if it is received with gratitude — NASB

when gratefully received — Ber

if only it is received with thankfulness
— Mon

provided it is accepted with thanksgiving — Gspd

**5. For it is sanctified by the word of God
and prayer.**

For it is hallowed by the word of God
and intercession — Rhm

since it is hallowed by God's own word
and by prayer — NEB

it is made holy by the word . . . — Wey

for in this way it is consecrated by the
word . . . — Wms

for then it is consecrated by God's
word, by the prayer uttered over it
— Mof

. . . consecrated by prayer and the
Scripture used in it — Gspd

**6. If thou put the brethren in remem-
brance of these things,**

In pointing out these things to the
brethren — NASB

By setting forth these things to . . . —
Alf

As you lay these things before the
brethren — Mon

In thus instructing . . . — Con

If you continue to put these things before . . . — Wms

If you explain this to the others —
Tay

**thou shalt be a good minister of Jesus
Christ,**

Thou shalt be a noble minister of
Christ Jesus — Rhm

you will be a good servant of . . . —
Wey

you will be an excellent minister of . . .
— Ber

you will prove a good servant of . . . —
NEB

and thou wilt shew thyself a true servant of . . . — Knox

You will be doing your duty as Christ's
minister — Phi

**nourished up in the words of faith and
of good doctrine,**

Nourishing thyself with the words of
the faith and of the noble teaching
— Rhm

while you continue nurturing on the
messages of faith and the noble
teachings — Ber

ever feeding your own soul on the
truths of the faith and the fine teaching — Wms

sustained by the precepts of the Faith
and of that Good Teaching — TCNT

brought up on the truths of the faith
and on . . . — Mof

bred in the precepts of our faith and
of the sound instruction — NEB

trained in the words of the faith, and
of the right teaching — Bas

living on the principles of the faith
and the excellent teaching — Gspd

whereunto thou hast attained.

which you have closely followed —
Amp

which thou hast strictly followed —
ABUV

which you have faithfully followed —
Wey

whose course thou hast followed — Alf

which thou hast closely studied — Rhm

to which you have been conforming
your life — Ber

by which you have guided your life —
TCNT

which you have so faithfully practiced
— Nor

**7. But refuse profane and old wives'
fables,**

But from the profane and old-wives'

stories excuse thyself — Rhm

As for profane legends and old wives' tales, leave them alone — TCNT

Ever reject those profane and old womanish myths — Mon

But make it your habit to let worldly and old women's stories alone — Wms

But shun these unholy and old-womanish tales — Ber

Have nothing to do with godless and silly myths — RSV

But steer clear of all these stupid Godless fictions — Phi

Shut your mind against those profane, drivelling myths — Mof

Reject the fables of profane and doting teachers — Con

. . . irreverent legends — profane and impure and godless fictions, mere grandmothers' tales—and silly myths — Amp

and exercise thyself rather unto godliness.

And be training thyself unto godliness — Rhm

On the other hand, discipline yourself for the purpose of godliness — NASB

and continually train yourself for the contest of godliness — Mon

Train yourself in godliness — RSV

Keep yourself in training for the practice of religion — NEB

Spend your time and energy in the exercise of keeping spiritually fit — Tay

8. For bodily exercise profiteth little:

for bodily discipline is only of little profit — NASB

For the training of the body is profitable for a little — Con

for while bodily training is of some value — RSV

because while physical training is to some benefit — Ber

Physical training, indeed, is of some service — Wms

Bodily fitness has a certain value — Phi

but godliness is profitable unto all things,

but godliness is useful in every respect — Wey

godliness is of value in every way — RSV

godliness is beneficial all around — Ber

but godliness [spiritual training] is useful . . . — Amp

but religion is of service in all directions — Mof

but the benefits of religion are without limit — NEB

but spiritual fitness is essential — Phi

having promise of the life that now is, and of that which is to come.

Having promise of life — The present and the coming — Rhm

it holds promise for this present and for the future life — Ber

for it contains a promise for the present life as well as the future — Wms

since it carries with it a promise of life, both here and hereafter — Mon

9. This is a faithful saying and worthy of all acceptation.[3]

10. For therefore we both labour and suffer reproach,

For to this end we labor and strive — ASV

To this end we are toiling and struggling — Wms

With this before us we labour and struggle — NEB

and this is the motive of our toiling and wrestling — Wey

For this purpose we labor and wrestle — Ber

We toil and agonize — Mon

It is because we realize the paramount importance of the spiritual that we labor and struggle — Phi

because we trust in the living God,

because we have our hope set on the living God — ASV

because we have placed our hope in . . . — Ber

because our hope is fixed upon . . . — Mof

We place our whole confidence in . . . — Phi

. . . the ever-living God — Mon

who is the Saviour of all men,

Who is Saviour of all men — Rhm

who is the Savior of all people — Ber

who is the saviour of all mankind — Con

Who is the Savior (Preserver, Maintainer, Deliverer) of all men — Amp

specially of those that believe.

---

[3]See I Tim. 1:15.

975

especially of believers — Alf
— of believers in particular — Mof
and above all of those who believe in him — Knox
and particularly for those who have accepted His salvation — Tay
and especially of those who hold the Faith — TCNT
. . . believe — trust in, rely on and adhere to Him — Amp

11. These things command and teach.

Prescribe and teach these things — NASB
Charge and teach these things — ABUV
These things enjoin and teach — Con
Continue to give these orders and to teach these truths — Wms
Give these orders and teach these lessons — Mof
Pass on these orders and these teachings — NEB
Dwell upon these things in your teaching — TCNT
This is what you must urge and teach — Gspd

12. Let no man despise thy youth;

Let no one look down on your youthfulness — NASB
. . . despise you on account of your youth — Mon
. . . think little of you because you are young — Wms
. . . think slightingly of you because you are a young man — Wey
. . . slight you because you are a youth — Mof
. . . make little of you because you are young — Bas

but be thou an example of the believers,

but become an example of the believers — ABUV
but make thyself a pattern of the faithful — Con
but always set an example for believers — Wms
make thyself a model . . . for the faithful — Knox
instead, become . . . an example before the believers — Ber
see that they look up to you because you are an example to them — Phi

in word, in conversation, in charity, in spirit, in faith, in purity.

in word, in manner of life, in love, in faith, in purity — ASV
In discourse in behaviour in love in faith in chastity — Rhm
by your conversation, your conduct, your love, your faith, and your purity — TCNT
. . . in love, fidelity, and purity — NEB
. . . in your love, your faith, and your clean thoughts — Tay

13. Till I come, give attendance to

Until I come, devote yourself to — Gspd
Until I arrive devote your attention to — NEB
. . . go ahead with — Ber
. . . take care of — Beck

reading, to exhortation, to doctrine.

the reading, to the exhortation, to the doctrine — Alf
the public reading, the preaching and the teaching — Ber
your Scripture-reading, your preaching, and your teaching — Mof
the reading of the holy Writings, to comforting the saints, . . . — Bas
Reading, preaching, instruction—Knox

14. Neglect not the gift that is in thee,

Be not careless of the gift of favour that is in thee — Rhm
Never neglect the gift within you — Mon
Do not neglect the spiritual endowment you possess — NEB
. . . the spiritual gift within you—NASB
. . . the abilities God gave you — Tay

which was given thee by prophecy,

which was bestowed upon you through prophetic utterance — NASB
. . . conferred on you by prophetic indication — Wey
. . . given thee through means of prophesying — Rhm
. . . under the guidance of prophecy — NEB
. . . prophetically granted you — Ber
. . . given you, amid many a prediction — TCNT
. . . with predictions of your work — Gspd

with the laying on of the hands of the presbytery.

with the laying on of the hands of the eldership — ABUV

when the hands of the elders were placed upon you — Wey

when the hands of the Officers of the Church . . . — TCNT

and the imposition of the presbyters' hands . . . — Knox

. . . the hands of the elders as a body — NEB

. . . their hands upon you [at your ordination] — Amp

5. Meditate upon these things; give thyself wholly to them;

Be diligent in these things; . . . — ASV

Take pains with these things; be absorbed in them — NASB

These things be thy care, In these things be thou — Rhm

Make these things thy care; in these things be employed — Alf

Cultivate these matters, live in them — Ber

Continue cultivating these things; be devoted to them — Wms

Practice these duties and be absorbed in them — Wey

Make these matters your business and your absorbing interest — NEB

Give your whole attention, all your energies, to these things — Phi

. . . give yourself to them with all your heart — Bas

. . . throw yourself wholly into them [your ministry] — Amp

Let this be thy study, these thy employments — Knox

that thy profiting may appear to all.

that thy progress may be manifest . . . — ASV

so that your advance may be evident to everyone — Ber

that thy improvement may be manifest to all men — Con

so that all men may note your progress — Mof

16. Take heed unto thyself, and unto the doctrine;

Be giving heed to thyself and to thy teaching — Rhm

Pay close attention to yourself . . . — NASB

Make it your habit to pay close attention to . . . — Wms

Look well to yourself (to your own personality) . . . — Amp

Keep a critical eye both upon your own life and on the teaching you give — Phi

continue in them:

Persevere in these things — Wey

— Abide still in them — Rhm

Keep right on in these things — Beck

continue steadfast therein — Con

stick to your work — Mof

for in doing this

for as you do this — NASB

For in so doing — Con

for by doing this — Wey

thou shalt both save thyself, and them that hear thee.

Both thyself shalt thou save And them that hearken to thee — Rhm

you will further the salvation of yourself and your hearers — NEB

. . . insure salvation both for yourself and for those who hear you — NASB

. . . secure your own and your hearers' salvation — Wey

. . . save both yourself and those who listen to you — Gspd

CHAPTER 5

1. Rebuke not an elder,

Rebuke not an aged man — Con

An elderly man do not thou reprimand — Rhm

Never administer a sharp reprimand to an older man — Wey

Never censure an older man harshly — Mof

Never speak sharply to . . . — Tay

Do not chide . . . — Ber

Don't reprimand a senior member of your church — Phi

Never be harsh with an elder — NEB

. . . one who has authority in the church — Bas

but intreat him as a father;

but exhort him as thou wouldst a father — Con

But beseech him as [though he were thy] father — Rhm

but plead with him as if he were your father — TCNT

but appeal to him as to a father — Gspd

but address him as a father — Ber

but continue pleading with him . . . — Mon

but plead with him respectfully . . . — Tay

and the younger men as brethren;

and those younger as brothers — Ber

Treat younger men like brothers — Mof

Talk to the younger men as you would to much-loved brothers — Tay

2. **The elder women as mothers;**

Elderly women as mothers — Rhm

Treat the older women as mothers — Tay

In like manner, deal with older women as mothers — Nor

the younger as sisters, with all purity.

Younger women as sisters, in all chastity — Rhm

to the younger (but with all modesty) as sisters — Knox

and the girls as your sisters, thinking only pure thoughts about them — Tay

. . . with perfect propriety — Mof

. . . with absolute purity — Gspd

3. **Honour widows that are widows indeed.**

Give honour to widows who are truly widows — Bas

Treat with respect widows who are all alone — Beck

Pay due regard to the widows who are friendless in their widowhood — Con

Look after widows who are really dependent — Gspd

Relieve widows who are really in need — Wey

Widows in real need must be supported from the funds — Mof

4. **But if any widow have children or nephews,**

. . . hath children or grandchildren — ASV

. . . has children or children's children — Bas

let them learn first to shew piety at home,

. . . learn first to show piety towards their own family — ASV

. . . first learn to practice piety in regard to their own family — NASB

. . . to show their godliness first towards their own household — Con

. . . to show their filial piety at home — Wey

. . . to practice piety in the treatment of their own families — Wms

. . . to practice religion at home — Ber

and to requite their parents;

And returns to be making unto their progenitors — Rhm

and so to return a remuneration for those who nurtured them — Ber

and to return the care of those who brought them up — Gspd

and to pay the debt they owe their parents or grandparents — Wms

so that the children have the opportunity to repay their obligations to their parents — Lam

for that is good and acceptable before God.

for this is acceptable in the sight of God — ASV

for that is what God approves — Gspd

for God looks with favor on such action — Nor

In God's sight this is a commendable deed.) — Mof

5. **Now she that is a widow indeed, and desolate,**

But she who is indeed a widow and is left alone — Rhm

She who is a real widow, and is left all alone — RSV

. . . and desolate in her widowhood — Con

. . . and has no children — Gspd

. . . one who is alone in the world — NEB

trusteth in God,

hath her hope set on God — ASV

Hath turned her hope towards God — Rhm

puts her hope in God — Bas

has her hopes fixed on God — Wey

and continueth in supplications and prayers night and day.

and continues in entreaties and prayers . . . — NASB

and is steadfast in her petitions and prayers . . . — Ber

and perseveres in supplications and prayers . . . — Amp

and devotes herself to prayers and entreaties . . . — Gspd

6. **But she that liveth in pleasure**

But she that giveth herself to pleasure
— ASV
but a pleasure-loving widow — Wey
whereas she who is self-indulgent —
RSV
while one who lives voluptuously—Ber
But she who lives in wantonness —
Mon
whereas the widow who plunges into
dissipation — Mof
. . . gives herself up to luxury — Wms
is dead while she liveth.
is dead while existing — Ber
is dead even while still alive — Wey
is really dead though still alive — Wms

7. And these things give in charge,
These things also command — ASV
Prescribe these things as well — NASB
Press these facts upon them — Wey
Add these orders to the rest — NEB
Continue to give these directions —
Wms
Drive home these suggestions — Ber
Insist upon these points — Gspd
that they may be blameless.
that they may be irreproachable — Alf
so that the people may be without reproach — Wms
so that they may live lives free from
reproach — Wey
so that no evil may be said of anyone
— Bas
that there may be no call for your censure — TCNT

8. But if any provide not for his own,
If a man makes no provision for his
own relations — Wey
Whoever fails to provide for his own
relatives — Wms
If however anyone for his own . . .
taketh not forethought — Rhm
**and specially for those of his own
house,**
and specially his own household—ASV
and particularly for his own family —
Mof
. . . for those of his immediate family
— Wms
. . . for those under his own roof —
TCNT
he hath denied the faith,
he has disowned the faith — Wey
has repudiated the faith — Mof
His faith hath he denied — Rhm

has contradicted the teaching of the
faith — Knox
has no right to say he is a Christian —
Tay
and is worse than an infidel.
. . . than an unbeliever — ASV
. . . than one who has no faith — Bas
and is behaving worse than an unbeliever — Wey
. . . than the heathen — Tay

**9. Let not a widow be taken into the
number under threescore years old,**
Let no one be enrolled as a widow under sixty years old — ABUV
Let a widow not be put on the list if
she is less than . . . — NASB
Let no one be put on the roll of widows
[who are to receive church support]
who is under sixty years of age —
Amp
having been the wife of one man,
the wife of one husband — Alf
One man's wife — Rhm
She must have been faithful in marriage to one man — NEB
and she must have been only once married — Mof

10. Well reported of for good works;
In noble works well-attested — Rhm
must have a reputation for doing good
deeds — Wms
and have a good reputation for Christian service — Gspd
if she have brought up children,
If she hath nourished children — Rhm
if she has had the care of children —
Bas
who has reared children — Ber
as one who has brought up a family
— Mon
for having brought up her children
properly — Nor
if she have lodged strangers,
if she has shown hospitality to strangers
— NASB
if she entertained strangers — Alf
if she has been kind to travellers —
Bas
who has practiced hospitality to strangers [of the brotherhood] — Amp
if she have washed the saints' feet,
washing the feet of God's people —
Gspd
. . . willing to serve fellow Christians in
menial ways — Phi

if she have relieved the afflicted,

if she relieved afflicted ones — ABUV

if she assisted those in distress — NASB

If them who were in tribulation she hath succoured — Rhm

helping those who are in trouble — Bas

for having given relief to the oppressed — Nor

if she have diligently followed every good work.

if she followed after every good work — Alf

and has been devoted to all kinds of good works — Ber

and devoted herself to every kind of good action — TCNT

and interested herself in all good works — Mof

and was busy doing every kind of good work — Beck

11. But the younger widows refuse:

But younger widows decline — Alf

. . . reject — Con

. . . you must not enrol — Wey

But turn down younger widows — Ber

But exclude from the list . . . — Mon

. . . should not become members of this special group — Tay

for when they have begun to wax wanton against Christ,

For as soon as they wax wanton against the Christ — Rhm

for when they feel sensual desires in disregard of Christ — NASB

for when their wanton desires make them chafe against Christ — Mof

. . . their youthful vigor comes between them and Christ — Gspd

. . . their passions draw them away from Christ — NEB

. . . they get to indulging their lower nature in opposition to Christ — Wms

. . . their affections stray wantonly from Christ — Wey

. . . they grow restive under the yoke of the Christ — TCNT

they will marry;

they wish to marry — ABUV

they have a desire to be married — Bas

To marry are they determined — Rhm

they hanker after marriage — NEB

12. Having damnation,

Having as sentence — Rhm

bearing a judgment — Alf

thus incurring condemnation — NASB

and they incur the censure — Wey

and thus are guilty — Mof

because they have cast off their first faith.

That their first faith they have set at nought — Rhm

because they made void their first faith — Alf

because they have been untrue to their first faith — Lam

because they have set aside their previous pledge — NASB

because they have broken their former promise — Con

of having broken their first plighted faith — Wey

for having violated their first pledge — RSV

of breaking their first troth to Him — Mof

of breaking their prime engagement — Ber

13. And withal they learn to be idle,

At the same time to be idlers are they learning — Rhm

Presently they acquire habits of idleness — Ber

Besides, they are likely to be lazy — Tay

Moreover, they get into habits of slackness — Phi

wandering about from house to house;

going about from house to house—ASV

by gadding about from one house to another — Mof

as they go about visiting their neighbors — Nor

and not only idle, but tattlers also and busybodies,

and not merely idle, but also gossips and busybodies — NASB

and not only doing no work, but talking foolishly, being over-interested in the business of others — Bas

. . . they gossip and interfere — Knox

. . . but gossiping and meddling — Beck

. . . getting into other people's business — Tay

speaking things which they ought not.

talking about things not proper to mention — NASB

saying things which they have no right to say — Bas

repeating things they ought not — Mon

speaking of things that ought not to be
spoken of — Wey

speaking of things better left unspoken
— NEB

**14. I will therefore that the younger
women marry,**

I wish therefore that younger widows
should marry — Con

Therefore, I want younger widows to
get married — NASB

Therefore I advise . . . — TCNT

bear children, guide the house,

have children, and preside over a home
— NEB

. . . be mistress of the house — Rhm

. . . manage their own households —
Lam

. . . controlling their families — Bas

**give none occasion to the adversary to
speak reproachfully.**

Giving no single occasion unto the op-
poser as a cause of reviling — Rhm

and afford the opponent no incentive
whatever for slandering — Ber

and so avoid giving the enemy an opportunity for scandal — TCNT

. . . any excuse for abusing us — Gspd

. . . no handle for speaking ill of us —
Knox

**15. For some are already turned aside
after Satan.**

For already some of them have gone
astray after Satan — Con

. . . some widows have already strayed
. . . — Mof

. . . have gone astray, following Satan
— Wey

. . . have already played into the enemy's hands — Phi

**16. If any man or woman that believeth
have widows,**

If any believing woman has widows —
— ABUV

If any woman who is a believer has dependent widows — NASB

Any Christian woman who has widowed relatives — Gspd

let them relieve them,

let her relieve them — ASV

let her assist them — RSV

Let her be giving them succour — Rhm

she should help them — Wms

should look after them — Gspd

and let not the church be charged;

and let not the church be burdened —
ASV

And not suffer the assembly to be burdened — Rhm

and let the church be free from the
burden — Wms

the congregation must be relieved of
the burden — NEB

**that it may relieve them that are
widows indeed.**

so that it may assist those who are real
widows — RSV

That them who are indeed widows it
may itself succour — Rhm

and so it may give help to those who
are truly widowed — Bas

so that the church may relieve the
really destitute widows — Mon

. . . be free to support those who are
widows in the full sense of the term
— NEB

. . . can look after widows who are
really dependent — Gspd

17. Let the elders that rule well

Let the Elders who preside well —
Wey

Let the presbyters that rule well —
Alf

Let the well presiding elders — Rhm

Presbyters who are efficient presidents
— Mof

Those Officers of the Church who fill
their office well — TCNT

The elders who conduct their office
well — Ber

. . . who do their duties well — Gspd

. . . with a gift of leadership — Phi

be counted worthy of double honour,

be held worthy of twofold honor —
Mon

be honoured twice over — Bas

should be held deserving of especial
consideration — TCNT

. . . considered worthy of a double reward — Nor

. . . considered as deserving twice the
salary they get — Wms

. . . reckoned worthy of a double
stipend — NEB

**especially they who labour in the word
and doctrine.**

Especially they who toil in discourse
and teaching — Rhm

particularly those who labor in preaching and teaching — Ber

... who work hard at their preaching and teaching — NASB

... who labor faithfully in preaching ... — Amp

18. For the scripture saith,

For the Writings say — Bas

The words of Scripture are — TCNT

Remember the scriptural principle — Phi

Thou shalt not muzzle the ox that treadeth out the corn.

A threshing ox shalt thou not muzzle — Rhm

Never tie up the mouth of an ox when it is treading out the grain — let him eat as he goes along! — Tay

It is not right to keep the ox from taking the grain when he is crushing it — Bas

And, The labourer is worthy of his reward.

And — Worthy is the workman of his hire — Rhm

and again — The worker is worth his wages — TCNT

And in another place, Those who work deserve their pay! — Tay

And Scripture says also: A laborer deserves to get his pay — Nor

and the workman deserves his pay — Wey

and the labourer has a right to expect his maintenance — Knox

19. Against an elder receive not an accusation,

Against a presbyter receive not ... — Alf

Do not receive a charge against an Officer of the Church — TCNT

Never entertain an accusation against an Elder — Wey

Make it a rule not to consider a charge preferred against ... — Wms

Do not take cognizance of any charge made against ... — Knox

Don't accept an accusation against a pastor — Beck

but before two or three witnesses.

except at the mouth of two ... — ASV

except on the evidence of ... — Wey

except it be confirmed by the testimony of ... — Amp

unless it is certified by ... — Mof

unless there are two or three witnesses to accuse him — Tay

20. Them that sin rebuke before all,

But them who are sinning before all do thou reprove — Rhm

Those who continue in sin, rebuke in the presence of all — NASB

Give a public rebuke to those who are living amiss — Knox

but rebuke offenders publicly — TCNT

those who are guilty of sin you should expose in public — Mof

... in front of the whole church — Tay

... in the presence of all men — Lam

that others also may fear.

that the rest also may be in fear — ASV

so that the rest may be awed — Ber

so that the rest also may be afraid to sin — Wey

as a salutary warning to others — Phi

so that the rest may be warned and stand in wholesome awe and fear — Amp

21. I charge thee

I adjure thee — Alf

I charge you solemnly — TCNT

I solemnly call upon you — Wey

I solemnly command you — Tay

before God, and the Lord Jesus Christ, and the elect angels,

in the sight of God, and Christ Jesus, and ... — ASV

in the presence of God and of Christ Jesus and of ... — Wey

... and of His chosen angels — NASB

... and the angels of God's selection — Bas

... and the angels who are his chosen — NEB

before God and Christ Jesus and the chosen messengers — Rhm

that thou observe these things without preferring one before another,

that thou guard these things without prejudging — ABUV

That these things thou observe apart from prejudgment — Rhm

to carry out these instructions without prejudice — Wey

to maintain these principles without bias — NASB

to carry out these directions, unswayed by prejudice — TCNT

that you observe these suggestions without discrimination — Ber

to follow these orders with the strictest impartiality — Phi maintain these rules, and never pre-judge the issue — NEB

to do this whether the pastor is a spe-cial friend of yours or not — Tay

doing nothing by partiality.

never acting with partiality — TCNT

and with perfect impartiality — Wms

that you act with no favoritism — Ber

and without a preference for anyone in anything you do — Beck

All must be treated exactly the same — Tay

22. Lay hands suddenly on no man,

Lay hands hastily on no man — ASV

As for the imposition of hands, do not bestow it inconsiderately — Knox

Do not be over-hasty in laying on hands in ordination — NEB

Never be in a hurry to ordain a pres-byter — Mof

. . . a hurry about choosing a pastor — Tay

neither be partaker of other men's sins:

neither share in other men's sins — ABUV

nor participate in another man's sins — RSV

Neither have fellowship with sins of strangers — Rhm

neither make common cause with the sins of others — Ber

and thus share responsibility for the sins of others — NASB

and so share the blame for the sins of others — Knox

keep thyself pure.

Thyself keep chaste — Rhm

keep yourself free from sin — NASB

keep your own hands clean — NEB

Keep thyself clear of fault — Knox

23. Drink no longer water,

(No longer be a water drinker — Wey

No longer drink water exclusively — NASB

Do not continue to drink water only — TCNT

Stop drinking nothing but water — Gspd

but use a little wine

but take a little wine — TCNT

But of a little wine make use — Rhm

for thy stomach's sake and thine often infirmities.

Because of thy stomach and thy fre-quent sicknesses — Rhm

for the good of your stomach and your recurring illness — Ber

to strengthen your stomach and relieve its frequent attacks — Wms

for your digestion, for your frequent ailments — NEB

. . . and thy frequent maladies — Con

. . . and help you to get over your fre-quent spells of illness.) — Phi

24. Some men's sins are open beforehand,

The sins of some men are clearly seen — Bas

Some men's sins are openly evident — Rhm

The sins of some people are soon in evidence — Ber

There are some men whose sins are conspicuous — TCNT

. . . are notorious — Mof

[In thy decisions remember that] the sins of some men are manifest be-forehand — Con

going before to judgment;

leading on into judgment — Rhm

going before them to be judged — Bas

and lead them straight on the way to condemnation — Mon

. . . obviously bringing them to judg-ment — Phi

going before them to the judgment [seat] and proclaiming their sentence in advance — Amp

and some men they follow after.

for others, their sins follow after — NASB

In the case of others, their sins show up later — Nor

but the sins of others appear later — RSV

but in some cases sin only comes out afterwards — Mof

with others, discovery follows upon the heels of enquiry — Knox

there are others whose offenses have not yet overtaken them — NEB

. . . whose sins only dog their steps — Gspd

but the sins of others appear later — following the offender to the bar of judgment and coming into view there — Amp

25. Likewise also the good works of some are manifest beforehand;

In like manner also there are good works that are evident — ASV

In the same way the noble works also are openly evident — Rhm

So also the right actions of some are obvious — Wey

Equally so are good works readily observed — Ber

Similarly some virtues are plain to see — Phi

Good works are equally conspicuous — Mof

In the same way noble deeds become conspicuous — TCNT

and they that are otherwise cannot be hid.

and those which they conceal cannot be kept hidden — Con

and those [works] that are otherwise cannot be hid — Alf

or when they are not, they cannot be wholly concealed — Gspd

and even when they are not, they cannot escape notice for ever — Mof

CHAPTER 6

1. Let as many servants as are under the yoke

Let as many as are bondmen under the yoke — Alf

Let those who are under the yolk as slaves — Mon

All who wear the yoke of slavery — NEB

count their own masters worthy of all honour,

regard their masters as worthy . . . — RSV

esteem their masters worthy . . . — Con

must treat their masters with the greatest respect — Gspd

remember that their masters are entitled to perfect respect — Mof

should think of their masters as men who deserve every respect — Beck

that the name of God and his doctrine be not blasphemed.

Lest the name of God and the teaching be defamed — Rhm

so that God's name and what we teach isn't slandered — Beck

— otherwise it will be a scandal to the Name of . . . — Mof

so that the name of God, and our Teaching, may not be maligned — TCNT

. . . and the Christian teaching are not brought into disrepute — NEB

. . . and our doctrine will be ill spoken of — Knox

2. And they that have believing masters,

They however that have . . . — Rhm

Those who have Christian believers as their masters — Mof

And let those whose masters are of the faith — Bas

let them not despise them, because they are brethren;

must not treat them with disrespect, because they are brothers — Mon

must not be disrespectful on the ground that they are brothers — RSV

must not think lightly of them because they . . . — Gspd

must honor them no less because they . . . — Ber

must not take liberties with them because they . . . — Mof

but rather do them service,

but serve them all the more — Alf

nay, rather slave for them the better — Mon

Quite the contrary; they must be all the better servants — NEB

they must serve them all the more faithfully — Gspd

. . . with the more subjection — Con

. . . more zealously — Lam

because they are faithful and beloved, partakers of the benefit.

because believing and beloved are they who from the good workmanship receive advantage — Rhm

since those who benefit by their service are believers and beloved — RSV

. . . are dear to them as their fellow Christians — TCNT

These things teach and exhort.

These things be teaching and exhorting — Rhm

Continue to teach and preach this — Mon

Teach and preach these principles — NASB

Teach and urge these duties — RSV

Teach this! Preach it! — Nor

Teach them, and encourage them, so to act — Knox

3. If any man teach otherwise,

If any one teaches differently — Wey

If any one advocates a different doctrine — NASB

If any one teaches heterodoxy — Mon

Anyone who teaches different views — Gspd

... teaches novelties — Mof

... teach falsely — Con

and consent not to wholesome words,

and assents not to healthful words — ABUV

and refuses his assent to sound instruction — TCNT

and refuses to agree with the wholesome messages — Wms

And doth not adhere to healthful discourses — Rhm

and will not give his mind to wholesome precepts — NEB

... the wholesome sayings — Ber

even the words of our Lord Jesus Christ,

— those of our Lord Jesus Christ — Rhm

which comes from our ... — Gspd

— the instruction of our ... — TCNT

and to the doctrine which is according to godliness;

and with the doctrine conforming to godliness — NASB

and the teaching that harmonizes with true godliness — Wey

... that tallies with godliness — Mof

... that fosters godliness — Ber

... which is in agreement with true religion — Bas

4. He is proud, knowing nothing,

he is puffed up, ... — ASV

He is beclouded, knowing nothing rightly — Rhm

is puffed up with conceit, not really knowing anything — TCNT

He has an over-high opinion of himself; being without knowledge — Bas

he is blinded with pride, and understands nothing — Con

he is a conceited ignoramus — Wms

... a pompous ignoramus — NEB

but doting about questions and strifes of words,

... about questionings and disputes of words — ASV

But is diseased about questionings and word-battles — Rhm

but is filled with a sickly appetite for disputations and contentions about words — Con

with a morbid appetite for discussions and controversies — Wms

with a morbid craving for speculations and arguments — Gspd

... an unhealthy love of questionings and wars of words — Bas

... morbidly keen on mere verbal questions and quibbles — NEB

... quibbling over the meaning of Christ's words and stirring up arguments — Tay

whereof cometh envy, strife, railings, evil surmisings,

Out of which spring envy strife defamations wicked surmisings — Rhm

which give rise to envy, quarrellings, revilings, ill-natured suspicions — Wey

such as result in envy, wrangling, slander, bad suspicions — Ber

which leads only to envy, dissension, insults, insinuations — Mof

... jealousy, quarrelling, recriminations and base suspicions — Knox

... jealousy, quarreling, insults and malicious innuendoes — Phi

... envy, strife, abusive language, evil suspicions — NASB

5. Perverse disputings of men of corrupt minds,

wranglings of men corrupted in mind — ASV

incessant quarrellings of men depraved ... — Alf

perpetual contention between people of depraved minds — Ber

and persistent wranglings on the part of people perverted ... — Wey

and constant friction between people who are ... — Mof

and mutual irritation between people ... — Gspd

... their minds warped by sin — Tay

... of men who have let their reasoning powers become atrophied — NEB

and destitute of the truth,

and robbed of the truth — ABUV

and bereft of ... — ASV

and so deprived of ... — Wey

and defrauded of ... — Ber

and have lost grip of . . . — NEB

who have lost all hold on the Truth — TCNT

who have lost the truth — Beck

supposing that gain is godliness: from such withdraw thyself.

— Supposing godliness to be a means of gain! — Rhm

who imagine that godliness means gain — Wey

who think of godliness in terms of acquisition — Ber

and who think religion is a way to make money — Beck

. . . is a gainful trade — Con

. . . should yield dividends — NEB

. . . is a source of profit — a money-making business, a means of livelihood. . . . — Amp

6. But godliness with contentment is great gain.

There is great gain in godliness with contentment — RSV

Godliness is indeed great gain when accompanied by . . . — Wey

Of course, there's a big profit in religion if we're satisfied — Beck

. . . provided that it goes with a contented spirit — Mof

and of course religion does yield high dividends, but only to the man whose resources are within him — NEB

— that contentment which is a sense of inward sufficiency — . . . — Amp

7. For we brought nothing into this world,

For nothing brought we into the world — Rhm

Empty-handed we came into the world — Knox

After all we didn't bring any money with us when we came . . . — Tay

and it is certain we can carry nothing out.

Neither to take anything out are we able — Rhm

and surely we can take nothing out of it — Wms

and empty-handed, beyond question, we must leave it — Knox

and we can't carry away a single penny when we die — Tay

8. And having food and raiment let us be therewith content.

and having food and covering, with these we shall be content — ABUV

And having sustenance and covering we shall be . . . — Rhm

If we have food and clothing we will be satisfied — Gspd

When we have nourishment and covering, let us be content with these — Ber

So, with food and shelter, we will be . . . — TCNT

So we should be well satisfied without money if we have enough food and clothing — Tay

9. But they that will be rich

But they that are minded to be rich — ASV

But they who are determined to be rich — Rhm

But men who keep planning to get rich — Wms

But those who have a desire for wealth — Bas

. . . crave to be rich — Amp

. . . are eager to be rich — Mof

. . . set their hearts on being wealthy — Phi

fall into temptation and a snare,

are falling into danger, and are taken as in a net — Bas

get tempted and trapped — Mof

fall into temptation, the devil's trap for them — Knox

expose themselves to temptation . . . — Phi

and into many foolish and hurtful lusts,

into many senseless and hurtful desires — RSV

and into numerous thoughtless and hurtful cravings — Ber

and many foolish and hurtful covetings — Rhm

and into many unwise and pernicious cravings — Wey

and become the prey of many foolish and harmful ambitions — TCNT

and lay themselves open to all sorts of silly and wicked desires — Phi

which drown men in destruction and perdition.

The which sink men into ruin and destruction — Rhm

which plunge people into Destruction and Ruin — TCNT

that drags men down to . . . — Mof
. . . ruin and destruction and miserable perishing — Amp

10. For the love of money is the root of all evil:

For a root of all the vices is the love of money — Rhm

For the love of money is a root of all the evils — Ber

. . . a source of all kinds of evil — TCNT

. . . a root from which every kind of evil springs — Knox

From love of money all sorts of evils arise — Wey

For loving money leads to all kinds of evil — Phi

which while some coveted after,

which some reaching after — ASV

Which some being eager for — Rhm

it is through this craving — RSV

after which while some were lusting — Alf

and in their eagerness to be rich — TCNT

and some have so hankered after money — Wey

it is by aspiring to be rich that certain individuals — Mof

they have erred from the faith,

have been led astray from . . . — ASV

have been seduced from their faith — Nor

have been turned away from . . . — Bas

that some have wandered away from . . . — RSV

Some people have even turned away from God — Tay

and pierced themselves through with many sorrows.

and spiked themselves on many thorny griefs — NEB

and pierce themselves to the heart with many a pang — Gspd

and found themselves pierced with many a pang of remorse — Mof

and been wounded with unnumbered sorrows — Bas

and caused themselves untold agonies of mind — Phi

. . . with many acute [mental] pangs — Amp

11. But thou, O man of God, flee these things;

But thou O Man of God! From these things flee! — Rhm

But you, as a man of God, must be fleeing always from . . . — Wms

. . . must fly from these things — Gspd

. . . shun all this — RSV

. . . keep clear of such things — Phi

. . . Run from all these evil things — Tay

and follow after

and pursue after — NASB

and run after — Mon

Aim at — TCNT

you must constantly strive for — Wms

righteousness, godliness, faith, love, patience, meekness.

righteousness, piety, faith, love, endurance, gentleness — TCNT

uprightness, godliness, faith, love, fortitude, . . . — Wey

integrity, piety, faith, love, stedfastness, . . . — Mon

justice, piety, fidelity, love, . . . — NEB

12. Fight the good fight of faith,

Keep contending in the noble contest of the faith — Mon

Keep up the good fight for the faith — Wms

Take part in the great contest of faith! — Gspd

Struggle your hardest in the good contest for the faith — Wey

Run the great race of the Faith — TCNT

Fight the worthwhile battle . . . — Phi

lay hold on eternal life,

take hold of the everlasting life—Beck

seize hold of eternal Life — Wey

lay thy grasp on . . . — Knox

keep your grip on that life eternal — Phi

Hold tightly to . . . — Tay

secure that life eternal — Mof

. . . the age-abiding life — Rhm

whereunto thou art also called,

to which you were called — Wey

to which you were summoned — Amp

to which God called you — Gspd

It was for this that you received the Call — TCNT

for you were called to this end — Nor

and hast professed a good profession before many witnesses.

and didst confess the good confession in the sight of . . . — ASV

And didst make the noble confession before . . . — Rhm

and you confessed your faith nobly
... — NEB

as you made a beautiful confession in
the presence of ... — Ber

and to which you boldly professed your
loyalty ... — Phi

... confessed with such a ringing confession ... — Tay

13. I give thee charge in the sight of God,
I give you orders before God — Bas
I command thee ... — Alf
I solemnly charge you ... — Wms
I urge you, as in the sight of God —
TCNT
I adjure thee before the God — Knox
who quickeneth all things,
who giveth life to all things — ASV
who endueth all things with life — Alf
who causes all things to live — Ber
the source of all life — TCNT
who maintains all life — Gspd
who preserves the life of all His creatures — Wms
and before Christ Jesus,
**who before Pontius Pilate witnessed a
good confession;**
who at the bar of Pontius Pilate made
the noble confession — Wey
who bore witness to the good confession before ... — Mon
who in testifying before Pontius Pilate
made his great confession — Gspd
who fearlessly witnessed to the truth
before ... — Phi

**14. That thou keep this commandment
without spot, unrebukeable,**
that thou keep the commandment without spot, irreproachable — Alf
to keep his Command free from stain
or reproach — TCNT
to keep all His precepts unsullied and
flawless, irreproachable — Amp
to keep the principles stainless and irreproachable — Ber
to keep your commission clean and
above reproach — Phi
to obey your orders irreproachably and
without fault — NEB
... without spot, blameless — ABUV
... untouched by evil, clear from all
shame — Bas
**until the appearing of our Lord Jesus
Christ:**
till the appearance of ... — Mof
Until the forthshining of ... — Rhm

until our Lord Jesus Christ shall make
His appearance — Nor

until our Lord Jesus Christ returns —
Tay

15. Which in his times he shall shew,
which in his own seasons he shall shew
— Alf
which He will bring about at the proper
time — NASB
which in due time He shall show forth
— Ber
That appearance God will bring to pass
in his own good time — NEB
For in due season Christ will be revealed from heaven by — Tay
This will be, in his own time, the final
dénouement of God — Phi
who is the blessed and only Potentate,
who is the blissful and only Potentate
— ABUV
the happy and only Potentate — Rhm
that blessed and only Sovereign — Mof
— He, the blessed and only Ruler —
Beck
who is the blessed controller of all
things — Phi
— God who in eternal felicity alone
holds sway — NEB
the King of kings, and Lord of lords;
The King of them that reign And Lord
of them that wield lordship — Rhm
the king over all kings and the master
of all masters — Phi

16. Who only hath immortality,
who alone possesses immortality —
Wey
Who alone can never die — Tay
the only source of immortality — Phi
**dwelling in the light which no man can
approach unto;**
dwelling in light unapproachable —
ASV
living in light to which no man may
come near — Bas
He lives in a house of unapproachable
light — Nor
... so terrible that no human being can
approach Him — Tay
whom no man hath seen, nor can see:
whom no man has seen or is able to
see — Bas
whom no human being has ever seen
... — Ber

No mere man has ever seen Him, nor ever will — Tay

the one whom no mortal eye has ever seen . . . — Phi

to whom be honour and power everlasting. Amen.

. . . honor and power eternal. Amen — ASV

. . . honour and might age-abiding. Amen. — Rhm

To Him be eternal honour and power! Amen — Wey

— to whom be ascribed honour and power for ever. Amen — TCNT

To Him be honor and eternal dominion! Amen — NASB

. . . So be it — Bas

17. Charge them that are rich in this world,

Upon them who are rich in the present age lay thou charge — Rhm

Them that are rich in this present world, command — Alf

Instruct those who are rich in this world's goods — NEB

Urge upon those who are wealthy in this life — TCNT

Continue charging the rich . . . — Wms

Enjoin upon those who are rich . . . — Ber

Impress on those who are rich . . . — Wey

that they be not highminded,

that they be not proud — Lam

to stop being haughty — Wms

not to be arrogant — Gspd

not to be supercilious — Mof

not to be conceited — NASB

not to be lifted up in their minds — Bas

not to set their minds on their elevation — Ber

nor trust in uncertain riches,

nor have their hope set on the uncertainty of riches — ASV

or set their hopes on an uncertain thing like riches — Wey

or to put their hope in the uncertain chances of wealth — Bas

and not to rest the weight of their confidence on the transitory power of wealth — Phi

and not to trust in their money which will soon be gone — Tay

but in the living God, who giveth us richly all things to enjoy;

But on God who offereth us all things richly for enjoying — Rhm

. . . who provides us richly with all things for our enjoyment — Wey

. . . who richly furnishes us with everything to enjoy — RSV

. . . who richly and ceaselessly provides us with everything for our enjoyment — Wms

. . . who richly provides us with all the joys of life — Mof

. . . who generously gives us everything . . . — Phi

. . . who endows us richly with . . . — NEB

. . . who gives us in full measure all things for our use — Bas

18. That they do good, that they be rich in good works,

To be doing good To be rich in noble works — Rhm

They must be beneficent, rich in good deeds — Wey

charge them to continue doing good and being rich in good deeds — Wms

Charge them to practice benevolence, . . . — Con

Urge upon them to show kindness, to exhibit a wealth of good actions — TCNT

Tell them to use their money to do good . . . — Tay

ready to distribute, willing to communicate;

to be free in imparting, . . . — ABUV

free in distributing, . . . — Alf

To be generous in giving Ready for fellowship — Rhm

open-handed and generous-hearted — Wms

to be generous givers, to practice sharing — Ber

always ready to give, and to share the common burden — Knox

. . . and to sympathize with those in distress — Phi

19. Laying up in store for themselves

Treasuring up for themselves — Rhm

thus laying up for themselves — RSV

in this way amassing for themselves — Wms

and so acquire a treasure — NEB

a good foundation against the time to come,

a good foundation for the future — Rhm

a sound foundation for the future — Ber

what shall form a solid foundation for the future — Wey

what in the future will prove to be a good foundation — TCNT

the riches that forever endure in the life to come — Wms

that they may lay hold on eternal life.

and to take hold of the life that is real — Beck

so that they may gain the only true life — TCNT

in order that they may obtain the Life which is life indeed — Mon

and the life that is life indeed may be theirs at last — Nor

so as to have life which is true life within their grasp — Knox

And they will be living a fruitful Christian life down here — Tay

20. O Timothy, keep that which is committed to thy trust,

O Timothy, guard the deposit — Ber

. . . keep safe that which has been entrusted to you — NEB

. . . take good care of that which is given to you — Bas

O Timotheus, guard the treasure which is committed to thy trust — Con

. . . guard the truths entrusted to you — Wey

. . . keep the securities of the faith intact — Mof

. . . guard most carefully your divine commission — Phi

avoiding profane and vain babblings,

turning away from the profane babblings — ASV

shunning irreligious and frivolous talk — Wey

Avoiding the profane pratings — Rhm

continue to turn away from the worldly, futile phrases — Wms

Keep away from the irreligious and empty discussions — Ber

Turn a deaf ear to empty and worldly chatter — NEB

. . . the profane jargon — Mof

. . . empty, unholy talk — Beck

. . . the irreverent babble and godless chatter — Amp

and oppositions of science falsely so called:

and oppositions of falsely named knowledge — Rhm

and objections from what is falsely called 'knowledge' — Wey

and the contradictions of so-called 'knowledge' — NEB

. . . of pseudo-science — Nor

. . . of what some miscall 'theology' — TCNT

21. Which some professing

which some have claimed to possess — Wey

by professing which some individuals — Wms

For those professing this — Lam

Through which some, who gave their minds to it — Bas

have erred concerning the faith.

concerning the faith have missed the mark! — Rhm

and so have missed the faith — Ber

have shot far wide of the faith — NEB

and thus gone astray from the faith — NASB

have failed in the faith — Wms

Grace be with thee. Amen.

Favour be with you — Rhm

Spiritual blessing be with you all — Wms

God bless you all — TCNT

. . . Amen — so be it — Amp

THE
SECOND EPISTLE OF PAUL TO TIMOTHY

CHAPTER 1

1. Paul, an apostle of Jesus Christ by the will of God,

Paul, an apostle of Christ Jesus through the will of God — ASV

Paul, an Apostle (special messenger) of . . . — Amp

Paul, sent as an apostle of . . . — Knox

. . . by the purpose of God — Bas

according to the promise of life

in accordance with the promise of the life — Wms

in fulfilment of the promise of that life — Gspd

in furtherance of that promise of life — Knox

for the announcing of the life — Ber

to proclaim the promise of the Life — Wey

in the service of the Life — Mof

because God promised life — Beck

which is in Christ Jesus,

that comes through union with . . . — Wms

that is in fellowship with . . . — Ber

that is to be had in . . . — Nor

which is given us in . . . — Knox

2. To Timothy, my dearly beloved son:

to Timothy, a beloved child — ABUV

to my dearly loved child Timothy — Wms

Grace, mercy, and peace, from God the Father and Christ Jesus our Lord.[1]

3. I thank God,

whom I serve from my forefathers with pure conscience,

Unto whom I am rendering divine service from my progenitors in a . . . — Rhm

whom I serve, as my ancestors did, with a clear . . . — TCNT

(whom I worship, as did my forefathers, with a pure . . . — Con

whom, in line with my ancestors, I worship with clear . . . — Ber

. . . the way my forefathers did—NASB

whom I serve with a clear conscience in the way my fathers taught me — Knox

that without ceasing I have remembrance of thee

as I ceaselessly remember you — Wms

as without omission I remember you — Ber

when I remember you constantly — RSV

when I remember you, as I never fail to do — TCNT

how unceasingly I have remembrance of thee — ABUV

at all times the thought of you is with me — Bas

in my prayers night and day;

in my supplications night and day — ABUV

in my prayers, as I never fail to do day and night — Beck

in my prayers. Night and day — Mon

4. Greatly desiring to see thee, being mindful of thy tears,

longing to see thee, remembering thy tears — ASV

I yearn to see you, when I remember the tears you shed — Ber

I am anxious to see you; I still remember your tears — Lam

. . . remembering thy [parting] tears — Con

I keep the memory of thy tears, and long to see thee again — Knox

that I may be filled with joy;

In order that with joy I may be filled — Rhm

that I may feel the fullest joy — Wms

and to have you with me again would be the greatest possible joy — Phi

5. When I call to remembrance the unfeigned faith that is in thee,

For I have been reminded of thy undissembled faith — Con

on being reminded of your genuine faith — Wms

I bring back to mind your unalloyed faith — Ber

I am calling up memories of your sincere and unqualified . . . — Amp

. . . that sincere faith which is in your heart — Mon

. . . the sincere faith that you have shown — TCNT

---

[1]See I Tim. 1:2.

which dwelt first in thy grandmother Lois, and thy mother Eunice;

such as first dwelt in thy . . . — Alf

that lived first in your . . . — Ber

just as it lived in . . . before you — Beck

a faith that first found a home in the heart of . . . — Wms

That faith was seen first in . . . — TCNT

and I am persuaded that in thee also.

and I am sure that it is in you as well — NASB

— I am persuaded moreover that [it dwelleth] in thee also — Rhm

6. Wherefore I put thee in remembrance

For this reason I now remind you — Wms

For which cause I put thee in mind — Alf

For this reason let me remind you — Wey

that thou stir up the gift of God,

to be stirring up God's gift of favour — Rhm

to keep ever blazing that gift of God — Mon

to keep alive the flame of God's gracious gift — Ber

to fan the flame of that special grace — Knox

to stir into flame . . . — TCNT

that thou kindle up . . . — ABUV

to kindle afresh . . . — NASB

. . . the fire of the divine gift — Wms

which is in thee by the putting on of my hands.

that is in you through the imposition of my hands — Ber

which came upon you when I laid my hands upon you — Wms

which is yours through your ordination at my hands — TCNT

7. For God hath not given us the spirit of fear;

For God gave us not a spirit of fearfulness — ASV

for God did not give us a spirit of timidity — RSV

For the Spirit that God has given us does not impart timidity — Wms

The spirit he has bestowed on us is not one that shrinks from danger — Knox

. . . not the spirit of cowardice — Alf

but of power, and of love, and of a sound mind.

but of power, and of love, and of sobriety — ABUV

but one of power and of love and of sound judgement — Wey

but a spirit of power, love, and self-control — TCNT

but one to inspire strength, love, and self-discipline — NEB

. . . and self-restraint — Con

. . . and wise discretion — Nor

. . . and of correction — Alf

but [He has given us a spirit] of power and of love and of calm and well-balanced mind and discipline and self-control — Amp

8. Be not thou therefore ashamed of the testimony of our Lord,

Therefore do not be ashamed of the testimony of . . . — NASB

Feel no shame, therefore, about bearing witness to our Lord — Ber

So never be ashamed of your testimony to our Lord — NEB

Do not blush, then, for the witness thou bearest to . . . — Knox

So you must not be ashamed to testify to . . . — Gspd

So don't be ashamed to tell about our Lord — Beck

nor of me his prisoner:

nor yet of me who am a prisoner for him — TCNT

nor be ashamed of me who am in prison for his sake — Gspd

or to let them know that I am your friend even though I am here in jail for Christ's sake — Tay

but be thou partaker of the afflictions of the gospel

but suffer hardship with the gospel — ASV

But suffer hardship together with the glad-message — Rhm

but endure hardship with me for . . . — ABUV

but suffer for the good news in fellowship with me — Wms

join me in bearing suffering for the gospel — Mof

but take your share of suffering for the sake of . . . — NEB

but share the affliction of them who publish the Glad-tidings — Con according to the power of God;

in reliance on the power of God—Wey

in the strength that comes from God — NEB

by virtue of the power of God — Ber

with the power of God to back us — Nor

for He will give you strength in suffering — Tay

9. Who hath saved us,
and called us with an holy calling,

and called us with a call for dedication — Ber

and from him we received our solemn Call — TCNT

and called us to a dedicated life — NEB

and called us to a life of holiness — Phi

. . . a calling in itself holy and leading to holiness . . . — Amp

and chose us for His holy work — Tay

not according to our works,

not in accordance with anything that we had done — Wms

not on account of our works — Bas

not dealing with us according to our own works — Con

not for any merit of ours — NEB

not as a reward for anything that we had done — TCNT

but according to his own purpose and grace,

but in accordance with His own purpose and unmerited favor — Wms

But according to the peculiar purpose and favour — Rhm

but due to His own purpose and the grace — Ber

but in the measure of his purpose . . . — Bas

but because of His own design . . . — Nor

but in fulfilment of his own loving purpose — TCNT

but because of and to further His own purpose . . . — Amp

which was given us in Christ Jesus before the world began.

which was granted us in Christ Jesus from all eternity — NASB

which was bestowed upon us . . . before eternal times — Con

which was shown us through union with Christ Jesus eternal ages ago — Wms

which he gave us ages ago in Christ Jesus — Mof

. . . before eternal ages — ABUV

. . . before the beginning of time — Mon

. . . planned before the beginning of time — Nor

10. But is now made manifest by the appearing of our Saviour Jesus Christ,

but now has been revealed by . . . — NASB

and has now been made apparent through . . . — TCNT

But now it has been realized through . . . — Ber

but has only recently been made known through the appearance of . . . — Wms

but has now at length been brought fully into view by . . . — NEB

But hath now been made manifest through means of the forthshining of our Saviour Christ Jesus — Rhm

who hath abolished death,

who on the one hand rendered death ineffectual — Ber

who . . . has put a stop to the power of death — Wms

For he has broken the power of death — NEB

now he has annulled death — Knox

who destroyed death — ABUV

who has made an end of Death—TCNT

and hath brought life and immortality to light

And hath thrown light upon life and incorruptibility — Rhm

and has revealed life and . . . — Lam

. . . and immortality — that is, immunity from eternal death . . . — Amp

through the gospel:

through means of the glad-message — Rhm

by the Glad-tidings — Con

by that Good News — TCNT

11. Whereunto I am appointed a preacher, and an apostle, and a teacher of the Gentiles.

of which I was myself appointed a Herald and Apostle, and Teacher — TCNT

Of this Gospel I, by his appointment, am herald, apostle, and teacher — NEB

For [the proclaiming of] this [Gospel], I was appointed . . . — Amp

12. For the which cause I also suffer these things:

That is why I am undergoing these sufferings — TCNT

and this is why I suffer as I do — Mof

nevertheless I am not ashamed:

Yet I am not in the least ashamed — Phi

and I am certainly not ashamed of it — Tay

for I know whom I have believed,

for I know him whom I have believed — ASV

for I know whom I have fully believed — Mon

and am persuaded that he is able to keep

and I am confident that He is . . . — Wey

and I am thoroughly persuaded that . . . — Mon

and I am absolutely sure that He is able to guard — Wms

and am convinced that He is able to guard safely — Ber

and am confident of his power to keep safe — NEB

that which I have committed unto him against that day.

my deposit, entrusted to Him against that Day — Ber

the treasure which I have committed to Him, even unto that day — Con

what I have entrusted to him until That Day — TCNT

until that Day what has been entrusted to me — RSV

what he has put into my charge, until the great Day — NEB

the work he has committed to me . . . — Phi

. . . until the day of His return — Tay

13. Hold fast the form of sound words,

Hold the pattern of healthful words — ABUV

An outline have thou of healthful discourses — Rhm

Keep to the example of the sound teaching — Wey

Retain the standard of sound words — NASB

As your example in wholesome instructions, keep before you — Gspd

Follow the pattern of the sound words — RSV

Continue to be an example in wholesome instructions — Wms

which thou hast heard of me,

which from me thou hast heard — Rhm

what you learned from me — Gspd

all that you learnt from me as you listened — TCNT

in faith and love which is in Christ Jesus.

— With the faith and love which are in . . . — Rhm

in the faith and love that come through union with . . . — Gspd

living by the faith and love which are ours in . . . — NEB

14. That good thing which was committed unto thee keep

Guard that precious entrusted deposit — Ber

The goodly trust committed unto thee keep — Alf

The noble thing entrusted [to thee] do thou guard — Rhm

That goodly treasure which is committed to thy charge, guard — Con

Guard that splendid trust — Gspd

Guard this fine deposit of truth — Wms

Keep the great securities of your faith intact — Mof

by the Holy Ghost which dwelleth in us.

Through means of the Holy Spirit which dwelleth within us — Rhm

by the help of the indwelling Holy Spirit within us — Ber

by the aid of the Holy Spirit who makes his home in us — Mon

. . . that lives in our hearts — Gspd

15. This thou knowest,

You are aware — Mof

You already know — Mon

You have no doubt heard — Nor

that all they which are in Asia be turned away from me;

that all those in Asia went away from me — Bas

that I was abandoned by all the Asiatics — Con

that everyone in the province of Asia has deserted me — Gspd

that all our friends in Roman Asia turned their backs on me — TCNT that all the Christians in Asia have deserted me — Wey

. . . have treated me coldly — Knox

. . . have discarded me — Mof

of whom are Phygellus and Hermogenes.

among them Phygellus and Hermogenes — Mon

including Phygelus and Hermogenes — Mof

16. **The Lord give mercy unto the house of Onesiphorus;**

The Lord grant mercy unto the house . . . — ASV

May the Lord show favour to the household . . . — Mof

. . . to the Onesiphorus family — Ber

for he oft refreshed me,

for many a time he refreshed me — Mon

because he often cheered me — Wms

often enough he revived my spirits — Knox

. . . gave me fresh vigour — Wey

. . . put fresh heart into me — Phi

. . . relieved me in my troubles — NEB

for he often showed me kindness and ministered to my needs — comforting and reviving and bracing me like fresh air! — Amp

His visits revived me like a breath of fresh air — Tay

and was not ashamed of my chain:

and was not ashamed of my being a prisoner — Ber

and had no feeling of shame because I was in chains — Bas

He was not ashamed to visit a prisoner — NEB

. . . of my chains and imprisonment [for Christ's sake] — Amp

17. **But, when he was in Rome,**

but coming to Rome — Beck

Instead, on arriving in Rome — Ber

Yes, when he got to Rome — Wms

Nay, when he was here in Rome — Wey

he sought me out very diligently, and found me.

he eagerly searched for me, . . . — NASB

he searched hard for me . . . — Beck

he searched everywhere trying to find me, and finally did — Tay

he took great pains to inquire for me, and he found me — Wey

. . . and succeeded in finding me — Knox

18. **The Lord grant unto him that he may find mercy of the Lord in that day:**

. . . to find mercy from the Lord in that day — Rhm

. . . that he may be shown mercy by the Lord on that Day! — Mof

. . . that he may obtain mercy at His hands on that Day! — Wey

. . . that he may find the Lord's mercy . . . — Beck

(may he find favour with the Lord on the great Day! The Lord grant it!) — Gspd

May the Lord give him a special blessing at the day of Christ's return — Tay

and in how many things he ministered unto me at Ephesus,

how many services he rendered in Ephesus — Mon

And all his services at Ephesus — Con

And how many times in Ephesus he hath ministered — Rhm

thou knowest very well.

thou knowest better than I — Alf

you know better than I can tell you — NEB

you have full knowledge — Bas

CHAPTER 2

1. **Thou therefore, my son, be strong**

Thou therefore, my child, be strengthened — ASV

So you, my son, must keep renewing your strength — Wms

. . . be strong — strengthened inwardly — Amp

. . . be empowering thyself — Rhm

in the grace that is in Christ Jesus.

. . . in the favour that is in . . . — Rhm

in the spiritual blessing that comes through union with . . . — Wms

in the help which comes from union with . . . — TCNT

by means of the grace that is in . . . — Ber

. . . that is [to be found only] in . . . — Amp

2. **And the things that thou hast heard of me**

The teachings which you have heard . . . — Mon

The things you learned from me — Mof

Everything that you have heard me teach — Phi

and, as for the instructions I gave you — Gspd

among many witnesses,

through many witnesses — ABUV

before many witnesses — Mof

in the presence of many listeners — TCNT

along with many witnesses — Amp

with the help of . . . — Ber

attested by . . . — Con

the same commit thou to faithful men,

The same entrust thou unto faithful men — Rhm

transmit them to trustworthy men — Gspd

you must hand on to trusty men — Wey

this you commit to reliable men — Ber

deliver into the keeping of . . . — Con

give to those of the faith — Bas

transmit and entrust (as a deposit) . . . — Amp

who shall be able to teach others also.

Such as shall be competent to teach . . . — Rhm

such as shall be qualified to teach others as well — Ber

who will be capable of teaching others — Mof

who will be able to pass it on . . . — Phi

3. **Thou therefore endure hardness,**

Suffer hardship with me — ASV

Take thy part in suffering hardship — Rhm

Share hardships with me — TCNT

Join the ranks of those who bear suffering — Gspd

accept your share of suffering — Wey

Suffer afflictions with me — Alf

as a good soldier of Jesus Christ.

As a noble soldier of Christ Jesus — Ber

as a brave soldier . . . — Rhm

as a true soldier . . . — TCNT

as a good (first class) soldier . . . — Amp

like a loyal soldier . . . — Gspd

4. **No man that warreth**

No one that is serving as a soldier — Rhm

No soldier in active service — NASB

No enlisted recruit — Ber

A fighting man, when he is with the army — Bas

entangleth himself with the affairs of this life;

entangleth himself with the matters of his livelihood — Rhm

gets involved in enterprises for making a living — Ber

. . . in the every-day affairs of life — Mon

. . . in the business affairs of life — Wms

. . . in civilian pursuits — RSV

that he may please him who hath chosen him to be a soldier.

that he may please him who enrolled him as . . . — ASV

so that he may satisfy the officer who enlisted him — Wey

. . . him who has taken him into his army — Bas

since his aim is to satisfy the one who enlisted him — RSV

he must be wholly at his commanding officer's disposal — NEB

5. **And if a man also strive for masteries,**

And if any one takes part in an athletic contest — Wey

And if also a man contend in the games — ASV

And if anyone enters competitive games — Amp

Again, a competitor in the games — Gspd

yet is he not crowned, except he strive lawfully.

he is not crowned, except he have contended lawfully — ASV

he does not win the prize unless he competes according to the rules — NASB

he does not get the crown if he has not kept the rules — Bas

. . . awarded the wreath of victory unless . . . — TCNT

. . . unless he competes fairly — Ber

. . . obeys the rules of the game — Mon

6. **The husbandman that laboureth**

The toiling husbandman — Rhm

The hard-working farmer — NASB

The labourer who does the work —
TCNT

The harvestman who labours — Wey

must be first partaker of the fruits.

ought first of the fruits to partake —
Rhm

must have first share of the produce —
Ber

ought to be the first to share the crop
— Wms

should be the first to be sustained by
the fruits — Lam

has first claim on the crop — NEB

7. Consider what I say;

Keep on thinking about what I am saying — Wms

Reflect on what I am telling you —
Mon

Grasp the sense of what I am saying —
Knox

Consider these three illustrations of
mine — Phi

**and the Lord give thee understanding
in all things.**

. . . will give thee discernment in all
things — ABUV

. . . shall give thee clear apprehension
. . . — Alf

. . . will give you understanding in
everything — Wey

. . . will grant you understanding of it
in all its phases — Wms

. . . will help you to understand it perfectly — Mof

. . . will help you to full understanding
— NEB

8. Remember that Jesus Christ

Continue to remember Jesus Christ —
Wms

Keep before your mind Jesus Christ —
TCNT

**of the seed of David was raised from
the dead**

Raised from among the dead, Of the
seed of David — Rhm

risen from the dead, a descendant of
David — Wey

as risen from the dead, and descended
from David — Mof

. . . born of David's line — NEB

with David as a human ancestor, was
raised from the dead — Nor

according to my gospel:

According to my joyful message—Rhm

as told in the Good News entrusted to
me — TCNT

as is declared in the gospel which I
preach — Wey

according to the Glad-tidings which I
proclaim — Con

This is the theme of my gospel — NEB

9. Wherein I suffer trouble,

In which I am suffering hardship —
Rhm

in whose service I am exposed to hardship — NEB

For that [Gospel] I am suffering affliction — Amp

as an evil doer, even unto bonds;

even unto chains, as a malefactor —
Con

even to being put in fetters as a criminal — TCNT

even to the extent of wearing chains as
though I were a criminal — Wms

even to imprisonment as a criminal —
NASB

but the word of God is not bound.

but the word of God hath not been
bound — Alf

But the Message of God is not fettered
— TCNT

yet the word of God is not chained —
Wey

(But there is no prison for the word
of God.) — Gspd

But God's message is not imprisoned!
— Mof

but the word of God is not shackled —
Ber

10. Therefore I endure all things

For this cause am I enduring all things
— Rhm

For this reason I am bearing anything
— Wms

and that is why I submit to anything
— TCNT

Therefore I [am ready to] persevere
and stand my ground with patience
and endure everything — Amp

for the elect's sakes,

for the sake of the chosen — Rhm

for the sake of His chosen people —
Wms

. . . those whom God has chosen —
Mof

. . . God's chosen ones — NEB

on behalf of the elect — Ber

that they may also obtain the salvation

In order that they also may obtain . . . — Rhm

so that they, too, may gain possession of . . . — Ber

that they, like us, may win salvation — Knox

with this end in view, that they too may . . . — NEB

which is in Christ Jesus with eternal glory.

. . . with glory everlasting — Con

. . . along with glory age-abiding — Rhm

which comes from union with Christ Jesus, and imperishable glory — TCNT

which union with Christ Jesus affords, with . . . — Ber

which in Christ Jesus goes with eternal glory — RSV

through Christ Jesus, and the everlasting glory that follows — Nor

. . . with [the reward of] eternal glory — Amp

11. **It is a faithful saying:**[2]

For if we be dead with him, we shall also live with him:

If we have died together we shall also live together — Rhm

If we indeed have died with Him, we will live with Him too — Wms

If we undergo death with him, then we will be living with him — Bas

12. **If we suffer, we shall also reign with him:**

If we endure we shall also reign together — Rhm

If we patiently endure, we will reign with Him too — Wms

If we continue to endure, we shall also share his throne — TCNT

If we go on to the end, then we will be ruling with him — Bas

if we deny him, he also will deny us:

If we disown Him, He will also disown us — Wey

if we say we have no knowledge of him, then he will say he has no knowledge of us — Bas

If we go back on Him, then He will also personally go back on us — Ber

. . . disown and reject [Him], . . . — Amp

13. **If we believe not, yet he abideth faithful:**

If we're disloyal, he stays loyal — Beck

If we are unfaithful, he will remain faithful — Mof

If we play him false, he remains true to his word — Knox

If we prove faithless, he abides faithful — Mon

if we disbelieve, yet he remaineth faithful — Alf

If we are without faith, still he keeps faith — Bas

he cannot deny himself.

For deny himself he cannot! — Rhm

for he cannot be false to himself! — Mof

for He cannot prove false to Himself — Wms

for he cannot be untrue to himself — Gspd

for He cannot deny His own nature! — Nor

He cannot disown Himself — Wey

14. **Of these things put them in remembrance,**

Of these things remind them — ABUV

Keep on reminding men of these things — Wms

Remind them of these facts — Ber

Bring this to men's remembrances — Wey

Always call these truths to men's mind — Mon

charging them before the Lord

solemnly charging them in the presence of God — Wey

Adjuring them before God — Rhm

urge them solemnly, as in the sight of God — TCNT

giving them orders in the name of the Lord — Bas

that they strive not about words to no profit,

to avoid disputing about words, which does no good — RSV

not to contend about words, with no profitable end — Con

not to wrangle about words, which is useless — NASB

to indulge in no wars of words; it helps no one — Ber

---

[2]See I Tim. 1:15.

Not to be waging word-battles, — Useful for nothing — Rhm

to avoid petty controversy over words, . . . — Amp

not to bandy arguments — no good comes out of that — Gspd

to stop petty debating, . . . — Wms

but to the subverting of the hearers.

and the ruin of those who listen to it — TCNT

but brings destruction on those who hear it — Wms

Occasioning a subversion of them that hearken — Rhm

and it completely upsets the listeners — Ber

it only means the undoing of your audience — Gspd

but rather unsettles the minds of . . . — Nor

15. Study to shew thyself approved unto God,

Give diligence to present thyself . . . — ASV

Earnestly endeavor to present thyself . . . — ABUV

Earnestly seek to commend yourself to God — Wey

Do your best to present yourself to God as one approved — RSV

Try hard to show yourself worthy of God's approval — NEB

Let it be your care to get the approval of God — Bas

Aim first at winning God's approval — Knox

Be diligent to present thyself unto God as one proved trustworthy by trial — Con

a workman that needeth not to be ashamed,

a workman not ashamed — Alf

a workman with no reason to be ashamed — TCNT

. . . who does not need to be ashamed of his work — Knox

. . . who doesn't have to feel ashamed — Beck

rightly dividing the word of truth.

handling aright the word of truth — ASV

ever cutting a straight path for the message of the truth — Mon

driving a straight furrow, in your proclamation of the truth — NEB

rightly laying out the word of . . . — Alf

correctly analyzing the message of the truth — Ber

Skilfully handling the word . . . — Rhm

accurate in delivering the Message of the Truth — TCNT

because of his straightforward dealing with the word . . . — Wey

declaring the word of truth without distortion — Con

16. But shun profane and vain babblings:

But avoid worldly and empty chatter — NASB

But the profane pratings shun — Rhm

But stand aloof from godless and idle chatter — Nor

Avoid all that profane jargon — Gspd

But from irreligious and frivolous talk hold aloof — Wey

But keep away from those unholy, empty discussions — Ber

Continue shunning worldly, futile phrases — Wms

for they will increase unto more ungodliness.

for they will advance unto a greater measure of . . . — Alf

for they will go on to more . . . — ABUV

for those who indulge in it will proceed from bad to worse in impiety — Wey

for they lead on to greater depths of godlessness — Wms

for it leads people still further into irreligion — Gspd

17. And their word will eat as doth a canker:

and their teaching will spread like a cancer — TCNT

And their discourse as a gangrene will eat its way — Rhm

And their words will be like poisoned wounds in the flesh — Bas

For their teachings are as dangerous as blood poisoning to the body, and spread like sepsis from a wound — Phi

of whom is Hymenaeus and Philetus;

Among whom are . . . — Con

men like . . . — Wms

. . . are instances of this — TCNT

. . . are men of that stamp — Wey

18. Who concerning the truth have erred,

who have gone astray concerning the truth — Mon

that have missed out on the truth — Ber

who have swerved from the truth — RSV

They have left the path of truth — Tay

they have failed in the Truth — Gspd

they have shot wide of the truth — NEB

. . . are palpable traitors to the truth — Phi

saying that the resurrection is past already;

Affirming a resurrection already to have taken place — Rhm

when they say that the resurrection has already occurred — Ber

by contending that the resurrection has come about already — Knox

who say that the coming back from the dead has even now taken place — Bas

preaching the lie that the resurrection is already over — Tay

and overthrow the faith of some.

and they are upsetting the faith . . . — Wey

and they are undermining some people's faith — Gspd

and they play havoc with the faith . . . — Ber

thus destroying the faith . . . — Lam

19. **Nevertheless the foundation of God standeth sure,**

Howbeit the firm foundation of God standeth — ASV

Yet God's solid foundation stands unmoved — Wey

But God's strong base is unchanging — Bas

. . . foundation [laid by] God stands — Amp

having this seal,

bearing this seal — RSV

bearing this inscription — Mof

having this sign — Bas

and this is the legend on it — Knox

bearing this guarantee — Wey

The Lord knoweth them that are his.

The Lord knew them that were His — Con

The Lord knows those who belong to Him — Wey

The Lord hath acknowledged them who are his — Rhm

The Lord knows his own — NEB

. . . those who are really His — Tay

And,

And this also — Wey

and again — Knox

Let everyone that nameth the name of Christ depart from iniquity.

Let every one that nameth the name of the Lord stand aloof from unrighteousness — Rhm

Let all those who use the Name of the Lord turn away from wickedness — TCNT

Let everyone who names himself by the Lord's name . . . — Ber

. . . takes the Lord's name upon his lips must forsake . . . — NEB

. . . renounce wickedness — Wey

. . . give up evil — Mof

. . . have no dealings with evil — Phi

20. **But in a great house there are not only vessels of gold and of silver,**

In any large house there are not only gold and silver dishes — Mof

In any big household there are naturally not only gold and silver vessels — Phi

In a wealthy home there are dishes made of . . . — Tay

. . . not only gold and silver utensils — Ber

. . . not only gold and silver articles — Wms

but also of wood and of earth;

but also of wood and clay — Con

but also wooden and earthen — Rhm

but also others of wood and earthenware — TCNT

and some to honour, and some to dishonour.

and some for noble use, some for ignoble — RSV

some for honorable uses and some for lowly uses — Wms

some for great occasions and some for ordinary use — Mof

some for noble, some for menial service — Gspd

21. **If a man therefore purge himself from these,**

If one therefore cleanse himself from these — ABUV

If then a man shall purify himself from these — Alf

... makes himself clean from these — Bas

... keeps himself clear of these latter — Mon

... keeps himself clean from the contaminations of evil — Phi

So whoever cleanses himself [from what is ignoble and unclean] . . . — Amp

he shall be a vessel unto honour,

will be a utensil for noble use — Ber

he will be a vessel used for honorable purposes — Phi

... an instrument for honorable uses — Wms

sanctified, and meet for the master's use,

set apart and useful for the Master — Ber

sanctified, and fitted for the Master's use — Con

consecrated, fit for the Master's service — Wey

made holy, ready for the master's use — Bas

... and useful to the Owner of the House — Mof

... the master of the household — Phi

and prepared unto every good work.

for every good work prepared — Rhm

and equipped for . . . — Wey

and ready for any good service — Wms

and fit for all honourable employment — Knox

... for good service of every sort — Ber

... for any honourable purpose — NEB

22. Flee also youthful lusts:

But flee youthful desires — ABUV

But from the youthful covetings flee! — Rhm

Fly from the cravings of youth — Gspd

You must keep on fleeing from the evil impulses of youth — Wms

But avoid by flight the lusts of youth — Ber

So shun youthful passions — RSV

but follow righteousness, faith, charity, peace,

but pursue righteousness, faith, love, and peace — TCNT

but ever strive for uprightness, faith, . . . — Wms

and aim at integrity, faith, . . . — Mof

but run after righteousness, faith, love, and peace — Mon

with them that call on the Lord out of a pure heart.

in fellowship with those who invoke the Lord . . . — Ber

in association with those who call upon the Lord with pure hearts — Wms

in company with all those who approach God in sincerity — Phi

with those whose prayers go up to the Lord from a clean heart — Bas

23. But foolish and unlearned questions avoid,

But foolish and ignorant questionings refuse — ASV

But from the foolish and undisciplined questionings excuse thyself — Rhm

Ever shun foolish and puerile discussions — Mon

Decline those foolish and uncultural discussions — Ber

Have nothing to do with stupid, senseless controversies — RSV

... silly and ill informed controversies — Phi

... foolish and ignorant speculations — NEB

knowing that they do gender strifes.

knowing that they beget strifes — ABUV

knowing that they produce quarrels — NASB

for you know that they only breed quarrels — TCNT

... they foster strife . . . — Amp

24. And the servant of the Lord must not strive;

and a slave of the Lord must not quarrel — Gspd

And the Lord's bond-servant must not be quarrelsome — NASB

And the Lord's servant must not be a man of strife — Mof

... has no business with quarrelling — Knox

but be gentle unto all men,

but must be gentle to everybody—Wms

but treat everyone kindly — Gspd

instead, he must be affable toward everyone — Ber

but must be inoffensive towards all men — Wey

He ought, on the contrary, to be courteous to every one — TCNT

apt to teach, patient,

skilful in teaching, patient of wrong — Con

able to teach, patient when wronged — NASB

apt in teaching ready to endure malice — Rhm

he must be a skillful teacher, and not resentful under injuries — Wms

. . . willing to suffer wrong — Ber

. . . and ready to overlook grievances — Nor

25. In meekness instructing those that oppose themselves;

In a gentle way he must discipline those who put themselves in opposition — Ber

correcting his opponents with gentleness — Gspd

he must be gentle in his admonitions to the opposition — Mof

in meekness teaching those . . . — ABUV

Gently guiding those who go against the teaching — Bas

if God peradventure will give them repentance

if perhaps God may give them repentance — ABUV

for possibly God may give them a change of mind — Mon

in the hope that God may give them a change of heart — Nor

to the acknowledging of the truth;

to a full knowledge of the truth — ABUV

unto a personal knowledge of truth — Rhm

that leads to acknowledgment of . . . — Ber

for the recognition of the truth — Mon

26. And that they may recover themselves

and that they may return to soberness — Alf

And they should wake up to sobriety — Rhm

and they may come to their senses — NASB

and they might recover their senses — Wms

and they may yet come to a sober mind — TCNT

out of the snare of the devil,

out of the adversary's snare — Rhm

and escape from the devil's trap—Wms

and be freed from the snare of . . . — Ber

and be rescued from the snare of . . . — Phi

who are taken captive by him at his will.

having been taken captive by him unto his will — ASV

Though they have been taken alive by him for that one's will — Rhm

who has caught them to make them do his will — Gspd

though they are now entrapped by him to do his will — Wey

under whom they have been taken captive, to do His will — Ber

. . . [henceforth] to do His [God's] will — Amp

when captured by the Lord's Servant to do the will of God — TCNT

being made the prisoners of the Lord's servant for the purpose of God — Bas

CHAPTER 3

1. This know also,

But realize this — NASB

But this be taking note of — Rhm

But understand this — RSV

But of this be assured — Wey

that in the last days perilous times shall come,

That in last days there will set in perilous seasons — Rhm

that in the last days difficult times will come — TCNT

that in the last days there are troublesome times impending — Ber

. . . there will come times of stress — RSV

. . . there are going to be hard times — Gspd

. . . the times will be dangerous — Nor

the final age of this world is to be a time of troubles — NEB

that in the last days it is going to be very difficult to be a Christian — Tay

2. For men shall be lovers of their own selves,

For men will be — fond of themselves — Rhm

For people will be self-lovers — Ber

For men shall be selfish — Con

Men will become utterly self-centered — Phi

covetous, boasters, proud, blasphemers,

lovers of money, boastful, haughty, railers — ASV

fond of money ostentatious arrogant defamers — Rhm

avaricious, boasters, haughty, abusive — Ber

mercenary, boastful, haughty, and blasphemous — TCNT

greedy for money, full of big words . . . proud and contemptuous — Phi

lovers of money, uplifted in pride, given to bitter words — Bas

disobedient to parents, unthankful, unholy,

to parents unyielding unthankful unkind — Rhm

with no respect for parents, no gratitude, no piety — NEB

undutiful, ungrateful, irreverent—Gspd

going against the authority of their fathers, never giving praise, having no religion — Bas

. . . thankless, irreligious — Wey

. . . ungrateful, wicked — Lam

3. **Without natural affection, trucebreakers, false accusers,**

unloving, irreconcilable, malicious gossips — NASB

without natural affection accepting no truce given to intrigue — Rhm

lacking in love for kinsmen, irreconcilable, slanderers — Wms

hard-hearted, unforgiving, slanderers — Wey

inhuman, implacable, slanderers—RSV

without love, never forgiving an enemy, slandering — Beck

callous, relentless, scurrilous — Mof

. . . implacable in their hatreds, scandal-mongers — NEB

incontinent, fierce, despisers of those that are good,

without self-control, fierce, no lovers of good — ASV

dissolute, and savage; they will hate goodness — Mof

uncontrolled, brutal, with no love for the good — Ber

profligates, fierce, haters of good — RSV

intemperate and fierce, strangers to all goodness — NEB

. . . brutal and hostile to what is good — Nor

. . . uncivilized unfriendly to good men — Rhm

4. **Traitors, heady, highminded,**

betrayers, headstrong, puffed up — ABUV

treacherous, reckless, conceited—Gspd

False to their friends, acting without thought, lifted up in mind — Bas

traitors, adventurers, swollen with self-importance — NEB

. . . rash, conceited — Ber

. . . headlong with passion, blinded with pride — Con

They will betray their friends; they will be hot-headed, puffed up with pride — Tay

lovers of pleasure more than lovers of God;

pleasure-loving rather than God-loving — Ber

loving pleasure more than God—Wms

preferring pleasure to God — Mof

and prefer good times to worshipping God — Tay

They will be men who put pleasure in the place of God — NEB

[They will be] lovers of sensual pleasures and vain amusements more than and other than lovers of God — Amp

5. **Having a form of godliness,**

having an outward form of godliness — Alf

They will maintain a façade of "religion" — Phi

and will keep up a make-believe of piety — Wey

They will go to church, yes — Tay

but denying the power thereof:

but having denied . . . — ASV

but are a standing denial of its reality — NEB

they are strangers to its power — Ber

but turning their backs on the power of it — Bas

but refuse to let it be a power — Beck

but resisting its influence — Gspd

but not giving expression to its power — Wms

from such turn away.

And from these turn away — Rhm

and avoid such men as these — NASB

Keep away from these people! — Nor

6. **For of this sort are they which creep into houses,**

For among them are those who enter into households — NASB

For some of them practice going into people's houses — Wms

For some of that ilk sneak into the homes — Ber

Some of them worm their way into families — Mof

They are the sort that insinuate themselves into private houses — NEB

... go secretly into houses — Bas

and lead captive silly women

and capturing weak and silly women — Wms

And captivate silly women — Rhm

and find easy prey in silly women — Phi

and get hold of women-folk — Mof

and there get miserable women into their clutches — NEB

laden with sins,

weighted down with sin — Bas

loaded down with their sins — Gspd

who are overwhelmed with the weight of their sins — Wms

who feel crushed by the burden of their sins — Mof

loaded down with the consciousness of sin — Ber

women burdened with a sinful past — NEB

with an exaggerated sense of sin — Phi

led away with divers lusts,

and led on by all kinds of desires — NEB

and controlled by all sorts of impulses — Ber

led on by manifold covetings — Rhm

turned from the way by their evil desires — Bas

and swayed by many lustful cravings — Nor

— wayward creatures of impulse — Mof

7. **Ever learning,**

perpetually learning — Con

forever getting information — Ber

who are for ever inquiring — Knox

always curious to learn — Mof

who are always trying to learn — Wms

who are always wanting to be taught — NEB

Women of that kind are forever following new teachers — Tay

and never able to come to the knowledge of the truth.

and yet never able to arrive at knowledge of ... — Wey

and never unto a personal knowledge of truth able to come — Rhm

and never able to reach an understanding of ... — Ber

... to grasp the truth — Phi

... to comprehend the truth — Gspd

but are incapable of reaching a knowledge of ... — NEB

yet never attain to recognition of the truth — Knox

8. **Now as Jannes and Jambres withstood Moses,**

Just as Jannes and Jambres opposed Moses — TCNT

And as Iannes and Iambres resisted Moses — Con

... stood up against Moses — Lam

... were hostile to Moses — Mof

... defied Moses — NEB

so do these also resist the truth:

so do these withstand ... — ASV

so do these people, in their turn, oppose the Truth — TCNT

so these men also are hostile to ... — Amp

... defy the truth — NEB

... set themselves up in rivalry against the truth — Knox

... go against what is true — Bas

men of corrupt minds,

Men utterly corrupted in their mind — Rhm

— being men of debased mind — Wey

they are depraved in mind — Mof

Their minds are distorted — Phi

they have lost the power to reason — NEB

reprobate concerning the faith.

rejected as regards the faith — NASB

Disapproved concerning their faith — Rhm

and they cannot pass the tests of faith — NEB

who, tested by faith, are seen to be false — Bas

and counterfeits so far as faith is concerned — Ber

and useless for any purpose of faith —
Mof

and, as regards the Faith, they are utterly worthless — TCNT

9. But they shall proceed no further:

But they shall not advance farther —
Con

However, they will not get very far —
Ber

... will not make any more progress —
Wms

... will have no further success —
Wey

But their successes will be short-lived
— NEB

**for their folly shall be manifest unto
all men,**

for their folly will be fully manifest to
all — ABUV

for their shallowness will be obvious to
everyone — Ber

for their aberrations will be detected
by ... — Mof

for their foolish behaviour will be clear
to all men — Bas

Some day their deceit will be well-
known ... — Tay

as theirs also was.

as was the case with those mentioned
— Ber

just as that of Jannes and Jambres was
— TCNT

10. But thou hast fully known

But thou didst accurately trace — ABUV

But thou hast closely studied — Rhm

Now you have observed — RSV

... have followed, step by step — NEB

... on your part, have faithfully followed — Wms

... have known intimately — Phi

**my doctrine, manner of life, purpose,
faith,**

my teaching, my conduct, my purpose,
my faith — Ber

my teaching, my practice, my aims, my
faith — Mof

my teaching and behavior, my resolution, ... — Con

... my aim in life, my faith — RSV

longsuffering, charity, patience,

my forbearance, my love, and my patient endurance — TCNT

my long waiting, my love, my quiet
undergoing of trouble — Bas

my patience, my love, my stedfastness
— Mof

**11. Persecutions, afflictions, which came
unto me at Antioch, at Iconium, at
Lystra;**

my persecutions, my sufferings, such as
befell me at ... — Wms

... — the things that happened to me
at ... — Gspd

... — all that I went through at ... —
NEB

what persecutions I endured:

What matter of persecutions ... —
Rhm

all the persecutions I had to undergo —
Mof

What terrible persecution I had to live
through! — Nor

**but out of them all the Lord delivered
me.**

And out of all the Lord rescued me —
Rhm

and yet the Lord brought me safe out
of all! — TCNT

**12. Yea, and all that will live godly in
Christ Jesus shall suffer persecution.**

Yea, and all who wish to live godly ...
— ABUV

In fact, all who want to live devoutly
in Christ Jesus will be persecuted —
Ber

Yes, and all who aim at living a religious life in union with ... — TCNT

... who purpose to live a godly life ...
— Mon

... who are determined to live in a
godly manner ... — Rhm

... who are resolved to live a holy life
... — Knox

Persecution is inevitable for those who
are determined to live really Christian lives — Phi

**13. But evil men and seducers shall wax
worse and worse,**

But wicked men and impostors will
advance from bad to worse — Con

Wicked men and pretenders, on the
other hand, will keep on going from
... — Nor

But bad men and swindlers will get
worse — Beck

whereas wicked men and charlatans will make progress from bad to worse — NEB

while the rogues and the mountebanks go on from . . . — Knox

But bad and deceptive men shall grow worse and worse — Lam

deceiving, and being deceived.

misleading others and misled themselves — Wms

deluding others and deluding themselves — Phi

using deceit and themselves overcome by deceit — Bas

as they cheat and are cheated — Beck

14. **But continue thou in the things which thou hast learned**

But thou — abide in the things . . . — Rhm

You, however, must remain faithful in what you have learned — Ber

Yet you must go on steadily in those things that . . . — Phi

But for your part, stand by the truths you . . . — NEB

But see that you keep to the teaching you have been given — Bas

But do you hold fast what . . . — Mon

and hast been assured of,

and of which you are convinced — Wey

and the things of which you are certain — Bas

and which you know are true — Phi

and been led to rely upon — Wms

and have firmly believed — RSV

knowing of whom thou hast learned them,

knowing from what persons thou didst learn — ABUV

well aware from whom you learned — Ber

knowing who your teachers were — Wey

Remember from what sort of people your knowledge has come — Phi

15. **And that from a child thou hast known the holy scriptures,**

and that from a babe thou hast known the sacred writings — ASV

and how from infancy you have known the sacred Scriptures — Ber

and how from early childhood your mind has been familiar with . . . — Phi

which are able to make thee wise unto salvation

. . . to make you wise to obtain salvation — Wey

. . . to instruct you for salvation — RSV

which can give you wisdom that leads to salvation — Wms

that can impart saving wisdom — Mof

and it is these that make you wise to accept God's salvation — Tay

through faith which is in Christ Jesus.

by the faith which is in . . . — Con

through the faith that leans on . . . — Wms

through the faith which rests in . . . — Knox

by trusting in . . . — Tay

16. **All scripture is given by inspiration of God, and is profitable**

Every scripture [is] God-breathed, And profitable — Rhm

Every Scripture is God-inspired and is helpful — TCNT

All Scripture is divinely inspired, and useful — Gspd

Every scripture inspired of God is also profitable — ASV

Every holy Writing which comes from God is of profit — Bas

for doctrine, for reproof, for correction,

for teaching, for refutation, for correction — Mon

for teaching, for reproof, for amendment — Mof

for teaching, for refuting error, for giving guidance — TCNT

unto teaching unto conviction unto correction — Rhm

for teaching, for training, for guiding — Bas

for teaching the faith and correcting error, for resetting the direction of a man's life — Phi

for instruction in righteousness:

for discipline which is in righteousness — Alf

and in training in uprightness — Gspd

and for moral discipline — Mof

and for instruction in right doing — Wey

and training him in good living — Phi

for education in righteousness — Bas

17. **That the man of God may be perfect,**

that the man of God may be complete
— ASV

In order that ready may be the man of
God — Rhm

to make the man of God proficient —
Mof

so that the man who belongs to God
may be efficient — NEB

... will be adequate — Gspd

... may be perfectly fit — Wms

... well-prepared at every point —
Tay

... may himself be complete — Mon

**throughly furnished unto all good
works.**

furnished completely unto every good
work — ASV

Unto every good work being well-prepared — Rhm

and adequately equipped for all good
work — Ber

thoroughly equipped for every good
enterprise — Wms

CHAPTER 4

**1. I charge thee therefore before God,
and the Lord Jesus Christ,**

I solemnly charge you, in the sight of
God and of Christ Jesus — TCNT

I adjure you, in the presence of ... —
Wey

And so I solemnly urge you before ...
— Tay

who shall judge the quick and the dead

who shall judge the living and the dead
— ASV

Who is about to be judging living and
dead — Rhm

at his appearing and his kingdom;

and by his appearing ... — ASV

in the light of his appearance and his
reign — Mof

in view of His coming and ruling over
us — Beck

I adjure you by his coming appearance
and ... — NEB

2. Preach the word;

Herald the message — Ber

— proclaim the tidings — Con

be instant in season, out of season;

Take thy position — in season, ... —
Rhm

and stand by it zealously in season and
... — Lam

be urgent in season, ... — ASV

be at it when it is and when it is not
convenient — Ber

press it home on all occasions, convenient or inconvenient — NEB

dwelling upon it continually, welcome
or unwelcome — Knox

Never lose your sense of urgency, ...
— Phi

... whether the opportunity seems to

be favorable or unfavorable ... —
Amp

reprove, rebuke, exhort

convict, rebuke, exhort — Alf

Convince, rebuke, encourage — Rhm

correct, rebuke, ... — Beck

use argument, reproof, and appeal —
NEB

make protests, say sharp words, give
comfort — Bas

bring home wrongdoing, comfort the
waverer, rebuke the sinner — Knox

with all longsuffering and doctrine.

with neverfailing patience and teaching
— Mon

with the utmost patience and instruction — Wey

with unqualified patience and willingness to teach — Ber

with all the patience that the work of
teaching requires — NEB

with perfect patience as a teacher —
Wms

being unflagging and inexhaustible in
patience and teaching — Amp

3. For the time will come

For there will be a season — Rhm

For a period will come — ABUV

For a time is coming — Wey

**when they will not endure sound doc-
trine;**

When the healthful teaching they will
not endure — Rhm

when men will not tolerate wholesome
instruction — Wey

when people decline to be taught sound
doctrine — Mof

when people won't listen to the truth
— Tay

but after their own lusts

but according to their own inclinations
— Con

but, moved by their desires — Bas

but to gratify their own evil desires —
Wms

But according to their own covetings
— Rhm

to satisfy their own fancies — Wey

but . . . to suit their whims — Gspd

shall they heap to themselves teachers,

they will accumulate for themselves
teachers — RSV

they will get for themselves a great
number of teachers — Bas

. . . procure themselves a crowd of
teachers — TCNT

. . . find a multitude of teachers —
Wey

. . . provide themselves with a continuous succession of new teachers —
Knox

having itching ears;

Because they have an itching ear —
Rhm

because their ears are itching so to be
tickled — Wms

in their itching for novelty — TCNT

to satisfy their own fancies — Wey

having ears itching [for something
pleasing and gratifying] — Amp

being lured by enticing words — Lam

**4. And they shall turn away their ears
from the truth,**

And from the truth indeed their ear
will they turn away — Rhm

And will turn aside from hearing the
truth — Amp

they will give up listening to the Truth
— Mof

. . . turn their attention away from the
truth — Ber

. . . turn a deaf ear to the Truth —
TCNT

. . . refuse to listen to the truth — Beck

And shutting their ears to what is true
— Bas

and shall be turned unto fables.

and turn aside to fable-lore — Nor

will be turned away to belief in foolish
stories — Bas

and will turn to listen to myths —
Wms

and give their attention to legends instead — TCNT

. . . wander off after man-made fictions
— Phi

**5. But watch thou in all things, endure
afflictions,**

But thou — be sober in all things, suffer hardship — Rhm

But as for you, be always self-controlled, face hardships — Mon

As for you, always be steady, . . . —
RSV

But amid it all, you keep your head;
. . . — Ber

Whatever happens, be self-possessed,
flinch from no suffering — Mof

But you must always be composed; do
not shrink from hardship — Gspd

do the work of an evangelist,

do the work of a Missionary — TCNT

do your work as a herald of the good
news — Wms

work to spread the Gospel — NEB

make full proof of thy ministry.

fully accomplish thy ministry — ABUV

thy ministry completely fulfil — Rhm

and so fill your ministry to the brim
— Wms

discharge all the duties of your ministry — Mon

and do all the duties of your calling
— NEB

Leave nothing undone that you ought
to do — Tay

6. For I am now ready to be offered,

For I am already being offered — ASV

For I am already being poured out as
a drink offering — Ber

I for my part am a libation already being poured in sacrifice — Mon

As for me, already my life is being
poured out on the altar — NEB

My life, indeed, is already ebbing out
— Wms

**and the time of my departure is at
hand.**

And the season of my release is at hand
— Rhm

and the time of my unmooring is at
hand — Mon

and the time has come for me to sail
away — Wms

the time of my [spirit's] release [from
the body] . . . — Amp

and the hour for my departure is upon
me — NEB

7. I have fought a good fight,

The noble contest have I contested —
Rhm

I have fought in the glorious contest —
Mon

I have fought the grand fight — Ber

The glorious fight that God gave me I
have fought — Phi

I have run the great Race — TCNT

I have finished my course,

The race have I finished — Rhm

the course that I was set I have finished
— Phi

I have run my course — Mof

I have kept the faith:

The faith have I kept — Rhm

I have preserved the faith — Gspd

. . . kept (firmly held) the faith—Amp

8. **Henceforth there is laid up for me a
crown of righteousness,**

in the future there is laid up for me the
crown . . . — NASB

Hereafter there is reserved for me the
crown . . . — Wey

And now the prize awaits me, the garland of righteousness — NEB

. . . the [victor's] crown of righteousness — for being right with God and
doing right — Amp

**which the Lord, the righteous judge,
shall give me at that day:**

which the Lord, the upright judge, will
award me on that Day — Gspd

The Lord, the judge whose award
never goes amiss, will grant it to . . .
— Knox

. . . on that great day of His return —
Tay

and not to me only,

Yet not alone unto me — Rhm

And not just to me — Tay

**but unto all them also that love his
appearing.**

but also to all them that have loved
his appearing — ASV

. . . who have loved his forthshining —
Rhm

. . . who have set their hearts on his
coming appearance — NEB

. . . who eagerly await his appearance
— Lam

. . . who have loved the thought of His
appearing — Wey

. . . yearned for and welcomed His appearing [His return] — Amp

9. **Do thy diligence to come shortly unto
me:**

Earnestly endeavor to come to me
shortly — ABUV

Make every effort to come to me soon
— NASB

Do thy utmost to come to me speedily
— Con

Do your best to join me soon — NEB

Make haste to visit me soon — Ber

10. **For Demas hath forsaken me,**

for Demas forsook me — ASV

. . . has deserted me — Wey

. . . has gone away from me — Bas

having loved this present world,

having loved the present age — ABUV

because he loved the present world —
Wms

because his heart was set on this world
— NEB

for love of this present life — Bas

and is departed unto Thessalonica:

and went to . . . — ASV

And hath journeyed unto . . . — Rhm

and is now in . . . — Nor

**Crescens to Galatia, Titus unto Dal-
matia.**

Crescens has gone to Galatia, Titus to
. . . — NASB

Crescens is off to Gaul, . . . — Mof

11. **Only Luke is with me.**

Luke alone is with me — Con

No one but Luke is with me — Gspd

and Luke is my only companion —
Knox

Take Mark, and bring him with thee:

Pick up Mark and bring him along
with you — Mof

Get hold of Mark and bring him along
— Ber

Join company with Mark, and bring
him here with thee — Knox

**for he is profitable to me for the min-
istry.**

for he is useful to me for ministering
— ASV

. . . helpful to me in service — Ber

. . . of great assistance to me — Gspd

. . . very useful in serving me — RSV

12. **And Tychicus have I sent to Ephesus.**

But Tychicus I sent to Ephesus — ASV

(Tychicus is gone too, as I sent him . . .
— Tay

13. **The cloke that I left at Troas with
Carpus,**

the cloak which I left behind at Troas
at the house of Carpus — Wey
the mantle I left . . . — Mof
the travel-cloak I left . . . — Ber
the warm coat I left with Carpus in
Troas — Beck
when thou comest, bring with thee,
bring when thou comest — ASV
When you come, bring along — Ber
**and the books, but especially the
parchments.**
And the scrolls, especially . . . — Rhm
and the books, especially the parch-
ment scrolls — Lam
. . . especially the manuscripts — Phi
. . . and particularly my papers — Mof
. . . above all my notebooks — NEB

14. **Alexander the coppersmith did me
much evil:**
. . . the coppersmith, manifested bitter
hostility toward me — Mon
. . . the metalworker, has displayed considerable ill will towards me — Ber
. . . the smith did me much mischief —
Wey
. . . the blacksmith has done me great
harm — Mof
. . . the copperworker did me much
wrong — Bas
. . . the brass-founder charged me with
much evil in his declaration — Con
. . . has done many wicked things
against me — Nor
**the Lord reward him according to his
works:**
The Lord will render to him . . . — ASV
. . . will repay him according to his
deeds — NASB
. . . will requite him according to his
doing — Wey
. . . will pay him back to the measure
of his doings — Ber
. . . will give him what his actions deserve — TCNT
Retribution will fall upon him from the
Lord — NEB

15. **Of whom be thou ware also;**
You too must be on your guard against
him — Wms
(beware of him) — Mof
But be on the watch for him — Bas
**for he hath greatly withstood our
words.**
. . . has violently opposed our words —
Wey

. . . strongly opposed our message —
RSV
. . . vehemently opposed my teaching
— Gspd
. . . has been bitterly hostile to anything I have said — Mof
. . . resisted our message very strongly
and exceedingly — Amp
. . . has been a great opponent of my
arguments — Con

16. **At my first answer no man stood with
me,**
At my first defence I had no one at
my side — Wey
At my first appearance in court no one
came to help me — Gspd
At my first meeting with my judges, no
one took my part — Bas
At the first hearing of my case no one
came into court to support me —
NEB
At my first trial no one acted in my
defense (as my advocate) . . . —
Amp
but all men forsook me:
on the contrary they all deserted me —
Mon
they all left me in the lurch — NEB
Everyone had run away — Tay
**I pray God that it may not be laid to
their charge.**
Unto them may it not be reckoned! —
Rhm
May it never be counted against them!
TCNT
May it never be charged to their ac-
count — Wms
I pray that it may not be held against
them — NEB
(God grant it may not be brought up
against them!) — Mof
I hope that they will not be blamed
for it — Tay

17. **Notwithstanding the Lord stood with
me, and strengthened me;**
But the Lord stood by me and empowered me — Rhm
But the Lord came to my help and . . .
— TCNT
But the Lord supported me and gave
me strength — Mof
. . . and filled me with strength — Wey
**that by me the preaching might be
fully known,**

that through me the message might be fully proclaimed — ASV

so that I might make a full presentation of the message — Gspd

so that through me the news might be given out in full measure — Bas

so that I might be his instrument in making the full proclamation of the Gospel — NEB

. . . the preaching might be fully accomplished — ABUV

. . . might have its full effect — Wms

and that all the Gentiles might hear:

and all the heathen might hear it — Wms

for the whole pagan world to hear — NEB

and I was delivered out of the mouth of the lion.

and I was rescued out of the Lion's mouth — TCNT

and I was rescued from the jaws of the lion — Mof

18. **And the Lord shall deliver me from every evil work,**

The Lord will rescue me from every wicked work — Rhm

. . . will deliver me from every evil deed — NASB

. . . will henceforth protect me from every wicked scheme — Nor

. . . will keep me safe from . . . — Bas

. . . from every assault of evil — Mof

. . . from every malicious attack—Wey

. . . from every evil plot — Phi

. . . from every attempt to do me harm — NEB

and will preserve me unto his heavenly kingdom:

and will save me unto . . . — ASV

and will preserve me for . . . — Mon

and will bring me safe to His heavenly Kingdom — Wey

he will bring me safe to his own realm in heaven — Mof

and will give me salvation in his kingdom in heaven — Bas

and keep me safe until his heavenly reign begins — NEB

to whom be glory for ever and ever. Amen.

Unto whom be the glory unto the ages of ages. Amen — Rhm

To him be the glory forever and ever! Amen! — Mon

glory be to him through endless ages,

Amen — Knox

To Him be everlasting glory! Amen! — Nor

. . . So be it — Bas

19. **Salute Prisca and Aquila, and the household of Onesiphorus.**

Greet Prisca and Aquila, and . . . — Wey

Remember me to Prisca and Aquila, and to the members of . . . — Gspd

Give my love to Prisca and Aquila and those of the house of . . . — Bas

My greetings to Prisca and Aquila and to the Onesiphorus family — Ber

20. **Erastus abode at Corinth:**

. . . remained at Corinth — ASV

. . . stayed in Corinth — Wey

. . . stayed behind at Corinth — NEB

but Trophimus have I left at Miletum sick.

but Trophimus I left at Miletus sick — ASV

Trophimus I left behind me at Miletus, ill — Wey

21. **Do thy diligence to come before winter.**

Earnestly endeavor to come . . . — ABUV

Make every effort to come . . . — NASB

Do your utmost to come . . . — TCNT

Hurry to arrive . . . — Ber

Do your best to get here . . . — Wms

Do try to be here . . . — Tay

Eubulus greeteth thee, and Pudens, and Linus, and Claudia,

Eubulus saluteth thee, and . . . — ASV

Eubulus wishes to be remembered to you, and so do . . . — Gspd

. . . sends you his love, and . . . — Bas

. . . sends greetings to you, as do . . . — RSV

and all the brethren.

and all the brothers — Gspd

and all the fellow Christians greet you — Beck

and from all the brotherhood here — NEB

22. **The Lord Jesus Christ be with thy spirit.**

The Lord be with your spirit — Wey

May the Lord be with your soul—TCNT

Grace be with you, Amen.

Favour be with you — Rhm

Spiritual blessing be with you all — Wms

God bless you all — TCNT

THE
EPISTLE OF PAUL TO TITUS

CHAPTER 1

1. Paul, a servant of God,
Paul, a bondsman of God — Con
. . . a slave of God — Gspd

and an apostle of Jesus Christ,
— an apostle moreover of . . . — Rhm
and messenger of . . . — Phi
and an apostle (a special messenger)
of Jesus Christ, the Messiah — Amp

according to the faith of God's elect,
According to the faith of the chosen
ones of God — Rhm
in agreement with the faith of the
saints of God — Bas
for the faith of God's elect — Alf
to stimulate faith in God's chosen people — Wms
— sent forth to bring God's chosen to
faith — Con
charged to strengthen the faith of . . .
— TCNT
with the faith of God's elect for his
care — Knox
in the faith God gives to his chosen —
Phi

**and the acknowledging of the truth
which is after godliness;**
and the knowledge of the truth which
is according to godliness — ASV
and the full knowledge of what is true
in harmony with religion — Bas
and for an understanding of the truth
that effects godliness — Ber
and to lead them on to a full knowledge of religious truth — Wms
. . . the Truth that goes with a religious
life — Mof
. . . God's truth — the kind of truth
that changes lives — Tay

2. In hope of eternal life,
In hope of life age-abiding — Rhm
(Resting) in the hope of . . . — Amp
and is based on the hope of Immortal
Life — TCNT
Sent also in hope of everlasting life —
Nor
and fix their hopes on . . . — Knox
so that they can have eternal life —
Tay

**which God, that cannot lie, promised
before the world began;**
which God, who never lies, promised

before the ages began — TCNT
which God, who never deceives, promised from all eternity — Wey
which was made certain before eternal
time, by the word of God who is ever
true — Bas

**3. But hath in due times manifested his
word**
But hath manifested in its fitting seasons, Even his word — Rhm
and has revealed at his own time in his
Message — TCNT
and at the appointed time He made
known His word — Wey
Who, in his time, made clear his word
— Bas
— he gave effect to his word in due
time — Mof
and now in his own good time he has
openly declared himself — NEB
. . . He has revealed this Good News
— Tay

**through preaching, which is commit-
ted unto me**
in the message, wherewith I was intrusted — ASV
in the proclamation with which entrusted am I — Rhm

**according to the commandment of
God our Saviour;**
By injunction of . . . — Rhm
by the command of . . . — Con
by the order of . . . — Bas
by ordinance of . . . — NEB
God our Saviour commanded that I be
allowed to do this work for Him —
Tay

**4. To Titus, mine own son after the com-
mon faith:**
. . . my true child after a common faith
— ASV
. . . my genuine child in our common
faith — Wms
. . . my true-born son in the faith which
we share — NEB
. . . my lawful son in the faith we hold
in common — Mof
. . . truly my son in the affairs of the
Lord — Tay

Grace, mercy, and peace,
Grace and peace — ASV

Favour and peace — Rhm
spiritual blessing and peace — Wms
. . . and heart peace — Amp
from God the Father and the Lord Jesus Christ our Saviour.
. . . and Christ Jesus our Saviour — ASV

5. For this cause left I thee in Crete,
This is why I left you in Crete — RSV
My reason for leaving you in Crete was — TCNT
My intention in leaving you behind in Crete was — NEB
I left you in Crete for this express purpose — Wms
that thou shouldest set in order the things that are wanting,
That the things remaining undone thou mightest completely set in order — Rhm
that you may set right the things still requiring attention — Wey
that you might straighten out unfinished business — Ber
. . . further correct what is deficient — Con
. . . put in order what has been left unsettled — TCNT
to make the improvements still needed — Beck
and ordain elders in every city,
and mightest establish in every city elders — Rhm
and appoint elders . . . — ASV
and appoint Presbyters . . . — Con
and in particular should institute elders in each town — NEB
. . . Officers of the Church in the various towns — TCNT
. . . pastors in every city — Tay
. . . elders and set them over the churches (assemblies) — Amp
as I had appointed thee:
as I gave thee charge — ASV
. . . prescribed to thee — Alf
. . . had instructed you — Mon
. . . myself directed you — TCNT
. . . with thee arranged — Rhm
In doing so, observe the tests I prescribed — NEB

6. If any be blameless,
If anyone is unaccusable — Rhm
if any be under no imputation — Alf
namely, if any man be above reproach — NASB

. . . of irreproachable character — TCNT
. . . of unquestionable integrity — Phi
. . . have a reputation beyond reproach — Nor
. . . well thought of for their good lives — Tay
the husband of one wife,[1]
having faithful children
having children that believe — ASV
one whose children hold the faith — Knox
whose children are Christians — TCNT
and their children must love the Lord — Tay
whose children are [well-trained and are] believers — Amp
not accused of riot or unruly.
who are not charged with riotous excess, nor insubordinate — Rhm
and are free from every reproach of profligacy or of disorderliness — Wey
not accused of reckless living, not wanting in obedience — Knox
not open to charges of reckless living and unwillingness to obey — Nor
and not likely to be accused of loose living or lawbreaking — Phi

7. For a bishop must be blameless, as the steward of God;
For it is needful that the overseer be — Unaccusable as God's steward — Rhm
For a Presiding-Officer, as God's steward, ought to be a man of irreproachable character — TCNT
For as God's overseer a superintendent must be irreproachable — Gspd
For as God's trustee a pastor must be above reproach — Wms
As a manager appointed by God, . . . — Beck
. . . be of unimpeachable virtue, for he is God's agent in the affairs of his household — Phi
not selfwilled, not soon angry,
not stubborn or quick-tempered — Wms
not arrogant or . . . — Gspd
— he must not be presumptuous or hot-tempered — Mof
He must not be overbearing or short-tempered — NEB

[1]See 1 Tim. 3:2.

He must not be an obstinate or quarrel-some man — Knox

He shouldn't do as he pleases, get angry easily — Beck

ready to give way to others, not quickly moved to wrath — Bas

not given to wine, no striker,

not a lover of wine, not given to brawls — Con

or addicted to strong drink or pug-nacious — Wms

not a drunkard or violent — Mof

or a hard drinker, not given to blows — Wey

not excessive in the use of wine, not too ready to strike with his hand — Lam

. . . He must not be ever ready to come to blows — Nor

. . . not ready to wound — Rhm

not given to filthy lucre;

not greedy of base gain — ABUV

not seeking gain by base means—Rhm

not addicted to dishonest gain — Nor

or to questionable money-making — TCNT

no money-grubber — NEB

or addicted to pilfering — Mof

8. But a lover of hospitality, a lover of good men,

but given to hospitality, a lover of good — ASV

But opening his house freely to guests; a lover of what is good — Bas

but hospitable, a lover of goodness — Gspd

but hospitable, right-minded — NEB

But he must be hospitable—loving and a friend to believers, especially to the strangers and foreigners [He must be] a lover of goodness — Amp

sober, just, holy, temperate;

sober-minded, just, holy, self-con-trolled — ASV

sensible, upright, of pure life, . . . — Wms

self-restrained, just, holy, continent — Con

master of himself, a just man, a reli-gious man, and abstemious — Mof

discreet, upright, a man of holy life . . . — TCNT

use good judgment, live right and holy. He should control himself — Beck

9. Holding fast the faithful word as he hath been taught,

holding to the faithful word which is according to the teaching — ASV

Holding fast in the matter of his teach-ing the faithful word — Rhm

and a man who continues to cling to the trustworthy message . . . — Wms

he must hold by the sure truths of doctrine — Mof

. . . the words which are faithful to our teaching — Con

that he may be able by sound doctrine both to exhort

. . . able both to exhort in the healthful teaching — ABUV

. . . able both to encourage with his healthful instruction — Rhm

. . . competent to encourage others with wholesome teaching — Wms

. . . able to give instruction in sound doctrine — RSV

. . . able to give comfort by right teach-ing — Bas

so that he may be well able to move his hearers with wholesome teaching . . . — NEB

and to convince the gainsayers.

and the gainsayers to refute — Rhm

and to convict those who oppose him — Wms

and also to confute those who contra-dict it — RSV

and to show the error of those who oppose him — Gspd

as well as to refute our opponents — TCNT

and overcome the arguments of the doubters — Bas

and correct those who oppose him — Beck

10. For there are many unruly

. . . many undisciplined people — Gspd

. . . many disorderly persons — Wey

. . . plenty of insubordinate creatures — Mof

For there are men who are not ruled by law — Bas

For there are many rebellious spirits abroad — Knox

There are far too many who are out of all control — NEB

. . . who do not readily submit to au-thority — Nor

and vain talkers and deceivers,

disobedient babblers and . . . — Con

mere talkers with nothing to say, but deceivers of their own minds—Wms

given to idle and misleading talk—Wey

they talk wildly and lead men's minds astray — NEB

who impose on people with their empty arguments — Mof

specially they of the circumcision:

particularly those who have come over from Judaism — Mof

especially those of the circumcision party — Wms

who, for the most part, are of the Jewish party — Wey

those especially who hold by circumcision — Knox

This is especially true among those who say that all Christians must obey the Jewish laws — Tay

11. Whose mouths must be stopped,

they must be silenced — Mof

Such men must be curbed — NEB

whose mouths need bit and bridle — Con

who subvert whole houses,

men who overthrow whole houses — ASV

for they upset whole households — TCNT

for they are undermining whole families — Mof

because they are ruining . . . — NEB

because by it whole families are turned away from the grace of God — Tay

teaching things which they ought not,

Teaching the things which ought not to be taught — Rhm

by teaching things they ought not to think — Wms

by teaching objectionable doctrine — Mof

by teaching evil — Con

. . . what they have no right to teach — RSV

for filthy lucre's sake.

for the sake of sordid gain — NASB

for the love of shameful gain — Con

for the sake of dishonest gain — Gspd

with an eye to their own base profits — Knox

only to make money in such a shameful way — Beck

12. One of themselves, even a prophet of their own, said,

One of them, a prophet of their own countrymen, has said — Wms

It was a Cretan — one of their own teachers — who said — TCNT

One of their own men, a prophet born in Crete, . . . — Tay

The Cretians are always liars, evil beasts, slow bellies.

Cretans! always false, mischievous wild-beasts, idle gluttons — Rhm

Cretans are always liars, wicked brutes, lazy bellies — Wms

. . . savage brutes, lazy gluttons—Gspd

. . . vicious beasts with empty bellies — Lam

venomous creatures, all hungry belly and nothing besides — Knox

. . . evil beasts, lovers of food, hating work — Bas

13. This witness is true.

This testimony . . . — ASV

and his statement . . . — TCNT

and he told the truth! — NEB

and that is a true account of them — Knox

Wherefore rebuke them sharply,

For which cause reprove them sharply — ASV

So continue correcting them severely — Wms

Therefore correct them rigorously — Gspd

Be strict, then, in taking them to task — Knox

So speak to them as sternly as necessary — Tay

All the more reason why you should pull them up sharply — NEB

that they may be sound in the faith;

That they may be healthy in their faith — Rhm

that they may keep sound in their faith — Wey

so that they may be soundly established in . . . — Knox

to make them strong in . . . — Tay

14. Not giving heed to Jewish fables,

instead of applying their minds to . . . — Ber

and may pay no attention to Jewish legends — TCNT

by ceasing to give attention to Jewish myths — Wms

and not study Jewish fictions — Gspd

with a proper contempt for Jewish fairy tales — Phi

and commandments of men, that turn from the truth.

and commandments of men that turn themselves away from . . . — Alf

or to the directions of those who turn their backs upon . . . — TCNT

and the rules laid down by men who have discarded . . . — Mof

and orders issued by men who have forsaken the path of truth — Phi

15. **Unto the pure all things are pure:**

Everything is pure to the pure-minded — TCNT

To the pure [in heart and conscience] . . . — Amp

Everything is wholesome to those who are themselves wholesome — Phi

A person who is pure of heart sees goodness and purity in everything — Tay

To the clean in heart all things are clean — Bas

but unto them that are defiled and unbelieving is nothing pure;

But unto the polluted and faithless . . . — Rhm

but to the evil-minded and unbelieving . . . — Gspd

but to the contaminated and the faithless . . . — Mon

But nothing is wholesome to those who are themselves unwholesome and who have no faith in God — Phi

but nothing is pure to the tainted minds of disbelievers — NEB

but a person whose own heart is evil and untrusting finds evil in everything — Tay

but even their mind and conscience is defiled.

but both their mind and their conscience are defiled — ASV

but both their understanding and their conscience is polluted — Con

nay, their very minds and consciences are tainted — Mon

defilement has entered their very thought, their very conscience — Knox

they become unclean in mind and in thought — Bas

for his dirty mind and rebellious heart color all he sees and hears — Tay

16. **They profess that they know God;**

God they confess that they know — Rhm

They openly claim to know God — Beck

They profess to acknowledge God — NEB

They profess recognition of God — Knox

They profess to know God — to recognize, perceive and be acquainted with Him — Amp

but in works they deny him,

but in their actions they disown Him — Wey

but they deny him by their deeds — RSV

but their practice contradicts it — Knox

while by their acts they are turning their backs on him — Bas

but their actual behavior denies their profession — Phi

being abominable, and disobedient,

Being abominable and obdurate—Rhm

for they are detestable, disobedient men — Wey

They are degraded and self-willed — TCNT

for they are obviously vile and rebellious — Phi

They are rotten and disobedient — Tay

Their detestable obstinacy — NEB

and unto every good work reprobate.

And as to any good work found worthless — Rhm

and useless for good work of any kind — Mof

and unfit for any good enterprise — Ber

worthless for any good purpose — Gspd

and when it comes to doing any real good they are palpable frauds — Phi

CHAPTER 2

1. But speak thou the things which become sound doctrine:

But do thou speak the things which become the healthful instruction — Rhm

. . . in a manner that befits wholesome teaching — Wey

. . . conformably to the sound doctrine — Con

. . . of such subjects as properly have a place in sound Christian teaching — TCNT

You must continue telling the people what is proper for wholesome teaching — Wms

But as for you, speak up for the right living that goes along with true Christianity — Tay

2. That the aged men be sober, grave, temperate,

that aged men be temperate, grave, sober-minded — ASV

. . . temperate, dignified, sensible — NASB

. . . temperate, serious, and discreet — TCNT

Exhort the aged men to be sober, grave, self-restrained — Con

. . . sober, high-principled, and temperate — NEB

. . . simple in their tastes, serious, wise — Bas

Teach the older men to be sober, decent, orderly — Knox

sound in faith, in charity, in patience.

healthy in their faith, love, endurance Rhm

sound in faith, in love, in perseverance — NASB

soundly established in faith, in charity, in patience — Knox

sound in faith, in love, in steadfastness — Con

3. The aged women likewise,

Aged women in the same way — Rhm

So, too, that the older women — TCNT

Bid the older women likewise — RSV

that they be in behaviour as becometh holiness,

be reverent in demeanor — ASV

in deportment as becometh sacred persons — Rhm

should be reverent in their bearing — NEB

to let their deportment testify of holiness — Con

to behave as becomes the worship of God — Lam

not false accusers, not given to much wine,

not slanderers, nor enslaved to much wine — ASV

not scandal-mongers or slaves to strong drink — NEB

not malicious gossips, . . . — NASB

not given to intrigue, . . . — Rhm

and that they should avoid scandal, and beware of becoming slaves to drink — TCNT

teachers of good things;

teachers of that which is good — ASV

teachers of virtue — Rhm

but teachers of what is right — Mon

They should be teachers of what is noble — Ber

teaching others by their good example — Knox

they must set a high standard — NEB

4. That they may teach the young women to be sober,

that they may train the young women — ASV

that they may teach discretion to the younger women — Con

From them the younger women must learn orderly behaviour — Knox

to love their husbands, to love their children,

to be affectionate to their husbands and children — Wey

leading them to be loving wives and loving mothers — Con

how to treat their husbands and their children lovingly — Knox

5. To be discreet, chaste, keepers at home, good,

to be sober-minded, chaste, workers at home, kind — ASV

to be serious, pure, homekeepers, kind — Wms

sensible, chaste, good house-keepers, good-natured — Ber

and to be discreet, pure-minded, domesticated, good women — TCNT

to use good judgment and be pure, to keep house, to be good — Beck

. . . home lovers, kindhearted — Phi

obedient to their own husbands,

being in subjection to . . . — ASV

submitting themselves to . . . — Alf

respecting the authority of . . . — NEB

and subordinate to their husbands — Wms

and willing to adapt themselves to their husbands — Phi

that the word of God be not blasphemed.

— That the word of God be not defamed — Rhm

in order that God's Message may not be maligned — TCNT

so that the word of God may not be slandered — Ber

that the word of God may not be discredited — RSV

so as not to cause God's message to suffer reproach — Wms

that the word of God may not be dishonored — NASB

— otherwise it will be a scandal to the gospel — Mof

— a good advertisement for the Christian faith — Phi

6. **Young men likewise exhort to be sober minded.**

In the same way exhort the younger men to be self-restrained — Wey

Keep urging the younger men to be sensible — Wms

Encourage the young men, too, to live orderly lives — Knox

Tell the young men also to be masters of themselves at all points — Mof

. . . to behave prudently — Ber

. . . to be temperate in all things — NEB

. . . to use good judgment — Beck

7. **In all things shewing thyself a pattern of good works:**

In everything you yourself continue to set them a worthy example of doing good — Wms

And, above all, exhibit in your own life a pattern of right conduct — Wey

. . . an all-round example of doing what is lovely — Ber

. . . the model of a life nobly lived — Knox

in doctrine shewing uncorruptness, gravity, sincerity,

in thy doctrine showing uncorruptness, gravity — ASV

In thine instruction . . . — Rhm

of teaching what is unadulterated and dignified — Ber

In your teaching, you must show integrity and high principle — NEB

be sincere and serious in your teaching — Mof

8. **Sound speech, that cannot be condemned;**

healthful speech, that . . . — ABUV

and sound speech that cannot be censured — RSV

and present a wholesome, unobjectionable message — Gspd

let the instruction that you give be sound and above reproach — TCNT

Your speech should be unaffected and logical — Phi

Your message should be true, your language correct and not open to criticism — Nor

that he that is of the contrary part may be ashamed,

In that way your opponent may be put to shame — Nor

so that the opposite side may be confounded — Mof

that our adversaries may be ashamed — Con

so that anyone who opposes us will feel foolish — Beck

. . . may relent — Rhm

having no evil thing to say of you.

Having nothing to say concerning us that is disparaging — Rhm

when he fails to find anything bad to say about us — TCNT

by finding nothing that they can say to our discredit — Mof

. . . no opportunity for speaking ill of us — Knox

. . . nothing in which to pick holes — Phi

9. **Exhort servants to be obedient unto their own masters,**

Exhort bond-servants to submit themselves . . . — Alf

Continue urging slaves to practice perfect submission . . . — Wms

Urge slaves to be submissive to their owners in all circumstances — TCNT

Tell slaves to respect their masters' authority in everything — NEB

. . . to be in subjection to their own masters — ASV

... that it is their duty as Christians to obey their masters — Phi

and to please them well in all things;
to be well-pleasing — Rhm
and to give them perfect satisfaction — Wms
and to comply with their demands — NEB
and try to please them in every task — Nor
so as to content them in every way — Knox

not answering again;
not gainsaying — ASV
not contradicting — Alf
not argumentative — NASB
not contentious — Lam
and don't talk back — Beck
to stop resisting them — Wms

10. **Not purloining,**
not taking anything away — Rhm
Not taking what is not theirs — Bas
not to embezzle — Mof
nor pilfer — Mon
or to be light-fingered — Phi
Nor to steal by taking things of small value — Amp

but shewing all good fidelity;
but manifesting perfect good faith — Wey
but to exhibit praiseworthy trustworthiness in everything — Mon
but to prove themselves faithful at all points — Mof
but to evidence such complete reliableness — Ber
but to show such praiseworthy fidelity in everything — TCNT
but to prove themselves truly loyal and entirely reliable ... — Amp

that they may adorn the doctrine of God our Saviour in all things.
that the instruction which is of our Saviour God they may adorn ... — Rhm
so as to be an ornament to the doctrine ... — Mof
for in all such ways they add lustre to the doctrine ... — NEB
as to recommend the teaching about God our Saviour by all that they do — TCNT
that altogether they shall beautify the teaching ... — Ber

a living testimonial to the teaching ... — Phi

11. **For the grace of God that bringeth salvation hath appeared to all men,**
for the favour of God bringing salvation for all men hath shone forth — Rhm
For the grace of God has displayed itself with saving power to all mankind — Wey
For the loving-kindness of God has been revealed, bringing salvation for all — TCNT
For God's mercy has appeared with salvation for all men — Gspd
... has now come, offering salvation to everyone — Nor
... has dawned upon the world with healing for all mankind — NEB
... — His unmerited favor and blessing — has come forward ... — Amp

12. **Teaching us that,**
instructing us, to the intent that — ASV
disciplining us, in order that — Alf
And schooling us — Mon
training us — Wey

denying ungodliness and worldly lusts,
denying ourselves of ungodliness and worldly covetings — Rhm
to renounce ungodliness and worldly desires — Wey
to give up godless ways and worldly cravings — Wms
to forego irreverent thoughts and worldly appetites — Knox
to say no to ... — Beck
to remove impiety and evil passions — Mon
... irreligious ways and worldly ambitions — TCNT

we should live soberly, righteously, and godly,
In a soberminded and righteous and godly manner we should live — Rhm
and to live discreet, upright, and religious lives — TCNT
and to live a life of self-mastery, of integrity, and of piety — Mof
to use good judgment, and to live right and godly — Beck
... a life of temperance, honesty, and godliness — NEB
... responsible, honorable, and God-fearing lives — Phi

in this present world;
in this present age — ABUV
in this present life — Bas
here and now — Phi
day after day — Tay

13. Looking for that blessed hope, and the glorious appearing
looking for the blessed hope and appearing of the glory — ASV
Prepared to welcome the happy hope and forthshining of the glory — Rhm
awaiting fulfilment of our blessed hope — the Appearing in glory — Wey
While we look for the blessed hope and epiphany — Mon
while we are waiting for the realization of our blessed hope at the glorious appearing — Wms
looking for the happy fulfilment of our hopes when the splendour . . . will appear — NEB

of the great God and our Saviour Jesus Christ;
of our great God and Saviour, Christ Jesus — TCNT
. . . Christ Jesus, the Messiah, the Anointed One — Amp

14. Who gave himself for us,
Who gave himself up in our behalf — Rhm
He it is who sacrificed himself for us — NEB
Who died under God's judgment against our sins — Tay

that he might redeem us from all iniquity,
. . . redeem us from all manner of lawlessness — Rhm
. . . make us free from all wrongdoing — Bas
. . . rescue us from all our evil ways — Phi
to purchase our freedom from all iniquity — Wey
to free us from all wickedness — Gspd

and purify unto himself a peculiar people,
. . . unto himself a people for his own possession — ASV
. . . for himself a people as his own treasure — Rhm
. . . for Himself a people to be His very own — Wms
and to make us a pure people marked out for his own — NEB
and secure himself a clean people — Mof

zealous of good works.
— Zealous of noble works — Rhm
eager to do right — Gspd
with a zest for good works — Mof
ambitious of noble deeds — Knox
with our hearts set upon living a life that is good — Phi
and real enthusiasm for doing kind things for others — Tay

15. These things speak, and exhort, and rebuke
Declare these things; exhort and reprove — RSV
You must continue teaching this, and continue exhorting and reproving people — Wms
Tell them all this, exhort and reprove them — Mof
This is what you must teach and urge and insist upon — Gspd
These, then, are your themes; urge them and argue them — NEB

with all authority.
with full authority — Gspd
with all impressiveness — Wey
with all manner of precept — Rhm
And speak with authority — NEB
with all the authority of God's minister — Phi

Let no man despise thee.
No one is to look down on you — Gspd
Let no one make light of you — Wey
. . . slight you — NEB
. . . belittle you — Wms
. . . disregard thee! — Rhm
— and as such let no one treat you with contempt — Phi

CHAPTER 3

1. Put them in mind
Remind your hearers — TCNT
Constantly remind people — Wms
Make clear to them — Bas

to be subject to principalities and powers, to obey magistrates,
to be in subjection to rulers, to authorities, to be obedient — ASV
to submit themselves to governments, . . . — Alf

to render submission to magistrates and authorities, to obey the Government — Con

to respect and obey the Powers that be — TCNT

that they have a duty of submissive loyalty to governments and to those in authority — Knox

to be ready to every good work,

. . . for every kind of good work — TCNT

. . . for any useful service — Gspd

. . . for any honest work — RSV

. . . for any good enterprise — Wms

2. To speak evil of no man, to be no brawlers,

To be defaming no one, to be averse to strife — Rhm

to speak ill of no one, to avoid quarrelling — TCNT

to slander no one, not to pick quarrels — NEB

not to insult anyone or fight — Beck

to abuse nobody, to be peaceful — Gspd

. . . not to be contentious — ASV

. . . they must not be argumentative — Phi

but gentle, shewing all meekness unto all men.

but be yielding, and constantly manifesting a gentle spirit towards . . . — Wey

fair-minded, showing perfect gentleness to everybody — Wms

but lenient, showing unqualified mildness toward all people — Ber

to be forbearing, and under all circumstances to show a gentle spirit in dealing with others, whoever they may be — TCNT

but be conciliatory and display perfect gentleness . . . — Mof

to show forbearance and a consistently gentle disposition towards . . . — NEB

they must be considerate, and lose no opportunity of shewing courtesy to the world around them — Knox

3. For we ourselves also were sometimes

For we also once were — ASV

For even we used at one time to be — Rhm

There was you remember a time when we ourselves were — TCNT

We, after all, were once like the rest of them — Knox

foolish, disobedient, deceived,

— Thoughtless, unyielding, deceived — Rhm

unintelligent, obstinate, deluded — Wey

without understanding, disobedient, misled — Wms

senseless, disobedient, astray — Mof

reckless, rebellious, the dupes of error — Knox

foolish, hard in heart, turned from the true way — Bas

foolish and disobedient ourselves; we were misled by others — Tay

serving divers lusts and pleasures,

the slaves of various cravings and pleasures — Wey

habitual slaves to all sorts of passions . . . — Wms

slaves to all kinds of passions and vices — TCNT

. . . many evil pleasures and wicked desires — Tay

living in malice and envy,

living in a spirit of . . . — TCNT

wasting our time in . . . — Ber

spending our lives in . . . — Wey

We lived in wickedness and jealousy — Beck

our lives full of meanness and of envy — Knox

. . . full of resentment and envy — Tay

hateful, and hating one another.

detested ourselves and hating one another — TCNT

deserving hatred ourselves and . . . — Wey

we were odious ourselves and we hated . . . — NEB

4. But after that the kindness and love of God our Saviour toward men appeared,

But when the graciousness and affection for man of our Saviour God shone forth — Rhm

But when God our Saviour made manifest His kindness and love of men — Con

But when the goodness and lovingkindness of . . . were brought to light — Wms

But when the kindness and generosity of . . . dawned upon the world — NEB

5. **Not by works of righteousness which we have done,**

not by works done in righteousness, which we did ourselves — ASV

not as the result of any righteous actions . . . — TCNT

not for any upright actions we had performed — Gspd

— not by virtue of any moral achievements of ours — Phi

— not because we were good enough to be saved — Tay

but according to his mercy he saved us,

but in agreement with His mercy, He saved us — Ber

but in the measure of his mercy, he gave us salvation — Bas

but because he was merciful, he . . . — NEB

In accordance with his own merciful design he saved us — Knox

. . . in fulfilment of his merciful purpose — TCNT

. . . from his own pity for us — Mof

by the washing of regeneration,

by the laver of regeneration — Con

Through means of the bathing of a new birth — Rhm

by means of the bath of . . . — Wey

through the water of rebirth — NEB

with the cleansing power which gives us a new birth — Knox

— by washing away our sins — Tay

and renewing of the Holy Ghost;

And the moulding anew of Holy Spirit — Rhm

and by the renewing power of the Holy Spirit — TCNT

and the moral renewal of . . . — Phi

and the giving of new life in . . . — Bas

6. **Which he shed on us abundantly**

which he poured out upon us richly — ASV

which he gave us so generously — Phi

who was given to us freely — Nor

whom He poured out upon us with wonderful fullness — Tay

He poured a rich measure of this Spirit on us — Beck

For he sent down the Spirit upon us plentifully — NEB

through Jesus Christ our Saviour;

by Jesus Christ . . . — Con

for the sake of Jesus Christ, our Saviour — Nor

— and all because of what Jesus Christ our Saviour did — Tay

7. **That being justified by his grace,**

In order that having been declared righteous by his favour — Rhm

so that we might come into right standing with God through His unmerited favor — Wms

that, having been pronounced righteous through his loving-kindness — TCNT

so that, counted righteous by His personal grace — Ber

we should be made heirs according to the hope of eternal life.

we should be made inheritors according to hope of life age-abiding — Rhm

. . . become heirs to eternal life in fulfilment of our hopes — Wey

. . . enter on our inheritance with the hope of Immortal life — TCNT

. . . have a part in the heritage, the hope of . . . — Bas

and have been made heirs of eternal life, to which we look forward in hope — Nor

8. **This is a faithful saying,[2]**
and these things I will that thou affirm constantly,

And on these points I would have you insist strenuously — Wey

And it is on these subjects that I desire you to lay special stress — TCNT

I want you to speak about these matters with absolute certainty — Phi

On this I want you to firmly insist — Mon

and these things I desire thee to affirm — Con

that they which have believed in God

to the end that they who have believed God — ASV

so that those who have become believers in God — Ber

in order that those who have their faith fixed on God — Wey

. . . believed in (trusted, relied on) God — Amp

Let them that have believed in God — Con

---

[2] See I Tim. 1:15.

might be careful to maintain good works.

may be careful to be forward in noble works — Rhm

... to take the lead in doing good — Wms

... to devote themselves to doing good — TCNT

may concentrate on a life of goodness — Phi

may make it their business to do good — Gspd

make a point of practicing honourable occupations — Mof

be careful to practice good works — Con

These things are good and profitable unto men.

Such subjects are excellent in themselves, and of real use to mankind — TCNT

Such counsels are right and good for men — Mof

That is their duty, and the world will benefit by it — Knox

which is excellent and beneficial for all people — Ber

9. But avoid foolish questions, and genealogies,

but shun foolish questionings, ... — ASV

but avoid foolish disputations, ... — Con

But hold yourself aloof from foolish controversies, pedigrees — Wms

But keep away from foolish arguments, lists of ancestors — Beck

But take no part in vain researches into pedigrees — Knox

and contentions, and strivings about the law;

and strifes, and fightings about ... — ASV

or with controversy, or disputes ... — TCNT

and dissensions and strife over the Law alone — Mof

and controversies that wrangle over points of the law — Knox

keep out of arguments and quarrels about obedience to Jewish laws — Tay

for they are unprofitable and vain.

for they are futile and purposeless — Ber

for these are fruitless and futile — Mof

... unprofitable and empty — Mon

... unprofitable and worthless — NASB

They settle nothing and lead nowhere — Phi

10. A man that is an heretick

A factious man — ASV

A sectarian — Con

If a man is causing divisions among you — TCNT

after the first and second admonition reject;

after a first and second admonition refuse — ASV

after warning him once or twice, have nothing more to say to him — TCNT

... excuse thyself — Rhm

... shun him — Lam

... refuse to have anything to do with — Nor

11. Knowing that he that is such is subverted,

... such a one is perverted — ASV

... such a man is crooked — Wms

recognizing that a man of that sort has a distorted mind — NEB

... that such a man has forsaken the Truth — TCNT

... that a man of that kind is corrupt — Gspd

because you know such a man is set in his wrong way — Beck

and sinneth, being condemned of himself.

and sins, being self-condemned—ABUV

and by his sins is self-condemned — Con

he is sinning and he knows it — Mof

and is, when he sins, his own condemner — Ber

and stands self-condemned in his sin — NEB

and sinful, for his own actions condemn him — Gspd

12. When I shall send Artemas unto thee, or Tychicus,

After I have sent ... — Wey

I will send either ... — Nor

As soon as I send Artemas to you (or perhaps it will be Tychicus) — Phi

be diligent to come unto me to Nicopolis:

earnestly endeavor to come to me at ... — ABUV

do your best to come to me at . . . —
Mof

make every effort to . . . — NASB

join me as quickly as possible at . . . —
TCNT

then do your utmost to visit me at . . .
— Ber

for I have determined there to winter.

. . . arranged to spend the winter there
— TCNT

. . . decided to pass the winter there —
Wey

. . . decided to settle there for the winter — Gspd

. . . made up my mind to spend the
winter there — Phi

13. **Bring Zenas the lawyer and Apollos
on their journey diligently,**

Set forward Zenas . . . — ASV

Forward zealously on their journey . . .
— Alf

Speed Zenas . . . — Mon

Give a hearty send-off to Zenas the
jurist and Apollos — Mof

Equip Zenas, the jurist and Apollos
carefully for their journey — Ber

Do your best to help Zenas the lawyer
and Apollos to get on their way —
Beck

. . . Zenas the expert in the Law . . . —
Gspd

that nothing be wanting unto them.

that nothing be lacking to them—ABUV

and see that they are not short of anything — NEB

and see that they have everything they
need — Gspd

14. **And let ours also learn to maintain
good works**

Moreover let our own learn to be forward in honourable works — Rhm

Moreover, let our people also learn to
practice . . . — Alf

Our people too must set examples of
doing good — Wms

Let all our People learn to devote
themselves to . . . — TCNT

. . . learn to make it their business to
do good — Gspd

. . . learn to follow honest occupations
— Wey

for necessary uses,

for necessary wants — ABUV

for the supply of their necessities —
Wey

so as to meet the most pressing needs
— TCNT

so as to be able to meet such special
occasions — Mof

to supply the necessities of their teachers — Mon

that they be not unfruitful.

so they may not be unproductive —
Ber

so that they may not live useless lives
— Wey

and so as not to be unfruitful in helping others — Nor

and not waste their lives — Beck

15. **All that are with me salute thee.**

All who are with me here send you
their greeting — TCNT

. . . wish to be remembered to you —
Gspd

. . . send you their love — Bas

Greet them that love us in the faith.

Give our greetings to our friends in the
Faith — TCNT

Salute thou them who regard us with
faithful affection — Rhm

Greet the believers who hold us dear —
Wey

My greetings to those who are our
friends in truth — NEB

Greet those who love us as fellow believers — Beck

Grace be with you all. Amen.

Favour be with you all — Rhm

May grace be with you all! (Amen) —
Ber

Spiritual blessing be with you all —
Wms

God bless you all — TCNT

THE
EPISTLE OF PAUL TO PHILEMON

1. Paul, a prisoner of Jesus Christ,
. . . for Christ Jesus — Wey
. . . because of Christ Jesus — Nor
. . . for the sake of Jesus Christ — Phi
From: Paul, in jail for preaching the Good News about . . . — Tay

and Timothy our brother,
and Timotheus the brother — Con
and Timothy my brother — Rhm
and our colleague Timothy — NEB

unto Philemon our dearly beloved, and fellowlabourer,
Unto Philemon the beloved and fellow-worker of ours — Rhm
To my beloved friend and coworker Philemon — Mon
to our dear fellow-worker Philemon — Gspd
to the well beloved Philemon, who shares our labours — Knox
. . . our dear helper in the faith — Bas

2. And to our beloved Apphia,
and to Apphia the sister — ABUV
and to Apphia our sister — ASV
to my sister Apphia — Mon
to our dear sister Appia — Knox

and Archippus our fellowsoldier,
and Archippus our comrade-in-arms — NEB
and Archippus who is with us in the fight — Phi
and to Archippus our brother in God's army — Bas
. . . our fellow soldier [in the Christian warfare] — Amp
. . . who fights the same battle with ourselves, and the rest — Knox

and to the church in thy house:
and to the church that meets at your home — Ber
And unto the assembly which meeteth at thy house — Rhm
and to the congregation in your house — Lam
and to all the church that is in his household — Knox

3. Grace to you, and peace,
Favour unto you and peace — Rhm
spiritual blessing be with you and peace — Wms
Grace (spiritual blessing and favor) be to you all and heart peace — Amp

from God our Father and the Lord Jesus Christ.
. . . and the Lord Jesus Christ, the Messiah — Amp

4. I thank my God,
I am giving thanks unto my God — Rhm
I thank my God always — ASV
I give continual thanks to my God — Wey
I always offer thanks to my God — Ber

making mention of thee always in my prayers,
I am ever mentioning you in my prayers — Mon
every time I mention you . . . — Wms
when I mention you . . . — Mof
while making mention of you . . . — Wey

5. Hearing of thy love and faith, which thou hast
hearing of thy love, and of the faith which thou hast — ASV
because I continue to hear of the love and faith you have — Wms
for I hear of the love and the faith you practice — Ber
. . . of the love and the faith which you show — TCNT
. . . of your love and your loyal faith — Amp
. . . of your love and loyalty — Mof
. . . how you love and trust — Phi

toward the Lord Jesus, and toward all saints;
toward the Lord Jesus, and to all the saints — ABUV
not only to the Lord Jesus, but also to all his People — TCNT
both the Lord Jesus himself and those who believe in him — Phi
. . . and all the holy people — Beck
. . . and for all the Christians — Nor
. . . all the saints — God's consecrated people — Amp

6. That the communication of thy faith
that the fellowship of thy faith — ASV
That the faith which you have in common with them — Bas
and I pray that your participation in the Faith — TCNT

1025

... that your fellowship with us in our common faith — NEB

... that the sharing of your faith — RSV

... that thy faith may communicate itself to others — Con

may become effectual by the acknowledging of

may become effectual, in the knowledge of — ASV

may become energetic by a personal knowledge of — Rhm

may result in the full recognition of — Wey

may result in action, as you come to a fuller realization of — TCNT

may result in their recognition in us of — Wms

will grip their lives too, as they see — Tay

every good thing which is in you in Christ Jesus.

every good thing which is in you, unto Christ — ASV

everything that is right with reference to Christ — Wms

the wealth of good things in you that come from ... — Tay

... in you for Christ's sake — NASB

all the blessings that our union with Christ brings us[1] — NEB

everything that is good and Christlike in us — TCNT

how much good we Christians can attain — Mof

... in us, for Christ's service — Con

7. **For we have great joy and consolation in thy love,**

For I had much joy and comfort in thy love — ASV

For I have derived much joy and comfort from your love — RSV

Your love delighted and encouraged me very much — Beck

because the bowels of the saints

because the hearts of the saints — ASV

In that the tender affections of the saints — Rhm

how the heart of Christ's People — TCNT

... of our holy people — Beck

... of your fellow Christians — Phi

are refreshed by thee, brother.

have been refreshed through thee, brother — ASV

have had rest given them by thee, brother — Rhm

have been comforted by ... — Con

have been, and are, refreshed through you, my brother — Wey

have been cheered, Brother, by you — TCNT

8. **Wherefore, though I might be much bold in Christ**

Wherefore, though having much boldness in Christ — ABUV

So, although through union with Christ I have full freedom — Wms

Therefore, although in Christ I feel very free — Ber

... I have much freedom of speech in Christ — Rhm

... I might with Christ's authority speak very freely — Wey

... I could rely on my authority in Christ — Phi

to enjoin thee that which is convenient,

to command thee that which is becoming — ABUV

to order you to do that which is proper — NASB

to dictate the course that you should adopt — TCNT

to give you directions as to your duty — Ber

9. **Yet for love's sake I rather beseech thee,**

Yet for love's sake I rather exhort — Rhm

I prefer to appeal to you on the ground of love — Mof

I am moved by love just to urge you — Beck

yet the claims of love make me prefer to plead with you — TCNT

Nevertheless, my argument will be that you do it for love's sake — Nor

Still, because of love, in place of an order, I make a request to you — Bas

being such an one as Paul the aged,

— since I am such a person as Paul the aged — NASB

— although I am none other than Paul the aged — Wey

even I, Paul, an old man as you know — Lam

---

[1]Alternative reading.

— yes, even me, Paul, though I am an ambassador for Christ Jesus[2]—TCNT

and now also a prisoner of Jesus Christ.

Now also even a prisoner of Christ Jesus — Rhm

now in prison for the sake of Jesus Christ — Nor

10. I beseech thee for my son Onesimus,

I beseech thee for my child . . . Onesimus — ASV

I entreat you on behalf of my own child — Wey

I exhort thee concerning my own child — Rhm

I appeal to you on behalf of my spiritual son — Mof

I plead with you for this Child of mine, Onesimus — TCNT

My request is for my child Onesimus — Bas

whom I have begotten in my bonds:

Whom I have begotten in my bonds, — Onesimus — Rhm

whose father I have become while in my chains — I mean, Onesimus — Wey

born while I was in prison. It is Onesimus (Worth)! — Mof

to whom, in my prison, I have become a Father — TCNT

for I have become his spiritual father here in my imprisonment — Nor

whom I converted during my imprisonment — Lam

11. Which in time past was to thee unprofitable,

who once was unprofitable to thee — ASV

Formerly he was useless to you — Wey

Him who at one time was unto thee unserviceable — Rhm

Once you found him a worthless character — Mof

He did thee an ill service once — Knox

but now profitable to thee and to me:

But now unto thee and unto me serviceable — Rhm

but now he is helpful both to you and to me — Ber

but now — true to his name — he is of great use to you and to me — Wey

but now he is going to be of real use to both of us — Tay

12. Whom I have sent again: thou therefore receive him,

whom I have sent back to thee in his own person — ASV

and I am sending him back to you with this letter — TCNT

Whom I have sent back unto thee — Him — Rhm

that is, mine own bowels:

that is, my very heart — ASV

— though it is like tearing out my very heart — TCNT

though in so doing I send part of myself — Wey

He is, as it were, a part of me, an innermost part — Nor

for my heart goes with him — Knox

13. Whom I would have retained with me,

whom I would fain have kept with me — ASV

whom I would have desired to keep with myself — ABUV

Whom I was minded with myself to detain — Rhm

whom I was purposing to retain with myself — Alf

It was my wish to keep him at my side — Wey

I would have been glad to keep him with me — RSV

I should have dearly loved to have kept him with me — Phi

that in thy stead he might have ministered unto me

That in thy behalf unto me he might be ministering — Rhm

in order that he might serve me on your behalf — RSV

that as your deputy he might serve me — Mof

for him to attend to my wants, as your representative — Wey

to wait on me in your place — Gspd

to look after me as you would wish — NEB

in the bonds of the gospel:

in the bonds of the joyful message — Rhm

during my imprisonment for the gospel — Wey

while I am here in prison for the sake of the Gospel — Nor

---

[2]Alternative reading.

while I wear these chains for the good news — Wms

while I am a prisoner for declaring the Glad-tidings — Con

14. But without thy mind would I do nothing;

But without thy consent I wished to do nothing — ABUV

but I preferred to do nothing without your consent — RSV

But I did not wish to do anything without consulting you — Lam

but I am unwilling to do any thing without thy decision — Con

But without your approval I would do nothing — Bas

that thy benefit should not be as it were of necessity,

That not as by necessity thy goodness should be — Rhm

that thy kindness may not be constrained — Con

so that your kind action may not be compulsory — Ber

. . . might not be done under pressure — Wey

. . . not forced from you by circumstances — Phi

but willingly.

but voluntarily — Wms

but of free will — ASV

but by choice — Rhm

but of your own desire — Lam

but because you wanted to — Tay

15. For perhaps he therefore departed for a season,

For peradventure for this cause was he separated for an hour — Rhm

For perhaps he departed for a time on this account — ABUV

For perhaps to this very end he was parted from thee . . . — Con

Perhaps this was the reason why he left you for a while — Lam

. . . why you lost him for a time — NEB

that thou shouldest receive him for ever;

that thou mightest have him back forever — ABUV

That as an age-abiding possession thou mightest . . . — Rhm

so that you might get him back permanently — Nor

. . . receive him back wholly and for ever yours — Wey

. . . have him always by thee — Knox

. . . receive him eternally — Alf

16. Not now as a servant,

no longer as a servant — ASV

. . . as a bondsman — Con

. . . as a slave — TCNT

. . . as a mere slave — Mof

Do not think of him any longer as a slave — Knox

but above a servant, a brother beloved,

but above a bondsman, . . . — Con

but something more than a slave — a beloved brother — Mof

but as something better than a slave — a brother peculiarly dear — Wey

. . . a dear fellow Christian — Beck

specially to me, but now much more unto thee,

very dear to me, but how much more to thee — Con

Very greatly to me, But how much rather to thee — Rhm

He is already especially loved by me — how much more will you be able to love him — Phi

both in the flesh, and in the Lord?

being thine both in the flesh and in the Lord! — Con

both personally and in the Lord — Ber

both as a servant and as a fellow Christian — Wey

not only as your fellow man, but as your fellow Christian! — TCNT

now that both nature and Christ make him thy own — Knox

17. If thou count me therefore a partner,

If therefore you regard me as a comrade — Wey

If therefore thou holdest me as one in thy fellowship — Rhm

Now then, if you consider me as a bosom friend — Nor

As thou dost value thy fellowship with me — Knox

receive him as myself.

receive him as if he were I myself — Wey

then welcome him as you would me — Ber

take him in as myself — Bas

take him to your bosom as you would me — Wms

18. If he hath wronged thee, or oweth thee ought,

But if he hath wronged thee at all, . . . — ASV

If he has caused you any loss, or owes you anything — TCNT

But whatsoever he has wronged thee of, or owes thee — Con

If he has harmed you in any way or stolen anything from you — Tay

put that on mine account;

set that down on mine account — Alf

The same unto me do thou reckon — Rhm

charge it to me — TCNT

make me answerable for it — Knox

19. I Paul have written it with mine own hand,

(I, Paul, write this with my own hand) — Con

I Paul, writing this myself, say — Bas

This is in my own handwriting — Mof

Here is my signature, PAUL — NEB

(I, Paul, personally guarantee this promise by writing it here with my own hand) — Tay

I will repay it:

I will refund it — Ber

— I will pay you in full — Wey

I will make it good — Knox

albeit I do not say to thee

That I may not tell thee — Rhm

that I say not unto thee — ASV

for I would not say to thee — Con

(I say nothing of the fact — Wey

not reminding you — Lam

(Of course I'm not stressing the fact — — Phi

how thou owest unto me even thine own self besides.

That thyself unto me thou still owest — Rhm

that you are in debt to me even for your life — Bas

that thou owest me a debt already, thyself — Knox

that you owe me, over and above, your very soul — Mof

that you owe me more than that — your own self — Beck

20. Yea, brother, let me have joy of thee in the Lord:

Yea, brother, let me have profit of thee . . . — Alf

Yes, brother, I want some benefit from you . . . — RSV

Brother, let me gain something from you because of your union with the Lord — TCNT

Come, brother, let me have some return from you in the Lord! — Mof

Yes, brother, do me this favour for the Lord's sake — Wey

Now brother, as a Christian, be generous with me — NEB

refresh my bowels in the Lord.

refresh my heart in Christ — ASV

buoy up my deepest feelings in Christ — Ber

Through Christ refresh my heart — Wms

comfort my heart in Christ — Con

Cheer my heart by your Christlike spirit — TCNT

Give rest unto my tender affections . . . — Rhm

give new life to my heart . . . — Bas

— such an act of love will do my old heart good — Phi

and relieve my anxiety; we are both in Christ! — NEB

21. Having confidence in thy obedience I wrote unto thee,

Confident of thine obedience I have written . . . — Rhm

Because I am thoroughly persuaded of your obedience, . . . — Mon

I write in full reliance upon your obedience — Gspd

Being certain that you will do my desire, I am writing . . . — Bas

knowing that thou wilt also do more than I say.

. . . do even beyond what I say — ASV

. . . do more than I request — Ber

I know that you will in fact do better than I ask — NEB

because I am positive that you will do what I ask and even more! — Tay

22. But withal prepare me also a lodging:

. . . be also getting ready for me a lodging — Rhm

And have a guest-room ready for me, too — Wms

But, moreover, prepare to receive me as thy guest — Con

And get ready to entertain me too — Gspd

And one thing more: have a room

ready for me — NEB

At the same time I want to ask you to find lodging for me, too — Nor

for I trust that through your prayers

for I hope that through your prayers — ASV

for I have great hopes that . . . — Phi

because I hope by the prayers of all of you — Beck

. . . in answer to your prayers — TCNT

I shall be given unto you.

I shall be granted-unto you — ASV

. . . be granted as a favour unto you — Rhm

. . . be permitted to come to you—Wey

. . . be given back to you all — TCNT

. . . have the gracious privilege of coming to you — Wms

. . . be restored to you — Mof

I myself will be returned to you as well! — Phi

23. There salute thee Epaphras,

Epaphras, . . . saluteth thee — ASV

. . . sends you his greetings — TCNT

. . . sends you his best regards — Nor

. . . wishes to be remembered to you — Gspd

my fellowprisoner in Christ Jesus;

my fellow-captive in Christ Jesus — Rhm

my fellow-prisoner in the cause of . . . — Wms

Christ's captive like myself — NEB

24. Marcus, Aristarchus, Demas, Lucas, my fellowlabourers.

as do Mark, Aristarchus, Demas, Luke, my fellow-workers — NASB

. . . my brother-workers — Bas

. . . who share my labours — Knox

. . . all fellow workers for God — Phi

25. The grace of our Lord Jesus Christ be with your spirit. Amen.

The favour of the Lord Jesus Christ . . . — Rhm

The spiritual blessing of the Lord . . . — Wms

May the blessing of the Lord Jesus Christ rest on your souls — TCNT

. . . be with the spirit of every one of you — Wey

. . . be with your spirit. So be it — Bas

THE EPISTLE TO THE HEBREWS

CHAPTER 1

1. God, who at sundry times and in divers manners spake in time past

God, having of old time spoken . . . by divers portions and in divers manners — ASV

Whereas in many parts and in many ways of old God spoke — Rhm

God, who of old spoke . . . in many fragments and by various methods —Wey

Many were the forms and fashions in which God spoke of old — Mof

It was bit by bit and in many different ways that God in olden times spoke — Wms

In many and various ways God spoke of old — RSV

In many separate revelations — each of which set forth a portion of the Truth — and in different ways God spoke of old — Amp

unto the fathers by the prophets,

unto the fathers in the prophets — ASV

to our ancestors, by the Prophets — TCNT

to our forefathers . . . through the Prophets — Wey

. . . by means of the prophets — Ber

. . . in the words of the prophets — Phi

2. Hath in these last days spoken unto us

hath at the end of these days spoken unto us — ASV

now at last in these times he has spoken to us — Knox

has now, at the end of the present age, given us the truth — Phi

But in this final age he has spoken to us — NEB

by his Son,

in his Son — ASV

through a Son — Wey

with a Son to speak for him — Knox

in [the person of a] Son — Amp

whom he hath appointed heir of all things,

whom he has appointed heir of the universe — Mof

who is the predestined Lord of the universe — Wey

whom He had appointed lawful owner of everything — Wms

to whom he has given all things for a heritage — Bas

whom he made the heir of everything — Beck

and to the Son he has ordained that all creation shall ultimately belong — Phi

by whom also he made the worlds;

Through whom also he hath made the ages — Rhm

by whom also He made the universe — Con

and through whom he created all orders of existence — NEB

just as it was through him that he created this world of time — Knox

3. Who being the brightness of his glory,

who being the effulgence of his glory — ASV

Who being an eradiated brightness of his glory — Rhm

Who, being the outshining of his glory — Bas

For he is the radiance of the Glory of God — TCNT

He is the reflection of God's glory — Gspd

who, being an emanation of His glory — Con

and the express image of his person,

and the very image of his substance — ASV

And an exact representation of his very being — Rhm

flawless expression of the nature of God — Phi

and stamped with God's own character — Mof

and is the copy of His being — Beck

and upholding all things by the word of his power,

and continues to uphold the universe by His mighty word — Wms

supporting all things by the word of his power — Bas

Also bearing up all things by the utterance of his power — Rhm

He sustains the universe by His almighty word — Ber

upholding and maintaining and guiding and propelling the universe by His mighty word of power — Amp when he had by himself purged our sins,

when he had made purification of sins — ASV

After He had procured purification from sins — Wms

And when He had effected our cleansing from sin — Ber

When he had brought about the purgation of sins — NEB

having given himself as an offering making clean from sins — Bas

and, when he had made an expiation for the sins of men — TCNT

. . . accomplished our cleansing of sins and riddance of guilt — Amp

sat down on the right hand of the Majesty on high;

He took His seat at the right hand of God's majesty — Wms

took his seat at the right hand of God in heaven — Bas

and then sat down in highest honor beside the great God of heaven — Tay

4. **Being made so much better than the angels,**

having become by so much better than the angels — ASV

By so much becoming superior to the messengers — Rhm

He became as much mightier than the angels — Ber

being made so much greater than the Angels — Con

having shown himself as much greater than the angels — TCNT

thus proving Himself to be as much superior to the angels — Wms

raised as far above the angels — NEB

He is as much superior to the angels — Mon

as he hath by inheritance obtained a more excellent name than they.

as he hath inherited a more excellent name than they — ASV

. . . he hath inherited a more distinguished name — Rhm

as the Name that he has inherited surpasses theirs — TCNT

as the title He has inherited is superior to theirs — Wms

as the name that was given Him is more excellent than theirs — Nor

as the name which is his heritage is more noble than theirs — Bas

5. **For unto which of the angels said he at any time,**

For to whom of the angels said he ever — ABUV

For unto which of the messengers said he at any time — Rhm

For to what angel did God ever say — Wms

. . . ever say such words as these — Phi

Thou art my Son, this day have I begotten thee?

My Son art thou, I this day have begotten thee — Rhm

You are my Son! I have today become your Father — Gspd

. . . this day I have given you being — Bas

. . . and today I have given you the honor that goes with that Name — Tay

. . . begotten You [that is, established You in an official Sonship relation, with kingly dignity] — Amp

And again, I will be to him a Father, and he shall be to me a Son?

. . . I will be to him as a father, and he shall be to me as a son — Alf

. . . I will become his father, And he shall become my Son — Rhm

Another time He said, I am His Father and He is my Son — Tay

6. **And again, when he bringeth in the firstbegotten into the world,**

And when he again bringeth in the firstborn into the world — ASV

But when he shall again have brought the first-born . . . — ABUV

But of the time when he is to bring his firstborn Son back . . . — Gspd

But whensoever he again introduceth the first-begotten into the habitable earth — Rhm

And further, when he brought the first-born into the habitable world — Mon

Once more, when He introduces the First-born into the world — Ber

he saith, And let all the angels of God worship him.

he saith — And let all God's messengers worship him! — Rhm

. . . Let all the angels of God bow down before him — TCNT

. . . And let all God's angels fall before Him — Ber

7. And of the angels he saith,

However, regarding the angels He says — Wms

Referring to the angels He says — Ber

This is what he says of the angels — Phi

In speaking of the angels he says — Gspd

God speaks of His angels — Tay

Who maketh his angels spirits,

Who maketh his angels winds — ASV

Who turns his angels into winds—Mof

He makes His angels to be like winds — Nor

He makes the winds his angels — TCNT

as messengers swift as the wind — Tay

and his ministers a flame of fire.

And his ministers of state a fiery flame — Rhm

And His ministering servants into a flame of fire — Wey

And the fiery flames his servants — TCNT

And his attendants into blazing fire! — Gspd

and his servants flames of fire — Bas

and as servants made of flaming fire — Tay

8. But unto the Son he saith,

but of the Son he saith — ASV

But regarding the Son He says — Wms

but as to the Son — Rhm

Thy throne, O God, is for ever and ever:

Your throne, O God, will stand forever and ever — Wms

O God, Your throne is from everlasting to everlasting — Nor

Your seat of power, O God, is for ever and ever — Bas

Thy throne, O God, is unto times age-abiding — Rhm

God is thy throne for ever and ever — Mof

a sceptre of righteousness is the sceptre of thy kingdom.

And the sceptre of uprightness is the sceptre of thy kingdom — ASV

and the rod of your kingdom is a rod of righteousness — Bas

A sceptre of rectitude is . . . — ABUV

and the scepter of Thy kingdom is a scepter of absolute fairness — Ber

. . . is a sceptre of absolute justice — Wey

the sceptre of thy kingship is a rod that rules true — Knox

9. Thou hast loved righteousness, and hated iniquity;

You have loved right and hated wrong! — Gspd

You have loved what is right and hated what is wrong — Nor

thou hast loved justice and hated lawlessness — Mof

You have been a lover of righteousness and a hater of evil — Bas

Thou hast been a friend to right, an enemy to wrong — Knox

You have loved righteousness — You have delighted in integrity, virtue and uprightness in purpose, thought, and action . . . — Amp

therefore God, even thy God, hath anointed thee

For this cause hath God, thy God, anointed thee — Rhm

So God, Your God, has for that reason anointed You — Nor

therefore God, thy God, has consecrated thee — Mof

and so God, your God, has put — Bas

with the oil of gladness above thy fellows.

with the oil of exultation beyond thy partners — Rhm

with the oil of rejoicing beyond thy comrades — Mof

with the festal oil more abundantly than thy peers — TCNT

the oil of joy on your head more than on the heads of those who are with you — Bas

. . . and set You above Your companions — Nor

10. And,

Further: — Ber

He also says: — Phi

It is also of His Son that God says — Wey

Thou, Lord, in the beginning hast laid the foundation of the earth;

Thou by way of beginning, Lord, the earth didst found — Rhm

You, Lord, in the beginning founded the earth — Gspd

You, Lord, at the first did put the earth on its basis — Bas

By thee, Lord, were earth's foundations laid of old — NEB

and the heavens are the works of thine hands:

And the works of thy hands are the heavens — Rhm

And the sky is the work of your hands! — Gspd

and the heavens are made by Your hands — Nor

11. They shall perish; but thou remainest;

They shall perish; but thou continuest — ASV

They will come to their end; but you are for ever — Bas

They will perish, but thou abidest — ABUV

They will perish, but you always remain — Wms

They shall pass away, but thou endurest — NEB

and they all shall wax old as doth a garment;

And all as a mantle shall be worn out — Rhm

And they will all wear out like a coat — Gspd

they will all be like a cloak that grows threadbare — Knox

Like clothes they shall all grow old — NEB

12. And as a vesture shalt thou fold them up,

And as a mantle shalt thou roll them up — ASV

And as if a robe wilt thou fold them up — Rhm

You will roll them up like a blanket — Beck

Like a mantle [thrown about one's self] You will roll them up — Amp

and they shall be changed:

As a garment, and they shall be changed — ASV

Yet, they shall be changed like any garment — NEB

Yes, like a garment, and they will undergo change — Wey

And change them as one changes his coat — Gspd

but thou art the same, and thy years shall not fail.

But you are always the same, and your years will have no end! — Gspd

but thou art he who never changes, thy years will not come to an end — Knox

But You will remain the same, and Your years will never end — Nor

. . . and your years will never cease — Wms

. . . and Thy years shall not come to failure — Ber

13. But to which of the angels said he at any time,

But to whom of the angels has he ever said — ABUV

Did he ever say to one of the angels — Knox

But to which of the messengers hath he said at any time — Rhm

Sit on my right hand,

Just keep your seat at my right hand — Wms

Be seated at My right hand — Ber

Sit here beside Me in honor — Tay

Sit at My right hand — associated with Me in My royal dignity — Amp

until I make thine enemies thy footstool?

Until I put thy enemies as a stool for thy feet — TCNT

till I put all those who are against you under your feet — Bas

Until I make thy foes thy footstool — Rhm

until I put down your enemies for a footstool of your feet — Ber

14. Are they not all ministering spirits,

Are they not all spirits doing public service — Rhm

Are not the angels all attending spirits — Wms

Are not all the angels spirits in the service of God — TCNT

. . . merely spirits in the divine service — Mof

sent forth to minister

sent forth to do service — ASV

— for ministry sent forth — Rhm

commissioned to serve — Phi

sent forth to execute [His] service — Con

whom he sends on his errands — Gspd

for them who shall be heirs of salvation?

for the sake of them that shall inherit salvation — ASV

on account of them who shall be heirs of salvation — Alf

for the benefit of those who are to inherit salvation — Wey

for the assistance of those who are to inherit salvation — Ber

. . . those who are destined to obtain Salvation — TCNT

. . . who are going to be unceasing possessors of salvation — Wms

CHAPTER 2

1. Therefore we ought to give the more earnest heed

This is why we must pay much closer attention — Wms

Thus we are bound to pay all the more heed — NEB

We should therefore pay the more careful attention — Ber

We ought, therefore, to pay the greatest attention — Phi

Since all this is true, we ought to pay much closer attention than ever — Amp

to the things which we have heard,

to the things that were heard — ASV

to the message once heard — Wms

to the things which have come to our ears — Bas

to what we have been told — NEB

to the truth that we have heard — Phi

lest at any time we should let them slip.

lest haply we drift away from them — ASV

lest perhaps we drift past them — ABUV

to keep from drifting to one side — Wms

so we may nowise drift by — Ber

for fear of drifting from our course — NEB

for fear that by chance we might be slipping away — Bas

lest we be diverted from them — Alf

2. For if the word spoken by angels was stedfast,

For if the word uttered through angels stood firm — Mon

For if the message spoken through angels proved to be valid — Wms

For if the message delivered through angels proved to be true — Wey

. . . became binding — Alf

. . . was fixed — Bas

. . . proved unalterable — NASB

. . . through angels [that is, the Law spoken by them to Moses] was authentic and proved sure — Amp

and every transgression and disobedience

so that every offence against it, or neglect of it — TCNT

and every violation and infraction of it — Wms

every transgression of it, every refusal to listen to it — Knox

so that defiance of it and disobedience to it — Phi

received a just recompence of reward;

met with a fitting requital — TCNT

met with just retribution — Wey

led to a corresponding penalty — Gspd

had its adequate penalty — Wms

has met with a just punishment — Nor

received an appropriate (just and adequate) penalty — Amp

3. How shall we escape,

how can we, of all people, expect to escape — TCNT

how can we escape — Wms

what escape can there be for us — NEB

What makes us think that we can escape — Tay

if we neglect so great salvation;

if so great a salvation as this we have neglected — Rhm

if we disregard so great a Salvation — TCNT

if we pay no attention at all to a salvation that is so great — Wms

if we ignore a deliverance so great — NEB

which at the first began to be spoken by the Lord,

which had its beginning in being spoken through the Lord — ABUV

which was declared at first by the Lord — Con

which was originally proclaimed by the Lord himself — Mof

a salvation of which our fathers first had knowledge through the words of the Lord — Bas

For this deliverance was first announced through the lips of the Lord himself — NEB

and was confirmed unto us by them that heard him;

and was made sure to us by those who
heard — ABUV

by them who heard unto us was confirmed — Rhm

was confirmed unto us by them that
heard it — Alf

and which was made certain to us by
those to whom his words came—Bas

and was established unto us on firm
foundations by those who heard Him
— Con

had its truth made sure to us by those
who heard Him — Wey

and then it was proved to us to be
valid by the very men who heard
Him themselves — Wms

4. God also bearing them witness,

God also bearing witness with them
— ASV

God jointly witnessing also — Rhm

God also bearing witness to it — Alf

while God corroborated their testimony — Wey

while God continued to confirm their
testimony — Wms

and God moreover has plainly endorsed their witness — Phi

**both with signs and wonders, and with
divers miracles,**

both by signs and wonders, and by
manifold powers — ASV

by signs, and marvels, and many different miracles — TCNT

by signs and portents, manifesting his
power so variously — Knox

by supernatural proofs, wonders, different kinds of miracles — Bas

. . . and a great variety of miraculous
powers — Ber

**and gifts of the Holy Ghost, according
to his own will?**

and distributions of the Holy Spirit,
according to his own will — Alf

and with gifts of the Holy Spirit, which
He distributed . . . — Con

as distributed by the Holy Spirit according to His will — Ber

as well as by imparting the Holy Spirit
as he saw fit — TCNT

and by giving the Holy Spirit as He
wanted to give Him — Beck

and by imparting the gifts of the Holy
Spirit [to the believers] . . . — Amp

**5. For unto the angels hath he not put in
subjection the world to come,**

For not unto messengers hath he subjected the coming habitable earth —
Rhm

God has not given to angels the control
of that Future World — TCNT

For he did not make the angels rulers
over the world to come — Bas

It is not to angels that God has assigned
the sovereignty of that coming world
— Wey

. . . destined the control of that world
to come — Gspd

For it was not to angels that He gave
authority over that world to be —
Wms

And it is not the angels who will be
in charge of the future world — Tay

whereof we speak.

of which we are speaking — Rhm

which is our theme — NEB

and it is this world that we are now
talking about — Phi

**6. But one in a certain place testified, say-
ing,**

But one somewhere hath borne witness,
saying — Rhm

For someone somewhere has solemnly
said: — Wms

But a certain writer has given his witness, saying — Bas

But there is somewhere a solemn assurance which runs: — NEB

It has been solemnly and earnestly said
in a certain place — Amp

**What is man, that thou art mindful of
him?**

What is Man that thou should'st remember him — TCNT

What is man that you should think of
him — Wms

What is man, that you keep him in
mind — Bas

How poor a creature is man, and yet
Thou dost remember him — Wey

What is man, since You are concerned
about him — Nor

**or the son of man, that thou visitest
him?**

or a son of man that Thou lookest after
him — Ber

Or the son of man, that Thou art concerned about him — NASB

or the son of man that thou regardest
him — Con

And a son of man, and yet Thou dost come to him! — Wey

7. Thou madest him a little lower than the angels;

Thou hast made him only a little lower than the angels — Wey

For a little while thou hast made him lower than the angels — Con

You made him for a little while inferior to angels — Gspd

For a little while Thou hast ranked him lower than the angels — Ber

thou crownedst him with glory and honour,

With glory and honour hast thou crowned him — Rhm

Yet you have crowned him with glory and honor — Gspd

now You have crowned Him with glory and honor — Tay

and didst set him over the works of thy hands:

And you have put him in charge of the works of your hands! — Gspd

And hast set him to govern the works of thy hands — Mon

and made him ruler over all the works of your hands — Bas

setting him in authority over . . . — Knox

8. Thou hast put all things in subjection under his feet.

All things hast thou subjected beneath his feet — Rhm

You have put everything under his feet! — Gspd

And You have put Him in complete charge of everything there is — Tay

For in that he put all in subjection under him,

For in subjecting [to him] the all things — Rhm

For this subjecting of the universe to man — Wey

Now when He gave Him authority over everything — Wms

For in making man the ruler over all things — Bas

Notice that the writer puts "all things" under the sovereignty of man — Phi

he left nothing that is not put under him.

he left nothing that is not subject to him — ASV

Nothing left he to him unsubjected — Rhm

implies the leaving nothing not subject to him — Wey

He did not leave a single thing that was not put under His authority — Wms

he left nothing outside his control — Phi

But now we see not yet all things put under him.

But now not yet do we see to him the all things subjected — Rhm

But as yet we do not see everything actually under His authority — Wms

But, as it is, we do not yet see all things controlled by man — Mof

But at present we do not yet see . . . — Amp

9. But we see Jesus, who was made a little lower than the angels[1]

But we behold him who hath been made a little lower than the angels, even Jesus — ASV

What our eyes do see is Jesus, who . . . — TCNT

What we actually see is Jesus, after being made . . . — Phi

In Jesus, however, we do see one who . . . — NEB

But we can see this; we can see one who . . ., I mean Jesus — Knox

for the suffering of death, crowned with glory and honour;

because of the suffering of death crowned . . . — ASV

By reason of the suffering of death crowned . . . — Rhm

on account of the suffering of death, crowned . . . — ABUV

to suffer death, and who has been crowned . . . — Mof

crowned with glory and honor because He suffered death — Wms

that he by the grace of God

in order that he by the grace of God — Alf

To the end that by favour of God — Rhm

that by the free gift of God He — Con

in God's gracious design — Knox

in order that by the grace (unmerited favor) of God [to us sinners]—Amp

so that, by God's gracious will — NEB

---

[1]Compare verse 7.

should taste death for every man.

in behalf of every one he might taste
of death — Rhm

he might taste the bitterness of death
on behalf of every human being —
Gspd

He might experience death for every
human being — Wms

in tasting death he should stand for us
all — NEB

he was to taste death, and taste it on
behalf of all — Knox

10. For it became him,

For it was fitting that He — Wey

For it was appropriate that he — Gspd

For it was an act worthy [of God] and
fitting [to the divine nature] that He
— Amp

**for whom are all things, and by whom
are all things,**

For the sake of whom are the all things
And by means of whom are the all
things — Rhm

for whom and through whom all things
exist — TCNT

for whom and by whom the universe
exists — Mof

who is the Final Goal and the First
Cause of the universe — Wms

in bringing many sons unto glory,

when leading many sons to glory —
TCNT

in guiding his many children to his
glorious salvation — Gspd

while He was bringing vast multitudes
of God's people to heaven — Tay

to make the captain of their salvation

to make the author of their salvation —
ASV

The Princely Leader of their salvation
. . . — Rhm

to make the Pioneer of their salvation
— Mon

to make the Leader in their salvation
— Wms

. . . that Prince who was to lead them
into salvation — Knox

. . . the leader who delivers them —
NEB

perfect through sufferings.

perfect through the process of suffering — Wms

fully qualified through what he suffered — Gspd

a perfect leader through the fact that
he suffered — Phi

perfect [that is, should bring to maturity the human experience necessary
for a perfect equipment for His office as High Priest], through suffering — Amp

**11. For both he that sanctifieth and they
who are sanctified**

For both the sanctifier and the sanctified — ABUV

For both he that maketh holy and they
who are being made holy — Rhm

For both He who is purifying them
and those who are being purified —
Wms

For a consecrating priest and those
whom he consecrates — NEB

are all of one:

Are all of One — Rhm

have all one Father — Con

are all of one family — Bas

are all of one stock — NEB

have all one origin — Mof

all spring from One — TCNT

share a common humanity — Phi

**for which cause he is not ashamed to
call them brethren,**

and for this reason He is not ashamed
to speak of them as His brothers —
Wey

and that is why the Son does not shrink
from calling men his brothers —
NEB

he is not ashamed, then, to own them
as his brethren — Knox

**12. Saying, I will declare thy name unto
my brethren,**

as when He says: I will proclaim Thy
name to my brothers — Wey

when He says: I will announce your
name to my brothers — Wms

He says, I will tell My brothers Your
name — Beck

. . . I will talk to my brothers about
God My Father — Tay

**in the midst of the church will I sing
praise unto thee.**

In the midst of the congregation will I
sing thy praise — ASV

in the midst of the assembly will I sing
of thee — Alf

. . . I will hymn thy praises — Wey

. . . I will praise thee — RSV

13. And again, I will put my trust in him.

and again, I too will put my trust in God — Wms

. . . I will be one whose trust reposes in God — Wey

. . . I will keep my trust fixed on him — NEB

. . . My trust and assured reliance and confident hope shall be fixed in Him — Amp

And again, Behold I and the children which God hath given me.

. . . Lo! I and the children which unto me God hath given — Rhm

. . . See, here am I and the children whom God gave me — TCNT

14. Forasmuch then as the children

Since then the children referred to — Wey

Since then the children mentioned — Wms

The children of a family — NEB

are partakers of flesh and blood,

are sharers in flesh and blood — ASV

share flesh and blood — Ber

have a common inheritance of flesh and blood — Knox

are all alike sharers in perishable human nature — Wey

have the same mortal nature — Gspd

have a common physical nature as human beings — Phi

he also himself likewise took part of the same;

He Himself also, in the same way, took on Him a share of it — Wey

he himself participated in their nature — Mof

he too shared that inheritance with them — Knox

he took a body himself and became like them — Bas

he also became a human being — Phi

that through death he might destroy him

. . . he might bring to nought him — ASV

in order that by death he might render powerless him — TCNT

. . . might put a stop to the power of him — Wms

so that through death he might break the power of him — NEB

. . . He might neutralize the one — Ber

in order that by his death he might dethrone — Gspd

. . . He might paralyse him — Rhm

so that by dying he might crush him — Mof

that had the power of death, that is, the devil;

that held the dominion of death, That is the Adversary — Rhm

whose power lies in death — that is, the Devil — TCNT

who had authority over death . . . — Wey

who wields the power of death . . . — Mof

who had death at his command . . . — NEB

the lord of death, that is, the Devil — Con

15. And deliver them who through fear of death

and might deliver as many as through fear of death — Alf

and set at liberty those who . . . because of their dread of death — Wms

and to free those who, terrified by death — Beck

. . . completely set free all those who through the (haunting) fear of death — Amp

were all their lifetime subject to bondage.

were all their lifetime liable to bondage — Rhm

had been subject to lifelong slavery — Wey

lived their whole lives a prey — Phi

lived all the while as slaves — Knox

had all their lifetime been in servitude — NEB

16. For verily he took not on him the nature of angels;

For verily not to angels doth he give help — ASV

For not surely of messengers is he laying hold — Rhm

For surely it is not with angels that he is concerned — RSV

For assuredly it is not to angels that He reaches a helping hand — Wey

It was not, surely, to the help of the angels that Jesus came — TCNT

After all, he does not make himself the

angels' champion, no sign of that —
Knox

It is plain that for this purpose he did
not become an angel — Phi

but he took on him the seed of Abraham.

but he giveth help to the seed of Abraham — ASV

But of Abraham's seed he is laying
hold — Rhm

but to the help of the descendants of
Abraham — TCNT

nay, it is the offspring of Abraham,
whom he is taking by the hand —
Wey

it is the sons of Abraham that he champions — Knox

he became a man, in actual fact a descendant of Abraham — Phi

17. **Wherefore in all things it behoved him**

Whence he was obligated in every way
— Rhm

And for this purpose it was necessary
that in all respects He should—Wey

And so it was necessary that he should
in all points — Mon

It was imperative that he should . . . —
Phi

to be made like unto his brethren,

unto the brethren to be made like —
Rhm

be made to resemble His brothers —
Wey

to be like us, His brothers — Tay

that he might be

in order to become — Ber

so that he could be — Wms

so that He might prove Himself—Wey

**a merciful and faithful high priest in
things pertaining to God,**

a merciful as well as a faithful High
Priest in man's relations to God —
TCNT

a compassionate and faithful High
Priest in things relating to God —
Wey

. . . in all that relates to God — Mon

. . . in things divine — Mof

. . . in his service to God — Gspd

. . . before God — NEB

. . . Who would be both merciful to us
and faithful to God — Tay

**to make reconciliation for the sins of
the people.**

to make propitiation for the sins of the
people — ASV

to make expiation for the sins of the
people — Alf

in order to atone for the sins of the
people — Wey

and pay for the sins of the people —
Beck

18. **For in that he himself hath suffered
being tempted,**

For inasmuch as He has suffered Himself by being tempted — Wms

For in that he suffered when tested —
Rhm

For insofar as He personally suffered
in being tempted — Ber

For whereas He hath himself been
tried by suffering — Con

. . . He has Himself felt the pain of
temptation and trial — Wey

. . . because He himself has experienced suffering and temptation —
Nor

For since he himself has passed
through the test of suffering — NEB

For because He himself [in His humanity] has suffered . . . — Amp

**he is able to succour them that are
tempted.**

he is also able instantly to succor those
who are tempted — Mon

He is able to give immediate help to
any that are tempted — Wms

He is able unto them who are being
tested to give succour — Rhm

he is able to help those who are exposed to temptation — Phi

. . . them that are in trial — Con

He is able (immediately) to run to the
cry of (assist, relieve) those who
are being tempted and tested and
tried — Amp

CHAPTER 3

1. **Wherefore, holy brethren,**

For this reason, holy brothers — Bas

So then, my brothers in holiness —
Ber

Therefore, brothers in the family of

God — NEB

So then, brethren, consecrated and set
apart for God — Amp

partakers of the heavenly calling,

comrades of a heavenly calling — Mon

partners in a heavenly calling — Rhm

sharers with others in a heavenly calling — Wey

you who participate in a heavenly calling — Mof

who have likewise heard the heavenly invitation — Gspd

you who, all alike, have received the Call from Heaven — TCNT

consider the Apostle and High Priest of our profession, Christ Jesus;

Attentively consider the Apostle and High-priest of our confession — Jesus — Rhm

fix your attention on Jesus, the Apostle and High Priest of our Religion — TCNT

fix your thoughts on Jesus, the Messenger and High Priest whom we profess to follow — Wms

give thought to Jesus the representative and High Priest of our faith — Bas

Think carefully now of Christ Jesus. He is . . . — Nor

thoughtfully and attentively consider Jesus, the Apostle and High Priest Whom we confessed as ours [when we embraced the Christian faith] — Amp

2. Who was faithful to him that appointed him,

As one faithful to him who made him — Rhm

to see how faithful He was to God who appointed Him — Wms

How faithful he was to the God who appointed him! — Mon

and how loyal he was to . . . — Knox

Who kept faith with God who gave him his place — Bas

[See how] faithful He was to Him Who appointed Him [Apostle and High Priest] — Amp

as also Moses was faithful in all his house.

as also was Moses in all His house — Alf

as Moses also was faithful in all the household of God — Con

. . . also was faithful in every department of God's house — Mof

. . . was loyal in all the management of God's house — Knox

. . . also faithfully discharged his duty in the household of God — Phi

just as Moses also faithfully served in God's house — Tay

3. For this man was counted worthy of more glory than Moses,

For of more glory than Moses hath this one been counted worthy — Rhm

For greater glory is due to Him than unto Moses — Con

He has been deemed worthy of far higher honour than Moses — TCNT

For Jesus is entitled to as much more honour than Moses — Gspd

He deserves greater glory than Moses — Beck

inasmuch as he who hath builded the house

inasmuch as he who established the house — Alf

By as much as . . . he that prepared it — Rhm

inasmuch as the founder of the household — Con

even as the builder of a house — Bas

just as a man who builds a fine house — Tay

hath more honour than the house.

is held in greater regard than the House itself — TCNT

enjoys greater honour than the house itself — Mof

gets more praise than his house does — Tay

is honored above the household — Con

4. For every house is builded by some man;

For every house is prepared by some one — Rhm

For every house is established by some one — Alf

For every house has a builder — Wey

For every household hath some founder — Con

For, [of course], every house is built and furnished by someone — Amp

but he that built all things is God.

But he that hath prepared all things is God — Rhm

but he that established all things is God — Alf

the Builder of all things being God — Wey

and the founder of the universe is God — TCNT

but the builder and furnisher of the universe is God — Wms

5. And Moses verily was faithful in all his house, as a servant,

And Moses indeed was faithful in all his house as a servant — ASV

While the faithful service of Moses in the whole House of God was that of a servant — TCNT

Besides, while Moses was faithful in every department of God's house as an attendant — Mof

Now Moses was faithful . . . yet only as a servant — Wms

Thus the loyalty of Moses in the management of all God's house was the loyalty of a servant — Knox

Moses, then, was faithful as a servitor in God's whole household — NEB

for a testimony of those things which were to be spoken after;

for a witness of the things which were to be spoken — Rhm

whose duty was to bear testimony to the Message still to come — TCNT

— by way of witness to the coming revelation — Mof

to bear witness to the things that were to be announced — Ber

to bear witness to the words that God would speak — NEB

6. But Christ as a son over his own house;

but Christ as a son, over his house — ASV

but Christ as a Son over His own household — Con

Christ was faithful as a Son in charge of His own household — Ber

but Christ's faithfulness was that of a son set over the house of God — Gspd

but Christ as a Son set over the house of God was faithful — Wms

. . . faithful as the Son in charge of God's family — Beck

But Christ, the Messiah, was faithful over His [own Father's] house as a Son [and Master of it] — Amp

whose house are we,

And we are his House — TCNT

And His household are we — Con

And we are members of this household — Phi

We are His family — Beck

And we Christians are God's house — He lives in us — Tay

if we hold fast

if only we retain — TCNT

if we will only hold on — Mof

if only we will keep — Knox

the confidence and the rejoicing of the hope

our boldness and the glorying of our hope — ASV

the freedom of speech and boast of the hope — Rhm

the courage and confidence inspired by our hope — TCNT

the boldness and the hope which we boast of as ours — Wey

the cheerful courage and pride of our hope — Mon

the confidence and sense of triumph which our hope inspires — Ber

our trust and joyful hope — Phi

firm unto the end.

unshaken to the end — TCNT

firmly unto the end — Con

steadfast to the end — Phi

to the very end — Gspd

7. Wherefore (as the Holy Ghost saith,

Wherefore, — According as saith the Holy Spirit — Rhm

For this reason — as the Holy Spirit warns us — Wey

Therefore, just as the Holy Spirit says — NASB

To day if ye will hear his voice,

To-day if unto his voice ye would hearken — Rhm

To-day, if you should hear His voice — Wey

If to-day you hear God's voice — TCNT

To-day, when you hear his voice — Mof

If you but hear His voice today — Wms

Today if you let his voice come to your ears — Bas

8. Harden not your hearts, as in the provocation,

Do not harden your hearts, — As in the embitterment — Rhm

Continue not to harden your hearts as in the Provocation — Mon

You must not harden your hearts as they did in provoking me — Wms

don't close your minds as happened when the people provoked Me — Beck

Do not grow stubborn as in those days of rebellion — NEB

and not let our hearts become set against Him . . . — Tay

. . . as in that provoking situation — Ber

in the day of temptation in the wilderness:

Like as in the day of the trial in the wilderness — ASV

In the day of testing in the desert — Rhm

at the time of the desert ordeal — Ber

On the day when they tried my patience in the desert — TCNT

9. When your fathers tempted me, proved me,

When your fathers tried me by proving me — ASV

Your fathers put me to the test, made trial of me — Knox

as they tried My patience and tested Me — Nor

Where your ancestors tried my forbearance — TCNT

Where your forefathers put my doings to the proof — Gspd

when your fathers . . . tried Me by putting Me to the proof — Ber

Where your forefathers found I stood their test — Wms

and saw my works forty years.

And saw my mighty deeds for forty years — TCNT

and they saw all that I did during forty years — Wey

Because they saw my works for forty years — Wms

and for forty years felt what I could do — Mof

For forty years they saw My reactions — Nor

10. Wherefore I was grieved with that generation,

Wherefore I was displeased with this generation — ASV

Wherefore I was sore vexed with this generation — Rhm

Therefore I was provoked . . . — RSV

Therefore I grew exasperated . . . — Mof

That was why I was angry with that generation — Gspd

So I was indignant . . . — Wms

and said, They do always err in their heart;

And I said — Their hearts are always straying — TCNT

And I said, In their hearts they are ever astray — Wey

. . . They are always wandering in their hearts — Mon

. . . Their minds are always wandering — Gspd

. . . In their hearts they always wander around — Beck

. . . Their hearts are always off the track — Ber

. . . Their hearts are in error at all times — Bas

These, I said, are ever wayward hearts — Knox

for their hearts were always looking somewhere else instead of up to Me — Tay

and they have not known my ways.

And they have never come to know my ways — Wms

they have not recognized My paths — Ber

Howbeit they learned not my ways — Rhm

They would not discern my ways — NEB

And they have never found my paths — Gspd

11. So I sware in my wrath,

While in my wrath I swore — TCNT

So I sware in mine anger — Rhm

But as I made oath in my anger — Gspd

So in My indignation I swore — Ber

As I vowed in my anger — NEB

Then God, full of His anger against them, bound Himself with an oath — Tay

They shall not enter into my rest.)

They shall never enter upon my Rest — TCNT

They shall not be admitted to My rest — Wey

they will never come to My place of rest! — Beck

They shall never attain my rest — Knox

12. Take heed, brethren, lest there be

Take heed, brethren, lest haply there shall be — ASV

1043

Be taking heed brethren, Lest at any time there shall be — Rhm

Be careful, Brothers, that there is never found — TCNT

See to it, brethren, that there is never — Wey

See to it, brothers, that — NEB

My brothers, take care that there is not by chance — Bas

Look out, brothers, so there may not be — Ber

Take care, brethren, that there is — Knox

Beware then . . . — Tay

in any of you an evil heart of unbelief,

in any one of you A wicked heart of unbelief — Rhm

in any one of you — as perhaps there is — a sinful and unbelieving heart — Wey

. . . a wicked and faithless heart — TCNT

. . . that wickedness of heart which refuses to trust — Phi

. . . an evil heart without belief — Bas

no one among you has the wicked, faithless heart — NEB

no heart among you so warped by unbelief — Knox

. . . a wicked, unbelieving heart — which refuses to cleave to, trust in and rely on Him — Amp

in departing from the living God.

in falling away from the living God — ASV

shown by his separating himself from the Living God — TCNT

as shown by your turning away from the ever-living God — Wms

In revolting from a Living God — Rhm

moving you to be apostates from the living God — Mof

and deserts the cause of the living God — Phi

of a deserter from the living God — NEB

. . . desert or stand aloof from the living God — Amp

13. **But exhort one another daily,**

But be exhorting one another on each successive day — Rhm

On the contrary encourage one another, day after day — Wey

Rather admonish one another daily — Mof

Instead, give daily warning to one another — Ber

Help one another to stand firm in the faith every day — Phi

Each day, . . ., strengthen your own resolution — Knox

But give comfort to one another every day — Bas

while it is called To day;

so long as it is called To-day — ASV

while there is a 'To-day' — TCNT

so long as 'to-day' lasts — Wey

as long as we can still speak of Today — Gspd

while that word 'Today' still sounds in your ears — NEB

while there is still time — Tay

lest any of you be hardened

so that no one of you may be hardened — Wey

. . . may have his heart hardened — Gspd

— to prevent any one among you from being hardened — TCNT

to make sure that none of you grows hardened — Knox

so that no one of you is made stubborn — NEB

that none of you may be hardened [into settled rebellion] — Amp

through the deceitfulness of sin.

through the deceitful character of sin — Wey

by sin's deceiving ways — Wms

by the wiles of sin — NEB

in the delusion of sin — Ber

through the delusive glamour of sin — Phi

by the pleasantness of sin — Gspd

. . . by the fraudulence, the stratagem, the trickery which the delusive glamor of his sin may play on him — Amp

14. **For we are made partakers of Christ,**

For partners of the Christ have we become — Rhm

For we have become real sharers in Christ — Wms

For we are become comrades of the Christ — Mon

For we only participate in Christ — Mof

For we continue to share in all that Christ has for us — Phi

For we have become fellows with Christ, the Messiah, and share in all He has for us — Amp

if we hold the beginning of our confidence stedfast unto the end;

if indeed we retain, unshaken to the end, the confidence that we had at the first — TCNT

if we really hold our first confidence firm to the end — Wey

provided that we hold firm to the very end the confidence with which we started — Mof

if we really keep the conviction that we had at first unshaken to the very end — Gspd

. . . maintain firmly to the very end that original assurance — Ber

if we hold our first title deed firm unto the very end — Mon

if we keep firm to the end the faith we had at the first — Wms

For if we keep the substance of the faith which we had at the start — Bas

15. While it is said,

So long as it is said — Rhm

To use the words of Scripture — TCNT

this word ever sounding in our ears — Mof

with this in mind — Ber

seeing that the warning still comes to us — Wey

These words still hold true — Nor

To day if ye will hear his voice, harden not your hearts, as in the provocation.[2]

16. For some, when they had heard, did provoke:

For who, when they heard, did provoke? — ASV

For who were they that heard, and yet provoked God? — Wey

For who though they heard caused embitterment? — Rhm

. . . heard the Word of God and yet provoked his indignation? — Phi

Who were they that heard and yet were rebellious? — RSV

howbeit not all that came out of Egypt by Moses.

nay, did not all they that came out of Egypt by Moses? — ASV

Were they not all whom Moses brought forth out of Egypt? — Con

. . . who left Egypt under the leadership of Moses? — Mof

. . . who had escaped from Egypt under Moses' leadership? — Gspd

Had they not all gotten out of Egypt under Moses? — Ber

All those, surely, whom Moses had led out of Egypt — NEB

17. But with whom was he grieved forty years?

And with whom was he displeased forty years — ASV

And with whom was he provoked forty years — RSV

And with whom was he exasperated . . . — Mof

With whom was He disgusted . . . — Wms

And with whom was God incensed . . . — Nor

And with whom was God indignant . . . — NEB

And who was it with whom God was angry forty whole years — Gspd

Who was it, during all those forty years, that incurred his enmity — Knox

was it not with them that had sinned,

Was it not with those who sinned — ABUV

With those, surely, who had sinned — NEB

Those who sinned — Knox

whose carcases fell in the wilderness?

whose dead bodies fell in the desert — Rhm

whose carcasses fell in the wilderness — ABUV

whose corpses fell in the desert — Mof

it was their corpses that lay scattered in the wilderness — Knox

whose bodies lay where they fell in the desert — NEB

who dropped dead in the desert — Gspd

18. And to whom sware he[3]

And who were they to whom God swore — TCNT

And who was it to whom God made oath — Gspd

---

[2]See verses 7,8.

[3]Compare verse 11.

And to whom did he vow — NEB

that they should not enter into his rest,

that they would never enter his Rest — Mof

that they should not be admitted to His rest — Wey

they would not come to His place of rest — Beck

that they should never attain his rest — Knox

but to them that believed not?

but to them that were disobedient — ASV

Save unto them who were obstinate — Rhm

if not those who had proved faithless — TCNT

but to those who were disbelieving — ABUV

Was it not these very men who refused to trust him — Phi

19. So we see that they could not enter in

And we see that they were not able to enter in — ASV

We see, then, that they failed to enter upon it — TCNT

. . . that they could not be admitted — Wey

because of unbelief.

owing to unbelief — Mof

on account of unbelief — Ber

because of their want of faith — TCNT

owing to lack of faith — Wey

because of their unwillingness to adhere to and trust and rely on God — unbelief had shut them out — Amp

CHAPTER 4

1. Let us therefore fear, lest,

Let us fear therefore, lest haply — ASV

. . . lest at any time — Rhm

We should be fearful then — Beck

Then let us have the proper fear lest — Nor

We must, therefore, be very careful — TCNT

Therefore let us be on our guard lest perhaps — Wey

So let us fear that — Wms

a promise being left us of entering into his rest,

since a promise still remaineth of entering into His rest — Con

though there is a promise still standing that we shall enter into God's Rest — TCNT

when the promise for us to be admitted to His rest is still remaining valid — Wms

while the promise of entering into His rest still holds — Ber

any of you should seem to come short of it.

any one of you should seem to have come short of it — ASV

. . . should be deemed to have come short — Rhm

. . . even appear to have missed it — TCNT

none of you may be found to be delinquent — Ber

any one of you should be found to have failed to obtain it — Wey

. . . be found to have missed his chance — Knox

. . . should think he has come too late and has come short of [reaching] it — Amp

2. For unto us was the gospel preached,

For indeed we have had good tidings preached unto us — ASV

For we have had delivered to us the joyful message — Rhm

For we have had the Good News told us — TCNT

For we, too, have had the Good News announced to us — Nor

For a gospel has been brought to us — Wey

For we have received glad tidings — Con

as well as unto them:

even as also they — ASV

just as they had — TCNT

as truly as to them — Wey

as those men had — Phi

just as it was to those who lived in the time of Moses — Tay

but the word preached did not profit them,

but the word of hearing did not profit them — ASV

But the word which was heard did not profit them — Rhm

But the Message which they heard did

them no good — TCNT

... failed to benefit them — Wey

... was of no use to them — Mof

not being mixed with faith in them that heard it.

because it was not united by faith with them that heard — ASV

They not having been blended by faith with the things heard — Rhm

because it did not meet with faith in the hearers — Mof

because they brought no admixture of faith to the hearing of it — NEB

unmingled as they were in faith with those that heard it[4] — Alf

since they did not share the faith of those who were attentive to it — TCNT

because they were not by faith made one with those who heeded it — Wms

3. For we which have believed do enter into rest,

For we that have believed are entering into the [promised] rest — Con

We are actually entering into that rest, we who have believed — Mon

For we who have believed are being admitted to that rest — Wms

For only as believers do we enter into His rest — Ber

It is only as a result of our faith and trust that we are experiencing that rest — Phi

For only we who believe God can enter into His place of rest — Tay

... — who have adhered to and trusted and relied on God ... — Amp

as he said,

even as he hath said — ASV

As God has said — TCNT

in accordance with his declaration ... — Amp

As I have sworn in my wrath, if they shall enter into my rest:[5]

although the works were finished from the foundation of the world.

although God's works had been completed at the creation of the world — Wms

Although his works were finished since the foundation of the world — Mon

And yet God's work was finished at the creation of the world, — Gspd

And yet God finished His work when He made the world, — Beck

4. For he spake in a certain place of the seventh day on this wise,

For he has spoken in a certain place of the seventh day thus — ABUV

for, in a passage referring to the seventh day, you will find these words — TCNT

For he says this somewhere about the seventh day: — Mof

For he has somewhere spoken of the seventh day in this way — RSV

because in one place He said about the seventh day — Beck

as he says elsewhere in the scriptures, speaking of the seventh day of creation — Phi

And God did rest the seventh day from all his works.

On the seventh day God rested after all his work — Gspd

And God rested from all his works on the seventh day — Mof

On the seventh day God rested from all He had done — Beck

God rested on the seventh day of creation, having finished all that He had planned to make — Tay

5. And in this place again,

And again in this passage — Mof

and He has also declared — Wey

and yet in this passage he is still saying — Knox

If they shall enter into my rest.

They shall not enter into my rest — Con

They shall never enter upon my Rest — TCNT

They shall not be admitted to My rest — Wey

They will never come to My place of rest — Beck

They shall not attain my rest — Knox

6. Seeing therefore it remaineth that some must enter therein,

Since then it remains for some to enter into it — ABUV

Seeing therefore that it is left over for some to enter into it — Rhm

Since, then, there is still a promise that

---

[4]Based on a variant reading.
[5]See Heb. 3:11.

some shall enter upon this Rest — TCNT

Since, then, it is still true that some will be admitted to it — Wey

and they to whom it was first preached

and they to whom the good tidings were before preached — ASV

And they who formerly had delivered to them the joyful message — Rhm

and since those who formerly got the good news — Mof

and, since the previous hearers of the message — Phi

entered not in because of unbelief:

failed to enter in because of disobedience — ASV

entered not in by reason of obstinancy — Rhm

were not admitted because of their disobedience — Gspd

have been excluded by their unbelief — Knox

7. Again, he limiteth a certain day,

he again defineth a certain day — ASV

Again he marketh out a certain day — Rhm

again he designates a certain day — ABUV

again he sets a certain day — RSV

he proclaims a further opportunity — Phi

saying in David, To day, after so long a time;

To-day, saying in David so long a time afterward — ASV

To-day — as he says in David after so long an interval — Mof

. . . speaking after a long interval through the mouth of David — TCNT

as it is said,

(even as hath been said before) — ASV

in the passage already quoted — TCNT

To day if ye will hear his voice, harden not your hearts.[6]

8. For if Jesus had given them rest,

For if Joshua had given them rest — ASV

For if Joshua had really brought them rest — Gspd

This new place of rest He is talking about is not what Joshua gave to those he led into Palestine. If God had meant that — Tay

then would he not afterward have spoken of another day.

God would not have continued to speak later about another still future day — Wey

God would not still be talking of a fresh To-day, long afterwards — Knox

He would not have spoken long afterwards about "today" being the time to get in — Tay

9. There remaineth therefore

It follows that there still remains — Wey

Hence there is left over — Rhm

Consequently, there is . . . reserved — Ber

So there must still be — Gspd

There still exists, therefore — Phi

a rest to the people of God.

a sabbath rest for the people of God — ASV

a keeping of sabbath for . . . — Alf

a promised Sabbath of Rest for God's people — Gspd

a full and complete rest for the people of God — Phi

. . . for the [true] people of God — Amp

10. For he that is entered into his rest,

For the one who has entered His rest — NASB

For whoever has been admitted to His rest — Wey

And anyone who attains to this rest — Nor

For he that is entered into God's rest — Con

he also hath ceased from his own works, as God did from his.

hath himself also rested from his works, as God did from his — ASV

He too hath rested from his works, — just as from his own God [rested] — Rhm

does himself rest after his work, just as God did — TCNT

is resting from his own work as fully as God from his — Phi

11. Let us labour therefore to enter into that rest,

Let us therefore give diligence to enter into that rest — ASV

---

[6]See Heb. 3:7,8.

Let us therefore earnestly strive to enter . . . — Alf

Let us, therefore, make every effort to enter . . . — TCNT

Let us then exert ourselves to enter . . . — Ber

So let us do our best to be admitted to that rest — Wms

Let us then be eager to know this rest for ourselves — Phi

lest any man fall

that no man fall — ASV

so that none of us fall — TCNT

so that none of us may fail — Gspd

and let us beware that no one misses it through falling — Phi

so that no one may perish — Wey

after the same example of unbelief.

after the same example of disobedience — ASV

into the same example of obstinacy — Rhm

into the same sort of disobedience — Mof

on account of such disobedience as they exemplified — Ber

after the example of those who went against God's orders — Bas

through such disbelief as that of which we have had an example — TCNT

12. **For the word of God is quick, and powerful,**

For the word of God is living, and active — ASV

For living is the word of God and energetic — Rhm

For the word of God is full of life and power — Wey

For the word of God is living, and effectual — ABUV

For the Logos of God is a living thing, active — Mof

For God's message is alive and full of power in action — Wms

For the Word that God speaks is alive and active — Phi

For whatever God says to us is full of living power — Tay

and sharper than any twoedged sword,

And more cutting than any knife with two edges — Rhm

and is keener than the sharpest two-edged sword — Wey

and more cutting than any sword with double edge — Mof

It cuts better than any two-edged sword — Beck

It is sharper than the sharpest dagger — Tay

piercing even to the dividing asunder of soul and spirit,

And penetrating as far as a dividing asunder of soul and spirit — Rhm

it penetrates deeply, making a distinction between . . . — Nor

it strikes through to the place where soul and spirit meet — Phi

It pierces even to the severance of soul from spirit — Wey

penetrating to the dividing line of the breath of life (soul) and [the immortal] spirit — Amp

and of the joints and marrow,

— not the joints only but the very marrow — TCNT

to the dividing of joints and marrow — Wms

yea, to the inmost parts thereof — Wey

to the innermost intimacies of a man's being — Phi

and is a discerner of the thoughts and intents of the heart.

And able to judge the impulses and designs of the heart — Rhm

and it can discern the secret thoughts and purposes . . . — Wey

— and detecting the inmost thoughts and purposes of the mind — TCNT

— scrutinizing the very thoughts and conceptions of the heart — Mof

It sifts the purposes and thoughts of the heart — NEB

and passing judgment on the thoughts and purposes . . . — Wms

and is skilled in judging the heart's ponderings and meditations — Ber

it exposes the very thoughts and motives of a man's heart — Phi

13. **Neither is there any creature that is not manifest in his sight:**

And no created thing is hidden from him — Mof

And there is no created thing can be secreted before him — Rhm

There is no created thing that can hide itself from the sight of God — TCNT

And no created thing is able to escape its scrutiny — Wey

And there is not a creature hidden from him — Mon

No being created can escape God's sight — Gspd

Not a creature exists that is hidden from Him — Ber

No creature has any cover from the sight of God — Phi

but all things are naked and open unto the eyes of him

but everything lies bare and completely exposed before the eyes of Him — Wey

all things lie open and exposed before the eyes of him — Mof

but all things are naked and laid prostrate before the eyes of him — Mon

but everything is bare and helpless before the eyes of him — Gspd

everything lies bare, everything is brought face to face with him — Knox

with whom we have to do.

with whom we have to reckon — Mof

As to whom is our discourse — Rhm

to whom we are to answer — Lam

to whom we have to give account — TCNT

to Whom we must explain all that we have done — Tay

14. **Seeing then that we have a great high priest,**

Having then a great high priest — ASV

Since then we have a great high priest — RSV

Inasmuch, then, as we have . . . a great High Priest — Wey

that is passed into the heavens, Jesus the Son of God,

who hath passed through the heavens, Jesus . . . — ASV

who has ascended into heaven, Jesus Christ, the Son of God — Lam

. . . who has gone right up to heaven itself — Wms

. . . who has passed into the highest Heaven — TCNT

let us hold fast our profession.

let us hold fast our confession — ASV

let us hold firmly to our profession of faith — Wey

let us continue to keep a firm hold on our profession of faith in Him — Wms

let us cling to what we confess — Beck

therefore let us never stop trusting Him — Tay

15. **For we have not an high priest which cannot**

For we have not an high priest unable — Alf

Our High Priest is not one unable — TCNT

For our high priest is not one who is incapable — Gspd

be touched with the feeling of our infirmities;

to sympathize with our infirmities — Alf

to have fellow-feeling with our weaknesses — Rhm

to feel for us in our weaknesses — Wey

to be touched by the feelings of our feeble flesh — Bas

share our infirmities — Lam

but was in all points tempted like as we are,

but who bore in all things the likeness of our trials — Con

But one tested in all respects by way of likeness — Rhm

but one who has in every way been tempted, exactly as we have been — TCNT

but we have one who has been tested in all points as we ourselves are tested — Bas

yet without sin.

apart from sin — Rhm

but without sinning — TCNT

without committing any sin — Gspd

16. **Let us therefore come boldly unto the throne of grace,**

Let us therefore draw near with boldness unto . . . — ASV

Let us then be approaching with freedom of speech unto the throne of favour — Rhm

So let us approach the throne of grace with confidence — Mof

So let us continue coming with courage to the throne of God's unmerited favor — Wms

Let us then approach the throne of grace with assurance — Ber

Then let us come near to the seat of grace without fear — Bas

that we may obtain mercy,

that we may receive mercy — ASV

to obtain His mercy — Wms

so that mercy may be given to us — Bas

that we may receive mercy for our failures — Phi

and find grace to help in time of need.

and find grace for well-timed help — ABUV

And favour may find for seasonable succour — Rhm

and in his grace find timely help — NEB

and find him responsive when we need his help — Gspd

and to find His spiritual strength to help us when we need it — Wms

CHAPTER 5

1. For every high priest taken from among men

For every high priest, being taken from among men — ASV

For every High Priest, chosen as he is from among men — Wey

For every high priest chosen from time to time from among men — Mon

Every high priest who is selected from men — Mof

is ordained for men in things pertaining to God,

is appointed to act on behalf of men in relation to God — RSV

is appointed to represent his fellowmen in their relations to God—Gspd

is appointed to officiate on behalf of men in matters relating to God — Wms

that he may offer both gifts and sacrifices for sins:

That he may be offering . . . — Rhm

It is his business to make offerings — gifts and sacrifices — for sins — Nor

in order to offer both gifts and sin-offerings — Wey

— he offers gifts to God and makes the necessary sacrifices for sins on behalf of his fellow men — Phi

2. Who can have compassion on

who can bear gently with — ASV

Able to have a measure of feeling for — Rhm

and he must be one who is able to bear patiently with — Wey

And he is able to sympathize with — TCNT

He must be able to deal sympathetically with — Phi

the ignorant, and on them that are out of the way;

the ignorant and erring — ASV

the ignorant and deluded — TCNT

the ignorant and misguided — Gspd

the ignorant and foolish — Phi

the ignorant and wayward — Ber

for those who have no knowledge and for those who are wandering from the true way — Bas

for that he himself also is compassed with infirmity.

Since he also is compassed with weakness — Rhm

since he himself also is encompassed with moral weakness — Mon

because he himself also is beset with infirmity — Wey

since he is himself liable to weakness — Ber

because he realizes that he is himself prone to human weakness — Phi

Since he himself is human and frail — Nor

3. And by reason hereof he ought,

and by reason thereof is bound — ASV

And for this cause is he obligated — Rhm

And for this reason he is required — Wey

And because of his own sinful nature, he must necessarily — Nor

as for the people, so also for himself, to offer for sins.

— As for the people, So also for himself, — To be offering for sins — Rhm

to offer sacrifices for sins, not only for the People, but equally so for himself — TCNT

offer sin-offerings for himself as well as for the people he serves — Nor

. . . on his own personal behalf as well as on behalf of those whom he represents — Phi

4. And no man taketh this honour unto himself,

And not unto himself doth one take the honour — Rhm

No one of his own accord assumes this honor — Nor

Besides, no one appropriates the honor for himself — Ber

And nobody arrogates the honour to himself — NEB

And no one takes this honourable office upon himself — Wey

Also, it is an office which no one elects to take for himself — Mof

Another thing to remember is that no one could be a high priest just because he wanted to — Tay

but he that is called of God, as was Aaron.

but when he is called of God, even as was Aaron — ASV

but only when called of God, as indeed was Aaron — Alf

but only accepts it when called to it by God, . . . — Wey

but receives it when he is called by God, . . . — NASB

It is God who calls a high priest, even as He called Aaron — Nor

5. So also Christ

Thus also the Christ — Rhm

Similarly Christ — Mof

So it is with Christ — Knox

It was so with Christ, too — Nor

glorified not himself to be made an high priest;

did not claim for Himself the honour of being made High Priest — Wey

did not claim for himself the dignity of the high priesthood — Gspd

did not take upon Himself the glory of being appointed . . . — Wms

did not confer upon himself the glory of becoming . . . — NEB

did not exalt himself to be made a high priest — RSV

did not raise himself to the dignity of the high priesthood — Knox

did not elect Himself to the honor of being High Priest — Tay

was not raised to the high glory of the priesthood by himself — Mon

He did not claim for Himself the honor of being a High Priest — Nor

but he that said unto him,

but on the contrary by Him who said to Him — Mon

but He did, who said to Him — Ber

but by Him who declared to him — — Mof

but was appointed to it by Him who said to Him — Wey

it was granted by God, who said to him — NEB

it was God that raised him to it, when he said — Knox

Thou art my Son, to day have I begotten thee.[7]

6. As he saith also in another place,

Even as he saith also in another place — Alf

as also in another passage He says — Wey

Just as elsewhere he says — Mof

and on another occasion also — TCNT

Thou art a priest for ever after the order of Melchisedec.

Thou art a priest age-abidingly, According to the rank of Melchizedek — Rhm

Thou art a priest for all time of the order of Melchizedek — TCNT

. . . Belonging to the order of Melchizedek — Wey

. . . for ever, of the rank of Melchizedek! — Nor

. . . for ever, in the succession of Melchizedek — NEB

. . . for ever, in the line of Melchisedech — Knox

You are a priest forever of the priesthood of Melchizedek — Gspd

You are like Melchizedek a priest forever — Beck

You have been chosen forever as a priest with the same rank as Melchizedek — Tay

You are a Priest [appointed] forever . . . — Amp

7. Who in the days of his flesh,

Jesus, in the days of his earthly life — TCNT

For Jesus during His earthly life — Wey

For during His human life — Wms

Even when he was clothed in the flesh — Lam

In His humble life on earth Jesus — Beck

---

[7]See Heb. 1:5.

Christ, in the days when he was a man on earth — Phi

when he had offered up prayers and supplications

Having offered up both supplications and entreaties — Rhm

offered up prayers and entreaties — Wey

He has offered prayers and petitions — Ber

having sent up prayers and requests — Bas

with strong crying and tears

With mighty outcries and tears — Rhm

with earnest cries and with tears — TCNT

with bitter cries and tears — Mof

crying aloud and weeping as He pleaded — Wey

with vehement cries and tears — Lam

not without a piercing cry, not without tears — Knox

in desperate prayer and the agony of tears — Phi

unto him that was able to save him from death,

Unto him that was able to save him out of death — Rhm

to Him who was always able to save Him out of death — Wms

to God who was able to deliver him from the grave — NEB

to Him who could save Him from death — Ber

to the only One Who could save Him from (premature) death — Tay

and was heard in that he feared;

and having been heard for his godly fear — ASV

and was heard because He feared God — Con

And been hearkened to by reason of his devoutness — Rhm

and because of His beautiful spirit of worship His prayer was heard — Wms

and having been heard by reason of his reverent submission — Alf

. . . because of His strong desire to obey God at all times — Tay

and in response He was eased from His dread — Ber

. . . he was freed from his shrinking from death — Phi

8. Though he were a Son,

Even though he was a son — Rhm

Thus, Son though he was — Mof

Although He was God's Son — Wey

yet learned he obedience by the things which he suffered;

yet learned he his obedience from the things which he suffered — Alf

yet He learned obedience from the sufferings which He endured — Wey

he learned by all he suffered how to obey — Mof

he had to prove the meaning of obedience through all that he suffered — Phi

He found out from what He suffered what it means to obey — Beck

through the pain which he underwent, the knowledge came to him of what it was to be under God's orders — Bas

9. And being made perfect, he became

and having been made perfect, he became — ASV

And when His consecration was accomplished . . . — Con

And because He had finished His task . . . — Nor

and when he was fully qualified, . . . — Gspd

It was after He had proved Himself perfect in this experience that Jesus became — Tay

the author of eternal salvation unto all them that obey him;

to all them that obey him Author of salvation age-abiding — Rhm

to all those who obey him the source of eternal Salvation — TCNT

the cause of eternal salvation unto all . . . — Alf

the author of endless salvation for all . . . — Wms

the source of enduring salvation to all . . . — Mon

to all who obey Him the source and giver of eternal salvation — Wey

. . . for all those who render obedience to him — Knox

10. Called of God an high priest

being addressed by God as high priest — Alf

having been named by God a High Priest — Con

while God himself pronounced him a High Priest — TCNT

being designated by God high priest
— Mof

since He had received from God the
title of a High Priest — Wms

Being designated and recognized and
saluted by God as . . . — Amp

after the order of Melchisedec.[8]

11. Of whom we have many things to say,

Concerning whom what we have to say
is much — Alf

I have much to say to you about Him
— Wms

Concerning whom great is our discourse — Rhm

About this we have much to say —
RSV

Now on this subject I have much to say
— TCNT

On this point I have a great deal to say
— Mof

There is a great deal that we should
like to say about this high priesthood
— Phi

and hard to be uttered,

and hard of interpretation — ASV

and hard to be explained — ABUV

but it is difficult to make it clear to you
— Gspd

which it is hard to make intelligible to
you — Mof

seeing ye are dull of hearing.

For you have grown dull of hearing —
Mof

since you have become so dull of apprehension — Wey

since ye have grown dull in understanding — Con

because you have shown yourselves so
slow to learn — TCNT

since you have become so dull in your
spiritual senses — Wms

. . . so slow to grasp spiritual truth —
Phi

. . . sluggish in spiritual understanding
— Nor

Seeing that slothful have ye become in
the hearing — Rhm

**12. For when for the time ye ought to be
teachers,**

For even when ye ought to be teachers
by reason of the time — Rhm

For though ye ought, on account of the
time, to be teachers — ABUV

Though by this time you should be
teaching other people — Mof

For whereas, considering the time that
has elapsed, you ought to be teaching others — TCNT

ye have need that one teach you again

ye again have need that some one teach
you — Alf

you still need someone to teach you
once more — Mof

you actually need someone to teach
you over and over again — Wms

but instead you have dropped back to
the place where you need someone
to teach you all over again — Tay

**which be the first principles of the
oracles of God;**

the rudiments of the first principles of
the oracles of God — ASV

the rudimentary principles of the divine
revelation — Mof

the very elements of the truths that
God has given us — Wms

about the first simple rules of God's
revelation — Bas

the elementary beginnings of God's
lessons — Ber

the very alphabet of the Divine Revelation — TCNT

the ABC of God's revelation to men
— Phi

**and are become such as have need
of milk, and not of strong meat.**

. . . have need of milk, and not of
solid food — ASV

and need again to be fed with 'milk' instead of with 'solid food' — TCNT

and you have come to require milk
instead of solid food — Wey

and you have gotten into such a state
that you are in constant need of milk
instead of solid food — Wms

You have become people who need a
milk diet and cannot face solid food!
— Phi

13. For every one that useth milk

For every one that partaketh of milk
— ASV

For every one who still has to take
milk — TCNT

For anyone who is limited to milk —
Gspd

Those who have milk for their diet —
Knox

---

[8]See verse 6.

For anyone who continues to live on milk — Phi

is unskilful in the word of righteousness:

is without experience of the word of righteousness — ASV

are imperfectly acquainted with the doctrine of righteousness — Wey

is not accustomed to the word of righteousness — NASB

is inexperienced in the doctrine of being righteous — Ber

is inexperienced in the message of rightdoing — Wms

is unacquainted with Christian teaching — Gspd

knows nothing of the Teaching of Righteousness — TCNT

does not know what is right — NEB

doesn't have enough experience to talk of what is right — Beck

for he is a babe.

for he is an infant — Ber

He is still an infant — Mon

he is a mere babe — Mof

— he simply has not grown up — Phi

for he is a mere infant — not able to talk yet! — Amp

14. **But strong meat belongeth to them that are of full age,**

But solid food is for fullgrown men — ASV

But to such as are mature pertaineth the strong food — Rhm

But solid food is for grown-up people — Beck

But grown men can take solid food — NEB

But 'solid food' is for Christians of mature faith — TCNT

even those who by reason of use have their senses exercised

To them who by reason of habit have their organs of perception well trained — Rhm

— those whose faculties have been trained by practice — TCNT

who on account of constant use have their faculties trained — Wms

whose senses are habitually in training — Nor

— that is, for those who through constant practice have their spiritual faculties carefully trained — Wey

that is, for the man who has developed by experience his power — Phi

to discern both good and evil.

with a view to discernment of good and evil — Alf

for discriminating both good and evil — Rhm

to distinguish right from wrong — TCNT

to discriminate between what is good and what is bad for him — Phi

CHAPTER 6

1. **Therefore leaving the principles of the doctrine of Christ,**

Wherefore leaving the doctrine of the first principles of Christ — ASV

Wherefore dismissing the elementary discourse concerning the Christ — Rhm

Therefore leaving elementary instruction about the Christ — Wey

Therefore, let us leave behind the elementary teaching about the Christ — TCNT

So then let us once for all quit the elementary teaching . . . — Wms

So let us get beyond the teaching of the elementary doctrines of Christ — Mon

leaving elementary Christian doctrine behind — Mof

Let us then stop discussing the rudiments of Christianity — NEB

We must leave on one side then, all discussion of our first lessons in Christ — Knox

Therefore let us go on and get past the elementary stage in the teachings and doctrine of Christ — Amp

let us go on unto perfection;

let us press on unto perfection — ASV

and let us be borne along toward what is mature — Mon

and continue progressing toward maturity — Wms

Let us pass on then to what is mature — Mof

and go forward to adult understanding — Phi

But let us go on to be mature — Beck

and pass on to our full growth — Knox

let us advance to mature manhood — Wey

not laying again the foundation

Not again a foundation laying down —
Rhm

and not be continually re-laying a
foundation — Wey

let us stop re-laying a foundation —
Wms

Let us not lay over and over again the
foundation truths — Phi

**of repentance from dead works, and
of faith toward God,**

that is, the turning of the heart from
dead works, and faith in God—Bas

of repentance from lifeless works and
of faith in God — Wey

of repentance for a lifeless formality,
of faith in God — TCNT

. . . and of repentance from the deadness of our former ways — NEB

of repentance from works that mean
only death, . . . — Wms

the change of heart which turns away
from lifeless observances, the faith
which turns towards God — Knox

**2. Of the doctrine of baptisms, and of
laying on of hands,**

of teaching of immersions and . . . —
ABUV

or of teaching about ceremonial washings, . . . — Wey

by instruction about cleansing rites and
. . . — NEB

with instruction about ablutions and
. . . — Mof

instructions about the different kinds of
baptism, about . . . — Knox

— Baptism, Instruction, and Laying-
on of hands — Con

— teaching concerning baptisms and
the laying on of hands — TCNT

**and of resurrection of the dead, and of
eternal judgment.**

raising the dead, and everlasting judgment — Beck

. . . and final judgment — Gspd

. . . And of judgement age-abiding —
Rhm

. . . and our sentence in eternity —
Knox

. . . and eternal punishment — Mof

3. And this will we do, if God permit.

Yes and, with God's help, we will —
TCNT

With God's permission we will take this
step — Mof

And advance we will, if God permits us
to do so — Wey

The Lord willing, we will go on now to
other things — Tay

. . . we will [now] proceed [to advanced
teaching] — Amp

**4. For it is impossible for those who were
once enlightened,**

For it is impossible — As to those who
have been once for all illuminated
— Rhm

For as touching those who were once
enlightened — ASV

As for those who at one time saw
the light — Bas

For if those who were once for all
brought into the light — TCNT

For in the case of those who have once
been enlightened — NASB

and have tasted of the heavenly gift,

Who have tasted also of the heavenly
free-gift — Rhm

and had a taste of the gift from heaven
— Gspd

and have tasted the sweetness of the
heavenly gift — Wey

and have experienced the gift from
heaven — Wms

and learnt to appreciate the gift from
Heaven — TCNT

who have consciously tasted the heavenly gift — Amp

**and were made partakers of the Holy
Ghost,**

and came to share in the Holy Spirit —
TCNT

and having their part in the Holy Spirit
— Bas

who participated in the holy Spirit —
Mof

who have been made sharers of the
Holy Spirit — Wms

have become participants of the Holy
Spirit — Ber

and received the Holy Spirit — Phi

**5. And have tasted the good word of
God,**

and have tasted the goodness of the
word of God — Con

And have tasted God's utterance to be
sweet — Rhm

and have realized how good the word
of God is — Wey

and have experienced how good God's
message is — Wms

have felt the ennobling word of God
— Ber

and learnt to appreciate the beauty of
the Divine Message — TCNT

who have known the wholesome nourishment of the Word of God — Phi

and the powers of the world to come,

and the powers of the age to come —
ASV

Mighty works also of a coming age —
Rhm

and the spiritual energies of the age
to come — NEB

and the strong influences of the coming age — Gspd

and touched the spiritual resources of
the eternal world — Phi

and felt the mighty powers of the world
to come — Tay

6. If they shall fall away,

and then fell away — ASV

and have fallen away — Alf

and after all this have fallen away —
NEB

and yet have fallen back — Gspd

and then have fallen by the wayside —
Wms

if they then commit apostasy — RSV

If they then deviate from the faith and
turn away from their allegiance —
Amp

to renew them again unto repentance;

Again to be remoulding them into repentance — Rhm

to renew them again unto repentance
— ASV

to bring them again to repentance —
TCNT

to make them repent afresh — Mof

. . . to keep on restoring them to their
first repentance — Wms

to make them repent as they did at
first — Phi

**seeing they crucify to themselves the
Son of God afresh,**

Seeing they are again crucifying unto
themselves the Son of God — Rhm

since they continue to crucify the Son
of God to their detriment — Wms

for they repeat so far as they are concerned the crucifying of the Son of
God — Ber

for they crucify the Son of God on
their own account — Gspd

for with their own hands they are crucifying . . . — NEB

since they crucify the Son of God in
their own persons — Mof

For they are recrucifying . . . in their
own souls — Phi

and put him to an open shame.

And holding him up as an example —
Rhm

and exposing him to open contempt —
TCNT

and are exposing Him to public disgrace — Ber

and hold Him up for mockery — Beck

and making mock of his death — NEB

**7. For the earth which drinketh in the
rain that cometh oft upon it,**

For land which hath drunk in the rain
thereupon ofttimes coming — Rhm

For land which absorbs the rain that
often falls on it — Mof

Ground that drinks in frequent showers
— Gspd

It is so, too, with a piece of ground that
has drunk in the downpouring rain
repeatedly — Nor

. . . the rains so frequently falling on
it — Wms

. . . the rain which falls abundantly on
it — Lam

and bringeth forth herbs

And bringeth forth vegetation — Rhm

and continues yielding vegetation —
Wms

and producing good plants — Bas

and yields a useful crop — NEB

meet for them by whom it is dressed,

fit for them for whom it is even cultivated — Rhm

profitable to those for whom it is tilled
— Con

useful to those for whose benefit it is
cultivated — Amp

receiveth blessing from God:

receives from God His blessings—Wms

has a share in God's blessing — Wey

is ground which has the blessing of God
— Phi

**8. But that which beareth thorns and
briers**

But should it be bringing forth thorns
and briars — Rhm

But if it only yields a mass of thorns
and thistles — Wey

whereas, if it produces thorns and thistles — Mof

But if it continues to yield . . . — Wms

But if [that same soil] persistently bears
. . . — Amp

is rejected, and is nigh unto cursing;

it is rejected and nigh unto a curse —
ASV

It is disapproved, and unto cursing
nigh — Rhm

it is regarded as worthless, it is in danger of being 'cursed' — TCNT

it is reprobate and on the verge of being cursed — Mof

it has lost its value; a curse hangs over
it — Knox

whose end is to be burned.

and its end will be the fire — TCNT

and its final fate is burning — Wms

and the end is to burn it all down —
Nor

the only thing to do is to burn it clean
— Phi

and at the end this crop will be used
for fuel — Lam

9. **But, beloved, we are persuaded better
things of you,**

But about you, dear friends, . . . we
are confident of better things—TCNT

But we . . . have a happier conviction
concerning you — Wey

yet in your case, beloved, we feel sure
of better things — RSV

yet in your case, beloved, we are now
firmly convinced of better things —
Amp

and things that accompany salvation,

things which go with salvation — Bas

things that have to do with salvation —
Nor

yea, things that point to salvation —
Wms

that promise salvation — Gspd

that are near to salvation and accompany it — Amp

though we thus speak.

even though we speak in this way —
TCNT

even while we speak in this tone —
Wey

Even if we give this warning — Nor

10. **For God is not unrighteous to forget
your work**

For not unrighteous is God to be forgetful of your work — Rhm

For God is not unjust so as to be
unmindful of your labour — Wey

God is not unfair; he will not forget
. . . — Mof

. . . so unjust as to overlook your work
— RSV

God is not unfair: he will not lose
sight of all that you have done —
Phi

. . . How can He forget your hard work
for Him — Tay

**and labour of love, which ye have
shewed toward his name,**

and of the love which ye have shewn
forth for his name — Rhm

and the love you have shown His name
— Wms

and of the love which you have manifested towards Himself — Wey

. . . shown for his sake — Mof

. . . showed for his cause — Gspd

**in that ye have ministered to the saints,
and do minister.**

in having rendered services to His people and in still rendering them —
Wey

in the help which you gave and still
give to the saints — Bas

in sending help to your fellow Christians — as you are still doing—TCNT

as you helped His holy people and still
help them — Beck

. . . the saints — His own consecrated
people . . . — Amp

11. **And we desire that every one of you**

But we earnestly desire that . . . — Alf

It is my heart's desire that each of you
— Mof

It is our earnest wish that . . . — Phi

But we long for each of you — Wey

But we covet . . . — Rhm

do shew the same diligence

be shewing forth the same diligence —
Rhm

to continue to manifest the same earnestness — Wey

would prove equally keen — Mof

to show the same eager concern — NEB

might show the same zeal — Con

**to the full assurance of hope unto the
end:**

unto the fulness of hope even to the
end — ASV

in realizing the full assurance of hope
until the end — RSV

to realize the fulness of your hope, even to the end — Mon

in fully grasping the hope that is within you . . . — Phi

to secure the full possession of your hope . . . — Con

with a view to your enjoying fulness of hope to the very end — Wey

to attain to a full conviction that our hope will be fulfilled, and that you should keep that hope to the end — TCNT

12. That ye be not slothful,

that ye be not sluggish — ASV

In order that not slothful ye may become — Rhm

so that you may not become half-hearted — Wey

so that you may not grow careless — Wms

Then you will not show yourselves slow to learn — TCNT

so you may not grow disinterested — Ber

We want you not to become lazy — NEB

but followers of them who through faith and patience

but imitators of them who through . . . — ASV

but follow the example of them who through faith and steadfastness — Con

. . . because of their faith and their long waiting — Bas

. . . through their faith and patient endurance — Wms

. . . through faith and long-suffering — ABUV

. . . through sheer patient faith — Phi

inherit the promises.

were becoming heirs of the promises — Rhm

are heirs to the promises — Wey

are now possessors of the blessings promised — Wms

are now inheriting the promises—Mon

are now entering upon the enjoyment of God's promises — TCNT

13. For when God made promise to Abraham,

When God gave his promise to Abraham — TCNT

For instance, there was God's promise to Abraham — Tay

Such was Abraham. God made him a promise — Knox

because he could swear by no greater, he sware by himself,

Seeing he had no one greater by whom to swear . . . — Rhm

since there was no one greater for him to make oath by, he did so by himself — Gspd

because there was no greater oath, he made it by himself — Bas

. . . since there was no greater name by which He could swear — Nor

14. Saying, Surely blessing I will bless thee,

saying — Truly if blessing I will bless thee — Rhm

. . . Surely I will bless you, and bless you — Mon

His words were—I will assuredly bless thee — TCNT

. . . I will certainly bless you richly — Gspd

. . . I will certainly bless you over and over again — Wms

. . . I certainly will bless you with blessings — Ber

and multiplying I will multiply thee.

I will increase you, and increase you — Mon

and greatly increase your numbers — Gspd

I will extensively increase your numbers — Wms

and multiply you abundantly — Ber

15. And so, after he had patiently endured,

And thus being patient — Rhm

And so, when he had been waiting calmly for a long time — Bas

And so by patiently waiting — Wms

and so, having steadfastly endured — Con

he obtained the promise.

he attained unto the promise — Rhm

he received what God had promised him — Gspd

Abraham obtained the fulfilment of God's promise — TCNT

[Abraham] . . . realized and obtained [in the birth of Isaac as a pledge of what was to come] . . . — Amp

16. For men verily swear by the greater:

For men by the greater one swear — Rhm

For men swear by one greater than themselves — NASB

People swear by Someone greater — Beck

Men, of course, swear by what is greater than themselves — TCNT

Among men it is customary to swear by something greater than themselves — Phi

and an oath for confirmation is to them an end of all strife.

and in every dispute of theirs the oath is final for confirmation — ASV

And with them an end of all gainsaying by way of confirmation is the oath — Rhm

and with them an oath is accepted as putting a matter beyond all dispute — TCNT

and as an oath means to them a guarantee that ends any dispute — Mof

And if a statement is confirmed by an oath, that is the end of all quibbling — Phi

17. Wherein God, willing more abundantly to shew

On which principle God, wishing to show more convincingly — Mon

In this way God, in His extreme desire to show — Ber

In the same way, since it was God's desire to display more convincingly — Wey

So in this matter, God, wishing to show beyond doubt — Phi

Therefore, because God wanted to make the strongest demonstration of — Wms

And therefore God, in his desire to show, with unmistakable plainness — TCNT

. . . in his desire to make it perfectly clear — Gspd

. . . in his desire to afford . . . a special proof of — Mof

unto the heirs of promise

unto the heirs of the promise — ASV

to those to whom he made his promise — Gspd

to those who were to enter on the enjoyment of what he had promised — TCNT

the immutability of his counsel,

the unchangeableness of his counsel — Rhm

the unchangeable character of His purpose — Wms

the solid character of his purpose — Mof

that his purpose was unalterable — Gspd

that his design was irrevocable — Knox

that his purpose was fixed — Bas

confirmed it by an oath:

interposed with an oath — ASV

Mediated with an oath — Rhm

set an oath between himself and them — Con

made it more certain with an oath — Bas

gave surety with an oath — Ber

bound himself with an oath — TCNT

guaranteed it by oath — NEB

18. That by two immutable things,

in order that, through two unchangeable things — Wey

so that by these two solid facts (The Promise and the Oath) — Mof

so that by these two unalterable things — Gspd

Here, then, are two irrevocable acts — NEB

in which it was impossible for God to lie,

in which it is impossible for God to prove false — Wms

. . . to make himself false — Rhm

. . . to play false — Ber

. . . to break his promise — Gspd

over which there could be no question of God deceiving us — Knox

we might have a strong consolation,

we may have a strong encouragement — ASV

A mighty consolation we might have — Rhm

we . . . might enjoy mighty encouragement — Ber

we . . . might have mighty indwelling strength and strong encouragement — Amp

who have fled for refuge

Who have fled along — Rhm

we who have taken refuge with him — Gspd

who have claimed his protection — NEB

who have fled the world — Ber

to lay hold upon the hope set before us:

to grasp the forelying hope — Rhm

to seize the hope set before us — Mof

to get hold of the hope that lies ahead of us — Ber

to seize upon the hope that is offered to us — Gspd

to grasp and hold fast the hope appointed for us and set before [us] — Amp

19. Which hope we have as an anchor of the soul, both sure and stedfast,

Which we have as an anchor of the soul, Both secure and firm — Rhm

This hope is a very anchor for our souls, secure and strong — TCNT

We have this hope like an anchor for our lives, . . . — Beck

To this hope we anchor the soul safely and securely — Ber

We have this as a sure and steadfast anchor of the soul — RSV

This certain hope of being saved is a strong and trustworthy anchor for our souls — Tay

. . . — an anchor that can neither break nor drag — Wey

. . . it cannot slip and it cannot break down under whoever steps out upon it — Amp

and which entereth into that within the veil;

And entering into the interior of the veil — Rhm

It passes in behind the veil — Wey

a hope that enters into the inner shrine behind the curtain — RSV.

and it 'reaches into the Sanctuary that lies behind the Curtain' — TCNT

and it reaches on into the Holy of Holies — Ber

as it enters the inner Presence behind the veil — Mof

connecting us with God Himself behind the sacred curtains of heaven — Tay

20. Whither the forerunner is for us entered, even Jesus,

whither as a forerunner Jesus entered for us — ASV

There Jesus entered for us in advance — Mof

where Jesus has gone for us, ahead of us — Beck

where Jesus has blazed the way for us — Wms

made an high priest for ever after the order of Melchisedec.

Who according to the rank of Melchizedek hath become a high-priest unto times age-abiding — Rhm

having become, like Melchizedek, a High Priest for ever — Wey

after being made for all time a High Priest of the order . . . — Tay

when He became a High Priest forever of the Melchizedek order — Ber

. . . for ever in the succession of Melchizedek — NEB

. . . with the honor and rank of Melchizedek — Tay

CHAPTER 7

1. For this Melchisedec, king of Salem, priest of the most high God,

It was this Melchizedek, King . . . — TCNT

For this man Melchizedek, king . . . — Wms

This Melchizedek was king of the city of Salem, . . . — Tay

. . . priest of God Most High — ASV

who met Abraham returning from the slaughter of the kings,

who met Abraham as he was on his way back from defeating the kings — Gspd

met Abraham returning from the rout of the kings — NEB

and blessed him;

and gave him his blessing — TCNT

and put his blessing on him — Wms

2. To whom also Abraham gave a tenth part of all;

To whom even a tenth of all Abraham apportioned — Rhm

and Abraham gave him a tithe of everything as his portion — NEB

to whom also Abraham divided a tenth part of all — ASV

. . . allotted a tithe of all the spoil — TCNT

. . . assigned a tenth part of all the spoil — Wey

. . . contributed a tenth of all his spoils — Wms

first being by interpretation King of righteousness,

First, indeed, when translated, King of Righteousness — Rhm

was in the first place, as his name means, King . . . — Wey

He was first, as his name signifies, King . . . — Mon

— This Melchizedek is primarily a king of righteousness (such is the meaning of his name) — Mof

Melchizedek's name means "Justice," so he is the King of Justice — Tay

and after that also King of Salem, which is, King of peace;

and besides that, King of Salem (that is, King of peace) — Wey

and, secondly, king of Salem, which is KING OF PEACE — Con

and his other title is "king of peace" [for Salem means peace] — Phi

3. **Without father, without mother, without descent,**

without father, without mother, without genealogy — ASV

. . . without table of descent — Con

. . . without pedigree — Rhm

. . . or ancestry — Gspd

There is no record of his father, or mother, or lineage — TCNT

Being without father or mother or ancestry — Wey

He has neither father nor mother nor genealogy — Mof

He had no father or mother and no family tree — Phi

having neither beginning of days, nor end of life;

having no birth or end to his life — Bas

no date of birth or of death — Knox

nor again of any beginning of his days, or end of his life — TCNT

his years have no beginning, his life no end — NEB

He was not born nor did he die — Phi

but made like unto the Son of God;

but resembling the Son of God — Mon

but likened unto the Son of God — Alf

but his life is like that of the Son of God — Tay

and is a true symbol of the Son of God — Nor

abideth a priest continually.

— remaineth a priest forever — Con

he remains a priest in perpetuity — Wey

he abides a priest perpetually — NASB

continues to be priest permanently — Mof

as priest continues on and on with no successor — Wms

he remains a priest for all time — NEB

he continues to be a priest without interruption . . . — Amp

4. **Now consider how great this man was,**

Now behold how great this man was — ABUV

But observe how great this man was — Mon

Consider, then, the importance of this Melchizedek — TCNT

Mark the dignity of this man — Mof

Now think how great this man must have been — Wey

unto whom even the patriarch Abraham gave the tenth of the spoils.

to whom a tenth Abraham gave out of the choicest spoils Yea Abraham the Patriarch — Rhm

unto whom Abraham, even the patriarch, paid tithes from the best of the spoil — Alf

. . . out of the chief spoils — ASV

. . . of the finest of the spoil — NEB

. . . of what he had got in the fight — Bas

. . . gave a tithe of his first fruits — Ber

to whom even Abraham the patriarch gave a tenth — the topmost [the pick] of the heap — of the spoils — Amp

5. **And verily they that are of the sons of Levi,**

And they, indeed, from among the sons of Levi — Rhm

Now, those of Levi's descendants — Nor

And it is true that those descendants of Levi — Amp

who receive the office of the priesthood,

who the priesthood receive — Rhm

who accept the priesthood — Wms

who take the priestly office — NEB

who are charged with the priestly office — Ber

who became priests — Nor

who are from time to time appointed to the priesthood — TCNT

have a commandment to take tithes of the people according to the law,

have commandment in the law to collect a tenth from the people — NASB

are directed to collect tithes . . .—TCNT

are authorized by the law to collect a tenth . . . — Wms

are enjoined by law to tithe the people — Ber

have the right to demand a "tenth" from the people — Phi

that is, of their brethren, though they come out of the loins of Abraham:

— that is from their own Brothers, although they also are descended from Abraham — TCNT

that is, their kinsmen, although they too are descendants . . . — NEB

that is, from other Israelites, although . . . — Beck

. . . although sprung from the loins of Abraham — Rhm

6. But he whose descent is not counted from them

but he whose genealogy is not counted from them — ASV

But he who deriveth not his pedigree from among them — Rhm

But, in this instance, one who does not trace his origin from them — Wey

But this man, whose ancestry is not connected with theirs — Gspd

but he who had no Levitical genealogy — Mof

received tithes of Abraham,

hath taken tithes of Abraham — ASV

actually tithed Abraham — Mof

collected a tenth from Abraham — Wms

and blessed him that had the promises.

And the holder of the promises hath he blessed — Rhm

and blessed the possessor of the promises! — Mof

and blessed him to whom the promises belong — Mon

and put his blessing on the man who had the promises of God — Wms

Then Melchizedek placed a blessing upon mighty Abraham — Tay

7. And without all contradiction

But without any dispute — ASV

But apart from all gainsaying — Rhm

Now it is beyond all controversy that — Mon

But, beyond any doubt — Gspd

And there is no question that — Mof

the less is blessed of the better.

The less by the greater is blessed — Rhm

it is always the inferior who is blessed by the superior — Wey

the receiver of a blessing is inferior to the one who gives it — Phi

it is the superior who blesses the inferior — TCNT

8. And here men that die receive tithes;

And here indeed dying men take tithes — Rhm

And here those who take a tenth are people who die — Beck

. . . tithes are received by men who must die — NEB

. . . men over whom death has power take the tenth — Bas

In the one case the tithes are received by mortal men — TCNT

but there he receiveth them, of whom it is witnessed

while in the other it is one of whom the witness is — Mof

but here, by him of whom it is testified — Con

in the other case by one about whom there is the statement — TCNT

that he liveth.

that his life still continues — TCNT

that he lives [perpetually] — Amp

9. And as I may so say,

And so to speak — ABUV

And — so to say a word — Rhm

In fact, we might almost say — Mof

In one way of putting it — Gspd

One might even say that — RSV

Levi also, who receiveth tithes, payed tithes in Abraham.

through Abraham even Levi, who receiveth tithes, hath paid tithes — ASV

And Levi also, the receiver of tithes, hath paid tithes — Con

Levi himself, the collector of the tithes, through Abraham paid him tithes — Gspd

10. For he was yet in the loins of his father,

For even then was he in the loins of his father — Rhm

for Levi was still in the body of his ancestor — TCNT

for he was a vital part of his forefather though yet unborn — Wms

for none of Abraham's posterity was yet begotten — Gspd

Although Levi wasn't born yet, the seed from which he came was in Abraham — Tay

when Melchisedec met him.

at the time of his meeting with Melchizedek — Gspd

when Abraham paid the tithes to Melchizedek — Tay

11. **If therefore perfection were by the Levitical priesthood,**

If indeed therefore there had been a perfecting through means of the Levitical priesthood — Rhm

If, then, Perfection had been attainable through . . . — TCNT

Now if perfection had been reached through . . . —Wms

Now if anything final had been really accomplished through . . . — Gspd

Now if perfection [that is, a perfect fellowship between God and the worshipper], had been attainable by . . . — Amp

(for under it the people received the law,)

(for on the ground of it the people hath received the law,) — Alf

For the people thereon have had based a code of laws — Rhm

— for on it as a basis even the law was enacted for the people — Wms

and it was under this priesthood that the people received the Law — TCNT

(for that is the system under which the people were given . . . — Phi

what further need was there that another priest should rise

What further need was there for a different priest to be raised up — Rhm

why was it still necessary that a priest of a different order should appear — TCNT

. . . for another sort of priest to emerge — Mof

. . . of appointing a different priest — Gspd

— why was it required to have another Priest appointed — Ber

after the order of Melchisedec,[9]
and not be called after the order of Aaron?

and not be called after the order of Aaron — Con

and not be reckoned after . . . — ASV

instead of being said to belong to . . . — Wey

And not according to the rank of Aaron to be designated — Rhm

instead of choosing one of the Aaronic order — Ber

instead of the succession of Aaron — NEB

instead of following the normal priestly calling of Aaron — Phi

12. **For the priesthood being changed,**

For when the priesthood is changed — Ber

With the change of the priesthood — TCNT

For seeing there is to be a change of the priesthood — Rhm

When the priesthood is altered — Knox

there is made of necessity a change also of the law.

Of necessity of law too a change cometh — Rhm

a change of Law also of necessity takes place — Wey

a change in its law necessarily takes place — Wms

there will necessarily follow an alteration of the law regarding priesthood — Phi

the law, necessarily, is altered with it — Knox

13. **For he of whom these things are spoken**

For the one concerning whom these things are spoken — NASB

The Man of whom these things . . . — Nor

He who is thus described — Mof

After all, he to whom the prophecy relates — Knox

pertaineth to another tribe,

With a different tribe hath taken partnership — Rhm

_____
[9]See Heb. 5:6.

has taken part in a different tribe —
ABUV
became a member of . . . — Wms
belongeth to . . . — ASV
is connected with . . . — Wey

**of which no man gave attendance at
the altar.**

from which no man hath given attendance . . . — ASV
no member of which has ever served
. . . — TCNT
not one man of which has anything to
do with the altar — Wey
no member of which ever devoted himself to . . . — Mof
from which no one has officiated at
the altar — NASB
of which no man has ever made offerings . . . — Bas

14. **For it is evident that our Lord sprang
out of Juda;**
For it is very evident that out of Ju-
dah hath sprung our Lord — Rhm
For it is plain that our Lord . . . —
TCNT
For it is perfectly clear that . . . —
Gspd
for obviously our Lord sprang from
Judah — Ber
For it is a matter of history that our
Lord was a descendant of Judah —
Phi
For it is evident that our Lord hath
arisen out of Judah — Alf
Everybody knows our Lord came from
Judah — Beck

**of which tribe Moses spake nothing
concerning priesthood.**

Respecting which tribe concerning
priests nothing did Moses speak —
Rhm
a tribe concerning which Moses said
nothing about priests — Wey
regarding which tribe Moses never
mentioned priests — Ber

15. **And it is yet far more evident:**
And what we say is yet more abundant-
ly evident — ASV
And yet more abundantly evident it is
— Rhm
This becomes all the more plain —
Mof
And it is still more overwhelmingly
clear — Wms

This point is made still more clear —
Nor
The argument becomes still clearer —
— NEB
All this becomes even yet plainer when
we remember — TCNT
. . . still more clear in view of the fact
— Gspd
. . . still more abundantly clear when
we read — Wey

**for that after the similitude of Mel-
chisedec**

if after the likeness of Melchizedek —
ASV
that it is as belonging to the order of
Melchizedek — Wey
since . . . in the likeness of Melchizedek — Wms

there ariseth another priest,

there is to be raised up a different
priest — Rhm
that a priest of a different kind is to
arise — Wey
that a new priest has appeared — TCNT
a different priest . . . is appointed —
Wms
when another priest emerges — Mof

16. **Who is made,**
who hath been made — ASV
who has become such — Mon
and that he was appointed — TCNT
who has been made a priest — ABUV
Who has been constituted a Priest —
Amp
and deriving his priesthood — Phi

**not after the law of a carnal command-
ment,**

not after the law of a fleshly commandment — ABUV
not according to a law of commandment dealing with the flesh — Rhm
not on the basis of a law of physical
requirements — NASB
not according to a legal requirement
concerning bodily descent — RSV
not under a Law regulating only earthly matters — TCNT

but after the power of an endless life.

But according to the power of an indis-
soluble life — Rhm
but by virtue of an indestructible Life
— Wey
but according to the energy of an in-
dissoluble life — Mon

but with the power of an imperishable life — Con

but on the basis of a power flowing from a life that cannot end — Wms

but by virtue of a life beyond the reach of death — TCNT

17. For he testifieth,

for it is witnessed of him — ASV

For the Scripture bears witness:—Wms

For here is the testimony: — NEB

for that is the meaning of the declaration — TCNT

Thou art a priest for ever after the order of Melchisedec.[10]

18. For there is verily a disannulling of the commandment going before

For a setting aside doth indeed take place, of a foregoing commandment — Rhm

Quite plainly, then, there is a definite cancellation of . . . — Phi

So an earlier regulation is abrogated — Gspd

A previous command is set aside — Mof

So the law which went before is put on one side — Bas

On the one hand, an old commandment is annulled — Con

on the one hand we have here the abrogation of an earlier code — Wey

for the weakness and unprofitableness thereof.

By reason of its own weakness and unprofitableness — Rhm

because it was weak and profitless — Con

because it was weak and ineffective — Wey

as being both inefficient and useless — TCNT

as impotent and useless — NEB

because it was feeble and without profit — Bas

19. For the law made nothing perfect,

For the law perfected nothing — Rhm

(for the Law never brought anything to perfection) — TCNT

— for the law completed nothing — ABUV

(for there was nothing final about the Law) — Gspd

the law had nothing in it of final achievement — Knox

— the Law was incapable of bringing anyone to real maturity — Phi

It never made anyone really right with God — Tay

but the bringing in of a better hope did;

But there is the superinducing of a better hope — Rhm

and on the other hand, a better hope is brought in — Con

and, on the other hand, we have the introduction of a better hope — TCNT

but there has come in its place a better hope — Lam

— and so a better hope is brought to us — Wms

But now we have a far better hope — Tay

by the which we draw nigh unto God.

through which we draw nigh unto God — ASV

by means of which we draw near to God — Wey

through which we approach our God — Phi

which enables us to draw near to God — TCNT

enabling us to come close to God — Knox

20. And inasmuch as not without an oath he was made priest:

And inasmuch as it is not without the taking of an oath — ASV

And since this was effected not without an oath — Wey

And it was not without an oath — Ber

And inasmuch as this Priesthood hath the confirmation of an oath — Con

Then again, the appointment of this new priest was ratified by an oath — TCNT

A better Hope, because it was not promised apart from an oath — Mof

21. (For those priests were made without an oath;

(for they indeed have been made priests without an oath — ASV

— for those others became priests apart from any oath — Wey

Those who formerly became priests

_____
[10]See Heb. 5:6.

took their office without an oath —
RSV

For the Levites became priests without
an oath — Ber

for God took no oath in appointing the
old priests — Gspd

**but this with an oath by him that said
unto him,**

But he with an oath-taking,—Through
him that was saying unto him —
Rhm

but his appointment was ratified by an
oath, when God said to him — TCNT

but he has an oath from Him who said
to him — Mof

but this one was addressed with an oath
— RSV

but this One was designated and addressed and saluted with . . . — Amp

The Lord sware and will not repent,

The Lord sware and will not regret —
Rhm

The Lord has sworn and will not rue
it — Ber

The Lord took oath and will not
change — Wms

. . . and he will not change his mind
— Mof

. . . and will not recall His words —
Wey

The Lord has sworn an irrevocable
oath — Knox

**Thou art a priest for ever after the
order of Melchisedec:)**[11]

22. By so much

by so much also — ASV

— so much the more also — Wey

By as much as this — Rhm

And to the degree of the oath's greater
validity — Ber

In keeping with [the oath's greater
strength and force] — Amp

**was Jesus made a surety of a better
testament.**

hath Jesus become the surety of a better covenant — ASV

Jesus has become the guarantee of a
better covenant — Wms

is the Covenant of which Jesus has become the guarantor, a better covenant — Wey

the agreement which he guarantees is
better than the old one — Gspd

And this makes Jesus surety for a superior covenant — Mof

Jesus has become the Guarantee of a
better (stronger) agreement — a
more excellent and more advan-
tageous covenant — Amp

23. And they truly were many priests,

And they indeed in greater numbers
have been made priests — Rhm

Also, while they became priests in
large numbers — Mof

And the former priests, on the one
hand, existed in greater numbers —
NASB

And the Levitical priests, on the one
hand, have become numerous —
Wms

And they, indeed, are many priests
[one succeeding to another's office]
— Con

Those other priests are appointed in
numerous succession — NEB

**because they were not suffered to con-
tinue by reason of death:**

because that by death they are hindered from continuing — ASV

because they were forbidden by death
to continue — ABUV

because death prevents their remaining
in office — TCNT

because death does not let them go on
for ever — Bas

because they kept dying off — Tay

since death denied them permanence
— Knox

**24. But this man, because he continueth
ever,**

but he, because he abideth for ever —
ASV

But he, because He remaineth forever
— Con

but He, on the other hand, because He
Himself lives on forever — Wms

But this priest, because his life goes on
for ever — Bas

hath an unchangeable priesthood.

hath his priesthood unchangeable —
ASV

and his priestly office is unchanging —
Knox

Untransmissible holdeth the priesthood
— Rhm

---

[11]See Heb. 5:6.

and so his priesthood is untransferable — Gspd

holds his priesthood permanently — RSV

holds his priesthood inviolable — Mon

has a priesthood which does not pass to any successor — Wey

enjoys the only priesthood that has no successors in office — Wms

25. Wherefore he is able also to save them to the uttermost

Whence he is able even to be saving unto the very end — Rhm

Hence also he is able to continue saving to the uttermost — Mon

Therefore, He is also fully able to save all those — Nor

Therefore, . . . He is able to save completely any and all — Wms

That is why he is also able to save absolutely — NEB

Therefore, he is forever able to save all — Gspd

that come unto God by him,

that draw near unto God through him — ASV

Them who approach through him unto God — Rhm

those who are ever drawing near to God through him — Mon

seeing he ever liveth to make intercession for them.

Since he evermore liveth to be interceding in their behalf — Rhm

living for ever, as he does, to intercede on their behalf — TCNT

because He Himself lives always to intercede for them always — Wms

he is always living to plead on their behalf — NEB

for He will always live to make intercession for them — Nor

26. For such an high priest became us,

For it was fitting that we should have such a high priest — RSV

For we needed just such a high priest — Mon

Such a High Priest as this was exactly suited to our need — Wey

Such a high priest does indeed fit our condition — NEB

Here is the High Priest we needed — Beck

[Here is] the High Priest [perfectly adapted] to our needs — Amp

who is holy, harmless, undefiled,

holy, guileless, undefiled — ASV

holy, innocent, spotless — TCNT

holy, blameless, unstained — RSV

— devout, guileless, undefiled — NEB

saintly, innocent, unstained — Mof

— godly, blameless, unstained — Gspd

separate from sinners,

separated from sinners — ASV

Set apart from sinners — Rhm

withdrawn from sinners — TCNT

far removed from sinful men — Wey

far from all contact with the sinful — Mof

having no part with sinners — Bas

beyond the very reach of sin — Phi

in a different class from sinners — Ber

and made higher than the heavens;

And become higher than the heavens — Rhm

lifted high above the heavens — Mof

and raised above the very heavens — Gspd

and elevated far above the very heavens — Wms

exalted above the highest Heaven — TCNT

and to Him has been given the place of honor in heaven — Tay

27. Who needeth not daily, as those high priests,

Who hath no daily necessity like the high-priests — Rhm

who, unlike other High Priests, is not under the necessity — Wey

one who has no need, like yonder high priests, day by day — Mof

who does not need, as did the Levitical priests — Wms

to offer up sacrifice, first for his own sins,

Beforehand over his own sins to be offering sacrifices — Rhm

to offer up sacrifices day after day, first for his own sins — Wey

to bring sacrifices every day . . . — Beck

. . . first of all for his own [personal] sins — Amp

and then for the people's:

and then for the sins of the people — ASV

After that over those of the people — Rhm

for this he did once, when he offered up himself.

For this he did once for all when himself he offered up — Rhm

— he did that once for all in offering up himself — Mof

For his sacrifice was made once for all, when he . . . — Mon

this latter is just what He did once for all when . . . — Wms

. . . when he offered himself as the sacrifice — TCNT

. . . when He brought Himself as an offering — Ber

28. **For the law maketh men high priests which have infirmity;**

For the law constituteth men high-priests having weakness — Rhm

For the Law constitutes men — men with all their infirmity as . . . — Wey

For the Law appoints weak, human beings to the priesthood — Ber

For the law appoints imperfect men as high priests — Wms

The high priests made by the Law are men in all their frailty — NEB

. . . men full of imperfection — Gspd

For the Law sets up men in their weakness [frail, sinful, dying human beings] as high priests — Amp

but the word of the oath, which was since the law,

But the word of the oath-taking which cometh after the law — Rhm

but this utterance about the making of the oath, which came . . . — Gspd

but the assertion about the taking of an oath, which was spoken after the time of the law — Wms

but the words of God's oath, which was later than the Law — TCNT

maketh the Son, who is consecrated for evermore.

appointeth a Son, perfected for evermore — ASV

appoints the forever-perfect Son — Ber

constitutes as High Priest a Son who has been made for ever perfect — Wey

name the Son as, for all time, the perfect Priest — TCNT

appoints a son, fully qualified to be high priest forever — Gspd

CHAPTER 8

1. **Now of the things which we have spoken this is the sum:**

Now in the things which we are saying the chief point is this — ASV

A crowning point on the things being spoken: — Rhm

Now of the things which we are saying this is the chief — Alf

Now the main point of what we have been saying is this — Ber

The pith of all that we have been saying is this — Mon

To sum up what I have been saying — TCNT

We have such an high priest,

Such a one as this have we as high-priest — Rhm

— Such is the High Priest that we have — TCNT

we do have such a high priest — Mof

we have an ideal High Priest such as has been described above — Phi

who is set on the right hand

Who hath sat down on the right hand — Rhm

one who has taken his seat at the right hand — TCNT

who has taken his place at the right hand — Bas

one who is seated at the right hand — Mof

of the throne of the Majesty in the heavens;

of the throne of God's Majesty in the heavens — Wey

of God's majestic throne in heaven — Wms

of God's high seat of glory in heaven — Bas

of the throne of the Almighty in heaven — Nor

2. **A minister of the sanctuary,**

a minister of the holy places — ABUV

Of the Holy place a public minister — Rhm

a ministrant in the real sanctuary — NEB

as officiating Priest in that sanctuary — Wms

as Administrator of things holy — Ber

where he ministers in the Sanctuary — TCNT

and of the true tabernacle, which the Lord pitched, and not man.

And of the Real Tent which the Lord pitched and not man — Rhm

and of the true tent, which was put up by God, not by man — Bas

yes, of the real tabernacle which not a man, but the Lord pitched — Ber

the true place of worship built by the Lord and not by human hands — Tay

3. For every high priest is ordained to offer gifts and sacrifices:

. . . is appointed to offer both gifts and sacrifices — ASV

. . . for the offering of both gifts and sacrifices is constituted — Rhm

. . . is given authority to take to God the things which are given and to make offerings — Bas

. . . is appointed to offer both bloodless gifts and sacrifices — Wey

wherefore it is of necessity that this man

whence it was necessary for this one — Rhm

wherefore it is necessary that this high priest — ASV

it follows, therefore, that this High Priest — TCNT

so it is essential for this [High Priest] — Amp

have somewhat also to offer.

also to have something which he might offer — Rhm

also must have something to offer — Con

also must have some offering to present — Wey

also must have some sacrifice to offer — Gspd

4. For if he were on earth,

Now if he were on earth — ASV

If indeed therefore he had been on earth — Rhm

If then He were still on earth — Wey

Now if he were still living on earth — Phi

Were he on earth — Mof

he should not be a priest,

he would not be a priest at all — ASV

He had not in that case even been a priest — Rhm

he would not even be a priest — Alf

they wouldn't even let him be a priest — Tay

seeing that there are priests that offer gifts according to the law:

seeing there are those who offer the gifts . . . — ASV

Since there are those who are offering the gifts . . . — Rhm

since there are here those who present the gifts . . . — Mon

because there are those who officiate in accordance with the law in offering the gifts — Wms

since there are already priests who offer the gifts as the Law directs — TCNT

because there are other priests who make the offerings ordered by the law — Bas

for there are priests enough provided to offer the gifts the Law prescribes — Gspd

. . . the gifts demanded by the Law — Beck

. . . the offerings in obedience to the Law — Wey

5. Who serve unto the example and shadow of heavenly things,

who serve that which is a copy and shadow of the heavenly things — ASV

Who indeed are rendering divine service with a glimpse and shadow of . . . — Rhm

such as serve the delineation and shadow . . . — Alf

(men who serve a mere outline and shadow . . . — Mof

who minister to that which is a figure and shadow . . . — Con

These men are serving what is only a pattern or reproduction of things that exist in Heaven — Phi

. . . engaged in a service which is only a copy and shadow of heavenly realities — TCNT

though the service they engage in is only a shadow and imitation of that in heaven — Gspd

and yet they officiate in a sanctuary that is a mere copy and shadow of the heavenly one — Wms

Their work is connected with a mere earthly model of the real tabernacle in heaven — Tay

as Moses was admonished of God

Even as Moses hath received intimation — Rhm

as is shown by the directions given to Moses — TCNT

just as Moses was instructed — Ber

just as Moses was divinely instructed — Wey

as Moses, . . . had special orders from God — Bas

even as Moses is warned of God — ASV

Moses, you will remember, . . . was cautioned by God — Phi

when he was about to make the tabernacle:

when about to complete the tent — Rhm

when he was about to construct the Tabernacle — TCNT

when about to build the tabernacle — Wey

for when Moses was about to erect the tent — RSV

. . . going to make the tent of worship — Gspd

for, See, saith he, that thou make all things

For see! saith he — Thou shalt make all things — Rhm

God said, See that you make everything — Wey

according to the pattern shewed to thee in the mount.

according to the model which hath been pointed out to thee . . . — Rhm

in accordance with the pattern shown thee on the mountain — TCNT

just like the pattern you were shown . . . — Gspd

according to the example which was showed thee . . . — ABUV

like the design which you saw in the mountain — Bas

6. **But now hath he obtained a more excellent ministry,**

But now hath he attained unto a more distinguished public ministry—Rhm

As it is, however, the divine service he has obtained is superior — Mof

But, as it is, the priestly service to which Christ has been appointed . . . — Gspd

But now He has acquired a ministry as far superior — Ber

. . . a higher ministry — Con

. . . all the nobler a ministry — Wey

. . . a ministry as far excelling theirs — TCNT

by how much also he is the mediator of a better covenant,

By as much as of a better covenant also he is mediator — Rhm

in proportion as he is also mediator . . . — Alf

as the Covenant of which he is the intermediary — TCNT

in that He is at the same time the negotiator of a sublimer covenant — Wey

owing to the fact that he mediates a superior covenant — Mof

. . . a nobler covenant — Knox

. . . a higher agreement — Phi

. . . a better agreement with man — Bas

. . . the Mediator (the Arbiter, Agent) . . . — Amp

which was established upon better promises.

which hath been enacted upon better promises — ASV

Which indeed upon better promises hath been legislated — Rhm

which in turn rests upon higher promises — Phi

based upon sublimer promises — Wey

with nobler promises for its sanction — Knox

. . . superior promises — Wms

. . . more excellent promises — Ber

7. **For if that first covenant had been faultless,**

For if that first covenant had been flawless — Ber

. . . free from imperfection — Wey

. . . without defect — Amp

if there had been no fault to find with the first — Knox

If the first agreement had proved satisfactory — Phi

then should no place have been sought for the second.

Not in that case for a second had there been sought a place — Rhm

there would have been no need for a second — Mon

. . . no occasion for a second — TCNT

. . . no room for a second one — Wms

. . . no occasion sought for a second — NASB

... no occasion to introduce a second — Wey

8. For finding fault with them, he saith,

But, finding fault with the people, God says — TCNT

Whereas God does find fault with the people of that covenant, when he says — Mof

But in his dissatisfaction with them he says — Gspd

But Scripture says that God was dissatisfied with His people — Wey

whereas He findeth fault, and saith unto them — Con

But, finding fault with it, He says — Ber

Behold, the days come, saith the Lord,

Lo! days are coming, saith the Lord — Rhm

Behold, a time is coming, says the Lord — TCNT

There are days coming, says the Lord — Wey

See! the time is coming, ... — Gspd

The days will come, says the Lord — RSV

when I will make a new covenant

When I will conclude ... A covenant of a new sort — Rhm

When I will conclude a new agreement — Gspd

When I will complete ... — ABUV

when I will accomplish ... — Alf

When I will effect ... — NASB

When I will establish ... — Wey

When I will ratify ... — TCNT

with the house of Israel and with the house of Judah:

upon the house of Israel and upon the house of Judah — Alf

for the house of Israel and the house of Judah — Rhm

with the People of Israel and with the People of Judah — TCNT

9. Not according to the covenant that I made with their fathers

Not such a Covenant as I made with their ancestors — TCNT

not according to the covenant that I appointed to ... — Alf

Not like the one that I made with their forefathers — Gspd

It will not be on the lines of the covenant I made ... — Mof

This new agreement will not be like the old one I gave ... — Tay

in the day when I took them by the hand

In the day when I took hold of their hand — ABUV

when I took them by the hand — Bas

at the time when I took them — Nor

on the day when I grasped them by the hand — Amp

to lead them out of the land of Egypt;

to lead them forth out of the land of Egypt — ASV

to lead them out from ... — Wey

because they continued not in my covenant,

Because they abode not in my covenant — Rhm

For they did not abide by their Covenant with me — TCNT

for they would not hold to my covenant — Mof

For they would not remain faithful to ... — Wey

because they did not abide by the terms of that covenant — NEB

... did not stick to their agreement — Nor

they did not keep their part in that agreement — Tay

and I regarded them not, saith the Lord.

And I disregarded them, saith the Lord — Rhm

And so I turned away from them, says the Lord — Beck

and I also turned my face from them, ... — Con

So I paid no attention to them, ... — Gspd

so I let them alone, ... — Mof

So I did not care for them, ... — Wms

and so I withdrew My favor and disregarded them, ... — Amp

and I abandoned them, ... — NEB

10. For this is the covenant that I will make with the house of Israel

Because this the covenant that I will covenant with ... — ABUV

For this is the agreement that I will make with ... — Gspd

For this is the covenant that I will establish to ... — Alf

... on which I will agree with the house of Israel — Ber

. . . . that I will make with the People of Israel — TCNT

after those days, saith the Lord;

In those later days, says the Lord — Gspd

when the day comes, . . . — Mof

I will put my law into their mind,

Putting my laws into their mind — ABUV

Giving my laws into their understanding — Rhm

I will impress my laws on their minds — TCNT

I will imprint My laws upon their minds, . . . — Amp

I will implant my law in their innermost thoughts — Knox

I will fix My laws into the minds — Ber

and write them in their hearts:

And upon their heart also will I write them — ASV

Upon their hearts also will I inscribe them — Rhm

engrave it in their hearts — Knox

and I will be to them a God,

and I will be God to them — Ber

And I will be their God — TCNT

I will indeed be their God — Wey

And they will have me for their God — Gspd

And I will become their God — Rhm

and they shall be to me a people:

and they shall be My people — Ber

And they shall be my People — TCNT

and they shall be a People to me—Mof

And I will have them for my people — Gspd

And they shall become my people — Rhm

11. **And they shall not teach every man his neighbour,**

And in nowise shall they teach — Every one his fellow-citizen — Rhm

And nevermore will each one need to teach his fellow-citizen — Wms

There shall be no need for every man to instruct his fellow-citizen—TCNT

And they will not have to teach their townsmen — Gspd

No longer shall each citizen be teaching his neighbor — Ber

one citizen will no longer teach his fellow — Mof

and every man his brother, saying, Know the Lord:

And every one his brother, Saying, — Get to know the Lord! — Rhm

Or for a man to say to his Brother Learn to know the Lord — TCNT

and each person his brother, saying, Get acquainted with the Lord — Ber

for all shall know me, from the least to the greatest.

For all of them shall know me, from small to great — NEB

for all are to know me, low and high together — Mof

Because all shall know me, From the least unto the greatest of them — Rhm

because everyone, great and small, will know Me already — Tay

12. **For I will be merciful to their unrighteousness,**

Because propitious will I be to their unrighteousnesses — Rhm

For I will be merciful to their iniquities — ASV

For I will be merciful and gracious toward their sins — Amp

And I will forgive their wickedness — Lam

. . . merciful to their wicked deeds — — NEB

. . . to their wrong-doings — TCNT

. . . to their misdeeds — Gspd

and their sins and their iniquities will I remember no more.

And of their sins in nowise will I be mindful any more — Rhm

And never, never any more will I recall their sins — Wms

and their sins I will remember no more at all — NEB

And their sins I will remember no longer — Wey

and I will not keep their sins in mind — Bas

13. **In that he saith, A new covenant,**

By saying, "new" — Ber

In speaking of a new covenant — Wms

By using the words, 'a new Covenant,' — Wey

By calling the covenant "new" — Mon

Now when he speaks of a new agreement — Gspd

he hath made the first old.

he has pronounced the first one old —
— NEB

he hath made obsolete the first — Rhm

he is treating the first one as obsolete
— Gspd

God at once renders the former Covenant obsolete — TCNT

he puts the first out of date — Ber

he antiquates the first — Mof

he has superannuated the old — Knox

He makes the first one obsolete — out
of use — Amp

**Now that which decayeth and waxeth
old**

But the thing that is becoming obsolete
and aged — Rhm

But that which is becoming old and
waxeth aged — ASV

and that which is old and stricken in
years — Con

But what is decaying and showing signs
of old age — Wey

Now that which is growing old, and
wearing out with age — ABUV

And when a thing grows weak and out
of date — Phi

and whatever becomes obsolete and
loses its force — TCNT

is ready to vanish away.

is nigh unto vanishing away — ASV

Is near disappearing! — Rhm

is not far from disappearing altogether
— Wey

is on the verge of vanishing — Mof

approaches the vanishing point — Ber

will shortly disappear — NEB

it is obviously soon going to be dispensed with altogether — Phi

is ripe for disappearance and to be dispensed with altogether — Amp

CHAPTER 9

1. Then verily the first covenant had also

Now even the first covenant had — ASV

Even the first indeed therefore used to
have — Rhm

It is true that even the first Covenant
had — TCNT

Even the first agreement provided —
Gspd

ordinances of divine service,

righteous appointments of divine service — Rhm

certain rules for the service of God —
Phi

its rules of worship — Bas

its ordinances of public worship—Mon

its regulations for divine worship —
TCNT

its forms of worship — Nor

its own ceremonial observances —
Knox

and a worldly sanctuary.

and its sanctuary, a sanctuary of this
world — ASV

and had also its sanctuary — a sanctuary belonging to this material world
— Wey

and its Holy Place was in this world —
Con

and the earthly holy place — Beck

and a mundane sanctuary — Mof

and its Sanctuary — though only a material one — TCNT

Even the holy ritual well arranged —
Rhm

and a sanctuary that was fully equipped
— Gspd

**2. For there was a tabernacle made; the
first,**

For a tent was prepared, the first —
Rhm

For the tabernacle was established, the
first one — Alf

For a tabernacle was made [in two portions]: the first — Con

For a Tabernacle was constructed, with
an outer part — TCNT

A sacred tent was constructed — the
outer one — Wey

A tent was erected: in the outer compartment — Phi

A tabernacle was set up. In the first
part — Beck

for the first tabernacle was thus finished: — Ber

**wherein was the candlestick, and the
table, and the shewbread;**

In which were both the lampstand and
the table and the setting forth of the
loaves — Rhm

was equipped with the lamp and table
and the presentation bread — Wms

which contained the stand for the
lamps, and the table, and the consecrated bread — TCNT

having in it the vessels for the lights

and the table and the ordering of the bread — Bas

were placed the lamp standard, the table and the sacred loaves — Phi

. . . and a table with special loaves of holy bread upon it — Tay

. . . and the loaves of the Presence — Mof

. . . and the loaves set out before God — Knox

which is called the sanctuary.

which is called the Holy place — ASV

This part was called the Holy Place — Nor

[This portion] is called the Holy [Place] — Amp

3. And after the second veil,

and, behind the second veil — Con

And inside the second veil — Bas

And beyond the second curtain — Gspd

The part of the Tabernacle behind the second Curtain — TCNT

the tabernacle which is called the Holiest of all;

the tabernacle which is called the Holy of holies — ASV

a tent, that which is called Most Holy — Rhm

was a sacred tent called the Holy of Holies — Wey

is called the inner sanctuary — Gspd

was a room called . . . — Nor

4. Which had the golden censer,

having a golden altar of incense — ASV

with its golden incense-altar — Wms

Having a vessel of gold in it for burning perfumes — Bas

and the ark of the covenant overlaid round about with gold,

and the Ark containing the Covenant, completely covered with gold — TCNT

and the chest that contained the agreement, entirely covered with gold — Gspd

and the gold-covered ark of the agreement — Phi

. . . covered around on every side with gold — Rhm

. . . plated all over with gold — NEB

. . . covered over with wrought gold — Amp

wherein was the golden pot that had manna,

wherein was a golden pot holding the manna — ASV

In which was a golden jar holding the manna — Rhm

In the Ark is a gold casket containing the manna — TCNT

in the ark rested the golden urn with the manna in it — Knox

and Aaron's rod that budded,

And the rod of Aaron that sprouted — Rhm

the rod of Aaron that once blossomed — Mof

and Aaron's rod, which put out buds — Bas

Aaron's rod that had budded — Nor

and Aaron's staff that budded — Gspd

and Aaron's wooden cane . . . — Tay

and the tables of the covenant;

and the tablets of the covenant — Mof

and the tablets containing the agreement — Gspd

and the tablets on which the Covenant was written — TCNT

and the stones with the writing of the agreement — Bas

and the tables on which the covenant was inscribed — Knox

and the [two stone] slabs of the covenant, [bearing the Ten Commandments] — Amp

5. And over it the cherubims of glory

and above it cherubim of glory — ASV

But over-above it Cherubim of glory — Rhm

above this were the cherubim of the Glory — Mof

while above it . . . are the Cherubim of the Presence — TCNT

And over it were the winged ones of glory — Bas

and above the chest were the winged creatures of the Divine Presence — Gspd

. . . the winged creatures, the symbols of God's glorious presence — Wms

shadowing the mercyseat;

overshadowing the mercy seat — ASV

with their wings covering the mercy-seat — Bas

spreading their wings over the throne of mercy — Knox

casting their shadow over the ark's covering — Phi

overshadowing the propitiatory — Rhm

and overshadowing the Cover on which atonement was made — TCNT

overshadowing the lid on which the blood was sprinkled — Gspd

overshadowing the place of expiation — NEB

of which we cannot now speak particularly.

of which things we cannot now speak severally — ASV

— about which we cannot now go into detail — Ber

We have no time to treat of these more particularly — Knox

On these we cannot now enlarge — NEB

6. Now when these things were thus ordained,

Now these things having been thus prepared — ASV

Now these things being thus arranged — Alf

Now these things being thus ordered — Con

These arrangements having been completed — Wey

With these arrangements for worship — Gspd

Such, then, was the arrangement of the Tabernacle — TCNT

the priests went always into the first tabernacle,

the priests go in continually into the first tabernacle — ASV

Into the first tent indeed continually do the priests enter — Rhm

The priests are always going into the first part of the tabernacle— Beck

. . . regularly go into the outer part of the tent of worship — Wms

the outer tent was habitually used by the priests — Phi

accomplishing the service of God.

accomplishing the services — ASV

performing their service — ABUV

The divine services completing — Rhm

accomplishing the offices of their worship — Con

when conducting the divine services — Wey

in the discharge of their ritual duties — Mof

in the performance of their rites — Gspd

7. But into the second

but into the inner tent — Mon

but into the second or inner part — Wms

But into the inner room — Nor

But into the second [division of the tabernacle] — Amp

went the high priest alone once every year,

the High Priest goes only on one day of the year, and goes alone — Wey

nobody but the high priest may go, and he only once a year — Wms

only the high priest could go, and that only once a year — Nor

not without blood,

not without taking blood — NASB

and never without blood — Wms

— and it must not be without blood — Mof

and never without taking the blood of a victim — TCNT

bearing a sacrifice of shed blood — Phi

and even then he must take with him the blood — NEB

which he offered for himself,

which he offereth for himself — ASV

which he offers on his own behalf — TCNT

which he presents on behalf of himself — Mof

to be offered for his own sins — Phi

which he sprinkled on the mercy seat as an offering to God to cover his own mistakes and sins — Tay

and for the errors of the people:

and for the sins of ignorance of the people — ABUV

and for the ignorances of the people — Alf

and on account of the sins which the people have ignorantly committed — Wey

and for the sins committed through ignorance by the people — Gspd

and for the thoughtless sins of the people — Ber

for the faults . . . committed unknowingly — Knox

8. The Holy Ghost this signifying,

The Holy Spirit making this evident — Rhm

By this the Holy Spirit indicates — RSV

And so the Holy Spirit clearly tells us — Beck

By this the Holy Spirit is teaching — TCNT

The lesson which the Holy Spirit teaches is this — Wey

In all this the holy Spirit was seeking to show — Gspd

that the way into the holiest of all was not yet made manifest,

that the way into the Holiest has not yet been disclosed — Mon

. . . is not yet made fully manifest — Con

. . . remains unrevealed — NEB

that the way into the Sanctuary was hidden — TCNT

. . . into the true Holy Place is not yet open — Wey

. . . into the Holy of Holies was not yet open to us — Nor

. . . is not yet thrown open — Amp

that there was as yet no access to the real sanctuary — Wms

that the way into the Holiest Presence was not disclosed — Mof

while as the first tabernacle was yet standing:

So long as the first tent hath a standing — Rhm

while still the outer tabernacle standeth — Con

as long as the outer part of the Tabernacle still remained — TCNT

while the outer tent was still in existence — Wms

as long as the former tabernacle maintained its standing — Knox

that is, so long as the first tent and all it stands for still exist — Phi

while the old covenant was still in force — Nor

. . . the outer room and the old system it represents was still in use — Tay

as long as the former [the outer portion of the] tabernacle remains a recognized institution and is still standing — Amp

9. Which was a figure for the time then present,

which is a figure for the time present — ASV

for it is merely a symbol of the present time — Wms

the which tabernacle is a parable for the time now present — Alf

The which is a similitude for the present season — Rhm

(All this is symbolic, pointing to the present time) — NEB

(which foreshadowed the present age) — Mof

For that was only a type, to continue down to the present time — TCNT

This was a symbol of that current time — Ber

in which were offered both gifts and sacrifices,

According to which both gifts and sacrifices are offered — Rhm

under which gifts and sacrifices are offered — Con

and, in keeping with it, both gifts . . . — TCNT

in connection with which gifts . . . are repeatedly offered — Wms

According to this arrangement, gifts . . . — RSV

According to that symbol both gifts . . . — Wey

For under the old system, gifts . . . — Tay

that could not make him that did the service perfect, as pertaining to the conscience;

that cannot, as touching the conscience, make the worshipper perfect — ASV

Which cannot as to the conscience perfect him that rendereth the divine service — Rhm

having no power to perfect in conscience him that serveth — Alf

could not render the worshiper's conscience perfect — Ber

cannot give the worshipper inward perfection — NEB

cannot inwardly qualify the worshiper to approach God — Gspd

. . . make the worshiper feel perfect in his conscience — Beck

and yet are incapable of perfecting the conscience or of cleansing and renewing the inner man of the worshipper — Amp

10. Which stood only in meats and drinks, and divers washings,

being only (with meats and drinks and divers washings) — ASV

Only as to eatings and drinkings and diversified immersions — Rhm as they consist only of food and drink and various ablutions — Ber

since they relate merely to . . . — Mof

since they deal only with . . . — Wms

For [the ceremonies] deal only with clean and unclean meats . . . — Amp

the whole system being concerned only with . . . — TCNT

and carnal ordinances,

ordinances of the flesh — Alf

— regulations for the body — Wey

— outward regulations for the body — Mof

that is, with mere material regulations — Wms

[mere] external rules and regulations for the body — Amp

imposed on them until the time of reformation.

imposed until a time of reformation — ASV

Which until a season of rectifying are in force — Rhm

which are in force only until the time of setting things straight — Wms

which have their place till the time comes when things will be put right — Bas

imposed until the coming of the New Order — TCNT

in force only until the time for the new order — Gspd

11. **But Christ being come an high priest of good things to come,**

But when Christ approached as high-priest of the coming good things — Rhm

But when Christ arrived as the high priest of the bliss that was to come — Mof

But Christ having appeared an high priest . . . — Alf

But [that appointed time came] when Christ, the Messiah, appeared as a High Priest . . . — Amp

. . . of the good things that have come[12] — RSV

. . . of good things already in being — — NEB

. . . of the good things which he wrought — Lam

But, when Christ came, he appeared as High Priest of that Better System which was established — TCNT

He came as High Priest of this better system we now have — Tay

by a greater and more perfect tabernacle,

Through the greater and more perfect tent — Rhm

and he entered through that nobler and more perfect Tabernacle, — TCNT

He went by way of that greater and more perfect tent of worship — Wms

His was a greater and more perfect tabernacle — Nor

The tent of his priesthood is a greater and more perfect one — NEB

not made with hands,

not made by hand — Rhm

which no hands had made — Mof

not made by human hands — TCNT

which human hands never fashioned — Knox

(a tent not built with hands — Wey

that is to say, not of this building;

(that is, not of this creation) — ABUV

(no part, that is to say, of the present order) — Mof

— that is to say, which does not belong to this material creation) — Wey

it does not belong to this order of creation at all — Knox

that is to say, not of this world — Bas

that is, not belonging to this created world — NEB

(that is, not of man's building) — Con

12. **Neither by the blood of goats and calves,**

nor yet through the blood of goats and calves — ASV

not through the blood of goats and young oxen — Bas

not taking any blood of goats and oxen — Mof

Nor was it with . . . — TCNT

And He didn't use . . . — Beck

but by his own blood he entered in

but through his own blood he entered — Alf

but with his own blood, . . . — TCNT

but his own blood, and so entered — Mof

It is his own blood . . . that has enabled him to enter — Knox

once into the holy place,

---

[12]Alternate reading.

once for all into the holy places —
ABUV

once for all, into the Holy Place —
Con

. . . into the Sanctuary — TCNT

. . . into the real sanctuary — Wms

into the [Holy of] Holies [of heaven]
— Amp

**having obtained eternal redemption
for us.**

Age-abiding redemption discovering —
Rhm

thus finding and securing a complete
redemption . . . — Amp

procuring eternal redemption — Ber

and securing our permanent deliverance — Gspd

having obtained an everlasting redemption — Con

and pay a price that frees us forever —
Beck

the ransom he has won lasts for ever
— Knox

13. **For if the blood of bulls and of goats,**
For if the blood of goats and bulls —
ASV

For if the blood of goats and oxen —
Bas

And if under the old system the blood
of . . . — Tay

**and the ashes of an heifer sprinkling
the unclean,**

. . . sprinkling them that have been defiled — ASV

. . . sprinkling those who have contracted defilement — Wey

. . . sprinkling ceremonially defiled persons — Gspd

. . . sprinkling those who are ceremonially unclean — Wms

. . . as it sprinkles those who were
stained — Ber

. . . sprinkling the profaned — Rhm

. . . when sprinkled on the unholy —
Phi

sanctifieth to the purifying of the flesh:

Halloweth unto the purity of the flesh
— Rhm

sanctify unto the cleanness of the flesh
— ASV

purifies them with physical cleansing—
Wms

is sufficient for the purification of the
body — Amp

make them holy so as to bring about
ceremonial purity — Wey

14. **How much more shall the blood of
Christ,**
How much rather shall the blood of
the Christ — Rhm

how much more certainly shall . . . —
Wey

how much more surely will . . . —
Gspd

who through the eternal Spirit
Who through an age-abiding spirit —
Rhm

who through the Spirit Eternal — Ber

who . . . through the Holy Spirit —
Knox

who with an eternal Spirit — Wms

who in the spirit of the eternal — Mof

who, through his eternal Spirit — TCNT

Who by virtue of [His] eternal Spirit
[His own preexistent personality] —
Amp

offered himself without spot to God,
offered himself without blemish unto
God — ASV

Offered himself unspotted unto God —
Rhm

. . . without fault to God — Alf

offered Himself to God, free from
blemish — Wey

offered Himself a flawless sacrifice to
God — Ber

. . . as an unblemished sacrifice to God
— Mof

. . . as a victim without blemish —
TCNT

gave Himself a spotless offering to God
— Wms

**purge your conscience from dead
works**
cleanse your conscience from dead
works — ASV

purify your consciences from lifeless
works — Wey

purify our conscience from a lifeless
formality — TCNT

cleanse our conscience from the deadness of our former ways — NEB

to serve the living God?
To the rendering of divine-service unto
a Living God — Rhm

unto the service of an ever-living God!
— Mon

and fit us for the service of the Living
God! — TCNT

that we may worship the living God! — Con

for the worship of the ever-living God — Gspd

15. And for this cause he is the mediator of the new testament,

And for this cause of a new covenant is he mediator — Rhm

And that is why he is the intermediary of a new Covenant — TCNT

And that is why he is the negotiator of a new agreement — Gspd

Thus, through his intervention, a new covenant has been bequeathed to us — Knox

Christ is consequently the administrator of an entirely new agreement — Phi

that by means of death, for the redemption

in order that, death having taken place for the redemption — ABUV

To the end that death coming to pass for the redemption — Rhm

in order that, as a death has taken place to effect a deliverance — TCNT

now that a death has occurred which redeems them — Mof

in order that as someone has died to deliver them — Gspd

in order that, since a life has been given in atonement — Wey

in order that, after He had suffered death for securing redemption — Wms

of the transgressions that were under the first testament,

of the transgressions that were committed under the first covenant — NASB

of the transgressions against the first covenant — Rhm

from the offences committed under . . . — TCNT

for the offences committed under . . . — Wey

from sins committed under the former covenant — NEB

from transgressions involved in the first covenant — Mof

they which are called might receive

they that have been called may receive — ASV

those who have received the Call may obtain — TCNT

those who had been invited to share it might obtain — Wms

those who have been offered it may receive — Gspd

those whom God has called may receive — NEB

all who are invited may come and have forever — Tay

the promise of eternal inheritance.

the promise of the age-abiding inheritance — Rhm

the promised eternal inheritance — RSV

the eternal inheritance promised to them — TCNT

the eternal heritage that was promised — Ber

the unending inheritance they have been promised — Gspd

all the wonders God has promised them — Tay

16. For where a testament is,

For where a covenant is — Rhm

Whenever such a Covenant as a will is in question — TCNT

For when a will is made — Wms

For where there is a legal 'will' — Wey

Thus, in the case of a will — Mof

For where there is a [last] will and testament involved — Amp

there must also of necessity be the death of the testator.

there must of necessity be the death of him that made it — ASV

It is necessary for the death to be brought in of him that hath covenanted — Rhm

there has to be the death of the man who made it — Bas

the death of the testator must be declared — Con

it is necessary that the death of him who made it be proved — Wms

17. For a testament is of force after men are dead:

For a testament is of force where there hath been death — ASV

For a covenant over dead persons is firm — Rhm

For such a Covenant takes effect only upon death — TCNT

For a covenant is valid only when men are dead — NASB

And a will is only of force in the case of a deceased person — Wey

for a will only holds in cases of death
— Mof

otherwise it is of no strength at all while the testator liveth.

for it doth never avail while he that made it liveth — ASV

Since it is not then of force when he is living that hath covenanted — Rhm

since it is of no strength at all while the testator is living — ABUV

it is never valid so long as . . . — Mof

it cannot possibly have force while . . . — NEB

for what power has it while the man who made it is living? — Bas

18. Whereupon neither the first testament was dedicated without blood.

Whence not even the first apart from blood hath been consecrated — Rhm

Wherefore even the first covenant hath not been dedicated without blood — ASV

So that even the first agreement was not made . . . — Bas

. . . was not inaugurated without blood — Ber

. . . could not be ratified without the use of blood — Gspd

. . . not put into force without the shedding of blood — Phi

Accordingly we find that not without blood was the first testament enacted — Mon

19. For when Moses had spoken

Thus when Moses had proclaimed — Wey

for after Moses had announced — Mof

For when Moses had given — Bas

every precept to all the people according to the law,

every commandment according to the law . . . unto all the people — Rhm

all the regulations of the Law to all the people — Gspd

every injunction found in the Law . . . — Ber

all the rules of the law . . . — Bas

the provision of the law to the assembled people — Knox

he took the blood of calves and of goats,

Taking the blood of the calves and the goats — Rhm

he took calves' and goats' blood — Gspd

. . . the blood of goats and young oxen — Bas

. . . the blood of slain calves and goats — Amp

with water, and scarlet wool, and hyssop,

along with water, crimson wool, and a bunch of hyssop — Gspd

. . . and scarlet-dyed wool, and hyssop — Knox

. . . scarlet wool and marjoram — NEB

. . . some scarlet wool and a hyssop sprinkler — Nor

and sprinkled both the book, and all the people

Both the scroll itself and all the people he sprinkled — Rhm

and sprinkled the roll of the Law and all the people — Gspd

and sprinkled the book containing the law and . . . — Wms

. . . both the book itself and the people generally — Wey

20. Saying, This is the blood of the testament

Saying — This is the blood of the covenant — Rhm

saying, as he did so — This is the blood that renders valid the Covenant — TCNT

. . . This is the blood which confirms the Covenant — Wey

. . . This blood ratifies the agreement — Gspd

. . . This is the blood that seals and ratifies . . . — Amp

. . . the blood that marks the beginning of the agreement between you and God — Tay

which God hath enjoined unto you.

which God commanded to you-ward — ASV

which God hath sent in command unto you — Rhm

which God has commanded to be made with you — TCNT

That God has made binding upon you — Wey

which has been ordained for you by God — Lam

which God has prescribed to you — Knox

21. Moreover he sprinkled with blood

Moreover he in like manner sprinkled with the blood — Alf

And in the same way he also sprinkled
... — TCNT

He even sprinkled with blood — Mof

both the tabernacle, and all the vessels of the ministry.

the tent and all the vessels of divine service — NEB

upon the Tent of worship and upon all the vessels used in the ministry — Wey

... and all the things that were used in the public worship — TCNT

... and all the sacred vessels — Phi

... and all the appliances used in the priestly service — Gspd

22. And almost all things are by the law purged with blood;

And nearly all things with blood are purified according to the law—Rhm

And nearly all things are cleansed according to the law with blood — ABUV

In fact, under the Law, almost everything is ... — Gspd

and the law enjoins that blood shall be used in almost every act of purification — Knox

And according to the Law, one may almost say, all things are ... — NASB

Indeed we may almost say that in obedience to the Law everything is ... — Wey

and without shedding of blood is no remission.

And apart from blood-shedding cometh no remission — Rhm

and, unless blood is shed, no forgiveness is to be obtained — TCNT

and unless blood is poured out nothing is forgiven — Gspd

No blood shed, no remission of sins! — Mof

... there is neither release from sin and its guilt nor the remission of the due and merited punishment for sins — Amp

23. It was therefore necessary

It was indeed therefore necessary — Rhm

It was needful therefore — Wey

For this cause it was necessary — Bas

By such means, therefore — Gspd

that the patterns of things in the heavens

that the copies of the things in the heavens — ASV

that the figures of the things ... — Alf

that the outlines of the things ... — ABUV

these things that were only copied from the originals in heaven — Gspd

the earthly reproductions of heavenly realities — Phi

should be purified with these;

should be cleansed with these — ASV

... by such means as these — TCNT

... with sacrifices like these — Mof

... with these rites — RSV

... by such methods — Phi

had to be purified — Gspd

but the heavenly things themselves with better sacrifices than these.

the heavenly realities themselves required better sacrifices — TCNT

but the heavenly originals themselves required far better ... — Gspd

the heavenly world itself will need sacrifices more availing still — Knox

... required nobler sacrifices — Mof

... should be cleansed with more costly sacrifices — Wey

24. For Christ is not entered into the holy places made with hands,

For not into a Holy place made by hands entered Christ — Rhm

For Christ entered not into holy places ... — Alf

For Christ, the Messiah, has not entered ... — Amp

which are the figures of the true;

like in pattern to the true — ASV

Counterpart of the real Holy place — Rhm

— a mere copy of the reality — Wey

(a mere type of the reality!) — Mof

which is only a symbol of the reality — NEB

which merely foreshadowed the true one — TCNT

but into heaven itself,

But into the heaven itself — Rhm

but it was into heaven itself that He went — Wms

now to appear in the presence of God for us:

now to appear before the face of God for us — ASV

in order to appear now on our behalf in the very presence of God — Gspd

Now to be plainly manifested before the face of God . . . — Rhm

to appear now before God as our friend — Tay

to make his appearance before God as High Priest on our behalf — Phi

25. Nor yet that he should offer himself often,

Nor yet that ofttimes he should be offering himself — Rhm

Nor was it for the purpose of many times offering Himself in sacrifice — Wey

Nor did he enter to offer himself repeatedly — Mon

Nor does he go in to offer himself over and over again — Gspd

Nor did He [enter into the heavenly sanctuary to] offer . . . — Amp

as the high priest entereth into the holy place every year

. . . enters into the holy places every year — ABUV

. . . enters the [Holy of] Holies every year — Amp

. . . enters annually into the sanctuary — Ber

. . . enters the Holy Place, year after year — Wey

with blood of others;

with blood not his own — ASV

with alien blood — Rhm

with the blood of another creature — Phi

taking with him blood not his own — Wey

with an offering of blood — but not his own blood — TCNT

26. For then must he often have suffered

Else hath it been needful for him ofttimes to suffer — Rhm

(for in that case he would have needed to suffer repeatedly — Mon

If that were so, he would have had to suffer many times — NEB

For then Christ would have had to undergo death many times — TCNT

. . . to suffer death over and over — Gspd

since the foundation of the world:

from the foundation of the world — Rhm

ever since the world was founded — Mof

from the very beginning of the world — Lam

since the creation of the world — TCNT

from the creation of the world onwards — Wey

but now once

But now once for all — Rhm

But now, once and for all — TCNT

But, as it is, once for all — Gspd

in the end of the world hath he appeared

at the end of the ages hath he been manifested — ASV

Upon the conjunction of the ages, . . . — Rhm

at the close of the ages He has appeared — Wms

He has shown Himself . . . at the close of the ages — Ber

at the consummation He has been manifested — NASB

he has come to us at the end of the old order — Bas

. . . at the moment when history reached its fulfilment — Knox

. . . at the climax of history — NEB

to put away sin by the sacrifice of himself.

for the putting away of sin by His sacrifice — Alf

For a setting aside of sin through means of his sacrifice — Rhm

in order to do away with sin by the sacrifice of Himself — Wey

to put an end to sin by his sacrifice — Gspd

in order to abolish sin by the sacrifice of himself — TCNT

to eliminate sin by His self-sacrifice — Ber

annulling our sin by his sacrifice — Knox

to put away the power of sin forever by dying for us — Tay

27. And as it is appointed unto men once to die,

And inasmuch as it is in store for men — Once for all to die — Rhm

And since it is reserved for all mankind once to die — Wey

And as it is the lot of men to die once — NEB

And just as men are destined to die once — Gspd

And, as it is ordained for men to die but once — TCNT

but after this the judgment:

but after this, judgment — ABUV

and after this cometh judgment — ASV

with judgment following — Ber

(death being followed by judgement) — TCNT

and afterwards to be judged — Wey

nothing remains after that but judgement — Knox

and after that the [certain] judgment — Amp

28. So Christ

so also the Christ — ABUV

Thus the Christ also — Rhm

so it is with the Christ — TCNT

Even so it is that Christ — Amp

so it is certain that Christ — Phi

was once offered to bear the sins of many;

having been once offered to bear the sins of many — ASV

Once for all has been offered For the bearing of the sins of many — Rhm

He was offered up once and for all, to bear away the sins of many — TCNT

having at his first coming taken on himself the sins of men — Bas

. . . to bear the burden of men's sins — NEB

and unto them that look for him

to them that wait for him — ASV

To them who for him are ardently waiting — Rhm

to those who are eagerly expecting Him — Wey

. . . are (eagerly, constantly and patiently) waiting for and expecting Him — Amp

shall he appear the second time without sin

A second time apart from sin will appear — Rhm

shall . . . show Himself the second time, with no reference to sin — Ber

. . . — but without any burden of sin — TCNT

. . . not to deal with sin — Mof

. . . not to bear sin — NASB

. . . not as a sin-bearer — Nor

unto salvation.

and that for their salvation — Ber

to bring Salvation — TCNT

to bring them final salvation — Wms

but to bring to full salvation — Phi

to make their salvation complete — Wey

CHAPTER 10

1. For the law having a shadow of good things to come,

For while the Law foreshadowed the blessings that were to come — Gspd

For since the law cast only a shadow of the blessings . . . — Wms

The Law gives only a shadow of the benefits in store for the godly — Nor

The Law possessed only a dim outline of the benefits Christ would bring — Phi

The Law, though able to foreshadow the Better System which was coming — TCNT

The old system of Jewish laws gave only a dim foretaste of the good things Christ would do for us — Tay

and not the very image of the things,

and not the true image of those things — Bas

and not a perfect representation of the realities — Wey

instead of the true form of these realities — RSV

instead of representing the reality of that bliss — Mof

and did not possess the reality itself of those blessings — Wms

can never with those sacrifices

can never with the same sacrifices — ASV

it can never, by the same sacrifices — RSV

its priests can never, by repeating the same sacrifices — Wey

which they offered year by year continually

year by year, which they offer continually — ASV

which year by year they offer evermore — Rhm

that are perpetually offered year after year — Wms

make the comers thereunto perfect.

make perfect them that draw nigh — ASV

Make them who approach perfect — Rhm

make perfect those who approach [its altars] — Amp

make those who come to worship perfect — TCNT

bring the worshippers to perfection for all time — NEB

give complete freedom from sin to those who draw near — Wey

make the people who come to the altar . . . completely clean — Bas

2. For then would they not have ceased to be offered?

Otherwise would they not have ceased to be offered — Mon

Else, would they not have quit bringing their offerings, — Ber

Otherwise, would not the offering of these sacrifices have been abandoned, — TCNT

Otherwise, they would surely have ceased to be offered; — Mof

. . . surely the sacrifices would have been discontinued — Phi

because that the worshippers once purged

as the worshippers, having been once purified — TCNT

because those who offered them, . . . — Gspd

. . . having been once cleansed — ASV

. . . having been really cleansed — Phi

. . . . made completely clean — Bas

should have had no more conscience of sins.

would have had no more consciousness of sins — ASV

would no longer have any consciousness of sin — Ber

would have had their consciences clear from sins — TCNT

would no longer be conscious of sin! — Mof

their consciences would no longer reproach them of sin — Nor

. . . would no longer be burdened with sins — Wey

they would no longer have any guilt or consciousness of sin — Amp

3. But in those sacrifices

But in them — Rhm

But, on the contrary, these sacrifices — TCNT

On the other hand, through these sacrifices — Wms

As it is, the sacrifices — Mof

In practice, however, the sacrifices — Phi

there is a remembrance again made of sins every year.

is a recalling to mind of sins year by year — Rhm

are an annual reminder of sins — Mof

amounted to an annual reminder of sins — Phi

there is given a real reminder of their sins — Wms

. . . a fresh remembrance of sins [to be atoned for] — Amp

4. For it is not possible that the blood of bulls and of goats

For it is impossible for blood of bulls and goats — Rhm

Because it is not possible for the blood of oxen and goats — Bas

for bulls' and goats' blood is powerless — Gspd

should take away sins.

to be taking away sins — Rhm

to remove sins — TCNT

5. Wherefore when he cometh into the world, he saith,

Wherefore coming into the world he saith — Rhm

As He enters into the world, He therefore says — Ber

Hence, on entering the world . . . — Mof

Consequently, when Christ came . . . — RSV

. . . the Christ, on coming into the world, declared — Mon

Sacrifice and offering thou wouldest not,

Sacrifice and offering thou didst not wish — ABUV

Sacrifice and offering thou dost not desire — TCNT

Thou hast no desire for sacrifice or offering — Mof

O God, the blood of bulls and goats cannot satisfy You — Tay

but a body hast thou prepared me:

But a body didst thou prepare for me — ASV

But a body hast thou fitted for me — Rhm

but thou dost provide for me a body — TCNT

but instead You have made ready a body for Me [to offer] — Amp

6. In burnt offerings and sacrifices for sin thou hast had no pleasure.

In whole-burnt-offerings and sacrifices for sins thou didst not delight—Rhm

in holocausts and sin-offerings thou takest no delight — Mof

You never cared for burnt-offerings and sacrifices for sin! — Gspd

You had no joy in burned offerings, or in offerings for sin — Bas

You were not satisfied with the animal sacrifices, slain and burnt before You as offerings for sin — Tay

7. Then said I, Lo, I come

Then said I, Lo, I am come — ASV

So I said, See, I have come! — Gspd

. . . Here am I: — NEB

(in the volume of the book it is written of me,)

(In the roll of the book . . . — ASV

(the writing in the scroll of the book tells about Me) — Beck

(as is written of me in the pages of the Book) — TCNT

just as the Scripture writes about me in the book — Wms

In the heading of the scroll it is written concerning me — Rhm

to do thy will, O God.

To do, O God, thy will — Rhm

O God, to do your will! — Gspd

I'm here to do what you want, O God — Beck

— I come to do thy will, O God—Mof

to do your pleasure, O God — Bas

8. Above when he said,

Saying above — ASV

After saying the words I have just quoted — Wey

Sacrifice and offering and burnt offerings and offerings for sin

Sacrifices and offerings, and whole-burnt-offerings and sacrifices for sins — Rhm

thou wouldest not, neither hadst pleasure therein;

thou didst not wish, nor hadst pleasure therein — ABUV

You never wished or cared for — Gspd

You never wished or took delight in — Wms

Thou hast no longing for, thou takest no delight in — Mon

which are offered by the law:

(the which are offered according to the law) — ASV

— all of which the Law prescribes — Gspd

— all of which are repeatedly offered in accordance with the law — Wms

(offerings regularly made under the Law) — TCNT

9. Then said he, Lo, I come to do thy will, O God.

then hath he said, Lo, I am come to do thy will — ASV

then he added, Lo, I have come to do thy will — RSV

He then went on to say, Lo, [here] I am, come to do Your will — Amp

He taketh away the first, that he may establish the second.

He does away with the first in order to establish the second — Wey

He is taking away the first to let the second take its place — Wms

He thus annuls the former to establish the latter — NEB

The former sacrifices are set aside to be replaced by the latter — TCNT

He took away the old order, so that he might put the new order in its place — Bas

He cancels the first system in favor of a far better one — Tay

10. By the which will we are sanctified

In which will we have been sanctified — ABUV

By which will we have been made holy — Rhm

And in accordance with this will [of God] . . . — Amp

Under this new plan we have been forgiven and made clean — Tay

And it is through his doing of God's will that we . . . — Gspd

through the offering of the body of Jesus Christ once for all.

through the offering of the body of Jesus Christ once for all — Rhm

by means of the offering up once for all of the body . . . — Ber

by the sacrifice, once and for all, of the body of . . . — TCNT

11. And every priest standeth daily ministering

And every priest indeed standeth day by day ministering — ASV

Every priest stands performing his service daily — NEB

Every other priest stands officiating day after day — Gspd

Every human priest stands day by day performing his religious duties — Phi

and offering oftentimes the same sacrifices,

And the same sacrifices ofttimes offering — Rhm

offering the same sacrifice repeatedly — Mof

offering over and over again the same sacrifices — Gspd

and constantly offering . . . — Wey

and offering time after time . . . — Phi

which can never take away sins:

the which can never take away sins — ASV

such as possess no power whatever to strip off our sins — Ber

The which never can clear away sins — Rhm

— though these can never rid us of our sins — Wey

which can never actually remove sins — Phi

though they were powerless ever to remove people's sins — Gspd

12. But this man,

But this One — Wms

— this Priest, on the contrary — Wey

after he had offered one sacrifice for sins for ever,

having offered one sacrifice for sins evermore — Rhm

has offered for all time one sacrifice for sin — Gspd

offered up once for all and for all time one sacrifice for sins — Wms

after offering for sins a single sacrifice of perpetual efficacy — Wey

after he had offered one sacrifice for sins, which should serve for ever — TCNT

. . . good forever — Beck

sat down on the right hand of God;

took his seat at the right hand of God — TCNT

and once for all took His seat at God's right hand — Wms

and then sat down in the place of highest honor at God's right hand — Tay

13. From henceforth expecting

from then on anticipating — Ber

and has since then been waiting—TCNT

from that time offering no more sacrifice, but waiting — Phi

till his enemies be made his footstool.

until His enemies are placed a footstool for His feet — Ber

till all who are against him are made a footrest for his feet — Bas

Until his foes be made his footstool — Rhm

14. For by one offering he hath perfected for ever

For with a single offering He has forever perfected — Ber

For by that one sacrifice He has made perfect for all time — Wms

Because by one offering he has made complete for ever — Bas

. . . he has forever qualified . . . to approach God — Gspd

. . . He has forever completely cleansed and perfected — Amp

them that are sanctified.

them that are being sanctified — Alf

them who are being made holy — Rhm

those who are consecrated to Him — Wms

those who are purified from sin — Gspd

those who are being purified — TCNT

15. Whereof the Holy Ghost also is a witness to us:

And the Holy Spirit also beareth witness to us — ASV

And the Holy Spirit also gives us His testimony — Wey

The Holy Spirit, too, affirms it to us — Ber

The Holy Spirit himself endorses this truth for us — Phi

And here the Holy Spirit adds his testimony — Knox

for after that he had said before,

For after having said — Rhm

for when He had said — Wey

16. This is the covenant that I will make with them

This is the covenant that I will covenant with them — ABUV

This is the agreement that I will make with them — Gspd

after those days, saith the Lord,

In those later days, says the Lord — Gspd

I will put my laws into their hearts,

putting my laws on their hearts — ABUV

Giving my laws upon their hearts — Rhm

I will set my laws upon their hearts — Mon

I will impress my laws on their hearts — TCNT

and in their minds will I write them;

And upon their mind also will I write them — ASV

Upon their understanding also will I inscribe them — Rhm

engrave them in their innermost thoughts — Knox

17. And their sins and iniquities

and their sins and their transgressions — ABUV

and their sins and their lawbreakings — Ber

[He] also [saith] — Of their sins, and of their lawlessnesses — Rhm

then saith he, And their sins and their iniquities — ASV

will I remember no more.

I will never, never any more recall — Wms

I will in nowise be mindful any more — Rhm

I will no longer remember — TCNT

I will never again remember — Tay

18. Now where remission of these is,

Now where there is forgiveness of these — Bas

Now, when sins have once been forever forgiven and forgotten — Tay

there is no more offering for sin.

there is no longer a sin-offering — ABUV

there is no more sacrificing for sin — Beck

there is no further need of an offering for sin — TCNT

19. Having therefore, brethren,

Therefore, brethren, since we have — RSV

boldness to enter into the holiest by the blood of Jesus,

boldness for the entrance into the holy places by the . . . — ABUV

a cheerful confidence . . . to enter into the Holiest by . . . — Mon

free access to the sanctuary through . . . — Gspd

freedom of speech for the entrance

through the Holy place by . . . — Rhm

20. By a new and living way, which he hath consecrated for us,

which he instituted for us, a new and living way — ABUV

Which entrance he hath consecrated for us as a way recent and living — Rhm

by the way which he dedicated for us, a new and living way — ASV

by the way which he inaugurated for us — a new . . . — TCNT

by a new and living way which He hath opened for us — Con

He has opened up for us a new, a living approach — Knox

through the veil, that is to say, his flesh;

Through the veil, that is, his flesh — Rhm

through the curtain, that is, through his flesh — RSV

through the separating curtain [veil of the Holy of Holies], . . . — Amp

a way through the Sanctuary Curtain (that is, his human nature) — TCNT

by way of the veil, I mean, his mortality — Knox

21. And having an high priest over the house of God;

and having a great priest over . . . — ASV

and since we have a great Priest who has authority over . . . — Wey

and, since we have in him a great priest set over . . . — TCNT

. . . set over the household of God — NEB

. . . in charge of God's family — Beck

And since this great High Priest of ours rules over God's household — Tay

22. Let us draw near with a true heart in full assurance of faith,

Let us approach with a genuine heart in full assurance of faith — Rhm

let us come with a true heart in fullness of faith — ABUV

let us draw near to God in all sincerity of heart and perfect faith — TCNT

let us continue to draw near to God with sincere hearts and perfect faith — Wms let us draw near with sincerity and un-faltering faith — Wey

. . . with honest hearts and with un-qualified assurance of faith — Ber

. . . with a sincere heart and with un-wavering faith — Nor

. . . with true hearts fully trusting Him to receive us — Tay

having our hearts sprinkled from an evil conscience,

Having been sprinkled as to our hearts from an evil conscience — Rhm

as our hearts have been sprinkled from the stain of an evil conscience — Con

. . . sprinkled clean from a bad con-science — Mof

. . . sprinkled clean from consciences oppressed with sin — Wey

. . . purified by the sprinkled blood from all consciousness of wrong — TCNT

. . . sprinkled to take away our guilty feelings — Beck

with our hearts cleansed from the sense of sin — Wms

and our bodies washed with pure water.

And bathed as to our bodies with pure water — Rhm

and our bodies have been washed with pure water — Con

. . . bathed in clean water — Wms

23. Let us hold fast the profession of our faith without wavering;

let us hold fast the confession of our hope that it waver not — ASV

let us, without ever wavering, keep on holding to the hope that we profess — Wms

Let us maintain the confession of our hope unshaken — TCNT

. . . hold the hope we avow without wavering — Mof

. . . hold firmly to an unflinching avowal of our hope — Wey

. . . hold unwavering our grip on the hope we confess — Ber

Do not let us waver in acknowledging the hope we cherish — Knox

(for he is faithful that promised;)

For faithful is he that hath promised — Rhm

for He is to be trusted who has made the promise — Wms

for he who has given us his promise will not fail us — TCNT

(for we can rely on him who gave us the Promise) — Mof

for there is no question that He will do what He says — Tay

24. And let us consider one another

And let us attentively consider one an-other — Rhm

Let us continue so to consider one an-other — Wms

And let us consider the example one of another — Con

And let us bestow thought on one an-other — Wey

Let us vie with one another — TCNT

And let us consider and give attentive, continuous care to watching over one another — Amp

to provoke unto love and to good works:

to incite to love and to good works — ABUV

as to stimulate one another to love and good deeds — Wms

with a view to arousing one another to brotherly love and right conduct — Wey

in a rivalry of love and noble actions — TCNT

25. Not forsaking the assembling of our-selves together,

not forsaking the gathering of ourselves together — ABUV

not abandoning . . . our common as-sembly — Knox

not neglecting our own church meeting — Ber

not staying away from our meetings — NEB

And let us not hold aloof from our church meetings — Phi

as the manner of some is;

as the custom of some is — ASV

According to the custom of some — Rhm

as some do — TCNT

— as some habitually do — Wey

but exhorting one another:

but encouraging one another — Wey

but giving mutual encouragement — Ber

but using exhortation — Alf

but admonishing one another — Mof

and so much the more, as ye see the day approaching.

and all the more, now that you see the Day drawing near — TCNT

and this the more earnestly as we see the final day drawing ever nearer — Phi

especially now that the Day of His coming back again is drawing near — Tay

26. For if we sin wilfully

For if we are willfully sinning — ABUV

For if we wilfully persist in sin — Wey

For if by choice we be sinning — Rhm

For if we sin deliberately — Mof

For if we do evil on purpose — Bas

after that we have received the knowledge of the truth,

after the receiving of the full-knowledge of . . . — Rhm

after we have gained a full knowledge of . . . — TCNT

after acquiring the knowledge of . . . — Ber

after we have so fully learned the truth — Gspd

after we have known and accepted the truth — Phi

there remaineth no more sacrifice for sins,

No longer for sins is there left over a sacrifice — Rhm

there is no sacrifice left to be offered for our sins — Gspd

there can be no further sacrifice . . . — TCNT

there no longer remains a sin-offering — ABUV

. . . to atone for [our] sins — Amp

27. But a certain fearful looking for of judgment

but a certain fearful expectation of judgment — ASV

nothing but an awful outlook of doom — Mof

only a terrifying prospect of judgment — Wms

only a terrible waiting for . . . — Beck

and fiery indignation, which shall devour the adversaries.

and a fierceness of fire which shall devour . . . — ASV

and a wrathful fire that shall devour . . . — Con

and the fury of fire which is to consume the enemies of God — Wey

and a burning indignation which will destroy all opponents — TCNT

and that blazing indignation which is to . . . — Gspd

and fiery jealousy About to devour the opposers — Rhm

a fire that will eagerly consume the rebellious — Knox

. . . those who put themselves in opposition [to God] — Amp

28. He that despised Moses' law

Any one having set aside a law of Moses — Rhm

When a man disregarded the Law of Moses, he — TCNT

A man that hath set at nought Moses' law — ASV

One who has rejected . . . — ABUV

Anyone who breaks . . . — Gspd

A man who has violated . . . — RSV

Any one who bids defiance to . . . — Wey

The man who showed contempt for . . . — Phi

died without mercy under two or three witnesses:

dieth without compassion on the word of two or . . . — ASV

is put to death without mercy on the testimony of . . . — Wey

dies without mercy, on the evidence of . . . — Mof

was killed without mercy if there were two or three witnesses to his sin — Tay

29. Of how much sorer punishment, suppose ye,

Of how much worse punishment, think ye — ABUV

How much severer punishment, think you — Wey

How much heavier, do you suppose, . . . — Mof

shall he be thought worthy,

shall he be judged worthy — ASV

shall he be accounted worthy — Rhm

will he be held to deserve — Wey

shall he be found worthy — Alf

who hath trodden under foot the Son of God,

who has trampled under foot . . . — Wey

who has spurned the Son . . . — Mof

who has poured scorn on the Son . . .
— Phi

and hath counted the blood of the covenant, wherewith he was sanctified,

and has accounted the blood . . . —
ABUV

and has regarded . . . — NASB

and treats . . . the blood of the agreement by which he has been purified — Gspd

who have treated the blood that rendered the Covenant valid — TCNT

and counts . . . the blood of the covenant . . . — Wms

an unholy thing,

as a common thing — Wms

as ordinary blood — Lam

a profane thing — Rhm

as worthless . . . by which he has been purified — Gspd

— as of no account — TCNT

as though it were common and unhallowed — Tay

and hath done despite unto the Spirit of grace?

And unto the Spirit of favour hath offered wanton insult — Rhm

and has insulted the Spirit of grace —
ABUV

and affronted God's gracious Spirit! —
NEB

and who has outraged the Spirit . . . —
Ber

mocked at the Spirit that brought him grace — Knox

. . . the Spirit from whom comes grace — Wey

. . . the Spirit that grants God's unmerited favor — Wms

. . . the (Holy) Spirit [Who imparts] grace — the unmerited favor and blessing of God — Amp

30. **For we know him that hath said,**

For we know who it is that has said —
Wey

For we have had experience of him who says — Bas

Vengeance belongeth unto me, I will recompense, saith the Lord.

To me belongeth avenging, I will recompense — Rhm

Vengeance is mine, I will exact a requital — Mof

It is for me to avenge, I will requite —
TCNT

Retribution rests with Me; I will pay back — Ber

And again, The Lord shall judge his people.

. . . will judge and determine and solve and settle the cause and the cases of His people — Amp

31. **It is a fearful thing to fall into the hands of the living God.**

It is dreadful to fall into the hands of the living God! — Ber

It is an awful thing to fall . . . — Wey

It is a terrifying thing to fall . . . of the ever living God! — Wms

It is a fearful (formidable and terrible) thing to incur the divine penalties and be cast into . . . — Amp

32. **But call to remembrance the former days, in which,**

But be calling to mind the former days, . . . — Rhm

Call to mind those previous days when — Ber

But you must continue to remember . . . — Wms

Don't ever forget those wonderful days of old when — Tay

after ye were illuminated,

after having been enlightened — Mon

after you were first spiritually enlightened — Amp

when first you received the light — Wms

after you had received the Light — TCNT

when you first learned about Christ — Tay

ye endured a great fight of afflictions;

A great combat of sufferings ye endured — Rhm

ye endured a great conflict of sufferings ASV

you endured a hard struggle of suffering — Mof

you had to go through a great struggle with persecution — Gspd

you patiently underwent a long and painful conflict — TCNT

you successfully came through a hard and painful struggle — Beck

you met the challenge of great sufferings and held firm — NEB

33. Partly, whilst ye were made a gazing-stock

partly, being made a gazingstock—ASV

Partly indeed because . . . ye were being made a spectacle — Rhm

Sometimes . . . you became a public spectacle — TCNT

This was partly through allowing yourselves to be made a public spectacle — Wey

. . . made a public show — Beck

. . . made an object of ridicule — Lam

both by reproaches and afflictions;

both with reproaches and tribulations — Rhm

amid reproaches and persecutions — Wey

in consequence of the taunts and injuries heaped upon you — TCNT

by angry words and cruel acts — Bas

. . . insults and violent sufferings — Wms

. . . calumny and persecution — Knox

. . . obloquy and anguish — Mof

and partly, whilst ye became companions of them that were so used.

and partly, becoming partakers with them that were so used — ASV

and partly by becoming sharers with those who were so treated — NASB

But partly because into fellowship with them who were so involved ye were brought — Rhm

but ye took part also in the sufferings of others who bore the like — Con

and partly through coming forward to share the sufferings . . . — Wey

partly by making common cause with those who fared thus — Mof

and sometimes showing yourselves ready to share the lot of those in that condition — Gspd

34. For ye had compassion on me in my bonds,

For ye both had compassion on them that were in bonds — ASV

For ye showed compassion to the prisoners — Con

For even with them who were in bonds ye sympathised — Rhm

For indeed you shared the sufferings of . . . — NEB

and took joyfully the spoiling of your goods,

And unto the seizure of your goods with joy ye bade welcome — Rhm

and accepted joyfully the seizure of your property — NASB

and cheerfully submitted to the violent seizure of . . . — Wms

and you did take joyfully the confiscation of . . . — Mon

and ye took joyfully the plundering of . . . — ABUV

knowing in yourselves that ye have in heaven

knowing that ye have for yourselves — ASV

knowing that ye have of your own — Alf

conscious that elsewhere you had — Mof

knowing well that (in heaven) you personally have — Ber

knowing, as you did, that you had in yourselves — TCNT

a better and an enduring substance.

a better possession and an abiding one — ASV

a greater possession and a lasting one — TCNT

a more valuable possession and one which will remain — Wey

a better property and one which you would keep for ever — Bas

a much more solid and lasting treasure in Heaven — Phi

something better that is permanent — Beck

35. Cast not away therefore your confidence,

Therefore do not throw away your confidence — RSV

Now do not drop that confidence of yours — Mof

Do not, therefore, abandon the confidence that you have gained — TCNT

Therefore do not cast from you your confident hope — Wey

Now do not fling away your bold confidence — Mon

Cast not away therefore your boldness — ASV

So you must never give up your confident courage — Wms

. . . your fearless confidence — Amp

which hath great recompence of reward.

The which hath a great recompense — Rhm

for it will receive a vast reward — Wey

for it has a great reward awaiting it — TCNT

for it holds a rich reward for you — Wms

it carries with it a rich hope of reward — Mof

. . . a rich reward in the world to come — Phi

36. For ye have need of patience,

For of endurance ye have need — Rhm

You still have need of patient endurance — TCNT

Steady patience is what you need — Mof

For ye have need of steadfastness — Con

that, after ye have done the will of God,

In order that the will of God having done — Rhm

so that when you have done the will of God — NASB

so that, as the result of having done . . . — Wey

if you are to carry out God's will — Gspd

that ye may do the will . . . — Alf

ye might receive the promise.

Ye may bear away the promise — Rhm

you may obtain the fulfilment of his promise — TCNT

you may receive what you were promised — Mof

you may receive the promised blessing — Wey

and receive the blessing he has promised — Gspd

and thus receive and carry away [and enjoy to the full] what is promised — Amp

37. For yet a little while,

For yet a very little while — ASV

For yet a little while how short! how short! — Rhm

For there is indeed but a very little while — TCNT

For in a little, a very little now — Mof

and he that shall come will come, and will not tarry.

He that cometh shall come, and shall not tarry — ASV

The Coming One will be here and will . . . — Rhm

the Coming One will come, and will not delay — ABUV

Ere He who is Coming will have come, without delay — TCNT

. . . he will not be slow — Bas

. . . he will not linger on the way — Knox

His coming will not be much longer delayed — Tay

38. Now the just shall live by faith:

But my righteous one by faith shall live — Rhm

But my just man shall live by faith — Alf

Meantime my just man is to live on by his faith — Mof

But the upright man will be living by his faith — Bas

Now By faith shall the righteous live — Con

And through faith the Righteous man shall find his Life — TCNT

Meantime my righteous servant will live on by faith — Wms

but He whom I find righteous shall live by faith — Ber

And he whom I accept as righteous will find life through his faith — Gspd

And those whose faith has made them good in God's sight must live by faith — Tay

but if any man draw back, my soul shall have no pleasure in him.

And if he draw back my soul delighteth not in him — Rhm

and If he draw back through fear, my soul hath no pleasure in him — Con

And if he shrink back, my soul hath . . . — ASV

. . . my heart can find no pleasure in him — TCNT

. . . My soul is not pleased with him — Ber

. . . he shall win no favour with me — Knox

39. But we are not of them who draw back unto perdition;

We however are not of a drawing back unto destruction — Rhm

But we are not of defections unto perdition — Mon

But we are not of backsliding unto . . . — Alf

But we are not men of fear unto . . . — Con

But we are not of those who shrink back and are destroyed — RSV

Surely we are not going to be men who cower back and are lost — Phi

But we are not of a disposition to draw back so as to perish — Wms

. . . who draw back, to their Ruin — TCNT

. . . who draw back to eternal misery (perdition) and are utterly destroyed — Amp

but of them that believe to the saving of the soul.

but of faith unto the saving of the soul — Alf

but of them that have faith unto . . . — ASV

but we have faith that leads to the saving . . . — Wms

but of those who have faith to the preserving . . . — NASB

but men who maintain their faith until the salvation of their souls is complete! — Phi

but of faith unto the gaining of the soul — Mon

but are of those who believe and so win possession of their souls — Wey

But of faith unto an acquisition of life — Rhm

we have the faith to make life our own — NEB

No, our faith in Him assures our soul's salvation — Tay

CHAPTER 11

1. Now faith is the substance of things hoped for,

Now faith is assurance of things hoped for — ASV

Now faith is a confident assurance of that for which we hope — Wey

But faith is of things hoped for a confidence — Rhm

Now faith means that we are confident of what we hope for — Mof

But faith forms a solid ground for what is hoped for — Ber

Faith is being sure of the things we hope for — Beck

Now faith is the title-deed of things hoped for — Mon

And what is Faith? Faith gives substance to our hopes — NEB

Faith is the realization of things hoped for — TCNT

the evidence of things not seen.

a conviction of things not seen — ASV

a conviction of the reality of things we do not see — Wey

and makes us certain of realities we do not see — NEB

the proof of the reality of the things we cannot see — Wms

the putting to the proof of things not seen — Mon

being the proof of things [we] do not see and the conviction of their reality — faith perceiving as real what is not revealed to the senses — Amp

2. For by it the elders obtained a good report.

For therein the elders had witness borne to them — ASV

For in this the elders obtained a good testimony — ABUV

For thereby well-attested were the ancients — Rhm

It is for their faith that the men of old stand on record — NEB

And it was for faith that the men of old were renowned — TCNT

For by it the men of old gained approval — NASB

By it the saints of old won God's approval — Wey

3. Through faith we understand

By faith we perceive — ABUV

Faith enables us to perceive — TCNT

It is faith that enables us to see — Gspd

that the worlds were framed by the word of God,

that the ages have been framed by God's word — ABUV

the ages to have been fitted together by declaration of God — Rhm

that the worlds were prepared by the word of God — NASB

that the world came into being by the command . . . — Wey

that the world was fashioned by the word . . . — Mof

that the worlds were put in order at God's command — Ber

that the universe was created at the bidding of God — TCNT

that the whole scheme of time and space was created . . . — Phi

. . . created, beautifully co-ordinated, and now exist, at God's command — Wms

so that things which are seen were not made of things which do appear.

so that what is seen has not arisen out of things which appear — ABUV

. . . what we now see did not come from visible things — Ber

. . . what is seen does not owe its existence to that which is visible — Wey

. . . the world which we behold springs not from things that can be seen — Con

To the end that not out of things appearing should that which is seen have come into existence — Rhm

. . . did not evolve out of existing matter — Nor

and that they were made from nothing! — Tay

4. By faith Abel offered unto God a more excellent sacrifice than Cain,

By faith a fuller sacrifice did Abel offer unto God than Cain — Rhm

Through faith Abel offered to God a more acceptable sacrifice . . . — Wey

Faith made Abel's sacrifice greater in the sight of God than Cain's — Gspd

[Prompted, actuated] by faith Abel brought God . . . — Amp

. . . a better sacrifice than Cain's — TCNT

. . . a sacrifice superior to that of Cain — Ber

. . . a richer sacrifice than Cain did — Mof

. . . an offering that pleased God more than Cain's offering did — Tay

by which he obtained witness that he was righteous,

through which he had witness borne to him that he was righteous — ASV

. . . that he was upright and in right standing with God — Amp

whereby he obtained testimony that . . . — Con

through faith he gained God's approval as an upright man — Gspd

Through it, God approved of him as

being righteous — Nor

and won his renown as a righteous man — TCNT

God testifying of his gifts:

God bearing witness in respect of his gifts — ASV

there being a witnessing upon his gifts by God — Rhm

God giving the testimony by accepting his gifts — Mon

for God acknowledged his gifts — Ber

since God approved him for the offering he made — Wms

God himself establishing his renown by accepting his gifts — TCNT

and by it he being dead yet speaketh.

And through it though he died he yet is speaking — Rhm

and by it he still continues to speak, though dead — Wms

and it is by the example of his faith that Abel, though dead, still speaks — TCNT

he died, but by his faith he is speaking to us still — Mof

through that offering of his he still speaks in death — Knox

5. By faith Enoch was translated

By faith Enoch was transferred — Ber

By faith Enoch was transplanted from earth — Wms

Through faith Enoch was taken from the earth — Wey

Faith led to Enoch's removal from earth — TCNT

Enoch trusted God too and that is why He took him away to heaven — Tay

that he should not see death;

so as not to see death — Rhm

so that he did not see death — Wey

so that he never died — Mof

and was not found, because God had translated him:

and he was not found, because God translated him — Con

He could not be found because God had removed him — TCNT

He disappeared from this world because God promoted him — Phi

for before his translation he had this testimony,

For before the translation he had received witness — Rhm

for before he was taken he had witness borne to him — Wey

For before he was transplanted from earth evidence was given him — Wms

For before he was taken to heaven, his record was — Mof

Now before he was taken he was attested — RSV

For, before his removal, he was renowned — TCNT

for he hath had witness borne to him that before his translation — ASV

for he obtained the witness that before his being taken up — NASB

For it is the testimony of Scripture that before he was taken — NEB

that he pleased God.

that he had become well-pleasing unto God — Rhm

he had been well-pleasing unto God — ASV

as having pleased God — TCNT

6. But without faith it is impossible to please him:

But apart from faith it is impossible to be well-pleasing — Rhm

Where there is no faith it is impossible truly to please Him — Wey

Without faith, man cannot please God — Lam

You can never please God without faith, without depending on Him — Tay

for he that cometh to God must believe

for the man who draws near to God must believe — Wey

for anyone who approaches God must believe — Wms

for whoever cometh unto God must have faith — Con

Nobody reaches God's presence until he has learned to believe — Knox

that he is,

that he exists — Mof

that there is a God — Wey

and that he is a rewarder of them that diligently seek him.

And that to them who seek him out a rewarder he becometh — Rhm

and that he ever rewards those who are seeking — Mon

and that He gives rewards to all who earnestly try to find Him — Wms

and that He will reveal Himself to those who sincerely look for Him — Tay

7. By faith Noah,

Through faith Noah — Wey

[Prompted] by faith Noah — Amp

It was faith that enabled Noah — TCNT

being warned of God of things not seen as yet,

having received intimation concerning the things not yet seen — Rhm

being divinely instructed concerning things not yet seen — ABUV

being divinely warned about things as yet unseen — Wey

being forewarned of God concerning events of which as yet there was no visible sign — Amp

... of the dangers in the offing — Nor

... of impending disaster — Phi

moved with fear, prepared an ark to the saving of his house;

moved with godly fear, prepared an ark ... — ASV

Filled with reverence prepared an ark ... — Rhm

reverently constructed an ark to save his household — Mof

took heed and constructed an ark for the saving of ... — RSV

taking forethought, prepared an ark ... — Alf

... an ark to preserve his family — Knox

... an ark for the deliverance of his own family — Amp

by the which he condemned the world,

through which he condemned ... — ASV

and through it the world was judged by him — Bas

and by this act he condemned ... — Wey

This action of faith condemned the unbelief of the rest of ... — Phi

By his faith he condemned ... — TCNT

by which faith he passed sentence on ... — Ber

and became heir of the righteousness which is by faith.

And of the righteousness by way of faith became heir — Rhm

while he fell heir to the righteousness that springs from faith — Ber

and became possessor of the uprightness that results from faith — Wms

and got the righteousness that is to be had by faith — Beck

. . . the righteousness which depends on faith — Wey

. . . that uprightness which faith produces — Gspd

. . . of righteousness, [that relation of being right into which God puts the person who has faith] — Amp

and . . . he became one of those God accepts — Tay

8. By faith Abraham, when he was called

By faith Abraham, on being called — Wms

[Urged on] by faith Abraham when he was called — Amp

Faith enabled Abraham . . . when God summoned him — Gspd

to go out into a place which he should after receive for an inheritance, obeyed;

obeyed to go out unto a place which he was to receive . . . — ASV

obeyed, to go forth into a place which he was about to receive for an inheritance — ABUV

obeyed the command to go forth into a place . . . — Con

. . . a place which was to be given to him as a heritage — Bas

. . . a place which he would eventually possess — Phi

. . . a land destined for himself and his heirs — NEB

and he went out, not knowing whither he went.

And he came forth not well knowing whither he was coming — Rhm

and he set out not knowing where he was going — TCNT

and he migrated without any idea . . . — Ber

and he did it in spite of the fact that he did not know . . . — Wms

. . . in complete ignorance of his destination — Phi

9. By faith he sojourned in the land of promise,

By faith he lived around in the land of promise — Ber

By faith he made his temporary home in the land that God had promised him — Wms

It was faith that made him go to live as an emigrant in the Promised Land — TCNT

By faith he became a sojourner in the land . . . — ASV

By faith he was a wanderer in the land of the agreement — Bas

It was faith that kept him journeying . . . through the land . . . — Phi

as in a strange country,

as in a land not his own — ASV

as a foreign land — Rhm

as an alien — Mon

dwelling in tabernacles with Isaac and Jacob,

living merely in tents with . . . — Wms

he lived in tents like a mere visitor — Tay

with no more home than the tents which he shared with . . . — Phi

the heirs with him of the same promise:

the joint-heirs of the same promise — Rhm

who were to share the promise with him — Wms

to whom God gave the same promise — Tay

10. For he looked for a city which hath foundations,

For he was awaiting the city having foundations — Rhm

For he was looking for the City with the sure foundations — TCNT

For he was confidently looking forward to that city with the solid foundations — Wms

For he continually looked for . . . — Mon

For he was waiting expectantly and confidently, looking . . . — Amp

. . . waiting for God to bring him to that strong heavenly city — Tay

whose builder and maker is God.

Whose architect and builder is God — Rhm

the one God built and made — Beck

designed and built by God — Gspd

which is God's design and God's fashioning — Knox

11. Through faith also Sara herself received strength to conceive seed,

By faith even Sarah herself received power to . . . — ASV

It was by faith that even Sara got strength . . . — Mof

By faith even Sarah herself received power for founding a seed — Rhm

. . . received strength to become pregnant — Wms

. . . personally received potency for conception — Ber

. . . received strength to become a mother — Wey

. . . gained the physical vitality to become a mother — Phi

It was faith that enabled Sara, barren till then, to conceive offspring — Knox

and was delivered of a child when she was past age,

even when she was past age — Alf

and that when past the normal age — Ber

Even beyond the season of life's prime — Rhm

— although she was past the time of life for this — Wey

(though she was past the age for childbearing) — TCNT

because she judged him faithful who had promised.

since she counted him faithful who . . . — ASV

Seeing that faithful she reckoned him that . . . — Rhm

— because she considered that she could rely on Him who gave the promise — Mof

. . . that he who had made the promise would keep it — Gspd

. . . that God would be faithful to his word — Knox

. . . that God, Who gave her His promise, would certainly do what He said — Tay

12. **Therefore sprang there even of one,**

wherefore also there sprang of one — ASV

And thus there sprang from one man — Wey

Wherefore even from one were born — Rhm

And so a whole nation came from Abraham — Tay

and him as good as dead,

and him become as dead — ABUV

and him as good as dead at that — NASB

— and that when his powers were dead — TCNT

and he already impotent — Ber

for any prospect of descendants as good as dead — Gspd

who as a potential father was already considered dead — Phi

so many as the stars of the sky in multitude,

Like the stars of the heaven for multitude — Rhm

a people as numerous as the stars in the heavens — TCNT

a race whose numbers rival the stars of heaven — Knox

a people as numberless as the stars in the sky — Wms

and as the sand which is by the sea shore innumerable.

And as the sand that is by the lip of the sea that cannot be numbered — Rhm

or the countless grains of sand upon the shore — TCNT

13. **These all died in faith,**

In faith these all died — ABUV

All these persons died in faith — NEB

All these people lived all their lives in faith, and died — Gspd

All these died sustained by faith — TCNT

Controlled by faith all these went to their death — Ber

It was faith they lived by, all of them, and in faith they died — Knox

These people all died victoriously as a result of their faith — Wms

not having received the promises,

without obtaining the promises — Mof

without realizing the promises — Ber

although they did not receive the blessings promised — Wms

not having received what was promised — RSV

for them, the promises were not fulfilled — Knox

but not having received the tangible fulfillment of . . . — Amp

but having seen them afar off, and were persuaded of them, and embraced them,

But from afar beholding and saluting them — Rhm

but having seen them and greeted them from afar — ASV

they only saw them far away and hailed them — Mof

but scanning and hailing them from a distance — Ber

. . . glimpsed the fulfillment in the distance; they hailed it with delight — Nor

and confessed that they were strangers and pilgrims on the earth.

And confessing that strangers and sojourners were they upon the land — Rhm

and having acknowledged that they were strangers and exiles on the earth — RSV

recognizing that they themselves were only foreigners and strangers here on earth — Gspd

They freely admitted that they lived on this earth as . . . — Phi

. . . strangers who had no permanent home on earth — Beck

14. For they that say such things declare plainly

For those who say such things make it clear — NASB

Now people who speak in this way plainly show — Mof

men who acknowledge this make it manifest — Wey

For men who recognize that show — Gspd

For people who make such a profession as this show — Wms

that they seek a country.

that they are seeking a Fatherland — Mon

that they are seeking a homeland — RSV

that of a paternal home they are in quest — Rhm

that they are looking for a home country — Ber

. . . are searching for a country for themselves — Bas

. . . are seeking elsewhere a country of their own — Wey

. . . were looking forward to their real home in heaven — Tay

15. And truly, if they had been mindful of

And if indeed of that they had been mindful — Rhm

And indeed if they had been thinking of — NASB

. . . had been cherishing the memory of — Wms

. . . had been thinking with [homesick] remembrance of — Amp

. . . had been longing for — Nor

If their hearts had been in — NEB

that country from whence they came out,

that land from which they had gone out — RSV

that country from which they came away — Ber

the particular country they had left behind — Phi

they might have had opportunity to have returned.

They might in that case have had an opportunity to return — Rhm

they would have had chances of turning back — Bas

they would have found an opportunity to return — Wey

they would have found constant opportunity to return to it — Amp

they had ample opportunity to return — Phi

16. But now they desire a better country, that is, an heavenly:

But now after a better one are they reaching, . . . — Rhm

But now they desire a better home, . . . — Alf

but now they are longing for a better homeland, . . . — Mon

but, as it is, we see them eager for a better land, . . . — Wey

But the truth is that they were yearning for and aspiring to a better and more desirable country . . . — Amp

. . . a better, a heavenly, land! — TCNT

wherefore God is not ashamed to be called their God:

wherefore God is not ashamed of them, to be called their God — ASV

For this reason God is not ashamed to be called . . . — Wey

and so it is no shame to God to be named their God — Bas

God does not disdain to take his title from such names as these — Knox

for he hath prepared for them a city.

indeed he had already prepared them a city — TCNT

In fact, He has gotten a city ready for them — Ber

for he has prepared a city to receive them — Gspd

he has a city ready for them to dwell in — Knox

. . . a heavenly city for them — Tay

17. By faith Abraham, when he was tried, offered up Isaac:

By faith Abraham, being tried, has offered Isaac — ABUV

Through faith Abraham, when he was being put to the test, . . . — Wey

Faith enabled Abraham, when he was put to the test, to offer Isaac as a sacrifice — Gspd

Abraham shewed faith, when he was put to the test, by offering up Isaac — Knox

. . . while the testing of his faith was still in progress — had already brought Isaac for an offering—Amp

and he that had received the promises

and he who had gladly received the promises — ABUV

Yes, he who had joyfully welcomed . . . — Wey

He who had accepted God's promises — Gspd

this man who had made the promises his own — Knox

offered up his only begotten son.

was offering up his only begotten son — ASV

was ready to sacrifice his only son — Mof

was about to offer up his only son — Mon

was on the point of offering . . . — NEB

was starting to offer as a sacrifice his . . . — Wms

lifted upon the altar his only begotten son — Lam

18. Of whom it was said,

even he to whom it was said — ASV

though it was said unto him — Con

Even him of whom it had been said — Rhm

It was the son concerning whom it had been promised — Nor

That in Isaac shall thy seed be called;

In Isaac shall there be called to thee a seed — Rhm

From Isaac will your seed take their name — Bas

Through Isaac shall your descendants be named — RSV

It is through Isaac that your posterity will be traced — Mon

19. Accounting that God was able to raise him up, even from the dead;

accounting that God is able even to raise from the dead — ABUV

Accounting that even from among the dead God was able to raise him — Rhm

For he reckoned that God had power even to raise . . . — NEB

For he considered the fact that God was able to raise people . . . — Wms

For he reasoned that God was able to raise him . . . — Ber

For he argued that God was able even to raise a man . . . — TCNT

Judging that God was able to give life even to the dead — Bas

He believed that God could raise his son up, even if he were dead — Phi

from whence also he received him in a figure.

from whence he did also in a figure receive him back — ASV

Whence even in similitude he bare him away — Rhm

from which he also received him back as a type — NASB

Hence he did get him back, by what was a parable of the resurrection — Mof

hence, figuratively speaking, he did receive him back — RSV

and indeed, in a hidden sense, he did so recover him — Knox

. . . he did get him back as if from death — Bas

. . . Isaac was doomed to death, but he came back again alive! — Tay

20. By faith Isaac blessed Jacob and Esau

It was faith that enabled Isaac to bless . . . — TCNT

Faith enabled Isaac to bequeath to Jacob and Esau blessings — Gspd

By faith Isaac gave Jacob and Esau his blessing — Ber

[With eyes of] faith Isaac, . . . invoked blessings upon . . . — Amp

concerning things to come.

concerning things about to be — ABUV

even with regard to the future — TCNT

and spoke of things to come — NEB

for his words dealt with what should happen in the future — Phi

in regard to their future — Beck

21. By faith Jacob, when he was a dying,

By faith Jacob when about to die — Rhm

Faith enabled Jacob, when dying — TCNT

Faith caused Jacob, on his deathbed — Nor

[Prompted] by faith Jacob, when . . . — Amp

. . . when he was near to death — Bas

. . . at the point of death — Ber

blessed both the sons of Joseph;

blessed each of the sons of Joseph — ASV

put his blessing on each of Joseph's sons — Wms

to give his blessing to each of . . . — TCNT

and worshipped, leaning upon the top of his staff.

And bowed in worship on the top of his staff — Rhm

and, bowing upon the top of his staff, worshipped God — Wey

and gave God worship, supported by his staff — Bas

as he stood and prayed, leaning on the top of his cane — Tay

and to bow himself in worship as he leant upon the top of his staff — TCNT

22. By faith Joseph, when he died,

By faith Joseph, when his end was nigh — ASV

Through faith Joseph, when he was near his end — Wey

It was by faith that Joseph at his end — Mof

Faith induced Joseph, as he was dying — Nor

[Actuated] by faith Joseph, when nearing the end of his life — Amp

Faith inspired Joseph when he was dying — Gspd

. . . in the hour of his death — Con

made mention of the departing of the children of Israel;

made mention of the departure of the children of Israel — ASV

made mention of the future migration of the Israelites — Wms

thought about the exodus of the sons of Israel — Mof

said that the children of Israel would go out of Egypt — Bas

confidently spoke of God bringing the people of Israel out of Egypt — Tay

spoke of the Israelites' escape from Egypt — Knox

to tell of the future migration of the Israelites — Gspd

and gave commandment concerning his bones.

and commanded concerning his bones — ABUV

and gave instructions in regard to his bones — Mon

and gave orders about his own body — Wey

and gave directions what to do with his body — Wms

and gave directions concerning his burial — RSV

and gave orders for the removal of his bones — Knox

23. By faith Moses, when he was born,

By faith, Moses, at his birth — Wms

[Prompted] by faith Moses after his birth — Amp

Through faith the child Moses — Wey

was hid three months of his parents,

was hidden three months by his parents — Alf

was kept concealed for . . . — Amp

was kept secretly by his father and mother for . . . — Bas

because they saw he was a proper child;

because they saw he was a goodly child — ASV

for they saw that he was a beautiful child — TCNT

when they saw what a fine child he was — Knox

. . . that the child was fair — ABUV

. . . that the child was comely — Alf

. . . that he was a handsome child — Nor

. . . his rare beauty — Wey

. . . that God had given them an unusual child — Tay

and they were not afraid of the king's commandment.

And were not affrighted at the decree of the king — Rhm

and they were not awed by the king's order — Ber

and had no dread of the royal decree — Mof

and the king's edict had no terror for them — Wey

and refused to be daunted by . . . — Phi

and they would not respect . . . — TCNT

24. By faith Moses, when he was come to years,

By faith Moses when grown up—Rhm

Through faith Moses, when he grew to manhood — Wey

[Aroused] by faith Moses, when he had grown to maturity and become great — Amp

refused to be called the son of Pharaoh's daughter;

. . . to be known as a son of Pharaoh's daughter — Gspd

. . . to pass for the son of Pharao's daughter — Knox

. . . the title of 'Son of a Daughter of Pharaoh' — TCNT

25. Choosing rather to suffer affliction with the people of God,

preferring rather to endure ill-treatment along with . . . — Wey

because he preferred to suffer hardships with . . . — Wms

He preferred ill usage, shared with . . . — Knox

and preferred sharing maltreatment with . . . — Ber

Feeling that it was better to undergo pain with . . . — Bas

than to enjoy the pleasures of sin for a season;

Than for a season to be having sin's enjoyment — Rhm

than to enjoy the short-lived pleasures of sin — Wey

than to have the passing enjoyment that results from sin — Wms

. . . the fleeting pleasures of sin — RSV

. . . the transient pleasures of sin — NEB

. . . the temporary enjoyment of sinful pleasures — Nor

. . . the fleeting enjoyment of a sinful life — Amp

. . . the temporary advantages of alliance with a sinful nation — Phi

26. Esteeming the reproach of Christ

accounting the reproach of the Christ — ABUV

Judging a part in the shame of Christ — Bas

He considered the abuse suffered by Christ — Beck

He considered the stigma that rested on God's Anointed — NEB

and thought such contempt as the Christ endured — Gspd

. . . The reproach of the Anointed One — Rhm

. . . the reproaches that are heaped upon the Christ — TCNT

. . . the despised lot of God's anointed — Knox

. . . the reproach endured for the Christ — Wms

. . . the reproaches which he might meet with in the service of Christ — Wey

. . . that it was better to suffer for Christ — Tay

greater riches than the treasures of Egypt:

As greater riches than Egypt's treasures — Rhm

to be richer wealth than Egypt's treasures — Mof

of greater value than the treasures of Egypt — TCNT

was truer wealth than the treasures . . . — Gspd

more precious than all the wealth of Egypt — Phi

was greater wealth than all the treasures in Egypt — Wms

than to own all the money in Egypt — Tay

for he had respect unto the recompence of the reward.

For he was looking away unto the recompense — Rhm

for he fixed his gaze on the coming reward — Wey

for he looked beyond unto the reward — Con

for he kept his eye upon the reward — Wms

looking forward, as he did, to the reward awaiting him — TCNT

for he looked steadily at the ultimate, not the immediate, reward — Phi

27. By faith he forsook Egypt,

Through faith he left Egypt — Wey

Faith caused him to leave Egypt — TCNT

It was in faith that he left Egypt behind — Knox

1102

[Motivated] by faith he left Egypt behind him — Amp

And it was because he trusted God that he . . . — Tay

not fearing the wrath of the king:

not being afraid of the king's anger — Wey

Not put in fear of the wrath of the king — Rhm

unawed by the king's anger — Ber

though undaunted by the King's anger — TCNT

— not from any fear of the king's wrath — Mof

not because he feared the wrath of the king — Mon

defying the royal anger — Knox

for he endured, as seeing him who is invisible.

For as seeing him who cannot be seen he persevered — Rhm

for he persevered as though he were actually seeing Him who is unseen — Wms

He persisted as one who was constantly seeing Him who can't be seen — Beck

for he held on his course as seeing the unseen One — Wey

for he was resolute, as one who saw the invisible God — NEB

like one who saw the King Invisible, he never flinched — Mof

for he was strengthened in his endurance by the vision of the invisible God — TCNT

28. **Through faith he kept the passover,**

By faith he hath kept the passover — Alf

By faith he hath established the passover — Con

Through faith he instituted the Passover — Wey

By faith (simple trust and confidence in God) he instituted and carried out . . . — Amp

. . . kept the first Passover — Phi

. . . performed the paschal rite — Knox

and the sprinkling of blood,

and the sprinkling of the blood — ASV

and the besmearing of the blood — Rhm

and the affusion of the blood — ABUV

and performed the sprinkling of blood — Mof

and splash the blood upon the doorposts — Gspd

and the pouring of blood upon the doorposts — Wms

lest he that destroyed the firstborn should touch them.

that the destroyer of the first-born should not touch them — ASV

Lest he that was destroying the firstborn should be touching them — Rhm

in order that the Destroying Angel might not touch the firstborn — Mon

. . . might not touch the children of Israel — Con

. . . might not touch the eldest children of the Israelites — TCNT

. . . the oldest child in those homes, as he did among the Egyptians — Tay

29. **By faith they passed through the Red sea as by dry land:**

Through faith they passed through the Red Sea as though they were passing over dry land — Wey

By faith the people crossed the Red Sea as on dry land — Mon

Faith enabled the people to cross the Red Sea, as if it had been dry land — TCNT

[Urged on] by faith the people crossed . . . — Amp

which the Egyptians assaying to do were drowned.

which the Egyptians attempting were swallowed up — ABUV

Which the Egyptians seizing an attempt to do were swallowed up — Rhm

but the Egyptians, when they tried to do the same, . . . — Wey

while the Egyptians, in attempting it, were drowned — Wms

though the Egyptians were overcome by the water when they made an attempt to do the same — Bas

30. **By faith the walls of Jericho fell down,**

By faith the walls of Jericho collapsed — Wms

Faith caused the walls of Jericho to fall — TCNT

Because of faith the walls of . . . — Amp

Faith pulled down the walls of . . . — Knox

It was faith that brought the walls of Jericho tumbling down — Tay

after they were compassed about seven days.

after they had been encompassed for seven days — ABUV

Having been surrounded for . . . — Rhm

after being encircled for . . . — TCNT

after they had marched around them each day for . . . — Gspd

. . . on seven successive days — NEB

31. By faith the harlot Rahab

Through faith Rahab the harlot—Wey

By faith Rahab the prostitute — Wms

It was because of her faith that Rahab . . . — Phi

It was by faith that Rahab . . . — Mof

[Prompted] by faith Rahab . . . — Amp

. . . Rahab the loose woman — Bas

. . . Rahab the innkeeper — Ber

By faith — because she believed in God and His power — Rahab . . . — Tay

perished not with them that believed not,

did not perish along with the disobedient — Wey

perished not with them who refused to yield — Rhm

did not share the fate of the disobedient — Phi

was not put to death with those who had gone against God's orders — Bas

didn't perish with her disobedient people — Beck

was not destroyed along with those who refused to believe and obey — Amp

escaped the doom of the unbelievers — NEB

when she had received the spies with peace.

having received the spies with peace — ASV

because she had received the spies . . . — Alf

She having welcomed the spies . . . — Rhm

because she had taken into her house in peace those sent to see the land — Bas

after she had entertained the spies with friendliness — TCNT

as she had given a friendly welcome to the scouts — Mof

. . . given the spies a peaceable welcome — Knox

. . . welcomed the scouts as friends — Wms

. . . welcomed the Israelites sent out to reconnoiter — Phi

. . . received the spies in peace (without enmity) — Amp

32. And what shall I more say?

And what more shall I say — ABUV

And what shall I say further — Amp

Need I add anything more — TCNT

And what other examples shall I give — Phi

And why need I say more — Wey

And why should I continue to mention more — Wms

for the time would fail me to tell

For time would fail me to go on narrating — Ber

For time will fail me while I go on telling — Rhm

. . . if I attempted to relate the stories of — TCNT

There is simply not time to continue by telling the stories — Phi

Time is too short for me to tell the stories of — NEB

of Gedeon, and of Barak, and of Samson, and of Jephthae;

of Gideon, Barak, Samson, Jephthah — ASV

about Gideon, . . . — ABUV

of David also, and Samuel, and of the prophets:

of David and Samuel and the prophets — ASV

33. Who through faith subdued kingdoms, wrought righteousness,

who through faith overcame kingdoms, . . . — ABUV

— men who by faith conquered kingdoms, administered justice — Mof

Through faith they overthrew kingdoms, established justice — NEB

By their faith they subdued kingdoms, ruled righteously — TCNT

Theirs was the faith which subdued kingdoms, which served the cause of right — Knox

. . . performed acts of righteousness — NASB

. . . did righteous works — Beck

obtained promises, stopped the mouths of lions,

procured promised blessings, . . . — Ber

received new promises, . . . — Gspd

gained the fulfilment of God's promises, . . . — TCNT

saw God's promises fulfilled. They muzzled ravening lions — NEB

and received what God had promised them; they were kept from harm in a den of lions — Tay

34. Quenched the violence of fire,

quenched the power of fire — ASV

stopped the force of fire — Wms

quelled the fury of flames — TCNT

Extinguished the power of raging fire — Amp

put out furious fires — Gspd

escaped the edge of the sword,

Escaped the mouths of the sword — Rhm

escaped the biting of . . . — Ber

escaped the devourings of . . . — Amp

got safely away from the edge of . . . — Bas

swords were drawn on them, and they escaped — Knox

out of weakness were made strong,

Were made powerful from weakness — Rhm

were made powerful when they had been weak — Ber

were made strong when they had been feeble — Bas

out of weakness found great strength — Wms

Their weakness was turned to strength — NEB

out of frailty and weakness won strength and became stalwart—Amp

From being weaklings they became strong men — Phi

waxed valiant in fight, turned to flight the armies of the aliens.

waxed mighty in war, turned to flight armies of aliens — ASV

became mighty in war, put to flight foreign armies — Wey

proved valiant in warfare, and routed hosts of foreigners — Mof

displayed their prowess in war, and routed hostile armies — TCNT

proved to be mighty in battle, . . . — Beck

they became mighty warriors . . . — Nor

even mighty and resistless in battle, routing alien hosts — Amp

what courage they shewed in battle, how they routed invading armies! — Knox

. . . hurled back foreign armies — Ber

. . . Overturned camps of aliens — Rhm

. . . and routed the camps of enemies — Lam

. . . made whole armies turn and run away — Tay

35. Women received their dead raised to life again:

Women received their dead by a resurrection — ASV

Women had their dead restored to them by resurrection — Gspd

Women received back their dead raised to life — TCNT

and others were tortured, not accepting deliverance;

Others endured torture, and refused to accept release — Gspd

and others were put to death with torture, refusing the deliverance offered to them — Wey

while others were tortured and refused to be ransomed — Phi

others let themselves be cruelly attacked, having no desire to go free — Bas

Some were tortured on the wheel, and refused release — TCNT

Others, who refused release, . . . were stretched and broken on the wheel — Ber

Others were tortured to death with clubs, refusing to accept release [offered on the terms of denying their faith] — Amp

that they might obtain a better resurrection:

That unto a better resurrection they might attain — Rhm

—that they might secure a better resurrection — Wey

that they might be resurrected to a better life — Amp

that they might rise again to the better life — Gspd

looking forward to a better resurrection still — Knox

— trusting that they would rise again to a better life afterwards — Tay because they wanted to deserve a more honorable resurrection in the world to come — Phi

36. And others had trial of cruel mockings and scourgings,

Others again of mockings and scourgings received trial — Rhm

Still others stood the test of taunts and tortures — Wms

. . . were tested by being laughed at or by blows — Bas

. . . took the test of mockings and floggings — Ber

. . . had to face jeers and flogging — NEB

. . . experienced mockery and scourging — Knox

. . . were exposed to the test of public mockery and flogging — Phi

yea, moreover of bonds and imprisonment:

and even fetters and prison — Gspd

Nay! further of bonds and imprisonments — Rhm

and even chains and prisons — Wms

yes, of shackles and prisons, too — Ber

and to the torture of being left bound in prison — Phi

37. They were stoned,

They were stoned to death — TCNT

They were killed by stoning — Phi

they were sawn asunder,

. . . they were cut in pieces — Knox

. . . they were cut up with knives — Bas

were tempted, were slain with the sword:

they were tested, they were put to death with . . . — Bas

they were tried by temptation, they were killed with . . . — Wey

they were tempted to sin; . . . they were murdered with . . . — Ber

. . . lured with tempting offers [to renounce their faith]; . . . — Amp

. . . tempted by specious promises of release and then were killed with . . . — Phi

they wandered about in sheepskins and goatskins;

Went about in sheep-skins in goat-hides — Rhm

they had to roam about in sheepskins and . . . — Mof

they wandered about clothed in the skins of sheep or goats — TCNT

[while they were alive] they had to go about wrapped in . . . — Amp

Many became refugees with nothing but sheepskins or goatskins to cover them — Phi

being destitute, afflicted, tormented;

Being in want suffering tribulation, enduring ill-treatment — Rhm

being poor, and in pain, and cruelly attacked — Bas

needy, oppressed, mistreated — Beck

destitute, persecuted, misused — Gspd

forlorn, oppressed, ill-treated — Mof

utterly destitute, oppressed, cruelly treated — Amp

enduring want, oppression, and cruelty — Wey

in poverty, distress, and misery — NEB

They lost everything and yet were spurned and ill-treated — Phi

38. (Of whom the world was not worthy:)

— men of whom the world was not worthy — TCNT

— the world was not worthy of them — Ber

men whom the world was unworthy to contain — Knox

They were too good for this world — NEB

by a world that was too evil to see their worth — Phi

they wandered in deserts, and in mountains,

Wandering in waste places, and in mountains — Bas

— roaming in lonely places, and on the mountains — TCNT

They were refugees in deserts and on the hills — NEB

living a hunted life in deserts and on mountain sides — Knox

They lived as vagrants in . . . — Phi

and in dens and caves of the earth.

and caves, and the holes of the earth — ASV

and in caves, — and in the caverns of . . . — Rhm

and in caves and holes in the ground — TCNT

in rock-fastnesses and caverns underground — Knox

or hid themselves in . . . — Wey

39. And these all, having obtained a good report through faith,

. . . having had witness borne to them through their faith — ASV

. . . having obtained a good testimony through . . . — ABUV

. . . though well attested by . . . — RSV

These also, one and all, are commemorated for their faith — NEB

Yet, though they all won renown by their faith — TCNT

Though all these people by their faith won God's approval — Wms

received not the promise:

Yet bare not away the promise — Rhm

but the Promise they did not obtain — — Mof

did not receive what was promised — RSV

none of them received the fulfilment of His promise — Wey

they did not obtain the final fulfilment of God's promise — TCNT

did not procure the promised blessing — Ber

and yet they did not enter upon the promised inheritance — NEB

40. God having provided some better thing for us,

God for us something better providing — Rhm

for God had provided something still better for us — Wms

God had something better in store for us — Mof

since God had foreseen something better for us — RSV

For God had resolved upon something still better for us — Gspd

because, with us in mind, God had made a better plan — NEB

God had something better planned for our day — Phi

that they without us should not be made perfect.

that apart from us they should not be perfected — ABUV

That not apart from us should they be made perfect — Rhm

so that without us their consummation might not be attained — Ber

that they, apart from us, should not attain perfection — TCNT

that only in company with us should they reach their perfection — NEB

in order to have them reach their goal with us — Beck

CHAPTER 12

1. Wherefore seeing we also

Seeing then that we — Mon

Therefore, let us also — ABUV

Seeing, therefore — TCNT

And what of ourselves? — NEB

are compassed about with so great a cloud of witnesses,

have encircling us so great a cloud of witnesses — Rhm

having so great a cloud of witnesses surrounding us — ABUV

with such a crowd of witnesses about us — Gspd

that there is on every side of us such a throng of witnesses — TCNT

. . . so vast a crowd of spectators in the grandstands — Wms

With all these witnesses to faith around us like a cloud — NEB

. . . of witnesses [who have borne testimony of the Truth] — Amp

let us lay aside every weight,

laying aside every weight — Alf

Stripping off every incumbrance—Rhm

let us fling aside every encumbrance — Wey

let us throw off every impediment — Wms

let us also lay aside everything that hinders us — TCNT

let us rid ourselves of all that weighs us down — Knox

and the sin which doth so easily beset us,

and the easily entangling sin — Rhm

and our besetting sin — Ber

and the sin which clingeth closely round us — Con

and the sin into which we come so readily — Bas

and sin, which doth naturally enwrap us — Alf

and the entanglement of sin — Gspd

and the sin that so readily entangles our feet — Wey

and that sin which so readily (deftly and cleverly) clings to . . . — Amp

. . . sin with its clinging folds — Mof

and let us run with patience the race that is set before us,

With endurance let us be running the race that is lying before us — Rhm

And let us run with patient endurance the race that lies before us — Wey

and run with determination the race for which we are entered — Gspd

and let us run steadily the course mapped out for us — Ber

and let us run with perseverance the race . . . — RSV

and run with resolution the race . . . — NEB

and run with courage the race . . . — Con

let us keep on running in the way which is marked out for us — Bas

. . . the particular race that God has set before us — Tay

2. Looking unto Jesus the author and finisher of our faith;

looking away to the author and perfecter of the faith, Jesus — ABUV

Looking away unto our faith's Princely-leader and perfecter Jesus — Rhm

with our eyes on Jesus, the Cause and Completer of our faith — Ber

simply fixing our gaze upon Jesus, the Leader and Perfecter of faith — Wey

looking onward unto Jesus, the forerunner and the finisher of our faith — Con

. . . the pioneer and perfecter of our faith — Mon

. . . as the pioneer and the perfection of faith — Mof

. . . the guide and end of our faith — Bas

. . . our leader and example in faith — Gspd

. . . the source and the goal of our faith — Phi

. . . Jesus, on whom faith depends from start to finish — NEB

who for the joy that was set before him

who, in view of the joy that lay ahead for Him — Ber

Who in consideration of the joy lying before him — Rhm

He, for the sake of the joy which lay before Him — Wey

who, in order to reach his own appointed joy — Mof

who, to win his prize of blessedness — Knox

because of the joy he knew would follow his suffering — Phi

who, instead of the joy which lay before Him — Wms

who in place of the happiness that belonged to him — Gspd

and who, instead of the joy which he could have had — Lam

endured the cross, despising the shame,

Endured a cross shame depising! — Rhm

patiently endured the cross, looking with contempt upon its shame — Wey

steadily endured the cross, thinking nothing of its shame — Mof

submitted to a cross, caring nothing for its shame — Gspd

. . . heedless of its shame — TCNT

. . . making light of its disgrace — NEB

. . . and scorned its shame — Nor

and is set down at the right hand of the throne of God.

And on the right hand of the throne of God hath taken his seat — Rhm

and now has taken his seat at the right hand of . . . — TCNT

and is now seated at the right hand of . . . — Wey

and since has taken His seat . . . — Wms

and who has now taken his place at the right hand of God's seat of power — Bas

and now He sits in the place of honor by the throne . . . — Tay

3. For consider him

Give thought to him — Bas

Think constantly of him — Phi

consider Him carefully — Nor

Compare yourselves with him — Mon

Compare your experience with His — Ber

Take your standard from him — Knox

that endured such contradiction of sinners against himself,

that hath endured such gainsaying of sinners . . . — ASV

who endured such hostility directed against Him by sinners — Wey

who steadily endured all that hostility from sinful men — Mof

who was willing to stand so much contradicting from the sinners against
Himself — Ber

who submitted to such opposition from
sinners — NEB

. . . so great opposition aimed at Him
by sinful men! — Wms

. . . such grievous opposition and bitter hostility . . . — Amp

**lest ye be wearied and faint in your
minds.**

that ye wax not weary, fainting in your
souls — ASV

so that you should not grow weary or
faint-hearted — TCNT

so that you may not grow weary and
lose heart — NASB

so that your souls may not wear out
with despondency — Ber

Lest ye be wearied in your souls becoming exhausted — Rhm

so as to keep your own hearts from
fainting and failing — Mof

. . . get tired and give up — Beck

. . . lose your purpose or your courage
— Phi

**4. Ye have not yet resisted unto blood,
striving against sin.**

Not yet did ye resist unto blood, contending against sin — ABUV

Not yet unto blood have ye resisted
against sin waging a contest — Rhm

You have not had to shed blood yet
in the struggle against sin — Mof

. . . resisted unto death in your struggle with sin — Gspd

. . . struggled and fought agonizingly
against sin, . . . — Amp

5. And ye have forgotten the exhortation

And ye have quite forgotten the exhortation — Alf

And you have not kept in mind the
word — Bas

and you have perhaps lost sight of that
piece of advice — Phi

And have you forgotten the word of
appeal — Mof

. . . forgotten the challenge — Gspd

. . . forgotten the encouraging words —
TCNT

. . . forgotten the text of Scripture —
NEB

**which speaketh unto you as unto chil-
dren,**

which reasoneth with you as with sons
— ASV

which discourses with you as with sons
— ABUV

which addresses you as sons? — RSV

which reminds you of your sonship in
God — Phi

**My son, despise not thou the chasten-
ing of the Lord,**

My son, regard not lightly the chastening . . . — ASV

My son! be not slighting the discipline
. . . — Rhm

My child, think not lightly of the
Lord's discipline — TCNT

. . . refrain from thinking lightly of the
discipline the Lord inflicts — Wms

. . . do not undervalue the correction
which the Lord sends thee — Knox

. . . do not despise the training of the
Lord — Mon

. . . don't be angry when the Lord punishes you — Tay

**nor faint when thou art rebuked of
him:**

Nor faint when reproved by him —
ABUV

neither feel fainthearted under His reproof — Ber

Do not despond when he rebukes you
— TCNT

Nor lose heart when he corrects you —
NEB

and do not lose courage when He repri-
mands you — Nor

Don't be discouraged when He has to
show you where you are wrong —
Tay

Or give up when he corrects you —
Gspd

**6. For whom the Lord loveth he chas-
teneth,**

For whom the Lord loveth he doth
discipline — Rhm

for the Lord disciplines the person He
loves — Ber

For it is him whom he loves that he
disciplines — TCNT

It is where he loves that he bestows
correction — Knox

For when He punishes you, it proves
that He loves you — Tay

**and scourgeth every son whom he re-
ceiveth.**

And he chastises every son that he acknowledges — Gspd

And chastises every son whom He heartily receives — Wms

And scourgeth every son whom he doth welcome home — Rhm

He lays the rod on every son whom he acknowledges — NEB

everyone whom he takes as his son has experience of his rod — Bas

there is no recognition for any child of his, without chastisement — Knox

7. If ye endure chastening,

It is for chastisement that ye are enduring — Alf

It is for discipline that you have to endure — Mof

The sufferings that you are enduring are for your discipline — Wey

What you endure is to correct you — Beck

For the sake of discipline persevere! — Rhm

You must endure for the sake of correction — Ber

You must submit to discipline — Wms

Let God train you — Tay

Be patient, then, while correction lasts — Knox

God dealeth with you as with sons;

God is dealing with you as sons — Wey

God is treating you as sons — Mof

for He is doing what any loving father does for his children — Tay

for what son is he whom the father chasteneth not?

For who is a son whom a father doth not discipline — Rhm

For what sort of son is it whom the father . . . — Ber

Can anyone be a son, who is not disciplined by his father — NEB

for what son does not have punishment from his father — Bas

No true son ever grows up uncorrected by his father — Phi

8. But if ye be without chastisement,

But if ye are without chastisement — Alf

If however ye are without discipline — Rhm

If you receive no correction — Ber

If you are left without that discipline — TCNT

If God doesn't punish you when you need it — Tay

whereof all are partakers,

whereof all have been made partakers — ASV

of which all have had a share — Wey

in which all have participated — RSV

which all sons undergo — Gspd

in which all true sons share — Wms

which all sons have to bear — Phi

that very discipline by which every man is trained — Lam

then are ye bastards, and not sons.

that shows that you are . . . — Wey

then you are illegitimates and not sons — Ber

you are only illegitimate children and not true sons — Wms

. . . illegitimate offspring and not true sons [at all] — Amp

. . . not true sons, but the children of shame — Bas

then it means that you aren't really God's son at all — that you don't really belong in His family — Tay

9. Furthermore we have had fathers of our flesh which corrected us,

Furthermore, we had the fathers of our flesh as chasteners — ABUV

Furthermore indeed the fathers of our flesh we used to have as administrators of discipline — Rhm

Besides this, our earthly fathers used to discipline us — Wey

Now, if we were corrected by our human fathers — Ber

and we gave them reverence:

and we reverenced them — ABUV

And we used to pay deference — Rhm

and we respected them — RSV

and we treated them with respect — Wey

and we yielded to them! — Mof

shall we not much rather

shall we not far rather — Ber

and shall we not still more — Wey

should we not . . . even more readily — NEB

Can we not much more readily — Phi

how much more cheerfully should we — Wms

be in subjection unto the Father of spirits, and live?

submit ourselves to the Father of our spirits and live — Rhm willingly be under subjection to our Spiritual Father, . . . — Lam

yield submission to the Father of souls, . . . — TCNT

be under the authority of the Father of spirits, and have life — Bas

. . . and learn how to live — Phi

. . . and live a better life — Nor

. . . and enjoy life — Ber

10. For they verily for a few days chastened us

For they indeed for a few days, . . . were administering discipline—Rhm

For they disciplined us for a short time — Gspd

They, after all, only corrected us for a short while — Knox

For they truly gave us punishment for a short time — Bas

Our earthly fathers trained us for a few brief years — Tay

for our fathers used to correct us . . . during the brief days of childhood — Phi

after their own pleasure; but he for our profit,

as it seemed proper to them; but He does it for our good — Wms

according to that which seemed good to them . . . But he unto that which is profitable — Rhm

according as they thought fit; but He does it for our certain good — Wey

and as seemed best to them; but God disciplines us for our true good — TCNT

according to their own ideas . . . But God corrects us all our days for our own benefit — Phi

doing the best for us that they knew how, but God's correction is always right and for our best good — Tay

that we might be partakers of his holiness.

so that we may share in His holiness — Ber

with a view to our partaking of his holiness — Rhm

to enable us to share his holiness — TCNT

in order that we may share His holy character — Wms

so that we may become holy as he is — Bas

11. Now no chastening for the present seemeth to be joyous,

All chastening seemeth for the present to be not joyous — ASV

Of course, all discipline seems at the time not enjoyable — Ber

Naturally, all discipline seems hard to take at the time — Nor

But no discipline for the present indeed seemeth to be of joy — Rhm

Now for the time being no discipline seems to be pleasant — Wms

While we're being corrected, it always seems unpleasant — Beck

Being punished isn't enjoyable while it is happening — Tay

but grievous: nevertheless afterward

but of sorrow: Afterward however — Rhm

but of grief: nevertheless afterward — Alf

but painful; later on, however — Ber

— it hurts! But afterwards — Tay

it is in fact most unpleasant. Yet when it is all over we can see that — Phi

it yieldeth the peaceable fruit of righteousness

it yieldeth peaceable fruit, . . . even the fruit of righteousness — ASV

it affords . . . the peaceful fruitage of an upright life — Ber

its fruit is seen in the peacefulness of a righteous life — TCNT

. . . the fruit of peace which grows from upright character — Wms

. . . the peaceful harvest of an honest life — NEB

. . . — a harvest of fruit which consists in righteousness . . . — Amp

unto them which are exercised thereby.

. . . that have been exercised thereby — ASV

. . . who thereby have been well trained — Rhm

. . . who have been trained by it — RSV

. . . who have passed through its training — Wey

those schooled in it — Ber

12. Wherefore lift up the hands which hang down,

Wherefore the slackened hands . . . restore ye — Rhm

Wherefore lift up the relaxed hands! — ABUV

So up with your listless hands! — Mof

Therefore lift again the down-dropped hands — TCNT

Therefore, up with your hands that are now dangling down — Nor

Therefore strengthen the drooping hands — Wey

Come, then, stiffen your drooping arms — NEB

So tighten the grip of your slipping hands — Wms

So take a new grip with your tired hands — Tay

So then, brace up and reinvigorate and set right your . . . — Amp

and the feeble knees;

and the palsied knees — ASV

and paralysed knees — Rhm

and your shaky knees — Ber

and straighten the weakened knees — TCNT

Strengthen your weak knees! — Mof

stand firm on your shaky legs — Tay

stiffen the stand of your knocking knees — Wms

13. And make straight paths for your feet,

And straight tracks be making for your feet — Rhm

And keep your feet in straight paths — Gspd

step out straight ahead with your feet — Ber

and march on without wavering — Beck

and plant your footprints in a straight track — Knox

Don't wander away from the path but forge steadily onward — Phi

lest that which is lame be turned out of the way;

that that which is lame be not turned . . . — ASV

so that the feeble may not be turned . . . — Bas

so that the man who goes lame may not stumble out of the path — Knox

Then a cripple will not be turned away — Beck

That the lame members may not be dislocated — Rhm

so that the lame limb may not be put out of joint — TCNT

so that lame legs may not be dislocated — Ber

Then the disabled limb will not be put out of joint — NEB

Let no lame souls be dislocated — Mof

but let it rather be healed.

but be healed rather — Rhm

but rather be cured — TCNT

but be made well — Beck

but rather grow healthy — Ber

but regain strength instead — Knox

but may rather be restored — Wey

rather set them right — Mof

14. Follow peace with all men,

Peace be pursuing with all — Rhm

Run swiftly after peace with all men — Mon

Ever strive for peace with . . . — Wey

Seek eagerly for peace with everyone — Ber

Try earnestly to live at peace with every one — TCNT

Aim at peace with all — Mof

Let it be your ambition to live at peace . . . — Phi

Continue to live in peace with everybody — Wms

Try to stay out of all quarrels — Tay

and holiness, without which no man shall see the Lord:

and the sanctification without which . . . — ASV

and for that sanctification apart from which no one will see . . . — Wey

and the obtaining of holiness, . . . — Rhm

and a holy life, for without that . . . — NEB

and to attain to that purity without which . . . — TCNT

and strive for that consecration without which no one can see . . . — Gspd

15. Looking diligently

looking carefully — ASV

Looking with care to see — Bas

Using oversight — Rhm

See to it — Ber

Continue to look after one another — Wms

lest any man fail of the grace of God;

lest there be any one coming short of . . . — ABUV

Lest any one be falling behind from the favour of God — Rhm

that no one misses the grace of God — Mof

that no one falls short of divine grace
— Ber

. . . fails to avail himself of the grace
of God — Wey

. . . fails to gain God's favor — Gspd

. . . fails to respond to the grace which
God gives — Phi

. . . fails to use the loving help of God
— TCNT

. . . forfeits the grace of God — NEB

**lest any root of bitterness springing
up trouble you,**

Lest any root of bitterness springing up
above be causing trouble — Rhm

that no root of bitterness grows up to
be a trouble — Mof

that no root with bitter fruit grows up
to trouble you — Beck

that no one cultures a root of bitterness to cause a disturbance — Ber

that no poisonous shoot is allowed to
spring up — Knox

in order that no root of resentment
(rancor, bitterness or hatred) shoot
forth . . . — Amp

that no bitterness is allowed to take
root and spring up, . . . — TCNT

and thereby many be defiled;

and thereby the greater number be defiled — Alf

and by its means many become defiled
— Mon

and through it the whole brotherhood
be defiled — Wey

by which the majority shall be contaminated — Ber

and be a poison to many — Nor

and so poison the whole community —
TCNT

16. **Lest there be any fornicator, or profane person, as Esau,**

that there be no immoral or godless
person like Esau — NASB

that no one turn to sexual vice or to a
profane life as Esau did — Mof

that no one be immoral or irreligious
. . . — RSV

Let no one be immoral or irreverent,
as Esau — Nor

. . . become involved in sexual sin or
becomes careless about God as . . .
— Tay

**who for one morsel of meat sold his
birthright.**

who for one meal sold his own birthright — Alf

who, in return for a single meal, parted
with his birthright — Wey

Who for the sake of one meal yielded
up his own firstborn rights — Rhm

who let his birthright go for a plate of
food — Bas

. . . sold his rights as the oldest son —
Tay

17. **For ye know how that afterward,**

For ye know that even when afterward
— ABUV

For ye know that afterwards — Rhm

For you know that when later — Wms

For you understand that later on —
Amp

**when he would have inherited the
blessing, he was rejected:**

wishing to inherit the blessing, . . . —
ABUV

when he desired to inherit the blessing,
. . . — Con

when he wished to claim his father's
blessing, . . . — TCNT

when he wanted to obtain his inheritance of blessing, he was set aside —
Mof

. . . he was refused it — Gspd

. . . he was turned away — Bas

. . . he was rejected (disqualified and
set aside) — Amp

for he found no place of repentance,

he found no opportunity for repentance
— Wey

for he found no place for a change of
mind in his father — ASV

He had no chance to change his mind
— Beck

for he found no way open for second
thoughts — NEB

because he found no place for recalling the decision — Ber

. . . to repent of what he had done —
Gspd

. . . to repent of his foolish deed —
Nor

. . . to repair his error — TCNT

**though he sought it carefully with
tears.**

Even though with tears he diligently
sought it — Rhm

though he sought it earnestly, with
tears — Mon

though he sought it desperately and with tears — Phi

although with tears he sought for the blessing — Ber

— though he begged for the blessing . . . — TCNT

He pleaded for it in tears — Knox

18. For ye are not come unto the mount that might be touched,

For ye have not drawn near unto the mount . . . — Alf

For ye are not come unto a mount that might be touched — ASV

You have not come to what you can touch — Mof

In fact, you have not come up to something tangible — Ber

No, you have not come near to something material — Wey

You have not had to approach things which your senses could experience as they did in the old days — Phi

and that burned with fire,

and burning with fire — ABUV

and to a blazing fire — NASB

all ablaze with fire — Wey

[a mountain] that is ablaze with fire — Amp

nor unto blackness, and darkness, and tempest,

nor to gloom, and darkness, and storm — TCNT

to mist and gloom and stormy blasts — Mof

and darkness, and gloom, and a tempest — RSV

and to darkness and gloom and whirlwind — NASB

. . . and a raging storm — Amp

19. And the sound of a trumpet, and the voice of words;

and trumpet-blast and the sound of words — Wey

and the blare of a trumpet and an audible voice — Mon

the blast of a trumpet, or the speaking of a voice — Beck

And a trumpet's peal, — And a sound of things spoken — Rhm

. . . and the oracular voice — NEB

. . . a voice speaking human words — Phi

which voice they that heard intreated

— the hearers whereof entreated — Con

the hearers of which made request — Bas

the hearers of which implored — Ber

Those who heard that voice entreated — TCNT

which sound was such that those who heard begged — NASB

From which they who heard excused themselves — Rhm

that the word should not be spoken to them any more:

that no word more should be spoken unto them — ASV

that no further word should be added — Wey

that no further message be brought them — Ber

that they might hear no more — TCNT

that nothing more be said to them — Amp

Lest there should be added to them a word — Rhm

that it might stop speaking — Phi

20. (For they could not endure that which was commanded,

For they could not bear that which was being enjoined — Rhm

. . . could not endure the order that was given — RSV

. . . could not bear the injunction — Ber

. . . could not bear that which was charged — ABUV

. . . could not bear the command — Mof

. . . staggered back under God's command — Tay

And if so much as a beast touch the mountain,

If even a beast touch . . . — ASV

And should a beast be touching . . . — Rhm

Even if a wild beast touches . . . — Mon

it shall be stoned, or thrust through with a dart:

it shall be stoned — ASV

it must be stoned — Mof

it is to be stoned to death — TCNT

21. And so terrible was the sight,

and so fearful was the appearance — ASV

And so fearful was that which was showing itself — Rhm

So appalling was the sight — NEB

indeed, so awful was the sight — Mof

and so terrible was the scene — Wey

and so terrifying was the sight — Wms

So fearful was the spectacle — Phi

And the phenomenon was so dreadful — Ber

And the vision was so over-powering — Bas

that Moses said, I exceedingly fear and quake:)

. . . I am terrified, and trembling — ABUV

. . . I am terrified and do tremble! — Rhm

. . . I am terrified and terror-stricken! — Wms

. . . I am aghast and appalled! — Gspd

. . . I am full of fear and trembling — NASB

. . . I shudder with fear — NEB

22. **But ye are come unto mount Sion,**

but ye have drawn near unto . . . — Alf

But ye have approached — Unto Zion's mountain — Rhm

Instead, you have come up to Mount Zion — Nor

On the contrary you are come to . . . — Mon

No, you stand before . . . — NEB

No, you have been allowed to approach the true Mount Zion — Phi

and unto the city of the living God, the heavenly Jerusalem,

And unto the city of a Living God a heavenly Jerusalem — Rhm

even to the city of the living God, . . . — Wms

to the place of the living God, to the Jerusalem which is in heaven — Bas

and to an innumerable company of angels,

and to myriads of angels — ABUV

to countless hosts of angels — TCNT

and to an army of angels which may not be numbered — Bas

here are gathered thousands upon thousands . . . — Knox

to ten thousands of angels — Ber

and to countless multitudes of angels in festal gathering — Amp

and to myriads of angels — Con

23. **To the general assembly and church of the firstborn,**

to the festal gathering and Church of

the first-born — Wey

to the festal assemblage and church of the firstborn — Mon

the festal assembly of Heaven and the Church . . . — Phi

the full concourse and assembly of the first-born — NEB

to the solemn gathering of all God's elder sons — Gspd

And unto an assembly of firstborn ones — Rhm

in full assembly, and to the congregation of the firstborn — Con[13]

in festal gathering, and to the church of the first-born — Ber

which are written in heaven,

who are enrolled in heaven — ASV

enrolled as citizens in heaven — Gspd

registered in heaven — Mof

whose names are written in heaven — Con

and to God the Judge of all,

to God the Judge of all men — TCNT

and to the God of all as Judge — Wey

to a Judge who is God of all — Mon

here is God sitting in judgement on all men — Knox

and to the spirits of just men made perfect,

And unto the spirits of righteous ones made perfect — Rhm

. . . of the righteous who have reached perfection — Ber

. . . of just men, now made perfect — Knox

. . . of the redeemed in heaven, already made perfect — Tay

. . . of upright men now at last enjoying the fulfilment of their hopes — Gspd

24. **And to Jesus the mediator of the new covenant,**

And unto the mediator of a new covenant, Jesus — Rhm

and to Jesus, mediator of a new agreement — Phi

to Jesus, the intermediary of a new Covenant — TCNT

to Jesus the negotiator of a new agreement — Gspd

And to Jesus by whom the new agreement has been made between God and man — Bas

---

[13]Note the punctuation of Con and Ber.

and to Jesus Himself, Who has brought us His wonderful new agreement — Tay

and to the blood of sprinkling,

and to the Sprinkled Blood — TCNT

and to the sprinkling of his blood — Lam

that speaketh better things than that of Abel.

that speaks better than Abel — ABUV

that tells of better things than that of Abel — Ber

which speaks a better message than even Abel's did — Wms

that speaks more graciously than the blood of Abel — RSV

which speaks in more gracious tones than . . . — Wey

whose message is nobler than Abel's — Mof

that speaks more powerfully than even Abel's — Gspd

whose message cries louder than that of Abel — Mon

which graciously forgives instead of crying out for vengeance as the blood of Abel did — Tay

25. **See that ye refuse not him that speaketh.**

See that you do not refuse him who is speaking — Mon

Beware how you refuse to hear him . . . — TCNT

Take care not to refuse to listen to him . . . — Gspd

Be careful not to reject the Speaker — Ber

So be sure you do not refuse to hear the voice of God! — Phi

Beware lest ye excuse yourselves from him that speaketh — Rhm

So see to it that you obey Him Who is speaking to you — Tay

For if they escaped not

for if those people did not escape — Ber

For if they of old did not escape unpunished — Wey

For if the people of Israel did not escape — Tay

. . . failed to escape — Mof

. . . found no escape — NEB

. . . could not escape — Gspd

who refused him that spake on earth,

when they refused him that warned them on earth — ASV

refusing him who declared the divine will on earth — ABUV

when they refused to listen to Him who spoke on earth — Wey

who excused themselves from him who on earth was warning — Rhm

because they would not listen to him . . . — Gspd

who rejected him that spake on earth — Con

. . . the teacher of God's will on earth — Ber

. . . their instructor upon earth — Mof

. . . the man who here on earth instructed them in God's law — Nor

. . . Moses, the earthly messenger — Tay

much more shall not we escape,

much more shall not we — ABUV

How much less shall we — Rhm

still less shall we escape — NEB

how little chance of escape is there for us — Phi

far worse will it be for us — TCNT

how terrible our danger — Tay

if we turn away from him that speaketh from heaven:

who turn away from him that warneth from heaven — ASV

who from him that warneth from the heavens do turn ourselves away — Rhm

who turn a deaf ear to Him who now speaks from heaven — Wey

if we discard the Speaker from heaven — Ber

who reject him who is from heaven! — Gspd

if we refuse to hear Him who came from heaven to teach us — Nor

. . . him who is teaching us from Heaven — TCNT

26. **Whose voice then shook the earth:**

Whose voice shook the earth then — Rhm

His voice, even then, made the earth rock — Knox

Then [at Mount Sinai] His voice shook . . . — Amp

but now he hath promised, saying,

. . . He has given a promise — Amp

. . . we have His promise — Wey

. . . it is announced — Ber

. . . his declaration is — TCNT

. . . the assurance is — Mof

Yet once more I shake
Yet once for all I will shake — Rhm
Yet once more only will I shake — Con
Still once more I will cause . . . to tremble — TCNT
once again I will make . . . to quake — Mof

not the earth only, but also heaven.
Not only the earth But also the heaven — Rhm
. . . but the heaven as well — Ber
. . . but heaven itself — Wms
. . . but the very heaven — Gspd
. . . but also the (starry) heavens — Amp

27. And this word, Yet once more,
And this "yet once more only" — Con
Now that expression, "Once more" — Wms
And those words 'still once more' — TCNT

signifieth the removing of those things that are shaken,
signifies the removing of the things shaken — ABUV
Maketh clear the removal of things which can be shaken — Rhm
indicate the passing away of all that is shaken — TCNT
show clearly He will take away what is shaken — Beck
indicates the final removal of everything shaken — Ber
. . . all that is impermanent will be removed — Phi
. . . that He will sift out everything without solid foundation — Tay

as of things that are made,
as of things that have been made — ASV
as of created things — NASB
this created universe — Knox
(as no more than created) — Mof

that those things which cannot be shaken may remain.
so that the unshaken things may remain — Ber
that the things which are not shaken may abide — ABUV
that the things unshaken may remain immovable — Con
leaving only what is unshaken to be permanent — Gspd
and only the unshakable things will remain — Phi

to let remain the things that cannot be shaken — Wms
only the things which cannot be shaken are to stand firm — Knox
. . . may remain and continue — Amp

28. Wherefore we receiving a kingdom which cannot be moved,
Wherefore, receiving a kingdom that cannot be shaken — ASV
. . . Seeing that of a kingdom not to be shaken we are receiving possession — Rhm
. . . since we are receiving a kingdom which is unshakable — Mon
. . . a kingdom which will never be moved — Bas
. . . a kingdom nothing can destroy — Tay
. . . a kingdom that is firm and stable and cannot be shaken — Amp

let us have grace,
let us have thankfulness — Alf
. . . cherish thankfulness — Wey
. . . show gratitude — NASB
. . . render thanks — Mof
. . . be filled with thankfulness — Con

whereby we may serve God acceptably
whereby we may offer service well-pleasing to God — ASV
and in this way continue to serve God acceptably — Wms
so that we may offer to God an acceptable service — Wey
. . . offer acceptable worship unto God — Con
. . . give God such worship as is pleasing to him — Bas

with reverence and godly fear:
with reverence and awe — ASV
with godly reverence and awe — Wey
with holy awe and fear — Mon
with fear and respect — Bas
— though with godly fear and awe — Mof
with modesty and pious care and godly fear and awe — Amp

29. For our God is a consuming fire.
For our God is indeed a consuming fire — Wey
For even our God is a consuming fire — Rhm
for our God is a devouring fire — NEB
For our God is an all-burning fire — Bas

CHAPTER 13

1. Let brotherly love continue.

Let love of the brethren continue — ASV

Let brotherly love abide — ABUV

Let your love for the Brethren continue — TCNT

Never cease to love your fellow-Christians — NEB

. . . continue and be a fixed practice with you — never let it fail — Amp

2. Be not forgetful to entertain strangers:

Forget not to show love unto strangers — ASV

Of the entertaining of strangers be not forgetful — Rhm

Don't neglect to welcome guests — Beck

Do not forget hospitality — ABUV

Do not remain neglectful of hospitality to strangers — Wms

Do not grow negligent in the hospitality — Ber

Take care to keep open house — Bas

for thereby some have entertained angels unawares.

for by it some have entertained angels without knowing it — Wms

For hereby unawares have some entertained messengers — Rhm

for, through being hospitable, men have all unawares entertained angels — TCNT

. . . some, without knowing it, have had angels as their guests — Gspd

3. Remember them that are in bonds, as bound with them;

Bear in mind them who are in bonds As having become jointly bound — Rhm

Keep in mind those who are in chains, as if you were chained with them — Bas

Continue to remember those who are in prison, as though you were in prison with them — Wms

Remember the prisoners, as though ye shared their prison — Con

. . . as if you were their fellow-prisoners — TCNT

. . . as if you were in prison yourselves — Mof

. . . Suffer with them as though you were there yourselves — Tay

and them which suffer adversity,

them that are ill-treated — ASV

and the maltreated — Ber

and remember those suffering ill-treatment — Wey

those who endure suffering — Knox

and the afflicted — Con

as being yourselves also in the body.

for you yourselves also are still in the body — Wey

since you, too, have mortal bodies — Nor

because you are human also — Lam

as suffering physically yourselves — Ber

as being yourselves liable to the same trials — Gspd

since you, too, are liable to similar physical punishment — Wms

for you like them are still in the world — NEB

4. Marriage is honourable in all,

Let marriage be had in honor among all — ASV

Let marriage be honoured by all — TCNT

Let your marriage be held in honour in all things — Alf

Marriage should be respected by everyone — Gspd

Marriage, in every way, must be held in honour — Knox

Everybody should think highly of marriage — Beck

. . . in honor — esteemed worthy, precious, [that is], of great price and especially dear . . . — Amp

and the bed undefiled:

and let the bed be undefiled — ASV

and the marriage bed unpolluted — Ber

and the marriage-bed kept free from stain — Knox

and the married life be pure — TCNT

and the marriage relation kept sacred — Gspd

and the marriage-bond inviolate—NEB

but whoremongers and adulterers God will judge.

for fornicators and adulterers God will judge — ASV

but God will judge those who practice vice and adultery — Lam

. . . the unchaste and adulterous — Ber

. . . those who are immoral and those who commit adultery — TCNT

. . . those who sin sexually whether single or married — Beck

Persons who are sexually vicious and immoral God will punish — Wms

5. Let your conversation be without covetousness;

Let your way of life be free from the love of money — NASB

Without fondness for money be your way of life — Rhm

Let your conduct be free from covetousness — Con

Do not let your conduct be ruled by the love of money — TCNT

Let your disposition be without . . . — ABUV

You must have a turn of mind that is free from avarice — Wms

Keep your life free from . . . — Mof

Do not live for money — NEB

and be content with such things as ye have:

being content with what you have — NASB

Being content with the present things — Rhm

Let what there is suffice — Ber

Be satisfied with what you have — Beck

for he hath said,

For he himself hath said — Alf

for God himself has said — TCNT

God Himself has told us — Knox

I will never leave thee, nor forsake thee.

I will in no wise fail thee, neither will I in any wise forsake thee — ASV

In nowise thee will I leave, No indeed! in nowise thee will I forsake — Rhm

I will neither give you up nor ever at all desert you — Ber

I will never let go of you or desert you! — Gspd

I will never forsake you, nor will I ever abandon you — TCNT

. . . [I will] not in any degree leave you helpless, nor forsake nor let [you] down . . . — Amp

6. So that we may boldly say,

So that with good courage we say — ASV

So that taking courage we may be saying — Rhm

So that we confidently say — ABUV

Hence we can confidently say — RSV

. . . can boldly claim — Nor

. . . we fearlessly say — Wey

. . . can say without any doubt or fear — Tay

The Lord is my helper, and I will not fear

The Lord is my Helper, I will not fear! — Ber

The Lord hasteth to my cry, — I will not be put in fear! — Rhm

The Lord is my champion; . . . —Knox

. . . I will not be afraid — TCNT

. . . I will have no fear: — Bas

what man shall do unto me.

What shall man do unto me? — ASV

what is man able to do to me? — Bas

7. Remember them which have the rule over you,

Remember your leaders — Mof

Do not forget your Leaders — TCNT

Remember your leaders and superiors in authority — Amp

Be mindful of them who are guiding you — Rhm

. . . that had the rule over you — ASV

. . . your former leaders — Wey

. . . those who have had charge of you — Knox

who have spoken unto you the word of God:

men that spake unto you the word of God — ASV

such as spoke unto you . . . — Alf

Who indeed have spoken unto you . . . — Rhm

— it was they who brought you . . . — Wey

who first spoke to you . . . — Phi

. . . told you God's Message — TCNT

. . . taught you the Word of God — Tay

whose faith follow, considering the end of their conversation.

and considering the issue of their life, imitate their faith — ASV

and observing the issue of their manner of life, . . . — ABUV

The outgoing of whose behaviour reviewing Be imitating . . . — Rhm

seeing the outcome of their way of life, let your faith be like theirs — Bas

the end of whose life considering, imitate their faith — Alf

Bear in mind how they ended their lives, and imitate ... — Wey

look back upon the close of their career, and copy ... — Mof

observe how they closed a well-spent life, and copy ... — Ber

contemplate the happy issue of the life they lived, ... — Knox

... and follow the example of their faith — Con

8. Jesus Christ the same yesterday, and to day, and for ever.

Jesus Christ is the same yesterday and to-day, yea and for ever — ASV

Jesus Christ is always the same, yesterday, ... — Mof

What Jesus Christ was yesterday, and is to-day, he remains for ever — Knox

Jesus Christ is the same today that he was yesterday, and he will be so forever — Gspd

9. Be not carried about with divers and strange doctrines.

Be not carried away with manifold and strange teachings — ABUV

With teachings manifold and strange be not carried aside — Rhm

Do not be drawn aside by all sorts of strange teaching — Wey

You must stop being carried away with varied and ... — Wms

Do not allow yourselves to be swept away by various and ... — Mon

Be not moved from your moorings by all sorts of strange teachings — Ber

... swept off your course by all sorts of outlandish teachings — NEB

... by the various novel forms of teaching — TCNT

... by a maze of new doctrines—Knox

For it is a good thing

for it is good — ASV

because it is good — Bas

for it is well — Wey

For it is noble — Rhm

For it is a beautiful thing — Mon

for the right thing is — Mof

that the heart be established with grace;

that the heart be confirmed with grace — ABUV

that the heart is made stable by grace — Nor

that with gratitude should the heart be getting confirmed — Rhm

to have the heart strengthened by grace — Ber

for the heart to be strengthened by God's spiritual strength — Wms

to rely for spiritual strength upon the divine help — TCNT

that our souls should gain their strength from the grace of God — NEB

... strengthened by means of grace (God's favor and spiritual blessing) — Amp

not with meats,

not with foods — ABUV

Not with matters of food — Rhm

not through scruples about food—Gspd

not by the eating of food — Mof

not by special kinds of food — Wms

and not by regulations regarding food — Mon

and not on rules of diet — Phi

not from ceremonial rules about eating certain foods — Tay

rather than by ritualistic meals — Ber

which have not profited them that have been occupied therein.

which did not profit those who walked therein — ABUV

which never yet proved useful to those who followed them — Knox

which have never done any good to those who were governed by them — NEB

for those whose lives are guided by such regulations have not found them of service — TCNT

which have not benefited their adherents — RSV

from which those who place dependence upon them have derived no benefit — Wey

10. We have an altar,

We Christians have an altar — Wey

We have an altar of our own — Knox

Ours is a spiritual altar — Nor

We are not without an altar — TCNT

whereof they have no right to eat which serve the tabernacle.

from which those have no right to eat who minister in ... — Mon

whereof they that minister unto the tabernacle have no right to eat — Con

from which those priests who are servants in the tent may not take food — Bas from which the priests of the sacred tent have no . . . — NEB

at which the ministers of the Jewish tent of worship . . . — Wms

of which those that worshiped in the tabernacle have no . . . — Ber

but it is one at which those who still worship in the Tabernacle have no right to eat — TCNT

11. For the bodies of those beasts,

For the bodies of those animals — Wey

For in the case of those living creatures — Rhm

For the flesh of the beasts — Lam

whose blood is brought into the sanctuary

whose blood is brought into the holy places — ABUV

whose blood was carried . . . into the Holiest — Ber

of which the blood is carried . . . into the Holy Place — Wey

by the high priest for sin,

by the high priest as an offering for sin — ASV

through the high priest as an offering for sin — ABUV

. . . as a sin-offering — Mof

. . . as a sacrifice for sin — RSV

are burned without the camp.

are burned outside the camp — Wey

The bodies of these are burned up outside the camp — Rhm

have to be burned away from the camp — Knox

. . . outside the circle of the tents — Bas

. . . outside the limits of the camp — Amp

. . . outside the precincts of the camp — Phi

12. Wherefore Jesus also,

And for this reason Jesus also — Wey

And so Jesus, also — TCNT

That is why Jesus — Phi

and thus it was that Jesus — Knox

that he might sanctify the people with his own blood,

in order to sanctify the people by . . . — Mof

That he might hallow the people through means of . . . — Rhm

to consecrate the people by . . . — NEB

so that he might make the people holy

by his blood — Bas

to purify the People by his own blood — TCNT

suffered without the gate.

suffered outside the gate — Alf

suffered beyond the city gate — Knox

suffered death outside the city gate — Gspd

was put to death outside the walls — Bas

13. Let us go forth therefore unto him without the camp,

Now therefore let us be going forth unto him outside the camp — Rhm

Accordingly, let us go out to Him . . . — Ber

Let us then go out to him outside the circle of the tents — Bas

. . . beyond the boundaries of the camp — Phi

bearing his reproach.

bearing the same reproach as He — Wey

enduring the reproach that He endured — Wms

sharing the shame with Him — Nor

sharing the contempt that he endured — Gspd

bearing His disgrace — Ber

. . . the ignominy he bore — Knox

. . . the stigma that he bore — NEB

. . . abuse for him — RSV

14. For here have we no continuing city,

For we have not here an abiding city — ASV

for here we have no permanent city — TCNT

(for we have no lasting city here below — Mof

. . . no permanent home — NEB

. . . no fixed resting-place — Bas

but we seek one to come.

but are seeking for the one that is to be — ABUV

instead, we are seeking the future one — Ber

But unto that which is to be are we seeking our way — Rhm

but we are earnestly seeking the city that is to be — Mon

our goal is the city that is one day to be — Knox

we are looking forward to our everlasting home in heaven — Tay

15. By him therefore

Through him then — ASV
So then, through Christ — Wms
In his name, then — Mon
With Jesus' help — Tay

let us offer the sacrifice of praise to God continually,

. . . be offering up a sacrifice of praise continually unto God — Rhm
. . . at all times present a praise offering to God — Ber
. . . offer, as our sacrifice, continual praise to God — TCNT
. . . continually lay on the altar a sacrifice of praise to God — Wey
. . . always offer God the sacrifice of praise — Wms

that is, the fruit of our lips giving thanks to his name.

that is, the fruit of lips which make confession to his name — ASV
which is the fruit of lips that make confession in His name — Ber
that is, the tribute of lips which acknowledge his name — NEB
. . . the fruit of lips that celebrate his Name — Mof
. . . the speech of lips that glorify the name of God — Wms

16. But to do good and to communicate forget not:

But of the doing good and of fellowship be not forgetful — Rhm
But to do good and to distribute forget not — ABUV
Do not neglect to do good and to share what you have — RSV
And stop neglecting to do good and to be generous — Wms
And forget not to be kind and liberal — Mon
And be not unmindful of benevolence and liberality — Con
Do not forget beneficence and charity, either — Mof
. . . and contribute to the needy [of the church as embodiment and proof of fellowship] — Amp

for with such sacrifices God is well pleased.

for with sacrifices of that sort God is greatly pleased — Wey
for God is highly pleased with just such sacrifices as these — Wms

for such are the sacrifices which God approves — NEB
for such are the sacrifices which are acceptable unto God — Con

17. Obey them that have the rule over you, and submit yourselves:

Be yielding unto them who are guiding you and submit yourselves — Rhm
Continue to obey and to be submissive to your leaders — Wms
Give ear to those who are rulers over you, and do as they say — Bas
Obey your Leaders, and submit to their control — TCNT
. . . and recognize their authority — Phi
. . . and give way to them — Gspd
. . . and be willing to do what they say — Tay

for they watch for your souls,

For they are watching over your souls — Rhm
for they are attentive about . . . — Ber
for they are alive to the interests of . . . — Mof
for they on their part watch for the good of . . . — Con
for they are ever watching in defense of . . . — Wms
for they are watchful guardians of . . . — Lam
They are like men standing guard over your spiritual good — Phi

as they that must give account,

as having an account to render — Rhm
as those who are to give account — ABUV
as men who will have to give account of their trust — Wms
as men accountable for the trust — Gspd
and God will judge them on how well they do this — Tay

that they may do it with joy, and not with grief:

that they may do this with joy, and not with sighing — ABUV
so that they may be happy in their work and not groaning — Beck
that they may keep their watch with joy, and not with lamentation — Con
[Do your part to] let them do this with gladness, . . . — Amp
Have them do so joyfully and not with regrets — Ber

Make their work a joy and not a grief
— Gspd

Try to make their work a pleasure and
not a burden — Phi

Let it be a happy task for them, and
not pain and grief — NEB

Give them reason to report joyfully
about you to the Lord and not with
sorrow — Tay

for that is unprofitable for you.

because that would be of no profit to
you — Bas

That would not be to your advantage
— TCNT

which would not be to your credit —
Nor

for that would be hurtful to you — Ber

— which would be a sore loss to yourselves — Mof

for that would be the worse for you —
Gspd

18. Pray for us:

Be praying for us — Rhm

Keep on praying for me — Mon

for we trust we have a good conscience,

for we are persuaded that we have a
good conscience — ASV

For we persuade ourselves that an honourable conscience have we — Rhm

for we are confident of having a clear
conscience — Ber

for we are convinced that our conscience is clear — NEB

for we are sure that we have a good
conscience — NASB

for we are certain that our hearts are
free from the sense of sin — Bas

for I am confident that my conscience
is clean — Mof

Our conscience is clear before God —
Phi

in all things willing to live honestly.

desiring to live honorably in all things
— ASV

desiring to conduct ourselves honorably in all things — NASB

in all things wishing to deport ourselves
well — ABUV

desiring in all things to behave ourselves with seemliness — Alf

and in everything I want to live a noble
life — Wms

for we want to be honorable in all our
conduct — Nor

and I mean in every way to live an upright life — Gspd

my desire is to be perfectly straight and
clean — Mof

our one desire is always to do what is
right — NEB

19. But I beseech you the rather to do this,

And I exhort you the more exceedingly
to do this — ASV

I urge you the more earnestly to do
this — RSV

I specially urge this upon you all the
more — Wey

And more especially do I beg you to do
so — Wms

I make this request more strongly —
Bas

I beg of you to do this now specially —
Ber

I urge you all the more to pray for me
— Mof

All the more earnestly I ask for your
prayers — NEB

**that I may be restored to you the
sooner.**

That more speedily I may be restored
unto you — Rhm

that I may the more quickly be restored
to you — ABUV

so that I may be the sooner restored to
you — Ber

that I may very soon be brought back
to you — Wms

20. Now the God of peace,

Now may the God of peace — Wey

May God, the source of all peace —
TCNT

. . . the author of peace — Knox

. . . who gives us peace — Wms

**that brought again from the dead our
Lord Jesus,**

who brought up from the dead . . .
even Jesus our Lord — Wey

who has raised our Lord Jesus Christ
from the dead — Knox

who made . . . even our Lord Jesus,
come back from the dead — Bas

that great shepherd of the sheep,

the great Shepherd of the sheep — Con

that great keeper of his flock — Bas

who . . . is the Great Shepherd of God's
Sheep — TCNT

who . . . has become the great shepherd
. . . — Gspd

who . . . is now the Great Shepherd . . .
— Wms

through the blood of the everlasting covenant,

with the blood of an eternal covenant
— ASV

in virtue of the blood of an eternal covenant — ABUV

through the blood of the eternal agreement — Bas

who by His blood made an everlasting covenant — Beck

through the blood by which he ratified the everlasting agreement — Gspd

by virtue of the blood that rendered valid the . . . — TCNT

21. **Make you perfect in every good work to do his will,**

fit you out with everything good to do His will — Ber

furnish you with everything that is good for the doing of his will — Mof

equip you with every good for the doing of . . . — Wey

equip you thoroughly for the doing of his will! — Phi

make you perfect in all goodness so that you may do his will — NEB

grant you every capacity for good, to do . . . — Knox

Strengthen (complete, perfect) and make you what you ought to be, . . . — Amp

working in you that which is wellpleasing in his sight,

effecting in us that which is pleasing in His sight — Wey

Doing within us that which is well-pleasing before him — Rhm

working in us whatever is pleasing in his eyes — Bas

creating in your lives . . . what is acceptable . . . — Mof

and . . . carry out in us what will please him — Gspd

[while He Himself] works in you and accomplishes that . . . — Amp

and may he make of us what he would have us be — NEB

through Jesus Christ;

by Jesus Christ — Con

through Jesus Christ, the Messiah — Amp

through the power of Christ — Tay

to whom be glory for ever and ever. Amen.

to whom be the glory, forever and ever. Amen — ABUV

To him be the glory unto the ages of the ages! Amen! — Mon

Glory be to Him for ever and ever! Amen! — Nor

and may the glory be given to him for ever and ever. So be it — Bas

to whom glory belongs throughout all ages, Amen — Knox

22. **And I beseech you, brethren, suffer the word of exhortation:**

But I exhort you, brethren, bear with the word . . . — ASV

I appeal to you, brothers, bear with this appeal of mine — Mof

I beg you, Brothers, to bear with these words of advice — TCNT

I urge you, fellow Christians, listen patiently to what I say to encourage you — Beck

. . . to listen patiently to this message — Wms

. . . take kindly the words which I have said for your profit — Bas

. . . bear patiently with all these words of warning — Knox

for I have written a letter unto you in few words.

for I have written you but briefly — Gspd

for I have written unto you in few words — ASV

for I have written you only a short letter — Wms

For even with brief words have I sent unto you — Rhm

although I have compressed it into a short letter — Phi

23. **Know ye that our brother Timothy is set at liberty;**

Take notice that our brother Timothy has been released — NASB

You must understand that our brother Timotheus is now free — Mof

You must know that our brother Timothy has been released from prison — Gspd

You will be glad to hear that our Brother, Timothy, has been set free — TCNT

You know that our brother Timothy has been set free — Mon

with whom, if he come shortly, I will see you.

with whom, if he comes soon, I shall see you — NASB

Along with him, if he comes here shortly, I will see you — Ber

If he comes here soon, we will visit you together — TCNT

24. Salute all them that have the rule over you, and all the saints.

Salute all them who are guiding you, and all the saints — Rhm

Salute all them that are your leaders, . . . — Con

Extend our greetings to all your leaders and . . . — Ber

Greet all your leaders and all the holy people — Beck

Remember us to all your leaders and to all the Christians — Wms

Greet all the pastors and all the Christian lay-members — Nor

. . . all of (God's consecrated believers, your fellow) saints — Amp

They of Italy salute you.

They from Italy salute you — Alf

Those who come from Italy send you greetings — RSV

The Christians from Italy wish to be remembered to you — Wms

The Italian believers send you greetings — Ber

The Christians of Italy send their greeting — Phi

Those who are in Italy send you their love — Bas

25. Grace be with you all. Amen.

Favour be with you all — Rhm

Grace be with all of you. Amen — RSV

God's grace be with you all! — NEB

May God bless you all — TCNT

God's spiritual blessings be with you all. Amen — Wms

. . . Amen — so be it — Amp

THE EPISTLE OF JAMES

CHAPTER 1

1. James, a servant of God and of the Lord Jesus Christ,
. . . a slave . . . — Gspd
to the twelve tribes which are scattered abroad, greeting.
to the twelve tribes which are of the Dispersion, greeting — ASV
. . . dispersed throughout the world . . . — NEB
. . . living abroad . . . — TCNT

2. My brethren, count it all joy
. . . consider yourselves happy indeed — Knox
Reckon it nothing but joy . . . — Wey
You must find the greatest joy . . . — Gspd
when ye fall into divers temptations;
. . . manifold temptations — ASV
. . . various trials — RSV
. . . trials of every sort — Knox
whenever you find yourselves surrounded by various temptations — Wey

3. Knowing this, that the trying of your faith
knowing that the proving of your faith — ASV
. . . the testing . . . — TCNT
worketh patience.
produces steadfastness — RSV
leads to steadfastness — Gspd
develops endurance — TCNT
breeds fortitude — NEB

4. But let patience[1] have her perfect work,
. . . have mature work — Rhm
. . . finish its work — Beck
. . . do a thorough work — Amp
that ye may be perfect and entire,
. . . mature and complete — ABUV
. . . fully developed and perfectly equipped — Wms
so that you may be [people] perfectly and fully developed — Amp
wanting nothing.
lacking in nothing — ASV
without any defect — Gspd
in no respect deficient — TCNT
In nothing coming short — Rhm

5. If any of you lack wisdom, let him ask of God,
But if any of you is coming short of wisdom . . . — Rhm
. . . is deficient in . . . — Gspd

that giveth to all men liberally, and upbraideth not;
who gives freely to everyone without reproaches — TCNT
who gives generously and does not reproach one with it afterwards — Gspd
who gives with open hand — Wey
and it shall be given him.

6. But let him ask in faith, nothing wavering.
. . . with confidence, never doubting — TCNT
. . . nothing doubting — ASV
. . . with never a doubt — Mof
For he that wavereth is like a wave of the sea
. . . is like the surge of the sea — ASV
. . . the surf . . . — NASB
. . . the billowing sea — Gspd
driven with the wind and tossed.
driven and blown about by the wind — Gspd
whirled and swayed by the wind — Mof

7. For let not that man think that he shall receive any thing of the Lord.
Such a man must not expect to get anything from the Lord — Gspd
A person of that sort must not expect to receive anything from the Lord — Wey
that man need not imagine he will get anything from the Lord — Mof
Such a man should not expect to get anything from the Lord — Beck

8. A double minded man is unstable in all his ways.
— an irresolute person like him, who is uncertain about everything he does — Gspd
being a man of two minds, undecided in every step he takes — Wey
double-minded creature that he is, wavering at every turn! — Mof
He's half-hearted—wavering in everything he does — Beck

9. Let the brother of low degree
. . . in humble circumstances — Mon
. . . of low position — Bas
But let the lowly brother — ABUV

[1]See verse 3.

rejoice in that he is exalted:
glory in his high estate — ASV
be glad that he is lifted up — Bas
rejoice when he is promoted — Wey
rejoice in his exalted station as a Christian — Wms

10. **But the rich, in that he is made low:**
    . . . at being reduced in circumstances — Gspd
    . . . in his humiliation — Mon
    . . . in being humbled — Amp
    because as the flower of the grass he shall pass away.
    . . . will disappear — NEB

11. **For the sun is no sooner risen**
    once the sun is up — NEB
    — up comes the sun — Mof
    with a burning heat,
    . . . scorching wind — ASV
    . . . scorching heat — Gspd
    but it withereth the grass, and the flower thereof falleth,
    and dries up the grass, and the flower withers — Gspd
    . . . drops off — Mof
    and the grace of the fashion of it perisheth:
    and the beauty of its appearance perishes — ABUV
    . . . its lovely appearance is ruined — Ber
    . . . all its beauty is gone — Gspd
    so also shall the rich man fade away in his ways.
    That is the way the rich man will fade and die in the midst of his pursuits — Gspd

12. **Blessed is the man that endureth temptation:**
    Happy the man who endureth temptation! — Rhm
    . . . remains firm under . . . — TCNT
    . . . endures under trial — Mof
    . . . perseveres under trial — NASB
    . . . endures trial — Gspd
    for when he is tried,
    for when he hath been approved—ASV
    For once his testing is complete — Phi
    for when he has stood the test — Wey
    When he has proved his worth — Knox
    he shall receive the crown of life, which the Lord hath promised to them that love him.
    . . . which God has promised to those that love him — RSV

13. **Let no man say when he is tempted,**
    . . . passing through a trial — Wey
    . . . under trial or temptation — NEB
    . . . tested — Bas
    I am tempted of God:
    It is God who is tempting me — TCNT
    My temptation comes from God — Mof
    for God cannot be tempted with evil,
    . . . is incapable of being tempted by evil — Wey
    . . . cannot be tempted to do wrong — TCNT
    . . . never wants to do wrong — Tay
    neither tempteth he any man:
    and he himself tempteth no man — ASV
    and he himself puts no man to such a test — Bas
    does not himself tempt any one — TCNT

14. **But every man is tempted, when he is drawn away of his own lust, and enticed.**
    . . . when he is drawn away, enticed and baited by his own evil desire . . . — Amp
    . . . as he is beguiled and lured by his own desire — Mof
    . . . when he is allured by his own evil desire and enticed by a bait — Wms
    A man is in every case tempted by his own passions — allured and enticed by them — TCNT

15. **Then when lust hath conceived, it bringeth forth sin:**
    Then Passion conceives and gives birth to Sin — TCNT
    Then desire conceives . . . — Gspd
    and sin, when it is finished,
    . . . when it has run its course — Nor
    . . . when fully matured — Wey
    . . . on reaching maturity — TCNT
    bringeth forth death.
    gives birth to death — Wey
    breeds . . . — NEB
    produces . . . — Beck
    means . . . — Phi

16. **Do not err, my beloved brethren.**
    Be not deceived . . . — ASV
    Be not led astray . . . — ABUV
    Make no mistake about this . . . — Mof
    Do not be misled, my dear brothers — Gspd

17. **Every good gift and every perfect gift is from above,**

All good giving and every perfect gift comes from above — NEB

Every beneficent gift and every perfect present . . . — Ber

and cometh down from the Father of lights,

. . . the Father of the heavenly lights — Mof

. . . the Father, who is the source of all light — Wey

with whom is no variableness,

with whom can be no variation — ASV

about whom there is no variation — Gspd

In Him there is no variation — Wey

who is himself never subject to change — TCNT

who knows no change of rising or of setting — Mof

neither shadow of turning.

neither shadow that is cast by turning — ASV

nor shadow of eclipse — Mon

who casts no shadow on the earth — Mof

18. **Of his own will begat he us with the word of truth,**

Of his own accord he brought us into being through the message of truth — Gspd

Of his set purpose . . . — NEB

Voluntarily . . . — Ber

that we should be a kind of firstfruits of his creatures.

that we might be in a sense the first fruits of all the things which he has made — Bas

and we became, as it were, the first children of His new family — Tay

. . . so to speak, the first specimens of his new creation — Phi

. . . as it were, an earnest of still further creation — TCNT

19. **Wherefore, my beloved brethren,**

Ye know this, my beloved brethren — ASV

Know this . . . — RSV

You must understand this . . . — Gspd

Of that you may be certain, my friends — NEB

Mark this . . . — TCNT

let every man be swift to hear, slow to speak, slow to wrath:

. . . quick to listen but slow to use his

tongue and slow to lose his temper — Phi

. . . quick to listen, slow to talk, slow to be angry — Mof

20. **For the wrath of man worketh not the righteousness of God.**

A man's anger does not accomplish God's righteousness — Wey

. . . does not further the righteous purpose of God — Mon

. . . cannot promote the justice of God — NEB

. . . does not produce the uprightness God wishes — Gspd

human anger does not promote divine righteousness — Mof

Anger is not the way to arrive at the justice God demands — Nor

An angry man doesn't do what is right before God — Beck

man's temper is never the means of the achieving of God's true goodness — Phi

21. **Wherefore lay apart all filthiness and superfluity of naughtiness,**

Wherefore putting away all filthiness and overflowing of wickedness — ASV

So strip yourselves of everything that soils you, and of every evil growth — Gspd

Therefore, have done with all filthiness and whatever wickedness still remains — TCNT

Away then with all that is sordid, and the malice that hurries to excess — NEB

Ridding yourselves, therefore, of all that is vile and of the excesses of malice — Wey

and receive with meekness the engrafted word,

. . . the implanted word — RSV

and in a humble spirit receive that Message which has been implanted in your hearts — TCNT

make a soil of humble modesty for the Word which roots itself inwardly — Mof

which is able to save your souls.

with power to . . . — Mof

22. **But be ye doers of the word,**

Keep on obeying this message — Wms

Act on the word — Mof

Put that Message into practice — TCNT

and not hearers only,
do not merely listen to it — TCNT
instead of merely listening to it — Mof
deceiving your own selves.
deluding . . . — ASV
for that would be to mislead yourselves
— NEB

23. **For if any be a hearer of the word,**
For when any one listens to it — TCNT
The man who simply hears — Phi
and not a doer,
and does not practice it — TCNT
without obeying it — Wms
and does nothing about it — Phi
**he is like unto a man beholding his
natural face in a glass:**
he is like a man looking at his own
face in a mirror — TCNT
. . . who carefully looks at his own . . .
— Wey
. . . who glances at his natural face . . .
— Mof
. . . who looks in a mirror at the face
nature gave him — NEB
. . . the face he was born with . . . —
Knox

24. **For he beholdeth himself, and goeth
his way,**
For he thoughtfully observes himself,
then goes off —-Amp
For he beheld himself, and has gone
away — ABUV
He glances at himself and goes away
— NEB
He looks at himself and then goes off
— Gspd
. . . takes a look at . . . — Ber
For once he has looked at himself and
gone away — NASB
and straightway forgetteth
and at once forgets — Mof
. . . immediately forgets — Gspd
. . . in a short time he has no memory
— Bas
what manner of man he was.
what he was like — Mof
what he looked like — Gspd
what kind of person he was — NASB

25. **But whoso looketh into**
. . . he who looks into — ABUV
. . . looks carefully into — TCNT
. . . looks closely into — Wey
. . . looks seriously into — Ber
. . . gazes into — Mof

the perfect law of liberty,
. . . faultless law of freedom — Mof
. . . flawless law that makes men free —
Gspd
and continueth therein,
. . . perseveres — RSV
. . . keeps on looking — Wms
. . . continues to do so — TCNT
. . . makes a habit of so doing — Phi
. . . lives in its company — NEB
. . . abides by it — NASB
. . . perseveres in looking into it —
Amp
he being not a forgetful hearer,
proving himself to be no forgetful list-
ener — Mof
not listening to it and then forgetting
it — TCNT
so that he does not just listen and then
forget — Gspd
but a doer of the work,
but obeys and acts upon it — Gspd
but an active agent — Mof
this man shall be blessed in his deed.
. . . in his doing — ASV
. . . in the very act of obedience—Wey
. . . in his practice — Ber

26. **If any man among you seem to be
religious,**
. . . thinketh himself to be . . . — ASV
. . . thinks he is . . . — Gspd
. . . appears to be . . . — TCNT
and bridleth not his tongue,
without bridling his own . . . — Ber
yet does not bridle . . . — TCNT
but if he has no control over his own
. . . — NEB
but deceiveth his own heart,
. . . imposes upon his own conscience
— TCNT
he is just fooling himself — Tay
this man's religion is vain.
. . . of no value — Bas
. . . futile — Mof
. . . worthless — Wms

27. **Pure religion and undefiled before God
and the Father**
The religion which is pure and stainless
in the sight of our God and Father
— Wey
Pure, unsoiled religion in the judgment
of . . . — Mof
A pure and undefiled religious service
before God and the Father — ABUV
The religious observance which is pure

and spotless in the eyes of God our Father — TCNT

is this, To visit the fatherless and widows

. . . to care for . . . — Mof

. . . to look after orphans and . . . — Gspd

. . . to go to the help of . . . — NEB

in their affliction,

. . . distress — NEB

. . . trouble — TCNT

. . . time of trouble — Wey

and to keep himself unspotted from the world.

. . . untarnished by . . . — NEB

. . . uncontaminated by . . . — TCNT

. . . unstained by . . . — Gspd

. . . free from the smut of . . . — Ber

CHAPTER 2

1. **My brethren, have not the faith of our Lord Jesus Christ, the Lord of glory, with respect of persons.**

   My brethren, do not hold your faith in our glorious Lord Jesus Christ with an attitude of personal favoritism — NASB

   My brothers, stop trying to maintain your faith in our Lord Jesus Christ, the glorious presence of God on earth, along with acts of partiality to certain ones — Wms

   Brethren, you believe that all glory belongs to our Lord Jesus Christ; do not combine this faith of yours with flattery of human greatness — Knox

   My brethren, while holding to your faith in our Lord Jesus Christ who is the Glory, do not exhibit partiality — Wey

   . . . the King of Glory . . . — Nor

   My Brothers, believing as you do in our Lord Jesus Christ, who reigns in glory, you must never show snobbery — NEB

   My Brothers, are you really trying to combine faith in Jesus Christ, our glorified Lord with the worship of rank? — TCNT

2. **For if there come unto your assembly a man with a gold ring,**

   . . . synagogue . . . — Rhm

   . . . place of worship . . . — NEB

   . . . congregation . . . — Nor

   . . . church . . . — Tay

   in goodly apparel,

   . . . splendid apparel — Amp

   . . . fine clothing — ASV

   . . . handsome clothes — Mof

   and there come in also a poor man in vile raiment;

   And there enter a destitute man also in soiled clothing — Rhm

   . . . in dirty clothes — NASB

   . . . in shabby clothes — TCNT

3. **And ye have respect to him that weareth the gay clothing,**

   and you are deferential to the man who is wearing grand clothes — TCNT

   . . . you pay special attention to the well-dressed man — NEB

   and say unto him, Sit thou here in a good place;

   . . . Sit here; this is a good place — Wey

   . . . There is a good seat for you here — TCNT

   and say to the poor, Stand thou there,

   . . . You must stand — TCNT

   or sit here under my footstool:

   or, Sit at my feet — RSV

   . . . on the floor at my feet — Wey

4. **Are ye not then partial in yourselves,**

   do ye not make distinctions among yourselves — ASV

   are you not discriminating among your own? — Ber

   Are you not drawing distinctions in your minds? — Mof

   is it not plain that in your hearts you have little faith — Wey

   is not this to doubt within yourselves? — Alf

   and are become judges of evil thoughts?

   . . . evil-thinking judges — ABUV

   . . . prejudiced judges — TCNT

   and judge by false standards — NEB

   . . . prove to be critics with evil motives — Wms

5. **Hearken, my beloved brethren,**

   Listen . . . — RSV

   Hath not God chosen

   did not God choose — ASV

   the poor of this world rich in faith,

   them that are poor in this world to be rich in faith — ASV

   . . . to be rich through their faith — TCNT

poor men, whose only wealth was their
faith — Phi

and heirs of the kingdom
and to possess the Kingdom — TCNT
**which he hath promised to them that
love him?**

6. But ye have despised the poor.
. . . dishonored the poor man — ASV
But you humiliate the poor — Gspd
. . . insult . . . — TCNT
But you [in contrast] have insulted —
humiliated, dishonored and shown
your contempt for — the poor —
Amp

Do not rich men oppress you,
Yet is it not the rich who grind you
down? — Wey
. . . lord it over you — Mof
. . . domineer you — Ber

**and draw you before the judgment
seats?**
Are not they the people who drag you
into the law courts — Wey
. . . into courts of justice — Rhm

**7. Do not they blaspheme that worthy
name**
. . . the honorable name — ASV
. . . defame the noble name — Rhm
. . . speak evil of . . . — Wey
. . . pour contempt on . . . — NEB

by the which ye are called?
which hath been invoked upon you —
Rhm
. . . has been bestowed upon you —
TCNT
by which God has claimed you — NEB

**8. If ye fulfil the royal law according to
the scripture,**
If ye are indeed fulfilling a royal law
. . . — Rhm
. . . the supreme law . . . — Gspd
. . . the sovereign law . . . — NEB
. . . laid down by scripture — Mof

**Thou shalt love thy neighbour as thy-
self, ye do well:**
. . . you are doing well — TCNT
. . . that is excellent — NEB
. . . well and good — Mof
. . . all is well — Phi

**9. But if ye have respect to persons,[2] ye
commit sin, and are convinced of the
law as transgressors.**

**10. For whosoever shall keep the whole
law, and yet offend in one point, he is
guilty of all.**

. . . but fails in a single point, has become guilty of violating all — Wey
. . . and only makes a single slip, is
guilty of everything — Mof
. . . except to slip in a single instance,
is guilty of breaking it all — Wms
. . . becomes guilty in every respect —
Ber
. . . is liable to all its penalties — Knox

**11. For he that said, Do not commit adul-
tery, said also, Do not kill.**
**Now if thou commit no adultery, yet
if thou kill,**
Now if thou dost not commit adultery,
but killest — ASV
**thou art become a transgressor of the
law.**

12. So speak ye, and so do,
You must continue talking and acting
— Wms
**as they that shall be judged by the
law of liberty.**
as men that are to be judged by a law
of liberty — ASV
. . . through means of a law of freedom
— Rhm
. . . under a law of freedom — NEB
. . . a law that brings liberty — Beck
. . . the law which makes free . . . — Bas
. . . the law that treats men as free —
Gspd

**13. For he shall have judgment without
mercy, that hath shewed no mercy;**
For judgment is without mercy to him
that hath showed no mercy — ASV
For he who shows no mercy will incur
judgement without mercy — Wey
For there will be justice without mercy
for him who has not acted mercifully — TCNT
and mercy rejoiceth against judgment.
. . . glorieth . . . — ASV
. . . boasteth over . . . — Rhm
. . . triumphs over . . . — RSV
. . . glories in the face of . . . — Mon

**14. What doth it profit, my brethren,
though a man say he hath faith, and
have not works?**
What good is it, my brethren, if a man
professes to have faith, and yet his
actions do not correspond — Wey

---

[2]See verse 1.

My brothers, what is the use of anyone declaring that he has faith, if he has no deeds to show — Mof

My Brothers, what is the good of a man's saying that he has faith, if he does not prove it by actions — TCNT

What is the use, my brothers, for anyone to say he has faith, if he fails to act on it — Ber

can faith save him?

Can [such] faith save [his soul] — Amp

can that faith save him — ASV

Can such faith save him — TCNT

15. If a brother or sister be naked,

... is ill-clad — Mof

... be in want of clothes — TCNT

and destitute of daily food,

or lack daily food — Wey

and has no food for the day — Wms

16. And one of you say unto them, Depart in peace, be ye warmed and filled;

... Fare you well; keep yourselves warm and well fed — Wey

... Good-bye, keep warm and have plenty to eat — Gspd

... Go, and peace be with you; find warmth and food for yourselves — TCNT

... Blessings on you, keep warm, eat until you have plenty — Wms

... Good luck to you, keep yourselves warm, and have plenty to eat — NEB

notwithstanding ye give them not those things which are needful to the body;

without giving them the necessaries of life — Gspd

and yet you do not supply their bodily needs — Wey

what doth it profit?

what good does it do — Gspd

what good would it be to them — TCNT

what is the use of that — Wey

17. Even so faith, if it hath not works,

So also faith, if it is unaccompanied by obedience — Wey

In just the same way faith, if not followed by actions — TCNT

... if it does not lead to action — NEB

Exactly so the faith that issues in no works — Ber

is dead, being alone.

is dead in itself — ASV

is, by itself, a lifeless thing — TCNT

18. Yea, a man may say, Thou hast faith, and I have works:

But some one may object, Here is one who claims to have faith and another who points to his deeds — NEB

Some one indeed may say, You are a man of faith, and I am a man of action — TCNT

shew me thy faith without thy works, and I will shew thee my faith by my works.

show me thy faith apart from thy works and I by my works will show thee my faith — ASV

Then show me your faith, I reply, apart from any actions, and I will show you my faith by my actions — TCNT

prove to me your faith apart from corresponding actions and I will prove mine to you by my actions — Wey

19. Thou believest that there is one God;

Thou believest that God is one — ASV

It is a part of your faith, is it not, that there is one God? — TCNT

thou doest well: the devils also believe, and tremble.

Good; yet even the demons have that faith, and tremble at the thought — TCNT

Excellent! The devils have faith like that, and it makes them tremble — NEB

and you are quite right: evil spirits also believe this and shudder — Wey

20. But wilt thou know, O vain man,

But do you want proof, my senseless friend — Gspd

Do you want to be shown, you foolish fellow — RSV

But do you want to be convinced ... — Mon

Now do you really want to understand ... — TCNT

But, idle boaster, are you willing to be taught — Wey

that faith without works is dead?

... barren — RSV

that faith apart from [good] works is inactive and ineffective and worthless — Amp

... apart from obedience is worthless — Wey

... without good deeds amounts to nothing — Gspd

... divorced from good deeds is barren — NEB

Faith that does not result in good deeds is not real faith — Tay

21. Was not Abraham our father justified by works, when he had offered Isaac his son upon the altar?

Was not our forefather Abraham shown to be upright by his good deeds, namely, by offering Isaac his son upon the altar — Wms

22. Seest thou how faith wrought with his works,

You see that faith was active along with his works — RSV

You see how, in his case, faith and actions went together — TCNT

You notice that his faith was co-operating with his actions — Wey

Surely you can see that faith was at work in his actions — NEB

You see his faith was active with works — Beck

You see that faith was spurring him on to do good works — Nor

and by works was faith made perfect?

and by works reached its goal — Beck

And by his works did his faith become full grown — Rhm

and that by these actions the integrity of his faith was fully proved — NEB

faith found its highest expression in good deeds — Gspd

faith was completed by deeds — Mof

and his faith was completed and reached its supreme expression [when he implemented it] by [good] works — Amp

23. And the scripture was fulfilled which saith, Abraham believed God,

... Abraham believed — adhered to, trusted in and relied on — God — Amp

and it was imputed unto him for righteousness:

and it was reckoned unto him ... — ASV

and it was credited to him for uprightness — Wms

and that was regarded by God as righteousness — TCNT

and this was accounted to him for righteousness — Amp

and he was called the Friend of God.

24. Ye see then how that by works a man is justified,

You see, then, that it is as a result of his actions that a man is pronounced righteous — TCNT

You see that a man is shown to be upright by his good deeds — Wms

and not by faith only.

not simply by what he believes — Mof

and not merely by his faith — Wms

25. Likewise also was not Rahab the harlot justified by works, when she had received the messengers,

The same is true of Rahab the prostitute also. Was she not justified by her action in welcoming the messengers into her house — NEB

Was not it the same with the prostitute, Rahab? Was not it as the result of her actions that she was pronounced righteous, after she had welcomed the messengers — TCNT

Was not even Rahab the prostitute shown to be upright by her good deeds, namely by entertaining the scouts — Wms

and had sent them out another way?

and sending them away by a different route — NEB

and by another way urged them forth — Rhm

and hastened them away by a different road — TCNT

26. For as the body without the spirit is dead,

... apart from the spirit ... — ASV

... when separated from ... — Nor

... is lifeless — Wey

Exactly as a body is dead without a spirit — TCNT

so faith without works is dead also.

so faith divorced from deeds is lifeless as a corpse — NEB

so faith is dead without actions—TCNT

CHAPTER 3

1. My brethren, be not many masters,

Be not many of you teachers, my brethren — ASV

Let not many of you become teachers

... — RSV

My brothers, do not crowd in to be teachers — Mof

My brothers, not many of you should

become teachers — NEB

knowing that we shall receive the greater condemnation.

. . . incur a stricter judgment — NASB

. . . be judged by a more severe standard — TCNT

. . . be judged with special strictness — Mof

2. For in many things we offend all.

. . . we all sin — ABUV

. . . we all stumble — ASV

For we all go wrong in a number of things — Bas

We all make many a slip — Mof

We often make mistakes, every one of us — TCNT

If any man offend not in word,

If any one sins not in word — ABUV

but whoever avoids slips of speech — Mof

Any one who does not make mistakes when speaking — TCNT

the same is a perfect man, and able also to bridle the whole body.

The same is a mature man . . . — Rhm

. . . has a character that is fully developed and is able to control his whole body as well — Gspd

3. Behold, we put bits in the horses' mouths, that they may obey us;

Now if we put the horses' bridles into their mouths that they may obey us — ASV

and we turn about their whole body.

we turn about their whole body also — ASV

we control the rest of their bodies also — TCNT

we can direct their whole body — NEB

4. Behold also the ships, which though they be so great, and are driven of fierce winds,

. . . rough winds — ASV

. . . strong gales — Wey

. . . violent winds — Wms

Look at the ships also; though they are so great and are driven by strong winds — RSV

yet are they turned about with a very small helm,

. . . controlled by a very small rudder — TCNT

. . . steered with . . . — Wey

withersoever the governor listeth.

whither the impulse of the steersman willeth — ASV

wherever the will of the pilot directs — RSV

in whatever direction the will of the man at the helm determines — Wey

wherever the mind of the steersman chooses — Mof

on whatever course the helmsman chooses — NEB

5. Even so the tongue is a little member, and boasteth great things.

So the tongue is a small organ and can talk big — Ber

So the tongue is a small member of the body, but it can boast of great exploits — Mof

. . . but can boast of great achievements — Wms

So is it with the tongue. Small as it is, it is a great boaster — TCNT

So with the tongue. It is a small member but it can make huge claims — NEB

Behold, how great a matter a little fire kindleth!

. . . how much wood is kindled by how small a fire! — ASV

Lo! how small a fire kindleth how great a forest — Rhm

What a great forest a spark will set on fire! — Gspd

Remember how a mere spark may set a vast forest in flames — Wey

Think how tiny a spark may set the largest forest ablaze! — TCNT

What a huge stack of timber can be set ablaze by the tiniest spark! — NEB

6. And the tongue is a fire, a world of iniquity; so is the tongue among our members, that it defileth the whole body,

And the tongue is in effect a fire. It represents among our members the world with all its wickedness; it pollutes our whole being — NEB

And the tongue is like a spark. Among the members of our body it proves itself a very world of mischief; it contaminates the whole body—TCNT

And the tongue is a fire. The tongue is an unrighteous world among our members, staining the whole body — RSV

... and takes its place among the parts of our bodies as a world of evil ... — Wms

and setteth on fire the course of nature;
... wheel of nature — ASV
... wheel of our natural life — Rhm
... the cycle of nature — RSV
it sets the wheels of life on fire — TCNT
setting fire to the round circle of existence — Mof

and it is set on fire of hell.
with a flame fed from hell — Mof

7. **For every kind of beasts, and of birds, and of serpents, and of things in the sea, is tamed, and hath been tamed of mankind:**
... are tameable, and actually have been tamed by man — TCNT
... by human genius — Amp

8. **But the tongue can no man tame; it is an unruly evil,**
... a restless evil — RSV
... restless mischief — Alf
... an irreconcilable evil — Gspd
... an intractable evil — NEB
... an evil incapable of being quieted — Wms

full of deadly poison.
full of deadly venom — Mof
It is charged with deadly poison — TCNT

9. **Therewith bless we God, even the Father;**
With it we continually bless our Lord and Father — Mon
We use it to sing the praises of our Lord and Father — NEB

and therewith curse we men,
and we use it to invoke curses upon our fellow-men — NEB

which are made after the similitude of God.
... likeness of God — ASV
... image ... — Mon
who are made in God's likeness — NEB

10. **Out of the same mouth proceedeth blessing and cursing. My brethren, these things ought not so to be.**
... This is not right, my brothers — Gspd
... this is the sort of thing that never ought to happen! — Phi
... it ought not to be like this — Wms

11. **Doth a fountain send forth at the same place**
... from the same opening — ASV
... from the same crevice — Gspd
sweet water and bitter?

12. **Can a fig tree, my brethren, bear olive berries? either a vine, figs? so can no fountain both yield salt water and fresh.**
... neither can salt water yield sweet — ASV
... No, nor can a brackish well give good water — TCNT

13. **Who is a wise man and endued with knowledge among you?**
Who among you is wise and learned — Mof
Who among you claims to be wise and intelligent — TCNT
Who among you is wise or clever — NEB
Which of you is a wise and well-instructed man — Wey

let him shew out of a good conversation
let him show by his good life — ASV
... out of his good conduct — Alf

his works with meekness of wisdom.
his conduct to be guided by a wise gentleness — Wey
that what he does is done in the humility of wisdom — Gspd
that his good deeds are done in humility which wisdom prompts — Wms

14. **But if ye have bitter envying and strife in your hearts,**
But if ye have bitter jealousy and faction ... — ASV
But while you harbour envy and bitterness and a spirit of rivalry in your hearts — TCNT
But if ye have bitter jealousy and party spirit in your hearts — ABUV

glory not, and lie not against the truth.
do not be arrogant and so lie against the truth — NASB
do not pride yourselves on that and be false to the truth — Mof
do not boast or lie to the detriment of the Truth — TCNT
do not speak boastfully and falsely, in defiance of the truth — Wey
stop being proud of it and stop being false to the standard of truth — Wms

15. This wisdom descendeth not from above, but is earthly, sensual, devilish.

That is not the wisdom which comes down from above: it belongs to earth, to the unspiritual nature and to evil spirits — Wey

. . . it comes from this world, from your own lower nature, even from the devil — Phi

. . . it is earth-bound, sensual, demonic — NEB

16. For where envying and strife is,

For where jealousy and faction are — ASV

. . . envying and rivalry . . . — Alf

. . . jealousy and party spirit . . . — ABUV

. . . jealous and selfish ambition . . . — NEB

For wherever you find jealousy and rivalry — Phi

there is confusion and every evil work.

. . . confusion and every vile deed — ASV

. . . unrest and every vile deed — Wey

. . . anarchy and every ignoble deed — Rhm

. . . disorder and all kinds of base actions — TCNT

. . . disharmony and all other kinds of evil — Phi

17. But the wisdom that is from above is

first pure, then peaceable, gentle,

. . . reasonable — Rhm

. . . forbearing — Mof

. . . courteous — Wey

and easy to be intreated,

. . . open to reason — RSV

. . . conciliatory — Mof

. . . compliant — Wey

. . . easily persuaded — Alf

. . . willing to yield — Gspd

. . . ready to be convinced — Knox

full of mercy and good fruits,

rich in compassion and good deeds — TCNT

. . . kind actions — Wey

without partiality, and without hypocrisy.

. . . variance . . . — ASV

— free from doubts, wavering and insincerity — Amp

free from partiality and insincerity — TCNT

unambiguous, straightforward — Mof

18. And the fruit of righteousness is sown in peace

The harvest uprightness yields must be sown in peace — Gspd

The harvest uprightness yields is grown from the seed of peace — Wms

of them that make peace.

by peacemakers — Gspd

by those who work for peace — TCNT

CHAPTER 4

1. From whence come wars and fightings among you?

But what about the feuds and struggles that exist among you — Phi

What is the cause of the fighting and quarrelling that goes on among you — TCNT

Where do the conflicts, where do the wrangles come from, in your society — Mof

come they not hence, even of your lusts that war in your members?

Is it not the passions which are ever at war in your natures — Wey

Is it not to be found in the desires which are always at war within you — TCNT

2. Ye lust, and have not: ye kill, and desire to have,

. . . ye kill, and covet — ASV

You crave, yet do not obtain. You murder and rage — TCNT

and cannot obtain:

yet cannot gain your end — TCNT

ye fight and war, yet ye have not, because ye ask not.

you wrangle and fight — you miss what you want because you do not ask God for it — Mof

you fight and you battle and you do not possess, because — you do not pray — Ber

You quarrel and fight. You do not obtain, because you do not ask — TCNT

3. Ye ask, and receive not, because ye ask amiss,

You ask and fail to get . . . — Wms

. . . because you ask it with wrong motives — Gspd

... because you ask for it with ill intent
— Knox

... because you pray wrongly — Wey

that ye may consume it upon your lusts.

... spend it on your pleasures — ASV

your object being to waste on your pleasures what you acquire — Wey

4. Ye adulterers and adulteresses, know ye not

Ye adulteresses, know ye not — ASV

Unfaithful people! Do you not know — TCNT

You faithless wives! ... — Wms

that the friendship of the world is enmity with God?

that to be friends with the world means to be at enmity with God — TCNT

whosoever therefore will be a friend of the world

... determines to be a friend of the world — Ber

... is bent on being friendly with the world — Wey

... chooses to be friends with the world — TCNT

is the enemy of God.

makes himself an enemy of God—RSV

doth constitute himself ... — Rhm

turns enemy to ... — Mof

takes his stand as God's enemy — Ber

5. Do ye think that the scripture saith in vain,

Or do you think that the Scripture speaks to no purpose — NASB

Do you suppose that it is to no purpose that the Scripture says — Wey

What, do you consider this an idle word of Scripture? — Mof

The spirit that dwelleth in us lusteth to envy?

Doth the spirit which he made to dwell in us long unto envying? — ASV

The Spirit that he placed in us jealously desireth us — Alf

... He yearns for the Spirit [to be welcome] ... — Amp

The Spirit which He has caused to dwell in us yearns jealously over us — Wey

The Spirit which God has put in our hearts has a strong desire for us — Bas

The Spirit he made to dwell in us has jealous longings — ABUV

He yearns jealously for the spirit he set within us — Mof

He yearns jealously over the Spirit he has put in our hearts — Gspd

The spirit which God implanted in man turns towards envious desires — NEB

6. But he giveth more grace.

Howbeit he giveth greater favour — Rhm

And He shows more abundant grace — Wey

And yet the grace he gives is stronger — NEB

Wherefore he saith,

Wherefore the scripture saith — ASV

God resisteth the proud, but giveth grace unto the humble.

God sets Himself against the haughty, but to the lowly He shows grace — Wey

God opposes haughty persons, but he blesses humble-minded ones—Gspd

God ever resists the proud; but to the humble he gives grace continually — Mon

God against the haughty arrayeth himself, Whereas unto the lowly he giveth favour — Rhm

7. Submit yourselves therefore to God.

Be subject therefore unto God — ASV

Range yourselves therefore under God — Rhm

Resist the devil, and he will flee from you.

Stand firm against the devil . . . — Knox

Stand up to the devil and he will turn and run — NEB

8. Draw nigh to God, and he will draw nigh to you.

... near ... near ... — Alf

come close ... come close ... — Knox

Cleanse your hands, ye sinners;

Wash your hands, you sinners!—Gspd

Make your hands clean, you sinners — TCNT

and purify your hearts, ye double-minded.

and your hearts pure, you vacillating men! — TCNT

put away deceit from your hearts, you false in mind — Bas

you who are double-minded, see that your motives are pure — NEB

9. Be afflicted, and mourn, and weep:

Sorrow, and mourn, and weep — ABUV

Be wretched and mourn and weep — RSV

Be miserable and lament and weep — Rhm

... be deeply penitent and grieve, even weep [over your disloyalty] — Amp

Grieve, mourn, and lament! — TCNT

... weep aloud — Gspd

let your laughter be turned to mourning,

Let your laughter into lamentation be turned — Rhm

Let there be sadness instead of laughter — Tay

and your joy to heaviness.

and your happiness to gloom! — TCNT

and your gaiety into gloom — NEB

... humiliation — Alf

... dejection — RSV

... depression — Mof

10. Humble yourselves in the sight of the Lord,

Be made low in presence of the Lord — Rhm

and he shall lift you up.

... exalt you — ASV

11. Speak not evil one of another, brethren.

Do not malign one another ... — Ber

Do not disparage ... — TCNT

Stop talking against ... — Wms

He that speaketh evil of his brother, and judgeth his brother,

Whosoever is in the haibt of talking against his brother or criticizing his brother — Wms

speaketh evil of the law, and judgeth the law: but if thou judge the law, thou art not a doer of the law, but a judge.

... you are not a practicer but a critic of the law — Wms

... thou art setting thyself up to be its censor, instead of obeying it — Knox

12. There is one lawgiver, who is able to save and to destroy:

One only is lawgiver and judge, even he who is ... — ASV

... he who has power of salvation and destruction — Bas

who art thou that judgest another?

but who art thou that judgest thy neighbor — ASV

who are you to judge your neighbor — Lam

But who are you to be your neighbour's judge — Bas

13. Go to now, ye that say,

Come now ... — RSV

To day or to morrow we will go into such a city, and continue there a year, and buy and sell, and get gain:

To-day or to-morrow we will go into this city, and spend a year there, and trade, and get gain — ASV

... and carry on a successful business — Wey

... go into business and make money — Wms

... and make profit by trading — Knox

14. Whereas ye know not what shall be on the morrow.

you who know nothing about to-morrow! — Mof

when you do not know what will happen to-morrow — Wey

although you do not have the slightest knowledge of tomorrow — Wms

For what is your life? It is even a vapour,

What is your life? For ye are a vapor — ASV

... For you are but a mist — TCNT

Your life, what is it? You are no more than a mist — NEB

that appeareth for a little time, and then vanisheth away.

seen for a little while and then dispersing — NEB

visible for a little while and then dissolving into thin air — Phi

which shows for a little moment and then must vanish into nothing — Knox

appearing for a little while and then disappearing — TCNT

15. For that ye ought to say, If the Lord will, we shall live, and do this, or that.

You ought instead to say, If the Lord is willing, we shall live and we shall do this or that [thing] — Amp

16. But now ye rejoice in your boastings:

But now ye glory in your vauntings — ASV

But, as it is, you pride yourselves on your pretensions — Gspd

But, as it is, you are constantly boasting presumptuously! — TCNT

But here you are, boasting in your proud pretensions! — Mof

As it is, you boast in your arrogance — RSV

But now you are glorying in these insolent boastings — Mon

all such rejoicing is evil.

All such pride is wrong — Gspd

All such boasting is wicked — TCNT

17. **Therefore to him that knoweth to do good,**

He, then, who knows what is right — TCNT

The principle is this, that whosoever knows what is right to do — Nor

and doeth it not, to him it is sin.

but fails to do it ... — TCNT

... he is guilty of sin — Gspd

CHAPTER 5

1. **Go to now, ye rich men, weep and howl**

Come now, you rich, weep and howl — RSV

Listen to me, you rich men, weep and wail — TCNT

And now, you plutocrats, is the time for you to weep and moan — Phi

for your miseries that shall come upon you.

for your hardships which are coming on you — Rhm

over the miseries — the woes — that are surely coming upon you — Amp

over the miseries that are going to overtake you! — Gspd

over your impending miseries! — Mof

2. **Your riches are corrupted,**

Your wealth has rotted — Gspd

Your treasures are rotten — Wey

For your riches lie rotting — Mon

and your garments are motheaten.

your fine clothes are moth-eaten — NEB

3. **Your gold and silver is cankered;**

... rusted — ASV

... corroded — Wey

... tarnished — Lam

and the rust of them shall be a witness against you,

and their rust shall be for a testimony against you — ASV

... evidence against you — RSV

and shall eat your flesh as it were fire.

will bite into your flesh like flame — Knox

burning into your flesh — Bas

Ye have heaped treasure together for the last days.

Ye have laid up your treasure in the last days — ASV

It is in the last days that you have stored up your treasure — NASB

You have piled up wealth in an age that is near its close — NEB

4. **Behold, the hire of the labourers**

... the wages ... — Mof

... the pay ... — Wey

who have reaped down your fields,

who mowed your fields — ASV

which is of you kept back by fraud, crieth:

which you have been fraudulently keeping back, are crying out against you — TCNT

... are crying aloud! — Mon

and the cries of them which have reaped are entered into the ears of the Lord of sabaoth.

... the Lord of Hosts! — TCNT

5. **Ye have lived in pleasure on the earth, and been wanton;**

You have revelled on earth and plunged into dissipation — Mof

Here on earth you have lived self-indulgent and profligate lives — Wey

You have lived luxuriously and voluptuously here on earth — Gspd

Ye have luxuriated upon the land and run riot — Rhm

ye have nourished your hearts, as in a day of slaughter.

Ye have pampered your hearts in a day full of slaughter — Rhm

You have gratified your appetite with a day of slaughter! — Wey

You have indulged your fancies in a time of bloodshed — TCNT

You have fattened yourselves as for the Day of slaughter — Mof

You have comforted your hearts with luxuries on this day that dooms you to slaughter — Knox

fattening yourselves like cattle — and the day for slaughter has come — NEB

6. Ye have condemned and killed the just;

Ye sentenced, ye murdered the Righteous one! — Rhm

. . . the upright — Gspd

You have condemned, you have murdered, the Righteous One — TCNT

and he doth not resist you.

he offers no resistance — Wey

Is he not arraying himself against you?
— Rhm

Must not God be opposed to you? —
TCNT

Will he make no resistance? — Gspd

**7. Be patient therefore, brethren, unto
the coming of the Lord.**

. . . until the Presence of the Lord —
Rhm

**Behold, the husbandman waiteth for
the precious fruit of the earth, and
hath long patience for it,**

. . . being patient over it — ASV

Even the farmer has to wait for the
precious fruit of the earth, watching
over it patiently — TCNT

**until he receive the early and latter
rain.**

till it has had spring and summer rains
— TCNT

for it to get the fall and spring rains —
Beck

until the winter and spring rains have
fallen — NEB

8. Be ye also patient; stablish your hearts:

You too must be patient and stout-
hearted — NEB

You also be patient. Establish your
hearts — RSV

So you also must be patient, keeping
up your courage — Wey

**for the coming of the Lord draweth
nigh.**

for the Lord's Coming is near — TCNT

**9. Grudge not one against another, breth-
ren,**

Do not complain, brethren, against one
another — Amp

Murmur not, brethren, one against another — ASV

Do not make complaints . . . — TCNT

Say no hard things . . . — Bas

Do not grumble . . . — RSV

Don't blame your troubles on one another . . . — Beck

Stop muttering against one another . . .
— Wms

lest ye be condemned:

or judgement will be passed upon you
— TCNT

**behold, the judge standeth before the
door.**

. . . has stationed Himself at . . . — Ber

. . . is already standing at the door! —
TCNT

. . . is standing before the very door! —
Mon

**10. Take, my brethren, the prophets, who
have spoken in the name of the Lord,
for an example of suffering affliction,
and of patience.**

Brothers, as an example of the patient
endurance of suffering, take the
Prophets who spoke in the name of
the Lord — TCNT

**11. Behold, we count them happy which
endure.**

Behold, we call them blessed that endured — ASV

Lo! we pronounce them happy who
have endured — Rhm

Why, we call those who showed such
endurance happy! — Gspd

Just see how we esteem as blessed
those who endured the test — Nor

**Ye have heard of the patience of Job,
and have seen the end of the Lord;**

You have heard of the steadfastness of
Job, and you have seen the purpose
of the Lord — RSV

. . . and you have seen what the Lord
brought out of it — Gspd

. . . and have seen the issue of the
Lord's dealings with him — Wey

. . . how the Lord treated him in the
end — NEB

**that the Lord is very pitiful, and of
tender mercy.**

. . . full of pity, and merciful — ASV

for the Lord is full of pity and compassion — TCNT

— how full of tenderness and pity the
Lord is — Wey

**12. But above all things, my brethren,
swear not,**

. . . never take an oath — TCNT

. . . do not use oaths — NEB

. . . stop swearing — Wms

It is of the highest importance, my
brothers, that your speech should be

free from oaths — Phi

neither by heaven, neither by the earth, neither by any other oath:

(whether they are "by" Heaven or earth or anything else) — Phi

but let your yea be yea; and your nay, nay;

let your "Yes" be a plain Yes and your "No" a plain No — Gspd

Let your 'yes' be simply 'yes,' and your 'no' simply 'no' — Wey

With you let 'Yes' suffice for 'yes' and 'No' for 'no' — TCNT

lest ye fall into condemnation.

. . . under judgment — ASV

for fear that you expose yourselves to judgement — NEB

13. Is any among you afflicted?

. . . suffering — ASV

let him pray.

— he should turn to prayer — NEB

Is any merry?

. . . cheerful — ASV

. . . in good spirits — Wey

. . . in a happy mood — Wms

. . . in good heart — NEB

let him sing psalms.

He should sing praises — NEB

14. Is any sick among you? let him call for the elders of the church;

. . . Let him send for the Officers of the Church — TCNT

. . . the elders of the assembly — Rhm

and let them pray over him, anointing him with oil in the name of the Lord:

. . . and pour oil on him in the name of the Lord — Gspd

. . . after anointing him with oil in the name of the Lord — Mon

15. And the prayer of faith shall save the sick,

The prayer offered in faith will save the man who is sick — TCNT

and the Lord shall raise him up; and if he have committed sins, they shall be forgiven him.

and the Lord will restore him; and if he has committed sins, he will be forgiven — Amp

16. Confess your faults one to another,

Confess therefore your sins one to another — ASV

and pray one for another, that ye may be healed.

. . . cured — TCNT

. . . restored — Nor

The effectual fervent prayer of a righteous man availeth much.

The supplication of a righteous man availeth much in its working — ASV

Powerful is the heartfelt supplication of a righteous man — Wey

The prayers of the righteous have a powerful effect — Mof

Tremendous power is made available through a good man's earnest prayer — Phi

Great is the power of a good man's fervent prayer — TCNT

The prayer of a righteous man has great power in its effects — RSV

When a just man prays fervently there is great virtue in his prayer — Knox

An upright man's prayer, when it keeps at work, is very powerful — Wms

The prayer of a righteous man can bring powerful results — Nor

. . . makes tremendous power available — dynamic in its working — Amp

17. Elias was a man subject to like passions as we are,

Elijah was only a man like ourselves — TCNT

. . . a man with human frailties like our own — NEB

. . . a man with feelings just like ours — Wms

. . . a man with a nature similar to ours — Wey

. . . a man of flesh and blood as we are — Bas

. . . a mortal man like ourselves — Knox

and he prayed earnestly that it might not rain: and it rained not on the earth by the space of three years and six months.

. . . no rain fell upon the land for three years and a half — TCNT

18. And he prayed again, and the heaven gave rain,

And, when he prayed again, the clouds brought rain — TCNT

. . . the sky gave rain — Wey

and the earth brought forth her fruit.

. . . produced crops — Gspd

. . . yielded its crops — Wey

. . . bore crops — TCNT

JAMES 5

19. Brethren, if any of you do err from the truth,
... be seduced from the truth — Alf
My brothers, should any of you be led astray from the Truth — TCNT
... strays from the truth — Wey
... wanders from the truth — RSV
and one convert him;
... turn him back — Rhm
and some one bring him back again — TCNT

20. Let him know, that he which converteth the sinner
Be sure that he who brings a sinner back — TCNT

Be sure of this: any man who brings a sinner back — NEB

from the error of his way
from his misguided way — Gspd
from his evil course — Amp
from his mistaken ways — TCNT
from his crooked ways — NEB

shall save a soul from death,
will save the man's soul from death — Gspd

and shall hide a multitude of sins.
and cover up a host of sins — Gspd
and throw a veil over countless sins — TCNT

1142

THE FIRST EPISTLE OF PETER

CHAPTER 1

1. Peter, an apostle of Jesus Christ, to the strangers scattered throughout Pontus, Galatia, Cappadocia, Asia, and Bithynia,

. . . to the elect who are sojourners of the Dispersion in Pontus . . . — ASV

. . . to those who reside as aliens, scattered throughout Pontus . . . — NASB

. . . Unto the chosen pilgrims of the dispersion, throughout Pontus . . . — Rhm

To the People of God who are living abroad, dispersed throughout Pontus . . ., From Peter, an Apostle of Jesus Christ — TCNT

. . . to those who are scattered as foreigners over Pontus . . . — Gspd

. . . to the exiles of the Dispersion in Pontus . . . — RSV

2. Elect according to the foreknowledge of God the Father,

whom God the Father knew and chose — Phi

whom God the Father has predestined and chosen — Mof

chosen of old in the purpose of God the Father — NEB

chosen and destined by God the Father — RSV

through sanctification of the Spirit,

through the consecration of the Spirit — TCNT

through the sanctifying work of the Spirit — Wey

unto obedience and sprinkling of the blood of Jesus Christ:

to learn obedience, and to be purified by the sprinkling of the Blood of Jesus Christ — TCNT

to obey Jesus Christ and be sprinkled with his blood — Mof

Grace unto you, and peace, be multiplied.

May blessing and peace be yours in ever increasing measure — TCNT

May more and more grace and peace be granted to you — Wey

3. Blessed be the God and Father of our Lord Jesus Christ,

Let us praise the God and Father of our Lord Jesus Christ — Beck

which according to his abundant mercy

hath begotten us again unto a lively hope by the resurrection of Jesus Christ from the dead,

By his great mercy we have been born anew to a living hope through the resurrection . . . — RSV

by whose great mercy we have been born anew into a living hope, through the resurrection . . . — Mon

who has, in his great mercy, through the resurrection of Jesus Christ from the dead, given us the new life of undying hope — TCNT

. . . into a life full of hope, through Christ's rising again from the dead! — Phi

4. To an inheritance incorruptible, and undefiled, and that fadeth not away,

. . . a perfect inheritance beyond the reach of change and decay — Phi

. . . an inheritance, imperishable, stainless, unfading — TCNT

reserved in heaven for you,

which has been reserved for you in Heaven — TCNT

which is kept safe for you in heaven — Gspd

5. Who are kept by the power of God through faith

. . . for you who, through faith, are being guarded by the power of God — TCNT

and the power of God protects you by faith — Mof

and meanwhile, through faith, the power of God affords you safe-conduct till you reach it — Knox

unto salvation ready to be revealed in the last time.

. . . to be unveiled at the end of the world — Wey

. . . to be disclosed at the last time — Gspd

. . . to be revealed at the last hour — Mof

6. Wherein ye greatly rejoice,

At the thought of this you are full of exultation — TCNT

This means tremendous joy to you — Phi

This is great cause for joy — NEB

In such a hope keep on rejoicing — Wms

Exult in the prospect of this — Wey

though now for a season, if need be, ye are in heaviness through manifold temptations:

though now for a little while, if need be, ye have been put to grief in manifold trials — ASV

though (if it has been necessary) you have suffered for the moment somewhat from various trials — TCNT

though for the passing moment you may need to suffer various trials — Mof

even if now, for a short time, you are compelled to sorrow amid various trials — Wey

even though now you smart for a little, if need be, under trials of many kinds — NEB

7. That the trial of your faith, being much more precious than of gold that perisheth,

These things happen in order that the testing of your faith — being more precious than that of gold, which perishes — Wey

that is only to prove your faith is sterling (far more precious than gold which is perishable — Mof

that the genuineness of your faith — a thing far more precious than gold, which is perishable — TCNT

though it be tried with fire,

yet has to be tested by fire — TCNT

might be found unto praise and honour and glory at the appearing of Jesus Christ:

may win praise and glory and honour at . . . — TCNT

and it redounds to your praise and glory and honour at the revelation of Jesus Christ — Mof

8. Whom having not seen, ye love;

Without having seen him you love him — RSV

You love Him though you have never seen Him — Wey

Though you have never seen him yet you love him — TCNT

You must continue to love Him although you have never seen Him — Wms

in whom, though now ye see him not, yet believing,

though you do not even now see him, yet you believe in him — TCNT

in him you ever believe, though even now you see him not — Mon

ye rejoice with joy unspeakable and full of glory:

and you are rejoicing with joy unspeakable and full of glory — Mon

and triumph with a joy unspeakable and crowned with glory — Wey

you will thrill with an unspeakable and glorious joy — Mof

you are transported with a joy too great for words — NEB

9. Receiving the end of your faith, even the salvation of your souls.

As the outcome of your faith you obtain the salvation of your souls — RSV

while you procure the salvation of your souls as the goal of your faith — Ber

while you reap the harvest of your faith, that is, salvation for your souls — NEB

10. Of which salvation the prophets have enquired and searched diligently,

This salvation was the theme which prophets pondered and explored — NEB

who prophesied of the grace that should come unto you:

. . . that was to be yours — RSV

. . . that was destined for you — Gspd

. . . which was intended for you — Amp

11. Searching what, or what manner of time the Spirit of Christ which was in them did signify,

They tried to find out what was the time, and what the circumstances, to which the spirit of Christ in them pointed — NEB

earnestly trying to find out the time, and the nature of the times, which the Spirit of the Christ within them pointed to — Wms

they inquired what person or time was indicated by the Spirit of Christ within them — RSV

They investigated the time which the Spirit of Christ within them kept indicating, or its characteristics — Wey

when it testified beforehand the sufferings of Christ, and the glory that
should follow.
when predicting the sufferings of Christ
and the subsequent glory — RSV
when He solemnly made known beforehand the sufferings that were
destined for Christ and the glories
that would follow — Wey
foretelling the sufferings in store for
Christ and the splendours to follow
— NEB

12. **Unto whom it was revealed, that not
unto themselves, but unto us they did
minister the things,**
It was disclosed to them that they were
serving not themselves but you in
dealing with these things — Gspd

**which are now reported unto you by
them that have preached the gospel
unto you with the Holy Ghost sent
down from heaven;**
which have now been told to you, by
those who, with the help of the Holy
Spirit sent from Heaven, have
brought you the Good News — TCNT

**which things the angels desire to look
into.**
The very angels long to get a glimpse
of this! — Mof
The angels long to take a peep into
these things — Wms
truths into which even angels long to
look — TCNT

13. **Wherefore gird up the loins of your
mind, be sober, and hope to the end
for the grace that is to be brought unto
you**
You must therefore be like men
stripped for action, perfectly self-
controlled. Fix your hopes on the
grace which is to be yours — NEB
So then brace up your minds, be steady
in spirit, and fix your hope firmly
in the grace that is coming to you
— Mon
Brace up your minds, then, keep cool,
and put your hope for good and all
in the grace that is coming to you —
Mof
Therefore concentrate your minds,
with the strictest self-control, and fix
your hopes on the blessing that is
coming for you — TCNT

Therefore, prepare your minds for action, and with perfect calmness fix
your hopes on the mercy that you
are to experience — Gspd
Therefore, gird your minds for action,
keep sober in spirit, fix your hope
completely on the grace to be
brought to you — NASB
at the revelation of Jesus Christ;
at the Appearing of Jesus Christ —
TCNT
when Jesus Christ is revealed — Gspd

14. **As obedient children, not fashioning
yourselves**
Be like obedient children; do not let
your lives be shaped — TCNT
. . . stop molding your character —
Wms
. . . do not adapt yourselves to — Gspd
. . . do not be conformed to — RSV
**according to the former lusts in your
ignorance:**
by the passions which once swayed you
in the days of your ignorance —
TCNT
by the evil desires you used to cherish
when you did not know any better
— Wms
the cravings you used to follow when
you were ignorant — Gspd
. . . the passions of your former ignorance — RSV

15. **But as he which hath called you is
holy,**
rather after the pattern of the Holy
One which called you — Alf
but, in imitation of the holy One who
has called you — Wey
**so be ye holy in all manner of con-
versation;**
. . . in all manner of living — ASV
. . . in all your behaviour — Wey
. . . in every department of your lives
— Phi

16. **Because it is written,**
For Scripture says — TCNT
Be ye holy; for I am holy.
Ye shall be holy; for I am holy — ASV

17. **And if ye call on the Father,**
And if ye call on him as Father — ASV
. . . address him as Father — Gspd
who without respect of persons
. . . without the slightest favoritism —
Phi

... without preferring one to another — Beck

judgeth according to every man's work,
judges men by their actions — Phi

pass the time of your sojourning here in fear:
let reverence be the spirit of your lives during the time of your stay upon earth — TCNT

be reverent in your conduct while you sojourn here below — Mof

spend the time of your stay here on earth with reverent fear — Phi

You must stand in awe of him while you live out your time on earth — NEB

You must live reverently all your fleeting stay on earth — Wms

18. **Forasmuch as ye know that ye were not redeemed with corruptible things, as silver and gold,**
For you know that it was not by perishable things, such as silver and gold, that you were ransomed — TCNT

from your vain conversation received by tradition from your fathers;
from the aimless way of living which was handed down to you from your ancestors — TCNT

... futile way of living in which you have been brought up — Gspd

... the emptiness of your manner of life, received by tradition from your ancestors — Mon

... the empty folly of your traditional ways — NEB

19. **But with the precious blood of Christ, as of a lamb without blemish and without spot:**
but by precious blood, as it were of a lamb, unblemished and spotless, the Blood of Christ — TCNT

20. **Who verily was foreordained before the foundation of the world,**
who was foreknown indeed ... — ASV

He was pre-destined indeed to this work, even before the creation of the world — Wey

but was manifest in these last times for you,
but was manifested at the end of the times for your sake — ASV

but it was for your benefit that he was revealed in these last days — Phi

but was brought out to public view at the end of the ages — Wms

21. **Who by him do believe in God, that raised him up from the dead, and gave him glory;**
who, through him, are faithful to God who raised him from the dead and gave him honour — TCNT

that your faith and hope might be in God.
and so your faith and hope are fixed on God — NEB

... are resting upon ... — Wey

... are directed towards ... — Rhm

22. **Seeing ye have purified your souls in obeying the truth**
Now that, by your obedience to the Truth, you have purified your lives — TCNT

... through your obedience to the truth, you have prepared your souls by purification — Wey

through the Spirit[1] unto unfeigned love of the brethren,
so that there is growing up among you a genuine brotherly affection—TCNT

see that ye love one another with a pure heart fervently:
love one another earnestly with all your hearts — TCNT

... heartily and fervently — Wey

... intensely and heartily — Gspd

... most cordially and consistently — Ber

... whole-heartedly with all your strength — NEB

23. **Being born again, not of corruptible seed, but of incorruptible,**
You are born anew of immortal, not of mortal seed — Mof

since your new Life has come, not from perishable, but imperishable seed — TCNT

by the word of God, which liveth and abideth for ever.
... the word of the living and abiding God — Rhm

through the message of the living, everlasting God — Gspd

... through the message of the Everlasting God — TCNT

---

[1]The words "through the Spirit" are now recognized as not adequately supported by original manuscripts.

. . . by God's living and enduring word — Wey

. . . the living and abiding word of God — RSV

. . . the living, lasting word of God — Mof

24. For all flesh is as grass, and all the glory of man as the flower of the grass.

All mankind is like herbage and all their beauty like its flowers — Wey

. . . All earthly life is but as grass, And all its splendour as the flower of grass — TCNT

. . . All mortals are like grass; All their splendour like the flower of the field — NEB

The grass withereth, and the flower thereof falleth away:

The herbage dries up and its flowers drop off — Wey

The grass fades, Its flower falls — TCNT

The grass dries up, The flowers drop off — Wms

25. But the word of the Lord endureth forever.

But the declaration of the Lord age-abidingly remaineth — Rhm

But the word of the Lord lives on forever — Wms

. . . the Teaching of the Lord remains forever — TCNT

And this is the word which by the gospel is preached unto you.

And that is the word of the Gospel for you — Mof

And that means the message which has been proclaimed to you in the Gospel — Wey

And that is the Teaching of the Good News which has been told to you — TCNT

And this word is nothing other than the Gospel which has been preached to you — Knox

That word is the good news that has been brought to you — Gspd

CHAPTER 2

1. Wherefore laying aside all malice, and all guile,

Rid yourselves therefore of all ill-will and all deceitfulness — Wey

Free yourselves, therefore, from all malice, deceit — Gspd

So once for all get rid of all malice, deceit — Wms

Now that you have done with all malice, all deceitfulness — TCNT

and hypocrisies, and envies, and all evil speakings,

insincerity, jealous feelings, and all back-biting — TCNT

hypocrisy, envy, and all sorts of slander — Wms

and insincerity and envy and slander of every kind! — Mof

. . . recrimination of every kind! — NEB

2. As newborn babes, desire the sincere milk of the word,

. . . long for spiritual milk which is without guile — ASV

. . . for the pure milk that is for the mind eagerly crave — Rhm

like newly born infants, crave pure spiritual milk — TCNT

Thirst, like newly-born infants, for pure milk for the soul — Wey

that ye may grow thereby:

that ye may grow thereby unto salvation — ASV

so that you may thrive upon it to your souls' health — NEB

that you may grow up to salvation — Wey

that you may be enabled by it to grow till you attain Salvation — TCNT

3. If so be ye have tasted that the Lord is gracious.

Since you have tasted the Lord's kindness — Gspd

You have had a taste of the kindness of the Lord — Mof

Surely you have tasted that the Lord is good — NEB

since you have found by experience that the Lord is kind — TCNT

If you have had any taste of the goodness of the Lord — Wey

4. To whom coming, as unto a living stone,

Come to Him then, the living Stone — Wey

Keep on coming to Him, as to a living stone — Wms

disallowed indeed of men,

rejected indeed by men — Wey

but chosen of God, and precious,

but with God elect, precious — ASV

but in God's eyes choice and precious
— TCNT

but in God's esteem chosen and valuable — Wey

but chosen and prized in the sight of
God — Gspd

5. **Ye also, as lively stones, are built up a
spiritual house,**
and, as living stones form yourselves
into a spiritual House — TCNT
. . . keep on building yourselves up . . .
— Wms

an holy priesthood,
to be a holy priesthood — ASV
to be a consecrated priesthood — TCNT
to offer up spiritual sacrifices,
for the offering of . . . — TCNT
acceptable to God by Jesus Christ.
that God gladly accepts through Jesus
Christ — Beck

6. **Wherefore also it is contained in the
scripture,**
For there is a passage of Scripture that
runs — TCNT
Behold, I lay in Sion
Behold I am setting down in Sion —
Knox
See, I am placing in Zion — Wey

a chief corner stone, elect, precious:
a choice corner-stone of great worth
— NEB
a Cornerstone, chosen and valuable —
Wey
a choice and precious corner-stone —
TCNT
**and he that believeth on him shall not
be confounded.**
. . . put to shame — ASV
. . . shall have no cause for shame —
TCNT
. . . shall never be disappointed — Wey

7. **Unto you therefore which believe he
is precious:**
You believers, therefore, feel His
value — Wey
The great worth of which it speaks is
for you who have faith — NEB
It is you, therefore, who believe who
see its value — Gspd
It is to you who believe, therefore, that
this honour is given — Lam
It is to you, then, who believe in him
that he is precious — TCNT

but unto them which be disobedient,
but for such as disbelieve — ASV
**the stone which the builders dis-
allowed,**
The stone which the builders refused
— Gspd
The very stone which the builders rejected — RSV
**the same is made the head of the cor-
ner,**
is now the cornerstone — Mof
has now itself become the corner-stone
— TCNT

8. **And a stone of stumbling, and a rock
of offence,**
And, a stone of falling, a rock of trouble — Bas
a stumbling-block, and a rock that shall
prove a hindrance — TCNT
A stone that will make men stumble,
a rock that will make them fall —
RSV
A Stone to trip over, and a Rock to
stumble at — Wey
**even to them which stumble at the
word, being disobedient:**
They keep on stumbling over the message, because they are disobedient to
it — Wms
for they stumble because they disobey
the word — RSV
They stumble when they disbelieve the
Word — NEB
they stumble over God's word, and refuse to believe it — Knox
whereunto also they were appointed.
as they were destined to do — RSV
and this is their appointed doom —
Wms
Such was their appointed lot! — NEB
which makes stumbling a foregone
conclusion — Phi

9. **But ye are a chosen generation, a royal
priesthood,**
But ye are an elect race . . . — ASV
an holy nation, a peculiar people;
a dedicated nation, and a people
claimed by God for his own — NEB
a consecrated nation, God's own People — TCNT
. . . a people for a possession — ABUV
. . . a purchased people — Mon
that ye should shew forth the praises
that the excellence ye may tell forth
— Rhm

that you may proclaim the wondrous deeds — Mof

that you may show forth the virtues — Mon

entrusted with the proclamation of the goodness — TCNT

that you may make known the perfections — Wey

of him who hath called you out of darkness into his marvellous light:

... his amazing light — Phi

... his wonderful light — TCNT

10. **Which in time past were not a people, but are now the people of God:**

Who at one time were a No-people, But now are a people of God — Rhm

which had not obtained mercy, but now have obtained mercy.

outside his mercy once, you have now received his mercy — NEB

who once experienced no mercy but are now enjoying mercy — Ber

11. **Dearly beloved, I beseech you as strangers and pilgrims,**

Dear friends, I beg you, as aliens and exiles here — Gspd

I implore you, dear friends ... — Ber

Dear Friends, I beg you, as aliens in a foreign land — NEB

abstain from fleshly lusts, which war against the soul;

not to indulge the physical cravings that are at war with the soul — Gspd

to restrain the cravings of your lower natures which war upon the soul — Wey

to refrain from indulging the cravings of your earthly nature, for they make war upon the soul — TCNT

12. **Having your conversation honest among the Gentiles:**

Maintain good conduct among the Gentiles — RSV

Live honourable lives among ... — Wey

bear yourselves uprightly before pagans — Mof

Live upright lives among the heathen — Gspd

Let your manner of life before the Gentiles be honest — Mon

that, whereas they speak against you as evildoers,

and then, whereas they malign you as criminals now — NEB

so that, for all their slander of you as bad characters — Mof

in order that, although they speak against you as evildoers — Wey

they may by your good works, which they shall behold, glorify God

they may learn, as they watch, from the uprightness of your conduct, to praise God — TCNT

they may, by beholding your noble conduct, come to glorify God — Mon

in the day of visitation.

when he comes to be their judge — Bas

on the day when he comes to hold assize — NEB

on the Day of Judgment — Gspd

when his time comes to have mercy on them — Knox

in the day of inspection — Amp

when Christ returns — Tay

13. **Submit yourselves to every ordinance of man for the Lord's sake:**

Submit to all human institutions ... — TCNT

Submit, for the Lord's sake, to every authority set up by man — Wey

For the Lord's sake, submit to all human authority — Wms

Submit yourselves to every human creation for the Lord's sake — Rhm

For the Lord's sake, obey every law of your government — Tay

whether it be to the king, as supreme;

... to the emperor as the supreme authority — TCNT

14. **Or unto governors, as unto them that are sent by him for the punishment of evildoers,**

or to the governor as his deputy for the punishment of criminals — NEB

and to the magistrates who hold his commission to punish criminals — Knox

or to governors as commissioned by him to bring criminals to justice — Ber

and for the praise of them that do well.

and encourage honest men — Knox

and to encourage the well-behaved — Ber

and to commend those who do right — TCNT

15. For so is the will of God, that with well doing ye may put to silence the ignorance of foolish men:

For God's will is this—that you should silence the ignorance of foolish people by doing what is right — TCNT

For it is the will of God that by your good conduct you should put ignorance and stupidity to silence — NEB

For this is God's intention, that by behaving well you should silence the foolishness of thoughtless people — Ber

For it is the will of God that by well-doing you should silence the ignorant talk of foolish men — Mon

16. As free, and not using your liberty for a cloke of maliciousness,

Be free men, and yet do not make your freedom a screen for base conduct — Wey

Live like free men, only never make your freedom a pretext for misconduct — Mof

Live like free men, only do not make your freedom an excuse for doing wrong — Gspd

Act as free men, but do not use your freedom as a cloak to cover up some wickedness — Nor

but as the servants of God.

but be slaves of God — Gspd

17. Honour all men. Love the brotherhood. Fear God. Honour the king.

Show honor to everyone. Practice love for the brotherhood; practice reverence to God and honor to the Emperor — Wms

18. Servants, be subject to your masters with all fear;

Those of you who are domestic servants should always be submissive and respectful to their masters — TCNT

Household slaves, submit yourselves to your masters in all reverence—Mon

... with the utmost respect — Wey

not only to the good and gentle, but also to the froward.

not only if they are kind and thoughtful, but also if they are unreasonable — Wey

... surly — Mof

... overbearing — RSV

... arbitrary — TCNT

... cruel — Wms

19. For this is thankworthy,

For this wins God's approval — TCNT

For it is pleasing in the sight of God — Wms

if a man for conscience toward God endure grief, suffering wrongfully.

when from a sense of God one bears the pain of unjust suffering — Mof

when, because conscious of God's presence, a man who is suffering unjustly bears his troubles patiently — TCNT

if from a sense of duty to him [God], a man endures a wrong, even suffering unjustly — Mon

20. For what glory is it, if, when ye be buffeted for your faults, ye shall take it patiently?

Where is the credit in standing punishment for having done wrong — Mof

What credit is there in fortitude when you have done wrong and are beaten for it — NEB

If you do wrong and receive a blow for it, what credit is there in your bearing it patiently — Wey

but if, when ye do well, and suffer for it, ye take it patiently, this is acceptable with God.

But, on the other hand, if, after doing right, you take your sufferings patiently, that does win the approval of God — TCNT

21. For even hereunto were ye called:

That is the life to which you have been called — Gspd

Indeed it was to this kind of living that you were called — Wms

To such an experience you have been called — Ber

because Christ also suffered for us,

because Christ also suffered on your behalf — Wey

for when Christ suffered for you — Mof

leaving us an example, that ye should follow his steps:

leaving you an example, so that you should follow in his footsteps—Mon

... a pattern ... — Alf

he left you an example, and you must be following in his footsteps — Mof

22. Who did no sin, neither was guile found in his mouth:

He did no wrong, no treachery was found on his lips — Knox

He never sinned, nor was anything deceitful ever heard from his lips — TCNT

23. **Who, when he was reviled, reviled not again;**

he was reviled and he made no retort — Mof

Yet when he was insulted he offered no insult in return — Phi

when he suffered, he threatened not; but committed himself to him that judgeth righteously:

. . . left His cause in the hands of the righteous Judge — Wey

. . . committed his case to him who judges justly — Gspd

. . . He turned the matter over to Him who judges justly — Nor

. . . kept entrusting Himself to Him who judges righteously — NASB

24. **Who his own self bare our sins in his own body on the tree,**

And he himself carried our sins . . . — TCNT

he personally bore . . . — Phi

He carried the burden of our sins in his own body . . . — Gspd

that we, being dead to sins, should live unto righteousness:

that we might break with sin and live the good life — Mof

so that we might cease to live for sin and begin to live for righteousness — NEB

that we might abandon our sins . . . — Ber

by whose stripes ye were healed.

His bruising was your healing — TCNT

By his wounds you have been healed — NEB

It was the suffering that he bore which has healed you — Phi

25. **For ye were as sheep going astray;**

For you were continually straying like sheep — NASB

but are now returned unto the Shepherd and Bishop of your souls.

now, you have been brought back to him, your shepherd, who keeps watch over your souls — Knox

but now you have returned to the Shepherd and Guardian of your souls — TCNT

but now you have returned to your Shepherd, the Guardian who keeps you safe from all attacks — Tay

CHAPTER 3

1. **Likewise, ye wives, be in subjection to your own husbands;**

Again, you married women should submit to your husbands — TCNT

Wives, fit in with your husband's plans — Tay

that, if any obey not the word,

so that even if some of them disbelieve — Wey

so that if any of them reject the Message — TCNT

they also may without the word be won by the conversation of the wives;

they may, apart from the word, be won over by the daily life of their wives — Wey

2. **While they behold your chaste conversation coupled with fear.**

Having been permitted to behold your reverently chaste behaviour — Rhm

. . . how chaste and respectful you are — Wms

. . . how pure and god-fearing you are — Nor

. . . your submissive and blameless conduct — TCNT

3. **Whose adorning let it not be that outward adorning**

You are not to adorn yourselves on the outside — Mof

Don't be concerned about the outward beauty — Tay

Your beauty should reside, not in outward adornment — NEB

of plaiting the hair, and of wearing of gold, or of putting on of apparel;

with braids of hair and ornaments of gold and changes of dress — Mof

of the arrangement of the hair, the wearing of jewelry, or the putting on of dresses — TCNT

4. **But let it be the hidden man of the heart, in that which is not corruptible, even the ornament of a meek and quiet spirit,**

but rather that hidden personality of the heart, the imperishable ornament of a quiet and gentle spirit — Mon

but the inner life, with the imperishable beauty of a quiet and gentle Spirit — TCNT

Your beauty should, rather, be from within — it should be the inner loveliness of the heart, the imperishable jewel of a gentle and quiet spirit — Nor

but an inward beauty of nature, the imperishable ornament of a gentle and peaceful spirit — Wey

. . . with the immortal beauty of a gentle, modest spirit — Mof

. . . with the lasting charm of a gentle and quiet spirit — Tay

which is in the sight of God of great price.

to God's eyes, beyond price — Knox

which in the sight of God is of rare value — Mof

for this is very precious in God's sight — TCNT

5. For after this manner

Thus it was — NEB

It was in this way — Mof

in the old time

in ancient times — Gspd

the holy women also, who trusted in God, adorned themselves,

that those pious women who set their hopes on God made themselves attractive — Gspd

. . . used to make themselves beautiful — Beck

being in subjection unto their own husbands:

by their submission to their husbands — NEB

They were submissive to their husbands — Mof

and paid their husbands such respect — Knox

and fitted in with their husband's plans — Tay

6. Even as Sara obeyed Abraham, calling him lord:

As Sarah, for example, obeyed Abraham and called him master — Wms

whose daughters ye are, as long as ye do well,

And you have become Sarah's children if you do right — Wey

and are not afraid with any amazement.

and permit nothing to make you afraid — Mon

. . . yield to no panic — Mof

. . . let nothing terrify you — TCNT

. . . let no anxious thoughts disturb you — Knox

7. Likewise, ye husbands, dwell with them according to knowledge,

Again, those of you who are married men should live considerately with their wives — TCNT

In the same way, you husbands must conduct your married life with understanding — NEB

giving honour unto the wife, as unto the weaker vessel, and as being heirs together of the grace of life;

You must show deference to women as the weaker sex, sharing the gift of life with you — Gspd

since they are the weaker sex; you must honor them as heirs equally with yourselves of the grace of Life — Mof

that your prayers be not hindered.

so that your prayers may be unrestrained — Wey

so that nothing may interfere with your prayers — Gspd

so that your praying may not be disturbed — Ber

and your prayers must not suffer interruption — Knox

8. Finally, be ye all of one mind, having compassion one of another, love as brethren, be pitiful, be courteous:

To sum up: . . . — NEB

And now this word to each of you: . . . — Tay

Finally, be ye all likeminded, compassionate, loving as brethren, tenderhearted, humbleminded — ASV

Lastly, you should all be united, sympathetic, full of brotherly love, kind-hearted, humble-minded—TCNT

Finally, all of you, have unity of spirit, sympathy, love of the brethren, a tender heart and a humble mind — RSV

9. Not rendering evil for evil, or railing for railing:

. . . reviling for reviling — ASV

. . . an insult with another insult — Phi

. . . hard words with hard words — Knox

. . . curse for curse — Bas

. . . abuse for abuse — TCNT

. . . reproach for reproach — Alf

but contrariwise blessing; knowing that ye are thereunto called, that ye should inherit a blessing.

but on the contrary, blessing. For this is your vocation, to bless and to inherit a blessing — Mof

but, on the contrary, blessing. It was to that that you were called—to obtain a blessing! — TCNT

10. **For he that will love life, and see good days, let him refrain his tongue from evil, and his lips that they speak no guile:**

He that would enjoy life And see happy days —Let him keep his tongue from evil And his lips from deceitful words — TCNT

11. **Let him eschew evil, and do good;**
. . . shun wrong and do right — Mof
let him seek peace, and ensue it.
. . . and pursue it — ASV
let him seek peace, making peace his aim — Mof
searching for peace and going after it with all his heart — Bas
try to live in peace even if you must run after it to catch and hold it — Tay

12. **For the eyes of the Lord are over the righteous, and his ears are open unto their prayers:**

Because the eyes of the Lord are on upright men, And His ears listen to their pleading cries — Wms
. . . And his ears are attentive to their prayers — TCNT
but the face of the Lord is against them that do evil.

13. **And who is he that will harm you,**
And who is there that can hurt you — Gspd
if ye be followers of that which is good?
if you are eager to do what is right — Gspd
if you prove yourselves to be eager for what is good — TCNT
if you have a passion for goodness — Mof
. . . are devoted to what is good — NEB
if only what is good inspires your ambitions — Knox

14. **But and if ye suffer for righteousness' sake, happy are ye:**

Even supposing you have to suffer for the sake of what is right; still you are blessed — Mof
. . . you are to be envied — Wey
and be not afraid of their terror, neither be troubled;
So do not be alarmed by their threats, nor be troubled — Wey
Have no fear of their threats, never let that trouble you — Mof
Do not fear their intimidation, and do not be troubled — NASB

15. **But sanctify the Lord God in your hearts:**

Revere the Christ as Lord in your hearts — TCNT
. . . hold the Lord Christ in reverence in your hearts — NEB
. . . in your hearts be consecrated to Christ as Lord — Wms
. . . give honour to Christ in your hearts as your Lord — Bas
and be ready always to give an answer to every man that asketh you a reason of the hope that is in you
being always ready to make your defence to any one who asks from you a reason for the hope which you cherish — Wey
And always be ready with a reply for anyone who calls you to account for the hope you cherish — Mof
Be always ready with your defence whenever you are called to account for the hope that is in you — NEB
with meekness and fear:
with modesty and respect — NEB
in a gentle and respectful way — Tay
in a humble and reverent manner — Nor
Yet argue gently and cautiously—Wey
but courteously and with due reverence — Knox
but do it gently and respectfully — Ber

16. **Having a good conscience;**

and keeping your consciences clear — TCNT
and see that you have a clean conscience — Mof
Maintain a clear conscience — Ber
that, whereas they speak evil of you, as of evildoers,

that, wherein ye are spoken against —
ASV

so that, for all their slander of you —
Mof

so that, whenever you are maligned —
TCNT

so that if men should speak slanderously of you as rogues — Phi

**they may be ashamed that falsely
accuse**

they may be put to shame who revile
— ASV

... cast wanton insult on — Rhm

your good conversation in Christ.

your manner of life in Christ — ASV

your good Christian behaviour — Mof

your excellent conduct as Christians —
Wms

17. For it is better, if the will of God be so,

For it is better, if the will of God
should so will — ASV

... if God wants it that way — Beck

... if God wants you to suffer — Tay

**that ye suffer for well doing, than for
evil doing.**

... for doing right, than for doing
wrong — TCNT

**18. For Christ also hath once suffered for
sins,**

because Christ also once for all died
for sins — Wey

For Christ himself died to atone for
sins once for all — TCNT

the just for the unjust,

a just man for unjust men — Mof

the innocent One for the guilty many
— Wey

an upright man for unrighteous men
— Gspd

the Righteous One for the guilty —
Beck

that he might bring us to God,

so as to present us in God's sight —
Knox

that he might bring us near to God —
Mof

being put to death in the flesh,

and was physically put to death —
Gspd

his body being put to death — TCNT

being put to death in physical form —
Wms

But though His body died — Tay

but quickened by the Spirit:

but made alive in the spirit — ASV

but made alive in the Spirit — Wms

but his spirit entering upon new Life
— TCNT

in the spirit he was brought to life —
NEB

His spirit lived on — Tay

**19. By which also he went and preached
unto the spirits in prison;**

in which also ... — ASV

By whom he went to the spirits in
prison, preaching to those — Bas

And it was then that he went and
preached to the imprisoned spirits —
TCNT

And in the spirit he went and made his
proclamation to the imprisoned spirits — NEB

20. Which sometime were disobedient,

They had refused obedience long ago
— NEB

unyielding at one time — Rhm

**when once the longsuffering of God
waited**

when the longsuffering of God was
holding forth a welcome — Rhm

at the time when God patiently waited
— TCNT

at the time when God's patience held
out — Mof

**in the days of Noah, while the ark was
a preparing,**

during the construction of the ark in
the days of Noah — Mof

**wherein few, that is, eight souls were
saved by water.**

... were brought safely through by
means of water — Rhm

... were brought safely through the
water — Wey

... found refuge as they passed through
the waves — Knox

**21. The like figure whereunto even bap-
tism doth also now save us**

This water prefigured the water of baptism through which you are now
brought to safety — NEB

And, corresponding to that figure, baptism now saves you — Wey

And baptism, which this foreshadowed,
now saves you — TCNT

Baptism, the counterpart of that, saves
you to-day — Mof

**(not the putting away of the filth of
the flesh,**

not as the mere removing of physical stain — Gspd

not the mere washing of dirt from the flesh — Mof

not the mere cleansing of the body — TCNT

but the answer of a good conscience toward God,)

. . . the craving for a conscience right with God — Gspd

. . . the prayer for a clean conscience before God — Mof

. . . the request unto God for a good conscience — Rhm

. . . an appeal to God for a clear conscience — RSV

. . . the appeal made to God by a good conscience — NEB

it means the ability to face God with a clear conscience — Phi

by the resurrection of Jesus Christ:

22. **Who is gone into heaven, and is on the right hand of God;**
angels and authorities and powers being made subject unto him.

where Angels and Archangels and the Powers of heaven now yield submission to him — TCNT

CHAPTER 4

1. **Forasmuch then as Christ hath suffered for us in the flesh,**

Remembering that Christ endured bodily suffering — NEB

Since, then, Christ suffered in body — TCNT

arm yourselves likewise with the same mind:

. . . the same resolve as he — TCNT

. . . the same determination — Wms

. . . the same attitude — Nor

for he that hath suffered in the flesh hath ceased from sin;

. . . hath done with sins — Rhm

. . . gets quit of sin — Mof

2. **That he no longer should live the rest of his time in the flesh to the lusts of men, but to the will of God.**

and so will live the rest of his earthly life, guided not by human passions, but by the will of God — TCNT

so that he no longer can spend the rest of his earthly life in harmony with human desires but in accordance with God's will — Wms

so to live for the rest of the time in the flesh no longer by human passions but by the will of God — RSV

. . . in satisfying human appetites, but in doing God's will — Nor

. . . for the things that men desire, but for what God wills — NEB

3. **For the time past of our life may suffice us**

For sufficient is the bygone time — Rhm

You have spent time enough in the past — Gspd

You had time enough in the past — NEB

Surely in the past you have spent time enough — TCNT

Let the time that is past suffice — RSV

to have wrought the will of the Gentiles,

in doing as the heathen like to do — Gspd

to do all the things that men want to do in the pagan world — NEB

to have done as pagans choose to do — Mof

living as the Gentiles delight to live — TCNT

for doing what the Gentiles like to do — RSV

when we walked in lasciviousness, lusts,

leading lives that are steeped in sensuality, lustful desires — Wms

pursuing, as you did, a course of licence, debauchery — Wey

Then you lived in licence and debauchery — NEB

excess of wine, revellings, banquetings, and abominable idolatries:

drunkenness, riot, and tippling, and the forbidden worship of idols — NEB

drunkenness, revelry, hard drinking and profane idolatry — TCNT

getting drunk, wild parties, drinking bouts, and worship of idols — Tay

4. **Wherein they think it strange that ye run not with them**

Indeed your former companions may think it very queer that you will no longer join with them — Phi and it astonishes pagans that you will not plunge with them — Mof

to the same excess of riot,

into the same flood of profligacy — Mof

. . . flood of dissipation — Gspd

in the same wild profligacy — RSV

. . . unbridled dissipation — Ber

. . . welter of debauch — Knox

. . . violent wasting of life — Bas

speaking evil of you:

uttering defamation — Rhm

and malign you — TCNT

and they vilify you accordingly — NEB

and they abuse you — Wey

5. **Who shall give account to him that is ready to judge the quick and the dead.**

But they will have to give account to Him who is ready to pronounce judgement on the living and the dead — Wey

6. **For for this cause was the gospel preached also to them that are dead,**

Why was the Gospel preached to those who are dead? — NEB

that they might be judged according to men in the flesh,

that it might judge the lives they lived as men — Phi

that though they are judged in their physical nature as men are — Gspd

that though judged in the flesh like men — RSV

that, after they have been judged in the body, as men are judged — TCNT

In order that, although in the body they received the sentence common to men — NEB

but live according to God in the spirit.

they might in the spirit be alive with the life of God — NEB

and give them also the opportunity to share the eternal life of God in the spirit — Phi

they might live in the spirit, as God lives — TCNT

7. **But the end of all things is at hand:**

. . . hath drawn near — Rhm

. . . of everything is near — Beck

be ye therefore sober, and watch unto prayer.

be ye therefore of sound mind, and be sober unto prayer — ASV

Be serious and collected, therefore, and pray — Gspd

Steady then, keep cool and pray! — Mof

therefore be sober-minded and temperate, that you may give yourselves to prayer — Wey

so you must lead an ordered and sober life, given to prayer — NEB

Therefore be earnest, thoughtful men of prayer — Tay

8. **And above all things have fervent charity among yourselves:**

above all things being fervent in your love among yourselves — ASV

. . . keep your love for one another strong — Gspd

. . . preserve constant charity among yourselves — Knox

. . . have intense and unfailing love for one another — Amp

for charity shall cover the multitude of sins.

for Love throws a veil over countless sins — TCNT

. . . love hides a host of sins — Mof

. . . love cancels innumerable sins — NEB

9. **Use hospitality one to another without grudging.**

Extend ungrudging hospitality towards one another — Wey

Welcome one another as guests without grumbling — Beck

Keep open house for all with a glad heart — Bas

10. **As every man hath received the gift,**

Whatever the endowment God has given you — Gspd

Whatever the gift that each has received — TCNT

even so minister the same one to another,

use it in service to one another . . . — Gspd

you must keep on using them in serving one another — Wms

you must use them for another's benefit — Wey

as good stewards of the manifold grace of God.

. . . good trustees of God's many-sided favour — Wms

. . . efficient stewards of God's varied grace — Mof

. . . careful stewards of the manifold favour of God — Rhm

. . . the grace of God in its varied forms — NEB

. . . the unmeasured grace of God — Bas

11. If any man speak, let him speak as the oracles of God;

. . . he must preach as one who utters the words of God — Mof

. . . let it be as uttering God's oracles — Wey

When any one speaks, let him speak as one who is delivering the oracles of God — TCNT

if any man minister, let him do it as of the ability which God giveth:

When any one is endeavouring to serve others, let him do so in reliance on the strength which God supplies — TCNT

that God in all things may be glorified through Jesus Christ,

In all things so act as that the glory may be God's through Jesus Christ — NEB

to whom be praise and dominion for ever and ever. Amen.

. . . through endless ages, Amen — Knox

12. Beloved, think it not strange

. . . do not be bewildered — NEB

. . . I beg you not to be unduly alarmed — Phi

. . . do not be surprised — Wey

. . . do not be astonished — TCNT

concerning the fiery trial which is to try you,

that a test of fire is being applied to you — Gspd

at the fiery test taking place among you to prove you — ABUV

at the fiery ordeal coming among you to put you to the test — Wey

at the fiery trials that you are passing through, to test you — TCNT

as though some strange thing happened unto you:

as though this were some abnormal experience — Phi

as though some foreign thing befell you — Mof

13. But rejoice, inasmuch as ye are partakers of Christ's sufferings;

No, in the degree that you share in the sufferings of Christ rejoice — Wey

You are sharing what Christ suffered; so rejoice in it — Mof

that, when his glory shall be revealed,

that, when the time comes for the manifestation of his Glory — TCNT

ye may be glad also with exceeding joy.

you may be triumphantly happy — Gspd

you may rejoice and exult — TCNT

14. If ye be reproached for the name of Christ,

If you are suffering abuse because you bear the name of Christ — Wms

. . . are denounced for the sake of Christ — Mof

happy are ye;

blessed are ye — ASV

count yourselves blessed — TCNT

for the spirit of glory and of God resteth upon you:

because the Spirit of glory and the Spirit of God resteth upon you — ASV

because the glorious Spirit of God is resting upon you — Gspd

because the divine Glory and the Spirit of God are resting upon you — TCNT

on their part he is evil spoken of, but on your part he is glorified.[2]

15. But let none of you suffer as a murderer, or as a thief, or as an evildoer, or as a busybody in other men's matters.

Let it not be said that any of you underwent punishment for murder, or theft, or slander, or infringing other men's rights — Knox

. . . or as a spy upon other people's business — Mon

. . . a mischief-maker — RSV

. . . a busybody and prying into other people's affairs — Tay

. . . for interfering in matters which do not concern Christians — TCNT

16. Yet if any man suffer as a Christian,

because he is a Christian — Wey

let him not be ashamed;

he should feel it no disgrace — NEB

---

[2]Now recognized as not adequately supported by original manuscripts.

but let him glorify God on this behalf.

but confess that name to the honour of God — NEB

but let him glorify God through that very name — Lam

but under that name let him glorify God — RSV

17. For the time is come that judgment must begin at the house of God:

For it is the ripe time for the judgment to begin with the house of God — Rhm

. . . to begin from the house of God — ABUV

. . . among God's own children — Tay

and if it first begin at us, what shall the end be of them that obey not the gospel of God?

And if even we who are Christians must be judged, what terrible fate waits those who have never believed in the Lord — Tay

and if our turn comes first, what will

be its issue for those who refuse credence to God's message — Knox

18. And if the righteous scarcely be saved,

If it is hard for the upright man to be saved — Gspd

If a good man is saved only with difficulty — TCNT

where shall the ungodly and the sinner appear?

what will become of irreligious men and sinners — Wey

what chance will the godless have — Tay

19. Wherefore let them that suffer according to the will of God commit the keeping of their souls to him in well doing, as unto a faithful Creator.

. . . do right and entrust their souls to a faithful Creator — RSV

. . . commit their lives into the hands of a faithful Creator, and persevere in doing right — TCNT

CHAPTER 5

1. The elders which are among you I exhort,

Now to you who are presbyters I make this appeal — Mon

And now I appeal to the elders of your community — NEB

who am also an elder, and a witness of the sufferings of Christ,

. . . who am a fellow-elder and a witness . . . — ASV

for I myself am a presbyter, and was a witness of the sufferings of Christ — Mon

and also a partaker of the glory that shall be revealed:

who shall also share in the glory that is to be revealed — TCNT

. . . the glory about to be revealed — Mon

2. Feed the flock of God which is among you,

Tend that flock of God whose shepherds you are — NEB

be shepherds of God's flock which is among you — Wey

taking the oversight thereof, not by constraint, but willingly;

exercising the oversight, not of constraint, but willingly, according to the will of God — ASV

. . . not as though it were forced upon you but of your own free will — Gspd

. . . not because you are compelled, but of your own free will — TCNT

. . . not reluctantly, but voluntarily, in accordance with the will of God — Wey

not for filthy lucre, but of a ready mind;

not from a base love of gain, but with a ready spirit — TCNT

. . . not from the motive of personal profit but freely — Wms

3. Neither as being lords over God's heritage,

neither as lording it over the charge allotted to you — ASV

not as lords of your charges — TCNT

but being ensamples to the flock.

but as examples to your flock — TCNT

but proving yourselves patterns to the flock — Wey

but be models for them to copy — Nor

4. And when the chief Shepherd shall appear, ye shall receive a crown of glory that fadeth not away.

. . . the unfading garland of glory — NEB

... the eternal crown of glory — Bas

... the never-withering wreath of glory — Wey

... the glorious wreath that will never fade — Gspd

5. Likewise, ye younger, submit yourselves unto the elder.

You younger men must also submit to the presbyters — Mof

Again, you younger men should shew deference to the older — TCNT

Yea, all of you be subject one to another, and be clothed with humility:

Yea, all of you gird yourselves with humility to serve one another — ASV

Indeed you must all put on the apron of humility to serve one another — Mof

Indeed, all of you should wrap yourselves in the garment of humility towards each other — NEB

And all of you should put on the badge of humility in mutual service—TCNT

for God resisteth the proud,

Because God against the haughty arrayeth himself — Rhm

... God opposes the proud — Beck

and giveth grace to the humble.

but to the humble he gives grace — Mof

whereas unto the lowly he giveth favour — Rhm

but is kind to the humble — Beck

but gives his help to the humble — TCNT

6. Humble yourselves therefore under the mighty hand of God,

Bow down, then, before the strong hand of God — Knox

that he may exalt you in due time:

so that He may honor you when his time comes — NASB

so that at the right time He may set you on high — Wey

He will raise you up, when his time to deliver you comes — Knox

7. Casting all your care upon him;

Let all your anxieties fall upon him — Mof

Cast every worry you have upon Him — Wms

Throw back on him the burden of all your anxiety — Knox

Casting the whole of your care — all your anxieties, all your worries, all your concerns, once and for all — on Him — Amp

for he careth for you.

... he makes you his care — TCNT

... He takes care of you — Beck

... you are his personal concern — Phi

... his great interest is in you — Mof

... you are his charge — NEB

... he is concerned for you — Knox

for He cares for you affectionately, and cares about you watchfully — Amp

8. Be sober, be vigilant;

Be calm and watchful — Gspd

Exercise self-control, be watchful — TCNT

Awake! be on the alert! — NEB

because your adversary the devil, as a roaring lion, walketh about,

... roams around like a lion roaring — Amp

... is prowling about — TCNT

seeking whom he may devour:

looking for someone to devour — NEB

eager to devour you — TCNT

9. Whom resist stedfast in the faith,

Resist him and be strong in the faith — Gspd

Resist him; keep your foothold in the faith — Mof

Withstand him, firm in your faith — Wey

knowing that the same afflictions are accomplished in your brethren that are in the world.

in the knowledge that your brothers who are in the world undergo the same troubles — Bas

for you know that your brotherhood all over the world is having the same experience of suffering—Gspd

and remember that your brother Christians are going through the same kinds of suffering while they are in the world — NEB

10. But the God of all grace,

And God, the giver of all grace — Knox

And God, the giver of every spiritual blessing — Wms

who hath called us unto his eternal glory by Christ Jesus,

who has called us by Christ Jesus to share in his eternal glory — Mon

after that ye have suffered a while, make you perfect, stablish, strengthen, settle you.

. . . will himself make you perfect, steadfast, and strong — Gspd

. . . will himself give you mastery, and steadiness, and strength — Knox

will himself, after your brief suffering, restore, establish, and strengthen you on a firm foundation — NEB

11. To him be glory and dominion for ever and ever. Amen.

His is the power, for ever and ever! Amen. — Wey

His is the power for ever. So be it — Bas

12. By Silvanus, a faithful brother unto you, as I suppose,

. . . as I account him — ASV

. . . for such I regard him — Wey

. . . whom I know to be a faithful brother — Phi

I have written briefly, exhorting, and testifying

I have written these few lines of encouragement, to testify — Mof

I have written you this short letter to encourage you and bear my testimony — Gspd

that this is the true grace of God wherein ye stand.

that this is what God's grace means. Stand in that grace — Mof

that the grace in which you are so firmly established is the true grace of God — Knox

13. The church that is at Babylon, elected together with you, saluteth you;

She that is in Babylon, elect together with you, saluteth you — ASV

She who is in Babylon, chosen together with you, sends you greetings — NASB

and so doth Marcus my son.

and so does Mark my son — Wey

14. Greet ye one another with a kiss of charity.

Greet one another with the kiss of love — TCNT

Greet one another with the kiss of fellowship — Knox

Peace be with you all that are in Christ Jesus. Amen.

Peace to you all who belong to Christ! — NEB

Peace to all of you that are in union with Christ — Gspd

THE SECOND EPISTLE OF PETER

CHAPTER 1

1. Simon Peter, a servant and an apostle of Jesus Christ,

... a slave and apostle ... — Mon

... a servant and messenger ... — Phi

... a bond-servant and apostle ... — NASB

to them that have obtained like precious faith with us

to those who share with us the common privilege of faith — Knox

to those to whom there has been allotted a faith of equal privilege with ours — Wey

to those who . . . have been given a faith as privileged as ours — Gspd

to those who . . . share our faith and enjoy equal privilege with ourselves — NEB

To those who have obtained a faith of equal standing with ours — RSV

to those who have been given a faith as valuable as ours — Phi

through the righteousness of God and our Saviour Jesus Christ:

through the justice of our God and Saviour Jesus Christ — NEB

in the righteousness of our God and Savior . . . — RSV

2. Grace and peace be multiplied unto you

May you know more and more of grace and peace — Phi

May blessing and peace be yours in ever-increasing measure — TCNT

God bless you and give you perfect peace — Gspd

spiritual blessing and peace be to you in increasing abundance — Wms

through the knowledge of God, and of Jesus our Lord,

as you gain fuller knowledge of God, and of Christ Jesus our Lord—Knox

as you advance in the knowledge of God and of Jesus, our Lord — TCNT

through intimate acquaintance with God and with Jesus our Lord — Ber

3. According as his divine power hath given unto us

seeing that his divine power hath granted unto us — ASV

For his divine power has given us — TCNT

Inasmuch as his power divine has bestowed upon us — Mof

all things that pertain to life and godliness,

everything that makes for life and true religion — NEB

every requisite for life and godliness — Mof

everything that is needful for a life of piety — TCNT

through the knowledge of him that hath called us to glory and virtue:

through our coming to know him who through his glory and excellence called us to him — Gspd

as we advance in the knowledge of him who called us by a glorious manifestation of his goodness — TCNT

enabling us to know the One who called us by his own splendour and might — NEB

by the knowledge of him who called us to his own glory and excellence — Mof

through our getting to know Him who has called us to share His glory and virtue — Nor

through the knowledge of Him who called us by His own glory and perfection — Wey

4. Whereby are given unto us exceeding great and precious promises:

For it was through this that he gave us what we prize as the greatest of his promises — TCNT

Thus he has given us his precious and splendid promises — Gspd

. . . high and treasured promises — Knox

Through this might and splendour he has given us his promises, great beyond all price — NEB

that by these ye might be partakers of the divine nature,

that by means of these . . . — Alf

in order that through these ye might become sharers in a divine nature — Rhm

that through them you might participate in the divine nature — TCNT

having escaped the corruption that is in the world through lust.

having escaped the corruption which is now in the world by reason of lustful passions — Wey

now that you have fled from the corruption in the world, resulting from human passions — TCNT

. . . produced within the world by lust — Mof

. . . the moral decay (rottenness and corruption) that is in the world because of covetousness (lust and greed) — Amp

5. And beside this, giving all diligence, add to your faith virtue;

Yea, and for this very cause adding on your part all diligence, in your faith supply virtue — ASV

— for this very reason, do you contrive to make it your whole concern to furnish your faith with resolution — Mof

For this very reason make every effort to supplement your faith with goodness — Gspd

Now for this very reason you must do your level best to supplement your faith with moral character — Wms

With all this in view, you should try your hardest to supplement your faith with virtue — NEB

For this very reason do your best to add to your faith manliness — Mon

Now for this reason also, applying all diligence, in your faith supply moral excellence — NASB

. . . with your faith exhibit also a noble character — Wey

and to virtue knowledge;

. . . intelligence — Mof

6. And to knowledge temperance;

. . . self-control — ASV

. . . self-restraint — Alf

and to temperance patience;

. . . endurance — Rhm

. . . steadfastness — Mof

. . . fortitude — NEB

. . . perseverance — NASB

. . . patient endurance — Wms

and to patience godliness;

. . . piety — TCNT

. . . devotion to God — Phi

. . . the fear of God — Bas

7. And to godliness brotherly kindness;

. . . brotherly affection — Rhm

. . . love to the brethren — Wey

. . . a spirit of brotherhood — Gspd

and to brotherly kindness and charity.

. . . love — ASV

. . . Christian love — Mof

. . . love itself — Mon

. . . universal love — Wms

8. For if these things be in you, and abound,

For these things being in you, and multiplying — Alf

For as these qualities exist and increase with you — Mof

For if you have these qualities in their fulness — Gspd

For, when these virtues are yours, in increasing measure — TCNT

they make you that ye shall neither be barren nor unfruitful

they make you to be not idle nor unfruitful — ASV

they will keep you from being either useless or barren — NEB

they keep you from being ineffective or unfruitful — RSV

they will make you neither idle nor unproductive — Gspd

they render you active and fruitful — Mof

they will not let you remain inactive or unfruitful — Nor

in the knowledge of our Lord Jesus Christ.

unto the knowledge of . . . — ASV

in advancing towards a full knowledge . . . — Wey

when it comes to the understanding of . . . — Gspd

until you come unto the full knowledge of . . . — Mon

reaching ever closer knowledge of . . . — Knox

9. But he that lacketh these things is blind, and cannot see afar off,

Surely the man who has not these virtues is shortsighted even to blindness — TCNT

For he that lacketh these things is blind, seeing only what is near — ASV

For whoever lacks these qualities is blind — or short-sighted — Wms

and hath forgotten that he was purged from his old sins.

having forgotten the cleansing of his old sins — ASV

having no memory of how he was
made clean from his old sins — Bas

oblivious that he has been cleansed
from his erstwhile sins — Mof

and has chosen to forget that he has
been purified from his sins of the
past — TCNT

10. Wherefore the rather, brethren, give diligence

For this cause, my brothers, take all
the more care — Bas

Therefore, brothers, make all the
greater efforts — Gspd

Therefore, Brothers, do your best —
TCNT

For this reason, brethren, be all the
more in earnest — Wey

So be the more eager, brothers — Mof

Therefore, brethren, be the more zealous — RSV

Exert yourselves the more then, brothers — Ber

to make your calling and election sure:

to make certain of your calling and
election — Wey

to make God's call and choice of you
certain — Gspd

to put God's Call and Selection of you
beyond all doubt — TCNT

for if ye do these things, ye shall never fall:

for, so long as you practise these things,
you will never stumble — Wey

for as you exercise these qualities you
will never make a slip — Mof

If you behave so you will never come
to grief — NEB

11. For so an entrance shall be ministered unto you abundantly

for thus shall be richly supplied unto
you the entrance — ASV

so there will be richly provided for you
an entrance — RSV

for then you will be triumphantly admitted — Gspd

you will thus be richly furnished with
the right of entry — Mof

For thus you will be given a triumphant
admission — TCNT

and it will be no grudging entrance that
is afforded to you — Knox

into the everlasting kingdom of our Lord and Saviour Jesus Christ.

into the eternal realm . . . — Mof

12. Wherefore I will not be negligent

. . . I shall be ready — ASV

And so I will not hesitate — NEB

Hence I mean to keep on — Mof

I shall never fail, then — Knox

to put you always in remembrance of these things,

to remind you of this again and again
— NEB

reminding you of this — Mof

though ye know them, and be established in the present truth.

even though you know it and are firmly established in the Truth that you
now hold — TCNT

although you know them and are steadfast believers in the truth which you
possess — Wey

although you are aware of it and are
fixed in your experience of the Truth
— Mof

although you know it and are firmly
grounded in the truth that you have
— Gspd

. . . are well grounded in the truth that
has already reached you — NEB

13. Yea, I think it meet, as long as I am in this tabernacle,

So long as I am in this tent, I deem it
proper — Mof

But I think it right, so long as I sojourn
in this body — Wey

. . . so long as I still lodge in this body
— NEB

to stir you up by putting you in remembrance;

to keep refreshing your memory —
NEB

to rouse you by awakening memories
of the past — TCNT

to stir you up by way of reminder —
Mof

to stimulate you by these reminders —
Phi

14. Knowing that shortly I must put off this my tabernacle,

knowing that the putting off of my
tabernacle cometh swiftly — ASV

For I know that soon my body must
be laid aside — Wey

since I know my tent must be folded
up very soon — Mof

since I know that the time for me to
strike tent comes swiftly on — Mon

even as our Lord Jesus Christ hath shewed me.
. . . pointed out to me — Mon
. . . revealed to me — Wey
. . . made clear to me — Rhm

15. **Moreover I will endeavour that ye may be able after my decease to have these things always in remembrance.**
Yea, I will give diligence that at every time ye may be able after my decease to call these things to remembrance — ASV
And I will also earnestly endeavor that at all times ye may be able after my departure to call these things to mind — ABUV
So I will do my best to enable you, at any time after my departure, to call these truths to mind — TCNT
I will also take care that after I am gone you will be able at any time to call these things to mind — Gspd
But I will see to it that after I am gone you will have means of remembering these things at all times — NEB

16. **For we have not followed cunningly devised fables,**
. . . we were not following cleverly devised legends — Wey
For they were no fictitious stories that we followed — Gspd
It was not on tales artfully spun that we relied — NEB
We were not crediting fables of man's invention — Knox
when we made known unto you the power and coming of our Lord Jesus Christ,
when we told you of the Coming in power of our Lord Jesus Christ — TCNT
when we preached to you about the power of our Lord Jesus Christ, and about his coming — Knox
but were eyewitnesses of his majesty.
we saw him with our own eyes in majesty — NEB
we actually saw his majesty with our own eyes — Phi
we were admitted to the spectacle of his sovereignty — Mof

17. **For he received from God the Father honour and glory, when there came such a voice to him from the excellent glory,**
when he was invested with honour and glory by God the Father, and when the following voice was borne to him from the sublime Glory — Mof
For he received honour and glory from God the Father, when from the Glory of the Divine Majesty there were borne to his ears words such as these — TCNT
. . . when there was borne such a voice to him by the Majestic Glory — ASV
. . . by the magnificent glory — Rhm
. . . and out of the wondrous glory words such as these were conveyed to Him — Wey
Such honour, such glory was bestowed on him by God the Father that a voice came out of the splendour which dazzles human eyes — Knox
This is my beloved Son, in whom I am well pleased.
. . . in whom I delight — Rhm
. . . I take delight — Wey
. . . on whom my favour rests — NEB
This is my Son, my Beloved! He is my Chosen! — Gspd

18. **And this voice which came from heaven we heard,**
. . . we ourselves heard borne out of heaven — ASV
We actually heard that voice speaking from Heaven — Phi
when we were with him in the holy mount.
we who were beside him on the sacred hill — Mof

19. **We have also a more sure word of prophecy;**
And we have the word of prophecy made more sure — ASV
So we have the word of prophecy confirmed — Wey
and thus we have gained fresh confirmation of the prophetic word—Mof
And we have the prophetic word made more sure — RSV
So we have the message of the prophets more fully guaranteed — Gspd
All this only confirms for us the message of the prophets — NEB
whereunto ye do well that ye take heed, as unto a light that shineth in a dark place, until the day dawn, and the day star arise in your hearts:

to which you will do well to pay attention (as if it were a lamp shining in a gloomy place), until the Day dawns and the Morning Star arises in your hearts — TCNT

Pray attend to that word; it shines like a lamp within a darksome spot, till the Day dawns and the day-star rises within your hearts — Mof

to which you do well to attend, because it is like a lamp shining in a murky place, until the day breaks and the morning star rises to illuminate your minds — NEB

20. Knowing this first, that no prophecy of the scripture

— understanding this, at the outset, that no prophetic scripture — Mof

But above all, remember that no prophecy in Scripture — Wey

is of any private interpretation.

can be understood through one's own powers — Gspd

allows a man to interpret it by himself — Mof

is to be interpreted by one's own mind — Wms

is the subject of private interpretation — Knox

is a matter of one's own interpretation — NASB

arose from an individual's interpretation of truth — Phi

was ever thought up by the prophet himself — Tay

21. For the prophecy came not in old time by the will of man:

For no prophecy ever came by the will of man — ASV

for no prophecy ever originated in human will — Gspd

for no prophetic teaching ever came in the days of old at the mere wish of man — TCNT

Because no prophecy ever resulted from human design — Ber

For it was not through any human whim that men prophesied of old — NEB

For no prophecy ever originated because some man willed it — Amp

but holy men of God spake as they were moved by the Holy Ghost.

but men spake from God, being moved by the Holy Spirit — ASV

but under the influence of the holy Spirit men spoke for God — Gspd

but men, moved by the Holy Spirit, spoke direct from God — TCNT

it was when carried away by the holy Spirit that the holy men of God spoke — Mof

men they were, but, impelled by the Holy Spirit, they spoke the words of God — NEB

CHAPTER 2

1. But there were false prophets also among the people,

But also [in those days] there arose false prophets among the people — Amp

even as there shall be false teachers among you,

as there will be teachers of falsehood among you too — Wey

who privily shall bring in damnable heresies,

... destructive heresies — ASV

who will cunningly introduce fatal heresies — Wey

They will import disastrous heresies — NEB

who will secretly introduce ruinous divisions — TCNT

even denying the Lord that bought them,

disowning even ... — TCNT

and bring upon themselves swift destruction.

bringing rapid destruction on themselves — Mof

bringing swift disaster on their own heads — NEB

bringing speedy Ruin upon themselves — TCNT

2. And many shall follow their pernicious ways;

... lascivious ... — ASV

... licentious ... — Alf

... wanton ... — Rhm

... licentiousness — RSV

And in their immoral ways they will have many disciples — Wey

They will gain many adherents to their dissolute practices — NEB

by reason of whom the way of truth

shall be evil spoken of.

and thereby bring discredit on the way of truth — Phi

through whom the true way will be brought into disrepute — Wey

and cause the Way of Truth to be maligned — TCNT

3. **And through covetousness shall they with feigned words make merchandise of you:**

Motivated by greed, they will exploit you with their counterfeit arguments — Ber

In their covetousness they will try to make you a source of profit by their fabrications — TCNT

in their lust they will exploit you with cunning arguments — Mof

In their greed for money they will trade on your credulity with sheer fabrications — NEB

whose judgment now of a long time lingereth not,

whose punishment has been ready for a long time — Bas

From of old their sentence has been hanging over them — Ber

men whose doom comes apace from of old — Mof

but for a long time past their Sentence has not been standing idle — TCNT

and their damnation slumbereth not.

nor their Ruin slumbering — TCNT

and on their trail destruction is awake — Mof

and their destruction is watching for them — Bas

4. **For if God spared not the angels that sinned, but cast them down to hell,**

For if God did not spare angels when they had sinned, but hurled them down to Tartarus — Wey

and delivered them into chains of darkness, to be reserved unto judgment;

and committed them to pits[1] of darkness, to be reserved . . . — ASV

and committed them to dark dungeons to await their doom — Gspd

and committed them to caverns of darkness, to be kept under guard for judgement — TCNT

5. **And spared not the old world,**

if he did not spare the ancient world — RSV

but saved Noah the eighth person, a preacher of righteousness,

but preserved Noah with seven others, a preacher of righteousness — ASV

but kept Noah, the herald of righteousness, safe with seven others — Mof

bringing in the flood upon the world of the ungodly;

when he brought a flood upon the world of the ungodly — ASV

when he brought the flood upon the world in its wickedness — Phi

. . . the godless world — Gspd

6. **And turning the cities of Sodom and Gomorrha into ashes condemned them with an overthrow,**

if He reduced to ashes the cities of Sodom and Gomorrah, and condemned them to overthrow — Wey

if by turning the cities of Sodom and Gomorrah to ashes he condemned them to extinction — RSV

making them an ensample unto those that after should live ungodly;

holding them up as a warning to the godless of what was in store for them — TCNT

as a warning to ungodly men of what was to come — Gspd

making them an object-lesson for godless men in future days — NEB

for an example to the godless of a later time — Knox

7. **And delivered just Lot,**

and if he rescued righteous Lot — RSV

vexed with the filthy conversation of the wicked:

sore distressed by the lascivious life of the wicked — ASV

wearied out with the lewd conduct of the lawless — ABUV

who was so distressed by the immoral conduct of unprincipled men—Gspd

shocked by the dissolute habits of lawless society — NEB

8. **(For that righteous man dwelling among them, in seeing and hearing,**

for, seeing and hearing what he did, as he lived his righteous life among them — TCNT

(for by what that righteous man saw and heard as he lived among them — RSV

---

[1]Variant reading.

vexed his righteous soul from day to day with their unlawful deeds;)

his righteous soul was vexed day after day with their unlawful doings — Mof

day after day, Lot's righteous soul was tortured by their wicked doings — TCNT

he was vexed in his righteous soul day after day with their lawless deeds) — RSV

9. The Lord knoweth how to deliver the godly out of temptations,

. . . to rescue the godly from trial — Mof

. . . God-fearing people from trial — Gspd

and to reserve the unjust unto the day of judgment to be punished:

and to keep the unrighteous under punishment unto the day of judgment — ASV

and to keep the wicked, who are even now suffering punishment, in readiness for the Day of Judgement — TCNT

10. But chiefly them that walk after the flesh in the lust of uncleanness, and despise government.

and especially those who are abandoned to sensuality — craving for polluted things, and scorning control — Wey

particularly those who fall in with the polluting appetites of the flesh and despise the powers Celestial — Mof

especially those who yield to their physical nature and indulge in passions that defile them, and despise authority — Gspd

Presumptuous are they, selfwilled,

Daring, selfwilled — ASV

These men are arrogant and presumptuous — Phi

Daring, presumptuous creatures!—Mof

Rash, headstrong men! — Gspd

Audacious and self-willed — TCNT

In their boldness and wilfulness—Nor

they are not afraid to speak evil of dignities.

they tremble not to rail at dignities — ASV

they think nothing of scoffing at the glories of the unseen world — Phi

they are not afraid to insult celestial beings — NEB

they are not afraid to revile the glorious ones — RSV

they stand in no awe of majesty — Gspd

They do not tremble when they abuse persons of majesty — Wms

they have no fear as to speaking evil of those in high repute — Nor

11. Whereas angels, which are greater in power and might,

even where angels, though excelling them in strength and power — TCNT

even angels, far superior to these beings in strength and power — Gspd

bring not railing accusation against them before the Lord.

employ no insults in seeking judgement against them before the Lord — NEB

do not make use of violent language against them . . . — Bas

bring no abusive charge before the Lord — Gspd

12. But these, as natural brute beasts, made to be taken and destroyed,

But these, as creatures without reason, born mere animals to be taken and destroyed — ASV

These men, however, like animals without reason, intended by nature to be caught and killed — TCNT

But these people! — like irrational animals, creatures of mere instinct, born for capture and corruption — Mof

But these men, with no more sense than the unreasoning brute beasts which are born to be caught and killed — Phi

speak evil of the things that they understand not;

abuse what they do not understand — Gspd

sneer at what they can not understand — Knox

scoff at things outside their own experience — Phi

and shall utterly perish in their own corruption;

shall in their destroying surely be destroyed — ASV

and in their corruption they will perish — Wey

and will assuredly perish through their own corruption — TCNT

13. And shall receive the reward of unrighteousness,

suffering wrong as the hire of wrongdoing — ASV

suffering themselves, as the penalty for the suffering they have inflicted — TCNT

receiving injury in retribution for the injuries they do — Wey

suffering hurt for the hurt they have inflicted — NEB

and so lose what they hope to gain by their wrongdoing — Beck

they will have the reward their wickedness has deserved — Knox

as they that count it pleasure to riot in the day time.

They take pleasure in spending the day in carousing — Nor

To carouse in broad daylight is their idea of pleasure — NEB

They think that pleasure consists in the indulgence of the moment — TCNT

Spots they are and blemishes, sporting themselves with their own deceivings while they feast with you;

foul blots and blemishes that stuff themselves at your tables by means of their deceptions — Ber

They are a stain and a disgrace, indulging, as they do, in their wanton revelry, even while joining you at your feasts — TCNT

they are foul spots and blots, playing their tricks at your very dinner tables — Phi

14. Having eyes full of adultery, and that cannot cease from sin;

Having eyes full of an adulteress and that cannot rest from sin — Rhm

They have eyes for nothing but women, eyes never at rest from sin — NEB

They have eyes for nobody but adulterous women — eyes insatiable in sin — Gspd

They have eyes only for adulteresses, eyes never tired of sin — TCNT

beguiling unstable souls:

enticing unsteadfast souls — ASV

They lure the unstable to their ruin — NEB

they captivate the unstable ones — Phi

They practice enticing unsteady souls — Wms

They know how to win wavering souls to their purpose — Knox

an heart they have exercised with covetous practices; cursed children:

having a heart exercised in covetousness; children of cursing — ASV

Their hearts are trained to be greedy. Cursed people! — Beck

past masters in mercenary greed, God's curse is on them! — NEB

their minds are trained to covet; they live under a curse — TCNT

15. Which have forsaken the right way, and are gone astray,

forsaking the right way, they went astray — ASV

Leaving the straight road, they have gone astray — TCNT

following the way of Balaam the son of Bosor, who loved the wages of unrighteousness;

having followed the way of Balaam the son of Beor, who loved the hire of wrong-doing — ASV

. . . set his heart on dishonest gain — Gspd

. . . fell in love with the profits of wrong-doing — Wms

16. But was rebuked for his iniquity:

but he got reproved for his mal-practice — Mof

. . . his offence — TCNT

the dumb ass speaking with man's voice forbad the madness of the prophet.

a dumb beast of burden spoke with a human voice and checked the madness of the prophet — Wey

. . . checked the prophet's infatuation — Mof

. . . halted the folly of the prophet — Lam

. . . put a stop to the prophet's madness — NEB

17. These are wells without water, clouds that are carried with a tempest;

These are springs without water, and mists driven by a storm — ASV

These people are waterless fountains and mists driven by a squall — Mof

Such men are dried-up springs, clouds driven before the storm — Gspd to whom the mist of darkness is reserved for ever.

and for them the blackest darkness has been reserved — TCNT

men for whom the densest darkness has been reserved — Wey

18. For when they speak great swelling words of vanity, they allure through the lusts of the flesh, through much wantonness,

They utter big, empty words, and make of sensual lusts and debauchery a bait to catch — NEB

For, uttering loud boasts of folly, they entice with licentious passions of the flesh — RSV

They utter arrogant nonsense and use physical cravings to lure into immorality — Gspd

Using fine phrases that have no meaning, they bait their hook with wanton appetites of sense — Knox

those that were clean escaped from them who live in error.

those who are just[2] escaping from them that live in error — ASV

those who have barely begun to escape from their heathen environment — NEB

men who have barely escaped from those who live in error — RSV

those who have had but a short respite from false teaching — Knox

19. While they promise them liberty, they themselves are the servants of corruption:

They promise them freedom, while they themselves are slaves to corrupt habits — TCNT

. . . while they themselves are slaves of rottenness! — Mon

promising them freedom when they are themselves slaves of destruction — Gspd

for of whom a man is overcome, of the same is he brought in bondage.

for by what one is overcome, by this he is also enslaved — ABUV

(for a man is a slave of whatever overpowers him) — Mof

(For indeed a man is the slave of anything which masters him.) — Mon

because whatever gets the better of a man makes a servant of him — Bas

20. For if after they have escaped the pollutions of the world through the knowledge of the Lord and Saviour Jesus Christ, they are again entangled therein, and overcome,

. . . the polluting influences of the world . . . — TCNT

. . . the world's contaminations . . . — Phi

For if, after they have escaped the defilements of the world through the knowledge of our Lord and Savior Jesus Christ, they are again entangled in them and overpowered — RSV

the latter end is worse with them than the beginning.

the last state has become worse for them than the first — RSV

these people are worse off in the end than they were before — Beck

their plight in the end is worse than before — NEB

their final condition is worse than their former one — Gspd

21. For it had been better for them not to have known the way of righteousness, than, after they had known it, to turn from the holy commandment delivered unto them.

For it would have been better for them never to have known the way of righteousness than after knowing it to turn back from the holy commandment delivered to them — RSV

22. But it is happened unto them according to the true proverb,

What has happened to them proves the truth of the proverb — Knox

In them is verified the truth of the proverb — Wms

There has befallen them the thing spoken in the true proverb — Amp

The dog is turned to his own vomit again;

A dog returns to what he has vomited — TCNT

and the sow that was washed to her wallowing in the mire.

and the sow that had washed to wallowing in the mire — ASV

and The sow after a wash rolls in the mud again — NEB

_____

[2]Variant reading.

CHAPTER 3

1. **This second epistle, beloved, I now write unto you;**

    This is now, beloved, the second epistle that I write . . . — ASV

    This, dear friends, is my second letter to you — TCNT

    in both which I stir up your pure minds by way of remembrance:

    In both I seek to revive in your sincere minds certain memories — Wey

    and in this as in the first, I am attempting to keep your true minds awake — Bas

    In both of them I have been recalling to you what you already know, to rouse you to honest thought — NEB

    In both of them I have tried, by appealing to your remembrance to arouse your better feelings — TCNT

2. **That ye may be mindful of the words which were spoken before by the holy prophets,**

    so that you may recall the words spoken beforehand by the holy Prophets — Wey

    and of the commandment of us the apostles of the Lord and Saviour:

    and the commandment of the Lord and Saviour through your apostles — ASV

    . . . given by your apostles from the Lord and saviour — Mof

3. **Knowing this first, that there shall come in the last days scoffers,**

    To begin with, you know that mockers will come with their mockeries in the last days — Mof

    walking after their own lusts,

    going where their own passions lead — Gspd

    behaving in line with their own lusts — Ber

    — men governed by their own passions — Wey

    ruled by their evil desires — Bas

4. **And saying, Where is the promise of his coming?**

    . . . What has become of the promise that he would appear — Knox

    . . . Where is his promised Return — Wey

    for since the fathers fell asleep, all

things continue as they were from the beginning of the creation.

    Ever since our fathers passed to their rest, everything remains just as it was when the world was first created! — TCNT

5. **For this they willingly are ignorant of,**

    For this they wilfully forget — ASV

    They deliberately ignore this fact — RSV

    In taking this view they lose sight of the fact — NEB

    For when they maintain this, it escapes their notice — NASB

    For they wilfully shut their eyes to the fact — TCNT

    For they are fain to forget how — Knox

    that by the word of God the heavens were of old, and the earth standing out of the water and in the water:

    that there were heavens from of old, and an earth compacted out of water and amidst water, by the word of God — ASV

    that long ago the heavens existed; and the earth, also — formed out of water and by the action of water, by the fiat of God — TCNT

    that there were heavens of old and an earth rising from and extended through water, by the word of God — Wey

    . . . standing partly above and partly amidst water by the word of God — Ber

    . . . lifted out of the water and circled by water, by the word of God — Bas

6. **Whereby the world that then was, being overflowed with water, perished:**

    and by water that first world was destroyed, the water of the deluge — NEB

    and that by the same means the world which then existed was destroyed in a deluge of water — TCNT

7. **But the heavens and the earth, which are now,**

    But the present heavens and earth — TCNT

    by the same word are kept in store, reserved unto fire

by the same fiat, have been reserved
for fire, and are being kept — TCNT

are, also by God's command, being
carefully kept — Phi

by the same word have been stored up
for fire, being reserved — ASV

**against the day of judgment and perdi-
tion of ungodly men.**

for the day when the impious are
doomed and destroyed — Mof

for the day of the judgement and destruction of the godless — TCNT

**8. But, beloved, be not ignorant of this
one thing,**

But do not overlook this one fact, dear
friends — Gspd

But this one thing, beloved, you must
not forget — Wey

Beloved, you must not ignore this one
fact — Mof

**that one day is with the Lord as a thou-
sand years, and a thousand years as
one day.**

that with the Lord a day counts as a
thousand years, and a thousand
years count as a day — Knox

with the Lord one day is like a thousand years and a thousand years like
one day — NEB

**9. The Lord is not slack concerning his
promise,**

. . . is not negligent concerning . . . —
Lam

. . . is not being dilatory over . . . —
Knox

. . . does not loiter over . . . — Mon

. . . is not slow to fulfil his promise —
TCNT

as some men count slackness;

in the sense that some men think —
Gspd

according to some people's conception
of slowness — Amp

but is longsuffering to us-ward,

He bears patiently with you — Wey

**not willing that any should perish, but
that all should come to repentance.**

because it is not his will for any to be
lost, but for all to come to repentance — NEB

His desire being that no one should
perish . . . — Wey

. . . but that all should reach repentance
— RSV

**10. But the day of the Lord will come as
a thief in the night;**

But the Day of the Lord will come;
it will come, unexpected as a thief
— NEB

**in the which the heavens shall pass
away with a great noise,**

On that day the heavens will disappear
with a great rushing sound — NEB

. . . with a rush and a roar — Wey

. . . the heavens will vanish with crack-
ling roar — Mof

Then with a tremendous crash the
heavens will pass away — Ber

**and the elements shall melt with ferv-
ent heat,**

. . . the heavenly bodies shall be
scorched up and dissolved — Alf

. . . the stars will be set ablaze and melt
— Mof

. . . the elements will disintegrate in
flames — NEB

**the earth also and the works that are
therein shall be burned up.**

and the earth and the works that are
upon it will be burned up — RSV

. . . will be discovered — Rhm

. . . will be disclosed — TCNT

. . . will be laid bare — NEB

**11. Seeing then that all these things shall
be dissolved,**

Seeing that these things are thus all to
be dissolved — ASV

. . . are in the process of dissolution —
TCNT

. . . are on the verge of dissolution —
Wey

**what manner of persons ought ye to
be in all holy conversation and godliness,**

what holy and pious lives you ought
to lead — Gspd

what devout and dedicated lives you
should live! — NEB

**12. Looking for and hasting unto the com-
ing of the day of God,**

looking for and earnestly desiring the
coming of . . . — ASV

expecting and helping to hasten the
coming of . . . — Wey

Look eagerly for the coming of the day
of God and work to hasten it on —
NEB

**wherein the heavens being on fire shall
be dissolved,**

because of which the heavens will be kindled and dissolved — RSV

which will cause the heavens to blaze and dissolve — Wms

and the elements shall melt with fervent heat?

While the elements becoming intensely hot are to be melted — Rhm

and the elements disintegrate in fearful heat — Phi

13. **Nevertheless we, according to his promise, look for new heavens and a new earth, wherein dwelleth righteousness.**

. . . where righteousness shall have its home — TCNT

. . . in which uprightness will have its permanent home — Wms

14. **Wherefore, beloved, seeing that ye look for such things,**

Therefore, dear friends, in expectation of these things — TCNT

be diligent that ye may be found of him in peace, without spot, and blameless.

make every effort to be found of him spotless, blameless, and at peace — TCNT

. . . at peace with him, unblemished and above reproach in his sight — NEB

15. **And account that the longsuffering of our Lord is salvation;**

Look upon our Lord's patience as salvation — Gspd

And regard the forbearance of our Lord as salvation — Wey

and consider that the long-suffering of our Lord means salvation — Mof

even as our beloved brother Paul also according to the wisdom given unto him hath written unto you;

16. **As also in all his epistles, speaking in them of these things;**

and as well in all the letters in which he mentions these subjects — Ber

And so he does in all his other letters, wherever he speaks of this subject — NEB

in which are some things hard to be understood,

There are some things in them hard to understand — Gspd

though they contain some obscure passages — NEB

which they that are unlearned and unstable wrest,

which untaught and weak people distort — TCNT

and which, unhappily, ill informed and unbalanced people distort — Phi

as they do also the other scriptures, unto their own destruction.

. . . to their own undoing — Knox

. . . to their own Ruin — TCNT

17. **Ye therefore, beloved, seeing ye know these things before,**

. . . being warned beforehand — Wey

beware lest ye also, being led away with the error of the wicked,

Be on your guard lest . . . — Rhm

fall from your own stedfastness.

lose your own stability — RSV

. . . your proper foothold — Phi

. . . your own safe foothold — NEB

18. **But grow in grace, and in the knowledge of our Lord and Saviour Jesus Christ.**

. . . continue to grow . . . — Wms

. . . and become better acquainted with . . . — Tay

To him be glory both now and for ever. Amen.

Glory be to him now and forever — Gspd

. . . now and for all eternity . . . — Knox

. . . and to the day of eternity! — Wey

THE FIRST EPISTLE OF JOHN

CHAPTER 1

1. That which was from the beginning, which we have heard, which we have seen with our eyes, which we have looked upon, and our hands have handled, of the Word of life;

It is of what has been in existence from the Beginning, of what we have heard, of what we have seen with our eyes, of what we watched reverently and touched with our hands — it is about the Word who is the Life that we are now writing — TCNT

It is what existed from the beginning, that we announce; what we have heard, what we have seen with our own eyes, what we have beheld, and touched with our hands; it is the very message of life — Gspd

What was from the beginning, what we have heard, what we have seen with our eyes, what we beheld and our hands handled, concerning the Word of life — NASB

[We are writing] about the Word of Life [in] Him Who existed from the beginning, Whom we have heard, Whom we have seen with our own eyes, Whom we have gazed upon [for ourselves] and have touched with our [own] hands — Amp

It is of what has existed from the beginning, of what we have listened to, of what we have seen with our own eyes, of what we have witnessed and touched with our own hands, it is concerning the Logos of Life that we are now writing — Mon

Christ was alive when the world began, yet I myself have seen Him with my own eyes and listened to Him speak. I have touched Him with my own hands. He is God's message of Life — Tay

2. (For the life was manifested, and we have seen it, and bear witness, and shew unto you that eternal life,

— for life has been revealed and we have seen it and testify to it and announce to you that eternal life — Gspd

(the Life has appeared; we saw it, we testify to it, we bring you word of that eternal Life — Mof

That Life was made visible, and we have seen it, and now bear our testimony to it, and tell you of that Immortal Life — TCNT

And the Life [an aspect of His being] was revealed, . . . — Amp

which was with the Father, and was manifested unto us;)

which was face to face with the Father and was made visible to us — Mon

which existed with the Father and was disclosed to us) — Mof

which ever abode with the Father and has dawned, now, upon us — Knox

3. That which we have seen and heard declare we unto you, that ye also may have fellowship with us:

. . . so that you may share our fellowship — Mof

. . . in order that you may have partnership with us — Mon

. . . so that you may have communion with us — TCNT

. . . so that we together may share in a common life — NEB

and truly our fellowship is with the Father, and with his Son Jesus Christ.

4. And these things write we unto you, that your joy may be full.

. . . that our joy may be made full — ASV

. . . so that joy may be yours in full measure — Knox

. . . that our joy in you may be complete — Lam

5. This then is the message which we have heard of him, and declare unto you,

These, then, are the Tidings that we have heard from him and now tell you — TCNT

. . . and are reporting unto you — Rhm

. . . and announce unto you — ASV

that God is light, and in him is no darkness at all.

. . . and no darkness can find any place in him — Knox

. . . and no shadow of darkness can exist in him — Phi

. . . and in him there is nothing dark — Bas

6. If we say that we have fellowship with him, and walk in darkness,

If, while we are living in darkness, we profess to have fellowship with him — Wey

If we say that we have communion with him, and yet continue to live in darkness — TCNT

we lie, and do not the truth:

we are dealing falsely and not doing the truth — Rhm

our words are false and our acts are untrue — Bas

then we are lying, we are not practising the truth — Mof

we are liars both in word and deed — Nor

7. But if we walk in the light, as he is in the light,

But, if our lives are lived in the Light, as God himself is in the Light — TCNT

we have fellowship[1] one with another, and the blood of Jesus Christ his Son cleanseth us from all sin.

. . . is cleansing us from all sin — Rhm

. . . continues to cleanse us from every sin — Wms

8. If we say that we have no sin,

If we refuse to admit that we are sinners — Phi

If we say, We have no sin — Mon

If we claim to be sinless — NEB

we deceive ourselves, and the truth is not in us.

we are self-deceived and strangers to the truth — NEB

we are only fooling ourselves, and refusing to accept the truth — Tay

9. If we confess our sins,

If we acknowledge our sins — Gspd

If we freely admit that we have sinned — Amp

he is faithful and just to forgive us our sins,

God may be trusted, in his righteousness, to forgive us our sins — TCNT

he is upright and can be depended on to forgive us our sins — Gspd

He is to be depended on, since He is just, to forgive us our sins — Wms

and to cleanse us from all unrighteousness.

. . . iniquity — Mof

. . . everything wrong — Gspd

and purify us from all wickedness — Nor

10. If we say that we have not sinned,

If we deny that we have sinned — Wey

we make him a liar, and his word is not in us.

it means that we are treating him as a liar; it means that his word does not dwell in our hearts — Knox

we make him out to be a liar, and then his word has no place in us — NEB

we contradict His Word and make Him out to be false and a liar, and His Word is not in us — the divine message of the Gospel is not in our hearts — Amp

CHAPTER 2

1. My little children, these things write I unto you,

My dear children! . . . — Rhm

that ye sin not.

that ye may not sin — ASV

that you may not continue in sin — Mon

to keep you clear of sin — Knox

to help you avoid sin — Phi

And if any man sin, we have an advocate with the Father, Jesus Christ the righteous:

but if any one should sin, we have one who can plead for us with the Father — Jesus Christ, the Righteous — TCNT

yet if anyone does sin, we have in Jesus

Christ one who is upright and will intercede for us with the Father — Gspd

. . . we have a Counsel for defense in the Father's presence, Jesus Christ, the Righteous — Ber

2. And he is the propitiation for our sins:

the one who made personal atonement for our sins — Phi

He, in his own person, is the atonement made for our sins — Knox

and he is the expiation for our sins — RSV

And He is Himself the atoning sacrifice

[1]See verse 3 for variants of "fellowship."

for our sins — Wms

and not for ours only, but also for the sins of the whole world.

. . . but for those of the whole world besides — TCNT

(and for those of the rest of the world as well) — Phi

3. And hereby we do know that we know him, if we keep his commandments.

This is how we may be sure that we know him, by obeying his commands — Mof

And by this we know that we have learnt to know him — by our laying his commands to heart — TCNT

It is only when we obey God's laws that we can be quite sure that we really know him — Phi

4. He that saith, I know him, and keepeth not his commandments,

He who professes to know Him, and does not obey His commands — Wey

is a liar, and the truth is not in him.

is a liar, and there is no truth in his heart — Gspd

. . . and the Truth has no place in him — TCNT

5. But whoso keepeth his word, in him verily is the love of God perfected:

but, whenever a man lays his Message to heart, in that man the love of God has indeed reached its perfection — TCNT

. . . has reached its full stature in him — Knox

But if you do what He says, God's love has in you really accomplished what He wants — Beck

But everyone who obeys His Word will truly have the love of God find perfect expression in his heart — Nor

hereby know we that we are in him.

Hereby perceive we . . . — Rhm

This is the way we can be sure that we are in union with him — Gspd

6. He that saith he abideth in him

The man who professes to continue in Him — Wey

whoever says I am always in union with him — Gspd

One who claims to dwell in him — Knox

ought himself also so to walk, even as he walked.

binds himself to live as Christ himself lived — NEB

ought to be living as he lived — Mof

must live just as he lived — Gspd

must needs live and move as he lived and moved — Knox

7. Brethren, I write no new commandment unto you, but an old commandment which ye had from the beginning. The old commandment is the word which ye have heard from the beginning.

8. Again, a new commandment I write unto you, which thing is true in him and in you:

Yet, again, it is a new Command that I am writing to you — manifest in Christ's life and in your own — TCNT

Yet it is a new command that I am writing you; it is newly realized in him and in yourselves — Gspd

because the darkness is past, and the true light now shineth.

for the darkness is passing away and the true Light is already shining — TCNT

. . . has passed away now, and true light shines instead — Knox

9. He that saith he is in the light,

Any one who professes to be in the light — Wey

He who claims enlightenment — Knox

and hateth his brother,

. . . continues to hate . . . — Wms

is in darkness even until now.

is still in darkness — Wey

10. He that loveth his brother abideth in the light,

. . . continues in the light — Wey

. . . remains in the light — Mof

. . . lives in light — Knox

and there is none occasion of stumbling in him.

and there is nothing within him to cause him to stumble — TCNT

and puts no hindrance in anyone's way — Gspd

. . . he is no hindrance to others — Wms

. . . there is nothing to make him stumble — NEB

1175

— and in the light there is no pitfall —
Mof

no fear of stumbling haunts him —
Knox

11. **But he that hateth his brother is in
darkness, and walketh in darkness,**

... is shut off from the light and gropes
his way in the dark — Phi

... and is spending his life in the darkness — Mon

**and knoweth not whither he goeth, be-
cause that darkness hath blinded his
eyes.**

and does not know where he is going,
because the Darkness prevents his
seeing — TCNT

and has no idea where he is going,
because the darkness has made him
blind — NEB

12. **I write unto you, little children, because your sins are forgiven you for his
name's sake.**

13. **I have written unto you, fathers, because ye have known him that is from
the beginning.**

... you have come to know ... — Nor

... you have learnt to know ...—TCNT

... you have known him who has always existed — Phi

**I write unto you, young men, because
ye have overcome the wicked one.**

... the evil one — ASV

**I write unto you, little children, be-
cause ye have known the Father.**

... have learnt to know ... — TCNT

14. **I have written unto you, fathers, because ye have known him that is from
the beginning.**

**I have written unto you, young men,
because ye are strong,**

... because you are vigorous — Ber

and the word of God abideth in you,

... is treasured in your hearts — Nor

... you have a hold on God's truth —
Phi

and ye have overcome the wicked one.

... conquered ... — Wms

... mastered ... — NEB

15. **Love not the world, neither the things
that are in the world.**

Stop loving the world, or the things
... — Wms

Do not love the world or what the
world can offer — TCNT

**If any man love the world, the love of
the Father is not in him.**

... persists in loving ... — Wms

When any one loves the world, there is
no love for the Father in him —
TCNT

16. **For all that is in the world,**

For the whole world system — Phi

Everything the world affords — NEB

for all that the world can offer — TCNT

**the lust of the flesh, and the lust of the
eyes, and the pride of life,**

the things our physical nature and our
eyes crave for, and the proud display
of life — Mof

The coveting of the flesh, The coveting
of the eyes, And the vain grandeur
of life — Rhm

— the gratification of the earthly nature, the gratification of the eye, the
pretentious life — TCNT

all that panders to the appetites, or entices the eyes, all the glamour of its
life — NEB

is not of the Father, but is of the world.

belongs, not to the Father, but to the
world — TCNT

these do not come from the Father, but
from the world — Gspd

17. **And the world passeth away, and the
lust thereof:**

and the world with its cravings is passing away — Gspd

The world and all its passionate desires
will one day disappear — Phi

**but he that doeth the will of God abid-
eth for ever.**

but whoever perseveres in doing God's
will lives on forever — Wms

18. **Little children, it is the last time:**

Little children, it is the last hour —
ASV

Dear children, the last hour has come
— Wey

My Children, these are the last days
— TCNT

My children, it is the final age of the
world — Nor

**and as ye have heard that antichrist
shall come, even now are there many
antichrists;**

You were told that an Anti-Christ was
coming; and many Anti-Christs have
already arisen — TCNT

. . . and many AntiChrists have indeed appeared — Wey

whereby we know that it is the last time.

So that we may be sure that it is the last hour — Gspd

19. They went out from us, but they were not of us;

They have gone out from our number, but they did not really belong to us — Gspd

They came of our company, but they never belonged to our company — Knox

for if they had been of us, they would no doubt have continued with us:

. . . they would have persevered at our side — Knox

. . . would have stayed with us — Beck

had they belonged to us, they would have remained with us — Mof

but they went out, that they might be made manifest

but they withdrew — to make it plain — Mof

They left us that it might be made clear — TCNT

that they were not all of us.

that they are none of us — Mof

that they do not, any of them, belong to us — TCNT

20. But ye have an unction from the Holy One,

Besides, you hold your anointing from the Holy One — Ber

But you have been anointed by the Holy One — RSV

and ye know all things.

and you all know — RSV

and now all of you know — Beck

21. I have not written unto you because ye know not the truth,

The reason I wrote to you was not that you do not know the truth — Ber

but because ye know it, and that no lie is of the truth.

but because you do know it, and that no lie comes from the truth — Wey

. . . and [know positively] that nothing false — no deception, no lie — is of the Truth — Amp

. . . and because that which is false has nothing in common with that which is true — Bas

22. Who is a liar but he that denieth that Jesus is the Christ?

Who is the real liar? . . . — Mof

Who is the notorious liar, if it is not the man who denies that Jesus is the Christ — Wms

Who is [such a] liar as he who denies that Jesus is the Christ, the Messiah — Amp

He is antichrist, that denieth the Father and the Son.

He is the real Antichrist — the man who disowns the Father and the Son — Gspd

He who disowns the Father and the Son is the antichrist — Wey

23. Whosoever denieth the Son, the same hath not the Father:

No one who habitually denies (disowns) the Son even has the Father — Amp

No one who denies the Son has the Father — RSV

[but] he that acknowledgeth the Son hath the Father also.

He who confesses the Son has the Father also — RSV

24. Let that therefore abide in you, which ye have heard from the beginning.

Keep what you have heard from the beginning in your hearts — Gspd

Enough for you, that the message which was first brought you should dwell in you — Knox

For yourselves I beg you to stick to the original teaching — Phi

If that which ye have heard from the beginning shall remain in you, ye also shall continue in the Son, and in the Father.

25. And this is the promise that he hath promised us, even eternal life.

And what he himself hath promised us is eternal life — Gspd

26. These things have I written unto you concerning them that seduce you.

. . . them that would lead you astray — ASV

. . . who are trying to mislead you — TCNT

27. But the anointing which ye have received of him abideth in you, and ye need not that any man teach you:

. . . [so] then you have no need that anyone should instruct you — Amp but as the same anointing teacheth you of all things, and is truth, and is no lie,

but, since his consecration of you teaches you about everything, and since it is a real consecration, and no lie — TCNT

... and as it is true and no falsehood — Gspd

... no illusion — NEB

and even as it hath taught you, ye shall abide in him.

keep in union with him just as it has taught you to do — Gspd

28. And now, little children, abide in him;

... continue to live in union with Him — Nor

that, when he shall appear, we may have confidence,

... boldness — ASV

... cheerful confidence — Mon

... unshaken confidence — Wms

and not be ashamed before him at his coming.

... shrink with shame from him ... — Alf

... shrink back in shame ... — Nor

... at his arrival — Mof

and not be shamed away from him by his presence — Rhm

and we may not be ashamed to meet him at his coming — TCNT

29. If ye know that he is righteous, ye know that every one that doeth righteousness is born of him.

... be sure that everyone who practises righteousness is born of him — Mof

... be assured that everyone also who acts righteously is a child of His — Wey

... you know also that everyone who habitually practises righteousness has been born of him — Mon

... is his offspring — Ber

CHAPTER 3

1. Behold, what manner of love the Father hath bestowed upon us,

Think what love the Father has shown us — TCNT

How great is the love that the Father has shown to us! — NEB

that we should be called the sons of God:

... children of God; and such we are[2] — ASV

therefore the world knoweth us not, because it knew him not.

The world does not recognise us? That is simply because it did not recognise him — Mof

2. Beloved, now are we the sons of God, and it doth not yet appear what we shall be:

Dear friends, we are God's Children now; what we shall be has not yet been revealed — TCNT

... it has not yet been disclosed what we are to be — Gspd

but we know that, when he shall appear, we shall be like him;

... if he shall be manifested, we shall be like him — ASV

What we do know is that, when it is revealed, we shall be like Christ — TCNT

for we shall see him as he is.

3. And every man that hath this hope in him purifieth himself, even as he is pure.

And every one that hath this hope set on him purifieth himself ... — ASV

And every one who has this hope with regard to Christ tries to make himself pure — as Christ is pure — TCNT

4. Whosoever committeth sin transgresseth also the law:

Every one who lives sinfully is living in violation of Law — TCNT

Every one that doeth sin doeth also lawlessness — ASV

for sin is the transgression of the law.

and sin is lawlessness — ASV

Sin is violation of Law — TCNT

5. And ye know that he was manifested to take away our sins; and in him is no sin.

... and in him Sin has no place — TCNT

6. Whosoever abideth in him sinneth not:

Whoever continually abides in him does not habitually sin — Mon

No one who maintains union with him lives in sin — TCNT

---

[2]Variant reading.

I JOHN 3

whosoever sinneth hath not seen him, neither known him.

whoever lives in sin has not seen him, nor come to know him — Mon

The regular sinner has never seen nor known him — Phi

7. Little children, let no man deceive you:

. . . lead you astray — ASV

. . . do not allow anybody to mislead you — Knox

he that doeth righteousness is righteous, even as he is righteous.

Whoever acts uprightly is upright, just as he is upright — Gspd

The man who lives a consistently good life is a good man, as surely as God is good — Phi

8. He that committeth sin is of the devil; for the devil sinneth from the beginning.

But the man whose life is habitually sinful is spiritually a son of the devil . . . — Phi

. . . belongs to the Devil . . . — TCNT

For this purpose the Son of God was manifested,

To this end . . . — ASV

This is why the Son of God appeared — Gspd

that he might destroy the works of the devil.

. . . undo . . . — Rhm

. . . put an end to . . . — Bas

9. Whosoever is born of God doth not commit sin;

Whoever is a child of God cannot go on sinning — Mon

for his seed remaineth in him:

because the very nature of God dwells within him — TCNT

for God's nature abides in him — RSV

A divine germ remains in him — Wey

because the God-given life-principle continues to live in him — Wms

and he cannot sin, because he is born of God.

and he cannot practice sinning, because he is born of God — Wms

and he cannot go on sinning because he is a child of God — Mon

10. In this the children of God are manifest, and the children of the devil.

By this the Children of God are distinguished from the Children of the Devil — TCNT

In this way it is clear who are the children of God and who are the children of the evil one — Bas

whosoever doeth not righteousness is not of God,

no one who fails to act righteously is a child of God — Wey

The man who does not lead a good life is no son of God — Phi

neither he that loveth not his brother.

nor is he who does not love his brother — Mon

11. For this is the message that ye heard from the beginning, that we should love one another.

12. Not as Cain, who was of that wicked one, and slew his brother.

We must not be like Cain . . . — TCNT

We are not to resemble Cain . . . — Wey

And wherefore slew he him?

And why did he kill him — TCNT

Because his own works were evil, and his brother's righteous.

It was because his life was bad while his brother's was good — TCNT

Because his own actions were wicked and his brother's righteous — Wey

13. Marvel not, my brethren, if the world hate you.

Do not be surprised . . . — Wey

Do not wonder, brothers, if the world continues to hate you — Mon

14. We know that we have passed from death unto life,

We know that we have migrated, out of death into life — Mon

because we love the brethren.

because we love our brothers — Mon

He that loveth not his brother abideth in death.

Anyone who does not love is still in death — Gspd

The man who does not love remains in a state of death — TCNT

. . . is still in the realm of death — NEB

15. Whosoever hateth his brother is a murderer: and ye know that no murderer hath eternal life abiding in him.

Anyone who keeps on hating his brother . . . — Wms

16. Hereby perceive we the love of God, because he laid down his life for us:

1179

... know we love, because ... — ASV

... have we the knowledge of love ... — Alf

We have learnt to know what love is from this — that Christ laid down his life on our behalf — TCNT

and we ought to lay down our lives for the brethren.

17. **But whoso hath this world's good, and seeth his brother have need,**

Whoever possesses this world's resources and notices that his brother suffers need — Ber

and shutteth up his bowels of compassion from him,

... steels his heart against him — TCNT

... closes his heart against him — Wey

how dwelleth the love of God in him?

how is it possible for the love of God to be in him — Bas

18. **My little children, let us not love in word, neither in tongue; but in deed and in truth.**

... let us put our love not into words or into talk but into deeds, and make it real — Mof

... let us not parade our love in word and speech only, but let us show it in deed and in truth — Nor

19. **And hereby we know that we are of the truth, and shall assure our hearts before him.**

20. **For if our heart condemn us, God is greater than our heart, and knoweth all things.**

By that we shall know that we are on the side of the Truth; and we shall satisfy ourselves in God's sight, that if our conscience condemns us, yet God is greater than our conscience and knows everything — TCNT

In this way we may be certain that we are true, and may give our heart comfort before him, When our heart says that we have done wrong; be-

cause God is greater than our heart, and has knowledge of all things — Bas

Thus it is that we may be sure we belong to the truth and reassure ourselves before him whenever our heart may condemn us; for God is greater than our heart, and he knows all — Mof

21. **Beloved, if our heart condemn us not, then have we confidence toward God.**

Dear friends, if our conscience does not condemn us, then we approach God with confidence — TCNT

... we have boldness toward God — ASV

... in approaching God — Gspd

22. **And whatsoever we ask, we receive of him,**

And he gives us all our requests — Bas

because we keep his commandments,

... practise obedience to ... — Wms

and do those things that are pleasing in his sight.

23. **And this is his commandment, That we should believe on the name of his Son Jesus Christ,**

... have faith in ... — Bas

... put your trust in ... — Phi

and love one another, as he gave us commandment.

24. **And he that keepeth his commandments dwelleth in him, and he in him.**

All who keep his commandments abide in him, and he in them — RSV

And hereby we know that he abideth in us, by the Spirit which he hath given us.

This is our proof that he is really dwelling in us, through the gift of his Spirit — Knox

and the guarantee of his presence within us is the Spirit he has given us — Phi

CHAPTER 4

1. **Beloved, believe not every spirit,**

But do not trust any and every spirit, my friends — NEB

Dear friends, do not believe every inspired utterance — Gspd

Not all prophetic spirits, brethren, deserve your credence — Knox

but try the spirits whether they are of God:

... test the spirits to see if they come from God — Mof

because many false prophets are gone out into the world.

2. **Hereby know ye the Spirit of God:**

The test by which you may recognize the Spirit of God is that — Wey

You can recognize the Spirit of God by this — Mof

This is how we may recognise the Spirit of God — NEB

Every spirit that confesseth that Jesus Christ is come in the flesh is of God:

every spirit which confesses Jesus as the Christ incarnate comes from God — Mof

every inspired utterance that acknowledges that Jesus Christ has come in human form, comes from God — Gspd

3. **And every spirit that confesseth not that Jesus Christ is come in the flesh is not of God:**

. . . does not thus acknowledge Jesus . . . — NEB

and this is that spirit of antichrist, whereof ye have heard that it should come; and even now already is it in the world.

. . . Right now he is in the world — Ber

4. **Ye are of God, little children, and have overcome them:**

But you, my children, are of God's family and you have the mastery over these false prophets — NEB

because greater is he that is in you, than he that is in the world.

5. **They are of the world: therefore speak they of the world,**

These men belong to the world . . . — Beck

. . . and so their language is that of the world — Wey

and the world heareth them.

. . . listens to them — TCNT

. . . pays attention to what they say — Phi

6. **We are of God: he that knoweth God heareth us;**

We, on the other hand, are God's people . . . — Nor

. . . Whoever has acquaintance with God, listens to us — Ber

he that is not of God heareth not us.

. . . refuses us a hearing — NEB

Hereby know we the spirit of truth, and the spirit of error.

By this test we can distinguish the spirit of truth from the spirit of error — Wey

This is how we recognize the spirit of truth and the spirit of error — Mof

7. **Beloved, let us love one another: for love is of God;**

. . . springs from God — Knox

. . . originates with God — Wms

and every one that loveth is born of God, and knoweth God.

8. **He that loveth not knoweth not God; for God is love.**

. . . has no knowledge of . . . — Wey

. . . Doth not understand . . . — Rhm

9. **In this was manifested the love of God toward us,**

In this the love of God was made manifest among us — RSV

God's love to us has been revealed in this way — Gspd

This is how the love of God has appeared for us — Mof

In this was the love of God clearly shown toward us — Mon

because that God sent his only begotten Son into the world,

that God sent his only Son . . . — RSV

that we might live through him.

that we might find Life through him — TCNT

10. **Herein is love, not that we loved God, but that he loved us,**

Love lies in this, not in our love for God but in his love for us — Mof

The love consists not in our having loved God, but in his loving us — Gspd

In this is love, not that we loved God but that he loved us — RSV

and sent his Son to be the propitiation for our sins.

and sending his Son as an atoning sacrifice for our sins — Gspd

and sent his Son to be the expiation for our sins — RSV

. . . to make personal atonement for . . . — Phi

11. **Beloved, if God so loved us, we ought also to love one another.**

If God thus loved us, dear friends, we in turn are bound to love one another — NEB

Dear Friends, if that's how God loved us, then we should love one another — Beck

12. No man hath seen God at any time.
No one has ever seen God — Wey
No human eyes have ever seen God — TCNT
If we love one another, God dwelleth in us, and his love is perfected in us.
. . . God then remains within us, and love for him is complete in us — Mof
. . . God does actually live within us, and his love grows in us toward perfection — Phi

13. Hereby know we that we dwell in him, and he in us, because he hath given us of his Spirit.
This is how we may be sure we remain in him and he in us, because he has given us a share in his own Spirit — Mof
We know that we remain in union with him, and he with us, by this — by his having given us some measure of his Spirit — TCNT
. . . a portion of . . . — Wey

14. And we have seen and do testify
And we have beheld and bear witness — ASV
We ourselves are eyewitnesses able and willing to testify to the fact — Phi
that the Father sent the Son to be the Saviour of the world.
. . . to save the world — Beck

15. Whosoever shall confess that Jesus is the Son of God,
If anyone will acknowledge . . . — Nor
Whoever acknowledges that Jesus Christ is the Son of God — TCNT
God dwelleth in him, and he in God.
God remains in union with him and he in union with God — Wms

16. And we have known and believed the love that God hath to us.
And we have come to understand and to trust the love which God hath in us — Rhm
So we know by experience and trust the love that God has for us — Wms
God is love; and he that dwelleth in love dwelleth in God, and God in him.

. . . and he who continues in love continues in God and God continues in him — Ber

17. Herein is our love made perfect,
It is through this that love has attained its perfection in us — TCNT
In this will love in its perfection be displayed in us — Wey
that we may have boldness in the day of judgment:
in our being fearless on the day of judgement — Wey
. . . when we have absolute confidence about . . . — Mof
. . . when we have perfect confidence about . . . — Gspd
because as he is, so are we in this world.
since in this world we are living as he is — Mof
— for we realize that our life in this world is actually his life lived in us — Phi

18. There is no fear in love; but perfect love casteth out fear:
Love has no dread in it . . . — Mof
. . . instead, perfect love expels fear — Ber
. . . No! Love, when perfect, drives out fear — TCNT
There is no room for fear in love; perfect love banishes fear — NEB
because fear hath torment.
. . . implies punishment — TCNT
. . . involves punishment — Wey
. . . suggests punishment — Gspd
He that feareth is not made perfect in love.
and the man who feels fear has not attained to perfect love — TCNT
and if a man fears, there is something imperfect in his love — Wey
The man who is still afraid has not yet reached the full measure of love — Knox

19. We love him, because he first loved us.
We love, because . . . — RSV

20. If a man say, I love God, and hateth his brother,
. . . habitually hates . . . — Wms
. . . while hating . . . — NEB
he is a liar:
his words are false — Bas
for he that loveth not his brother whom

he hath seen, how can he love God whom he hath not seen?

21. **And this commandment have we from him, That he who loveth God love his brother also.**

. . . He who loves God must also love his brother — TCNT

. . . the lover of God shall love his brother too — Ber

. . . the man who loves God must be one who loves his brother as well — Knox

CHAPTER 5

1. **Whosoever believeth that Jesus is the Christ is born of God:**

Every one who believes that Jesus is the Christ is a child of God — Wey

and every one that loveth him that begat

and every one who loves the Father — Wey

loveth him also that is begotten of him.

loves Him who is the Father's Child — Wey

loves his child — Gspd

loves the sons born of him — Mof

2. **By this we know that we love the children of God,**

This is how we can be sure . . . — Gspd

when we love God, and keep his commandments:

by continuing to love . . . — Wms

3. **For this is the love of God, that we keep his commandments:**

For loving God means obeying his commands — Gspd

and his commandments are not grievous.

. . . burdensome — Rhm

. . . irksome — Wey

. . . hard to keep — Bas

4. **For whatsoever is born of God overcometh the world:**

because all that is begotten of God . . . — Alf

Because all that has received new life from God conquers the world — TCNT

Whatsoever takes it origin from God must needs triumph over the world — Knox

Every child of God continues to conquer . . . — Wms

and this is the victory that overcometh the world, even our faith.

The victory that defeats the world is our faith — NEB

Our faith, that is the conquest which conquers the world — Mof

And this is the power that has conquered the world — our faith! — TCNT

5. **Who is he that overcometh the world,**

for who is victor over the world — NEB

Who is the world's conqueror — Mof

but he that believeth that Jesus is the Son of God?

6. **This is he that came by water and blood, even Jesus Christ;**

He it is whose Coming was attested by means of Water and Blood — TCNT

not by water only, but by water and blood.

And it is the Spirit that beareth witness, because the Spirit is truth.

. . . And there is the Spirit also to bear testimony, and the Spirit is Truth itself — TCNT

7. **For there are three that bear record[3] in heaven, the Father, the Word, and the Holy Ghost: and these three are one.**

8. **And there are three that bear witness in earth, the spirit, and the water, and the blood: and these three agree in one.**

. . . and the three have the same purport — Wey

. . . and these three are in agreement — NEB

. . . and the three of them are in accord — Mof

9. **If we receive the witness of men, the witness of God is greater:**

If we accept human testimony . . . — Mof

If we take the witness of men to be true . . . — Bas

. . . surely divine testimony is stronger — NEB

---

[3]The words between "bear record" (verse 7) and "the spirit" (verse 8) are now recognized as not adequately supported by original manuscripts.

for this is the witness of God which he hath testified of his Son.

for the witness of God is this, that he hath borne witness concerning his Son — ASV

For God's witness is what he has testified about his Son — Wey

for God's testimony consists in the testimony he has borne to his Son — Mof

10. **He that believeth on the Son of God hath the witness in himself:**

    . . . has this testimony in his own heart — NEB

    he that believeth not God hath made him a liar;

    but he who disbelieves God, makes him out to be a liar — NEB

    because he believeth not the record that God gave of his Son.

    by refusing to believe the testimony which God has borne to his Son — Mof

    because he has put no faith in the evidence God has adduced regarding His Son — Ber

11. **And this is the record, that God hath given to us eternal life,**

    And this is the evidence: God has granted us eternal life — Ber

    The witness is this: that God has given us eternal life — NEB

    and this life is in his Son.

    and that this life is found in his Son — NEB

12. **He that hath the Son hath life; and he that hath not the Son of God hath not life.**

13. **These things have I written unto you that believe on the name of the Son of God; that ye may know that ye have eternal life, and that ye may believe on the name of the Son of God.**

    I have written in this way to you who believe in the name of the Son of God, that you may be sure you have life eternal — Mof

    I write this to you, that you may realize that you have found Immortal Life — you who believe in the Name of the Son of God — TCNT

14. **And this is the confidence that we have in him,**

And this is the confidence with which we approach him — TCNT

that, if we ask any thing according to his will, he heareth us:

that whenever we ask anything that is in accordance with his will, he listens to us — TCNT

15. **And if we know that he hear us, whatsoever we ask, we know that we have the petitions that we desired of him.**

    . . . we can rest assured that He will give us what we have asked for — Nor

    And if we realize that he listens to us —whatever we ask—we realize that we have what we have asked from him — TCNT

16. **If any man see his brother sin a sin which is not unto death,**

    . . . which is not mortal — Wey

    . . . which is not deadly — Mof

    . . . that does not lead to death — Wms

    he shall ask, and he shall give him life for them that sin not unto death.

    he will ask, and so be the means of giving Life to him — to any whose sin is not deadly — TCNT

    There is a sin unto death: I do not say that he shall pray for it.

    . . . not concerning this do I say that he should make request — ASV

    There is such a thing as deadly sin, and I do not suggest that he should pray about that — NEB

    . . . I do not mean that he is to pray for that — Mof

    . . . for that I do not bid him make request — Wey

    . . . I advise no prayer for that — Ber

17. **All unrighteousness is sin: and there is a sin not unto death.**

    Every wrong action is sin, and there is sin that is not deadly — TCNT

    Any wrongdoing is sin; and there are sins that do not lead to death — Wms

18. **We know that whosoever is born of God sinneth not;**

    . . . that no one who has received the new Life from God lives in sin — TCNT

    . . . that whoever is a child of God is not habitually committing sin — Mon

... will not practise sin — Nor

but he that is begotten of God keepeth himself,

but He who was born of God keeps him — RSV

For the Son of God will guard him — Nor

but the Son who was born of God continues to keep him — Wms

it is the Son of God who keeps him safe — NEB

and that wicked one toucheth him not.

and the evil one ... — ASV

... does not get a grip of him — Ber

... cannot get his hands on him — Tay

19. **And we know that we are of God, and the whole world lieth in wickedness.**

We realize that we have come from God, while all the world is under the influence of the Evil One — TCNT

... in the power of the evil one — Wey

20. **And we know that the Son of God is come, and hath given us an under-**standing, that we may know him that is true,

We realize, too, that the Son of God has come among us, and has given us the discernment to know the true God — TCNT

... the true One — Alf

... him that is Real — Rhm

and we are in him that is true, even in his Son Jesus Christ.

This is the true God, and eternal life.

21. **Little children, keep yourselves from idols. Amen.**

Little children, keep yourselves from idols — false gods, [from anything and everything that would occupy the place in your heart due to God, from any sort of substitute for Him that would take first place in your life]. Amen. So let it be. — Amp

... guard yourselves ... — ASV

... keep clear of ... — Mof

... keep away from ... — Gspd

... beware of false gods! — Nor

My children, be on the watch against false gods — NEB

THE SECOND EPISTLE OF JOHN

1. The elder unto the elect lady and her children,
The presbyter . . . — Mof
The pastor . . . — Beck
. . . the chosen lady . . . — Gspd
. . . the Lady chosen by God . . . — NEB
. . . an eminent Christian lady . . . — TCNT
whom I love in the truth; and not I only,
whom I love in truth . . . — Wey
whom I truly love . . . — Wey
I sincerely love you all, and not I only — TCNT
held in the highest affection not only by me — Phi
but also all they that have known the truth;
. . . all who know . . . — Gspd
. . . all those who recognize . . . — Ber

2. For the truth's sake, which dwelleth in us,
. . . abides . . . — Wey
. . . remains within . . . — Mof
. . . stays in our hearts . . . — Gspd
. . . dwells among . . . — NEB
and shall be with us for ever.
yes, and it will be ours for ever — TCNT

3. Grace be with you, mercy, and peace,
Grace, mercy, peace shall be with us — ASV
. . . will be ours — TCNT
from God the Father, and from the Lord Jesus Christ, the Son of the Father, in truth and love.
. . . in all true love — Bas
. . . in all sincerity . . . — Amp

4. I rejoiced greatly that I found
I was very glad . . . — NASB
I was delighted to find — NEB
It was a great joy to me to find — TCNT
of thy children walking in truth
some of your children leading the true life — Mof
the lives of some of your children guided by the Truth — TCNT
as we have received a commandment from the Father.
in obedience to the commandment that we received . . . — TCNT

as we were ordered by the Father — Bas

5. And now I beseech thee, lady,
. . . request . . . — Rhm
. . . entreat . . . — Mof
. . . pray you . . . — TCNT
not as though I wrote a new commandment unto thee,
— not as though I were writing . . . — TCNT
but that which we had from the beginning,
no, it is the command which we had from the first — TCNT
that we love one another.
Let us love . . . — TCNT
that we continue to . . . — Wms

6. And this is love, that we walk after his commandments.
The love I mean consists in obedience to . . . — Wey
Love means this, that we be guided by . . . — Gspd
To live by his commandments, that is what love means — Mof
This is the commandment, That, as ye have heard from the beginning,
. . . even as ye heard . . . — ASV
. . . you learnt from the first — TCNT
ye should walk in it.
that you follow love — RSV
to be guided by love — Gspd
to live in a spirit of love — TCNT

7. For many deceivers are entered into the world,
Because . . . went forth . . . — Alf
. . . many impostors have left us to go . . . — TCNT
. . . false teachers . . . — Bas
who confess not
who do not acknowledge — TCNT
who will not admit — Phi
those who deny — Mon
that Jesus Christ is come in the flesh.
the coming of . . . — Mon
Jesus Christ as coming . . . — NEB
. . . in our human nature — TCNT
This is a deceiver and an antichrist.
Such a one is 'the deceiver' and 'the antichrist' — Wey
that is the mark of the impostor and the Antichrist — Gspd
These are the persons described as the Antichrist, the arch-deceiver — NEB

Such people are against the truth and against Christ — Tay

8. Look to yourselves,
Keep watch over yourselves — Bas
Be on your guard — Knox
Take care — TCNT

that we lose not those things which we have wrought,
not to lose what we have worked for — Gspd
that you do not lose the fruit of all our work — TCNT
don't throw away all the labor that has been spent on you — Phi

but that we receive a full reward.
but that ye . . . — ASV
rather, reap the benefit of it in full — TCNT
instead, make sure of a full reward — Ber

9. Whosoever transgresseth, and abideth not in the doctrine of Christ,
. . . goeth onward and abideth not in the teaching of Christ — ASV
. . . goes beyond the limits of the Teaching of the Christ — TCNT
. . . runs ahead too far, and does not stand by the doctrine of the Christ — NEB
. . . assumes leadership, and does not remain in the doctrine of Christ — Ber

hath not God.
does not have hold of God — Nor

He that abideth in the doctrine of Christ,
he that abideth in the teaching — ASV
he who remains true to that teaching — Wey
the man who keeps to that Teaching — TCNT
It is the man who holds to the teaching — Gspd
he who stands by that doctrine — NEB

he hath both the Father and the Son.
he has found . . . — TCNT
keeps hold both of . . . — Knox

10. If there come any unto you,
If any one comes to you — TCNT
If you are visited by one — Knox
If anyone continuously comes to see you — Wms

and bring not this doctrine,

and does not bring this Teaching — — TCNT

receive him not into your house,
do not admit him to the house — Mof
you must stop welcoming him to . . . — Wms

neither bid him God speed:
do not even greet him — Mof
and give him no greeting — ASV
or welcome him — TCNT

11. For he that biddeth him God speed
. . . that giveth him his greeting — ASV
. . . who wishes him success — Amp
. . . gives him a friendly greeting — Nor
is partaker of his evil deeds.
partaketh in his evil works — ASV
is sharing with him in his wicked work — TCNT
is an accomplice in his wicked deeds — NEB

12. Having many things to write unto you,
I have a great deal to write to you — Wey
Though I have a great deal to say to you — TCNT
I would not write with paper and ink:
I would rather not write it . . . — Gspd
. . . rather not trust it to paper and ink — TCNT
but I do not care to put it down in black and white — NEB
but I trust to come unto you,
. . . I hope to visit you — Mof
. . . I hope to come and see you personally — Phi
and speak face to face,
and to speak with you face to face — TCNT
and we shall have a heart-to-heart talk together — Phi
that our joy may be full.
. . . your joy may be complete — TCNT

13. The children of thy elect sister greet thee. Amen.
The children of your Sister, chosen by God, send their greetings — NEB
. . . send you their greetings — TCNT
. . . wish to be remembered to you — Gspd
. . . send you their best wishes . . . — Nor
Greetings from the children of your sister, another choice child of God — Tay

THE THIRD EPISTLE OF JOHN

1. The elder unto the wellbeloved Gaius,
The elder unto Gaius the beloved —
ASV
From the pastor, to the beloved Gaius
— Nor
The presbyter . . . — Mof
. . . to my dear friend Gaius — Gspd
whom I love in the truth.
whom he sincerely loves — TCNT
whom I truly love — Wey

**2. Beloved, I wish above all things that
thou mayest prosper and be in health,**
Beloved, I pray that in all things thou
mayest . . . — ASV
Dearly loved one, I pray that you may
in all respects prosper and keep well
— Wey
Dear friend, I pray that all may be well
with you and that you may have
good health — TCNT
even as thy soul prospereth.
as indeed your soul is keeping well —
Mof
— I know that all is well with your
soul — TCNT

3. For I rejoiced greatly,
. . . I was delighted — NEB
. . . I felt extremely happy — Ber
. . . it was a great joy to me — TCNT
What happiness it gave me — Knox
when the brethren came
when some Brothers came — TCNT
and testified of the truth that is in thee,
and bare witness unto thy truth — ASV
and testified to your fidelity to the
Truth — TCNT
and spoke so highly of the sincerity of
your life — Phi
even as thou walkest in the truth.
as indeed you do follow the truth —
RSV
since you are living by the truth —
Wms
how you live in obedience to the truth
— Wey
as indeed you do lead the true life —
Mof

4. I have no greater joy
Greater joy have I none — ASV
Nothing gives me greater pleasure —
TCNT
No greater joy can I have — RSV
Nothing affords me more enjoyment —
Ber

**than to hear that my children walk in
truth.**
than to hear from time to time that the
lives of my Children are guided by
the Truth — TCNT
. . . to hear that my children follow the
truth — RSV
. . . to hear that my children are living
by the truth — Wms

**5. Beloved, thou doest faithfully whatso-
ever thou doest**
Beloved, thou doest a faithful work in
whatsoever thou doest — ASV
My dear friend, you show a fine loyalty
in everything that you do — NEB
Beloved, you are acting faithfully in all
your behaviour — Wey
Beloved, it is a loyal thing you do when
you render any service — RSV
Dearly beloved, you are acting faithfully in doing what you can — Wms
to the brethren, and to strangers;
to the brethren, especially to strangers
— RSV
to the brethren, who besides are strangers — Alf
for these our fellow-Christians, strangers though they are to you — NEB

**6. Which have borne witness of thy char-
ity before the church:**
They have testified before the church
to your love — Wms
They have testified, in the presence of
the Church, to your love — Wey
**whom if thou bring forward on their
journey after a godly sort, thou shalt
do well:**
whom thou wilt do well to set forward
on their journey worthily of God —
ASV
and you will do well to help them on
their way in a manner worthy of
the service of God — TCNT
. . . in a manner worthy of your fellowship with God — Wey
Pray speed them on their journey
worthily of God — Mof
Please help them on their journey in a
manner worthy of the God we serve
— NEB

**7. Because that for his name's sake they
went forth,**
they have started out for his sake —
Mof

For they went out for love of the Name
— Bas

taking nothing of the Gentiles.

accepting nothing from the heathen —
Gspd

taking nothing from the people of the
world — Beck

and declined to take anything from
pagans — Mof

and they accept no help from non-
Christians — Phi

8. We therefore ought to receive such,

We therefore ought to welcome such
— ASV

It is therefore our duty to entertain
such men — Wey

So we ought to show hospitality to such
men — Wms

hence we are bound to support such
men — Mof

**that we might be fellowhelpers to the
truth.**

to prove ourselves allies of the Truth
— Mof

and so play our part in spreading the
truth — NEB

9. I wrote unto the church:

I wrote somewhat unto the church —
ASV

I wrote something unto the assembly
— Rhm

I sent a letter to the congregation —
NEB

**but Diotrephes, who loveth to have
the pre-eminence among them,**

. . . who loves to have the foremost
place among them — Wey

. . . who likes to take the lead . . . —
Mof

. . . loves to push himself forward . . .
— Tay

. . . who is eager to be a leader — Nor

but he who is fond of taking the first
place among them — Diotrephes —
Rhm

but Diotrephes, their would-be leader
— NEB

receiveth us not.

does not acknowledge our authority
RSV

doth not make us welcome — Rhm

declines to recognize us — TCNT

refuses to listen to us — Wey

will not accept what I say — Gspd

**10. Wherefore, if I come, I will remember
his deeds which he doeth,**

Therefore, when I come, I shall not
forget his conduct — TCNT

. . . I shall call attention to his conduct
— Wey

**prating against us with malicious
words:**

in ridiculing us with his wicked tongue
— TCNT

and how he is maliciously accusing me
— Gspd

his idle and mischievous talk against
us — Wey

He lays baseless and spiteful charges
against us — NEB

He maligns us with his foolish gossip
— Knox

**and not content therewith, neither doth
he himself receive the brethren,**

and as if this was not enough, he does
not take the brothers into his house
— Bas

and not content with these he neither
himself maketh the brethren welcome — Rhm

not satisfied with that, he refuses to
receive our friends — NEB

and forbiddeth them that would,

and them that would he forbiddeth —
ASV

and he interferes with those who would
do so — NEB

but actually prevents those who would
— TCNT

and casteth them out of the church.

and expels them from the Church —
TCNT

and tries to expel them from the congregation — NEB

**11. Beloved, follow not that which is evil,
but that which is good.**

. . . imitate not . . . — ASV

. . . do not copy evil, but good — Wey

. . . do not follow bad examples, but
good ones — Wms

He that doeth good is of God:

He who does good is a child of God —
Wey

The man who does what is good is
from God — TCNT

the man who does right . . . — Gspd

. . . is God's man — Phi

**but he that doeth evil hath not seen
God.**

he who does evil has not seen God — Wey

the man who does what is bad has never seen God — TCNT

the wrong-doer has caught no glimpse of him — Knox

12. Demetrius hath good report of all men, and of the truth itself:

Everyone speaks well of Demetrius, even the truth itself approves of him — Nor

Every one has always had a good word for Demetrius, and the Truth itself speaks for him — TCNT

Demetrius has a good word from all men, and the witness of the truth itself — Wey

yea, and we also bear record; and ye know that our record is true.

I testify of him too, and you know my testimony is true — Mof

He has our warm commendation also, and you know you can trust what we say about anyone — Phi

13. I had many things to write,

I have a great deal to write to you — Gspd

I have a great deal to say to you — TCNT

but I will not with ink and pen write unto thee:

but it is not my purpose to put it all down with ink and pen — Bas

but I do not care to set it down with pen and ink — NEB

14. But I trust I shall shortly see thee,

I hope, however, it will not be long before I see you — TCNT

and we shall speak face to face.

and we will have a talk — Mof

and we will have a heart-to-heart talk — Phi

Peace be to thee. Our friends salute thee.

. . . Our friends here send you their greetings — TCNT

. . . Our friends wish to be remembered to you — Gspd

Greet the friends by name.

Greet our friends individually — NEB

Remember me to our friends, every one — Gspd

Remember me to the friends personally — Ber

THE EPISTLE OF JUDE

1. Jude, the servant of Jesus Christ, and brother of James,

Jude, a slave of Jesus Christ, and a brother of James — Mon

to them that are sanctified by God the Father, and preserved in Jesus Christ, and called:

to them that are called, beloved in God the Father, and kept for Jesus Christ — ASV

to those who have been called, who are dear to God the Father and have been kept through union with Jesus Christ — Gspd

2. Mercy unto you, and peace, and love, be multiplied.

May mercy, peace, and love be yours in ever-increasing measure — TCNT

. . . be abundantly granted you — Wey

May you ever experience more and more mercy . . . — Phi

3. Beloved, when I gave all diligence to write unto you

. . . while I was giving all diligence to write unto you — ASV

. . . being very eager to write to you — RSV

. . . although I was making all haste to write to you — Mon

Dear friends, I was just on the point of writing to you — Gspd

of the common salvation,

on the subject of our common salvation — Wey

about our salvation — which is yours no less than ours — NEB

it was needful for me to write unto you,

I was constrained . . . — ASV

I felt that I must write to you at once — TCNT

when it became urgently necessary to write at once — NEB

and exhort you that ye should earnestly contend for the faith

to urge you to fight in defence of the Faith — TCNT

and appeal to you to join in the struggle in defence of the faith — NEB

. . . to carry on a vigorous defense of . . . — Wms

. . . to stoutly defend . . . — Tay

which was once delivered unto the saints.

which was once for all . . . — ASV

that has once for all been entrusted to . . . — TCNT

4. For there are certain men crept in unawares,

For there crept in unobserved certain men — Rhm

For certain persons have crept in unnoticed — Wey

. . . have slipped in by stealth — Mof

For some people have sneaked in among us — Gspd

who were before of old ordained to this condemnation,

even they who were of old written of beforehand unto this condemnation — ASV

. . . before written down in prophecy for this judgment — Alf

the very men whom Scripture long ago marked down for the doom they have incurred — NEB

whose sentence has long since been pronounced — TCNT

ungodly men, turning the grace of our God into lasciviousness,

godless persons . . . — Gspd

impious creatures . . . — Mof

They have no real reverence for God, and they abuse his grace as an opportunity for immorality — Phi

ungodly men, who pervert the grace of our God into immorality — Wey

. . . who make the mercy of God an excuse for profligacy — TCNT

and denying the only Lord God, and our Lord Jesus Christ.

. . . our only Master and Lord, Jesus Christ — ASV

. . . disown our only lord and master, Jesus Christ — TCNT

. . . our sole liege and Lord, Jesus Christ — Mof

. . . disown Jesus Christ, our only Sovereign and Lord — Wey

5. I will therefore put you in remembrance,

Now I desire to . . . — ASV

I wish to remind you — Mon

though ye once knew this,

though ye know all things once for all — ASV

of what you already know right well — Mon

of what you are perfectly aware — Mof

although the whole matter is sufficiently familiar to you — Wey

how that the Lord, having saved the people out of the land of Egypt,

that though the Lord delivered the people from . . . — TCNT

afterward destroyed them that believed not.

went on to destroy those who had proved unfaithful — Knox

. . . those who had no faith — Wey

. . . those who were guilty of unbelief — NEB

6. And the angels which kept not their first estate,

. . . their own principality — ASV

. . . who abandoned their own domain — Mof

. . . who did not keep to their appointed spheres — TCNT

. . . who neglected their responsibilities — Gspd

. . . who did not preserve their original rank — Wms

but left their own habitation,

. . . their proper habitation — ASV

. . . their proper home — Wms

. . . deserted their proper abode — Wey

he hath reserved in everlasting chains under darkness unto the judgment of the great day.

unto the judgment of the great day in perpetual bonds under thick gloom hath he reserved — Rhm

and God has reserved them for judgement on the great Day, bound beneath the darkness in everlasting chains — NEB

7. Even as Sodom and Gomorrha, and the cities about them

. . . the adjacent cities — Mof

. . . the neighboring towns — Gspd

in like manner, giving themselves over to fornication,

having in the same manner been guilty of gross immorality — Wey

which similarly glutted themselves with vice — Mof

which fell into the same debauchery as their neighbours — Knox

which likewise acted immorally — RSV

and going after strange flesh,

and indulged in unnatural lust — RSV

and fell into unnatural vice — TCNT

and sensual perversity — Mof

and homosexuality — Nor

and pursued unnatural lust — Knox

are set forth for an example, suffering the vengeance of eternal fire.

are now before us as an example of eternal fire in the punishment which they are undergoing — Wey

are exhibited as a warning of the everlasting fire they are sentenced to suffer — Mof

and they paid the penalty of eternal fire, as an example for all to see — NEB

8. Likewise also these filthy dreamers

Yet in like manner these also in their dreamings — ASV

Yet in the very same way these men, too, cherishing vain dreams — TCNT

So too with these men today. Their dreams lead them to — NEB

defile the flesh, despise dominion, and speak evil of dignities.

. . . set at nought dominion, and rail at dignities — ASV

pollute our human nature, reject control, and malign the Mighty — TCNT

pollute the body, while they set Authority at naught and speak evil of the angelic Orders — Wey

pollute their flesh, scorn the Powers celestial, and scoff at angelic Glories — Mof

defile the body, make light of authority, and deride majesty — Gspd

to defile the body, to flout authority, and to insult celestial beings — NEB

9. Yet Michael the archangel,

Now the very archangel Michael — Mof

. . . Michael, one of the chief angels — Bas

Whereas Michael, the chief-messenger — Rhm

when contending with the devil he disputed about the body of Moses,

when contending with the devil and disputing with him about the body of Moses — Wey

when, in his dispute with the Devil, he was arguing about the body of Moses — TCNT

durst not bring against him a railing accusation,

did not dare to pronounce judgement on him in abusive terms — Wey

did not presume to condemn him in insulting words — NEB

dared not (presume to) bring an abusive condemnation against him — Amp

did not venture to condemn him for blasphemy — Gspd

did not dare to bring against him a charge of blasphemy — Wms

did not dare to pronounce sentence for blasphemy — Mon

but said, The Lord rebuke thee.

he only said, May the Lord rebuke you — Gspd

he was content to say . . . — Knox

He simply said . . . — Phi

10. **But these speak evil of those things which they know not:**

But these rail at whatsoever things they know not — ASV

But these men malign whatever they do not understand — TCNT

. . . are abusive in matters of which they know nothing — Wey

. . . pour out abuse on things they do not understand — NEB

but what they know naturally, as brute beasts,

and the things they know by instinct, like unreasoning animals — Gspd

and whatever they do understand (like irrational animals) by mere instinct — Mof

in those things they corrupt themselves.

in these things are they destroyed — ASV

they use for their own destruction — Gspd

prove their undoing — NEB

11. **Woe unto them! for they have gone in the way of Cain,**

. . . they trod the road that Cain did — Wms

. . . they follow Cain's path — Gspd

Alas for them! They walk in the steps of Cain — TCNT

and ran greedily after the error of Balaam for reward,

running uncontrolled into the error of Balaam, for reward — Bas

and abandon themselves for the sake of gain to Balaam's error — RSV

For a profit they've rushed into the error of Balaam — Beck

they plunge into Balaam's error for gain — Gspd

for the sake of gain they have rushed on headlong into the errors of Balaam — Wey

led astray by Balaam's love of gain, they plunge into sin — TCNT

and perished in the gainsaying of Core.

and they perish in rebelliousness like Korah's — Gspd

and meet their ruin through rebellion like that of Korah — TCNT

they have rebelled like Korah, and they share his doom — NEB

they've rebelled like Korah and perished — Beck

12. **These are spots in your feasts of charity,**

These are they who are hidden rocks in your love-feasts — ASV

These are the men — sunken rocks — who in your love feasts — Wey

These men are those who are hidden reefs in your love-feasts — NASB

when they feast with you, feeding themselves without fear:

when they feast with you, shepherds that without fear feed themselves — ASV

when they feast with you without fear, pasturing their own selves — Alf

when they feast together and provide without scruple for themselves alone — TCNT

are not afraid to feast with you, caring only for themselves — Wey

they have no qualms about carousing in your midst, they look after none but themselves — Mof

where they eat and drink without reverence. They are shepherds who take care only for themselves — NEB

clouds they are without water, carried about of winds;

They are clouds without rain, driven before the winds — TCNT

rainless clouds, swept along by the wind — Mof

trees whose fruit withereth, without fruit,

autumn trees without fruit — ASV

fruitless trees in late autumn — RSV

trees that in late fall have no fruit —
Beck

trees in autumn, fruitless — Wey

they are leafless trees without a vestige
of fruit — TCNT

trees that in season bear no fruit — NEB

twice dead, plucked up by the roots;

doubly dead . . . — Wey

dead through and through, torn up by
the roots — TCNT

13. Raging waves of the sea,

Violent waves of the sea — Bas

they are wild sea waves — TCNT

foaming out their own shame;

foaming shameful deeds — NEB

that foam up their own disgrace — Ber

producing only the spume of their own
evil deeds — Phi

flinging up the foam of their own
shame and disgrace — Amp

wandering stars,

They are stars that have wandered
from their course — NEB

They are like stars which follow no
orbit — Phi

**to whom is reserved the blackness of
darkness for ever.**

for whom the nether gloom of darkness has been reserved eternally —
Mof

that are forever doomed to utter darkness — Wms

**14. And Enoch also, the seventh from
Adam, prophesied of these, saying,**

And to these also Enoch, the seventh
from Adam . . . — ASV

To these men, as to others, Enoch the
seventh in descent from Adam, declared — TCNT

**Behold, the Lord cometh with ten
thousands of his saints,**

See! the Lord has come with his hosts
of holy ones around him — TCNT

15. To execute judgment upon all,

to bring all men to judgment — NEB

to carry out his sentence on all men —
Knox

**and to convince all that are ungodly
among them**

and to convict all godless people —
TCNT

**of all their ungodly deeds which they
have ungodly committed,**

of all their godless acts, which in their

ungodliness they have committed —
TCNT

and of all their hard speeches

and of all the harsh words — TCNT

. . . all the defiant words — NEB

**which ungodly sinners have spoken
against him.**

which they have spoken against him,
godless sinners that they are — TCNT

16. These are murmurers, complainers,

These persons are grumblers, ever complaining about their lot — Wms

. . . dissatisfied with life — Gspd

walking after their own lusts;

Their lives are guided by their evil passions — Wey

they follow where their passions lead
them — TCNT

**and their mouth speaketh great swell-
ing words,**

Big words come rolling from their lips
— NEB

loud-mouthed boasters — RSV

their mouths are full of big and boastful words — Wey

their talk is arrogant — Mof

**having men's persons in admiration
because of advantage.**

showing respect of persons for the sake
of advantage — ASV

admiring men's persons for the sake of
profit — ABUV

and they flatter men for the sake of
what they can get from them —
TCNT

flattering people to gain advantage —
RSV

17. But, beloved, remember ye the words

But you, dear friends, must remember
the words — Gspd

**which were spoken before of the apos-
tles of our Lord Jesus Christ;**

that the messengers of Jesus Christ
gave us beforehand — Phi

**18. How that they told you there should
be mockers in the last time,**

This was the warning they gave you:
In the final age there will be men
who will pour scorn on religion —
NEB

how they used to say to you — As the
time draws near the end there will
be scoffers — TCNT

**who should walk after their own un-
godly lusts.**

who will go where their own godless passions lead — Gspd

obeying only their own ungodly passions — Wey

who will live to satisfy their own godless passions — Wms

who would make their own ungodly appetites into a rule of life — Knox

19. These be they who separate themselves,

... who make separations — ASV

... who cause divisions — TCNT

sensual, having not the Spirit.

the worldly, who lack the Spirit — Ber

they are men of the world, devoid of the Spirit — Wey

animal and unspiritual — TCNT

20. But ye, beloved, building up yourselves on your most holy faith,

It is for you, beloved, to make your most holy faith the foundation of your lives — Knox

But you, my friends, must fortify yourselves in your most sacred faith — NEB

... must continue to build yourselves up on the groundwork of your most holy faith — Wms

... do you, dear friends, build up your characters on the foundation of your most holy faith — TCNT

praying in the Holy Ghost,

pray under the guidance of the Holy Spirit — TCNT

Continue to pray in the power of the Holy Spirit — NEB

and ever praying ... — Mon

21. Keep yourselves in the love of God,

and keep within the love of God — TCNT

Stay always within the boundaries where the love of God can reach and bless you — Tay

looking for the mercy of our Lord Jesus Christ unto eternal life.

Awaiting the ... — Rhm

while waiting for the mercy of our Lord Jesus Christ, to bring you to Immortal Life — TCNT

... which issues in ... — Wey

22. And of some have compassion, making a difference:

And on some have mercy, who are in doubt — ASV

On some who are in doubt, you should have pity — Wey

To some show pity, because they are in doubt — TCNT

and have mercy on the waverers — Mof

23. And others save with fear, pulling them out of the fire;

and save some, snatching them out of the fire — ASV

hating even the garment spotted by the flesh.

while you hate even the garment stained by the flesh — Wey

... the very clothing that is contaminated with sensuality — NEB

... the very clothing polluted by their touch — TCNT

24. Now unto him that is able to keep you from falling,

... to guard you from stumbling — ASV

... slipping — Mof

and to present you faultless

... without blemish — ASV

... irreproachable — Gspd

before the presence of his glory with exceeding joy,

in the presence of ... — Mon

... with exultation — Rhm

... jubilant — NEB

25. To the only wise God our Saviour,

... through Jesus Christ our Lord[1] — ASV

be glory and majesty, dominion and power,

Be glory, greatness, dominion, and authority — Rhm

both now and ever. Amen.

before all time, and now, and for evermore. Amen — ASV

as it was before time began, is now, and shall be for all time to come. Amen — TCNT

[1]Variant reading.

THE
REVELATION OF JOHN

CHAPTER 1

1. The Revelation of Jesus Christ, which God gave unto him,

The unveiling [Apocalypse] of Jesus Christ which God gave him — Mon

This is a revelation from Jesus Christ, which God has allowed him — Knox

to shew unto his servants things which must shortly come to pass;

so that his servants might have knowledge of the things which will quickly take place — Bas

to show them what must come to pass very soon — Mof

. . . certain events which must shortly come to pass — Wey

to make known to his servants, of things which must soon find their due accomplishment — Knox

and he sent and signified it by his angel unto his servant John:

He made it known by sending his angel to his servant John — Phi

and he shewed them by signs sending through his messenger unto his servant John — Rhm

2. Who bare record of the word of God, and of the testimony of Jesus Christ, and of all things that he saw.

who bare witness of . . . — ASV

He in turn testifies to the Word of God and the testimony of Jesus Christ, telling both what he heard and what he saw — Nor

. . . omitting nothing of what he had seen — TCNT

3. Blessed is he that readeth, and they that hear the words of this prophecy,

Blessed is he who reads aloud and blessed they who hear . . . — Mof

Happy is the man who reads, and happy those who listen . . . — NEB

and keep those things which are written therein:

and keep true to their message — Knox

and heed what is written in it — Gspd

for the time is at hand.

for The Time is near — TCNT

for the time for fulfillment is now close at hand — Wey

For the crisis is at hand — Mon

For the time is near when these things will all come true — Tay

4. John to the seven churches which are in Asia: Grace be unto you, and peace, from him which is, and which was, and which is to come;

. . . from He who is and was and is coming — Mof

. . . from him who is, and ever was, and is still to come — Knox

and from the seven Spirits which are before his throne;

. . . the seven Spirits — that is, the seven-fold Holy Spirit — before His throne — Amp

5. And from Jesus Christ, who is the faithful witness,

and the first begotten of the dead, and the prince of the kings of the earth.

. . . the firstborn of the dead, and the ruler of . . . — ASV

. . . the first of the dead to be born to life, . . . — Wey

. . . the first to come back from the dead, . . . — Bas

. . . the First of the dead to live again, . . . — Beck

. . . first-born of the risen dead, who rules over all earthly kings — Knox

Unto him that loved us, and washed[1] us from our sins in his own blood,

Unto him that loveth us, and loosed us . . . by his blood — ASV

To Him who ever loves us and once for all released us from . . . — Wms

To him who loves us and freed us from our sins by his own blood — TCNT

He has proved his love for us, by washing us clean from . . . — Knox

6. And hath made us kings and priests unto God and his Father;

and he made us to be a kingdom, to be priests unto his God and Father — ASV

and he made us a kingdom, even priests unto . . . — Alf

---

[1]Some manuscripts read "wash"; others read "loose." The Greek words are very similar in spelling.

and has formed us into a Kingdom, to
be priests to God, His Father—Wey
. . . a realm of priests for his God and
Father — Mof
. . . a royal race of priests, to serve
God, his Father — Knox
. . . a royal house, to serve as the priests
of his God and Father — NEB
**to him be glory and dominion for ever
and ever. Amen.**
Give to Him everlasting glory! He rules
forever! Amen! — Tay

7. **Behold, he cometh with clouds; and
every eye shall see him, and they also
which pierced him:**
**and all kindreds of the earth shall wail
because of him.**
and all the tribes of the earth shall
mourn over him — ASV
. . . shall wail for fear of him — TCNT
. . . shall lament in remorse — NEB
All the nations will weep in sorrow and
in terror when He comes — Tay
Even so, Amen.
So it is to be. Amen! — Nor

8. **I am Alpha and Omega, the beginning
and the ending, saith the Lord,**
I am the A and the Z, saith the Lord —
Rhm
I am Alpha, I am Omega, the beginning of all things and their end, says
the Lord God — Knox
**which is, and which was, and which is
to come,[2] the Almighty.**
. . . the sovereign Lord of all — NEB
the God who Is and who Was and who
is Coming, The Almighty — Rhm

9. **I John, who also am your brother, and
companion in tribulation, and in the
kingdom and patience of Jesus Christ,**
. . . your brother and partaker with you
in the tribulation and kingdom and
patience which are in Jesus — ASV
. . . your companion in the distress, the
kingdom and the faithful endurance
to which Jesus calls us — Phi
. . . your fellow Christian, who in Jesus
share with you suffering and ruling
and enduring — Beck
. . . who share with you in the suffering
and kingship and endurance of Jesus
— TCNT
. . . a sharer with you in the sorrows
. . . — Wey

**was in the isle that is called Patmos,
for the word of God, and for the testimony of Jesus Christ.**
on account of the word of God . . . —
Alf
for the sake of the Message of God . . .
— TCNT
for my loyalty to the Word of God . . .
— Wey
for preaching God's message and testifying to Jesus — Wms
for love of God's word and of the truth
concerning Jesus — Knox
because I had spoken God's message
and borne witness to Jesus — Phi

10. **I was in the Spirit on the Lord's day,**
I fell into a trance . . . — TCNT
I came under the Spirit's power . . . —
Beck
On the Lord's day I found myself rapt
in the Spirit — Mof
On the Lord's day I was inspired by
the Spirit — Wey
. . . I was in the Spirit's power — Wms
. . . I became Spirit-possessed — Ber
It was Sunday and I was worshiping —
Tay
**and heard behind me a great voice,
as of a trumpet,**
loud as the call of a trumpet — Knox
like the blast of a trumpet — Wey

11. **Saying, I am Alpha and Omega,[3] the
first and the last:**
and, What thou seest, write in a book,
. . . write in a scroll — Rhm
Write your vision in a book — Wey
**and send it unto the seven churches
which are in Asia; unto Ephesus,
and unto Smyrna, and unto Pergamos, and unto Thyatira, and unto
Sardis, and unto Philadelphia, and
unto Laodicea.**

12. **And I turned to see the voice that
spake with me. And being turned, I
saw seven golden candlesticks;**
. . . Seven Lamps of gold — Rhm
. . . seven golden lampstands — Wey

13. **And in the midst of the seven candle-
sticks one like unto the Son of man,**
. . . One resembling the Son of Man —
Wey

---

[2]Compare verse 4.
[3]Compare verse 8.

. . . Someone like the Son of man —
Beck

**clothed with a garment down to the
foot, and girt about the paps with a
golden girdle.**

. . . and girt about at the breasts . . . —
ASV

. . . and a belt of gold round his breast
— Mof

He wore a long robe that reached to
His feet and He had a gold band
around His chest — Nor

**14. His head and his hairs were white like
wool, as white as snow;**

The hair on his head was like wool
snow-white — Knox

and his eyes were as a flame of fire;

his eyes were like flaming fire — TCNT

. . . like coals of fire — Wms

and His eyes penetrated like flames of
fire — Tay

**15. And his feet like unto fine brass, as if
they burned in a furnace;**

. . . like unto burnished brass, as if it
had been refined in a furnace — ASV

. . . like unto glowing copper . . . —
Rhm

. . . like polished brass . . . — Nor

. . . like burnished bronze . . . — NASB

. . . like the fine brass of Lebanon[4] . . .
— Lam

. . . as if it were glowing in . . . — ABUV

. . . when it is white-hot in . . . — Wey

**and his voice as the sound of many
waters.**

His voice had the sound of a great
waterfall — Phi

and His voice thundered like the waves
against the shore — Tay

**16. And he had in his right hand seven
stars: and out of his mouth went a
sharp twoedged sword:**

**and his countenance was as the sun
shineth in his strength.**

. . . his face was shining like the sun
at midday — Wms

. . . his face was ablaze like the sun at
its height — Phi

and his whole appearance as when the
sun shineth in its strength — Rhm

and His face shone like the power of
the sun in unclouded brilliance —
Tay

**17. And when I saw him, I fell at his feet
as dead.**

. . . as one dead — ASV

. . . as if dead — Wey

. . . like a dead man — Mof

**and he laid his right hand upon me,
saying unto me,**

Fear not; I am the first and the last:

Do not be afraid any more. I am the
First and the Last — Wms

. . . I am before all, I am at the end
of all — Knox

**18. I am he that liveth, and was dead; and
behold, I am alive for evermore,
Amen;**

. . . the Living one; and I was dead,
and behold, I am alive for evermore
— ASV

. . . the ever-living One . . . — Wey

I, who underwent death, am alive, as
thou seest, to endless ages — Knox

and have the keys of hell and of death.

. . . the keys of death and of Hades —
ASV

. . . the keys of the gates of Death and
of Hades — Wey

. . . the keys of death and the underworld — Gspd

. . . the keys of death and the grave —
Phi

. . . the keys that unlock death and
Hades — Mof

**19. Write the things which thou hast seen,
and the things which are, and the
things which shall be hereafter;**

Therefore, write of what you have seen
and of what is happening now and
of what is about to take place —
TCNT

. . . the things which are, and the things
which are about to take place after
these — ABUV

. . . what is now, and what will be hereafter — Phi

**20. The mystery of the seven stars which
thou sawest in my right hand, and the
seven golden candlesticks.[5]**

— the mystic meaning of . . . — TCNT

the secret symbol of . . . — Mof

the open secret of . . . — Wms

---

[4]This is the reading in the Aramaic source
from which Lamsa translated.

[5]Compare verse 12.

The seven stars are the angels of the seven churches:

The seven stars are messengers of the seven assemblies — Rhm

The seven stars are the leaders of the seven churches — Tay

and the seven candlesticks[6] which thou sawest are the seven churches.

and the seven lights are the seven churches — Bas

And the seven lamps are seven assemblies — Rhm

CHAPTER 2

1. **Unto the angel of the church of Ephesus write;**

Write a letter to the leader of the church at Ephesus — Tay

These things saith he that holdeth the seven stars in his right hand,

A message to thee from him who bears the seven stars . . . — Knox

. . . who holds the seven stars safe in his right hand — Phi

who walketh in the midst of the seven golden candlesticks;[7]

who walks to and fro among . . . — Wey

2. **I know thy works, and thy labour, and thy patience,**

. . . thy works, and thy toil, and . . . — ASV

. . . your activities, your fatiguing toil . . . — Ber

I know what you have done; your hard work and your endurance — Gspd

. . . what you have done, how hard you have worked, how you have endured — Beck

and how thou canst not bear them which are evil:

. . . you cannot tolerate evil-doers — TCNT

and thou hast tried them which say they are apostles, and are not, and hast found them liars:

. . . didst find them false — ASV

3. **And hast borne, and hast patience, and for my name's sake hast laboured, and hast not fainted.**

and thou hast patience and didst bear for my name's sake, and hast not grown weary — ASV

And you have the power of waiting . . . — Bas

And you endure patiently and have borne burdens for . . . and have never flagged — Wey

Yes, thou endurest, and all thou hast borne for the love of my name has not made thee despair — Knox

4. **Nevertheless I have somewhat against thee, because thou hast left thy first love.**

But I have this against thee, that thou didst leave . . . — ASV

But this I have against you — You have abandoned your first love — TCNT

. . . you no longer love Me as you did at first — Wey

. . . you have abandoned the love you had at first — RSV

. . . you have given up loving one another as you did at first — Mof

Yet there is one thing wrong: you don't love Me as at first! — Tay

5. **Remember therefore from whence thou art fallen,**

Be mindful, therefore, of the height from which you have fallen — Wey

and repent, and do the first works;

and repent, and live the life that you lived before — TCNT

Repent and live as you lived at first — Phi

repent, and do as you once did — NEB

. . . And work as you did at first — Nor

. . . and do the works you did previously [when first you knew the Lord] — Amp

or else I will come unto thee quickly, and will remove thy candlestick[8] out of his place, except thou repent.

. . . if your heart remains unchanged — Phi

6. **But this thou hast, that thou hatest the deeds of the Nicolaitanes, which I also hate.**

. . . hatest the works of the Nicolaitans . . . — ASV

But this is in your favor — You hate the life lived by the . . . — TCNT

---

[6]Compare verse 12.

[7]Compare Rev. 1:12.

[8]Compare Rev. 1:12.

7. He that hath an ear, let him hear what the Spirit saith unto the churches;

Listen, you who have ears, to the message which the Spirit has for the churches — Knox

You have ears; then listen to what . . . — Beck

Let anyone who has an ear listen to . . . — Mof

To him that overcometh will I give to eat of the tree of life,

To him who conquers . . . — TCNT

To the victorious . . . — Phi

To the victor I will give the privilege of eating . . . — Wey

which is in the midst of the paradise of God.

that stands in the Garden of God — NEB

which is in the Paradise of God — NASB

8. And unto the angel of the church in Smyrna write; These things[9] saith the first and the last, which was dead and is alive;

9. I know thy works, and tribulation, and poverty,

. . . tribulation and destitution — Rhm

I know how sorely tried thou art, how stricken with poverty — Knox

I know how hard pressed you are, and poor — NEB

(but thou art rich)

but you have true wealth — Bas

(yet, all the while, so rich) — Knox

and I know the blasphemy of them

. . . the slandering of thee by them — Alf

and the evil name given you by those — Wey

and the insolence of . . . — Ber

and how you are abused and reviled and slandered by those — Amp

which say they are Jews, and are not, but are the synagogue of Satan.

who style themselves Jews (no Jews are they, but a mere synagogue of Satan!) — Mof

. . . though they are not, but are a Congregation of Satan — TCNT

. . . (though they are no true Jews; they are rather the chosen people of Satan) — Knox

10. Fear none of those things which thou shalt suffer:

Stop being afraid of what you are about to suffer — Tay

behold, the devil shall cast some of you into prison,

. . . the devil is about to cast . . . — ASV

that ye may be tried;

to have your faith tested there — Knox

This is to test you — Beck

and ye shall have tribulation ten days:

and for ten days you will have to endure persecution — Wey

be thou faithful unto death, and I will give thee a crown of life.

Be faithful, even if you have to die for it . . . — Wey

Each one of you must prove to be faithful, even if you have to die . . . — Wms

Keep faith with me to the point of death, and I will crown thee with life — Knox

11. He that hath an ear,[10] let him hear what the Spirit saith unto the churches; He that overcometh[11] shall not be hurt of the second death.

The victorious cannot suffer the slightest hurt from the second death — Phi

12. And to the angel of the church in Pergamos write: These things said he which hath the sharp sword with two edges;

This message is from Him who wields the sharp and double-bladed sword — Tay

13. I know thy works,[12] and where thou dwellest,

even where Satan's seat is:

where Satan's throne is — ASV

where the Throne of Satan stands — TCNT

where Satan sits enthroned — Mof

and thou holdest fast my name, and hast not denied my faith,

And yet you hold to my name, and you did not disown my Faith — TCNT

and yet you are true to Me and did not

---

[9]Compare verse 1.

[10]Compare verse 7.

[11]Compare verse 1.

[12]Compare verse 2.

deny your faith in Me — Wey
. . . you have not renounced your faith in me — Mof

even in those days wherein Antipas was my faithful martyr,
even in the days of Antipas my witness, my faithful one — ASV

who was slain among you, where Satan dwelleth.
who was martyred among you, in the place where Satan dwells — Wey
. . . martyred before your eyes in the very house of Satan — Phi
. . . killed in your city, the home of Satan — NEB
who was killed among you — you have the devil living there! — Beck

14. But I have a few things against thee, because thou hast there them that hold the doctrine of Balaam,
. . . some that hold the teaching of . . . — ASV

who taught Balac to cast a stumbling-block before the children of Israel,
. . . to put temptation in the way of . . . — TCNT

to eat things sacrificed unto idols, and to commit fornication.
by involving them in sexual sin, and encouraging them to go to idol feasts — Tay

15. So hast thou also them that hold the doctrine[13] of the Nicolaitanes, which thing I hate.
. . . some that hold the teaching of . . . — ASV

16. Repent; or else I will come unto thee quickly,
Repent therefore; or else . . . — ASV

and will fight against them with the sword of my mouth.
. . . will make war against . . . — ASV
. . . will contend with such men with words that will cut like a sword — TCNT

17. He that hath an ear,[14] let him hear what the Spirit saith unto the churches; To him that overcometh[15] will I give to eat of the hidden manna, and will give him a white stone, and in the stone a new name written, which no man knoweth saving he that receiveth it.

18. And unto the angel of the church in Thyatira write; These things[16] saith the Son of God, who hath his eyes like unto a flame of fire, and his feet are like fine brass;[17]

19. I know thy works,[18] and charity, and service, and faith, and thy patience, and thy works;
. . . works, and love and faith and ministry and patience — ASV
. . . your works, your love and faith and service and patient endurance — RSV

and the last to be more than the first.
and that thy last works are more than the first — ASV
and that your latter works exceed the first — RSV
. . . your life of late has been better than it was at first — TCNT
. . . of late you have toiled harder than you did at first — Wey
. . . of late you have done even better than at first — NEB
I know you are doing more than you did at first — Mof

20. Notwithstanding I have a few things against thee, because thou sufferest that woman Jezebel, which calleth herself a prophetess,
But I have this against you, that you tolerate the woman . . . — RSV
. . . that Jezebel of a woman who calls herself a prophetess — Mof
. . . who claims to be inspired — Gspd
. . . who claims the gift of prophecy — Knox

to teach and to seduce my servants to commit fornication, and to eat things sacrificed unto idols.
but who by her teaching deceives my servants into sexual immorality and eating idols'-meat — Phi

21. And I gave her space to repent of her fornication; and she repented not.
And I gave her time that she should repent; and she willeth not to repent of her fornication — ASV

---

[13]Compare verse 14.
[14]Compare verse 7.
[15]Compare verse 1.
[16]Compare Rev. 1:14.
[17]Compare Rev. 1:15.
[18]Compare verse 2.

. . . she is determined not to turn from her licentiousness — TCNT

. . . she has shown no desire to repent of her immorality — Phi

. . . she will not mend her harlot's ways — Knox

22. Behold, I will cast her into a bed,

Therefore, I am laying her upon a bed of sickness — TCNT

. . . on a bed of pain — NEB

and them that commit adultery with her into great tribulation,

and plunge her lovers into terrible suffering — NEB

and bringing great suffering upon those who are unfaithful with her — TCNT

except they repent of their[19] deeds.

. . . repent of her works — ASV

. . . repent and turn from a life like hers — TCNT

. . . repent of conduct such as hers — Wey

23. And I will kill her children with death;

As for her children, I shall strike them dead — Phi

and all the churches shall know that I am he which searcheth the reins and hearts:

. . . who looks into the hearts and souls of men — TCNT

. . . who searches into men's inmost thoughts — Wey

. . . who searches men's hearts and minds — Gspd

. . . the searcher of men's hearts and thoughts — NEB

and I will give unto every one of you according to your works.

. . . what his deeds have earned—Knox

. . . as your works deserve — RSV

24. But unto you I say, and unto the rest in Thyatira,

But to you I say, to the rest that are in Thyatira — ASV

as many as have not this doctrine,

— all who do not accept such teaching — TCNT

and which have not known the depths of Satan, as they speak;

who know not the deep things of Satan, as they are wont to say — ASV

. . . the depths of Satan, as they call them — Alf

. . . the 'secrets of Satan' as men call them — TCNT

. . . have not learnt the 'deep things,' as they call them (the deep things of Satan!) — Wey

. . . the deep mysteries (as they are called) which Satan offers — Knox

I will put upon you none other burden.

I impose no fresh burden on you — Mof

25. But that which ye have already hold fast till I come.

except that you hold on to what you have until I come! — Phi

26. And he that overcometh,[20] and keepeth my works unto the end, to him will I give power over the nations:

. . . authority over . . . — ASV

27. And he shall rule them with a rod of iron;

and he shall shepherd them with a sceptre of iron — Rhm

as the vessels of a potter shall they be broken to shivers:

as vessels of earthenware are dashed in pieces — Rhm

and shatter them like earthen jars! — Gspd

even as I received of my Father.

(as I myself have received from my father) — TCNT

28. And I will give him the morning star.[21]

. . . the Morning Star — TCNT

29. He that hath an ear,[22] let him hear what the Spirit saith unto the churches.

CHAPTER 3

1. And unto the angel of the church in Sardis write; These things[23] saith he that hath the seven Spirits[24] of God, and the seven stars;

I know thy works,[25] that thou hast a name that thou livest, and art dead.

. . . men say that you are living, though

---

[19]Some manuscripts read "her."

[20]Compare verse 7.

[21]Compare Rev. 22:16.

[22]Compare verse 7.

[23]Compare Rev. 2:1.

[24]Compare Rev. 1:4.

[25]Compare Rev. 2:2.

... — TCNT

... you are supposed to be alive, but in reality ... — Wey

... how thou dost pass for a living man, and all the while art a corpse — Knox

I know your reputation as a live and active church, but you are dead — Tay

2. Be watchful, and strengthen the things which remain, that are ready to die:

Wake up, rally what is still left to you, though it is on the very point of death — Mof

Now wake up! Strengthen what you have before it dies! — Phi

... strengthen what still survives, though once it was all but dead — TCNT

... that which still remains though it is at the point of death — Wey

... put some strength into what is left, which must otherwise die! — NEB

Wake up and strengthen the rest that are dying — Beck

for I have not found thy works perfect before God.

... I have found no works of thine perfected before my God — ASV

... I have found none of your works meeting the requirements of my God — Ber

... nothing you have done is complete in the eyes of my God — Mof

There are tasks my God expects of thee, and I find them unfulfilled — Knox

3. Remember therefore how thou hast received and heard,
and hold fast, and repent.

Take it to heart and repent — Beck

If therefore thou shalt not watch, I will come on thee as a thief, and thou shalt not know what hour I will come upon thee.

4. Thou hast a few names even in Sardis which have not defiled their garments;

Yet even there in Sardis some haven't soiled their garments with the world's filth — Tay

and they shall walk with me in white: for they are worthy.

5. He that overcometh,[26] the same shall be clothed in white raiment;

Be victorious and that's how you will be dressed — Beck

He that overcometh shall thus be arrayed in white garments — ASV

and I will not blot out his name out of the book of life,

... never will I erase his name from the Book of Life — Wey

but I will confess his name before my Father, and before his angels.

but I will own him before my Father ... — TCNT

... acknowledge him as mine ... — Gspd

Indeed, I will speak his name ... — Phi

but I will announce before My Father and His angels that he is Mine — Tay

6. He that hath an ear,[27] let him hear what the Spirit saith unto the churches.

7. And to the angel of the church in Philadelphia write;

These things[28] saith he that is holy, he that is true, he that hath the key of David, he that openeth, and no man shutteth; and shutteth, and no man openeth;

... so that none may shut when he opens, none open when he shuts — Knox

8. I know thy works:[29]

behold, I have set before thee an open door,

... I have put a door wide open in front of you — Wey

... I have given you a door flung wide open — Phi

and no man can shut it:

... there is no shutting it — Knox

for thou hast a little strength, and hast kept my word and hast not denied my name.

Your strength, I know, is small, yet you ... — NEB

because, while possessing little strength, you have observed My Word and you have not renounced My Name — Ber

---

[26]Compare Rev. 2:7.

[27]Compare Rev. 2:7.

[28]Compare Rev. 2:2.

[29]Compare Rev. 2:2.

9. **Behold, I will make them of the synagogue[30] of Satan, which say they are Jews, and are not, but do lie;**

See how I deal with those of Satan's synagogue who claim to be Jews, yet are no Jews but liars — Phi

. . . who claim to be Jews but are lying frauds — NEB

behold I will make them to come and worship before thy feet,

— I will make them come and bow down at your feet — TCNT

and to know that I have loved thee.

and they shall learn that I loved you — TCNT

. . . that you are my beloved people — NEB

10. **Because thou hast kept the word of my patience, I also will keep thee from the hour of temptation,**

. . . from the hour of trial — ASV

which shall come upon all the world, to try them that dwell upon the earth.

11. **Behold, I come quickly: hold that fast which thou hast,[31] that no man take thy crown.**

12. **Him that overcometh[32] will I make a pillar in the temple of my God, and he shall go no more out:**

. . . he shall never go out from it again — Wey

. . . he shall never be put out of it — Amp

and I will write upon him the name of my God, and the name of the city of my God, which is new Jerusalem, which cometh down out of heaven from my God: and I will write upon him my new name.

13. **He that hath an ear,[33] let him hear what the Spirit saith unto the churches.**

14. **And unto the angel of the church of the Laodiceans write; These things saith the Amen, the faithful and true witness,**

. . . These are the words of the Unchanging One . . . — TCNT

the beginning of the creation of God;

the head of God's new order — Bas

The Origin of God's creation — Beck

15. **I know thy works, that thou art neither cold nor hot: I would thou wert cold or hot.**

. . . it would be better if you were cold or hot — Bas

16. **So then because thou art lukewarm, and neither cold nor hot,**

So because you are not one or the other — Bas

I will spue thee out of my mouth.

I am about to vomit thee out of . . . — Rhm

I am about to spit thee out of . . . — TCNT

I will have no more to do with you — Bas

17. **Because thou sayest,**

I am rich, and increased with goods, and have need of nothing:

I am rich, and have gotten riches . . . — ASV

I am rich, and I have become wealthy . . . — Alf

I am rich, and have wealth stored up . . . — Wey

I am rich, I am well off, I lack nothing! — Mof

and knowest not that thou art wretched, and miserable, and poor, and blind, and naked:

. . . that thou of all others art the wretched one, and the pitiable one, and poor and blind and naked — Alf

. . . that if there is a wretched creature it is you — pitiable, poor, blind, naked — Wey

18. **I counsel thee to buy of me**

If you are wise you will get from me — Bas

gold tried in the fire, that thou mayest be rich;

gold refined by fire, that thou mayest become rich — ASV

. . . that you may be [truly] wealthy — Amp

and white raiment, that thou mayest be clothed, and that the shame of thy nakedness do not appear; and anoint thine eyes with eyesalve, that thou mayest see.

19. **As many as I love, I rebuke and chasten:**

---

[30]Compare Rev. 2:9.

[31]Compare Rev. 2:25.

[32]Compare Rev. 2:7.

[33]Compare Rev. 2:1.

It is those I love that I correct and chasten — Knox

I correct and discipline all whom I love — Beck

All whom I love I rebuke and discipline — TCNT

be zealous therefore, and repent.

Therefore, shake off your complacency and repent — Phi

20. Behold, I stand at the door, and knock:

Lo! I am standing at the door and knocking — Rhm

if any man hear my voice, and open the door, I will come in to him,

and will sup with him, and he with me.

and will feast with him, and he shall feast with me — TCNT

21. To him that overcometh[34] will I grant to sit with me in my throne,

As for the victorious, I will give him the honor of sitting beside me on my throne — Phi

even as I also overcame, and am set down with my Father in his throne.

just as I myself have won the victory and have taken my seat beside my Father on his throne — Phi

22. He that hath an ear,[35] let him hear what the Spirit saith unto the churches.

CHAPTER 4

1. After this I looked, and, behold, a door was opened in heaven:

After this I looked, and lo, in heaven an open door! — RSV

... a door set open in heaven — Alf

... a door in heaven standing open — Wey

... an open door to heaven — Nor

and the first voice which I heard was as it were of a trumpet talking with me;

and the former voice which I heard as of a trumpet talking with me — Alf

and the first voice I heard, a voice as of a trumpet speaking with me — ASV

and the first voice came to my ears, like the sound of a horn — Bas

which said, Come up hither,

It said — Come up here — TCNT

and I will shew thee things which must be hereafter.

and I will make clear to you the things which are to come — Bas

... which are to happen in the future — Wey

2. And immediately I was in the Spirit:[36]

Immediately I found myself in the Spirit — Wey

... I came under the Spirit's power — Ber

... I knew myself to be inspired by the Spirit — Phi

At once I was caught up by the Spirit — NEB

and, behold, a throne was set in heaven, and one sat on the throne.

and saw — oh the glory of it! — a throne and someone sitting on it — Tay

3. And he that sat was to look upon like a jasper and a sardine stone:

... appeared like [the crystalline brightness of] jasper and [the fiery] sardius — Amp

and there was a rainbow round about the throne, in sight like unto an emerald.

and around the throne was a halo of the color of an emerald — Gspd

and there was a circle of coloured light ... like an emerald — Bas

and all around the throne shone a halo like an emerald rainbow — Phi

4. And round about the throne were four and twenty seats:

... four and twenty thrones — ASV

Twenty-four smaller thrones surrounded His — Tay

and upon the seats I saw four and twenty elders sitting, clothed in white raiment;

and upon the thrones ... — ASV

and they had on their heads crowns of gold.

5. And out of the throne proceeded lightnings and thunderings and voices:

and there were seven lamps of fire

[34]Compare Rev. 2:7.

[35]Compare Rev. 2:7.

[36]See Rev. 1:10 for other translations of this expression.

burning before the throne,

... seven torches of fire burning ... — Rhm

which are the seven Spirits of God.[37]

6. **And before the throne there was a sea of glass like unto crystal:**

... there seemed to be a sea of glass, resembling crystal — Wey

... a sea of glass, like a sheet of ice — NEB

and in the midst of the throne, and round about the throne, were four beasts

while within the space before the throne and round the throne are four creatures — TCNT

... four living creatures — ASV

... four beings — Alf

full of eyes before and behind.

that had eyes everywhere to see before them and behind them — Knox

7. **And the first beast was like a lion, and the second beast like a calf, and the third beast had a face as a man, and the fourth beast was like a flying eagle.**

And the first creature ... — ASV

And the first being ... — Alf

8. **And the four beasts had each of them six wings about him; and they were full of eyes within:**

And the four living creatures, having each one of them six wings, are full of eyes round about and within — ASV

And each of the four living creatures has six wings, and these are covered with eyes, both on top and underneath — Nor

and they rest not day and night, saying,

and day and night they never cease to say — TCNT

... they never cease to sing — RSV

Holy, holy, holy, Lord God almighty, which was, and is, and is to come.

... Lord God, the Almighty, who was and who is and who is to come — ASV

9. **And when those beasts[38] give glory and honour and thanks to him that sat on the throne, who liveth for ever and ever,**

And as often as ... — Knox

And whenever ... — Ber

10. **The four and twenty elders fall down before him that sat on the throne,**

the twenty-four elders prostrate themselves before ... — Phi

and worship him that liveth for ever and ever, and cast their crowns before the throne, saying,

11. **Thou art worthy, O Lord, to receive glory and honour and power:**

Worthy art thou, our Lord and our God, to receive the glory and the honor and the power — ASV

for thou hast created all things, and for thy pleasure they are and were created.

... and because of thy will they were, and were created — ASV

... And it was by Thy will that they came into existence, and were created — Wey

by thee all things were created; nothing ever was, nothing was even created, but in obedience to thy will — Knox

CHAPTER 5

1. **And I saw in the right hand of him that sat on the throne a book written within and on the backside,**

a scroll; written within and on the back — Rhm

a scroll with writing on the back as well as inside — Mof

sealed with seven seals.

shut with seven stamps of wax — Bas

2. **And I saw a strong angel proclaiming with a loud voice,**

Who is worthy to open the book, and to loose the seals thereof?

Who claims the right to open the book,

and break the seals on it — Knox

Who is worthy to open the scroll? And — who is entitled and deserves and is morally fit — to break its seals — Amp

3. **And no man in heaven, nor in earth, neither under the earth,**

... under the earth [in the realm of the dead, Hades] — Amp

was able to open the book, neither to look thereon.

---

[37]Compare Rev. 1:4.

[38]See verse 6.

... to open the scroll, or to look thereon — Rhm

4. And I wept much,
And I began to weep much — Rhm
At this I wept long — TCNT
And while I was weeping bitterly —
Wey
I was in tears — NEB
And I wept audibly and bitterly —
Amp
**because no man was found worthy
to open and to read the book, neither
to look thereon.**
to open the scroll or to look thereon
— Rhm
No one was able to get the book open,
or to take a look at it — Bas

**5. And one of the elders saith unto me,
Weep not:**
No need for tears — Knox
Stop weeping! — Wms
**behold the Lion of the tribe of Juda,
the Root of David,**
the Descendant of David — Beck
has prevailed to open the book,
has overcome to open ... — ASV
has won a victory, and He can open
... — Beck
here is one who has gained the right to
open ... — Knox
and to loose the seven seals thereof.

**6. And I beheld, and, lo, in the midst of
the throne and of the four beasts, and
in the midst of the elders,**
Then, within the space between the
throne and the four Creatures, and
in the midst of the Councillors, I
saw — TCNT
stood a Lamb as it had been slain,
a Lamb standing, as though it had been
slain — ASV
a Lamb standing, showing that it ...
— Rhm
a Lamb standing, looking as if it ... —
Wey
a Lamb, which seemed to have been
sacrificed — TCNT
a Lamb standing upright, yet slain (as
I thought) in sacrifice — Knox
**having seven horns and seven eyes,
which are the seven Spirits[39] of God
sent forth into all the earth.**
He had seven horns and seven eyes;
these are the seven Spirits of God,

which are sent on errands to all parts
of the earth — Gspd
... which are sent on duty to every
portion of ... — Wms
... that go out to do his bidding everywhere on earth — Knox

**7. And he came and took the book out
of the right hand of him that sat upon
the throne.**
And he came, and at once took ... —
Rhm

**8. And when he had taken the book, the
four beasts[40] and four and twenty elders fell down before the Lamb, having every one of them harps, and
golden vials full of odours,**
... golden bowls full of incense — ASV
which are the prayers of saints.
(These are the prayers of Christ's people) — TCNT

9. And they sung a new song, saying,
And now it was a new hymn they sang
— Knox
**Thou art worthy to take the book, and
to open the seals thereof:**
It is right for you to take ... — Bas
for thou wast slain,
Thou was slain in sacrifice — Knox
**and hast redeemed us to God by thy
blood.**
and didst purchase unto God with thy
blood — ASV
... with thy blood thou didst buy for
God — TCNT
**out of every kindred, and tongue, and
people, and nation;**
men of every tribe ... — ASV

**10. And hast made us unto our God kings
and priests:[41] and we shall reign on
the earth.**
and madest them to be unto our God a
kingdom and priests; and they reign
... — ASV
... a kingdom of Priests in the service
of our God, and they are reigning
upon the earth — TCNT
Thou hast made us a royal race of
priests, to serve God; we shall reign
as kings over the earth — Knox

[39]See Rev. 1:4.
[40]See Rev. 4:6.
[41]See Rev. 1:6 for other translations of the
same expression.

11. **And I beheld, and I heard the voice of many angels round about the throne and the beasts**[42] **and the elders:**

Then, in my vision, I heard the voices of . . . — TCNT

and the number of them was ten thousand times ten thousand, and thousands of thousands;

. . . myriads of myriads, and thousands of thousands — Alf

12. **Saying with a loud voice, Worthy is the Lamb that was slain**

The Lamb who was sacrificed deserves — Beck

to receive power, and riches, and wisdom, and strength, and honour, and glory, and blessing.

and wisdom, and might . . . — ASV

13. **And every creature which is in heaven, and on earth, and under the earth,**[43]

and such as are in the sea, and all that are in them, heard I saying,

Then I heard the voice of everything created in Heaven, upon earth, under the earth and upon the sea, and all that are in them saying — Phi

Blessing, and honour, and glory, and power, be unto him that sitteth upon the throne, and unto the Lamb

Unto him that sitteth on the throne, and unto the Lamb, be the blessing, and the honor, and the glory, and the dominion — ASV

for ever and ever.

Unto the ages of ages! — Rhm

through the eternities of eternities! — Amp

14. **And the four beasts**[44] **said, Amen. And the four and twenty elders fell down and worshipped him that liveth for ever and ever.**

CHAPTER 6

1. **And I saw when the Lamb opened one of the seals, and I heard, as it were the noise of thunder, one of the four beasts saying, Come**[45] **and see.**

. . . one of the four living creatures saying with a voice of thunder, Come — ASV

. . . saying . . . Go! — Rhm

Then I saw the Lamb break one of the seven seals, and I heard one of the four Creatures crying with a voice like thunder — Come — TCNT

2. **And I saw, and behold a white horse: and he that sat on him had a bow; and a crown was given unto him: and he went forth conquering, and to conquer.**

. . . conquering and bent on conquest — Phi

. . . he set forth as a conqueror, to win victories — Nor

3. **And when he had opened the second seal, I heard the second beast say, Come and see.**[46]

4. **And there went out another horse that was red: and power was given to him that sat thereon to take peace from the earth, and that they should kill one another: and there was given unto him a great sword.**

5. **And when he had opened the third seal, I heard the third beast say, Come and see.**[47] **And I beheld, and lo a black horse; and he that sat on him had a pair of balances in his hand.**

6. **And I heard a voice in the midst of the four beasts say,**

A measure of wheat for a penny, and three measures of barley for a penny;

A whole day's wage for a loaf of bread, a whole day's wage for three barley cakes — Wey

Wheat at a dollar a quart, and barley three quarts for a dollar — Gspd

A silver piece, it said, for a quart of wheat, a silver piece for three quarts of barley — Knox

A quart of wheat for a day's pay . . . — Beck

and see thou hurt not the oil and the wine.

but do not damage the oil or the wine — Wey

---

[42]See Rev. 4:6 for variants of "beasts."

[43]Compare verse 3.

[44]Compare Rev. 4:3.

[45]Some manuscripts have a single imperative, "Come."

[46]See footnote on verse 1.

[47]See footnote on verse 1.

— but no tampering with . . . — Phi

7. And when he had opened the fourth seal, I heard the voice of the fourth beast say, Come and see.[48]

8. And I looked, and behold a pale horse:
. . . a livid horse — Rhm
. . . a grey horse — TCNT
. . . a pale-coloured horse — Wey
. . . a cream-white horse — Knox
. . . an ash-colored horse — Ber
. . . a horse sickly green — Phi
. . . a horse sickly pale — NEB
. . . an ashen horse — NASB
. . . a pale-green horse — Beck
. . . an ashy pale horse — Amp
and his name that sat on him was Death,
and Hell followed with him.
Hades followed . . . — ASV
the grave followed . . . — Phi
the Lord of the Place of Death rode behind him — TCNT
And power was given unto them over the fourth part of the earth,
And there was given unto them authority over . . . — ASV
to kill with sword, and with hunger,
. . . sword, and with famine — ASV
and with death, and with the beasts of the earth.

9. And when he had opened the fifth seal, I saw under the altar
. . . at the foot of the altar — Amp
the souls of them that were slain for the word of God, and for the testimony which they held:
. . . slain for adhering to God's word and to the testimony which they bore — Mof
. . . because of the Word of God and because of the stand they had taken — Nor
. . . because of the word of God, and because of the testimony which they had maintained — NASB

10. And they cried with a loud voice, saying,
How long, O Lord, holy and true,
How long will it be . . . — Bas
How long, O Sovereign Lord, the holy One and the true — Wey
dost thou not judge and avenge our blood on them that dwell on the earth?

dost Thou delay judgement and the taking of vengeance upon the inhabitants of the earth for our blood — Wey
before you take your place as judge and give punishment for our blood to those on the earth — Bas
wilt Thou refrain from judging . . . — NASB

11. And white robes were given unto every one of them;
and it was said unto them, that they should rest yet for a little season,
and they were bidden to wait patiently for a short time longer — Wey
. . . remain quiet a little longer — Mof
. . . wait quietly a little while longer — Ber
. . . be patient a little longer — Phi
. . . for a little time — ASV
until their fellowservants also and their brethren, that should be killed as they were,
should be fulfilled.
should have fulfilled their course — ASV

12. And I beheld when he had opened the sixth seal, and, lo, there was a great earthquake; and the sun became black as sackcloth of hair, and the moon became as blood;
Then I watched while he broke the sixth seal. There was a tremendous earthquake, the sun turned dark like coarse black cloth, and the full moon was red as blood — Phi

13. And the stars of heaven fell unto the earth, even as a fig tree casteth her untimely figs, when she is shaken of a mighty wind.
. . . unripe figs . . . — ASV
. . . winter figs . . . — Rhm
like green fruit from fig trees buffeted by mighty winds — Tay

14. And the heaven departed as a scroll when it is rolled together;
and the heaven was withdrawn as a scroll rolling itself up — Rhm
The heavens disappeared like a scroll when it is rolled up — TCNT
The sky too passed away, as if a scroll were being rolled up — Wey

------

[48]See footnote on verse 1.

and every mountain and island were moved out of their places.

15. And the kings of the earth, and the great men, and the rich men, and the chief captains, and the mighty men, and every bondman, and every free man, hid themselves in the dens and in the rocks of the mountains;

16. And said to the mountains and rocks, Fall on us, and hide us from the face of him that sitteth on the throne, and from the wrath of the Lamb:

Fall on us and hide us from the face of

the One who sits on the throne and from the vengeance of the Lamb — NEB

17. For the great day of his[49] wrath is come;

for the great day of their wrath is come — ASV

For the great day of their vengeance . . . — NEB

and who shall be able to stand?

and who is able . . . — ASV

. . . who can escape — Gspd

. . . who can stand it — Wms

. . . who can survive it — Tay

CHAPTER 7

1. And after these things I saw four angels standing on the four corners of the earth,

. . . at the four corners . . . — ASV

holding the four winds of the earth,

restraining the four winds . . . — TCNT

that the wind should not blow on the earth, nor on the sea, nor on any tree.

2. And I saw another angel ascending from the east,

. . . from the sunrising — ASV

. . . coming up from the rising of the sun — Alf

having the seal of the living God: and he cried with a loud voice to the four angels, to whom it was given to hurt the earth and the sea,

3. Saying, Hurt not the earth, neither the sea, nor the trees, till we have sealed the servants of our God in their foreheads.

4. And I heard the number of them which were sealed:

. . . sealed (marked) — Amp

and there were sealed an hundred and forty and four thousand

When the sealing was finished, I heard how many were sealed. . . . There were 144,000 — Wey

of all the tribes of the children of Israel.

out of all the tribes of the descendants of Israel — Wey

5. Of the tribe of Juda were sealed twelve thousand. Of the tribe of Reuben were sealed twelve thousand. Of the tribe of Gad were sealed twelve thousand.

Of the tribe of Judah, 12,000 were sealed; Of the tribe of Reuben, 12,000; Of the tribe of Gad, 12,000[50] — Wey

6. Of the tribe of Aser were sealed twelve thousand. Of the tribe of Nephthalim were sealed twelve thousand. Of the tribe of Manasses were sealed twelve thousand.

7. Of the tribe of Simeon were sealed twelve thousand. Of the tribe of Levi were sealed twelve thousand. Of the tribe of Issachar were sealed twelve thousand.

8. Of the tribe of Zabulon were sealed twelve thousand. Of the tribe of Joseph were sealed twelve thousand. Of the tribe of Benjamin were sealed twelve thousand.

9. After this I beheld, and, lo,

After this, in my vision, I saw — TCNT

a great multitude, which no man could number,

a vast crowd beyond man's power to number — Phi

of all nations, and kindreds, and people, and tongues, stood before the throne, and before the Lamb,

. . . standing before the throne . . . — ASV

clothed with white robes, and palms in their hands;

. . . palm-branches in their hands — Rhm

---

[49]Variant reading is "their."

[50]Wey puts verses 5-8 in table form.

... carrying palm-branches in ... — Wey

10. **And cried with a loud voice, saying, Salvation to our God which sitteth upon the throne, and unto the Lamb.**

With a great voice they shouted these words: Salvation belongs to our God ... — Phi

... To our God seated on the throne, and to the Lamb, we owe our salvation! — Wey

11. **And all the angels stood round about the throne, and about the elders and the four beasts,[51]**

and fell before the throne on their faces, and worshipped God,

... prostrated themselves with heads bowed before the throne and worshiped God — Phi

12. **Saying, Amen: Blessing, and glory, and wisdom, and thanksgiving, and honour, and power, and might, be unto our God for ever and ever. Amen.**

13. **And one of the elders answered, saying unto me, What are these which are arrayed in white robes? and whence came they?**

14. **And I said unto him, Sir, thou knowest.**

... My Lord, you know, not I — NEB

My Lord, said I, thou canst tell me — Knox

I answered him, My Lord, you must know — Nor

And he said to me, These are they which came out of great tribulation,

that come out of the great tribulation — ASV

who come through the Great Persecution — TCNT

who are coming through the great persecution — Wms

... have come here out of great affliction — Knox

... through the great oppression — Phi

... through the great ordeal — NEB

... out of great distress — Wey

and have washed their robes, and made them white in the blood of the Lamb.

15. **Therefore are they before the throne of God,**

That is why they now have their places before ... — Phi

For this reason they are before ... — NASB

and serve him day and night in his temple: and he that sitteth on the throne

shall dwell among them.

shall spread his tabernacle over them — ASV

shall spread his tent over them — Rhm

will be a tent over them — Bas

will shelter them with his presence — Amp

16. **They shall hunger no more, neither thirst any more;**

They will never be hungry again, nor thirsty — Tay

neither shall the sun light on them, nor any heat.

neither shall the sun strike upon them ... — ASV

neither shall they be stricken by the sun, nor by heat — Lam

and they will be fully protected from the scorching noontime heat — Tay

17. **For the Lamb which is in the midst of the throne shall feed them,**

... shall be their shepherd — ASV

... shall tend them — Alf

and shall lead them unto living fountains of waters:

... fountains of water of life — ASV

and God shall wipe away all tears from their eyes.

CHAPTER 8

1. **And when he had opened the seventh seal,**

And as soon as he opened the seventh seal — Rhm

there was silence in heaven about the space of half an hour.

there came to be silence ... — Rhm

there was utter silence in Heaven for

what seemed to me half an hour — Phi

2. **And I saw the seven angels which stood before God; and to them were given seven trumpets.**

---

[51]See Rev. 4:6 for other translations of "beasts."

3. **And another angel came and stood at the altar,**
having a golden censer;
having a gold vessel for burning perfume — Bas
and there was given unto him much incense,
that he should offer it with the prayers of all saints upon the golden altar which was before the throne.
that he should add it unto the prayers . . . — ASV
to offer with the prayers of all God's people . . . — NEB
so that he could make an offering on the golden altar before the throne, out of the prayers said by all the saints — Knox

4. **And the smoke of the incense, which came with the prayers of the saints, ascended up before God out of the angel's hand.**
And the smoke of the incense rose up before God from the angel's hand, mingled with the prayers of the saints — Phi

5. **And the angel took the censer, and filled it with fire of the altar, and cast it into the earth:**
. . . upon the earth — ASV
and there were voices, and thunderings, and lightnings, and an earthquake.

6. **And the seven angels which had the seven trumpets prepared themselves to sound.**

7. **The first angel sounded,**
The first angel blew his trumpet — RSV
and there followed hail and fire mingled with blood,
and there followed a rain of hail and fire mingled with blood — Nor
and they were cast upon the earth: and the third part of trees was burnt up, and all green grass was burnt up.

8. **And the second angel sounded,**
The second angel blew his trumpet — RSV
and as it were a great mountain burning with fire was cast into the sea:
and what appeared to be a huge burning mountain was thrown into the sea — Tay

and the third part of the sea became blood:

9. **And the third part of the creatures which were in the sea, and had life, died; and the third part of the ships were destroyed.**

10. **And the third angel sounded,**
The third angel blew his trumpet — RSV
and there fell a great star from heaven, burning as it were a lamp.
. . . burning as a torch — ASV
. . . blazing as a torch — RSV
and a great star shot from the sky, flaming like a torch — NEB
and it fell upon the third part of the rivers, and upon the fountains of waters:

11. **And the name of the star is called Wormwood: and the third part of the waters became wormwood; and many men died of the waters, because they were made bitter.**

12. **And the fourth angel sounded,**
The fourth angel blew his trumpet — RSV
and the third part of the sun was smitten, and the third part of the moon, and the third part of the stars;
so as the third part of them was darkened, and the day shone not for a third part of it, and the night likewise.
that the third part of them should be darkened, and the day should not shine for the third part of it, and the night in like manner — ASV
. . . and for the third part of the day there was no light, and at night it was the same — TCNT
so that light by day and light by night were both diminished by a third part — Phi

13. **And I beheld, and heard an angel[52] flying through the midst of heaven, saying with a loud voice,**
. . . I heard an eagle — ASV
. . . an eagle having a tail[53] red as it were blood — Lam
Woe, woe, woe, to the inhabiters of the earth

---

[52]Variant reading is "eagle."
[53]This is from Lamsa's Aramaic source.

Trouble, trouble, trouble . . . — Bas

. . . for them that dwell on the earth —
ASV

**by reason of the other voices of the
trumpet of the three angels, which
are yet to sound!**

for there are three more trumpet blasts
which the three angels shall sound!
— Phi

when the trumpets sound which the
three angels must now blow — NEB

CHAPTER 9

1. And the fifth angel sounded,

And the fifth angel blew his trumpet —
RSV

**and I saw a star fall from heaven unto
the earth: and to him was given the
key of the bottomless pit.**

. . . the key of the pit of the abyss —
ASV

. . . the key of the shaft of the abyss —
Rhm

**2. And he opened the bottomless pit;
and there arose a smoke out of the pit,
as the smoke of a great furnace;**

and there came up a smoke out of the
shaft as the smoke of a great furnace
— Rhm

. . . smoke whirled upward from the pit
like the smoke of a gigantic furnace
— Ber

. . . as smoke belching from a great
furnace — Lam

**and the sun and the air were darkened
by reason of the smoke of the pit.**

**3. And there came out of the smoke
locusts upon the earth:**

. . . grasshoppers . . . — Beck

**and unto them was given power, as the
scorpions of the earth have power.**

and they received the same power as
that possessed by scorpions — TCNT

**4. And it was commanded them that they
should not hurt the grass of the earth,
neither any green thing, neither any
tree; but only those men which have
not the seal of God in their foreheads.**

**5. And to them it was given that they
should not kill them, but that they
should be tormented five months: and
their torment was as the torment of a
scorpion, when he striketh a man.**

**6. And in those days shall men seek
death, and shall not find it;**

In those days men will try to kill themselves but won't be able to — death
will not come — Tay

**and shall desire to die, and death shall
flee from them.**

they will long to die, but death ever
flees from them — Mon

**7. And the shapes of the locusts[54] were
like unto horses prepared unto battle;**

In appearance the locusts were like
horses arrayed for battle — RSV

These locusts looked to me in my vision like horses prepared for battle
— Phi

**and on their heads were as it were
crowns like gold, and their faces
were as the faces of men.**

on their heads were what looked like
crowns of gold; their faces were like
human faces — RSV

**8. And they had hair as the hair of
women, and their teeth were as the
teeth of lions.**

**9. And they had breastplates, as it were
breastplates of iron;**

they had scales like iron breastplates —
RSV

**and the sound of their wings was as
the sound of chariots of many
horses running to battle.**

and their wings roared like an army of
chariots rushing into battle — Tay

**10. And they had tails like unto scor-
pions, and there were stings in their
tails: and their power was to hurt men
five months.**

**11. And they had a king over them, which
is the angel of the bottomless pit,[55]
whose name in the Hebrew tongue is
Abaddon, but in the Greek tongue
hath his name Apollyon.**

They have over them as king the messenger of the abyss, whose name in
Hebrew is Abaddon ["Destroyer"]
and in the Greek he hath for name
Destroyer — Rhm

---

[54]See verse 3.
[55]See verse 1.

They have as their king the Angel of the bottomless pit, whose name, in Hebrew, is 'Abaddon,' while, in Greek, his name is 'Apollyon' (the Destroyer) — TCNT

... in Greek Apollyon, that is ... the Exterminator — Knox

12. One woe is past; and, behold, there come two woes more hereafter.

The first calamity is past ... — Ber

The first disaster is now past, but I see two more approaching — Phi

One terror now ends, but there are two more coming — Tay

13. And the sixth angel sounded,

Then the sixth angel blew his trumpet — RSV

and I heard a voice from the four horns of the golden altar which is before God,

and from the four horns of the altar of gold which stands before God I heard a solitary voice — Amp

14. Saying to the sixth angel which had the trumpet, Loose the four angels which are bound in the great river Euphrates.

... at the great river, Euphrates — ASV

15. And the four angels were loosed, which were prepared for an hour, and a day, and a month, and a year,

that had been prepared for the hour and day and month and year — ASV

who had been ready for the hour, the day, the month, and the year — RSV

for to slay the third part of men.

that they should kill ... — ASV

16. And the number of the army of the horsemen

The number of the squadrons of their cavalry — Wey

... troops of their cavalry — Mof

were two hundred thousand thousand:

... twice ten thousand times ten thousand — ASV

... two hundred million — Wey

... twenty thousand armies of ten thousand — Knox

and I heard the number of them.

I heard their number — RSV

17. And thus I saw the horses in the vision, and them that sat on them, having

breastplates of fire, and of jacinth, and brimstone:

In my vision the horses and their riders looked this way: The riders wore fire-red, sky-blue, sulphur-yellow breastplates — Ber

And after this manner I saw the horses in the vision, and them that sat on them, having breastplates red, as fire, and blue, as smoke, and yellow, as brimstone — Alf

... of fire, and of hyacinth ... — ASV

and the heads of the horses were as the heads of lions; and out of their mouths issued fire and smoke and brimstone.

The horses' heads resembled lions' heads, and from their mouths issued forth fire and smoke and sulphur — Ber

The horses' heads looked much like lions', and smoke and fire and flaming sulphur bellowed from their mouths — Tay

18. By these three was the third part of men killed, by the fire, and by the smoke, and by the brimstone, which issued out of their mouths.

Through these three Curses a third of mankind perished — because of the fire, and the smoke, and the sulphur that issued from their mouths — TCNT

19. For their power is in their mouth, and in their tails:

for the power of the horses lies in their mouths and in their tails — TCNT

for their tails were like unto serpents, and had heads, and with them they do hurt.

For their tails are like snakes, with heads, and it is with them that they do harm — TCNT

20. And the rest of the men which were not killed by these plagues yet repented not of the works of their hands, that they should not worship devils, and idols of gold, and silver, and brass, and stone, and of wood: which neither can see, nor hear, nor walk:

But those who were left of mankind, who had not perished through these Curses, did not repent and turn away from what their own hands had made; they would not abandon the worship of demons, and of idols made of . . . — TCNT

21. Neither repented they of their mur-

ders, nor of their sorceries, nor of their fornication, nor of their thefts.

. . . or their immorality or their thefts — RSV

CHAPTER 10

1. And I saw another mighty angel come down from heaven, clothed with a cloud:
   and a rainbow was upon his head,
   and the rainbow of the cloud was upon his head — Lam
   with a [halo like a] rainbow over his head — Amp
   and his face was as it were the sun, and his feet as pillars of fire:
   his face was like the sun, and his feet like pillars of fire — TCNT

2. And he had in his hand a little book open:
   . . . a little scroll opened — Rhm
   . . . a small scroll unrolled — Wey
   and he set his right foot upon the sea, and his left foot on the earth,

3. And cried with a loud voice, as when a lion roareth:
   And gave a great shout — it was like the roar of a lion — Tay
   and when he had cried, seven thunders uttered their voices.
   At his cry the seven peals of thunder spoke, each with its own voice — TCNT
   and the seven thunders crashed their reply — Tay

4. And when the seven thunders had uttered their voices, I was about to write:
   When the seven thunders had rolled I was on the point of writing — Phi
   and I heard a voice from heaven saying unto me, Seal up those things which the seven thunders uttered, and write them not.
   . . . but I heard a voice from Heaven say — Keep secret what the seven peals of thunder said, and do not write it down — TCNT

5. And the angel which I saw stand upon the sea and upon the earth lifted up his hand to heaven,

6. And sware by him that liveth for ever and ever, who created heaven, and the

things that therein are, and the earth, and the things that therein are, and the sea, and the things which are therein, that there should be time no longer:
. . . delay no longer — ASV
. . . no further delay — Wey
. . . no more waiting — Bas

7. But in the days of the voice of the seventh angel, when he shall begin to sound,
   In the days which shall soon be announced by the trumpet blast of the seventh angel — Phi
   Moreover at the time when the seventh angel shall speak, when he is ready to blow his blast — TCNT
   but when the time comes for the seventh angel to sound his trumpet — NEB
   the mystery of God should be finished, as he hath declared to his servants the prophets.
   then the hidden purposes of God, of which he told the good news to his servants, the Prophets, are at once fulfilled — TCNT
   then shall have been completed the sacred secret of God, as he told the good-news unto his own servants the prophets — Rhm
   . . . the secret purpose . . . — Wey
   . . . the hidden purpose . . . — NEB

8. And the voice which I heard from heaven spake unto me again, and said,
   Then came the voice which I had heard from Heaven. It spoke to me again, and said — TCNT
   Go and take the little book which is open in the hand of the angel which standeth upon the sea and upon the earth.
   Go and take the opened scroll . . . — Rhm

9. And I went unto the angel, and said unto him, Give me the little book.
   . . . the little scroll — Rhm

And he said unto me, Take it, and eat
it up;

... eat the whole of it — Wey

... eat all of it — Beck

and it shall make thy belly bitter,

It will give you great pain when you
have eaten it — Wey

but it will be bitter to digest — Mof

It will turn your stomach sour — NEB

**but it shall be in thy mouth sweet as
honey.**

10. **And I took the little book out of the
angel's hand,**

And I took the little scroll out of the
hand of the messenger — Rhm

**and ate it up; and it was in my mouth
sweet as honey: and as soon as I had
eaten it, my belly was bitter.**

11. **And he said unto me, Thou must
prophesy again before many peoples,
and nations, and tongues, and kings.**

CHAPTER 11

1. **And there was given me a reed like
unto a rod:**

Then I was given a measuring rod like
a staff — RSV

**and the angel stood, saying, Rise, and
measure the temple of God, and the
altar, and them that worship therein.**

2. **But the court which is without the
temple leave out, and measure it not;**

but do not measure the court outside
the temple — RSV

**for it is given unto the Gentiles: and
the holy city shall they tread under
foot forty and two months.**

... forty-two months [three and one-
half years] — Amp

3. **And I will give power unto my two
witnesses, and they shall prophesy a
thousand two hundred and threescore
days, clothed in sackcloth.**

And I have two witnesses, whom I will
appoint to prophesy, dressed in sackcloth all through those twelve hundred and sixty days — NEB

... all through those twelve hundred
and sixty days [forty-two months;
three and one-half years] — Amp

4. **These are the two olive trees,**

**and the two candlesticks standing be-
fore the God of the earth.**

and the two lampstands which stand
before the Lord of the earth — RSV

5. **And if any man will hurt them, fire
proceedeth out of their mouth, and
devoureth their enemies:**

And if any man desireth to hurt them
... — ASV

**and if any man will hurt them, he must
in this manner be killed.**

if any one would harm them, thus he
is doomed to be killed — RSV

6. **These have power to shut heaven, that
it rain not in the days of their prophecy:**

... power to control the sky, so that
it will not rain in those days — Lam

**and have power over waters to turn
them to blood, and to smite the
earth with all plagues, as often as
they will.**

7. **And when they shall have finished
their testimony, the beast that ascendeth out of the bottomless pit[56]**

... the monster that comes up from
... — Ber

**shall make war against them, and
shall overcome them, and kill them.**

8. **And their dead bodies shall lie in the
street of the great city,**

**which spiritually is called Sodom and
Egypt,**

which is mystically spoken of as ... —
TCNT

whose mystical name is ... — Mof

that is figuratively called ... — Gspd

which is allegorically called ... — RSV

whose name is called in allegory ... —
NEB

which is called by those with spiritual
understanding ... — Phi

... called Sodom and Egypt, to show
what kind of city it is — Beck

where also our[57] Lord was crucified.

... their Lord ... — ASV

there, too, their Lord was crucified —
Knox

9. **And they of the people and kindreds
and tongues and nations shall see their
dead bodies three days and an half,**

---

[56]See Rev. 9:1.

[57]Some manuscripts read "their."

And from among the peoples and tribes and tongues and nations do men look upon their . . . — ASV

and shall not suffer their dead bodies to be put in graves.

and do not allow them to be laid in a grave — TCNT

10. **And they that dwell upon the earth shall rejoice over them, and make merry, and shall send gifts one to another;**

. . . will gloat over them and will hold celebrations and send one another presents — Phi

And there will be a worldwide holiday — people everywhere will rejoice and give presents to each other and throw parties — Tay

because these two prophets tormented them that dwelt on the earth.

. . . had brought such misery to the inhabitants of the earth — Phi

to celebrate the death of the two prophets who had tormented them so much — Tay

11. **And after three days and an half the spirit of life from God**

. . . the breath of life from God — ASV

entered into them, and they stood upon their feet;

and great fear fell upon them which saw them.

and consternation seized those who saw them — Wms

This struck terror into the hearts of . . . — Phi

12. **And they heard a great voice from heaven saying unto them, Come up hither.**

Come up here — TCNT

And they ascended up to heaven in a cloud; and their enemies beheld them.

. . . in full view of their enemies — Phi

13. **And the same hour was there a great earthquake,**

And at that hour there was a great earthquake — RSV

and the tenth part of the city fell, and in the earthquake were slain of men seven thousand:

A tenth part of the city fell, and seven thousand people perished in the earthquake — TCNT

and the remnant were affrighted,

and the rest were terrified — ASV

and gave glory to the God of heaven.

and acknowledged the glory of the God of Heaven — Phi

14. **The second woe is past;**[58]

The second disaster is now past — Phi

and behold, the third woe cometh quickly.

and there is a third woe soon to follow — TCNT

and I see the third disaster following hard upon the heels of the second — Phi

15. **And the seventh angel sounded;**

Then the seventh angel blew his trumpet — RSV

and there were great voices in heaven, saying,

The kingdoms of this world are become the kingdoms of our Lord, and of his Christ;

The kingdom of the world is become the kingdom of . . . — ASV

The sovereignty of the world now belongs to . . . — Wey

The rule of the world has passed to . . . — Mof

The dominion of the world has passed to . . . — Knox

. . . has passed into the possession of . . . — Gspd

and he shall reign for ever and ever.

He will be King . . . — Wey

16. **And the four and twenty elders, which sat before God on their seats,**

. . . on their thrones — ASV

fell upon their faces, and worshipped God,

17. **Saying, We give thee thanks, O Lord God Almighty, which art, and wast, and art to come; because thou hast taken to thee thy great power, and hast reigned.**

. . . and hast become king — Rhm

18. **And the nations were angry, and thy wrath is come, and the time of the dead, that they should be judged,**

And the nations were angered; and

---

[58]Compare Rev. 9:12.

thine anger came, and the fit time of the dead to be vindicated — Rhm

and that thou shouldest give reward unto thy servants the prophets, and to the saints, and them that fear thy name, small and great;

and the time to give their rewards to . . . — ASV

and shouldest destroy them which destroy the earth.

and to destroy them that destroy . . . — ASV

19. And the temple of God was opened in heaven, and there was seen in his temple

the ark of his testament:

the ark of his covenant — ASV

the chest containing God's covenant — Wms

and the Ark, in which His Covenant was — Wey

and there were lightnings, and voices, and thunderings, and an earthquake, and great hail.

CHAPTER 12

1. And there appeared a great wonder in heaven;

. . . a great sign was seen in heaven — ASV

Then a huge sign became visible in the sky — Phi

Then a great pageant appeared in heaven — Tay

a woman clothed with the sun, and the moon under her feet, and upon her head a crown of twelve stars:

and with a crownlike garland (tiara) of twelve stars on her head — Amp

2. And she being with child cried, travailing in birth, and pained to be delivered.

and she was with child, and crieth out being in pangs and in anguish to bring forth — Rhm

She was pregnant and screamed in the pain of her labor, awaiting delivery — Tay

3. And there appeared another wonder in heaven;

. . . another sign . . . — ASV

and behold a great red dragon,

. . . a gigantic, fiery dragon — Ber

. . . a monstrous red dragon — Nor

having seven heads and ten horns, and seven crowns upon his heads.

4. And his tail drew the third part of the stars of heaven, and did cast them to the earth: and the dragon stood before the woman which was ready to be delivered, for to devour her child as soon as it was born.

5. And she brought forth a man child,

The woman gave birth to a son, a male child — TCNT

who was to rule all nations with a rod of iron:

who is destined to rule all the nations with an iron rod — TCNT

who was about to shepherd all the nations with a sceptre of iron — Rhm

who is to shepherd all the nations . . . — Phi

. . . with an iron staff — Ber

and her child was caught up unto God, and to his throne.

6. And the woman fled into the wilderness,

And the woman fled into the desert — Rhm

where she hath a place prepared of God,

where there is a place prepared for her by God — TCNT

that they should feed her there a thousand two hundred and three score days.[59]

that there they may nourish her . . . — ASV

7. And there was war in heaven:

Then a battle took place in the heavens — TCNT

Fierce war broke out . . . — Knox

Then war developed in . . . — Ber

Michael and his angels fought against the dragon; and the dragon fought and his angels,

Michael and his messengers . . . — Rhm

8. And prevailed not;

but they were defeated — Wey

neither was their place found any more in heaven.

---

[59]Compare Rev. 11:3.

neither was place found for them any longer in heaven — Rhm

9. And the great dragon was cast out,

... the great dragon was cast down — ASV

that old serpent, called the Devil, and Satan, which deceiveth the whole world:

— the ancient serpent, he that is called Adversary and the Satan, that deceiveth the whole habitable world — Rhm

... serpent of the primal age ... the whole world's seducer — Knox

he was cast out into the earth, and his angels were cast out with him.

he was cast down to the earth, and his angels were cast down with him — ASV

... and his messengers ... — Rhm

10. And I heard a loud voice saying in heaven,

Now is come salvation, and strength, and the kingdom of our God, and the power of his Christ:

... the salvation, and the power, and the kingdom of our God, and the authority of his Christ — ASV

This is the hour of victory for our God, the hour of his sovereignty and power, when his Christ comes to his rightful rule — NEB

for the accuser of our brethren is cast down, which accused them before our God day and night.

11. And they overcame him by the blood of the Lamb, and by the word of their testimony;

... because of the blood ... and because of the word of ... — ASV

And they conquered him by the blood of the Lamb ... — Lam

... by means of the blood of ... — Ber

They defeated him by the blood of the Lamb and by the preaching of the Word — Nor

and they loved not their lives unto the death.

and not by loving their own lives; they were willing to die — Nor

they had to die for it, but they did not cling to life — Mof

they did not hold their lives too dear to lay them down — NEB

they did not spare themselves even unto death — Lam

In their love of life they shrank not from death — TCNT

and because they held their lives cheap and did not shrink even from death — Wey

they loved not their lives even in the face of death — Ber

12. Therefore rejoice, ye heavens, and ye that dwell in them.

So celebrate your triumph ... — Wms

Woe to the inhabiters of the earth and of the sea! for the devil is come down unto you, having great wrath, because he knoweth that he hath but a short time.

13. And when the dragon saw that he was cast unto the earth, he persecuted the woman which brought forth the man child.

14. And to the woman were given two wings of a great eagle, that she might fly

into the wilderness, into her place,

into the desert ... — Rhm

where she is nourished for a time, and times, and half a time, from the face of the serpent.

where for a year, two years, and half a year she will be kept hidden from the serpent's view — Knox

where she is to be kept safe and fed for a time, and times, and half a time [three and one-half years, or twelve hundred sixty days][60] — Amp

15. And the serpent cast out of his mouth water as a flood after the woman,

And the serpent cast out of his mouth after the woman water as a river — ASV

that he might cause her to be carried away of the flood.

... by the river — Alf

... by the stream — ASV

16. And the earth helped the woman, and the earth opened her mouth, and swallowed up the flood which the dragon cast out of his mouth.

---

[60]Compare Rev. 11:3.

But Earth came to her help, and opened her mouth and drank up the river which the Dragon had poured out of its mouth — TCNT

17. **And the dragon was wroth with the woman, and went to make war with the remnant of her seed,**
... the rest of her seed — ASV
... the rest of her off-spring — TCNT
... her other children — Wey
which keep the commandments of God, and have the testimony of

Jesus Christ.
that is, on those who keep God's commandments and maintain their testimony to Jesus — NEB
who were keeping ... and holding the witness of Jesus — Rhm
... who hold the testimony of Jesus — ASV
... bear their testimony to Jesus — TCNT
... hold fast the testimony of Jesus — Wey

CHAPTER 13

1. **And I**[61] **stood upon the sand of the sea,**
And he stood there waiting on the sea beach — Knox
He took his stand on the sea-shore — NEB
And he stood on the sand of the sea-shore — NASB
He stopped on the sandy shore of the sea — Beck
and saw a beast rise up out of the sea,
And out of the sea, in my vision, a beast came up to land — Knox
having seven heads and ten horns, and upon his horns ten crowns, and upon his heads the name of blasphemy.
... names of blasphemy — ASV
... blasphemous names — TCNT

2. **And the beast which I saw was like a leopard, and his feet were as the feet of a bear, and his mouth as the mouth of a lion:**
This Creature looked like a leopard but had bear's feet and a lion's mouth — Tay
and the dragon gave him his power, and his seat, and great authority.
... his power, and his throne, and great authority — ASV

3. **And I saw one of his heads as it were wounded to death; and his deadly wound was healed:**
One of his heads seemed to me to have been mortally wounded, but its deadly wound had been healed — TCNT
and all the world wondered after the beast.
and the whole earth went after the beast in amazement and admiration — Amp

4. **And they worshipped the dragon which gave power unto the beast:**
... because he gave his authority unto the beast — ASV
and they worshipped the beast, saying,
they worshipped the beast also, and chanted — NEB
Who is like unto the beast? who is able to make war with him?
Who matches the beast? ... — Ber
Who is like the Beast? Who can fight against it — NEB

5. **And there was given unto him a mouth speaking great things and blasphemies;**
... haughty and blasphemous words — RSV
... arrogant words and blasphemies — NASB
and power was given unto him
... authority ... — ASV
to continue forty and two months.[62]
to work forty-two months — Alf
to work his will forty-two months — TCNT

6. **And he opened his mouth in blasphemy against God, to blaspheme his name, and his tabernacle, and them that dwell in heaven.**
So it poured out blasphemies against God ... his name ... his dwelling-place ... those who live in Heaven — Phi

7. **And it was given unto him to make war with the saints, and to overcome them:**
... to fight with Christ's People and to conquer them — TCNT

---

[61]Some manuscripts read "he."
[62]See Rev. 11:2.

and power was given him

and there was given to him authority
— ASV

over all kindreds, and tongues, and nations.

8. **And all that dwell upon the earth shall worship him, whose names are not written in the book of life of the Lamb slain from the foundation of the world.**

... written from the foundation of the world in the book of life of the Lamb that has been slain — ASV

9. **If any man have an ear, let him hear.**[63]

10. **He that leadeth into captivity shall go into captivity:**

If any man is for captivity, into captivity he goeth — ASV

he that killeth with the sword must be killed with the sword.

If any man shall kill with the sword, with the sword must he be killed — ASV

Here is the patience and the faith of the saints.

Here is a call for the endurance and faith of ... — RSV

Here is where the holy people will need to endure and trust — Beck

(Here there is need for endurance and faith on the part of Christ's People) — TCNT

11. **And I beheld another beast coming up out of the earth; and he had two horns like a lamb,**

and he spake as a dragon.

but it spoke like a dragon — Gspd

but it roared like a dragon — Knox

12. **And he exerciseth all the power of the first beast before him,**

He is acting for the first animal with all his authority — Beck

It wielded all the authority of the first beast — NEB

He exercises the full authority of the first wild beast in his presence — Wms

and causeth the earth and them which dwell therein to worship the first beast, whose deadly wound was healed.

13. **And he doeth great wonders, so that he maketh fire come down from**

heaven on the earth in the sight of men,

He performed amazing miracles ... — Mof

It also performs impressive miracles ... — Ber

And he doeth great signs, that he should even make fire ... — ASV

14. **And deceiveth them that dwell on the earth by the means of those miracles which he had power to do in the sight of the beast;**

it leads those living on the earth astray ... — Ber

saying to them that dwell on the earth, that they should make an image to the beast,

telling the earth's inhabitants to erect a statue to the beast — Ber

which had the wound by a sword, and did live.

15. **And he had power to give life unto the image of the beast,**

... to give breath to ... — ASV

that the image of the beast should both speak, and cause that as many as would not worship the image of the beast should be killed.

so that the statue of the Beast should actually speak. He has everyone put to death who will not worship the statue of ... — Mof

16. **And he causeth all, both small and great, rich and poor, free and bond, to receive a mark in their right hand, or in their foreheads:**

High and low, rich and poor, freemen and slaves — it causes a brand to be put on the right hand or on the forehead of every one of them — TCNT

17. **And that no man might buy or sell, save he that had the mark, or the name of the beast, or the number of his name.**

save he that hath the mark, even the name of the beast or ... — ASV

The purpose of this is that no one should be able to buy or sell unless ... — Phi

18. **Here is wisdom.**

---

[63]Compare Rev. 2:7.

This calls for wisdom — RSV

Here is the key — NEB

There is wisdom hidden here! — Gspd

(Here there is need for discernment) — TCNT

Let him that hath understanding count the number of the beast:

let him who has understanding reckon ... — RSV

let every thinking man calculate ... — Phi

and anyone who has intelligence may work out the number ... — NEB

for it is the number of a man;

... it indicates a certain man — Wey

... it is the code number of the name of a man — Lam

and his number is Six hundred threescore and six.

and his number is 666 — Rhm

CHAPTER 14

1. And I looked, and, lo, a Lamb stood on the mount Sion,

... and behold, the Lamb standing ... — ASV

and with him an hundred forty and four thousand,

... 144,000 — Wey

having his Father's name written in their foreheads.

having his name, and the name of his Father ... — ASV

2. And I heard a voice from heaven, as the voice of many waters, and as the voice of a great thunder:

... louder than water in full flood, or heavy thunder — Knox

and I heard the voice of harpers harping with their harps:

It was the singing of a choir accompanied by harps — Tay

3. And they sung as it were a new song before the throne, and before the four beasts, and the elders: and no man could learn that song but the hundred and forty and four thousand,

which were redeemed from the earth.

even they that had been purchased out of the earth — ASV

4. These are they which were not defiled with women; for they are virgins. These are they which follow the Lamb whithersoever he goeth.

These were redeemed from among men, being the firstfruits unto God and to the Lamb.

These were purchased from among men, to be the first fruits unto God and unto the Lamb — ASV

5. And in their mouth was found no guile: for they are without fault before the throne of God.

... was found no lie: they are without blemish ... — ASV

No lie was ever heard upon their lips. They are beyond the reach of blame — TCNT

6. And I saw another angel fly in the midst of heaven,

... flying high in mid-air — Beck

having the everlasting gospel to preach

having eternal good news to proclaim — ASV

He had the Good News, decreed from eternity, to announce — TCNT

unto them that dwell on the earth, and to every nation, and kindred, and tongue, and people,

7. Saying with a loud voice, Fear God, and give glory to him; for the hour of his judgment is come: and worship him that made heaven, and earth, and the sea, and the fountains of waters.

8. And there followed another angel, saying, Babylon is fallen, is fallen, that great city, because she made all nations drink of the wine of the wrath of her fornication.

9. And the third angel followed them, saying with a loud voice, If any man worship the beast and his image,

... If any one worships the Wild Beast and his statue — Wey

and receive his mark in his forehead, or in his hand,

10. The same shall drink of the wine of the wrath of God,

which is poured out without mixture into the cup of his indignation;

which is prepared unmixed in the cup of his anger — ASV

and he shall be tormented with fire and

brimstone in the presence of the holy angels, and in the presence of the Lamb:

11. And the smoke of their torment ascendeth up for ever and ever: and they have no rest day nor night, who worship the beast and his image, and whosoever receiveth the mark of his name.

12. Here is the patience of the saints:
Here is a call for the saints . . . to hold out — Nor
Here the fortitude of God's people has its place — NEB
here are they that keep the commandments of God, and the faith of Jesus.
— in keeping God's commands and remaining loyal to Jesus — NEB

13. And I heard a voice from heaven saying unto me, Write, Blessed are the dead
. . . Happy are the dead — NEB
which die in the Lord from henceforth:
who from this hour die in union with the Lord — TCNT
who from this time forth die as Christians — Gspd
who die in the faith of Christ — NEB
who die in the Lord from now on! — NASB
Yea, saith the Spirit, that they may rest from their labours;
and their works do follow them.
Their good deeds go with them — TCNT
for what they have done goes with them — Mof
for they take with them the record of their deeds — NEB
for their works will follow them — — Lam

14. And I looked, and behold a white cloud, and upon the cloud one sat like unto the Son of man, having on his head a golden crown, and in his hand a sharp sickle.

15. And another angel came out of the temple, crying with a loud voice to him that sat on the cloud, Thrust in thy sickle, and reap: for the time is come for thee to reap; for the harvest of the earth is ripe.

16. And he that sat on the cloud thrust in his sickle on the earth; and the earth was reaped.

17. And another angel came out of the temple which is in heaven, he also having a sharp sickle.

18. And another angel came out from the altar, which had power over fire;
. . . he that hath power over fire — ASV
and cried with a loud cry to him that had the sharp sickle, saying, Thrust in thy sharp sickle, and gather the clusters of the vine of the earth; for her grapes are fully ripe.

19. And the angel thrust in his sickle into the earth, and gathered the vine of the earth, and cast it into the great winepress of the wrath of God.

20. And the winepress was trodden without the city,
and blood came out of the winepress, even unto the horse bridles, by the space of a thousand and six hundred furlongs.
and out of the winepress flowed blood for two hundred miles in a stream as high as the horses' bridles — Phi
and for two hundred miles around blood flowed from the press to the height of . . . — NEB
and blood came out of the press, rising as high as the bridles of the horses for a distance of two hundred miles — TCNT

CHAPTER 15

1. And I saw another sign in heaven, great and marvellous, seven angels having the seven last plagues;
. . . the seven last punishments — Bas
for in them is filled up the wrath of God.
. . . in them is finished the wrath of God — ASV
. . . with them the Wrath of God is ended — TCNT
. . . in them the wrath of God has reached its climax — Wey
. . . by which the vengeance of God is finally achieved — Knox
. . . with them God's wrath (indignation) is completely expressed —

reaches its climax and is ended —
Amp

2. And I saw as it were a sea of glass mingled with fire:

. . . a sea of glass, tinged with fire —
Knox

. . . something like a glassy sea mixed
with fire — Ber

. . . a sea of glass shot through with
fire — Phi

. . . a glassy sea blended with fire —
Amp

and them that had gotten the victory over the beast,

and the conquerors of the beast — Alf

those who had come victorious out of
the conflict with the Beast — TCNT

and over his image, and over his mark, and over the number of his name, stand on the sea of glass,

. . . standing on the sea of glass — Alf

. . . standing upon the glassy sea —
Rhm

having the harps of God.

3. And they sing the song of Moses the servant of God, and the song of the Lamb, saying, Great and marvellous are thy works, Lord God Almighty; just and true are thy ways, thou King of saints.[64]

. . . King of the ages — ASV

. . . King of the nations — Alf

. . . Eternal King — TCNT

4. Who shall not fear thee, O Lord, and glorify thy name? for thou only art

holy: for all nations shall come and
worship before thee; for thy judgments
are made manifest.

. . . for thy righteous acts have been
made manifest — ASV

5. And after that I looked, and, behold, the temple of the tabernacle of the testimony in heaven was opened:

And after these things I saw, and the
sanctuary of The Tent of Witness
in heaven was opened — Rhm

6. And the seven angels came out of the temple, having the seven plagues, clothed in pure and white linen, and having their breasts girded with golden girdles.

7. And one of the four beasts[65] gave unto the seven angels seven golden vials

. . . seven golden bowls — ASV

. . . seven golden cups — Knox

full of the wrath of God,

filled with the vengeance of God —
Knox

who liveth for ever and ever.

8. And the temple was filled with smoke from the glory of God, and from his power;

. . . from the Glory and Majesty of
God — TCNT

and no man was able to enter into the temple, till the seven plagues of the seven angels were fulfilled.

. . . should be finished — ASV

CHAPTER 16

1. And I heard a great voice out of the temple saying to the seven angels, Go your ways, and pour out the vials of the wrath of God upon the earth.

. . . pour out the seven bowls . . . —
ASV

2. And the first went, and poured out his vial[66] upon the earth;

. . . bowl . . . — ASV

and there fell a noisome and grievous sore

. . . loathsome and painful sores —
TCNT

. . . foul and painful ulcers — Amp

. . . a baneful and painful ulcer — Rhm

. . . a severe and malignant sore — Lam

Whereupon loathsome and malignant

ulcers attacked — Phi

upon the men which had the mark of the beast, and upon them which worshipped his image.

upon the men that had the mark of the
beast, and that worshipped his image
— ASV

all those who bore the mark of the
animal and worshiped its statue —
Phi

3. And the second angel poured out his

---

[64]Some manuscripts read "nations" and "ages."

[65]Compare Rev. 4:6.

[66]See Rev. 16:3, 4, 8, 10, 12, 17.

vial upon the sea; and it became as the
blood of a dead man:

... turned into a fluid like the blood of
a corpse — Phi

... turned into blood like that of a
corpse [thick, corrupt, ill-smelling
and disgusting] — Amp

and every living soul died in the sea.

4. **And the third angel poured out his vial
upon the rivers and fountains of
waters; and they became blood.**

... into the rivers and springs of water,
and they turned into blood — Phi

5. **And I heard the angel of the waters
say, Thou art righteous, O Lord, which
art, and wast, and shalt be, because
thou hast judged thus.**

... You are just in passing such a sentence ... — Wms

6. **For they have shed the blood of saints
and prophets,**

for they poured out the blood of ...
— ASV

For they made the blood of saints and
prophets come out like a stream —
Bas

**and thou hast given them blood to
drink;**

and blood have you given them for
drink — Bas

for they are worthy.

It is what they deserve — TCNT

7. **And I heard another out of the altar
say, Even so, Lord God Almighty, true
and righteous are thy judgments.**

8. **And the fourth angel poured out his
vial upon the sun; and power was given
unto him to scorch men with fire.**

9. **And men were scorched with great
heat, and blasphemed the name of
God, which hath power over these
plagues; and they repented not to give
him glory.**

10. **And the fifth angel poured out his vial
upon the seat of the beast;**

... upon the throne of the beast — ASV

and his kingdom was full of darkness;

and his kingdom was darkened — ASV

... plunged into darkness — Phi

**and they gnawed their tongues for
pain,**

... in agony — Phi

11. **And blasphemed the God of heaven**

... cursed the God of Heaven — Phi

**because of their pains and their sores,
and repented not of their deeds.**

... but refused to repent of what they
had done — Phi

12. **And the sixth angel poured out his
vial upon the great river Euphrates;
and the water thereof was dried up,
that the way of the kings of the east
might be prepared.**

in order to clear the way for the kings
who are to come from the east —
Wey

so that the road for the Kings of the
East might be made ready — TCNT

so that the highway of the kings from
the rising sun might be made ready
— Ber

13. **And I saw three unclean spirits like
frogs come out of the mouth of the
dragon, and out of the mouth of the
beast, and out of the mouth of the
false prophet.**

... three foul spirits leap like frogs
from ... — Wms

... three unclean spirits in the form of
frogs ... — Knox

... three impure spirits as frogs ... —
Rhm

... three foul spirits, like frogs ... —
TCNT

... emerge from the mouth ... —Gspd

14. **For they are the spirits of devils, working miracles,**

They really are the spirits of demons
... — Ber

They are diabolical spirits ... — Phi

**which go forth unto the kings of the
earth and of the whole world, to
gather them to the battle of that
great day of God Almighty.**

15. **Behold, I come as a thief. Blessed is
he that watcheth, and keepeth his garments.**

(That is the day when I come like a
thief! Happy the man who stays
awake and keeps on his clothes —
NEB ..

... stays awake and keeps his clothes
at his side — Phi

**lest he walk naked, and they see his
shame.**

so that he will not have to go naked and ashamed for all to see! — NEB

16. And he[67] gathered them together
... they gathered them together — ASV
into a place called in the Hebrew tongue Armageddon.
... Har Magedon — Rhm

17. And the seventh angel poured out his vial into the air: and there came a great voice out of the temple of heaven, from the throne, saying, It is done.
It is all over! — Gspd
It is all accomplished — Wey
The end has come! — Phi

18. And there were voices, and thunders, and lightnings; and there was a great earthquake, such as was not since men were upon the earth, so mighty an earthquake, and so great.

19. And the great city was divided into three parts, and the cities of the nations fell:
... split into three parts ... — Phi
and great Babylon came to remembrance before God,
and Babylon the great was remembered

in the sight of God — ASV
and God did not forget Babylon the great — NEB
to give unto her the cup of the wine of the fierceness of his wrath.
but made her drink the cup which was filled with the fierce wine of his vengeance — NEB

20. And every island fled away, and the mountains were not found.
and every island vanished, and the mountains disappeared — TCNT
And islands vanished, and mountains flattened out — Tay

21. And there fell upon men a great hail out of heaven, every stone about the weight of a talent:
Hailstones, big as hundredweights, fell down from the sky onto the people — Ber
Great hailstones like heavy weights fell from the sky — Phi
And huge hailstones, about one hundred pounds each, came down from heaven upon men — NASB
and men blasphemed God because of the plague of the hail; for the plague thereof was exceeding great.

CHAPTER 17

1. And there came one of the seven angels which had the seven vials[68] and talked with me, saying unto me, Come hither;
I will shew unto thee the judgment of the great whore that sitteth upon many waters:
and I will show you the sentence passed upon the Great Harlot who is seated at the meeting of many waters — TCNT
... the doom of the great idolatress ... — Gspd
... the condemnation of ... — Lam
and I will show you what is going to happen to the Notorious Prostitute, who sits upon the many waters of the world — Tay

2. With whom the kings of the earth have committed fornication, and the inhabitants of the earth have been made drunk with the wine of her fornication.

3. So he carried me away in the spirit into the wilderness:
So he carried me away in spiritual rapture to a desert — Wms
And he bore me away in a trance to a lonely place — TCNT
and I saw a woman sit upon a scarlet coloured beast,
and I saw a woman sitting upon a scarlet-coloured wild-beast — Alf
... riding on ... — Knox
full of names of blasphemy,
covered with blasphemous names — TCNT
having seven heads and ten horns.

4. And the woman was arrayed in purple and scarlet colour,
and decked with gold and precious stones and pearls,
and gilded with gold and precious

---

[67]Variant reading is "they."
[68]Compare Rev. 15:7.

stones and pearls — Alf

and glittering with gold ornaments, precious stones, and pearls — TCNT

having a golden cup in her hand full of abomination and filthiness of her fornication:

having in her hand a golden cup full of abominations, even the unclean things of her fornication — ASV

In her hand she held a gold cup, full of idolatrous abominations and the unclean fruits of her licentiousness — TCNT

and held in her hand a golden goblet full of obscenities — Tay

5. And upon her forehead was a name written, MYSTERY, BABYLON THE GREAT, THE MOTHER OF HAR-LOTS AND ABOMINATIONS OF THE EARTH.

. . . a symbolic title was inscribed . . . — Ber

and written on her forehead was a name with a secret meaning: Baby-lon the great, the mother of whores and of every obscenity on earth — NEB

There was a title written over her fore-head, The mystic Babylon, great mother-city of all harlots, and all that is abominable on earth — Knox

6. And I saw the woman drunken with the blood of the saints, and with the blood of the martyrs of Jesus:

. . . drinking herself drunk with . . . — Wey

and when I saw her, I wondered with great admiration.

. . . with a great wonder — ASV

. . . I was amazed beyond measure — TCNT

And I was astonished . . . with great astonishment — Rhm

7. And the angel said unto me, Where-fore didst thou marvel?

. . . didst thou wonder — ASV

I will tell thee the mystery of the woman,

. . . the symbolic meaning of . . . — Wms

. . . the mystic meaning of . . . — TCNT

. . . the secret of the woman — Rhm

and of the beast that carrieth her, which hath the seven heads and ten horns.

and of the seven-headed, ten-horned Wild Beast which carries her — Wey

8. The beast that thou sawest was, and is not; and shall ascend out of the bottomless pit,[69] and go into perdition:

The animal, which you saw, once lived but now he is no more — it will come up out of the pit only to meet destruction — Phi

. . . is about to come up . . . — ASV

. . . and go to be destroyed — Lam

and they that dwell on the earth shall wonder, whose names were not writ-ten in the book of life from the foundation of the world,

Those who are living on earth will be amazed — those whose names have not been written . . . — TCNT

when they behold the beast that was, and is not, and yet is.

when they behold the beast, how that he was, and is not, and shall come — ASV

. . . and shall come again — Alf

9. And here is the mind which hath wis-dom.

But here is the clue for those who can interpret it — NEB

Here is a problem for a profound mind! — Gspd

Here is something for the intelligent to ponder — Ber

The seven heads are seven mountains, on which the woman sitteth.

The seven heads are seven hills . . . — NEB

10. And there are seven kings: five are fallen, and one is, and the other is not yet come; and when he cometh, he must continue a short space.

and they are seven kings, the five are fallen, the one is, the other is not yet come; and when he cometh, he must continue a little while — ASV

They are also seven kings; of whom five have fallen and one remains, while one is not yet come. When he comes, he must stay for a little while — TCNT

11. And the beast that was, and is not, even he is the eighth, and is of the seven,

---

[69]Compare Rev. 9:1.

So must the Beast that was, but is not.
He counts as an eighth king, al-
though he is one of the seven —
TCNT

And the beast which lived once and
now is dead must be reckoned as the
eighth, yet it is one of the seven —
Knox

. . . he springs from the seven — Ber

and goeth into perdition.

and is on his way to destruction —
TCNT

and goes on to ruin — Ber

and he is going to be destroyed — Wms

**12. And the ten horns which thou sawest
are ten kings, which have received no
kingdom as yet;
but receive power as kings one hour
with the beast.**

but they receive authority as kings,
with the beast, for one hour — ASV

. . . will receive authority to be kings
. . . — Phi

**13. These have one mind, and shall give
their power and strength unto the
beast.**

All of them have a single policy; they
surrender to the beast the power and
dominion which is theirs — Knox

. . . one common policy . . . — Wey

. . . and they give their power and authority unto the beast — ASV

14. These shall make war with the Lamb,

**and the Lamb shall overcome them:
for he is Lord of lords, and King of
kings:
and they that are with him are called,
and chosen, and faithful.**

And those who accompany Him —
called as they are, and chosen and
faithful — shall share in the victory
— Wey

**15. And he saith unto me, The waters[70]
which thou sawest, where the whore
sitteth, are peoples, and multitudes,
and nations, and tongues.**

**16. And the ten horns which thou sawest
upon the beast, these shall hate the
whore,**

. . . the ten horns . . . will become the
harlot's enemies — Knox

**and shall make her desolate and naked,
and shall eat her flesh, and burn her
with fire.**

**17. For God hath put in their hearts to
fulfil his will, and to agree,**

. . . to carry out his design — Knox

. . . to do his mind, and to come to one
mind — ASV

**and give their kingdom unto the beast,
until the words of God shall be fulfilled.**

. . . shall be accomplished — ASV

**18. And the woman which thou sawest is
that great city, which reigneth over the
kings of the earth.**

CHAPTER 18

**1. And after these things I saw another
angel come down from heaven,
having great power;**

having great authority — ASV

**and the earth was lightened with his
glory.**

and the earth was illuminated by his
splendour — TCNT

**2. And he cried mightily with a strong
voice, saying, Babylon the great is
fallen, is fallen,**

**and is become the habitation of devils,
and the hold of every foul spirit, and
a cage of every unclean and hateful
bird.**

She has become a resort for demons; a
fort for every unclean spirit; a refuge
for every filthy and detestable bird
— Ber

She has become an abode of demons,
a stronghold of every wicked spirit,
a stronghold of every foul and hateful bird — TCNT

. . . a dwelling for demons, a haunt
for every unclean spirit, for every
foul and loathesome bird — NEB

**3. For all nations have drunk of the wine
of the wrath of her fornication, and
the kings of the earth have committed
fornication with her,**

For by the wine of the wrath of her
fornication all the nations are fallen
. . . — ASV

**and the merchants of the earth are
waxed rich through the abundance**

---

[70]See verse 1, TCNT translation.

of her delicacies.

... waxed rich by the power of her wantonness — ASV

... have grown rich through the excess of her luxury — TCNT

4. **And I heard another voice from heaven, saying, Come out of her, my people,**
that ye be not partakers of her sins,
that ye have no fellowship with her sins — ASV

... may not share in her sins — Wms

... may not be involved in her guilt — Knox

lest you become accomplices in her sins — Phi

and that ye receive not of her plagues.

... suffer from her plagues — Wms

... share in her punishment — Phi

5. **For her sins have reached unto heaven,**

... her sins are piled up to the sky — Gspd

... her sins are heaped up to the heavens — TCNT

and God hath remembered her iniquities.

6. **Reward her even as she rewarded you,**
Pay her back in her own coin — Wms

and double unto her double according to her works:

repay twice over what her actions deserve — TCNT

in the cup which she hath filled fill to her double.

in the cup which she mingled, mingle unto her double — ASV

mix her a drink of double strength! — Phi

7. **How much she hath glorified herself, and lived deliciously, so much torment and sorrow give her:**

How much soever she glorified herself, and waxed wanton, so much give her of torment and mourning — ASV

for her self-glorification and luxury, give her now an equal measure of torture and misery — TCNT

for she saith in her heart,

I sit a queen, and am no widow, and shall see no sorrow.

I am a queen on my throne! No mourning for me, no widow's weeds! — NEB

8. **Therefore shall her plagues come in**
one day, death, and mourning, and famine; and she shall be utterly burned with fire: for strong is the Lord God who judgeth her.

9. **And the kings of the earth, who have committed fornication and lived deliciously with her,**

... lived wantonly with her — ASV

... lived luxuriously with her — Alf

shall bewail her, and lament for her,

shall weep and wail over her — ASV

when they shall see the smoke of her burning,

10. **Standing afar off for the fear of her torment,**

while they stand at a distance, horrified at her torture — TCNT

saying, Alas, alas, that great city Babylon, that mighty city! for in one hour is thy judgment come.

... Alas! Alas! Great City! O mighty City of Babylon! In a single hour your judgment fell — TCNT

11. **And the merchants of the earth shall weep and mourn over her; for no man buyeth their merchandise any more:**

12. **The merchandise of gold, and silver, and precious stones, and of pearls, and fine linen, and purple, and silk, and scarlet, and all thyine wood,**

... citron wood — Alf

... scented woods — TCNT

and all manner vessels of ivory, and all manner vessels of most precious wood, and of brass, and iron, and marble,

13. **And cinnamon, and odours,[71] and ointments, and frankincense, and wine, and oil, and fine flour, and wheat, and beasts,**

... cattle — ASV

and sheep, and horses, and chariots, and slaves, and souls of men.

... bodies and souls of men — TCNT

... slaves — and human lives — Gspd

... slaves, that is, human souls — RSV

... slaves, the very souls of men — Phi

... slaves, and human lives — NASB

14. **And the fruits that thy soul lusteth after are departed from thee,**

The fruit that your soul craved is no

---

[71]Compare Rev. 5:8.

longer within your reach — TCNT

And the fruit of the coveting of thy soul . . . — Rhm

and all things which were dainty and goodly

. . . dainty and sumptuous — ASV

are departed from thee, and thou shalt find them no more at all.

15. **The merchants of these things, which were made rich by her, shall stand afar off for the fear of her torment,[72] weeping and wailing.**

16. **And saying, Alas, alas that great city, that was clothed in fine linen, and purple, and scarlet, and decked[73] with gold, and precious stones, and pearls!**

17. **For in one hour so great riches is come to nought.**

. . . so great riches is made desolate — ASV

In one moment, all the wealth of the city is gone! — Tay

And every shipmaster,

. . . pilot — Alf

. . . ship's captain — TCNT

and all the company in ships,

and every passenger — Rhm

and sailors,

and mariners — Rhm

and as many as trade by sea,

. . . carry on traffic afar off — Rhm

and all who get their living from the sea — TCNT

stood afar off,

18. **And cried when they saw the smoke of her burning, saying, What city is like unto this great city!**

19. **And they cast dust on their heads, and cried, weeping and wailing, saying, Alas, alas that great city,**

wherein were made rich all that had ships in the sea by reason of her costliness!

wherein all that had their ships in the sea were made rich by reason of her costliness — ASV

. . . grew rich by her extravagance! — Gspd

for in one hour is she made desolate.

For in a single hour she has been laid waste! — Gspd

20. **Rejoice over her, thou heaven, and ye holy apostles and prophets;**

. . . thou heaven, and ye saints, and ye apostles, and ye prophets — ASV

for God hath avenged you on her.

21. **And a mighty angel took up a stone like a great millstone, and cast it into the sea, saying,**

Thus with violence shall that great city Babylon be thrown down,

Thus with a mighty fall shall Babylon . . . — ASV

. . . Babylon the great city will be hurled to ruin — Wms

So, with one crash of ruin, will Babylon fall, the great city — Knox

and shall be found no more at all.

never more to be seen — TCNT

22. **And the voice of harpers, and musicians, and of pipers, and trumpeters, shall be heard no more at all in thee; and no craftsman, of whatsoever craft he be, shall be found any more in thee; and the sound of a millstone shall be heard no more at all in thee;**

23. **And the light of a candle**

and the light of a lamp — ASV

shall shine no more at all in thee; and the voice of the bridegroom and of the bride shall be heard no more at all in thee: for thy merchants were the great men of the earth; for by thy sorceries were all nations deceived.

24. **And in her was found the blood of prophets, and of saints, and of all that were slain upon the earth.**

The blood of prophet and saint lay at her doors; the blood of all that were ever slain on the earth — Knox

CHAPTER 19

1. **And after these things**

I heard a great voice of much people in heaven, saying,

I heard what sounded like the roar of a vast throng in heaven, and they were shouting: — NEB

Alleluia;

Praise the Lord! — Gspd

Salvation, and glory, and honour, and power, unto the Lord our God:

the salvation and the glory belong unto

[72]Compare verse 10.

[73]Compare Rev. 17:4.

our God — Alf
Victory and glory and power belong to
our God — NEB

2. For true and righteous are his judgments:
for he hath judged the great whore,
now he has given sentence against the
great harlot — Knox
which did corrupt the earth with her fornication,
who was corrupting the earth by her
licentiousness — TCNT
and hath avenged the blood of his servants at her hand.
he has taken vengeance upon her for
the blood of . . . — TCNT
now he has called her to account for
. . . — Knox

3. And again they said, Alleluia.[74] And her smoke rose up for ever and ever.
Again and again their voices rang,
Praise the Lord! The smoke from
her burning ascends forever and
forever! — Tay

4. And the four and twenty elders and the four beasts[75] fell down and worshipped God that sat on the throne, saying, Amen; Alleluia.

5. And a voice came out of the throne, saying, Praise our God, all ye his servants, and ye that fear him, both small and great.

6. And I heard as it were the voice of a great multitude,
and as the voice of many waters,[76]
like the boom of many pounding waves
— Amp
and as the voice of mighty thunderings, saying, Alleluia: for the Lord God omnipotent reigneth.

7. Let us be glad and rejoice, and give honour to him: for the marriage of the Lamb is come,
. . . the marriage day of . . . — Wey
and his wife hath made herself ready.

8. And to her was granted that she should be arrayed in fine linen, clean and white:
for the fine linen is the righteousness of saints.
(Now the fine linen signifies the righteous deeds of God's people.) — NEB

9. And he saith unto me, Write, Blessed are they which are called

. . . they that are bidden — ASV
. . . those who have been invited—Wey
unto the marriage supper of the Lamb.
And he saith unto me, These are the true sayings of God.
And he added, These are the very
words of God — NEB

10. And I fell at his feet to worship him. And he said unto me, See thou do it not:
. . . Never that — Knox
. . . No, be careful! — Ber
. . . You must not do thát! — RSV
I am thy fellowservant, and of thy brethren that have the testimony of Jesus:
. . . thy brethren that hold . . . — ASV
worship God:
keep thy worship for God — Knox
for the testimony of Jesus is the spirit of prophecy.
Those who bear testimony to Jesus are
inspired like the prophets — NEB
For to bear testimony to Jesus needs
the inspiration of the Prophets —
TCNT
For the truth revealed by Jesus is the
inspiration of all prophecy — Wey
For the testimony of Jesus is what inspires prophecy — Gspd
It is the truth concerning Jesus which
inspires all prophecy — Knox

11. And I saw heaven opened,
Then I saw heaven thrown open — Ber
and behold a white horse;
and he that sat upon him was called Faithful and True, and in righteousness he doth judge and make war.
whose rider is called faithful and true,
for his judgments and his warfare
are just — Phi
. . . for he is just in judgement and just
in war — NEB

12. His eyes were as a flame of fire[77] and on his head were many crowns; and he had a name written, that no man knew, but he himself.

13. And he was clothed with a vesture dipped in blood:

[74]See verse 1.
[75]Compare Rev. 4:6.
[76]Compare Rev. 1:15.
[77]Compare Rev. 1:14.

... a garment deep dyed with ... —
Knox

... a robe dyed by dipping in ... —
Amp

... a garment sprinkled with ... —
TCNT

... a garment spattered with ... —
Gspd

... a garment drenched in ... — NEB
He was clothed with garments dipped
in blood — Tay

**and his name is called The Word of
God.**

14. **And the armies which were in heaven
followed him upon white horses,
clothed in fine linen, white and clean.**

15. **And out of his mouth goeth a sharp
sword, that with it he should smite the
nations:**
**and he shall rule them with a rod of
iron:**[78]
... shepherd them with a staff of iron
— Gspd
and he treadeth the winepress
and it is His work to tread ... — Wey
**of the fierceness and wrath of Al-
mighty God.**
of the fierce anger of God, the Ruler of
all — Wey

16. **And he hath on his vesture and on his
thigh a name written, KING OF
KINGS, AND LORD OF LORDS.**

17. **And I saw an angel standing in the
sun;**
... in the blazing light of the sun —
Phi
**and he cried with a loud voice,
saying to all the fowls that fly in the**

midst of heaven,
calling to all the birds flying in mid-air
— Phi
**Come and gather yourselves together
unto the supper of the great God;**

18. **That ye may eat the flesh of kings, and
the flesh of captains, and the flesh of
mighty men, and the flesh of horses,
and of them that sit on them, and the
flesh of all men, both free and bond,
both small and great.**

19. **And I saw the beast, and the kings of
the earth, and their armies, gathered
together to make war against him that
sat on the horse, and against his army.**
And then I saw the beast and the kings
of the earth muster their armies, to
join battle with the rider on the white
horse and the army which followed
him — Knox
... massed together for battle against
... — Phi

20. **And the beast was taken,**
... captured — NEB
**and with him the false prophet that
wrought miracles before him, with
which he deceived them that had
received the mark of the beast, and
them that worshipped his image.**
**These both were cast alive into a lake
of fire burning with brimstone.**
... into the fiery lake of burning
sulphur — TCNT

21. **And the remnant were slain with the
sword of him that sat upon the horse,
which sword proceeded out of his
mouth; and all the fowls were filled
with their flesh.**

CHAPTER 20

1. **And I saw an angel come down from
heaven, having the key of the bottomless pit**[79] **and a great chain in his hand.**

2. **And he laid hold on the dragon,**
He seized the dragon — NEB
He overpowered the dragon — Ber
that old serpent,[80] **which is the Devil,
and Satan, and bound him a thou-
sand years.**
... chained him up for ... — NEB

3. **And cast him into the bottomless pit,
and shut him up, and set a seal upon
him,**

... shut it, and sealed it over him —
ASV
**that he should deceive the nations no
more,**
that he might not lead the nations
astray any more — Wey
**till the thousand years should be ful-
filled:**
... should be finished — ASV

---

[78]Compare Rev. 2:27.

[79]Compare Rev. 9:1.

[80]Compare Rev. 12:9.

and after that he must be loosed a little season.

4. **And I saw thrones, and they sat upon them, and judgment was given unto them:**

Then I saw thrones prepared for those to whom judgment was committed — Knox

Then I saw thrones with beings seated on them, who were empowered to act as judges — Gspd

and I saw the souls of them that were beheaded for the witness of Jesus, and for the word of God,

Then I saw the souls of those who had been executed . . . — Phi

and which had not worshipped the beast, neither his image,

— those who never worshipped . . . — Phi

those who would not worship the Beast or his statue — Mof

neither had received his mark upon their foreheads, or in their hands; and they lived and reigned with Christ a thousand years.

They came to life and reigned . . . — Phi

5. **But the rest of the dead lived not again** . . . did not come to life — Phi.

until the thousand years were finished. This is the first resurrection.

6. **Blessed and holy is he that hath part in the first resurrection: on such the second death[81] hath no power, but they shall be priests of God and of Christ, and shall reign with him a thousand years.**

7. **And when the thousand years are expired, Satan shall be loosed out of his prison,**

8. **And shall go out to deceive[82] the nations**

and will set out to deceive the nations — Phi

which are in the four quarters of the earth, Gog and Magog,

. . . even to China and Mongolia — Lam

to gather them together to battle: the number of whom is as the sand of the sea.

9. **And they went up on the breadth of the earth, and compassed the camp of the saints about, and the beloved city: and fire came down from God out of heaven,**

. . . fire came down from the sky — Phi **and devoured them.**

10. **And the devil that deceived them was cast into the lake of fire and brimstone, where the beast and the false prophet are, and shall be tormented**

. . . and they shall be tormented — ASV

day and night for ever and ever.

11. **And I saw a great white throne, and him that sat on it, from whose face the earth and the heaven flew away;**

. . . at whose glance earth and heaven vanished — Knox

and there was found no place for them.

and were found no more — Knox

12. **And I saw the dead, small and great, stand before God;**

. . . standing before God — ASV

and the books were opened; and another book was opened, which is the book of life: and the dead were judged

out of those things which were written in the books, according to their works.

by what was written in the books about what they had done — Gspd

13. **And the sea gave up the dead which were in it; and death and hell delivered up the dead which were in them:**

. . . death and Hades . . . — ASV

. . . death and the underworld . . . — Gspd

and they were judged every man according to their works.

. . . they were judged, one by one, each according to his actions — TCNT

. . . all were tried and their cases determined by . . . — Amp

14. **And death and hell were cast into the lake of fire. This is the second death.**

And death and Hades. . . . This is the second death, even the lake of fire[83] — ASV

. . . death and Sheol . . . — Lam

. . . death and the grave were themselves hurled into . . . — Phi

15. **And whosoever was not found written in the book of life was cast into the lake of fire.**

---

[81]Compare Rev. 2:11.
[82]Compare verse 3.
[83]"Even the lake of fire" represents a variant reading.

CHAPTER 21

1. **And I saw a new heaven and a new earth:**
   for the first heaven and the first earth were passed away;
   The old heaven, and old earth had vanished — Knox
   The former heavens and the former earth had passed away — TCNT
   and there was no more sea.
   and the sea had ceased to be — TCNT

2. **And I John saw the holy city, new Jerusalem, coming down from God out of heaven,**
   prepared as a bride adorned for her husband.
   . . . like a bride attired to meet her husband — Wey
   It was a glorious sight, beautiful as a bride at her wedding — Tay

3. **And I heard a great voice out of heaven saying,**
   Behold, the tabernacle of God is with men,
   Now at last God has his dwelling among men — NEB
   Lo! the tent of God is with men — Rhm
   See! the house of God is . . . — Phi
   Lo! God's dwelling place is . . . — Wey
   See! the Tabernacle of God is set up among men — TCNT
   and he will dwell with them,
   . . . will make his living-place with them — Bas
   and they shall be his people, and God himself shall be with them, and be their God.

4. **And God shall wipe away all tears from their eyes; and there shall be no more death, neither sorrow, nor crying, neither shall there be any more pain:**
   for the former things are passed away.
   The old order has passed away — TCNT
   For all those former things are past and gone — Phi

5. **And he that sat upon the throne said, Behold, I make all things new.**
   See! I am making everything new — Wms
   And he said unto me, Write: for these words are true and faithful.

6. **And he said unto me, It is done.**[84] **I am Alpha and Omega,**[85] **the beginning and the end. I will give unto him that is athirst of the fountain of the water of life freely.**

7. **He that overcometh shall inherit all things;**
   . . . shall inherit these things — ASV
   and I will be his God, and he shall be my son.

8. **But the fearful,**
   But as for cowards — TCNT
   and unbelieving, and the abominable, and murderers, and whore-mongers, and sorcerers, and idolaters, and all liars, shall have their part in the lake which burneth with fire and brimstone:
   which is the second death.
   That is the second death — TCNT

9. **And there came unto me one of the seven angels which had the seven vials**[86] **full of the seven last plagues,**[87] **and talked with me, saying, Come hither, I will shew thee the bride, the Lamb's wife.**

10. **And he carried me away in the spirit to a great and high mountain,**
    . . . to the top of a vast, lofty mountain — Wey
    and shewed me that great city, the holy Jerusalem, descending out of heaven from God,
    and pointed out to me the holy city . . . — Rhm

11. **Having the glory of God:**
    clothed in God's glory — Knox
    and her light was like unto a stone most precious,
    The light that shone over it was bright as any precious stone — Knox
    Her luster resembled . . . — Ber
    it had the radiance of some priceless jewel — NEB
    Her brilliance was like a very costly stone — NASB

---

[84]Compare Rev. 16:17.
[85]Compare Rev. 1:8.
[86]Compare Rev. 15:7.
[87]Compare Rev. 15:6.

even like a jasper stone, clear as crystal;

12. And had a wall great and high, and had twelve gates, and at the gates twelve angels, and names written thereon, which are the names of the twelve tribes of the children of Israel:

13. On the east three gates; on the north three gates; on the south three gates; and on the west three gates.

14. And the wall of the city had twelve foundations, and in them the names of the twelve apostles of the Lamb.

15. And he that talked with me had a golden reed to measure the city, and the gates thereof, and the wall thereof.

16. And the city lieth foursquare, and the length is as large as the breadth:
The City is square; the length and the breadth are the same — TCNT
The city is laid out as a quadrangle with its length equal to its width — Ber
and he measured the city with the reed, twelve thousand furlongs. The length and the breadth and the height of it are equal.
. . . it was twelve hundred miles . . . — TCNT
. . . it was fifteen hundred miles . . . — Ber
. . . one thousand five hundred miles in length, and exactly the same in breadth and height — Nor

17. And he measured the wall thereof, an hundred and forty and four cubits,
. . . two hundred and eighty-five feet — TCNT
according to the measure of a man, that is, of the angel.
as men measure, that is as the angel measured — TCNT

18. And the building of the wall of it was of jasper: and the city was pure gold, like unto clear glass.

19. And the foundations of the wall of the city were garnished with all manner of precious stones. The first foundation was jasper; the second, sapphire; the third, a chalcedony; the fourth, an emerald;

20. The fifth, sardonyx; the sixth, sardius;
. . . the sixth a carnelian — TCNT

the seventh, chrysolyte; the eighth, beryl; the ninth, a topaz; the tenth, a chrysoprasus; the eleventh, a jacinth;
. . . the eleventh a hyacinth — TCNT
. . . the eleventh turquoise — NEB
the twelfth, an amethyst.

21. And the twelve gates were twelve pearls; every several gate was of one pearl: and the street of the city was pure gold,
. . . the main street of the city was made of pure gold — Wey
as it were transparent glass.

22. And I saw no temple therein: for the Lord God Almighty and the Lamb are the temple of it.

23. And the city had no need of the sun, neither of the moon, to shine in it: for the glory of God did lighten it,
and the Lamb is the light thereof.
. . . the lamp thereof is the Lamb — ASV
. . . its Lamp was the Lamb — TCNT

24. And the nations of them which are saved
And the people who have been saved — Lam
shall walk in the light of it: and the kings of the earth do bring their glory and honour into it.

25. And the gates of it shall not be shut at all by day: for there shall be no night there.
All day the gates will never be shut (there will be no night there) — Knox
And in the daytime (for there shall be no night there) its gates shall never be closed — NASB

26. And they shall bring the glory and honour of the nations into it.
as the nations flock into it with their honour and their praise — Knox

27. And there shall in no wise enter into it anything that defileth, neither whatsoever worketh abomination, or maketh a lie:
Never shall any unhallowed thing enter it, nor he whose life is shameful and false — TCNT
but they which are written in the Lamb's book of life.
there is no entrance but for those whose names are . . . — Knox

CHAPTER 22

1. And he shewed me a pure river of water of life,

... a river whose waters give life — Knox

clear as crystal, proceeding out of the throne of God and of the Lamb.

... gushing out of the throne ... — — Lam

sparkling like crystal, flaming from the throne of God and of the Lamb — NEB

2. In the midst of the street of it,

in the middle of the street of the City — TCNT

down the middle of the city's street — NEB

and on either side of the river, was there the tree of life,

On each side of the river was a Tree of Life — Mon

which bare twelve manner of fruits, and yielded her fruit every month:

... bearing twelve crops of fruit ... — Rhm

It produced twelve kinds of fruit, yielding a fresh crop month by month — Wey

and the leaves of the tree were for the healing of the nations.

... served as medicine for ... — Wey

... served to heal ... — Mof

... contained the remedy to heal ... — Wms

3. And there shall be no more curse: but the throne of God and of the Lamb

... God's throne (which is the Lamb's throne) — Knox

shall be in it; and his servants shall serve him:

4. And they shall see his face; and his name shall be in their foreheads.

5. And there shall be no night there; and they need no candle,

... no light of lamp — ASV

neither light of the sun; for the Lord God giveth them light:

... because the Lord God will shine on them — Beck

and they shall reign for ever and ever.

6. And he said unto me, These sayings are faithful and true:

You can trust these words ... they are true — Beck

and the Lord God of the holy prophets sent his angel to shew unto his servants the things which must shortly[88] be done.

7. Behold, I come quickly:[89]

And remember, I am coming soon! — NEB

blessed is he that keepeth the sayings of the prophecy of this book.

Blessed will he be who lays to heart the words of prophecy contained in this book — TCNT

8. And I John saw these things, and heard them.

And I John am he that heard and saw these things — ASV

And when I had heard and seen, I fell down to worship before the feet of the angel which shewed me these things.

9. Then saith he unto me, See thou do it not:[90] for I am thy fellowservant, and of thy brethren the prophets, and of them which keep the sayings of this book: worship God.

10. And he saith unto me, Seal not the sayings of the prophecy of this book:

Make no secret ... of the meaning of the prophecies contained in this book — Wey

... Do not keep secret the words of ... — TCNT

for the time is at hand.

The Time is near — TCNT

for the time of their fulfillment is now close at hand — Wey

... the time of their coming true is near — Wms

... the time is near when it will come true — Beck

... for the hour of fulfilment is near — NEB

11. He that is unjust, let him be unjust still:

He who is unjust will continue to be unjust — Lam

---

[88]Compare Rev. 1:1.

[89]Compare Rev. 3:11.

[90]Compare Rev. 19:10.

Meanwhile, let the evil-doer go on doing evil — NEB

Until then let the unrighteous keep on being unrighteous — Nor

and he which is filthy, let him be filthy still:

and he who is filthy will continue to be filthy — Lam

and he that is righteous, let him be righteous still:

But let also the righteous still be . . . — Nor

and he who is righteous will continue to be . . . — Lam

and he that is holy, let him be holy still.

and he who is holy will continue to be holy — Lam

12. **And, behold, I come quickly;**[91]

Yes, I am coming soon — NEB

and my reward is with me,

bringing my recompense — RSV

to give every man according as his work[92] **shall be.**

to give each man what his actions deserve — TCNT

to repay every one for what he has done — RSV

13. **I am Alpha and Omega,**[93] **the beginning and the end, the first and the last.**

14. **Blessed are they that do his commandments,**

Blessed are they that wash their robes[94] — ASV

Happy are they who are washing . . . — Rhm

Blessed will they be who wash . . . — TCNT

that they may have right to the tree of life,

that their right may be unto . . . — Rhm

that they may have the right to approach . . . — TCNT

and may enter in through the gates into the city.

15. **For without are dogs, and sorcerers, and whoremongers, and murderers, and idolaters,**

and whosoever loveth and maketh a lie.

. . . all who love the false and live by it — TCNT

. . . whoever loves to tell lies — Lam

16. **I Jesus have sent mine angel to testify**

unto you these things in the churches.

. . . for the churches — ASV

I am the root[95] **and the offspring of David, and the bright and morning star.**[96]

. . . the bright Star of the Morning — TCNT

17. **And the Spirit and the bride say, Come. And let him that heareth say, Come. And let him that is athirst come. And whosoever will, let him take the water of life freely.**

Come! say the Spirit and the bride. Come! let each hearer reply. Come forward, you who are thirsty; accept the water of life, a free gift to all who desire it — NEB

Come, you who are thirsty, take, you who will, the water of life; it is my free gift — Knox

. . . let every one who wishes come and take the water of life without any cost — Wms

. . . without payment — Wey

18. **For I testify unto every man that heareth the words of the prophecy of this book, If any man shall add unto these things, God shall add unto him the plagues that are written in this book:**

I declare to all who hear the words of the prophecy contained in this book — If anyone adds to it, God will add to his troubles the Curses described in this book — TCNT

19. **And if any man shall take away from the words of the book of this prophecy, God shall take away his part out of the book of life, and out of the holy city, and from the things which are written in this book.**

20. **He which testifieth these things**

He whose testimony this is — TCNT

saith, Surely I come quickly.[97] **Amen. Even so, come, Lord Jesus.**

21. **The grace of our Lord Jesus Christ be with you all. Amen.**

. . . Amen — so let it be! — Amp

---

[91]Compare Rev. 3:11; 22:7.

[92]Compare Rev. 20:12-13.

[93]Compare Rev. 1:8.

[94]Variant reading.

[95]Compare Rev. 5:5.

[96]Compare Rev. 2:28.

[97]Compare Rev. 3:11; 22:7, 12.